THE NEW TESTAMENT: SINAITIC VERSION

The monastery of St. Catherine, on the eastern
slope of Mt.Sinai:

John 1.1-38 (Page 48):
Courtesy The British Library, London.

Η ΚΑΙΝΗ ΔΙΑΘΗΚΗ

THE NEW COVENANT

THE NEW TESTAMENT: SINAITIC VERSION

In Greek and English

Ancient Text Edited and Translated by: Dalmer R. Ford

VANTAGE PRESS
New York

Η ΚΑΙΝΗ ΔΙΑΘΗΚΗ

The New Testament: Sinaitic Version

PREFACE

Introduction. The Codex Sinaiticus is the *only* ancient manuscript containing the entire New Testament without a break. It is presented here in Greek and English on facing pages, in the unpolished form, so that any student knowing the Greek alphabet can examine the text of the famous Codex Sinaiticus for himself. In fact, that fourth century manuscript contains 29 books in the New Testament portion, though the last one is incomplete due to deterioration of the last leaves. All of those books are included here, in the same order as in the Codex.

Most editions of the New Testament consider multiple manuscripts and former versions, usually including *all* the stories from the Textus Receptus while preserving much of the traditional wording of previous editions. Finally, the translation or paraphrase is polished for smooth reading in English.

This work is a direct translation of the Codex Sinaiticus, the fourth century Greek manuscript that was preserved for many centuries at Mount Sinai and is now owned by the British Museum in London. First, it was translated from the uncial to standard Greek letters with the words separated and chapter and verse numbers added as in *The Greek New Testament,* 3rd edition. Next, it was converted to minuscule, complete with accents and punctuation. However, if a word were misspelled in the manuscript, it is misspelled here; if the "wrong" tense or case were used in the manuscript, it is also "wrong" here. This is a letter-by-letter and word-by-word edition of the original text, presented in a more readable form. Finally, it was translated literally into English, though not "polished" as required in literature. I have specifically avoided Elizabethan English. However, in Greek, the second person pronoun "you" is different in the plural than it is in the singular, and it does make a difference in the meaning. Therefore, I have used the archaic English form "ye" for the plural and "you" only for the singular.

PREFACE

This literal English is included here, printed on facing pages with the Greek. The English, though rather literal, is arranged so as to make sense to the non-reader of Greek. But with the "word of God" printed on the facing page, the motivation, or challenge, will always be present for the student to learn to read it! And one does not have to learn much Greek to learn how to pick out some key words and look them up in one of the less expensive lexicons, especially *The Analytical Greek Lexicon Revised* (Zondervan), or one that is keyed to Strong's Concordance.

The oldest manuscripts had no punctuation, so all punctuation of the Greek has but questionable authority. The capital letter edition is presented without punctuation so that the serious scholar can consider that for himself. The minuscule edition is punctuated as in *The Greek New Testament*, 3rd edition (1975). However, both editions are broken, or paragraphed, as in the manuscript.

There are 16 complete verses from the Byzantine *Textus Receptus* that are "missing" from the best ancient manuscripts of the New Testament. These are:

Matt. 17.21	Matt. 18.11	Matt. 23.14	Mark 7.16
Mark 9.44	Mark 9.46	Mark 11.26	Mark 15.28
Luke 17.36	Luke 23.17	John 5.4	Acts 8.37
Acts 15.34	Acts 24.7	Acts 28.29	Rom. 16.24

These verse numbers are simply skipped in the *Sinaitic New Testament*, except for Luke 23.17. I have no apology for the contents or "omissions" of this book. This is the *Sinaitic New Testament*, translated directly from that manuscript only.

Concerning the many corrections shown in the facsimile of the manuscript, this policy was adopted: If *The Greek New Testament,* 3rd edition, allowed the correction, it was allowed here; otherwise, the original text of the codex was retained. In the few, rare cases where a letter, word, or correction is not clear in the facsimile, the spelling given for Sinaiticus in the *Concordant Greek Text* is used.

PREFACE

Concerning the Old Testament, *any* version in
Greek or English is adequate for reference purposes as
needed. The writer's primary reference is the Septua-
gint or LXX (Greek), secondary is the Masoretic Text
(Hebrew), tertiary is the Vulgate (Latin), while *any*
version whatever in English is a very poor fourth
choice. The Index of Old Testament Quotations is from
The Greek New Testament, 3rd edition (1975).

The call, purpose, and preparation. I became a
Christian in 1944, and God inspired me in 1946 to do
this work. But I studied the subject for 38 years and
studied the Greek language for 23 years before beginning the serious work of translating, or even reading
any scriptures in Greek. By studying religion and
language separately for all those years, then applying
my Greek to the Bible, it was immediately apparent
that the usual ecclesiastical language (church lingo)
written into it by the traditional translators is not
what the scriptures say!

This work was done for God and for the truth-
loving believer, to offer an alternative to the lingo
and doctrines that became frozen during the Dark Ages
--the Latin era of the church. This scholar does not
believe there was any church lingo in the first century A.D. Such lingo was developed during the Dark Ages
by Latin-loving interpreters. It was not until 1824
that a serious scholar (Winer) first suggested that
the Bible was written in the common language of the
people of the Hellenistic era, and the discovery of
the meanings of that common language took place between 1890 and the present day --the process of that
discovery continues at this very time. But the lingo
and doctrines of the 20th century churches remain
frozen to the Latin era!

In the final stages of preparation, I read *The
Amplified Bible* and Wuest's *The New Testament*, and I
read the great and useful interlinear New Testaments
by George Ricker Berry, Alfred Marshal, and Jay P.
Greene. I also studied other literature and writings

PREFACE

in Greek from the Biblical age and nine different
Greek grammars of the New Testament. Then I translated
by use of Bauer's lexicon, Moulton's *The Analytical
Greek Lexicon Revised*, and Moulton-Milligan's *The
Vocabulary of the Greek Testament*. My translation
favors the meaning of the terms as used during the
Hellenistic age (300 B.C. to 330 A.D.), sans ecclesi-
astical jargon and church lingo.

Translation Policies. Translate each construc-
tion intact rather than scattering alleged "agnate"
constructions for the sake of variety. Make a direct,
literal translation, not an exercise in variety of
either traditional Elizabethan or contemporary English
expression. Use the two word form of anyone, everyone, etc, when appropriate--there *is* a difference.
For example: everyone = all, while every one = each
one.

Many grammatical analysts declare that the arti-
cular participle is the same as a relative clause.
But the participle is the one idiom that is virtually
the same in English as in Greek, though Greek uses it
much more often. I have translated the participle as
a participle and the relative as a relative, with no
transposing of grammatical forms. This is a general
rule that I followed throughout the translation,
including all the other so-called "parallel" constructions.

Use of shall and will. Shall is used for simple
future time in the first person, but it is emphatic
when used with the second and third persons (see any
good dictionary). For the simple future tense, shall
is used in the first person, will in the second and
third persons. Most English language Bibles consistently use "shall" in *all* persons, which injects a
strong emphasis to most future tense verbs where there
really is none. Thus, the actual emphases present in
the Greek is lost and replaced by the misconceived
emphases of men! Throughout this translation, I used
shall and will in the proper sense to avoid adding

strong emphases to passages that are actually given in the moods of dubious uncertainty.

When used in Greek, the first and second person pronouns in the nominative case are emphatic. I usually indicate this by simple repetition of the emphasized pronoun, such as: We, we.... The reader might handle this by raising the voice on the first, perhaps even omitting the second when reading aloud.

Capitalization. I have capitalized only proper names in the minuscule Greek text. I made one exception to this rule: When a new chapter coincides with a new paragraph, the first letter is capitalized. However, the English translation is capitalized in the conventional manner, except for pronouns and some appositives referring to deity.

I use a few different translation techniques than are usually found in literal translations, which results in literal translation even where most translators substitute an English/American idiom instead. For the most part this translation makes good sense from direct left-to-right reading, but there is an occasional passage that lacks, or seems ambiguous in, sense. But bear in mind that this is a direct translation from the ancient manuscript, which lacks the grammatical nicety of the edited editions of the Greek New Testament or of traditional translations "interpreted" from conjecture.

I have translated the Greek word ἀγάπη (love) as "agape", in all 116 occurrences of it, because agape is an English word that most are now familiar with. But I translated other Greek words for love as "love". On another very important point, most people seem to be unaware that pagan, heathen, nations, and Gentiles are actually one and the same word! I have translated that word with the noun "ethnics" throughout. This is fitting, because nations as we know them did not exist until the 18th or 19th centuries, and they only began about the 14th century, almost concurrent with the

Renaissance, i.e., the revival of Greek science and learning.

There are no "Jews" in my translation--just Judeans, who were citizens of, or ethnics from, the province of Judea.

Translation devices. Many of the prepositions in English are added as aids in translation--helper words. Conversely, many Greek prepositions are omitted in the English translations. Why? Tradition! The definite article is used much more frequently in Greek. Many are omitted in English for smoothness and better "sense". Unexplainedly, and sadly, the usual English translators omit the article where truly needed and insert it where there is none, following the Latin traditions (Latin has *no* definite article). I tried instead to use the article as in Hellenistic Greek. Words such as (one), (man), (woman), (who), (thing), (time) are often inserted where there is only an adjective, or just an article. These are implied substantives.

The terms (thing) and (one) generally fit, and they tend to degenderize the text, though often another noun would be appropriate in a given context: purpose, man, woman, etc, etc. Let each reader judge for himself!

Where the definite article is used alone as a pronoun, as: the (he), the (they), etc, it only signifies a change of speaker, and the (*pronoun*) is most often the appropriate word to use.

Many discourses, especially in the gospels, begin with "answering" or "answered", even if no question was asked. The Greek word actually means more like: Replying, taking up a/the discourse, after careful thought, having considered, etc.

Other helper words commonly used: Would, ever-- indicates an indefinite clause, from the Greek parti-

cle ἄν. Let us, let him/her/it, let them--indicate
the imperative mood, first person plural, third person
singular and plural. Shall, will--simple future
tense. Should, would--future tense subordinate to an
imperfect verb, or for contingency. May, might--used
to indicate contingency of the subjunctive or optative
moods, may for present and might for aorist. Was,
were--Often used as a helper word to indicate the
imperfect tense. I have consistently used them so,
for example, "they were serving". Some translators
also employ "used to", "went on", "kept on", etc, for
the imperfect tense.

I also use some translation devices that are
quite different from those customarily used. For
example, Greek often uses the definite article with
whole clauses and included sentences, not just with
single words. This indicates that the entire following clause is definite, sometimes called the bracket
force of the article. I render these: to or for the
(thing), in or at the (time), of the (thing), from the
(thing), etc. Also, the Greek particle ἄν is used in
much the same way, but it renders the entire clause
indefinite. It is usually rendered as "ever" or
"would" in English, as I also did here. And further,
the subject of the infinitive in Greek is in the
accusative (objective) case. I add the preposition
"for" so that the accusative noun or pronoun becomes
object of the preposition and the phrase becomes
subject of the infinitive in English, as: *for* him to
go out. J.P. Greene also did this often in his *Interlinear Bible*. Moreover, a Greek sentence often begins
with or includes the genitive absolute, which is any
or all of an article, noun or pronoun, and participle
in the genitive case. I usually render this: from
them having gone out, or from the (thing or time) of
him having come, etc.

I arranged the word order of my English translation so that they make sense when read normally in
English, though this is a literal and not a full
idiomatic translation. A few other devices are used

which may warrant a brief explanation: Old Testament quotations are printed in small capitals in the English translation, and in quotation marks in the Greek minuscule. Italics indicate words supplied by the translator, while words in parentheses are implied substantives. The fraction bar is used often, in the standard way--it means and/or. Two or more translations are often given for the same Greek word, and the reader may read any one or all of those at that point.

Errors. I thoroughly understand the fact that the scribes made errors in their hand-copying of the scriptures. In the course of this work, I was amazed at the multitude of human errors that I made myself. In the middle of the work, I used two years just for proofreading and correcting the errors I had made in both Greek and English. God inspired me throughout the preparation and the work, but He seldom if ever inspires a man beyond his own knowledge, ability, and culture. The individual's culture and education shows through the work of each writer of the scriptures. Also, the legends that the scribes and translators preserved the scriptures letter-perfect and infallible through the ages are just that--legends! However inspired, we too are men and prone to make the human errors of men.

Conclusion. The writer makes no claims for this work to be "better" or more accurate than the scholarly editions now in existence. The big difference is the fact that this work is done in the common language of the biblical age and not in the church lingo of this age! He has merely presented the one complete ancient version directly, but in a more readable and referencable form. Any failure to accomplish that is his own error.

Every effort has been made to present this work free from all biases, traditions, and -isms. I sincerely hope this edition will be useful and a blessing to many Christians everywhere, regardless of creed, doctrine, or denomination. Being called by God to

PREFACE

accomplish this work, I pray that it might prove useful to you the scholar, and you the minister, and you the reader.

Credits. This work has spanned several decades, and to mention every individual or organization who has been helpful would be impossible. I gladly accepted and built upon the works of many other scholars who preceded me. I do want to express especial thanks to the staffs of The British Library, The Vatican Library, The New York International Bible Society, and the Mosher Library and Seminary Book Room of Dallas Theological Seminary, to United Bible Societies (UBS) for most of the material in Appendix I, and to Ms. Sheila Cummings, resident librarian at the public library in Warner Robins, Georgia.

Η ΚΑΙΝΗ ΔΙΑΘΗΚΗ

The New Testament: Sinaitic Version

INDEX

This is the Sinaitic New Testament, book of Matthew.

1.1 Βίβλος γενέσεως Ἰησοῦ χριστοῦ υἱοῦ Δαυὶδ υἱοῦ Ἀβραάμ. 1.2 Ἀβραὰμ ἐγέννησεν τὸν Ἰσαάκ, Ἰσαὰκ δὲ ἐγέννησεν τὸν Ἰακώβ, Ἰακὼβ δὲ ἐγέννησεν τὸν Ἰούδαν καὶ τοὺς ἀδελφοὺς αὐτοῦ, 1.3 Ἰούδας δὲ ἐγέννησεν τὸν Φάρες καὶ τὸν Ζάρα ἐκ τῆς Θαμάρ, Φάρες δὲ ἐγέννησεν τὸν Ἑσρώμ, Ἑσρὼμ δὲ ἐγέννησεν τὸν Ἀράμ, 1.4 Ἀρὰμ δὲ ἐγέννησεν τὸν Ἀμιναδάβ, Ἀμιναδὰβ δὲ ἐγέννησεν τὸν Ναασσών, Ναασσὼν δὲ ἐγέννησεν τὸν Σαλμών, 1.5 Σαλμὼν δὲ ἐγέννησεν τὸν Βόες ἐκ τῆς Ῥαχάβ, Βόες δὲ ἐγέννησεν τὸν Ἰωβὴδ ἐκ τῆς Ῥούθ, Ἰωβὴδ δὲ ἐγέννησεν τὸν Ἰεσσαί, 1.6 Ἰεσσαὶ δὲ ἐγέννησεν τὸν Δαυὶδ τὸν βασιλέα. Δαυεὶδ δὲ ἐγέννησεν τὸν Σολομῶνα ἐκ τῆς τοῦ Οὐρίου,

1.7 Σολομὼν δὲ ἐγέννησεν τὸν Ῥοβοάμ, Ῥοβοὰμ δὲ ἐγέννησεν τὸν Ἀβιά, Ἀβιὰ δὲ ἐγέννησεν τὸν Ἀσάφ, 1.8 Ἀσάφ δὲ ἐγέννησεν τὸν Ἰωσαφάτ, Ἰωσαφὰτ δὲ ἐγέννησεν τὸν Ἰωράμ, Ἰωρὰμ δὲ ἐγέννησεν τὸν Ὀζείαν, 1.9 Ὀζίας δὲ ἐγέννησεν τὸν Ἰωαθάμ, Ἰωαθὰμ δὲ ἐγέννησεν τὸν Ἀχάς, Ἀχὰς δὲ ἐγέννησεν τὸν Ἑζεκίαν,

1.10 Ἑζεκίας δὲ ἐγέννησεν τὸν Μανασσῆ, Μανασσῆς δὲ ἐγέννησεν τὸν Ἀμώς, Ἀμὼς δὲ ἐγέννησεν τὸν Ἰωσείαν, 1.11 Ἰωσείας δὲ ἐγέννησεν τὸν Ἰεχονίαν καὶ τοὺς ἀδελφοὺς αὐτοῦ ἐπὶ τῆς μετοικεσίας Βαβυλῶνος.

1.12 μετὰ δὲ τὴν μετοικεσίαν Βαβυλῶνος Ἰεχονίας ἐγέννησεν τὸν Σαλαθιήλ, Σαλαθιὴλ δὲ ἐγέννησεν τὸν Ζοροβαβέλ, 1.13 Ζοροβαβὲλ δὲ ἐγέννησεν τὸν Ἀβιούδ, Ἀβιοὺδ δὲ ἐγέννησεν τὸν Ἐλιακείμ, Ἐλιακεὶμ δὲ ἐγέννησεν τὸν Ἀζώρ, 1.14 Ἀζὼρ δὲ ἐγέννησεν τὸν Σαδώκ, Σαδὼκ δὲ ἐγέννησεν τὸν Ἀχείμ, Ἀχεὶμ δὲ ἐγέννησεν τὸν Ἐλιούδ, 1.15 Ἐλιοὺδ δὲ ἐγέννησεν τὸν Ἐλεάζαρ, Ἐλεάζαρ δὲ ἐγέννησεν τὸν Ματθάν, Ματθὰν δὲ ἐγέννησεν τὸν Ἰακώβ, 1.16 Ἰακὼβ δὲ ἐγέννησεν τὸν Ἰωσὴφ τὸν ἄνδρα Μαρίας, ἐξ ἧς ἐγεννήθη Ἰησοῦς ὁ λεγόμενος χριστός.

1.17 Πᾶσαι οὖν αἱ γενεαὶ ἀπὸ Ἀβραὰμ ἕως Δαυὶδ γενεαὶ δεκατέσσαρες, καὶ ἀπὸ Δαυὶδ ἕως τῆς μετοικεσίας Βαβυλῶνος γενεαὶ δεκατέσσαρες, καὶ ἀπὸ τῆς μετοικεσίας Βαβυλῶνος ἕως τοῦ χριστοῦ γενεαὶ δεκατέσσαρες.

1.18 τοῦ δὲ Ἰησοῦ χριστοῦ ἡ γένεσις οὕτως ἦν.

ACCORDING TO MATTHEW

1.1 A scroll of generations of Jesus the anointed (one), a son of David, a son of Abraham.

1.2 Abraham generated Isaac, and Isaac generated Jacob, and Jacob generated Judas and his brothers, 1.3 and Judas generated Phares and Zara out of Thamar, and Phares generated Esrom, and Esrom generated Aram, 1.4 and Aram generated Aminadab, and Aminadab generated Naasson, and Naasson generated Salmon, 1.5 and Salmon generated Booz out of Rachab, and Booz generated Obed out of Ruth, and Obed generated Jesse, 1.6 and Jesse generated David the king. And David generated Solomon out of the (one) from Uriah.

1.7 And Solomon generated Roboam, and Roboam generated Abia, and Abia generated Asaph, 1.8 and Asaph generated Josaphat, and Josaphat generated Joram, and Joram generated Ozias, 1.9 and Ozias generated Joatham, and Joatham generated Achaz,

And Achaz generated Hezekias,

1.10 And Hezekias generated Manasses, and Manasses generated Amos, and Amos generated Josias, 1.11 and Josias generated Jechonias and his brothers up to the deportation/captivity of Babylon.

1.12 And after the deportation/captivity of Babylon, Jechonias generated Salathiel, and Salathiel generated Zorobabel, 1.13 and Zorobabel generated Abiud, and Abiud generated Eliakim.

And Eliakim generated Azor, 1.14 and Azor generated Sadok.

And Sadok generated Achim, and Achim generated Eliud, 1.15 and Eliud generated Eleazar, and Eleazar generated Matthan, and Matthan generated Jacob, 1.16 and Jacob generated Joseph the man of Mary, from whom was generated Jesus, the (one) being called the anointed (one).

1.17 Therefore, all the generations from Abraham until David *were* fourteen generations, and from David until the deportation/captivity of Babylon *were* fourteen generations,

and from the deportation/captivity of Babylon until the anointed (one) *were* fourteen generations.

1.18 And the birth of Jesus the anointed (one) was thus: Mary, the mother of him, being betrothed to

μνηστευθίσης τῆς μητρὸς αὐτοῦ Μαρίας τῷ Ἰωσήφ, πρὶν ἢ συνελθῖν αὐτοὺς εὑρέθη ἐν γαστρὶ ἔχουσα ἐκ πνεύματος ἁγίου. 1.19 Ἰωσὴφ δὲ ὁ ἀνὴρ αὐτῆς, δίκαιος ὢν καὶ μὴ θέλων αὐτὴν παραδιγματίσαι, ἐβουλήθη λάθρα ἀπολῦσε αὐτήν.

1.20 ταῦτα δὲ αὐτοῦ ἐνθυμηθέντος ἰδοὺ ἄγγελος κυρίου κατ᾿ ὄναρ ἐφάνη αὐτῷ λέγων, Ἰωσὴφ υἱὸς Δαυίδ, μὴ φοβηθῇς παραλαβεῖν Μαριὰμ τὴν γυναῖκά σου, τὸ γὰρ ἐν αὐτῇ γεννηθὲν ἐκ πνεύματός ἐστιν ἁγίου· 1.21 τέξεται δὲ υἱὸν καὶ καλέσεις τὸ ὄνομα αὐτοῦ Ἰησοῦν, αὐτὸς γὰρ σώσι τὸν λαὸν αὐτοῦ ἀπὸ τῶν ἁμαρτιῶν αὐτῶν. 1.22 τοῦτο δὲ ὅλον γέγονεν ἵνα πληρωθῇ τὸ ῥηθὲν ὑπὸ κυρίου διὰ τοῦ προφήτου λέγοντος, 1.23 «ἰδοὺ ἡ παρθένος ἐν γαστρὶ ἕξι καὶ τέξεται υἱόν, καὶ καλέσουσιν τὸ ὄνομα αὐτοῦ Ἐμμανουήλ,» ὅ ἐστιν μεθερμηνευόμενον «μεθ᾿ ἡμῶν ὁ θεός.» 1.24 ἐγερθεὶς δὲ Ἰωσὴφ ἀπὸ τοῦ ὕπνου ἐποίησεν ὡς προσέταξεν αὐτῷ ὁ ἄγγελος κυρίου καὶ παρέλαβεν τὴν γυναῖκα αὐτοῦ· 1.25 καὶ οὐκ ἐγίνωσκεν αὐτὴν ἕως οὗ ἔτεκεν υἱόν· καὶ ἐκάλεσεν τὸ ὄνομα αὐτοῦ Ἰησοῦν.

2.1 Τοῦ δὲ Ἰησοῦ γεννηθέντος ἐν Βηθλέεμ τῆς Ἰουδαίας ἐν ἡμέραις Ἡρώδου τοῦ βασιλέως, ἰδοὺ μάγοι ἀπὸ ἀνατολῶν παρεγένοντο εἰς Ἱεροσόλυμα 2.2 λέγοντες, ποῦ ἐστιν ὁ τεχθεὶς βασιλεὺς τῶν Ἰουδαίων; εἴδομεν γὰρ αὐτοῦ τὸν ἀστέρα ἐν τῇ ἀνατολῇ καὶ ἤλθομεν προσκυνῆσαι αὐτῷ.

2.3 ἀκούσας δὲ ὁ βασιλεὺς Ἡρώδης ἐταράχθη καὶ πᾶσα Ἱεροσόλυμα μετ᾿ αὐτοῦ, 2.4 καὶ συναγαγὼν πάντας τοὺς ἀρχιερεῖς καὶ γραμματεῖς τοῦ λαοῦ ἐπυνθάνετο παρ᾿ αὐτῶν ποῦ ὁ χριστὸς γεννᾶται. 2.5 οἱ δὲ εἶπαν αὐτῷ, ἐν Βηθλέεμ τῆς Ἰουδαίας· οὕτως γὰρ γέγραπται διὰ τοῦ προφήτου· 2.6 «καὶ σύ, Βηθλέεμ» γῆ Ἰούδα, οὐδαμῶς «ἐλαχίστη εἶ ἐν τοῖς ἡγεμόσιν Ἰούδα· ἐξ οὗ ἐξελεύσεται ἡγούμενος, ὅστις ποιμανεῖ τὸν λαόν μου τὸν Ἰσραήλ.»

2.7 τότε Ἡρώδης λάθρα καλέσας τοὺς μάγους ἠκρίβωσεν

Joseph, before the (thing) for them to come together she was found/discovered having in a belly/womb from a holy spirit. 1.19 But Joseph, being a just (one) and not wishing to expose her to contempt, was decided to release/dismiss her quietly.

1.20 And from him pondering on these (things), behold, a messenger/angel from the Lord was manifested to him by a dream, saying: Joseph, son of David, fear not to take along Mary, your woman, for the (thing) in her, having been generated from a spirit, is holy; 1.21 and she will give birth to a son and you will call his name Jesus, for he will save his people from their faults/sins. 1.22 And all this happened that it might be fulfilled, the (thing) having been spoken by the Lord through the prophet, saying: 1.23 BEHOLD, THE MAIDEN WILL HAVE IN A PREGNANCY AND SHE WILL BIRTH/BEAR A SON, AND THEY WILL CALL HIS NAME EMMANU- AL, which is, being translated, GOD WITH US. 1.24 And being wakened from the sleep, Joseph did as the an- gel/messenger of the Lord commanded him and he took along his woman; 1.25 and he knew not her until which (time) she bore a son; and he called the name of him Jesus.

2.1 And from Jesus having been born in Bethlehem of Judea in the days of Herod the king, behold, ma- gicians/wise men from the east arrived in Jerusalem 2.2 saying: Where is the (one) having been born king of the Judeans? For we saw his star in the east and we came to worship him.

2.3 And having heard, the king Herod was trou- bled, and all Jerusalem with him, 2.4 and having assembled all the high priests and scribes of the people, he inquired from them where the anointed (one) was being born. 2.5 And they said to him: In Bethlehem of Judea; for so it has been written through the prophet: 2.6 AND YOU, BETHLEHEM, LAND OF JUDA, YOU ARE CERTAINLY NOT LEAST AMONG THE LEADERS OF JUDA: OUT OF YOU WILL COME FORTH A LEADER/GOVERNOR, WHO WILL SHEPHERD MY PEOPLE ISRAEL.

2.7 Then Herod, having secretly called the magicians/wise men, he inquired exactly from them the

παρ' αὐτῶν τὸν χρόνον τοῦ φαινομένου ἀστέρος, 2.8 καὶ πέμψας αὐτοὺς εἰς Βηθλέεμ εἶπεν, πορευθέντες ἐξετάσατε ἀκριβῶς περὶ τοῦ πεδίου· ἐπὰν δὲ εὕρητε ἀπαγγίλατέ μοι, ὅπως κἀγὼ ἐλθὼν προσκυνήσω αὐτῷ.

2.9 οἱ δὲ ἀκούσαντες τοῦ βασιλέως ἐπορεύθησαν, καὶ ἰδοὺ ὁ ἀστὴρ ὃν εἶδον ἐν τῇ ἀνατολῇ προῆγεν αὐτοὺς ἕως ἐλθὼν ἐστάθη ἐπάνω οὗ ἦν τὸ παιδίον. 2.10 ἰδόντες δὲ τὸν ἀστέρα ἐχάρησαν χαρὰν μεγάλην σφόδρα. 2.11 καὶ ἐλθόντες εἰς τὴν οἰκίαν ἦδον τὸ παιδίον μετὰ Μαρίας τῆς μητρὸς αὐτοῦ, καὶ πεσόντες προσεκύνησαν αὐτῷ, καὶ ἀνοίξαντες τοὺς θησαυροὺς αὐτῶν προσήνεγκαν αὐτῷ δῶρα, χρυσὸν καὶ λίβανον καὶ σμύρναν. 2.12 καὶ χρηματισθέντες κατ' ὄναρ μὴ ἀνακάμψαι πρὸς Ἡρώδην, δι' ἄλλης ὁδοῦ ἀνεχώρησαν εἰς τὴν ἑαυτῶν χώραν.

2.13 ἀναχωρησάντων δὲ αὐτῶν ἰδοὺ ἄγγελος κυρίου φαίνεται κατ' ὄναρ τῷ Ἰωσὴφ λέγων, ἐγερθεὶς παράλαβε τὸ πεδίον καὶ τὴν μητέρα αὐτοῦ καὶ φεῦγε εἰς Αἴγυπτον, καὶ ἴσθι ἐκεῖ ἕως ἂν εἴπω σοι· μέλλει γὰρ Ἡρώδης ζητῖν τὸ παιδίον τοῦ ἀπολέσε αὐτό. 2.14 ὁ δὲ ἐγερθεὶς παρέλαβε τὸ πεδίον καὶ τὴν μητέρα αὐτοῦ νυκτὸς καὶ ἀνεχώρησεν εἰς Αἴγυπτον, 2.15 καὶ ἦν ἐκῖ ἕως τῆς τελευτῆς Ἡρώδου· ἵνα πληρωθῇ τὸ ῥηθὲν ὑπὸ κυρίου διὰ τοῦ προφήτου λέγοντος, «ἐξ Αἰγύπτου ἐκάλεσα τὸν υἱόν μου.»

2.16   τότε Ἡρώδης ἰδὼν ὅτι ἐνεπέχθη ὑπὸ τῶν μάγων ἐθυμώθη λείαν, καὶ ἀποστίλας ἀνεῖλεν πάντας τοὺς παῖδας τοὺς ἐν Βηθλέεμ καὶ ἐν πᾶσι τοῖς ὁρίοις αὐτῆς ἀπὸ διετοῦς καὶ κατωτέρω, κατὰ τὸν χρόνον ὃν ἠκρίβωσεν παρὰ τῶν μάγων. 2.17 τότε ἐπληρώθη τὸ ῥηθὲν διὰ Ἰερεμίου τοῦ προφήτου λέγοντος,

2.18 «φωνὴ ἐν Ῥαμὰ ἠκούσθη, κλαυθμὸς καὶ ὀδυρμὸς» πολύς· «Ῥαχὴλ κλαίουσα τὰ τέκνα αὐτῆς, καὶ οὐκ ἤθελεν παρακληθῆναι, ὅτι οὐκ εἰσίν.»

2.19   τελευτήσαντος δὲ τοῦ Ἡρώδου ἰδοὺ ἄγγελος κυρίου φαίνεται κατ' ὄναρ τῷ Ἰωσὴφ ἐν Αἰγύπτῳ 2.20 λέγων, ἐγερθεὶς

time of the star appearing, 2.8 and sending them to Bethlehem, he said: Be going, question ye exactly concerning the child; and when ye might find *it* report ye to me, so that I also, going, may worship him.

2.9 And the (they), having heard the king, they went *out*, and behold, the star which they saw in the east went before them until it was stood/stopped above where the child was. 2.10 And seeing the star, they rejoiced an exceedingly great joy. 2.11 And going into the house they saw the child with Mary his mother, and falling *down* they worshiped him, and opening their stores (packages) they offered gifts to him, gold and frankincense and myrrh. 2.12 And having been instructed/warned by a dream not to return to Herod, they departed through another way/road into/to the country of themselves.

2.13 And from them having departed, behold, a messenger/angel from *the* Lord appeared by a dream to Joseph, saying: Be rising, take along the child and his mother, and you flee into Egypt, and you be there until I would speak to you; for Herod is about to seek the child from the (thing) to destroy it. 2.14 And the (one)/*he*, arising, he took along the child and his mother of/at night and he departed into Egypt, 2.15 and he was there until the death of Herod; that might be fulfilled the (thing) having been spoken by *the* Lord through the prophet, saying: OUT OF EGYPT I CALLED MY SON.

2.16 Then Herod, seeing that he was mocked by the magicians/wise men, was very angered, and having sent forth he took up all the boys, those in Bethlehem and in all her boundaries, from two years *old* and less, according to the time that he ascertained from the magicians/wise men. 2.17 Then was fulfilled the (thing) having been spoken through Jeremiah the prophet, saying:

2.18 A SOUND WAS HEARD IN RAMA, MUCH WEEPING AND MOURNING; RACHEL CRYING FOR HER CHILDREN, AND SHE WAS NOT WILLING TO BE COMFORTED, BECAUSE THEY WERE NOT.

2.19 But from the (thing) of Herod having died, behold, a messenger from *the* Lord appeared with/by a dream to Joseph in Egypt, 2.20 saying: Be rising, you

3

παράλαβε τὸ παιδίον καὶ τὴν μητέρα αὐτοῦ καὶ πορεύου εἰς γῆν Ἰσραήλ, τεθνήκασιν γὰρ οἱ ζητοῦντες τὴν ψυχὴν τοῦ πεδίου. 2.21 ὁ δὲ ἐγερθεὶς παρέλαβε τὸ παιδίον καὶ τὴν μητέρα αὐτοῦ καὶ εἰσῆλθεν εἰς γῆν Ἰσραήλ.

2.22 ἀκούσας δὲ ὅτι Ἀρχέλαος βασιλεύει τῆς Ἰουδαίας ἀντὶ τοῦ πατρὸς αὐτοῦ Ἡρώδου ἐφοβήθη ἐκεῖ ἀπελθεῖν· χρηματισθεὶς δὲ κατ' ὄναρ ἀνεχώρησεν εἰς τὰ μέρη τῆς Γαλιλαίας, 2.23 καὶ ἐλθὼν κατῴκησεν εἰς πόλιν λεγομένην Ναζαρέτ, ὅπως πληρωθῇ τὸ ῥηθὲν διὰ τῶν προφητῶν ὅτι Ναζωραῖος κληθήσεται.

3.1 Ἐν δὲ ταῖς ἡμέρες ἐκείναις παραγείνεται Ἰωάννης ὁ βαπτιστὴς κηρύσσων ἐν τῇ ἐρήμῳ τῆς Ἰουδέας 3.2 λέγων, μετανοεῖτε, ἤγγικεν γὰρ ἡ βασιλεία τῶν οὐρανῶν. 3.3 οὗτος γάρ ἐστιν ὁ ῥηθὶς διὰ Ἠσαΐου τοῦ προφήτου λέγοντος, «φωνὴ βοῶντος ἐν τῇ ἐρήμῳ, ἑτοιμάσατε τὴν ὁδὸν κυρίου, εὐθίας ποιεῖται τὰς τρίβους» αὐτοῦ.

3.4 αὐτὸς δὲ ὁ Ἰωάννης εἶχεν τὸ ἔνδυμα αὐτοῦ ἀπὸ τριχῶν καμήλου καὶ ζώνην δερματίνην περὶ τὴν ὀσφὺν αὐτοῦ, ἡ δὲ τροφὴ ἦν αὐτοῦ ἀκρίδες καὶ μέλι ἄγριον.

3.5 τότε ἐξεπορεύετο πρὸς αὐτὸν Ἱεροσόλυμα καὶ πᾶσα ἡ Ἰουδέα καὶ πᾶσα ἡ περίχωρος τοῦ Ἰορδάνου, 3.6 καὶ ἐβαπτίζοντο ἐν τῷ Ἰορδάνῃ ποταμῷ ἐξομολογούμενοι τὰς ἁμαρτίας αὐτῶν.

3.7 ἰδὼν δὲ πολλοὺς τῶν Φαρισαίων καὶ Σαδδουκαίων ἐρχομένους ἐπὶ τὸ βάπτισμα αὐτοῦ εἶπεν αὐτοῖς, γεννήματα ἐχιδνῶν, τίς ὑπέδειξεν ὑμῖν φυγῖν ἀπὸ τῆς μελλούσης ὀργῆς;

3.8 ποιήσατε οὖν καρπὸν ἄξιον τῆς μετανοίας· 3.9 καὶ μὴ δόξητε λέγιν ἐν ἑαυτοῖς, πατέρα ἔχομεν τὸν Ἀβραάμ, λέγω γὰρ ὑμῖν ὅτι δύναται ὁ θεὸς ἐκ τῶν λίθων τούτων ἐγεῖραι τέκνα τῷ Ἀβραάμ. 3.10 ἤδη δὲ ἡ ἀξίνη πρὸς τὴν ῥίζαν τῶν δένδρων κεῖται· πᾶν οὖν δένδρον μὴ ποιοῦν καρπὸν καλὸν ἐκκόπτεται καὶ εἰς πῦρ βάλλεται.

3.11 ἐγὼ μὲν γὰρ ὑμᾶς βαπτίζω ἐν ὕδατι εἰς μετάνοιαν· ὁ

take along the child and his mother and go into a land of Israel, for they have died, those seeking the life/soul of the child.   2.21 And the (he), having been aroused, he took the child and his mother and went into a land of Israel.

2.22 But having heard that Archelaus rules Judea instead of his father Herod, he was afraid to go there; and having been instructed with/by a dream, he departed into the parts of Galilee,   2.23 and having come he settled in a city being called Nazareth, so that might be fulfilled the (thing) having been spoken through the prophets that he will be called a Nazarene.

3.1 And in those days arrives John the baptizer, preaching/heralding in the desert/wilderness of Judea, 3.2 saying: Repent ye, for the kingdom of the heavens/skies has come near.   3.3 For this (one) is the (one) having been spoken *of* through Isaiah the prophet, saying: A VOICE CRYING IN THE DESERT/WILDERNESS, PREPARE YE THE ROAD/WAY OF *the* LORD, MAKE YE STRAIGHT HIS PATHS.

3.4 And John himself had his garment from hairs of a camel and a leather belt around his loin, and the food of him was grasshoppers and wild honey.

3.5 Then they went out to him, Jerusalem and all Judea and all the surrounding region of the Jordan, 3.6 and they were baptized in the Jordan River, confessing their faults/sins.

3.7 And seeing many of the Pharisees and Sadducees coming to the baptism of him/his baptism, he said to them: Generated (things) from snakes, who warned ye to flee from the coming anger/wrath?

3.8 Therefore, make ye fruit worthy of the repentance; 3.9 and think ye not to say among yourselves, we hold/have the father Abraham, for I say to ye that God is able out of these stones to raise up children for Abraham.   3.10 And already the axe is laid to the root of the trees; therefore, every tree making not good fruit is cut out and put to fire/ thrown into a fire.

3.11 I, indeed, I baptize ye, in repentance,

δὲ ὀπίσω μου ἐρχόμενος ἰσχυρότερός μού ἐστιν, οὗ οὐκ εἰμὶ ἱκανὸς τὰ ὑποδήματα βαστάσαι· αὐτὸς ὑμᾶς βαπτίσι ἐν πνεύματι ἁγίῳ καὶ πυρί· 3.12 οὗ τὸ πτύον ἐν τῇ χειρὶ αὐτοῦ, καὶ διακαθαριεῖ τὴν ἅλωνα αὐτοῦ, καὶ συνάξει τὸν σῖτον αὐτοῦ εἰς τὴν ἀποθήκην, τὸ δὲ ἄχυρον κατακαύσι πυρὶ ἀσβέστῳ.

3.13 τότε παραγίνεται ὁ Ἰησοῦς ἀπὸ τῆς Γαλιλαίας ἐπὶ τὸν Ἰορδάνην πρὸς τὸν Ἰωάννην τοῦ βαπτισθῆναι ὑπ' αὐτοῦ. 3.14 ὁ δὲ Ἰωάννης διεκώλυεν αὐτὸν λέγων, Ἐγὼ χρείαν ἔχω ὑπὸ σοῦ βαπτισθῆναι, καὶ σὺ ἔρχῃ πρός με;

3.15 ἀποκριθεὶς δὲ ὁ Ἰησοῦς εἶπεν πρὸς αὐτόν, ἄφες ἄρτι, οὕτως γὰρ πρέπον ἐστὶν ἡμῖν πληρῶσαι πᾶσαν δικαιοσύνην. τότε ἀφίησιν αὐτόν. 3.16 βαπτισθεὶς δὲ ὁ Ἰησοῦς εὐθὺς ἀνέβη ἀπὸ τοῦ ὕδατος· καὶ ἰδοὺ ἀνεῴχθησαν οἱ οὐρανοί, καὶ εἶδεν πνεῦμα θεοῦ καταβαῖνον ὡσεὶ περιστερὰν καὶ ἐρχόμενον ἐπ' αὐτόν· 3.17 καὶ ἰδοὺ φωνὴ ἐκ τῶν οὐρανῶν λέγουσα, οὗτός ἐστιν ὁ υἱός μου ὁ ἀγαπητός, ἐν ᾧ εὐδόκησα.

4.1 Τότε ὁ Ἰησοῦς ἀνήχθη ὑπὸ τοῦ πνεύματος εἰς τὴν ἔρημον, πειρασθῆναι ὑπὸ τοῦ διαβόλου. 4.2 καὶ νηστεύσας ἡμέρας τεσσεράκοντα καὶ τεσσεράκοντα νύκτας ὕστερον ἐπίνασεν.

4.3 καὶ προσελθὼν ὁ πιράζων εἶπεν αὐτῷ, εἰ υἱὸς εἶ τοῦ θεοῦ, εἰπὸν ἵνα οἱ λίθοι οὗτοι ἄρτοι γένωνται.

4.4 ὁ δὲ ἀποκριθεὶς εἶπεν, γέγραπται, «οὐκ ἐπ' ἄρτῳ μόνῳ ζήσεται ὁ ἄνθρωπος, ἀλλ' ἐπὶ παντὶ ῥήματι ἐκπορευομένῳ διὰ στόματος θεοῦ.»

4.5 τότε παραλαμβάνι αὐτὸν ὁ διάβολος εἰς τὴν ἁγίαν πόλιν, καὶ ἔστησεν αὐτὸν ἐπὶ τὸ πτερύγιον τοῦ ἱεροῦ, 4.6 καὶ λέγει αὐτῷ,. εἰ υἱὸς εἶ τοῦ θεοῦ, βάλε σεαυτὸν κάτω· γέγραπται γὰρ ὅτι «τοῖς ἀγγέλοις αὐτοῦ ἐντελεῖτε περὶ σοῦ» καὶ «ἐπὶ χειρῶν ἀροῦσίν σε, μήποτε προσκόψῃς πρὸς λίθον τὸν πόδα σου.» 4.7 ἔφη αὐτῷ ὁ Ἰησοῦς, πάλιν γέγραπται, «οὐκ ἐκπιράσεις κύριον τὸν θεόν σου.» 4.8 πάλιν παραλαμβάνει αὐτὸν ὁ διάβολος εἰς ὄρος ὑψηλὸν λίαν, καὶ δίκνυει αὐτῷ πάσας

with water; but the (one) coming behind me is greater than me, of whom I am not fit/sufficient to bear the sandals; he, he will baptize ye with a holy spirit and with fire; 3.12 of whom the fan *is* in his hand, and he will cleanse/sift his threshing floor/threshing, and he will gather his grain into the storehouse, but the chaff he will burn up with inextinguishable fire.

3.13 Then Jesus arrives from Galilee upon the Jordan to John from the (thing) to be baptized by him. 3.14 But John was restraining him, saying: I, I have a need to be baptized by you; and you, you would come to me?

3.15 But, answering, Jesus said to him: Let it be now, for thus it is proper for us to fulfill all justness. Then he allows him. 3.16 And Jesus, having been baptized, came up immediately from the water; and behold, the skies were opened and he saw a spirit of God/God's spirit descending as a dove and coming upon him; 3.17 and behold, a voice out of the skies, saying: This (one) is my beloved son, with whom I was well pleased.

4.1 Then Jesus was led up by the spirit into the desert/wilderness, to be tempted/tested by the devil. 4.2 And having fasted forty days and forty nights, he hungered afterwards.

4.3 And approaching, the (one) testing *him* said to him: If you are a son of God, you say to the stones that they might become loaves.

4.4 But the (he) answering, he said: It has been written: NOT BY BREAD ALONE WILL THE MAN/HUMAN LIVE, BUT BY EVERY WORD PROCEEDING THROUGH GOD'S MOUTH.

4.5 Then the devil takes him along into the holy city, and he stood him upon the wing/pinion of the *outer* temple, 4.6 and he says to him: If you are a son of God, you throw yourself down; for it has been written that HE WILL COMMAND HIS MESSENGERS/ANGELS CONCERNING YOU AND THEY WILL BEAR YOU UPON HANDS, LEST YOU MIGHT STRIKE YOUR FOOT TO A STONE. 4.7 Jesus said to him: Again, it has been written: YOU WILL NOT TEST *the* LORD YOUR GOD. 4.8 Again the devil takes him along to a very high mountain, and he shows to him all

5

τὰς βασιλίας τοῦ κόσμου καὶ τὴν δόξαν αὐτῶν, 4.9 καὶ εἶπεν αὐτῷ, ταῦτά σοι πάντα δώσω ἐὰν πεσὼν προσκυνήσῃς μοι.

4.10 τότε λέγει αὐτῷ ὁ Ἰησοῦς, ὕπαγε, Σατανᾶ· γέγραπται γάρ, «κύριον τὸν θεόν σου προσκυνήσῃς καὶ αὐτῷ» μόνῳ «λατρεύσις.»

4.11 τότε ἀφίησιν αὐτὸν ὁ διάβολος, καὶ ἰδοὺ ἄγγελοι προσῆλθον καὶ διηκόνουν αὐτῷ. 4.12 ἀκούσας δὲ Ἰωάννης ὅτι παρεδόθη ἀνεχώρησεν εἰς τὴν Γαλιλαίαν. 4.13 καὶ καταλιπὼν τὴν Ναζαρὰ ἐλθὼν κατώκησεν εἰς Καφαρναοὺμ τὴν παραθαλασσίαν ἐν ὁρίοις Ζαβουλὼν καὶ Νεφθαλείμ· 4.14 ἵνα πληρωθῇ τὸ ῥηθὲν διὰ Ἡσαΐου τοῦ προφήτου λέγοντος, 4.15 «γῆ Ζαβουλὼν καὶ γῆ Νεφθαλείμ, ὁδὸν θαλάσσης, πέραν τοῦ Ἰορδάνου, Γαλιλαία τῶν ἐθνῶν, 4.16 ὁ λαὸς ὁ καθήμενος ἐν σκότι φῶς ἶδεν μέγα, καὶ τοῖς καθημένοις ἐν χώρᾳ καὶ σκιᾷ θανάτου φῶς ἀνέτιλεν αὐτοῖς.»

4.17 ἀπὸ τότε ἤρξατο ὁ Ἰησοῦς κηρύσσιν καὶ λέγιν, μετανοεῖτε, ἤγγικεν γὰρ ἡ βασιλεία τῶν οὐρανῶν.

4.18 περιπατῶν δὲ παρὰ τὴν θάλασσαν τῆς Γαλιλαίας εἶδεν δύο ἀδελφούς, Σίμωνα τὸν λεγόμενον Πέτρον καὶ Ἀνδρέαν τὸν ἀδελφὸν αὐτοῦ, βάλλοντας ἀμφίβληστρον εἰς τὴν θάλασσαν· ἦσαν γὰρ ἁλιεῖς. 4.19 καὶ λέγει αὐτοῖς, δεῦτε ὀπίσω μου, καὶ ποιήσω ὑμᾶς ἁλιεῖς ἀνθρώπων. 4.20 οἱ δὲ εὐθέως ἀφέντες τὰ δίκτυα ἠκολούθησαν αὐτῷ.

4.21 καὶ προβὰς ἐκεῖθεν ἶδεν ἄλλους δύο ἀδελφούς, Ἰάκωβον τὸν τοῦ Ζεβεδαίου καὶ Ἰωάννην τὸν ἀδελφὸν αὐτοῦ, ἐν τῷ πλοίῳ μετὰ Ζεβεδαίου τοῦ πατρὸς αὐτῶν καταρτίζοντας τὰ δίκτυα αὐτῶν· καὶ ἐκάλεσεν αὐτούς. 4.22 οἱ δὲ εὐθέως ἀφέντες τὸ πλοῖον καὶ τὸν πατέρα αὐτῶν ἠκολούθησαν αὐτῷ.

4.23 καὶ περιῆγεν ὁ Ἰησοῦς ἐν τῇ Γαλιλαίᾳ, διδάσκων ἐν ταῖς συναγωγαῖς αὐτῶν καὶ κηρύσσων τὸ εὐαγγέλιον τῆς βασιλίας καὶ θεραπεύων πᾶσαν νόσον καὶ πᾶσαν μαλακίαν ἐν τῷ λαῷ. 4.24 καὶ ἀξῆλθεν ἡ ἀκοὴ αὐτοῦ εἰς πᾶσαν τὴν Συρίαν· καὶ προσήνεγκαν αὐτῷ πάντας τοὺς κακῶς ἔχοντας ποικίλαις

the kingdoms of the world and the glory/fame/reputa-
tion of them,   4.9 and he said to him: All these
(things) I will give to you if you would fall *down* and
worship me.

4.10   Then Jesus says to him: You go away, Satan;
for it has been written: *the* LORD YOUR GOD YOU WILL
WORSHIP AND FOR HIM ALONE YOU WILL SERVE.

4.11   Then the devil leaves him, and behold,
messengers/angels came near and were ministering to
him.   4.12 And having heard that John was delivered up
he withdrew into Galilee.   4.13 And having left Nazareth, going, he settled in Capernaum, the (one) beside
the sea in boundaries of Zebulon and Naphthali;
4.14 that might be fulfilled the (thing) having been
spoken through Isaiah the prophet, saying: 4.15 A
LAND OF ZEBULON AND A LAND OF NAPHTHALI, A ROAD FROM A
SEA, BEYOND THE JORDAN, GALILEE OF THE ETHNICS;   4.16
THE PEOPLE, THE (ONE) SITTING IN DARKNESS, SAW A GREAT
LIGHT, AND TO THOSE SITTING IN A REGION AND IN A
SHADOW OF DEATH, A LIGHT SPRANG UP FOR THEM.

4.17   From then/that time Jesus began to herald/
preach and to say: Repent ye, for the kingdom of the
skies/heavens has come near.

4.18   And walking alongside the sea of Galilee he
saw two brothers, Simon, the (one) being called Peter,
and Andrew his brother, casting a net into the sea,
for they were fishers.   4.19 And he says to them: Ye
come behind me, and I will make ye fishers of men.
4.20 And the (they), immediately leaving the nets,
they followed with him.

4.21   And going on from there, he saw two other
brothers, James the (one) from Zebedee and John his
brother, in the boat with Zebedee their father, mend-
ing/fitting their nets; and he called them.   4.22 And
the (they), immediately leaving the boat and their
father, they followed with him.

4.23   And Jesus went about in Galilee, teaching
in/among their congregations and heralding/preaching
the good message/gospel of the kingdom and healing
every disease and every ailment among the people.
4.24 And the report of him went out into all Syria;
and they brought forward to him all those having badly

νόσοις καὶ βασάνου συνεχομένους καὶ δεμονιαζομένους καὶ σεληνιαζομένους καὶ παραλυτικούς, καὶ ἐθεράπευσεν αὐτούς.

4.25 καὶ ἠκολούθησαν αὐτῷ ὄχλοι πολλοὶ ἀπὸ τῆς Γαλιλαίας καὶ Δεκαπόλεως καὶ Ἱεροσολύμων καὶ Ἰουδαίας καὶ πέραν τοῦ Ἰορδάνου.

5.1 Ἰδὼν δὲ τοὺς ὄχλους ἀνέβη εἰς τὸ ὄρος· καὶ καθίσαντος αὐτοῦ προσῆλθαν αὐτῷ οἱ μαθηταὶ αὐτοῦ· 5.2 καὶ ἀνοίξας τὸ στόμα αὐτοῦ ἐδίδασκεν αὐτοὺς λέγων, 5.3 μακάριοι οἱ πτωχοὶ τῷ πνεύματι, ὅτι αὐτῶν ἐστιν ἡ βασιλία τῶν οὐρανῶν. 5.4 μακάριοι οἱ πενθοῦντες, ὅτι αὐτοὶ παρακληθήσονται. 5.5 μακάριοι οἱ πραεῖς, ὅτι αὐτοὶ κληρονομήσουσιν τὴν γῆν. 5.6 μακάριοι οἱ πινῶντες καὶ διψῶντες τὴν δικαιοσύνην, ὅτι αὐτοὶ χορτασθήσονται.

5.7 μακάριοι οἱ ἐλεήμονες, ὅτι αὐτοὶ ἐλεηθήσονται.

5.8 μακάριοι οἱ καθαροὶ τῇ καρδίᾳ, ὅτι αὐτοὶ τὸν θεὸν ὄψονται.

5.9 μακάριοι οἱ ἰρηνοποιοί, ὅτι αὐτοὶ υἱοὶ θεοῦ κληθήσονται.

5.10 μακάριοι οἱ δεδιωγμένοι ἕνεκεν δικαιοσύνης, ὅτι αὐτῶν ἐστιν ἡ βασιλεία τῶν οὐρανῶν. 5.11 μακάριοί ἐστε ὅταν ὀνειδίσωσιν ὑμᾶς καὶ διώξουσιν καὶ εἴπωσιν πᾶν πονηρὸν καθ' ὑμῶν ψευδόμενοι ἕνεκεν ἐμοῦ· 5.12 χαίρεται καὶ ἀγαλλιᾶσθε, ὅτι ὁ μισθὸς ὑμῶν πολὺς ἐν τοῖς οὐρανοῖς· οὕτως γὰρ ἐδίωξαν τοὺς προφήτας τοὺς πρὸ ὑμῶν. 5.13 ὑμῖς ἐστε τὸ ἅλας τῆς γῆς· ἐὰν δὲ τὸ ἅλα μωρανθῇ, ἐν τίνι ἁλισθήσεται; εἰς οὐδὲν ἰσχύει ἔτι εἰ μὴ βληθὲν ἔξω καταπατῖσθε ὑπὸ τῶν ἀνθρώπων.

5.14 ὑμεῖς ἐσται τὸ φῶς τοῦ κόσμου. οὐ δύναται πόλις κρυβῆναι ἐπάνω ὄρους κειμένη· 5.15 οὐδὲ κέουσιν λύχνον καὶ τιθέασιν αὐτὸν ὑπὸ τὸν μόδιον ἀλλ' ἐπὶ τὴν λυχνίαν, καὶ λάμπι

various diseases and (those) suffering from torments and *those* being demon-possessed and *those* being moon-struck and *those* being paralyzed, and he healed/treated them.

4.25   And many crowds followed with him, from Galilee and Decapolis and Jerusalem and Judea and beyond the Jordan.

5.1   And having seen the crowds, he went up to the mountain; and from him having been seated, his learners/pupils came near to him;   5.2 and opening his mouth, he taught them, saying: 5.3 The poor (ones) in the spirit *are* happy (ones), because of them is the kingdom of the skies/heavens.   5.4 The (ones) mourning *are* happy (ones), because they will be comforted.   5.5 The gentle (ones) *are* happy (ones), because they will inherit the land.   5.6 The (ones)   hungering and thirsting for   justness/justice   *are*   happy   (ones), because they will be satisfied.

5.7   The merciful (ones) *are* happy (ones), because they will be shown mercy.

5.8   The clean (ones) in the heart *are* happy (ones), because they will see God.

5.9   The peacemakers *are* happy (ones), because they will be called sons of God.

5.10   Those/the (ones) having been prosecuted for the sake of justness/justice *are* happy (ones), because of them is the kingdom of the skies/heavens.   5.11 Happy are ye when they might reproach ye and they will prosecute *ye* and they might say every evil (thing) against ye, lying, for the sake of/on account of me; 5.12 rejoice ye and exult ye, because the reward of ye *is* much in the skies/heavens, for so they prosecuted/persecuted the prophets before ye.   5.13 Ye, ye are the salt of the earth; but if the salt become tasteless, by what will it be salted/seasoned?   In/for nothing is it strong still except from throwing out to be trodden down by the men/humans.

5.14   Ye, ye are the light of the world. A city being set upon a mountain is not able to be hidden; 5.15 neither light they a lamp and place it under the dry-measure but upon the lampstand, and it lightens

7

πᾶσιν τοῖς ἐν τῇ οἰκίᾳ. 5.16 οὕτως λαμψάτω τὸ φῶς ὑμῶν ἔμπροσθεν τῶν ἀνθρώπων, ὅπως ἴδωσιν ὑμῶν τὰ καλὰ ἔργα καὶ δοξάσωσιν τὸν πατέρα ὑμῶν τὸν ἐν τοῖς οὐρανοῖς.

5.17 μὴ νομίσητε ὅτι ἦλθον καταλῦσαι τὸν νόμον ἢ τοὺς προφήτας· οὐκ ἦλθον καταλῦσαι ἀλλὰ πληρῶσαι.

5.18 ἀμὴν γὰρ λέγω ὑμῖν, ἕως ἂν παρέλθῃ ὁ οὐρανὸς καὶ ἡ γῆ, ἰῶτα ἓν ἢ μία κεραία οὐ μὴ παρέλθῃ ἀπὸ τοῦ νόμου ἕως ἂν πάντα γένηται. 5.19 ὃς ἐὰν οὖν λύσῃ μίαν τῶν ἐντολῶν τούτων τῶν ἐλαχίστων καὶ διδάξῃ οὕτως τοὺς ἀνθρώπους, ἐλάχιστος κληθήσεται ἐν τῇ βασιλίᾳ τῶν οὐρανῶν· ὃς δ' ἂν ποιήσῃ καὶ διδάξῃ, οὗτος μέγας κληθήσετε ἐν τῇ βασιλίᾳ τῶν οὐρανῶν. 5.20 λέγω γὰρ ὑμῖν ὅτι ἐὰν μὴ περισσεύσῃ ὑμῶν ἡ δικαιοσύνη πλεῖον τῶν γραμματέων καὶ Φαρισαίων, οὐ μὴ εἰσέλθηται εἰς τὴν βασιλείαν τῶν οὐρανῶν.

5.21 ἠκούσατε ὅτι ἐρρέθη τοῖς ἀρχαίοις, «οὐ φονεύσεις·» ὃς δ' ἂν φονεύσῃ, ἔνοχος ἔσται τῇ κρίσει. 5.22 ἐγὼ δὲ λέγω ὑμῖν ὅτι πᾶς ὁ ὀργιζόμενος τῷ ἀδελφῷ αὐτοῦ ἔνοχος ἔστε τῇ κρίσει· ὃς δ' ἂν εἴπῃ τῷ ἀδελφῷ αὐτοῦ, ῥακά, ἔνοχος ἔσται τῷ συνεδρίῳ· ὃς δ' ἂν εἴπῃ, μωρέ, ἔνοχος ἔστε εἰς τὴν γέενναν τοῦ πυρός.

5.23 ἐὰν οὖν προσφέρῃς τὸ δῶρόν σου ἐπὶ τὸ θυσιαστήριον κἀκεῖ μνησθῇς ὅτι ὁ ἀδελφός σου ἔχι τι κατὰ σοῦ, 5.24 ἄφες ἐκῖ τὸ δῶρόν σου ἔμπροσθεν τοῦ θυσιαστηρίου, καὶ ὕπαγε πρῶτον διαλλάγηθι τῷ ἀδελφῷ σου, καὶ τότε ἐλθὼν πρόσφερε τὸ δῶρόν σου.

5.25 ἴσθι εὐνοῶν τῷ ἀντιδίκῳ σου ταχὺ ἕως ὅτου εἶ μετ' αὐτοῦ ἐν τῇ ὁδῷ, μήποτέ σε παραδῷ ὁ ἀντίδικος τῷ κριτῇ, καὶ ὁ κριτὴς τῷ ὑπηρέτῃ, καὶ εἰς φυλακὴν βληθήσῃ·

5.26 ἀμὴν λέγω σοι, οὐ μὴ ἐξέλθῃς ἐκῖθεν ἕως ἂν ἀποδῷς τὸν ἔσχατον κοδράντην.

5.27 ἠκούσατε ὅτι ἐρρέθη, «οὐ μοιχεύσεις.» 5.28 ἐγὼ δὲ

for all those in the house. 5.16 So/thus let shine the light of ye/your light before the men/humans, so that they might see your good works and they might glorify the father of ye/your father, the (one) in the skies/heavens.

5.17 Think ye not that I came to destroy the law or the prophets; I came not to destroy but to fulfill.

5.18 For truly I say to ye: Until the sky/heaven and the earth would pass away, one iota or one hook by no means may pass away from the law until all (things) might happen. 5.19 Therefore, whoever might destroy/loose one of the least of these commands and might teach the men/humans so, he will be called least in the kingdom of the skies/heavens; but who ever might do and might teach *them*, this (one) will be called great in the kingdom of the heavens. 5.20 For I say to ye that unless the justness/justice of ye might abound more than *that* of the scribes and Pharisees, by no means might ye enter into the kingdom of the heavens/skies.

5.21 Ye heard that it was said to the ancients: YOU WILL NOT MURDER; and who ever might murder, he will be bound for the judgment. 5.22 But I, I say to ye that every one being angry with his brother will be guilty/bound for the judgment; and who ever might say to his brother: Numbskull, he will be liable/bound to the council; and who ever might say: Fool, he will be liable to the hell of the fire.

5.23 Then, if you may offer your gift upon the altar and there you might remember that your brother holds something against you, 5.24 leave your gift there before the altar, and you go first, be reconciled with your brother, and then, coming, you offer your gift.

5.25 Be you agreeing with your adversary quickly while you are with him on the road, lest your adversary might deliver you to the judge, and the judge to the servant/assistant and you be thrown into prison.

5.26 Truly I say to you, by no means might you come out from there until you would repay the last quadrans/penny.

5.27 Ye heard that it was said: YOU WILL NOT *do*

λέγω ὑμῖν ὅτι πᾶς ὁ βλέπων γυναῖκα πρὸς τὸ ἐπιθυμῆσε αὐτὴν ἤδη ἐμοίχευσεν αὐτὴν ἐν τῇ καρδίᾳ αὐτοῦ.

5.29 εἰ δὲ ὁ ὀφθαλμός σου ὁ δεξιὸς σκανδαλίζι σε, ἔξελε αὐτὸν καὶ βάλε ἀπὸ σοῦ· συμφέρι γάρ σοι ἵνα ἀπόληται ἓν τῶν μελῶν σου καὶ μὴ ὅλον τὸ σῶμά σου βληθῇ εἰς γέενναν. 5.30 καὶ εἰ ἡ δεξιά σου χεὶρ σκανδαλίζι σε, ἔκκοψον αὐτὴν καὶ βάλε ἀπὸ σοῦ· συμφέρει γάρ σοι ἵνα ἀπόληται ἓν τῶν μελῶν σου καὶ μὴ ὅλον τὸ σῶμά σου εἰς γέενναν ἀπέλθῃ. 5.31 ἐρρέθη δέ, « ὃς ἂν ἀπολύσῃ τὴν γυναῖκα αὐτοῦ, δότω αὐτῇ ἀποστάσιον.» 5.32 ἐγὼ δὲ λέγω ὑμῖν ὅτι πᾶς ὁ ἀπολύων τὴν γυναῖκα αὐτοῦ παρεκτὸς λόγου πορνίας ποιεῖ αὐτὴν μοιχευθῆναι, καὶ ὃς ἐὰν ἀπολελυμένην γαμήσῃ μοιχᾶτε.

5.33 πάλιν ἠκούσατε ὅτι ἐρρέθη τοῖς ἀρχαίοις, «οὐκ ἐφιορκήσεις, ἀποδώσεις» δὲ «τῷ κυρίῳ τοὺς ὅρκους σου.»

5.34 ἐγὼ δὲ λέγω ὑμῖν μὴ ὀμόσαι ὅλως· μήτε ἐν τῷ οὐρανῷ, ὅτι θρόνος ἐστὶν τοῦ θεοῦ· 5.35 μήτε ἐν τῇ γῇ, ὅτι ὑποπόδιόν ἐστιν τῶν ποδῶν αὐτοῦ· μήτε εἰς Ἱεροσόλυμα, ὅτι πόλις ἐστὶν τοῦ μεγάλου βασιλέως· 5.36 μήτε ἐν τῇ κεφαλῇ σου ὀμόσῃς, ὅτι οὐ δύνασαι μίαν τρίχα λευκὴν ποιῆσαι ἢ μέλαιναν. 5.37 ἔστω δὲ ὁ λόγος ὑμῶν ναὶ ναί, οὒ οὔ· τὸ δὲ περισσὸν τούτων ἐκ τοῦ πονηροῦ ἐστιν.

5.38 ἠκούσατε ὅτι ἐρρέθη, « ὀφθαλμὸν ἀντὶ ὀφθαλμοῦ» καὶ «ὀδόντα ἀντὶ ὀδόντος.» 5.39 ἐγὼ δὲ λέγω ὑμῖν μὴ ἀντισταθῆναι τῷ πονηρῷ· ἀλλ’ ὅστις σε ραπίζι εἰς τὴν δεξιὰν σιαγόνα, στρέψον αὐτῷ καὶ τὴν ἄλλην· 5.40 καὶ τῷ θέλοντί σοι κριθῆναι καὶ τὸν χιτῶνά σου λαβῖν, ἄφες αὐτῷ καὶ τὸ ἱμάτιόν σου· 5.41 καὶ ὅστις σε ἐὰν ἐγγαρεύσει μίλιον ἕν, ὕπαγε μετ’ αὐτοῦ δύο. 5.42 τῷ αἰτοῦντί σε δός, καὶ τὸν θέλοντα ἀπὸ σοῦ δανίσασθαι μὴ ἀποστραφῇς.

5.43 ἠκούσατε ὅτι ἐρρέθη, « ἀγαπήσεις τὸν πλησίον σου»

ADULTERY. 5.28 But I, I say to ye that every one looking at a woman toward the (thing) to desire her has already *done* adultery *with* her in his heart.

5.29 And if your right eye causes you to stumble, take it out and throw (it) away from you; for it is an advantage for you that one of your members should itself perish and not your entire body be thrown into hell. 5.30 And if your right hand causes you to stumble, cut it off and throw it away from you; for it is an advantage for you that one of your members should itself perish and not your entire body should be gone away into hell. 5.31 And it was said: WHO EVER WOULD RELEASE/DISMISS HIS WOMAN, LET HIM GIVE HER A BILL OF SEPARATION. 5.32 But I, I say to ye that every one dismissing his woman, except from a reason of unchastity/prostitution, he makes her to *do* adultery, and who ever might marry a woman having been dismissed *does* adultery.

5.33 Again, ye heard that it was said to the ancients: YOU WILL NOT FAIL YOUR OATH, AND YOU WILL REPAY TO THE LORD YOUR OATHS.

5.34 But I, I say to ye not to swear at all; neither by the sky, because it is a throne of God; 5.35 nor by the earth, because it is a footstool of his feet; nor to Jerusalem, because it is a city of the great king; 5.36 nor might you swear by your head, because you are not able to make one hair white or black. 5.37 Let the saying/word of ye be: yes, yes; no, no; and the (thing) exceeding these is from the evil (one).

5.38 Ye heard that it was said: AN EYE FOR AN EYE AND A TOOTH FOR A TOOTH. 5.39 But I, I say to ye not to resist the evil (one); but whoever strikes you to the right cheek, you turn for him the other also; 5.40 And for the (one) wanting to judge you and to take your shirt, let go to him also your cloak; 5.41 And whoever would compel you for one mile, go you with him *for* two. 5.42 Give you to the (one) asking you, and you might not turn away from the (one) wanting to borrow from you.

5.43 Ye heard that it was said: YOU WILL LOVE YOUR NEIGHBOR/NEAR (ONE) AND YOU WILL HATE YOUR ENEMY.

καὶ μισήσεις τὸν ἐχθρόν σου. 5.44 ἐγὼ δὲ λέγω ὑμῖν, ἀγαπᾶτε τοὺς ἐχθροὺς ὑμῶν καὶ προσεύχεσθαι ὑπὲρ τῶν διωκόντων ὑμᾶς, 5.45 ὅπως γένησθε υἱοὶ τοῦ πατρὸς ὑμῶν τοῦ ἐν οὐρανοῖς, ὅτι τὸν ἥλιον αὐτοῦ ἀνατέλλι ἐπὶ πονηροὺς καὶ ἀγαθοὺς καὶ βρέχι ἐπὶ --. 5.46 ἐὰν γὰρ ἀγαπήσητε τοὺς ἀγαπῶντας ὑμᾶς, τίνα μισθὸν ἔχετε; οὐχὶ καὶ οἱ τελῶναι τὸ αὐτὸ ποιοῦσιν;

5.47 καὶ ἐὰν ἀσπάσησθε τοὺς ἀδελφοὺς ὑμῶν μόνον, τί περισσὸν ποιεῖται; οὐχὶ καὶ οἱ ἐθνικοὶ τὸ αὐτὸ ποιοῦσιν;

5.48 ἔσεσθε οὖν ὑμῖς τέλιοι ὡς ὁ πατὴρ ὑμῶν ὁ οὐράνιος τέλιός ἐστιν. 6.1 προσέχετε δὲ τὴν δικαιοσύνην ὑμῶν μὴ ποιεῖν ἔμπροσθεν τῶν ἀνθρώπων πρὸς τὸ θεαθῆνε αὐτοῖς· εἰ δὲ μή γε, μισθὸν οὐκ ἔχετε παρὰ τῷ πατρὶ ὑμῶν τῷ ἐν τοῖς οὐρανοῖς.

6.2 ὅταν οὖν ποιῇς ἐλεημοσύνην, μὴ σαλπίσῃς ἔμπροσθέν σου, ὥσπερ οἱ ὑποκριταὶ ποιοῦσιν ἐν τές συναγωγὲς καὶ ἐν ταῖς ῥύμαις, ὅπως δοξασθῶσιν ὑπὸ τῶν ἀνθρώπων· ἀμὴν ἀμὴν λέγω ὑμῖν, ἀπέχουσιν τὸν μισθὸν αὐτῶν. 6.3 σοῦ δὲ ποιοῦντος ἐλαιημοσύνην μὴ γνώτω ἡ ἀριστερά σου τί ποιεῖ ἡ δεξιά σου, 6.4 ὅπως ᾖ σου ἡ ἐλεημοσύνη ἐν τῷ κρυπτῷ· καὶ ὁ πατροῦ ὁ βλέπων ἐν τῷ κρυπτῷ ἀποδώσει σοι.

6.5 καὶ ὅταν προσεύχησθε, οὐκ ἔσεσθε ὡς οἱ ὑποκριταί· ὅτι φιλοῦσιν ἐν ταῖς συναγωγαῖς καὶ ἐν ταῖς γωνίαις τῶν πλατειῶν ἑστῶτες προσεύχεσθαι, ὅπως φανῶσιν τοῖς ἀνθρώποις· ἀμὴν λέγω ὑμῖν, ἀπέχουσιν τὸν μισθὸν αὐτῶν. 6.6 σὺ δὲ ὅταν προσεύχῃ, εἴσελθε εἰς τὸ ταμῖόν σου καὶ κλίσας τὴν θύραν σου πρόσευξε τῷ πατρί σου τῷ ἐν τῷ κρυπτῷ· καὶ ὁ πατήρ σου ὁ βλέπων ἐν τῷ κρυπτῷ ἀποδώσι σοι. 6.7 προσευχόμενοι δὲ μὴ βατταλογήσηται ὥσπερ οἱ ἐθνικοί, δοκοῦσιν γὰρ ὅτι ἐν τῇ πολυλογίᾳ αὐτῶν εἰσακουσθήσονται. 6.8 μὴ οὖν ὁμοιωθῆτε αὐτοῖς, οἶδεν γὰρ ὁ πατὴρ ὑμῶν ὧν χρίαν ἔχετε πρὸ τοῦ ὑμᾶς αἰτῆσαι αὐτόν.

6.9 οὕτως οὖν προσεύχεσθαι ὑμεῖς· πάτερ ἡμῶν ὁ ἐν τοῖς

5.44 But I, I say to ye: Love ye the enemies of ye and be ye praying in behalf of those pursuing/prosecuting ye, 5.45 so that ye may become sons of the father of ye, of the (one) in skies/heavens, because he causes his sun to rise upon evil (ones) and good (ones), and it rains upon *both*. 5.46 For if ye might love those loving ye, what reward have ye? Even the tax collectors, do they not the same?

5.47 And if ye might greet your brothers only, what excess do ye? Even the ethnics, do they not the same?

5.48 Ye, therefore, be ye complete/mature as your heavenly father is complete/mature. 6.1 And heed ye not to do your justness before the men/humans toward the (thing) to be beheld by them; otherwise, ye have not a reward with your father, with the (one) in the skies/heavens.

6.2 Then/therefore, when you may do charity, you might not sound a trumpet before you, as the pretenders/hypocrites do in the congregations and in the narrow streets, so that they might be glorified by the men; truly, truly I say to ye, they have their reward. 6.3 And of you doing charity, let not your left (hand) know what your right (hand) does, 6.4 so that your charity may be in secret; and the father, the (one) seeing in secret, he will repay to you.

6.5 And when ye may pray, be ye not as the pretenders/hypocrites; because they love to pray standing in the congregations and on the corners of the streets, so that they may be visible to the men/humans; truly I say to ye, they have their reward. 6.6 But you, whenever you may pray, enter you into your private room, and having closed your door, you pray to your father, to the (one) in secret; and your father, the (one) seeing in secret, he will repay to you. 6.7 And praying, babble ye not empty words as the ethnics *do*, for they think they will be heard in/by their many reasonings/much speaking. 6.8 Then/therefore ye should not be like them, for the father of ye/your father knows what need ye have before the (thing) of ye to ask him.

6.9 Therefore, ye, ye will pray thus: Our

οὐρανοῖς, ἁγιασθήτω τὸ ὄνομά σου, 6.10 ἐλθέτω ἡ βασιλεία σου, γενηθήτω τὸ θέλημά σου, ὡς ἐν οὐρανῷ καὶ ἐπὶ γῆς. 6.11 τὸν ἄρτον ἡμῶν τὸν ἐπιούσιον δὸς ἡμῖν σήμερον· 6.12 καὶ ἄφες ἡμῖν τὰ ὀφιλήματα ἡμῶν, ὡς καὶ ἡμῖς ἀφήκαμεν τοῖς ὀφιλέταις ἡμῶν· 6.13 καὶ μὴ εἰσενέγκῃς ἡμᾶς εἰς πειρασμόν, ἀλλὰ ῥῦσαι ἡμᾶς ἀπὸ τοῦ πονηροῦ. 6.14 ἐὰν γὰρ ἀφῆται τοῖς ἀνθρώποις τὰ παραπτώματα αὐτῶν, ἀφήσι καὶ ὑμῖν ὁ πατὴρ ὑμῶν ὁ οὐράνιος· 6.15 ἐὰν δὲ μὴ ἀφῆτε τοῖς ἀνθρώποις, οὐδὲ ὁ πατὴρ ὑμῶν ἀφήσει τὰ παραπτώματα ὑμῶν.

6.16 ὅταν δὲ νηστεύητε, μὴ γίνεσθε ὡς οἱ ὑποκριταὶ σκυθρωποί, ἀφανίζουσι γὰρ τὰ πρόσωπα αὐτῶν ὅπως φανῶσιν τοῖς ἀνθρώποις νηστεύοντες· ἀμὴν γὰρ λέγω ὑμῖν, ἀπέχουσιν τὸν μισθὸν αὐτῶν. 6.17 σὺ δὲ νηστεύων ἄλιψέ σου τὴν κεφαλὴν καὶ τὸ πρόσωπόν σου νίψαι, 6.18 ὅπως μὴ φανῇς τοῖς ἀνθρώποις νηστεύων ἀλλὰ τῷ πατρί σου τῷ ἐν τῷ κρυφαίῳ· καὶ ὁ πατήρ σου ὁ βλέπων ἐν τῷ κρυφαίῳ ἀποδώσι σοι. 6.19 μὴ θησαυρίζετε ὑμῖν θησαυροὺς ἐπὶ τῆς γῆς, ὅπου σὴς καὶ βρῶσις ἀφανίζει, καὶ ὅπου κλέπται διορύσσουσι καὶ κλέπτουσιν· 6.20 θησαυρίζετε δὲ ὑμῖν θησαυροὺς ἐν οὐρανῷ, ὅπου οὔτε σὴς οὔτε βρῶσις ἀφανίζει, καὶ ὅπου κλέπται οὐ διορύσσουσι καὶ κλέπτουσιν· 6.21 ὅπου γάρ ἐστιν ὁ θησαυρός σου, ἐκῖ ἔσται καὶ ἡ καρδία σου.

6.22 ὁ λύχνος τοῦ σώματός ἐστιν ὁ ὀφθαλμός. ἐὰν ᾖ ὁ ὀφθαλμός σου ἁπλοῦς, ὅλον τὸ σῶμά σου φωτινὸν ἔστε· 6.23 ἐὰν δὲ ὁ ὀφθαλμός σου πονηρὸς ᾖ, ὅλον τὸ σῶμά σου σκοτινὸν ἔσται. εἰ οὖν τὸ φῶς τὸ ἐν σοὶ σκότος ἐστίν, τὸ σκότος πόσον.

6.24 οὐδεὶς δύναται δυσὶ κυρίοις δουλεύειν· εἰ γὰρ τὸν ἕνα μισήσι καὶ τὸν ἕτερον ἀγαπήσι, ἢ ἑνὸς ἀνθέξετε καὶ τοῦ ἑτέρου καταφρονήσει· οὐ δύνασθε θεῷ δουλεύειν καὶ μαμωνᾷ.

6.25 διὰ τοῦτο λέγω ὑμῖν, μὴ μεριμνᾶται τῇ ψυχῇ ὑμῶν τί

father, the (one) in the skies/heavens, let your name be holy, 6.10 let your kingdom come, let your will be generated, as in heaven, also upon earth. 6.11 Our bread, that being necessary, give you to us today; 6.12 and forgive us our debts, as also we, we forgave to/for those debtors of us; 6.13 and bring us not into temptation/testing, but rescue us from the evil. 6.14 For if ye might forgive to/for the men the trespasses from them, the heavenly father of ye will also forgive ye; 6.15 but if ye might not forgive to/for the men/humans, neither will your heavenly father forgive your trespasses/the trespasses of ye.

6.16 And whenever ye may fast, become ye not sad (ones), as the pretenders/hypocrites *do*, for they disfigure their faces so that they might appear to the men *to be* fasting (ones); for truly I say to ye, they have their reward. 6.17 And you, *when* fasting, you anoint your head and you wash your face, 6.18 so that you might not appear to the men *to be* fasting, but to your father, to the (one) in secret; and your father, the (one) seeing in secret, he will repay you. 6.19 Store ye not up for ye stores *of things* upon the earth, where moth and rust disfigures *them,* and where thieves break through and steal; 6.20 but store ye up for ye stores/treasures in heaven, where neither moth nor rust disfigures *them*, and where thieves break not through and steal; 6.21 for where the store/treasure of you is, there will be also the heart of you/your heart.

6.22 The lamp of the body is the eye. If the eye of you/your eye may be sincere/sound, your entire body will be lightened; 6.23 but if the eye of you may be evil, your entire body will be darkened. Therefore, if the light, the (one) in you, is darkness, how great *is* the darkness.

6.24 No one is able to slave/be a slave for two lords; for either he will hate the one and love the other/different (one), or of one he will be devoted to and of the other/different (one) he will despise *him;* ye are not able to slave/be a slave to God and to money/riches/property.

6.25 Because of this I say to ye: Be ye not

11

φάγηται, μηδὲ τῷ σώματι ὑμῶν τί ἐνδύσησθε· οὐχὶ ἡ ψυχὴ πλεῖόν ἐστι τῆς τροφῆς καὶ τὸ σῶμα τοῦ ἐνδύματος; 6.26 ἐμβλέψαται εἰς τὰ πετινὰ τοῦ οὐρανοῦ ὅτι οὐ σπίρουσιν οὐδὲ θερίζουσιν οὐδὲ συνάγουσιν εἰς ἀποθήκας, καὶ ὁ πατὴρ ὑμῶν ὁ οὐράνιος τρέφι αὐτά· οὐχ ὑμεῖς μᾶλλον διαφέρεται αὐτῶν; 6.27 τίς δὲ ἐξ ὑμῶν μεριμνῶν δύναται προσθεῖναι ἐπὶ τὴν ἡλικίαν αὐτοῦ πῆχυν ἕνα; 6.28 καὶ περὶ ἐνδύματος τί μεριμνᾶται; καταμάθεται τὰ κρίνα τοῦ ἀγροῦ πῶς αὐξάνουσιν· οὐ κοπιῶσιν οὐδὲ νήθουσιν·

6.29 λέγω δὲ ὑμῖν ὅτι οὐδὲ Σολομὼν ἐν πάσῃ τῇ δόξῃ αὐτοῦ περιεβάλετο ὡς ἐν τούτων. 6.30 ἰ δὲ τὸν χόρτον τοῦ ἀγροῦ σήμερον ὄντα καὶ αὔριον εἰς κλίβανον βαλλόμενον ὁ θεὸς οὕτως ἀμφιέννυσιν, οὐ πολλῷ μᾶλλον ὑμᾶς, ὀλιγόπιστοι; 6.31 μὴ οὖν μεριμνήσητε λέγοντες, τί φάγωμεν; ἢ, τί πίωμεν; ἢ, τί περιβαλώμεθα; 6.32 ταῦτα γὰρ πάντα τὰ ἔθνη ἐπιζητοῦσιν· οἶδεν γὰρ ὁ θεὸς ὁ πατὴρ ὑμῶν ὅτι χρήζετε τούτων ἁπάντων. 6.33 ζητεῖτε δὲ πρῶτον τὴν βασιλείαν καὶ τὴν δικαιοσύνην αὐτοῦ, καὶ ταῦτα πάντα προστεθήσεται ὑμῖν. 6.34 μὴ οὖν μεριμνήσητε εἰς τὴν αὔριον, ἡ γὰρ αὔριον μεριμνήσι ἑαυτῆς· ἀρκετὸν τῇ ἡμέρᾳ ἡ κακία αὐτῆς.

7.1 Μὴ κρίνεται, ἵνα μὴ κριθῆτε· 7.2 ἐν ᾧ γὰρ κρίματι κρίνετε κριθήσεσθαι, καὶ ἐν ᾧ μέτρῳ μετρῖται μετρηθήσεται ὑμῖν.

7.3 τί δὲ βλέπεις τὸ κάρφος τὸ ἐν τῷ ὀφθαλμῷ τοῦ ἀδελφοῦ σου, τὴν δὲ δοκὸν ἐν τῷ σῷ ὀφθαλμῷ οὐ κατανοεῖς; 7.4 ἢ πῶς ἐρῖς τῷ ἀδελφῷ σου, ἀδελφέ, ἄφες ἐκβάλω τὸ κάρφος ἐκ τοῦ ὀφθαλμοῦ σου, καὶ ἰδοὺ ἡ δοκὸς ἐν τῷ ὀφθαλμῷ σου; 7.5 ὑποκριτά, ἔκβαλε πρῶτον ἐκ τοῦ ὀφθαλμοῦ σου τὴν δοκόν, καὶ τότε διαβλέψις ἐκβαλεῖν τὸ κάρφος ἐκ τοῦ ὀφθαλμοῦ τοῦ ἀδελφοῦ σου.

7.6 μὴ δῶτε τὸ ἅγιον τοῖς κυσίν, μηδὲ βάλητε τοὺς

anxious for the life/soul of ye, what ye may eat, neither for the body of ye, what ye may put on; is not the life/soul more *than* the food and the body *more than* the clothing? 6.26 Look ye carefully to the birds of the sky/heaven, because they sow not, neither *do* they reap nor *do* they gather into storehouses, and your heavenly father nourishes them; ye, *are* ye not of more value *than* them? 6.27 And who out of ye, being anxious, is able to add to his span of life/maturity one cubit? 6.28 And concerning clothing, why be ye anxious? Consider ye the lilies of the field, how they grow; they toil not nor *do* they spin;

6.29 but I say to ye that Solomon in all his reputation/glory/fame was certainly not dressed/clothed as one of them. 6.30 And if God so dresses/clothes the grass/hay, being of/from the field today and being thrown into a furnace tomorrow, not much more *for* ye, (ones) of little faith? 6.31 Therefore, be ye not worried, saying: What might we eat? Or, what might we drink? Or, what might we wear/put on? 6.32 For all these (things) the ethnics seek after; for God the father of ye/your father knows that ye have need of all these (things). 6.33 But seek ye first the kingdom and the justness/justice of him, and all these (things) will be added for ye. 6.34 Therefore, be ye not anxious in/*for* the morrow, for the morrow will be anxious of itself; sufficient for the day *is* the badness/evil of it.

7.1 Judge ye not, in order that ye be not judged; 7.2 for with what judgment ye judge ye will be judged, and with what measure ye measure, it will be measured to ye.

7.3 And why see you the splinter, the (one) in the eye of your brother, but you consider not the log in your eye? 7.4 Or how will you say to your brother: Brother, let me remove the splinter out of your eye, and behold, the log *is* in your eye? 7.5 Pretender/hypocrite, first remove the log out of the eye of you/ your eye, and then you will see clearly to remove the splinter out of the eye of your brother.

7.6 Give ye not the holy (thing) to the dogs,

μαργαρίτας ὑμῶν ἔμπροσθεν τῶν χοίρων, μήποτε καταπατήσωσιν αὐτοὺς ἐν τοῖς ποσὶν αὐτῶν καὶ στραφέντες ῥήξωσιν ὑμᾶς.

7.7 αἰτεῖτε, καὶ δοθήσεται ὑμῖν· ζητεῖτε, καὶ εὑρήσετε· κρούεται, καὶ ἀνοιγήσεται ὑμῖν. 7.8 πᾶς γὰρ ὁ αἰτῶν λαμβάνει καὶ ὁ ζητῶν εὑρίσκει καὶ τῷ κρούοντι ἀνοιγήσεται. 7.9 ἢ τίς ἐστιν ἐξ ὑμῶν ἄνθρωπος, ὃν αἰτήσει ὁ υἱὸς αὐτοῦ ἄρτον μὴ λίθον ἐπιδώσι αὐτῷ; 7.10 ἢ καὶ ἰχθὺν αἰτήσι μὴ ὄφιν ἐπιδώσει αὐτῷ; 7.11 εἰ οὖν ὑμῖς πονηροὶ ὄντες οἴδαται δόματα ἀγαθὰ διδόναι τοῖς τέκνοις ὑμῶν, πόσῳ μᾶλλον ὁ πατὴρ ὑμῶν ὁ ἐν τοῖς οὐρανοῖς δώσει ἀγαθὰ τοῖς αἰτοῦσιν αὐτόν. 7.12 πάντα οὖν ὅσα ἐὰν θέληται ἵνα ποιῶσιν ὑμῖν οἱ ἄνθρωποι, οὕτως καὶ ὑμῖς ποιεῖται αὐτοῖς· οὗτος γάρ ἐστιν ὁ νόμος καὶ οἱ προφῆται. 7.13 εἰσέλθατε διὰ τῆς στενῆς πύλης· ὅτι πλατῖα ἡ πύλη καὶ εὐρύχωρος ἡ ὁδὸς ἡ ἀπάγουσα εἰς τὴν ἀπώλιαν, καὶ πολλοί εἰσιν οἱ εἰσερχόμενοι δι' αὐτῆς· 7.14 τί στενὴ ἡ πύλη καὶ τεθλιμμένη ἡ ὁδὸς ἡ ἀπάγουσα εἰς τὴν ζωήν, καὶ ὀλίγοι εἰσὶν οἱ εὑρίσκοντες αὐτήν.

7.15 προσέχεται ἀπὸ τῶν ψευδοπροφητῶν, οἵτινες ἔρχονται πρὸς ὑμᾶς ἐν ἐνδύμασι προβάτων, ἔσωθεν δέ εἰσιν λύκοι ἅρπαγες. 7.16 ἀπὸ τῶν καρπῶν αὐτῶν ἐπιγνώσεσθε αὐτούς·

μήτι συλλέγουσιν ἀπὸ ἀκανθῶν σταφυλὰς ἢ ἀπὸ τριβόλων σῦκα;

7.17 οὕτω πᾶν δένδρον ἀγαθὸν καρποὺς καλοὺς ποιεῖ, τὸ δὲ σαπρὸν δένδρον καρποὺς πονηροὺς ποιεῖ· 7.18 οὐ δύναται δένδρον ἀγαθὸν καρποὺς πονηροὺς ποιεῖν, οὐδὲ δένδρον σαπρὸν καρποὺς καλοὺς ποιεῖν. 7.19 πᾶν δένδρον μὴ ποιοῦν καρπὸν καλὸν ἐκκόπτεται καὶ εἰς πῦρ βάλλεται. 7.20 ἄρα γε ἀπὸ τῶν καρπῶν αὐτῶν ἐπιγνώσεσθαι αὐτούς.

7.21 οὐ πᾶς ὁ λέγων μοι, κύριε κύριε, εἰσελεύσεται εἰς τὴν βασιλίαν τῶν οὐρανῶν, ἀλλ' ὁ ποιῶν τὰ θελήματα τοῦ πατρός μου τοῦ ἐν τοῖς οὐρανοῖς.

7.22 πολλοὶ ἐροῦσίν μοι ἐν ἐκείνῃ τῇ ἡμέρᾳ, κύριε κύριε, οὐ

neither throw ye your pearls before the pigs, lest they might trample them down with their feet and, turning, they might rend ye.

7.7 Ask ye, and it will be given to ye; seek ye, and ye will find; knock ye, and it will be opened to ye. 7.8 For every one asking receives, and the (one) seeking finds, and for the (one) knocking, it will be opened. 7.9 Or what man/human is out of ye, whom his son might ask *for* bread/a loaf -- he will not give a stone to him? 7.10 Or also he will ask *for* a fish -- he will not give a serpent to him? 7.11 Then if ye, being evil (ones), ye know to give good gifts to the children of ye, how much more the father of ye, the (one) in the skies/heavens, he will give good (things) to those asking him. 7.12 Therefore, all (things) what ever ye may wish that the men may do for ye, so also ye, ye do/be doing for them; for this is the law and the prophets. 7.13 Enter ye in through the narrow gate; because wide *is* the gate and broad *is* the road, the (one) leading off to the destruction, and many are the (ones) going in through it; 7.14 a narrow thing *is* the gate and having been made narrow *is* the (one) leading to the life, and few are those/the (ones) finding it.

7.15 Beware ye from the lying prophets, which/ who come to ye in garments of sheep, but from within they are greedy/rapacious wolves. 7.16 From their fruits/products ye will know them;

they gather not grapes from thorns or figs from thistles, *do they*?

7.17 Thus/so, every good tree makes good fruits, but the corrupt/rotten tree makes evil fruits/prod- ucts; 7.18 a good tree is not able to make evil fruits, neither *for* a corrupt tree to make good fruits. 7.19 Every tree not making good fruit is cut out/off and is thrown into a fire. 7.20 Then, indeed, ye recognize them from their fruits/products.

7.21 Not every one saying to me: Lord, lord, will enter into the kingdom of the skies/heavens, but the (one) doing the wishes/willed things of my father, of the (one) in the heavens/skies.

7.22 Many will say to me in that day: Lord,

13

τῷ σῷ ὀνόματι ἐπροφητεύσαμεν, καὶ τῷ σῷ ὀνόματι δεμόνια ἐξεβάλομεν, καὶ τῷ σῷ ὀνόματι δυνάμις πολλὰς ἐποιήσαμεν; 7.23 καὶ τότε ὁμολογήσω αὐτοῖς ὅτι οὐδέποτε ἔγνων ὑμᾶς· ἀποχωρεῖτε ἀπ' ἐμοῦ οἱ ἐργαζόμενοι τὴν ἀνομίαν. 7.24 πᾶς οὖν ὅστις ἀκούει μου τοὺς λόγους τούτους καὶ ποιεῖ αὐτοὺς ὁμοιωθήσεται ἀνδρὶ φρονίμῳ, ὅστις ᾠκοδόμησεν αὐτοῦ τὴν οἰκίαν ἐπὶ τὴν πέτραν. 7.25 καὶ κατέβη ἡ βροχὴ καὶ ἦλθον οἱ ποταμοὶ καὶ ἔπνευσαν οἱ ἄνεμοι καὶ προσέπεσαν τῇ οἰκίᾳ ἐκίνῃ, καὶ οὐκ ἔπεσεν, τεθεμελίωτο γὰρ ἐπὶ τὴν πέτραν.

7.26 καὶ πᾶς ὁ ἀκούων μου τοὺς λόγους τούτους καὶ μὴ ποιῶν αὐτοὺς ὁμοιωθήσεται ἀνδρὶ μωρῷ, ὅστις ᾠκοδόμησεν αὐτοῦ τὴν οἰκίαν ἐπὶ τὴν ἄμμον. 7.27 καὶ κατέβη ἡ βροχὴ καὶ ἦλθον οἱ ποταμοὶ καὶ -- καὶ προσέκοψαν τῇ οἰκίᾳ ἐκίνῃ, καὶ ἔπεσεν, καὶ ἦν ἡ πτῶσις αὐτῆς μεγάλη. 7.28 καὶ ἐγένετο ὅτε ἐτέλεσεν ὁ Ἰησοῦς τοὺς λόγους τούτους ἐξεπλήσσοντο ἐπὶ τῇ διδαχῇ αὐτοῦ οἱ ὄχλοι· 7.29 ἦν γὰρ διδάσκων αὐτοὺς ὡς ἐξουσίαν ἔχων καὶ οὐχ ὡς οἱ γραμματεῖς αὐτῶν.

8.1 Καταβάντος δὲ αὐτοῦ ἀπὸ τοῦ ὄρους ἠκολούθησαν αὐτῷ ὄχλοι πολλοί.

8.2 καὶ ἰδοὺ λεπρὸς προσελθὼν προσεκύνει αὐτῷ λέγων, κύριε, ἐὰν θέλῃς δύνασαί με καθαρίσαι. 8.3 καὶ ἐκτείνας τὴν χεῖρα αὐτοῦ ἥψατο αὐτοῦ λέγων, Θέλω, καθαρίσθητι· καὶ εὐθέως ἐκαθαρίσθη αὐτοῦ ἡ λέπρα. 8.4 καὶ λέγι αὐτῷ ὁ Ἰησοῦς, ὅρα μηδενὶ εἴπῃς, ἀλλὰ ὕπαγε σεαυτὸν δῖξον τῷ ἱερεῖ, καὶ προσένεγκε τὸ δῶρον ὃ προσέταξεν Μωϋσῆς, εἰς μαρτύριον αὐτοῖς.

8.5 εἰσελθόντος δὲ αὐτοῦ εἰς Καφαρναοὺμ προσῆλθεν αὐτῷ ἑκατόνταρχος παρακαλῶν αὐτὸν 8.6 καὶ λέγων, κύριε, ὁ παῖς μου βέβληται ἐν τῇ οἰκίᾳ παραλυτικός, δινῶς βασανιζόμενος. 8.7 καὶ λέγι αὐτῷ, ἀκολουθι μοι, ἐγὼ ἐλθὼν θεραπεύσω αὐτόν. 8.8 καὶ ἀποκριθεὶς ὁ ἑκατόνταρχος ἔφη, κύριε, οὐκ εἰμὶ ἱκανὸς ἵνα μου ὑπὸ τὴν στέγην εἰσέλθῃς· ἀλλὰ μόνον εἰπὲ λόγῳ, καὶ ἰαθήσεται ὁ παῖς μου. 8.9 καὶ γὰρ ἐγὼ ἄνθρωπός εἰμι ὑπὸ

14

lord, *was it* not in your name we prophesied, and in your name we put out demons, and in your name we made/did many powers? 7.23 And then I will profess to them: I never knew ye; go ye away from me, those working the lawlessness. 7.24 Therefore every (one) who hears these reasonings/sayings from me and does them will be likened to a prudent man, who built his house on the rock. 7.25 And the rain came down and the rivers came and the winds blew and they fell upon that house, and it fell not, for it had been founded on the rock.

7.26 And every one hearing these reasonings/sayings from me and not doing them, will be likened to a foolish man who built his house upon the sand. 7.27 And the rain came down and the rivers came also -- and they beat against that house, and it fell, and the falling of it was great. 7.28 And it happened/became, when Jesus finished these reasonings/sayings, *that* the crowds were astounded by the teaching/doctrine of him; 7.29 for he was teaching them as (one) holding authority, and not as/like their scribes.

8.1 And of him coming down from the mountain, many crowds followed him.

8.2 And behold a leper, coming near, worshiped him, saying: Lord, if you may want/wish, you are able to cleanse me. 8.3 And stretching forth his hand, he touched of him, saying: I want/wish, be you cleansed; and immediately his leprosy was cleansed. 8.4 And Jesus says to him: See *that* you might tell *it* to no one, but you go, show yourself to the priest, and you offer the gift which Moses commanded, in/for a testimony to them.

8.5 And from him having entered into Capernaum, a centurion came near to him, beseeching him 8.6 and saying: Lord, my boy has been laid in the house, a paralytic, being tormented terribly. 8.7 And he says to him: You follow me. I, going, I shall heal/treat him. 8.8 And answering, the centurion was saying: Lord, I am not fit/sufficient that you might enter under my roof; but you only speak by a word/saying and my boy will be healed. 8.9 For I also, I am a man

ἐξουσίαν τασσομένος, ἔχων ὑπ' ἐμαυτὸν στρατιώτας, καὶ λέγω τούτω, πορεύθητι, καὶ πορεύετε, καὶ ἄλλῳ, ἔρχου, καὶ ἔρχετε, καὶ τῷ δούλῳ μου, ποίησον τοῦτο, καὶ ποιεῖ.

8.10 ἀκούσας δὲ ὁ Ἰησοῦς ἐθαύμασεν καὶ εἶπεν τοῖς ἀκολουθοῦσιν, ἀμὴν λέγω ὑμῖν, οὐδὲ ἐν τῷ Ἰσραὴλ τοσαύτην πίστιν εὗρον.

8.11 λέγω δὲ ὑμῖν ὅτι πολλοὶ ἀπὸ ἀνατολῶν καὶ δυσμῶν ἥξουσιν καὶ ἀνακλιθήσονται μετὰ Ἀβραὰμ καὶ Ἰσὰκ καὶ Ἰακὼβ ἐν τῇ βασιλείᾳ τῶν οὐρανῶν· 8.12 οἱ δὲ υἱοὶ τῆς βασιλείας ἐκβληθήσονται εἰς τὸ σκότος τὸ ἐξώτερον· ἐκεῖ ἔστε ὁ κλαυθμὸς καὶ ὁ βρυγμὸς τῶν ὀδόντων. 8.13 καὶ εἶπεν ὁ Ἰησοῦς τῷ ἑκατοντάρχῃ, ὕπαγε, ὡς ἐπίστευσας γενηθήτω σοι. καὶ ἰάθη ὁ παῖς ἐν τῇ ὥρᾳ ἐκείνῃ. 8.14 καὶ ἐλθὼν ὁ Ἰησοῦς εἰς τὴν οἰκίαν Πέτρου εἶδεν τὴν πενθερὰν αὐτοῦ βεβλημένην καὶ πυρέσσουσαν· 8.15 καὶ ἥψατο τῆς χιρὸς αὐτῆς, καὶ ἀφῆκεν αὐτὴν ὁ πυρετός· καὶ ἠγέρθη καὶ διηκόνι αὐτοῖς. 8.16 ὀψίας δὲ γενομένης προσήνεγκαν αὐτῷ δαιμονιζομένους πολλούς· καὶ ἐξέβαλεν τὰ πνεύματα λόγῳ, καὶ πάντας τοὺς κακῶς ἔχοντας ἐθεράπευσεν· 8.17 ὅπως πληρωθῇ τὸ ῥηθὲν διὰ Ἠσαΐου τοῦ προφήτου λέγοντος, «αὐτὸς τὰς ἀσθενίας ἡμῶν ἔλαβεν καὶ τὰς νόσους ἐβάστασεν.» 8.18 ἰδὼν δὲ ὁ Ἰησοῦς ὄχλον περὶ αὐτὸν ἐκέλευσεν ἀπελθεῖν εἰς τὸ πέραν.

8.19 καὶ προσελθὼν εἷς γραμματεὺς εἶπεν αὐτῷ, διδάσκαλε, ἀκολουθήσω σοι ὅπου ἐὰν ἀπέρχῃ. 8.20 καὶ λέγει αὐτῷ ὁ Ἰησοῦς, αἱ ἀλώπεκες φωλεοὺς ἔχουσιν καὶ τὰ πετεινὰ τοῦ οὐρανοῦ κατασκηνώσις, ὁ δὲ υἱὸς τοῦ ἀνθρώπου οὐκ ἔχει ποῦ τὴν κεφαλὴν κλίνῃ.

8.21 ἕτερος δὲ τῶν μαθητῶν εἶπεν αὐτῷ, κύριε, ἐπίτρεψόν μοι πρῶτον ἀπελθεῖν καὶ θάψε τὸν πατέρα μου.

8.22 ὁ δὲ λέγει αὐτῷ, ἀκολούθι μοι, καὶ ἄφες τοὺς νεκροὺς θάψε τοὺς ἑαυτῶν νεκρούς.

8.23 καὶ ἐμβάντι αὐτῷ εἰς τὸ πλοῖον ἠκολούθησαν αὐτῷ οἱ μαθητὲ αὐτοῦ. 8.24 καὶ ἰδοὺ σισμὸς μέγας ἐγένετο ἐν τῇ

under ordering authority, having soldiers under my-self, and I say to this (one): you go, and he goes; and to another (one): you come, and he comes; and to my slave: you do this, and he does *it*.

8.10 And having heard *him*, Jesus was astonished, and he said to those following: Truly I say to ye, not even in Israel found I such faith.

8.11 And I say to ye that many from sunrises and sunsets will come and they will be reclined with Abraham and Isaac and Jacob in the kingdom of the skies/heavens; 8.12 but the sons of the kingdom will be thrown out into the outer darkness; *in that place* there will be the wailing and the gritting of the teeth. 8.13 And Jesus said to the centurion: You go, as you believed, let it become for you. And the boy was healed at that hour/time. 8.14 And going into the house of Peter, Jesus saw the mother-in-law of him, having been laid up and having fever; 8.15 and he touched the hand of her, and the fever left her; and she arose and was ministering to them. 8.16 And from evening having come, they brought to him many being demon-possessed; and he put out the spirits by a saying/word, and he healed/treated all those having *it* badly; 8.17 so that *it* might be fulfilled, the (thing) having been spoken through Isaiah the prophet, saying: HE, HE TOOK THE SICKNESSES/WEAKNESSES OF US AND HE BORE THE DISEASES. 8.18. But Jesus, seeing a crowd around him, ordered to go away to the other side/beyond.

8.19 And coming near, one scribe said to him: Teacher, I will follow with you where ever you may go. 8.20 And Jesus says to him: The foxes have dens and the birds of the sky/heaven dwelling places, but the son of man has not where he might lay the/*his* head.

8.21 And a different (one)/another from the learners said to him: Lord, allow me first to go away and to bury my father.

8.22 But the (he) says to him: You follow me, and leave the dead (ones) to bury the dead (ones) of themselves.

8.23 And with him embarking in the boat, his learners/pupils followed with him. 8.24 And behold, a

θαλάσσῃ, ὥστε τὸ πλοῖον καλύπτεσθε ὑπὸ τῶν κυμάτων· αὐτὸς δὲ ἐκάθευδεν. 8.25 καὶ προσελθόντες ἤγιραν αὐτὸν λέγοντες, κύριε, σῶσον, ἀπολλύμεθα.

8.26 καὶ λέγι αὐτοῖς, τί δειλοί ἐστε, ὀλιγόπιστοι; τότε ἐγερθεὶς ἐπετίμησεν τοῖς ἀνέμοις καὶ τῇ θαλάσσῃ, καὶ ἐγένετο γαλήνη μεγάλη. 8.27 οἱ δὲ ἄνθρωποι ἐθαύμασαν λέγοντες, ποταπός ἐστιν οὗτος ὅτι καὶ οἱ ἄνεμοι καὶ ἡ θάλασσα αὐτῷ ὑπακούουσιν; 8.28 καὶ ἐλθόντος αὐτοῦ εἰς τὸ πέραν εἰς τὴν χώραν τῶν Γαδαρηνῶν ὑπήντησαν αὐτῷ δύο δεμονιζόμενοι ἐκ τῶν μνημείων ἐξερχόμενοι, χαλεποὶ λίαν, ὥστε μὴ ἰσχύειν τινὰ παρελθεῖν διὰ τῆς ὁδοῦ ἐκίνης. 8.29 καὶ ἰδοὺ ἔκραξαν λέγοντες, τί ἡμῖν καὶ σοί, υἱὲ τοῦ θεοῦ; ἦλθες ὧδε πρὸ καιροῦ βασανίσαι ἡμᾶς; 8.30 ἦν δὲ μακρὰν ἀπ' αὐτῶν ἀγέλη χοίρων πολλῶν βοσκομένη. 8.31 οἱ δὲ δαίμονες παρεκάλουν αὐτὸν λέγοντες, εἰ ἐκβάλλις ἡμᾶς, ἀπόστιλον ἡμᾶς εἰς τὴν ἀγέλην τῶν χοίρων. 8.32 καὶ εἶπεν αὐτοῖς, ὑπάγετε.

οἱ δὲ ἐξελθόντες ἀπῆλθον εἰς τοὺς χοίρους· καὶ ἰδοὺ ὥρμησεν πᾶσα ἡ ἀγέλη κατὰ τοῦ κρημνοῦ εἰς τὴν θάλασσαν, καὶ ἀπέθανον ἐν τοῖς ὕδασιν. 8.33 οἱ δὲ βόσκοντες ἔφυγον, καὶ ἀπελθόντες εἰς τὴν πόλιν ἀπήγγιλαν πάντα καὶ τὰ τῶν δαιμονιζομένων. 8.34 καὶ ἰδοὺ πᾶσα ἡ πόλις ἐξῆλθεν εἰς ὑπάντησιν τοῦ Ἰησοῦ, καὶ εἰδόντες αὐτὸν παρεκάλεσαν ὅπως μεταβῇ ἀπὸ τῶν ὁρίων αὐτῶν. 9.1 καὶ ἐμβὰς εἰς πλοῖον διεπέρασεν καὶ ἦλθεν εἰς τὴν ἰδίαν πόλιν.

9.2 καὶ ἰδοὺ προσέφερον αὐτῷ παραλυτικὸν ἐπὶ κλίνης βεβλημένον. καὶ ἰδὼν ὁ Ἰησοῦς τὴν πίστιν αὐτῶν εἶπεν τῷ παραλυτικῷ, θάρσει, τέκνον· ἀφίενταί σου αἱ ἁμαρτίαι.

9.3 καὶ ἰδού τινες τῶν γραμματέων εἶπον ἐν ἑαυτοῖς, οὗτος βλασφημεῖ. 9.4 καὶ ἰδὼν ὁ Ἰησοῦς τὰς ἐνθυμήσεις αὐτῶν εἶπεν, ἱνατί ἐνθυμεῖσθε πονηρὰ ἐν ταῖς καρδίαις ὑμῶν; 9.5 τί γάρ ἐστιν εὐκοπώτερον, εἰπεῖν, ἀφίενταί σου αἱ ἁμαρτίαι,

great earthquake/shaking happened in the sea, so as
for the boat to be hidden/covered by the waves; but
he, he was sleeping.   8.25 And approaching, they
wakened him, saying: Lord, you rescue/save us; we
perish!

8.26   And he says to them: Why are ye cowards,
(men) of little faith?   Then, arising, he rebuked the
winds and the sea, and there became a great calm.
8.27 And the men/humans were astonished, saying: of
what sort is this (one), that even the winds and the
sea obey him?   8.28 And of him having come to the
other side into the region of the Gadarenes, (there)
met with him two(men) being demon-possessed, coming
forth out of the tombs, very violent (ones), so that
anyone was not to be strong/able to pass through that
road.   8.29 And behold, they cried out, saying: What
is for us and you, son of God? Came you here to torment us before the time/season?   8.30 And a herd of
many grazing swine was far/a long way from them.   8.31
And the demons besought him, saying: If you put us
out, you send us into the herd of the swine.   8.32 And
he said to them: Go ye away/depart ye.

And they, coming out, went away into the swine;
and behold, all the herd rushed down the precipice
into the sea, and they died in the waters.   8.33 But
those tending them fled, and going away to the city,
they reported all (things) and the (things) of those
being demon-possessed.   8.34 And behold, all the city
went out to a meeting of Jesus, and having seen, they
entreated him so that he might depart from their
borders.   9.1   And embarking in a boat, he crossed
over and went to his own city.

9.2   And behold, they brought to him a paralytic,
having been laid upon a cot. And Jesus, seeing their
faith, said to the paralytic: Be of good courage,
child, the faults/sins of you/your faults are forgiven.

9.3   And behold, some of the scribes said among
themselves: This (one) blasphemes.   9.4 And Jesus,
seeing the thoughts of them/their thoughts, said: Why
think ye evil (things) in your hearts?   9.5 For what
is easier, to say: Your faults/sins are forgiven,

16

ἢ εἰπεῖν, ἔγειρε καὶ περιπάτι; 9.6 ἵνα δὲ εἰδῆτε ὅτι ἐξουσίαν ἔχι ὁ υἱὸς τοῦ ἀνθρώπου ἐπὶ τῆς γῆς ἀφιέναι ἁμαρτίας

τότε λέγει τῷ παραλυτικῷ, ἐγερθεὶς ἆρόν σου τὴν κλίνην καὶ ὕπαγε πορεύου εἰς τὸν οἶκόν σου. 9.7 καὶ ἐγερθεὶς ἀπῆλθεν εἰς τὸν οἶκον αὐτοῦ.

9.8 ἰδόντες δὲ οἱ ὄχλοι ἐφοβήθησαν καὶ ἐδόξασαν τὸν θεὸν τὸν δόντα ἐξουσίαν τοιαύτην τοῖς ἀνθρώποις.

9.9 καὶ παράγων ὁ Ἰησοῦς ἐκεῖθεν εἶδεν ἄνθρωπον καθήμενον ἐπὶ τὸ τελώνιον, Μαθθαῖον λεγόμενον, καὶ λέγει αὐτῷ, ἀκολούθει μοι. καὶ ἀναστὰς ἠκολούθει αὐτῷ. 9.10 καὶ ἐγένετο ἀνακειμένου αὐτοῦ ἐν τῇ οἰκίᾳ, ἰδοὺ πολλοὶ τελῶναι καὶ ἁμαρτωλοὶ ἐλθόντες συνανέκιντο τῷ Ἰησοῦ καὶ τοῖς μαθηταῖς αὐτοῦ. 9.11 καὶ ἰδόντες οἱ Φαρισαῖοι ἔλεγον τοῖς μαθηταῖς αὐτοῦ, διὰ τί μετὰ τῶν τελωνῶν καὶ ἁμαρτωλῶν ἐσθίει ὁ διδάσκαλος ὑμῶν;

9.12 ὁ δὲ ἀκούσας εἶπεν, οὐ χρίαν ἔχουσιν οἱ ἰσχύοντες ἰατρῶν ἀλλ᾿ οἱ κακῶς ἔχοντες. 9.13 πορευθέντες δὲ μάθεται τί ἐστιν, «ἔλεος θέλω καὶ οὐ θυσίαν» οὐ γὰρ ἦλθον καλέσαι δικαίους ἀλλὰ ἁμαρτωλούς. 9.14 τότε προσέρχονται αὐτῷ οἱ μαθηταὶ Ἰωάννου λέγοντες, διὰ τί ἡμεῖς καὶ οἱ Φαρισαῖοι νηστεύομεν πολλά, οἱ δὲ μαθηταί σου οὐ νηστεύουσιν; 9.15 καὶ εἶπεν αὐτοῖς ὁ Ἰησοῦς, μὴ δύνανται οἱ υἱοὶ τοῦ νυμφῶνος πενθεῖν ἐφ᾿ ὅσον μετ᾿ αὐτῶν ἐστιν ὁ νυμφίος; ἐλεύσονται δὲ ἡμέραι ὅταν ἀπαρθῇ ἀπ᾿ αὐτῶν ὁ νυμφίος, καὶ τότε νηστεύσουσιν.

9.16 οὐδεὶς δὲ ἐπιβάλλει ἐπίβλημα ῥάκους ἀγνάφου ἐπὶ ἱματίῳ παλεῷ· αἴρι γὰρ τὸ πλήρωμα αὐτοῦ ἀπὸ τοῦ ἱματίου, καὶ χεῖρον σχίσμα γείνεται.

9.17 οὐδὲ βάλλουσιν οἶνον νέον εἰς ἀσκοὺς παλαιούς· εἰ δὲ μή γε, ῥήγνυνται οἱ ἀσκοί, καὶ ὁ οἶνος ἐκχεῖται καὶ οἱ ἀσκοὶ ἀπόλλυνται·

ἀλλ᾿ οἶνον νέον εἰς ἀσκοὺς καινοὺς βλήτεον, καὶ ἀμφότεροι συντηροῦνται.

9.18 ταῦτα αὐτοῦ λαλοῦντος αὐτοῖς ἰδοὺ ἄρχων εἷς ἐλθὼν προσεκύνι αὐτῷ λέγων ἡ θυγάτηρ μου ἄρτι ἐτελεύτησεν· ἀλλὰ

or to say: Arise and walk? 9.6 But in order that
ye may know that the son of man has authority upon the
earth to forgive faults/sins--

he then says to the paralytic: You arise, take up
your cot, and depart. Go to your house. 9.7 And
arising, he went away to his house.

9.8 And having seen, the crowds were afraid and
they glorified God, the (one) giving such authority to
the men/humans.

9.9 And Jesus, passing by from there, saw a man
sitting at the tax office, (one) being called Matthew,
and he says to him: you follow me, and rising up he
followed with him. 9.10 And it happened of him reclining in the house, behold, many tax collectors and
sinners, coming *there* reclined at table with Jesus and
his learners/pupils. 9.11 And having seen, the Pharisees said to his learners/pupils: Why eats your teacher with tax collectors and sinners?

9.12 But the (he), hearing, he said: Those being
strong have not need of a physician, but those having
it badly. 9.13 But going, learn ye what it is: I WANT
MERCY AND NOT SACRIFICE; for I came not to call/invite
just (ones), but sinners. 9.14 Then the learners/pu-
pils of John approach/come near to him, saying: Why *do*
we and the Pharisees fast much, but your learners/pu-
pils fast not? 9.15 And Jesus said to them: The sons
of the marriage hall are not able to mourn for so long
as the bridegroom is with them, *are they?* But days
will come when the bridegroom might be snatched away
from them, and then they will fast.

9.16 And no one puts a patch of unshrunken cloth
on an old garment; for the fullness (*curing*) of it
takes away from the garment, and a tear becomes worse.

9.17 Neither put they new wine into old wineskins; otherwise, the wineskins are burst, and the
wine is spilled and the wineskins are destroyed/per-
ish;

but new wine *is* put into new wineskins, and both
are preserved.

9.18 From him speaking these things to them,
behold one ruler, coming, worshiping/kneeling to him,
saying: My daughter died just now; but be coming, you

ἐλθὼν ἐπίθες τὴν χεῖρά σου ἐπ᾽ αὐτήν, καὶ ζήσεται.

9.19 καὶ ἐγερθεὶς ὁ Ἰησοῦς ἠκολούθει αὐτῷ καὶ οἱ μαθηταὶ αὐτοῦ. 9.20 καὶ ἰδοὺ γυνὴ αἱμοροοῦσα δώδεκα ἔτη προσελθοῦσα ὄπισθεν ἤψατο τοῦ κρασπέδου τοῦ ἱματίου αὐτοῦ· 9.21 ἔλεγεν γὰρ ἐν ἑαυτῇ, ἐὰν μόνον ἅψωμαι τοῦ ἱματίου αὐτοῦ σωθήσομαι.

9.22 ὁ δὲ Ἰησοῦς στραφεὶς καὶ ἰδὼν αὐτὴν εἶπεν, θάρσει, θύγατερ· ἡ πίστις σου σέσωκέν σε. καὶ ἐσώθη ἡ γυνὴ ἀπὸ τῆς ὥρας ἐκίνης. 9.23 καὶ ἐλθὼν ὁ Ἰησοῦς εἰς τὴν οἰκίαν τοῦ ἄρχοντος καὶ ἰδὼν τοὺς αὐλητὰς καὶ τὸν ὄχλον θορυβούμενον 9.24 ἔλεγεν, ἀναχωρῖτε, οὐ γὰρ ἀπέθανε τὸ κοράσιον ἀλλὰ καθεύδει. καὶ κατεγέλων αὐτοῦ εἰδόντες ὅτι ἀπέθανεν. 9.25 ὅτε δὲ ἐξεβλήθη ὁ ὄχλος, εἰσελθὼν ἐκράτησεν τῆς χιρὸς αὐτῆς, καὶ ἠγέρθη τὸ κοράσιον. 9.26 καὶ ἐξῆλθεν ἡ φήμη αὔτης εἰς ὅλην τὴν γῆν ἐκείνην.

9.27 καὶ παράγοντι ἐκεῖθεν τῷ Ἰησοῦ ἠκολούθησαν αὐτῷ δύο τυφλοὶ κραυγάζοντες καὶ λέγοντες, ἐλέησον ἡμᾶς, υἱὸς Δαυίδ. 9.28 ἐλθόντι δὲ αὐτῷ εἰς τὴν οἰκίαν προσῆλθον αὐτῷ οἱ δύο τυφλοί, καὶ λέγει αὐτοῖς ὁ Ἰησοῦς, πιστεύετε ὅτι δύναμαι τοῦτο ποιῆσαι; λέγουσιν αὐτῷ, ναί, κύριε. 9.29 τότε ἤψατο τῶν ὀφθαλμῶν αὐτῶν λέγων, κατὰ τὴν πίστιν ὑμῶν γενηθήτω ὑμῖν. 9.30 καὶ ἀνεῴχθησαν αὐτῶν οἱ ὀφθαλμοί.

καὶ ἐνεβριμήθη αὐτοῖς ὁ Ἰησοῦς λέγων, ὁρᾶτε μηδὶς γινωσκέτω. 9.31 οἱ δὲ ἐξελθόντες διεφήμισαν αὐτὸν ἐν ὅλῃ τῇ γῇ ἐκείνῃ.

9.32 αὐτῶν δὲ ἐξερχομένων ἰδοὺ προσήνεγκαν αὐτῷ κωφὸν δαιμονιζόμενον· 9.33 καὶ ἐκβληθέντος τοῦ δαιμονίου ἐλάλησεν ὁ κωφός. καὶ ἐθαύμασαν οἱ ὄχλοι λέγοντες, οὐδέποτε ἐφάνη οὕτως ἐν τῷ Ἰσραήλ. 9.34 οἱ δὲ Φαρισαῖοι ἔλεγον, ἐν τῷ ἄρχοντι τῶν δαιμονίων ἐκβάλλει τὰ δεμόνια.

9.35 καὶ περιῆγεν ὁ Ἰησοῦς τὰς πόλις πάσας καὶ τὰς κώμας, διδάσκων ἐν ταῖς συναγωγαῖς αὐτῶν κηρύσσων τὸ εὐαγγέλιον τῆς βασιλείας καὶ θεραπεύων πᾶσαν νόσον καὶ πᾶσαν μαλακίαν.

9.36 ἰδὼν δὲ τοὺς ὄχλους ἐσπλαγχνίσθη περὶ αὐτῶν ὅτι

lay your hand upon her, and she will live.
9.19 And arising, Jesus followed with him, also his learners/pupils. 9.20 And behold, a woman having a flow of blood twelve years, coming near from behind, she touched the hem of his garment; 9.21 for she was saying in herself: If only I might touch of his garment, I will be saved/delivered.

9.22 And Jesus, turning and seeing her, said: Daughter, be of good courage; your faith has saved/delivered you. And the woman was saved/delivered from that hour/time. 9.23 And Jesus, going into the house of the ruler and seeing the flute-players and the crowd being fearful, 9.24 he said: Make ye room, for the girl died not but she sleeps. And they were laughing from this, knowing that she died. 9.25 But when the crowd was put out, entering, he took hold of her hand, and the girl was raised. 9.26 And the voice of her/this went out into that entire land.

9.27 And going on from there with Jesus, two blind (ones) followed him, crying out and saying: Son of David, have mercy *for* us. 9.28 And coming to the house with him, the two blind (ones) came near to him, and Jesus says to them: Believe ye that I am able to do this/it? They say to him: Yes, Lord. 9.29 Then he touched their eyes, saying: According to your faith, let it become for ye. 9.30 And the eyes of them/their eyes were opened.

And Jesus sternly charged them, saying: See *that* ye let no one know. 9.31 But going out, they told about him in all that land.

9.32 And from them going out, behold they brought to him a dumb (one) being demon-possessed; 9.33 and from the demon being put out, the dumb (one) spoke. And the crowds were astonished, saying: Never it appeared thus in Israel. 9.34 But the Pharisees said: He puts out the demons by the ruler of the demons.

9.35 And Jesus went about all the cities and the villages, teaching among their congregations, heralding the good message of the kingdom and healing every disease and every ailment.

9.36 And seeing the crowds he felt compassion

ἦσαν ἐσκυλμένοι καὶ ἐριμμένοι ὡσεὶ πρόβατα μὴ ἔχοντα ποιμένα. 9.37 τότε λέγι τοῖς μαθητὲς αὐτοῦ, Ὁ μὲν θερισμὸς πολύς, οἱ δὲ ἐργάτε ὀλίγοι· 9.38 δεήθητε οὖν τοῦ κυρίου τοῦ θερισμοῦ ὅπως ἐκβάλῃ ἐργάτας εἰς τὸν θερισμὸν αὐτοῦ. 10.1 καὶ προσκαλεσάμενος τοὺς δώδεκα μαθητὰς αὐτοῦ ἔδωκεν αὐτοῖς ἐξουσίαν πνευμάτων ἀκαθάρτων ὥστε ἐκβάλλιν αὐτὰ καὶ θεραπεύειν πᾶσαν νόσον καὶ πᾶσαν μαλακίαν. 10.2 τῶν δὲ δώδεκα ἀποστόλων τὰ ὀνόματά ἐστιν ταῦτα·

πρῶτος Σίμων ὁ λεγόμενος Πέτρος καὶ Ἀνδρέας ὁ ἀδελφὸς αὐτοῦ, Ἰάκωβος ὁ τοῦ Ζεβεδαίου καὶ Ἰωάννης ὁ ἀδελφὸς αὐτοῦ, 10.3 Φίλιππος καὶ Βαρθολομαῖος, Θωμᾶς καὶ Μαθθέος ὁ τελώνης, Ἰάκωβος ὁ τοῦ Ἁλφαίου καὶ Θαδδαῖος, 10.4 Σίμων ὁ Κανανίτας καὶ Ἰούδας ὁ Ἰσκαριώτης ὁ καὶ παραδοὺς αὐτόν. 10.5 τούτους τοὺς δώδεκα ἀπέστιλεν ὁ Ἰησοῦς παραγγίλας αὐτοῖς λέγων, εἰς ὁδὸν ἐθνῶν μὴ ἀπέλθηται, καὶ εἰς πόλιν Σαμαριτῶν μὴ εἰσέλθηται· 10.6 πορεύεσθε δὲ μᾶλλον πρὸς τὰ πρόβατα τὰ ἀπολωλότα οἴκου Ἰσραήλ. 10.7 πορευόμενοι δὲ κηρύσσετε λέγοντες ὅτι ἤγγικεν ἡ βασιλία τῶν οὐρανῶν. 10.8 ἀσθενοῦντας θεραπεύετε, νεκροὺς ἐγείρεται, λεπροὺς καθαρίζεται, δαιμόνια ἐκβάλλετε· δωρεὰν ἐλάβετε, δωρεὰν δότε. 10.9 Μὴ κτήσησθαι χρυσὸν μηδὲ ἄργυρον μηδὲ χαλκὸν εἰς τὰς ζώνας ὑμῶν,

10.10 μὴ πήραν εἰς ὁδὸν μηδὲ δύο χιτῶνας μηδὲ ὑποδήματα μηδὲ ῥάβδον· ἄξιος γὰρ ὁ ἐργάτης τῆς τροφῆς αὐτοῦ. 10.11 εἰς ἣν δ᾽ ἂν πόλιν ἢ κώμην εἰσέλθηται, ἐξετάσαται ἐν τῇ τὶς ἄξιός ἐστιν· κἀκεῖ μίνατε ἕως ἂν ἐξέλθηται. 10.12 εἰσερχόμενοι δὲ εἰς τὴν οἰκίαν ἀσπάσασθε αὐτὴν λέγοντες εἰρήνη τῷ οἴκῳ τούτῳ·

10.13 καὶ ἐὰν μὲν ᾖ ἡ οἰκία ἀξία, ἐλθάτω ἡ ἰρήνη ὑμῶν ἐπ᾽ αὐτήν· ἐὰν δὲ μὴ ᾖ ἀξία, ἡ ἰρήνη ὑμῶν ἐφ᾽ ὑμᾶς ἐπιστραφήτω. 10.14 καὶ ὃς ἂν μὴ δέξηται ὑμᾶς μηδὲ ἀκούσῃ τοὺς λόγους ὑμῶν, ἐξερχόμενοι ἔξω τῆς οἰκίας ἢ πόλεως ἢ κώμης ἐκίνης ἐκτινάξατε τὸν κονιορτὸν ἐκ τῶν ποδῶν ὑμῶν. 10.15 ἀμὴν λέγω ὑμῖν, ἀνεκτότερον ἔσται γῇ Σοδόμων καὶ γῇ Γομόρρων ἐν

concerning them because they were tired (ones) and having been let down as sheep having not a shepherd. 9.37 Then he says to his pupils/learners: The harvest *is* much indeed, but the laborers *are* few; 9.38 therefore, entreat ye from the lord of the harvest so that he may put forth workers into/for his harvest. 10.1 And calling forward his twelve learners/pupils, he gave to them authority *over* unclean spirits so as to put them out and to heal/treat every disease and every ailment. 10.2 And the names of the twelve apostles/ sent ones are these:

first Simon, the (one) being called Peter, and Andrew his brother, James the (one) of Zebedee and John his brother, 10.3 Philip and Bartholomew, Thomas and Matthew the tax collector, James the (one) of Alphaeus, and Thaddaeus, 10.4 Simon the Canaanite and Judas the Iscariot, the (one) also betraying him. 10.5 These twelve Jesus sent forth, having given a charge to them, saying: Go ye not in a road of ethnics, and enter ye not in a city of Samaritans; 10.6 But go ye rather to the sheep, those having been lost from *the* house of Israel, 10.7 And going, herald/ preach ye, saying: The kingdom of the skies/heavens has come near. 10.8 Heal/treat ye (those) being sick, raise ye dead (ones), cleanse ye leprous (ones), put ye out demons; ye received freely/for nothing, give ye freely/for nothing. 10.9 Provide ye not gold nor silver nor copper in your belts,

10.10 not a bag for a/*the* road, neither two shirts nor sandals nor a staff/rod; for the workman is worthy of his food. 10.11 And into what ever city or village ye may enter, ask ye who in the (it) is worthy; and there abide ye until ye would go out. 10.12 And going into the house, salute/greet ye it, saying: Peace to this house;

10.13 and if indeed the house may be worthy, let your peace come upon it; but if it may be not worthy, let your peace return to ye. 10.14 And who ever might not receive ye nor hear your sayings/words, going away outside that house or city or village, ye shake off *once* the dust from your feet. 10.15 Truly I say to ye: It will be more tolerable for a land of Sodom and

ἡμέρᾳ κρίσεως ἢ τῇ πόλι ἐκίνῃ. 10.16 ἰδοὺ ἐγὼ ἀποστέλλω ὑμᾶς ὡς πρόβατα ἐν μέσῳ λύκων· γίνεσθε οὖν φρόνιμοι ὡς οἱ ὄφις καὶ ἀκέραιοι ὡς αἱ περιστεραί. 10.17 προσέχετε δὲ ἀπὸ τῶν ἀνθρώπων· παραδώσουσιν γὰρ ὑμᾶς εἰς συνέδρια, καὶ ἐν ταῖς συναγωγαῖς αὐτῶν μαστιγώσουσιν ὑμᾶς· 10.18 καὶ ἐπὶ ἡγεμόνας δὲ καὶ βασιλῖς ἀχθήσεσθαι ἕνεκεν ἐμοῦ εἰς μαρτύριον αὐτοῖς καὶ τοῖς ἔθνεσιν. 10.19 ὅταν δὲ παραδῶσιν ὑμᾶς, μὴ μεριμνήσητε πῶς ἢ τί λαλήσητε· δοθήσεται γὰρ ὑμῖν ἐν ἐκίνῃ τῇ ὥρᾳ τί λαλήσητε· 10.20 οὐ γὰρ ὑμῖς ἐστε οἱ λαλοῦντες ἀλλὰ τὸ πνεῦμα τοῦ πατρὸς ὑμῶν τὸ λαλοῦν ἐν ὑμῖν. 10.21 παραδώσι δὲ ἀδελφὸς ἀδελφὸν εἰς θάνατον καὶ πατὴρ τέκνον, καὶ ἐπαναστήσονται τέκνα ἐπὶ γονῖς καὶ θανατώσουσιν αὐτούς. 10.22 καὶ ἔσεσθε μισούμενοι ὑπὸ πάντων διὰ τὸ ὄνομά μου· ὁ δὲ ὑπομίνας εἰς τέλος οὗτος σωθήσεται. 10.23 ὅταν δὲ διώκωσιν ὑμᾶς ἐν τῇ πόλι ταύτῃ, φεύγεται εἰς τὴν ἑτέραν·

ἀμὴν γὰρ λέγω ὑμῖν, οὐ μὴ τελέσητε τὰς πόλις τοῦ Ἰσραὴλ ἕως οὗ ἔλθῃ ὁ υἱὸς τοῦ ἀνθρώπου. 10.24 οὐκ ἔστιν μαθητὴς ὑπὲρ τὸν διδάσκαλον αὐτοῦ οὐδὲ δοῦλος ὑπὲρ τὸν κύριον αὐτοῦ. 10.25 ἀρκετὸν τῷ μαθητῇ ἵνα γένηται ὡς ὁ διδάσκαλος αὐτοῦ, καὶ ὁ δοῦλος ὡς ὁ κύριος αὐτοῦ. εἰ τὸν οἰκοδεσπότην Βεελζεβοὺλ ἐπεκάλεσαν, πόσῳ μᾶλλον τοὺς οἰκιακοὺς αὐτοῦ. 10.26 μὴ οὖν φοβηθῆτε αὐτούς· οὐδὲν γάρ ἐστιν κεκαλυμμένον ὃ οὐκ ἀποκαλυφθήσετε, καὶ κρυπτὸν ὃ οὐ γνωσθήσετε. 10.27 ὃ λέγω ὑμῖν ἐν τῇ σκοτίᾳ, εἴπατε ἐν τῷ φωτί· καὶ ὃ εἰς τὸ οὖς ἀκούετε, κηρύξατε ἐπὶ τῶν δωμάτων. 10.28 καὶ μὴ φοβῖσθε ἀπὸ τῶν ἀποκτεννόντων τὸ σῶμα, τὴν δὲ ψυχὴν μὴ δυναμένων ἀποκτεῖναι· φοβῖσθε δὲ μᾶλλον τὸν δυνάμενον καὶ ψυχὴν καὶ τὸ σῶμα ἀπολέσε ἐν γεέννῃ. 10.29 οὐχὶ δύο στρουθία ἀσσαρίου πωλῖται; καὶ ἓν ἐξ αὐτῶν οὐ πεσῖται ἐπὶ τὴν γῆν ἄνευ τοῦ πατρὸς ὑμῶν. 10.30 ὑμῶν δὲ καὶ αἱ τρίχες τῆς κεφαλῆς πᾶσαι

a land of Gomorra in a day of judgment than for that city. 10.16 Behold, I, I send ye forth as sheep in the midst of wolves; therefore, become ye prudent (ones) as the serpents and pure/innocent (ones) as the doves. 10.17 And ye take heed from the men/humans; for they will betray ye/deliver ye over to councils, and they will scourge ye in their congregations; 10.18 and ye will be brought to both governors and kings on account of me to/for a testimony/witness to them and to the ethnics. 10.19 But when they betray ye/deliver ye up, worry ye not how or what ye might speak; for it will be given to ye at that time/hour what ye might speak; 10.20 for ye, ye are not the (ones) speaking, but the spirit from your father *is* the thing speaking in ye. 10.21 And a brother will betray/deliver up a brother to death, and a father a child, and children will raise themselves up against parents and they will put them to death. 10.22 And ye will be hated (ones) by all because of my name; but the (one) enduring to *the* end, this (one) will be saved/delivered. 10.23 But whenever they prosecute ye in this city, flee ye to another (different);

for truly I say to ye, by no means will ye finish the cities of Israel until which *time* the son of man might come. 10.24 A pupil/learner is not over his teacher, nor a slave over his lord. 10.25 Sufficient *it is* for the learner/pupil that he might become like his teacher, and the slave like his lord. If they called Beelzebub the housemaster, how much more *are* the members of his household. 10.26 Then be ye not afraid *for* them; for there is nothing having been hidden which will not be revealed, and secret which will not be made known. 10.27 What I say to ye in the darkness, say ye in the light; and what ye hear in the ear, herald/preach ye upon/over the housetops. 10.28 And be ye not afraid from those killing the body, but being not able to kill the soul/life; but fear ye rather the (one) being able to destroy both soul/life and the body in hell. 10.29 Were not two sparrows being sold for a penny? And one out of them will not fall to the earth without your father. 10.30 But of ye, even all the hairs of the head have been numbered.

ἠριθμημένε εἰσίν. 10.31 μὴ οὖν φοβῖσθε· πολλῶν στρουθίων διαφέρετε ὑμῖς. 10.32 πᾶς οὖν ὅστις ὁμολογήσι ἐν ἐμοὶ ἔμπροσθεν τῶν ἀνθρώπων, ὁμολογήσω κἀγὼ ἐν αὐτῷ ἔμπροσθεν τοῦ πατρός μου τοῦ ἐν οὐρανοῖς· 10.33 ὅστις δ' ἂν ἀρνήσηταί με ἔμπροσθεν τῶν ἀνθρώπων, ἀρνήσομε κἀγὼ αὐτὸν ἔμπροσθεν τοῦ πατρός μου τοῦ ἐν οὐρανοῖς. 10.34 μὴ νομίσηται ὅτι ἦλθον ἰρήνην βαλῖν ἐπὶ τὴν γῆν· οὐκ ἦλθον βαλῖν ἰρήνην ἀλλὰ μάχαιραν. 10.35 ἦλθον γὰρ διχάσαι ἄνθρωπον «κατὰ τοῦ πατρὸς αὐτοῦ καὶ θυγατέρα κατὰ τῆς μητρὸς αὐτῆς καὶ νύμφην κατὰ τῆς πενθερᾶς αὐτῆς,» 10.36 καὶ «ἐχθροὶ τοῦ ἀνθρώπου οἱ οἰκιακοὶ αὐτοῦ.» 10.37 ὁ φιλῶν πατέρα ἢ μητέρα ὑπὲρ ἐμὲ οὐκ ἔστιν μου ἄξιος· καὶ ὁ φιλῶν υἱὸν ἢ θυγατέρα ὑπὲρ ἐμὲ οὐκ ἔστιν μου ἄξιος· 10.38 καὶ ὃς οὐ λαμβάνι τὸν σταυρὸν αὐτοῦ καὶ ἀκολουθῖ ὀπίσω μου, οὐκ ἔστιν μου ἄξιος. 10.39 ὁ εὑρὼν τὴν ψυχὴν αὐτοῦ ἀπολέσι αὐτήν, καὶ ὁ ἀπολέσας τὴν ψυχὴν αὐτοῦ ἕνεκεν ἐμοῦ εὑρήσει αὐτήν.

10.40 ὁ δεχόμενος ὑμᾶς ἐμὲ δέχετε, καὶ ὁ ἐμὲ δεχόμενος δέχετε τὸν ἀποστίλαντά με. 10.41 ὁ δεχόμενος προφήτην εἰς ὄνομα προφήτου μισθὸν προφήτου λήμψετε, καὶ ὁ δεχόμενος δίκαιον εἰς ὄνομα δικαίου μισθὸν δικέου λήμψετε.

10.42 καὶ ὃς ἐὰν ποτίσῃ ἕνα τῶν μικρῶν τούτων ποτήριον ψυχροῦ μόνον εἰς ὄνομα μαθητοῦ,

ἀμὴν λέγω ὑμῖν, οὐ μὴ ἀπολέσῃ τὸν μισθὸν αὐτοῦ. 11.1 καὶ ἐγένετο ὅτε ἐτέλεσεν ὁ Ἰησοῦς διατάσσων τοῖς δώδεκα μαθηταῖς αὐτοῦ, μετέβη ἐκεῖθεν τοῦ διδάσκιν καὶ κηρύσσιν ἐν ταῖς πόλεσιν αὐτῶν. 11.2 ὁ δὲ Ἰωάννης ἀκούσας ἐν τῷ δεσμωτηρίῳ τὰ ἔργα τοῦ χριστοῦ πέμψας διὰ τῶν μαθητῶν αὐτοῦ 11.3 εἶπεν αὐτῷ, σὺ εἶ ὁ ἐρχόμενος ἢ ἕτερον προσδοκῶμεν;

11.4 καὶ ἀποκριθὶς ὁ Ἰησοῦς εἶπεν αὐτοῖς, πορευθέντες ἀπαγγίλατε Ἰωάννῃ ἃ ἀκούετε καὶ βλέπετε· 11.5 τυφλοὶ ἀναβλέπουσιν καὶ χωλοὶ περιπατοῦσιν, λεπροὶ καθαρίζοντε καὶ

10.31 Therefore, be not afraid; ye, ye excel from many sparrows.   10.32 Then each *one* who will profess/confess in me before the men/humans, I also, I shall profess/confess in him before my father, the (one) in heavens/skies;   10.33 and who ever might deny me before the men, also I, I shall deny him before my father, the (one) in skies/heavens.   10.34 Suppose ye not that I came to put peace upon the earth; I came not to put peace, but a sword/fight.   10.35 For I came to contend/split a man AGAINST HIS FATHER AND A DAUGHTER AGAINST HER MOTHER AND A BRIDE AGAINST HER MOTHER-IN-LAW,   10.36 AND ENEMIES OF THE MAN *are/will be* THE MEMBERS OF HIS HOUSEHOLD.   10.37 The (one) loving father or mother over me is not worthy of me; and the (one) loving son or daughter over me is not worthy of me;   10.38 and (one) who takes not his cross and follows behind/after me is not worthy of me.   10.39 The (one) finding his soul/life will lose/perish/destroy it, but the (one) losing his soul/life on account of me will find it.

10.40   The (one) receiving ye receives me, and the (one) receiving me receives the (one) having sent me.   10.41 The (one) receiving a prophet in a prophet's name, he will receive a prophet's reward/wage, and the (one) receiving a just (one) in a just (one's) name, he will receive a just (one's) reward/wage.

10.42 And who ever might give drink to one of these little (ones), only a cup of cold (water) in a learn-er/pupil's name, truly I say to ye, will certainly not lose his wage/reward.   11.1   And it happened when Jesus finished directing to his twelve learners/pu-pils, *that* he departed from there for the (thing) to teach and to herald/preach among their cities.   11.2 And John, having heard in the prison the works of the anointed (one), having sent through his pupils/learn-ers,   11.3   he said to him: You, are you the (one) coming, or should we expect another/different (one)?

11.4   And answering, Jesus said to them: Be going, report ye to John what ye hear and ye see: 11.5 blind (ones) look up/see and lame (ones) walk, lepers are cleansed and deaf (ones) hear, and dead

κωφοὶ ἀκούουσιν, καὶ νεκροὶ ἐγίρονται καὶ πτωχοὶ εὐαγγελίζονται·
11.6 καὶ μακάριός ἐστιν ὃς ἐὰν μὴ σκανδαλισθῇ ἐν ἐμοί. 11.7
τούτων δὲ πορευομένων ἤρξατο ὁ Ἰησοῦς λέγιν τοῖς ὄχλοις περὶ
Ἰωάννου, τί ἐξήλθατε εἰς τὴν ἔρημον θεάσασθε; κάλαμον ὑπὸ
ἀνέμου σαλευόμενον; 11.8 ἀλλὰ τί ἐξήλθατε; ἄνθρωπον ἰδῖν ἐν
μαλακοῖς ἠμφιεσμένον; ἰδοὺ οἱ τὰ μαλακὰ φοροῦντες ἐν τοῖς
οἴκοις τῶν βασιλέων εἰσίν. 11.9 ἀλλὰ τί ἐξήλθατε, προφήτην ἰδῖν;
ναί, λέγω ὑμῖν, καὶ περισσότερον προφήτου. 11.10 οὗτός ἐστιν
περὶ οὗ γέγραπται,

«ἰδοὺ ἐγὼ ἀποστέλλω τὸν ἄγγελόν μου πρὸ προσώπου
σου, ὃς κατασκευάσι τὴν ὁδόν» σου «ἔμπροσθέν» σου. 11.11
ἀμὴν λέγω ὑμῖν, οὐκ ἐγήγερτε ἐν γεννητοῖς γυνεκῶν μίζων
Ἰωάννου τοῦ βαπτιστοῦ· ὁ δὲ μικρότερος ἐν τῇ βασιλίᾳ τῶν
οὐρανῶν μίζων αὐτοῦ ἐστιν.

11.12 ἀπὸ δὲ τῶν ἡμερῶν Ἰωάννου τοῦ βαπτιστοῦ ἕως ἄρτι
ἡ βασιλία τῶν οὐρανῶν βιάζετε, καὶ βιασταὶ ἁρπάζουσιν αὐτήν.

11.13 πάντες γὰρ οἱ προφῆται καὶ ὁ νόμος ἕως Ἰωάννου
ἐπροφήτευσαν· 11.14 καὶ εἰ θέλετε δέξασθε, αὐτός ἐστιν Ἠλίας ὁ
μέλλων ἔρχεσθε. 11.15 ὁ ἔχων ὦτα ἀκούειν, ἀκουέτω.

11.16 τίνι δὲ ὁμοιώσω τὴν γενεὰν ταύτην; ὁμοία ἐστὶν
παιδίοις καθημένοις ἐν ταῖς ἀγοραῖς ἃ προσφωνοῦντα τοῖς
ἑτέροις 11.17 λέγουσιν, ηὐλήσαμεν ὑμῖν καὶ οὐκ ὠρχήσασθε·
ἐθρηνήσαμεν καὶ οὐκ ἐκόψασθε. 11.18 ἦλθεν γὰρ Ἰωάννης μήτε
ἐσθίων μήτε πίνων, καὶ λέγουσιν, δεμόνιον ἔχει· 11.19 ἦλθεν ὁ
υἱὸς τοῦ ἀνθρώπου ἐσθίων καὶ πίνων, καὶ λέγουσιν, ἰδοὺ
ἄνθρωπος φάγος καὶ οἰνοπότης, τελωνῶν φίλος καὶ ἁμαρτωλῶν.
καὶ ἐδικαιώθη ἡ σοφία ἀπὸ τῶν ἔργων αὐτῆς.

11.20 τότε ἤρξατο ὀνιδίζειν τὰς πόλεις ἐν αἷς ἐγένοντο αἱ
πλῖσται δυνάμις αὐτοῦ, ὅτι οὐ μετενόησαν·

11.21 οὐαί σοι, Χοραζείν· οὐαί σοι, Βηθσαϊδά· ὅτι εἰ ἐν
Τύρῳ καὶ Σιδῶνι ἐγένοντο αἱ δυνάμις αἱ γενόμεναι ἐν ὑμῖν,
πάλαι ἂν ἐν σάκκῳ καὶ σποδῷ καθήμενοι μετενόησαν.

(ones) are raised and poor (ones) are evangelized; 11.6 and happy is who ever is not offended in/by me. 11.7 And from these *pupils* going, Jesus began to say to the crowds concerning John: What went ye out to the wilderness/desert to behold? A reed/cane being shaken by a wind? 11.8 But what went ye out to see, a man having dressed in soft (things)? Behold, those wearing the soft (things) are in the houses of the kings. 11.9 But why went ye out, to see a prophet? Yes, I say to ye, and much more than a prophet. 11.10 This is concerning *the one* of whom it has been written:
BEHOLD I, I SEND FORTH MY MESSENGER BEFORE YOUR FACE, WHO WILL PREPARE your ROAD/WAY BEFORE you. 11.11 Truly I say to ye: (One) greater than John the baptizer has not arisen among born (ones) from women; but the lesser (one) in the kingdom of the skies/heavens is greater than he.

11.12 And from the days of John the baptizer until now the kingdom of the skies/heavens suffers violence, and violent (ones) snatch it away.

11.13 For all the prophets and the law prophesied until John; 11.14 and if ye want/wish to receive *it*, he is Elias, the (one) being about to come. 11.15 The (one) having ears to hear, let him hear.

11.16 But to what shall I liken this generation? It is like children sitting in the markets who, calling to the others/different (ones), 11.17 they say: We played flutes for ye and ye danced not; we mourned and ye wailed not. 11.18 For John came neither eating nor drinking, and they say: He has a demon; 11.19 the son of man came eating and drinking, and they say: Behold, a man *being* a glutton and a wine guzzler/drunkard, a friend of tax collectors and sinners. And the wisdom was vindicated from all her/*its* works.

11.20 Then he began to reproach the cities in which his many powers happened/came about, because they repented not;

11.21 Woe to you, Chorazin; woe to you, Bethsaida; because if in Tyre and Sidon happened/came about the powers having happened/came about in ye, they would have repented long ago, sitting in sackcloth and ashes.

11.22 πλὴν λέγω ὑμῖν, Τύρῳ καὶ Σιδῶνι ἀνεκτότερον ἔστε ἐν ἡμέρᾳ κρίσεως ἢ ὑμῖν.

11.23 καὶ σύ, Καφαρναούμ,

11.21 οὐαί σοι, Χοραζείν· οὐαί σοι, Βηθσαϊδά· ὅτι εἰ ἐν Τύρῳ καὶ Σιδῶνι ἐγένοντο αἱ δυνάμις αἱ γενόμεναι ἐν ὑμῖν, πάλαι ἂν ἐν σάκκῳ καὶ σποδῷ καθήμενοι μετενόησαν.

11.22 πλὴν λέγω ὑμῖν, Τύρῳ καὶ Σιδῶνι ἀνεκτότερον ἔστε ἐν ἡμέρᾳ κρίσεως ἢ ὑμῖν.

11.23 καὶ σύ, Καφαρναούμ, μὴ ἕως οὐρανοῦ ὑψωθήσῃ; ἕως ἅδου καταβιβασθήσῃ. ὅτι εἰ ἐν Σοδόμοις ἐγενήθησαν αἱ δυνάμις αἱ γενόμεναι ἐν σοί, ἔμεινεν ἂν μέχρι τῆς σήμερον.

11.24 πλὴν λέγω ὑμῖν ἀνεκτότερον ἔστε γῇ Σοδόμων ἐν ἡμέρᾳ κρίσεως ἢ σοί. 11.25 ἐν ἐκίνῳ τῷ καιρῷ ἀποκριθὶς ὁ Ἰησοῦς εἶπεν, ἐξομολογοῦμαί σοι, πάτερ, κύριε τοῦ οὐρανοῦ καὶ τῆς γῆς, ὅτι ἔκρυψας ταῦτα ἀπὸ σοφῶν καὶ συνετῶν καὶ ἀπεκάλυψας αὐτὰ νηπίοις· 11.26 ναί, ὁ πατήρ, ὅτι οὕτως εὐδοκία ἐγένετο ἔμπροσθέν σου.

11.27 πάντα μοι παρεδόθη ὑπὸ τοῦ πατρός μου, καὶ οὐδὶς ἐπιγινώσκι τὸν υἱὸν εἰ μὴ ὁ πατήρ, οὐδὲ τὸν πατέρα τις ἐπιγινώσκι εἰ μὴ ὁ υἱὸς καὶ ᾧ ἐὰν βούλητε ὁ υἱὸς ἀποκαλύψε.

11.28 δεῦτε πρός με πάντες οἱ κοπιῶντες καὶ πεφορτισμένοι, κἀγὼ ἀναπαύσω ὑμᾶς.

11.29 ἄρατε τὸν ζυγόν μου ἐφ᾽ ὑμᾶς καὶ μάθετε ἀπ᾽ ἐμοῦ, ὅτι πραΰς εἰμι καὶ ταπινὸς τῇ καρδίᾳ, καὶ εὑρήσετε ἀνάπαυσιν ταῖς ψυχαῖς ὑμῶν·

11.30 ὁ γὰρ ζυγός μου χρηστὸς καὶ τὸ φορτίον μου ἐλαφρόν ἐστιν. 12.1 ἐν ἐκείνῳ τῷ καιρῷ ἐπορεύθη ὁ Ἰησοῦς τοῖς σάββασιν διὰ τῶν σπορίμων· οἱ δὲ μαθητὲ αὐτοῦ ἐπίνασαν, καὶ ἤρξαντο τίλλιν στάχυας καὶ ἐσθίειν. 12.2 οἱ δὲ Φαρισαῖοι ἰδόντες εἶπαν αὐτῷ, ἰδοὺ οἱ μαθηταί σου ποιοῦσιν ὃ οὐκ ἔξεστιν ποιεῖν ἐν σαββάτῳ.

12.3 ὁ δὲ εἶπεν αὐτοῖς, οὐκ ἀνέγνωτε τί ἐποίησεν Δαυὶδ ὅτε ἐπίνασεν καὶ οἱ μετ᾽ αὐτοῦ; 12.4 πῶς εἰσῆλθεν εἰς τὸν οἶκον τοῦ θεοῦ καὶ τοὺς ἄρτους τῆς προθέσεως ἔφαγον, οὓς οὐκ ἐξὸν ἦν αὐτῷ φαγῖν οὐδὲ τοῖς μετ᾽ αὐτοῦ, εἰ μὴ τοῖς ἱερεῦσιν μόνοις; 12.5 ἢ οὐκ ἀνέγνωτε ἐν τῷ νόμῳ ὅτι τοῖς σάββασιν οἱ ἱερῖς ἐν τῷ ἱερῷ τὸ σάββατον βεβηλοῦσιν καὶ ἀναίτιοί εἰσιν;

11.22   However, I say to ye: It will be more tolerable for Tyre and Sidon in a day of judgment than for ye.

11.23   And you, Capernaum, were you not exalted to/until heaven? You will descend to/until hades. Because if the powers having come about in you were come about in Sodom, it would have remained until the present/today.

11.24   However, I say to ye: It will be more tolerable for a land of Sodom in a day of judgment than for you.   11.25 Jesus, answering in that time, said: I give thanks to you, Father, Lord of the heaven/sky and the earth, because you concealed these (things) from wise (ones) and intelligent (ones), but you revealed them to infants;   11.26 yes, Father, for so it became a pleasure before you.

11.27   All (things) were delivered to me by my father, and no one completely knows the son except the father, neither knows anyone completely the father, except the son and to who ever the son wills/wishes to reveal *him*.

11.28   Come to me. all the (ones) toiling and having been burdened, and I, I shall rest/refresh ye.

11.29   Take ye my yoke upon ye and learn ye from **me**, because I am gentle and lowly in the heart, and ye will find rest for your souls/lives;

11.30   for my yoke *is* good/kind and my burden is light.   12.1   In that season/time Jesus went on the sabbaths through the grainfields; and his learners/pupils were hungry, and they began to pick stalks/heads of grain and to eat.   12.2 But having seen *them*, the Pharisees said to him: Behold, your learners/pupils do what is not lawful to do on a sabbath.

12.3   And the (he) said to them: Read ye not what David did when he was hungry, and those with him? 12.4 How he went in, into the house of God, and they ate the loaves of the setting before/forth, which was not being lawful for him to eat, neither for those with him, except for the priests only?   12.5 Or read ye not in the law that on the sabbaths the priests in the temple profane/make common the sabbath, and they are guiltless?

23

12.6 λέγω δὲ ὑμῖν ὅτι τοῦ ἱεροῦ μῖζόν ἐστιν ὧδε.

12.7 εἰ δὲ ἐγνώκειτε τί ἐστιν, « ἔλεος θέλω καὶ οὐ θυσίαν,» οὐκ ἂν κατεδικάσατε τοὺς ἀναιτίους. 12.8 κύριος γάρ ἐστιν τοῦ σαββάτου ὁ υἱὸς τοῦ ἀνθρώπου. 12.9 καὶ μεταβὰς ἐκῖθεν ἦλθεν εἰς τὴν συναγωγὴν αὐτῶν· 12.10 καὶ ἰδοὺ ἄνθρωπος χῖρα ἔχων ξηράν. καὶ ἐπηρώτησαν αὐτὸν λέγοντες, εἰ ἔξεστιν τοῖς σάββασιν θεραπεῦσε; ἵνα κατηγορήσωσιν αὐτοῦ.

12.11 ὁ δὲ εἶπεν αὐτοῖς, τίς ἔσται ἐξ ὑμῶν ἄνθρωπος ὃς ἔξι πρόβατον ἕν, καὶ ἐὰν ἐμπέσῃ τοῦτο τοῖς σάββασιν εἰς βόθυνον, οὐχὶ κρατήσας ἐγερεῖ αὐτὸ;

12.12 πόσῳ οὖν διαφέρι ἄνθρωπος προβάτου. ὥστε ἔξεστιν τοῖς σάββασιν καλῶς ποιεῖν.

12.13 τότε λέγι τῷ ἀνθρώπῳ, ἔκτινόν σου τὴν χεῖρα. καὶ ἐξέτινεν, καὶ ἀπεκατεστάθη ὑγιής.

12.14 ἐξελθόντες δὲ οἱ Φαρισέοι συμβούλιον ἔλαβον κατ᾽ αὐτοῦ ὅπως αὐτὸν ἀπολέσωσιν. 12.15 ὁ δὲ Ἰησοῦς γνοὺς ἀνεχώρησεν ἐκῖθεν. καὶ ἠκολούθησαν αὐτῷ πολλοί, καὶ ἐθεράπευσεν αὐτοὺς πάντας,

12.16 καὶ ἐπετίμησεν αὐτοῖς ἵνα μὴ φανερὸν αὐτὸν ποιήσωσιν· 12.17 ἵνα πληρωθῇ τὸ ῥηθὲν διὰ Ἡσαΐου τοῦ προφήτου λέγοντος, 12.18 « ἰδοὺ ὁ παῖς μου ὃν ᾑρέτισα, ὁ ἀγαπητός μου εἰς ὃν ηὐδόκησεν ἡ ψυχή μου· θήσω τὸ πνεῦμά μου ἐπ᾽ αὐτόν, καὶ κρίσιν τοῖς ἔθνεσιν ἀπαγγελεῖ. 12.19 οὐκ ἐρίσει οὐδὲ κραυγάσει, οὐδὲ ἀκούσει τις ἐν ταῖς πλατίαις τὴν φωνὴν αὐτοῦ. 12.20 κάλαμον συντετριμμένον οὐ κατεάξει καὶ λίνον τυφόμενον οὐ σβέσι, ἕως ἂν ἐκβάλῃ εἰς νῖκος τὴν κρίσιν. 12.21 καὶ τῷ ὀνόματι αὐτοῦ ἔθνη ἐλπιοῦσιν.»

12.22 τότε προσηνέχθη αὐτῷ δαιμονιζόμενος τυφλὸς καὶ κωφός· καὶ ἐθεράπευσεν αὐτόν, ὥστε τὸν κωφὸν λαλεῖν καὶ βλέπειν. 12.23 καὶ ἐξίσταντο πάντες οἱ ὄχλοι καὶ ἔλεγον, μήτι

12.6 And I say to ye that the temple is greater than here/this place.

12.7 And if ye had known what it is: I WANT MERCY AND NOT SACRIFICE/OFFERING, ye would condemn not the guiltless (ones). 12.8 For the son of the man/human is lord of the sabbath. 12.9 And departing from there, he went to their congregation; 12.10 and behold, a man having a withered hand. And they questioned him, saying: If it is/is it lawful to heal on the sabbaths? in order that they might accuse him.

12.11 And the (he) said to them: Who out of ye will be a man who will have one sheep, and if it/this (one) might fall into a pit on the sabbaths, taking hold of *it*, will not raise it?

12.12 By how much then surpasses/excels a man/human from a sheep. So it is lawful to do well on the sabbaths.

12.13 Then he says to the man: Stretch forth your hand. And he stretched *it* forth and it was restored healthy.

12.14 And going out, the Pharisees took a consensus/counsel against him so that they might destroy him. 12.15 But Jesus, knowing *this*, withdrew from there. And many followed with him, and he healed/treated them all,

12.16 and he warned to them that they should not make him known; 12.17 that it might be fulfilled, the (thing) having been spoken through Isaiah the prophet, saying: 12.18 BEHOLD, MY BOY WHOM I CHOSE, MY BELOVED (ONE) IN WHOM MY LIFE/SOUL WAS WELL PLEASED; I SHALL PUT MY SPIRIT UPON HIM, AND HE WILL ANNOUNCE A JUDGMENT FOR THE ETHNICS. 12.19 HE WILL NOT QUARREL, NEITHER WILL HE SHOUT, NOR WILL ANYONE HEAR HIS VOICE IN THE BROAD STREETS. 12.20 A REED/CANE HAVING BEEN BRUISED HE WILL NOT BREAK, AND SMOKING FLAX HE WILL NOT QUENCH, UNTIL HE MIGHT PUT FORTH THE JUDGMENT IN VICTORY. 12.21 AND ETHNICS WILL HOPE IN/BY HIS NAME.

12.22 Then (one) was brought to him, being demon-possessed, blind and mute; and he healed/treated him, so as *for* the mute (one) to speak and to see. 12.23 And all the crowds were astonished, and they said: Is not this (one) the son of David/David's son?

οὗτός ἐστιν ὁ υἱὸς Δαυίδ;   12.24 οἱ δὲ Φαρισαῖοι ἀκούσαντες εἶπον, οὗτος οὐκ ἐκβάλλι τὰ δαιμόνια εἰ μὴ ἐν τῷ Βεελζεβοὺλ ἄρχοντι τῶν δαιμονίων.

12.25 ἰδὼς δὲ τὰς ἐνθυμήσεις αὐτῶν εἶπεν αὐτοῖς, πᾶσα βασιλία μερισθῖσα καθ' ἑαυτῆς ἐρημοῦται,

καὶ πᾶσα πόλις ἢ οἰκία μερισθῖσα καθ' ἑαυτῆς οὐ σταθήσεται.

12.26 καὶ εἰ ὁ Σατανᾶς τὸν Σατανᾶν ἐκβάλλι, ἐφ' ἑαυτὸν ἐμερίσθη·

πῶς οὖν σταθήσετε ἡ βασιλία αὐτοῦ; 12.27 καὶ εἰ ἐγὼ ἐν Βεελζεβοὺλ ἐκβάλλω τὰ δαιμόνια, οἱ υἱοὶ ὑμῶν ἐν τίνι ἐκβάλλουσιν;

διὰ τοῦτο αὐτοὶ κριταὶ ἔσονται ὑμῶν. 12.28 εἰ δὲ ἐν πνεύματι θεοῦ ἐγὼ ἐκβάλλω τὰ δεμόνια, ἄρα ἔφθασεν ἐφ' ὑμᾶς ἡ βασιλία τοῦ θεοῦ.

12.29 ἢ πῶς δύναταί τις εἰσελθῖν εἰς τὴν οἰκίαν τοῦ ἰσχυροῦ καὶ τὰ σκεύη αὐτοῦ διαρπάσαι, ἐὰν μὴ πρῶτον δήσῃ τὸν ἰσχυρόν; καὶ τότε τὴν οἰκίαν αὐτοῦ διαρπάσῃ.

12.30 ὁ μὴ ὢν μετ' ἐμοῦ κατ' ἐμοῦ ἐστιν, καὶ ὁ μὴ συνάγων μετ' ἐμοῦ σκορπίζι με.

12.31 διὰ τοῦτο λέγω ὑμῖν, πᾶσα ἁμαρτία καὶ βλασφημία ἀφεθήσετε τοῖς ἀνθρώποις, ἡ δὲ τοῦ πνεύματος βλασφημία οὐκ ἀφεθήσετε. 12.32 καὶ ὃς ἐὰν εἴπῃ λόγον κατὰ τοῦ υἱοῦ τοῦ ἀνθρώπου, ἀφεθήσετε αὐτῷ· ὃς δ' ἂν εἴπῃ κατὰ τοῦ πνεύματος τοῦ ἁγίου, οὐκ ἢ ἀφεθήσετε αὐτῷ οὔτε ἐν τούτῳ τῷ αἰῶνι οὔτε ἐν τῷ μέλλοντι. 12.33 ἢ ποιήσαται τὸ δένδρον καλὸν καὶ τὸν καρπὸν αὐτοῦ καλόν,

ἢ ποιήσατε τὸ δένδρον σαπρὸν καὶ τὸν καρπὸν αὐτοῦ σαπρόν·

ἐκ γὰρ τοῦ καρποῦ τὸ δένδρον γινώσκετε.

12.34 γεννήματα ἐχιδνῶν, πῶς δύνασθε ἀγαθὰ λαλῖν πονηροὶ ὄντες; ἐκ γὰρ τοῦ περισσεύματος τῆς καρδίας τὸ στόμα λαλεῖ.

12.35 ὁ ἀγαθὸς ἄνθρωπος ἐκ τοῦ ἀγαθοῦ θησαυροῦ ἐκβάλλει τὰ ἀγαθά, καὶ ὁ πονηρὸς ἄνθρωπος ἐκ τοῦ πονηροῦ θησαυροῦ ἐκβάλλει πονηρά.

12.24 But having heard, the Pharisees said: This (one) puts not out demons except by Beelzebub, the ruler/ leader of the demons.

12.25   And knowing their thoughts, he said to them: Every kingdom having been divided against itself will be laid waste/depopulated.

And every city or house having been divided against itself will not be standing.

12.26   And if Satan puts/throws out Satan, he was divided upon/against himself.

How then will his kingdom stand?   12.27 And I, if I put out the demons by Beelzebub, by whom *do* your sons put/throw them out?

Because of this they will be judges of ye/your judges.   12.28 But if I, I put out the demons by a spirit from God, then the kingdom of God came upon/to ye.

12.29   Or how is a certain one able to enter into the house of the strong (one) and to plunder his vessels/goods, unless he might first bound/tied the strong (one)? And then he will plunder his house.

12.30   The (one) not being with me is against me, and the (one) not gathering with me scatters me.

12.31   Because of this I say to ye: Every fault/ sin and slander/abusive speech will be forgiven for the men/humans, but the slander/abusive speech of the spirit will not be forgiven.   12.32 And who ever might speak a saying/word against the son of man, it will be forgiven for him; but who ever might speak against the holy spirit, truly it will not be forgiven for him, neither in this age nor in the (one) about to come. 12.33 Either make ye the tree good and it's fruit good,

or make ye the tree rotten and it's fruit rotten; for the tree is known from the fruit.

12.34   Generated (things) from snakes, how are ye able to speak good things, being evil (ones)? For the mouth speaks from the fullness of the heart.

12.35   The good man/human out of the good store/ treasure puts forth the good (things), and the evil man/human out of the evil store/treasure puts forth evil (things).

ΚΑΤΑ ΜΑΘΘΑΙΟΝ

12.36 λέγω δὲ ὑμῖν ὅτι πᾶν ῥῆμα ἀργὸν ὃ λαλήσουσιν οἱ ἄνθρωποι ἀποδώσουσιν περὶ αὐτοῦ λόγον ἐν ἡμέρᾳ κρίσεως· 12.37 ἐκ γὰρ τῶν λόγων σου δικεωθήσῃ, καὶ ἐκ τῶν λόγων καταδικασθήσῃ. 12.38 τότε ἀπεκρίθησαν αὐτῷ τινες τῶν γραμματέων καὶ Φαρισαίων λέγοντες, διδάσκαλε, θέλομεν ἀπὸ σοῦ σημῖον ἰδῖν.

12.39 ὁ δὲ ἀποκριθὶς εἶπεν αὐτοῖς, γενεὰ πονηρὰ καὶ μοιχαλὶς σημῖον ἐπιζητῖ, καὶ σημῖον οὐ δοθήσετε αὐτῇ εἰ μὴ τὸ σημῖον Ἰωνᾶ τοῦ προφήτου. 12.40 ὥσπερ γὰρ «ἦν Ἰωνᾶς ἐν τῇ κοιλίᾳ τοῦ κήτους τρῖς ἡμέρας καὶ τρῖς νύκτας,» οὕτως ἔστε ὁ υἱὸς τοῦ ἀνθρώπου ἐν τῇ καρδίᾳ τῆς γῆς τρῖς ἡμέρας καὶ τρεῖς νύκτας.

12.41 ἄνδρες Νινευεῖτε ἀναστήσοντε ἐν τῇ κρίσι μετὰ τῆς γενεᾶς ταύτης καὶ κατακρινοῦσιν αὐτήν· ὅτι μετενόησαν εἰς τὸ κήρυγμα Ἰωνᾶ, καὶ ἰδοὺ πλεῖον Ἰωνᾶ ὧδε. 12.42 βασίλισσα νότου ἐγερθήσετε ἐν τῇ κρίσει μετὰ τῆς γενεᾶς ταύτης καὶ κατακρινῖ αὐτήν· ὅτι ἦλθεν ἐκ τῶν περάτων τῆς γῆς ἀκοῦσε τὴν σοφίαν Σολομῶνος, καὶ ἰδοὺ πλεῖον Σολομῶνος ὧδε.

12.43 ὅταν δὲ τὸ ἀκάθαρτον πνεῦμα ἐξέλθῃ ἀπὸ τοῦ ἀνθρώπου, διέρχετε δι' ἀνύδρων τόπων ζητοῦν ἀνάπαυσιν, καὶ οὐχ εὑρίσκει. 12.44 τότε λέγι, εἰς τὸν οἶκόν μου ἐπιστρέψω ὅθεν ἐξῆλθον· καὶ ἐλθὸν εὑρίσκει σχολάζοντα καὶ σεσαρωμένον καὶ κεκοσμημένον. 12.45 τότε πορεύετε καὶ παραλαμβάνι μεθ' ἑαυτοῦ ἑπτὰ ἕτερα πνεύματα πονηρότερα ἑαυτοῦ, καὶ εἰσελθόντα κατοικῖ ἐκῖ· καὶ γίνετε τὰ ἔσχατα τοῦ ἀνθρώπου ἐκίνου χίρονα τῶν πρώτων. οὕτως ἔστε καὶ τῇ γενεᾷ ταύτῃ τῇ πονηρᾷ. 12.46 ἔτι αὐτοῦ λαλοῦντος τοῖς ὄχλοις ἰδοὺ ἡ μήτηρ καὶ οἱ ἀδελφοὶ αὐτοῦ ἱστήκισαν ἔξω ζητοῦντες αὐτῷ λαλῆσαι. 12.47 εἶπεν δέ τις τῶν μαθητῶν αὐτοῦ ἰδοὺ ἡ μήτηρ σου καὶ οἱ ἀδελφοί σου ἔξω ἑστήκασιν ζητοῦντές σε.

12.48 ὁ δὲ ἀποκριθεὶς εἶπεν τῷ λέγοντι αὐτῷ, τίς ἐστιν ἡ μήτηρ μου, καὶ τίνες εἰσὶν οἱ ἀδελφοί μου; 12.49 καὶ ἐκτίνας τὴν χῖρα αὐτοῦ ἐπὶ τοὺς μαθητὰς αὐτοῦ εἶπεν, ἰδοὺ ἡ μήτηρ μου

12.36 But I say to ye that every idle word that the men will speak, they will give an account concerning it in a day of judgment; 12.37 for from your sayings/words you will be vindicated, and from the sayings/words you will be condemned. 12.38 Then some of the scribes and Pharisees replied to him, saying: Teacher, we wish to see a sign from you.

12.39 And answering, the (he) said to them: An evil and adulterous generation seeks for a sign, and a sign will not be given to it except the sign of Jonas the prophet. 12.40 For just as JONAS WAS IN THE BELLY OF THE SEA-MONSTER THREE DAYS AND THREE NIGHTS, so the son of man will be in the heart of the earth three days and three nights.

12.41 Men, Ninevites, will stand up in the judgment with/after this generation, and they will condemn it; because they repented in/to the heralding/preaching of Jonas, and behold, (one) greater than Jonas *is* here. 12.42 *The* queen from *the* south will be raised in the judgment with/after this generation, and she will condemn it; because she came from the ends of the land/earth to hear the wisdom of Solomon, and behold, (one) greater than Solomon *is* here.

12.43 And whenever the unclean spirit might go out from the man, it goes through waterless places seeking rest, and it finds not. 12.44 Then it says: I shall return to my house/abode from which I came out; and coming, it finds *it* standing empty, both having been cleaned and having been furnished. 12.45 Then it goes and takes with itself seven other/different spirits more evil from itself, and having entered, it dwells there; and the last (things) from/of that man becomes worse from the first (things). And thus it will be for this evil generation. 12.46 From him yet speaking to the crowds, behold, the mother and the brothers of him stood outside seeking to speak with him. 12.47 And someone of his learners said: Behold, your mother and your brothers *are* outside seeking you.

12.48 And the (he) answering, he said to the (one) speaking to him: Who is my mother, and who are my brothers? 12.49 And stretching forth his hand to his learners/pupils, he said: Behold my mother and my

καὶ οἱ ἀδελφοί μου·

12.50 ὅστις γὰρ ἂν ποιήσῃ τὸ θέλημα τοῦ πατρός μου τοῦ ἐν οὐρανοῖς αὐτός μου ἀδελφὸς καὶ ἀδελφὴ καὶ μήτηρ ἐστίν. 13.1 ἐν τῇ ἡμέρᾳ ἐκίνῃ ἐξελθὼν ὁ Ἰησοῦς ἐκ τῆς οἰκίας ἐκάθητο παρὰ τὴν θάλασσαν· 13.2 καὶ συνήχθησαν πρὸς αὐτὸν ὄχλοι πολλοί, ὥστε αὐτὸν εἰς πλοῖον ἐμβάτα καθῆσθε, καὶ πᾶς ὁ ὄχλος ἐπὶ τὸν αἰγιαλὸν ἱστήκι.

13.3 καὶ ἐλάλησεν αὐτοῖς πολλὰ ἐν παραβολαῖς λέγων, ἰδοὺ ἐξῆλθεν ὁ σπίρων τοῦ σπίρε. 13.4 καὶ ἐν τῷ σπίριν αὐτὸν ἃ μὲν ἔπεσεν παρὰ τὴν ὁδόν, καὶ ἦλθεν τὰ πετινὰ καὶ κατέφαγεν αὐτά.

13.5 ἄλλα δὲ ἔπεσεν ἐπὶ τὰ πετρώδη ὅπου οὐκ εἶχεν γῆν πολλήν, καὶ εὐθέως ἐξανέτιλεν διὰ τὸ μὴ ἔχιν βάθος γῆς. 13.6 ἡλίου δὲ ἀνατίλαντος ἐκαυματίσθη καὶ διὰ τὸ μὴ ἔχειν ῥίζαν ἐξηράνθη.

13.7 ἄλλα δὲ ἔπεσεν ἐπὶ τὰς ἀκάνθας, καὶ ἀνέβησαν αἱ ἄκανθαι καὶ ἔπνιξαν αὐτά.

13.8 ἄλλα δὲ ἔπεσεν ἐπὶ τὴν γῆν τὴν καλὴν καὶ ἐδίδου καρπόν, ὃ μὲν ἑκατόν, ὃ δὲ ἑξήκοντα, ὃ δὲ τριάκοντα. 13.9 ὁ ἔχων ὦτα ἀκουέτω. 13.10 καὶ προσελθόντες οἱ μαθηταὶ εἶπαν αὐτῷ, διὰ τί ἐν παραβολαῖς αὐτοῖς λαλεῖς ; 13.11 ὁ δὲ ἀποκριθεὶς εἶπεν ὅτι ὑμῖν δέδοται γνῶνε τὰ μυστήρια τῆς βασιλίας τῶν οὐρανῶν, ἐκίνοις δὲ οὐ δέδοται.

13.12 ὅστις γὰρ ἔχει, δοθήσετε αὐτῷ καὶ περισσευθήσετε· ὅστις δὲ οὐκ ἔχι, καὶ ὃ ἔχει ἀρθήσετε ἀπ᾽ αὐτοῦ. 13.13 διὰ τοῦτο ἐν παραβολαῖς αὐτοῖς λαλῶ, ὅτι βλέποντες οὐ βλέπουσιν καὶ ἀκούοντες οὐκ ἀκούουσιν οὐδὲ συνίουσιν·

13.14 καὶ ἀναπληροῦται αὐτοῖς ἡ προφητία Ἡσαΐου ἡ λέγουσα, « ἀκοῇ ἀκούσετε καὶ οὐ μὴ συνῆτε, καὶ βλέποντες βλέψητε καὶ οὐ μὴ ἴδητε. 13.15 ἐπαχύνθη γὰρ ἡ καρδία τοῦ λαοῦ τούτου, καὶ τοῖς ὠσὶν αὐτῶν βαρέως ἤκουσαν, καὶ τοὺς

brothers;

12.50 for who ever might do the will of my father, of the (one) in heavens/skies, this (one) is my brother and sister and mother. 13.1 On that day Jesus, going out of the house, was sitting beside the sea; 13.2 and many crowds were gathered near him, so as for him having embarked in a boat to sit, and all the crowd was standing on the seashore.

13.3 And he spoke many (things) to them in parables, saying: Behold, the (one) sowing went out from the (thing) to sow. 13.4 And in the (thing)/at the time *for* him to sow, some on the one hand fell beside the road, and the birds came and devoured them.

13.5 And others fell upon the rocky (places) where it had not much earth, and immediately it sprang up because of the (thing) not to have depth of earth. 13.6 But from *the* sun having risen, it was scorched, and because of the (thing) not to have a root, it was withered.

13.7 And others fell upon the thorns, and the thorns came up and choked them.

13.8 But others (different) fell upon the good land and gave produce/fruit, the one a hundred, the other sixty, the other thirty. 13.9 The (one) having ears, let him hear. 13.10 And coming near, the learners/pupils said to him: Why *do* you speak to them in/by parables? 13.11 And the (he) answering, he said: It has been given to ye to know the mysteries of the kingdom of the skies/heavens, but to those it has not been given.

13.12 For whoever has, it will be given to him and he will be made abundant; but whoever has not, even what he has will be taken up from him. 13.13 Because of this I speak to them in parables, because seeing they see not and hearing they hear not, neither *do* they understand.

13.14 And it is fulfilled for them, the prophesy of Isaiah, the (one) saying: IN A HEARING/BY A REPORT YE WILL HEAR AND BY NO MEANS MIGHT YE UNDERSTAND, AND SEEING, YE MAY SEE AND BY NO MEANS MIGHT YE PERCEIVE. 13.15 FOR THE HEART OF THIS PEOPLE WAS FATTENED, THEY HEARD HEAVILY WITH THEIR EARS, AND THEY CLOSED THEIR

ὀφθαλμοὺς αὐτῶν ἐκάμμυσαν· μήποτε ἴδωσιν τοῖς ὀφθαλμοῖς καὶ τοῖς ὠσὶν ἀκούσωσιν καὶ τῇ καρδίᾳ συνῶσιν καὶ ἐπιστρέψωσιν, καὶ ἰάσομε αὐτούς.»

13.16 ὑμῶν δὲ μακάριοι οἱ ὀφθαλμοὶ ὅτι βλέπουσιν, καὶ τὰ ὦτα ὑμῶν ὅτι ἀκούουσιν.

13.17 ἀμὴν λέγω ὑμῖν ὅτι πολλοὶ προφῆτε καὶ δίκαιοι ἐπεθύμησαν ἰδῖν ἃ βλέπετε καὶ οὐκ ἴδαν, καὶ ἀκοῦσε ἃ ἀκούετε καὶ οὐκ ἤκουσαν.

13.18 ὑμῖς οὖν ἀκούσατε τὴν παραβολὴν τοῦ σπίραντος. 13.19 παντὸς ἀκούοντος τὸν λόγον τῆς βασιλίας καὶ μὴ συνιέντος, ἔρχετε ὁ πονηρὸς καὶ ἁρπάζι τὸ ἐσπαρμένον ἐν τῇ καρδίᾳ αὐτοῦ· οὗτός ἐστιν ὁ παρὰ τὴν ὁδὸν σπαρίς.

13.20 ὁ δὲ ἐπὶ τὰ πετρώδη σπαρίς, οὗτός ἐστιν ὁ τὸν λόγον ἀκούων καὶ εὐθὺς μετὰ χαρᾶς λαμβάνων αὐτόν· 13.21 οὐκ ἔχι δὲ ῥίζαν ἐν ἑαυτῷ ἀλλὰ πρόσκαιρός ἐστιν, γενομένης δὲ θλίψεως ἢ διωγμοῦ διὰ τὸν λόγον εὐθὺς σκανδαλίζεται.

13.22 ὁ δὲ εἰς τὰς ἀκάνθας σπαρείς, οὗτός ἐστιν ὁ τὸν λόγον ἀκούων καὶ ἡ μέριμνα τοῦ αἰῶνος καὶ ἡ ἀπάτη τοῦ πλούτου συνπνίγει τὸν λόγον, καὶ ἄκαρπος γίνετε.

13.23 ὁ δὲ ἐπὶ τὴν καλὴν γῆν σπαρίς, οὗτός ἐστιν ὁ τὸν λόγον ἀκούων καὶ συνιείς, ὃς δὴ καρποφορῖ καὶ ποιεῖ ὃ μὲν ἑκατόν, ὃ δὲ ἑξήκοντα, ὃ δὲ τριάκοντα. 13.24 ἄλλην παραβολὴν παρέθηκεν αὐτοῖς λέγων, ὡμοιώθη ἡ βασιλία τῶν οὐρανῶν ἀνθρώπῳ σπίραντι καλὸν σπέρμα ἐν τῷ ἀγρῷ αὐτοῦ. 13.25 ἐν δὲ τῷ καθεύδιν τοὺς ἀνθρώπους ἦλθεν αὐτοῦ ὁ ἐχθρὸς καὶ ἐπέσπειρεν ζιζάνια ἀνὰ μέσον τοῦ σίτου καὶ ἀπῆλθεν.

13.26 ὅτε δὲ ἐβλάστησεν ὁ χόρτος καὶ καρπὸν ἐποίησεν, τότε ἐφάνη καὶ τὰ ζιζάνια. 13.27 προσελθόντες δὲ οἱ δοῦλοι τοῦ οἰκοδεσπότου εἶπον αὐτῷ, κύριε, οὐχὶ καλὸν σπέρμα ἔσπιρας ἐν τῷ σῷ ἀγρῷ; πόθεν οὖν ἔχι ζιζάνια;

EYES; LEST THEY MIGHT PERCEIVE WITH THE EYES AND THEY MIGHT HEAR WITH THE EARS AND THEY MIGHT UNDERSTAND IN THE HEART AND THEY MIGHT TURN BACK/REPENT, AND I SHALL HEAL THEM.

13.16 But the eyes of ye *are* happy (ones), because they see, and the ears of ye because they hear.

13.17 For truly I say to ye that many prophets and just (ones) desired to see what ye see and they saw not, and to hear what ye hear and they heard not.

13.18 Therefore ye, hear ye the parable of the (one) having sown. 13.19 Each (one) hearing the saying/word of the kingdom and not understanding *it*, the evil (one) comes and snatches away the (thing) having been sown in his heart; this is the (one) having been sown beside the road.

13.20 And that having been sown upon the rocky places, this is the (one) hearing the saying and quickly receiving it with joy; 13.21 but he has not a root in himself, but he is temporary, and from tribulation/oppression or prosecution having been generated because of the saying, he is quickly offended/caused to stumble.

13.22 And that having been sown in the thorns, this is the (one) hearing the saying and the burden of the age and the deceit of the wealth chokes to death the saying/word, and he becomes unfruitful/unproductive.

13.23 And that having been sown upon the good land, this is the (one) hearing and understanding the saying/word, who then produces, and makes the one a hundred, the other sixty, the other thirty. 13.24 He put to them another parable, saying: The kingdom of the skies/heavens was likened to a man having sown good seed in his field. 13.25 But in the (time) *for* the men to sleep, his enemy came and sowed grasses/darnel in the midst of the grain, and he went away.

13.26 And when the blade/stalk grew and made fruit/produce, then was made clear the grasses/darnel. 13.27 And having come near, the slaves of the housemaster said to him: Lord, sowed you not good seed in your field? Then from where has it grasses/darnel?

13.28 ὁ δὲ ἔφη αὐτοῖς, ἐχθρὸς ἄνθρωπος τοῦτο ἐποίησεν. οἱ δὲ δοῦλοι λέγουσιν αὐτῷ, θέλις οὖν ἀπελθόντες συλλέξωμεν αὐτά; 13.29 ὁ δέ φησιν, οὔ, μήποτε συλλέγοτες τὰ ζιζάνια ἐκριζώσητε ἅμα αὐτοῖς τὸν σῖτον. 13.30 ἄφετε συναυξάνεσθε ἀμφότερα ἄχρι τοῦ θερισμοῦ· καὶ ἐν τῷ καιρῷ τοῦ θερισμοῦ ἐρῶ τοῖς θερισταές, συλλέξατε πρῶτον τὰ ζιζάνια καὶ δήσατε αὐτὰ εἰς δέσμας πρὸς τὸ κατακαῦσε αὐτά, τὸν δὲ σῖτον συναγάγετε εἰς τὴν ἀποθήκην μου.

13.31 ἄλλην παραβολὴν παρέθηκεν αὐτοῖς λέγων, ὁμοία ἐστὶν ἡ βασιλεία τῶν οὐρανῶν κόκκῳ σινάπεως, ὃν λαβὼν ἄνθρωπος ἔσπιρεν ἐν τῷ ἀγρῷ αὐτοῦ· 13.32 ὃ μικρότερον μέν ἐστιν πάντων τῶν σπερμάτων, ὅταν δὲ αὐξηθῇ μεῖζον τῶν λαχάνων ἐστὶν καὶ γίνετε δένδρον, ὥστε ἐλθεῖν τὰ πετινὰ τοῦ οὐρανοῦ καὶ κατασκηνοῦν ἐν τοῖς κλάδοις αὐτοῦ.

13.33 ἄλλην παραβολὴν ἐλάλησεν αὐτοῖς λέγων· ὁμοία ἐστὶν ἡ βασιλεία τῶν οὐρανῶν ζύμῃ, ἣν λαβοῦσα γυνὴ ἐνέκρυψεν εἰς ἀλεύρου σάτα τρία ἕως οὗ ἐζυμώθη ὅλον. 13.34 ταῦτα πάντα ἐλάλησεν ὁ Ἰησοῦς ἐν παραβολαῖς τοῖς ὄχλοις, καὶ χωρὶς παραβολῆς οὐδὲν ἐλάλι αὐτοῖς· 13.35 ὅπως πληρωθῇ τὸ ῥηθὲν διὰ τοῦ προφήτου λέγοντος, « ἀνοίξω ἐν παραβολαῖς τὸ στόμα μου, ἐρεύξομαι κεκρυμμένα ἀπὸ καταβολῆς» κόσμου. 13.36 τότε ἀφὶς τοὺς ὄχλους εἰσῆλθεν εἰς τὴν οἰκίαν. καὶ προσῆλθον αὐτῷ οἱ μαθητε αὐτοῦ λέγοντες, διασάφησον ἡμῖν τὴν παραβολὴν τῶν ζιζανίων τοῦ ἀγροῦ.

13.37 ὁ δὲ ἀποκριθεὶς εἶπεν, ὁ σπίρων τὸ καλὸν σπέρμα ἐστὶν ὁ υἱὸς τοῦ ἀνθρώπου· 13.38 ὁ δὲ ἀγρός ἐστιν ὁ κόσμος· τὸ δὲ καλὸν σπέρμα, οὗτοί εἰσιν οἱ υἱοὶ τῆς βασιλίας· τὰ δὲ ζιζάνιά εἰσιν οἱ υἱοὶ τοῦ πονηροῦ, 13.39 ὁ δὲ ἐχθρὸς ὁ σπίρας αὐτὰ ἐστιν ὁ διάβολος· ὁ δὲ θερισμὸς συντέλεια αἰῶνός ἐστιν, οἱ δὲ θερισταὶ ἄγγελοί εἰσιν. 13.40 ὥσπερ οὖν συλλέγετε τὰ ζιζάνια καὶ πυρὶ κατακαίεται, οὕτως ἔστε ἐν τῇ συντελίᾳ τοῦ αἰῶνος· 13.41 ἀποστελῖ ὁ υἱὸς τοῦ ἀνθρώπου τοὺς ἀγγέλους, καὶ

13.28   And the (he) said to them: A man, an enemy, did this. And the slaves say to him: *Do* you want then, going out, *that* we should gather them? 13.29 But the (he) says: No, lest gathering the grasses/darnel ye might uproot the grain together with them.   13.30 Leave both to grow together until the harvest; and in/at the season/time of the harvest I shall say to the reapers: Gather ye first the grasses/darnel and bind ye them in bundles toward/for the (thing) to burn them, but gather ye the grain into my storehouse/barn.

13.31   He put another parable to them, saying: The kingdom of the skies/heavens is like a seed of mustard, which having taken, a man sowed in his field; 13.32 which indeed is smaller from all the seeds, but when it might grow, it is greater of the herbs and it becomes a tree, so as to come the birds of the sky/heaven and they settle/dwell among its branches.

13.33   He spoke another parable to them, saying: The kingdom of the skies/heavens is like leaven, which a woman having taken she concealed *it* in three measures of flour until which *time* all was leavened. 13.34 All these (things) Jesus spoke in/by parables to the crowds, and without a parable he spoke nothing to them;   13.35 so that was fulfilled the (thing) having been spoken through the prophet, saying: I SHALL OPEN MY MOUTH WITH/IN PARABLES, I SHALL DECLARE (THINGS) HAVING BEEN HIDDEN FROM *the* FOUNDING/FOUNDATION of a world.   13.36 Then, having sent away the crowds, he went into the house. And his learners/pupils came near to him, saying: Explain you for us the parable of the grasses/darnel/weeds of the field.

13.37   And the (he) answering, he said: The (one) sowing the good seed is the son of man,   13.38 and the field is the world; and the good seed: these are the sons of the kingdom; and the grasses/darnel/weeds are the sons of the evil (one),   13.39 and the enemy, the (one) having sown them, is the devil; and the harvest is completion of an age, and the reapers are messengers/angels. 13.40 Therefore, even as the grasses/weeds are gathered and consumed by fire, so it will be in the ending of the age;   13.41 the son of man will

συλλέξουσιν ἐκ τῆς βασιλίας αὐτοῦ πάντα τὰ σκάνδαλα καὶ τοὺς ποιοῦντας τὴν ἀνομίαν, 13.42 καὶ βαλοῦσιν αὐτοὺς εἰς τὴν κάμινον τοῦ πυρός· ἐκῖ ἔσται ὁ κλαυθμὸς καὶ ὁ βρυγμὸς τῶν ὀδόντων. 13.43 τότε οἱ δίκαιοι ἐκλάμψουσιν ὡς ὁ ἥλιος ἐν τῇ βασιλείᾳ τοῦ πατρὸς αὐτῶν. ὁ ἔχων ὦτα ἀκουέτω.

13.44 ὁμοία ἐστὶν ἡ βασιλεία τῶν οὐρανῶν θησαυρῷ κεκρυμμένῳ ἐν τῷ ἀγρῷ, ὃν εὑρὼν ἄνθρωπος ἔκρυψεν, καὶ ἀπὸ τῆς χαρᾶς αὐτοῦ ὑπάγι καὶ πωλῖ πάντα ὅσα ἔχι καὶ ἀγοράζει τὸν ἀγρὸν ἐκῖνον.

13.45 πάλιν ὁμοία ἐστὶν ἡ βασιλεία τῶν οὐρανῶν ἐμπόρῳ ζητοῦντι καλοὺς μαργαρίτας· 13.46 εὑρὼν δὲ ἕνα πολύτιμον μαργαρίτην ἀπελθὼν πέπρακεν πάντα ὅσα εἶχεν καὶ ἠγόρασεν αὐτόν. 13.47 πάλιν ὁμοία ἐστὶν ἡ βασιλία τῶν οὐρανῶν σαγήνῃ βληθίσῃ εἰς τὴν θάλασσαν καὶ ἐκ παντὸς γένους συναγαγούσῃ· 13.48 ἣν ὅτε ἐπληρώθη ἀναβιβάσαντες ἐπὶ τὸν αἰγιαλὸν καὶ καθίσαντες συνέλεξαν τὰ καλὰ εἰς ἄγγη, τὰ δὲ σαπρὰ ἔξω ἔβαλλον. 13.49 οὕτως ἔστε ἐν τῇ συντελίᾳ τοῦ αἰῶνος· ἐξελεύσοντε οἱ ἄγγελοι καὶ ἀφοριοῦσι τοὺς πονηροὺς ἐκ μέσου τῶν δικαίων 13.50 καὶ βαλοῦσιν αὐτοὺς εἰς τὴν κάμινον τοῦ πυρός· ἐκεῖ ἔστε ὁ κλαυθμὸς καὶ ὁ βρυγμὸς τῶν ὀδόντων. 13.51 συνήκατε ταῦτα πάντα; λέγουσιν αὐτῷ, ναί.

13.52 ὁ δὲ εἶπεν αὐτοῖς, διὰ τοῦτο πᾶς γραμματεὺς μαθητευθὶς τῇ βασιλίᾳ τῶν οὐρανῶν ὅμοιός ἐστιν ἀνθρώπῳ οἰκοδεσπότῃ ὅστις ἐκβάλλει ἐκ τοῦ θησαυροῦ αὐτοῦ καινὰ καὶ παλαιά.

13.53 καὶ ἐγένετο ὅτε ἐτέλεσεν ὁ Ἰησοῦς τὰς παραβολὰς ταύτας, μετῆρεν ἐκῖθεν. 13.54 καὶ ἐλθὼν εἰς τὴν πατρίδα αὐτοῦ ἐδίδασκεν αὐτοὺς ἐν τῇ συναγωγῇ αὐτῶν, ὥστε ἐκπλήσσεσθαι αὐτοὺς καὶ λέγειν, πόθεν τούτῳ ἡ σοφία αὕτη καὶ αἱ δυνάμις; 13.55 οὐχ οὗτός ἐστιν ὁ τοῦ τέκτονος υἱός; οὐχ ἡ μήτηρ αὐτοῦ λέγεται Μαριὰμ καὶ οἱ ἀδελφοὶ αὐτοῦ Ἰάκωβος καὶ Ἰωσὴφ καὶ

send forth the messengers/angels, and they will gather out of his kingdom all the (things) offending and those doing the lawlessness, 13.42 and they will throw them into the furnace of the fire; there will be the wailing and the gritting of the teeth. 13.43 Then the just (ones) will shine forth as the sun in the kingdom of their father. The (one) having ears, let him hear.

13.44 The kingdom of the skies/heavens is similar to a store/treasure having been hidden in the field, which a man having found, he concealed, and from his joy he goes and sells all (things) whatever he has and he buys that field.

13.45 Again, the kingdom of the skies/heavens is similar to a merchant seeking good pearls; 13.46 and having found one very valuable pearl, having gone away, he sold all (things) whatever he had and he bought it. 13.47 Again, the kingdom of the skies/heavens is similar/like to a net having been thrown into the sea and having gathered out of every kind; 13.48 which when it was filled, bringing it up to the seashore and sitting *there*, they gathered the good (things) into vessels, but they threw the corrupt (things) out. 13.49 So it will be in/at completion/ending of the age; the messengers/angels will go forth and they will set apart the evil (ones) from the midst of the just (ones) 13.50 and they will throw them into the furnace of the fire; there will be the wailing and the gritting of the teeth. 13.51 Understood ye all these (things)? They said to him: Yes.

13.52 And the (he) said to them: Because of this every scribe being made a learner/pupil for the kingdom of the heavens is similar to a man, to a housemaster, who puts out from his storehouse new (things) and old (things).

13.53 And it happened when Jesus finished these parables, *that* he removed from there. 13.54 And having gone into his native place/land, he taught them in their congregation, so as *for* them to be astonished and to say: From where *are* for this (one) this wisdom and the powers? 13.55 Is not this (one) the son of the craftsman/carpenter? *Is* not his mother called Mary

Σίμων καὶ Ἰούδας; 13.56 καὶ αἱ ἀδελφαὶ αὐτοῦ οὐχὶ πᾶσαι πρὸς ἡμᾶς εἰσιν; πόθεν οὖν τούτῳ ταῦτα πάντα; 13.57 καὶ ἐσκανδαλίζοντο ἐν αὐτῷ.

ὁ δὲ εἶπεν αὐτοῖς, οὐκ ἔστιν προφήτης ἄτιμος εἰ μὴ ἐν τῇ ἰδίᾳ πατρίδι καὶ ἐν τῇ οἰκίᾳ αὐτοῦ. 13.58 καὶ οὐκ ἐποίησεν ἐκῖ δυνάμις πολλὰς διὰ τὴν ἀπιστίαν αὐτῶν.

14.1 ἤκουσεν Ἡρώδης ἐν ἐκίνῳ τῷ καιρῷ ὁ τετραάρχης τὴν ἀκοὴν Ἰησοῦ, 14.2 καὶ εἶπεν τοῖς παισὶν αὐτοῦ, οὗτός ἐστιν Ἰωάννης ὁ βαπτιστής· αὐτὸς ἠγέρθη ἀπὸ τῶν νεκρῶν, καὶ διὰ τοῦτο αἱ δυνάμις ἐνεργοῦσιν ἐν αὐτῷ. 14.3 ὁ γὰρ Ἡρώδης κρατήσας τὸν Ἰωάννην ἔδησεν καὶ ἐν φυλακῇ ἀπέθετο διὰ Ἡρῳδιάδα τὴν γυναῖκα Φιλίππου τοῦ ἀδελφοῦ αὐτοῦ·

14.4 ἔλεγεν γὰρ Ἰωάννης αὐτῷ, οὐκ ἔξεστίν σοι ἔχιν αὐτήν. 14.5 καὶ θέλων αὐτὸν ἀποκτῖναι ἐφοβήθη τὸν ὄχλον, ὅτι ὡς προφήτην αὐτὸν εἶχον.

14.6 γενεσίοις δὲ γενομένοις τοῦ Ἡρώδου ὠρχήσατο ἡ θυγάτηρ τῆς Ἡρῳδιάδος ἐν τῷ μέσῳ καὶ ἤρεσεν τῷ Ἡρώδῃ, 14.7 ὅθεν μετὰ ὅρκου ὡμολόγησεν αὐτῇ δοῦναι ὃ ἐὰν αἰτήσηται. 14.8 ἡ δὲ προβιβασθῖσα ὑπὸ τῆς μητρὸς αὐτῆς, δός μοι, φησίν, ὧδε ἐπὶ πίνακι τὴν κεφαλὴν Ἰωάννου τοῦ βαπτιστοῦ. 14.9 καὶ ἐλυπήθη ὁ βασιλεὺς διὰ τοὺς ὅρκους καὶ τοὺς συνανακιμένους ἐκέλευσεν δοθῆναι, 14.10 καὶ πέμψας ἀπεκεφάλισεν Ἰωάννην ἐν τῇ φυλακῇ· 14.11 καὶ ἠνέχθη ἡ κεφαλὴ αὐτοῦ ἐπὶ πίνακι καὶ ἐδόθη τῷ κορασίῳ, καὶ ἤνεγκεν τῇ μητρὶ αὐτῆς. 14.12 καὶ προσελθόντες οἱ μαθηταὶ αὐτοῦ ἦραν τὸ πτῶμα καὶ ἔθαψαν αὐτόν, καὶ ἐλθόντες ἀπήγγιλαν τῷ Ἰησοῦ.

14.13 ἀκούσας δὲ ὁ Ἰησοῦς ἀνεχώρησεν ἐκῖθεν ἐν πλοίῳ εἰς ἔρημον τόπον κατ' ἰδίαν· καὶ ἀκούσαντες οἱ ὄχλοι ἠκολούθησαν αὐτῷ πεζοὶ ἀπὸ τῶν πόλεων. 14.14 καὶ ἐξελθὼν εἶδεν πολὺν ὄχλον, καὶ ἐσπλαγχνίσθη ἐπ' αὐτοῖς καὶ ἐθεράπευσεν τοὺς ἀρρώστους αὐτῶν.

14.15 ὀψίας δὲ γενομένης προσῆλθον αὐτῷ οἱ μαθητὲ

and his brothers James and Joseph and Simon and Judas? 13.56 And are not his sisters all near us? From where then *are* all these things for this (one)? 13.57 And they were offended by/in him.

But the (he) said to them: A prophet is not without honor, except in his own native place and in his house. 13.58 And he did/made not many powers because of their unbelief/lack of faith.

14.1 In that season/at that time Herod the tetrarch heard the report of Jesus, 14.2 and he said to his boys/servants: This (one) is John the baptizer; he was raised from the dead (ones), and because of this the powers are working in/by him. 14.3 For Herod, having seized *him*, bound and put John in prison because of Herodias, the woman of Philip his brother.

14.4 For John was saying to him: It is not lawful for you to have her. 14.5 And wanting to kill him, he feared the crowd, because they held him as a prophet.

14.6 And *when* having become the birthdays of Herod, the daughter of Herodias danced in the middle/midst and pleased Herod, 14.7 from what he professed with an oath to give to her what ever she might ask. 14.8 And the (she), having been told beforehand by her mother, she says: Give you to me, here on a platter, the head of John the baptizer. 14.9 And the king was grieved; because of the oaths and those reclining together at table, he ordered *it* to be given, 14.10 and having sent, he beheaded John in the prison; 14.11 and his head was brought on a platter and it was given to the girl/maiden, and she brought *it* to her mother. 14.12 And having come near, his learners/pupils took the corpse and they buried him, and having come, they reported *it* to Jesus.

14.13 And having heard, Jesus withdrew privately from there by boat to an uninhabited place; and hearing *this* the crowds followed him on foot from the cities. 14.14 And going forth, he saw a great crowd, and he was filled with compassion toward them, and he healed/treated their sick (ones).

14.15 And from evening having become, the learn-

λέγοντες, ἔρημός ἐστιν ὁ τόπος καὶ ἡ ὥρα παρῆλθεν ἤδη· ἀπόλυσον οὖν τοὺς ὄχλους, ἵνα ἀπελθόντες εἰς τὰς κώρας ἀγοράσωσιν ἑαυτοῖς βρώματα.

14.16 ὁ δὲ εἶπεν αὐτοῖς, οὐ χρίαν ἔχουσιν ἀπελθῖν· δότε αὐτοῖς ὑμῖς φαγῖν. 14.17 οἱ δὲ λέγουσιν αὐτῷ, οὐκ ἔχομεν ὧδε ἄρτους εἰ μὴ πέντε καὶ δύο ἰχθύας. 14.18 ὁ δὲ εἶπεν, Φέρετέ μοι ὧδε αὐτούς. 14.19 καὶ ἐκελεύσεν τοὺς ὄχλους ἀνακλιθῆναι ἐπὶ τοῦ χόρτου, καὶ λαβὼν τοὺς πέντε ἄρτους καὶ τοὺς δύο ἰχθύας, ἀναβλέψας εἰς τὸν οὐρανὸν εὐλόγησεν καὶ κλάσας ἔδωκεν τοῖς μαθηταῖς τοὺς ἄρτους οἱ δὲ μαθηταὶ τοῖς ὄχλοις. 14.20 καὶ ἔφαγον πάντες καὶ ἐχορτάσθησαν, καὶ ἦραν τὸ περισσεῦον τῶν κλασμάτων δώδεκα κοφίνους πλήρεις. 14.21 οἱ δὲ ἐσθίοντες ἦσαν ἄνδρες ὡσὶ πεντακισχίλιοι χωρὶς γυναικῶν καὶ παιδίων. 14.22 καὶ εὐθέως ἠνάγκασεν τοὺς μαθητὰς ἐμβῆνε εἰς τὸ πλοῖον καὶ προάγιν αὐτὸν εἰς τὸ πέραν, ἕως οὖ ἀπολύσῃ τοὺς ὄχλους. 14.23 καὶ ἀπολύσας τοὺς ὄχλους ἀνέβη εἰς τὸ ὄρος κατ' ἰδίαν προσεύξασθε.

ὀψίας δὲ γενομένης μόνος ἦν ἐκεῖ. 14.24 τὸ δὲ πλοῖον ἤδη μέσον τῆς θαλάσσης ἦν, βασανιζόμενον ὑπὸ τῶν κυμάτων, ἦν γὰρ ἐναντίος ὁ ἄνεμος.

14.25 τετάρτῃ δὲ φυλακῇ τῆς νυκτὸς ἦλθεν πρὸς αὐτοὺς περιπατῶν ἐπὶ τὴν θάλασσαν. 14.26 οἱ δὲ μαθηταὶ ἰδόντες αὐτὸν ἐπὶ τῆς θαλάσσης περιπατοῦντα ἐταράχθησαν λέγοντες ὅτι φάντασμά ἐστιν, καὶ ἀπὸ τοῦ φόβου ἔκραξαν. 14.27 εὐθὺς δὲ ἐλάλησεν ὁ Ἰησοῦς αὐτοῖς λέγων, θαρσῖτε, ἐγώ εἰμι· μὴ φοβῖσθε.

14.28 ἀποκριθὶς δὲ αὐτῷ ὁ Πέτρος εἶπεν, εἰ σὺ εἶ, κύριε, κέλευσόν με ἐλθῖν πρὸς σὲ ἐπὶ τὰ ὕδατα· 14.29 ὁ δὲ εἶπεν, ἐλθέ. καὶ καταβὰς ἀπὸ τοῦ πλοίου Πέτρος περιεπάτησεν ἐπὶ τὰ ὕδατα ἐλθῖν, ἦλθεν οὖν πρὸς τὸν Ἰησοῦν. 14.30 βλέπων δὲ τὸν ἄνεμον ἐφοβήθη, καὶ ἀρξάμενος καταποντίζεσθε ἔκραξεν λέγων, κύριε, σῶσόν με. 14.31 εὐθὺς δὲ ὁ Ἰησοῦς ἐκτίνα τὴν χεῖρα ἐπελάβετο αὐτοῦ καὶ λέγει αὐτῷ, ὀλιγόπιστε, εἰς τί ἐδίστασας;

ers/pupils came near to him, saying: The place is a desert and the hour passed already; therefore, dismiss you the crowds in order that, going away into the villages, they might buy foods for themselves.

14.16 But Jesus said to them: They have not a need to go away; ye, ye give for them to eat. 14.17 But they, they say to him: We have not loaves here, except five, and two fish. 14.18 And the (he) said: Ye bring them here to me. 14.19 And having ordered the crowds to recline on the grass, and taking the five loaves and the two fishes, looking up into the sky, he blessed *them* and, having broken *them*, he gave the loaves to the learners/pupils and the learners/pupils *gave* to the crowds. 14.20 And all ate and they were satisfied, and they took up the excess of the fragments twelve baskets full. 14.21 And those eating were about five thousand men, apart from women and children. 14.22 And immediately he compelled the learners/pupils to embark in the boat and to go before him to the other side, until which (time) he should dismiss the crowds. 14.23 And having dismissed the crowds, he went up to the mountain to pray privately.

And from evening having become, only he was there. 14.24 And the boat was already in the midst of the sea, being tortured by the waves, for the wind was contrary.

14.25 And in the fourth watch of the night, he went to them, walking on the sea. 14.26 And the learners/pupils, seeing him walking on the sea, they were troubled, saying that it is a phantom, and they cried out from the fear. 14.27 But Jesus spoke quickly to them, saying: Be ye of good courage, I, I am; fear ye not.

14.28 And answering, Peter said to him: If you, you are, Lord, you order me to go to you upon the waters: 14.29 and the (he) said: You come. And, going down from the boat, Peter walked upon the waters to go, then he came near/to Jesus. 14.30 But seeing the wind, he was afraid, and beginning to be submerged, he cried out, saying: Lord, you rescue/save me. 14.31 And Jesus, quickly stretching forth the hand, he took hold of him, and he says to him: One of little faith,

14.32 καὶ ἀναβάντων αὐτῶν εἰς τὸ πλοῖον ἐκόπασεν ὁ ἄνεμος. 14.33 οἱ δὲ ἐν τῷ πλοίῳ προσεκύνησαν αὐτῷ λέγοντες, ἀληθῶς θεοῦ υἱὸς εἶ. 14.34 καὶ διαπεράσαντες ἦλθον ἐπὶ τὴν γῆν εἰς Γεννησαρέτ. 14.35 καὶ ἐπιγνόντες αὐτὸν οἱ ἄνδρες τοῦ τόπου ἀπέστιλαν εἰς ὅλην τὴν περίχωρον ἐκίνην, καὶ προσήνεγκαν αὐτῷ πάντας τοὺς κακῶς ἔχοντας, 14.36 καὶ παρεκάλουν αὐτὸν ἵνα μόνον ἅψωνται τοῦ κρασπέδου τοῦ ἱματίου αὐτοῦ· καὶ ὅσοι ἥψαντο ἐσώθησαν.

15.1 Τότε προσέρχοντε τῷ Ἰησοῦ ἀπὸ Ἱεροσολύμων Φαρισαῖοι καὶ γραμματεῖς λέγοντες, 15.2 διὰ τί οἱ μαθητέ σου παραβαίνουσι τὴν παράδοσιν τῶν πρεσβυτέρων; οὐ γὰρ νίπτονται τὰς χῖρας ὅταν ἄρτον ἐσθίωσιν.

15.3 ὁ δὲ ἀποκριθεὶς εἶπεν αὐτοῖς, διὰ τί καὶ ὑμεῖς παραβαίνετε τὴν ἐντολὴν τοῦ θεοῦ διὰ τὴν παράδοσιν ὑμῶν; 15.4 ὁ γὰρ θεὸς ἐνετίλατο λόγων· «τίμα τὸν πατέρα καὶ τὴν μητέρα,» καί, « ὁ κακολογῶν πατέρα ἢ μητέρα θανάτῳ τελευτάτω»

15.5 ὑμῖς δὲ λέγετε, ὃς ἂν εἴπῃ τῷ πατρὶ ἢ τῇ μητρί, δῶρον ὃ ἐὰν ἐξ ἐμοῦ ὠφεληθῇς, 15.6 οὐδέν ἐστιν οὖν ἀτιμῆσι τὸν πατέρα αὐτοῦ· καὶ ἠκυρώσατε τὸν λόγον τοῦ θεοῦ διὰ τὴν παράδοσιν ὑμῶν.

15.7 ὑποκριταί, καλῶς ἐπροφήτευσεν περὶ ὑμῶν Ἡσαΐας λέγων,

15.8 « ὁ λαὸς οὗτος τοῖς χίλεσίν με τιμᾷ, ἡ δὲ καρδία αὐτῶν πόρρω ἀπέχει ἀπ' ἐμοῦ·

15.9 μάτην δὲ σέβονταί με, διδάσκοντες διδασκαλίας ἐντάλματα ἀνθρώπων.» 15.10 καὶ προσκαλεσάμενος τὸν ὄχλον εἶπεν αὐτοῖς, ἀκούετε καὶ συνίετε· 15.11 οὐ τὸ εἰσερχόμενον εἰς τὸ στόμα τοῦτο κοινοῖ τὸν ἄνθρωπον,

ἀλλὰ τὸ ἐκπορευόμενον ἐκ τοῦ στόματος τοῦτο κοινοῖ τὸν ἄνθρωπον.

15.12 τότε προσελθόντες οἱ μαθηταὶ εἶπαν αὐτῷ, οἶδας ὅτι οἱ Φαρισαῖοι ἀκούσαντες τὸν λόγον ἐσκανδαλίσθησαν;

15.13 ὁ δὲ ἀποκριθὶς εἶπεν, πᾶσα φυτία ἣν οὐκ ἐφύτευσεν

in what doubted you? 14.32 And from them going up into the boat, the wind ceased. 14.33 And those in the boat worshiped/genuflexed to him, saying: You are truly a son of God. 14.34 And crossing over, they came to the land in Gennesaret. 14.35 And recognizing him, the men of the place sent into all that surrounding region and they brought near to him all those having *it* badly, 14.36 and they besought him that they might touch only the hem of his garment; and as many as touched *it* were saved/delivered.

15.1 Then Pharisees and scribes from Jerusalem came near to Jesus, saying: 15.2 Why *do* your learners/pupils violate/deviate from the tradition of the elders? For they wash not the hands whenever they eat bread/a loaf.

15.3 And the (he) answering, he said to them: Why also *do* ye, ye violate/deviate from the command of God on account of your tradition? 15.4 For God enjoined/charged from sayings: HONOR THE FATHER AND THE MOTHER, and: THE (ONE) SPEAKING BAD OF FATHER OR MOTHER, LET HIM FINISH/END/DIE IN/BY DEATH.

15.5 But ye, ye say: Who ever might say to the father or the mother, *it is* a gift, what ever you might be owed from me, 15.6 there is certainly nothing dishonoring his father; and ye annulled the word/*law* of God on account of your tradition!

15.7 Pretenders/hypocrites, Isaiah prophesied well concerning ye, saying:

15.8 THIS PEOPLE HONORS ME WITH THE LIPS, BUT THEIR HEART IS FAR DISTANT FROM ME.

15.9 AND THEY REVERE ME IN VAIN, TEACHING *for* TEACHINGS/DOCTRINES PRECEPTS OF MEN. 15.10 And calling forward the crowd, he said to them: Hear ye and understand ye: 15.11 The (thing) entering into the mouth, this defiles not the man/human;

but the (thing) proceeding forth out of the mouth, this defiles the man.

15.12 Then the learners/pupils, coming near, say to him: Know you that the Pharisees hearing the saying/word were offended/caused to stumble?

15.13 And the (he), answering, he said: Every

ὁ πατήρ μου ὁ οὐράνιος ἐκριζωθήσετε.

15.14 ἄφετε αὐτούς· ὁδηγοί εἰσιν τυφλοί τυφλὸς δὲ τυφλὸν ἐὰν ὁδηγῇ, ἀμφότεροι εἰς βόθυνον πεσοῦνται.

15.15 ἀποκριθεὶς δὲ ὁ Πέτρος εἶπεν αὐτῷ, φράσον ἡμῖν τὴν παραβολήν.

15.16 ὁ δὲ εἶπεν, ἀκμὴν καὶ ὑμῖς ἀσύνετοί ἐστε; 15.17 οὐ νοεῖτε ὅτι πᾶν τὸ εἰσπορευόμενον εἰς τὸ στόμα εἰς τὴν κοιλίαν χωρῖ καὶ εἰς τὸν ἀφεδρῶνα ἐκβάλλετε; 15.18 τὰ δὲ ἐκπορευόμενα ἐκ τοῦ στόματος ἐκ τῆς καρδίας ἐξέρχεται, κἀκεῖνα κοινοῖ τὸν ἄνθρωπον. 15.19 ἐκ γὰρ τῆς καρδίας ἐξέρχονται διαλογισμοὶ πονηροί, φόνοι, μοιχεῖαι, πορνεῖαι, κλοπαί, ψευδομαρτυρίαι, βλασφημίαι.

15.20 ταῦτά ἐστιν τὰ κοινοῦντα τὸν ἄνθρωπον, τὸ δὲ ἀνίπτοις χερσὶν φαγῖν οὐ κοινοῖ τὸν ἄνθρωπον.

15.21 καὶ ἐξελθὼν ἐκῖθεν ὁ Ἰησοῦς ἀνεχώρησεν εἰς τὰ μέρη Τύρου καὶ Σιδῶνος. 15.22 καὶ ἰδοὺ γυνὴ Χαναναία ἀπὸ τῶν ὁρίων ἐκίνων ἐξελθοῦσα ἔκραζεν λέγουσα, ἐλέησόν με, κύριε, υἱὲ Δαυίδ· ἡ θυγάτηρ μου κακῶς δαιμονίζετε. 15.23 ὁ δὲ οὐκ ἀπεκρίθη αὐτῇ λόγον. καὶ προσελθόντες οἱ μαθηταὶ αὐτοῦ ἠρώτουν αὐτὸν λέγοντες, ἀπόλυσον αὐτήν, ὅτι κράζει ὄπισθεν ἡμῶν. 15.24 ὁ δὲ ἀποκριθὶς εἶπεν, οὐκ ἀπεστάλην εἰ μὴ εἰς τὰ πρόβατα τὰ ἀπολωλότα οἴκου Ἰσραήλ. 15.25 ἡ δὲ ἐλθοῦσα προσεκύνι αὐτῷ λέγουσα, κύριε, βοήθι μοι. 15.26 ὁ δὲ ἀποκριθεὶς εἶπεν, οὐκ ἔστιν καλὸν λαβῖν τὸν ἄρτον τῶν τέκνων καὶ βαλῖν τοῖς κυναρίοις. 15.27 ἡ δὲ εἶπεν, ναί, κύριε, καὶ γὰρ τὰ κυνάρια ἐσθίει ἀπὸ τῶν ψιχίων τῶν πιπτόντων ἀπὸ τῆς τραπέζης τῶν κυρίων αὐτῶν. 15.28 τότε ἀποκριθεὶς ὁ Ἰησοῦς εἶπεν αὐτῇ, ὦ γύναι, μεγάλη σου ἡ πίστις· γενηθήτω σοι ὡς θέλις. καὶ ἰάθη ἡ θυγάτηρ αὐτῆς ἀπὸ τῆς ὥρας ἐκίνης. 15.29 καὶ μεταβὰς

ἐκῖθεν ὁ Ἰησοῦς ἦλθεν παρὰ τὴν θάλασσαν τῆς Γαλιλαίας, καὶ ἀναβὰς εἰς τὸ ὄρος ἐκάθητο ἐκεῖ.

plant which my heavenly father planted not will be uprooted.

15.14 Leave ye them; leaders/guides are blind (ones), and if a blind (one) might guide a blind (one), both will fall into a ditch.

15.15 And answering, Peter said to him: Explain you to us the parable.

15.16 And the (he) said: Ye, are ye also still senseless (ones)? 15.17 Perceive ye not that every thing entering into the mouth proceeds into the belly and is put out in the drain? 15.18 But the (things) going forth out of the mouth comes forth from the heart, and those (things) defile the man. 15.19 For out of the heart come forth evil reasonings/opinions/ arguments, murders, adulteries, prostitutions, thefts, lying testimonies, *and* slanderings/blasphemies.

15.20 These are the (things) defiling the human/man, but the (thing) to eat with unwashed hands defiles not the man.

15.21 And going forth from there, Jesus withdrew into the parts of Tyre and Sidon. 15.22 And behold, a Canaanite woman having come forth from those borders, she cried out, saying: You have mercy on me, Lord, son of David; my daughter is badly demon-possessed. 15.23 But the (he) answered not a word to her. And coming near, his pupils/learners were entreating him, saying: Send her away, because she cries out behind us. 15.24 And the (he) answering, he said: I was sent not except to the lost sheep of *the* house of Israel. 15.25 But the (she) having come, she worshiped/genuflexed to him, saying: Lord, you help me. 15.26 But the (he) answering, he said: It is not good to take the loaf/ bread from the children and to throw *it* to the dogs. 15.27 But the (she)said: Yes, Lord, for even the dogs eat from the crumbs, those falling from the tables of their lords. 15.28 Then answering, Jesus said to her: O woman, great *is* your faith; let it become for you as you want. And her daughter was healed from that hour/ time. 15.29 And having departed

from there, Jesus went beside the sea of Galilee, and having gone up to the mountain, he was sitting there.

15.30 καὶ προσῆλθον αὐτῷ ὄχλοι πολλοὶ ἔχοντες μεθ' ἑαυτῶν χωλούς, τυφλούς, κυλλούς, κωφούς, καὶ ἑτέρους πολλούς, καὶ ἔριψαν αὐτοὺς παρὰ τοὺς πόδας αὐτοῦ, καὶ ἐθεράπευσεν αὐτούς·

15.31 ὥστε τὸν ὄχλον θαυμάσαι βλέποντας

κωφοὺς λαλοῦντας, κυλλοὺς καὶ χωλοὺς περιπατοῦντας καὶ, τυφλοὺς βλέποντας·

καὶ ἐδόξασον τὸν θεὸν Ἰσραήλ.

15.32 ὁ δὲ Ἰησοῦς προσκαλεσάμενος τοὺς μαθητὰς εἶπεν αὐτοῖς, σπλαγχνίζομε ἐπὶ τὸν ὄχλον, ὅτι ἤδη ἡμέρας τρεῖς προσμένουσί μοι καὶ οὐκ ἔχουσιν τί φάγωσιν· καὶ ἀπολῦσε αὐτοὺς νήστις οὐ θέλω, μὴ ἐκλυθῶσιν ἐν τῇ ὁδῷ. 15.33 καὶ λέγουσιν αὐτῷ οἱ μαθηταί, πόθεν ἡμῖν ἐν ἐρημίᾳ ἄρτοι τοσοῦτοι ὥστε χορτάσε ὄχλον τοσοῦτον; 15.34 καὶ λέγει αὐτοῖς ὁ Ἰησοῦς, πόσους ἄρτους ἔχετε; οἱ δὲ εἶπαν, ἑπτά, καὶ ὀλίγα ἰχθύδια.

15.35 καὶ παραγγίλας τῷ ὄχλῳ ἀναπεσεῖν ἐπὶ τὴν γῆν 15.35 ἔλαβεν τοὺς ἑπτὰ ἄρτους καὶ τοὺς δύο ἰχθύας καὶ εὐχαριστήσας ἔκλασεν καὶ ἐδίδου τοῖς μαθηταῖς, οἱ δὲ μαθηταὶ τοῖς ὄχλοις. 15.37 καὶ ἔφαγον πάντες καὶ ἐχορτάσθησαν, καὶ ἦραν τὸ περισσεῦον τῶν κλασμάτων, ἑπτὰ σπυρίδας πλήρις. 15.38 οἱ δὲ ἐσθίοντες ἦσαν ἄνδρες ὧσι τετρακισχίλιοι χωρὶς πεδίων καὶ γυνεκῶν.

15.39 καὶ ἀπολύσας τοὺς ὄχλους ἐνέβη εἰς τὸ πλοῖον, καὶ ἦλθεν εἰς τὰ ὅρια Μαγαδάν. 16.1 καὶ προσελθόντες οἱ Φαρισαῖοι καὶ οἱ Σαδδουκαῖοι πιράζοντες ἐπηρώτησαν αὐτὸν σημῖον ἐκ τοῦ οὐρανοῦ ἐπιδῖξε αὐτοῖς.

16.2 ὁ δὲ ἀποκριθεὶς εἶπεν αὐτοῖς, — 16.4 γενεὰ πονηρὰ καὶ μοιχαλὶς σημῖον ἐπιζητεῖ, καὶ σημῖον οὐ δοθήσετε αὐτῇ εἰ μὴ τὸ σημῖον Ἰωνᾶ. καὶ καταλιπὼν αὐτοὺς ἀπῆλθεν. 16.5 καὶ ἐλθόντες οἱ μαθηταὶ εἰς τὸ πέραν ἐπελάθοντο ἄρτους λαβεῖν.

16.6 ὁ δὲ Ἰησοῦς εἶπεν, ὁρᾶτε καὶ προσέχετε ἀπὸ τῆς ζύμης τῶν Φαρισαίων καὶ Σαδδουκαίων. 16.7 οἱ δὲ διελογίζοντο

15.30 And many crowds came near to him, having with themselves lame (ones), blind (ones), crippled (ones), mute (ones), and many other/different (ones), and they let them down beside his feet, and he heal-ed/treated them;

15.31 So as *for* the crowd to wonder, seeing mute (ones) speaking, crippled (ones) and lame (ones) walking, and blind (ones) seeing. and they glorified/praised the God of Israel.

15.32 And Jesus, calling forward the learners/pupils, he said to them: I am compassionate to the crowd, because already they stay with me three days, and they have not eaten anything; and I want not to dismiss them starving/fasting; might not they be fainted on the way/road? 15.33 And the learners/pupils say to him: From where, for us in a desert (place), *are* so many loaves so as to satisfy/fill so great a crowd? 15.34 And Jesus says to them: How many loaves have ye? And they said: Seven, and a few little fish.

15.35 And having charged for the crowd to recline on the earth/ground, 15.36 he took the seven loaves and the two fishes and having given thanks, he broke *it* and he was giving to the learners/pupils, and the learners/pupils to the crowds. 15.37 And all ate and they were filled/satisfied, and they took up the overflow/excess of the fragments, seven baskets full. 15.38 And those eating were about four thousand men, apart from children and women.

15.39 And having dismissed the crowds, he embarked in the boat, and he went into the borders of Magadan. 16.1 And coming near, the Pharisees and the Sadducees, trying/testing him, they asked *for* him to demonstrate a sign out of the sky\heaven for them.

16.2 But the (he) answering, he said to them: -- 16.4 An evil and adulterous generation seeks for a sign, and a sign will not be given to it except the sign of Jonah. And leaving them, he went away. 16.5 And the learners/pupils, going to the other side, they forgot to take loaves.

16.6 And Jesus said: Observe ye and ye take heed from the leaven of the Pharisees and Sadducees. 16.7

ἐν ἑαυτοῖς λέγοντες ὅτι ἄρτους οὐκ ἐλάβομεν.

16.8 γνοὺς δὲ ὁ Ἰησοῦς εἶπεν, τί διαλογίζεσθε ἐν ἑαυτοῖς, ὀλιγόπιστοι, ὅτι ἄρτους οὐκ ἔχετε;

16.9 οὔπω νοεῖτε, οὐδὲ μνημονεύεται τοὺς πέντε ἄρτους τῶν πεντακισχιλίων καὶ πόσους κοφίνους ἐλάβετε; 16.10 οὐδὲ τοὺς ἑπτὰ ἄρτους τῶν τετρακισχιλίων καὶ πόσας σπυρίδας ἐλάβετε; 16.11 πῶς οὐ νοεῖτε ὅτι οὐ περὶ ἄρτων εἶπον ὑμῖν; προσέχετε δὲ ἀπὸ τῆς ζύμης τῶν Φαρεισαίων καὶ Σαδδουκαίων. 16.12 τότε συνῆκαν ὅτι οὐκ εἶπεν προσέχειν ἀπὸ τῆς ζύμης τῶν ἄρτων Φαρεισαίων καὶ Σαδδουκαίων ἀλλὰ ἀπὸ τῆς διδαχῆς τῶν Φαρισαίων καὶ Σαδδουκαίων.

16.13 ἐλθὼν δὲ ὁ Ἰησοῦς εἰς τὰ μέρη Καισαρείας τῆς Φιλίππου ἠρώτα τοὺς μαθητὰς αὐτοῦ λέγων, τίνα οἱ ἄνθρωποι εἶναι λέγουσιν τὸν υἱὸν τοῦ ἀνθρώπου; 16.14 οἱ δὲ εἶπον, οἱ μὲν Ἰωάννην τὸν βαπτιστήν, ἄλλοι δὲ Ἠλίαν, ἕτεροι δὲ Ἰερεμίαν ἢ ἕνα τῶν προφητῶν. 16.15 λέγει αὐτοῖς, ὑμεῖς δὲ τίνα με λέγετε εἶναι; 16.16 ἀποκριθεὶς δὲ Σίμων Πέτρος εἶπεν, σὺ εἶ ὁ χριστὸς ὁ υἱὸς τοῦ θεοῦ τοῦ ζῶντος. 16.17 ἀποκριθεὶς δὲ ὁ Ἰησοῦς εἶπεν αὐτῷ, μακάριος εἶ, Σίμων Βαριωνᾶ, ὅτι σὰρξ καὶ αἷμα οὐκ ἀπεκάλυψέν σοι ἀλλὰ ὁ πατήρ μου ὁ ἐν τοῖς οὐρανοῖς. 16.18 κἀγὼ δέ σοι λέγω ὅτι σὺ εἶ Πέτρος, καὶ ἐπὶ ταύτη τῇ πέτρα οἰκοδομήσω μου τὴν ἐκκλησίαν, καὶ πύλαι ἄδου οὐ κατισχύσουσιν αὐτῆς. 16.19 δώσω σοι τὰς κλῖδας τῆς βασιλείας τῶν οὐρανῶν, καὶ ὃ ἐὰν δήσῃς ἐπὶ τῆς γῆς ἔσται δεδυμένον ἐν τοῖς οὐρανοῖς, καὶ ὃ ἐὰν λύσῃς ἐπὶ τῆς γῆς ἔσται λελυμένον ἐν τοῖς οὐρανοῖς. 16.20 τότε διεστείλατο τοῖς μαθηταῖς ἵνα μηδενὶ εἴπωσιν ὅτι αὐτός ἐστιν ὁ χριστός.

16.21 ἀπὸ τότε ἤρξατο ὁ Ἰησοῦς δικνύειν τοῖς μαθηταῖς αὐτοῦ ὅτι δεῖ αὐτὸν εἰς Ἱεροσόλυμα ἀπελθεῖν καὶ πολλὰ παθεῖν ἀπὸ τῶν πρεσβυτέρων καὶ ἀρχιερέων καὶ γραμματέων καὶ ἀποκτανθῆναι καὶ τῇ τρίτῃ ἡμέρᾳ ἐγερθῆναι.

And they were reasoning among themselves, saying: We took not loaves.

16.8 And knowing, Jesus said: Why discuss ye among yourselves, (ones) of little faith, because ye have not loaves?

16.9 *Do* ye not yet perceive, neither remember, the five loaves of the five thousand and how many baskets ye took up? 16.10 Nor the seven loaves of the four thousand and how many hampers ye took up? 16.11 How *do* ye perceive not that I spoke not to ye about loaves? But take ye heed from the leaven of the Pharisees and Sadducees. 16.12 Then they understood that he said not to take heed from the leaven of the loaves of Pharisees and Sadducees, but from the doctrine/teaching of the Pharisees and Sadducees.

16.13 And Jesus, going into the parts of Caesarea Philippi, he questioned his learners/pupils, saying: Who *do* men say *for* the son of the man/human to be? 16.14 And they said: Some *say* John the baptizer, and others *say* Elias, and others *say* Jeremias or one of the prophets. 16.15 He says to them: But ye, who say ye *for* me to be? 16.16 And answering, Simon Peter said: You, you are the anointed (one), the son of the living God! 16.17 And answering, Jesus said to him: You are a happy (one), Simon Barjonas, because flesh and blood revealed *it* not to you, but my father, the (one) in the skies/heavens. 16.18 And I also, I say that you, you are Peter, and upon this the rock I will build my assembly, and the gates of Hades will not overpower/prevail against it. 16.19 I will give to you the keys of the kingdom of the skies/heavens, and what ever you might bind upon the earth, it will have been bound in the skies/heavens, and what ever you might loose upon the earth it will have been loosed in the skies/heavens. 16.20 Then he issued a decision/gave orders to the learners/pupils that they should say to no one that he is the anointed (one).

16.21 From then Jesus began to show to his learners/pupils that it is necessary *for* him to go to Jerusalem and to suffer many (things) from the elders and chief/high priests and scribes, and to be killed, and on the third day to be raised.

16.22 καὶ προσλαβόμενος αὐτὸν ὁ Πέτρος ἤρξατο ἐπιτιμᾶν αὐτῷ λέγων, ἵλεώς σοι, κύριε· οὐ μὴ ἔσται σοι τοῦτο. 16.23 ὁ δὲ στραφεὶς εἶπεν τῷ Πέτρῳ, ὕπαγε ὀπίσω μου, Σατανᾶ· σκάνδαλον εἶ ἐμοῦ, ὅτι οὐ φρονεῖς τὰ τοῦ θεοῦ ἀλλὰ τὰ τῶν ἀνθρώπων.

16.24 τότε ὁ Ἰησοῦς εἶπεν τοῖς μαθηταῖς αὐτοῦ, εἴ τις θέλει ὀπίσω μου ἐλθεῖν, ἀπαρνησάσθω ἑαυτὸν καὶ ἀράτω τὸν σταυρὸν αὐτοῦ καὶ ἀκολουθείτω μοι. 16.25 ὃς γὰρ ἐὰν θέλῃ τὴν ψυχὴν αὐτοῦ σῶσαι ἀπολέσει αὐτήν· ὃς δ' ἂν ἀπολέσῃ τὴν ψυχὴν αὐτοῦ ἕνεκεν ἐμοῦ εὑρήσει αὐτήν. 16.26 τί γὰρ ὠφεληθήσεται ἄνθρωπος ἐὰν τὸν κόσμον ὅλον κερδήσῃ τὴν δὲ ψυχὴν αὐτοῦ ζημιωθῇ; ἢ τί δώσει ἄνθρωπος ἀντάλλαγμα τῆς ψυχῆς αὐτοῦ; 16.27 μέλλει γὰρ ὁ υἱὸς τοῦ ἀνθρώπου ἔρχεσθαι ἐν τῇ δόξῃ τοῦ πατρὸς αὐτοῦ μετὰ τῶν ἀγγέλων αὐτοῦ, καὶ τότε ἀποδώσει ἑκάστῳ κατὰ τὴν πρᾶξιν αὐτοῦ. 16.28 ἀμὴν λέγω ὑμῖν ὅτι εἰσίν τινες τῶν ὧδε ἑστώτων οἵτινες οὐ μὴ γεύσωνται θανάτου ἕως ἂν ἴδωσιν τὸν υἱὸν τοῦ ἀνθρώπου ἐρχόμενον ἐν τῇ δόξῃ τοῦ πατρὸς αὐτοῦ βασιλείᾳ αὐτοῦ.

17.1 Καὶ μεθ' ἡμέρας ἓξ παραλαμβάνει ὁ Ἰησοῦς τὸν Πέτρον καὶ τὸν Ἰάκωβον καὶ Ἰωάννην τὸν ἀδελφὸν αὐτοῦ, καὶ ἀναφέρει αὐτοὺς εἰς ὄρος ὑψηλὸν κατ' ἰδίαν. 17.2 καὶ μετεμορφώθη ἔμπροσθεν αὐτῶν, καὶ ἔλαμψεν τὸ πρόσωπον αὐτοῦ ὡς ὁ ἥλιος, τὰ δὲ ἱμάτια αὐτοῦ ἐγένετο λευκὰ ὡς τὸ φῶς. 17.3 καὶ ἰδοὺ ὤφθη αὐτοῖς Μωϋσῆς καὶ Ἡλείας συλλαλοῦντες μετ' αὐτοῦ. 17.4 ἀποκριθεὶς δὲ ὁ Πέτρος εἶπεν τῷ Ἰησοῦ, κύριε, καλόν ἐστιν ἡμᾶς ὧδε εἶναι· εἰ θέλεις, ποιήσω ὧδε τρεῖς σκηνάς, σοὶ μίαν καὶ Μωϋσεῖ μίαν καὶ Ἡλείᾳ μίαν. 17.5 ἔτι αὐτοῦ λαλοῦντος ἰδοὺ νεφέλη φωτεινὴ ἐπεσκίασεν αὐτούς, καὶ ἰδοὺ φωνὴ ἐκ τῆς νεφέλης λέγουσα, οὗτός ἐστιν ὁ υἱός μου ὁ ἀγαπητός, ἐν ᾧ εὐδόκησα· ἀκούετε αὐτοῦ. 17.6 καὶ ἀκούσαντες οἱ μαθηταὶ ἔπεσαν ἐπὶ πρόσωπον αὐτῶν καὶ ἐφοβήθησαν σφόδρα. 17.7 καὶ προσῆλθεν ὁ Ἰησοῦς καὶ ἁψάμενος αὐτῶν εἶπεν, ἐγέρθητε καὶ μὴ φοβεῖσθε. 17.8 ἐπάραντες δὲ τοὺς

16.22 And taking exception to him, Peter began to rebuke him, saying: Mercy for you, Lord, this (thing) will certainly not be for you. 16.23 But the (he) turning, he said to Peter: You go/depart behind me, Satan; you are an offense/stumbling block of me because you think not the (things) of God but the (things) of the men/humans.

16.24 Then Jesus said to his learners/pupils: If anyone wants to come after/behind me, let him/her deny himself and let him/her take up his cross and let him follow me. 16.25 For who ever may want to save his life/soul, he will lose it; but who ever might lose his life/soul on account of me, he will find it. 16.26 For what will a man be profited if he might gain the entire world, but his life/soul might be lost? Or, what will a man give *as* an exchange for his life/soul? 16.27 For the son of man is about to come in the glory/reputation of his father with the messengers/angels of him, and then he will give back/repay to each (one) according to his practice. 16.28 Truly I say to ye that there are some of those standing here who will certainly not taste of death until they might see the son of the man/human coming/going in the glory/reputation of his father, of his kingdom.

17.1 And after six days, Jesus takes along Peter and James and his brother John, and he brings them privately to a high mountain. 17.2 And he was transformed before them, and his face shone as the sun, and his garments became white as the light. 17.3 And behold, Moses and Elias were seen by them, conferring with him. 17.4 And answering, Peter said to Jesus: Lord, it is good *for* us to be here; if you want, we will make three tents/shrines here, for you one, and for Moses one, and for Elias one. 17.5 From him yet/still speaking, behold, a bright cloud covered them, and behold a voice from the cloud, saying: This (one) is my beloved son, in whom I was well pleased; hear ye him. 17.6 And hearing, the learners/pupils fell upon their face and they were exceedingly afraid. 17.7 And Jesus came near and having touched them, he said: Rise ye and fear ye not. 17.8 And having lift

ὀφθαλμοὺς αὐτῶν οὐδένα εἶδον εἰ μὴ Ἰησοῦν αὐτὸν μόνον. 17.9 καὶ καταβαινόντων αὐτῶν ἐκ τοῦ ὄρους ἐνετείλατο αὐτοῖς ὁ Ἰησοῦς λέγων, μηδενὶ εἴπητε τὸ ὅραμα ἕως οὗ ὁ υἱὸς τοῦ ἀνθρώπου ἐκ νεκρῶν ἀναστῇ.

17.10 καὶ ἐπηρώτησαν αὐτὸν οἱ μαθηταὶ λέγοντες, τί οὖν οἱ γραμματεῖς λέγουσιν ὅτι Ἡλείαν δεῖ ἐλθεῖν πρῶτον;

17.11 ὁ δὲ ἀποκριθεὶς εἶπεν αὐτοῖς ὅτι, Ἡλείας μὲν ἔρχεται καὶ ἀποκαταστήσει πάντα· 17.12 λέγω δὲ ὑμῖν ὅτι Ἡλείας ἤδη ἦλθεν, καὶ οὐκ ἐπέγνωσαν αὐτὸν ἀλλ᾽ ἐποίησαν αὐτῷ ὅσα ἠθέλησαν· οὕτως καὶ ὁ υἱὸς τοῦ ἀνθρώπου μέλλει πάσχειν ὑπ᾽ αὐτῶν. 17.13 τότε συνῆκαν οἱ μαθηταὶ ὅτι περὶ Ἰωάνου τοῦ βαπτιστοῦ εἶπεν αὐτοῖς. 17.14 καὶ ἐλθόντων πρὸς τὸν ὄχλον προσῆλθεν αὐτῷ ἄνθρωπος γονυπετῶν αὐτὸν 17.15 καὶ λέγων, ἐλέησόν μου τὸν υἱόν, ὅτι σεληνιάζεται καὶ κακῶς ἔχει· πολλάκις γὰρ πίπτει εἰς τὸ πῦρ καὶ πολλάκις εἰς τὸ ὕδωρ. 17.16 καὶ προσήνεγκα αὐτὸν τοῖς μαθηταῖς σου, καὶ οὐκ ἠδυνήθησαν αὐτὸν θεραπεῦσαι.

17.17 ὁ δὲ ἀποκριθεὶς ὁ Ἰησοῦς εἶπεν αὐτοῖς, ὦ γενεὰ ἄπιστος καὶ διεστραμμένη, ἕως πότε μεθ᾽ ὑμῶν ἔσομαι; ἕως πότε ἀνέξομαι ὑμῶν; φέρετέ μοι αὐτὸν ὧδε. 17.18 καὶ ἐπετίμησεν αὐτῷ ὁ Ἰησοῦς, καὶ ἐξῆλθεν ἀπ᾽ αὐτοῦ τὸ δαιμόνιον· καὶ ἐθεραπεύθη ἀπὸ τῆς ὥρας ἐκείνης.

17.19 τότε προσελθόντες οἱ μαθηταὶ τῷ Ἰησοῦ κατ᾽ ἰδίαν εἶπαν, διὰ τί ἡμεῖς οὐκ ἠδυνήθημεν ἐκβαλεῖν αὐτό; 17.20 ὁ δὲ λέγει αὐτοῖς, διὰ τὴν ὀλιγοπιστίαν ὑμῶν· ἀμὴν γὰρ λέγω ὑμῖν, ἐὰν ἔχητε πίστιν ὡς κόκκον σινάπεως, ἐρεῖτε τῷ ὄρει τούτῳ, μετάβα ἔνθεν ἐκεῖ, καὶ μεταβήσεται· καὶ οὐδὲν ἀδυνατήσει ὑμῖν. 17.22 συστρεφομένων δὲ αὐτῶν ἐν τῇ Γαλιλαίᾳ εἶπεν αὐτοῖς ὁ Ἰησοῦς, μέλλει ὁ υἱὸς τοῦ ἀνθρώπου παραδίδοσθαι εἰς χεῖρας ἀνθρώπων, 17.23 καὶ ἀποκτενοῦσιν αὐτόν, καὶ τῇ τρίτῃ ἡμέρᾳ ἐγερθήσεται. καὶ ἐλυπήθησαν σφόδρα. 17.24 ἐλθόντων δὲ αὐτῶν εἰς Καφαρναοὺμ προσῆλθον οἱ τὰ δίδραχμα λαμβάνοντες τῷ

up their eyes, they saw no one except Jesus himself alone. 17.9 And from them coming down from the mountain, Jesus commanded to them, saying: Ye should tell the vision to no one until which *time* the son of man be risen out of dead (ones).

17.10 And the learners/pupils questioned him, saying: Then why *do* the scribes say that it is necessary *for* Elias to come first?

17.11 And the (he) answering, he said to them: Elias indeed comes and he will restore all (things); 17.12 but I say to ye that Elias already came, and they recognized him not, but they did to him whatever they wanted; so also the son of man is about to suffer by/under them. 17.13 Then the learners/pupils understood that he spoke to them about John the baptizer. 17.14 And from them having come near the crowd, a man came near to him, kneeling *to* him 17.15 and saying: (You) have pity on my son, because he is moonstruck and he has *it* badly; for he falls often into the fire and often into the water. 17.16 And I brought him to your learners/pupils, and they were not able to heal/treat him.

17.17 And the (he) answering, Jesus said to them: O faithless generation, also having been misled, until when shall I be with ye? Until when shall I endure ye? Bring ye him to me here. 17.18 And Jesus rebuked to it, and the demon came out from him; and he was healed from that hour/time.

17.19 Then the pupils/learners, coming near to Jesus, they said privately: Because of what/why were we, we not able to put it out? 17.20 And the (he) says to them: Because of the little faith of ye; for truly I say to ye, if ye may have faith as a seed of mustard, ye will say to this mountain: Remove from here to there, and it will move itself; and nothing will be impossible for ye. -- 17.22 And of them turning/strolling together in Galilee, Jesus said to them: The son of man is about to be delivered over/betrayed into hands of men, 17.23 and they will kill him, and on the third day he will be raised. And they were exceedingly grieved. 17.24 And from them coming/going into Capernaum, those taking up the two-drachma came

Πέτρῳ καὶ εἶπαν, ὁ διδάσκαλος ὑμῶν οὐ τελεῖ τὰ δίδραχμα; 17.25 λέγει, ναί.

καὶ εἰσελθόντα εἰς τὴν οἰκίαν προέφθασεν αὐτὸν ὁ Ἰησοῦς λέγων, τί σοι δοκεῖ, Σίμων; οἱ βασιλεῖς τῆς γῆς ἀπὸ τίνων λαμβάνουσιν τέλη ἢ κῆνσον; ἀπὸ τῶν υἱῶν αὐτῶν ἢ ἀπὸ τῶν ἀλλοτρίων; 17.26 ὁ δὲ ἔφη, ἀπὸ τῶν ἀλλοτρίων εἰπόντος δέ, ἀπὸ τῶν ἀλλοτρίων, ἔφη αὐτῷ ὁ Ἰησοῦς, ἄρα γε ἐλεύθεροί εἰσιν οἱ υἱοί. 17.27 ἵνα δὲ μὴ σκανδαλίσωμεν αὐτούς, πορευθεὶς εἰς θάλασσαν βάλε ἄγκιστρον καὶ τὸν ἀναβάντα πρῶτον ἰχθὺν ἆρον, καὶ ἀνοίξας τὸ στόμα αὐτοῦ εὑρήσεις στατῆρα· ἐκεῖνον λαβὼν δὸς αὐτοῖς ἀντὶ ἐμοῦ καὶ σοῦ. 18.1 ἐν ἐκείνῃ τῇ ὥρᾳ προσῆλθον οἱ μαθηταὶ τῷ Ἰησοῦ λέγοντες, τίς ἄρα μείζων ἐστὶν ἐν τῇ βασιλείᾳ τῶν οὐρανῶν;

18.2 καὶ προσκαλεσάμενος παιδίον ἔστησεν αὐτὸ ἐν μέσῳ αὐτῶν 18.3 καὶ εἶπεν, ἀμὴν λέγω ὑμῖν, ἐὰν μὴ στραφῆτε καὶ γένησθε ὡς τὰ παιδία, οὐ μὴ εἰσέλθητε εἰς τὴν βασιλείαν τῶν οὐρανῶν. 18.4 ὅστις οὖν ταπινώσει ἑαυτὸν ὡς τὸ παιδίον τοῦτο, οὗτός ἐστιν ὁ μείζων ἐν τῇ βασιλείᾳ τῶν οὐρανῶν. 18.5 καὶ ὃς ἐὰν δέξηται ἓν παιδίον τοιοῦτο ἐπὶ τῷ ὀνόματί μου, ἐμὲ δέχεται. 18.6 ὃς δ' ἂν σκανδαλίσῃ ἕνα τῶν μεικρῶν τούτων τῶν πιστευόντων εἰς ἐμέ, συμφέρει αὐτῷ ἵνα κρεμασθῇ μύλος ὀνικὸς περὶ τὸν τράχηλον αὐτοῦ καὶ καταποντισθῇ ἐν τῷ πελάγι τῆς θαλάσσης.

18.7 οὐαὶ τῷ κόσμῳ ἀπὸ τῶν σκανδάλων· ἀνάγκη γάρ ἐστιν ἐλθεῖν τὰ σκάνδαλα, πλὴν οὐαὶ τῷ ἀνθρώπῳ δι' οὗ τὸ σκάνδαλον ἔρχεται. 18.8 εἰ δὲ ἡ χείρ σου ἢ ὁ πούς σου σκανδαλίζει σε, ἔξελε αὐτὸν καὶ βάλε ἀπὸ σοῦ· καλόν σοί ἐστιν εἰσελθεῖν εἰς τὴν ζωὴν κυλλὸν ἢ χωλόν, ἢ δύο χεῖρας ἢ δύο πόδας ἔχοντα βληθῆναι εἰς τὸ πῦρ τὸ αἰώνιον. 18.9 καὶ εἰ ὁ ὀφθαλμός σου σκανδαλίζει σε, ἔξελε αὐτὸν καὶ βάλε ἀπὸ σοῦ· καλόν σοί ἐστιν μονόφθαλμον εἰς τὴν ζωὴν εἰσελθεῖν, ἢ δύο ὀφθαλμοὺς ἔχοντα βληθῆναι εἰς τὴν γένναν τοῦ πυρός.

near to Peter and said: Does not the teacher of ye pay the two-drachma? 17.25 He says: Yes.

And in having gone into the house, Jesus preceded him, saying: What seems it to you, Simon? From whom *do* the kings of the land/earth take toll/tribute or poll-tax? From their sons or from the foreigners/aliens? 17.26 And the (he) said: From the aliens. And from having said: From aliens, Jesus said to him: Then indeed the sons are free (ones/men). 17.27 But in order that we should not offend them/cause them to stumble, you be going *and* throw a hook in a sea and take the first fish having come up, and having opened its mouth, you will find a stater; you be taking that -- give *it* to them for me and you. 18.1 At/in that same hour/time the learners/pupils came near to Jesus, saying: So who is greater in the kingdom of the skies/heavens?

18.2 And calling forward a little child, he stood it in the midst of them 18.3 and said: Truly I say to ye, except ye might be turned and become as the little children ye may certainly not enter into the kingdom of the heavens. 18.4 Therefore, *the one* who will humble himself as this little child, this (one) is the greater (one) in the kingdom of the heavens. 18.5 And who ever receives one such little child upon the name of me, he receives me. 18.6 And who ever might cause to stumble one of the least of these, the (ones) believing in me, it is better for him that an upper millstone be hanged around his neck and he be drowned in the depths of the sea.

18.7 Woe to the world from the offenses/stumbling blocks/scandals; for it is a necessity to come the offenses/scandals, but woe to the man/human through whom the stumbling block/offense comes. 18.8 And if your hand or yourfoot causes you to stumble, be taking it off and throw *it* from you; it is good for you to enter into the life crippled or lame, than to be thrown into the eternal fire having two hands and two feet. 18.9 And if your eye scandalizes you/causes you to stumble, be taking it out and throw *it* from you; for it is good for you to enter into the life one-eyed than to be thrown into the hell of the fire

18.10 ὁρᾶτε μὴ καταφρονήσητε ἑνὸς τῶν μεικρῶν τούτων· λέγω γὰρ ὑμῖν ὅτι οἱ ἄγγελοι αὐτῶν ἐν οὐρανοῖς διὰ παντὸς βλέπουσι τὸ πρόσωπον τοῦ πατρός μου τοῦ ἐν οὐρανοῖς. 18.12 τί ὑμῖν δοκεῖ; ἐὰν γένηταί τινι ἀνθρώπῳ ἑκατὸν πρόβατα καὶ πλανηθῇ ἓν ἐξ αὐτῶν, οὐχὶ ἀφήσει τὰ ἐνενήκοντα ἐννέα ἐπὶ τὰ ὄρη καὶ πορευθεὶς ζητεῖ τὸ πλανώμενον; 18.13 καὶ ἐὰν γένηται εὑρῖν αὐτό,

ἀμὴν λέγω ὑμῖν ὅτι χαίρι ἐπ᾽ αὐτῷ μᾶλλον ἢ ἐπὶ τοῖς ἐνενήκοντα ἐννέα τοῖς μὴ πεπλανημένοις. 18.14 οὕτως οὐκ ἔστιν θέλημα ἔμπροσθεν τοῦ πατρὸς ὑμῶν τοῦ ἐν οὐρανοῖς ἵνα ἀπόληται ἓν τῶν μικρῶν τούτων.

18.15 ἐὰν δὲ ἁμαρτήσῃ ὁ ἀδελφός σου, ὕπαγε ἔλεγξον αὐτὸν μεταξὺ σοῦ καὶ αὐτοῦ μόνου. ἐὰν σου ἀκούσῃ, ἐκέρδησας τὸν ἀδελφόν σου· 18.16 ἐὰν δὲ μὴ ἀκούσῃ, παράλαβε μετὰ σεαυτοῦ ἔτι ἕνα ἢ δύο, ἵνα «ἐπὶ στόματος δύο ἢ τριῶν μαρτύρων σταθῇ πᾶν ῥῆμα·» 18.17 ἐὰν δὲ παρακούσῃ αὐτῶν, εἶπον τῇ ἐκκλησίᾳ· ἐὰν δὲ καὶ τῆς ἐκκλησίας παρακούσῃ, ἔστω σοι ὥσπερ ὁ ἐθνικὸς καὶ ὁ τελώνης. 18.18 ἀμὴν λέγω ὑμῖν, ὅσα ἐὰν δήσητε ἐπὶ τῆς γῆς ἔσται δεδεμένα ἐν τοῖς οὐρανοῖς καὶ ὅσα ἐὰν λύσητε ἐπὶ τῆς γῆς ἔσται λελυμένα ἐν οὐρανῷ.

18.19 πάλιν λέγω ὑμῖν ὅτι ἐὰν δύο συμφωνήσωσιν ἐξ ὑμῶν ἐπὶ τῆς γῆς περὶ παντὸς πράγματος οὗ ἐὰν αἰτήσωνται, αὐτοῖς γενήσεται παρὰ τοῦ πατρός μου τοῦ ἐν οὐρανοῖς. 18.20 οὗ γάρ εἰσιν δύο ἢ τρεῖς συνηγμένοι εἰς τὸ ἐμὸν ὄνομα, ἐκεῖ εἰμι ἐν μέσῳ αὐτῶν.

18.21 τότε προσελθὼν ὁ Πέτρος εἶπεν αὐτῷ, κύριε,

ποσάκις ἁμαρτήσι εἰς ἐμὲ ὁ ἀδελφός μου καὶ ἀφήσω αὐτῷ; ἕως ἑπτάκις; 18.22 λέγι αὐτῷ ὁ Ἰησοῦς, οὐ λέγω σοι ἕως ἑπτάκις ἀλλ᾽ ἕως ἑβδομηκοντάκις ἑπτά.

18.23 διὰ τοῦτο ὡμοιώθη ἡ βασιλία τῶν οὐρανῶν ἀνθρώπῳ βασιλῖ ὃς ἠθέλησεν συνᾶραι λόγον μετὰ τῶν δούλων

having two eyes.

18.10 See ye *that* ye might not despise one of these little (ones); for I say to ye that the messengers/angels of them in heavens see through every (man) the face of my father, of the (one) in heavens/skies. 18.12 What seems it to ye? If there might become for a certain man a hundred sheep, and one out of them might stray, will he not leave the ninety-nine on the mountains, *and* going, he will seek the straying (one)? 18.13 And if he might happen to find it,

truly I say to ye that he rejoices over it more than over the ninety nine, for those having not strayed. 18.14 Thus it is not a will/wish before your father, the (one) in heavens/skies, that one of these little (ones) should perish.

18.15 And if your brother might sin/fail, go you *and* reprove him between you and him only. If he might hear you, you gained your brother; 18.16 but if he might not listen, you take with yourself yet one or two, that ON A MOUTH OF TWO OR THREE WITNESSES EVERY WORD MIGHT BE ESTABLISHED; 18.17 and if he might fail to hear them, (you) speak to the assembly; and if also he might fail to hear the assembly, let him be to you as the ethnic/foreigner and the tax collector. 18.18 Truly I say to ye: What ever ye might bind on the earth, it will be having been bound in the skies/heavens, and what ever ye might loose on the earth, it will be having been loosed in heaven.

18.19 Again, I say to ye that if two out of ye might agree on the earth about every practical (thing), what ever they might request, it will become for them from my father, from the (one) in skies/heavens. 18.20 For where two or three are, having been gathered in my name, I am there in the midst of them.

18.21 Then, coming near, Peter said to him: Lord,

how often will my brother sin to/against me and I shall dismiss *it* for him? Until seven times? 18.22 Jesus says to him: I say not to you until seven times, but until seventy times seven.

18.23 Because of this the kingdom of the skies/heavens was likened to a man, a king, who wanted to

40

αὐτοῦ. 18.24 ἀρξαμένου δὲ αὐτοῦ συναίριν προσηνέχθη εἷς αὐτῷ ὀφειλέτης μυρίων πολλῶν ταλάντων. 18.25 μὴ ἔχοντος δὲ αὐτοῦ ἀποδοῦνε ἐκέλευσεν αὐτὸν ὁ κύριος πραθῆνε καὶ τὴν γυναῖκα καὶ τὰ πεδία καὶ πάντα ὅσα εἶχεν, καὶ ἀποδοθῆνε. 18.26 πεσὼν οὖν ὁ δοῦλος προσεκύνι αὐτῷ λέγων, κύριε, μακροθύμησον ἐπ᾽ ἐμοί, καὶ πάντα ἀποδώσω σοι. 18.27 σπλαγχνισθὶς δὲ ὁ κύριος τοῦ δούλου ἐκίνου ἀπέλυσεν αὐτόν, καὶ τὸ δάνιον ἀφῆκεν αὐτῷ. 18.28 ἐξελθὼν δὲ ὁ δοῦλος ἐκῖνος εὗρεν ἕνα τῶν συνδούλων αὐτοῦ ὃς ὤφιλεν αὐτῷ ἑκατὸν δηνάρια, καὶ κρατήσας αὐτὸν ἔπνιγεν λέγων, ἀπόδος εἴ τι ὀφίλις. 18.29 πεσὼν οὖν ὁ σύνδουλος αὐτοῦ παρεκάλι αὐτὸν λέγων, μακροθύμησον ἐπ᾽ ἐμοί, καὶ ἀποδώσω σοι. 18.30 ὁ δὲ οὐκ ἤθελεν, ἀλλὰ ἀπελθὼν ἔβαλεν αὐτὸν εἰς φυλακὴν ἕως ἀποδῷ τὸ ὀφιλόμενον. 18.31 ἰδόντες οὖν οἱ σύνδουλοι αὐτοῦ τὰ γενόμενα ἐλυπήθησαν σφόδρα, καὶ οἱ δὲ ἐλθόντες διεσάφησαν τῷ κυρίῳ ἑαυτῶν πάντα τὰ γενόμενα.

18.32 τότε προσκαλεσάμενος αὐτὸν ὁ κύριος αὐτοῦ λέγι αὐτῷ, δοῦλε πονηρέ, πᾶσαν τὴν ὀφιλὴν ἐκίνην ἀφῆκά σοι, ἐπὶ παρεκάλεσάς με· 18.33 οὐκ ἔδει καὶ σὲ ἐλεῆσαι τὸν σύνδουλόν σου, ὡς κἀγὼ σὲ ἠλέησα; 18.34 καὶ ὀργισθὶς ὁ κύριος αὐτοῦ παρέδωκεν αὐτὸν τοῖς βασανισταῖς ἕως οὗ ἀποδῷ πᾶν τὸ ὀφιλόμενον αὐτῷ. 18.35 οὕτως καὶ ὁ πατήρ μου ὁ οὐράνιος ποιήσι ὑμῖν ἐὰν μὴ ἀφῆτε ἕκαστος τῷ ἀδελφῷ αὐτοῦ ἀπὸ τῶν καρδιῶν ὑμῶν. 19.1 καὶ ἐγένετο ὅτε ἐτέλεσεν ὁ Ἰησοῦς τοὺς λόγους τούτους, μετῆρεν ἀπὸ τῆς Γαλιλαίας καὶ ἦλθεν εἰς τὰ ὅρια τῆς Ἰουδαίας πέραν τοῦ Ἰορδάνου. 19.2 καὶ ἠκολούθησαν αὐτῷ ὄχλοι πολλοί, καὶ ἐθεράπευσεν αὐτοὺς ἐκῖ. 19.3 καὶ προσῆλθον αὐτῷ οἱ Φαρισαῖοι πιράζοντες αὐτὸν καὶ λέγοντες, εἰ ἔξεστιν ἀνθρώπῳ ἀπολῦσαι τὴν γυνέκα αὐτοῦ κατὰ πᾶσαν αἰτίαν;

19.4 ὁ δὲ ἀποκριθεὶς εἶπεν, οὐκ ἀνέγνωτε ὅτι ὁ ποιήσας ἀπ᾽ ἀρχῆς «ἄρσεν καὶ θῆλυ ἐποίησεν αὐτούς;» 19.5 καὶ εἶπεν,

settle an accounting with his slaves. 18.24 And from him having begun to settle, one was brought to him, a debtor of a myriad of talents. 18.25 And from him having not to repay, the lord ordered *for* him to be sold, also the woman and the children and all whatever he had, and to be repaid. 18.26 Then, falling down, the slave worshiped/genuflexed to him, saying: Lord, be forbearing/patient to me, and I shall repay all to you. 18.27 And having compassion, the lord of that slave dismissed him and forgave the loan for him. 18.28 But going out, that slave found one of his fellow slaves who owed to him a hundred denarii, and having seized him, he choked him, saying: Repay *me* if you owe something. 18.29 Then falling *down*, his fellow slave besought him, saying: Be forbearing/patient to me, and I shall repay *it* to you. 18.30 But the (he) wanted not, but going away, he threw him into prison until he might repay the (thing) being owed. 18.31 Having seen, his fellow slaves then were grieved exceedingly *for* the things having happened, and they also, going, they explained to the lord of themselves all the (things) having happened.

18.32 Then, calling him forward/having summoned him, his lord says to him: Evil slave, all that debt I forgave for you, since you besought me; 18.33 was it not necessary *for* you also to have mercy on your fellow slave, even as I had mercy on you? 18.34 And being angry, his lord delivered him up to the tormentors until which *time* he might repay every thing being owed to him. 18.35 Thus also my heavenly father will do to ye, unless ye might forgive each (one) his brother from your hearts. 19.1 And it happened, when Jesus finished these sayings, he departed from Galilee and went into the borders of Judea, beyond the Jordan. 19.2 And many crowds followed with him, and he healed/treated them there. 19.3 And the Pharisees came near to him, trying/testing him and saying/asking: Is it lawful for a man to dismiss his woman according to every cause/accusation?

19.4 And the (he) answering, he said: Read ye not that the (one) having made them from the beginning, HE MADE THEM MALE AND FEMALE? 19.5 And he said:

« ἕνεκα τούτου καταλίψι ἄνθρωπος τὸν πατέρα καὶ τὴν μητέρα καὶ προσκολληθήσετε τῇ γυνεκὶ αὐτοῦ, καὶ ἔσοντε οἱ δύο εἰς σάρκα μίαν.» 19.6 ὥστε οὐκέτι εἰσὶν δύο ἀλλὰ μία σάρξ. ὃ οὖν ὁ θεὸς συνέζευξεν ἄνθρωπος μὴ χωριζέτω. 19.7 λέγουσιν αὐτῷ, τί οὖν Μωϋσῆς ἐνετίλατο «δοῦνε βιβλίον ἀποστασίου καὶ ἀπολῦσε;» 19.8 λέγι αὐτοῖς ὁ Ἰησοῦς ὅτι Μωϋσῆς πρὸς τὴν σκληροκαρδίαν ὑμῶν ἐπέτρεψεν ὑμῖν ἀπολῦσαι τὰς γυναῖκας ὑμῶν, ἀπ' ἀρχῆς δὲ οὐ γέγονεν οὕτως. 19.9 λέγω δὲ ὑμῖν ὅτι ὃς ἐὰν ἀπολύσῃ τὴν γυναῖκα αὐτοῦ μὴ ἐπὶ πορνίᾳ καὶ γαμήσῃ ἄλλην μοιχᾶτε.

19.10 λέγουσιν αὐτῷ οἱ μαθηταί, εἰ οὕτως ἐστὶν ἡ αἰτία τοῦ ἀνθρώπου μετὰ τῆς γυναικός, οὐ συμφέρι γαμῆσαι. 19.11 ὁ δὲ εἶπεν αὐτοῖς, οὐ πάντες χωροῦσι τὸν λόγον τοῦτον, ἀλλ' οἷς δέδοτε. 19.12 εἰσὶν γὰρ εὐνοῦχοι οἵτινες ἐκ κοιλίας μητρὸς ἐγεννήθησαν οὕτως, καὶ εἰσὶν εὐνοῦχοι οἵτινες εὐνουχίσθησαν ὑπὸ τῶν ἀνθρώπων, καὶ εἰσὶν εὐνοῦχοι οἵτινες εὐνούχισαν ἑαυτοὺς διὰ τὴν βασιλείαν τῶν οὐρανῶν.

ὁ δυνάμενος χωρῖν χωρίτω.

19.13 τότε προσηνέχθησαν αὐτῷ πεδία, ἵνα τὰς χῖρας ἐπιθῇ αὐτοῖς καὶ προσεύξητε· οἱ δὲ μαθητε ἐπετίμησαν αὐτοῖς.

19.14 ὁ δὲ Ἰησοῦς εἶπεν αὐτοῖς, ἄφετε τὰ πεδία καὶ μὴ κωλύετε αὐτὰ ἐλθῖν πρός ἐμέ, τῶν γὰρ τοιούτων ἐστὶν ἡ βασιλία τῶν οὐρανῶν. 19.15 καὶ ἐπιθὶς τὰς χῖρας ἐν αὐτοὺς ἐπορεύθη ἐκεῖθεν.

19.16 καὶ ἰδοὺ εἷς προσελθὼν αὐτῷ εἶπεν, διδάσκαλε, τί ἀγαθὸν ποιήσας ζωὴν αἰώνιον κληρονομήσω;

19.17 ὁ δὲ εἶπεν αὐτῷ, τί με ἐρωτᾷς περὶ τοῦ ἀγαθοῦ; εἷς ἐστιν ὁ ἀγαθός. εἰ δὲ θέλις εἰς τὴν ζωὴν εἰσελθῖν, τήρησον τὰς ἐντολάς.

19.18 ποίας; φησιν. ὁ δὲ Ἰησοῦς εἶπεν, τὸ «οὐ φονεύσις, οὐ μοιχεύσεις, οὐ κλέψεις, οὐ ψευδομαρτυρήσεις, 19.19 τίμα τὸν πατέρα καὶ τὴν μητέρα,» καί, «ἀγαπήσεις τὸν πλησίον σου ὡς

ON ACCOUNT OF THIS A MAN WILL LEAVE THE FATHER AND THE MOTHER AND HE WILL BE JOINED TO HIS WOMAN, AND THE TWO WILL BE IN ONE FLESH. 19.6 So they are no longer two but one flesh. Therefore, what God yoked together, let not a man separate. 19.7 They say to him: Why then did Moses command TO GIVE A SCROLL OF ABANDONMENT AND TO DISMISS/RELEASE *her*? 19.8 Jesus says to them: Moses, to/for your hardness of heart, allowed ye to dismiss/release your women, but from the beginning it has not been so. 19.9 And I say to ye that who ever might dismiss his woman, not for prostitution/unchastity, and might marry another, does adultery.

19.10 The pupils/learners say to him: If thus/so is the cause/reason of the man with the woman, it is not profitable to marry. 19.11 And the (he) said to them: Not all make room for/grasp this saying, but to whom it has been given. 19.12 For there are eunuchs who were generated so from a mother's belly, and there are eunuchs who were made eunuchs by the men, and there are eunuchs who made themselves eunuchs because of the kingdom of the heavens.

The (one) being able to make room/grasp *it*, let him make room/grasp.

19.13 Then children were brought to him, that he might put the hands on them and pray; but the learners/pupils rebuked them.

19.14 But Jesus said to them: Leave/let the children and forbid them not to come near/to me, for of such is the kingdom of the heavens. 19.15 And laying the hands on them, he went/departed from there.

19.16 And behold, one coming near to him, said: Teacher, having done what good (thing) might I inherit eternal life?

19.17 And the (he) said to him: Why *do* you ask me about the good (thing)? One is the good (one). But if you want to enter into the life, you keep the commands.

19.18 Which (ones)? he says. And Jesus said: The (thing) YOU MURDER NOT, YOU DO NOT ADULTERY, YOU STEAL NOT, YOU TESTIFY NOT TO A LIE, 19.19 YOU HONOR THE FATHER AND THE MOTHER, and YOU LOVE YOUR NEIGHBOR AS

σεαυτόν.»

19.20 λέγι αὐτῷ ὁ νεανίσκος, πάντα ταῦτα ἐφύλαξα· τί ἔτι ὑστερῶ; 19.21 ἔφη αὐτῷ ὁ Ἰησοῦς, εἰ θέλις τέλιος εἶναι, ὕπαγε πώλησόν σου τὰ ὑπάρχοντα καὶ δὸς πτωχοῖς, καὶ ἕξεις θησαυρὸν ἐν οὐρανοῖς, καὶ δεῦρο ἀκολούθι μοι. 19.22 ἀκούσας δὲ ὁ νεανίσκος ἀπῆλθεν λυπούμενος, ἦν γὰρ ἔχων κτήματα πολλά.

19.23 ὁ δὲ Ἰησοῦς εἶπεν τοῖς μαθηταῖς αὐτοῦ, ἀμὴν λέγω ὑμῖν ὅτι πλούσιος δυσκόλως εἰσελεύσετε εἰς τὴν βασιλίαν τῶν οὐρανῶν. 19.24 πάλιν δὲ λέγω ὑμῖν ὅτι εὐκοπώτερόν ἐστιν κάμηλον διὰ τρυπήματος ῥαφίδος εἰσελθεῖν ἢ πλούσιον εἰς τὴν βασιλίαν τοῦ θεοῦ. 19.25 ἀκούσαντες δὲ οἱ μαθηταὶ ἐξεπλήσσοντο σφόδρα λέγοντες, τίς ἄρα δύνατε σωθῆνε;

19.26 ἐμβλέψας δὲ ὁ Ἰησοῦς εἶπεν αὐτοῖς, τοῦτο παρὰ ἀνθρώποις ἀδύνατόν ἐστιν, παρὰ δὲ θεῷ δυνατὰ πάντα.

19.27 τότε ἀποκριθεὶς ὁ Πέτρος εἶπεν αὐτῷ, ἰδοὺ ἡμεῖς ἀφήκαμεν πάντα καὶ ἠκολουθήσαμέν σοι· τί ἄρα ἔσται ἡμῖν;

19.28 ὁ δὲ Ἰησοῦς εἶπεν αὐτοῖς, ἀμὴν λέγω ὑμῖν ὅτι ὑμεῖς οἱ ἀκολουθήσαντές μοι, ἐν τῇ παλινγενεσίᾳ, ὅταν καθίσῃ ὁ υἱὸς τοῦ ἀνθρώπου ἐπὶ θρόνου δόξης αὐτοῦ, καθήσεσθε καὶ αὐτοὶ ἐπὶ δώδεκα θρόνους κρίνοντες τὰς δώδεκα φυλὰς τοῦ Ἰσραήλ. 19.29 καὶ πᾶς ὅστις ἀφῆκεν ἀδελφοὺς ἢ ἀδελφὰς ἢ πατέρα ἢ μητέρα ἢ γυναῖκα ἢ τέκνα ἢ ἀγροὺς ἢ οἰκίας ἕνεκα τοῦ ἐμοῦ ὀνόματός ἑκατονταπλασίονα λήμψετε καὶ ζωὴν αἰώνιον κληρονομήσι.

19.30 πολλοὶ δὲ ἔσοντε ἔσχατοι πρῶτοι καὶ πρῶτοι ἔσχατοι. 20.1 ὁμοία γάρ ἐστιν ἡ βασιλία τῶν οὐρανῶν

ἀνθρώπῳ οἰκοδεσπότῃ ὅστις ἐξῆλθεν ἅμα πρωῒ μισθώσασθε ἐργάτας εἰς τὸν ἀμπελῶνα αὐτοῦ·

20.2 συμφωνήσας δὲ μετὰ τῶν ἐργατῶν ἐκ δηναρίου τὴν ἡμέραν ἀπέστιλεν αὐτοὺς εἰς τὸν ἀμπελῶνα αὐτοῦ.

20.3 καὶ ἐξελθὼν περὶ τρίτην ὥραν εἶδεν ἄλλους ἑστῶτας ἐν τῇ ἀγορᾷ ἀργούς· 20.4 καὶ ἐκείνοις εἶπεν, ὑπάγετε καὶ ὑμεῖς εἰς

YOURSELF.

19.20   The young man says to him: All these (things) I guarded/kept; what yet/else *do* I lack? 19.21 Jesus said to him: If you want to be complete/mature, you go *and* sell all your possessions and give *it* to poor (ones), and you will have a store/treasure in heavens/skies, and you come *and* follow me.   19.22 But having heard *this* the youth went away grieving, for he was holding many fields/possessions.

19.23   And Jesus said to his learners/pupils: Truly I say to ye that a rich (one) will enter with difficulty into the kingdom of the skies/heavens. 19.24 And again I say to ye that it is easier *for* a camel to enter a hole of a needle than *for* a rich (one) to enter the kingdom of God.   19.25 And hearing, the learners/pupils were very astonished, saying: Then, who is able to be saved?

19.26   And considering (this) Jesus said to them: With men this is impossible, but with God all things are possible.

19.27   Answering then, Peter said to him: Behold, we, we left all (things) and we followed with you; then what will be for us?

19.28   And Jesus said to them: Truly I say to ye that ye, the (ones) having followed with me, in the regeneration, when the son of man might sit upon a throne of his glory/reputation, ye will sit also, these upon twelve thrones, judging the twelve tribes of Israel.   19.29 And every (one) who left brothers or sisters or father or mother or a woman or children or fields or houses for the sake of my name, he/she will receive a hundred times more and will inherit eternal life.

19.30   But many last (ones) will be first (ones) and first (ones) last (ones).   20.1   For the kingdom of the heavens/skies is similar

to a man, a house master, who went in the early morning to hire workers in his vineyard;

20.2   And having agreed with the workers from a denarius *for* the day, he sent them into his vineyard.

20.3   And going out about *the* third hour, he saw others standing idle in/at the market;   20.4 and he

τὸν ἀμπελῶνα μου, καὶ ὃ ἐὰν ᾖ δίκαιον δώσω ὑμῖν. 20.5 οἱ δὲ ἀπῆλθον.

πάλιν δὲ ἐξελθὼν περὶ ἕκτην καὶ ἐνάτην ὥραν ἐποίησεν ὡσαύτως.

20.6 περὶ δὲ τὴν ἐνδεκάτην ἐξελθὼν εὗρεν ἄλλους ἑστῶτας, καὶ λέγει αὐτοῖς, τί ὧδε ἑστήκατε ὅλην τὴν ἡμέραν ἀργοί; 20.7 λέγουσιν αὐτῷ, ὅτι οὐδὶς ἡμᾶς ἐμισθώσατο. λέγει αὐτοῖς, ὑπάγετε καὶ ὑμῖς εἰς τὸν ἀμπελῶνα.

20.8 ὀψίας δὲ γενομένης λέγι ὁ κύριος τοῦ ἀμπελῶνος τῷ ἐπιτρόπῳ αὐτοῦ, κάλεσον τοὺς ἐργάτας καὶ ἀπόδος τὸν μισθὸν ἀρξάμενος ἀπὸ τῶν ἐσχάτων ἕως τῶν πρώτων. 20.9 καὶ ἐλθόντες οἱ περὶ τὴν ἐνδεκάτην ὥραν ἔλαβον ἀνὰ δηνάριον.

20.10 ἐλθόντες δὲ οἱ πρῶτοι ἐνόμισαν ὅτι πλῖον ἃ λήμψονται· καὶ ἔλαβον τὸ ἀνὰ δηνάριον καὶ αὐτοί. 20.11 λαβόντες δὲ ἐγόγγυζον κατὰ τοῦ οἰκοδεσπότου 20.12 λέγοντες, οὗτοι οἱ ἔσχατοι μίαν ὥραν ἐποίησαν, καὶ ἴσους αὐτοὺς ἡμῖν ἐποίησας τοῖς βαστάσασι τὸ βάρος τῆς ἡμέρας καὶ τὸν καύσωνα.

20.13 ὁ δὲ ἀποκριθεὶς ἑνὶ αὐτῶν εἶπεν, ἑτὲρε, οὐχ ἀδικῶ σε· οὐχὶ δηναρίου συνεφώνησάς μοι; 20.14 ἆρον τὸ σὸν καὶ ὕπαγε· θέλω δὲ τούτῳ τῷ ἐσχάτῳ δοῦναι ὡς καὶ σύ. 20.15 ἢ οὐκ ἔξεστίν μοι ὃ θέλω ποιῆσε ἐν τοῖς ἐμοῖς; ἢ ὁ ὀφθαλμός σου πονηρός ἐστιν ὅτι ἐγὼ ἀγαθός εἰμι; 20.16 οὕτως ἔσοντε οἱ ἔσχατοι πρῶτοι καὶ οἱ πρῶτοι ἔσχατοι.

20.17 καὶ ἀναβαίνων ὁ Ἰησοῦς εἰς Ἱεροσόλυμα παρέλαβεν τοὺς δώδεκα κατ' ἰδίαν, καὶ ἐν τῇ ὁδῷ εἶπεν αὐτοῖς, 20.18 ἰδοὺ ἀναβαίνομεν εἰς Ἱεροσόλυμα, καὶ ὁ υἱὸς τοῦ ἀνθρώπου παραδοθήσετε τοῖς ἀρχιερεῦσιν καὶ γραμματεῦσιν, καὶ κατακρινοῦσιν αὐτὸν εἰς θανάτῳ, 20.19 καὶ παραδώσουσιν αὐτὸν τοῖς ἔθνεσιν εἰς τὸ ἐμπῖξε καὶ μαστιγῶσαι καὶ σταυρῶσε, καὶ τῇ τρίτῃ ἡμέρᾳ ἐγερθήσετε.

20.20 τότε προσῆλθεν αὐτῷ ἡ μήτηρ τῶν υἱῶν Ζεβεδαίου

said to those: Ye, go ye also into my vineyard, and what ever may be just, I shall give to ye. 20.5 And they went.

And again going out about *the* sixth, also *the* ninth hour, he did likewise.

20.6 And about the eleventh (hour), going out, he found others standing, and he says to them: Why have ye stood here idle *for* the whole day? 20.7 They say to him: Because no one hired us. He says to them: Ye, go ye also into the vineyard.

20.8 And from it having become evening/late, the lord of the vineyard says to his foreman: You call the workers and pay the wage, beginning from the last (ones) until the first (ones). 20.9 And coming, those about the eleventh hour, they received each a denarius.

20.10 But coming, the first (ones) supposed that from the beginning they will receive more; and they themselves also received the (thing/wage), each a denarius. 20.11 And taking *it* they grumbled against the house master, 20.12 saying: These, the last (ones), did one hour, and you made them equal to us, to the (ones) having borne the burden of the day, and the heat.
20.13 But the (he), answering to one of them, said: Friend, I wronged you not; did you not agree with me of a denarius? 20.14 Take you your thing/wage and go; but I want to give to this (one), to the last (one), even as you. 20.15 Or is it not lawful for me to do what I want with the (things) *being* my *own*? Or is your eye evil because I, I am good? 20.16 So the last (ones) will be first (ones) and the first (ones) last (ones).

20.17 And Jesus, going up to Jerusalem, took along the twelve privately, and on the road he said to them: 20.18 Behold, we go up to Jerusalem, and the son of man will be delivered up/betrayed to the high priests and scribes, and they will condemn him to death, 20.19 and they will deliver him up to the ethnics in/for the (thing) to mock and to scourge and to crucify, and in/on the third day he will be raised.

20.20 Then the mother of the sons of Zebedee

μετὰ τῶν υἱῶν αὐτῆς προσκυνοῦσα καὶ αἰτοῦσά τι παρ' αὐτοῦ. 20.21 ὁ δὲ εἶπεν αὐτῇ, τί θέλις; λέγι αὐτῷ, εἰπὲ ἵνα καθίσωσιν οὗτοι οἱ δύο υἱοί μου εἷς ἐκ δεξιῶν καὶ εἷς ἐξ εὐωνύμων σου ἐν τῇ βασιλίᾳ σου.

20.22 ἀποκριθὶς δὲ ὁ Ἰησοῦς εἶπεν, οὐκ οἴδατε τί αἰτῖσθε· δύνασθε πιεῖν τὸ ποτήριον ὃ ἐγὼ μέλλω πίνιν; λέγουσιν αὐτῷ, δυνάμεθα.

20.23 λέγι αὐτοῖς, τὸ μὲν ποτήριόν μου πίεσθε, τὸ δὲ καθίσαι ἐκ δεξιῶν μου καὶ ἐξ εὐωνύμων οὐκ ἔστιν ἐμὸν δοῦνε, ἀλλ' οἷς ἡτοίμασται ὑπὸ τοῦ πατρός μου.

20.24 καὶ ἀκούσαντες οἱ δέκα ἤξαντο ἀγανάκτιν περὶ τῶν δύο ἀδελφῶν. 20.25 ὁ δὲ Ἰησοῦς προσκαλεσάμενος αὐτοὺς εἶπεν, οἴδατε ὅτι οἱ ἄρχοντες τῶν ἐθνῶν κατακυριεύουσιν αὐτῶν καὶ οἱ μεγάλοι κατεξουσιάζουσιν αὐτῶν. 20.26 οὐχ οὕτως ἔστε ἐν ὑμῖν· ἀλλ' ὃς ἐὰν θέλῃ ἐν ὑμῖν μέγας γενέσθε ἔσται ὑμῶν διάκονος, 20.27 καὶ ὃς ἂν θέλῃ ἐν ὑμῖν εἶνε πρῶτος ἔστε ὑμῶν δοῦλος·

20.28 ὥσπερ ὁ υἱὸς τοῦ ἀνθρώπου οὐκ ἦλθεν διακονηθῆναι ἀλλὰ διακονῆσε καὶ δοῦνε τὴν ψυχὴν αὐτοῦ λύτρον ἀντὶ πολλῶν.

20.29 καὶ ἐκπορευομένων αὐτῶν ἀπὸ Ἰεριχὼ ἠκολούθησεν αὐτῷ ὄχλος πολύς. 20.30 καὶ ἰδοὺ δύο τυφλοὶ καθήμενοι παρὰ τὴν ὁδόν, ἀκούσαντες ὅτι Ἰησοῦς παράγει, ἔκραξαν λέγοντες, ἐλέησον ἡμᾶς, Ἰησοῦς, υἱὲ Δαυίδ.

20.31 ὁ δὲ ὄχλος ἐπετίμησεν αὐτοῖς ἵνα σιωπήσωσιν· οἱ δὲ πολλῶν ἄλλον ἔκραξαν λέγοντες, κύριε, ἐλέησον ἡμᾶς, υἱὸς Δαυίδ.

20.32 καὶ στὰς ὁ Ἰησοῦς ἐφώνησεν αὐτοὺς καὶ εἶπεν, τί θέλετε ποιήσω ὑμῖν; 20.33 λέγουσιν αὐτῷ, κύριε, ἵνα ἀνυγῶσιν οἱ ὀφθαλμοὶ ἡμῶν.

20.34 σπλαγχνισθεὶς δὲ ὁ Ἰησοῦς ἥψατο τῶν ὀφθαλμῶν αὐτῶν, καὶ εὐθέως ἀνέβλεψαν καὶ ἠκολούθησαν αὐτῷ. 21.1 καὶ ὅτε ἤγγισαν εἰς Ἰεροσόλυμα καὶ ἦλθον εἰς Βηθφαγὴ πρὸς τὸ ὄρος τῶν ἐλεῶν,

came near to him with her sons, worshiping/genuflexing and asking something from him. 20.21 And the (he) said to her: What *do* you want? She says to him: You say/speak that these, my two sons, might sit one from *the* right *hand* and one from *the* left of you in your kingdom.

20.22 And answering, Jesus said: Ye know not what ye ask; are ye able to drink the cup that I, I am about to drink? They say to him: We are able.

20.23 He says to them: The one (thing) ye will drink my cup, but the (other), to sit from/at my right and left *hand* is not mine to give, but for (those) whom it has been prepared by my father.

20.24 And hearing, the ten were beginning to anger about the two brothers. 20.25 But Jesus, having called them near/forward, he said: Ye know that the rulers of the ethnics lord it over them and the great (ones)/magistrates exercise authority over them. 20.26 It is not so among ye; but who ever among ye may want to become great, he will be your waiter/servant, 20.27 and who ever among ye may want to be first, he will be your slave;

20.28 just as the son of the man came not to be served but to serve and to give his life/soul a ransom for/instead of many.

20.29 And of them going out from Jericho, a much crowd followed with him. 20.30 And behold, two blind (ones) *were* sitting beside the road, having heard that Jesus passes by, they cried out saying: Have mercy on us, Jesus, a son of David.

20.31 And the crowd warned them that they should be quiet; but they cried out much another *time*, saying: Lord, have mercy on us, son of David.

20.32 And standing (still)/stopping, Jesus addressed them and said: What *do* ye want *that* I might do for ye? 20.33 They say to him: Lord, that our eyes might be opened.

20.34 And having compassion, Jesus touched their eyes, and immediately they looked up/received sight, and they followed with him. 21.1 And when they drew near to Jerusalem and went into Bethphage near the mountain of the olives,

45

τότε ὁ Ἰησοῦς ἀπέστιλεν δύο μαθητὰς 21.2 λέγων αὐτοῖς,

πορεύεσθε εἰς τὴν κώμην τὴν κατέναντει ὑμῶν, καὶ εὐθοὺς εὑρήσετε ὄνον δεδεμένην καὶ πῶλον μετ' αὐτῆς· λύσαντες ἀγάγετέ μοι. 21.3 καὶ ἐάν τις ὑμῖν εἴπῃ τι, ἐρεῖτε ὅτι ὁ κύριος αὐτοῦ χρείαν ἔχει·

εὐθὺς δὲ ἀποστελῖ αὐτούς.

21.4 τοῦτο δὲ γέγονεν ἵνα πληρωθῇ τὸ ῥηθὲν διὰ τοῦ προφήτου λέγοντος, 21.5 «εἴπατε τῇ θυγατρὶ Σιών,

ἰδοὺ ὁ βασιλεύς σου ἔρχετε σοι, πραὺς καὶ ἐπιβεβηκὼς ἐπὶ ὄνον, καὶ ἐπὶ πῶλον υἱὸν ὑποζυγίου.»

21.6 πορευθέντες δὲ οἱ μαθηταὶ καὶ ποιήσαντες καθὼς προσέταξεν αὐτοῖς ὁ Ἰησοῦς 21.7 ἤγαγον τὴν ὄνον καὶ τὸν πῶλον, καὶ ἐπέθηκαν ἐπ' αὐτῶν τὰ ἱμάτια, καὶ ἐκάθισαν ἐπάνω αὐτῶν. 21.8 ὁ δὲ πλῖστος ὄχλος ἔστρωσαν ἑαυτῶν τὰ ἱμάτια ἐν τῇ ὁδῷ, ἄλλοι δὲ ἔκοπτον κλάδους ἀπὸ τῶν δένδρων καὶ ἐστρώννυον ἐν τῇ ὁδῷ. 21.9 οἱ δὲ ὄχλοι οἱ προάγοντες αὐτὸν καὶ οἱ ἀκολουθοῦντες ἔκραζον λέγοντες, «ὡσαννὰ» τῷ υἱῷ Δαυίδ·

«εὐλογημένος ὁ ἐρχόμενος ἐν ὀνόματι κυρίου· ὡσαννὰ» ἐν τοῖς ὑψίστοις.

21.10 καὶ ἰσελθόντος αὐτοῦ ἰς Ἱεροσόλυμα ἐσίσθη πᾶσα ἡ πόλις λέγουσα, τίς ἐστιν οὗτος;

21.11 οἱ δὲ ὄχλοι ἔλεγον, οὗτός ἐστιν ὁ προφήτης Ἰησοῦς ὁ ἀπὸ Ναζαρὲθ τῆς Γαλιλέας.

21.12 καὶ εἰσῆλθεν Ἰησοῦς εἰς τὸ ἱερόν, καὶ ἐξέβαλεν πάντας τοὺς πωλοῦντας καὶ ἀγοράζοντας ἐν τῷ ἱερῷ, καὶ τὰς τραπέζας τῶν κολλυβιστῶν κατέστρεψεν καὶ τὰς καθέδρας τῶν πωλούντων τὰς περιστεράς, 21.13 καὶ λέγι αὐτοῖς, γέγραπται, «ὁ οἶκός μου οἶκος προσευχῆς κληθήσετε », ὑμῖς δὲ αὐτὸν ποιεῖτε σπήλαιον λῃστῶν.

21.14 καὶ προσῆλθον αὐτῷ τυφλοὶ καὶ χωλοὶ ἐν τῷ ἱερῷ, καὶ ἐθεράπευσεν αὐτούς.

21.15 ἰδόντες δὲ οἱ ἀρχιερῖς καὶ οἱ γραμματῖς τὰ θαυμάσια ἃ ἐποίησεν καὶ τοὺς παῖδας τοὺς κράζοντας ἐν τῷ

then Jesus sent two learners/pupils, 21.2 saying to them:

Go ye into the village, the (one) opposite from ye, and ye will soon find an ass having been tied *there*, also a colt with her; loosing *them* bring them to me. 21.3 And if someone might say something to ye, ye will say that the Lord has a need of it;

and he will send them quickly.

21.4 And this (thing) has happened that might be fulfilled the (thing) having been spoken through the prophet, saying: 21.5 SAY YE TO THE DAUGHTER OF ZION:

BEHOLD, YOUR KING COMES TO YOU, GENTLE AND HAVING BEEN MOUNTED UPON AN ASS, AND ON A COLT, A SON OF/BY A DONKEY.

21.6 And the learners/pupils, going and doing as Jesus commanded to them, 21.7 they brought the ass and the colt, and they placed the/*their* garments upon them, and he sat on/above them. 21.8 And the very large crowd spread the garments of themselves in the road, and others cut off branches from the trees and were spreading *them* in the road. 21.9 And the crowds, those going before him and those following, cried out, saying: HOSANNA to the son of David; HAVING BEEN BLES-SED *is* THE (ONE) COMING IN/BY NAME OF THE LORD; HOSAN-NA in the highest (places).

21.10 And from him entering into Jerusalem, all the city was shaken, saying: Who is this (one)?

21.11 And the crowds said: This (one) is the prophet Jesus, the (one) from Nazareth of Galilee.

21.12 And Jesus went into the *outer* temple, and he threw out all those selling and buying in the temple (area)/*outer* temple, and he overturned the tables of the money-changers and the seats of those selling the doves/pigeons, 21.13 and he says to them: It has been written: MY HOUSE WILL BE CALLED A HOUSE OF PRAYER, but ye, ye make it a cave of robbers.

21.14 And blind (ones) and lame (ones) came near to him in the temple (area), and he healed them.

21.15 But the high priests and the scribes, seeing the wonders that he did and the children/ser-vants, those crying out in the temple (area*)/outer* temple and saying: Hosanna to the son of David, they

ἱερῷ καὶ λέγοντας, ὡσαννὰ τῷ υἱῷ Δαυίδ, ἠγανάκτησαν 21.16 καὶ εἶπαν αὐτῷ, ἀκούεις τί οὗτοι λέγουσιν; ὁ δὲ Ἰησοῦς λέγι αὐτοῖς, ναί· οὐδέποτε ἀνέγνωτε

«ἐκ στόματος νηπίων καὶ θηλαζόντων κατηρτίσω αἶνον;» 21.17 καὶ καταλιπὼν αὐτοὺς ἐξῆλθεν ἔξω τῆς πόλεως εἰς Βηθανίαν, καὶ ηὐλίσθη ἐκεῖ.

21.18 πρωὶ δὲ ἐπανάγων εἰς τὴν πόλιν ἐπείνασεν. 21.19 καὶ ἰδὼν συκῆν μίαν ἐπὶ τῆς ὁδοῦ ἦλθεν ἐπ᾽ αὐτήν, καὶ οὐδὲν εὗρεν ἐν αὐτῇ εἰ μὴ φύλλα μόνον, καὶ λέγει αὐτῇ, μηκέτι ἐκ σοῦ καρπὸς γένητο εἰς τὸν αἰῶνα. καὶ ἐξηράνθη παραχρῆμα ἡ συκῆ.

21.20 καὶ ἰδόντες οἱ μαθητὲ ἐθαύμασαν λέγοντες, πῶς παραχρῆμα ἐξηράνθη ἡ συκῆ;

21.21 ἀποκριθεὶς δὲ ὁ Ἰησοῦς εἶπεν αὐτοῖς, ἀμὴν λέγω ὑμῖν, ἐὰν ἔχητε πίστιν καὶ μὴ διακριθῆτε, οὐ μόνον τὸ τῆς συκῆς ποιήσετε, ἀλλὰ κἂν τῷ ὄρι τούτῳ εἴπητε, ἄρθητι καὶ βλήθητι εἰς τὴν θάλασσαν, γενήσετε 21.22 καὶ πάντα ὅσα ἂν αἰτήσητε ἐν τῇ προσευχῇ πιστεύοντες λήμψεσθε. 21.23 καὶ ἐλθόντος αὐτοῦ εἰς τὸ ἱερὸν προσῆλθον αὐτῷ διδάσκοντι οἱ ἀρχιερεῖς καὶ οἱ πρεσβύτεροι τοῦ λαοῦ λέγοντες, ἐν ποίᾳ ἐξουσίᾳ ταῦτα ποιεῖς; καὶ τίς σοι ἔδωκεν τὴν ἐξουσίαν ταύτην;

21.24 ἀποκριθεὶς δὲ ὁ Ἰησοῦς εἶπεν αὐτοῖς, ἐρωτήσω ὑμᾶς κἀγὼ λόγον ἕνα, ὃν ἐὰν εἴπητέ μοι κἀγὼ ὑμῖν ἐρῶ ἐν ποίᾳ ἐξουσίᾳ ταῦτα ποιῶ·

21.25 τὸ βάπτισμα τὸ Ἰωάννου πόθεν ἦν; ἐξ οὐρανοῦ ἢ ἐξ ἀνθρώπων;

οἱ δὲ διελογίζοντο παρ᾽ ἑαυτοῖς λέγοντες, ἐὰν εἴπωμεν, ἐξ οὐρανοῦ, ἐρεῖ ἡμῖν, διὰ τί οὖν οὐκ ἐπιστεύσατε αὐτῷ;

21.26 ἐὰν δὲ εἴπωμεν, ἐξ ἀνθρώπων, φοβούμεθα τὸν ὄχλον, πάντες γὰρ ὡς προφήτην ἔχουσι τὸν Ἰωάννην.

21.27 καὶ ἀποκριθέντες τῷ Ἰησοῦ εἶπαν, οὐκ οἴδαμεν. ἔφη αὐτοῖς ὁ Ἰησοῦς, οὐδὲ ἐγὼ λέγω ὑμῖν ἐν ποίᾳ ἐξουσίᾳ ταῦτα ποιῶ.

21.28 τί δὲ ὑμῖν δοκεῖ; ἄνθρωπος εἶχεν τέκνα δύο. καὶ προσελθὼν τῷ πρώτῳ εἶπεν, τέκνον, ὕπαγε σήμερον ἐργάζου ἐν τῷ ἀμπελῶνι. 21.29 ὁ δὲ ἀποκριθεὶς εἶπεν, οὐ θέλω, ὕστερον

angered   21.16 and said to him: *Do* you hear what these say? And Jesus says to them: Yes; read ye never:

OUT OF A MOUTH OF BABES AND SUCKLINGS YOU PREPAR-ED PRAISE?   21.17 And leaving them he went away outside the city to Bethany, and he camped there.

21.18   And returning early into the city, he hungered.   21.19 And seeing one fig tree on/by the road, he went to it, and he found nothing on/in it except leaves only, and he says to it: No longer from you may become fruit into the age. And the fig tree was withered immediately.

21.20   And having seen, the learners/pupils wondered, saying: How was the fig tree withered immediately?

21.21   And answering, Jesus said to them: Truly I say to ye, if ye may have faith and ye may not be doubting, ye will do not only the (thing) of the fig tree, but also ye might say to this mountain: You be taken up and be thrown into the sea, it will happen. 21.22 And all things, what ever ye would ask in the prayer, believing, ye will receive.   21.23 And from him going into the temple *court* for teaching, the high/chief priests and the elders of the people came near to him, saying: By what authority do you these (things)? And who gave to you this authority?

21.24   And answering, Jesus said to them: I, I ask ye also *for* one saying, which if ye might say to me, also I, I shall say to ye by what authority I do these (things):

21.25 The baptism, the (one) of John, from where was *it*? From heaven or from men?

And they were reasoning with/beside themselves, saying: If we might say: From heaven, he will say to us: Then why believed ye not in him?

21.26   And if we might say: From men, we fear the crowd, for all (them) hold John as a prophet.

21.27   And answering to Jesus, they said: We know not. Jesus said to them: Neither I, I say to ye by what authority I do these (things).

21.28   But what seems it to ye? A man had two children. And going near the first, he said: Child, go you today *and* work in the vineyard.   21.29 And the

μεταμεληθὶς ἀπῆλθεν. 21.30 προσελθὼν δὲ τῷ ἑτέρῳ εἶπεν ὡσαύτως. ὁ δὲ ἀποκριθὶς εἶπεν, ἐγώ, κύριε· καὶ οὐκ ἀπῆλθεν. 21.31 τίς ἐκ τῶν δύο ἐποίησεν τὸ θέλημα τοῦ πατρός; λέγουσιν, ὁ πρῶτος. λέγι αὐτοῖς ὁ Ἰησοῦς, ἀμὴν λέγω ὑμῖν ὅτι οἱ τελῶναι καὶ αἱ πόρναι προάγουσιν ὑμᾶς εἰς τὴν βασιλίαν τοῦ θεοῦ.

21.32 ἦλθεν γὰρ Ἰωάννης πρὸς ὑμᾶς ἐν ὁδῷ δικαιοσύνης, καὶ οὐκ ἐπιστεύσατε αὐτῷ· οἱ δὲ τελῶνε καὶ αἱ πόρναι ἐπίστευσαν αὐτῷ· ὑμῖς δὲ ἰδόντες οὐ μετεμελήθητε ὕστερον τοῦ πιστεῦσαι αὐτῷ.

21.33 ἄλλην παραβολὴν ἀκούσατε. ἄνθρωπος ἦν οἰκοδεσπότης ὅστις «ἐφύτευσεν ἀμπελῶνα καὶ φραγμὸν αὐτῷ περιέθηκεν καὶ ὤρυξεν ἐν αὐτῷ ληνὸν καὶ ᾠκοδόμησεν πύργον,» καὶ ἐξέδετο αὐτὸν γεωργοῖς, καὶ ἀπεδήμησεν. 21.34 ὅτε δὲ ἤγγισεν ὁ καιρὸς τῶν καρπῶν, ἀπέστιλεν τοὺς δούλους αὐτοῦ πρὸς τοὺς γεωργοὺς λαβεῖν τοὺς καρποὺς αὐτοῦ. 21.35 καὶ λαβόντες οἱ γεωργοὶ τοὺς δούλους αὐτοῦ ὃν μὲν ἔδιραν, ὃν δὲ ἀπέκτιναν, ὃν δὲ ἐλιθοβόλησαν.

21.36 καὶ πάλιν ἀπέστιλεν ἄλλους δούλους πλίονας τῶν πρώτων, καὶ ἐποίησαν αὐτοῖς ὡσαύτως. 21.37 ὕστερον δὲ ἀπέστιλεν πρὸς αὐτοὺς τὸν υἱὸν αὐτοῦ λέγων, ἐντραπήσονται τὸν υἱόν μου. 21.38 οἱ δὲ γεωργοὶ ἰδόντες τὸν υἱὸν εἶπον ἐν ἑαυτοῖς, οὗτός ἐστιν ὁ κληρονόμος· δεῦτε ἀποκτίνωμεν αὐτὸν καὶ σχῶμεν τὴν κληρονομίαν αὐτοῦ. 21.39 καὶ λαβόντες αὐτὸν ἔβαλον ἔξω τοῦ ἀμπελῶνος καὶ ἀπέκτιναν. 21.40 ὅταν οὖν ἔλθῃ ὁ κύριος τοῦ ἀμπελῶνος, τί ποιήσι τοῖς γεωργοῖς ἐκίνοις; 21.41 λέγουσιν αὐτῷ, κακοὺς κακῶς ἀπολέσι αὐτούς, καὶ τὸν ἀμπελῶνα ἐκδώσετε ἄλλοις γεωργοῖς, οἵτινες ἀποδώσουσιν αὐτῷ τοὺς καρποὺς ἐν τοῖς καιροῖς αὐτῶν.

21.42 λέγει αὐτοῖς ὁ Ἰησοῦς, οὐδέποτε ἀνέγνωτε ἐν ταῖς γραφαῖς, «λίθον ὃν ἀπεδοκίμασαν οἱ οἰκοδομοῦντες οὗτος ἐγενήθη εἰς κεφαλὴν γωνίας· παρὰ κυρίου ἐγένετο αὕτη, καὶ ἔστιν θαυμαστὴ ἐν ὀφθαλμοῖς ἡμῶν;»

(he) answering, he said: I shall not; later, changing his mind/repenting, he went. 21.30 And going near to the other, he said likewise. And the (he) answering, he said: I *go*, Lord; and he went not. 21.31 Which out of the two did the will of the father? They say: The first. Jesus says to them: Truly I say to ye that the tax collectors and the prostitutes precede ye into the kingdom of God.

21.32 For John came to ye on/with a road/way of justness, and ye believed not in him; but the tax collectors and the prostitutes believed in him; but ye, seeing, ye repented not afterwards from the (thing) to believe in him.

21.33 Hear ye another parable: A man was a house master who planted a vineyard and he put a fence/wall around it and he dug a winepress/vat in it and he built a fortress/tower, and he leased it to vinedressers/farmers, and he went abroad. 21.34 And when the season of the products/fruits was near, he sent his slaves to the farmers/vinedressers to take the fruits from it. 21.35 But the vinedressers, taking his slaves, they beat one and killed another and hurled stones at another.

21.36 And again he sent other slaves, more than the first (ones), and they did to them likewise. 21.37 And afterwards, he sent to them his son, saying: They will respect/revere my son. 21.38 But the vinedressers, seeing the son, said among themselves: This (one) is the heir; come (ye), we might/let us kill him and we might have/hold his inheritance. 21.39 And taking him, they threw *him* outside the vineyard and they killed *him*. 21.40 Therefore, when the lord of the vineyard might come, what will he do to those vinedressers? 21.41 They say to him: He will destroy/treat those bad (ones) badly, and he will lease out the vineyard to other vinedressers/farmers who will give to him the products/fruits in their seasons.

21.42 Jesus says to them: Read ye never in the writings: A STONE WHICH THOSE BUILDING REJECTED, THIS (ONE) BECAME INTO/HAPPENED TO *be* A HEAD/CORNER STONE OF A CORNER; IT BECAME/HAPPENED FROM *the* LORD, AND IT IS WONDERFUL IN OUR EYES?

21.43 διὰ τοῦτο λέγω ὑμῖν ὅτι ἀρθήσετε ἀφ' ὑμῶν ἡ βασιλία τοῦ θεοῦ καὶ δοθήσετε ἔθνι ποιοῦντι τοὺς καρ- καρποὺς αὐτῆς. 21.44 καὶ ὁ πεσὼν ἐπὶ τὸν λίθον τοῦτον συνθλασθήσετε· ἐφ' ὃν δ' ἂν πέσῃ λικμήσι αὐτόν.

21.45 ἀκούσαντες δὲ οἱ ἀρχιερῖς καὶ οἱ Φαρισαῖοι τὰς παραβολὰς αὐτοῦ ἔγνωσαν ὅτι περὶ αὐτῶν λέγει· 21.46 καὶ ζητοῦντες αὐτὸν κρατῆσαι ἐφοβήθησαν τοὺς ὄχλους, ἐπὶ εἰς προφήτην αὐτὸν εἶχον.

22.1 Καὶ ἀποκριθεὶς ὁ Ἰησοῦς πάλιν εἶπεν ἐν παραβολαῖς αὐτοῖς λέγων,

22.2 ὡμοιώθη ἡ βασιλεία τῶν οὐρανῶν ἀνθρώπῳ βασιλῖ, ὅστις ἐποίησεν γάμους τῷ υἱῷ αὐτοῦ. 22.3 καὶ ἀπέστιλεν τοὺς δούλους αὐτοῦ καλέσε τοὺς κεκλημένους εἰς τοὺς γάμους, καὶ οὐκ ἤθελον ἐλθῖν.

22.4 πάλιν ἀπέστιλεν ἄλλους δούλους λέγων, εἴπατε τοῖς κεκλημένοις, ἰδοὺ τὸ ἄριστόν μου ἡτοίμακα, οἱ ταῦροί μου καὶ τὰ σιτιστὰ τεθυμένα, καὶ πάντα ἕτοιμα· δεῦτε εἰς τοὺς γάμους. 22.5 οἱ δὲ ἀμελήσαντες ἀπῆλθον, ὃ μὲν εἰς τὸν ἴδιον ἀγρόν, ὃς δὲ ἐπὶ τὴν ἐμπορίαν αὐτοῦ· 22.6 οἱ δὲ λοιποὶ κρατήσαντες τοὺς δούλους αὐτοῦ ὕβρισαν καὶ ἀπέκτιναν.

22.7 ὁ δὲ βασιλεὺς ὠργίσθη, καὶ πέμψας τὰ στρατεύματα αὐτοῦ ἀπώλεσεν τοὺς φονῖς ἐκίνους καὶ τὴν πόλιν αὐτῶν ἐνέπρησεν. 22.8 τότε λέγι τοῖς δούλοις αὐτοῦ, ὁ μὲν γάμος ἕτοιμός ἐστιν, οἱ δὲ κεκλημένοι οὐκ ἦσαν ἄξιοι· 22.9 πορεύεσθε οὖν ἐπὶ τὰς διεξόδους τῶν ὁδῶν, καὶ ὅσους ἐὰν εὕρητε καλέσατε εἰς τοὺς γάμους. 22.10 καὶ ἐξελθόντες οἱ δοῦλοι ἐκῖνοι εἰς τὰς ὁδοὺς συνήγαγον πάντας οὓς εὗρον, πονηρούς τε καὶ ἀγαθούς· καὶ ἐπλήσθη ὁ νύμφων ἀνακιμένων.

22.11 εἰσελθὼν δὲ ὁ βασιλεὺς θεάσασθαι τοὺς ἀνακιμένους εἶδεν ἐκεῖ ἄνθρωπον οὐκ ἐνδεδυμένον ἔνδυμα γάμου· 22.12 καὶ λέγι αὐτῷ, ἑταῖρε, πῶς εἰσῆλθες ὧδε μὴ ἔχων ἔνδυμα γάμου; ὁ δὲ ἐφιμώθη. 22.13 τότε ὁ βασιλεὺς εἶπεν τοῖς διακόνοις, δήσαντες

21.43   Because of this I say to ye that the kingdom of God will be taken from ye and given to a nation/ethnic making/doing the fruits/products of it. 21.44   And the (one) falling on this stone will be broken in fragments; but on whom ever it might fall, it will crush him.

21.45   And the high priests and the Pharisees, hearing his parables, they knew that he speaks about them;   21.46 and seeking to seize him, they feared the crowds, since they were holding him to *be* a prophet.

22.1   And answering, Jesus again spoke to them by/in parables, saying:

22.2   The kingdom of the heavens/skies was likened to a man, a king, who made a wedding for his son. 22.3 And he sent his slaves to call those having been invited to the marriage, and they wanted not to come.

22.4   Again he sent other slaves, saying: Say ye to those having been invited: Behold, I have prepared my dinner, my bulls and the fatted *calves* having been killed, and all (things) are ready; come ye to the marriage.   22.5 And they went off, not caring, one into his own field, another to his trading (mercantile);   22.6 and the rest/others, seizing his slaves, they insulted andkilled *them*.

22.7   And the king was angered, and sending his soldiers, he destroyed those murderers and he burned their city.   22.8 Then he says to his *other* slaves: Indeed the marriage is prepared, but those having been invited/called were not worthy;   22.9 therefore, go ye to the thoroughfares from the roads, as many as ever ye might find, call/invite ye *them* to the marriage (festivities).   22.10 And those slaves, going forth into the roads, they gathered all whom they found, both evil (ones) and good (ones); and the wedding hall was filled of/with reclining (ones).

22.11   But the king, having entered to view/behold those reclining, he saw a man there having not been dressed *in* a garment of a wedding;   22.12 and he says to him: Friend, how entered you here having not a garment of a wedding? And the (he) was silenced. 22.13 Then the king said to the waiters/servants:

αὐτοῦ πόδας καὶ χῖρας ἐκβάλετε αὐτὸν εἰς τὸ σκότος τὸ ἐξώτερον· ἐκῖ ἔσται ὁ κλαυθμὸς καὶ ὁ βρυγμὸς τῶν ὀδόντων. 22.14 πολλοὶ γάρ εἰσιν κλητοὶ ὀλίγοι δὲ ἐκλεκτοί. 22.15 τότε πορευθέντες οἱ Φαρισέοι συμβούλιον ἔλαβον ὅπως αὐτὸν παγιδεύσωσιν ἐν λόγῳ.

22.16 καὶ ἀποστέλλουσιν αὐτῷ τοὺς μαθητὰς αὐτῶν μετὰ τῶν Ἡρῳδιανῶν λέγοντας, διδάσκαλε, οἴδαμεν ὅτι ἀληθὴς εἶ καὶ τὴν ὁδὸν τοῦ θεοῦ ἐν ἀληθίᾳ διδάσκεις, καὶ οὐ μέλι σοι περὶ οὐδενός, οὐ γὰρ βλέπις εἰς πρόσωπον ἀνθρώπων. 22.17 εἰπὲ οὖν ἡμῖν τί σοι δοκῖ· ἔξεστιν δοῦναι κῆνσον Καίσαρι ἢ οὔ; 22.18 γνοὺς δὲ ὁ Ἰησοῦς τὴν πονηρίαν αὐτῶν εἶπεν, τί με πιράζετε, ὑποκριταί; 22.19 ἐπιδίξατέ μοι τὸ νόμισμα τοῦ κήνσου. οἱ δὲ προσήνεγκαν αὐτῷ δηνάριον. 22.20 καὶ λέγι αὐτοῖς, τίνος ἡ ἰκὼν αὕτη καὶ ἡ ἐπιγραφή; 22.21 λέγουσιν, Κέσαρος.

τότε λέγι αὐτοῖς, ἀπόδοτε οὖν τὰ Κέσαρος Καίσαρι καὶ τὰ τοῦ θεοῦ τῷ θεῷ. 22.22 καὶ ἀκούσαντες ἐθαύμασαν, καὶ ἀφέντες αὐτὸν ἀπῆλθον. 22.23 ἐν ἐκίνῃ τῇ ἡμέρᾳ προσῆλθον αὐτῷ Σαδδουκαῖοι, λέγοντες μὴ εἶναι ἀνάστασιν, καὶ ἐπηρώτησαν αὐτὸν 22.24 λέγοντες, διδάσκαλε, Μωϋσῆς εἶπεν,

«ἐάν τις ἀποθάνῃ μὴ ἔχων τέκνα, ἐπιγαμβρεύσι ὁ ἀδελφὸς αὐτοῦ τὴν γυναῖκα αὐτοῦ καὶ ἀναστήσι σπέρμα τῷ ἀδελφῷ αὐτοῦ.» 22.25 ἦσαν δὲ παρ' ἡμῖν ἑπτὰ ἀδελφοί· καὶ ὁ πρῶτος γήμας ἐτελεύτησεν, καὶ μὴ ἔχων σπέρμα ἀφῆκεν τὴν γυναῖκα αὐτοῦ τῷ ἀδελφῷ αὐτοῦ· 22.26 ὁμοίως καὶ ὁ δεύτερος καὶ ὁ τρίτος, ἕως τῶν ἑπτά. 22.27 ὕστερον δὲ πάντων ἀπέθανεν ἡ γυνή. 22.28 ἐν τῇ ἀναστάσι οὖν τίνος τῶν ἑπτὰ ἔστε γυνή; πάντες γὰρ ἔσχον αὐτήν. 22.29 καὶ ἀποκριθὶς ὁ Ἰησοῦς εἶπεν αὐτοῖς, πλανᾶσθαι μὴ εἰδότες τὰς γραφὰς μηδὲ τὴν δύναμιν τοῦ θεοῦ· 22.30 ἐν γὰρ τῇ ἀναστάσι οὔτε γαμοῦσι οὔτε γαμίζονται, ἀλλ' ὡς ἄγγελοι ἐν τῷ οὐρανῷ εἰσιν.

22.31 περὶ δὲ τῆς ἀναστάσεως τῶν νεκρῶν οὐκ ἀνέγνωτε τὸ ῥηθὲν ὑμῖν ὑπὸ τοῦ θεοῦ λέγοντος, 22.32 «ἐγώ εἰμι ὁ θεὸς

Having bound his feet and hands, ye throw him out into the outermost darkness; the wailing/weeping and the gritting of the teeth will be there. 22.14 For many are called but few chosen. 22.15 Then, having gone, the Pharisees took a consultation/plot in order that they might trap him in/by a saying/word.

22.16 And they send to him their learners/pupils with the Herodians, saying: Teacher, we know that you are truthful and you teach the road/way of God in truth, and it is not a care for you about no one, for you look not to a face/front of men. 22.17 Therefore, you say to us what it seems to you: Is it lawful to give tribute to Caesar, or not? 22.18 But Jesus, knowing their evil intent, said: Why prove/test ye me, pretenders/hypocrites? 22.19 Show ye to me the coin of the tribute. And they brought to him a denarius. 22.20 And he says to them: Of whom *is* this image and the inscription? 22.21 They say: Of Caesar/Caesar's.

Then he says to them: Then ye give back the (things) of Caesar to Caesar and the (things) of God to God. 22.22 And, hearing *this*, they wondered/marveled, and leaving him, they went away. 22.23 In that *same* day, Sadducees, *those* saying to be not a resurrection, came near to him/approached him and they questioned him, 22.24 saying: Teacher, Moses said:
IF SOMEONE MIGHT DIE NOT HAVING CHILDREN, HIS BROTHER WILL MATE UPON HIS WOMAN AND HE WILL RAISE UP SEED FOR HIS BROTHER. 22.25 But seven brothers were with us; and the first, having married, he died and, not having seed, he left his woman to his brother; 22.26 similarly, also the second and the third, until the seven. 22.27 And afterwards from all, the woman died. 22.28 Therefore, in the resurrection, of whom from the seven will she be a woman? For all had her. 22.29 And answering, Jesus said to them: Ye deceive/ lead astray, not knowing the writings nor the power of God; 22.30 for in the resurrection, they neither marry not are given in marriage, but they are as messengers/angels of God in the sky/heaven.

22.31 And concerning the resurrection of the dead (ones), read ye not the (thing) having been said to ye by God, saying: 22.32 I, I AM THE GOD OF ABRA-

Ἀβραὰμ καὶ θεὸς Ἰσαὰκ καὶ θεὸς Ἰακώβ;» οὐκ ἔστιν θεὸς νεκρῶν ἀλλὰ ζώντων.

22.33 καὶ ἀκούσαντες οἱ ὄχλοι ἐξεπλήσσοντο ἐπὶ τῇ διδαχῇ αὐτοῦ. 22.34 οἱ δὲ Φαρισαῖοι ἀκούσαντες ὅτι ἐφίμωσε τοὺς Σαδδουκέους συνήχθησαν ἐπὶ τὸ αὐτό. 22.35 καὶ ἐπηρώτησεν εἷς ἐξ αὐτῶν νομικὸς πιράζων αὐτόν, 22.36 διδάσκαλε, ποία ἐντολὴ μεγάλη ἐν τῷ νόμῳ;

22.37 ὁ δὲ ἔφη αὐτῷ, « ἀγαπήσις κύριον τὸν θεόν σου ἐν ὅλῃ τῇ καρδίᾳ σου καὶ ἐν ὅλῃ τῇ ψυχῇ σου» καὶ ἐν ὅλῃ τῇ διανοίᾳ σου· 22.38 αὕτη ἐστὶν ἡ μεγάλη καὶ πρώτη ἐντολή.

22.39 δευτέρα δὲ ὁμοία αὐτῇ, « ἀγαπήσις τὸν πλησίον σου ὡς σεαυτόν.»

22.40 ἐν ταύταις ταῖς δυσὶν ἐντολαῖς ὅλος ὁ νόμος κρέμαται καὶ οἱ προφῆται.

22.41 συνηγμένων δὲ τῶν Φαρισέων ἐπηρώτησεν αὐτοὺς ὁ Ἰησοῦς 22.42 λέγων, τί ὑμῖν δοκεῖ περὶ τοῦ χριστοῦ; τίνος υἱός ἐστιν; λέγουσιν αὐτῷ, Δαυίδ.

22.43 λέγι αὐτοῖς, πῶς οὖν Δαυὶδ ἐν πνεύματι καλῖ κύριον αὐτὸν λέγων,

22.44 «εἶπεν κύριος τῷ κυρίῳ μου, κάθου ἐκ δεξιῶν μου ἕως ἂν θῶ τοὺς ἐχθρούς σου ὑποκάτω τῶν ποδῶν σου;»

22.45 εἰ οὖν Δαυὶδ καλῖ αὐτὸν κύριον, πῶς υἱὸς αὐτοῦ ἐστιν;

22.46 καὶ οὐδεὶς ἐδύνατο ἀποκριθῆναι αὐτῷ λόγον, οὐδὲ ἐτόλμησέν τις ἀπ᾽ ἐκίνης τῆς ἡμέρας ἐπερωτῆσε αὐτὸν οὐκέτι.

23.1 Τότε ὁ Ἰησοῦς ἐλάλησεν τοῖς ὄχλοις καὶ τοῖς μαθηταῖς αὐτοῦ 23.2 λέγων,

ἐπὶ τῆς Μωϋσέως καθέδρας ἐκάθισαν οἱ γραμματεῖς καὶ οἱ Φαρισέοι. 23.3 πάντα οὖν ὅσα ἐὰν εἴπωσιν ὑμῖν ποιήσατε καὶ τηρεῖτε, κατὰ δὲ τὰ ἔργα αὐτῶν μὴ ποιεῖτε· λέγουσιν γὰρ καὶ οὐ ποιοῦσιν. 23.4 δεσμεύουσιν δὲ φορτία μεγάλα βαρέα καὶ ἐπιτιθέασιν ἐπὶ τοὺς ὤμους τῶν ἀνθρώπων, αὐτοὶ δὲ τῷ δακτύλῳ αὐτῶν οὐ θέλουσιν κινῆσε αὐτά.

23.5 πάντα δὲ τὰ ἔργα αὐτῶν ποιοῦσιν πρὸς τὸ θεαθῆνε

HAM AND GOD OF ISAAC AND GOD OF JACOB? He is not a God of dead (ones) butof living (ones).

22.33 And hearing, the crowds were astounded at his teaching/doctrine. 22.34 And the Pharisees, hearing that he silenced the Sadducees, were gathered together. 22.35 And one out of them, a lawyer, proving/testing him, asked: 22.36 Teacher, what command *is* great in the law?

22.37 And the (he) said to him: YOU WILL LOVE THE LORD YOUR GOD WITH YOUR WHOLE HEART AND WITH YOUR WHOLE LIFE/SOUL and with your whole mind; 22.38 this is the great and first command.

22.39 And a second is like to it: YOU WILL LOVE YOUR NEAR ONE/NEIGHBOR AS YOURSELF.

22.40 On these two commands depends the entire law and the prophets.

22.41 And from the Pharisees having assembled together, Jesus questioned them 22.42 saying: What seems it to ye concerning the anointed (one)? Of whom is he a son? They say to him: Of David.

22.43 He says to them: Then how, by a spirit, does David call him Lord, saying:

22.44 THE LORD SAID TO MY LORD: YOU SIT AT MY RIGHT (HAND) UNTIL I WOULD PUT YOUR ENEMIES UNDERNEATH YOUR FEET?

22.45 Therefore, if David calls him Lord, how is he his son?

22.46 And no one was able to answer to him a word/saying, nor dared anyone from that day to question him no longer.

23.1 Then Jesus spoke to the crowds and to his learners/pupils 23.2 saying:

The scribes and Pharisees sat upon the seat of Moses. 23.3 Therefore all (things) what ever they might speak to ye, do and observe ye, but do ye not according to their works; for they say/speak but they do not. 23.4 And they bind up large, heavy burdens and they place *them* upon the shoulders of the men/humans, but they, with their finger, are not willing to move them.

23.5 But they do all their works toward the

τοῖς ἀνθρώποις· πλατύνουσι γὰρ τὰ φυλακτήρια αὐτῶν καὶ μεγαλύνουσι τὰ κράσπεδα, 23.6 φιλοῦσι δὲ τὴν πρωτοκλισίαν ἐν τοῖς δίπνοις καὶ τὰς πρωτοκαθεδρίας ἐν τὲς συναγωγὲς

23.7 καὶ τοὺς ἀσπασμοὺς ἐν ταῖς ἀγοραῖς καὶ καλεῖσθε ὑπὸ τῶν ἀνθρώπων, ῥαββεί. 23.8 ὑμεῖς δὲ μὴ κληθῆτε, ῥαββεί, εἷς γάρ ἐστιν ὑμῶν ὁ διδάσκαλος, πάντες δὲ ὑμῖς ἀδελφοί ἐστε.

23.9 καὶ πατέρα μὴ καλέσητε ὑμῶν ἐπὶ τῆς γῆς, εἷς γάρ ἐστιν ὑμῶν ὁ πατὴρ ὁ οὐράνιος. 23.10 μηδὲ κληθῆτε καθηγηταί, εἷς γάρ ἐστιν ὑμῶν ὁ καθηγητὴς χριστός.

23.11 ὁ δὲ μίζων ὑμῶν ἔσται διάκονος. 23.12 ὅστις δὲ ὑψώσει ἑαυτὸν ταπινωθήσετε, καὶ ὅστις ταπινώσει ἑαυτὸν ὑψωθήσετε.

23.13 οὐαὶ δὲ ὑμῖν, γραμματῖς καὶ Φαρισαῖοι ὑποκριτε, ὅτι κλίετε τὴν βασιλίαν τῶν οὐρανῶν ἔμπροσθεν τῶν ἀνθρώπων· ὑμεῖς γὰρ οὐκ εἰσέρχεσθε, οὐδὲ τοὺς εἰσερχομένους ἀφίετε εἰσελθεῖν. 23.15 οὐαὶ ὑμῖν, γραμματῖς καὶ Φαρισαῖοι ὑποκριταί, ὅτι περιάγετε τὴν θάλασσαν καὶ τὴν ξηρὰν ποιῆσε ἕνα προσήλυτον, καὶ ὅταν γένηται ποιεῖτε αὐτὸν υἱὸν γεέννης διπλότερον ὑμῶν.

23.16 οὐαὶ ὑμῖν, ὁδηγοὶ τυφλοὶ οἱ λέγοντες, ὃς ἂν ὀμόση ἐν τῷ ναῷ, οὐδέν ἐστιν· ὃς δ' ἂν ὀμόσῃ ἐν τῷ χρυσῷ τοῦ ναοῦ ὀφίλει. 23.17 μωροὶ καὶ τυφλοί, τίς γὰρ μείζων ἐστίν, ὁ χρυσὸς ἢ ὁ ναὸς ὁ ἁγιάσας τὸν χρυσόν; 23.18 καί, ὃς ἂν ὀμόσῃ ἐν τῷ θυσιαστηρίῳ, οὐδέν ἐστιν· ὃς δ' ἂν ὀμόσῃ ἐν τῷ δώρῳ τῷ ἐπάνω αὐτοῦ ὀφίλι. 23.19 τυφλοί, τί γὰρ μῖζον, τὸ δῶρον ἢ τὸ θυσιαστήριον τὸ ἁγιάζον τὸ δῶρον; 23.20 ὁ οὖν ὀμόσας ἐν τῷ θυσιαστηρίῳ ὀμνύι ἐν αὐτῷ καὶ ἐν πᾶσι τοῖς ἐπάνω αὐτοῦ·

23.21 καὶ ὁ ὀμόσας ἐν τῷ ναῷ ὀμνύει ἐν αὐτῷ καὶ ἐν τῷ κατοικοῦντι αὐτόν·

(thing)/purpose to be seen by the men; for they broaden their phylacteries and enlarge the fringes *of their garments,* 23.6 and they love the place of honor in/at the banquets (dinners) and the chief seats in the congregations

23.7 and the salutations/greetings in the markets and to be called rabbi (respected teacher) by the men/humans. 23.8 But ye, ye be not called rabbi, for one is your teacher, and all ye, ye are brothers.

23.9 And ye might not call your father on the earth, for one is your father, the heavenly (one). 23.10 Neither might ye be called instructors, for one is the instructor/teacher of ye, the anointed (one).

23.11 And the greater (one) of ye will be a waiter/servant. 23.12 And whoever will exalt himself will be humbled, and whoever will humble himself will be exalted.

23.13 But woe to ye, scribes and Pharisees, pretenders/hypocrites, because ye close/shut the kingdom of the heavens before/in front of the men; for ye, ye are not entering, neither allow/permit ye those entering to enter/to go in. 23.15 Woe to ye, scribes and Pharisees, pretenders, because ye go about the sea and the dry *land* to make one convert/proselyte, and whenever he might become (one), ye make him a son of hell twice as much from/as ye.

23.16 Woe to ye, blind guides, those saying: Who ever might swear in/by the *inner* temple, it is nothing; but who ever might swear by the gold of the *inner* temple, he owes *it.* 23.17 Foolish and blind (ones), for which is greater: the gold or the *inner* temple, the (one) having sanctified the gold? 23.18 And who ever might swear on/by the altar, it is nothing; but who ever might swear by the gift, the (thing) over/above it, he owes *it*/is obligated. 23.19 Blind (ones), for what *is* greater: the gift or the altar, the (thing) sanctifying the gift? 23.20 Therefore, the (one) having sworn by the altar, he swears by it and by all the (things) above/over it;

23.21 and the (one) having sworn by the *inner* temple, he swears by it and the (one) dwelling in/inhabiting it.

23.22 καὶ ὁ ὀμόσας ἐν τῷ οὐρανῷ ὀμνύι ἐν τῷ θρόνῳ τοῦ θεοῦ καὶ ἐν τῷ καθημένῳ ἐπάνω αὐτοῦ. 23.23 οὐαὶ ὑμῖν, γραμματῖς καὶ Φαρισαῖοι ὑποκριτέ, ὅτι ἀποδεκατοῦτε τὸ ἡδύοσμον καὶ τὸ ἄνηθον καὶ τὸ κύμινον, καὶ ἀφήκατε τὰ βαρύτερα τοῦ νόμου, τὴν κρίσιν καὶ τὸ ἔλεος καὶ τὴν πίστιν· ταῦτα ἔδει ποιῆσε κἀκῖνα μὴ ἀφίνε.

23.24 ὁδηγοὶ τυφλοί, οἱ διϋλίζοντες τὸν κώνωπα τὴν δὲ κάμηλον καταπίνοντες.

23.25 οὐαὶ ὑμῖν, γραμματῖς καὶ Φαρισέοι ὑποκριτέ, ὅτι καθαρίζετε τὸ ἔξωθεν τοῦ ποτηρίου κὲ τῆς παροψίδος, ἔσωθεν δὲ γέμουσιν ἐξ ἁρπαγῆς καὶ ἀκρασίας.

23.26 Φαρισαῖε τυφλέ, καθάρισον πρῶτον τὸ ἐντὸς τοῦ ποτηρίου καὶ τῆς παροψίδος, ἵνα γένηται καὶ τὸ ἐκτὸς αὐτοῦ καθαρόν.

23.27 οὐαὶ ὑμῖν, γραμματῖς καὶ Φαρισαῖοι ὑποκριτέ, ὅτι παρομοιάζετε τάφοις κεκονιαμένοις, οἵτινες ἔξωθεν μὲν φένοντε ὡρεῖοι ἔσωθεν δὲ γέμουσιν ὀστέων νεκρῶν καὶ πάσης ἀκαθαρσίας. 23.28 οὕτως καὶ ὑμῖς ἔξωθεν μὲν φένεσθε τοῖς ἀνθρώποις δίκαιοι, ἔσωθεν δέ ἐστε μεστοὶ ὑποκρίσεως κὲ ἀνομίας.

23.29 οὐαὶ ὑμῖν, γραμματῖς καὶ Φαρισαῖοι ὑποκριτέ, ὅτι οἰκοδομεῖτε τοὺς τάφους τῶν προφητῶν καὶ κοσμῖτε τὰ μνημῖα τῶν δικαίων, 23.30 καὶ λέγεται, εἰ ἤμεθα ἐν ταῖς ἡμέραις τῶν πατέρων ἡμῶν, οὐκ ἂν ἤμεθα κοινωνοὶ αὐτῶν ἐν τῷ αἵματι τῶν προφητῶν. 23.31 ὥστε μαρτυρῖτε ἑαυτοῖς ὅτι υἱοί ἐστε τῶν φονευσάντων τοὺς προφήτας. 23.32 καὶ ὑμῖς πληρώσατε τὸ μέτρον τῶν πατέρων ὑμῶν.

23.33 ὄφις γεννήματα ἐχιδνῶν,

πῶς φύγητε ἀπὸ τῆς κρίσεως τῆς γεέννης;

23.34 διὰ τοῦτο ἰδοὺ ἐγὼ ἀποστέλλω πρὸς ὑμᾶς προφήτας καὶ σοφοὺς καὶ γραμματῖς· ἐξ αὐτῶν ἀποκτενῖτε καὶ σταυρώσετε, ἐξ καὶ αὐτῶν μαστιγώσετε ἐν τὲς συναγωγὲς ὑμῶν

23.22 And the (one) having sworn by the sky/ heaven, he swears by the throne of God and by the (one) sitting above/over it. 23.23 Woe to ye, scribes and Pharisees, pretenders/hypocrites, because ye give a tenth from the mint and the dill and the cummin, and ye have left the weightier (things) of the law: the justice/judgment and the mercy and the faith/trust; these (things) it was necessary to do and those (things) not to leave/let go.

23.24 Blind guides, those straining out the gnat but swallowing the camel.

23.25 Woe to ye, scribes and Pharisees, pretenders, because ye cleanse the (thing) from outside of the cup and the dish, but from within they are filled out of/from plunder/greed and self-indulgences.

23.26 Blind Pharisee, cleanse you first the inside of the cup and the dish, in order that the outside of it might also become clean.

23.27 Woe to ye, scribes and Pharisees, pretenders, because ye are like tombs having been whitewash- ed, which indeed appear beautiful from outside but from within they are full of bones of dead (ones) and of every uncleanness. 23.28 So also ye, from outside ye indeed appear just to the men, but from within ye are full of pretense/hypocrisy and lawlessness.

23.29 Woe to ye, scribes and Pharisees, pretenders, because ye build the tombs of the prophets and ye decorate the memorials of the just (ones), 23.30 and ye say: If we were being in the days of our fathers, we would not be being sharers of them in the blood of the prophets. 23.31 So that ye testify for yourselves that ye are sons of those having murdered the pro- phets. 23.32 And ye, ye filled up the measure of your fathers.

23.33 Serpents, offsprings from snakes, how might ye escape from the judgment of the hell?

23.34 Because of this, behold I, I send to ye prophets and wise (ones) and scribes; (some) out of them ye will kill and crucify, and (some) out of them ye will scourge/whip/flog in your congregations, and ye will prosecute/pursue *them* from city to city;

καὶ διώξετε ἀπὸ πόλεως εἰς πόλιν· 23.35 ὅπως ἔλθῃ ἐφ' ὑμᾶς πᾶν αἷμα δίκαιον ἐκχυννόμενον ἐπὶ τῆς γῆς ἀπὸ τοῦ αἵματος Ἄβελ τοῦ δικαίου ἕως τοῦ αἵματος Ζαχαρίου υἱοῦ Βαραχίου, ὃν ἐφονεύσατε μεταξὺ τοῦ ναοῦ καὶ τοῦ θυσιαστηρίου.

23.36 ἀμὴν λέγω ὑμῖν, ἥξι ταῦτα πάντα ἐπὶ τὴν γενεὰν ταύτην.

23.37 Ἰερουσαλὴμ Ἰερουσαλήμ, ἡ τοὺς προφήτας ἀποκτίνουσα καὶ λιθοβολοῦσα τοὺς ἀπεσταλμένους πρὸς αὐτήν,

ποσάκις ἠθέλησα ἐπισυναγαγεῖν τὰ τέκνα σου, ὃν τρόπον ὄρνις ἐπισυνάγει τὰ νοσσία αὐτῆς ὑπὸ τὰς πτέρυγας, καὶ οὐκ ἠθελήσατε. 23.38 ἰδοὺ ἀφίεται ὑμῖν ὁ οἶκος ὑμῶν ἔρημος.

23.39 λέγω γὰρ ὑμῖν, οὐ μή με ἴδητε ἀπ' ἄρτι ἕως ἂν εἴπητε, «εὐλογημένος ὁ ἐρχόμενος ἐν ὀνόματι κυρίου.»

24.1 Καὶ ἐξελθὼν ὁ Ἰησοῦς ἀπὸ τοῦ ἱεροῦ ἐπορεύετο, καὶ προσῆλθον οἱ μαθητὲ αὐτοῦ ἐπιδῖξε αὐτῷ τὰς οἰκοδομὰς τοῦ ἱεροῦ·

24.2 ὁ δὲ ἀποκριθεὶς εἶπεν αὐτοῖς, οὐ βλέπετε ταῦτα πάντα; ἀμὴν λέγω ὑμῖν, οὐ μὴ ἀφεθῇ ὧδε λίθος ἐπὶ λίθον ὃς οὐ καταλυθήσεται.

24.3 καθημένου δὲ αὐτοῦ ἐπὶ τοῦ ὄρους τῶν ἐλεῶν προσῆλθον αὐτῷ οἱ μαθηταὶ καθ' ἰδίαν λέγοντες, εἰπὲ ἡμῖν πότε ταῦτα ἔστε, καὶ τί τὸ σημῖον τῆς σῆς παρουσίας καὶ συντελίας τοῦ αἰῶνος. 24.4 καὶ ἀποκριθεὶς ὁ Ἰησοῦς εἶπεν αὐτοῖς, Βλέπετε μή τις ὑμᾶς πλανήσῃ· 24.5 πολλοὶ γὰρ ἐλεύσοντε ἐπὶ τῷ ὀνόματί μου λέγοντες, ἐγώ εἰμι ὁ χριστός, καὶ πολλοὺς πλανήσουσιν.

24.6 μελλήσετε δὲ ἀκούειν πολέμους καὶ ἀκοὰς πολέμων· ὁρᾶτε, μὴ θροεῖσθε· δῖ γὰρ γενέσθαι, ἀλλ' οὔπω ἐστὶν τὸ τέλος.

24.7 ἐγερθήσετε γὰρ ἔθνος ἐπ' ἔθνος καὶ βασιλία ἐπὶ

23.35 thus it might come upon ye every just blood being poured out upon the earth from the blood of Abel, the just (one), until the blood of Zacharias, a son of Barachias, whom ye murdered between the *inner* temple and the altar.

23.36 Truly I say to ye, all these (things) will come upon this generation.

23.37 Jerusalem, Jerusalem, the (one) killing the prophets and stoning those having been sent to her,

how often I wanted to gather your children, *in* which manner a bird/fowl gathers the young (ones) of her under the wings, but ye wanted *it* not. 23.38 Behold, your house is left deserted/depopulated for ye.

23.39 For I say to ye, by no means might ye see me from now until ye might ever say: HAVING BEEN BLESSED/PRAISED *is* THE (ONE) COMING IN *the* NAME OF *the* LORD.

24.1 And Jesus, going out from the *outer* temple, he departed, and his learners/pupils came near to exhibit/show to him the buildings of the *outer* temple/temple area.

24.2 And the (he) answering, he said to them: See ye not all these (things)? truly, I say to ye, by no means will there be left here a stone upon a stone which will not be thrown down.

24.3 And from him being seated on the mountain of the olives, the learners/pupils came near to him privately, saying: Say you to us when these (things) will be, and what *is* the sign of your coming/presence and of the ending/completion or the age. 24.4 And answering, Jesus said to them: See ye *that* anyone should not deceive ye/beware ye lest anyone might deceive ye; 24.5 for many will come upon my name, saying: I, I am the anointed (one), and they will deceive/lead astray many.

24.6 And ye will be about to hear wars and reports of wars; see ye, be ye not disturbed; for it is necessary to happen, but the end is not yet.

24.7 For an ethnic will be raised upon/against

βασιλίαν, καὶ ἔσοντε σισμοὶ καὶ λιμοὶ κατὰ τόπους· 24.8 πάντα δὲ ταῦτα ἀρχὴ ὠδίνων.

24.9 τότε παραδώσουσιν ὑμᾶς εἰς θλῖψιν καὶ ἀποκτενοῦσιν ὑμᾶς, καὶ ἔσεσθε μισούμενοι ὑπὸ πάντων τῶν ἐθνῶν διὰ τὸ ὄνομά μου.

24.10 καὶ τότε σκανδαλισθήσονται πολλοὶ καὶ ἀλλήλους παραδώσουσιν εἰς θλιψιν·

24.11 καὶ πολλοὶ ψευδοπροφῆται ἐγερθήσονται καὶ πολλοὺς πλανήσουσιν·

24.12 καὶ διὰ τὸ πληθυνθῆναι τὴν ἀνομίαν ψυγήσετε ἡ ἀγάπη τῶν πολλῶν.

24.13 ὁ δὲ ὑπομείνας εἰς τέλος οὗτος σωθήσεται.

24.14 καὶ κηρυχθήσετε τοῦτο τὸ εὐαγγέλιον τῆς βασιλίας ἰς ὅλην τὴν οἰκουμένην εἰς μαρτύριον πᾶσι τοῖς ἔθνεσιν, καὶ τότε ἥξι τὸ τέλος.   24.15 ὅταν οὖν ἴδητε τὸ βδέλυγμα τῆς ἐρημώσεως τὸ ῥηθὲν διὰ Δανιὴλ τοῦ προφήτου ἑστὸς ἐν τόπῳ ἁγίῳ, ὁ ἀναγινώσκων νοείτω, 24.16 τότε οἱ ἐν τῇ Ἰουδαίᾳ φευγέτωσαν ἐπὶ τὰ ὄρη, 24.17 ὁ ἐπὶ τοῦ δώματος μὴ καταβάτω ἆραι τὰ ἐκ τῆς οἰκίας αὐτοῦ, 24.18 καὶ ὁ ἐν τῷ ἀγρῷ μὴ ἐπιστρεψάτω ὀπίσω ἆραι τὸ ἱμάτιον αὐτοῦ.

24.19 οὐαὶ δὲ ταῖς ἐν γαστρὶ ἐχούσαις καὶ ταῖς θηλαζούσαις ἐν ἐκίναις ταῖς ἡμέραις. 24.20 προσεύχεσθε δὲ ἵνα μὴ γένηται ἡ φυγὴ ὑμῶν χιμῶνος μηδὲ σαββάτῳ·

24.21 ἔσται γὰρ τότε θλῖψις μεγάλη οἵα οὐκ ἐγένετο ἀπ' ἀρχῆς κόσμου ἕως τοῦ νῦν οὐδ' οὐ μὴ γένητε. 24.22 καὶ εἰ μὴ ἐκολοβώθησαν αἱ ἡμέραι ἐκῖναι, οὐκ ἂν ἐσώθη πᾶσα σάρξ· διὰ δὲ τοὺς ἐκλεκτοὺς ἐκολοβωθήσονται αἱ ἡμέραι ἐκῖναι.

an ethnic and a kingdom upon/against a kingdom, and there will be earthquakes and famines against/according to places/from place to place; 24.8 but all these things *are* the beginning of woes/pains.

24.9 Then they will deliver ye into tribulation and they will kill ye, and ye will be (ones) being hated by all the ethnics because of my name.

24.10 And then many will be caused to stumble/be offended and they will deliver up/betray one another into tribulation/affliction;

14.11 and many lying prophets will be raised up and they will deceive many;

24.12 and because of the (thing) *of* the lawlessness to be multiplied, the agape of the many will become cold.

24.13 But the (one) having endured to an/*the* end, this (one) will be saved.

24.14 And this (thing), the good message/gospel of the kingdom, will be heralded/preached to the entire empire/inhabited earth in/for a testimony to all the ethnics, and then the end will come. 24.15 Then when ye might see the abomination of the desolation, the (thing) having been spoken through Daniel the prophet, having been stood in a holy place, the (one) reading, let him understand; 24.16 then let those in Judea flee to the mountains; 24.17 the (one) on the roof top, let him not come down to take the (things) out of his house; 24.18 and the (one) in the field, let him not turn back behind to take his garment.

24.19 And woe to those (women) holding in a belly/being pregnant and to those (women) nursing sucklings in those days. 24.20 And pray ye that your fleeing/escape might not happen of a winter/foul weather nor in/on a sabbath;

24.21 for then there will be a great tribulation/oppression such as has not happened from the beginning of a world until the present, neither by no means might it happen. 24.22 And unless those days were shortened/curtailed, all flesh could not be saved/delivered; but on account of the chosen (ones) those days will be shortened/curtailed.

24.23 τότε ἐάν τις ὑμῖν εἴπῃ, ἰδοὺ ὧδε ὁ χριστός, ἤ, ὧδε, μὴ πιστεύσητε· 24.24 ἐγερθήσονται γὰρ ψευδόχριστοι καὶ ψευδοπροφῆτε, καὶ δώσουσιν σημῖα μεγάλα καὶ τέρατα ὥστε πλανῆναι, εἰ δυνατόν, καὶ τοὺς ἐκλεκτούς· 24.25 ἰδοὺ προείρηκα ὑμῖν. 24.26 ἐὰν οὖν εἴπωσιν ὑμῖν, ἰδοὺ ἐν τῇ ἐρήμῳ ἐστίν, μὴ ἐξέλθητε· ἰδοὺ ἐν τοῖς ταμίοις, μὴ πιστεύσητε· 24.27 ὥσπερ γὰρ ἡ ἀστραπὴ ἐξέρχετε ἀπὸ ἀνατολῶν καὶ φαίνετε ἕως δυσμῶν, οὕτως ἔστε ἡ παρουσία τοῦ υἱοῦ τοῦ ἀνθρώπου. 24.28 ὅπου ἐὰν ᾖ τὸ πτῶμα, ἐκῖ συναχθήσονται οἱ ἀετοί.

24.29 εὐθέως δὲ μετὰ τὴν θλῖψιν τῶν ἡμερῶν ἐκίνων, ὁ ἥλιος σκοτισθήσετε, καὶ ἡ σελήνη οὐ δώσι τὸ φέγγος αὐτῆς, καὶ οἱ ἀστέρες πεσοῦνται ἐκ τοῦ οὐρανοῦ, καὶ αἱ δυνάμις τῶν οὐρανῶν σαλευθήσονται. 24.30 καὶ τότε φανήσετε τὸ σημῖον τοῦ υἱοῦ τοῦ ἀνθρώπου ἐν οὐρανῷ, καὶ τότε κόψοντε πᾶσαι αἱ φυλαὶ τῆς γῆς καὶ ὄψοντε «τὸν υἱὸν τοῦ ἀνθρώπου ἐρχόμενον ἐπὶ τῶν νεφελῶν τοῦ οὐρανοῦ» μετὰ δυνάμεως καὶ δόξης πολλῆς·

24.31 καὶ ἀποστελῖ τοὺς ἀγγέλους αὐτοῦ μετὰ σάλπιγγος μεγάλης, καὶ ἐπισυνάξουσιν τοὺς ἐκλεκτοὺς αὐτοῦ ἐκ τῶν τεσσάρων ἀνέμων ἀπ' ἄκρων οὐρανῶν ἕως ἄκρων αὐτῶν. 24.32 ἀπὸ δὲ τῆς συκῆς μάθετε τὴν παραβολήν· ὅταν ἤδη ὁ κλάδος αὐτῆς γένητε ἀπαλὸς καὶ τὰ φύλλα ἐκφύῃ, γινώσκετε ὅτι ἐγγὺς τὸ θέρος· 24.33 οὕτως καὶ ὑμῖς, ὅταν ἴδητε ταῦτα πάντα, γινώσκετε ὅτι ἐγγύς ἐστιν ἐπὶ θύραις.

24.34 ἀμὴν λέγω ὑμῖν οὐ μὴ παρέλθῃ ἡ γενεὰ αὕτη ἕως πάντα ταῦτα γένητε. 24.35 ὁ οὐρανὸς καὶ ἡ γῆ παρελεύσεται, οἱ δὲ λόγοι μου οὐ μὴ παρέλθωσιν.

24.36 περὶ δὲ τῆς ἡμέρας ἐκείνης καὶ ὥρας οὐδεὶς οἶδεν, οὐδὲ οἱ ἄγγελοι τῶν οὐρανῶν οὐδὲ ὁ υἱός, εἰ μὴ ὁ πατὴρ μόνος.

24.23 Then if someone might say to ye: Behold, the anointed (one) *is* here, or: Here/there, believe ye not; 24.24 for false anointed (ones) and false/lying prophets will be raised, and they will give signs and wonders so as to deceive/lead astray, if able/possible, even the chosen(ones); 24.25 behold, I have foretold *it* to ye. 24.26 Therefore, if they might say to ye: Behold, he is in the desert/wilderness, go ye not out; behold, he is in the inner/secret rooms, believe ye not; 24.27 for even as the ray/lighting comes forth from the sunrise and shines until sunset, so will be the coming of the son of man. 24.28 Where ever the corpse may be, the eagles/vultures will be gathered there.

24.29 And immediately/soon after the tribulation of those days, the sun will be darkened, and the moon will not give its light, and the stars will be falling out of the sky/heaven, and the powers of the skies heavens will be shaken. 24.30 And then the sign of the son of the man/human will appear/shine in heaven/a sky, and then all the tribes of the earth will be cut down and they will observe/behold THE SON OF MAN COMING UPON THE CLOUDS OF THE SKY/HEAVEN with much power and glory/fame/reputation;

24.31 and he will send his messengers/angels with a great trumpet *sound,* and they will gather together his chosen/elect (ones) out of the four winds, from the extremities of skies/heavens until their extremities. 24.32 And from the fig tree, learn ye the parable: Whenever its branch might already become tender and it grows out the leaves, you know that the summer *is* near; 24.33 so also ye, when ye might see all these (things), ye know that it is near to/at *the* doors.

24.34 Truly I say to ye: By no means might this generation pass by until all these (things) might happen. 24.35 The sky/heaven and the land/earth will pass on/by, but my sayings/words might by no means pass away/by.

24.36 But concerning that day and hour/time, no one knows, neither the messengers/angels of the skies/heavens nor the son, except the father alone/on-

24.37 ὥσπερ δὲ αἱ ἡμέραι τοῦ Νῶε, οὕτως ἔσται ἡ παρουσία τοῦ υἱοῦ τοῦ ἀνθρώπου. 24.38 ὡς γὰρ ἦσαν ἐν ταῖς ἡμέραις ταῖς πρὸ τοῦ κατακλυσμοῦ τρώγοντες καὶ πίνοντες, γαμοῦντες καὶ γαμίζοντες, ἄχρι ἧς ἡμέρας εἰσῆλθεν Νῶε εἰς τὴν κιβωτόν, 24.39 καὶ οὐκ ἔγνωσαν ἕως ἦλθεν ὁ κατακλυσμὸς καὶ ἦρεν ἅπαντας, οὕτως ἔσται καὶ ἡ παρουσία τοῦ υἱοῦ τοῦ ἀνθρώπου.

24.40 τότε δύο ἔσονται ἐν τῷ ἀγρῷ, εἷς παραλαμβάνετε καὶ εἷς ἀφίετε· 24.41 δύο ἀλήθουσαι ἐν τῷ μύλῳ, μία παραλαμβάνεται καὶ μία ἀφίεται. 24.42 γρηγορεῖτε οὖν, ὅτι οὐκ οἴδατε ποίᾳ ἡμέρᾳ ὁ κύριος ὑμῶν ἔρχεται.

24.43 ἐκεῖνο δὲ γινώσκετε ὅτι εἰ ᾔδει ὁ οἰκοδεσπότης ποίᾳ φυλακῇ ὁ κλέπτης ἔρχεται, ἐγρηγόρησεν ἂν καὶ οὐκ ἂν εἴασεν διορυχθῆναι τὴν οἰκίαν αὐτοῦ. 24.44 διὰ τοῦτο καὶ ὑμεῖς γίνεσθε ἕτοιμοι, ὅτι ᾗ οὐ δοκεῖτε ὥρᾳ ὁ υἱὸς τοῦ ἀνθρώπου ἔρχεται.

24.45 τίς ἄρα ἐστὶν ὁ πιστὸς δοῦλος καὶ φρόνιμος ὃν κατέστησεν ὁ κύριος ἐπὶ τῆς οἰκίας αὐτοῦ τοῦ δοῦναι αὐτοῖς τὴν τροφὴν ἐν καιρῷ;

24.46 μακάριος ὁ δοῦλος ἐκεῖνος ὃν ἐλθὼν ὁ κύριος αὐτοῦ εὑρήσει οὕτως ποιοῦντα· 24.47 ἀμὴν λέγω ὑμῖν ὅτι ἐπὶ πᾶσιν τοῖς ὑπάρχουσιν αὐτοῦ καταστήσει αὐτόν. 24.48 ἐὰν δὲ εἴπῃ ὁ κακὸς δοῦλος ἐκῖνος ἐν τῇ καρδίᾳ ἑαυτοῦ, χρονίζει μου ὁ κύριος, 24.49 καὶ ἄρξηται τύπτειν τοὺς συνδούλους ἑαυτοῦ, ἐσθίῃ δὲ καὶ πίνῃ μετὰ τῶν μεθυόντων, 24.50 ἥξει ὁ κύριος τοῦ δούλου ἐκείνου ἐν ἡμέρᾳ ᾗ οὐ προσδοκᾷ καὶ ἐν ὥρᾳ ᾗ οὐ γινώσκει, 24.51 καὶ διχοτομήσει αὐτὸν καὶ τὸ μέρος αὐτοῦ μετὰ τῶν ὑποκριτῶν θήσει· ἐκεῖ ἔσται ὁ κλαυθμὸς καὶ ὁ βρυγμὸς τῶν ὀδόντων.

25.1 Τότε ὁμοιωθήσεται ἡ βασιλεία τῶν οὐρανῶν δέκα παρθένοις, αἵτινες λαβοῦσαι τὰς λαμπάδας αὐτῶν ἐξῆλθον εἰς ὑπάντησιν τοῦ νυμφίου. 25.2 πέντε δὲ ἐξ αὐτῶν ἦσαν μωραὶ καὶ πέντε φρόνιμοι. 25.3 αἱ γὰρ μωραὶ λαβοῦσαι τὰς λαμπάδας οὐκ ἔλαβον μεθ' ἑαυτῶν ἔλαιον· 25.4 αἱ δὲ φρόνιμοι ἔλαβον ἔλαιον ἐν

ly. 24.37 For even as the days of Noah, so will be the coming/advent of the son of the man/human. 24.38 For as they were in those days, those before the flood, eating and drinking, marrying and being given in marriage, until which day Noah entered into the ark, 24.39 and they knew not until the flood came and took *them* all away, thus/so will be also the coming/advent of the son of the man.

24.40 Then two (mem) will be in the field, one is taken along and one is left; 24.41 two (women) *will be* grinding at/in the mill, one is taken along and one is left. 24.42 Therefore, ye watch, because ye know not in what day your Lord comes/is coming.

24.43 And that (thing) ye know, because if the house master had known in what watch the thief comes, he would have watched and would not have allowed his house to be broken into. 24.44 Because of this, ye also, ye become ready, because *in* which hour/time ye think not, the son of man comes/is coming.

24.45 Then who is the faithful slave, also prudent, whom the lord appoints to his house of/from the (thing) to give to them the food in/at a season/time?

24.46 Happy *is* that slave whom, having come, his lord will find thus/so having done; 24.47 truly I say to ye that he will appoint him to/over all his goods. 24.48 But if that bad slave might say in the heart of himself: My Lord tarries/lingers, 24.49 and he begins to strike the fellow slaves of himself, and he may eat and drink with those being drunk, 24.50 the lord of that slave will come in/on a day *in* which he expects not, and *in* an hour/time which he knows not. 24.51 and he will cut him in two and he will put his part with the pretenders/hypocrites; the wailing and the gritting of the teeth will be there.

25.1 Then the kingdom of the heavens will be likened to ten maidens, who having taken their lamps, they went out to a meeting of the bridegroom. 25.2 And five out of them were foolish and five thoughtful/prudent. 25.3 For the foolish (ones), having taken the lamps, they took not olive oil with themselves; 25.4 but the thoughtful (ones) took olive oil

τοῖς ἀγγείοις μετὰ τῶν λαμπάδων ἑαυτῶν. 25.5 χρονίζοντος δὲ τοῦ νυμφίου ἐνύσταξαν πᾶσαι καὶ ἐκάθευδον. 25.6 μέσης δὲ νυκτὸς κραυγὴ γέγονεν, ἰδοὺ ὁ νυμφίος, ἐξέρχεσθε εἰς ἀπάντησιν.

25.7 τότε ἠγέρθησαν πᾶσαι αἱ παρθένοι ἐκεῖναι καὶ ἐκόσμησαν τὰς λαμπάδας ἑαυτῶν. 25.8 αἱ δὲ μωραὶ ταῖς φρονίμοις εἶπον, δότε ἡμῖν ἐκ τοῦ ἐλαίου ὑμῶν, ὅτι αἱ λαμπάδες ἡμῶν σβέννυνται.

25.9 ἀπεκρίθησαν δὲ αἱ φρόνιμοι λέγουσαι, μήποτε οὐκ ἀρκέσῃ ἡμῖν καὶ ὑμῖν· πορεύεσθε μᾶλλον πρὸς τοὺς πωλοῦντας καὶ ἀγοράσατε ἑαυταῖς. 25.10 ἀπερχομένων δὲ αὐτῶν ἀγοράσαι ἦλθεν ὁ νυμφίος, καὶ αἱ ἕτοιμοι εἰσῆλθον μετ' αὐτοῦ εἰς τοὺς γάμους, καὶ ἐκλείσθη ἡ θύρα. 25.11 ὕστερον δὲ ἔρχονται καὶ αἱ λοιπαὶ παρθένοι λέγουσαι, κύριε κύριε, ἄνοιξον ἡμῖν.

25.12 ὁ δὲ ἀποκριθεὶς εἶπεν, ἀμὴν λέγω ὑμῖν, οὐκ οἶδα ὑμᾶς. 25.13 γρηγορεῖτε οὖν, ὅτι οὐκ οἴδατε τὴν ἡμέραν οὐδὲ τὴν ὥραν.

25.14 ὥσπερ γὰρ ἄνθρωπος ἀποδημῶν ἐκάλεσεν τοὺς ἰδίους δούλους καὶ παρέδωκεν αὐτοῖς τὰ ὑπάρχοντα αὐτοῦ, 25.15 καὶ ᾧ μὲν ἔδωκεν πέντε τάλαντα, ᾧ δὲ δύο, ᾧ δὲ ἕν, ἑκάστῳ κατὰ τὴν ἰδίαν δύναμιν, καὶ ἀπεδήμησεν. εὐθέως 25.16 πορευθεὶς ὁ τὰ πέντε τάλαντα λαβὼν εἰργάσατο ἐν αὐτοῖς καὶ ἐκέρδησεν ἄλλα πέντε τάλαντα· 25.17 ὡσαύτως ὁ τὰ δύο ἐκέρδησεν ἄλλα δύο. 25.18 ὁ δὲ τὸ ἓν λαβὼν ἀπελθὼν ὤρυξεν γῆν καὶ ἔκρυψεν τὸ ἀργύριον τοῦ κυρίου αὐτοῦ.

25.19 μετὰ δὲ πολὺν χρόνον ἔρχεται ὁ κύριος τῶν δούλων ἐκείνων καὶ συναίρει λόγον μετ' αὐτῶν.

25.20 καὶ προσελθὼν ὁ τὰ πέντε λαβὼν προσήνεγκεν ἄλλα πέντε τάλαντα λέγων, κύριε, πέντε τάλαντά μοι παρέδωκας· ἴδε ἄλλα πέντε τάλαντα ἐκέρδησα.

25.21 ἔφη αὐτῷ ὁ κύριος αὐτοῦ, εὖ, δοῦλε ἀγαθὲ καὶ πιστέ, ἐπὶ ὀλίγα ἦς πιστός, ἐπὶ πολλῶν σε καταστήσω· εἴσελθε εἰς τὴν χαρὰν τοῦ κυρίου σου.

in the utensils with the lamps of themselves. 25.5 But from the bridegroom lingering/delaying they all slumbered and fell asleep. 25.6 And from the middle of night there has become an outcry: Behold the bridegroom, come ye forth to a meeting!

25.7 Then all those maidens were awakened and they trimmed the lamps of themselves. 25.8 And the foolish (ones) said to the thoughtful/prudent (ones): Give us out of your olive oil, because our lamps are being extinguished/going out.

25.9 But the thoughtful/prudent (ones) answered, saying: Never! It might not be enough for us and for ye; rather, go ye to those selling *it* and buy ye for yourselves. 25.10 And from them going away to buy *it*, the bridegroom came, and the (ones) prepared went in with him to the wedding, and the door was closed. 25.11 And later, the remaining maidens come also, saying: Lord, lord, open you for us.

25.12 But the (he) answering, he said: Truly I say to ye, I know ye not. 25.13 Therefore, ye watch, because ye know not the day nor the hour/time.

25.14 For just as a man going abroad called his own slaves and delivered over to them his possessions, 25.15 and to one he gave five talents, to another two, and to another one, to each according to his own ability/power, and he journeyed abroad. Going 25.16 at once, the (one) having received the five talents, he traded/did business with them and he gained another five talents; 25.17 similarly, the (one) *having received* the two gained another two. 25.18 But the (one) having received one, going away, he dug earth and hid the silver/money of his lord.

25.19 And after much time, the lord of those slaves comes and settles an accounting with them.

25.20 And coming near, the (one) having received the five, he brought forward another five talents, saying: Lord, you delivered to me five talents; behold, I gained another five talents.

25.21 His lord said to him: Well *done* good and faithful slave, you were faithful on/over a few (things), I will stand you over many (things); enter you into the joy of your lord.

58

25.22 προσελθὼν καὶ ὁ τὰ δύο τάλαντα λαβὼν εἶπεν, δύο τάλαντά μοι παρέδωκας· ἴδε ἄλλα δύο τάλαντα ἐκέρδησα.

25.23 ἔφη αὐτῷ ὁ κύριος αὐτοῦ, εὖ, δοῦλε ἀγαθὲ καὶ πιστέ, ἐπὶ ὀλίγα ἦς πιστός, ἐπὶ πολλῶν σε καταστήσω· εἴσελθε εἰς τὴν χαρὰν τοῦ κυρίου σου.

25.24 προσελθὼν δὲ καὶ ὁ τὸ ἓν τάλαντον εἰληφὼς εἶπεν, κύριε, ἔγνων σε ὅτι ἄνθρωπος αὐστηρὸς εἶ, θερίζων ὅπου οὐκ ἔσπειρας καὶ συνάγων ὅθεν οὐ διεσκόρπισας· 25.25 καὶ φοβηθεὶς ἀπελθὼν ἔκρυψα τὸ τάλαντόν σου ἐν τῇ γῇ· ἴδε ἔχεις τὸ σόν.

25.26 ἀποκριθεὶς δὲ ὁ κύριος αὐτοῦ εἶπεν αὐτῷ, πονηρὲ δοῦλε καὶ ὀκνηρέ, ᾔδεις ὅτι θερίζω ὅπου οὐκ ἔσπειρα καὶ συνάγω ὅθεν οὐ διεσκόρπισα; 25.27 ἔδει σε οὖν βαλεῖν τὰ ἀργύριά μου τοῖς τραπεζίταις, καὶ ἐλθὼν ἐγὼ ἐκομισάμην ἂν τὸ ἐμὸν σὺν τόκῳ. 25.28 ἄρατε οὖν ἀπ' αὐτοῦ τὸ τάλαντον καὶ δότε τῷ ἔχοντι τὰ δέκα τάλαντα· 25.29 τῷ γὰρ ἔχοντι παντὶ δοθήσεται καὶ περισσευθήσεται· τοῦ δὲ μὴ ἔχοντος καὶ ὃ ἔχει ἀρθήσεται ἀπ' αὐτοῦ. 25.30 καὶ τὸν ἀχρῖον δοῦλον ἐκβάλετε εἰς τὸ σκότος τὸ ἐξώτερον· ἐκεῖ ἔσται ὁ κλαυθμὸς καὶ ὁ βρυγμὸς τῶν ὀδόντων.

25.31 ὅταν δὲ ἔλθῃ ὁ υἱὸς τοῦ ἀνθρώπου ἐν τῇ δόξῃ αὐτοῦ καὶ πάντες οἱ ἄγγελοι μετ' αὐτοῦ, τότε καθίσει ἐπὶ θρόνου δόξης αὐτοῦ· 25.32 καὶ συναχθήσονται ἔμπροσθεν αὐτοῦ πάντα τὰ ἔθνη, καὶ ἀφορίσει αὐτοὺς ἀπ' ἀλλήλων, ὥσπερ ὁ ποιμὴν ἀφορίζει τὰ πρόβατα ἀπὸ τῶν ἐρίφων, 25.33 καὶ στήσει τὰ μὲν πρόβατα ἐκ δεξιῶν τὰ δὲ ἐρίφια ἐξ εὐωνύμων αὐτοῦ. 25.34 τότε ἐρεῖ ὁ βασιλεὺς τοῖς ἐκ δεξιῶν αὐτοῦ, δεῦτε, οἱ εὐλογημένοι τοῦ πατρός μου, κληρονομήσατε τὴν ἡτοιμασμένην ὑμῖν βασιλείαν ἀπὸ καταβολῆς κόσμου· 25.35 ἐπείνασα γὰρ καὶ ἐδώκατέ μοι φαγεῖν, ἐδίψησα καὶ ἐποτίσατέ με, ξένος ἤμην καὶ συνηγάγετέ με, 25.36 γυμνὸς καὶ περιεβάλετέ με, ἠσθένησα καὶ ἐπεσκέψασθέ με,

25.22 Also coming near, the (one) having received the two talents said: You delivered to me two
talents; behold, I gained another two talents.

25.23 His lord said to him: Well *done* good and
faithful slave, you were faithful on/over a few
(things), I will stand/set you over many (things);
enter you into the joy of your lord.

25.24 And the (one) having received the one
talent, approaching *him*, he said: Lord, I knew you,
that you are a hard man, reaping where you sowed not
and gathering from where you scattered not; 25.25 and
going away, fearing, I buried your talent in the
earth; behold, you have that/the (thing) *being* yours.

25.26 And answering, his lord said to him: Evil
slave, also *being* lazy, knew you that I reap where I
sowed not and I gather from where I scattered not?
25.27 Therefore, it was necessary *for* you to put my
silver things with the money-changers; and I, coming,
would have recovered that *being* mine, with interest.
25.28 Therefore, take the talent from him and give *it*
to the (one) having the ten talents; 25.29 for to the
(one) having, to each (one), will be given and he will
have abundance; but from the (one) having not, even
what he has will be taken from him. 25.30 And cast ye
out the useless slave into the outer darkness; the
lamentation/weeping and the gritting of the teeth will
be there.

25.31 And whenever the son of the man may come
in his glory/fame, and all the messengers/angels with
him, then he will sit upon a throne of his glory;
25.32 and all the ethnics/Gentiles will be gathered
together in front of him, and he will separate them
from one another as the shepherd separates the sheep
from the goats, 25.33 and he will stand/put/set the
sheep at the right but the goats at the left of him.
25.34 Then the king will say to those on his right:
Come, the (ones) being blessed of my father, inherit
ye the kingdom having been prepared for ye from a
founding of a world; 25.35 for I hungered and ye gave
me to eat, I thirsted and ye gave me drink, I was a
stranger and ye were hospitable *to* me, 25.36 strip-
ped/naked and ye clothed me, I was sick/weak and ye

ἐν φυλακῇ ἤμην καὶ ἤλθατε πρός ἐμέ.

25.37 τότε ἀποκριθήσονται αὐτῷ οἱ δίκαιοι λέγοντες, κύριε, πότε σε εἴδομεν πεινῶντα καὶ ἐθρέψαμεν, ἢ διψῶντα καὶ ἐποτίσαμεν; 25.38 πότε δέ σε εἴδομεν ξένον καὶ συνηγάγομεν, ἢ γυμνὸν καὶ περιεβάλομεν; 25.39 πότε δέ σε εἴδομεν ἀσθένη ἢ ἐν φυλακῇ καὶ ἤλθομεν πρός σε;

25.40 καὶ ἀποκριθεὶς ὁ βασιλεὺς ἐρεῖ αὐτοῖς, ἀμὴν λέγω ὑμῖν, ἐφ᾽ ὅσον ἐποιήσατε ἑνὶ τούτων τῶν ἀδελφῶν μου τῶν ἐλαχίστων, ἐμοὶ ἐποιήσατε.

25.41 τότε ἐρεῖ καὶ τοῖς ἐξ εὐωνύμων, ὑπάγετε ἀπ᾽ ἐμοῦ κατηραμένοι εἰς τὸ πῦρ τὸ αἰώνιον τὸ ἡτοιμασμένον τῷ διαβόλῳ καὶ τοῖς ἀγγέλοις αὐτοῦ· 25.42 ἐπίνασα γὰρ καὶ οὐκ ἐδώκατέ μοι φαγεῖν, ἐδίψησα καὶ οὐκ ἐποτίσατέ με, 25.43 ξένος ἤμην καὶ οὐ συνηγάγετέ με, γυμνὸς καὶ οὐ περιεβάλεταί, ἀσθενὴς καὶ ἐν φυλακῇ καὶ οὐκ ἐπεσκέψασθέ με.

25.44 τότε ἀποκριθήσονται καὶ αὐτοὶ λέγοντες, κύριε, πότε σε εἴδομεν πεινῶντα ἢ διψῶντα ἢ ξένον ἢ γυμνὸν ἢ ἀσθενῆ ἢ ἐν φυλακῇ καὶ οὐκ ἠδικονήσαμέν σοι;

25.45 τότε ἀποκριθήσεται αὐτοῖς λέγων, ἀμὴν λέγω ὑμῖν, ἐφ᾽ ὅσον οὐκ ἐποιήσατε ἑνὶ τούτων τῶν ἐλαχίστων, οὐδὲ ἐμοὶ ἐποιήσατε. 25.46 καὶ ἀπελεύσονται οὗτοι εἰς κόλασιν αἰώνιον, οἱ δὲ δίκαιοι εἰς ζωὴν αἰώνιον.

26.1 Καὶ ἐγένετο ὅτε ἐτέλεσεν ὁ Ἰησοῦς πάντας τοὺς λόγους τούτους, εἶπεν τοῖς μαθηταῖς αὐτοῦ, 26.2 οἴδατε ὅτι μετὰ δύο ἡμέρας τὸ πάσχα γίνεται, καὶ ὁ υἱὸς τοῦ ἀνθρώπου παραδίδοται εἰς τὸ σταυρωθῆναι.

26.3 τότε συνήχθησαν οἱ ἀρχιερεῖς καὶ οἱ πρεσβύτεροι τοῦ λαοῦ εἰς τὴν αὐλὴν τοῦ ἀρχιερέως τοῦ λεγομένου Καϊάφα, 26.4 καὶ συνεβουλεύσαντο ἵνα τὸν Ἰησοῦν δόλῳ κρατήσωσιν καὶ ἀποκτείνωσιν·

visited/cared for me, I was in prison and ye came to me.

25.37 Then the just (ones) will answer to him, saying: Lord, when saw we you having hungered and we nourished *you*, or having thirsted and we gave drink to *you*? 25.38 And when saw we you a stranger and we were hospitable *to you*, or naked and we clothed *you*? 25.39 And when saw we you sick or in prison and we came to you?

25.40 And answering, the king will say to them: Truly I say to ye. on/for as much as ye did *it* for one of these my brothers, of the least (ones), ye did *it* for me.

25.41 And then he will say to those from the left (hand): Go ye away from me, (ones) having been cursed, into the eternal fire, the (thing) having been prepared for the devil and for his messengers/angels; 25.42 for I hungered and ye gave not for me to eat, I thirsted and ye gave not drink to me, 25.43 I was a stranger and ye were not hospitable *to* me, naked and ye clothed *me* not, sick and in prison and ye visited/cared not for me.

25.44 And then those, they will answer, saying: Lord, when saw we you having hungered or having thirsted or a stranger or naked or sick or in prison and we waited not on/ministered not to you?

25.45 Then he will answer to them, saying: Truly I say to ye, on/for as much as ye did *it* not for one of these, of the least (ones), neither did ye for me. 25.46 And these, they will go away into eternal punishment, and/but the just (ones) into eternal life.

26.1 And it happened, when Jesus ended/finished all these sayings/words/reasonings, he said to his learners/pupils: 26.2 Ye know that after two days it becomes the passover, and the son of man will be delivered up to/for the (thing) to be crucified.

26.3 Then the high priests and the elders of the people were gathered in the court *yard* of the high priest named Caiaphas, 26.4 and they consulted together in order that by cunning/guile they might apprehend/arrest and they might kill Jesus.

26.5 ἔλεγον δέ, μὴ ἐν τῇ ἑορτῇ, ἵνα μὴ θόρυβος γένηται ἐν τῷ λαῷ.

26.6 τοῦ δὲ Ἰησοῦ γενομένου ἐν Βηθανίᾳ ἐν οἰκίᾳ Σίμωνος τοῦ λεπροῦ,   26.7 προσῆλθεν αὐτῷ γυνὴ ἔχουσα ἀλάβαστρον μύρου πολυτίμου καὶ κατέχεεν ἐπὶ τῆς κεφαλῆς αὐτοῦ ἀνακιμένου.

26.8 ἰδόντες δὲ οἱ μαθηταὶ ἠγανάκτησαν λέγοντες, εἰς τί ἡ ἀπώλια αὕτη; 26.9 ἐδύνατο γὰρ τοῦτο πραθῆναι πολλοῦ καὶ δοθῆναι πτωχοῖς.

26.10 γνοὺς δὲ ὁ Ἰησοῦς εἶπεν αὐτοῖς, τί κόπους παρέχετε τῇ γυναικί; ἔργον γὰρ καλὸν ἠργάσατο εἰς ἐμέ· 26.11 πάντοτε γὰρ τοὺς πτωχοὺς ἔχετε μεθ' ἑαυτῶν, ἐμὲ δὲ οὐ πάντοτε ἔχετε· 26.12 βαλοῦσα γὰρ αὕτη τὸ μύρον τοῦτο ἐπὶ τοῦ σώματός μου πρὸς τὸ ἐνταφιάσαι με ἐποίησεν.

26.13 ἀμὴν λέγω ὑμῖν, ὅπου ἐὰν κηρυχθῇ τὸ εὐαγγέλιον τοῦτο ἐν ὅλῳ τῷ κόσμῳ, λαληθήσετε καὶ ὃ ἐποίησεν αὕτη εἰς μνημόσυνον αὐτῆς. 26.14 τότε πορευθὶς εἷς τῶν δώδεκα, ὁ λεγόμενος Ἰούδας Ἰσκαριώτης, πρὸς τοὺς ἀρχιερῖς 26.15 εἶπεν, τί θέλεταί μοι δῶνε καὶ ἐγὼ ὑμῖν παραδώσω αὐτόν; οἱ δὲ ἔστησαν αὐτῷ τριάκοντα ἀργύρια. 26.16 καὶ ἀπὸ τότε ἐζήτι εὐκαιρίαν ἵνα αὐτὸν παραδῶ.

26.17 τῇ δὲ πρώτῃ τῶν ἀζύμων προσῆλθον οἱ μαθηταὶ τῷ Ἰησοῦ λέγοντες, ποῦ θέλις ἑτοιμάσωμέν σοι φαγῖν τὸ πάσχα;

26.18 ὁ δὲ εἶπεν, ὑπάγετε εἰς τὴν πόλιν πρὸς τὸν δῖνα καὶ εἴπατε αὐτῷ, ὁ διδάσκαλος λέγει, ὁ καιρός μου ἐγγύς ἐστιν· πρὸς σὲ ποιῶ τὸ πάσχα μετὰ τῶν μαθητῶν μου. 26.19 καὶ ἐποίησαν οἱ μαθηταὶ ὡς συνέταξεν αὐτοῖς ὁ Ἰησοῦς, καὶ ἡτοίμασαν τὸ πάσχα. 26.20 ὀψίας δὲ γενομένης ἀνέκιτο μετὰ τῶν δώδεκα μαθητῶν. 26.21 καὶ ἐσθιόντων αὐτῶν λέγι, ἀμὴν λέγω ὑμῖν ὅτι

26.5 But they said: Not in/at the festival, in order that an uproar might not happen among the people.

26.6 And from Jesus having become at Bethany in *the* house of Simon the leper, 26.7 a woman came near to him having an alabaster/flask of very valuable ointment, and she poured it upon the head of him, being reclined.

26.8 And having seen *this*, the learners/pupils were indignant, saying: To/for what *is* this ruin/waste? 26.9 For this was able to be sold for much and to be given to poor (ones).

26.10 And knowing, Jesus said to them: Why *do* ye offer troubles for the woman? For she worked a good work/deed to/for me; 26.11 for ye always have the poor (ones) with yourselves, but me ye have not always; 26.12 for this (woman), having put this ointment upon my body, she did it toward the (thing) to bury me.

26.13 Truly I say to ye, where ever this good message/gospel might be heralded/preached in the entire world, it will be spoken also what this (one) did, in her memory. 26.14 Then one of the twelve, the (one) being called Judas Iscariot, going to the high priests, 26.15 he said: What want ye to give to me, and I, I will deliver him over to ye? And they set forth for him thirty silver coins/shekels. 26.16 And from then/that (time) he was seeking a good time/an opportunity in order that he might deliver him/hand him over.

26.17 And on the first day of the unleavened (bread), the learners/pupils came near to Jesus, saying: Where *do* you want *that* we might prepare for you to eat the passover (lamb)?

26.18 And the (he) said: Go ye into the city to the such/somebody and say ye to him: The teacher says: My time is near; with/near you I shall do/make the passover with my learners/pupils. 26.19 And the learners/pupils did as Jesus ordered to them, and they prepared the passover (lamb). 26.20 And from it having become evening, he reclined with the twelve learners/pupils. 26.21 And from them having eaten, he

εἷς ἐξ ὑμῶν παραδώσι με. 26.22 καὶ λυπούμενοι σφόδρα ἤρξαντο λέγιν αὐτῷ εἷς ἕκαστος, μήτι ἐγώ εἰμι, κύριε;

26.23 ὁ δὲ ἀποκριθὶς εἶπεν, ὁ ἐμβάψας μετ' ἐμοῦ τὴν χῖρα ἐν τῷ τρυβλίῳ οὗτός με παραδώσει.

26.24 ὁ μὲν υἱὸς τοῦ ἀνθρώπου ὑπάγι καθὼς γέγραπται περὶ αὐτοῦ, οὐαὶ δὲ τῷ ἀνθρώπῳ ἐκείνῳ δι' οὗ ὁ υἱὸς τοῦ ἀνθρώπου παραδίδοται· καλὸν ἦν αὐτῷ εἰ οὐκ ἐγεννήθη ὁ ἄνθρωπος ἐκῖνος.

26.25 ἀποκριθὶς δὲ Ἰούδας ὁ παραδιδοὺς αὐτὸν εἶπεν, μήτι ἐγώ εἰμι, ῥαββεί; λέγει αὐτῷ ὁ Ἰησοῦς, σὺ εἶπας.

26.26 ἐσθιόντων δὲ αὐτῶν λαβὼν ὁ Ἰησοῦς ἄρτον καὶ εὐλογήσας ἔκλασεν καὶ δοὺς τοῖς μαθηταῖς εἶπεν, λάβετε φάγετε, τοῦτό ἐστιν τὸ σῶμά μου.

26.27 καὶ λαβὼν ποτήριον καὶ εὐχαριστήσας ἔδωκεν αὐτοῖς λέγων, πίετε ἐξ αὐτοῦ πάντες, 26.28 τοῦτο γάρ ἐστιν τὸ αἷμά μου τῆς διαθήκης τὸ περὶ πολλῶν ἐκχυννόμενον εἰς ἄφεσιν ἁμαρτιῶν.

26.29 λέγω δὲ ὑμῖν, οὐ μὴ πίω ἀπ' ἄρτι ἐκ τούτου τοῦ γενήματος τῆς ἀμπέλου ἕως τῆς ἡμέρας ἐκίνης ὅταν αὐτὸ πίνω μεθ' ὑμῶν κενὸν ἐν τῇ βασιλείᾳ τοῦ πατρός μου. 26.30 καὶ ὑμνήσαντες ἐξῆλθον εἰς τὸ ὄρος τῶν ἐλαιῶν. 26.31 τότε λέγι αὐτοῖς ὁ Ἰησοῦς, πάντες ὑμῖς σκανδαλισθήσεσθαι ἐν ἐμοὶ ἐν τῇ νυκτὶ ταύτῃ,

γέγραπται γάρ, «πατάξω τὸν ποιμένα, καὶ διασκορπισθήσονται τὰ πρόβατα τῆς ποίμνης»

26.32 μετὰ δὲ τὸ ἐγερθῆνέ με προάξω ὑμᾶς εἰς τὴν Γαλιλαίαν. 26.33 ἀποκριθεὶς δὲ ὁ Πέτρος εἶπεν αὐτῷ, εἰ πάντες σκανδαλισθήσονται ἐν σοί, ἐγὼ οὐδέποτε σκανδαλισθήσομαι. 26.34 ἔφη αὐτῷ ὁ Ἰησοῦς, ἀμὴν λέγω σοι ὅτι ἐν ταύτῃ τῇ νυκτὶ πρὶν ἀλέκτορα φωνῆσαι τρίς με ἀπαρνήσῃ.

26.35 λέγι αὐτῷ ὁ Πέτρος, κἂν δέῃ με σὺν σοὶ ἀποθανῖν, οὐ μή σε ἀπαρνήσομαι. ὁμοίως καὶ πάντες οἱ μαθηταὶ εἶπον.

said: Truly I say to ye that one out of ye will deliver me over/betray me.   26.22 And grieving exceedingly, they began to say to him, each one: I, it is not I, Lord?

26.23 And the (he) answering, he said: The (one) dipping with me the hand in the dish, this (one) will deliver up/betray me.

26.24 Indeed, the son of the man departs, even as it has been written concerning him, but woe to that man through whom the son of man is handed over/betrayed; it was good for him if that man was not generated/born.

26.25 And answering, Judas, the (one) betraying him, said: I, it is not I, Rabbi?   Jesus says to him: You, you said *it*.

26.26 And from them having eaten, Jesus, taking a loaf and blessing *it*, he broke *it* and giving to the learners/pupils, he said: Take ye, eat ye, this is my body.

26.27 And taking a cup and giving thanks, he gave *it* to them, saying: All ye drink out of it, 26.28 for this is my blood of the covenant, the (one) concerning many, being poured out to/for a remission/forgiveness of faults/sins.

26.29 And I say to ye, by no means shall I drink out of this, the product/fruit of the vine, from just now until that day when I drink it new with ye in the kingdom of my father.   26.30 And having sung a hymn, they went out to the mountain of the olives.   26.31 Then Jesus says to them: All ye, ye will be offended/caused to stumble in me during/in this night,

for it has been written: I SHALL SMITE THE SHEPHERD, AND THE SHEEP OF THE FLOCK WILL BE SCATTERED;

26.32 but after the (thing) for me to be raised, I shall go before ye into Galilee.   26.33 And answering, Peter said to him: If all (men) will be offended/caused to stumble by/in you, I, never shall I be offended.   26.34 Jesus said to him: Truly I say to you that in/during this night, prior/before to crow a rooster/cock, you will deny me thrice.

26.35 Peter says to him: Even if it be necessary *for* me to die with you, by no means shall I deny you.

26.36 τότε ἔρχεται μετ' αὐτῶν ὁ Ἰησοῦς εἰς χωρίον λεγόμενον Γεθσημανί, καὶ λέγι τοῖς μαθηταῖς αὐτοῦ, καθίσατε ἕως ἀπελθὼν ἐκῖ προσεύξωμαι.

26.37 καὶ παραλαβὼν τὸν Πέτρον καὶ τοὺς δύο υἱοὺς Ζεβεδέου ἤρξατο λυπῖσθε καὶ ἀδημονῖν. 26.38 τότε λέγει αὐτοῖς, περίλυπός ἐστιν ἡ ψυχή μου ἕως θανάτου· μίνατε ὧδε καὶ γρηγορῖτε μετ' ἐμοῦ.

26.39 καὶ προσελθὼν μικρὸν ἔπεσεν ἐπὶ πρόσωπον αὐτοῦ προσευχόμενος καὶ λέγων, πάτερ μου, εἰ δυνατόν ἐστιν, παρελθάτω ἀπ' ἐμοῦ τὸ ποτήριον τοῦτο· πλὴν οὐχ ὡς ἐγὼ θέλω ἀλλ' ὡς σύ.

26.40 καὶ ἔρχετε πρὸς τοὺς μαθητὰς καὶ εὑρίσκι αὐτοὺς καθεύδοντας, καὶ λέγι τῷ Πέτρῳ, οὕτως οὐκ ἰσχύσατε μίαν ὥραν γρηγορῆσε μετ' ἐμοῦ; 26.41 γρηγορεῖτε καὶ προσεύχεσθε, ἵνα μὴ εἰσέλθηται εἰς πιρασμόν· τὸ μὲν πνεῦμα πρόθυμον ἡ δὲ σὰρξ ἀσθενής.

26.42 πάλιν ἐκ δευτέρου ἀπελθὼν προσηύξατο λέγων, πάτερ μου, εἰ οὐ δύνατε τοῦτο παρελθῖν ἐὰν μὴ αὐτὸ πίω, γενηθήτω τὸ θέλημά σου. 26.43 καὶ ἐλθὼν πάλιν εὖρεν αὐτοὺς καθεύδοντας, ἦσαν γὰρ αὐτῶν οἱ ὀφθαλμοὶ βεβαρημένοι.

26.44 καὶ ἀφὶς αὐτοὺς πάλιν ἀπελθὼν προσηύξατο ἐκ τρίτου τὸν αὐτὸν λόγον εἰπὼν πάλιν.

26.45 τότε ἔρχεται πρὸς τοὺς μαθητὰς καὶ λέγι αὐτοῖς, καθεύδετε τὸ λοιπὸν καὶ ἀναπαύεσθε; ἰδοὺ ἤγγικεν ἡ ὥρα καὶ ὁ υἱὸς τοῦ ἀνθρώπου παραδίδοται εἰς χῖρας ἁμαρτωλῶν.

26.46 ἐγείρεσθε, ἄγωμεν· ἰδοὺ ἤγγικεν ὁ παραδιδούς με.

26.47 καὶ ἔτι αὐτοῦ λαλοῦντος ἰδοὺ Ἰούδας εἷς τῶν δώδεκα ἦλθεν καὶ μετ' αὐτοῦ ὄχλος πολὺς μετὰ μαχερῶν καὶ ξύλων ἀπὸ τῶν ἀρχιερέων καὶ πρεσβυτέρων τοῦ λαοῦ. 26.48 ὁ δὲ παραδιδοὺς αὐτὸν ἔδωκεν αὐτοῖς σημεῖον λέγων, ὃν ἐὰν φιλήσω αὐτός ἐστιν· κρατήσαται αὐτόν. 26.49 καὶ εὐθέως προσελθὼν τῷ Ἰησοῦ εἶπεν, χαῖρε, ῥαββεί· καὶ κατεφίλησεν αὐτόν. 26.50 ὁ δὲ εἶπεν αὐτῷ, ἑταῖρε, ἐφ' ὃ πάρει.

τότε προσελθόντες ἐπέβαλον τὰς χῖρας ἐπὶ τὸν Ἰησοῦν καὶ

And all the learners/pupils spoke likewise.

26.36   Then Jesus goes with them to a place being named Gethsemane, and he says to his learners/pupils: Sit ye until, going away *over* there, I might pray.

26.37   And taking along Peter and the two sons of Zebedee, he began to grieve and to be inwardly troubled.   26.38 Then he says to them: My life/soul is very sad until death; stay ye here and watch ye with me.

26.39   And going ahead a little *way*, he fell upon his face praying and saying: My father, if it is possible, let this cup pass by from me; however, not as I, I want, but as you *do*.

26.40   And he comes to the learners/pupils and he finds them sleeping, and he says to Peter: So, were ye not able to watch *for* one hour with me?   26.41   Watch ye and pray ye, in order that ye might not enter into trying/temptation; the spirit indeed *is* willing/eager but the flesh *is* weak.

26.42   Again, from a second going away, he prayed, saying: My father, if this *cup* is not able to pass by unless I might drink it, let your will be generated/done.   26.43 And going/coming again he found them sleeping, for their eyes had been weighted down.

26.44   And forgiving/leaving them, again going away, he prayed from a third *time*, speaking the same saying again.

26.45   Then he comes to the learners/pupils and he says to them: *Do* ye sleep from now on and take ye rest? Behold, the time/hour has drawn near and the son of man is betrayed/handed over into hands of sinners.

26.46   Rise ye, let us go; behold, the (one) betraying me has drawn near.

26.47   And of him yet speaking, behold Judas, one of the twelve, came and with him *was* a much crowd with swords and clubs, from the high priests and elders of the people.   26.48 And the (one) betraying him gave to them a sign, saying: Whom ever I might kiss is he; grasp/arrest him.   26.49 And immediately/soon coming near to Jesus, he said: Greetings, Rabbi; and he kissed him.   26.50 And the (he) said to him: Friend/comrade, for/on what you *are* here.

Then having come near, they threw the hands upon

ἐκράτησαν αὐτόν. 26.51 καὶ ἰδοὺ εἷς τῶν μετὰ Ἰησοῦ ἐκτίνας τὴν χῖρα ἀπέσπασε τὴν μάχαιραν αὐτοῦ καὶ πατάξας τὸν δοῦλον τοῦ ἀρχιερέως ἀφῖλεν αὐτοῦ τὸ ὠτίον. 26.52 τότε λέγει αὐτῷ ὁ Ἰησοῦς, ἀπόστρεψον τὴν μάχαιράν σου εἰς τὸν τόπον αὐτῆς, πάντες γὰρ οἱ λαβόντες μάχαιραν ἐν μαχαίρῃ ἀπολοῦνται. 26.53 ἢ δοκεῖς ὅτι οὐ δύναμαι παρακαλέσε τὸν πατέρα μου, καὶ παραστήσει μοι ὧδε ἄρτι πλείω δώδεκα λεγιῶνων ἀγγέλους; 26.54 πῶς οὖν πληρωθῶσιν αἱ γραφαὶ ὅτι οὕτως δεῖ γενέσθε;

26.55 ἐν ἐκείνῃ τῇ ὥρᾳ εἶπεν ὁ Ἰησοῦς τοῖς ὄχλοις, ὡς ἐπὶ λῃστὴν ἐξήλθατε μετὰ μαχαιρῶν καὶ ξύλων συλλαβεῖν με; καθ᾽ ἡμέραν ἐν τῷ ἱερῷ ἐκαθεζόμην διδάσκων καὶ οὐκ ἐκρατήσατέ με. 26.56 τοῦτο δὲ ὅλον γέγονεν ἵνα πληρωθῶσιν αἱ γραφαὶ τῶν προφητῶν.

τότε οἱ μαθηταὶ πάντες ἀφέντες αὐτὸν ἔφυγον. 26.57 οἱ δὲ κρατήσαντες τὸν Ἰησοῦν ἀπήγαγον πρὸς Καιάφαν τὸν ἀρχιερέα, ὅπου οἱ γραμματῖς καὶ οἱ πρεσβύτεροι συνήχθησαν.

26.58 ὁ δὲ Πέτρος ἠκολούθι αὐτῷ ἀπὸ μακρόθεν ἕως τῆς αὐλῆς τοῦ ἀρχιερέως, καὶ εἰσελθὼν ἔσω ἐκάθητο μετὰ τῶν ὑπηρετῶν ἰδεῖν τὸ τέλος.

26.59 οἱ δὲ ἀρχιερῖς καὶ τὸ συνέδριον ὅλον ἐζήτουν ψευδομαρτυρίαν κατὰ τοῦ Ἰησοῦ ὅπως αὐτὸν θανατώσωσιν, 26.60 καὶ οὐχ εὗρον πολλῶν προσελθόντων ψευδομαρτύρων. ὕστερον δὲ προσελθόντες δύο 26.61 εἶπαν, οὗτος ἔφη, δύναμαι καταλῦσε τὸν ναὸν τοῦ θεοῦ καὶ διὰ τριῶν ἡμερῶν αὐτὸν οἰκοδομῆσαι.

26.62 καὶ ἀναστὰς ὁ ἀρχιερεὺς εἶπεν αὐτῷ, οὐδὲν ἀποκρίνῃ; τί οὗτοί σου καταμαρτυροῦσιν; 26.63 ὁ δὲ Ἰησοῦς ἐσιώπα. καὶ ὁ ἀρχιερεὺς εἶπεν αὐτῷ, ἐξορκίζω σε κατὰ τοῦ θεοῦ τοῦ ζῶντο ἵνα ἡμῖν εἴπῃς εἰ σὺ εἶ ὁ χριστὸς ὁ υἱὸς τοῦ θεοῦ. 26.64 λέγει αὐτῷ ὁ Ἰησοῦς, σὺ εἶπας· πλὴν λέγω ὑμῖν, ἀπ᾽ ἄρτι ὄψεσθε «τὸν υἱὸν τοῦ ἀνθρώπου καθήμενον ἐκ δεξιῶν τῆς δυνάμεως» καὶ «ἐρχόμενον ἐπὶ τῶν νεφελῶν τοῦ οὐρανοῦ.»

Jesus and they seized him. 26.51 And behold, one of those with Jesus, stretching forth the hand, he drew his sword, and smiting the slave of the high priest, he cut off his ear. 26.52 Then Jesus says to him: Return your sword to its place, for all those taking up a sword they will perish by a sword. 26.53 Or *do* you think that I am not able to call my father and he will stand more than ten legions of angels/messengers beside me here, just now? 26.54 How then would the writings be fulfilled that thus it is necessary to become/happen?

26.55 In/at that hour/time Jesus said to the crowds: As upon/against a robber came ye out with swords/weapons and clubs to take me? Day by day I sat in the *outer* temple teaching, and ye seized me not. 26.56 But this whole (thing) has happened in order that the writings of the prophets might be fulfilled.

Then the learners/pupils all fled/ran away, leaving him. 26.57 But those having seized Jesus led him away to Caiaphas the high priest, where the scribes and the elders were gathered together.

26.58 And Peter was following after him from afar until/as far as the court/yard of the high priest, and going in, he sat within with the servants (assistants) to see the end.

26.59 And the high priests and the whole council were seeking a false witness against Jesus so that they might put him to death, 26.60 and they found not many false witnesses coming near. But later, coming near, two 26.61 said: This (one) said: I am able to destroy the *inner* temple of God and to rebuild it through *only* three days.

26.62 And arising, the high priest said to him: *Do* you answer nothing? What are these testifying against you? 26.63 But Jesus remained silent. And the high priest said to him: I charge you under oath from the living God that you might say to us if you, you are the anointed (one), the son of God. 26.64 Jesus says to him: You, you said *it*; nevertheless, I say to ye: From now *on* ye will observe the son of man SITTING FROM/AT A/(*the*) RIGHT *hand* OF THE POWER and COMING UPON THE CLOUDS OF THE SKY/HEAVEN.

26.65 τότε ὁ ἀρχιερεὺς διέρρηξεν τὰ ἱμάτια αὐτοῦ λέγον, δὲ ἐβλασφήμησεν· τί ἔτι χρίαν ἔχομεν μαρτύρων; ἴδε νῦν ἠκούσατε τὴν βλασφημίαν· 26.66 τί ὑμῖν δοκεῖ; οἱ δὲ ἀποκριθέντες εἶπαν, ἔνοχος θανάτου ἐστίν. 26.67 τότε ἐνέπτυσαν εἰς τὸ πρόσωπον αὐτοῦ καὶ ἐκολάφισαν αὐτόν, οἱ δὲ ἐράπισαν 26.68 λέγοντες, προφήτευσον ἡμῖν, χριστέ, τίς ἐστιν ὁ παίσας σε; 26.69 ὁ δὲ Πέτρος ἐκάθητο ἔξω ἐν τῇ αὐλῇ· καὶ προσῆλθεν αὐτῷ μία παιδίσκη λέγουσα, καὶ σὺ ἦσθα μετὰ Ἰησοῦ τοῦ Γαλιλαίου. 26.70 ὁ δὲ ἠρνήσατο ἔμπροσθεν πάντων λέγων, οὐκ οἶδα τί λέγεις. 26.71 ἐξελθόντα δὲ εἰς τὸν πυλῶνα εἶδεν αὐτὸν ἄλλη καὶ λέγει τοῖς ἐκεῖ, οὗτος ἦν μετὰ Ἰησοῦ τοῦ Ναζωραίου. 26.72 καὶ πάλιν ἠρνήσατο μετὰ ὅρκου οὐκ οἶδα τὸν ἄνθρωπον. 26.73 μετὰ μικρὸν δὲ προσελθόντες οἱ ἑστῶτες εἶπον τῷ Πέτρῳ, ἀληθῶς καὶ σὺ ἐξ αὐτῶν εἶ, καὶ γὰρ ἡ λαλιά σου δῆλόν σε ποιεῖ. 26.74 τότε ἤρξατο καταθεματίζειν καὶ ὀμνύειν ὅτι οὐκ οἶδα τὸν ἄνθρωπον. καὶ εὐθέως ἀλέκτωρ ἐφώνησεν. 26.75 καὶ ἐμνήσθη ὁ Πέτρος τοῦ ῥήματος Ἰησοῦ εἰρηκότος ὅτι πρὶν ἀλέκτορα φωνῆσαι τρὶς ἀπαρνήσῃ με·

καὶ ἐξελθὼν ἔξω ἔκλαυσεν πικρῶς. 27.1 πρωίας δὲ γενομένης συμβούλιον ἔλαβον πάντες οἱ ἀρχιερῖς καὶ οἱ πρεσβύτεροι τοῦ λαοῦ κατὰ τοῦ Ἰησοῦ ὥστε θανατῶσαι αὐτόν· 27.2 καὶ δήσαντες αὐτὸν ἀπήγαγον καὶ παρέδωκαν Πιλάτῳ τῷ ἡγεμόνι.

27.3 τότε ἰδὼν Ἰούδας ὁ παραδιδοὺς αὐτὸν ὅτι κατεκρίθη μεταμεληθεὶς ἀπ᾽ ἔστρεψεν τὰ τριάκοντα ἀργύρια τοῖς ἀρχιερεῦσι καὶ πρεσβυτέροις 27.4 λέγων, ἥμαρτον παραδοὺς αἷμα ἀθῶον.

οἱ δὲ εἶπαν, τί πρὸς ἡμᾶς; σὺ ὄψῃ. 27.5 καὶ ῥίψας τὰ τριάκοντα ἀργύρια εἰς τὸν ναὸν ἀνεχώρησεν, καὶ ἀπελθὼν ἀπήγξατο.

27.6 οἱ δὲ ἀρχιερεῖς λαβόντες τὰ ἀργύρια εἶπον, οὐκ ἔξεστιν βαλῖν αὐτὰ εἰς τὸν κορβανᾶν, ἐπὶ τιμὴ αἵματός ἐστιν.

26.65   Then the high priest was tearing his garments asunder, and he said: He slandered/blasphemed; what need have we still of witnesses? Behold, ye now heard the blasphemy.   26.66 What seems *it* to ye? And the (they), answering, they said: He is guilty/deserving of death.   26.67 Then they spit into the face of him and beat him with *their* fists, and they slapped *him,*   26.68   saying: You prophesy for us, anointed (one), who is the (one) having hit you?   26.69 And Peter was sitting outside in the court/yard; and one maidservant came near to him saying: You, you also were being with Jesus, the (one) from Galilee.   26.70 But the (he) denied *it* before *them* all, saying: I know not what you say.   26.71 And having gone out to the gateway/vestibule, another maid saw him and she says to those there: This (one) was with Jesus from Nazareth.   26.72 And again he denied *it* with an oath: I know not the man. 26.73   And after a little *time* those having been standing, coming near, they said to Peter: Truly you, you also are out of them, for even your speech makes you clear/plain.   26.74 Then he began to curse and to swear: I know not the man. And immediately a rooster crowed.   26.75 And Peter remembered from the word of Jesus having been declared: Prior to a rooster to crow, you will deny me thrice;

and going outside, he wept/wailed bitterly.   27.1 And from *it* having become early morning, all the high priests and the elders of the people took a consensus/counsel against Jesus so as to put him to death; 27.2 and, having tied him, they led *him* away and they handed *him* over to Pilate, the governor.

27.3   Then Judas, the (one) having given him up/betrayed him, seeing that he was condemned, repenting from *it* he returned the thirty silver (coins/shekels) to the high priests and elders,   27.4 saying: I sinned, handing over/betraying innocent blood.

But those, they said: What *is it* to us? You, you will see.   27.5 And having thrown the thirty silver shekels into the *inner* temple, he departed, and having gone away, he hanged himself.

27.6   And the chief priests, taking the silver (shekels), they said: It is not lawful to put them

27.7 συμβούλιον δὲ λαβόντες ἠγόρασαν ἐξ αὐτῶν τὸν ἀγρὸν τοῦ κεραμέως εἰς ταφὴν τοῖς ξένοις. 27.8 διὸ ἐκλήθη ὁ ἀγρὸς ἐκῖνος ἀγρὸς αἵματος ἕως τῆς σήμερον.

27.9 κατ᾽ ἐπληρώθη τὸ ῥηθὲν διὰ Ἰερεμίου τοῦ προφήτου λέγοντος, «καὶ ἔλαβον τὰ τριάκοντα ἀργύρια, τὴν τιμὴν τοῦ τετιμημένου ὃν ἐτιμήσαντο ἀπὸ υἱῶν Ἰσραήλ, 27.10 καὶ ἔδωκα αὐτὰ εἰς τὸν ἀγρὸν τοῦ κεραμέως, καθὰ συνέταξέν μοι κύριος.» 27.11 ὁ δὲ Ἰησοῦς ἐστάθη ἔμπροσθεν τοῦ ἡγεμόνος· καὶ ἐπηρώτησεν αὐτὸν ὁ ἡγεμὼν λέγων, σὺ εἶ ὁ βασιλεὺς τῶν Ἰουδαίων;

ὁ δὲ Ἰησοῦς ἔφη, σὺ λέγις. 27.12 καὶ ἐν τῷ κατηγορῖσθε αὐτὸν ὑπὸ τῶν ἀρχιερέων καὶ πρεσβυτέρων οὐδὲν ἀπεκρίνατο.

27.13 τότε λέγι αὐτῷ ὁ Πιλᾶτος, οὐκ ἀκούεις πόσα σου καταμαρτυροῦσιν; 27.14 καὶ οὐκ ἀπεκρίθη αὐτῷ πρὸς οὐδὲ ἓν ῥῆμα, ὥστε θαυμάζιν τὸν ἡγεμόνα λίαν. 27.15 κατὰ δὲ ἑορτὴν εἰώθει ὁ ἡγεμὼν ἀπολύειν ἕνα τῷ ὄχλῳ δέσμιον ὃν ἤθελον. 27.16 εἶχον δὲ τότε δέσμιον ἐπίσημον λεγόμενον Βαραββᾶν. 27.17 συνηγμένων οὖν αὐτῶν εἶπεν αὐτοῖς ὁ Πιλᾶτος, τίνα θέλετε ἀπολύσω ὑμῖν, Βαραββᾶν ἢ Ἰησοῦν τὸν λεγόμενον χριστόν; 27.18 ἤδι γὰρ ὅτι διὰ φθόνον παρέδωκαν αὐτόν. 27.19 καθημένου δὲ αὐτοῦ ἐπὶ τοῦ βήματος ἀπέστιλεν πρὸς αὐτὸν ἡ γυνὴ αὐτοῦ λέγουσα, μηδὲν σοὶ καὶ τῷ δικαίῳ ἐκίνῳ, πολλὰ γὰρ ἔπαθον σήμερον κατ᾽ ὄναρ δι᾽ αὐτόν.

27.20 οἱ δὲ ἀρχιερῖς καὶ οἱ πρεσβύτεροι ἔπισαν τοὺς ὄχλους ἵνα αἰτήσωνται τὸν Βαραββᾶν τὸν δὲ Ἰησοῦν ἀπολέσωσιν.

27.21 ἀποκριθεὶς δὲ ὁ ἡγεμὼν εἶπεν αὐτοῖς, τίνα θέλετε ἀπὸ τῶν δύο ἀπολύσω ὑμῖν; οἱ δὲ εἶπαν, τὸν Βαραββᾶν.

27.22 λέγι αὐτοῖς ὁ Πιλᾶτος, τί οὖν ποιήσω Ἰησοῦν τὸν λεγόμενον χριστόν; λέγουσιν πάντες, σταυρωθήτω. 27.23 ὁ δὲ

into the treasury, since it is a price of blood.   27.7
And taking a counsel/consensus, they bought out of
them the field of the potter for a grave for the
strangers.   27.8 Wherefore that field was called a
field of blood until the today.

   27.9   Accordingly, it was fulfilled, the (thing)
having been spoken through Jeremiah the prophet,
saying: AND   THEY   TOOK   THE   THIRTY   SILVER   (SHEKELS/
COINS),   THE   PRICE   OF   THE   (ONE)   HAVING   BEEN   VALUED,
WHOM   THEY   VALUED   FROM/BY   *the*   SONS   OF   ISRAEL,   27.10
AND   THEY   GAVE   THEM   TO/FOR   THE   FIELD   OF   THE   POTTER,   AS
THE LORD COMMANDED TO ME.   27.11   And Jesus was stood
before the governor; and the governor questioned him,
saying: You, are you the king of the Judeans?

   And Jesus said: You, you say *it*.   27.12 And in
the (thing) *for* him to be accused by the high priests
and elders, he answered nothing.

   27.13   Then Pilate says to him: *Do* you not hear
what (things) they testify against you?   27.14 And he
answered not to him, to not even one word, so as *for*
the governor to wonder/marvel very much.   27.15 And
from festival to festival the governor was accustomed
to release to the crowd one prisoner whom they were
wanting.   27.16 And they were holding then a renowned
prisoner being named Barabbas.   27.17 Therefore,
having gathered them together, Pilate said to them:
Whom *do* ye want *that* I might release for ye: Barabbas
or Jesus, the (one) being called the anointed (one)?
27.18 For he knew that they betrayed/delivered him up
because of envy.   27.19 And of him sitting upon the
judgment seat, his woman sent to him, saying: Nothing
for/between you and that just (one), for I suffered
many (things) today through a dream because of him.

   27.20   And the high priests and the elders persuaded the crowds that they might request Barabbas,
but destroy Jesus.

   27.21   And answering, the governor said to them:
Whom *do* ye want from the two *that* I might release for
ye? And they said: Barabbas!

   27.22   Pilate says to them: Then what might I do
to Jesus, the (one) being called the anointed (one)?
They all say: Let him be crucified!   27.23 But the

ἔφη, τί γὰρ κακὸν ἐποίησεν;

οἱ δὲ περισσῶς ἔκραζον λέγοντες, σταυρωθήτω.

27.24 ἰδὼν δὲ ὁ Πιλᾶτος ὅτι οὐδὲν ὠφελεῖ ἀλλὰ μᾶλλον θόρυβος γείνεται, λαβὼν ὕδωρ ἀπενίψατο τὰς χῖρας ἀπέναντι τοῦ ὄχλου, λέγων, ἀθῶός εἰμι ἀπὸ τοῦ αἵματος τοῦ δικαίου τούτου· ὑμεῖς ὄψεσθε.

27.25 καὶ ἀποκριθεὶς πᾶς ὁ λαὸς εἶπεν, τὸ αἷμα αὐτοῦ ἐφ' ἡμᾶς καὶ ἐπὶ τὰ τέκνα ἡμῶν. 27.26 τότε ἀπέλυσεν αὐτοῖς τὸν Βαραββᾶν, τὸν δὲ Ἰησοῦν φραγελλώσας παρέδωκεν ἵνα σταυρωθῇ.

27.27 τότε οἱ στρατιῶται τοῦ ἡγεμόνος παραλαβόντες τὸν Ἰησοῦν εἰς τὸ πραιτώριον συνήγαγον ἐπ' αὐτὸν ὅλην τὴν σπῖραν. 27.28 καὶ ἐκδύσαντες αὐτὸν χλαμύδα κοκκίνην περιέθηκαν αὐτῷ, 27.29 καὶ πλέξαντες στέφανον ἐξ ἀκανθῶν ἐπέθηκαν ἐπὶ τῆς κεφαλῆς αὐτοῦ καὶ κάλαμον ἐν τῇ δεξιᾷ αὐτοῦ, καὶ γονυπετήσαντες ἔμπροσθεν αὐτοῦ ἐνέπεξαν αὐτῷ λέγοντες, χαῖρε, βασιλεῦς τῶν Ἰουδαίων, 27.30 καὶ ἐμπτύσαντες εἰς αὐτὸν ἔλαβον τὸν κάλαμον καὶ ἔτυπτον εἰς τὴν κεφαλὴν αὐτοῦ. 27.31 καὶ ὅτε ἐνέπεξαν αὐτῷ, ἐκδύσαντες αὐτὸν τὴν χλαμύδα ἐνέδυσαν αὐτὸν τὰ ἱμάτια αὐτοῦ, καὶ ἀπήγαγον αὐτὸν εἰς τὸ σταυρῶσαι.

27.32 ἐξερχόμενοι δὲ εὗρον ἄνθρωπον Κυρηνεῖον ὀνόματι Σίμωνα· τοῦτον ἠγγάρευσαν ἵνα ἄρῃ τὸν σταυρὸν αὐτοῦ.

27.33 καὶ ἐλθόντες εἰς τόπον λεγόμενον Γολγοθᾶ, ὅ ἐστιν κρανίου τόπος λεγόμενος, 27.34 ἔδωκαν αὐτῷ πιεῖν οἶνον μετὰ χολῆς μεμιγμένον· καὶ γευσάμενος οὐκ ἠθέλησεν πιεῖν. 27.35 σταυρώσαντες δὲ αὐτὸν διεμερίσαντο τὰ ἱμάτια αὐτοῦ βάλλοντες κλῆρον, 27.36 καὶ καθήμενοι ἐτήρουν αὐτὸν ἐκεῖ.

27.37 καὶ ἐπέθηκαν ἐπάνω τῆς κεφαλῆς αὐτοῦ τὴν αἰτίαν αὐτοῦ γεγραμμένην· οὗτός ἐστιν Ἰησοῦς ὁ βασιλεῦς τῶν Ἰουδαίων. 27.38 τότε σταυροῦνται σὺν αὐτῷ δύο λῃσταί, εἷς ἐκ δεξιῶν καὶ εἷς ἐξ εὐωνύμων. 27.39 οἱ δὲ παραπορευόμενοι ἐβλασφήμουν αὐτὸν κινοῦντες τὰς κεφαλὰς αὐτῶν 27.40 καὶ

(he) said: For what bad (thing) did he *do*?

But the (they) cried out more, saying: Let him be crucified!

27.24   And Pilate, seeing that he profits/gains nothing, but rather it becomes an uproar, having taken water, he washed the hands before the crowd, saying: I am guiltless from the blood of this just (one); ye, ye will observe/behold.

27.25   And answering, all the people said: The blood of him *be* upon us and upon our children.   27.26 Then he released Barabbas to them: but Jesus, having been scourged/whipped, he delivered/handed over in order that he might be crucified.

27.27   Then the soldiers of the governor, having taken along Jesus into the praetorium, gathered upon/ against him the entire detachment/cohort.   27.28 And having stripped him, they put a purple cloak around him,   27.29 and having plaited a crown/wreath out of thorns, they put *it* upon his head and a staff/reed in his right *hand*, and kneeling down before him, they mocked him, saying: Greetings, king of the Judeans, 27.30   and having spit in/on him, they took the staff and they beat *him* in/on his head.   27.31 And when/af- ter they ridiculed him, taking the cloak off *of* him, they clothed him *in* his garments, and they led him away to/for the (thing) to crucify *him*.

27.32   And going forth, they found a Cyrenian man by name of Simon; this (one) they pressed into service that he might take up the cross of him.

27.33   And having come to a place being called Golgotha, which is being called a place of a skull, 27.34 they gave to him wine to drink, *it* having been mixed with gall; and having tasted *it*, he wanted not to drink *it*.   27.35 And having crucified him, they divided his garments, casting a lot,   27.36 and sitting, they were guarding him there.

27.37   And they put above his head his charge/ac- cusation, having been written: This is Jesus the King of the Judeans.   27.38 Then two robbers are crucified with him, one on the right and one on the left.   27.39 And those passing by were blaspheming/reviling him, shaking their heads   27.40 and saying: The (one)

λέγοντες, ὁ καταλύων τὸν ναὸν καὶ ἐν τρισὶν ἡμέραις οἰκοδομῶν, σῶσον σεαυτόν, εἰ υἱὸς εἶ τοῦ θεοῦ, καὶ κατάβηθι ἀπὸ τοῦ σταυροῦ. 27.41 ὁμοίως οἱ ἀρχιερῖς ἐμπαίζοντες μετὰ τῶν πρεσβυτέρων καὶ γραμματαίων ἔλεγον, 27.42 ἄλλους ἔσωσεν, ἑαυτὸν οὐ δύναται σῶσαι· βασιλεὺς Ἰσραήλ ἐστιν, καταβάτω νῦν ἀπὸ τοῦ σταυροῦ καὶ πιστεύσομεν ἐπ' αὐτόν. 27.43 πέποιθεν ἐπὶ τὸν θεόν, ῥυσάσθω νῦν εἰ θέλι αὐτόν· εἶπεν γὰρ ὅτι θεοῦ εἰμι υἱός. 27.44 τὸ δ' αὐτὸ καὶ οἱ λησταὶ οἱ συσταυρωθέντες σὺν αὐτῷ ὠνείδιζον αὐτόν.

27.45 ἀπὸ δὲ ἕκτης ὥρας σκότος ἐγένετο — ἕως ὥρας ἐνάτης. 27.46 περὶ δὲ τὴν ἐνάτην ὥραν ἀνεβόησεν ὁ Ἰησοῦς φωνῇ μεγάλῃ λέγων, «ἐλωΐ ἐλωΐ λέμα σαβάχθανι;» τοῦτ' ἔστιν, «θεέ μου θεέ μου, ἱνατί με ἐγκατέλιπες;»

27.47 τινὲς δὲ τῶν ἐκεῖ ἑστηκότων ἀκούσαντες ἔλεγον Ἡλίαν φωνῖ οὗτος. 27.48 καὶ εὐθέως δραμὼν εἷς καὶ λαβὼν σπόγγον πλήσας τε ὄξους καὶ περιθεὶς καλάμῳ ἐπότιζεν αὐτόν.

27.49 οἱ δὲ λοιποὶ ἔλεγον, ἄφες ἴδωμεν εἰ ἔρχεται Ἡλίας σώσων αὐτόν, ἄλλος δὲ λαβὼν λόγχην ἔνυξεν αὐτοῦ τὴν πλεύραν, καὶ ἔξηλθεν ὕδωρ καὶ αἷμα.

27.50 ὁ δὲ Ἰησοῦς πάλιν κράξας φωνῇ μεγάλῃ ἀφῆκεν τὸ πνεῦμα. 27.51 καὶ ἰδοὺ τὸ καταπέτασμα τοῦ ναοῦ ἐσχίσθη εἰς δύο ἄνωθεν ἕως κάτω, καὶ ἡ γῆ ἐσίσθη, καὶ αἱ πέτραι ἐσχίσθησαν, 27.52 καὶ τὰ μνημῖα ἀνεῴχθησαν καὶ πολλὰ σώματα τῶν κεκοιμημένων ἁγίων ἠγέρθησαν, 27.53 καὶ ἐξελθόντες ἐκ τῶν μνημίων μετὰ τὴν ἔγερσιν αὐτοῦ εἰς τὴν ἁγίαν πόλιν ἐνεφανίσθησαν πολλοῖς.

27.54 ὁ δὲ ἑκατοντάρχης καὶ οἱ μετ' αὐτοῦ τηροῦντες τὸν Ἰησοῦν ἰδόντες τὸν σισμὸν καὶ τὰ γενόμενα ἐφοβήθησαν σφόδρα, λέγοντες, ἀληθῶς υἱὸς ἦν τοῦ θεοῦ οὗτος. 27.55 ἦσαν δὲ κἀκεῖ γυναῖκες πολλαὶ ἀπὸ μακρόθεν θεωροῦσαι, αἵτινες ἠκολούθησαν τῷ Ἰησοῦ ἀπὸ τῆς Γαλιλαίας διακονοῦσαι αὐτῷ· 27.56 ἐν αἷς ἦν Μαρία ἡ Μαγδαληνὴ καὶ Μαρία ἡ τοῦ Ἰακώβου καὶ Ἰωσὴφ καὶ ἡ μήτηρ τῶν υἱῶν Ζεβεδαίου.

destroying the *inner* temple and building *it* in three days, save yourself, if you are a son of God, and come down from the cross. 27.41 Likewise, the high priests, ridiculing *him* with the elders and scribes, they were saying: 27.42 He saved others, he is not able to save himself; he is a king of Israel, let him come down now from the cross, and we shall believe on him. 27.43 He trusted upon God, now let him rescue him, if he wants him; for he said: I am a son of God. 27.44 And the same (thing), the robbers also being crucified together with him were reviling him.

27.45 And from *the* sixth hour, it became dark -- until *the* ninth hour. 27.46 And about the ninth hour Jesus cried aloud in a great voice, saying: ELI, ELI, LEMA SABACHTHANI? This is: MY GOD, MY GOD, WHY DID YOU FORSAKE ME?

27.47 And some of those standing there, hearing, said: This (one) calls Elias. 27.48 And one, having run straightway -- and taking a sponge and filling *it* from sour wine, and putting it around a reed/cane, he gave him a drink.

27.49 But the rest said: Leave, let us see if Elias comes, saving him; but another, taking a spear, pierced the side of him, and water and blood came out.

27.50 And Jesus, again crying out with a great voice, sent away the spirit. 27.51 And behold, the curtain of the *inner* temple was split in two, from above until below, and the earth was shaken, and the rocks were split, 27.52 and the tombs were opened, and many bodies of the saints, having been sleeping, were raised; 27.53 and going forth from the tombs into the holy city, after the raising of him, they were made visible to many.

27.54 And the centurion and those with him guarding Jesus, seeing the earthquake and the (things) having happened, they were exceedingly afraid, saying: Truly this (one) was a son of God 27.55 And many women were also there, observing/beholding from afar, who followed with Jesus from Galilee serving/waiting on/ministering for him; 27.56 among whom was Mary the Magdalene, and Mary the (one) of James and Joseph, and the mother of the sons of Zebedee.

27.57 ὀψίας δὲ γενομένης ἦλθεν ἄνθρωπος πλούσιος ἀπὸ Ἀριμαθαίας, τοὔνομα Ἰωσήφ, ὃς καὶ αὐτὸς ἐμαθητεύθη τῷ Ἰησοῦ· 27.58 οὗτος προσελθὼν τῷ Πιλάτῳ ᾐτήσατο τὸ σῶμα τοῦ Ἰησοῦ. τότε ὁ Πιλᾶτος ἐκέλευσεν ἀποδοθῆναι.

27.59 καὶ λαβὼν τὸ σῶμα ὁ Ἰωσὴφ ἐνετύλιξεν αὐτὸ σινδόνι καθαρᾷ, 27.60 καὶ ἔθηκεν αὐτὸ ἐν τῷ καινῷ αὐτοῦ μνημίῳ ὃ ἐλατόμησεν ἐν τῇ πέτρᾳ, καὶ προσκυλίσας λίθον μέγαν τῇ θύρᾳ τοῦ μνημίου ἀπῆλθεν.

27.61 ἦν δὲ ἐκεῖ Μαριὰμ ἡ Μαγδαληνὴ καὶ ἡ ἄλλη Μαρία καθήμεναι ἀπέναντι τοῦ τάφου. 27.62 τῇ δὲ ἐπαύριον, ἥτις ἐστὶν μετὰ τὴν παρασκευήν, συνήχθησαν οἱ ἀρχιερεῖς καὶ οἱ Φαρισαῖοι πρὸς Πιλᾶτον 27.63 λέγοντες, κύριε, ἐμνήσθημεν ὅτι ἐκῖνος ὁ πλάνος εἶπεν ἔτι ζῶν, μετὰ τρῖς ἡμέρας ἐγίρομαι. 27.64 κέλευσον οὖν ἀσφαλισθῆναι τὸν τάφον ἕως τῆς τρίτης ἡμέρας, μήποτε ἐλθόντες οἱ μαθηταὶ κλέψωσιν αὐτὸν καὶ εἴπωσιν τῷ λαῷ, ἠγέρθη ἀπὸ τῶν νεκρῶν, καὶ ἔσται ἡ ἐσχάτη πλάνη χείρων τῆς πρώτης.

27.65 ἔφη δὲ αὐτοῖς ὁ Πιλᾶτος, ἔχετε κουστωδίαν· ὑπάγετε ἀσφαλίσασθαι ὡς οἴδατε. 27.66 οἱ δὲ πορευθέντες ἠσφαλίσαντο τὸν τάφον σφραγίσαντες τὸν λίθον μετὰ τῆς κουστωδίας.

28.1 Ὀψὲ δὲ σαββάτων, τῇ ἐπιφωσκούσῃ εἰς μίαν σαββάτων, ἦλθεν Μαριὰμ ἡ Μαγδαληνὴ καὶ ἡ ἄλλη Μαρία θεωρῆσαι τὸν τάφον. 28.2 καὶ ἰδοὺ σισμὸς ἐγένετο μέγας· ἄγγελος γὰρ κυρίου καταβὰς ἐξ οὐρανοῦ καὶ προσελθὼν ἀπεκύλισε τὸν λίθον καὶ ἐκάθητο ἐπάνω αὐτοῦ. 28.3 ἦν δὲ ἡ εἰδέα αὐτοῦ ὡς ἀστραπὴ καὶ τὸ ἔνδυμα αὐτοῦ λευκὸν ὡς χιών. 28.4 ἀπὸ δὲ τοῦ φόβου αὐτοῦ ἐσίσθησαν οἱ τηροῦντες καὶ ἐγενήθησαν ὡς νεκροί.

28.5 ἀποκριθεὶς δὲ ὁ ἄγγελος εἶπεν ταῖς γυναιξίν, μὴ φοβῖσθαι ὑμῖς, οἶδα γὰρ ὅτι Ἰησοῦν τὸν ἐσταυρωμένον ζητεῖτε· 28.6 οὐκ ἔστιν ὧδε, ἠγέρθη γὰρ καθὼς εἶπεν· δεῦτε ἴδετε τὸν

27.57 And from evening having come, a rich man came from Arimathea, of the name Joseph, who also himself was made a learner/pupil for Jesus; 27.58 this (one), coming near to Pilate, he requested the body of Jesus. Then Pilate ordered it to be given/ handed over.

27.59 And taking the body, Joseph wrapped it in a clean linen *sheet*, 27.60 and he put it in his new tomb which he hewed in the rock, and having rolled forward a large stone to the door of the tomb, he went away.

27.61 And Mary the Magdalene and the other Mary were there, sitting opposite/before the grave. 27.62 And on the morrow, which is after the preparation *day*/Friday, the high priests and the Pharisees were gathered together near/to Pilate, 27.63 saying: Lord, we remembered that that impostor/deceiver said while living: After three days, I am raised up. 27.64 You order, therefore, to make secure the grave/tomb until the third day, lest coming, the learners/pupils might steal him and say to the people: He was raised from the dead (ones), and the last deceit will be worse than the first.

27.65 And Pilate was saying to them: Ye have a guard/watch; go ye *and* make ye secure as ye know. 27.66 And the (those), going with the guard, they secured the grave/tomb, having sealed the stone.

28.1 But late of sabbaths, in/at the dawning to one of sabbaths, Mary the Magdalene and the other Mary came/went to behold/view the tomb/grave. 28.2 And behold, a great earthquake happened/came about; for a messenger (angel) from the Lord, descending out of heaven and coming near, he rolled away the stone and sat above/upon it. 28.3 And his appearance/face was like lightning/a ray *of light* and his garment *was* white as snow. 28.4 And from the fear of him, those keeping/guarding were shaken and caused to become as dead (ones).

28.5 And answering, the messenger/angel said to the women: Ye, fear ye not, for I know that ye seek Jesus, the (one) having been crucified. 28.6 He is

τόπον ὅπου ἔκειτο. 28.7 καὶ ταχὺ πορευθῖσαι εἴπατε τοῖς μαθηταῖς αὐτοῦ ὅτι ἠγέρθη ἀπὸ τῶν νεκρῶν, καὶ ἰδοὺ προάγει ὑμᾶς εἰς τὴν Γαλιλαίαν, ἐκεῖ αὐτὸν ὄψεσθαι· ἰδοὺ εἶπον ὑμῖν.

28.8 καὶ ἀπελθοῦσαι ταχὺ ἀπὸ τοῦ μνημίου μετὰ φόβου καὶ χαρᾶς μεγάλης ἔδραμον ἀπαγγῖλαι τοῖς μαθηταῖς αὐτοῦ.

28.9 καὶ ἰδοὺ Ἰησοῦς ὑπήντησεν αὐταῖς λέγων, χαίρετε. αἱ δὲ προσελθοῦσαι ἐκράτησαν αὐτοῦ τοὺς πόδας καὶ προσεκύνησαν αὐτῷ.

28.10 τότε λέγει αὐταῖς ὁ Ἰησοῦς, μὴ φοβεῖσθε· ὑπάγεται ἀπαγγίλατε τοῖς ἀδελφοῖς μου ἵνα ἀπέλθωσιν εἰς τὴν Γαλιλαίαν, καὶ ἐκεῖ με ὄψονται. 28.11 πορευομένων δὲ αὐτῶν ἰδού τινες τῆς κουστωδίας ἐλθόντες εἰς τὴν πόλιν ἀπήγγιλαν τοῖς ἀρχιερεῦσιν ἅπαντα τὰ γενόμενα. 28.12 καὶ συναχθέντες μετὰ τῶν πρεσβυτέρων συμβούλιόν τε ἐποίησαν καὶ λαβόντες ἀργύρια ἱκανὰ ἔδωκαν τοῖς στρατιώταις 28.13 λέγοντες, ὅτι εἴπατε οἱ μαθηταὶ αὐτοῦ νυκτὸς ἐλθόντες ἔκλεψαν αὐτὸν ἡμῶν κοιμωμένων. 28.14 καὶ ἐὰν ἀκουσθῇ τοῦτο ἐπὶ τοῦ ἡγεμόνος, ἡμεῖς πείσομεν καὶ ὑμᾶς ἀμερίμνους ποιήσομεν. 28.15 οἱ δὲ λαβόντες τὰ ἀργύρια ἐποίησαν ὡς ἐδιδάχθησαν. καὶ ἐφημίσθη ὁ λόγος οὗτος παρὰ Ἰουδαίοις μέχρι τῆς σήμερον.

28.16 οἱ δὲ ἕνδεκα μαθηταὶ ἐπορεύθησαν εἰς τὴν Γαλιλαίαν εἰς τὸ ὄρος οὗ ἐτάξατο αὐτοῖς ὁ Ἰησοῦς, 28.17 καὶ ἰδόντες αὐτὸν προσεκύνησαν, οἱ δὲ ἐδίστασαν. 28.18 καὶ προσελθὼν ὁ Ἰησοῦς ἐλάλησεν αὐτοῖς λέγων, ἐδόθη μοι πᾶσα ἐξουσία ἐν οὐρανῷ καὶ ἐπὶ γῆς. 28.19 πορευθέντες μαθητεύσατε πάντα τὰ ἔθνη, βαπτίζοντες αὐτοὺς εἰς τὸ ὄνομα τοῦ πατρὸς καὶ τοῦ υἱοῦ καὶ τοῦ ἁγίου πνεύματος, 28.20 διδάσκοντες αὐτοὺς τηρῖν πάντα ὅσα ἐνετιλάμην ὑμῖν·

καὶ ἰδοὺ ἐγὼ μεθ' ὑμῶν εἰμι πάσας τὰς ἡμέρας ἕως τῆς συντελείας τοῦ αἰῶνος.

not here, for he was raised even as he said; come, see ye the place where he was lying. 28.7 And *be* ye going quickly, ye say to his learners/pupils that he was raised from the dead (ones), and behold, he goes before ye into Galilee; there ye will observe/see him; behold, I said *it* to ye.

28.8 And, having gone away quickly from the tomb with fear and a great joy, they ran to announce *the* message to his learners/pupils.

28.9 And behold, Jesus met them, saying: Greetings *to* ye! And they, having come near, they grasped his feet and worshiped/genuflexed to him.

28.10 Then Jesus says to them: Fear ye not; go ye, announce *the* message to my brothers, that I might go away into Galilee, and they will see/observe me there. 28.11 And from them going, behold some from the security guard, having gone into the city, they reported to the high priests all the (things) having happened. 28.12 And, being gathered together with the elders, they both made a counsel/plan and taking adequate silver/money, they gave *it* to the soldiers, 28.13 saying: Say/tell ye that his learners/pupils, having come of/at night, they stole him from us, being asleep. 28.14 And if this might be heard/reported to the governor, we, we shall persuade *him* and we shall make ye free from care. 28.15 And they, taking/receiving the moneys/silver (coins), they did as they were taught. And this saying was spread about from Judeans until the today.

28.16 And the eleven learners/pupils went into Galilee, to the mountain which Jesus appointed for them, 28.17 and seeing him, they worshiped *him*, but they doubted. 28.18 And coming near, Jesus spoke to them, saying: Every/all authority was given to me, in heaven and on earth. 28.19 Ye be going, make ye learners of/disciple ye all the ethnics, baptizing them in the name of the father and of the son and of the holy spirit, 28.20 teaching them to keep/observe all (things) whatever I commanded to ye;

and behold I, I am with ye all the days until the completion/ending of the age.

This is the Sinaitic New Testament, book of Mark.

1.1 Ἀρχὴ τοῦ εὐαγγελίου Ἰησοῦ χριστοῦ υἱοῦ θεοῦ. 1.2 καθὼς γέγραπται ἐν τῷ Ἠσαΐᾳ τῷ προφήτη, «ἰδοὺ ἐγὼ ἀποστέλω τὸν ἄγγελόν μου πρὸ προσώπου σου, ὃς κατασκευάσει τὴν ὁδόν σου· 1.3 φωνὴ βοῶντος ἐν τῇ ἐρήμῳ, ἑτοιμάσατε τὴν ὁδὸν κυρίου, εὐθίας ποιεῖτε τὰς τρίβους» αὐτοῦ 1.4 καὶ ἐγένετο Ἰωάννης ὁ βαπτίζων ἐν τῇ ἐρήμῳ καὶ κηρύσσων βάπτισμα μετανοίας εἰς ἄφεσιν ἁμαρτιῶν.

1.5 καὶ ἐξεπορεύετο πρὸς αὐτὸν πᾶσα ἡ Ἰουδαία χώρα καὶ οἱ Ἱεροσολυμεῖται πάντες, καὶ ἐβαπτίζοντο ὑπ' αὐτοῦ ἐν τῷ Ἰορδάνη ποταμῷ ἐξομολογούμενοι τὰς ἁμαρτίας αὐτῶν. 1.6 καὶ ἦν ὁ Ἰωάννης ἐνδεδυμένος τρίχας καμήλου καὶ ζώνην δερματίνην περὶ τὴν ὀσφὺν αὐτοῦ, καὶ ἐσθῶν ἀκρίδας καὶ μέλι ἄγριον.

1.7 καὶ ἐκήρυσσεν λέγων, ἔρχεται ὁ ἰσχυρότερός μου ὀπίσω μου, οὗ οὐκ εἰμὶ ἱκανὸς κύψας λῦσαι τὸν ἱμάντα τῶν ὑποδημάτων αὐτοῦ· 1.8 ἐγὼ ἐβάπτισα ὑμᾶς ὕδατι, αὐτὸς δὲ βαπτίσει ὑμᾶς ἐν πνεύματι ἁγίῳ.

1.9 καὶ ἐγένετο ἐν ἐκείναις ταῖς ἡμέραις ἦλθεν Ἰησοῦς ἀπὸ Ναζαρὲτ τῆς Γαλιλαίας καὶ ἐβαπτίσθη εἰς τὸν Ἰορδάνην ὑπὸ Ἰωάννου. 1.10 καὶ εὐθὺς ἀναβαίνων ἐκ τοῦ ὕδατος εἶδεν σχιζομένους τοὺς οὐρανοὺς καὶ τὸ πνεῦμα ὡς περιστερὰν καταβαῖνον καὶ μένον ἐπ' αὐτόν·

1.11 καὶ φωνὴ ἐγένετο ἐκ τῶν οὐρανῶν, σὺ εἶ ὁ υἱός μου ὁ ἀγαπητός, ἐν σοὶ εὐδόκησα. 1.12 καὶ εὐθὺς τὸ πνεῦμα αὐτὸν ἐκβάλλει εἰς τὴν ἔρημον. 1.13 καὶ ἦν ἐν τῇ ἐρήμῳ τεσσεράκοντα ἡμέρας πιραζόμενος ὑπὸ τοῦ Σατανᾶ, καὶ ἦν μετὰ τῶν θηρίων, καὶ οἱ ἄγγελοι διηκόνουν αὐτῷ.

1.14 μετὰ δὲ τὸ παραδοθῆναι τὸν Ἰωάννην ἦλθεν ὁ Ἰησοῦς εἰς τὴν Γαλιλαίαν κηρύσσων τὸ εὐαγγέλιον τοῦ θεοῦ 1.15 ὅτι πεπλήρωται ὁ καιρὸς καὶ ἤγγεικεν ἡ βασιλεία τοῦ θεοῦ· μετανοεῖτε καὶ πιστεύεται ἐν τῷ εὐαγγελίῳ.

1.16 καὶ παράγων παρὰ τὴν θάλασσαν τῆς Γαλιλαίας

1.1   The beginning of the good message/gospel of Jesus the anointed (one), a son of God.   1.2 As it has been written in Isaiah the prophet: BEHOLD, I SEND MY MESSENGER BEFORE YOUR FACE. WHO WILL PREPARE YOUR ROAD/WAY;

1.3   A VOICE OF (ONE) CRYING IN THE DESOLATE (PLACE): PREPARE YE THE ROAD/WAY OF *the* LORD, MAKE YE STRAIGHT HIS PATHS.-- 1.4 And John came into being/became, the (one) baptizing in the desolate place/desert, heralding a baptism of repentance to/for remission/forgiveness of faults/sins.

1.5   And all the Judean country and all the Jerusalemites went out to him and they were baptized by him in the Jordan river, confessing their faults/sins.   1.6 And John was having been clothed in/with hairs of a camel and a leather girdle/belt around his loin, and eating locusts/grasshoppers and wild honey.

1.7   And he was heralding/preaching, saying: One stronger than me comes after/behind me, of whom I am not sufficient, having stooped over, to loose the strap of his sandals;

1.8   I, I baptized ye in/with water, but he, he will baptize ye in/with a holy spirit.

1.9   And it happened in those days *that* Jesus came from Nazareth of Galilee, and he was baptized in the Jordan by John.   1.10 And going up immediately out of the water, he saw the skies/heavens being divided/split and The Spirit coming/going down as a dove and remaining/abiding upon him;

1.11   and a voice became out of the skies/heavens: You, you are my beloved son, with/in you I was well pleased.   1.12 And immediately The Spirit put him out into the desert/desolate place.   1.13 And he was in the desert forty days being tempted/tested by Satan, and he was with the beasts, and the messengers/angels served/waited on him.

1.14   And after the (thing) *for* John to be delivered up, Jesus went into Galilee, heralding the good message/gospel from God   1.15 that the time has been fulfilled and the kingdom of God has come near: Repent ye and believe ye in the good message/gospel.

1.16   And going along beside the Sea of Galilee,

εἶδεν Σίμωνα καὶ Ἀνδρέαν τὸν ἀδελφὸν Σίμωνος ἀμφιβάλλοντας ἐν τῇ θαλάσσῃ· ἦσαν γὰρ ἁλιεῖς. 1.17 καὶ εἶπεν αὐτοῖς ὁ Ἰησοῦς, δεῦτε ὀπίσω μου, καὶ ποιήσω ὑμᾶς γενέσθε ἁλιεῖς ἀνθρώπων. 1.18 καὶ εὐθὺς ἀφέντες τὰ δίκτυα ἠκολούθησαν αὐτῷ.

1.19 καὶ προβὰς ὀλίγον ἐκεῖδεν ἴδεν Ἰάκωβον τὸν τοῦ Ζεβεδέου καὶ Ἰωάννην τὸν ἀδελφὸν αὐτοῦ, καὶ αὐτοὺς ἐν τῷ πλοίῳ καταρτίζοντας τὰ δίκτυα, 1.20 καὶ εὐθὺς ἐκάλεσεν αὐτούς. καὶ ἀφέντες τὸν πατέρα αὐτῶν Ζεβεδέον ἐν τῷ πλοίῳ μετὰ τῶν μισθωτῶν ἀπῆλθον ὀπίσω αὐτοῦ.

1.21 καὶ εἰσπορεύονται εἰς Καφαρναούμ. καὶ εὐθὺς τοῖς σάββασιν ἐδίδασκεν εἰς τὴν συναγωγήν. 1.22 καὶ ἐξεπλήσσοντο ἐπὶ τῇ διδαχῇ αὐτοῦ, ἦν γὰρ διδάσκων αὐτοὺς ὡς ἐξουσίαν ἔχων καὶ οὐχ ὡς οἱ γραμματεῖς. 1.23 καὶ εὐθὺς ἦν ἐν τῇ συναγωγῇ αὐτῶν ἄνθρωπος ἐν πνεύματι ἀκαθάρτῳ, καὶ ἀνέκραξεν 1.24 λέγων, τί ἡμῖν καὶ σοί, Ἰησοῦ Ναζαρηνέ; ἦλθες ἀπολέσαι ἡμᾶς; οἴδαμέν σε τίς εἶ, ὁ ἅγιος τοῦ θεοῦ. 1.25 καὶ ἐπετίμησεν αὐτῷ ὁ Ἰησοῦς λέγων, φιμώθητι καὶ ἔξελθε ἐξ αὐτοῦ. 1.26 καὶ σπαράξαν αὐτὸν τὸ πνεῦμα τὸ ἀκάθαρτον καὶ φωνῆσαν φωνῇ μεγάλῃ ἐξῆλθεν ἐξ αὐτοῦ. 1.27 καὶ ἐθαμβήθησαν ἅπαντες, ὥστε συνζητῖν αὐτοὺς λέγοντας, τί ἐστιν τοῦτο; διδαχὴ καινὴ κατ᾽ ἐξουσίαν· καὶ τοῖς πνεύμασι τοῖς ἀκαθάρτοις ἐπιτάσσι, καὶ ὑπακούουσιν αὐτῷ.

1.28 καὶ ἐξῆλθεν ἡ ἀκοὴ αὐτοῦ εὐθὺς πανταχῆ εἰς ὅλην τὴν περίχωρον τῆς Γαλιλαίας. 1.29 καὶ εὐθὺς ἐκ τῆς συναγωγῆς ἐξελθόντες ἦλθον εἰς τὴν οἰκίαν Σίμωνος καὶ Ἀνδρέου μετὰ Ἰακώβου καὶ Ἰωάννου. 1.30 ἡ δὲ πενθερὰ Σίμωνος κατέκειτο πυρέσσουσα, καὶ εὐθὺς λέγουσιν αὐτῷ περὶ αὐτῆς. 1.31 καὶ προσελθὼν ἤγειρεν αὐτὴν κρατήσας τῆς χιρός· καὶ ἀφῆκεν αὐτὴν ὁ πυρετός, καὶ διηκόνει αὐτοῖς.

1.32 ὀψίας δὲ γενομένης, ὅτε ἔδυ ὁ ἥλιος, ἔφερον πρὸς

he saw Simon and Andrew the brother of Simon, casting *a net* in the sea; for they were fishermen.   1.17 And Jesus said to them: Ye come behind me, and I shall make ye to become fishers of men.   1.18 And immediately/at once, having left the nets, they followed with him.

1.19   And going on a little (way) from there, behold, he saw James, the (one) of Zebedee, and John the brother of him/his brother, and them in the boat fitting/mending the nets,   1.20 and immediately/at once he called them.   And having left their father Zebedee in the boat with the hired hands, they went away behind him.

1.21   And they enter into Capernaum. And at once in/on the sabbaths, he taught in/to the congregation. 1.22 And they were being astounded at/upon his doc- trine/teaching, for he was teaching them as (one) holding authority and not as the scribes.   1.23 And at once one was in their congregation, a man with an unclean spirit, and he cried out,   1.24 saying: What *is* for us and for you, Jesus, *you* Nazarene? Came you to destroy us? We know you, who you are, the holy (one) from God.   1.25 And Jesus rebuked him, saying: Be you muzzled/gagged   and come forth out of him. 1.26 Both having convulsed him and having shouted with a great sound/voice, the unclean spirit came forth out of him.   1.27   And all were astounded/amazed, so as *for* them to discuss *it* together, saying: What is this (thing)? A new doctrine/teaching down from/by autho- rity; he even orders/commands to the unclean spirits, and they obey him.

1.28   And at once the report of him went forth everywhere in all the surrounding region of Galilee. 1.29 And going forth out of the congregation, they went at once/straight to the house of Simon and An- drew, with James and John.   1.30 And Simon's mother- in-law was lying down, having a fever, and they speak at once to him concerning her.   1.31 And coming near, having grasped her hand, he raised her up; and the fever left her, and she was serving/waiting on them.

1.32   And from evening having become, when the sun set,   they were bringing near/to   him   all   those

αὐτὸν πάντας τοὺς κακῶς ἔχοντας καὶ τοὺς δαιμονιζομένους· 1.33 καὶ ἦν ὅλη ἡ πόλις ἐπισυνηγμένη πρὸς τὴν θύραν. 1.34 καὶ ἐθεράπευσεν πολλοὺς κακῶς ἔχοντας ποικίλαις νόσοις, καὶ δαιμόνια πολλὰ ἐξέβαλλεν, καὶ οὐκ ἤφιεν λαλῖν τὰ δαιμόνια, ὅτι ᾔδισαν αὐτόν.

1.35 καὶ πρωῒ ἔννυχα λείαν ἀναστὰς ἐξῆλθεν καὶ ἀπῆλθεν εἰς ἔρημον τόπον κἀκῖ προσηύχετο. 1.36 καὶ κατεδίωξεν αὐτὸν Σίμων καὶ οἱ μετ' αὐτοῦ, 1.37 καὶ εὗρον αὐτὸν καὶ λέγουσιν αὐτῷ ὅτι πάντες ζητοῦσίν σε.

1.38 καὶ λέγει αὐτοῖς, ἄγωμεν ἀλλαχοῦ εἰς τὰς ἐχομένας κωμοπόλις, ἵνα κἀκῖ κηρύξω· εἰς τοῦτο γὰρ ἐξῆλθον. 1.39 καὶ ἦλθεν κηρύσσων εἰς τὰς συναγωγὰς αὐτῶν εἰς ὅλην τὴν Γαλιλαίαν καὶ τὰ δαιμόνια ἐκβάλλων.

1.40 καὶ ἔρχεται πρὸς αὐτὸν λεπρὸς παρακαλῶν αὐτὸν καὶ γονυπετῶν καὶ λέγων αὐτῷ ὅτι ἐὰν θέλῃς δύνασαί με καθαρίσαι. 1.41 καὶ σπλαγχνισθεὶς ἐκτίνας τὴν χεῖρα αὐτοῦ ἥψατο καὶ λέγει, θέλω, καθαρίσθητι· 1.42 καὶ εὐθὺς ἀπῆλθεν ἀπ' αὐτοῦ ἡ λέπρα, καὶ ἐκαθαρίσθη. 1.43 καὶ ἐμβριμησάμενος αὐτῷ εὐθὺς ἐξέβαλεν αὐτόν, 1.44 καὶ λέγει αὐτῷ, Ὅρα μηδενὶ μηδὲν εἴπῃς, ἀλλὰ ὕπαγε σεαυτὸν δεῖξον τῷ ἱερεῖ καὶ προσσένεγκε περὶ τοῦ καθαρισμοῦ σου ἃ προσέταξεν Μωϋσῆς, εἰς μαρτύριον αὐτοῖς.

1.45 ὁ δὲ ἐξελθὼν ἤρξατο κηρύσσιν πολλὰ καὶ διαφημίζιν τὸν λόγον, ὥστε μηκέτι δύνασθαι αὐτὸν εἰς πόλιν φανερῶς εἰσελθῖν, ἀλλ' ἔξω ἐπ' ἐρήμοις τόποις ἦν· καὶ ἤρχοντο πρὸς αὐτὸν πάντοθεν.

2.1 Καὶ εἰσελθὼν πάλιν εἰς Καφαρναοὺμ δι' ἡμερῶν ἠκούσθη ὅτι ἐν οἴκῳ ἐστίν. 2.2 καὶ συνήχθησαν πολλοὶ ὥστε μηκέτι χωρῖν μηδὲ τὰ πρὸς τὴν θύραν, καὶ ἐλάλει αὐτοῖς τὸν λόγον.

2.3 καὶ ἔρχονται φέροντες πρὸς αὐτὸν παραλυτικὸν

having *it* badly/being sick and those being demon-possessed; 1.33 and the entire city, having been congregated, was near the door. 1.34 And he healed many having *it* badly/being ill with various diseases, and he threw/put out many demons, and he was not allowing the demons to speak, because they knew/had known him.

1.35 And having arose very early in the night, he went out and went away to a desert/desolate place, and there he was praying. 1.36 And Simon and those with him hunted him down, 1.37 and they found him and they say to him: All are seeking you.

1.38 And he says to them: Let us go elsewhere into the neighboring towns, that I might herald/preach there also; for I came forth for this. 1.39 And he went, heralding/preaching in their congregations in all Galilee, and/also putting out the demons.

1.40 And a leper comes near/to him, beseeching him and kneeling down and saying to him: If you might want, you are able to cleanse me. 1.41 And being compassionate, having stretched forth his hand, he touched *him* and says: I will/want, be cleansed; 1.42 and the leprosy went away from him at once, and he was cleansed. 1.43 And having admonished him, he put him out at once, 1.44 and he says to him: See *that* you say nothing to no one, but you go, show yourself to the priest and bring an offering concerning your cleansing, *the things* which Moses appointed/directed, into/for a testimony to them.

1.45 But the (he), going out/forth, he began to herald/preach many things and to spread the saying/word around, so as *for* him no longer to be able to enter a city openly, but he was being outside at/upon desolate/desert places, and they were coming to him from all directions/sides.

2.1 And having gone again into Capernaum, it was heard through/after *some* days that he was in a house/at home. 2.2 And many were gathered so as no longer to be room, not even the *places* near the door, and he spoke to them the saying/reason/word.

2.3 And they come, carrying to him a paralytic,

αἰρόμενον ὑπὸ τεσσάρων. 2.4 καὶ μὴ δυνάμενοι προσενέγκαι αὐτῷ διὰ τὸν ὄχλον ἀπεστέγασαν τὴν στέγην ὅπου ἦν, καὶ ἐξορύξαντες χαλῶσι τὸν κράβαττον ὅπου ὁ παραλυτικὸς κατέκειτο.

2.5 καὶ ἰδὼν ὁ Ἰησοῦς τὴν πίστιν αὐτῶν λέγει τῷ παραλυτικῷ, τέκνον μου, ἀφέωνταί σου αἱ ἁμαρτίαι. 2.6 ἦσαν δέ τινες τῶν γραμματέων ἐκεῖ καθήμενοι καὶ διαλογιζόμενοι ἐν ταῖς καρδίες αὐτῶν, 2.7 τί οὗτος οὕτως λαλεῖ; βλασφημεῖ· τίς δύναται ἀφιέναι ἁμαρτίας εἰ μὴ εἷς ὁ θεός; 2.8 καὶ εὐθὺς ὁ Ἰησοῦς ἐπιγνοὺς τῷ πνεύματι αὐτοῦ ὅτι οὕτως διαλογίζονται ἐν ἑαυτοῖς λέγει αὐτοῖς, τί ταῦτα διαλογίζεσθε ἐν ταῖς καρδίες ὑμῶν; 2.9 τί ἐστιν εὐκοπώτερον, εἰπεῖν τῷ παραλυτικῷ, ἀφίενταί σου αἱ ἁμαρτίαι, ἢ εἰπεῖν, ἔγειρε καὶ ἆρον τὸν κράβακτόν σου καὶ ὕπαγε; 2.10 ἵνα δὲ εἰδῆτε ὅτι ἐξουσίαν ἔχι ὁ υἱὸς τοῦ ἀνθρώπου ἐπὶ τῆς γῆς ἀφιέναι ἁμαρτίας

λέγει τῷ παραλυτικῷ, 2.11 ἔγειρε σοὶ λέγω, ἆρον τὸν κράβακτόν σου καὶ ὕπαγε εἰς τὸν οἶκόν σου.

2.12 καὶ ἠγέρθη καὶ εὐθὺς ἄρας τὸν κράβακτον ἐξῆλθεν ἔμπροσθεν πάντων, ὥστε ἐξίστασθαι πάντας καὶ δοξάζιν τὸν θεὸν λέγοντας ὅτι οὕτως οὐδέποτε εἴδομεν. ἐφάνη ἐν τῷ Ἰσραήλ. 2.13 καὶ ἐξῆλθεν πάλιν εἰς τὴν θάλασσαν· καὶ πᾶς ὁ ὄχλος ἤρχετο πρὸς αὐτόν, καὶ ἐδίδασκεν αὐτούς.

2.14 καὶ παράγων εἶδεν Λευεὶ τὸν τοῦ Ἀλφαίου καθήμενον ἐπὶ τὸ τελώνιον, καὶ λέγει αὐτῷ, ἀκολούθι μοι. καὶ ἀναστὰς ἠκολούθησεν αὐτῷ.

2.15 καὶ γίνεται κατακῖσθαι αὐτὸν ἐν τῇ οἰκίᾳ αὐτοῦ, καὶ πολλοὶ τελῶναι καὶ ἁμαρτωλοὶ συνανέκιντο τῷ Ἰησοῦ καὶ τοῖς μαθηταῖς αὐτοῦ· ἦσαν γὰρ πολλοὶ καὶ ἠκολούθουν αὐτῷ. 2.16 καὶ γραμματεῖς τῶν Φαρισαίων καὶ ἰδόντες ὅτι ἤσθίεν μετὰ τῶν τελωνῶν καὶ ἁμαρτωλῶν ἔλεγον τοῖς μαθηταῖς αὐτοῦ, διάτι μετὰ

being taken up by four (men). 2.4 And not being able to bring *him* near to him through/because of the crowd, they removed the roof where he was, and having dug through, they lowered the mattress where the paralytic was lying.

2.5 And Jesus, seeing their faith, says to the paralytic: My child, the faults/sins are forgiven/dismissed from you. 2.6 But some of the scribes were there, sitting and reasoning/considering/arguing in their hearts: 2.7 Why *does* this (one) speak so? He slanders/blasphemes; who is able to forgive/dismiss faults/sins, except one, God? 2.8 And Jesus, immediately knowing in/by his spirit/the spirit of him that they reason/discuss thus among themselves, says to them: Why *do* ye reason/discuss these (things) in your hearts? 2.9 What is easier, to say to the paralytic: The faults/sins are dismissed from you, or to say: You arise and take up your mattress and go away? 2.10 But in order that ye might know that the son of the man has/holds authority on the earth to forgive/dismiss faults/sins,

he says to the paralytic: 2.11 Arise, I say to you, take up your mattress/bed and go away to your house.

2.12 And he arose and immediately taking up the mattress he went out before *them* all, so as *for* all to be astonished and to glorify/acknowledge God, saying: Thus we never saw revealed/made manifest in Israel. 2.13 And he went out again to the sea; and all the crowd came to him, and he was teaching them.

2.14 And passing by/going along he saw Levi, the (one) of Alphaeus, sitting on/at the tax office/place, and he says to him: You follow with me. And having risen/stood up, he followed with him.

2.15 And it becomes *time for* him to recline in his house, and many tax collectors and sinners reclined together with Jesus and his learners/pupils; for there were many and they were following with him. 2.16 And scribes from the Pharisees, also seeing that he was eating with the tax collectors and sinners, they said to his pupils/learners: Why/because of what *does* your teacher eat with tax collectors and sinners?

τῶν τελωνῶν καὶ ἁμαρτωλῶν ἐσθίει ὁ διδασκαλὸς ἡμῶν; 2.17 καὶ ἀκούσας ὁ Ἰησοῦς λέγει αὐτοῖς οὐ χρίαν ἔχουσιν οἱ ἰσχύοντες ἰατροῦ ἀλλ' οἱ κακῶς ἔχοντες· οὐκ ἦλθον καλέσαι δικαίους ἀλλὰ ἁμαρτωλούς.

2.18 καὶ ἦσαν οἱ μαθηταὶ Ἰωάννου καὶ οἱ Φαρισαῖοι νηστεύοντες. καὶ ἔρχονται καὶ λέγουσιν αὐτῷ, διὰ τί οἱ μαθηταὶ Ἰωάννου καὶ οἱ μαθηταὶ τῶν Φαρισαίων νηστεύουσιν, οἱ δὲ σοὶ μαθηταὶ οὐ νηστεύουσιν;

2.19 καὶ εἶπεν αὐτοῖς ὁ Ἰησοῦς, μὴ δύνανται οἱ υἱοὶ τοῦ νυμφῶνος ἐν ᾧ ὁ νυμφίος μετ' αὐτῶν ἐστιν νηστεύειν; ὅσον χρόνον ἔχουσι τὸν νυμφίον μετ' αὐτῶν οὐ δύνανται νηστεύειν· 2.20 ἐλεύσονται δὲ ἡμέραι ὅταν ἀπαρθῇ ἀπ' αὐτῶν ὁ νυμφίος, καὶ τότε νηστεύσουσιν ἐν ἐκείνῃ τῇ ἡμέρᾳ.

2.21 οὐδεὶς ἐπίβλημα ῥάκους ἀγνάφου ἐπιράπτι ἐπὶ ἱμάτιον παλαιόν· εἰ δὲ μή, αἴρει πλήρωμα ἀπ' αὐτοῦ τὸ καινὸν τοῦ παλαιοῦ, καὶ χεῖρον σχίσμα γείνεται.

2.22 καὶ οὐδεὶς βάλλει οἶνον νέον εἰς ἀσκοὺς παλαιούς εἰ δὲ μή, ῥήξει ὁ οἶνος τοὺς ἀσκούς, καὶ ὁ οἶνος ἐκχεῖται καὶ οἱ ἀσκοὶ ἀπόλλυται — ἀλλὰ οἶνον νέον εἰς ἀσκοὺς καινούς.

2.23 καὶ ἐγένετο αὐτὸν ἐν τοῖς σάββασιν παραπορεύεσθαι διὰ τῶν σπορίμων, καὶ οἱ μαθηταὶ αὐτοῦ ἤρξαντο ὁδὸν ποιεῖν τίλλοντες τοὺς στάχυας. 2.24 καὶ οἱ Φαρισαῖοι ἔλεγον αὐτῷ, ἴδε τί ποιοῦσιν τοῖς σάββασιν ὃ οὐκ ἔξεστι; 2.25 καὶ λέγει αὐτοῖς, οὐδέποτε ἀνέγνωτε τί ἐποίησεν Δαυίδ, ὅτε χρίαν ἔσχεν καὶ ἐπίνασεν αὐτὸς καὶ οἱ μετ' αὐτοῦ; 2.26 πῶς εἰσῆλθεν εἰς τὸν οἶκον τοῦ θεοῦ ἐπὶ Ἀβιαθὰρ ἀρχιερέως καὶ τοὺς ἄρτους τῆς προθέσεως ἔφαγεν, οὓς οὐκ ἔξεστιν φαγῖν εἰ μὴ τοὺς ἱερεῖς, καὶ ἔδωκεν καὶ τοῖς σὺν αὐτῷ οὖσιν; 2.27 καὶ ἔλεγεν αὐτοῖς, τὸ σάββατον διὰ τὸν ἄνθρωπον ἐγένετο καὶ οὐχ ὁ ἄνθρωπος διὰ τὸ σάββατον· 2.28 ὥστε κύριός ἐστιν ὁ υἱὸς τοῦ ἀνθρώπου καὶ τοῦ σαββάτου.

3.1 Καὶ εἰσῆλθεν πάλιν εἰς συναγωγήν. καὶ ἦν ἐκεῖ

2.17 And having heard, Jesus says to them: The strong/able (ones) have not a need of a physician/doctor, but those having *it* badly/being sick; I came not to call just (ones) but sinners.

2.18 Both the pupils/learners of John and the Pharisees were fasting. And they come and say to him: Why *do* the pupils/learners of John and the pupils/learners of the Pharisees fast, but the pupils/learners for you *do* not fast?

2.19 And Jesus said to them: The sons of the wedding hall are not able to fast in what (time) the bridegroom is with them; *for* as much time as they have the bridegroom with them, they are not able to fast; 2.20 but days will come when the bridegroom might be taken away from them, and then they will fast in that day.

2.21 No one sews a piece/patch of unshrunken cloth upon an old garment; otherwise, the new takes away filling from the old, and a split/tear becomes worse.

2.22 And no one puts new wine into old wineskins; otherwise, the wine will burst the wineskins, and the wine is poured out and the wineskins perish, -- but *he puts* new wine into new wineskins.

2.23 And it happened on/in the sabbaths *for* him to pass/go along through the grainfields, and his learners/pupils began to make a way/road, plucking (picking) the grainstalks. 2.24 And the Pharisees said to him: Look, why *do* they do what is not lawful on/in the sabbaths? 2.25 And he says to them: Never read ye what David did, when he had a need and he hungered, himself and those with him? 2.26 How he entered into the house of God on/against Abiather, a high priest, and he ate the loaves of the setting before/shewbread, which is not lawful to eat, except *for* the priests, and he gave also to those being with him? 2.27 And he said to them: The sabbath came to be because of the man/human and not the man/human because of the sabbath; 2.28 so the son of the man is lord also/even or the sabbath.

3.1 And he went again into a congregation. And a

ἄνθρωπος ἐξηραμμένην ἔχων τὴν χεῖρα·

3.2 καὶ παρετήρουν αὐτὸν εἰ ἐν τοῖς σάββασι θεραπεύσι αὐτόν, ἵνα κατηγορήσωσιν αὐτοῦ. 3.3 καὶ λέγει τῷ ἀνθρώπῳ τῷ τὴν ξηρὰν χῖρα ἔχοντι, ἔγειρε εἰς τὸ μέσον.

3.4 καὶ λέγει αὐτοῖς, ἔξεστιν τοῖς σάββασιν ἀγαθὸν ποιῆσαι ἢ κακοποιῆσαι, ψυχὴν σῶσαι ἢ ἀποκτῖναι; οἱ δὲ ἐσιώπων. 3.5 καὶ περιβλεψάμενος αὐτοὺς μετ᾽ ὀργῆς, συνλυπούμενος ἐπὶ τῇ πωρώσει τῆς καρδί᾽ αὐτῶν,

λέγει τῷ ἀνθρώπῳ, ἔκτινον τὴν χῖρά σου. καὶ ἐξέτινεν, καὶ ἀπεκατεστάθη ἡ χὶρ αὐτοῦ.

3.6 καὶ ἐξελθόντες οἱ Φαρισαῖοι εὐθὺς μετὰ τῶν Ἡρῳδιανῶν συμβούλιον ἐποίησαν κατ᾽ αὐτοῦ ὅπως αὐτὸν ἀπολέσωσιν.

3.7 καὶ ὁ Ἰησοῦς μετὰ τῶν μαθητῶν αὐτοῦ ἀνεχώρησεν πρὸς τὴν θάλασσαν· καὶ πολὺ πλῆθος ἀπὸ τῆς Γαλιλαίας καὶ ἀπὸ τῆς Ἰουδαίας ἠκολούθησεν· 3.8 καὶ ἀπὸ Ἱεροσολύμων καὶ ἀπὸ τῆς Ἰδουμαίας καὶ πέραν τοῦ Ἰορδάνου καὶ περὶ Τύρον καὶ Σιδῶνα, πλῆθος πολύ, ἀκούοντες ὅσα ἐποίει ἦλθον πρὸς αὐτόν. 3.9 καὶ εἶπεν τοῖς μαθηταῖς αὐτοῦ ἵνα πλοιάριον προσκαρτερῇ αὐτῷ διὰ τὸν ὄχλον ἵνα μὴ θλίβωσιν αὐτόν· 3.10 πολλοὺς γὰρ ἐθεράπευσεν, ὥστε ἐπιπίπτειν αὐτῷ ἵνα αὐτοῦ ἅψωνται ὅσοι εἶχον μάστιγας.

3.11 καὶ τὰ πνεύματα τὰ ἀκάθαρτα, ὅταν αὐτὸν ἐθεώρουν, προσέπιπτον αὐτῷ καὶ ἔκραζον λέγοντες ὅτι σὺ εἶ ὁ υἱὸς τοῦ θεοῦ. 3.12 καὶ πολλὰ ἐπετίμα αὐτοῖς ἵνα μὴ αὐτὸν φανερὸν ποιήσωσιν. 3.13 καὶ ἀναβαίνει εἰς τὸ ὄρος καὶ προσκαλεῖται οὓς ἤθελεν αὐτός, οἱ δὲ ἀπῆλθον πρὸς αὐτόν.

3.14 καὶ ἐποίησεν δώδεκα, οὓς καὶ ἀποστόλους ὠνόμασεν, ἵνα ὦσι μετ᾽ αὐτοῦ καὶ ἵνα ἀποστέλλῃ αὐτοὺς κηρύσσειν 3.15 καὶ ἔχειν ἐξουσία ἐκβάλλειν τὰ δαιμόνια· 3.16 καὶ ἐποίησεν τοὺς δώδεκα,

καὶ ἐπέθηκεν ὄνομα τῷ Σίμωνι Πέτρον, 3.17 καὶ Ἰάκωβον

man was there having the hand dried up/withered;

3.2 and they were watching him carefully if in/on the sabbaths he will heal/treat him, in order that they might accuse/charge him. 3.3 And he says to the man, to the (one) having the dried/withered hand: Rise up in the midst.

3.4 And he says to him: Is it lawful on/in the sabbaths to do a good (thing) or to do bad, to save a soul/life, or to kill? But they were being silent. 3.5 And having looked around/about *at* them with anger, being deeply grieved over the hardness of their heart,

he says to the man: Stretch forth/hold out your hand. And he stretched *it* forth, and his hand was restored/cured.

3.6 And the Pharisees, going out at once, they made a plot/plan with the Herodians against him, that they might kill him.

3.7 And Jesus, with his pupils/learners, withdrew to/near the sea; and a much multitude from Galilee and from Judea followed; 3.8 also from Jerusalem and from Idumea and beyond the Jordan and around Tyre and Sidon, a much/great multitude, they came to/near him, hearing whatever he does/makes. 3.9 And he spoke to his learners/pupils in order that a little boat may remain near for him because of the crowd, that they may not press upon him; 3.10 for he healed/treated many, so as to fall eagerly upon him in order that as many as were having plagues might touch of him.

3.11 And the unclean spirits, when they were beholding him, fell *down* near to him and cried out, saying: You, you are the Son of God. 3.12 And he was warning many (things/times) to them that they should not make him evident/manifest. 3.13 And he went up to the mountain and he calls forward *those* whom he, he wanted, and they came near/to him.

3.14 And he made twelve, whom he also named apostles, that they may be with him and that he may send them forth/away to herald/preach 3.15 and to have authority to put out/expel the demons; 3.16 and he made the twelve,

and he layed/put a name upon the (one) Simon: Peter; 3.17 also James the (one) of Zebedee and John

τὸν τοῦ Ζεβεδαίου καὶ Ἰωάννην τὸν ἀδελφὸν τοῦ Ἰακώβου, καὶ ἐπέθηκεν αὐτοῖς ὀνόματα Βοανηργές, ὅ ἐστιν υἱοὶ βροντῆς· 3.18 καὶ Ἀνδραίαν καὶ Φίλιππον καὶ Βαρθολομαῖον καὶ Μαθαῖον καὶ Θωμᾶν καὶ Ἰάκωβον τὸν τοῦ Ἀλφαίου καὶ Θαδδαῖον καὶ Σίμωνα τὸν Κανανᾶτον 3.19 καὶ Ἰούδαν Ἰσκαριώ, ὃς καὶ παρέδωκεν αὐτόν. 3.20 καὶ ἔρχεται εἰς οἶκον·

καὶ συνέρχεται πάλιν ὁ ὄχλος, ὥστε μὴ δύνασθαι αὐτοὺς μητὲ ἄρτον φαγῖν. 3.21 καὶ ἀκούσαντες οἱ παρ' αὐτοῦ ἐξῆλθον κρατῆσαι αὐτόν, ἔλεγον γὰρ ὅτι ἐξέστη.

3.22 καὶ οἱ γραμματεῖς οἱ ἀπὸ Ἱεροσολύμων καταβάντες ἔλεγον ὅτι Βεελζεβοὺλ ἔχει, καὶ ὅτι ἐν τῷ ἄρχοντι τῶν δαιμονίων ἐκβάλλει τὰ δαιμόνια.

3.23 καὶ προσκαλεσάμενος αὐτοὺς ἐν παραβολαῖς ἔλεγεν αὐτοῖς, πῶς δύναται Σατανᾶς Σατανᾶν ἐκβάλλειν; 3.24 καὶ ἐὰν βασιλεία ἐφ' ἑαυτὴν μερισθῇ, οὐ δύναται σταθῆναι ἡ βασιλεία ἐκείνη· 3.25 καὶ ἐὰν οἰκία ἐφ' ἑαυτὴν μερισθῇ, οὐ δυνήσεται ἡ οἰκία ἐκείνη σταθῆναι. 3.26 καὶ εἰ ὁ Σατανᾶς ἀνέστη ἐφ' ἑαυτὸν ἐμερίσθη καὶ, οὐ δύναται στῆναι ἀλλὰ τέλος ἔχει. 3.27 ἀλλ' οὐ δύναται οὐδὶς εἰσελθὼν εἰς τὴν οἰκίαν τοῦ ἰσχυροῦ τὰ σκεύη αὐτοῦ διαρπάσαι ἐὰν μὴ πρῶτον τὸν ἰσχυρὸν δήσῃ, καὶ τότε τὴν οἰκίαν αὐτοῦ διαρπάσει.

3.28 ἀμὴν λέγω ὑμῖν ὅτι πάντα ἀφεθήσετε τοῖς υἱοῖς τῶν ἀνθρώπων, τὰ ἁμαρτήματα καὶ αἱ βλασφημίαι ὅσα ἂν βλασφημήσωσιν· 3.29 ὃς δ' ἂν βλασφημήσῃ εἰς τὸ πνεῦμα τὸ ἅγιον οὐκ ἔχι ἄφεσιν εἰς τὸν αἰῶνα, ἀλλὰ ἔνοχός ἐσται αἰωνίου ἁμαρτήματος 3.30 ὅτι ἔλεγον, πνεῦμα ἀκάθαρτον ἔχει.

3.31 καὶ ἔρχεται ἡ μήτηρ αὐτοῦ καὶ οἱ ἀδελφοὶ αὐτοῦ καὶ ἔξω στάντες ἀπέστειλαν πρὸς αὐτὸν καλοῦντες αὐτόν. 3.32 καὶ ἐκάθητο περὶ αὐτὸν ὄχλος, καὶ λέγουσιν αὐτῷ, ἰδοὺ ἡ μήτηρ σου καὶ οἱ ἀδελφοί σου ἔξω ζητοῦσίν σε. 3.33 καὶ ἀποκριθεὶς αὐτοῖς λέγει, τίς ἐστιν ἡ μήτηρ μου καὶ οἱ ἀδελφοί μου; 3.34 καὶ περιβλεψάμενος τοὺς περὶ αὐτὸν κύκλῳ καθημένους λέγει, εἶδε ἡ

the brother of James, and he layed/put upon them names: Boanerges, which is sons of thunder; 3.18 also Andrew and Philip and Bartholomew and Matthew and Thomas and James, the (one) of Alphaeus, and Thaddaeus and Simon the Cananaean 3.19 and Judas Iscariot, who also delivered up/betrayed him 3.20 And he comes/goes to/into a house;

and the crowd comes together again, so as *for* them not to be able to eat bread/a loaf. 3.21 And having heard, those with him went forth to seize him, for they were saying that he was ecstatic.

3.22 And the scribes, the (ones) having come down from Jerusalem, were saying that he has Beelzebub, and that by the ruler/leader of the demons he puts out/expels the demons.

3.23 And having called them near, he was saying to them in/by parables: How is Satan able to put out/expel Satan? 3.24 And if a kingdom be divided against/upon itself, that kingdom is not able to stand; 3.25 and if a house be divided against/upon itself, that house will not be able to stand. 3.26 And if Satan rose up against himself and was divided/separated, he is not able to stand, but he has an end. 3.27 But no one is not able, entering into the house of the strong (one), to plunder/steal his vessels/goods, except first he might bind the strong (one), and then he will plunder/rob his house.

3.28 Truly I say to ye that all (things) will be forgiven for the sons of the men, the faults/sins and the revilings/blasphemies, what ever they may blaspheme; 3.29 but who ever might slander/blaspheme to/against the Holy Spirit, he has not forgiveness into the age, but he will be guilty of an eternal sin. -- 3.30 because they were saying: He has an unclean spirit.

3.31 And his mother and his brothers come and having stood outside they sent to him, calling him. 3.32 And a crowd was sitting around him, and they say to him: Behold, your mother and your brothers *are* outside, they seek you. 3.33 And answering to them he says: Who is my mother and my brothers? 3.34 And having looked around *at* those around him, sitting

77

μήτηρ μου καὶ οἱ ἀδελφοί μου. 3.35 ὃς γὰρ ἂν ποιήσῃ τὸ θέλημα τοῦ θεοῦ, οὗτος ἀδελφός μου καὶ ἀδελφὴ καὶ μήτηρ ἐστίν.

4.1 Καὶ πάλιν ἤρξατο διδάσκιν παρὰ τὴν θάλασσαν. καὶ συνάγεται πρὸς αὐτὸν ὄχλος πλῖστος, ὥστε αὐτὸν εἰς πλοῖον ἐμβάντα καθῆσθε ἐν τῇ θαλάσσῃ, καὶ πᾶς ὁ ὄχλος πρὸς τὴν θάλασσαν ἐπὶ τῆς γῆς ἦσαν. 4.2 καὶ ἐδίδασκεν αὐτοὺς πολλά ἐν παραβολαῖς, καὶ ἔλεγεν αὐτοῖς ἐν τῇ διδαχῇ αὐτοῦ, 4.3 ἀκούετε.

ἰδοὺ ἐξῆλθεν ὁ σπίρων σπεῖραι. 4.4 καὶ ἐγένετο ἐν τῷ σπίρειν ὃ μὲν ἔπεσεν παρὰ τὴν ὁδόν, καὶ ἦλθεν τὰ πετινὰ καὶ κατέφαγεν αὐτό.

4.5 καὶ ἄλλο ἔπεσεν ἐπὶ τὸ πετρῶδες ὅπου οὐκ εἶχεν γῆν πολλήν, καὶ εὐθὺς ἐξανέτιλεν διὰ τὸ μὴ ἔχιν βάθος γῆς· 4.6 καὶ ὅτε ἀνέτιλεν ὁ ἥλιος ἐκαυματίσθη, καὶ διὰ τὸ μὴ ἔχιν ρίζαν ἐξηράνθη. 4.7 καὶ ἄλλο ἔπεσεν εἰς τὰς ἀκάνθας, καὶ ἀνέβησαν αἱ ἄκανθαι καὶ συνέπνιξαν αὐτό, καὶ καρπὸν οὐκ ἔδωκεν.

4.8 καὶ ἄλλα ἔπεσεν εἰς τὴν γῆν τὴν καλήν, καὶ ἐδίδου καρπὸν ἀναβαίνοντα καὶ αὐξανόμενα, καὶ ἔφερον εἰς τριάκοντα καὶ εἰς ἑξήκοντα καὶ εἰς ἑκατόν. 4.9 καὶ ἔλεγεν, ὃς ἔχει ὦτα ἀκούειν ἀκουέτω.

4.10 καὶ ὅτε ἐγένετο κατὰ μόνας, ἠρώτουν αὐτὸν οἱ περὶ αὐτὸν σὺν τοῖς δώδεκα τὰς παραβολάς. 4.11 καὶ ἔλεγεν αὐτοῖς, ὑμῖν τὸ μυστήριον δέδοται τῆς βασιλίας τοῦ θεοῦ· ἐκείνοις δὲ τοῖς ἔξω ἐν παραβολαῖς πάντα γίνεται, 4.12 ἵνα «βλέποντες βλέπωσιν καὶ μὴ ἴδωσιν, καὶ ἀκούοντες ἀκούωσιν καὶ μὴ συνιῶσιν, μήποτε ἐπιστρέψωσιν καὶ ἀφεθῇ αὐτοῖς.» 4.13 καὶ λέγει αὐτοῖς, οὐκ οἴδατε τὴν παραβολὴν ταύτην, καὶ πῶς πάσας τὰς παραβολὰς γνώσεσθε;

4.14 ὁ σπίρων τὸν λόγον σπέρει. 4.15 οὗτοι δέ εἰσιν οἱ παρὰ τὴν ὁδὸν ὅπου σπίρεται ὁ λόγος, καὶ ὅταν ἀκούσωσιν

round about/all around, he says: Behold my mother and
my brothers.   3.35 For who ever might do the will of
God, this (one) is my brother and sister and mother.

4.1   And again he began to teach beside the sea.
And a very great crowd gathered near him, so that
having embarked in a boat *for* him to sit in/on the
sea, and all the crowd were on the land near the sea.
4.2 And he taught them many (things) in/by parables,
and he spoke   to   them in/by his doctrine/teaching:
4.3 Hear/listen ye!
    behold, the (one) sowing went out to sow.   4.4
And it happened in the (thing) to sow, some *seed* fell
beside the road/way, and the birds came and devoured
it.
    4.5   And   other/another fell upon the stony
(place) where it had not much earth, and it sprang up
at once because of the (thing) not to have depth of
earth;   4.6 and when the sun rose it was scorched, and
because of the (thing) to have not a root, it was
withered/dried   up.   4.7 And other fell into   the
thorns, and the thorns came up and choked it *to death*,
and it gave not a produce/fruit.
    4.8   But others fell in the good earth/land, and
it gave a product/fruit, coming up and growing, and
they were bearing, one thirty, and one sixty, and one
a hundred.   4.9 And he was saying: Who has ears to
hear, let him listen/hear.
    4.10   And when he became in private/alone, those
around him with the twelve were asking him *about* the
parables.   4.11 And he said to them: The mystery of
the kingdom of God has been given to ye; but to those,
the (ones) outside, all (things) are in/by parables,
4.12   that SEEING, THEY SEE AND PERCEIVE NOT, AND
HEARING, THEY HEAR BUT UNDERSTAND NOT, LEST THEN THEY
MIGHT TURN/BEHAVE AND IT BE FORGIVEN FOR THEM.   4.13
And he says to them: Know/perceive ye not this parable, and how ye will know all the parables?
    4.14   The (one) sowing/scattering, he sows/scat-
ters the saying/word.   4.15   And these are those
beside the road/way where he sows the saying/logos/
word, and when they might hear, Satan comes at once

εὐθὺς ἔρχεται ὁ Σατανᾶς καὶ ἁρπάζει τὸν λόγον τὸν ἐσπαρμένον ἐν αὐτούς.

4.16 καὶ οὗτοι ὁμοίως εἰσιν οἱ ἐπὶ τὰ πετρώδη σπιρόμενοι, οἳ ὅταν ἀκούσωσιν τὸν λόγον εὐθὺς μετὰ χαρᾶς λαμβάνουσιν αὐτόν, 4.17 καὶ οὐκ ἔχουσιν ῥίζαν ἐν ἑαυτοῖς ἀλλὰ πρόσκαιροί εἰσιν· εἶτα γενομένης θλίψεως ἢ διωγμοῦ διὰ τὸν λόγον εὐθὺς σκανδαλίζονται. 4.18 καὶ ἄλλοι εἰσιν οἱ ἐπὶ τὰς ἀκάνθας σπιρόμενοι· οὗτοί εἰσιν οἱ ἀκούσαντες τὸν λόγον, 4.19 καὶ αἱ μέριμναι τοῦ αἰῶνος καὶ ἡ ἀπάτη τοῦ πλούτου συμπνίγει τὸν λόγον καὶ αἱ περὶ τὰ λοιπὰ ἐπιθυμίαι εἰσπορευόμεναι, καὶ ἄκαρπος γείνεται. 4.20 καὶ ἐκεῖνοί εἰσιν οἱ ἐπὶ τὴν γῆν τὴν καλὴν σπαρέντες, οἵτινες ἀκούουσι τὸν λόγον καὶ παραδέχονται καὶ καρποφοροῦσιν ἓν τριάκοντα καὶ ἓν ἑξήκοντα καὶ ἓν ἑκατόν. 4.21 καὶ ἔλεγεν αὐτοῖς, μήτι ἔρχεται ὁ λύχνος ἵνα ὑπὸ τὸν μόδιον τεθῇ ἢ ὑπὸ τὴν κλίνην; οὐχ ἵνα ὑπὸ τὴν λυχνίαν τεθῇ; 4.22 οὐ γάρ ἐστιν κρυπτὸν ἐὰν μὴ ἵνα φανερωθῇ, οὐδὲ ἐγένετο ἀπόκρυφον ἀλλ’ ἵνα ἔλθῃ εἰς φανερόν. 4.23 εἴ τις ἔχει ὦτα ἀκούειν ἀκουέτω.

4.24 καὶ ἔλεγεν αὐτοῖς, βλέπετε τί ἀκούετε. ἐν ᾧ μέτρῳ μετρῖτε μετρηθήσεται ὑμῖν καὶ προστεθήσετε ὑμῖν. 4.25 ὃς γὰρ ἔχει, δοθήσεται αὐτῷ· καὶ ὃς οὐκ ἔχει, καὶ ὃ ἔχει ἀρθήσεται ἀπ’ αὐτοῦ. 4.26

καὶ ἔλεγεν, οὕτως ἐστὶν ἡ βασιλεία τοῦ θεοῦ ὡς ἄνθρωπος βάλῃ τὸν σπόρον ἐπὶ τῆς γῆς 4.27 καὶ καθεύδῃ καὶ ἐγείρεται νύκτα καὶ ἡμέραν, καὶ ὁ σπόρος βλαστάνῃ καὶ μηκύνηται ὡς οὐκ οἶδεν αὐτός. 4.28 αὐτομάτη ἡ γῆ καρποφορεῖ, πρῶτον χόρτον, εἶτα στάχυν, εἶτα πλήρη σῖτον ἐν τῷ στάχυϊ.

4.29 ὅταν δὲ παραδοῖ ὁ καρπός, εὐθὺς ἀποστέλλει τὸ δρέπανον, ὅτι παρέστηκεν ὁ θερισμός. 4.30 καὶ ἔλεγεν, πῶς

and snatches away the saying/word having been sown in/among them.

4.16   And these likewise/similarly are those being sown on the stony places, who when they might hear the saying/word, they receive it immediately with joy,   4.17 and they have not a root in themselves, but they are temporary/transitory (ones); then from oppression or prosecution having happened/become because of the saying/word, they are at once offended/caused to fall away.   4.18 And others are those being sown upon the thorns/thorny (places); these are those having heard the saying/word,   4.19 and the cares of the age and the deceit of the wealth chokes the saying/word, even/also the desires concerning/about the remaining (things) coming in, and it becomes barren/without fruit.   4.20 And those are the (ones) having been sown upon thegood land/earth, who hear the saying/logos/word and they accept *it* and they bear fruit, one thirty and one sixty and one a hundred.   4.21 And he was saying to them: Comes not the lamp that it might be placed under the peck measure or under the bed/cot?   Not that it might be put beneath the lampstand? 4.22   For it is not hidden except that it might be revealed, nor *did* it become secret but that it may come into *the* open/public.   4.23 If anyone has ears to hear, let him hear/listen.

4.24   And he was saying to them: See/heed ye what ye hear/obey. With what measure ye measure/apportion it will be measured to ye and it will be added for ye. 4.25 For *the one* who has, it will be given to him; and *the one* who has not, even what he has will be taken from him.   4.26 And he was saying: So/thus is the kingdom of God, as a man might throw the sowing/seed upon the land   4.27   and he might sleep and awaken/rise up night and day, and the seed may germinate/sprout and might be lengthened as he, he has not known.   4.28 The land/earth produces/bears fruit by itself, first a grass/blade, then a bunch/head, then full grain in the head/bunch.

4.29   But when the product/fruit might mature, he sends at once the scythe, because the harvest has become.   4.30 And he was saying: How might we liken

ὁμοιώσωμεν τὴν βασιλείαν τοῦ θεοῦ, ἢ ἐν τίνι αὐτὴν παραβολῇ θῶμεν; 4.31 ὡς κόκκῳ σινάπεως, ὃς ὅταν σπαρῇ ἐπὶ τῆς γῆς, ὁ μικρότερον ὂν πάντων τῶν σπερμάτων τῶν ἐπὶ τῆς γῆς, 4.32 καὶ ὅταν σπαρῇ, ἀναβαίνι καὶ γείνεται μεῖζον πάντων τῶν λαχάνων καὶ ποιεῖ κλάδους μεγάλους, ὥστε δύνασθαι ὑπὸ τὴν σκιὰν αὐτοῦ τὰ πετινὰ τοῦ οὐρανοῦ κατασκηνοῦν.

4.33 καὶ τοιαύταις παραβολαῖς πολλαῖς ἐλάλει αὐτοῖς τὸν λόγον, καθὼς ἠδύναντο ἀκούειν· 4.34 χωρὶς δὲ παραβολῆς οὐκ ἐλάλει αὐτοῖς,

κατ᾽ ἰδίαν δὲ τοῖς ἰδίοις μαθηταῖς ἐπέλυεν πάντα. 4.35 καὶ λέγει αὐτοῖς ἐν ἐκίνῃ τῇ ἡμέρᾳ ὀψίας γενομένης, διέλθωμεν εἰς τὸ πέραν. 4.36 καὶ ἀφέντες τὸν ὄχλον παραλαμβάνουσιν αὐτὸν ὡς ἦν ἐν τῷ πλοίῳ, καὶ ἄλλα πλοῖα ἦσαν μετ᾽ αὐτοῦ. 4.37 καὶ γείνεται λαῖλαψ μεγάλη ἀνέμου, καὶ τὰ κύματα ἐπέβαλλεν εἰς τὸ πλοῖον, ὥστε ἤδη γεμίζεσθαι τὸ πλοῖον. 4.38 καὶ αὐτὸς ἦν ἐν τῇ πρύμνῃ ἐπὶ τὸ προσκεφάλαιον καθεύδων·

καὶ ἐγείρουσιν αὐτὸν καὶ λέγουσιν αὐτῷ, διδάσκαλε, οὐ μέλι σοι ὅτι ἀπολλύμεθα;

4.39 καὶ διεγερθεὶς ἐπετίμησεν τῷ ἀνέμῳ καὶ εἶπεν τῇ θαλάσσῃ, σιώπα, πεφίμωσο. καὶ ἐκόπασεν ὁ ἄνεμος, καὶ ἐγένετο γαλήνη μεγάλη.

4.40 καὶ εἶπεν αὐτοῖς, τί δειλοί ἐστε; οὔπω ἔχετε πίστιν; 4.41 καὶ ἐφοβήθησαν φόβον μέγαν, καὶ ἔλεγον πρὸς ἀλλήλους, τίς ἄρα οὗτός ἐστιν ὅτι καὶ ὁ ἄνεμος καὶ ἡ θάλασσα αὐτῷ ὑπακούει; 5.1 καὶ ἦλθον εἰς τὸ πέραν τῆς θαλάσσης εἰς τὴν χώραν τῶν Γερασηνῶν. 5.2 καὶ ἐξελθόντος αὐτοῦ ἐκ τοῦ πλοίου εὐθὺς ὑπήντησεν αὐτῷ ἐκ τῶν μνημίων ἄνθρωπος ἐν πνεύματι ἀκαθάρτῳ, 5.3 ὃς τὴν κατοίκησιν εἶχεν ἐν τοῖς μνήμασιν· καὶ οὐδὲ ἁλύσεσιν οὐκέτι οὐδεὶς ἐδύνατο αὐτὸν δῆσαι, 5.4 διὰ τὸ αὐτὸν πολλάκις πέδαις καὶ ἁλύσεσι δεδέσθαι καὶ διεσπάσθαι ὑπ᾽ αὐτοῦ τὰς ἁλύσεις καὶ τὰς παίδας συντετρῖφθαι, καὶ οὐδὶς ἴσχυσεν αὐτὸν δαμάσαι· 5.5 καὶ διὰ παντὸς νυκτὸς καὶ ἡμέρας

the kingdom of God or in/by what parable might we put it?   4.31 As a grain/seed of mustard, which when it might be sown upon the land, being the smaller of all the seeds, of the (ones) upon the earth/land,   4.32 and when it might be sown, it comes up and becomes greater than all the garden herbs and it makes great branches, so as *for* the birds of the sky/heaven to be able to dwell/settle under its shade/shadow.

4.33 And he was speaking the saying/word to them in many such parables, as they were being able to listen/hear;   4.34 and without a parable he spoke not to them,

but alone/in private with his own learners/pupils he was explaining all.   4.35   And he says to them in/on that *same* day, it having become evening: Let us cross over to the other side/beyond.   4.36 And leaving the crowd, they take him along as he was in the boat, and other boats were with him.   4.37 And there happened a great storm of wind, and the waves were being thrown up into the boat, so as already *for* the boat to be filled.   4.38 But he, he was in the stern sleeping upon the pillow;

and they arouse him and say to him: Teacher, is it not a care to you that we perish?

4.39   And having been awakened, he rebuked the wind and he said to the sea: You be quiet, you have been muzzled. And the wind abated/was stilled, and there became a great calm.

4.40   And he said to them: Why are ye cowards? Have ye not yet faith? 4.41   And they feared a great fear, and they were saying to one another: Then who is this (one), that both the wind and the sea obey him? 5.1   And they came to the other side of the sea to the land/region of Gerasenes.   5.2 And from him having gone forth out of the boat, immediately a man with an unclean spirit met him, out of the tombs/monuments, 5.3 who had the dwelling/home among the tombs; and not any longer was anyone being able to bind him with/in chains,   5.4 because of the (thing) *for* him to have been bound many times with/in fetters and chains, and *for* the chains and the fetters to have been broken by him, and no one had strength to subdue him;   5.5 and

ἐν τοῖς μνήμασιν καὶ ἐν τοῖς ὄρεσιν ἦν κράζων καὶ κατακόπτων ἑαυτὸν λίθοις.

5.6 καὶ ἰδὼν τὸν Ἰησοῦν ἀπὸ μακρόθεν ἔδραμεν καὶ προσεκύνησεν αὐτῷ, 5.7 καὶ κράξας φωνῇ μεγάλῃ λέγει, τί ἐμοὶ καὶ σοί, Ἰησοῦ υἱὲ τοῦ θεοῦ τοῦ ὑψίστου; ὁρκίζω σε τὸν θεόν, μή με βασανίσῃς. 5.8 καὶ ἔλεγεν αὐτῷ, ἔξελθε τὸ πνεῦμα τὸ ἀκάθαρτον ἐκ τοῦ ἀνθρώπου.

5.9 καὶ ἐπηρώτα αὐτόν, τί ὄνομά σοι; καὶ λέγι αὐτῷ, Λεγιὼν ὄνομά μοι, ὅτι πολλοί ἐσμεν. 5.10 καὶ παρεκάλει αὐτὸν πολλὰ ἵνα μὴ αὐτὸν ἀποστίλῃ ἔξω τῆς χώρας.

5.11 ἦν δὲ ἐκεῖ πρὸς τῷ ὄρι ἀγέλη χοίρων μεγάλη βοσκομένη· 5.12 καὶ παρεκάλεσαν αὐτὸν λέγοντες, πέμψον ἡμᾶς εἰς τοὺς χοίρους, ἵνα εἰς αὐτοὺς εἰσέλθωμεν. 5.13 καὶ ἐπέτρεψεν αὐτοῖς.

καὶ ἐξελθόντα τὰ πνεύματα τὰ ἀκάθαρτα εἰσῆλθον εἰς τοὺς χοίρους, καὶ ὥρμησεν ἡ ἀγέλη κατὰ τοῦ κρημνοῦ εἰς τὴν θάλασσαν, ὡς δισχίλιοι, καὶ ἐπνίγοντο ἐν τῇ θαλάσσῃ. 5.14 καὶ οἱ βόσκοντες αὐτοὺς ἔφυγον καὶ ἀπήγγιλαν εἰς τὴν πόλιν καὶ εἰς τοὺς ἀγρούς· καὶ ἐξῆλθον ἰδεῖν τί ἐστιν τὸ γεγονός.

5.15 καὶ ἤρχοντο πρὸς τὸν Ἰησοῦν, καὶ θεωροῦσι τὸν δαιμονιζόμενον καθήμενον ἱματισμένον καὶ σωφρονοῦντα, τὸν ἐσχηκότα τὸν λεγιῶνα, καὶ ἐφοβήθησαν.

5.16 καὶ διηγήσαντο αὐτοῖς οἱ ἰδόντες πῶς ἐγένετο τῷ δαιμονιζομίνῳ καὶ περὶ τῶν χοίρων. 5.17 καὶ ἤρξαντο παρακαλῖν αὐτὸν ἀπελθῖν ἀπὸ τῶν ὁρίων αὐτῶν.

5.18 καὶ ἐμβαίνοντος αὐτοῦ εἰς τὸ πλοῖον παρεκάλει αὐτὸν ὁ δαιμονισθεὶς ἵνα μετ' αὐτοῦ ᾖ.

5.19 καὶ οὐκ ἀφῆκεν αὐτόν, ἀλλὰ λέγει αὐτῷ, ὕπαγε εἰς τὸν οἶκόν σου πρὸς τοὺς σούς, καὶ ἀπάγγειλον αὐτοῖς ὅσα ὁ

through every night and day among the tombs/monuments and in/on the mountains he was crying out and cutting against himself with stones.

5.6 And having seen Jesus from afar, he ran and worshiped/genuflexed to him, 5.7 and crying out with a great voice, he says: What *is it* to/for me and to/for you, Jesus, son of the high God? I implore *for* you, the God, *that* you might not torment me. 5.8 And he was saying to him: You come out, the unclean spirit, out of the man.

5.9 And he was asking him: What *is* a name for you? And he says to him: Legion *is* a name for me, because we are many. 5.10 And he besought him much that he might not send him away out of the country/region/land.

5.11 And a large herd of pigs were there, being grazed/tended near the mountain; 5.12 And they besought him, saying: You send us into the pigs, in order that we might enter into them. 5.13 And he permitted them.

And having come out, the unclean spirits entered into the pigs, and the herd ran headlong down the precipice/cliff into the sea, about two thousands, and they were being drowned in the sea. 5.14 And those tending them ran away/fled and they reported *it* in the city and in the fields; and they went out to see what is the (thing) having happened.

5.15 And they were coming to/near Jesus, and they view/gaze on the (one) being demon-possessed sitting, having been clothed, and being of sound mind, the (one) having had the legion, and they were made to fear.

5.16 And those having seen how it happened/came about for the (one) demon-possessed recounted/related *it* to them, also concerning the pigs. 5.17 And they began to beseech him to go away from their borders (leave their country/region).

5.18 And of him embarking into the boat, the (one) being demon-possessed was beseeching him that he may be with him.

5.19 And he *did* not let him, but he says to him: You go to your house, to those yours, and report to

κύριος πεποίηκέν σοι καὶ ἠλέησέν σε.

5.20 καὶ ἀπῆλθεν καὶ ἤρξατο κηρύσσειν ἐν τῇ Δεκαπόλι ὅσα ἐποίησεν αὐτῷ ὁ Ἰησοῦς, καὶ πάντες ἐθαύμαζον.

5.21 καὶ διαπεράσαντος τοῦ Ἰησοῦ ἐν τῷ πλοίῳ εἰς τὸ πέραν πάλιν συνήχθη ὄχλος πολὺς ἐπ᾽ αὐτόν, καὶ ἦν παρὰ τὴν θάλασσαν.

5.22 καὶ ἔρχεται εἷς τῶν ἀρχισυναγώγων, ὀνόματι Ἰάϊρος, καὶ ἰδὼν αὐτὸν πίπτι πρὸς τοὺς πόδας αὐτοῦ 5.23 καὶ παρακαλεῖ αὐτὸν πολλὰ λέγων ὅτι τὸ θυγάτριόν μου ἐσχάτως ἔχει, ἵνα ἐλθὼν ἐπιθῇς τὰς χῖρας αὐτῇ ἵνα σωθῇ καὶ ζήσῃ. 5.24 καὶ ἀπῆλθεν μετ᾽ αὐτοῦ. καὶ ἠκολούθι αὐτῷ ὄχλος πολύς, καὶ συνέθλιβον αὐτόν.

5.25 καὶ γυνὴ οὖσα ἐν ῥύσει αἵματος δώδεκα ἔτη 5.26 καὶ πολλὰ παθοῦσα ὑπὸ πολλῶν ἰατρῶν καὶ δαπανήσασα τὰ παρ᾽ ἑαυτῆς πάντα καὶ μηδὲν ὠφεληθῖσα ἀλλὰ μᾶλλον εἰς τὸ χεῖρον ἐλθοῦσα, 5.27 ἀκούσασα περὶ τοῦ Ἰησοῦ, ἐλθοῦσα ἐν τῷ ὄχλῳ ὄπισθεν ἥψατο τοῦ ἱματίου αὐτοῦ· 5.28 ἔλεγεν γὰρ ὅτι ἐὰν ἅψωμαι κἂν τοῦ ἱματίου αὐτοῦ σωθήσομαι. 5.29 καὶ εὐθὺς ἐξηράνθη ἡ πηγὴ τοῦ αἵματος αὐτῆς, καὶ ἔγνω τῷ σώματι ὅτι ἴαται ἀπὸ τῆς μάστιγος.

5.30 καὶ εὐθὺς ὁ Ἰησοῦς ἐπιγνοὺς ἐν ἑαυτῷ τὴν ἐξ αὐτοῦ δύναμιν ἐξελθοῦσαν ἐπιστραφεὶς ἐν τῷ ὄχλῳ ἔλεγεν, τίς μου ἥψατο τῶν ἱματίων;

5.31 καὶ ἔλεγον αὐτῷ οἱ μαθηταὶ αὐτοῦ, βλέπεις τὸν ὄχλον συνθλίβοντά σε, καὶ λέγις, τίς μου ἥψατο; 5.32 καὶ περιεβλέπετο ἰδεῖν τὴν τοῦτο ποιήσασαν. 5.33 ἡ δὲ γυνὴ φοβηθῖσα καὶ τρέμουσα, καὶ ἰδυῖα ὃ γέγονεν αὐτῇ, ἦλθεν καὶ προσέπεσεν αὐτῷ καὶ εἶπεν αὐτῷ πᾶσαν τὴν ἀλήθιαν.

5.34 ὁ δὲ εἶπεν αὐτῇ, θυγάτερ, ἡ πίστις σου σέσωκέν σε· ὕπαγε εἰς ἰρήνην, καὶ ἴσθι ὑγιὴς ἀπὸ τῆς μάστιγός σου.

them what (things) the Lord has done for you and had mercy on you.

5.20 And he went away and began to herald/preach in Decapolis what (things) Jesus did for him, and all were marveling.

5.21 And from Jesus having crossed over in the boat to the other side, a much crowd was gathered again to him, and he was beside the sea.

5.22 And there comes one of the congregation leaders, by name of Jairus, and having seen him, he falls near his feet 5.23 and he beseeches him much, saying: My daughter has *it* finally/is about to die, that having come you might lay the hands on her that she might be saved and she might live. 5.24 And he went away with him. And a much crowd followed with him, and they were pressing/crowding with him.

5.25 And a woman being with an issue of blood *for* twelve years, 5.26 and having suffered many (things) under/by many doctors and having spent all things from herself and having been benefited nothing, but rather having come into the worse, 5.27 having heard the (things) concerning Jesus, having come in the crowd from behind, she touched his garment; 5.28 for she was saying: If I might at least touch his garment, I shall be saved/delivered. 5.29 And the fountain of her blood was immediately dried up, and she knew that she had been healed in the body from the plague/scourge.

5.30 And at once Jesus, having known/sensed in himself the power having gone forth out of him, having been turned in/with the crowd, he was saying: Who touched my garments?

5.31 And his learners/pupils were saying to him: You see the crowd pressing with you, and you say: Who touched me? 5.32 And he was looking about to see the (one) having done this (thing). 5.33 And the woman, having fear and trembling, and having known what has happened to her, she came and fell near to him, and she spoke to him all the truth.

5.34 And the (he) said to her: Daughter, your faith has saved/delivered you; you go in peace, and be you healthy from your plague.

82

5.35 ἔτι αὐτοῦ λαλοῦντος ἔρχονται ἀπὸ τοῦ ἀρχισυναγώγου λέγοντες ὅτι ἡ θυγάτηρ σου ἀπέθανεν· τί ἔτι σκύλλεις τὸν διδάσκαλον;

5.36 ὁ δὲ Ἰησοῦς παρακούσας τὸν λόγον λαλούμενον λέγει τῷ ἀρχισυναγώγῳ, μὴ φοβοῦ, μόνον πίστευε.

5.37 καὶ οὐκ ἀφῆκεν οὐδένα μετ' αὐτοῦ συνακολουθῆσαι εἰ μὴ τὸν Πέτρον καὶ Ἰάκωβον καὶ Ἰωάννην τὸν ἀδελφὸν Ἰακώβου.

5.38 καὶ ἔρχονται εἰς τὸν οἶκον τοῦ ἀρχισυναγώγου, καὶ θεωρεῖ θόρυβον καὶ κλαίοντας καὶ ἀλαλάζοντας πολλά, 5.39 καὶ εἰσελθὼν λέγει αὐτοῖς, τί θορυβεῖσθε καὶ κλαίετε; τὸ παιδίον οὐκ ἀπέθανεν ἀλλὰ καθεύδι. 5.40 καὶ κατεγέλων αὐτοῦ.

αὐτὸς δὲ ἐκβαλὼν πάντας παραλαμβάνει τὸν πατέρα τοῦ παιδίου καὶ τὴν μητέρα καὶ τοὺς μετ' αὐτοῦ, καὶ εἰσπορεύεται ὅπου ἦν τὸ παιδίον· 5.41 καὶ κρατήσας τῆς χιρὸς τοῦ πεδίου λέγει αὐτῇ, ταλιθα κουμ, ὅ ἐστιν μεθερμηνευόμενον τὸ κοράσιον, σοί λέγω, ἔγειρε. 5.42 καὶ εὐθὺς ἀνέστη τὸ κοράσιον καὶ περιεπάτι, ἦν γὰρ ὥσει ἐτῶν δώδεκα. καὶ ἐξέστησαν εὐθὺς ἐκστάσι μεγάλῃ. 5.43 καὶ διεστείλατο αὐτοῖς πολλὰ ἵνα μηδὶς γνῶ τοῦτο, καὶ εἶπεν δοθῆναι αὐτῇ φαγῖν.

6.1 Καὶ ἐξῆλθεν ἐκῖθεν, καὶ ἔρχεται εἰς τὴν πατρίδα αὐτοῦ, καὶ ἀκολουθοῦσιν αὐτῷ οἱ μαθηταὶ αὐτοῦ.

6.2 καὶ γενομένου σαββάτου ἤρξατο διδάσκειν ἐν τῇ συναγωγῇ· καὶ πολλοὶ ἀκούοντες ἐξεπλήσσοντο λέγοντες, πόθεν τούτῳ ταῦτα, καὶ τίς ἡ σοφία ἡ δοθῖσα τούτῳ καὶ αἱ δυνάμις τοιαῦται διὰ τῶν χειρῶν αὐτοῦ γινόμεναι;

6.3 οὐχ οὗτός ἐστιν ὁ τέκτων, ὁ υἱὸς τῆς Μαρίας καὶ ὁ ἀδελφὸς Ἰακώβου καὶ Ἰωσῆφ καὶ Ἰούδα καὶ Σίμωνος; καὶ οὐκ εἰσὶν αἱ ἀδελφαὶ αὐτοῦ ὧδε πρὸς ἡμᾶς; καὶ ἐσκανδαλίζοντο ἐν αὐτῷ.

6.4 καὶ ἔλεγεν αὐτοῖς ὁ Ἰησοῦς ὅτι οὐκ ἔστιν προφήτης ἄτιμος εἰ μὴ ἐν τῇ πατρίδι αὐτοῦ καὶ ἐν τοῖς συνγενέσιν καὶ ἐν

5.35 Of him still speaking, they come from the ruler/chief of the congregation, saying: Your daughter died; why *do* you still trouble the teacher?

5.36 But Jesus, having overheard the saying/word being spoken, says to the chief of the congregation: Fear you not, only believe!

5.37 And he let/allowed not no one with him to follow with *him* except Peter and James and John, the brother of James.

5.38 And they go into the house of the chief of the congregation, and he beholds an uproar, both weeping and many wailing loudly,   5.39 and having gone in, he says to them: Why *do* ye make an uproar and weep? The child *did* not die, but she sleeps.   5.40 And they were laughing against/at him.

But he, having put *them* all out, he takes along the father of the child and the mother and the (ones) with him, and he goes in where the child was;   5.41 And having grasped the hand of the child, he says to her: Talitha koum, which being interpreted/translated is the *words:* Maiden, I say to you, rise up.   5.42 And the maiden rose up at once and was walking, for she was about twelve years *old.* And they were astonished immediately in a great ecstasy.   5.43 And he commanded to them many *times* that no one should know this (thing), and he said to be given to her to eat.

6.1 And he went out from there, and comes to his native place/country, and his pupils/learners follow with him.

6.2 And from it becoming a sabbath, he began to teach in the congregation; and hearing, many were being amazed, saying: From where *are* these (things) for this (one), and what *is* the wisdom having been given to this (one), and the powers to become/happen through his hands?

6.3 Is not this (one) the craftsman, the son of Mary, and the brother of James and Joseph and Judas and Simon? And are not his sisters here near us? And they were being offended/caused to stumble in/by him.

6.4 And Jesus was saying to them that a prophet is not unhonored except in his native place, and among

τῇ οἰκίᾳ αὐτοῦ. 6.5 καὶ οὐκ ἐδύνατο ἐκεῖ ποιῆσαι οὐδεμίαν δύναμιν, εἰ μὴ ὀλίγοις ἀρρώστοις ἐπιθεὶς τὰς χῖρας ἐθεράπευσεν· 6.6 καὶ ἐθαύμαζεν διὰ τὴν ἀπιστίαν αὐτῶν. καὶ περιῆγεν ὁ Ἰησοῦς τὰς κώμας κύκλῳ διδάσκων.

6.7 καὶ προσκαλεῖται τοὺς δώδεκα, καὶ ἤρξατο αὐτοὺς ἀποστέλλιν δύο δύο, καὶ ἐδίδου αὐτοῖς ἐξουσίαν τῶν πνευμάτων τῶν ἀκαθάρτων· 6.8 καὶ παρήγγειλεν αὐτοῖς ἵνα μηδὲν ἄρωσιν εἰς ὁδὸν εἰ μὴ ῥάβδον μόνον, μὴ ἄρτον,

μὴ πήραν, μὴ εἰς τὴν ζώνην χαλκόν, 6.9 ἀλλὰ ὑποδεδεμένους σανδάλια καὶ μὴ ἐνδύσησθε δύο χιτῶνας. 6.10 καὶ ἔλεγεν αὐτοῖς, ὅπου ἐὰν εἰσέλθητε εἰς οἰκίαν, ἐκεῖ μίνατε ἕως ἂν ἐξέλθητε ἐκῖθεν.

6.11 καὶ ὃς ἂν τόπος μὴ δέξηται ὑμᾶς μηδὲ ἀκούσωσιν ὑμῶν, ἐκπορευόμενοι ἐκεῖθεν ἐκτινάξατε τὸν χοῦν τὸν ὑποκάτω τῶν ποδῶν ὑμῶν εἰς μαρτύριον αὐτοῖς.

6.12 καὶ ἐξελθόντες ἐκήρυξαν ἵνα μετανοῆσιν, 6.13 καὶ δαιμόνια πολλὰ ἐξέβαλλον, καὶ ἤλειφον ἐλαίῳ πολλοὺς ἀρρώστους καὶ ἐθεράπευον. 6.14 καὶ ἤκουσεν ὁ βασιλεὺς Ἡρώδης, φανερὸν γὰρ ἐγένετο τὸ ὄνομα αὐτοῦ, καὶ ἔλεγον ὅτι Ἰωάννης ὁ βαπτίζων ἐγήγερται ἐκ νεκρῶν, καὶ διὰ τοῦτο ἐνεργοῦσιν αἱ δυνάμις ἐν αὐτῷ. 6.15 ἄλλοι δὲ ἔλεγον ὅτι Ἡλίας ἐστίν·

ἄλλοι δὲ ὅτι προφήτης ὡς εἷς τῶν προφητῶν.

6.16 ἀκούσας δὲ ὁ Ἡρώδης ἔλεγεν, ὃν ἐγὼ ἀπεκεφάλισα οὗτος Ἰωάννην ἠγέρθη. 6.17 αὐτὸς γὰρ ὁ Ἡρώδης ἀποστίλας ἐκράτησε τὸν Ἰωάννην καὶ ἔδησεν αὐτὸν ἐν φυλακῇ διὰ Ἡρῳδιάδα τὴν γυναῖκα Φιλίππου τοῦ ἀδελφοῦ αὐτοῦ, ὅτι αὐτὴν ἐγάμησεν·

6.18 ἔλεγεν γὰρ ὁ Ἰωάννης τῷ Ἡρώδῃ ὅτι οὐκ ἔξεστίν σοι ἔχιν τὴν γυναῖκα τοῦ ἀδελφοῦ σου.

6.19 ἡ δὲ Ἡρῳδιὰς ἐνεῖχεν αὐτῷ καὶ ἤθελεν αὐτὸν ἀποκτῖναι, καὶ οὐκ ἠδύνατο· 6.20 ὁ γὰρ Ἡρώδης ἐφοβεῖτο τὸν Ἰωάννην, εἰδὼς αὐτὸν ἄνδρα δίκαιον καὶ ἅγιον, καὶ συνετήρει

the relatives, and in his house/household. 6.5 And he was not being able to do not one power there, except for a few sick (ones), having layed on the hands, he healed/treated *them*; 6.6 and he wondered because of their unbelief/lack of faith. And Jesus was going about the villages round about, teaching.

6.7 And he calls the twelve forward, and he began to send them away two *by* two, and he gave to them authority of/over the unclean spirits; 6.8 and he charged them that they may take nothing to/for the road except a rod/staff only, not a loaf,

not a bag/knapsack, not a copper in the money-belt, 6.9 but sandals having been tied on, and put ye not on two tunics/shirts. 6.10 And he was saying to them: Where ever ye might enter into a house, abide ye there until ye would go out from there.

6.11 And what ever place might not receive ye neither might they hear from ye, be ye going out from there, shake ye off the dust under your feet in/for a testimony to/for/against them.

6.12 And going forth, they heralded/preached that they might repent, 6.13 and they were putting out/expelling many demons, and they were anointing with olive oil and were healing/treating many sick (ones). 6.14 And the king, Herod, heard, for his name became public/manifest, and he was saying that John, the (one) baptizing, has been raised out of dead (ones), and because of this the powers work in/by him. 6.15 But others were saying that he is Elias;

and others that *he is* a prophet, as one of the prophets.

6.16 But having heard, Herod was saying: This John whom I, I beheaded was raised up. 6.17 For Herod himself, having sent away, he seized John and bound him in prison because of Herodias the woman of Philip his brother, because he married her;

6.18 for John was saying to Herod: It is not lawful for you to have the woman of your brother.

6.19 And Herodias had a grudge for him and was wanting to kill him, but she was not being able; 6.20 for Herod was fearing John, having known him *to be* a just and holy man, and he was protecting him, also

αὐτόν, καὶ ἀκούσας αὐτοῦ πολλὰ ἠπόρει, καὶ ἡδέως αὐτοῦ ἤκουεν. 6.21 καὶ γενομένης ἡμέρας εὐκαίρου ὅτε Ἡρώδης τοῖς γενεσίοις αὐτοῦ δῖπνον ἐποίησεν τοῖς μεγιστᾶσιν αὐτοῦ καὶ τοῖς χιλιάρχοις καὶ τοῖς πρώτοις τῆς Γαλιλαίας,

6.22 καὶ εἰσελθούσης τῆς θυγατρὸς αὐτοῦ Ἡρωδιάδος καὶ ὀρχησαμένης, ἤρεσεν τῷ Ἡρώδῃ καὶ τοῖς συνανακειμένοις.

ὁ δὲ βασιλεὺς εἶπεν τῷ κορασίῳ, αἴτησαί με ὃ ἐὰν θέλῃς, καὶ δώσω σοι· 6.23 καὶ ὤμοσεν αὐτῇ, ὅ τι ὃ ἐάν αἰτήσῃς δώσω σοι ἕως ἡμίσους τῆς βασιλείας μου.

6.24 καὶ ἐξελθοῦσα εἶπεν τῇ μητρὶ αὐτῆς, τί αἰτήσωμαι; ἡ δὲ εἶπεν, τὴν κεφαλὴν Ἰωάννου τοῦ βαπτίζοντος.

6.25 καὶ εἰσελθοῦσα εὐθὺς μετὰ σπουδῆς πρὸς τὸν βασιλέα ᾐτήσατο λέγουσα, θέλω ἵνα ἐξαυτῆς δῷς μοι ἐπὶ πίνακι τὴν κεφαλὴν Ἰωάννου τοῦ βαπτιστοῦ. 6.26 καὶ περίλυπος γενόμενος ὁ βασιλεὺς διὰ τοὺς ὅρκους καὶ τοὺς σὺν ἀνακειμένους οὐκ ἠθέλησεν ἀθετῆσαι αὐτήν·

6.27 καὶ εὐθὺς ἀποστίλας ὁ βασιλεὺς σπεκουλάτορα ἐπέταξεν ἐνέγκε τὴν κεφαλὴν αὐτοῦ. -- 6.28 -- ἐπὶ πίνακι καὶ ἔδωκεν αὐτὴν τῷ κορασίῳ, καὶ τὸ κοράσιον ἔδωκεν αὐτὴν τῇ μητρὶ αὐτῆς.

6.29 καὶ ἀκούσαντες οἱ μαθηταὶ αὐτοῦ ἦλθον καὶ ἦραν τὸ πτῶμα αὐτοῦ καὶ ἔθηκαν αὐτὸν ἐν μνημείῳ. 6.30 καὶ συνάγονται οἱ ἀπόστολοι πρὸς τὸν Ἰησοῦν, καὶ ἀπήγγιλαν αὐτῷ πάντα ὅσα ἐποίησαν καὶ ὅσα ἐδίδαξαν.

6.31 καὶ λέγει αὐτοῖς, δεῦτε ὑμῖς αὐτοὶ κατ' ἰδίαν εἰς ἔρημον τόπον καὶ ἀναπαύεσθαι ὀλίγον.

ἦσαν γὰρ οἱ ἐρχόμενοι καὶ οἱ ὑπάγοντες πολλοί, καὶ οὐδὲ φαγεῖν εὐκαίρουν.

6.32 καὶ ἀπῆλθον ἐν πλοίῳ εἰς ἔρημον τόπον κατ' ἰδίαν. 6.33 καὶ εἶδον αὐτοὺς ὑπάγοντας καὶ ἐπέγνωσαν αὐτοὺς πολλοί, καὶ πεζῇ ἀπὸ πασῶν τῶν πόλεων συνέδραμον ἐκεῖ καὶ προῆλθον αὐτούς.

6.34 καὶ ἐξελθὼν εἶδεν ὄχλον πολὺν, καὶ ἐσπλαγχνίσθη ἐπ' αὐτοὺς ὅτι ἦσαν ὡς πρόβατα μὴ ἔχοντα ποιμένα, καὶ ἤρξατο

having heard many things from him, he was visiting/being perplexed and gladly hearing from him. 6.21 And having come a day of good time, when Herod made a dinner for his birthday festivities for his magistrates and captains and the chief (ones) of Galilee,

6.22 and from his daughter of Herodias having entered and danced, she was pleasing to Herod and to those reclining together.

And the king said to the maiden: What ever you may want to ask me, I will also give to you; 6.23 and he swore to her: What ever you might ask, I will give to you, until half of my kingdom.

6.24 And having gone out, she said to her mother: What might I ask? and the (she) said: The head of John, of the (one) baptizing.

6.25 And having gone in at once with haste to the king, she requested, saying: I want that you might give immediately to me the head of John the baptizer upon a platter. 6.26 And the king was becoming deeply grieved; he wished/wanted not to annul/abrogate her, because of the oaths and those reclining with *him*;

6.27 and the king, having sent at once, he charged an executioner to bring the head of him -- 6.28 -- upon a platter, and he gave it to the maiden, and the maiden gave it to her mother.

6.29 And having heard, his learners/pupils came and took his corpse and placed him in a tomb. 6.30 And the apostles were gathered near Jesus, and they reported to him all (things) whatever they did and whatever they taught.

6.31 And he says to them: Ye, ye come privately to a desert/desolate place and rest ye a little.

For those coming and those going were many, and they were having not time to eat.

6.32 And they went away privately by themselves in a boat to a desolate place. 6.33 And many saw them departing and they knew them, and they ran together by land/on foot from all the cities and they preceded them there.

6.34 And having come forth, he saw a much crowd, and he had compassion on them because they were as sheep not having a shepherd, and he began to teach

διδάσκιν αὐτοὺς πολλά.

6.35 καὶ ἤδη ὥρας πολλῆς γινομένης προσελθόντες αὐτῷ οἱ μαθηταὶ αὐτοῦ ἔλεγον ὅτι ἔρημός ἐστιν ὁ τόπος, καὶ ἤδη ὥρα πολλή· 6.36 ἀπόλυσον αὐτούς, ἵνα ἀπελθόντες εἰς τοὺς κύκλῳ ἀγροὺς καὶ κώμας ἀγοράσωσιν ἑαυτοῖς βρώματα τί φάγωσιν.

6.37 ὁ δὲ ἀποκριθεὶς εἶπεν αὐτοῖς, δότε αὐτοῖς ὑμεῖς φαγῖν. καὶ λέγουσιν αὐτῷ, ἀπελθόντες ἀγοράσωμεν δηναρίων διακοσίων ἄρτους καὶ δώσομεν αὐτοῖς φαγεῖν; 6.38 ὁ δὲ λέγει αὐτοῖς, πόσους ἄρτους ἔχετε; ὑπάγετε ἴδετε. καὶ γνόντες λέγουσιν, πέντε, καὶ δύο ἰχθύας.

6.39 καὶ ἐπέταξεν αὐτοῖς ἀνακλίθηναι πάντας συμπόσια συμπόσια ἐπὶ τῷ χλωρῷ χόρτῳ. 6.40 καὶ ἀνέπεσαν πρασιαὶ πρασιαὶ κατὰ ἑκατὸν καὶ κατὰ πεντήκοντα.

6.41 καὶ λαβὼν τοὺς πέντε ἄρτους καὶ τοὺς δύο ἰχθύας ἀναβλέψας εἰς τὸν οὐρανὸν εὐλόγησεν καὶ κλάσας τοὺς ἄρτους καὶ ἐδίδου τοῖς μαθηταῖς ἵνα παρατιθῶσιν αὐτοῖς, καὶ τοὺς δύο ἰχθύας ἐμέρισεν πᾶσιν. 6.42 καὶ ἔφαγον πάντες καὶ ἐχορτάσθησαν· 6.43 καὶ ἦραν κλασμάτων δώδεκα κοφίνων πληρώματα καὶ ἀπὸ τῶν δύο ἰχθύων. 6.44 καὶ ἦσαν οἱ φαγόντες ὡς πεντακισχίλιοι ἄνδρες. 6.45 καὶ εὐθὺς ἠνάγκασε τοὺς μαθητὰς αὐτοῦ ἐμβῆναι εἰς πλοῖον καὶ προάγειν εἰς τὸ πέραν πρὸς Βηθσαϊδάν, ἕως αὐτὸς ἀπολύει τὸν ὄχλον. 6.46 καὶ ἀποταξάμενος αὐτοῖς ἀπῆλθεν εἰς τὸ ὄρος προσεύξασθαι.

6.47 καὶ ὀψίας γενομένης ἦν τὸ πλοῖον ἐν μέσῳ τῆς θαλάσσης, καὶ αὐτὸς μόνος ἐπὶ τῆς γῆς. 6.48 καὶ ἰδὼν αὐτοὺς βασανιζομένους ἐν τῷ ἐλαύνειν, ἦν γὰρ ἐναντίος ὁ ἄνεμος αὐτοῖς, περὶ τετάρτην φυλακὴν τῆς νυκτὸς ἔρχεται πρὸς αὐτοὺς περιπατῶν ἐπὶ τῆς θαλάσσης· καὶ ἤθελεν παρελθεῖν αὐτούς.

6.49 οἱ δὲ ἰδόντες αὐτὸν ἐπὶ τῆς θαλάσσης περιπατοῦντα ἔδοξαν ὅτι φάντασμά ἐστιν, καὶ ἀνέκραξαν· 6.50 πάντες γὰρ

them many (things).

6.35 And from it having become of a much hour already, his learners/pupils having come near to him, they were saying: The place is a desert, and *it is* now a much hour; 6.36 you dismiss them, that having gone away into the surrounding fields and villages they might buy foods for themselves, something to eat.

6.37 But the (he) answering, he said to them: Ye, ye give for them to eat. And they say to him: Having gone away, we might buy loaves from/of two hundred denarii, and shall we give to them to eat? 6.38 And the (he) says to them: How many loaves have ye? Go ye and see. And having known, they say: Five, and two fishes.

6.39 And he enjoined upon them for all to be reclined in groups/parties upon the pale green grass. 6.40 And they reclined by groups according to/by a hundred and according to fifty.

6.41 And having taken the five loaves and the two fishes, having looked up into the sky/heaven, he blessed *them* and having broken the loaves also, he was giving to the learners/pupils that they might set *it* before them, and he divided the two dishes for all. 6.42 And they all ate and they were filled/satisfied; 6.43 and they took up of fragments twelve baskets, full (ones), and from the two fishes. 6.44 And those having eaten were about five thousand men. 6.45 And he compelled his pupils/learners to embark at once into a boat and go before to the other side to Bethsaida, until/while he, he dismisses the crowd. 6.46 And having said farewell to them, he went away to the mountain to pray.

6.47 And from it having become evening, the boat was in the midst of the sea, and he alone *was* upon the land/ground. 6.48 And having seen them being tormented in/by the (thing) to row, for the wind was contrary to/for them, about *the* fourth watch of the night, he comes to/toward them, walking upon the sea; and he was wanting to pass by them.

6.49 But the (they), having seen him walking upon the sea, they thought that he was a phantom, and they cried out. 6.50 For all saw him and they were

αὐτὸν εἶδαν καὶ ἐταράχθησαν. ὁ δὲ εὐθὺς ἐλάλησεν μετ' αὐτῶν, καὶ λέγει αὐτοῖς, θαρσεῖτε, ἐγώ εἰμι· μὴ φοβεῖσθε.

6.51 καὶ ἀνέβη πρὸς αὐτοὺς εἰς τὸ πλοῖον, καὶ ἐκόπασεν ὁ ἄνεμος. καὶ λίαν ἐν ἑαυτοῖς ἐξίσταντο, 6.52 οὐ γὰρ συνῆκαν ἐπὶ τοῖς ἄρτοις, ἀλλ' ἦν αὐτῶν ἡ καρδία πεπωρωμένη. 6.53 καὶ διαπεράσαντες ἐπὶ τὴν γῆν ἦλθον εἰς Γεννησαρὲτ καὶ προσωρμίσθησαν. 6.54 καὶ ἐξελθόντων αὐτῶν ἐκ τοῦ πλοίου εὐθὺς ἐπιγνόντες αὐτὸν 6.55 περιέδραμον ὅλην τὴν χώραν ἐκείνην καὶ ἤρξαντο ἐπὶ τοῖς κραβάττοις τοὺς κακῶς ἔχοντας περιφέρειν ὅπου ἠκούσθη ὅτι ἐστίν.

6.56 καὶ ὅπου ἂν εἰσεπορεύετο εἰς κώμας ἢ εἰς πόλις ἢ εἰς ἀγροὺς ἢ ἐν ταῖς ἀγοραῖς ἐτίθεσαν τοὺς ἀσθενοῦντας, καὶ παρεκάλουν αὐτὸν ἵνα κἂν τοῦ κρασπέδου τοῦ ἱματίου αὐτοῦ ἅψωνται· καὶ ὅσοι ἥψαντο αὐτοῦ ἐσώζοντο.

7.1 Καὶ συνάγονται πρὸς αὐτὸν οἱ Φαρισαῖοι καί τινες τῶν γραμματαίων ἐλθόντες ἀπὸ Ἱεροσολύμων 7.2 καὶ ἰδόντες τινὰς τῶν μαθητῶν αὐτοῦ ὅτι κοιναῖς χερσίν, τοῦτ' ἔστιν ἀνίπτοις, ἐσθίουσιν ἄρτον

7.3 οἱ γὰρ Φαρισαῖοι καὶ πάντες οἱ Ἰουδαῖοι ἐὰν μὴ πύκνα νίψωνται τὰς χεῖρας οὐκ ἐσθίωσιν, κρατοῦντες τὴν παράδοσιν τῶν πρεσβυτέρων, 7.4 καὶ ἀπὸ ἀγορᾶς ἐὰν μὴ ῥαπντίσωνται οὐκ ἐσθίουσιν,

καὶ ἄλλα πολλά ἐστιν ἃ παρέλαβον κρατῖν, βαπτισμοὺς ποτηρίων καὶ ξεστῶν καὶ χαλκίων

7.5 καὶ ἐπερωτῶσιν αὐτὸν οἱ Φαρισαῖοι καὶ οἱ γραμματῖς, διὰ τί οὐ περιπατοῦσιν οἱ μαθηταί σου κατὰ τὴν παράδοσιν τῶν πρεσβυτέρων, ἀλλὰ κοιναῖς χερσὶν ἐσθίουσιν τὸν ἄρτον; 7.6 ὁ δὲ εἶπεν αὐτοῖς, καλῶς ἐπροφήτευσεν Ἡσαΐας περὶ ὑμῶν τῶν ὑποκριτῶν, ὡς γέγραπται ὅτι «οὗτος ὁ λαὸς τοῖς χείλεσίν με τιμᾷ, ἡ δὲ καρδία αὐτῶν πόρρω ἀπέχει ἀπ' ἐμοῦ· 7.7 μάτην δὲ

troubled. But the (he) spoke at once with them, and he says to them: Be of good cheer, I, I am; be ye not afraid.

6.51 And he went up to/near them into the boat, and the wind abated. And they were being very much astonished in/among themselves, 6.52 for they understood not on the loaves, but the heart of them had been hardened. 6.53 And having crossed over to the land, they came to Gennesaret and they were landed. 6.54 And from them having gone forth out of the boat, having recognized him immediately, 6.55 they ran around all that country/district and they began to carry around those having *it* badly/being ill upon the beds/matts, where they heard that he is.

6.56 And where ever he was entering into villages or into cities or into fields or in the markets, they were placing those being sick, and they were beseeching him that if they might touch even the hem of his garment; and as many as touched him were being saved/delivered.

7.1 And the Pharisees gather near him, and also some of the scribes having come from Jerusalem. 7.2 And having seen some of his learners/pupils that with common/defiled hands, this is with unwashed (ones), they eat bread

-- for the Pharisees and all the Judeans, unless they might wash the hands frequently, they may not eat, holding fast the tradition of the elders, 7.4 and from markets, unless they purify by sprinkling, they eat not;

and many other (things) there are which they received to hold fast, washings/baptisms of cups and of pots and of copper/bronze utensils/vessels,

7.5 and the Pharisees and the scribes question him: Why *do* not your pupils/learners walk according to the tradition of the elders, but they eat the loaf with common/defiled hands? 7.6 And the (he) said to them: Well prophesied Isaiah concerning ye, the pretenders/hypocrites, as it has been written: THIS PEOPLE HONORS ME WITH THE LIPS, BUT THEIR HEART IS FAR AWAY FROM ME; 7.7 AND IN VAIN THEY REVERENCE ME,

σέβονταί με, διδάσκοντες διδασκαλίας ἐντάλματα ἀνθρώπων.»

7.8 ἀφέντες τὴν ἐντολὴν τοῦ θεοῦ κρατεῖτε τὴν παράδοσιν τῶν ἀνθρώπων.

7.9 καὶ ἔλεγεν αὐτοῖς, καλῶς ἀθετῖτε τὴν ἐντολὴν τοῦ θεοῦ, ἵνα τὴν παράδοσιν ὑμῶν τηρήσητε. 7.10 Μωϋσῆς γὰρ εἶπεν, «τίμα τὸν πατέρα σου καὶ τὴν μητέρα σου,» καί, « ὁ κακολογῶν πατέρα ἢ μητέρα θανάτῳ τελευτάτω»

7.11 ὑμεῖς δὲ λέγετε, ἐὰν εἴπῃ ἄνθρωπος τῷ πατρὶ ἢ τῇ μητρί, κορβᾶν, ὅ ἐστιν, δῶρον, ὃ ἐὰν ἐξ ἐμοῦ ὠφεληθῇς, 7.12 οὐκέτι ἀφίετε αὐτὸν οὐδὲν ποιῆσαι τῷ πατρὶ ἢ τῇ μητρί, 7.13 ἀκυροῦντες τὸν λόγον τοῦ θεοῦ τῇ παραδόσει ὑμῶν ᾗ παρεδώκατε· καὶ παρόμοια πολλὰ τοιαῦτα ποιεῖτε. 7.14 καὶ προσκαλεσάμενος πάλιν τὸν ὄχλον ἔλεγεν αὐτοῖς, ἀκούετέ καὶ σύνετε. 7.15 οὐδέν ἐστιν ἔξωθεν τοῦ ἀνθρώπου εἰσπορευόμενον εἰς αὐτὸν ὃ δύναται κοινῶσαι αὐτόν· ἀλλὰ τὰ ἐκ τοῦ ἀνθρώπου ἐκπορευόμενά ἐστιν τὰ κοινοῦντα τὸν ἄνθρωπον.

7.17 καὶ ὅτε εἰσῆλθον εἰς τὸν οἶκον ἀπὸ τοῦ ὄχλου, ἐπηρώτων αὐτὸν οἱ μαθηταὶ αὐτοῦ τὴν παραβολήν.

7.18 καὶ λέγει αὐτοῖς, οὕτως καὶ ὑμῖς ἀσύνετοί ἐστε; οὔπω νοεῖτε ὅτι πᾶν τὸ ἔξωθεν εἰσπορευόμενον οὐ κοίνοι τὸν ἄνθρωπον, 7.19 ὅτι οὐκ εἰσπορεύετε αὐτοῦ εἰς τὴν καρδίαν ἀλλ᾽ εἰς τὴν κοιλίαν, καὶ εἰς τὸν ἀφεδρῶνα ἐκβάλλετε; καθαρίζων πάντα τὰ βρώματα.

7.20 ἔλεγεν δὲ ὅτι τὸ ἐκ τοῦ ἀνθρώπου ἐκπορευόμενον ἐκῖνο κοινοῖ τὸν ἄνθρωπον· 7.21 ἔσωθεν γὰρ ἐκ τῆς καρδίας τῶν ἀνθρώπων οἱ διαλογισμοὶ οἱ κακοὶ ἐκπορεύονται, πορνῖαι, κλοπαί, φόνοι, 7.22 μοιχῖαι, πλεονεξίαι, πονηρίαι, δόλος, ἀσέλγια, ὀφθαλμὸς πονηρός, βλασφημία, ὑπερηφανία, ἀφροσύνη·

7.23 πάντα ταῦτα τὰ πονηρὰ ἔσωθεν ἐκπορεύεται κακεῖνα κοινοῖ τὸν ἄνθρωπον.

TEACHING TEACHINGS/DOCTRINES *which are* COMMANDS OF/ FROM MEN.

7.8 Dismissing the command from God, ye hold fast the tradition from/of the men.

7.9 And he was saying to them: Well ye reject/ annul the command from God, that ye may keep your tradition. 7.10 For Moses said: YOU HONOR YOUR FATHER AND YOUR MOTHER, and: THE (ONE) ASSERTING AGAINST/SPEAKING BAD OF FATHER OR MOTHER, LET HIM FINISH/END BY DEATH.

7.11 But ye, ye say: If a man might say to the father or to the mother: Korban, which is: A gift, what ever you might profit out of me, 7.12 ye no longer allow *for* him to do anything for the father or for the mother, 7.13 voiding the saying/word from God by/in your tradition which ye handed over; and ye do many such similar (things). 7.14 And having called the crowd near again, he was saying to them: Hear/listen ye and understand. 7.15 From outside the man/human there is nothing going into him that is able to defile him; but the (things) going forth out of the man/human are the (things) defiling the man/human.

7.17 And when they went into the house from the crowd, his learners/pupils asked him the parable.

7.18 And he says to them: So ye, ye also are misunderstanding/senseless (ones)? *Do* ye not yet understand that every thing from outside going into the man makes common/defiles not, 7.19 because it goes not into the heart of him, but into the belly, and is expelled/cast out in the privy/drain? -- cleansing all the foods.

7.20 And he was saying: The (thing) going forth out of the man/human, that (thing) defiles/makes common the man/human. 7.21 For from within, out of the heart of the men, the evil/bad reasonings/disputes go/come forth: prostitutions, thefts, murders, 7.22 adulteries, greeds, evil deeds, deceit/treachery, orgy/revelry/wantonness, an evil eye, slander/blasphemy/reviling, haughtiness/arrogance, foolishness/lack of sense;

7.23 all these evil (things) come/go forth from within/inside and these things defile/make common the

7.24 ἐκεῖθεν δὲ ἀναστὰς ἀπῆλθεν εἰς τὰ ὅρια Τύρου καὶ Σιδῶνος. καὶ εἰσελθὼν εἰς οἰκίαν οὐδένα ἠθέλησεν γνῶναι, καὶ οὐκ ἠδυνάσθη λαθεῖν·

7.25 ἀλλ᾽ εὐθὺς ἀκούσασα γυνὴ περὶ αὐτοῦ, ἧς εἶχεν τὸ θυγάτριον πνεῦμα ἀκάθαρτον, εἰσελθοῦσα προσέπεσεν πρὸς τοὺς πόδας αὐτοῦ·

7.26 ἡ δὲ γυνὴ ἦν Ἑλληνίς, Συροφοινίκισσα τῷ γένι· καὶ ἠρώτα αὐτὸν ἵνα τὸ δαιμόνιον ἐκβάλῃ ἐκ τῆς θυγατρὸς αὐτῆς.

7.27 καὶ ἔλεγεν αὐτῇ, ἄφες πρῶτον χορτασθῆναι τὰ τέκνα, οὐ γάρ ἐστιν καλὸν λαβεῖν τὸν ἄρτον τῶν τέκνων καὶ τοῖς κυναρίοις βαλεῖν.

7.28 ἡ δὲ ἀπεκρίθη καὶ λέγει αὐτῷ, ναί, κύριε, καὶ τὰ κυνάρια ἐσθίουσιν ὑποκάτω τῆς τραπέζης ἀπὸ τῶν ψιχίων τῶν παιδίων.

7.29 καὶ εἶπεν αὐτῇ, διὰ τοῦτον τὸν λόγον ὕπαγε, ἐξελήλυθεν ἐκ τῆς θυγατρός σου τὸ δαιμόνιον. 7.30 καὶ ἀπελθοῦσα εἰς τὸν οἶκον ἑαυτῆς εὗρεν τὸ παιδίον βεβλημένον ἐπὶ τὴν κλίνην καὶ τὸ δαιμόνιον ἐξεληλυθός.

7.31 καὶ πάλιν ἐξελθὼν ἐκ τῶν ὁρίων Τύρου ἦλθεν διὰ Σιδῶνος εἰς τὴν θάλασσαν τῆς Γαλιλαίας ἀνὰ μέσον τῶν ὁρίων Δεκαπόλεως.

7.32 καὶ φέρουσιν αὐτῷ κωφὸν καὶ μογιλάλον, καὶ παρακαλοῦσιν αὐτὸν ἵνα ἐπιθῇ αὐτῷ τὴν χῖρας.

7.33 καὶ ἀπολαβόμενος αὐτὸν κατ᾽ ἰδίαν ἀπὸ τοῦ ὄχλου ἔβαλεν τοὺς δακτύλους εἰς τὰ ὦτα αὐτοῦ καὶ πτύσας ἥψατο τῆς γλώσσης αὐτοῦ, 7.34 καὶ ἀναβλέψας εἰς τὸν οὐρανὸν ἐστέναξεν, καὶ λέγει αὐτῷ, Εφφαθα, ὅ ἐστιν, διανοίχθητι.

7.35 καὶ ἠνύγησαν αὐτοῦ αἱ ἀκοαί, καὶ εὐθὴς ἐλύθη ὁ δεσμὸς τῆς γλώσσης αὐτοῦ, καὶ ἐλάλει ὀρθῶς. 7.36 καὶ διεστίλατο αὐτοῖς ἵνα μηδενὶ λέγωσιν·

ὅσον δὲ αὐτοῖς διεστέλλετο, αὐτοὶ μᾶλλον περισσοτέρως ἐκήρυσσον. 7.37 καὶ ὑπερπερισσῶς ἐξεπλήσσοντο λέγοντες, καλῶς

man/human.

7.24   And having risen up, he went away from there into the borders/districts of Tyre and Sidon. And having gone into a house, he was wanting no one to know, but he was not able to ignore/be unaware;

7.25   but immediately, having heard about him, a woman of whom the daughter of her had an unclean spirit, having gone in, she fell near his feet;

7.26   but the woman was a Greek, a Syrophenician for the race/kind; and she was asking him that he might expel/put out the demon out ot her daughter.

7.27   And he was saying to her: You let/permit first the children to be filled/satisfied, for it is not good to take the loaf/bread from the children and to throw it to the dogs.

7.28   But the (she) answered and says to him: Yes, Lord, but even the dogs eat beneath the table of the fragments/crumbs of/from the children.

7.29   And he said to her: Because of this saying/word, you go; the demon has gone forth out of your daughter.   7.30 And having gone away to the house of herself, she found the child having been laid upon the couch and the demon having gone out.

7.31   And again having gone forth out of the borders of Tyre, he went through Sidon to the sea of Galilee in the midst of the borders/regions of Decapolis.

7.32   And they bring to him a deaf (one) and speaking with difficulty, and they besought him that he might place the hand on him.

7.33   And having taken him aside privately from the crowd, he put the fingers in his ears and, having spit, he touched his tongue,   7.34 and having looked up into the sky/heaven he groaned, and he says to him: Ephphatha, which is: Be you opened.

7.35   And his ears were opened, and the bond of his tongue was loosed immediately, and he spoke plainly.   7.36 And he directed/admonished them that they may tell it to no one;

but as much as he admonished to them, they were heralding/preaching it more abundantly.   7.37 And they were astounded/amazed beyond measure, saying: All

πάντα πεποίηκεν· καὶ τοὺς κωφοὺς ποιεῖ ἀκούειν καὶ ἀλάλους λαλῖν. 8.1 ἐν ἐκείναις ταῖς ἡμέραις πάλιν πολλοῦ ὄχλου ὄντος καὶ μὴ ἐχόντων τί φάγωσιν, προσκαλεσάμενος τοὺς μαθητὰς λέγει αὐτοῖς, 8.2 σπλαγχνίζομε ἐπὶ τὸν ὄχλον ὅτι ἤδη ἡμέραι τρῖς προσμένουσί μοι καὶ οὐκ ἔχουσι τί φάγωσιν· 8.3 καὶ ἐὰν ἀπολύσω αὐτοὺς νήστις εἰς οἶκον αὐτῶν, ἐκλυθήσονται ἐν τῇ ὁδῷ· καί τινες αὐτῶν ἀπὸ μακρόθεν ἥκασιν.

8.4 καὶ ἀπεκρίθησαν οἱ μαθηταὶ αὐτοῦ καὶ εἶπαν πόθεν τούτους δυνήσετέ τις ὧδε χορτάσαι ἄρτων ἐπ' ἐρημίας; 8.5 καὶ ἠρώτα αὐτούς, πόσους ἄρτους ἔχετε; οἱ δὲ εἶπαν, ἑπτά. 8.6 καὶ παραγγέλλι τῷ ὄχλῳ ἀναπεσεῖν ἐπὶ τῆς γῆς· καὶ λαβὼν τοὺς ἑπτὰ ἄρτους εὐχαριστήσας ἔκλασεν καὶ ἐδίδου τοῖς μαθηταῖς αὐτοῦ ἵνα παρατιθῶσιν καὶ παρέθηκαν τῷ ὄχλῳ. 8.7 καὶ εἶχαν ἰχεύδια ὀλίγα· καὶ εὐλογήσας αὐτὰ εἶπε καὶ ταῦτα τιθένσεν. 8.8 καὶ ἔφαγον πάντες ἐχορτάσθησαν, καὶ ἦραν τὰ περισσεύματα κλασμάτων ἑπτὰ σφυρίδας. 8.9 ἦσαν δὲ τετρακισχίλιοι. καὶ ἀπέλυσεν αὐτούς. 8.10 καὶ εὐθὺς ἐμβὰς εἰς τὸ πλοῖον μετὰ τῶν μαθητῶν αὐτοῦ ἦλθεν ὁ Ἰησοῦς εἰς τὰ μέρη Δαλμανουθά.

8.11 καὶ ἐξῆλθον οἱ Φαρισαῖοι καὶ ἤρξαντο συνζητεῖν αὐτῷ, ζητοῦντες παρ' αὐτοῦ σημῖον ἴδιν ἀπὸ τοῦ οὐρανοῦ, πιράζοντες αὐτόν.

8.12 καὶ ἀναστενάξας τῷ πνεύματι αὐτοῦ λέγει, τί ἡ γενεὰ αὕτη ζητῖ σημῖον; ἀμὴν λέγω ὑμῖν, εἰ δοθήσεται τῇ γενεᾷ ταύτῃ σημῖον. 8.13 καὶ ἀφὶς αὐτοὺς πάλιν ἐμβὰς ἀπῆλθεν εἰς τὸ πέραν.

8.14 καὶ ἐπελάθοντο λαβεῖν ἄρτους, καὶ εἰ μὴ ἕνα ἄρτον οὐκ εἶχον μεθ' ἑαυτῶν ἐν τῷ πλοίῳ.

8.15 καὶ διεστέλλετο αὐτοῖς λέγων, ὁρᾶτε, βλέπετε ἀπὸ τῆς ζύμης τῶν Φαρισαίων καὶ τῆς ζύμης Ἡρώδου.

8.16 καὶ διελογίζοντο πρὸς ἀλλήλους ὅτι ἄρτους οὐκ ἔχομεν.

(things) he has done well; he makes both the deaf (ones) to hear and (ones) without speech to speak. 8.1 Again in those days from there being a much crowd, also having not anything they might eat, having summoned the learners/pupils he says to them: 8.2 I have compassion on the crowd, because already/now three days they stay/remain with me, and they have not something to eat; 8.3 and if I might dismiss them hungry to their house, they will faint on the road/ way, and some of them have come from afar.

8.4 And the learners/pupils answered him and said: From where will anyone be able to fill these with loaves here on a desert? 8.5 And he was asking them: How many loaves have ye? And they said: Seven. 8.6 And he ordered for the crowd to recline on the land/ground; and having taken the seven loaves, giving thanks, he broke *them* and he was giving to his learners/pupils that they may set before and they set *it* before the crowd. 8.7 And they had a few small fishes; and having blessed them, he said also they will put these. 8.8 And all ate and they were filled/satisfied, and they took up the excesses, seven baskets of fragments. 8.9 And they were four thousand. And he dismissed them. 8.10 And having embarked at once in the boatwith his learners/pupils, Jesus went into the parts of Dalmanutha.

8.11 And the Pharisees came forth and began to dispute/argue with him, seeking from him to see/view a sign from the sky/heaven, testing/trying him.

8.12 And having groaned in his spirit, he says: Why seeks this generation a sign? Truly I say to ye, if a sign/*no sign* will be given to this generation. 8.13 And leaving them, again having embarked, he went away to the other side.

8.14 And they forgot to take loaves, and except *for* one loaf they had not *bread* with themselves in the boat.

8.15 And he admonished them, saying: View ye, see ye/beware ye from the leaven of the Pharisees and the leaven of Herod.

8.16 And they were reasoning/discussing to/with one another because they had not loaves.

8.17 καὶ γνοὺς ὁ Ἰησοῦς λέγει αὐτοῖς, τί διαλογίζεσθε ὅτι ἄρτους οὐκ ἔχετε; οὔπω νοεῖτε οὐδὲ συνίετε; πεπωρωμένην ἔχετε τὴν καρδίαν ὑμῶν;

8.18 ὀφθαλμοὺς ἔχοντες οὐ βλέπεται καὶ ὦτα ἔχοντες οὐκ ἀκούετε; καὶ οὐ μνημονεύετε, 8.19 ὅτε τοὺς πέντε ἄρτους ἔκλασα εἰς τοὺς πεντακισχιλίους, καὶ πόσους κοφίνους κλασμάτων πλήρις ἤρατε; λέγουσιν, δώδεκα.

8.20 ὅτε καὶ τοὺς ἑπτὰ ἄρτους εἰς τοὺς τετρακισχιλίους, πόσων σπυρίδων πληρώματα κλασμάτων ἤρατε; καὶ λέγουσιν, ἑπτά. 8.21 καὶ ἔλεγεν αὐτοῖς, οὔπω συνίετε; 8.22 καὶ ἔρχονται εἰς Βηθσαϊδάν. καὶ φέρουσιν αὐτῷ τυφλὸν καὶ παρακαλοῦσιν αὐτὸν ἵνα αὐτοῦ ἅψηται. 8.23 καὶ ἐπιλαβόμενος τῆς χειρὸς τοῦ τυφλοῦ ἐξήνεγκεν αὐτὸν ἔξω τῆς κώμης, καὶ πτύσας εἰς τὰ ὄμματα αὐτοῦ, ἐπιθεὶς τὰς χῖρας αὐτῷ, ἐπηρώτα αὐτόν, εἴ τι βλέπει; 8.24 καὶ ἀναβλέψας εἶπεν, βλέπω τοὺς ἀνθρώπους, ὅτι ὡς δένδρα ὁρῶ περιπατοῦντας. 8.25 εἶτα πάλιν ἐπέθηκεν τὰς χῖρας ἐπὶ τοὺς ὀφθαλμοὺς αὐτοῦ, καὶ διέβλεψεν, καὶ ἀπεκατέστη, καὶ ἐνέβλεπεν τηλαυγῶς ἅπαντα.

8.26 καὶ ἀπέστιλεν εἰς τὸν οἶκον αὐτὸν αὐτοῦ λέγων, μηδὲ εἰς τὴν κώμην εἰσέλθῃς. 8.27 καὶ ἐξῆλθεν ὁ Ἰησοῦς καὶ οἱ μαθηταὶ αὐτοῦ εἰς τὰς κώμας Καισαρείας τῆς Φιλίππου· καὶ ἐν τῇ ὁδῷ ἐπηρώτα τοὺς μαθητὰς αὐτοῦ λέγων αὐτοῖς, τίνα με λέγουσιν οἱ ἄνθρωποι εἶναι;

8.28 οἱ δὲ εἶπαν αὐτῷ λέγοντες ὅτι Ἰωάννην τὸν βαπτιστήν, καὶ ἄλλοι, Ἡλείαν, ἄλλοι δὲ ὅτι εἷς τῶν προφητῶν.

8.29 καὶ αὐτὸς ἐπηρώτα αὐτούς, ὑμεῖς δὲ τίνα με λέγεται εἶναι; ἀποκριθεὶς δὲ ὁ Πέτρος λέγει αὐτῷ, σὺ εἶ ὁ χριστός ὁ υἱὸς τοῦ θεοῦ. 8.30 καὶ ἐπετίμησεν αὐτοῖς ἵνα μηδενὶ λέγωσιν περὶ αὐτοῦ.

8.31 καὶ ἤρξατο διδάσκιν αὐτοὺς ὅτι δεῖ τὸν υἱὸν τοῦ ἀνθρώπου πολλὰ παθεῖν καὶ ἀποδοκιμασθῆναι ὑπὸ τῶν πρεσβυτέρων καὶ τῶν ἀρχιερέων καὶ τῶν γραμματέων καὶ

8.17 And knowing, Jesus says to them: Why *do* ye reason/debate because ye have not loaves? Perceive ye not yet, neither ye understand? Have ye completely hardened your heart?

8.18 Having eyes see ye not, and having ears hear ye not? And remember ye not, 8.19 when I broke the five loaves to/for the five thousand, and how many baskets ye took up full of fragments? They say to him: Twelve.

8.20 When also the seven loaves to/for the four thousand, ye took up fullnesses of how many baskets of fragments? And they say: Seven. 8.21 And he was saying to them: *Do* ye not yet understand? 8.22 And they went into Bethsaida. And they bring a blind (one) to him and they beseech him that he might touch him. 8.23 And having taken hold of the hand of the blind (one), he led him forth outside the village, and having spit in his eyes, having layed the hands on him, he was asking him if he sees anything? 8.24 And having looked up, he said: I see the men, because I behold *them* as trees walking. 8.25 Then he again put the hands upon his eyes, and he opened the eyes/saw clearly, and he was restored, and he was seeing all things plainly.

8.26 And he sent him to his house, saying: And you might not go into the village. 8.27 And Jesus and his learners/pupils went out into the villages of Caesarea, the (one) of Philip; and on the road, he was questioning his pupils/learners, saying to them: Whom *do* the men say *for* me to be?

8.28 And they said to him, saying: John the baptizer, and others: Elias, and others: One of the prophets.

8.29 And he, he was asking them: But ye, whom *do* ye say *for* me to be? And answering, Peter says to him: You, you are the anointed (one), the son of God. 8.30 And he warned them that they might say it to no one about him.

8.31 And he began to teach them that it is necessary *for* the son of the man to suffer many (things), and to be rejected by the elders and the high priests and the scribes, and to be killed, and

ἀποκτανθῆναι καὶ μετὰ τρεῖς ἡμέρας ἀναστῆναι· 8.32 καὶ παρρησίᾳ τὸν λόγον ἐλάλει.

καὶ προσλαβόμενος αὐτὸν ὁ Πέτρος ἤρξατο ἐπιτιμᾶν αὐτῷ.

8.33 ὁ δὲ ἐπιστραφὶς καὶ ἰδὼν τοὺς μαθητὰς αὐτοῦ ἐπετίμησεν Πέτρῳ καὶ λέγει, ὕπαγε ὀπίσω μου, Σατανᾶ, ὅτι οὐ φρονεῖς τὰ τοῦ θεοῦ ἀλλὰ τὰ τῶν ἀνθρώπων. 8.34 καὶ προσκαλεσάμενος τὸν ὄχλον σὺν τοῖς μαθηταῖς αὐτοῦ εἶπεν αὐτοῖς, εἴ τις θέλει ὀπίσω μου ἐλθεῖν, ἀπαρνησάσθω ἑαυτὸν καὶ ἀράτω τὸν σταυρὸν αὐτοῦ καὶ ἀκολουθίτω μοι.

8.35 ὃς γὰρ ἐὰν θέλῃ τὴν ψυχὴν αὐτοῦ σῶσαι ἀπολέσει αὐτήν· ὃς δ' ἂν ἀπολέσει τὴν ψυχὴν αὐτοῦ ἕνεκεν ἐμοῦ καὶ τοῦ εὐαγγελίου σώσει αὐτήν.

8.36 τί γὰρ ὠφελῖ ἄνθρωπον κερδῆσαι τὸν κόσμον ὅλον καὶ ζημιωθῆναι τὴν ψυχὴν αὐτοῦ;

8.37 τί γὰρ δοῖ ἄνθρωπος ἀντάλλαγμα τῆς ψυχῆς αὐτοῦ;

8.38 ὃς γὰρ ἐὰν ἐπαισχυνθῇ με καὶ τοὺς ἐμοὺς λόγους ἐν τῇ γενεᾷ ταύτῃ τῇ μοιχαλίδι καὶ ἁμαρτωλῷ, καὶ ὁ υἱὸς τοῦ ἀνθρώπου ἐπαισχυνθήσετε αὐτὸν ὅταν ἔλθη ἐν τῇ δόξῃ τοῦ πατρὸς αὐτοῦ μετὰ τῶν ἀγγέλων τῶν ἁγίων.

9.1 Καὶ ἔλεγεν αὐτοῖς, ἀμὴν λέγω ὑμῖν ὅτι εἰσίν τινες τῶν ὧδε ἑστώτων οἵτινες οὐ μὴ γεύσωνται θανάτου ἕως ἂν ἴδωσιν τὴν βασιλίαν τοῦ θεοῦ ἐληλυθυῖαν ἐν δυνάμει.

9.2 καὶ μετὰ ἡμέρας ἓξ παραλαμβάνει ὁ Ἰησοῦς τὸν Πέτρον καὶ τὸν Ἰάκωβον καὶ τὸν Ἰωάννην, καὶ ἀναφέρι αὐτοὺς εἰς ὄρος ὑψηλὸν λίαν κατ' ἰδίαν μόνους. καὶ μετεμορφώθη ἔμπροσθεν αὐτῶν, 9.3 καὶ τὰ ἱμάτια αὐτοῦ ἐγένετο στίλβοντα λευκὰ λίαν οἷα γναφεὺς ἐπὶ τῆς γῆς οὐ δύναται οὕτως λευκᾶναι. 9.4 καὶ ὤφθη αὐτοῖς Ἠλίας σὺν Μωϋσῆ, καὶ ἦσαν λαλοῦντες τῷ Ἰησοῦ.

9.5 καὶ ἀποκριθεὶς ὁ Πέτρος λέγει τῷ Ἰησοῦ, ῥαββεί, καλόν ἐστιν ἡμᾶς ὧδε εἶναι, καὶ ποιήσωμεν τρεῖς σκηνάς, σοὶ μίαν καὶ Μωϋσεῖ μίαν καὶ Ἠλίᾳ μίαν. 9.6 οὐ γὰρ ἤδι τί ἀπεκριθῆ, ἔκφοβοι γὰρ ἐγένοντο.

after three days to rise. 8.32 And he spoke the saying/word plainly.

But Peter, having taken him aside, he began to rebuke him.

8.33 But the (he), having turned around and having seen his learners/pupils, he rebuked Peter and says: Depart you behind me, Satan, because you regard not the (things) of God but the (things) of the men. 8.34 And having summoned the crowd with his learners/pupils, he said to them: If anyone wants to come after/behind me, let him deny himself and let him take up the cross of himself and let him follow with me.

8.35 For who ever may want to save his soul/life will lose it; but who ever loses his soul/life on account of me and the good message/gospel will save it.

8.36 For what profits/benefits a man/human to gain the whole world and *for* his soul/life to be lost?

8.37 For what might a man/human give an exchange of his soul/life?

8.38 For who ever might be ashamed of me and my sayings/words in this adulterous and sinful generation, also the son of the man will be ashamed of him, whenever he might come in/by the glory/reputation of his father with all the holy messengers/angels.

9.1 And he was saying to them: Truly I say to ye that there are some of those standing here who by no means might taste of death until they might see the kingdom of God having been come in/with/by power.

9.2 And after six days, Jesus takes along Peter and James and John, and he leads/brings them up to a very high mountain privately, only *them*. And he was transformed/changed in form in front of them, 9.3 and his garments became white, shining exceedingly such as a bleacher/cleaner/fuller upon the earth is not able to whiten. 9.4 And Elias was made visible to them with Moses, and they were speaking to/with Jesus.

9.5 And answering Peter says to Jesus: Rabbi, it is good *for* us to be here, and we might make three tents/shrines, for you one and for Moses one and for Elias one. 9.6 For he had not known what he answered, for they became terrified.

92

9.7 καὶ ἐγένετο νεφέλη ἐπεισκιάζουσα αὐτοῖς, καὶ ἐγένετο ἐκ τῆς νεφέλης φωνή, οὗτός ἐστιν ὁ υἱός μου ὁ ἀγαπητός, ἀκούετε αὐτοῦ.

9.8 καὶ ἐξάπινα περιβλεψάμενοι οὐκέτι οὐδένα εἶδον εἰ μὴ τὸν Ἰησοῦν μόνον μεθ' ἑαυτῶν. 9.9 καὶ καταβαινόντων αὐτῶν ἀπὸ τοῦ ὄρους διεστίλατο αὐτοῖς ἵνα μηδενὶ ἃ εἶδον διηγήσωνται, εἰ μὴ ὅταν ὁ υἱὸς τοῦ ἀνθρώπου ἐκ νεκρῶν ἀναστῇ. 9.10 καὶ τὸν λόγον ἐκράτησαν πρὸς ἑαυτοὺς συνζητοῦντες τί ἐστιν τὸ ἐκ νεκρῶν ἀναστῆναι.

9.11 καὶ ἐπηρώτων αὐτὸν λέγοντες, ὅτι λέγουσιν οἱ Φαρισαῖοι καὶ οἱ γραμματῖς ὅτι Ἡλίαν δῖ ἐλθεῖν πρῶτον;

9.12 ὁ δὲ ἔφη αὐτοῖς, Ἡλίας μὲν ἐλθὼν πρῶτον ἀποκαθιστάνι πάντα, καὶ πῶς γέγραπται ἐπὶ τὸν υἱὸν τοῦ ἀνθρώπου ἵνα πολλὰ πάθῃ καὶ ἐξουδενηθῇ; 9.13 ἀλλὰ λέγω ὑμῖν ὅτι καὶ Ἡλίας ἐλήλυθεν, καὶ ἐποίησαν αὐτῷ ὅσα ἤθελον, καθὼς γέγραπτε ἐπ' αὐτόν.

9.14 καὶ ἐλθόντες πρὸς τοὺς μαθητὰς εἶδον ὄχλον πολὺν περὶ αὐτοὺς καὶ γραμματεῖς συνζητοῦντας πρὸς αὐτούς. 9.15 καὶ εὐθὺς πᾶς ὁ ὄχλος ἰδόντες αὐτὸν ἐξεθαμβήθησαν, καὶ προστρέχοντες ἠσπάζοντο αὐτόν.

9.16 καὶ ἐπηρώτησεν αὐτούς, τί συνζητεῖτε πρὸς αὐτούς; 9.17 καὶ ἀπεκρίθη αὐτῷ εἷς ἐκ τοῦ ὄχλου, διδάσκαλε, ἤνεγκα τὸν υἱόν μου πρὸς σέ, ἔχοντα πνεῦμα ἄλαλον· 9.18 καὶ ὅπου ἐὰν αὐτὸν καταλάβῃ ῥήσσει, καὶ ἀφρίζει καὶ τρίζει τοὺς ὀδόντας καὶ ξηραίνεται· καὶ εἶπα τοῖς μαθηταῖς σου ἵνα αὐτὸ ἐκβάλωσι, καὶ οὐκ ἴσχυσαν.

9.19 ὁ δὲ ἀποκριθεὶς αὐτοῖς λέγει, ὦ γενεὰ ἄπιστος, ἕως πότε πρὸς ὑμᾶς ἔσομαι; ἕως πότε ἀνέξομαι ὑμῶν; φέρετε αὐτὸν πρός ἐμέ. 9.20 καὶ ἤνεγκαν αὐτὸν πρὸς αὐτόν.

καὶ ἰδὼν αὐτὸν τὸ πνεῦμα εὐθὺς συνεσπάραξεν αὐτόν, καὶ πεσὼν ἐπὶ τῆς γῆς ἐκυλίετο ἀφρίζων.

9.21 καὶ ἐπηρώτησεν τὸν πατέρα αὐτοῦ, πόσος χρόνος

9. 7   And there became a cloud overshadowing them, and there became a voice out of the cloud: This (one) is my beloved son, hear ye from him.

9. 8   And suddenly, having looked around, they no longer saw no one except Jesus, alone with himself.

9. 9 And of them coming down from the mountain, he ordered them   that   they should relate to no one (things) which they saw, except whenever the son of the man might rise out of dead (ones).   9. 10 And they held fast the saying to themselves, seeking/discussing what is the (thing) to arise out of dead (ones).

9. 11   And they were questioning him, saying: Because *why do* the Pharisees and the scribes say that it is necessary *for* Elias to come first?

9. 12   And the (he) said to them: Elias indeed, having   come first, will   restore/reestablish all (things), and how has it been written upon/for the son of the man that he should suffer many (things)/much and to be despised/contemned?   9. 13 But I   say to ye that Elias has indeed come, and they did to him what they were wanting, as it has been written on him.

9. 14   And having come near/to the learners/pupils, they saw a much crowd around them, and/also scribes arguing/debating to/with them.   9. 15 And having seen him immediately, all the crowd were astonished, and running near, they were greeting him.

9. 16   And he questioned them: Why/what argue/debate ye to/with them?   9. 17   And one out of the crowd answered to him: Teacher, I brought my son to you, having a dumb/speechless spirit;   9. 18 and where ever it might overtake him, he convulses and he froths and grinds the teeth and he is dried up/withered;   and we spoke to your pupils/learners that they might expel it/might put it out, and they could not.

9. 19   And the (he), answering to them, says: O generation without faith/belief, until when shall I be with/near ye? Until when shall I endure from ye? Ye bring him to me.   9. 20 And they brought him to him.

And having seen him, the spirit immediately tore him to and fro, and having fallen upon the ground/ earth he was wallowing, foaming/frothing.

9. 21   And he questioned his father: How long is

ἐστὶν ὡς τοῦτο γέγονεν αὐτῷ; ὁ δὲ εἶπεν, ἐκ παιδιόθεν· 9.22 καὶ πολλάκις καὶ εἰς πῦρ αὐτὸν ἔβαλεν καὶ εἰς ὕδατα ἵνα ἀπολέσῃ αὐτόν· ἀλλὰ εἴ τι δύνῃ, βοήθησον ἡμῖν σπλαγχνισθεὶς ἐφ' ἡμᾶς.

9.23 ὁ δὲ Ἰησοῦς εἶπεν αὐτῷ, τὸ εἰ δύνῃ πάντα δυνατὰ τῷ πιστεύοντι. 9.24 εὐθὺς κράξας ὁ πατὴρ τοῦ παιδίου ἔλεγεν, πιστεύω· βοήθει μου τῇ ἀπιστίᾳ.

9.25 ἰδὼν δὲ ὁ Ἰησοῦς ὅτι ἐπισυντρέχει ὄχλος ἐπετίμησεν τῷ πνεύματι τῷ ἀκαθάρτῳ λέγων αὐτῷ, τὸ ἄλαλον καὶ κωφὸν πνεῦμα, ἐγὼ ἐπιτάσσω σοι, ἔξελθε ἐξ αὐτοῦ καὶ μηκέτι εἰσέλθῃς εἰς αὐτόν. 9.26 καὶ κράξας καὶ πολλὰ σπαράξας αὐτὸν ἐξῆλθεν·

καὶ ἐγένετο ὡσεὶ νεκρός, ὥστε τοὺς πολλοὺς λέγειν ὅτι ἀπέθανεν.

9.27 ὁ δὲ Ἰησοῦς κρατήσας τῆς χιρὸς αὐτοῦ ἤγειρεν αὐτόν, καὶ ἀνέστη.

9.28 καὶ εἰσελθόντος αὐτοῦ εἰς οἶκον οἱ μαθηταὶ αὐτοῦ κατ' ἰδίαν ἐπηρώτων αὐτόν, ὅτι ἡμῖς οὐκ ἠδυνήθημεν ἐκβαλεῖν αὐτό;

9.29 καὶ εἶπεν αὐτοῖς, τοῦτο τὸ γένος ἐν οὐδενὶ δύνατε ἐξελθεῖν εἰ μὴ ἐν προσευχῇ.

9.30 κἀκεῖθεν ἐξελθόντες παρεπορεύοντο διὰ τῆς Γαλιλαίας, καὶ οὐκ ἤθελεν ἵνα τις γνοῖ· 9.31 ἐδίδασκεν γὰρ τοὺς μαθητὰς αὐτοῦ καὶ ἔλεγεν αὐτοῖς ὅτι ὁ υἱὸς τοῦ ἀνθρώπου παραδίδοται εἰς χῖρας ἀνθρώπων, καὶ ἀποκτενοῦσιν αὐτόν, καὶ ἀποκτανθεὶς μετὰ τρῖς ἡμέρας ἀναστήσεται.

9.32 οἱ δὲ ἠγνόουν τὸ ῥῆμα, καὶ ἐφοβοῦντο αὐτὸν ἐπερωτῆσαι.

9.33 καὶ ἦλθον εἰς Καφαρναούμ. καὶ ἐν τῇ οἰκίᾳ γενόμενος ἐπηρώτα αὐτούς, τί ἐν τῇ ὁδῷ διελογίζεσθε;

9.34 οἱ δὲ ἐσιώπων, πρὸς ἀλλήλους γὰρ διελέχθησαν ἐν τῇ ὁδῷ τίς μείζων ἐστίν.

9.35 καὶ καθίσας ἐφώνησεν τοὺς δώδεκα καὶ λέγει αὐτοῖς,

it since this (thing) has happened to him? And the (he) said: From childhood; 9.22 and often it threw him both into fire and into waters that it might destroy him; but if something you are able, you help us, having compassion on us.

9.23 And Jesus said to him: The thing, "If you are able"-- All (things) are possible/able to the (one) believing. 9.24 Having cried out at once, the father of the child was saying: I believe; you help from me for the distrust/lack of faith.

9.25 And Jesus, having seen that a crowd is running together, he rebuked the unclean spirit, saying to it: The speechless and deaf spirit, I, I order to you: Come forth out of him and no longer might you enter into him. 9.26 Both having cried out and having torn/convulsed him much, it came out;

and he became like a dead (one), so as *for* the many to say that he died.

9.27 But Jesus, having taken hold of his hand, raised him up, and he stood up.

9.28 And from him going into a house, his learners/pupils were questioning him privately: For what reason were we, we not able to expel it/put it out?

9.29 And he said to them: This kind is able to come out by nothing except by prayer.

9.30 And having gone forth from there, they were passing through Galilee, and he was not wanting that anyone might know; 9.31 for he was teaching his learners/pupils and he was saying to them that the son of the man is delivered over/betrayed into hands of men, and they will kill him, and having been killed, he will stand up/arise after three days.

9.32 But the (they) were not perceiving the word/rhetoric, and they were being afraid to question him.

9.33 And they went into Capernaum. And having become at/in the house, he was asking them: What were ye discussing on the road?

9.34 But the (they) were being silent, for they discussed/debated to/with one another on the road: Who is greater.

9.35 And having sat *down* he called the twelve

εἴ τις θέλει πρῶτος εἶναι ἔσται πάντων ἔσχατος καὶ πάντων διάκονος.

9.36 καὶ λαβὼν παιδίον ἔστησεν αὐτὸ ἐν μέσῳ αὐτῶν καὶ ἐναγκαλισάμενος αὐτὸ εἶπεν αὐτοῖς, 9.37 ὃς ἂν ἓν τῶν παιδίων τούτων δέξηται ἐπὶ τῷ ὀνόματί μου, ἐμὲ δέχεται· καὶ ὃς ἐμὲ δέχετε, οὐκ ἐμὲ δέχετε ἀλλὰ τὸν ἀποστίλαντά με.

9.38 ἔφη αὐτῷ ὁ Ἰωάννης, διδάσκαλε, εἴδομέν τινα ἐν τῷ ὀνόματί σου ἐκβάλλοντα δαιμόνια, καὶ ἐκωλύομεν αὐτόν, ὅτι οὐκ ἠκολούθει ἡμῖν.

9.39 ὁ δὲ Ἰησοῦς εἶπεν, μὴ κωλύετε αὐτόν, οὐδὶς γάρ ἐστιν ὃς ποιήσει δύναμιν ἐπὶ τῷ ὀνόματί μου καὶ δυνήσετε ταχὺ κακολογῆσαί με· 9.40 ὃς γὰρ οὐκ ἔστιν καθ᾽ ἡμῶν, ὑπὲρ ἡμῶν ἐστιν.

9.41 ὃς γὰρ ἐὰν ποτίσῃ ὑμᾶς ποτήριον ὕδατος ἐν ὀνόματί μου ὅτι ἐμὸν χριστοῦ ἐσται, ἀμὴν λέγω ὑμῖν ὅτι οὐ μὴ ἀπολέσῃ τὸν μισθὸν αὐτοῦ.

9.42 καὶ ὃς ἂν σκανδαλίσῃ ἕνα τῶν μικρῶν τούτων τῶν πιστευόντων, καλόν ἐστιν αὐτῷ μᾶλλον εἰ περίκιται μύλος ὀνικὸς περὶ τὸν τράχηλον αὐτοῦ καὶ βέβλητε εἰς τὴν θάλασσαν. 9.43 καὶ ἐὰν σκανδαλίσῃ σε ἡ χείρ σου, ἀπόκοψον αὐτήν· καλόν ἐστίν σε κυλλὸν εἰσελθεῖν εἰς τὴν ζωὴν ἢ τὰς δύο χεῖρας ἔχοντα ἀπελθεῖν εἰς τὴν γέενναν, εἰς τὸ πῦρ τὸ ἄσβεστον.

9.45 καὶ ἐὰν ὁ πούς σου σκανδαλίζει σε, ἀπόκοψον αὐτόν· καλόν ἐστίν σε εἰς τὴν ζωὴν εἰσελθεῖν κυλλὸν ἢ χωλὸν ἢ τοὺς δύο πόδας ἔχοντα εἰς τὴν γέενναν βληθῆναι. 9.47 καὶ ἐὰν ὁ ὀφθαλμός σου σκανδαλίζῃ σε, ἔκβαλε αὐτόν· καλόν σέ ἐστιν μονόφθαλμον εἰσελθῖν εἰς τὴν βασιλείαν τοῦ θεοῦ ἢ δύο ὀφθαλμοὺς ἔχοντα βληθῆναι εἰς τὴν γέενναν, 9.48 ὅπου ὁ σκώληξ αὐτῶν οὐ τελευτᾷ καὶ τὸ πῦρ οὐ σβέννυται· 9.49 πᾶς γὰρ ἐν πυρὶ ἁλισθήσεται.

9.50 καλὸν τὸ ἅλας· ἐὰν δὲ τὸ ἅλας ἄναλον γένηται, ἐν τίνι αὐτὸ ἀρτύσετε; ἔχετε ἐν ἑαυτοῖς ἅλα, καὶ εἰρηνεύετε ἐν

and he says to them: If anyone/someone wants to be first, he will be last of all and a waiter/servant of all.

9.36 And having taken a little child, he stood/ put it in the midst of them, and having taken it in his arms, he said to them: 9.37 Who ever might receive/accept one of these children on my name, he receives me; and *the one* who receives me receives not me, but the (one) having sent me.

9.38 John said/spoke to him: Teacher, we saw a certain (one)/someone expelling demons in your name, and we were hindering/forbidding him, because he was not following with us.

9.39 But Jesus said: forbid ye not him, for no one who will do/make a power on my name is also able quickly/soon to speak bad of me; 9.40 for *the one* who is not against us, he is in our behalf.

9.41 For who ever might give drink to ye, a cup of water in my name, because ye are of my anointing, truly I say to ye that by no means might he lose his reward/wages.

9.42 And who ever might cause to stumble one of these little (ones), of those believing, it is more good for him if an ass-powered millstone be laid around his neck and he have been thrown into the sea. 9.43 And if your hand might cause you to stumble, cut it off; it is good *for* you to go in/to enter into the life crippled than, having two hands, to go away into the hell, into the unquenchable fire.

9.45 And if your foot might cause you to stumble, cut it off; it is good *for* you to go into the life crippled or lame than, having the two feet, to be thrown into the hell. 9.47 And if your eye might cause you to stumble, throw it out; it is good *for* you to go into the kingdom of God one-eyed than having two eyes to be thrown into the hell, 9.48 where their worm ends/dies not and the fire is not extinguished; 9.49 for every/each (one) will be salted/seasoned in/by fire;

9.50 the salt *is* good; but if the salt might become without salt/unsalty, by what will it be salted? Hold/have ye salt among yourselves, and be ye at

ἀλλήλοις.

10.1 Καὶ ἐκεῖθεν ἀναστὰς ἔρχεται εἰς τὰ ὅρια τῆς Ἰουδαίας καὶ πέραν τοῦ Ἰορδάνου, καὶ συνπορεύονται πάλιν ὄχλοι πρὸς αὐτόν, καὶ ὡς εἰώθει πάλιν ἐδέδασκεν αὐτούς. 10.2 καὶ προσελθόντες οἱ Φαρισαῖοι ἐπηρώτων αὐτὸν εἰ ἔξεστιν ἀνδρὶ γυναῖκα ἀπολῦσαι, πιράζοντες αὐτόν. 10.3 ὁ δὲ ἀποκριθεὶς εἶπεν αὐτοῖς, τί ὑμῖν ἐνετείλατο Μωϋσῆς;

10.4 οἱ δὲ εἶπαν, ἐπέτρεψεν Μωϋσῆς «βιβλίον ἀποστασίου γράψαι καὶ ἀπολῦσαι.»

10.5 ὁ δὲ Ἰησοῦς εἶπεν αὐτοῖς, πρὸς τὴν σκληροκαρδίαν ὑμῶν ἔγραψεν ὑμῖν τὴν ἐντολὴν ταύτην. 10.6 ἀπὸ δὲ ἀρχῆς κτίσεως «ἄρσεν καὶ θῆλυ ἐποίησεν αὐτούς· 10.7 ἕνεκεν τούτου καταλίψι ἀνθρώπων τὸν πατέρα αὐτοῦ καὶ τὴν μητέρα, 10.8 καὶ ἔσονται οἱ δύο εἰς σάρκα μίαν» ὥστε οὐκέτι εἰσὶν δύο ἀλλὰ σάρξ μία. 10.9 ὃ οὖν ὁ θεὸς συνέζευξεν ἄνθρωπος μὴ χωριζέτω.

10.10 καὶ εἰς τὴν οἰκίαν πάλιν οἱ μαθηταὶ περὶ τούτων ἐπηρώτων αὐτόν.

10.11 καὶ λέγει αὐτοῖς, ὃς ἂν ἀπολύσῃ τὴν γυναῖκα αὐτοῦ καὶ γαμήσῃ ἄλλην μοιχᾶτε ἐπ’ αὐτήν, 10.12 καὶ ἐὰν αὐτὴ ἀπολύσασα τὸν ἄνδρα αὐτῆς γαμήσῃ ἄλλον μοιχᾶται.

10.13 καὶ προσέφερον αὐτῷ παιδία ἵνα αὐτῶν ἅψηται· οἱ δὲ μαθηταὶ ἐπετίμησαν αὐτοῖς. 10.14 ἰδὼν δὲ ὁ Ἰησοῦς ἠγανάκτησεν καὶ εἶπεν αὐτοῖς, ἄφετε τὰ παιδία ἔρχεσθαι πρός με, καὶ μὴ κωλύετε αὐτά, τῶν γὰρ τοιούτων ἐστὶν ἡ βασιλία τοῦ θεοῦ. 10.15 ἀμὴν λέγω ὑμῖν, ὃς ἂν μὴ δέξηται τὴν βασιλίαν τοῦ θεοῦ ὡς παιδίον, οὐ μὴ εἰσέλθῃ εἰς αὐτήν.

10.16 καὶ ἐναγκαλισάμενος αὐτὰ κατευλόγει τιθεὶς τὰς χῖρας ἐπ’ αὐτά. 10.17 καὶ ἐκπορευομένου αὐτοῦ εἰς ὁδὸν προσδραμὼν εἷς καὶ γονυπετήσας αὐτὸν ἐπηρώτα αὐτόν, διδάσκαλε ἀγαθέ, τί ποιήσω ἵνα ζωὴν αἰώνιον κληρονομήσω;

10.18 ὁ δὲ Ἰησοῦς εἶπεν αὐτῷ, τί με λέγεις ἀγαθόν; οὐδεὶς

peace in/with one another.

10.1 And having rose up, he goes from there into the boundaries of Judea and beyond the Jordan, and again crowds accompany/go together with/near him, and as he is accustomed, again he was teaching them. 10.2 And having come near, the Pharisees were questioning him if it is lawful for a man to dismiss/release a woman, testing/trying him. 10.3 But the (he) answering, he said to them: What commanded Moses to/for ye?

10.4 And the (they) said: Moses permitted TO WRITE A SCROLL OF DIVORCE AND TO DISMISS/RELEASE.

10.5 And Jesus said to them: Toward/to your hardheartedness he wrote this command for ye. 10.6 But from the beginning of creation HE MADE THEM MALE AND FEMALE; 10.7 ON ACCOUNT OF THIS A MAN/HUMAN WILL LEAVE HIS FATHER AND THE MOTHER, 10.8 AND THE TWO WILL BE ONE IN FLESH; so that no longer are they two but one flesh. 10.9 Therefore, what God yoked together let not a man separate.

10.10 And in the house, again the learners/pupils were asking him about these (things).

10.11 And he says to them: Who ever might/would release/dismiss his woman and might marry another, he *does* adultery to/against her, 10.12 and if ever she, having released/dismissed her man, might/would marry another, she *does* adultery.

10.13 And they were bringing children near to him in order that he might touch them; but the pupils/learners rebuked them. 10.14 But having seen, Jesus was angered and he said to them: Let/permit ye the children to come near/to me, ye forbid not them, for of such (ones) is the kingdom of God. 10.15 Truly I say to ye, who ever might not receive/take the kingdom of God as a child, by no means might he go in/enter into it.

10.16 And having embraced (them) in his arms, he was blessing them, placing/laying the hands on them. 10.17 And from him going out into the road, one having run and having knelt *to* him, was asking him: Good teacher, what might I do that I might inherit everlasting life?

10.18 And Jesus said to him: Why *do* you call me

ἀγαθὸς εἰ μὴ εἷς ὁ θεός.

10.19 τὰς ἐντολὰς οἶδας· «μὴ φονεύσῃς, μὴ μοιχεύσῃς, μὴ κλέψῃς, μὴ ψευδομαρτυρήσῃς,» μὴ ἀποστερήσῃς, «τίμα τὸν πατέρα σου καὶ τὴν μητέρα.» 10.20 ὁ δὲ ἔφη αὐτῷ, διδάσκαλε, ταῦτα πάντα ἐφυλαξάμην ἐκ νεότητός μου. 10.21 ὁ δὲ Ἰησοῦς ἐμβλέψας αὐτῷ ἠγάπησεν αὐτὸν καὶ εἶπεν αὐτῷ, ἐτι ἕν σε ὑστερῖ· ὕπαγε ὅσα ἔχεις πώλησον καὶ δὸς τοῖς πτωχοῖς, καὶ ἕξεις θησαυρὸν ἐν οὐρανῷ, καὶ δεῦρο ἀκολούθι μοι.

10.22 ὁ δὲ στυγνάσας ἐπὶ τῷ λόγῳ ἀπῆλθεν λυπούμενος, ἦν γὰρ ἔχων κτήματα πολλά. 10.23 καὶ περιβλεψάμενος ὁ Ἰησοῦς ἔλεγεν τοῖς μαθηταῖς αὐτοῦ, πῶς δυσκόλως οἱ τὰ χρήματα ἔχοντες εἰς τὴν βασιλίαν τοῦ θεοῦ εἰσελεύσοντε. 10.24 οἱ δὲ μαθηταὶ ἐθαμβοῦντο ἐπὶ τοῖς λόγοις αὐτοῦ.

ὁ δὲ Ἰησοῦς πάλιν ἀποκριθεὶς λέγει αὐτοῖς, τέκνα, πῶς δύσκολόν ἐστιν εἰς τὴν βασιλείαν τοῦ θεοῦ εἰσελθεῖν· 10.25 εὐκοπώτερόν ἐστιν κάμηλον διὰ τῆς τρυμαλιᾶς τῆς ῥαφίδος διελθεῖν ἢ πλούσιον εἰς τὴν βασιλείαν τοῦ θεοῦ εἰσελθεῖν. 10.26 οἱ δὲ περισσῶς ἐξεπλήσσοντο λέγοντες πρὸς αὐτούς, καὶ τίς δύναται σωθῆναι; 10.27 ἐμβλέψας αὐτοῖς ὁ Ἰησοῦς εἶπεν, παρὰ ἀνθρώποις ἀδύνατον ἀλλ' οὐ παρὰ θεῷ, πάντα γὰρ δυνατὰ παρὰ τῷ θεῷ. 10.28 ἤρξατο λέγιν ὁ Πέτρος αὐτῷ, ἰδοὺ ἡμῖς ἀφήκαμεν πάντα καὶ ἠκολουθήκαμέν σοι, τί ἄρα ἔσται ἡμῖν; 10.29 ἔφη αὐτῷ ὁ Ἰησοῦς, ἀμὴν λέγω ὑμῖν, οὐδίς ἐστιν ὃς ἀφῆκεν οἰκίαν ἢ ἀδελφοὺς ἢ ἀδελφὰς ἢ μητέρα ἢ πατέρα ἢ τέκνα ἢ ἀγροὺς ἕνεκεν ἐμοῦ καὶ ἕνεκεν τοῦ εὐαγγελίου, 10.30 ἐὰν μὴ ἀπὸ λάβῃ ἑκατονταπλασίονα νῦν ἐν τῷ καιρῷ τούτῳ οἰκίας καὶ ἀδελφοὺς καὶ ἀδελφὰς καὶ μητέρας καὶ τέκνα καὶ ἀγροὺς μετὰ διωγμῶν, καὶ ἐν τῷ αἰῶνι τῷ ἐρχομένῳ ζωὴν αἰώνιον. 10.31 πολλοὶ δὲ ἔσονται πρῶτοι ἔσχατοι καὶ ἔσχατοι πρῶτοι.

10.32 ἦσαν δὲ ἐν τῇ ὁδῷ ἀναβαίνοντες εἰς Ἱεροσόλυμα, καὶ ἦν προάγων αὐτοὺς ὁ Ἰησοῦς, καὶ ἐθαμβοῦντο, οἱ δὲ

good? No one *is* good except one: God.

    10.19   You know the commands: YOU MAY NOT MURDER, YOU MAY NOT *do* ADULTERY, YOU MAY NOT STEAL, YOU MAY NOT GIVE FALSE TESTIMONY, you may not defraud, HONOR YOU YOUR FATHER AND THE MOTHER.   10.20 And the (he) said to him: Teacher, all these I guarded/kept from my youth.   10.21 But Jesus, having looked on him, loved him, and he said to him: Yet one (thing) is lacking *for* you: You depart, sell what (things) you have and give to the poor (ones), and you will have a store/ treasure in heaven, and you come, follow with me.

    10.22   But the (he), being shocked at the saying/word, went away grieving, for he was having many possessions.   10.23 And having looked around himself, Jesus was saying to his learners/pupils: How hardly will those holding/having the riches/wealth enter into the kingdom of God.   10.24 And the learners/pupils were being astounded at his sayings/words.

    And Jesus, answering again, says to them: Children, how hard/difficult it is to enter into the kingdom of God;   10.25 it is easier *for* a camel to go through the eye of the needle than *for* a rich (one) to enter into the kingdom of God.   10.26 But they were being astonished/amazed exceedingly, saying to them-(selves): And who is able to be saved?   10.27 Having looked at/to them, Jesus said: With/from men *it is* impossible, but not with God; for all (things) *are* possible with God.   10.28 Peter began to say to him: Behold, we, we let go/left all (things) and we have followed with you. From *what* is it for us?   10.29 Jesus said to him: Truly I say to ye, there is no one who let go/left a house or brothers or sisters or mother or father or children or lands/fields for the sake of me and for the sake of the good message/gospel,   10.30 except he might receive a hundredfold now, houses and brothers and sisters and mothers and children and fields, in at this time/season with prosecutions/persecutions, and life eternal in the coming age.   10.31 And manyfirst (ones) will be last (ones) and last (ones) first (ones).

    10.32   And they were on/in the road going up to Jerusalem, and Jesus was leading forth/preceding them,

ἀκολουθοῦντες ἐφοβοῦντο.

καὶ παραλαβὼν πάλιν τοὺς δώδεκα ἤρξατο αὐτοῖς λέγιν τὰ μέλλοντα αὐτῷ συμβαίνιν, 10.33 ὅτι ἰδοὺ ἀναβένομεν ἰς Ἱεροσόλυμα, καὶ ὁ υἱὸς τοῦ ἀνθρώπου παραδοθήσεται τοῖς ἀρχιερεῦσι καὶ τοῖς γραμματεῦσιν, καὶ κατακρινοῦσιν αὐτὸν θανάτῳ καὶ παραδώσουσιν αὐτὸν τοῖς ἔθνεσιν 10.34 καὶ ἐμπαίξουσιν αὐτῷ καὶ ἐμπτύσουσιν αὐτῷ καὶ μαστιγώσουσιν αὐτὸν καὶ ἀποκτενοῦσιν, καὶ μετὰ τρῖς ἡμέρας ἀναστήσεται.

10.35 καὶ παραπορεύονται αὐτῷ Ἰάκωβος καὶ Ἰωάννης οἱ υἱοὶ Ζεβεδαίου λέγοντες αὐτῷ, διδάσκαλε, θέλομεν ἵνα ὃ ἐὰν αἰτήσωμέν σε ποιήσῃς ἡμῖν. 10.36 ὁ δὲ εἶπεν αὐτοῖς, τί θέλετέ με ποιήσω ὑμῖν; 10.37 οἱ δὲ εἶπαν αὐτῷ, δὸς ἡμῖν ἵνα εἷς σου ἐκ δεξιῶν καὶ εἷς σου ἐξ εὐωνύμων καθίσωμεν ἐν τῇ δόξῃ σου. 10.38 ὁ δὲ Ἰησοῦς εἶπεν αὐτοῖς, οὐκ οἴδαται τί αἰτῖσθε. δύνασθαι πειῖν τὸ ποτήριον ὃ ἐγὼ πίνω, ἢ τὸ βάπτισμα ὃ ἐγὼ βαπτίζομε βαπτισθῆναι; 10.39 οἱ δὲ εἶπαν αὐτῷ, δυνάμεθα. ὁ δὲ Ἰησοῦς εἶπεν αὐτοῖς, τὸ ποτήριον ὃ ἐγὼ πίνω πίεσθε καὶ τὸ βάπτισμα ὃ ἐγὼ βαπτίζομε βαπτισθήσεσθε, 10.40 τὸ δὲ καθίσαι ἐκ δεξιῶν μου ἢ ἐξ εὐωνύμων οὐκ ἔστιν ἐμὸν δοῦναι, ἀλλ' οἷς ἡτοίμασται ὑπὸ τοῦ πατρός μου. 10.41 καὶ ἀκούσαντες οἱ δέκα ἤρξαντο ἀγανακτεῖν καὶ περὶ Ἰακώβου καὶ Ἰωάννου.

10.42 καὶ προσκαλεσάμενος αὐτοὺς ὁ Ἰησοῦς λέγει αὐτοῖς, οἴδατε ὅτι οἱ δοκοῦντες ἄρχειν τῶν ἐθνῶν κατακυριεύουσιν αὐτῶν καὶ οἱ βασιλεῖς κατεξουσιάζουσιν αὐτῶν. 10.43 οὐχ οὕτως δέ ἐστιν ἐν ὑμῖν· ἀλλ' ὃς ἂν θέλῃ μέγας γενέσθαι ἐν ὑμῖν, ἔστω ὑμῶν διάκονος, 10.44 καὶ ὃς ἂν θέλῃ ἐν ὑμῖν εἶναι πρῶτος, ἔσται πάντων δοῦλος·

10.45 καὶ γὰρ ὁ υἱὸς τοῦ ἀνθρώπου οὐκ ἦλθεν διακονηθῆναι ἀλλὰ διακονῆσαι καὶ δοῦναι τὴν ψυχὴν αὐτοῦ λύτρον ἀντὶ πολλῶν. 10.46 καὶ ἔρχονται εἰς Ἰεριχώ.

καὶ ἐκπορευομένου αὐτοῦ ἀπὸ Ἰεριχὼ καὶ τῶν μαθητῶν

and they were being astounded/distressed, and those following were being afraid/fearing.

And having taken again the twelve, he began to say to them the (things) being about to happen to him: 10.33 Behold, we are going up to Jerusalem, and the son of the man will be handed over/betrayed to the high priests and the scribes, and they will condemn him to death and will hand him over to the ethnics, 10.34 and they will mock/ridicule him and spit on him and scourge/whip him   and they will kill *him*, and after three days he will stand up/arise.

10.35 Both James and John, the sons of Zebedee, go along beside/with him, saying to him: Teacher, we wish/want that what (thing) we might ask you if you might do *it* for us.   10.36 And the (he) said to them: What wish/want ye *of* me *that* I might do for ye?   10.37 And they said to him: You give to us that we might sit, one out of your right (ones) and one out of your left (ones) in your glory/fame.   10.38 But Jesus said to them: Ye know not what ye ask. Are ye able to drink the cup that I, I drink, or to be baptized *with* the baptism which I, I am baptized?   10.39 And they said to him: We are able.   And Jesus said to them: The cup which I, I drink, ye will drink, and the baptism which I, I am baptized, ye will be baptized,   10.40 but the (thing) to sit out of my right (ones) or out of left (ones) is not mine to give, but for *those* whom it has been prepared by my father.   10.41 And having heard, the ten began also to be angry about James and John.

10.42 And having called them near, Jesus says to them: Ye know that those thinking/seeming to rule the ethnics, they lord it over them and the kings exercise authority against/over them.   10.43 But it is not so among ye; but who ever may want/wish to be great among ye, let him be your waiter/servant,   10.44 and who ever may want/wish to be first/foremost among ye, he will be a slave of all;

10.45 For even the son of the man came not to be waited on/served but to serve/wait on and to give his soul/life a ransom instead of/for many.   10.46 And they come/go to Jericho.

And of him going out from Jericho, also of his

αὐτοῦ καὶ ὄχλου ἱκανοῦ ὁ υἱὸς Τιμαίου Βαρτιμαῖος τυφλὸς καὶ προσαίτης ἐκάθητο παρὰ τὴν ὁδόν. 10.47 καὶ ἀκούσας ὅτι Ἰησοῦς ὁ Ναζωραιός ἐστιν ἤρξατο κράζειν καὶ λέγειν, υἱὲ Δαυὶδ Ἰησοῦ, ἐλέησόν με. 10.48 καὶ ἐπετίμων αὐτῷ πολλοὶ ἵνα σιωπήσῃ ὁ δὲ πολλῷ μᾶλλον ἔκραζεν, υἱὲ Δαυίδ, ἐλέησόν με. 10.49 καὶ στὰς ὁ Ἰησοῦς εἶπεν, Φωνήσατε αὐτόν. καὶ φωνοῦσι τὸν τυφλὸν λέγοντες αὐτῷ, θάρσει, ἔγειρε, φωνεῖ σε.

10.50 ὁ δὲ ἀποβαλὼν τὸ ἱμάτιον αὐτοῦ ἀναπηδήσας ἦλθεν πρὸς τὸν Ἰησοῦν. 10.51 καὶ ἀποκριθεὶς αὐτῷ ὁ Ἰησοῦς εἶπεν, τί σοι θέλεις ποιήσω; ὁ δὲ τυφλὸς εἶπεν αὐτῷ, ῥαββουνι, ἵνα ἀναβλέψω. 10.52 ὁ δὲ Ἰησοῦς εἶπεν αὐτῷ, ὕπαγε, ἡ πίστις σου σέσωκέν σε. καὶ εὐθὺς ἀνέβλεψεν, καὶ ἠκολούθει αὐτῷ ἐν τῇ ὁδῷ.

11.1 Καὶ ὅτε ἐγγίζουσιν εἰς Ἱεροσόλυμα εἰς Βηθφαγὴ καὶ εἰς Βηθανίαν πρὸς τὸ ὄρος τῶν ἐλαιῶν, ἀποστέλλει δύο τῶν μαθητῶν αὐτοῦ 11.2 καὶ λέγι αὐτοῖς, ὑπάγετε εἰς τὴν κώμην τὴν κατέναντι ὑμῶν, καὶ εὐθὺς εἰσπορευόμενοι εἰς αὐτὴν εὑρήσετε πῶλον δεδεμένον ἐφ' ὃν οὐδὶς ἀνθρώπων οὔπω ἐκάθισεν· λύσατε αὐτὸν καὶ φέρετε.

11.3 καὶ ἐάν τις ὑμῖν εἴπῃ, τί ποιεῖτε τοῦτο; εἴπατε ὅτι ὁ κύριος αὐτοῦ χρίαν ἔχει, καὶ εὐθὺς αὐτὸν ἀποστέλλει πάλιν ὧδε.

11.4 καὶ ἀπῆλθον καὶ εὗρον τὸν πῶλον δεδεμένον πρὸς τὴν θύραν ἔξω ἐπὶ τοῦ ἀμφόδου, καὶ λύουσιν αὐτόν. 11.5 καὶ τινες τῶν ἐκεῖ ἑστηκότων ἔλεγον αὐτοῖς, τί ποιεῖτε λύοντες τὸν πῶλον; 11.6 οἱ δὲ εἶπαν αὐτοῖς καθὼς εἶπεν ὁ Ἰησοῦς· καὶ ἀφῆκαν αὐτούς. 11.7 καὶ φέρουσιν τὸν πῶλον πρὸς τὸν Ἰησοῦν, καὶ ἐπιβάλλουσιν αὐτῷ τὰ ἱμάτια αὐτῶν, καὶ ἐκάθισεν ἐπ' αὐτόν. 11.8 καὶ πολλοὶ τὰ ἱμάτια αὐτῶν ἔστρωσαν εἰς τὴν ὁδόν, ἄλλοι δὲ στιβάδας κόψαντες ἐκ τῶν ἀγρῶν.

11.9 καὶ οἱ προάγοντες καὶ οἱ ἀκολουθοῦντες ἔκραζον, «

learners/pupils and a considerable crowd, the son of Timaeus Bartimaeus, a blind (one) and a beggar, was sitting beside the road. 10.47 And having heard that Jesus the Nazarite is *near/coming*, he began to cry out and to say: Son of David, Jesus, have mercy on me. 10.48 And many were rebuking him in order that he might be quiet; but the (he) was crying out with much more: Son of David, have mercy on me. 10.49 And having stopped, Jesus said: Call ye him. And they called the blind (one), saying to him: Be of good cheer, you arise, he calls you.

10.50 And the (he), throwing off/away his garment, having sprang up, he came to/near Jesus. 10.51 And answering to him, Jesus said: What *do* you want/wish *that* I might do for you? And the blind (one) said to him: Rabboni, that I might receive *my* sight. 10.52 And Jesus said to him: Go you away, your faith has saved/delivered you. And immediately he looked up/received sight, and he was following with him on the road.

11.1 And when they draw near to Jerusalem, to Bethphage and into Bethany near the mountain of the olives, he sends forth two of his learners/pupils 11.2 and he says to them: Depart ye into the village opposite/before ye, and going into it quickly/at once ye will find a colt having been tied, upon which not yet no one of men sat; loose ye it and ye bring *it*.

11.3 And if anyone might say to ye: Why do ye this? Say ye that the Lord has a need of it, and at once he sends it here again.

11.4 And they went and found the colt having been tied near the door, outside on the open street, and they loose it. 11.5 And a certain one of those having been standing there was saying to them: What do ye, loosing the colt? 11.6 And they said to them as Jesus said; and they let them go. 11.7 And they bring the colt to Jesus, and they throw their garments upon it, and he sat upon it. 11.8 And many spread their garments in the road, and others *were* having cut branches out of the fields.

11.9 Both those going ahead and those following

ὡσαννά· εὐλογημένος ὁ ἐρχόμενος ἐν ὀνόματι κυρίου» 11.10 εὐλογημένη ἡ ἐρχομένη βασιλεία τοῦ πατρὸς ἡμῶν Δαυίδ· «ὡσαννὰ» ἐν τοῖς ὑψίστοις.

11.11 καὶ εἰσῆλθεν ἰς Ἱεροσόλυμα εἰς τὸ ἱερόν· καὶ περιβλεψάμενος πάντα, ὀψὲ ἤδη οὔσης τῆς ὥρας, ἐξῆλθεν εἰς Βηθανίαν μετὰ τῶν δώδεκα. 11.12 καὶ τῇ ἐπαύριον ἐξελθόντων αὐτῶν ἀπὸ Βηθανίας ἐπείνασεν. 11.13 καὶ ἰδὼν συκῆν μιὰ ἀπὸ μακρόθεν ἔχουσαν φύλλα ἦλθεν εἰ ἄρα τι εὑρήσι ἐν αὐτῇ, καὶ ἐλθὼν ἐπ' αὐτὴν οὐδὲν εὗρεν εἰ μὴ φύλλα· ὁ γὰρ καιρὸς οὐκ ἦν σύκων. 11.14 καὶ ἀποκριθεὶς εἶπεν αὐτῇ, μηκέτι εἰς τὸν αἰῶνα ἐκ σοῦ μηδὶς καρπὸν φάγοι.

καὶ ἤκουον οἱ μαθηταὶ αὐτοῦ. 11.15 καὶ ἔρχονται εἰς Ἱεροσόλυμα. καὶ εἰσελθὼν εἰς τὸ ἱερὸν ἤρξατο ἐκβάλλειν τοὺς πωλοῦντας καὶ τοὺς ἀγοράζοντας ἐν τῷ ἱερῷ, καὶ τὰς τραπέζας τῶν κολλυβιστῶν καὶ τὰς καθέδρας τῶν πωλούντων τὰς περιστερὰς κατέστρεψεν, 11.16 καὶ οὐκ ἤφιεν ἵνα τις διενέγκη σκεῦος διὰ τοῦ ἱεροῦ. 11.17 καὶ ἐδίδασκεν καὶ ἔλεγεν αὐτοῖς, οὐ γέγραπται ὅτι «ὁ οἶκός μου οἶκος προσευχῆς κληθήσεται πᾶσιν τοῖς ἔθνεσιν;» ὑμεῖς δὲ ἐποιήσατε αὐτὸν σπήλαιον λῃστῶν.

11.18 καὶ ἤκουσαν οἱ ἀρχιερῖς καὶ οἱ γραμματῖς, καὶ ἐζήτου πῶς αὐτὸν ἀπολέσωσιν· ἐφοβοῦντο γὰρ αὐτόν, πᾶς γὰρ ὁ ὄχλος ἐξεπλήσσετο ἐπὶ τῇ διδαχῇ αὐτοῦ.   11.19 καὶ ὅταν ὀψὲ ἐγένετο, ἐξεπορεύετο ἔξω τῆς πόλεως. 11.20 καὶ παραπορευόμενοι πρωΐ καὶ ἶδον τὴν συκῆν ἐξηραμμένην ἐκ ῥιζῶν. 11.21 καὶ ἀναμνησθεὶς ὁ Πέτρος λέγει αὐτῷ, ῥαββεί, εἶδε ἡ συκῆ ἣν κατηράσω ἐξήρανται.

11.22 καὶ ἀποκριθεὶς ὁ Ἰησοῦς λέγει αὐτοῖς, εἰ ἔχετε πίστιν θεοῦ, 11.23 ἀμὴν λέγω ὑμῖν ὃς ἂν εἴπῃ τῷ ὄρι τούτῳ, ἄρθητι καὶ βλήθητι εἰς τὴν θάλασσαν, καὶ μὴ διακριθῇ ἐν τῇ καρδίᾳ

were crying out: HOSANNA! HAVING BEEN BLESSED/PRAISED *is* THE (ONE) COMING BY/IN NAME OF THE LORD; 11.10 Having been blessed *is* the coming kingdom of our father David; HOSANNA in the high (places).

11.11 And he went/entered into Jerusalem to the *outer* temple; and having looked around all (things), the hour already being late, he went out to Bethany with the twelve. 11.12 And from them having gone out on the morrow from Bethany, he was hungry. 11.13 And having seen one fig tree from afar having leaves, he went if perhaps he would find something on it, and having come up to it, he found nothing except leaves; for it was not a season/time of figs. 11.14 And answering/from judging he said to it: No longer into the age might no one wish to eat fruit out of/from you.

And his learners/pupils were hearing/listening. 11.15 And they come into Jerusalem. And having gone into the *outer* temple he began to throw out those selling and those buying in the *outer* temple, and he overturned the tables of the moneychangers and the seats/chairs of those selling the pigeons/doves, 11.16 and he was not allowing/letting that anyone might bring/carry a vessel through the *outer* temple/ temple area. 11.17 And he was teaching and he was saying to them: Has it not been written that MY HOUSE WILL BE CALLED A HOUSE OF PRAYER FOR ALL THE ETHNICS? But ye, ye have made it a cave/den of robbers.

11.18 Both the high priests and the scribes heard, and they were seeking how they might destroy him; for they were fearing him, for all the crowd was being amazed/astonished at his doctrine/teaching. 11.19 And when it became late, he was going forth outside the city. 11.20 And going along early in the morning they also saw the fig tree, having been withered/dried up from *the* roots. 11.21 And having remembered, Peter says to him: Rabbi, see the fig tree that you cursed, it has been dried up.

11.22 And answering, Jesus says to them: If ye have faith from God, 11.23 truly I say to ye, who ever might say to this mountain: Be you taken up and be thrown into the sea, and it not be doubted in his

αὐτοῦ ἀλλὰ πιστεύῃ ὅτι ὃ λαλεῖ γίνεται, ἔστε αὐτῷ.

11.24 διὰ τοῦτο λέγω ὑμῖν, πάντα ὅσα προσεύχεσθε καὶ αἰτῖσθε, πιστεύετε ὅτι ἐλάβετε, καὶ ἔστε ὑμῖν.

11.25 καὶ ὅταν στῆτε προσευχόμενοι, ἀφίεται εἴ τι ἔχεται κατά τινος, ἵνα καὶ ὁ πατὴρ ὑμῶν ὁ ἐν τοῖς οὐρανοῖς ἀφῇ ὑμῖν τὰ παραπτώματα ὑμῶν.

11.27 καὶ ἔρχονται πάλιν εἰς Ἱεροσόλυμα. καὶ ἐν τῷ ἱερῷ περιπατοῦντος αὐτοῦ ἔρχονται πρὸς αὐτὸν οἱ ἀρχιερεῖς καὶ οἱ γραμματῖς καὶ οἱ πρεσβύτεροι 11.28 καὶ ἔλεγον αὐτῷ, ἐν ποίᾳ ἐξουσίᾳ ταῦτα ποιεῖς; ἢ τίς σοι ἔδωκεν τὴν ἐξουσίαν ταύτην ἵνα ταῦτα ποιῇς; 11.29 ὁ δὲ Ἰησοῦς εἶπεν αὐτοῖς, ἐπερωτήσω ὑμᾶς κἀγὼ ἕνα λόγον, καὶ ἀποκρίθητέ μοι, καὶ ἐρῶ ὑμῖν ἐν ποίᾳ ἐξουσίᾳ ταῦτα ποιῶ· 11.30 τὸ βάπτισμα τὸ Ἰωάννου πόθεν ἦν ἐξ οὐρανοῦ ἢ ἐξ ἀνθρώπων; ἀποκρίθητέ μοι. 11.31 καὶ διελογίζοντο πρὸς ἑαυτοὺς λέγοντες, ἐὰν εἴπωμεν, ἐξ οὐρανοῦ, ἐρεῖ, διὰ τί οὖν οὐκ ἐπιστεύσατε αὐτῷ; 11.32 ἀλλὰ εἴπωμεν, ἐξ ἀνθρώπων; ἐφοβοῦντο τὸν ὄχλον, ἅπαντες γὰρ εἶχον τὸν Ἰωάννην ὄντως ὅτι προφήτης ἦν. 11.33 καὶ ἀποκριθέντες τῷ Ἰησοῦ λέγουσιν, οὐκ οἴδαμεν. καὶ ὁ Ἰησοῦς λέγι αὐτοῖς, οὐδὲ ἐγὼ λέγω ὑμῖν ἐν ποίᾳ ἐξουσίᾳ ταῦτα ποιῶ.

12.1 Καὶ ἤρξατο αὐτοῖς ἐν παραβολαῖς λαλῖν, ἀμπελῶνα ἄνθρωπος ἐφύτευσεν, καὶ περιέθηκεν φραγμὸν καὶ ὤρυξεν ὑπολήνιον καὶ ᾠκοδόμησεν πύργον, καὶ ἐξέδετο αὐτὸν γεωργοῖς, καὶ ἀπεδήμησεν. 12.2 καὶ ἀπέστιλεν πρὸς τοὺς γεωργοὺς τῷ καιρῷ δοῦλον, ἵνα παρὰ τῶν γεωργῶν λάβῃ ἀπὸ τῶν καρπῶν τοῦ ἀμπελῶνος· 12.3 καὶ λαβόντες αὐτὸν ἔδειραν καὶ ἀπέστιλαν καινόν. 12.4 καὶ πάλιν ἀπέστιλεν πρὸς αὐτοὺς ἄλλον δοῦλον· κἀκεῖνον ἐκεφαλίωσαν καὶ ἠτίμασαν. 12.5 καὶ ἄλλον ἀπέστιλεν,

heart but he might believe that what he speaks happens, it will be *so* for him.

11.24 Because of this I say to ye: All (things) whatever ye pray and ask for yourselves, believe ye that ye received, and it will be for ye.

11.25 And when ye might stand praying, ye forgive/dismiss if ye have something against someone, in order that also your father, the (one) in the skies/heavens, might forgive for ye your trespasses.

11.27 And they come again into Jerusalem. And from him walking in the *outer* temple, the high priests and the scribes and the elders come near/to him, 11.28 and they were saying to him: By what authority do you these (things)? Or who gave to you this authority in order that you may do these (things)? 11.29 But Jesus said to them: I also, I shall ask ye one saying/reason/word, and ye reply to me, and I say to ye by what authority I do these (things): 11.30 The baptism, the (one) of John, from where was it, out of/from heaven or out of/from men? Ye reply/answer to me. 11.31 And they were reasoning/debating to/with themselves, saying: If we might say: Out of/from heaven, he will say: Then why did ye not believe in him? 11.32 But we might say: out of/from men? -- they were fearing the crowd, for all (men) were holding John that certainly he was a prophet. 11.33 And replying to Jesus, they say: We know not. And Jesus says to them: Neither *do* I, I say/tell to ye by what authority I do these (things).

12.1 And he began to speak to them in parables: A man planted a vineyard, and he put a fence/wall around *it* and he dug out a wine vat and he built a tower/fortress, and he leased it out to farmers/vinedressers, and he took a journey. 12.2 And he sent a slave to the vinedressers/farmers at/in the season, in order that beside/from the vinedressers he might receive from the fruits of the vineyard; 12.3 And having taken him, they beat *him* and sent *him* away empty. 12.4 And again he sent another slave to them; and that (one) they wounded in the head and dishonored. 12.5 And he sent another, and that (one) they

κἀκεῖνον ἀπέκτιναν, καὶ πολλοὺς ἄλλους, οὓς μὲν δέροντες οὓς δὲ ἀποκτέννουντες. 12.6 ἔτι ἕνα εἶχεν, υἱὸν ἀγαπητόν· ἀπέστιλεν αὐτὸν ἔσχατον πρὸς αὐτοὺς λέγων ὅτι ἐντραπήσονται τὸν υἱόν μου. 12.7 ἐκῖνοι δὲ οἱ γεωργοὶ πρὸς ἑαυτοὺς εἶπαν ὅτι οὗτός ἐστιν ὁ κληρονόμος· δεῦτε ἀποκτίνωμεν αὐτόν, καὶ ἡμῶν ἔστε ἡ κληρονομία. 12.8 καὶ λαβόντες ἀπέκτιναν αὐτόν, καὶ ἐξέβαλον αὐτὸν ἔξω τοῦ ἀμπελῶνος.

12.9 τί ποιήσει ὁ κύριος τοῦ ἀμπελῶνος; ἐλεύσεται καὶ ἀπολέσει τοὺς γεωργούς, καὶ δώσει τὸν ἀμπελῶνα ἄλλοις. 12.10 οὐδὲ τὴν γραφὴν ταύτην ἀνέγνωτε, « λίθον ὃν ἀπεδοκίμασαν οἱ οἰκοδομοῦντες, οὗτος ἐγενήθη εἰς κεφαλὴν γωνίας· 12.11 παρὰ κυρίου ἐγένετο αὕτη, καὶ ἔστιν θαυμαστὴ ἐν ὀφθαλμοῖς ἡμῶν;»

12.12 καὶ ἐζήτουν αὐτὸν κρατῆσαι, καὶ ἐφοβήθησαν τὸν ὄχλον, ἔγνωσαν γὰρ ὅτι πρὸς αὐτοὺς τὴν παραβολὴν εἶπεν. καὶ ἀφέντες αὐτὸν ἀπῆλθον.

12.13 καὶ ἀποστέλλουσιν πρὸς αὐτόν τινας τῶν Φαρισαίων καὶ τῶν Ἡρωδιανῶν ἵνα αὐτὸν ἀγρεύσωσιν λόγῳ. 12.14 καὶ ἐλθόντες λέγουσιν αὐτῷ, διδάσκαλε, οἴδαμεν ὅτι ἀληθὴς εἶ καὶ οὐ μέλι σοι περὶ οὐδενός, οὐ γὰρ βλέπις εἰς πρόσωπον ἀνθρώπων, ἀλλ' ἐπ' ἀληθείας τὴν ὁδὸν τοῦ θεοῦ διδάσκις· ἔξεστιν δοῦναι κῆνσον Καίσαρι ἢ οὔ; δῶμεν ἢ μὴ δῶμεν; 12.15 ὁ δὲ εἰδὼς αὐτῶν τὴν ὑπόκρισιν εἶπεν αὐτοῖς, τί με πιράζετε; φέρετέ μοι δηνάριον ἵνα εἴδω. 12.16 οἱ δὲ ἤνεγκαν. καὶ λέγει αὐτοῖς, τίνος ἡ εἰκὼν αὕτη καὶ ἡ ἐπιγραφή; οἱ δὲ εἶπαν αὐτῷ, Καίσαρος. 12.17 ὁ δὲ Ἰησοῦς εἶπεν αὐτοῖς, τὰ Καίσαρος ἀπόδοτε Καίσαρι καὶ τὰ τοῦ θεοῦ τῷ θεῷ. καὶ ἐξεθαύμαζον ἐπ' αὐτῷ. 12.18 καὶ ἔρχονται Σαδδουκαῖοι πρὸς αὐτόν, οἵτινες λέγουσιν ἀνάστασιν μὴ εἶναι, καὶ ἐπηρώτων αὐτὸν λέγοντες, 12.19 διδάσκαλε, Μωϋσῆς ἔγραψεν ἡμῖν ὅτι « ἐάν τινος ἀδελφὸς ἀποθάνῃ» καὶ καταλίψῃ γυναῖκα « καὶ μὴ ἀφῇ τέκνα,» ἵνα «λάβῃ ὁ ἀδελφὸς αὐτοῦ τὴν γυναῖκα καὶ ἐξαναστήσῃ σπέρμα τῷ ἀδελφῷ αὐτοῦ.» 12.20 ἑπτὰ ἀδελφοὶ

killed, also many others, beating some, and killing others. 12.6 He still had one, a beloved son; he sent him lastly to them, saying: They will respect my son. 12.7 But those vinedressers/farmers said to themselves: This (one) is the heir; come, let us kill him, and the inheritance will be ours. 12.8 And having taken/received *him*, they killed him, and they threw him out outside the vineyard.

12.9 What will the lord of the vineyard do? He will come and will destroy the farmers/vinedressers, and he will give the vineyard to others. 12.10 And read ye not this writing: A STONE WHICH THE (ONES) BUILDING REJECTED, THIS (ONE)/THE *same* WAS MADE INTO A HEAD OF A CORNER; 12.11 THIS (THING) HAPPENED FROM THE LORD, AND IT IS WONDERFUL IN OUR EYES?

12.12 And they were seeking to seize him, but they feared the crowd, for they knew that he said/ spoke the parable to them. And having left him they went away.

12.13 And they sent to him some of the Pharisees and of the Herodians that they might catch him by/in a saying/word. 12.14 And having come/arrived they say to him: Teacher, we know that you are truthful and it is not a care to you about no one, for you see/look not in a face of men, but you teach the way/road of God upon truth; is it lawful to give tribute to Caesar, or not? Should we give or should we not give? 12.15 But the (he), having known their pretense, said to them: Why do ye try/test me? Bring ye a denarius to me that I might see. 12.16 And they brought *one*. And he says to them: Of whom *is* this image and the inscription? And the (they) said to him: Of Caesar. 12.17 And Jesus said to them: The (things) of Caesar, pay ye back to Caesar and the (things) of God to God. And they were wondering at/on him. 12.18 And Sadducees come to/near him, who say *for* a resurrection not to be, and they were questioning him, saying: 12.19 Teacher, Moses wrote for us that IF A BROTHER OF SOMEONE MIGHT DIE and might leave behind a woman AND MIGHT NOT LEAVE CHILDREN, that THE BROTHER OF HIM SHOULD TAKE THE WOMAN AND SHOULD RAISE UP SEED FOR HIS BROTHER. 12.20 There were seven brothers; and the

ἦσαν· καὶ ὁ εἷς ἔλαβεν γυναῖκα, καὶ ἀποθνῄσκων οὐκ ἀφῆκεν σπέρμα· 12.21 καὶ ὁ δεύτερος ἔλαβεν αὐτήν, καὶ ἀπέθανεν μὴ καταλιπὼν σπέρμα· καὶ ὁ τρίτος ὡσαύτως· 12.22 καὶ οἱ ἑπτὰ οὐκ ἀφῆκαν σπέρμα. ἔσχατον πάντων καὶ ἡ γυνὴ ἀπέθανεν. 12.23 ἐν τῇ ἀναστάσει τίνος αὐτῶν ἔσται γυνή; οἱ γὰρ ἑπτὰ ἔσχον αὐτὴν γυναῖκα.

12.24 ἔφη αὐτοῖς ὁ Ἰησοῦς, οὐ διὰ τοῦτο πλανᾶσθαι μὴ εἰδότες τὰς γραφὰς μηδὲ τὴν δύναμιν τοῦ θεοῦ; 12.25 ὅταν γὰρ ἐκ νεκρῶν ἀναστῶσιν, οὔτε γαμοῦσιν οὔτε γαμίζονται, ἀλλ᾽ εἰσὶν ὡς ἄγγελοι ἐν τοῖς οὐρανοῖς. 12.26 περὶ δὲ τῶν νεκρῶν ὅτι ἐγείρονται οὐκ ἀνέγνωτε ἐν τῇ βίβλῳ Μωϋσέως ἐπὶ τοῦ βάτου πῶς εἶπεν αὐτῷ ὁ θεὸς λέγων, « ἐγὼ ὁ θεὸς Ἀβραὰμ καὶ ὁ θεὸς Ἰσαὰκ καὶ ὁ θεὸς Ἰακώβ;» 12.27 οὐκ ἔστιν ὁ θεὸς νεκρῶν ἀλλὰ ζώντων· πολὺ πλανᾶσθε.

12.28 καὶ προσελθὼν εἷς τῶν γραμματέων ἀκούσας αὐτῶν συζητούντων, ἰδὼν ὅτι καλῶς ἀπεκρίθη αὐτοῖς, ἐπηρώτησεν αὐτόν, ποία ἐστὶν ἐντολὴ πρώτη πάντων; 12.29 ἀπεκρίθη ὁ Ἰησοῦς ὅτι πρώτη ἐστίν, « ἄκουε, Ἰσραήλ, κύριος ὁ θεὸς ἡμῶν κύριος εἷς ἐστιν, 12.30 καὶ ἀγαπήσεις κύριον τὸν θεόν σου ἐξ ὅλης τῆς καρδίας σου καὶ ἐξ ὅλης τῆς ψυχῆς σου» καὶ ἐξ ὅλης τῆς διανοίας σου «καὶ ἐξ ὅλης τῆς ἰσχύος σου.» 12.31 δευτέρα αὕτη ἐστίν, « ἀγαπήσεις τὸν πλησίον σου ὡς σεαυτόν.» μείζων δὲ τούτων ἄλλη ἐντολὴ οὐκ ἔστιν.

12.32 καὶ εἶπεν αὐτῷ ὁ γραμματεύς, καλῶς, διδάσκαλε, ἐπ᾽ ἀληθίας εἶπες ὅτι «εἷς ἐστιν καὶ οὐκ ἔστιν ἄλλος πλὴν αὐτοῦ» 12.33 καὶ τὸ «ἀγαπᾶν αὐτὸν ἐξ ὅλης τῆς καρδίας σου καὶ ἐξ ὅλης τῆς συνέσεως καὶ ἐξ ὅλης τῆς ἰσχύος» καὶ τὸ «ἀγαπᾶν τὸν πλησίον ὡς ἑαυτὸν» περισσότερόν ἐστιν πάντων τῶν ὁλοκαυτωμάτων καὶ τῶν θυσιῶν. 12.34 καὶ ὁ Ἰησοῦς εἰδὼν ὅτι νουνεχῶς ἀπεκρίθη εἶπεν αὐτῷ, οὐ μακρὰν εἶ ἀπὸ τῆς βασιλίας τοῦ θεοῦ. καὶ οὐδὶς οὐκέτι ἐτόλμα ἐπερωτῆσαι αὐτόν.

12.35 καὶ ἀποκριθεὶς ὁ Ἰησοῦς ἔλεγεν διδάσκων ἐν τῷ

(one) took a woman, but dying, he left not a seed/off-spring; 12.21 and the second took her, and died not having left behind a seed/offspring; and the third likewise; 12.22 and the seven left not a seed. Last of all the woman also died. 12.23 In the resurrection, of which of them will she be a woman? For the seven had her *for* a woman.

12.24 Jesus said to them: Are ye not deceived/led astray because of this (thing), having known not the writings, neither the power of God? 12.25 For whenever they might arise out of dead (ones), they neither marry nor are given in marriage, but they are as/like angels/messengers in the skies/heavens. 12.26 But concerning the dead (ones) that they are raised up, read ye not in the scroll of Moses how God spoke to him at the bush, saying: I *am* THE GOD OF ABRAHAM AND THE GOD OF ISAAC AND THE GOD OF JACOB? 12.27 He is not the God of dead (ones) but of living (ones); ye are much deceived.

12.28 And having come near, one of the scribes, having heard from their discussions/debatings, having known that he answered well to them, questioned him: What is a first command of all? 12.29 Jesus answered that *the* first is: YOU HEAR, ISRAEL, THE LORD OUR GOD IS ONE LORD, 12.30 AND YOU WILL LOVE THE LORD YOUR GOD OUT OF YOUR WHOLE HEART AND OUT OF YOUR WHOLE SOUL/LIFE and out of your whole mind AND OUT OF YOUR WHOLE STRENGTH. 12.31 A second is this: YOU WILL LOVE YOUR NEIGHBOR/NEAR (ONE) AS YOURSELF. There is not another command greater than these.

12.32 And the scribe said to him: Well, teacher, you said on a truth that THERE IS ONE AND THAT THERE IS NOT ANOTHER EXCEPT HIM; 12.33 and the (thing) TO LOVE HIM OUT OF YOUR WHOLE HEART AND OUT OF THE WHOLE UNDERSTANDING AND OUT OF THE WHOLE STRENGTH and the (thing) TO LOVE THE NEIGHBOR AS YOURSELF is more *than* all the whole burnt offerings and the sacrifices. 12.34 And Jesus, having seen that he answered sensibly, said to him: You are not far from the kingdom of God. And no one no longer was daring to question him.

12.35 And answering, Jesus was speaking, teaching in the *outer* temple: How say the scribes that the

ἱερῷ, πῶς λέγουσιν οἱ γραμματῖς ὅτι ὁ χριστὸς υἱὸς Δαυίδ ἐστιν; 12.36 αὐτὸς Δαυὶδ εἶπεν ἐν τῷ πνεύματι τῷ ἁγίῳ, « εἶπεν ὁ κύριος τῷ κυρίῳ μου, κάθου ἐκ δεξιῶν μου ἕως ἂν θῶ τοὺς ἐχθρούς σου ὑποπόδιον τῶν ποδῶν σου.» 12.37 αὐτὸς Δαυὶδ λέγει αὐτὸν κύριον, καὶ πόθεν υἱός αὐτοῦ ἐστιν; καὶ πολὺς ὄχλος ἤκουεν αὐτοῦ ἡδέως.

12.38 καὶ ἐν τῇ διδαχῇ αὐτοῦ ἔλεγεν, βλέπετε ἀπὸ τῶν γραμματαίων τῶν θελόντων ἐν στολαῖς περιπατῖν καὶ ἀσπασμοὺς ἐν ταῖς ἀγοραῖς 12.39 καὶ πρωτοκαθεδρίας ἐν ταῖς συναγωγαῖς καὶ πρωτοκλισίας ἐν τοῖς δίπνοις·

12.40 οἱ κατεσθίοντες τὰς οἰκίας τῶν χηρῶν καὶ προφάσει μακρὰ προσευχόμενοι, οὗτοι λήμψονται περισσότερον κρίμα. 12.41 καὶ καθίσας κατέναντι τοῦ γαζοφυλακίου ἐθεώρει πῶς ὁ ὄχλος βάλλει τὸν χαλκὸν εἰς τὸ γαζοφυλάκιον· καὶ πολλοὶ πλούσιοι ἔβαλλον πολλά· 12.42 καὶ ἐλθοῦσα μία γυνὴ χήρα πτωχὴ ἔβαλε λεπτὰ δύο, ὅ ἐστι κοδράντης. 12.43 καὶ προσκαλεσάμενος τοὺς μαθητὰς αὐτοῦ εἶπεν αὐτοῖς, ἀμὴν λέγω ὑμῖν ὅτι ἡ χήρα αὕτη ἡ πτωχὴ πλέον πάντων ἔβαλεν τῶν βαλλόντων εἰς τὸ γαζοφυλάκιον· 12.44 πάντες γὰρ ἐκ τοῦ περισσεύοντος αὐτοῖς ἔβαλον, αὕτη δὲ ἐκ τῆς ὑστερήσεως αὐτῆς πάντα ὅσα εἶχεν ἔβαλεν, ὅλον τὸν βίον αὐτῆς.

13.1 Καὶ ἐκπορευομένου αὐτοῦ ἐκ τοῦ ἱεροῦ λέγει αὐτῷ εἷς τῶν μαθητῶν αὐτοῦ, διδάσκαλε, ἴδε ποταποὶ λίθοι καὶ ποταπαὶ οἰκοδομαί. 13.2 καὶ ὁ Ἰησοῦς εἶπεν αὐτῷ, βλέπις ταύτας τὰς μεγάλας οἰκοδομάς; οὐ μὴ ἀφεθῇ ὧδε λίθος ἐπὶ λίθον ὃς οὐ μὴ καταλυθῇ. 13.3 καὶ καθημένου αὐτοῦ εἰς τὸ ὄρος τῶν ἐλαιῶν κατέναντι τοῦ ἱεροῦ ἐπηρώτα αὐτὸν

κατ' ἰδίαν ὁ Πέτρος καὶ Ἰάκωβος καὶ Ἰωάννης καὶ Ἀνδρέας, 13.4 εἰπὸν ἡμῖν πότε ταῦτα ἔσται, καὶ τί τὸ σημῖον

anointed (one) is a son of David? 12.36 David himself said in/by the Holy Spirit: THE LORD SAID TO MY LORD: YOU SIT OUT OF MY RIGHT (ONES)/AT MY RIGHT HAND UNTIL I WOULD GIVE YOUR ENEMIES A FOOTSTOOL OF YOUR FEET. 12.37 David himself says/calls him Lord, and from where/how is he his son? And a much crowd was hearing him gladly.

12.38 And he was saying in/by his teaching/doctrine: See/observe/beware ye from the scribes, those wanting/wishing to walk around in long robes, and greetings in/at the markets, 12.39 and chief seats in the congregations, and places of honor in/at the dinners/suppers/banquets;

12.40 the (ones) devouring the houses/households of the widows, and praying long *prayers* by pretext, these will receive to themselves more abundant judgment. 12.41 And sitting opposite the contribution box, he was observing how the crowd puts the copper/money into the contribution box; and many rich (ones) were putting *in* much, 12.42 and having come, one woman, a poor widow, put *in* two lepton, which is a quadrans. 12.43 And having summoned/called near his pupils/learners, he said to them: Truly I say to ye that this poor widow put in more from/than all those putting into the contribution box; 12.44 for all *men* put *in* out of the (thing) being abundant/excess to them, but she, out of her poverty, she put in all (things) whatever she was having, her whole livelihood.

13.1 And from him going forth out of the temple *area*, one of his learners/pupils says to him: Teacher, behold what sort of stones and what sort of buildings. 13.2 And Jesus said to him: *Do* you see these great buildings? By no means might there be left here a stone upon a stone which might not be certainly destroyed/thrown down. 13.3 And from him sitting in the mountain of the olives, opposite from the temple *area*, Peter and James

and John and Andrew were questioning him privately: 13.4 Say you to us when these (things) will be, and what the sign *is* whenever all these (things) might

ὅταν μέλλῃ ταῦτα συντελῖσθαι πάντα. 13.5 ὁ δὲ Ἰησοῦς ἤρξατο λέγιν αὐτοῖς, βλέπετε μή τις ὑμᾶς πλανήσῃ· 13.6 πολλοὶ ἐλεύσονται ἐπὶ τῷ ὀνόματί μου λέγοντες ὅτι ἐγώ εἰμι, καὶ πολλοὺς πλανήσουσιν. 13.7 ὅταν δὲ ἀκούσητε πολέμους καὶ ἀκοὰς πολέμων ἔρατε, μὴ θροεῖσθαι· δεῖ γενέσθαι, ἀλλ' οὔπω τὸ τέλος. 13.8 ἐγερθήσεται γὰρ ἔθνος ἐπ' ἔθνος καὶ βασιλία ἐπὶ βασιλείαν, ἔσονται σισμοὶ κατὰ τόπους, ἔσονται λιμοί· ἀρχὴ ὠδίνων ταῦτα.

13.9 βλέπετε δὲ ὑμεῖς ἑαυτούς· παραδώσουσιν γὰρ ὑμᾶς εἰς συνέδρια καὶ εἰς συναγωγὰς δαρήσεσθε καὶ ἐπὶ ἡγεμόνων καὶ βασιλέων σταθήσεσθε ἕνεκεν ἐμοῦ εἰς μαρτύριον αὐτοῖς. 13.10 καὶ εἰς πάντα τὰ ἔθνη πρῶτον δεῖ κηρυχθῆναι τὸ εὐαγγέλιον.

13.11 καὶ ὅταν ἄγωσιν ὑμᾶς παραδιδόντες, μὴ προμεριμνᾶται τί λαλήσητε, ἀλλ' ὃ ἐὰν δοθῇ ὑμῖν ἐν ἐκείνῃ τῇ ὥρᾳ τοῦτο λαλῖτε, οὐ γάρ ἐστε ὑμῖς οἱ λαλοῦντες ἀλλὰ τὸ πνεῦμα τὸ ἅγιον. 13.12 καὶ παραδώσει ἀδελφὸς ἀδελφὸν εἰς θάνατον καὶ πατὴρ τέκνον, καὶ ἐπαναστήσονται τέκνα ἐπὶ γονῖς καὶ θανατώσουσιν αὐτούς· 13.13 καὶ ἔσεσθε μισούμενοι ὑπὸ πάντων διὰ τὸ ὄνομά μου. ὁ δὲ ὑπομίνας εἰς τέλος οὗτος σωθήσεται.

13.14 ὅταν δὲ ἴδητε τὸ βδέλυγμα τῆς ἐρημώσεως ἑστηκότα ὅπου οὐ δῖ, ὁ ἀναγινώσκων νοείτω,

τότε οἱ ἐν τῇ Ἰουδαίᾳ φευγέτωσαν εἰς τὰ ὄρη, 13.15 ὁ δὲ ἐπὶ τοῦ δώματος μὴ καταβάτω μηδὲ εἰσελθάτω ἆραί τι ἐκ τῆς οἰκίας αὐτοῦ, 13.16 καὶ ὁ εἰς τὸν ἀγρὸν μὴ ἐπιστρεψάτω ὀπίσω ἆραι τὸ ἱμάτιον αὐτοῦ.

13.17 οὐαὶ δὲ ταῖς ἐν γαστρὶ ἐχούσαις καὶ ταῖς θηλαζούσαις ἐν ἐκείναις ταῖς ἡμέραις. 13.18 προσεύχεσθε δὲ ἵνα

be about to be completed/accomplished. 13.5 And Jesus began to say to them: See/beware ye lest someone might deceive ye; 13.6 many will come upon/at the name of me, saying that I, I am --, and they will deceive/lead astray many. 13.7 But whenever ye might hear wars and reports of wars *and* ye are passionate, be ye not disturbed/fear ye not; it is necessary to happen, but the end *is* not yet. 13.8 For ethnic will be raised up against ethnic and kingdom upon/against kingdom, there will be earthquakes according to places/from place to place, there will be famines; these (things) *are* the beginning of woes/birthpains.

13.9 But ye, ye see/beware *for* yourselves; for they will hand over/betray ye to councils and ye will be beaten in congregations, and ye will be stood upon/against governors and kings on account of me in/for a testimony to them. 13.10 And it is necessary first *for* the good message/gospel to be heralded/preached to all the ethnics.

13.11 And whenever they may lead ye, delivering over/betraying *ye*, worry ye not beforehand what ye might speak, but what ever might be given to ye in/at that hour/time, speak ye this, for ye, ye are not the (ones) speaking, but *it is* the Holy Spirit. 13.12 And a brother will betray/deliver over a brother to death and a father a child, and children will raise themselves up against parents, and they will put them to death; 13.13 and ye will be being hated by all because of my name. But the (one) enduring to an end, this (one) will be saved.

13.14 And whenever ye might see the detestable/abominable thing of the destruction/desolation having been stood/put where it is not necessary, the (one) reading, let him understand,

then let those in Judea flee to the mountains, 13.15 but the (one) on the roof/housetop let him not come down, neither let him go in to take anything out of his house. 13.16 And the (one) in the field, let him not return back to take his garment/cloak.

13.17 But woe to the (women) having in a belly/being pregnant and to those giving suck in those days. 13.18 But pray ye that it might not happen of/from

μὴ γένηται χειμῶνος·

13.19 ἔσονται γὰρ αἱ ἡμέραι ἐκεῖναι θλῖψις οἷα οὐ γέγονεν τοιαύτη ἀπ᾽ ἀρχῆς κτίσεως ἣν ἔκτισεν ὁ θεὸς ἕως τοῦ νῦν καὶ οὐ μὴ γένηται.

13.20 καὶ εἰ μὴ ἐκολόβωσεν κύριος τὰς ἡμέρας, οὐκ ἂν ἐσώθη πᾶσα σάρξ. ἀλλὰ διὰ τοὺς ἐκλεκτοὺς οὓς ἐξελέξατο ἐκολόβωσεν τὰς ἡμέρας.

13.21 καὶ τότε ἐάν τις ὑμῖν εἴπῃ, εἴδε ὧδε ὁ χριστός, εἴδε ἐκεῖ, μὴ πιστεύετε· 13.22 ἐγερθήσονται δὲ ψευδόχριστοι καὶ ψευδοπροφῆτε καὶ δώσουσιν σημῖα καὶ τέρατα πρὸς τὸ ἀποπλανᾶν, εἰ δυνατόν, τοὺς ἐκλεκτούς. 13.23 ὑμεῖς δὲ βλέπετε· ἰδοὺ προείρηκα ὑμῖν πάντα.

13.24 ἀλλὰ ἐν ἐκείναις ταῖς ἡμέραις μετὰ τὴν θλῖψιν ἐκείνην ὁ ἥλιος σκοτισθήσεται, καὶ ἡ σελήνη οὐ δώσι τὸ φέγγος αὐτῆς, 13.25 καὶ οἱ ἀστέρες ἔσονται ἐκ τοῦ οὐρανοῦ πίπτοντες, καὶ αἱ δυνάμεις αἱ ἐν τοῖς οὐρανοῖς σαλευθήσονται. 13.26 καὶ τότε ὄψονται « τὸν υἱὸν τοῦ ἀνθρώπου ἐρχόμενον ἐν νεφέλαις» μετὰ δυνάμεως πολλῆς καὶ δόξης. 13.27 καὶ τότε ἀποστελῖ τοὺς ἀγγέλους αὐτοῦ καὶ ἐπισυνάξει τοὺς ἐκλεκτοὺς αὐτοῦ ἐκ τῶν τεσσάρων ἀνέμων ἀπ᾽ ἄκρου γῆς ἕως ἄκρου οὐρανοῦ. 13.28 ἀπὸ δὲ τῆς συκῆς μάθετε τὴν παραβολήν· ὅταν ἤδη ὁ κλάδος αὐτῆς ἁπαλὸς γένηται καὶ ἐκφύῃ τὰ φύλλα, γινώσκετε ὅτι ἐγγὺς τὸ θέρος ἐστίν. 13.29 οὕτως καὶ ὑμῖς, ὅταν ἴδητε ταῦτα γινόμενα, γινώσκετε ὅτι ἐγγύς ἐστιν ἐπὶ θύραις. 13.30 ἀμὴν λέγω ὑμῖν ὅτι οὐ μὴ παρέλθῃ ἡ γενεὰ αὕτη μέχρι ταῦτα πάντα γένηται. 13.31 ὁ οὐρανὸς καὶ ἡ γῆ παρελεύσονται, οἱ δὲ λόγοι μου οὐ μὴ παρελεύσονται.

13.32 περὶ δὲ τῆς ἡμέρας ἐκείνης ἢ τῆς ὥρας οὐδεὶς οἶδεν, οὐδὲ οἱ ἄγγελοι ἐν οὐρανῷ οὐδὲ ὁ υἱός, εἰ μὴ ὁ πατήρ.

13.33 βλέπετε ἀγρυπνῖτε καὶ προσεύχεσθε· οὐκ οἴδαται γὰρ πότε ὁ καιρός ἐστιν.

stormy weather/winter;

13.19   for those days will be an oppression/tribulation such as has not happened from the beginning of creation which   God created until the present (time), and might it by no means happen.

13.20   And unless/except the Lord shortened/cut short the days, every flesh would not be saved.   But he shortened/cut short the days because of the chosen/elect (ones) whom he chose.

13.21   And then if anyone might say to ye: Behold, the anointed (one) *is* here, behold there, believe ye not;   13.22 but false anointed (ones) and lying/false prophets will be raised up, and they will give signs and wonders toward the (thing) to deceive/lead astray, if possible, the chosen/elect (ones). 13.23 But ye, ye see/beware; behold I have said all (things) to ye beforehand.

13.24   But in those days after   that oppression/affliction, the sun will be darkened, and the moon will not give her light,   13.25 and the stars will be falling out of the sky, and the powers in   the skies/heavens will be shaken. 13.26   And then they will see/behold THE SON OF THE MAN COMING IN/ON CLOUDS with much power and glory/fame.   13.27 And then he will send his messengers/angels and they   will gather his chosen/elect (ones) out of the four winds from the tip/point of earth until a tip/point of sky/heaven. 13.28 And from the fig tree learn ye the parable/illustration: Whenever her branch might become   already/now tender and may put out the leaves, ye know that the summer is near.   13.29 So also ye, whenever ye might see these (things) happening, ye know that it is near, at *the* doors.   13.30 Truly I say to ye that by no means might this generation go by until all these (things) might happen/become.   13.31   The sky/heaven and the land/earth will pass/go by, but my sayings/words will by no means pass by/away.

13.32   But concerning that day or the hour/time, no one knows, neither the messengers/angels in heaven nor the son, except the father.

13.33   See/look ye, be ye watching, and be ye praying; for ye know not when the season/time is.

13.34 ὡς ἄνθρωπος ἀπόδημος ἀφὶς τὴν οἰκίαν αὐτοῦ καὶ δοὺς τοῖς δούλοις αὐτοῦ τὴν ἐξουσίαν, ἑκάστῳ τὸ ἔργον αὐτοῦ, καὶ τῷ θυρωρῷ ἐνετίλατο ἵνα γρηγορῇ. 13.35 γρηγορῖτε οὖν, οὐκ οἴδατε γὰρ πότε ὁ κύριος τῆς οἰκίας ἔρχεται, ἢ ὀψὲ ἢ μεσονύκτιον ἢ ἀλεκτοροφωνίας ἢ πρωΐ, 13.36 μὴ ἐλθὼν ἐξαίφνης εὕρῃ ὑμᾶς καθεύδοντας. 13.37 ὃ δὲ ὑμῖν λέγω, πᾶσιν λέγω, γρηγορεῖτε. 14.1 ἦν δὲ τὸ πάσχα καὶ τὰ ἄζυμα μετὰ δύο ἡμέρας. καὶ ἐζήτουν οἱ ἀρχιερῖς καὶ οἱ γραμματῖς πῶς αὐτὸν ἐν δόλῳ κρατήσαντες ἀποκτίνωσι· 14.2 ἔλεγον γάρ, μὴ ἐν τῇ ἑορτῇ, μήποτε ἔσται θόρυβος τοῦ λαοῦ. 14.3 καὶ ὄντος αὐτοῦ ἐν Βηθανίᾳ ἐν τῇ οἰκίᾳ Σίμωνος τοῦ λεπροῦ κατακειμένου αὐτοῦ ἦλθεν γυνὴ ἔχουσα ἀλάβαστρον μύρου νάρδου πιστικῆς πολυτελοῦς· συντρίψασα τὴν ἀλάβαστρον κατέχεεν αὐτοῦ τῆς κεφαλῆς. 14.4 ἦσαν δέ τινες ἀγανακτοῦντες πρὸς ἑαυτούς, εἰς τί ἡ ἀπώλια αὕτη τοῦ μύρου γέγονεν; 14.5 ἠδύνατο γὰρ τὸ μύρον πραθῆναι ἐπάνω δηναρίων τριακοσίων καὶ δοθῆνε τοῖς πτωχοῖς· καὶ ἐνεβριμοῦντο αὐτῇ. 14.6 ὁ δὲ Ἰησοῦς εἶπεν, ἄφετε αὐτήν· τί αὐτῇ κόπους παρέχετε; καλὸν γὰρ ἔργον ἠργάσατο ἐν ἐμοί. 14.7 πάντοτε γὰρ τοὺς πτωχοὺς ἔχετε μεθ' ἑαυτῶν, καὶ ὅταν θέλητε δύνασθαι αὐτοῖς εὖ ποιῆσαι, ἐμὲ δὲ οὐ πάντοτε ἔχετε. 14.8 ὃ ἔσχεν ἐποίησεν· προέλαβεν μυρίσαι τὸ σῶμά μου εἰς τὸν ἐνταφιασμόν.

14.9 ἀμὴν δὲ λέγω ὑμῖν, ὅπου ἐὰν κηρυχθῇ τὸ εὐαγγέλιον εἰς ὅλον τὸν κόσμον, καὶ ὃ ἐποίησεν αὕτη λαληθήσεται εἰς μνημόσυνον αὐτῆς. 14.10 καὶ Ἰούδας Ἰσκαριὼθ εἷς τῶν δώδεκα ἀπῆλθεν πρὸς τοὺς ἀρχιερῖς ἵνα αὐτὸν παραδῷ αὐτοῖς.

14.11 οἱ δὲ ἀκούσαντες ἐχάρησαν καὶ ἐπηγγίλαντο αὐτῷ ἀργύριον δοῦναι. καὶ ἐζήτι πῶς αὐτὸν εὐκαίρως παραδῷ. 14.12 καὶ τῇ πρώτῃ ἡμέρᾳ τῶν ἀζύμων, ὅτε τὸ πάσχα ἔθυον, λέγουσιν

13.34 As a man away on a journey, having left his house and having given the authority to his slaves, to each his work, and he commanded to the doorkeeper that he should watch. 13.35 Therefore watch ye, for ye know not when the lord of the house comes, either late (evening) or midnight or at cock-crowing or early in *the* morning, 13.36 lest having come suddenly, he might find ye sleeping. 13.37 And what I say to ye, I say to all: Be ye watching. 14.1 And it was the passover and the unleavened (loaves) after two days. And the high priests and the scribes were seeking how they might kill him, having seized him by cunning/treachery; 14.2 for they were saying: Not in/at the festival, lest there will be then an uproar from the people. 14.3 And of him being in Bethany in the house of Simon the leper, of him re-clining, a woman came having an alabaster flask of very costly ointment of genuine nard; having broken the alabaster flask, she poured it out *over* his head, 14.4 and there were some being angry to themselves: To/for what has become this destruction/waste of the ointment? 14.5 For it was being possible *for* the ointment to be sold from above three hundred denarii and to be given to the poor (ones); and they were being angry with her. 14.6 But Jesus said: Ye forgive her; why cause ye troubles for her? For she worked a good work in/on me. 14.7 For ye always have the poor (ones) with yourselves, and whenever ye might want/ wish ye are able to do well for them, but me ye have not always. 14.8 What she had, she did; she took beforehand to anoint my body to/for the entombment.

14.9 And truly I say to ye: Where ever the good message/gospel might be heralded/preached in the entire world, also what this (one/woman) did will be spoken in memory of her. 14.10 And Judas the Iscari-ot, one of the twelve, went to the high priests in order that he might betray him/hand him over to them.

14.11 And they, having listened, they rejoiced and promised to give silver/money to him. And he was seeking/debating how he might opportunely betray/de-liver him. 14.12 And in/on the first day of the unleavenings (loaves), when they were sacrificing the

αὐτῷ οἱ μαθηταὶ αὐτοῦ, ποῦ θέλις ἀπελθόντες ἑτοιμάσωμεν ἵνα φάγῃς τὸ πάσχα; 14.13 καὶ ἀποστέλλει δύο τῶν μαθητῶν αὐτοῦ καὶ λέγει αὐτοῖς, ὑπάγεται εἰς τὴν πόλιν, καὶ ἀπαντήσι ὑμῖν ἄνθρωπος κεράμιον ὕδατος βαστάζων· ἀκολουθήσατε αὐτῷ, 14.14 καὶ ὅπου ἐὰν εἰσέλθῃ εἴπατε τῷ οἰκοδεσπότῃ ὅτι ὁ διδάσκαλος λέγει, ποῦ ἐστιν τὸ κατάλυμά μου ὅπου τὸ πάσχα μετὰ τῶν μαθητῶν μου φάγω; 14.15 καὶ αὐτὸς ὑμῖν δείξει ἀνάγαιον μέγα ἐστρωμένον ἕτοιμον· κἀκεῖ ἑτοιμάσατε ἡμῖν. 14.16 καὶ ἐξῆλθον οἱ μαθηταὶ καὶ ἦλθον εἰς τὴν πόλιν καὶ εὗρον καθὼς εἶπεν αὐτοῖς, καὶ ἡτοίμασαν τὸ πάσχα. 14.17 καὶ ὀψίας γενομένης ἔρχεται μετὰ τῶν δώδεκα. 14.18 καὶ ἀνακειμένων αὐτῶν καὶ ἐσθιόντων ὁ Ἰησοῦς εἶπεν, ἀμὴν λέγω ὑμῖν ὅτι εἷς ἐξ ὑμῶν παραδώσει με, ὁ ἐσθίων μετ' ἐμοῦ. 14.19 ἤρξαντο λυπῖσθαι καὶ λέγιν αὐτῷ εἷς κατὰ εἷς, μήτι ἐγώ; 14.20 ὁ δὲ εἶπεν αὐτοῖς, εἷς τῶν δώδεκα, ὁ ἐμβαπτόμενος μετ' ἐμοῦ εἰς τὸ τρύβλιον.

14.21 ὅτι ὁ μὲν υἱὸς τοῦ ἀνθρώπου ὑπάγι καθὼς γέγραπται περὶ αὐτοῦ, οὐαὶ δὲ τῷ ἀνθρώπῳ ἐκίνῳ δι' οὗ ὁ υἱὸς τοῦ ἀνθρώπου παραδίδοται· καλὸν αὐτῷ εἰ οὐκ ἐγεννήθη ὁ ἄνθρωπος ἐκεῖνος. 14.22 καὶ ἐσθιόντων αὐτῶν λαβὼν ὁ Ἰησοῦς ἄρτον ἔκλασεν εὐλογήσας καὶ ἔδωκεν αὐτοῖς καὶ εἶπεν, λάβετε, τοῦτό ἐστιν τὸ σῶμά μου. 14.23 καὶ λαβὼν ποτήριον εὐχαριστήσας ἔδωκεν αὐτοῖς, καὶ ἔπιον ἐξ αὐτοῦ πάντες. 14.24 καὶ εἶπεν αὐτοῖς, τοῦτό ἐστιν τὸ αἷμά μου τῆς διαθήκης τὸ ἐκχυννόμενον ὑπὲρ πολλῶν· 14.25 ἀμὴν λέγω ὑμῖν ὅτι οὐ μὴ πίω ἐκ τοῦ γενήματος τῆς ἀμπέλου ἕως τῆς ἡμέρας ἐκείνης ὅταν αὐτὸ πίνω καινὸν ἐν τῇ βασιλείᾳ τοῦ θεοῦ. 14.26 καὶ ὑμνήσαντες ἐξῆλθον εἰς τὸ ὄρος τῶν ἐλαιῶν. 14.27 καὶ λέγει αὐτοῖς ὁ Ἰησοῦς ὅτι πάντες σκανδαλισθήσεσθαι, ὅτι γέγραπται, « πατάξω τὸν ποιμένα, καὶ τὰ πρόβατα διασκορπισθήσονται» 14.28 ἀλλὰ μετὰ τὸ ἐγερθῆναί με προάξω ὑμᾶς εἰς τὴν Γαλιλαίαν. 14.29 ὁ δὲ

passover (lamb), his learners/pupils say to him: Where *do* you want/wish *that* having gone, we might prepare/ make ready in order that you might eat the passover (lamb)? 14.13 And he sends away two of his learners/ pupils, and he says to them: Depart/go ye into the city, and a man bearing a clay/pottery jar of water will meet you; ye follow with him, 14.14 and wherever he might go in/enter, say ye to the housemaster: The teacher says: Where is my guest room, where I might eat the passover (lamb) with my learners/pupils? 14.15 And he, he will show to ye a large upper room, having been spread ready; and ye prepare *it* there for us. 14.16 And the learners/pupils went forth and came into the city and found even as he said to them, and they prepared the passover (lamb). 14.17 And from evening having become, he comes with the twelve. 14.18 And from them reclining and eating, Jesus said: Truly I say to ye that one out of ye will deliver me up/betray me, the (one) eating with me. 14.19 They began to grieve and to say to him one by one: Not I? 14.20 But he said to them: One of the twelve, the (one) dipping into the dish with me.

14.21 Because indeed the son of the man goes away as it has been written about him, but woe to that man through whom the son of the man is betrayed/handed over; *it is* better for him if that man was not generated/born. 14.22 And from them eating, Jesus having taken a loaf, he broke *it*, and he gave to them and said: Take/receive ye, this is my body. 14.23 And having taken a cup, having given thanks, he gave to them, and they all drank out of it. 14.24 And he said to them: This is my blood of the covenant, the (blood) being poured out in behalf of many; 14.25 Truly I say to ye that by no means shall I drink out of/from the product/fruit of the vine until that day when I may drink it new in the kingdom of God. 14.26 And having sung a hymn, they went out to the mountain of the olives. 14.27 And Jesus says to them: Ye will all be caused to stumble, because it has been written: I SHALL SMITE THE SHEPHERD AND THE SHEEP WILL BE SCATTERED; 14.28 but after the (thing) *for* me to be raised up, I shall go before/precede ye into Galilee.

Πέτρος ἔφη αὐτῷ, εἰ καὶ πάντες σκανδαλισθήσονται, ἀλλ' οὐκ ἐγώ.

14.30 καὶ λέγει αὐτῷ ὁ Ἰησοῦς, ἀμὴν λέγω σοι ὅτι σὺ σήμερον ταύτῃ τῇ νυκτὶ πρὶν ἀλέκτορα φωνῆσαι τρίς με ἀπαρνήσει. 14.31 ὁ δὲ ἐκπερισσῶς ἐλάλει, ἐὰν δέῃ με συναποθανῖν σοι, οὐ μή σε ἀπαρνήσομε. ὡσαύτως δὲ καὶ πάντες ἔλεγον. 14.32 καὶ ἔρχονται εἰς χωρίον οὗ τὸ ὄνομα Γεθσημανεί, καὶ λέγει τοῖς μαθηταῖς αὐτοῦ, καθίσατε ὧδε ἕως προσεύξωμαι. 14.33 καὶ παραλαμβάνει τὸν Πέτρον καὶ Ἰάκωβον καὶ Ἰωάννην μετ' αὐτοῦ, καὶ ἤρξατο ἐκθαμβεῖσθαι καὶ ἀδημονῖν,

14.34 καὶ λέγει αὐτοῖς, περίλυπός ἐστιν ἡ ψυχή μου ἕως θανάτου· μίνατε ὧδε καὶ γρηγορεῖτε. 14.35 καὶ προελθὼν μικρὸν ἔπιπτεν ἐπὶ τῆς γῆς, καὶ προσηύχετο εἰ δυνατόν ἐστιν παρέλθιν ἀπ' αὐτοῦ ἡ ὥρα, 14.36 καὶ ἔλεγεν, ἀββά ὁ πατήρ, πάντα δυνατά σοι· παρένεγκαι τὸ ποτήριον τοῦτο ἀπ' ἐμοῦ· ἀλλ' οὐ τί ἐγὼ θέλω ἀλλὰ τί σύ. 14.37 καὶ ἔρχεται καὶ εὑρίσκει αὐτοὺς καθεύδοντας, καὶ λέγει τῷ Πέτρῳ, Σίμων, καθεύδις; οὐκ ἴσχυσας μίαν ὥραν γρηγορῆσαι; 14.38 γρηγορεῖτε καὶ προσεύχεσθαι, ἵνα μὴ ἔλθηται εἰς πιρασμόν· τὸ μὲν πνεῦμα πρόθυμον ἡ δὲ σὰρξ ἀσθενής. 14.39 καὶ πάλιν ἀπελθὼν προσηύξατο τὸν αὐτὸν λόγον εἰπών. 14.40 καὶ πάλιν ἐλθὼν εὗρεν αὐτοὺς καθεύδοντας, ἦσαν γὰρ αὐτῶν οἱ ὀφθαλμοὶ καταβαρυνόμενοι, καὶ οὐκ ἤδισαν τί ἀποκριθῶσιν αὐτῷ. 14.41 καὶ ἔρχεται τὸ τρίτον καὶ λέγει αὐτοῖς, καθεύδετε τὸ λοιπὸν καὶ ἀναπαύεσθε; ἀπέχει· ἦλθεν ἡ ὥρα, ἰδοὺ παραδίδοται ὁ υἱὸς τοῦ ἀνθρώπου εἰς τὰς χῖρας τῶν ἁμαρτωλῶν. 14.42 ἐγείρεσθε ἄγωμεν· ἰδοὺ ὁ παραδιδούς με ἤγγισεν.

14.43 καὶ εὐθὺς ἔτι αὐτοῦ λαλοῦντος παραγείνεται Ἰούδας εἷς τῶν δώδεκα καὶ μετ' αὐτοῦ ὄχλος μετὰ μαχαιρῶν καὶ ξύλων παρὰ τῶν ἀρχιερέων καὶ τῶν γραμματέων καὶ πρεσβυτέρων. 14.44 δεδώκει δὲ ὁ παραδιδοὺς αὐτὸν σύσσημον αὐτοῖς λέγων, ὃν ἂν φιλήσω αὐτός ἐστιν· κρατήσατε αὐτὸν καὶ ἀπάγετε

14.29 And Peter said to him: Even if all are caused to stumble, but not I.

14.30 And Jesus says to him: Truly I say to you that you today, in this very night before a cock to crow, three times you will deny me. 14.31 But the (he) spoke more vehemently: If it be necessary *for* me to die with you, by no means shall I deny you. And all were also saying likewise. 14.32 And they come into a region/district of which the name *is* Gethsemane, and he says to his learners/pupils: Sit ye here until I might pray. 14.33 And he takes along Peter and James and John with him, and he began to be distressed and to be dejected,

14.34 and he says to them: My life/soul is deeply grieved until death; ye stay here and watch. 14.35 And having gone on a little (way), he was fallen upon the earth and he was praying if it is possible *for* the hour to pass away from him, 14.36 and he was saying: Abba, the father, all (things) are possible for you; remove this cup from me; but not what I, I will/wish but what you *will*. 14.37 And he comes and finds them sleeping, and he says to Peter: Simon, *do* you sleep? *Are* you not strong/able to watch *for* one hour? 14.38 Ye watch and ye pray, in order that ye might not come into temptation/testing; the spirit indeed *is* ready/willing but the flesh *is* weak. 14.39 And again having gone away, he prayed, having spoken the same saying/word. 14.40 And again having come, he found them sleeping, for their eyes had become very heavy, and they knew not what they might answer to him. 14.41 And he comes the third (time) and says to them: Sleep ye and rest ye *for* the remaining (time); it is sufficient; the hour/time came, behold the son of the man is betrayed/handed over into the hands of the sinners. 14.42 Rise ye up, let us go; behold/look, the (one) betraying me has drawn near.

14.43 And at once, from him still speaking, Judas, one of the twelve, arrives and with him a crowd with swords and woods/clubs, from the high priests and the scribes and the elders. 14.44 And the one betraying him had given a signal to them, saying: Whom ever I might kiss is he; seize ye him and lead away secure-

ἀσφαλῶς. 14.45 καὶ ἐλθὼν εὐθὺς προσελθὼν αὐτῷ λέγει, ῥαββεί, καὶ κατεφίλησεν αὐτόν. 14.46 οἱ δὲ ἐπέβαλαν τὰς χῖρας αὐτῶν καὶ ἐκράτησαν αὐτόν. 14.47 εἷς δέ τῶν παρεστηκότων σπασάμενος τὴν μάχαιραν ἔπαισεν τὸν δοῦλον τοῦ ἀρχιερέως καὶ ἀφῖλεν αὐτοῦ τὸ ὠτάριον.

14.48 καὶ ἀποκριθεὶς ὁ Ἰησοῦς εἶπεν αὐτοῖς, ὡς ἐπὶ λῃστὴν ἐξήλθαται μετὰ μαχαιρῶν καὶ ξύλων συλλαβῖν με; 14.49 καθ' ἡμέραν ἤμην πρὸς ὑμᾶς ἐν τῷ ἱερῷ διδάσκων καὶ οὐκ ἐκρατήσαταί με· ἀλλ' ἵνα πληρωθῶσιν αἱ γραφαί. 14.50 καὶ ἀφέντες αὐτὸν ἔφυγον πάντες.

14.51 καὶ νεανίσκος τις συνηκολούθει αὐτῷ περιβεβλημένος σινδόνα ἐπὶ γυμνοῦ, καὶ κρατοῦσιν αὐτόν·

14.52 ὁ δὲ καταλιπὼν τὴν σινδόνα γυμνὸς ἔφυγεν. 14.53 καὶ ἀπήγαγον τὸν Ἰησοῦν πρὸς τὸν ἀρχιερέα, καὶ συνέρχονται πάντες οἱ ἀρχιερῖς καὶ οἱ πρεσβύτεροι καὶ οἱ γραμματεῖς. 14.54 καὶ ὁ Πέτρος ἀπὸ μακρόθεν ἠκολούθησεν αὐτῷ ἕως ἔσω εἰς τὴν αὐλὴν τοῦ ἀρχιερέως, καὶ ἦν συγκαθήμενος μετὰ τῶν ὑπηρετῶν καὶ θερμαινόμενος πρὸς τὸ φῶς.

14.55 οἱ δὲ ἀρχιερεῖς καὶ ὅλον τὸ συνέδριον ἐζήτουν κατὰ τοῦ Ἰησοῦ μαρτυρίαν εἰς τὸ θανατῶσαι αὐτόν, καὶ οὐχ εὕρισκον· 14.56 πολλοὶ γὰρ ἐψευδομαρτύρουν κατ' αὐτοῦ, καὶ ἴσαι αἱ μαρτυρίαι οὐκ ἦσαν.

14.57 καί τινες ἀναστάντες ἐψευδομαρτύρουν κατ' αὐτοῦ λέγοντες 14.58 ὅτι -- εἶπεν ὅτι ἐγὼ καταλύσω τὸν ναὸν τοῦτον τὸν χειροποίητον καὶ διὰ τριῶν ἡμερῶν ἄλλον ἀχειροποίητον οἰκοδομήσω· 14.59 καὶ οὐδὲ οὕτως ἴση ἦν ἡ μαρτυρία αὐτῶν.

14.60 καὶ ἀναστὰς ὁ ἀρχιερεὺς εἰς μέσον ἐπηρώτησεν τὸν Ἰησοῦν λέγων, οὐκ ἀποκρίνῃ οὐδέν; τί οὗτοί σου καταμαρτυροῦσιν;

14.61 ὁ δὲ Ἰησοῦς ἐσιώπα καὶ οὐκ ἀπεκρίνατο οὐδέν. πάλιν ὁ ἀρχιερεὺς ἐπηρώτα αὐτὸν καὶ λέγει αὐτῷ, σὺ εἶ ὁ

ly.   14.45 And having come, immediately having come near him, he says: Rabbi, and he kissed him.   14.46 And they layed their hands upon and seized him.   14.47 But a certain one of those having been standing, having drawn the sword, he struck/hit the slave of the high priest and he took off from him the ear/cut off his ear.

14.48   And answering, Jesus said to them: As against a robber came ye out with swords and woods/clubs to apprehend me?   14.49 I was near/with ye daily, teaching in the *outer* temple/temple court and ye did not seize me; but that the writings might be fulfilled.   14.50 And having left him, they all fled.

14.51   And a certain youth was following with him, having been clothed *with* a linen sheet over nakedness/bare skin, and they seize him.

14.52   But the (he), having left the sheet behind, he escaped/ran away naked.   14.53 And they led Jesus away to the high priest, and all the high priests and the elders and the scribes come together. 14.54 And Peter followed him from afar until he *was* inside, in the yard/court of the high priest, and he was sitting with the servants/attendants and warming himself near the light.

14.55   But the high priests and the whole council/sanhedrin were seeking a witness against Jesus in/for the (thing) to put him to death, and they were not finding (one);   14.56 for many were testifying falsely against him, and the testimonies were not alike/in agreement.

14.57   And some having stood up were testifying falsely against him, saying 14.58 that -- he said: I, I shall destroy/overthrow this handmade *inner* temple and through three days I shall build another not made by hand;   14.59 And thus/so neither was their testimony equal/alike.

14.60   And having stood up in the middle, the high priest asked Jesus, saying: Answer you not nothing? Why/what *do* these (men) testify against you?

14.61   But Jesus was being silent and he answered not nothing. Again the high priest was questioning him and says to him: You, are you the anointed (one), the

χριστὸς ὁ υἱὸς τοῦ εὐλογητοῦ;

14.62 ὁ δὲ Ἰησοῦς εἶπεν, ἐγώ εἰμι, καὶ «ὄψεσθε τὸν υἱὸν τοῦ ἀνθρώπου ἐκ δεξιῶν καθήμενον τῆς δυνάμεως» καὶ «ἐρχόμενον μετὰ τῶν νεφελῶν τοῦ οὐρανοῦ.»

14.63 ὁ δὲ ἀρχιερεὺς διαρρήξας τοὺς χιτῶνας αὐτοῦ λέγει, τί ἔτι χρείαν ἔχομεν μαρτύρων; 14.64 ἰδὲ νῦν ἠκούσατε τῆς βλασφημίας· τί ὑμῖν φαίνεται;

οἱ δὲ πάντες κατέκριναν αὐτὸν ἔνοχον εἶναι θανάτου.

14.65 καὶ ἤρξαντό τινες ἐμπτύειν αὐτῷ καὶ περικαλύπτειν αὐτοῦ τὸ πρόσωπον καὶ κολαφίζειν αὐτὸν καὶ λέγειν αὐτῷ, προφήτευσον, καὶ οἱ ὑπηρέται ῥαπίσμασιν αὐτὸν ἔλαβον.

14.66 καὶ ὄντος τοῦ Πέτρου κάτω ἐν τῇ αὐλῇ ἔρχεται μία παιδίσκη τοῦ ἀρχιερέως, 14.67 καὶ ἰδοῦσα τὸν Πέτρον θερμαινόμενον ἐμβλέψασα αὐτῷ λέγει, καὶ σὺ μετὰ τοῦ Ἰησοῦ ἦσθα τοῦ Ναζαρηνοῦ.

14.68 ὁ δὲ ἠρνήσατο λέγων, οὔτε οἶδα οὔτε ἐπίσταμαι σὺ τί λέγεις. καὶ ἐξῆλθεν ἔξω εἰς τὸ προαύλιον. 14.69 καὶ ἡ παιδίσκη ἰδοῦσα αὐτὸν ἤρξατο πάλιν λέγειν τοῖς παρεστῶσιν ὅτι οὗτος ἐξ αὐτῶν ἐστιν.

14.70 ὁ δὲ πάλιν ἠρνεῖτο. καὶ μετὰ μεικρὸν πάλιν οἱ παρεστῶτες ἔλεγον τῷ Πέτρῳ, ἀληθῶς ἐξ αὐτῶν εἶ, καὶ γὰρ Γαλιλαῖος εἶ.

14.71 ὁ δὲ ἤρξατο ἀναθεματίζειν καὶ ὀμνύειν ὅτι οὐκ οἶδα τὸν ἄνθρωπον.

14.72 καὶ εὐθὺς ἀλέκτωρ ἐφώνησεν. καὶ ἀνεμνήσθη ὁ Πέτρος τὸ ῥῆμα ὡς εἶπεν αὐτῷ ὁ Ἰησοῦς ὅτι πρὶν ἀλέκτορα φωνῆσαι τρίς με ἀπαρνήσῃ· καὶ ἐπιβαλὼν ἔκλαιεν. 15.1 καὶ εὐθὺς πρωῒ συμβούλιον ἑτοιμάσαντες οἱ ἀρχιερεῖς μετὰ τῶν πρεσβυτέρων καὶ τῶν γραμματέων καὶ ὅλον τὸ συνέδριον δήσαντες τὸν Ἰησοῦν ἀπήνεγκαν καὶ παρέδωκαν Πειλάτῳ.

15.2 καὶ ἐπηρώτησεν αὐτὸν ὁ Πειλᾶτος, σὺ εἶ ὁ βασιλεὺς τῶν Ἰουδαίων;

son of the blessed/praised (one)?

14.62 And Jesus said: I, I am, and YE WILL BEHOLD THE SON OF THE MAN SITTING OUT OF RIGHT (ONES) OF THE POWER/POWERFUL (ONE) AND COMING WITH THE CLOUDS OF THE SKY/HEAVEN.

14.63 And the high priest, having torn his tunics, says: What need have we yet for witnesses? 14.64 Behold, ye now heard of the blasphemy/slander; what appears/seems *it* to ye?

And the (they) all condemned him to be guilty/ deserving of death.

14.65 And some began to spit on him and to cover his face and to hit him with the fist, and to say to him: You prophesy, and the servants/attendants took him *for* blows/handslaps.

14.66 And of Peter being below in the yard/ court, one maidservant of the high priest comes, 14.67 and having beheld Peter warming himself, having looked closely at him, she says: And you, you were with Jesus the Nazarene.

14.68 But the (he) denied *it*, saying: I neither know nor understand what you, you say. And he went out to the forecourt outside. 14.69 And the maidservant having seen/beheld him, she began again to say to those having been standing: This (one) is out of them.

14.70 But the (he) again was denying *it*. And after a little *time*, again those having been standing *by* were saying to Peter: You are truly out of/from them, for you are also a Galilean.

14.71 And the (he) began to declare with a curse and to swear: I know not the man.

14.72 And immediately a cock/rooster crowed. And Peter was reminded of the word as Jesus said to him: Before to crow a cock/rooster, you will deny me three times; and having pondered *it* he was weeping. 15.1 And early in the morning, the high priests, having readied/prepared a plot/plan with the elders and the scribes and the entire council/sanhedrin, having bound Jesus, they led/brought him away and delivered *him* to Pilate.

15.2 And Pilate questioned him: You, are you the king of the Judeans?

ὁ δὲ ἀποκριθεὶς αὐτῷ λέγει, σὺ λέγεις. 15.3 καὶ κατηγόρουν αὐτοῦ οἱ ἀρχιερεῖς πολλά.

15.4 ὁ δὲ Πειλᾶτος πάλιν ἐπηρώτησεν αὐτὸν λέγων, οὐκ ἀποκρίνῃ οὐδέν; ἴδε πόσα σου κατηγοροῦσιν.

15.5 ὁ δὲ Ἰησοῦς οὐκέτι οὐδὲν ἀπεκρίθη, ὥστε θαυμάζειν τὸν Πειλᾶτον.

15.6 κατὰ δὲ ἑορτὴν ἀπέλυεν αὐτοῖς ἕνα δέσμιον ὃν παρῃτοῦντο. 15.7 ἦν δὲ ὁ λεγόμενος Βαραββᾶς μετὰ τῶν στασιαστῶν δεδεμένος οἵτινες ἐν τῇ στάσι φόνον τινὰ πεποιήκεισαν. 15.8 καὶ ἀναβὰς ὁ ὄχλος ἤρξατο αἰτεῖσθαι καθὼς ἐποίει αὐτοῖς.

15.9 ὁ δὲ Πειλᾶτος ἀπεκρίθη αὐτοῖς λέγων, θέλετε ἀπολύσω ὑμῖν τὸν βασιλέα τῶν Ἰουδαίων; 15.10 ἐγίνωσκει γὰρ ὅτι διὰ φθόνον παραδεδώκεισαν αὐτὸν οἱ ἀρχιερεῖς.

15.11 οἱ δὲ ἀρχιερεῖς ἀνέσεισαν τὸν ὄχλον ἵνα μᾶλλον τὸν Βαραββᾶν ἀπολύσῃ αὐτοῖς. 15.12 ὁ δὲ Πειλᾶτος πάλιν ἀποκριθεὶς ἔλεγεν αὐτοῖς, τί οὖν ποιήσω ὃν λέγετε τὸν βασιλέα τῶν Ἰουδαίων; 15.13 οἱ δὲ πάλιν ἔκραξαν, σταύρωσον αὐτόν. 15.14 ὁ δὲ Πειλᾶτος ἔλεγεν αὐτοῖς, τί γὰρ κακὸν ἐποίησεν; οἱ δὲ περισσῶς ἔκραξαν λέγοντες, σταύρωσον αὐτόν.

15.15 ὁ δὲ Πειλᾶτος βουλόμενος ποιῆσαι τὸ ἱκανὸν τῷ ὄχλῳ ἀπέλυσεν αὐτοῖς τὸν Βαραββᾶν, καὶ παρέδωκεν τὸν Ἰησοῦν φραγελλώσας ἵνα σταυρωθῇ.

15.16 οἱ δὲ στρατιῶται ἀπήγαγον αὐτὸν ἔσω τῆς αὐλῆς, ὅ ἐστιν πραιτώριον, καὶ συγκαλοῦσιν ὅλην τὴν σπεῖραν. 15.17 καὶ ἐνδιδύσκουσιν αὐτὸν πορφύραν καὶ περιτιθέασιν αὐτῷ πλέξαντες ἀκάνθινον στέφανον· 15.18 καὶ ἤρξαντο ἀσπάζεσθαι αὐτὸν καὶ λέγειν, χαῖρε, βασιλεῦ τῶν Ἰουδαίων·

15.19 καὶ ἔτυπτον αὐτοῦ τὴν κεφαλὴν καλάμῳ καὶ ἐνέπτυον αὐτῷ, καὶ τιθέντες τὰ γόνατα προσεκύνουν αὐτῷ.

15.20 καὶ ὅτε ἐνέπαιξαν αὐτῷ, ἐξέδυσαν αὐτὸν τὴν

And the (he) answering to him, he says: You, you say *it*. 15.3 And the high priests were accusing many (things) of him.

15.4 But Pilate again questioned him, saying: *Do* you not answer nothing? Behold how many things they accuse of you.

15.5 But Jesus no longer answered nothing, so as *for* Pilate to wonder/marvel.

15.6 And according to a festival, he was releasing for them one prisoner whom they were requesting. 15.7 And there was the (one) being called Barabbas, having been bound with the insurrectionists who had done a certain murder in the insurrection. 15.8 And having gone up, the crowd began to petition according as he was doing for them.

15.9 But Pilate answered to them, saying: *Do* ye want/wish I might release for ye the king of the Judeans? 15.10 for he was knowing that the high priests had delivered him over because of envy.

15.11 But the high priests instigated/stirred up the crowd in order that he might rather release Barabbas for them. 15.12 And Pilate, answering again, was saying to them: Then what might I do *with him* whom ye call the king of the Judeans? 15.13 And they again cried out: You crucify him! 15.14 But Pilate was saying to them: For what bad did he? And they cried out more, saying: You crucify him!

15.15 And Pilate, willing to do that/the (thing) sufficient for the crowd, released Barabbas for them, and he handed over Jesus, having scourged/whipped *him*, in order that he might be crucified.

15.16 And the soldiers led him away inside the court, which is a praetorium, and they call together/muster the entire cohort/detachment. 15.17 And they clothed him *with* purple and having woven a thorny crown/wreathe, they placed it on/around him; 15.18 and they began to salute/greet him and to say: Greetings, king of the Judeans.

15.19 And they were hitting his head with a staff and spitting on him, and putting *down* the knees, they were worshiping him.

15.20 And when/*after* they mocked/ridiculed him,

πορφύραν καὶ ἐνέδυσαν αὐτὸν τὰ ἴδια ἱμάτια αὐτοῦ. καὶ ἐξάγουσιν αὐτὸν ἵνα σταυρώσωσιν.

15.21 καὶ ἀγγαρεύουσιν παράγοντά τινα Σίμωνα Κυρηναῖον ἐρχόμενον ἀπ' ἀγροῦ, τὸν πατέρα Ἀλεξάνδρου καὶ Ῥούφου, ἵνα ἄρῃ τὸν σταυρὸν αὐτοῦ.

15.22 καὶ φέρουσιν αὐτὸν ἐπὶ τὸν Γολγοθᾶν τόπον, ὅπερ ἔστιν μεθερμηνευόμενον κρανίου τόπος.

15.23 καὶ ἐδίδουν αὐτῷ ἐσμυρνισμένον οἶνον, ὃς δὲ οὐκ ἔλαβεν.

15.24 καὶ σταυρώσαντες αὐτὸν διαμερίζονται τὰ ἱμάτια ἑαυτοῦ, βάλλοντες κλῆρον ἐπ' αὐτὰ τίς τί ἄρῃ.

15.25 ἦν δὲ ὥρα τρίτη καὶ ἐσταύρωσαν αὐτόν.

15.26 καὶ ἦν ἡ ἐπιγραφὴ τῆς αἰτίας αὐτοῦ ἐπιγεγραμμένη, ὁ βασιλεὺς τῶν Ἰουδαίων.

15.27 καὶ σὺν αὐτῷ σταυροῦσιν δύο λῃστάς, ἕνα ἐκ δεξιῶν καὶ ἕνα ἐξ εὐωνύμων αὐτοῦ.

15.29 καὶ οἱ παραπορευόμενοι ἐβλασφήμουν αὐτὸν κεινοῦντες τὰς κεφαλὰς αὐτῶν καὶ λέγοντες, οὐὰ ὁ καταλύων τὸν ναὸν καὶ ἐν τρισὶν ἡμέραις οἰκοδομῶν, 15.30 σῶσον σεαυτὸν καταβὰς ἀπὸ τοῦ σταυροῦ.

15.31 ὁμοίως καὶ οἱ ἀρχιερεῖς ἐμπαίζοντες πρὸς ἀλλήλους μετὰ τῶν γραμματέων ἔλεγον, ἄλλους ἔσωσεν, ἑαυτὸν οὐ δύναται σῶσαι· 15.32 ὁ χριστὸς ὁ βασιλεὺς Ἰσραὴλ καταβάτω νῦν ἀπὸ τοῦ σταυροῦ, ἵνα ἴδωμεν καὶ πιστεύσωμεν. καὶ οἱ συνεσταυρωμένοι σὺν αὐτῷ ὠνείδιζον αὐτόν.

15.33 καὶ γενομένης ὥρας ἕκτης σκότος ἐγένετο ἐφ' ὅλην τὴν γῆν ἕως ὥρας ἐνάτης.

15.34 καὶ τῇ ἐνάτῃ ὥρᾳ ἐβόησεν ὁ Ἰησοῦς φωνῇ μεγάλῃ, « ἐλωΐ ἐλωΐ λεμὰ σαβαχθάνει;» ὅ ἐστιν μεθερμηνευόμενον « ὁ θεός μου ὁ θεός μου, εἰς τί ἐγκατέλιπές με;»

15.35 καὶ τινες τῶν παρεστώτων ἀκούσαντες ἔλεγον, ἴδε

they stripped from him the purple and put his own garments *on* him. And they lead him forth in order that they might crucify *him*.

15.21   And they compel/press into service a certain Simon, a Cyrenian passing by, coming from a field, the father of Alexander and Rufus, that he might take up/carry his cross.

15.22   And they bring him to the place Golgotha, which is indeed, being translated, a place of a skull.

15.23   And they were giving wine having been spiced with myrrh to him, but which he took/received not.

15.24   And having crucified him, they divide the garments of himself, casting/throwing a lot on them *for* who might take up/receive what.

15.25   And it was *the* third hour and they crucified him.

15.26   And the superscription of his charges/accusations were having been written above *him*: The king of the Judeans.

15.27   And they crucify two robbers with him, one from *the* right and one from *the* left of him.

15.29   And those passing by were reviling/blaspheming him, moving/shaking their heads and saying: Ah, the (one) destroying the *inner* temple and building it in three days,   15.30 you save yourself, coming down from the cross.

15.31   Similarly, the high priests also were mocking to/with one another with the scribes, they were saying: He saved others, he is not able to save himself;   15.32 the anointed (one), the king of Israel, let him come down now from the cross, that we might see and we might believe.   Even those having been crucified with him were reproaching him.

15.33   And from *it* having become *the* sixth hour, darkness became/came about upon/over all the land/ earth until *the* ninth hour.

15.34   And in/at the ninth hour Jesus yelled in a great voice: ELOI, ELOI, LEMA SABACHTHANI? Which is, being translated: MY GOD, MY GOD, IN/FOR WHY *did* YOU ABANDON/FORSAKE ME?

15.35   And some of those having been standing by,

Ἡλείαν φωνεῖ. 15.36 δραμὼν δέ τις καὶ γεμίσας σπόγγον ὄξους περιθεὶς καλάμῳ ἐπότιζεν αὐτόν, λέγων, ἄφες ἴδωμεν εἰ ἔρχεται Ἡλείας καθελεῖν αὐτόν.

15.37 ὁ δὲ Ἰησοῦς ἀφεὶς φωνὴν μεγάλην ἐξέπνευσεν.

15.38 καὶ τὸ καταπέτασμα τοῦ ναοῦ ἐσχίσθη εἰς δύο ἀπὸ ἄνωθεν ἕως κάτω.

15.39 ἰδὼν δὲ ὁ κεντυρίων ὁ παρεστηκὼς ἐξ ἐναντίας αὐτοῦ ὅτι οὕτως ἐξέπνευσεν εἶπεν, ἀληθῶς οὗτος ὁ ἄνθρωπος υἱὸς θεοῦ ἦν.

15.40 ἦσαν δὲ καὶ γυναῖκες ἀπὸ μακρόθεν θεωροῦσαι, ἐν αἷς καὶ Μαρία ἡ Μαγδαληνὴ καὶ Μαρία ἡ Ἰακώβου τοῦ μικροῦ καὶ Ἰωσῆτος μήτηρ καὶ Σαλώμη, 15.41 αἳ ὅτε ἦν ἐν τῇ Γαλειλαίᾳ ἠκολούθουν αὐτῷ καὶ διηκόνουν αὐτῷ, καὶ ἄλλαι πολλαὶ αἱ συναναβᾶσαι αὐτῷ εἰς Ἱεροσόλυμα.

15.42 καὶ ἤδη ὀψείας γενομένης, ἐπεὶ ἦν παρασκευή, ὅ ἐστιν προσάββατον, 15.43 ἐλθὼν Ἰωσὴφ ὁ ἀπὸ Ἁριμαθαίας εὐσχήμων βουλευτής, ὃς καὶ αὐτὸς ἦν προσδεχόμενος τὴν βασιλείαν τοῦ θεοῦ, τολμήσας εἰσῆλθεν πρὸς τὸν Πειλᾶτον καὶ ᾐτήσατο τὸ σῶμα τοῦ Ἰησοῦ. 15.44 ὁ δὲ Πειλᾶτος ἐθαύμασεν εἰ ἤδη τέθνηκεν, καὶ προσκαλεσάμενος τὸν κεντυρίωνα ἐπηρώτησεν αὐτὸν εἰ πάλαι ἀπέθανεν· 15.45 καὶ γνοὺς ἀπὸ τοῦ κεντυρίωνος ἐδωρήσατο τὸ πτῶμα τῷ Ἰωσήφ.

15.46 καὶ ἀγοράσας σινδόνα καθελὼν αὐτὸν ἐνείλησεν τῇ σινδόνι καὶ ἔθηκεν αὐτὸν ἐν μνήματι ὃ ἦν λελατομημένον ἐκ πέτρας, καὶ προσεκύλισεν λίθον μέγαν ἐπὶ τὴν θύραν τοῦ μνημείου. 15.47 ἡ δὲ Μαρία ἡ Μαγδαληνὴ καὶ Μαρία ἡ Ἰωσῆτος ἐθεώρουν ποῦ τέθειται.

16.1 Καὶ διαγενομένου τοῦ σαββάτου ἡ Μαρία ἡ Μαγδαληνὴ καὶ Μαρία ἡ τοῦ Ἰακώβου καὶ Σαλώμη ἠγόρασαν ἀρώματα ἵνα ἐλθοῦσαι ἀλίψωσιν αὐτόν. 16.2 καὶ λίαν πρωῒ τῇ

having heard, were saying: Behold, he calls Elias. 15.36 And a certain one, having run and filled a sponge *with* sour wine, having put *it* on a staff/cane pole, he gave him a drink, saying: You leave/wait, let us see if Elias comes to take him down.

15.37 But Jesus, having let go a great sound/ voice, breathed his last/died/expired.

15.38 And the veil/curtain of the *inner* temple was split/torn in two from above until below.

15.39 And having seen that he thus died, the centurion, having been standing by opposite from him, said: Truly this (one) was a son of God.

15.40 And there were also women there, observing from afar, among whom *were* both Mary the Magdalene, and Mary the mother of the little/lesser James and Joses, and Salome, 15.41 who were following with him and were serving/ministering to him when he was in Galilee, and the many others (women) having come up with him to Jerusalem.

15.42 And from/of it having become late already, since it was Friday/preparation (day), which is before a sabbath, 15.43 having come Joseph, the (one) from Arimathaea, a decent/becoming councilman, who was also himself awaiting/expecting the kingdom of God, having dared, he went in to Pilate and he requested the body of Jesus. 15.44 But Pilate was wondering if he has/ had already died, and having summoned the centurion he questioned him if he died long ago/in the past; 15.45 and having learned/known from the centurion, he grant-ed the corpse to Joseph.

15.46 And having bought a linen sheet, having taken him down, he wrapped *him* in the linen sheet and put him in a tomb which had been hewed out of rock. And he rolled forward a great stone over the door of the tomb. 15.47 And Mary the Magdalene and Mary the (one) of Joses were observing where he has been layed.

16.1 And of/from the sabbath having passed, Mary the Magdalene and Mary the (one) of James, and Salome bought spices/ointments in order that having come they might anoint him. 16.2 And very early in the morning on the one (day) of the sabbaths/first day of the

μιᾷ τῶν σαββάτων ἔρχονται ἐπὶ τὸ μνημὰ ἀνατίλαντος τοῦ ἡλίου. 16.3 καὶ ἔλεγον πρὸς ἑαυτάς, τίς ἀποκυλίσει ἡμῖν τὸν λίθον ἐκ τῆς θύρας τοῦ μνημείου; 16.4 καὶ ἀναβλέψασαι θεωροῦσιν ἀποκεκυλίσμενον τὸν λίθον, ἦν γὰρ μέγας σφόδρα.

16.5 καὶ εἰσελθοῦσαι εἰς τὸ μνημεῖον εἶδον νεανίσκον καθήμενον ἐν τοῖς δεξιοῖς περιβεβλημένον στολὴν λευκήν, καὶ ἐξεθαμβήθησαν.

16.6 ὁ δὲ λέγει αὐταῖς, μὴ ἐκθαμβεῖσθε· Ἰησοῦν ζητεῖτε τὸν Ναζαρηνὸν τὸν ἐσταυρωμένον· ἠγέρθη, οὐκ ἔστιν ὧδε· ἴδε ὁ τόπος ὅπου ἔθηκαν αὐτόν.

16.7 ἀλλὰ ὑπάγετε εἴπατε τοῖς μαθηταῖς αὐτοῦ καὶ τῷ Πέτρῳ ὅτι προάγει ὑμᾶς εἰς τὴν Γαλιλαίαν· ἐκεῖ αὐτὸν ὄψεσθε, καθὼς εἶπεν ὑμῖν.

16.8 καὶ ἐξελθοῦσαι ἔφυγον ἀπὸ τοῦ μνημείου, εἶχεν γὰρ αὐτὰς τρόμος καὶ ἔκστασις· καὶ οὐδενὶ οὐδὲν εἶπον, ἐφοβοῦντο γάρ.

Εὐαγγέλιον Κατὰ Μάρκον

week, they came to the grave/tomb from the sun having risen. 16.3 And they were saying to themselves: Who will roll away for us the stone out of/from the door/ entrance of the tomb? 16.4 And having looked up, they behold the stone having been rolled away, for it was exceedingly big/great.

16.5 And having entered into the tomb, they saw a young (man) sitting among the right (ones/things), having been clothed *in* a long white robe, and they were greatly amazed/distressed.

16.6 But the (he) says to them: Be ye not distressed; ye seek Jesus the Nazarene, the (one) having been crucified; he was raised up, he is not here; behold the place where they put/layed him.

16.7 But ye go away, say ye to his learners/pupils and to Peter that he goes before/precedes ye into Galilee; ye will see/behold him there, even as he said to ye.

16.8 And having gone out, they ran away/fled from the tomb, for trembling and ecstasy/amazement was holding/having them; and they said nothing to no one, for they were fearing/being afraid.

A Good Message According to Mark

This is the Sinaitic New Testament, book of Luke.

1.1 Ἐπειδήπερ πολλοὶ ἐπεχείρησαν ἀνατάξασθαι διήγησιν περὶ τῶν πεπληροφορημένων ἐν ἡμῖν πραγμάτων, 1.2 καθὼς παρέδοσαν ἡμῖν οἱ ἀπ᾽ ἀρχῆς αὐτόπται καὶ ὑπηρέται γενόμενοι τοῦ λόγου, 1.3 ἔδοξε κἀμοὶ παρηκολουθηκότι ἄνωθεν πᾶσιν ἀκριβῶς καθεξῆς σοι γράψαι, κράτιστε Θεόφιλε, 1.4 ἵνα ἐπιγνῷς περὶ ὧν κατηχήθης λόγων τὴν ἀσφάλιαν. 1.5 ἐγένετο ἐν ταῖς ἡμέραις Ἡρῴδου βασιλέως τῆς Ἰουδαίας ἱερεύς τις ὀνόματι Ζαχαρίας ἐξ ἐφημερίας Ἀβιά, καὶ γυνὴ αὐτῷ ἐκ τῶν θυγατέρων Ἀαρών, καὶ τὸ ὄνομα αὐτῆς Ἐλισάβετ.

1.6 ἦσαν δὲ δίκαιοι ἀμφότεροι ἐναντίον τοῦ θεοῦ, πορευόμενοι ἐν πάσαις ταῖς ἐντολαῖς καὶ δικαιώμασιν τοῦ κυρίου ἄμεμπτοι. 1.7 καὶ οὐκ ἦν αὐτοῖς τέκνον, καθότι ἦν ἡ Ἐλεισάβετ στεῖρα, καὶ ἀμφότεροι προβεβηκότες ἐν ταῖς ἡμέραις αὐτῶν ἦσαν.

1.8 ἐγένετο δὲ ἐν τῷ ἱερατεύειν αὐτὸν ἐν τῇ τάξει τῆς ἐφημερίας αὐτοῦ ἐνάντιον τοῦ θεοῦ, 1.9 κατὰ τὸ ἔθος τῆς ἱερατείας ἔλαχε τοῦ θυμιᾶσαι εἰσελθὼν εἰς τὸν ναὸν τοῦ κυρίου, 1.10 καὶ πᾶν τὸ πλῆθος ἦν τοῦ λαοῦ προσευχόμενον ἔξω τῇ ὥρᾳ τοῦ θυμιάματος· 1.11 ὤφθη δὲ αὐτῷ ἄγγελος κυρίου ἑστὼς ἐκ δεξιῶν τοῦ θυσιαστηρίου τοῦ θυμιάματος. 1.12 καὶ ἐταράχθη Ζαχαρίας ἰδών, καὶ φόβος ἐπέπεσεν ἐπ᾽ αὐτόν.

1.13 εἶπεν δὲ πρὸς αὐτὸν ὁ ἄγγελος, μὴ φοβοῦ, Ζαχαρία, διότι εἰσηκούσθη ἡ δέησίς σου, καὶ ἡ γυνή σου Ἐλεισάβετ γεννήσει υἱόν σοι, καὶ καλέσεις τὸ ὄνομα αὐτοῦ Ἰωάννην. 1.14 καὶ ἔσται χαρά σοι καὶ ἀγαλλίασις, καὶ πολλοὶ ἐπὶ τῇ γενέσει αὐτοῦ χαρήσονται· 1.15 ἔσται γὰρ μέγας ἐνώπιον κυρίου, καὶ οἶνον καὶ σίκερα οὐ μὴ πίῃ, καὶ πνεύματος ἁγίου πλησθήσεται ἔτι ἐκ κοιλίας μητρὸς αὐτοῦ, 1.16 καὶ πολλοὺς τῶν υἱῶν Ἰσραὴλ

1.1 Since many took in hand/attempted to arrange/compose a narration/relation concerning things/matters having been fully accomplished/established among us, 1.2 as the eyewitnesses and servants/assistants, having become (men) of the logos/word from the beginning, delivered *them* to me, 1.3 it seemed *good* for me also, having investigated accurately all (things) from above, to write them in order for you, most noble Theophilus, 1.4 in order that you might know the certainty concerning sayings/words which you were told/informed. 1.5 There became, in the days of Herod *the* king of Judea, a certain priest by name of Zacharias, from the daily service of Abia, and a woman for him from the daughters of Aaron, and her name *was* Elizabeth.

1.6 And they were both just before God, going by all the commands and justnesses/just laws of the Lord, blameless (ones). 1.7 And there was not a child for them, because Elizabeth was barren, and both were having advanced in their days.

1.8 And it came about in the (thing) *for* him to serve as a priest in the order/manner of the daily service of him before God, 1.9 according to the custom of the priesthood he obtained by lot from the (thing) to offer incense, having entered into the *inner* temple of the Lord, 1.10 and all the multitude of the people was praying outside at the hour of the incense (offering); 1.11 and a messenger/angel from *the* Lord was made visible to him, having stood from *the* right of the altar of the incense (offering). 1.12 And having seen *him*, Zacharias was troubled, and a fear fell upon him.

1.13 But the messenger said to him: Fear not, Zacharias, because you entreaty was heard, and your woman Elizabeth will generate a son for you, and you will call the name of him John. 1.14 Both joy and gladness/exultation will be for you, and many will rejoice over the generating/birth of him; 1.15 for he will be great before *the* Lord, both wine and strong drink he might by no means drink, and he will be filled from a holy spirit, even from his mother's belly, 1.16 and he will turn many of the sons of

ἐπιστρέψει ἐπὶ κύριον τὸν θεὸν αὐτῶν. 1.17 καὶ αὐτὸς προελεύσεται ἐνώπιον αὐτοῦ ἐν πνεύματι καὶ δυνάμει Ἠλίου, ἐπιστρέψαι καρδίας πατέρων ἐπὶ τέκνα καὶ ἀπειθεῖς ἐν φρονήσει δικαίων, ἑτοιμάσαι κυρίῳ λαὸν κατεσκευασμένον.

1.18 καὶ εἶπεν Ζαχαρίας πρὸς τὸν ἄγγελον, κατὰ τί γνώσομαι τοῦτο; ἐγὼ γάρ εἰμι πρεσβύτης καὶ ἡ γυνή μου προβεβηκυῖα ἐν ταῖς ἡμέραις αὐτῆς. 1.19 καὶ ἀποκριθεὶς ὁ ἄγγελος εἶπεν αὐτῷ, ἐγώ εἰμι Γαβριὴλ ὁ παρεστηκὼς ἐνώπιον τοῦ θεοῦ, καὶ ἀπεστάλην λαλῆσαι πρὸς σὲ καὶ εὐαγγελίσασθαί σοι ταῦτα· 1.20 καὶ ἰδοὺ ἔσῃ σιωπῶν καὶ μὴ δυνάμενος λαλῆσαι ἄχρι ἧς ἡμέρας γένηται ταῦτα, ἀνθ' ὧν οὐκ ἐπίστευσας τοῖς λόγοις μου, οἵτινες πληρωθήσονται εἰς τὸν καιρὸν αὐτῶν. 1.21 καὶ ἦν ὁ λαὸς προσδοκῶν τὸν Ζαχαρίαν, καὶ ἐθαύμαζον ἐν τῷ χρονίζειν αὐτόν ἐν τῷ ναῷ. 1.22 ἐξελθὼν δὲ οὐκ ἐδύνατο λαλῆσαι αὐτοῖς, καὶ ἐπέγνωσαν ὅτι ὀπτασίαν ἑώρακεν ἐν τῷ ναῷ· καὶ αὐτὸς ἦν διανεύων αὐτοῖς, καὶ διέμενεν κωφός. 1.23 καὶ ἐγένετο ὡς ἐπλήσθησαν αἱ ἡμέραι τῆς λειτουργίας αὐτοῦ ἀπῆλθεν εἰς τὸν οἶκον αὐτοῦ.

1.24 μετὰ δὲ ταύτας τὰς ἡμέρας συνέλαβεν Ἐλεισάβετ ἡ γυνὴ αὐτοῦ· καὶ περιέκρυβεν ἑαυτὴν μῆνας πέντε, λέγουσα 1.25 ὅτι οὕτως μοι πεποίηκεν κύριος ἐν ἡμέραις αἷς ἐπεῖδεν ἀφελεῖν ὄνειδός μου ἐν ἀνθρώποις.

1.26 ἐν δὲ τῷ μηνὶ τῷ ἕκτῳ ἀπεστάλη ὁ ἄγγελος Γαβριὴλ ἀπὸ τοῦ θεοῦ εἰς πόλιν τῆς Γαλιλαίας ᾗ ὄνομα Ναζαρὲτ 1.27 πρὸς παρθένον ἐμνηστευμένην ἀνδρὶ ᾧ ὄνομα Ἰωσὴφ ἐξ οἴκου καὶ πατρίας Δαυίδ, καὶ τὸ ὄνομα τῆς παρθένου Μαριάμ.

1.28 καὶ εἰσελθὼν πρὸς αὐτὴν ὁ ἄγγελος εἶπεν, χαῖρε, κεχαριτωμένη, ὁ κύριος μετὰ σοῦ. 1.29 ἡ δὲ ἐπὶ τῷ λόγῳ διεταράχθη καὶ διελογίζετο ποταπὸς εἴη ὁ ἀσπασμὸς οὗτος. 1.30

Israel to *the* Lord their God.   1.17 And he himself
will go before him in spirit and power of Elias, to
turn back hearts of fathers to children and uncompli-
ant (ones) by opinions of just (ones), to prepare/get
ready a people having been furnished/prepared for *the*
Lord.

    1.18   And Zacharias said to the messenger: Ac-
cording to/by what shall I know this?   For I, I am
aged, and my woman having been advanced in her days.
1.19   And answering, the messenger/angel said to him:
I, I am Gabriel, the (one) standing before God, and I
was sent to speak to you and to announce/report these
(things) to you;   1.20 and behold, you will be being
silent and not being able to speak until which day
these (things) become/happen, because/for which you
believed not in my sayings/words, which will be fulfilled in their time/season.   1.21 And the people was
waiting for Zacharias, and they were wondering in/at
the (time) *for*   him   to linger/tarry in the *inner*
temple.   1.22 But having come out, he was not being
able to speak to them, and they recognized/perceived
that he has seen a vision in the *inner* temple; and he
was nodding/making signs to them, and he remained
dumb/silent.   1.23 And it became/happened as the days
of his service/liturgy were fulfilled, *that* he departed to his house.

    1.24   And after these days, Elizabeth, his woman,
conceived; and she concealed/hid herself five months,
saying: 1.25 Thus *the* Lord has done for me in days
which he looked upon *me* to take away my reproach among
men/humans.

    1.26   And in the sixth month, the messenger/angel
Gabriel was sent from God to a city of Galilee, for
which *the* name *is* Nazareth,   1.27 to a maiden having
been betrothed to a man for whom *the* name *was* Joseph,
from a house and ancestry of David, and the maiden's
name *was* Mary.

    1.28   And having entered to her, the messenger/
angel said: Greeting/you rejoice, *lady* having been
favored, the Lord *is* with you.   1.29 And the (she) was
greatly troubled over the saying/word, and she was
considering of what sort this salutation/greeting may

καὶ εἶπεν ὁ ἄγγελος αὐτῇ, μὴ φοβοῦ, Μαριάμ, εὗρες γὰρ χάριν παρὰ τῷ θεῷ· 1.31 καὶ ἰδοὺ συλλήμψῃ ἐν γαστρὶ καὶ τέξῃ υἱόν, καὶ καλέσεις τὸ ὄνομα αὐτοῦ Ἰησοῦν. 1.32 οὗτος ἔσται μέγας καὶ υἱὸς ὑψίστου κληθήσεται, καὶ δώσει αὐτῷ κύριος ὁ θεὸς τὸν θρόνον Δαυὶδ τοῦ πατρὸς αὐτοῦ, 1.33 καὶ βασιλεύσει ἐπὶ τὸν οἶκον Ἰακὼβ εἰς τοὺς αἰῶνας, καὶ τῆς βασιλείας αὐτοῦ οὐκ ἔσται τέλος.

1.34 εἶπεν δὲ Μαριὰμ πρὸς τὸν ἄγγελον, πῶς ἔσται τοῦτο, ἐπεὶ ἄνδρα οὐ γινώσκω;

1.35 καὶ ἀποκριθεὶς ὁ ἄγγελος εἶπεν αὐτῇ, πνεῦμα ἅγιον ἐπελεύσεται ἐπὶ σέ, καὶ δύναμις ὑψίστου ἐπισκιάσει σοι· διὸ καὶ τὸ γεννώμενον ἅγιον κληθήσεται, υἱὸς θεοῦ. 1.36 καὶ ἰδοὺ Ἐλεισάβετ ἡ συγγενίς σου καὶ αὐτὴ συνείληφεν υἱὸν ἐν γήρει αὐτῆς, καὶ οὗτος μὴν ἕκτος ἐστὶν αὐτῇ τῇ καλουμένῃ στείρᾳ· 1.37 ὅτι οὐκ ἀδυνατήσει παρὰ τοῦ θεοῦ πᾶν ῥῆμα.

1.38 εἶπεν δὲ Μαριάμ, ἰδοὺ ἡ δούλη κυρίου· γένοιτό μοι κατὰ τὸ ῥῆμά σου. καὶ ἀπῆλθεν ἀπ᾽ αὐτῆς ὁ ἄγγελος. 1.39 ἀναστᾶσα δὲ Μαριὰμ ἐν ταῖς ἡμέραις ταύταις ἐπορεύετο εἰς τὴν ὀρεινὴν μετὰ σπουδῆς εἰς πόλιν Ἰούδα, 1.40 καὶ εἰσῆλθεν εἰς τὸν οἶκον Ζαχαρίου καὶ ἠσπάσατο τὴν Ἐλεισάβετ.

1.41 καὶ ἐγένετο ὡς ἤκουσεν τὸν ἀσπασμὸν τῆς Μαρίας ἡ Ἐλεισάβετ, ἐσκίρτησεν τὸ βρέφος ἐν τῇ κοιλίᾳ αὐτῆς, καὶ ἐπλήσθη πνεύματος ἁγίου ἡ Ἐλεισάβετ, 1.42 καὶ ἀνεβόησεν φωνῇ μεγάλῃ καὶ εἶπεν, εὐλογημένη σὺ ἐν γυναιξίν, καὶ εὐλογημένος ὁ καρπὸς τῆς κοιλίας σου. 1.43 καὶ πόθεν μοι τοῦτο ἵνα ἔλθῃ ἡ μήτηρ τοῦ κυρίου μου πρὸς ἐμέ; 1.44 ἰδοὺ γὰρ ὡς ἐγένετο ἡ φωνὴ τοῦ ἀσπασμοῦ σου εἰς τὰ ὦτά μου, ἐσκίρτησεν ἐν ἀγαλλιάσει τὸ βρέφος ἐν τῇ κοιλίᾳ μου. 1.45 καὶ μακαρία ἡ πιστεύσασα ὅτι ἔσται τελείωσις τοῖς λελαλημένοις αὐτῇ παρὰ κυρίου.

1.46 καὶ εἶπεν Μαριάμ, 1.47 μεγαλύνει ἡ ψυχή μου τὸν

be.   1.30 And the messenger said to her: Fear not, Mary, for you found favor/grace beside/from God.   1.31 And behold, you will conceive in a belly/pregnancy and will bear a son, and you will call the name of him/his name Jesus.   1.32 This (one) will be great, and he will be called a son of *the* most high, and *the* Lord God will give to him the throne of David, the father of him,   1.33 and he will reign over the house of Jacob into the ages, and of his kingdom, there will not be an end.

1.34   And Mary said to the messenger/angel: How will this be, since I know not a man?

1.35   And answering, the messenger said to her: A holy spirit will come upon/over you, and power from *the* most high will overshadow you; wherefore the (thing) being generated/born will also be called holy/sacred, a son of God.   1.36 And behold, Elizabeth your relative, she also conceived a son in her old age, and this is *the* sixth month for her, the (one) being called barren;   1.37 because every/each word from God will not be impossible.

1.38   And Mary said: Behold, the slave of *the* Lord; may it be to me according to your word. And the messenger departed/went away from her.   1.39 And Mary, having arose in these days, went/journeyed to the mountain region with haste to a city of Juda,   1.40 and she entered into the house of Zacharias and greeted/saluted Elizabeth.

1.41   And it happened, as Elizabeth heard the salutation of Mary, the unborn baby leaped in her belly, and Elizabeth was filled from a holy spirit, 1.42   and she called out with a great voice and said: You *are* having been blessed among women, and the fruit of your belly *is* having been blessed.   1.43 And from where *is* this (thing) for me, that the mother of my Lord might come to me?   1.44 For behold, as the sound/voice of your greeting became/happened in my ears, the unborn baby in my belly leaped in exultation/extreme joy.   1.45   And happy *is* the (woman) having believed that a completion will be for the (things) having been spoken to her from *the* Lord.

1.46   And Mary said: 1.47 My soul/life magni-

118

κύριον, καὶ ἠγαλλίασεν τὸ πνεῦμά μου ἐπὶ τῷ θεῷ τῷ σωτῆρί μου, 1.48 ὅτι ἐπέβλεψεν ἐπὶ τὴν ταπίνωσιν τῆς δούλης αὐτοῦ. ἰδοὺ γὰρ ἀπὸ τοῦ νῦν μακαριοῦσίν με πᾶσαι αἱ γενεαί· 1.49 ὅτι ἐποίησέν μοι μεγάλα ὁ δυνατός, καὶ ἅγιον τὸ ὄνομα αὐτοῦ, 1.50 καὶ τὸ ἔλεος αὐτοῦ εἰς γενεὰν καὶ γενεὰν τοῖς φοβουμένοις αὐτόν. 1.51 ἐποίησεν κράτος ἐν βραχίονι αὐτοῦ, διεσκόρπισεν ὑπερηφάνους διανοίᾳ καρδίας αὐτῶν· 1.52 καθεῖλεν δυνάστας ἀπὸ θρόνων καὶ ὕψωσεν ταπεινούς, 1.53 πεινῶντας ἐνέπλησεν ἀγαθῶν καὶ πλουτοῦντας ἐξαπέστειλεν κενούς. 1.54 ἀντελάβετο Ἰσραὴλ παιδὸς αὐτοῦ, μνησθῆναι ἐλέους, 1.55 καθὼς ἐλάλησεν πρὸς τοὺς πατέρας ἡμῶν, τῷ Ἀβραὰμ καὶ τῷ σπέρματι αὐτοῦ εἰς τὸν αἰῶνα.

1.56 ἔμεινεν δὲ Μαριὰμ σὺν αὐτῇ ὡς μῆνας τρεῖς, καὶ ὑπέστρεψεν εἰς τὸν οἶκον αὐτῆς. 1.57 τῇ δὲ Ἐλισάβετ ἐπλήσθη ὁ χρόνος τοῦ τεκεῖν αὐτήν, καὶ ἐγέννησεν υἱόν. 1.58 καὶ ἤκουσαν οἱ περίοικοι καὶ οἱ συγγενεῖς αὐτῆς ὅτι ἐμεγάλυνεν κύριος τὸ ἔλεος αὐτοῦ μετ' αὐτῆς, καὶ συνέχαιρον αὐτῇ.

1.59 καὶ ἐγένετο ἐν τῇ ἡμέρᾳ τῇ ὀγδόῃ ἦλθον περιτεμῖν τὸ παιδίον, καὶ ἐκάλουν αὐτὸ ἐπὶ τῷ ὀνόματι τοῦ πατρὸς αὐτοῦ Ζαχαρίαν.

1.60 καὶ ἀποκριθεῖσα ἡ μήτηρ αὐτοῦ εἶπεν, οὐχί, ἀλλὰ κληθήσεται Ἰωάννης. 1.61 καὶ εἶπαν πρὸς αὐτὴν ὅτι οὐδίς ἐστιν ἐκ τῆς συγγενίας σου ὃς καλεῖται τῷ ὀνόματι τούτῳ. 1.62 ἐνένευον δὲ τῷ πατρὶ αὐτοῦ τὸ τί ἂν θέλοι καλῖσθε αὐτό. 1.63 καὶ αἰτήσας πινακίδιον ἔγραψεν λέγων, Ἰωάννης ἐστὶν τὸ ὄνομα αὐτοῦ. καὶ ἐθαύμασαν πάντες. 1.64 ἀνεῴχθη δὲ τὸ στόμα αὐτοῦ παραχρῆμα καὶ ἡ γλῶσσα αὐτοῦ, καὶ ἐλάλι εὐλογῶν τὸν θεόν.

1.65 καὶ ἐγένετο ἐπὶ πάντας φόβος τοὺς περιοικοῦντας αὐτούς, καὶ ἐν ὅλῃ τῇ ὀρεινῇ τῆς Ἰουδαίας διελαλεῖτο πάντα τὰ ῥήματα ταῦτα, 1.66 καὶ ἔθεντο πάντες οἱ ἀκούσαντες ἐν τῇ

fies/extols the Lord, and my spirit exulted over/upon God, the savior of me, 1.48 because he looked upon the humility of his *female* slave. For behold, from the present (time) all the generations will pronounce me happy; 1.49 because the mighty (one) made/did great (things) for/to me, and the name of him *is* holy/sacred, 1.50 and his mercy *is* into/for generation and generation for those fearing him. 1.51 He made power/might/dominion with his arm, he dispersed proud/haughty (ones) in an understanding of their heart; 1.52 he pulled down potentates/sovereigns from thrones and exalted humble (ones), 1.53 he filled/satisfied hungering (ones) from good (things) and he sent away empty (ones) being rich. 1.54 He helped/assisted Israel, his boy/child, to remember mercy, 1.55 as he spoke to our fathers, to Abraham and to his seed/descendant into the age.

1.56 And Mary stayed with her about three months, and returned to her house. 1.57 And for Elizabeth, the time was fulfilled from the (thing) *for* her to give birth, and she generated/birthed a son. 1.58 And the neighbors and her relatives heard that *the* Lord extended/enlarged his mercy with her, and rejoiced together with her.

1.59 And it became/came about in the eighth day *that* they went to circumcise the child, and they were calling it for/by the name of his father Zacharias,

1.60 And answering, his mother said: No, but he will be called John. 1.61 And they say to her: There is no one out of your kindred/family who is called by this name. 1.62 But they were nodding/making signs to his father *for* the (thing) what ever he may want *for* him to be called. 1.63 And having requested a little wood tablet he wrote, saying: John is his name And they all marveled/wondered. 1.64 And his mouth was opened immediately, and his tongue, and he spoke, blessing/praising God.

1.65 And there became a fear upon all those dwelling around them, and these words were being spread around in the entire mountain region/hill country of Judea, 1.66 and all those having heard put/laid *it* in their heart, saying: What then will

καρδία αὐτῶν, λέγοντες, τί ἄρα τὸ παιδίον τοῦτο ἔσται; καὶ γὰρ χὶρ κυρίου ἦν μετ᾽ αὐτοῦ.

1.67 καὶ Ζαχαρίας ὁ πατὴρ αὐτοῦ ἐπλήσθη πνεύματος ἁγίου καὶ ἐπροφήτευσεν λέγων, 1.68 εὐλογητὸς κύριος ὁ θεὸς τοῦ Ἰσραήλ, ὅτι ἐπεσκέψατο καὶ ἐποίησεν λύτρωσιν τῷ λαῷ αὐτοῦ, 1.69 καὶ ἤγειρεν κέρας σωτηρίας ἡμῖν ἐν οἴκῳ Δαυὶδ παιδὸς αὐτοῦ, 1.70 καθὼς ἐλάλησεν διὰ στόματος τῶν ἁγίων ἀπ᾽ αἰῶνος αὐτοῦ προφητῶν, 1.71 σωτηρίαν ἐξ ἐχθρῶν ἡμῶν καὶ ἐκ χειρὸς πάντων τῶν μισούντων ἡμᾶς· 1.72 ποιῆσαι ἔλεος μετὰ τῶν πατέρων ἡμῶν καὶ μνησθῆναι διαθήκης ἁγίας αὐτοῦ, 1.73 ὅρκον ὃν ὤμοσεν πρὸς Ἀβραὰμ τὸν πατέρα ἡμῶν, τοῦ δοῦναι ἡμῖν 1.74 ἀφόβως ἐκ χιρὸς ἐχθρῶν ῥυσθέντας λατρεύειν αὐτῷ 1.75 ἐν ὁσιότητι καὶ δικαιοσύνῃ ἐνώπιον αὐτοῦ πάσας τὰς ἡμέρας ἡμῶν. 1.76 καὶ σὺ δέ, παιδίον, προφήτης ὑψίστου κληθήσῃ, προπορεύσῃ γὰρ ἐνώπιον κυρίου ἑτοιμάσαι ὁδοὺς αὐτοῦ, 1.77 τοῦ δοῦναι γνῶσιν σωτηρίας τῷ λαῷ αὐτοῦ ἐν ἀφέσι ἁμαρτιῶν αὐτῶν, 1.78 διὰ σπλάγχνα ἐλέους θεοῦ ἡμῶν, ἐν οἷς ἐπισκέψεται ἡμᾶς ἀνατολὴ ἐξ ὕψους, 1.79 ἐπιφᾶναι τοῖς ἐν σκότι καὶ σκιᾷ θανάτου καθημένοις, τοῦ κατευθῦναι τοὺς πόδας ἡμῶν εἰς ὁδὸν ἰρήνης.

1.80 τὸ δὲ παιδίον ηὔξανεν καὶ ἐκρατεοῦτο πνεύματι, καὶ ἦν ἐν ταῖς ἐρήμοις ἕως ἡμέρας ἀναδείξεως αὐτοῦ πρὸς τὸν Ἰσραήλ.

2.1 Ἐγένετο δὲ ἐν ταῖς ἡμέραις ἐκίναις ἐξῆλθεν δόγμα παρὰ Καίσαρος Ἀγούστου ἀπογράφεσθε πᾶσαν τὴν οἰκουμένην. 2.2 αὕτη ἡ ἀπογραφὴ πρώτη ἐγένετο ἡγεμονεύοντος τῆς Συρίας Κυρηνίου. 2.3 καὶ ἐπορεύοντο πάντες ἀπογράφεσθαι, ἕκαστος εἰς τὴν ἑαυτοῦ πόλιν.

2.4 ἀνέβη δὲ καὶ Ἰωσὴφ ἀπὸ τῆς Γαλιλαίας ἐκ πόλεως Ναζαρὲθ εἰς τὴν Ἰουδαίαν εἰς πόλιν Δαυὶδ ἥτις καλεῖται Βηθλέεμ, διὰ τὸ εἶναι αὐτὸν ἐξ οἴκου καὶ πατριᾶς Δαυίδ, 2.5

this child be? For even *the* hand of *the* Lord was with him.

1.67 And Zacharias, his father, was filled from a holy spirit and he prophesied, saying: 1.68 Blessed/praised *be the* Lord God of Israel, because he looked after/cared for and made a redemption/releasing for his people, 1.69 and he raised up a horn of salvation for us in/by *the* house of David, his boy/child, 1.70 as he spoke through a mouth of his holy prophets from an age, 1.71 a deliverance/salvation from our enemies and out of *the* hand of all those hating us; 1.72 to do/make mercy with our fathers and to remember his holy/sacred covenant, 1.73 an oath which he swore to Abraham our father, of the (thing) to give to us 1.74 having been rescued out of *the* hand of enemies to serve/worship for him without fear, 1.75 in sacred observance and justness before him all of our days. 1.76 And even you, child, you will be called a prophet of the most high, for you will go before *the* Lord to prepare his road/way, 1.77 of the (thing) to give a knowledge of salvation to his people by forgiveness/releasing from their sins/faults, 1.78 because of compassions of mercy from our God, by which he will visit/look after us, a sunrise from a height/on high, 1.79 to appear for/upon those sitting in darkness and in *the* shadow of death, of the (thing) to direct straight our feet into a road/way of peace.

1.80 And the child was growing and being strengthened in spirit, and he was in the deserts until a day of his showing/manifestation to Israel.

2.1 And it happened/came about in those days *that* a decree went forth from Caesar Augustus *for* all the empire/civilized world to be enrolled/registered. 2.2 This became the first enrollment/registration from Cyrenius governing Syria. 2.3 And all (men) were going to be enrolled/registered, each (one) to the city of himself.

2.4 And Joseph also went up from Galilee out of a city, Nazareth, into Judea to a city of David which is called Bethlehem, because of the (thing) *for* him to be from a house and lineage of David, 2.5 to be

ἀπογράψασθαι σὺν Μαριὰμ τῇ ἐμνηστευμένῃ αὐτῷ, οὔσῃ ἐνκύῳ. 2.6 ἐγένετο δὲ ἐν τῷ εἶναι αὐτοὺς ἐκεῖ ἐπλήσθησαν αἱ ἡμέραι τοῦ τεκῖν αὐτήν, 2.7 καὶ ἔτεκεν τὸν υἱὸν αὐτῆς τὸν πρωτότοκον· καὶ ἐσπαργάνωσεν αὐτὸν καὶ ἀνέκλινεν αὐτὸν ἐν φάτνῃ, διότι οὐκ ἦν αὐτοῖς τόπος ἐν τῷ καταλύματι. 2.8 καὶ ποιμένες ἦσαν ἐν τῇ χώρᾳ τῇ αὐτῇ ἀγραυλοῦντες καὶ φυλάσσοντες φυλακὰς τῆς νυκτὸς ἐπὶ τὴν ποίμνην αὐτῶν. 2.9 καὶ ἄγγελος κυρίου ἐπέστη αὐτοῖς καὶ δόξα κυρίου περιέλαμψεν αὐτούς, καὶ ἐφοβήθησαν φόβον μέγαν. 2.10 καὶ εἶπεν αὐτοῖς ὁ ἄγγελος, μὴ φοβῖσθε, ἰδοὺ γὰρ εὐαγγελίζομαι ὑμῖν χαρὰν μεγάλην ἥτις ἔσται παντὶ τῷ λαῷ, 2.11 ὅτι ἐτέχθη ὑμῖν σήμερον σωτὴρ ὅς ἐστιν χριστὸς κύριος ἐν πόλι Δαυίδ· 2.12 καὶ τοῦτο ὑμῖν τὸ σημῖον, εὑρήσεται βρέφος ἐσσπαργανωμένον καὶ κείμενον ἐν φάτνῃ. 2.13 καὶ ἐξαίφνης ἐγένετο σὺν τῷ ἀγγέλῳ πλῆθος στρατιᾶς οὐρανίου αἰνούντων τὸν θεὸν καὶ λεγόντων, 2.14 δόξα ἐν ὑψίστοις θεῷ καὶ ἐπὶ γῆς ἰρήνη ἐν ἀνθρώποις εὐδοκίας.

2.15 καὶ ἐγένετο ὡς ἀπῆλθον ἀπ' αὐτῶν εἰς τὸν οὐρανὸν οἱ ἄγγελοι, οἱ ποιμαίνες ἐλάλουν πρὸς ἀλλήλους λέγοντες, διέλθωμεν δὴ ἕως Βηθλέεμ καὶ ἴδωμεν τὸ ῥῆμα τοῦτο τὸ γεγονὸς ὃ ὁ κύριος ἐγνώρισεν ἡμῖν. 2.16 καὶ ἦλθον σπεύσαντες καὶ ἀνεῦραν τήν τε Μαριὰμ καὶ τὸν Ἰωσὴφ καὶ τὸ βρέφος κείμενον ἐν τῇ φάτνῃ· 2.17 ἰδόντες δὲ ἐγνώρισαν περὶ τοῦ ῥήματος τοῦ λαληθέντος αὐτοῖς περὶ τοῦ παιδίου τούτου. 2.18 καὶ πάντες οἱ ἀκούσαντες ἐθαύμασαν περὶ τῶν λαληθέντων ὑπὸ τῶν ποιμένων πρὸς αὐτούς· 2.19 ἡ δὲ Μαριὰμ πάντα συνετήρι τὰ ῥήματα ταῦτα συμβάλλουσα ἐν τῇ καρδίᾳ αὐτῆς. 2.20 καὶ ὑπέστρεψαν οἱ ποιμαίνες δοξάζοντες καὶ αἰνοῦντες τὸν θεὸν ἐπὶ πᾶσιν οἷς ἤκουσαν καὶ ἴδον καθὼς ἐλαλήθη πρὸς αὐτούς. 2.21 καὶ ὅτε ἐπλήσθησαν ἡμέραι ὀκτὼ τοῦ περιτεμῖν αὐτόν, καὶ ἐκλήθη τὸ

enrolled with Mary, the (one) having been betrothed to him, *she* being pregnant. 2.6 And it happened at/in the (time) *for* them to be there *that* the days were fulfilled from the (thing) *for* her to give birth, 2.7 and she birthed her firstborn son; and she wrapped him in swaddling cloths and laid him in a stable/stall, because there was not a place for them in the inn. 2.8 And there were shepherds in the same country living in fields and keeping watch over their flock from the night. 2.9 And a messenger/angel from *the* Lord stood over/near them and glory of *the* Lord shone around them, and they feared a great fear. 2.10 And the messenger said to them: Fear ye not, for behold I announce/report a great joy to ye which will be for all the people, 2.11 because today a savior/deliverer was birthed for ye, who is the anointed Lord, in *the* city of David; 2.12 and this *is* the sign for ye: Ye will find a baby, having been wrapped in swaddling cloths and lying in a stall/manger, 2.13 and suddenly there became with the messenger/angel a multitude from a heavenly army/host, praising God and saying: 2.14 Glory/fame to God in the highest (places), and upon earth peace, good will, among men/humans.

2.15 And it came about, as the messengers/angels went away from them into the sky/heaven, *that* the shepherds were speaking to one another, saying: Let us go over now until/as far as Bethlehem and let us see this word/thing having happened, which the Lord made known to us. 2.16 And having hastened they went and found both Mary and Joseph, and the infant/baby lying in the stall/manger; 2.17 and having seen, they made *it* known about the word having been spoken to them concerning this child. 2.18 And all those having heard marveled/wondered about the (things) having been spoken to them by the shepherds; 2.19 but Mary kept all (things) carefully in mind, pondering with all these words/sayings in her heart. 2.20 And the shepherds returned, glorifying and praising God over all (things) which they heard and saw, as it was spoken to them. 2.21 And when eight days were completed, from the (thing) to circumcise him, the name of him was called Jesus, the (one) having been called by the

ὄνομα αὐτοῦ Ἰησοῦς, τὸ κληθὲν ὑπὸ τοῦ ἀγγέλου πρὸ τοῦ συλλημφθῆναι αὐτὸν ἐν τῇ κοιλίᾳ. 2.22 καὶ ὅτε ἐπλήσθησαν αἱ ἡμέραι τοῦ καθαρισμοῦ αὐτῶν κατὰ τὸν νόμον Μωϋσέως, ἀνήγαγον αὐτὸν εἰς Ἱεροσόλυμα παραστῆσαι τῷ κυρίῳ, 2.23 καθὼς γέγραπται ἐν νόμῳ κυρίου ὅτι « πᾶν ἄρσεν διανοῖγον μήτραν ἅγιον τῷ κυρίῳ κληθήσεται,» 2.24 καὶ τοῦ δοῦναι θυσίαν κατὰ τὸ εἰρημένον ἐν τῷ νόμῳ κυρίου, « ζεῦγος τρυγόνων ἢ δύο νοσσοὺς περιστερῶν.» 2.25 καὶ ἰδοὺ ἄνθρωπος ἦν ἐν Ἱερουσαλὴμ ᾧ ὄνομα Συμεών, καὶ ὁ ἄνθρωπος οὗτος δίκαιος καὶ εὐλαβής, προσδεχόμενος παράκλησιν τοῦ Ἰσραήλ, καὶ πνεῦμα ἦν ἅγιον ἐπ᾽ αὐτόν· 2.26 καὶ ἦν αὐτῷ κεχρηματισμένον ὑπὸ τοῦ πνεύματος τοῦ ἁγίου μὴ ἰδῖν θάνατον πρὶν ἢ ἂν ἴδῃ τὸν χριστὸν κυρίου. 2.27 καὶ ἦλθεν ἐν τῷ πνεύματι εἰς τὸ ἱερόν· καὶ ἐν τῷ εἰσαγαγεῖν τοὺς γονεῖς τὸ παιδίον Ἰησοῦν τοῦ ποιῆσαι αὐτοὺς κατὰ τὸ εἰθισμένον τοῦ νόμου περὶ αὐτοῦ 2.28 καὶ αὐτὸς ἐδέξατο αὐτὸ εἰς τὰς ἀγκάλας καὶ εὐλόγησεν τὸν θεὸν καὶ εἶπεν, 2.29 νῦν ἀπολύεις τὸν δοῦλόν σου, δέσποτα, κατὰ τὸ ῥῆμά σου ἐν εἰρήνῃ· 2.30 ὅτι εἶδον οἱ ὀφθαλμοί μου τὸ σωτήριόν σου 2.31 ὃ ἡτοίμασας κατὰ πρόσωπον πάντων τῶν λαῶν, 2.32 φῶς εἰς ἀποκάλυψιν ἐθνῶν καὶ δόξαν λαοῦ σου Ἰσραήλ. 2.33 καὶ ἦν ὁ πατὴρ αὐτοῦ καὶ ἡ μήτηρ θαυμάζοντες ἐπὶ τοῖς λαλουμένοις περὶ αὐτοῦ. 2.34 καὶ ηὐλόγησεν αὐτοὺς Συμεὼν καὶ εἶπεν πρὸς Μαριὰμ τὴν μητέρα αὐτοῦ, ἰδοὺ οὗτος κεῖται εἰς πτῶσιν καὶ ἀνάστασιν πολλῶν ἐν τῷ Ἰσραὴλ καὶ εἰς σημῖον ἀντιλεγόμενον 2.35 καὶ σοῦ δὲ αὐτῆς τὴν ψυχὴν διελεύσεται ῥομφαία, ὅπως ἂν ἀποκαλυφθῶσιν ἐκ πολλῶν καρδιῶν διαλογισμοί.

2.36 καὶ ἦν Ἄννα προφῆτις, θυγάτηρ Φανουήλ, ἐκ φυλῆς Ἀσήρ· αὕτη προβεβηκυῖα ἐν ἡμέραις πολλαῖς, ζήσασα μετὰ ἀνδρὸς ἔτη ἑπτὰ ἀπὸ τῆς παρθενίας αὐτῆς, 2.37 καὶ αὐτὴ χήρα ἕως ἐτῶν ὀγδοήκοντα τεσσάρων, ἣ οὐκ ἀφίστατο ἐκ τοῦ ἱεροῦ

messenger before the (thing) *for* him to be conceived in the belly/womb.   2.22 And when the days of their purifications according to the law of Moses were completed, they brought him up to Jerusalem to present *him* to the Lord,   2.23 as it has been written in the law of *the* Lord: EVERY MALE OPENING A WOMB WILL BE CALLED HOLY/SACRED FOR *the* LORD;   2.24 and from the (thing) to give a sacrifice according to the (thing) having been said in the law of *the* Lord: A YOKE/PAIR OF TURTLEDOVES OR TWO YOUNG PIGEONS/DOVES.   2.25 And behold, a man was in Jerusalem, for whom a name *is* Simeon, and this man *was* just and devout/reverent, waiting for/expecting a consolation of Israel, and a holy spirit was upon him;   2.26 and it had been re-vealed/imparted to him by the Holy Spirit not to see death before he would see the anointed Lord.   2.27 And he went by the spirit into the *outer* temple; and at the (time) *for* the parents to bring in the child Jesus from the (thing) *for* them to do according to the (thing) having been customary from the law concerning it/him   2.28 and he also took it/(the child) in the arms and he blessed/praised God and said: 2.29 Now, Master, you dismiss/release your slave in peace ac-cording to your word;   2.30 because my eyes saw your deliverance/salvation   2.31 which you prepared by/ac-cording to a face of all the people,   2.32 a light into/for a revelation of ethnics and a glory/reputa-tion of your people Israel.   2.33 And his father and mother were marveling/wondering at the (things) being spoken about him.   2.34 And Simeon blessed them and said to Mary, his mother: Behold, this (one) is laid/ set to/for a fall and a rising/resurrection of many in Israel, and to/for a sign being opposed/slandered, 2.35 and a sword also will go through the life/soul of you yourself, in order that the reasonings/opinions out of many hearts might ever be revealed.
    2.36   And Anna was a prophetess, a daughter of Phanuel, out of a tribe of Asher; this (one) having advanced by/in many days, having lived with a man seven years from her virginity,   2.37 and she *was* a widow until eighty-four years, who withdrew not out of the *outer* temple, serving/worshiping night and day in

νηστείαις καὶ δεήσεσιν λατρεύουσα νύκτα καὶ ἡμέραν. 2.38 καὶ αὐτῇ τῇ ὥρᾳ ἐπιστᾶσα ἀνθωμολογῖτο τῷ θεῷ καὶ ἐλάλει περὶ αὐτοῦ πᾶσιν τοῖς προσδεχομένοις λύτρωσιν Ἰερουσαλήμ.

2.39 καὶ ὡς ἐτέλεσαν πάντα κατὰ τὸν νόμον κυρίου, ἐπέστρεψαν εἰς τὴν Γαλιλαίαν εἰς πόλιν ἑαυτῶν Ναζαρέτ. 2.40 τὸ δὲ παιδίον ηὔξανεν καὶ ἐκραταιοῦτο πληρούμενον σοφίᾳ, καὶ χάρις θεοῦ ἦν ἐπ᾽ αὐτό. 2.41 καὶ ἐπορεύοντο οἱ γονῖς αὐτοῦ κατ᾽ ἔτος ἰς Ἰερουσαλὴμ τῇ ἑορτῇ τοῦ πάσχα.

2.42 καὶ ὅτε ἐγένετο ἐτῶν δώδεκα, ἀναβαινόντων αὐτῶν κατὰ τὸ ἔθος τῆς ἑορτῆς 2.43 καὶ τελιωσάντων τὰς ἡμέρας, ἐν τῷ ὑποστρέφειν αὐτοὺς ὑπέμεινεν Ἰησοῦς ὁ παῖς ἐν Ἰερουσαλήμ, καὶ οὐκ ἔγνωσαν οἱ γονῖς αὐτοῦ. 2.44 νομίσαντες δὲ αὐτὸν εἶναι ἐν τῇ συνοδίᾳ ἦλθον ἡμέρας ὁδὸν καὶ ἀνεζήτουν αὐτὸν ἐν τοῖς συγγενέσιν καὶ τοῖς γνωστοῖς, 2.45 καὶ μὴ εὑρόντες ὑπέστρεψαν εἰς Ἰερουσαλὴμ ἀναζητοῦντες αὐτόν. 2.46 καὶ ἐγένετο μετὰ ἡμέρας τρεῖς εὗρον αὐτὸν ἐν τῷ ἱερῷ καθεζόμενον ἐν μέσῳ τῶν διδασκάλων καὶ ἀκούοντα αὐτῶν καὶ ἐπερωτῶντα αὐτούς· 2.47 ἐξίσταντο δὲ πάντες οἱ ἀκούοντες αὐτοῦ ἐπὶ τῇ συνέσι καὶ ταῖς ἀποκρίσεσιν αὐτοῦ. 2.48 καὶ ἰδόντες αὐτὸν ἐξεπλάγησαν, καὶ εἶπεν πρὸς αὐτὸν ἡ μήτηρ αὐτοῦ, τέκνον, τί ἐποίησας ἡμῖν οὕτως; ἰδοὺ ὁ πατήρ σου κἀγὼ ὀδυνώμενοι ἐζητοῦμέν σε.

2.49 καὶ εἶπεν πρὸς αὐτούς, τί ὅτι ἐζητεῖτέ με; οὐκ ἤδειτε ὅτι ἐν τοῖς τοῦ πατρός μου δῖ εἶναί με; 2.50 καὶ αὐτοὶ οὐ συνῆκαν τὸ ῥῆμα ὃ ἐλάλησεν αὐτοῖς. 2.51 καὶ κατέβη μετ᾽ αὐτῶν καὶ ἦλθεν εἰς Ναζαρέτ, καὶ ἦν ὑποτασσόμενος αὐτοῖς. καὶ ἡ μήτηρ αὐτοῦ διετήρι πάντα τὰ ῥήματα ἐν τῇ καρδίᾳ αὐτῆς. 2.52 καὶ ὁ Ἰησοῦς προέκοπτεν ἐν τῇ σοφίᾳ καὶ ἡλικίᾳ καὶ χάριτι παρὰ θεῷ καὶ ἀνθρώποις.

3.1 Ἐν ἔτι δὲ πεντεκαιδεκάτῳ τῆς ἡγεμονίας Τιβερίου Καίσαρος, ἡγεμονεύοντος Ποντίου Πιλάτου τῆς Ἰουδαίας, καὶ

fastings and supplications.   2.38 And having stood near at this very hour, she was confessing openly to God, and she spoke about him to all those waiting for/expecting a redemption/ransoming of Jerusalem.

2.39 And as they finished all (things) according to the law of *the* Lord, they returned to Galilee to a city of themselves, Nazareth.   2.40 And the child grew and was being strengthened, being filled with wisdom, and grace/favor from God was upon it/him.   2.41 And his parents were going each year to Jerusalem to the festival of the Passover.

2.42   And when he became of years twelve, from their going up according to the custom of the festival 2.43 and having finished/completed the days, at/in the (time) *for* them to return, the boy Jesus remained in Jerusalem, and his parents did not know.   2.44 But supposing him to be in the company/caravan they went a road/way of a day and were looking for him among the relatives and the known (ones)/acquaintances,   2.45 and having not found *him*, they returned to Jerusalem looking for him.   2.46 And it happened *that* after three days they found him in the *outer* temple sitting in the midst of the teachers, both hearing from them and questioning them;   2.47 and all those hearing from him were being amazed at the insight/understanding and the answers from him.   2.48 And having seen him they were astounded, and his mother said to him: Child, why did you thus to us? Behold, your father and I, suffering pains/being in distress, were seeking you.

2.49 And he said to them: Why *is it* that ye were seeking me? Know ye not that it is necessary *for* me to be in the (things) of my father?   2.50 And they, they understood not the word which he spoke to them.   2.51 And he went down with them and went to Nazareth, and he was being subjected/subordinated to them. And his mother carefully kept all the words in her heart. 2.52 And Jesus progressed in the wisdom, both in maturity/time of life and in grace/favor beside/with God and men/humans.

3.1   And in the fifteenth year of the leadership/governorship of Tiberias Caesar, from Pontius

τετρααρχοῦντος τῆς Γαλιλαίας Ἡρώδου, Φιλίππου δὲ τοῦ ἀδελφοῦ αὐτοῦ τετρααρχοῦντος τῆς Ἰτουραίας καὶ Τραχωνίτιδος χώρας, καὶ Λυσανίου τῆς Ἀβιληνῆς τετρααρχοῦντος, 3.2 ἐπὶ ἀρχιερέως Ἄννα καὶ Καϊάφα, ἐγένετο ῥῆμα θεοῦ ἐπὶ Ἰωάννην τὸν Ζαχαρίου υἱὸν ἐν τῇ ἐρήμῳ. 3.3 καὶ ἦλθεν εἰς πᾶσαν τὴν περίχωρον τοῦ Ἰορδάνου κηρύσσων βάπτισμα μετανοίας εἰς ἄφεσιν ἁμαρτιῶν, 3.4 ὡς γέγραπται ἐν βίβλῳ λόγων Ἡσαΐου τοῦ προφήτου, « φωνὴ βοῶντος ἐν τῇ ἐρήμῳ, ἑτοιμάσατε τὴν ὁδὸν κυρίου, εὐθίας ποιεῖται τὰς τρίβους αὐτοῦ. 3.5 πᾶσα φάραγξ πληρωθήσεται καὶ πᾶν ὄρος καὶ βουνὸς ταπινωθήσετε, καὶ ἔσται τὰ σκολιὰ εἰς εὐθίαν καὶ αἱ τραχῖαι εἰς ὁδοὺς λίας· 3.6 καὶ ὄψεται πᾶσα σάρξ τὸ σωτήριον τοῦ θεοῦ.»

3.7 ἔλεγεν οὖν τοῖς ἐκπορευομένοις ὄχλοις βαπτισθῆναι ὑπ' αὐτοῦ, γεννήματα ἐχιδνῶν, τίς ὑπέδιξεν ὑμῖν φυγεῖν ἀπὸ τῆς μελλούσης ὀργῆς; 3.8 ποιήσατε οὖν καρποὺς ἀξίους τῆς μετανοίας· καὶ μὴ ἄρξησθε λέγειν ἐν ἑαυτοῖς, πατέρα ἔχομεν τὸν Ἀβραάμ, λέγω γὰρ ὑμῖν ὅτι δύναται ὁ θεὸς ἐκ τῶν λίθων τούτων ἐγεῖραι τέκνα τῷ Ἀβραάμ. 3.9 ἤδη δὲ καὶ ἡ ἀξίνη πρὸς τὴν ῥίζαν τῶν δένδρων κεῖται· πᾶν οὖν δένδρον μὴ ποιοῦν καρπὸν καλὸν ἐκκόπτεται καὶ εἰς πῦρ βάλλεται. 3.10 καὶ ἐπηρώτων αὐτὸν οἱ ὄχλοι λέγοντες, τί οὖν ποιήσωμεν; 3.11 ἀποκριθεὶς δὲ ἔλεγεν αὐτοῖς, ὁ ἔχων δύο χιτῶνας μεταδότω τῷ μὴ ἔχοντι, καὶ ὁ ἔχων βρώματα ὁμοίως ποιείτω. 3.12 ἦλθον δὲ καὶ τελῶναι βαπτισθῆναι καὶ εἶπον πρὸς αὐτόν, διδάσκαλε, τί ποιήσωμεν; 3.13 ὁ δὲ εἶπεν πρὸς αὐτούς, μηδὲν πλέον παρὰ τὸ διατεταγμένον ὑμῖν πράσσετε. 3.14 ἐπηρώτων δὲ αὐτὸν καὶ στρατευόμενοι λέγοντες, τί ποιήσωμεν καὶ ἡμῖς; καὶ εἶπεν πρὸς αὐτοῦ, μηδένα διασείσητε μηδὲ συκοφαντήσητε, καὶ ἀρκῖσθαι τοῖς ὀψωνίοις ὑμῶν.

Pilate being governor of Judea and from Herod being tetrarch of Galilee, and from Philip his brother being tetrarch of the country of Ituraea and Trachonitis, from Lysanias being tetrarch of Abilene, 3.2 in the time of a high priest Annas and Caiaphas, a word from god became to/upon John the son of Zacharias in the desert/wilderness. 3.3 And he went into all the surrounding country of the Jordan, heralding/preaching a baptism of repentance into/for forgiveness/remission of sins/faults, 3.4 as it has been written in a scroll of sayings of Esaias the prophet: A SOUND/VOICE OF (ONE) CRYING IN THE DESERT/WILDERNESS: PREPARE YE THE ROAD/WAY OF *the* LORD, MAKE YE STRAIGHT THE PATHS OF HIM. 3.5 EVERY RAVINE/VALLEY WILL BE FILLED UP AND EVERY MOUNTAIN AND HILL WILL BE LEVELED/LOWERED, AND THE CROOKED (PLACES) WILL BE INTO/FOR SMOOTH (ONES) AND THE ROUGH (ONES) INTO SMOOTH ROADS/WAYS; 3.6 AND EVERY FLESH WILL SEE/VIEW THE DELIVERANCE OF/FROM GOD.

3.7 Then he was saying to the crowds going out to be baptized by him: Products of vipers/offsprings from snakes, who warned for ye to flee from the anger/wrath being about to come? 3.8 Therefore, make/do ye fruits worthy of the repentance; and ye should not begin to say among/in yourselves: We have/hold Abraham the father, for I say to ye that God is able to raise up children for Abraham out of these stones. 3.9 But also the ax is already laid to the root of the trees; therefore, every tree not making beautiful/good fruit is cut out and thrown into a fire. 3.10 And the crowds were asking/questioning him, saying: What then should we do? 3.11 And answering, he was saying to them: Let the (one) having two tunics give/impart to the (one) not having, and let the (one) having foods do likewise. 3.12 And tax-collectors also came to be baptized and said to him: Teacher, what should we do? 3.13 And he said to them: Practice ye nothing more besides the (thing) having been prescribed/charged to ye. 3.14 And *the ones* serving as soldiers were asking him, saying: Even/also we, what should we do? And he said to them: Ye should shake/harass no one, neither should ye accuse falsely, and be ye content with your wages.

124

3.15 προσδοκῶντος δὲ τοῦ λαοῦ καὶ διαλογιζομένων πάντων ἐν ταῖς καρδίαις αὐτῶν περὶ τοῦ Ἰωάννου, μήποτε αὐτὸς εἴη ὁ χριστός, 3.16 ἀπεκρίνατο λέγων πᾶσιν ὁ Ἰωάννης, ἐγὼ μὲν ὕδατι βαπτίζω ὑμᾶς· ἔρχεται δὲ ὁ ἰσχυρότερός μου, οὗ οὐκ ἰμὶ ἱκανὸς λῦσαι τὸν ἱμάντα τῶν ὑποδημάτων αὐτοῦ· αὐτὸς ὑμᾶς βαπτίσει ἐν πνεύματι ἁγίῳ καὶ πυρί· 3.17 οὗ τὸ πτύον ἐν τῇ χειρὶ αὐτοῦ διακαθᾶρε τὴν ἅλωνα αὐτοῦ καὶ συναγαγεῖν τὸν σῖτον εἰς τὴν ἀποθήκην αὐτοῦ, τὸ δὲ ἄχυρον κατακαύσι πυρὶ ἀσβέστῳ.

3.18 πολλὰ μὲν οὖν καὶ ἔτερα παρακαλῶν εὐηγγέλιζε τὸν λαόν· 3.19 ὁ δὲ Ἡρώδης ὁ τετραάρχης, ἐλεγχόμενος ὑπ' αὐτοῦ περὶ Ἡρωδιάδος τῆς γυναικὸς τοῦ ἀδελφοῦ αὐτοῦ καὶ περὶ πάντων τῶν πονηρῶν ὧν ἐποίησεν ὁ Ἡρώδης, 3.20 προσέθηκεν καὶ τοῦτο ἐπὶ πᾶσιν καὶ κατέκλισεν τὸν Ἰωάννην ἐν φυλακῇ.

3.21 ἐγένετο δὲ ἐν τῷ βαπτισθῆναι πάντα τὸν λαὸν καὶ Ἰησοῦ βαπτισθέντος καὶ προσευχομένου ἀνεῳχθῆνε τὸν οὐρανὸν 3.22 καὶ καταβῆναι τὸ πνεῦμα τὸ ἅγιον σωματικῷ εἴδι ὡς περιστερὰν ἐπ' αὐτόν, καὶ φωνὴν ἐξ οὐρανοῦ γενέσθαι, σὺ εἶ ὁ υἱός μου ὁ ἀγαπητός, ἐν σοὶ εὐδόκησα. 3.23 καὶ αὐτὸς ἦν Ἰησοῦς ἀρχόμενος ὡσεὶ ἐτῶν τριάκοντα, ὢν υἱός, ὡς ἐνομίζετο, Ἰωσὴφ τοῦ Ἡλεὶ 3.24 τοῦ Μαθθὰθ τοῦ Λευεὶ τοῦ Μελχεὶ τοῦ Ἰανναὶ τοῦ Ἰωσὴφ 3.25 τοῦ Ματταθίου τοῦ Ἀμὼς τοῦ Ναοὺμ τοῦ Ἑσλεὶ τοῦ Ναγγαὶ 3.26 τοῦ Μάαθ τοῦ Ματταθίου τοῦ Σεμεεῒν τοῦ Ἰωσὴχ τοῦ Ἰωδὰ 3.27 τοῦ Ἰωανὰν τοῦ Ῥησὰ τοῦ Ζοροβαβὲλ τοῦ Σαλαθιὴλ τοῦ Νηρεὶ 3.28 τοῦ Μελχεὶ τοῦ Ἀδδεὶ τοῦ Κωσὰμ τοῦ Ἑλμαδὰμ τοῦ Ἢρ 3.29 τοῦ Ἰησοῦ τοῦ Ἐλιέζερ τοῦ Ἰωρὶμ τοῦ Μαθθὰθ τοῦ Λευεὶ 3.30 τοῦ Συμεὼν τοῦ Ἰούδα τοῦ Ἰωσὴφ τοῦ Ἰωνὰμ τοῦ Ἐλιακεὶμ 3.31 τοῦ Μελεὰ τοῦ Μεννὰ τοῦ Ματταθὰ τοῦ Ναθὰμ τοῦ Δαυὶδ 3.32 τοῦ Ἰεσσαὶ τοῦ Ἰωβὴδ τοῦ Βόος τοῦ Σαλὰ τοῦ Ναασσὼν 3.33 τοῦ Ἀμιναδὰβ τοῦ Ἀδμὶν τοῦ Ἀρνεὶ τοῦ Ἑσρὼμ τοῦ Φάρες τοῦ Ἰούδα 3.34 τοῦ Ἰακὼβ τοῦ Ἰσαὰκ τοῦ Ἀβραὰμ τοῦ Θάρα τοῦ Ναχὼρ 3.35 τοῦ Σεροὺχ τοῦ Ῥαγαὺ τοῦ Φάλεκ τοῦ Ἕβερ τοῦ Σαλὰ 3.36 τοῦ Καϊνὰμ τοῦ Ἀρφαξὰδ τοῦ Σὴμ τοῦ Νῶε τοῦ Λάμεχ 3.37 τοῦ Μαθουσαλὰ τοῦ Ἐνὼχ τοῦ Ἰάρετ τοῦ

3.15 And from the people waiting for/expecting and from all reasoning/debating in their hearts about John, whether he, he may be the anointed (one), 3.16 John himself answered, saying to all: I, indeed I baptize ye in/with water; but the (one) stronger than me comes, of whom I am not sufficient to loose the strap of his sandals; He, he will baptize ye in/with a holy spirit and fire; 3.17 of whom the winnowing-shovel *is* in his hand to cleanse his threshing floor and to gather the wheat into his storehouse/granary, but he will burn up the chaff in unquenchable fire.

3.18 Then he was announcing many and different (things), exhorting/beseeching the people; 3.19 but Herod, the tetrarch, being reproved by him concerning Herodias, his brother's woman, and concerning all the evil (things) which Herod did, 3.20 he added also this to/over all and he shut up John in prison.

3.21 And it came about in the (thing) *for* all the people to be baptized *that* Jesus also, having been baptized and himself praying, *for* the sky/heaven to be opened 3.22 and *for* the Holy Spirit to come down in a bodily form like a dove/pigeon upon him, and *for* a voice to become out of heaven: You, you are my beloved son, I was well pleased with/by you. 3.23 And Jesus himself was beginning from about thirty years, being a son, as it was being supposed, of Joseph, the (one) of Eli, 3.24 of Matthat, of Levi, of Melchi, of Jannai, of Joseph, 3.25 of/from Mattathias, of Amos, of Naum, of Hesli, of Naggai, 3.26 of Maath, of Mattathias, of Semein, of Josech, of Jodah, 3.27 of Joanan, of Rhesa, of Zorobabel, of Salathiel, of Neri, 3.28 of Melchi, of Addi, of Kosam, of Ellmadam, of Er, 3.29 of Jesus, of Eliezer, of Jorim, of Matthat, of Levi, 3.30 of Simeon, of Juda, of Joseph, of Jonam, of Eliakim, 3.31 of Melea, of Menna, of Mattatha, of Natham, of David, 3.32 of Jesse, of Jobed, of Boos, of Sala, of Naasson, 3.33 of Aminadab, of Admin, of Arni, of Hesrom, of Phares, of Juda, 3.34 of Jacob, of Isaac, of Abraham, of Thara, of Nachor, 3.35 of Seruch, of Rhagan, of Phalek, of Eber, of Sala, 3.36 of Cainam, of Arphaxad, of Sem, of Noe, of Lamech, 3.37 of Mathusala, of Henoch, of Jaret, of Maleleel,

Μαλελεὴλ τοῦ Καϊνάμ 3.38 τοῦ Ἐνὼς τοῦ Σὴθ τοῦ Ἀδάμ τοῦ θεοῦ.

4.1 Ἰησοῦς δὲ πλήρης πνεύματος ἁγίου ὑπέστρεψεν ἀπὸ τοῦ Ἰορδάνου, καὶ ἤγετο τὸ ἐν τῷ πνεύματι ἐν τῇ ἐρήμῳ 4.2 ἡμέρας τεσσεράκοντα πειραζόμενος ὑπὸ τοῦ διαβόλου. καὶ οὐκ ἔφαγεν οὐδὲν, οὐδὲν ἐν ταῖς ἡμέραις ἐκείναις, καὶ συντελεσθεισῶν αὐτῶν ἐπείνασεν. 4.3 εἶπεν δὲ αὐτῷ ὁ διάβολος, εἰ υἱὸς εἶ τοῦ θεοῦ, εἰπὲ τῷ λίθῳ τούτῳ ἵνα γένηται ἄρτος.

4.4 καὶ ἀπεκρίθη πρὸς αὐτὸν ὁ Ἰησοῦς, γέγραπται ὅτι « οὐκ ἐπ’ ἄρτῳ μόνῳ ζήσεται ὁ ἄνθρωπος.» 4.5 καὶ ἀναγαγὼν αὐτὸν ἔδειξεν αὐτῷ πάσας τὰς βασιλίας τῆς οἰκουμένης ἐν στιγμῇ χρόνου· 4.6 καὶ εἶπεν αὐτῷ ὁ διάβολος, σοὶ δώσω τὴν ἐξουσίαν ταύτην πᾶσαν καὶ τὴν δόξαν αὐτῶν, ὅτι ἐμοὶ παραδέδοται καὶ ᾧ ἐὰν θέλω δίδωμι αὐτήν· 4.7 σὺ οὖν ἐὰν προσκυνήσῃς ἐνώπιον ἐμοῦ, ἔστε σοῦ πᾶσα. 4.8 καὶ ἀποκριθεὶς ὁ Ἰησοῦς εἶπεν αὐτῷ, γέγραπται, «κύριον τὸν θεόν σου προσκυνήσεις καὶ αὐτῷ» μόνῳ «λατρεύσεις.» 4.9 Ἤγαγεν δὲ αὐτὸν εἰς Ἰερουσαλὴμ καὶ ἔστησεν ἐπὶ τὸ πτερύγιον τοῦ ἱεροῦ, καὶ εἶπεν αὐτῷ, εἰ υἱὸς εἶ τοῦ θεοῦ, βάλε σεαυτὸν ἐντεῦθεν κάτω· 4.10 γέγραπται γὰρ ὅτι «τοῖς ἀγγέλοις αὐτοῦ ἐντελῖται περὶ σοῦ τοῦ διαφυλάξαι σε,» 4.11 καὶ ὅτι « ἐπὶ χειρῶν ἀροῦσίν σε μήποτε προσκόψῃς πρὸς λίθον τὸν πόδα σου.»

4.12 καὶ ἀποκριθεὶς εἶπεν αὐτῷ ὁ Ἰησοῦς ὅτι εἴρηται, « οὐκ ἐκπιράσεις κύριον τὸν θεόν σου.» 4.13 καὶ συντελέσας πάντα πιρασμὸν ὁ διάβολος ἀπέστη ἀπ’ αὐτοῦ ἄχρι καιροῦ. 4.14 καὶ ὑπέστρεψεν ὁ Ἰησοῦς ἐν τῇ δυνάμι τοῦ πνεύματος εἰς τὴν Γαλιλαίαν. καὶ φήμη ἐξῆλθεν καθ’ ὅλης τῆς χώρας περι περὶ αὐτοῦ. 4.15 καὶ αὐτὸς ἐδίδασκεν ἐν ταῖς συναγωγαῖς αὐτῶν, δοξαζόμενος ὑπὸ πάντων. 4.16 καὶ ἦλθεν εἰς Ναζαρά, οὗ ἦν ἀνατεθραμμένος, καὶ εἰσῆλθεν κατὰ τὸ εἰωθὸς αὐτῷ ἐν τῇ ἡμέρᾳ

of Cainam, 3.38 of Enos, of Seth, of Adam, of/from God.

4.1 And Jesus, *being* full of a holy spirit, returned from the Jordan, and was being led by the Spirit in the desert/wilderness 4.2 being tempted/ tested forty days by the devil. And he ate not no-thing, nothing in those days, and from them having been ended/finished, he hungered. 4.3 But the devil said to him: If you are a son of God, speak to this stone in order that it might become a loaf.
4.4 And Jesus answered to him: It has been written: THE MAN/HUMAN WILL NOT LIVE ON/FOR A LOAF/ BREAD ONLY/ALONE. 4.5 And having brought/led him up, he showed to him all the kingdoms of the empire/civil-ized world in an instant/at a point of time; 4.6 and the devil said to him: I shall give all this authority to you, and the glory/fame of them, because it has been delivered to me and I give it to whom ever I want/wish; 4.7 therefore you, if you might kneel down/worship before me, it all will be yours. 4.8 And answering, Jesus said to him: It has been written: YOU WILL WORSHIP *the* LORD YOUR GOD, AND YOU WILL SERVE/ WORSHIP FOR HIM ALONE/ONLY. 4.9 But he brought him to Jerusalem and stood *him* upon the edge/summit of the *outer* temple, and said to him: If you are a son of God, throw yourself down from here; 4.10 for it has been written: HE WILL COMMAND/CHARGE TO HIS MESSEN-GERS/ANGELS CONCERNING YOU, OF THE (THING) TO GUARD/ KEEP YOU, 4.11 and: THEY WILL TAKE YOU UPON HANDS, LEST YOU MIGHT STRIKE YOUR FOOT AGAINST A STONE.
4.12 And answering, Jesus said to him: It has been said: YOU WILL NOT TRY/TEST/TEMPT *the* LORD YOUR GOD. 4.13 And having completed every temptation/ test, the devil withdrew from him until a time/season. 4.14 And Jesus returned to Galilee in/by the power of the spirit. And a rumor/report about him went forth throughout the whole country. 4.15 And he himself was teaching in/among their congregations, being acknow-ledged/glorified by all. 4.16 And he went to Nazar-eth, where he had been brought up/reared, and he went into the congregation, according to the custom for him

τῶν σαββάτων εἰς τὴν συναγωγήν, καὶ ἀνέστη ἀναγνῶναι. 4.17 καὶ ἐπεδόθη αὐτῷ βιβλίον τοῦ προφήτου Ἡσαΐου, καὶ ἀναπτύξας τὸ βιβλίον εὗρεν τόπον οὗ ἦν γεγραμμένον, 4.18 « πνεῦμα κυρίου ἐπ᾽ ἐμέ, οὗ εἵνεκεν ἔχρισέν με εὐαγγελίσασθαι πτωχοῖς, ἀπέσταλκέν με κηρύξαι αἰχμαλώτοις ἄφεσιν καὶ τυφλοῖς ἀνάβλεψιν, ἀποστῖλαι τεθραυσμένους ἐν ἀφέσι, 4.19 κηρύξαι ἐνιαυτὸν κυρίου δεκτόν.» 4.20 καὶ πτύξας τὸ βιβλίον ἀποδοὺς τῷ ὑπηρέτῃ ἐκάθισεν· καὶ πάντων οἱ ὀφθαλμοὶ ἐν τῇ συναγωγῇ ἦσαν ἀτενίζοντες αὐτῷ. 4.21 ἤρξατο δὲ λέγιν πρὸς αὐτοὺς ὅτι σήμερον πεπλήρωται ἡ γραφὴ αὕτη ἐν τοῖς ὠσὶν ὑμῶν. 4.22 καὶ πάντες ἐμαρτύρουν αὐτῷ καὶ ἐθαύμαζον ἐπὶ τοῖς λόγοις τῆς χάριτος τοῖς ἐκπορευομένοις ἐκ τοῦ στόματος αὐτοῦ, καὶ ἔλεγον, οὐχὶ υἱός ἐστιν Ἰωσὴφ οὗτος; 4.23 καὶ εἶπεν πρὸς αὐτούς, πάντως ἐρεῖτέ μοι τὴν παραβολὴν ταύτην· ἰατρέ, θεράπευσον σεαυτόν· ὅσα ἠκούσαμεν γενόμενα εἰς τὴν Καφαρναοὺμ ποίησον καὶ ὧδε ἐν τῇ πατρίδι σου.

4.24 εἶπεν δέ, ἀμὴν λέγω ὑμῖν ὅτι οὐδὶς προφήτης δεκτός ἐστιν ἐν τῇ πατρίδι αὐτοῦ. 4.25 ἐπ᾽ ἀληθίας δὲ λέγω ὑμῖν, ὅτι πολλαὶ χῆραι ἦσαν ἐν ταῖς ἡμέραις Ἡλίου ἐν τῷ Ἰσραήλ, ὅτε ἐκλίσθη ὁ οὐρανὸς ἐπὶ ἔτη τρία καὶ μῆνας ἕξ, ὡς ἐγένετο λιμὸς μέγας ἐπὶ πᾶσαν τὴν γῆν, 4.26 καὶ πρὸς οὐδεμίαν αὐτῶν ἐπέμφθη Ἡλείας εἰ μὴ εἰς Σάρεπτα τῆς Σιδωνίας πρὸς γυναῖκα χήραν. 4.27 καὶ πολλοὶ λεπροὶ ἦσαν ἐν τῷ Ἰσραήλ ἐπὶ Ἐλισαίου τοῦ προφήτου, καὶ οὐδὶς αὐτῶν ἐκαθαρίσθη εἰ μὴ Ναιμὰν ὁ Σύρος. 4.28 καὶ ἐπλήσθησαν πάντες θυμοῦ ἐν τῇ συναγωγῇ ἀκούοντες ταῦτα, 4.29 καὶ ἀναστάντες ἐξέβαλον αὐτὸν ἔξω τῆς πόλεως, καὶ ἤγαγον αὐτὸν ἕως ὀφρύος τοῦ ὄρους ἐφ᾽ οὗ ἡ πόλις ᾠκοδόμητο αὐτῶν, ὥστε κατακρημνίσαι αὐτόν· 4.30 αὐτὸς δὲ διελθὼν διὰ μέσου αὐτῶν ἐπορεύετο.

4.31 καὶ κατῆλθεν εἰς Καφαρναοὺμ πόλιν τῆς Γαλιλαίας.

on the day of the sabbaths, and he stood up to read. 4.17 And a scroll of the prophet Esaias was given to him, and having unrolled the scroll, he found a place where it had been written: 4.18 A SPIRIT FROM *the* LORD *is* UPON ME, ON ACCOUNT OF WHICH HE ANOINTED ME TO ANNOUNCE A GOOD MESSAGE TO POOR (ONES), HE HAS SENT ME TO HERALD/PREACH A RELEASE . .r CAPTIVES/PRISONERS AND RECEIVING SIGHT FOR BLIND (ONES), TO SENd AWAY (THOSE) HAVING BEEN CRUELLY CRUSHED IN RELEASE, 4.19 TO HERALD/PREACH A FAVORABLE YEAR/PERIOD OF TIME OF *the* LORD. 4.20 And having rolled up the scroll, having given *it* back to the assistant/servant, he sat down; and the eyes of all in the congregation were gazing at him. 4.21 And he began to speak to them: This writing has been fulfilled today in your ears. 4.22 And all were witnessing for him and they were marveling over the words of the grace proceeding/going forth out of his mouth, and they were saying: Is this (one) not a son of Joseph? 4.23 And he said to them: Ye will surely say this parable to/for me: Doctor, treat/heal yourself; as many (things) as we heard happening in Capernaum, do you also here in your native place/ homeland.

4.24 And he said: Truly I say to ye that no prophet is accepted in his native place. 4.25 But I say to ye on/for a truth that many widows were in Israel in the days of Elias, when the sky was closed over/for three years and six months, as a great famine became on/over all the land, 4.26 and Elias was sent to no one of them except to Sarepta of Sidon, to a woman, a widow. 4.27 And there were many lepers in Israel at *the time* of Elisaeus the prophet, and no one of them was cleansed except Naaman the Syrian. 4.28 And hearing these (things), all in the congregation were filled with wrath, 4.29 and having rose up, they threw him out, outside the city, and they led him until *the* brow/edge of the hill on which their city had been built, so as to throw him down a cliff; 4.30 but he, he was going/departing, having passed through the midst of them.

4.31 And he went down into Capernaum, a city of Galilee, and he was teaching them on the sabbaths;

καὶ ἦν διδάσκων αὐτοὺς ἐν τοῖς σάββασιν· 4.32 καὶ ἐξεπλήσσοντο ἐπὶ τῇ διδαχῇ αὐτοῦ, ὅτι ἐν ἐξουσίᾳ ἦν ὁ λόγος αὐτοῦ. 4.33 καὶ ἐν τῇ συναγωγῇ ἦν ἄνθρωπος ἔχων πνεῦμα δαιμονίου ἀκαθάρτου, καὶ ἀνέκραξεν φωνῇ μεγάλῃ, 4.34 ἔα, τί ἡμῖν καὶ σοί, Ἰησοῦ Ναζαρηνέ; ἦλθες ἀπολέσαι ἡμᾶς; οἶδά σε τίς εἶ, ὁ ἅγιος τοῦ θεοῦ. 4.35 καὶ ἐπετίμησεν αὐτῷ ὁ Ἰησοῦς λέγων, φιμώθητι καὶ ἔξελθε ἀπ' αὐτοῦ. καὶ ῥίψαν αὐτὸν τὸ δαιμόνιον εἰς τὸ μέσον ἐξῆλθεν ἀπ' αὐτοῦ μηδὲν βλάψαν αὐτόν. 4.36 καὶ ἐγένετο θάμβος ἐπὶ πάντας, καὶ συνελάλουν πρὸς ἀλλήλους λέγοντες, τίς ὁ λόγος οὗτος, ὅτι ἐν ἐξουσίᾳ καὶ δυνάμι ἐπιτάσσει τοῖς ἀκαθάρτοις πνεύμασιν, καὶ ἐξέρχονται; 4.37 καὶ ἐξεπορεύετο ἦχος περὶ αὐτοῦ εἰς πάντα τόπον τῆς περιχώρου. 4.38 ἀναστὰς δὲ ἀπὸ τῆς συναγωγῆς εἰσῆλθεν εἰς τὴν οἰκίαν τοῦ Σίμωνος. πενθερὰ δὲ τοῦ Σίμωνος ἦν συνεχομένη πυρετῷ μεγάλῳ, καὶ ἠρώτησαν αὐτὸν περὶ αὐτῆς. 4.39 καὶ ἐπιστὰς ἐπάνω αὐτῆς ἐπετίμησεν τῷ πυρετῷ, καὶ ἀφῆκεν αὐτήν ὁ πυρετός· παραχρῆμα δὲ ἀναστᾶσα διηκόνι αὐτοῖς. 4.40 δύνοντος δὲ τοῦ ἡλίου πάντες ὅσοι εἶχον ἀσθενοῦντας νόσοις ποικίλαις ἤγαγον αὐτοὺς πρὸς αὐτόν· ὁ δὲ ἑνὶ ἑκάστῳ αὐτῶν ἐπιτιθεὶς τὰς χῖρας ἐθεράπευσεν αὐτούς. 4.41 ἐξήρχοντο δὲ καὶ δαιμόνια πολλῶν, κράζοντα καὶ λέγοντα ὅτι σὺ εἶ ὁ υἱὸς τοῦ θεοῦ. καὶ ἐπιτιμῶν οὐκ εἴα αὐτὰ λαλῖν, ὅτι ᾔδισαν τὸν χριστὸν αὐτὸν εἶναι.

4.42 γενομένης δὲ ἡμέρας ἐξελθὼν ἐπορεύθη εἰς ἔρημον τόπον· καὶ οἱ ὄχλοι ἐπεζήτουν αὐτόν, καὶ ἦλθον ἕως αὐτοῦ, καὶ κατεῖχον αὐτὸν τοῦ μὴ πορεύεσθαι ἀπ' αὐτῶν. 4.43 ὁ δὲ εἶπεν πρὸς αὐτοὺς ὅτι καὶ ταῖς ἑτέραις πόλεσιν εὐαγγελίσασθαί με δεῖ τὸ εὐαγγέλιον τὴν βασιλίαν τοῦ θεοῦ, ὅτι ἐπὶ τοῦτο ἀπεστάλην. 4.44 καὶ ἦν κηρύσσων εἰς τὰς συναγωγὰς τῆς Ἰουδαίας.

5.1 Ἐγένετο δὲ ἐν τῷ τὸν ὄχλον ἐπικεῖσθαι αὐτῷ καὶ

4.32 And they were astounded at/over his doctrine/ teaching, because the reason/word of him was with authority. 4.33 And there was a man in the congregation having a spirit from/of an unclean demon, and he cried out with a great voice: 4.34 Ah, what *is* for us and you, Jesus, Nazarene? Did you come to destroy us? I know you, who you are: The holy (one) from God. 4.35 And Jesus rebuked it, saying: Be muzzled and come out from him. And the demon, having thrown him down in the midst, it came out from him, not having harmed him. 4.36 And astonishment/fear became upon all, and they were speaking to/with one another, saying: What *is* this logos/saying/word, because he gives orders to the unclean spirits with authority and power, and they come out? 4.37 And news about him was going out into every place of the surrounding country. 4.38 And having arose from the congregation, he entered into the house of Simon. And Simon's mother-in-law was being confined/constrained with a great fever, and they asked him about her. 4.39 And having stood above her, he rebuked the fever, and the fever left her; and having immediately arose, she was serving/ministering to them. 4.40 And from the sun going down, all, as many as were having (ones) being sick with various diseases, brought them to/near him; and the (he), laying on the hands for each one of them, he treated/ healed them. 4.41 And also demons were coming out from many, crying aloud and saying: You, you are the son of God. And rebuking *them*, he was not allowing them to speak, because they knew him to be the anointed (one).

4.42 And from day having become, having gone out, he went to a desert/uninhabited place; and the crowds were looking for him, and they went until him, and they were detaining him from the (thing) not to go from them. 4.43 And the (he) said to them: It is necessary *for* me to announce the good message/gospel, the kingdom of God, to the other/different cities, because I was sent for this. 4.44 And he was heralding/preaching in the congregations of Judea.

5.1 And it happened in the (thing) *for* the crowd to press upon him and to hear the saying/word of God,

ἀκούειν τὸν λόγον τοῦ θεοῦ καὶ αὐτὸς ἦν ἑστὼς παρὰ τὴν λίμνην Γεννησαρέτ, 5.2 καὶ εἶδεν δύο πλοῖα ἑστῶτα παρὰ τὴν λίμνην· οἱ δὲ ἁλιεῖς ἀπ' αὐτῶν ἀποβάντες ἔπλυναν τὰ δίκτυα. 5.3 ἐμβὰς δὲ εἰς ἓν τῶν πλοίων, ὃ ἦν Σίμωνος, ἠρώτησεν αὐτὸν ἀπὸ τῆς γῆς ἐπαναγαγῖν ὀλίγον, καθίσας δὲ ἐν τῷ πλοίῳ ἐδίδασκεν τοὺς ὄχλους. 5.4 ὡς δὲ ἐπαύσατο λαλῶν, εἶπεν πρὸς τὸν Σίμωνα, ἐπανάγαγε εἰς τὸ βάθος καὶ χαλάσατε τὰ δίκτυα ὑμῶν εἰς ἄγραν.

5.5 καὶ ἀποκριθεὶς Σίμων εἶπεν, ἐπιστάτα, δι' ὅλης νυκτὸς κοπιάσαντες οὐδὲν ἐλάβομεν, ἐπὶ δὲ τῷ ῥήματί σου χαλάσω τὰ δίκτυα. 5.6 καὶ τοῦτο ποιήσαντες συνέκλεισαν πλῆθος ἰχθύων πολύ, διερρήσσετο δὲ τὰ δίκτυα αὐτῶν. 5.7 καὶ κατένευσαν τοῖς μετόχοις ἐν τῷ ἑτέρῳ πλοίῳ τοῦ ἐλθόντας συλλαβέσθε αὐτοῖς· καὶ ἦλθαν, καὶ ἔπλησαν ἀμφότερα τὰ πλοῖα ὥστε βυθίζεσθαι αὐτά. 5.8 ἰδὼν δὲ Σίμων Πέτρος προσέπεσεν τοῖς γόνασιν Ἰησοῦ λέγων, ἔξελθε ἀπ' ἐμοῦ, ὅτι ἀνὴρ ἁμαρτωλός εἰμι, κύριε· 5.9 θάμβος γὰρ περιέσχεν αὐτὸν καὶ πάντας τοὺς σὺν αὐτῷ ἐπὶ τῇ ἄγρᾳ τῶν ἰχθύων ἧ συνέλαβον, 5.10 ὁμοίως δὲ καὶ Ἰάκωβος καὶ Ἰωάννης οἱ υἱοὶ Ζεβεδαίου, οἳ ἦσαν κοινωνοὶ τῷ Σίμωνι. καὶ εἶπεν πρὸς τὸν Σίμωνα ὁ Ἰησοῦς, μὴ φοβοῦ· ἀπὸ τοῦ νῦν ἀνθρώπους ἔσῃ ζωγρῶν. 5.11 καὶ καταγαγόντες τὰ πλοῖα ἐπὶ τὴν γῆν ἀφέντες πάντα ἠκολούθησαν αὐτῷ.

5.12 καὶ ἐγένετο ἐν τῷ εἶναι αὐτὸν ἐν μιᾷ τῶν πόλεων καὶ ἰδοὺ ἀνὴρ πλήρης λέπρας· ἰδὼν δὲ τὸν Ἰησοῦν πεσὼν ἐπὶ πρόσωπον ἐδεήθη αὐτοῦ λέγων, κύριε, ἐὰν θέλῃς δύνασαί με καθαρίσαι. 5.13 καὶ ἐκτίνας τὴν χεῖρα ἥψατο αὐτοῦ λέγων, θέλω, καθαρίσθητι· καὶ εὐθέως ἡ λέπρα ἀπῆλθεν ἀπ' αὐτοῦ. 5.14 καὶ αὐτὸς παρήγγιλεν αὐτῷ μηδενὶ εἰπῖν, ἀλλὰ ἀπελθὼν δῖξον σεαυτὸν τῷ ἱερῖ, προσένεγκαι περὶ τοῦ καθαρισμοῦ σου καθὼς προσέταξεν Μωϋσῆς, εἰς μαρτύριον αὐτοῖς. 5.15 διήρχετο δὲ μᾶλλον ὁ λόγος περὶ αὐτοῦ, καὶ συνήρχοντο ὄχλοι πολλοὶ

and he himself had been standing beside the lake Gennesaret, 5.2 and he saw two boats having been set beside the lake; but the fishermen, having gone away from them, washed the nets. 5.3 And having embarked in one of the boats, which was Simon's, he asked *for* him to put off a little from the land, and having sat down in the boat, he was teaching the crowds. 5.4 And when he stopped speaking, he said to Simon: Put out into the deep and let down your nets for a catch.

5.5 And answering, Simon said: Commander/master, having labored an entire night, we took nothing, but on the word from you, I shall lower the nets. 5.6 And having done this, they enclosed a much multitude of fishes, but their nets were being torn. 5.7 And they motioned/waved for the partners in the other/different boat, from the (thing) having come, to assist with them; and they came, and they filled both the boats so as *for* them to sink. 5.8 And having seen, Simon Peter fell near the knees of Jesus, saying: Go away from me, because I am a sinful man, Lord. 5.9 For astonishment/fear encompassed him and all those with him over the catch of the fishes which they caught/took, 5.10 and likewise *did* both James and John, the sons of Zebedee, who were companions/sharers with Peter. And Jesus said to Simon: Fear not; from the present (time) you will be catching men. 5.11 And having brought down the boats upon the land, having left all (things), they followed with him.

5.12 And it came about by the (thing) *for* him to be in one of the cities, and behold, a man full of leprosy; and having seen Jesus, having fallen upon *his* face, he petitioned him, saying: Lord, if you may will/wish to be able yourself to cleanse me. 5.13 And having reached out, he touched his hand, saying: I will, be cleansed; and immediately the leprosy went away from him. 5.14 And he, he enjoined to him to tell no one, but going away, show yourself to the priest, and bring *an* offering concerning your purification as Moses ordered/commanded, in/for a testimony to them. 5.15 But rather, the saying/word was going throughout concerning him, and many crowds were coming together to hear/listen and to be treated/healed from

ἀκούειν καὶ θεραπεύεσθαι ἀπὸ τῶν ἀσθενιῶν αὐτῶν· 5.16 αὐτὸς δὲ ἦν ὑποχωρῶν ἐν ταῖς ἐρήμοις καὶ προσευχόμενος.

5.17 καὶ ἐγένετο ἐν μιᾷ τῶν ἡμερῶν καὶ αὐτὸς ἦν διδάσκων, καὶ ἦσαν καθήμενοι Φαρισαῖοι καὶ νομοδιδάσκαλοι οἳ ἦσαν ἐληλυθότες ἐκ πάσης κώμης τῆς Γαλιλαίας καὶ Ἰουδαίας καὶ Ἰερουσαλήμ· καὶ δύναμις κυρίου ἦν εἰς τὸ ἰᾶσθαι αὐτόν.

5.18 καὶ ἰδοὺ ἄνδρες φέροντες ἄνθρωπον ἐπὶ κλίνης βεβλημένον ὃς ἦν παραλελυμένος, καὶ ἐζήτουν αὐτὸν εἰσενεγκεῖν καὶ θεῖναι ἐνώπιον αὐτοῦ. 5.19 καὶ μὴ εὑρόντες ποίας εἰσενέγκωσιν αὐτὸν διὰ τὸν ὄχλον ἀναβάντες ἐπὶ τὸ δῶμα διὰ τῶν κεράμων καθῆκαν αὐτὸν σὺν τῷ κλινιδίῳ εἰς τὸ μέσον ἔμπροσθεν τοῦ Ἰησοῦ. 5.20 καὶ ἰδὼν τὴν πίστιν αὐτῶν εἶπεν, ἄνθρωπε, ἀφέωντέ σου αἱ ἁμαρτίαι. 5.21 καὶ ἤρξαντο διαλογίζεσθε οἱ γραμματεῖς καὶ οἱ Φαρισαῖοι λέγοντες, τίς ἐστιν οὗτος ὃς λαλεῖ βλασφημίας; τίς δύναται ἀφεῖναι ἁμαρτίας εἰ μὴ μόνος ὁ θεός; 5.22 ἐπιγνοὺς δὲ ὁ Ἰησοῦς τοὺς διαλογισμοὺς αὐτῶν ἀποκριθεὶς εἶπεν πρὸς αὐτούς, τί διαλογίζεσθε ἐν ταῖς καρδίαις ὑμῶν; 5.23 τί ἐστιν εὐκοπώτερον, εἰπεῖν, ἀφέωνταί σου αἱ ἁμαρτίαι, ἢ εἰπεῖν, ἔγειρε καὶ περιπάτι; 5.24 ἵνα δὲ εἰδῆτε ὅτι ἐξουσίαν ἔχει ὁ υἱὸς τοῦ ἀνθρώπου ἐπὶ τῆς γῆς ἀφιέναι ἁμαρτίας εἶπεν τῷ παραλυτικῷ, σοὶ λέγω, ἔγειρε καὶ ἆρον τὸ κλινίδιόν σου καὶ πορεύου εἰς τὸν οἶκόν σου. 5.25 καὶ παραχρῆμα ἀναστὰς ἐνώπιον αὐτοῦ, ἄρας ἐφ᾽ ὃ κατέκειτο, ἀπῆλθεν εἰς τὸν οἶκον αὐτοῦ δοξάζων τὸν θεόν. 5.26 καὶ ἔκστασις ἔλαβεν ἅπαντας καὶ ἐδόξαζον τὸν θεόν, καὶ ἐπλήσθησαν φόβου λέγοντες ὅτι εἴδομεν παράδοξα σήμερον. 5.27 καὶ μετὰ ταῦτα ἐξῆλθεν καὶ ἐθεάσατο τελώνην ὀνόματι Λευεὶν καθήμενον· ἐπὶ τὸ τελώνιον, καὶ λέγει αὐτῷ, ἀκολούθι μοι. 5.28 καὶ καταλιπὼν ἅπαντα ἀναστὰς ἠκολούθησεν αὐτῷ. 5.29 καὶ ἐποίησεν δοχὴν μεγάλην Λευεὶς αὐτῷ ἐν τῷ οἴκῳ αὐτοῦ· καὶ ἦν ὄχλος πολὺς τελωνῶν καὶ ἄλλων οἳ ἦσαν μετ᾽ αὐτῶν κατακείμενοι. 5.30 καὶ ἐγόγγυζον οἱ Φαρισαῖοι καὶ οἱ

their sicknesses/weaknesses; 5.16 but he, he was withdrawing in the deserts and praying.

5.17 And it happened on one of the days; both he, he was teaching, and there were sitting Pharisees and teachers of law who had come out of every village of Galilee and Judea and Jerusalem; and power from *the* Lord was in the (thing) *for* him to heal.

5.18 And behold, men *were* carrying a man having been placed on a stretcher, who had been paralyzed, and they were seeking to bring and to lay him before him. 5.19 And not having found of what (way)/how they might carry him in because of the crowd, having gone up on the roof, they lowered him through the tiles with the stretcher into the midst before/in front of Jesus. 5.20 And having seen the faith of them, he said: Man, the sins/faults have been forgiven/sent away from you. 5.21 And the scribes and the Pharisees began to reason/dispute, saying: Who is this (one) who speaks slander/blasphemy? Who is able to dismiss/forgive sins/faults, except God alone? 5.22 But Jesus, having known their reasonings/disputings, answering, he said to them: Why do ye argue/dispute in your hearts? 5.23 What is easier to say: The sins/faults have been dismissed/forgiven from you, or to say: Rise up and walk? 5.24 But in order that ye may know that the son of the man holds/has authority on the earth to dismiss/forgive sins, -- he said to the paralytic: I say to you: arise and take up your cot/stretcher and go to your house. 5.25 And having rose up at once before him, having taken up *that* on which he was laid down, he went away to his house, glorifying/acknowledging God. 5.26 And ecstasy/amazement took all, and they were glorifying/acknowledging God, and they were filled from a fear/awe, saying: We saw/beheld unexpected/strange (things) today. 5.27 And after these (things) he went forth and beheld a tax-collector, Levi by name, sitting at the revenue/tax office, and he says to him: Follow with me. 5.28 And leaving all behind, having arose, he followed with him. 5.29 And Levi made a great banquet for him in/at his house; and there was a much crowd of tax-collectors/publicans and others who were reclining with them. 5.30 And the

γραμματεῖς πρὸς τοὺς μαθητὰς αὐτοῦ λέγοντες, διὰ τί μετὰ τῶν τελωνῶν καὶ ἁμαρτωλῶν ἐσθίεται καὶ πίνετε;

5.31 καὶ ἀποκριθεὶς ὁ Ἰησοῦς εἶπεν πρὸς αὐτούς, οὐ χρίαν ἔχουσιν οἱ ὑγιαίνοντες ἰατροῦ ἀλλ᾽ οἱ κακῶς ἔχοντες· 5.32 οὐκ ἐλήλυθα καλέσαι δικαίους ἀλλὰ ἁμαρτωλοὺς εἰς μετάνοιαν. 5.33 οἱ δὲ εἶπον πρὸς αὐτόν, διάτι οἱ μαθηταὶ Ἰωάννου νηστεύουσιν πυκνὰ καὶ δεήσεις ποιοῦνται, ὁμοίως καὶ οἱ τῶν Φαρισαίων, οἱ δὲ σοὶ ἐσθίουσιν καὶ πίνουσιν;

5.34 ὁ δὲ Ἰησοῦς εἶπεν πρὸς αὐτούς, μὴ δύνασθε τοὺς υἱοὺς τοῦ νυμφῶνος ἐν ᾧ ὁ νυμφίος μετ᾽ αὐτῶν ἐστιν ποιῆσαι νηστεύειν; 5.35 ἐλεύσονται δὲ ἡμέραι, ὅταν ἀπαρθῇ ἀπ᾽ αὐτῶν ὁ νυμφίος καὶ τότε νηστεύσουσιν ἐν ἐκείναις ταῖς ἡμέραις. 5.36 ἔλεγεν δὲ πρὸς αὐτοὺς παραβολὴν ὅτι οὐδὶς ἐπίβλημα ἀπὸ ἱματίου καινοῦ σχίσας ἐπιβάλλει ἐπὶ ἱμάτιον παλαιόν· εἰ δὲ μή γε, καὶ τὸ καινὸν σχίσει καὶ τῷ παλαιῷ οὐ συμφωνήσει τὸ ἐπίβλημα τὸ ἀπὸ τοῦ καινοῦ. 5.37 καὶ οὐδεὶς βάλλει οἶνον νέον εἰς ἀσκοὺς παλαιούς· εἰ δὲ μή γε, ῥήξει ὁ οἶνος τοὺς ἀσκούς, καὶ αὐτὸς ἐκχυθήσεται καὶ οἱ ἀσκοὶ ἀπολοῦνται· 5.38 ἀλλὰ οἶνον νέον εἰς ἀσκοὺς καινοὺς βλητέον. 5.39 καὶ οὐδεὶς πιὼν παλαιὸν θέλει νέον· λέγει γάρ, ὁ παλαιὸς χρηστός ἐστιν.

6.1 Ἐγένετο δὲ ἐν σαββάτῳ διαπορεύεσθαι αὐτὸν διὰ σπορίμων, καὶ ἔτιλλον οἱ μαθηταὶ αὐτοῦ στάχυας καὶ ἤσθιον ψώχοντες ταῖς χερσίν.

6.2 τινὲς δὲ τῶν Φαρισαίων εἶπον, τί ποιεῖται ὃ οὐκ ἔξεστιν ποιεῖν τοῖς σάββασιν; 6.3 καὶ ἀποκριθεὶς ὁ Ἰησοῦς πρὸς αὐτοὺς εἶπεν, οὐδὲ τοῦτο ἀνέγνωτε ὃ ἐποίησεν Δαυὶδ ὅτε ἐπίνασεν αὐτὸς καὶ οἱ μετ᾽ αὐτοῦ; 6.4 ὡς εἰσῆλθεν εἰς τὸν οἶκον τοῦ θεοῦ καὶ τοὺς ἄρτους τῆς προθέσεως ἔφαγεν καὶ ἔδωκεν καὶ τοῖς μετ᾽ αὐτοῦ, οὓς οὐκ ἔξεστιν φαγεῖν εἰ μὴ μόνους τοὺς ἱερεῖς; 6.5 καὶ ἔλεγεν αὐτοῖς, κύριός ἐστιν τοῦ σαββάτου ὁ υἱὸς τοῦ ἀνθρώπου.

6.6 ἐγένετο δὲ ἐν ἑτέρῳ σαββάτῳ εἰσελθῖν αὐτὸν εἰς τὴν

Pharisees and the scribes were grumbling to his learn-ers/pupils, saying: Why do ye eat and drink with the tax-collectors and sinners?

5.31 And answering, Jesus said to them: Those being healthy have not a need of a doctor, but those having *it* badly; 5.32 I have not come to call just (ones), but sinners into repentance. 5.33 And they said to him: Why do the learners/pupils of John fast frequently and make entreaties/supplications, and those of the Pharisees *do* likewise, but those with you eat and drink?

5.34 And Jesus said to them: Ye are not able to make the sons of the wedding hall to fast in *time* which the bridegroom is with them, *are you*? 5.35 But days will come, when the bridegroom might be taken away from them, and then they will fast in those days. 5.36 And he was saying a parable to them: No one, having torn a piece/patch from a new garment puts *it* on an old garment; otherwise, both the new will tear and the patch from the new will not harmonize/agree with the old. 5.37 And no one puts new wine into old wineskins; otherwise, the wine will break/burst the wineskins, and it will be poured out and the wineskins will perish; 5.38 but one must put new wine into new wineskins. 5.39 And no one having drunk old wants new; for he says: The old is good/useful.

6.1 And it came about on a sabbath *for* him to travel through grainfields, and his learners/pupils were picking and eating heads of grain, rubbing with/ in the hands. 6.2 And some of the Pharisees said: Why do ye what is not lawful to do on the sabbaths? 6.3 And answering, Jesus said to them: Did ye not read what David did when he hungered, he and those with him? 6.4 When he entered into the house of God and he ate the loaves of presentation, and he also gave *it* to those with him, which is not lawful to eat, except *for* the priests only? 6.5 And he was saying to them: The son of the man is lord of the sabbath.

6.6 And it came about on another/different sabbath *for* him to enter into the congregation and to

συναγωγὴν καὶ διδάσκιν· καὶ ἦν ἄνθρωπος ἐκεῖ καὶ ἡ χεὶρ αὐτοῦ ἡ δεξιὰ ἦν ξηρά· 6.7 παρετηροῦν δὲ αὐτὸν οἱ γραμματεῖς καὶ οἱ Φαρισαῖοι εἰ ἐν τῷ σαββάτῳ θεραπεύει, ἵνα εὕρωσιν κατηγορῖν αὐτοῦ. 6.8 αὐτὸς δὲ ᾔδει τοὺς διαλογισμοὺς αὐτῶν,

εἶπεν δὲ τῷ ἀνδρὶ τῷ τὴν ξηρὰν ἔχοντι τὴν χεῖρα, ἔγειρε καὶ στῆθι εἰς τὸ μέσον· καὶ ἀναστὰς ἔστη.

6.9 εἶπεν δὲ ὁ Ἰησοῦς πρὸς αὐτούς, ἐπερωτῶ ὑμᾶς, εἰ ἔξεστιν τῷ σαββάτῳ ἀγαθοποιῆσαι ἢ κακοποιῆσαι, ψυχὴν σῶσαι ἢ ἀπολέσαι; 6.10 καὶ περιβλεψάμενος πάντας αὐτοὺς εἶπεν τῷ ἀνθρώπῳ, ἔκτινον τὴν χεῖρά σου. ὁ δὲ ἐξέτινεν, καὶ ἀπεκατεστάθη ἡ χεὶρ αὐτοῦ. 6.11 αὐτοὶ δὲ ἐπλήσθησαν ἀνοίας, καὶ διελάλουν πρὸς ἀλλήλους τί ἂν ποιήσιεν τῷ Ἰησοῦ. 6.12 ἐγένετο δὲ ἐν ταῖς ἡμέραις ταύταις ἐξελθεῖν αὐτὸν εἰς τὸ ὄρος προσεύξασθαι, καὶ ἦν διανυκτερεύων ἐν τῇ προσευχῇ τοῦ θεοῦ.

6.13 καὶ ὅτε ἐγένετο ἡμέρα, προσεφώνησεν τοὺς μαθητὰς αὐτοῦ, καὶ ἐκλεξάμενος ἀπ᾽ αὐτῶν δώδεκα, οὓς καὶ ἀποστόλους ὠνόμασεν, 6.14 Σίμωνα, ὃν καὶ ὠνόμασεν Πέτρον, καὶ Ἀνδρέαν τὸν ἀδελφὸν αὐτοῦ, καὶ Ἰάκωβον καὶ Ἰωάννην καὶ Φίλιππον καὶ Βαρθολομαῖον 6.15 καὶ Μαθθαῖον καὶ Θωμᾶν καὶ Ἰάκωβον Ἁλφαίου καὶ Σίμωνα τὸν καλούμενον Ζηλωτὴν 6.16 καὶ Ἰούδαν Ἰακώβου καὶ Ἰούδαν Ἰσκαριώθ, ὃς ἐγένετο προδότης. 6.17 καὶ καταβὰς μετ᾽ αὐτῶν ἔστη ἐπὶ τόπου πεδινοῦ, καὶ ὄχλος πολὺς μαθητῶν αὐτοῦ, καὶ πλῆθος πολὺ τοῦ λαοῦ ἀπὸ πάσης τῆς Ἰουδαίας καὶ Ἰερουσαλὴμ καὶ τῆς παραλίου Τύρου καὶ Σειδῶνος, 6.18 οἳ ἦλθον ἀκοῦσαι αὐτοῦ καὶ ἰαθῆναι ἀπὸ τῶν νόσων αὐτῶν· καὶ οἱ ἐνοχλούμενοι ἀπὸ πνευμάτων ἀκαθάρτων ἐθεραπεύοντο. 6.19 καὶ πᾶς ὁ ὄχλος ἐζήτουν ἅπτεσθαι αὐτοῦ, ὅτι δύναμις παρ᾽ αὐτοῦ ἐξήρχετο καὶ ἰᾶτο πάντας. 6.20 καὶ αὐτὸς ἐπάρας τοὺς ὀφθαλμοὺς αὐτοῦ εἰς τοὺς μαθητὰς αὐτοῦ ἔλεγεν,

μακάριοι οἱ πτωχοί, ὅτι ὑμετέρα ἐστὶν ἡ βασιλία τοῦ θεοῦ.
6.21 μακάριοι οἱ πινῶντες νῦν, ὅτι χορτασθήσεσθε.

teach; and a man was there and his right hand was dried/withered; 6.7 but the scribes and the Pharisees were watching him closely, if he treats/heals on the sabbath, in order that they might find *something* of him to accuse. 6.8 But he, he knew their reasonings, and he said to the man having the withered hand: Arise and stand in the midst; and having arose, he stood.

6.9 And Jesus said to them: I ask ye, if it is lawful to do good on the sabbath, or to do bad; to save a life/soul, or to destroy? 6.10 And having looked around *at* them all, he said to the man: Stretch forth your hand. And the (he) stretched it forth, and his hand was restored. 6.11 But they were filled from senseless fury, and were deliberating to/with one another what ever they might do to Jesus. 6.12 And it came about in those days *for* him to go out to the mountain to pray, and he was being *there* through the night in the prayer of God.

6.13 And when it became day, he called to his learners/pupils, and having chosen twelve from them, whom he also named apostles, 6.14 Simon, whom he also named Peter, and Andrew his brother, and James, and John, and Philip, and Bartholomew, 6.15 and Matthew, and Thomas, and James of Alphaeus, and Simon the (one) being called a Zealot, 6.16 and Judas of James, and Judas Iscariot, who became a traitor. 6.17 And having come down with them, he stood on a level place, and a much crowd of his learners/pupils and a much multitude of the people from all of Judea and Jerusalem and the seacoast of Tyre and Sidon, 6.18 who came to hear from him and to be healed from their diseases; and the (ones) being troubled/annoyed from unclean spirits were being treated/healed. 6.19 And all the crowd were seeking to touch him, because power was going forth from him and was healing all. 6.20 And he, having lifted up his eyes to the learners/pupils, he was saying:

Happy *are* the poor (ones), because the kingdom of God is yours.

6.21 Happy *are* the (ones) hungering now, because ye will be filled/satisfied.

132

μακάριοι οἱ κλαίοντες νῦν, ὅτι γελάσετε.

6.22 μακάριοί ἐστε ὅταν μισήσωσιν ὑμᾶς οἱ ἄνθρωποι, καὶ ὅταν ἀφορίσωσιν ὑμᾶς καὶ ὀνειδίσωσιν καὶ ἐκβάλωσιν τὸ ὄνομα ὑμῶν ὡς πονηρὸν ἕνεκα τοῦ υἱοῦ τοῦ ἀνθρώπου· 6.23 χάρητε ἐν ἐκείνῃ τῇ ἡμέρᾳ καὶ σκιρτήσατε, ἰδοὺ γὰρ ὁ μισθὸς ὑμῶν πολὺς ἐν τῷ οὐρανῷ· κατὰ τ᾽ αὐτὰ γὰρ ἐποίουν τοῖς προφήταις οἱ πατέρες αὐτῶν. 6.24 πλὴν οὐαὶ ὑμῖν τοῖς πλουσίοις, ὅτι ἀπέχεται τὴν παράκλησιν ὑμῶν.

6.25 οὐαὶ ὑμῖν, οἱ ἐμπεπλησμένοι νῦν, ὅτι πεινάσετε.

οὐαί, οἱ γελῶντες νῦν, ὅτι πενθήσεται καὶ κλαύσεται.

6.26 οὐαὶ ὅταν καλῶς εἴπωσιν ὑμᾶς οἱ ἄνθρωποι πάντες, κατὰ τὰ αὐτὰ γὰρ ἐποίουν τοῖς ψευδοπροφήταις οἱ πατέρες αὐτῶν. 6.27 ἀλλὰ ὑμῖν λέγω τοῖς ἀκούουσιν, ἀγαπᾶται τοὺς ἐχθροὺς ὑμῶν, καλῶς ποιεῖται τοῖς μισοῦσιν ὑμᾶς, 6.28 εὐλογῖται τοὺς καταρωμένους ὑμᾶς, προσεύχεσθαι περὶ τῶν ἐπηρεαζόντων ὑμᾶς. 6.29 τῷ τύπτοντί σε ἐπὶ τὴν σιαγόνα πάρεχε καὶ τὴν ἄλλην, καὶ ἀπὸ τοῦ αἴροντός σου τὸ ἱμάτιον καὶ τὸν χιτῶνα μὴ κωλύσῃς. 6.30 παντὶ αἰτοῦντί σε δίδου, καὶ ἀπὸ τοῦ αἴροντος τὰ σὰ μὴ ἀπαίτει. 6.31 καὶ καθὼς θέλετε ἵνα ποιῶσιν ὑμῖν οἱ ἄνθρωποι καὶ ὑμῖς ποιεῖται αὐτοῖς ὁμοίως. 6.32 καὶ εἰ ἀγαπᾶτε τοὺς ἀγαπῶντας ὑμᾶς, ποία ὑμῖν χάρις ἐστίν; καὶ γὰρ οἱ ἁμαρτωλοὶ τοὺς ἀγαπῶντας αὐτοὺς ἀγαπῶσιν.

6.33 καὶ γὰρ ἐὰν ἀγαθοποιῆτε τοὺς ἀγαθοποιοῦντας ὑμᾶς, ποία ὑμῖν χάρις ἐστίν; καὶ οἱ ἁμαρτωλοὶ τὸ αὐτὸ ποιοῦσιν. 6.34 καὶ ἐὰν δανίσηται παρ᾽ ὧν ἐλπίζεται λαβῖν, ποία ὑμῖν χάρις ἐστίν; καὶ ἁμαρτωλοὶ ἁμαρτωλοῖς δανίζουσιν ἵνα ἀπολάβωσιν τὰ εἴσα.

6.35 πλὴν ἀγαπᾶται τοὺς ἐχθροὺς ὑμῶν καὶ ἀγαθοποιεῖται καὶ δανίζεται μηδὲν ἀπελπίζοντες· καὶ ἔσται ὁ μισθὸς ὑμῶν πολύς, καὶ ἔσεσθαι υἱοὶ ὑψίστου, ὅτι αὐτὸς

Happy *are* the (ones) weeping now, because ye will laugh.

6.22 Happy ye are whenever the men/humans might hate ye, and whenever they might ostracize ye and they might reproach and throw out the name of ye as evil/wicked on account of the son of the man; 6.23 rejoice ye in that day and leap ye for joy, for behold, the reward of ye *is* much in the sky/heaven; for their fathers were doing according to the same (things) to the prophets. 6.24 However, woe to ye, the wealthy/rich (ones), because ye have in full your consolation/comfort.

6.25 Woe to ye, the (ones) having been filled/satisfied now, because ye will hunger.

Woe, those/the (ones) laughing now, because ye will morn and lament/weep.

6.26 Woe whenever all men might speak well *of* ye, for their fathers were doing according to the same (things) to the lying/false prophets. 6.27 But I say to ye, the (ones) hearing: Love ye your enemies, do ye well to the (ones) hating ye, 6.28 bless ye/speak ye well of the (ones) cursing ye, pray ye concerning those harassing/insulting ye. 6.29 To the (one) striking you on the cheek, offer the other also, and from the (one) taking away from you the garment and the tunic, you may not hinder/forbid. 6.30 Give to every (one) asking you, and demand not back from the (one) taking away your things. 6.31 And as ye want/wish that the men may do for ye; ye also, do ye likewise for them. 6.32 And if ye love those loving ye, what is grace to ye/what grace/thanks is for ye? For even the sinners love those loving them.

6.33 For even if ye may do good *for* those doing good *for* ye, what is grace to ye? Even the sinners do the same. 6.34 And if ye might lend *to those* from whom ye hope to receive, what is grace to ye? Even sinners lend to sinners in order that they might receive back equal things.

6.35 However, love ye your enemies and do ye good and lend ye, hoping for nothing in return; and the reward of ye will be much, and ye will be sons of *the* most high, because he, he is kind to the unthank-

χρηστός ἐστιν ἐπὶ τοὺς ἀχαρίστους καὶ πονηρούς.

6.36 γείνεσθε οἰκτίρμονες καθὼς ὁ πατὴρ ὑμῶν οἰκτίρμων ἐστίν. 6.37 καὶ μὴ κρίνετε, καὶ οὐ μὴ κριθῆτε· καὶ μὴ καταδικάζετε, καὶ οὐ μὴ καταδικασθῆται.

ἀπολύεται, καὶ ἀπολυθήσεσθαι·

6.38 δίδοται, καὶ δοθήσεται ὑμῖν· μέτρον καλὸν πεπιεσμένον σεσαλευμένον ὑπερεκχυννόμενον δώσουσιν εἰς τὸν κόλπον ὑμῶν· ᾧ γὰρ μέτρῳ μετρῖται ἀντιμετρηθήσεται ὑμῖν.

6.39 εἶπεν δὲ καὶ παραβολὴν αὐτοῖς· μήτι δύναται τυφλὸς τυφλὸν ὁδηγεῖν; οὐκ ἀμφότεροι εἰς βόθυνον πεσοῦνται;

6.40 οὐκ ἔστιν μαθητὴς ὑπὲρ τὸν διδάσκαλον, κατηρτισμένος δὲ ἔστω ὡς ὁ διδάσκαλος αὐτοῦ.

6.41 τί δὲ βλέπεις τὸ κάρφος τὸ ἐν τῷ ὀφθαλμῷ τοῦ ἀδελφοῦ σου, τὴν δὲ δοκὸν τὴν ἐν τῷ ἰδίῳ ὀφθαλμῷ οὐ κατανοεῖς; 6.42 πῶς δὲ δύνασαι λέγειν τῷ ἀδελφῷ σου, ἀδελφέ, ἄφες ἐκβάλω τὸ κάρφος τὸ ἐν τῷ ὀφθαλμῷ σου, αὐτὸς τὴν ἐν τῷ ὀφθαλμῷ σοῦ δοκὸν οὐ βλέπων;

ὑποκριτά, ἔκβαλε πρῶτον τὴν δοκὸν ἐκ τοῦ ὀφθαλμοῦ σοῦ, καὶ τότε διαβλέψεις ἐκβαλῖν τὸ κάρφος τὸ ἐν τῷ ὀφθαλμῷ τοῦ ἀδελφοῦ σου. 6.43 οὐ γάρ ἐστιν δένδρον καλὸν ποιοῦν καρπὸν σαπρόν, οὐδὲ πάλιν δένδρον σαπρὸν ποιοῦν καρπὸν καλόν. 6.44 ἕκαστον γὰρ δένδρον ἐκ τοῦ ἰδίου καρποῦ γεινώσκεται· οὐ γὰρ ἐξ ἀκανθῶν συλλέγουσιν σῦκα, οὐδὲ ἐκ βάτου σταφυλὴν τρυγῶσιν.

6.45 ὁ ἀγαθὸς ἄνθρωπος ἐκ τοῦ ἀγαθοῦ θησαυροῦ τῆς καρδίας προφέρει τὸ ἀγαθόν, καὶ ὁ πονηρὸς ἐκ τοῦ πονηροῦ προφέρει τὸ πονηρόν· ἐκ γὰρ περισσεύματος καρδίας τὸ στόμα αὐτοῦ λαλεῖ. 6.46 τί δέ με καλεῖται, κύριε κύριε, καὶ οὐ ποιεῖται ἃ λέγω;

6.47 πᾶς ὁ ἐρχόμενος πρός με καὶ ἀκούων μου τῶν λόγων καὶ ποιῶν αὐτούς, ὑποδίξω ὑμῖν τίνι ἐστὶν ὅμοιος·

6.48 ὅμοιός ἐστιν ἀνθρώπῳ οἰκοδομοῦντι οἰκίαν ὃς

ful/ungraceful and evil/wicked (ones).

6.36 Become ye compassionate as the father of ye is compassionate. 6.37 And judge ye not, and ye might by no means be judged; and condemn ye not, and ye might by no means be condemned.

Release/dismiss ye, and ye will be released/dismissed;

6.38 give ye, and it will be given to ye; they will give good measure, having been pressed down, having been shaken, being poured beyond measure, in the bosom/pocket of ye; for with what measure ye measure, it will be measured in return to ye.

6.39 And he also said/told a parable to them: Is a blind (one) not able to guide a blind (one)? Will not both fall into a ditch?

6.40 A learner/pupil is not above the teacher, but let him be having been fully trained/prepared as/like his teacher.

6.41 But why do you see the splinter in your brothers eye, but you do not notice the timber/log in your own eye? 6.42 And how are you able to say to your brother: Brother, allow *that* I might put out the splinter in your eye, yourself not seeing observing the timber in your eye?

Pretender/hypocrite, first put out the timber out of your eye, and then you will see clearly to put out the splinter in your brother's eye. 6.43 For a good tree is not making rotten fruit, nor again a rotten tree making good fruit. 6.44 For each tree is known from its own fruit; for they do not gather figs out of/from thorn bushes, neither do they pick a bunch of grapes from a bramble (bush).

6.45 The good man out of the good storehouse of the heart offers/produces the good (thing), and the evil (man) offers/produces the evil (thing) out of the evil (store); for his mouth speaks out of *the* abundance of *his* heart. 6.46 But why do ye call me: Lord, Lord, and ye do not *the things* which I say?

6.47 Every one coming to/near/with me and hearing the sayings/words of me and doing them, I shall show/demonstrate for ye to whom he is like:

6.48 He is like/similar to a man building a

ἔσκαψεν καὶ ἐβάθυνεν καὶ ἔθηκεν θεμέλιον ἐπὶ τὴν πέτραν· πλημμύρης δὲ γενομένης προσέρηξεν ὁ ποταμὸς τῇ οἰκίᾳ ἐκίνῃ, καὶ οὐκ ἴσχυσεν σαλεῦσαι αὐτὴν διὰ τὸ καλῶς οἰκοδομῆσθαι αὐτήν.

6.49 ὁ δὲ ἀκούσας καὶ μὴ ποιήσας ὅμοιός ἐστιν ἀνθρώπῳ οἰκοδομήσαντι οἰκίαν ἐπὶ τὴν γῆν χωρὶς θεμελίου, ᾗ προσέρρηξεν ὁ ποταμός, καὶ εὐθὺς συνέπεσεν, καὶ ἐγένετο τὸ ῥῆγμα τῆς οἰκίας ἐκείνης μέγα.

7.1 Ἐπειδὲ ἐπλήρωσεν πάντα τὰ ῥήματα αὐτοῦ εἰς τὰς ἀκοὰς τοῦ λαοῦ, εἰσῆλθεν εἰς Καφαρναούμ.

7.2 ἑκατοντάρχου δέ τινος δοῦλος κακῶς ἔχων ἤμελλεν τελευτᾶν, ὃς ἦν αὐτῷ ἔντιμος. 7.3 ἀκούσας δὲ περὶ τοῦ Ἰησοῦ ἀπέστιλεν πρὸς αὐτὸν πρεσβυτέρους τῶν Ἰουδαίων, ἐρωτῶν αὐτὸν ὅπως αὐτὸς ἐλθὼν διασώσῃ τὸν δοῦλον αὐτοῦ.

7.4 οἱ δὲ παραγενόμενοι πρὸς τὸν Ἰησοῦν ἠρωτῶν αὐτὸν σπουδαίως, λέγοντες ὅτι ἄξιός ἐστιν ᾧ παρέξῃ τοῦτο, 7.5 ἀγαπᾷ γὰρ τὸ ἔθνος ἡμῶν καὶ τὴν συναγωγὴν αὐτὸς ᾠκοδόμησεν ἡμῖν.

7.6 ὁ δὲ Ἰησοῦς ἐπορεύετο σὺν αὐτοῖς. ἤδη δὲ αὐτοῦ οὐ μακρὰν ἀπέχοντος τῆς οἰκίας ἔπεμψεν φίλους ὁ ἑκατοντάρχος λέγων αὐτῷ, κύριε, μὴ σκύλλου, οὐ γὰρ ἱκανός εἰμι ἵνα μου ὑπὸ τὴν στέγην εἰσέλθῃς· 7.7 διὸ οὐδὲ ἐμαυτὸν ἠξίωσα πρὸς σὲ ἐλθεῖν· ἀλλ᾽ εἰπὲ λόγῳ, καὶ ἰαθήσεται ὁ παῖς μου.

7.8 καὶ γὰρ ἐγὼ ἄνθρωπός εἰμι ὑπὸ ἐξουσίαν τασσόμενος, ἔχων ὑπ᾽ ἐμαυτὸν στρατιώτας, καὶ λέγω τούτῳ, πορεύθητι, καὶ πορεύεται, καὶ ἄλλῳ, ἔρχου, καὶ ἔρχεται, καὶ τῷ δούλῳ μου, ποίησον τοῦτο, καὶ ποιεῖ.

7.9 ἀκούσας δὲ ταῦτα ὁ Ἰησοῦς ἐθαύμασεν αὐτόν, καὶ στραφεὶς τῷ ἀκολουθοῦντι αὐτῷ ὄχλῳ εἶπεν, λέγω ὑμῖν, οὐδὲ ἐν τῷ Ἰσραὴλ τοσαύτην πίστιν εὗρον. 7.10 καὶ ὑποστρέψαντες εἰς τὸν οἶκον οἱ πεμφθέντες εὗρον τὸν δοῦλον ὑγιαίνοντα.

7.11 καὶ ἐγένετο ἐν τῷ ἑξῆς ἐπορεύθη εἰς πόλιν καλουμένην

house, who excavated and deepened and laid a foundation upon the rock; and from a flood/deluge having
happened, the river burst upon/dashed against that
house, and it was not strong/able to shake it because
of the (thing) *for* it to be built well.

6.49   But the (one) having heard and not having
done is similar to a man having built a house upon the
land without a foundation, which the river burst
upon/dashed against, and immediately it fell in ruins,
and the crash/ruin of that house became great.

7.1   Since/when he ended all his words to/for the
ears of the people, he entered into Capernaum.

7.2   And a slave of a certain centurion *was*
having *it* badly, being about to die, who was preci-
ous/valuable to him.   7.3 And having heard about
Jesus, he sent to him elders of the Judeans, asking
him that, coming, he might save/deliver his slave.

7.4   And the (elders), having come to Jesus, were
asking him earnestly, saying: He is worthy for whom
you should render this,   7.5 for he loves the ethnic/
nation of us and he himself built the synagogue/con-
gregation for us.

7.6   And Jesus was going with them. And from him
being not far distant from the house, the centurion
sent friends, saying to him: Lord, do not trouble, for
I am not sufficient that you should enter under my
roof/cover; 7.7   wherefore, having considered myself
not worthy to come near you; but speak with a saying/
word and my boy will be healed.

7.8   For I, I also am a man being appointed under
authority, having soldiers under myself, and I say to
this (one): Go! And he goes, and to another: Come! And
he comes, and to my slave: Do this! And he does *it*.

7.9   And having heard these (things), Jesus
marveled/wondered at him, and having been turned to
the crowd following with him, he said: I say to ye, I
found not such faith in Israel.   7.10 And having
returned to the house, those having been sent found
the slave being healthy.

7.11   And it came about on the next day *that* he
was going to a city being called Nain, both his learn-

Ναΐν, καὶ συνεπορεύοντο αὐτῷ οἱ μαθηταὶ αὐτοῦ καὶ ὄχλος πολύς. 7.12 ὡς δὲ ἤγγισεν τῇ πύλῃ τῆς πόλεως, καὶ ἰδοὺ ἐξεκομίζετο τεθνηκὼς μονογενὴς υἱὸς τῇ μητρὶ αὐτοῦ, καὶ αὐτὴ ἦν χήρα, καὶ ὄχλος τῆς πόλεως ἱκανὸς ἦν σὺν αὐτῇ. 7.13 καὶ ἰδὼν αὐτὴν ὁ κύριος ἐσπλαγχνίσθη ἐπ᾿ αὐτὴν καὶ εἶπεν αὐτῇ, μὴ κλαῖε. 7.14 καὶ προσελθὼν ἥψατο τῆς σοροῦ, οἱ δὲ βαστάζοντες ἔστησαν, καὶ εἶπεν, νεανίσκε, σοὶ λέγω, ἐγέρθητι. 7.15 καὶ ἀνεκάθισεν ὁ νεκρὸς καὶ ἤρξατο λαλῖν, καὶ ἔδωκεν αὐτὸν τῇ μητρὶ αὐτοῦ.

7.16 ἔλαβεν δὲ φόβος ἅπαντας, καὶ ἐδόξαζον τὸν θεὸν λέγοντες ὅτι προφήτης μέγας ἠγέρθη ἐν ἡμῖν, καὶ ὅτι ἐπεσκέψατο ὁ θεὸς τὸν λαὸν αὐτοῦ. 7.17 καὶ ἐξῆλθεν ὁ λόγος οὗτος ἐν ὅλῃ τῇ Ἰουδαίᾳ περὶ αὐτοῦ καὶ πάσῃ τῇ περιχώρῳ. 7.18 καὶ ἀπήγγιλαν Ἰωάννει οἱ μαθηταὶ αὐτοῦ περὶ πάντων τούτων.

καὶ προσκαλεσάμενος δύο τινὰς τῶν μαθητῶν αὐτοῦ ὁ Ἰωάννης 7.19 ἔπεμψεν πρὸς τὸν Ἰησοῦν λέγων, σὺ εἶ ὁ ἐρχόμενος ἢ ἕτερον προσδοκῶμεν; 7.20 παραγενόμενοι δὲ οἱ ἄνδρες πρὸς αὐτὸν εἶπαν, Ἰωάννης ὁ βαπτιστὴς ἀπέστιλεν ἡμᾶς πρὸς σὲ λέγων, σὺ εἶ ὁ ἐρχόμενος ἢ ἕτερον προσδοκῶμεν; 7.21 ἐν ἐκείνῃ τῇ ὥρᾳ ἐθεράπευσεν πολλοὺς ἀπὸ νόσων καὶ μαστίγων καὶ πνευμάτων πονηρῶν, καὶ τυφλοῖς πολλοῖς ἐχαρίσατο βλέπειν. 7.22 καὶ ἀποκριθεὶς εἶπεν αὐτοῖς, πορευθέντες ἀπαγγίλατε Ἰωάννει ἃ εἴδετε καὶ ἠκούσατε· τυφλοὶ ἀναβλέπουσιν, χωλοὶ περιπατοῦσιν, λεπροὶ καθαρίζονται καὶ κωφοὶ ἀκούουσιν, νεκροὶ ἐγείρονται, πτωχοὶ εὐαγγελίζονται· 7.23 καὶ μακάριός ἐστιν ὃς ἂν μὴ σκανδαλισθῇ ἐν ἐμοί.

7.24 ἀπελθόντων δὲ τῶν ἀγγέλων Ἰωάννου ἤρξατο λέγειν πρὸς τοὺς ὄχλους περὶ Ἰωάννου, τί ἐξήλθαται εἰς τὴν ἔρημον θεάσασθε; κάλαμον ὑπὸ ἀνέμου σαλευόμενον; 7.25 ἀλλὰ τί ἐξήλθαται ἰδεῖν; ἄνθρωπον ἐν μαλακοῖς ἱματίοις ἠμφιεσμένον; ἰδοὺ οἱ ἐν ἱματισμῷ ἐνδόξῳ καὶ τρυφῇ ὑπάρχοντες ἐν τοῖς

ers/pupils and a much crowd were traveling with him.
7.12 And as he drew near to the gate of the city, and
behold, (one) having died was being carried out, an
only born son to his mother, and she was a widow, and
a considerable crowd from the city was with her. 7.13
And having seen her, the Lord was moved with compassion on/to her, and he said to her: Weep/lament not.
7.14 And having come near, he touched of the bier, and
those bearing *it* stood *still*/stopped, and he said:
Young man, I say to you: Be raised up. 7.15 And the
youth sat up and began to speak, and he gave him to
his mother.

7.16 But all took a fear/terror, and they were
glorifying/acknowledging God, saying: A great prophet
was raised up among us, and: God himself visited/
cared for his people. 7.17 And this saying/word
concerning him went out in all Judea and all the
surrounding country. 7.18 And his learners/pupils
reported to John about all these (things).

And having summoned a certain two/pair of his
learners/pupils, John 7.19 sent *them* to Jesus, saying: You, are you the (one) coming, or should we
expect/wait for another/different (one)? 7.20 And
having arrived near him, they said: John, the baptizer, sent us to you, saying: You, are you the (one)
coming, or should we expect/wait for another/different
(one)? 7.21 In that hour he treated/healed many from
diseases and plagues and evil spirits, and to many
blind (ones) he gave freely to see. 7.22 And answering he said to them: Be going *back*, report ye to John
the things which ye saw and heard: Blind (ones) receive sight, lame (ones) walk, lepers are being
cleansed, and deaf (ones) hear, dead (ones) are being
raised up, poor (ones) are being preached to; 7.23
and happy is *the one* who would/who ever will not be
offended/caused to stumble in/by me.

7.24 And from the messengers of John having gone
away, he began to say to the crowds about John: What
went ye out into the desert to behold? A reed being
shaken by wind? 7.25 But what went ye out to see? A
man having been clothed in soft garments? Behold,
those in/with an honored/glorious garment and existing

βασιλείοις εἰσίν. 7.26 ἀλλὰ τί ἐξήλθατε ἰδεῖν; προφήτην; ναί, λέγω ὑμῖν, καὶ περισσότερον προφήτου. 7.27 οὗτός ἐστιν περὶ οὗ γέγραπται, « ἰδοὺ ἀποστέλλω τὸν ἄγγελόν μου πρὸ προσώπου σου, ὃς κατασκευάσει τὴν ὁδόν» σου «ἔμπροσθέν» σου. 7.28 ἀμὴν λέγω ὑμῖν, μείζων ἐν γεννητοῖς γυναικῶν Ἰωάννου οὐδείς ἐστιν· ὁ δὲ μεικρότερος ἐν τῇ βασιλείᾳ τοῦ θεοῦ μείζων αὐτοῦ ἐστιν. 7.29 καὶ πᾶς ὁ λαὸς ἀκούσας καὶ οἱ τελῶναι ἐδικαίωσαν τὸν θεόν, βαπτισθέντες τὸ βάπτισμα Ἰωάννου· 7.30 οἱ δὲ Φαρισαῖοι καὶ οἱ νομικοὶ τὴν βουλὴν τοῦ θεοῦ ἠθέτησαν, μὴ βαπτισθέντες ὑπ' αὐτοῦ.

7.31 τίνι δὲ ὁμοιώσω τοὺς ἀνθρώπους τῆς γενεᾶς ταύτης, καὶ τίνι εἰσὶν ὅμοιοι; 7.32 ὅμοιοί εἰσιν παιδίοις τοῖς ἐν ἀγορᾷ καθημένοις καὶ προσφωνοῦσιν ἀλλήλοις, ἃ λέγει, ηὐλήσαμεν ὑμῖν καὶ οὐκ ὠρχήσασθε· ἐθρηνήσαμεν καὶ οὐκ ἐκλαύσατε. 7.33 ἐλήλυθεν γὰρ Ἰωάννης ὁ βαπτιστὴς μὴ ἐσθίων ἄρτον μήτε πίνων οἶνον, καὶ λέγεται, δαιμόνιον ἔχει· 7.34 ἐλήλυθεν ὁ υἱὸς τοῦ ἀνθρώπου ἐσθίων καὶ πίνων, καὶ λέγεται, ἰδοὺ ἄνθρωπος φάγος καὶ οἰνοπότης, φίλος τελωνῶν καὶ ἁμαρτωλῶν. 7.35 καὶ ἐδικαιώθη ἡ σοφία ἀπὸ πάντων τῶν ἔργων αὐτῆς. 7.36 ἠρώτα δέ τις αὐτὸν τῶν Φαρισαίων ἵνα φάγῃ μετ' αὐτοῦ· καὶ εἰσελθὼν εἰς τὸν οἶκον τοῦ Φαρισαίου κατεκλίθη.

7.37 καὶ ἰδοὺ γυνὴ ἥτις ἦν ἐν τῇ πόλει ἁμαρτωλός, καὶ ἐπιγνοῦσα ὅτι κατάκειται ἐν τῇ οἰκίᾳ τοῦ Φαρισαίου, κομίσασα ἀλάβαστρον μύρου 7.38 καὶ στᾶσα ὀπίσω παρὰ τοὺς πόδας αὐτοῦ κλαίουσα, τοῖς δάκρυσιν ἤρξατο βρέχειν τοὺς πόδας αὐτοῦ καὶ ταῖς θριξὶν τῆς κεφαλῆς αὐτῆς ἐξέμασσεν, καὶ κατεφίλει τοὺς πόδας αὐτοῦ καὶ ἤλειφεν τῷ μύρῳ. 7.39 ἰδὼν δὲ ὁ Φαρισαῖος ὁ καλέσας αὐτὸν εἶπεν ἐν ἑαυτῷ λέγων, οὗτος εἰ ἦν προφήτης, ἐγείνωσκεν ἂν τίς καὶ ποταπὴ ἡ γυνὴ ἥτις ἅπτεται αὐτοῦ, ὅτι ἁμαρτωλός ἐστιν. 7.40 καὶ ἀποκριθεὶς ὁ Ἰησοῦς εἶπεν

for luxury are in the royal (places)/palaces.   7.26
But what went ye out to see? A prophet? Yes, I say to
ye, and even more than a prophet.   7.27 This (one) is
he about whom it has been written: BEHOLD I SEND MY
MESSENGER/ANGEL   BEFORE   YOUR   FACE,   WHO   WILL   PREPARE/
FURNISH YOUR ROAD/WAY BEFORE YOU.   7.28 Truly I say to
ye, no one among *those* generated from women is greater
than John; but the (one) *being* less/more small in the
kingdom of God is greater than he.   7.29 Both all the
people and the tax-collectors/publicans having heard
acknowledged God's justice, *and* were being baptized *by*
the baptism of John;   7.30 but the Pharisees and the
lawyers rejected/nullified the will/purpose of God,
not being baptized by him.

7.31   And to what shall I liken the men/humans of
this generation, and to what are they like? 7.32 They
are similar to children, sitting in a market and
calling to one another, which/who says: We played on
the flute for ye and ye danced not; we mourned for *ye*
and ye lamented/wept not. 7.33 For John, the baptizer, has come not eating a loaf nor drinking wine, and
ye say: He has a demon; 7.34 the son of the man has
come eating and drinking, and ye say: Behold, a man
being a glutton and a drunkard/wino, a friend of
tax-collectors/publicans and sinners.   7.35 And the
wisdom was vindicated from all her/*its* works.   7.36
And a certain one of the Pharisees was asking/request-
ing that he might eat with him; and having entered
into the Pharisee's house, he was reclined.

7.37   And behold, a woman who *was* a sinner was in
the city, and having known that he was reclined in the
Pharisee's house, having provided an alabaster of
ointment 7.38 and having stood behind *him* beside his
feet weeping, she began to wet his feet with the tears
and she was drying *them* with the hairs of her head,
and she was affectionately kissing his feet and was
anointing *them* with the ointment.   7.39 But having
seen, the Pharisee having invited him spoke in himself
saying: If this (one) were a prophet, he would be
knowing who and of what sort *is* the woman who touch-
es/fastens to him, because she is a sinner.   7.40 And
answering, Jesus said to him: Simon, I have something

πρὸς αὐτόν, Σίμων, ἔχω σοί τι εἰπῖν. ὁ δέ, διδάσκαλε, εἰπέ, φησίν. 7.41 δύο χρεοφιλέται ἦσαν δανιστῇ τινι· ὁ εἷς ὤφιλεν δηνάρια πεντακόσια, ὁ δὲ ἕτερος πεντήκοντα. 7.42 μὴ ἐχόντων δὲ αὐτῶν ἀποδοῦναι ἀμφοτέροις ἐχαρίσατο. τίς οὖν αὐτῶν πλεῖον ἀγαπήσει αὐτόν; 7.43 ἀποκριθεὶς δὲ Σίμων εἶπεν, ὑπολαμβάνω ὅτι ᾧ τὸ πλῖον ἐχαρίσατο. ὁ δὲ εἶπεν αὐτῷ, ὀρθῶς ἔκρινας. 7.44 καὶ στραφεὶς πρὸς τὴν γυναῖκα τῷ Σίμωνι ἔφη, βλέπεις ταύτην τὴν γυναῖκα; εἰσῆλθόν σου εἰς τὴν οἰκίαν, ὕδωρ μου ἐπὶ τοὺς πόδας οὐκ ἔδωκας· αὕτη δὲ τοῖς δάκρυσιν ἔβρεξέν μου τοὺς πόδας καὶ ταῖς θριξὶν αὐτῆς ἐξέμαξεν. 7.45 φίλημά μοι οὐκ ἔδωκας· αὕτη δὲ ἀφ' ἧς εἰσῆλθον οὐ διέλιπεν καταφιλοῦσά μου τοὺς πόδας. 7.46 ἐλαίῳ τὴν κεφαλήν μου οὐκ ἤλειψας· αὐτὴ δὲ μύρῳ ἤλιψέν μου τοὺς πόδας. 7.47 οὗ χάριν λέγω σοι, ἀφέωνται αὐτῆς αἱ ἁμαρτίαι αἱ πολλαί, ὅτι ἠγάπησεν πολύ· ᾧ δὲ ὀλίγον ἀφίεται, ὀλίγον ἀγαπᾷ.

7.48 εἶπεν δὲ αὐτῇ, ἀφέωνταί σου αἱ ἁμαρτίαι. 7.49 καὶ ἤρξαντο οἱ συνανακείμενοι λέγειν ἐν ἑαυτοῖς, τίς οὗτός ἐστιν ὃς καὶ ἁμαρτίας ἀφίησιν;

7.50 εἶπεν δὲ πρὸς τὴν γυναῖκα, ἡ πίστις σου σέσωκέν σε· πορεύου εἰς εἰρήνην.

8.1 Καὶ ἐγένετο ἐν τῷ καθεξῆς καὶ αὐτὸς διώδευσεν κατὰ πόλιν καὶ κώμην κηρύσσων καὶ εὐαγγελιζόμενος τὴν βασιλείαν τοῦ θεοῦ, καὶ οἱ δώδεκα σὺν αὐτῷ,

8.2 καὶ γυναῖκές τινες αἳ ἦσαν τεθεραπευμέναι ἀπὸ πνευμάτων ἀκαθαρτῶν καὶ ἀσθενειῶν, Μαρία ἡ καλουμένη Μαγδαληνή, ἀφ' ἧς δαιμόνια ἑπτὰ ἐξεληλύθει, 8.3 καὶ Ἰωάνναι γυνὴ Χουζᾶ ἐπιτρόπου Ἡρώδου καὶ Σουσάννα καὶ ἕτεραι πολλαί, αἵτινες διηκόνουν αὐτῷ ἐκ τῶν ὑπαρχόντων αὐταῖς.

8.4 συνιόντος δὲ ὄχλου πολλοῦ καὶ τῶν κατὰ πόλιν ἐπιπορευομένων πρὸς αὐτὸν εἶπεν διὰ παραβολῆς,

8.5 ἐξῆλθεν ὁ σπίρων τοῦ σπῖραι τὸν σπόρον αὐτοῦ. καὶ

to say to you. And the (he): Teacher, he says, speak. 7.41 There were two debtors to a certain lender; the one was owing five hundred denarii, and the other/different fifty. 7.42 From them not having to pay back, he gave/forgave freely to both. Then who/which of them will love him more? 7.43 And answering, Simon said: I suppose that (he) to whom he freely forgave/gave the more. And the (he) said to him: You judged correctly. 7.44 And having been turned toward the woman, he was saying to Simon: Do you see this woman? I entered into your house, you gave not water for my feet; but she, she wet my feet with the tears and dried (them) with her hairs. 7.45 You gave not a kiss to me; but this (woman), from *the time* which I came in, she ceased not tenderly kissing my feet. 7.46 You anointed not my head with olive oil; but she, she anointed my feet with ointment/perfume. 7.47 On account of which I say to you: The many sins/faults of her have been forgiven/sent away, because she loved much; but (one) for whom little is forgiven loves little.

    7.48 And he said to her: Your sins/faults have been forgiven/sent away. 7.49 And those reclining together began to say among themselves: Who is this (one) who even forgives/dismisses sins/faults?

    7.50 But he said to the woman: Your faith has saved you; go in peace.

    8.1 And it happened in the (thing) *that* he himself was going through city and village in order/one after another, heralding/preaching and announcing the kingdom of God, and the twelve *were* with him,

    8.2 also certain/some women who had been healed from unclean spirits and sicknesses, Mary the (one) being called Magdalene, from whom seven demons had gone out, 8.3 and Joanna a woman of Chuza, Herod's manager/foreman, and Susanna and many others/different (ones), who were serving/ministering to him out of the goods/possessions to/for them.

    8.4 And from a much crowd accompanying and of those from city to city traveling near/with him, he said through a parable:

    8.5 The (one) sowing went out from the (thing)

ἐν τῷ σπίρειν αὐτὸν ὃ μὲν ἔπεσεν παρὰ τὴν ὁδόν, καὶ κατεπατήθη καὶ τὰ πετεινὰ τοῦ οὐρανοῦ κατέφαγεν αὐτό. 8.6 καὶ ἕτερον ἔπεσεν ἐπὶ τὴν πέτραν, καὶ φυὲν ἐξηράνθη καὶ διὰ τὸ μὴ ἔχιν ἰκμάδα.

8.7 καὶ ἕτερον ἔπεσεν ἐν μέσῳ τῶν ἀκανθῶν, καὶ συμφυεῖσαι αἱ ἄκανθαι ἀπέπνιξαν αὐτό. 8.8 καὶ ἕτερον ἔπεσεν εἰς τὴν γῆν τὴν ἀγαθήν, καὶ φυὲν ἐποίησεν καρπὸν ἑκατονταπλασίονα. ταῦτα λέγων ἐφώνει, ὁ ἔχων ὦτα ἀκούειν ἀκουέτω.

8.9 ἐπηρώτων δὲ αὐτὸν οἱ μαθηταὶ αὐτοῦ τίς αὕτη εἴη ἡ παραβολή.

8.10 ὁ δὲ εἶπεν, ὑμῖν δέδοται γνῶναι τὰ μυστήρια τῆς βασιλείας τοῦ θεοῦ, τοῖς δὲ λοιποῖς ἐν παραβολαῖς, ἵνα «βλέποντες μὴ βλέπωσιν καὶ ἀκούοντες καὶ μὴ συνιῶσιν.» 8.11 ἔστιν δὲ αὕτη ἡ παραβολή· ὁ σπόρος ἐστὶν ὁ λόγος τοῦ θεοῦ. 8.12 οἱ δὲ παρὰ τὴν ὁδόν εἰσιν οἱ ἀκούσαντες, εἶτα ἔρχεται ὁ διάβολος καὶ αἴρει τὸν λόγον ἀπὸ τῆς καρδίας αὐτῶν, ἵνα μὴ πιστεύσαντες σωθῶσιν.

8.13 οἱ δὲ ἐπὶ τῆς πέτρας οἳ ὅταν ἀκούσωσιν μετὰ χαρᾶς δέχονται τὸν λόγον τοῦ θεοῦ, καὶ οὗτοι ῥίζαν οὐκ ἔχουσιν, οἳ πρὸς καιρὸν πιστεύουσιν καὶ ἐν καιρῷ πειρασμοῦ ἀφίστανται.

8.14 τὸ δὲ εἰς τὰς ἀκάνθας πεσόν, οὗτοί εἰσιν οἱ ἀκούσαντες, καὶ ὑπὸ μεριμνῶν καὶ πλούτου καὶ ἡδονῶν τοῦ βίου πορευόμενοι συμπνίγονται καὶ οὐ τελεσφοροῦσιν. 8.15 τὸ δὲ ἐν τῇ καλῇ γῇ, οὗτοί εἰσιν οἵτινες ἐν καρδίᾳ καλῇ καὶ ἀγαθῇ ἀκούσαντες τὸν λόγον κατέχουσιν καὶ καρποφοροῦσιν ἐν ὑπομονῇ.

8.16 οὐδεὶς δὲ λύχνον ἅψας καλύπτι αὐτὸν σκεύει ἢ ὑποκάτω κλίνης τίθησιν, ἀλλ’ ἐπὶ τὴν λυχνίαν τίθησιν, ἵνα οἱ εἰσπορευόμενοι βλέπωσιν τὸ φῶς.

to sow his seed. And by the (thing)/at the (time) *for* him to sow, some fell beside the road, and was trampled down and the birds of the sky/heaven devoured it. 8.6 And other/different fell on the rock, and having grown/come up, it was withered also because of the (thing) not to have moisture.

8.7 And other/different fell in the midst of the thorns/thorn bushes, and having been growing together, the thorns/thorn bushes choked/strangled it. 8.8 And other/different fell into the good land/earth, and having been growing, it made fruit/a yield, a hundredfold. Saying these things, he was emphasizing: The (one) having ears to hear, let him hear.

8.9 And his learners/pupils were questioning him, what this parable may be.

8.10 And he said: It has been given to ye to know the mysteries of the kingdom of God, but to the rest (others) in/by parables, in order that SEEING THEY MAY NOT SEE AND HEARING THEY ALSO MAY NOT UNDERSTAND. 8.11 And this is the parable: The seed/sowing is the logos/word of God. 8.12 And the (ones) beside the road are those having heard, then the devil comes and takes away the saying/word from their heart, lest having believed they might be saved.

8.13 And the (ones) on the rock *are those* who, whenever they might hear, they receive the word of God with joy, and these have not a root, who believe to/for a time, and in a time of temptation/testing, they withdraw.

8.14 And the (thing) that having fallen in the thorns, these are those having heard, and going themselves under cares and wealth and pleasures/enjoyments of the daily life, they are choked/strangled and do not bear mature fruit. 8.15 But the (thing) that in/on the good earth/land, these are *those* who having heard/listened in/with a beautiful and good heart, they hold fast the saying/word and they bear fruit/are productive in/by patient endurance.

8.16 And no one having lit a lamp covers/conceals it with a vessel or puts it under a couch/cot, but he puts it on the lampstand, in order that those going in may see the light.

8.17 οὐ γάρ ἐστιν κρυπτὸν ὃ οὐ φανερὸν γενήσεται, οὐδὲ ἀπόκρυφον ὃ οὐ μὴ γνωσθῇ καὶ εἰς φανερὸν ἔλθῃ. 8.18 βλέπεται οὖν πῶς ἀκούεται· ὃς ἂν γὰρ ἔχῃ, δοθήσεται αὐτῷ, καὶ ὃς ἂν μὴ ἔχῃ, καὶ ὃ δοκεῖ ἔχιν ἀρθήσεται ἀπ᾽ αὐτοῦ.

8.19 παρεγένοντο δὲ πρὸς αὐτὸν ἡ μήτηρ αὐτοῦ καὶ οἱ ἀδελφοὶ αὐτοῦ, καὶ οὐκ ἠδύναντο συντυχῖν αὐτῷ διὰ τὸν ὄχλον.

8.20 ἀπηγγέλη δὲ αὐτῷ, ὅτι ἡ μήτηρ καὶ οἱ ἀδελφοί σου ἑστήκασιν ἔξω ἰδῖν σε θέλοντες. 8.21 ὁ δὲ ἀποκριθεὶς εἶπεν πρὸς αὐτούς, μήτηρ μου καὶ ἀδελφοί μου οὗτοί εἰσιν οἱ τὸν λόγον ἀκούοντες καὶ ποιοῦντες.

8.22 ἐγένετο δὲ ἐν μιᾷ τῶν ἡμερῶν ἐνέβη εἰς πλοῖον καὶ οἱ μαθηταὶ αὐτοῦ, καὶ εἶπεν πρὸς αὐτούς, διέλθωμεν εἰς τὸ πέραν τῆς λίμνης· καὶ ἀνήχθησαν.

8.23 πλεόντων δὲ αὐτῶν ἀφύπνωσεν. καὶ κατέβη λαῖλαψ ἀνέμου εἰς τὴν λίμνην, καὶ συνεπληροῦντο καὶ ἐκινδύνευον. 8.24 προσελθόντες δὲ διήγειραν αὐτὸν λέγοντες, ἐπιστάτα ἐπιστάτα, ἀπολλύμεθα.

ὁ δὲ διεγερθεὶς ἐπετίμησεν τῷ ἀνέμῳ καὶ τῷ κλύδωνι τοῦ ὕδατος· καὶ ἐπαύσατο, καὶ ἐγένετο γαλήνη.

8.25 εἶπεν δὲ αὐτοῖς, ποῦ ἡ πίστις ὑμῶν; οἱ δὲ φοβηθέντες ἐθαύμασαν, λέγοντες, τίς ἄρα οὗτός ἐστιν ὅτι καὶ τοῖς ἀνέμοις ἐπιτάσσει καὶ τῷ ὕδατι, καὶ ὑπακούουσιν αὐτῷ; 8.26 καὶ κατέπλυσαν εἰς τὴν χώραν τῶν Γεριεσηνῶν, ἥτις ἐστὶν ἀντιπέρα τῆς Γαλιλαίας.

8.27 ἐξελθόντι δὲ αὐτῷ ἐπὶ τὴν γῆν ὑπήντησεν ἀνήρ τις ἐκ τῆς πόλεως ἔχων δαιμόνια· καὶ χρόνῳ ἱκανῷ οὐκ ἐνεδύσατο ἱμάτιον, καὶ ἐν οἰκίᾳ οὐκ ἔμενεν ἀλλ᾽ ἐν τοῖς μνήμασιν.

8.28 ἰδὼν δὲ τὸν Ἰησοῦν ἀνακράξας προσέπεσεν αὐτῷ καὶ φωνῇ μεγάλῃ εἶπεν, τί ἐμοὶ καὶ σοί, Ἰησοῦ υἱὲ τοῦ θεοῦ τοῦ

8.17   For *a thing* is not hidden which will not become open/visible, nor secret which will not certainly be made known and might come into *the* open/public.   8.18 Therefore, see ye/take care how ye hear; for who ever would have/hold, it will be given to him, and who ever would not hold/have, even what he seems to have/hold will be taken away from him.

8.19   And his mother and brothers arrived/were coming near/to him, and they were not being able to get to him because of the crowd.

8.20   And it was reported to him: Your mother and brothers have stood outside, wanting to see you.   8.21 But the (he) answering said to them: My mother and my brothers are these, the (ones) hearing the saying/word and doing *it*.

8.22   And it came about on one of the days *that* he and his learners/pupils embarked in a boat, and he said to them: Let us go over to the other side of the lake; and they put out *to sea*.

8.23   And from them sailing he fell asleep. And a storm of wind came down in the lake, and they were being swamped and were being in danger.   8.24 And coming near, they aroused him, saying: Master, master, we are perishing!

And the (he), having been awakened, he rebuked/spoke sharply to the wind and to the billowing of the water; and it ceased, and it became calm.

8.25   And he said to them: Where *is* the faith of ye? And they, having been stricken by fear, marveled, saying: Then who is this (one) that even gives orders/commands to the winds and to the water, and they are obedient to him?   8.26 And they sailed down to the country of the Gerasenes, which is opposite from Galilee.

8.27   And to him, having gone forth upon the land, a certain man came to meet him out of the city, having demons; and he put not on a garment for a considerable time, and he did not live in a house but among the tombs.

8.28   And having seen Jesus, having cried out, he fell down toward him and said in a great voice: What *is it* for me and for you, Jesus, son of the most high

ὑψίστου; δαίομέ σου, μή με βασανίσῃς. 8.29 παρήγγελεν γὰρ τῷ πνεύματι τῷ ἀκαθάρτῳ ἐξελθεῖν ἀπὸ τοῦ ἀνθρώπου. πολλοῖς γὰρ χρόνοις συνηρπάκει αὐτόν, καὶ ἐδεσμεύετο ἁλύσεσιν καὶ παίδες φυλασσόμενος, καὶ διαρρήσσων τὰ δεσμὰ ἠλαύνετο ὑπὸ τοῦ δαιμονίου εἰς τὰς ἐρήμους. 8.30 ἐπηρώτησεν δὲ αὐτὸν ὁ Ἰησοῦς, τί σοι ὄνομά ἐστιν; ὁ δὲ εἶπεν, Λεκιών, ὅτι εἰσῆλθεν δαιμόνια πολλὰ εἰς αὐτόν.

8.31 καὶ παρεκάλουν αὐτὸν ἵνα μὴ ἐπιτάξῃ αὐτοῖς εἰς τὴν ἄβυσσον ἀπελθῖν.

8.32 ἦν δὲ ἐκεῖ ἀγέλη χοίρων ἱκανῶν βοσκομένη ἐν τῷ ὄρει· καὶ παρεκάλεσα αὐτὸν ἵνα ἐπιτρέψῃ αὐτοῖς εἰς ἐκείνους εἰσελθεῖν·

καὶ ἐπέτρεψεν αὐτοῖς. 8.33 ἐξελθόντα δὲ τὰ δαιμόνια ἀπὸ τοῦ ἀνθρώπου εἰσῆλθον εἰς τοὺς χοίρους, καὶ ὥρμησεν ἡ ἀγγέλη κατὰ τοῦ κρημνοῦ εἰς τὴν θάλασσαν καὶ ἀπεπνίγη.

8.34 ἰδόντες δὲ οἱ βόσκοντες τὸ γεγονὸς ἔφυγον καὶ ἀπήγγειλαν εἰς τὴν πόλιν καὶ εἰς τοὺς ἀγρούς. 8.35 ἐξῆλθον δὲ ἰδῖν τὸ γεγονὸς καὶ ἦλθον πρὸς τὸν Ἰησοῦν,

καὶ εὗρον καθήμενον τὸν ἄνθρωπον ἀφ᾽ οὗ τὰ δαιμόνια ἐξῆλθεν ἱματισμένον καὶ σωφρονοῦντα παρὰ τοὺς πόδας τοῦ Ἰησοῦ, καὶ ἐφοβήθησαν. 8.36 ἀπήγγειλαν δὲ λέφοντες αὐτοῖς οἱ ἰδόντες πῶς ἐσώθη ὁ δαιμονισθείς.

8.37 καὶ ἠρώτησεν αὐτὸν πᾶν τὸ πλῆθος τῆς περιχώρου τῶν Γεργεσηνῶν ἀπελθῖν ἀπ᾽ αὐτῶν, ὅτι φόβῳ μεγάλῳ συνείχοντο·

αὐτὸς δὲ ἐμβὰς εἰς πλοῖον ὑπέστρεψεν. 8.38 ἐδέετο δὲ αὐτοῦ ὁ ἀνὴρ ἀφ᾽ οὗ ἐξεληλύθει τὰ δαιμόνια εἶναι σὺν αὐτῷ·

ἀπέλυσεν δὲ αὐτὸν λέγων, 8.39 ὑπόστρεφε εἰς τὸν οἶκόν σου, καὶ διηγοῦ ὅσα σοι ἐποίησεν ὁ θεός.

καὶ ἀπῆλθεν καθ᾽ ὅλην τὴν πόλιν κηρύσσων ὅσα ἐποίησεν

God? I request/beg of you: Do not torment me.   8.29
For he ordered/charged to the unclean spirit to come
out from the man. For it had violently seized him
in/on many times, and he was being bound with chains
and fetters, being guarded/kept; and breaking the
bonds asunder, he was being driven by the demon into
the deserts.   8.30 But Jesus questioned/asked him:
What is a name for you? And the (he) said: Legion,
because many demons entered into him.

    8.31   And they were beseeching him in order that
he might not enjoin upon them to go away into the
abyss/bottomless pit.

    8.32   And a sufficient heard of pigs/swine was
there, grazing/being tended on the mountain;

    and they beseeched him that he might permit for
then to enter into those; and he permitted them.   8.33
And having come out from the man, the demons entered
into the pigs/swine, and the herd ran headlong down
from   the   cliff/precipice   into   the   sea and   was
drowned.

    8.34   But having seen the (thing) having happen-
ed, those tending *them* fled and reported *it* in the
city and in the fields.   8.35 And they went out to see
the (thing) having happened, and they came to/near
Jesus.

    and they found the man from whom the demons went
out, having been clothed and being soberminded, sitting beside the feet of Jesus, and they were caused to
fear.   8.36 And those having seen *it* reported *it* to
them, telling how the (one) having been demon-
possessed was saved/delivered.

    8.37   And all the multitude of the surrounding
country of the Gerasenes asked him to go away from
them, because they were being influenced by a great
fear;

    and he, having embarked into a boat, he return-
ed/turned back.   8.38 And the man from whom the demons
had gone out was obligating himself to be with him;

    but he released/dismissed him, saying: 8.39 You
return to your house, and relate fully what (things)
God did for you.

    And he went away throughout the entire city,

αὐτῷ ὁ Ἰησοῦς.   8.40 ἐγένετο δὲ ἐν τῷ ὑποστρέφειν τὸν Ἰησοῦν ἀπεδέξατο αὐτὸν ὁ ὄχλος, ἦσαν γὰρ πάντες προσδοκῶντες αὐτόν.

8.41 καὶ ἰδοὺ ἦλθεν ἀνὴρ ᾧ ὄνομα Ἰάειρος, καὶ οὗτος ἄρχων τῆς συναγωγῆς ὑπῆρχεν,

καὶ πεσὼν παρὰ τοὺς πόδας Ἰησοῦ παρεκάλει αὐτὸν εἰσελθεῖν εἰς τὸν οἶκον αὐτοῦ, 8.42 ὅτι θυγάτηρ μονογενὴς ἦν αὐτῷ ὡς ἐτῶν δώδεκα

καὶ αὕτη ἀπέθνῃσκεν. ἐν δὲ τῷ ὑπάγειν αὐτὸν οἱ ὄχλοι συνέπνιγον αὐτόν. 8.43 καὶ γυνὴ οὖσα ἐν ῥύσει αἵματος ἀπὸ ἐτῶν δώδεκα,

ἥτις ἰατροῖς προσαναλώσασα ὅλον τὸν βίον οὐκ ἴσχυσεν ὑπ᾽ οὐδενὸς θεραπευθῆναι, 8.44 προσελθοῦσα ὄπισθεν ἥψατο τοῦ κρασπέδου τοῦ ἱματίου αὐτοῦ,

καὶ παραχρῆμα ἔστη ἡ ῥύσις τοῦ αἵματος αὐτῆς.

8.45 καὶ εἶπεν ὁ Ἰησοῦς, τίς ὁ ἁψάμενός μου; ἀρνουμένων δὲ πάντων εἶπεν ὁ Πέτρος καὶ οἱ σὺν αὐτῷ, ἐπιστάτα, οἱ ὄχλοι συνέχουσίν σε καὶ ἀποθλίβουσιν. 8.46 ὁ δὲ Ἰησοῦς εἶπεν, ἥψατό μού τις, ἐγὼ γὰρ ἔγνων δύναμιν ἐξεληλυθυῖαν ἀπ᾽ ἐμοῦ. 8.47 ἰδοῦσα δὲ ἡ γυνὴ ὅτι οὐκ ἔλαθεν τρέμουσα ἦλθεν καὶ προσπεσοῦσα αὐτῷ δι᾽ — ἤγγειλεν ἐνώπιον παντὸς τοῦ λαοῦ καὶ ὡς ἰάθη παραχρῆμα.

8.48 ὁ δὲ εἶπεν, θυγάτερ, ἡ πίστις σου σέσωκέν σε· πορεύου εἰς εἰρήνην.

8.49 ἔτι αὐτοῦ λαλοῦντος ἔρχεταί τις παρὰ τοῦ ἀρχισυναγώγου λέγων ὅτι τέθνηκεν ἡ θυγάτηρ σου, μηκέτι σκύλλε τὸν διδάσκαλον. 8.50 ὁ δὲ Ἰησοῦς ἀκούσας ἀπεκρίθη εἶπεν αὐτῷ, μὴ φοβοῦ, μόνον πίστευε, καὶ σωθήσεται. 8.51 ἐλθὼν δὲ εἰς τὴν οἰκίαν οὐδένα ἀφῆκεν σὺν εἰσελθεῖν αὐτῷ εἰ μὴ Πέτρον καὶ Ἰάκωβον καὶ Ἰωάννην καὶ τὸν πατέρα τῆς παιδὸς καὶ τὴν μητέρα.

8.52 ἔκλαιον δὲ πάντες καὶ ἐκόπτοντο αὐτήν. ὁ δὲ εἶπεν,

heralding/preaching what (things) Jesus did for him. 8.40 And it happened at the (time) *for* Jesus to return, *that* the crowd welcomed him, for they were all waiting for/expecting him.

8.41 And behold, a man came, for whom a name *was* Jairus, and this (one) was being a ruler/leader of a congregation,

and falling beside Jesus' feet, he was inviting/appealing to him to enter into his house, 8.42 because there was an only born daughter to him, about twelve of years,

and she was dying. And in the (thing) *for* him to go, the crowds were pressing upon him. 8.43 And *there was* a woman, being with an issue of blood from twelve years *ago*,

who having expended the entire livelihood for doctors, she was not able to be treated/healed by no one, 8.44 having come near/approached from behind, she touched herself from the hem of his garment.

And the flow of her blood immediately stood *still*/stopped.

8.45 And Jesus said: Who *is* the (one) having touched himself from me? And from denying *it*, Peter and those with him said: Master, the crowds are hemming you in and pressing upon you. 8.46 But Jesus said: Who touched himself from/of me? For I, I knew *there was* power having gone out from me. 8.47 And the woman, having seen that she did not escape detection, she came trembling and having fallen *down* near to him, because of *it*, she reported/related *it* before all the people and how she was healed immediately.

8.48 And the (he) said: Daughter, your faith has saved/delivered you; go in peace.

8.49 From him still speaking, someone comes beside the synagogue/congregation leader, saying: Your daughter has died, no longer trouble you the teacher. 8.50 But Jesus answered, having heard, he said to him: Fear not, only believe, and she will be saved. 8.51 And having come to the house, he allowed no one to go in with him except Peter and James and John, and the father of the girl, and the mother.

8.52 And all were weeping and bewailing them-

μὴ κλαίετε, οὐ γὰρ ἀπέθανεν ἀλλὰ καθεύδει. 8.53 καὶ κατεγέλων αὐτοῦ, εἰδότες ὅτι ἀπέθανεν. 8.54 αὐτὸς δὲ κρατήσας τῆς χειρὸς αὐτῆς ἐφώνησεν λέγων, ἡ παῖς, ἔγειρε. 8.55 καὶ ἐπέστρεψεν τὸ πνεῦμα αὐτῆς, καὶ ἀνέστη παραχρῆμα, καὶ διέταξεν αὐτῇ δοθῆναι φαγεῖν.

8.56 καὶ ἐξέστησαν οἱ γονεῖς αὐτῆς· ὁ δὲ παρήγγειλεν αὐτοῖς μηδενὶ εἰπῖν τὸ γεγονός.

9.1 Συγκαλεσάμενος δὲ τοὺς δώδεκα ἀποστόλους δέδωκεν αὐτοῖς δύναμιν καὶ ἐξουσίαν ἐπὶ πάντα τὰ δαιμόνια καὶ νόσους θεραπεύειν, 9.2 καὶ ἀπέστιλεν αὐτοὺς κηρύσσειν τὴν βασιλείαν τοῦ θεοῦ καὶ ἰᾶσθαι τοὺς ἀσθενῖς,

9.3 καὶ εἶπεν πρὸς αὐτούς, μηδὲν αἴρετε εἰς τὴν ὁδόν, μήτε ῥάβδον μήτε πήραν μήδε ἄρτον μήτε ἀργύριον, μήδε δύο χιτῶνας ἔχειν. 9.4 καὶ εἰς ἣν ἂν οἰκίαν εἰσέλθητε, ἐκεῖ μίνατε καὶ ἐκεῖθεν ἐξέρχεσθε. 9.5 καὶ ὅσοι ἂν μὴ δέχωνται ὑμᾶς, ἐξερχόμενοι ἐκ τῆς πόλεως ἐκίνης τὸν κονιορτὸν ἀπὸ τῶν ποδῶν ὑμῶν ἀποτινάσσετε εἰς μαρτύριον ἐπ' αὐτούς.

9.6 ἐξερχόμενοι δὲ διήρχοντο κατὰ κώμας εὐαγγελιζόμενοι καὶ θεραπεύοντες πανταχοῦ. 9.7 ἤκουσεν δὲ Ἡρώδης ὁ τετραάρχης τὰ γεινόμενα πάντα, καὶ διηπόρει διὰ τὸ λέγεσθαι ὑπό τινων ὅτι Ἰωάννης ἠγέρθη ἐκ νεκρῶν, 9.8 ὑπό τινων δὲ ὅτι Ἡλίας ἐφάνη,

ἄλλων δὲ ὅτι προφήτης τις τῶν ἀρχαίων ἀνέστη. 9.9 εἶπεν δὲ Ἡρώδης, Ἰωάννην ἐγὼ ἀπεκεφάλισα· τίς δέ ἐστιν οὗτος περὶ οὗ ἀκούω τοιαῦτα; καὶ ἐζήτει ἰδῖν αὐτόν.

9.10 καὶ ὑποστρέψαντες οἱ ἀπόστολοι διηγήσαντο αὐτῷ ἃ ἐποίησαν.

καὶ παραλαβὼν αὐτοὺς ὑπεχώρησεν κατ' ἰδίαν εἰς τόπον ἔρημον πόλιν καλουμένην Βηθσαϊδά. 9.11 οἱ δὲ ὄχλοι γνόντες ἠκολούθησαν αὐτῷ.

καὶ ἀποδεξάμενος αὐτοὺς ἐλάλησεν αὐτοῖς περὶ τῆς

selves *for* her. But the (he) said: Weep ye not, for she died not, but she sleeps. 8.53 And they were laughing at him, having known that she died. 8.54 But he, having grasped her hand, he called out, saying: Girl, rise up. 8.55 And her breath/spirit returned, and she stood up immediately, and he ordered *them* to give for her to eat.

8.56 And her parents were amazed/astounded. But the (he) enjoined upon/charged them to tell to no one the (thing) having happened.

9.1 And having called the twelve apostles together, he gave to them power and authority over all the demons and to treat/heal diseases, 9.2 and he sent them away to herald/preach the kingdom of God and to heal the sicknesses/weaknesses,

9.3 and he said to them: Take ye nothing in/for the road/way, neither a staff nor a traveler's bag nor a loaf nor silver/money, nor to have two tunics. 9.4 And into which house ye would enter, stay ye there and from there go ye forth *again*. 9.5 And as many as might/would not receive ye, going forth out of that city, shake ye off the dust from your feet in/for a testimony against them.

9.6 And going forth, they were going through village by village announcing a good message and treating/healing everywhere. 9.7 But Herod the tetrarch heard *of* all the things happening, and he was being perplexed becauseof the (thing) to be said by some that John was raised out of dead (ones), 9.8 and by some that Elias appeared,

but *by* others that a certain prophet of the ancients rose up. 9.9 But Herod said: I, I beheaded John; but who is this (one) about whom I hear such (things)? And he was seeking to see him.

9.10 And having returned, the apostles related to him what (things) they did.

And taking them along, he departed privately into a desert place/*or* a city being called Bethsaida. 9.11 But the crowds, having known, followed with him.

And having welcomed them he spoke to them about the kingdom of God, and he healed those having a need

βασιλίας τοῦ θεοῦ, καὶ τοὺς χρείαν ἔχοντας θεραπείας ἰᾶτο.

9.12 ἡ δὲ ἡμέρα ἤρξατο κλίνειν· προσελθόντες δὲ οἱ δώδεκα εἶπον αὐτῷ, ἀπόλυσον τὸν ὄχλον, ἵνα πορευθέντες εἰς τὰς κύκλῳ κώμας καὶ ἀγροὺς καταλύσωσιν καὶ εὕρωσιν ἐπισιτισμόν, ὅτι ὧδε ἐν ἐρήμῳ τόπῳ ἐσμέν.

9.13 εἶπεν δὲ αὐτοῖς, δότε αὐτοῖς ὑμεῖς φαγεῖν. οἱ δὲ εἶπαν, οὐκ εἰσὶν ἡμῖν πλεῖον ἢ ἄρτοι πέντε καὶ ἰχθύες δύο, εἰ μήτι πορευθέντες ἡμῖς ἀγοράσωμεν εἰς πάντα τὸν λαὸν τοῦτον βρώματα.

9.14 ἦσαν δὲ ὡσεὶ ἄνδρες πεντακισχίλιοι. εἶπεν δὲ πρὸς τοὺς μαθητὰς αὐτοῦ, κατακλίνατε αὐτοὺς κλισίας ὡσεὶ ἀνὰ πεντήκοντα. 9.15 καὶ ἐποίησαν οὕτως καὶ κατέκλιναν πάντας. 9.16 λαβὼν δὲ τοὺς πέντε ἄρτους καὶ τοὺς δύο ἰχθύας ἀναβλέψας εἰς τὸν οὐρανὸν εὐλόγησεν καὶ κατέκλασεν καὶ ἐδίδου τοῖς μαθηταῖς παραθεῖναι τῷ ὄχλῳ. 9.17 καὶ ἔφαγον καὶ ἐχορτάσθησαν πάντες, καὶ ἤρθη τὸ περισσεῦσαν τῶν κλασμάτων κόφινοι δώδεκα.

9.18 καὶ ἐγένετο ἐν τῷ εἶναι αὐτὸν προσευχόμενον κατὰ μόνας συνῆσαν αὐτῷ οἱ μαθηταί,

καὶ ἐπηρώτησεν αὐτοὺς ὁ Ἰησοῦς λέγων, τίνα με λέγουσιν οἱ ὄχλοι εἶναι; 9.19 οἱ δὲ ἀποκριθέντες εἶπαν, Ἰωάννην τὸν βαπτιστήν, ἄλλοι δὲ Ἠλίαν, ἄλλοι δὲ ὅτι προφήτης τις τῶν ἀρχαίων ἀνέστη.

9.20 εἶπεν δὲ αὐτοῖς, ὑμεῖς δὲ τίνα με λέγεται εἶναι; Πέτρος δὲ ἀποκριθεὶς εἶπεν, τὸν χριστὸν τοῦ θεοῦ. 9.21 ὁ δὲ ἐπιτιμήσας αὐτοῖς παρήγγειλεν μηδενὶ λέγειν τοῦτο,

9.22 εἰπὼν ὅτι δεῖ τὸν υἱὸν τοῦ ἀνθρώπου πολλὰ παθεῖν καὶ ἀποδοκιμασθῆναι ἀπὸ τῶν πρεσβυτέρων καὶ ἀρχιερέων καὶ γραμματέων καὶ ἀποκτανθῆναι καὶ τῇ τρίτῃ ἡμέρᾳ ἐγερθῆναι.

9.23 ἔλεγεν δὲ πρὸς πάντας, εἴ τις θέλι ὀπίσω μου ἔρχεσθαι, ἀρνησάσθω ἑαυτὸν καὶ ἀράτω τὸν σταυρὸν αὐτοῦ καθ᾽ ἡμέραν, καὶ ἀκολουθίτω μοι.

9.24 ὃς γὰρ ἐὰν θέλῃ τὴν ψυχὴν αὐτοῦ σῶσαι, ἀπολέσει

of treatment/healing.

9.12 But the day began to wear away; and approaching, the twelve were saying to him: Dismiss the crowd, in order that being gone into the villages and fields round about, they might lodge and find something to eat, because here we are in a desert place.

9.13 And he said to them: Ye, give ye to them to eat. But they said: There is not for us more than five loaves and two fishes, unless having gone ourselves, we, we might buy foods to/for all this people.

9.14 And there were about five thousand men. But he said to his pupils/learners: Ye make them to recline *in* companies, about fifty each. 9.15 And they did so and they caused all to recline. 9.16 And having taken the five loaves and the two fishes, having looked up into the sky, he blessed and broke *them* and was giving to the learners/pupils to distribute to the crowd. 9.17 And they all ate and were filled/satisfied; and the excess/overflow was taken up, twelve baskets of the fragments.

9.18 And it happened in/at the *time for* him to be praying alone, only the learners/pupils were being with him,

and Jesus questioned them, saying: Whom do the crowds say *for* me to be? 9.19 And the (they) answering, they said: John the baptizer, but others Elias, and others that some/a certain prophet of the ancients rose up.

9.20 And he said to them: But ye, whom say ye *for* me to be? And answering, Peter said: The anointed one from God. 9.21 But the (he) having warned *them,* he charged to them to say this to no one,

9.22 having said that it is necessary *for* the son of the man to suffer many (things)/much and to be rejected/declared useless from the elders and high priests and scribes, and to be killed and to be raised on the third day.

9.23 And he was saying to all: If anyone wants/ wishes to come after me, let him deny himself and take up the cross of him/his cross day by day, and let him follow with me.

9.24 For who ever may want to save his soul/

αὐτήν· ὃς δ᾽ ἂν ἀπολέσῃ τὴν ψυχὴν αὐτοῦ ἕνεκεν ἐμοῦ, οὗτος σώσει αὐτήν.

9.25 τί γὰρ ὠφελεῖ ἄνθρωπος κερδήσας τὸν κόσμον ὅλον ἑαυτὸν δὲ ἀπολέσας ἢ ζημιωθείς; 9.26 ὃς γὰρ ἂν ἐπαισχυνθῇ με καὶ τοὺς ἐμοὺς λόγους, τοῦτον ὁ υἱὸς τοῦ ἀνθρώπου ἐπαισχυνθήσεται, ὅταν ἔλθῃ ἐν τῇ δόξῃ αὐτοῦ καὶ τοῦ πατρὸς καὶ τῶν ἁγίων ἀγγέλων. 9.27 λέγω δὲ ὑμῖν ἀληθῶς, εἰσίν τινες τῶν αὐτοῦ ἑστηκότων οἳ οὐ μὴ γεύσωνται θανάτου ἕως ἂν ἴδωσι τὴν βασιλίαν τοῦ θεοῦ.

9.28 ἐγένετο δὲ μετὰ τοὺς λόγους τούτους ὡσεὶ ἡμέραι ὀκτὼ καὶ παραλαβὼν Πέτρον καὶ Ἰωάννην καὶ Ἰάκωβον ἀνέβη εἰς τὸ ὄρος προσεύχεσθαι. 9.29 καὶ ἐγένετο ἐν τῷ προσεύχεσθαι αὐτὸν τὸ εἶδος τοῦ προσώπου αὐτοῦ ἐγένετο ἕτερον καὶ ὁ εἱματισμὸς αὐτοῦ λευκὸς ἐξαστράπτων. 9.30 καὶ ἰδοὺ ἄνδρες δύο συνελάλουν αὐτῷ, οἵτινες ἦσαν Μωϋσῆς καὶ Ἠλείας, 9.31 οἳ ὀφθέντες ἐν δόξῃ ἔλεγον τὴν ἔξοδον αὐτοῦ ἣν ἤμελλεν πληροῦν ἐν Ἰερουσαλήμ. 9.32 ὁ δὲ Πέτρος καὶ οἱ σὺν αὐτῷ ἦσαν βεβαρημένοι ὕπνῳ· διαγρηγορήσαντες δὲ εἶδαν τὴν δόξαν αὐτοῦ καὶ τοὺς δύο ἄνδρας τοὺς συνεστῶτας αὐτῷ. 9.33 καὶ ἐγένετο ἐν τῷ διαχωρίζεσθε αὐτοὺς ἀπ᾽ αὐτοῦ εἶπεν ὁ Πέτρος πρὸς τὸν Ἰησοῦν, ἐπιστάτα, καλόν ἐστιν ἡμᾶς ὧδε εἶναι, καὶ ποιήσομεν σκηνὰς τρῖς, σοὶ μίαν καὶ Μωσεῖ μίαν καὶ μίαν Ἠλίᾳ, μὴ εἰδὼς ὃ λέγει. 9.34 ταῦτα δὲ αὐτοῦ λέγοντος ἐγένετο νεφέλη καὶ ἐπεσκίαζεν αὐτούς· ἐφοβήθησαν δὲ ἐν τῷ εἰσελθεῖν αὐτοὺς εἰς τὴν νεφέλην. 9.35 καὶ φωνὴ ἐγένετο ἐκ τῆς νεφέλης λέγουσα, οὗτός ἐστιν ὁ υἱός μου ὁ ἐκλελεγμένος, αὐτοῦ ἀκούετε. 9.36 καὶ ἐν τῷ γενέσθαι τὴν φωνὴν εὑρέθη Ἰησοῦς μόνος. καὶ αὐτοὶ ἐσίγησαν καὶ οὐδενὶ ἀπήγγιλαν ἐν ἐκείναις ταῖς ἡμέραις οὐδὲν ὧν ἑωράκασιν. 9.37 ἐγένετο δὲ τῇ ἑξῆς ἡμέρᾳ κατελθόντων αὐτῶν ἀπὸ τοῦ ὄρους συνήντησεν αὐτῷ ὄχλος πολύς. 9.38 καὶ ἰδοὺ

life, he will lose it; but who ever might lose his soul/life on account of me, this (one) will save it.

9.25 For what does a man profit, having gained the entire world but having lost himself or having been forfeited? 9.26 For who ever might be ashamed of me and my sayings/words, the son of the man will be ashamed of this (one), whenever he might come in/with the glory/fame of himself and of the father and of the holy messengers/angels. 9.27 But truly I say to ye: There are some of those of him/his own having been standing/established who might by no means taste of death until they would see the kingdom of God.

9.28 And it happened about eight days after these sayings/words, also having taken along Peter and John and James, he went up to the mountain to pray. 9.29 And it happened in/by the (thing) *for* him to pray, *that* the form/appearance of his face became different and his clothing *was* glistening/flashing white. 9.30 And behold, two men were conversing with him, who were Moses and Elias, 9.31 who having been seen in/with fame/glory were telling his exodus/departure which he was about to fulfill in Jerusalem. 9.32 But Peter and the (ones) with him had been burdened with sleep; but having thoroughly awakened, they saw his glory and the two men having been standing with him. 9.33 And it happened in the (thing)/at the (time) *for* them to depart from him, *that* Peter said to Jesus: Master, it is good *for* us to be here, and we shall make three tents/tabernacles, one for you and one for Moses and one for Elias, not knowing what he says. 9.34 And from him saying these (things), there became a cloud and it was covering/falling upon them; and they became afraid in/by the (thing) *for* them to enter into the cloud. 9.35 And a voice happened/became out of/from the cloud: This (one) is my son, the (one) having been chosen; hear ye from him. 9.36 And in/by the (thing) *for* the voice to happen, Jesus was found alone. And they, they were silent and they reported to no one in those days, nothing which they have seen. 9.37 And it happened on the next day, from them having come down from the mountain, *that* a much crowd met with him. 9.38 And behold, a man from the

ἀνὴρ ἀπὸ τοῦ ὄχλου ἐβόησεν λέγων, διδάσκαλε, δέομαί σου ἐπιβλέψον ἐπὶ τὸν υἱόν μου, ὅτι μονογενής μοί ἐστιν, 9.39 καὶ πνεῦμα λαμβάνει αὐτόν, καὶ ἐξαίφνης κράζει, καὶ ῥάσσει καὶ σπαράσσει αὐτὸν μετὰ ἀφροῦ καὶ μόγις ἀποχωρεῖ ἀπ' αὐτοῦ συντρῖβον αὐτόν· 9.40 καὶ ἐδεήθην τῶν μαθητῶν σου ἵνα ἐκβάλωσιν αὐτό, καὶ οὐκ ἠδυνήθησαν.

9.41 ἀποκριθεὶς δὲ ὁ Ἰησοῦς εἶπεν, ὦ γεναιὰ ἄπιστος καὶ διεστραμμένη, ἕως πότε μεθ' ὑμῶν ἔσομαι καὶ ἀνέξομαι ὑμῶν; προσάγαγε ὧδε τὸν υἱόν σου. 9.42 ἔτι δὲ προσερχομένου αὐτοῦ ἔρρηξεν αὐτὸν τὸ δαιμόνιον καὶ συνεσπάραξεν· ἐπετίμησεν δὲ ὁ Ἰησοῦς τῷ πνεύματι τῷ ἀκαθάρτῳ, καὶ ἰάσατο τὸν παῖδα καὶ ἀπέδωκεν αὐτὸν τῷ πατρὶ αὐτοῦ. 9.43 ἐξεπλήσσοντο δὲ πάντες ἐπὶ τῇ μεγαλιότητι τοῦ θεοῦ. πάντων δὲ θαυμαζόντων ἐπὶ πᾶσιν οἷς ἐποίει εἶπεν πρὸς τοὺς μαθητὰς αὐτοῦ, 9.44 θέσθε ὑμεῖς εἰς τὰ ὦτα ὑμῶν τοὺς λόγους τούτους, ὁ γὰρ υἱὸς τοῦ ἀνθρώπου μέλλει παραδίδοσθαι εἰς χῖρας ἀνθρώπων. 9.45 οἱ δὲ ἠγνόουν τὸ ῥῆμα τοῦτο, καὶ ἦν παρακεκαλυμμένον ἀπ' αὐτῶν ἵνα μὴ ἔσθωνται αὐτό, καὶ ἐφοβοῦντο ἐρωτῆσαι αὐτὸν περὶ τοῦ ῥήματος τούτου. 9.46 εἰσῆλθεν δὲ διαλογισμὸς ἐν αὐτοῖς, τὸ τίς ἂν εἴη μίζον αὐτῶν. 9.47 ὁ δὲ Ἰησοῦς εἰδὼς τὸν διαλογισμὸν τῆς καρδίας αὐτῶν ἐπιλαβόμενος παιδίου ἔστησεν αὐτὸ παρ' ἑαυτῷ, 9.48 καὶ εἶπεν αὐτοῖς, ὃς ἐὰν δέξηται τοῦτο τὸ πεδίον ἐπὶ τῷ ὀνόματί μου ἐμὲ δέχεται, καὶ ὃς ἐμὲ δέξεται δέχεται τὸν ἀποστίλαντά με· ὁ γὰρ μεικρότερος ἐν πᾶσιν ὑμῖν ὑπάρχων οὗτός ἐστιν μέγας.

9.49 ἀποκριθεὶς δὲ ὁ Ἰωάννης εἶπεν, ἐπιστάτα, εἴδομέν τινα ἐν τῷ ὀνόματί σου ἐκβάλλοντα δαιμόνια, καὶ ἐκωλύομεν αὐτὸν ὅτι οὐκ ἀκολουθεῖ μεθ' ἡμῶν. 9.50 εἶπεν δὲ πρὸς αὐτὸν ὁ Ἰησοῦς, μὴ κωλύετε, ὃς γὰρ οὐκ ἔστιν καθ' ὑμῶν ὑπὲρ ὑμῶν ἐστιν.

9.51 ἐγένετο δὲ ἐν τῷ συμπληροῦσθαι τὰς ἡμέρας τῆς ἀναλήμψεως αὐτοῦ καὶ αὐτὸς τὸ πρόσωπον αὐτοῦ ἐστήρισεν τοῦ

crowd called out, saying: Teacher, I beg/entreat of you, look upon my son, because he is an only born to me, 9.39 and a spirit takes him, and he suddenly cries out, and it throws down and convulses him with froth/foam, and it scarcely departs from him, bruising him; 9.40 and I entreated from your learners/pupils that they might expel it, and they were not able.

9.41 And answering, Jesus said: O faithless generation, even having been perverted, until when shall I be with ye and endure from ye? Bring forward your son here. 9.42 But from him still coming forward, the demon threw him down and convulsed *him* altogether; but Jesus rebuked to the unclean spirit, and he healed the boy and gave him away/restored him to his father. 9.43 And they were all astounded over the greatness/majesty of God. And from all marveling/wondering at all (things) which he was doing, he said to his pupils/learners: 9.44 Ye, ye put these sayings/words into your ears, for the son of the man is about to be delivered up/betrayed into hands of men/humans. 9.45 But they, they were not knowing this word, and it had been veiled/concealed from them in order that they should not perceive it, and they were fearing to ask him about this word/rhetoric. 9.46 And a discussion/debate entered among them, the (thing) which of them would be greatest. 9.47 But Jesus, knowing the discussion/dispute of their heart, having received from a child, he stood it beside him, 9.48 and he said to them: Who ever might receive this child on the name of me, receives me, and *the one* who might receive me receives the (one) having sent me; for the (one) being smaller/lesser among all ye, this (one) is great.

9.49 And answering, John said: Master, we saw a certain (one) throwing out/expelling demons in your name, and we hindered/forbade him because he follows not with us. 9.50 But Jesus said to him: Forbid ye not, for (one) who is not against us is in behalf of us/in our behalf.

9.51 And it happened in/by the (thing) *for* the days of his receiving/taking up/assumption to be fulfilled, he, he also set his face from the (thing)

πορεύεσθαι εἰς Ἰερουσαλήμ, 9.52 καὶ ἀπέστιλεν ἀγγέλους πρὸ προσώπου αὐτοῦ. καὶ πορευθέντες εἰσῆλθον εἰς κώμην Σαμαριτῶν, ὡς ἑτοιμάσαι αὐτῷ· 9.53 καὶ οὐκ ἐδέξαντο αὐτόν, ὅτι τὸ πρόσωπον αὐτοῦ ἦν πορευόμενον εἰς Ἰερουσαλήμ. 9.54 ἰδόντες δὲ οἱ μαθηταὶ Ἰάκωβος καὶ Ἰωάννης εἶπαν, κύριε, θέλεις εἴπωμεν πῦρ καταβῆναι ἀπὸ τοῦ οὐρανοῦ καὶ ἀναλῶσαι αὐτούς;

9.55 στραφεὶς δὲ ἐπετίμησεν αὐτοῖς. 9.56 καὶ ἐπορεύθησαν εἰς ἑτέραν κώμην. 9.57 καὶ πορευομένων αὐτῶν ἐν τῇ ὁδῷ εἶπέν τις πρὸς αὐτόν, ἀκολουθήσω σοι ὅπου ἂν ἀπέρχῃ.

9.58 καὶ εἶπεν αὐτῷ ὁ Ἰησοῦς, αἱ ἀλώπεκες φωλεοὺς ἔχουσιν καὶ τὰ πετινὰ τοῦ οὐρανοῦ κατασκηνώσεις, ὁ δὲ υἱὸς τοῦ ἀνθρώπου οὐκ ἔχει ποῦ τὴν κεφαλὴν κλίνῃ.

9.59 εἶπεν δὲ πρὸς ἕτερον, ἀκολούθει μοι. ὁ δὲ εἶπεν, κύριε, ἐπίτρεψόν μοι πρῶτον ἀπελθόντι θάψαι τὸν πατέρα μου.

9.60 εἶπεν δὲ αὐτῷ, ἄφες τοὺς νεκροὺς θάψαι τοὺς ἑαυτῶν νεκρούς, σὺ δὲ ἀπελθὼν διάγγελλε τὴν βασιλίαν τοῦ θεοῦ. 9.61 εἶπεν δὲ καὶ ἕτερος, ἀκολουθήσω σοι, κύριε· πρῶτον δὲ ἐπίτρεψόν μοι ἀποτάξασθαι τοῖς εἰς τὸν οἶκόν μου.

9.62 εἶπεν δὲ πρὸς αὐτὸν ὁ Ἰησοῦς, οὐδὶς ἐπιβαλὼν τὴν χεῖρα ἐπ' ἄροτρον καὶ βλέπων εἰς τὰ ὀπίσω εὔθετός ἐστιν τῇ βασιλείᾳ τοῦ θεοῦ. 10.1 μετὰ δὲ ταῦτα ἀνέδιξεν ὁ κύριος καὶ ἑτέρους ἑβδομήκοντα, καὶ ἀπέστιλεν αὐτοὺς ἀνὰ δύο πρὸ προσώπου αὐτοῦ εἰς πᾶσαν πόλιν καὶ τόπον οὗ ἤμελλεν αὐτὸς ἔρχεσθαι. 10.2 ἔλεγεν δὲ πρὸς αὐτούς, ὁ μὲν θερισμὸς πολύς, οἱ δὲ ἐργάται ὀλίγοι· δεήθηται οὖν τοῦ κυρίου τοῦ θερισμοῦ ὅπως ἐκβάλῃ ἐργάτας εἰς τὸν θερισμὸν αὐτοῦ. 10.3 ὑπάγετε· ἰδοὺ ἀποστέλλω ὑμᾶς ὡς ἄρνας ἐν μέσῳ λύκων. 10.4 μὴ βαστάζετε βαλλάντιον, μὴ πήραν, μὴ ὑποδήματα, καὶ μηδένα κατὰ τὴν ὁδὸν ἀσπάσησθε. 10.5 εἰς ἣν δ' ἂν εἰσέλθητε οἰκίαν, πρῶτον λέγεται,

to go into Jerusalem, 9.52 and he sent messengers/angels before his face. And being gone, they entered into a village of Samaritans, as to get ready for him; 9.53 and they received him not themselves, because the face of him was going into Jerusalem. 9.54 And having seen, the learners/pupils, James and John, said: Lord, do you want/wish *that* we might speak *for* fire to come down from the sky/heaven and to consume them?

9.55 But having been turned, he rebuked to them. 9.56 And they went to another/different village. 9.57 And from them going on the road/way, someone said to him: I shall follow with you where ever you may go.

9.58 And Jesus said to him: The foxes have dens/lairs and the birds of the sky nests, but the son of the man has not where he may lay down/recline the head.

9.59 And he said to another/different (one): Follow with me. But the (he) said: Lord, allow/permit for me, by going first, to bury my father.

9.60 But he said to him: Leave the dead (ones) to bury the dead (ones) of themselves, but you, having gone forth, you announce the kingdom of God. 9.61 And another/different also said: I shall follow with you, Lord; but first permit for me to say farewell to those in my house.

9.62 But Jesus said to him: No one, having put the hand on a plow and looking to/for the (things) behind, is suitable/useful for the kingdom of God.

10.1 And after these things, the Lord appointed also seventy others/different (ones), and he sent them by twos/pairs before his face into every city and place where he, he was being about to go/come. 10.2 And he was saying to them: The harvest, on one hand, *is* much, but on the other, the workers *are* few; entreat/petition ye, therefore, from the lord of the harvest, that he might put out workers into/for his harvest. 10.3 Go ye, behold, I send ye forth as lambs in the midst of wolves. 10.4 Carry ye not a money bag, nor a traveler's bag, nor sandals, and greet/salute ye no one along the road/way. 10.5 And into which ever house ye might enter, first say ye: Peace *be* to this

εἰρήνη τῷ οἴκῳ τούτῳ. 10.6 καὶ ἐὰν ᾖ ἐκῖ ὁ υἱὸς εἰρήνης, ἐπαναπαήσεται ἐπ᾽ αὐτὸν ἡ εἰρήνη ὑμῶν· εἰ δὲ μή γε, ἐφ᾽ ὑμᾶς ἀνακάμψει. 10.7 ἐν αὐτῇ δὲ τῇ οἰκίᾳ μένετε, ἐσθίοντες καὶ πίνοντες τὰ παρ᾽ αὐτῶν, ἄξιος γὰρ ὁ ἐργάτης τοῦ μισθοῦ αὐτοῦ. μὴ μεταβαίνετε ἐξ οἰκίας εἰς οἰκίαν. 10.8 καὶ εἰς ἣν ἂν πόλιν εἰσέρχησθε καὶ δέχωνται ὑμᾶς, ἐσθίετε τὰ παρατιθέμενα ὑμῖν, 10.9 καὶ θεραπεύετε τοὺς ἐν αὐτῇ ἀσθενεῖς, καὶ λέγετε αὐτοῖς, ἤγγικεν ἐφ᾽ ὑμᾶς ἡ βασιλία τοῦ θεοῦ. 10.10 εἰς ἣν δ᾽ ἂν πόλιν εἰσέλθητε καὶ μὴ δέχωνται ὑμᾶς, ἐξελθόντες εἰς τὰς πλατίας αὐτῆς εἴπατε, 10.11 καὶ τὸν κονιορτὸν τὸν κολληθέντα ἡμῖν ἐκ τῆς πόλεως ὑμῶν εἰς τοὺς πόδας ἀπομασσόμεθα ὑμῖν· πλὴν τοῦτο γεινώσκετε ὅτι ἤγγικεν ἡ βασιλεία τοῦ θεοῦ. 10.12 λέγω δὲ ὑμῖν ὅτι Σοδόμοις ἐν τῇ ἡμέρᾳ ἐκείνῃ ἀνεκτότερον ἔσται ἢ τῇ πόλει ἐκίνῃ.

10.13 οὐαί σοι, Χοραζείν· οὐαί σοι, Βηθσαϊδάν· ὅτι εἰ ἐν Τύρῳ καὶ Σιδῶνι ἐγενήθησαν αἱ δυνάμις αἱ γενόμεναι ἐν ὑμῖν, πάλαι ἂν ἐν σάκκῳ καὶ σποδῷ καθήμενοι μετενόησαν.

10.14 πλὴν Τύρῳ καὶ Σιδῶνι ἀνεκτότερον ἔσται ἐν τῇ κρίσει ἢ ὑμῖν. 10.15 καὶ σύ, Καφαρναούμ, μὴ ἕως οὐρανοῦ ὑψωθήσῃ; ἕως ᾅδου καταβιβασθήσῃ. 10.16 ὁ ἀκούων ὑμῶν ἐμοῦ ἀκούει, καὶ ὁ ἀθετῶν ὑμᾶς ἐμὲ ἀθετεῖ· ὁ δὲ ἐμὲ ἀθετῶν ἀθετεῖ τὸν ἀποστίλαντά με.

10.17 ὑπέστρεψαν δὲ οἱ ἑβδομήκοντα μετὰ χαρᾶς λέγοντες, κύριε, καὶ τὰ δαιμόνια ὑποτάσσεται ἡμῖν ἐν τῷ ὀνόματί σου. 10.18 εἶπεν δὲ αὐτοῖς, ἐθεώρουν τὸν Σατανᾶν ὡς ἀστραπὴν ἐκ τοῦ οὐρανοῦ πεσόντα. 10.19 ἰδοὺ δέδωκα ὑμῖν τὴν ἐξουσίαν τοῦ πατεῖν ἐπάνω ὄφεων καὶ σκορπίων, καὶ ἐπὶ πᾶσαν τὴν δύναμιν τοῦ ἐχθροῦ, καὶ οὐδὲν ὑμᾶς ἀδικήσει. 10.20 πλὴν ἐν τούτῳ μὴ χαίρετε ὅτι τὰ πνεύματα ὑμῖν ὑποτάσσεται, χέρετε δὲ ὅτι τὰ ὀνόματα ὑμῶν ἐνγέγραπται ἐν τοῖς οὐρανοῖς. 10.21 ἐν αὐτῇ τῇ ὥρᾳ ἠγαλλιάσατο ἐν τῷ πνεύματι τῷ ἁγίῳ καὶ εἶπεν,

house.   10.6 And if a son of peace be there, your
peace shall rest/repose on him; otherwise, it shall
turn back on ye.   10.7 And stay ye in the same house,
eating and drinking the (things) from them, for the
worker *is* worthy of his reward/pay.   Change/remove ye
not from house to house.   10.8 And into which ever
city ye may enter and they may receive ye, eat ye the
(things) being set before ye,   10.9 and treat/heal ye
those being sick in her/it, and say ye to them: The
kingdom of God has drawn near to/upon ye.   10.10 And
into what ever city ye might enter and they receive ye
not,   having gone forth into her streets,   say ye:
10.11 Even the dust cleaving to us, to the feet, out
of/from your city, we shall shake off to ye; however
know ye this, that the kingdom of God has drawn near.
10.12 But I say to ye that in that day it will be more
tolerable for Sodomites than for that city.

10.13 Woe to you, Chorazin; woe to you, Bethsaida; because if the powers having happened in ye had
been caused to happen in Tyre and Sidon, they would
have repented long ago, sitting in sackcloth and
ashes.

10.14   Nevertheless, it will be more tolerable
for Tyre and Sidon in that day than for ye.   10.15 And
you, Capernaum, was you not exalted until/as far as
heaven? You will be caused to descend until/as far as
Hades/the nether world.   10.16 The (one) hearing from
ye hears from me, and the (one) rejecting ye rejects
me; but the (one) rejecting me rejects the (one)
having sent me.

10.17 And the seventy returned with joy, saying:
Lord, even the demons are subjected to us in the name
of you/in your name.   10.18 And he said to them: I was
beholding Satan as lightning having fallen out of the
sky/heaven.   10.19   Behold, I have given to ye the
authority of the (thing) to tread over serpents and
scorpions, and over/above all the power of the enemy,
and nothing will harm ye.   10.20 However, rejoice ye
not in this (thing) that/because the spirits are
subject to ye, but rejoice ye because your names have
been recorded in the skies/heavens.   10.21 In the same
hour he exulted himself/had extreme joy in/with the

ἐξομολογοῦμαί σοι, πάτερ, κύριε τοῦ οὐρανοῦ καὶ τῆς γῆς, ὅτι ἀπέκρυψας ταῦτα ἀπὸ σοφῶν καὶ συνετῶν, καὶ ἀπεκάλυψας αὐτὰ νηπίοις· ναί, ὁ πατήρ, ὅτι οὕτως ἐγένετο εὐδοκία ἔμπροσθέν σου. 10.22 πάντα μοι παρεδόθη ὑπὸ τοῦ πατρός μου, καὶ οὐδὶς γινώσκει τίς ἐστιν ὁ υἱὸς εἰ μὴ ὁ πατήρ, καὶ τίς ἐστιν ὁ πατὴρ εἰ μὴ ὁ υἱὸς καὶ ᾧ ἐὰν βούληται ὁ υἱὸς ἀποκαλύψαι. 10.23 καὶ στραφεὶς πρὸς τοὺς μαθητὰς κατ' ἰδίαν εἶπεν, μακάριοι οἱ ὀφθαλμοὶ οἱ βλέποντες ἃ βλέπετε. 10.24 λέγω γὰρ ὑμῖν ὅτι πολλοὶ προφῆται καὶ βασιλεῖς ἠθέλησαν ἰδεῖν ἃ ὑμεῖς βλέπεται καὶ οὐκ εἶδαν, καὶ ἀκοῦσαι ἃ ἀκούεται καὶ οὐκ ἤκουσαν.

10.25 καὶ ἰδοὺ νομικός τις ἀνέστη ἐκπειράζων αὐτὸν λέγων, διδάσκαλε, τί ποιήσας ἵνα ζωὴν αἰώνιον κληρονομήσω; 10.26 ὁ δὲ εἶπεν πρὸς αὐτόν, ἐν τῷ νόμῳ τί γέγραπται; πῶς ἀναγινώσκις;

10.27 ὁ δὲ ἀποκριθεὶς εἶπεν, « ἀγαπήσεις κύριον τὸν θεόν σου ἐξ ὅλης τῆς καρδίας σου καὶ ἐν ὅλῃ τῇ ψυχῇ σου καὶ ἐν ὅλῃ τῇ ἰσχύϊ σου» καὶ ἐν ὅλῃ τῇ διανοίᾳ σου, καὶ «τὸν πλησίον σου ὡς σεαυτόν.» 10.28 εἶπεν δὲ αὐτῷ, ὀρθῶς ἀπεκρίθης· τοῦτο ποίει καὶ ζήσῃ. 10.29 ὁ δὲ θέλων δικαιῶσαι ἑαυτὸν εἶπεν πρὸς τὸν Ἰησοῦν, καὶ τίς ἐστίν μου πλησίον; 10.30 ὑπολαβὼν δὲ ὁ Ἰησοῦς εἶπεν, ἄνθρωπός τις κατέβαινεν ἀπὸ Ἰερουσαλὴμ εἰς Ἰεριχὼ καὶ λῃσταῖς περιέπεσεν, οἳ καὶ ἐκδύσαντες αὐτὸν καὶ πληγὰς ἐπιθέντες ἀπῆλθον ἀφέντες ἡμιθανῆ. 10.31 κατὰ συγκυρίαν δὲ ἱερεύς τις κατέβαινεν ἐν τῇ ὁδῷ ἐκείνῃ, καὶ ἰδὼν αὐτὸν ἀντιπαρῆλθεν· 10.32 ὁμοίως δὲ καὶ Λευίτης κατὰ τὸν τόπον ἐλθὼν καὶ ἰδὼν ἀντιπαρῆλθεν. 10.33 Σαμαρίτης δέ τις ὁδεύων ἦλθεν κατ' αὐτὸν καὶ ἰδὼν ἐσπλαγχνίσθη, 10.34 καὶ προσελθὼν κατέδησεν τὰ τραύματα αὐτοῦ ἐπιχέων ἔλεον καὶ οἶνον, ἐπιβιβάσας δὲ αὐτὸν ἐπὶ τὸ

149

holy spirit, and said: I give praise/blessing to you, father, Lord of the sky/heaven and of the earth/land, because you concealed these (things) from sophists/ wise (ones) and intelligent (ones), and revealed them to infants; yes, father, because thus it became a pleasure/delight before you. 10.22 All (things) were delivered over to me by my father, and no one knows who is the son except the father, and who is the father except the son and *the one* to whom ever the son wills to reveal *him*. 10.23 And having been turned toward the learners/pupils, he said privately: Happy *are* the eyes seeing what (things) ye see. 10.24 For I say to ye that many prophets and kings wanted/wished to see what (things) ye, ye see and they saw not, and to hear what (things) ye hear and they heard not.

10.25 And behold, a certain lawyer stood up, testing/trying him, saying: Teacher, what should I do in order that I shall inherit eternal life? 10.26 But the (he) said to him: What has been written in the law? How do you read *it*?

10.27 And the (he) answering, he said: YOU WILL LOVE THE LORD YOUR GOD FROM YOUR ENTIRE HEART AND WITH YOUR ENTIRE LIFE/SOUL AND WITH YOUR WHOLE/ENTIRE STRENGTH and with your whole mind/thinking, and YOUR NEAR (ONE)/NEIGHBOR AS YOURSELF. 10.28 And he said to him: You answered correctly; do this and you will live. 10.29 But the (he), wanting/wishing to justify himself, he said to Jesus: And who is my near (one)/ neighbor? 10.30 And taking *it* up/replying, Jesus said: A certain man was going down from Jerusalem to Jericho and he fell in with robbers, who both having unclothed him and having laid blows on *him*, they went away leaving *him* half dead. 10.31 And according to/by a coincidence a certain priest was going down on that road, and having seen him, he passed by opposite; 10.32 and likewise, a Levite also, having come down to/along the place and having seen, he passed by opposite/*on the other side*. 10.33 But a certain traveling Samaritan came by/down to him, and having seen, he was moved with compassion, 10.34 and having come near, he bound up his wounds, pouring on olive oil and wine, and having mounted him upon his own

ἴδιον κτῆνος ἤγαγεν αὐτὸν εἰς πανδοχῖον καὶ ἐπεμελήθη αὐτοῦ. 10.35 καὶ ἐπὶ τὴν αὔριον ἐκβαλὼν δύο δηνάρια ἔδωκεν τῷ πανδοχεῖ καὶ εἶπεν αὐτῷ, ἐπιμελήθητι αὐτοῦ, καὶ ὅ τι ἂν προσδαπανήσῃς ἐγὼ ἐν τῷ ἐπανέρχεσθαί με ἀποδώσω σοι. 10.36 τίς τούτων τῶν τριῶν πλησίον δοκεῖ σοι γεγονέναι τοῦ ἐμπεσόντος εἰς τοὺς λῃστάς; 10.37 ὁ δὲ εἶπεν, ὁ ποιήσας τὸ ἔλεος μετ᾽ αὐτοῦ. εἶπεν δὲ αὐτῷ ὁ Ἰησοῦς, πορεύου καὶ σοὶ ποίει ὁμοίως. 10.38 ἐν δὲ τῷ πορεύεσθαι αὐτοὺς αὐτὸς εἰσῆλθεν εἰς κώμην τινά·

γυνὴ δέ τις ὀνόματι Μάρθα ὑπεδέξατο αὐτόν εἰς τὴν οἰκίαν. 10.39 καὶ τῇδε ἦν ἀδελφὴ καλουμένη Μαριάμ, καὶ παρακαθεσθῖσα πρὸς τοὺς πόδας τοῦ κυρίου ἤκουεν τὸν λόγον αὐτοῦ. 10.40 ἡ δὲ Μάρθα περιεσπᾶτο περὶ πολλὴν διακονίαν·

ἐπιστᾶσα δὲ εἶπεν, κύριε, οὐ μέλι σοι ὅτι ἡ ἀδελφή μου μόνην με κατέλιπεν διακονῖν; εἰπὲ οὖν αὐτῇ ἵνα μοι συναντιλάβηται.

10.41 ἀποκριθεὶς δὲ εἶπεν αὐτῇ ὁ κύριος, Μάρθα Μάρθα, μεριμνᾷς καὶ θορυβάζῃ περὶ πολλά, 10.42 ὀλίγον δέ ἐστιν χρία ἡ ἑνός· Μαριὰ γὰρ τὴν ἀγαθὴν μερίδα ἐξελέξατο ἥτις οὐκ ἀφαιρεθήσεται αὐτῆς. 11.1 καὶ ἐγένετο ἐν τῷ εἶναι αὐτὸν ἐν τόπῳ τινὶ προσευχόμενον, ὡς ἐπαύσατο, εἶπέν τις τῶν μαθητῶν αὐτοῦ πρὸς αὐτόν, κύριε, δίδαξον ἡμᾶς προσεύχεσθαι, καθὼς καὶ Ἰωάννης ἐδίδαξεν τοὺς μαθητὰς αὐτοῦ. 11.2 εἶπεν δὲ αὐτοῖς, ὅταν προσεύχησθε, λέγετε,

πάτερ, ἁγιασθήτω τὸ ὄνομά σου· ἐλθάτω ἡ βασιλία σου· γενηθήτω τὸ θέλημά σου ὡς ἐν οὐρανῷ καὶ ἐπὶ τῆς γῆς. 11.3 τὸν ἄρτον ἡμῶν τὸν ἐπιούσιον δὸς ἡμῖν τὸ καθ᾽ ἡμέραν· 11.4 καὶ ἄφες ἡμῖν τὰς ἁμαρτίας ἡμῶν, καὶ γὰρ αὐτοὶ ἀφίομεν παντὶ ὀφίλοντι ἡμῖν· καὶ μὴ εἰσενέγκῃς ἡμᾶς εἰς πιρασμόν.

11.5 καὶ εἶπεν πρὸς αὐτούς, τίς ἐξ ὑμῶν ἕξει φίλον καὶ πορεύσεται πρὸς αὐτὸν μεσονυκτίου καὶ εἴπῃ αὐτῷ, φίλε, χρῆσόν

animal, he led him to an inn and took care of him. 10.35 And on the morrow, having taken out two denarii, he gave *it* to the innkeeper and said to him: You care for him, and anything what ever you might spend in addition, I, at the (time) *for* me to return, I shall repay *it* to you. 10.36 Who of these three seems to you to have become a neighbor of the (one) having fallen to the robbers? 10.37 And the (he) said: The (one) having done the mercy with him. And Jesus said to him: You go and do you likewise. 10.38 And at/in the (time/thing) *for* them to travel/be going, he entered into a certain village;

and a certain woman, Martha be name, welcomed him into the house. 10.39 And with this (one) was a sister being called Mary, and having been seated alongside near the feet of the Lord, she was hearing the word/saying from him. 10.40 But Martha was being drawn off around/about much service/ministry;

and having stood by, she said: Lord, is it not a care to you that my sister left me alone to serve? Then speak to her in order that she might help me.

10.41 But answering, the Lord said to her: Martha, Martha, you worry and are distressed about much, 10.42 but the one need is little/small; for Mary herself picked out the good part, which will not be taken away from her. 11.1 And it happened at the (time) *for* him to be in/at a certain place praying, as he ceased/stopped, a certain one of his learners/pupils said to him: Lord, teach us to pray, as John also taught his learners/pupils. 11.2 And he said to them: Whenever ye may pray, say ye:

Father, let your name be holy; let your kingdom come; let your purpose/will come about, as in heaven, also upon the earth. 11.3 Give to us our necessary loaf by a day/day by day; 11.4 and forgive/send away for us our sins/faults, for we ourselves also forgive to every (one) being obligated/indebted to us; and bring us not/you might not bring us into temptation/testing.

11.5 And he said to them: Who out of ye will have a friend and will go to him of a midnight and might say to him: Friend, lend three loaves to me,

μοι τρῖς ἄρτους, 11.6 ἐπιδὴ φίλος μου παρεγένετο ἐξ ὁδοῦ πρός με καὶ οὐκ ἔχω ὃ παραθήσω αὐτῷ· 11.7 κἀκεῖνος ἔσωθεν ἀποκριθεὶς εἴπῃ, μή μοι κόπους πάρεχε· ἤδη ἡ θύρα κέκλισται, καὶ τὰ παιδία μου εἰς τὴν κοίτην μετ' ἐμοῦ εἰσίν· καὶ οὐ δύναμαι ἀναστὰς δοῦναί σοι.

11.8 λέγω ὑμῖν, εἰ καὶ οὐ δώσει αὐτῷ ἀναστὰς διὰ τὸ εἶναι φίλον αὐτοῦ, διά γε τὴν ἀναίδιαν αὐτοῦ ἐγερθεὶς δώσει αὐτῷ ὅσων χρῄζει. 11.9 κἀγὼ ὑμῖν λέγω, αἰτεῖτε, καὶ δοθήσεται ὑμῖν· ζητεῖτε, καὶ εὑρήσετε· κρούετε, καὶ ἀνυγήσεται ὑμῖν. 11.10 πᾶς γὰρ ὁ αἰτῶν λαμβάνει, καὶ ὁ ζητῶν εὑρίσκει, καὶ τῷ κρούοντι ἀνυγήσεται.

11.11 τίς δὲ ἐξ ὑμῶν τὸν πατέρα αἰτήσει ἄρτον μὴ λίθον ἐπιδώσει αὐτῷ, ἢ ἰχθυν, μὴ ἀντὶ ἰχθύος ὄφιν ἐπιδώσει αὐτῷ; 11.12 ἢ καὶ αἰτήσει ᾠόν, μὴ ἐπιδώσει αὐτῷ σκορπίον; 11.13 εἰ οὖν ὑμῖς πονηροὶ ὄντες οἴδαται δόματα ἀγαθὰ διδόναι τοῖς τέκνοις ὑμῶν, πόσῳ μᾶλλον ὁ πατὴρ ἐξ οὐρανοῦ δώσει πνεῦμα ἅγιον τοῖς αἰτοῦσιν αὐτόν.

11.14 καὶ ἦν ἐκβάλλων δαιμόνιον κωφόν· ἐγένετο δὲ τοῦ δαιμονίου ἐξελθόντος ἐλάλησεν ὁ κωφός. καὶ ἐθαύμασαν οἱ ὄχλοι· 11.15 τινὲς δὲ ἐξ αὐτῶν εἶπον, ἐν Βεελζεβοὺλ τῷ ἄρχοντι τῶν δαιμονίων ἐκβάλλει τὰ δαιμόνια· 11.16 ἕτεροι δὲ πιράζοντες σημεῖον ἐξ οὐρανοῦ ἐζήτουν παρ' αὐτοῦ. 11.17 αὐτὸς δὲ εἰδὼς αὐτῶν τὰ διανοήματα εἶπεν αὐτοῖς, πᾶσα βασιλεία διαμερισθεῖσα ἐφ' ἑαυτὴν ἐρημοῦται, καὶ οἶκος ἐπὶ οἶκον πίπτει. 11.18 εἰ δὲ καὶ ὁ Σατανᾶς ἐφ' ἑαυτὸν διεμερίσθη, πῶς σταθήσεται ἡ βασιλεία αὐτοῦ; ὅτι λέγετε ἐν Βεελζεβοὺλ ἐκβάλλειν με τὰ δαιμόνια. 11.19 εἰ δὲ ἐγὼ ἐν Βεελζεβοὺλ ἐκβάλλω τὰ δαιμόνια, οἱ υἱοὶ ὑμῶν ἐν τίνι ἐκβάλλουσιν; διὰ τοῦτο αὐτοὶ κριταὶ ἔσονται ὑμῶν. 11.20 εἰ δὲ ἐν δακτύλῳ θεοῦ ἐκβάλλω τὰ δαιμόνια, ἄρα ἔφθασεν ἐφ' ὑμᾶς ἡ βασιλεία τοῦ θεοῦ. 11.21 ὅταν ὁ ἰσχυρὸς

11.6 since a friend of mine arrived to me from a road/way, and I have not *a thing* which I shall set before him;   11.7 and that (one), answering from within, might say: Cause not troubles for me; the door has already been closed, and my children are in the bed with me; and having rose up I am not able to give to you.

11.8 I say to ye: Even if having risen he will not give to him because of the (thing) to be his friend, at least because of the importunity of his having been aroused he will give to him from as much as he has a need.   11.9 And I, I say to ye: Ask, and it will be given to ye; seek, and ye will find; knock, and it will be opened for ye.   11.10 For every one asking receives, and the (one) seeking finds, and it will be opened for the (one) knocking.

11.11 And who out of ye will ask the father *for* a loaf, he will not give a stone to him, or *for* a fish, he will not give to him a serpent instead of a fish?   11.12 Or even he will ask *for* an egg, he will not give a scorpion to him?   11.13 Therefore if ye, being evil (ones), ye know to give good gifts to the children of ye, how much more the father out of heaven will give a holy spirit to those asking him.

11.14 And he was expelling/putting out a demon *for* a dumb (one); and it happened, from the demon having gone out *that* the dumb (one) spoke. And the crowds marveled;   11.15 but some out of them said: He puts out the demons by Beelzebub, the ruler/chief of the demons;   11.16 and others, tempting/testing/ trying, were seeking a sign out of heaven from him. 11.17 But he, knowing their thoughts, he said to them: Every kingdom having been divided against itself is laid waste, and a house against a house falls.   11.18 And if even/also Satan were divided against himself, how will his kingdom be established? That/because ye say *for* me to put out the demons by Beelzebub.   11.19 But if I, I put out the demons by Beelzebub, by whom do your sons put *them* out? Because of this, they themselves will be your judges.   11.20 But if I put out/expel the demons by a finger of God, then the kingdom of God arrived/came upon ye.   11.21 Whenever

καθωπλισμένος φυλάσσῃ τὴν ἑαυτοῦ αὐλήν, ἐν εἰρήνῃ ἔσται τὰ ὑπάρχοντα αὐτοῦ· 11.22 ἐπὰν δὲ ἰσχυρότερος αὐτοῦ ἐπελθὼν νικήσῃ αὐτόν, τὴν πανοπλίαν αὐτοῦ αἴρει ἐφ' ᾗ ἐπεποίθει, καὶ τὰ σκῦλα αὐτοῦ διαδίδωσιν. 11.23 ὁ μὴ ὢν μετ' ἐμοῦ κατ' ἐμοῦ ἐστιν, καὶ ὁ μὴ συνάγων μετ' ἐμοῦ σκορπίζει. 11.24 ὅταν τὸ ἀκάθαρτον πνεῦμα ἐξέλθῃ ἀπὸ τοῦ ἀνθρώπου, διέρχεται δι' ἀνύδρων τόπων ζητοῦν ἀνάπαυσιν, καὶ μὴ εὑρίσκον, λέγει, ὑποστρέψω εἰς τὸν οἶκόν μου ὅθεν ἐξῆλθον· 11.25 καὶ ἐλθὸν εὑρίσκι σεσαρωμένον καὶ κεκοσμημένον.

11.26 τότε πορεύετε καὶ παραλαμβάνι αὐτοῦ ἕτερα πνεύματα πονηρότερα ἑαυτοῦ ἑπτά, καὶ εἰσελθόντα κατοικεῖ ἐκεῖ, καὶ γίνετε τὰ ἔσχατα τοῦ ἀνθρώπου ἐκείνου χείρονα τῶν πρώτων. 11.27 ἐγένετο δὲ ἐν τῷ λέγειν αὐτὸν ταῦτα ἐπάρασά τις φωνὴν γυνὴ ἐκ τοῦ ὄχλου εἶπεν αὐτῷ, μακαρία κοιλία ἡ βαστάσασά σε καὶ μαστοὶ οὓς ἐθήλασας. 11.28 αὐτὸς δὲ εἶπεν, μενοῦν μακάριοι οἱ ἀκούοντες τὸν λόγον τοῦ θεοῦ καὶ φυλάσσοντες. 11.29 τῶν δὲ ὄχλων ἐπαθροιζομένων ἤρξατο λέγειν, ἡ γενεὰ αὕτη γενεὰ πονηρά ἐστιν· σημῖον ζητεῖ, καὶ σημῖον οὐ δοθήσεται αὐτῇ εἰ μὴ τὸ σημῖον Ἰωνᾶ. 11.30 καθὼς ἐγένετο Ἰωνᾶς τοῖς Νινευείταις σημεῖον, οὕτως ἔσται καὶ ὁ υἱὸς τοῦ ἀνθρώπου τῇ γενεᾷ ταύτῃ. 11.31 βασίλισσα νότου ἐγερθήσεται ἐν τῇ κρίσει μετὰ τῶν ἀνδρῶν τῆς γενεᾶς ταύτης καὶ κατακρινεῖ αὐτούς· ὅτι ἦλθεν ἐκ τῶν περάτων τῆς γῆς ἀκοῦσαι τὴν σοφίαν Σολομῶνος, καὶ ἰδοὺ πλεῖον Σολομῶνος ὧδε. 11.32 ἄνδρες Νινευεῖται ἀναστήσονται ἐν τῇ κρίσι μετὰ τῆς γενεᾶς ταύτης καὶ κατακρινοῦσιν αὐτήν· ὅτι μετενόησαν εἰς τὸ κήρυγμα Ἰωνᾶ, καὶ ἰδοὺ πλεῖον Ἰωνᾶ ὧδε.

11.33 οὐδεὶς λύχνον ἅψας εἰς κρύπτην τίθησιν οὐδὲ ὑπὸ

the strong (one) *is* having himself armed well he may guard/protect the court/yard of himself, the goods of him is in peace; 11.22 but as soon as a stronger (one) from/than himself having come upon (him) might conquer/overcome him, he takes from him the armor/panoply on which he had trusted, and he distributes/divides the spoils of/from him. 11.23 The (one) not being with me is against me, and the (one) not gathering with me scatters. 11.24 Whenever the unclean spirit goes out from the man/human, it wanders about through waterless places seeking rest/a repose, and not finding *it*, it says: I shall return to my house from where I went out; 11.25 and having come, it finds *it* having been swept and having been furnished/prepared.

11.26 Then it goes and takes along its seven other/different spirits more wicked from/than itself, and having entered, it dwells there, and the last (things) of that man/human becomes worse than the first (things). 11.27 And it came about by the (thing) *for* him to say these (things), *that* a certain woman out of the crowd, having raised up a voice, said to him: Happy *is* a belly/womb having produced you and breasts which you nursed. 11.28 But he, he said: On the contrary/other hand, happy *are* those hearing and observing/keeping the saying/word of God. 11.29 And from the crowds being gathered close by, he began to say: This generation is an evil/wicked generation; it seeks a sign, and a sign will not be given to it except the sign of Jonas. 11.30 Even as Jonas became a sign for the Nenevites, so also will the son of the man be for this generation. 11.31 A/*the* queen from *the* south will be raised up in/at the judgment with the men of this generation, and she will condemn them; because she came from the bounds/limits of the land/earth to hear the wisdom of Solomon, and behold, *one* greater from/than Solomon *is* here. 11.32 Men, Nenevites, will be raised up in/at the judgment with this generation and they will condemn her/it; because they repented in/for the preaching/message of Jonas, and behold, *one* greater than Jonas *is* here.

11.33 No one having lit a lamp places it in

152

τὸν μόδιον ἀλλ' ἐπὶ τὴν λυχνίαν, ἵνα οἱ εἰσπορευόμενοι τὸ φῶς βλέπουσιν. 11.34 ὁ λύχνος τοῦ σώματός ἐστιν ὁ ὀφθαλμός σου. ὅταν ὁ ὀφθαλμός σου ἁπλοῦς ᾖ, καὶ ὅλον τὸ σῶμά σου φωτινόν ἐστιν· ἐπὰν δὲ πονηρὸς ᾖ, καὶ τὸ σῶμά σου σκοτινόν. 11.35 σκόπι οὖν μὴ τὸ φῶς τὸ ἐν σοὶ σκότος ἐστίν. 11.36 εἰ οὖν τὸ σῶμά σου ὅλον φωτινόν, μὴ ἔχον τι μέρος σκοτινόν, ἔσται φωτινὸν ὅλον ὡς ὅταν ὁ λύχνος τῇ ἀστραπῇ φωτίζῃ σε. 11.37 ἐν δὲ τῷ λαλῆσαι ἐρωτᾷ αὐτὸν Φαρισαῖος ὅπως ἀριστήσῃ παρ' αὐτῷ· εἰσελθὼν δὲ ἀνέπεσεν. 11.38 ὁ δὲ Φαρισαῖος ἰδὼν ἐθαύμασεν ὅτι οὐ πρῶτον ἐβαπτίσθη πρὸ τοῦ ἀρίστου.

11.39 εἶπεν δὲ ὁ κύριος πρὸς αὐτόν, νῦν ὑμεῖς οἱ Φαρισαῖοι τὸ ἔξωθεν τοῦ ποτηρίου καὶ τοῦ πίνακος καθαρίζεται, τὸ δὲ ἔσωθεν ὑμῶν γέμει ἁρπαγῆς καὶ πονηρίας. 11.40 ἄφρονες, οὐχ ὁ ποιήσας τὸ ἔξωθεν καὶ τὸ ἔσωθεν ἐποίησεν; 11.41 πλὴν τὰ ἐνόντα δότε ἐλεημοσύνην, καὶ ἰδοὺ πάντα καθαρὰ ὑμῖν ἐστιν.

11.42 ἀλλὰ οὐαὶ ὑμῖν τοῖς Φαρισαίοις, ὅτι ἀποδεκατοῦται τὸ ἡδύοσμον καὶ τὸ πήγανον καὶ πᾶν λάχανον, καὶ παρέρχεσθαι τὴν κρίσιν καὶ τὴν ἀγάπην τοῦ θεοῦ· ταῦτα δὲ ἔδει ποίσαι κἀκεῖνα μὴ παρεῖναι.

11.43 οὐαὶ ὑμῖν, Φαρισαίοι, ὅτι ἀγαπᾶτε τὴν πρωτοκαθεδρίαν ἐν ταῖς συναγωγαῖς καὶ τοὺς ἀσπασμοὺς ἐν ταῖς ἀγοραῖς.

11.44 οὐαὶ ὑμῖν, ὅτι ἐστὲ ὡς τὰ μνημῖα τὰ ἄδηλα, καὶ οἱ ἄνθρωποι οἱ περιπατοῦντες ἐπάνω οὐκ οἴδασιν. 11.45 ἀποκριθεὶς δέ τις τῶν νομικῶν λέγει αὐτῷ, διδάσκαλε, ταῦτα λέγων καὶ ἡμᾶς ὑβρίζεις. 11.46 ὁ δὲ εἶπεν, καὶ ὑμῖν τοῖς νομικοῖς οὐαί, ὅτι φορτίζετε τοὺς ἀνθρώπους φορτία δυσβάστακτα, καὶ αὐτοὶ ἑνὶ τῶν δακτύλων ὑμῶν οὐ προσψαύετε τοῖς φορτίοις.

11.47 οὐαὶ ὑμῖν, ὅτι οἰκοδομεῖτε τὰ μνημῖα τῶν προφητῶν,

hiding/secret nor under the dry/peck measure, but on the lampstand, in order that those going in may see the light. 11.34 The lamp of the body is your eye. Whenever your eye may be simple/sound, your whole body is also enlightened; but when it may be evil/wicked, your whole body *is* also dark. 11.35 Therefore, be careful/take care lest the light in you is darkness. 11.36 Therefore, if your whole body *be* enlightened, having not any part dark, *the* whole will be enlightened as when the lamp may lighten/illuminate you by the ray/beam. 11.37 And in the (thing/time) *for* him to speak, a Pharisee asks that he might dine beside/with him; and having entered, he reclined *at table*. 11.38 But the Pharisee having seen marveled/wondered because he was not first dipped/washed before the meal/dinner.

11.39 But the Lord said to him: Now ye, the Pharisees, ye cleanse the outside ot the cup and the dish/plate, but the inside of ye is full of plunder and evil/wickedness. 11.40 Foolish (ones), did not the (one) having made the (thing)/that from without also made the (thing) from within? 11.41 However, give ye the (things) being within *for* charity, and behold, all (things) are clean/pure for ye.

11.42 But woe to ye, the Pharisees, because ye tithe the mint and the rue and every garden herb, and ye neglect/disregard the judgment/justice and the agape of/from God; but it was necessary to do these (things) and those not to neglect.

11.43 Woe to ye, Pharisees, because ye love the chief seat in the congregations and the greetings/salutations in/at the markets.

11.44 Woe to ye, because ye are like the uncertain/indistinct tombs/graves, and the men walking above/over do not know. 11.45 And answering, a certain one of the lawyers says to him: Teacher, you insult us also, saying these (things). 11.46 But the (he) said: Woe also to ye, the lawyers, because ye burden the men *with* loads/burdens difficult to carry, and ye yourselves touch not the burdens with one of your fingers.

11.47 Woe to ye, because ye build the tombs of

οἱ δὲ πατέρες ὑμῶν ἀπέκτιναν αὐτούς. 11.48 ἄρα μάρτυρές ἐστε καὶ συνευδοκεῖτε τοῖς ἔργοις τῶν πατέρων ὑμῶν, ὅτι αὐτοὶ μὲν ἀπέκτιναν αὐτοὺς ὑμεῖς δὲ οἰκοδομεῖτε. 11.49 διὰ τοῦτο καὶ ἡ σοφία τοῦ θεοῦ εἶπεν, ἀποστελῶ εἰς αὐτοὺς προφήτας καὶ ἀποστόλους, καὶ ἐξ αὐτῶν ἀποκτενοῦσιν καὶ διώξουσιν, 11.50 ἵνα ἐκζητηθῇ τὸ αἷμα πάντων τῶν προφητῶν τὸ ἐκχυννόμενον ἀπὸ καταβολῆς κόσμου ἀπὸ τῆς γενεᾶς ταύτης, 11.51 ἀπὸ αἵματος Ἄβελ ἕως αἵματος Ζαχαρίου τοῦ ἀπολομένου μεταξὺ τοῦ θυσιαστηρίου καὶ τοῦ οἴκου· ναί, λέγω ὑμῖν, ἐκζητηθήσεται ἀπὸ τῆς γενεᾶς ταύτης.

11.52 οὐαὶ ὑμῖν τοῖς νομικοῖς, ὅτι ἤρατε τὴν κλεῖδα τῆς γνώσεως· αὐτοὶ οὐκ εἰσήλθατε καὶ τοὺς εἰσερχομένους ἐκωλύσατε. 11.53 κἀκεῖθεν ἐξελθόντος αὐτοῦ ἤρξαντο οἱ γραμματεῖς καὶ οἱ Φαρισαῖοι δινῶς ἐνέχειν καὶ ἀποστοματίζειν αὐτὸν περὶ πλειόνων, 11.54 ἐνεδρεύοντες θηρεῦσαί τι ἐκ τοῦ στόματος αὐτοῦ. 12.1 ἐν οἷς ἐπισυναχθεισῶν τῶν μυριάδων τοῦ ὄχλου, ὥστε καταπατεῖν ἀλλήλους, ἤρξατο λέγειν πρὸς τοὺς μαθητὰς αὐτοῦ πρῶτον,

προσέχετε ἑαυτοῖς ἀπὸ τῆς ζύμης τῶν Φαρισαίων, ἥτις ἐστὶν ὑπόκρισις, 12.2 οὐδὲν κεκαλυμμένον ἐστὶν ὃ οὐκ ἀποκαλυφθήσεται, καὶ κρυπτὸν ὃ οὐ γνωσθήσεται. 12.3 ἀνθ' ὧν ὅσα ἐν τῇ σκοτίᾳ εἴπατε ἐν τῷ φωτὶ ἀκουσθήσεται, καὶ ὃ πρὸς τὸ οὖς ἐλαλήσατε ἐν τοῖς ταμίοις κηρυχθήσεται ἐπὶ τῶν δωμάτων. 12.4 λέγω δὲ ὑμῖν τοῖς φίλοις μου, μὴ φοβηθῆτε ἀπὸ τῶν ἀποκτεννόντων τὸ σῶμα καὶ μετὰ ταῦτα μὴ ἐχόντων περισσότερόν τι ποιῆσαι. 12.5 ὑποδείξω ὑμῖν τίνα φοβηθῆτε· φοβήθητε τὸν μετὰ τὸ ἀποκτεῖναι ἔχοντα ἐξουσίαν ἐμβαλεῖν εἰς τὴν γέενναν· ναί, λέγω ὑμῖν, τοῦτον φοβήθητι. 12.6 οὐχὶ πέντε στρουθία πωλοῦνται ἀσσαρίων δύο; καὶ ἓν ἐξ αὐτῶν οὐκ ἔστιν ἐπιλελησμένον ἐνώπιον τοῦ θεοῦ. 12.7 ἀλλὰ καὶ αἱ τρίχες τῆς κεφαλῆς ὑμῶν πᾶσαι ἠρίθμηνται. μὴ οὖν φοβεῖσθε· πολλῶν

the prophets, but your fathers killed them. 11.48 Therefore ye are witnesses and ye consent to the works of your fathers, because they, on one hand, they killed them; and ye, on the other, ye build (monuments). 11.49 Because of this, the wisdom of God also said: I shall send to them prophets and apostles, and from/out of them they will kill and prosecute/pursue, 11.50 in order that the blood of all the prophets, that having been poured out from foundation of a world, might be required from this generation, 11.51 from blood of Abel until blood of Zacharias, the (one) having been destroyed between the altar and the house; yes, I say to ye, it will be required from this generation.

11.52 Woe to ye, the lawyers, because ye took away the key of/from the knowledge; ye yourselves entered not, and ye hindered/prevented those entering/going in. 11.53 And from him having gone out from there, the scribesand the Pharisees began to be fearfully hostile and to draw him out about more (things), 11.54 trying to entrap *him*, to seize upon something out of his mouth. 12.1 In/by which, from the myriads of the crowd having been assembled, so as to trample down one another, he began to say to his learners/pupils first:

Take heed for yourselves from the leaven of the Pharisees, which is pretense/hypocrisy. 12.2 There is nothing having been covered/concealed which will not be revealed, and hidden/secret which will not be made known. 12.3 On which account, what ever (things) ye said in the darkness will be heard in the light, and what ye spoke to the ears in the inner/private rooms will be heralded/preached upon the housetops. 12.4 But I say to ye my friends, fear ye not from those killing the body, and after these (things) having not anything more to do. 12.5 I show to ye secretly whom ye should fear: Ye should fear the (one), after the (thing) to kill, having authority to throw into the hell; yes, I say to ye: Fear ye this (one). 12.6 Are not five sparrows being sold *for* two sixteenths of a denarius? And one out of/from them has not been forgotten before/in the sight of God. 12.7 But even the hairs of the head of ye have all been numbered. There-

στρουθίων διαφέρεται.

12.8 λέγω δὲ ὑμῖν, ὅτι πᾶς ὃς ἂν ὁμολογήσῃ ἐν ἐμοὶ ἔμπροσθεν τῶν ἀνθρώπων, καὶ ὁ υἱὸς τοῦ ἀνθρώπου ὁμολογήσει ἐν αὐτῷ ἔμπροσθεν τῶν ἀγγέλων τοῦ θεοῦ· 12.9 ὁ δὲ ἀρνησάμενός με ἐνώπιον τῶν ἀνθρώπων ἀπαρνηθήσεται ἐνώπιον τῶν ἀγγέλων τοῦ θεοῦ. 12.10 καὶ πᾶς ὃς ἐρεῖ λόγον εἰς τὸν υἱὸν τοῦ ἀνθρώπου, ἀφεθήσεται αὐτῷ· τῷ δὲ εἰς τὸ ἅγιον πνεῦμα βλασφημοῦντι οὐκ ἀφεθήσεται. 12.11 ὅταν δὲ εἰσφέρωσιν ὑμᾶς εἰς τὰς συναγωγὰς καὶ τὰς ἀρχὰς καὶ τὰς ἐξουσίας, μὴ μεριμνήσητε πῶς ἢ τί ἀπολογήσησθε ἢ τί εἴπητε· 12.12 τὸ γὰρ ἅγιον πνεῦμα διδάξει ὑμᾶς ἐν αὐτῇ τῇ ὥρᾳ ἃ δεῖ εἰπεῖν. 12.13 εἶπεν δέ τις ἐκ τοῦ ὄχλου αὐτῷ, διδάσκαλε, εἰπὲ τῷ ἀδελφῷ μου μερίσασθε μετ᾽ ἐμοῦ τὴν κληρονομίαν.

12.14 ὁ δὲ εἶπεν αὐτῷ, ἄνθρωπε, τίς με κατέστησεν κριτὴν ἢ μεριστὴν ἐφ᾽ ὑμᾶς; 12.15 εἶπεν δὲ πρὸς αὐτούς, ὁρᾶται καὶ φυλάσσεσθαι ἀπὸ πάσης πλεονεξίας, ὅτι οὐκ ἐν τῷ περισσεύειν τινὶ ἡ ζωὴ αὐτοῦ ἐστιν ἐκ τῶν ὑπαρχόντων αὐτῷ. 12.16 εἶπεν δὲ παραβολὴν πρὸς αὐτοὺς λέγων, ἀνθρώπου τινὸς πλουσίου εὐφόρησεν ἡ χώρα. 12.17 καὶ διελογίζετο ἐν ἑαυτῷ λέγων, τί ποιήσω, ὅτι οὐκ ἔχω ποῦ συνάξω τοὺς καρπούς μου; 12.18 καὶ εἶπεν, τοῦτο ποιήσω· καθελῶ μου τὰς ἀποθήκας καὶ μείζονας οἰκοδομήσω, καὶ συνάξω ἐκεῖ πάντα τὸν σῖτον καὶ τὰ ἀγαθά μου, 12.19 καὶ ἐρῶ τῇ ψυχῇ μου, ψυχή, ἔχεις πολλὰ ἀγαθὰ κείμενα εἰς ἔτη πολλά· ἀναπαύου, φάγε, πίε, εὐφρένου.

12.20 εἶπεν δὲ αὐτῷ ὁ θεός, ἄφρων, ταύτῃ τῇ νυκτὶ τὴν ψυχήν σου ἀπαιτοῦσιν ἀπὸ σοῦ· ἃ δὲ ἡτοίμασας, τίνι ἔσται; 12.21 οὕτως ὁ θησαυρίζων ἑαυτῷ καὶ μὴ εἰς θεὸν πλουτῶν. 12.22 εἶπεν δὲ πρὸς τοὺς μαθητὰς αὐτοῦ, διὰ τοῦτο λέγω ὑμῖν, μὴ

fore, fear ye not; ye differ/excel from many sparrows.

12.8 But I say to ye that every (one) who ever might confess in me before the men/humans, the son of the man will also confess in him before the messengers/angels of god; 12.9 but the (one) having himself denied me before the men/humans will be denied before the messengers/angels of God. 12.10 And every (one) who will speak a saying/word in/to/against the son of the man, it will be forgiven for him; but for the (one) slandering/blaspheming to/in/against the holy spirit it will not be forgiven. 12.11 And whenever they may bring ye to the congregations and the rulers and the authorities, be ye not anxious how or what ye might answer or what ye might say; 12.12 for the holy spirit will teach ye in the same hour what it is necessary to say. 12.13 But someone out of the crowd said to him: Teacher, speak to my brother to divide/share the inheritance with me.

12.14 But the (he) said to him: Man, who appointed me a judge or divider over ye? 12.15 And he said to them: Observe/see ye and guard/keep ye from every greed/greediness, because the life of him is not in the (thing) for anyone to abound/increase/overflow from the possessions/existing (things) for himself. 12.16 And he spoke a parable to them, saying: The country/region of a certain rich (man) produced well. 12.17 And he reasoned with himself, saying: What should I do, because I have not where I shall gather my fruits/products? 12.18 And he said: I shall do this: I shall pull down my barns/storehouses and I shall build larger (ones), and I shall gather there all the wheat and my good (things), 12.19 and I shall say to my life/soul: Soul, you have many good (things) being laid up into/for many years; you rest, eat, drink, be glad.

12.20 But God said to him: Foolish (one), in this very night they will require your life/soul from you; but what (things) you prepared, for whom will it be? 12.21 So *is* the (one) treasuring/storing up for himself and not being wealthy/rich in God. 12.22 And he said to his learners/pupils: Because of this, I say to ye: Be ye not anxious for the life/soul, what ye

μεριμνᾶται τῇ ψυχῇ τί φάγητε, μηδὲ τῷ σώματι τί ἐνδύσησθε. 12.23 ἡ γὰρ ψυχὴ πλεῖόν ἐστιν τῆς τροφῆς καὶ τὸ σῶμα τοῦ ἐνδύματος. 12.24 κατανοήσατε τοὺς κόρακας ὅτι οὔτε σπείρουσιν οὔτε θερίζουσιν, οἷς οὐκ ἔστιν ταμῖον οὐδὲ ἀποθήκη, καὶ ὁ θεὸς τρέφει αὐτούς· πόσῳ μᾶλλον ὑμεῖς διαφέρετε τῶν πετινῶν. 12.25 τίς δὲ ἐξ ὑμῶν μεριμνῶν δύναται προσθεῖναι ἐπὶ τὴν ἡλικίαν αὐτοῦ πῆχυν; 12.26 εἰ οὖν οὐδὲ ἐλάχιστον δύνασθαι, τί περὶ τῶν λοιπῶν μεριμνᾶται; 12.27 κατανοήσαται τὰ κρίνα πῶς αὐξάνι· οὐ κοπιᾷ οὐδὲ νήθει· λέγω δὲ ὑμῖν ὅτι οὐδὲ Σολομῶν ἐν πάσῃ τῇ δόξῃ αὐτοῦ περιεβάλετο ὡς ἓν τούτων. 12.28 ἴδε ἐν ἀγρῷ τὸν χόρτον ὄντα σήμερον καὶ αὔριον εἰς κλίβανον βαλλόμενον ὁ θεὸς οὕτως ἀμφιέννυσιν, πόσῳ μᾶλλον ὑμᾶς, ὀλιγόπιστοι. 12.29 καὶ ὑμεῖς μὴ ζητεῖτε τί φάγητε καὶ τί πίητε, καὶ μὴ μετεωρίζεσθε· 12.30 ταῦτα γὰρ πάντα τὰ ἔθνη τοῦ κόσμου ἐπιζητοῦσιν· ὑμῶν δὲ ὁ πατὴρ οἶδεν ὅτι χρῄζετε τούτων. 12.31 πλὴν ζητεῖτε τὴν βασιλείαν αὐτοῦ, καὶ ταῦτα προστεθήσετε ὑμῖν. 12.32 μὴ φοβοῦ, τὸ μικρὸν ποίμνιον, ὅτι εὐδόκησεν ὑμῶν ὁ πατὴρ δοῦναι ὑμῖν τὴν βασιλείαν. 12.33 πωλήσατε τὰ ὑπάρχοντα ὑμῶν καὶ δότε ἐλεημοσύνην· ποιήσατε ἑαυτοῖς βαλλάντια μὴ παλαιούμενα, θησαυρὸν ἀνέκλιπτον ἐν τοῖς οὐρανοῖς, ὅπου κλέπτης οὐκ ἐνγίζει οὐδὲ σὴς διαφθείρει· 12.34 ὅπου γάρ ἐστιν ὁ θησαυρὸς ὑμῶν, ἐκεῖ καὶ ἡ καρδία ὑμῶν ἔσται. 12.35 ἔστωσαν ὑμῶν αἱ ὀσφύες περιεζωσμέναι καὶ οἱ λύχνοι καιόμενοι, 12.36 καὶ ὑμεῖς ὅμοιοι ἀνθρώποις προσδεχομένοις τὸν κύριον ἑαυτῶν πότε ἀναλύσῃ ἐκ τῶν γάμων, ἵνα ἐλθόντος καὶ κρούσαντος εὐθέως ἀνοίξωσιν αὐτῷ.

12.37 μακάριοι οἱ δοῦλοι ἐκεῖνοι, οὓς ἐλθὼν ὁ κύριος εὑρήσει γρηγοροῦντας· ἀμὴν λέγω ὑμῖν ὅτι περιζώσεται καὶ ἀνακλινεῖ αὐτοὺς καὶ παρελθὼν διακονήσει αὐτοῖς. 12.38 κᾶν

might eat; nor for the body, what ye might put on. 12.23 For the life/soul is more than the food and the body *than* the clothing. 12.24 Consider ye the crows/ ravens, that/because they neither sow nor reap/harvest, for whom/which there is not a storeroom nor a barn/storehouse, and God rears/nourishes them; by how much more ye, ye differ *in values* from the birds. 12.25 And who out of ye being anxious/caring is able to add a cubit to/on his span of life? 12.26 Then if ye are not able *for* the least (thing), why are ye anxious/caring about the rest/remaining (things)? 12.27 Consider ye the lilies, how it grows; it toils/ labors not, nor spins; but I say to ye that Solomon in all his fame/glory was not clothed like one of these. 12.28 Behold/and if God so clothes/dresses the grass being in a field today and being thrown into a furnace tomorrow, by how much more *for* ye, (ones) of little faith! 12.29 And ye, seek ye not what ye might eat and what ye might drink, and be ye not in anxious suspense; 12.30 for all the ethnics/nations of the world are seeking for these (things); but your father knows that ye have need of these/them. 12.31 But seek ye his kingdom, and these (things) will be added for ye. 12.32 Fear not, the little flock, because your father was well pleased to give the kingdom to ye. 12.33 Sell ye (once) your goods/possessions and give ye *for* charity; make ye for yourselves purses not becoming old, an unfailing store/deposit in the heavens/skies, where a thief comes not near nor a moth corrupts; 12.34 for where the treasure/deposit of ye is, the heart of ye will be there also. 12.35 Let the loins of ye be having been girded/made ready and the lamps being lighted, 12.36 and ye *be* similar to men awaiting/expecting the lord of themselves when he might depart from the wedding (festivities), in order that having come and knocked, they might open for him quickly.

12.37 Happy *are* those slaves, whom the lord, having come, will find watching; truly I say to ye that he will gird himself and make them recline, and passing along, he will serve/minister to them. 12.38 And if in the second and if in the third watch he

ἐν τῇ δευτέρᾳ κἂν ἐν τῇ τρίτῃ φυλακῇ ἔλθῃ καὶ εὕρῃ οὕτως, μακάριοί εἰσιν ἐκεῖνοι. 12.39 τοῦτο δὲ γινώσκετε ὅτι εἰ ᾔδει ὁ οἰκοδεσπότης ποίᾳ ὥρᾳ ὁ κλέπτης ἔρχεται, οὐκ ἂν ἀφῆκεν διορυχθῆναι τὸν οἶκον αὐτοῦ. 12.40 καὶ ὑμεῖς γίνεσθε ἕτοιμοι, ὅτι ᾗ ὥρᾳ οὐ δοκεῖτε ὁ υἱὸς τοῦ ἀνθρώπου ἔρχεται. 12.41 εἶπεν δὲ αὐτῷ ὁ Πέτρος, κύριε, πρὸς ἡμᾶς τὴν παραβολὴν ταύτην λέγεις ἢ καὶ πρὸς πάντας; 12.42 καὶ εἶπεν ὁ κύριος, τίς ἄρα ἐστὶν ὁ πιστὸς οἰκονόμος καὶ φρόνιμος, ὃν καταστήσει ὁ κύριος ἐπὶ τῆς θεραπείας αὐτοῦ τοῦ διδόναι ἐν καιρῷ τὸ σιτομέτριον;

12.43 μακάριος ὁ δοῦλος ἐκεῖνος, ὃν ἐλθὼν ὁ κύριος αὐτοῦ εὑρήσει οὕτως ποιοῦντα· 12.44 ἀληθῶς λέγω ὑμῖν ὅτι ἐπὶ πᾶσιν τοῖς ὑπάρχουσιν αὐτοῦ καταστήσει αὐτόν. 12.45 ἐὰν δὲ εἴπῃ ὁ δοῦλος ἐκεῖνος ἐν τῇ καρδίᾳ αὐτοῦ, χρονίζει μου ὁ κύριος ἔρχεσθαι, καὶ ἄρξηται τύπτειν τοὺς παῖδας καὶ τὰς παιδίσκας, ἐσθίειν τε καὶ πίνειν καὶ μεθύσκεσθαι, 12.46 ἥξει ὁ κύριος τοῦ δούλου ἐκείνου ἐν ἡμέρᾳ ᾗ οὐ προσδοκᾷ καὶ ἐν ὥρᾳ ᾗ οὐ γινώσκει, καὶ διχοτομήσει αὐτὸν καὶ τὸ μέρος αὐτοῦ μετὰ τῶν ἀπίστων θήσει. 12.47 ἐκεῖνος δὲ ὁ δοῦλος ὁ γνοὺς τὸ θέλημα τοῦ κυρίου αὐτοῦ καὶ μὴ ἑτοιμάσας ἢ ποιήσας πρὸς τὸ θέλημα αὐτοῦ δαρήσεται πολλάς· 12.48 ὁ δὲ μὴ γνούς, ποιήσας δὲ ἄξια πληγῶν, δαρήσεται ὀλίγας. παντὶ δὲ ᾧ ἐδόθη πολύ, πολὺ ζητηθήσεται παρ' αὐτοῦ, καὶ ᾧ παρέθεντο πολύ, περισσότερον αἰτήσουσιν αὐτόν.

12.49 πῦρ ἦλθον βαλεῖν ἐπὶ τὴν γῆν, καὶ τί θέλω εἰ ἤδη ἀνήφθη. 12.50 βάπτισμα δὲ ἔχω βαπτισθῆναι, καὶ πῶς συνέχομαι ἕως ὅτου τελεσθῇ. 12.51 δοκεῖτε ὅτι εἰρήνην παρεγενόμην δοῦναι ἐν τῇ γῇ; οὐχί, λέγω ὑμῖν, ἀλλ' ἢ διαμερισμόν. 12.52 ἔσονται γὰρ ἀπὸ τοῦ νῦν πέντε ἐν ἑνὶ οἴκῳ διαμεμερισμένοι, τρεῖς ἐπὶ δυσὶν καὶ δύο ἐπὶ τρισίν, 12.53 διαμερισθήσονται πατὴρ ἐπὶ υἱῷ καὶ

might come and might find thus, happy (ones) are those. 12.39 But know ye this, that if the housemaster knew in what hour the thief comes, he would not have let his house to be broken into. 12.40 And ye, ye become prepared, because ye think/suppose not in which hour the son of the man comes. 12.41 But Peter said to him: Lord, do you say this parable to us or also to all? 12.42 And the Lord said: Who then is the faithful and prudent manager/housemaster, whom the Lord will appoint over his service from the (thing) to give the measure of wheat/grain in season?

12.43 Happy *is* that slave, whom the lord of him, having come, will find thus doing. 12.44 Truly I say to ye that he will appoint him over all his goods/possessions. 12.45 But if that slave might say in his heart: My lord delays to come, and he begins *himself* to beat the boys and the girls/maidservants, both to eat and to drink and to be intoxicated, 12.46 the lord of that slave will arrive in a day in which he expects not and at an hour which he knows not, and will cut him asunder/punish him severely, and he will put his part with the unbelieving/unfaithful (ones). 12.47 But that slave, the (one) having known the will/purpose of his lord and not having prepared or having done toward the will/purpose of him will be beaten much; 12.48 and the (one) not having known, but having done (things) worthy of blows/stripes, he will be beaten little/few. And to every (one) to whom much was given, much will be required from him, and from whom much was set before/entrusted they will ask/demand more abundantly *of* him.

12.49 I came to put/throw fire upon/over the land, and what I want/wish if it were already kindled. 12.50 But I have a baptism to be baptized, and how I am urged/constrained until whatever *time* it might be finished. 12.51 *Do* ye think/suppose that I arrived to give peace in the land? No, I say to ye, but rather a dissension/division. 12.52 For from the present, there will be five in one house having been divided/-separated, three against two and two against three, 12.53 they will be divided/separated, father against son and son against father, and mother against daugh-

υἱὸς ἐπὶ πατρί, καὶ μήτηρ ἐπὶ θυγατέρα καὶ θυγάτηρ ἐπὶ μητέρα, πενθερὰ ἐπὶ τὴν νύμφην αὐτῆς καὶ νύμφη ἐπὶ τὴν πενθεράν. 12.54 ἔλεγεν δὲ καὶ τοῖς ὄχλοις, ὅταν ἴδητε νεφέλην ἀνατέλλουσαν ἐπὶ δυσμῶν, εὐθέως λέγεται ὅτι ὄμβρος ἔρχεται, καὶ γείνεται οὕτως· 12.55 καὶ ὅταν νότον πνέοντα, λέγετε ὅτι καύσων ἔσται, καὶ γείνεται. 12.56 ὑποκριταί, τὸ πρόσωπον τῆς γῆς καὶ τοῦ οὐρανοῦ οἴδαται δοκιμάζειν, τὸν δὲ καιρὸν τοῦτον πῶς οὐκ οἴδαται δοκιμάζειν; 12.57 τί δὲ καὶ ἀφ᾽ ἑαυτῶν οὐ κρίνετε τὸ δίκαιον; 12.58 ὡς γὰρ ὑπάγεις μετὰ τοῦ ἀντιδίκου σου ἐπ᾽ ἄρχοντα, ἐν τῇ ὁδῷ δὸς ἐργασίαν ἀπηλλάχθαι ἀπ᾽ αὐτοῦ, μήποτε κατασύρῃ σε πρὸς τὸν κριτήν, καὶ ὁ κριτής σε παραδώσει τῷ πράκτορι, καὶ ὁ πράκτωρ σε βαλεῖ εἰς φυλακήν. 12.59 λέγω σοι, οὐ μὴ ἐξέλθῃς ἐκεῖθεν ἕως καὶ τὸ ἔσχατον λεπτὸν ἀποδῷς. 13.1 παρῆσαν δέ τινες ἐν αὐτῷ τῷ καιρῷ ἀπαγγέλλοντες αὐτῷ περὶ τῶν Γαλιλαίων ὧν τὸ αἷμα Πειλᾶτος ἔμιξεν μετὰ τῶν θυσιῶν αὐτῶν.

13.2 καὶ ἀποκριθεὶς εἶπεν αὐτοῖς, δοκεῖτε ὅτι οἱ Γαλιλαῖοι οὗτοι ἁμαρτωλοὶ παρὰ πάντας τοὺς Γαλιλαίους ἐγένοντο, ὅτι ταῦτα πεπόνθασιν; 13.3 οὐχί, λέγω ὑμῖν, ἀλλ᾽ ἐὰν μὴ μετανοῆτε πάντες ὁμοίως ἀπολεῖσθε. 13.4 ἢ ἐκεῖνοι οἱ δεκαοκτὼ ἐφ᾽ οὓς ἔπεσεν ὁ πύργος ἐν τῷ Σιλωὰμ καὶ ἀπέκτεινεν αὐτούς, δοκεῖται ὅτι αὐτοὶ ὀφιλέται ἐγένοντο παρὰ πάντας τοὺς ἀνθρώπους τοὺς κατοικοῦντας ἐν Ἰερουσαλήμ; 13.5 οὐχί, λέγω ὑμῖν, ἀλλ᾽ ἐὰν μὴ μετανοήσητε πάντες ὡσαύτως ἀπολεῖσθαι. 13.6 ἔλεγεν δὲ ταύτην τὴν παραβολήν· συκῆν εἶχέν τις πεφυτευμένην ἐν τῷ ἀμπελῶνι αὐτοῦ, καὶ ἦλθεν ζητῶν καρπὸν ἐν αὐτῇ καὶ οὐχ εὗρεν. 13.7 εἶπεν δὲ πρὸς τὸν ἀμπελουργόν, ἰδοὺ τρία ἔτη ἀφ᾽ οὗ ἔρχομαι ζητῶν καρπὸν ἐν τῇ συκῇ ταύτῃ καὶ οὐχ εὑρίσκω. ἔκκοψον αὐτήν· ἱνατί καὶ τὴν γῆν καταργεῖ;

13.8 ὁ δὲ ἀποκριθεὶς λέγει αὐτῷ, κύριε, ἄφες αὐτὴν καὶ

ter and daughter against mother, mother-in-law against her daughter-in-law, and bride/daughter-in-law against the mother-in-law.   12.54 And he was saying to the crowds: Whenever ye might see a cloud rising over a sunset, ye say quickly that a rainstorm comes/is coming, and so it happens;   12.55 and whenever it is blowing a south wind, ye say that it is a hot wind, and it happens/becomes *so*.   12.56 Pretenders/hypocrites, ye know to be testing/proving the face of the earth and of the sky/heaven, but how do ye not know to test/prove this time/season?   12.57 And also, why judge ye not the just (thing) from yourselves?   12.58 For as ye go away/depart with your adversary/opponent to a ruler, on the road/way give a work/effort to be freed/released from him, lest he then may drag you down to the judge, and the judge will deliver you over to the officer/jailer, and the jailer/officer will put/throw you in prison.   12.59 I say to you: By no means might you come out from there until you might repay even the last lepton/mite.   13.1 And some were present at the same time, reporting to him about the Galileans of whom Pilate mixed the blood with their sacrifices.

13.2   And answering, he said to them: Do ye think/suppose that these Galileans became sinners alongside/in the presence of all the Galileans, because they have suffered these (things)?   13.3 No, I say to ye, but unless ye may repent ye will all perish similarly.   13.4 Or those, the eighteen, on whom the tower fell upon in Siloam and killed them, do ye think/suppose that they became debtors alongside/in the presence of all the men dwelling in Jerusalem? 13.5 No, I say to ye, but unless ye might repent, ye will all perish likewise.   13.6 And he was speaking this parable: A certain (one) had a fig tree having been planted in his vineyard, and he came seeking fruit on it and found not.   13.7 And he said to the vinedresser: Behold, *it is* three years from which I come seeking fruit on this fig tree, and I find not. Cut it out/down; why does it even occupy the land unprofitably?

13.8   But the (he) answering, he says to him:

τοῦτο τὸ ἔτος, ἕως ὅτου σκάψω περὶ αὐτὴν καὶ βάλω κόπρια· 13.9 κἂν μὲν ποιήσῃ καρπὸν εἰς τὸ μέλλον εἰ δὲ μή γε, ἐκκόψεις αὐτήν.

13.10 ἦν δὲ διδάσκων ἐν μιᾷ τῶν συναγωγῶν ἐν τοῖς σάββασιν. 13.11 καὶ ἰδοὺ γυνὴ πνεῦμα ἔχουσα ἀσθενίας ἔτη δεκαοκτώ, καὶ ἦν συγκύπτουσα καὶ μὴ δυναμένη ἀνακύψαι εἰς τὸ παντελές. 13.12 ἰδὼν δὲ αὐτὴν ὁ Ἰησοῦς προσεφώνησεν καὶ εἶπεν αὐτῇ, γύναι, ἀπολέλυσαι ἀπὸ τῆς ἀσθενίας σου, 13.13 καὶ ἐπέθηκεν αὐτῇ τὰς χῖρας· καὶ παραχρῆμα ἀνωρθώθη, καὶ ἐδόξαζεν τὸν θεόν.

13.14 ἀποκριθεὶς δὲ ὁ ἀρχισυνάγωγος, ἀγανακτῶν ὅτι τῷ σαββάτῳ ἐθεράπευσεν ὁ Ἰησοῦς, ἔλεγεν τῷ ὄχλῳ ὅτι ἓξ ἡμέραι εἰσὶν ἐν αἷς δεῖ ἐργάζεσθαι· ἐν αὐταῖς οὖν ἐρχόμενοι θεραπεύεσθε καὶ μὴ τῇ ἡμέρᾳ τοῦ σαββάτου. 13.15 ἀπεκρίθη δὲ αὐτῷ ὁ κύριος καὶ εἶπεν, ὑποκριταί, ἕκαστος ὑμῶν τῷ σαββάτῳ οὐ λύει τὸν βοῦν αὐτοῦ ἢ τὸν ὄνον ἀπὸ τῆς φάτνης καὶ ἀπαγαγὼν ποτίζει; 13.16 ταύτην δὲ θυγατέρα Ἀβραὰμ οὖσαν, ἣν ἔδησεν ὁ Σατανᾶς ἰδοὺ δέκα καὶ ὀκτὼ ἔτη, οὐκ ἔδι λυθῆναι ἀπὸ τοῦ δεσμοῦ τούτου τῇ ἡμέρᾳ τοῦ σαββάτου; 13.17 καὶ ταῦτα λέγοντος αὐτοῦ κατῃσχύνοντο πάντες οἱ ἀντικείμενοι αὐτῷ, καὶ πᾶς ὁ ὄχλος ἔχαιρεν ἐπὶ πᾶσιν τοῖς ἐνδόξοις τοῖς γινομένοις ὑπ' αὐτοῦ. 13.18 ἔλεγεν οὖν, τίνι ὁμοία ἐστὶν ἡ βασιλία τοῦ θεοῦ, καὶ τίνι ὁμοιώσω αὐτήν; 13.19 ὁμοία ἐστὶν κόκκῳ σινάπεως, ὃν λαβὼν ἄνθρωπος ἔβαλεν εἰς κῆπον αὐτοῦ, καὶ ηὔξησεν καὶ ἐγένετο εἰς δένδρον, καὶ τὰ πετινὰ τοῦ οὐρανοῦ κατεσκήνωσεν ἐν τοῖς κλάδοις αὐτοῦ. 13.20 καὶ πάλιν εἶπεν, τίνι ὁμοιώσω τὴν βασιλείαν τοῦ θεοῦ; 13.21 ὁμοία ἐστὶν ζύμῃ, ἣν λαβοῦσα γυνὴ ἐνέκρυψεν εἰς ἀλεύρου σάτα τρία ἕως οὗ ἐζυμώθη ὅλον. 13.22 καὶ διεπορεύετο κατὰ πόλις καὶ κώμας διδάσκων καὶ

Lord, leave/forgive it also this year, until which (time) I might dig around it and put a dung hill; 13.9 and if indeed it might make fruit in the *year* being about to -- otherwise you cut it out/down.

13.10   And he was teaching in one of the congregations on the sabbaths.   13.11   And behold, a woman having a spirit of weakness/sickness *for* eighteen years, and she was being bent over and not being able to stand erect ever/through all time.   13.12   And having seen her, Jesus called *her* forward and said to her: Woman, you have been released from your sickness/weakness,   13.13   and he placed the hands on her; and she was straightened immediately, and she acknowledged/glorified God.

13.14   But answering, the leader of the congregation, being indignant because Jesus treated/healed on the sabbath, was saying to the crowd: There are six days in which it is necessary to work; therefore, coming in/on them, be ye treated/healed, and not on the day of the sabbath.   13.15 But the Lord answered to him and said: Pretenders/hypocrites, does not each (one) of ye loose his ox or the ass from the stall/ stable and, having led it away, give it drink on the sabbath? 13.16 But this (woman), being a daughter of Abraham, whom, behold, Satan bound for ten and eight years, is it not necessary to be loosed from this bond on the day of the sabbath? 13.17 And from him saying these (things), all those being opposed to him were being put to shame, and all the crowd rejoiced over the glorious (things) coming about/happening by him. 13.18 Then he was saying: To what is the kingdom of God like/similar, and to what shall I liken it? 13.19 It is similar to a grain of mustard seed, which having taken, a man threw into his garden, and it grew and became a tree, and the birds of the sky/heaven nested/lodged among the branches of it.   13.20   And again he said: To what shall I liken the kingdom of God? 13.21 It is similar to leaven, which a woman having taken,   she   concealed/hid *it* in   three   measures of farina/meal until which (time) all was leavened. 13.22 And he was traveling through by cities and villages, teaching and making a trip to Jerusalem.

πορίαν ποιούμενος εἰς Ἱεροσόλυμα. 13.23 εἶπεν δέ τις αὐτῷ, κύριε, εἰ ὀλίγοι οἱ σῳζόμενοι;

ὁ δὲ εἶπεν πρὸς αὐτούς, 13.24 ἀγωνίζεσθαι εἰσελθεῖν διὰ τῆς στενῆς θύρας, ὅτι πολλοί, λέγω ὑμῖν, ζητήσουσιν εἰσελθεῖν καὶ οὐκ ἰσχύσουσιν. 13.25 ἀφ' οὗ ἂν ἐγερθῇ ὁ οἰκοδεσπότης καὶ ἀποκλίσῃ τὴν θύραν, καὶ ἄρξησθε ἔξω ἑστάναι καὶ κρούειν τὴν θύραν λέγοντες, κύριε, ἄνοιξον ἡμῖν· καὶ ἀποκριθεὶς ἐρεῖ ὑμῖν, οὐκ οἶδα ὑμᾶς πόθεν ἐστέ. 13.26 τότε ἄρξησθαι λέγειν, ἐφάγομεν ἐνώπιόν σου καὶ ἐπίομεν, καὶ ἐν ταῖς πλατίαις ἡμῶν ἐδίδαξας· 13.27 καὶ ἐρεῖ ὑμῖν, οὐκ οἶδα ὑμᾶς πόθεν ἐστέ· ἀπόστητε ἀπ' ἐμοῦ, πάντες ἐργάται ἀδικίας. 13.28 ἐκεῖ ἔστε ὁ κλαυθμὸς καὶ ὁ βρυγμὸς τῶν ὀδόντων, ὅταν ἴδητε Ἀβραὰμ καὶ Ἰσαὰκ καὶ Ἰακὼβ καὶ πάντας τοὺς προφήτας ἐν τῇ βασιλείᾳ τοῦ θεοῦ, ὑμᾶς δὲ ἐκβαλλομένους ἔξω. 13.29 καὶ ἥξουσιν ἀπὸ ἀνατολῶν καὶ δυσμῶν καὶ βορρᾶ καὶ νότου καὶ ἀνακλιθήσονται ἐν τῇ βασιλείᾳ τοῦ θεοῦ. 13.30 καὶ ἰδοὺ εἰσὶν ἔσχατοι οἳ ἔσονται πρῶτοι, καὶ εἰσὶν πρῶτοι οἳ ἔσονται ἔσχατοι. 13.31 ἐν αὐτῇ τῇ ὥρᾳ προσῆλθόν τινες Φαρισαῖοι λέγοντες αὐτῷ, ἔξελθε καὶ πορεύου ἐντεῦθεν, ὅτι Ἡρῴδης θέλει σε ἀποκτεῖναι.

13.32 καὶ εἶπεν αὐτοῖς, πορευθέντες εἴπατε τῇ ἀλώπεκι ταύτῃ, ἰδοὺ ἐκβάλλω δαιμόνια καὶ ἰάσεις ἀποτελῶ σήμερον καὶ αὔριον, καὶ τῇ τρίτῃ τελειοῦμαι. 13.33 πλὴν δεῖ με σήμερον καὶ αὔριον καὶ τῇ ἐχομένῃ πορεύεσθαι, ὅτι οὐκ ἐνδέχεται προφήτην ἀπολέσθαι ἔξω Ἱερουσαλήμ. 13.34 Ἱερουσαλὴμ Ἱερουσαλήμ, ἡ ἀποκτείνουσα τοὺς προφήτας καὶ λιθοβολοῦσα τοὺς ἀπεσταλμένους πρὸς αὐτήν, ποσάκις ἠθέλησα ἐπισυνάξαι τὰ τέκνα σου ὃν τρόπον ὄρνιξ τὴν ἑαυτῆς νοσσιὰν ὑπὸ τὰς πτέρυγας, καὶ οὐκ ἠθελήσατε. 13.35 ἰδοὺ ἀφίεται ὑμῖν ὁ οἶκος ὑμῶν. λέγω ὑμῖν, οὐ μὴ ἴδητέ με ἕως ἂν εἴπητε, « εὐλογημένος ὁ

13.23 And someone said to him: Lord, if few *are* the (ones) being saved?

And the (he) said to them: 13.24 Strive/struggle ye to enter through the narrow door, because many, I say to ye, will seek to enter and they will not be strong/able. 13.25 From which *time* the housemaster would be raised/wakened and would close the door, and ye would begin to stand outside and to knock *on* the door, saying: Lord, open *it* for us; and answering, he will say to ye: I know ye not, from where ye are. 13.26 Then ye will begin to say: We ate and drank in the sight/presence of you, and you taught in our streets; 13.27 and he will say to ye: I know ye not, from where ye are; stand ye away from me, all workers of injustice/wrong. 13.28 There will be there/at that place the wailing/weeping and the gritting/gnashing of the teeth, whenever ye might see Abraham and Isaac and Jacob and all the prophets in the kingdom of God, but *for* ye being put/thrown outside. 13.29 And they will arrive from east (ones) and from west (ones), both north and south, and they will be reclined in the kingdom of God. 13.30 And behold, there are last (ones) who will be first, and there are first (ones) who will be last. 13.31 In the same hour/at the same time some Pharisees came near/approached, saying to him: You depart and go from here/this place, because Herod wants/wishes to kill you.

13.32 And he said to them: Having gone your- selves, ye say to this fox: Behold, I put out/expel demons and I complete healings today and tomorrow, and I am finished on the third (day). 13.33 However, it is necessary *for* me to travel today and tomorrow and the coming (one), because it is not possible/accepta- ble *for* a prophet to perish outside Jerusalem. 13.34 Jerusalem, Jerusalem, the (one) killing the prophets and stoning those having been sent to her, how often I wanted/wished to gather together your children *in* which manner a bird *collects* the brood of herself under the wings, and ye wanted/wished not. 13.35 Behold, the house of ye is left to ye. I say to ye: By no means might ye see me until ye would say: HAVING BEEN BLESSED/PRAISED *is* THE (ONE) COMING IN *the* NAME

ἐρχόμενος ἐν ὀνόματι κυρίου.»

14.1 Καὶ ἐγένετο ἐν τῷ ἐλθεῖν αὐτὸν εἰς οἶκόν τινος τῶν ἀρχόντων Φαρισαίων σαββάτῳ φαγεῖν ἄρτον καὶ αὐτοὶ ἦσαν παρατηρούμενοι αὐτόν. 14.2 καὶ ἰδοὺ ἄνθρωπός τις ἦν ὑδρωπικὸς ἔμπροσθεν αὐτοῦ. 14.3 καὶ ἀποκριθεὶς ὁ Ἰησοῦς εἶπεν πρὸς τοὺς νομικοὺς καὶ Φαρισαίους λέγων, ἔξεστιν τῷ σαββάτῳ θεραπεῦσαι ἢ οὔ; 14.4 οἱ δὲ ἡσύχασαν. καὶ ἐπιλαβόμενος ἰάσατο αὐτὸν καὶ ἀπέλυσεν. 14.5 καὶ ἀποκριθεὶς πρὸς αὐτοὺς εἶπεν, τίνος ὑμῶν ὄνος ἢ βοῦς εἰς φρέαρ πεσεῖτε, καὶ οὐκ εὐθέως ἀνασπάσει αὐτὸν ἐν ἡμέρᾳ τοῦ σαββάτου; 14.6 καὶ οὐκ ἴσχυσαν ἀποκριθῆναι πρὸς ταῦτα. 14.7 ἔλεγεν δὲ πρὸς τοὺς κεκλημένους παραβολήν, ἐπέχων πῶς τὰς πρωτοκλισίας ἐξελέγοντο, λέγων πρὸς αὐτούς, 14.8 ὅταν κληθῇς ὑπό τινος εἰς γάμους, μὴ κατακλιθῇς εἰς τὴν πρωτοκλισίαν, μήποτε ἐντιμότερός σου ᾖ κεκλημένος ὑπ᾽ αὐτοῦ, 14.9 καὶ ἐλθὼν ὁ σὲ καὶ αὐτὸν καλέσας ἐρεῖ σοι, δὸς τούτῳ τόπον, καὶ τότε ἄρξῃ μετὰ αἰσχύνης τὸν ἔσχατον τόπον κατέχιν. 14.10 ἀλλ᾽ ὅταν κληθῇς πορευθεὶς ἀνάπεσε εἰς τὸν ἔσχατον τόπον, ἵνα ὅταν ἔλθῃ ὁ κεκληκώς σε ἐρῖ σοι, φίλε, προσανάβηθι ἀνώτερον· τότε σοί ἐστε δόξα ἐνώπιον πάντων τῶν συνανακειμένων σοι. 14.11 ὅτι πᾶς ὁ ὑψῶν ἑαυτὸν ταπινωθήσεται καὶ ὁ ταπινῶν ἑαυτὸν ὑψωθήσεται. 14.12 ἔλεγεν δὲ καὶ τῷ κεκληκότι αὐτόν, ὅταν ποιῇς ἄριστον ἢ δῖπνον, μὴ φώνει τοὺς φίλους σου μηδὲ τοὺς ἀδελφούς σου μηδὲ τοὺς συγγενεῖς μηδὲ γίτονας πλουσίους, μήποτε καὶ αὐτοὶ ἀντικαλέσωσίν σε καὶ γένηται ἀνταπόδομά σοι. 14.13 ἀλλ᾽ ὅταν δοχὴν ποιῇς ἧς κάλει πτωχούς, ἀναπίρους, χωλούς, τυφλούς·

14.14 καὶ μακάριος ἔσῃ, ὅτι οὐκ ἔχουσιν ἀνταποδοῦναί

OF *the* LORD.

14.1   And it happened in/by the (thing) *for* him to go into a house of a certain one of the leaders/ rulers of Pharisees on a sabbath to eat a loaf, and they themselves were watching him closely.   14.2 And behold, a certain man afflicted with dropsy was before him.   14.3 And answering/taking up a discourse, Jesus spoke to the lawyers and Pharisees, saying: Is it lawful to treat/heal (one) on the sabbath, or not? 14.4 But they were silent. And having taken *him* up, he healed him and released *him*.   14.5 And answering, he said to them: Of which of ye will an ass or an ox be fallen into a well/pit, and he will not pull him/*it* up quickly on a day of the sabbath?   14.6 And they were not able to reply to these (things).   14.7 And he was saying a parable to/toward those having been invited, noticing how they were choosing the places of honor, saying to them: 14.8 Whenever you might be invited by someone to wedding (festivities)/weddings, recline not yourself in the place of honor, lest (one) more honor- able than you may have been invited by him,   14.9 and having come, the (one) having invited you and him will say to you: Give place to this (one), and then you will begin with shame to have the last place. 14.10 But whenever you might be invited, having gone, re- cline in the last place, in order that whenever the (one) having invited you might come, he will say to you: Friend, go up higher; then there will be fame/- glory for you before all those reclining with you. 14.11 Because every one exalting himself will be humbled and the (one) humbling himself will be exalt- ed.   14.12 And he was also saying to the (one) having invited him: Whenever you may make a noon meal or a dinner, call ye not your friends, neither your broth- ers nor the relatives, nor wealthy neighbors, lest they also might invite you in return and it might become a recompense/pay-back to you.   14.13 But when- ever you might make a party/reception/banquet invite poor (ones), maimed (ones), lame (ones), blind (ones); 14.14   and you will be happy/blessed, because they have not to recompense/repay to you, but it will

σοι, ἀνταποδοθήσεται δὲ σοι ἐν τῇ ἀναστάσι τῶν δικαίων. 14.15 ἀκούσας δέ τις ταῦτα τῶν συνανακειμένων εἶπεν αὐτῷ, μακάριος ὅστις φάγεται ἄρτον ἐν τῇ βασιλείᾳ τοῦ θεοῦ. 14.16 ὁ δὲ εἶπεν αὐτῷ, ἄνθρωπός τις ἐποίει δῖπνον μέγα, καὶ ἐκάλεσεν πολλούς, 14.17 καὶ ἀπέστιλεν τὸν δοῦλον αὐτοῦ τῇ ὥρᾳ τοῦ δίπνου εἰπεῖν τοῖς κεκλημένοις, ἔρχεσθαι, ὅτι ἤδη ἕτοιμά εἰσιν. 14.18 καὶ ἤρξαντο ἀπὸ μιᾶς πάντες παρετῖσθαι. ὁ πρῶτος εἶπεν αὐτῷ, ἀγρὸν ἠγόρασα καὶ ἔχω ἀνάγκην ἐξελθὼν ἰδεῖν αὐτόν· ἐρωτῶ σε, ἔχε με παρητημένον. 14.19 καὶ ἕτερος εἶπεν, ζεύγη βοῶν ἠγόρασα πέντε καὶ πορεύομαι δοκιμάσαι αὐτά· ἐρωτῶ σε, ἔχε με παρητημένον. 14.20 καὶ ἕτερος εἶπεν, γυναῖκα ἔγημα καὶ διὰ τοῦτο οὐ δύναμαι ἐλθῖν. 14.21 καὶ παραγενόμενος ὁ δοῦλος ἀπήγγιλεν τῷ κυρίῳ αὐτοῦ ταῦτα. τότε ὀργισθεὶς ὁ οἰκοδεσπότης εἶπεν τῷ δούλῳ αὐτοῦ, ἔξελθε ταχέως εἰς τὰς πλατείας καὶ ῥύμας τῆς πόλεως, καὶ τοὺς πτωχοὺς καὶ ἀναπίρους καὶ τυφλοὺς καὶ χωλοὺς εἰσάγαγε ὧδε. 14.22 καὶ εἶπεν ὁ δοῦλος, κύριε, γέγονεν ὃ ἐπέταξας, καὶ ἔτι τόπος ἐστίν. 14.23 καὶ εἶπεν ὁ κύριος πρὸς τὸν δοῦλον, ἔξελθε εἰς τὰς ὁδοὺς καὶ φραγμοὺς καὶ ἀνάγκασον εἰσελθῖν, ἵνα γεμισθῇ μου ὁ οἶκος· 14.24 λέγω γὰρ ὑμῖν ὅτι οὐδὶς τῶν ἀνθρώπων ἐκείνων τῶν κεκλημένων γεύσεταί μου τοῦ δίπνου.

14.25 συνεπορεύοντο δὲ αὐτῷ ὄχλοι πολλοί, καὶ στραφὶς εἶπεν πρὸς αὐτούς, 14.26 εἴ τις ἔρχεται πρός ἐμὲ καὶ οὐ μισεῖ τὸν πατέρα αὐτοῦ καὶ τὴν μητέρα καὶ τὴν γυναῖκα καὶ τὰ τέκνα καὶ τοὺς ἀδελφοὺς καὶ τὰς ἀδελφάς, ἔτι δὲ καὶ τὴν ψυχὴν ἑαυτοῦ, οὐ δύναται εἶναί μου μαθητής. 14.27 ὅστις οὐ βαστάζει τὸν σταυρὸν αὐτοῦ καὶ ἔρχεται ὀπίσω μου οὐ δύναται εἶναί μου μαθητής.

14.28 τίς γὰρ ἐξ ὑμῶν θέλων πύργον οἰκοδομῆσαι οὐχὶ πρῶτον καθίσας ψηφίζει τὴν δαπάνην, εἰ ἔχει τὰ εἰς ἀπαρτισμόν;

be repaid to you in/at the resurrection of the just (ones). 14.15 And having heard these (things), a certain one of those reclining together said to him: Happy *is the one* who eats a loaf in the kingdom of God. 14.16 And the (he) said to him: A certain man was making a great dinner/supper, and he called/invited many, 14.17 and he sent his slave at the hour of the dinner to say to those having been invited: Ye come, because it is already prepared. 14.18 And they began from one, all to beg off/decline. The first said to him: I bought a field and I have a necessity, going out, to see it; I ask you, hold me having been excused. 14.19 And another/different said: I bought five yokes of oxen and I am going to prove/test them; I ask you, hold me having been excused. 14.20 And another/different (one) said: I married a woman and because of this I am not able to come. 14.21 And having approached/arrived, the slave reported these (things) to his lord. Then the housemaster, being angry, said to his slave: Go forth quickly into the streets and alleys/lanes of the city, and bring the poor (ones) and maimed (ones) and blind (ones) and lame (ones) in here. 14.22 And the slave said: Lord, what you commanded has happened and *there* is still a place. 14.23 And the lord said to the slave: Go forth into the roads and hedges and compel *them* to come in, in order that my house may be filled; 14.24 for I say to ye that no one of those men having been invited will taste of my dinner/supper.

14.25 But many crowds were going/traveling together with him, and having been turned he said to them: 14.26 If anyone comes to/with me and hates not his father and the mother and the woman and the children and the brothers and the sisters, and yet even/also the soul/life of himself, he is not able to be my learner/pupil. 14.27 Whoever bears/carries not his cross and comes after/behind me is not able to be my learner/pupil.

14.28 For who out of ye wanting/wishing to build a tower/fortress, having first sat down, reckons/calculates not the spending/cost, if he has the (things) into/for completion? 14.29 In order that never, from

14.29 ἵνα μήποτε θέντος αὐτοῦ θεμέλιον καὶ μὴ ἰσχύοντος ἐκτελέσαι πάντες οἱ θεωροῦντες ἄρξωνται αὐτῷ ἐμπέζιν 14.30 λέγοντες ὅτι οὗτος ὁ ἄνθρωπος ἤρξατο οἰκοδομῖν καὶ οὐκ ἴσχυσεν ἐκτελέσαι. 14.31 ἢ τίς βασιλεὺς πορευόμενος ἑτέρῳ βασιλεῖ συμβαλλεῖν εἰς πόλεμον οὐχὶ καθίσας πρῶτον βουλεύσεται εἰ δυνατός ἐστιν ἐν δέκα χιλιάσιν ὑπαντῆσαι τῷ μετὰ εἴκοσι χειλιάδων ἐρχομένῳ ἐπ' αὐτόν; 14.32 εἰ δὲ μή γε, ἔτι αὐτοῦ πόρρω ὄντος πρεσβείαν ἀποστίλας ἐρωτᾷ τὰ πρὸς εἰρήνην. 14.33 οὕτως οὖν πᾶς ἐξ ὑμῶν ὃς οὐκ ἀποτάσσεται πᾶσι τοῖς ἑαυτοῦ ὑπάρχουσιν οὐ δύναται εἶναί μου μαθητής. 14.34 καλὸν οὖν τὸ ἅλας· ἐὰν δὲ καὶ τὸ ἅλας μωρανθῇ, ἐν τίνι ἀρτυθήσεται; 14.35 οὔτε εἰς γῆν οὔτε εἰς κοπρίαν εὔθετόν ἐστιν· ἔξω βάλλουσιν αὐτό. ὁ ἔχων ὦτα ἀκούειν ἀκουέτω. 15.1 ἦσαν δὲ αὐτῷ ἐγγίζοντες πάντες οἱ τελῶναι καὶ οἱ ἁμαρτωλοὶ ἀκούειν αὐτοῦ. 15.2 καὶ διεγόγγυζον οἵ τε Φαρισαῖοι καὶ οἱ γραμματεῖς λέγοντες ὅτι ἁμαρτωλοὺς προσδέχετε καὶ συνεσθίει αὐτοῖς. 15.3 εἶπεν δὲ πρὸς αὐτοὺς τὴν παραβολὴν ταύτην λέγων, 15.4 τίς ἄνθρωπος ἐξ ὑμῶν ἔχων ἑκατὸν πρόβατα καὶ ἀπολέσας ἐξ αὐτῶν ἓν οὐ καταλίπει τὰ ἐνενήκοντα ἐννέα ἐν τῇ ἐρήμῳ καὶ πορεύεται ἐπὶ τὸ ἀπολωλὸς ἕως οὗ εὕρῃ αὐτό; 15.5 καὶ εὑρὼν ἐπιτίθησιν ἐπὶ τοὺς ὤμους αὐτοῦ χαίρων, 15.6 καὶ ἐλθὼν εἰς τὸν οἶκον συνκαλεῖ τοὺς φίλους καὶ τοὺς γείτονας λέγων αὐτοῖς, συνχάρητέ μοι, ὅτι εὗρον τὸ πρόβατόν μου τὸ ἀπολωλός.

15.7 λέγω ὑμῖν ὅτι οὕτως χαρὰ ἐν τῷ οὐρανῷ ἔστε ἐπὶ ἑνὶ ἁμαρτωλῷ μετανοοῦντι ἢ ἐπὶ ἐνενήκοντα ἐννέα δικαίοις οἵτινες οὐ χρίαν ἔχουσι μετανοίας.

15.8 ἢ τίς γυνὴ δραχμὰς ἔχουσα δέκα, ἐὰν ἀπολέσῃ δραχμὴν μίαν, οὐχὶ ἅπτι λύχνον καὶ σαροῖ τὴν οἰκίαν καὶ ζητῖ ἐπιμελῶς ἕως οὗ εὕρῃ; 15.9 καὶ εὑροῦσα συγκαλεῖ τὰς φίλας καὶ

him having laid a foundation and not having strength/ being able to finish *it*, might all those beholding/ viewing *it* begin to ridicule/mock to him, 14.30 saying: This man began to build and was not strong/ able to finish *it*. 14.31 Or what king, going to engage with another/different king in a war, will not first having sat down plan/decide if he is able with ten thousands to meet with the (one) coming against him with twenty thousands? 14.32 Otherwise, from him still being afar, having sent an ambassador/envoy, he asks the (things) toward/*terms for* peace. 14.33 So therefore every (one) out of ye who parts not with/ bids not farewell to all the goods/possessions of himself is not able to be my learner/pupil. 14.34 Then good/beautiful is the salt; but if even the salt might be made insipid, with what will it be seasoned? 14.35 It is useful neither in/for land nor in/for dung; they throw it out. The one having ears to hear, let him hear. 15.1 And all the tax collectors and the sinners had drawn near to him to hear from him. 15.2 And both the Pharisees and the scribes were complaining/grumbling aloud, saying: He receives/welcomes sinners, and he eats with them. 15.3 But he spoke this parable to them, saying: 15.4 What man out of ye, having a hundred sheep and having lost one out of them, leaves not the ninety-nine behind in the desert/wilderness and goes to/for the (one) having been lost until which *time* he might find it? 15.5 And having found *it*, he puts it upon his shoulders rejoicing, 15.6 and having come to the house, he calls together the friends and the neighbors (men) saying to them: Rejoice ye with me, because I found my sheep, the (one) having been lost.

15.7 I say to ye that thus there will be joy in the sky/heaven over one sinner repenting than over ninety-nine just (ones) who have not a need of repentance.

15.8 Or what woman having ten drachmae, if she might lose one drachma, lights not a lamp and sweeps the house and seeks/searches carefully until which *time* she might find *it*? 15.9 And having found *it* she calls together the friends and neighbors (women),

γείτονας λέγουσα, συγχάρητέ μοι, ὅτι εὗρον τὴν δραχμὴν ἣν ἀπώλεσα. 15.10 οὕτως, λέγω ὑμῖν, γείνεται χαρὰ ἐνώπιον τῶν ἀγγέλων τοῦ θεοῦ ἐπὶ ἑνὶ ἁμαρτωλῷ μετανοοῦντι.

15.11 εἶπεν δέ, ἄνθρωπός τις εἶχεν δύο υἱούς. 15.12 καὶ εἶπεν ὁ νεώτερος αὐτῶν τῷ πατρί, πάτερ, δός μοι τὸ ἐπιβάλλον μέρος τῆς οὐσίας. ὁ δὲ διεῖλεν αὐτοῖς τὸν βίον. 15.13 καὶ μετ' οὐ πολλὰς ἡμέρας συναγαγὼν ἅπαντα ὁ νεώτερος υἱὸς ἀπεδήμησεν εἰς χώραν μακράν, καὶ ἐκεῖ διεσκόρπισε τὴν οὐσίαν ἑαυτοῦ ζῶν ἀσώτως. 15.14 δαπανήσαντος δὲ αὐτοῦ πάντα ἐγένετο λειμὸς ἰσχυρὰ κατὰ τὴν χώραν ἐκείνην, καὶ αὐτὸς ἤρξατο ὑστερῖσθαι. 15.15 καὶ πορευθὶς ἐκολλήθη ἑνὶ τῶν πολειτῶν τῆς χώρας ἐκείνης, καὶ ἔπεμψεν αὐτὸν εἰς τοὺς ἀγροὺς αὐτοῦ βόσκειν χοίρους· 15.16 καὶ ἐπεθύμει χορτασθῆναι ἐκ τῶν κερατίων ὧν ἤσθιον οἱ χοῖροι, καὶ οὐδεὶς ἐδίδου αὐτῷ. 15.17 εἰς ἑαυτὸν δὲ ἐλθὼν ἔφη, πόσοι μίσθιοι τοῦ πατρός μου περισσεύουσιν ἄρτων, ἐγὼ δὲ λειμῷ ὧδε ἀπόλλυμαι.

15.18 ἀναστὰς πορεύσομαι πρὸς τὸν πατέρα μου καὶ ἐρῶ αὐτῷ, πάτερ, ἥμαρτον εἰς τὸν οὐρανὸν καὶ ἐνώπιόν σου, 15.19 οὐκέτι εἰμὶ ἄξιος κληθῆναι υἱός σου· ποίησόν με ὡς ἕνα τῶν μισθίων σου. 15.20 καὶ ἀναστὰς ἦλθεν πρὸς τὸν πατέρα αὐτοῦ. ἔτι δὲ αὐτοῦ μακρὰν ἀπέχοντος εἶδεν αὐτὸν ὁ πατὴρ αὐτοῦ καὶ ἐσπλαγχνίσθη καὶ δραμὼν ἐπέπεσεν ἐπὶ τὸν τράχηλον αὐτοῦ καὶ κατεφίλησεν αὐτόν. 15.21 εἶπεν δὲ αὐτῷ ὁ υἱός, πάτερ, ἥμαρτον εἰς τὸν οὐρανὸν καὶ ἐνώπιόν σου, οὐκέτι εἰμὶ ἄξιος κληθῆναι υἱός σου. ποίησόν με ὡς ἕνα τῶν μισθίων σου.

15.22 εἶπεν δὲ ὁ πατὴρ πρὸς τοὺς δούλους ἑαυτοῦ, ταχὺ ἐξενέγκατε στολὴν τὴν πρώτην καὶ ἐνδύσατε αὐτόν, καὶ δότε δακτύλιον εἰς τὴν χεῖρα αὐτοῦ καὶ ὑποδήματα εἰς τοὺς πόδας, 15.23 καὶ φέρετε τὸν μόσχον τὸν σιτευτόν, θύσατε καὶ φαγόντες εὐφρανθῶμεν, 15.24 ὅτι ὁ υἱός μου οὗτος νεκρὸς ἦν καὶ

saying: Rejoice ye with me, because I found the drachma which I lost. 15.10 So, I say to ye, there becomes
joy before the messengers/angels of God over one
sinner repenting.

15.11 And he said: A certain man had two sons.
15.12 And the younger (one) of them said to the father: Father, give to me the part of the property
being put upon/to me. And the (he) divided the liv-
ing/goods for them. 15.13 And after not many days,
having gathered together all (things), the younger son
went abroad into a far country, and there he scatter-
ed/squandered the property/proceeds of himself, living
riotously. 15.14 But from him having spent all, a
mighty famine happened throughout that country, and he
himself began to be lacking. 15.15 And having been
gone, he was joined to one of the citizens of that
country, and he sent him into his fields to tend
pigs/swine; 15.16 and he desired/longed to be filled
from the husks which the pigs were eating, and no one
gave to him. 15.17 But having come to himself, he was
saying: How many hired hands/servants of my father
abound/overflow from loaves, but I, I perish here
by/in famine.

15.18 Having risen, I shall go to my father, and
I shall say to him: Father, I sinned/missed the mark
in/against the sky/heaven and before you, 15.19 I am
no longer worthy to be called your son; make me as one
of your hired servants. 15.20 And having risen, he
went to the father of himself. And of him yet being
far distant, his father saw him and was moved with
compassion, and having run, he fell upon his neck and
kissed him affectionately. 15.21 And the son said to
him: Father, I sinned/failed in/against the sky/heav-
en and before you, I am no longer worthy to be called
your son. Make me as one of your hired hands/servants.

15.22 But the father said to the slaves of
himself: Quickly, bring ye out the first/chief robe
and clothe him, and give a ring to/for his hand and
sandals to/for the feet, 15.23 and bring ye the
fatted calf, kill ye *it* and having eaten we should be
gladdened, 15.24 because my son, this (one), was dead
and he lived again, he had been lost and was found.

ἀνέζησεν, ἦν ἀπολωλὸς καὶ εὑρέθη. καὶ ἤρξαντο εὐφρένεσθαι. 15.25 ἦν δὲ ὁ υἱὸς αὐτοῦ ὁ πρεσβύτερος ἐν ἀγρῷ· καὶ ὡς ἐρχόμενος ἤγγισεν τῇ οἰκίᾳ, ἤκουσεν συμφωνίας καὶ χορῶν, 15.26 καὶ προσκαλεσάμενος ἕνα τῶν παίδων ἐπυνθάνετο τί εἴη ταῦτα. 15.27 ὁ δὲ εἶπεν αὐτῷ ὅτι ὁ ἀδελφός σου ἥκει, καὶ ἔθυσεν ὁ πατήρ σου τὸν μόσχον τὸν σιτευτόν, ὅτι ὑγιαίνοντα αὐτὸν ἀπέλαβεν. 15.28 ὠργίσθη δὲ καὶ οὐκ ἤθελεν εἰσελθῖν. ὁ δὲ πατὴρ αὐτοῦ ἐξελθὼν παρεκάλει αὐτόν.

15.29 ὁ δὲ ἀποκριθεὶς εἶπεν τῷ πατρί, ἰδοὺ τοσαῦτα ἔτη δουλεύω σοι καὶ οὐδέποτε ἐντολήν σου παρῆλθον, καὶ ἐμοὶ οὐδέποτε ἔδωκας ἔριφον ἵνα μετὰ τῶν φίλων μου εὐφρανθῶ· 15.30 ὅτε δὲ ὁ υἱός σου οὗτος ὁ καταφαγών σου τὸν βίον μετὰ πορνῶν ἦλθεν, ἔθυσας αὐτῷ τὸν σιτευτὸν μόσχον. 15.31 ὁ δὲ εἶπεν αὐτῷ, τέκνον, σὺ πάντοτε μετ' ἐμοῦ εἶ, καὶ πάντα τὰ ἐμὰ σά ἐστιν· 15.32 εὐφρανθῆναι δὲ καὶ χαρῆναι ἔδει, ὅτι ὁ ἀδελφός σου οὗτος νεκρὸς ἦν καὶ ἔζησεν, ἀπολωλὼς ἦν καὶ εὑρέθη.

16.1 Ἔλεγεν δὲ καὶ πρὸς τοὺς μαθητάς, ἄνθρωπός τις ἦν πλούσιος ὃς εἶχεν οἰκονόμον, καὶ οὗτος διεβλήθη αὐτῷ ὡς διασκορπίζων τὰ ὑπάρχοντα αὐτοῦ. 16.2 καὶ φωνήσας αὐτὸν εἶπεν, τί τοῦτο ἀκούω περὶ σοῦ; ἀπόδος τὸν λόγον τῆς οἰκονομίας σου, οὐ γὰρ ἔτι δύνῃ οἰκονομῖν. 16.3 εἶπεν δὲ ἐν ἑαυτῷ ὁ οἰκονόμος, τί ποιήσω, ὅτι ὁ κύριός μου ἀφαιρῖται τὴν οἰκονομίαν ἀπ' ἐμοῦ; σκάπτιν οὐκ ἰσχύω, ἐπαιτῖν αἰσχύνομαι. 16.4 ἔγνων τί ποιήσω, ἵνα ἂν μετασταθῶ ἐκ τῆς οἰκονομίας δέξωνταί με εἰς τοὺς οἴκους ἑαυτῶν. 16.5 καὶ προσκαλεσάμενος ἕνα ἕκαστον τῶν χρεοφιλετῶν τοῦ κυρίου ἑαυτοῦ ἔλεγεν τῷ πρώτῳ, πόσον ὀφίλεις τῷ κυρίῳ μου; 16.6 ὁ δὲ εἶπεν αὐτῷ, ἑκατὸν βάδους ἐλαίου. ὁ δὲ εἶπεν αὐτῷ, δέξαι σου τὰ γράμματα καὶ καθίσας ταχέως γράψον πεντήκοντα. 16.7 ἔπειτα ἑτέρῳ εἶπεν,

And they began to be gladdened/cheered. 15.25 But his elder son was in a field; and coming, as he drew near to the house, he heard a symphony/music and dances/dancers, 15.26 and summoning/calling to one of the boys, he inquired what these (things) may be. 15.27 And the (he) said to him: Your brother has come, and your father killed the fatted calf, because he received him back being healthy. 15.28 But he was angered and he was not wanting to go in. But his father, having come out, was appealing to/beseeching him.

15.29 But the (he) answering said to the father: Behold, so many years I am a slave for you, and I never passed by/disregarded a command from you, and you never gave a goat to me in order that I might rejoice/be glad with my friends; 15.30 but when your son, this (one) having devoured your living/goods with prostitutes, came, you killed the fatted calf for him. 15.31 And the (he) said to him: Child, you, you are always with me, and all my things are yours; 15.32 and it was being necessary to be gladdened and to rejoice, because your brother, this (one), was dead and he lived, he had been lost and he was found.

16.1 And he was also saying to the learners/pupils: A certain man was wealthy, who had a manager/steward/foreman, and this (one) was informed against to him as scattering/wasting his possessions/goods. 16.2 And having called/summoned him, he said: What *is* this I hear about you? You render the account of you responsibility/stewardship, for you are not able still to be manager. 16.3 And the manager said in himself: What should I do, because my lord takes away the work/responsibility from me? I am not strong/able to dig/excavate, I am ashamed to beg. 16.4 I knew what I might do in order that, *if* I would be removed from the responsibility/stewardship, they might receive me into their houses. 16.5 And having summoned each one of the debtors of the lord of himself, he was saying to the first: How much do you owe to my lord? 16.6 And the (he) said to him: A hundred baths of olive oil And the (he) said to him: Take your letters, and having sat down, quickly write fifty. 16.7 Then he said to

σὺ δὲ πόσον ὀφίλεις; ὁ δὲ εἶπεν, ἑκατὸν κόρους σίτου. λέγει δὲ αὐτῷ, δέξαι σου τὰ γράμματα καὶ γράψον ὀγδοήκοντα. 16.8 καὶ ἐπήνεσεν ὁ κύριος τὸν οἰκονόμον τῆς ἀδικίας ὅτι φρονίμως ἐποίησεν· φρονιμώτεροι ὅτι οἱ υἱοὶ τοῦ αἰῶνος τούτου ὑπὲρ τοὺς υἱοὺς τοῦ φωτὸς εἰς τὴν γενεὰν τὴν ἑαυτῶν εἰσιν. 16.9 καὶ ἐγὼ ὑμῖν λέγω, ἑαυτοῖς ποιήσατε φίλους ἐκ τοῦ μαμωνᾶ τῆς ἀδικίας, ἵνα ὅταν ἐκλίπῃ δέξωνται ὑμᾶς εἰς τὰς αἰωνίους σκηνάς. 16.10 ὁ πιστὸς ἐν ἐλαχίστῳ καὶ ἐν πολλῷ πιστός ἐστιν, καὶ ὁ ἐν ἐλαχίστῳ ἄδικος καὶ ἐν πολλῷ ἄδικός ἐστιν. 16.11 εἰ οὖν ἐν τῷ ἀδίκῳ μαμωνᾷ πιστοὶ οὐκ ἐγένεσθαι, τὸ ἀληθινὸν τίς ὑμῖν πιστεύσει; 16.12 καὶ εἰ ἐν τῷ ἀλλοτρίῳ πιστοὶ οὐκ ἐγένεσθαι, τὸ ὑμέτερον τίς δώσει ὑμῖν;

16.13 οὐδεὶς οἰκέτης δύναται δυσὶ κυρίοις δουλεύειν· εἰ γὰρ τὸν ἕνα μισήσι καὶ τὸν ἕτερον ἀγαπήσει, ἢ ἑνὸς ἀνθέξεται καὶ τοῦ ἑτέρου καταφρονήσει. οὐ δύνασθε θεῷ δουλεύειν καὶ μαμωνᾷ.

16.14 ἤκουον δὲ ταῦτα πάντα οἱ Φαρισαῖοι φιλάργυροι ὑπάρχοντες, καὶ ἐξεμυκτήριζον αὐτόν.

16.15 καὶ εἶπεν αὐτοῖς, ὑμεῖς ἐστε οἱ δικαιοῦντες ἑαυτοὺς ἐνώπιον τῶν ἀνθρώπων, ὁ δὲ θεὸς γινώσκει τὰς καρδίας ὑμῶν· ὅτι τὸ ἐν ἀνθρώποις ὑψηλὸν βδέλυγμα ἐνώπιον τοῦ θεοῦ. 16.16 ὁ νόμος καὶ οἱ προφῆται μέχρι Ἰωάννου· ἀπὸ τότε ἡ βασιλεία τοῦ θεοῦ εὐαγγελίζεται καὶ πᾶς εἰς αὐτὴν βιάζεται. 16.17 εὐκοπώτερον δέ ἐστιν τὸν οὐρανὸν καὶ τὴν γῆν παρελθῖν ἢ τοῦ νόμου μίαν καιρέαν πεσῖν. 16.18 πᾶς ὁ ἀπολύων τὴν γυναῖκα αὐτοῦ καὶ γαμῶν ἑτέραν μοιχεύει, καὶ πᾶς ὁ ἀπολελυμένην ἀπὸ ἀνδρὸς γαμῶν μοιχεύει.

16.19 ἄνθρωπος δέ τις ἦν πλούσιος, καὶ ἐνεδιδύσκετο

another/different: And you, how much do you owe? And the (he) said: A hundred cors of wheat. And he says to him: Take your letters and write eighty. 16.8 And the lord praised/commended the manager of the injustice/wrong because he did prudently; because the sons of this age are more prudent in behalf of the sons of the light in the generation of themselves. 16.9 And I, I say to ye: Make ye friends for yourselves out of/from the money/wealth of the injustice/wrong, in order that whenever it might fail they might receive ye into the eternal tents. 16.10 The (one) faithful in/with a least (thing) is also faithful in/with much, and the (one) unjust/wrong in/with a least (thing) is also unjust/wrong in/with much. 16.11 Therefore, if ye became not faithful in/with the unjust/wicked property/money, who will entrust the true (thing) to/with ye? 16.12 And if ye did not become faithful/trustworthy in the (thing) belonging to another, who will give the (thing) your own to ye?

16.13 No one *being* a domestic/house servant is able to be a slave for two lords; for either he will hate the one and love the other/different, or he will take interest of/from one and scorn/despise from the other/different. Ye are not able to be a slave for God and for money/property/wealth.

16.14 But the Pharisees existing as/being lovers of money/silver were hearing all these (things), and they were deriding/scoffing at him.

16.15 And he said to them: Ye, ye are the (ones) justifying yourselves before the men/humans, but God knows your hearts; because the high/exalted (thing) among men *is* an abominable/detestable (thing) before God. 16.16 The law and the prophets *were* until John; from then/that time the kingdom of God is being announced and every (one) is being urged into it. 16.17 But it is easier *for* the sky/heaven and the earth to pass away than for one little horn/hook to fall from the law. 16.18 Every (one) dismissing/releasing his woman and marrying another/different does adultery, and every (one) marrying her having been released from a man does adultery.

16.19 And a certain man was wealthy/rich, and he

πορφύραν καὶ βύσσον εὐφραινόμενος καθ' ἡμέραν λαμπρῶς. 16.20 πτωχὸς δέ τις ὀνόματι Λάζαρος ἐβέβλητο πρὸς τὸν πυλῶνα αὐτοῦ εἱλκωμένος 16.21 καὶ ἐπιθυμῶν χορτασθῆναι ἀπὸ τῶν πιπτόντων ἀπὸ τῆς τραπέζης τοῦ πλουσίου· ἀλλὰ καὶ οἱ κύνες ἐρχόμενοι ἐπέλειχον τὰ ἕλκη αὐτοῦ. 16.22 ἐγένετο δὲ ἀποθανεῖν τὸν πτωχὸν καὶ ἀπενεχθῆναι αὐτὸν ὑπὸ τῶν ἀγγέλων εἰς τὸν κόλπον Ἀβραάμ· ἀπέθανεν δὲ καὶ ὁ πλούσιος καὶ ἐτάφη. 16.23 καὶ ἐν τῷ ᾅδῃ ἐπάρας τοὺς ὀφθαλμοὺς αὐτοῦ, ὑπάρχων ἐν βασάνοις, ὁρᾷ Ἀβραὰμ ἀπὸ μακρόθεν καὶ Λάζαρον ἐν τοῖς κόλποις αὐτοῦ. 16.24 καὶ αὐτὸς φωνήσας εἶπεν, πάτερ Ἀβραάμ, ἐλέησόν με καὶ πέμψον Λάζαρον ἵνα βάψῃ τὸ ἄκρον τοῦ δακτύλου αὐτοῦ ὕδατι καὶ καταψύξῃ τὴν γλῶσσάν μου, ὅτι ὀδυνῶμαι ἐν τῇ φλογὶ ταύτῃ. 16.25 εἶπεν δὲ Ἀβραάμ, μνήσθητι, τέκνον, ὅτι ἀπέλαβες τὰ ἀγαθά σου ἐν τῇ ζωῇ σου, καὶ Λάζαρος ὁμοίως τὰ κακά· νῦν δὲ ὧδε παρακαλεῖται σὺ δὲ ὀδυνᾶσαι. 16.26 καὶ ἐν πᾶσι τούτοις μεταξὺ ἡμῶν καὶ ὑμῶν χάσμα μέγα ἐστήρικται, ὅπως οἱ θέλοντες διαβῆναι ἔνθεν πρὸς ὑμᾶς μὴ δύνωνται, μηδὲ ἐκεῖθεν πρὸς ἡμᾶς διαπερῶσιν. 16.27 εἶπεν δέ, ἐρωτῶ οὖν σε, πάτερ, ἵνα πέμψῃς αὐτὸν εἰς τὸν οἶκον τοῦ πατρός μου, 16.28 ἔχω γὰρ πέντε ἀδελφούς, ὅπως διαμαρτύρηται αὐτοῖς, ἵνα μὴ καὶ αὐτοὶ ἔλθωσιν εἰς τὸν τόπον τοῦτον τῆς βασάνου. 16.29 λέγει δὲ Ἀβραάμ, ἔχουσι Μωσέα καὶ τοὺς προφήτας· ἀκουσάτωσαν αὐτῶν.

16.30 ὁ δὲ εἶπεν, οὐχί, πάτερ Ἀβραάμ, ἀλλ' ἐάν τις ἀπὸ νεκρῶν ἀναστῇ πρὸς αὐτοὺς μετανοήσουσιν. 16.31 εἶπεν δὲ αὐτῷ, εἰ Μωσέως καὶ τῶν προφητῶν οὐκ ἀκούουσιν, οὐδὲ ἐάν τις ἐκ νεκρῶν ἀναστῇ πισθήσονται.

17.1 Εἶπεν δὲ πρὸς τοὺς μαθητὰς αὐτοῦ, ἀνένδεκτόν ἐστιν

was clothing himself with purple and fine linen, being sumptuously gladdened/cheered day by day. 16.20 And a certain poor (one), Lazarus by name, had been laid/put near his gate having been afflicted with sores 16.21 and desiring to be satisfied/filled from the (thing) falling from the table of the rich (one); but the dogs coming also were licking his sores. 16.22 And it happened *for* the poor (one) to die, and *for* him to be carried away by the messengers/angels to the bosom/inlet of Abraham, and the rich (one) also died and was buried. 16.23 And having lifted up his eyes in the abode of the dead/hades, existing in torments/tortures, he sees Abraham from afar and Lazarus in the bosom/inlet/haven of him. 16.24 And he, having called out, he said: Father Abraham, have mercy on me and send Lazarus in order that he might dip the tip of his finger in water and might cool down my tongue, because I am tormented in/by this flame. 16.25 But Abraham said: You be reminded, child, that you took/received your good (things) in your life, and Lazarus likewise the bad (things). But now he is comforted/consoled here, but you, you are tormented. 16.26 And among all these (things), between us and ye a great chasm has been fixed firmly, so that those wanting/wishing to cross over from here to ye are not able, neither may they cross over from there to us. 16.27 And he said: Then I ask you, father, that you might send him to my father's house, 16.28 for I have five brothers, so that he may testify solemnly to them, lest also they themselves might come to this place of the torment/torture. 16.29 But Abraham says: They have Moses and the prophets; let them hear from them.

16.30 But the (he) said: No, father Abraham, but if someone might raise up from dead (ones) to them, they will repent. 16.31 But he said to him: If they hear/listen not from Moses and the prophets, neither will they be persuaded if someone might raise up out of dead (ones).

17.1 And he said to his learners/pupils/students: It is impossible from the (thing) *for* the offenses/stumbling blocks not to come, but woe *to the*

τοῦ τὰ σκάνδαλα μὴ ἐλθῖν, πλὴν οὐαὶ δι' οὗ ἔρχεται· 17.2 λυσιτελεῖ αὐτῷ εἰ λίθος μυλικὸς περίκειται περὶ τὸν τράχηλον αὐτοῦ καὶ ἔρριπται εἰς τὴν θάλασσαν ἢ ἵνα σκανδαλίσῃ τῶν μικρῶν τούτων ἕνα. 17.3 προσέχετε ἑαυτοῖς. ἐὰν ἁμάρτῃ ὁ ἀδελφός σου ἐπιτίμησον αὐτῷ, καὶ ἐὰν μετανοήσῃ ἄφες αὐτῷ· 17.4 καὶ ἐὰν ἑπτάκις τῆς ἡμέρας ἁμαρτῇ εἰς σὲ καὶ ἑπτάκις ἐπιστρέψῃ πρὸς σὲ λέγων, μετανοῶ, ἀφήσεις αὐτῷ. 17.5 καὶ εἶπαν οἱ ἀπόστολοι τῷ κυρίῳ, πρόσθες ἡμῖν πίστιν. 17.6 εἶπεν δὲ ὁ κύριος, εἰ ἔχετε πίστιν ὡς κόκκον σινάπεως, ἐλέγετε ἂν τῇ συκαμίνῳ, ἐκριζώθητι καὶ φυτεύθητι ἐν τῇ θαλάσσῃ· καὶ ὑπήκουσεν ἂν ὑμῖν.

17.7 τίς δὲ ἐξ ὑμῶν δοῦλον ἔχων ἀροτριῶντα ἢ ποιμαίνοντα, ὃς εἰσελθόντι ἐκ τοῦ ἀγροῦ ἐρεῖ αὐτῷ, εὐθέως παρελθὼν ἀνάπεισε, 17.8 ἀλλ' οὐχὶ ἐρεῖ αὐτῷ, ἑτοίμασόν μοι τί διπνήσω, καὶ περιζωσάμενος διακόνι μοι ἕως φάγω καὶ πίω, καὶ μετὰ ταῦτα φάγεσε καὶ πίεσε σύ; 17.9 μὴ ἔχι χάριν τῷ δούλῳ ὅτι ἐποίησεν τὰ διαταχθέντα; 17.10 οὕτως καὶ ὑμεῖς, ὅταν ποιήσηται πάντα τὰ διαταχθέντα ὑμῖν, λέγετε ὅτι δοῦλοι ἀχρῖοί ἐσμεν, ὃ ὠφείλομεν ποιῆσαι πεποιήκαμεν.

17.11 καὶ ἐγένετο ἐν τῷ πορεύεσθαι εἰς Ἰερουσαλὴμ καὶ αὐτὸς διήρχετο διὰ μέσον Σαμαρίας καὶ Γαλιλαίας.

17.12 καὶ εἰσερχομένου αὐτοῦ εἴς τινα κώμην ἀπήντησαν αὐτῷ δέκα λεπροὶ ἄνδρες, οἳ ἔστησαν πόρρωθεν, 17.13 καὶ αὐτοὶ ἦραν τὴν φωνὴν λέγοντες, Ἰησοῦ ἐπιστάτα, ἐλέησον ἡμᾶς.

17.14 καὶ ἰδὼν εἶπεν αὐτοῖς, πορευθέντες ἐπιδείξατε ἑαυτοὺς τοῖς ἱερεῦσιν. καὶ ἐγένετο ἐν τῷ ὑπάγιν αὐτοὺς ἐκαθαρίσθησαν. 17.15 εἷς δὲ ἐξ αὐτῶν, ἰδὼν ὅτι ἰάθη, ὑπέστρεψεν μετὰ φωνῆς μεγάλης δοξάζων τὸν θεόν, 17.16 καὶ ἔπεσεν ἐπὶ πρόσωπον παρὰ τοὺς πόδας αὐτοῦ εὐχαριστῶν αὐτῷ· καὶ αὐτὸς

one through whom it comes.   17.2 It is gain/advantage
for him if a mill stone is laid/placed around his neck
and he has been thrown into the sea than that he
should cause one of these little (ones) to stumble/
fall into *sin*.   17.3 Take heed for yourselves. If your
brother might sin/miss the   mark   be rebuking/warning
to him, and if he might repent, yield to him/forgive
him;   17.4 even if he might sin/fail to you seven
times of the day, and he might turn seven times toward
you, saying: I repent, you yield to him/forgive him.
17.5 And the apostles said to the Lord: Add faith to
us.   17.6 But the Lord said: If ye have faith as a
grain of mustard seed, ye would have been saying to
the sycamore tree: Be uprooted and be planted by the
sea; and it would obey for ye.
    17.7   But who out of ye, having a slave plowing
or shepherding, who will say to him on coming in from
the field: Having arrived, you recline quickly,   17.8
but will he not say to him: You prepare something for
me *that* I might dine, and having girded around yourself, you wait on/serve me until I eat and drink, and
after these (things) you, you eat and drink?   17.9
Does he not have grace/thanks/favor for the slave
because he did the (things) having been ordered?
17.10 So also ye, whenever ye might do all (things)
ordered/ordained to ye, say ye: Because we are worth-
less/useless slaves, we have done what we were being
obligated/indebted to do.
    17.11   And it happened in the (thing)/at the
(time) to go to Jerusalem, he himself was also passing
through the midst of Samaria and Galilee.
    17.12   And from him entering into a certain
village, ten leprous men met him, who stood from afar,
17.13   and they themselves lifted up the voice, saying: Jesus, master, have mercy on us.
    17.14   And having seen, he said to them: Be
going, exhibit/show yourselves to the priests. And it
came about in the (thing)/at the (time) *for* them to go
away *that* they were cleansed.   17.15 And one out of
them, having seen that he was healed, he returned,
acknowledging/glorifying God with a great voice,
17.16   and he fell on *his* face beside the feet of him,

ἦν Σαμαρίτης.

17.17 ἀποκριθεὶς δὲ ὁ Ἰησοῦς εἶπεν, οὐχὶ οἱ δέκα ἐκαθαρίσθησαν; οἱ δὲ ἐννέα ποῦ; 17.18 οὐχ εὑρέθησαν ὑποστρέψαντες δοῦναι δόξαν τῷ θεῷ εἰ μὴ ὁ ἀλλογενὴς οὗτος; 17.19 καὶ εἶπεν αὐτῷ, ἀναστὰς πορεύου· ἡ πίστις σου σέσωκέν σε.

17.20 ἐπερωτηθεὶς δὲ ὑπὸ τῶν Φαρισαίων πότε ἔρχεται ἡ βασιλία τοῦ θεοῦ ἀπεκρίθη αὐτοῖς καὶ εἶπεν, οὐκ ἔρχεται ἡ βασιλία τοῦ θεοῦ μετὰ παρατηρήσεως, 17.21 οὐδὲ ἐροῦσιν, ἰδοὺ ὧδε· ἤ, ἐκεῖ· ἰδοὺ γὰρ ἡ βασιλεία τοῦ θεοῦ ἐντὸς ὑμῶν ἐστιν. 17.22 εἶπεν δὲ πρὸς τοὺς μαθητάς, ἐλεύσονται ἡμέραι ὅτε ἐπιθυμήσετε μίαν τῶν ἡμερῶν τοῦ υἱοῦ τοῦ ἀνθρώπου ἰδεῖν καὶ οὐκ ὄψεσθαι. 17.23 καὶ ἐροῦσιν ὑμῖν, ἰδοὺ ἐκεῖ· καὶ ἰδοὺ ὧδε· μὴ ἀπέλθητε μήτε διώξητε. 17.24 ὥσπερ γὰρ ἡ ἀστραπὴ ἀστράπτουσα ἐκ τῆς ὑπὸ τὸν οὐρανὸν εἰς τὴν ὑπ' οὐρανὸν λάμπει, οὕτως ἔσται ὁ υἱὸς τοῦ ἀνθρώπου ἐν τῇ ἡμέρᾳ αὐτοῦ. 17.25 πρῶτον δὲ δεῖ αὐτὸν πολλὰ παθεῖν καὶ ἀποδοκιμασθῆναι ἀπὸ τῆς γενεᾶς ταύτης.

17.26 καὶ καθὼς ἐγένετο ἐν ταῖς ἡμέραις Νῶε, οὕτως ἔσται καὶ ἐν ταῖς ἡμέραις τοῦ υἱοῦ τοῦ ἀνθρώπου· 17.27 ἤσθιον, ἔπινον, ἐγάμουν, ἐγαμίζοντο, ἄχρι ἧς ἡμέρας εἰσῆλθεν Νῶε εἰς τὴν κιβωτόν, καὶ ἦλθεν ὁ κατακλυσμὸς καὶ ἦρεν ἅπαντας. 17.28 ὁμοίως καθὼς ἐγένετο ἐν ταῖς ἡμέραις Λώτ· ἤσθιον, ἔπινον, ἠγόραζον, ἐπώλουν, ἐφύτευον, ᾠκοδόμουν· 17.29 ᾗ δὲ ἡμέρᾳ ἐξῆλθεν Λὼτ ἀπὸ Σοδόμων, ἔβρεξεν πῦρ καὶ θῖον ἀπ' οὐρανοῦ καὶ ἀπώλεσεν ἅπαντας. 17.30 κατὰ τὰ αὐτὰ ἔσται ᾗ ἡμέρᾳ ὁ υἱὸς τοῦ ἀνθρώπου ἀποκαλύπτεται. 17.31 ἐν ἐκείνῃ τῇ ἡμέρᾳ ὃς ἔσται ἐπὶ τοῦ δώματος καὶ τὰ σκεύη αὐτοῦ ἐν τῇ οἰκίᾳ αὐτοῦ, μὴ καταβάτω ἆραι αὐτά, καὶ ὁ ἐν ἀγρῷ ὁμοίως μὴ ἐπιστρεψάτω εἰς τὰ ὀπίσω. 17.32 μνημονεύετε τῆς γυναικὸς Λώτ. 17.33 ὃς ἐὰν ζητήσῃ τὴν ψυχὴν αὐτοῦ σῶσαι ἀπολέσει αὐτήν, ὃς δ' ἂν ἀπολέσῃ ζωογονήσει αὐτήν.

17.34 λέγω ὑμῖν, ταύτῃ τῇ νυκτὶ ἔσονται δύο ἐπὶ κλίνης

giving thanks to him; and he himself was a Samaritan.
17.17   And answering, Jesus said: Were not the ten cleansed? But where *are* the nine?   17.18 Were they not found having returned to give glory/fame to God, except this (one) born of another race/tribe?   17.19 And he said to him: Having rose up, you go; your faith has saved/delivered you.

17.20   And having been asked by the Pharisees when the kingdom of God comes/is coming, answering, he said to them: The kingdom of God comes not with intent observation,   17.21 neither will they say: Behold/see here; or, there; for behold, the kingdom of God is inside of ye.   17.22 But he said to the learners/pupils: Days will come when ye will desire to see one of the days of the son of the man, and ye will not view *it*.   17.23 And they will say to ye: Behold, there; and behold, here; go ye not away nor pursue ye.   17.24 For just as the lightning flashing out of the (space) under the sky/heaven shines into the (place) under heaven, so the son of the man will be in his day. 17.25 But it is first necessary *for* him to suffer much and to be disapproved/rejected from this generation.

17.26   And even as it happened in the days of Noe/Noah, so also will it be in the days of the son of the man: 17.27 They were eating, drinking, marrying, being given in marriage, until which day Noah entered into the ark, and the flood/deluge came and destroyed all.   17.28 As it happened similarly in the days of Lot: They were eating, drinking, buying, selling, planting, building;   17.29 but in which day Lot went away from Sodom, it rained fire and sulphur from heaven and destroyed all.   17.30 It will be according to the same (things) in a day in which the son of the man is revealed.   17.31 In that day *the one* who will be upon the roof and his vessels in his house, let him not come down to take them, and the (one) in a field, likewise let him not turn back to/for the (things) behind.   17.32 Remember ye Lot's woman!   17.33 Who ever might seek to save his life/soul will lose it, but who ever will lose *it* will preserve it alive.

17.34   I say to ye, in the same night two will be on one bed/cot, the one (masculine) will be taken

μιᾶς, ὁ εἷς παραλημφθήσεται καὶ ὁ ἕτερος ἀφεθήσεται·

17.35 ἔσονται δύο ἀλήθουσαι ἐπὶ τὸ αὐτό, ἡ μία παραλημφθήσεται ἡ δὲ ἑτέρα ἀφεθήσεται.

17.37 καὶ ἀποκριθέντες λέγουσιν αὐτῷ, ποῦ, κύριε; ὁ δὲ εἶπεν αὐτοῖς, ὅπου τὸ σῶμα, ἐκεῖ καὶ οἱ ἀετοὶ ἐπισυναχθήσονται.

18.1 Ἔλεγεν δὲ παραβολὴν αὐτοῖς πρὸς τὸ δεῖν πάντοτε προσεύχεσθαι αὐτοὺς καὶ μὴ ἐνκακεῖν, 18.2 λέγων, κριτής τις ἦν ἔν τινι πόλει τὸν θεὸν μὴ φοβούμενος καὶ ἄνθρωπον μὴ ἐντρεπόμενος. 18.3 χήρα δὲ ἦν ἐν τῇ πόλει ἐκίνῃ καὶ ἤρχετο πρὸς αὐτὸν λέγουσα, ἐκδίκησόν με ἀπὸ τοῦ ἀντιδίκου μου. 18.4 καὶ οὐκ ἤθελεν ἐπὶ χρόνον, μετὰ δὲ ταῦτα εἶπεν ἐν ἑαυτῷ, εἰ καὶ τὸν θεὸν οὐ φοβοῦμαι οὐδὲ ἄνθρωπον ἐντρέπομαι, 18.5 διά γε τὸ παρέχειν μοι κόπον τὴν χήραν ταύτην ἐκδικήσω αὐτήν, ἵνα μὴ εἰς τέλος ἐρχομένη ὑπωπιάζῃ με.

18.6 εἶπεν δὲ ὁ κύριος, τί ὁ ἀκούσατε κριτὴς τῆς ἀδικίας λέγει· 18.7 ὁ δὲ θεὸς οὐ μὴ ποιήσῃ τὴν ἐκδίκησιν τῶν ἐκλεκτῶν αὐτοῦ τῶν βοώντων αὐτῷ ἡμέρας καὶ νυκτός, καὶ μακροθυμεῖ ἐπ᾽ αὐτοῖς; 18.8 λέγω ὑμῖν ὅτι ποιήσει τὴν ἐκδίκησιν αὐτῶν ἐν τάχει. πλὴν ὁ υἱὸς τοῦ ἀνθρώπου ἐλθὼν ἆρα εὑρήσει τὴν πίστιν ἐπὶ τῆς γῆς;

18.9 εἶπεν δὲ καὶ πρός τινας τοὺς πεποιθότας ἐφ᾽ ἑαυτοῖς ὅτι εἰσὶν δίκαιοι καὶ ἐξουδενοῦντας τοὺς λοιποὺς τὴν παραβολὴν ταύτην· 18.10 ἄνθρωποι δύο ἀνέβησαν εἰς τὸ ἱερὸν προσεύξασθε,

ὁ εἷς Φαρισαῖος καὶ ὁ ἕτερος τελώνης. 18.11 ὁ Φαρισαῖος σταθεὶς ταῦτα πρὸς ἑαυτὸν προσηύχετο, ὁ θεός, εὐχαριστῶ σοι ὅτι οὐκ εἰμὶ ὥσπερ οἱ λοιποὶ τῶν ἀνθρώπων, ἅρπαγες, ἄδικοι, μοιχοί, ἢ καὶ ὡς οὗτος ὁ τελώνης· 18.12 νηστεύω δὶς τοῦ σαββάτου, ἀποδεκατῶ πάντα ὅσα κτῶμαι.

along and the other/different will be left;

17.35   two will be grinding on the same (thing), the one (feminine) will be taken along but the other/different will be left.

17.37   And having considered it/answering, they say to him: Where, Lord? But the (he) said to them: Where the body *is*, there the eagles/vultures will also be gathered together.

18.1   And he was saying a parable to them toward the (thing) *for* it always to be necessary *for* them to pray and not to accuse,   18.2 saying: There was a certain judge in a certain city, not fearing God and not regarding/respecting man.   18.3   And there was a widow in that city, and she was coming to him saying: Vindicate/avenge me from my adversary.   18.4 And he was not wanting/wishing *to* over a time, but after these (things) he said in himself: If I do not even fear God, neither do I regard/respect a man,   18.5 at least because of the (thing) *for* this widow to offer/occasion toil/trouble for me, I shall vindicate/avenge her, lest, coming, she may pester/weary me to an end.

18.6   And the Lord said: Hear ye what the judge says of the injustice/wrong: 18.7   Might God by no means make the vindication/vengeance of his chosen (ones), those crying to him day and night, and be patient to/for them?   18.8   I say to ye that he will do the vindication/vengeance of them with speed. However, the son to the man having come, will he then find the faith upon/over the land/earth?

18.9   And he also said to some, those having persuaded to/for themselves that they are just, and despising/rejecting the rest/other (ones) with contempt, this parable: 18.10 Two men went up to the *outer* temple to pray, the one a Pharisee and the other/different a tax-collector.   18.11 The Pharisee having stood to/near himself was praying these (things): God, I give thanks to you because I am not like the rest of the men, greedy (ones), unjust (ones), adulterers, or even like this tax-collector;   18.12 I fast twice of/from the sabbath, I tithe all (things) as much as whatever

18.13 ὁ δὲ τελώνης μακρόθεν ἑστὼς οὐκ ἤθελεν οὐδὲ τοὺς ὀφθαλμοὺς ἐπᾶραι εἰς τὸν οὐρανόν, ἀλλ' ἔτυπτε τὸ στῆθος αὐτοῦ λέγων, ἱλάσθητί μοι τῷ ἁμαρτωλῷ.

18.14 λέγω ὑμῖν, κατέβη οὗτος δεδικαιωμένος εἰς τὸν οἶκον αὐτοῦ παρ' ἐκῖνον· ὅτι πᾶς ὁ ὑψῶν ἑαυτὸν ταπινωθήσεται, ὁ δὲ ταπινῶν ἑαυτὸν ὑψωθήσεται.

18.15 προσέφερον δὲ αὐτῷ καὶ τὰ βρέφη ἵνα αὐτῶν ἅπτηται·

ἰδόντες δὲ οἱ μαθηταὶ ἐπετίμων αὐτοῖς. 18.16 ὁ δὲ Ἰησοῦς προσεκαλέσατο αὐτὰ λέγων, ἄφετε τὰ παιδία ἔρχεσθαι πρός με καὶ μὴ κωλύετε αὐτά, τῶν γὰρ τοιούτων ἐστὶν ἡ βασιλεία τοῦ θεοῦ.

18.17 ἀμὴν λέγω ὑμῖν, ὃς ἂν μὴ δέξηται τὴν βασιλίαν τοῦ θεοῦ ὡς παιδίον, οὐ μὴ εἰσέλθῃ εἰς αὐτήν. 18.18 καὶ ἐπηρώτησέν τις αὐτὸν ἄρχων λέγων, διδάσκαλε ἀγαθέ, τί ποιήσας ζωὴν αἰώνιον κληρονομήσω;

18.19 εἶπεν δὲ αὐτῷ ὁ Ἰησοῦς, τί με λέγεις ἀγαθόν; οὐδὶς ἀγαθὸς εἰ μὴ εἷς θεός. 18.20 τὰς ἐντολὰς οἶδας· «μὴ μοιχεύσῃς, μὴ φονεύσῃς, μὴ κλέψῃς, μὴ ψευδομαρτυρήσῃς, τίμα τὸν πατέρα σου καὶ τὴν μητέρα» σου.

18.21 ὁ δὲ εἶπεν, ταῦτα πάντα ἐφύλαξα ἐκ νεότητός μου. 18.22 ἀκούσας δὲ ὁ Ἰησοῦς εἶπεν αὐτῷ, ἔτι ἕν σοι λίπει· πάντα ὅσα ἔχις πώλησον καὶ δὸς πτωχοῖς, καὶ ἕξεις θησαυρὸν ἐν οὐρανοῖς, καὶ δεῦρο ἀκολούθι μοι. 18.23 ὁ δὲ ἀκούσας ταῦτα πάντα περίλυπος ἐγενήθη, ἦν γὰρ πλούσιος σφόδρα.

18.24 ἰδὼν δὲ αὐτὸν ὁ Ἰησοῦς εἶπεν, πῶς δυσκόλως οἱ τὰ χρήματα ἔχοντες εἰς τὴν βασιλείαν τοῦ θεοῦ εἰσελεύσονται· 18.25 εὐκοπώτερον γάρ ἐστιν κάμηλον διὰ τρήματος βελόνης εἰσελθεῖν ἢ πλούσιον εἰς τὴν βασιλείαν τοῦ θεοῦ εἰσελθεῖν.

I get/acquire.

18.13   But the tax-collector/publican having stood from afar, was not wanting/wishing, nor to lift up the eyes to/into the sky, but he beat his chest, saying: Be an atonement/sin offering for me, the sinner.

18.14   I say to ye, this (one) went down to his house having been justified by/from/*instead of* that (one); because every one exalting himself will be humbled, but the (one) humbling himself will be exalted.

18.15   And they were bringing even the babies to him in order that he might touch of them;

and having seen, the learners/pupils were rebuking/warning to them.   18.16   But Jesus called to them, saying: Let/allow ye the children to come to me, and do not forbid/hinder them, for of the such is the kingdom of God.

18.17   Truly I say to ye, who ever receives not the kingdom of God like/as a child might by no means enter into it.   18.18 And a certain ruler asked him, saying: Good teacher, what having done shall I inherit eternal life?

18.19   And Jesus said to him: Why do you say/call me good? No one *is* good except one -- God.   18.20 You know the commands: YOU MIGHT NOT DO ADULTERY, YOU MIGHT NOT MURDER, YOU MIGHT NOT STEAL, YOU MIGHT NOT TESTIFY FALSELY, HONOR YOUR FATHER AND YOUR MOTHER.

18.21   And the (he) said: I guarded/kept all these (things) from my youth.   18.22 But having heard, Jesus said to him: Yet one (thing) is left for you: Sell all (things) whatever you have, and give to poor (ones), and you will have a treasure/deposit in skies/heavens, and you come, follow with me.   18.23 But the (he) having heard all these (things) was caused to become deeply grieved, for he was exceedingly wealthy/rich.

18.24   And having seen him, Jesus said: How difficultly those having the wealth/money enter into the kingdom of God;   18.25 for it is easier *for* a camel to enter through an eye of a needle than *for* a rich (one) to enter into the kingdom of God.

18.26 εἶπαν δὲ οἱ ἀκούσαντες, καὶ τίς δύναται σωθῆναι; 18.27 ὁ δὲ εἶπεν, τὰ ἀδύνατα παρὰ ἀνθρώποις δυνατὰ παρὰ τῷ θεῷ ἐστιν.

18.28 εἶπεν δὲ ὁ Πέτρος, ἰδοὺ ἡμεῖς ἀφέντες τὰ ἴδια ἠκολουθήσαμέν σοι.

18.29 ὁ δὲ εἶπεν αὐτοῖς, ἀμὴν λέγω ὑμῖν ὅτι οὐδείς ἐστιν ὃς ἀφῆκεν οἰκίαν ἢ γυναῖκα ἢ ἀδελφοὺς ἢ γονεῖς ἢ τέκνα εἴνεκεν τῆς βασιλείας τοῦ θεοῦ, 18.30 ὃς οὐχὶ μὴ ἀπολάβῃ πολλαπλασίονα ἐν τῷ καιρῷ τούτῳ καὶ ἐν τῷ αἰῶνι τῷ ἐρχομένῳ ζωὴν αἰώνιον.

18.31 παραλαβὼν δὲ τοὺς δώδεκα εἶπεν πρὸς αὐτούς, ἰδοὺ ἀναβαίνομεν εἰς Ἰερουσαλήμ, καὶ τελεσθήσεται πάντα τὰ γεγραμμένα διὰ τῶν προφητῶν τῷ υἱῷ τοῦ ἀνθρώπου·

18.32 παραδοθήσεται γὰρ τοῖς ἔθνεσιν καὶ ἐμπαιχθήσεται καὶ ὑβρισθήσεται καὶ ἐμπτυσθήσεται, 18.33 καὶ μαστιγώσαντες ἀποκτενοῦσιν αὐτόν, καὶ τῇ ἡμέρᾳ τῇ τρίτῃ ἀναστήσεται. 18.34 καὶ αὐτοὶ οὐδὲν τούτων συνῆκαν, καὶ ἦν τὸ ῥῆμα τοῦτο κεκρυμμένον ἀπ' αὐτῶν, καὶ οὐκ ἐγίνωσκον τὰ λεγόμενα.

18.35 ἐγένετο δὲ ἐν τῷ ἐγγίζειν αὐτὸν εἰς Ἰεριχὼ τυφλός τις ἐκάθητο παρὰ τὴν ὁδὸν ἐπαιτῶν. 18.36 ἀκούσας δὲ ὄχλου διαπορευομένου ἐπυνθάνετο τί εἴη τοῦτο· 18.37 ἀπήγγιλαν δὲ αὐτῷ ὅτι Ἰησοῦς ὁ Ναζωραῖος παρέρχετε. 18.38 καὶ ἐβόησεν λέγων, Ἰησοῦ, υἱὲ Δαυίδ, ἐλέησόν με.

18.39 καὶ οἱ προάγοντες ἐπετίμων αὐτῷ ἵνα σιωπήσῃ· ὁ δὲ πολλῷ μᾶλλον ἔκραζεν, Ἰησοῦ, υἱὲ Δαυίδ, ἐλέησόν με. 18.40 σταθεὶς δὲ ὁ Ἰησοῦς ἐκέλευσεν αὐτὸν ἀχθῆναι πρὸς αὐτόν. ἐγγίσαντος δὲ αὐτοῦ ἐπηρώτησεν αὐτόν, 18.41 τί σοι θέλεις ποιήσω; ὁ δὲ εἶπεν, κύριε, ἵνα ἀναβλέψω. 18.42 καὶ ὁ Ἰησοῦς εἶπεν αὐτῷ, ἀνάβλεψον· ἡ πίστις σου σέσωκέν σε. 18.43 καὶ

18.26 And those having heard said: And who is able to be saved? 18.27 And the (he) said: The (things) *being* impossible with men are possible with God.

18.28 And Peter said: Behold, we, having left all our own things, we followed with you.

18.29 And the (he) said to them: truly I say to ye that there is no one who left a house or a woman or brothers or parents or children for the sake of the kingdom of God, 18.30 who may certainly not receive back many times more in this time, and eternal life in the coming age.

18.31 And having taken along the twelve, he said to them: Behold, we go up to Jerusalem, and all the (things) having been written through the prophets for the son of the man, it will be finished/completed;

18.32 for he will be betrayed/handed over to the ethnics, and he will be mocked and insulted and spit on, 18.33 and having scourged *him* they will kill him, and he will arise on the third day. 18.34 And they themselves understood nothing of these (things), and this was the word having been hidden from them, and they knew/understood not the (things) being said.

18.35 And it happened in the (thing)/at the (time) *for* him to draw near to Jericho *that* a certain blind (one) was sitting beside the road begging. 18.36 And having heard of a crowd passing through, he was inquiring what this may be; 18.37 and they announced to him that Jesus the Nazarene passes by. 18.38 And he cried out, saying: Jesus, son of David, have mercy on me.

18.39 And the (those) preceding were rebuking/warning to him that he should be quiet; but the (he) cried out by much more: Jesus, son of David, have mercy on me. 18.40 And having been stood/stopped, Jesus ordered *for* him to be brought/led near him. And from him having drawn near, he questioned him: 18.41 What do you want/wish *that* I might do for you? And the (he) said: Lord, that I might receive sight. 18.42 And Jesus said to him: receive *your* sight; your faith has saved/delivered you. 18.43 And immediately he received sight, and he followed with him, glorifying/

παραχρῆμα ἀνέβλεψεν, καὶ ἠκολούθει αὐτῷ δοξάζων τὸν θεόν. καὶ πᾶς ὁ λαὸς ἰδὼν ἔδωκεν αἶνον τῷ θεῷ. 19.1 καὶ εἰσελθὼν διήρχετο τὴν Ἰερειχώ. 19.2 καὶ ἰδοὺ ἀνὴρ ὀνόματι καλούμενος Ζακχαῖος, καὶ αὐτὸς ἦν ἀρχιτελώνης καὶ ἦν πλούσιος. 19.3 καὶ ἐζήτει ἰδῖν τὸν Ἰησοῦν τίς ἐστιν, καὶ οὐκ ἠδύνατο ἀπὸ τοῦ ὄχλου ὅτι τῇ ἡλικίᾳ μικρὸς ἦν.

19.4 καὶ προδραμὼν εἰς τὸ ἔμπροσθεν ἀνέβη ἐπὶ συκομορέαν ἵνα τοῦ ἴδῃ αὐτόν, ὅτι ἐκείνης ἤμελλεν διέρχεσθαι. 19.5 καὶ ὡς ἦλθεν ἐπὶ τὸν τόπον, ἀναβλέψας ὁ Ἰησοῦς εἶπεν πρὸς αὐτόν, Ζακχαῖε, σπεύσας κατάβηθι, σήμερον γὰρ ἐν τῷ οἴκῳ σου δῖ με μεῖναι. 19.6 καὶ σπεύσας κατέβη, καὶ ὑπεδέξατο αὐτὸν χαίρων. 19.7 καὶ ἰδόντες πάντες διεγόγγυζον λέγοντες ὅτι παρὰ ἀνδρὶ ἁμαρτωλῷ εἰσῆλθεν καταλῦσαι. 19.8 σταθεὶς δὲ ὁ Ζακχαῖος εἶπεν πρὸς τὸν κύριον, ἰδοὺ τὰ ἡμίσιά μου τῶν ὑπαρχόντων, κύριε, τοῖς πτωχοῖς δίδωμι, καὶ εἴ τινός τι ἐσυκοφάντησα ἀποδίδωμι τετραπλοῦν.

19.9 εἶπεν δὲ πρὸς αὐτὸν ὁ Ἰησοῦς ὅτι σήμερον σωτηρία τῷ οἴκῳ τούτῳ ἐγένετο, καθότι καὶ αὐτὸς υἱὸς Ἀβραάμ ἐστιν· 19.10 ἦλθεν γὰρ ὁ υἱὸς τοῦ ἀνθρώπου ζητῆσαι καὶ σῶσαι τὸ ἀπὸ ἀπολωλός. 19.11 ἀκουόντων δὲ αὐτῶν ταῦτα προσθεὶς εἶπεν παραβολὴν διὰ τὸ ἐγγὺς εἶναι Ἰερουσαλὴμ αὐτὸν καὶ δοκεῖν αὐτοὺς ὅτι παραχρῆμα ἡ βασιλεία τοῦ θεοῦ μέλλει ἀναφαίνεσθαι.

19.12 εἶπεν οὖν, ἄνθρωπός τις εὐγενὴς ἐπορεύθη εἰς χώραν μακρὰν λαβεῖν ἑαυτῷ βασιλείαν καὶ ὑποστρέψαι. 19.13 καλέσας δὲ δέκα δούλους ἑαυτοῦ ἔδωκεν αὐτοῖς δέκα μνᾶς

καὶ εἶπεν πρὸς αὐτούς, πραγματεύσασθαι ἐν ᾧ ἔρχομαι. 19.14 οἱ δὲ πολεῖται αὐτοῦ ἐμίσουν αὐτόν, καὶ ἀπέστιλαν πρεσβείαν ὀπίσω αὐτοῦ λέγοντες, οὐ θέλομεν τοῦτον βασιλεῦσαι ἐφ᾿ ἡμᾶς. 19.15 καὶ ἐγένετο ἐν τῷ ἐπανελθῖν αὐτὸν λαβόντα τὴν

praising God. And all the people having seen gave praise to God. 19.1 And having entered, he was passing through Jericho. 19.2 And behold, a man by name being called Zacchaeus, and he himself was a chief tax-collector, and he was rich. 19.3 And he was seeking to see Jesus, who he is, and he was not able from the crowd, because he was small in stature.

19.4 And having run ahead to the (place) in front of (him), he went up on a sycamore tree, in order that of the (thing) *for* him to see, because of that he was being about to pass through. 19.5 And as he came upon/to the place, having looked up, Jesus said to him: Zacchaeus, making haste, come down, for today it is necessary *for* me to stay in your house. 19.6 And making haste he came down, and he welcomed him/received him as a guest, rejoicing. 19.7 And having seen, all (men) were murmuring/grumbling, saying: He went in to lodge with/beside a sinful man. 19.8 And having stood up, Zacchaeus said to the Lord: Behold, the half of my goods/possessions, Lord, I shall give to the poor (ones), and if I extorted anything from anyone by false information, I shall repay *it* fourfold.

19.9 And Jesus said to him: Salvation came about/became for this house today, because he himself is also a son of Abraham; 19.10 for the son of the man came to seek and to save the (thing)/that from having been lost. 19.11 And from them hearing these (things) having been added, he spoke a parable on account of the (thing) *for* him to be near Jerusalem and *for* them to think that the kingdom of God was about to appear soon/immediately.

19.12 Therefore he said: A certain well-born/high-born man went/journeyed to a far country to receive a kingdom for himself and to return. 19.13 And having called ten slaves of himself he gave ten minas to them,

and he said to them: Ye engage in business in (time) which I am gone. 19.14 But his citizens were hating him, and they sent an ambassador after/behind him, saying: We want/wish not *for* this (one) to reign over us. 19.15 And it came about at the (time) *for*

173

βασιλείαν καὶ εἶπεν φωνηθῆναι αὐτῷ τοὺς δούλους τούτους οἷς δεδώκει τὸ ἀργύριον, ἵνα γνοῖ τί διεπραγματεύσαντο. 19.16 παρεγένετο δὲ ὁ πρῶτος λέγων, κύριε, ἡ μνᾶ σου δέκα προσηργάσατο μνᾶς. 19.17 καὶ εἶπεν αὐτῷ, εὖ, δοῦλε ἀγαθέ, ὅτι ἐν ἐλαχίστῳ πιστὸς ἐγένου, ἴσθι ἐξουσίαν ἔχων ἐπάνω δέκα πόλεων. 19.18 καὶ ἦλθεν ὁ δεύτερος λέγων, ἡ μνᾶ σου, κύριε, ἐποίησεν πέντε μνᾶς. 19.19 εἶπεν δὲ καὶ τούτῳ, καὶ σὺ ἐπάνω γείνου πέντε πόλεων.

19.20 καὶ ὁ ἕτερος ἦλθεν λέγων, κύριε, ἰδοὺ ἡ μνᾶ σου ἣν εἶχον ἀποκειμένην ἐν σουδαρίῳ· 19.21 ἐφοβούμην γάρ σε, ὅτι ἄνθρωπος αὐστηρὸς εἶ, αἴρις ὃ οὐκ ἔθηκας καὶ θερίζεις ὃ οὐκ ἔσπιρας. 19.22 λέγει αὐτῷ, ἐκ τοῦ στόματός σου κρίνω σε, πονηρὲ δοῦλε. ᾔδις ὅτι ἐγὼ ἄνθρωπος αὐστηρός εἰμι, αἴρων ὃ οὐκ ἔθηκα καὶ θερίζων ὃ οὐκ ἔσπιρα; 19.23 καὶ διὰ τί οὐκ ἔδωκάς μου τὸ ἀργύριον ἐπὶ τράπεζαν; κἀγὼ ἐλθὼν σὺν τόκῳ ἂν αὐτὸ ἔπραξα. 19.24 καὶ τοῖς παρεστῶσιν εἶπεν, ἄρατε ἀπ' αὐτοῦ τὴν μνᾶν καὶ δότε τῷ τὰς δέκα μνᾶς ἔχοντι 19.25 καὶ εἶπαν αὐτῷ, κύριε, ἔχει δέκα μνᾶς 19.26 λέγω ὑμῖν ὅτι παντὶ τῷ ἔχοντι δοθήσεται, ἀπὸ δὲ τοῦ μὴ ἔχοντος καὶ ὃ ἔχει ἀρθήσεται. 19.27 πλὴν τοὺς ἐχθρούς μου τούτους τοὺς μὴ θελήσαντάς με βασιλεῦσαι ἐπ' αὐτοὺς ἀγάγετε ὧδε καὶ κατασφάξετε αὐτοὺς ἔμπροσθέν μου. 19.28 καὶ εἰπὼν ταῦτα ἐπορεύετο ἔμπροσθεν ἀναβαίνων εἰς Ἱεροσόλυμα. 19.29 καὶ ἐγένετο ὡς ἤγγισεν εἰς Βηθφαγὴ καὶ Βηθανίαν πρὸς τὸ ὄρος τὸ καλούμενον ἐλεῶν,

ἀπέστιλεν δύο τῶν μαθητῶν 19.30 λέγων, ὑπάγετε εἰς τὴν κατέναντι κώμην, ἐν ᾗ εἰσπορευόμενοι εὑρήσετε πῶλον δεδεμένον, ἐφ' ὃν οὐδὶς πώποτε ἀνθρώπων ἐκάθισεν, λύσαντες αὐτὸν ἀγάγετε.

19.31 καὶ ἐάν τις ὑμᾶς ἐρωτᾷ, διὰ τί λύετε; οὕτως ἐρεῖτε ὅτι ὁ κύριος αὐτοῦ χρείαν ἔχει. 19.32 ἀπελθόντες δὲ οἱ ἀπεσταλμένοι

him having received the kingdom to return, and he said to him *for* these slaves to whom he had given the silver/money to be called, in order that he may know what they did through trading. 19.16 And the first arrived, saying: Lord, your mina added ten minas in trading. 19.17 And he said to him: Well, good slave, because you became faithful in a least (thing), be you (one) having authority over ten cities. 19.18 And the second came, saying: Your mina. Lord, made five minas. 19.19 And he said also to this (one): And you, become you over five cities.

19.20 And the other/different came, saying: Lord, behold your mina, which I had laid away/up in a napkin; 19.21 for I was fearing you, because you are a severe/austere man, you take up what you laid not and you reap what you sowed not. 19.22 He says to him: I shall judge you out of/from your mouth, evil/-wicked slave. Did you know that I, I am a severe/aus-tere man, taking up what I laid not and reaping what I sowed not? 19.23 And why did you not give my silver/-money on a table *of a money changer*? And I, having come, would collect it with interest. 19.24 And he said to those having been present: Take ye the mina from him and give *it* to the one having the ten minas. -- 19.25 And they said to him: Lord, he has ten minas! -- 19.26 I say to ye that *it* will be given to every one having, but from the (one) having not, even what he has will be taken. 19.27 Nevertheless, bring ye here my enemies, these (men) not wanting *for* me to reign over them, and slaughter them before/in front of me. 19.28 And having said/told these (things), he was going before/in front of *them*, going up to Jerusalem. 19.29 And it happened as he drew near to Bethphage and Bethany, toward the mountain, the (one) being called of olives, *that*

he sent two of the learners/pupils, 19.30 say-ing: Go ye into the opposite village, in which going into ye will find a colt having been tied, on which no one of men ever sat, having loosed him, bring ye *him*.

19.31 And if anyone may ask ye: Why do ye loose *it*? Ye will thus say: Because the Lord has a need of him. 19.32 And having gone away, those having been

εὗρον καθὼς εἶπεν αὐτοῖς. 19.33 λυόντων δὲ αὐτῶν τὸν πῶλον εἶπαν οἱ κύριοι αὐτοῦ πρὸς αὐτούς, τί λύετε τὸν πῶλον; 19.34 οἱ δὲ εἶπαν ὅτι ὁ κύριος αὐτοῦ χρίαν ἔχει. 19.35 καὶ ἤγαγον αὐτὸν πρὸς τὸν Ἰησοῦν, καὶ ἐπιρίψαντες αὐτῶν τὰ ἱμάτια ἐπὶ τὸν πῶλον ἐπεβίβασαν τὸν Ἰησοῦν. 19.36 πορευομένου δὲ αὐτοῦ ὑπεστρώννυον τὰ ἱμάτια αὐτῶν ἐν τῇ ὁδῷ.

19.37 ἐγγίζοντος δὲ αὐτοῦ ἤδη πρὸς τῇ καταβάσει τοῦ ὄρους τῶν ἐλαιῶν ἤρξαντο ἅπαν τὸ πλῆθος τῶν μαθητῶν χαίροντες αἰνῖν τὸν θεὸν φωνῇ μεγάλῃ περὶ πασῶν ὧν εἶδον δυνάμεων, 19.38 λέγοντες, « εὐλογημένος ὁ ἐρχόμενος» βασιλεὺς «ἐν ὀνόματι κυρίου» ἐν οὐρανῷ ἰρήνη καὶ δόξα ἐν ὑψίστοις. 19.39 καί τινες τῶν Φαρισαίων ἀπὸ τοῦ ὄχλου εἶπαν πρὸς αὐτόν, διδάσκαλε, ἐπιτίμησον τοῖς μαθηταῖς σου.

19.40 καὶ ἀποκριθεὶς εἶπεν, λέγω ὑμῖν ὅτι ἐὰν οὗτοι σιωπήσουσιν, οἱ λίθοι κράξουσιν. 19.41 καὶ ὡς ἤγγισεν, ἰδὼν τὴν πόλιν ἔκλαυσεν ἐπ᾽ αὐτήν, 19.42 λέγων ὅτι εἰ ἔγνως ἐν τῇ ἡμέρᾳ ταύτῃ καὶ σὺ τὰ πρὸς ἰρήνην νῦν δὲ ἐκρύβη ἀπὸ ὀφθαλμῶν σου. 19.43 ὅτι ἥξουσιν ἡμέραι ἐπὶ σὲ καὶ παρεμβαλοῦσιν οἱ ἐχθροί σου χάρακά σοι καὶ περικυκλώσουσίν σε καὶ συνέξουσίν σε πάντοθεν, 19.44 καὶ ἐδαφιοῦσίν σε καὶ τὰ τέκνα σου ἐν σοί, καὶ οὐκ ἀφήσουσιν λίθον ἐπὶ λίθον ἐν σοί, ἀνθ᾽ ὧν οὐκ ἔγνως τὸν καιρὸν τῆς ἐπισκοπῆς σου.

19.45 καὶ εἰσελθὼν εἰς τὸ ἱερὸν ἤρξατο ἐκβάλλειν τοὺς πωλοῦντας, 19.46 λέγων αὐτοῖς, γέγραπται, «καὶ ἔσται ὁ οἶκός μου οἶκος προσευχῆς,»

ὑμεῖς δὲ αὐτὸν ἐποιήσατε σπήλαιον ληστῶν. 19.47 καὶ ἦν διδάσκων τὸ καθ᾽ ἡμέραν ἐν τῷ ἱερῷ. οἱ δὲ ἀρχιερεῖς καὶ οἱ γραμματεῖς ἐξήτουν αὐτὸν ἀπολέσε καὶ οἱ πρῶτοι τοῦ λαοῦ· 19.48 καὶ οὐχ εὕρισκον τὸ τί ποιήσωσιν, ὁ λαὸς γὰρ ἅπας ἐξεκρέμετο αὐτοῦ ἀκούων.

sent found *it* even as he said to them. 19.33 But of them loosing the colt, the lords of him/it said to them: Why do ye loose the colt? 19.34 And they said: Because the Lord has a need of him. 19.35 And they led him to Jesus, and having thrown their garments upon the colt, they mounted Jesus on *it*. 19.36 And from him going, they were spreading their garments in the road/on the way.

19.37 And of him now drawing near to the desert from the mountain of the olives, all the multitude of the learners/pupils, rejoicing, began to praise God with a great sound/voice about all the powers which they saw, 19.38 saying: HAVING BEEN BLESSED/PRAISED *is* THE (ONE) COMING, a king IN *the* NAME OF *the* LORD; peace *be* in heaven and glory/fame in highest (places). 19.39 And some of the Pharisees from the crowd said to him: Teacher, rebuke/give warning to your learners/pupils.

19.40 And answering he said: I say to ye that if these should be silent, the stones will cry out. 19.41 And as he drew near, having seen the city, he wept/lamented over her, 19.42 saying: You, if you even knew the (things) toward peace in this day, -- but now they were hidden from you eyes. 19.43 Because days will arrive upon you, and your enemies will mount/muster a palisade to you and they will surround you and besiege/press upon you from all sides, 19.44 and will level/raze you to the ground and your children with you, and will not leave a stone upon a stone in you, on account of which you knew/recognized not the time of your visitation.

19.45 And having gone into the *outer* temple he began to throw out/expel those selling, 19.46 saying to them: It has been written: AND MY HOUSE WILL BE A HOUSE OF PRAYER,

but ye, ye made it a cave/hideout of robbers. 19.47 And he was teaching the (thing) day by day in the *outer* temple. But the high priests and the scribes and the first (ones) of the people were seeking to destroy him; 19.48 and they were not finding the (thing) which they might do, for all the people were earnestly hearing from him.

20.1 καὶ ἐγένετο ἐν μιᾷ τῶν ἡμερῶν διδάσκοντος αὐτοῦ τὸν λαὸν ἐν τῷ ἱερῷ καὶ εὐαγγελιζομένου ἐπέστησαν οἱ ἀρχιερεῖς καὶ οἱ γραμματεῖς σὺν τοῖς πρεσβυτέροις, 20.2 καὶ εἶπαν λέγοντες πρὸς αὐτόν, εἰπὸν μῖν ἐν ποίᾳ ἐξουσίᾳ ταῦτα ποιεῖς, ἢ τίς ἐστιν ὁ δούς σοι τὴν ἐξουσίαν ταύτην. 20.3 ἀποκριθεὶς δὲ εἶπεν πρὸς αὐτούς, ἐρωτήσω ὑμᾶς κἀγὼ λόγον, καὶ εἴπατέ μοι· 20.4 τὸ βάπτισμα τὸ Ἰωάννου ἐξ οὐρανοῦ ἦν ἢ ἐξ ἀνθρώπων; 20.5 οἱ δὲ συνελογίζοντο πρὸς ἑαυτοὺς λέγοντες ὅτι ἐὰν εἴπωμεν, ἐξ οὐρανοῦ, ἐρεῖ, διὰ τί οὐκ ἐπιστεύσατε αὐτῷ; 20.6 ἐὰν δὲ εἴπωμεν, ἐξ ἀνθρώπων, ὁ λαὸς ἅπας καταλιθάσει ἡμᾶς, πεπεισμένος γάρ ἐστιν Ἰωάννην προφήτην εἶναι. 20.7 καὶ ἀπεκρίθησαν μὴ εἰδέναι πόθεν.

20.8 καὶ ὁ Ἰησοῦς εἶπεν αὐτοῖς, οὐδὲ ἐγὼ λέγω ὑμῖν ἐν ποίᾳ ἐξουσίᾳ ταῦτα ποιῶ.

20.9 ἤρξατο δὲ πρὸς τὸν λαὸν λέγειν τὴν παραβολὴν ταύτην·

ἄνθρωπός ἐφύτευσεν ἀμπελῶνα, καὶ ἐξέδοτο αὐτὸν γεωργοῖς, καὶ ἀπεδήμησεν χρόνους ἱκανούς. 20.10 καὶ καιρῷ ἀπέστιλεν πρὸς τοὺς γεωργοὺς δοῦλον, ἵνα ἀπὸ τοῦ καρποῦ τοῦ ἀμπελῶνος δώσουσιν αὐτῷ·

οἱ δὲ γεωργοὶ ἐξαπέστιλαν αὐτὸν δίραντες καινόν. 20.11 καὶ προσέθετο ἕτερον πέμψαι δοῦλον· οἱ δὲ κἀκῖνον δίραντες καὶ ἀτιμάσαντες ἐξαπέστιλαν καινόν. 20.12 καὶ προσέθετο τρίτον πέμψαι· οἱ δὲ καὶ τοῦτον τραυματίσαντες ἐξέβαλον.

20.13 εἶπεν δὲ ὁ κύριος τοῦ ἀμπελῶνος, τί ποιήσω; πέμψω τὸν υἱόν μου τὸν ἀγαπητόν· ἴσως τοῦτον ἐντραπήσονται. 20.14 ἰδόντες δὲ αὐτὸν οἱ γεωργοὶ διελογίζοντο πρὸς ἀλλήλους λέγοντες, οὗτός ἐστιν ὁ κληρονόμος· δεῦτε, ἀποκτίνωμεν αὐτόν, ἵνα ἡμῶν γένηται ἡ κληρονομία. 20.15 καὶ ἐκβαλόντες αὐτὸν ἔξω τοῦ ἀμπελῶνος ἀπέκτιναν.

τί οὖν ποιήσει αὐτοῖς ὁ κύριος τοῦ ἀμπελῶνος; 20.16 ἐλεύσεται καὶ ἀπολέσει τοὺς γεωργοὺς τούτους, καὶ δώσει τὸν

20.1 And it happened on one of the days of him teaching the people in the *outer* temple and announcing the good message/gospel *that* the high priests and the scribes came upon *him* with the elders, 20.2 and they spoke to him, saying: Say to us by what authority you do these (things), or who is the (one) giving this authority to you. 20.3 And answering, he said to them: Also I, I shall ask ye a word/reason, and ye say to me: 20.4 The baptism of John, was it from heaven or from men? 20.5 And they reasoned with themselves, saying: If we should say: From heaven, he will say: Why did ye not believe in him? 20.6 But if we should say: From men, all the people will stone us, for *the people* is/are having been persuaded *for* John to be a prophet. 20.7 And they answered to know not from where.

20.8 And Jesus said to them: I, neither say I to ye by what authority I do these (things).

20.9 And he began to speak this parable to the people:

A man planted a vineyard, and leased it out to farmers, and he journeyed away *for* considerable times. 20.10 And in season/at a season he sent a slave to the farmers, in order that they will give from the fruit of the vineyard to him;

but the farmers, having beat him, sent *him* out empty. 20.11 And he added another/different slave to send; but they, having beat and dishonored that one also, they sent *him* out empty. 20.12 And he added a third (one) to send; but they, also having wounded this (one), they threw *him* out.

20.13 And the lord of the vineyard said: What should I do? I shall send my beloved son; they will respect/regard him equally. 20.14 But having seen him, the farmers were reasoning to one another, saying: This (one) is the heir; come, let us kill him, in order that the inheritance may become ours. 20.15 And having thrown him outside the vineyard, they killed *him*.

What therefore will the lord of the vineyard do to them? 20.16 He will come and destroy these farmers, and he will give the vineyard to others. And

ἀμπελῶνα ἄλλοις. ἀκούσαντες δὲ εἶπαν, μὴ γένοιτο. 20.17 ὁ δὲ ἐμβλέψας αὐτοῖς εἶπεν, τί οὖν ἐστιν τὸ γεγραμμένον τοῦτο· « λίθον ὃν ἀπεδοκίμασαν οἱ οἰκοδομοῦντες, οὗτος ἐγενήθη εἰς κεφαλὴν γωνίας;» 20.18 πᾶς ὁ πεσὼν ἐπ' ἐκῖνον τὸν λίθον συνθλασθήσεται· ἐφ' ὃν δ' ἂν πέσῃ, λικμήσει αὐτόν. 20.19 καὶ ἐζήτησαν οἱ ἀρχιερεῖς καὶ οἱ γραμματεῖς ἐπιβαλεῖν ἐπ' αὐτὸν τὰς χῖρας ἐν αὐτῇ τῇ ὥρᾳ, καὶ ἐφοβήθησαν τὸν λαόν· ἔγνωσαν γὰρ ὅτι πρὸς αὐτοὺς εἶπεν τὴν παραβολὴν ταύτην. 20.20 καὶ παρατηρήσαντες ἀπέστιλαν ἐγκαθέτους ὑποκρινομένους ἑαυτοὺς δικαίους εἶναι, ἵνα ἐπιλάβωνται αὐτοῦ λόγου, ὥστε παραδοῦναι αὐτὸν τῇ ἀρχῇ καὶ ἐξουσίᾳ τοῦ ἡγεμόνος.

20.21 καὶ ἐπηρώτησαν αὐτὸν λέγοντες, διδάσκαλε, οἴδαμεν ὅτι ὀρθῶς λέγεις καὶ διδάσκις καὶ οὐ λαμβάνεις πρόσωπον, ἀλλ' ἐπ' ἀληθείας τὴν ὁδὸν τοῦ θεοῦ διδάσκις· 20.22 ἔξεστιν ἡμᾶς Καίσαρι φόρον δοῦναι ἢ οὔ; 20.23 κατανοήσας δὲ αὐτῶν τὴν πανουργίαν εἶπεν πρὸς αὐτούς, 20.24 δείξατέ μοι δηνάριον· οἱ δὲ ἔδειξαν αὐτῷ καὶ εἶπαν, τίνος ἔχει εἰκόνα καὶ ἐπιγραφήν; οἱ δὲ εἶπαν, Καίσαρος.

20.25 ὁ δὲ εἶπεν πρὸς αὐτούς, τοίνυν ἀπόδοτε τὰ Καίσαρος Καίσαρι καὶ τὰ τοῦ θεοῦ τῷ θεῷ. 20.26 καὶ οὐκ ἴσχυσαν ἐπιλαβέσθαι τοῦ ῥήματος ἐναντίον τοῦ λαοῦ, καὶ θαυμάσαντες ἐπὶ τῇ ἀποκρίσει αὐτοῦ ἐσίγησαν.

20.27 προσελθόντες δέ τινες τῶν Σαδδουκαίων, οἱ λέγοντες ἀνάστασιν μὴ εἶναι, ἐπηρώτησαν αὐτὸν 20.28 λέγοντες, διδάσκαλε, Μωσῆς ἔγραψεν ἡμῖν, «ἐάν τινος ἀδελφὸς ἀποθάνῃ» ἔχων γυναῖκα, «καὶ οὗτος ἄτεκνος ᾖ,» ἵνα «λάβῃ ὁ ἀδελφὸς αὐτοῦ τὴν γυναῖκα καὶ ἐξαναστήσῃ σπέρμα τῷ ἀδελφῷ αὐτοῦ.» 20.29 ἑπτὰ οὖν ἀδελφοὶ ἦσαν· καὶ ὁ πρῶτος λαβὼν γυναῖκα ἀπέθανεν ἄτεκνος· 20.30 καὶ ὁ δεύτερος 20.31 καὶ ὁ τρίτος ἔλαβεν αὐτήν, ὡσαύτως δὲ καὶ οἱ ἑπτὰ οὐ κατέλιπον τέκνα καὶ ἀπέθανον. 20.32 ὕστερον καὶ ἡ γυνὴ ἀπέθανεν. 20.33 ἐν τῇ οὖν ἀναστάσι τίνος αὐτῶν ἔσται γυνή; οἱ γὰρ ἑπτὰ

having heard, they said: May it not happen!   20.17 And the (he), having looked carefully at them, he said: Then what is this thing having been written: A STONE WHICH THOSE BUILDING REJECTED, THIS (ONE) CAME TO BE IN A HEAD OF A CORNER?   20.18 Every one falling on that stone will be broken in pieces; and on who ever it might fall, it will scatter him like chaff.   20.19 And in the same hour, the high priests and the scribes sought to lay the hands upon him, and they feared the people; for they knew that he spoke this parable to/toward them.   20.20 And having observed carefully, they sent bribed (men) pretending *for* themselves to be just (ones), in order that they might take hold of a saying/word from him, so as to betray/deliver him over to the rule and authority of the governor.

20.21   And they questioned him, saying: Teacher, we know that you speak and teach correctly and you receive not a face, but you teach the way/road of God on *the basis* of truth;   20.22 is it lawful *for* us to give tribute to Caesar, or not?   20.23 And having perceived their shrewdness, he said to them: 20.24 Show to me a denarius; and they showed (one) to him, and he said: of whom has it an image and inscription? And they said: Of Caesar.

20.25   And the (he) said to them: Then render ye the (things) of Caesar to Caesar and the (things) of God to God.   20.26 And they were not able to take hold of the word/rhetoric before the people, and marveling/wondering at his answer, they were silent.

20.27   And having come near, some of the Sadducees, those saying *for* a resurrection not to be, questioned him,   20.28 saying: Teacher, Moses wrote for us: IF ANYONE'S BROTHER MIGHT DIE, having a woman, AND THIS (MAN) MAY BE WITHOUT A CHILD, that HIS BROTHER MIGHT TAKE THE WOMAN AND MIGHT RAISE UP A SEED/OFFSPRING FOR HIS BROTHER.   20.29 Therefore, there were seven brothers; and the first, having taken a woman, died childless;   20.30 both the second   20.31 and the third took her, and likewise also the seven left not a child and died.   20.32 Afterwards, the woman also died.   20.33 Therefore, in/at the resurrection, of which of them will she be a woman? For seven had her a

ἔσχον αὐτὴν γυναῖκα. 20.34 καὶ εἶπεν αὐτοῖς ὁ Ἰησοῦς, οἱ υἱοὶ τοῦ αἰῶνος τούτου γαμοῦσι καὶ γαμίσκονται, 20.35 οἱ δὲ καταξιωθέντες τοῦ αἰῶνος ἐκείνου τυχεῖν καὶ τῆς ἀναστάσεως τῆς ἐκ νεκρῶν οὔτε γαμοῦσιν οὔτε γαμίζονται· 20.36 οὐτὲ γὰρ ἀποθανῖν ἔτι δύνανται, ἰσάγγελοι γάρ εἰσιν, καὶ υἱοί θεοῦ εἰσιν, τῆς ἀναστάσεως υἱοὶ ὄντες. 20.37 ὅτι δὲ ἐγείρονται οἱ νεκροὶ καὶ Μωσῆς ἐμήνυσεν ἐπὶ τῆς βάτου, ὡς λέγει «κύριον τὸν θεὸν Ἀβραὰμ καὶ θεὸν Ἰσαὰκ καὶ θεὸν Ἰακώβ» 20.38 θεὸς δὲ οὐκ ἔστιν νεκρῶν ἀλλὰ ζώντων, πάντες γὰρ αὐτῷ ζῶσιν.

20.39 ἀποκριθέντες δέ τινες τῶν γραμματέων εἶπαν αὐτῷ, διδάσκαλε, καλῶς εἶπας· 20.40 οὐκέτι γὰρ ἐτόλμων ἐπερωτᾶν αὐτὸν οὐδέν. 20.41 εἶπεν δὲ πρὸς αὐτούς, πῶς λέγουσι τὸν χριστὸν εἶναι Δαυὶδ υἱόν; 20.42 αὐτὸς γὰρ Δαυὶδ λέγει ἐν βίβλῳ ψαλμῶν, «εἶπεν ὁ κύριος τῷ κυρίῳ μου, κάθου ἐκ δεξιῶν μου 20.43 ἕως ἂν θῶ τοὺς ἐχθρούς σου ὑποπόδιον τῶν ποδῶν σου.» 20.44 Δαυὶδ οὖν κύριον αὐτὸν καλεῖ, καὶ πῶς υἱός αὐτοῦ ἐστιν;

20.45 ἀκούοντος δὲ παντὸς τοῦ λαοῦ εἶπεν τοῖς μαθηταῖς αὐτοῦ, 20.46 προσέχετε ἀπὸ τῶν γραμματέων τῶν θελόντων ἐν στολαῖς περιπατεῖν

καὶ φιλούντων ἀσπασμοὺς ἐν ταῖς ἀγοραῖς καὶ πρωτοκαθεδρίας ἐν ταῖς συναγωγαῖς καὶ πρωτοκλισίας ἐν τοῖς δίπνοις, 20.47 οἳ κατεσθίουσι τὰς οἰκίας τῶν χηρῶν καὶ προφάσει μακρὰ προσεύχονται· οὗτοι λήμψονται περισσότερον κρίμα. 21.1 ἀναβλέψας δὲ εἶδεν τοὺς βάλλοντας εἰς τὸ γαζοφυλάκιον τὰ δῶρα αὐτῶν πλουσίους. 21.2 εἶδεν δέ τινα χήραν πενιχρὰν βάλλουσαν ἐκεῖ λεπτὰ δύο,

21.3 καὶ εἶπεν, ἀληθῶς λέγω ὑμῖν ὅτι ἡ χήρα αὕτη ἡ πτωχὴ πλέον πάντων ἔβαλεν· 21.4 πάντες γὰρ οὗτοι ἐκ τοῦ περισσεύοντος αὐτοῖς ἔβαλον εἰς τὰ δῶρα, αὕτη δὲ ἐκ τοῦ

woman. 20.34 And Jesus said to them: The sons of this age marry and are given in marriage, 20.35 but those having been considered worthy to obtain/enjoy of that age and of the resurrection out of dead (ones) neither marry not are given in marriage; 20.36 for they are not even able to die, for they are like messengers/angels, and they are sons of God, being sons from the resurrection. 20.37 But that the dead (ones) are raised, even Moses indicated at the time of the bush, since he says: THE LORD GOD OF ABRAHAM AND GOD OF ISAAC AND GOD OF JACOB; 20.38 but he is not God of dead (ones) but of living (ones), for all live for him.

20.39 And answering, some of the scribes said to him: Teacher, you spoke well; 20.40 for they were no longer daring to question him *for* nothing. 20.41 And he said to them: How do they say *for* the anointed (one) to be David's son? 20.42 For David himself says in a scroll of psalms: THE LORD SAID TO MY LORD: SIT (YOU) FROM MY RIGHT (HAND)/OUT OF MY RIGHT (ONES) 20.43 UNTIL I WOULD PLACE YOUR ENEMIES A FOOTSTOOL OF YOU FEET. 20.44 David therefore speaks/calls him lord, and how is he his son?

20.45 And from all the people hearing, he said to his learners/pupils: 20.46 Beware ye/take heed from the scribes, the (ones) wanting/wishing to walk around in long robes,

and loving greetings in/at the markets and chief seats in/among the congregations and chief couches at the dinners/suppers, 20.47 who devour the houses/households of the widows and pray a long (prayer) by pretext; they themselves will receive more abundant/greater judgment. 21.1 And having looked carefully, he saw the wealthy (ones) putting their gifts into the contribution box/receptacle. 21.2 And he saw a certain widow, one who works for her bread, putting two lepta there,

21.3 and he said: Truly I say to ye that this poor widow put more than all; 21.4 for all these put in the gifts out of the (thing) being abundant/excess to them, but this (woman), she put all the living/livelihood which she was having out of her deficien-

178

ὑστερήματος αὐτῆς πάντα τὸν βίον ὃν εἶχεν ἔβαλεν. 21.5 καί τινων λεγόντων περὶ τοῦ ἱεροῦ, ὅτι λίθοις καλοῖς καὶ ἀναθέμασιν κεκόσμηται, εἶπεν, 21.6 ταῦτα ἃ θεωρεῖτε, ἐλεύσονται ἡμέραι ἐν αἷς οὐκ ἀφεθήσεται λίθος ἐπὶ λίθῳ ὧδε ὃς οὐ καταλυθήσεται. 21.7 ἐπηρώτησαν δὲ αὐτὸν λέγοντες, διδάσκαλε, πότε οὖν ταῦτα ἔσται, καὶ τί τὸ σημῖον ὅταν μέλλῃ ταῦτα γείνεσθαι; 21.8 ὁ δὲ εἶπεν, βλέπετε μὴ πλανηθῆτε· πολλοὶ γὰρ ἐλεύσονται ἐπὶ τῷ ὀνόματί μου λέγοντες, ἐγώ εἰμι· καί, ὁ καιρὸς ἤγγικεν· μὴ πορευθῆται ὀπίσω αὐτῶν.

21.9 ὅταν δὲ ἀκούσηται πολέμους καὶ ἀκαταστασίας, μὴ πτοηθῆτε· δεῖ γὰρ ταῦτα γενέσθαι πρῶτον, ἀλλ' οὐκ εὐθέως τὸ τέλος. 21.10 τότε ἔλεγεν αὐτοῖς, ἐγερθήσετε ἔθνος ἐπ' ἔθνος καὶ βασιλεία ἐπὶ βασιλείαν, 21.11 σεισμοί τε μεγάλοι καὶ κατὰ τόπους λειμοὶ καὶ λοιμοὶ ἔσονται, φόβητρά τε καὶ σημῖα μεγάλα ἀπ' οὐρανοῦ ἔσται. 21.12 πρὸ δὲ τούτων πάντων ἐπιβαλοῦσιν ἐφ' ὑμᾶς τὰς χῖρας αὐτῶν καὶ διώξουσιν, παραδιδόντες εἰς τὰς συναγωγὰς καὶ φυλακάς, ἀπαγομένους ἐπὶ βασιλεῖς καὶ ἡγεμόνας ἕνεκεν τοῦ ὀνόματός μου· 21.13 ἀποβήσεται ὑμῖν εἰς μαρτύριον. 21.14 θέτε οὖν ἐν ταῖς καρδίαις ὑμῶν μὴ προμελετᾶν ἀπολογηθῆναι,

21.15 ἐγὼ γὰρ δώσω ὑμῖν στόμα καὶ σοφίαν ᾗ οὐ δυνήσονται ἀντιστῆναι ἢ ἀντειπῖν πάντες οἱ ἀντικείμενοι ὑμῖν. 21.16 παραδοθήσεσθε δὲ καὶ ὑπὸ γονέων καὶ ἀδελφῶν καὶ συγγενῶν καὶ φίλων, καὶ θανατώσουσιν ἐξ ὑμῶν, 21.17 καὶ ἔσεσθαι μισούμενοι ὑπὸ πάντων διὰ τὸ ὄνομά μου. 21.18 καὶ θρὶξ ἐκ τῆς κεφαλῆς ὑμῶν οὐ μὴ ἀπόληται. 21.19 ἐν τῇ ὑπομονῇ ὑμῶν κτήσασθαι τὰς ψυχὰς ὑμῶν. 21.20 ὅταν δὲ ἴδητε κυκλουμένην ὑπὸ στρατοπαίδων Ἰερουσαλήμ, τότε γνῶτε ὅτι ἤγγικεν ἡ ἐρήμωσις αὐτῆς.

21.21 τότε οἱ ἐν τῇ Ἰουδαίᾳ φευγέτωσαν εἰς τὰ ὄρη, καὶ οἱ

cy/poverty.   21.5 And from some speaking about the *outer* temple, that it has been adorned/decorated with beautiful stones and devoted things, he said: 21.6 These (things) which ye behold, days will come in which there will not be left here a stone upon a stone which will not be thrown down.   21.7 And they questioned him, saying: Teacher, when then will these (things) *be*, and what *is* the sign when these things are about to happen? 21.8   And the (he) said: Beware/ see ye lest ye might be led astray; for many will come at/upon my name, saying: I, I am; and: The time has drawn near; go ye not after them.

21.9   And whenever ye might hear wars and insurrections, be ye not terrified; for it is necessary *for* these (things) to happen first, but the end *is* not immediate/soon.   21.10 Then he was saying to them: Ethnic will be raised up against ethnic and kingdom against kingdom,   21.11 both great earthquakes and famines and pestilences will be according to places/by place to place, there will be both things inspiring terror and great signs from heaven.   21.12 But before all these (things), they will lay their hands upon ye and they will prosecute *ye*, being delivered over/betrayed into the congregations and prisons, being led away to kings and governors on account of my name; 21.13 it will become/happen to ye in/for a testimony. 21.14 Therefore, put ye in your hearts not to premeditate/practice beforehand to be defended.

21.15   for I, I shall give a mouth and wisdom to ye, which all those being opposed to ye will not be able to resist or to contradict.   21.16 And ye will also be betrayed by parents and brothers and relatives and friends, and they will put to death (some) out of ye,   21.17 and ye will be (ones) being hated by all because of my name.   21.18 And a hair from the head of ye might by no means perish.   21.19 By your patience/ endurance ye purchase/gain/acquire your souls/lives. 21.20 But whenever ye might see Jerusalem being surrounded by troops/armed camps, then know ye that her desolation has drawn near.

21.21   Then let those in Judea flee/run away to the hills/mountains and let those in the midst of her

ἐν μέσῳ αὐτῆς ἐκχωρίτωσαν, καὶ οἱ ἐν ταῖς χώραις μὴ εἰσερχέσθωσαν εἰς αὐτήν, 21.22 ὅτι ἡμέραι ἐκδικήσεως αὗταί τοῦ πλησθῆναι πάντα τὰ γεγραμμένα.

21.23 οὐαὶ δὲ ταῖς ἐν γαστρὶ ἐχούσαις καὶ ταῖς θηλαζούσαις ἐν ἐκείναις ταῖς ἡμέραις· ἔστε γὰρ ἀνάγκη μεγάλη ἐπὶ τῆς γῆς καὶ ὀργὴ τῷ λαῷ τούτῳ,

21.24 καὶ πεσοῦνται στόματι μαχαίρας καὶ αἰχμαλωτισθήσονται εἰς τὰ ἔθνη πάντα, καὶ Ἰερουσαλὴμ ἔσται πατουμένη ὑπὸ ἐθνῶν, ἄχρι οὗ πληρωθῶσιν καιροὶ ἐθνῶν.

21.25 καὶ ἔσονται σημῖα ἐν ἡλίῳ καὶ σελήνῃ καὶ ἄστροις, καὶ ἐπὶ τῆς γῆς συνοχὴ ἐθνῶν καὶ ἐν ἀπορίᾳ ἤχους θαλάσσης καὶ σάλου, 21.26 ἀποψυχόντων ἀνθρώπων ἀπὸ φόβου καὶ προσδοκίας τῶν ἐπερχομένων τῇ οἰκουμένῃ, αἱ γὰρ δυνάμις τῶν οὐρανῶν σαλευθήσονται.

21.27 καὶ τότε ὄψονται «τὸν υἱὸν τοῦ ἀνθρώπου ἐρχόμενον ἐν νεφέλῃ» μετὰ δυνάμεως καὶ δόξης πολλῆς. 21.28 ἀρχομένων δὲ τούτων γείνεσθαι ἀνακύψατε καὶ ἐπάρατε τὰς κεφαλὰς ὑμῶν, διότι ἐγγίζει ἡ ἀπολύτρωσις ὑμῶν. 21.29 καὶ εἶπεν παραβολὴν αὐτοῖς· ἴδετε τὴν συκὴν καὶ πάντα τὰ δένδρα· 21.30 ὅταν προβάλωσιν ἤδη, βλέποντες ἀφ' ἑαυτῶν γεινώσκετε ὅτι ἐγγὺς ἐστίν ἤδη τὸ θέρος· 21.31 οὕτως καὶ ὑμῖς, ὅταν ἴδητε ταῦτα γεινόμενα, γεινώσκετε ὅτι ἐγγύς ἐστιν ἡ βασιλεία τοῦ θεοῦ.

21.32 ἀμὴν λέγω ὑμῖν ὅτι οὐ μὴ παρέλθῃ ἡ γενεὰ αὕτη ἕως πάντα γένηται. 21.33 ὁ οὐρανὸς καὶ ἡ γῆ παρελεύσονται, οἱ δὲ λόγοι μου οὐ μὴ παρελεύσονται. 21.34 προσέχετε ἑαυτοῖς μήποτε βαρηθῶσιν ὑμῶν αἱ καρδίαι ἐν κρεπάλῃ καὶ μέθῃ καὶ μερίμναις βιωτικαῖς, καὶ ἐπιστῇ ἐφ' ὑμᾶς ἐφνίδιος ἡ ἡμέρα ἐκείνη 21.35 ὡς παγίς. ἐπισελεύσεται γὰρ ἐπὶ πάντας τοὺς καθημένους ἐπὶ πρόσωπον πάσης τῆς γῆς. 21.36 ἀγρυπνεῖτε δὲ ἐν παντὶ καιρῷ

depart out, and let those in the countries/regions enter not into her, 21.22 because these days of vengeance *are* of the (thing) *for* all the (things) having been written to be fulfilled.

21.23 But woe to those (women) having in belly/ being pregnant and to those (women) suckling in those days; for there will be a great affliction on the land and anger/wrath for this people,

21.24 and they will fall by *the* mouth/*edge* of a sword and they will be led captive to/for all the ethnics, and Jerusalem will be being trampled by ethnics, until *a time* which *the* times/seasons of ethnics might be fulfilled.

21.25 And there will be signs by/in sun and moon and stars, and anxiety of ethnics on/over the land, and sounds/noises of sea and surf in perplexity, 21.26 of men/humans fainting from fear and anticipation of the (things) being caused to come upon the empire/inhabited earth, for the powers of the skies/heavens will be shaken.

21.27 And then they will behold THE SON OF THE MAN COMING IN/ON A CLOUD with power and much fame/glory. 21.28 And from these (things) beginning to happen, stand ye up and lift up your heads, because your redemption/release draws near, 21.29 And he spoke a parable to them: Behold ye the fig tree and all the trees/woods; 21.30 whenever they might put forth *leaves* already, seeing *it* ye know from yourselves that the summer is already near; 21.31 so also ye, whenever ye might see these (things) happening, ye will know that the kingdom of God is near.

21.32 Truly I say to ye that by no means will this generation pass by until all might come to be/happen. 21.33 The sky/heaven and the earth will pass by, but the sayings/words from me will by no means pass by/away. 21.34 Take heed/beware ye for yourselves lest your hearts might be weighted down in/with dereliction of duty and drunkenness and anxieties of daily life, and that day might come upon ye unexpected 21.35 as a snare trap. For it will come as a surprise upon all those sitting over *the* face of all the land/earth. 21.36 But watch ye in every time/season,

δεόμενοι ἵνα κατισχύσητε ἐκφυγεῖν ταῦτα πάντα τὰ μέλλοντα γείνεσθαι, καὶ σταθῆναι ἔμπροσθεν τοῦ υἱοῦ τοῦ ἀνθρώπου.

21.37 ἦν δὲ τὰς ἡμέρας ἐν τῷ ἱερῷ διδάσκων, τὰς δὲ νύκτας ἐξερχόμενος ηὐλίζετο εἰς τὸ ὄρος τὸ καλούμενον ἐλαιῶν· 21.38 καὶ πᾶς ὁ λαὸς ὤρθριζεν πρὸς αὐτὸν ἐν τῷ ἱερῷ ἀκούειν αὐτοῦ.

22.1 Ἤγγιζεν δὲ ἡ ἑορτὴ τῶν ἀζύμων ἡ λεγομένη πάσχα. 22.2 καὶ ἐζήτουν οἱ ἀρχιερεῖς καὶ οἱ γραμματῖς τὸ πῶς ἀνέλωσιν αὐτόν, ἐφοβοῦντο γὰρ τὸν λαόν.

22.3 εἰσῆλθεν δὲ Σατανᾶς εἰς Ἰούδαν τὸν καλούμενον Ἰσκαριώτην, ὄντα ἐκ τοῦ ἀριθμοῦ τῶν δώδεκα·

22.4 καὶ ἀπελθὼν συνελάλησεν τοῖς ἀρχιερεῦσιν καὶ στρατηγοῖς τὸ πῶς αὐτοῖς παραδῷ αὐτόν. 22.5 καὶ ἐχάρησαν καὶ συνέθεντο αὐτῷ ἀργύριον δοῦναι. 22.6 καὶ ἐξωμολόγησεν, καὶ ἐζήτει εὐκαιρίαν τοῦ παραδοῦναι αὐτὸν ἄτερ ὄχλου αὐτοῖς. 22.7 ἦλθεν δὲ ἡ ἡμέρα τῶν ἀζύμων, ἐν ᾗ ἔδει θύεσθαι τὸ πάσχα. 22.8 καὶ ἀπέστιλεν Πέτρον καὶ Ἰωάννην εἰπών, πορευθέντες ἑτοιμάσατε ἡμῖν τὸ πάσχα ἵνα φάγωμεν. 22.9 οἱ δὲ εἶπαν αὐτῷ, ποῦ θέλις ἑτοιμάσωμεν; 22.10 ὁ δὲ εἶπεν αὐτοῖς, ἰδοὺ εἰσελθόντων ὑμῶν εἰς τὴν πόλιν συναντήσι ὑμῖν ἄνθρωπος κεράμειον ὕδατος βαστάζων· ἀκολουθήσατε αὐτῷ εἰς τὴν οἰκίαν εἰς ἣν εἰσπορεύεται. 22.11 καὶ ἐρεῖτε τῷ οἰκοδεσπότῃ τῆς οἰκίας λέγοντες, λέγει σοι ὁ διδάσκαλος, ποῦ ἐστιν τὸ κατάλυμά μου ὅπου τὸ πάσχα μετὰ τῶν μαθητῶν μου φάγω; 22.12 κἀκεῖνος ὑμῖν δείξει ἀνάγαιον μέγα ἐστρωμένον· κἀκεῖ ἑτοιμάσατε. 22.13 ἀπελθόντες δὲ εὗρον καθὼς εἰρήκει αὐτοῖς, καὶ ἡτοίμασαν τὸ πάσχα. 22.14 καὶ ὅτε ἐγένετο ἡ ὥρα, ἀνέπεσεν καὶ οἱ ἀπόστολοι

praying/entreating that ye might be strong/prevail to escape from all these things being about to happen, and to be stood in front of/before the son of the man.

21.37   And *in* the days he was teaching in the *outer* temple, but he was spending the nights going out to the mountain being called of olives/named from olives.   21.38 And all the people were coming to him at dawn to hear from him in the *outer* temple.

22.1   And the festival of the unleavened (loaves), being called Passover, was drawing near. 22.2 And the high priests and the scribes were seeking the (thing) how they might destroy him, for they were fearing the people.

22.3   But Satan entered into Judas, the (one) being called Iscariot, being out of the number of the twelve;

22.4   and having gone away, he conferred with the high priests and military commanders the (thing) how he might betray/deliver him over to them.   22.5   And they rejoiced, and they agreed to give money/silver to him.   22.6 And he professed/bound himself, and was seeking an opportunity apart from the crowd to be- tray/deliver him over to them.   22.7 And the day of the unleavened loaves came, on which it was necessary to kill the passover (lamb).   22.8 And he sent Peter and John, saying: Having gone, prepare ye the passover (lamb) for us in order that we might eat.   22.9 But the (they) said to him: Where do you want/wish we should prepare *it*?   22.10 And the (he) said to them: Behold, from ye having entered into the city, a man will meet ye bearing/carrying an earthenware jar of water; follow ye with him to the house in which he enters.   22.11   And ye will speak to the housemaster of the house, saying: The teacher says to you: Where is my guest room/dining room where I might eat the passover (lamb) with my learners/pupils?   22.12 And that (one) will show to ye a large room upstairs having been furnished; and ye prepare *it* there.   22.13 And having gone away, they found *it* just as he had said to them, and they prepared the passover (lamb). 22.14 And when it became the hour, he reclined, and

σὺν αὐτῷ.

22.15 καὶ εἶπεν πρὸς αὐτούς, ἐπιθυμίᾳ ἐπεθύμησα τοῦτο τὸ πάσχα φαγεῖν μεθ᾽ ὑμῶν πρὸ τοῦ με παθεῖν·

22.16 λέγω γὰρ ὑμῖν ὅτι οὐ μὴ φάγω αὐτὸ ἕως ὅτου πληρωθῇ ἐν τῇ βασιλείᾳ τοῦ θεοῦ. 22.17 καὶ δεξάμενος ποτήριον εὐχαριστήσας εἶπεν, λάβετε τοῦτο καὶ διαμερίσατε εἰς ἑαυτούς· 22.18 λέγω γὰρ ὑμῖν ὅτι οὐ μὴ πίω ἀπὸ τοῦ νῦν ἀπὸ τοῦ γενήματος τῆς ἀμπέλου ἕως οὗ ἡ βασιλεία τοῦ θεοῦ ἔλθῃ. 22.19 καὶ λαβὼν ἄρτον εὐχαριστήσας ἔκλασεν καὶ ἔδωκεν αὐτοῖς λέγων, τοῦτό ἐστιν τὸ σῶμά μου τὸ ὑπὲρ ὑμῶν διδόμενον· τοῦτο ποιεῖται εἰς τὴν ἐμὴν ἀνάμνησιν.

22.20 καὶ τὸ ποτήριον ὡσαύτως μετὰ τὸ διπνῆσαι, λέγων, τοῦτο τὸ ποτήριον ἡ καινὴ διαθήκη ἐν τῷ αἵματί μου, τὸ ὑπὲρ ὑμῶν ἐκχυννόμενον.

22.21 πλὴν ἰδοὺ ἡ χεὶρ τοῦ παραδιδόντος με μετ᾽ ἐμοῦ ἐπὶ τῆς τραπέζης· 22.22 ὅτι ὁ υἱὸς μὲν τοῦ ἀνθρώπου κατὰ τὸ ὡρισμένον πορεύεται, πλὴν οὐαὶ τῷ ἀνθρώπῳ ἐκείνῳ δι᾽ οὗ παραδίδοται. 22.23 καὶ αὐτοὶ ἤρξαντο συνζητεῖν πρὸς ἑαυτοὺς τὸ τίς ἄρα εἴη ἐξ αὐτῶν ὁ τοῦτο μέλλων πράσσειν.

22.24 ἐγένετο δὲ φιλονικία ἐν αὐτοῖς, τὸ τίς αὐτῶν δοκεῖ εἶναι μίζων. 22.25 ὁ δὲ εἶπεν αὐτοῖς, οἱ βασιλεῖς τῶν ἐθνῶν κυριεύουσιν αὐτῶν καὶ οἱ ἐξουσιάζοντες αὐτῶν εὐεργέται καλοῦνται. 22.26 ὑμεῖς δὲ οὐχ οὕτως, ἀλλ᾽ ὁ μείζων ἐν ὑμῖν γεινέσθω ὡς ὁ νεώτερος, καὶ ὁ ἡγούμενος ὡς ὁ διακονῶν.

22.27 τίς γὰρ μείζων, ὁ ἀνακείμενος ἢ ὁ διακονῶν; οὐχὶ ὁ ἀνακείμενος; ἐγὼ δὲ ἐν μέσῳ ὑμῶν εἰμι ὡς ὁ διακονῶν. 22.28 ὑμεῖς δέ ἐστε οἱ διαμεμενηκότες μετ᾽ ἐμοῦ ἐν τοῖς πειρασμοῖς μου· 22.29 κἀγὼ διατίθεμαι ὑμῖν καθὼς διέθετό μοι ὁ πατήρ μου βασιλείαν 22.30 ἵνα ἔσθίηται καὶ πίνηται ἐπὶ τῆς τραπέζης μου

the apostles with him.

22.15 And he said to them: I desired/longed with a desire to eat this, the Passover, with ye before the (thing) *for* me to suffer.

22.16 For I say to ye that by no means might I eat it until which (time) *it* might be fulfilled in the kingdom of God. 22.17 And having received a cup, having given thanks, he said: Take ye this and divide *it* to/for yourselves; 22.18 for I say to ye that by no means might I drink from the yield/fruit of the vine, from now until which (time) the kingdom of God might come. 22.19 And having taken a loaf, having given thanks, he broke and gave *it* to them, saying: This is my body, the (one) being given in behalf of ye; do ye this in my memory/remembrance.

22.20 And likewise the cup, after the (thing) to dine, saying: This cup *is* the new covenant in my blood, the (blood) being poured out in behalf of ye.

22.21 But behold, the hand of the (one) betraying me/delivering me over *is* with me on the table; 22.22 because indeed the son of the man goes according to the (thing) having been appointed, but woe to that man through whom he is betrayed/handed over. 22.23 And they began to discuss *it* with themselves, the (thing) who then/indeed out of them may be the (one) being about to perform this (thing).

22.24 But a contention/dispute became among them, the (thing) who of them seems to be greater. 22.25 And the (he) said to them: The kings of the ethnics lord it over them and those having their authority are being called benefactors. 22.26 But ye *are* not so, but let the greater/older (one) among ye become as the newer/younger, and the (one) governing/leading as the (one) serving/waiting on.

22.27 For who is greater, the (one) being reclined or the (one) serving? *Is it* not the (one) being reclined? But I, I am in the midst of ye as the (one) serving. 22.28 But ye, ye are the (ones) having stayed with me throughout in my trials/temptations; 22.29 and I, I assign/confer my kingdom to ye even as my father assigned *it* to me, 22.30 in order that ye may eat and drink on/at my table in my kingdom, and ye

ἐν τῇ βασιλείᾳ μου, καὶ καθήσεσθε ἐπὶ θρόνων κρίνοντες τὰς δώδεκα φυλὰς τοῦ Ἰσραήλ.

22.31 εἶπεν δὲ ὁ κύριος, Σίμων, ἰδοὺ ὁ Σατανᾶς ἐξῃτήσατο ὑμᾶς τοῦ σινιάσαι ὡς τὸν σῖτον· 22.32 ἐγὼ δὲ ἐδεήθην περὶ σοῦ ἵνα μὴ ἐκλίπῃ ἡ πίστις σου· καὶ σύ ποτε ἐπιστρέψας στήρισον τοὺς ἀδελφούς σου.

22.33 ὁ δὲ εἶπεν αὐτῷ, κύριε, μετὰ σοῦ ἕτοιμός εἰμι καὶ εἰς φυλακὴν καὶ εἰς θάνατον πορεύεσθαι.

22.34 ὁ δὲ εἶπεν, λέγω σοι, Πέτρε, οὐ φωνήσει σήμερον ἀλέκτωρ ἕως τρεῖς με ἀπαρνήσῃ εἰδέναι.

22.35 καὶ εἶπεν αὐτοῖς, ὅτε ἀπέστιλα ὑμᾶς ἄτερ βαλλαντίου καὶ πήρας καὶ ὑποδημάτων, μή τινος ὑστερήσατε; οἱ δὲ εἶπον, οὐδενός. 22.36 εἶπεν δὲ αὐτοῖς, ἀλλὰ νῦν ὁ ἔχων βαλλάντιον ἀράτω, ὁμοίως καὶ πήραν, καὶ ὁ μὴ ἔχων πωλησάτω τὸ ἱμάτιον αὐτοῦ καὶ ἀγορασάτω μάχαιραν.

22.37 λέγω γὰρ ὑμῖν ὅτι τοῦτο τὸ γεγραμμένον δεῖ τελεσθῆναι ἐν ἐμοί, τὸ «καὶ μετὰ ἀνόμων ἐλογίσθη» καὶ γὰρ τὸ περὶ ἐμοῦ τέλος ἔχει.

22.38 οἱ δὲ εἶπαν, κύριε, ἰδοὺ μάχαιραι ὧδε δύο. ὁ δὲ εἶπεν αὐτοῖς, ἱκανόν ἐστιν.

22.39 καὶ ἐξελθὼν ἐπορεύθη κατὰ τὸ ἔθος εἰς τὸ ὄρος τῶν ἐλαιῶν· ἠκολούθησαν δὲ αὐτῷ καὶ οἱ μαθηταί.

22.40 γενόμενος δὲ ἐπὶ τοῦ τόπου εἶπεν αὐτοῖς, προσεύχεσθαι μὴ εἰσελθεῖν εἰς πειρασμόν.

22.41 καὶ αὐτὸς ἀπεσπάσθη ἀπ' αὐτῶν ὡσεὶ λίθου βολήν, καὶ θεὶς τὰ γόνατα προσηύξατο 22.42 λέγων,

πάτερ, εἰ βούλι παρένεγκαι τοῦτο τὸ ποτήριον ἀπ' ἐμοῦ· πλὴν μὴ τὸ θέλημά μου ἀλλὰ τὸ σὸν γεινέσθω. 22.43 ὤφθη δὲ αὐτῷ ἄγγελος ἀπ' οὐρανοῦ ἐνισχύων αὐτόν. 22.44 καὶ γενάμενος ἐν ἀγωνίᾳ ἐκτενέστερον προσηύχετο· καὶ ἐγένετο ἱδρὼς αὐτοῦ ὡσὶ θρόμβοι αἵματος καταβαίνοντος ἐπὶ τὴν γῆν.

22.45 καὶ ἀναστὰς ἀπὸ τῆς προσευχῆς ἐλθὼν πρὸς τοὺς

will sit on thrones judging the twelve tribes of Israel.

22.31   And the Lord said: Simon, behold, Satan himself demanded/requested ye from the (thing) to sift as the wheat;   22.32 but I myself entreated concerning you in order that your faith/trust might fail/die not; and you, when having returned, you strengthen your brothers.

22.33   And the (he) said to him: Lord, with you I am ready to go both into prison and to death.

22.34   But the (he) said: I say to you, Peter, a cock/rooster will not sound/crow today until you might thrice deny to know me.

22.35 But the (he) said to them: When I sent ye without a purse and traveler's bag and sandals, were ye deficient/lacking of anything? And they said: Of nothing.   22.36 And he said to them: But now, let the (one) having take a purse, and likewise a traveler's bag, and let the (one) not having sell his garment and let him buy a sword.

22.37   For I say to ye that it is necessary *for* this thing having been written to be finished by me, the (thing): AND HE WAS ACCOUNTED WITH LAWLESS (ONES); for even the (thing) concerning me has an end.

22.38   And they said: Lord, behold, here *are* two swords. And the (he) said to them: *It* is sufficient.

22.39   And having gone out, he went/traveled according to the custom to the mountain of the olives; and the learners pupils also followed with him.

22.40   And having become at the place, he said to them: Pray ye to enter not into trial/temptation.

22.41   And he himself was withdrawn from them about a stone's throw, and having put *down* the knees, he was praying,   22.42 saying:

Father, if you will, remove this cup from me; however let not my will but yours come about/become. 22.43 And a messenger/angel from heaven was seen by him, strengthening him.   22.44 And having become in agony, he was praying more fervently; and his sweat became like drops of blood going down upon the ground/earth.

22.45   And having risen from the prayer, having

μαθητὰς εὗρεν κοιμωμένους αὐτοὺς ἀπὸ τῆς λύπης, 22.46 καὶ εἶπεν αὐτοῖς, τί καθεύδετε; ἀναστάντες προσεύχεσθαι, ἵνα μὴ εἰσέλθηται εἰς πιρασμόν.

22.47 ἔτι αὐτοῦ λαλοῦντος ἰδοὺ ὄχλος, καὶ ὁ λεγόμενος Ἰούδας εἷς τῶν δώδεκα προήρχετο αὐτούς,

καὶ ἤγγισεν τῷ Ἰησοῦ φιλῆσαι αὐτόν. 22.48 Ἰησοῦς δὲ εἶπεν αὐτῷ, Ἰούδα, φιλήματι τὸν υἱὸν τοῦ ἀνθρώπου παραδίδως;

22.49 εἰδόντες δὲ οἱ περὶ αὐτὸν τὸ ἐσόμενον εἶπαν, κύριε, εἰ πατάξομεν ἐν μαχαίρῃ; 22.50 καὶ ἐπάταξεν εἷς τις ἐξ αὐτῶν τοῦ ἀρχιερέως τὸν δοῦλον καὶ ἀφῖλεν τὸ οὖς αὐτοῦ τὸ δεξιόν. 22.51 ἀποκριθεὶς δὲ ὁ Ἰησοῦς εἶπεν, ἐᾶτε ἕως τούτου· καὶ ἁψάμενος τοῦ ὠτίου ἰάσατο αὐτόν.

22.52 εἶπεν δὲ Ἰησοῦς πρὸς τοὺς παραγενομένους ἐπ᾽ αὐτὸν ἀρχιερεῖς καὶ στρατηγοὺς τοῦ ἱεροῦ καὶ πρεσβυτέρους, ὡς ἐπὶ λῃστὴν ἐξήλθαται μετὰ μαχαιρῶν καὶ ξύλων; 22.53 καθ᾽ ἡμέραν ὄντος μου μεθ᾽ ὑμῶν ἐν τῷ ἱερῷ οὐκ ἐξετίνατε τὰς χεῖρας ἐπ᾽ ἐμέ· ἀλλ᾽ αὕτη ἐστὶν ὑμῶν ἡ ὥρα καὶ ἡ ἐξουσία τοῦ σκότους.

22.54 συλλαβόντες δὲ αὐτὸν ἤγαγον καὶ εἰσήγαγον εἰς τὴν οἰκίαν τοῦ ἀρχιερέως·

ὁ δὲ Πέτρος ἠκολούθι μακρόθεν. 22.55 περιαψάντων δὲ πῦρ ἐν μέσῳ τῆς αὐλῆς καὶ συνκαθισάντων ἐκάθητο ὁ Πέτρος ἐν μέσῳ αὐτῶν. 22.56 ἰδοῦσα δὲ αὐτὸν παιδίσκη τις καθήμενον πρὸς τὸ φῶς καὶ ἀτενίσασα αὐτῷ εἶπεν, καὶ οὗτος σὺν αὐτῷ ἦν· 22.57 ὁ δὲ ἠρνήσατο λέγων, οὐκ οἶδα αὐτόν, γύναι. 22.58 καὶ μετὰ βραχὺ ἕτερος ἰδὼν αὐτὸν ἔφη, καὶ σὺ ἐξ αὐτῶν εἶ· ὁ δὲ Πέτρος ἔφη· ἄνθρωπε, οὐκ εἰμί. 22.59 καὶ διαστάσης ὡσεὶ ὥρας μιᾶς ἄλλος τις διϊσχυρίζετο λέγων, ἐπ᾽ ἀληθίας καὶ οὗτος μετ᾽ αὐτοῦ ἦν, καὶ γὰρ Γαλιλαῖός ἐστιν· 22.60 εἶπεν δὲ ὁ Πέτρος, ἄνθρωπε, οὐκ οἶδα τι λέγεις. καὶ παραχρῆμα ἔτι λαλοῦντος

gone to the learners/pupils, he found them being fallen asleep from the grief, 22.46 and he said to them: Why do ye sleep? Be rising up, pray ye, lest ye might come into trial/temptation.

22.47 Of him yet speaking, behold, a crowd, and the (one) being called Judas, one of the twelve, were approaching them,

and he drew near to Jesus to kiss him. 22.48 But Jesus said to him: Judas, do you betray/hand over the son of the man with a kiss?

22.49 And those around him, having seen the (thing) going to be, they said: Lord, shall we smite with a sword? 22.50 And one, a certain one out of them, struck the high priest's slave and cut off his right ear. 22.51 But answering, Jesus said: Stop/let ye until this;

and having himself touched *his* ear, he healed him.

22.52 And Jesus said to the high priests and commanders and elders having come against him from the *outer* temple: Came ye out with swords and woods/clubs as against a robber? 22.53 Day by day from me being with ye in the *outer* temple ye stretched not out the hands against me; but this is your hour and the authority of/from the darkness.

22.54 And having seized him, they led *him* and brought him to/into the house of the high priest;

and Peter followed from afar. 22.55 And from them having kindled/lit a fire in the middle of the yard and having sat down together, Peter was sitting in their midst. 22.56 But having seen him, a certain maidservant sitting near the light, and having gazed at him, said: This (one) was also with him; 22.57 but the (he) denied *it*, saying: I do not know him, woman. 22.58 And after a short *time* another/different, having seen him, was saying: You, you are also out of them; but Peter was saying: Man, I am not. 22.59 And from having intervened about one hour, a certain other *man* was being insistent, saying: On a truth/reality, this (one) was also with him, for he also is a Galilean; 22.60 but Peter said: Man, I know not what you say. And immediately, from him yet speaking, a cock/rooster

αὐτοῦ ἐφώνησεν ἀλέκτωρ. 22.61 καὶ στραφεὶς ὁ κύριος ἐνέβλεψεν τῷ Πέτρῳ, καὶ ὑπεμνήσθη ὁ Πέτρος τοῦ ῥήματος τοῦ κυρίου ὡς εἶπεν αὐτῷ ὅτι πρὶν ἀλέκτορα φωνῆσε σήμερον ἀπαρνήσῃ με τρίς· 22.62 καὶ ἐξελθὼν ἔξω ἔκλαυσεν πικρῶς.

22.63 καὶ οἱ ἄνδρες οἱ συνέχοντες αὐτὸν ἐνέπεζον αὐτῷ δέροντες, 22.64 καὶ περικαλύψαντες ἐπηρώτων αὐτὸν λέγοντες, προφήτευσον, τίς ἐστιν ὁ παίσας σε; 22.65 καὶ ἕτερα πολλὰ βλασφημοῦντες ἔλεγον εἰς αὐτόν.

22.66 καὶ ὡς ἡμέρα ἐγένετο, συνήχθη τὸ πρεσβυτέριον τοῦ λαοῦ, ἀρχιερεῖς τε καὶ γραμματῖς, καὶ ἀπήγαγον αὐτὸν εἰς τὸ συνέδριον αὐτῶν, 22.67 λέγοντες, εἰ σὺ εἶ ὁ χριστός, εἰπὸν ἡμῖν.

εἶπεν δὲ αὐτοῖς, ἐὰν ὑμῖν εἴπω οὐ μὴ πιστεύσητε· 22.68 ἐὰν δὲ ἐρωτήσω οὐ μὴ ἀποκριθῆτε.

22.69 ἀπὸ τοῦ νῦν δὲ ἔσται «ὁ υἱὸς τοῦ ἀνθρώπου καθήμενος ἐκ δεξιῶν τῆς δυνάμεως τοῦ θεοῦ.» 22.70 εἶπαν δὲ πάντες, σὺ οὖν εἶ ὁ υἱὸς τοῦ θεοῦ; ὁ δὲ πρὸς αὐτοὺς ἔφη, ὑμεῖς λέγετε ὅτι ἐγώ εἰμι.

22.71 οἱ δὲ εἶπαν, τί ἔτι χρείαν ἔχομεν μαρτυρίας; αὐτοὶ γὰρ ἠκούσαμεν ἀπὸ τοῦ στόματος αὐτοῦ.

23.1 Καὶ ἀναστὰν ἅπαν τὸ πλῆθος αὐτῶν ἤγαγον αὐτὸν ἐπὶ τὸν Πιλᾶτον.

23.2 ἤρξαντο δὲ κατηγορῖν αὐτοῦ λέγοντες, τοῦτον εὕρομεν διαστρέφοντα τὸ ἔθνος ἡμῶν καὶ κωλύοντα φόρους Καίσαρι διδόναι καὶ λέγοντα ἑαυτὸν χριστὸν βασιλέα εἶναι. 23.3 ὁ δὲ Πιλᾶτος ἠρώτησεν αὐτὸν λέγων, σὺ εἶ ὁ βασιλεὺς τῶν Ἰουδαίων; ὁ δὲ ἀποκριθεὶς αὐτῷ λέγει, σὺ λέγεις.

23.4 ὁ δὲ Πιλᾶτος εἶπεν πρὸς τοὺς ἀρχιερῖς καὶ τοὺς ὄχλους, οὐδὲν εὑρίσκω αἴτιον ἐν τῷ ἀνθρώπῳ τούτῳ. 23.5 οἱ δὲ ἐπίσχυον λέγοντες ὅτι ἀνασείει τὸν ὄχλον διδάσκων καθ' ὅλης τῆς Ἰουδαίας, καὶ ἀρξάμενος ἀπὸ τῆς Γαλιλαίας ἕως ὧδε.

sounded/crowed.   22.61 And having been turned/having turned around, the Lord looked intently at/to Peter, and he was reminded of the Lord's word as/when he said to him that before a cock *is* to crow today, you will yourself deny me thrice/three times; 22.62 and having gone outside, he wept bitterly.

22.63   And the men holding him in custody were mocking at him, beating *him*,   22.64 and having covered around *him*, they were entreating him, saying: You prophesy, who is the (one) having hit you?   22.65 And they were saying many other/different blaspheming/reviling (things) to him.

22.66   And as/when it became day, the presbytery of the people were gathered, both high priests and scribes, and they led him away to their council/Sanhedrin,   22.67 saying: You, if you are the anointed (one), speak tous.

And he said to them: If I should speak to ye, ye would by no means believe;   22.68 and if I should question, ye would by no means answer.

22.69   But from the present (time), THE SON OF THE MAN will be SITTING OUT OF RIGHT (ONES) FROM THE POWER OF GOD.   22.70 And they all said: You, then are you the son of God? And the (he) was saying to them: Ye, ye say that I, I am.

22.71   And they said: Why have we yet need of testimony? For we ourselves heard *it* from his mouth!

23.1   And having risen up, all the multitude of them led him to Pilate.

23.2   And they began to accuse of him, saying: We found this (one) perverting our ethnic/race and forbidding to give tribute to Caesar, and saying *for* himself to be an anointed king.   23.3 And Pilate questioned him, saying: You, are you the king of the Judeans? And the (he), answering, he says to them: You, you say.

23.4   And Pilate said to the high priests and the crowds: I find no cause/guilt/complaint in this man. 23.5 But they were insisting, saying: He incites the crowd, teaching throughout all Judea, even having begun from Galilee until here.

23.6 Πειλᾶτος δὲ ἀκούσας ἐπηρώτησεν εἰ ὁ ἄνθρωπος Γαλιλαῖός ἐστιν· 23.7 καὶ ἐπιγνοὺς ὅτι ἐκ τῆς ἐξουσίας Ἡρώδου ἐστὶν ἀνέπεμψεν αὐτὸν πρὸς Ἡρώδην, ὄντα καὶ αὐτὸν ἐν Ἱεροσολύμοις ἐν ταύταις ταῖς ἡμέραις. 23.8 ὁ δὲ Ἡρώδης ἰδὼν τὸν Ἰησοῦν ἐχάρη λίαν, ἦν γὰρ ἐξ ἱκανῶν χρόνων θέλων ἰδῖν αὐτὸν διὰ τὸ ἀκούειν περὶ αὐτοῦ, καὶ ἤλπιζέν τι σημῖον ἰδῖν ὑπ' αὐτοῦ γεινόμενον. 23.9 ἐπηρώτα δὲ αὐτὸν ἐν λόγοις ἱκανοῖς· αὐτὸς δὲ οὐκ ἀπεκρίνατο αὐτῷ. 23.10 ἱστήκεισαν δὲ οἱ ἀρχιερεῖς καὶ οἱ γραμματεῖς εὐτόνως κατηγοροῦντες αὐτοῦ.

23.11 ἐξουθενήσας τὲ αὐτὸν καὶ ὁ Ἡρώδης σὺν τοῖς στρατεύμασιν αὐτοῦ καὶ ἐνπέξας περιβαλὼν αἰσθῆτα λαμπρὰν ἀνέπεμψεν αὐτὸν τῷ Πιλάτῳ. 23.12 ἐγένοντο δὲ φίλοι ὅ τε Ἡρώδης καὶ ὁ Πιλᾶτος ἐν αὐτῇ τῇ ἡμέρᾳ μετ' ἀλλήλων· προϋπῆρχον γὰρ ἐν ἔχθρᾳ ὄντες πρὸς αὐτούς. 23.13 Πιλᾶτος δὲ συγκαλεσάμενος τοὺς ἀρχιερεῖς καὶ τοὺς ἄρχοντας καὶ τὸν λαὸν 23.14 εἶπεν πρὸς αὐτούς, προσηνέγκατέ μοι τὸν ἄνθρωπον τοῦτον ὡς ἀποστρέφοντα τὸν λαόν, καὶ ἰδοὺ ἐγὼ ἐνώπιον ὑμῶν ἀνακρίνας οὐθὲν εὗρον ἐν τῷ ἀνθρώπῳ τούτῳ αἴτιον ὧν κατηγορεῖτε αὐτοῦ, 23.15 ἀλλ' οὐδὲ Ἡρώδης· ἀνέπεμψε γὰρ αὐτὸν πρὸς ἡμᾶς· καὶ ἰδοὺ οὐδὲν ἄξιον θανάτου ἐστὶν πεπραγμένον αὐτῷ. 23.16 παιδεύσας οὖν αὐτὸν ἀπολύσω.

23.17 ἄναικην δὲ εἶχεν ἀπολυεῖν αὐτοῖς κατὰ ἑορτὴν ἵνα 23.18 ἀνέκραγον δὲ πανπληθεὶ λέγοντες, αἶρε τοῦτον, ἀπόλυσον δὲ ἡμῖν τὸν Βαραββᾶν· 23.19 ὅστις ἦν διὰ στάσιν τινὰ γενομένην ἐν τῇ πόλει καὶ φόνον βεβλημένος ἐν τῇ φυλακῇ.

23.20 πάλιν δὲ ὁ Πιλᾶτος προφώνησεν αὐτοῖς, θέλων ἀπολῦσαι τὸν Ἰησοῦν· 23.21 οἱ δὲ ἐπεφώνουν λέγοντες, σταύρου, σταύρου αὐτόν. 23.22 ὁ δὲ τρίτον εἶπεν πρὸς αὐτούς, τί γὰρ κακὸν ἐποίησεν οὗτος; οὐδὲν αἴτιον θανάτου εὗρον ἐν αὐτῷ·

παιδεύσας οὖν αὐτὸν ἀπολύσω. 23.23 οἱ δὲ ἔκειντο φωναῖς μεγάλαις αἰτούμενοι αὐτὸν σταυρωθῆναι, καὶ κατίσχυον αἱ φωναὶ αὐτῶν.

23.6 And having heard, Pilate asked if the man is a Galilean; 23.7 and having recognized that he is from Herod's authority, he sent him up to Herod, *for* him also being in Jerusalem in those days. 23.8 And having seen Jesus, Herod was very joyed/gladdened, for he had wanted/wished to see him because of the (thing) to hear about him from considerable times, and he was hoping to see some sign coming about by him. 23.9 And he questioned him with sufficient reasonings/words; but he himself replied not to him. 23.10 And the high priests and the scribes were present, accusing of him vehemently.

23.11 And having despised him, even Herod with his soldiers, and having mocked *him*, having put brilliant clothing around him, he sent him back to Pilate. 23.12 And both Herod and Pilate became friends with one another in the same day; for they formerly were being in enmity toward/with themselves. 23.13 And Pilate, having called together the high priests and the leaders and the people, 23.14 he said to them: Ye brought this man to me as perverting/misleading the people, and behold I, having examined *him* before ye, I found no guilt/cause in this man of which ye accuse him of, 23.15 but neither *did* Herod; for he sent him back to us; and behold, there is nothing worthy of death having been practiced by him. 23.16 Therefore, having disciplined him, 23.17 I shall release *him*.

And he was having an idea to release *him* to them, *the custom* according to a festival. 23.18 But they shouted all together, saying: Take this (one) away, and release for us Barabbas; 23.19 who had been thrown in the prison because of a certain insurrection having happened in the city, and *for* murder. 23.20 But again Pilate called/spoke to them, wanting to release Jesus; 23.21 but they were shouting, saying: Crucify, crucify him! 23.22 And he said to them a third time: For what bad did this (one)? I found no guilt/cause of death in him;

Therefore I shall release him, having chastised *him*. 23.23 But they were urging/insisting with great voices, requesting *for* him to be crucified, and their voices were prevailing.

23.24 καὶ Πιλᾶτος ἐπέκρινεν γενέσθαι τὸ αἴτημα αὐτῶν· 23.25 ἀπέλυσεν δὲ τὸν διὰ στάσιν καὶ φόνον βεβλημένον εἰς φυλακὴν ὃν ᾐτοῦντο, τὸν δὲ Ἰησοῦν παρέδωκεν τῷ θελήματι αὐτῶν.

23.26 καὶ ὡς ἀπήγαγον αὐτόν, ἐπιλαβόμενοι Σίμωνά τινα Κυρηναῖον ἐρχόμενον ἀπ' ἀγροῦ ἐπέθηκαν αὐτῷ τὸν σταυρὸν φέρειν ὄπισθεν τοῦ Ἰησοῦ. 23.27 ἠκολούθει δὲ αὐτῷ πολὺ πλῆθος τοῦ λαοῦ καὶ γυναικῶν ἐκόπτοντο καὶ ἐθρήνουν αὐτόν. 23.28 στραφεὶς δὲ πρὸς αὐτὰς Ἰησοῦς εἶπεν, θυγατέραις Ἰερουσαλήμ, μὴ κλαίετε ἐπ' ἐμέ· πλὴν ἐφ' ἑαυτὰς κλαίετε καὶ ἐπὶ τὰ τέκνα ὑμῶν, 23.29 ὅτι ἰδοὺ ἡμέραι ἔρχονται ἐν αἷς ἐροῦσιν, μακάριαι στεῖραι καὶ αἱ κοιλίαι αἳ οὐκ ἐγέννησαν καὶ μαστοὶ οἳ οὐκ ἔθρεψαν. 23.20 τότε ἄρξονται «λέγειν τοῖς ὄρεσιν, πέσετε ἐφ' ἡμᾶς, καὶ τοῖς βουνοῖς, καλύψατε ἡμᾶς·» 23.31 ὅτι εἰ ἐν τῷ ὑγρῷ ξύλῳ ταῦτα ποιοῦσιν, ἐν τῷ ξηρῷ τί γένηται;

23.32 ἤγοντο δὲ καὶ ἕτεροι κακοῦργοι δύο σὺν αὐτῷ ἀναιρεθῆναι.

23.33 καὶ ὅτε ἦλθον ἐπὶ τὸν τόπον τὸν καλούμενον κρανίον, ἐκεῖ ἐσταύρωσαν αὐτὸν

καὶ τοὺς κακούργους, ὃν μὲν ἐκ δεξιῶν ὃν δὲ ἐξ ἀριστερῶν. 23.34 ὁ δὲ Ἰησοῦς ἔλεγεν, πάτερ, ἄφες αὐτοῖς, οὐ γὰρ οἴδασιν τί ποιοῦσιν.

διαμεριζόμενοι δὲ τὰ ἱμάτια αὐτοῦ ἔβαλον κλῆρον. 23.35 καὶ ἱστήκει ὁ λαὸς θεωρῶν.

ἐξεμυκτήριζον δὲ οἱ ἄρχοντες λέγοντες, ἄλλους ἔσωσεν, σωσάτω ἑαυτόν, εἰ οὗτός ἐστιν ὁ χριστὸς τοῦ θεοῦ ὁ ἐκλεκτός.

23.36 ἐνέπαιξαν δὲ αὐτῷ οἱ στρατιῶται προσερχόμενοι, ὄξος προσφέροντες αὐτῷ 23.37 καὶ λέγοντες, εἰ σὺ εἶ ὁ βασιλεὺς τῶν Ἰουδαίων, σῶσον σεαυτόν. 23.38 ἦν δὲ καὶ ἐπιγραφὴ ἐπ' αὐτῷ, γράμμασιν Ἑλληνικοῖς, Ῥωμαικοῖς, Ἑβραικοῖς, ὁ βασιλεὺς τῶν Ἰουδαίων οὗτος. 23.39 εἷς δὲ τῶν κρεμασθέντων κακούργων ἐβλασφήμι αὐτὸν λέγων,

23.24   And Pilate decided *for* their request to come about;   23.25 and he released the (one) having been thrown into prison because of insurrection and murder, *for* whom they were asking, and he delivered Jesus over to their will.

23.26   And as they brought him, having taken hold of a certain Simon, a Cyrenian coming from a field, they pressed upon him to carry/bear the cross behind Jesus.   23.27 And a much multitude of the people followed with him, also of women *who* were mourning and bewailing him.   23.28 And turning toward them, Jesus said: Daughters of Jerusalem, weep ye not over me; but weep ye over yourselves and over your children,   23.29 because behold, days are coming in which they will say: Happy *are* the barren (ones) and the bellies/wombs which did not generate/bear and breasts which did not suckle.   23.30 Then they will begin TO SAY TO THE MOUNTAINS: FALL YE UPON US, AND TO THE HILLS: COVER/ CONCEAL US;   23.31 because if they do these things with the green/moist wood/tree, what will become/ happen with/to the dry/withered (one)?

23.32   And two other/different criminals were being brought to be crucified with him.

23.33   And when they came to the place being called a skull, they crucified him there, also the bad doers/criminals, one on the right, the other on the left.   23.34   And Jesus was saying: Father, forgive to them, for they know not what they do. And dividing his garments, they threw a lot/die. 23.35 And the people had stood beholding/observing.

And the rulers/leaders were ridiculing/sneering, saying: He saved others, let him save himself, if this (one) is the anointed (one) from God, the chosen (one).

23.36   And the soldiers, coming near, mocked to him, offering sour wine to him 23.37 and saying: You, if you are the king of the Judeans, save yourself. 23.38 And there was also a superscription over him, in Greek, Roman, *and* Hebrew letters: The King of the Judeans *is* this (one).   23.39 And one of the bad doers/criminals having been hanging was reviling/blaspheming him, saying:

οὐχὶ σὺ εἶ ὁ χριστός; σῶσον σεαυτὸν καὶ ἡμᾶς. 23.40 ἀποκριθεὶς δὲ ὁ ἕτερος ἐπιτιμῶν αὐτῷ ἔφη, οὐδὲ φοβῇ σὺ τὸν θεόν, ὅτι ἐν τῷ αὐτῷ κρίματι εἶ; 23.41 καὶ ἡμῖς μὲν δικαίως, ἄξια γὰρ ὧν ἐπράξαμεν ἀπολαμβάνομεν· οὗτος δὲ οὐδὲν ἄτοπον ἔπραξεν. 23.42 καὶ ἔλεγεν, Ἰησοῦ, μνήσθητί μου ὅταν ἔλθῃς ἐν τῇ βασιλείᾳ σου. 23.43 καὶ εἶπεν αὐτῷ, ἀμήν λέγω σοι, σήμερον μετ' ἐμοῦ ἔσῃ ἐν τῷ παραδίσῳ.

23.44 καὶ ἦν ἤδη ὥρα ὡσεὶ ἕκτη καὶ σκότος ἐγένετο ἐφ' ὅλην τὴν γῆν ἕως ὥρας ἐνάτης 23.45 τοῦ ἡλίου ἐκλιπόντος, ἐσχίσθη δὲ τὸ καταπέτασμα τοῦ ναοῦ μέσον. 23.46 καὶ φωνήσας φωνῇ μεγάλῃ ὁ Ἰησοῦς εἶπεν,

πάτερ, «εἰς χῖράς σου παρατίθεμαι τὸ πνεῦμά μου·» τοῦτο δὲ εἰπὼν ἐξέπνευσεν.

23.47 ἰδὼν δὲ ὁ ἑκατοντάρχης τὸ γενόμενον ἐδόξαζεν τὸν θεὸν λέγων ὅτι ὄντως ὁ ἄνθρωπος οὗτος δίκαιος ἦν.

23.48 καὶ πάντες οἱ συνπαραγενόμενοι ὄχλοι εἰς τὴν θεωρίαν ταύτην, θεωρήσαντες τὰ γενόμενα, τύπτοντες τὰ στήθη ὑπέστρεφον.

23.49 εἰστήκισαν δὲ πάντες οἱ γνωστοὶ αὐτοῦ ἀπὸ μακρόθεν, καὶ γυναῖκες αἱ συνακολουθοῦσαι αὐτῷ ἀπὸ τῆς Γαλιλαίας, ὁρῶσαι ταῦτα.

23.50 καὶ ἰδοὺ ἀνὴρ ὀνόματι Ἰωσὴφ βουλευτὴς ὑπάρχων καὶ ἀνὴρ ἀγαθὸς καὶ δίκαιος 23.51 οὗτος οὐκ ἦν συγκατατιθεμένος τῇ βουλῇ καὶ τῇ πράξει αὐτῶν ἀπὸ Ἀριμαθαίας πόλεως τῶν Ἰουδαίων, ὃς προσεδέχετο τὴν βασιλείαν τοῦ θεοῦ, 23.52 οὗτος προσελθὼν τῷ Πιλάτῳ ᾐτήσατο τὸ σῶμα τοῦ Ἰησοῦ, 23.53 καὶ καθελὼν ἐνετύλιξεν αὐτὸ σινδόνι, καὶ ἔθηκεν αὐτὸν ἐν μνήματι λαξευτῷ οὗ οὐκ ἦν οὐδεὶς οὐδέπω κείμενος. 23.54 καὶ ἡμέρα ἦν παρασκευῆς, καὶ σάββατον ἐπέφωσκεν. 23.55 κατακολουθήσασαι δὲ γυναῖκες, αἵτινες ἦσαν συνεληλυθυῖαι ἐκ τῆς Γαλιλαίας αὐτῷ, ἐθεάσαντο τὸ μνημῖον καὶ ὡς ἐτέθη τὸ σῶμα αὐτοῦ,

You, are you not the anointed (one)? Save your-self and us. 23.40 But answering, the other/differ-ent, rebuking to him, was saying: You, do you not fear God, because you are in the same judgment? 23.41 And we indeed justly, for we practiced (things) worthy of *that* which we receive back; but this (one) practiced nothing improper/out of place. 23.42 And he was saying: Jesus, be mindful of me whenever you might come in your kingdom. 23.43 And he said to him: Truly I say to you, you will be with me today in the gar-den/paradise.

23.44 And it was now about *the* sixth hour, and darkness became over the entire land until *the* ninth hour 23.45 from the sun having failed, and the veil of the *inner* temple was split in the middle. 23.46 And having cried out in a great voice, Jesus said:

Father, I PLACE/GIVE OVER THE SPIRIT OF/FROM ME INTO YOUR HANDS; and having said this, he breathed his last/expired.

23.47 And having seen the (thing) having happen-ed, the centurion glorified/acknowledged God, saying: This man was certainly/surely a just (one).

23.48 And all the crowds having come together to this spectacle/sight, having beheld the (things) having happened, were returning, beating the breasts.

23.49 And all the (men) known of him had stood from afar, also the women following with him from Galilee, beholding these (things).

23.50 And behold, a man by name of Joseph, being a councilman and a good and just man 23.51 -- this (one) had not agreed with the council and the act/action of them -- from Arimathaea, a city of the Judeans, who was awaiting/expecting the kingdom of God, 23.52 this (one), having gone near to Pilate, requested the body of Jesus, 23.53 and having taken *it* down, he wrapped it in linen cloth, and put him in a tomb hewn in rock, where no one had not yet been laid. 23.54 And it was a day of preparation/Friday, and a sabbath was coming on. 23.55 And the women having followed, who had come out of Galilee with him, were also beholding/observing the tomb as his body was placed,

23.56 ὑποστρέψασαι δὲ ἡτοίμασαν ἀρώματα καὶ μύρα. καὶ τὸ μὲν σάββατον ἡσύχασαν κατὰ τὴν ἐντολήν,

24.1 Τῇ δὲ μιᾷ τῶν σαββάτων ὄρθρου βαθέως ἐπὶ τὸ μνημῖον ἦλθον φέρουσαι ἃ ἡτοίμασαν ἀρώματα. 24.2 εὗρον δὲ τὸν λίθον ἀποκεκυλισμένον ἀπὸ τοῦ μνημίου, 24.3 εἰσελθοῦσαι δὲ οὐκ εὗρον τὸ σῶμα τοῦ κυρίου Ἰησοῦ. 24.4 καὶ ἐγένετο ἐν τῷ ἀπορῖσθαι αὐτὰς περὶ τούτου καὶ ἰδοὺ ἄνδρες δύο ἐπέστησαν αὐταῖς ἐν ἐσθῆτι ἀστραπτούσῃ.

24.5 ἐμφόβων δὲ γενομένων αὐτῶν καὶ κλινουσῶν τὰ πρόσωπα εἰς τὴν γῆν εἶπαν πρὸς αὐτάς, τί ζητεῖτε τὸν ζῶντα μετὰ τῶν νεκρῶν; 24.6 οὐκ ἔστιν ὧδε, ἀλλὰ ἠγέρθη. μνήσθητι ὡς ἐλάλησεν ὑμῖν ἔτι ὢν ἐν τῇ Γαλιλαίᾳ, 24.7 λέγων τὸν υἱὸν τοῦ ἀνθρώπου ὅτι δεῖ παραδοθῆναι εἰς χῖρας ἀνθρώπων ἁμαρτωλῶν καὶ σταυρωθῆναι καὶ τῇ τρίτῃ ἡμέρᾳ ἀναστῆναι. 24.8 καὶ ἐμνήσθησαν τῶν ῥημάτων αὐτοῦ,

24.9 καὶ ὑποστρέψασαι ἀπὸ τοῦ μνημίου ἀπήγγιλαν πάντα ταῦτα τοῖς ἕνδεκα καὶ πᾶσιν τοῖς λοιποῖς.

24.10 ἦσαν δὲ ἡ Μαγδαληνὴ Μαρίαμ καὶ Ἰωάννα καὶ Μαρία ἡ Ἰακώβου· καὶ αἱ λοιπαὶ σὺν αὐταῖς ἔλεγον πρὸς τοὺς ἀποστόλους ταῦτα. 24.11 καὶ ἐφάνησαν ἐνώπιον αὐτῶν ὡσεὶ λῆρος τὰ ῥήματα ταῦτα, καὶ ἠπίστουν αὐταῖς. 24.12 ὁ δὲ Πέτρος ἀναστὰς ἔδραμεν ἐπὶ τὸ μνημῖον, καὶ παρακύψας βλέπει τὰ ὀθόνια μόνα· καὶ ἀπῆλθεν πρὸς ἑαυτὸν θαυμάζων τὸ γεγονός. 24.13 καὶ ἰδοὺ δύο ἐξ αὐτῶν ἐν τῇ αὐτῇ ἡμέρᾳ ἦσαν πορευόμενοι εἰς κώμην ἀπέχουσαν σταδίους ἑκατὸν ἑξήκοντα ἀπὸ Ἰερουσαλήμ, ᾗ ὄνομα Ἐμμαοῦς, 24.14 καὶ αὐτοὶ ὡμίλουν πρὸς ἀλλήλους περὶ πάντων τῶν συμβεβηκότων τούτων. 24.15 καὶ ἐγένετο ἐν τῷ ὁμιλεῖν αὐτοὺς καὶ συνζητεῖν καὶ αὐτὸς Ἰησοῦς ἐγγίσας συνεπορεύετο αὐτοῖς, 24.16 οἱ δὲ ὀφθαλμοὶ αὐτῶν

23.56 and having returned, they prepared spices and ointments. And they indeed rested/were still *for* the sabbath, according to the command.

24.1 And on the one of the sabbaths/*first day of the week*, from very early dawn, they went to the tomb carrying spices which they prepared. 24.2 And they found the stone having been rolled away from the tomb, 24.3 but having entered they found not the body of the Lord Jesus. 24.4 And it happened at/in the (time) *for* them to be in doubt about this, and behold, two men came upon/stood by them in flashing/shining clothing.
24.5 And from them having become afraid and bowing the faces to the ground, they said to them (the women): Why do ye seek the (one) living with the dead (ones)? 24.6 He is not here, but he was raised. Remember ye as he spoke to ye, being still in Galilee, 24.7 saying: It is necessary *for* the son of the man to be delivered over into hands of sinful men and to be crucified and to rise up on the third day. 24.8 And they were reminded of his words,
24.9 and having returned from the tomb they reported all these (things) to the eleven and to all the rest (men).
24.10 And they were the Magdalene Mary and Joanna and the Mary of James; and the rest (women) with them, they were saying these (things) to the apostles. 24.11 And these words appeared like folly in their sight, and they were not believing for them (women). 24.12 But Peter, having risen up, ran to the tomb, and having stooped over, he sees only the linens; and he went away to himself, wondering at the (thing) having happened. 24.13 And behold, on the same day two out of them were going to a village being distant a hundred sixty stadia from Jerusalem, for which a name *is* Emmaus, 24.14 and they themselves were conversing to one another about all these (things) having happened/come together. 24.15 And it happened in the (time) *for* them to talk and to discuss (them) *that* also Jesus himself, having drawn near, was going/traveling with them. 24.16 but their eyes were being hindered from the (thing) not to recognize him.

189

ἐκρατοῦντο τοῦ μὴ ἐπιγνῶναι αὐτόν. 24.17 εἶπεν δὲ πρὸς αὐτούς, τίνες οἱ λόγοι οὗτοι οὓς ἀντιβάλλεται πρὸς ἀλλήλους περιπατοῦντες; καὶ ἐστάθησαν σκυθρωποί. 24.18 ἀποκριθεὶς δὲ εἷς ὀνόματι Κλεοπᾶς εἶπεν πρὸς αὐτόν, σὺ μόνος παροικεῖς Ἰερουσαλὴμ καὶ ταῦτα οὐκ ἔγνως τὰ γενόμενα ἐν αὐτῇ ἐν ταῖς ἡμέραις ταύταις; 24.19 καὶ εἶπεν αὐτοῖς, ποῖα; οἱ δὲ εἶπαν αὐτῷ, τὰ περὶ Ἰησοῦ τοῦ Ναζαρηνοῦ, ὃς ἐγένετο ἀνὴρ προφήτης δυνατὸς ἐν λόγῳ καὶ ἔργῳ ἐναντίον τοῦ θεοῦ καὶ παντὸς τοῦ λαοῦ, 24.20 ὅπως τε παρέδωκαν αὐτὸν οἱ ἀρχιερεῖς καὶ οἱ ἄρχοντες ἡμῶν εἰς κρίμα θανάτου καὶ ἐσταύρωσαν αὐτόν. 24.21 ἡμεῖς δὲ ἐλπίζομεν ὅτι αὐτός ἐστιν ὁ μέλλων λυτροῦσθαι τὸν Ἰσραήλ· ἀλλά γε καὶ σὺν πᾶσι τούτοις τρίτην ταύτην ἡμέραν ἄγι ἀφ' οὗ ταῦτα ἐγένετο. 24.22 ἀλλὰ καὶ γυναῖκές τινες ἐξ ἡμῶν ἐξέστησαν ἡμᾶς· γενόμεναι ὀρθριναὶ ἐπὶ τὸ μνημῖον 24.23 καὶ μὴ εὑροῦσαι τὸ σῶμα αὐτοῦ ἦλθον λέγουσαι καὶ ὀπτασίαν ἀγγέλων ἑωρακέναι, οἳ λέγουσιν αὐτὸν ζῆν. 24.24 καὶ ἀπῆλθόν τινες τῶν σὺν ἡμῖν ἐπὶ τὸ μνημῖον, καὶ εὗρον οὕτως καθὼς καὶ αἱ γυναῖκες εἶπον, αὐτὸν δὲ οὐκ εἶδον. 24.25 καὶ αὐτὸς εἶπεν πρὸς αὐτούς, ὦ ἀνόητοι καὶ βραδεῖς τῇ καρδίᾳ τοῦ πιστεύειν ἐπὶ πᾶσιν οἷς ἐλάλησαν οἱ προφῆται· 24.26 οὐχὶ ταῦτα ἔδει παθεῖν τὸν χριστὸν καὶ εἰσελθεῖν εἰς τὴν δόξαν αὐτοῦ; 24.27 καὶ ἀρξάμενος ἀπὸ Μωσέως καὶ ἀπὸ πάντων τῶν προφητῶν διερμήνευσεν αὐτοῖς τί ἦν ἐν ταῖς γραφαῖς τὰ περὶ ἑαυτοῦ. 24.28 καὶ ἤγγισαν εἰς τὴν κώμην οὗ ἐπορεύοντο, καὶ αὐτὸς προσεποιήσατο πορρωτέρω πορεύεσθαι. 24.29 καὶ παρεβιάσαντο αὐτὸν λέγοντες, μῖνον μεθ' ἡμῶν, ὅτι πρὸς ἑσπέραν ἐστὶν καὶ κέκλικεν ἤδη ἡ ἡμέρα. καὶ εἰσῆλθεν τοῦ μῖναι σὺν αὐτοῖς. 24.30 καὶ ἐγένετο ἐν τῷ κατακλιθῆναι αὐτὸν μετ' αὐτῶν καὶ λαβὼν τὸν ἄρτον ηὐλόγησεν καὶ κλάσας ἐδίδου αὐτοῖς· 24.31 αὐτῶν δὲ διηνοίχθησαν οἱ ὀφθαλμοὶ καὶ ἐπέγνωσαν αὐτόν· καὶ αὐτὸς ἄφαντος ἐγένετο ἀπ' αὐτῶν.

24.32 καὶ εἶπαν πρὸς ἀλλήλους, οὐχὶ ἡ καρδία ἡμῶν

24.17 And he said to them: What *are* these sayings/rea-
sonings which ye throw back and forth to one another,
walking? And they were stopped, sad faced (ones).
24.18 And answering, one by name of Cleopas said to
him: You, are you only a stranger *in* Jerusalem and
knew not these (things) having happened in her in
these days? 24.19 And he said to them: What (things)?
And they said to him: The (things) about Jesus the
Nazarene, who became a man, a powerful prophet in
reasoning/word and work before God and all the people,
24.20 and that the high priests and our leaders hand-
ed/delivered him over into a judgment of death and
they crucified him. 24.21 But we, we were hoping
that he himself is the (one) being about to redeem
Israel; but even so with all these (things), it brings
this third day from *the time* which these (things)
happened. 24.22 But also some women from us amazed
us, having been to the tomb at dawn/daybreak 24.23
and not having found his body, they came saying also
to have beheld a vision of messengers/angels, who say
for him to live. 24.24 And some of those with us went
to the tomb, and they found thus even as the women
said, but they saw not him. 24.25 And he himself said
to them: O foolish (ones) and slow in the heart of the
(thing) to believe on all (things) which the prophets
spoke; 24.26 was it not necessary *for* the anointed
(one) to suffer these (things) and to enter into his
glory/reputation? 24.27 And having himself begun from
Moses and from all the prophets he interpreted/ex-
plained to them what was in the writings, the (things)
about himself. 24.28 And they drew near to the village where they were going, and he himself made as if
to go/journey to a further place. 24.29 And they
prevailed upon him, saying: You stay with us, because
it is toward evening and the day has already declin-
ed/worn away. And he went in from the (thing) to stay
with them. 24.30 And it happened at the (time) *for*
him to recline with them, and having taken the loaf he
blessed *it* and having broken he was giving to them;
24.31 and their eyes were opened and they recognized
him; and he himself became invisible from them.
24.32 And they said to one another: Was not our

κεομένη ἦν ἐν ἡμῖν ὡς ἐλάλει ἡμῖν ἐν τῇ ὁδῷ, ὡς διήνυγεν ἡμῖν τὰς γραφάς; 24.33 καὶ ἀναστάντες αὐτῇ τῇ ὥρᾳ ὑπέστρεψαν εἰς Ἰερουσαλήμ, καὶ εὗρον ἠθροισμένους τοὺς ἕνδεκα καὶ τοὺς σὺν αὐτοῖς, 24.34 λέγοντας ὅτι ὄντως ἠγέρθη ὁ κύριος καὶ ὤφθη τῷ Σίμωνι. 24.35 καὶ αὐτοὶ ἐξηγοῦντο τὰ ἐν τῇ ὁδῷ καὶ ὡς ἐγνώσθη αὐτοῖς ἐν τῇ κλάσει τοῦ ἄρτου.

24.36 ταῦτα δὲ αὐτῶν λαλούντων αὐτὸς ἔστη ἐν μέσῳ αὐτῶν καὶ λέγει αὐτοῖς, εἰρήνη ὑμῖν. 24.37 φοβηθέντες δὲ καὶ ἔμφοβοι γενόμενοι ἐδόκουν πνεῦμα θεωρεῖν. 24.38 καὶ εἶπεν αὐτοῖς, τί τεταραγμένοι ἐστέ, καὶ διὰ τί διαλογισμοὶ ἀναβαίνουσιν ἐν ταῖς καρδίαις ὑμῶν; 24.39 εἴδετε τοὺς πόδας μου καὶ τὰς χῖράς μου ὅτι ἐγώ εἰμι αὐτός· ψηλαφήσατέ με καὶ ἴδετε, ὅτι πνεῦμα σάρκα καὶ ὀστέα οὐκ ἔχει καθὼς ἐμὲ θεωρεῖται ἔχοντα. 24.40 καὶ τοῦτο εἰπὼν ἔδιξεν αὐτοῖς τὰς χῖρας καὶ τοὺς πόδας.

24.41 ἔτι δὲ ἀπιστούντων αὐτῶν ἀπὸ τῆς χαρᾶς καὶ θαυμαζόντων εἶπεν αὐτοῖς, ἔχετέ τι βρώσιμον ἐνθάδε; 24.42 οἱ δὲ ἐπέδωκαν αὐτῷ ἰχθύος ὀπτοῦ μέρος· 24.43 καὶ λαβὼν ἐνώπιον αὐτῶν ἔφαγεν. 24.44 εἶπεν δὲ πρὸς αὐτούς,

οὗτοι οἱ λόγοι οὓς ἐλάλησα πρὸς ὑμᾶς ἔτι ὢν σὺν ὑμῖν, ὅτι δεῖ πληρωθῆναι πάντα τὰ γεγραμμένα ἐν τῷ νόμῳ Μωσέως ἐν τοῖς προφήταις καὶ ψαλμοῖς περὶ ἐμοῦ.

24.45 τότε διήνυξεν αὐτῶν τὸν νοῦν τοῦ συνιέναι τὰς γραφάς. 24.46 καὶ εἶπεν αὐτοῖς ὅτι οὕτως γέγραπται παθεῖν τὸν χριστὸν καὶ ἀναστῆναι ἐκ νεκρῶν τῇ τρίτῃ ἡμέρᾳ, 24.47 καὶ κηρυχθῆναι ἐπὶ τῷ ὀνόματι αὐτοῦ μετάνοιαν εἰς ἄφεσιν ἁμαρτιῶν εἰς πάντα τὰ ἔθνη ἀρξάμενοι ἀπὸ Ἰερουσαλήμ· 24.48 ὑμεῖς ἐστε μάρτυρες τούτων. 24.49 κἀγὼ ἀποστέλλω τὴν ἐπαγγελίαν τοῦ πατρός μου ἐφ' ὑμᾶς· ὑμεῖς δὲ καθίσατε ἐν τῇ πόλει ἕως οὗ ἐνδύσησθε ἐξ ὕψους δύναμιν.

24.50 ἐξήγαγεν δὲ αὐτοὺς ἕως πρὸς Βηθανίαν, καὶ ἐπάρας

heart being burned in us as he was speaking to us on the road/way, as he was explaining the writings to us? 24.33 And having rose up in the same hour, they returned to Jerusalem, and they found the eleven and those having been collected with them, 24.34 saying: The Lord really was raised and was made visible to Simon. 24.35 And they themselves were relating the (things) on the road and how he was made known to them by the breaking of the loaf.

24.36 And from them saying these (things), he himself stood in the midst of them and says to them: Peace to ye. 24.37 But having been fearing and having become startled, they were thinking to behold a spirit. 24.38 And he said to them: Why have ye been troubled, and why do reasonings/doubts come up in your hearts? 24.39 See ye my feet and my hands, that I, I am he/myself; feel ye me and see, because a spirit has not flesh and bones as ye behold me having. 24.40 And having said this, he gave to them the hands and the feet.

24.41 And of them yet/still disbelieving from the joy and marveling, he said to them: Have ye any food here? 24.42 And they gave to him a part of a broiled fish; 24.43 and having taken *it* he ate before them. 24.44 And he said to them:

These *are* my words/sayings which I spoke to ye being still with ye, that it is necessary *for* all the (things) having been written about me in the law of Moses, in the prophets and psalms, to be fulfilled.

24.45 Then he opened the mind of them of the (thing) to understand the writings. 24.46 And he said to them: Thus it has been written *for* the anointed (one) to suffer and to rise up out of dead (ones) on the third day, 24.47 and *for* repentance into/for remission/forgiveness of sins/failures to be heralded/preached on his name to all the ethnics, having begun from Jerusalem; 24.48 ye, ye are witnesses of these (things). 24.49 And I, I sent forth the promise from/of my father upon ye; but ye, ye sit in the city until which *time* ye might be clothed *with* power out of/from a height/*on high*.

24.50 And he led them out until near Bethany,

τὰς χῖρας αὐτοῦ ηὐλόγησεν αὐτούς. 24.51 καὶ ἐγένετο ἐν τῷ εὐλογῖν αὐτὸν αὐτοὺς διέστη ἀπ' αὐτῶν καὶ ἀνεφέρετο εἰς τὸν οὐρανόν. 24.52 καὶ αὐτοὶ προσκυνήσαντες αὐτὸν ὑπέστρεψαν εἰς Ἰερουσαλὴμ μετὰ χαρᾶς μεγάλης, 24.53 καὶ ἦσαν διὰ παντὸς ἐν τῷ ἱερῷ εὐλογοῦντες τὸν θεόν.

Εὐαγγέλιον κατὰ Λοῦκαν

and having lifted up his hands, he blessed them. 24.51 And it happened in the (time) *for* him to bless them *that* he parted from them and he was being carried up into the sky/heaven. 24.52 And they themselves having worshiped him, they returned to Jerusalem with great joy, 24.53 and they were through all/continually in the *outer* temple blessing/praising God.

A Good Message According to Luke

This is the Sinaitic New Testament, book of John.

1.1 Ἐν ἀρχῇ ἦν ὁ λόγος, καὶ ὁ λόγος ἦν πρὸς τὸν θεόν, καὶ θεὸς ἦν ὁ λόγος. 1.2 οὗτος ἦν ἐν ἀρχῇ πρὸς τὸν θεόν. 1.3 πάντα δι᾽ αὐτοῦ ἐγένετο, καὶ χωρὶς αὐτοῦ ἐγένετο οὐδὲ ἕν. ὃ γέγονεν 1.4 ἐν αὐτῷ ζωή ἐστίν, καὶ ἡ ζωὴ ἦν τὸ φῶς τῶν ἀνθρώπων· 1.5 καὶ τὸ φῶς ἐν τῇ σκοτίᾳ φαίνει, καὶ ἡ σκοτία αὐτὸ οὐ κατέλαβεν.

1.6 ἐγένετο ἄνθρωπος ἀπεσταλμένος παρὰ θεοῦ, ἦν ὄνομα αὐτῷ Ἰωάννης· 1.7 οὗτος ἦλθεν εἰς μαρτυρίαν, ἵνα μαρτυρήσῃ περὶ τοῦ φωτός, ἵνα πάντες πιστεύσωσιν δι᾽ αὐτοῦ. 1.8 οὐκ ἦν ἐκῖνος τὸ φῶς, ἀλλ᾽ ἵνα μαρτυρήσῃ περὶ τοῦ φωτός. 1.9 ἦν τὸ φῶς τὸ ἀληθεινόν, ὃ φωτίζει πάντα ἄνθρωπον, ἐρχόμενον εἰς τὸν κόσμον. 1.10 ἐν τῷ κόσμῳ ἦν, καὶ ὁ κόσμος δι᾽ αὐτὸν ἐγένετο, καὶ ὁ κόσμος αὐτὸν οὐκ ἔγνω. 1.11 εἰς τὰ ἴδια ἦλθεν, καὶ οἱ ἴδιοι αὐτὸν οὐ παρέλαβον. 1.12 ὅσοι δὲ ἔλαβον αὐτόν, ἔδωκεν αὐτοῖς ἐξουσίαν τέκνα θεοῦ γενέσθε, τοῖς πιστεύουσιν εἰς τὸ ὄνομα αὐτοῦ, 1.13 οἳ οὐκ ἐξ αἱμάτων οὐδὲ ἐκ θελήματος σαρκὸς οὐδὲ ἐκ θελήματος ἀνδρὸς ἀλλ᾽ ἐκ θεοῦ ἐγεννήθησαν. 1.14 καὶ ὁ λόγος σὰρξ ἐγένετο καὶ ἐσκήνωσεν ἐν ἡμῖν, καὶ ἐθεασάμεθα τὴν δόξαν αὐτοῦ, δόξαν ὡς μονογενοῦς παρὰ πατρός, πλήρης χάριτος καὶ ἀληθία. 1.15 Ἰωάννης μαρτυρῖ περὶ αὐτοῦ καὶ κέκραγεν λέγων, οὗτος ἦν ὃν εἶπον, ὁ ὀπίσω μου ἐρχόμενος ἔμπροσθέν μου γέγονεν, ὅτι πρῶτός μου ἦν. 1.16 ὅτι ἐκ τοῦ πληρώματος αὐτοῦ ἡμεῖς πάντες ἐλάβομεν, καὶ χάριν ἀντὶ χάριτος· 1.17 ὅτι ὁ νόμος διὰ Μωϋσέως ἐδόθη, ἡ χάρις καὶ ἡ ἀλήθια διὰ Ἰησοῦ ἐγένετο. 1.18 θεὸν οὐδεὶς ἑώρακεν πώποτε· μονογενὴς θεὸς ὁ ὢν εἰς τὸν κόλπον τοῦ πατρὸς ἐκεῖνος ἐξηγήσατο. 1.19 καὶ αὕτη ἐστὶν ἡ μαρτυρία τοῦ Ἰωάννου, ὅτε ἀπέστιλαν οἱ Ἰουδαῖοι ἐξ Ἱεροσολύμων ἱερῖς καὶ Λευείτας ἵνα ἐπερωτήσωσιν αὐτόν, σὺ τίς εἶ; 1.20 καὶ ὡμολόγησεν καὶ οὐκ ἠρνήσατο, — ὅτι ἐγὼ οὐκ ἰμὶ ὁ χριστός. 1.21 καὶ ἐπ᾽ ἠρώτησαν

1.1   In *the* beginning was the logos, and the logos was near/with God, and the logos was God.   1.2 This (one) was in *the* beginning with God.   1.3 All (things) became through him, and without him there became not one (thing). What became   1.4 by him is a life, and the life was the light   of   the men/humans. 1.5 And the light shines in the darkness, and the darkness overcame it not.

1.6   *There* became a man, being sent from God, a name for him was John;   1.7   this (one) came into/for a testimony, that he might testify about the light, in order that all might believe through him.   1.8 That (one) was not the light, but that he might testify about the light.   1.9   The light was the truth, which enlightens every man coming into the cosmos/world. 1.10 He was in the cosmos/world, and the cosmos/world became because of him, and the cosmos/world knew him not.   1.11 He came to the (things) his own, and those his own received him not.   1.12 But to as many as received him, he gave to them a right/authority to become children of God, to those believing in his name, 1.13 who were not generated/born out of bloods, neither out of a will of flesh, nor out of a will of man, but from/out of God.   1.14 And the logos became flesh and dwelt/tented among us, and we beheld his glory/fame, a glory as of an only born (one) from a father, full of grace and truth.   1.15 John testifies about him and has cried out, saying: This was the (one) of whom I spoke, the (one) coming after me, having become before me, because he was my first/before me.   1.16 Because we, we all received out of his fullness, and grace for a gift/grace;   1.17 because the law was given through Moses, the grace and the truth became/came about through Jesus.   1.18 No one has seen God at any time; an only born/generated God, the (one) being in the bosom/haven of the father, that (one) explained/described *himself*.   1.19 And this is the testimony/witness   from John, when the Judeans sent priests and Levites out of Jerusalem that they might ask him one (thing): You, who are you?   1.20 And he confessed and denied not: -- I, I am not the a-nointed (one).   1.21 And they besought   to/upon him

αὐτόν, πάλιν τί οὖν; Ἡλίας εἶ; λέγει, οὐκ εἰμί. ὁ προφήτης εἶ σύ; καὶ ἀπεκρίθη, οὔ. 1.22 εἶπον οὖν αὐτῷ, τίς εἶ; ἵνα ἀπόκρισιν δῶμεν τοῖς πέμψασιν ἡμᾶς· τί λέγεις περὶ σεαυτοῦ; 1.23 ἔφη, ἐγὼ « φωνὴ βοῶντος ἐν τῇ ἐρήμῳ, εὐθύνατε τὴν ὁδὸν κυρίου,» καθὼς εἶπεν Ἡσαΐας ὁ προφήτης. 1.24 καὶ ἀπεσταλμένοι ἦσαν ἐκ τῶν Φαρισαίων. 1.25 καὶ — εἶπον αὐτῷ, τί οὖν βαπτίζεις εἰ σὺ οὐκ εἶ ὁ χριστὸς οὐδὲ Ἡλίας οὐδὲ ὁ προφήτης;

1.26 ἀπεκρίθη αὐτοῖς ὁ Ἰωάννης λέγων, ἐγὼ βαπτίζω ἐν ὕδατι· μέσος ὑμῶν ἕστηκει ὃν ὑμεῖς οὐκ οἴδατε, 1.27 ὁ ὀπίσω μου ἐρχόμενος, οὗ οὐκ εἰμὶ ἄξιος ἵνα λύσω αὐτοῦ τὸν ἱμάντα τοῦ ὑποδήματος.

1.28 ταῦτα ἐγένετο ἐν Βηθανίᾳ πέραν τοῦ Ἰορδάνου ποταμοῦ, ὅπου ἦν ὁ Ἰωάννης βαπτίζων. 1.29 τῇ ἐπαύριον βλέπι τὸν Ἰησοῦν ἐρχόμενον πρὸς αὐτόν, καὶ λέγει, ἴδε ὁ ἀμνὸς τοῦ θεοῦ ὁ ἔρων τὴν ἁμαρτίαν τοῦ κόσμου. 1.30 οὗτός ἐστιν ὑπὲρ οὗ ἐγὼ εἶπον, ὀπίσω μου ἔρχεται ἀνὴρ ὃς ἔμπροσθέν μου γέγονεν, ὅτι πρῶτός μου ἦν. 1.31 κἀγὼ οὐκ ᾔδειν αὐτόν, ἀλλ᾽ ἵνα φανερωθῇ τῷ Ἰσραὴλ διὰ τοῦτο ἦλθον ἐγὼ ἐν ὕδατι βαπτίζων. 1.32 καὶ ἐμαρτύρησεν Ἰωάννης λέγων ὅτι τεθέαμαι τὸ πνεῦμα ὡς περιστερὰν καταβαῖνον ἐκ τοῦ οὐρανοῦ, καὶ μένον ἐπ᾽ αὐτόν· 1.33 καὶ ἐγὼ οὐκ ᾔδειν αὐτόν, ἀλλ᾽ ὁ πέμψας με βαπτίζειν ἐν τῷ ὕδατι ἐκῖνός μοι εἶπεν, ἐφ᾽ ὃν ἂν ἴδῃς τὸ πνεῦμα καταβαῖνον καὶ μένον ἐπ᾽ αὐτόν, οὗτός ἐστιν ὁ βαπτίζων ἐν πνεύματι ἁγίῳ. 1.34 κἀγὼ ἑώρακα, καὶ μεμαρτύρηκα ὅτι οὗτός ἐστιν ὁ ἐκλεκτὸς τοῦ θεοῦ.

1.35 τῇ ἐπαύριον πάλιν ἱστήκι ὁ Ἰωάννης καὶ ἐκ τῶν μαθητῶν αὐτοῦ δύο, 1.36 καὶ ἐμβλέψας τῷ Ἰησοῦ περιπατοῦντι λέγει, ἴδε ὁ ἀμνὸς τοῦ θεοῦ. 1.37 καὶ ἤκουσαν οἱ δύο μαθηταὶ αὐτοῦ λαλοῦντος καὶ ἠκολούθησαν τῷ Ἰησοῦ.

1.38 στραφεὶς δὲ ὁ Ἰησοῦς καὶ θεασάμενος αὐτοὺς

again: What then? Are you Elias? He says: I am not. You, are you the prophet? And he replied: No.   1.22 They said then to him: Who are you? In order that we might give an answer to those having sent us; what say you about yourself?   1.23 He was saying: I *am* A VOICE OF (ONE) CRYING IN THE DESERT/WILDERNESS: MAKE YE STRAIGHT THE ROAD/PATH OF THE LORD,   as   Isaiah/Esaias the prophet said.   1.24 And they had been/were being sent from the Pharisees.   1.25 And they said to him: Then why *do* you baptize if you, you are not the a-nointed (one) nor Elias nor the prophet?

1.26   John answered to them saying: I, I baptize in/with water; in the midst of ye (one) stands whom ye, ye know not,   1.27 the (one) coming after me, of whom I am not worthy that I might loose from him the strap of the sandal.

1.28   These (things) happened in Bethany beyond the Jordan river, where John was baptizing.   1.29 On the morrow he sees Jesus coming to/toward him, and he says: Behold, the lamb of God, the (one) taking away/bearing the sin/fault of the cosmos/world.   1.30 This (one) is he in behalf of whom I, I said: A man comes after me who has become before me, because he was my former/before me.   1.31 And I knew not him, but in order that he/it might be revealed/made known to Israel, because of this I, I came baptizing in/with water.   1.32 And John testified, saying: I have beheld the spirit coming down/descending as a dove out of the sky/heaven, and remaining/abiding upon him;   1.33 and I, I knew not him, but the (one) having sent me to baptize in/with water, that (one) said to me: Upon who ever you might see the spirit coming down and remain-ing/abiding upon him, this (one)/he is the (one) baptizing in/with a holy spirit.   1.34 I, I have both seen and witnessed/testified that this (one)/he is the chosen/elect (one) from God.

1.35   On the morrow John and two out of his learners/pupils again had stood,   1.36 and having seen Jesus walking, he says: Behold the lamb of God.   1.37 And the two learners/pupils of him heard *his* speaking and they followed with Jesus.

1.38   But Jesus, having turned and having himself

ἀκολουθοῦντας λέγει αὐτοῖς, τί ζητεῖτε; οἱ δὲ εἶπον αὐτῷ, ῥαββεί ὃ λέγεται μεθερμηνευόμενον διδάσκαλε, ποῦ μένεις; 1.39 λέγει αὐτοῖς, ἔρχεσθε καὶ ἴδετε. ἦλθον οὖν καὶ εἶδον ποῦ μαίνει, καὶ παρ' αὐτῷ ἔμιναν τὴν ἡμέραν ἐκείνην· ὥρα ἦν ὡς δεκάτη. 1.40 ἦν Ἀνδρέας ὁ ἀδελφὸς Σίμωνος Πέτρου εἷς ἐκ τῶν δύο τῶν ἀκουσάντων παρὰ Ἰωάννου καὶ ἀκολουθησάντων αὐτῷ·

1.41 εὑρίσκει οὗτος πρῶτον τὸν ἀδελφὸν τὸν ἴδιον Σίμωνα καὶ λέγει αὐτῷ, εὑρήκαμεν τὸν μεσσίαν, ὅ ἐστιν μεθερμηνευόμενον χριστός· 1.42 ἤγαγεν αὐτὸν πρὸς τὸν Ἰησοῦν. ἐμβλέψας αὐτῷ ὁ Ἰησοῦς εἶπεν, σὺ εἶ Σίμων ὁ υἱὸς Ἰωάννου· σὺ κληθήσῃ Κηφᾶς, ὃ ἑρμηνεύεται Πέτρος.

1.43 τῇ ἐπαύριον ἠθέλησεν ἐξελθῖν εἰς τὴν Γαλιλαίαν, καὶ εὑρίσκει Φίλιππον. καὶ λέγει αὐτῷ ὁ Ἰησοῦς, ἀκολούθι μοι. 1.44 ἦν δὲ ὁ Φίλιππος ἀπὸ Βηθσαϊδάν, ἐκ τῆς πόλεως Ἀνδρέου καὶ Πέτρου. 1.45 εὑρίσκει Φίλιππος τὸν Ναθαναὴλ καὶ λέγει αὐτῷ, ὃν ἔγραψεν Μωσῆς ἐν τῷ νόμῳ καὶ οἱ προφῆται εὑρήκαμεν, Ἰησοῦν υἱὸν τοῦ Ἰωσὴφ τὸν ἀπὸ Ναζαρέτ. 1.46 εἶπεν αὐτῷ Ναθαναήλ, ἐκ Ναζαρὲτ δύναται ἀγαθόν τι εἶναι; λέγει αὐτῷ Φίλιππος, ἔρχου καὶ ἴδε. 1.47 εἶδεν ὁ Ἰησοῦς τὸν Ναθαναὴλ ἐρχόμενον πρὸς αὐτὸν καὶ λέγει περὶ περὶ τοῦ Ναθαναήλ, ἴδε ἀληθῶς Ἰσδραηλείτης ἐν ᾧ δόλος οὐκ ἔστιν. 1.48 λέγει αὐτῷ Ναθαναήλ, πόθεν με γινώσκεις; ἀπεκρίθη ὁ Ἰησοῦς καὶ εἶπεν αὐτῷ, πρὸ τοῦ σε Φίλιππον φωνῆσαι ὄντα ὑπὸ τὴν συκῆν ἴδόν σε.

1.49 ἀπεκρίθη Ναθαναήλ καὶ εἶπεν, ῥαββεί, σὺ εἶ ὁ υἱὸς τοῦ θεοῦ, σὺ εἶ ὁ βασιλεὺς τοῦ Ἰσραήλ.

1.50 ἀπεκρίθη Ἰησοῦς καὶ εἶπεν αὐτῷ, ὅτι εἶπόν σοι ὅτι εἶδόν σε ὑποκάτω τῆς συκῆς πιστεύεις; μείζονα τούτων ὄψῃ. 1.51 καὶ λέγει αὐτῷ, ἀμὴν ἀμὴν λέγω ὑμῖν, ὄψεσθε τὸν οὐρανὸν ἀνεῳγότα καὶ τοὺς ἀγγέλους τοῦ θεοῦ ἀναβαίνοντας καὶ καταβαίνοντας ἐπὶ τὸν υἱὸν τοῦ ἀνθρώπου. 2.1 καὶ τῇ ἡμέρᾳ τῇ τρίτῃ γάμος ἐγένετο ἐν Κανὰ τῆς Γαλιλαίας, καὶ ἦν ἡ μήτηρ

beheld them following, he says to them: What seek ye? And they said to him: Rabbi, which being translated is called teacher, where *do* you stay/live? 1.39 He says to them: Come ye and see. Then they went and saw where he stays/lives, and they stayed/remained beside/with him that day; it was about *the* tenth hour. 1.40 Andrew the brother of Simon Peter was one out of the two of those having heard from John and having followed with him;

    1.41 this (one)/he first finds his own brother Simon and he says to him: We have found the messiah, which being translated is the anointed (one); 1.42 he led/brought him to Jesus. Having looked at him, Jesus said: You, you are Simon the son of John; you will be called Cephas, which is translated Peter.

    1.43 On the morrow he wanted/wished to go forth to Galilee, and he finds Philip. And Jesus says to him: Follow me. 1.44 And Philip was from Bethsaida, out of the city of Andrew and Peter. 1.45 Philip finds Nathanael and says to him: We have found *the one* whom Moses wrote *of* in the law and the prophets, Jesus, a son of Joseph, the (one) from Nazareth. 1.46 Nathanael said to him: Is anything good able to be from/out of Nazareth? Philip says to him: Come and see/behold. 1.47 Jesus saw Nathanael coming toward him, and he says concerning Nathanael: Behold, truly an Israelite, in whom guile is not. 1.48 Nathanael says to him: From where *do* you know me? Jesus answered and said to him: Before the (thing) *for* Philip to call you, I saw you being under the fig tree.

    1.49 Nathanael answered and said : Rabbi, you, you are the son of God; you, you are the king of Israel.

    1.50 Jesus answered and said to him: *Do* you believe because I said to you that I saw you underneath the fig tree? You will see greater (things) than these. 1.51 And he says to him: Truly, truly I say to ye, ye will see the sky/heaven having been opened and the messengers/angels of God going up/ascending and going down/descending upon/to the son of the man. 2.1 And on the third day a wedding/marriage happened in Cana of Galilee, and the mother of Jesus was there;

τοῦ Ἰησοῦ ἐκεῖ· 2.2 ἐκλήθη δὲ καὶ ὁ Ἰησοῦς καὶ οἱ μαθηταὶ αὐτοῦ εἰς τὸν γάμον. 2.3 καὶ ὑστερήσαντος οἴνου λέγει ἡ μήτηρ τοῦ Ἰησοῦ πρὸς αὐτόν, οἶνον οὐκ ἔχουσιν. 2.4 λέγει αὐτῇ ὁ Ἰησοῦς, τί ἐμοὶ καὶ σοί, γύναι; οὔπω ἥκει ἡ ὥρα μου.

2.5 λέγει ἡ μήτηρ αὐτοῦ τοῖς διακόνοις, ὅ τι ὁ ἂν λέγῃ ὑμῖν ποιήσατε. 2.6 ἦσαν δὲ ἐκεῖ λίθιναι ὑδρίαι ἓξ κατὰ τὸν καθαρισμὸν τῶν Ἰουδαίων κίμεναι, χωροῦσαι ἀνὰ μετρητὰς δύο ἢ τρεῖς. 2.7 καὶ λέγει αὐτοῖς ὁ Ἰησοῦς, γεμίσατε τὰς ὑδρίας ὕδατος. καὶ ἐγέμισαν αὐτὰς ἕως ἄνω. 2.8 καὶ λέγει αὐτοῖς, ἀντλήσατε νῦν καὶ φέρετε τῷ ἀρχιτρικλίνῳ· οἱ δὲ ἤνεγκαν. 2.9 ὡς δὲ ἐγεύσατο ὁ ἀρχιτρίκλινος τὸ ὕδωρ οἶνον γεγενημένον, καὶ οὐκ ἤδει πόθεν ἐστίν, οἱ δὲ διάκονοι ἤδεισαν οἱ ἠντληκότες τὸ ὕδωρ, φωνεῖ τὸν νυμφίον ὁ ἀρχιτρίκλινος 2.10 καὶ λέγει, πᾶς ἄνθρωπος πρῶτον τὸν καλὸν οἶνον τίθησιν, καὶ ὅταν μεθυσθῶσιν τὸν ἐλάσσω· σὺ δὲ τετήρηκας τὸν καλὸν οἶνον ἕως ἄρτι. 2.11 ταύτην ἐποίησεν τὴν ἀρχὴν τῶν σημίων ὁ Ἰησοῦς ἐν Κανὰ τῆς Γαλιλαίας πρώτην καὶ ἐφανέρωσεν τὴν δόξαν αὐτοῦ, καὶ ἐπίστευσαν οἱ μαθηταὶ αὐτοῦ εἰς αὐτόν. 2.12 μετὰ τοῦτο κατέβη εἰς Καφαρναοὺμ αὐτὸς καὶ ἡ μήτηρ αὐτοῦ καὶ οἱ ἀδελφοὶ αὐτοῦ —, καὶ ἐκεῖ ἔμιναν οὐ πολλὰς ἡμέρας.

2.13 ἐγγὺς δὲ ἦν τὸ πάσχα τῶν Ἰουδαίων, καὶ ἀνέβη ις Ἱεροσόλυμα ὁ Ἰησοῦς. 2.14 καὶ εὗρεν ἐν τῷ ἱερῷ τοὺς πωλοῦντας καὶ τὰ πρόβατα καὶ βόας καὶ περιστερὰς καὶ τοὺς κερματιστὰς καθημένους, 2.15 καὶ ποιήσας φραγέλλιον ἐκ σχοινίων καὶ πάντας ἐξέβαλεν ἐκ τοῦ ἱεροῦ, τά πρόβατα καὶ τοὺς βόας, καὶ τῶν κολλυβιστῶν ἐξέχεεν τὸ κέρμα καὶ τὰς τραπέζας κατέστρεψεν, 2.16 καὶ τοῖς τὰς περιστερὰς πωλοῦσιν εἶπεν, ἄρατε ταῦτα ἐντεῦθεν, μὴ ποιεῖται τὸν οἶκον τοῦ πατρός μου οἶκον ἐμπορίου. 2.17 ἐμνήσθησαν οἱ μαθηταὶ αὐτοῦ ὅτι γεγραμμένον ἐστίν, « ὁ ζῆλος τοῦ οἴκου σου καταφάγεταί με.»

2.18 ἀπεκρίθησαν οὖν οἱ Ἰουδαῖοι καὶ εἶπον αὐτῷ, τί

2.2 and both Jesus and his pupils/learners were invited/called to the wedding. 2.3 And from wine having been failing/lacking the mother of Jesus says to him: They have not wine. 2.4 Jesus says to her: What *is it* to me and to you, woman? My hour is not yet come.

2.5 His mother says to the servants/waiters/ministers: Do ye anything what ever the (he) may say to ye. 2.6 And there were six stone water jars, being laid/placed there according to the cleansing/purification of the Judeans, each (one) holding two or three measures. 2.7 And Jesus says to them: Fill ye the water jars with water. And they filled them until above (full). 2.8 And he says to them: Draw ye now and carry to the headwaiter; and they brought/carried *it*. 2.9 But as the headwaiter/caterer himself tasted the water having been generated/become wine, and he knew not from where it is, but the servants/ministers knew, those having drawn the water; the headwaiter calls the bridegroom 2.10 and says: Every man puts *forth* the good wine first, and when they are made drunk, the lesser/inferior; but you, you have kept the good wine until just now. 2.11 This, the beginning of the signs, Jesus did in Cana of Galilee first, and he revealed/made public his glory/fame. And his learners/pupils believed in him. 2.12 After this, he and his mother and his brothers went down into Capernaum, and they stayed/remained there not many days.

2.13 And the passover of the Judeans was near, and Jesus went up to Jerusalem. 2.14 And he found those selling both the sheep and oxen and doves and the moneychangers sitting in the *outer* temple, 2.15 and he made a whip/lash out of rope and he threw *them* all out of the *outer* temple, the sheep and the oxen, and he poured out the coins of the moneychangers and overturned/upset the tables, 2.16 and he said to those selling the doves/pigeons: Take ye these (things) from this place, make ye not the house of my father a house of merchandise. 2.17 His pupils/learners were reminded that it is having been written: THE ZEAL/JEALOUSY OF YOUR HOUSE WILL DEVOUR ME.

2.18 Then the Judeans answered and said to him: What sign *do* you show to us, that you do these

σημῖον δικνύεις ἡμῖν, ὅτι ταῦτα ποιεῖς; 2.19 ἀπεκρίθη ὁ Ἰησοῦς καὶ εἶπεν αὐτοῖς, λύσατε τὸν ναὸν τοῦτον καὶ ἐν τρισὶν ἡμέραις ἐγερῶ αὐτόν. 2.20 εἶπον οὖν οἱ Ἰουδαῖοι, τεσσεράκοντα καὶ ἓξ ἔτεσιν οἰκοδομήθη ὁ ναὸς οὗτος, καὶ σὺ τρισὶν ἡμέραις ἐγερεῖς αὐτόν; 2.21 ἐκεῖνος δὲ ἔλεγεν περὶ τοῦ ναοῦ τοῦ σώματος αὐτοῦ. 2.22 ὅτε οὖν ἠγέρθη ἐκ νεκρῶν, ἐμνήσθησαν οἱ μαθηταὶ αὐτοῦ ὅτι τοῦτο ἔλεγεν, καὶ ἐπίστευσαν τῇ γραφῇ καὶ τῷ λόγῳ ὃν εἶπεν ὁ Ἰησοῦς. 2.23 ὡς δὲ ἦν ἐν τοῖς Ἱεροσολύμοις ἐν τῷ πάσχα ἐν τῇ ἑορτῇ, πολλοὶ ἐπίστευσαν εἰς τὸ ὄνομα αὐτοῦ, θεωροῦντες αὐτοῦ τὰ σημῖα ἃ ἐποίει· 2.24 αὐτὸς δὲ ὁ Ἰησοῦς οὐκ ἐπίστευεν αὐτὸν αὐτοῖς διὰ τὸ γινώσκιν πάντας, 2.25 καὶ ὅτι χρίαν οὐκ εἶχεν ἵνα τις μαρτυρήσῃ περὶ τοῦ ἀνθρώπου· αὐτὸς γὰρ ἐγίνωσκεν τί ἦν ἐν, τί ἦν ἐν τῷ ἀνθρώπῳ.

3.1 Ἦν δὲ ἄνθρωπος ἐκ τῶν Φαρισαίων, Νικόδημος ὀνόματι αὐτῷ, ἄρχων τῶν Ἰουδαίων· 3.2 οὗτος ἦλθεν νυκτὸς πρὸς αὐτὸν καὶ εἶπεν αὐτῷ, ῥαββεί, οἴδαμεν ὅτι ἀπὸ θεοῦ ἐλήλυθας διδάσκαλος· καὶ οὐδεὶς δύναται ταῦτα τὰ σημῖα ποιεῖν ἃ σὺ ποιεῖς, ἐὰν μὴ ᾖ ὁ θεὸς μετ' αὐτοῦ. 3.3 ἀπεκρίθη ὁ Ἰησοῦς καὶ εἶπεν αὐτῷ, ἀμὴν ἀμὴν λέγω σοι, ἐὰν μή τις γεννηθῇ ἄνωθεν, οὐ δύναται ἰδεῖν τὴν βασιλείαν τοῦ θεοῦ.

3.4 λέγει πρὸς αὐτὸν ὁ Νικόδημος, πῶς δύναται ἄνθρωπος γέρων ὢν γεννηθῆναι; μὴ δύναται εἰς τὴν κοιλίαν τῆς μητρὸς αὐτοῦ δεύτερον εἰσελθῖν καὶ γεννηθῆναι; 3.5 ἀπεκρίθη Ἰησοῦς, ἀμὴν ἀμὴν λέγω σοι, ἐὰν μή τις ἐξ ὕδατος καὶ πνεύματος γεννηθῇ, οὐ δύναται εἰσελθῖν τὴν βασιλίαν τοῦ θεοῦ. 3.6 τὸ γεγεννημένον ἐκ τῆς σαρκὸς σάρξ ἐστιν, καὶ τὸ γεγεννημένον ἐκ τοῦ πνεύματος πνεῦμά ἐστιν. 3.7 μὴ θαυμάσῃς ὅτι εἶπόν σοι, δῖ ὑμᾶς γεννηθῆναι ἄνωθεν. 3.8 τὸ πνεῦμα ὅπου θέλει πνῖ, καὶ τὴν φωνὴν αὐτοῦ ἀκούεις, ἀλλ' οὐκ οἶδας πόθεν ἔρχεται καὶ ποῦ

(things)?   2.19 Jesus answered and said to them:
Destroy ye this *inner* temple and I shall raise it up
in three days.   2.20 Then the Judeans said: This *inner*
temple was built *in* forty and six years, and you, you
will raise it up in three days?   2.21 But that (one)
was saying/speaking about the temple of his body.
2.22 Then when he was raised out of dead (ones), his
learners/pupils were reminded that he was saying this,
and they believed in the writing and the saying/word
which Jesus said.   2.23 And as he was among the Jerusalemites at the passover at the festival, many believed in his name, observing/beholding from him the
signs which he was doing;   2.24 but Jesus himself was
not believing by/for them because of the (thing) *for*
him to know all (men),   2.25 and because he had not a
need that anyone might testify about the man/human;
for he, he was knowing what was in *them*, what was in
the man/human.

3.1   And *there* was a man out of the Pharisees,
Nicodemus by name for him, a ruler/leader of the
Judeans;   3.2 this (one) came of a night to him and
said to him: Rabbi, we know that you have come from
God a teacher;   and   no   one   is able to do these
(things), the signs which you, you do, unless God be
with him.   3.3 Jesus answered and said to him: Truly,
truly I say to you, unless someone might be generat-
ed/born from above, he is not able to see the kingdom
of God.
3.4   Nicodemus says to him: How is a man/human,
being an old (one), able to be generated/born? He is
not able to enter a second *time* into the belly of his
mother and to be generated/born?   3.5 Jesus answered:
Truly, truly I say to you, except someone be generated
out of water and spirit, he is not able to enter the
kingdom of God.   3.6 That having been generated out of
flesh is flesh, and that having been generated out of
the spirit is spirit.   3.7 Wonder/marvel ye not because I said to you: It is necessary for ye to be
generated/born from above.   3.8 The wind/spirit blows
where it wants/wills, and you hear the sound/voice of
it, but you know not from where it comes and where it

ὑπάγει· οὕτως ἐστὶν πᾶς ὁ γεγεννημένος ἐκ τοῦ ὕδατος καὶ τοῦ πνεύματος. 3.9 ἀπεκρίθη Νικόδημος καὶ εἶπεν αὐτῷ, πῶς δύναται ταῦτα γενέσθαι; 3.10 ἀπεκρίθη ὁ Ἰησοῦς καὶ εἶπεν αὐτῷ, σὺ εἶ ὁ διδάσκαλος τοῦ Ἰσραὴλ καὶ ταῦτα οὐ γινώσκις; 3.11 ἀμὴν ἀμὴν λέγω σοι ὅτι ὃ οἴδαμεν λαλοῦμεν καὶ ὃ ἑωράκαμεν μαρτυροῦμεν, καὶ τὴν μαρτυρίαν ἡμῶν οὐ λαμβάνεται. 3.12 εἰ τὰ ἐπίγια εἶπον ὑμῖν καὶ οὐ πιστεύεται, πῶς ἐὰν εἴπω ὑμῖν τὰ ἐπουράνια πιστεύσεται; 3.13 καὶ οὐδεὶς ἀναβέβηκεν εἰς τὸν οὐρανὸν εἰ μὴ ὁ ἐκ τοῦ οὐρανοῦ καταβάς, ὁ υἱὸς τοῦ ἀνθρώπου.

3.14 καὶ καθὼς Μωϋσῆς ὕψωσεν τὸν ὄφιν ἐν τῇ ἐρήμῳ, οὕτως ὑψωθῆναι δῖ τὸν υἱὸν τοῦ ἀνθρώπου, 3.15 ἵνα πᾶς ὁ πιστεύων εἰς αὐτὸν ἔχῃ ζωὴν αἰώνιον. 3.16 οὕτως γὰρ ἠγάπησεν ὁ θεὸς τὸν κόσμον, ὥστε τὸν υἱὸν τὸν μονογενῆ —, ἵνα πᾶς ὁ πιστεύων εἰς αὐτὸν μὴ ἀπόληται ἀλλ' ἔχῃ ζωὴν αἰώνιον. 3.17 οὐ γὰρ ἀπέστιλεν ὁ θεὸς τὸν υἱὸν εἰς τὸν κόσμον ἵνα κρίνῃ τὸν κόσμον, ἀλλ' ἵνα σωθῇ ὁ κόσμος δι' αὐτοῦ. 3.18 ὁ πιστεύων εἰς αὐτὸν οὐ κρίνεται· ὁ μὴ πιστεύων ἤδη κέκριται, ὅτι μὴ πεπίστευκεν εἰς τὸ ὄνομα τοῦ μονογενοῦς υἱοῦ τοῦ θεοῦ. 3.19 αὕτη δέ ἐστιν ἡ κρίσις, ὅτι τὸ φῶς ἐλήλυθεν εἰς τὸν κόσμον καὶ οἱ ἄνθρωποι ἠγάπησαν τὸ σκότος μᾶλλον ἢ τὸ φῶς, ἦν γὰρ αὐτῶν πονηρὰ τὰ ἔργα. 3.20 πᾶς γὰρ ὁ φαῦλα πράσσων μεισεῖ τὸ φῶς καὶ οὐκ ἔρχεται πρὸς τὸ φῶς, ἵνα μὴ ἐλεγχθῇ τὰ ἔργα αὐτοῦ· 3.21 ὁ δὲ ποιῶν τὴν ἀλήθιαν ἔρχεται πρὸς τὸ φῶς, ἵνα φανερωθῇ τὰ ἔργα αὐτοῦ ὅτι ἐν θεῷ ἐστιν εἰργασμένα. 3.22 μετὰ ταῦτα ἦλθεν ὁ Ἰησοῦς εἰς τὴν Ἰουδαίαν γῆν καὶ οἱ μαθηταὶ αὐτοῦ, κἀκεῖ διέτριβεν μετ' αὐτῶν καὶ ἐβάπτιζεν. 3.23 ἦν δὲ καὶ Ἰωάννης βαπτίζων ἐν Αἰνὼν ἐγγὺς τοῦ Σαλείμ, ὅτι ὕδατα πολλὰ ἦν ἐκεῖ, καὶ παρεγείνοντο καὶ ἐβαπτίζοντο· 3.24 οὔπω γὰρ ἦν

goes; so is every one having been generated out of the water and the spirit. 3.9 Nicodemus answered and said to him: How *are* these (things) able to happen/come about? 3.10 Jesus answered and said to him: You, you are the teacher from/of Israel, and you don't know these (things)? 3.11 Truly, truly I say to you that we speak what we know and we testify what we have seen, and you receive not the testimony from us. 3.12 If I said the earthly (things) to ye and ye believe not, how will ye believe if I say the heavenly (things) to ye? 3.13 And no one has gone up/ascended into the sky/heaven except the (one) having come down/descended out of the sky/heaven, the son of the man/human.

3.14 And as Moses lifted up/exalted the serpent in the wilderness/desert, so it is necessary *for* the son of the man to be lifted up, 3.15 that every one believing in him may have eternal life. 3.16 For God so loved the world, so that *he gave* the only generated son, in order that every one believing in him might not perish but may have eternal life. 3.17 For God sent not the son into the world that he might judge the world, but that the world might be saved through him. 3.18 The (one) believing in him is not being judged; the (one) not believing has been judged already, because he has not believed in the name of the only generated/born son of God. 3.19 And this is the judgment, because the light has come into the world and/but the men/humans loved the darkness rather/more than the light, for their works were evil. 3.20 For every one practicing the worthless/vile (things) hates the light and comes not near/to the light, in order that his works might not be reproved; 3.21 but the (one) doing the truth comes to the light, in order that the works of him might be revealed/exposed, because they have been worked in/with God. 3.22 After these (things) Jesus and his learners/pupils came into the Judean land, and there he was spending time with them and he was baptizing. 3.23 And John also was baptizing in Ainon near Salim, because many waters were/much water was there, and they were arriving/coming and were being baptized; 3.24 for John had not

βεβλημένος εἰς τὴν φυλακὴν ὁ Ἰωάννης. 3.25 ἐγένετο οὖν δὲ ζήτησις ἐκ τῶν μαθητῶν Ἰωάννου μετὰ Ἰουδαίου περὶ καθαρισμοῦ. 3.26 καὶ ἦλθον πρὸς τὸν Ἰωάννην καὶ εἶπον αὐτῷ, ῥαββεί, ὃς ἦν μετὰ σοῦ πέραν τοῦ Ἰορδάνου, ᾧ σὺ μεμαρτύρηκας, ἴδε οὗτος βαπτίζι καὶ πάντες ἔρχονται πρὸς αὐτόν.

3.27 ἀπεκρίθη Ἰωάννης καὶ εἶπεν, οὐ δύναται ἄνθρωπος λαβῖν οὐδ' ἓν ἐὰν μὴ ᾖ δεδομένον αὐτῷ ἐκ τοῦ οὐρανοῦ. 3.28 αὐτοὶ ὑμῖς μαρτυρῖται ὅτι εἶπον οὐκ εἰμὶ ἐγὼ ὁ χριστός, ἀλλ' ὅτι ἀπεσταλμένος εἰμὶ ἔμπροσθεν ἐκείνου. 3.29 ὁ ἔχων τὴν νύμφην νυμφίος ἐστίν· ὁ δὲ φίλος τοῦ νυμφίου, ὁ ἑστηκὼς αὐτοῦ καὶ ἀκούων, χαρᾷ χαίρει διὰ τὴν φωνὴν τοῦ νυμφίου. αὕτη οὖν ἡ χαρὰ ἡ ἐμὴ πεπλήρωται. 3.30 ἐκεῖνον δεῖ αὐξάνιν, ἐμὲ δὲ ἐλαττοῦσθαι.

3.31 ὁ ἄνωθεν ἐρχόμενος ἐπάνω πάντων ἐστίν· ὁ ὢν ἐπὶ τῆς γῆς ἐκ τῆς γῆς ἐστιν καὶ ἐκ τῆς γῆς λαλεῖ. ὁ ἐκ τοῦ οὐρανοῦ ἐρχόμενος ἐπάνω πάντων ἐστίν· 3.32 ὃν ἑώρακεν καὶ ἤκουσεν μαρτυρεῖ, καὶ τὴν μαρτυρίαν αὐτοῦ οὐδὶς λαμβάνει. 3.33 ὁ λαβὼν αὐτοῦ τὴν μαρτυρίαν ἐσφράγισεν ὅτι ὁ θεὸς ἀληθής ἐστιν. 3.34 ὃν γὰρ ἀπέστιλεν ὁ θεὸς τὰ ῥήματα τοῦ θεοῦ λαλεῖ, οὐ γὰρ ἐκ μέτρου δίδωσι τὸ πνεῦμα.

3.35 ὁ πατὴρ ἀγαπᾷ τὸν υἱόν, καὶ πάντα δέδωκεν ἐν τῇ χειρὶ αὐτοῦ. 3.36 ὁ πιστεύων εἰς τὸν υἱὸν ἔχει ζωὴν αἰώνιον· ὁ δὲ ἀπιθῶν τῷ υἱῷ οὐκ ὄψεται ἔχει ζωήν, ἀλλ' ἡ ὀργὴ τοῦ θεοῦ ἐπ' αὐτόν μένει.

4.1 Ὡς οὖν ἔγνω ὁ Ἰησοῦς ὅτι ἤκουσαν οἱ φαρισαῖοι ὅτι Ἰησοῦς πλείονας μαθητὰς ποιεῖ καὶ βαπτίζει ἢ Ἰωάννης 4.2 καίτοιγε Ἰησοῦς αὐτὸς οὐκ ἐβάπτιζεν ἀλλ' οἱ μαθηταὶ αὐτοῦ 4.3 ἀφῆκεν τὴν Ἰουδαίαν καὶ ἀπῆλθεν πάλιν εἰς τὴν Γαλιλαίαν. 4.4 ἔδει δὲ αὐτὸν διέρχεσθαι διὰ τῆς Σαμαρίας. 4.5 ἔρχεται οὖν εἰς πόλιν τῆς Σαμαρίας λεγομένην Συχὰρ πλησίον τοῦ χωρίου ὃ

yet been thrown into the prison. 3.25 But then there became an issue/debate out of the learners/pupils of John with a Judean about purification. 3.26 And they came to John and said to him: Rabbi, *the one* who was with you beyond the Jordan, for whom you, you have testified, behold this (one)/he is baptizing and all (men) are going to him.

3.27 John answered and said: A man is not able to receive/take nothing unless it has been given to him out of the sky/heaven. 3.28 Ye yourselves, ye witness/testify that I said: I, I am not the anointed (one), but that I have/am having been sent before that (one). 3.29 The (one) having the bride is a bridegroom; but the friend of the bridegroom, the (one) standing with him and hearing, he rejoices with joy because of the voice of the bridegroom. Then this, the joy my own, has been fulfilled. 3.30 It is necessary *for* that (one) to increase/grow, but *for* me to decrease/become lesser.

3.31 The (one) coming from above is above/over all; the (one) being on the earth is from the earth and he speaks from the earth. The (one) coming out of the sky/heaven is above all (men/things); 3.32 whom he has seen and heard he testifies, and/but no one receives his testimony/witness. 3.33 The (one) having received his witness/testimony he sealed/secured, because God is true. 3.34 For *the one* whom God sent speaks the words from God, for he gives not the spirit out of a measure.

3.35 The father loves the son, and he has given all (things) in/by the hand of him. 3.36 The (one) believing in the son has eternal life; but the (one) disobeying to/for the son will not see *or* have life, but the anger/wrath of/from God abides upon him.

4.1 Therefore, since Jesus knew that the Pharisees heard that Jesus makes and baptizes more learners/pupils than John 4.2 -- and indeed Jesus himself was not baptizing, but his learners/pupils -- 4.3 he left Judea and went away again into Galilee. 4.4 And it was necessary *for* him to go/pass through Samaria. 4.5 He goes then into a city of Samaria being called

ἔδωκεν Ἰακὼβ τῷ Ἰωσῆφ τῷ υἱῷ αὐτοῦ· 4.6 ἦν δὲ ἐκεῖ πηγὴ τοῦ Ἰακώβ. ὁ οὖν Ἰησοῦς κεκοπιακὼς ἐκ τῆς ὁδοιπορίας ἐκαθέζετο οὕτως ἐπὶ τῇ πηγῇ· ὥρα ἦν ὡς ἕκτη. 4.7 ἔρχεταί τις γυνὴ ἐκ τῆς Σαμαρίας ἀντλῆσαι ὕδωρ. λέγει αὐτῇ ὁ Ἰησοῦς, δός μοι πεῖν· 4.8 οἱ γὰρ μαθηταὶ αὐτοῦ ἀπεληλύθισαν εἰς τὴν πόλιν, ἵνα τροφὰς ἀγοράσωσιν. 4.9 λέγει οὖν αὐτῷ ἡ γυνὴ ἡ Σαμαρῖτις, πῶς σὺ Ἰουδαῖος ὢν παρ' ἐμοῦ πεῖν αἰτῖς γυναικὸς Σαμαρίτιδος οὔσης; οὐ γὰρ συγχρῶνται Ἰουδαῖοι Σαμαρίταις.

4.10 ἀπεκρίθη Ἰησοῦς καὶ εἶπεν αὐτῇ, εἰ ᾔδις τὴν δωρεὰν τοῦ θεοῦ καὶ τίς ἐστιν ὁ λέγων σοι, δός μοι πεῖν, σὺ ἂν ᾔτησας αὐτὸν καὶ ἔδωκεν ἄν σοι ὕδωρ ζῶν. 4.11 λέγει αὐτῷ ἡ γυνή, κύριε, οὔτε ἄντλημα ἔχεις καὶ τὸ φρέαρ ἐστὶν βαθύ· πόθεν ἔχεις τὸ ὕδωρ τὸ ζῶν; 4.12 μὴ σὺ μείζων εἶ τοῦ πατρὸς ἡμῶν Ἰακώβ, ὅστις ἔδωκεν ἡμῖν τὸ φρέαρ καὶ αὐτὸς καὶ ἐξ αὐτοῦ ἔπιεν καὶ οἱ υἱοὶ αὐτοῦ καὶ τὰ θρέμματα αὐτοῦ; 4.13 ἀπεκρίθη Ἰησοῦς καὶ εἶπεν αὐτῇ, πᾶς ὁ πίνων ἐκ τοῦ ὕδατος τούτου διψήσει πάλιν· 4.14 ὃς δ' ἂν πίῃ ἐκ τοῦ ὕδατος οὗ ἐγὼ δώσω αὐτῷ, οὐ μὴ διψήσει εἰς τὸν αἰῶνα, ἀλλὰ τὸ ὕδωρ ὃ ἐγὼ δώσω γενήσεται ἐν αὐτῷ πηγὴ ὕδατος ἁλλομένου εἰς ζωὴν αἰώνιον. 4.15 λέγει πρὸς αὐτὸν ἡ γυνή, κύριε, δός μοι τοῦτο τὸ ὕδωρ, ἵνα μὴ δειψῶ μηδὲ διέρχωμαι ὧδε ἀντλεῖν. 4.16 λέγει αὐτῇ ὁ Ἰησοῦς, ὕπαγε φώνησον τὸν ἄνδρα σου καὶ ἐλθὲ ἐνθάδε. 4.17 ἀπεκρίθη ἡ γυνὴ καὶ εἶπεν αὐτῷ, ἄνδρα οὐκ ἔχω. λέγει αὐτῇ ὁ Ἰησοῦς, καλῶς εἶπες ὅτι ἄνδρα οὐκ ἔχις· 4.18 πέντε γὰρ ἄνδρας ἔσχες, καὶ νῦν ὃν ἔχις οὐκ ἔστιν σου ἀνήρ· τοῦτο ἀληθῶς εἴρηκας. 4.19 λέγει αὐτῷ ἡ γυνή, κύριε, θεωρῶ ὅτι προφήτης εἶ σύ. 4.20 οἱ πατέρες ἡμῶν ἐν τῷ ὄρι τούτῳ προσεκύνησαν· καὶ ὑμεῖς λέγεται ὅτι ἐν Ἱεροσολύμοις ἐστὶν ὅπου προσκυνῖν δεῖ. 4.21 λέγει αὐτῇ ὁ Ἰησοῦς, πίστευέ μοι, γύναι, ὅτι ἔρχεται ὥρα ὅτε οὔτε ἐν τῷ ὄρει τούτῳ οὔτε ἐν Ἱεροσολύμοις προσκυνήσεται τῷ πατρί.

Sychar, a neighbor of the possession/field which Jacob gave to his son Joseph; 4.6 and a well of/from Jacob was there, then Jesus having grown weary from the journey was thus sitting at/upon the well; it was about *the* sixth hour. 4.7 A certain woman comes out of Samaria to draw water. Jesus says to her: Give for me to drink; 4.8 for his learners/pupils had gone away into the city, in order that they might buy foods. 4.9 Then the Samaritan woman says to him: How *do* you, being a Judean, you ask to drink from me, being a Samaritan woman? For Judeans deal/associate not with Samaritans.

4.10 Jesus answered and said to her: If you knew the gift of God and who is the (one) saying to you: Give for me to drink, you, you would *have* asked him and he would *have* gave to you living water. 4.11 The woman says to him: Lord/sir, you have not a bucket and the well is deep. From where have you the living water? 4.12 You, you are not greater than our father Jacob, who gave the well to us, and even he, he drank out of it, and/also his sons and his cattle? 4.13 Jesus answered and said to her: Every one drinking from this water will thirst again; 4.14 but who ever might drink out of the water from which I, I shall give to him, by no means will he thirst into the age, but the water which I, I shall give will become a spring of water in him springing up into eternal life. 4.15 The woman says to him: Lord/sir, give to me this water, in order that I may not thirst nor come here to draw. 4.16 Jesus says to her: Go you, call your man and come to this place. 4.17 The woman answered and said to him: I have not a man. Jesus to her: You said well that you have not a man; 4.18 for you had five men, and *the one* whom you have now is not your man; this you have said truly. 4.19 The woman says to him: Lord/sir, I perceive that you, you are a prophet. 4.20 Our fathers worshiped on/at this mountain; and ye, ye say that in Jerusalem is where it is necessary to worship. 4.21 Jesus says to her: Believe me, woman, that an hour/time comes when neither at/on this mountain nor in/at Jerusalem will ye worship to the father.

4.22 ὑμεῖς προσκυνεῖτε ὃ οὐκ οἴδατε· ἡμεῖς προσκυνοῦμεν ὃ οἴδαμεν, ὅτι ἡ σωτηρία ἐκ τῶν Ἰουδαίων ἐστίν. 4.23 ἀλλὰ ἔρχεται ὥρα, καὶ νῦν ἐστιν, ὅτε οἱ ἀληθινοὶ προσκυνηταὶ προσκυνήσουσιν τῷ πατρὶ ἐν πνεύματι καὶ ἀληθείᾳ· καὶ γὰρ ὁ πατὴρ τοιούτους ζητεῖ τοὺς προσκυνοῦντας αὐτόν. 4.24 πνεῦμα ὁ θεός, καὶ τοὺς προσκυνοῦντας αὐτὸν ἐν πνεύματι ἀληθείᾳ προσκυνῖν δεῖ. 4.25 λέγει αὐτῷ ἡ γυνή, οἶδα ὅτι μεσσίας ἔρχεται, ὁ λεγόμενος χριστός· ὅταν ἔλθῃ ἐκεῖνος, ἀναγγελεῖ ἡμῖν ἅπαντα. 4.26 λέγει αὐτῇ ὁ Ἰησοῦς, ἐγώ εἰμι, ὁ λαλῶν σοι. 4.27 καὶ ἐπὶ τούτῳ ἦλθαν οἱ μαθηταὶ αὐτοῦ, καὶ ἐθαύμαζον ὅτι μετὰ γυναικὸς ἐλάλει· οὐδεὶς μέντοι εἶπεν αὐτῷ, τί ζητεῖς; ἤ, τί λαλεῖς μετ᾽ αὐτῆς; 4.28 ἀφῆκεν οὖν τὴν ὑδρίαν αὐτῆς ἡ γυνὴ καὶ ἀπῆλθεν εἰς τὴν πόλιν καὶ λέγει τοῖς ἀνθρώποις, 4.29 δεῦτε ἴδετε ἄνθρωπον ὃς εἶπέν μοι πάντα ἃ ἐποίησα· μήτι οὗτός ἐστιν ὁ χριστός;

4.30 ἐξῆλθον οὖν ἐκ τῆς πόλεως καὶ ἤρχοντο πρὸς αὐτόν. 4.31 ἐν τῷ μεταξὺ ἠρώτων αὐτὸν οἱ μαθηταὶ λέγοντες, ῥαββεί, φάγε. 4.32 ὁ δὲ εἶπεν αὐτοῖς, ἐγὼ βρῶσιν ἔχω φαγῖν ἣν ὑμῖ οὐκ οἴδατε. 4.33 ἔλεγον οὖν οἱ μαθηταὶ πρὸς ἀλλήλους, μή τις ἤνεγκεν αὐτῷ φαγεῖν; 4.34 λέγει αὐτοῖς ὁ Ἰησοῦς, ἐμὸν βρῶμά ἐστιν ἵνα ποιῶ τὸ θέλημα τοῦ πέμψαντός με καὶ τελιώσω αὐτοῦ τὸ ἔργον. 4.35 οὐχ ὑμεῖς λέγεται ὅτι ἔτι τετράμηνός ἐστιν καὶ ὁ θερισμὸς ἔρχεται; ἰδοὺ λέγω ὑμῖν, ἐπάρατε τοὺς ὀφθαλμοὺς ὑμῶν καὶ θεάσασθε τὰς χώρας ὅτι λευκαί εἰσιν πρὸς θερισμόν. ἤδη 4.36 ὁ θερίζων μισθὸν λαμβάνει καὶ συνάγι καρπὸν εἰς ζωὴν αἰώνιον, ἵνα καὶ ὁ σπίρων ὁμοῦ χαίρῃ καὶ ὁ θερίζων. 4.37 ἐν γὰρ τούτῳ ὁ λόγος ἐστὶν ὁ ἀληθινὸς ὅτι ἄλλος ἐστὶν ὁ σπίρων καὶ ἄλλος ὁ θερίζων. 4.38 ἐγὼ ἀπέσταλκα ὑμᾶς θερίζειν ὃ οὐχ ὑμεῖς κεκοπιάκατε· ἄλλοι κεκοπιάκασιν, καὶ ὑμεῖς εἰς τὸν κόπον αὐτῶν εἰσεληλύθατε.

4.39 ἐκ δὲ τῆς πόλεως ἐκίνης πολλοὶ ἐπίστευσαν εἰς αὐτὸν

4.22 Ye, ye worship what ye know not; we, we worship what we know, because the salvation is out of/from the Judeans. 4.23 But an hour/time comes, and now is, when the true worshipers will worship to the father in spirit and truth; for the father also seeks the such (ones) worshiping to him. 4.24 God *is* a spirit, and it is necessary *for* those worshiping to worship in/with a spirit of truth. 4.25 The woman says to him: I know that a messias comes, the (one) being called the anointed (one); whenever that (one) might come, he will announce to us all (things). 4.26 Jesus says to her: I, I am, the (one) speaking to you. 4.27 And his learners/pupils came upon this/at this (time) and they were wondering/astonished that he was speaking with a woman; however, no one said to him: What seek you? Or, why *do* you speak with her? 4.28 Then the woman left her water jar and went away into the city and she says to the men: 4.29 Come! Behold/ see ye a man who said/told to me all (things) which I did; is this (one) not the anointed (one)?

4.30 Then they went forth out of the city and they were going to/near him. 4.31 In the meantime the learners/pupils were entreating him, saying: Rabbi, you eat. 4.32 But the (he) said to them: I, I have food to eat which ye, ye know not. 4.33 Then the learners/pupils were saying to one another: Someone brought him not to eat? 4.34 Jesus says to them: My food is that I may do the will of the (one) having sent me and I might complete the work from/of him. 4.35 Ye, say ye not that it is yet four months and the harvest comes? Behold, I say to ye, ye lift up your eyes and behold the fields, because they are white to harvest. Already 4.36 the (one) reaping takes wages and gathers fruit/products into eternal life, in order that both the (one) sowing and the (one) reaping may rejoice together. 4.37 For in this the logos/saying is the true (one) because another/one is the (one) sowing and another the (one) reaping. 4.38 I, I have sent ye to reap what ye, ye have not labored; others have labored, and ye, ye have entered into their toil/labor.

4.39 And many of the Samaritans out of that city

τῶν Σαμαριτῶν διὰ τὸν λόγον τῆς γυναικὸς μαρτυρούσης ὅτι εἶπέν μοι πάντα ἃ ἐποίησα. 4.40 ὡς οὖν ἦλθον πρὸς αὐτὸν οἱ Σαμαρῖται, ἠρώτων αὐτὸν μεῖναι παρ' αὐτοῖς· καὶ ἔμινεν παρ' αὐτοῖς ἡμέρας δύο. 4.41 καὶ πολλῷ πλείους ἐπίστευσαν διὰ τὸν λόγον αὐτοῦ, 4.42 καὶ ἔλεγον τῇ γυναικὶ ὅτι οὐκέτι διὰ τὴν σὴν λαλιὰν πιστεύομεν· αὐτοὶ γὰρ ἀκηκόαμεν παρ' αὐτοῦ, καὶ οἴδαμεν ὅτι ἀληθῶς οὗτός ἐστιν ὁ σωτὴρ τοῦ κόσμου.

4.43 μετὰ δὲ τὰς δύο ἡμέρας ἐξῆλθεν ἐκεῖθεν εἰς τὴν Γαλιλαίαν· 4.44 αὐτὸς γὰρ Ἰησοῦς ἐμαρτύρησεν ὅτι προφήτης ἐν τῇ ἰδίᾳ πατρίδι τιμὴν οὐκ ἔχει. 4.45 ὡς οὖν ἦλθεν εἰς τὴν Γαλιλαίαν, ἐδέξαντο αὐτὸν οἱ Γαλιλαῖοι, πάντα ἑωρακότες ὅσα ἐποίησεν ἐν Ἱεροσολύμοις ἐν τῇ ἑορτῇ, καὶ αὐτοὶ γὰρ ἐληλύθισαν εἰς τὴν ἑορτήν. 4.46 ἦλθαν οὖν πάλιν εἰς τὴν Κανὰ τῆς Γαλιλαίας, ὅπου ἐποίησεν τὸ ὕδωρ οἶνον.

ἦν δέ τις βασιλικὸς οὗ ὁ υἱὸς ἠσθένι ἐν Καφαρναούμ· 4.47 οὗτος ἀκούσας ὅτι ὁ Ἰησοῦς ἥκι ἐκ τῆς Ἰουδαίας εἰς τὴν Γαλιλαίαν ἀπῆλθεν πρὸς αὐτὸν καὶ ἠρώτα ἵνα καταβῇ καὶ ἰάσηται αὐτοῦ τὸν υἱόν, ἤμελλεν γὰρ ἀποθνῄσκειν.

4.48 εἶπεν οὖν ὁ Ἰησοῦς πρὸς αὐτόν, ἐὰν μὴ σημῖα καὶ τέρατα ἴδητε, οὐ μὴ πιστεύσηται. 4.49 λέγει πρὸς αὐτὸν ὁ βασιλικός, κύριε, κατάβηθι πρὶν ἀποθανῖν τὸν παιδά μου.

4.50 λέγει αὐτῷ ὁ Ἰησοῦς, πορεύου· ὁ υἱός σου ζῇ. ἐπίστευσεν ὁ ἄνθρωπος τῷ λόγῳ ὃν εἶπεν αὐτῷ τοῦ Ἰησοῦ καὶ ἐπορεύετο. 4.51 ἤδη δὲ αὐτοῦ καταβαίνοντος οἱ δοῦλοι ὑπήντησαν αὐτῷ καὶ ἤγγειλαν ὅτι ὁ παῖς αὐτοῦ ζῇ. 4.52 ἐπύθετο οὖν τὴν ὥραν παρ' αὐτῶν ἐν ᾗ κομψότερον ἔσχεν· καὶ εἶπον αὐτῷ ὅτι ἐχθὲς ὥραν ἑβδόμην ἀφῆκεν αὐτὸν ὁ πυρετός. 4.53 ἔγνω οὖν ὁ πατὴρ ὅτι ἐν ἐκείνῃ τῇ ὥρᾳ ἐν ᾗ εἶπεν αὐτῷ, ὁ υἱός σου ζῇ, καὶ ἐπίστευσεν αὐτὸς καὶ ἡ οἰκία αὐτοῦ ὅλη. 4.54 τοῦτο πάλιν δεύτερον ἐποίησεν σημῖον ὁ Ἰησοῦς ἐλθὼν ἐκ τῆς Ἰουδαίας εἰς τὴν Γαλιλαίαν. 5.1 μετὰ ταῦτα ἦν ἡ ἑορτὴ τῶν

believed in him because of the saying/word of the woman testifying: He said/told to me all (things) which I did. 4.40 Therefore, as the Samaritans came to him, they were entreating him to abide/stay with them; and he stayed with them two days. 4.41 And many more believed because of the saying/word of him, 4.42 and they were saying to the woman: No longer *do* we believe because of your speaking, for we ourselves have heard from him, and we know that truly this (one) is the savior of the world.

4.43 And after the two days he went forth from there into Galilee; 4.44 for Jesus himself testified that a prophet has not honor in his own country/ native place. 4.45 Then as he came into Galilee, the Galileans received him, having seen/beheld all (things) whatever he did in Jerusalem at the festival, for they also had gone to the festival. 4.46 Then he went again into Cana of Galilee, where he made the water wine.

And there was a certain royal (one), the son of whom was ailing in Capernaum; 4.47 this (one), having heard that Jesus has come out of Judea into Galilee, he therefore went away to him and was requesting that he might come down and heal his son, for he was about to die.

4.48 Then Jesus said to him: Unless ye might behold signs and wonders, by no means will/might ye believe. 4.49 The royal (one) says to him: Lord/sir, you come down before my child *is* to die.

4.50 Jesus says to him: You go, your son lives. The man believed/obeyed the saying/word which Jesus said to him, and he was going. 4.51 But already of him going down, the slaves met him and drew near because his boy lives. 4.52 He inquired therefore from them the time in/at which he had *it* better; and they said to him: The fever left him yesterday, *the* seventh hour. 4.53 Then the father knew that *it was* in/at that very hour in which he said to him: Your son lives, and he believed/obeyed, himself and his whole house/household. 4.54 Again, Jesus did this second sign, having gone out of Judea into Galilee. 5.1 After these (things) there was the festival of the

Ἰουδαίων, καὶ ἀνέβη ὁ Ἰησοῦς εἰς Ἱεροσόλυμα. 5.2 ἔστιν δὲ ἐν τοῖς Ἱεροσολύμοις ἐν τῇ προβατικῇ κολυμβήθρα ἡ ἐπιλεγομένη Ἑβραϊστὶ Βηθζαθά, πέντε στοὰς ἔχουσα. 5.3 ἐν ταύταις κατέκειτο πλῆθος τῶν ἀσθενούντων, τυφλῶν, χωλῶν, ξηρῶν.

5.5 ἦν δέ τις ἄνθρωπος τριάκοντα καὶ ὀκτὼ ἔτη ἔχων ἐν τῇ ἀσθενίᾳ αὐτοῦ· 5.6 τοῦτον ἰδὼν ὁ Ἰησοῦς κατακείμενον, καὶ γνοὺς ὅτι πολὺν χρόνον ἔχει, λέγει αὐτῷ, θέλις ὑγιὴς γενέσθαι; 5.7 ἀπεκρίθη αὐτῷ ὁ ἀσθενῶν, κύριε, ἄνθρωπον οὐκ ἔχω ἵνα ὅταν ταραχθῇ τὸ ὕδωρ βάλῃ με εἰς τὴν κολυμβήθραν· ἐν ᾧ δὲ ἔρχομαι ἐγὼ ἄλλος πρὸ ἐμοῦ καταβαίνι. 5.8 λέγει αὐτῷ ὁ Ἰησοῦς, ἔγειρε ἆρον τὸν κράβακτόν σου καὶ περιπάτει. 5.9 καὶ εὐθέως ἐγένετο ὑγιὴς ὁ ἄνθρωπος, καὶ ἠγέρθη καὶ ἦρε τὸν κράβαττον αὐτοῦ καὶ περιεπάτει. ἦν δὲ σάββατον ἐν ἐκίνῃ τῇ ἡμέρᾳ. 5.10 ἔλεγον οὖν οἱ Ἰουδαῖοι τῷ τεθεραπευμένῳ, σάββατόν ἐστιν, καὶ οὐκ ἔξεστίν σοι ἆραι τὸν κράβαττόν σου. 5.11 ὁ δὲ ἀπεκρίθη αὐτοῖς, ὁ ποιήσας με ὑγιῆν ἐκεῖνός μοι εἶπεν, ἆρον τὸν κράβαττόν σου καὶ περιπάτει.

5.12 ἠρώτησαν αὐτόν, τίς ἐστιν ὁ ἄνθρωπος ὁ εἰπών σοι, ἆρον καὶ περιπάτιν; 5.13 ὁ δὲ ἰαθεὶς οὐκ ᾔδει τίς ἐστιν, ὁ γὰρ Ἰησοῦς ἐξένευσεν ὄχλου ὄντος ἐν τῷ τόπῳ. 5.14 μετὰ ταῦτα εὑρίσκει αὐτὸν ὁ Ἰησοῦς ἐν τῷ ἱερῷ καὶ λέγει αὐτῷ, ἴδε ὑγιὴς γέγονας· μηκέτι ἁμάρτανε, ἵνα μὴ χεῖρον τί σοι γένηται.

5.15 ἀπῆλθεν ὁ ἄνθρωπος καὶ εἶπεν τοῖς Ἰουδαίοις ὅτι Ἰησοῦς ἐστιν ὁ ποιήσας αὐτὸν ὑγιῆ. 5.16 καὶ διὰ τοῦτο ἐδίωκον οἱ Ἰουδαῖοι τὸν Ἰησοῦν, ὅτι ταῦτα ἐποίει ἐν σαββάτῳ.

5.17 ὁ δὲ ἀπεκρίνετο αὐτοῖς, ὁ πατήρ μου ἕως ἄρτι ἐργάζετε, κἀγὼ ἐργάζομαι. 5.18 διὰ τοῦτο μᾶλλον ἐζήτουν αὐτὸν οἱ Ἰουδαῖοι ἀποκτῖναι, ὅτι οὐ μόνον ἔλυε τὸ σάββατον

Judeans, and Jesus went up to Jerusalem.   5.2 And
there is among the Jerusalemites a pool at the sheep-
gate, the one being called Bethzatha in Hebrew, having
five colonades/porticos.   5.3 In these was lying a
multitude of the sick/ailing (ones), blind, lame,
withered.
     5.5 And *there* was a certain man having *it* in his
sickness/ailment *for* thirty and eight years;   5.6
Jesus, having seen this (one) lying down, and knowing
that he has *it for* much time, says to him: *Do* you
want/wish to become healthy/whole?   5.7 The (one)
ailing answered to him: Lord/sir, I have not a man in
order that whenever the water might be troubled to put
me into the pool; but in what (time) I, I am going,
another goes down before me.   5.8 Jesus says to him:
Rise up, take up your mattress/bed and walk.   5.9 And
immediately the man became whole/healthy, and he was
raised up and he took up his mattress/bed and he was
walking. But it was a sabbath on that day.   5.10
Therefore, the Judeans were saying to the (one) having
been treated/healed: It is a sabbath, and it is not
lawful for you to take up your mattress/bed.   5.11 But
the (he) answered to them: The (one) having made me
whole, that (one) said to me: You take up your mat-
tress/bed and walk.
     5.12   They asked him: Who is the man, the (one)
having said to you: You take *it* up and to walk?   5.13
But the (one) having been healed knew not who he is,
for Jesus withdrew from a crowd being in the place.
5.14 After these (things) Jesus finds him in the *outer*
temple and says   to   him: Behold, you have become
whole/well; sin no longer, lest something worse might
happen to you.
     5.15   The man went away/out and said to the
Judeans that Jesus is the (one) having made him whole.
5.16 And because of this the Judeans were pursuing/
prosecuting Jesus, because he was doing these (things)
on a sabbath.
     5.17   But the (he) answered to them: My father
works until just now, and I, I work.   5.18 Because of
this the Judeans were seeking more to kill him, because he not only was loosing/infringing the sabbath,

ἀλλὰ καὶ πατέρα ἴδιον ἔλεγε τὸν θεόν, ἴσον ἑαυτὸν ποιῶν τῷ θεῷ. 5.19 ἀπεκρίνατο οὖν ὁ Ἰησοῦς καὶ ἔλεγεν αὐτοῖς, ἀμὴν ἀμὴν λέγω ὑμῖν, οὐ δύναται ὁ υἱὸς ποιεῖν ἀφ᾽ ἑαυτοῦ οὐδὲν ἂν μή τι βλέπῃ τὸν πατέρα ποιοῦντα· ἃ γὰρ ἂν ἐκεῖνος ποιῇ, ταῦτα καὶ ὁ υἱὸς ποιεῖ ὁμοίως. 5.20 ὁ γὰρ πατὴρ φιλῖ τὸν υἱὸν καὶ πάντα δίκνυσιν αὐτῷ ἃ αὐτὸς ποιεῖ, καὶ μίζονα τούτων ἔργα δείξει αὐτῷ, ἵνα ὑμεῖς θαυμάζετε. 5.21 ὡς γὰρ ὁ πατὴρ ἐγείρει τοὺς νεκροὺς καὶ ζωοποιεῖ, οὕτως καὶ ὁ υἱὸς οὓς θέλει ζωοποιεῖ. 5.22 οὐδὲ γὰρ ὁ πατὴρ κρίνει οὐδένα, ἀλλὰ τὴν κρίσιν πᾶσαν δέδωκεν τῷ υἱῷ, 5.23 ἵνα πάντες τιμῶσι τὸν υἱὸν καθὼς τιμῶσι τὸν πατέρα. ὁ μὴ τιμῶν τὸν υἱὸν οὐ τειμᾷ τὸν πατέρα τὸν πέμψαντα αὐτόν.

5.24 ἀμὴν ἀμὴν λέγω ὑμῖν ὅτι ὁ τὸν λόγον μου ἀκούων καὶ πιστεύων τῷ πέμψαντί με ἔχει ζωὴν αἰώνιον, καὶ εἰς κρίσιν οὐκ ἔρχεται ἀλλὰ μεταβέβηκεν ἐκ τοῦ θανάτου εἰς τὴν ζωήν.

5.25 ἀμὴν ἀμὴν λέγω ὑμῖν ὅτι ἔρχεται ὥρα καὶ νῦν ἐστιν ὅτε οἱ νεκροὶ ἀκούσουσι τῆς φωνῆς τοῦ υἱοῦ τοῦ θεοῦ καὶ οἱ ἀκούσαντες ζήσουσιν. 5.26 ὥσπερ γὰρ ὁ πατὴρ ζωὴν ἔχει ἐν ἑαυτῷ, οὕτως καὶ τῷ υἱῷ ἔδωκεν ζωὴν ἔχιν ἐν ἑαυτῷ· 5.27 καὶ κρίσιν ἔδωκεν αὐτῷ ἐξουσίαν ποιεῖν, ὅτι υἱὸς ἀνθρώπου ἐστίν. 5.28 μὴ θαυμάζεται τοῦτο, ὅτι ἔρχεται ὥρα ἐν ᾗ πάντες οἱ ἐν τοῖς μνημίοις ἀκούσουσιν τῆς φωνῆς αὐτοῦ 5.29 καὶ ἐκπορεύσονται, οἱ τὰ ἀγαθὰ ποιήσαντες εἰς ἀνάστασιν ζωῆς, οἱ δὲ τὰ φαῦλα πράξαντες εἰς ἀνάστασιν κρίσεως. 5.30 οὐ δύναμαι ποιεῖν ἐγὼ ἀπ᾽ ἐμαυτοῦ οὐδέν· καθὼς ἀκούω κρίνω, καὶ ἡ κρίσις ἡ ἐμὴ δικαία ἐστίν, ὅτι οὐ ζητῶ τὸ θέλημα τὸ ἐμὸν ἀλλὰ τὸ θέλημα τοῦ πέμψαντός με. 5.31 ἐὰν ἐγὼ μαρτυρῶ περὶ ἐμαυτοῦ, ἡ μαρτυρία μου οὐκ ἔστιν ἀληθής· 5.32 ἄλλος ἐστὶν ὁ μαρτυρῶν περὶ ἐμοῦ, καὶ οἶδα ὅτι ἀληθής ἐστιν ἡ μαρτυρία ἣν μαρτυρῖ

but he was also saying his own father *is* God, making himself equal to God. 5.19 Then Jesus answered/ replied and Jesus was saying to them: Truly, truly I say to ye, the son is not able to do/make nothing from/of himself except what he may see the father doing; for what ever (things) that (one) may do, the son also does these (things) similarly/likewise. 5.20 For the father loves/φιλέω the son and shows to him all (things) which he, he does, and he will show to him works greater than these, in order that ye, ye wonder/marvel. 5.21 For as the father raises up the dead (ones) and makes *them* alive, so also the son makes alive (those) whom he wants/wishes. 5.22 For the father judges no one, but he has given the every judgment to the son, 5.23 in order that all (men) may honor the son just as they may honor the father. The (one) honoring not the son honors not the father, the (one) having sent him.

5.24 Truly, truly I say to ye that the (one) hearing my saying/word and believing/obeying the (one) having sent me has eternal life, and he comes not into judgment but has crossed over out of the death into the life.

5.25 Truly, truly I say to ye that an hour comes and now is when the dead (ones) will hear the voice of/sound from the son of God and the (ones) having heard will live. 5.26 For just as the father has/ holds life in himself, so also he gave life to the son to have/hold in himself; 5.27 and he gave judgment to him to do/make authority, because he is a son of man. 5.28 Wonder/marvel ye not *at* this, because an hour comes in which all the (ones) in the tombs will hear the voice/sound of him 5.29 and they will come forth/out, those having made the good (things) into a resurrection of life, but those having practiced the vile/worthless (things) into a resurrection of judg- ment. 5.30 I, I am not able to do nothing from myself; I judge just as I hear, and my judgment is just, because I seek not my own will but the will of the (one) having sent me. 5.31 If I, I testify about myself, my testimony is not true; 5.32 there is another one testifying about me and ye know that the

περὶ ἐμοῦ. 5.33 ὑμεῖς ἀπεστάλκατε πρὸς Ἰωάννην, καὶ μεμαρτύρηκε τῇ ἀληθίᾳ· 5.34 ἐγὼ δὲ οὐ παρὰ ἀνθρώπου τὴν μαρτυρίαν λαμβάνω, ἀλλὰ ταῦτα λέγω ἵνα ὑμεῖς σωθῆτε. 5.35 ἐκεῖνος ἦν ὁ λύχνος ὁ καιόμενος καὶ φαίνων, ὑμῖς δὲ ἠθελήσαται ἀγαλλιαθῆναι πρὸς ὥραν ἐν τῷ φωτὶ αὐτοῦ. 5.36 ἐγὼ δὲ ἔχω μαρτυρίαν μείζω τοῦ Ἰωάννου· τὰ γὰρ ἔργα ἃ δέδωκέν μοι ὁ πατὴρ ἵνα τελιώσω αὐτά, αὐτὰ τὰ ἔργα ἃ ποιῶ, μαρτυρῖ περὶ ἐμοῦ ὅτι ὁ πατήρ ἐμὲ ἀπέσταλκεν· 5.37 καὶ ὁ πέμψας με πατὴρ ἐκεῖνος μεμαρτύρηκεν περὶ ἐμοῦ. οὔτε φωνὴν αὐτοῦ πώποτε ἀκηκόατε οὔτε εἶδος αὐτοῦ ἑωράκατε, 5.38 καὶ τὸν λόγον αὐτοῦ οὐκ ἔχετε ἐν ὑμῖν μένοντα, ὅτι ὃν ἀπέστιλεν ἐκῖνος τούτῳ ὑμῖς οὐ πιστεύετε. 5.39 ἐραυνᾶτε τὰς γραφάς, ὅτι ὑμεῖς δοκεῖται ἐν αὐταῖς ζωὴν αἰώνιον ἔχιν· καὶ ἐκεῖναί εἰσιν αἱ μαρτυροῦσαι περὶ ἐμοῦ· 5.40 καὶ οὐ θέλετε ἐλθεῖν πρός με ἵνα ζωὴν ἔχητε. 5.41 δόξαν παρὰ ἀνθρώπων οὐ λαμβάνω, 5.42 ἀλλ᾽ ἔγνωκα ὑμᾶς ὅτι τὴν ἀγάπην τοῦ θεοῦ οὐκ ἔχετε ἐν ἑαυτοῖς. 5.43 ἐγὼ ἐλήλυθα ἐν τῷ ὀνόματι τοῦ πατρός μου καὶ οὐ λαμβάνετέ με· ἐὰν ἄλλος ἔλθῃ τῷ ὀνόματι τῷ ἰδίῳ, ἐκεῖνον λήμψεσθαι. 5.44 πῶς δύνασθαι ὑμῖς πιστεῦσαι, δόξαν παρὰ ἀλλήλων λαμβάνοντες καὶ τὴν δόξαν τὴν παρὰ τοῦ μόνου θεοῦ οὐ ζητῖτε; 5.45 μὴ δοκεῖται ὅτι ἐγὼ κατηγορήσω ὑμῶν πρὸς τὸν πατέρα· ἔστιν ὁ κατηγορῶν ὑμῶν Μωϋσῆς, εἰς ὃν ὑμεῖς ἠλπίκατε. 5.46 εἰ γὰρ ἐπιστεύετε Μωσεῖ, ἐπιστεύετε ἂν ἐμοί, περὶ γὰρ ἐμοῦ ἐκεῖνος ἔγραψεν. 5.47 εἰ δὲ τοῖς ἐκείνου γράμμασιν οὐ πιστεύεται, πῶς τοῖς ἐμοῖς ῥήμασιν πιστεύσετε; 6.1 μετὰ ταῦτα ἀπῆλθεν ὁ Ἰησοῦς πέραν τῆς θαλάσσης τῆς Γαλιλαίας τῆς Τιβεριάδος. 6.2 ἠκολούθει δὲ αὐτῷ πολύς ὄχλος, ὅτι ἑώρων τὰ σημεῖα ἃ ἐποίει περὶ τῶν ἀσθενούντων. 6.3 ἀνῆλθεν δὲ εἰς τὸ ὄρος Ἰησοῦς, καὶ ἐκῖ ἐκαθέζετο μετὰ τῶν μαθητῶν αὐτοῦ. 6.4 ἦν δὲ ἐγγὺς τὸ πάσχα, ἡ ἑορτὴ τῶν Ἰουδαίων.

testimony which he testifies about me is true.   5.33
Ye, ye have sent to John, and he has testified to the
truth;   5.34 but I, I take/receive not the testimony
from a man, but I say these (things) in order that ye,
ye might be saved.   5.35 That (one) was the burning
and shining lamp, and ye, ye wanted/wished to be
exulted toward an hour/time in the light of him.   5.36
But I, I have a testimony greater than the (one) of
John; for the works which the father has given to me
that I might complete/finish them, the works themselves which I do, testifies/witnesses about me that
the father has sent me;   5.37 and the father having
sent me, that (one) has testified/witnessed about me.
Ye have neither heard his voice at any time nor have
ye seen his form/appearance,   5.38   and ye have not
his saying/word abiding in ye, because *the one* whom
that (one) sent, ye, ye believe/obey not for this
(one).   5.39 Ye search the writings, because ye, ye
think/suppose to have eternal life in/by them; and
those are the (ones) witnessing/testifying about me.
5.40 And ye want/wish not to come to me in order that
ye may have life.   5.41 I take/receive not fame/glory
from men,   5.42 but I have known ye that ye have not
the agape of/from God in yourselves.   5.43 I, I have
come in the name of my father and ye *do* not receive
me; if another might come in/for his own name, ye will
receive that (one).   5.44 How are ye able to believe,
receiving fame/glory from one another and not seeking
the fame/glory from the only God?   5.45 Think ye not
that I, I shall accuse ye to the father; there is one
accusing ye, Moses, in whom ye, ye have hoped.   5.46
For if ye were believing in Moses, ye would have been
believing in me, for that (one) has written about me.
5.47 But if ye believe not in the writings/letters
from that (one), how will ye believe in my words?   6.1
After these (things) Jesus went away beyond/across the
sea of Galilee from/of Tiberias.   6.2 And a much crowd
followed with him, because they were seeing/observing
the signs which he was doing about the ailing/sick
(ones).   6.3 And Jesus went up to the mountain, and he
was sitting there with his learners/pupils.   6.4 And
the passover was near, the festival of the Judeans.

6.5 ἐπάρας οὖν τοὺς ὀφθαλμοὺς Ἰησοῦς καὶ θεασάμενος ὅτι ὄχλος πολὺς ἔρχεται πρὸς αὐτὸν λέγει πρὸς Φίλιππον, πόθεν ἀγοράσωμεν ἄρτους ἵνα οὗτοι φάγωσιν; 6.6 τοῦτο δὲ ἔλεγεν πιράζων αὐτόν, αὐτὸς γὰρ ᾔδει τί ἔμελλεν ποιεῖν.

6.7 ἀποκρίνετε οὖν ὁ Φίλιππος, διακοσίων δηναρίων ἄρτοι οὐκ ἀρκοῦσιν ἵνα ἕκαστος βραχύ τι λάβῃ. 6.8 λέγει αὐτῷ εἷς ἐκ τῶν μαθητῶν αὐτοῦ, Ἀνδρέας ὁ ἀδελφὸς Σίμωνος Πέτρου, 6.9 ἔστιν παιδάριον ὧδε ὃ ἔχει πέντε ἄρτους κριθίνους καὶ δύο ὀψάρια· ἀλλὰ ταῦτα τί ἐστιν εἰς τοσούτους; 6.10 εἶπεν ὁ Ἰησοῦς, ποιήσατε τοὺς ἀνθρώπους ἀναπεσῖν. ἦν δὲ χόρτος πολὺς ἐν τῷ τόπῳ. ἀνέπεσαν οὖν οἱ ἄνδρες τὸν ἀριθμὸν ὡς πεντακισχίλιοι. 6.11 ἔλαβεν οὖν τοὺς ἄρτους ὁ Ἰησοῦς καὶ εὐχαριστήσεν καὶ ἔδωκεν τοῖς ἀνακειμένοις, ὁμοίως καὶ ἐκ τῶν ὀψαρίων ὅσον ἤθελον. 6.12 ὡς δὲ ἐνεπλήσθησαν λέγι τοῖς μαθηταῖς αὐτοῦ, συναγάγετε τὰ περισσεύσαντα κλάσματα, ἵνα μή τι ἀπόληται. 6.13 συνήγαγον οὖν, καὶ ἐγέμισαν δώδεκα κοφίνους κλασμάτων ἐκ τῶν πέντε ἄρτων τῶν κριθίνων ἃ ἐπερίσσευσεν τοῖς βεβρωκόσιν. 6.14 οἱ οὖν ἄνθρωποι ἰδόντες ὃ ἐποίησεν σημεῖον ἔλεγον οὗτός ἐστιν ἀληθῶς ὁ προφήτης ὁ εἰς τὸν κόσμον ἐρχόμενος.

6.15 Ἰησοῦς οὖν γνοὺς ὅτι μέλλουσιν ἔρχεσθαι καὶ ἁρπάζειν αὐτὸν ἵνα ποιήσωσιν βασιλέα ἀνεχώρησεν πάλιν εἰς τὸ ὄρος μόνος αὐτός. 6.16 ὡς ὀψία ἐγένετο κατέβησαν οἱ μαθηταὶ αὐτοῦ ἐπὶ τὴν θάλασσαν, 6.17 καὶ ἐμβάντες εἰς πλοῖον ἔρχονται πέραν τῆς θαλάσσης εἰς Καφαρναούμ. κατέλαβεν δὲ αὐτοὺς ἡ σκοτία καὶ οὔπω ἐληλύθει Ἰησοῦς πρὸς αὐτούς, 6.18 ἥ τε θάλασσα ἀνέμου μεγάλου πνέοντος διηγείρετο. 6.19 ἐληλακότες οὖν ὡς στάδια εἴκοσι πέντε ἢ τριάκοντα θεωροῦσιν τὸν Ἰησοῦν περιπατοῦντα ἐπὶ τῆς θαλάσσης καὶ ἐγγὺς τοῦ πλοίου γινόμενον, καὶ ἐφοβήθησαν. 6.20 καὶ λέγει αὐτοῖς, ἐγώ εἰμι, μὴ φοβῖσθε. 6.21 ἦλθον οὖν λαβῖν αὐτὸν εἰς τὸ πλοῖον, καὶ εὐθέως τὸ πλοῖον ἐγένετο ἐπὶ τῆς γῆς εἰς ἣν ὑπῆγον. 6.22 τῇ ἐπαύριον ὁ

6.5 And Jesus, having lifted up the eyes and having beheld/observed that a much crowd comes to him, he says to Philip: From where might we buy loaves in order that these might eat? 6.6 But he was saying this testing him, for he, he knew what he was about to do.

6.7 Philip then responds/answers: Loaves from two hundred denarii are not enough in order that each (one) might take/receive a little something. 6.8 One out of his learners/pupils, Andrew the brother of Simon Peter, says to him: 6.9 A little boy is here who has five barley loaves and two fishes; but what is these to/for so many? 6.10 Jesus said: Make ye the men/humans to recline. And much grass was in the place. Then the men/males reclined, the number about five thousand. 6.11 Then Jesus took the loaves and gave thanks and he gave *it* to the (ones) being reclined, and likewise as much as they wanted/wished from the fishes. 6.12 And when they were filled/satisfied he says to his learners/pupils: Gather ye the excess/left over fragments, that anything might not perish. 6.13 Therefore they gathered and filled twelve baskets of fragments from the five barley loaves which were left over for those having eaten. 6.14 Then the men, having seen what sign he did, were saying: This (one)/he is truly the prophet, the (one) coming to/into the world.

6.15 Then Jesus, knowing that they were about to come and to seize/snatch him in order that they might make *him* a king, he withdrew again to the mountain, himself alone. 6.16 As it became evening, his learners/pupils went down to the sea, 6.17 and having embarked in a boat they were going beyond/across the sea to Capernaum. But the darkness overtook them and Jesus had not yet come to them, 6.18 and the sea was being aroused from a great wind blowing. 6.19 Then, having rowed about twenty-five or thirty stadia, they behold/see Jesus walking on the sea and becoming near the boat, and they were afraid. 6.20 And he says to them: I, I am, fear ye not. 6.21 Then they came/went to take him into the boat, and immediately the boat became on/at the land to which they were going. 6.22

ὄχλος ὁ ἑστὼς πέραν τῆς θαλάσσης εἶδεν ὅτι πλοιάριον ἄλλο οὐκ ἦν ἐκεῖ εἰ μὴ ἕν, καὶ ὅτι οὐ συνεισῆλθεν τοῖς μαθηταῖς αὐτοῦ ὁ Ἰησοῦς εἰς τὸ πλοῖον ἀλλὰ μόνοι οἱ μαθηταὶ αὐτοῦ ἀπῆλθον·

6.23 ἐπέλθον τῶν οὖν τῶν πλοίων ἐκ Τιβεριάδος ἐγγὺς τοῦ τόπου ὅπου καὶ ἔφαγον ἄρτον εὐχαριστήσαντος τοῦ κυρίου. 6.24 καὶ ἴδοντες ὅτι οὐκ ἔστιν ἐκεῖ ὁ Ἰησοῦς οὐδὲ οἱ μαθηταὶ αὐτοῦ, ἀνέβησαν αὐτοὶ εἰς τὰ πλοιάρια καὶ ἦλθον εἰς Καφαρναοὺμ ζητοῦντες τὸν Ἰησοῦν. 6.25 καὶ εὑρόντες αὐτὸν πέραν τῆς θαλάσσης εἶπον αὐτῷ, ῥαββεί, πότε ὧδε ἦλθες; 6.26 ἀπεκρίθη αὐτοῖς Ἰησοῦς καὶ εἶπεν, ἀμὴν ἀμὴν λέγω ὑμῖν, ζητῖτέ με οὐχ ὅτι εἴδετε σημῖα ἀλλ’ ὅτι ἐφάγετε ἐκ τῶν ἄρτων καὶ ἐχορτάσθητε.

6.27 ἐργάζεσθαι βρῶσιν μὴ τὴν ἀπολλυμένην ἀλλὰ τὴν μένουσαν εἰς ζωὴν αἰώνιον, ἣν ὁ υἱὸς τοῦ ἀνθρώπου δίδωσιν ὑμῖν· τοῦτον γὰρ ὁ πατὴρ ἐσφράγισεν ὁ θεός. 6.28 εἶπον οὖν πρὸς αὐτόν, τί ποιῶμεν ἵνα ἐργαζώμεθα τὰ ἔργα τοῦ θεοῦ; 6.29 ἀπεκρίθη Ἰησοῦς καὶ εἶπεν αὐτοῖς, τοῦτό ἐστιν τὸ ἔργον τοῦ θεοῦ, ἵνα πιστεύηται εἰς ὃν ἀπέστιλεν ἐκεῖνος. 6.30 εἶπον οὖν αὐτῷ, τί οὖν ποιεῖς σὺ σημῖον σύ, ἵνα ἴδωμεν καὶ πιστεύσωμέν σοι; τί ἐργάζῃ; 6.31 οἱ πατέρες ἡμῶν τὸ μάννα ἔφαγον ἐν τῇ ἐρήμῳ, καθώς ἐστιν γεγραμμένον, « ἄρτον ἐκ τοῦ οὐρανοῦ δέδωκεν αὐτοῖς φαγεῖν.» 6.32 εἶπεν οὖν αὐτοῖς ὁ Ἰησοῦς,

ἀμὴν ἀμὴν λέγω ὑμῖν, οὐ Μωϋσῆς δέδωκεν ὑμῖν τὸν ἄρτον ἐκ τοῦ οὐρανοῦ, ἀλλ’ ὁ πατήρ μου δίδωσιν ὑμῖν τὸν ἄρτον ἐκ τοῦ οὐρανοῦ τὸν ἀληθινόν· 6.33 ὁ γὰρ ἄρτος ὃ τοῦ θεοῦ ἐστιν ὁ καταβαίνων ἐκ τοῦ οὐρανοῦ καὶ ζωὴν διδοὺς τῷ κόσμῳ. 6.34 εἶπον οὖν πρὸς αὐτόν, πάντοτε κύριε, δὸς ἡμῖν τὸν ἄρτον τοῦτον. 6.35 εἶπεν οὖν αὐτοῖς ὁ Ἰησοῦς, ἐγώ εἰμι ὁ ἄρτος τῆς ζωῆς· ὁ ἐρχόμενος πρός ἐμὲ οὐ μὴ πινάσῃ, καὶ ὁ πιστεύων εἰς ἐμὲ οὐ μὴ διψήσει πώποτε. 6.36 ἀλλ’ εἶπον ὑμῖν ὅτι καὶ ἑωράκατέ καὶ οὐ πιστεύεται. 6.37 πᾶν ὃ δίδωσίν μοι ὁ πατὴρ πρὸς ἐμὲ ἥξει,

On the morrow the crowd having been beyond the sea saw that another boat was not there, except one, and that Jesus went not in the boat with his learners/pupils, but his learners/pupils went away alone; 6.23 therefore they came to those from the boats out of Tiberias near the place where they also ate bread/a loaf from the Lord, having given thanks. 6.24 And seeing that Jesus is not there, neither his learners/pupils, they themselves embarked in the boats and.went/came to Capernaum seeking Jesus. 6.25 And having found him beyond/across the sea, they said to him: Rabbi, when *did* you come here? 6.26 Jesus answered to them and said: Truly, truly I say to ye, ye seek me not because ye saw signs but because ye ate from the loaves and were filled/satisfied.

6.27 Work ye not *for* the perishing/spoiling food but *for* the (one) abiding into eternal life, which the son of the man/human will give to ye; for God the father sealed/secured this (one/food). 6.28 Then they said to him: What may we do that we may work the works of God? 6.29 Jesus answered and said to them: This is the work of God, that ye may believe in *the one* whom that (one) sent. 6.30 Therefore they said to him: Then you, what sign do you, in order that we might see and might believe in you? What *do* you work? 6.31 Our fathers ate the manna in the desert/wilderness, as it is having been written: HE HAS GIVEN TO THEM A LOAF/ BREAD OUT OT THE SKY/HEAVEN TO EAT. 6.32 Therefore Jesus said to them:

Truly, truly I say to ye: Moses has not given to ye the loaf/bread out of the sky/heaven, but my father gives to ye the true bread/loaf out of the sky/heaven; 6.33 for the loaf/bread, the (one) from God, is the (one) coming down out of the sky/heaven and giving life to the world. 6.34 Then they said to him: Lord, always give to us this loaf/bread. 6.35 Then Jesus said to them: I, I am the loaf/bread of the life; the (one) coming to me by no means might he hunger, and the (one) believing in me by no means will he ever thirst. 6.36 But I said to ye that ye have both seen and ye believe not. 6.37 Each (one) which the father gives to me will come to me, and the (one) coming to

καὶ τὸν ἐρχόμενον πρὸς ἐμὲ οὐ μὴ ἐκβάλω ἔξω, 6.38 ὅτι οὐ καταβέβηκα ἐκ τοῦ οὐρανοῦ οὐχ ἵνα ποιήσω τὸ θέλημα τὸ ἐμὸν ἀλλὰ τὸ θέλημα τοῦ πέμψαντός με· 6.39 —, ἵνα πᾶν ὃ δέδωκέν μοι μὴ ἀπολέσω ἐξ αὐτοῦ ἀλλὰ ἀναστήσω αὐτὸ ἐν τῇ ἐσχάτῃ ἡμέρᾳ. 6.40 τοῦτο γάρ ἐστιν τὸ θέλημα τοῦ πατρός μου, ἵνα πᾶς ὁ θεωρῶν τὸν υἱὸν καὶ πιστεύων εἰς αὐτὸν ἔχῃ ζωὴν αἰώνιον, καὶ ἀναστήσω αὐτὸν ἐγὼ ἐν τῇ ἐσχάτῃ ἡμέρᾳ.

6.41 ἐγόγγυζον οὖν οἱ Ἰουδαῖοι περὶ αὐτοῦ ὅτι εἶπεν, ἐγώ εἰμι ὁ ἄρτος ὁ καταβὰς ἐκ τοῦ οὐρανοῦ, 6.42 καὶ ἔλεγον, οὐχ οὗτός ἐστιν Ἰησοῦς ὁ υἱὸς Ἰωσήφ, οὗ ἡμῖς οἴδαμεν καὶ τὸν πατέρα καὶ τὴν μητέρα; πῶς οὖν οὗτὸς λέγει ὅτι ἐκ τοῦ οὐρανοῦ καταβέβηκα;

6.43 ἀπεκρίθη οὖν Ἰησοῦς αὐτοῖς καὶ εἶπεν, μὴ γογγύζεται μετ' ἀλλήλων. 6.44 οὐδὶς δύναται ἐλθῖν πρός με ἐὰν μὴ ὁ πατὴρ ὁ πέμψας με ἑλκύσῃ αὐτόν, κἀγὼ ἀναστήσω αὐτὸν ἐν τῇ ἐσχάτῃ ἡμέρᾳ.

6.45 ἔστι γεγραμμένον ἐν τοῖς προφήταις, « καὶ ἔσονται πάντες διδακτοὶ θεοῦ» πᾶς ὁ ἀκούσας παρὰ τοῦ πατρὸς καὶ μαθὼν ἔρχεται πρὸς ἐμέ. 6.46 οὐχ ὅτι τὸν πατέρα ἑώρακέν τις εἰ μὴ ὁ ὢν παρὰ τοῦ πατρός, οὗτος ἑώρακεν τὸν θεὸν πατέρα.

6.47 ἀμὴν ἀμὴν λέγω ὑμῖν, ὅτι ὁ πιστεύων ἔχει ζωὴν αἰώνιον. 6.48 ἐγώ εἰμι ὁ ἄρτος τῆς ζωῆς. 6.49 οἱ πατέρες ὑμῶν ἔφαγον τὸ μάννα ἐν τῇ ἐρήμῳ καὶ ἀπέθανον· 6.50 οὗτός ἐστιν ὁ ἄρτος ὁ ἐκ τοῦ οὐρανοῦ καταβαίνων ἵνα τις ἐξ αὐτοῦ φάγῃ καὶ μὴ ἀποθάνῃ.

6.51 ἐγώ εἰμι ὁ ἄρτος ὁ ζῶν ὁ ἐκ τοῦ οὐρανοῦ καταβάς· ἐάν τις φάγῃ ἐκ τοῦ ἐμοῦ ἄρτου ζήσει εἰς τὸν αἰῶνα· καὶ ὁ ἄρτος ὃν ἐγὼ δώσω ὑπὲρ τῆς τοῦ κόσμου ζωῆς ἡ σάρξ μού ἐστιν. 6.52 ἐμάχοντο οὖν πρὸς ἀλλήλους οἱ Ἰουδαῖοι λέγοντες, πῶς οὖν δύναται ἡμῖν οὗτος δοῦναι τὴν σάρκα φαγῖν;

me, by no means might/shall I throw out, 6.38 because I have come down out of the sky/heaven not in order that I may do my will but the will of the (one) having sent me; 6.39 --, in order that each (thing) which he has given to me, I might not lose out of/from it, but I might raise it up in the last day. 6.40 For this is the will of my father, that every one beholding the son and believing in him may have eternal life, and I, I shall raise him up in/at/on the last day.

6.41 Then the Judeans were grumbling about him because he said: I, I am the bread/loaf, the (one) having come down out of the sky/heaven, 6.42 and they were saying: Is not this (one) Jesus, the son of Joseph, of whom we, we know both the father and the mother? How then says he: I have come down out of the sky/heaven?

6.43 Then Jesus answered and said to them: Grumble/murmur ye not with one another. 6.44 No one is able to come to me unless the father, the (one) having sent me might draw him, and I, I shall raise him up in the last day.

6.45 It is having been written/it has been written in the prophets: AND THEY ALL WILL BE TAUGHT OF GOD; every one hearing from the father and learning comes to me. 6.46 Not that anyone has seen the father except the (one) being from/beside the father, this (one) has seen God the father.

6.47 Truly, truly I say to ye that the (one) believing has eternal life. 6.48 I, I am the loaf/-bread of the life. 6.49 Our fathers ate the manna in the desert/wilderness and they died; 6.50 this (one) is the loaf/bread, the (one) coming down out of the sky/heaven in order that anyone might eat from it and might not die.

6.51 I, I am the living loaf/bread, the (one) having come down out of the sky/heaven; if anyone might eat from my loaf/bread he will live in/into the age; and the loaf/bread which I, I shall give in behalf of the life of the world is my flesh. 6.52 Then the Judeans were fighting/quarreling with one another, saying: Then how is this (one) able to give the flesh to us to eat?

6.53 εἶπεν οὖν αὐτοῖς ὁ Ἰησοῦς, ἀμὴν ἀμὴν λέγω ὑμῖν, ἂν μὴ φάγηται τὴν σάρκα τοῦ υἱοῦ τοῦ ἀνθρώπου καὶ πίητε τὸ αἷμα αὐτοῦ, οὐκ ἔχετε ζωὴν αἰώνιον ἐν ἑαυτοῖς.

6.54 ὁ τρώγων μου τὴν σάρκα καὶ πίνων μου τὸ αἷμα ἔχει ζωὴν αἰώνιον, κἀγὼ ἀναστήσω αὐτὸν τῇ ἐσχάτῃ ἡμέρᾳ· 6.55 ἡ γὰρ σάρξ μου ἀληθής ἐστιν βρῶσις, καὶ τὸ αἷμά μου ἀληθής ἐστι πόσις. 6.56 ὁ τρώγων μου τὴν σάρκα καὶ πίνων μου τὸ αἷμα ἐν ἐμοὶ μένει κἀγὼ ἐν αὐτῷ. 6.57 καθὼς ἀπέστιλέν με ὁ ζῶν πατὴρ κἀγὼ ζῶ διὰ τὸν πατέρα, καὶ ὁ τρώγων με κἀκεῖνος ζήσει δι’ ἐμέ. 6.58 οὗτός ἐστιν ὁ ἄρτος ὁ ἐκ τοῦ οὐρανοῦ καταβάς, οὐ καθὼς οἱ πατέρες ἔφαγον καὶ ἀπέθανον· ὁ τρώγων τοῦτον τὸν ἄρτον ζήσει εἰς τὸν αἰῶνα.

6.59 ταῦτα εἶπεν ἐν συναγωγῇ διδάσκων ἐν Καφαρναούμ. 6.60 πολλοὶ οὖν ἀκούσαντες ἐκ τῶν μαθητῶν αὐτοῦ εἶπον, σκληρός ἐστιν ὁ λόγος οὗτος· τίς δύναται αὐτοῦ ἀκούειν; 6.61 ἔγνω οὖν Ἰησοῦς ἐν ἑαυτῷ ὅτι γογγύζουσιν περὶ τούτου οἱ μαθηταὶ αὐτοῦ καὶ εἶπεν αὐτοῖς, τοῦτο ὑμᾶς σκανδαλίζι; 6.62 ἐὰν οὖν θεωρῆται ἀναβαίνοντα τὸν υἱὸν τοῦ ἀνθρώπου ὅπου ἦν τὸ πρότερον; 6.63 τὸ πνεῦμά ἐστιν τὸ ζῳοποιοῦν, ἡ σάρξ οὐκ ὠφελεῖ οὐδέν· τὰ ῥήματα ἃ ἐγὼ λελάληκα ὑμῖν πνεῦμά ἐστιν καὶ ζωή. 6.64 ἀλλ’ ἐξ ὑμῶν εἰσιν τινες οἳ οὐ πιστεύουσιν. ᾔδει γὰρ ἀπ’ ἀρχῆς ὁ σωτὴρ τίνες εἰσὶν οἱ πιστεύοντες καὶ τίς ἦν ὁ μέλλον αὐτὸν παραδίδοναι. 6.65 καὶ ἔλεγεν, διὰ τοῦτο εἴρηκα ὑμῖν ὅτι οὐδὶς δύναται ἐλθεῖν πρός ἐμὲ ἐὰν μὴ ᾖ δεδομένον αὐτῷ ἐκ τοῦ πατρός. 6.66 ἐκ τούτου οὖν πολλοὶ τῶν μαθητῶν ἀπῆλθον εἰς τὰ ὀπίσω καὶ οὐκέτι μετ’ αὐτοῦ περιεπάτουν. 6.67 εἶπεν οὖν ὁ Ἰησοῦς τοῖς δώδεκα, μὴ καὶ ὑμῖς θέλεται ὑπάγειν; 6.68 ἀπεκρίθη αὐτῷ Σίμων Πέτρος, κύριε, πρὸς τίνα ἀπελευσόμεθα; ῥήματα ζωῆς αἰωνίου ἔχεις, 6.69 καὶ ἡμῖς πεπιστεύκαμεν καὶ

6.53 Therefore Jesus said to them: Truly, truly I say to ye: Unless ye might eat the flesh of the son of the man/human and might drink his blood, ye have not eternal life in yourselves.

6.54 The (one) eating my flesh and drinking my blood has eternal life, and I, I shall raise him up in/at/on the last day; 6.55 for my flesh is true food/eating, and my blood is true drink. 6.56 The (one) eating my flesh/of me the flesh and drinking my blood/of me the blood abides in/with me and I in/with him. 6.57 Just as the living father sent me and I, I live through the father, also the (one) eating me, even that (one) will live through me. 6.58 This (one) is the loaf/bread, the (one) coming down out of the sky/heaven, not as the fathers ate and died; the (one) eating this loaf/bread will live in/into the age.

6.59 He said these (things) teaching in/among a congregation in Capernaum. 6.60 Therefore, many out of his learners/pupils, having heard, said: This saying/word/reasoning is hard/rough/cruel; who is able to hear/heed it? 6.61 Then Jesus knew in himself that his learners/pupils murmur/whisper about this, and he said to them: *Does* this offend ye/cause ye to stumble? 6.62 Therefore, if ye may behold the son of the man/human going up/ascending where he was the first/-former (time), 6.63 the spirit is the (thing) giving life/making alive, the flesh does not profit nothing; the words which I, I have spoken to ye are spirit and life. 6.64 But there are some out of ye who believe not. For the savior knew from *the* beginning who were the (ones) believing/obeying and who was the (one) being about to betray him/hand him over. 6.65 And he was saying: Because of this I have said to ye that no one is able to come to me unless it be given to him from the father. 6.66 Therefore, out of this (thing), many of the learners/pupils went away to the (things) behind and they were no longer walking with him. 6.67 Then Jesus said to the twelve: Ye, *do* ye not want/wish to depart/go away also? 6.68 Simon Peter answered to him: Lord, to whom shall we go away? You have/hold words of eternal life, 6.69 and we, we have believed and have known/understood that you, you are the holy

ἐγνώκαμεν ὅτι σὺ εἶ ὁ ἅγιος τοῦ θεοῦ. 6.70 ἀπεκρίθη Ἰησοῦς καὶ εἶπεν αὐτοῖς, οὐκὶ ἐγὼ ὑμᾶς ἐξελεξάμην τοὺς δώδεκα, καὶ εἷς ἐξ ὑμῶν διάβολός ἐστιν; 6.71 ἔλεγεν δὲ τὸν Ἰούδαν Σίμωνος ἀπὸ Ἰσκαριώτου· οὗτος γὰρ καὶ ἔμελλεν αὐτὸν παραδιδόναι, εἷς ὢν ἐκ τῶν δώδεκα.

7.1 Μετὰ ταῦτα περιεπάτει ὁ Ἰησοῦς ἐν τῇ Γαλιλαίᾳ· οὐ γὰρ ἤθελεν ἐν τῇ Ἰουδαίᾳ περιπατεῖν, ὅτι ἐζήτουν αὐτὸν οἱ Ἰουδαῖοι ἀποκτῖναι. 7.2 ἦν δὲ ἐγγὺς ἡ ἑορτὴ τῶν Ἰουδαίων ἡ σκηνοπηγία. 7.3 εἶπον οὖν οἱ ἀδελφοὶ αὐτοῦ πρὸς αὐτόν, μετάβηθι ἐντεῦθεν καὶ ὕπαγε εἰς τὴν Ἰουδαίαν, ἵνα καὶ οἱ μαθηταί σου θεωρήσουσιν τὰ ἔργα σου ἃ ποιεῖς· 7.4 οὐδὶς γάρ τι ἐν κρυπτῷ ποιῶν ζητῖ αὐτὸς ἐν παρρησίᾳ εἶναι. εἰ ταῦτα ποιεῖς, φανέρωσον σεαυτὸν τῷ κόσμῳ. 7.5 οὐδὲ γὰρ οἱ ἀδελφοὶ αὐτοῦ ἐπίστευον εἰς αὐτόν.

7.6 λέγει οὖν αὐτοῖς ὁ Ἰησοῦς, ὁ καιρὸς ὁ ἐμὸς οὔπω πάρεστιν, ὁ δὲ καιρὸς ὁ ὑμέτερος πάντοτέ ἐστιν ἔτοιμος.

7.7 ὁ κόσμος οὐ δύναται μισεῖν ὑμᾶς, ἐμὲ δὲ μισεῖ, ὅτι μαρτυρῶ ὅτι τὰ ἔργα αὐτοῦ πονηρά ἐστιν. 7.8 ὑμεῖς ἀνάβηται εἰς τὴν ἑορτήν· ἐγὼ οὐκ ἀναβαίνω εἰς τὴν ἑορτὴν ταύτην, ὅτι ὁ ἐμὸς καιρὸς οὔπω πεπλήρωται. 7.9 ταῦτα εἰπὼν αὐτὸς ἔμινεν ἐν τῇ Γαλιλαίᾳ. 7.10 ὡς δὲ ἀνέβησαν οἱ ἀδελφοὶ αὐτοῦ εἰς τὴν ἑορτήν, τότε καὶ αὐτὸς ἀνέβη, οὐ φανερῶς ἀλλ᾽ ἐν κρυπτῷ. 7.11 οἱ οὖν Ἰουδαῖοι ἐζήτουν αὐτὸν ἐν τῇ ἑορτῇ καὶ ἔλεγον, ποῦ ἐστιν ἐκῖνος; 7.12 καὶ γογγυσμὸς πολὺς ἦν περὶ αὐτοῦ ἐν τῷ ὄχλῳ· οἱ μὲν ἔλεγον ὅτι ἀγαθός ἐστιν, ἄλλοι ἔλεγον, οὔ, ἀλλὰ πλανᾷ τὸν ὄχλον. 7.13 οὐδὶς μέντοι παρρησίᾳ περὶ αὐτοῦ ἐλάλει διὰ τὸν φόβον τῶν Ἰουδαίων. 7.14 ἤδη δὲ τῆς ἑορτῆς μεσούσης ἀνέβη Ἰησοῦς εἰς τὸ ἱερὸν καὶ ἐδίδασκεν.

7.15 ἐθαύμαζον οὖν οἱ Ἰουδαῖοι λέγοντες, πῶς οὗτος γράμματα οἶδεν μὴ μεμαθηκώς; 7.16 ἀπεκρίθη οὖν αὐτοῖς

(one) from God.   6.70 Jesus answered and said to them:
Did not I, I choose ye, the twelve, and one out of ye
is a devil?   6.71 And he was speaking *of* Judas of
Simon from Iscariot; for this (one) also was being
about to betray him/hand him over, being one out of
the twelve.

    7.1   After these (things) Jesus was walking in
Galilee; for he was not wanting/wishing to walk in
Judea, because the Judeans were seeking to kill him.
    7.2   And the festival of the Judeans, the taber-
nacles, was near.   7.3 Therefore his brothers said to
him: Depart you from this place and go into Judea, in
order that your pupils/learners also will observe/-
behold your works which you do;   7.4 for no one doing
something in secret seeks himself/this to be in bold-
ness/freedom of speech. If you do these (things), make
yourself plain/clear to the world.   7.5 For his brothers were not believing in him.
    7.6   Therefore Jesus says to them: My time/season
is not yet arrived, but your time is always ready.
    7.7   The world is not able to hate ye, but it
hates me, because I, I testify that the works of it
are evil.   7.8 Go ye up to the festival; I, I go not
up to this festival, because my time has not yet been
fulfilled.   7.9 Having said these (things), he, he
stayed/remained in Galilee.   7.10 But since his brothers went up to the festival, then he, he also went up,
not openly but in secret.   7.11 The Judeans therefore
were seeking him at the festival and they were saying:
Where is that (one)?   7.12 And there was much murmur-
ing/whispering about him among/in the crowd; those on
one hand were saying that he is a good (man), others
were saying: No, but he deceives the crowd.   7.13 No
one, however, was speaking freely/boldly about him
because of the fear of/from the Judeans.   7.14 And
from the festival already in its midst, Jesus went up
to the *outer* temple/temple compound and he was
teaching.
    7.15   Then the Judeans were wondering/astonished,
saying: How *does* this (one)/he know letters, having
not learned?   7.16 Therefore Jesus answered to them

Ἰησοῦς καὶ εἶπεν, ἡ ἐμὴ διδαχὴ οὐκ ἔστιν ἐμὴ ἀλλὰ τοῦ πέμψαντός με· 7.17 ἐάν τις θέλῃ τὸ θέλημα αὐτοῦ ποιεῖν, γνώσεται περὶ τῆς διδαχῆς πότερον ἐκ θεοῦ ἐστιν ἢ ἐγὼ ἀπ' ἐμαυτοῦ λαλῶ. 7.18 ὁ ἀφ' ἑαυτοῦ λαλῶν τὴν δόξαν τὴν ἰδίαν ζητῖ· καὶ ὁ ζητῶν τὴν δόξαν τοῦ πέμψαντος αὐτόν, οὗτος ἀληθής ἐστιν καὶ ἀδικία ἐν αὐτῷ οὐκ ἔστιν. 7.19 οὐ Μωϋσῆς δέδωκεν ὑμῖν τὸν νόμον; καὶ οὐδὶς ἐξ ὑμῶν ποιεῖ τὸν νόμον. τί με ζητεῖτε ἀποκτῖναι; 7.20 ἀπεκρίθη ὁ ὄχλος, δαιμόνιον ἔχεις· τίς σε ζητῖ ἀποκτῖναι;

7.21 ἀπεκρίθη Ἰησοῦς καὶ εἶπεν αὐτοῖς, ἓν ἔργον ἐποίησα καὶ πάντες θαυμάζετε. 7.22 διὰ τοῦτο Μωϋσῆς δέδωκεν ὑμῖν τὴν περιτομήν οὐχ ὅτι ἐκ τοῦ Μωσέως ἐστὶν ἀλλ' ὅτι ἐκ τῶν πατέρων καὶ ἐν σαββάτῳ περιτέμνετε ἄνθρωπον.

7.23 εἰ περιτομὴν λαμβάνι ἄνθρωπος ἐν σαββάτῳ ἵνα μὴ λυθῇ ὁ νόμος ὁ Μωϋσέως, ἐμοὶ χολᾶται ὅτι ὅλον ἄνθρωπον ὑγιῆ ἐποίησα ἐν σαββάτῳ; 7.24 μὴ κρίνετε κατ' ὄψιν, ἀλλὰ τὴν δικαίαν κρίσιν κρίνατε. 7.25 ἔλεγον οὖν τινες τῶν Ἱεροσολυμειτῶν, οὐκ οὗτός ἐστιν ὃν ζητοῦσιν ἀποκτῖναι; 7.26 καὶ ἴδε παρρησίᾳ λαλῖ καὶ οὐδὲν αὐτῷ λέγουσιν. μήτι ἀληθῶς ἔγνωσαν οἱ ἀρχιερεῖς ὅτι οὗτός ἐστιν ὁ χριστός; 7.27 ἀλλὰ τοῦτον οἴδαμεν πόθεν ἐστίν· ὁ χριστὸς ὅταν ἔρχηται οὐδὶς γινώσκει αὐτὸν πόθεν ἐστίν.

7.28 ἔκραξεν οὖν ὁ Ἰησοῦς ἐν τῷ ἱερῷ διδάσκων καὶ λέγων, καὶ ἐμὲ οἴδατε καὶ οἴδατε πόθεν εἰμί· καὶ ἀπ' ἐμαυτοῦ οὐκ ἐλήλυθα, ἀλλά ἔστιν ἀληθής ὁ πέμψας με, ὃν ὑμεῖς οὐκ οἴδαται· 7.29 ἐγὼ δὲ οἶδα αὐτόν, ὅτι παρ' αὐτοῦ εἰμι κἀκεῖνός με ἀπέστακεν. 7.30 οἱ δὲ ἐξήτουν αὐτὸν πιάσαι, καὶ οὐδεὶς ἐπέβαλεν ἐπ' αὐτὸν τὴν χεῖρα, ὅτι οὔπω ἐληλύθει ἡ ὥρα αὐτοῦ. 7.31 πολλοὶ δὲ ἐπίστευσαν ἐκ τοῦ ὄχλου εἰς αὐτόν, καὶ ἔλεγον, ὁ χριστὸς ὅταν ἔλθῃ μὴ πλίονα σημεῖα ποιήσει ὧν οὗτος ἐποίησεν; 7.32 ἤκουσαν δὲ οἱ Φαρισαῖοι τοῦ ὄχλου γογγύζοντος ταῦτα

and said: My doctrine is not mine but from the (one) having sent me; 7.17 if anyone may want/wish to do the will of him, he will know about the doctrine, whether it is from God or I, I speak from myself. 7.18 The (one) speaking from himself seeks his own fame/glory; and the (one) seeking the fame/glory of the (one) having sent him, this (one)/he is true and unjustness is not in him. 7.19 Did not Moses give the law to ye? And no one out of ye does the law. Why seek ye to kill me? 7.20 The crowd answered: You have a demon; who seeks to kill you?

7.21 Jesus answered and said to them: I did one work and ye all wonder at *it*. 7.22 Because of this Moses has given the circumcision to ye -- not that it is out of/from Moses but that it is out of/from the fathers -- and ye circumcise a man on a sabbath.

7.23 If a man takes/receives circumcision on a sabbath in order that the law of Moses might not be loosed/infringed, are ye mad with me because I made a whole man healthy on a sabbath? 7.24 Be ye not judging according to appearance/aspect/face, but judge ye the just judgment. 7.25 Then some of the Jerusalemites were saying: Is not this (one)/he *the one* whom they seek to kill? 7.26 And behold, he speaks boldly/freely and they say nothing to him. Did not the high priests truly know that this (one)/he is the anointed (one)? 7.27 But we know this (one) from where he is; whenever the anointed (one) may come, no one knows him from where he is.

7.28 Jesus therefore cried out in the *outer* temple, teaching and saying: Ye know both me and from where I am; and I have not come from myself, but the (one) having sent me is true, *the one* whom ye, ye know not; 7.29 but I, I know him, because I am from him, and that (one) has sent me forth. 7.30 But they were seeking to arrest him, and no one laid the hand upon him, because his hour had not yet come. 7.31 And many out of the crowd believed in him, and they were saying: Whenever the anointed (one) might come, will he do greater signs than *those* which this (one) did? 7.32 But the Pharisees heard of the crowd murmuring/whispering these (things) about him, and the high

περὶ αὐτοῦ, καὶ ἀπέστιλαν τοὺς ὑπηρέτας οἱ ἀρχιερεῖς καὶ οἱ Φαρισαῖοι ἵνα πιάσωσιν αὐτόν.

7.33 εἶπεν οὖν ὁ Ἰησοῦς, ἔτι χρόνον μικρὸν μεθ᾽ ὑμῶν εἰμι καὶ ὑπάγω πρὸς τὸν πέμψαντά με. 7.34 ζητήσετέ με καὶ οὐχ εὑρήσετέ, καὶ ὅπου εἰμὶ ἐγὼ ὑμῖς οὐ δύνασθαι ἐλθῖν. 7.35 εἶπον οὖν οἱ Ἰουδαῖοι πρὸς ἑαυτούς, ποῦ οὗτος μέλλει πορεύεσθε ὅτι οὐχ εὑρήσομεν αὐτόν; μὴ εἰς τὴν διασπορὰν τῶν Ἑλλήνων μέλλει πορεύεσθε καὶ διδάσκιν τοὺς Ἕλληνας; 7.36 τί ἐστιν οὗτος ὁ λόγος ὃν εἶπεν, ζητήσετε καὶ οὐχ εὑρήσετέ με, καὶ ὅπου εἰμὶ ἐγὼ ὑμῖς οὐ δύνασθαι ἐλθῖν; 7.37 ἐν δὲ τῇ ἐσχάτῃ ἡμέρα τῇ μεγάλῃ τῆς ἑορτῆς ἱστήκει ὁ Ἰησοῦς καὶ ἔκραξεν λέγων, ἐάν τις διψᾷ ἐρχέσθω πρός με καὶ πινέτω. 7.38 ὁ πιστεύων εἰς ἐμέ, καθὼς εἶπεν ἡ γραφή, ποταμοὶ ἐκ τῆς κοιλίας αὐτοῦ ῥεύσουσιν ὕδατος ζῶντος. 7.39 τοῦτο δὲ ἔλεγεν περὶ τοῦ πνεύματος οὗ ἤμελλον λαμβάνιν οἱ πιστεύοντες εἰς αὐτόν· οὔπω γὰρ ἦν πνεῦμα, ὅτι Ἰησοῦς οὔπω ἐδοξάσθη. 7.40 ἐκ τοῦ ὄχλου οὖν ἀκούσαντες αὐτοῦ τῶν λόγων τούτων ἔλεγον, ἀληθῶς οὗτός ἐστιν ὁ προφήτης· 7.41 ἄλλοι ἔλεγον, οὗτός ἐστιν ὁ χριστός· ἄλλοι ἔλεγον, μὴ γὰρ ἐκ τῆς Γαλιλαίας ὁ χριστὸς ἔρχεται; 7.43 οὐχὶ ἡ γραφὴ εἶπεν ὅτι ἐκ τοῦ σπέρματος Δαυίδ, καὶ ἀπὸ Βηθλέεμ τῆς κώμης ὅπου ἦν ὁ Δαυίδ, ὁ χριστὸς ἔρχεται; 7.43 σχίσμα οὖν ἐγένετο ἐν τῷ ὄχλῳ δι᾽ αὐτόν. 7.44 τινὲς δὲ ἤθελον ἐξ αὐτῶν πιάσαι αὐτόν, ἀλλ᾽ οὐδὶς ἐπέβαλεν ἐπ᾽ αὐτὸν τὰς χῖρας.

7.45 ἦλθον οὖν οἱ ὑπηρέται πρὸς τοὺς ἀρχιερεῖς καὶ Φαρισαίους, καὶ λέγουσιν αὐτοῖς ἐκεῖνοι, διὰ τί οὐκ ἠγάγετε αὐτόν; 7.46 οἱ δὲ ὑπηρέται ἀπεκρίθησαν, οὐδέποτε οὕτως ἄνθρωπος ἐλάλησεν. 7.47 ἀπεκρίθησαν οὖν αὐτοῖς οἱ Φαρισαῖοι, μὴ καὶ ὑμῖς πεπλάνησθαι; 7.48 μή τις ἐκ τῶν ἀρχόντων ἐπίστευσεν εἰς αὐτὸν ἢ ἐκ τῶν Φαρισαίων; 7.49 ἀλλ᾽ ὁ ὄχλος οὗτος ὁ μὴ γινώσκων τὸν νόμον ἐπάρατοί εἰσιν.

7.50 εἶπεν δὲ Νικόδημος πρὸς αὐτούς, ὁ ἐλθὼν πρὸς αὐτὸν

priests and the Pharisees sent the servants/assistants in order that they might arrest him.

7.33 Therefore Jesus said: I am still with ye a little time and I go/depart to the (one) having sent me. 7.34 Ye will seek me and ye will not find me, and where I, I am, ye, ye are not able to come/go. 7.35 Therefore the Judeans said to themselves: Where is this (one)/he about to go that we, we shall not find him? Is he not about to go to the dispersion of the Greeks and to teach the Greeks? 7.36 What is the saying/reasoning which this (one)/he said: Ye will seek me and ye will not find *me*, and where I, I am, ye, ye are not able to come? 7.37 And in/on the last day, the great (one) of the festival, Jesus had stood and he cried out, saying: If anyone may thirst, let him come to me and drink. 7.38 The (one) believing in me, even as the writing said, rivers of living water will flow out of his belly. 7.39 But he was saying this about the spirit which those believing in him were being about to receive; for there was not yet a spirit, because Jesus was not yet glorified. 7.40 Therefore out of/from the crowd having heard these sayings/words from him, they were saying: This (one)/he is truly the prophet; 7.41 others were saying: This (one)/he is the anointed (one); others were saying: For the anointed (one) comes not out of Galilee, *does he?* 7.42 Did not the writing say that the anointed (one) comes out of the seed of David, and from Bethlehem, the village where David was? 7.43 A split/division therefore happened among the crowd because of him. 7.44 And some out of them were wanting/wishing to lay hold of/arrest him, but no one laid the hands upon him. 7.45 Then the servants/assistants went to the high priests and Pharisees, and those say to them: Because of what/why did ye not bring him? 7.46 But the servants/assistants answered: A man never spoke thus. 7.47 Therefore the Pharisees answered to them: Ye, ye have not also been deceived? 7.48 Not anyone out of the rulers/leaders or out of the Pharisees believed in him? 7.49 But this crowd, the (one) not knowing the law, are execrations/cursed (ones).

7.50 And Nicodemus said to them, the (one)

πρότερον, εἷς ὢν ἐξ αὐτῶν, 7.51 μὴ ὁ νόμος ἡμῶν κρίνι τὸν ἄνθρωπον ἐὰν μὴ ἀκούσῃ πρῶτον παρ' αὐτοῦ καὶ γνῷ τί ποιεῖ; 7.52 ἀπεκρίθησαν καὶ εἶπον αὐτῷ, μὴ καὶ σὺ ἐκ τῆς Γαλιλαίας εἶ; ἐραύνησον καὶ ἴδε ὅτι προφήτης ἐκ τῆς Γαλιλαίας οὐκ ἐγείρεται. — 8.12 πάλιν οὖν αὐτοῖς ἐλάλησεν ὁ Ἰησοῦς λέγων, ἐγώ τὸ φῶς εἰμι τοῦ κόσμου· ὁ ἀκολουθῶν ἐμοὶ οὐ μὴ περιπατήσῃ ἐν τῇ σκοτίᾳ, ἀλλ' ἕξει τὸ φῶς τῆς ζωῆς. 8.13 εἶπον οὖν αὐτῷ οἱ Φαρισαῖοι, σὺ περὶ σεαυτοῦ μαρτυρεῖς· ἡ μαρτυρία σου οὐκ ἔστιν ἀληθής. 8.14 εἶπεν αὐτοῖς ὁ Ἰησοῦς, κἂν ἐγώ μαρτυρῶ περὶ ἐμαυτοῦ, ἀληθής ἐστιν ἡ μαρτυρία μου, ὅτι οἶδα πόθεν ἦλθον καὶ ποῦ ὑπάγω· ὑμῖς οὐκ οἴδαται πόθεν ἔρχομαι καὶ ποῦ ὑπάγω. 8.15 ὑμεῖς κατὰ τὴν σάρκα κρίνετε, ἐγώ οὐ κρίνω οὐδένα. 8.16 κἂν κρίνω δὲ ἐγώ, ἡ κρίσις ἡ ἐμὴ ἀληθής ἐστιν, ὅτι μόνος οὐκ εἰμί, ἀλλ' ἐγώ καὶ ὁ πέμψας με πατήρ. 8.17 καὶ ἐν τῷ νόμῳ δὲ τῷ ὑμετέρῳ γέγραμμένον ἐστιν ὅτι δύο ἀνθρώπων ἡ μαρτυρία ἀληθής ἐστιν. 8.18 ἐγώ εἰμι ὁ μαρτυρῶν περὶ ἐμαυτοῦ καὶ μαρτυρεῖ περὶ ἐμοῦ ὁ πέμψας με πατήρ. 8.19 ἔλεγον οὖν αὐτῷ, ποῦ ἐστιν ὁ πατήρ σου; ἀπεκρίθη ὁ Ἰησοῦς καὶ εἶπεν, οὔτε ἐμὲ οἴδαται οὔτε τὸν πατέρα μου· εἰ ἐμὲ ᾔδειται, καὶ τὸν πατέρα ᾔδειται ἄν.

8.20 ταῦτα τὰ ῥήματα ἐλάλησεν ἐν τῷ γαζοφυλακίῳ —· καὶ οὐδὶς ἐπίασεν αὐτόν, ὅτι οὔπω ἐληλύθει ἡ ὥρα αὐτοῦ. 8.21 ἔλεγεν οὖν αὐτοῖς, ἐγώ ὑπάγω καὶ ζητήσεταί με, καὶ ἐν τῇ ἁμαρτίᾳ ὑμῶν ἀποθανῖσθαι· ὅπου ἐγώ ὑπάγω ὑμῖς οὐ δύνασθαι ἐλθῖν. 8.22 ἔλεγον οὖν οἱ Ἰουδαῖοι, μήτι ἀποκτενεῖ ἑαυτόν, ὅτι λέγει, ὅπου ἂν ἐγώ ὑπάγω ὑμῖς οὐ δύνασθαι ἐλθῖν; 8.23 ἔλεγεν οὖν αὐτοῖς, ὑμεῖς ἐκ τῶν κάτω ἐστέ, ἐγώ ἐκ τῶν ἄνω εἰμί· ὑμεῖς ἐκ τοῦ κόσμου τούτου ἐστέ, ἐγώ οὐκ εἰμὶ ἐκ τοῦ κόσμου τούτου. 8.24 εἶπον ὑμῖν ὅτι ἀποθανῖσθαι ἐν ταῖς ἁμαρτίαις ὑμῶν· ἐὰν γὰρ μὴ πιστεύσηταί μοι ὅτι ἐγώ εἰμι, ἀποθανῖσθαι ἐν ταῖς ἁμαρτίαις ὑμῶν. 8.25 ἔλεγον αὐτῷ, σὺ τίς

having formerly come to him, being one from/out of them: 7.51 Our law judges not the man/human unless it might first hear from him and might know what he does, *does it*? 7.52 They answered and said to him: You, are you not also from Galilee? You search and behold that a prophet is not raised up out of Galilee. --. 8.12 Therefore Jesus again spoke to them, saying: I, I am the light of the world; the (one) following me, by no means might he walk in the darkness, but he has the light of the life. 8.13 Therefore the Pharisees said to him: You, you testify/witness about yourself; your testimony is not true. 8.14 Jesus said to them: Even if I, I testify/witness about myself, my testimony is true, because I know from where I came and where I go; ye, ye know not from where I came and where I go. 8.15 Ye, ye judge according to the flesh; I, I *do* not judge no one. 8.16 But even if I, I may judge, my judgment is true, because I am not alone, but I and the father having sent me. 8.17 And even in your law it is having been written that the testimony/witness from two men/humans is true. 8.18 I, I am the (one) testifying about myself and the father having sent me testifies about me. 8.19 Then they were saying to him: Where is your father? Jesus answered and said: Ye know neither me nor my father; if ye knew me, ye would know the father.

8.20 He spoke these words/rhetorics at the contribution box/treasury --; and no one laid hold of/arrested him, because his hour had not yet come. 8.21 Then he was saying to them: I, I go away and ye will seek me, and ye will die in your faults/sins; where I, I go ye, ye are not able to come/go. 8.22 Then the Judeans were saying: Will he not kill him-self, because he says: Where I, I would go, ye, ye are not able to go/come? 8.23 Therefore/then he was saying to them: Ye, ye are out of the (things) below; I, I am out of the (things) above; ye, ye are out of/from this world; I, I am not from this world. 8.24 I said to ye that ye will die in your faults/sins; for if ye might not believe in me that I, I am, ye will die in your faults/sins. 8.25 They were saying to him: You, who are you? Then Jesus said to them: Why *do*

εἶ; εἶπεν οὖν αὐτοῖς ὁ Ἰησοῦς, τὴν ἀρχὴν ὅ τι καὶ ἐν λαλῶ ὑμῖν; 8.26 πολλὰ ἔχω περὶ ὑμῶν λαλῖν καὶ κρίνιν· ἀλλ᾽ ὁ πέμψας με πατήρ ἀληθής ἐστιν, κἀγὼ ἃ ἤκουσα παρ᾽ αὐτοῦ ταῦτα λαλῶ εἰς τὸν κόσμον. 8.27 οὐκ ἔγνωσαν ὅτι τὸν πατέρα αὐτοῖς ἔλεγεν τὸν θεόν.

8.28 εἶπεν οὖν αὐτοῖς ὁ Ἰησοῦς πάλιν, ὅταν ὑψώσητε τὸν υἱὸν τοῦ ἀνθρώπου, τότε γνώσεσθαι ὅτι ἐγώ εἰμι, καὶ ἀπ᾽ ἐμαυτοῦ ποιῶ οὐδέν, ἀλλὰ καθὼς ἐδίδαξέν με ὁ πατὴρ οὕτως λαλῶ. 8.29 καὶ ὁ πέμψας με οὐκ ἀφῆκέν με μόνον μετ᾽ ἐμοῦ ἐστιν· ὅτι ἐγὼ τὰ ἀρεστὰ αὐτῷ ποιῶ πάντοτε. 8.30 ταῦτα αὐτοῦ λαλοῦντος πολλοὶ ἐπίστευσαν εἰς αὐτόν.

8.31 ἔλεγεν οὖν ὁ Ἰησοῦς πρὸς τοὺς πεπιστευκότας αὐτῷ Ἰουδαίους, ἐὰν ὑμεῖς μίνητε ἐν τῷ λόγῳ τῷ ἐμῷ, ἀληθῶς μαθηταί μού ἐστε, 8.32 καὶ γνώσεσθαι τὴν ἀλήθειαν, καὶ ἡ ἀλήθια ἐλευθερώσει ὑμᾶς. 8.33 ἀπεκρίθησαν πρὸς αὐτόν, σπέρμα Ἀβραάμ ἐσμεν καὶ οὐδενὶ δεδουλεύκαμεν πώποτε· πῶς σὺ λέγεις ὅτι ἐλεύθεροι γενήσεσθε; 8.34 ἀπεκρίθη αὐτοῖς ὁ Ἰησοῦς, ἀμὴν ἀμὴν λέγω ὑμῖν ὅτι πᾶς ὁ ποιῶν τὴν ἁμαρτίαν δοῦλός ἐστιν τῆς ἁμαρτίας. 8.35 ὁ δὲ δοῦλος οὐ μένει ἐν τῇ οἰκίᾳ εἰς τὸν αἰῶνα· --. 8.36 ἐὰν οὖν ὁ υἱὸς ὑμᾶς ἐλευθερώσῃ, ὄντως ἐλεύθεροι ἔσεσθαι. 8.37 οἶδα ὅτι σπέρμα Ἀβραάμ ἐστε· ἀλλὰ ζητεῖτέ με ἀποκτῖναι, ὅτι ὁ λόγος ὁ ἐμὸς οὐ χωρεῖ ἐν ὑμῖν. 8.38 ἃ ἐγὼ ἑώρακα παρὰ τῷ πατρί μου λαλῶ· καὶ ὑμεῖς οὖν ὃ ἠκούσαται ἃ ἑωράκατε παρὰ τοῦ πατρὸς ὑμῶν ποιεῖται. 8.39 ἀπεκρίθησαν καὶ εἶπαν αὐτῷ, ὁ πατὴρ ἡμῶν Ἀβραάμ ἐστιν. ἀπεκρίθη αὐτοῖς ὁ Ἰησοῦς, εἰ τέκνα τοῦ Ἀβραάμ ἐστε, τὰ ἔργα τοῦ Ἀβραὰμ ἐποιεῖται· 8.40 νῦν δὲ ζητῖτέ με ἀποκτῖναι, ἄνθρωπον ὃς τὴν ἀλήθιαν ὑμῖν λελάληκα ἣν ἤκουσα παρὰ τοῦ θεοῦ· τοῦτο Ἀβραὰμ οὐκ ἐποίησεν. 8.41 ὑμεῖς ποιεῖται τὰ ἔργα τοῦ πατρὸς ὑμῶν. εἶπαν αὐτῷ, ἡμεῖς ἐκ πορνίας οὐ γεγεννήμεθα· ἕνα πατέρα ἔχομεν τὸν θεόν. 8.42 εἶπεν οὖν αὐτοῖς ὁ Ἰησοῦς, εἰ ὁ θεὸς πατὴρ ὑμῶν ἦν, ἠγαπᾶτε ἂν ἐμέ, ἐγὼ γὰρ ἐκ τοῦ θεοῦ ἐξῆλθον

I even speak the beginning/first (thing) with ye?
8.26 I have much to speak and to judge about ye; but
the father having sent me is true, and what (things)
I, I heard from him, these (things) I speak to the
world.   8.27 They knew not that he was speaking to
them *of* God the father.

8.28   Therefore Jesus said to them again: Whenever ye might exalt/lift up the son of the man, then
ye will know that I, I am, and I do nothing from
myself, but just as the father taught me, thus/so I
speak.   8.29 And the (one) having sent me, he left/
sent away not me alone; he is with me, because I, I
always do the (things) pleasing to him.   8.30 From him
saying these (things) many believed in him.

8.31   Then Jesus was saying to the Judeans having
believed in him: If ye, ye might abide in/by my say-
ing/word, ye are truly my learners/pupils,   8.32 and
ye will know the truth, and the truth will set ye
free.   8.33 They answered/replied to him: We are
seed/posterity of Abraham and we have never been
enslaved to no one; how *do* you, you say that we shall
become free (ones/men)? 8.34 Jesus answered to them:
Truly, truly I say to ye that every one doing the sin
is a slave of the sin.   8.35 But the slave *does* not
abide in the house into the age; --. 8.36 If therefore
the son might free ye, ye will really be free (ones/-
men).   8.37 I know that ye are seed/posterity of
Abraham; but ye seek to kill me, because my saying/-
reason has not room/place in/with ye.   8.38 I speak
what (things) I, I have seen with/beside my father;
and ye therefore, ye do what ye heard and what -
(things) ye have heard from your father.   8.39 They
answered and said to him: The father of us is Abraham.
Jesus answered to them: If ye are children of Abraham,
ye were doing the works of Abraham;   8.40 but now ye
seek to kill me, a man who has spoken the truth to ye,
which I heard from God; Abraham did not do this.   8.41
Ye, ye do the works of your father. They said to him:
We,we have not been generated out of prostitution; we
have one father, God.   8.42 Then Jesus said to them:
If God were your your father, ye would be loving me,
for I, I came forth from God, and I have come; for I

καὶ ἥκω· οὐδὲ γὰρ ἀπ' ἐμαυτοῦ ἐλήλυθα, ἀλλ' ἐκεῖνός με ἀπέστιλεν. 8.43 διὰ τί τὴν λαλιὰν τὴν ἐμὴν οὐ γινώσκεται; ὅτι οὐ δύνασθε ἀκούειν τὸν λόγον τὸν ἐμόν. 8.44 ὑμεῖς ἐκ τοῦ πατρὸς τοῦ διαβόλου ἐσταὶ καὶ τὰς ἐπιθυμίας τοῦ πατρὸς ὑμῶν θέλετε ποιεῖν. ἐκῖνος ἀνθρωποκτόνος ἦν ἀπ' ἀρχῆς, καὶ ἐν τῇ ἀληθίᾳ οὐκ ἔστηκεν, ὅτι οὐκ ἔστιν ἀλήθια ἐν αὐτῷ. ὅταν λαλῇ τὸ ψεῦδος, ἐκ τῶν ἰδίων λαλεῖ, ὅτι ψεύστης ἐστὶν καὶ ὁ πατὴρ αὐτοῦ. 8.45 ἐγὼ δὲ ὅτι τὴν ἀλήθιαν λέγω, οὐ πιστεύετέ μοι. 8.46 τίς ἐξ ὑμῶν ἐλέγχει με περὶ ἁμαρτίας; εἰ ἀλήθειαν λέγω, διὰ τί ὑμεῖς οὐ πιστεύεταί μοι; 8.47 ὁ ὢν ἐκ τοῦ θεοῦ τὰ ῥήματα τοῦ θεοῦ ἀκούει· διὰ τοῦτο ὑμεῖς οὐκ ἀκούετε, ὅτι ἐκ τοῦ θεοῦ οὐκ ἐστέ. 8.48 ἀπεκρίθησαν οἱ Ἰουδαῖοι καὶ εἶπαν αὐτῷ, οὐ καλῶς λέγομεν ἡμεῖς ὅτι Σαμαρίτης εἶ σὺ καὶ δαιμόνιον ἔχεις; 8.49 ἀπεκρίθη Ἰησοῦς καὶ εἶπεν, ἐγὼ δαιμόνιον οὐκ ἔχω, ἀλλὰ τιμῶ τὸν πατέρα μου, καὶ ὑμῖς ἀτιμάζετέ με. 8.50 ἐγὼ δὲ οὐ ζητῶ τὴν δόξαν μου· ἔστιν ὁ ζητῶν καὶ κρίνων. 8.51 ἀμὴν ἀμὴν λέγω ὑμῖν, ἐάν τις τὸν ἐμὸν λόγον τηρήσει, θάνατον οὐ μὴ θεωρήσει εἰς τὸν αἰῶνα. 8.52 εἶπαν αὐτῷ οἱ Ἰουδαῖοι, νῦν ἐγνώκαμεν ὅτι δαιμόνιον ἔχεις. Ἀβραὰμ ἀπέθανεν καὶ οἱ προφῆται, καὶ σὺ λέγεις, ἐάν τις τὸν λόγον μου τηρήσῃ, οὐ μὴ γεύσηται θανάτου εἰς τὸν αἰῶνα. 8.53 μὴ σὺ μίζων εἶ τοῦ πατρὸς ἡμῶν Ἀβραάμ, ὅστις ἀπέθανεν; καὶ οἱ προφῆται ἀπέθανον· τίνα σεαυτὸν ποιεῖς; 8.54 ἀπεκρίθη ὁ Ἰησοῦς, ἐὰν ἐγὼ δοξάσω ἐμαυτόν, ἡ δόξα μου οὐδέν ἐστιν· ἔστιν ὁ πατήρ μου ὁ δοξάζων με, ὃν ὑμεῖς λέγεται ὅτι θεὸς ἡμῶν ἐστιν· 8.55 καὶ οὐκ ἐγνώκαται αὐτόν, ἐγὼ δὲ οἶδα αὐτόν. κἂν εἴπω ὅτι οὐκ οἶδα αὐτόν, ἔσομαι ὅμοιος ὑμῖν ψεύστης· ἀλλ' οἶδα αὐτὸν καὶ τὸν λόγον αὐτοῦ τηρῶ. 8.56 Ἀβραὰμ ὁ πατὴρ ὑμῶν ἠγαλλιάσατο ἵνα εἴδῃ τὴν ἡμέραν τὴν ἐμήν, καὶ εἶδεν καὶ ἐχάρη. 8.57 εἶπαν οὖν οἱ Ἰουδαῖοι πρὸς αὐτόν, πεντήκοντα ἔτη οὔπω ἔχεις καὶ Ἀβραὰμ ἑώρακέν σε; 8.58 εἶπεν αὐτοῖς ὁ Ἰησοῦς, ἀμὴν ἀμὴν λέγω ὑμῖν, πρὶν Ἀβραὰμ γενέσθαι ἐγὼ εἰμί. 8.59 ἦραν οὖν λίθους ἵνα βάλωσιν ἐπ' αὐτόν·

have not come from myself, but that (one) sent me.
8.43 Because of what *do* ye not know my speech/-speaking? Because ye are not able to hear/listen to my saying/word.   8.44 Ye, ye are from the father the devil, and ye want/wish to do the desires of your father. That (one) was a murderer/man-killer from the beginning, and he stood not in/by the truth, because truth is not in him. Whenever he may speak the lie, he speaks out of the (things) his own, because he is a liar and the father of it.   8.45 But because I, I say/speak the truth, ye do not believe in me.   8.46 Who out of ye convicts/reproves   me   about sin/fault? If I say/speak truth, why *do* ye not believe in me? 8.47 The (one) being from God hears the words from God; because of this ye, ye hear/listen not, because ye are not from God.   8.48 The Judeans answered and said to him: We, say we not well that you, you are a Samaritan and you have a demon?   8.49 Jesus answered and said: I, I have not a demon, but I honor my father, and ye, ye dishonor me.   8.50 But I, I seek not my fame/glory; there is the (one) seeking and judging. 8.51 truly, truly I say to ye: If anyone will keep my saying/word, by no means will he see/behold death into the age.   8.52 The Judeans said to him: Now we have known that you have a demon. Abraham and the prophets died, and you, you say: If anyone might keep my saying/word, by no means might he taste death into the age.   8.53 You, you are not greater than our father Abraham, who died? The prophets also died; who *do* you make yourself? 8.54 Jesus answered: If I, I might glorify myself, my glory/fame is nothing; my father is the (one) glorifying me, whom ye, ye say: He is our God; 8.55   and ye have not known him, but I, I know him. Even if I might say that I *do* not know him, I shall be a liar like ye; but I know him and I keep the saying/word from him.   8.56 Abraham, the father of ye, himself rejoiced exceedingly that he might see my day, he both saw and rejoiced.   8.57 Then the Judeans said to him: You have not yet fifty years, and Abraham has seen you?   8.58 Jesus said to them: Truly, truly I say to ye: Before to be generated Abraham, I, I am.   8.59 Therefore they took up stones in order that they might

Ἰησοῦς δὲ ἐκρύβη καὶ ἐξῆλθεν ἐκ τοῦ ἱεροῦ. 9.1 καὶ παράγων εἶδεν ἄνθρωπον τυφλὸν ἐκ γενετῆς. 9.2 καὶ ἠρώτησαν αὐτὸν οἱ μαθηταὶ αὐτοῦ λέγοντες, ῥαββεί, τίς ἥμαρτεν, οὗτος ἢ οἱ γονὶς αὐτοῦ, ἵνα τυφλὸς γεννηθῇ; 9.3 ἀπεκρίθη Ἰησοῦς, οὔτε οὗτος ἥμαρτεν οὔτε οἱ γονὶς αὐτοῦ, ἀλλ' ἵνα φανερωθῇ τὰ ἔργα τοῦ θεοῦ ἐν αὐτῷ. 9.4 ἡμᾶς δεῖ ἐργάζεσθαι τὰ ἔργα τοῦ πέμψαντός ἡμᾶς ἕως ἡμέρα ἐστίν· ἔρχεται νὺξ ὅτε οὐδεὶς δύναται ἐργάζεσθαι. 9.5 ὅταν ἐν τῷ κόσμῳ ὦ, φῶς εἰμι τοῦ κόσμου. 9.6 ταῦτα εἰπὼν ἔπτυσεν χαμαὶ καὶ ἐποίησεν πηλὸν ἐκ τοῦ πτύσματος, καὶ ἐπέχρισεν αὐτοῦ τὸν πηλὸν ἐπὶ τοὺς ὀφθαλμοὺς 9.7 καὶ εἶπεν αὐτῷ, ὕπαγε νίψαι εἰς τὴν κολυμβήθραν τοῦ Σιλωάμ ὃ ἑρμηνεύεται ἀπεσταλμένος. ἀπῆλθεν οὖν καὶ ἐνίψατο, καὶ ἦλθεν βλέπων. 9.8 οἱ οὖν γείτονες καὶ οἱ θεωροῦντες αὐτὸν τὸ πρότερον ὅτι προσαίτης ἦν ἔλεγον, οὐχ οὗτός ἐστιν ὁ καθήμενος καὶ προσαιτῶν; 9.9 ἄλλοι ἔλεγον ὅτι οὗτός ἐστιν· ἄλλοι δὲ ἔλεγον, οὐχί, ἀλλὰ ὅμοιος αὐτῷ ἐστιν. ἐκεῖνος δὲ ἔλεγεν ὅτι ἐγώ εἰμι. 9.10 ἔλεγον οὖν αὐτῷ, πῶς οὖν ἠνεῴχθησάν σου οἱ ὀφθαλμοί; 9.11 ἀπεκρίθη ἐκεῖνος, ὁ ἄνθρωπος ὁ λεγόμενος Ἰησοῦς πηλὸν ἐποίησεν καὶ ἐπέχρισέν μου τοὺς ὀφθαλμοὺς καὶ εἶπέν μοι ὅτι ὕπαγε εἰς τὸν Σιλωὰμ καὶ νίψαι· ἀπελθὼν οὖν καὶ νιψάμενος ἀνέβλεψα. 9.12 καὶ εἶπαν αὐτῷ, ποῦ ἐστιν ἐκεῖνος; λέγει, οὐκ οἶδα. 9.13 ἄγουσιν αὐτὸν πρὸς τοὺς Φαρισαίους τόν ποτε τυφλόν. 9.14 ἦν δὲ σάββατον ἐν ᾗ ἡμέρᾳ τὸν πηλὸν ἐποίησεν ὁ Ἰησοῦς καὶ ἀνέῳξεν αὐτοῦ τοὺς ὀφθαλμούς. 9.15 πάλιν οὖν ἠρώτων αὐτὸν καὶ οἱ Φαρισαῖοι πῶς ἀνέβλεψεν. ὁ δὲ εἶπεν αὐτοῖς, πηλὸν ἐπέθηκέν μου ἐπὶ τοὺς ὀφθαλμούς, καὶ ἐνιψάμην, καὶ βλέπω. 9.16 ἔλεγον οὖν ἐκ τῶν Φαρισαίων τινές, οὐκ ἔστιν οὗτος παρὰ θεοῦ ὁ ἄνθρωπος, ὅτι τὸ σάββατον οὐ τηρεῖ. ἄλλοι δὲ ἔλεγον, πῶς δύναται ἄνθρωπος ἁμαρτωλὸς τοιαῦτα σημῖα ποιεῖν; καὶ σχίσμα ἦν ἐν αὐτοῖς. 9.17 λέγουσιν οὖν τῷ ποτὲ τυφλῷ πάλιν, οὖν τί σὺ λέγεις περὶ σεαυτοῦ, ὅτι

throw *them* upon him; but Jesus was hidden and he went forth out of the temple compound. 9.1 And passing along/by he saw a man, a blind (one) from birth. 9.2 And his learners/pupils questioned him, saying: Rabbi, who sinned, this (one) or his parents, in order that he was generated/born blind? 9.3 Jesus answered: Neither this (one)/he sinned nor his parents, but in order that the works of God might be manifested in him. 9.4 It is necessary *for* us to work the works of the (one) having sent us until/while it is day; when night comes, no one is able to work/to be working. 9.5 Whenever I may be in the world, I am a/*the* light of the world. 9.6 Having said these things, he spat on the ground and made clay from the spittle, and smeared/anointed the clay on his eyes, 9.7 and he said to him: You go wash in the pool of Siloam, which is translated: having been sent. Then he went away and washed, and he came seeing. 9.8 then the neighbors and those seeing/beholding him formerly that he was a beggar were saying: Is not this (one)/he the (one) being seated and begging? 9.9 Others were saying that this is he/he is; but others were saying: No, but he is similar to him. And that (one)was saying: I, I am. 9.10 Therefore they were saying to him: How then were your eyes opened? 9.11 That (one) answered: The man being called Jesus made clay/mud and rubbed it upon my eyes and said to me: You go to Siloam and wash; then having gone away and having washed myself, I looked up/received sight. 9.12 And they said to him: Where is that (one)? He says: I know not. 9.13 They bring/ lead him, the (one) once blind, to the Pharisees. 9.14 But it was a sabbath on which day Jesus made the clay and opened his eyes. 9.15 Then the Pharisees were also asking him again how he received sight. And the (he) said to them: He put clay on my eyes, and I washed myself, and I see. 9.16 Then some out of the Pharisees were saying: This man is not from God, because he keeps not the sabbath. But others were saying: How is a sinful man able to do such signs? And there was a division among them. 9.17 Therefore they say/speak again to the once blind (one): Then you, what *do* you say about/concerning yourself, because he

ἤνοιξέν σου τοὺς ὀφθαλμούς; ὁ δὲ εἶπεν ὅτι προφήτης ἐστίν. 9.18 οὐκ ἐπίστευσαν οὖν οἱ Ἰουδαῖοι περὶ αὐτοῦ ὅτι ἦν τυφλὸς καὶ ἀνέβλεψεν, ἕως ὅτου ἐφώνησαν τοὺς γονῖς αὐτοῦ τοῦ ἀναβλέψαντος 9.19 καὶ ἠρώτησαν αὐτοὺς εἰ οὗτός ἐστιν ὁ υἱὸς ὑμῶν, ὃν ὑμεῖς λέγεται ὅτι τυφλὸς ἐγεννήθη; πῶς οὖν βλέπι ἄρτι; 9.20 ἀπεκρίθησαν οὖν οἱ γονῖς αὐτοῦ καὶ εἶπαν, οἴδαμεν ὅτι οὗτός ἐστιν ὁ υἱὸς ἡμῶν καὶ ὅτι τυφλὸς ἐγεννήθη· 9.21 πῶς δὲ νῦν βλέπει οὐκ οἴδαμεν, ἢ τίς ἤνυξεν αὐτοῦ τοὺς ὀφθαλμοὺς ἡμεῖς οὐκ οἴδαμεν· αὐτὸν ἐρωτήσατai, ἡλικίαν ἔχει, αὐτὸς περὶ ἑαυτοῦ λαλήσει. 9.22 ταῦτα εἶπαν οἱ γονῖς αὐτοῦ ὅτι ἐφοβοῦντο τοὺς Ἰουδαίους, ἤδη γὰρ συνετέθιντο οἱ Ἰουδαῖοι ἵνα ἐάν τις αὐτὸν ὁμολογήσῃ χριστόν, ἀποσυνάγωγος γένηται. 9.23 διὰ τοῦτο οἱ γονῖς αὐτοῦ εἶπαν ὅτι ἡλικίαν ἔχι, αὐτὸν ἐπερωτήσαται.

9.24 ἐφώνησαν οὖν τὸν ἄνθρωπον ἐκ δευτέρου ὃς ἦν τυφλὸς καὶ εἶπαν αὐτῷ, δὸς δόξαν τῷ θεῷ· ἡμῖς οἴδαμεν ὅτι οὗτος ὁ ἄνθρωπος ὁ ἁμαρτωλός ἐστιν. 9.25 ἀπεκρίθη οὖν ἐκεῖνος, εἰ ἁμαρτωλός ἐστιν οὐκ οἶδα· ἓν δὲ οἶδα, ὅτι τυφλὸς ὢν ἄρτι βλέπω. 9.26 εἶπον οὖν αὐτῷ, τί ἐποίησέν σοι; πῶς ἤνυξέν σου τοὺς ὀφθαλμούς; 9.27 ἀπεκρίθη αὐτοῖς, εἶπον ὑμῖν ἤδη καὶ οὐκ ἠκούσατε· τί πάλιν θέλεται ἀκούειν; μὴ καὶ ὑμῖς θέλεται μαθηταὶ αὐτοῦ γενέσθαι; 9.28 καὶ ἐλοιδόρησαν αὐτὸν καὶ εἶπαν, σὺ μαθητὴς εἶ ἐκίνου, ἡμεῖς δὲ τοῦ Μωϋσέως ἐσμὲν μαθηταί· 9.29 ἡμῖς οἴδαμεν ὅτι Μωϋσεῖ λελάληκεν ὁ θεός, τοῦτον δὲ οὐκ οἴδαμεν πόθεν ἐστίν. 9.30 ἀπεκρίθη ὁ ἄνθρωπος καὶ εἶπεν αὐτοῖς, ἐν τούτῳ γὰρ τὸ θαυμαστόν ἐστιν ὅτι ὑμεῖς οὐκ οἴδαται πόθεν ἐστίν, καὶ ἤνοιξέν μου τοὺς ὀφθαλμούς. 9.31 οἴδαμεν ὅτι ἁμαρτωλῶν ὁ θεὸς οὐκ ἀκούει, ἀλλ' ἐάν τις θεοσεβὴς ᾖ καὶ τὸ θέλημα αὐτοῦ ποιῇ τούτου ἀκούει. 9.32 ἐκ τοῦ αἰῶνος οὐκ ἠκούσθη ὅτι ἤνοιξέν τις ὀφθαλμοὺς τυφλοῦ γεγεννημένου· 9.33 εἰ

opened your eyes? And the (he) said: He is a prophet.
9.18 Then the Judeans believe not about him that he
was blind and received sight, until which *time* they
summoned the parents of him, the (one) having received
sight,   9.19 and they asked them if this (one)/he is
your son, whom ye, ye say that he   was born/generated
blind; how then *does* he see now?   9.20 Then his parents answered and said: We know that this (one)/he is
our son and that he was generated/born blind;   9.21
but we know not how he sees now, or we know not who
opened his eyes; ask ye him, he has maturity/majori-
ty/is of age; he, he will speak concerning himself.
9.22 His parents said these (things) because they were
fearing the Judeans, for the Judeans had already
decided/agreed that if anyone might confess him the
anointed (one), he might himself become excommunicat-
ed/expelled from the   congregation.   9.23 Because of
this his parents said: He has maturity/legal age,
interrogate/question ye him.
    9.24   Therefore from a second *time* they summoned
the man who was blind and said to him: You give   fame/
glory to God; we, we know that this (one)/he is a
sinful man.   9.25 Then that (one) answered: I know not
if he is a sinner; but one (thing) I know, that being
blind, now I see.   9.26 Therefore they said to him:
What did he to/for you? How opened he your eyes?   9.27
He replied to them: I   said   to ye already and ye
heard/listened not; why *do* ye want/wish to hear again?
Ye, do ye not want/wish also to become   his learners/
pupils?   9.28 And they reviled/cursed him and said:
You, you are a learner/pupil of that (one), but we, we
are learners/pupils of Moses;   9.29 we, we know that
God has spoken to/by Moses, but we know not from where
this (one) is.   9.30 The man answered and said to
them: For the astonishment/wonderment is in this
(thing) that/because ye, ye know not from where he is,
and/but he opened my eyes.   9.31   We know that God
hears not sinners, but if anyone may be godfearing and
may do his will, from this (one) he hears/listens.
9.32 Out of the age it was not heard that anyone
opened eyes from having been generated/born blind;
9.33 unless this (one)/he was from God, he was not

μὴ ἦν οὗτος παρὰ θεοῦ, οὐκ ἠδύνατο ποιεῖν οὐδέν. 9.34 ἀπεκρίθησαν καὶ εἶπαν αὐτῷ, ἐν ἁμαρτίαις σὺ ἐγεννήθης ὅλος, καὶ σὺ διδάσκεις ἡμᾶς; καὶ ἐξέβαλον αὐτὸν ἔξω. 9.35 καὶ ἤκουσεν Ἰησοῦς ὅτι ἐξέβαλον αὐτὸν ἔξω, καὶ εὑρὼν αὐτὸν εἶπεν, σὺ πιστεύεις εἰς τὸν υἱὸν τοῦ ἀνθρώπου; 9.36 ἀπεκρίθη ἐκεῖνος καὶ εἶπεν, κύριε, τίς ἐστιν ἵνα πιστεύσω εἰς αὐτόν; 9.37 ἔφη αὐτῷ ὁ Ἰησοῦς, καὶ ἑώρακας αὐτὸν καὶ ὁ λαλῶν μετὰ σοῦ ἐκεῖνός ἐστιν.9.38 ὁ δὲ ἔφη, πιστεύω, κύριε· καὶ προσεκύνησεν αὐτῷ. 9.39 καὶ εἶπεν Ἰησοῦς, εἰς κρίμα ἐγὼ εἰς τὸν κόσμον τοῦτον ἦλθον, ἵνα οἱ μὴ βλέποντες βλέπωσιν καὶ οἱ βλέποντες τυφλοὶ γένωνται. 9.40 ἤκουσαν ἐκ τῶν Φαρισαίων οἱ μετ᾽ αὐτοῦ ὄντες, καὶ εἶπαν αὐτῷ, μὴ καὶ ἡμεῖς τυφλοί ἐσμεν; 9.41 εἶπεν αὐτοῖς ὁ Ἰησοῦς, εἰ τυφλοὶ ἦτε, οὐκ ἂν εἴχετε ἁμαρτίαν· νῦν δὲ λέγετε ὅτι Βλέπομεν· ἡ ἁμαρτία ὑμῶν μένει.

10.1 Ἀμὴν ἀμὴν λέγω ὑμῖν, ὁ μὴ εἰσερχόμενος διὰ τῆς θύρας εἰς τὴν αὐλὴν τῶν προβάτων ἀλλὰ ἀναβαίνων ἀλλαχόθεν ἐκεῖνος κλέπτης ἐστὶν καὶ λῃστής· 10.2 ὁ δὲ εἰσερχόμενος διὰ τῆς θύρας ποιμήν ἐστιν τῶν προβάτων. 10.3 τούτῳ ὁ θυρωρὸς ἀνύγει, καὶ τὰ πρόβατα τῆς φωνῆς αὐτοῦ ἀκούει, καὶ τὰ ἴδια πρόβατα φωνεῖ κατ᾽ ὄνομα καὶ ἐξάγει αὐτά. 10.4 ὅταν τὰ ἴδια πάντα ἐκβάλῃ, ἔμπροσθεν αὐτῶν πορεύεται, καὶ τὰ πρόβατα αὐτῷ ἀκολουθεῖ, ὅτι οἴδασιν τὴν φωνὴν αὐτοῦ· 10.5 ἀλλοτρίῳ δὲ οὐ μὴ ἀκολουθήσωσιν ἀλλὰ φεύξονται ἀπ᾽ αὐτοῦ, ὅτι οὐκ οἴδασι τῶν ἀλλοτρίων τὴν φωνήν. 10.6 ταύτην τὴν παροιμίαν εἶπεν αὐτοῖς ὁ Ἰησοῦς· ἐκεῖνοι καὶ οὐκ ἔγνωσαν τίνα ἦν ἃ ἐλάλει αὐτοῖς. 10.7 εἶπεν οὖν αὐτοῖς πάλιν ὁ Ἰησοῦς, ἀμὴν ἀμὴν λέγω ὑμῖν ὅτι ἐγώ εἰμι ἡ θύρα τῶν προβάτων. 10.8 πάντες ὅσοι ἦλθον πρὸ ἐμοῦ κλέπται εἰσὶν καὶ λῃσταί· ἀλλ᾽ οὐκ ἤκουσαν αὐτῶν τὰ πρόβατα. 10.9 ἐγώ ἡ εἰμι ἡ θύρα· δι᾽ ἐμοῦ ἐάν τις εἰσέλθῃ σωθήσεται καὶ

being able to do nothing. 9.34 They answered and said to him: You, you were generated wholly in sins, and you, you teach/are teaching us? And they threw him out. 9.35 And Jesus heard that they threw him out, and having found him, he said: You, *do* you believe in the son of the man? 9.36 That (one) answered and said: Lord, sir, who is *he* in order that I might believe in him? 9.37 Jesus was saying to him: You have both seen him and the (one) speaking with you is that (one). 9.38 And the (he) was saying: I believe, Lord/sir; and he worshiped/knelt to him. 9.39 And Jesus said: I, I came into this world into/for judgment, in order that the (ones) seeing not may see and the (ones) seeing might themselves become blind. 9.40 They heard, the (ones) being with him out of the Pharisees, and they said to him: We, are we not also blind? 9.41 Jesus said to them: If ye were blind (ones), ye would not be having sin; but now ye say: We see; your fault/sin remains/stays.

10.1 Truly, truly I say to ye, the (one) not entering into the enclosure/courtyard of the sheep through the door but going up/ascending from another place, that (one) is a thief and a robber; 10.2 but the (one) going in through the door is a shepherd of the sheep. 10.3 The door opens for this (one), and the sheep hear his voice/sound, and he calls his own sheep by/according to name and he leads/brings them forth. 10.4 Whenever he might put out/forth all his own (sheep), he goes before them, and the sheep follow with him, because they know his voice; 10.5 but by no means will they follow for another/stranger but they will flee from him, because they know not the voice/sound of strangers. 10.6 Jesus said this proverb/allegory to them; and/but those (men) knew not what (things) they were which he was speaking to them. 10.7 Therefore, Jesus said/spoke to them again: Truly, truly I say to ye that I, I am the door of the sheep. 10.8 All (men), as many as came before me, are thieves and robbers; but the sheep heard not from them. 10.9 I, truly I am the door; if anyone might enter through me he will be saved and he himself will

εἰσελεύσεται καὶ ἐξελεύσεται καὶ νομὴν εὑρήσει. 10.10 ὁ κλέπτης οὐκ ἔρχεται εἰ μὴ ἵνα κλέψῃ καὶ θύσῃ καὶ ἀπολέσῃ· ἐγὼ ἦλθον ἵνα ζωὴν αἰώνιον ἔχωσιν καὶ περισσὸν ἔχωσιν. 10.11 ἐγώ εἰμι ὁ ποιμὴν ὁ καλός· ὁ ποιμὴν ὁ καλὸς τὴν ψυχὴν αὐτοῦ τίθησιν ὑπὲρ τῶν προβάτων· 10.12 ὁ δὲ μισθωτὸς καὶ οὐκ ὢν ποιμήν, οὗ οὐκ ἔστιν τὰ πρόβατα ἴδια, θεωρεῖ τὸν λύκον ἐρχόμενον καὶ ἀφίησιν τὰ πρόβατα καὶ φεύγει καὶ ὁ λύκος ἁρπάζει αὐτὰ καὶ σκορπίζει 10.13 ὅτι μισθωτός ἐστιν καὶ οὐ μέλει αὐτῷ περὶ τῶν προβάτων. 10.14 ἐγώ εἰμι ὁ ποιμὴν ὁ καλός, καὶ γεινώσκω τὰ ἐμὰ καὶ γεινώσκουσί με τὰ ἐμά, 10.15 καθὼς γινώσκι με ὁ πατὴρ κἀγὼ γινώσκω τὸν πατέρα· καὶ τὴν ψυχήν μου τίθημι ὑπὲρ τῶν προβάτων. 10.16 καὶ ἄλλα πρόβατα ἔχω ἃ οὐκ ἔστιν ἐκ τῆς αὐλῆς ταύτης· κἀκεῖνα δεῖ με ἀγαγῖν, καὶ τῆς φωνῆς μου ἀκούσωσιν, καὶ γενήσονται μία ποίμνη, εἷς ποιμήν. 10.17 διὰ τοῦτό με ὁ πατὴρ ἀγαπᾷ ὅτι ἐγὼ τίθημι τὴν ψυχήν μου, ἵνα πάλιν λάβω αὐτήν. 10.18 οὐδὶς ἔρει αὐτὴν ἀπ’ ἐμοῦ, ἀλλ’ ἐγὼ τίθημι αὐτὴν ἀπ’ ἐμαυτοῦ. ἐξουσίαν ἔχω θεῖναι αὐτήν, καὶ ἐξουσίαν ἔχω πάλιν λαβῖν αὐτήν· ταύτην τὴν ἐντολὴν ἔλαβον παρὰ τοῦ πατρός μου. 10.19 σχίσμα πάλιν ἐγένετο ἐν τοῖς Ἰουδαίοις διὰ τοὺς λόγους τούτους. 10.20 ἔλεγον οὖν πολλοὶ ἐξ αὐτῶν, δαιμόνιον ἔχει καὶ μαίνεται· τί αὐτοῦ ἀκούεται; 10.21 ἄλλοι δὲ ἔλεγον, ταῦτα τὰ ῥήματα οὐκ ἔστιν δαιμονιζομένου· μὴ δαιμόνιον δύναται τυφλῶν ὀφθαλμοὺς ἀνῦξαι;

10.22 ἐγένετο δὲ τὰ ἐνκαίνια ἐν Ἰεροσολύμοις· χειμὼν ἦν, 10.23 καὶ περιεπάτει ὁ Ἰησοῦς ἐν τῷ ἱερῷ ἐν τῇ στοᾷ Σολομῶνος. 10.24 ἐκύκλωσαν οὖν αὐτὸν οἱ Ἰουδαῖοι καὶ ἔλεγον αὐτῷ, ἕως πότε τὴν ψυχὴν ἡμῶν ἔρεις; εἰ σὺ εἶ ὁ χριστός, εἰπὸν ἡμῖν παρρησίᾳ. 10.25 ἀπεκρίθη αὐτοῖς ὁ Ἰησοῦς, εἶπον

go in and will go out and he will find a pasture.
10.10 The thief comes not except that he might steal
and slay/slaughter and destroy; I, I came that they
may nave eternal life and may have abundance. 10.11
I, I am the good shepherd; the good shepherd puts/lays
down his soul/life in behalf of the sheep; 10.12 but
the hired servant/wage earner, also/even being not a
shepherd, of whom the sheep are not his own, he ob-
serves/beholds the wolf coming and he leaves the sheep
and flees -- and the wolf seizes/snatches and scatters
them -- 10.13 because he is a hired (man) and it is
not a care to him concerning the sheep. 10.14 I, I am
the good shepherd, and I know my *sheep* and my *sheep*
know me, 10.15 just as the father knows me and I know
the father; and I give my soul/life in behalf of the
sheep. 10.16 I also have other sheep which are not
from this enclosure/courtyard; it is necessary *for* me
to bring/lead those also, and they will hear my voice,
they will become one flock, one shepherd. 10.17
Because of this the father loves me, because I, I
put/lay down my soul/life, in order that I might
receive/take it again. 10.18 No one takes/is taking
it from me, but I, I put it down from myself. I have/
hold authority to put/lay it down, and I have/hold
authority to take it again; I received/took this
from/beside my father. 10.19 Again there came to
be/came about a split/division among the Judeans
because of these sayings/words. 10.20 Then many out
of them said: He has a demon and he is mad/insane;
why do we hear/listen from him? 10.21 But others were
saying: These words are not from (one) being demon-
possessed; a demon is not able to open eyes of blind
(ones), *is it*?
     10.22 And the festival of the lights/rededica-
tion became among the Jerusalemites; it was winter,
10.23 and Jesus walked in the *outer* temple in/at the
portico/colonnade of Solomon. 10.24 Then the Judeans
encircled him and were saying to him: Until when/how
long *do* you bear/take away/remove our life/soul? If
you, you are the anointed (one), speak to us freely/
plainly. 10.25 Jesus answered to them: I said *so* to

ὑμῖν καὶ οὐ πιστεύεται· τὰ ἔργα ἃ ἐγὼ ποιῶ ἐν ὀνόματι τοῦ πατρός μου ταῦτα μαρτυρῖ περὶ ἐμοῦ· 10.26 ἀλλὰ ὑμῖς οὐ πιστεύετε, ὅτι οὐκ ἐσταὶ ἐκ τῶν προβάτων τῶν ἐμῶν. 10.27 τὰ πρόβατα τὰ ἐμὰ τῆς φωνῆς μου ἀκούουσιν, καὶ γινώσκω αὐτά, καὶ ἀκολουθοῦσίν μοι, 10.28 κἀγὼ δίδωμι αὐτοῖς ζωὴν αἰώνιον, καὶ οὐ μὴ ἀπόλωνται εἰς τὸν αἰῶνα, καὶ οὐ μὴ ἁρπάση τις αὐτὰ ἐκ τῆς χειρός μου. 10.29 ὁ πατήρ μου ὃ δέδωκέν μοι πάντων μεῖζόν ἐστιν, καὶ οὐδὶς δύναται ἁρπάζειν ἐκ τῆς χειρὸς τοῦ πατρός. 10.30 ἐγὼ καὶ ὁ πατὴρ ἕν ἐσμεν. 10.31 ἐβάστασαν πάλιν λίθους οἱ Ἰουδαῖοι ἵνα λιθάσωσιν αὐτόν. 10.32 ἀπεκρίθη αὐτοῖς ὁ Ἰησοῦς, πολλὰ ἔργα καλὰ ἔδιξα ὑμῖν ἐκ τοῦ πατρός· διὰ ποῖον αὐτῶν ἔργον ἐμὲ λιθάζετε; 10.33 ἀπεκρίθησαν αὐτῷ οἱ Ἰουδαῖοι, περὶ καλοῦ ἔργου οὐ λιθάζομέν σε ἀλλὰ περὶ βλασφημίας, ὅτι σὺ ἄνθρωπος ὢν ποιεῖς σεαυτὸν θεόν.

10.34 ἀπεκρίθη αὐτοῖς ὁ Ἰησοῦς, οὐκ ἔστιν γεγραμμένον ἐν τῷ νόμῳ ὑμῶν ὅτι «ἐγὼ εἶπα, Θεοί ἐστε;» 10.35 εἰ ἐκείνους εἶπεν θεοὺς πρὸς οὓς ὁ λόγος τοῦ θεοῦ ἐγένετο, καὶ οὐ δύναται λυθῆναι ἡ γραφή, 10.36 ὃν ὁ πατὴρ ἡγίασεν καὶ ἀπέστιλεν εἰς τὸν κόσμον ὑμεῖς λέγετε ὅτι βλασφημῖς, ὅτι εἶπον, υἱὸς θεοῦ εἰμι; 10.37 εἰ οὐ ποιῶ τὰ ἔργα τοῦ πατρός μου, μὴ πιστεύετέ μοι· 10.38 εἰ δὲ ποιῶ, κἂν ἐμοὶ μὴ πιστεύεται, τοῖς ἔργοις πιστεύεται, ἵνα γνῶτε καὶ πιστεύητε ὅτι ἐν ἐμοὶ ὁ πατὴρ κἀγὼ ἐν τῷ πατρί. 10.39 ἐζήτουν οὖν αὐτὸν πάλιν πιάσαι· καὶ ἐξῆλθεν ἐκ τῆς χειρὸς αὐτῶν. 10.40 καὶ ἀπῆλθεν πάλιν πέραν τοῦ Ἰορδάνου εἰς τὸν τόπον ὅπου ἦν Ἰωάννης τὸ πρῶτερον βαπτίζων, καὶ ἔμινεν ἐκεῖ. 10.41 καὶ πολλοὶ ἦλθον πρὸς αὐτὸν καὶ ἔλεγον Ἰωάννης μὲν σημῖον ἐποίησεν οὐδέν, πάντα δὲ ὅσα εἶπεν Ἰωάννης περὶ τούτου ἀληθῆ ἦν. 10.42 καὶ πολλοὶ ἐπίστευσαν εἰς αὐτὸν ἐκεῖ.

11.1 Ἦν δέ τις ἀσθενῶν, Λάζαρος ἀπὸ Βηθανίας, ἐκ τῆς

ye and/but ye believe not; the works which I, I do in
the name of my father, they/these testify/witness
about me; 10.26 but ye, ye believe not, because ye
are not out of/part of my sheep. 10.27 My sheep hear
my voice, and I know them, and they follow with me,
10.28 and I, I give eternal life to them, and by no
means might they perish into the age, and by no means
may anyone snatch them out of my hand. 10.29 My
father, who has given *them* to me is greater than all
(men), and no one is able to snatch *them* out of the
hand of the father. 10.30 I and the father, we are
one. 10.31 The Judeans again lifted up stones in
order that they might stone him. 10.32 Jesus answered
to them: I showed to ye many good works from the
father; because of what work of them *do* ye stone me?
10.33 The Judeans answered to him: We indeed stone you
not concerning a good work but concerning slandering/
blasphemy, because you, being a man, you make yourself
God.

10.34 Jesus answered to them: Is it not having
been written in your law: I, I SAID: YE ARE GODS?
10.35 If he called those Gods to/for whom the logos/
word of God became/came to be, and the writing is not
able to be loosed/repealed, 10.36 ye, say ye of *him*
whom the father sanctified and sent into the world:
You slander/blaspheme, because I said: I am a son of
God? 10.37 If I do not the works of my father, *do* ye
not believe in me? 10.38 But if I do, even if ye
believe not in me, believe ye in the works, that ye
might know and ye may believe that the father *is* in me
and I in the father. 10.39 Therefore they were again
seeking to arrest him; and he went forth out of their
hand. 10.40 And he went away again beyond/across the
Jordan to the place where John was the first/former
(one) baptizing, and he stayed/remained there. 10.41
And many came to him and they were saying: John indeed
did no sign, but all (things) whatever John said about
this (one) was true. 10.42 And many believed in him
there.

11.1 And a certain (man) was being sick/ailing,
Lazarus from Bethany, from the village of Mary and

κώμης Μαρίας καὶ τῆς Μάρθας τῆς ἀδελφῆς αὐτῆς. 11.2 ἦν δὲ Μαριὰ ἡ ἀλίψασα τὸν κύριον μύρῳ καὶ ἐκμάξασα τοὺς πόδας αὐτοῦ ταῖς θριξὶν αὐτῆς, ἧς ὁ ἀδελφὸς Λάζαρος ἠσθένι. 11.3 ἀπέστιλαν οὖν πρὸς αὐτὸν αἱ ἀδελφαὶ λέγουσαι, κύριε, ἴδε ὃν φιλεῖς ἀσθενεῖ.

11.4 ἀκούσας δὲ ὁ Ἰησοῦς εἶπεν, αὕτη ἡ ἀσθένεια οὐκ ἔστιν πρὸς θάνατον ἀλλ᾽ ὑπὲρ τῆς δόξης τοῦ θεοῦ, ἀλλ᾽ ἵνα δοξασθῇ ὁ υἱὸς τοῦ θεοῦ δι᾽ αὐτῆς. 11.5 ἠγάπα δὲ ὁ Ἰησοῦς τὴν Μάρθαν καὶ τὴν ἀδελφὴν αὐτῆς καὶ τὸν Λάζαρον. 11.6 ὡς οὖν ἤκουσεν ὅτι ἀσθενεῖ, τότε μὲν ἔμινεν ἐν ᾧ ἦν τόπῳ δύο ἡμέρας· 11.7 ἔπιτα μετὰ τοῦτο λέγει τοῖς μαθηταῖς, ἄγωμεν εἰς τὴν Ἰουδαίαν πάλιν. 11.8 λέγουσιν αὐτῷ οἱ μαθηταί, ῥαββεί, νῦν ἐζήτουν σε λιθάσε οἱ Ἰουδαῖοι, καὶ πάλιν ὑπάγεις ἐκεῖ;

11.9 ἀπεκρίθη Ἰησοῦς, οὐχὶ δώδεκα ὧραί εἰσιν τῆς ἡμέρας; ἐάν τις περιπατῇ ἐν τῇ ἡμέρᾳ, οὐ προσκόπτει, ὅτι τὸ φῶς τοῦ κόσμου τούτου βλέπει· 11.10 ἐὰν δέ τις περιπατῇ ἐν τῇ νυκτεί, προσκόπτει, ὅτι τὸ φῶς οὐκ ἔστιν ἐν αὐτῷ. 11.11 ταῦτα εἶπεν, καὶ μετὰ τοῦτο λέγει αὐτοῖς, Λάζαρος ὁ φίλος ἡμῶν κεκοίμηται, ἀλλὰ πορεύομαι ἵνα ἐξυπνίσω αὐτόν. 11.12 εἶπαν οὖν αὐτῷ οἱ μαθηταί, κύριε, εἰ κεκοίμηται σωθήσεται. 11.13 εἰρήκι δὲ ὁ Ἰησοῦς περὶ τοῦ θανάτου αὐτοῦ. ἐκεῖνοι δὲ ἔδοξαν ὅτι περὶ τῆς κοιμήσεως τοῦ ὕπνου λέγει. 11.14 τότε οὖν εἶπεν αὐτοῖς Ἰησοῦς παρρησίᾳ, Λάζαρος ἀπέθανεν, 11.15 καὶ χαίρω δι᾽ ὑμᾶς, ἵνα πιστεύσητε, ὅτι οὐκ ἤμην ἐκῖ· ἀλλὰ ἄγωμεν πρὸς αὐτόν.

11.16 εἶπεν οὖν Θωμᾶς ὁ λεγόμενος Δίδυμος τοῖς συμμαθηταῖς, ἄγωμεν καὶ ἡμῖς ἵνα ἀποθάνωμεν μετ᾽ αὐτοῦ. 11.17 ἐλθὼν οὖν ὁ Ἰησοῦς εὗρεν αὐτὸν τέσσαρες ἡμέρας ἤδη ἔχοντα ἐν τῷ μνημίῳ. 11.18 ἦν δὲ ἡ Βηθανία ἐγγὺς τῶν Ἱεροσολύμων ὡς ἀπὸ σταδίων δεκαπέντε. 11.19 πολλοὶ δὲ ἐκ τῶν Ἰουδαίων ἐληλύθισαν πρὸς τὴν Μάρθαν καὶ Μαριὰν ἵνα

Martha, her sister.   11.2 And Mary was the (one) having anointed the Lord with ointment and having dried his feet with her hairs, of whom the brother Lazarus was ailing.   11.3 Therefore they sent the sisters to him saying: Lord, behold, (he) whom you love is sick/weak/ailing.

11.4 And having heard, Jesus said: This sickness is not to death but in behalf of the fame/glory of God, but that the son of God might be glorified/ acknowledged through it.   11.5 And Jesus was loving (*agape*) Martha and her sister and Lazarus.   11.6 Then, since he heard that he is sick, then indeed he stayed two days in/at the place where he was;   11.7 then after this, he says to the learners/pupils: We may go/let us go to Judea again.   11.8 The pupils/learn- ers say to him: Rabbi, the Judeans were now/presently seeking to stone you, and you go/are going there again?

11.9 Jesus answered: Are there not twelve hours of the day? If anyone may walk in the day, he stumbles not, because he sees the light of this world; 11.10 but if anyone may walk in the night, he stumbles, because the light is not in/with him.   11.11 He said these (things), and after this he says to them: Lazar- us our friend has fallen asleep, but I go/am going in order that I might awaken him.   11.12 Then the learn- ers/pupils said to him: Lord, if he has fallen asleep, he will be saved/healed.   11.13 But Jesus had spoken about his death. But those thought that he speaks about the sleep of the slumber.   11.14 Therefore Jesus then spoke to them freely/plainly: Lazarus died, 11.15 and I rejoice because of ye, that ye might believe, because I was not there; but we may go/let us go to him.

11.16   Then Thomas, the (one) being called a twin/Twin, said to the fellow learners/students: May we, we go also that we might die with him.   11.17 Therefore, having come, Jesus found him having been in the tomb/grave four days already/now.   11.18 And Bethany was near from the Jerusalemites, about fifteen stadia from *them*.   11.19 And many out of/from the Judeans had come to Martha and Mary in order that they

παραμυθήσωνται αὐτὰς περὶ τοῦ ἀδελφοῦ.

11.20 ἡ οὖν Μάρθα ὡς ἤκουσεν ὅτι Ἰησοῦς ἔρχεται ὑπήντησεν αὐτῷ· Μαριὰ δὲ ἐν τῷ οἴκῳ ἐκαθέζετο. 11.21 εἶπεν οὖν ἡ Μάρθα πρὸς Ἰησοῦν, κύριε, εἰ ἦς ὧδε οὐκ ἂν ἀπέθανεν ὁ ἀδελφός μου· 11.22 ἀλλὰ καὶ νῦν οἶδα ὅτι ὅσα ἂν αἰτήσει τὸν θεὸν δώσει σοι ὁ θεός. 11.23 λέγει αὐτῇ ὁ Ἰησοῦς, ἀναστήσεται ὁ ἀδελφός σου. 11.24 λέγι αὐτῷ Μάρθα, οἶδα ὅτι ἀναστήσεται ἐν τῇ ἀναστάσει ἐν τῇ ἐσχάτῃ ἡμέρᾳ. 11.25 εἶπεν δὲ αὐτῇ ὁ Ἰησοῦς, ἐγώ εἰμι ἡ ἀνάστασις καὶ ἡ ζωή· ὁ πιστεύων εἰς ἐμὲ κἂν ἀποθάνῃ ζήσεται, 11.26 καὶ πᾶς ὁ ζῶν καὶ πιστεύων εἰς ἐμὲ οὐ μὴ ἀποθάνῃ εἰς τὸν αἰῶνα· πιστεύεις τοῦτο; 11.27 λέγει αὐτῷ, ναί, κύριε· ἐγὼ πεπίστευκα ὅτι σὺ εἶ ὁ χριστὸς ὁ υἱὸς τοῦ θεοῦ ὁ εἰς τὸν κόσμον ἐρχόμενος. 11.28 καὶ τοῦτο εἰποῦσα ἀπῆλθεν καὶ ἐφώνησεν Μαριὰν τὴν ἀδελφὴν αὐτῆς λάθρᾳ εἰποῦσα, ὁ διδάσκαλος πάρεστιν καὶ φωνεῖ σε. 11.29 ἐκείνη δὲ ὡς ἤκουσεν ἠγέρθη ταχὺ καὶ ἤρχετο πρὸς αὐτόν· 11.30 οὔπω δὲ ἐληλύθει ὁ Ἰησοῦς εἰς τὴν κώμην, ἀλλ᾽ ἦν ἔτι ἐν τῷ τόπῳ ὅπου ὑπήντησεν αὐτῷ ἡ Μάρθα.

11.31 οἱ οὖν Ἰουδαῖοι οἱ ὄντες μετ᾽ αὐτῆς ἐν τῇ οἰκίᾳ καὶ παραμυθούμενοι αὐτήν, ἰδόντες τὴν Μαριὰν ὅτι ταχέως ἀνέστη καὶ ἐξῆλθεν, ἠκολούθησαν αὐτῇ, δόξαντες ὅτι Ἰησοῦς ὑπάγει εἰς τὸ μνημεῖον ἵνα κλαύσῃ ἐκεῖ. 11.32 ἡ οὖν Μαριὰ ὡς ἦλθεν ὅπου ἦν ὁ Ἰησοῦς ἰδοῦσα αὐτὸν ἔπεσεν αὐτοῦ πρὸς τοὺς πόδας, λέγουσα αὐτῷ, κύριε, εἰ ἦς ὧδε οὐκ ἄν μου ἀπέθανεν ὁ ἀδελφός. 11.33 Ἰησοῦς οὖν ὡς εἶδεν αὐτὴν κλαίουσαν καὶ τοὺς συνελθόντας αὐτῇ Ἰουδαίους κλαίοντας, ἐβριμήσατο τῷ πνεύματι καὶ ἐτάραξεν ἑαυτόν, 11.34 καὶ εἶπεν, ποῦ τεθίκατε αὐτόν; λέγουσιν αὐτῷ, κύριε, ἔρχου καὶ ἴδε. 11.35 ἐδάκρυσεν ὁ Ἰησοῦς. 11.36 ἔλεγον οὖν οἱ Ἰουδαῖοι, ἴδε πῶς ἐφίλει αὐτόν. 11.37 τινὲς δὲ ἐξ αὐτῶν εἶπαν, οὐκ ἠδύνατο οὗτος ὁ ἀνοίξας τοὺς ὀφθαλμοὺς τοῦ τυφλοῦ ποιῆσαι ἵνα καὶ οὗτος μὴ ἀποθάνῃ;

might console/comfort them concerning the brother.

11.20   Then Martha, as she heard that Jesus comes, went to meet him; but Mary was sitting in the house.   11.21 Then Martha said to Jesus: Lord, if you was being here, my brother would not *have* died;   11.22 but even now I know that whatever you would ask God, God will give to you.   11.23 Jesus says to her: Your brother will himself rise up.   11.24 Martha says to him: I know that he will rise up in/at the resurrection in/on the last day.   11.25 But Jesus said to her: I, I am the resurrection and the life; the (one) believing in me, even if he should/might die, he will live himself,   11.26 and every one living and believing in me, by no means might he die in/into the age; *do* you believe this?   11.27 She says to him: Yes, Lord; I, I have believed that you, you are the anointed (one), the son of God, the (one) coming into the world.   11.28 And having said this, she went away and called Mary her sister, having said quietly: The teacher is present/here and he calls for you.   11.29 And as that (one) heard, she arose quickly and was going to him;   11.30 and Jesus had not yet come into the village, but he was still at the place where Martha met him.

11.31   Therefore the Judeans, those being with her in the house and consoling/comforting her, seeing that Mary rose up quickly and went out, they followed her, thinking that Jesus is going to the tomb in order that he might weep there.

11.32   Then as Mary came where Jesus was, having beheld him, she fell near his feet, saying to him: Lord, if you was here, my brother would not *have* died. 11.33 Then Jesus, as he saw her weeping and the Judeans having gathered with/to her weeping, was moved in the spirit and troubled *in* himself,   11.34 and he said: Where have ye put him? They say to him: Lord, come and see.   11.35 Jesus wept.   11.36 Then the Judeans were saying: Behold how he was loving him. 11.37   But some out of them said: Was not this (one)/he, the (one) having opened the eyes of the blind (one), being able even to make *it* that this (one) might not *have* died?

11.38 Ἰησοῦς οὖν πάλιν ἐμβριμούμενος ἐν ἑαυτῷ ἔρχεται εἰς τὸ μνημῖον· ἦν δὲ σπήλαιον, καὶ λίθος ἐπέκειτο ἐπ᾽ αὐτῷ. 11.39 λέγει ὁ Ἰησοῦς, ἄρατε τὸν λίθον. λέγι αὐτῷ ἡ ἀδελφὴ τοῦ τετελευτηκότος Μάρθα, κύριε, ἤδη ὄζει, τεταρταῖος γάρ ἐστιν. 11.40 λέγει αὐτῇ ὁ Ἰησοῦς, οὐκ εἶπόν σοι ὅτι ἐὰν πιστεύσῃς ὄψῃ τὴν δόξαν τοῦ θεοῦ; 11.41 ἦραν οὖν τὸν λίθον. ὁ δὲ Ἰησοῦς ἦρεν τοὺς ὀφθαλμοὺς ἄνω καὶ εἶπεν, πάτερ, εὐχαριστῶ σοι ὅτι ἤκουσάς μου. 11.42 ἐγὼ δὲ ᾔδειν ὅτι πάντοτέ μου ἀκούεις· ἀλλὰ διὰ τὸν ὄχλον τὸν περιεστῶτα εἶπον, ἵνα πιστεύσωσιν ὅτι σύ με ἀπέστιλας. 11.43 καὶ ταῦτα εἰπὼν φωνῇ μεγάλῃ ἐκραύγασεν, Λάζαρε, δεῦρο ἔξω. 11.44 καὶ ἐξῆλθεν ὁ τεθνηκὼς δεδεμένος τοὺς πόδας καὶ τὰς χῖρας κιρίαις, καὶ ἡ ὄψις αὐτοῦ σουδαρίῳ περιεδέδετο. λέγει αὐτοῖς ὁ Ἰησοῦς, λύσατε αὐτὸν καὶ ἄφεται ὑπάγειν.

11.45 πολλοὶ δὲ ἐκ τῶν Ἰουδαίων, οἱ ἐλθόντες πρὸς τὴν Μαριὰν καὶ θεασάμενοι ἃ ἐποίησεν Ἰησοῦς, ἐπίστευσαν εἰς αὐτόν· 11.46 τινὲς δὲ ἐξ αὐτῶν ἀπῆλθον πρὸς τοὺς Φαρισαίους καὶ εἶπαν αὐτοῖς ἃ ἐποίησεν ὁ Ἰησοῦς. 11.47 συνήγαγον οὖν οἱ ἀρχιερεῖς καὶ οἱ Φαρισαῖοι συνέδριον, καὶ ἔλεγαν, τί ποιοῦμεν, ὅτι οὗτος ὁ ἄνθρωπος πολλὰ ποιεῖ σημῖα; 11.48 ἐὰν ἀφῶμεν αὐτὸν οὕτως, πάντες πιστεύσουσιν εἰς αὐτόν, καὶ ἐλεύσονται οἱ Ῥωμαῖοι καὶ ἀροῦσιν ἡμῶν καὶ τὸν τόπον καὶ τὸ ἔθνος.

11.49 εἷς δέ τις ἐξ αὐτῶν Καϊάφας, ἀρχιερεὺς ὢν τοῦ ἐνιαυτοῦ ἐκείνου, εἶπεν αὐτοῖς, ὑμῖς οὐκ οἴδατε οὐδέν, 11.50 οὐδὲ λογίζεσθε ὅτι συμφέρει ἵνα εἷς ἄνθρωπος ἀποθάνῃ ὑπὲρ τοῦ λαοῦ καὶ μὴ ὅλον τὸ ἔθνος ἀπόληται. 11.51 τοῦτο δὲ ἀφ᾽ ἑαυτοῦ οὐκ εἶπεν, ἀλλὰ ἀρχιερεὺς ὢν τοῦ ἐνιαυτοῦ ἐκίνου ἐπροφήτευσεν ὅτι ἔμελλεν Ἰησοῦς ἀποθνήσκιν ὑπὲρ τοῦ ἔθνους, 11.52 καὶ οὐχ ὑπὲρ τοῦ ἔθνους μόνον ἀλλ᾽ ἵνα καὶ τὰ τέκνα τοῦ θεοῦ τὰ διεσκορπισμένα συναγάγῃ εἰς ἕν. 11.53 ἀπ᾽ ἐκείνης οὖν τῆς ἡμέρας ἐβουλεύσαντο ἵνα ἀποκτίνωσιν αὐτόν.

11.38   Then Jesus, again being deeply moved in himself, goes/comes to the tomb; but it was a cave, and a stone was laying on/over it.   11.39 Jesus says: remove ye the stone. The sister of the (one) having died, Martha, says to him: Lord, he stinks/smells already, for it is *the* fourth (day).   11.40 Jesus says to her: Said I not to you that if you might believe, you will yourself see the fame/glory of God?   11.41 Therefore/then they removed the stone. And Jesus lifted up the eyes above and said: Father, I give thanks to you because you heard me.   11.42 But I, I knew that you always hear me; but because of the crowd having stood/standing around I spoke, in order that they might believe that you, you sent me.   11.43 And having said these (things), he cried out with a great voice: Lazarus, come out!   11.44 And the (one) having died came out, the feet and the hands having been bound with grave cloths, and his face had been tied around with a handkerchief/facecloth. Jesus says to them: Loose ye him and give *him* to eat.

11.45   And many out of the Judeans, the (ones) having come to Mary and having beheld what Jesus did, believed in him;   11.46 but some out of them went away to the Pharisees and said/told to them what (things) Jesus did.   11.47   Then the high priests and the Pharisees gathered/convened a council, and they said: What do we, because this man does/makes many signs?   11.48 If we might leave him thus, all (men) will believe in him, and the Romans will come and they will take from us both the place and the nation/ethnic.

11.49   But a certain one of them, Caiaphas, being a/*the* high priest of that year, said to them: Ye, ye know not nothing,   11.50 neither reckon ye that it is profitable/expedient that one man might die in behalf of the people and the entire nation/ethnic might not perish.   11.51 But he spoke not this from himself, but being a high priest of that year he prophesied that Jesus was being about to die in behalf of the nation/ ethnic,   11.52 and not in behalf of the nation only, but also in order that he might gather/collect the children of God, having been dispersed, into one.   11.53 Therefore, from that day they planned/plotted

11.54 ὁ οὖν Ἰησοῦς οὐκέτι παρρησίᾳ περιεπάτει ἐν τοῖς Ἰουδαίοις, ἀλλὰ ἀπῆλθεν ἐκεῖθεν εἰς τὴν χώραν ἐγγὺς τῆς ἐρήμου, εἰς Ἐφρὲμ λεγομένην πόλιν, κἀκεῖ ἔμινεν μετὰ τῶν μαθητῶν. 11.55 ἦν δὲ ἐγγὺς τὸ πάσχα τῶν Ἰουδαίων, καὶ ἀνέβησαν πολλοὶ εἰς Ἱεροσόλυμα ἐκ τῆς χώρας πρὸ τοῦ πάσχα ἵνα ἁγνίσωσιν ἑαυτούς. 11.56 ἐζήτουν οὖν τὸν Ἰησοῦν καὶ ἔλεγαν μετ' ἀλλήλων ἐν τῷ ἱερῷ ἑστηκότες, τί δοκεῖ ὑμῖν; ὅτι οὐ μὴ ἔλθῃ εἰς τὴν ἑορτήν; 11.57 δεδώκισαν δὲ οἱ ἀρχιερῖς καὶ οἱ Φαρισαῖοι ἐντολὰς ἵνα ἐάν τις γνῷ ποῦ ἐστιν μηνύσῃ, ὅπως πιάσωσιν αὐτόν.

12.1 Ὁ οὖν Ἰησοῦς πρὸ ἓξ ἡμερῶν τοῦ πάσχα ἦλθεν εἰς Βηθανίαν, ὅπου ἦν Λάζαρος, ὃν ἤγειρεν Ἰησοῦς ἐκ νεκρῶν. 12.2 ἐποίησαν οὖν αὐτῷ δεῖπνον ἐκεῖ, καὶ ἡ Μάρθα διηκόνι, ὁ δὲ Λάζαρος εἷς ἦν ἐκ τῶν ἀνακειμένων σὺν αὐτῷ.

12.3 ἡ οὖν Μαριὰ λαβοῦσα λίτραν μύρου νάρδου πιστικῆς πολυτίμου ἤλιψεν τοὺς πόδας τοῦ Ἰησοῦ καὶ ἐξέμαξεν ταῖς θριξὶν αὐτῆς τοὺς πόδας αὐτοῦ· ἡ δὲ οἰκία ἐπληρώθη ἐκ τῆς ὀσμῆς τοῦ μύρου. 12.4 λέγει δὲ Ἰούδας ὁ Ἰσκαριώτης εἷς ἐκ τῶν μαθητῶν αὐτοῦ, ὁ μέλλων αὐτὸν παραδιδόναι, 12.5 διὰ τί τοῦτο τὸ μύρον οὐκ ἐπράθη τριακοσίων δηναρίων καὶ ἐδόθη πτωχοῖς; 12.6 εἶπεν δὲ τοῦτο οὐχ ὅτι περὶ τῶν πτωχῶν ἔμελεν αὐτῷ ἀλλ' ὅτι κλέπτης ἦν καὶ τὸ γλωσσόκομον ἔχων τὰ βαλλόμενα ἐβάσταζεν. 12.7 εἶπεν οὖν ὁ Ἰησοῦς, ἄφες αὐτήν, ἵνα εἰς τὴν ἡμέραν τοῦ ἐνταφιασμοῦ μου τηρήσῃ αὐτό· 12.8 τοὺς πτωχοὺς γὰρ πάντοτε ἔχετε μεθ' ἑαυτῶν, ἐμὲ δὲ οὐ πάντοτε ἔχετε. 12.9 ἔγνω οὖν ὁ ὄχλος πολὺς ἐκ τῶν Ἰουδαίων ὅτι ἐκεῖ ἐστιν, καὶ ἦλθον οὐ διὰ τὸν Ἰησοῦν μόνον ἀλλ' ἵνα καὶ τὸν Λάζαρον ἴδωσιν ὃν ἤγειρεν ἐκ νεκρῶν. 12.10 ἐβουλεύσαντο δὲ οἱ ἀρχιερεῖς ἵνα καὶ τὸν Λάζαρον ἀποκτίνωσιν, 12.11 ὅτι πολλοὶ δι' αὐτὸν

that they might kill him.

11.54   Therefore, Jesus was no longer walking freely among the Judeans, but he went away from there into the country near the desert, to a city being called Ephraim, and he stayed there with the learners/pupils.   11.55 And the Passover of the Judeans was near, and many out of the country went up to Jerusalem before the Passover in order that they might purify themselves.   11.56   Then they were seeking Jesus and speaking with one another standing in the *outer* temple: What seems it to ye? That he might by no means come to the festival?   11.57 And the high priests and the Pharisees had given commands that if anyone might know where he is, he should disclose *it* in order that they might lay hold of/arrest him.

12.1   Then Jesus went to Bethany six days before the Passover, where Lazarus was, whom Jesus raised out of dead (ones).   12.2 Therefore they made a meal/supper for him there, and Martha was serving, but Lazarus was one of those reclining with him.

12.3   Then Martha, having taken a libra/12 oz of pure, very expensive spikenard ointment, anointed the feet of Jesus and dried/wiped off his feet with her hairs; and the house was filled up from the odor of the ointment.   12.4   And Judas the Iscariot, one out of his learners/pupils, the (one) being about to hand him over/betray him, says: 12.5 Why was this ointment not sold *for* three hundred of denarii and given to poor (ones)?   12.6 But he said this, not because it was being a care to him about the poor (ones), but because he was a thief and holding the money bag, he carried the (things) being put *in*.   12.7   Then Jesus said: Leave/let her *alone*, in order that she might keep it to/for the day of my burial/entombment;   12.8 for ye always have the poor (ones) with yourselves, but ye have me not always.   12.9 Then the much crowd out of the Judeans knew that he is there, and they came not only because of Jesus but that they might also see/observe Lazarus whom he raised out of dead (ones).   12.10 But the high priests plotted/planned that they might kill Lazarus also,   12.11 because many

ὑπῆγον τῶν Ἰουδαίων καὶ ἐπίστευον εἰς τὸν Ἰησοῦν.

12.12 τῇ ἐπαύριον ὄχλος πολὺς ὁ ἐλθὼν εἰς τὴν ἑορτήν, ἀκούσαντες ὅτι ἔρχεται Ἰησοῦς εἰς Ἱεροσόλυμα, 12.13 ἔλαβον τὰ βαΐα τῶν φοινίκων καὶ ἐξῆλθον εἰς ὑπάντησιν αὐτῷ, καὶ ἐκραύγαζον λέγοντες, « ὡσαννά· εὐλογημένος ὁ ἐρχόμενος ἐν ὀνόματι κυρίου,» καὶ ὁ βασιλεὺς τοῦ Ἰσραήλ. 12.14 εὑρὼν δὲ ὁ Ἰησοῦς ὀνάριον ἐκάθισεν ἐπ' αὐτό, καθώς ἐστι γεγραμμένον, 12.15 « μὴ φοβοῦ, θυγάτε Σιών· ἰδοὺ ὁ βασιλεύς σου ἔρχεται, καθήμενος ἐπὶ πῶλον ὄνου.» 12.16 ταῦτα οὐκ ἔγνωσαν αὐτοῦ οἱ μαθηταὶ τὸ πρῶτον, ἀλλ' ὅτε ἐδοξάσθη Ἰησοῦς τότε ἐμνήσθησαν ὅτι ταῦτα ἐπ' αὐτῷ ἦν γεγραμμένα καὶ ταῦτα ἐποίησαν αὐτῷ. 12.17 ἐμαρτύρι οὖν ὁ ὄχλος ὁ ὢν μετ' αὐτοῦ ὅτε τὸν Λάζαρον ἐφώνησεν ἐκ τοῦ μνημίου καὶ ἤγειρεν αὐτὸν ἐκ νεκρῶν. 12.18 διὰ τοῦτο καὶ ὑπήντησεν αὐτῷ ὄχλος πολύς ὅτι ἤκουσαν αὐτὸν τοῦτο πεποιηκέναι τὸ σημεῖον. 12.19 οἱ οὖν Φαρισαῖοι εἶπαν πρὸς ἑαυτούς, Θεωρεῖτε ὅτι οὐκ ὠφελεῖτε οὐδέν· εἶδε ὁ κόσμος ὀπίσω αὐτοῦ ἀπῆλθεν. 12.20 ἦσαν δὲ Ἕλληνές τινες ἐκ τῶν ἀναβαινόντων ἵνα προσκυνήσωσιν ἐν τῇ ἑορτῇ· 12.21 οὗτοι οὖν προσῆλθον Φιλίππῳ τῷ ἀπὸ Βηθσαϊδὰ τῆς Γαλιλαίας, καὶ ἠρώτων αὐτὸν λέγοντες, κύριε, θέλομεν τὸν Ἰησοῦν ἰδῖν. 12.22 ἔρχεται Φίλιππος καὶ λέγει τῷ Ἀνδρέᾳ· καί πάλιν ἔρχεται Ἀνδρέας καὶ Φίλιππος καὶ λέγουσιν τῷ Ἰησοῦ. 12.23 ὁ δὲ Ἰησοῦς ἀποκρίνεται αὐτοῖς λέγων, ἐλήλυθεν ἡ ὥρα ἵνα δοξασθῇ ὁ υἱὸς τοῦ ἀνθρώπου. 12.24 ἀμὴν ἀμὴν λέγω ὑμῖν, ἐὰν μὴ ὁ κόκκος τοῦ σίτου πεσὼν εἰς τὴν γῆν ἀποθάνῃ, αὐτὸς μόνος μένει· ἐὰν δὲ ἀποθάνῃ, πολὺν καρπὸν φέρει. 12.25 ὁ φιλῶν τὴν ψυχὴν αὐτοῦ ἀπολλύει αὐτήν, καὶ ὁ μεισῶν τὴν ψυχὴν αὐτοῦ ἐν τῷ κόσμῳ τούτῳ εἰς ζωὴν αἰώνιον φυλάξει αὐτήν. 12.26 ἐάν ἐμοί τις διακονῇ, ἐμοὶ ἀκολουθίτω, καὶ ὅπου εἰμὶ ἐγὼ ἐκεῖ καὶ ὁ διάκονος ὁ ἐμὸς ἔσται· ἐάν τις ἐμοὶ διακονῇ τεμήσει αὐτὸν ὁ πατήρ. 12.27 νῦν ἡ ψυχή μου τετάρακται. καὶ τί εἴπω;

of the Judeans were departing and believing in Jesus because of him.

12.12 On the morrow a much crowd having come to the festival, having heard that Jesus comes to Jerusalem, 12.13 they took branches from the palms and went to/for a meeting with him, and they were crying out, saying: HOSANNA; HAVING BEEN BLESSED *is* THE (ONE) COMING BY/IN *the* NAME OF *the* LORD, even the king of Israel. 12.14 And Jesus, having found a young ass, sat upon it, as it is having been written: 12.15 FEAR NOT, DAUGHTER OF SION; BEHOLD, YOUR KING COMES, SITTING UPON A COLT/FOAL OF AN ASS. 12.16 The learners/pupils knew not these (things) of him *at* the first, but when Jesus was glorified, then they were reminded that these (things) were having been written on/for him and they did these (things) to him. 12.17 Therefore the crowd was witnessing/testifying, the (one) being with him when he summoned Lazarus out of the tomb and raised him out of dead (ones). 12.18 Because of this a much crowd also met with him, because they heard *of* him to have done this sign. 12.19 Then the Pharisees said to themselves: behold/observe ye that ye profit/gain nothing; behold! The world went after/behind him. 12.20 And there were some Greeks out of those going up in order that they might worship in/at the festival; 12.21 then these came to Philip, the (one) from Bethsaida of Galilee, and they were asking him, saying: Lord/sir, we want/wish to see Jesus. 12.22 Philip comes and speaks to Andrew; and again Andrew and Philip come and they speak to Jesus. 12.23 But Jesus answers to them, saying: The hour has come that the son of the man might be glorified. 12.24 Truly, truly I say to ye, unless the kernel/grain of wheat having fallen to the earth/ground might die, it remains alone; but if it might die, it bears much fruit. 12.25 The (one) loving his soul/life loses it, and the (one) hating his soul/life in this world will guard/keep it in eternal life. 12.26 If anyone may serve/wait on me, let him follow/obey me, and where I, I am, there will my servant/waiter also be; if anyone may serve/wait on me, the father will honor him. 12.27 Now my soul/life has been troubled. And

πάτερ, σῶσόν με ἐκ τῆς ὥρας τούτης; ἀλλὰ διὰ τοῦτο ἦλθον εἰς τὴν ὥραν ταύτην. 12.28 πάτερ, δόξασόν σου τὸ ὄνομα. ἦλθεν οὖν φωνὴ ἐκ τοῦ οὐρανοῦ, καὶ ἐδόξασα καὶ πάλιν δοξάσω. 12.29 ὁ οὖν ὄχλος ὁ ἑστὼς ἀκούσας ἔλεγεν βροντὴν γεγονέναι· ἄλλοι ἔλεγον, ἄγγελος αὐτῷ λελάληκεν. 12.30 ἀπεκρίθη Ἰησοῦς, οὐ δι᾽ ἐμὲ ἡ φωνὴ αὕτη γέγονεν ἀλλὰ δι᾽ ὑμᾶς. 12.31 νῦν κρίσις ἐστὶν τοῦ κόσμου τούτου, καὶ νῦν ὁ ἄρχων τοῦ κόσμου τούτου ἐκβληθήσεται ἔξω· 12.32 κἀγὼ ἐὰν ὑψωθῶ ἐκ τῆς γῆς, πάντας ἑλκύσω πρὸς ἐμαυτόν. 12.33 τοῦτο δὲ ἔλεγεν σημαίνων ποίῳ θανάτῳ ἔμελλεν ἀποθνῄσκειν. 12.34 ἀπεκρίθη οὖν αὐτῷ ὁ ὄχλος, ἡμεῖς ἠκούσαμεν ἐκ τοῦ νόμου ὅτι ὁ χριστὸς μένει εἰς τὸν αἰῶνα, καὶ πῶς σὺ λέγις ὅτι δεῖ ὑψωθῆναι τὸν υἱὸν τοῦ ἀνθρώπου; τίς ἐστιν οὗτος ὁ υἱὸς τοῦ ἀνθρώπου;   12.35 εἶπεν οὖν αὐτοῖς ὁ Ἰησοῦς, ἔτι μικρὸν χρόνον τὸ φῶς ἐν ὑμῖν ἐστιν. περιπατεῖτε ἕως τὸ φῶς ἔχετε, ἵνα μὴ σκοτία ὑμᾶς καταλάβῃ· καὶ ὁ περιπατῶν ἐν τῇ σκοτίᾳ οὐκ οἶδεν ποῦ ὑπάγει. 12.36 ὡς τὸ φῶς ἔχετε, πιστεύεται εἰς τὸ φῶς, ἵνα υἱοὶ φωτὸς γένησθε. ταῦτα ἐλάλησεν Ἰησοῦς, καὶ ἀπελθὼν ἐκρύβη ἀπ᾽ αὐτῶν. 12.37 τοσαῦτα δὲ αὐτοῦ σημῖα πεποιηκότος ἔμπροσθεν αὐτῶν οὐκ ἐπίστευον εἰς αὐτόν, 12.38 ἵνα ὁ λόγος Ἡσαΐου τοῦ προφήτου πληρωθῇ ὃν εἶπεν, « κύριε, τίς ἐπίστευσεν τῇ ἀκοῇ ἡμῶν; καὶ ὁ βραχίων κυρίου τίνι ἀπεκαλύφθη;» 12.39 διὰ τοῦτο οὐκ ἠδύναντο πιστεύειν, ὅτι πάλιν εἶπεν Ἡσαΐας, 12.40 « τετύφλωκεν αὐτῶν τοὺς ὀφθαλμοὺς καὶ ἐπήρωσεν αὐτῶν τὴν καρδίαν, ἵνα μὴ εἴδωσιν τοῖς ὀφθαλμοῖς καὶ τῇ καρδίᾳ σύνωσιν καὶ στραφῶσιν, καὶ ἰάσομαι αὐτούς.» 12.41 ταῦτα εἶπεν Ἡσαΐας, ὅτι εἶδεν τὴν δόξαν αὐτοῦ, καὶ ἐλάλησεν περὶ αὐτοῦ. 12.42 ὅμως μέντοι καὶ ἐκ τῶν ἀρχόντων πολλοὶ ἐπίστευσαν εἰς αὐτόν, ἀλλὰ διὰ τοὺς Φαρισαίους οὐχ ὡμολόγουν ἵνα μὴ ἀποσυνάγωγοι γένωνται·

what might I say? Father, save me from this hour? But because of this I came to/for this hour. 12.28 Father, glorify your name. Then a voice came out of the sky/heaven: I both glorified and I shall glorify again. 12.29 Then the crowd having been standing listening were saying *for* thunder to have happened; others were saying: A messenger/angel has spoken to him. 12.30 Jesus answered: This voice has happened not because of me but because of ye. 12.31 Judgment is now/presently of this world, and now/presently the ruler of this world will be thrown out; 12.32 and I, if I be lifted up/exalted out of the earth/land, I shall draw all (men) to myself. 12.33 And he was saying this signifying by what kind of death he was being about to die. 12.34 Then the crowd answered to him: We, we heard out of the law that the anointed (one) abides into the age, and how do you, you say that it is necessary *for* the son of the man to be lifted up/exalted? Who is this (one), the son of the man/human? 12.35 Therefore Jesus said to them: The light is still with/among ye *for* a little time. Walk ye as long as ye have the light, in order that darkness might not overtake ye; and the (one) walking in the darkness knows not where he goes. 12.36 Since/as ye have the light, believe ye in the light, that ye might become sons of light. Jesus spoke these (things), and having gone away he was hidden from them. 12.37 But from him having done so many signs before them, they were not believing in him, 12.38 that the saying/word/reason of Esaias the prophet might be fulfilled, which said: LORD, WHO BELIEVED IN OUR REPORT? AND THE ARM OF *the* LORD, TO WHOM WAS IT REVEALED? 12.39 Because of this they were not able to believe, because again Esaias said: 12.40 HE HAS BLINDED THEIR EYES AND HARDENED THEIR HEART, LEST HAVING SEEN WITH THE EYES THEY MIGHT ALSO UNDERSTAND WITH THE HEART AND BE TURNED (AROUND), AND I SHALL HEAL THEM. 12.41 These (things) Esaias said, because he saw his glory/fame/reputation, and he spoke about him. 12.42 Nevertheless, even/also many of the rulers believed in him, but they were not confessing *him* because of the Pharisees, in order that they might not

12.43 ἠγάπησαν γὰρ τὴν δόξαν τῶν ἀνθρώπων μᾶλλον ὑπὲρ τὴν δόξαν τοῦ θεοῦ.

12.44 Ἰησοῦς δὲ ἔκραξεν καὶ εἶπεν, ὁ πιστεύων εἰς ἐμὲ οὐ πιστεύει εἰς ἐμὲ ἀλλὰ εἰς τὸν πέμψαντά με, 12.45 καὶ ὁ θεωρῶν ἐμὲ θεωρεῖ τὸν πέμψαντά με. 12.46 ἐγὼ φῶς εἰς τὸν κόσμον ἐλήλυθα, ἵνα πᾶς ὁ πιστεύων εἰς ἐμὲ ἐν τῇ σκοτίᾳ μὴ μίνῃ. 12.47 καὶ ἐάν τίς μου ἀκούσῃ τῶν ῥημάτων καὶ μὴ φυλάξῃ, ἐγὼ οὐ κρίνω αὐτόν, οὐ γὰρ ἦλθον ἵνα κρίνω τὸν κόσμον ἀλλ' ἵνα σώσω τὸν κόσμον. 12.48 ὁ ἀθετῶν ἐμὲ καὶ μὴ λαμβάνων τὰ ῥήματά μου ἔχει τὸν κρίνοντα αὐτόν· ὁ λόγος ὃν ἐλάλησα ἐκεῖνος κρινεῖ αὐτὸν ἐν τῇ ἐσχάτῃ ἡμέρᾳ· 12.49 ὅτι ἐγὼ ἐξ ἐμαυτοῦ οὐκ ἐλάλησα, ἀλλ' ὁ πέμψας με πατὴρ αὐτός μοι ἐντολὴν δέδωκεν τί εἴπω καὶ τί λαλήσω. 12.50 καὶ οἶδα ὅτι ἡ ἐντολὴ αὐτοῦ ζωὴ αἰώνιός ἐστιν. ἃ οὖν ἐγὼ λαλῶ, καθὼς εἴρηκέν μοι ὁ πατήρ, οὕτως λαλῶ.

13.1 Πρὸ δὲ τῆς ἑορτῆς τοῦ πάσχα εἰδὼς ὁ Ἰησοῦς ὅτι ἦλθεν αὐτοῦ ἡ ὥρα ἵνα μεταβῇ ἐκ τοῦ κόσμου τούτου πρὸς τὸν πατέρα, ἀγαπήσας τοὺς Ἰουδαίους τοὺς ἐν τῷ κόσμῳ, εἰς τέλος ἠγάπησεν αὐτούς. 13.2 καὶ δίπνου γεινομένου, τοῦ διαβόλου ἤδη βεβληκότος εἰς τὴν καρδίαν ἵνα παραδοῖ αὐτὸν Ἰούδας Σίμωνος Ἰσκαριώτης, 13.3 εἰδὼς ὅτι πάντα ἔδωκεν αὐτῷ ὁ πατὴρ εἰς τὰς χῖρας καὶ ὅτι ἀπὸ θεοῦ ἐξῆλθεν καὶ πρὸς τὸν θεὸν ὑπάγει, 13.4 ἐγείρεται ἐκ τοῦ δίπνου καὶ τίθησιν τὰ ἱμάτια, καὶ λαβὼν λέντιον διέζωσεν ἑαυτόν. 13.5 εἶτα βάλλει ὕδωρ εἰς τὸν νιπτῆρα καὶ ἤρξατο νίπτειν τοὺς πόδας τῶν μαθητῶν καὶ ἐκμάσσειν τῷ λεντίῳ ᾧ ἦν διεζωσμένος. 13.6 ἔρχεται οὖν πρὸς Σίμωνα Πέτρον. καὶ λέγει αὐτῷ, σύ μου νίπτις τοὺς πόδας; 13.7 ἀπεκρίθη Ἰησοῦς καὶ εἶπεν αὐτῷ, ὃ ἐγὼ ποιῶ σὺ οὐκ οἶδας ἄρτι, γνώσῃ δὲ μετὰ

become expelled from the congregations; 12.43 for they loved the fame/glory from the men more than the fame/glory from God.

12.44 But Jesus cried out and said: The (one) believing in me, believes not in me but in the (one) having sent me, 12.45 and the (one) beholding me beholds the (one) having sent me. 12.46 I, a light, have come into the world, that every one believing in me might not abide in the darkness. 12.47 And if anyone might hear of my words and might not guard/keep *them*, I, I judge him not, for I came not in order that I might judge the world, but in order that I might save the world. 12.48 The (one) rejecting me and receiving not the words from me has/holds the (one) judging him: The logos/word/reason which I spoke, that (one) will judge him in/on/at the last day; 12.49 because I, I spoke not from myself, but the father having sent me, he himself has given a command to me, what I might say and what I might speak. 12.50 And I know that the command from him is eternal life. What (things) therefore I, I speak, as the father has spoken to me, so/thus I speak.

13.1 And before the festival of the Passover, Jesus, having known that his hour came that he would depart out of this world to the father, having loved the Judeans/his own, those in the world, he loved them to/in *the* end. 13.2 And from supper becoming/taking place, from the devil already having put *it* in the heart that Judas of Simon Iscariot might deliver him up/betray him, 13.3 having known that the father gave all (things) to him in the hands and that he came from God and he goes/departs to God, 13.4 he rises from the supper/meal and places the garments, and having taken a linen towel, he girded himself. 13.5 Then he puts water into the wash basin and he began to wash the feet of the learners/pupils and to wipe off/dry with the towel with which he had been girded. 13.6 Then he comes to Simon Peter. And that (one) says to him: Lord, you yourself wash the feet of me? 13.7 Jesus answered and said to him: What I, I do, you, you know not just now, but you will know after these

ταῦτα. 13.8 λέγει αὐτῷ Πέτρος, οὐ μὴ νίψῃς τοὺς πόδας μου εἰς τὸν αἰῶνα. ἀπεκρίθη αὐτῷ ὁ Ἰησοῦς, ἐὰν μὴ νίψω σε, οὐκ ἔχεις μέρος μετ’ ἐμοῦ. 13.9 λέγει αὐτῷ Σίμων Πέτρος, κύριε, μὴ τοὺς πόδας μου μόνον ἀλλὰ καὶ τὰς χῖρας καὶ τὴν κεφαλήν. 13.10 λέγει αὐτῷ ὁ Ἰησοῦς, ὁ λελουμένος οὐκ ἔχει χρείαν νίψασθαι, ἀλλὰ ἔστιν καθαρὸς ὅλος· καὶ ὑμεῖς καθαροί ἐστε, ἀλλ’ οὐχὶ πάντες. 13.11 ᾔδει γὰρ τὸν παραδιδόντα αὐτόν· διὰ τοῦτο εἶπεν οὐχὶ πάντες καθαροί ἐστε. 13.12 ὅτε οὖν ἔνιψεν τοὺς πόδας αὐτῶν ἔλαβεν τὰ ἱμάτια αὐτοῦ καὶ ἀνέπεσεν πάλιν, εἶπεν αὐτοῖς, γεινώσκεται τί πεποίηκα ὑμῖν; 13.13 ὑμεῖς φωνεῖτέ με ὁ διδάσκαλος καὶ ὁ κύριος, καὶ καλῶς λέγεται, εἰμὶ γάρ. 13.14 εἰ οὖν ἐγὼ ἔνιψα ὑμῶν τοὺς πόδας ὁ κύριος καὶ ὁ διδάσκαλος, καὶ ὑμεῖς ὀφίλεται νίπτειν ἀλλήλων τοὺς πόδας· 13.15 ὑπόδιγμα γὰρ δέδωκα ὑμῖν ἵνα καθὼς ἐγὼ ἐποίησα ὑμῖν καὶ ὑμῖς ποιῆται.

13.16 ἀμὴν ἀμὴν λέγω ὑμῖν, οὐκ ἔστιν δοῦλος μίζων τοῦ κυρίου αὐτοῦ οὐδὲ ἀπόστολος μείζων τοῦ πέμψαντος αὐτόν. 13.17 εἰ ταῦτα οἴδατε, μακάριοί ἐστε ἐὰν ποιῆτε αὐτά. 13.18 οὐ περὶ πάντων ὑμῶν λέγω· ἐγὼ γὰρ οἶδα τίνας ἐξελεξάμην· ἀλλ’ ἵνα ἡ γραφὴ πληρωθῇ, « ὁ τρώγων μετ’ ἐμοῦ τὸν ἄρτον ἐπῆρκεν ἐπ’ ἐμὲ τὴν πτέρναν αὐτοῦ.» 13.19 ἀπ’ ἄρτι λέγω ὑμῖν πρὸ τοῦ γενέσθαι, ἵνα πιστεύσηται ὅταν γένηται ὅτι ἐγώ εἰμι.

13.20 ἀμὴν ἀμὴν λέγω ὑμῖν, ὁ λαμβάνων ἄν τινα πέμψω ἐμὲ λαμβάνει, ὁ δὲ ἐμὲ λαμβάνων λαμβάνι τὸν πέμψαντά με.

13.21 ταῦτα εἰπὼν Ἰησοῦς ἐταράχθη τῷ πνεύματι καὶ ἐμαρτύρησεν καὶ εἶπεν, ἀμὴν ἀμὴν λέγω ὑμῖν ὅτι εἷς ἐξ ὑμῶν παραδώσει με. 13.22 ἔβλεπον οὖν εἰς ἀλλήλους οἱ μαθηταὶ ἀπορούμενοι περὶ τίνος λέγει.

13.23 ἦν δὲ ἀνακείμενος εἷς ἐκ τῶν μαθητῶν αὐτοῦ ἐν τῷ κόλπῳ τοῦ Ἰησοῦ, ὃν ἠγάπα ὁ Ἰησοῦς·

13.24 νεύει οὖν τούτῳ Σίμων Πέτρος πυθέσθαι τίς ἂν εἴη

(things). 13.8 Peter says to him: By no means may
you wash my feet into the age. Jesus answered to him:
Unless I might wash you, you have not a part with me.
13.9 Simon Peter says to him: Lord, not only my feet
but also the hands and the head. 13.10 Jesus says to
him: The (one) having bathed has not a need to wash
himself, but he is wholly clean; and ye, ye are clean,
but not all. 13.11 Forhe knew the (one) delivering
him up/betraying him; because of this he said: Ye are
not all clean. 13.12 Then when he washed their feet,
he took *up* his garments and reclined again, he said to
them: Do ye know what I have done for ye? 13.13 Ye,
ye call me the teacher and the Lord, and well ye say,
for I am. 13.14 If therefore I, I washed the feet of
ye, *being* the Lord and teacher; ye, ye also are obligated to wash the feet of one another; 13.15 for I
gave an example to ye that even as I, I did for ye;
ye, ye may do also.

13.16 Truly, truly I say to ye, a slave is not
greater than his lord, nor a sent one/apostle greater
than the (one) having sent him. 13.17 If ye know
these (things), happy are ye if ye may do them. 13.18
I speak not about all of ye; for I, I know whom I
chose; but in order that the writing might be fulfilled: THE (ONE) EATING THE LOAF/BREAD WITH ME LIFTED UP
HIS HEEL AGAINST ME. 13.19 From just now I say *it* to
ye before the (thing) *is* to happen, in order that
whenever it might happen ye might believe that I, I
am.

13.20 Truly, truly I say to ye, the (one) receiving whom ever I might send receives me, and the
(one) receiving me receives the (one) having sent me.

13.21 Having said these (things) Jesus was
troubled in the spirit and he testified/witnessed and
said: Truly, truly I say to ye that one out of ye will
deliver me over/betray me. 13.22 The learners/pupils
therefore looked to one another, being in doubt about
whom he speaks.

13.23 One out of his learners/pupils was reclining on the bosom of Jesus, *the one* whom Jesus was
loving;

13.24 Simon Peter nodded/motioned to this (one)

περὶ οὗ ἔλεγεν καὶ λέγει αὐτῷ εἰπὲ τίς ἐστιν περὶ οὗ λέγει. 13.25 ἀναπεσὼν οὖν ἐκεῖνος οὕτως ἐπὶ τὸ στῆθος τοῦ Ἰησοῦ λέγει αὐτῷ, κύριε, τίς ἐστιν; 13.26 ἀποκρίνεται ὁ Ἰησοῦς καὶ λέγει, ἐκεῖνός ἐστιν ᾧ ἐγὼ βάψας τὸ ψωμίον ἐπὶ δώσω. βάψας οὖν τὸ ψωμίον δίδωσιν Ἰούδᾳ Σίμωνος Ἰσκαριώτου. 13.27 καὶ μετὰ τὸ ψωμίον εἰσῆλθεν εἰς ἐκεῖνον ὁ Σατανᾶς. λέγει οὖν αὐτῷ ὁ Ἰησοῦς, ὃ ποιεῖς ποίησον τάχειον. 13.28 τοῦτο δὲ οὐδεὶς ἔγνω τῶν ἀνακειμένων πρὸς τί εἶπεν αὐτῷ· 13.29 τινὲς γὰρ ἐδόκουν, ἐπὶ τὸ γλωσσόκομον εἶχεν Ἰούδας, ὅτι λέγει αὐτῷ Ἰησοῦς, ἀγόρασον ὧν χρίαν ἔχομεν εἰς τὴν ἑορτήν, ἢ τοῖς πτωχοῖς ἵνα τι δῷ. 13.30 λαβὼν οὖν τὸ ψωμίον ἐκεῖνος ἐξῆλθεν εὐθύς· ἦν δὲ νύξ. 13.31 ὅτε οὖν ἐξῆλθεν λέγει Ἰησοῦς, νῦν ἐδοξάσθη ὁ υἱὸς τοῦ ἀνθρώπου, καὶ ὁ θεὸς ἐδοξάσθη ἐν αὐτῷ· 13.32 εἰ ὁ θεὸς ἐδοξάσθη ἐν αὐτῷ καὶ ὁ θεὸς δοξάσει αὐτὸν ἐν αὐτῷ, καὶ εὐθὺς δοξάσει αὐτόν.

13.33 τεκνία, ἔτι μεικρὸν κρόνον μεθ' ὑμῶν εἰμι· ζητήσεταί με, καὶ καθὼς εἶπον τοῖς Ἰουδαίοις ὅτι ὅπου ἐγὼ ὑπάγω ὑμεῖς οὐ δύνασθαι ἐλθῖν, καὶ ὑμῖν λέγω ἄρτι. 13.34 ἐντολὴν καινὴν δίδωμι ὑμῖν, ἵνα ἀγαπᾶτε ἀλλήλους· καθὼς ἠγάπησα ὑμᾶς καὶ ὑμεῖς ἀγαπᾶτε ἀλλήλους. 13.35 ἐν τούτῳ γνώσονται πάντες ὅτι ἐμοὶ μαθηταί ἐστε, ἐὰν ἀγάπην ἔχηται ἐν ἀλλήλων. 13.36 λέγει αὐτῷ Σίμων Πέτρος, κύριε, ποῦ ὑπάγεις; ἀπεκρίθη αὐτῷ ὁ Ἰησοῦς, ὅπου ἐγὼ ὑπάγω οὐ δύνασαί μοι νῦν ἀκολουθῆσαι, ἀκολουθήσεις δὲ ὕστερον. 13.37 λέγει αὐτῷ Πέτρος, κύριε, διὰ τί οὐ δύναμέ σοι ἀκολουθῆσαι ἄρτι; ὑπὲρ σοῦ τὴν ψυχήν μου θήσω.

13.38 ἀποκρίνεται Ἰησοῦς, τὴν ψυχήν σου ὑπὲρ ἐμοῦ θήσεις; ἀμὴν ἀμὴν λέγω σοι, οὐ μὴ ἀλέκτωρ φωνήσῃ ἕως οὗ ἀπαρνήσῃ με τρίς.

14.1 Μὴ ταρασσέσθω ὑμῶν ἡ καρδία· πιστεύεται εἰς τὸν

to inquire who it may be, about whom he was speaking, and he says to him: Say who it is about whom he speaks. 13.25 Then that (one), having thus fallen back upon the breast of Jesus, says to him: Lord, who is *it*? 13.26 Jesus answers and says: He is that (one) for whom I, having dipped the morsel/piece of bread, I shall give to. Then, having dipped the morsel/piece of bread, he gave *it* to Judas of Simon Iscariot. 13.27 And after the morsel, Satan entered into that (one). Then Jesus says to him: What you do, do at once. 13.28 But no one of those reclining knew toward what/*for* why he said this to him; 13.29 for some were thinking, since Judas held the bag, that Jesus says to him: Buy what (things) we have need of in/for the festival, or that he might give something to the poor (ones). 13.30 Having therefore received the morsel, that (one) went out quickly, and it was night. 13.31 Then, when he went out, Jesus says: The son of the man was now glorified, and God was glorified in him; 13.32 if God was glorified in him, God will also glorify him in/by himself, and he will glorify him quickly.

13.33 Little children, I am with ye still a little time; ye will seek me, and as I said to the Judeans that where I, I go/depart, ye, ye are not able to go, I say just now to ye also. 13.34 I give a new command to ye, that ye may/should love one another; even as I loved ye, also ye, ye may/should love one another. 13.35 By this will all *men* know that ye are learners/pupils for me, if ye may have/hold agape in one another. 13.36 Simon Peter says to him: Lord, where do you go/depart? Jesus answered to him: Where I, I go, you are not able to follow with me now, but you will follow later. 13.37 Peter says to him: Lord, why am I not able to follow with you just now? I shall put/lay down my soul/life in behalf of you.

13.38 Jesus answers: You will put down you soul/life in behalf of me? Truly, truly I say to you, by no means might a cock crow until which *time* you will deny me thrice/three times.

14.1 Let not the heart of ye be troubled; be-

θεόν, καὶ εἰς ἐμὲ πιστεύετε. 14.2 ἐν τῇ οἰκίᾳ τοῦ πατρός μου μοναὶ πολλαί εἰσιν· εἰ δὲ μή, εἶπον ὑμῖν ὅτι πορεύομαι ἑτοιμάσαι τόπον ὑμῖν; 14.3 καὶ ἐὰν πορευθῶ καὶ ἑτοιμάσω τόπον ὑμῖν, πάλιν ἔρχομαι καὶ παραλήμψομαι ὑμᾶς πρὸς ἐμαυτόν, ἵνα ὅπου εἰμὶ ἐγὼ καὶ ὑμῖς ἦτε. 14.4 καὶ ὅπου ἐγὼ ὑπάγω οἴδατε τὴν ὁδόν. 14.5 λέγει αὐτῷ Θωμᾶς, κύριε, οὐκ οἴδαμεν ποῦ ὑπάγεις· καὶ πῶς τὴν ὁδὸν εἰδέναι δυνάμεθα; 14.6 λέγει αὐτῷ Ἰησοῦς, ἐγώ εἰμι ἡ ὁδὸς καὶ ἡ ἀλήθεια καὶ ἡ ζωή· οὐδὶς ἔρχεται πρὸς τὸν πατέρα εἰ μὴ δι' ἐμοῦ. 14.7 εἰ ἐγνώκατε ἐμέ, καὶ τὸν πατέρα μου γνώσεσθαι· καὶ ἀπ' ἄρτι γινώσεσθαι αὐτὸν καὶ ἑωράκαται αὐτόν. 14.8 λέγει αὐτῷ ὁ Φίλιππος, κύριε, δεῖξον ἡμῖν τὸν πατέρα, καὶ ἀρκεῖ ἡμῖν. 14.9 λέγει αὐτῷ ὁ Ἰησοῦς, τοσούτῳ χρόνῳ μεθ' ὑμῶν εἰμι καὶ οὐκ ἔγνωκάς με, Φίλιππε; ὁ ἑωρακὼς ἐμὲ ἑώρακεν τὸν πατέρα· πῶς σὺ λέγις, ὅτι δεῖξον ἡμῖν τὸν πατέρα; 14.10 οὐ πιστεύεις ὅτι ἐγὼ ἐν τῷ πατρὶ καὶ ὁ πατὴρ ἐν ἐμοί ἐστιν;

τὰ ῥήματα ἃ ἐγὼ λέγω ὑμῖν ἀπ' ἐμαυτοῦ οὐ λαλῶ· ὁ δὲ πατὴρ ὁ ἐν ἐμοὶ μένων ποιεῖ τὰ ἔργα αὐτοῦ. 14.11 πιστεύεταί μοι ὅτι ἐγὼ ἐν τῷ πατρὶ καὶ ὁ πατὴρ ὁ ἐν ἐμοί· εἰ δὲ μή, διὰ τὰ ἔργα αὐτὰ πιστεύετε.

14.12 ἀμὴν ἀμὴν λέγω ὑμῖν, ὁ πιστεύων εἰς ἐμὲ τὰ ἔργα ἃ ἐγὼ ποιῶ κἀκεῖνος ποιήσει, καὶ μείζονα τούτων ποιήσει, ὅτι ἐγὼ πρὸς τὸν πατέρα πορεύομαι· 14.13 καὶ ὅ τι ἂν αἰτήσητε ἐν τῷ ὀνόματί μου τοῦτο ποιήσω, ἵνα δοξασθῇ ὁ πατὴρ ἐν τῷ υἱῷ· 14.14 ἐάν τι αἰτήσητέ με ἐν τῷ ὀνόματί μου ἐγὼ ποιήσω.

14.15 ἐὰν ἀγαπᾶτέ με, τὰς ἐντολὰς τὰς ἐμὰς τηρήσητε· 14.16 κἀγὼ ἐρωτήσω τὸν πατέρα καὶ ἄλλον παράκλητον δώσει ὑμῖν ἵνα μεθ' ὑμῶν ᾖ εἰς τὸν αἰῶνα, 14.17 τὸ πνεῦμα τῆς ἀληθίας, ὃ ὁ κόσμος οὐ δύναται λαβεῖν, ὅτι οὐ θεωρεῖ αὐτὸ οὐδὲ γινώσκει· ὑμῖς γεινώσκετε αὐτό, ὅτι παρ' ὑμῖν μένει καὶ ἐν ὑμῖν ἔσται. 14.18 οὐκ ἀφήσω ὑμᾶς ὀρφανούς, ἔρχομαι πρὸς ὑμᾶς. 14.19 ἔτι μικρὸν καὶ ὁ κόσμος με οὐκέτι θεωρεῖ, ὑμεῖς δὲ

lieve ye in God and believe ye in me.   14.2 In the
house of my father are many rooms/abodes; and if not,
I said *so* to ye, because I go to prepare a place for
ye;   14.3 and if I may go and prepare a place for ye,
I come/am coming again and I shall take ye to myself,
that where I, I am; ye, ye may be also.   14.4 And
where I, I go/depart, ye know the road/way.   14.5
Thomas says to him: Lord, we know not where you go;
and how are we able to have known the road/way?   14.6
Jesus says to him: I, I am the road/way and the truth
and the life;   no   one   comes to the father except
through me.   14.7 If ye have known me, ye will also
know my father; and from just now ye yourselves know
him and ye have seen him.   14.8 Philip says to him:
Lord, show the father to us, and it is enough for us.
14.9   Jesus says to him: For so great a time I am with
ye,   and you have not known me, Philip? The (one)
having seen me has seen the father; how *do* you, you
say: Show the father to us?   14.10 Believe you not
that I *am* in the father and the father is in me?

The words which I, I say to ye, I speak not from
myself; but the father, the (one) abiding in me; I do
the works of him.   14.11 Believe ye in me, that/
because I *am* in the father and the father in me; and
if not, believe ye because of the works themselves.

14.12   Truly, truly I say to ye, the one believing in me, the works which I, I do, that (one) will do
also, and he will do greater than these, because I, I
go to the father;   14.13 and what ever that ye might
ask in my name, this I shall do, that the father might
be glorified in/by the son;   14.14 if ye might ask me
something in my name, I, I shall do it.

14.15   If ye love me, ye will keep my commands;
14.16 I, I also will petition the father and he will
send another paraclete to ye in order that he may be
with ye into the age,   14.17 the spirit of the truth,
which the world is not able to receive, because it
beholds/perceives it not, not knows; ye, ye know it,
because it abides beside/with ye and it will be in/-
among ye.   14.18 I shall not leave ye/let ye be orphans, I come/am coming to ye.   14.19 Yet a little
time, and the world beholds me no longer; but ye, ye

θεωρεῖτέ με, ὅτι ἐγὼ ζῶ καὶ ὑμεῖς ζήσεσθαι.

14.20 ἐν ἐκίνῃ τῇ ἡμέρᾳ γνώσεσθαι ὑμῖς ὅτι ἐγὼ ἐν τῷ πατρί μου καὶ ὑμῖς ἐν ἐμοὶ κἀγὼ ἐν ὑμῖν.

14.21 ὁ ἔχων τὰς ἐντολάς μου καὶ τηρῶν αὐτὰς ἐκεῖνός ἐστιν ὁ ἀγαπῶν με· ὁ δὲ ἀγαπῶν με ἀγαπηθήσεται ὑπὸ τοῦ πατρός μου, κἀγὼ ἀγαπήσω αὐτὸν καὶ ἐμφανίσω αὐτῷ ἐμαυτόν.

14.22 λέγει αὐτῷ Ἰούδας, οὐχ ὁ Ἰσκαριώτης, κύριε, καὶ τί γέγονεν ὅτι ἡμῖν μέλλεις ἐμφανίζειν σεαυτὸν καὶ οὐχὶ τῷ κόσμῳ; 14.23 ἀπεκρίθη Ἰησοῦς καὶ εἶπεν αὐτῷ, ἐάν τις ἀγαπᾷ με τὸν λόγον μου τηρήσῃ, καὶ ὁ πατήρ μου ἀγαπήσει αὐτόν, καὶ πρὸς αὐτὸν ἐλευσόμεθα καὶ μονὴν παρ' αὐτῷ ποιησόμεθα. 14.24 ὁ μὴ ἀγαπῶν με τοὺς λόγους μου οὐ τηρεῖ· καὶ ὁ λόγος ὃν ἀκούεται οὐκ ἔστιν ἐμὸς ἀλλὰ τοῦ πέμψαντός με πατρός. 14.25 ταῦτα λελάληκα ὑμῖν παρ' ὑμῖν μένων· 14.26 ὁ δὲ παράκλητος, πέμψει τὸ πνεῦμα τὸ ἅγιον ὁ πατὴρ ἐν τῷ ὀνόματί μου, ἐκεῖνος ὑμᾶς διδάξει πάντα καὶ ὑπομνήσει ὑμᾶς πάντα ἃ εἶπον ὑμῖν.

14.27 εἰρήνην ἀφίημι ὑμῖν, εἰρήνην τὴν ἐμὴν δίδωμι ὑμῖν· οὐ καθὼς ὁ κόσμος δίδωσιν ὑμῖν ἐγὼ δίδωμι ὑμῖν. μὴ ταρασσέσθω ὑμῶν ἡ καρδία μηδὲ διλιάτω. 14.28 ἠκούσατε ὅτι ἐγὼ εἶπον ὑμῖν, ὑπάγω καὶ ἔρχομαι πρὸς ὑμᾶς. εἰ ἠγαπᾶτέ με ἐχάρητε ἄν, ὅτι πορεύομαι πρὸς τὸν πατέρα, ὅτι ὁ πατήρ μου μείζων μού ἐστιν. 14.29 καὶ νῦν εἴρηκα ὑμῖν πρὶν γενέσθε, ἵν' ὅταν γένηται πιστεύσητε. 14.30 οὐκέτι πολλὰ λαλήσω μεθ' ὑμῶν, ἔρχεται γὰρ ὁ τοῦ κόσμου ἄρχων· καὶ ἐν ἐμοὶ οὐκ ἔχει οὐδέν, 14.31 ἀλλ' ἵνα γνῷ ὁ κόσμος ὅτι ἀγαπῶ τὸν πατέρα, καὶ καθὼς ἐνετίλατο μοι ὁ πατήρ, οὕτως ποιῶ. ἐγείρεσθε, ἄγωμεν ἐντεῦθεν.

15.1 Ἐγώ εἰμι ἡ ἄμπελος ἡ ἀληθινή, καὶ ὁ πατήρ μου ὁ γεωργός ἐστιν. 15.2 πᾶν κλῆμα ἐν ἐμοὶ μὴ φέρον καρπόν, αἴρει αὐτό, καὶ πᾶν τὸ καρπὸν φέρον καθαίρει αὐτὸ ἵνα καρπὸν

behold me, because I live and ye will live yourselves.

14.20   In that day ye, ye will know that I *am* in my father and ye *are* in me and I in ye.

14.21   The (one) having/holding my commands and keeping them, that (one) is the (one) loving me; and the (one) loving me will be loved by my father, and I, I shall love him and I shall manifest/reveal myself to him.

14.22   Judas, not the (one) of Iscariot, says to him: Lord, what has happened that you are about to manifest/reveal yourself to us and not to the world? 14.23 Jesus answered and said to him: If anyone may love me, he will keep my saying/word, and my father will love him, and we shall come near to him and we shall make a room/abode beside/with him.   14.24 The (one) not loving me keeps not my sayings/words; and the saying/word which ye hear is not from me but from the father having sent me.   14.25 I have spoken these (things) to ye living/abiding beside/with ye;   14.26 but the paraclete, the holy spirit, which *the* father will send in my name, that (one) will teach ye all (things) and will remind ye *of* all (things) which I said to ye.

14.27   I leave peace to ye, my peace I give to ye; I, I give to ye not as/like the world gives to ye. Let not the heart of ye be troubled nor   timid/cowardly.   14.28 Ye heard that I, I said to ye: I go away/depart and I come near/to ye. If ye were loving me ye would rejoice that I go to the father, because my father is greater than me.   14.29 And now I have said *it* to ye before *it is* to happen, in order that whenever it might happen ye might believe.   14.30 No longer shall I speak many (things) with ye, for the ruler of the world comes; and he has not anything in/with me, 14.31 but in order that the world may know that I love the father, and as the father commanded/enjoined to me, so I do. Arise ye, let us go from here/this place.

15.1   I, I am the true vine, and my father is the vinedresser/farmer.   15.2   Every branch in me not bearing fruit, he takes it away, and every (one) bearing the fruit he cleanses (*prunes*) it in order

πλείω φέρῃ. 15.3 ἤδη ὑμεῖς καθαροί ἐστε διὰ τὸν λόγον ὃν λελάληκα ὑμῖν· 15.4 μίνατε ἐν ἐμοί, κἀγὼ ἐν ὑμῖν. καθὼς τὸ κλῆμα οὐ δύναται καρπὸν φέρειν ἀφ’ ἑαυτοῦ ἐὰν μὴ μένῃ ἐν τῇ ἀμπέλῳ, οὕτως οὐδὲ ὑμῖς ἐὰν μὴ ἐν ἐμοὶ μένητε. 15.5 ἐγώ εἰμι ἡ ἄμπελος, ὑμῖς τὰ κλήματα. ὁ μένων ἐν ἐμοὶ κἀγὼ ἐν αὐτῷ οὗτος φέρει καρπὸν πολύν, ὅτι χωρὶς ἐμοῦ οὐ δύνασθαι ποιεῖν οὐδέν. 15.6 ἐὰν μή τις μένῃ ἐν ἐμοί, ἐβλήθη ἔξω ὡς τὸ κλῆμα καὶ ἐξηράνθη, καὶ συνάγουσιν αὐτὸ καὶ εἰς τὸ πῦρ βάλλουσιν καὶ καίεται. 15.7 ἐὰν μείνητε ἐν ἐμοὶ καὶ τὰ ῥήματά μου ἐν ὑμῖν μίνῃ, ὅσα ἐὰν θέλητε αἰτήσεσθε καὶ γενήσεται ὑμῖν. 15.8 ἐν τούτῳ ἐδοξάσθη ὁ πατήρ μου, ἵνα καρπὸν πολὺν φέρηται καὶ γένησεσθαι μοι μαθηταί. 15.9 καθὼς ἠγάπησέν με ὁ πατήρ, κἀγὼ ἠγάπησα ὑμᾶς· μείνατε ἐν τῇ ἀγάπῃ τῇ ἐμῇ. 15.10 ἐὰν τὰς ἐντολάς μου τηρήσεται, μενῖται ἐν τῇ ἀγάπῃ μου, καθὼς κἀγὼ τοῦ πατρός μου τὰς ἐντολὰς μου ἐτήρησα καὶ μένω αὐτοῦ ἐν τῇ ἀγάπῃ. 15.11 ταῦτα λελάληκα ὑμῖν ἵνα ἡ χαρὰ ἡ ἐμὴ ἐν ὑμῖν μείνῃ καὶ ἡ χαρὰ ὑμῶν πληρωθῇ. 15.12 αὕτη ἐστὶν ἡ ἐντολὴ ἡ ἐμή, ἵνα ἀγαπᾶτε ἀλλήλους καθὼς ἠγάπησα ὑμᾶς· 15.13 μείζονα ταύτης ἀγάπην οὐδὶς ἔχει, ἵνα τις τὴν ψυχὴν αὐτοῦ θῇ ὑπὲρ τῶν φίλων αὐτοῦ.

15.14 ὑμεῖς φίλοι μού ἐστε ἐὰν ποιῆται ἃ ἐγὼ ἐντέλλομαι ὑμῖν. 15.15 οὐκέτι λέγω ὑμᾶς δούλους, ὅτι ὁ δοῦλος οὐκ οἶδεν τί ποιεῖ αὐτοῦ ὁ κύριος· ὑμᾶς δὲ εἴρηκα φίλους, ὅτι πάντα ἃ ἤκουσα παρὰ τοῦ πατρός μου ἐγνώρισα ὑμῖν. 15.16 οὐχ ὑμῖς με ἐξελέξασθαι, ἀλλ’ ἐγὼ ἐξελεξάμην ὑμᾶς καὶ ἔθηκα ὑμᾶς ἵνα ὑμῖς ὑπάγητε καὶ καρπὸν φέρηται καὶ ὁ καρπὸς ὑμῶν μένῃ, ἵνα ὅ τι ἐὰν αἰτήσηται τὸν πατέρα ἐν τῷ ὀνόματί μου δῶσει ὑμῖν. 15.17 ταῦτα ἐντέλλομαι ὑμῖν, ἵνα ἀγαπᾶτε ἀλλήλους. 15.18 εἰ ὁ κόσμος ὑμᾶς· μεισεῖ, γινώσκετε ὅτι ἐμὲ πρῶτον ὑμῶν μεμίσηκεν. 15.19 εἰ ἐκ τοῦ κόσμου ἦτε, ὁ κόσμος ἂν τὸ ἴδιον ἐφίλει· ὅτι δὲ ἐκ τοῦ κόσμου οὐκ ἐστέ, ἀλλ’ ἐγὼ ἐξελεξάμην ὑμᾶς ἐκ τοῦ κόσμου, διὰ τοῦτο ὁ κόσμος μισεῖ ὑμᾶς. 15.20 μνημονεύεται

that it may bear more. 15.3 Already ye, ye are clean because of the saying/word which I have spoken to ye. 15.4 Abide/stay ye in/with me, and I in ye. As the branch is not able to bear fruit from itself unless it abides/remains on the vine, so neither ye unless ye may abide in me. 15.5 I, I am the vine, ye *are* the branches. The (one) abiding in me and I in him, this (one) bears much fruit, because apart from me ye are not able to do nothing. 15.6 Unless someone may abide in me, he was thrown out like the branch and was withered, and they gather together and throw it into the fire and it is burned. 15.7 If ye might abide in me and my words might abide in ye, what ever ye may want, ask ye, and it will become/happen for ye. 15.8 In/by this my father was glorified, that ye may bear much fruit and ye will become learners/pupils for me. 15.9 As the father loved me, I also loved ye; abide ye in my agape. 15.10 If ye might keep my commands, ye will abide/stay in my agape, as also I, I kept my commands from my father and I abide in his agape. 15.11 I have spoken these (things) to ye in order that my joy may abide in ye and your joy might be fulfilled. 15.12 This is my command, that ye may/should love one another as I loved ye. 15.13 No one has greater love than this, that someone might put down his soul/life in behalf of his friends.

15.14 Ye, ye are my friends if ye may do what (things) I, I command ye. 15.15 I no longer call ye slaves, because the slave knows not what his lord does; but I have called ye friends, because I made known to ye all (things) which I heard from my father. 15.16 Ye, ye chose not me, but I, I chose ye and I appointed/committed ye that ye may go and bear fruit and the fruit of ye may abide/stay, in order that what ever ye may ask the father in my name, he will give to ye. 15.17 I command these (things) to ye, that ye may/should love one another. 15.18 If the world hates ye, ye know that it has hated me before ye. 15.19 If ye be out of/from the world, the world would love its own (thing); but because ye are not out of/from the world, but I, I chose ye out of the world, the world hates ye because of this. 15.20 Remember ye the

τὸν λόγον ὃν ἐγὼ ἐλάλησα ὑμάσιν, οὐκ ἔστιν δοῦλος μείζων τοῦ κυρίου αὐτοῦ. εἰ ἐμὲ ἐδίωξαν, καὶ ὑμᾶς διώξουσιν· εἰ τὸν λόγον μου ἐτήρησαν, καὶ τὸν ὑμέτερον τηρήσωσιν. 15.21 ἀλλὰ ταῦτα πάντα ποιήσουσιν εἰς ὑμᾶς διὰ τὸ ὄνομά μου, ὅτι οὐκ οἴδασιν τὸν πέμψαντά με. 15.22 εἰ μὴ ἦλθον καὶ ἐλάλησα αὐτοῖς, ἁμαρτίαν οὐκ εἴχοσαν· νῦν πρόφασιν οὐκ ἔχουσιν περὶ τῆς ἁμαρτίας αὐτῶν. 15.23 ὁ ἐμὲ μισῶν καὶ τὸν πατέρα μου μισεῖ. 15.24 εἰ τὰ ἔργα μὴ ἐποίησα ἐν αὐτοῖς ἃ οὐδὶς ἄλλος ἐποίησεν, ἁμαρτίαν οὐκ εἴχοσαν· νῦν δὲ καὶ ἑωράκασιν καὶ μεμισήκασιν καὶ ἐμὲ καὶ τὸν πατέρα μου. 15.25 ἀλλ᾿ ἵνα πληρωθῇ ὁ λόγος ὁ ἐν τῷ νόμῳ αὐτῶν γεγραμμένος ὅτι « ἐμίσησάν με δωρεάν.» 15.26 ὅταν ἔλθῃ ὁ παράκλητος ὃν ἐγὼ πέμψω ὑμῖν παρὰ τοῦ πατρός, τὸ πνεῦμα τῆς ἀληθείας ὃ παρὰ τοῦ πατρὸς ἐκπορεύεται, ἐκεῖνος μαρτυρήσει περὶ ἐμοῦ· 15.27 καὶ ὑμεῖς δὲ μαρτυρῖτε, ὅτι ἀπ᾿ ἀρχῆς μετ᾿ ἐμοῦ ἐστε. 16.1 ταῦτα λελάληκα ὑμῖν ἵνα μὴ σκανδαλισθῆτε. 16.2 ἀποσυναγώγους γὰρ ποιήσουσιν ὑμᾶς· ἀλλὰ ἔρχεται ὥρα ἵνα πᾶς ὁ ἀποκτίνας ὑμᾶς δόξῃ λατρίαν προσφέριν τῷ θεῷ. 16.3 καὶ ταῦτα ποιήσωσιν ἡμῖν ὅτι οὐκ ἔγνωσαν τὸν πατέρα οὐδὲ ἐμέ. 16.4 ἀλλὰ ταῦτα λελάληκα ὑμῖν ἵνα ἐὰν ἔλθῃ ἡ ὥρα αὐτῶν μνημονεύηται αὐτῶν ὅτι ἐγὼ εἶπον ὑμῖν. ταῦτα δὲ ὑμῖν ἐξ ἀρχῆς οὐκ εἶπον, ὅτι μεθ᾿ ὑμῶν ἤμην. 16.5 νῦν δὲ ἐγὼ ὑπάγω πρὸς τὸν πέμψαντά με, καὶ οὐδὶς ἐξ ὑμῶν ἐρωτᾷ με, ποῦ ὑπάγεις; 16.6 ἀλλ᾿ ὅτι ταῦτα λελάληκα ὑμῖν ἡ λύπη πεπλήρωκεν ὑμῶν τὴν καρδίαν. 16.7 ἀλλ᾿ ἐγὼ τὴν ἀλήθειαν λέγω ὑμῖν, συμφέρει ὑμῖν ἵνα ἐγὼ ἀπέλθω. ἐὰν γὰρ μὴ ἀπέλθω, ὁ παράκλητος οὐκ ἐλεύσεται πρὸς ὑμᾶς· ἐὰν δὲ πορευθῶ, πέμψω αὐτὸν πρὸς ὑμᾶς. 16.8 καὶ ἐλθὼν ἐκεῖνος ἐλέγξει τὸν κόσμον

περὶ ἁμαρτίας καὶ περὶ δικαιοσύνης καὶ περὶ κρίσεως· 16.9

saying/word which I, I spoke to ye: A slave is not greater than his lord. If they prosecuted/pursued me, they will also prosecute/pursue ye; if they kept my saying/word, they will keep yours also.   15.21 But they will do all these (things) to ye because of my name, because they know not the (one) having sent me. 15.22 Except I came and spoke to them, they were not having sin; now they have not an excuse concerning their sin.   15.23 The (one) hating me also hates my father.   15.24 If I did not the works among them which no one else did, they were not having sin; but now they have both seen and hated both me and my father. 15.25 But in order that the saying/word, the (one) having been written in their law might be fulfilled: THEY HATED ME FOR NOTHING.   15.26 Whenever the paraclete might come, *the one* which I, I shall send to ye from the father, the spirit of the truth which proceeds/goes forth from the father, that (one) will testify/witness about me;   15.27 and ye, ye will witness also because ye are with me from the beginning.   16.1 I have spoken these (things) to ye in order that ye may not be offended/ caused to stumble.   16.2 For they will make ye expel-led (ones) from the congregation; but an hour comes that every one having killed ye might think *it*/seem to offer service/worship to God. 16.3   And they will do these (things) to ye because they knew not the father nor me.   16.4 But I have spoken these (things) to ye in order that whenever their hour might come ye may remember *them* because I, I spoke of them to ye. But I spoke not these (things) to ye from the beginning, because I was with ye.   16.5 But now I, I go away/-depart to the (one) having sent me, and no one out of ye asks me: Where *do* you go? 16.6 But because I have spoken these (things) to ye, the pain/grief has filled the heart of ye.   16.7 But I, I say the truth to ye, it is beneficial/profitable for ye that I, I might go away. For except/unless I might go away, the paraclete will not come near/to ye; but if I might go, I shall send him to ye.   16.8 And having come, that (one) will reprove/convict the world

about sin and about justice and about judgment;

233

περὶ ἁμαρτίας μέν, ὅτι οὐ πιστεύουσιν εἰς ἐμέ· 16.10 περὶ δικαιοσύνης δέ, ὅτι πρὸς τὸν πατέρα ὑπάγω καὶ οὐκέτι θεωρεῖτέ με· 16.11 περὶ δὲ κρίσεως, ὅτι ὁ ἄρχων τοῦ κόσμου τούτου κέκριται. 16.12 ἔτι πολλὰ ἔχω ὑμῖν λέγειν, ἀλλ᾽ οὐ δύνασθαι βαστάζειν ἄρτι· 16.13 ὅταν δὲ ἔλθῃ ἐκεῖνος, τὸ πνεῦμα τῆς ἀληθίας, ὁδηγήσει ὑμᾶς ἐν τῇ ἀληθείᾳ πάσῃ· οὐ γὰρ λαλήσει ἀφ᾽ ἑαυτοῦ, ἀλλ᾽ ὅσα ἀκούει λαλήσει, καὶ τὰ ἐρχόμενα ἀναγγελεῖ ὑμῖν. 16.14 ἐκεῖνος ἐμὲ δοξάσει, ὅτι ἐκ τοῦ ἐμοῦ λήμψεται καὶ ἀναγγελεῖ ὑμῖν. 16.15 πάντα ὅσα ἔχι ὁ πατὴρ ἐμά ἐστιν· διὰ τοῦτο εἶπον ὑμῖν ὅτι ἐκ τοῦ ἐμοῦ λαμβάνει καὶ ἀναγγελεῖ ὑμῖν. 16.16 μεικρὸν καὶ οὐκέτι θεωρεῖτέ με, καὶ πάλιν μικρὸν καὶ ὄψεσθέ με. 16.17 εἶπαν οὖν ἐκ τῶν μαθητῶν αὐτοῦ πρὸς ἀλλήλους, τί ἐστιν τοῦτο ὃ λέγει ἡμῖν, μικρὸν καὶ οὐ θεωρῖταί με, καὶ πάλιν μικρὸν καὶ ὄψεσθέ με; καί, ὅτι ὑπάγω πρὸς τὸν πατέρα; 16.18 ἔλεγον οὖν, τί ἐστιν τοῦτο ὃ λέγι, τὸ μικρόν; οὐκ οἴδαμεν τί λαλεῖ. 16.19 ἔγνω ὁ Ἰησοῦς ὅτι ἤμελλον αὐτὸν ἐρωτᾶν, καὶ εἶπεν αὐτοῖς, περὶ τούτου ζητεῖτε μετ᾽ ἀλλήλων ὅτι εἶπον, μικρὸν καὶ οὐ θεωρεῖτέ με, καὶ πάλιν μικρὸν καὶ ὄψεσθέ με; 16.20 ἀμὴν ἀμὴν λέγω ὑμῖν ὅτι κλαύσετε καὶ θρηνήσητε ὑμῖς, ὁ δὲ κόσμος χαρήσεται· ὑμῖς λυπηθήσεσθαι, ἀλλ᾽ ἡ λύπη ὑμῶν εἰς χαρὰν γενήσεται. 16.21 ἡ γυνὴ ὅταν τίκτῃ λύπην ἔχει, ὅτι ἦλθεν ἡ ὥρα αὐτῆς· ὅταν δὲ γεννήσῃ τὸ παιδίον, οὐκέτι μνημονεύει τῆς θλίψεως διὰ τὴν χαρὰν ὅτι ἐγεννήθη ἄνθρωπος εἰς τὸν κόσμον. 16.22 καὶ ὑμεῖς νῦν μὲν οὖν λύπην ἔχεται· πάλιν δὲ ὄψομαι ὑμᾶς, καὶ χαρήσεται ὑμῶν ἡ καρδία, καὶ τὴν χαρὰν ὑμῶν οὐδὶς αἴρει ἀφ᾽ ὑμῶν. 16.23 καὶ ἐν ἐκείνῃ τῇ ἡμέρᾳ ἐμὲ οὐκ ἐρωτήσηται οὐδέν.

ἀμὴν ἀμὴν λέγω ὑμῖν, ὅτι ὃ ἂν αἰτήσηται τὸν πατέρα

16.9 concerning sin on one hand, because they believe not in me; 16.10 and concerning justice, because I depart to the father and ye no longer behold me; 16.11 and concerning judgment, because the ruler of this world has been judged. 16.12 I still have many things to say to ye, but ye are not able to bear *it* just now; 16.13 but whenever that (one) might come, the spirit of the truth, he/it will guide ye in/by every truth; for he/it will speak not from himself/it-self, but it will speak whatever it hears, and it will announce the coming (things) to ye. 16.14 That (one) will glorify me, because it will receive *it* from me and will announce *it* to ye. 16.15 All (things) as many as the father has are mine; because of this I said to ye that out of the (thing) from me it receives and will announce *it* to ye. 16.16 A little (time) and ye behold me no longer, and again a little (time) and ye will see me. 16.17 Therefore, they out of his learners/pupils said to one another: What is this which he says to us: A little (time) and ye behold me not, and again a little (time) and ye will see me? And: Because I depart to the father? 16.18 Therefore, they were saying: What is this which he says, the little (time)? We know not what he speaks. 16.19 Jesus knew that they were being about to question him, and he said to them: Are ye discussing with one another this (thing) that I said: A little (time) and ye behold me not, and again a little (time) and ye will see me? 16.20 Truly, truly I say to ye that ye, ye will weep and lament/morn, but the world will rejoice; ye, ye will be grieved, but the grief of ye will become into/for joy. 16.21 The woman has pain/grief whenever she may give birth, because her hour came; but whenever she might generate/birth the child, she remembers no more of the affliction because of the joy that a man/human has been generated/born into the world. 16.22 And ye therefore, ye will indeed have pain/grief now; but I shall see ye again, and the heart of ye will rejoice, and no one takes your joy away from ye. 16.23 And in that day ye will not question me for nothing.

Truly, truly I say to ye, that what ever ye might

δώσει ὑμῖν ἐν τῷ ὀνόματί μου. 16.24 ἕως ἄρτι οὐκ ᾐτήσατε οὐδὲν ἐν τῷ ὀνόματί μου· αἰτήσασθαι καὶ λήμψεσθε, ἵνα ἡ χαρὰ ὑμῶν ᾖ πεπληρωμένη. 16.25 ταῦτα ἐν παροιμίαις λελάληκα ὑμῖν· ἔρχεται ὥρα ὅτε οὐκέτι ἐν παροιμίαις λαλήσω ὑμῖν ἀλλὰ παρρησίᾳ περὶ τοῦ πατρὸς ἀπαγγελῶ ὑμῖν.

16.26 ἐν ἐκείνῃ τῇ ἡμέρᾳ αἰτήσασθαι ἐν τῷ ὀνόματί μου, καὶ οὐ λέγω ὑμῖν ὅτι ἐγὼ ἐρωτήσω τὸν πατέρα περὶ ὑμῶν· 16.27 αὐτὸς γὰρ ὁ πατὴρ φιλεῖ ὑμᾶς, ὅτι ὑμεῖς με πεφιλήκατε καὶ πεπιστεύκατε ὅτι ἐγὼ παρὰ θεοῦ ἐξῆλθον. 16.28 ἐξῆλθον παρὰ τοῦ πατρὸς καὶ ἐλήλυθα εἰς τὸν κόσμον· πάλιν ἀφίημι τὸν κόσμον καὶ πορεύομαι πρὸς τὸν πατέρα. 16.29 λέγουσιν οἱ μαθηταὶ αὐτοῦ, ἴδε νῦν ἐν παρρησίᾳ λαλεῖς, καὶ παροιμίαν οὐδεμίαν λέγεις. 16.30 νῦν οἴδαμεν ὅτι οἶδας πάντα καὶ οὐ χρίαν ἔχεις ἵνα τίς σε ἐρωτᾷ· ἐν τούτῳ πιστεύομεν ὅτι ἀπὸ θεοῦ ἐξῆλθες. 16.31 ἀπεκρίθη αὐτοῖς ὁ Ἰησοῦς, ἄρτι πιστεύεται; 16.32 ἰδοὺ ἔρχεται ὥρα καὶ ἐλήλυθεν ἡ ὥρα ἵνα σκορπισθῆτε ἕκαστος εἰς τὰ ἴδια κἀμὲ μόνον ἀφῆτε· καὶ οὐκ εἰμὶ μόνος, ὅτι ὁ πατὴρ μετ' ἐμοῦ ἐστιν. 16.33 ταῦτα λελάληκα ὑμῖν ἵνα ἐν ἐμοὶ εἰρήνην ἔχηται· ἐν τῷ κόσμῳ θλῖψιν ἔχετε, ἀλλὰ θαρσεῖται, ἐγὼ νενίκηκα τὸν κόσμον.

17.1 Ταῦτα λελάληκεν Ἰησοῦς, καὶ ἐπάρας τοὺς ὀφθαλμοὺς αὐτοῦ εἰς τὸν οὐρανὸν εἶπεν, πάτερ, ἐλήλυθεν ἡ ὥρα· δόξασόν σου τὸν υἱόν, ἵνα ὁ υἱὸς δοξάσῃ σέ, 17.2 καθὼς ἔδωκας αὐτῷ ἐξουσίαν πάσης σαρκός, ἵνα πᾶν ὃ δέδωκας αὐτῷ δώσω αὐτῷ ζωὴν αἰώνιον. 17.3 αὕτη δέ ἐστιν ἡ αἰώνιος ζωή, ἵνα γινώσκωσι σὲ τὸν μόνον ἀληθινὸν θεὸν καὶ ὃν ἀπέστιλας Ἰησοῦν χριστόν. 17.4 ἐγώ σε ἐδόξασα ἐπὶ τῆς γῆς, τὸ ἔργον τελιώσας ὃ δέδωκάς μοι ἵνα ποιήσω· 17.5 καὶ νῦν δόξασόν με σύ, πάτερ, παρὰ σεαυτῷ τῇ δόξῃ ᾗ εἶχον πρὸ τοῦ τὸν κόσμον εἶναι παρὰ σοί. 17.6 ἐφανέρωσά σου τὸ ὄνομα τοῖς ἀνθρώποις

ask the father, he will give *it* to ye in/by my name. 16.24 Until just now ye asked not nothing in my name; ask ye and ye will receive, in order that the joy of ye may be, having been fulfilled. 16.25 I have spoken these (things) to ye in proverbs/enigmas; an hour/time comes when I shall no longer speak to ye in proverbs, but I shall proclaim plainly to ye about the father.

16.26 In that day ye will ask/petition in my name, and I say not to ye that I, I shall question the father concerning ye; 16.27 for the father loves ye, because ye, ye have loved me and ye have believed that I, I came forth from God. 16.28 I came forth from the father and I have come into the world; again I leave the world and go to the father. 16.29 His learners/pupils say: Behold, you now speak with boldness/plainness, and you say nothing proverbial. 16.30 We know now that you know all (things) and you have not a need that anyone may question you; in/by this we believe that you came forth from God. 16.31 Jesus answered to them: Now *do* ye believe? 16.32 Behold, an hour comes and the hour/time has come that ye might be scattered, each (one) to his own (things), and ye might leave me alone; and I am not alone, because the father is with me. 16.33 I have spoken these (things) to ye in order that ye may have peace in me; in the world ye have tribulation/oppression, but be ye of good cheer, I, I have overcome the world.

17.1 Jesus had spoken these (things), and having lifted up his eyes to the sky/heaven, he said: Father, the hour has come: glorify your son, in order that the son might glorify you, 17.2 as you gave authority of/*over* every flesh to him, that every (one) which you have given to him, I shall give eternal life to him. 17.3 And this is the eternal life, that they may know/discern you, the only true God, and Jesus the anointed (one) whom you sent. 17.4 I, I glorified you on the earth, having finished/completed the work which you have given to me that I might do; 17.5 and now you, you glorify me, father, beside yourself with/in the glory which I was having beside you before the (thing) *for* the world to be. 17.6 I manifested your name to

οὓς ἔδωκάς μοι ἐκ τοῦ κόσμου. σοὶ ἦσαν καὶ ἐμοὶ αὐτοὺς ἔδωκας, καὶ τὸν λόγον σου ἐτήρησαν. 17.7 νῦν ἔγνων ὅτι πάντα ὅσα δέδωκάς μοι παρὰ σοῦ εἰσιν· 17.8 ὅτι τὰ ῥήματα ἃ δέδωκάς μοι δέδωκα αὐτοῖς, καὶ αὐτοὶ ἔλαβον καὶ ἔγνωσαν ἀληθῶς ὅτι παρὰ σοῦ ἐξῆλθον, καὶ ἐπίστευσαν ὅτι σύ με ἀπέστιλας. 17.9 ἐγὼ περὶ αὐτῶν ἐρωτῶ· οὐ περὶ τοῦ κόσμου ἐρωτῶ ἀλλὰ περὶ ὧν δέδωκάς μοι, ὅτι σοί εἰσιν, 17.10 καὶ ἐμοὶ αὐτοὺς ἔδωκας, καὶ δεδόξασμε ἐν αὐτοῖς. 17.11 καὶ οὐκέτι εἰμὶ ἐν τῷ κόσμῳ, καὶ αὐτοὶ ἐν τῷ κόσμῳ εἰσίν, κἀγὼ πρὸς σὲ ἔρχομαι. πάτερ ἅγιε, τήρησον αὐτοὺς ἐν τῷ ὀνόματί σου ᾧ δέδωκάς μοι, ἵνα ὦσιν ἓν καθὼς ἡμεῖς. 17.12 ὅτε ἤμην μετ᾽ αὐτῶν ἐγὼ ἐτήρουν αὐτοὺς ἐν τῷ ὀνόματί σου ὃ δέδωκάς μοι, καὶ ἐφύλαξα, καὶ οὐδὶς ἐξ αὐτῶν ἀπώλετο εἰ μὴ ὁ υἱὸς τῆς ἀπωλίας, ἵνα ἡ γραφὴ πληρωθῇ. 17.13 νῦν δὲ πρὸς σὲ ἔρχομαι, καὶ ταῦτα λαλῶ ἐν τῷ κόσμῳ ἵνα ἔχωσιν τὴν χαρὰν τὴν ἐμὴν πεπληρωμένην ἐν ἑαυτοῖς. 17.14 ἐγὼ δέδωκα αὐτοῖς τὸν λόγον σου, καὶ ὁ κόσμος ἐμίσησεν αὐτούς, ὅτι οὐκ εἰσὶν ἐκ τοῦ κόσμου καθὼς ἐγὼ οὐκ εἰμὶ ἐκ τοῦ κόσμου. 17.15 οὐκ ἐρωτῶ ἵνα ἄρῃς αὐτοὺς ἐκ τοῦ κόσμου ἀλλ᾽ ἵνα τηρήσῃς αὐτοὺς ἐκ τοῦ πονηροῦ. 17.16 ἐκ τοῦ κόσμου οὐκ εἰσὶν καθὼς ἐγὼ οὐκ εἰμὶ ἐκ τοῦ κόσμου. 17.17 ἁγίασον αὐτοὺς ἐν τῇ ἀληθίᾳ· ὁ λόγος ὁ σὸς ἀλήθιά ἐστιν. 17.18 καθὼς ἐμὲ ἀπέστιλας εἰς τὸν κόσμον, κἀγὼ ἀπέστιλα αὐτοὺς εἰς τὸν κόσμον· 17.19 καὶ ὑπὲρ αὐτῶν ἁγιάζω ἐμαυτόν, ἵνα ὦσιν καὶ αὐτοὶ ἡγιασμένοι ἐν ἀληθίᾳ. 17.20 οὐ περὶ τούτων δὲ ἐρωτῶ μόνον, ἀλλὰ καὶ περὶ τῶν πιστευόντων διὰ τοῦ λόγου αὐτῶν εἰς ἐμέ, 17.21 ἵνα πάντες ἓν ὦσιν, καθὼς σύ, πάτερ, ἐν ἐμοὶ κἀγὼ ἐν σοί, ἵνα καὶ αὐτοὶ ἐν ἡμῖν ἓν ὦσιν, ἵνα ὁ κόσμος πιστεύσῃ ὅτι σύ με ἀπέστιλας. 17.22 κἀγὼ τὴν δόξαν ἣν δέδωκάς μοι ἔδωκα αὐτοῖς, ἵνα ὦσιν ἓν καθὼς ἡμεῖς ἕν, 17.23 ἐγὼ ἐν αὐτοῖς καὶ σὺ

the men whom you gave to me out of the world. They were for you and you gave them to me, and they have kept your saying/word.   17.7 Now I knew that all (things) as many as you have given to me are from you; 17.8 because the words which you gave to me I have given to them, and they, they received *them* and they knew truly that I came forth from you, and they believed that you, you sent me.   17.9 I, I petition/ask concerning them; I ask not about the world but about *those* whom you have given to me, because they are for you,   17.10 and you gave them to me, and I have been glorified in/by them.   17.11 And I am no longer in the world, and they, they are in the world, and I, I come to you. holy father, keep them in your name, which you have given to me, in order that they may be one as we *are*.   17.12 When I was with them, I, I was keeping them which you have given to me in your name, and I guarded *them*, and no one out of them perished except the son of the destruction, in order that the writing might be fulfilled.   17.13 But now I come to you, and I speak these (things) in the world in order that they may have my joy having been fulfilled/filled up in themselves.   17.14 I, I have given your saying/word to them, and the world hated them, because they are not from the world as I, I am not from the world. 17.15 I petition not that you might take them out of the world but that you might keep them out of/from the evil. 17.16 They are not from the world as I, I am not from the world.   17.17 Sanctify them/set them apart in the truth; your logos/word is truth.   17.18 Even as you sent me into the world, I also, I sent them into the world;   17.19 and I sanctify/set apart myself in behalf of them, in order that they also, they may be having been set apart/sanctified in/by truth.   17.20 But I petition not concerning them only, but also concerning those believing in me through their saying/word,   17.21 in order that all may be one, as you, father, in me and I in you, in order that they also may be one in us, in order that the world might believe that you sent me. 17.22   And I, I gave to them the glory/fame which you have given me, that they may be one as we *are* one,   17.23 I in them and you in me,

ἐν ἐμοί, ἵνα ὦσιν τετελιωμένοι εἰς ἕν, καὶ γινώσκῃ ὁ κόσμος ὅτι σύ με ἀπέστιλας καὶ ἠγάπησας αὐτοὺς καθὼς ἐμὲ ἠγάπησας. 17.24 πάτερ, ὃ δέδωκάς μοι, θέλω ἵνα ὅπου εἰμὶ ἐγὼ κἀκεῖνοι ὦσιν μετ᾽ ἐμοῦ, ἵνα θεωρῶσιν τὴν δόξαν τὴν ἐμὴν ἣν δέδωκάς μοι, ὅτι ἠγάπησάς με πρὸ καταβολῆς κόσμου. 17.25 πάτερ δίκαιε, καὶ ὁ κόσμος σε οὐκ ἔγνω, ἐγὼ δέ σε ἔγνων, καὶ οὗτοι ἔγνωσαν ὅτι σύ με ἀπέστιλας, 17.26 καὶ ἐγνώρισα αὐτοῖς τὸ ὄνομά σου καὶ γνωρίσω, ἵνα ἡ ἀγάπη ἣν ἠγάπησάς αὐτούς ἐν αὐτοῖς ᾖ κἀγὼ ἐν αὐτοῖς.

18.1 Ταῦτα εἰπὼν Ἰησοῦς ἐξῆλθεν σὺν τοῖς μαθηταῖς αὐτοῦ πέραν τοῦ χιμάρρου τοῦ Κεδρὼν ὅπου ἦν κῆπος, εἰς ὃν εἰσῆλθεν αὐτὸς καὶ οἱ μαθηταὶ αὐτοῦ. 18.2 ᾔδει δὲ καὶ Ἰούδας ὁ παραδιδοὺς αὐτὸν τὸν τόπον, ὅτι πολλάκις συνήχθη Ἰησοῦς ἐκεῖ μετὰ τῶν μαθητῶν αὐτοῦ. 18.3 ὁ οὖν Ἰούδας λαβὼν τὴν σπεῖραν καὶ ἐκ τῶν ἀρχιερέων καὶ ἐκ τῶν Φαρισαίων ὑπηρέτας ἔρχεται ἐκῖ μετὰ φανῶν καὶ λαμπάδων καὶ ὅπλων.

18.4 Ἰησοῦς δὲ εἰδὼς πάντα τὰ ἐρχόμενα ἐπ᾽ αὐτὸν ἐξελθὼν εἶπεν αὐτοῖς, τίνα ζητεῖτε; 18.5 ἀπεκρίθησαν αὐτῷ, Ἰησοῦν τὸν Ναζωραῖον. λέγει αὐτοῖς Ἰησοῦς, ἐγώ εἰμι. εἱστήκει δὲ καὶ Ἰούδας ὁ παραδιδοὺς αὐτὸν μετ᾽ αὐτῶν. 18.6 ὡς οὖν εἶπεν αὐτοῖς, ἐγώ εἰμι, ἀπῆλθαν εἰς τὰ ὀπίσω καὶ ἔπεσαν χαμαί. 18.7 πάλιν οὖν αὐτοὺς ἐπηρώτησεν, τίνα ζητεῖτε; οἱ δὲ εἶπον, Ἰησοῦν τὸν Ναζωραῖον. 18.8 ἀπεκρίθη Ἰησοῦς, εἶπον ὑμῖν ὅτι ἐγώ εἰμι· εἰ οὖν ἐμὲ ζητεῖτε, ἄφετε τούτους ὑπάγειν· 18.9 ἵνα πληρωθῇ ὁ λόγος ὃν εἶπεν ὅτι οὓς δέδωκάς μοι οὐκ ἀπώλεσα ἐξ αὐτῶν οὐδένα. 18.10 Σίμων οὖν Πέτρος ἔχων μάχαιραν εἵλκυσεν αὐτὴν καὶ ἔπεσεν τὸν δοῦλον τοῦ ἀρχιερέως καὶ ἀπέκοψεν αὐτοῦ τὸ ὠτάριον τὸ δεξιόν. ἦν δὲ ὄνομα τῷ δούλῳ Μάλχος.

18.11 εἶπεν οὖν ὁ Ἰησοῦς τῷ Πέτρῳ, βάλε τὴν μάχαιραν

in order that they may be having been completed into one, and the world may know that you, you sent me and you loved them even as you loved me. 17.24 Father, what you have given to me, I want/wish that where I, I am, those also may be with me, in order that they may behold my glory/fame which you have given to me, because you loved me before foundation of a world. 17.25 Just father, the world also knew not you, but I, I knew you, and they, they knew that you, you sent me, 17.26 and I made your name known to them and I shall make *it* known, in order that the agape *with* which you loved them may be in them and I in them.

18.1 Having said these (things), Jesus went forth with his learners/pupils beyond/across the winter-flowing of the Cedron where there was a garden, into which he entered, he and his pupils/learners. 18.2 But Judas, the (one) delivering him over/betraying him also knew the place, because Jesus was often gathered there with his learners/pupils. 18.3 Then Judas, having taken the cohort of soldiers and servants/assistants from the high priests and from the Pharisees comes there with torches and lamps and weapons.
18.4 But Jesus, having known all things coming upon him, having gone forth, he said to them: Whom *do* ye seek? 18.5 They answered to him: Jesus, the Nazarene. Jesus says to them: I, I am *he*. And Judas, the (one) delivering him over, had also stood with them. 18.6 Then when he said to them: I, I am *he*, they went away to the (places) behind and fell to the ground. 18.7 Then he asked them again: Whom *do* ye seek? And the (ones)/they said: Jesus, the Nazarene. 18.8 Jesus answered: I said to ye that I, I am *he*; therefore, if ye seek me, allow ye these (men) to depart; 18.9 that the logos/word which he said might be fulfilled: *Those* whom you have given to me, I lost/destroyed no one out of them. 18.10 Then Simon Peter, having a sword, he drew it and struck the slave of the high priest and cut off the right ear of him. And a name for the slave was Malchus.
18.11 Then Jesus said to Peter: Put the sword

εἰς τὴν θήκην· τὸ ποτήριον ὃ δέδωκέν μοι ὁ πατὴρ οὐ μὴ πίω αὐτό; 18.12 ἡ οὖν σπῖρα καὶ ὁ χιλίαρχος καὶ οἱ ὑπηρέται τῶν Ἰουδαίων συνέλαβον τὸν Ἰησοῦν καὶ ἔδησαν αὐτὸν 18.13 καὶ ἤγαγον πρὸς Ἄνναν πρῶτον· ἦν γὰρ πενθερὸς τοῦ Καϊάφα, ὃς ἦν ἀρχιερεὺς τοῦ ἐνιαυτοῦ ἐκείνου· 18.14 ἦν δὲ Καϊάφας ὁ συμβουλεύσας τοῖς Ἰουδαίοις ὅτι συμφέρει ἕνα ἄνθρωπον ἀποθανεῖν ὑπὲρ τοῦ λαοῦ. 18.15 ἠκολούθι δὲ τῷ Ἰησοῦ Σίμων Πέτρος καὶ ὁ ἄλλος μαθητής. ὁ δὲ μαθητὴς ἐκεῖνος ἦν γνωστὸς τῷ ἀρχιερεῖ, καὶ συνεισῆλθεν τῷ Ἰησοῦ εἰς τὴν αὐλὴν τοῦ ἀρχιερέως, 18.16 ὁ δὲ Πέτρος εἱστήκει ἔξω πρὸς τῇ θύρᾳ. ἐξῆλθεν οὖν ὁ μαθητὴς ὁ ἄλλος ὃς ἦν γνωστὸς τῷ ἀρχιερεῖ καὶ εἶπεν τῇ θυρωρῷ καὶ εἰσήνεγκε τὸν Πέτρον. 18.17 λέγει οὖν ἡ παιδίσκη ἡ θυρωρός τῷ Πέτρῳ, μὴ καὶ σὺ ἐκ τῶν μαθητῶν εἶ τοῦ ἀνθρώπου τούτου; λέγει ἐκεῖνος, οὐκ εἰμί. 18.18 ἱστήκισαν δὲ καὶ οἱ δοῦλοι καὶ οἱ ὑπηρέται ἀνθρακιὰν πεποιηκότες, ὅτι ψῦχος ἦν, καὶ ἐθερμαίνοντο· ἦν δὲ καὶ ὁ Πέτρος μετ' αὐτῶν ἑστὼς καὶ θερμαινόμενος. 18.19 ὁ οὖν ἀρχιερεὺς ἠρώτησε τὸν Ἰησοῦν περὶ τῶν μαθητῶν αὐτοῦ καὶ περὶ τῆς διδαχῆς αὐτοῦ. 18.20 καὶ ἀπεκρίθη Ἰησοῦς αὐτῷ, ἐγὼ παρρησίᾳ λελάληκα τῷ κόσμῳ· ἐγὼ πάντοτε ἐδίδαξα ἐν συναγωγῇ καὶ ἐν τῷ ἱερῷ, ὅπου πάντες οἱ Ἰουδαῖοι συνέρχονται, καὶ ἐν κρυπτῷ ἐλάλησα οὐδέν. 18.21 τί με ἐρωτᾷς; ἐρώτησον τοὺς ἀκηκοότας τί ἐλάλησα αὐτοῖς· ἴδε οὗτοι οἴδασιν ἃ εἶπον ἐγώ.

18.22 ταῦτα δὲ αὐτοῦ εἰπόντος εἷς παρεστηκὼς τῶν ὑπηρετῶν ἔδωκεν ῥάπισμα τῷ Ἰησοῦ εἰπών, οὕτως ἀποκρίνῃ τῷ ἀρχιερεῖ;

18.23 ὁ δὲ Ἰησοῦς εἶπεν αὐτῷ, εἰ κακῶς ἐλάλησα, μαρτύρησον περὶ τοῦ κακοῦ· εἰ δὲ καλῶς, τί με δέρις; 18.24 ἀπέστιλεν δὲ αὐτὸν ὁ Ἄννας δεδεμένον πρὸς Καϊάφαν τὸν ἀρχιερέα. 18.25 ἦν δὲ Σίμων Πέτρος ἑστὼς καὶ θερμαινόμενος. εἶπον οὖν αὐτῷ, μὴ καὶ σὺ ἐκ τῶν μαθητῶν αὐτοῦ εἶ; ἠρνήσατο

into the sheath; the cup which the father has given to me, should I not certainly drink it? 18.12 Then the cohort of soldiers and the chiliarch/captain and the servants/assistants of the Judeans took Jesus and bound him 18.13 and they led *him* first to Annas; for he was the father-in-law of Caiaphas, who was high priest of that year; 18.14 but Caiaphas was the (one) having counselled/plotted with the Judeans that it is beneficial *for* one man to die in behalf of the people. 18.15 And Simon Peter and the other learner/pupil were following with/after Jesus. And that learner/pupil was known to the high priest, and he went in with Jesus into the court/yard of the high priest, 18.16 but Peter had stood outside near the door. Then the other learner/pupil, who was known to the high priest, went out and spoke to the doorkeeper and brought Peter in. 18.17 Then the maidservant, the doorkeeper, says to Peter: You, are you not also from the learners/-pupils of this man? That (one) says: I am not. 18.18 And both the slaves and the servants/assistants had stood *there* , having built a mass of coals, because it was cold, and they were warming themselves; and Peter, having also stood with them, was warming himself. 18.19 Then the high priest questioned Jesus about his learners/pupils and about his doctrine/ teaching. 18.20 And Jesus answered to him: I, I have spoken freely/plainly to the world; I always taught in a congregation and in the *outer* temple, where all the Judeans come together, and I spoke nothing in secret. 18.21 Why *do* you ask me? Ask the (ones) having heard what I spoke to them; behold, they, they know what (things) I, I said.

18.22 And from him having said these (things), one of the servants/assistants having been present gave a hand-slap to Jesus, saying: Should you so answer to the high priest?

18.23 But Jesus said to him: If I spoke badly, you testify concerning the bad/evil; but if well, why *do* you beat me? 18.24 But Annas sent him, having been bound, to Caiaphas the high priest. 18.25 And Simon Peter was standing *there* and warming himself. Then they said to him: You, are you not also out of the

ἐκεῖνος καὶ εἶπεν, οὐκ εἰμί. 18.26 λέγει εἷς ἐκ τῶν δούλων τοῦ ἀρχιερέως, συγγενὴς ὢν οὗ ἀπέκοψεν Πέτρος τὸ ὠτίον, οὐκ ἐγώ σε ἶδον ἐν τῷ κήπῳ μετ' αὐτοῦ; 18.27 πάλιν οὖν ἠρνήσατο ὁ Πέτρος· καὶ εὐθέως ἀλέκτωρ ἐφώνησεν. 18.28 ἄγουσιν οὖν τὸν Ἰησοῦν ἀπὸ τοῦ Καϊάφα εἰς τὸ πραιτώριον· ἦν δὲ πρωΐ· καὶ αὐτοὶ οὐκ εἰσῆλθον εἰς τὸ πραιτώριον, ἵνα μὴ μιανθῶσιν ἀλλὰ φάγωσιν τὸ πάσχα. 18.29 ἐξῆλθεν οὖν πρὸς αὐτοὺς ὁ Πιλᾶτος ἔξω καὶ φησίν, τίνα κατηγορίαν φέρετε τοῦ ἀνθρώπου τούτου; 18.30 ἀπεκρίθησαν καὶ εἶπαν αὐτῷ, εἰ μὴ ἦν οὗτος κακὸν ποιήσας, οὐκ ἄν σοι παρεδώκειμεν αὐτόν. 18.31 εἶπεν οὖν αὐτοῖς ὁ Πιλᾶτος, λάβετε αὐτὸν ὑμεῖς, καὶ κατὰ τὸν νόμον ὑμῶν κρίνατε αὐτόν. εἶπον οὖν αὐτῷ οἱ Ἰουδαῖοι, ἡμῖν οὐκ ἔξεστιν ἀποκτῖναι οὐδένα· 18.32 ἵνα ὁ λόγος τοῦ Ἰησοῦ πληρωθῇ ὃν εἶπεν σημαίνων ποίῳ θανάτῳ ἤμελλεν ἀποθνήσκιν. 18.33 εἰσῆλθεν οὖν εἰς τὸ πραιτώριον πάλιν ὁ Πιλᾶτος καὶ ἐφώνησεν τὸν Ἰησοῦν καὶ εἶπεν αὐτῷ, σὺ εἶ ὁ βασιλεὺς τῶν Ἰουδαίων; 18.34 ἀπεκρίθη αὐτῷ ὁ Ἰησοῦς, ἀπὸ σεαυτοῦ σὺ τοῦτο λέγις ἢ ἄλλοι σοι εἶπόν περὶ ἐμοῦ; 18.35 ἀπεκρίθη ὁ Πιλᾶτος, μήτι ἐγὼ Ἰουδαῖός εἰμι; τὸ ἔθνος τὸ σὸν καὶ οἱ ἀρχιερεῖς παρέδωκάν σε ἐμοί· τί ἐποίησας; 18.36 ἀπεκρίθη Ἰησοῦς, ἡ ἐμὴ βασιλεία οὐκ ἔστιν ἐκ τοῦ κόσμου τούτου· εἰ ἐκ τοῦ κόσμου τούτου ἦν ἡ ἐμὴ βασιλία, καὶ οἱ ὑπηρέται οἱ ἐμοὶ ἠγωνίζοντο ἄν, ἵνα μὴ παραδοθῶ τοῖς Ἰουδαίοις· νῦν δὲ ἡ ἐμὴ βασιλεία οὐκ ἔστιν ἐντεῦθεν. 18.37 εἶπεν οὖν αὐτῷ ὁ Πιλᾶτος, οὐκοῦν βασιλεὺς εἶ σύ; ἀπεκρίθη ὁ Ἰησοῦς, σὺ λέγεις ὅτι βασιλεύς εἰμι. ἐγὼ εἰς τοῦτο γεγέννημαι καὶ εἰς τοῦτο ἐλήλυθα εἰς τὸν κόσμον, ἵνα μαρτυρήσω τῇ ἀληθίᾳ· πᾶς ὁ ὢν τῆς ἀληθίας ἀκούει μου τῆς φωνῆς. 18.38 λέγει αὐτῷ ὁ Πιλᾶτος, τίς ἐστιν ἀλήθεια;

καὶ τοῦτο εἰπὼν πάλιν ἐξῆλθεν πρὸς τοὺς Ἰουδαίους, καὶ λέγει αὐτοῖς, ἐγὼ οὐδεμίαν αἰτίαν εὑρίσκω ἐν αὐτῷ. 18.39 ἔστιν

learners/pupils of him? That (one) denied *it* and said: I am not. 18.26 One out of the slaves of the high priest, being a relative of *the one* of whom Peter cut off the ear, says: I, did I not see you in the garden with him? 18.27 Then Peter denied *it* again; and immediately a cock sounded/crowed. 18.28 Then they lead Jesus away from Caiaphas into the praetorium/ palace guard; and it was early in the morning; and they, they entered not into the praetorium, in order that they might not be defiled, but might eat the Passover (lamb). 18.29 Then Pilate went outside to them and says: What accusation/charge do ye bring of this man? 18.30 They answered and said to him: Except this (one) was doing evil/bad, indeed we would not have delivered him to you. 18.31 Therefore Pilate said to them: Ye, ye take him, and ye judge him according to your law. Then the Judeans said to him: It is not lawful for us to kill no one; 18.32 in order that the saying/word of Jesus which he said signifying by what sort of death he was about to die might be fulfilled. 18.33 Then Pilate entered again into the praetorium and called Jesus and said to him: You, are you the king of the Judeans? 18.34 Jesus answered to him: You, *do* you say this from yourself, or did others say it to you about me? 18.35 Pilate answered: I, I am not a Judean, *am I*? Your nation/ethnic *group* and the high priests delivered you to me; what did you *do*? 18.36 Jesus answered: My kingdom is not from/out of this world; if my kingdom were from/out of this world, my servants/assistants also would have fought/struggled, in order that I might not be delivered up to the Judeans; but now my kingdom is not from here. 18.37 Therefore Pilate said to him: You then, are you not a king? Jesus answered: You, you say that I am a king. I, I have been generated/born to/for this, and to/for this I have come into the world, in order that I might testify to the truth; every one being of the truth hears my voice. 18.38 Pilate says to him: Who/what is truth?

And having said this, he went out again to the Judeans, and he says to them: I, I find no cause for accusation in him. 18.39 But there is a custom for ye

δὲ συνήθια ὑμῖν ἵνα ἕνα ἀπολύσω ὑμῖν ἐν τῷ πάσχα· βούλεσθε οὖν ἵνα ἀπολύσω ὑμῖν τὸν βασιλέα τῶν Ἰουδαίων; 18.40 ἐκραύγασαν οὖν πάλιν λέγοντες, μὴ τοῦτον ἀλλὰ τὸν Βαραββᾶν. ἦν δὲ ὁ Βαραββᾶς λῃστής. 19.1 τότε οὖν λαβὼν ὁ Πιλᾶτος τὸν Ἰησοῦν ἐμαστίγωσεν. 19.2 καὶ οἱ στρατιῶται πλέξαντες στέφανον ἐξ ἀκανθῶν ἐπέθηκαν αὐτοῦ τῇ κεφαλῇ, καὶ ἱμάτιον πορφυροῦν περιέβαλον αὐτόν, 19.3 καὶ ἤρχοντο πρὸς αὐτὸν καὶ ἔλεγον, χαῖρε, βασιλεῦ τῶν Ἰουδαίων· καὶ ἐδίδοσαν αὐτῷ ῥαπίσματα. 19.4 ἐξῆλθεν πάλιν ὁ Πιλᾶτος ἔξω καὶ λέγει αὐτοῖς, ἴδε ἄγω ὑμῖν αὐτὸν ἔξω, ἵνα γνῶτε ὅτι αἰτίαν οὐδεμίαν εὑρίσκω ἐν αὐτῷ. 19.5 ἐξῆλθεν οὖν ὁ Ἰησοῦς ἔξω, φορῶν τὸν ἀκάνθινον στέφανον καὶ τὸ πορφυροῦν ἱμάτιον. καὶ λέγει αὐτοῖς, ἰδοὺ ὁ ἄνθρωπος. 19.6 ὅτε οὖν ἴδον αὐτὸν οἱ ἀρχιερεῖς καὶ οἱ ὑπηρέται ἐκραύγασαν, σταύρωσον σταύρωσον αὐτόν. καὶ λέγει αὐτοῖς ὁ Πιλᾶτος, λάβετε αὐτὸν ὑμεῖς καὶ σταυρώσατε, ἐγὼ γὰρ οὐχ εὑρίσκω ἐν αὐτῷ αἰτίαν. 19.7 ἀπεκρίθησαν οἱ Ἰουδαῖοι, ἡμεῖς νόμον ἔχομεν, καὶ κατὰ τὸν νόμον ὀφίλει ἀποθανῖν, ὅτι υἱὸν θεοῦ ἑαυτὸν ἐποίησεν. 19.8 ὅτε οὖν ἤκουσεν ὁ Πιλᾶτος τὸν λόγον τοῦτον, μᾶλλον ἐφοβήθη, 19.9 καὶ εἰσῆλθεν εἰς τὸ πραιτώριον πάλιν καὶ λέγει τῷ Ἰησοῦ, πόθεν εἶ σύ; ὁ δὲ Ἰησοῦς ἀπόκρισιν οὐκ ἔδωκεν αὐτῷ. 19.10 λέγει οὖν αὐτῷ ὁ Πιλᾶτος, ἐμοὶ οὐ λαλῖς; οὐκ οἶδας ὅτι ἐξουσίαν ἔχω ἀπολῦσαί σε καὶ ἐξουσίαν ἔχω σταυρῶσαί σε; 19.11 ἀπεκρίθη αὐτῷ ὁ Ἰησοῦς, οὐκ ἔχις ἐξουσίαν κατ᾽ ἐμοῦ οὐδεμίαν εἰ μὴ ἦν δεδομένον σοι ἄνωθεν· διὰ τοῦτο ὁ παραδούς μέ σοι μείζονα ἁμαρτίαν ἔχει. 19.12 ἐκ τούτου ὁ Πιλᾶτος ἐζήτει ἀπολῦσαι αὐτόν· οἱ δὲ Ἰουδαῖοι ἔλεγον, ἐὰν τοῦτον ἀπολύσῃς, οὐκ εἶ φίλος τοῦ Καίσαρος· πᾶς ὁ βασιλέα ἑαυτὸν ποιῶν ἀντιλέγει τῷ Καίσαρι.

19.13 ὁ οὖν Πειλᾶτος ἀκούσας τῶν λόγων τούτων ἤγαγεν ἔξω τὸν Ἰησοῦν, καὶ ἐκάθισεν ἐπὶ βήματος εἰς τόπον λεγόμενον λιθόστρωτον, Ἑβραϊστὶ Γαββαθα.

that I might release one for ye in/at the Passover; therefore, will ye that I might release the king of the Judeans for ye? 18.40 Then they cried aloud again, saying: Not this (one), but Barabbas. But Barabbas was a robber. 19.1 Therefore at that time, Pilate, having taken Jesus, he scourged/flogged *him*. 19.2 And the soldiers, having plaited a crown/wreath out of thorns, they placed it upon his head, and they threw a purple garment around him, 19.3 and they were coming near him and saying: Greetings, king of the Judeans; and they were giving slaps/blows to him. 19.4 Pilate went outside again and says to them: Behold, I bring him out to ye, in order that ye might know that I find not a cause for accusation in him. 19.5 Therefore Jesus went outside, wearing the thorny crown and a purple garment. And he says to them: Behold the man/human. 19.6 Then, when the high priests and the servants/assistants saw him, they cried aloud: You crucify *him*, you crucify *him*! And Pilate says to them: Ye, ye take him and ye crucify *him*, for I, I find not a reason/cause in him. 19.7 The Judeans answered: We, we have a law, and according to the law he ought to die, because he made himself a son of God. 19.8 Therefore, when Pilate heard this saying/word, he was more afraid, 19.9 and he entered into the praetorium again and says to Jesus: You, from where are you? But Jesus gave not an answer to him. 19.10 Then Pilate says to him: *Do* you not speak to me? *Do* you not know that I hold authority to release you and I hold authority to crucify you? 19.11 Jesus answered to him: You held not any authority against me, except it had been given to you from above; because of this, the (one) having delivered/betrayed me to you has a greater sin. 19.12 From this *time* Pilate was seeking to release him; but the Judeans were saying: If you might/should release this (one), you are not a friend of Caesar; every one making himself a king speaks against Caesar.

19.13 Therefore Pilate, having heard these sayings/words, brought Jesus outside, and he sat upon a judgment seat in a place being called a stone pavement, in Hebrew, Gabbatha.

19.14 ἦν δὲ παρασκευὴ τοῦ πάσχα, ὥρα ἦν ὡς ἕκτη. καὶ λέγει τοῖς Ἰουδαίοις, ἴδε ὁ βασιλεὺς ὑμῶν. 19.15 ἐκραύγασαν οὖν ἐκῖνοι, ἆρον ἆρον, σταύρωσον αὐτόν. λέγει αὐτοῖς ὁ Πιλᾶτος, τὸν βασιλέα ὑμῶν σταυρώσω; ἀπεκρίθησαν οἱ ἀρχιερεῖς, οὐκ ἔχομεν βασιλέα εἰ μὴ Καίσαρα. 19.16 τότε οὖν παρέδωκεν αὐτοῖς αὐτὸν ἵνα σταυρωθῇ.

οἱ δὲ λάβοντες τὸν Ἰησοῦν· 19.17 ἀπήγαγον αὐτὸν καὶ βαστάζων ἑαυτῷ τὸν σταυρὸν ἐξῆλθεν εἰς τὸν λεγόμενον κρανίου τόπον, ὃ λέγεται Ἑβραϊστὶ γολγοθα, 19.18 ὅπου αὐτὸν ἐσταύρωσαν, καὶ μετ᾽ αὐτοῦ ἄλλους δύο ἐντεῦθεν καὶ ἐντεῦθεν, μέσον δὲ τὸν Ἰησοῦν. 19.19 ἔγραψεν δὲ καὶ τίτλον ὁ Πιλᾶτος καὶ ἔθηκεν ἐπὶ τοῦ σταυροῦ· ἦν δὲ γεγραμμένον, Ἰησοῦς ὁ Ναζωραῖος ὁ βασιλεὺς τῶν Ἰουδαίων. 19.20 τοῦτον οὖν τὸν τίτλον πολλοὶ ἀνέγνωσαν τῶν Ἰουδαίων, ὅτι ἐγγὺς ἦν ὁ τόπος τῆς πόλεως ὅπου ἐσταυρώθη ὁ Ἰησοῦς· καὶ ἦν γεγραμμένον Ἑβραϊστί, Ῥωμαϊστί, Ἑλληνιστί. 19.21 ἔλεγον οὖν τῷ Πειλάτῳ οἱ ἀρχιερεῖς τῶν Ἰουδαίων, μὴ γράφε, ὁ βασιλεὺς τῶν Ἰουδαίων, ἀλλ᾽ ὅτι ἐκεῖνος εἶπεν, βασιλεύς εἰμι τῶν Ἰουδαίων. 19.22 ἀπεκρίθη ὁ Πιλᾶτος, ὃ γέγραφα, γέγραφα. 19.23 οἱ οὖν στρατιῶται οἱ σταυρώσαντες τὸν Ἰησοῦν ἔλαβον τὰ ἱμάτια αὐτοῦ καὶ ἐποίησαν τέσσαρα μέρη, ἑκάστῳ στρατιώτῃ μέρος, καὶ τὸν χιτῶνα. ἦν δὲ ὁ χιτὼν ἄραφος, ἐκ τῶν ἄνωθεν ὑφαντὸς δι᾽ ὅλου. 19.24 εἶπαν οὖν πρὸς αὐτούς, μὴ σχίσωμεν αὐτόν, ἀλλὰ λάχωμεν περὶ αὐτοῦ τίνος ἔσται· ἵνα ἡ γραφὴ πληρωθῇ, « διεμερίσαντό μου τὰ ἱμάτιά ἑαυτοῖς καὶ ἐπὶ τὸν ἱματισμόν μου ἔβαλον κλῆρον.» οἱ μὲν οὖν στρατιῶται ταῦτα ἐποίησαν. 19.25 εἱστήκισαν δὲ παρὰ τῷ σταυρῷ τοῦ Ἰησοῦ ἡ μήτηρ αὐτοῦ καὶ ἡ ἀδελφὴ τῆς μητρὸς αὐτοῦ, Μαριὰμ ἡ τοῦ Κλωπᾶ καὶ Μαριὰμ ἡ Μαγδαληνή. 19.26 Ἰησοῦς δὲ ἰδὼν τὴν μητέρα καὶ τὸν μαθητὴν παρεστῶτα ὃν ἠγάπα, καὶ λέγει τῇ μητρί, γύναι, ἰδοὺ ὁ υἱός σου. 19.27 εἶτα λέγει τῷ μαθητῇ, εἴδε ἡ μήτηρ σου. καὶ ἀπ᾽ ἐκίνης τῆς

19.14   And it was Friday/preparation of the Passover, it was about *the* sixth hour. And he says to the Judeans: Behold your king.   19.15 Then those cried aloud: Take away, take away, crucify him! Pilate says to them: Might/should I crucify your king? The high priests answered: We have not a king except Caesar. 19.16 Therefore at that time he delivered him over to them in order that he might be crucified.

And the (they), having taken/received Jesus, 19.17 they led him away, and carrying the cross for himself, he went forth to the place being named from a skull, which in Hebrew is called Golgotha,   19.18 where they crucified him and two others with him, two from here and from here/on this side and that side, and Jesus in the middle.   19.19 And Pilate also wrote a notice, and placed it over/upon the cross; and it had been written: Jesus the Nazarene, the King of the Judeans.   19.20 Therefore, many from the Judeans read this notice, because the place was near from the city, where Jesus was crucified; and it had been written in Hebrew, in Roman (Latin), and in Greek.   19.21   Then the high priests of the Judeans were saying to Pilate: Write not: The King of the Judeans, but that that (one) said: I am a king of the Judeans. 19.22   Pilate answered: What I have written, I have written.   19.23 Then the soldiers, the (ones) having crucified Jesus, took his garments and made four parts/shares, a part for each soldier, even the tunic. But the tunic/under thing was seamless, woven out of the (holes) from above through all.   19.24   Therefore they said to themselves: We should not split/divide it, but we should cast lots concerning whose it will be; in order that the writing might be fulfilled: THEY DIVIDED MY GARMENTS FOR THEMSELVES AND THEY THREW A LOT OVER/UP- ON/FOR MY CLOTHING. Indeed, then, the soldiers did these (things).   19.25 And his mother and her sister, Mary of Clopas, and Mary the Magdalene had stood beside the cross of Jesus.   19.26 And Jesus, having seen the mother and the learner/pupil whom he was loving having stood by, and he says to the mother: Woman, behold your son.   19.27 Then/next he says to the learner/pupil: Behold your mother. And from that

ὥρας ἔλαβεν αὐτὴν ὁ μαθητὴς εἰς τὰ ἴδια.

19.28 μετὰ τοῦτο εἰδὼς ὁ Ἰησοῦς ὅτι πάντα ἤδη τετέλεσται, ἵνα πληρωθῇ ἡ γραφή, λέγει, διψῶ. 19.29 σκεῦος δὲ ἔκειτο ὄξους μεστόν· σπόγγον οὖν μεστὸν τοῦ ὄξους ὑσσώπῳ περιθέντες προσήνεγκαν αὐτοῦ τῷ στόματι. 19.30 ὅτε οὖν ἔλαβεν τὸ ὄξος ὁ Ἰησοῦς εἶπεν, τετέλεσται· καὶ κλείνας τὴν κεφαλὴν παρέδωκεν τὸ πνεῦμα. 19.31 οἱ οὖν Ἰουδαῖοι, ἐπεὶ παρασκευὴ ἦν, ἵνα μὴ μίνῃ ἐπὶ τοῦ σταυροῦ τὰ σώματα ἐν τῷ σαββάτῳ, ἦν γὰρ μεγάλη ἡμέρα ἐκείνου τοῦ σαββάτου, ἠρώτησαν οὖν τὸν Πιλᾶτον ἵνα κατεαγῶσιν αὐτῶν τὰ σκέλη καὶ ἀρθῶσιν. 19.32 ἦλθον οὖν οἱ στρατιῶται, καὶ τοῦ μὲν πρώτου κατέαξαν τὰ σκέλη καὶ τοῦ ἄλλου τοῦ συνσταυρωθέντος αὐτῷ· 19.33 ἐπὶ δὲ τὸν Ἰησοῦν ἐλθόντες, ὡς εἶδον αὐτὸν ἤδη τεθνηκότα, καὶ οὐ κατέαξαν αὐτοῦ τὰ σκέλη, 19.34 ἀλλ᾽ εἷς τῶν στρατιωτῶν λόγχῃ αὐτοῦ τὴν πλευρὰν ἔνυξεν, καὶ ἐξῆλθεν εὐθὺς αἷμα καὶ ὕδωρ. 19.35 καὶ ὁ ἑωρακὼς μεμαρτύρηκεν, καὶ ἀληθὴς αὐτοῦ ἐστιν ἡ μαρτυρία, κἀκεῖνος οἶδεν ὅτι ἀληθῆ λέγει, ἵνα καὶ ὑμεῖς πιστεύητε. 19.36 ἐγένετο γὰρ ταῦτα ἵνα ἡ γραφὴ πληρωθῇ, « ὀστοῦν οὐ συντριβήσεται ἀπ᾽ αὐτοῦ.» 19.37 καὶ πάλιν ἑτέρα γραφὴ λέγει, « ὄψονται εἰς ὃν ἐξεκέντησαν.»

19.38 μετὰ δὲ ταῦτα ἠρώτησεν τὸν Πιλᾶτον Ἰωσὴφ ὁ ἀπὸ Ἁριμαθαίας, ὢν μαθητὴς τοῦ Ἰησοῦ κεκρυμμένος δὲ διὰ τὸν φόβον τῶν Ἰουδαίων, ἵνα ἄρῃ τὸ σῶμα τοῦ Ἰησοῦ· καὶ ἐπέτρεψεν ὁ Πιλᾶτος. ἦλθεν οὖν καὶ ἦρεν αὐτόν. 19.39 ἦλθεν δὲ καὶ Νικόδημος, ὁ ἐλθὼν πρὸς τὸν Ἰησοῦν νυκτὸς τὸ πρῶτον, φέρων μίγμας σμύρνης καὶ ἀλόης ὡς λίτρας ἑκατόν. 19.40 ἔλαβον οὖν τὸ σῶμα τοῦ Ἰησοῦ καὶ ἔδησαν αὐτὸ ὀθονίοις μετὰ τῶν ἀρωμάτων, καθὼς ἔθος ἐστὶν τοῖς Ἰουδαίοις ἐνταφιάζειν.

19.41 ἦν δὲ ἐν τῷ τόπῳ ὅπου ἐσταυρώθη κῆπος, καὶ ἐν τῷ

hour the learner/pupil took/received her into the
(things) his own.

19.28 Jesus, knowing after this that all had now
been finished, in order that the writing might be
fulfilled, he says: I thirst. 19.29 And a vessel full
of sour wine was setting *there*; therefore, having put
a sponge full of sour wine around a hyssop stalk, they
brought it to his mouth. 19.30 Then, when he received
the sour wine, Jesus said: It has been finished; and
having reclined/bent down the head, he delivered up
the spirit. 19.31 Then, since it was Friday/prepara-
tion (day), in order that the bodies might not stay on
the cross in/on the sabbath, for it was a great day
of/from that sabbath, the Judeans therefore asked/pe-
titioned Pilate that their legs might be broken and
they might be removed. 19.32 Therefore, the soldiers
came and they indeed broke the legs of the first (one)
and of the other having been crucified with him;
19.33 but having come to Jesus, since they saw him
having died already, and they broke not the legs of
him, 19.34 but one of the soldiers pierced his side
with a spear, and there immediately came out blood and
water. 19.35 And the one having seen has testified,
and his testimony is true, and that (one) knows that
he speaks truly, that ye, ye also may believe. 19.36
For these (things) happened in order that the writing
might be fulfilled: A BONE WILL NOT BE BROKEN FROM
HIM. 19.37 And again another/different writing says:
THEY WILL LOOK TO *the one* WHOM THEY PIERCED.

19.38 And after these (things), Joseph from
Arimathaea, being a learner/pupil of Jesus, but having
been so in secret because of the fear of the Judeans,
asked Pilate that he might remove the body of Jesus;
and Pilate permitted *him*. Therefore, he went and
removed him. 19.39 And Nicodemus, the (one) having
come to Jesus at night the first *time*, went also,
carrying a mixture of myrrh and aloes, about a hundred
libra (75 lbs). 19.40 Then they took the body of
Jesus and bound it in linen wrappings with the spices,
as it is a custom for the Judeans to entomb/bury.

19.41 And there was a garden in/at the place
where he was crucified, and in the garden *was* a new

242

κήπῳ μνημῖον καινὸν ἐν ᾧ οὐδὶς οὐδέπω ἦν τεθειμένος· 19.42 ἐκεῖ οὖν διὰ τὴν παρασκευὴν τῶν Ἰουδαίων, ὅτι ἐγγὺς ἦν τὸ μνημῖον, ἔθηκαν τὸν Ἰησοῦν.

20.1 Τῇ δὲ μιᾷ τῶν σαββάτων Μαριὰμ ἡ Μαγδαληνὴ ἔρχεται πρωῒ σκοτίας ἔτι οὔσης εἰς τὸ μνημεῖον, καὶ βλέπει τὸν λίθον ἠρμένον ἀπὸ τῆς θύρας ἐκ τοῦ μνημίου. 20.2 τρέχει οὖν καὶ ἔρχεται πρὸς τὸν Σίμωνα Πέτρον καὶ πρὸς τὸν ἄλλον μαθητὴν ὃν ἐφίλει ὁ Ἰησοῦς, καὶ λέγει αὐτοῖς, ἦραν τὸν κύριον ἐκ τοῦ μνημίου, καὶ οὐκ οἴδαμεν ποῦ ἔθηκαν αὐτόν. 20.3 ἐξῆλθεν οὖν ὁ Πέτρος καὶ ὁ ἄλλος μαθητής, καὶ ἤρχοντο εἰς τὸ μνημῖον. 20.4 ἔτρεχον δὲ οἱ δύο ὁμοῦ· καὶ ὁ ἄλλος μαθητὴς προέδραμεν δὲ τάχιον τοῦ Πέτρου καὶ ἦλθεν εἰς τὸ μνημῖον πρῶτος, 20.5 καὶ παρακύψας βλέπει τὰ ὀθόνια κείμενα, οὐ μέντοι εἰσῆλθεν. 20.6 ἔρχεται οὖν καὶ Σίμων Πέτρος ἀκολουθῶν αὐτῷ, καὶ εἰσῆλθεν εἰς τὸ μνημῖον· καὶ θεωρεῖ τὰ ὀθόνια κείμενα, 20.7 καὶ τὸ σουδάριον, ὃ ἦν ἐπὶ τῆς κεφαλῆς αὐτοῦ, οὐ μετὰ τῶν ὀθονίων κείμενον ἀλλὰ χωρὶς ἐντετυλιγμένον εἰς ἕνα τόπον. 20.8 τότε οὖν εἰσῆλθεν καὶ ὁ ἄλλος μαθητὴς ὁ ἐλθὼν πρῶτος εἰς τὸ μνημῖον, καὶ εἶδεν καὶ ἐπίστευσεν· 20.9 οὐδέπω γὰρ ᾔδεισαν τὴν γραφὴν ὅτι δεῖ αὐτὸν ἐκ νεκρῶν ἀναστῆναι.

20.10 ἀπῆλθον οὖν πάλιν πρὸς αὐτοὺς οἱ μαθηταί. 20.11 Μαριὰμ δὲ εἱστήκει ἐν τῷ μνημίῳ ἔξω κλαίουσα. ὡς οὖν ἔκλαιεν παρέκυψεν εἰς τὸ μνημῖον, 20.12 καὶ θεωρεῖ δύο ἀγγέλους καθεζομένους ἐν λευκοῖς, ἕνα πρὸς τῇ κεφαλῇ καὶ ἕνα πρὸς τοῖς ποσίν, ὅπου ἔκειτο τὸ σῶμα τοῦ Ἰησοῦ. 20.13 λέγουσιν αὐτῇ ἐκεῖνοι, γύναι, τί κλαίεις; λέγει αὐτοῖς ὅτι ἦραν τὸν κύριόν μου, καὶ οὐκ οἶδα ποῦ ἔθηκαν αὐτόν.

20.14 ταῦτα εἰποῦσα ἐστράφη εἰς τὰ ὀπίσω, καὶ θεωρεῖ τὸν Ἰησοῦν ἑστῶτα, καὶ οὐκ ᾔδει ὅτι Ἰησοῦς ἐστιν. 20.15 λέγει αὐτῇ Ἰησοῦς, γύναι, τί κλαίεις; τίνα ζητεῖς; ἐκείνη δὲ δοκοῦσα ὅτι ὁ

tomb in which no one had not yet been placed; 19.42 therefore, because of the preparation (day) of the Judeans, they placed/put Jesus *there*, because the tomb was near.

20.1 And on the first day of the weeks/sabbaths, Mary the Magdalene comes early in the morning, darkness still being, to the tomb, and she sees the stone having been removed from the door of/from the tomb. 20.2 She runs therefore and goes to Simon Peter and to the other learner/pupil whom Jesus was loving, and she says to them: They took the Lord out of the tomb, and we know not where they put him. 20.3 Then Peter and the other learner/pupil went out, and were going to the tomb. 20.4 And the two were running together; and the other learner/pupil ran ahead and more quickly than Peter and he went to the tomb first, 20.5 and having stooped over he sees the linen wrappings lying, but he did not enter. 20.6 Then Simon Peter also comes, following him, and he entered into the tomb; and he beholds the linen wrappings lying, 20.7 and the face cloth, which was over his head, not lying with the linen wrappings but having been folded up apart from *them* in one place. 20.8 Then the other learner/pupil also entered/went in, the (one) having come first to the tomb, and he saw and believed; 20.9 for they not yet knew the writing that it is necessary for him to arise out of dead (ones).
20.10 Then the learners/pupils went away again to themselves. 20.11 But Mary had stood by the tomb, weeping outside. Then as she was weeping, she stooped over into the tomb, 20.12 and she beholds two messengers/angels sitting in white (things), one near the head and one near the feet, where the body of Jesus was lying. 20.13 Those say to her: Woman, why *do* you weep? She says to them: They took my Lord, and I know not where they put him.
20.14 Having said these (things) she turned to the (things) behind, and she observes/beholds Jesus having stood *there*, and she knew not that it is Jesus. 20.15 Jesus says to her: Woman, why *do* you weep? Whom *do* you seek? And that (woman), supposing that he is

243

κηπουρός ἐστιν λέγει αὐτῷ, κύριε, εἰ σὺ ἐβάστασας αὐτόν, εἰπέ μοι ποῦ ἔθηκας αὐτόν, κἀγὼ αὐτὸν ἀρῶ. 20.16 λέγει αὐτῇ ὁ Ἰησοῦς, Μαριάμ. στραφεῖσα δὲ ἐκείνη λέγει αὐτῷ Ἑβραϊστί, ῥαββουνί, ὃ λέγεται διδάσκαλε. 20.17 λέγει αὐτῇ ὁ Ἰησοῦς, μή μου ἅπτου, οὔπω γὰρ ἀναβέβηκα πρὸς τὸν πατέρα· πορεύου δὲ πρὸς τοὺς ἀδελφούς μου καὶ εἰπὲ αὐτοῖς, ἰδοὺ ἀναβαίνω πρὸς τὸν πατέρα μου καὶ πατέρα ὑμῶν καὶ θεόν μου καὶ θεὸν ὑμῶν. 20.18 ἔρχεται Μαριὰμ ἡ Μαγδαληνὴ ἀγγέλλουσα τοῖς μαθηταῖς ὅτι ἑώρακα τὸν κύριον, καὶ ταῦτα εἶπεν αὐτῇ. 20.19 οὔσης οὖν ὀψίας τῇ ἡμέρᾳ ἐκείνῃ τῇ μιᾷ σαββάτων, καὶ τῶν θυρῶν κεκλισμένων ὅπου ἦσαν οἱ μαθηταὶ διὰ τὸν φόβον τῶν Ἰουδαίων, ἦλθεν ὁ Ἰησοῦς καὶ ἔστη εἰς τὸ μέσον καὶ λέγει αὐτοῖς, ἰρήνη ὑμῖν. 20.20 καὶ τοῦτο εἰπὼν ἔδιξεν τὰς χῖρας καὶ τὴν πλευρὰν αὐτοῖς. ἐχάρησαν οὖν οἱ μαθηταὶ ἰδόντες τὸν κύριον. 20.21 εἶπεν οὖν αὐτοῖς πάλιν, εἰρήνη ὑμῖν· καθὼς ἀπέσταλκέν με ὁ πατήρ, κἀγὼ πέμπω ὑμᾶς. 20.22 καὶ τοῦτο εἰπὼν ἐνεφύσησεν καὶ λέγει αὐτοῖς, λάβετε πνεῦμα ἅγιον· 20.23 ἄν τινων ἀφῆται τὰς ἁμαρτίας ἀφέθήσεται αὐτοῖς, ἐὰν δέ τινων κρατῆνται κεκράτηνται. 20.24 Θωμᾶς δὲ εἷς ἐκ τῶν δώδεκα, ὁ λεγόμενος Δίδυμος, οὐκ ἦν μετ' αὐτῶν ὅτε ἦλθεν Ἰησοῦς. 20.25 ἔλεγον οὖν αὐτῷ οἱ ἄλλοι μαθηταί, ἑωράκαμεν τὸν κύριον. ὁ δὲ εἶπεν αὐτοῖς, ἐὰν μὴ εἴδω ἐν ταῖς χερσὶν αὐτοῦ τὸν τύπον τῶν ἥλων καὶ βάλω μου τὸν δάκτυλόν εἰς ἥ χεῖραν αὐτοῦ καὶ βάλω μου τὴν χεῖρα εἰς τὴν πλευρὰν αὐτοῦ, οὐ μὴ πιστεύσω. 20.26 καὶ μετ' ἡμέρας ὀκτὼ πάλιν ἦσαν ἔσω οἱ μαθηταὶ καὶ Θωμᾶς μετ' αὐτῶν.

ἔρχεται ὁ Ἰησοῦς τῶν θυρῶν κεκλισμένων, καὶ ἔστη εἰς τὸ μέσον καὶ εἶπεν, ἰρήνη ὑμῖν. 20.27 εἶτα λέγει τῷ Θωμᾷ, φέρε τὸν δάκτυλόν σου ὧδε καὶ ἴδε τὰς χεῖράς μου, καὶ φέρε τὴν χεῖρά σου καὶ βάλε εἰς τὴν πλευράν μου, καὶ μὴ γίνου ἄπιστος ἀλλὰ πιστός. 20.28 ἀπεκρίθη Θωμᾶς καὶ εἶπεν αὐτῷ, ὁ κύριός

the gardener, she says to him: Lord/sir, if you, you removed him, say to me where you put him, and I, I shall take him away.

20.16 Jesus says to her: Mary! And that (woman) having been turned, she says to him in Hebrew: Rabboni, which is said: Teacher. 20.17 Jesus says to her: Touch you not of me, for I have not yet ascended to the father; but you go to the brothers of me and you speak to them: Behold, I go up/ascend to the father of me/my father and a father of ye/your father, both my God and your God.

20.18 Mary the Magdalene comes, reporting to the learners/pupils that she has seen the Lord, and he said these (things) to her. 20.19 Then, from it being late for/on that day, on the one (first) of sabbaths/weeks, and from the doors having been shut where the learners/pupils were, because of the fear of the Judeans, Jesus came and stood in the midst and says to them: Peace to ye. 20.20 And having said this, he showed the hands and the side to them. Then the learners/pupils rejoiced, having seen the Lord. 20.21 Therefore/then he said to them again: Peace to ye; even as the father sent me, I also send ye. 20.22 And having said this, he breathed in/blew breath and says to them: Receive ye a holy spirit. 20.23 Of whom ever ye would dismiss/forgive the sins, it will be forgiven for them, and of whom ever ye would hold fast, they have been held fast. 20.24 But Thomas, one out of the twelve, the (one) being called a twin, was not with them then when Jesus came. 20.25 Therefore, the other learners/pupils were saying to him: We have seen the Lord. But the (he) said to them: Unless I might see the mark of the nails in his hands and might put my finger into his hand and might put my hand into his side, by no means shall I believe. 20.26 And after eight days, the learners/pupils were again inside, and Thomas *was* with them.

From the doors having been shut, Jesus comes and stands in the midst and he says: Peace to ye. 20.27 Next he says to Thomas: Bring you finger here and see my hands, and bring your hand and put *it* into my side, and become not unfaithful but faithful. 20.28 Thomas

μου καὶ ὁ θεός μου. 20.29 εἶπεν δὲ αὐτῷ ὁ Ἰησοῦς, ὅτι ἑώρακάς με πεπίστευκας; μακάριοι οἱ μὴ ἰδόντες καὶ πιστεύσαντες. 20.30 πολλὰ μὲν οὖν καὶ ἄλλα σημεῖα ἐποίησεν ὁ Ἰησοῦς ἐνώπιον τῶν μαθητῶν αὐτοῦ, ἃ οὐκ ἔστιν γεγραμμένα ἐν τῷ βιβλίῳ τούτῳ· 20.31 ταῦτα δὲ γέγραπται ἵνα πιστεύσητε ὅτι Ἰησοῦς ἐστιν ὁ χριστὸς ὁ υἱὸς τοῦ θεοῦ, καὶ ἵνα πιστεύοντες ζωὴν αἰώνιον ἔχητε ἐν τῷ ὀνόματι αὐτοῦ.

21.1 Μετὰ ταῦτα ἐφανέρωσεν πάλιν ἑαυτὸν ὁ Ἰησοῦς τοῖς μαθηταῖς ἐπὶ τῆς θαλάσσης τῆς Τιβεριάδος· ἐφανέρωσεν δὲ οὕτως. 21.2 ἦσαν ὁμοῦ Σίμων Πέτρος καὶ Θωμᾶς ὁ λεγόμενος Δίδυμος καὶ Ναθαναὴλ ὁ ἀπὸ Κανὰ τῆς Γαλιλαίας καὶ οἱ υἱοὶ Ζεβεδαίου καὶ ἄλλοι ἐκ τῶν μαθητῶν αὐτοῦ δύο. 21.3 λέγει αὐτοῖς Σίμων Πέτρος, ὑπάγω ἁλιεύειν. λέγουσιν αὐτῷ, ἐρχόμεθα καὶ ἡμεῖς σὺν σοί. ἐξῆλθον οὖν καὶ ἐνέβησαν εἰς τὸ πλοῖον, καὶ ἐν ἐκίνῃ τῇ νυκτὶ ἐπίασαν οὐδέν. 21.4 πρωΐας δὲ ἤδη γενομένης ἔστη Ἰησοῦς ἐπὶ τὸν αἰγιαλόν· οὐ μέντοι ἔγνωσαν οἱ μαθηταὶ ὅτι Ἰησοῦς ἐστιν. 21.5 λέγει οὖν αὐτοῖς Ἰησοῦς, παιδία, μή τι προσφάγιον ἔχετε; ἀπεκρίθησαν αὐτῷ, οὔ. 21.6 λέγει αὐτοῖς, βάλετε εἰς τὰ δεξιὰ μέρη τοῦ πλοίου τὸ δίκτυον, καὶ εὑρήσετε. ἔβαλον οὖν, καὶ οὐκέτι αὐτὸ ἑλκύσαι ἴσχυον ἀπὸ τοῦ πλήθους τῶν ἰχθύων. 21.7 λέγει οὖν ὁ μαθητὴς ἐκεῖνος ὃν ἠγάπα ὁ Ἰησοῦς τῷ Πέτρῳ, ὁ κύριός ἐστιν. Σίμων οὖν Πέτρος, ἀκούσας ὅτι ὁ κύριός ἐστιν, τὸν ἐπενδύτην διεζώσατο, ἦν γὰρ γυμνός, καὶ ἔβαλεν ἑαυτὸν εἰς τὴν θάλασσαν· 21.8 οἱ δὲ ἄλλοι μαθηταὶ τῷ ἄλλῳ πλοιαρίῳ ἦλθον, οὐ γὰρ ἦσαν μακρὰν ἀπὸ τῆς γῆς ἀλλὰ ὡς ἀπὸ πηχῶν διακοσίων, σύροντες τὸ δίκτυον τῶν ἰχθύων. 21.9 ὡς οὖν ἀπέβησαν εἰς τὴν γῆν βλέπουσιν ἀνθρακιὰν κειμένην καὶ ὀψάριον ἐπικείμενον καὶ ἄρτον. 21.10 λέγει αὐτοῖς ὁ Ἰησοῦς, ἐνέγκατε ἀπὸ τῶν ὀψαρίων ὧν ἐπιάσατε νῦν.

answered and said to him: My Lord and my God. 20.29 Jesus said to him: Because you have seen me, have you also believed? Happy *are* the (ones) not having seen and having believed. 20.30 Then Jesus indeed did also many other signs before/in the presence of his learners/pupils, which is not having been written in this scroll; 20.31 but these (things) have been written in order that ye might believe that Jesus is the anointed (one), the son of God, and that believing, ye may have eternal life in/by his name.

21.1 After these (things) Jesus again revealed/ manifested himself to the learners/pupils on the sea of Tiberias; and he appeared thus. 21.2 They were together, Simon Peter and Thomas, the (one) being called a twin, and Nathanael, the (one) from Cana of Galilee, and the sons of Zebedee, and two others out of his learners/pupils.
21.3 Simon Peter says to them: I go to fish. They say to him: We, we also go with you. Therefore, they went forth and embarked in the boat, and they caught nothing in that night. 21.4 But from early morning already having become, Jesus stood on the shore; the learners/pupils, however, knew not that it is Jesus.
21.5 Then Jesus says to them: Children, have ye not anything to eat? They answered to him: No. 21.6 He says to them: Cast ye the net into the right *hand* parts from the boat, and ye will find *some*. Therefore they cast *it*, and they were no longer able to drag/ haul it from the multitudes of the fishes. 21.7 Then that learner/pupil whom Jesus was loving says to Peter: It is the Lord. Then Simon Peter, having heard that it is the Lord, girded the outer shirt around himself, for he was naked, and he threw himself into the sea; 21.8 but the other learners/pupils came in the little boat, for they were not far from the land but from about two hundred cubits, dragging the net of the fishes. 21.9 Then, as they disembarked to the land, they see a heap of coals lying, and a fish lying on *it*, and a loaf/bread. 21.10 Jesus says to them: Bring ye from the fishes which ye caught now.

21.11 ἐνέβη οὖν Σίμων Πέτρος καὶ εἵλκυσεν τὸ δίκτυον εἰς τὴν γῆν μεστὸν ἰχθύων μεγάλων ἑκατὸν πεντήκοντα τριῶν· καὶ τοσούτων ὄντων οὐκ ἐσχίσθη τὸ δίκτυον. 21.12 λέγει αὐτοῖς ὁ Ἰησοῦς, δεῦτε ἀριστήσατε. οὐδὶς δὲ ἐτόλμα τῶν μαθητῶν ἐξετάσαι αὐτόν, σὺ τίς εἶ; εἰδότες ὅτι ὁ κύριός ἐστιν. 21.13 ἔρχεται ὁ Ἰησοῦς καὶ λαμβάνει τὸν ἄρτον καὶ δίδωσιν αὐτοῖς, καὶ τὸ ὀψάριον ὁμοίως. 21.14 τοῦτο δὲ ἤδη τρίτον ἐφανερώθη ὁ Ἰησοῦς τοῖς μαθηταῖς ἐγερθεὶς ἐκ νεκρῶν. 21.15 ὅτε οὖν ἠρίστησαν λέγει τῷ Σίμωνι Πέτρῳ ὁ Ἰησοῦς, Σίμων Ἰωάννου, ἀγαπᾷς με πλέον τούτων; λέγει αὐτῷ, ναί, κύριε, σὺ οἶδας ὅτι φιλῶ σε. λέγει αὐτῷ, βόσκε τὰ ἀρνία μου. 21.16 πάλιν λέγει αὐτῷ τὸ δεύτερον, Σίμων Ἰωάννου, ἀγαπᾷς με; λέγει αὐτῷ, ναί, κύριε, σὺ οἶδας ὅτι φιλῶ σε. λέγει αὐτῷ, ποίμαινε τὰ πρόβατά μου. 21.17 λέγει αὐτῷ τὸ τρίτον, Σίμων Ἰωάννου, φιλεῖς με; ἐλυπήθη ὁ Πέτρος ὅτι εἶπεν αὐτῷ τὸ τρίτον, φιλεῖς με; καὶ λέγει αὐτῷ, κύριε, πάντα σὺ οἶδας, σὺ γινώσκεις ὅτι φιλῶ σε. λέγει αὐτῷ, βόσκε τὰ πρόβατά μου.

21.18 ἀμὴν ἀμὴν λέγω σοι, ὅτε ἦς νεώτερος, ἐζώννυες σεαυτὸν καὶ περιεπάτεις ὅπου ἤθελες· ὅταν δὲ γηράσῃς, ἐκτενεῖς τὰς χῖράς σου, καὶ ἄλλοι ζώσουσίν σε καὶ ἀποίσουσιν σε ὅπου οὐ θέλις. 21.19 τοῦτο δὲ εἶπεν σημαίνων ποίῳ θανάτῳ δοξάσει τὸν θεόν. καὶ τοῦτο εἰπὼν λέγει αὐτῷ, ἀκολούθι μοι. 21.20 ἐπιστραφεὶς δὲ ὁ Πέτρος βλέπι τὸν μαθητὴν ὃν ἠγάπα ὁ Ἰησοῦς ἀκολουθοῦντα, ὃς καὶ ἀνέπεσεν ἐν τῷ δείπνῳ ἐπὶ τὸ στῆθος αὐτοῦ καὶ εἶπεν, κύριε, τίς ἐστιν ὁ παραδιδούς σε; 21.21 τοῦτον οὖν ἰδὼν ὁ Πέτρος εἶπεν τῷ Ἰησοῦ, οὗτος δὲ τί; 21.22 λέγει αὐτῷ ὁ Ἰησοῦς, ἐὰν αὐτὸν θέλω μένιν ἕως ἔρχομαι, τί πρὸς σέ; σύ μοι ἀκολούθι. 21.23 ἐξῆλθεν οὖν οὗτος ὁ λόγος εἰς τοὺς ἀδελφοὺς ὅτι ὁ μαθητὴς ἐκεῖνος οὐκ ἀποθνήσκει. οὐκ εἶπεν δὲ αὐτῷ ὁ

21.11 Therefore Simon Peter embarked and dragged the net to the land, full of great fishes, a hundred fifty-three; and the net was not split/torn from *there* being so many. 21.12 Jesus says to them: Come, ye dine. And no one of the learners/pupils was daring to ask/interrogate him: You, who are you? Having known that he is the Lord. 21.13 Jesus comes and takes the loaf/bread and gives *it* to them, and the fish likewise. 21.14 And this *was* already a third (time) *that* Jesus, having been raised out of dead (ones), was revealed/manifested to the learners/pupils. 21.15 When they dined, Jesus then says to Simon Peter: Simon of John, *do* you love me more than these? He says to him: Yes, Lord, you, you know that I love you. He says to him: Feed/tend my lambs. 21.16 Again he says to him the second (time): Simon of John, *do* you love me? He says to him: Yes, Lord, you, you know that I love you. He says to him: Shepherd my sheep. 21.17 He says to him the third (time): Simon of John, *do* you love/ have affection for me? But Peter was grieved because he said also to him the third (time): *Do* you love/have affection for me? And he says to him: Lord, you, you know all; you, you know that I love you. And he says to him: Feed/tend my sheep.

21.18 Truly, truly I say to you, when you was younger, you was dressing/girding yourself and walking where you were wanting/wishing; but when you might become old, you will stretch forth your hands, and others will dress/gird you and will carry/bear you away where you want/wish not. 21.19 And he said this indicating by what kind of death he will glorify God. And having said this, he says to him: Follow with me. 21.20 And having been turned, Peter sees the learner/ pupil whom Jesus was loving following, who also reclined upon his breast at the supper, and he says: Lord, who is the (one) delivering/betraying you? 21.21 Then Peter, having seen this (one), said to Jesus: And what *is* this (one)? 21.22 Jesus says to him: If I will/wish *for* him to abide/remain until I come, what *is it* to you? You, you follow with me. 21.23 Therefore this saying/word went forth to the brothers that that pupil/learner dies not. But Jesus

Ἰησοῦς ὅτι οὐκ ἀποθνήσκει, ἀλλ᾽, ἐὰν αὐτὸν θέλω μένειν ἕως ἔρχομαι, τί πρὸς σέ; 21.24 οὗτός ἐστιν ὁ μαθητὴς ὁ μαρτυρῶν περὶ τούτων καὶ γράψας ταῦτα, καὶ οἴδαμεν ὅτι ἀληθὴς ἐστίν ἡ μαρτυρία αὐτοῦ .

21.25 ἔστιν δὲ καὶ ἄλλα πολλὰ ἃ ἐποίησεν ὁ Ἰησοῦς, ἅτινα ἐὰν γράφηται καθ᾽ ἕν, οὐδ᾽ αὐτὸν οἶμαι τὸν κόσμον χωρῆσειν τὰ γραφόμενα βιβλία.

Εὐαγγέλιον κατα Ἰωάννην

said not to him that he dies not, but: If I will/wish *for* him to abide/remain until I come, what *is it* to you? 21.24 This (one) is the learner/pupil testifying about these (things) and having written these (things), and we know that the testimony/witness of him is true. 21.25 And there is also many other (things) which Jesus did, which if it were written one by one, I suppose the world itself had not room for the scrolls being written.

A Good Message According to John

ΠΡΟΣ ΡΩΜΑΙΟΥΣ

This is the Sinaitic New Testament, book of Romans.

1.1 Παῦλος δοῦλος Ἰησοῦ χριστοῦ, κλητὸς ἀπόστολος, ἀφωρισμένος εἰς εὐαγγέλιον θεοῦ, 1.2 ὃ προεπηγγίλατο διὰ τῶν προφητῶν αὐτοῦ ἐν γραφαῖς ἁγίαις, 1.3 περὶ τοῦ υἱοῦ αὐτοῦ τοῦ γενομένου ἐκ σπέρματος Δαυὶδ κατὰ σάρκα, 1.4 τοῦ ὁρισθέντος υἱοῦ θεοῦ ἐν δυνάμι κατὰ πνεῦμα ἁγιωσύνης ἐξ ἀναστάσεως νεκρῶν, Ἰησοῦ χριστοῦ τοῦ κυρίου ἡμῶν, 1.5 δι' οὗ ἐλάβομεν χάριν καὶ ἀποστολὴν εἰς ὑπακοὴν πίστεως ἐν πᾶσιν τοῖς ἔθνεσιν ὑπὲρ τοῦ ὀνόματος αὐτοῦ, 1.6 ἐν οἷς ἐστε καὶ ὑμῖς κλητοὶ Ἰησοῦ χριστοῦ, 1.7 πᾶσιν τοῖς οὖσιν ἐν Ῥώμῃ ἀγαπητοῖς θεοῦ, κλητοῖς ἁγίοις· χάρις ὑμῖν καὶ εἰρήνη ἀπὸ θεοῦ πατρὸς ἡμῶν καὶ κυρίου Ἰησοῦ χριστοῦ.

1.8 πρῶτον μὲν εὐχαριστῶ τῷ θεῷ μου διὰ Ἰησοῦ χριστοῦ περὶ πάντων ὑμῶν, ὅτι ἡ πίστις ὑμῶν καταγγέλλεται ἐν ὅλῳ τῷ κόσμῳ. 1.9 μάρτυς γάρ μού ἐστιν ὁ θεός, ᾧ λατρεύω ἐν τῷ πνεύματί μου ἐν τῷ εὐαγγελίῳ τοῦ υἱοῦ αὐτοῦ, ὡς ἀδιαλείπτως μνίαν ὑμῶν ποιοῦμαι 1.10 πάντοτε ἐπὶ τῶν προσευχῶν μου, δεόμενος εἴ πως ἤδη ποτὲ εὐοδωθήσομε ἐν τῷ θελήματι τοῦ θεοῦ ἐλθῖν πρὸς ὑμᾶς. 1.11 ἐπιποθῶ γὰρ ἰδῖν ὑμᾶς, ἵνα τι μεταδῶ χάρισμα ὑμῖν πνευματικὸν εἰς τὸ στηριχθῆναι ὑμᾶς,

1.12 τοῦτο δέ ἐστιν συνπαρακληθῆναι ἐν ὑμῖν διὰ τῆς ἐν ἀλλήλοις πίστεως ὑμῶν τε καὶ ἐμοῦ.

1.13 οὐ θέλω δὲ ὑμᾶς ἀγνοεῖν, ἀδελφοί, ὅτι πολλάκις προεθέμην ἐλθῖν πρὸς ὑμᾶς, καὶ ἐκωλύθην ἄχρι τοῦ δεῦρο, ἵνα τινὰ καρπὸν σχῶ καὶ ἐν ὑμῖν καθὼς καὶ ἐν τοῖς λοιποῖς ἔθνεσιν. 1.14 Ἕλλησίν τε καὶ βαρβάροις, σοφοῖς τε καὶ ἀνοήτοις ὀφιλέτης εἰμί· 1.15 οὕτω τὸ κατ' ἐμὲ πρόθυμον καὶ ὑμῖν τοῖς ἐν Ῥώμῃ εὐαγγελίσασθαι.

1.16 οὐ γὰρ ἐπαισχύνομαι τὸ εὐαγγέλιον, δύναμις γὰρ

1.1 Paul, a slave of Jesus the anointed (one), a called apostle, having been set apart into/for a good message/gospel from God, 1.2 which he promised beforehand through his prophets in/by holy writings, 1.3 concerning his son, the (one) having come about from a seed of David according to flesh, 1.4 the (one) having been destined, a son of God with power according to a spirit of consecration from resurrection out of dead (ones), Jesus, the anointed (one), our Lord, 1.5 through whom we received grace/favor and apostleship into/for obedience from faith among all the ethnics in behalf of his name, 1.6 among whom ye, ye are also called (ones) of Jesus, the anointed (one), 1.7 to all those being in Rome, beloved (ones) of God, called saints; grace *be* to ye and peace from God our father and *the* Lord Jesus, the anointed (one).

1.8 First indeed I give thanks to my God through Jesus the anointed (one) concerning/about all of ye, because the faith of ye is being proclaimed in the whole world. 1.9 For God is my witness, for whom I serve/worship in/with my spirit in/by the good message/gospel of his son, since I constantly make mention of ye 1.10 always upon/at my prayers, requesting if somehow now at any time I shall be given a prosperous journey in/by the will of God to come to ye. 1.11 For I desire earnestly to see ye, in order that I might bestow a certain spiritual gift to ye into/for the (thing) *for* ye to be established/confirmed,

1.12 and this is to be mutually exhorted among ye through the faith in one another, both of ye and of/from me.

1.13 But I want/wish not *for* ye to be ignorant, brothers, because I often purposed/intended to come to ye, and was hindered/prevented until the now/present, in order that I might also have some fruit/produce among ye as also among the rest/other ethnics. 1.14 Both to Greeks and to barbarians/foreigners, both to sophists/wise (ones) and to unknowing (ones), I am a debtor; 1.15 so the (thing) with me *is*: *I am* eager to announce/proclaim the good message/gospel also to those in Rome.

1.16 For I am not ashamed of the good message,

θεοῦ ἐστιν εἰς σωτηρίαν παντὶ τῷ πιστεύοντι, Ἰουδαίῳ τε πρῶτον καὶ Ἕλληνι·

1.17 δικαιοσύνη γὰρ θεοῦ ἐν αὐτῷ ἀποκαλύπτεται ἐκ πίστεως εἰς πίστιν, καθὼς γέγραπται, « ὁ δὲ δίκαιος ἐκ πίστεως ζήσεται.»

1.18 ἀποκαλύπτεται γὰρ ὀργὴ θεοῦ ἀπ' οὐρανοῦ ἐπὶ πᾶσαν ἀσέβειαν καὶ ἀδικίαν ἀνθρώπων τῶν τὴν ἀλήθιαν ἐν ἀδικίᾳ κατεχόντων, 1.19 διότι τὸ γνωστὸν τοῦ θεοῦ φανερόν ἐστιν ἐν αὐτοῖς· ὁ θεὸς γὰρ αὐτοῖς ἐφανέρωσεν.

1.20 τὰ γὰρ ἀόρατα αὐτοῦ ἀπὸ κτίσεως κόσμου τοῖς ποιήμασιν νοούμενα καθορᾶτε, ἥ τε ἀίδιος αὐτοῦ δύναμις καὶ θειότης, εἰς τὸ εἶναι αὐτοὺς ἀναπολογήτους·

1.21 διότι γνόντες τὸν θεὸν οὐχ ὡς θεὸν ἐδόξασαν ἢ ηὐχαρίστησαν, ἀλλ' ἐματαιώθησαν ἐν τοῖς διαλογισμοῖς αὐτῶν καὶ ἐσκοτίσθη ἡ ἀσύνετος αὐτῶν καρδία. 1.22 φάσκοντες εἶναι σοφοὶ ἐμωράνθησαν, 1.23 καὶ ἤλλαξαν τὴν δόξαν τοῦ ἀφθάρτου θεοῦ ἐν ὁμοιώματι εἰκόνος φθαρτοῦ ἀνθρώπου καὶ πετινῶν καὶ τετραπόδων καὶ ἑρπετῶν. 1.24 Διὸ παρέδωκεν αὐτοὺς ὁ θεὸς ἐν ταῖς ἐπιθυμίαις τῶν καρδιῶν αὐτῶν εἰς ἀκαθαρσίαν τοῦ ἀτιμάζεσθαι τὰ σώματα αὐτῶν ἐν αὐτοῖς, 1.25 οἵτινες μετήλλαξαν τὴν ἀλήθιαν τοῦ θεοῦ ἐν τῷ ψεύδει, καὶ ἐσεβάσθησαν καὶ ἐλάτρευσαν τῇ κτίσει παρὰ τὸν κτίσαντα, ὅς ἐστιν εὐλογητὸς εἰς τοὺς αἰῶνας· ἀμήν.

1.26 διὰ τοῦτο παρέδωκεν αὐτοὺς ὁ θεὸς εἰς πάθη ἀτιμίας·

αἵ τε γὰρ θήλειαι αὐτῶν μετήλλαξαν τὴν φυσικὴν χρῆσιν εἰς τὴν παρὰ φύσιν,

1.27 ὁμοίως τε καὶ οἱ ἄρρενες ἀφέντες τὴν φυσικὴν χρῆσιν τῆς θηλείας ἐξεκαύθησαν ἐν τῇ ὀρέξι αὐτῶν εἰς ἀλλήλους, ἄρρενες ἐν ἄρρεσι τὴν ἀσχημοσύνην κατεργαζόμενοι καὶ τὴν ἀντιμισθίαν ἣν ἔδει τῆς πλάνης αὐτῶν ἐν ἑαυτοῖς

for it is power from God into/for salvation/deliver-
ance to/for every one believing, both to Judean first
and to Greek;

1.17 for justice of/from God is revealed in/by
it out of faith into/for faith, as it has been written: AND THE JUST (ONE) WILL LIVE OUT OF FAITH.

1.18 For anger from God/God's anger is revealed
from heaven upon/against every impiety/irreverence and
injustice of men, of those holding back/down the truth
by injustice/iniquity, 1.19 because the (thing) known
from God is plain/manifest in/among them; for God made
it plain/manifested it to them.

1.20 For his unseen/invisible (things) are
looked down on from creation of a world being understood by the made (things/ones), both his everlasting
power and divinity, in/for the (thing) *for* them to be
inexcusable;

1.21 because knowing God, they glorified/acknow-
ledged *him* not, as God, or gave thanks, but they
became vain/empty in their reasonings/disputes and the
senseless heart of them was darkened. 1.22 Asserting
to be sophists/wise (ones), they were made foolish,
1.23 and they changed the glory/reputation of the
immortal God in/by a figure/similarity of a mortal/
perishing man/human and of birds and quadrupeds and
reptiles. 1.24 Wherefore, God gave/delivered them
over in the desires of their hearts into uncleanness
from the (thing) *for* their bodies to be dishonored
among themselves, 1.25 who(pl) exchanged the truth
from God with/in the lie/falsehood, they both rever-
enced and served/worshiped the creation from/besides
the (one) having created *it*, *the one* who is blessed
into the ages; truly.

1.26 Because of this God delivered them over
into passions of dishonor;

for even their females exchanged the natural
use/employment into the *use* against nature,

1.27 and likewise also the males, having left
the natural use of the female, they were burned in/
with their longing for one another, males with males
working out the indecency and receiving back among/on
themselves the recompense which was necessary from

ἀπολαμβάνοντες.

1.28 καὶ καθὼς οὐκ ἐδοκίμασαν τὸν θεὸν ἔχειν ἐν ἐπιγνώσι, παρέδωκεν αὐτοὺς ὁ εἰς ἀδόκιμον νοῦν, ποιεῖν τὰ μὴ καθήκοντα, 1.29 πεπληρωμένους πάσῃ ἀδικίᾳ πονηρίᾳ κακίᾳ πλεονεξίᾳ, μεστοὺς φθόνου φόνου ἔριδος δόλου κακοηθίας, ψιθυριστάς, 1.30 καταλάλους, θεοστυγεῖς, ὑβριστάς, ὑπερηφάνους, ἀλαζόνας, ἐφευρετὰς κακῶν, γονεῦσιν ἀπιθεῖς, 1.31 ἀσυνέτους, ἀσυνθέτους, ἀστόργους, ἀνελεήμονας·

1.32 οἵτινες τὸ δικαίωμα τοῦ θεοῦ ἐπιγνόντες, ὅτι οἱ τὰ τοιαῦτα πράσσοντες ἄξιοι θανάτου εἰσίν, οὐ μόνον αὐτὰ ποιοῦσιν ἀλλὰ καὶ συνευδοκοῦσιν τοῖς πράσσουσιν.

2.1 Διὸ ἀναπολόγητος ἶ, ὦ ἄνθρωπε πᾶς ὁ κρίνων· ἐν ᾧ γὰρ κρίνις τὸν ἕτερον, σεαυτὸν κατακρίνις, τὰ γὰρ αὐτὰ πράσσεις ὁ κρίνων. 2.2 οἴδαμεν γὰρ ὅτι τὸ κρίμα τοῦ θεοῦ ἐστιν κατὰ ἀλήθειαν ἐπὶ τοὺς τὰ τοιαῦτα πράσσοντας.

2.3 λογίζῃ δὲ τοῦτο, ὦ ἄνθρωπε ὁ κρίνων τοὺς τὰ τοιαῦτα πράσσοντας καὶ ποιῶν αὐτά, ὅτι σὺ ἐκφεύξῃ τὸ κρίμα τοῦ θεοῦ; 2.4 ἢ τοῦ πλούτου τῆς χρηστότητος αὐτοῦ καὶ τῆς ἀνοχῆς καὶ τῆς μακροθυμίας καταφρονεῖς, ἀγνοῶν ὅτι τὸ χρηστὸν τοῦ θεοῦ εἰς μετάνοιάν σε ἄγει;

2.5 κατὰ δὲ τὴν σκληρότητά σου καὶ ἀμετανόητον καρδίαν θησαυρίζεις σεαυτῷ ὀργὴν ἐν ἡμέρᾳ ὀργῆς καὶ ἀποκαλύψεως δικαιοκρισίας τοῦ θεοῦ, 2.6 ὃς ἀποδώσει ἑκάστῳ κατὰ τὰ ἔργα αὐτοῦ, 2.7 τοῖς μὲν καθ᾽ ὑπομονὴν ἔργου ἀγαθοῦ δόξαν καὶ τιμὴν καὶ ἀφθαρσίαν ζητοῦσιν, ζωὴν αἰώνιον·

2.8 τοῖς δὲ ἐξ ἐριθείας καὶ ἀπιθοῦσι τῇ ἀληθίᾳ πιθομένοις δὲ τῇ ἀδικίᾳ, ὀργὴ καὶ θυμός 2.9 θλῖψις καὶ στενοχωρία ἐπὶ πᾶσαν ψυχὴν ἀνθρώπου τοῦ κατεργαζομένου τὸ κακόν,

their error/deceit.

1.28 And as they supposed not *for* God to hold *it* in knowledge, he gave/delivered them over/up into/to a worthless/vile mind, to do the (things) not being proper, 1.29 having been filled with every injustice/iniquity, evil/wickedness, malice/evil intent, greediness, full (ones) of envy, murder, strife, guile/deceit, malignity, whisperers, 1.30 slanderers, haters of God, insolent (ones), arrogant (ones), boasters/braggarts, inventors of bad (things), disobedient (ones) to parents, 1.31 senseless (ones), uncovenanting/untrustworthy (ones), (ones) without love/affection, without mercy;

1.32 who(pl) having known the just (thing) from God, that those practicing such things are worthy of death, they not only do them but they also consent to those practicing *them*.

2.1 Wherefore you are inexcusable, o man/human, every one judging; for in what you judge the other/different, you condemn yourself, for you, the (one) judging, practice the same (things). 2.2 For we know that the judgment of God is according to truth upon those practicing such things.

2.3 But do you reckon/account this, o man/human, the (one) judging those practicing such things and doing/making *the* same, that you yourself will escape the judgment of God? 2.4 Or do you despise the wealth/abundance of his kindness and the forbearance and the patience *of him*, not knowing that the kindness of God leads you to repentance?

2.5 But according to your hardness and unrepenting heart, you store up anger/wrath for yourself in a day of anger/wrath and of revelation of a just judgment from God, 2.6 who will repay/give back to each (one) according to his works, 2.7 to those on one hand by endurance of good work seeking fame/glory and honor and immortality, eternal life;

2.8 and to those on the other out of selfishness and disobeying the truth but obeying the unjustness/iniquity, anger and wrath -- 2.9 affliction and anguish upon every life/soul of man, of the (one) work-

Ἰουδαίου τε πρῶτον καὶ Ἕλληνος·

2.10 δόξα δὲ καὶ τιμὴ καὶ εἰρήνη παντὶ τῷ ἐργαζομένῳ τὸ ἀγαθόν, Ἰουδαίῳ τε πρῶτον καὶ Ἕλληνι· 2.11 οὐ γάρ ἐστιν προσωπολημψία παρὰ τῷ θεῷ.

2.12 ὅσοι γὰρ ἀνόμως ἥμαρτον, ἀνόμως καὶ ἀπολοῦνται· καὶ ὅσοι ἐν νόμῳ ἥμαρτον, διὰ νόμου κριθήσονται· 2.13 οὐ γὰρ οἱ ἀκροαταὶ νόμου δίκαιοι παρὰ τῷ θεῷ, ἀλλ' οἱ ποιηταὶ νόμου δικαιωθήσονται.

2.14 ὅταν γὰρ ἔθνη τὰ μὴ νόμον ἔχοντα φύσει τὰ τοῦ νόμου ποιῶσιν, οὗτοι νόμον μὴ ἔχοντες ἑαυτοῖς εἰσιν νόμος· 2.15 οἵτινες ἐνδίκνυνται τὸ ἔργον τοῦ νόμου γραπτὸν ἐν ταῖς καρδίαις αὐτῶν, συνμαρτυρούσης αὐτῶν τῆς συνειδήσεως καὶ μεταξὺ ἀλλήλων τῶν λογισμῶν κατηγορούντων ἢ καὶ ἀπολογουμένων, 2.16 ἐν ἡμέρᾳ ὅτε κρίνει ὁ θεὸς τὰ κρυπτὰ τῶν ἀνθρώπων κατὰ τὸ εὐαγγέλιόν μου διὰ Ἰησοῦ χριστοῦ.

2.17 εἰ δὲ σὺ Ἰουδαῖος ἐπονομάζῃ καὶ ἐπαναπαύῃ νόμῳ καὶ καυχᾶσαι ἐν θεῷ 2.18 καὶ γινώσκις τὸ θέλημα καὶ δοκιμάζεις τὰ διαφέροντα κατηχούμενος ἐκ τοῦ νόμου, 2.19 πέποιθάς τε σεαυτὸν ὁδηγὸν εἶναι τυφλῶν, φῶς τῶν ἐν σκότι, 2.20 παιδευτὴν ἀφρόνων, διδάσκαλον νηπίων, ἔχοντα τὴν μόρφωσιν τῆς γνώσεως καὶ τῆς ἀληθείας ἐν τῷ νόμῳ

2.21 ὁ οὖν διδάσκων ἕτερον σεαυτὸν οὐ διδάσκεις;

ὁ κηρύσσων μὴ κλέπτιν κλέπτις;

2.22 ὁ λέγων μὴ μοιχεύειν μοιχεύεις;

ὁ βδελυσσόμενος τὰ ἴδωλα ἱεροσυλεῖς; 2.23 ὃς ἐν νόμῳ καυχᾶσαι, διὰ τῆς παραβάσεως τοῦ νόμου τὸν θεὸν ἀτιμάζεις; 2.24 «τὸ» γὰρ «ὄνομα τοῦ θεοῦ δι' ὑμᾶς βλασφημῖται ἐν τοῖς ἔθνεσιν,» καθὼς γέγραπται. 2.25 περιτομὴ μὲν γὰρ ὠφελῖ ἐὰν νόμον πράσσῃς· ἐὰν δὲ παραβάτης νόμου ᾖς, ἡ περιτομή σου

ing out the bad, both of Judean first and of Greek;

2.10 but glory/fame and honor/worth and peace to every one working the good, both to Judean first and to Greek; 2.11 for there is not partiality from/beside God.

2.12 For as many as sinned without law, they will also perish without law; and as many as sinned in/by law, they will be judged through law; 2.13 for the hearers of law *are* not just (ones) beside God, but the doers of law will be justified.

2.14 For whenever the ethnics not having law do by nature the (things) of the law, these not having law for themselves are law; 2.15 who (pl) show/demonstrate the work of the law written in their hearts, witnessing together from their conscience and from accusing or ever/also excusing the reasonings between one another, 2.16 in a day when God judges the secret (things) of the men/humans according to the good message/gospel from me through Jesus the anointed (one).

2.17 But if you, a Judean, you be named and might rest on law and boast/triumph (yourself) in/by God, 2.18 and you know the will/purpose and you test/prove the excelling (things) being instructed/informed out of the law, 2.19 and having persuaded yourself to be a guide of blind (ones), a light of those in darkness, 2.20 a trainer of foolish (ones), a teacher of infants, having the form of the knowledge and of the truth in the law ...

2.21 The (one) therefore teaching another/different, do you not teach yourself?

The (one) preaching/heralding not to steal, do you steal?

2.22 The (one) saying not to *do* adultery, do you *do* adultery?

The (one) detesting the idols, do you rob/despoil temples? 2.23 *The one* who boasts in/by law, do you dishonor God through the transgression of the law? 2.24 For THE NAME OF GOD IS SLANDERED/BLASPHEMED AMONG THE ETHNICS BECAUSE OF YE, as it has been written. 2.25 For circumcision is indeed profitable if you may practice law; but if you were a transgressor of law,

ἀκροβυστία γέγονεν. 2.26 ἐὰν οὖν ἡ ἀκροβυστία τὰ δικαιώματα τοῦ νόμου φυλάσσῃ, οὐχ ἡ ἀκροβυστία αὐτοῦ εἰς περιτομὴν λογισθήσεται; 2.27 καὶ κρινεῖ ἡ ἐκ φύσεως ἀκροβυστία τὸν νόμον τελοῦσα σὲ τὸν διὰ γράμματος καὶ περιτομῆς παραβάτην νόμου.

2.28 οὐ γὰρ ὁ ἐν τῷ φανερῷ Ἰουδαῖός ἐστιν, οὐδὲ ἡ ἐν τῷ φανερῷ ἐν σαρκὶ περιτομή·

2.29 ἀλλ᾽ ὁ ἐν τῷ κρυπτῷ Ἰουδαῖος, καὶ περιτομὴ καρδίας ἐν πνεύματι οὐ γράμματι, οὗ ὁ ἔπαινος οὐκ ἐξ ἀνθρώπων ἀλλ᾽ ἐκ τοῦ θεοῦ.

3.1 Τί οὖν τὸ περισσὸν τοῦ Ἰουδαίου, ἢ τίς ἡ ὠφέλια τῆς περιτομῆς; 3.2 πολὺ κατὰ πάντα τρόπον. πρῶτον μὲν γὰρ ὅτι ἐπιστεύθησαν τὰ λόγια τοῦ θεοῦ. 3.3 τί γὰρ εἰ ἠπίστησάν τινες; μὴ ἡ ἀπιστία αὐτῶν τὴν πίστιν τοῦ θεοῦ καταργήσει; 3.4 μὴ γένοιτο·

γινέσθω δὲ ὁ θεὸς ἀληθής, πᾶς δὲ ἄνθρωπος ψεύστης, καθάπερ γέγραπτε, « ὅπως ἂν δικαιωθῇς ἐν τοῖς λόγοις σου καὶ νικήσεις ἐν τῷ κρίνεσθαί σε.»

3.5 εἰ δὲ ἡ ἀδικία ἡμῶν θεοῦ δικαιοσύνην συνίστησιν, τί ἐροῦμεν;

μὴ ἄδικος ὁ θεὸς ὁ ἐπιφέρων τὴν ὀργήν; κατὰ ἄνθρωπον λέγω. 3.6 μὴ γένοιτο· ἐπεὶ πῶς κρινεῖ ὁ θεὸς τὸν κόσμον;

3.7 εἰ δὲ ἡ ἀλήθια τοῦ θεοῦ ἐν τῷ ἐμῷ ψεύσματι ἐπερίσσευσεν εἰς τὴν δόξαν αὐτοῦ, τί ἔτι κἀγὼ ὡς ἁμαρτωλὸς κρίνομαι; 3.8 καὶ μὴ καθὼς βλασφημούμεθα καὶ καθὼς φασίν τινες ἡμᾶς λέγιν ὅτι ποιήσωμεν τὰ κακὰ ἵνα ἔλθῃ τὰ ἀγαθά; ὧν τὸ κρίμα ἔνδικόν ἐστιν.

3.9 τί οὖν; προεχόμεθα; οὐ πάντως, προῃτιασάμεθα γὰρ Ἰουδαίους τε καὶ Ἕλληνας πάντας ὑφ᾽ ἁμαρτίαν εἶναι, 3.10 καθὼς γέγραπται ὅτι « οὐκ ἔστιν δίκαιος οὐδὲ εἷς, 3.11 οὐκ

your circumcision has become a foreskin/uncircumcision. 2.26 If therefore the uncircumcision guards/keeps the just deeds/regulations of the law, will not the uncircumcision of him be reckoned/accounted into/for circumcision? 2.27 And the uncircumcision keeping the law out of nature will judge you, the transgressor of law through a letter and circumcision.

2.28 For the (he) is not a Judean in the open/public, nor is the circumcision in the open in flesh;

2.29 but the (he) is a Judean in the secret, and circumcision is from a heart in/by a spirit, not a letter, of whom the praise is not from men but from God.

3.1 What therefore is the advantage of the Judean, or what is the gain/profit from the circumcision? 3.2 It is much according to every manner/way. For first indeed because they were entrusted with the oracles/sayings from God. 3.3 For what if some disbelieved? Will the unbelief/disobedience of them not destroy/overturn the faith of God? 3.4 May it not happen!

But let God become true and every man/human a liar, even as it has been written, SO/THUS YOU WOULD BE JUSTIFIED IN YOUR SAYINGS/WORDS AND YOU WILL OVERCOME IN THE (THING) for YOU TO BE JUDGED.

3.5 And if our injustice recommends justice from God, what shall we say? God is not unjust, the (one) bearing upon/inflicting the anger, is he? I speak according to man. 3.6 May it not happen! Otherwise, how will God judge the world?

3.7 But if the truth of God abounded in/by my falsehood into/for his glory/fame, why am I also still judged as a sinner? 3.8 And not as we were slandered/blasphemed and as some assert for us to say: Should we do the bad (things) in order that the good (things) might come? Of whom the judgment is just/fair.

3.9 Then what? Do we excel? Not wholly, for we ourselves previously accused both Judeans and Greeks to be all under sin, 3.10 as it has been written: THERE IS NOT A JUST (ONE), NOT ONE, 3.11 THERE IS NOT THE (ONE) UNDERSTANDING, THERE IS NOT THE (ONE) SEEK-

ἔστιν ὁ συνίων, οὐκ ἔστιν ὁ ἐκζητῶν τὸν θεόν. 3.12 πάντες ἐξέκλιναν, ἅμα ἠχρεώθησαν· οὐκ ἔστιν ὁ ποιῶν χρηστότητα, οὐκ ἔστιν ἕως αἰνός. 3.13 τάφος ἀνεῳγμένος ὁ λάρυγξ αὐτῶν, ταῖς γλώσσαις αὐτῶν ἐδολιοῦσαν, ἰὸς ἀσπίδων ὑπὸ τὰ χίλη αὐτῶν, 3.14 ὧν τὸ στόμα ἀρᾶς καὶ πικρίας γέμει· 3.15 ὀξεῖς οἱ πόδες αὐτῶν ἐκχέαι αἷμα, 3.16 σύντριμμα καὶ ταλαιπωρία ἐν ταῖς ὁδοῖς αὐτῶν, 3.17 καὶ ὁδὸν ἰρήνης οὐκ ἔγνωσαν. 3.18 οὐκ ἔστιν φόβος θεοῦ ἀπέναντι τῶν ὀφθαλμῶν αὐτῶν.»

3.19 οἴδαμεν δὲ ὅτι ὅσα ὁ νόμος λέγει τοῖς ἐν τῷ νόμῳ λαλεῖ, ἵνα πᾶν στόμα φραγῇ καὶ ὑπόδικος γένηται πᾶς ὁ κόσμος τῷ θεῷ· 3.20 διότι ἐξ ἔργων νόμου οὐ δικαιωθήσεται πᾶσα σὰρξ ἐνώπιον αὐτοῦ,

διὰ γὰρ νόμου ἐπίγνωσις ἁμαρτίας. 3.21 νυνεὶ δὲ χωρὶς νόμου δικαιοσύνη θεοῦ πεφανέρωται, μαρτυρουμένη ὑπὸ τοῦ νόμου καὶ τῶν προφητῶν,

3.22 δικαιοσύνη δὲ θεοῦ διὰ πίστεως Ἰησοῦ χριστοῦ, εἰς πάντας τοὺς πιστεύοντας· οὐ γάρ ἐστιν διαστολή· 3.23 πάντες γὰρ ἥμαρτον καὶ ὑστεροῦνται τῆς δόξης τοῦ θεοῦ, 3.24 δικαιούμενοι δωρεὰν τῇ αὐτοῦ χάριτι διὰ τῆς ἀπολυτρώσεως τῆς ἐν χριστῷ Ἰησοῦ·

3.25 ὃν προέθετο ὁ θεὸς ἱλαστήριον διὰ πίστεως ἐν τῷ αὐτοῦ αἵματι εἰς ἔνδιξιν τῆς δικαιοσύνης αὐτοῦ διὰ τὴν πάρεσιν τῶν προγεγονότων ἁμαρτημάτων 3.26 ἐν τῇ ἀνοχῇ τοῦ θεοῦ, πρὸς τὴν ἔνδιξιν τῆς δικαιοσύνης αὐτοῦ ἐν τῷ νῦν καιρῷ, εἰς τὸ εἶναι αὐτὸν δίκαιον καὶ δικαιοῦντα τὸν ἐκ πίστεως Ἰησοῦ.

3.27 ποῦ οὖν ἡ καύχησις; ἐξεκλίσθη. διὰ ποίου νόμου; τῶν ἔργων; οὐχί, ἀλλὰ διὰ νόμου πίστεως.

3.28 λογιζόμεθα γὰρ δικαιοῦσθαι πίστι ἄνθρωπον χωρὶς ἔργων νόμου. 3.29 ἢ Ἰουδαίων ὁ θεὸς μόνον; οὐχὶ καὶ ἐθνῶν; ναὶ καὶ ἐθνῶν, 3.30 ἐπείπερ εἷς ὁ θεός, ὃς δικαιώσει περιτομὴν ἐκ

ING OUT GOD. 3.12 ALL TURNED AWAY, TOGETHER THEY WERE MADE UNPROFITABLE; THERE IS NOT THE (ONE) DOING KIND- NESS/KIND (THINGS), THERE IS NOT EVEN ONE. 3.13 THEIR THROAT/LARYNX *is* A GRAVE HAVING BEEN OPENED, THEY DECEIVED WITH THEIR LANGUAGES/TONGUES, POISON FROM ASPS *being* UNDER THEIR LIPS, 3.14 OF WHOM THE MOUTH IS FULL OF A PRAYER FOR EVIL, AND OF BITTERNESS; 3.15 THEIR FEET *are* SWIFT TO SHED BLOOD, 3.16 RUIN AND MISERY *are* IN/ON THEIR WAYS/ROADS, 3.17 AND THEY KNEW NOT A ROAD/WAY OF PEACE. 3.18 THERE IS NOT A FEAR OF GOD BEFORE THEIR EYES.

3.19 But we know that whatever (things) the law says, it speaks to those in the law, in order that every mouth might be stopped and all the world might become accountable to God; 3.20 because every flesh will not be justified before him from works of law,

for full knowledge of sin *is* through law. 3.21 But now justice/justness of/from God has been mani- fested/made clear without a law, being witnessed by the law and the prophets,

3.22 and justice/justness of/from God through faith from Jesus the anointed (one), to all the (ones) believing; for there is not a distinction/difference; 3.23 for all sinned and they fall short of the glory/ reputation of God, 3.24 being justified freely by his grace through the redemption in/by the anointed Jesus;

3.25 whom God set forth/pre-placed a *means of* conciliation/atonement through faith in his blood into/for a proof/showing of his justness/justice, because of the passing over of the sins/faults having previously been done 3.26 in/by the forbearance of God, toward the proof/showing of the justness/justice of him in the present time, in the (thing) *for* him to be just and justifying the (one) out of faith from/of Jesus.

3.27 Where then *is* the pride/boasting? It was shut out. Through what law? The (one) of works? No, but through a law of faith.

3.28 For we reckon/account a man/human to be justified by faith apart from works of law. 3.29 Or *is he* the God of Judeans only? Not also of ethnics? Yes, also of ethnics, 3.30 since indeed God *is* one,

πίστεως καὶ ἀκροβυστίαν διὰ τῆς πίστεως. 3.31 νόμον οὖν καταργοῦμεν διὰ τῆς πίστεως; μὴ γένοιτο, ἀλλὰ νόμον ἱστάνομεν.

4.1 Τί οὖν ἐροῦμεν εὑρηκέναι Ἀβραὰμ τὸν προπάτορα ἡμῶν κατὰ σάρκα; 4.2 εἰ γὰρ Ἀβραὰμ ἐξ ἔργων ἐδικαιώθη, ἔχει καύχημα· ἀλλ' οὐ πρὸς θεόν. 4.3 τί γὰρ ἡ γραφὴ λέγει; « ἐπίστευσεν δὲ Ἀβραὰμ τῷ θεῷ, καὶ ἐλογίσθη αὐτῷ εἰς δικαιοσύνην.» 4.4 τῷ δὲ ἐργαζομένῳ ὁ μισθὸς οὐ λογίζεται κατὰ χάριν ἀλλὰ κατὰ ὀφίλημα·

4.5 τῷ δὲ μὴ ἐργαζομένῳ, πιστεύοντι δὲ ἐπὶ τὸν δικαιοῦντα τὸν ἀσεβῆν, λογίζεται ἡ πίστις αὐτοῦ εἰς δικαιοσύνην, 4.6 καθάπερ καὶ Δαυὶδ λέγει τὸν μακαρισμὸν τοῦ ἀνθρώπου ᾧ ὁ θεὸς λογίζεται δικαιοσύνην χωρὶς ἔργων,

4.7 «μακάριοι ὧν ἀφέθησαν αἱ ἀνομίαι καὶ ὧν ἐπεκαλύφθησαν αἱ ἁμαρτίαι· 4.8 μακάριος ἀνὴρ οὗ οὐ μὴ λογίσηται κύριος ἁμαρτίαν.»

4.9 ὁ μακαρισμὸς οὖν οὗτος ἐπὶ τὴν περιτομὴν ἢ καὶ ἐπὶ τὴν ἀκροβυστίαν; λέγομεν γάρ, « ἐλογίσθη τῷ Ἀβραὰμ ἡ πίστις εἰς δικαιοσύνην.»

4.10 πῶς οὖν ἐλογίσθη; ἐν περιτομῇ ὄντι ἢ ἐν ἀκροβυστίᾳ; οὐκ ἐν περιτομῇ ἀλλ' ἐν ἀκροβυστίᾳ·

4.11 καὶ σημεῖον ἔλαβεν περιτομῆς, σφραγῖδα τῆς δικαιοσύνης τῆς πίστεως τῆς ἐν τῇ ἀκροβυστίᾳ, εἰς τὸ εἶναι αὐτὸν πατέρα πάντων τῶν πιστευόντων δι' ἀκροβυστίας, εἰς τὸ λογισθῆναι καὶ αὐτοῖς δικαιοσύνην, 4.12 καὶ πατέρα περιτομῆς τοῖς οὐκ ἐκ περιτομῆς μόνον ἀλλὰ καὶ τοῖς στοιχοῦσιν τοῖς ἴχνεσιν τῆς ἐν ἀκροβυστίᾳ πίστεως τοῦ πατρὸς ἡμῶν Ἀβραάμ.

4.13 οὐ γὰρ διὰ νόμου ἡ ἐπαγγελία τῷ Ἀβραὰμ ἢ τῷ

who will justify circumcision/a circumcised (one) out of faith and uncircumcision through the faith.   3.31 Do we therefore destroy/overturn law through the faith? May it not happen, but we confirm/establish law.

4.1   What then shall we say *for* Abraham, our forefather according to flesh, to have found? 4.2 For if Abraham was justified/vindicated from works, he has a boast/triumph; but not to/with God.   4.3 For what says the writing? AND ABRAHAM BELIEVED GOD, AND IT WAS RECKONED/ACCOUNTED   TO   HIM   INTO/FOR   JUSTNESS/JUSTICE. 4.4 And to the (one) working, the reward is not reckoned according to grace but according to debt;
4.5   but to the (one) not working, but believing on the (one) justifying the impious (one), the faith of him/his faith is reckoned/accounted into/for justness,   4.6 even as David also says/speaks the happiness/blessing of the man/human to whom God accounts justness apart from works:
4.7   HAPPY *are they* OF WHOM THE LAWLESSNESSES WERE FORGIVEN AND OF WHOM THE SINS/FAULTS WERE COVERED OVER;   4.8 HAPPY *is* A MAN OF WHOM *the* LORD BY NO MEANS MIGHT ACCOUNT SIN.
4.9   Then *is* this happiness upon/to the circumcision, or also upon/to the uncircumcision? For we say: THE FAITH WAS RECKONED/ACCOUNTED TO ABRAHAM INTO/FOR JUSTICE/JUSTNESS.
4.10   How then was it reckoned? Being in circumcision or in uncircumcision? Not in/by circumcision, but in/by uncircumcision;
4.11   and he received a sign of circumcision, a seal of the justness/justice of the faith, of the (one) in/by the uncircumcision, into/for the (thing) *for* him to be a father of all the (ones) believing through uncircumcision, into/for the (thing) *for* justice also to be reckoned/accounted to them,   4.12 and a father of circumcision to the (ones) not only from circumcision but also to those following the rudiments in the footsteps of the faith of our father Abraham in uncircumcision.
4.13   For the promise to Abraham or to his seed/

σπέρματι αὐτοῦ, τὸ κληρονόμον αὐτὸν εἶναι κόσμου, ἀλλὰ διὰ δικαιοσύνης πίστεως· 4.14 εἰ γὰρ οἱ ἐκ νόμου κληρονόμοι, κεκένωται ἡ πίστις καὶ κατήργηται ἡ ἐπαγγελία· 4.15 ὁ γὰρ νόμος ὀργὴν κατεργάζεται· οὗ δὲ οὐκ ἔστιν νόμος, οὐδὲ παράβασις. 4.16 διὰ τοῦτο ἐκ πίστεως, ἵνα κατὰ χάριν, εἰς τὸ εἶναι βεβαίαν τὴν ἐπαγγελίαν παντὶ τῷ σπέρματι, οὐ τῷ ἐκ τοῦ νόμου μόνον ἀλλὰ καὶ τῷ ἐκ πίστεως Ἀβραάμ ὅς ἐστιν πατὴρ πάντων ἡμῶν,

4.17 καθὼς γέγραπται ὅτι « πατέρα πολλῶν ἐθνῶν τέθικά σε» κατέναντι οὗ ἐπίστευσεν θεοῦ τοῦ ζῳοποιοῦντος τοὺς νεκροὺς καὶ καλοῦντος τὰ μὴ ὄντα ὡς ὄντα·

4.18 ὃς παρ᾽ ἐλπίδα ἐπ᾽ ἐλπίδι ἐπίστευσεν εἰς τὸ γενέσθαι αὐτὸν «πατέρα πολλῶν ἐθνῶν» κατὰ τὸ εἰρημένον, « οὕτως ἔσται τὸ σπέρμα σου·» 4.19 καὶ μὴ ἀσθενήσας τῇ πίστι κατενόησεν τὸ ἑαυτοῦ σῶμα ἤδη νενεκρωμένον, ἑκατονταετής που ὑπάρχων, καὶ τὴν νέκρωσιν τῆς μήτρας Σάρρας,

4.20 εἰς δὲ τὴν ἐπαγγελίαν τοῦ θεοῦ οὐ διεκρίθη τῇ ἀπιστίᾳ ἀλλ᾽ ἐνεδυναμώθη τῇ πίστι, δοὺς δόξαν τῷ θεῷ 4.21 καὶ πληροφορηθεὶς ὅτι ὃ ἐπήγγελται δυνατός ἐστιν καὶ ποιῆσαι. 4.22 διὸ καὶ «ἐλογίσθη αὐτῷ εἰς δικαιοσύνην.»

4.23 οὐκ ἐγράφη δὲ δι᾽ αὐτὸν μόνον ὅτι ἐλογίσθη αὐτῷ, 4.24 ἀλλὰ καὶ δι᾽ ἡμᾶς οἷς μέλλει λογίζεσθε, τοῖς πιστεύουσιν ἐπὶ τὸν ἐγίραντα Ἰησοῦν τὸν κύριον ἡμῶν ἐκ νεκρῶν, 4.25 ὃς παρεδόθη διὰ τὰ παραπτώματα ἡμῶν καὶ ἠγέρθη διὰ τὴν δικέωσιν ἡμῶν.

5.1 Δικαιωθέντες οὖν ἐκ πίστεως εἰρήνην ἔχομεν πρὸς τὸν θεὸν διὰ τοῦ κυρίου ἡμῶν Ἰησοῦ χριστοῦ, 5.2 δι᾽ οὗ καὶ τὴν προσαγωγὴν ἐσχήκαμεν τῇ πίστι εἰς τὴν χάριν ταύτην ἐν ᾗ ἑστήκαμεν, καὶ καυχώμεθα ἐπ᾽ ἐλπίδι τῆς δόξης τοῦ θεοῦ.

offspring *was* not through a law, the (one) *for* him to be a heir of a world, but through justice from faith; 4.14 for if the heirs *be* from law, the faith has been emptied and the promise has been destroyed; 4.15 for the law works out anger/wrath; and where there is not law, neither *is there* transgression, 4.16 because of this *it is* from faith, in order that *it may be* according to grace, in the (thing) *for* the promise to be firm/steadfast to all the seed/offspring, not only to the (one) from the law, but also to the (one) from faith of Abraham, who is a father of us all,

4.17 as it has been written: I HAVE APPOINTED YOU A FATHER OF MANY ETHNICS/NATIONS before God whom he believed, the (one) making the dead (ones) alive and calling the (things) not being as being;

4.18 who from hope to hope believed in the (thing) *for* him TO BECOME A FATHER OF MANY ETHNICS/NATIONS according to the (thing) having been said: THUS YOUR SEED WILL BE; 4.19 and not having weakened in the faith, he considered the body of himself having already died, from having existed about a hundred years, and the deadness of Sarah's womb;

4.20 but he doubted not in the promise of God in/by unbelief, but he was strengthened in/by the faith, giving glory/fame to God 4.21 and being fully persuaded that what he has promised, he is also able to do. 4.22 Wherefore IT WAS also RECKONED/ACCOUNTED TO HIM INTO/FOR JUSTICE.

4.23 But it was not written because of him alone, that it was reckoned to him, 4.24 but also because of us, to whom it is about to be reckoned, to the (ones) believing on the (one) having raised Jesus our Lord out of dead (ones), 4.25 who was delivered over/betrayed because of our trespasses and was raised up on account of our justification.

5.1 Therefore, having been justified out of faith, we have peace with God through our Lord Jesus the anointed (one), 5.2 through whom we also have had the freedom of access by the faith into this grace/favor in which we stand, and we triumph/boast over/on the hope of the glory/fame/reputation of God.

5.3 οὐ μόνον δέ, ἀλλὰ καὶ καυχώμεθα ἐν ταῖς θλίψεσιν, εἰδότες ὅτι ἡ θλῖψις ὑπομονὴν κατεργάζεται, 5.4 ἡ δὲ ὑπομονὴ δοκιμήν, ἡ δὲ δοκιμὴ ἐλπίδα· 5.5 ἡ δὲ ἐλπὶς οὐ καταισχύνει, ὅτι ἡ ἀγάπη τοῦ θεοῦ ἐκκέχυται ἐν ταῖς καρδίες ἡμῶν διὰ πνεύματος ἁγίου τοῦ δοθέντος ἡμῖν,

5.6 ἔτι γὰρ χριστὸς ὄντων ἡμῶν ἀσθενῶν ἔτι κατὰ καιρὸν ὑπὲρ ἀσεβῶν ἀπέθανεν.

5.7 μόλις γὰρ ὑπὲρ δικαίου τις ἀποθανεῖται· ὑπὲρ γὰρ τοῦ ἀγαθοῦ τάχα τις καὶ τολμᾷ ἀποθανεῖν·

5.8 συνίστησιν δὲ τὴν ἑαυτοῦ ἀγάπην εἰς ἡμᾶς ὁ θεὸς ὅτι ἔτι ἁμαρτωλῶν ὄντων ἡμῶν χριστὸς ὑπὲρ ἡμῶν ἀπέθανεν.

5.9 πολλῷ οὖν μᾶλλον δικαιωθέντες νῦν ἐν τῷ αἵματι αὐτοῦ σωθησόμεθα δι' αὐτοῦ ἀπὸ τῆς ὀργῆς. 5.10 εἰ γὰρ ἐχθροὶ ὄντες κατηλλάγημεν τῷ θεῷ διὰ τοῦ θανάτου τοῦ υἱοῦ αὐτοῦ,

πολλῷ μᾶλλον καταλλαγέντες σωθησόμεθα ἐν τῇ ζωῇ αὐτοῦ·

5.11 οὐ μόνον δέ, ἀλλὰ καὶ καυχώμενοι ἐν τῷ θεῷ διὰ τοῦ κυρίου ἡμῶν Ἰησοῦ χριστοῦ, δι' οὗ νῦν τὴν καταλλαγὴν ἐλάβομεν.

5.12 διὰ τοῦτο ὥσπερ δι' ἑνὸς ἀνθρώπου ἡ ἁμαρτία εἰς τὸν κόσμον εἰσῆλθεν καὶ διὰ τῆς ἁμαρτίας ὁ θάνατος, καὶ οὕτως εἰς πάντας ἀνθρώπους ὁ θάνατος διῆλθεν, ἐφ' ᾧ πάντες ἥμαρτον

5.13 ἄχρι γὰρ νόμου ἁμαρτία ἦν ἐν κόσμῳ, ἁμαρτία δὲ οὐκ ἐλλογεῖται μὴ ὄντος νόμου· 5.14 ἀλλ' ἐβασίλευσεν ὁ θάνατος ἀπὸ Ἀδὰμ μέχρι Μωϋσέως καὶ ἐπὶ τοὺς μὴ ἁμαρτήσαντας ἐπὶ τῷ ὁμοιώματι τῆς παραβάσεως Ἀδάμ, ὅς ἐστιν τύπος τοῦ μέλλοντος.

5.15 ἀλλ' οὐχ ὡς τὸ παράπτωμα, οὕτως καὶ τὸ χάρισμα· εἰ γὰρ τῷ τοῦ ἑνὸς παραπτώματι οἱ πολλοὶ ἀπέθανον, πολλῷ μᾶλλον ἡ χάρις τοῦ θεοῦ καὶ ἡ δωρεὰ ἐν χάριτι τῇ τοῦ ἑνὸς ἀνθρώπου Ἰησοῦ χριστοῦ εἰς τοὺς πολλοὺς ἐπερίσσευσεν. 5.16 καὶ οὐχ ὡσι δι' ἑνὸς ἁμαρτήσαντος τὸ δώρημα· τὸ μὲν γὰρ κρίμα

5.3 And not alone, but we also boast/triumph in the afflictions, knowing that the affliction works out endurance/patience, 5.4 and the patience proving, and the proving hope; 5.5 and the hope puts not to shame, because the agape of God has been poured out in our hearts through a holy spirit, the (one) having been given to us,

5.6 for from us yet being weak, the anointed (one) still died in behalf of impious/irreverent (ones) according to a time.

5.7 For hardly will anyone die in behalf of a just (one); for perhaps in behalf of a just (one) someone even dares to die;

5.8 but God commends the agape of himself to us, because from us still being sinners the anointed (one) died in behalf of us.

5.9 By much more, having now been justified by his blood, we shall be saved from the anger/wrath through him. 5.10 For if being enemies we were reconciled to God through the death of his son,

by much more, having been reconciled, we shall be saved by his life;

5.11 and not only *that*, but also triumphant/ boasting (ones) in God through our Lord Jesus, the anointed (one), through whom we now received the reconciliation.

5.12 Because of this, even as the sin came into the world through one man, and the death through the sin, so also the death proceeded to all men, over all who sinned;

5.13 for until law, sin was in the world, but sin is not reckoned/accounted, *there* being no law; 5.14 but the death reigned from Adam until Moses, even over/upon the (ones) having not sinned on/to the likeness of Adam's transgression, who is a type/example of the (one) being about to come.

5.15 But not as the trespass, so also the gift; for if the many died for the trespass of the one, by much more the grace/favor from God and the gift in/by grace, the (one) from the one man, Jesus the anointed (one), abounded in/for the many. 5.16 And not like the gift, through one having sinned; for indeed the

ἐξ ἑνὸς εἰς κατάκριμα, τὸ δὲ χάρισμα ἐκ πολλῶν παραπτωμάτων εἰς δικαίωμα.

5.17 εἰ γὰρ τῷ τοῦ ἑνὸς παραπτώματι ὁ θάνατος ἐβασίλευσεν διὰ τοῦ ἑνός, πολλῷ μᾶλλον οἱ τὴν περισσείαν τῆς χάριτος καὶ τῆς δωρεᾶς τῆς δικαιοσύνης λαμβάνοντες ἐν ζωῇ βασιλεύσουσιν διὰ τοῦ ἑνὸς Ἰησοῦ χριστοῦ. 5.18 ἄρα οὖν ὡς δι' ἑνὸς παραπτώματος εἰς πάντας ἀνθρώπους εἰς κατάκριμα, οὕτως καὶ δι' ἑνὸς δικαιώματος εἰς πάντας ἀνθρώπους εἰς δικαίωσιν ζωῆς·

5.19 ὥσπερ γὰρ διὰ τῆς παρακοῆς τοῦ ἑνὸς ἀνθρώπου ἁμαρτωλοὶ κατεστάθησαν οἱ πολλοί,

οὕτως καὶ διὰ τῆς ὑπακοῆς τοῦ ἑνὸς δίκαιοι κατασταθήσονται οἱ πολλοί.

5.20 νόμος δὲ παρεισῆλθεν ἵνα πλεονάσῃ τὸ παράπτωμα· οὗ δὲ ἐπλεόνασεν ἡ ἁμαρτία, ὑπερεπερίσσευσεν ἡ χάρις,

5.21 ἵνα ὥσπερ ἐβασίλευσεν ἡ ἁμαρτία ἐν τῷ θανάτῳ, οὕτως καὶ ἡ χάρις βασιλεύσῃ διὰ δικαιοσύνης εἰς ζωὴν αἰώνιον διὰ Ἰησοῦ χριστοῦ τοῦ κυρίου ἡμῶν.

6.1 Τί οὖν ἐροῦμεν; ἐπιμένομεν τῇ ἁμαρτίᾳ, ἵνα ἡ χάρις πλεονάσῃ; 6.2 μὴ γένοιτο·

οἵτινες ἀπεθάνομεν τῇ ἁμαρτίᾳ, πῶς ἔτι ζήσομεν ἐν αὐτῇ;

6.3 ἢ ἀγνοεῖτε ὅτι ὅσοι ἐβαπτίσθημεν εἰς χριστὸν Ἰησοῦν εἰς τὸν θάνατον αὐτοῦ ἐβαπτίσθημεν; 6.4 συνετάφημεν οὖν αὐτῷ διὰ τοῦ βαπτίσματος εἰς τὸν θάνατον,

ἵνα ὥσπερ ἠγέρθη χριστὸς ἐκ νεκρῶν διὰ τῆς δόξης τοῦ πατρός, οὕτως καὶ ἡμεῖς ἐν καινότητι ζωῆς περιπατήσωμεν.

6.5 εἰ γὰρ σύμφυτοι γεγόναμεν τῷ ὁμοιώματι τοῦ θανάτου αὐτοῦ, ἀλλὰ καὶ τῆς ἀναστάσεως ἐσόμεθα·

6.6 τοῦτο γινώσκοντες, ὅτι ὁ παλαιὸς ἡμῶν ἄνθρωπος συνεσταυρώθη, ἵνα καταργηθῇ τὸ σῶμα τῆς ἁμαρτίας, τοῦ

judgment *is* from one into condemnation, but also the gift *is* into/for justification out of/from many trespasses.

5.17 For if by the trespass of the one the death reigned through the one, by much more the (ones) receiving the abundance of the grace/favor and of the gift of the justice/justness will reign/rule in life through the one, Jesus the anointed (one). 5.18 So therefore as through one trespass to/for all men into condemnation, so also through one just deed to/for all men into justification of life;

5.19 for even as through the disobedience of the one man the many were constituted sinners,

so also through the obedience of the one the many will be constituted just (ones).

5.20 But law supervened in order that the trespass might increase; but where the sin increased/abounded, the grace surpassed/excelled/overflowed,

5.21 in order that even as the sin reigned by the death, so also the grace might reign through justice/justness into/for eternal life through Jesus, the anointed (one), our Lord.

6.1 What then shall we say? Should we continue in the sin in order that the grace might increase/abound? 6.2 May it not happen!

How shall we, who died to the sin, still live in her/it?

6.3 Or are ye ignorant that as many as we were baptized into the anointed Jesus, we were baptized into his death? 6.4 Then we were buried with him through the baptism into the death,

in order that just as the anointed (one) was raised out of dead (ones) through the glory/fame of the father, so also we, we should walk in newness of life.

6.5 For if we have become united with the likeness of his death, but we shall also be of the resurrection;

6.6 knowing this, that our old man was crucified with *him*, in order that the body of the sin might be destroyed, from the (thing) *for* us no longer to serve

μηκέτι δουλεύειν ἡμᾶς τῇ ἁμαρτίᾳ·

6.7 ὁ γὰρ ἀποθανὼν δεδικαίωται ἀπὸ τῆς ἁμαρτίας. 6.8 εἰ δὲ ἀπεθάνομεν σὺν χριστῷ, πιστεύομεν ὅτι καὶ συζήσομεν αὐτῷ· 6.9 εἰδότες ὅτι χριστὸς ἐγερθεὶς ἐκ νεκρῶν οὐκέτι ἀποθνήσκει, θάνατος αὐτοῦ οὐκέτι κυριεύει.

6.10 ὃ γὰρ ἀπέθανεν, τῇ ἁμαρτίᾳ ἀπέθανεν ἐφάπαξ· ὃ δὲ ζῇ, ζῇ τῷ θεῷ.

6.11 οὕτως καὶ ὑμεῖς λογίζεσθε ἑαυτοὺς εἶναι νεκροὺς μὲν τῇ ἁμαρτίᾳ ζῶντας δὲ τῷ θεῷ ἐν χριστῷ Ἰησοῦ τῷ κυρίῳ ἡμῶν.

6.12 μὴ οὖν βασιλευέτω ἡ ἁμαρτία ἐν τῷ θνητῷ ὑμῶν σώματι εἰς τὸ ὑπακούειν ταῖς ἐπιθυμίαις αὐτοῦ,

6.13 μηδὲ παριστάνετε τὰ μέλη ὑμῶν ὅπλα ἀδικίας τῇ ἁμαρτίᾳ,

ἀλλὰ παραστήσατε ἑαυτοὺς τῷ θεῷ ὡσεὶ ἐκ νεκρῶν ζῶντας καὶ τὰ μέλη ὑμῶν ὅπλα δικαιοσύνης τῷ θεῷ· 6.14 ἁμαρτία γὰρ ὑμῶν οὐ κυριεύσει, οὐ γάρ ἐστε ὑπὸ νόμον ἀλλὰ ὑπὸ χάριν.

6.15 τί οὖν; ἁμαρτήσωμεν ὅτι οὐκ ἐσμὲν ὑπὸ νόμον ἀλλὰ ὑπὸ χάριν; μὴ γένοιτο.

6.16 οὐκ οἴδατε ὅτι ᾧ παριστάνετε ἑαυτοὺς δούλους εἰς ὑπακοήν, δοῦλοί ἐστε ᾧ ὑπακούετε, ἤτοι ἁμαρτίας εἰς θάνατον ἢ ὑπακοῆς εἰς δικαιοσύνην; 6.17 χάρις δὲ τῷ θεῷ ὅτι ἦτε δοῦλοι τῆς ἁμαρτίας ὑπηκούσατε δὲ ἐκ καρδίας εἰς ὃν παρεδόθητε τύπον διδαχῆς, 6.18 ἐλευθερωθέντες δὲ ἀπὸ τῆς ἁμαρτίας ἐδουλώθητε τῇ δικαιοσύνῃ· 6.19 ἀνθρώπινον λέγω διὰ τὴν ἀσθένειαν τῆς σαρκὸς ὑμῶν. ὥσπερ γὰρ παρεστήσατε τὰ μέλη ὑμῶν δοῦλα τῇ ἀκαθαρσίᾳ καὶ τῇ ἀνομίᾳ εἰς τὴν ἀνομίαν,

οὕτω νῦν παραστήσατε τὰ μέλη ὑμῶν δοῦλα τῇ δικαιοσύνῃ εἰς ἁγιασμόν. 6.20 ὅτε γὰρ δοῦλοι ἦτε τῆς ἁμαρτίας, ἐλεύθεροι ἦτε τῇ δικαιοσύνῃ.

6.21 τίνα οὖν καρπὸν εἴχετε τότε ἐφ’ οἷς νῦν ἐπαισχύνεσθε;

as slaves to the sin;

6.7 for the (one) having died has been justified from the sin. 6.8 But if we died with the anointed (one), we believe that we shall also live with him; 6.9 knowing that the anointed (one), having been raised out of dead (ones), no longer dies, death no longer rules over him.

6.10 For *in* that he died, he died once/at one time for the sin; and *in* that he lives, he lives for God.

6.11 So also ye, count ye yourselves to be dead (ones) indeed to/for the sin, but living (ones) for God in/by the anointed Jesus, our Lord.

6.12 Therefore, let not the sin reign in the mortal body of ye into/for the (thing) to obey the desires of it,

6.13 neither present ye the members of ye weapons/tools of injustice for the sin,

but present ye yourselves to God as living out of dead (ones), and the members of ye weapons/tools of justice/justness for God; 6.14 for a sin of/from ye will not rule/be lord, for ye are not under law but under grace/favor.

6.15 Then what? Should we sin because we are not under law but under grace? May it not happen!

6.16 Know ye not that to whom ye present yourselves slaves in obedience, ye are slaves to whom ye obey, whether of sin into death or of obedience into justice/justness? 6.17 But grace/thanks *be* to God that ye were slaves of the sin, but ye obeyed from *the* heart in a type/example of teaching/doctrine *by* which ye were delivered up, 6.18 and having been freed from the sin, ye were enslaved for/to the justice/justness; 6.19 I speak humanly because of the weakness of your flesh. For even as ye presented your members slaves to the viciousness and the iniquity in the lawlessness,

so now present ye the members of ye/your members slaves to the justice/justness into/for sanctification. 6.20 For when ye were slaves of the sin, ye were free (ones) to the justice/justness.

6.21 Then what fruit/product had ye then/at any time over (things) which ye are now ashamed? For the

τὸ γὰρ τέλος ἐκίνων θάνατος. 6.22 νυνὶ δέ, ἐλευθερωθέντες ἀπὸ τῆς ἁμαρτίας δουλωθέντες δὲ τῷ θεῷ, ἔχετε τὸν καρπὸν ὑμῶν εἰς ἁγιασμόν, τὸ δὲ τέλος ζωὴν αἰώνιον.

6.23 τὰ γὰρ ὀψώνια τῆς ἁμαρτίας θάνατο, δὲ χάρισμα τοῦ θεοῦ ζωὴ αἰώνιος ἐν χριστῷ Ἰησοῦ τῷ κυρίῳ ἡμῶν.

7.1 Ἢ ἀγνοεῖτε, ἀδελφοί, γινώσκουσιν γὰρ νόμον λαλῶ, ὅτι ὁ νόμος κυριεύει τοῦ ἀνθρώπου ἐφ᾽ ὅσον χρόνον ζῇ; 7.2 ἡ γὰρ ὕπανδρος γυνὴ τῷ ζῶντι ἀνδρὶ δέδεται νόμῳ· ἐὰν δὲ ἀποθάνη ὁ ἀνήρ, κατήργηται ἀπὸ τοῦ νόμου τοῦ ἀνδρός. 7.3 ἄρα οὖν ζῶντος τοῦ ἀνδρὸς μοιχαλὶς χρηματίσει ἐὰν γένηται ἀνδρὶ ἑταίρῳ·

ἐὰν δὲ ἀποθάνη ὁ ἀνήρ, ἐλευθέρα ἐστὶν ἀπὸ τοῦ νόμου, τοῦ μὴ εἶναι αὐτὴν μοιχαλίδα γενομένην ἀνδρὶ ἑταίρῳ.

7.4 ὥστε καὶ ὑμεῖς, ἀδελφοί μου, ἐθανατώθητε τῷ νόμῳ διὰ τοῦ σώματος τοῦ χριστοῦ, εἰς τὸ γενέσθαι ὑμᾶς ἑτέρῳ, τῷ ἐκ νεκρῶν ἐγερθέντι, ἵνα καρποφορήσωμεν τῷ θεῷ.

7.5 ὅτε γὰρ ἦμεν ἐν τῇ σαρκί, τὰ παθήματα τῶν ἁμαρτιῶν τὰ διὰ τοῦ νόμου ἐνηργεῖτο ἐν τοῖς μέλεσιν ἡμῶν εἰς τὸ καρποφορῆσαι τῷ θανάτῳ·

7.6 νυνὶ δὲ κατηργήθημεν ἀπὸ τοῦ νόμου, ἀποθανόντες ἐν ᾧ κατειχόμεθα, ὥστε δουλεύειν ἡμᾶς ἐν καινότητι πνεύματος καὶ οὐ παλαιότητι γράμματος. 7.7 τί οὖν ἐροῦμεν; ὁ νόμος ἁμαρτία; μὴ γένοιτο·

ἀλλὰ τὴν ἁμαρτίαν οὐκ ἔγνων εἰ μὴ διὰ νόμου, τήν τε γὰρ ἐπιθυμίαν οὐκ ἤδιν εἰ μὴ ὁ νόμος ἔλεγεν, «οὐκ ἐπιθυμήσεις.» 7.8 ἀφορμὴν δὲ λαβοῦσα ἡ ἁμαρτία διὰ τῆς ἐντολῆς κατειργάσατο ἐν ἐμοὶ πᾶσαν ἐπιθυμίαν·

χωρὶς γὰρ νόμου ἁμαρτία νεκρά. 7.9 ἐγὼ δὲ ἔζων χωρὶς νόμου ποτέ· ἐλθούσης δὲ τῆς ἐντολῆς ἡ ἁμαρτία ἀνέζησεν, 7.10

end of those *is* death.   6.22 But now, having been
freed from the sin/fault and having been enslaved
to/for God, ye have your fruit into/for sanctifica-
tion/setting apart, and the end *is* eternal life.

6.23 For the wages from/of the sin *is* death, but
the gift from God *is* eternal life in/with the anointed
Jesus, the Lord of us/our Lord.

7.1 Or are ye ignorant. brothers, for I speak
law to those knowing *it*, because the law rules over
the man/human for as much time as he lives?   7.2 For
the woman married to the living man has been bound by
law; but if the man might die, she has been freed from
the law of the man.   7.3 So therefore, from the man
living she will be styled an adulteress if she becomes
with another/different man;

but if the man might die, she is free from the
law, from the (thing) *for* her not to be an adulteress,
having become with another/different man.

7.4 So that ye also, my brothers, ye were put to
death for the law through the body of the anointed
(one), into/for the (thing) *for* ye to become for a
different (one), for the (one) having been raised out
of dead (ones), in order that ye might be fruitful/
productive for God.

7.5 For when we were in the flesh, the passions
of the sins, the (ones) through the law, were working
in our members to/for the (thing) to bear fruit to the
death;

7.6 but now we were freed from the law, having
died in *that* which we were held fast, so as *for* us to
slave in newness of spirit and not in oldness of
letter.   7.7 What then shall we say? The law *is* sin?
May it not be;

but I know not the sin except through law, for
indeed I knew not the desire except the law was saying: YOU WILL NOT DESIRE/LUST.   7.8 But the sin having
taken an occasion through the command, worked out
every desire in me;

for sin *is* dead without/apart from law. 7.9 And
I, I was living without law then; but the sin lived
again from the command having come,   7.10 but I myself

ἐγὼ δὲ ἀπέθανον, καὶ εὑρέθη μοι ἡ ἐντολὴ ἡ εἰς ζωὴν αὕτη εἰς θάνατον·

7.11 ἡ γὰρ ἁμαρτία ἀφορμὴν λαβοῦσα διὰ τῆς ἐντολῆς ἐξηπάτησέν με καὶ δι᾽ αὐτῆς ἀπέκτινεν.

7.12 ὥστε ὁ μὲν νόμος ἅγιος, καὶ ἡ ἐντολὴ ἁγία καὶ δικαία καὶ ἀγαθή.

7.13 τὸ οὖν ἀγαθὸν ἐμοὶ ἐγένετο θάνατος; μὴ γένοιτο·

ἀλλὰ ἡ ἁμαρτία, ἵνα φανῇ ἁμαρτία, διὰ τοῦ ἀγαθοῦ μοι κατεργαζομένη θάνατον· ἵνα γένηται καθ᾽ ὑπερβολὴν ἁμαρτωλὸς ἡ ἁμαρτία διὰ τῆς ἐντολῆς. 7.14 οἴδαμεν γὰρ ὅτι ὁ νόμος πνευματικός ἐστιν· ἐγὼ δὲ σάρκινός εἰμι, πεπραμένος ὑπὸ τὴν ἁμαρτίαν. 7.15 ὃ γὰρ κατεργάζομαι οὐ γινώσκω·

οὐ γὰρ ὃ θέλω τοῦτο πράσσω, ἀλλὰ ὃ μισῶ τοῦτο ποιῶ. 7.16 εἰ δὲ ὃ οὐ θέλω τοῦτο ποιῶ, σύνφημι τῷ νόμῳ ὅτι καλός.

7.17 νυνὶ δὲ οὐκέτι ἐγὼ κατεργάζομαι αὐτὸ ἀλλ᾽ ἡ ἐνοικοῦσα ἐν ἐμοὶ ἁμαρτία. 7.18 οἶδα γὰρ ὅτι οὐκ οἰκεῖ ἐν ἐμοί, τοῦτ᾽ ἔστιν ἐν τῇ σαρκί μου, ἀγαθόν·

τὸ γὰρ θέλειν παράκειταί μοι, τὸ δὲ κατεργάζεσθε τὸ καλὸν οὔ·

7.19 οὐ γὰρ ὃ θέλω ποιῶ ἀγαθόν, ἀλλὰ ὃ οὐ θέλω κακὸν τοῦτο πράσσω. 7.20 εἰ δὲ ὃ οὐ θέλω ἐγὼ τοῦτο ποιῶ, οὐκέτι ἐγὼ κατεργάζομαι αὐτὸ ἀλλὰ ἡ οἰκοῦσα ἐν ἐμοὶ ἁμαρτία.

7.21 εὑρίσκω ἄρα τὸν νόμον τῷ θέλοντι ἐμοὶ ποιεῖν τὸ καλὸν ὅτι ἐμοὶ τὸ κακὸν παράκειται· 7.22 συνήδομαι γὰρ τῷ νόμῳ τοῦ θεοῦ κατὰ τὸν ἔσω ἄνθρωπον, 7.23 βλέπω δὲ ἕτερον νόμον ἐν τοῖς μέλεσίν μου ἀντιστρατευόμενον τῷ νόμῳ τοῦ νοός μου καὶ αἰχμαλωτίζοντά με ἐν τῷ νόμῳ τῆς ἁμαρτίας τῷ ὄντι ἐν τοῖς μέλεσίν μου. 7.24 ταλαίπωρος ἐγὼ ἄνθρωπος· τίς με ῥύσεται ἐκ τοῦ σώματος τοῦ θανάτου τούτου;

7.25 εὐχάριστῶ τῷ θεῷ διὰ Ἰησοῦ χριστοῦ τοῦ κυρίου ἡμῶν.

ἄρα οὖν αὐτὸς ἐγὼ τῷ μὲν νοΐ δουλεύω νόμῳ θεοῦ, τῇ δὲ σαρκὶ νόμῳ ἁμαρτίας.

died, and the command to/for life, this was found for me in death;

7.11   for the sin having taken an occasion through the command deceived me and killed *me* through it.

7.12   So that the law indeed *is* holy, and the command is holy and just and good.

7.13   Therefore, *did* the good (thing) become death to me? May it not be!

But the sin, in order that it might appear sin, through the good (thing) working out death to me; in order that the sin might become excessively sinful through the command.   7.14 For we know that the law is spiritual; but I, I am fleshy/carnal, having been sold under the sin.   7.15 For what I work out I know not;

for what I want/wish, I practice not this, but what I hate, I do this.   7.16   But if I do this which I want/wish not, I agree with the law that *it is* good.

7.17   But now I myself work it out no longer, but the sin dwelling in me. 7.18 For I know that a good (thing) dwells not in me, this/that is in my flesh.

for the (thing) to wish is present for me, but the (thing) to work out the beautiful (thing) *is* not,

7.19   for what I want/wish, I do not good, but what I want/wish not, I practice this bad (thing). 7.20 But if what I want/wish not, I, I do this, I myself no longer work it out, but the sin dwelling in me.

7.21   Therefore I find the law to me, the (one) wanting to do the beautiful (thing), because the bad (thing) is present for me;   7.22 for I delight in the law of God according to the man within,   7.23 but I see another/different law in my members battling against the law of my mind and taking me captive in/by the law of the sin being in my members.   7.24 I *am* a wretched man/human; who will rescue me out of the body from this death?

7.25   I give thanks to God through Jesus, the anointed (one), our Lord.

So then I myself, I indeed slave for law of God with the mind, but also to law of sin with the flesh.

8.1 Οὐδὲν ἄρα νῦν κατάκριμα τοῖς ἐν χριστῷ Ἰησοῦ·

8.2 ὁ γὰρ νόμος τοῦ πνεύματος τῆς ζωῆς ἐν χριστῷ Ἰησοῦ ἠλευθέρωσέ σε ἀπὸ τοῦ νόμου τῆς ἁμαρτίας καὶ τοῦ θανάτου.

8.3 τὸ γὰρ ἀδύνατον τοῦ νόμου, ἐν ᾧ ἠσθένει διὰ τῆς σαρκός, ὁ θεὸς τὸν ἑαυτοῦ υἱὸν πέμψας ἐν ὁμοιώματι σαρκὸς ἁμαρτίας καὶ περὶ ἁμαρτίας κατέκρινε τὴν ἁμαρτίαν ἐν τῇ σαρκί, 8.4 ἵνα τὸ δικαίωμα τοῦ νόμου πληρωθῇ ἐν ἡμῖν τοῖς μὴ κατὰ σάρκα περιπατοῦσιν ἀλλὰ κατὰ πνεῦμα. 8.5 οἱ γὰρ κατὰ σάρκα ὄντες τὰ τῆς σαρκὸς φρονοῦσιν, οἱ δὲ κατὰ πνεῦμα τὰ τοῦ πνεύματος.

8.6 τὸ γὰρ φρόνημα τῆς σαρκὸς θάνατος, τὸ δὲ φρόνημα τοῦ πνεύματος ζωὴ καὶ εἰρήνη·

8.7 διότι τὸ φρόνημα τῆς σαρκὸς ἔχθρα εἰς θεόν, τῷ γὰρ νόμῳ τοῦ θεοῦ οὐχ ὑποτάσσεται, οὐδὲ γὰρ δύναται· 8.8 οἱ δὲ ἐν σαρκὶ ὄντες θεῷ ἀρέσαι οὐ δύνανται. 8.9 ὑμεῖς δὲ οὐκ ἐστὲ ἐν σαρκὶ ἀλλὰ ἐν πνεύματι, εἴπερ πνεῦμα θεοῦ οἰκεῖ ἐν ὑμῖν.

εἰ δέ τις πνεῦμα χριστοῦ οὐκ ἔχει, οὗτος οὐκ ἔστιν αὐτοῦ.

8.10 εἰ δὲ χριστὸς ἐν ὑμῖν, τὸ μὲν σῶμα νεκρὸν δι᾽ ἁμαρτίαν, τὸ δὲ πνεῦμα ζωὴ διὰ δικαιοσύνην.

8.11 εἰ δὲ τὸ πνεῦμα τοῦ ἐγίραντος τὸν Ἰησοῦν ἐκ νεκρῶν οἰκεῖ ἐν ὑμῖν, ὁ ἐγίρας ἐκ νεκρῶν χριστὸν Ἰησοῦν ζωοποιήσει τὰ θνητὰ σώματα ὑμῶν διὰ τοῦ ἐνοικοῦντος αὐτοῦ πνεύματος ἐν ὑμῖν.

8.12 ἄρα οὖν, ἀδελφοί, ὀφιλέται ἐσμέν, οὐ τῇ σαρκὶ τοῦ κατὰ σάρκα ζῆν· 8.13 εἰ γὰρ κατὰ σάρκα ζῆτε μέλλετε ἀποθνήσκειν, εἰ δὲ πνεύματι τὰς πράξις τοῦ σώματος θανατοῦτε ζήσεσθε.

8.14 ὅσοι γὰρ πνεύματι θεοῦ ἄγονται, οὗτοι υἱοὶ θεοῦ εἰσιν. 8.15 οὐ γὰρ ἐλάβετε πνεῦμα δουλίας πάλιν εἰς φόβον, ἀλλὰ

8.1   Then there *is* now no condemnation to the
(ones) in the anointed Jesus;

8.2 for the law of the spirit of the life in the
anointed Jesus freed you from the law of the sin/fail-
ure and from the death.

8.3   For the impossible (thing) of the law, in
which it was weak through the flesh, God having sent
the son of himself in a likeness of sinful flesh, and
concerning sin, he condemned the sin/failure in the
flesh,   8.4 in order that the just (thing) of the law
might be fulfilled in/by us, the (ones) walking not
according to/by flesh, but according to/by a spirit.
8.5 For the (ones) being according to flesh mind/think
of the (things) of the flesh, but the (ones) by/ac-
cording to spirit the (things) of the spirit.

8.6   For the aim/aspiration/thinking from the
flesh *is* death, but the aim/thinking from the spirit
is life and peace;

8.7   because the thinking of/from the flesh *is*
enmity to God, for the law of God is not subjected/
subordinated, for it is not able *to be*;   8.8   and the
(ones) being in flesh are not able to please God.   8.9
But ye, ye are not in flesh but in spirit, since a
spirit from God lives/dwells in/among ye.

But if anyone has not a spirit from the anointed
(one), this (one) is not his.

8.10   But if the anointed (one) *be* in ye, the
body *is* indeed dead on account of sin, but also the
spirit *is* life through/because of justice.

8.11   But if the spirit from the (one) having
raised Jesus out of dead (ones) lives/dwells in/among
ye, the (one) having raised the anointed Jesus out of
dead (ones) will make alive your mortal bodies through
the indwelling of his spirit in/among ye.

8.12 So therefore, brothers, we are debtors, not
to the flesh, from the (thing) to live according to
flesh;   8.13 for if ye may live according to flesh, ye
are about to die, but if by a spirit ye put to death
the acts/practices of the body, ye will live.

8.14   For as many as are led by a spirit of/from
God, these are sons of God.   8.15 For ye received not
a spirit of slavery to fear again, but ye received a

ἐλάβετε πνεῦμα υἱοθεσίας, ἐν ᾧ κράζομεν, αββα ὁ πατήρ·

8.16 αὐτὸ τὸ πνεῦμα συνμαρτυρεῖ τῷ πνεύματι ἡμῶν ὅτι ἐσμὲν τέκνα θεοῦ. 8.17 εἰ δὲ τέκνα, καὶ κληρονόμοι· κληρονόμοι μὲν θεοῦ, συγκληρονόμοι δὲ χριστοῦ, εἴπερ συνπάσχομεν ἵνα καὶ συνδοξασθῶμεν.

8.18 λογίζομαι γὰρ ὅτι οὐκ ἄξια τὰ παθήματα τοῦ νῦν καιροῦ πρὸς τὴν μέλλουσαν δόξαν ἀποκαλυφθῆναι εἰς ἡμᾶς. 8.19 ἡ γὰρ ἀποκαραδοκία τῆς κτίσεως τὴν ἀποκάλυψιν τῶν υἱῶν τοῦ θεοῦ ἀπεκδέχεται·

8.20 τῇ γὰρ ματαιότητι ἡ κτίσις ὑπετάγη, οὐχ ἑκοῦσα ἀλλὰ διὰ τὸν ὑποτάξαντα, ἐφ' ἐλπίδι 8.21 διότι καὶ αὐτὴ ἡ κτίσις ἐλευθερωθήσεται ἀπὸ τῆς δουλίας τῆς φθορᾶς εἰς τὴν ἐλευθερίαν τῆς δόξης τῶν τέκνων τοῦ θεοῦ.

8.22 οἴδαμεν γὰρ ὅτι πᾶσα ἡ κτίσις συστενάζει καὶ συνωδίνει ἄχρι τοῦ νῦν·

8.23 οὐ μόνον δέ, ἀλλὰ καὶ αὐτοὶ τὴν ἀπαρχὴν τοῦ πνεύματος ἔχοντες ἡμεῖς καὶ αὐτοὶ ἐν ἑαυτοῖς στενάζομεν υἱοθεσίαν ἀπεκδεχόμενοι, τὴν ἀπολύτρωσιν τοῦ σώματος ἡμῶν. 8.24 τῇ γὰρ ἐλπίδι ἐσώθημεν·

ἐλπὶς δὲ βλεπομένη οὐκ ἔστιν ἐλπίς· ὃ γὰρ βλέπει τίς ἐλπίζι; 8.25 εἰ δὲ ὃ οὐ βλέπομεν ἐλπίζομεν, δι' ὑπομονῆς ἀπεκδεχόμεθα.

8.26 ὡσαύτως δὲ καὶ τὸ πνεῦμα συναντιλαμβάνεται τῇ ἀσθενείᾳ ἡμῶν· τὸ γὰρ τί προσευξώμεθα καθὸ δεῖ οὐκ οἴδαμεν, ἀλλὰ αὐτὸ τὸ πνεῦμα ὑπερεντυγχάνει στεναγμοῖς ἀλαλήτοις·

8.27 ὁ δὲ ἐραυνῶν τὰς καρδίας οἶδεν τί τὸ φρόνημα τοῦ πνεύματος, ὅτι κατὰ θεὸν ἐντυγχάνι ὑπὲρ ἁγίων.

8.28 οἴδαμεν δὲ ὅτι τοῖς ἀγαπῶσιν τὸν θεὸν πάντα συνεργεῖ εἰς ἀγαθόν, τοῖς κατὰ πρόθεσιν κλητοῖς οὖσιν.

8.29 ὅτι οὓς προέγνω, καὶ προώρισεν συνμόρφους τῆς

spirit of sonship, by which we cry out: Abba, the father;

8.16 the spirit itself witnesses/testifies with the spirit of us/our spirit that we are children of God/God's children. 8.17 And if children, also heirs; heirs indeed of God, and also joint heirs of the anointed (one), since we suffer together in order that we might also be glorified together.

8.18 For I reckon/account that the sufferings of the present time are not worthy to/toward the glory being about to be revealed to/in us. 8.19 For the eager watching from the creation awaits expectantly the revelation of/from the sons of God;

8.20 for the creation was influenced by the emptiness/vanity, but not voluntary because of the (one) having ordered/arranged *it*, on/for a hope 8.21 because even the creation itself will be set free from the slavery of the decay/corruption into the liberty/ freedom of the glory of the children of God.

8.22 For we know that all the creation groans and travails until the present (time);

8.23 and not only *that*, but we ourselves hav- ing/holding the firstfruit of/from the spirit, we ourselves also groan in ourselves expecting earnestly a sonship/an adoption, *for* the redemption of our body. 8.24 For we were saved for the hope;

but hope being seen is not hope; for does anyone hope *for* what he sees? 8.25 But if we hope *for* what we see not, we earnestly expect it through patience.

8.26 And likewise the spirit also takes hold of/supports us in the weakness; for we know not the (thing) which we should pray in so far as it is neces- sary, but the spirit itself intercedes for *us* with unspoken groanings;

8.27 but the (one) searching the hearts knows what *is* the thought/thinking of the spirit, because it intercedes according to God, in behalf of saints.

8.28 And we know that for those loving God, he operates/works all (things) together into/for good, to/for those being called according to a purpose.

8.29 Because (those) whom he knew beforehand, he also ordained beforehand in like form from the image

εἰκόνος τοῦ υἱοῦ αὐτοῦ, εἰς τὸ εἶναι αὐτὸν πρωτότοκον ἐν πολλοῖς ἀδελφοῖς·

8.30 οὓς δὲ προώρισεν, τούτους καὶ ἐκάλεσεν·

καὶ οὓς ἐκάλεσεν, τούτους καὶ ἐδικαίωσεν·

οὓς δὲ ἐδικαίωσεν, τούτους καὶ ἐδόξασεν.

8.31 τί οὖν ἐροῦμεν πρὸς ταῦτα; εἰ ὁ θεὸς ὑπὲρ ἡμῶν, τίς καθ᾽ ἡμῶν; 8.32 ὅς γε τοῦ ἰδίου υἱοῦ οὐκ ἐφίσατο, ἀλλὰ ὑπὲρ ἡμῶν πάντων παρέδωκεν αὐτόν, πῶς οὐχὶ καὶ σὺν αὐτῷ τὰ πάντα ἡμῖν χαρίσεται; 8.33 τίς ἐγκαλέσει κατὰ ἐκλεκτῶν θεοῦ; θεὸς ὁ δικαιῶν· 8.34 τίς ὁ κατακρινῶν; χριστὸς Ἰησοῦς ὁ ἀποθανών, μᾶλλον δὲ ἐγερθείς, καὶ ὅς ἐστιν ἐν δεξιᾷ τοῦ θεοῦ, ὃς καὶ ἐντυγχάνει ὑπὲρ ἡμῶν.

8.35 τίς ἡμᾶς χωρίσει ἀπὸ τῆς ἀγάπης τοῦ θεοῦ; θλῖψις ἢ στενοχωρία ἢ διωγμὸς ἢ λιμὸς ἢ γυμνότης ἢ κίνδυνος ἢ μάχαιρα;

8.36 καθὼς γέγραπται ὅτι «ἕνεκεν σοῦ θανατούμεθα ὅλην τὴν ἡμέραν, ἐλογίσθημεν ὡς πρόβατα σφαγῆς.» 8.37 ἀλλ᾽ ἐν τούτοις πᾶσιν ὑπερνικῶμεν διὰ τοῦ ἀγαπήσαντος ἡμᾶς.

8.38 πέπισμαι γὰρ ὅτι οὔτε θάνατος οὔτε ζωὴ οὔτε ἄγγελοι οὔτε ἀρχαὶ οὔτε ἐνεστῶτα οὔτε μέλλοντα οὔτε δυνάμεις 8.39 οὔτε ὕψωμα οὔτε βάθος οὔτε τις κτίσις ἑτέρα δυνήσεται ἡμᾶς χωρίσαι ἀπὸ τῆς ἀγάπης τοῦ θεοῦ τῆς ἐν χριστῷ Ἰησοῦ τῷ κυρίῳ ἡμῶν.

9.1 Ἀλήθειαν λέγω ἐν χριστῷ, οὐ ψεύδομαι, συνμαρτυρούσης μοι τῆς συνειδήσεώς μου ἐν πνεύματι ἁγίῳ, 9.2 ὅτι λύπη μοί ἐστιν μεγάλη καὶ ἀδιάλειπτος ὀδύνη τῇ καρδίᾳ μου.

9.3 ηὐχόμην γὰρ εἶναι ἀνάθεμα αὐτὸς ἐγὼ ἀπὸ τοῦ χριστοῦ ὑπὲρ τῶν ἀδελφῶν μου τῶν συγγενῶν μου κατὰ σάρκα, 9.4 οἵτινές εἰσιν Ἰσραηλεῖται, ὧν ἡ υἱοθεσία καὶ ἡ δόξα καὶ αἱ

of his son, to the (thing) *for* him to be a firstborn among many brothers;

8.30 But (those) whom he preordained/preappointed, he also called these; and (those) whom he called, he also justified/vindicated these;

and (those) whom he justified/vindicated, he also glorified these.

8.31 What then shall we say to these (things)? If God *be* in behalf of us, who *is* against us? 8.32 *The one* who even spared not his own son, but delivered him up in behalf of us all, how will he not also bestow/give freely all (things) to us with him? 8.33 Who will accuse against God's chosen (ones)? God *is* the one justifying; 8.34 who *is* the (one) condemning? The anointed Jesus, the (one) having died, but rather having been raised, and who is at *the* right *hand* of God, who also pleads/appeals in behalf of us.

8.35 Who/what will separate us from the agape of God? Affliction or distress or prosecution or famine or nakedness or danger or sword?

8.36 As it has been written: WE ARE BEING PUT TO DEATH ALL THE DAY ON ACCOUNT OF YOU, WE WERE COUNTED/ RECKONED AS SHEEP OF A SLAUGHTER. 8.37 But in these (things) we conquer over/overcome all (things) through the (one) having loved us.

8.38 For I have been persuaded that neither death not life nor angels/messengers nor rulers nor present things nor (things) being about to come nor powers 8.39 nor height nor depth nor any other/different creation will be able to separate us from the agape of God, the (one) in the anointed Jesus, our Lord.

9.1 I speak truth by the anointed (one), I lie not, from my conscience witnessing with me in/by a holy spirit, 9.2 because it is a great grief to me and an incessant pain in my heart.

9.3 For I myself, I was wishing/longing to be a curse from the anointed (one) in behalf of my brothers, of my kinsmen according to flesh, 9.4 who are Israelites, of whom *is* the sonship/adoption and the glory and the covenants and the given law and the

διαθῆκαι καὶ ἡ νομοθεσία καὶ ἡ λατρεία καὶ αἱ ἐπαγγελίαι,

9.5 ὧν οἱ πατέρες, καὶ ἐξ ὧν ὁ χριστὸς τὸ κατὰ σάρκα· ὁ ὢν ἐπὶ πάντων θεὸς εὐλογητὸς εἰς τοὺς αἰῶνας, ἀμήν.

9.6 οὐχ οἷον δὲ ὅτι ἐκπέπτωκεν ὁ λόγος τοῦ θεοῦ. οὐ γὰρ πάντες οἱ ἐξ Ἰσραήλ, οὗτοι Ἰσραήλ· 9.7 οὐδ᾽ ὅτι εἰσὶν σπέρμα Ἀβραάμ, πάντες τέκνα, ἀλλ᾽, «ἐν Ἰσαὰκ κληθήσεταί σοι σπέρμα.» 9.8 τοῦτ᾽ ἔστιν, οὐ τὰ τέκνα τῆς σαρκὸς ταῦτα τέκνα τοῦ θεοῦ, ἀλλὰ τὰ τέκνα τῆς ἐπαγγελίας λογίζεται εἰς σπέρμα· 9.9 ἐπαγγελίας γὰρ ὁ λόγος οὗτος, «κατὰ τὸν καιρὸν τοῦτον ἐλεύσομαι καὶ ἔσται τῇ Σάρρᾳ υἱός.»

9.10 οὐ μόνον δέ, ἀλλὰ καὶ Ῥεβέκκα ἐξ ἑνὸς κοίτην ἔχουσα, Ἰσαὰκ τοῦ πατρὸς ἡμῶν·

9.11 μήπω γὰρ γεννηθέντων μηδὲ πραξάντων τι ἀγαθὸν ἢ φαῦλον, ἵνα ἡ κατ᾽ ἐκλογὴν πρόθεσις τοῦ θεοῦ μένῃ, 9.12 οὐκ ἐξ ἔργων ἀλλ᾽ ἐκ τοῦ καλοῦντος, ἐρρέθη αὐτῇ ὅτι «ὁ μείζων δουλεύσει τῷ ἐλάσσονι·» 9.13 καθὼς γέγραπται, «τὸν Ἰακὼβ ἠγάπησα, τὸν δὲ Ἠσαῦ ἐμίσησα.»

9.14 τί οὖν ἐροῦμεν; μὴ ἀδικία παρὰ τῷ θεῷ; μὴ γένοιτο·

9.15 τῷ Μωϋσεῖ γὰρ λέγει, «ἐλεήσω ὃν ἂν ἐλεῶ, καὶ οἰκτιρήσω ὃν ἂν οἰκτίρω.» 9.16 ἄρα οὖν οὐ τοῦ θέλοντος οὐδὲ τοῦ τρέχοντος, ἀλλὰ τοῦ ἐλεῶντος θεοῦ. 9.17 λέγει γὰρ ἡ γραφὴ τῷ Φαραὼ ὅτι «εἰς αὐτὸ τοῦτο ἐξήγειρά σε ὅπως ἐνδίξωμαι ἐν σοὶ τὴν δύναμίν μου, καὶ ὅπως διαγγελῇ τὸ ὄνομά μου ἐν πάσῃ τῇ γῇ.»

9.18 ἄρα οὖν ὃν θέλει ἐλεεῖ, ὃν δὲ θέλει σκληρύνει.

9.19 ἐρεῖς μοι οὖν, τί ἔτι μέμφεται; τῷ γὰρ βουλήματι αὐτοῦ τίς ἀνθέστηκεν; 9.20 ὦ ἄνθρωπε, μενοῦνγε σὺ τίς εἶ ὁ ἀνταποκρινόμενος τῷ θεῷ; μὴ ἐρεῖ τὸ πλάσμα τῷ πλάσαντι, τί με ἐποίησας οὕτως; 9.21 ἢ οὐκ ἔχει ἐξουσίαν ὁ κεραμεὺς τοῦ πηλοῦ

worship/service and the promises,

9.5 of whom *are* the fathers, and out of whom the anointed (one) *is* that according to flesh; the (one) being over all God blessed into the ages, truly. 9.6 But not as implying that the reason/word of God has fallen away. For not all *are* the (ones) out of Israel, these *are* from Israel; 9.7 neither because they are seed of Abraham *are* all children, but: IN/BY ISAAC WILL SEED BE CALLED FOR YOU. 9.8 This is, not the children of the flesh *are* these children of God, but the children of the promise is accounted into/for seed; 9.9 for this is the saying/word of a promise: ACCORDING TO THIS SEASON I SHALL COME AND A SON WILL BE FOR SARAH.

9.10 And not only *this*, but also Rebecca having one from a conjugal bed, from Isaac the father of us;

9.11 for not yet having been generated/birthed not having practiced anything good or vile/worthless, in order that the purpose of God might abide by/according to choice, 9.12 not from works but from the (one) calling, it was said to her: THE GREATER WILL BE A SLAVE TO THE LESSER; 9.13 as it has been written: I LOVED JACOB, BUT I HATED ESAU.

9.14 What then shall we say? Not injustice beside/from God? May it not happen!

9.15 For he says to Moses: I SHALL HAVE MERCY ON WHOM I WOULD HAVE MERCY, AND I SHALL PITY WHOM I WOULD PITY. 9.16 So then *it is* not of the (one) wishing nor the (one) running, but of the (one) having mercy from God. 9.17 For the writing says to Pharaoh: INTO/FOR THIS VERY THING I RAISED YOU UP, SO THAT I MIGHT DEMONSTRATE MY POWER IN/BY YOU, AND SO THAT MY NAME MIGHT BE PROCLAIMED IN ALL THE LAND/EARTH.

9.18 So then he has mercy on whom he wishes, and/but he hardens whom he wishes.

9.19 Then you will say to me: Why does he still find fault? For who has stood against his counsel/will? 9.20 O man/human, yea truly, who are you, the (one) disputing against God? Will not the (thing) formed say to the (one) having been formed: Why did you make me thus? *No.* 9.21 Or has the potter not authority *over* the clay to make out of the same lump

ἐκ τοῦ αὐτοῦ φυράματος ποιῆσαι ὃ μὲν εἰς τιμὴν σκεῦος, ὃ δὲ εἰς ἀτιμίαν;

9.22 εἰ δὲ θέλων ὁ θεὸς ἐνδείξασθε τὴν ὀργὴν καὶ γνωρίσαι τὸ δυνατὸν αὐτοῦ ἤνεγκεν ἐν πολλῇ μακροθυμίᾳ σκεύη ὀργῆς κατηρτισμένα εἰς ἀπώλιαν, 9.23 καὶ ἵνα γνωρίσῃ τὸν πλοῦτον τῆς δόξης αὐτοῦ ἐπὶ σκεύη ἐλέους, ἃ προητοίμασεν εἰς δόξαν, 9.24 οὓς καὶ ἐκάλεσεν ἡμᾶς οὐ μόνον ἐξ Ἰουδαίων ἀλλὰ καὶ ἐξ ἐθνῶν;

9.25 ὡς καὶ ἐν τῷ Ὡσηὲ λέγι, «καλέσω τὸν οὐ λαόν μου λαόν μου καὶ τὴν οὐκ ἠγαπημένην ἠγαπημένην· 9.26 καὶ ἔσται ἐν τῷ τόπῳ οὗ ἐρρέθη αὐτοῖς, οὐ λαός μου ὑμεῖς, ἐκεῖ κληθήσονται υἱοὶ θεοῦ ζῶντος.»

9.27 Ἠσαΐας δὲ κράζει ὑπὲρ τοῦ Ἰσραήλ, «ἐὰν ᾖ ὁ ἀριθμὸς τῶν υἱῶν Ἰσραὴλ ὡς ἡ ἄμμος τῆς θαλάσσης, τὸ ὑπόλιμμα σωθήσεται· 9.28 λόγον γὰρ συντελῶν καὶ συντέμνων ποιήσει κύριος ἐπὶ τῆς γῆς.»

9.29 καὶ καθὼς προείρηκεν Ἠσαΐας, «εἰ μὴ κύριος Σαβαὼθ ἐνκατέλιπεν ἡμῖν σπέρμα, ὡς Σόδομα ἂν ἐγενήθημεν καὶ ὡς Γόμορρα ἂν ὡμοιώθημεν.»

9.30 τί οὖν ἐροῦμεν; ὅτι ἔθνη τὰ μὴ διώκοντα δικαιοσύνην κατέλαβεν δικαιοσύνην, δικαιοσύνην δὲ τὴν ἐκ πίστεως· 9.31 Ἰσραὴλ δὲ διώκων νόμον δικαιοσύνης εἰς νόμον οὐκ ἔφθασεν. 9.32 διὰ τί; ὅτι οὐκ ἐκ πίστεως ἀλλ᾽ ὡς ἐξ ἔργων· προσέκοψαν τῷ λίθῳ τοῦ προσκόμματος, 9.33 καθὼς γέγραπται, «ἰδοὺ τίθημι ἐν Σιὼν λίθον προσκόμματος καὶ πέτραν σκανδάλου, καὶ ὁ πιστεύων ἐπ᾽ αὐτῷ οὐ κατεσχυνθήσεται.»

10.1 Ἀδελφοί, ἡ μὲν εὐδοκία τῆς ἐμῆς καρδίας καὶ ἡ δέησις πρὸς τὸν θεὸν ὑπὲρ αὐτῶν εἰς σωτηρίαν. 10.2 μαρτυρῶ γὰρ αὐτοῖς ὅτι ζῆλον θεοῦ ἔχουσιν, ἀλλ᾽ οὐ κατ᾽ ἐπίγνωσιν· 10.3 ἀγνοοῦντες γὰρ τὴν τοῦ θεοῦ δικαιοσύνην, καὶ τὴν ἰδίαν

one vessel into/for honor, but another into/for dishonor?

9.22 But if God, wanting to demonstrate/show the anger and to make known his power/ability, brought by much patience vessels of wrath having been fitted to/for destruction, 9.23 and in order that he might make known the wealth of his glory/reputation upon/over vessels/tools of mercy, which he previously prepared in/for glory, 9.24 *from* whom he also called us, not only out of Judeans but also out of ethnics?

9.25 As he also says to Osee (Hosea): I SHALL NOT CALL THE PEOPLE OF ME MY PEOPLE, AND THE *people* HAVING NOT BEEN LOVED HAVING BEEN LOVED; 9.26 AND IT WILL BE IN/AT THE PLACE WHERE IT WAS SAID TO THEM: YE *are* NOT A PEOPLE OF ME; THERE THEY WILL BE CALLED SONS OF A LIVING GOD.

9.27 But Esaias cries in behalf of Israel: IF THE NUMBER OF THE SONS OF ISRAEL BE AS THE SAND OF THE SEA, THE REMNANT WILL BE SAVED; 9.28 FOR ACCOMPLISHING AND CUTTING SHORT, *the* LORD WILL MAKE A REASON/WORD UPON THE EARTH.

9.29 And as Esaias (Isaiah) said before: EXCEPT *the* LORD OF SABAOTH/ARMIES LEFT A SEED FOR US, WE WOULD HAVE BECOME AS SODOM AND WE WOULD HAVE BEEN LIKENED AS GOMORRA.

9.30 What then shall we say? That ethnics, the (ones) not pursuing justice apprehended/obtained justice, but the justice out of faith; 9.31 but Israel, pursuing a law of justice/justness attained not in law. 9.32 Why/because of what? Because not out of faith but as out of works; they stumbled *on* the stone of the stum-bling block/offense, 9.33 as it has been written: BEHOLD I PUT A STONE OF STUMBLING/OFFENSE IN SION (Zion) AND A ROCK OF OFFENSE/REVULSION, AND THE (ONE) BELIEVING ON HIM WILL NOT BE PUT TO SHAME.

10.1 Brothers, indeed the choice/pleasure of my heart and the petition to God in behalf of ye *is* into/for salvation/deliverance. 10.2 For I witness to them that they have zeal of God, but not according to knowledge; 10.3 for not knowing the justice/justness

δικαιοσύνην ζητοῦντες στῆσαι, τῇ δικαιοσύνῃ τοῦ θεοῦ οὐχ ὑπετάγησαν·

10.4 τέλος γὰρ νόμου χριστὸς εἰς δικαιοσύνην παντὶ τῷ πιστεύοντι.

10.5 Μωϋσῆς γὰρ γράφει τὴν δικαιοσύνην τὴν ἐκ νόμου ὅτι «ὁ ποιήσας» αὐτὰ «ἄνθρωπος ζήσεται ἐν αὐτοῖς.»

10.6 ἡ δὲ ἐκ πίστεως δικαιοσύνη οὕτως λέγει, «μὴ εἴπῃς ἐν τῇ καρδίᾳ σου, τίς ἀναβήσεται εἰς τὸν οὐρανόν;» τοῦτ' ἔστιν χριστὸν καταγαγεῖν· 10.7 ἤ, «τίς καταβήσεται εἰς τὴν ἄβυσσον;» τοῦτ' ἔστιν χριστὸν ἐκ νεκρῶν ἀναγαγεῖν. 10.8 ἀλλὰ τί λέγει; «ἐγγύς σου τὸ ῥῆμά ἐστιν, ἐν τῷ στόματί σου καὶ ἐν τῇ καρδίᾳ σου·» τοῦτ' ἔστιν τὸ ῥῆμα τῆς πίστεως ὃ κηρύσσομεν. 10.9 ὅτι ἐὰν ὁμολογήσῃς ἐν τῷ στόματί σου κύριον Ἰησοῦν, καὶ πιστεύσῃς ἐν τῇ καρδίᾳ σου ὅτι ὁ θεὸς αὐτὸν ἤγειρεν ἐκ νεκρῶν, σωθήσῃ· 10.10 καρδίᾳ γὰρ πιστεύεται εἰς δικαιοσύνην, στόματι δὲ ὁμολογεῖται εἰς σωτηρίαν. 10.11 λέγει γὰρ ἡ γραφή, πᾶς «ὁ πιστεύων ἐπ' αὐτῷ οὐ καταισχυνθήσεται.» 10.12 οὐ γάρ ἐστιν διαστολὴ Ἰουδαίου τε καὶ Ἕλληνος, ὁ γὰρ αὐτὸς κύριος πάντων, πλουτῶν εἰς πάντας τοὺς ἐπικαλουμένους αὐτόν· 10.13 «πᾶς» γὰρ «ὃς ἂν ἐπικαλέσηται τὸ ὄνομα κυρίου σωθήσεται.»

10.14 πῶς οὖν ἐπικαλέσωνται εἰς ὃν οὐκ ἐπίστευσαν; πῶς δὲ πιστεύσωσιν οὗ οὐκ ἤκουσαν; πῶς δὲ ἀκούσωσιν χωρὶς κηρύσσοντος; 10.15 πῶς δὲ κηρύξωσιν ἐὰν μὴ ἀποσταλῶσιν; καθὼς γέγραπται, «ὡς ὡρέοι οἱ πόδες τῶν εὐαγγελιζομένων τὰ ἀγαθά.»

10.16 ἀλλ' οὐ πάντες ὑπήκουσαν ἐν τῷ εὐαγγελίῳ·

Ἠσαΐας γὰρ λέγει, «κύριε, τίς ἐπίστευσεν τῇ ἀκοῇ ἡμῶν;»

10.17 ἄρα ἡ πίστις ἐξ ἀκοῆς, ἡ δὲ ἀκοὴ διὰ ῥήματος χριστοῦ.

of God, and seeking to establish *their* own justness/ justice, they were not subjected/subordinated to the justness of God;

10.4 for the anointed (one) is an end of law into/for justice/justness for every one believing.

10.5 For Moses writes the justice from the law, that THE MAN DOING them WILL LIVE BY THEM.

10.6 But the justness/justice from faith says thus: YOU MAY NOT SAY IN YOUR HEART: WHO WILL GO UP INTO THE SKY/HEAVEN? This is *for* the anointed (one) to bring down; 10.7 or: WHO WILL GO DOWN INTO THE ABYSS? This is *for* the anointed (one) to bring up out of dead (ones). 10.8 But what does it say? THE WORD/RHETORIC IS NEAR YOU, IN YOUR MOUTH AND IN YOUR HEART; this is the word of the faith which we herald/proclaim. 10.9 Because if you might confess *the* Lord Jesus with your mouth, and might believe in your heart that God raised him out of dead (ones), you will be saved; 10.10 for in/with heart (one) believes in justice, and by mouth (one) confesses into salvation. 10.11 For the writing says: Every ONE BELIEVING ON HIM WILL NOT BE PUT TO SHAME. 10.12 For there is not a distinction/difference, both from Judean and from Greek, for the same (one) *is* Lord of all, being rich/ wealthy to/for all the (ones) calling upon him; 10.13 for EVERY (ONE) WHO WOULD CALL UPON THE NAME OF *the* LORD WILL BE SAVED.

10.14 How then should they call upon (one) in whom they did not believe? And how might they believe *the one* of whom they heard not? And how might they hear apart from/without (one) heralding/preaching? 10.15 And how might they herald/preach unless they might be sent? As it has been written: HOW HANDSOME/ MATURE *are* THE FEET OF THOSE ANNOUNCING THE GOOD (THINGS).

10.16 But not all obeyed in/at the good message/gospel;

for Esaias says: LORD, WHO BELIEVED IN OUR RE-PORT?

10.17 Therefore the faith *is* from a report, and the report/hearing *is* through a word/rhetoric from the anointed (one).

10.18 ἀλλὰ λέγω, μὴ οὐκ ἤκουσαν; μενοῦνγε, «εἰς πᾶσαν τὴν γῆν ἐξῆλθεν ὁ φθόγγος αὐτῶν, καὶ εἰς τὰ πέρατα τῆς οἰκουμένης τὰ ῥήματα αὐτῶν.» 10.19 ἀλλὰ λέγω, μὴ Ἰσραὴλ οὐκ ἔγνω; πρῶτος Μωϋσῆς λέγει, «ἐγὼ παραζηλώσω» ὑμᾶς «ἐπ᾽ οὐκ ἔθνι, ἐπ᾽ ἔθνι ἀσυνέτῳ παροργιῶ» ὑμᾶς.

10.20 Ἡσαΐας δὲ ἀποτολμᾷ καὶ λέγει, «εὑρέθην τοῖς ἐμὲ μὴ» ζητοῦσιν, ἐμφανὴς ἐγενόμην τοῖς ἐμὲ μὴ «ἐπερωτῶσιν.»

10.21 πρὸς δὲ τὸν Ἰσραὴλ λέγι, «ὅλην τὴν ἡμέραν ἐξεπέτασα τὰς χεῖράς μου πρὸς λαὸν ἀπιθοῦντα καὶ ἀντιλέγοντα.»

11.1 Λέγω οὖν, μὴ ἀπώσατο ὁ θεὸς τὸν λαὸν αὐτοῦ; μὴ γένοιτο· καὶ γὰρ ἐγὼ Ἰσδραηλείτης εἰμί, ἐκ σπέρματος Ἀβραάμ, φυλῆς Βενιαμείν. 11.2 οὐκ ἀπώσατο ὁ θεὸς τὸν λαὸν αὐτοῦ ὃν προέγνω.

ἢ οὐκ οἴδατε ἐν Ἠλίᾳ τί λέγει ἡ γραφή; ὡς ἐντυγχάνει τῷ θεῷ κατὰ τοῦ Ἰσραήλ, 11.3 κύριε, «τοὺς προφήτας σου ἀπέκτιναν, τὰ θυσιαστήριά σου κατέσκαψαν, κἀγὼ ὑπελίφθην μόνος, καὶ ζητοῦσιν τὴν ψυχήν μου.»

11.4 ἀλλὰ τί λέγει αὐτῷ ὁ χρηματισμός; «κατέλιπον» ἐμαυτῷ «ἑπτακισχιλίους ἄνδρας, οἵτινες οὐκ ἔκαμψαν γόνυ τῇ Βάαλ.»

11.5 οὕτως οὖν καὶ ἐν τῷ νῦν καιρῷ λῖμμα κατ᾽ ἐκλογὴν χάριτος γέγονεν· 11.6 εἰ δὲ χάριτι, οὐκέτι ἐξ ἔργων, ἐπὶ ἡ χάρις οὐκέτι γείνεται χάρις. 11.7 τί οὖν; ὃ ἐπιζητεῖ Ἰσραήλ, τοῦτο οὐκ ἐπέτυχεν, ἡ δὲ ἐκλογὴ ἐπέτυχεν· οἱ δὲ λοιποὶ ἐπωρώθησαν,

11.8 καθάπερ γέγραπται, «ἔδωκεν αὐτοῖς ὁ ὁ θεὸς πνεῦμα κατανύξεως, ὀφθαλμοὺς τοῦ μὴ βλέπειν καὶ ὦτα τοῦ μὴ ἀκούειν, ἕως τῆς σήμερον ἡμέρας.»

11.9 καὶ Δαυὶδ λέγει, «γενηθήτω ἡ τράπεζα αὐτῶν εἰς παγίδα» καὶ εἰς θήραν «καὶ εἰς σκάνδαλον καὶ εἰς ἀνταπόδομα αὐτοῖς, 11.10 σκοτισθήτωσαν οἱ ὀφθαλμοὶ αὐτῶν τοῦ μὴ βλέπειν,

10.18 But I say: Did not they hear/listen? *No.* On the contrary, THEIR SOUND/TONE WENT OUT INTO ALL THE LAND/EARTH, AND THEIR WORDS TO THE ENDS OF THE INHABITED EARTH (Roman Empire). 10.19 But I say: Did Israel not know? *No.* First Moses says: I, I SHALL PROVOKE YE TO JEALOUSY NOT AGAINST AN ETHNIC/NATION, I SHALL ANGER YE AGAINST A SENSELESS ETHNIC/NATION.

10.20 But Esaias dares and says: I WAS FOUND BY/AMONG THOSE NOT SEEKING ME, I BECAME VISIBLE/MANIFEST/PLAIN TO THOSE NOT QUESTIONING ME.

10.21 But he says to Israel: I STRETCHED OUT MY HANDS THE ENTIRE DAY TO/TOWARD A DISOBEYING AND CONTRADICTING PEOPLE.

11.1 Therefore I say: Did not God reject his people? May it not happen; for I, even I am an Israelite, out of seed/descendants from Abraham, from *the* tribe of Benjamin. 11.2 God rejected not/thrust not away his people whom he knew before.

Or know ye not what the writing says by/in Elias? How he pleads/converses with God against Israel: 11.3 Lord, THEY KILLED YOUR PROPHETS, THEY DUG DOWN YOUR ALTARS, AND I, I ALONE WAS LEFT, AND THEY SEEK MY LIFE/SOUL.

11.4 But what says the response to him: I RESERVED SEVEN THOUSAND MEN for myself, WHO DID NOT BOW A KNEE TO BAAL.

11.5 So then there has also become a remnant in the present time according to a choice of grace; 11.6 and if by grace/a gift, *it is* no longer from/out of works, since the grace becomes no longer a gift/grace. 11.7 Then what? What Israel seeks for, this he obtained not, but the choice/choosing/selection obtained; and the rest were hardened,

11.8 even as it has been written: GOD GAVE A SPIRIT OF STUPOR/DULLNESS TO THEM, FROM THE (THING) *for* EYES TO SEE NOT AND OF THE (THING) *for* EARS TO HEAR NOT, UNTIL THE DAY, TODAY.

11.9 And David says: LET THEIR TABLE BECOME IN/FOR A SNARE and a net AND A STUMBLING BLOCK/OFFENSE AND A RETRIBUTION TO THEM, 11.10 LET THEIR EYES BE DARKENED FROM THE (THING) TO SEE NOT, AND THE BACK OF

καὶ τὸν νῶτον αὐτῶν διὰ παντὸς σύνκαμψον.»

11.11 λέγω οὖν, μὴ ἔπταισαν ἵνα πέσωσιν; μὴ γένοιτο·

ἀλλὰ τῷ αὐτῶν παραπτώματι ἡ σωτηρία τοῖς ἔθνεσιν, εἰς τὸ παραζηλῶσαι αὐτούς. 11.12 εἰ δὲ τὸ παράπτωμα αὐτῶν πλοῦτος κόσμου καὶ τὸ ἥττημα αὐτῶν πλοῦτος ἐθνῶν, πόσῳ μᾶλλον τὸ πλήρωμα αὐτῶν.

11.13 ὑμῖν δὲ λέγω τοῖς ἔθνεσιν. ἐφ' ὅσον μὲν οὖν εἰμι ἐγὼ ἐθνῶν ἀπόστολος, τὴν διακονίαν μου δοξάζω, 11.14 εἴ πως παραζηλώσω μου τὴν σάρκα καὶ σώσω τινὰς ἐξ αὐτῶν.

11.15 εἰ γὰρ ἡ ἀποβολὴ αὐτῶν καταλλαγὴ κόσμου, τίς ἡ πρόσλημψις εἰ μὴ ζωὴ ἐκ νεκρῶν;

11.16 εἰ δὲ ἡ ἀπαρχὴ ἁγία, καὶ τὸ φύραμα· καὶ εἰ ἡ ῥίζα ἁγία, καὶ οἱ κλάδοι.

11.17 εἰ δέ τινες τῶν κλάδων ἐξεκλάσθησαν, σὺ δὲ ἀγριέλαιος ὢν ἐνεκεντρίσθης ἐν αὐτοῖς καὶ συνκοινωνὸς τῆς ῥίζης τῆς πιότητος τῆς ἐλέας ἐγένου, 11.18 μὴ κατακαυχῶ τῶν κλάδων· εἰ δὲ κατακαυχᾶσαι, οὐ σὺ τὴν ῥίζαν βαστάζεις ἀλλὰ ἡ ῥίζα σέ.

11.19 ἐρεῖς οὖν, ἐξεκλάσθησαν κλάδοι ἵνα ἐγὼ ἐνκεντρισθῶ. 11.20 καλῶς· τῇ ἀπιστίᾳ ἐξεκλάσθησαν, σὺ δὲ τῇ πίστι ἕστηκας. μὴ ὑψηλὰ φρόνει, ἀλλὰ φοβοῦ· 11.21 εἰ γὰρ ὁ θεὸς τῶν κατὰ φύσιν κλάδων οὐκ ἐφίσατο, οὐδὲ σοῦ φίσεται.

11.22 ἴδε οὖν χρηστότητα καὶ ἀποτομίαν θεοῦ· ἐπὶ μὲν τοὺς πεσόντας ἀποτομία, ἐπὶ δὲ σὲ χρηστότητος θεοῦ, ἐὰν ἐπιμένῃς τῇ χρηστότητι, ἐπεὶ καὶ σὺ ἐκκοπήσῃ. 11.23 κἀκεῖνοι δέ, ἐὰν μὴ ἐπιμένωσιν τῇ ἀπιστίᾳ, ἐνκεντρισθήσονται· δυνατὸς γάρ ἐστιν ὁ θεὸς πάλιν ἐνκεντρίσαι αὐτούς.

11.24 εἰ γὰρ σὺ ἐκ τῆς κατὰ φύσιν ἐξεκόπης ἀγριελαίου καὶ παρὰ φύσιν ἐνεκεντρίσθης εἰς καλλιέλαιον, πόσῳ μᾶλλον

THEM CAUSED TO BEND THROUGH/BECAUSE OF EVERY (THING).

11.11   Therefore, I say: Did they not trip that they might fall? May it not become;

but in/by the trespass of them *is* the salvation for the ethnics. in/for the (thing) to provoke them to jealousy.   11.12 But if their trespass *be* the wealth of a world and their defeat *be* wealth of ethnics, by how much more the fullness of them.

11.13   But I speak to ye, to the ethnics: Then indeed in as much as I, I am an apostle of ethnics, I glorify/acknowledge my service/ministry,   11.14 if somehow I shall/might provoke my flesh to zeal and I shall/might save some out of them.

11.15   For if the throwing off of them *be* a reconciliation of *the* world, what *is* the reception except life out of dead (ones)?

11.16   And if the firstfruit *be* holy, also the lump/dough; and if the root *be* holy, also the branches.

11.17   But if some of the branches were broken off, and you being a wild olive tree was grafted in among them and you became a partner/sharer from the root of the fatness of the olive tree,   11.18 boast you not over the branches; but if you do boast, you, you bear/carry not the root, but the root you.

11.19   Therefore you will say: Branches were broken off in order that I, I might be grafted in. 11.20 Well, they were broken off for the unbelief/ disobedience, and you, you stand in/by the faith. Think not high (things), but fear;   11.21 for if God spared not the branches according to nature, neither will he spare you.

11.22   Behold then a kindness and a severity from God: On one hand, severity *is* upon those having fallen; on the other, kindness from God *is* upon you, if you may continue in/for the kindness, since, even you will be cut off.   11.23 And those also, if they continue not in the unbelief/disobedience, will be grafted in; for God is able to graft them in again.

11.24   For if you, you was cut off from the wild olive tree according to nature and was grafted in against nature into a cultivated olive tree, by how

οὗτοι οἱ κατὰ φύσιν ἐνκεντρισθήσονται τῇ ἰδίᾳ ἐλαίᾳ.

11.25 οὐ θέλω γὰρ ὑμᾶς ἀγνοεῖν, ἀδελφοί, τὸ μυστήριον τοῦτο, ἵνα μὴ ἦτε παρ' ἑαυτοῖς φρόνιμοι, ὅτι πώρωσις ἀπὸ μέρους τῷ Ἰσραὴλ γέγονεν ἄχρις οὗ τὸ πλήρωμα τῶν ἐθνῶν εἰσέλθῃ, 11.26 καὶ οὕτω πᾶς Ἰσραὴλ σωθήσεται· καθὼς γέγραπται, «ἥξει ἐκ Σιὼν ὁ ῥυόμενος, ἀποστρέψει ἀσεβίας ἀπὸ Ἰακώβ· 11.27 καὶ αὕτη αὐτοῖς ἡ παρ' ἐμοῦ διαθήκη, ὅταν ἀφέλωμαι τὰς ἁμαρτίας αὐτῶν.»

11.28 κατὰ μὲν τὸ εὐαγγέλιον ἐχθροὶ δι' ὑμᾶς, κατὰ δὲ τὴν ἐκλογὴν ἀγαπητοὶ διὰ τοὺς πατέρας· 11.29 ἀμεταμέλητα γὰρ τὰ χαρίσματα καὶ ἡ κλῆσις τοῦ θεοῦ. 11.30 ὥσπερ γὰρ ὑμεῖς ποτε ἠπειθήσατε τῷ θεῷ, νῦν δὲ ἠλεήθητε τῇ τούτων ἀπειθείᾳ,

11.31 οὕτως καὶ οὗτοι νῦν ἠπίθησαν τῷ ὑμετέρῳ ἐλέει ἵνα καὶ αὐτοὶ νῦν ἐλεηθῶσιν· 11.32 συνέκλισεν γὰρ ὁ θεὸς τοὺς πάντας εἰς ἀπίθιαν ἵνα τοὺς πάντας ἐλεήσῃ.

11.33 ὦ βάθος πλούτου καὶ σοφίας καὶ γνώσεως θεοῦ· ὡς ἀνεξεραύνητα τὰ κρίματα αὐτοῦ καὶ ἀνεξιχνίαστοι αἱ ὁδοὶ αὐτοῦ. 11.34 «τίς» γὰρ «ἔγνω νοῦν κυρίου; ἢ τίς σύμβουλος αὐτοῦ ἐγένετο; 11.35 ἢ τίς προέδωκεν αὐτῷ, καὶ ἀνταποδοθήσετε αὐτῷ;» 11.36 ὅτι ἐξ αὐτοῦ καὶ δι' αὐτοῦ καὶ εἰς αὐτὸν τὰ πάντα· αὐτῷ ἡ δόξα εἰς τοὺς αἰῶνας· ἀμήν.

12.1 Παρακαλῶ οὖν ὑμᾶς, ἀδελφοί, διὰ τῶν οἰκτιρμῶν τοῦ θεοῦ, παραστῆσαι τὰ σώματα ὑμῶν θυσίαν ζῶσαν ἁγίαν εὐάρεστον τῷ θεῷ, τὴν λογικὴν λατρίαν ὑμῶν·

much more will these, the (ones) according to nature, be grafted in their own olive tree.

11.25 For I want/wish not *for* ye to be ignorant, brothers, *of* this mystery (religion), in order that ye may not be wise (ones) with/beside yourselves, dullness/insensitivity from a part has become for/to Israel until which (time) the fullness of the ethnics/Gentiles might come in, 11.26 and thus all Israel/every (one) of Israel will be saved/delivered; as it has been written: THE (ONE) RESCUING/RANSOMING WILL COME OUT OF SION, HE WILL TURN AWAY IMPIETY/IRREVERENCE FROM JACOB; 11.27 AND THIS *is* THE COVENANT FROM ME TO THEM, WHENEVER I MIGHT SEND AWAY/FORGIVE THEIR SINS/THE SINS OF THEM.

11.28 On one hand, *they are* enemies according to the good message/gospel because of ye; on the other, according to the choice/election, *they are* beloved (ones) because of the fathers; 11.29 for the gifts and the invitation/calling from God *are* without repentance/change. 11.30 For just as ye, ye formerly might be disobedient to God, and now ye were shown mercy for the disobedience of these,

11.31 so also these now disobeyed for your mercy in order that they now might also be shown mercy; 11.32 for God hemmed in/enclosed all the (ones) in disobedience in order that he might have mercy on them all.

11.33 O depth of wealth and wisdom and knowledge of God! How unsearchable *are* the judgments of him, and the roads/ways of him *are* incomprehensible. 11.34 For WHO KNEW A THOUGHT/MIND OF *the* LORD? OR WHO BECAME HIS COUNSELOR/ADVISER? 11.35 OR WHO PREVIOUSLY GAVE TO HIM, AND IT WILL BE REPAID TO HIM? 11.36 Because all the (things) are from him and through him and in/for him; to him *be* the glory/reputation into the ages; truly.

12.1 Therefore I beseech ye, brothers, through the compassions of God, to present your bodies a holy, well-pleasing sacrifice, living for God, the reasonable service/worship from ye/your reasonable service/worship;

12.2 καὶ μὴ συνσχηματίζεσθαι τῷ αἰῶνι τούτῳ, ἀλλὰ μεταμορφοῦσθε τῇ ἀνακαινώσει τοῦ νοός ὑμῶν, εἰς τὸ δοκιμάζειν ὑμᾶς τί τὸ θέλημα τοῦ θεοῦ, τὸ ἀγαθὸν καὶ εὐάρεστον καὶ τέλειον. 12.3 λέγω γὰρ διὰ τῆς χάριτος τῆς δοθίσης μοι παντὶ τῷ ὄντι ἐν ὑμῖν μὴ ὑπερφρονῖν παρ' ὃ δεῖ φρονῖν, ἀλλὰ φρονῖν εἰς τὸ σωφρονῖν, ἑκάστῳ ὡς ὁ θεὸς ἐμέρισεν μέτρον πίστεως.

12.4 καθάπερ γὰρ ἐν ἑνὶ σώματι πολλὰ μέλη ἔχομεν, τὰ δὲ μέλη πάντα οὐ τὴν αὐτὴν ἔχει πρᾶξιν, 12.5 οὕτως οἱ πολλοὶ ἓν σῶμά ἐσμεν ἐν χριστῷ, τὸ δὲ καθ' ἷς ἀλλήλων μέλη.

12.6 ἔχοντες δὲ χαρίσματα κατὰ τὴν χάριν τὴν δοθῖσαν ἡμῖν διάφορα, εἴτε προφητίαν κατὰ τὴν ἀναλογίαν τῆς πίστεως, 12.7 εἴτε διακονίαν ἐν τῇ διακονίᾳ, εἴτε ὁ διδάσκων ἐν τῇ διδασκαλίᾳ, 12.8 εἴτε ὁ παρακαλῶν ἐν τῇ παρακλήσει,

ὁ μεταδιδοὺς ἐν ἁπλότητι, ὁ προϊστανόμενος ἐν σπουδῇ, ὁ ἐλαιῶν ἐν ἱλαρότητι.

12.9 ἡ ἀγάπη ἀνυπόκριτος. ἀποστυγοῦντες τὸ πονηρόν, κολλώμενοι τῷ ἀγαθῷ·

12.10 τῇ φιλαδελφίᾳ εἰς ἀλλήλους φιλόστοργοι, τῇ τιμῇ ἀλλήλους προηγούμενοι,

12.11 τῇ σπουδῇ μὴ ὀκνηροί, τῷ πνεύματι ζέοντες, τῷ κυρίῳ δουλεύοντες, 12.12 τῇ ἐλπίδι χαίροντες, τῇ θλίψι ὑπομένοντες, τῇ προσευχῇ προσκαρτεροῦντες, 12.13 ταῖς χρίαις τῶν ἁγίων κοινωνοῦντες, τὴν φιλοξενίαν διώκοντες. 12.14 εὐλογεῖτε τοὺς διώκοντας ὑμᾶς, εὐλογεῖτε καὶ μὴ καταρᾶσθε.

12.15 χαίρειν μετὰ χαιρόντων, κλαίειν μετὰ κλαιόντων. 12.16 τὸ αὐτὸ εἰς ἀλλήλους φρονοῦντες,

μὴ τὰ ὑψηλὰ φρονοῦντες ἀλλὰ τοῖς ταπινοῖς

12.2 and be ye not conformed to this age, but be ye transformed by the renewing of your mind/thinking, in/to the (thing) *for* ye to prove/test what *is* the will/purpose of God, the (thing) *being* good and acceptable and mature/complete. 12.3 For I say through the gift/grace having been given to me for every one being among ye, not thinking above/beyond what it is necessary to think, but to think in the (thing) to be sober-minded, as God bestowed to each (one) a measure of faith.

12.4 For even as we are many members in one body, but all the members have not the same practice/activity, 12.5 so *being* the many, we are one body in the anointed (one), but *for* the (thing) one by one *we are* members of one another.

12.6 And having the different gifts according to the grace/favor having been given to us: whether prophecy, according to the agreement/sound reasoning of the faith; 12.7 or a service, in the ministry/service; or the (one) teaching, by/in the teaching; 12.8 or the (one) exhorting, in the exhortation;

the (one) sharing, in simplicity/with sincerity; the (one) presiding, with diligence; the (one) showing mercy, with/in cheerfulness.

12.9 The agape *is* without pretense/hypocrisy, detesting/abhorring the evil, being joined to the good;

12.10 *Be ye* affectionate (ones) in brotherly love to one another, giving precedence to one another in honor,

12.11 *Be ye* not slothful (ones) in the diligence, being fervent/zealous in the spirit, slaving for the Lord, 12.12 rejoicing in the hope, bearing up under/enduring in the affliction, attending constantly to the prayer, 12.13 contributing to/jointly participating in the needs of the saints, pursuing the hospitality. 12.14 Bless ye/speak well of the (ones) prosecuting ye, bless ye/speak well and do not curse.

12.15 To rejoice with rejoicing (ones), to weep with weeping (ones), 12.16 having the same/thinking the same thought/(thing) to/for one another,

thinking not the high/exalted (things) but con-

συναπαγόμενοι. μὴ γίνεσθαι φρόνιμοι παρ᾽ ἑαυτοῖς.

12.17 μηδενὶ κακὸν ἀντὶ κακοῦ ἀποδιδόντες· προνοούμενοι καλὰ ἐνώπιον πάντων ἀνθρώπων·

12.18 εἰ δυνατόν, τὸ ἐξ ὑμῶν μετὰ πάντων ἀνθρώπων εἰρηνεύοντες·

12.19 μὴ ἑαυτοὺς ἐκδικοῦντες, ἀγαπητοί, ἀλλὰ δότε τόπον τῇ ὀργῇ, γέγραπται γάρ, «ἐμοὶ ἐκδίκησεις, ἐγὼ ἀνταποδώσω,» λέγει κύριος.

12.20 ἀλλ᾽ «ἐὰν πινᾷ ὁ ἐχθρός σου, ψώμιζε αὐτόν· ἐὰν διψᾷ, πότιζε αὐτόν· τοῦτο γὰρ ποιῶν ἄνθρακας πυρὸς σωρεύσεις ἐπὶ τὴν κεφαλὴν αὐτοῦ.» 12.21 μὴ νικῶ ὑπὸ τοῦ κακοῦ, ἀλλὰ νίκα ἐν τῷ ἀγαθῷ τὸ κακόν.

13.1 Πᾶσα ψυχὴ ἐξουσίαις ὑπερεχούσαις ὑποτασσέσθω. οὐ γὰρ ἔστιν ἐξουσία εἰ μὴ ὑπὸ θεοῦ, αἱ δὲ οὖσαι ὑπὸ θεοῦ τεταγμέναι εἰσίν· 13.2 ὥστε ὁ ἀντιτασσόμενος τῇ ἐξουσίᾳ τῇ τοῦ θεοῦ διαταγῇ ἀνθέστηκεν, οἱ δὲ ἀνθεστηκότες ἑαυτοῖς κρίμα λήμψονται.

13.3 οἱ γὰρ ἄρχοντες οὐκ εἰσὶν φόβος τῷ ἀγαθῷ ἔργῳ ἀλλὰ τῷ κακῷ. θέλεις δὲ μὴ φοβεῖσθε τὴν ἐξουσίαν; τὸ ἀγαθὸν ποίει, καὶ ἕξις ἔπαινον ἐξ αὐτῆς· 13.4 θεοῦ γὰρ διάκονός ἐστιν σοὶ εἰς τὸ ἀγαθόν. ἐὰν δὲ τὸ κακὸν ποιῇς, φοβοῦ· οὐ γὰρ εἰκῇ τὴν μάχαιραν φορεῖ· θεοῦ γὰρ διάκονός ἐστιν, ἔκδικος εἰς ὀργὴν τῷ τὸ κακὸν πράσσοντι.

13.5 διὸ ἀνάγκη ὑποτάσσεσθαι, οὐ μόνον διὰ τὴν ὀργὴν ἀλλὰ καὶ διὰ τὴν συνίδησιν. 13.6 διὰ τοῦτο γὰρ καὶ φόρους τελεῖτε, λιτουργοὶ γὰρ θεοῦ εἰσιν εἰς αὐτὸ τοῦτο προσκαρτεροῦντες.

13.7 ἀπόδοτε πᾶσιν τὰς ὀφιλάς, τῷ τὸν φόρον τὸν φόρον,

forming yourselves willingly to the humble (ones). Become ye not wise (ones) beside/by yourselves.

12.17 Repaying no one evil for evil; striving to practice good/beautiful (things) before/in the sight of all men;

12.18 If possible, the (thing) from/of ye *is* seeking peace/being at peace with all men;

12.19 avenging not yourselves, beloved (ones), but give place to the anger, for it has been written: VENGEANCE *is* FOR ME, I, I SHALL REPAY, says *the* Lord.

12.20 But IF YOUR ENEMY BE HUNGRY, FEED HIM; IF HE BE THIRSTY, GIVE HIM DRINK; FOR DOING THIS, YOU WILL PILE UP COALS OF FIRE UPON HIS HEAD. 12.21 Be not overcome/conquered by the bad, but overcome/conquer the bad by the good.

13.1 Let every life/soul be subjected/subordinated to authorities being superior. For there is not authority except by/under God, and the (ones) being have been ordained by God; 13.2 So that the (one) being opposed to the authority has stood against the institute/ordinance of God, but the (ones) having opposed/stood against *it* will receive a judgment for themselves.

13.3 For the (ones) ruling/leading are not a terror/fear for the good work but for the bad. And do you want/wish not to fear the authority? Do the good (thing), and you will have lauding/approbation from her; 13.4 for a servant/minister of/from God is for you in the good (thing). But if you may do the bad, you must fear; for he bears not the sword for no purpose; for he is a servant/minister/deacon/waiter of God, an avenger in anger/wrath to the (one) practicing the bad.

13.5 Wherefore *it is* a necessity to be subjected to, not only because of the anger/wrath but also because of the conscience. 13.6 For because of this, ye also accomplish/pay tribute/tax, for they are public servants/liturgists of God, attending constantly to this very thing.

13.7 Pay ye back the debts to all, to the (one) the tribute, the tax; to the (one) the end, the end;

τῷ τὸ τέλος τὸ τέλος, τῷ τὸν φόβον τὸν φόβον, τῷ τὴν τιμὴν τὴν τιμήν. 13.8 μηδενὶ μηδὲν ὀφίλοντε, εἰ μὴ τὸ ἀλλήλους ἀγαπᾶν·

ὁ γὰρ ἀγαπῶν τὸν ἕτερον νόμον πεπλήρωκεν. 13.9 τὸ γὰρ «οὐ μοιχεύσις, οὐ φονεύσεις, οὐ κλέψεις, οὐ ψευδομαρτηρήεις, οὐκ ἐπιθυμήσεις,» καὶ εἴ τις ἑτέρα ἐντολή, ἐν τῷ λόγῳ τούτῳ ἀνακεφαλαιοῦται, ἐν τῷ «ἀγαπήσις τὸν πλησίον σου ὡς σεαυτόν.» 13.10 ἡ ἀγάπη τῷ πλησίον κακὸν οὐκ ἐργάζεται·

πλήρωμα οὖν νόμου ἡ ἀγάπη.

13.11 καὶ τοῦτο εἰδότες τὸν καιρόν, ὅτι ὥρα ἤδη ὑμᾶς ἐξ ὕπνου ἐγερθῆναι, νῦν γὰρ ἐγγύτερον ἡμῶν ἡ σωτηρία ἢ ὅτε ἐπιστεύσαμεν. 13.12 ἡ νὺξ προέκοψεν, ἡ δὲ ἡμέρα ἤγγικεν.

ἀποθώμεθα οὖν τὰ ἔργα τοῦ σκότους, καὶ ἐνδυσώμεθα τὰ ὅπλα τοῦ φωτός. 13.13 ὡς ἐν ἡμέρᾳ εὐσχημόνως περιπατήσωμεν, μὴ κώμοις καὶ μέθαις, μὴ κοίταις καὶ ἀσελγίαις, μὴ ἔριδι καὶ ζήλῳ· 13.14 ἀλλ᾽ ἐνδύσασθε τὸν κύριον Ἰησοῦν χριστόν,

καὶ τῆς σαρκὸς πρόνοιαν μὴ ποιεῖσθαι εἰς ἐπιθυμίας.

14.1 Τὸν δὲ ἀσθενοῦντα τῇ πίστι προσλαμβάνεσθε, μὴ εἰς διακρίσεις διαλογισμῶν. 14.2 ὃς μὲν πιστεύει φαγῖν πάντα, ὁ δὲ ἀσθενῶν λάχανα ἐσθίει.

14.3 ὁ ἐσθίων τὸν μὴ ἐσθίοντα μὴ ἐξουθενίτω, ὁ δὲ μὴ ἐσθίων τὸν ἐσθίοντα μὴ κρινέτω, ὁ θεὸς γὰρ αὐτὸν προσελάβετο. 14.4 σὺ τίς εἶ ὁ κρίνων ἀλλότριον οἰκέτην; τῷ ἰδίῳ κυρίῳ στήκει ἢ πίπτει· σταθήσεται δέ, δυνατῖ γὰρ ὁ κύριος στῆσαι αὐτόν.

14.5 ὃς μὲν γὰρ κρίνει ἡμέραν παρ᾽ ἡμέραν, ὃς δὲ κρίνει

to the (one) the fear, the fear; to the (one) the honor, the honor. 13.8 Owe ye nothing to no one, except the (thing) to love one another;

for the (one) loving the other/different (one) has fulfilled *the* law. 13.9 For the (thing): YOU WILL NOT DO ADULTERY, YOU WILL NOT MURDER, YOU WILL NOT STEAL, YOU WILL NOT TESTIFY TO A LIE, YOU WILL NOT DESIRE/LONG FOR/COVET, and if *there be* any other/different command, it is brought together under one heading by this saying, by the (saying): YOU WILL LOVE YOUR NEIGHBOR AS YOURSELF. 13.10 The agape works not bad to the neighbor;

The agape *is* therefore the fullness of law.

13.11 And this, knowing the time/season, because *it is* already a time/hour *for* ye to be raised up out of sleep/hypnosis, for the salvation *is* nearer now than when we believed. 13.12 The night progressed, and the day has drawn near.

Therefore, we should/let us throw off the works of the darkness, and we should/let us put on the weapons/tools of the light. 13.13 We should/let us walk decently as in/by day, not in carousings/orgies and drunkennesses, not in sexual indulgences and revelries/parties, not in strife and jealousy; 13.14 but put ye on the Lord Jesus, the anointed (one),

and make ye not a provision/care into/for desires of the flesh.

14.1 But take with yourselves the (one) being weak in the faith, not in/for judgments of thoughts/reasonings. 14.2 *The one* who believes *is* indeed to eat all (things), but the (one) being weak eats herbs/vegetables.

14.3 The (one) eating should not/let not the one eating despise/reject the (one) not eating, and let not the (one) not eating judge the (one) eating, for God took/accepted him. 14.4 You, who are you, the (one) judging another's house servant? He stands or falls for his own lord; and he will be stood/established, for the Lord is able to stand/establish him.

14.5 *There is* indeed (one) who judges day by day, but also *there is one* who judges every day; let

πᾶσαν ἡμέραν· ἕκαστος ἐν τῷ ἰδίῳ νοεῖ πληροφορίσθω.

14.6 ὁ φρονῶν τὴν ἡμέραν κυρίῳ φρονεῖ· καὶ ὁ ἐσθίων κυρίῳ ἐσθίει, εὐχαριστῖ γὰρ τῷ θεῷ·

14.7 οὐδὶς γὰρ ἡμῶν ἑαυτῷ ζῇ, καὶ οὐδὶς ἑαυτῷ ἀποθνῄσκι· 14.8 ἐάν τε γὰρ ζῶμεν, τῷ κυρίῳ ζῶμεν, ἐάν τε ἀποθνῄσκωμεν, τῷ κυρίῳ ἀποθνῄσκομεν. ἐάν τε οὖν ζῶμεν ἐάν τε ἀποθνῄσκωμεν, τοῦ κυρίου ἐσμέν. 14.9 εἰς τοῦτο γὰρ χριστὸς ἀπέθανεν καὶ ἔζησεν ἵνα καὶ νεκρῶν καὶ ζώντων κυριεύσῃ. 14.10 σὺ δὲ τί κρίνεις τὸν ἀδελφόν σου; ἢ καὶ σὺ τί ἐξουθενῖς τὸν ἀδελφόν σου; πάντες γὰρ παραστησόμεθα τῷ βήματι τοῦ θεοῦ·

14.11 γέγραπται γάρ, «ζῶ ἐγώ, λέγει κύριος, ὅτι ἐμοὶ κάμψει πᾶν γόνυ, καὶ πᾶσα γλῶσσα ἐξομολογήσεται τῷ θεῷ.» 14.12 ἄρα οὖν ἕκαστος ἡμῶν περὶ ἑαυτοῦ λόγον δώσει τῷ θεῷ.

14.13 μηκέτι οὖν ἀλλήλους κρίνωμεν· ἀλλὰ τοῦτο κρίνατε μᾶλλον, τὸ μὴ τιθέναι πρόσκομμα τῷ ἀδελφῷ ἢ σκάνδαλον.

14.14 οἶδα καὶ πέπεισμαι ἐν κυρίῳ Ἰησοῦ ὅτι οὐδὲν κοινὸν δι’ ἑαυτοῦ· εἰ μὴ τῷ λογιζομένῳ τι κοινὸν εἶναι, ἐκείνῳ κοινόν.

14.15 εἰ γὰρ διὰ βρῶμα ὁ ἀδελφός σου λυπεῖται, οὐκέτι κατὰ ἀγάπην περιπατεῖς. μὴ τῷ βρώματί σου ἐκεῖνον ἀπόλλυε ὑπὲρ οὗ χριστὸς ἀπέθανεν. 14.16 μὴ βλασφημίσθω οὖν ὑμῶν τὸ ἀγαθόν.

14.17 οὐ γάρ ἐστιν ἡ βασιλεία τοῦ θεοῦ βρῶσις καὶ πόσις, ἀλλὰ δικαιοσύνη καὶ εἰρήνη καὶ χαρὰ ἐν πνεύματι ἁγίῳ· 14.18 ὁ γὰρ ἐν τούτῳ δουλεύων τῷ χριστῷ εὐάρεστος τῷ θεῷ καὶ δόκιμος τοῖς ἀνθρώποις.

14.19 ἄρα οὖν τὰ τῆς εἰρήνης διώκωμεν καὶ τὰ τῆς

each (one) be fully persuaded in his own mind/understanding.

14.6 The (one) regarding the day regards it for the Lord; and the (one) eating eats for the Lord, for he gives thanks to God;

and the (one) not eating eats not for the Lord, and he gives thanks to God.

14.7 For no one of us lives for himself, and no one dies for himself; 14.8 for not only if we live, we live for the Lord, but also if we die, we die for the Lord. Then whether we may live and if we may die, we are the Lord's. 14.9 For the anointed (one) died in/for this (thing), and he lived in order that he might be Lord of both dead (ones) and living (ones). 14.10 But you, why do you judge your brother? Or you, why do you also despise/reject your brother? For we all shall stand beside the tribunal/judgment seat of God; 14.11 for it has been written: I, I LIVE/AM ALIVE, SAYS *the* LORD, BECAUSE EVERY KNEE WILL BOW TO ME, AND EVERY TONGUE WILL CONFESS TO GOD. 14.12 So therefore, each (one) of us will give an account about himself to God.

14.13 Therefore, let us no longer judge one another; but rather judge ye this, the (thing) not to put/place a stumbling-block or offense/cause to stumble for the brother.

14.14 I know and have been persuaded by *the* Lord Jesus that nothing *is* common/unclean through itself; except *for* something to be common/unclean to the (one) accounting *it* *so*, *it* *is* common/unclean to/for that (one).

14.15 For if your brother is grieved/pained because of food, you walk no longer according to agape. Destroy not that (one), in behalf of whom the anointed (one) died, for your food. 14.16 Then let not the good (thing) of ye be reviled/slandered/blasphemed.

14.17 For the kingdom of God is not food and drink, but justice and peace and joy in/by a holy spirit; 14.18 for the (one) slaving in this for the anointed (one) *is* acceptable to God and proven/approved by the men/humans. 14.19 So then, let us pursue

οἰκοδομῆς τῆς εἰς ἀλλήλους· 14.20 μὴ ἕνεκεν βρώματος κατάλυε τὸ ἔργον τοῦ θεοῦ. πάντα μὲν **καθαρά, ἀλλὰ κακὸν τῷ ἀνθρώπῳ τῷ διὰ προσκόμματος ἐσθίοντι**. 14.21 **καλὸν τὸ μὴ φαγεῖν κρέα μηδὲ πιεῖν οἶνον μηδὲ ἐν ᾧ ὁ ἀδελφός σου προσκόπτει**.

14.22 σὺ πίστιν ἣν ἔχεις κατὰ σεαυτὸν ἔχε ἐνώπιον τοῦ θεοῦ. μακάριος ὁ μὴ κρίνων ἑαυτὸν ἐν ᾧ δοκιμάζει· 14.23 ὁ δὲ διακρινόμενος ἐὰν φάγῃ κατακέκριται, ὅτι οὐκ ἐκ πίστεως· πᾶν δὲ ὃ οὐκ ἐκ πίστεως ἁμαρτία ἐστίν.

15.1 Ὀφίλομεν δὲ ἡμεῖς οἱ δυνατοὶ τὰ ἀσθενήματα τῶν ἀδυνάτων βαστάζειν, καὶ μὴ ἑαυτοῖς ἀρέσκιν. 15.2 ἕκαστος ἡμῶν τῷ πλησίον ἀρεσκέτω εἰς τὸ ἀγαθὸν πρὸς οἰκοδομήν· 15.3 καὶ γὰρ ὁ χριστὸς οὐχ ἑαυτῷ ἤρεσεν· ἀλλὰ καθὼς γέγραπται, «οἱ ὀνιδισμοὶ τῶν ὀνιδιζόντων σε ἐπέπεσαν ἐπ᾽ ἐμέ.»

15.4 ὅσα γὰρ προεγράφη, εἰς τὴν ἡμετέραν διδασκαλίαν ἐγράφη, ἵνα διὰ τῆς ὑπομονῆς καὶ διὰ τῆς παρακλήσεως τῶν γραφῶν τὴν ἐλπίδα ἔχωμεν. 15.5 ὁ δὲ θεὸς τῆς ὑπομονῆς καὶ τῆς παρακλήσεως δῴη ὑμῖν τὸ αὐτὸ φρονῖν ἐν ἀλλήλοις κατὰ Ἰησοῦν χριστόν, 15.6 ἵνα ὁμοθυμαδὸν ἐν ἑνὶ στόματι δοξάζητε τὸν θεὸν καὶ πατέρα τοῦ κυρίου ἡμῶν Ἰησοῦ χριστοῦ.

15.7 διὸ προσλαμβάνεσθαι ἀλλήλους, καθὼς καὶ ὁ χριστὸς προσελάβετο ὑμᾶς, εἰς δόξαν τοῦ θεοῦ. 15.8 λέγω γὰρ χριστὸν διάκονον γεγενῆσθαι περιτομῆς ὑπὲρ ἀληθίας θεοῦ, εἰς τὸ βεβαιῶσαι τὰς ἐπαγγελίας τῶν πατέρων, 15.9 τὰ δὲ ἔθνη ὑπὲρ ἐλέους δοξάσαι τὸν θεόν·

the (things) of the peace and the (things) of the building/edification, of the (one) in/for one another; 14.20 do not destroy the work of God for the sake of food. Indeed, all (things) *are* pure/clean, but bad to the man/human eating through/because of an offense/ stumbling-block. 14.21 Good/beautiful *is* the (thing) not to eat meat nor to drink wine nor *the thing* in/by which your brother stumbles.

14.22 You, you have faith, which you have according to yourself before God. Happy *is* the (one) not judging himself in/by *the thing* which he proves/ tests. 14.23 But the (one) doubting has been condemned if he might eat, because *it is* not from/out of faith, and every (thing) which *is* not from/out of faith is sin.

15.1 But we, the able/strong (ones), we are indebted to bear/carry the weaknesses/sicknesses of the unable (ones), and not to please ourselves. 15.2 Let each (one) of us be pleasing to the neighbor in the good toward building/edification; 15.3 for even the anointed (one) was not for pleasing himself, but as it has been written: THE REPROACHES/REVILINGS FROM THOSE REPROACHING YOU FELL UPON ME.

15.4 For what (things) were previously written, were written into/for our teaching, in order that we may have the hope through the endurance/patience and through the consolation of the writings. 15.5 And from the endurance and the consolation God may give to ye to think the same (thing) in/with one another according to Jesus, the anointed (one), 15.6 in order that with one mouth ye might unanimously glorify/acknowledge the God and father of our Lord Jesus, the anointed (one).

15.7 Wherefore tolerate/receive/accept ye one another, as the anointed (one) also received/accepted ye, in *the* glory/fame/reputation of God. 15.8 For I say the anointed (one) to have become a servant/minister of circumcision in behalf of truth from God, in/for the (thing) to confirm the promises from the fathers, 15.9 and *for* the ethnics to glorify/acknowledge God over/beyond mercy;

καθὼς γέγραπται, «διὰ τοῦτο ἐξομολογήσομαί σοι ἐν ἔθνεσιν, καὶ τῷ ὀνοματί σου ψαλῶ.»

15.10 καὶ πάλιν λέγει, «εὐφράνθητε, ἔθνη, μετὰ τοῦ λαοῦ αὐτοῦ.»

15.11 καὶ πάλιν, «αἰνεῖται, πάντα τὰ ἔθνη, τὸν κύριον, καὶ ἐπαινεσάτωσαν αὐτὸν πάντες οἱ λαοί.»

15.12 καὶ πάλιν λέγει Ἠσαΐας, «ἔσται ἡ ῥίζα τοῦ Ἰεσσαί, καὶ ὁ ἀνιστανόμενος ἄρχειν ἐθνῶν· ἐπ’ αὐτῷ ἔθνη ἐλπιοῦσιν.» 15.13 ὁ δὲ θεὸς τῆς ἐλπίδος πληρῶσαι ὑμᾶς πάσης χαρᾶς καὶ εἰρήνης ἐν τῷ πιστεύειν, εἰς τὸ περισσεύειν ὑμᾶς ἐν τῇ ἐλπίδι ἐν δυνάμι πνεύματος ἁγίου.

15.14 πέπισμαι δέ, ἀδελφοί μου, καὶ αὐτὸς ἐγὼ περὶ ὑμῶν, ὅτι καὶ αὐτοὶ μεστοί ἐστε ἀγαθωσύνης, πεπληρωμένοι πάσης τῆς γνώσεως, δυνάμενοι καὶ ἀλλήλους νουθετεῖν.

15.15 τολμηρότερον δὲ ἔγραψα ὑμῖν ἀπὸ μέρους, ὡς ἐπαναμιμνήσκων ὑμᾶς διὰ τὴν χάριν τὴν δοθεῖσάν μοι ὑπὸ τοῦ θεοῦ 15.16 εἰς τὸ εἶναί με λιτουργὸν χριστοῦ Ἰησοῦ εἰς τὰ ἔθνη, ἱερουργοῦντα τὸ εὐαγγέλιον τοῦ θεοῦ, ἵνα γένηται ἡ προσφορὰ τῶν ἐθνῶν εὐπρόσδεκτος, ἡγιασμένη ἐν πνεύματι ἁγίῳ.

15.17 ἔχω οὖν καύχησιν ἐν χριστῷ Ἰησοῦ τὰ πρὸς τὸν θεόν· 15.18 οὐ γὰρ τολμήσω τι λαλῖν ὧν οὐ κατειργάσατο χριστὸς δι’ ἐμοῦ εἰς ὑπακοὴν ἐθνῶν, λόγῳ καὶ ἔργῳ, 15.19 ἐν δυνάμει σημείων καὶ τεράτων, ἐν δυνάμει πνεύματος θεοῦ·

ὥστε με ἀπὸ Ἰερουσαλὴμ καὶ κύκλῳ μέχρι τοῦ Ἰλλυρικοῦ πεπληρωκέναι τὸ εὐαγγέλιον τοῦ χριστοῦ,

15.20 οὕτως δὲ φιλοτιμούμενον εὐαγγελίζεσθαι οὐχ ὅπου ὠνομάσθη χριστός, ἵνα μὴ ἐπ’ ἀλλότριον θεμέλιον οἰκοδομῶ, 15.21 ἀλλὰ καθὼς γέγραπται, «οἷς οὐκ ἀνηγγέλλη περὶ αὐτοῦ

as it has been written: BECAUSE OF THIS I SHALL CONFESS/ADMIT TO YOU AMONG ETHNICS, AND SHALL SING A PSALM/PRAISE TO YOUR NAME.

15.10 And it says again: BE YE GLAD, ETHNICS, WITH THE PEOPLE OF HIM.

15.11 And again: PRAISE YE THE LORD, ALL THE ETHNICS/NATIONS, AND LET ALL THE PEOPLES PRAISE HIM.

15.12 And again Esaias says: THERE WILL BE THE ROOT FROM JESSE, AND THE (ONE) RISING UP TO RULE over ETHNICS; ETHNICS WILL HOPE ON HIM. 15.13 And may the God of the hope fill ye with every joy and peace in/by the (thing) to believe, in/for the (thing) for ye to abound in the hope by power/ability from a holy spirit.

15.14 But I have been persuaded, my brothers, even I, myself, concerning ye, that also/even ye are yourselves full of goodness, having been filled from all knowledge, being able also to admonish/warn one another.

15.15 And I wrote more daringly to ye from a part, as reminding ye because of the grace/gift having been given to me by God 15.16 in/for the (thing) for me to be a public minister/liturgist of the the anointed Jesus to the ethnics, ministering/officiating the good message/gospel from God, in order that the offering/sacrifice from the ethnics might become acceptable, having been sanctified/consecrated in/by a holy spirit.

15.17 Therefore I have/hold triumph/boasting the things toward God in/by the anointed Jesus; 15.18 for I shall not dare to speak anything which the anointed (one) did not work out through me into/for obedience of ethnics, for a word/saying and for a work, 15.19 in/by power/ability of signs and wonders, in/by power of a spirit from God;

so as for me to have fulfilled the good message/gospel of the anointed (one) from Jerusalem and round about as far as the Illyricum, and 15.20 so loving the honor/being ambitious to announce the good message where the anointed (one) was not called upon/named, in order that I may not build on another's foundation, 15.21 but as it has been written: THEY WILL LOOK TO

ὄψονται, καὶ οἳ οὐκ ἀκηκόασιν συνήσουσιν.»

15.22 διὸ καὶ ἐνεκοπτόμην τὰ πολλὰ τοῦ ἐλθῖν πρὸς ὑμᾶς·

15.23 νυνὶ δὲ μηκέτι τόπον ἔχων ἐν τοῖς κλίμασι τούτοις, ἐπιποθίαν δὲ ἔχων τοῦ ἐλθῖν πρὸς ὑμᾶς ἀπὸ πολλῶν ἐτῶν, 15.24 ὡς ἂν πορεύωμαι εἰς τὴν Σπανίαν· ἐλπίζω γὰρ διαπορευόμενος θεάσασθαι ὑμᾶς καὶ ὑφ' ὑμῶν προπεμφθῆναι ἐκεῖ ἐὰν ὑμῶν πρῶτον ἀπὸ μέρους ἐμπλησθῶ

15.25 νυνὶ δὲ πορεύομαι εἰς Ἰερουσαλὴμ διακονήσων τοῖς ἁγίοις. 15.26 ηὐδόκησαν γὰρ Μακαιδονία καὶ Ἀχαΐα κοινωνίαν τινὰ ποιήσασθαι εἰς τοὺς πτωχοὺς τῶν ἁγίων τῶν ἐν Ἰερουσαλήμ. 15.27 ηὐδόκησαν γάρ, καὶ ὀφιλέται εἰσὶν αὐτῶν· εἰ γὰρ τοῖς πνευματικοῖς αὐτῶν ἐκοινώνησαν τὰ ἔθνη, ὀφίλουσιν καὶ ἐν τοῖς σαρκικοῖς λιτουργῆσαι αὐτοῖς.

15.28 τοῦτο οὖν ἐπιτελέσας, καὶ σφραγισάμενος αὐτοῖς τὸν καρπὸν τοῦτον, ἀπελεύσομαι δι' ὑμῶν εἰς Σπανίαν· 15.29 οἶδα δὲ ὅτι ἐρχόμενος πρὸς ὑμᾶς ἐν πληρώματι εὐλογίας χριστοῦ ἐλεύσομαι.

15.30 παρακαλῶ δὲ ὑμᾶς, ἀδελφοί, διὰ τοῦ κυρίου ἡμῶν Ἰησοῦ χριστοῦ καὶ διὰ τῆς ἀγάπης τοῦ πνεύματος, συναγωνίσασθαί μοι ἐν ταῖς προσευχαῖς ὑπὲρ ἐμοῦ πρὸς τὸν θεόν, 15.31 ἵνα ῥυσθῶ ἀπὸ τῶν ἀπιθούντων ἐν τῇ Ἰουδαίᾳ καὶ ἡ διακονία μου ἡ ἰς Ἰερουσαλὴμ εὐπρόσδεκτος τοῖς ἁγίοις γένηται, 15.32 ἵνα ἐν χαρᾷ ἐλθὼν πρὸς ὑμᾶς διὰ θελήματος Ἰησοῦ χριστοῦ συναναπαύσωμαι ὑμῖν. 15.33 ὁ δὲ θεὸς τῆς ἰρήνης μετὰ πάντων ὑμῶν· ἀμήν.

16.1 Συνίστημι δὲ ὑμῖν Φοίβην τὴν ἀδελφὴν ἡμῶν, οὖσαν διάκονον τῆς ἐκκλησίας τῆς ἐν Κενχραιαῖς, 16.2 ἵνα αὐτὴν προσδέξησθε ἐν κυρίῳ ἀξίως τῶν ἁγίων, καὶ παραστῆτε αὐτῇ ἐν ᾧ ἂν ὑμῶν χρῄζῃ πράγματι, καὶ γὰρ αὐτὴ προστάτις πολλῶν ἐγενήθη καὶ αὐτοῦ καὶ ἐμοῦ.

(THOSE) WHOM IT WAS NOT REPORTED CONCERNING HIM, AND (THOSE) WHO HAVE NOT HEARD WILL UNDERSTAND.

15.22 Wherefore I was also being interrupted *for* many things from the (thing) to come to ye;

15.23 but now no longer having a place in these climates/regions, and having a desire from many years of the (thing) to come/go to ye, 15.24 since I would travel to Spain; for I hope, going through/(on the way) to behold ye and to be sent on there by ye, if I may first be filled from a part of ye.

15.25 But now I go to Jerusalem, serving for/ ministering to the saints. 15.26 For Macedonia and Achaia thought it good to make a certain/some contribution to the poor (ones) of the saints in Jerusalem. 15.27 For they thought it good, and they are debtors of them; for if the ethnics participated/shared in the spiritual (things) of them, they are also obligated to serve/minister publicly to them in the fleshly (things).

15.28 Therefore, having completed this, and having sealed this fruit for them, I shall go away through ye to Spain; 15.29 and I know that coming to ye, I shall come in fullness of a blessing from the anointed (one).

15.30 But I beseech ye, brothers, through our Lord Jesus, the anointed (one), and through the agape of the spirit, to strive together with me in the prayers to God in behalf of me, 15.31 in order that I might be rescued from the unbelieving (ones) in Judea and my service/ministry in Jerusalem might become acceptable to the saints, 15.32 in order that having come to ye in joy through a will/purpose of Jesus, the anointed (one), I might have refreshment/rest with ye. 15.33 And the God of the peace *be* with ye all; truly.

16.1 And I recommend Phoebe our sister to ye, being a servant/minister/deacon from the assembly in Cenchrea, 16.2 in order that ye might receive her in *the* Lord, worthily of the saints, and ye might stand beside her in a matter which she would have need from ye, for she also became/came about both from him and from me.

16.3 ἀσπάσασθαι Πρίσκαν καὶ ᾿Ακύλαν τοὺς συνεργούς μου ἐν χριστῷ ᾿Ιησοῦ, 16.4 οἵτινες ὑπὲρ τῆς ψυχῆς μου τὸν ἑαυτῶν τράχηλον ὑπέθηκαν, οἷς οὐκ ἐγὼ μόνος εὐχαριστῶ ἀλλὰ καὶ πᾶσαι αἱ ἐκκλησίαι τῶν ἐθνῶν, 16.5 καὶ τὴν κατ᾿ οἶκον αὐτῶν ἐκκλησίαν.

ἀσπάσασθαι ᾿Επαίνετον τὸν ἀγαπητόν μου, ὅς ἐστιν ἀπαρχὴ τῆς ᾿Ασίας εἰς χριστόν. 16.6 ἀσπάσασθε Μαρίαμ, ἥτις πολλὰ ἐκοπίασεν εἰς ὑμᾶς.

16.7 ἀσπάσασθαι ᾿Ανδρόνικον καὶ ᾿Ιουνιᾶν τοὺς συγγενεῖς μου καὶ συνεχμαλώτους μου, οἵτινές εἰσιν ἐπίσημοι ἐν τοῖς ἀποστόλοις, οἳ καὶ πρὸ ἐμοῦ γέγοναν ἐν χριστῷ.

16.8 ἀσπάσασθαι ᾿Αμπλιᾶτον τὸν ἀγαπητόν μου ἐν κυρίῳ.

16.9 ἀσπάσασθε Οὐρβανὸν τὸν συνεργὸν ἡμῶν ἐν χριστῷ καὶ Στάχυν τὸν ἀγαπητόν μου.

16.10 ἀσπάσασθε ᾿Απελλῆν τὸν δόκιμον ἐν χριστῷ.

ἀσπάσασθε τοὺς ἐκ τῶν ᾿Αριστοβούλου.

16.11 ἀσπάσασθε Ἡρῳδίωνα τὸν συγγενῆ μου.

ἀσπάσασθε τοὺς ἐκ τῶν Ναρκίσσου τοὺς ὄντας ἐν κυρίῳ.

16.12 ἀσπάσασθαι Τρύφεναν καὶ Τρυφῶσαν τὰς κοπιώσας ἐν κυρίῳ.

ἀσπάσασθαι Περσίδα τὴν ἀγαπητήν, ἥτις πολλὰ ἐκοπίασεν ἐν κυρίῳ. 16.13 ἀσπάσασθε Ῥοῦφον τὸν ἐκλεκτὸν ἐν κυρίῳ καὶ τὴν μητέρα αὐτοῦ καὶ ἐμοῦ. 16.14 ἀσπάσασθε ᾿Ασύνκριτον, Φλέγοντα, Ἑρμῆν, Πατροβᾶν, Ἑρμᾶν, καὶ τοὺς σὺν αὐτοῖς ἀδελφούς. 16.15 ἀσπάσασθε Φιλόλογον καὶ ᾿Ιουλίαν, Νηρέα καὶ τὴν ἀδελφὴν αὐτοῦ, καὶ ᾿Ολυμπᾶν, καὶ τοὺς σὺν αὐτοῖς πάντας ἁγίους.

16.16 ἀσπάσασθε ἀλλήλους ἐν φιλήματι ἁγίῳ. ἀσπάζονται ὑμᾶς αἱ ἐκκλησίαι πᾶσαι τοῦ χριστοῦ.

16.17 παρακαλῶ δὲ ὑμᾶς, ἀδελφοί, σκοπεῖν τοὺς τὰς διχοστασίας καὶ τὰ σκάνδαλα παρὰ τὴν διδαχὴν ἣν ὑμεῖς ἐμάθετε ποιοῦντας, καὶ ἐκκλίνετε ἀπ᾿ αὐτῶν· 16.18 οἱ γὰρ

277

16.3 Greet ye Prisca and Aquila, my fellow workers in the anointed Jesus, 16.4 who put down/ risked the neck of themselves in behalf of the life/ soul of me, to whom not only I, I give thanks, but also all the assemblies of the ethnics, 16.5 and the assem-bly by their house.

Greet ye Eraenetus, my beloved (one), who is a firstfruit from Asia in/for the anointed (one). 16.6 Greet ye Mary, who labored/toiled much to/for ye.

16.7 Greet ye Andronicus and Junius, my rela- tives and my fellow prisoners/captives, who are nota- ble (men) among/by the apostles, who also have be- come/come about before me in the anointed (one).

16.8 Greet ye Ampliatus, my beloved (one) in *the* Lord.

16.9 Greet ye Urbanus, our fellow worker in the anointed (one), and Stachys, my beloved (one).

16.10 Greet ye Apelles, the proven (one) in the anointed (one).

Greet ye the (ones) out of/from those of Aristo- bulus.

16.11 Greet ye Herodion, my relative.

Greet ye the (ones) out of/from those of Narcis- sus, the (ones) being in *the* Lord.

16.12 Greet ye Tryphaena and Tryphosa, the (ones) laboring in *the* Lord.

Greet ye Persis, the beloved (woman), who labor- ed/toiled much in *the* Lord. 16.13 Greet ye Rufus, the chosen (one) in *the* Lord/the (one) chosen by *the* Lord and the mother of him and of me. 16.14 Greet ye Asyncritus, Phlegon, Hermes, Patrobas, Hermas, and the brothers with them. 16.15 Greet ye Philologus and Julia, Nerea and his sister, and Olympas, and all the saints with them.

16.16 Greet ye one another with a holy kiss. All the assemblies of the anointed (one) greets/salutes ye.

16.17 But I beseech ye, brothers, to beware of those making the divisions and the stumbling blocks from the doctrine which ye, ye learned, and turn ye away from them; 16.18 for the (those) such slave/are slaving not for the anointed (one) our Lord, but for

τοιοῦτοι τῷ κυρίῳ ἡμῶν χριστῷ οὐ δουλεύουσιν ἀλλὰ τῇ ἑαυτῶν κοιλίᾳ, καὶ διὰ τῆς χρηστολογίας καὶ εὐλογίας ἐξαπατῶσι τὰς καρδίας τῶν ἀκάκων.

16.19 ἡ γὰρ ὑμῶν ὑπακοὴ εἰς πάντας ἀφίκετο· ἐφ' ὑμῖν οὖν χαίρω,

θέλω δὲ ὑμᾶς σοφοὺς μὲν εἶναι εἰς τὸ ἀγαθόν, ἀκαιρέους δὲ εἰς τὸ κακόν.

16.20 ὁ δὲ θεὸς τῆς εἰρήνης συντρίψι τὸν Σατανᾶν ὑπὸ τοὺς πόδας ὑμῶν ἐν τάχι.

ἡ χάρις τοῦ κυρίου ἡμῶν Ἰησοῦ μεθ' ὑμῶν.

16.21 ἀσπάζεται ὑμᾶς Τιμόθεος ὁ συνεργός μου, καὶ Λούκιος καὶ Ἰάσων καὶ Σωσίπατρος οἱ συγγενεῖς μου.

16.22 ἀσπάζομαι ὑμᾶς ἐγὼ Τέρτιος ὁ γράψας τὴν ἐπιστολὴν ἐν κυρίῳ.

16.23 ἀσπάζεται ὑμᾶς Γάϊος ὁ ξένος μου καὶ ὅλης τῆς ἐκκλησίας.

ἀσπάζεται ὑμᾶς Ἔραστος ὁ οἰκονόμος τῆς πόλεως καὶ Κούαρτος ὁ ἀδελφός. 16.25 τῷ δὲ δυναμένῳ ὑμᾶς στηρίξαι κατὰ τὸ εὐαγγέλιόν μου καὶ τὸ κήρυγμα Ἰησοῦ χριστοῦ, κατὰ ἀποκάλυψιν μυστηρίου χρόνοις αἰωνίοις σεσιγημένου 16.26 φανερωθέντος δὲ νῦν διά τε γραφῶν προφητικῶν κατ' ἐπιταγὴν τοῦ αἰωνίου θεοῦ εἰς ὑπακοὴν πίστεως εἰς πάντα τὰ ἔθνη γνωρισθέντος, 16.27 μόνῳ σοφῷ θεῷ διὰ Ἰησοῦ χριστοῦ ᾧ ἡ δόξα εἰς τοὺς αἰῶνας τῶν αἰώνων· ἀμήν.

Πρὸς Ρωμαίους

the belly of themselves, and they deceive the hearts of the innocent/blameless simple (ones) through the smooth speech and praise/flattery.

16.19 For the obedience of ye reached/was reported to all; therefore, I rejoice over ye, and I want/wish *for* ye to be wise in the good, but unmixed/not mingled in the bad.

16.20 And the God of the peace will bruise/crush Satan under the feet of ye in quickness/with speed.

The grace of our Lord Jesus *be* with ye.

16.21 Timothy, my fellow worker, greets ye, also Lucius and Jason and Sosipater, the relatives of me.

16.22 I, Tertios, the (one) having written the epistle, I greet ye in *the* Lord.

16.23 Gaius, my host, and the entire assemble greets/salutes ye.

Erastus, the (house) manager of the city and Quartus, the brother, greets ye. 16.25 But to the (one) being able to stand/establish ye according to the good message/gospel from me and the preaching/proclamation of Jesus the anointed (one), according to a revelation of a mystery (religion) having been kept silent for eternal ages, 16.26 but now having been made plain/manifested and through writings from prophets according to/by a precept/order from the eternal God, having been made known to all the ethnics into/for obedience from faith, 16.27 to *the* only wise God, through Jesus the anointed (one), to whom *be* the glory into the ages of the ages; truly.

To Romans

This is the Sinaitic New Testament, book of 1 Corinthians.

1.1 Παῦλος κλητὸς ἀπόστολος χριστοῦ Ἰησοῦ διὰ θελήματος θεοῦ, καὶ Σωσθένης ὁ ἀδελφός, 1.2 τῇ ἐκκλησίᾳ τοῦ θεοῦ τῇ οὔσῃ ἐν Κορίνθῳ, ἡγιασμένοις ἐν χριστῷ Ἰησοῦ, κλητοῖς ἁγίοις, σὺν πᾶσι τοῖς ἐπικαλουμένοις τὸ ὄνομα τοῦ κυρίου ἡμῶν Ἰησοῦ χριστοῦ ἐν παντὶ τόπῳ, αὐτῶν καὶ ἡμῶν·

1.3 χάρις ὑμῖν καὶ εἰρήνη ἀπὸ θεοῦ πατρὸς ἡμῶν καὶ κυρίου Ἰησοῦ χριστοῦ.

1.4 εὐχαριστῶ τῷ θεῷ μου πάντοτε περὶ ὑμῶν ἐπὶ τῇ χάριτι τοῦ θεοῦ τῇ δοθίσῃ ὑμῖν ἐν χριστῷ Ἰησοῦ, 1.5 ὅτι ἐν παντὶ ἐπλουτίσθητε ἐν αὐτῷ, ἐν παντὶ λόγῳ καὶ πάσῃ γνώσει, 1.6 καθὼς τὸ μαρτύριον τοῦ χριστοῦ ἐβεβαιώθη ἐν ὑμῖν, 1.7 ὥστε ὑμᾶς μὴ ὑστερῖσθαι ἐν μηδενὶ χαρίσματι, ἀπεκδεχομένους τὴν ἀποκάλυψιν τοῦ κυρίου ἡμῶν Ἰησοῦ χριστοῦ· 1.8 ὃς καὶ βεβαιώσει ὑμᾶς ἕως τέλους ἀνεγκλήτους ἐν τῇ ἡμέρᾳ τοῦ κυρίου ἡμῶν Ἰησοῦ χριστοῦ. 1.9 πιστὸς ὁ θεὸς δι' οὗ ἐκλήθητε εἰς κοινωνίαν τοῦ υἱοῦ αὐτοῦ Ἰησοῦ χριστοῦ τοῦ κυρίου ἡμῶν.

1.10 παρακαλῶ δὲ ὑμᾶς, ἀδελφοί, διὰ τοῦ ὀνόματος τοῦ κυρίου ἡμῶν Ἰησοῦ χριστοῦ, ἵνα τὸ αὐτὸ λέγητε πάντες, καὶ μὴ ᾖ ἐν ὑμῖν σχίσματα, ἦτε δὲ κατηρτισμένοι ἐν τῷ αὐτῷ νοῒ καὶ ἐν τῇ αὐτῇ γνώμῃ. 1.11 ἐδηλώθη γάρ μοι περὶ ὑμῶν, ἀδελφοί μου, ὑπὸ τῶν Χλόης ὅτι ἔριδες ἐν ὑμῖν εἰσιν. 1.12 λέγω δὲ τοῦτο, ὅτι ἕκαστος ὑμῶν λέγει, ἐγὼ μέν εἰμι Παύλου, ἐγὼ δὲ Ἀπολλῶ, ἐγὼ δὲ Κηφᾶ, ἐγὼ δὲ χριστοῦ.

1.13 μεμέρισται ὁ χριστός; μὴ Παῦλος ἐσταυρώθη ὑπὲρ ὑμῶν, ἢ εἰς τὸ ὄνομα Παύλου ἐβαπτίσθητε; 1.14 εὐχαριστῶ ὅτι οὐδένα ὑμῶν ἐβάπτισα εἰ μὴ Κρίσπον καὶ Γάϊον, 1.15 ἵνα μή τις εἴπῃ ὅτι εἰς τὸ ἐμὸν ὄνομα ἐβαπτίσθητε. 1.16 ἐβάπτισα δὲ καὶ τὸν Στεφανᾶ οἶκον· λοιπὸν οὐκ οἶδα εἴ τινα ἄλλον ἐβάπτισα.

1.17 οὐ γὰρ ἀπέστιλέν με χριστὸς βαπτίζειν ἀλλὰ

1.1 Paul, a called apostle of Jesus, the anointed (one), through *the* will of God, and Sosthenes the brother, 1.2 to the assembly of God being in Corinth, to (those) having been sanctified/set apart in the anointed Jesus, to (those) called saints, with all (those) calling upon the name of our Lord Jesus, the anointed (one), in every place, of them and of us:

1.3 Grace to ye and peace from God our father and *the* Lord Jesus, the anointed (one).

1.4 I give thanks to my God always concerning ye upon/for the grace/gift of God being given to ye in/by the anointed Jesus, 1.5 because ye were enriched in every (thing) by him, by every saying/word and every knowledge, 1.6 as the witness/testimony of the anointed (one) was established in ye, 1.7 so as *for* ye not to be deficient in any grace/gift, earnestly expecting/awaiting the revelation from our Lord Jesus, the anointed (one); 1.8 who also establishes/confirms ye irreproachable (ones) until an end in the day of our Lord Jesus, the anointed (one). 1.9 God *is* faithful, through whom ye were called into a fellowship of his son Jesus, the anointed (one), our Lord.

1.10 And I call upon/beseech ye, brothers, through the name of our Lord Jesus, the anointed (one), that ye all may say the same (thing), and splits/divisions may not be among ye, but ye may have been mended/prepared/knitted together in the same mind and in the same decision/judgment. 1.11 For it was shown to me about ye, my brothers, by those of Chloe, that strifes/contentions are among ye. 1.12 And I say this, because each of ye says: I, indeed I am of Paul, but I of Apollos, but I of Cephas, but I of the anointed (one).

1.13 Has the anointed (one) been divided? Paul was not crucified in behalf of ye, or were ye baptized in the name of Paul? 1.14 I give thanks that I baptized no one of ye, except Crispus and Gaius, 1.15 in order that anyone might not say that ye were baptized in my name. 1.16 And I also baptized the house of Stephanus; *for* the rest, I know not if I baptized any other.

1.17 For the anointed (one) sent me not to

εὐαγγελίζεσθε, οὐκ ἐν σοφίᾳ λόγου, ἵνα μὴ κενωθῇ ὁ σταυρὸς τοῦ χριστοῦ.

1.18 ὁ λόγος γὰρ ὁ τοῦ σταυροῦ τοῖς μὲν ἀπολλυμένοις μωρία ἐστίν, τοῖς δὲ σῳζομένοις ἡμῖν δύναμις θεοῦ ἐστιν.

1.19 γέγραπται γάρ, «ἀπολῶ τὴν σοφίαν τῶν σοφῶν, καὶ τὴν σύνεσιν τῶν συνετῶν ἀθετήσω.» 1.20 ποῦ σοφός; ποῦ γραμματεύς; ποῦ συνζητητὴς τοῦ αἰῶνος τούτου; οὐχὶ ἐμώρανεν ὁ θεὸς τὴν σοφίαν τοῦ κόσμου;

1.21 ἐπιδὴ γὰρ ἐν τῇ σοφίᾳ τοῦ θεοῦ οὐκ ἔγνω ὁ κόσμος διὰ τῆς σοφίας τὸν θεόν, εὐδόκησεν ὁ θεὸς διὰ τῆς μωρίας τοῦ κηρύγματος σῶσαι τοὺς πιστεύοντας.

1.22 ἐπειδὴ καὶ Ἰουδαῖοι σημῖα αἰτοῦσιν καὶ Ἕλληνες σοφίαν ζητοῦσιν, 1.23 ἡμεῖς δὲ κηρύσσομεν χριστὸν ἐσταυρωμένον, Ἰουδαίοις μὲν σκάνδαλον ἔθνεσιν δὲ μωρίαν, 1.24 αὐτοῖς δὲ τοῖς κλητοῖς, Ἰουδαίοις τε καὶ Ἕλλησιν, χριστὸν θεοῦ δύναμιν καὶ θεοῦ σοφίαν·

1.25 ὅτι τὸ μωρὸν τοῦ θεοῦ σοφώτερον τῶν ἀνθρώπων ἐστίν, καὶ τὸ ἀσθενὲς τοῦ θεοῦ ἰσχυρότερον τῶν ἀνθρώπων.

1.26 βλέπεται γὰρ τὴν κλῆσιν ὑμῶν, ἀδελφοί, ὅτι οὐ πολλοὶ σοφοὶ κατὰ σάρκα, οὐ πολλοὶ δυνατοί, οὐ πολλοὶ εὐγενεῖς· 1.27 ἀλλὰ τὰ μωρὰ τοῦ κόσμου ἐξελέξατο ὁ θεὸς ἵνα κατεσχύνῃ τοὺς σοφούς, καὶ τὰ ἀσθενῆ τοῦ κόσμου ἐξελέξατο ὁ θεὸς ἵνα κατεσχύνῃ τὰ ἰσχυρά, 1.28 καὶ τὰ ἀσθενῆ τοῦ κόσμου καὶ τὰ ἐξουθενημένα ἐξελέξατο ὁ θεός, τὰ μὴ ὄντα, ἵνα τὰ ὄντα καταργήσῃ, 1.29 ὅπως μὴ καυχήσηται πᾶσα σὰρξ ἐνώπιον τοῦ θεοῦ.

1.30 ἐξ αὐτοῦ δὲ ὑμεῖς ἐστε ἐν χριστῷ Ἰησοῦ, ὃς ἐγενήθη σοφία ἡμῖν ἀπὸ θεοῦ, δικαιοσύνη τε καὶ ἁγιασμὸς καὶ

baptize, but to be an evangelist/to proclaim a good message, not in/by wisdom of saying/word, in order that the cross of the anointed (one) might not be made empty/falsified.

1.18 For the saying/word of the cross on the one hand is folly to the (ones) perishing, but on the other, it is power from God to us, to the (ones) being saved.

1.19 For it has been written: I SHALL DESTROY THE WISDOM OF THE WISE (ONES), AND I SHALL ANNUL/SET ASIDE THE UNDERSTANDING OF THE SENSIBLE (ONES). 1.20 Where *is* a wise one? Where *is* a scribe? Where *is* a disputant/debater of this age? Did not God make foolish the wisdom of the world?

1.21 For since in/by the wisdom of God, the world knew not God because of the wisdom, God thought it good to save the (ones) believing through the foolishness of the heralding/preaching/proclamation.

1.22 Since both Judeans request signs and Greeks seek wisdom, 1.23 and we, we herald/preach the anointed (one) having been crucified, to Judeans on one hand an offense/stumbling block, and to ethnics on the other, folly/foolishness, 1.24 but to these called (ones), both Judeans and Greeks, the anointed (one) of God, power and wisdom from God;

1.25 because the foolish (thing) from God is wiser than the men/humans, and the weak (thing) from God *is* stronger than the men/humans.

1.26 For ye see the calling/invitation of ye, brothers, that not many *are* wise according to flesh, not many *are* powerful, not many *are* well/high born; 1.27 but God chose the foolish (things) of the world, in order that he might shame the wise (ones), and God chose the weak (things) of the world, in order that he might shame the strong (things), 1.28 and God chose/selected the ignoble/basic (things) of the world and the (things) being despised, the (things) not being, in order that he might abolish the (things) being, 1.29 so that every/all flesh might not boast before God.

1.30 But ye, ye are out of/from him in/by the anointed Jesus, who became/was generated wisdom from

ἀπολύτρωσις, 1.31 ἵνα καθὼς γέγραπται, «ὁ καυχώμενος ἐν κυρίῳ καυχάσθω.»

2.1 Κἀγὼ ἐλθὼν πρὸς ὑμᾶς, ἀδελφοί, ἦλθον οὐ καθ' ὑπεροχὴν λόγου ἢ σοφίας καταγγέλλων ὑμῖν τὸ μυστήριον τοῦ θεοῦ. 2.2 οὐ γὰρ ἔκρινα εἰδέναι τι ἐν ὑμῖν εἰ μὴ Ἰησοῦν χριστὸν καὶ τοῦτον ἐσταυρωμένον. 2.3 κἀγὼ ἐν ἀσθενίᾳ καὶ ἐν φόβῳ καὶ ἐν τρόμῳ πολλῷ ἐγενόμην πρὸς ὑμᾶς,

2.4 καὶ ὁ λόγος μου καὶ τὸ κήρυγμά μου οὐκ ἐν πιθοῖς σοφίας λόγος ἀλλ' ἐν ἀποδείξει πνεύματος καὶ δυνάμεως, 2.5 ἵνα ἡ πίστις ὑμῶν μὴ ᾖ ἐν σοφίᾳ ἀνθρώπων ἀλλ' ἐν δυνάμι θεοῦ.

2.6 σοφίαν δὲ λαλοῦμεν ἐν τοῖς τελίοις, σοφίαν δὲ οὐ τοῦ αἰῶνος τούτου οὐδὲ τῶν ἀρχόντων τοῦ αἰῶνος τούτου τῶν καταργουμένων· 2.7 ἀλλὰ λαλοῦμεν θεοῦ σοφίαν ἐν μυστηρίῳ, τὴν ἀποκεκρυμμένην, ἣν προώρισεν ὁ θεὸς πρὸ τῶν αἰώνων εἰς δόξαν ἡμῶν·

2.8 ἣν οὐδεὶς τῶν ἀρχόντων τοῦ αἰῶνος τούτου ἔγνωκεν, εἰ γὰρ ἔγνωσαν, οὐκ ἂν τὸν κύριον τῆς δόξης ἐσταύρωσαν. 2.9 ἀλλὰ καθὼς γέγραπται, «ἃ ὀφθαλμὸς οὐκ εἶδεν καὶ οὓς οὐκ ἤκουσεν» καὶ ἐπὶ καρδίαν ἀνθρώπου οὐκ ἀνέβη, ἃ ἡτοίμασεν ὁ θεὸς τοῖς ἀγαπῶσιν αὐτόν.

2.10 ἡμῖν δὲ ἀπεκάλυψεν ὁ θεὸς διὰ τοῦ πνεύματος· τὸ γὰρ πνεῦμα πάντα ἐραυνᾷ, καὶ τὰ βάθη τοῦ θεοῦ.

2.11 τίς γὰρ οἶδεν ἀνθρώπων τὰ τοῦ ἀνθρώπου εἰ μὴ τὸ πνεῦμα τοῦ ἀνθρώπου τὸ ἐν αὐτῷ; οὕτως καὶ τὰ τοῦ θεοῦ οὐδεὶς ἔγνωκεν εἰ μὴ τὸ πνεῦμα τοῦ θεοῦ. 2.12 ἡμῖς δὲ οὐ τὸ πνεῦμα τοῦ κόσμου ἐλάβομεν ἀλλὰ τὸ πνεῦμα τὸ ἐκ τοῦ θεοῦ, ἵνα εἰδῶμεν τὰ ὑπὸ τοῦ θεοῦ χαρισθέντα ἡμῖν·

2.13 ἃ καὶ λαλοῦμεν οὐκ ἐν διδακτοῖς ἀνθρωπίνης σοφίας

God to us, both justice and consecration and redemption, 1.31 in order that as it has been written: THE (ONE) BOASTING, LET HIM BOAST IN *the* LORD.

2.1 And I, having come to ye, brothers, I came not according to an excellent quality of speech/word or wisdom, proclaiming to ye the mystery (religion) of/from God. 2.2 For I judged/decided not to know anything among ye, except Jesus, the anointed (one), and this (one) having been crucified. 2.3 And I, in/with weakness and in/with fear and in/with much trembling, became myself near/toward ye,
2.4 both my logos/word and my proclamation/preaching, not a logos/saying in/by persuasions from wisdom, but in/by a demonstration of spirit and power, 2.5 in order that the faith of ye may not be in wisdom of men but in power of/from God.
2.6 And we speak wisdom among the mature (ones), but not wisdom of this age nor of the rulers/leaders of this age, of those being abrogated/rendered null; 2.7 but we speak a wisdom from God in a mystery (religion), the (one) having been hidden, which God predefined/determined before the ages in/for his glory/fame;
2.8 which no one of the rulers/leaders of this age has known, for if they knew, they would not *have* crucified the Lord of the glory/fame. 2.9 But as it has been written: (THINGS) WHICH AN EYE SAW NOT AND AN EAR HEARD NOT and came not upon a man's heart, (things) which God prepared for the (ones)/those loving him.
2.10 But God revealed *it* to us through the spirit; for the spirit searches/examines all (things), even the deep (things) of God.
2.11 For who of men/humans knows the (things) of a man except the spirit of the man, the (one) in him? So also no one has known the (things) of God except the spirit of/from God. 2.12 And we, we received/took not the spirit of the world, but the spirit, the (one) out of/from God, in order that we may know the (things) having been freely given to us by God;
2.13 (things) which also we speak not by impart-

λόγοις ἀλλ᾽ ἐν διδακτοῖς πνεύματος, πνευματικοῖς πνευματικὰ συγκρίνοντες.

2.14 ψυχικὸς δὲ ἄνθρωπος οὐ δέχεται τὰ τοῦ πνεύματος τοῦ θεοῦ, μωρία γὰρ αὐτῷ ἐστιν, καὶ οὐ δύναται γνῶναι, ὅτι πνευματικῶς ἀνακρίνεται· 2.15 ὁ δὲ πνευματικὸς ἀνακρίνει πάντα, αὐτὸς δὲ ὑπ᾽ οὐδενὸς ἀνακρίνεται. 2.16 «τίς» γὰρ «ἔγνω νοῦν κυρίου, ὃς συμβιβάσει αὐτόν;» ἡμεῖς δὲ νοῦν χριστοῦ ἔχομεν.

3.1 Κἀγώ, ἀδελφοί, οὐκ ἠδυνήθην λαλῆσαι ὑμῖν ὡς πνευματικοῖς ἀλλ᾽ ὡς σαρκίνοις, ὡς νηπίοις ἐν χριστῷ. 3.2 γάλα ὑμᾶς ἐπότισα, οὐ βρῶμα, οὔπω γὰρ ἐδύνασθε. ἀλλ᾽ οὐδὲ ἔτι νῦν δύνασθε, 3.3 ἔτι γὰρ σαρκικοί ἐστε.

ὅπου γὰρ ἐν ὑμῖν ζῆλος καὶ ἔρις, οὐχὶ σαρκικοί ἐστε καὶ κατὰ ἄνθρωπον περιπατεῖτε;

3.4 ὅταν γὰρ λέγῃ τις, ἐγὼ μέν εἰμι Παύλου, ἕτερος δέ, ἐγὼ Ἀπολλῶ, οὐκ ἄνθρωποί ἐστε; 3.5 τί οὖν ἐστιν Ἀπολλῶς; τί δέ ἐστιν Παῦλος; διάκονοι δι᾽ ὧν ἐπιστεύσατε, καὶ ἑκάστῳ ὡς ὁ κύριος ἔδωκεν. 3.6 ἐγὼ ἐφύτευσα, Ἀπολλῶς ἐπότισεν, ἀλλὰ ὁ θεὸς ηὔξανεν·

3.7 ὥστε οὔτε ὁ φυτεύων ἐστίν τι οὐδὲ ὁ ποτίζων, ἀλλ᾽ ὁ αὐξάνων θεός. 3.8 ὁ φυτεύων δὲ καὶ ὁ ποτίζων ἕν εἰσιν, ἕκαστος δὲ τὸν ἴδιον μισθὸν λήμψεται κατὰ τὸν ἴδιον κόπον.

3.9 θεοῦ γάρ ἐσμεν συνεργοί· θεοῦ γεώργιον, θεοῦ οἰκοδομή ἐστε. 3.10 κατὰ τὴν χάριν τοῦ θεοῦ τὴν δοθεῖσάν μοι ὡς σοφὸς ἀρχιτέκτων θεμέλιον ἔθηκα, ἄλλος δὲ ἐποικοδομεῖ. ἕκαστος δὲ βλεπέτω πῶς ἐποικοδομεῖ· 3.11 θεμέλιον γὰρ ἄλλον οὐδεὶς δύναται θεῖναι παρὰ τὸν κείμενον, ὅς ἐστιν Ἰησοῦς χριστός.

3.12 εἰ δέ τις ἐποικοδομεῖ ἐπὶ τὸν θεμέλιον χρυσίον,

ed sayings/words of human wisdom, but by (ones) im-
parted/taught from a spirit, comparing/combining
spiritual (things) to/with spiritual *sayings/words*.

2.14 But a natural man/human receives not the
(things) from the spirit of God, for it is foolishness
to him, and he is not able to know, because they are
discerned/examined spiritually; 2.15 and the spiritual (one) discerns/examines all (things), but he, he
is judged/examined by no one. 2.16 For WHO KNEW A
MIND/THOUGHT OF *the* LORD, WHO WILL UNITE/INSTRUCT HIM?
But we, we have a mind from the anointed (one).

3.1 And I, brothers, I was not able to speak to
ye as to spiritual (ones), but as to fleshly (ones),
as to babies in the anointed (one) 3.2 I gave milk
for ye to drink, not food, for ye were not yet able.
But ye are still not able now, 3.3 for ye are still
fleshly (ones).

For where jealousy and strife *are* among ye, are
ye not fleshly (ones) and ye walk according to a
man/human?

3.4 For whenever anyone may say: I, I am indeed
of Paul; and another (one): I *am* of Apollos, are ye
not men/humans? 3.5 Therefore, what is Apollos? And
what is Paul? Servants/ministers through whom ye
believed, even as the Lord gave to each. 3.6 I, I
planted, Apollos gave drink to/watered, but God caused
to grow;

3.7 So that neither the (one) planting is anything nor the (one) irrigating, but the (one) causing
to grow *is* God. 3.8 But the (one) planting and the
(one) irrigating are one, and each will receive his
own reward/wage according to his own toil/labor.

3.9 For we are fellow workers of God; ye are a
building of God, a cultivated field/farm of God. 3.10
According to the grace of God having been given to me,
I laid a foundation as a wise chief-craftsman, but
another builds upon *it*. But let each (one) see/(be
careful) how he builds upon *it*; 3.11 for no one is
able to lay another foundation from the (one) being
laid, who/which is Jesus the anointed (one).

3.12 And if anyone builds upon the foundation,

ἀργύριον, λίθους τιμίους, ξύλα, χόρτον, καλάμην, 3.13 ἑκάστου τὸ ἔργον φανερὸν γενήσεται, ἡ γὰρ ἡμέρα δηλώσει· ὅτι ἐν πυρὶ ἀποκαλύπτεται, καὶ ἑκάστου τὸ ἔργον ὁποῖόν ἐστιν τὸ πῦρ δοκιμάσει.

3.14 εἴ τινος τὸ ἔργον μενεῖ ὃ ἐποικοδόμησεν, μισθὸν λήμψεται· 3.15 εἴ τινος τὸ ἔργον κατακαήσεται, ζημιωθήσεται, αὐτὸς δὲ σωθήσεται, οὕτως δὲ ὡς διὰ πυρός.

3.16 οὐκ οἴδατε ὅτι ναὸς θεοῦ ἐστε καὶ τὸ πνεῦμα τοῦ θεοῦ οἰκεῖ ἐν ὑμῖν; 3.17 εἴ τις τὸν ναὸν τοῦ θεοῦ φθείρει, φθερεῖ τοῦτον ὁ θεός· ὁ γὰρ ναὸς τοῦ θεοῦ ἅγιός ἐστιν, οἵτινές ἐστε ὑμεῖς.

3.18 μηδεὶς ἑαυτὸν ἐξαπατάτω· εἴ τις δοκεῖ σοφὸς εἶναι ἐν ὑμῖν ἐν τῷ αἰῶνι τούτῳ, μωρὸς γενέσθω, ἵνα γένηται σοφός. 3.19 ἡ γὰρ σοφία τοῦ κόσμου τούτου μωρία παρὰ τῷ θεῷ ἐστιν·

γέγραπται γάρ, «ὁ δρασσόμενος τοὺς σοφοὺς ἐν τῇ πανουργίᾳ αὐτῶν·» 3.20 καὶ πάλιν, «κύριος γινώσκι τοὺς διαλογισμοὺς τῶν» σοφῶν «ὅτι εἰσὶν μάταιοι.» 3.21 ὥστε μηδὶς καυχάσθω ἐν ἀνθρώποις·

πάντα γὰρ ὑμῶν ἐστιν, 3.22 εἴτε Παῦλος εἴτε Ἀπολλῶς εἴτε Κηφᾶς εἴτε κόσμος εἴτε ζωὴ εἴτε θάνατος εἴτε ἐνεστῶτα εἴτε μέλλοντα, πάντα ὑμῶν, 3.23 ὑμεῖς δὲ χριστοῦ, χριστὸς δὲ θεοῦ.

4.1 Οὕτως ἡμᾶς λογιζέσθω ἄνθρωπος ὡς ὑπηρέτας χριστοῦ καὶ οἰκονόμους μυστηρίων θεοῦ. 4.2 ὧδε λοιπὸν ζητεῖτε ἐν τοῖς οἰκονόμοις ἵνα πιστός τις εὑρεθῇ. 4.3 ἐμοὶ δὲ εἰς ἐλάχιστόν ἐστιν ἵνα ὑφ᾽ ὑμῶν ἀνακριθῶ ἢ ὑπὸ ἀνθρωπίνης ἡμέρας· ἀλλ᾽ οὐδὲ ἐμαυτὸν ἀνακρίνω· 4.4 οὐδὲν γὰρ ἐμαυτῷ σύνοιδα, ἀλλ᾽ οὐκ ἐν τούτῳ δεδικαίωμαι, ὁ δὲ ἀνακρίνων με κύριός ἐστιν.

gold, silver, precious stones, woods, grass/hay, straw/stubble, 3.13 the work of each (one) will become plain/evident, for the day will manifest *it*/make it known; because it is revealed by fire, and the fire will prove/test the work of each (one), what sort it is.

3.14 If the work of anyone, which he built on, abides, he will receive a reward/wages; 3.15 if the work of anyone will be burned/consumed, he will be punished/suffer loss, but he, he will be saved, but so as through fire.

3.16 Know ye not that ye are an *inner* temple of God and the spirit from God dwells in/among ye? 3.17 If anyone corrupts/ruins the *inner* temple of God, God will corrupt/ruin this (one); for the *inner* temple of God is holy/set apart, which ye, ye are.

3.18 Let no one deceive himself; if anyone seems to be wise/a sophist among ye in this age, let him become foolish, in order that he might become wise. 3.19 For the wisdom of this world is folly in the presence/alongside of God. For it has been written: THE (ONE) HIMSELF CATCHING THE WISE (ONES) IN THEIR SHREWDNESS; 3.20 and again: *The* LORD KNOWS THE REASONINGS/ARGUMENTS OF THE WISE (ONES)/SOPHISTS, THAT THEY ARE EMPTY/VAIN. 3.21 Therefore, let no one boast among men;

for all is yours, 3.22 whether Paul or Apollos or Cephas or a world or life or death or things having existed or things about to be, all *are* yours, 3.23 but ye *are* the anointed one's, and the anointed (one) is God's.

4.1 So let a man reckon/count us as servants/assistants of the anointed (one) and managers of God's mysteries. 4.2 Here it is sought *for* the rest among the managers in order that someone might be found faithful. 4.3 But to me it is in *the* least (thing) that I should be judged/examined by ye or by a human day; but I judge/examine not myself; 4.4 for I know nothing to/for myself, but I have not been vindicated by this, and the (one) judging/examining me is *the* Lord.

4.5 ὥστε μὴ πρὸ καιροῦ τι κρίνεται, ἕως ἂν ἔλθῃ ὁ κύριος, ὃς καὶ φωτίσει τὰ κρυπτὰ τοῦ σκότους καὶ φανερώσει τὰς βουλὰς τῶν καρδιῶν· καὶ τότε ὁ ἔπαινος γενήσεται ἑκάστῳ ἀπὸ τοῦ θεοῦ.

4.6 ταῦτα δέ, ἀδελφοί, μετεσχημάτισα εἰς ἐμαυτὸν καὶ Ἀπολλῶν δι' ὑμᾶς, ἵνα ἐν ἡμῖν μάθητε τὸ μὴ ὑπὲρ ἃ γέγραπτε, ἵνα μὴ εἷς ὑπὲρ τοῦ ἑνὸς φυσιοῦσθαι κατὰ τοῦ ἑτέρου.

4.7 τίς γάρ σε διακρίνει; τί δὲ ἔχεις ὃ οὐκ ἔλαβες; εἰ δὲ καὶ ἔλαβες, τί καυχᾶσαι ὡς μὴ λαβών;

4.8 ἤδη κεκορεσμένοι ἐστέ· ἤδη ἐπλουτήσατε· χωρὶς ἡμῶν ἐβασιλεύσατε· καὶ ὄφελόν γε ἐβασιλεύσατε, ἵνα καὶ ἡμεῖς ὑμῖν συνβασιλεύσωμεν.

4.9 δοκῶ γάρ, ὁ θεὸς ἡμᾶς τοὺς ἀποστόλους ἐσχάτους ἀπέδιξεν ὡς ἐπιθανατίους, ὅτι θέατρον ἐγενήθημεν τῷ κόσμῳ καὶ ἀγγέλοις καὶ ἀνθρώποις.

4.10 ἡμεῖς μωροὶ διὰ χριστόν, ὑμεῖς δὲ φρόνιμοι ἐν χριστῷ· ἡμεῖς ἀσθενεῖς, ὑμεῖς δὲ ἰσχυροί· ὑμεῖς ἔνδοξοι, ἡμεῖς δὲ ἄτιμοι. 4.11 ἄχρι τῆς ἄρτι ὥρας καὶ πεινῶμεν καὶ διψῶμεν καὶ γυμνιτεύομεν καὶ κολαφιζόμεθα καὶ ἀστατοῦμεν 4.12 καὶ κοπιῶμεν ἐργαζόμενοι ταῖς ἰδίαις χερσίν· λοιδορούμενοι εὐλογοῦμεν, διωκόμενοι ἀνεχόμεθα, 4.13 δυσφημούμενοι παρακαλοῦμεν· ὡς περικαθάρματα τοῦ κόσμου ἐγενήθημεν, πάντων περίψημα, ἕως ἄρτι.

4.14 οὐκ ἐντρέπων ὑμᾶς γράφω ταῦτα, ἀλλ' ὡς τέκνα μου ἀγαπητὰ νουθετῶν· 4.15 ἐὰν γὰρ μυρίους παιδαγωγοὺς ἔχητε ἐν χριστῷ, ἀλλ' οὐ πολλοὺς πατέρας, ἐν γὰρ χριστῷ Ἰησοῦ διὰ τοῦ εὐαγγελίου ἐγὼ ὑμᾶς ἐγέννησα. 4.16 παρακαλῶ οὖν ὑμᾶς, μιμηταί μου γίνεσθε. 4.17 διὰ τοῦτο ἔπεμψα ὑμῖν Τιμόθεον, ὅς

4.5 Therefore, judge ye not anything before a time/season, until the Lord would come, who both will light the hidden (things) of the darkness and will make plain/public the wills/wishes of the hearts; and then the praise/approbation for each will come about/ happen from God.

4.6 And these (things), brothers, I have changed/transformed to/for myself and Apollos because of ye, in order that ye may learn by us the (thing) *being* not beyond what (things) have been written, lest ye be puffed up/conceited, one in behalf of the one, against the other/different.

4.7 For who discerns/doubts you? And what have you which you received not? But even if you did receive, why boast you as not having received/taken?

4.8 Ye are already having been satisfied; ye already became rich; ye reigned without us; and would that ye reigned indeed, in order that we also, we might reign together with ye.

4.9 For I think God designated/appointed us, the last apostles, as (ones) under sentence of death, because we were generated/became a spectacle to/for the world, both to messengers/angels and to men.

4.10 We *are* fools because of the anointed (one), but ye *are* prudent in the anointed (one); we *are* weak, but ye *are* strong; ye *are* respected/renowned, but we *are* dishonored. 4.11 Until the present hour, we both hunger and thirst and we are naked and being buffeted with fists and are unsettled, 4.12 and we labor/toil, working with our own hands; being reviled/abused, we bless/speak well of; being prosecuted/persecuted, we endure; 4.13 being reproached with ill words, we encourage/console/beseech; we were generated/became like refuse/filth of the world, offscouring/(sewer water) from all (things), until just now.

4.14 I write not these (things) shaming ye, but as admonishing my beloved children; 4.15 for if ye may have myriads of attendants/guides in the anointed (one), but not many fathers, for in/by the anointed Jesus, I generated/begat ye through the good message/ gospel. 4.16 Therefore I beseech/call upon ye, become ye imitators of me. 4.17 Because of this, I sent

ἐστίν μου τέκνον ἀγαπητὸν καὶ πιστὸν ἐν κυρίῳ, ὃς ὑμᾶς ἀναμνήσει τὰς ὁδούς μου τὰς ἐν χριστῷ Ἰησοῦ, καθὼς πανταχοῦ ἐν πάσῃ ἐκκλησίᾳ διδάσκω.

4.18 ὡς μὴ ἐρχομένου δέ μου πρὸς ὑμᾶς ἐφυσιώθησάν τινες· 4.19 ἐλεύσομαι δὲ ταχέως πρὸς ὑμᾶς, ἐὰν ὁ κύριος θελήσῃ, καὶ γνώσομαι οὐ τὸν λόγον τῶν πεφυσιωμένων ἀλλὰ τὴν δύναμιν, 4.20 οὐ γὰρ ἐν λόγῳ ἡ βασιλεία τοῦ θεοῦ ἀλλ᾽ ἐν δυνάμι. 4.21 τί θέλετε; ἐν ῥάβδῳ ἔλθω πρὸς ὑμᾶς, ἢ ἐν ἀγάπῃ πνεύματί τε πραότητος;

5.1 Ὅλως ἀκούετε ἐν ὑμῖν πορνία, καὶ τοιαύτη πορνία ἥτις οὐδὲ ἐν τοῖς ἔθνεσιν, ὥστε γυναῖκά τινα τοῦ πατρὸς ἔχιν. 5.2 καὶ ὑμῖς πεφυσιωμένοι ἐστέ, καὶ οὐχὶ μᾶλλον ἐπενθήσατε, ἵνα ἀρθῇ ἐκ μέσου ὑμῶν ὁ τὸ ἔργον τοῦτο πράξας; 5.3 ἐγὼ μὲν γάρ, ἀπὼν τῷ σώματι παρὼν δὲ τῷ πνεύματι, ἤδη κέκρικα ὡς παρὼν τὸν οὕτως τοῦτο κατεργασάμενον 5.4 ἐν τῷ ὀνόματι τοῦ κυρίου Ἰησοῦ χριστοῦ, συναχθέντων ὑμῶν καὶ τοῦ ἐμοῦ πνεύματος σὺν τῇ δυνάμι τοῦ κυρίου ἡμῶν Ἰησοῦ, 5.5 παραδοῦναι τὸν τοιοῦτον τῷ Σατανᾷ εἰς ὄλεθρον τῆς σαρκός, ἵνα τὸ πνεῦμα σωθῇ ἐν τῇ ἡμέρᾳ τοῦ κυρίου Ἰησοῦ.

5.6 οὐ καλὸν τὸ καύχημα ὑμῶν. οὐκ οἴδατε ὅτι μικρὰ ζύμη ὅλον τὸ φύραμα ζυμοῖ; 5.7 ἐκκαθάρατε τὴν παλαιὰν ζύμην, ἵνα ἦτε νέον φύραμα, καθώς ἐστε ἄζυμοι.

καὶ γὰρ τὸ πάσχα ἡμῶν ἐτύθη χριστός· 5.8 ὥστε ἑορτάζωμεν, μὴ ἐν ζύμῃ παλαιᾷ μηδὲ ἐν ζύμῃ κακίας καὶ πονηρίας, ἀλλ᾽ ἐν ἀζύμοις εἰλικρινίας καὶ ἀληθίας.

5.9 ἔγραψα ὑμῖν ἐν τῇ ἐπιστολῇ μὴ συναναμίγνυσθαι πόρνοις, 5.10 οὐ πάντως τοῖς πόρνοις τοῦ κόσμου τούτου ἢ τοῖς πλεονέκταις καὶ ἅρπαξιν ἢ εἰδωλολάτραις, ἐπεὶ ὠφίλετε ἄρα ἐκ

Timothy to ye, who is my beloved child, and faithful in *the* Lord, who will cause ye to remember the ways of me, the (ones) in the anointed Jesus, as I teach everywhere in every assembly/ecclesia. 4.18 But as for my coming not to ye, some were puffed up; 4.19 but I shall come quickly to ye, if the Lord might will *it*, and I shall know not the saying/ word of those having been puffed up, but the power, 4.20 for the kingdom of God is not in/by logos/word, but in/by power. 4.21 What want/wish ye? Should I come to ye with a staff/rod, or with agape and a spirit of gentleness?

5.1 Prostitution is actually heard *of* among ye, and such prostitution which *is* not among the ethnics, so as for someone to have/hold a woman of the father. 5.2 And ye, are ye having been puffed up, and ye mourned/grieved not more, in order that the (one) having practiced this work/deed might be removed from the midst of ye? 5.3 For I indeed, being absent in the body but present in the spirit, I have already judged, as being present, the (one) so working this (thing) 5.4 in the name of the Lord Jesus, the a- nointed (one), from ye having been gathered and from my spirit, with the power of our Lord Jesus, 5.5 to deliver over the (one) such to Satan into/for destruc- tion of the flesh, in order that the spirit might be saved in the day of the Lord Jesus.

5.6 Your boast *is* not good/beautiful. Know ye not that a little leaven leavens all the dough/lump? 5.7 Purge ye out/eliminate the old leaven, in order that ye may be a new kneaded lump, as ye are unleavened.

For even *at* our passover, the anointed (one) was sacrificed; 5.8 so that we may keep the festival, not with old leaven, not with leaven from bad and evil, but with unleavened (things) from sincerity/a pure motive and from truth. 5.9 I wrote to ye in the epistle/letter not to mingle with whoremongers, 5.10 certainly not with the whoremongers of this world or with the greedy (ones) and rapacious (ones) or idolaters, since ye are there-

τοῦ κόσμου ἐξελθῖν.

5.11 νῦν δὲ ἔγραψα ὑμῖν μὴ συναναμίγνυσθαι ἐάν τις ἀδελφὸς ὀνομαζόμενος ᾖ πόρνος ἢ πλεονέκτης ἢ εἰδωλολάτρης ἢ λοίδορος ἢ μέθυσος ἢ ἅρπαξ, τῷ τοιούτῳ μηδὲ συνεσθίειν.

5.12 τί γάρ μοι τοὺς ἔξω κρίνειν; οὐχὶ τοὺς ἔσω ὑμεῖς κρίνετε; 5.13 τοὺς δὲ ἔξω ὁ θεὸς κρινεῖ. «ἐξάρατε τὸν πονηρὸν ἐξ ὑμῶν αὐτῶν.»

6.1 Τολμᾷ τις ὑμῶν πρᾶγμα ἔχων πρὸς τὸν ἕτερον κρίνεσθαι ἐπὶ τῶν ἀδίκων, καὶ οὐχὶ ἐπὶ τῶν ἁγίων;

6.2 ἢ οὐκ οἴδατε ὅτι οἱ ἅγιοι τὸν κόσμον κρινοῦσιν; καὶ εἰ ἐν ὑμῖν κρίνεται ὁ κόσμος, ἀνάξιοί ἐστε κριτηρίων ἐλαχίστων;

6.3 οὐκ οἴδατε ὅτι ἀγγέλους κρινοῦμεν, μήτιγε βιωτικά;

6.4 βιωτικὰ μὲν οὖν κριτήρια ἐὰν ἔχητε, τοὺς ἐξουθενημένους ἐν τῇ ἐκκλησίᾳ τούτους καθίζετε; 6.5 πρὸς ἐντροπὴν ὑμῖν λέγω. οὕτως οὐκ ἔνι ἐν ὑμῖν οὐδεὶς σοφὸς ὃς δυνήσεται διακρῖναι ἀνὰ μέσον τοῦ ἀδελφοῦ αὐτοῦ; 6.6 ἀλλὰ ἀδελφὸς μετὰ ἀδελφοῦ κρίνεται, καὶ τοῦτο ἐπὶ ἀπίστων; 6.7 ἤδη μὲν οὖν ὅλως ἥττημα ὑμῖν ἐστιν ὅτι κρίμα ἔχετε μεθ᾽ ἑαυτῶν· διὰ τί οὐχὶ μᾶλλον ἀδικεῖσθε; διὰ τί οὐχὶ μᾶλλον ἀποστερεῖσθε; 6.8 ἀλλὰ ὑμεῖς ἀδικεῖτε καὶ ἀποστερεῖτε, καὶ τοῦτο ἀδελφούς. 6.9 ἢ οὐκ οἴδατε ὅτι ἄδικοι θεοῦ βασιλείαν οὐ κληρονομήσουσιν;

μὴ πλανᾶσθε· οὔτε πόρνοι οὔτε εἰδωλολάτραι οὔτε μοιχοὶ οὔτε μαλακοὶ οὔτε ἀρσενοκοῖται 6.10 οὔτε κλέπται οὔτε πλεονέκται, οὐ μέθυσοι, οὐ λοίδοροι, οὐχ ἅρπαγες βασιλείαν θεοῦ κληρονομήσουσιν. 6.11 καὶ ταῦτά τινες ἦτε· ἀλλὰ ἀπελούσασθε, ἀλλὰ ἡγιάσθητε, ἀλλὰ ἐδικαιώθητε ἐν τῷ ὀνόματι τοῦ κυρίου Ἰησοῦ χριστοῦ καὶ ἐν τῷ πνεύματι τοῦ θεοῦ ἡμῶν.

fore obligated to go forth out of the world.

5.11 But I wrote to ye now not to mingle/mix together if anyone being named/called a brother may be a whoremonger/male prostitute or a greedy (one) or an idolater or a curser/abuser or a drunkard or a rapacious (one), not to eat together with the such.

5.12 For what/why *is it* for me to judge the (ones) outside? Ye, *do* ye not judge the (ones) within? 5.13 But God will judge the (ones) without. REMOVE YE THE EVIL (ONE) OUT OF YE YOURSELVES.

6.1 Dares anyone of ye, having a matter/thing toward/against the other to be judged upon/*before* the unjust (ones), and not upon/*before* the saints?

6.2 Know ye not that the saints will judge the world? And if the world is judged by ye, are ye unworthy of judgments of least (things)?

6.3 Know ye not that we shall judge messengers, not to speak of (things) pertaining to daily life?

6.4 If therefore ye indeed may have/hold criteria/judgments pertaining to daily life, sit ye *for* these, the (ones) being rejected/despised in/by the assembly? 6.5 I speak to ye with/to shame. So *is* there not one among ye, no one *being* wise, who will be able to judge/discern between/in turn his brother? 6.6 But is a brother judged with a brother, and this upon/*before* unbelievers? 6.7 Then indeed there is actually a failure/defeat for ye because ye have judgment with yourselves; why not rather be ye wronged? Why not rather be ye defrauded? 6.8 But ye, ye do wrong and ye defraud, and this *to* brothers. 6.9 Or know ye not that unjust (ones) will not inherit a kingdom from God?

Be ye not deceived; neither whoremongers nor idolaters nor adulterers nor effeminate/homosexual (ones) nor sodomites (male lying with male) 6.10 nor thieves nor greedy (ones), not drunkards, not cursers/abusers, not rapacious (ones) will inherit a kingdom from God. 6.11 And some were being these (things); but ye washed yourselves, but ye were sanctified/set apart, but ye were vindicated in/by the name of the Lord Jesus, the anointed (one), and by the

6.12 πάντα μοι ἔξεστιν, ἀλλ' οὐ πάντα συμφέρει. πάντα μοι ἔξεστιν, ἀλλ' οὐκ ἐγὼ ἐξουσιασθήσομαι ὑπό τινος.

6.13 τὰ βρώματα τῇ κοιλίᾳ, καὶ ἡ κοιλία τοῖς βρώμασιν· ὁ δὲ θεὸς καὶ ταύτην καὶ ταῦτα καταργήσει. τὸ δὲ σῶμα οὐ τῇ πορνίᾳ ἀλλὰ τῷ κυρίῳ, καὶ ὁ κύριος τῷ σώματι· 6.14 ὁ δὲ θεὸς καὶ τὸν κύριον ἤγειρεν καὶ ἡμᾶς ἐξεγερεῖ διὰ τῆς δυμέως αὐτοῦ.

6.15 οὐκ οἴδατε ὅτι τὰ σώματα ὑμῶν μέλη χριστοῦ ἐστιν; ἄρας οὖν τὰ μέλη τοῦ χριστοῦ ποιήσω πόρνης μέλη; μὴ γένοιτο.

6.16 ἢ οὐκ οἴδατε ὅτι ὁ κολλώμενος τῇ πόρνῃ ἓν σῶμά ἐστιν; «ἔσονται» γάρ, φησίν, «οἱ δύο εἰς σάρκα μίαν.» 6.17 ὁ δὲ κολλώμενος τῷ κυρίῳ ἓν πνεῦμά ἐστιν.

6.18 φεύγετε τὴν πορνίαν· πᾶν ἁμάρτημα ὃ ἐὰν ποιήσῃ ἄνθρωπος ἐκτὸς τοῦ σώματός ἐστιν, ὁ δὲ πορνεύων εἰς τὸ ἴδιον σῶμα ἁμαρτάνι.

6.19 ἢ οὐκ οἴδαται ὅτι τὸ σῶμα ὑμῶν ναὸς τοῦ ἐν ὑμῖν ἁγίου πνεύματός ἐστιν, οὗ ἔχετε ἀπὸ θεοῦ, καὶ οὐκ ἐστὲ ἑαυτῶν; 6.20 ἠγοράσθητε γὰρ τιμῆς· δοξάσατε δὴ τὸν θεὸν ἐν τῷ σώματι ὑμῶν.

7.1 Περὶ δὲ ὧν ἐγράψατε, καλὸν ἀνθρώπῳ γυναικὸς μὴ ἅπτεσθαι·

7.2 διὰ δὲ τὰς πορνίας ἕκαστος τὴν ἑαυτοῦ γυναῖκα ἐχέτω, καὶ ἑκάστη τὸν ἴδιον ἄνδρα ἐχέτω. 7.3 τῇ γυναικὶ ὁ ἀνὴρ τὴν ὀφιλὴν ἀποδιδότω, ὁμοίως δὲ καὶ ἡ γυνὴ τῷ ἀδρί. 7.4 ἡ γυνὴ τοῦ ἰδίου σώματος οὐκ ἐξουσιάζει ἀλλὰ ὁ ἀνήρ· ὁμοίως δὲ καὶ ὁ ἀνὴρ τοῦ ἰδίου σώματος οὐκ ἐξουσιάζει ἀλλὰ ἡ γυνή.

7.5 μὴ ἀποστερῖτε ἀλλήλους, εἰ μήτι ἂν ἐκ συμφώνου πρὸς καιρὸν ἵνα σχολάσητε τῇ προσευχῇ καὶ πάλιν ἐπὶ τὸ αὐτὸ ἦτε,

spirit from our God.

6.12 All (things) are lawful for me, but not all (things) are beneficial/profitable. All (things) are lawful for me, but I, I shall not be enslaved/subjected by anyone/anything.

6.13 The foods for the belly, and the belly for the foods; but God will abolish/do away with both this/(the belly) and these (things)/(the foods). But the body *is* not for the prostitution but for the Lord, and the Lord for the body; 6.14 and God both raised up the Lord and he will raise us up through his power.

6.15 Know ye not that your bodies are members of the anointed (one)? Therefore, having taken the members of the anointed (one), shall I make *them* members of a harlot? May it not happen!

6.16 Or know ye not that the (one) being joined to the harlot is one body? For he says: THE TWO WILL BE IN ONE FLESH.   6.17 But the (one) being joined to the Lord is one spirit.

6.18 Ye flee/escape the prostitution; every sin (object of) which a man/human might do is outside the body, but the (one) prostituting sins in/to/against his own body.

6.19 Or know ye not that the body of ye is an *inner* temple of the holy spirit in/among ye, which ye have from god, and ye are not of yourselves?   6.20 For ye were bought/redeemed of/from a price; now ye glorify God in the body of ye.

7.1 And concerning (things) which ye wrote, *it is* good for a man not to fasten/touch of a woman;

7.2 but because of the prostitutions, let each (man) have the woman of himself, and let each (woman) have the man her own.   7.3 Let the man give away/pay the duty/obligation to the woman, and likewise also the woman to the man.   7.4 The woman has not authority over her own body, but the man; and likewise also the man has not authority over his own body, but the woman.

7.5 Deprive ye not one another, unless out of agreement toward/for a time in order that ye would be at leisure for the prayer, and ye may be again upon/

ἵνα μὴ πιράζῃ ὑμᾶς ὁ Σατανᾶς διὰ τὴν ἀκρασίαν ὑμῶν.

7.6 τοῦτο δὲ λέγω κατὰ συγγνώμην, οὐ κατ᾽ ἐπιταγήν.

7.7 θέλω δὲ πάντας ἀνθρώπους εἶναι ὡς καὶ ἐμαυτόν· ἀλλ᾽ ἕκαστος ἴδιον ἔχει χάρισμα ἐκ θεοῦ, ὁ μὲν οὕτως, ὁ δὲ οὕτως.

7.8 λέγω δὲ τοῖς ἀγάμοις καὶ ταῖς χήραις, καλὸν αὐτοῖς ἐὰν μίνωσιν ὡς κἀγώ· 7.9 εἰ δὲ οὐκ ἐγκρατεύονται γαμησάτωσαν, κρῖττον γάρ ἐστιν γαμῆσαι ἢ πυροῦσθε. 7.10 τοῖς δὲ γεγαμηκόσιν παραγγέλλω, οὐκ ἐγὼ ἀλλὰ ὁ κύριος, γυναῖκα ἀπὸ ἀνδρὸς μὴ χωρισθῆναι 7.11 ἐὰν δὲ καὶ χωρισθῇ, μενέτω ἄγαμος ἢ τῷ ἀνδρὶ καταλλαγήτω καὶ ἄνδρα γυναῖκα μὴ ἀφιέναι.

7.12 τοῖς δὲ λοιποῖς λέγω ἐγώ, οὐχ ὁ κύριος· εἴ τις ἀδελφὸς γυναῖκα ἔχει ἄπιστον, καὶ αὕτη συνευδοκεῖ οἰκεῖν μετ᾽ αὐτοῦ, μὴ ἀφιέτω αὐτήν·

7.13 καὶ γυνὴ εἴ τις ἔχει ἄνδρα ἄπιστον, καὶ οὗτος συνευδοκεῖ οἰκεῖν μετ᾽ αὐτῆς, μὴ ἀφιέτω τὸν ἄνδρα. 7.14 ἡγίασται γὰρ ὁ ἀνὴρ ὁ ἄπιστος ἐν τῇ γυναικί, καὶ ἡγίασται ἡ γυνὴ ἡ ἄπιστος ἐν τῷ ἀδελφῷ· ἐπεὶ ἄρα τὰ τέκνα ὑμῶν ἀκάθαρτά ἐστιν, νῦν δὲ ἅγιά ἐστιν.

7.15 εἰ δὲ ὁ ἄπιστος χωρίζετε, χωριζέσθω· οὐ δεδούλωται ὁ ἀδελφὸς ἢ ἡ ἀδελφὴ ἐν τοῖς τοιούτοις·

ἐν δὲ εἰρήνῃ κέκληκεν ὑμᾶς ὁ θεός. 7.16 τί γὰρ οἶδας, γύναι, εἰ τὸν ἄνδρα σώσεις; ἢ τί οἶδας, ἄνερ, εἰ τὴν γυναῖκα σώσεις; 7.17 εἰ μὴ ἑκάστῳ ὡς ἐμέρισεν ὁ κύριος, ἕκαστον ὡς κέκληκεν ὁ θεός, οὕτως περιπατείτω·

καὶ οὕτως ἐν πάσαις ταῖς ἐκκλησίαις διατάσσομαι. 7.18 περιτετμημένος τις ἐκλήθη; μὴ ἐπισπάσθω. ἐν ἀκροβυστίᾳ κέκληταί τις; μὴ περιτεμνέσθω.

7.19 ἡ περιτομὴ οὐδέν ἐστιν, καὶ ἡ ἀκροβυστία οὐδέν ἐστιν, ἀλλὰ τήρησις ἐντολῶν θεοῦ.

for the same (thing), lest Satan tempt ye because of your incontinence/lack of self-control.

7.6 But I say this according to permission/concession, not according to/by a command.

7.7 And I want/wish *for* all men to be also as myself; but each (one) has his own gift from God, one thus, another so.

7.8 And I say to the unmarried (ones) and to the widows, *it is* good for them if they abide as I also; 7.9 but if they be not temperate/control not themselves, let them marry, for it is better to marry than to be on fire/set on fire. 7.10 But I charge/enjoin to those having married, not I but the Lord, *for* a woman not to be separated/parted from a man, 7.11 but even if she be separated, let her abide/remain single or let her be reconciled to the man, and *for* a man not to send away/dismiss a woman.

7.12 And I speak/say to the rest, I, not the Lord: If a certain brother has an unbelieving woman, and she consents/thinks it good to dwell with him, let him not dismiss/release her;

7.13 And if a woman has an unbelieving man, and he consents/thinks it good to dwell with her, let her not dismiss/release the man. 7.14 For the unbelieving man has been sanctified/set apart in/by the woman, and the unbelieving woman has been sanctified/set apart in/by the brother; since then the children from ye are unclean, but now are holy/hallowed.

7.15 But if the unbelieving (one) withdraws/departs, let him be withdrawn; the brother or the sister has not been enslaved in/by the (things) such;

but God has called ye in peace. 7.16 For what do you know, woman, if you will save the man? Or what do you know, man, if you will save the woman? 7.17 Except as the Lord divided to each (one), as God has called each (one), so let him walk;

And so I ordain/order in all the assemblies/ecclesiae. 7.18 Was anyone having been circumcised called? Let him not obliterate *it*. Has anyone been called in uncircumcision? Let him not be circumcised.

7.19 The circumcision is nothing, and the uncircumcision is nothing, but keeping of commands from

7.20 ἕκαστος ἐν τῇ κλήσει ᾗ ἐκλήθη ἐν ταύτῃ μενέτω. 7.21 δοῦλος ἐκλήθης; μή σοι μελέτω· ἀλλ' εἰ καὶ δύνασαι ἐλεύθερος γενέσθαι, μᾶλλον χρῆσαι.

7.22 ὁ γὰρ ἐν κυρίῳ κληθεὶς δοῦλος ἀπελεύθερος κυρίου ἐστίν· ὁμοίως ὁ ἐλεύθερος κληθεὶς δοῦλος χριστοῦ ἐστιν. 7.23 τιμῆς ἠγοράσθητε· μὴ γείνεσθε δοῦλοι ἀνθρώπων. 7.24 ἕκαστος ἐν ᾧ ἐκλήθη, ἀδελφοί, ἐν τούτῳ μενέτω παρὰ θεῷ.

7.25 περὶ δὲ τῶν παρθένων ἐπιταγὴν κυρίου οὐκ ἔχω, γνώμην δὲ δίδωμι ὡς ἠλεημένος ὑπὸ κυρίου πιστὸς εἶναι. 7.26 νομίζω οὖν τοῦτο καλὸν ὑπάρχειν διὰ τὴν ἐνεστῶσαν ἀνάγκην, ὅτι καλὸν ἀνθρώπῳ τὸ οὕτως εἶναι. 7.27 δέδεσε γυναικί; μὴ ζήτι λύσιν· λέλυσαι ἀπὸ γυναικός; μὴ ζήτι γυναῖκα. 7.28 ἐὰν δὲ καὶ γαμήσῃς, οὐχ ἥμαρτες· καὶ ἐὰν γήμῃ ἡ παρθένος, οὐχ ἥμαρτεν. θλῖψιν δὲ τῇ σαρκὶ ἕξουσιν οἱ τοιοῦτοι, ἐγὼ δὲ ὑμῶν φίδομαι.

7.29 τοῦτο δέ φημι, ἀδελφοί, ὁ καιρὸς συννεσταλμένος ἐστίν· τὸ λοιπὸν ἵνα καὶ οἱ ἔχοντες γυναῖκας ὡς μὴ ἔχοντες ὦσιν,

7.30 καὶ οἱ κλαίοντες ὡς μὴ κλαίοντες, καὶ οἱ χαίροντες ὡς μὴ χαίροντες, καὶ οἱ ἀγοράζοντες ὡς μὴ κατέχοντες, 7.31 καὶ οἱ χρώμενοι τὸν κόσμον ὡς μὴ καταχρώμενοι· παράγει γὰρ τὸ σχῆμα τοῦ κόσμου τούτου.

7.32 θέλω δὲ ὑμᾶς ἀμερίμνους εἶναι. ὁ ἄγαμος μεριμνᾷ τὰ τοῦ κυρίου, πῶς ἀρέσῃ τῷ κυρίῳ· 7.33 ὁ δὲ γαμήσας μεριμνᾷ τὰ τοῦ κόσμου, πῶς ἀρέσῃ τῇ γυναικί, 7.34 καὶ μεμέρισται. καὶ ἡ γυνὴ ἡ ἄγαμος καὶ ἡ παρθένος ἡ ἄγαμος μεριμνᾷ τὰ τοῦ

God.

7.20 Each (one) in/by the calling in which he was called, let him abide in/by this. 7.21 Was a slave called? Let it not be a care to you; but even if you are able to become free, avail yourself more.

7.22 For the (one) having been called a slave in *the* Lord is a free (one) of *the* Lord; likewise, the (one) having been called a free (one) is a slave of the anointed (one). 7.23 Of what price were ye bought? Become ye not slaves of men/humans. 7.24 Each (one) in/by what he was called, brothers, let him abide/stay in this (thing) with/by God.

7.25 And concerning the maidens/virgins, I have not a command from *the* Lord, but I give a decision/judgment as having been shown mercy by *the* Lord, to be faithful. 7.26 Therefore I think/consider this good (thing) to exist because of the necessity having been placed, because *it is* good for a man to be so. 7.27 Have you been bound to a woman? Seek not a loosing/release; have you been loosed/released from a woman? Seek not a woman. 7.28 But even if you should/might marry, you sinned not; and if the maiden/virgin might marry, she sinned not. But the (ones) such will have oppression/affliction for/in the flesh, but I, I refrain from ye.

7.29 But I say this, brothers: The time/season has been shortened; the (time) remaining in order that both those having women may be as/like (ones) having not,

7.30 and those weeping as (ones) weeping not, and those rejoicing as (ones) rejoicing not, and those buying as (ones) not holding down, 7.31 and those availing themselves of the world as (ones) not using *it* downright; for the scheme/form of this world passes by/away.

7.32 But I want/wish *for* ye to be without a care. The unmarried (man) cares *for* the (things) of the Lord, how he might please the Lord; 7.33 but the (one) having married cares *for* the (things) of the world, how he might please the woman, 7.34 and he has been divided. Both the unmarried woman and unmarried maiden/virgin cares *for* the (things) of the Lord, in

κυρίου, ἵνα ᾖ ἁγία καὶ τῷ σώματι καὶ τῷ πνεύματι· ἡ δὲ γαμήσασα μεριμνᾷ τὰ τοῦ κόσμου, πῶς ἀρέσῃ τῷ ἀνδρί. 7.35 τοῦτο δὲ πρὸς τὸ ὑμῶν αὐτῶν σύμφερον λέγω, οὐχ ἵνα βρόχον ὑμῖν ἐπιβάλω, ἀλλὰ πρὸς τὸ εὔσχημον καὶ εὐπάρεδρον τῷ κυρίῳ ἀπερισπάστως.

7.36 εἰ δέ τις ἀσχημονεῖ ἐπὶ τὴν παρθένον αὐτοῦ νομίζει ἐὰν ᾖ ὑπέρακμος, καὶ οὕτως ὀφίλει γίνεσθε, ὃ θέλει ποιείτω· οὐχ ἁμαρτάνει· γαμίτωσαν.

7.37 ὃς δὲ ἕστηκεν ἐν τῇ καρδίᾳ αὐτοῦ ἑδραῖος, μὴ ἔχων ἀνάγκην, ἐξουσίαν δὲ ἔχει περὶ τοῦ ἰδίου θελήματος, καὶ τοῦτο κέκρικεν ἐν τῇ ἰδίᾳ καρδίᾳ, τηρῖν τὴν ἑαυτοῦ παρθένον, καλῶς ποιήσει· 7.38 ὥστε καὶ ὁ γαμίζων τὴν ἑαυτοῦ παρθένον καλῶς ποιεῖ, καὶ ὁ μὴ γαμίζων κρῖσσον ποιήσει.

7.39 γυνὴ δέδεται ἐφ' ὅσον χρόνον ζῇ ὁ ἀνὴρ αὐτῆς· ἐὰν δὲ κοιμηθῇ ὁ ἀνήρ, ἐλευθέρα ἐστὶν ᾧ θέλει γαμηθῆναι, μόνον ἐν κυρίῳ. 7.40 μακαριωτέρα δέ ἐστιν ἐὰν οὕτως μίνῃ, κατὰ τὴν ἐμὴν γνώμην, δοκῶ δὲ κἀγὼ πνεῦμα θεοῦ ἔχειν.

8.1 Περὶ δὲ τῶν ἰδωλοθύτων, οἴδαμεν ὅτι πάντες γνῶσιν ἔχομεν. ἡ γνῶσις φυσιοῖ, ἡ δὲ ἀγάπη οἰκοδομεῖ. 8.2 εἴ τις δοκεῖ ἐγνωκέναι τι, οὔπω ἔγνω καθὼς δεῖ γνῶναι· 8.3 εἰ δέ τις ἀγαπᾷ τὸν θεόν, οὗτος ἔγνωσται ὑπ' αὐτοῦ.

8.4 περὶ τῆς βρώσεως οὖν τῶν εἰδωλοθύτων οἴδαμεν ὅτι οὐδὲν εἴδωλον ἐν κόσμῳ, καὶ ὅτι οὐδὶς θεὸς εἰ μὴ εἷς.

8.5 καὶ γὰρ εἴπερ εἰσὶν λεγόμενοι θεοὶ εἴτε ἐν οὐρανῷ εἴτε ἐπὶ γῆς, ὥσπερ εἰσὶν θεοὶ πολλοὶ καὶ κύριοι πολλοί, 8.6 ἀλλ' ἡμῖν εἷς θεὸς ὁ πατήρ, ἐξ οὗ τὰ πάντα καὶ ἡμῖς εἰς αὐτόν, καὶ εἷς κύριος Ἰησοῦς χριστός, δι' οὗ τὰ πάντα καὶ ἡμῖς δι' αὐτοῦ.

order that she may be holy/set apart both in the body and in the spirit; but the (one) having married cares *for* the (things) of the world, how she might please the man.   7.35   And I say this to/for the (thing) being to the advantage of ye yourselves, not that I might put a noose upon ye, but to/for the decent/proper (thing) and devotedness/dedication to the Lord without distraction.

7.36   But if anyone behaves in an indecent manner to/on his maiden/virgin, he thinks/supposes if she may be past the bloom of youth, and she is obliged to become so, what he wants/wishes, let him do; he sins not; let them marry.

7.37   But (he) who has stood firm in his heart, having not a necessity, but he has authority concerning his own will/want, and has decided this in his own heart, to keep the maiden/virgin of himself, he will do well;   7.38 so that both the (one) marrying the maiden/virgin of himself does well, and the (one) not marrying will do better.

7.39   A woman has been bound for as long a time as her man lives; but if the man be fallen asleep, she is free to be married to whom she wants/wishes, only in *the* Lord.   7.40 But she is more happy if she abides/remains so, according to my judgment/decision, and I think I also have a spirit from God.

8.1   And about the (things) sacrificed to idols, we know that we all have knowledge. The knowledge inflates/puffs up, but the agape builds up/edifies. 8.2   If anyone seems to have known anything, he not yet knew as it is necessary to know;   8.3 but if anyone loves God, this (one) has been known by him.

8.4   Therefore, about the eating of the (things) sacrificed to idols, we know that an idol *is* nothing in a world, and that no one *is* God except one.

8.5 For even if there indeed are (ones) being called gods, whether in heaven or upon earth, just as there are many gods and many lords,   8.6 but for us one is God the father, out from whom all things *are* , and we *are* in/for him, and/also one *is* Lord, Jesus the anointed (one), through whom *are* all things, and we

8.7 ἀλλ' οὐκ ἐν πᾶσιν ἡ γνῶσις· τινὲς δὲ τῇ συνηθίᾳ ἕως ἄρτι τοῦ εἰδώλου ὡς εἰδωλόθυτόν ἐστιν, καὶ ἡ συνίδησεις αὐτῶν ἀσθενὴς οὖσα μολύνεται.

8.8 βρῶμα δὲ ἡμᾶς οὐ παραστήσει τῷ θεῷ· οὔτε ἐὰν φάγωμεν περισσεύομεν, οὔτε ἐὰν μὴ φάγωμεν ὑστερούμεθα.

8.9 βλέπετε δὲ μή πως ἡ ἐξουσία ὑμῶν αὕτη πρόσκομμα γένηται τοῖς ἀσθενέσιν.

8.10 ἐὰν γάρ τις ἴδῃ σὲ τὸν γνῶσιν ἔχοντα ἐν ἰδωλίῳ κατακείμενον, οὐχὶ ἡ συνίδησεις αὐτοῦ ἀσθενοῦς ὄντος οἰκοδομηθήσεται εἰς τὸ τὰ ἰδωλόθυτα ἐσθίειν; 8.11 ἀπόλλυται γὰρ ὁ ἀσθενῶν ἐν τῇ σῇ γνώσει, ὁ ἀδελφὸς δι' ὃν χριστὸς ἀπέθανεν.

8.12 οὕτως δὲ ἁμαρτάνοντες εἰς τοὺς ἀδελφοὺς καὶ τύπτοντες αὐτῶν τὴν συνίδησιν ἀσθενοῦσαν εἰς χριστὸν ἁμαρτάνετε.

8.13 διόπερ εἰ βρῶμα σκανδαλίζει τὸν ἀδελφόν μου, οὐ μὴ φάγω κρέας εἰς τὸν αἰῶνα, ἵνα μὴ τὸν ἀδελφόν μου σκανδαλίσω.

9.1 Οὐκ εἰμὶ ἐλεύθερος; οὐκ εἰμὶ ἀπόστολος; οὐχὶ Ἰησοῦν τὸν κύριον ἡμῶν ἑόρακα; οὐ τὸ ἔργον μου ὑμεῖς ἐστε ἐν κυρίῳ; 9.2 εἰ ἄλλοις οὐκ εἰμὶ ἀπόστολος, ἀλλά γε ὑμῖν εἰμι· ἡ γὰρ σφραγίς μου τῆς ἀποστολῆς ὑμεῖς ἐστε ἐν κυρίῳ.

9.3 ἡ ἐμὴ ἀπολογία τοῖς ἐμὲ ἀνακρίνουσίν ἐστιν αὕτη. 9.4 μὴ οὐκ ἔχομεν ἐξουσίαν φαγεῖν καὶ πῖν; 9.5 μὴ οὐκ ἔχομεν ἐξουσίαν ἀδελφὴν γυναῖκα περιάγειν, ὡς καὶ οἱ λοιποὶ ἀπόστολοι καὶ οἱ ἀδελφοὶ τοῦ κυρίου καὶ Κηφᾶς; 9.6 ἢ μόνος ἐγὼ καὶ Βαρναβᾶς οὐκ ἔχομεν ἐξουσίαν μὴ ἐργάζεσθαι;

9.7 τίς στρατεύεται ἰδίοις ὀψωνίοις ποτέ; τίς φυτεύει ἀμπελῶνα καὶ τὸν καρπὸν αὐτοῦ οὐκ ἐσθίει; ἢ τίς ποιμαίνει ποίμνην καὶ ἐκ τοῦ γάλακτος τῆς ποίμνης οὐκ ἐσθίει;

through him.

8.7 But the knowledge is not in all; but some (men), by custom/habit until now, are the idol's, as meat offered to an idol, and the conscience of them/ their conscience, being weak, is polluted.

8.8 But food will not devote/recommend us to God; neither do we abound if we might eat, nor do we lack if we might not eat.

8.9 But see/beware ye lest somehow this authority of ye/your authority might become an offense/stumbling block to the weak (ones).

8.10 For if anyone might see you, the (one) having knowledge, reclining *at table* in an idol's temple, will not his conscience, being weak, be emboldened/built up into the (thing) to eat the (things) sacrificed to an idol? 8.11 For the (one) being weak perishes in/by your knowledge, the brother because of whom the anointed (one) died.

8.12 And so, sinning to/against the brothers and smiting/beating their conscience, they being weak, ye sin to/against the anointed (one).

8.13 Therefore, if food/eating offends/causes to stumble your brother, by no means should I eat meat into the age, in order that I might not cause my brother to stumble/fall into sinful ways.

9.1 Am I not free? Am I not an apostle? Have I not seen Jesus our Lord? Ye, are ye not my work in *the* Lord? 9.2 If I am not an apostle to others, but at least I am to ye; for ye, ye are the seal of my apostleship in *the* Lord.

9.3 My defense to those examining/judging me is this: 9.4 Have we not a right/authority to eat and to drink? 9.5 Have we not a right/authority to bring along/accompany a sister, a woman, as also the remaining apostles *do*, and/also the brothers of the Lord and Cephas? 9.6 Or only I and Barnabas, have we not a right/authority not to work?

9.7 Who battles/serves as a soldier for his own pay at some time, who plants a vineyard and eats not the fruit/product from it? Or who shepherds a flock and eats not from the milk of the flock?

9.8 μὴ κατὰ ἄνθρωπον ταῦτα λαλῶ, ἢ καὶ ὁ νόμος ταῦτα οὐ λέγει; 9.9 ἐν γὰρ τῷ Μωϋσέως νόμῳ γέγραπται, «οὐ φιμώσεις βοῦν ἀλοῶντα.» μὴ τῶν βοῶν μέλει τῷ θεῷ; 9.10 ἢ δι᾽ ἡμᾶς πάντως λέγει; δι᾽ ἡμᾶς γὰρ ἐγράφη, ὅτι ὀφίλει ἐπ᾽ ἐλπίδι ὁ ἀροτριῶν ἀροτριᾶν, καὶ ὁ ἀλοῶν ἐπ᾽ ἐλπίδι τοῦ μετέχειν.

9.11 εἰ ἡμῖς ὑμῖν τὰ πνευματικὰ ἐσπείραμεν, μέγα εἰ ἡμῖς ὑμῶν τὰ σαρκικὰ θερίσομεν; 9.12 εἰ ἄλλοι τῆς ὑμῶν ἐξουσίας μετέχουσιν, οὐχὶ μᾶλλον ἡμῖς;

ἀλλ᾽ οὐκ ἐχρησάμεθα τῇ ἐξουσίᾳ ταύτῃ, ἀλλὰ πάντα στέγομεν ἵνα μή τινα ἐγκοπὴν δῶμεν τῷ εὐαγγελίῳ τοῦ χριστοῦ. 9.13 οὐκ οἴδατε ὅτι οἱ τὰ ἱερὰ ἐργαζόμενοι τὰ ἐκ τοῦ ἱεροῦ ἐσθίουσιν, οἱ τῷ θυσιαστηρίῳ παρεδρεύοντες τῷ θυσιαστηρίῳ συμμερίζονται; 9.14 οὕτως καὶ ὁ κύριος διέταξεν τοῖς τὸ εὐαγγέλιον καταγγέλλουσιν ἐκ τοῦ εὐαγγελίου ζῆν. 9.15 ἐγὼ δὲ οὐ κεχρήσαμαι οὐδενὶ τούτων. οὐκ ἔγραψα δὲ ταῦτα ἵνα οὕτως γένηται ἐν ἐμοί, καλὸν γάρ μοι μᾶλλον ἀποθανῖν ἢ τὸ καύχημά μου οὐδὶς κενώσει.

9.16 ἐὰν γὰρ εὐαγγελίζωμαι, οὐκ ἔστιν μοι καύχημα· ἀνάγκη γάρ μοι ἐπίκειται· οὐαὶ γάρ μοί ἐστιν ἐὰν μὴ εὐαγγελίσωμαι. 9.17 εἰ γὰρ ἑκὼν τοῦτο πράσσω, μισθὸν ἔχω· εἰ δὲ ἄκων, οἰκονομίαν πεπίστευμαι.

9.18 τίς οὖν μού ἐστιν ὁ μισθός; ἵνα εὐαγγελιζόμενος ἀδάπανον θήσω τὸ εὐαγγέλιον, εἰς τὸ μὴ καταχρήσασθαι ἐν τῇ ἐξουσίᾳ μου ἐν τῷ εὐαγγελίῳ.

9.19 ἐλεύθερος γὰρ ὢν ἐκ πάντων πᾶσιν ἐμαυτὸν ἐδούλωσα, ἵνα τοὺς πλίονας κερδήσω· 9.20 καὶ ἐγενόμην τοῖς Ἰουδαίοις ὡς Ἰουδαῖος, ἵνα Ἰουδαίους κερδήσω· τοῖς ὑπὸ νόμον ὡς ὑπὸ νόμον, μὴ ὢν αὐτὸς ὑπὸ νόμον, ἵνα τοὺς ὑπὸ

9.8 Speak I not these (things) according to a man, or the law also says not these (things)? 9.9 For it has been written in the law of Moses: YOU WILL NOT MUZZLE A THRESHING OX. Are not the oxen a care to God? 9.10 Or certainly he speaks because of us? For it was written because of us, the (one) plowing is obliged to plow on/for a hope, and the (one) threshing on/for a hope of the (thing) to partake.

9.11 If we, we sowed not the spiritual (things) for ye, *is it* a great thing if we, we shall reap the fleshly (things)? 9.12 If others partake of/share your right/authority, *are* we not more?

But we did not employ/use this right/authority, but we covered/endured all (things) in order that we might not give anyone a hindrance to the good message/gospel of the anointed (one). 9.13 Know ye not that the (ones) working the sacred (things) eat the (things) out of the *outer* temple, the (ones) sitting by/attending to the altar partake together at the altar? 9.14 So also the Lord ordained/commanded the (ones) proclaiming the good message/gospel to live out of the good message/gospel. 9.15 But I, I have not employed/used nothing from these. But I wrote not these (things) in order that it might become so in me, for *it is* more good for me to die than *that* no one will empty/falsify the object of my boast.

9.16 For if I may announce a good message, it is not a boast for me; for a necessity is laid upon me; for woe is for me if I should not announce a good message. 9.17 For if I willingly practice this, I have a reward; but if unwillingly, I have been entrusted *with* a responsibility.

9.18 What then is my reward? That announcing *the* good message I might place the good message/gospel free of charge, in the (thing) not to employ/use in full my authority in the good message/gospel.

9.19 For being free from all (men) I enslaved myself for all, in order that I might gain the more/greater (men); 9.20 and I became like a Judean to the Judeans, in order that I might gain Judeans; as under *the* law for those under *the* law, not being under *the* law myself, in order that I might gain those under *the*

νόμον κερδήσω· 9.21 τοῖς ἀνόμοις ὡς ἄνομος, μὴ ὢν ἄνομος θεοῦ ἀλλ᾽ ἔννομος χριστοῦ, ἵνα κερδάνω τοὺς ἀνόμους· 9.22 ἐγενόμην τοῖς ἀσθενέσιν ἀσθενής, ἵνα τοὺς ἀσθενεῖς κερδήσω·

τοῖς πᾶσιν γέγονα πάντα, ἵνα πάντως τινὰς σώσω. 9.23 πάντα δὲ ποιῶ διὰ τὸ εὐαγγέλιον, ἵνα συγκοινωνὸς αὐτοῦ γένωμαι.

9.24 οὐκ οἴδατε ὅτι οἱ ἐν σταδίῳ τρέχοντες πάντες μὲν τρέχουσιν, εἷς δὲ λαμβάνι τὸ βραβῖον; οὕτως τρέχετε ἵνα καταλάβητε. 9.25 πᾶς δὲ ὁ ἀγωνιζόμενος πάντα ἐγκρατεύεται, ἐκεῖνοι μὲν οὖν ἵνα φθαρτὸν στέφανον λάβωσιν, ἡμεῖς δὲ ἄφθαρτον. 9.26 ἐγὼ τοίνυν οὕτως τρέχω ὡς οὐκ ἀδήλως, οὕτως πυκτεύω ὡς οὐκ ἀέρα δέρων· 9.27 ἀλλ᾽ ὑπωπιάζω μου τὸ σῶμα καὶ δουλαγωγῶ, μή πως ἄλλοις κηρύξας αὐτὸς ἀδόκιμος γένωμαι.

10.1 Οὐ θέλω γὰρ ὑμᾶς ἀγνοεῖν, ἀδελφοί, ὅτι οἱ πατέρες ἡμῶν πάντες ὑπὸ τὴν νεφέλην ἦσαν καὶ πάντες διὰ τῆς θαλάσσης διῆλθον, 10.2 καὶ πάντες εἰς τὸν Μωϋσῆν ἐβαπτίσθησαν ἐν τῇ νεφέλῃ καὶ ἐν τῇ θαλάσσῃ, 10.3 καὶ πάντες τὸ αὐτὸ πνευματικὸν βρῶμα ἔφαγον, 10.4 καὶ πάντες τὸ αὐτὸ πνευματικὸν ἔπιον πόμα· ἔπινον γὰρ ἐκ πνευματικῆς ἀκολουθούσης πέτρας· ἡ πέτρα δὲ ἦν ὁ χριστός. 10.5 ἀλλ᾽ οὐκ ἐν τοῖς πλείοσιν αὐτῶν εὐδόκησεν ὁ θεός, κατεστρώθησαν γὰρ ἐν τῇ ἐρήμῳ.

10.6 ταῦτα δὲ τύποι ἡμῶν ἐγενήθησαν, εἰς τὸ μὴ εἶναι ἡμᾶς ἐπιθυμητὰς κακῶν, καθὼς κἀκεῖνοι ἐπεθύμησαν.

10.7 μηδὲ εἰδωλολάτραι γίνεσθε, καθώς τινες αὐτῶν· ὥσπερ γέγραπται, « ἐκάθισεν ὁ λαὸς φαγεῖν καὶ πῖν, καὶ ἀνέστησαν πέζιν.» 10.8 μηδὲ πορνεύωμεν, καθώς τινες αὐτῶν ἐπόρνευσαν,

law;   9.21 to the lawless (ones) as without law, not being without a law from God, but true to *the* law of the anointed (one), in order that I might gain the lawless (ones);   9.22 I became weak for the (ones) being weak, in order that I might gain those being weak themselves;

I have become all (things) for all (men), in order that I might certainly save some.   9.23 But I do all (things) because of the good message/gospel, in order that I might become a joint partaker of it.

9.24   Know ye not that those running in a stadium/on a track/course, all (men) indeed run, but one takes/receives the prize? So run ye in order that ye might receive *it*.   9.25 And every one contending/competing *for* all (things) exercises self control, those indeed therefore in order that they might receive a decayable wreath/crown, but we an undecaying/incorruptible (one).   9.26   I, I so run hence as not uncertainly/without a goal, so I fight with fists not as beating air;   9.27 but I browbeat/treat roughly my body and enslave *it*, lest perhaps/somehow *from* others having heralded I myself might become unproven/rejected.

10.1   For I want/wish not *for* ye to be ignorant, brothers, that our fathers were all under the cloud, and all went through the sea,   10.2 and all were baptized into/for Moses in the cloud and in the sea, 10.3 and all ate the same spiritual food,   10.4 and all drank the same spiritual drink; for they were drinking out of/from following a spiritual rock. And the rock was the anointed (one).   10.5 But in/by the most of them, God was not well pleased, for they were strewn down in the desert/wilderness.

10.6   But these (things) happened *for* types/examples of us, in the (thing) *for* us not to be desirers of bad (things), as those also desired.

10.7   Neither become ye idolaters, as/like some of them; as it has been written: THE PEOPLE SAT TO EAT AND TO DRINK, AND THEY STOOD UP TO PLAY.   10.8 Neither may/should we do prostitution, as some of them indulged in prostitution, and twenty-three thousands fell in

καὶ ἔπεσαν μιᾷ ἡμέρᾳ εἴκοσι τρῖς χιλιάδες.

10.9 μηδὲ ἐκπιράζωμεν τὸν χριστόν, καθώς τινες αὐτῶν ἐπείρασαν, καὶ ὑπὸ τῶν ὄφεων ἀπώλλυντο.

10.10 μηδὲ γογγύζωμε, καθάπερ τινὲς αὐτῶν ἐγόγγυσαν, καὶ ἀπώλοντο ὑπὸ τοῦ ὀλοθρευτοῦ.

10.11 πάντα δὲ ταῦτα τυπικῶς συνέβαινεν ἐκείνοις, ἐγράφη δὲ εἰς νουθεσίαν ἡμῶν, εἰς οὓς τὰ τέλη τῶν αἰώνων κατήντηκεν.

10.12 ὥστε ὁ δοκῶν ἑστάναι βλεπέτω μὴ πέσῃ. 10.13 πιρασμὸς ὑμᾶς οὐκ εἴληφεν εἰ μὴ ἀνθρώπινος· πιστὸς δὲ ὁ θεός, ὃς οὐκ ἐάσει ὑμᾶς πιρασθῆναι ὑπὲρ ὃ δύνασθαι, ἀλλὰ ποιήσει σὺν τῷ πιρασμῷ καὶ τὴν ἔκβασιν τοῦ δύνασθαι ὑπενεγκεῖν. 10.14 διόπερ, ἀγαπητοί μου, φεύγετε ἀπὸ τῆς ἰδωλολατρίας.

10.15 ὡς φρονίμοις λέγω· κρίνατε ὑμεῖς ὅ φημι. 10.16 τὸ ποτήριον τῆς εὐλογίας ὃ εὐλογοῦμεν, οὐχὶ κοινωνία τοῦ αἵματος τοῦ χριστοῦ ἐστιν; τὸν ἄρτον ὃν κλῶμεν, οὐχὶ κοινωνία τοῦ σώματος τοῦ χριστοῦ ἐστιν; 10.17 ὅτι εἷς ἄρτος, ἓν σῶμα οἱ πολλοί ἐσμεν, οἱ γὰρ πάντες ἐκ τοῦ ἑνὸς ἄρτου μετέχομεν.

10.18 βλέπετε τὸν Ἰσραὴλ κατὰ σάρκα· οὐχ οἱ ἐσθίοντες τὰς θυσίας κοινωνοὶ τοῦ θυσιαστηρίου εἰσίν; 10.19 τί οὖν φημι; ὅτι εἰδωλόθυτόν τί ἐστιν; ἢ ὅτι εἴδωλόν τί ἐστιν; 10.20 ἀλλ᾽ ὅτι ἃ θύουσιν τὰ ἔθνη, δαιμονίοις καὶ οὐ θεῷ θύουσιν,

οὐ θέλω δὲ ὑμᾶς κοινωνοὺς τῶν δαιμονίων γείνεσθαι. 10.21 οὐ δύνασθε ποτήριον κυρίου πίνιν καὶ ποτήριον δαιμονίων· οὐ δύνασθε τραπέζης κυρίου μετέχιν καὶ τραπέζης δαιμονίων. 10.22 ἢ παραζηλοῦμεν τὸν κύριον; μὴ ἰσχυρότεροι αὐτοῦ ἐσμεν; 10.23 πάντα ἔξεστιν, ἀλλ᾽ οὐ πάντα συμφέρει. πάντα ἔξεστιν, ἀλλ᾽ οὐ

one day.

10.9   Neither may/should we try/test the anointed (one), as some of them tried/tested, and they were destroyed by the serpents.

10.10   Neither grumble/murmur ye, even as some of them grumbled, and they were destroyed by the destroyer.

10.11   But all these (things) befell/happened to those (men) typically/symbolically, and was written to/for admonition of us, to/for whom the ends of the ages have arrived.

10.12   So that the (one) thinking to have stood, let him see/be careful lest he might fall.   10.13 A trial/temptation has not taken ye except a mannish/human; but God is faithful, who will not allow ye to be tempted/testedbeyond what ye are able, but he will make with the trial/temptation also the way out from the (thing) to be able to bear up under *it*.   10.14 Wherefore,   my   beloved (ones),   flee ye from the idolatry.

10.15   I speak as to prudent (ones); ye, ye judge what I say.   10.16 The cup of the blessing which we bless, is it not a fellowship from the blood of the anointed (one)? The loaf which we break, is it not a fellowship from the body of the anointed (one)?   10.17 Because *there is* one loaf, one body, we are the many, for all the (ones) *are* out of/from the one loaf we share.

10.18   See/consider ye Israel according to flesh; are not those eating the sacrifices companions/sharers of the altar?   10.19 What then say I? That a sacrifice to an idol is something? Or that an idol is something? 10.20 But that what (things) the ethnics sacrifice, they sacrifice to demons and not to God,

and I want/wish not *for* ye to become companions/ sharers of the demons.   10.21   Ye are not able to drink a cup of *the* Lord and a cup of demons; ye are not able to partake from a table of *the* Lord and from a table of demons.   10.22   Or do we provoke the Lord to jealousy? We are not stronger than he, *are we*? 10.23 All (things) are lawful, but not all are beneficial/useful. All (things) are lawful, but not all

πάντα οἰκοδομεῖ. 10.24 μηδεὶς τὸ ἑαυτοῦ ζητείτω ἀλλὰ τὸ τοῦ ἑτέρου. 10.25 πᾶν τὸ ἐν μακέλλῳ πωλούμενον ἐσθίετε μηδὲν ἀνακρίνοντες διὰ τὴν συνίδησιν, 10.26 «τοῦ κυρίου» γὰρ «ἡ γῆ καὶ τὸ πλήρωμα αὐτῆς.» 10.27 εἴ τις καλεῖ ὑμᾶς τῶν ἀπίστων καὶ θέλεται πορεύεσθε, πᾶν τὸ παρατιθέμενον ὑμῖν ἐσθίετε μηδὲν ἀνακρίνοντες διὰ τὴν συνίδησιν.

10.28 ἐὰν δέ τις ὑμῖν εἴπῃ, τοῦτο ἱερόθυτόν ἐστιν, μὴ ἐσθίετε δι' ἐκεῖνον τὸν μηνύσαντα καὶ τὴν συνίδησιν 10.29 συνίδησιν δὲ λέγω οὐχὶ τὴν ἑαυτοῦ ἀλλὰ τὴν τοῦ ἑτέρου.

ἰνατί γὰρ ἡ ἐλευθερία μου κρίνεται ὑπὸ ἄλλης συνειδήσεως; 10.30 εἰ ἐγὼ χάριτι μετέχω, τί βλασφημοῦμαι ὑπὲρ οὗ ἐγὼ εὐχαριστῶ;

10.31 εἴτε οὖν ἐσθίετε εἴτε πίνετε εἴτε τι ποιεῖτε, πάντα εἰς δόξαν θεοῦ ποιεῖτε. 10.32 ἀπρόσκοποι καὶ Ἰουδαίοις γείνεσθε καὶ Ἕλλησιν καὶ τῇ ἐκκλησίᾳ τοῦ θεοῦ, 10.33 καθὼς κἀγὼ πάντα πᾶσιν ἀρέσκω, μὴ ζητῶν τὸ ἐμαυτοῦ σύμφορον ἀλλὰ τὸ τῶν πολλῶν, ἵνα σωθῶσιν. 11.1 μιμηταί μου γείνεσθαι, καθὼς κἀγὼ χριστοῦ.

11.2 ἐπαινῶ δὲ ὑμᾶς ὅτι πάντα μου μέμνησθαι καὶ καθὼς παραδέδωκα ὑμῖν τὰς παραδόσεις κατέχετε.

11.3 θέλω δὲ ὑμᾶς εἰδέναι ὅτι παντὸς ἀνδρὸς ἡ κεφαλὴ ὁ χριστός ἐστιν, κεφαλὴ δὲ γυναικὸς ὁ ἀνήρ, κεφαλὴ δὲ τοῦ χριστοῦ ὁ θεός.

11.4 πᾶς ἀνὴρ προσευχόμενος ἢ προφητεύων κατὰ κεφαλῆς ἔχων καταισχύνει τὴν κεφαλὴν αὐτοῦ·

11.5 πᾶσα δὲ γυνὴ προσευχομένη ἢ προφητεύουσα ἀκατακαλύπτῳ τῇ κεφαλῇ καταισχύνει τὴν κεφαλὴν αὐτῆς· ἓν γάρ ἐστιν καὶ τὸ αὐτὸ τῇ ἐξυρημένῃ. 11.6 εἰ γὰρ οὐ κατακαλύπτεται γυνή, καὶ κειράσθω· εἰ δὲ αἰσχρὸν γυναικὶ τὸ

builds up/edifies. 10.24 Let no one seek the (thing) of himself but the (thing) of the other/different. 10.25 Eat ye every thing being sold in a meat/food market, examining nothing because/on account of the conscience, 10.26 for THE LAND/EARTH *is* THE LORD'S AND THE FULLNESS OF HER. 10.27 If anyone of the unbelievers calls/invites ye and ye want/wish to go, eat ye every thing being put before ye, examining nothing because of the conscience.

10.28 But if anyone might say to ye: This is meat sacrificed to an idol, eat ye not because of that one having disclosed it and the conscience; 10.29 but I say not the conscience of himself but the (one) of the other/different.

For why is my freedom/liberty judged by another's conscience? 10.30 If I, I partake in/with thanks/grace, why am I slandered/blasphemed over *that* which I, I give thanks?

10.31 Therefore, whether ye eat or drink or what ye do, do ye all (things) to/for fame/glory of God, 10.32 Become ye clear (ones)/without offense both to Judeans and to Greeks and to the assembly of God, 10.33 as even I, I please/agree with all *for* all (things), not seeking the benefit/advantage of myself but that of the many, in order that they might be saved. 11.1 Become ye imitators of me, as I also of the anointed (one).

11.2 But I praise ye because ye have remembered all (things) from me and ye hold fast the traditions as I delivered *them* to ye.

11.3 But I want/wish *for* ye to know that the anointed (one) is the head of every man, but the man *is* head of a woman, and God *is* head of the anointed (one).

11.4 Every man praying or prophesying having/holding against/down a head shames the head of him/his head.

11.5 But every woman praying or prophesying with the head unveiled/uncovered shames the head of her; for it is one and the same (thing) for the (woman) having shaved *it*. 11.6 For if a woman veils/covers not herself, let her also be shorn; but if the (thing)

κείρασθαι ἢ ξυρᾶσθαι, κατακαλυπτέσθω.

11.7 ἀνὴρ μὲν γὰρ οὐκ ὀφίλει κατακαλύπτεσθαι τὴν κεφαλήν, εἰκὼν καὶ δόξα θεοῦ ὑπάρχων· γυνὴ δὲ δόξα ἀνδρός ἐστιν. 11.8 οὐ γάρ ἐστιν ἀνὴρ ἐκ γυναικός, ἀλλὰ γυνὴ ἐξ ἀνδρός· 11.9 καὶ γὰρ οὐκ ἐκτίσθη ἀνὴρ διὰ τὴν γυναῖκα, ἀλλὰ γυνὴ διὰ τὸν ἄνδρα.

11.10 διὰ τοῦτο ὀφίλει ἡ γυνὴ ἐξουσίαν ἔχειν ἐπὶ τῆς κεφαλῆς διὰ τοὺς ἀγγέλους. 11.11 πλὴν οὔτε γυνὴ χωρὶς ἀνδρὸς οὔτε ἀνὴρ χωρὶς γυναικὸς ἐν κυρίῳ· 11.12 ὥσπερ γὰρ ἡ γυνὴ ἐκ τοῦ ἀνδρός, οὕτως καὶ ὁ ἀνὴρ διὰ τῆς γυναικός· τὰ δὲ πάντα ἐκ τοῦ θεοῦ.

11.13 ἐν ὑμῖν αὐτοῖς κρίνατε· πρέπον ἐστὶν γυναῖκα ἀκατακάλυπτον τῷ θεῷ προσεύχεσθαι; 11.14 οὐδὲ ἡ φύσις αὐτὴ διδάσκει ὑμᾶς ὅτι ἀνὴρ μὲν ἐὰν κομᾷ ἀτιμία αὐτῷ ἐστιν, 11.15 γυνὴ δὲ ἐὰν κομᾷ δόξα αὐτῇ ἐστιν; ὅτι ἡ κόμη ἀντὶ περιβολαίου δέδοται αὐτῇ.

11.16 εἰ δέ τις δοκεῖ φιλόνικος εἶναι, ἡμεῖς τοιαύτην συνήθιαν οὐκ ἔχομεν, οὐδὲ αἱ ἐκκλησίαι τοῦ θεοῦ. 11.17 τοῦτο δὲ παραγγέλλων οὐκ ἐπαινῶ ὅτι οὐκ εἰς τὸ κρῖσσον ἀλλ᾽ εἰς τὸ ἧσσον συνέρχεσθε. 11.18 πρῶτον μὲν γὰρ συνερχομένων ὑμῶν ἐν ἐκκλησίᾳ ἀκούω σχίσματα ἐν ὑμῖν ὑπάρχειν, καὶ μέρος τι πιστεύω. 11.19 δεῖ γὰρ καὶ αἱρέσις ἐν ὑμῖν εἶναι, ἵνα οἱ δόκιμοι φανεροὶ γένωνται ἐν ὑμῖν.

11.20 συνερχομένων οὖν ὑμῶν ἐπὶ τὸ αὐτὸ οὐκ ἔστιν κυριακὸν δῖπνον φαγεῖν, 11.21 ἕκαστος γὰρ τὸ ἴδιον δῖπνον προλαμβάνει ἐν τῷ φαγῖν, καὶ ὃς μὲν πινᾷ, ὃς δὲ μεθύει.

11.22 μὴ γὰρ οἰκίας οὐκ ἔχετε εἰς τὸ ἐσθίειν καὶ πίνιν; ἢ τῆς ἐκκλησίας τοῦ θεοῦ καταφρονῖτε, καὶ κατεσχύνετε τοὺς μὴ ἔχοντας;

to be shorn or to be shaved *is* a shame for a woman, let her be veiled/covered.

11.7 For indeed a man is obligated *for* the head not to be covered, existing/being an image and a glory of God; but also a woman is a glory of a man. 11.8 For man is not from woman, but woman from man; 11.9 for even/also man was not created because of the woman, but woman because of the man.

11.10 Because of this the woman is obliged to have authority upon/over the head on account of the messengers/angels. 11.11 However, neither is woman apart from man nor man apart from woman in *the* Lord; 11.12 for just as the woman *is* out of/from the man, so also *is* the man through the woman; but all things are out of/from God.

11.13 Judge/decide ye among ye yourselves: Is it proper for an uncovered woman to pray to God? 11.14 Does not the nature herself teach ye that if a man on one hand wears long hair, it is a dishonor for him, 11.15 but on the other if a woman wears long hair, it is a glory for her? Because the long hair has been given to her for a covering.

11.16 but if anyone think/seem to be quarrel-some, we, we have not such custom/habit, nor the assemblies of God. 11.17 But I praise/approve not *for* this charging, because ye come together not in/for the better but in/for the worse (thing). 11.18 For from/of your coming together in an assembly, I indeed hear first *of* divisions/splits to exist among ye, and I believe some part. 11.19 For it is even necessary *for* sects/choices/diversities to be among ye, in order that the tried/proven (ones) among ye might become manifest/made clear.

11.20 Then from your coming together for the same (thing), is it not *for* the Lord, to eat a supper? 11.21 For each (one) takes his own supper beforehand in the (thing) to eat, and *there is* (one) who hungers, but (another) who gets drunk.

11.22 For have ye not houses in/for the (thing) to eat and to drink? Or do ye despise/contemn of the assembly of God, and do ye put to shame those having not?

τί εἴπω ὑμῖν; ἐπαινέσω ὑμᾶς; ἐν τούτῳ οὐκ ἐπαινῶ. 11.23 ἐγὼ γὰρ παρέλαβον ἀπὸ τοῦ κυρίου, ὃ καὶ παρέδωκα ὑμῖν, ὅτι ὁ κύριος Ἰησοῦς ἐν τῇ νυκτὶ ᾗ παρεδίδετο ἔλαβεν ἄρτον 11.24 καὶ εὐχαριστήσας ἔκλασεν καὶ εἶπεν, τοῦτό μού ἐστιν τὸ σῶμα τὸ ὑπὲρ ὑμῶν· τοῦτο ποιεῖται εἰς τὴν ἐμὴν ἀνάμνησιν. 11.25 ὡσαύτως καὶ τὸ ποτήριον μετὰ τὸ διπνῆσαι, λέγων, τοῦτο τὸ ποτήριον ἡ καινὴ διαθήκη ἐστὶν ἐν τῷ ἐμῷ αἵματι· τοῦτο ποιεῖτε, ὁσάκις ἐὰν πίνητε, εἰς τὴν ἐμὴν ἀνάμνησιν.

11.26 ὁσάκις γὰρ ἐὰν ἐσθίητε τὸν ἄρτον τοῦτον καὶ τὸ ποτήριον πίνητε, τὸν θάνατον τοῦ κυρίου καταγγέλλετε, ἄχρις οὗ ἔλθῃ.

11.27 ὥστε ὃς ἂν ἐσθίῃ τὸν ἄρτον ἢ πίνῃ τὸ ποτήριον τοῦ κυρίου ἀναξίως τοῦ κυρίου, ἔνοχος ἔστε τοῦ σώματος καὶ τοῦ αἵματος τοῦ κυρίου.

11.28 δοκιμαζέτω δὲ ἄνθρωπος ἑαυτόν, καὶ οὕτως ἐκ τοῦ ἄρτου ἐσθιέτω καὶ ἐκ τοῦ ποτηρίου πινέτω· 11.29 ὁ γὰρ ἐσθίων καὶ πίνων ἀναξίως κρίμα ἑαυτῷ ἐσθίει καὶ πίνι μὴ διακρίνων τὸ σῶμα τοῦ κυρίου.

11.30 διὰ τοῦτο ἐν ὑμῖν πολλοὶ ἀσθενῖς καὶ ἄρρωστοι καὶ κοιμῶνται ἱκανοί. 11.31 εἰ δὲ ἑαυτοὺς διεκρίνομεν, οὐκ ἂν ἐκρινόμεθα· 11.32 κρινόμενοι δὲ ὑπὸ τοῦ κυρίου παιδευόμεθα, ἵνα μὴ σὺν τῷ κόσμῳ κατακριθῶμεν.

11.33 ὥστε, ἀδελφοί μου, συνερχόμενοι εἰς τὸ φαγῖν ἀλλήλους ἐκδέχεσθε. 11.34 εἴ τις πινᾷ, ἐν οἴκῳ ἐσθιέτω, ἵνα μὴ εἰς κρίμα συνέρχησθε. τὰ δὲ λοιπὰ ὡς ἂν ἔλθω διατάξομαι.

12.1 Περὶ δὲ τῶν πνευματικῶν, ἀδελφοί, οὐ θέλω ὑμᾶς ἀγνοεῖν. 12.2 οἴδατε ὅτι ὅτε ἔθνη ἦτε πρὸς τὰ ἴδωλα τὰ ἄφωνα ὡς ἂν ἤγεσθε ἀπαγόμενοι. 12.3 διὸ γνωρίζω ὑμῖν ὅτι οὐδὶς ἐν πνεύματι θεοῦ λαλῶν λέγει, ἀνάθεμα Ἰησοῦς, καὶ οὐδὶς δύναται

What might I say to ye? Shall I praise ye? I praise/approve not in/by this. 11.23 For I, I received from the Lord, what I also delivered over to ye, that the Lord Jesus, in the night which he was delivered over, took a loaf 11.24 and having given - thanks, he broke *it* and said: This is my body, the (one) in behalf of ye; do ye this in my memory. 11.25 Similarly, also the cup, after the (thing) to dine/sup, saying: This cup is the new covenant in/by my blood; do ye this, as many times if ye may drink *it*, in my memory.

11.26 For as many times if ye may eat this loaf and may drink the cup, ye proclaim the death of the Lord, until *a time* which he might come.

11.27 So that who ever may eat the loaf or may drink the cup of the Lord unworthily of the Lord, he will be guilty of the body and the blood of the Lord.

11.28 But let a man/human prove/test himself, and so let him eat from the loaf and let him drink from the cup; 11.29 for the (one) eating and drinking unworthily eats and drinks judgment for himself, not discerning/differentiating the body of the Lord.

11.30 Because of this, many among ye *are* weak and infirm/ill and insufficient, being asleep. 11.31 But if we discerned/judged ourselves, we would not be judged; 11.32 But being judged by the Lord, we are disciplined/chastised, in order that we might not be condemned with the world.

11.33 So, my brothers, coming together to/for the (thing) to eat, wait ye for one another. 11.34 If anyone hungers, let him eat in a house/at home, in order that ye may not come together in/for judgment. And I shall arrange myself the remaining (things), since I would come.

12.1 And concerning the spiritual (things), brothers, I want/wish not *for* ye to be ignorant. 12.2 Ye know that when ye were ethnics ye were being led away to the dumb idols as ever ye were being led. 12.3 Wherefore I make known to ye that no one speaking in/by a spirit from God says: Jesus *is* a curse, and no one is able to say: Jesus *is* Lord, except in/by a holy

εἰπεῖν, κύριος Ἰησοῦς, εἰ μὴ ἐν πνεύματι ἁγίῳ.

12.4 διαιρέσεις δὲ χαρισμάτων εἰσίν, τὸ δὲ αὐτὸ πνεῦμα· 12.5 καὶ διαιρέσεις διακονιῶν εἰσιν, καὶ ὁ αὐτὸς κύριος· 12.6 καὶ διερέσεις ἐνεργημάτων εἰσίν, ὁ δὲ αὐτὸς θεός, ὁ ἐνεργῶν τὰ πάντα ἐν πᾶσιν. 12.7 ἑκάστῳ δὲ δίδοται ἡ φανέρωσις τοῦ πνεύματος πρὸς τὸ συμφέρον. 12.8 ᾧ μὲν γὰρ διὰ τοῦ πνεύματος δίδοται λόγος σοφίας, ἄλλῳ δὲ λόγος γνώσεως κατὰ τὸ αὐτὸ πνεῦμα, 12.9 ἑτέρῳ πίστις ἐν τῷ αὐτῷ πνεύματι, ἄλλῳ δὲ χαρίσματα ἰαμάτων ἐν τῷ αὐτῷ πνεύματι, 12.10 ἄλλῳ δὲ ἐνεργήματα δυνάμεων, ἄλλῳ δὲ προφητία, ἄλλῳ δὲ διακρίσις πνευμάτων, ἑτέρῳ γένη γλωσσῶν, ἄλλῳ δὲ ἑρμηνία γλωσσῶν· 12.11 πάντα δὲ ταῦτα ἐνεργῖ τὸ ἓν καὶ τὸ αὐτὸ πνεῦμα, διαιροῦν ἰδίᾳ ἑκάστῳ καθὼς βούλεται.

12.12 καθάπερ γὰρ τὸ σῶμα ἕν ἐστιν καὶ μέλη πολλὰ ἔχει, πάντα δὲ τὰ μελήλη τοῦ σώματος πολλὰ ὄντα ἕν ἐστιν σῶμα, οὕτως καὶ ὁ χριστός· 12.13 καὶ γὰρ ἐν ἑνὶ πνεύματι ἡμεῖς πάντες εἰς ἓν σῶμα ἐβαπτίσθημεν, εἴτε Ἰουδαῖοι εἴτε Ἕλληνες, εἴτε δοῦλοι εἴτε ἐλεύθεροι, καὶ πάντες ἓν πνεῦμα ἐποτίσθημεν.

12.14 καὶ γὰρ τὸ σῶμα οὐκ ἔστιν ἓν μέλος ἀλλὰ πολλά. 12.15 ἐὰν εἴπῃ ὁ πούς, ὅτι οὐκ εἰμὶ χείρ, οὐκ εἰμὶ ἐκ τοῦ σώματος, οὐ παρὰ τοῦτο οὐκ ἔστιν ἐκ τοῦ σώματος· 12.16 καὶ ἐὰν εἴπῃ τὸ οὖς, ὅτι οὐκ εἰμὶ ὀφθαλμός, οὐκ εἰμὶ ἐκ τοῦ σώματος, οὐ παρὰ τοῦτο οὐκ ἔστιν ἐκ τοῦ σώματος· 12.17 εἰ ὅλον τὸ σῶμα ὀφθαλμός, ποῦ ἡ ἀκοή; εἰ ὅλον ἀκοή, ποῦ ἡ ὄσφρησις; 12.18 νυνὶ δὲ ὁ θεὸς ἔθετο τὰ μέλη, ἓν ἕκαστον αὐτῶν, ἐν τῷ σώματι καθὼς ἠθέλησεν. 12.19 εἰ δὲ ἦν τὰ πάντα ἓν μέλος, ποῦ τὸ σῶμα; 12.20 νῦν δὲ πολλὰ μὲν μέλη, ἓν δε σῶμα. 12.21 οὐ δύναται δὲ ὁ οφθαλμὸς εἰπῖν τῇ χειρί, χρίαν σου οὐκ ἔχω, ἢ πάλιν ἡ κεφαλὴ τοῖς ποσίν, χρίαν ὑμῶν οὐκ ἔχω·

spirit.

12.4 And there are distinctions/differences of gifts, but the same spirit; 12.5 there are also distinctions/differences of services/ministries, and the same Lord; 12.6 and there are distinctions/differences of effects/workings, but the same God, the (one) working/effecting all things in all. 12.7 But the manifestation/disclosure from the spirit is given to each (one) toward/for the profit/advantage. 12.8 For a logos/word of wisdom is given to one through the spirit, and a logos/word of knowledge to another down from/by the same spirit, 12.9 faith to another/different in/by the same spirit, and gifts of healings to another in/by the same spirit, 12.10 and workings/activities or/from powers/abilities to another, and prophecy to another, and discernings/separations of spirits to another, kinds/kindreds of languages to another/different, and interpretations/translations of languages to another; 12.11 but the one and the same spirit works/effects all these (things), distributing/bestowing to each his own as it wills/purposes.

12.12 For just as the body is one and has many members, and all the parts of the body, being many, are one body, so also *is* the anointed (one); 12.13 for we all, we were also baptized into one body in/by one spirit, whether Judeans or Greeks, whether slaves or free (ones), and we all were caused to drink in/by a spirit/one spirit.

12.14 for even the body is not one member, but many. 12.15 If the foot might say: Because I am not a hand, I am not from the body, not from this is it not out of the body; 12.16 and if the ear might say: Because I am not an eye, I am not from the body, it is not from this out of the body; 12.17 If the entire body *were* an eye, where *is* the hearing? If all *be* hearing, where *is* the smelling? 12.18 But now God placed the members, each one of them, in the body as he wanted/wished. 12.19 And if all the (things) was one member, where *is* the body? 12.20 But now indeed *are* many members, but one body. 12.21 And the eye is not able to say to the hand: I have not a need of you, or again the head to the feet: I have not a need of

12.22 ἀλλὰ πολλῷ μᾶλλον τὰ δοκοῦντα μέλη τοῦ σώματος ἀσθενέστερα ὑπάρχειν ἀναγκαῖά ἐστιν, 12.23 καὶ ἃ δοκοῦμεν ἀτιμότερα εἶναι τοῦ σώματος, τούτοις τιμὴν περισσοτέραν περιτίθεμεν, καὶ τὰ ἀσχήμονα ἡμῶν εὐσχημοσύνην περισσοτέραν ἔχει, 12.24 τὰ δὲ εὐσχήμονα ἡμῶν οὐ χρείαν ἔχει.

ἀλλὰ ὁ θεὸς συνεκέρασεν τὸ σῶμα, τῷ ὑστερουμένῳ περισσοτέραν δοὺς τιμήν, 12.25 ἵνα μὴ ᾖ σχίσματα ἐν τῷ σώματι, ἀλλὰ τὸ αὐτὸ ὑπὲρ ἀλλήλων μεριμνῶσι τὰ μέλη. 12.26 καὶ εἴτε πάσχει ἓν μέλος, συμπάσχει πάντα τὰ μέλη· εἴτε δοξάζεται μέλος, συγχαίρει πάντα τὰ μέλη.

12.27 ὑμεῖς δέ ἐστε σῶμα χριστοῦ καὶ μέλη ἐκ μέρους. 12.28 καὶ οὓς μὲν ἔθετο ὁ θεὸς ἐν τῇ ἐκκλησίᾳ πρῶτον ἀποστόλους, δεύτερον προφήτας, τρίτον διδασκάλους, ἔπειτα δυνάμις, ἔπειτα χαρίσματα ἰαμάτων, ἀντιλήμψεις, κυβερνήσις, γένη γλωσσῶν.

12.29 μὴ πάντες ἀπόστολοι; μὴ πάντες προφῆται; μὴ πάντες διδάσκαλοι; μὴ πάντες δυνάμις; 12.30 μὴ πάντες χαρίσματα ἔχουσιν ἰαμάτων; μὴ πάντες γλώσσαις λαλοῦσιν; μὴ πάντες διερμηνεύουσιν; 12.31 ζηλοῦτε δὲ τὰ χαρίσματα τὰ μίζονα.

καὶ ἔτι καθ᾽ ὑπερβολὴν ὁδὸν ὑμῖν δίκνυμι. 13.1 ἐὰν ταῖς γλώσσαις τῶν ἀνθρώπων λαλῶ καὶ τῶν ἀγγέλων, ἀγάπην δὲ μὴ ἔχω, γέγονα χαλκὸς ἠχῶν ἢ κύμβαλον ἀλαλάζον. 13.2 καὶ ἐὰν ἔχω προφητίαν καὶ εἰδῶ τὰ μυστήρια πάντα καὶ πᾶσαν τὴν γνῶσιν, καὶ ἐὰν ἔχω πᾶσαν τὴν πίστιν ὥστε ὄρη μεθιστάναι, ἀγάπην δὲ μὴ ἔχω, οὐθέν εἰμι.

13.3 καὶ ἐὰν ψωμίσω πάντα τὰ ὑπάρχοντά μου, καὶ ἐὰν παραδῶ τὸ σῶμά μου ἵνα καυχήσωμαι, ἀγάπην δὲ μὴ ἔχω,

ye;

12.22 But by much more the members of the body seeming more weak/weaker are necessary to exist, 12.23 and (members) of the body which we think to be less honorable, to these we attach/bestow more abundant honor, and our unbecoming/indecent (parts/things) have more abundant comeliness/decency, 12.24 but the decent/becoming members of us have not a need.

But God mixed together/combined the body, giving more abundant honor to the (member) lacking/being deficient, 12.25 in order that there may not be splits/divisions in the body, but the members should care the same in behalf of one another. 12.26 And whether one member suffers, all the members suffer together; or a member is glorified, all the members rejoice together.

12.27 And ye, ye are a body of the anointed (one) and members out of a part. 12.28 And God indeed put/placed (some) who *are* in the assembly: first apostles, second prophets, third teachers, then powers/abilities, then gifts of healing, helpers/assistants, officers/directors, kinds/sorts of languages/tongues.

12.29 Not all *are* apostles, *are they? No.* Not all *are* prophets, *are they? No.* Not all *are* teachers, *are they? No.* Not all *are* powers, *are they? No.* 12.30 Not all have gifts of healing, *do they? No.* Not all speak in tongues, *do they? No.* Not all interpret/translate, *do they? No.* 12.31 But be ye zealous for/desire ye earnestly the greater gifts.

And yet I show to ye a far better way/a way according to outstanding quality. 13.1 If I may speak in the tongues/languages of the men and of the messengers/angels, but I have not agape, I have become a sounding brass/gong or a clanging cymbal. 13.2 And if I may have prophecy and may know all the mysteries/mystery religions and all the knowledge/discernment, and if I may have all the faith so as to remove mountains, but I have not agape, I am nothing.

13.3 And if I might dole/piece out all my existing things/goods, and if I deliver up my body in order that it might be burned, but I have not agape, I am

οὐδὲν ὠφελοῦμαι.

13.4 ἡ ἀγάπη μακροθυμεῖ, χρηστεύεται ἡ ἀγάπη, οὐ ζηλοῖ, ἡ ἀγάπη οὐ περπερεύεται, οὐ φυσιοῦται, 13.5 οὐκ ἀσχημονεῖ, οὐ ζητῖ τὰ ἑαυτῆς, οὐ παροξύνεται, οὐ λογίζεται τὸ κακόν, 13.6 οὐ χαίρει ἐπὶ τῇ ἀδικίᾳ, συγχαίρι δὲ τῇ ἀληθίᾳ· 13.7 πάντα στέγει, πάντα πιστεύει, πάντα ἐλπίζει, πάντα ὑπομένει. 13.8 ἡ ἀγάπη οὐδέποτε πίπτει.

εἴτε δὲ προφητῖαι, καταργηθήσονται· εἴτε γλῶσσαι, παύσονται· εἴτε γνῶσις, καταργηθήσονται. 13.9 ἐκ μέρους γὰρ γινώσκομεν καὶ ἐκ μέρους προφητεύομεν· 13.10 ὅταν δὲ ἔλθῃ τὸ τέλιον, τὸ ἐκ μέρους καταργηθήσεται.

13.11 ὅτε ἤμην νήπιος, ἐλάλουν ὡς νήπιος, ἐφρόνουν ὡς νήπιος, ἐλογιζόμην ὡς νήπιος· ὅτε γέγονα ἀνήρ, κατήργηκα τὰ τοῦ νηπίου.

13.12 βλέπομεν γὰρ ἄρτι δι' ἐσόπτρου ἐν αἰνίγματι, τότε δὲ πρόσωπον πρὸς πρόσωπον· ἄρτι γινώσκω ἐκ μέρους, τότε δὲ ἐπιγνώσομαι καθὼς καὶ ἐπεγνώσθην. 13.13 νυνὶ δὲ μένει πίστις, ἐλπίς, ἀγάπη, τὰ τρία ταῦτα· μίζων δὲ τούτων ἡ ἀγάπη. 14.1 διώκετε τὴν ἀγάπην,

ζηλοῦτε δὲ τὰ πνευματικά, μᾶλλον δὲ ἵνα προφητεύητε. 14.2 ὁ γὰρ λαλῶν γλώσσῃ οὐχ ἀνθρώποις λαλεῖ ἀλλὰ θεῷ, οὐθὶς γὰρ ἀκούει, πνεύματι δὲ λαλεῖ μυστήρια· 14.3 ὁ δὲ προφητεύων ἀνθρώποις λαλεῖ οἰκοδομὴν καὶ παράκλησιν καὶ παραμυθίαν. 14.4 ὁ λαλῶν γλώσσῃ ἑαυτὸν οἰκοδομεῖ· ὁ δὲ προφητεύων ἐκκλησίαν οἰκοδομεῖ.

14.5 θέλω δὲ πάντας ὑμᾶς λαλῖν γλώσσαις, μᾶλλον δὲ ἵνα προφητεύητε· μείζων δὲ ὁ προφητεύων ἢ ὁ λαλῶν γλώσσαις, ἐκτὸς εἰ μὴ διερμηνεύῃ, ἵνα ἡ ἐκκλησία οἰκοδομὴν λάβῃ.

profited nothing.

13.4   The agape is patient, the agape is kind, she envies not, the agape vaunts not herself, she is not inflated/puffed up,   13.5 she is not shameful/indecent, she seeks not the (things) of herself, she is not irritated,   she accounts/reckons not the bad (thing),   13.6 she rejoices not over the injustice/wrong, but she rejoices *over* the truth;   13.7 she covers/keeps confidential all (things), she believes all (things), she hopes all (things), she endures all (things).   13.8 The agape never falls.

But whether *there are* prophecies, they will be abolished;   or tongues/languages, they will rest/cease; or knowledge, it will be abolished.   13.9 for we know from a part and we prophesy from a part;   13.10 but whenever the complete (thing) might come, the (thing) from a part will be abolished.

13.11   When I was a baby, I was speaking as a baby, I was thinking as a baby, I was reckoning as a baby/infant; when I have become a man, I have abrogated/annulled the (things) of the baby.

13.12   For we see/look now through a mirror in an enigma, but then face to face; just now I know from a part, but then I shall fully know as also I was fully known.   13.13 And now there abides faith, hope, agape, these three; but the agape *is* the greater of these. 14.1   Pursue ye the agape,

and   desire earnestly/seek ye the   spiritual (things), but more in order that ye may prophesy. 14.2 For the (one) speaking in a tongue speaks not to men but to God, for no one hears, but he speaks mysteries (religions) by a spirit;   14.3   but the (one) prophesying speaks to men *for* building up/edification and encouragement/comforting and consolation.   14.4 The (one) speaking in a tongue builds up/edifies himself; but the (one) prophesying builds up/edifies an assembly.

14.5   And I want/wish *for* ye all to speak in tongues/languages, but more that ye may prophesy; but the (one) prophesying *is* greater than the (one) speaking in tongues, except/unless he may interpret/translate, in order that the assembly might receive edifi-

300

14.6 νῦν δέ, ἀδελφοί, ἐὰν ἔλθω πρὸς ὑμᾶς γλώσσαις λαλῶν, τί ὑμᾶς ὠφελήσω, ἐὰν μὴ ὑμῖν λαλήσω ἐν ἀποκαλύψει ἢ ἐν γνώσει ἢ ἐν προφητείᾳ ἢ ἐν διδαχῇ;

14.7 ὅμως τὰ ἄψυχα φωνὴν διδόντα, εἴτε αὐλὸς εἴτε κιθάρα, ἐὰν διαστολὴν τοῖς φθόγγοις μὴ δῷ, πῶς γνωσθήσεται τὸ αὐλούμενον ἢ τὸ κιθαριζόμενον; 14.8 καὶ γὰρ ἐὰν ἄδηλον σάλπιγξ φωνὴν δῷ, τίς παρασκευάσεται εἰς πόλεμον; 14.9 οὕτως καὶ ὑμῖς διὰ τῆς γλώσσης ἐὰν μὴ εὔσημον λόγον δῶτε, πῶς γνωσθήσεται τὸ λαλούμενον; ἔσεσθε γὰρ εἰς ἀέρα λαλοῦντες. 14.10 τοσαῦτα εἰ τύχοι γένη φωνῶν εἰσιν ἐν κόσμῳ, καὶ οὐδὲν ἄφωνον· 14.11 ἐὰν οὖν μὴ εἰδῶ τὴν δύναμιν τῆς φωνῆς, ἔσομαι τῷ λαλοῦντι βάρβαρος καὶ ὁ λαλῶν ἐν ἐμοὶ βάρβαρος.

14.12 οὕτως καὶ ὑμεῖς, ἐπὶ ζηλωταί ἐστε πνευμάτων, πρὸς τὴν οἰκοδομὴν τῆς ἐκκλησίας ζητῖτε ἵνα περισσεύητε. 14.13 διὸ ὁ λαλῶν γλώσσῃ προσευχέσθω ἵνα διερμηνεύῃ.

14.14 ἐὰν γὰρ προσεύχωμαι γλώσσῃ, τὸ πνεῦμά μου προσεύχεται, ὁ δὲ νοῦς μου ἄκαρπός ἐστιν. 14.15 τί οὖν ἐστιν; προσεύξωμαι τῷ πνεύματι, προσεύξομαι δὲ καὶ τῷ νοΐ· ψαλῶ τῷ πνεύματι, ψαλῶ δὲ καὶ τῷ νοΐ.

14.16 ἐπεὶ ἐὰν εὐλογῇς ἐν πνεύματι, ὁ ἀναπληρῶν τὸν τόπον τοῦ ἰδιώτου πῶς ἐρεῖ τὸ ἀμήν ἐπὶ τῇ σῇ εὐχαριστίᾳ, ἐπειδὴ τί λέγεις οὐκ οἶδεν; 14.17 σὺ μὲν γὰρ καλῶς εὐχαριστῖς, ἀλλ᾽ ὁ ἕτερος οὐκ οἰκοδομεῖται.

14.18 εὐχαριστῶ τῷ θεῷ, πάντων ὑμῶν μᾶλλον γλώσσῃ λαλῶ· 14.19 ἀλλ᾽ ἐν ἐκκλησίᾳ θέλω πέντε λόγους τῷ νοΐ μου λαλῆσαι, ἵνα καὶ ἄλλους κατηχήσω, ἢ μυρίους λόγους ἐν γλώσσῃ.

cation.

14.6 But now, brothers, if I might come to ye speaking in tongues, what will I benefit/profit ye, unless I might speak by/in a revelation or by knowledge or by a prophecy or by a teaching?

14.7 Nevertheless, the lifeless (things) giving sound, whether a flute or a lyre/harp, if they may not give a difference in the sounds, how will the (thing) being played on the flute or the (thing) being played on the harp be known? 14.8 For also if a trumpet gives an indistinct sound, who will prepare himself to/for war/battle? 14.9 So also ye, unless ye might give a clear saying/word through the tongue, how will the (thing) being spoken be known? For ye will be speaking into air. 14.10 If it may be the case that there are so many sorts/kinds of sounds in the world, and nothing without sound; 14.11 if then I may not know the power of/from the sound, I shall be a non-Greek/barbarian to the one speaking and the (one) speaking in/by me *is* a non-Greek/barbarian.

14.12 So also ye, since ye are zealots of spiritual (things), seek/discuss ye toward the building up of the assembly in order that ye may abound. 14.13 Wherefore let the (one) speaking in a tongue pray in order that he may interpret/translate.

14.14 For if I may pray in a tongue, my spirit prays, but my mind is unfruitful/barren. 14.15 Then what is it? I shall pray in the spirit, but I shall also pray in the mind; I shall sing psalms to/for the spirit, but I shall also sing psalms in/for the mind.

14.16 Otherwise if you may bless by a spirit, the (one) filling up/occupying the place of the unlearned/layman, how will he say the truly/so be it (amen) over/for your thanksgiving, since he knows not what he says? 14.17 For indeed you, you give thanks well, but the other/different (one) is not built up/edified.

14.18 I give thanks to God, I speak in/with a tongue/language more than all of ye; 14.19 but in an assembly, I want/wish to speak five sayings/words with my mind, in order that I also might inform others, than myriads of sayings/words in a tongue/language.

14.20 ἀδελφοί, μὴ παιδία γείνεσθε ταῖς φρεσίν, ἀλλὰ τῇ κακίᾳ νηπιάζετε, ταῖς δὲ φρεσὶν τέλειοι γίνεσθε.

14.21 ἐν τῷ νόμῳ γέγραπται ὅτι « ἐν ἑτερογλώσσοις καὶ ἐν χείλεσιν ἑτέρων λαλήσω τῷ λαῷ τούτῳ, καὶ οὐδ᾽» οὕτως «εἰσακούσονταί» μου, λέγει κύριος. 14.22 ὥστε αἱ γλῶσσαι εἰς σημῖόν εἰσιν οὐ τοῖς πιστεύουσιν ἀλλὰ τοῖς ἀπίστοις, ἡ δὲ προφητία οὐ τοῖς ἀπίστοις ἀλλὰ τοῖς πιστεύουσιν. 14.23 ἐὰν οὖν συνέλθῃ ἡ ἐκκλησία ὅλη ἐπὶ τὸ αὐτὸ καὶ πάντες λαλῶσιν γλώσσαις, εἰσέλθωσιν δὲ ἰδιῶται ἢ ἄπιστοι, οὐκ ἐροῦσιν ὅτι μαίνεσθε; 14.24 ἐὰν δὲ πάντες προφητεύωσιν, εἰσέλθῃ δέ τις ἄπιστος ἢ ἰδιώτης, ἐλέγχεται ὑπὸ πάντων, ἀνακρίνεται ὑπὸ πάντων, 14.25 τὰ κρυπτὰ τῆς καρδίας αὐτοῦ φανερὰ γείνεται, καὶ οὕτως πεσὼν ἐπὶ πρόσωπον προσκυνήσει τῷ θεῷ, ἀπαγγέλλων ὅτι ὄντως ὁ θεὸς ἐν ὑμῖν ἐστιν.

14.26 τί οὖν ἐστιν, ἀδελφοί; ὅταν συνέρχησθε, ἕκαστος ψαλμὸν ἔχει, διδαχὴν ἔχει, ἀποκάλυψιν ἔχει, γλῶσσαν ἔχει, ἑρμηνίαν ἔχει· πάντα πρὸς οἰκοδομὴν γινέσθω. 14.27 εἴτε γλώσσῃ τις λαλῖ, κατὰ δύο ἢ τὸ πλῖστον τρῖς, καὶ ἀνὰ μέρος, καὶ εἷς διερμηνευέτω· 14.28 ἐὰν δὲ μὴ ᾖ διερμηνευτής, σιγάτω ἐν ἐκκλησίᾳ, ἑαυτῷ δὲ λαλείτω καὶ τῷ θεῷ. 14.29 προφῆται δὲ δύο ἢ τρῖς λαλείτωσαν, καὶ οἱ ἄλλοι διακρινέτωσαν· 14.30 ἐὰν δὲ ἄλλῳ ἀποκαλυφθῇ καθημένῳ, ὁ πρῶτος σιγάτω. 14.31 δύνασθε γὰρ καθ᾽ ἕνα πάντες προφητεύειν, ἵνα πάντες μανθάνωσιν καὶ πάντες παρακαλῶνται, 14.32 καὶ πνεύματα προφητῶν προφήταις ὑποτάσσεται· 14.33 οὐ γάρ ἐστιν ἀκαταστασίας ὁ θεὸς ἀλλὰ εἰρήνης. ὡς ἐν πάσαις ταῖς ἐκκλησίαις τῶν ἁγίων,

14.20 Brothers, become ye not children in the minds/intellects, but be ye childlike to the badness/ depravity, and become ye complete/mature in the minds/intellects.

14.21 It has been written in the law: I SHALL SPEAK TO THIS PEOPLE IN/BY OTHER/DIFFERENT TONGUES/ LANGUAGES AND BY OTHER/DIFFERENT LIPS, AND EVEN SO THEY WILL NOT LISTEN TO/OBEY ME, says *the* Lord. 14.22 So that the tongues/languages are into/for a sign, not for those believing but for the unfaithful/unbe- lieving (ones), and the prophecy *is* not for the un- faithful/unbelieving (ones) but for those believing. 14.23 Therefore, if the entire assembly might come together over/for the same (thing) and all speak in tongues, but untrained/unlearned (ones) or unbelievers might enter, will they not say that ye are mad? 14.24 But if all may prophesy, and a certain/some unbeliever or unlearned (one) might enter, he is reproved/con- vinced by all, he is examined by all (he hears), 14.25 the hidden/secret (things) of his heart becomes open/public, and so, having fallen upon *his* face, he will worship to God, announcing that God is really/ certainly among ye.

14.26 Then what/why is it, brothers? Whenever ye may come together, each (one) has a psalm/hymn, *each* has a teaching/doctrine, *each* has a revelation, *each* has a tongue/language, *each* has a translation/inter- pretation; let all (things) become toward/for build- ing/edification. 14.27 And if a certain (one)/someone speaks in a tongue, among two or the most three, and one at a time, and let one interpret/translate; 14.28 but if there may not be an interpreter/translator, let him be silent in an assembly, and let him speak to himself and to God. 14.29 And let two or three pro- phets speak, and let the others discern/differentiate; 14.30 but if *it* might be revealed to another sitting, let the first (one) be silent. 14.31 For ye are all able to prophesy one by one, in order that all may learn and all may be encouraged/comforted, 14.32 and spirits of prophets are subjected to prophets; 14.33 for God is not of/from an insurrection/instability, but of peace. As in all the assemblies of the saints,

14.34 αἱ γυναῖκες ἐν ταῖς ἐκκλησίαις σιγάτωσαν, οὐ γὰρ ἐπιτρέπεται αὐταῖς λαλεῖν· ἀλλὰ ὑποτασσέσθωσαν, καθὼς καὶ ὁ νόμος λέγει. 14.35 εἰ δέ τι μανθάνειν θέλουσιν, ἐν οἴκῳ τοὺς ἰδίους ἄνδρας ἐπερωτάτωσαν, αἰσχρὸν γάρ ἐστιν γυναικὶ λαλεῖν ἐν ἐκκλησίᾳ.

14.36 ἢ ἀφ’ ὑμῶν ὁ λόγος τοῦ θεοῦ ἐξῆλθεν, ἢ εἰς ὑμᾶς μόνους κατήντησεν;

14.37 εἴ τις δοκεῖ προφήτης εἶναι ἢ πνευματικός, ἐπιγινωσκέτω ἃ γράφω ὑμῖν ὅτι κυρίου ἐντολή ἐστιν· 14.38 εἰ δέ τις ἀγνοεῖ, ἀγνοεῖται.

14.39 ὥστε, ἀδελφοί μου, ζηλοῦτε τὸ προφητεύειν, καὶ τὸ λαλεῖν μὴ κωλύετε γλώσσαις· 14.40 πάντα δὲ εὐσχημόνως καὶ κατὰ τάξιν γινέσθω.

15.1 Γνωρίζω δὲ ὑμῖν, ἀδελφοί, τὸ εὐαγγέλιον ὃ εὐηγγελισάμην ὑμῖν, ὃ καὶ παρελάβετε, ἐν ᾧ καὶ ἑστήκατε, 15.2 δι’ οὗ καὶ σῴζεσθε, τίνι λόγῳ εὐηγγελισάμην ὑμῖν εἰ κατέχετε, ἐκτὸς εἰ μὴ εἰκῇ ἐπιστεύσατε. 15.3 παρέδωκα γὰρ ὑμῖν ἐν πρώτοις, ὃ καὶ παρέλαβον, ὅτι χριστὸς ἀπέθανεν ὑπὲρ τῶν ἁμαρτιῶν ἡμῶν κατὰ τὰς γραφάς, 15.4 καὶ ὅτι ἐτάφη, καὶ ὅτι ἐγήγερται τῇ ἡμέρᾳ τῇ τρίτῃ κατὰ τὰς γραφάς, 15.5 καὶ ὅτι ὤφθη Κηφᾷ, ἔπειτα τοῖς δώδεκα· 15.6 ἔπειτα ὤφθη ἐπάνω πεντακοσίοις ἀδελφοῖς ἐφάπαξ, ἐξ ὧν οἱ πλίονες μένουσιν ἕως ἄρτι, τινὲς δὲ ἐκοιμήθησαν· 15.7 ἔπειτα ὤφθη Ἰακώβῳ, εἶτα τοῖς ἀποστόλοις πᾶσιν· 15.8 ἔσχατον δὲ πάντων ὡσπερεὶ τῷ ἐκτρώματι ὤφθη κἀμοί. 15.9 ἐγὼ γάρ εἰμι ὁ ἐλάχιστος τῶν ἀποστόλων, ὃς οὐκ ἰμὶ ἱκανὸς καλεῖσθαι ἀπόστολος, διότι ἐδίωξα τὴν ἐκκλησίαν τοῦ θεοῦ· 15.10 χάριτι δὲ θεοῦ εἰμι ὅ εἰμι, καὶ ἡ χάρις αὐτοῦ ἡ εἰς ἐμὲ οὐ κενὴ ἐγενήθη, ἀλλὰ περισσότερον αὐτῶν ἁπάντων

14.34 let the women be silent in the assemblies, for it is not permitted for them to speak; but let them be subordinated/arranged beneath, as the law also says.   14.35 But if they want/wish to learn something, let them question/ask their own men at home/in a house, for it is a shame for a woman to speak in an assembly.

14.36 Or did the logos/word of God go forth from ye, or did it come to/reach ye alone/only?

14.37 If anyone seems to be a prophet or a spiritual (one), let him recognize/fully know that what (things) I write/am writing to ye is a command from *the* Lord;   14.38 but if anyone is ignorant, let him be ignorant.

14.39 Therefore, my brothers, desire ye earnestly the (thing) to prophesy, and forbid ye not the (thing) to speak in tongues/languages;   14.40 let all things become/come about properly/decently and according to good order.

15.1 And I make known to ye, brothers, the good message/gospel which I proclaimed/preached to ye, which ye also received, in which ye also stand,   15.2 through which ye are also saved, if ye hold fast what saying/word I preached to ye, unless ye received *it* in vain/to no purpose.   15.3 For I delivered to ye among *the* first, *that* which I received also: That the anointed (one) died in behalf of the sins of ye/your sins according to the writings,   15.4 and that he was buried, and that he was raised on the third day according to the writings,   15.5 and that he was seen by Cephas, then by the twelve;   15.6 then he was seen by over five hundred brothers at one time, out of whom the most abide/remain until now, but some were caused to sleep;   15.7 then he was seen by James, next by all the apostles;   15.8 and last of all, as it were by the puny birth, he was seen even by me.   15.9 For I, I am the least of the apostles, who is not sufficient to be called an apostle, because I prosecuted the assembly of God;   15.10 but by grace/a gift from God, I am what I am, and the grace/favor of him became not empty/vain to/for me, but I labored more abundantly from all of

ἐκοπίασα, οὐκ ἐγὼ δὲ ἀλλὰ ἡ χάρις τοῦ θεοῦ σὺν ἐμοί.

15.11 εἴτε οὖν ἐγὼ εἴτε ἐκεῖνοι, οὕτως κηρύσσομεν καὶ οὕτως ἐπιστεύσατε.

15.12 εἰ δὲ χριστὸς κηρύσσετε ὅτι ἐκ νεκρῶν ἐγήγερται, πῶς λέγουσιν ἐν ὑμῖν τινες ὅτι ἀνάστασις νεκρῶν οὐκ ἔστιν; 15.13 εἰ δὲ ἀνάστασις νεκρῶν οὐκ ἔστιν, οὐδὲ χριστὸς ἐγήγερται·

15.14 εἰ δὲ χριστὸς οὐκ ἐγήγερται, κενὸν ἄρα καὶ τὸ κήρυγμα ἡμῶν, καινὴ καὶ ἡ πίστις ὑμῶν, 15.15 εὑρισκόμεθα δὲ καὶ ψευδομάρτυρες τοῦ θεοῦ, ὅτι ἐμαρτυρήσαμεν κατὰ τοῦ θεοῦ ὅτι ἤγειρεν τὸν χριστόν, ὃν οὐκ ἔγειρεν εἴπερ ἄρα νεκροὶ οὐκ ἐγείρονται. 15.16 εἰ γὰρ νεκροὶ οὐκ ἐγίρονται, οὐδὲ χριστὸς ἐγήγερται· 15.17 εἰ δὲ χριστὸς οὐκ ἐγήγερται, ματαία ἡ πίστις ὑμῶν, καὶ ἔτι ἐστὲ ἐν ταῖς ἁμαρτίαις ὑμῶν.

15.18 ἄρα καὶ οἱ κοιμηθέντες ἐν χριστῷ ἀπώλοντο. 15.19 εἰ ἐν τῇ ζωῇ ταύτῃ ἐν χριστῷ ἠλπικότες ἐσμὲν μόνον, ἐλεεινότεροι πάντων ἀνθρώπων ἐσμέν.

15.20 νυνὶ δὲ χριστὸς ἐγήγερται ἐκ νεκρῶν, ἀπαρχὴ τῶν κεκοιμημένων. 15.21 ἐπιδὴ γὰρ δι᾽ ἀνθρώπου θάνατος, καὶ δι᾽ ἀνθρώπου ἀνάστασις νεκρῶν· 15.22 ὥσπερ γὰρ ἐν τῷ Ἀδὰμ πάντες ἀποθνήσκουσιν, οὕτως καὶ ἐν τῷ χριστῷ πάντες ζωοποιηθήσονται. 15.23 ἕκαστος δὲ ἐν τῷ ἰδίῳ τάγματι· ἀπαρχὴ χριστός, ἔπειτα οἱ τοῦ χριστοῦ ἐν τῇ παρουσίᾳ αὐτοῦ·

15.24 εἶτα τὸ τέλος, ὅταν παραδιδῷ τὴν βασιλίαν τῷ θεῷ καὶ πατρί, ὅταν καταργήσῃ πᾶσαν ἀρχὴν καὶ πᾶσαν ἐξουσίαν καὶ δύναμιν. 15.25 δεῖ γὰρ αὐτὸν βασιλεύειν ἄχρι οὗ θῇ πάντας τοὺς ἐχθροὺς ὑπὸ τοὺς πόδας αὐτοῦ. 15.26 ἔσχατος ἐχθρὸς καταργεῖται ὁ θάνατος· 15.27 «πάντα» γὰρ «ὑπέταξεν ὑπὸ τοὺς πόδας αὐτοῦ.»

ὅταν δὲ εἴπῃ ὅτι τὰ πάντα ὑποτέτακται, δῆλον ὅτι ἐκτὸς

them, and not I but the grace of God with me.

15.11   Therefore whether I or those, thus we herald/preach and thus ye believed.

15.12   But if the anointed (one) is heralded/preached because he   has   been raised out of dead (ones), how *do* some among ye say that there is not a resurrection of dead (ones)?   15.13 But if there is not a resurrection of dead (ones), neither has the anointed (one) been raised.

15.14   And if the anointed (one) has not been raised, then both the preaching/proclamation of us is empty/vain, and the faith of ye is empty/vain, 15.15 and we also are found to be false witnesses of God, because we witnessed/testified by God that he raised the anointed (one), whom he raised not if indeed dead (ones) are not raised.   15.16 For if dead (ones) are not raised,   neither   has the anointed (one) been raised;   15.17 but if the anointed (one) has not been raised, the faith of ye is worthless/empty, and ye are still in your sins/faults.

15.18   Then also the (ones) having been caused to sleep in the anointed (one) perished.   15.19 If we have hoped in the anointed (one) only in this life, we are of all men more pitiful.

15.20   But as a matter of fact the anointed (one) has been raised out of dead (ones). a firstfruit of those having been caused to sleep.   15.21 For since death *is* through a man, a resurrection of dead (ones) *is* also through a man;   15.22 for even as all die in/by Adam, so also will all be made alive in/by the anointed (one).   15.23 But each (one) in his own order; the anointed (one) *is* a firstfruit, next the (ones) of the anointed (one) in/at his coming/advent;

15.24   then *is* the end, whenever he may deliver up the kingdom to the God and father, whenever he might abolish every rule/ruler and every authority and power.   15.25 For it is necessary *for* him to reign until which (time) he might put all the enemies under his feet. 15.26 Death, the last enemy, is abrogated/canceled;   15.27 for HE SUBJECTED ALL (THINGS) UNDER HIS FEET.

But whenever he might say that all things has

τοῦ ὑποτάξαντος αὐτῷ τὰ πάντα. 15.28 ὅταν δὲ ὑποταγῇ αὐτῷ τὰ πάντα, τότε καὶ αὐτὸς ὁ υἱὸς ὑποταγήσεται τῷ ὑποτάξαντι αὐτῷ τὰ πάντα, ἵνα ᾖ ὁ θεὸς τὰ πάντα ἐν πᾶσιν.

15.29 ἐπεὶ τί ποιήσουσιν οἱ βαπτιζόμενοι ὑπὲρ τῶν νεκρῶν; εἰ ὅλως νεκροὶ οὐκ ἐγίρονται, τί καὶ βαπτίζονται ὑπὲρ αὐτῶν; 15.30 τί καὶ ἡμῖς κινδυνεύομεν πᾶσαν ὥραν;

15.31 καθ᾽ ἡμέραν ἀποθνήσκω, νὴ τὴν ὑμετέραν καύχησιν, ἀδελφοί, ἣν ἔχω ἐν χριστῷ Ἰησοῦ τῷ κυρίῳ ἡμῶν. 15.32 εἰ κατὰ ἄνθρωπον ἐθηριομάχησα ἐν Ἐφέσῳ, τί μοι τὸ ὄφελος; εἰ νεκροὶ οὐκ ἐγείρονται, «Φάγωμεν καὶ πίωμεν, αὔριον γὰρ ἀποθνήσκομεν.»

15.33 μὴ πλανᾶσθαι· Φθείρουσιν ἤθη χρηστὰ ὁμιλίαι κακαί. 15.34 ἐκνήψατε δικαίως καὶ μὴ ἁμαρτάνετε, ἀγνωσίαν γὰρ θεοῦ τινες ἔχουσιν· πρὸς ἐντροπὴν ὑμῖν λαλῶ.

15.35 ἀλλ᾽ ἐρῖ τις, πῶς ἐγείρονται οἱ νεκροί; ποίῳ δὲ σώματι ἔρχονται;

15.36 ἄφρων, σὺ ὃ σπίρεις οὐ ζωοποιεῖται τὴν ἐὰν μὴ ἀποθάνῃ· 15.37 καὶ ὃ σπίρεις, οὐ τὸ σῶμα τὸ γενησόμενον σπείρεις ἀλλὰ γυμνὸν κόκκον εἰ τύχοι σίτου ἤ τινος τῶν λοιπῶν· 15.38 ὁ δὲ θεὸς δίδωσιν αὐτῷ σῶμα καθὼς ἠθέλησεν, καὶ ἑκάστῳ τῶν σπερμάτων ἴδιον σῶμα.

15.39 οὐ πᾶσα σὰρξ ἡ αὐτὴ σάρξ, ἀλλὰ ἄλλη μὲν ἀνθρώπων,

ἄλλη δὲ σὰρξ κτηνῶν, ἄλλη δὲ σὰρξ πτηνῶν, ἄλλη δὲ ἰχθύων.

15.40 καὶ σώματα ἐπουράνια, καὶ σώματα ἐπίγεια· ἀλλ᾽ ἑτέρα μὲν ἡ τῶν ἐπουρανίων δόξα, ἑτέρα δὲ ἡ τῶν ἐπιγείων. 15.41 ἄλλη δόξα ἡλίου, καὶ ἄλλη δόξα σελήνης, καὶ ἄλλη δόξα

been subjected, *it is* plain that *it is* apart from the (one) having subjected all things to himself. 15.28 But whenever all things might be subjected to him, then even the son himself will be subjected to the (one) having subjected all things to himself, in order that God may be all things in all.

15.29 Otherwise what will the (ones) being baptized in behalf of the dead (ones) do? If dead (ones) actually are not raised, why are they even baptized in behalf of them? 15.30 We, why are we also in danger every hour?

15.31 I die day by day, by your own boasting/ triumph, brothers, which I have in the anointed Jesus, our Lord. 15.32 If I fought with beasts according to a man in Ephesus, what is the gain for me? If dead (ones) are not raised, WE SHOULD/LET US EAT AND DRINK, FOR TOMORROW WE DIE.

15.33 Be ye not deceived: Bad companies/associa-tions corrupt good customs/manners/habits. 15.34 Become ye sober/awake justly and sin ye not, for some have/hold ignorance of God; with/to shame I speak to ye/I speak for shame to ye.

15.35 But someone will say: How are the dead (ones) raised? And with what sort of body do they come?

15.36 You being foolish, what you sow is not made alive unless it might die; 15.37 and what you sow, you sow not the body being about to become, but a naked seed/kernel, if it may be of wheat of a certain one of the others; 15.38 but God gives a body to it as he wanted/wished, and to each of the seeds its own body.

15.39 Every flesh *is* not the same flesh, but one indeed of men/humans, and another a flesh of animals,

and another a flesh of birds, and another of fishes.

15.40 Also *there are* heavenly bodies and earthly bodies, but the glory/fame of the heavenly bodies *is* indeed another/different, and the (one)/(glory) of the earthly (one) *is* another/different. 15.41 *There is* another glory of a sun, and another glory of a moon, and another glory of stars; for a star differs in

ἀστέρων· ἀστὴρ γὰρ ἀστέρος διαφέρει ἐν δόξῃ.

15.42 οὕτως καὶ ἡ ἀνάστασις τῶν νεκρῶν. σπίρεται ἐν φθορᾷ, ἐγίρεται ἐν ἀφθαρσίᾳ· 15.43 σπείρεται ἐν ἀτιμίᾳ, ἐγείρεται ἐν δόξῃ· σπείρεται ἐν ἀσθενίᾳ, ἐγείρεται ἐν δυνάμι· 15.44 σπείρεται σῶμα ψυχικόν, ἐγείρεται σῶμα πνευματικόν. εἰ ἔστιν σῶμα ψυχικόν, ἔστιν καὶ πνευματικόν. 15.45 οὕτως καὶ γέγραπται, « ἐγένετο ὁ» πρῶτος «ἄνθρωπος» Ἀδὰμ «εἰς ψυχὴν ζῶσαν» ὁ ἔσχατος Ἀδὰμ εἰς πνεῦμα ζῳοποιοῦν.

15.46 ἀλλ᾽ οὐ πρῶτον τὸ πνευματικὸν ἀλλὰ τὸ ψυχικόν, ἔπειτα τὸ πνευματικόν.

15.47 ὁ πρῶτος ἄνθρωπος ἐκ γῆς χοϊκός, ὁ δεύτερος ἄνθρωπος ἐξ οὐρανοῦ. 15.48 οἷος ὁ χοϊκός, τοιοῦτοι καὶ οἱ χοϊκοί, καὶ οἷος ὁ ἐπουράνιος, τοιοῦτοι καὶ οἱ ἐπουράνιοι· 15.49 καὶ καθὼς ἐφορέσαμεν τὴν εἰκόνα τοῦ χοϊκοῦ, φορέσομεν καὶ τὴν εἰκόνα τοῦ ἐπουρανίου.

15.50 τοῦτο δέ φημι, ἀδελφοί, ὅτι σὰρξ καὶ αἷμα βασιλείαν θεοῦ κληρονομῆσαι οὐ δύναται, οὐδὲ ἡ φθορὰ τὴν ἀφθαρσίαν κληρονομεῖ.

15.51 ἰδοὺ μυστήριον ὑμῖν λέγω· πάντες μὲν κοιμηθησόμεθα, οὐ πάντες δὲ ἀλλαγησόμεθα, 15.52 ἐν ἀτόμῳ, ἐν ῥιπῇ ὀφθαλμοῦ, ἐν τῇ ἐσχάτῃ σάλπιγγι· σαλπίσει γάρ, καὶ οἱ νεκροὶ ἐγερθήσονται ἄφθαρτοι, καὶ ἡμεῖς ἀλλαγησόμεθα.

15.53 δεῖ γὰρ τὸ φθαρτὸν τοῦτο ἐνδύσασθαι ἀφθαρσίαν καὶ τὸ θνητὸν τοῦτο ἐνδύσασθαι ἀθανασίαν. 15.54 ὅταν δὲ τὸ φθαρτὸν τοῦτο ἐνδύσηται ἀφθαρσίαν καὶ τὸ θνητὸν τοῦτο ἐνδύσηται τὴν ἀθανασίαν, τότε γενήσεται ὁ λόγος ὁ γεγραμμένος, «κατεπόθη ὁ θάνατος εἰς νῖκος. 15.55 ποῦ σου, θάνατε, τὸ νῖκος; ποῦ σου, θάνατε, τὸ κέντρον;»

15.56 τὸ δὲ κέντρον τοῦ θανάτου ἡ ἁμαρτία, ἡ δὲ δύναμις τῆς ἁμαρτίας ὁ νόμος· 15.57 τῷ δὲ θεῷ χάρις τῷ διδόντι ἡμῖν τὸ

glory from a star/constellation.

15.42 So also *is* the resurrection of the dead (ones). It is sown in decay/corruption, raised in incorruption/immortality; 15.43 it is sown in dishonor, raised in glory/fame; it is sown in weakness, raised in power/strength; 15.44 it is sown a natural body, raised a spiritual body. If *there* is a natural body, there is also a spiritual (one). 15.45 So it also has been written: THE first MAN, Adam, WAS GENERATED INTO A LIVING SOUL/LIFE; the last Adam is making alive/life in a spirit.

15.46 But the spiritual (thing) *is* not first, but the natural (thing), then the spiritual (thing).

15.47 The first man/human *was* earthy, out of earth, the second man/human *is* out of a sky/heaven. 15.48 Of what sort the earthy (one) *is*, such *are* the earthy (ones) also, and of what sort the heavenly (one) *is*, such *are* the heavenly (ones) also; 15.49 and as we wore the image of the earthy (one), we wore also the image of the heavenly (one).

15.50 But I say this, brothers, that flesh and blood is not able to inherit a kingdom from God, nor does the corruption/decay inherit the incorruption/immortality.

15.51 Behold, I speak a mystery (religion) to ye: We all will indeed be caused to sleep, but not all will be transformed/changed in form, 15.52 in an instant, in/at the blink of an eye, at the last trumpet; for a trumpet will sound, and the dead (ones) will be raised unperishable/immortal, and we, we shall be changed.

15.53 For it is necessary *for* this perishable/decayable (thing) to put on incorruption/undecaying and *for* this mortal (thing) to put on immortality. 15.54 And whenever this perishable (thing) might put on incorruption and this mortal (thing) might put on immortality, then the saying/word having been written will become *so*: THE DEATH WAS SWALLOWED UP IN VICTORY. 15.55 WHERE FROM YOU, O DEATH, *is* THE VICTORY? WHERE FROM YOU, O DEATH, *is* THE STING?

15.56 But the sting of the death *is* the sin, and the power of the sin *is* the law; 15.57 but thanks/

νεῖκος διὰ τοῦ κυρίου ἡμῶν Ἰησοῦ χριστοῦ.

15.58 ὥστε, ἀδελφοί μου ἀγαπητοί, ἑδραῖοι γείνεσθε, ἀμετακίνητοι, περισσεύοντες ἐν τῷ ἔργῳ τοῦ κυρίου πάντοτε, εἰδότες ὅτι ὁ κόπος ὑμῶν οὐκ ἔστιν κενὸς ἐν κυρίῳ.

16.1 Περὶ δὲ τῆς λογίας τῆς εἰς τοὺς ἁγίους, ὥσπερ διέταξα ταῖς ἐκκλησίαις τῆς Γαλατείας, οὕτως καὶ ὑμῖς ποιήσατε. 16.2 κατὰ μίαν σαββάτω ἕκαστος ὑμῶν παρ᾽ ἑαυτῷ τιθέτω θησαυρίζων ὅ τι ἂν εὐοδῶται, ἵνα μὴ ὅταν ἔλθω τότε λογῖαι γίνωνται.

16.3 ὅταν δὲ παραγένωμαι, οὓς ἐὰν δοκιμάσηται, δι᾽ ἐπιστολῶν τούτους πέμψω ἀπενεγκῖν τὴν χάριν ὑμῶν ἰς Ἰερουσαλήμ· 16.4 ἐὰν δὲ ᾖ ἄξιον τοῦ κἀμὲ πορεύεσθαι, σὺν ἐμοὶ πορεύσονται.

16.5 ἐλεύσομαι δὲ πρὸς ὑμᾶς ὅταν Μακαιδονίαν διέλθω, Μακαιδονίαν γὰρ διέρχομαι· 16.6 πρὸς ὑμᾶς δὲ τυχὸν παραμενῶ ἢ καὶ παραχειμάσω, ἵνα ὑμεῖς με προπέμψητε οὗ ἐὰν πορεύωμαι. 16.7 οὐ θέλω γὰρ ὑμᾶς ἄρτι ἐν παρόδῳ εἰδῖν, ἐλπίζω γὰρ χρόνον τινὰ ἐπιμεῖναι πρὸς ὑμᾶς, ἐὰν ὁ κύριος ἐπιτρέψῃ. 16.8 ἐπιμενῶ δὲ ἐν Ἐφέσῳ ἕως τῆς πεντηκοστῆς· 16.9 θύρα γάρ μοι ἀνέῳγεν μεγάλη καὶ ἐνεργής, καὶ ἀντικίμενοι πολλοί.

16.10 ἐὰν δὲ ἔλθη Τιμόθεος, βλέπεται ἵνα ἀφόβως γένηται πρὸς ὑμᾶς, τὸ γὰρ ἔργον κυρίου ἐργάζεται ὡς κἀγώ· 16.11 μή τις οὖν αὐτὸν ἐξουθενήσῃ. προπέμψατε δὲ αὐτὸν ἐν ἰρήνῃ, ἵνα ἔλθη πρός με, ἐκδέχομαι γὰρ αὐτὸν μετὰ τῶν ἀδελφῶν.

16.12 περὶ δὲ Ἀπολλῶ τοῦ ἀδελφοῦ, πολλὰ παρεκάλεσα αὐτὸν ἵνα ἔλθη πρὸς ὑμᾶς μετὰ τῶν ἀδελφῶν· καὶ πάντως οὐκ ἦν θέλημα ἵνα νῦν ἔλθη, ἐλεύσεται δὲ ὅταν εὐκερήσῃ. 16.13 γρηγορεῖτε, στήκετε ἐν τῇ πίστι, ἀνδρίζεσθε, κραταιοῦσθαι· 16.14 πάντα ὑμῶν ἐν ἀγάπῃ γινέσθω.

grace *be* to God, the (one) giving the victory to us through our Lord Jesus, the anointed (one).

15.58 Therefore, my beloved brothers, become ye firm/steadfast, unmovable, always abounding in the work of the Lord, knowing that the toil/labor of ye is not in vain in *the* Lord.

16.1 And concerning the collection, the (one) to/for the saints, even as I charged the assemblies of Galatia, so ye, ye also do (once). 16.2 By/on one (day) of a sabbath/week let each (one) of ye place *it* by himself, storing up what ever he may be prospered, in order that whenever I might come, collections may not come about then.

16.3 And whenever I might arrive, whom ever ye might approve, through letters I shall send them to carry the gift/grace from ye to Jerusalem; 16.4 and if it be worthy/best of the (thing) *for* me also to go, they shall go with me.

16.5 And I shall come to ye whenever I might pass through Macedonia, for I am going through Macedonia; 16.6 and happening to be near ye I shall stay or even spent the winter, in order that ye, ye might send me forward where ever I may go. 16.7 For I want/wish not to see ye just now in passage, for I hope to stay some time near/with ye, if the Lord might permit *it*. 16.8 But I shall stay in Ephesus until the pentecost/ fiftieth (day); 16.9 for a great and effective door has opened for me, and many (men) are opposing.

16.10 And if Timothy might come/go, see ye/take ye care that he might become near/with ye fearlessly, for he works the work of *the* Lord as even I; 16.11 therefore anyone might not despise him. But ye send him forward in peace, in order that he might come to me, for I expect him with the brothers.

16.12 And concerning Apollos, the brother, I besought him much that he might go/come to ye with the brothers; and he was not at all willing in order that he might come now, but he will come whenever he might have time/opportunity. 16.13 Watch ye, stand ye in the faith, be ye as men, be ye strengthened; 16.14 Let all (things) of ye come about in/by agape.

16.15 παρακαλῶ δὲ ὑμᾶς, ἀδελφοί· οἴδατε τὴν οἰκίαν Στεφανᾶ, ὅτι ἐστὶν ἀπαρχὴ τῆς Ἀχαΐας καὶ εἰς διακονίαν τοῖς ἁγίοις ἔταξαν ἑαυτούς· 16.16 ἵνα καὶ ὑμεῖς ὑποτάσσησθε τοῖς τοιούτοις καὶ παντὶ τῷ συνεργοῦντι καὶ κοπιῶντι.

16.17 χαίρω δὲ ἐπὶ τῇ παρουσίᾳ Στεφανᾶ καὶ Φορτουνάτου καὶ Ἀχαϊκοῦ, ὅτι τὸ ὑμῶν ὑστέρημα οὗτοι ἀνεπλήρωσαν, 16.18 ἀνέπαυσαν γὰρ τὸ ἐμὸν πνεῦμα καὶ τὸ ὑμῶν. ἐπιγινώσκεται οὖν τοὺς τοιούτους.

16.19 ἀσπάζονται ὑμᾶς αἱ ἐκκλησίαι τῆς Ἀσίας.

ἀσπάζεται ὑμᾶς ἐν κυρίῳ πολλὰ Ἀκύλας καὶ Πρίσκα σὺν τῇ κατ᾽ οἶκον αὐτῶν ἐκκλησίᾳ.

16.20 ἀσπάζονται ὑμᾶς οἱ ἀδελφοὶ πάντες.

ἀσπάσασθε ἀλλήλους ἐν φιλήματι ἁγίῳ.

16.21 ὁ ἀσπασμὸς τῇ ἐμῇ χειρὶ Παύλου. 16.22 εἴ τις οὐ φιλεῖ τὸν κύριον, ἤτω ἀνάθεμα. μαράνα θά.

16.23 ἡ χάρις τοῦ κυρίου Ἰησοῦ μεθ᾽ ὑμῶν. 16.24 ἡ ἀγάπη μου μετὰ πάντων ὑμῶν ἐν χριστῷ Ἰησοῦ. αμην.

Πρὸς Κορινθιους Α΄

16.15 And I beseech ye, brothers: Know ye the house/household of Stephanas, that she/it is a first-fruit of Achaia and that they arranged/appointed themselves in/for service/ministry to the saints 16.16 in order that ye also, ye may be subjected to those such and to every one working together and toiling.

16.17 And I rejoice upon/for the coming/advent/presence of Stephanas and Fortunatus and Achaius, because these (men), they filled up your deficiency/lack, 16.18 for they refreshed/rested my spirit and the (spirit) of ye. Therefore, recognize ye the (ones) such.

16.19 The assemblies of Asia greets ye.

Aquila and Prisca greets ye much in the Lord, with the assembly by the house of them.

16.20 All the brothers greets ye.

Greet ye one another with a holy kiss.

16.21 The greeting from Paul by/in my hand. 16.22 If anyone loves not the Lord, let him be a curse. Marana tha.

16.23 The grace of the Lord Jesus the anointed (one) *be* with ye. 16.24 The agape of me *be* with all of ye in the anointed Jesus. Truly.

To Corinthians 1

This is the Sinaitic New Testament, book of 2 Corinthians.

1.1 Παῦλος ἀπόστολος χριστοῦ Ἰησοῦ διὰ θελήματος θεοῦ, καὶ Τιμόθεος ὁ ἀδελφός, τῇ ἐκκλησίᾳ τοῦ θεοῦ τῇ οὔσῃ ἐν Κορίνθῳ, σὺν τοῖς ἁγίοις πᾶσιν τοῖς οὖσιν ἐν ὅλῃ τῇ Ἀχαΐᾳ· 1.2 χάρις ὑμῖν καὶ εἰρήνη ἀπὸ θεοῦ πατρὸς ἡμῶν καὶ κυρίου Ἰησοῦ χριστοῦ.

1.3 εὐλογητὸς ὁ θεὸς καὶ πατὴρ τοῦ κυρίου ἡμῶν Ἰησοῦ χριστοῦ, ὁ πατὴρ τῶν οἰκτιρμῶν καὶ θεὸς πάσης παρακλήσεως, 1.4 ὁ παρακαλῶν ἡμᾶς ἐπὶ πάσῃ τῇ θλίψει ἡμῶν, εἰς τὸ δύνασθαι ἡμᾶς παρακαλεῖν τοὺς ἐν πάσῃ θλίψει διὰ τῆς παρακλήσεως ἧς παρακαλούμεθα αὐτοὶ ὑπὸ τοῦ θεοῦ·

1.5 ὅτι καθὼς περισσεύει τὰ παθήματα τοῦ χριστοῦ εἰς ἡμᾶς, οὕτως διὰ τοῦ χριστοῦ περισσεύει καὶ ἡ παράκλησις ἡμῶν.

1.6 εἴτε δὲ θλιβόμεθα, ὑπὲρ τῆς ὑμῶν παρακλήσεως καὶ σωτηρίας· εἴτε παρακαλούμεθα, ὑπὲρ τῆς ὑμῶν παρακλήσεως τῆς ἐνεργουμένης ἐν ὑπομονῇ τῶν αὐτῶν παθημάτων ὧν καὶ ἡμῖς πάσχομεν.

1.7 καὶ ἡ ἐλπὶς ἡμῶν βεβαία ὑπὲρ ὑμῶν, εἰδότες ὅτι ὡς κοινωνοί ἐστε τῶν παθημάτων, οὕτως καὶ τῆς παρακλήσεως.

1.8 οὐ γὰρ θέλομεν ὑμᾶς ἀγνοεῖν, ἀδελφοί, περὶ τῆς θλίψεως ἡμῶν τῆς γενομένης ἐν τῇ Ἀσίᾳ, ὅτι καθ᾽ ὑπερβολὴν ὑπὲρ δύναμιν ἐβαρήθημεν, ὥστε ἐξαπορηθῆναι ἡμᾶς καὶ τοῦ ζῆν· 1.9 ἀλλ᾽ αὐτοὶ ἐν ἑαυτοῖς τὸ ἀπόκριμα τοῦ θανάτου ἐσχήκαμεν, ἵνα μὴ πεποιθότες ὦμεν ἐφ᾽ ἑαυτοῖς ἀλλ᾽ ἐπὶ τῷ θεῷ τῷ ἐγίροντι τοὺς νεκρούς· 1.10 ὃς ἐκ τηλικούτου θανάτου ἐρρύσατο ἡμᾶς καὶ ῥύσεται, εἰς ὃν ἠλπίκαμεν ὅτι καὶ ἔτι ῥύσεται, 1.11 συνυπουργούντων καὶ ὑμῶν ὑπὲρ ἡμῶν τῇ δεήσει, ἵνα ἐκ πολλῶν προσώπων τὸ εἰς ἡμᾶς χάρισμα διὰ πολλῶν εὐχαριστηθῇ ὑπὲρ ἡμῶν.

1.12 ἡ γὰρ καύχησις ἡμῶν αὕτη ἐστίν, τὸ μαρτύριον τῆς συνειδήσεως ἡμῶν, ὅτι ἐν ἁπλότητι καὶ εἰλικρινίᾳ τοῦ θεοῦ, οὐκ

1.1   Paul, and apostle from/of the anointed
Jesus, through *the* will of God, and Timothy the bro-
ther, to the assembly of God, the (one) being in
Corinth, with all the saints, the (ones) being in all
Achaia: 1.2 Grace to ye and peace from God our father
and *the* Lord Jesus, the anointed (one).

1.3   Praised *be* the God and father of our Lord
Jesus the anointed (one), the father of the compas-
sions/pities and God of every solace/consolation,   1.4
the (one) consoling/comforting us upon our every
oppression/affliction, into the (thing) *for* us to be
able to encourage/console the (ones) in every affliction through the encouragement/consolation with which
we ourselves are consoled/comforted by God.

1.5   Because even as the suffering of the anointed (one) abounds in/for us, so our consolation also
abounds through the anointed (one).

1.6   But whether we are afflicted in behalf of
the consolation and salvation of ye; or we are consol-
ed/encouraged in behalf of the consolation of ye being
worked in/by patience/endurance of the same suffer-
ings/passions which we, we also suffer.

1.7   And our hope *is* firm in behalf of ye, having
seen that ye are as partners/companions of the sufferings, so also of the consolation.

1.8   For we want/wish not *for* ye to be ignorant,
brothers, about the affliction/tribulation of us, the
(one) having become/happened in Asia, because we were
burdened by an excess over/beyond *our* power/ability,
so as for *us* to be perplexed/despaired even of the
(thing) to live;   1.9 but we ourselves have had the
sentence of death in ourselves, in order that we may
not be having trusted upon ourselves but upon God, the
(one) raising the dead (ones);   1.10 who rescued us
from so great a death and he will rescue/deliver, in
whom we have hoped that he will also still rescue,
1.11 and from ye helping along with us in behalf of ye
in the petition, in order that thanks might be given
in behalf of us from many faces *for* the gift to us
through many.

1.12   For the boasting/triumph of us is this, the
testimony of our conscience, because in/by simplicity

309

ἐν σοφίᾳ σαρκικῇ ἀλλ' ἐν χάριτι θεοῦ, ἀνεστράφημεν ἐν τῷ κόσμῳ, περισσοτέρως δὲ πρὸς ὑμᾶς. 1.13 οὐ γὰρ ἄλλα γράφομεν ὑμῖν ἀλλ' ἢ ἃ ἀναγινώσκεται ἢ καὶ ἐπιγινώσκετε, ἐλπίζω δὲ ὅτι ἕως τέλους ἐπιγνώσεσθε, 1.14 καθὼς καὶ ἐπέγνωτε ἡμᾶς ἀπὸ μέρους, ὅτι καύχημα ὑμῶν ἐσμεν καθάπερ καὶ ὑμῖς ἡμῶν ἐν τῇ ἡμέρᾳ τοῦ κυρίου ἡμῶν Ἰησοῦ.

1.15 καὶ ταύτῃ τῇ πεποιθήσει ἐβουλόμην πρότερον πρὸς ὑμᾶς ἐλθεῖν, ἵνα δευτέραν χάριν σχῆτε, 1.16 καὶ δι' ὑμῶν διελθῖν εἰς Μακαιδονίαν, καὶ πάλιν ἀπὸ Μακαιδονίας ἐλθεῖν πρὸς ὑμᾶς καὶ ὑφ' ὑμῶν προπεμφθῆναι εἰς τὴν Ἰουδαίαν.

1.17 τοῦτο οὖν βουλόμενος μήτι ἄρα τῇ ἐλαφρίᾳ ἐχρησάμην; ἢ ἃ βουλεύομαι κατὰ σάρκα βουλεύομαι, ἵνα ᾖ παρ' ἐμοὶ τὸ ναὶ ναὶ καὶ τὸ οὒ οὔ;

1.18 πιστὸς δὲ ὁ θεὸς ὅτι ὁ λόγος ἡμῶν ὁ πρὸς ὑμᾶς οὐκ ἔστιν ναὶ καὶ οὔ. 1.19 ὁ τοῦ θεοῦ γὰρ υἱὸς χριστὸς Ἰησοῦς ὁ ἐν ὑμῖν δι' ἡμῶν κηρυχθείς, δι' ἐμοῦ καὶ Σιλουανοῦ καὶ Τιμοθέου, οὐκ ἐγένετο ναὶ καὶ οὔ, ἀλλὰ ναὶ ἐν αὐτῷ γέγονεν. 1.20 ὅσαι γὰρ ἐπαγγελίαι θεοῦ, ἐν αὐτῷ τὸ ναί· διὸ καὶ δι' αὐτοῦ τὸ ἀμὴν τῷ θεῷ πρὸς δόξαν δι' ἡμῶν.

1.21 ὁ δὲ βεβαιῶν ἡμᾶς σὺν ὑμῖν εἰς χριστὸν καὶ χρείσας ἡμᾶς θεός, 1.22 ὁ καὶ σφραγισάμενος ἡμᾶς καὶ δοὺς τὸν ἀραβῶνα τοῦ πνεύματος ἐν ταῖς καρδίες ἡμῶν.

1.23 ἐγὼ δὲ μάρτυρα τὸν θεὸν ἐπικαλοῦμαι ἐπὶ τὴν ἐμὴν ψυχήν, ὅτι φειδόμενος ὑμῶν οὐκέτι ἦλθον εἰς Κόρινθον. 1.24 οὐχ ὅτι κυριεύομεν ὑμῶν τῆς πίστεως, ἀλλὰ συνεργοί ἐσμεν τῆς χαρᾶς ὑμῶν, τῇ γὰρ πίστι ἑστήκατε.

2.1 Ἔκρινα δὲ ἐμαυτῷ τοῦτο, τὸ μὴ πάλιν ἐν λύπῃ πρὸς ὑμᾶς ἐλθεῖν· 2.2 ἰ γὰρ ἐγὼ ἐλυπῶ ὑμᾶς, καὶ τίς ὁ εὐφραίνων με εἰ μὴ ὁ λυπούμενος ἐξ ἐμοῦ;

2.3 καὶ ἔγραψα τοῦτο αὐτὸ ἵνα μὴ ἐλθὼν λύπην ἔχω ἀφ'

and sincerity of God, not by fleshly wisdom but by grace from God, we behaved in the world, and especially toward ye. 1.13 For we write not other (things) to ye other than what ye read or also perceive/understand, and I hope that ye will know fully until *the* end, 1.14 as ye also perceived/discerned us from part, because we are boasting of ye even as ye also of us in/at the day of our Lord Jesus.

1.15 And by this persuasion I was intending formerly to go to ye, in order that ye might have a second gift/grace, 1.16 and through ye to pass through into Macedonia, and again from Macedonia to come to ye and to be sent forward/on by ye to Judea.

1.17 Therefore, wishing/purposing this, did I not then use the fickleness/lightness? Or what (things) I desire/purpose according to flesh, I desire, in order that there may be with me the yes, yes and the no, no?

1.18 But God is faithful that our saying/word to ye is not yes and no. 1.19 For the son of God, Jesus the anointed (one), the (one) having been heralded/proclaimed to ye through us, through me and Silvanus and Timothy, because not yes and no, but has become yes in/by him. 1.20 For as many as *are* promises from God, by him is the yes; wherefore also through him *is* the truly/so be it/amen to fame/glory for God through us.

1.21 But the (one) confirming us with ye in the anointed (one) and having anointed us *is* God, 1.22 the (one) both having sealed us and given the pledge of the spirit in your hearts.

1.23 And I *being* witness *for* God, I call upon my life/soul, because refraining from ye, I went no longer to Corinth. 1.24 Not that we are lord over your faith, but we are fellow workers of your joy, for you have stood for the faith.

2.1 But I judged/decided this for myself, the (thing) not again to come to ye in/with grief/pain; 2.2 for if I, I might grieve ye, who also *is* the (one) gladdening me except the (one) being grieved from me?

2.3 And I wrote this very thing in order that

ὧν ἔδει με χαίρειν, πεποιθὼς ἐπὶ πάντας ὑμᾶς ὅτι ἡ ἐμὴ χαρὰ πάντων ὑμῶν ἐστιν.

2.4 ἐκ γὰρ πολλῆς θλίψεως καὶ συνοχῆς καρδίας ἔγραψα ὑμῖν διὰ πολλῶν δακρύων, οὐχ ἵνα λυπηθῆτε ἀλλὰ τὴν ἀγάπην ἵνα γνῶτε ἣν ἔχω περισσοτέρως εἰς ὑμᾶς.

2.5 εἰ δέ τις λελύπηκεν, οὐκ ἐμὲ λελύπηκεν, ἀλλὰ ἀπὸ μέρους, ἵνα μὴ ἐπιβαρῶ, πάντας ὑμᾶς. 2.6 ἱκανὸν τῷ τοιούτῳ ἡ ἐπιτιμία αὕτη ἡ ὑπὸ τῶν πλειόνων, 2.7 ὥστε τοὐναντίον μᾶλλον ὑμᾶς χαρίσασθαι καὶ παρακαλέσαι, μή πως τῇ περισσοτέρᾳ λύπῃ καταποθῇ ὁ τοιοῦτος. 2.8 διὸ παρακαλῶ ὑμᾶς κυρῶσαι εἰς αὐτὸν ἀγάπην·

2.9 εἰς τοῦτο γὰρ καὶ ἔγραψα ἵνα γνῶ τὴν δοκιμὴν ὑμῶν, εἰ εἰς πάντα ὑπήκοοί ἐστε.

2.10 ᾧ δέ τι χαρίζεσθε, κἀγώ· καὶ γὰρ ἐγὼ ὃ κεχάρισμαι, εἴ τι κεχάρισμαι, δι᾽ ὑμᾶς ἐν προσώπῳ χριστοῦ, 2.11 ἵνα μὴ πλεονεκτηθῶμεν ὑπὸ τοῦ Σατανᾶ, οὐ γὰρ αὐτοῦ τὰ νοήματα ἀγνοοῦμεν.

2.12 ἐλθὼν δὲ εἰς τὴν Τρῳάδα εἰς τὸ εὐαγγέλιον τοῦ χριστοῦ, καὶ θύρας μοι ἀνεῳγμένης ἐν κυρίῳ, 2.13 οὐκ ἔσχηκα ἄνεσιν τῷ πνεύματί μου τοῦ μὴ εὑρῖν με Τίτον τὸν ἀδελφόν μου, ἀλλὰ ἀποταξάμενος αὐτοῖς ἐξῆλθον εἰς Μακαιδονίαν.

2.14 τῷ δὲ θεῷ χάρις τῷ πάντοτε θριαμβεύοντι ἡμᾶς ἐν τῷ χριστῷ καὶ τὴν ὀσμὴν τῆς γνώσεως αὐτοῦ φανεροῦντι δι᾽ ἡμῶν ἐν παντὶ τόπῳ· 2.15 ὅτι χριστοῦ εὐωδία ἐσμὲν τῷ θεῷ ἐν τοῖς σωζομένοις καὶ ἐν τοῖς ἀπολλυμένοις, 2.16 οἷς μὲν ὀσμὴ ἐκ θανάτου εἰς θάνατον, οἷς δὲ ὀσμὴ ἐκ ζωῆς εἰς ζωήν.

καὶ πρὸς ταῦτα τίς ἱκανός; 2.17 οὐ γὰρ ἐσμεν ὡς οἱ πολλοὶ καπηλεύοντες τὸν λόγον τοῦ θεοῦ, ἀλλ᾽ ὡς ἐξ εἰλικρινίας, ἀλλ᾽ ὡς

coming, I might not have grief from (those) whom it was necessary *for* me to rejoice, having confidence on/for ye all that my joy is from ye all.

2.4 For out of much affliction and constriction of heart I wrote to ye through many tears, not in order that ye might be grieved but that ye might know the agape which I have abundantly in/for ye.

2.5 But if anyone has grieved, he has not grieved me, but from a part, lest I might be burdensome *for* all ye. 2.6 This punishment by the most/majority is sufficient for the (one) such, 2.7 so that on the other hand *it is* more *for* ye to forgive and to encourage/console, lest the (one) such be swallowed up *by* the more abundant grief. 2.8 Wherefore I beseech/call on ye to assure/ratify agape to/for him.

2.9 For in/to this I also wrote, in order that I might know your proof/worth, if ye are obedient (ones) in all (things).

2.10 But for whom ye forgive something, I also; for even I, what I have forgiven, if I have forgiven anything, *it is* on account of ye in *the* face of the anointed (one), 2.11 lest we might be taken advantage of by Satan, for we are not ignorant/unaware of his plots/thoughts.

2.12 But having come/gone to Troas in/for the good message/gospel of the anointed (one), and from a door having been opened for me by *the* Lord, 2.13 I had not relief/rest for my spirit from the (thing) *for* me not to find Titus my brother, but, having departed from them, I went forth into Macedonia.

2.14 But grace/thanks *be* to God, the one always causing us to triumph in the anointed (one) and manifesting/revealing through us the savor of the knowledge of him in every place; 2.15 because of the anointed (one) we are a fragrance to God in the (ones) being saved and in the (ones) perishing/destroying themselves, 2.16 for whom on the one hand an odor from death to death, for whom on the other an odor from life to life.

And who is sufficient to/for these (things)? 2.17 For we are not like/as the many, peddling/corrupting the saying/word of God, but as out of/from

ἐκ θεοῦ κατέναντι θεοῦ ἐν χριστῷ λαλοῦμεν.

3.1 Ἀρχόμεθα πάλιν ἑαυτοὺς συνιστάνιν; ἢ μὴ χρῄζομεν ὥς τινες συστατικῶν ἐπιστολῶν πρὸς ὑμᾶς ἢ ἐξ ὑμῶν;

3.2 ἡ ἐπιστολὴ ἡμῶν ὑμεῖς ἐστε, ἐνγεγραμμένη ἐν ταῖς καρδίες ὑμῶν, γινωσκομένη καὶ ἀναγινωσκομένη ὑπὸ πάντων ἀνθρώπων· 3.3 φανερούμενοι ὅτι ἐστὲ ἐπιστολὴ χριστοῦ διακονηθῖσα ὑφ᾽ ἡμῶν, ἐνγεγραμμένη οὐ μέλανι ἀλλὰ πνεύματι θεοῦ ζῶντος, οὐκ ἐν πλαξὶν λιθίναις ἀλλ᾽ ἐν πλαξὶν καρδίαις σαρκίναις.

3.4 πεποίθησιν δὲ τοιαύτην ἔχομεν διὰ τοῦ χριστοῦ πρὸς τὸν θεόν. 3.5 οὐχ ὅτι ἀφ᾽ ἑαυτῶν ἱκανοί ἐσμεν λογίσασθαί τι ὡς ἐξ ἑαυτῶν, ἀλλ᾽ ἡ ἱκανότης ἡμῶν ἐκ τοῦ θεοῦ,

3.6 ὃς καὶ ἱκάνωσεν ἡμᾶς διακόνους καινῆς διαθήκης, οὐ γράμματος ἀλλὰ πνεύματος· τὸ γὰρ γράμμα ἀποκτέννι, τὸ δὲ πνεῦμα ζῳοποιεῖ.

3.7 εἰ δὲ ἡ διακονία τοῦ θανάτου ἐν γράμμασιν ἐντετυπωμένι λίθοις ἐγενήθη ἐν δόξῃ, ὥστε μὴ δύνασθε ἀτενίσαι τοὺς υἱοὺς Ἰσραὴλ εἰς τὸ πρόσωπον Μωϋσέως διὰ τὴν δόξαν αὐτοῦ προσώπου αὐτοῦ τὴν καταργουμένην, 3.8 πῶς οὐχὶ μᾶλλον ἡ διακονία τοῦ πνεύματος ἔστε ἐν δόξῃ;

3.9 εἰ γὰρ τῇ διακονίᾳ τῆς κατακρίσεως δόξα, πολλῷ μᾶλλον περισσεύει ἡ διακονία τῆς δικεοσύνης δόξῃ.

3.10 καὶ γὰρ οὐ δεδόξασται τὸ δεδοξασμένον ἐν τούτῳ τῷ μέρει εἵνεκεν τῆς ὑπερβαλλούσης δόξης· 3.11 εἰ γὰρ τὸ καταργούμενον διὰ δόξης, πολλῷ μᾶλλον τὸ μένον ἐν δόξῃ.

3.12 ἔχοντες οὖν τοιαύτην ἐλπίδα πολλῇ παρρησίᾳ χρώμεθα, 3.13 καὶ οὐ καθάπερ Μωϋσῆς ἐτίθει κάλυμμα ἐπὶ τὸ

sincerity, but as from God we speak before God in/by the anointed (one).

3.1 *Do* we again begin to recommend/favor our- selves? Or may we not need as some recommending letters to ye or from ye?
3.2 Ye, ye are our epistle/letter, having been inscribed in your hearts, being known and being read by all men/humans; 3.3 being manifested/made clear that ye are a letter from the anointed (one), having been served/ministered by us, having been enscribed not by ink but by a spirit from a living God, not in/on stone tables/tablets but in fleshy heart ta- blets/tablets *of* fleshy hearts.
3.4 And we have such confidence/trust through the anointed (one) to/with God. 3.5 Not that we are sufficient from ourselves to reckon/account anything as out of/from ourselves, but our sufficiency *is* from God,
3.6 who also made us sufficient servants/minis- ters of a new covenant, not of/from a writing/letter but of/from a spirit; for the letter/character kills, but the spirit makes alive/imparts life.
3.7 And if the service/ministry of the death in/by letters/characters having been engraved in stones came about by a fame/glory, so as not to be able *for* the sons of Israel to gaze into the face of Moses because of the/his fame/glory of his face being rendered useless (fading away), 3.8 how will not the service/ministry from the spirit be more in/by fame/ glory?
3.9 For if fame/glory *be* in the service/ministry of the condemnation, the service/ministry of the justice/justness abounds by much more in fame/glory.
3.10 For even the (thing) that having been glorified has not been glorified in/by this part/des- tiny on account of the surpassing fame/glory; 3.11 for if the (thing)/that being rendered useless/cancel- ed through fame/glory, by much more the (thing)/that remaining/abiding in/by fame/glory.
3.12 Having the such a hope, we proceed in much boldness/frankness, 3.13 and not as Moses was put-

πρόσωπον αὐτοῦ, πρὸς τὸ μὴ ἀτενίσαι τοὺς υἱοὺς Ἰσραὴλ εἰς τὸ τέλος τοῦ καταργουμένου. 3.14 ἀλλ᾽ ἐπωρώθη τὰ νοήματα αὐτῶν. ἄχρι γὰρ τῆς σήμερον ἡμέρας τὸ αὐτὸ κάλυμμα ἐπὶ τῇ ἀναγνώσει τῆς παλαιᾶς διαθήκης μένει μὴ ἀνακαλυπτόμενον, ὅτι ἐν χριστῷ καταργεῖται· 3.15 ἀλλ᾽ ἕως σήμερον ἡνίκα ἂν ἀναγινώσκηται Μωϋσῆς κάλυμμα ἐπὶ τὴν καρδίαν αὐτῶν κεῖται· 3.16 ἡνίκα δὲ ἐὰν ἐπιστρέψῃ πρὸς κύριον, περιαιρεῖται τὸ κάλυμμα. 3.17 ὁ δὲ κύριος τὸ πνεῦμά ἐστιν· οὗ δὲ τὸ πνεῦμα κυρίου, ἐλευθερία.

3.18 ἡμεῖς δὲ πάντες ἀνακεκαλυμμένῳ προσώπῳ τὴν δόξαν κυρίου κατοπτριζόμενοι τὴν αὐτὴν εἰκόνα μεταφορμορφούμεθα ἀπὸ δόξης εἰς δόξαν, καθάπερ ἀπὸ κυρίου πνεύματος.

4.1 Διὰ τοῦτο, ἔχοντες τὴν διακονίαν ταύτην, καθὼς ἠλεήθημεν, οὐκ ἐγκακοῦμεν, 4.2 ἀλλὰ ἀπειπάμεθα τὰ κρυπτὰ τῆς αἰσχύνης, μὴ περιπατοῦντες ἐν πανουργίᾳ μηδὲ δολοῦντες τὸν λόγον τοῦ θεοῦ, ἀλλὰ τῇ φανερώσει τῆς ἀληθίας συνιστάντες ἑαυτοὺς πρὸς πᾶσαν συνίδησιν ἀνθρώπων ἐνώπιον τοῦ θεοῦ. 4.3 εἰ δὲ καὶ ἔστιν κεκαλυμμένον τὸ εὐαγγέλιον ἡμῶν, ἐν τοῖς ἀπολλυμένοις ἐστὶν κεκαλυμμένον, 4.4 ἐν οἷς ὁ θεὸς τοῦ αἰῶνος τούτου ἐτύφλωσεν τὰ νοήματα τῶν ἀπίστων εἰς τὸ μὴ αὐγάσαι τὸν φωτισμὸν τοῦ εὐαγγελίου τῆς δόξης τοῦ χριστοῦ, ὅς ἐστιν εἰκὼν τοῦ θεοῦ. 4.5 οὐ γὰρ ἑαυτοὺς κηρύσσομεν ἀλλὰ Ἰησοῦν χριστὸν κύριον, ἑαυτοὺς δὲ δούλους ἡμῶν διὰ χριστοῦ.

4.6 ὅτι ὁ θεὸς ὁ εἰπών, ἐκ σκότους φῶς λάμψαι, ὃς ἔλαμψεν ἐν ταῖς καρδίαις ἡμῶν πρὸς φωτισμὸν τῆς γνώσεως τῆς δόξης τοῦ θεοῦ ἐν προσώπῳ Ἰησοῦ χριστοῦ.

4.7 ἔχομεν δὲ τὸν θησαυρὸν τοῦτον ἐν ὀστρακίνοις σκεύεσιν, ἵνα ἡ ὑπερβολὴ τῆς δυνάμεως ᾖ τοῦ θεοῦ καὶ μὴ ἐξ ἡμῶν· 4.8 ἐν παντὶ θλιβόμενοι ἀλλ᾽ οὐ στενοχωρούμενοι,

ting a covering over his face, to/for the (thing) *for*
the sons of Israel not to gaze into the end of the
(thing) being rendered useless/(waning).   3.14 But
their thoughts were hardened. For until the day,
today, the same covering remains for the reading of
the old covenant, not being unveiled/uncovered, that
being abolished by the anointed (one);   3.15   but
until today, when ever Moses may be read, a veil/cov-
ering is laid over their heart;   3.16 but when ever
(one) might turn to *the* Lord, the covering/veil is
taken away.   3.17 But the Lord is the spirit;   and
where the spirit of *the* Lord *is*, liberty *is*.
     3.18   But we *are* all with a face having been
uncovered, ourselves beholding the glory/fame of *the*
Lord as in a mirror, being transformed into the same
image, from glory/fame into glory/fame, even as from a
spirit of *the* Lord.

     4.1   Because of this, having/holding this ser-
vice/ministry, even as we were given mercy,   we tire/
faint not .   4.2 But we ourselves renounced the hidden
(things) of the shame/disgrace, walking not in shrewdness nor corrupting the saying/word of God, but by the
revealing/appearing of the truth commending ourselves
to every conscience of men before God.   4.3 But if the
good message/gospel has also been hidden from us,   it
has been hidden in/by the (ones) perishing,   4.4 in/by
whom the god of this age blinded the thoughts of the
unbelieving (ones) to/for the (thing) not to shine the
enlightenment of the good message of the fame/glory of
the anointed (one), who is an image of God.   4.5 For
we herald/preach not ourselves, but Jesus, the anointed Lord, and ourselves *being* our/*your* slaves because
of Jesus.
     4.6   Because God, the (one) having said: A light
is to shine out of darkness, who shone in your hearts
toward enlightenment of the knowledge of the fame/glo-
ry of God in/by a face of Jesus, the anointed (one).
     4.7   But we have this store/precious deposit in
earthenware vessels, in order that the outstanding
quality of the power may be from God and not out of
us;   4.8 being oppressed in every (way) but not being

313

ἀπορούμενοι ἀλλ᾽ οὐκ ἐξαπορούμενοι, 4.9 διωκόμενοι ἀλλ᾽ οὐκ ἐγκαταλειπόμενοι, καταβαλλόμενοι ἀλλ᾽ οὐκ ἀπολλύμενοι, 4.10 πάντοτε τὴν νέκρωσιν τοῦ Ἰησοῦ ἐν τῷ σώματι περιφέροντες, ἵνα καὶ ἡ ζωὴ τοῦ Ἰησοῦ ἐν τοῖς σώμασιν ἡμῶν φανερωθῇ.

4.11 ἀεὶ γὰρ ἡμεῖς οἱ ζῶντες εἰς θάνατον παραδιδόμεθα διὰ Ἰησοῦν, ἵνα καὶ ἡ ζωὴ τοῦ Ἰησοῦ φανερωθῇ ἐν τῇ θνητῇ σαρκὶ ἡμῶν. 4.12 ὥστε ὁ θάνατος ἐν ἡμῖν ἐνεργεῖται, ἡ δὲ ζωὴ ἐν ὑμῖν.

4.13 ἔχοντες δὲ τὸ αὐτὸ πνεῦμα τῆς πίστεως, κατὰ τὸ γεγραμμένουνον, « ἐπίστευσα, διὸ καὶ ἐλάλησα,» καὶ ἡμῖς πιστεύομεν, διὸ καὶ λαλοῦμεν, 4.14 εἰδότες ὅτι ὁ ἐγείρας τὸν κύριον Ἰησοῦν καὶ ἡμᾶς σὺν θεοῦ ἐγερεῖ καὶ παραστήσει σὺν ὑμῖν. 4.15 τὰ γὰρ πάντα δι᾽ ὑμᾶς, ἵνα ἡ χάρις πλεονάσασα διὰ τῶν πλειόνων τὴν εὐχαριστίαν περισσεύσῃ εἰς τὴν δόξαν τοῦ θεοῦ.

4.16 διὸ οὐκ ἐγκακοῦμεν, ἀλλ᾽ εἰ καὶ ὁ ἔξω ἡμῶν ἄνθρωπος διαφθείρεται, ἀλλ᾽ ὁ ἔσω ἡμῶν ἀνακαινοῦται ἡμέρᾳ καὶ ἡμέρᾳ.

4.17 τὸ γὰρ παραυτίκα ἐλαφρὸν τῆς θλίψεως ἡμῶν καθ᾽ ὑπερβολὴν εἰς ὑπερβολὴν αἰώνιον βάρος δόξης κατεργάζεται ἡμῖν,

4.18 μὴ σκοπούντων ἡμῶν τὰ βλεπόμενα ἀλλὰ τὰ μὴ βλεπόμενα· τὰ γὰρ βλεπόμενα πρόσκαιρα, τὰ δὲ μὴ βλεπόμενα αἰώνια.

5.1 Οἴδαμεν γὰρ ὅτι ἐὰν ἡ ἐπίγιος ἡμῶν οἰκία τοῦ σκήνους καταλυθῇ, οἰκοδομὴν ἐκ θεοῦ ἔχομεν οἰκίαν ἀχιροποίητον αἰώνιον ἐν τοῖς οὐρανοῖς.

5.2 καὶ γὰρ ἐν τούτῳ στενάζομεν, τὸ οἰκητήριον ἡμῶν τὸ ἐξ οὐρανοῦ ἐπενδύσασθαι ἐπιποθοῦντες, 5.3 εἴ γε καὶ ἐνδυσάμενοι οὐ γυμνοὶ εὑρεθησόμεθα. 5.4 καὶ γὰρ οἱ ὄντες ἐν τῷ

confined/restricted, being without means/perplexed but not being in utmost despair, 4.9 being prosecuted but not being forsaken, being downcast but not being destroyed, 4.10 always carrying about the death of Jesus in the body, in order that also the life of Jesus might be manifested in the bodies of us/our bodies.

4.11 For we, the living (ones), are being unceasingly delivered up to death because of Jesus, in order that also the life of Jesus might be manifested in the mortal flesh or us. 4.12 So that the death is active in us, but the life in ye.

4.13 But having/holding the same spirit of the faith, according to the (thing) having been written, I BELIEVED, WHEREFORE I ALSO SPOKE, and we, we believe, wherefore we also speak, 4.14 having known that the (one) having raised the Lord Jesus also will raise us with Jesus and present us/stand us along with ye. 4.15 For all things are because of ye, in order that the grace/thanks, having increased through the many, may cause the thanksgiving to abound in/to/for the fame/glory of God.

4.16 Wherefore, we do not despair/become tired but if even the man outside of us is being destroyed, but the (one) within us is being renewed day by day/ for a day and a day.

4.17 For the momentary triviality of our oppression/affliction works for us beyond measure to/for an eternal extraordinary fullness of fame/glory,

4.18 from us not considering the (things) being seen but the (things) not being seen; for the (things) being seen are temporary, but the (things) not being seen are eternal.

5.1 For we know that if our earthly house of the tent/tabernacle might be destroyed, we have a building from God, a house not made by hand, eternal in the skies/heavens.

5.2 For we even groan in this, desiring earnestly to put on our habitation from heaven, 5.3 if indeed having been clothed, we shall not be found naked. 5.4 For we, the (ones) being in the tent/tab-

σκήνι στενάζομεν βαρούμενοι, ἐφ' ᾧ οὐ θέλομεν ἐκδύσασθαι ἀλλὰ ἐπενδύσασθαι, ἵνα καταποθῇ τὸ θνητὸν ὑπὸ τῆς ζωῆς. 5.5 ὁ δὲ κατεργασάμενος ἡμᾶς εἰς αὐτὸ τοῦτο θεός, ὁ δοὺς ἡμῖν τὸν ἀραβῶνα τοῦ πνεύματος.

5.6 θαρροῦντες οὖν πάντοτε καὶ εἰδότες ὅτι ἐνδημοῦντες ἐν τῷ σώματι ἐκδημοῦμεν ἀπὸ τοῦ κυρίου, 5.7 διὰ πίστεως γὰρ περιπατοῦμεν οὐ διὰ εἴδους 5.8 θαρροῦντες δὲ καὶ εὐδοκοῦμεν μᾶλλον ἐκδημῆσαι ἐκ τοῦ σώματος καὶ ἐνδημῆσαι πρὸς τὸν κύριον.

5.9 διὸ καὶ φιλοτιμούμεθα, εἴτε ἐνδημοῦντες εἴτε ἐκδημοῦντες, εὐάρεστοι αὐτῷ εἶναι.

5.10 τοὺς γὰρ πάντας ἡμᾶς φανερωθῆναι δεῖ ἔμπροσθεν τοῦ βήματος τοῦ χριστοῦ, ἵνα κομίσηται ἕκαστος τὰ διὰ τοῦ σώματος πρὸς ἃ ἔπραξεν, εἴτε ἀγαθὸν εἴτε φαῦλον. 5.11 εἰδότες οὖν τὸν φόβον τοῦ κυρίου ἀνθρώπους πείθομεν, θεῷ δὲ πεφανερώμεθα· ἐλπίζω δὲ καὶ ἐν ταῖς συνιδήσεσιν ὑμῶν πεφανερῶσθαι. 5.12 οὐ πάλιν ἑαυτοὺς συνιστάνομεν ὑμῖν, ἀλλὰ ἀφορμὴν διδόντες ὑμῖν καυχήματος ὑπὲρ ἡμῶν, ἵνα ἔχητε πρὸς τοὺς ἐν προσώπῳ καυχωμένους καὶ μὴ ἐν καρδίᾳ.

5.13 εἴτε γὰρ ἐξέστημεν, θεῷ· εἴτε σωφρονοῦμεν, ὑμῖν. 5.14 ἡ γὰρ ἀγάπη τοῦ χριστοῦ συνέχει ἡμᾶς, κρίναντας τοῦτο, ὅτι εἷς ὑπὲρ πάντων ἀπέθανεν· ἄρα οἱ πάντες ἀπέθανον· 5.15 καὶ ὑπὲρ πάντων ἀπέθανεν ἵνα οἱ ζῶντες μηκέτι ἑαυτοῖς ζῶσιν ἀλλὰ τῷ ὑπὲρ αὐτῶν ἀποθανόντι καὶ ἐγερθέντι.

5.16 ὥστε ἡμῖς ἀπὸ τοῦ νῦν οὐδένα οἴδαμεν κατὰ σάρκα· εἰ καὶ ἐγνώκαμεν κατὰ σάρκα χριστόν, ἀλλὰ νῦν οὐκέτι γινώσκομεν.

5.17 ὥστε εἴ τις ἐν χριστῷ, καινὴ κτίσις· τὰ ἀρχαῖα

ernacle, being burdened, we groan for (that) which we wish/want not to put off but to put on, in order that the mortal might by swallowed by the life.

5.5 And the (one) having worked us out in this very thing *is* God, the (one) having given to us the pledge/deposit of the spirit.

5.6 Therefore, being cheerful always and having known that being present/at home in the body we are absent/away from the Lord, 5.7 for we walk through faith, not through sight/perception -- 5.8 and also being cheerful, we think it good rather to journey/go abroad out of the body and to be at home near the Lord.

5.9 Wherefore we also love honor, whether being at home or journeying abroad, to be well pleasing/acceptable to him.

5.10 For it is necessary *for* the (ones), us all, to be manifested/made plain before the judgment seat of the anointed (one), in order that each (one) might receive back the (things) through the body according to what he practiced, whether good or vile/worthless. 5.11 Having known then the fear of the Lord, we persuade men, and we have been manifested by God; but I hope also to have been manifested in your consciences. 5.12 Again we commend not ourselves to ye, but giving to ye without form of a boast in behalf of us, in order that ye may have/hold *it* to the (ones) boasting in/by a face and not in heart.

5.13 For whether we are astonishing/amazing, for God; or we are soberminded/serious, for ye. 5.14 For the agape of the anointed (one) holds us together, having judged/decided this, that one died in behalf of all; then all the (ones) died; 5.15 and he died in behalf of all in order that the (ones) living may no longer live for themselves but for the (one) having died in behalf of them and having been raised up.

5.16 So that we, from the present (time), we know no one according to flesh; if we have even known the anointed (one) according to flesh, but now we know him no longer.

5.17 So that if anyone *be* in the anointed (one), *he is* a new creature; the old (things) passed by/away,

παρῆλθεν, ἰδοὺ γέγονεν καινά·

5.18 τὰ δὲ πάντα ἐκ τοῦ θεοῦ τοῦ καταλλάξαντος ἡμᾶς ἑαυτῷ διὰ χριστοῦ καὶ δόντος ἡμῖν τὴν διακονίαν τῆς καταλλαγῆς, 5.19 ὡς ὅτι θεὸς ἦν ἐν χριστῷ κόσμον καταλάσσων ἑαυτῷ, μὴ λογιζόμενος αὐτοῖς τὰ παραπτώματα αὐτῶν, καὶ θέμενος ἐν ἡμῖν τὸν λόγον τῆς καταλλαγῆς.

5.20 ὑπὲρ χριστοῦ οὖν πρεσβεύομεν ὡς τοῦ θεοῦ παρακαλοῦντος δι᾽ ἡμῶν· δεόμεθα ὑπὲρ χριστοῦ, καταλλάγητε τῷ θεῷ.

5.21 τὸν μὴ γνόντα ἁμαρτίαν ὑπὲρ ἡμῶν ἁμαρτίαν ἐποίησεν, ἵνα ἡμεῖς γενώμεθα δικαιοσύνη θεοῦ ἐν αὐτῷ.

6.1 Συνεργοῦντες δὲ καὶ παρακαλοῦμεν μὴ εἰς καινὸν τὴν χάριν τοῦ θεοῦ δέξασθαι ὑμᾶς

6.2 λέγει γάρ, «καιρῷ δεκτῷ ἐπήκουσά σου καὶ ἐν ἡμέρᾳ σωτηρίας ἐβοήθησά σοι·» ἰδοὺ νῦν καιρὸς εὐπρόσδεκτος, ἰδοὺ νῦν ἡμέρα σωτηρίας

6.3 μηδεμίαν ἐν μηδενὶ διδόντες προσκοπήν, ἵνα μὴ μωμηθῇ ἡ διακονία, 6.4 ἀλλ᾽ ἐν παντὶ συνίσταντες ἑαυτοὺς ὡς θεοῦ διάκονοι, ἐν ὑπομονῇ πολλῇ, ἐν θλίψεσιν, ἐν ἀνάγκαις, ἐν στενοχωρίαις, 6.5 ἐν πληγαῖς, ἐν φυλακαῖς, ἐν ἀκαταστασίαις, ἐν κόποις, ἐν ἀγρυπνίαις, ἐν νηστίαις, 6.6 ἐν ἁγνότητι, ἐν γνώσει, ἐν μακροθυμίᾳ, ἐν χρηστότητι, ἐν πνεύματι ἁγίῳ, ἐν ἀγάπῃ ἀνυποκρίτῳ, 6.7 ἐν λόγῳ ἀληθίας, ἐν δυνάμι θεοῦ·

διὰ τῶν ὅπλων τῆς δικαιοσύνης τῶν δεξιῶν καὶ ἀριστερῶν,

6.8 διὰ δόξης καὶ ἀτιμίας, διὰ δυσφημίας καὶ εὐφημίας· ὡς πλάνοι καὶ ἀληθεῖς, 6.9 ὡς ἀγνοούμενοι καὶ ἐπιγινωσκόμενοι, ὡς

behold they have become new;

5.18   and all the (things) *are* from God, the
(one) having reconciled us to himself through the
anointed (one) and having given to us the service/
ministry of the reconciliation,   5.19 since that God
was reconciling the world to himself by the anointed
(one), not accounting/reckoning their trespasses to
them, and having placed in us the saying/word of the
reconciliation.

5.20   Therefore we are elders/ambassadors in
behalf of the anointed (one) as from the (thing) of
God calling/beseeching through us; we ourselves bind
in behalf of the anointed (one); be ye reconciled to
God.

5.21   He made the (one) not having known sin *to
be* sin in behalf of us, in order that we, we might
ourselves become justice/justness of God by/in him.

6.1   But working together, we also beseech/en-
courage *for* ye not to receive the grace/favor of God
in vain;

6.2   for he says: I HEARD FROM YOU AT AN ACCEPTED
TIME AND I HELPED WITH/BY A DAY OF SALVATION FOR YOU;
behold, now is an acceptable time, behold, now *is* a
day of salvation;

6.3   giving no one an occasion for offense in
anything, in order that the service/ministry might not
be censured,   6.4 but in/by every (thing) recommending
ourselves as God's servants/ministers/deacons/waiters,
in/by much endurance, in afflictions/tribulations, in
necessities, in restrictions,   6.5 in blows/wounds, in
prisons, in insurrections/instabilities, in toils/la-
bors, in watchings, in fasts,   6.6 in purity/sinceri-
ty, in knowledge, in patience, in kindness, in/by a
holy spirit, in unpretended agape,   6.7 in/by a say-
ing/word of truth, in/by power from God;

through the weapons/tools of the justness from
the right (ones) and left (ones),

6.8   through fame/glory and dishonor, through
words of ill omen and words of good omen; as deceiv-
ing/erring (ones) and true (ones),   6.9 as being
unknown (ones) and being well-known (ones), as dying

ἀποθνῄσκοντες καὶ ἰδοὺ ζῶμεν, ὡς παιδευόμενοι καὶ μὴ θανατούμενοι, 6.10 ὡς λυπούμενοι ἀεὶ δὲ χαίροντες, ὡς πτωχοὶ πολλοὺς δὲ πλουτίζοντες, ὡς μηδὲν ἔχοντες καὶ πάντα κατέχοντες.

6.11 τὸ στόμα ἡμῶν ἀνέῳγεν πρὸς ὑμᾶς, Κορίνθιοι, ἡ καρδία ἡμῶν πεπλάτυνται· 6.12 οὐ στενοχωρεῖσθε ἐν ἡμῖν, στενοχωρεῖσθαι δὲ ἐν τοῖς σπλάγχνοις ὑμῶν· 6.13 τὴν δὲ αὐτὴν ἀντιμισθίαν, ὡς τέκνοις λέγω, πλατύνθητε καὶ ὑμῖς.

6.14 μὴ γίνεσθε ἑτεροζυγοῦντες ἀπίστοις· τίς γὰρ μετοχὴ δικαιοσύνῃ καὶ ἀνομίᾳ; ἢ τίς κοινωνία φωτὶ πρὸς σκότος; 6.15 τίς δὲ συμφώνησις χριστοῦ πρὸς Βελιάρ, ἢ τίς μερὶς πιστῷ μετὰ ἀπίστου; 6.16 τίς δὲ συγκατάθεσεις ναῷ θεοῦ μετὰ εἰδώλων; ἡμεῖς γὰρ ναὸς θεοῦ ἐσμεν ζῶντος· καθὼς εἶπεν ὁ θεὸς ὅτι «ἐνοικήσω ἐν αὐτοῖς καὶ ἐμπεριπατήσω, καὶ ἔσομαι αὐτῶν θεός, καὶ αὐτοὶ ἔσονταί μου λαός.» 6.17 διὸ «ἐξέλθαται ἐκ μέσου αὐτῶν καὶ ἀφορίσθητε,» λέγει κύριος, «καὶ ἀκαθάρτου μὴ ἅπτεσθε· κἀγὼ εἰσδέξομαι ὑμᾶς,» 6.18 καὶ «ἔσομαι» ὑμῖν «εἰς πατέρα, καὶ» ὑμεῖς ἔσεσθέ «μοι εἰς υἱοὺς» καὶ θυγατέρας, λέγει κύριος παντοκράτωρ.

7.1 Ταύτας οὖν ἔχοντες τὰς ἐπαγγελίας, ἀγαπητοί, καθαρίσωμεν ἑαυτοὺς ἀπὸ παντὸς μολυσμοῦ σαρκὸς καὶ πνεύματος, ἐπιτελοῦντες ἁγιωσύνην ἐν φόβῳ θεοῦ.

7.2 χωρήσατε ἡμᾶς· οὐδένα ἠδικήσαμεν, οὐδένα ἐφθίραμεν, οὐδένα ἐπλεονεκτήσαμεν. 7.3 πρὸς κατάκρισιν οὐ λέγω, προείρηκα γὰρ ὅτι ἐν ταῖς καρδίαις ἡμῶν ἐστε εἰς τὸ συναποθανῖν καὶ συνζῆν. 7.4 πολλή μοι παρρησία πρὸς ὑμᾶς, πολλή μοι καύχησις ὑπὲρ ὑμῶν· πεπλήρωμαι τῇ παρακλήσι, ὑπερπερισσεύομαι τῇ χαρᾷ ἐπὶ πάσῃ τῇ θλίψει ἡμῶν.

7.5 καὶ γὰρ ἐλθόντων ἡμῶν εἰς Μακαιδονίαν οὐδεμίαν ἔσχηκεν ἄνεσιν ἡ σὰρξ ἡμῶν, ἀλλ' ἐν παντὶ θλιβόμενοι ἔξωθεν

(ones), and behold we live, as (ones) being chastened and not being put to death, 6.10 as being grieved unceasingly but rejoicing, as poor (ones) but enriching many, as having/holding nothing and holding fast/ possessing all (things).

6.11 Our mouth has opened to ye, Corinthians, our heart has been enlarged; 6.12 ye are not restricted by us, but ye are restricted in your compassions; 6.13 but *for* the same exchange, I say as to children: Ye, be ye broadened/enlarged.

6.14 Become ye not unequally yoked to unbelievers; for what sharing/partnership *is* justice and lawlessness? Or what fellowship *is* light to/with darkness? 6.15 And what harmony/agreement of the anointed (one) to/with Beliar, or what part/share for a believer with an unbeliever? 6.16 And what assent/ accord for an *inner* temple of God with idols? For we, we are an *inner* temple of a living God; as God said: I SHALL LIVE/DWELL AND I SHALL WALK AMONG THEM, AND I SHALL BE THEIR GOD, AND THEY, THEY WILL BE MY PEOPLE. 6.17 Wherefore, COME YE FORTH OUT OF THEIR MIDST AND BE YE SET APART, says *the* Lord, AND PARTAKE YE NOT OF AN UNCLEAN THING; AND I, I SHALL ACCEPT YE KINDLY, 6.18 and I SHALL BE A FATHER TO/FOR YE, AND ye, ye will be SONS and daughters TO/FOR ME, says *the* Lord, *the* almighty/ ruler of all.

7.1 Therefore, having these promises, beloved (ones), we should cleanse ourselves from every pollution of flesh and of spirit, completing/finishing a sanctity/dedication/sanctuary in fear of God.

7.2 Make ye room *for* us; we wronged no one, we corrupted no one, we defrauded no one. 7.3 I say/- speak toward censure/for condemnation, for I have said before that in our hearts ye are in/for the (thing) to die together and to live together, 7.4 much bold- ness/confidence *is* for me near/with ye, much boasting *is* for me in behalf of ye; I have been filled with the consolation, I abound beyond all measure with the joy over our every affliction.

7.5 For even from us going to Macedonia, our flesh has had no rest/relief, but being afflicted in

μάχαι, ἔσωθεν φόβοι.

7.6 ἀλλ᾽ ὁ παρακαλῶν τοὺς ταπινοὺς παρεκάλεσεν ἡμᾶς ὁ θεὸς ἐν τῇ παρουσίᾳ Τίτου· 7.7 οὐ μόνον δὲ ἐν τῇ παρουσίᾳ αὐτοῦ ἀλλὰ καὶ ἐν τῇ παρακλήσει ᾗ παρεκλήθη ἐφ᾽ ὑμῖν, ἀναγγέλλων ἡμῖν τὴν ὑμῶν ἐπιπόθησιν, τὸν ὑμῶν ὀδυρμόν, τὸν ὑμῶν ζῆλον ὑπὲρ ἐμοῦ, ὥστε με μᾶλλον χαρῆναι. 7.8 ὅτι εἰ καὶ ἐλύπησα ὑμᾶς ἐν τῇ ἐπιστολῇ, οὐ μεταμέλομαι· εἰ καὶ μετεμελόμην· βλέπω γὰρ ὅτι ἡ ἐπιστολὴ ἐκίνη εἰ καὶ πρὸς ὥραν ἐλύπησεν ὑμᾶς, 7.9 νῦν χαίρω, οὐχ ὅτι ἐλυπήθητε, ἀλλ᾽ ὅτι ἐλυπήθητε εἰς μετάνοιαν· ἐλυπήθητε γὰρ κατὰ θεόν, ἵνα ἐν μηδενὶ ζημιωθῆτε ἐξ ἡμῶν.

7.10 ἡ γὰρ κατὰ θεὸν λύπη μετάνοιαν εἰς σωτηρίαν ἀμεταμέλητον ἐργάζεται· ἡ δὲ τοῦ κόσμου λύπη θάνατον κατεργάζεται.

7.11 ἰδοὺ γὰρ αὐτὸ τοῦτο τὸ κατὰ θεὸν λυπηθῆναι πόσην κατειργάσατο ὑμῖν σπουδήν, ἀλλὰ ἀπολογίαν, ἀλλὰ ἀγανάκτησιν, ἀλλὰ φόβον, ἀλλὰ ἐπιπόθησιν, ἀλλὰ ζῆλον, ἀλλὰ ἐκδίκησιν· ἐν παντὶ συνεστήσατε ἑαυτοὺς ἁγνοὺς εἶναι τῷ πράγματι. 7.12 ἄρα εἰ καὶ ἔγραψα ὑμῖν, οὐκ ἕνεκεν τοῦ ἀδικήσαντος, οὐδὲ ἕνεκεν τοῦ ἀδικηθέντος, ἀλλ᾽ ἕνεκεν τοῦ φανερωθῆναι τὴν σπουδὴν ὑμῶν τὴν ὑπὲρ ὑμῶν πρὸς ὑμᾶς ἐνώπιον τοῦ θεοῦ. 7.13 διὰ τοῦτο παρακεκλήμεθα.

ἐπὶ δὲ τῇ παρακλήσει ἡμῶν περισσοτέρως μᾶλλο ἐχάρημεν ἐπὶ τῇ χαρᾷ Τίτου, ὅτι ἀναπέπαυται τὸ πνεῦμα αὐτοῦ ἀπὸ πάντων ὑμῶν· 7.14 ὅτι εἴ τι αὐτῷ ὑπὲρ ὑμῶν κεκαύχημαι οὐ κατῃσχύνθην, ἀλλ᾽ ὡς πάντα ἐν ἀληθείᾳ ἐλαλήσαμεν ὑμῖν, οὕτως καὶ ἡ καύχησις ἡμῶν ἡ ἐπὶ Τίτου ἀλήθεια ἐγενήθη. 7.15 καὶ τὰ σπλάγχνα αὐτοῦ περισσοτέρως· εἰς ὑμᾶς ἐστιν ἀναμιμνησκομένου τὴν πάντων ὑμῶν ὑπακοήν, ὡς μετὰ φόβου καὶ τρόμου ἐδέξασθαι αὐτόν. 7.16 χαίρω ὅτι ἐν παντὶ θαρρῶ ἐν ὑμῖν.

every way -- fightings from without, fears from within.

7.6 But God, the (one) consoling/encouraging the humble (ones), consoled/encouraged us in/by the coming/presence of Titus; 7.7 and not only by his presence/advent/coming, but also in/by the consolation/encouragement with which he was consoled/encouraged over ye, reporting to us your earnest desire, your lamentation, your zeal in behalf of me, so as *for* me to rejoice more. 7.8 Because if I also grieved ye in/by the letter/epistle, I *do* not repent/change my mind; if I even repented for I see that the epistle, that if it even grieved ye for an hour, 7.9 I rejoice now, not because ye were grieved, but because ye were grieved in/to repentance; for ye were grieved according to/by God, in order that ye might not be punished from us.

7.10 For the grief/pain according to God works enduring repentance into salvation; but the grief of the world works out death.

7.11 For behold, this very thing according to God that *is* to be grieved, how much diligence it worked out in ye, but a reply/defense, but indignation, but fear, but earnest desire, but jealousy/zeal, but vengeance; in every (thing) ye commended yourselves to be clean/pure in the matter. 7.12 And then if I wrote to ye, not for the sake of the (one) having done wrong, neither for the sake of the (one) having been wronged, but for the sake of the (thing) *for* your diligence to be manifested, the (one) in your behalf to ye before God. 7.13 Through this we have been consoled/encouraged.

But upon our consolation we rejoiced more abundantly over the joy from Titus, because the spirit of him has been refreshed from all of ye; 7.14 because if I have boasted anything to him in behalf of ye, I was not ashamed, but as we spoke all (things) in truth to ye, so also our boasting, the (one) over Titus, became truth. 7.15 And his compassions are abundantly in ye from being reminded of the obedience of all ye, as ye received him with fear and trembling. 7.16 I rejoice because in every (thing) I am confident in ye.

8.1 Γνωρίζομεν δὲ ὑμῖν, ἀδελφοί, τὴν χάριν τοῦ θεοῦ τὴν δεδομένην ἐν ταῖς ἐκκλησίαις τῆς Μακαιδονίας, 8.2 ὅτι ἐν πολλῇ δοκιμῇ θλίψεως ἡ περισσεία τῆς χαρᾶς αὐτῶν καὶ ἡ κατὰ βάθους πτωχεία αὐτῶν ἐπερίσσευσεν εἰς τὸ πλοῦτος τῆς ἁπλότητος αὐτῶν· 8.3 ὅτι κατὰ δύναμιν, μαρτυρῶ, καὶ παρὰ δύναμιν, αὐθέρετοι 8.4 μετὰ πολλῆς παρακλήσεως δεόμενοι ἡμῶν τὴν χάριν καὶ τὴν κοινωνίαν τῆς διακονίας τῆς εἰς τοὺς ἁγίους 8.5 καὶ οὐ καθὼς ἠλπίσαμεν ἀλλ᾽ ἑαυτοὺς ἔδωκαν πρῶτον τῷ κυρίῳ καὶ ἡμῖν διὰ θελήματος θεοῦ, 8.6 εἰς τὸ παρακαλέσαι ἡμᾶς Τίτον ἵνα καθὼς προενήρξατο οὕτως καὶ ἐπιτελέσῃ εἰς ὑμᾶς καὶ τὴν χάριν ταύτην.

8.7 ἀλλ᾽ ὥσπερ ἐν παντὶ περισσεύετε, ἐν πίστι καὶ λόγῳ καὶ γνώσει καὶ πάσῃ σπουδῇ καὶ τῇ ἐξ ἡμῶν ἐν ὑμῖν ἀγάπῃ, ἵνα καὶ ἐν ταύτῃ τῇ χάριτι περισσεύητε.

8.8 οὐ κατ᾽ ἐπιταγὴν λέγω, ἀλλὰ διὰ τῆς ἑτέρων σπουδῆς καὶ τὸ τῆς ὑμετέρας ἀγάπης γνήσιον δοκιμάζων·

8.9 γινώσκετε γὰρ τὴν χάριν τοῦ κυρίου ἡμῶν Ἰησοῦ χριστοῦ, ὅτι δι᾽ ὑμᾶς ἐπτώχευσεν πλούσιος ὤν, ἵνα ὑμεῖς τῇ ἐκείνου πτωχίᾳ πλουτήσητε. 8.10 καὶ γνώμην ἐν τούτῳ δίδωμι· τοῦτο γὰρ ὑμῖν συμφέρει, οἵτινες οὐ μόνον τὸ ποιῆσαι ἀλλὰ καὶ τὸ θέλειν προενήρξασθε ἀπὸ πέρυσι· 8.11 νυνὶ δὲ καὶ τὸ ποιῆσαι ἐπιτελέσαται, ὅπως καθάπερ ἡ προθυμία τοῦ θέλειν οὕτως καὶ τὸ ἐπιτελέσε ἐκ τοῦ ἔχιν. 8.12 εἰ γὰρ ἡ προθυμία πρόκειται, καθὸ ἂν ἔχῃ εὐπρόσδεκτος, οὐ καθὸ οὐκ ἔχει. 8.13 οὐ γὰρ ἵνα ἄλλοις ἄνεσις, ὑμῖν θλῖψις· ἀλλ᾽ ἐξ ἰσότητος 8.14 ἐν τῷ νῦν καιρῷ τὸ ὑμῶν περίσσευμα εἰς τὸ ἐκείνων ὑστέρημα, ἵνα καὶ τὸ ἐκείνων περίσσευμα γένηται εἰς τὸ ὑμῶν ὑστέρημα, ὅπως γένηται ἰσότης·

8.15 καθὼς γέγραπται, «ὁ τὸ πολὺ οὐκ ἐπλεόνασεν, καὶ ὁ

8.1 And we make known to ye, brothers, the grace/favor of God having been given in/among the assemblies of Macedonia, 8.2 because, in much evidence of affliction, the abundance of their joy and their poverty accordingto depth abounded in the wealth of their generosity/sincerity; 8.3 because I testify/witness according to a power, and from a power, those acting spontaneously 8.4 with much persuasion entreating/requesting from us the grace and the fellowship of the service/ministry to the saints; 8.5 and not as we hoped, but they gave first themselves to the Lord and to us through *the* will of God, 8.6 in the (thing) *for* us to beseech/exhort Titus that as he previously began so also he should finish to/for ye and this grace/favor.

8.7 But even as ye abound in every (thing); in faith and in saying/word and in knowledge and in every diligence and in the agape in ye from us, that ye may abound also in this grace/gift.

8.8 I speak not according to a command, but through the diligence of others, also proving the legitimacy/sincerity of your agape;

8.9 for ye know the grace of our Lord Jesus, the anointed (one), because being rich, he became poor in order that ye, ye might become rich by the poverty of that (one). 8.10 And in/by this I give a judgment/decision; for this is expedient for ye, who not only *for* the (thing) to do but also to want/wish *for* the (thing) ye previously began from last year; 8.11 but now also finish ye the (thing) to do, so even as the readiness of the (thing) to will/wish so also *for* the (thing) to finish from the (thing) to hold. 8.12 For if the willingness/readiness be already there, according to *what* acceptance one may have, not according to *what* he has not. 8.13 For not in order that rest/relief *may be* for others, an affliction for ye; but out of fairness 8.14 in/at the present time/season the abundance from ye into/for the deficiency of those, in order that also the abundance of those may become into/for the deficiency of ye, so that there may become equality.

8.15 As it has been written: THE (HE) *having* THE

319

τὸ ὀλίγον οὐκ ἠλαττόνησεν.»

8.16 χάρις δὲ τῷ θεῷ τῷ δόντι τὴν αὐτὴν σπουδὴν ὑπὲρ ὑμῶν ἐν τῇ καρδίᾳ Τίτου, 8.17 ὅτι τὴν μὲν παράκλησιν ἐδέξατο, σπουδαιότερος δὲ ὑπάρχων αὐθαίρετος ἐξῆλθεν πρὸς ὑμᾶς.

8.18 συνεπέμψαμεν δὲ τὸν ἀδελφὸν μετ᾽ αὐτοῦ οὗ ὁ ἔπαινος ἐν τῷ εὐαγγελίῳ διὰ πασῶν τῶν ἐκκλησιῶν 8.19 οὐ μόνον δὲ ἀλλὰ καὶ χειροτονηθεὶς ὑπὸ τῶν ἐκκλησιῶν συνέκδημος ἡμῶν σὺν τῇ χάριτι ταύτῃ τῇ διακονουμένῃ ὑφ᾽ ἡμῶν πρὸς τὴν αὐτοῦ τοῦ κυρίου δόξαν καὶ προθυμίαν ἡμῶν 8.20 στελλόμενοι τοῦτο μή τις ἡμᾶς μωμήσηται ἐν τῇ ἁδρότητι ταύτῃ τῇ διακονουμένῃ ὑφ᾽ ἡμῶν· 8.21 προνοοῦμεν γὰρ καλὰ οὐ μόνον ἐνώπιον κυρίου ἀλλὰ καὶ ἐνώπιον ἀνθρώπων.

8.22 συνεπέμψαμεν δὲ αὐτοῖς τὸν ἀδελφὸν ἡμῶν ὃν ἐδοκιμάσαμεν ἐν πολλοῖς πολλάκις σπουδαῖον ὄντα, νυνὶ δὲ πολὺ σπουδαιότερον πεποιθήσει πολλῇ τῇ εἰς ὑμᾶς.

8.23 εἴτε ὑπὲρ Τίτου, κοινωνὸς ἐμὸς καὶ εἰς ὑμᾶς συνεργός· εἴτε ἀδελφοὶ ἡμῶν, ἀπόστολοι ἐκκλησιῶν, δόξα χριστοῦ.

8.24 τὴν οὖν ἔνδιξιν τῆς ἀγάπης ὑμῶν καὶ ἡμῶν καυχήσεως ὑπὲρ ὑμῶν εἰς αὐτοὺς ἐνδίξασθαι εἰς πρόσωπον τῶν ἐκκλησιῶν.

9.1 Περὶ μὲν γὰρ τῆς διακονίας τῆς εἰς τοὺς ἁγίους περισσόν μοί ἐστιν τὸ γράφειν ὑμῖν, 9.2 οἶδα γὰρ τὴν προθυμίαν ὑμῶν ἣν ὑπὲρ ὑμῶν καυχῶμαι Μακεδόσιν ὅτι Ἀχαΐα παρεσκεύασται ἀπὸ πέρυσι, καὶ τὸ ὑμῶν ζῆλος ἠρέθισε τοὺς πλείονας.

9.3 ἔπεμψα δὲ τοὺς ἀδελφούς, ἵνα μὴ τὸ καύχημα ἡμῶν τὸ ὑπὲρ ὑμῶν κενωθῇ ἐν τῷ μέρι τούτῳ, ἵνα καθὼς ἔλεγον παρεσκευασμένοι ἦτε, 9.4 μή πως ἐὰν ἔλθωσιν σὺν ἐμοὶ Μακαιδόνες καὶ εὕρωσιν ὑμᾶς ἀπαρασκευάστους καταισχυνθῶμεν ἡμεῖς, ἵνα μὴ λέγωμεν ὑμεῖς, ἐν τῇ ὑποστάσει

MUCH DID NOT SUPERABOUND, AND THE (HE) *having* THE LITTLE DID NOT HAVE LESS.

8.16 But grace/thanks *be* to God, the (one) giving the same diligence in behalf of ye in the heart of Titus, 8.17 because he indeed received the exhorting/beseeching, and being more diligent of his own accord, he went forthto ye.

8.18 And we sent together with him the brother of whom the approval in the good message *is* through all the assemblies, 8.19 and not only *this* but also our traveling companion having been appointed/voted in by the assemblies with this grace/gift being served/ministered by us to the fame/glory of the Lord himself and our willingness/good will, 8.20 avoiding this lest anyone might blame/ridicule us in this full abundance being served/ministered by us; 8.21 for we provide beforehand good (things) not only before *the* Lord but also before men/humans.

8.22 And we sent with them our brother whom we proved/tested, being diligent many times in many things, and now much more diligent in/by much confidence/trust, in the (one) in ye.

8.23 Whether in behalf of Titus, my partner and fellow worker to/for ye; or of our brothers, apostles of assemblies, *the* fame/glory *is* from the anointed (one).

8.24 Therefore demonstrate/show ye to them proof/evidence of your agape and of our boasting in behalf of ye in front of the assemblies.

9.1 For indeed concerning the service/ministry to/for the saints, it is unnecessary for me to write to ye, 9.2 for I know your willingness/readiness *for* which I boasted in behalf of ye to Macedonians that Achaia has prepared herself from last year, and your zeal stirred up/moved the greater *number*.

9.3 And I sent the brothers, lest our boast in behalf of ye might be made vain in this part/share, in order that as I was saying, ye may be having been prepared, 9.4 lest if Macedonians might come with me and they might find ye unprepared; we, we might be put to shame, that we may not say: Ye, in/by this assump-

ταύτη τῆς καυχησέως. 9.5 ἀναγκαῖον οὖν ἡγησάμην παρακαλέσαι τοὺς ἀδελφοὺς ἵνα προέλθωσιν εἰς ὑμᾶς καὶ προκαταρτίσωσι τὴν προεπηγγελμένην εὐλογίαν ὑμῶν, ταύτην ἑτοίμην εἶναι οὕτως ὡς εὐλογίαν καὶ μὴ ὡς πλεονεξίαν.

9.6 τοῦτο δέ, ὁ σπίρων φειδομένως φιδομένως καὶ θερίσει, καὶ ὁ σπίρων ἐπ᾽ εὐλογίαις ἐπ᾽ εὐλογίαις καὶ θερίσει. 9.7 ἕκαστος καθὼς προῄρηται τῇ καρδίᾳ, μὴ ἐκ λύπης ἢ ἐξ ἀνάγκης, ἱλαρὸν γὰρ δότην ἀγαπᾷ ὁ θεός.

9.8 δυνατεῖ δὲ ὁ θεὸς πᾶσαν χάριν περισσεῦσαι εἰς ὑμᾶς, ἵνα ἐν παντὶ πάντοτε πᾶσαν αὐτάρκειαν ἔχοντες περισσεύητε εἰς πᾶν ἔργον ἀγαθόν, 9.9 καθὼς γέγραπται, «ἐσκόρπισεν, ἔδωκεν τοῖς πένησιν, ἡ δικαιοσύνη αὐτοῦ μένει εἰς τὸν αἰῶνα.»

9.10 ὁ δὲ ἐπιχορηγῶν σπέρμα τῷ σπείροντι καὶ ἄρτον εἰς βρῶσιν χορηγήσει καὶ πληθυνεῖ τὸν σπόρον ὑμῶν καὶ αὐξήσει τὰ γενήματα τῆς δικαιοσύνης ὑμῶν· 9.11 ἐν παντὶ πλουτιζόμενοι εἰς πᾶσαν ἁπλότητα,

ἥτις κατεργάζεται δι᾽ ἡμῶν εὐχαριστίαν τῷ θεῷ 9.12 ὅτι ἡ διακονία τῆς λειτουργίας ταύτης οὐ μόνον ἐστὶν προσαναπληροῦσα τὰ ὑστερήματα τῶν ἁγίων, ἀλλὰ καὶ περισσεύουσα διὰ πολλῶν εὐχαριστιῶν τῷ θεῷ 9.13 διὰ τῆς δοκιμῆς τῆς διακονίας ταύτης δοξάζοντες τὸν θεὸν ἐπὶ τῇ ὑποταγῇ τῆς ὁμολογίας ὑμῶν εἰς τὸ εὐαγγέλιον τοῦ χριστοῦ καὶ ἁπλότητι τῆς κοινωνίας εἰς αὐτοὺς καὶ εἰς πάντας, 9.14 καὶ αὐτῶν δεήσει ὑπὲρ ὑμῶν ἐπιποθούντων ὑμᾶς διὰ τὴν ὑπερβάλλουσαν χάριν τοῦ θεοῦ ἐφ᾽ ὑμῖν. 9.15 χάρις τῷ θεῷ ἐπὶ τῇ ἀνεκδιηγήτῳ αὐτοῦ δωρεᾷ.

10.1 Αὐτὸς δὲ ἐγὼ Παῦλος παρακαλῶ ὑμᾶς διὰ τῆς πραΰτητος καὶ ἐπιεικίας τοῦ χριστοῦ, ὃς κατὰ πρόσωπον μὲν

tion of the boasting. 9.5 I considered *it* necessary therefore to exhort/beseech the brothers in order that they might go ahead to ye and arrange beforehand the blessing having been promised from ye, this to be ready thus as a blessing and not as greediness.

9.6 And this (thing), the (one) sowing sparingly will reap sparingly also, and the (one) sowing to/upon blessings will also reap upon blessings. 9.7 Each one as it was purposed by the heart, not out of pain/ grief or out of necessity, for God loves a cheerful giver.

9.8 But God is able to cause every grace/thanks to abound/overflow in ye, in order that having every sufficiency/contentment in every (thing) ye may over-flow/abound in every good work, 9.9 as it has been written: HE DISPERSED/SCATTERED, HE GAVE TO THE (ONES) BEING EMPTY, THE JUSTICE OF HIM/HIS JUSTNESS ABIDES INTO THE AGE.

9.10 But the (one) supplying seed for the (one) sowing will also supply bread/a loaf in/for food and will multiply/increase your sowing/seed and will cause to grow the fruits of your justness/justice; 9.11 being enriched/increased in every (thing) in every/ all sincerity/liberality,

which works out thanksgiving through us to God; 9.12 because the service/ministry of this liturgy/pub-lic service is not only supplying/filling up the deficiencies of the saints, but also abounding/over-flowing through many thanksgivings to God; 9.13 through the proof/evidence of this service/ministry glorifying God upon the submission of your profes-sion/confession to the good message/gospel of the anointed (one) and the sincerity/liberality of the fellowship to them and to all, 9.14 and from them desiring earnestly for ye by petition in behalf of ye because of the excelling grace/favor/gift of God upon ye. 9.15 Grace/thanks *be* to God for the inexpressible gift from him.

10.1 And I myself, Paul, I beseech/exhort ye through the gentleness and kindness of the anointed (one), who according to/by face *is* indeed humble among

ταπινὸς ἐν ὑμῖν, ἀπὼν δὲ θαρρῶ εἰς ὑμᾶς· 10.2 δέομαι δὲ τὸ μὴ παρὼν θαρρῆσαι τῇ πεποιθήσει ᾗ λογίζομαι τολμῆσαι ἐπί τινας τοὺς λογιζομένους ἡμᾶς ὡς κατὰ σάρκα περιπατοῦντας.

10.3 ἐν σαρκὶ γὰρ περιπατοῦντες οὐ κατὰ σάρκα στρατευόμεθα 10.4 τὰ γὰρ ὅπλα τῆς στρατείας ἡμῶν οὐ σαρκικὰ ἀλλὰ δυνατὰ τῷ θεῷ πρὸς καθέρεσιν ὀχυρωμάτων λογισμοὺς καθαιροῦντες 10.5 καὶ πᾶν ὕψωμα ἐπαιρόμενον κατὰ τῆς γνώσεως τοῦ θεοῦ, καὶ αἰχμαλωτίζοντες πᾶν νόημα εἰς τὴν ὑπακοὴν τοῦ χριστοῦ, 10.6 καὶ ἐν ἑτοίμῳ ἔχοντες ἐκδικῆσαι πᾶσαν παρακοήν, ὅταν πληρωθῇ ὑμῶν ἡ ὑπακοή. 10.7 τὰ κατὰ πρόσωπον βλέπετε. εἴ τις πέποιθεν ἑαυτῷ χριστοῦ εἶναι, τοῦτο λογιζέσθω πάλιν ἐφ᾽ ἑαυτοῦ ὅτι καθὼς αὐτὸς χριστοῦ οὕτως καὶ ἡμεῖς. 10.8 ἐάν τε γὰρ περισσότερόν τι καυχήσωμαι περὶ τῆς ἐξουσίας ἡμῶν, ἧς ἔδωκεν ὁ κύριος εἰς οἰκοδομὴν καὶ οὐκ εἰς καθαίρεσιν ὑμῶν, οὐκ αἰσχυνθήσομαι,

10.9 ἵνα μὴ δόξω ὡς ἂν ἐκφοβῖν ὑμᾶς διὰ τῶν ἐπιστολῶν· 10.10 ὅτι, αἱ ἐπιστολαὶ μέν, φησίν, βαρεῖαι καὶ ἰσχυραί, ἡ δὲ παρουσία τοῦ σώματος ἀσθενὴς καὶ ὁ λόγος ἐξουθενημένος. 10.11 τοῦτο λογιζέσθω ὁ τοιοῦτος, ὅτι οἷοί ἐσμεν τῷ λόγῳ δι᾽ ἐπιστολῶν ἀπόντες, τοιοῦτοι καὶ παρόντες τῷ ἔργῳ.

10.12 οὐ γὰρ τολμῶμεν ἐγκρῖναι ἢ συγκρῖναι ἑαυτούς τισιν τῶν ἑαυτοὺς συνιστανόντων· ἀλλὰ αὐτοὶ ἐν ἑαυτοῖς ἑαυτοὺς μετροῦντες καὶ συγκρίνοντες ἑαυτοὺς ἑαυτοῖς οὐ συνιᾶσιν.

10.13 ἡμεῖς δὲ οὐκ εἰς τὰ ἄμετρα καυχησόμεθα, ἀλλὰ κατὰ τὸ μέτρον τοῦ κανόνος οὗ ἐμέρισεν ἡμῖν ὁ θεὸς μέτρου, ἐφικέσθαι ἄχρι καὶ ὑμῶν.

10.14 οὐ γὰρ ὡς μὴ ἐφικνούμενοι εἰς ὑμᾶς ὑπερεκτίνομεν

ye, but being absent, I am bold to/for ye; 10.2 and I beg/pray *for* the (thing) of not being present to be bold/courageous in the confidence/trust which I reckon to be daring for some, the (ones)/those reckoning/accounting us as walking according to flesh.

10.3 For we serve/battle as soldiers in flesh, walking not according to flesh, 10.4 for the weapons/tools of our army/warfare *are* not worldly/fleshy but power/abilities for God to/toward a tearing down/destruction of strongholds, destroying thoughts/devices 10.5 and every exalted (thing) raising itself up against the knowledge of God, and taking captive every thought to/for the obedience of the anointed (one), 10.6 and holding in readiness to avenge every disobedience, whenever the patience/obedience of ye might be filled up. 10.7 Ye view the (things) according to face/appearance. If anyone has persuaded himself to be of the anointed (one), let him reckon/account this again upon himself, that as he *is* of the anointed (one), so also *are* we. 10.8 For even if I should boast something more abundantly about the authority of us, which the Lord gave into/for building/edification and not into/for tearing down/destruction of ye, I shall not be ashamed,

10.9 in order that I may not seem as ever to frighten ye through the epistles/letters; 10.10 because the letters indeed, he says, *are* heavy and strong, but the coming/advent/presence of the body *is* weak and the logos/word being despised. 10.11 Let the (one) such reckon/account this, that what sort we are for the logos/word through epistles/letters, being absent, such (ones) also being present for the work.

10.12 For we dare not to class with or to compare ourselves to some of those commending themselves; but they, measuring themselves among themselves and comparing themselves to themselves, they understand not.

10.13 But we, we shall triumph/boast, not in the (things) beyond measure, but according to the measure of the standard/canon/rule of measure which God divided for us, to reach even/also as far as from ye/yours.

10.14 For not as reaching not to ye do we over-

ἐαυτούς, ἄχρι γὰρ καὶ ὑμῶν ἐφθάσαμεν ἐν τῷ εὐαγγελίῳ τοῦ χριστοῦ· 10.15 οὐκ εἰς τὰ ἄμετρα καυχώμενοι ἐν ἀλλοτρίοις κόποις, ἐλπίδα δὲ ἔχοντες αὐξανομένης τῆς πίστεως ὑμῶν ἐν ὑμῖν μεγαλυνθῆναι κατὰ τὸν κανόνα ἡμῶν εἰς περισσίαν, 10.16 εἰς τὰ ὑπερέκεινα ὑμῶν εὐαγγελίσασθαι, οὐκ ἐν ἀλλοτρίῳ κανόνι εἰς τὰ ἕτοιμα καυχήσασθαι.

10.17 «ὁ» δὲ «καυχώμενος ἐν κυρίῳ καυχάσθω» 10.18 οὐ γὰρ ὁ ἑαυτὸν συνιστάνων, ἐκεῖνός δόκιμος ἐστιν, ἀλλ' ὃν ὁ κύριος συνίστησιν.

11.1 Ὄφελον ἀνείχεσθέ μου μικρόν τι ἀφροσύνης· ἀλλὰ καὶ ἀνάσχεσθέ μου. 11.2 ζηλῶ γὰρ ὑμᾶς θεοῦ ζήλῳ, ἡρμοσάμην γὰρ ὑμᾶς ἑνὶ ἀνδρὶ παρθένον ἁγνὴν παραστῆσαι τῷ χριστῷ· 11.3 φοβοῦμαι δὲ μή πως, ὡς ὁ ὄφις ἐξηπάτησεν Εὔαν ἐν τῇ πανουργίᾳ αὐτοῦ, φθαρῇ τὰ νοήματα ὑμῶν ἀπὸ τῆς ἁπλότητος καὶ τῆς ἁγνότητος τῆς εἰς χριστόν.

11.4 εἰ μὲν γὰρ ὁ ἐρχόμενος ἄλλον Ἰησοῦν κηρύσσει ὃν οὐκ ἐκηρύξαμεν, ἢ πνεῦμα ἕτερον λαμβάνετε ὃ οὐκ ἐλάβετε, ἢ εὐαγγέλιον ἕτερον ὃ οὐκ ἐδέξασθε, καλῶς ἀνείχεσθε.

11.5 λογίζομαι γὰρ μηδὲν ὑστερηκέναι τῶν ὑπερλίαν ἀποστόλων· 11.6 εἰ δὲ καὶ ἰδιώτης τῷ λόγῳ, ἀλλ' οὐ τῇ γνώσει, ἀλλ' ἐν παντὶ φανερώσαντες ἐν πᾶσιν εἰς ὑμᾶς. 11.7 ἢ ἁμαρτίαν ἐποίησα ἐμαυτὸν ταπινῶν ἵνα ὑμεῖς ὑψωθῆτε, ὅτι δωρεὰν τὸ τοῦ θεοῦ εὐαγγέλιον εὐηγγελισάμην ὑμῖν;

11.8 ἄλλας ἐκλησίας ἐσύλησα λαβὼν ὀψώνιον πρὸς τὴν ὑμῶν διακονία, 11.9 καὶ παρὼν πρὸς ὑμᾶς καὶ ὑστερηθεὶς οὐ κατενάρκησα οὐθενός· τὸ γὰρ ὑστέρημά μου προσανεπλήρωσαν οἱ ἀδελφοὶ ἐλθόντες ἀπὸ Μακαιδονίας· καὶ ἐν παντὶ ἀβαρῆ

extend ourselves, for as far as even from ye/yours we attained/achieved in/by the good message/gospel of the anointed (one); 10.15 not in the (things) beyond measure, boasting in others' labors, but having/holding a hope of your faith growing/increasing to be enlarged/magnified among ye according to your canon/standard/rule in abundance, 10.16 in the (places) beyond ye to announce the good message, not to boast/triumph in/by another's standard/canon/rule in the prepared (things).

10.17 But the (one) boasting in *the* Lord, let him boast; 10.18 for the (one) not commending himself, that (one) is proven, but whom the Lord commends.

11.1 O that ye were enduring from me a little something of foolishness; but ye even were enduring mine/of me. 11.2 For I am jealous *for* ye with a jealousy of God, for I betrothed ye to one man, to present a pure maiden/virgin to the anointed (one); 11.3 but I fear lest somehow, as the serpent deceived Eve by his shrewdness, your aspirations/thoughts might be corrupted from the sincerity and the purity of the (one) in the anointed (one).

11.4. For if indeed the (one) coming heralds/preaches another Jesus whom we heralded/preached not, or ye receive another/different spirit which ye received not, or another/different good message/gospel which ye yourselves received not, ye endure well.

11.5 For I reckon/count *it* nothing to be inferior from the superlative apostles; 11.6 but even if *I be* untrained in the logos/word, but not in the knowledge, but in every (thing) having revealed/manifested in all (things) to ye. 11.7 Or did I sin, humbling myself in order that ye, ye might be exalted, because I freely announced the good message/gospel from God to ye?

11.8 I robbed other assemblies, having taken wages to/for the service/ministry of ye, 11.9 both being present near ye and lacking/being deficient I was not anyone's burden; for the brothers coming from Macedonia filled up my deficiency/lacking; and in

ἐμαυτὸν ὑμῖν ἐτήρησα καὶ τηρήσω.

11.10 ἔστιν ἀλήθεια χριστοῦ ἐν ἐμοὶ ὅτι ἡ καύχησις αὕτη οὐ φραγήσεται εἰς ἐμὲ ἐν τοῖς κλίμασι τῆς Ἀχαΐας.

11.11 διὰ τί; ὅτι οὐκ ἀγαπῶ ὑμᾶς; ὁ θεὸς οἶδεν. 11.12 ὃ δὲ ποιῶ καὶ ποιήσω, ἵνα ἐκκόψω τὴν ἀφορμὴν τῶν θελόντων ἀφορμήν, ἵνα ἐν ᾧ καυχῶνται εὑρεθῶσιν καθὼς καὶ ἡμῖς.

11.13 οἱ γὰρ τοιοῦτοι ψευδαπόστολοι, ἐργάται δόλιοι, μετασχηματιζόμενοι εἰς ἀποστόλους χριστοῦ.

11.14 καὶ οὐ θαῦμα, αὐτὸς γὰρ ὁ Σατανᾶς μετασχηματίζεται εἰς ἄγγελον φωτός· 11.15 οὐ μέγα οὖν εἰ καὶ οἱ διάκονοι αὐτοῦ μετασχηματίζονται ὡς διάκονοι δικαιοσύνης, ὧν τὸ τέλος ἔσται κατὰ τὰ ἔργα αὐτῶν.

11.16 πάλιν λέγω, μή τίς με δόξῃ ἄφρονα εἶναι· εἰ δὲ μή γε, κἂν ὡς ἄφρονα δέξασθέ με, ἵνα κἀγὼ μικρόν τι καυχήσωμαι.

11.17 ὃ λαλῶ οὐ κατὰ κύριον λαλῶ, ἀλλ᾽ ὡς ἐν ἀφροσύνῃ, ἐν ταύτῃ τῇ ὑποστάσει τῆς καυχήσεως.

11.18 ἐπεὶ πολλοὶ καυχῶνται κατὰ σάρκα, κἀγὼ καυχήσομαι. 11.19 ἡδέως γὰρ ἀνέχεσθε τῶν ἀφρόνων φρόνιμοι ὄντες· 11.20 ἀνέχεσθε γὰρ εἴ τις ὑμᾶς καταδουλοῖ, εἴ τις κατεσθίει, εἴ τις λαμβάνει, εἴ τις ἐπαίρεται, εἴ τις εἰς πρόσωπον ὑμᾶς δέρι. 11.21 κατὰ ἀτιμίαν λέγω, ὡς ὅτι ἡμῖς ἠσθενήκαμεν· ἐν ᾧ δ᾽ ἄν τις τολμᾷ, ἐν ἀφροσύνῃ λέγω, τολμῶ κἀγώ. 11.22 Ἑβρέοί εἰσιν; κἀγώ. Ἰσδραηλῖταί εἰσιν; κἀγώ. σπέρμα Ἀβραάμ εἰσιν; κἀγώ. 11.23 διάκονοι χριστοῦ εἰσιν; παραφρονῶν λαλῶ, ὑπὲρ ἐγώ· ἐν κόποις περισσοτέρως, ἐν πληγαῖς περισσοτέρως, ἐν φυλακαῖς ὑπερβαλλόντως, ἐν θανάτοις πολλάκις· 11.24 ὑπὸ

every (way) I kept and shall keep myself unburdensome to ye.

11.10 Truth from the anointed (one) is in me, that this triumph/boasting will not be silenced/closed up in me in the regions of Achaia.

11.11 Why? Because I *do* not love ye? God knows. 11.12 But what I do, I also shall do, in order that I may cut off the occasion from those wanting an occasion, in order that in what they boast they might be found even as we.

11.13 For those such *are* false apostles, deceitful workers, disguising/transforming themselves into apostles of the anointed (one).

11.14 And no wonder, for Satan himself disguised/transforms himself into a messenger/angel of light; 11.15 no great (thing) then if also his servants/ministers are disguised/transformed as servants/ministers of justice/justness, of whom the end will be according to their works.

11.16 Again I say, think not anyone *for* me to be foolish; otherwise, even as foolish receive ye me, in order that even I, I might boast a little *for* something.

11.17 What I speak, I speak not according to the Lord, but as in foolishness, in this confidence/assumption of the boasting.

11.18 Since many are triumphing/boasting according to flesh, I also shall boast/triumph. 11.19 For ye endure with pleasure from the fools, being prudent/wise (ones) 11.20 for ye endure if anyone enslaves ye, if anyone devours *ye*, if anyone takes *ye* , if anyone lifts himself up, if anyone beats ye in *the* face. 11.21 I speak against/according to dishonor, as that we, we have been weak; but in what ever anyone would dare, I speak in/with foolishness; I also, I dare. 11.22 Are they Hebrews? I also. Are they Israelites? I also. Are they they seed of Abraham? I also. 11.23 Are they servants/ministers of the anointed (one)? I speak from madness, I *am* beyond/above: in toils more abundantly, in wounds/stripes more abundantly, in prisons excessively, in/by deaths many times; 11.24 five times by Judeans I received/took

Ἰουδαίων πεντάκις τεσσεράκοντα παρὰ μίαν ἔλαβον, 11.25 τρεὶς ἐραβδίσθην, ἅπαξ ἐλιθάσθην, τρεὶς ἐναυάγησα, νυχθήμερον ἐν τῷ βυθῷ πεποίηκα· 11.26 ὁδοιπορίαις πολλάκις, κινδύνοις ποταμῶν, κινδύνοις λῃστῶν, κινδύνοις ἐκ γένους, κινδύνοις ἐξ ἐθνῶν, κινδύνοις ἐν πόλει, κινδύνοις ἐν ἐρημίᾳ, κινδύνοις ἐν θαλάσσῃ, κινδύνοις ἐν ψευδαδέλφοις, 11.27 κόπῳ καὶ μόχθῳ, ἐν ἀγρυπνίαις πολλάκις, ἐν λειμῷ καὶ δίψει, ἐν νηστίαις πολλάκις, ἐν ψύχι καὶ γυμνότητι· 11.28 χωρὶς τῶν παρεκτὸς ἡ ἐπίστασίς μοι ἡ καθ᾽ ἡμέρα, ἡ μέριμνα πασῶν τῶν ἐκκλησιῶν. 11.29 τίς ἀσθενεῖ, καὶ οὐκ ἀσθενῶ; τίς σκανδαλείζεται, καὶ οὐκ ἐγὼ πυροῦμαι; 11.30 εἰ καυχᾶσθαι δεῖ, τὰ τῆς ἀσθενείας μου καυχήσομαι.

11.31 ὁ θεὸς καὶ πατὴρ τοῦ κυρίου Ἰησοῦ οἶδεν, ὁ ὢν εὐλογητὸς εἰς τοὺς αἰῶνας, ὅτι οὐ ψεύδομαι.

11.32 ἐν Δαμασκῷ ὁ ἐθνάρχης Ἀρέτα τοῦ βασιλέως ἐφρούρι τὴν πόλιν Δαμασκηνῶν πιάσαι με θέλων, 11.33 καὶ διὰ θυρίδος ἐν σαργάνῃ ἐχαλάσθην διὰ τοῦ τίχους καὶ ἐξέφυγον τὰς χῖρας αὐτοῦ.

12.1 Καυχᾶσθαι δέ· οὐ συμφέρον μέν, ἐλεύσομαι δὲ εἰς ὀπτασίας καὶ ἀποκαλύψεις κυρίου.

12.2 οἶδα ἄνθρωπον ἐν χριστῷ πρὸ ἐτῶν δεκατεσσάρων εἴτε ἐν σώματι οὐκ οἶδα, εἴτε ἐκτὸς τοῦ σώματος οὐκ οἶδα, ὁ θεὸς οἶδεν ἁρπαγέντα τὸν τοιοῦτον ἕως τρίτου οὐρανοῦ.

12.3 καὶ οἶδα τὸν τοιοῦτον ἄνθρωπον εἴτε ἐν σώματι εἴτε ἐκτὸς τοῦ σώματος οὐκ οἶδα, ὁ θεὸς οἶδεν 12.4 ὅτι ἡρπάγη εἰς τὸν παράδισον καὶ ἤκουσεν ἄρρητα ῥήματα ἃ οὐκ ἐξὸν ἀνθρώπῳ λαλῆσαι.

12.5 ὑπὲρ τοῦ τοιούτου καυχήσομαι, ὑπὲρ δὲ ἐμαυτοῦ οὐ καυχήσομαι εἰ μὴ ἐν ταῖς ἀσθενίαις μου.

12.6 ἐὰν γὰρ θελήσω καυχήσασθαι, οὐκ ἔσομαι ἄφρων,

forty less one (stripes), 11.25 three times I was beaten with staffs, once I was stoned, three times I was shipwrecked, I did/made a night and day in/on the deep (sea); 11.26 many times in travels, in perils from rivers, in perils from robbers, in perils from my race, in perils from ethnics, in perils in a city, in perils in a desert, in perils in/on a sea, in perils in/among false brothers, 11.27 by toil and hardship, in watchings/wakings many times, in famine and thirst, in starvings/fastings many times, in coldness and destitution/nakedness; 11.28 apart from the (things) besides the attack/pressure on me day by day, the burden of/from all the assemblies. 11.29 Who is being weak, and I am not weak? Who is being offended/caused to stumble, and I, I am not set on fire? 11.30 If it be necessary to boast, I shall boast for the (things) of my weakness.

11.31 The God and father of the Lord Jesus, the (one) being blessed into the ages, knows that I lie not.

11.32 In Damascus the ethnarc of Aretas the king was guarding the city of Damascus, wanting/wishing to arrest me, 11.33 and I was lowered through a window in a basket through the wall, and escaped the hands of him/his hands.

12.1 And to boast/triumph, being indeed not expedient, but I shall come into visions and revelations from the Lord.

12.2 I know a man in the anointed (one) from fourteen years before -- whether in a body I know not, or outside the body I know not; God knows -- for the (one) such having been snatched away until/as far as the third heaven/sky. 12.3 And I know the man such as this, -- whether in a body or outside the body I know not, God knows -- 12.4 that he was snatched away into the paradise and he heard unspeakable words which is not being lawful for a man/human to speak.

12.5 I shall boast in behalf of the (one) such, but I shall not boast in behalf of myself except in my weaknesses.

12.6 For if I shall want/wish to boast, I shall

ἀλήθειαν γὰρ ἐρῶ· φείδομαι δέ, μή τις εἰς ἐμὲ λογίσηται ὑπὲρ ὃ βλέπει με ἢ ἀκούει ἐξ ἐμοῦ 12.7 καὶ τῇ ὑπερβολῇ τῶν ἀποκαλύψεων. διό, ἵνα μὴ ὑπεραίρωμαι, ἐδόθη μοι σκόλοψ τῇ σαρκί, ἄγγελος Σατανᾶ, ἵνα με κολαφίζῃ, ἵνα μὴ ὑπεραίρωμαι. 12.8 ὑπὲρ τούτου τρὶς τὸν κύριον παρεκάλεσα ἵνα ἀποστῇ ἀπ' ἐμοῦ· 12.9 καὶ εἴρηκέν μοι, ἀρκεῖ σοι ἡ χάρις μου· ἡ γὰρ δύναμις ἐν ἀσθενίᾳ τελεῖται.

ἥδιστα οὖν μᾶλλον καυχήσομαι ἐν ταῖς ἀσθενίαις μου, ἵνα ἐπισκηνώσῃ ἐπ' ἐμὲ ἡ δύναμις τοῦ κριστοῦ. 12.10 διὸ εὐδοκῶ ἐν ἀσθενίαις, ἐν ὕβρεσιν, ἐν ἀνάγκαις, ἐν διωγμοῖς καὶ στενοχωρίαις, ὑπὲρ χριστοῦ· ὅταν γὰρ ἀσθενῶ, τότε δυνατός εἰμι.

12.11 γέγονα ἄφρων· ὑμεῖς με ἠναγκάσατε· ἐγὼ γὰρ ὤφειλον ὑφ' ὑμῶν συνίστασθαι. οὐδὲν γὰρ ὑστέρησα τῶν ὑπερλίαν ἀποστόλων, εἰ καὶ οὐδέν εἰμι· 12.12 τὰ μὲν σημεῖα τοῦ ἀποστόλου κατειργάσθη ἐν ὑμῖν ἐν πάσῃ ὑπομονῇ, σημίοις τε καὶ τέρασι καὶ δυνάμεσιν. 12.13 τί γάρ ἐστιν ὃ ἡσσώθητε ὑπὲρ τὰς λοιπὰς ἐκκλησίας, εἰ μὴ ὅτι αὐτὸς ἐγὼ οὐ κατενάρκησα ὑμῶν; χαρίσασθέ μοι τὴν ἀδικίαν ταύτην.

12.14 ἰδοὺ τρίτον τοῦτο ἑτοίμως ἔχω ἐλθεῖν πρὸς ὑμᾶς, καὶ οὐ καταναρκήσω· οὐ γὰρ ζητῶ τὰ ὑμῶν ἀλλὰ ὑμᾶς, οὐ γὰρ ὀφίλει τὰ τέκνα τοῖς γονεῦσι θησαυρίζειν, ἀλλὰ οἱ γονῖς τοῖς τέκνοις. 12.15 ἐγὼ δὲ ἥδιστα δαπανήσω καὶ ἐκδαπανηθήσομαι ὑπὲρ τῶν ψυχῶν ὑμῶν. εἰ περισσοτέρως ὑμᾶς ἀγαπῶ, ἧσσον ἀγαπῶμαι;

12.16 ἔστω δέ, ἐγὼ οὐ κατενάρκησα ὑμῶν· ἀλλὰ ὑπάρχων πανοῦργος δόλῳ ὑμᾶς ἔλαβον. 12.17 μή τινα ὧν ἀπέσταλκα πρὸς ὑμᾶς, δι' αὐτοῦ ἐπλεονέκτησα ὑμᾶς; 12.18 παρεκάλεσα Τίτον καὶ

not be foolish, for I shall speak truth; but I refrain, lest anyone might reckon/account to me beyond what he sees *in* me or hears from me   12.7 and in/by the outstanding quality of the revelations. Wherefore, in order that I may not be over-elated, a thorn in the flesh was given to me, a messenger/angel of Satan, in order that he might buffet me, in order that I may not be over-elated.   12.8 I called upon the Lord three times over this in order that it might withdraw from me;   12.9 and he has said to me: My grace is enough for you, for the power is finished/accomplished in/by weakness.

Therefore I shall most gladly boast more in my weaknesses, in order that the power of the anointed (one) might cover over/fall upon me.   12.10 Wherefore I am well-pleased in weaknesses, in/by insults, in constraints/compellings, in prosecutions and restrictions, in behalf of the anointed (one); for whenever I may be weak, then I am powerful/strong/able.

12.11   I have become foolish; ye constrained me; for I, I was deserving to be commended by ye, for I lacked nothing from the superlative apostles, even if I am nothing;   12.12 Indeed the signs from the apostle were worked among ye in/with every patience/endurance, both by signs and by wonders and by powers.   12.13 For what/why is *it* which/that ye were made less/lower beyond the remaining assemblies, except that I myself, I burdened ye not? Forgive ye this wrong/injustice to/for me.

12.14   Behold, I *am* prepared/have readily to come to ye this third (time), and I shall not be burdensome/torpid; for I seek not the (things) of ye but ye, for the children are not obligated to lay up a store/treasure for the parents, but the parents for the children.   12.15 But I, with pleasure I shall spend freely and I shall be expended in behalf of your souls/lives. If I love ye more abundantly, am I loved less?

12.16   But let it be; I, I was not burdensome to ye; but being shrewd/crafty I took ye by cunning/guile.   12.17 Not anyone whom I have sent to ye, did I defraud ye through him?   12.18 I called upon Titus and

συναπέστιλα τὸν ἀδελφόν· μήτι ἐπλεονέκτησεν ὑμᾶς Τίτος; οὐ τῷ αὐτῷ πνεύματι περιεπατήσαμεν; οὐ τοῖς αὐτοῖς ἴχνεσιν;

12.19 πάλαι δοκεῖτε ὅτι ὑμῖν ἀπολογούμεθα; κατέναντι θεοῦ ἐν χριστῷ λαλοῦμεν· τὰ δὲ πάντα, ἀγαπητοί, ὑπὲρ τῆς ὑμῶν οἰκοδομῆς. 12.20 φοβοῦμαι γὰρ μή πως ἐλθὼν οὐχ οἵους θέλω εὕρω ὑμᾶς, κἀγὼ εὑρεθῶ ὑμῖν οἷον οὐ θέλετε, μή πως ἔρις, ζῆλοι, θυμοί, ἐριθίαι, καταλαλιαί, ψιθυρισμοί, φυσιώσεις, ἀκαταστασίαι· 12.21 μὴ πάλιν ἐλθόντος μου ταπινώσῃ με ὁ θεός μου πρὸς ὑμᾶς, καὶ πενθήσω πολλοὺς τῶν προημαρτηκότων καὶ μὴ μετανοησάντων ἐπὶ τῇ ἀκαθαρσίᾳ καὶ πορνίᾳ καὶ ἀσελγείᾳ ᾗ ἔπραξαν.

13.1 Τρίτον τοῦτο ἔρχομαι πρὸς ὑμᾶς· «ἐπὶ στόματος δύο μαρτύρων ἢ τριῶν σταθήσεται πᾶν ῥῆμα.»

13.2 προείρηκα καὶ προλέγω ὡς παρὼν τὸ δεύτερον καὶ ἀπὼν νῦν τοῖς προημαρτηκόσιν καὶ τοῖς λοιποῖς πᾶσιν, ὅτι ἐὰν ἔλθω εἰς τὸ πάλιν οὐ φίσομαι,

13.3 ἐπεὶ δοκιμὴν ζητεῖτε τοῦ ἐν ἐμοὶ λαλοῦντος χριστοῦ· ὃς εἰς ὑμᾶς οὐκ ἀσθενεῖ ἀλλὰ δυνατεῖ ἐν ὑμῖν. 13.4 καὶ γὰρ ἐσταυρώθη ἐξ ἀσθενείας, ἀλλὰ ζῇ ἐκ δυνάμεως θεοῦ. καὶ γὰρ ἡμεῖς ἀσθενοῦμεν σὺν αὐτῷ, ἀλλὰ ζήσομεν σὺν αὐτῷ ἐκ δυνάμεως θεοῦ εἰς ὑμᾶς.

13.5 ἑαυτοὺς πιράζετε εἰ ἐστὲ ἐν τῇ πίστι, ἑαυτοὺς δοκιμάζετε· ἢ οὐκ ἐπιγινώσκετε ἑαυτοὺς ὅτι χριστὸς Ἰησοῦς ἐν ὑμῖν ἐστιν; εἰ μήτι ἀδόκιμοί ἐστε. 13.6 ἐλπίζω δὲ ὅτι γνώσεσθε ὅτι ἡμεῖς οὐκ ἐσμὲν ἀδόκιμοι. 13.7 εὐχόμεθα δὲ πρὸς τὸν θεὸν μὴ ποιῆσαι ὑμᾶς κακὸν μηδέν, οὐχ ἵνα ἡμεῖς δόκιμοι φανῶμεν, ἀλλ᾽ ἵνα ὑμεῖς τὸ καλὸν ποιεῖτε, ἡμεῖς δὲ ὡς ἀδόκιμοι ὦμεν. 13.8 οὐ

sent *him* forth with the brother; Titus did not defraud ye, *did he*? Did not we walk in/by the same spirit? Not in the same footsteps? *Yes*.

12.19 Do ye think that we are defending our- selves to ye from past time? We speak before God in the anointed (one); but all the (things), beloved (ones), *are* in behalf of the building up/edification of ye. 12.20 For I fear, lest having come, I may not find ye of what sort I want/wish; and I, I might be found by ye of a sort ye want/wish not, lest in any way strife, jealousies, wraths, rivalries, calumnies/ back-bitings, slanderous whisperings, arrogances, insurrections; 12.21 lest, from me having come again, my God might humble me to/toward ye, and I might grieve many of those having sinned before and not having repented for the uncleanness and prostitution and revelry/riotous living which they practiced.

13.1 I come to ye this third *time*; UPON THE MOUTH OF TWO OR THREE WITNESSES WILL EVERY WORD BE ESTABLISHED.

13.2 I have said before and I foretell/say beforehand, about/as being present the second *time* and being absent now, to those having sinned before and to all the rest, that if I might come into the (thing) again, I shall not refrain/forbear/spare, 13.3 since ye seek a evidence/proof of the anointed (one) speaking by me; *he* who in ye is not weak, but is powerful/strong among ye. 13.4 For even he was crucified out of weakness, but he lives out of/from God's power. For we also, we are weak with him, but we shall live with him from God's power in us. 13.5 Test/try ye yourselves, if ye are in the faith, prove ye yourselves; or do ye not understand/- fully know yourselves that the anointed Jesus is in/among ye? If not, ye are untested/unproven (ones). 13.6 But I hope that ye will know that we, we are not untested/unproved (ones). 13.7 And we pray to god *for* ye not to do nothing bad, not in order that we, we may appear proven (ones), but in order that ye, ye may do the good (thing), and we, we may be as untested (ones). 13.8 For we are not able *for* anything against

γὰρ δυνάμεθά τι κατὰ τῆς ἀληθίας, ἀλλὰ ὑπὲρ τῆς ἀληθίας.

13.9 χαίρομεν γὰρ ὅταν ἡμεῖς ἀσθενῶμεν, ὑμεῖς δὲ δυνατοὶ ἦτε· τοῦτο καὶ εὐχόμεθα, τὴν ὑμῶν κατάρτισιν.

13.10 διὰ τοῦτο ταῦτα ἀπὼν γράφω, ἵνα παρὼν μὴ ἀποτόμως χρήσωμαι κατὰ τὴν ἐξουσίαν ἣν ὁ κύριος ἔδωκέν μοι, εἰς οἰκοδομὴν καὶ οὐκ εἰς καθαίρεσιν.

13.11 λοιπόν, ἀδελφοί, χαίρετε, καταρτίζεσθαι, παρακαλεῖσθε, τὸ αὐτὸ φρονεῖτε, εἰρηνεύετε, καὶ ὁ θεὸς τῆς ἀγάπης καὶ εἰρήνης ἔσται μεθ᾽ ὑμῶν.

13.12 ἀσπάσασθε ἀλλήλους ἐν ἁγίῳ φιλήματι.

ἀσπάζονται ὑμᾶς οἱ ἅγιοι πάντες.

13.13 ἡ χάρις τοῦ κυρίου Ἰησοῦ χριστοῦ καὶ ἡ ἀγάπη τοῦ θεοῦ καὶ ἡ κοινωνία τοῦ ἁγίου πνεύματος μετὰ πάντων ὑμῶν.

Πρὸς Κορινθίους Β΄

the truth, but in behalf of the truth.

13.9 For we rejoice whenever we, we may be weak, and ye, ye may be powerful/strong (ones); this we also pray, *for* your adjustment/knitting together.

13.10 Because of this I write these (things) being absent, in order that being present I might not use/employ according to the authority which the Lord gave to me, into/for building up/edification and not in/for destruction/taking down.

13.11 Henceforth, brothers, rejoice ye, adjust/ mend yourselves, call upon/encourage yourselves, think ye the same (thing), be ye at peace, and the God of the agape and peace will be with ye.

13.12 Greet ye one another with a holy kiss.

All the saints greet ye.

13.13 The grace/favor of the Lord Jesus, the anointed (one), and the agape of God, and the fellow-ship of the holy spirit *be* with ye all.

To Corinthians 2

ΠΡΟΣ ΓΑΛΑΤΑΣ

This is the Sinaitic New Testament, book of Galatians.

1.1 Παῦλος ἀπόστολος, οὐκ ἀπ᾽ ἀνθρώπων οὐδὲ δι᾽ ἀνθρώπου ἀλλὰ διὰ Ἰησοῦ χριστοῦ καὶ θεοῦ πατρὸς τοῦ ἐγίραντος αὐτὸν ἐκ νεκρῶν, 1.2 καὶ οἱ σὺν ἐμοὶ πάντες ἀδελφοί, ταῖς ἐκκλησίαις τῆς Γαλατίας· 1.3 χάρις ὑμῖν καὶ εἰρήνη ἀπὸ θεοῦ πατρὸς ἡμῶν καὶ κυρίου Ἰησοῦ χριστοῦ, 1.4 τοῦ δόντος ἑαυτὸν ὑπὲρ τῶν ἁμαρτιῶν ἡμῶν ὅπως ἐξέληται ἡμᾶς ἐκ τοῦ αἰῶνος τοῦ ἐνεστῶτος πονηροῦ κατὰ τὸ θέλημα τοῦ θεοῦ καὶ πατρὸς ἡμῶν, 1.5 ᾧ ἡ δόξα εἰς τοὺς αἰῶνας τῶν αἰώνων· ἀμήν.

1.6 θαυμάζω ὅτι οὕτως ταχέως μετατίθεσθαι ἀπὸ τοῦ καλέσαντος ὑμᾶς ἐν χάριτι χριστοῦ εἰς ἕτερον εὐαγγέλιον, 1.7 ὃ οὐκ ἔστιν ἄλλο· εἰ μή τινές εἰσιν οἱ ταράσσοντες ὑμᾶς καὶ θέλοντες μεταστρέψαι τὸ εὐαγγέλιον τοῦ χριστοῦ. 1.8 ἀλλὰ καὶ ἐὰν ἡμεῖς ἢ ἄγγελος ἐξ οὐρανοῦ εὐαγγελίσηται παρ᾽ ὃ εὐηγγελισάμεθα ὑμῖν, ἀνάθεμα ἔστω.

1.9 ὡς προειρήκαμεν, καὶ ἄρτι πάλιν λέγω, εἴ τις ὑμᾶς εὐαγγελίζεται παρ᾽ ὃ παρελάβετε, ἀνάθεμα ἔστω. 1.10 ἄρτι γὰρ ἀνθρώπους πίθω ἢ τὸν θεόν; ἢ ζητῶ ἀνθρώποις ἀρέσκιν; εἰ ἔτι ἀνθρώποις ἤρεσκον, χριστοῦ δοῦλος οὐκ ἂν ἤμην.

1.11 γνωρίζω γὰρ ὑμῖν, ἀδελφοί, τὸ εὐαγγέλιον τὸ εὐαγγελισθὲν ὑπ᾽ ἐμοῦ ὅτι οὐκ ἔστιν κατὰ ἄνθρωπον· 1.12 οὐδὲ γὰρ ἐγὼ παρὰ ἀνθρώπου παρέλαβον αὐτό, οὐδὲ ἐδιδάχθην, ἀλλὰ δι᾽ ἀποκαλύψεως Ἰησοῦ χριστοῦ.

1.13 ἠκούσατε γὰρ τὴν ἐμὴν ἀναστροφήν ποτε ἐν τῷ Ἰουδαϊσμῷ, ὅτι καθ᾽ ὑπερβολὴν ἐδίωκον τὴν ἐκκλησίαν τοῦ θεοῦ καὶ ἐπόρθουν αὐτήν, 1.14 καὶ προέκοπτον ἐν τῷ Ἰουδαϊσμῷ ὑπὲρ πολλοὺς συνηλικιώτας ἐν τῷ γένι μου, περισσοτέρως ζηλωτὴς ὑπάρχων τῶν πατρικῶν μου παραδόσεων.

1.15 ὅτε δὲ εὐδόκησεν ὁ θεὸς ὁ ἀφορίσας με ἐκ κοιλίας

1.1 Paul an apostle, not from men not through a man but through Jesus the anointed (one) and God *the* father, the (one) having raised them/(him) up out of dead (ones), 1.2 and all the brothers with me, to the assemblies of Galatia: 1.3 Grace and peace to ye from God our father and *the* Lord Jesus, the anointed (one), 1.4 the (one) having given himself in behalf of our sins/faults/failures, that delivers us out of the age, the evil (one) having been standing, by/according to the will of our God and father, 1.5 to whom *be* the glory/fame into the ages of the ages, truly.

1.6 I wonder/marvel because so quickly ye are removing yourselves from the (one) having called ye by grace of the anointed (one) to another/different gospel/good message, 1.7 which is another (of same kind); except some are the (ones) troubling ye and wanting to distort/pervert the good message/gospel of the anointed (one). 1.8 But even if we or a messenger/angel out of heaven should announce a good message beside/alongside what we ourselves announced to ye, let him be an execration/curse.

1.9 As we have said before, even now I say again: If anyone announces a gospel/good message *for* ye besides what ye received, let him be an execration/curse. 1.10 For now *do* I persuade men or God? Or *do* I seek for men to please? If I were still/yet pleasing/agreeable to men, I would not be a slave of the anointed (one).

1.11 For I make known to ye, brothers, the good message/gospel, the (one) having been announced/preached by me that is not according to a man/human; 1.12 for I, I neither received it from a man nor was I taught *it*, but through a revelation from Jesus, the anointed (one).

1.13 For ye heard the (thing) *about* my conduct at one time in Judaism, that according to an excess/beyond measure I was prosecuting the assembly of God and was destroying/harassing it, 1.14 and I was advancing in Judaism above/beyond many contemporaries in my race/kind, being abundantly a zealot of my ancestral traditions.

1.15 But when God, the (one) having appointed/

μητρός μου καὶ καλέσας διὰ τῆς χάριτος αὐτοῦ 1.16 ἀποκαλύψαι τὸν υἱὸν αὐτοῦ ἐν ἐμοὶ ἵνα εὐαγγελίζωμαι αὐτὸν ἐν τοῖς ἔθνεσιν, εὐθέως οὐ προσανεθέμην σαρκὶ καὶ αἵματι, 1.17 οὐδὲ ἀνῆλθον εἰς Ἱεροσόλυμα πρὸς τοὺς πρὸ ἐμοῦ ἀποστόλους, ἀλλὰ ἀπῆλθον εἰς Ἀραβίαν, καὶ πάλιν ὑπέστρεψα εἰς Δαμασκόν.

1.18 ἔπειτα μετὰ τρία ἔτη ἀνῆλθον εἰς Ἱεροσόλυμα ἱστορῆσαι Κηφᾶν, καὶ ἐπέμεινα πρὸς αὐτὸν ἡμέρας δεκαπέντε· 1.19 ἕτερον δὲ τῶν ἀποστόλων οὐκ ἶδον, εἰ μὴ Ἰάκωβον τὸν ἀδελφὸν τοῦ κυρίου. 1.20 ἃ δὲ γράφω ὑμῖν, ἰδοὺ ἐνώπιον τοῦ θεοῦ ὅτι οὐ ψεύδομαι. 1.21 ἔπειτα ἦλθον εἰ τὰ κλίματα τῆς Συρίας καὶ τῆς Κιλικίας. 1.22 ἤμην δὲ ἀγνοούμενος τῷ προσώπῳ ταῖς ἐκκλησίαις τῆς Ἰουδαίας ταῖς ἐν χριστῷ, 1.23 μόνον δὲ ἀκούοντες ἦσαν ὅτι ὁ διώκων ἡμᾶς ποτε νῦν εὐαγγελίζεται τὴν πίστιν ἥν ποτε ἐπόρθει, 1.24 καὶ ἐδόξαζον ἐν ἐμοὶ τὸν θεόν.

2.1 Ἔπειτα διὰ δεκατεσσάρων ἐτῶν πάλιν ἀνέβην εἰς Ἱεροσόλυμα μετὰ Βαρναβᾶ, συνπαραλαβὼν καὶ Τίτον· 2.2 ἀνέβην δὲ κατὰ ἀποκάλυψιν· καὶ ἀνεθέμην αὐτοῖς τὸ εὐαγγέλιον ὃ κηρύσσω ἐν τοῖς ἔθνεσιν, κατ᾽ ἰδίαν δὲ τοῖς δοκοῦσιν, μή πως εἰς κενὸν τρέχω ἢ ἔδραμον. 2.3 ἀλλ᾽ οὐδὲ Τίτος ὁ σὺν ἐμοί, Ἕλλην ὤν, ἠναγκάσθη περιτμηθῆναι· 2.4 διὰ δὲ τοὺς παρισάκτους ψευδαδέλφους, οἵτινες παρεισῆλθον κατασκοπῆσαι τὴν ἐλευθερίαν ἡμῶν ἣν ἔχομεν ἐν χριστῷ Ἰησοῦ, ἵνα ἡμᾶς καταδουλώσουσιν· 2.5 οἷς οὐδὲ πρὸς ὥραν εἴξαμεν τῇ ὑποταγῇ, ἵνα ἡ ἀλήθια τοῦ εὐαγγελίου διαμείνῃ πρὸς ὑμᾶς.

2.6 ἀπὸ δὲ τῶν δοκούντων εἶναί τι ὁποῖοί ποτε ἦσαν οὐδέν μοι διαφέρι· πρόσωπον ὁ θεὸς ἀνθρώπου οὐ λαμβάνει· ἐμοὶ γὰρ οἱ δοκοῦντες οὐδὲν προσανέθεντο,

2.7 ἀλλὰ τοὐναντίον εἰδόντες ὅτι πεπίστευμαι τὸ εὐαγγέλιον

set apart me from my mother's womb and having called through his grace took pleasure/was pleased 1.16 to reveal his son in me in order that I might announce/preach him among the ethnics, I consulted not immediately with flesh and blood, 1.17 neither went I up to Jerusalem to the apostles before me, but I went away into Arabia, and I returned again to Damascus.

1.18 Then, after three years, I went up to Jerusalem to visit Cephas, and I stayed near/with him fifteen days; 1.19 but another/a different (one) of the apostles I saw not, except James the brother of the Lord. 1.20 And what (things) I write to ye, behold that I lie not before God. 1.21 Then/after that I went into the regions/districts of Syria and Cilicia. 1.22 And I was being unknown by the face to the assemblies of Judea, to those in the anointed (one), 1.23 but they were only hearing/had only been hearing that the (one) pursuing/prosecuting us at one time now/presently he announces/preaches the faith which he was destroying/harassing at one time, 1.24 and they were glorifying God in/by me.

2.1 Then/thereupon through fourteen years I again went up to Jerusalem with Barnabas, having taken along Titus also; 2.2 but I went up according to a revelation; and I laid before them the good message/gospel which I herald/preach among the ethnics, but privately to the (ones) seeing *influential*, lest perhaps I may be running, or did run, in vain. 2.3 But not Titus, the (one) with me, being a Greek, he was compelled to be circumcised; 2.4 but because of the smuggled-in false/lying brothers, who sneaked in to spy against the liberty/freedom of us which we have in the anointed Jesus, in order that they might reduce us to slavery; 2.5 to whom we yielded not even to an hour in the subjection, that the truth of the good message/gospel might continue near/with ye.

2.6 But from those seeming to be something -- what sort they were once makes not difference to me; God receives not a face of a man -- for to me the (ones) seeing *influential* added nothing,

2.7 but on the contrary seeing that I have been

τῆς ἀκροβυστίας καθὼς Πέτρος τῆς περιτομῆς, 2.8 ὁ γὰρ ἐνεργήσας Πέτρῳ εἰς ἀποστολὴν τῆς περιτομῆς ἐνήργησεν καὶ ἐμοὶ εἰς τὰ ἔθνη,

2.9 καὶ γνόντες τὴν χάριν τὴν δοθεῖσάν μοι, Ἰάκωβος καὶ Κηφᾶς καὶ Ἰωάννης, οἱ δοκοῦντες στῦλοι εἶναι, δεξιὰς ἔδωκαν ἐμοὶ καὶ Βαρναβᾷ κοινωνίας, ἵνα ἡμεῖς εἰς τὰ ἔθνη, αὐτοὶ δὲ εἰς τὴν περιτομήν· 2.10 μόνον τῶν πτωχῶν ἵνα μνημονεύωμεν, ὃ καὶ ἐσπούδασα αὐτὸ τοῦτο ποιῆσαι.

2.11 ὅτε δὲ ἦλθεν Κηφᾶς εἰς Ἀντιόχιαν, κατὰ πρόσωπον αὐτῷ ἀντέστην, ὅτι κατεγνωσμένος ἦν. 2.12 πρὸ τοῦ γὰρ ἐλθῖν τινας ἀπὸ Ἰακώβου μετὰ τῶν ἐθνῶν συνήσθιεν· ὅτε δὲ ἦλθεν, ὑπέστελλεν καὶ ἀφώριζεν ἑαυτόν, φοβούμενος τοὺς ἐκ περιτομῆς. 2.13 καὶ συνυπεκρίθησαν αὐτῷ καὶ οἱ λοιποὶ Ἰουδαῖοι πάντες, ὥστε καὶ Βαρναβᾶς συναπήχθη αὐτῶν τῇ ὑποκρίσι. 2.14 ἀλλ' ὅτε εἶδον ὅτι οὐκ ὀρθοποδοῦσι πρὸς τὴν ἀλήθειαν τοῦ εὐαγγελίου, εἶπον τῷ Κηφᾷ ἔμπροσθεν πάντων, εἰ σὺ Ἰουδαῖος ὑπάρχων ἐθνικῶς καὶ οὐχὶ Ἰουδαϊκῶς ζῇς, πῶς τὰ ἔθνη ἀναγκάζεις Ἰουδαΐζειν;

2.15 ἡμεῖς φύσει Ἰουδέοι καὶ οὐκ ἐξ ἐθνῶν ἁμαρτωλοί, 2.16 εἰδότες δὲ ὅτι οὐ δικαιοῦται ἄνθρωπος ἐξ ἔργων νόμου ἐὰν μὴ διὰ πίστεως Ἰησοῦ χριστοῦ, καὶ ἡμῖς εἰς χριστὸν Ἰησοῦν ἐπιστεύσαμεν, ἵνα δικαιωθῶμεν ἐκ πίστεως χριστοῦ καὶ οὐκ ἐξ ἔργων νόμου, ὅτι ἐξ ἔργων νόμου «οὐ δικαιωθήσεται πᾶσα» σάρξ. 2.17 εἰ δὲ ζητοῦντες δικαιωθῆναι ἐν χριστῷ εὑρέθημεν καὶ αὐτοὶ ἁμαρτωλοί, ἆρα χριστὸς ἁμαρτίας διάκονος; μὴ γένοιτο. 2.18 εἰ γὰρ ἃ κατέλυσα ταῦτα πάλιν οἰκοδομῶ, παραβάτην ἐμαυτὸν συνιστάνω.

2.19 ἐγὼ γὰρ διὰ νόμου νόμῳ ἀπέθανον ἵνα θεῷ ζήσω.

entrusted *with* the good message/gospel of the uncircumcision, as Peter *that* of circumcision, 2.8 for the (one) working/acting in Peter into/for an apostleship of the circumcision worked/acted also in me to/for the ethnics,

2.9 and knowing the grace having been given to me, James and Cephas and John, the (ones)/those seeming to be pillars, gave to me and to Barnabas right *hands* of fellowship, that we *may be* to/for the ethnics, but they *are* to/for the circumcision; 2.10 only that we may remember the poor (ones), which even this same thing I was eager/diligent to do.

2.11 But when Cephas came to Antioch, I opposed him against *the* face/to his face, because he had been blamed/shameful. 2.12 For from the (thing) to come beforehand some from James, he was eating with the ethnics; but when they came he drew back and separated himself, fearing the (ones) from/out of circumcision. 2.13 And all the remaining Judeans joined in the pretense with him so that even Barnabas was led away/fooled by their pretense. 2.14 But when I saw that they are not straight/progress not toward the truth of the good message/gospel, I said to Cephas before *them* all: If you, you being a Judean, are living as an ethnic and not as a Judean; how *do* you compel the ethnics to *be/live* as Judeans?

2.15 We by nature/birth *are* Judeans and not out of sinful ethnics, 2.16 but having known that a man is not vindicated/justified out of works of law except/unless through faith from Jesus the anointed (one), even we, we believed in the anointed Jesus, in order that we might be vindicated/justified out of/from faith from the anointed (one) and not out of/from works of law, because from works of law every flesh will hot be vindicated/justified. 2.17 But if, seeking to be justified in/by the anointed (one) we were found also ourselves *to be* sinners, then *is* the anointed (one) a servant/minister of sin? May it not be. 2.18 For what (things) I destroyed, if I build these (things) again, I demonstrate/present myself a transgressor.

2.19 For I, because of law, I died for/by law in

χριστῷ συνεσταύρωμαι· 2.20 ζῶ δὲ οὐκέτι ἐγώ, ζῇ δὲ ἐν ἐμοὶ χριστός· ὃ δὲ νῦν ζῶ ἐν σαρκί, ἐν πίστι ζῶ τῇ τοῦ υἱοῦ τοῦ θεοῦ τοῦ ἀγαπήσαντός με καὶ παραδόντος ἑαυτὸν ὑπὲρ ἐμοῦ. 2.21 οὐκ ἀθετῶ τὴν χάριν τοῦ θεοῦ· εἰ γὰρ διὰ νόμου δικαιοσύνη, ἄρα χριστὸς δωρεὰν ἀπέθανεν.

3.1 Ὦ ἀνόητοι Γαλάται, τίς ὑμᾶς ἐβάσκανεν, οἷς κατ' ὀφθαλμοὺς Ἰησοῦς χριστὸς προεγράφη ἐσταυρωμένος; 3.2 τοῦτο μόνον θέλω μαθεῖν ἀφ' ὑμῶν, ἐξ ἔργων νόμου τὸ πνεῦμα ἐλάβετε ἢ ἐξ ἀκοῆς πίστεως; 3.3 οὕτως ἀνόητοί ἐστε; ἐναρξάμενοι πνεύματι νῦν σαρκὶ ἐπιτελεῖσθαι; 3.4 τοσαῦτα ἐπάθετε εἰκῇ; εἴ γε καὶ εἰκῇ. 3.5 ὁ οὖν ἐπιχορηγῶν ὑμῖν τὸ πνεῦμα καὶ ἐνεργῶν δυνάμις ἐν ὑμῖν ἐξ ἔργων νόμου ἢ ἐξ ἀκοῆς πίστεως; 3.6 καθὼς Ἀβραὰμ «ἐπίστευσεν τῷ θεῷ, καὶ ἐλογίσθη αὐτῷ εἰς δικαιοσύνην.» 3.7 γινώσκετε ἄρα ὅτι οἱ ἐκ πίστεως, οὗτοι υἱοί εἰσιν Ἀβραάμ. 3.8 προϊδοῦσα δὲ ἡ γραφὴ ὅτι ἐκ πίστεως τὰ ἔθνη δικαιοῖ ὁ θεὸς προευηγγελίσατο τῷ Ἀβραὰμ ὅτι «ἐνευλογηθήσονται ἐν σοὶ πάντα τὰ ἔθνη.» 3.9 ὥστε οἱ ἐκ πίστεως εὐλογοῦνται σὺν τῷ πιστῷ Ἀβραάμ.

3.10 ὅσοι γὰρ ἐξ ἔργων νόμου εἰσὶν ὑπὸ κατάραν εἰσίν· γέγραπται γὰρ ὅτι «ἐπικατάρατος πᾶς ὃς οὐκ ἐμμένει ἐν πᾶσιν τοῖς γεγραμμένοις ἐν τῷ βιβλίῳ τοῦ νόμου τοῦ ποιῆσαι αὐτά.» 3.11 ὅτι δὲ ἐν νόμῳ οὐδεὶς δικαιοῦται παρὰ τῷ θεῷ δῆλον, ὅτι «ὁ δίκαιος ἐκ πίστεως ζήσεται·» 3.12 ὁ δὲ νόμος οὐκ ἔστιν ἐκ πίστεως, ἀλλὰ «ὁ ποιήσας» αὐτὰ «ζήσεται ἐν αὐτοῖς.» 3.13 χριστὸς ἡμᾶς ἐξηγόρασεν ἐκ τῆς κατάρας τοῦ νόμου γενόμενος ὑπὲρ ἡμῶν κατάρα, γέγραπται γάρ, «ἐπικατάρατος πᾶς ὁ

order that I might live for God. I have been crucified together with the anointed (one); 2.20 and I, I live no longer, but the anointed (one) lives in me; and what I now live in flesh, I live in/by faith, in the (faith) from the son of God, the (one) having loved me and having given himself up in behalf of me. 2.21 I nullify/reject not the grace of God; for if justness/ justice *is* through law, then the anointed (one) died for nothing/freely.

3.1 O senseless/foolish Galatians, who bewitched ye, to whom Jesus the anointed (one) having been crucified was portrayed before *the* eyes? 3.2 This alone I want to learn from ye: Did ye receive the spirit from works of law or from a hearing/report of faith? 3.3 Are ye so senseless/foolish? Having been begun in spirit, are ye not being finished/matured in flesh? 3.4 Suffered ye so many things in vain/without purpose? If *so*, also still in vain. 3.5 Therefore, the (one) granting the spirit to ye and working powers among ye, *is it* from works of law or from hearing of faith? 3.6 Even as Abraham BELIEVED/OBEYED IN/FOR GOD, AND IT WAS ACCOUNTED/RECKONED TO HIM IN/FOR JUST-NESS/JUSTICE. 3.7 Ye know then that the (ones) out of faith, these/they are sons of Abraham. 3.8 And the writing, having foreseen that God justifies the ethnics out of/from faith announced the good message to Abraham beforehand: IN/BY YOU ALL THE ETHNICS WILL BE BLESSED. 3.9 For this reason the (ones)/those out of faith are blessed with the faithful Abraham.

3.10 For as many as are from works of law, they are under a curse; for it has been written: EVERY (ONE) *is* CURSED WHO PERSEVERES/ABIDES NOT IN/BY ALL THE (THINGS) HAVING BEEN WRITTEN IN/ON THE SCROLL OF THE LAW, TO DO THEM. 3.11 But *it is* clear that no one in/by law is justified beside/in the presence of God, because THE JUST (ONE) WILL LIVE OUT OF/FROM FAITH; 3.12 and the law is not from faith, but THE (ONE) HAVING MADE them WILL HIMSELF LIVE IN/BY THEM. 3.13 The anointed (one) bought us back out of the curse of the law, having himself become a curse in behalf of us, for it has been written: CURSED *is* EVERY

332

κρεμάμενος ἐπὶ ξύλου,» 3.14 ἵνα εἰς τὰ ἔθνη ἡ εὐλογία τοῦ Ἀβραὰμ γένηται ἐν Ἰησοῦ χριστοῦ, ἵνα τὴν ἐπαγγελίαν τοῦ πνεύματος λάβωμεν διὰ τῆς πίστεως. 3.15 ἀδελφοί, κατὰ ἄνθρωπον λέγω· ὅμως ἀνθρώπου κεκυρωμένην διαθήκην οὐδὶς ἀθετῖ ἢ ἐπιδιατάσσεται. 3.16 τῷ δὲ Ἀβραὰμ ἐρρέθησαν αἱ ἐπαγγελίαι καὶ τῷ σπέρματι αὐτοῦ. οὐ λέγει, καὶ τοῖς σπέρμασι, ὡς ἐπὶ πολλῶν, ἀλλ᾽ ὡς ἐφ᾽ ἑνός, «καὶ τῷ σπέρματί σου,» ὅς ἐστιν χριστός. 3.17 τοῦτο δὲ λέγω· διαθήκην προκεκυρωμένην ὑπὸ τοῦ θεοῦ ὁ μετὰ τετρακόσια καὶ τριάκοντα ἔτη γεγονὼς νόμος οὐκ ἀκυροῖ, εἰς τὸ καταργῆσαι τὴν ἐπαγγελίαν. 3.18 εἰ γὰρ ἐκ νόμου ἡ κληρονομία, οὐκέτι ἐξ ἐπαγγελίας· τῷ δὲ Ἀβραὰμ δι᾽ ἐπαγγελίας κεχάρισται ὁ θεός.

3.19 τί οὖν ὁ νόμος; τῶν παραβάσεων χάριν προσετέθη, ἄχρις οὗ ἔλθῃ τὸ σπέρμα ᾧ ἐπήγγελται, διαταγεὶς δι᾽ ἀγγέλων ἐν χιρὶ μεσίτου. 3.20 ὁ δὲ μεσίτης ἑνὸς οὐκ ἔστιν, ὁ δὲ θεὸς εἷς ἐστιν.

3.21 ὁ οὖν νόμος κατὰ τῶν ἐπαγγελιῶν τοῦ θεοῦ; μὴ γένοιτο· εἰ γὰρ ἐδόθη νόμος ὁ δυνάμενος ζῳοποιῆσαι, ὄντως ἐκ νόμου ἦν ἂν ἡ δικαιοσύνη. 3.22 ἀλλὰ συνέκλισεν ἡ γραφὴ τὰ πάντα ὑπὸ ἁμαρτίαν ἵνα ἡ ἐπαγγελία ἐκ πίστεως Ἰησοῦ χριστοῦ δοθῇ τοῖς πιστεύουσιν.

3.23 πρὸ τοῦ δὲ ἐλθῖν τὴν πίστιν ὑπὸ νόμον ἐφρουρούμεθα συνκλιόμενοι εἰς τὴν μέλλουσαν πίστιν ἀποκαλυφθῆναι. 3.24 ὥστε ὁ νόμος παιδαγωγὸς ἡμῶν γέγονεν εἰς χριστόν, ἵνα ἐκ πίστεως δικαιωθῶμεν· 3.25 ἐλθούσης δὲ τῆς πίστεως οὐκέτι ὑπὸ παιδαγωγόν ἐσμεν. 3.26 πάντες γὰρ υἱοὶ θεοῦ ἐστε διὰ τῆς πίστεως ἐν χριστῷ Ἰησοῦ.

ONE HAVING HIMSELF HANGED ON A TREE, 3.14 in order that the blessing of/from Abraham might become in/for the ethnics in/by the anointed (one), in order that we might receive the promise of the spirit through the faith. 3.15 Brothers, I speak according to a man; all the same, no one voids/sets aside or adds codicil to a covenant having been validated. 3.16 But the promises were spoken to Abraham and to the seed/offspring of him. It says not: And to the seeds/descendants as to/for many, but as to/for one: AND TO YOUR SEED/DESCENDANT, who is the anointed (one). 3.17 And I say this: The law having come into being after four hundred and thirty years invalidates/makes void not a covenant having been previously ratified by God, in/for the (thing) to abolish/set aside the promise. 3.18 For if the inheritance *is* from a law, no longer *is it* from a promise; but God has freely given *it* to Abraham through a promise.

3.19 Therefore, why/what *is* the law? It was added on account of the transgressions, until which *time* the seed/descendant to whom it has been promised might come, having been ordained through angels/messengers in/by *the* hand of a mediator. 3.20 And the mediator is not of one, but God is one.

3.21 Then *is* the law against the promises from/of God? May it not be. For if a law was given, the (law) being able to make alive/to impart life, the justice/justness would certainly be from law. 3.22 But the writing confined/imprisoned all the (things) under sin in order that the promise might be given to the (ones) believing/obeying out of faith from Jesus, the anointed (one).

3.23 But before the (thing) *for* the faith to come we were being confined, imprisoned under law, to/for the faith being about to be revealed. 3.24 So that the law has become our custodian/attendant into the anointed (one), in order that we might be vindicated/justified out of faith; 3.25 but from the (thing) of faith having come, we are no longer under a custodian/schoolmaster 3.26 For all ye are sons of God/God's sons through the faith in the anointed Jesus.

3.27 ὅσοι γὰρ εἰς χριστὸν ἐβαπτίσθητε, χριστὸν ἐνεδύσασθε· 3.28 οὐκ ἔνι Ἰουδαῖος οὐδὲ Ἕλλην, οὐκ ἔνι δοῦλος οὐδὲ ἐλεύθερος, οὐκ ἔνι ἄρρεν καὶ θῆλυ· ἅπαντες γὰρ ὑμεῖς εἷς ἐστε ἐν χριστῷ Ἰησοῦ. 3.29 εἰ δὲ ὑμεῖς χριστοῦ, ἄρα τοῦ Ἀβραὰμ σπέρμα ἐστέ, κατὰ ἐπαγγελίαν κληρονόμοι. 4.1 λέγω δέ, ἐφ᾽ ὅσον χρόνον ὁ κληρονόμος νήπιός ἐστιν, οὐδὲν διαφέρι δούλου κύριος πάντων ὤν, 4.2 ἀλλὰ ὑπὸ ἐπιτρόπους ἐστὶ καὶ οἰκονόμους ἄχρι τῆς προθεσμίας τοῦ πατρός.

4.3 οὕτως καὶ ἡμῖς, ὅτε ἦμεν νήπιοι, ὑπὸ τὰ στοιχῖα τοῦ κόσμου ἤμεθα δεδουλωμένοι· 4.4 ὅτε δὲ ἦλθεν τὸ πλήρωμα τοῦ χρόνου, ἐξαπέστιλεν ὁ θεὸς τὸν υἱὸν αὐτοῦ, γενόμενον ἐκ γυναικός, γενόμενον ὑπὸ νόμον, 4.5 ἵνα τοὺς ὑπὸ νόμον ἐξαγοράσῃ, ἵνα τὴν υἱοθεσίαν ἀπολάβωμεν.

4.6 ὅτι δέ ἐστε υἱοί, ἐξαπέστιλεν ὁ θεὸς τὸ πνεῦμα τοῦ υἱοῦ αὐτοῦ εἰς τὰς καρδίας ἡμῶν, κρᾶζον, ἀββὰ ὁ πατήρ. 4.7 ὥστε οὐκέτι εἶ δοῦλος ἀλλὰ υἱός· εἰ δὲ υἱός, καὶ κληρονόμος διὰ θεοῦ.

4.8 ἀλλὰ τότε μὲν οὐκ εἰδότες θεὸν ἐδουλεύσατε τοῖς φύσει μὴ οὖσι θεοῖς· 4.9 νῦν δὲ γνόντες θεόν, μᾶλλον δὲ γνωσθέντες ὑπὸ θεοῦ, πῶς ἐπιστρέφετε πάλιν ἐπὶ τὰ ἀσθενῆ καὶ πτωχὰ στοιχῖα, οἷς πάλιν ἄνωθεν δουλεύσε θέλετε; 4.10 ἡμέρας παρατηρεῖσθε καὶ μῆνας καὶ καιροὺς καὶ ἐνιαυτούς. 4.11 φοβοῦμαι ὑμᾶς μή πως εἰκῇ κεκοπίακα εἰς ὑμᾶς.

4.12 γίνεσθε ὡς ἐγώ, ὅτι κἀγὼ ὡς ὑμῖς, ἀδελφοί, δέομαι ὑμῶν. οὐδέν με ἠδικήσαται· 4.13 οἴδαται δὲ ὅτι δι᾽ ἀσθένιαν τῆς σαρκὸς εὐηγγελισάμην ὑμῖν τὸ πρότερον, 4.14 καὶ τὸν πιρασμὸν ὑμῶν ἐν τῇ σαρκί μου οὐκ ἐξουθενήσατε οὐδὲ ἐξεπτύσατε, ἀλλ᾽ ὡς ἄγγελον θεοῦ ἐδέξασθέ με, ὡς χριστὸν Ἰησοῦν.

4.15 ποῦ οὖν ὁ μακαρισμὸς ὑμῶν; μαρτυρῶ γὰρ ὑμῖν ὅτι

3.27 For as much as ye were baptized into the anointed (one), ye put on *as a garment* the anointed (one). 3.28 There is not Judean nor Greek, there is not slave nor free (one), there is not male and female; for ye, ye are all one in the anointed Jesus. 3.29 But if ye *be* of the anointed (one), then ye are a seed/descendant of Abraham, heirs according to *the* promise. 4.1 But I say, over so much time as the heir is an infant, he differs nothing from a slave, being lord of all, 4.2 but he is under guardians and house-managers until the time appointed from the father.

4.3 So also we, when we were infants, we were being enslaved by the elements/rudiments of the world; 4.4 but when the fullness of the time/season came, God sent forth his son, having come into being out of a woman, having come into being under law, 4.5 in order that he might buy back the (ones) under law, in order that we might receive the sonship/adoption.

4.6 And because ye are sons, God sent forth the spirit of/from his son into our hearts, crying out: Abba, the father. 4.7 So that you are no longer a slave but a son; and if a son, also an heir through God.

4.8 But then indeed, knowing not God, ye served as slaves to the gods not being/those not being Gods by nature; 4.9 and now having known God, but rather/more having been known by God, how *do* ye turn/return again to the weak and poor elements/rudiments, to which ye want/wish to be slaves again from above/anew? 4.10 Ye observe closely days and months and seasons and years/periods of time. 4.11 I fear *for* ye lest perhaps I have labored/toiled in vain to/for ye.

4.12 Become ye as/like I *am*, because I also *am* like ye, brothers, I beg of ye. Ye did me no injustice; 4.13 and ye know that because of weakness of the flesh I announced glad tidings/the good message to ye the former (time), 4.14 and ye despised not, neither spit ye out, the testing/temptation of ye in/by the flesh of me, but ye received/welcomed me as a messenger/angel from God, as the anointed Jesus.

4.15 Where then *is* your happiness? For I testify

εἰ δυνατὸν τοὺς ὀφθαλμοὺς ὑμῶν ἐξορύξαντες ἐδώκατέ μοι.

4.16 ὥστε ἐχθρὸς ὑμῶν γέγονα ἀληθεύων ὑμῖν; 4.17 ζηλοῦσιν ὑμᾶς οὐ καλῶς, ἀλλὰ ἐκκλῖσαι ὑμᾶς θέλουσιν, ἵνα αὐτοὺς ζηλοῦτε. 4.18 καλὸν δὲ ζηλοῦσθαι ἐν καλῷ πάντοτε, καὶ μὴ μόνον ἐν τῷ παρεῖναί με πρὸς ὑμᾶς,

4.19 τέκνα μου, οὓς πάλιν ὠδίνω μέχρις οὗ μορφωθῇ χριστὸς ἐν ὑμῖν·

4.20 ἤθελον δὲ παρεῖναι πρὸς ὑμᾶς ἄρτι, καὶ ἀλλάξαι τὴν φωνήν μου, ὅτι ἀποροῦμαι ἐν ὑμῖν.

4.21 λέγετέ μοι, οἱ ὑπὸ νόμον θέλοντες εἶναι, τὸν νόμον οὐκ ἀκούετε; 4.22 γέγραπται γὰρ ὅτι Ἀβραὰμ δύο υἱοὺς ἔσχεν, ἕνα ἐκ τῆς παιδίσκης καὶ ἕνα ἐκ τῆς ἐλευθέρας. 4.23 ἀλλ᾿ ὁ μὲν ἐκ τῆς παιδίσκης κατὰ σάρκα γεγέννηται, ὁ δὲ ἐκ τῆς ἐλευθέριας δι᾿ ἐπαγγελίας.

4.24 ἅτινά ἐστιν ἀλληγορούμενα· αὗται γάρ εἰσιν δύο διαθῆκαι, μία μὲν ἀπὸ ὄρους Σινᾶ, εἰς δουλίαν γεννῶσα, ἥτις ἐστὶν Ἁγάρ. 4.25 τὸ γὰρ Σινᾶ ὄρος ἐστὶν ἐν τῇ Ἀραβίᾳ, συστοιχεῖ δὲ τῇ νῦν Ἰερουσαλήμ, δουλεύει γὰρ μετὰ τῶν τέκνων αὐτῆς.

4.26 ἡ δὲ ἄνω Ἰερουσαλὴμ ἐλευθέρα ἐστίν, ἥτις ἐστὶν μήτηρ ἡμῶν·

4.27 γέγραπται γάρ, «εὐφράνθητι, στῖρα ἡ οὐ τίκτουσα· ρῆξον καὶ βόησον, ἡ οὐκ ὠδίνουσα· ὅτι πολλὰ τὰ τέκνα τῆς ἐρήμου μᾶλλον ἢ τῆς ἐχούσης τὸν ἄνδρα.»

4.28 ὑμεῖς δέ, ἀδελφοί, κατὰ Ἰσαὰκ ἐπαγγελίας τέκνα ἐσμέν. 4.29 ἀλλ᾿ ὥσπερ τότε ὁ κατὰ σάρκα γεννηθεὶς ἐδίωκε τὸν κατὰ πνεῦμα, οὕτως καὶ νῦν. 4.30 ἀλλὰ τί λέγει ἡ γραφή; «ἔκβαλε τὴν παιδίσκην καὶ τὸν υἱὸν αὐτῆς, οὐ γὰρ μὴ

for ye that if possible, having dug out your eyes, ye gave to me.

4.16 So have I therefore become your enemy, speaking truth to ye? 4.17 They are not well concerned/envious *for* ye, but they want/wish to shut ye out, that ye may be jealous *for* them. 4.18 But *it is* good to be jealous/zealous in a good (thing) always, and not only in the (thing)/at the (time) *for* me to be present with/near ye,

4.19 my children, for whom I again suffer pain until which *time* the anointed (one) might be formed in ye.

4.20 And I wanted to be present with ye just now, and to alter/change my voice, because I am perplexed/in doubt in/with ye.

4.21 Say ye to me, the (ones) wanting to be under law, hear/heed ye not the law? 4.22 For it has been written that Abraham had two sons, one out of the maidservant and one out of the free (woman). 4.23 But indeed the (one) out of the maidservant has been generated according to flesh, but the (one) out of the free (woman) through a promise.

4.24 Which (things) is being an allegory; for these are two covenants, one indeed from mount Sina, in generating slavery, which is Hagar. 4.25 For it is the mount Sina in Arabia, and it agrees with/corresponds to the present Jerusalem, for she serves as a slave with her children.

4.26 But the Jerusalem above is free, who/which is our mother;

4.27 for it has been written: BE YOU GLADDENED/ CHEERED UP, THE BARREN (ONE) NOT GIVING BIRTH; BURST YOU FORTH AND SHOUT, THE (ONE) NOT HAVING BIRTHPAINS; BECAUSE THE CHILDREN OF THE DESOLATE (ONE) *are* MANY MORE THAN OF THE (ONE) HAVING THE MAN.

4.28 But ye, brothers, ye are children of promise down from Isaac. 4.29 But even as then the (one) having been generated according to flesh was pursuing/persecuting the (one) according to spirit, so also now. 4.30 But what says the writing? THROW/PUT OUT THE MAIDSERVANT AND THE SON OF HER/HER SON, FOR BY NO MEANS SHALL THE SON OF THE MAIDSERVANT INHERIT WITH

κληρονομήσει ὁ υἱὸς τῆς παιδίσκης μετὰ τοῦ υἱοῦ» τῆς ἐλευθέρας. 4.31 διό, ἀδελφοί, οὐκ ἐσμὲν παιδίσκης τέκνα ἀλλὰ τῆς ἐλευθέρας. 5.1 τῇ ἐλευθερίᾳ ἡμᾶς χριστὸς ἠλευθέρωσεν·

στήκετε οὖν καὶ μὴ πάλιν ζυγῷ δουλίας ἐνέχεσθε. 5.2 ἴδε ἐγὼ Παῦλος λέγω ὑμῖν ὅτι ἐὰν περιτέμνησθε χριστὸς ὑμᾶς οὐδὲν ὠφελήσει. 5.3 μαρτύρομαι δὲ πάλιν παντὶ ἀνθρώπῳ περιτεμνομένῳ ὀφιλέτης ἐστὶν ὅλον τὸν νόμον ποιῆσαι. 5.4 κατηργήθητε ἀπὸ χριστοῦ οἵτινες ἐν νόμῳ δικαιοῦσθε, τῆς χάριτος ἐξεπέσατε. 5.5 ἡμεῖς γὰρ πνεύματι ἐκ πίστεως ἐλπίδα δικαιοσύνης ἀπεκδεχόμεθα.

5.6 ἐν γὰρ χριστῷ Ἰησοῦ οὔτε περιτομή τι ἰσχύει οὔτε ἀκροβυστία, ἀλλὰ πίστις δι᾽ ἀγάπης ἐνεργουμένη.

5.7 ἐτρέχετε καλῶς· τίς ὑμᾶς ἐνέκοψεν τῇ ἀληθίᾳ μὴ πίθεσθαι; 5.8 ἡ πισμονὴ οὐκ ἐκ τοῦ καλοῦντας ὑμᾶς. 5.9 μικρὰ ζύμη ὅλον τὸ φύραμα ζυμοῖ.

5.10 ἐγὼ πέποιθα εἰς ὑμᾶς ἐν κυρίῳ ὅτι οὐδὲν ἄλλο φρονήσετε· ὁ δὲ ταράσσων ὑμᾶς βαστάσει τὸ κρίμα, ὅστις ἐὰν ᾖ. 5.11 ἐγὼ δέ, ἀδελφοί, εἰ περιτομὴν ἔτι κηρύσσω, τί ἔτι διώκομαι; ἄρα κατήργηται τὸ σκάνδαλον τοῦ σταυροῦ. 5.12 ὄφελον καὶ ἀποκόψονται οἱ ἀναστατοῦντες ὑμᾶς.

5.13 ὑμεῖς γὰρ ἐπ᾽ ἐλευθερίᾳ ἐκλήθητε, ἀδελφοί· μόνον μὴ τὴν ἐλευθερίαν εἰς ἀφορμὴν τῇ σαρκί, ἀλλὰ διὰ τῆς ἀγάπης δουλεύεται ἀλλήλοις. 5.14 ὁ γὰρ πᾶς νόμος ἐν ἑνὶ λόγῳ πεπλήρωται, ἐν τῷ «ἀγαπήσεις τὸν πλησίον σου ὡς σεαυτόν.»

5.15 εἰ δὲ ἀλλήλους δάκνετε καὶ κατεσθίετε, βλέπετε μὴ ὑπὸ ἀλλήλων ἀναλωθῆτε.

5.16 λέγω δέ, πνεύματι περιπατεῖτε καὶ ἐπιθυμίαν σαρκὸς οὐ μὴ τελέσητε. 5.17 ἡ γὰρ σὰρξ ἐπιθυμεῖ κατὰ τοῦ πνεύματος, τὸ δὲ πνεῦμα κατὰ τῆς σαρκός· ταῦτα γὰρ ἀντίκειται ἀλλήλοις,

THE SON of the free (woman). 4.31 Wherefore, brothers, we are not children of a maidservant but of the free (woman). 5.1 The anointed (one) freed us/set us free for the liberty/freedom;

therefore stand ye firm and be not again subject to a yoke of slavery. 5.2 Behold, I, Paul, I say to ye that if ye be circumcised, the anointed (one) will profit you nothing. 5.3 And I testify again to every man being circumcised, he is a debtor to do the whole/entire law. 5.4 Ye who *are* being justified by law, ye were released from the anointed (one), ye fell from the grace/gift. 5.5 For we in spirit we wait for/earnestly expect a hope of justice/justness from faith.

5.6 For in/by the anointed Jesus, neither circumcision nor uncircumcision is strong/able *for* anything, but faith working/acting through agape. 5.7 Ye were running well; who hindered/detained ye not to be persuaded in/by the truth? 5.8 The persuasion *is* not from the (one) calling ye. 5.9 A little leaven/yeast leavens the whole lump/all the dough.

5.10 I, I have trusted in ye by *the* Lord that ye will set your minds on nothing else/other; but the (one) troubling ye bears/carries the judgment, whoever he/it may be. 5.11 But I, brothers, if I still herald/preach circumcision, why am I still being pursued/prosecuted? Then the stumbling block/offense of the cross has been annulled/voided. 5.12 I would that also those unsettling ye will cut themselves off.

5.13 For ye were called to liberty, brothers; only *it is* not the liberty to/for an occasion/opportunity for the flesh, but through the agape serve ye as slaves to one another. 5.14 For all the law has been fulfilled in one saying, in the (one): YOU WILL LOVE YOUR NEIGHBOR AS YOURSELF.

5.15 But if ye bite and devour/eat up one another, see/beware ye lest ye might be consumed by one another.

5.16 And I say, walk ye in spirit and ye will by no means complete/finish a desire of flesh. 5.17 For the flesh desires against the spirit, and the spirit against the flesh; for these (two/things) are opposed

ἵνα μὴ ἃ ἐὰν θέλητε ταῦτα ποιῆτε. 5.18 εἰ δὲ πνεύματι ἄγεσθε, οὐκ ἐστὲ ὑπὸ νόμον.

5.19 φανερὰ δέ ἐστιν τὰ ἔργα τῆς σαρκός, ἅτινά ἐστιν πορνία, ἀκαθαρσία, ἀσέλγια, 5.20 εἰδωλολατρεία, φαρμακία, ἔχθραι, ἔρις, ζῆλοι, θυμοί, ἐριθεῖαι, διχοστασίαι, αἱρέσις, 5.21 φθόνοι, μέθαι, κῶμαι, καὶ τὰ ὅμοια τούτοις, ἃ προλέγω ὑμῖν καθὼς προεῖπον ὅτι οἱ τὰ τοιαῦτα πράσσοντες βασιλίαν θεοῦ οὐ κληρονομήσουσιν.

5.22 ὁ δὲ καρπὸς τοῦ πνεύματός ἐστιν ἀγάπη, χαρά, εἰρήνη, μακροθυμία, χρηστότης, ἀγαθωσύνη, πίστις, 5.23 πραΰτης, ἐγκράτεια· κατὰ τῶν τοιούτων οὐκ ἔστιν νόμος. 5.24 οἱ δὲ τοῦ χριστοῦ Ἰησοῦ τὴν σάρκα ἐσταύρωσαν σὺν τοῖς παθήμασι καὶ ταῖς ἐπιθυμίαις.

5.25 εἰ ζῶμεν πνεύματι, πνεύματι καὶ στοιχῶμεν. 5.26 μὴ γινώμεθα κενόδοξοι, ἀλλήλους προκαλούμενοι, ἀλλήλοις φθονοῦντες.

6.1 Ἀδελφοί, ἐὰν καὶ προλημφθῇ ἄνθρωπος ἔν τινι παραπτώματι, ὑμεῖς οἱ πνευματικοὶ καταρτίζετε τὸν τοιοῦτον ἐν πνεύματι πραΰτητος, σκοπῶν σεαυτόν, μὴ καὶ σὺ πιρασθῇς.

6.2 ἀλλήλων τὰ βάρη βαστάζετε, καὶ οὕτως ἀναπληρώσατε τὸν νόμον τοῦ χριστοῦ.

6.3 εἰ γὰρ δοκεῖ τις εἶναί τι μηδὲν ὤν, φρεναπατᾷ ἑαυτόν· 6.4 τὸ δὲ ἔργον ἑαυτοῦ δοκιμαζέτω ἕκαστος, καὶ τότε εἰς ἑαυτὸν μόνον τὸ καύχημα ἕξει καὶ οὐκ εἰς τὸν ἕτερον· 6.5 ἕκαστος γὰρ τὸ ἴδιον φορτίον βαστάσει. 6.6 κοινωνείτω δὲ ὁ κατηχούμενος τὸν λόγον τῷ κατηχοῦντι ἐν πᾶσιν ἀγαθοῖς.

6.7 μὴ πλανᾶσθε, θεὸς οὐ μυκτηρίζετε· ὃ γὰρ ἐὰν σπείρῃ

to one another, that what ever (things) ye may want/ wish, ye may not do these (things). 5.18 But if ye are led by a spirit, ye are not under law.

5.19 But the works of the flesh are plain/clear, which are: prostitution, uncleanness/viciousness, revelry/debauchery, 5.20 idolatry, sorcery/magic, hostili-ties/enmities, strife, jealousies, angers/ passions, rivalries/selfish ambitions, divisions/ dissensions, sects/denominations, 5.21 envies/ spites, intoxications/drunks, carousings/orgies, and the (things) similar to these, which (things) I say to ye before-hand as I said before that the (ones) practicing such things will not inherit *the* kingdom of God.

5.22 But the fruit/produce of the spirit is: agape, joy, peace, patience, kindness, goodness, faith/trust, 5.23 gentleness, self-control/temperance; there is not a law against such things. 5.24 But the (ones)/those of the anointed Jesus crucified the flesh with the passions and the desires.

5.25 If we live in/by spirit, we should also agree/follow in spirit. 5.26 We should not become vainglorious (ones), provoking/challenging one another, envying one another.

6.1 Brothers, even if a man be apprehended in some trespass, ye, the spiritual (ones), ye put in order/mend the such in/by a spirit of gentleness, noticing/considering yourself, lest you, you also be tried/tempted.

6.2 Bear/carry ye the burdens of one another, and thus ye will fulfill the law of the anointed (one).

6.3 For if anyone seems/thinks to be something, being nothing, he deceives himself; 6.4 but let each (one) test/prove the work of himself, and then he will have the triumph/boast to/for himself alone and not to/for another/different (one); 6.5 for each (one) will bear/carry his own burden/load. 6.6 And let the (one) being instructed *in* the saying/word participate with the (one) instructing in all good (things).

6.7 Be ye not deceived/led astray, God is not

ἄνθρωπος, τοῦτο καὶ θερίσει· 6.8 ὅτι ὁ σπίρων εἰς τὴν σάρκα ἑαυτοῦ ἐκ τῆς σαρκὸς θερίσει φθοράν, ὁ δὲ σπίρων εἰς τὸ πνεῦμα ἐκ τοῦ πνεύματος θερίσι ζωὴν αἰώνιον. 6.9 τὸ δὲ καλὸν ποιοῦντες μὴ ἐγκακῶμεν, καιρῷ γὰρ ἰδίῳ θερίσωμεν μὴ ἐκλυόμενοι. 6.10 ἄρα οὖν ὡς καιρὸν ἔχωμεν, ἐργαζώμεθα τὸ ἀγαθὸν πρὸς πάντας, μάλιστα δὲ πρὸς τοὺς οἰκείους τῆς πίστεως.

6.11 ἴδετε πηλίκοις ὑμῖν γράμμασιν ἔγραψα τῇ ἐμῇ χειρί. 6.12 ὅσοι θέλουσιν εὐπροσωπῆσαι ἐν σαρκί, οὗτοι ἀναγκάζουσιν ὑμᾶς περιτέμνεσθε, μόνον ἵνα τῷ σταυρῷ τοῦ χριστοῦ μὴ διώκωνται· 6.13 οὐδὲ γὰρ οἱ περιτεμνόμενοι αὐτοὶ νόμον φυλάσσουσιν, ἀλλὰ θέλουσιν ὑμᾶς περιτέμνεσθαι ἵνα ἐν τῇ ὑμετέρᾳ σαρκὶ καυχήσωνται.

6.14 ἐμοὶ δὲ μὴ γένοιτο καυχᾶσθαι εἰ μὴ ἐν τῷ σταυρῷ τοῦ κυρίου ἡμῶν Ἰησοῦ χριστοῦ, δι᾽ οὗ ἐμοὶ κόσμος ἐσταύρωται κἀγὼ κόσμῳ.

6.15 ἐν γὰρ χριστῷ Ἰησοῦ οὔτε περιτομή τί ἐστιν οὔτε ἀκροβυστία, ἀλλὰ καινὴ κτίσις. 6.16 καὶ ὅσοι τῷ κανόνι τούτῳ στοιχήσουσιν, ἰρήνη ἐπ᾽ αὐτοὺς καὶ ἔλεος, καὶ ἐπὶ τὸν Ἰσραὴλ τοῦ θεοῦ.

6.17 τοῦ λοιποῦ κόπους μοι μηδὶς παρεχέτω, ἐγὼ γὰρ τὰ στίγματα τοῦ κυρίου Ἰησοῦ χριστοῦ ἐν τῷ σώματί μου βαστάζω.

6.18 ἡ χάρις τοῦ κυρίου Ἰησοῦ χριστοῦ μετὰ τοῦ πνεύματος ὑμῶν, ἀδελφοί· ἀμήν.

Πρὸς Γαλάτας

outwitted/mocked; for what ever a man/human might sow, this/the same he will also reap; 6.8 because the (one) sowing in/to/for the flesh of himself, out of the flesh he will reap decay/rotting, but the (one) sowing in/to/for the spirit, out of/from the spirit he will reap eternal life. 6.9 And we may not lose heart/despair doing the good (thing), for not losing courage/becoming weary we shall reap in its own time/season. 6.10 So therefore, as we have a time/season, let us work the good (thing) to/toward all, and especially to the family/household members of the faith.

6.11 Behold ye how I wrote to ye in large letters by/in my *own* hand. 6.12 As many as want/wish to look well/make a good show in flesh, these compel/force ye to be circumcised, only in order that they be not pursued/prosecuted for the cross of the anointed (one); 6.13 for those being circumcised, they themselves guard/keep not *the* law, but they want/wish *for* ye to be circumcised in order that they themselves might boast in your flesh.

6.14 But may it not be for me to boast except in/by the cross of our Lord Jesus the anointed (one), through whom a/*the* world has been crucified to me and I to a/*the* world.

6.15 For in the anointed Jesus, something/anything is neither circumcision not uncircumcision, but a new creature/creation. 6.16 And as many as will agree with/follow by/in this standard/rule/canon, peace and mercy *be* on them, and on the Israel of God.

6.17 Of the rest, let no one offer/cause troubles/labors for me, for I bear the marks/brands of the Lord Jesus, the anointed (one), in/on my body.

6.18 The grace of the Lord Jesus, the anointed (one), *be* with the spirit of ye, brothers; truly.

To Galatians

This it the Sinaitic New Testament, book of Ephesians.

1.1 Παῦλος ἀπόστολος Ἰησοῦ χριστοῦ διὰ θελήματος θεοῦ τοῖς ἁγίοις τοῖς οὖσι ἐν Ἐφέσῳ καὶ πιστοῖς ἐν χριστῷ Ἰησοῦ· 1.2 χάρις ὑμῖν καὶ εἰρήνη ἀπὸ θεοῦ πατρὸς ἡμῶν καὶ κυρίου Ἰησοῦ χριστοῦ.

1.3 εὐλογητὸς ὁ θεὸς καὶ πατὴρ τοῦ κυρίου καὶ σωτῆρος ἡμῶν Ἰησοῦ χριστοῦ, ὁ εὐλογήσας ἡμᾶς ἐν πάσῃ εὐλογίᾳ πνευματικῇ ἐν τοῖς ἐπουρανίοις ἐν χριστῷ, 1.4 καθὼς ἐξελέξατο ἡμᾶς ἐν αὐτῷ πρὸ καταβολῆς κόσμου, εἶναι ἡμᾶς ἁγίους καὶ ἀμώμους κατενώπιον αὐτοῦ ἐν ἀγάπῃ, 1.5 προορίσας ἡμᾶς εἰς υἱοθεσίαν διὰ Ἰησοῦ χριστοῦ εἰς αὐτόν, κατὰ τὴν εὐδοκίαν τοῦ θελήματος αὐτοῦ, 1.6 εἰς ἔπαινον δόξης τῆς χάριτος αὐτοῦ ἧς ἐχαρίτωσεν ἡμᾶς ἐν τῷ ἠγαπημένῳ, 1.7 ἐν ᾧ ἔχομεν τὴν ἀπολύτρωσιν διὰ τοῦ αἵματος αὐτοῦ, τὴν ἄφεσιν τῶν παραπτωμάτων, κατὰ τὸ πλοῦτος τῆς χάριτος αὐτοῦ, 1.8 ἧς ἐπερίσσευσεν εἰς ἡμᾶς ἐν πάσῃ σοφίᾳ καὶ φρονήσει 1.9 γνωρίσας ἡμῖν τὸ μυστήριον τοῦ θελήματος αὐτοῦ, κατὰ τὴν εὐδοκίαν αὐτοῦ ἣν προέθετο ἐν αὐτῷ 1.10 εἰς οἰκονομίαν τοῦ πληρώματος τῶν καιρῶν, ἀνακεφαλαιώσασθε τὰ πάντα ἐν τῷ χριστῷ, τὰ ἐπὶ τοῖς οὐρανοῖς καὶ τὰ ἐπὶ τῆς γῆς· ἐν αὐτῷ,

1.11 ἐν ᾧ καὶ ἐκληρώθημεν προορισθέντες κατὰ πρόθεσιν τοῦ τὰ πάντα ἐνεργοῦντος κατὰ τὴν βουλὴν τοῦ θελήματος αὐτοῦ, 1.12 εἰς τὸ εἶναι ἡμᾶς εἰς ἔπαινον δόξης αὐτοῦ τοὺς προηλπικότας ἐν τῷ χριστῷ· 1.13 ἐν ᾧ καὶ ὑμῖς ἀκούσαντες τὸν λόγον τῆς ἀληθίας, τὸ εὐαγγέλιον τῆς σωτηρίας ὑμῶν, ἐν ᾧ καὶ πιστεύσαντες ἐσφραγίσθητε τῷ πνεύματι τῆς ἐπαγγελίας τῷ ἁγίῳ, 1.14 ὅς ἐστιν ἀρραβὼν τῆς κληρονομίας ἡμῶν, εἰς ἀπολύτρωσιν τῆς περιποιήσεως, εἰς ἔπαινον δόξης αὐτοῦ.

339

1.1 Paul, an apostle of Jesus the anointed (one) through *the* will of God, to the saints being in Ephesus and to faithful (ones) in the anointed Jesus: 1.2 Grace and peace *be* to ye from God our father and *the* Lord Jesus, the anointed (one).

1.3 Blessed/praised be the God and father of our Lord and savior, Jesus the anointed (one), the (one) having blessed us with every spiritual blessing in the heavenly (places) in/by the anointed (one), 1.4 as he chose us in/by himself before *the* foundation of a world, *for* us to be saints and blameless before him in/by agape, 1.5 having preappointed us into a sonship/adoption through Jesus, the anointed (one), in/for himself, according to the pleasure/good will of his will/purpose, 1.6 into/for praise from fame/glory of his grace of which he favored us in/by the one having been loved, 1.7 in/by whom we have the release/redemption through his blood, the forgiveness/remission of the trespasses, according to the wealth of his grace/favor, 1.8 which he caused to abound to/for us in/with every wisdom and prudence/understanding, 1.9 having made known to us the mystery (religion) of his will, according to his pleasure/good will which he planned/purposed in himself 1.10 to/for a responsibility from the fullness of the times, to sum up/list the headings all the things in/by the anointed (one), the (things) over the skies/heavens and the (things) over/upon the earth; in/by him,

1.11 in/by whom we were also chosen as heirs, having been preappointed according to a purpose of the (one) working all things according to the purpose/plan of his will, 1.12 in/for the (thing) *for* us to be in/for an approbation of his fame/glory, the ones having previously hoped in the anointed (one); 1.13 in/by whom ye also, having heard the reasoning/saying of/from the truth, the good message/gospel of our salvation, in/by whom also having believed/obeyed ye were sealed/secured in/by the holy spirit of/from the promise, 1.14 which is a deposit/down payment of our inheritance, into release/redemption of the preserving/gaining, in approval/recognition of his fame/glory.

1.15 διὰ τοῦτο κἀγώ, ἀκούσας τὴν καθ' ὑμᾶς πίστιν ἐν τῷ κυρίῳ Ἰησοῦ καὶ τὴν ἀγάπην τὴν εἰς πάντας τοὺς ἁγίους, 1.16 οὐ παύομαι εὐχαριστῶν ὑπὲρ ὑμῶν μνίαν ποιούμενος ἐπὶ τῶν προσευχῶν μου, 1.17 ἵνα ὁ θεὸς τοῦ κυρίου ἡμῶν Ἰησοῦ χριστοῦ, ὁ πατὴρ τῆς δόξης, δῴη ὑμῖν πνεῦμα σοφίας καὶ ἀποκαλύψεως ἐν ἐπιγνώσει αὐτοῦ, 1.18 πεφωτισμένους τοὺς ὀφθαλμοὺς τῆς καρδίας ὑμῶν εἰς τὸ εἰδέναι ὑμᾶς τίς ἐστιν ἡ ἐλπὶς τῆς κλήσεως αὐτοῦ, τίς ὁ πλοῦτος τῆς κληρονομίας τῆς δόξης αὐτοῦ ἐν τοῖς ἁγίοις, 1.19 καὶ τί τὸ ὑπερβάλλον μέγεθος τῆς δυνάμεως αὐτοῦ εἰς ἡμᾶς τοὺς πιστεύοντας κατὰ τὴν ἐνέργιαν τοῦ κράτους τῆς ἰσχύος αὐτοῦ 1.20 ἣν ἐνήργησεν ἐν τῷ χριστῷ ἐγείρας αὐτὸν ἐκ νεκρῶν, καὶ καθίσας αὐτὸν ἐν δεξιᾷ αὐτοῦ ἐν τοῖς ἐπουρανίοις 1.21 ὑπεράνω πάσης ἀρχῆς καὶ ἐξουσίας καὶ δυνάμεως καὶ κυριότητος καὶ παντὸς ὀνόματος ὀνομαζομένου οὐ μόνον ἐν τῷ αἰῶνι τούτῳ ἀλλὰ καὶ ἐν τῷ μέλλοντι· 1.22 καὶ πάντα ὑπέταξεν ὑπὸ τοὺς πόδας αὐτοῦ, καὶ αὐτὸν ἔδωκεν κεφαλὴν ὑπὲρ πάντα τῇ ἐκκλησίᾳ, 1.23 ἥτις ἐστὶν τὸ σῶμα αὐτοῦ, τὸ πλήρωμα τοῦ τὰ πάντα ἐν πᾶσιν πληρουμένου.

2.1 Καὶ ὑμᾶς ὄντας νεκροὺς τοῖς παραπτώμασιν καὶ ταῖς ἁμαρτίαις ὑμῶν, 2.2 ἐν αἷς ποτε περιεπατήσατε κατὰ τὸν αἰῶνα τοῦ κόσμου τούτου, κατὰ τὸν ἄρχοντα τῆς ἐξουσίας τοῦ ἀέρος, τοῦ πνεύματος τοῦ νῦν ἐνεργοῦντος ἐν τοῖς υἱοῖς τῆς ἀπιθίας· 2.3 ἐν οἷς καὶ ἡμεῖς πάντες ἀνεστράφημέν ποτε ἐν ταῖς ἐπιθυμίαις τῆς σαρκὸς ἡμῶν, ποιοῦντες τὰ θελήματα τῆς σαρκὸς καὶ τῶν διανοιῶν, καὶ ἤμεθα τέκνα φύσει ὀργῆς ὡς καὶ οἱ λοιποί· 2.4 ὁ δὲ θεὸς πλούσιος ὢν ἐν ἐλέει, διὰ τὴν πολλὴν ἀγάπην αὐτοῦ ἣν ἠγάπησεν ἡμᾶς, 2.5 καὶ ὄντας ἡμᾶς νεκροὺς τοῖς

1.15 Because of this I also, having heard the faith down from ye in the Lord Jesus and/also the agape, the (one)/that to/for all the saints, 1.16 I cease/stop not giving thanks in behalf of ye, making mention upon/*in* my prayers, 1.17 that the God of our Lord Jesus, the anointed (one), the father of the fame/glory, might give to ye a spirit of wisdom and revelation by/in his knowledge, 1.18 *for* the eyes of your hearts having been enlightened in the (thing) *for* ye to know who/which is the hope of his calling/invitation, who/which *is* the the wealth of the inheritance from his fame/glory in/with the saints; 1.19 and what *is* the surpassing/outstanding greatness of his power in/for us, the (ones) having believed/obeyed according to the working/efficiency of the might of his strength/ability 1.20 which he has worked in/with the anointed (one), having raised him out of dead (ones), and having seated him at his right (hand) in the - skies/heavens, 1.21 for above every ruler and authority and power and lordship and every name being named, not only in this age but also in the coming (age); 1.22 and all (things) *are* subordinated/subjected under his feet, and he gave him a head over all (things) to/for the assembly, 1.23 which is his body, the fullness of the (one) fulfilling all the (things) in/with all.

2.1 And *for* ye, being dead (ones) in the trespasses and in your faults/sins, 2.2 in which ye formerly/at one time walked according to the age of this world, according to the leader/prince of the authority from the air, of/from the spirit of the (one) now working among/in the sons of the unbelief/disobedience; 2.3 among whom we also, we all were conducted/caused to behave formerly/at one time by the desires of the flesh of us/our flesh, doing the wills/wishes of the flesh and from the impulses/senses/minds, and we were by nature children of anger/wrath as also *are* the remaining (ones);
2.4 but God, being rich/wealthy in mercy, because of the much agape of him *with* which he loved us, 2.5 even *for* us being dead (ones) in the trespasses,

παραπτώμασιν συνεζωοποίησεν τῷ χριστῷ χάριτί ἐστε σεσῳσμένοι 2.6 καὶ συνήγειρεν καὶ συνεκάθισεν ἐν τοῖς ἐπουρανίοις ἐν χριστῷ Ἰησοῦ, 2.7 ἵνα ἐνδείξηται ἐν τοῖς αἰῶσιν τοῖς ἐπερχομένοις τὸ ὑπερβάλλον πλοῦτος τῆς χάριτος αὐτοῦ ἐν χρηστότητι ἐφ᾿ ἡμᾶς ἐν χριστῷ Ἰησοῦ.

2.8 τῇ γὰρ χάριτί ἐστε σεσῳσμένοι διὰ πίστεως· καὶ τοῦτο οὐκ ἐξ ὑμῶν, θεοῦ τὸ δῶρον· 2.9 οὐκ ἐξ ἔργων, ἵνα μή τις καυχήσηται. 2.10 θεοῦ γάρ ἐσμεν ποιήματα, κτισθέντες ἐν χριστῷ Ἰησοῦ ἐπὶ ἔργοις ἀγαθοῖς οἷς προητοίμασεν ὁ θεὸς ἵνα ἐν αὐτοῖς περιπατήσωμεν. 2.11 διὸ μνημονεύετε ὅτι ποτὲ ὑμεῖς τὰ ἔθνη ἐν σαρκί, οἱ λεγόμενοι ἀκροβυστία ὑπὸ τῆς λεγομένης περιτομῆς ἐν σαρκὶ χειροποιήτου, 2.12 ὅτι ἦτε τῷ καιρῷ ἐκείνῳ χωρὶς χριστοῦ, ἀπηλλοτριωμένοι τῆς πολιτείας τοῦ Ἰσραὴλ καὶ ξένοι τῶν διαθηκῶν τῆς ἐλιαγγελίας, ἐλπίδα μὴ ἔχοντες καὶ ἄθεοι ἐν τῷ κόσμῳ.

2.13 νυνὶ δὲ ἐν χριστῷ Ἰησοῦ ὑμεῖς οἵ ποτε ὄντες μακρὰν ἐγενήθητε ἐγγὺς ἐν τῷ αἵματι τοῦ χριστοῦ. 2.14 αὐτὸς γάρ ἐστιν ἡ εἰρήνη ἡμῶν, ὁ ποιήσας τὰ ἀμφότερα ἓν καὶ τὸ μεσότοιχον τοῦ φραγμοῦ λύσας, τὴν ἔχθραν, ἐν τῇ σαρκὶ αὐτοῦ, 2.15 τὸν νόμον τῶν ἐντολῶν ἐν δόγμασιν καταργήσας, ἵνα τοὺς δύο κτίσῃ ἐν αὐτῷ εἰς ἕνα καινὸν ἄνθρωπον ποιῶν ἰρήνην, 2.16 καὶ ἀποκαταλλάξῃ τοὺς ἀμφοτέρους ἐν ἑνὶ σώματι τῷ θεῷ διὰ τοῦ σταυροῦ, ἀποκτίνας τὴν ἔχθραν ἐν αὐτῷ.

2.17 καὶ ἐλθὼν εὐηγγελίσατο ἰρήνην ὑμῖν τοῖς μακρὰν καὶ ἰρήνην τοῖς ἐγγύς· 2.18 ὅτι δι᾿ αὐτοῦ οἱ ἀμφότεροι ἐν ἑνὶ ἔχομεν τὴν προσαγωγὴν πνεύματι πρὸς τὸν πατέρα. 2.19 ἄρα οὖν οὐκέτι ἐστὲ ξένοι καὶ πάροικοι, ἀλλὰ ἐστὲ συνπολῖται τῶν ἁγίων καὶ

he made us alive together with/in the anointed (one) -- ye have been saved/rescued in/by grace -- 2.6 he both raised up together and seated together in the heavenly (places) in/by the anointed Jesus, 2.7 in order that he might demonstrate the outstanding/surpassing wealth of his grace in the approaching/coming ages in/by kindness/goodness to/on us in/by the anointed Jesus.

2.8 For ye have been saved/rescued by the grace/gift through faith; and this not out of ye, the gift *is* from God; 2.9 not out of works, that anyone/someone boast/exalt not himself. 2.10 For we are made of God, having been created by/in the anointed Jesus, to/upon good works which God prepared beforehand that we might/should walk in/by them. 2.11 Wherefore remember ye that once ye, the ethnics in flesh, the (ones) being called uncircumcision by the (one) being called circumcision made by hand in flesh, 2.12 because ye were without the anointed (one) in that time/season, having been alienated/estranged from the citizenship of Israel and strangers from the covenants of the promise, having not hope/a hope and *being* godless (ones)/atheists in the world.

2.13 But now in/by the anointed Jesus, ye, the (ones) being afar, ye were caused to become near by the blood of the anointed (one). 2.14 For he, he is our peace, the (one) having made both the (things) one and having loosed/torn down the dividing wall of the fence, the hostility/enmity, in/with his flesh, 2.15 having abolished the law of the commands in decrees/ordinances, in order that he might create the two into one new man/human, making peace in/with him, 2.16 and he might reconcile both the (ones) in one body for God through the cross, having killed the hostility/enmity in/by himself.

2.17 And having come, he announced/preached peace to ye, to the (ones) afar and peace to the (ones) near; 2.18 because through him the both *are* in one, we have the approach/free access by/in spirit to the father. 2.19 Consequently/as a result ye are no longer strangers and aliens, but ye are fellow citizens of the saints and household members of God/mem-

οἰκεῖοι τοῦ θεοῦ, 2.20 ἐποικοδομηθέντες ἐπὶ τῷ θεμελίῳ τῶν ἀποστόλων καὶ προφητῶν, ὄντος ἀκρογωνιαίου τοῦ χριστοῦ Ἰησοῦ, 2.21 ἐν ᾧ πᾶσα οἰκοδομὴ συναρμολογουμένη αὔξει εἰς ναὸν ἅγιον ἐν κυρίῳ, 2.22 ἐν ᾧ καὶ ὑμῖς συνοικοδομεῖσθε εἰς κατοικητήριον τοῦ θεοῦ ἐν πνεύματι.

3.1 Τούτου χάριν ἐγὼ Παῦλος ὁ δέσμιος τοῦ χριστοῦ ὑπὲρ ὑμῶν τῶν ἐθνῶν 3.2 εἴ γε ἠκούσατε τὴν οἰκονομίαν τῆς χάριτος τοῦ θεοῦ τῆς δοθίσης μοι εἰς ὑμᾶς, 3.3 ὅτι κατὰ ἀποκάλυψιν ἐγνωρίσθη μοι τὸ μυστήριον, καθὼς προέγραψα ἐν ὀλίγῳ, 3.4 πρὸς ὃ δύνασθε ἀναγινώσκοντες νοῆσαι τὴν σύνεσίν μου ἐν τῷ μυστηρίῳ τοῦ χριστοῦ,

3.5 ὃ ἑτέραις γενεαῖς οὐκ ἐγνωρίσθη τοῖς υἱοῖς τῶν ἀνθρώπων ὡς νῦν ἀπεκαλύφθη τοῖς ἁγίοις ἀποστόλοις αὐτοῦ καὶ προφήταις ἐν πνεύματι, 3.6 εἶναι τὰ ἔθνη συνκληρονόμα καὶ σύσσωμα καὶ συνμέτοχα τῆς ἐπαγγελίας ἐν χριστῷ Ἰησοῦ διὰ τοῦ εὐαγγελίου, 3.7 οὗ ἐγενήθην διάκονος κατὰ τὴν δωρεὰν τῆς χάριτος τοῦ θεοῦ τῆς δοθίσης μοι κατὰ τὴν ἐνέργειαν τῆς δυνάμεως αὐτοῦ.

3.8 ἐμοὶ τῷ ἐλαχιστοτέρῳ πάντων ἁγίων ἐδόθη ἡ χάρις αὕτη, τοῖς ἔθνεσιν εὐαγγελίσασθαι τὸ ἀνεξιχνίαστον πλοῦτος τοῦ χριστοῦ, 3.9 καὶ φωτίσαι πάντας τίς ἡ οἰκονομία τοῦ μυστηρίου τοῦ ἀποκεκρυμμένου ἀπὸ τῶν αἰώνων ἐν τῷ θεῷ τῷ τὰ πάντα κτίσαντι, 3.10 ἵνα γνωρισθῇ νῦν ταῖς ἀρχαῖς καὶ ταῖς ἐξουσίαις ἐν τοῖς ἐπουρανίοις διὰ τῆς ἐκκλησίας ἡ πολυποίκιλος σοφία τοῦ θεοῦ, 3.11 κατὰ πρόθεσιν τῶν αἰώνων ἣν ἐποίησεν ἐν χριστῷ Ἰησοῦ τῷ κυρίῳ ἡμῶν, 3.12 ἐν ᾧ ἔχομεν τὴν παρρησίαν

bers of God's household, 2.20 having been built upon the foundation of the apostles and prophets, from the anointed Jesus (himself) being a/*the* cornerstone, 2.21 by whom every building being fitted together grows/increases into a holy/consecrated temple in/by *the* Lord, 2.22 by whom ye also are being fit/built together into/for a habitation/dwelling place of God by a spirit/in spirit.

3.1 On account of this I, Paul, the prisoner of the anointed (one) in behalf of ye the ethnics -- 3.2 if even ye heard the responsibility of the grace/gift of God having been given to me to/for ye, 3.3 that according to a revelation the mystery (religion) was made known to me, as I wrote before in brief, 3.4 with which reading ye are able to perceive my insight in the mystery (religion) of the anointed (one),
3.5 which in other/different generations *it* was not made known to the sons of men as it was revealed not to his holy/set apart apostles and prophets by a spirit, 3.6 *for* the ethnics to be fellow heirs and a body together and fellow partakers/sharers of the promise in/by the anointed Jesus, through the good message/gospel, 3.7 of which I was caused to become a servant/minister according to the gift of the grace of God, the (grace) having been given to me according to the working/effectiveness of his power.
3.8 This grace/favor was given to me, the least of all the saints, to announce/preach the inscrutable/inexhaustible wealth/riches of the anointed (one) to the ethnics, 3.9 and to enlighten *for* all what *is* the management/responsibility of the mystery (religion), of the (one) having been kept secret/hidden from the ages by God, by the (one) having created all the (things), 3.10 in order that it might be made known now to the rulers/leaders and to the authorities in the heavenly/celestial (places) through the assembly, the manifold/varied wisdom of God, 3.11 according to a purpose/planfrom the ages which he made with/by the anointed Jesus, the Lord of us/our Lord, 3.12 in/by whom we have the confidence/boldness and free access/clear approach in/by trust/confidence

καὶ προσαγωγὴν ἐν πεποιθήσει διὰ τῆς πίστεως αὐτοῦ.

3.13 διὸ αἰτοῦμαι μὴ ἐγκακῖν ἐν ταῖς θλίψεσίν μου ὑπὲρ ὑμῶν, ἥτις ἐστὶν δόξα ὑμῶν. 3.14 τούτου χάριν κάμπτω τὰ γόνατά μου πρὸς τὸν πατέρα, 3.15 ἐξ οὗ πᾶσα πατριὰ ἐν οὐρανοῖς καὶ ἐπὶ γῆς ὀνομάζεται, 3.16 ἵνα δῷ ὑμῖν κατὰ τὸ πλοῦτος τῆς δόξης αὐτοῦ δυνάμι κραταιωθῆναι διὰ τοῦ πνεύματος αὐτοῦ εἰς τὸν ἔσω ἄνθρωπον, 3.17 κατοικῆσαι τὸν χριστὸν διὰ τῆς πίστεως ἐν ταῖς καρδίαις ὑμῶν, ἐν ἀγάπῃ ἐρριζωμένοι καὶ τεθεμελιωμένοι, 3.18 ἵνα ἐξισχύσηται καταλαβέσθαι σὺν πᾶσι τοῖς ἁγίοις τί τὸ πλάτος καὶ μῆκος καὶ βάθος καὶ ὕψος, 3.19 γνῶναί τε τὴν ὑπερβάλλουσαν τῆς γνώσεως ἀγάπην τοῦ χριστοῦ, ἵνα πληρωθῆτε εἰς πᾶν τὸ πλήρωμα τοῦ θεοῦ. 3.20 τῷ δὲ δυναμένῳ ὑπὲρ πάντα ποιῆσαι ὑπερεκπερισσοῦ ὧν αἰτούμεθα ἢ νοοῦμεν κατὰ τὴν δύναμιν τὴν ἐνεργουμένην ἐν ἡμῖν, 3.21 αὐτῷ ἡ δόξα ἐν τῇ ἐκκλησίᾳ καὶ ἐν χριστῷ Ἰησοῦ εἰς πάσας τὰς γενεὰς τοῦ αἰῶνος τῶν αἰώνων· ἀμήν.

4.1 Παρακαλῶ οὖν ὑμᾶς ἐγὼ ὁ δέσμιος ἐν χριστῷ ἀξίως περιπατῆσαι τῆς κλήσεως ἧς ἐκλήθητε, 4.2 μετὰ πάσης ταπινοφροσύνης καὶ πραΰτητος, μετὰ μακροθυμίας, ἀνεχόμενοι ἀλλήλων ἐν ἀγάπῃ, 4.3 σπουδάζοντες τηρῖν τὴν ἑνότητα τοῦ πνεύματος ἐν τῷ συνδέσμῳ τῆς εἰρήνης· 4.4 ἓν σῶμα καὶ ἓν πνεῦμα, καθὼς καὶ ἐκλήθητε ἐν μιᾷ ἐλπίδι τῆς κλήσεως ὑμῶν· 4.5 εἷς κύριος, μία πίστις, ἓν βάπτισμα· 4.6 εἷς θεὸς καὶ πατὴρ πάντων, ὁ ἐπὶ πάντων καὶ διὰ πάντων καὶ ἐν πᾶσιν.

4.7 ἑνὶ δὲ ἑκάστῳ ἡμῶν ἐδόθη ἡ χάρις κατὰ τὸ μέτρον τῆς δωρεᾶς τοῦ χριστοῦ. 4.8 διὸ λέγει, «ἀναβὰς εἰς ὕψος ᾐχμαλώτευσεν αἰχμαλωσίαν, ἔδωκεν δόματα τοῖς ἀνθρώποις.» 4.9 τὸ δὲ ἀνέβη τί ἐστιν εἰ μὴ ὅτι καὶ κατέβη εἰς τὰ κατώτερα

through the faith of/from him.

3.13 Wherefore I ask myself not to faint in my oppressions/afflictions in behalf of ye, which is your glory/fame. 3.14 On account of this I bow my knees to the father, 3.15 from whom every family/clan in heavens/skies and upon earth/land is named, 3.16 that he might give to ye according to the wealth/riches of his fame/glory to be strengthened by power through the spirit from him in the inner man/human, 3.17 *for* the anointed (one) to dwell in your hearts through the faith, having been rooted and having been founded in agape, 3.18 that ye might be strong enough to seize/-attain/apprehend with all the saints what *is* the breadth and length and depth and height, 3.19 and to know the agape of the anointed (one) surpassing/excelling the knowledge, that ye might be filled up/fully possessed in all the fullness/completion of God. 3.20 And to the (one) being himself able to make/do superabundantly beyond all (things) which we may ourselves ask or we may think/perceive according to the power, the (one) working/being effective in us, 3.21 for him *be* the fame/glory in the assembly and in the anointed Jesus, into/for the generations of the age of the ages; truly.

4.1 Therefore I, the prisoner in *the* anointed (one), I beseech ye to walk worthily of the calling of which ye were called, 4.2 with every humility/humiliation and gentleness, with patience, enduring/bearing with one another in agape, 4.3 being diligent/zealous to keep the unity of the spirit in/by the bond/binding of the peace; 4.4 in/one body and in/one spirit, as also/even ye were called/invited in one hope from the calling/invitation of ye; 4.5 one Lord, one faith, one baptism; 4.6 one God and father of all, the one over all and through all and in all.

4.7 But the grace was given to each one of us according to the measure of the gift from the anointed (one). 4.8 Wherefore he says: HAVING GONE UP TO A HEIGHT, HE LED CAPTIVE CAPTIVITY, HE GAVE GIFTS TO THE MEN/HUMANS. 4.9 But the (thing): He went up/ascended, what is it except that also he went down/descended

μέρη τῆς γῆς; 4.10 ὁ καταβὰς αὐτός ἐστιν καὶ ὁ ἀναβὰς ὑπεράνω πάντων τῶν οὐρανῶν, ἵνα πληρώσῃ τὰ πάντα.

4.11 καὶ αὐτὸς ἔδωκεν τοὺς μὲν ἀποστόλους, τοὺς δὲ προφήτας, τοὺς δὲ εὐαγγελιστάς, τοὺς δὲ ποιμένας καὶ διδασκάλους, 4.12 πρὸς τὸν καταρτισμὸν τῶν ἁγίων εἰς ἔργον διακονίας, εἰς οἰκοδομὴν τοῦ σώματος τοῦ χριστοῦ, 4.13 μέχρι καταντήσωμεν οἱ πάντες εἰς τὴν ἑνότητα τῆς πίστεως καὶ τῆς ἐπιγνώσεως τοῦ υἱοῦ τοῦ θεοῦ, εἰς ἄνδρα τέλιον, εἰς μέτρον ἡλικίας τοῦ πληρώματος τοῦ χριστοῦ,

4.14 ἵνα μηκέτι ὦμεν νήπιοι, κλυδωνιζόμενοι καὶ περιφερόμενοι παντὶ ἀνέμῳ τῆς διδασκαλίας ἐν τῇ κυβίᾳ τῶν ἀνθρώπων ἐν πανουργίᾳ πρὸς τὴν μεθοδίαν τῆς πλάνης, 4.15 ἀληθεύοντες δὲ ἐν ἀγάπῃ αὐξήσωμεν εἰς αὐτὸν τὰ πάντα, ὅς ἐστιν ἡ κεφαλή, χριστός, 4.16 ἐξ οὗ πᾶν τὸ σῶμα συναρμολογούμενον καὶ συμβιβαζόμενον διὰ πάσης ἁφῆς τῆς ἐπιχορηγίας κατ' ἐνέργιαν ἐν μέτρῳ ἑνὸς ἑκάστου μέρους τὴ αὔξησιν τοῦ σώματος ποιεῖται εἰς οἰκοδομὴν αὐτοῦ ἐν ἀγάπῃ.

4.17 τοῦτο οὖν λέγω καὶ μαρτύρομαι ἐν κυρίῳ, μηκέτι ὑμᾶς περιπατεῖν καθὼς καὶ τὰ ἔθνη περιπατεῖ ἐν ματαιότητι τοῦ νοὸς αὐτῶν, 4.18 ἐσκοτωμένοι τῇ διανοίᾳ ὄντες, ἀπηλλοτριωμένοι τῆς ζωῆς τοῦ θεοῦ, διὰ τὴν ἄγνοιαν τὴν οὖσαν ἐν αὐτοῖς, διὰ τὴν πώρωσιν τῆς καρδίας αὐτῶν, 4.19 οἵτινες ἀπηλγηκότες ἑαυτοὺς παρέδωκαν τῇ ἀσελγείᾳ εἰς ἐργασίαν ἀκαθαρσίας πάσης ἐν πλεονεξίᾳ.

4.20 ὑμεῖς δὲ οὐχ οὕτως ἐμάθετε τὸν χριστόν, 4.21 εἴ γε αὐτὸν ἠκούσατε καὶ ἐν αὐτῷ ἐδιδάχθητε, καθώς ἐστιν ἀλήθεια ἐν τῷ Ἰησοῦ, 4.22 ἀποθέσθαι ὑμᾶς κατὰ τὴν προτέραν ἀναστροφὴν

into the lower parts of the earth?   4.10 The (one) having gone down/descended is himself also the (one) having gone up/ascended far above all the skies/heavens, in order that he might fulfill all things.

4.11   And he, he gave indeed the apostles, and also the prophets, and the evangelists, and the shepherds and teachers,   4.12 toward the fitting/equipping of the saints into/for work of service/ministry, into/for a building of the body of the anointed (one), 4.13 until all the (ones)/those we may reach/attain to the unity of the faith and of the knowledge/recognition of the son of God, into a complete/mature man, to a measure of the maturity/time of life of the fullness of the anointed (one),

4.14   in order that we may no longer be infants/babies, being tossed by waves *here and there* and being carried about by every wind of the teaching/doctrine by the trickery/gambling/dice playing of the men in shrewdness/craftiness toward/with the scheming/methodology of the deception,   4.15 but speaking truth in agape we might increase all (things) to/for him, who is the head, the anointed (one),   4.16 from whom all the body, being fitted together and being united through every ligament of the provision according to a working in a measure of each one/single part, makes the growth/increase of the body in/for a building of itself in/by agape.

4.17   Therefore I say this and I testify by *the* Lord, *for* ye no longer to walk as also the ethnics walk in vanity of their mind,   4.18 being darkened in the sense/understanding, having been alienated/estranged from the life of God, through the ignorance being in them, because of the hardness of their hearts,   4.19 who having become callous, they betrayed/delivered up themselves to the revelry/lewdness into a pursuit/working of every uncleanness in/with greediness.

4.20   But ye, thus ye learned not the anointed (one),   4.21 if even ye heard him and were taught by him, as truth is in/by Jesus,   4.22 *for* ye to lay aside/put off according to the former behavior/conduct the old man, the (one) being corrupted according to

τὸν παλαιὸν ἄνθρωπον τὸν φθιρόμενον κατὰ τὰς ἐπιθυμίας τῆς ἀπάτης, 4.23 ἀνανεοῦσθαι δὲ τῷ πνεύματι τοῦ νοὸς ὑμῶν, 4.24 καὶ ἐνδύσασθε τὸν καινὸν ἄνθρωπον τὸν κατὰ θεὸν κτισθέντα ἐν ὁσιότητι καὶ δικαιοσύνῃ τῆς ἀληθείας.

4.25 διὸ ἀποθέμενοι τὸ ψεῦδος «λαλεῖτε ἕκαστος ἀλήθειαν πρὸς τὸν πλησίον αὐτοῦ,» ὅτι ἐσμὲν ἀλλήλων μέλη.

4.26 «ὀργίζεσθε καὶ μὴ ἁμαρτάνετε·» ὁ ἥλιος μὴ ἐπιδυέτω ἐπὶ παροργισμῷ ὑμῶν, 4.27 μηδὲ δίδοτε τόπον τῷ διαβόλῳ.

4.28 ὁ κλέπτων μηκέτι κλεπτέτω, μᾶλλον δὲ κοπιάτω ἐργαζόμενος ταῖς ἰδίαις χερσὶν τὸ ἀγαθόν, ἵνα ἔχηται μεταδιδόναι τῷ χρίαν ἔχοντι.

4.29 πᾶς λόγος σαπρὸς ἐκ τοῦ στόματος ὑμῶν μὴ ἐκπορευέσθω, ἀλλ' εἴ τις ἀγαθὸς πρὸς οἰκοδομὴν τῆς χρίας, ἵνα δῷ χάριν τοῖς ἀκούουσιν.

4.30 καὶ μὴ λυπεῖτε τὸ πνεῦμα τὸ ἅγιον τοῦ θεοῦ, ἐν ᾧ ἐσφραγίσθητε εἰς ἡμέραν ἀπολυτρώσεως.

4.31 πᾶσα πικρία καὶ θυμὸς καὶ ὀργὴ καὶ κραυγὴ καὶ βλασφημία ἀρθήτω ἀφ' ὑμῶν σὺμ πάσῃ κακίᾳ.

4.32 γείνεσθε δὲ εἰς ἀλλήλους χρηστοί, εὔσπλαγχνοι, χαριζόμενοι ἑαυτοῖς καθὼς καὶ ὁ θεὸς ἐν χριστῷ ἐχαρίσατο ὑμῖν. 5.1 γείνεσθε οὖν μιμητὲ τοῦ θεοῦ, ὡς τέκνα ἀγαπητά, 5.2 καὶ περιπατεῖτε ἐν ἀγάπῃ, καθὼς καὶ ὁ χριστὸς ἠγάπησεν ἡμᾶς καὶ παρέδωκεν ἑαυτὸν ὑπὲρ ἡμῶν θυσίαν καὶ προσφορὰν τῷ θεῷ εἰς ὀσμὴν εὐωδίας.

5.3 πορνία δὲ καὶ ἀκαθαρσία πᾶσα ἢ πλεονεξία μηδὲ ὀνομαζέσθω ἐν ὑμῖν, καθὼς πρέπει ἁγίοις,

5.4 καὶ αἰσχρότης καὶ ἡ μωρολογία ἢ εὐτραπελεία, ἃ οὐκ ἀνῆκεν, ἀλλὰ μᾶλλον εὐχαριστία.

5.5 τοῦτο γὰρ ἴστε γινώσκοντες ὅτι πᾶς πόρνος ἢ

the desires of the error/deceit, 4.23 and to be renewed in the spirit of your mind, 4.24 and to put on
as a garment the new man, the (one) having been created according to God in/by holiness and justice of/from
the truth.

4.25 Wherefore having laid aside/put off the
lie, SPEAK YE TRUTH, EACH (ONE) WITH/TO HIS NEIGHBOR,
because we are members of one another.

4.26 BE YE ANGRY BUT *do* NOT SIN/FAIL; let not
the sun set on your anger/angry mood, 4.27 neither
give ye a place for the devil.

4.28 The (one) stealing let him steal no longer,
but rather let him labor, working the good (thing)
with his own hands, in order that he may have to share
with/give to the (one) having need.

4.29 Every rotten/decayed saying/word, let it
not go forth out of your mouth, but if anyone *is* good
toward building/edifying of the need, in order that it
may give grace to those hearing.

4.30 And grieve ye not the holy spirit from God,
by which ye were sealed/secured in/for a day of redemption.

4.31 Let every bitterness and wrath and anger
and clamor and slander/blasphemy be removed from ye
with every malice/ill will.

4.32 And become ye kind (ones) to one another,
compassionate (ones), giving graciously/freely to
yourselves/each other as also God by the anointed
(one) gave freely/graciously to ye. 5.1 Become ye
therefore imitators of God, as beloved children, 5.2
and walk ye in agape, as also/even the anointed (one)
loved us and gave up/betrayed himself in behalf of us,
a sacrifice and an offering for God in/for an odor of
good smell/aroma.

5.3 But prostitution and every uncleanness/vi-
ciousness or greediness, neither let it be named/ap-
pealed to among ye, as is fitting/proper for saints,

5.4 both shamefulness/baseness and the foolish
talk or coarse jesting/horse play, which (things) are
not proper, but rather thanksgiving.

5.5 For this be ye knowing that every whoremong-
er/male prostitute or unclean (one) or greedy (one),

ἀκάθαρτος ἢ πλεονέκτης, ὅ ἐστιν εἰδωλολάτρης, οὐκ ἔχει κληρονομίαν ἐν τῇ βασιλείᾳ τοῦ χριστοῦ καὶ θεοῦ.

5.6 μηδεὶς ὑμᾶς ἀπατάτω καινοῖς λόγοις, διὰ ταῦτα ἔρχεται ἡ ὀργὴ τοῦ θεοῦ ἐπὶ τοὺς υἱοὺς τῆς ἀπιθίας.

5.7 μὴ οὖν γείνεσθαι συνμέτοχοι αὐτῶν· 5.8 ἦτε γάρ ποτε σκότος, νῦν δὲ φῶς ἐν κυρίῳ· ὡς τέκνα φωτὸς περιπατεῖτε 5.9 ὁ γὰρ καρπὸς τοῦ φωτὸς ἐν πάσῃ ἀγαθωσύνῃ καὶ δικαιοσύνῃ καὶ ἀληθείᾳ 5.10 δοκειμάζοντες τί ἐστιν εὐάρεστον τῷ κυρίῳ·

5.11 καὶ μὴ συνκοινωνεῖτε τοῖς ἔργοις τοῖς ἀκάρποις τοῦ σκότους, μᾶλλον δὲ καὶ ἐλέγχεται, 5.12 τὰ γὰρ κρυφῇ γινόμενα ὑπ᾽ αὐτῶν αἰσχρόν ἐστιν καὶ λέγειν· 5.13 τὰ δὲ πάντα ἐλεγχόμενα ὑπὸ τοῦ φωτὸς φανεροῦται,

5.14 πᾶν γὰρ τὸ φανερούμενον φῶς ἐστιν.

διὸ λέγι, ἔγιρε, ὁ καθεύδων, καὶ ἀνάστα ἐκ τῶν νεκρῶν, καὶ ἐπιφαύσι σοι ὁ χριστός.

5.15 βλέπετε οὖν ἀκριβῶς πῶς περιπατεῖτε, μὴ ὡς ἄσοφοι ἀλλ᾽ ὡς σοφοί, 5.16 ἐξαγοραζόμενοι τὸν καιρόν, ὅτι αἱ ἡμέραι πονηραί εἰσιν. 5.17 διὰ τοῦτο μὴ γίνεσθε ἄφρονες, ἀλλὰ συνίετε τί τὸ θέλημα τοῦ κυρίου.

5.18 καὶ μὴ μεθύσκεσθαι οἴνῳ, ἐν ᾧ ἐστιν ἀσωτία, ἀλλὰ πληροῦσθαι ἐν πνεύματι, 5.19 λαλοῦντες ἑαυτοῖς ψαλμοῖς καὶ ὕμνοις καὶ ᾠδαῖς πνευματικαῖς, ᾄδοντες καὶ ψάλλοντες τῇ καρδίᾳ ὑμῶν τῷ κυρίῳ, 5.20 εὐχαριστοῦντες πάντοτε ὑπὲρ πάντων ἐν ὀνόματι τοῦ κυρίου Ἰησοῦ χριστοῦ τῷ θεῷ καὶ πατρί, 5.21 ὑποτασσόμενοι ἀλλήλοις ἐν φόβῳ χριστοῦ.

5.22 αἱ γυναῖκες τοῖς ἰδίοις ἀνδράσιν ὑποτασσέσθωσαν ὡς τῷ κυρίῳ, 5.23 ὅτι ἀνήρ ἐστιν κεφαλὴ τῆς γυναικὸς ὡς καὶ ὁ χριστὸς κεφαλὴ τῆς ἐκκλησίας, αὐτὸς σωτὴρ τοῦ σώματος. 5.24 ἀλλ᾽ ὡς ἡ ἐκκλησία ὑποτάσσεται τῷ χριστῷ, οὕτως καὶ αἱ

which is an idolater, has not an inheritance in the kingdom of the anointed (one) and of God.

5.6 Let no one deceive ye with empty/vain sayings/words; because of these (things) the anger of God comes upon the sons of the unbelief/disobedience.

5.7 Therefore become ye not fellow sharers/partakers of them; 5.8 for ye were darkness at one time, but now a light in *the* Lord; walk ye as children of light 5.9 -- for the fruit/product of the light *is* in every goodness and justice and truth -- 5.10 proving/testing what is acceptable/well pleasing to the Lord;

5.11 and participate/share ye not in the unfruitful/unproductive works of/from the darkness, but rather even reprove ye *them*, 5.12 for it is shameful/base even to speak *of* the secret/hidden (things) being done/becoming created by them; 5.13 but all things *are* made public/revealed being reproved/convicted under the light, 5.14 for every thing being revealed/made public is light.

Wherefore he says: Rise up, the (one) sleeping, and stand up out of the dead (ones), and the anointed (one) will shine/appear for/to you.

5.15 Therefore see/beware ye how carefully ye walk, not as unwise (ones) but as wise (ones), 5.16 buying back/making good use of the time, because the days are evil. 5.17 Become ye not foolish (ones) because of this, but understand ye what *is* the will/purpose of the Lord.

5.18 And be ye not drunk on/with wine, in which is wantonness/wild dissipation, but be ye filled with/by a spirit, 5.19 speaking to yourselves in psalms and hymns and spiritual songs, singing odes and singing praise in your heart to the Lord, 5.20 giving thanks always in behalf of all in *the* name of the Lord Jesus, the anointed (one), to the God and father, 5.21 being subjected to one another in fear of the anointed (one).

5.22 Let the women subject themselves to their own men as to the Lord, 5.23 because a man is head of the woman as also the anointed (one) *is* head of the assembly, he *being* a savior of the body. 5.24 But as the assembly is subordinated to the anointed (one), so

γυναῖκες τοῖς ἀνδράσιν ἐν παντί.

5.25 οἱ ἄνδρες, ἀγαπᾶτε τὰς γυναῖκας, καθὼς καὶ ὁ χριστὸς ἠγάπησεν τὴν ἐκκλησίαν καὶ ἑαυτὸν παρέδωκεν ὑπὲρ αὐτῆς, 5.26 ἵνα αὐτὴν ἁγιάσῃ καθαρίσας τῷ λουτρῷ τοῦ ὕδατος ἐν ῥήματι, 5.27 ἵνα παραστήσῃ αὐτὸς ἑαυτῷ ἔνδοξον τὴν ἐκκλησίαν, μὴ ἔχουσαν σπίλον ἢ ῥυτίδα ἤ τι τῶν τοιούτων, ἀλλ' ἵνα ᾖ ἁγία καὶ ἄμωμος. 5.28 οὕτως ὀφίλουσιν οἱ ἄνδρες ἀγαπᾶν τὰς ἑαυτῶν γυναῖκας ὡς τὰ ἑαυτῶν σώματα. ὁ ἀγαπῶν τὴν ἑαυτοῦ γυναῖκα ἑαυτὸν ἀγαπᾷ, 5.29 οὐδὶς γάρ ποτε τὴν σάρκα αὐτοῦ ἐμίσησεν, ἀλλ' ἐκτρέφει καὶ θάλπει αὐτήν, καθὼς καὶ ὁ χριστὸς τὴν ἐκκλησίαν, 5.30 ὅτι μέλη ἐσμὲν τοῦ σώματος αὐτοῦ. 5.31 «ἀντὶ τούτου καταλίψι ἄνθρωπος τὸν πατέρα καὶ τὴν μητέρα καὶ προσκολληθήσεται πρὸς τῇ γυναῖκα, καὶ ἔσονται οἱ δύο εἰς σάρκα μίαν.»

5.32 τὸ μυστήριον τοῦτο μέγα ἐστίν, ἐγὼ δὲ λέγω εἰς χριστὸν καὶ εἰς τὴν ἐκκλησίαν. 5.33 πλὴν καὶ ὑμῖς οἱ καθ' ἕνα ἕκαστος τὴν ἑαυτοῦ γυναῖκα οὕτως ἀγαπάτω ὡς ἑαυτόν, ἡ δὲ γυνὴ ἵνα φοβῆται τὸν ἄνδρα.

6.1 Τὰ τέκνα, ὑπακούετε τοῖς γονεῦσιν ὑμῶν ἐν κυρίῳ, τοῦτο γάρ ἐστιν δίκαιον. 6.2 «τίμα τὸν πατέρα σου καὶ τὴν μητέρα,» ἥτις ἐστὶν ἐντολὴ πρώτη ἐν ἐπαγγελίᾳ, 6.3 «ἵνα εὖ σοι γένηται καὶ ἔσῃ μακροχρόνιος ἐπὶ τῆς γῆς.»

6.4 καὶ οἱ πατέρες, μὴ παροργίζετε τὰ τέκνα ὑμῶν, ἀλλὰ ἐκτρέφεται αὐτὰ ἐνὶ παιδίᾳ καὶ νουθεσίᾳ κυρίου.

6.5 οἱ δοῦλοι, ὑπακούετε τοῖς κατὰ σάρκα κυρίοις μετὰ φόβου καὶ τρόμου ἐν ἁπλότητι καρδίας ὑμῶν ὡς τῷ χριστῷ, 6.6 μὴ κατ' ὀφθαλμοδουλίαν ὡς ἀνθρωπάρεσκοι ἀλλ' ὡς δοῦλοι χριστοῦ ποιοῦντες τὸ θέλημα τοῦ θεοῦ ἐκ ψυχῆς, 6.7 μετ' εὐνοίας δουλεύοντες, ὡς τῷ κυρίῳ καὶ οὐκ ἀνθρώποις, 6.8 εἰδότες ὅτι, ἐάν ποιήσῃ ἕκαστος ἀγαθόν, τοῦτο κομίσεται παρὰ κυρίου, εἴτε

also *are* the women to the men in every (thing).

5.25 *For* the men, love ye the women, as also the anointed (one) loved the assembly and gave up/handed over himself in behalf of her, 5.26 in order that he might sanctify her, having cleansed *her* by the washing of the water in/by word/rhetoric, 5.27 in order that he, he might present to himself the honored/eminent assembly, not having a spot or wrinkle or any of the such (things), but that it may be holy and blameless. 5.28 Thus/so the men are obligated to love the women of themselves as the bodies of themselves. The (one) loving the woman of himself loves himself, 5.29 for no one/(man) at any time hated the flesh of himself, but he nourishes/feeds and cherishes/warms it, as also the anointed (one) the assembly, 5.30 because we are members of his body. 5.31 FOR THIS A MAN/HUMAN WILL LEAVE/FORSAKE THE FATHER AND THE MOTHER AND HE WILL BE JOINED/DEVOTED TO HIS WOMAN, AND THE TWO WILL BE IN ONE FLESH.

5.32 This mystery (religion) is great, and I, I say/speak in the anointed (one) and in/to the assembly. 5.33 But also/even ye, the (ones) one by one, let each (one) so love the woman of himself as himself, and the woman that she fears the man.

6.1 *For* the children. obey ye your parents in the Lord, for this is just, 6.2 HONOR YOUR FATHER AND/ALSO THE MOTHER, which is a/*the* first command with a promise, 6.3 IN ORDER THAT IT MIGHT BECOME WELL FOR YOU AND YOU WILL BE A LONG TIME UPON THE EARTH/LAND.

6.4 And *for* the fathers, make ye not angry your children, but raise/rear ye them in/by the training/discipline and admonition of *the* Lord.

6.5 *For* the slaves, obey ye the lords according to/by flesh with fear and trembling in/by sincerity of your heart as for the anointed (one), 6.6 not according to eye service/what appears as men-pleasers/good to people but as slaves of the anointed (one) doing the will of God out of life/soul, 6.7 serving as slaves with good will/enthusiasm, as for the Lord and not for men/humans, 6.8 knowing that if each (one) might do/make good, this he will get back from the

δοῦλος εἴτε ἐλεύθερος.

6.9 καὶ οἱ κύριοι, τὰ αὐτὰ ποιεῖτε πρὸς αὐτούς, ἀνιέντες τὴν ἀπιλήν, εἰδότες ὅτι καὶ αὐτῶν καὶ ὑμῶν ὁ κύριός ἐστιν ἐν οὐρανῶ, καὶ προσωπολημψία οὐκ ἔστιν παρ' αὐτῷ.

6.10 τοῦ λοιποῦ ἐνδυναμοῦσθαι ἐν κυρίῳ καὶ ἐν τῷ κράτι τῆς ἰσχύος αὐτοῦ. 6.11 ἐνδύσασθε τὴν πανοπλίαν τοῦ θεοῦ πρὸς τὸ δύνασθαι ὑμᾶς στῆναι πρὸς τὰς μεθοδίας τοῦ διαβόλου· 6.12 ὅτι οὐκ ἔστιν ἡμῖν ἡ πάλη πρὸς αἷμα καὶ σάρκα, ἀλλὰ πρὸς τὰς ἀρχάς, πρὸς τὰς ἐξουσίας, πρὸς τοὺς κοσμοκράτορας τοῦ σκότους τούτου, πρὸς τὰ πνευματικὰ τῆς πονηρίας ἐν τοῖς ἐπουρανίοις.

6.13 διὰ τοῦτο ἀναλάβετε τὴν πανοπλίαν τοῦ θεοῦ, ἵνα δυνηθῆτε ἀντιστῆναι ἐν τῇ ἡμέρᾳ τῇ πονηρᾷ καὶ ἅπαντα κατεργασάμενοι στῆναι.

6.14 στῆτε οὖν περιζωσάμενοι τὴν ὀσφὺν ὑμῶν ἐν ἀληθίᾳ, καὶ ἐνδυσάμενοι τὸν θώρακα τῆς δικαιοσύνης, 6.15 καὶ ὑποδησάμενοι τοὺς πόδας ἐν ἑτοιμασίᾳ τοῦ εὐαγγελίου τῆς εἰρήνης, 6.16 ἐν πᾶσιν ἀναλαβόντες τὸν θυρεὸν τῆς πίστεως, ἐν ᾧ δυνήσεσθαι πάντα τὰ βέλη τοῦ πονηροῦ τὰ πεπυρωμένα σβέσαι· 6.17 καὶ τὴν περικεφαλαίαν τοῦ σωτηρίου δέξασθε, καὶ τὴν μάχαιραν τοῦ πνεύματος, ὅ ἐστιν ῥῆμα θεοῦ, 6.18 διὰ πάσης προσευχῆς καὶ δεήσεως.

προσευχόμενοι ἐν παντὶ καιρῷ ἐν πνεύματι, καὶ εἰς αὐτὸ ἀγρυπνοῦντες ἐν πάσῃ προσκαρτερήσει καὶ δεήσει περὶ πάντων τῶν ἁγίων, 6.19 καὶ ὑπὲρ ἐμοῦ, ἵνα δοθῇ μοι λόγος ἐν ἀνοίξει τοῦ στόματός μου, ἐν παρρησίᾳ γνωρίσαι τὸ μυστήριον τοῦ εὐαγγελίου 6.20 ὑπὲρ οὗ πρεσβεύω ἐν ἁλύσει, ἵνα παρρησιάσωμαι ἐν αὐτῷ ὡς δεῖ με λαλῆσαι. 6.21 ἵνα δὲ καὶ

Lord, whether a slave or a free (one).

6.9 And the lords/masters, do ye the same to/toward them, ceasing from the threat, knowing that the Lord of both them and ye is in heaven, and there is not partiality with/beside him.

6.10 Of the rest, be ye strengthened/enabled in/by *the* Lord and in/by the might/dominion of his strength. 6.11 Put ye on/wear ye the armor/panoply of God toward the (thing) *for* ye to be able to stand with the methods/wiles of the devil; 6.12 because the struggle/wrestling is not with blood and flesh, but with the rulers, with the authorities, with the world rulers/powers of this darkness, with the spiritual (things) of the evil/wickedness in the heavenly (places).

6.13 Because of this, take ye up the armor/panoply of God, in order that ye might be enabled to resist in the evil day and to stand firm, having yourselves worked out/subdued all (things).

6.14 Therefore stand ye firm having girded around the loin of ye in/with truth, and having put on yourselves the breast plate of the justness/justice, 6.15 and having bound sandals on yourselves on the feet in/with a readiness of the good message/gospel of the peace, 6.16 in all (things) having taken up the shield of the faith, by which ye will be strengthened/enabled to put out/quench all the arrows having been fired/burning from the evil (one); 6.17 and receive ye/take ye in hand the helmet of the salvation/deliverance, and the sword of the spirit, which is a word from God, 6.18 through every prayer and petition

be ye praying in every season/time in spirit, and being watchful/alert in/to it/same by every perseverance and petition concerning all the saints, 6.19 and in behalf of me, that a saying/word might be given to me by an opening of my mouth, to make known with boldness/free speech the mystery (religion) of the good message/gospel 6.20 over which I am an ambassador in/with a chain, in order that I might speak freely/boldly in it/same as it is necessary *for* me to speak. 6.21 And in order that ye, ye also might know

ὑμεῖς εἰδῆτε τὰ κατ' ἐμέ, τί πράσσω, πάντα γνωρίσει ὑμῖν Τυχικὸς ὁ ἀγαπητὸς ἀδελφὸς καὶ πιστὸς διάκονος ἐν κυρίῳ, 6.22 ὃν ἔπεμψα πρὸς ὑμᾶς εἰς αὐτὸ τοῦτο ἵνα γνῶτε τὰ περὶ ἡμῶν καὶ παρακαλέσῃ τὰς καρδίας ὑμῶν. 6.23 εἰρήνη τοῖς ἀδελφοῖς καὶ ἀγάπη μετὰ πίστεως ἀπὸ θεοῦ πατρὸς καὶ κυρίου Ἰησοῦ χριστοῦ.

6.24 ἡ χάρις μετὰ πάντων τῶν ἀγαπώντων τὸν κύριον ἡμῶν Ἰησοῦν χριστὸν ἐν ἀφθαρσίᾳ. ἀμήν.

Πρὸς Ἐφεσιόυς

the (things) down from/by me, what I practice, Tychicus, the beloved brother and faithful servant/minister
in *the* Lord, will make known all (things) to ye, 6.22
whom I sent to ye in/for this very thing in order that
ye might know the (things) concerning us and he might
encourage your hearts.

6.23 Peace *be* to the brothers and agape with
faith from God *the* father and from *the* Lord Jesus, the
anointed (one).

6.24 The grace *be* with all those loving our Lord
Jesus, the anointed (one) in immortality. Truly.

To Ephesians

This is the Sinaitic New Testament, book of Philippians.

1.1 Παῦλος καὶ Τιμόθεος δοῦλοι χριστοῦ Ἰησοῦ πᾶσιν τοῖς ἁγίοις ἐν χριστῷ Ἰησοῦ τοῖς οὖσιν ἐν Φιλίπποις σὺν ἐπισκόποις καὶ διακόνοις· 1.2 χάρις ὑμῖν καὶ εἰρήνη ἀπὸ θεοῦ πατρὸς ἡμῶν καὶ κυρίου Ἰησοῦ χριστοῦ.

1.3 εὐχαριστῶ τῷ θεῷ μου ἐπὶ πάσῃ τῇ μνείᾳ ὑμῶν, 1.4 πάντοτε ἐν πάσῃ δεήσει μου ὑπὲρ πάντων ὑμῶν μετὰ χαρᾶς τὴν δέησιν ποιούμενος, 1.5 ἐπὶ τῇ κοινωνίᾳ ὑμῶν εἰς τὸ εὐαγγέλιον ἀπὸ τῆς πρώτης ἡμέρας ἄχρι τοῦ νῦν,

1.6 πεποιθὼς αὐτὸ τοῦτο, ὅτι ὁ ἐναρξάμενος ἐν ὑμῖν ἔργον ἀγαθὸν ἐπιτελέσι ἄχρι ἡμέρας χριστοῦ Ἰησοῦ· 1.7 καθώς ἐστιν δίκαιον ἐμοὶ τοῦτο φρονεῖν ὑπὲρ πάντων ὑμῶν, διὰ τὸ ἔχειν με ἐν τῇ καρδίᾳ ὑμᾶς, ἔν τε τοῖς δεσμοῖς μου καὶ ἐν τῇ ἀπολογίᾳ καὶ βεβαιώσει τοῦ εὐαγγελίου συνκοινωνούς μου τῆς χάριτος πάντας ὑμᾶς ὄντας.

1.8 μάρτυς γάρ μου ὁ θεός, ὡς ἐπιποθῶ πάντας ὑμᾶς ἐν σπλάγχνοις χριστοῦ Ἰησοῦ. 1.9 καὶ τοῦτο προσεύχομαι, ἵνα ἡ ἀγάπη ὑμῶν ἔτι μᾶλλον καὶ μᾶλλον περισσεύῃ ἐν ἐπιγνώσει καὶ πάσῃ αἰσθήσει, 1.10 εἰς τὸ δοκιμάζειν ὑμᾶς τὰ διαφέροντα, ἵνα ἦτε εἰλικρινεῖς καὶ ἀπρόσκοποι εἰς ἡμέραν χριστοῦ, 1.11 πεπληρωμένοι καρπὸν δικαιοσύνης τὸν διὰ Ἰησοῦ χριστοῦ εἰς δόξαν καὶ ἔπαινον θεοῦ.

1.12 γεινώσκιν δὲ ὑμᾶς βούλομαι, ἀδελφοί, ὅτι τὰ κατ᾽ ἐμὲ μᾶλλον εἰς προκοπὴν τοῦ εὐαγγελίου ἐλήλυθεν, 1.13 ὥστε τοὺς δεσμούς μου φανεροὺς ἐν τῷ χριστῷ γεγόνεναι ἐν ὅλῳ τῷ πραιτωρίῳ καὶ τοῖς λοιποῖς πάσιν, 1.14 καὶ τοὺς πλείονας τῶν ἀδελφῶν ἐν κυρίῳ πεποιθότας τοῖς δεσμοῖς μου περισσοτέρως τολμᾶν ἀφόβως τὸν λόγον τοῦ θεοῦ λαλῖν. 1.15 τινὲς μὲν καὶ διὰ φθόνον καὶ ἔριν, τινὲς δὲ καὶ δι᾽ εὐδοκίαν τὸν χριστὸν κηρύσσειν·

1.16 οἱ μὲν ἐξ ἀγάπης, εἰδότες ὅτι εἰς ἀπολογίαν τοῦ εὐαγγελίου κεῖμαι, 1.17 οἱ δὲ ἐξ ἐριθείας τὸν χριστὸν

1.1   Paul and Timothy, slaves of the anointed Jesus, to all the saints in the anointed Jesus, those being in Philippi with overseers and servants/waiters; 1.2 Grace to ye and peace from God our father and *the* Lord Jesus, the anointed (one).
1.3   I give thanks to my God at every mention/remembrance of ye,   1.4 always in every petition from me, making the petition in behalf of ye with joy,   1.5 over/on your fellowship in the good message/gospel from the first day until the present,
1.6   having trusted *for* this same (thing), that the (one) having begun a good work in you will finish/complete *it* until a day of the anointed Jesus; 1.7 as it is just for me to think this in behalf of ye all, because of the (thing) *for* me to have ye in the heart, both in/by my bonds and in/by the defense and firm establishment of the good message/gospel *for* all ye being partners of my grace/gift/favor.
1.8   For God *is* my witness, as I long for all ye in/with compassions of the anointed Jesus.   1.9 And I pray *for* this, that the agape of ye may still abound/increase more and more in recognition/full knowledge and every perception/experience,   1.10 in the (thing) *for* ye to prove/test the (things) being different in order that ye may be unmixed/pure and without offense in a/*the* day of the anointed (one),   1.11 having been filled *with* the fruit/product of justice through Jesus the anointed (one) in fame/glory and praise of God.
1.12   And I wish/will *for* ye to know, brothers, that the (things) by/down from me have come in/for advancement/progress of the good message/gospel.   1.13 so as *for* my bonds to become plain/clear in the anointed (one) in the whole praetorium and to all the rest, 1.14 and *for* the most of the brothers in *the* Lord, having trusted *me* in my bonds, to dare more abundantly to speak the saying/word of God fearlessly.   1.15 And some indeed herald/preach the anointed (one) because of envy and strife, but also some because of/through good will;
1.16   the (ones) indeed out of agape, knowing that I am laid *up/aside* to/for a defense of the good message/gospel,   1.17 but the (others) out of conten-

καταγγέλλουσιν, οὐχ ἁγνῶς, οἰόμενοι θλῖψιν ἐγείρειν τοῖς δεσμοῖς μου.

1.18 τί γάρ; πλὴν ὅτι παντὶ τρόπῳ, εἴτε προφάσει εἴτε ἀληθίᾳ, χριστὸς καταγγέλλεται, καὶ ἐν τούτῳ χαίρω· ἀλλὰ καὶ χαρήσομαι, 1.19 οἶδα γὰρ ὅτι τοῦτό μοι ἀποβήσεται εἰς σωτηρίαν διὰ τῆς ὑμῶν δεήσεως καὶ ἐπιχορηγίας τοῦ πνεύματος Ἰησοῦ χριστοῦ, 1.20 κατὰ τὴν ἀποκαραδοκίαν καὶ ἐλπίδα μου ὅτι ἐν οὐδενὶ αἰσχυνθήσομαι, ἀλλ' ἐν πάσῃ παρρησίᾳ ὡς πάντοτε καὶ νῦν μεγαλυνθήσεται χριστὸς ἐν τῷ σώματί μου, εἴτε διὰ ζωῆς εἴτε διὰ θανάτου. 1.21 ἐμοὶ γὰρ τὸ ζῆν χριστὸς καὶ τὸ ἀποθανεῖν κέρδος. 1.22 εἰ δὲ τὸ ζῆν ἐν σαρκί, τοῦτό μοι καρπὸς ἔργου· καὶ τί αἱρήσομαι οὐ γνωρίζω. 1.23 συνέχομαι δὲ ἐκ τῶν δύο, τὴν ἐπιθυμίαν ἔχων εἰς τὸ ἀναλῦσαι καὶ σὺν χριστῷ εἶναι, πολλῷ μᾶλλον κρῖσσον· 1.24 τὸ δὲ ἐπιμένειν τῇ σαρκὶ ἀναγκαιότερον δι' ὑμᾶς.

1.25 καὶ τοῦτο πεποιθὼς οἶδα ὅτι μενῶ καὶ παραμενῶ πᾶσιν ὑμῖν εἰς τὴν ὑμῶν προκοπὴν καὶ χαρὰν τῆς πίστεως ὑμῶν, 1.26 ἵνα τὸ καύχημα ὑμῶν περισσεύῃ ἐν χριστῷ Ἰησοῦ ἐν ἐμοὶ διὰ τῆς ἐμῆς παρουσίας πάλιν πρὸς ὑμᾶς.

1.27 μόνον ἀξίως τοῦ εὐαγγελίου τοῦ χριστοῦ πολιτεύεσθαι, ἵνα εἴτε ἐλθὼν καὶ εἰδὼν ὑμᾶς εἴτε ἀπὼν ἀκούω τὰ περὶ ὑμῶν, ὅτι στήκετε ἐν ἑνὶ πνεύματι, μιᾷ ψυχῇ συναθλοῦντες τῇ πίστι τοῦ εὐαγγελίου, 1.2δ καὶ μὴ πτυρόμενοι ἐν μηδενὶ ὑπὸ τῶν ἀντικειμένων, ἥτις ἐστὶν αὐτοῖς ἔνδειξις ἀπωλίας, ὑμῶν δὲ σωτηρίας, καὶ τοῦτο ἀπὸ θεοῦ· 1.29 ὅτι ὑμῖν ἐχαρίσθη τὸ ὑπὲρ χριστοῦ, οὐ μόνον τὸ εἰς αὐτὸν πιστεύειν ἀλλὰ καὶ τὸ ὑπὲρ αὐτοῦ πάσχειν, 1.30 τὸν αὐτὸν ἀγῶνα ἔχοντες οἷον εἴδετε ἐν ἐμοὶ καὶ νῦν ἀκούετε ἐν ἐμοί.

tion/self interest/rivalry proclaim the anointed (one), not sincerely/purely, supposing to raise up oppression/affliction for my bonds.

1.18 For what? Only that in every way/manner, whether in pretense or in truth, the anointed (one) is proclaimed, and I rejoice in this; but I shall also rejoice, 1.19 for I know that this will turn out/result in salvation for me through the entreaty of ye and support from the spirit of/from Jesus, the anointed (one), 1.20 according to the eager expectation and my hope that in/by nothing shall I be shamed, but as always with all confidence/free speaking also now the anointed (one) will be magnified in my body, whether through life or through death. 1.21 For to me the (thing) to live *is* the anointed (one) and the (thing) to die *is* gain. 1.22 But if the (thing) to live *is* in flesh, this to me *is* a fruit/product of work; and I make not known what I shall choose. 1.23 But I am distressed/hard pressed from the two, having the desire to/for the (thing) to depart and to be with the anointed (one), for much more better; 1.24 but the (thing) to continue in the flesh *is* more necessary because of ye.

1.25 And having trusted this I know that I shall abide/remain and shall continue alongside all ye in/for your advancement/progress and joy of/from your faith, 1.26 in order that your triumph/boast may abound in the anointed Jesus by me through my coming again to ye.

1.27 Only ye conduct yourselves worthily of the good message/gospel of the anointed (one), in order that whether having come and seen ye or being absent I hear the (things) about ye, that ye stand firmly in one spirit, in one life/soul struggling together for the faith of the good message/gospel, 1.28 and not being scared in nothing by those opposing, which is evidence of destruction to them, but of your salvation, and this *is* from God; 1.29 because the (thing) was given freely to ye in behalf of the anointed (one), not only *for* the (thing) to believe in him but also *for* the (thing) to suffer in behalf of him, 1.30 having the same struggle/race which sort ye saw in me

2.1 Εἴ τις οὖν παράκλησις ἐν χριστῷ, εἴ τι παραμύθιον ἀγάπης, εἴ τις κοινωνία πνεύματος, εἴ τις σπλάγχνα καὶ οἰκτιρμοί, 2.2 πληρώσατέ μου τὴν χαρὰν ἵνα τὸ αὐτὸ φρονῆτε, τὴν αὐτὴν ἀγάπην ἔχοντες, σύμψυχοι, τὸ αὐτὸ φρονοῦντες, 2.3 μηδὲν κατ' ἐριθίαν μηδὲ κατὰ κενοδοξίαν, ἀλλὰ τῇ ταπινοφροσύνῃ ἀλλήλους ἡγούμενοι ὑπερέχοντας ἑαυτῶν, 2.4 μὴ τὰ ἑαυτῶν ἕκαστος σκοποῦντες, ἀλλὰ καὶ τὰ ἑτέρων ἕκαστοι.

2.5 τοῦτο φρονεῖτε ἐν ὑμῖν ὃ καὶ ἐν χριστῷ Ἰησοῦ, 2.6 ὃς ἐν μορφῇ θεοῦ ὑπάρχων οὐχ ἁρπαγμὸν ἡγήσατο τὸ εἶναι ἴσα θεῷ, 2.7 ἀλλὰ ἑαυτὸν ἐκένωσεν μορφὴν δούλου λαβών, ἐν ὁμοιώματι ἀνθρώπων γενόμενος· καὶ σχήματι εὑρεθεὶς ὡς ἄνθρωπος 2.8 ἐταπίνωσεν ἑαυτὸν γενόμενος ὑπήκοος μέχρι θανάτου, θανάτου δὲ τοῦ σταυροῦ.

2.9 διὸ καὶ ὁ θεὸς αὐτὸν ὑπερύψωσεν καὶ ἐχαρίσατο αὐτῷ τὸ ὄνομα τὸ ὑπὲρ πᾶν ὄνομα, 2.10 ἵνα ἐν τῷ ὀνόματι Ἰησοῦ πᾶν γόνυ κάμψῃ ἐπουρανίων καὶ ἐπιγίων καὶ καταχθονίων, 2.11 καὶ πᾶσα γλῶσσα ἐξομολογήσητε ὅτι κύριος Ἰησοῦς χριστὸς εἰς δόξαν θεοῦ πατρός.

2.12 ὥστε, ἀγαπητοί μου, καθὼς πάντοτε ὑπηκούσατε, μὴ ὡς ἐν τῇ παρουσίᾳ μου μόνον ἀλλὰ νῦν πολλῷ μᾶλλον ἐν τῇ ἀπουσίᾳ μου, μετὰ φόβου καὶ τρόμου τὴν ἑαυτῶν σωτηρίαν κατεργάζεσθε· 2.13 θεὸς γάρ ἐστιν ὁ ἐνεργῶν ἐν ὑμῖν καὶ τὸ θέλειν καὶ τὸ ἐνεργεῖν ὑπὲρ τῆς εὐδοκίας.

2.14 πάντα ποιεῖτε χωρὶς γογγυσμῶν καὶ διαλογισμῶν, 2.15 ἵνα γένησθε ἄμεμπτοι καὶ ἀκαίρεοι, τέκνα θεοῦ ἄμωμα μέσον γενεᾶς σκολιᾶς καὶ διεστραμμένης, ἐν οἷς φαίνεσθε ὡς φωστῆρες ἐν κόσμῳ, 2.16 λόγον ζωῆς ἔχοντες, εἰς καύχημα ἐμοὶ

and now ye hear by me.

    2.1   If therefore any encouragement/comfort *be* in/with the anointed (one), if any encouragement/consolation *be* from agape, if any fellowship *be* from a spirit, if *there be* any compassions and pities, 2.2 fill ye up my joy that ye may think the same, having/holding the same agape, united (ones) in life/soul, by ye thinking the same, 2.3 nothing according to/down from a rivalry nor vainglory/empty fame, but in the humility of mind be ye considering/deeming one another excelling yourselves, 2.4 not each noticing/looking out for the (things) of yourselves, but each also the (things) of others.
    2.5 Think ye this among ye which *was* also in the anointed Jesus, 2.6 who existing in a form of God considered/thought *it* not plunder/booty the (thing) to be equal to God, 2.7 but he divested/emptied himself, having taken a form/appearance of a slave, he became in a form of men; and having been found in form as a man 2.8 he humbled himself, having become obedient until death, but of a death of/from the cross.
    2.9 Wherefore, God also exalted him and gave freely to him the name above every name, 2.10 in order that in/at the name of Jesus every knee might bend/bow, of heavenly (beings) and earthly (beings) and subterranean (beings), 2.11 and every tongue might confess/admit that *the* Lord is Jesus, the anointed (one), to *the* glory/fame of God *the* father.
    2.12 So that, my beloved (ones), ye obeyed as always, not as in/at my coming/presence only, but now by much more in my absence, ye work out/accomplish the salvation of yourselves from/with fear and trembling; 2.13 for God is the (one) working/effecting in/by ye both the (thing) to want/wish and the (thing) to work/effect in behalf of the good will.
    2.14 Do ye all (things) without grumblings and arguments/disputings, 2.15 in order that ye might become blameless and harmless, children of God without blame in the midst of a crooked/dishonest generation also/even having been perverted, among whom ye shine as light giving stars in a world, 2.16 holding/having

εἰς ἡμέραν χριστοῦ, ὅτι οὐκ εἰς κενὸν ἔδραμον οὐδὲ εἰς κενὸν ἐκοπίασα. 2.17 ἀλλ' εἰ καὶ σπένδομαι ἐπὶ τῇ θυσίᾳ καὶ λιτουργίᾳ τῆς πίστεως ὑμῶν, χαίρω καὶ συνχαίρω πᾶσιν ὑμῖν· 2.18 τὸ δὲ αὐτὸ καὶ ὑμεῖς χαίρετε καὶ συγχαίρετέ μοι.

2.19 ἐλπίζω δὲ ἐν κυρίῳ Ἰησοῦ Τιμόθεον ταχέως πέμψαι ὑμῖν, ἵνα κἀγὼ εὐψυχῶ γνοὺς τὰ περὶ ὑμῶν. 2.20 οὐδένα γὰρ ἔχω ἰσόψυχον ὅστις γνησίως τὰ περὶ ὑμῶν μεριμνήσει, 2.21 οἱ πάντες γὰρ τὰ ἑαυτῶν ζητοῦσιν, οὐ τὰ Ἰησοῦ χριστοῦ.

2.22 τὴν δὲ δοκιμὴν αὐτοῦ γινώσκετε, ὅτι ὡς πατρὶ τέκνον σὺν ἐμοὶ ἐδούλευσεν εἰς τὸ εὐαγγέλιον.

2.23 τοῦτον μὲν οὖν ἐλπίζω πέμψαι ὡς ἂν ἀφίδω τὰ περὶ ἐμὲ ἐξαυτῆς· 2.24 πέποιθα δὲ ἐν κυρίῳ ὅτι καὶ αὐτὸς ταχέως ἐλεύσομαι. 2.25 ἀναγκαῖον δὲ ἡγησάμην Ἐπαφρόδιτον τὸν ἀδελφὸν καὶ συνεργὸν καὶ συστρατιώτην μου, ὑμῶν δὲ ἀπόστολον καὶ λειτουργὸν τῆς χρείας μου, πέμψαι πρὸς ὑμᾶς, 2.26 ἐπειδὴ ἐπιποθῶν ἦν πάντας ὑμᾶς ἰδεῖν, καὶ ἀδημονῶν διότι ἠκούσατε ὅτι ἠσθένησεν. 2.27 καὶ γὰρ ἠσθένησεν παραπλήσιον θανάτῳ· ἀλλὰ ὁ θεὸς ἠλέησεν αὐτόν, οὐκ αὐτὸν δὲ μόνον ἀλλὰ καὶ ἐμέ, ἵνα μὴ λύπην ἐπὶ λύπην σχῶ. 2.28 σπουδαιοτέρως οὖν ἔπεμψα αὐτὸν ἵνα εἰδόντες αὐτὸν πάλιν χαρῆτε κἀγὼ ἀλυπότερος ὦ.

2.29 προσδέξασθαι οὖν αὐτὸν ἐν κυρίῳ μετὰ πάσης χαρᾶς, καὶ τοὺς τοιούτους ἐντίμους ἔχετε, 2.30 ὅτι διὰ τὸ ἔργον κυρίου μέχρι θανάτου ἤγγισεν, παραβολευσάμενος τῇ ψυχῇ ἵνα ἀναπληρώσει τὸ ὑμῶν ὑστέρημα τῆς πρός ἐμὲ λιτουργίας. 3.1 τὸ λοιπόν, ἀδελφοί μου, χαίρετε ἐν κυρίῳ. τὰ αὐτὰ γράφειν ὑμῖν

a saying/word of life, to/for a triumph for me in a/*the* day of the anointed (one), that I ran not in vain nor toiled/labored I in vain. 2.17 But if also I am poured out/sacrificed on/for the sacrifice and public service/liturgy of the faith of ye/of your faith, I rejoice, and I rejoice together with ye all; 2.18 and ye, ye also rejoice the same, and ye rejoice together with/for me.

2.19 But I hope in *the* Lord Jesus to sent Timothy to ye quickly/soon, in order that I also may have courage, knowing the (things) concerning ye. 2.20 For I have no one of like soul/life who will sincerely care of the (things) concerning ye, 2.21 for they all seek the (things) of themselves, not the (things) of Jesus, the anointed (one).

2.22 But ye know the test/proving of him, that as a child with a father he served as a slave with me in/for the good message/gospel.

2.23 Therefore, I indeed hope to sent this (one) immediately, as soon as I might see to the (things) concerning me; 2.24 but I have trusted in *the* Lord that I shall also come myself quickly/soon. 2.25 But I considered/thought it urgent/necessary to send to ye Epaphroditus, the brother and fellow worker and fellow soldier of me, and of/from ye an apostle and a public servant/minister of my need, 2.26 since he was earnestly desiring to see ye all, and *he was* being troubled because ye heard that he ailed/was weak. 2.27 For he also was sick/ailing, coming near to death; but God had mercy on him, and not him alone but also me, that I might not have grief/pain upon grief/pain. 2.28 Then I sent him more hastily in order that having seen him again ye might rejoice and I, I may be less grieved.

2.29 Therefore receive ye him in *the* Lord with every joy, and hold ye such ones honored/valuable, 2.30 because on account of the work of the anointed (one) he came near until death, having risked the soul/life in order that he might fill up the deficiency of ye of the service/ministry to/toward me. 3.1 *For* the rest/henceforth, my brothers, rejoice ye in *the* Lord. *It is* indeed not troublesome for me to write

ἐμοὶ μὲν οὐκ ὀκνηρόν, ὑμῖν δὲ ἀσφαλές.

3.2 βλέπετε τοὺς κύνας, βλέπετε τοὺς κακοὺς ἐργάτας, βλέπετε τὴν κατατομήν. 3.3 ἡμεῖς γάρ ἐσμεν ἡ περιτομή, οἱ πνεύματι θεοῦ λατρεύοντες καὶ καυχώμενοι ἐν χριστῷ Ἰησοῦ καὶ οὐκ ἐν σαρκὶ πεποιθότες, 3.4 καίπερ ἐγὼ ἔχων πεποίθησιν καὶ ἐν σαρκί. εἴ τις δοκεῖ ἄλλος πεποιθέναι ἐν σαρκί, ἐγὼ μᾶλλον· 3.5 περιτομῇ ὀκταήμερος, ἐκ γένους Ἰσραήλ, φυλῆς Βενιαμείν, Ἑβραῖος ἐξ Ἑβραίων, κατὰ νόμον Φαρισαῖος, 3.6 κατὰ ζῆλος διώκων τὴν ἐκκλησίαν, κατὰ δικαιοσύνην τὴν ἐν νόμῳ γενόμενος ἄμεμπτος.

3.7 ἅτινα ἦν μοι κέρδη, ταῦτα ἥγημαι διὰ τὸν χριστὸν ζημίαν. 3.8 ἀλλὰ μενοῦνγε καὶ ἡγοῦμαι πάντα ζημίαν εἶναι διὰ τὸ ὑπερέχον τῆς γνώσεως χριστοῦ Ἰησοῦ τοῦ κυρίου μου, δι' ὃν τὰ πάντα ἐζημιώθην, καὶ ἡγοῦμαι σκύβαλα ἵνα χριστὸν κερδήσω 3.9 καὶ εὑρεθῶ ἐν αὐτῷ, μὴ ἔχων δικαιοσύνην ἐμὴν τὴν ἐκ νόμου ἀλλὰ τὴν διὰ πίστεως χριστοῦ, τὴν ἐκ θεοῦ δικαιοσύνην ἐπὶ τῇ πίστι, 3.10 τοῦ γνῶναι αὐτὸν καὶ τὴν δύναμιν τῆς ἀναστάσεως αὐτοῦ καὶ τὴν κοινωνίαν τῶν παθημάτων αὐτοῦ, συνμορφιζόμενος τῷ θανάτῳ αὐτοῦ, 3.11 εἴ πως καταντήσω εἰς τὴν ἐξανάστασιν τὴν ἐκ νεκρῶν. 3.12 οὐχ ὅτι ἤδη ἔλαβον ἢ ἤδη τετελίωμαι, διώκω δὲ εἰ καὶ καταλάβω, ἐφ' ᾧ καὶ κατελήμφθην ὑπὸ χριστοῦ Ἰησοῦ.

3.13 ἀδελφοί, ἐγὼ ἐμαυτὸν οὔπω λογίζομαι κατειληφέναι· ἓν δέ, τὰ μὲν ὀπίσω ἐπιλανθανόμενος τοῖς δὲ ἔμπροσθεν ἐπεκτινόμενος, 3.14 κατὰ σκοπὸν διώκω εἰς τὸ βραβῖον τῆς ἄνω κλήσεως τοῦ θεοῦ ἐν χριστῷ Ἰησοῦ. 3.15 ὅσοι οὖν τέλιοι, τοῦτο

these things to ye, but also *it is* safe/secure for ye.

3.2 Ye see/beware the dogs, ye see/beware the evil workers, ye see/beware the mutilation. 3.3 For we, we are the circumcision, the (ones) serving/worshiping God in/by spirit and triumphing/boasting in the anointed Jesus and not having trusted in flesh, 3.4 although I *am* holding/having confidence/trust even in flesh. If any other (one)/anyone else seems to trust in flesh, I *do* more: 3.5 By circumcision *the* eighth day, out of *the* race of Israel, tribe of Benjamin, a Hebrew out of/from Hebrews, a Pharisee according to law, 3.6 prosecuting the assembly according to zeal/jealousy, having become blameless according to justice, the (one) by law.

3.7 But what things were gain for me, I have considered these (things) a loss/forfeit on account of the anointed (one). 3.8 But on the other hand, I also consider all (things) to be loss/forfeit on account of the surpassing greatness of the knowledge of the anointed Jesus, the Lord of me/my Lord, on account of whom I suffered loss *of* all things, and I consider *them* rubbishes in order that I might gain the anointed (one) 3.9 and I might be found in/by him, not having my justice, the (one) out of law, but the (one) through faith from the anointed (one), the justice from God upon/for the faith, 3.10 of the (thing) to know him and the power of his resurrection and the participation/fellowship of his sufferings, being conformed to/with the death of him, 3.11 if somehow/perhaps I might attain to/reach for the resurrection out of dead (ones). 3.12 Not that I received already or have already been completed/finished, but I pursue if even I might apprehend/lay hold of *it*, on *that* which also I was apprehended/laid hold of by the anointed Jesus.

3.13 Brothers, I not yet reckon/account myself to have apprehended/laid hold of *it*; but one (thing), indeed forgetting the (things) behind and also stretching forth to the (things) before/ahead, 3.14 according to a goal/mark I pursue to/for the prize/reward of the upward calling from God in/by the anointed Jesus. 3.15 Therefore, as many as are com-

φρονοῦμεν· καὶ εἴ τι ἑτέρως φρονεῖτε, καὶ τοῦτο ὁ θεὸς ὑμῖν ἀποκαλύψει· 3.16 πλὴν εἰς ὃ ἐφθάσαμεν, τῷ αὐτῷ στοιχεῖν. 3.17 συμμιμηταί μου γίνεσθε, ἀδελφοί, καὶ σκοπεῖτε τοὺς οὕτω περιπατοῦντας καθὼς ἔχετε τύπον ἡμᾶς.

3.18 πολλοὶ γὰρ περιπατοῦσιν οὓς πολλάκις ἔλεγον ὑμῖν, νῦν δὲ καὶ κλαίων λέγω, τοὺς ἐχθροὺς τοῦ σταυροῦ τοῦ χριστοῦ, 3.19 ὧν τὸ τέλος ἀπώλια, ὧν ὁ θεὸς ἡ κοιλία καὶ ἡ δόξα ἐν τῇ αἰσχύνῃ αὐτῶν, οἱ τὰ ἐπίγια φρονοῦντες. 3.20 ἡμῶν γὰρ τὸ πολίτευμα ἐν οὐρανοῖς ὑπάρχει, ἐξ οὗ καὶ σωτῆρα ἀπεκδεχόμεθα κύριον Ἰησοῦν χριστόν, 3.21 ὃς μετασχηματίσει τὸ σῶμα τῆς ταπινώσεως ἡμῶν σύμμορφον τῷ σώματι τῆς δόξης αὐτοῦ κατὰ τὴν ἐνέργειαν τοῦ δύνασθαι αὐτὸν καὶ ὑποτάξαι αὐτῷ τὰ πάντα.

4.1 Ὥστε, ἀδελφοί μου ἀγαπητοὶ καὶ ἐπιπόθητοι, χαρὰ καὶ στέφανός μου, οὕτως στήκετε ἐν κυρίῳ, ἀγαπητοί.

4.2 εὐοδίαν παρακαλῶ καὶ Συντύχην παρακαλῶ τὸ αὐτὸ φρονῖν ἐν κυρίῳ. 4.3 ναὶ ἐρωτῶ καὶ σέ, γνήσιε σύζυγε, συλαμβάνου αὐταῖς, αἵτινες ἐν τῷ εὐαγγελίῳ συνήθλησάν μοι μετὰ καὶ Κλήμεντος καὶ τῶν συνεργῶν μου λοιπῶν, ὧν τὰ ὀνόματα ἐν βίβλῳ ζωῆς.

4.4 χαίρετε ἐν κυρίῳ πάντοτε· πάλιν ἐρῶ, χαίρετε. 4.5 τὸ ἐπιεικὲς ὑμῶν γνωσθήτω πᾶσιν ἀνθρώποις. ὁ κύριος ἐγγύς. 4.6 μηδὲν μεριμνᾶτε, ἀλλ' ἐν παντὶ τῇ προσευχῇ καὶ τῇ δεήσει μετ' εὐχαριστίας τὰ αἰτήματα ὑμῶν γνωριζέσθω πρὸς τὸν θεόν. 4.7 καὶ ἡ εἰρήνη τοῦ θεοῦ ἡ ὑπερέχουσα πάντα νοῦν φρουρήσει τὰς καρδίας ὑμῶν καὶ τὰ νοήματα ὑμῶν ἐν χριστῷ Ἰησοῦ.

4.8 τὸ λοιπόν, ἀδελφοί, ὅσα ἐστὶν ἀληθῆ, ὅσα σεμνά, ὅσα

plete/mature (ones), we think of/consider this; and if ye think anything differently, God will also reveal this to ye;   3.16 however, in what we attained to/ reached, to the same to hold to/agree with.   3.17 Become ye my fellow imitators/emulators, brothers, and ye notice/look out for those so walking even as ye have/hold us an example/type.

3.18 For many walk/are walking, of whom I spoke often to ye, but now I say weeping: the enemies of the cross of the anointed (one),   3.19 of whom the end *is* destruction, of whom the God *is* the belly and the glory/fame in their shame/disgrace, the (ones) thinking the earthly (things).   3.20 For our citizenship in skies/heavens exists, out of which we also await/expect a savior, *the* Lord Jesus, the anointed (one), 3.21 who will transform our body from the humiliation/humble state, conformed to the body of his glory/fame according to the working/activity of the (thing) *for* him to be able and to subject all things to him.

4.1   So as, my beloved and earnestly desired brothers, my joy and crown, so stand ye firm in *the* Lord, beloved (ones).

4.2   I beseech/exhort Euodia and I beseech/exhort Syntyche to think/mind the same (thing) in *the* Lord. 4.3 Yes I also ask you, legitimate/true yoke- fellow, you help the (women), who struggled with me in the good message/gospel with both Clement and my fellow workers, *the* remaining (ones), of whom the names *are* in a scroll of life.

4.4   Rejoice ye always in *the* Lord; I shall say again: Rejoice ye.   4.5 Let the kindness/tolerance/ forbearance of ye be made known to all men/humans. The Lord *is* near.   4.6 Be ye not anxious for nothing, but in every (thing) by the prayer and the entreaty, with thanksgivings let the requests of ye be made known to God.   4.7 And the peace from God, the (one) surpassing all understanding/the mind will guard/keep your hearts and your thoughts/plans/minds in the anointed Jesus.

4.8   *For* the rest/Henceforth, brothers, what (things) are true, what (things) *are* honorable/venera-

δίκαια, ὅσα ἁγνά, ὅσα προσφιλῆ, ὅσα εὔφημα, εἴ τις ἀρετὴ καὶ εἴ τις ἔπενος, ταῦτα λογίζεσθε· 4.9 ἃ καὶ ἐμάθετε καὶ παρελάβετε καὶ ἠκούσατε καὶ εἴδετε ἐν ἐμοί, ταῦτα πράσσετε· καὶ ὁ θεὸς τῆς εἰρήνης ἔσται μεθ᾽ ὑμῶν.

4.10 ἐχάρην δὲ ἐν κυρίῳ μεγάλως ὅτι ἤδη ποτὲ ἀνεθάλετε τὸ ὑπὲρ ἐμοῦ φρονεῖν, ἐφ᾽ ᾧ καὶ ἐφρονεῖτε ἠκαιρεῖσθε δέ. 4.11 οὐχ ὅτι καθ᾽ ὑστέρησιν λέγω, ἐγὼ γὰρ ἔμαθον ἐν οἷς εἰμι αὐτάρκης εἶναι. 4.12 οἶδα καὶ ταπινοῦσθαι, οἶδα καὶ περισσεύειν· ἐν παντὶ καὶ ἐν πᾶσιν μεμύημαι καὶ χορτάζεσθαι καὶ πινᾶν, καὶ περισσεύειν καὶ ὑστερῖσθαι. 4.13 πάντα ἰσχύω ἐν τῷ ἐνδυναμοῦντί με χριστῷ.

4.14 πλὴν καλῶς ἐποιήσατε συγκοινωνήσαντές μου τῇ θλίψει.

4.15 οἴδαται δὲ καὶ ὑμῖς, Φιλιππήσιοι, ὅτι ἐν ἀρχῇ τοῦ εὐαγγελίου, ὅτε ἐξῆλθον ἀπὸ Μακαιδονίας, οὐδεμία μοι ἐκκλησία ἐκοινώνησεν εἰς λόγον δόσεως καὶ λήμψεως εἰ μὴ ὑμῖς μόνοι· 4.16 ὅτι καὶ ἐν Θεσσαλονίκῃ καὶ ἅπαξ καὶ δὶς εἰς τὴν χρίαν μοι ἐπέμψατε. 4.17 οὐχ ὅτι ἐπιζητῶ τὸ δόμα, ἀλλ᾽ ἐπιζητῶ τὸν καρπὸν τὸν πλεονάζοντα εἰς λόγον ὑμῶν.

4.18 ἀπέχω δὲ πάντα καὶ περισσεύω· πεπλήρωμαι δεξάμενος παρὰ Ἐπαφροδείτου τὰ παρ᾽ ὑμῶν, ὀσμὴν εὐωδίας, θυσίαν δεκτήν, εὐάρεστον τῷ θεῷ.

4.19 ὁ δὲ θεός μου πληρώσει πᾶσαν χρίαν ὑμῶν κατὰ τὸ πλοῦτος αὐτοῦ ἐν δόξῃ ἐν χριστῷ Ἰησοῦ. 4.20 τῷ δὲ θεῷ καὶ πατρὶ ἡμῶν ᾧ ἡ δόξα εἰς τοὺς αἰῶνας τῶν αἰώνων· ἀμήν.

4.21 ἀσπάσασθαι πάντα ἅγιον ἐν χριστῷ Ἰησοῦ. ἀσπάζονται ὑμᾶς οἱ σὺν ἐμοὶ ἀδελφοί.

4.22 ἀσπάζονται ὑμᾶς πάντες οἱ ἅγιοι, μάλιστα δὲ οἱ ἐκ

ble, what (things) *are* just, what (things) *are* pure, what (things) *are* lovable, what (things) *are* well-spoken of, if *there is* any virtue and if *there is* any praise, consider/reckon ye these (things); 4.9 which (things) ye both learned and ye received/accepted and ye heard and ye saw by/in me, practice ye these (things); and the God of the peace will be with ye.

4.10 And I rejoiced greatly in *the* Lord that now at last ye revived the (thing) to consider/think in behalf of me, and to/upon which ye were having time/opportunity and ye were considering/thinking. 4.11 Not that I speak according to/by deficiency/lack, for I, I learned in which/what I am to be content. 4.12 And I know to be humble, also I know to abound; I have been initiated in every (thing) and in all (things), both to be filled/satisfied and to hunger/be hungry, both to abound and to be lacking. 4.13 I can do all (things) in/by the (one) strengthening me, the a-nointed (one).

4.14 However, ye did well sharing together in my oppression/affliction.

4.15 And ye, ye also know, Philippians, that in the beginning of the good message/gospel when I went out from Macedonia, no/not one assembly shared/participated with me in a settlement/accounting of giving and receiving, except ye only; 4.16 because even in Thessalonica both once and again/repeatedly ye sent the need to me. 4.17 Not that I seek for the gift but I seek for fruit/result, the one abounding/increasing in/for your accounting/settlement.

4.18 But I have received all (things) and I abound; I have been filled, having received from Epaphroditus the (things) from ye, an odor of fragrance, an acceptable sacrifice, well-pleasing to God.

4.19 And my God will fill every need of ye according to his wealth/riches in/by fame/glory in/by the anointed Jesus. 4.20 But to our God and father be the fame/glory into the ages of the ages; truly.

4.21 Greet ye every consecrated (one)/saint in the anointed Jesus. The brothers with me greet ye.

4.22 All the saints greet ye, but especially the (ones) out of the house/household of Caesar. 4.23 The

τῆς Καίσαρος οἰκίας. 4.23 ἡ χάρις τοῦ κυρίου Ἰησοῦ χριστοῦ μετὰ τοῦ πνεύματος ὑμῶν. ἀμήν.

Πρὸς Φιλιππησίους

grace of the Lord Jesus, the anointed (one), *be* with the spirit of ye. Truly.

To Philippians

This is the Sinaitic New Testament, book of Colossians.

1.1 Παῦλος ἀπόστολος χριστοῦ Ἰησοῦ διὰ θελήματος θεοῦ καὶ Τιμόθεος ὁ ἀδελφὸς 1.2 τοῖς ἐν Κολοσσαῖς ἁγίοις καὶ πιστοῖς ἀδελφοῖς ἐν χριστῷ· χάρις ὑμῖν καὶ εἰρήνη ἀπὸ θεοῦ πατρὸς ἡμῶν καὶ κυρίου Ἰησοῦ χριστοῦ.

1.3 εὐχαριστοῦμεν τῷ θεῷ καὶ πατρὶ τοῦ κυρίου ἡμῶν Ἰησοῦ χριστοῦ πάντοτε περὶ ὑμῶν προσευχόμενοι, 1.4 ἀκούσαντες τὴν πίστιν ὑμῶν ἐν κυρίῳ Ἰησοῦ καὶ τὴν ἀγάπην ἣν ἔχετε εἰς πάντας τοὺς ἁγίους 1.5 διὰ τὴν ἐλπίδα τὴν ἀποκειμένην ὑμῖν ἐν τοῖς οὐρανοῖς, ἣν προηκούσατε ἐν τῷ λόγῳ τῆς ἀληθίας τοῦ εὐαγγελίου 1.6 τοῦ παρόντος εἰς ὑμᾶς, καθὼς καὶ ἐν παντὶ τῷ κόσμῳ ἐστὶν καρποφορούμενον καὶ αὐξανόμενον καθὼς καὶ ἐν ὑμῖν, ἀφ' ἧς ἡμέρας ἠκούσατε καὶ ἐπέγνωτε τὴν χάριν τοῦ θεοῦ ἐν ἀληθίᾳ· 1.7 καθὼς ἐμάθατε ἀπὸ Ἐπαφρᾶ τοῦ ἀγαπητοῦ συνδούλου ἡμῶν, ὅς ἐστιν πιστὸς ὑπὲρ ὑμῶν διάκονος τοῦ χριστοῦ, 1.8 ὁ καὶ δηλώσας ἡμῖν τὴν ὑμῶν ἀγάπην ἐν πνεύματι.

1.9 διὰ τοῦτο καὶ ἡμῖς, ἀφ' ἧς ἡμέρας ἠκούσαμεν, οὐ παυόμεθα ὑπὲρ ὑμῶν προσευχόμενοι καὶ αἰτούμενοι ἵνα πληρωθῆτε τὴν ἐπίγνωσιν τοῦ θελήματος αὐτοῦ ἐν πάσῃ σοφίᾳ καὶ συνέσει πνευματικῇ, 1.10 περιπατῆσαι ἀξίως τοῦ κυρίου εἰς πᾶσαν ἀρεσκίαν, ἐν παντὶ ἔργῳ ἀγαθῷ καρποφοροῦντες καὶ αὐξανόμενοι τῇ ἐπιγνώσει τοῦ θεοῦ, 1.11 ἐν πάσῃ δυνάμει δυναμούμενοι κατὰ τὸ κράτος τῆς δόξης αὐτοῦ εἰς πᾶσαν ὑπομονὴν καὶ μακροθυμίαν, μετὰ χαρᾶς 1.12 εὐχαριστοῦντες τῷ θεῷ πατρὶ τῷ ἱκανώσαντι ὑμᾶς εἰς τὴν μερίδα τοῦ κλήρου τῶν ἁγίων ἐν τῷ φωτί· 1.13 ὃς ἐρρύσατο ἡμᾶς ἐκ τῆς ἐξουσίας τοῦ σκότους καὶ μετέστησεν εἰς τὴν βασιλείαν τοῦ υἱοῦ τῆς ἀγάπης αὐτοῦ, 1.14 ἐν ᾧ ἔχομεν τὴν ἀπολύτρωσιν, τὴν ἄφεσιν τῶν ἁμαρτιῶν·

1.15 ὅς ἐστιν εἰκὼν τοῦ θεοῦ τοῦ ἀοράτου, πρωτότοκος πάσης κτίσεως,

1.16 ὅτι ἐν αὐτῷ ἐκτίσθη τὰ πάντα ἐν τοῖς οὐρανοῖς καὶ

1.1 Paul an apostle of the anointed Jesus, through *the* will of God, and Timothy the brother, 1.2 to the saints and faithful brothers in the anointed (one) in Colossae; grace to ye and peace from God our father and *the* Lord Jesus, the anointed (one).

1.3 We give thanks to God the father of our Lord Jesus, the anointed (one), always praying about ye, 1.4 having heard *of* the faith of ye in the Lord Jesus and the agape which ye have to/for all the saints 1.5 because of the hope, the (one) being laid up/reserved for ye in the skies/heavens, which ye heard before by the saying/word of the truth of the good message/gospel 1.6 from the (one) being present to/in ye, as also by every (thing) in the world, bearing fruit/producing results and increasing/growing as also in/among ye, from which day ye heard/listened and came to know the grace of God in truth; 1.7 as ye learned from Epaphras, our beloved fellow slave, who is a faithful servant/waiter of/from the anointed (one) in behalf of ye, 1.8 the (one) also having shown to us the agape of ye in spirit/by a spirit.

1.9 Because of this we also, from which day we heard, we cease not praying and petitioning in behalf of ye that ye might be filled *with* the knowledge of his will with every wisdom and spiritual insight/understanding, 1.10 to walk worthily of the Lord, in every (thing) desiring to please, in/by every good work bearing fruit/producing results and increasing/growing in the knowledge of God, 1.11 being strengthened with every power/ability according to the power/might of his fame/reputation into/for every/all endurance and patience, with joy 1.12 giving thanks to God the father, to the (one) making ye sufficient into/for the share of the lot of the saints in/with the light; 1.13 who rescued/delivered us out of the authority of the darkness and changed/removed into the kingdom of the son of/from his agape, 1.14 in whom we have the redemption, the forgiveness of the faults/sins;

1.15 who is an image of the unseen/invisible God, a firstborn of every creation,

1.16 because by him were created all the

ἐπὶ τῆς γῆς, τὰ ὁρατὰ καὶ τὰ ἀόρατα, εἴτε θρόνοι εἴτε κυριότητες εἴτε ἀρχαὶ εἴτε ἐξουσίαι· τὰ πάντα δι' αὐτοῦ καὶ εἰς αὐτὸν ἔκτισται, 1.17 καὶ αὐτός ἐστιν πρὸ πάντων καὶ τὰ πάντα ἐν αὐτῷ συνέστηκεν. 1.18 καὶ αὐτός ἐστιν ἡ κεφαλὴ τοῦ σώματος, τῆς ἐκκλησίας·

ὅς ἐστιν ἀρχή, πρωτότοκος τῶν νεκρῶν, ἵνα γένηται ἐν πᾶσιν αὐτὸς πρωτεύων, 1.19 ὅτι ἐν αὐτῷ εὐδόκησεν πᾶν τὸ πλήρωμα κατοικῆσαι 1.20 καὶ δι' αὐτοῦ ἀποκαταλλάξαι τὰ πάντα εἰς αὐτόν, εἰρηνοποιήσας διὰ τοῦ αἵματος τοῦ σταυροῦ αὐτοῦ, δι' αὐτοῦ εἴτε τὰ ἐπὶ τῆς γῆς εἴτε τὰ ἐν τοῖς οὐρανοῖς.

1.21 καὶ ὑμᾶς ποτε ὄντας ἀπηλλοτριωμένους καὶ ἐχθροὺς τῇ διανοίᾳ ἐν τοῖς ἔργοις τοῖς πονηροῖς, 1.22 νυνὶ δὲ ἀποκατήλλαξεν ἐν τῷ σώματι τῆς σαρκὸς αὐτοῦ διὰ τοῦ θανάτου αὐτοῦ, παραστῆσαι ὑμᾶς ἁγίους καὶ ἀμώμους καὶ ἀνεγκλήτους κατενώπιον αὐτοῦ,

1.23 εἴ γε ἐπιμένετε τῇ πίστι τεθεμελιωμένοι καὶ ἑδραῖοι καὶ μὴ μετακινούμενοι ἀπὸ τῆς ἐλπίδος τοῦ εὐαγγελίου οὗ ἠκούσατε, τοῦ κηρυχθέντος ἐν πάσῃ κτίσει τῇ ὑπὸ τὸν οὐρανόν, οὗ ἐγενόμην ἐγὼ Παῦλος διάκονος.

1.24 νῦν χαίρω ἐν τοῖς παθήμασιν ὑπὲρ ὑμῶν, καὶ ἀνταναπληρῶ τὰ ὑστερήματα τῶν θλίψεων τοῦ χριστοῦ ἐν τῇ σαρκί μου ὑπὲρ τοῦ σώματος αὐτοῦ, ὅ ἐστιν ἡ ἐκκλησία, 1.25 ἧς ἐγενόμην ἐγὼ Παῦλος διάκονος κατὰ τὴν οἰκονομίαν τοῦ θεοῦ τὴν δοθῖσάν μοι εἰς ὑμᾶς πληρῶσαι τὸν λόγον τοῦ θεοῦ, 1.26 τὸ μυστήριον τὸ ἀποκεκρυμμένον ἀπὸ τῶν αἰώνων καὶ ἀπὸ τῶν γενεῶν νῦν δὲ ἐφανερώθη τοῖς ἁγίοις αὐτοῦ, 1.27 οἷς ἠθέλησεν ὁ θεὸς γνωρίσαι τίς ὁ πλοῦτος τῆς δόξης τοῦ μυστηρίου τούτου ἐν τοῖς ἔθνεσιν,

(things) in the skies/heavens and on the earth, the visible (things) and the invisible (things), whether thrones or lordships/dominions or rulers or authorities; all the (things) were created through him and to/for him, 1.17 and he, he is/was before all (things) and all the (things) have continued/endured/existed in/by him. 1.18 Also he himself is the head of the body, of the assembly;

who is the beginning, *the* firstborn from the dead (ones), in order that he might generate himself being first in/among all (things), 1.19 because he took delight/pleasure *for* all the fullness to dwell in him 1.20 and through himself to reconcile all the (things) to/for him, having made peace through the blood of his cross, through him whether the (things) on the earth or the (things) in the skies/heavens.

1.21 And *for* ye, then/at one time being enemies and having been alienated/estranged in the mind in/by/with the evil works, 1.22 but now he reconciled in the body of his flesh through the death of himself, to present ye holy (ones)/saints both without fault/spot and blameless before him,

1.23 if indeed ye continue being founded in the faith, both steadfast and not being removed from the hope of the good message/gospel which ye heard, of the (one) having been heralded/preached in every creation under the sky/heaven, of which I, Paul, became a servant/minister/deacon/waiter.

1.24 Now I rejoice in the sufferings in behalf of ye, and I fill up completely the deficiencies of the oppressions/afflictions of the anointed (one) in my flesh in behalf of his body, which is the assembly, 1.25 of which I, Paul, became a servant/minister/deacon according to the responsibility from God, the (one) having been given to me to/for ye to fulfill the saying/word of God, 1.26 the mystery (religion), the (one) having been hidden from the ages and from the generations, but now it was made clear/plain to/for his saints, 1.27 to whom God wanted/wished to make known who *is* the wealthy/rich (one) of the fame/glory of this mystery (religion) among the ethnics,

which/who *is* the anointed (one) in ye, the hope

ὅς ἐστιν χριστὸς ἐν ὑμῖν, ἡ ἐλπὶς τῆς δόξης· 1.28 ὃν ἡμεῖς καταγγέλλομεν νουθετοῦντες πάντα ἄνθρωπον καὶ διδάσκοντες πάντα ἄνθρωπον ἐν πάσῃ σοφίᾳ, ἵνα παραστήσωμεν πάντα ἄνθρωπον τέλειον ἐν χριστῷ·

1.29 εἰς ὃ καὶ κοπιῶ ἀγωνιζόμενος κατὰ τὴν ἐνέργιαν αὐτοῦ τὴν ἐνεργουμένην ἐν ἐμοὶ ἐν δυνάμει.

2.1 Θέλω γὰρ ὑμᾶς εἰδέναι ἡλίκον ἀγῶνα ἔχω ὑπὲρ ὑμῶν καὶ τῶν ἐν Λαοδικίᾳ καὶ ὅσοι οὐχ ἑόρακαν τὸ πρόσωπόν μου ἐν σαρκί, 2.2 ἵνα παρακληθῶσιν αἱ καρδίαι αὐτῶν, συμβιβασθέντες ἐν ἀγάπῃ καὶ εἰς πάντα πλοῦτος τῆς πληροφορίας τῆς συνέσεως, εἰς ἐπίγνωσιν τοῦ μυστηρίου τοῦ θεοῦ καὶ πατρὸς χριστοῦ, 2.3 ἐν ᾧ εἰσιν πάντες οἱ θησαυροὶ τῆς σοφίας καὶ τῆς γνώσεως ἀπόκρυφοι.

2.4 τοῦτο λέγω ἵνα μηδεὶς ὑμᾶς παραλογίζηται ἐν πιθανολογίᾳ.

2.5 εἰ γὰρ καὶ τῇ σαρκὶ ἄπειμι, ἀλλὰ τῷ πνεύματι σὺν ὑμῖν εἰμι, χαίρων καὶ βλέπων ὑμῶν τὴν τάξιν καὶ τὸ στερέωμα τῆς εἰς χριστὸν πίστεως ὑμῶν.

2.6 Ὡς οὖν παρελάβετε τὸν χριστὸν Ἰησοῦν τὸν κύριον, ἐν αὐτῷ περιπατεῖτε, 2.7 ἐρριζωμένοι καὶ ἐποικοδομούμενοι καὶ βεβαιούμενοι τῇ πίστει καθὼς ἐδιδάχθητε, περισσεύοντες ἐν εὐχαριστίᾳ. 2.8 βλέπεται μή τις ἔσται ὑμᾶς ὁ συλαγωγῶν διὰ τῆς φιλοσοφίας καὶ κενῆς ἀπάτης κατὰ τὴν παράδοσιν τῶν ἀνθρώπων, κατὰ τὰ στοιχῖα τοῦ κόσμου καὶ οὐ κατὰ χριστόν·

2.9 ὅτι ἐν αὐτῷ κατοικεῖ πᾶν τὸ πλήρωμα τῆς θεότητος σωματικῶς, 2.10 καὶ ἐστὲ ἐν αὐτῷ πεπληρωμένοι, ὅς ἐστιν ἡ κεφαλὴ πάσης τῆς ἀρχῆς καὶ ἐξουσίας,

2.11 ἐν ᾧ καὶ περιετμήθητε περιτομῇ ἀχειροποιήτῳ ἐν τῇ ἀπεκδύσει τοῦ σώματος τῆς σαρκός, ἐν τῇ περιτομῇ τοῦ χριστοῦ, 2.12 συνταφέντες αὐτῷ ἐν τῷ βαπτισμῷ, ἐν ᾧ καὶ συνηγέρθητε

of the fame/glory; 1.28 whom we, we proclaim/ declare, admonishing/warning every man/human and teaching every man/human in/with every/all wisdom, in order
that we might present/establish every man complete/-
mature in/with the anointed (one);

1.29 in/for which also I labor/toil struggling
according to the working/energy of him, the (one)
working in me with power.

2.1 For I want/wish *for* ye to know how great a
struggle I have in behalf of ye and those in Laodicia
and as many as have not seen my face in flesh, 2.2
in order that their hearts might be encouraged/consol-
ed, being united in agape and into every abundance/
wealth of the full assurance/certainty from the
insight/understanding, in a knowledge of the mystery
(religion) of God *the* father *and* the anointed (one),
2.3 in/by whom are hidden all the stores/treasures of
the wisdom and the knowledge.

2.4 I say this in order that no one might deceive ye by/with persuasive argument.

2.5 For even if I am absent in the flesh, but I
am with ye in the spirit, rejoicing and seeing the
manner/order of ye and the firmness of your faith in
the anointed (one).

2.6 Therefore, as ye received the anointed
(one), Jesus the Lord, walk ye in him, 2.7 having
been rooted and being built up and being confirmed in
the faith as ye were taught, abounding in/with thanksgiving. 2.8 See/beware ye lest there will be anyone
leading ye away through the philosophy/love of wisdom
and empty deceit according to the tradition of the
men/humans, according to the elements/rudiments of the
world and not according to the anointed (one).

2.9 Because in him dwells bodily all the fullness of the deity/divinity, 2.10 and ye have been
fulfilled in/by him, who is the head of every (thing)
of the principle/rule/beginning and authority,

2.11 in whom also ye were circumcised with a
circumcision not done by hand, by the stripping off of
the body of flesh, by the circumcision from the a-
nointed (one), 2.12 having been buried with him in

360

διὰ τῆς πίστεως τῆς ἐνεργείας τοῦ θεοῦ τοῦ ἐγείραντος αὐτὸν ἐκ νεκρῶν· 2.13 καὶ ὑμᾶς νεκροὺς ὄντας ἐν τοῖς παραπτώμασιν καὶ τῇ ἀκροβυστίᾳ τῆς σαρκὸς ὑμῶν, συνεζωοποίησεν ὑμᾶς σὺν αὐτῷ, χαρισάμενος ἡμῖν πάντα τὰ παραπτώματα, 2.14 ἐξαλίψας τὸ καθ' ἡμῶν χειρόγραφον τοῖς δόγμασιν ὃ ἦν ὑπεναντίον ἡμῖν, καὶ αὐτὸ ἦρκεν ἐκ τοῦ μέσου προσηλώσας αὐτὸ τῷ σταυρῷ· 2.15 ἀπεκδυσάμενος τὰς ἀρχὰς καὶ τὰς ἐξουσίας ἐδιγμάτισεν ἐν παρρησίᾳ, θριαμβεύσας αὐτοὺς ἐν αὐτῷ.

2.16 μὴ οὖν τις ὑμᾶς κρινέτω ἐν βρώσι ἢ ἐν πόσει ἢ ἐν μέρει ἑορτῆς ἢ νουμηνίας ἢ σαββάτων, 2.17 ἅ ἐστιν σκιὰ τῶν μελλόντων, τὸ δὲ σῶμα τοῦ χριστοῦ. 2.18 μηδὶς ὑμᾶς καταβραβευέτω θέλων ἐν ταπινοφροσύνῃ καὶ θρησκείᾳ τῶν τῶν μέλλον τῶν ἀγγέλων, ἃ ἑόρακεν ἐμβατεύων, εἰκῇ φυσιούμενος ὑπὸ τοῦ νοὸς τῆς σαρκὸς αὐτοῦ,

2.19 καὶ οὐ κρατῶν τὴν κεφαλήν, ἐξ οὗ πᾶν τὸ σῶμα διὰ τῶν ἁφῶν καὶ συνδέσμων ἐπιχορηγούμενον καὶ συμβιβαζόμενον αὔξει τὴν αὔξησιν τοῦ θεοῦ.

2.20 εἰ ἀποθάνετε σὺν χριστῷ ἀπὸ τῶν στοιχίων τοῦ κόσμου, τί ὡς ζῶντες ἐν κόσμῳ δογματίζεσθε, 2.21 μὴ ἅψῃ μηδὲ γεύσῃ μηδὲ θίγῃς, 2.22 ἅ ἐστιν πάντα εἰς φθορὰν τῇ ἀποχρήσει, κατὰ τὰ ἐντάλματα καὶ διδασκαλίας τῶν ἀνθρώπων;

2.23 ἅτινά ἐστιν λόγον μὲν ἔχοντα σοφίας ἐν ἐθελοθρησκίᾳ καὶ ταπινοφροσύνῃ καὶ ἀφιδίᾳ σώματος, οὐκ ἐν τιμῇ τινι πρὸς πλησμονὴν τῆς σαρκός.

3.1 Εἰ οὖν συνηγέρθητε ἐν χριστῷ, τὰ ἄνω ζητεῖτε, οὗ ὁ

the baptism, in/with whom ye were also raised up through the faith of the working/action of God from the (thing) of having raised him up out of dead (ones); 2.13 and *for* ye, being dead (ones) in the trespasses and the uncircumcision of your flesh, he made ye alive together with him, having forgiven freely for ye all the trespasses, 2.14 having wiped away the handwriting/certificate of indebtedness against us in/by the ordinances/decrees which were opposite/opposed from us, and he has taken it out of the midst, having nailed it to the cross; 2.15 having stripped off the rulers/leaders and the authorities, he exposed/made an example of *them* with free speech/confidence, having triumphed over them by it.

2.16 Therefore, let not anyone judge ye in/by food/eating or in/by drink/drinking or in/by regard to a festival or a new moon or sabbaths, 2.17 which (things) are a shadow of those being about to come, but the body *is* of the anointed (one). 2.18 Let no one decide against/condemn ye, wanting/wishing *to* in humility and religion/worship of/from the messengers/angels being about to come, standing on what (things) he has seen, being conceited in vain by the mind of/from the flesh of him/his flesh, 2.19 and not holding fast/grasping the head, out of/from whom all the body *is* being furnished/supported and being united/joined together through the joints and tendons/sinews *it* grows/increases the growth/increase of/from God.

2.20 If ye died with the anointed (one) from the elements/principles of the world, why as living (ones) in a world are ye dogmatized/subject to decrees: 2.21 You touch not, neither taste nor handle/feel of, 2.22 which (things) are all into/for decay/ruin by the consumption/using up, according to the precepts/injunctions and teachings of the men/humans? 2.23 Whatever is indeed a saying/word having wisdom in would-be/self-made religion, with both humiliation and severe treatment of a body, not in any honor to/toward a gratification of the flesh.

3.1 Therefore, if ye were raised up with the anointed (one), seek ye the (things) above, where the

χριστός ἐστιν ἐν δεξιᾷ τοῦ θεοῦ καθήμενος· 3.2 τὰ ἄνω φρονεῖτε, μὴ τὰ ἐπὶ τῆς γῆς·

3.3 ἀπεθάνετε γάρ, καὶ ἡ ζωὴ ὑμῶν κέκρυπται σὺν τῷ χριστῷ ἐν τῷ θεῷ. 3.4 ὅταν ὁ χριστὸς φανερωθῇ, ἡ ζωὴ ὑμῶν, τότε καὶ ὑμῖς σὺν αὐτῷ φανερωθήσεσθε ἐν δόξῃ.

3.5 νεκρώσατε οὖν τὰ μέλη τὰ ἐπὶ τῆς γῆς, πορνίαν, ἀκαθαρσίαν, πάθος, ἐπιθυμίαν κακήν, καὶ τὴν πλεονεξείαν ἥτις ἐστὶν εἰδωλολατρία, 3.6 δι' ἃ ἔρχεται ἡ ὀργὴ τοῦ θεοῦ ἐπὶ τοὺς υἱοὺς τῆς ἀπιθίας)·

3.7 ἐν οἷς καὶ ὑμῖς περιεπατήσατέ ποτε ὅτε ἐζῆτε ἐν τούτοις.

3.8 νυνὶ δὲ ἀπόθεσθε καὶ ὑμεῖς τὰ πάντα, ὀργήν, θυμόν, κακίαν, βλασφημίαν, αἰσχρολογίαν ἐκ τοῦ στόματος ὑμῶν· 3.9 μὴ ψεύδεσθε εἰς ἀλλήλους,

ἀπεκδυσάμενοι τὸν παλαιὸν ἄνθρωπον σὺν ταῖς πράξεσιν αὐτοῦ, 3.10 καὶ ἐνδυσάμενοι τὸν νέον τὸν ἀνακαινούμενον εἰς ἐπίγνωσιν κατ' εἰκόνα τοῦ κτίσαντος αὐτόν,

3.11 ὅπου οὐκ ἔνι Ἕλλην καὶ Ἰουδαῖος, περιτομὴ καὶ ἀκροβυστία, βάρβαρος, Σκύθης, δοῦλος, ἐλεύθερος, ἀλλὰ πάντα καὶ ἐν πᾶσιν χριστός.

3.12 ἐνδύσασθε οὖν ὡς ἐκλεκτοὶ τοῦ θεοῦ, ἅγιοι καὶ ἠγαπημένοι, σπλάγχνα οἰκτιρμοῦ, χρηστότητα, ταπινοφροσύνην, πραΰτητα, μακροθυμίαν, 3.13 ἀνεχόμενοι ἀλλήλων καὶ χαριζόμενοι ἑαυτοῖς ἐάν τις πρός τινα ἔχῃ μομφή· καθὼς καὶ ὁ θεὸς ἐχαρίσατο ὑμῖν οὕτως καὶ ὑμῖς·

3.14 ἐπὶ πᾶσι δὲ τούτοις τὴν ἀγάπην, ὅς ἐστιν σύνδεσμος τῆς τελειότητός.

3.15 καὶ ἡ εἰρήνη τοῦ χριστοῦ βραβευέτω ἐν ταῖς καρδίαις ὑμῶν, εἰς ἣν καὶ ἐκλήθητε ἐν ἑνὶ σώματι· καὶ εὐχάριστοι γίνεσθε.

3.16 ὁ λόγος τοῦ χριστοῦ ἐνοικίτω ἐν ὑμῖν πλουσίως, ἐν

anointed (one) is being seated at the right (hand) of God; 3.2 think ye of the (things) above, not the (things) on the earth;

3.3 for ye died, and the life of ye has been hidden with the anointed (one) in/by God. 3.4 Whenever the anointed (one) might be manifested, the life of ye, then also ye will be manifested with him in glory/fame/reputation. 3.5 Therefore, make ye dead the members, the (things) upon the earth: Prostitution, uncleanness/viciousness, passion, bad/evil desire, and the greediness which is idolatry, 3.6 because of which (things) the anger of God comes upon the sons of the disobedience/unbelief;

3.7 in which even ye, ye walked then/at one time, when ye were living in them.

3.8 But now ye, ye also put away all the (things): Anger, wrath, malice/evil intention, slandering/blasphemy, shameful language out ot your mouth; 3.9 lie ye not to one another,

having stripped off the old man with his practices, 3.10 and having put on yourselves *as a garment* the new (one), the (one) being renewed in a full knowledge/recognition according to an image of the (one) having created him,

3.11 where there is not Greek and Judean, circumcision and uncircumcision, foreigner, Scythian, slave, free (man); but the anointed (one) *is* all (things) and in all.

3.12 Therefore, ye put on *as a garment*, as chosen ones of God, holy (ones)/saints and having been loved, compassions of mercy/pity, kindness/generosity, humility, gentleness, patience, 3.13 bearing with/ enduring one another and giving freely/forgiving for/*of* yourselves if anyone may have a complaint toward someone; as even the Lord gave freely/forgave ye, so also *do* ye;

3.14 and above all these (things) *is* the agape, which is a bond of the completeness/maturity.

3.15 And let the peace of the anointed (one) rule in your hearts, in/to which ye were also called in one body; and become ye thankful (ones).

3.16 Let the saying/reason/word of the anointed

πάση σοφία διδάσκοντες καὶ νουθετοῦντες ἑαυτοὺς

ψαλμοῖς, ὕμνοις, ᾠδαῖς πνευματικαῖς ἐν τῇ χάριτι ᾄδοντες ἐν ταῖς καρδίες ὑμῶν τῷ θεῷ· 3.17 καὶ πᾶν ὅ τι ἂν ποιῆτε ἐν λόγῳ ἢ ἐν ἔργῳ, πάντα ἐν ὀνόματι τοῦ κυρίου Ἰησοῦ χριστοῦ, εὐχαριστοῦντες τῷ θεῷ πατρὶ δι᾿ αὐτοῦ. 3.18 αἱ γυναῖκες, ὑποτάσσεσθαι τοῖς ἀνδράσιν, ὡς ἀνῆκεν ἐν κυρίῳ.

3.19 οἱ ἄνδρες, ἀγαπᾶτε τὰς γυναῖκας καὶ μὴ πικρένεσθε πρὸς αὐτάς.

3.20 τὰ τέκνα, ὑπακούετε τοῖς γονεῦσιν κατὰ πάντα, τοῦτο γὰρ εὐάρεστόν ἐστιν ἐν κυρίῳ.

3.21 οἱ πατέρες, μὴ παροργίζεται τὰ τέκνα ὑμῶν, ἵνα μὴ ἀθυμῶσιν.

3.22 οἱ δοῦλοι, ὑπακούετε κατὰ πάντα τοῖς κατὰ σάρκα κυρίοις, μὴ ἐν ὀφθαλμοδουλίαις ὡς ἀνθρωπάρεσκοι, ἀλλ᾿ ἐν ἁπλότητι καρδίας, φοβούμενοι τὸν κύριον. 3.23 ὃ ἐὰν ποιῆτε, ἐκ ψυχῆς ἐργάζεσθε, ὡς τῷ κυρίῳ καὶ οὐκ ἀνθρώποις, 3.24 εἰδότες ὅτι ἀπὸ κυρίου ἀπολήμψεσθε τὴν ἀνταπόδοσιν τῆς κληρονομίας. τῷ κυρίῳ χριστῷ δουλεύετε· 3.25 ὁ γὰρ ἀδικῶν κομίσεται ὃ ἠδίκησεν, καὶ οὐκ ἔστιν προσωπολημψία.

4.1 Οἱ κύριοι, τὸ δίκαιον καὶ τὴν ἰσότητα τοῖς δούλοις παρέχεσθαι, εἰδότες ὅτι καὶ ὑμεῖς ἔχετε κύριον ἐν οὐρανῷ.

4.2 τῇ προσευχῇ προσκαρτερεῖτε, γρηγοροῦντες ἐν αὐτῇ ἐν εὐχαριστίᾳ, 4.3 προσευχόμενοι ἅμα καὶ περὶ ἡμῶν, ἵνα ὁ θεὸς ἀνοίξῃ ἡμῖν θύραν τοῦ λόγου, λαλῆσαι τὸ μυστήριον τοῦ χριστοῦ, δι᾿ ὃ καὶ δέδεμαι, 4.4 ἵνα φανερώσω αὐτὸ ὡς δῖ με λαλῆσαι.

4.5 ἐν σοφίᾳ περιπατεῖτε πρὸς τοὺς ἔξω, τὸν καιρὸν ἐξαγοραζόμενοι.

4.6 ὁ λόγος ὑμῶν πάντοτε ἐν χάριτι, ἅλατι ἠρτυμένος, εἰδέναι πῶς δεῖ ὑμᾶς ἑνὶ ἑκάστῳ ἀποκρίνεσθαι.

(one) dwell in ye abundantly/richly, teaching and admonishing yourselves in/by every wisdom

with psalms, hymns, *and* spiritual songs with the grace in your hearts singing to God; 3.17 and every (thing) what ever ye may do in saying/word or in work, *do* all (things) in *the* name of the Lord Jesus, the anointed (one), giving thanks to God the father through him. 3.18 The women, be ye subordinate/subject to the men, as is proper/fitting in *the* Lord.

3.19 The men, love ye the women and be ye not embittered toward them.

3.20 The children, obey ye the parents according to all (things), for this is acceptable/well-pleasing in/by *the* Lord.

3.21 The fathers, irritate ye not your children, that they be not discouraged.

3.22 The slaves, obey ye according to all (things) to *the* lords according to the flesh, not in eye service as men-pleasers, but in simplicity of heart, fearing the Lord. 3.23 What ever ye may do, work ye out of the life/soul, as for the Lord and not for men, 3.24 knowing that from *the* Lord ye will receive the recompense of the inheritance. Serve ye as slaves for the Lord, the anointed (one); 3.25 for the (one) doing wrong/injustice will get back what he did wrong/unjust, and there is not partiality.

4.1 The lords, grant ye the just thing and the equity/fairness to the slaves, knowing that also/even ye, ye have a Lord in heaven.

4.2 Attend ye constantly/adhere ye to the prayer, watching in it with thanksgiving, 4.3 praying together also about us, that God may open a door of the saying/word for us, to speak the mystery (religion) of the anointed (one), through which I have also been bound, 4.4 in order that I might manifest it/ make it plain as it is necessary *for* me to speak.

4.5 Walk ye in wisdom to/with those outside/ without, making good use of the time/season.

4.6 The saying/reasoning from ye *be* always in/with grace, having been seasoned with salt, to know how it is necessary *for* ye to answer/reply to each

4.7 τὰ κατ' ἐμὲ πάντα γνωρίσει ὑμῖν Τυχικὸς ὁ ἀγαπητὸς ἀδελφὸς καὶ πιστὸς διάκονος καὶ σύνδουλος ἐν κυρίῳ, 4.8 ὃν ἔπεμψα πρὸς ὑμᾶς εἰς αὐτὸ τοῦτο, ἵνα γνῶτε τὰ περὶ ἡμῶν καὶ παρακαλέσῃ τὰς καρδίας ὑμῶν, 4.9 σὺν Ὀνησίμῳ τῷ πιστῷ καὶ ἀγαπητῷ ἀδελφῷ, ὅς ἐστιν ἐξ ὑμῶν· πάντα ὑμῖν γνωρίσουσιν τὰ ὧδε.

4.10 ἀσπάζεται ὑμᾶς Ἀρίσταρχος ὁ συναιχμάλωτός μου, καὶ Μᾶρκος ὁ ἀνεψιὸς Βαρναβᾶ περὶ οὗ ἐλάβετε ἐντολάς, ἐὰν ἔλθῃ πρὸς ὑμᾶς δέξασθε αὐτόν, 4.11 καὶ Ἰησοῦς ὁ λεγόμενος Ἰοῦστος, οἱ ὄντες ἐκ περιτομῆς οὗτοι μόνοι συνεργοὶ εἰς τὴν βασιλείαν τοῦ θεοῦ, οἵτινες ἐγενήθησάν μοι παρηγορία.

4.12 ἀσπάζετε ὑμᾶς Ἐπαφρᾶς ὁ ἐξ ὑμῶν, δοῦλος χριστοῦ Ἰησοῦ, πάντοτε ἀγωνιζόμενος ὑπὲρ ὑμῶν ἐν ταῖς προσευχαῖς, ἵνα σταθῆτε τέλειοι καὶ πεπληροφορημένοι ἐν παντὶ θελήματι τοῦ θεοῦ.

4.13 μαρτυρῶ γὰρ αὐτῷ ὅτι ἔχει πολὺν πόνον ὑπὲρ ὑμῶν καὶ τῶν ἐν Λαοδικίᾳ καὶ τῶν ἐν Ἱεραπόλει.

4.14 ἀσπάζεται ὑμᾶς Λουκᾶς ὁ ἰατρὸς ὁ ἀγαπητὸς καὶ Δημᾶς.

4.15 ἀσπάσασθε τοὺς ἐν Λαοδικίᾳ ἀδελφοὺς καὶ Νύμφαν καὶ τὴν κατ' οἶκον αὐτῶν ἐκκλησίαν.

4.16 καὶ ὅταν ἀναγνωσθῇ παρ' ὑμῖν ἡ ἐπιστολή, ποιήσατε ἵνα καὶ ἐν τῇ Λαοδικαίων ἐκκλησίᾳ ἀναγνωσθῇ, καὶ τὴν ἐκ Λαοδικίας ἵνα καὶ ὑμῖς ἀναγνῶτε.

4.17 καὶ εἴπατε Ἀρχίππῳ, βλέπε τὴν διακονίαν ἣν παρέλαβες ἐν κυρίῳ, ἵνα αὐτὴν πληροῖς.

4.18 ὁ ἀσπασμὸς τῇ ἐμῇ χειρὶ Παύλου. μνημονεύετέ μου τῶν δεσμῶν. ἡ χάρις μεθ' ὑμῶν. αμιν.

Πρὸς Κολοσσάεις

one.

4.7   Tychicus, the beloved brother and faithful servant/waiter/deacon and fellow slave in the Lord will make known to ye all the (things) down from me, 4.8   whom I sent to ye in/for this same (thing), in order that ye might know the (things) concerning us and he might console/encourage your hearts,   4.9 with Onesimus the faithful and beloved brother, who is out of/from ye; they will make known all the (things) here to ye.

4.10   Aristarchus, my fellow prisoner/captive greets ye, and Mark the cousin of Barnabas, concerning whom ye received commands, if he might come to ye, receive ye him,   4.11 and Jesus, the (one) being called Justus, the (ones) being out of/from circumcision, these only *are* fellow workers in the kingdom of God, who were generated a comfort for me.

4.12   Epaphras greets ye, the (one) out of ye, a slave of the anointed Jesus, always struggling in behalf of ye in/by the prayers, in order that ye might be firmly stood, complete and having been fulfilled in every (thing) by/in a will of God/God's will.

4.13   For I testify for him that he has much toil/pain in behalf of ye and of those in Laodicea and of those in Hierapolis.

4.14   Luke the beloved physician/doctor and Demas greets ye.

4.15   Greet/salute ye the brothers in Laodicia and Nymphas and the assembly by/down from/at her house.

4.16   And when the epistle might be read beside ye, make ye that it might also be read in/to the assembly of Laodicians, and that ye, ye also might read the (one) out of/from Laodicea.

4.17   And say ye to Archippus: See ye the service/ministry which ye took/received in/by *the* Lord, in order that you may fully perform it.

4.18   The salutation from Paul in/by my hand. Remember ye *for* the bonds of me/of my bonds. The grace *be* with ye. Truly.

To Colossians

This is the Sinaitic New Testament, book of 1 Thessalonians.

1.1 Παῦλος καὶ Σιλουανὸς καὶ Τιμόθεος τῇ ἐκκλησίᾳ Θεσσαλονικέων ἐν θεῷ πατρὶ καὶ κυρίῳ Ἰησοῦ χριστῷ· χάρις ὑμῖν καὶ εἰρήνη ἀπὸ θεοῦ πατρὸς ἡμῶν καὶ κυρίου Ἰησοῦ χριστοῦ. 1.2 εὐχαριστοῦμεν τῷ θεῷ πάντοτε περὶ πάντων ὑμῶν, μνίαν ποιούμενοι ἐπὶ τῶν προσευχῶν ἡμῶν, ἀδειαλίπτως 1.3 μνημονεύοντες ὑμῶν τοῦ ἔργου τῆς πίστεως καὶ τοῦ κόπου τῆς ἀγάπης καὶ τῆς ὑπομονῆς τῆς ἐλπίδος τοῦ κυρίου ἡμῶν Ἰησοῦ χριστοῦ ἔμπροσθεν τοῦ θεοῦ καὶ πατρὸς ἡμῶν,
1.4 εἰδότες, ἀδελφοὶ ἠγαπημένοι ὑπὸ τοῦ θεοῦ, τὴν ἐκλογὴν ὑμῶν, 1.5 ὅτι τὸ εὐαγγέλιον τοῦ θεοῦ ἡμῶν οὐκ ἐγενήθη εἰς ὑμᾶς ἐν λόγῳ μόνον ἀλλὰ καὶ ἐν δυνάμι καὶ ἐν πνεύματι ἁγίῳ καὶ πληροφορίᾳ πολλῇ, καθὼς οἴδατε οἷοι ἐγενήθημεν ὑμῖν δι᾽ ὑμᾶς.
1.6 καὶ ὑμεῖς μιμητὲ ἡμῶν ἐγενήθητε καὶ τοῦ κυρίου, δεξάμενοι τὸν λόγον ἐν θλίψει πολλῇ μετὰ χαρᾶς πνεύματος ἁγίου,
1.7 ὥστε γενέσθαι ὑμᾶς τύπους πᾶσιν τοῖς πιστεύουσιν ἐν τῇ Μακαιδονίᾳ καὶ ἐν τῇ Ἀχαΐᾳ. 1.8 ἀφ᾽ ὑμῶν γὰρ ἐξήχηται ὁ λόγος τοῦ κυρίου οὐ μόνον ἐν τῇ Μακαιδονίᾳ καὶ ἐν τῇ Ἀχαΐᾳ, ἀλλὰ ἐν παντὶ τόπῳ ἡ πίστις ὑμῶν ἡ πρὸς τὸν θεὸν ἐξελήλυθεν, ὥστε μὴ χρίαν ἔχιν ἡμᾶς λαλεῖν τι· 1.9 αὐτοὶ γὰρ περὶ ἡμῶν ἀπαγγέλλουσιν ὁποίαν εἴσοδον ἔσχομεν πρὸς ὑμᾶς, καὶ πῶς ἐπεστρέψατε πρὸς τὸν θεὸν ἀπὸ τῶν εἰδώλων δουλεύειν θεῷ ζῶντι καὶ ἀληθινῷ, 1.10 καὶ ἀναμένιν τὸν υἱὸν αὐτοῦ ἐκ τῶν οὐρανῶν, ὃν ἤγειρεν ἐκ τῶν νεκρῶν, Ἰησοῦν τὸν ῥυόμενον ἡμᾶς ἐκ τῆς ὀργῆς τῆς ἐρχομένης.

2.1 Αὐτοὶ γὰρ οἴδαται, ἀδελφοί, τὴν εἴσοδον ἡμῶν τὴν πρὸς ὑμᾶς ὅτι οὐ κενὴ γέγονεν, 2.2 ἀλλὰ προπαθόντες καὶ ὑβρισθέντες καθὼς οἴδαται ἐν Φιλίπποις ἐπαρρησιασάμεθα ἐν τῷ θεῷ ἡμῶν λαλῆσαι πρὸς ὑμᾶς τὸ εὐαγγέλιον τοῦ θεοῦ ἐν πολλῷ ἀγῶνι.

1.1 Paul and Silvanus and Timothy to the assembly of Thessalonians in God *the* father and *the* Lord Jesus, the anointed (one): Grace *be* to ye and peace from God our father and *the* Lord Jesus, the anointed (one). 1.2 We give thanks to God always concerning all of ye, making mention upon/at our prayers, unceasingly/constantly 1.3 remembering from ye of the works of the faith and of the toil/labor of the agape and of the endurance of the hope from our Lord Jesus, the anointed (one), before our God and father,

1.4 knowing, brothers having been loved by God/the deity, your choice, 1.5 because the good message/gospel from our God was not generated to/for ye by saying/word only but also by/in power and by/in a holy spirit and in/by much assurance, as ye know what sort of (ones) we were generated for ye because of ye.

1.6 And ye, ye were generated our imitators also of the Lord, having received the saying/word in much oppression/affliction with joy from a holy spirit.

1.7 So as *for* ye to be generated an example/type for all those believing in Macedonia and Achaia. 1.8 For from ye the saying/word of the Lord was caused to ring out, not only in Macedonia and in Achaia, but in every place your faith, the (one) toward God, has gone out, so as *for* us not to have a need to speak anything; 1.9 for they themselves proclaim about/around us what sort of access we had to ye, and how ye turned to God from the idols to be slaves for a living and true God, 1.10 and to await/expect the son of him out of the skies/heavens, whom he raised up out of the dead (ones), Jesus, the (one) delivering/rescuing us out of the coming anger/wrath.

2.1 For ye yourselves know, brothers, the entrance/visit from us, the (one) to/with ye, that it has not become vain/empty, 2.2 but having previously suffered and having been insulted, as ye know, in/at Philippi, we were bold/confident/exercised free speech in our God to speak to ye the good message/gospel of God in/by much struggle/agony.

2.3 For the exhortation/consolation from us *was*

2.3 ἡ γὰρ παράκλησις ἡμῶν οὐκ ἐκ πλάνης οὐδὲ ἐξ ἀκαθαρσίας οὐδὲ ἐν δόλῳ,

2.4 ἀλλὰ καθὼς δεδοκιμάσμεθα ὑπὸ τοῦ θεοῦ πιστευθῆναι τὸ εὐαγγέλιον οὕτως λαλοῦμεν, οὐχ ὡς ἀνθρώποις ἀρέσκοντες ἀλλὰ θεῷ τῷ δοκιμάζοντι τὰς καρδίας ἡμῶν.

2.5 οὔτε γάρ ποτε ἐν λόγῳ κολακίας ἐγενήθημεν, καθὼς οἴδατε, οὔτε ἐν προφάσει πλεονεξίας, θεὸς μάρτυς, 2.6 οὔτε ζητοῦντες ἐξ ἀνθρώπων δόξαν, οὔτε ἀφ᾽ ὑμῶν οὔτε ἀπ᾽ ἄλλων,

2.7 δυνάμενοι ἐν βάρει εἶναι ὡς χριστοῦ ἀπόστολοι,

ἀλλὰ ἐγενήθημεν νήπιοι ἐν μέσῳ ὑμῶν. ὡς ἂν τροφὸς θάλπῃ τὰ ἑαυτῆς τέκνα,

2.8 οὕτως ὁμειρόμενοι ὑμῶν εὐδοκοῦμεν μεταδοῦναι ὑμῖν οὐ μόνον τὸ εὐαγγέλιον τοῦ θεοῦ ἀλλὰ καὶ τὰς ἑαυτῶν ψυχάς, διότι ἀγαπητοὶ ἡμῖν ἐγενήθητε.

2.9 μνημονεύετε γάρ, ἀδελφοί, τὸν κόπον ἡμῶν καὶ τὸν μόχθον· νυκτὸς καὶ ἡμέρας ἐργαζόμενοι πρὸς τὸ μὴ ἐπιβαρῆσαί τινα ὑμῶν ἐκηρύξαμεν ὑμῖν τὸ εὐαγγέλιον τοῦ θεοῦ. 2.10 ὑμεῖς μάρτυρες καὶ ὁ θεός, ὡς ὁσίως καὶ δικαίως καὶ ἀμέμπτως ὑμῖν τοῖς πιστεύουσιν ἐγενήθημεν, 2.11 καθάπερ οἴδατε ὡς ἕνα ἕκαστον ὑμῶν ὡς πατὴρ τέκνα ἑαυτοῦ 2.12 παρακαλοῦντες καὶ παραμυθούμενοι καὶ μαρτυρόμενοι εἰς τὸ περιπατεῖν ὑμᾶς ἀξίως τοῦ θεοῦ τοῦ καλέσαντος ὑμᾶς εἰς τὴν ἑαυτοῦ βασιλείαν καὶ δόξαν.

2.13 καὶ διὰ τοῦτο καὶ ἡμεῖς εὐχαριστοῦμεν τῷ θεῷ ἀδιαλίπτως, ὅτι παραλαβόντες λόγον ἀκοῆς παρ᾽ ἡμῶν τοῦ θεοῦ ἐδέξασθε οὐ λόγον ἀνθρώπων ἀλλὰ καθώς ἐστιν λόγον θεοῦ, ὃς καὶ ἐνεργεῖται ἐν ἡμῖν τοῖς πιστεύουσιν. 2.14 ὑμῖς γὰρ μιμηταὶ ἐγενήθητε, ἀδελφοί, τῶν ἐκκλησιῶν τοῦ θεοῦ τῶν οὐσῶν ἐν τῇ Ἰουδαίᾳ ἐν χριστῷ Ἰησοῦ, ὅτι τὰ αὐτὰ ἐπάθετε καὶ ὑμῖς ὑπὸ

not out of deceit neither out of uncleanness nor in treachery/cunning,

2.4 but as we have been proved/tested by God to be entrusted *with* the good message/gospel, so/thus we speak, not as pleasing to men but to God, to the (one) testing/proving our hearts.

2.5 For neither were we generated then by a saying/word of flattery, as ye know, neither by an excuse/pretext of greediness, God *is* a witness, 2.6 nor seeking fame/glory from/out of men, neither from ye nor from others,

2.7 being able to be in heaviness/importance as apostles of the anointed (one),

but we were generated babies/infants in the midst of ye. As a nursing mother would cherish/comfort the children of herself,

2.8 so longing for ye we were well pleased to impart/share to/with ye not only the good message/gospel from God but also the souls/lives of us, because ye were generated beloved (ones) to us.

2.9 For ye remember, brothers, our toil/labor and the hardship; working night and day toward the (thing) not to burden/weigh down anyone of ye, we heralded/preached to ye the good message/gospel from God. 2.10 Ye and God *are* witnesses, as devoutly and justly and blamelessly we were generated for ye, the (ones) believing, 2.11 even as ye know, as each one of ye like a father *for* children of himself, 2.12 comforting/beseeching and encouraging and testifying/witnessing to/for the (thing) *for* ye to walk worthily of the God having called ye into the kingdom and fame/glory of himself.

2.13 And because of this we, we also give thanks to God constantly, that having received a saying/word of God from hearing us, ye accepted *it* not *as* a saying/word from men but as it is, a saying/word of God, which also works in/among us, the (ones) believing. 2.14 For ye were generated imitators/emulators, brothers, of the assemblies of God, of those being in Judea in the anointed Jesus, because ye, ye also suffered the same (things) by your own fellow tribesmen, as also they *suffered* by the Judeans, 2.15 from

τῶν ἰδίων συμφυλετῶν καθὼς καὶ αὐτοὶ ὑπὸ τῶν Ἰουδαίων, 2.15 τῶν καὶ τὸν κύριον ἀποκτεινάντων Ἰησοῦν καὶ τοὺς προφήτας, καὶ ἡμᾶς ἐκδιωξάντων, καὶ θεῷ μὴ ἀρεσκόντων, καὶ πᾶσιν ἀνθρώποις ἐναντίων, 2.16 κωλυόντων ἡμᾶς τοῖς ἔθνεσιν λαλῆσαι ἵνα σωθῶσιν, εἰς τὸ ἀναπληρῶσαι αὐτῶν τὰς ἁμαρτίας πάντοτε. ἔφθασεν δὲ ἐπ' αὐτοὺς ἡ ὀργὴ εἰς τέλος. 2.17 ἡμεῖς δέ, ἀδελφοί, ἀπορφανισθέντες ἀφ' ὑμῶν πρὸς καιρὸν ὥρας, προσώπῳ οὐ καρδίᾳ, περισσοτέρως ἐσπουδάσαμεν τὸ πρόσωπον ὑμῶν ἰδεῖν ἐν πολλῇ ἐπιθυμίᾳ. 2.18 διότι ἠθελήσαμεν ἐλθεῖν πρὸς ὑμᾶς, ἐγὼ μὲν Παῦλος καὶ ἅπαξ καὶ δίς, καὶ ἐνέκοψεν ἡμᾶς ὁ Σατανᾶς. 2.19 τίς γὰρ ἡμῶν ἐλπὶς ἢ χαρὰ ἢ στέφανος καυχήσεως ἢ οὐχὶ καὶ ὑμεῖς ἔμπροσθεν τοῦ κυρίου ἡμῶν Ἰησοῦ ἐν τῇ αὐτοῦ παρουσίᾳ; 2.20 ὑμεῖς γάρ ἐστε ἡ δόξα ἡμῶν καὶ ἡ χαρά. 3.1 διὸ μηκέτι στέγοντες ηὐδοκήσαμεν καταλιφθῆναι ἐν Ἀθήναις μόνοι, 3.2 καὶ ἐπέμψαμεν Τιμόθεον, τὸν ἀδελφὸν ἡμῶν καὶ διάκονον τοῦ θεοῦ ἐν τῷ εὐαγγελίῳ τοῦ χριστοῦ, εἰς τὸ στηρίξαι ὑμᾶς καὶ παρακαλέσαι ὑπὲρ τῆς πίστεως ὑμῶν 3.3 τὸ μηδένα σαίνεσθαι ἐν ταῖς θλίψεσι ταύταις. αὐτοὶ γὰρ οἴδατε ὅτι εἰς τοῦτο κείμεθα· 3.4 καὶ γὰρ ὅτε πρὸς ὑμᾶς ἦμεν, προελέγομεν ὑμῖν ὅτι μέλλομεν θλίβεσθαι, καθὼς καὶ ἐγένετο καὶ οἴδατε. 3.5 διὰ τοῦτο κἀγὼ μηκέτι στέγων ἔπεμψα εἰς τὸ γνῶναι τὴν πίστιν ὑμῶν, μή πως ἐπείρασεν ὑμᾶς ὁ πειράζων καὶ εἰς κενὸν γένηται ὁ κόπος ἡμῶν. 3.6 ἄρτι δὲ ἐλθόντος Τιμοθέου πρὸς ἡμᾶς ἀφ' ὑμῶν καὶ εὐαγγελισαμένου ἡμῖν τὴν ὑμῶν πίστιν καὶ τὴν ἀγάπην ὑμῶν, καὶ ὅτι ἔχετε μνίαν ἡμῶν ἀγαθὴν πάντοτε, ἐπιποθοῦντες ἡμᾶς ἰδεῖν καθάπερ καὶ ἡμεῖς ὑμᾶς, 3.7 διὰ τοῦτο παρεκλήθημεν, ἀδελφοί, ἐφ' ὑμῖν ἐπὶ πάσῃ τῇ ἀνάγκῃ καὶ θλίψει ἡμῶν διὰ τῆς ὑμῶν πίστεως, 3.8 ὅτι νῦν ζῶμεν ἐὰν ὑμεῖς στήκετε ἐν κυρίῳ. 3.9 τίνα γὰρ εὐχαριστίαν δυνάμεθα τῷ θεῷ ἀνταποδοῦναι περὶ ὑμῶν ἐπὶ πάσῃ τῇ χαρᾷ ᾗ χαίρομεν δι' ὑμᾶς ἔμπροσθεν τοῦ θεοῦ

those having killed both the Lord Jesus and the prophets and having severely pursued/prosecuted/persecut-
ed us, also not pleasing to God, and contrary to all
men, 2.16 forbidding *for* us to speak to the ethnics
in order that they might be saved, to/in the (thing)
for their sins always to be filled up. But the anger
came upon them in/to an end. 2.17 But we, brothers,
having been bereaved/deprived from/of ye to/for a
season of time, in face (presence) not in heart, we
were more abundantly eager/zealous with/in much desire
to see your face. 2.18 Therefore we wanted/wished to
come/go to ye, I Paul indeed both at one time and a
second, but Satan prevented us. 2.19 For what *is* our
hope or joy or crown/wreath of triumph -- or not even
ye -- before our Lord Jesus in/at the presence/coming
of him? 2.20 For ye, ye are our glory/fame and the
joy. 3.1 Wherefore, no longer forbearing/enduring,
we were well pleased to be left alone in Athens, 3.2
and we sent Timothy, our brother and a servant/dea-
con/waiter of God in/with the good message/gospel of
the anointed (one), to/for the (thing) to establish ye
and to beseech/comfort *ye* above/beyond your faith,
3.3 the (thing) for no one to be agitated/disturbed
by/in these oppressions/afflictions. For ye yourselves
know that we are exposed to this; 3.4 for even when
we were near ye, we foretold to ye that we were about
to be oppressed/afflicted, as even it happened and ye
know. 3.5 Because of this I also, no longer enduring,
I sent to/for the (thing) to know your faith, lest the
(one) tempting/testing somehow tempted/tried ye and
our toil/labor became in vain. 3.6 But Timothy,
having come just now to us from ye, and is announcing
the good message to us *of* your faith and your agape,
and that ye have always a good memory of us, desiring
earnestly to see us even as also we *for* ye, 3.7
because of this we were comforted, brothers, over ye
upon/against every calamity and oppression of us
because of your faith, 3.8 because we may now live if
ye, ye would stand in/by the Lord. 3.9 For what are
we able to return thanks to God concerning ye over/up-
on every joy which we rejoice because/on account of ye
before our God, 3.10 night and day petitioning super-

367

ἡμῶν, 3,10 νυκτὸς καὶ ἡμέρας ὑπερεκπερισσοῦ δεόμενοι εἰς τὸ ἰδεῖν ὑμῶν τὸ πρόσωπον καὶ καταρτίσαι τὰ ὑστερήματα τῆς πίστεως ὑμῶν; 3.11 αὐτὸς δὲ ὁ θεὸς καὶ πατὴρ ἡμῶν καὶ ὁ κύριος ἡμῶν Ἰησοῦς κατευθύναι τὴν ὁδὸν ἡμῶν πρὸς ὑμᾶς· 3.12 ὑμᾶς δὲ ὁ κύριος πλεονάσαι καὶ περισσεύσαι τῇ ἀγάπῃ εἰς ἀλλήλους καὶ εἰς πάντας, καθάπερ καὶ ἡμεῖς εἰς ὑμᾶς, 3.13 εἰς τὸ στηρίξαι ὑμῶν τὰς καρδίας ἀμέμπτους ἐν ἁγιωσύνῃ ἔμπροσθεν τοῦ θεοῦ καὶ πατρὸς ἡμῶν ἐν τῇ παρουσίᾳ τοῦ κυρίου ἡμῶν Ἰησοῦ μετὰ πάντων τῶν ἁγίων αὐτοῦ. ἀμήν.

4.1 Λοιπὸν οὖν, ἀδελφοί, ἐρωτῶμεν ὑμᾶς καὶ παρακαλοῦμεν ἐν τῷ κυρίῳ Ἰησοῦ, καθὼς παρελάβετε παρ' ἡμῶν τὸ πῶς δεῖ ὑμᾶς περιπατεῖν καὶ ἀρέσκειν θεῷ, καθὼς καὶ περιπατεῖτε, ἵνα περισσεύητε μᾶλλον. 4.2 οἴδατε γὰρ τίνας παραγγελίας δεδώκαμεν ὑμῖν διὰ τοῦ κυρίου Ἰησοῦ. 4.3 τοῦτο γάρ ἐστιν θέλημα τοῦ θεοῦ, ὁ ἁγιασμὸς ὑμῶν, ἀπέχεσθαι ὑμᾶς ἀπὸ τῆς πορνείας, 4.4 εἰδέναι ἕκαστον ὑμῶν τὸ ἑαυτοῦ σκεῦος κτᾶσθαι ἐν ἁγιασμῷ καὶ ἐν τιμῇ, 4.5 μὴ ἐν πάθει ἐπιθυμίας καθάπερ καὶ τὰ ἔθνη τὰ μὴ εἰδότα τὸν θεόν, 4.6 τὸ μὴ ὑπερβαίνειν καὶ πλεονεκτεῖν ἐν τῷ πράγματι τὸν ἀδελφὸν αὐτοῦ, διότι ἔκδικος κύριος περὶ πάντων τούτων, καθὼς καὶ προείπαμεν ὑμῖν καὶ διεμαρτυράμεθα. 4.7 οὐ γὰρ ἐκάλεσεν ἡμᾶς ὁ θεὸς ἐπὶ ἀκαθαρσίᾳ ἀλλ' ἐν ἁγιασμῷ. 4.8 τοιγαροῦν ὁ ἀθετῶν οὐκ ἄνθρωπον ἀθετεῖ ἀλλὰ τὸν θεὸν τὸν καὶ διδόντα τὸ πνεῦμα αὐτοῦ τὸ ἅγιον εἰς ὑμᾶς.

4.9 περὶ δὲ τῆς φιλαδελφίας οὐ χρείαν ἔχετε γράφειν ὑμῖν, αὐτοὶ γὰρ ὑμεῖς θεοδίδακτοί ἐστε εἰς τὸ ἀγαπᾶν ἀλλήλους· 4.10 καὶ γὰρ ποιεῖτε αὐτὸ εἰς πάντας τοὺς ἀδελφοὺς ὑμῶν ἐν ὅλῃ τῇ Μακεδονίᾳ.

παρακαλοῦμεν δὲ ὑμᾶς, ἀδελφοί, περισσεύειν μᾶλλον, 4.11 καὶ φιλοτιμεῖσθαι ἡσυχάζειν καὶ πράσσειν τὰ ἴδια καὶ

abundantly in/for the (thing) to see your face and to mend the deficiencies of your faith? 3.11 And our God and father himself and our Lord Jesus, may he make straight/direct our road/way to/toward ye; 3.12 and may the Lord cause ye to increase and abound in the agape to one another and to all, even as we also to ye, 3.13 in the (thing) to establish/confirm your hearts in consecration/holiness, blameless before the God and father of us in/at the presence/coming of our Lord Jesus with all the saints of him/all his saints. Truly/so be it.

4.1 Therefore, *for* the rest/henceforth, brothers, we ask and beseech ye in the Lord Jesus, as ye received from us the (thing) how it is necessary *for* ye to walk and to please God, as even ye do walk, in order that ye may abound more. 4.2 For ye know what commands/charges we have given to ye because of the Lord Jesus. 4.3 For this is a will/wish from God, the sanctification of ye, *for* ye to abstain from the prostitution, 4.4 *for* each (one) of ye to know to possess the instrument/vessel of himself in sanctity and in/with honor, 4.5 not in a passion from desire as even *do* the ethnics, the (ones) not knowing God, 4.6 the (thing) not to go beyond/trespass and to defraud his brother in the matter/deed, because *the* Lord *is* an avenger concerning all these (things), as also/even we foretold and solemnly testified/witnessed to ye. 4.7 For God called us not upon/to uncleanness but in/by consecration/holiness. 4.8 Then indeed the (one) rejecting rejects not a man/human but God, even the (one) giving the spirit from him/his spirit, the holy (one), to ye.
4.9 And concerning the brotherly love/love of brothers, ye have not a need *for me* to write to ye, for ye yourselves, ye are God-taught/taught by God in the (thing) to love one another; 4.10 for ye also do it to all your brothers in all Macedonia.
But we beseech ye, brothers, to abound more, 4.11 and to be ambitious/aspire to be quiet and to practice the (things) your own and to work with your own hands, as we ordered/commanded ye, 4.12 in order

ἐργάζεσθαι ταῖς ἰδίαις χερσὶν ὑμῶν, καθὼς ὑμῖν παρηγγίλαμεν, 4.12 ἵνα περιπατῆτε εὐσχημόνως πρὸς τοὺς ἔξω καὶ μηδενὸς χρείαν ἔχητε.

4.13 οὐ θέλομεν δὲ ὑμᾶς ἀγνοεῖν, ἀδελφοί, περὶ τῶν κοιμωμένων, ἵνα μὴ λυπῆσθε καθὼς καὶ οἱ λοιποὶ οἱ μὴ ἔχοντες ἐλπίδα. 4.14 εἰ γὰρ ἐπιστεύομεν ὅτι Ἰησοῦς ἀπέθανεν καὶ ἀνέστη, οὕτως καὶ ὁ θεὸς τοὺς κοιμηθέντας διὰ τοῦ Ἰησοῦ ἄξει σὺν αὐτῷ.

4.15 τοῦτο γὰρ ὑμῖν λέγομεν ἐν λόγῳ κυρίου, ὅτι ἡμεῖς οἱ ζῶντες οἱ περιλειπόμενοι εἰς τὴν παρουσίαν τοῦ κυρίου οὐ μὴ φθάσωμεν τοὺς κοιμηθέντας· 4.16 ὅτι αὐτὸς ὁ κύριος ἐν κελεύσματι, ἐν φωνῇ ἀρχαγγέλου καὶ ἐν σάλπιγγι θεοῦ, καταβήσεται ἀπ᾽ οὐρανοῦ, καὶ οἱ νεκροὶ ἐν χριστῷ ἀναστήσονται πρῶτον, 4.17 ἔπειτα ἡμεῖς οἱ ζῶντες οἱ περιλιπόμενοι ἅμα σὺν αὐτοῖς ἁρπαγησόμεθα ἐν νεφέλαις εἰς ἀπάντησιν τοῦ κυρίου εἰς ἀέρα· καὶ οὕτως πάντοτε σὺν κυρίῳ ἐσόμεθα.

4.18 ὥστε παρακαλεῖτε ἀλλήλους ἐν τοῖς λόγοις τούτοις. 5.1 περὶ δὲ τῶν χρόνων καὶ τῶν καιρῶν, ἀδελφοί, οὐ χρείαν ἔχετε τοῦ γράφεσθαι ὑμῖν, 5.2 αὐτοὶ γὰρ ἀκριβῶς οἴδατε ὅτι ἡμέρα κυρίου ὡς κλέπτης ἐν νυκτὶ οὕτως ἔρχεται. 5.3 ὅταν λέγωσιν, εἰρήνη καὶ ἀσφάλεια, τότε αἰφνίδιος αὐτοῖς ἐπίσταται ὄλεθρος ὥσπερ ἡ ὠδεὶν τῇ ἐν γαστρὶ ἐχούσῃ, καὶ οὐ μὴ ἐκφύγωσιν.

5.4 ὑμεῖς δέ, ἀδελφοί, οὐκ ἐσταὶ ἐν σκότει, ἵνα ἡ ἡμέρα ὑμᾶς ὡς κλέπτης καταλάβῃ, 5.5 πάντες γὰρ ὑμεῖς υἱοὶ φωτός ἐσται καὶ υἱοὶ ἡμέρας. οὐκ ἐσμὲν νυκτὸς οὐδὲ σκότους·

5.6 ἄρα οὖν μὴ καθεύδωμεν ὡς οἱ λοιποί, ἀλλὰ γρηγορῶμεν καὶ νήφωμεν. 5.7 οἱ γὰρ καθεύδοντες νυκτὸς καθεύδουσιν, καὶ οἱ μεθυσκόμενοι νυκτὸς μεθύουσιν· 5.8 ἡμεῖς δὲ ἡμέρας ὄντες νήφωμεν, ἐνδυσάμενοι θώρακα

that ye may walk/behave decently toward those outside and ye may have a need for nothing.

4.13 But we want/wish not *for* ye to be ignorant, brothers, about/concerning the sleeping (ones), that ye may not be grieved as also the rest/others, the (ones) not having hope. 4.14 For if we were believing that Jesus died and arose, so also God will bring the (ones) having fallen asleep through Jesus with him.

4.15 For we say this to ye in/by a saying/word from *the* Lord, that we, the (ones) living, the (ones) being left behind to the coming of the Lord, might by no means/certainly not precede the (ones) having been sleeping; 4.16 because the Lord himself at/with a signal/command, with a voice/sound from an archangel/ head messenger and with a trumpet of God, will come down from heaven, and the dead (ones) in the anointed (one) will arise (themselves) first, 4.17 then we, the (ones) living, the (ones) being left behind, we shall be snatched away together with them in/on clouds to a meeting of the Lord in air/space; and thus/so we shall always be with *the* Lord.

4.18 Therefore comfort/console ye one another with these sayings/words. 5.1 But concerning the times and the seasons, brothers, ye have not a need of the (thing) to be written to/for ye, 5.2 for ye yourselves know accurately that as a thief in/at night *time*, so comes a/*the* day of *the* Lord. 5.3 Whenever they may say: Peace and security, then sudden destruction comes upon them even as the travail/birthpain to the (one) having *it* in a belly/being pregnant, and by no means might they escape.

5.4 But ye, brothers, ye are not in darkness, that the day should overtake ye as a thief, 5.5 for all ye, ye are sons of light and sons of day. We are not of night nor of darkness;

5.6 so therefore we may/let us not sleep as the rest/other (ones) do, but we should/let us watch and be sober/temperate in wine. 5.7 For the (ones) sleeping, they sleep of/from night *time*, and the (ones) getting drunk/being intoxicated are drunk of/from night *time*;

5.8 but we being of day *time*, let us/we should

πίστεως καὶ ἀγάπης καὶ περικεφαλαίαν ἐλπίδα σωτηρίας·

5.9 ὅτι οὐκ ἔθετο ἡμᾶς ὁ θεὸς εἰς ὀργὴν ἀλλὰ εἰς περιποίησιν σωτηρίας διὰ τοῦ κυρίου ἡμῶν Ἰησοῦ χριστοῦ, 5.10 τοῦ ἀποθανόντος περὶ ἡμῶν ἵνα εἴτε γρηγορῶμεν εἴτε καθεύδωμεν ἅμα σὺν αὐτῷ ζήσωμεν. 5.11 διὸ παρακαλεῖτε ἀλλήλους καὶ οἰκοδομεῖτε εἷς τὸν ἕνα, καθὼς καὶ ποιεῖτε.

5.12 ἐρωτῶμεν δὲ ὑμᾶς, ἀδελφοί, εἰδέναι τοὺς κοπῶντας ἐν ὑμῖν καὶ προϊσταμένους ὑμῶν ἐν κυρίῳ καὶ νουθετοῦντας ὑμᾶς, 5.13 καὶ ἡγεῖσθαι αὐτοὺς ὑπερεκπερισσοῦ ἐν ἀγάπῃ διὰ τὸ ἔργον αὐτῶν. εἰρηνεύετε ἐν ἑαυτοῖς.

5.14 παρακαλοῦμεν δὲ ὑμᾶς, ἀδελφοί, νουθετεῖτε τοὺς ἀτάκτους, παραμυθεῖσθε τοὺς ὀλιγοψύχους, ἀντέχεσθε τῶν ἀσθενῶν, μακροθυμεῖτε πρὸς πάντας. 5.15 ὁρᾶτε μή τις κακὸν ἀντὶ κακοῦ τινι ἀποδῷ, ἀλλὰ πάντοτε τὸ ἀγαθὸν διώκετε καὶ εἰς ἀλλήλους καὶ εἰς πάντας.

5.16 πάντοτε χαίρετε, 5.17 ἀδιαλίπτως προσεύχεσθε, 5.18 ἐν παντὶ εὐχαριστεῖτε· τοῦτο γὰρ θέλημα θεοῦ ἐν χριστῷ Ἰησοῦ εἰς ὑμᾶς. 5.19 τὸ πνεῦμα μὴ σβέννυτε, 5.20 προφητείας μὴ ἐξουθενεῖτε· 5.21 πάντα δὲ δοκιμάζετε, τὸ καλὸν κατέχετε, 5.22 ἀπὸ παντὸς εἴδους πονηροῦ ἀπέχεσθε. 5.23 αὐτὸς δὲ ὁ θεὸς τῆς εἰρήνης ἁγιάσαι ὑμᾶς ὁλοτελεῖς, καὶ ὁλόκληρον ὑμῶν τὸ πνεῦμα καὶ ἡ ψυχὴ καὶ τὸ σῶμα ἀμέμπτως ἐν τῇ παρουσίᾳ τοῦ κυρίου ἡμῶν Ἰησοῦ χριστοῦ τηρηθείη. 5.24 πιστὸς ὁ καλῶν ὑμᾶς, ὃς καὶ ποιήσει. 5.25 ἀδελφοί, προσεύχεσθε περὶ ἡμῶν.

5.26 ἀσπάσασθε τοὺς ἀδελφοὺς πάντας ἐν φιλήματι ἁγίῳ. 5.27 ὁρκίζω ὑμᾶς τὸν κύριον ἀναγνωσθῆναι τὴν ἐπιστολὴν πᾶσι

be sober/temperate, having put on ourselves a breast plate of faith and agape and a helmet, a hope of salvation;

5.9   because God *did* not establish/set up us in/for anger, but in/for acquiring salvation through our Lord Jesus, the anointed (one),   5.10 the one having died concerning us in order that whether we may watch or we may sleep we might live together with him. 5.11 Wherefore exhort/comfort ye one another and build ye up/edify ye one *for* the one, as even ye are doing.

5.12   And we ask/request, brothers, *for* to know the (ones) toiling/laboring   among ye and presiding over ye in *the* Lord and admonishing ye,   5.13 and to consider them beyond all measure/most highly in agape because of their work. And ye be at peace/reconciled among yourselves.

5.14   And we beseech/exhort ye, brothers, admonish ye the disorderly/idle (ones), encourage ye the discouraged (ones), take ye interest in/hold firmly the weak/ailing (ones), by ye patient/forbearing to/toward all.   5.15 Observe ye lest anyone might give back/repay to someone evil for good, but always pursue/prosecute ye the good both in one another and in all.

5.16   Rejoice ye always,   5.17 pray ye constantly,   5.18 give ye thanks in every (thing); for this *is* a will/wish of God to/for ye in the anointed Jesus. 5.19 Extinguish ye not the spirit,   5.20 despise ye not prophecies;   5.21 and prove/test ye all (things), hold ye fast the good/beautiful,   5.22 avoid/abstain ye from every form/kind of evil.   5.23 And may the God of the peace himself sanctify/consecrate ye whole and complete, and may the spirit of ye be kept whole/intact, both the life/soul and the body blamelessly in/at the coming of our Lord Jesus, the anointed (one).   5.24 The (one) calling ye *is* faithful, who also/even will do *it*.   5.25 Brothers, pray ye about us.

5.26   Greet ye all the brothers with a holy kiss. 5.27 I cause ye to swear/adjure ye *by* the Lord *for* the epistle/letter to be publicly read to all the bro-

τοῖς ἀδελφοῖς. 5.28 ἡ χάρις τοῦ κυρίου ἡμῶν Ἰησοῦ χριστοῦ μεθ᾽ ὑμῶν. ἀμήν.

Πρὸς Θεσσαλονίκεις Α΄

thers.   5.28 The grace of our Lord Jesus the anointed (one) *be* with ye. Truly.

To Thessalonians 1

This is the Sinaitic New Testament, book of 2 Thessalonians.

1.1 Παῦλος καὶ Σιλουανὸς καὶ Τιμόθεος τῇ ἐκκλησίᾳ Θεσσαλονικέων ἐν θεῷ καὶ πατρὶ ἡμῶν καὶ κυρίῳ Ἰησοῦ χριστῷ· 1.2 χάρις ὑμῖν καὶ εἰρήνη ἀπὸ θεοῦ πατρὸς ἡμῶν καὶ κυρίου Ἰησοῦ χριστοῦ.

1.3 εὐχαριστεῖν ὀφίλομεν τῷ θεῷ πάντοτε περὶ ὑμῶν, ἀδελφοί, καθὼς ἄξιόν ἐστιν, ὅτι ὑπεραυξάνει ἡ πίστις ὑμῶν καὶ πλεονάζει ἡ ἀγάπη ἑνὸς ἑκάστου πάντων ὑμῶν εἰς ἀλλήλους,

1.4 ὥστε αὐτοὺς ἡμᾶς ἐν ὑμῖν ἐγκαυχᾶσθαι ἐν ταῖς ἐκκλησίαις τοῦ θεοῦ ὑπὲρ τῆς ὑπομονῆς ὑμῶν καὶ πίστεως ἐν πᾶσι τοῖς διωγμοῖς ὑμῶν καὶ ταῖς θλίψεσιν αἷς ἀνέχεσθε,

1.5 ἔνδιγμα τῆς δικαίας κρίσεως τοῦ θεοῦ, εἰς τὸ καταξιωθῆναι ὑμᾶς τῆς βασιλείας τοῦ θεοῦ, ὑπὲρ ἧς καὶ πάσχετε,

1.6 εἴπερ δίκαιον παρὰ θεῷ ἀνταποδοῦναι τοῖς θλίβουσιν ὑμᾶς θλῖψιν 1.7 καὶ ὑμῖν τοῖς θλιβομένοις ἄνεσιν μεθ᾽ ἡμῶν ἐν τῇ ἀποκαλύψει τοῦ κυρίου Ἰησοῦ ἀπ᾽ οὐρανοῦ μετ᾽ ἀγγέλων δυνάμεως αὐτοῦ 1.8 ἐν πυρὶ φλογός, διδόντος ἐκδίκησιν τοῖς μὴ εἰδόσι θεὸν καὶ τοῖς μὴ ὑπακούουσιν τῷ εὐαγγελίῳ τοῦ κυρίου ἡμῶν Ἰησοῦ χριστοῦ,

1.9 οἵτινες δίκην τίσουσιν ὄλεθρον αἰώνιον ἀπὸ προσώπου τοῦ κυρίου καὶ ἀπὸ τῆς δόξης τῆς ἰσχύος αὐτοῦ,

1.10 ὅταν ἔλθῃ ἐνδοξασθῆναι ἐν τοῖς ἁγίοις αὐτοῦ καὶ θαυμασθῆναι ἐν πᾶσι τοῖς πιστεύσασιν, ὅτι ἐπιστεύθη τὸ μαρτύριον ἡμῶν ἐφ᾽ ὑμᾶς, ἐν τῇ ἡμέρᾳ ἐκείνῃ.

1.11 εἰς ὃ καὶ προσευχόμεθα πάντοτε περὶ ὑμῶν, ἵνα ὑμᾶς ἀξιώσῃ τῆς κλήσεως ὁ θεὸς ἡμῶν καὶ πληρώσῃ πᾶσαν εὐδοκίαν ἀγαθωσύνης καὶ ἔργον πίστεως ἐν δυνάμει, 1.12 ὅπως ἐνδοξασθῇ τὸ ὄνομα τοῦ κυρίου ἡμῶν Ἰησοῦ ἐν ὑμῖν, καὶ ὑμεῖς ἐν αὐτῷ, κατὰ τὴν χάριν τοῦ θεοῦ ἡμῶν καὶ κυρίου Ἰησοῦ χριστοῦ.

1.1 Paul and Silvanus and Timothy to the assembly of Thessalonians in God and our father and *the* Lord Jesus, the anointed (one); 1.2 grace and peace *be* to ye from God our father and *the* Lord Jesus, the anointed (one).

1.3 We owe *it* to give thanks to God always concerning ye, brothers, as it is worthy, because the faith of ye increases exceedingly and the agape of each one of all ye to one another surperabounds,

1.4 so as *for* us ourselves to boast in/by ye in the assemblies of God in behalf of your endurance and faith in all your pursuits/prosecutions and the oppressions/afflictions which ye endure,

1.5 a plain evidence of the just judgment of God, in the (thing) *for* ye to be considered worthy of the kingdom of God, in behalf of which ye also suffer,

1.6 since *it is* a just (thing) with/beside God to recompense/give back oppression/affliction to those oppressing/afflicting ye 1.7 and relief with us to ye, the (ones) being oppressed/afflicted, by/in the revelation of the Lord Jesus from heaven with messengers/angels of his power 1.8 in/with a fire of flame/flaming fire, giving punishment to those not knowing God and to those not obeying the good message/gospel of our Lord Jesus,

1.9 who will undergo/pay a penalty/sentence, eternal destruction/ruin, from *the* face/presence of the Lord and from the fame/glory of his strength/might,

1.10 Whenever he might come to be glorified by his saints and to be wondered/marveled at by all those having believed, because our testimony to ye was believed, in/on that day.

1.11 In/for which we also pray always concerning ye, in order that our God might consider ye worthy of the calling/invitation and might fulfill every delight/choice of goodness and work of faith with power, 1.12 that the name of our Lord Jesus might be glorified by/in ye, and ye in/by him, according to the grace of our God and Lord, Jesus, the anointed (one).

2.1 And we ask ye, brothers, in behalf of the

2.1 Ἐρωτῶμεν δὲ ὑμᾶς, ἀδελφοί, ὑπὲρ τῆς παρουσίας τοῦ κυρίου ἡμῶν Ἰησοῦ χριστοῦ καὶ ἡμῶν ἐπισυναγωγῆς ἐπ' αὐτόν, 2.2 εἰς τὸ μὴ ταχέως σαλευθῆναι ὑμᾶς ἀπὸ τοῦ νοὸς μηδὲ θροεῖσθαι μήτε διὰ πνεύματος μήτε διὰ λόγου μήτε δι' ἐπιστολῆς ὡς δι' ἡμῶν, ὡς ὅτι ἐνέστηκεν ἡ ἡμέρα τοῦ κυρίου. 2.3 μή τις ὑμᾶς ἐξαπατήσῃ κατὰ μηδένα τρόπον· ὅτι ἐὰν μὴ ἔλθῃ ἡ ἀποστασία πρῶτον καὶ ἀποκαλυφθῇ ὁ ἄνθρωπος τῆς ἀνομίας, ὁ υἱὸς τῆς ἀπωλείας, 2.4 ὁ ἀντικείμενος καὶ ὑπεραιρόμενος ἐπὶ πάντα λεγόμενον θεὸν ἢ σέβασμα, ὥστε αὐτὸν εἰς τὸν ναὸν τοῦ θεοῦ καθίσαι, ἀποδικνύντα ἑαυτὸν ὅτι ἔστιν θεός. 2.5 οὐ μνημονεύετε ὅτι ἔτι ὢν πρὸς ὑμᾶς ταῦτα ἔλεγον ὑμῖν;

2.6 καὶ νῦν τὸ κατέχον οἴδαται, εἰς τὸ ἀποκαλυφθῆναι αὐτὸν ἐν τῷ ἑαυτοῦ καιρῷ. 2.7 τὸ γὰρ μυστήριον ἤδη γὰρ ἐνεργεῖται τῆς ἀνομίας· μόνον ὁ κατέχων ἄρτι ἕως ἐκ μέσου γένηται. 2.8 καὶ τότε ἀποκαλυφθήσεται ὁ ἄνομος, ὃν ὁ κύριος Ἰησοῦς ἀναλοῖ τῷ πνεύματι τοῦ στόματος αὐτοῦ καὶ καταργήσει τῇ ἐπιφανείᾳ τῆς παρουσίας αὐτοῦ,

2.9 οὗ ἐστιν ἡ παρουσία κατ' ἐνέργιαν τοῦ Σατανᾶ ἐν πάσῃ δυνάμι καὶ σημίοις καὶ τέρασιν ψεύδους 2.10 καὶ ἐν πάσῃ ἀπάτῃ ἀδικίας τοῖς ἀπολλυμένοις,

ἀνθ' ὧν τὴν ἀγάπην τῆς ἀληθείας οὐκ ἐδέξαντο εἰς τὸ σωθῆναι αὐτούς. 2.11 καὶ διὰ τοῦτο πέμπει αὐτοῖς ὁ θεὸς ἐνέργειαν πλάνης εἰς τὸ πιστεῦσαι αὐτοὺς τῷ ψεύδει, 2.12 ἵνα κριθῶσιν ἅπαντες οἱ μὴ πιστεύσαντες τῇ ἀληθείᾳ ἀλλὰ εὐδοκήσαντες τῇ ἀδεικίᾳ.

2.13 ἡμεῖς δὲ ὀφίλομεν εὐχαριστῖν τῷ θεῷ πάντοτε περὶ

coming/presence of our Lord Jesus, the anointed (one), and of our gathering together to/upon him, 2.2 into/for the (thing) *for* ye not quickly to be shaken from the mind/composure nor to be inwardly aroused/disturbed, neither through a spirit nor through a saying/word nor through an epistle/letter as through us, as that the day of the Lord has come. 2.3 May someone/anyone not deceive ye according to any guise/manner; because unless the rebellion/abandonment might come first and the man/human of the lawlessness might be revealed, the son of/from the destruction, 2.4 the (one) opposing and raising himself up against every (thing) being called God or an object of reverence/worship, so as *for* him to sit in the *inner* temple/sanctuary of God, proclaiming/exhibiting himself that he is God. 2.5 *Do* ye not remember that still being with ye I was saying these (things) to ye?

2.6 And now ye know the (thing) holding back/restraining, in/for the (thing) *for* him to be revealed in/at the time/season of himself. 2.7 For the mystery of the lawlessness is active already/now; only just now one *is* holding back/restraining until he might become out of the midst. 2.8 And then the lawless (one) will be revealed, whom the Lord Jesus may take away/kill by the spirit from his mouth and will abolish/render useless by the appearance/epiphany of his coming/presence,

2.9 of whom the coming/presence is according to the action/energy of Satan with every power and with signs and wonders from a lie 2.10 and with every deception from/of injustice/unjustness to those perishing,

for which they received not the love of the truth into/for the (thing) *for* them to be saved. 2.11 And because of this God sends to/for them a working/action of deceit into/for the (thing) *for* them to believe in the lie, 2.12 in order that all those which having not believed in the truth but having consented to the injustice may be judged.

2.13 But we, we owe *it*/are obligated to give thanks to God always concerning ye, brothers having been loved by the Lord, because God preferred/chose ye

ὑμῶν, ἀδελφοὶ ἠγαπημένοι ὑπὸ τοῦ κυρίου, ὅτι εἵλατο ὑμᾶς ὁ θεὸς ἀπαρχῆς εἰς σωτηρίαν ἐν ἁγιασμῷ πνεύματος καὶ πίστι ἀληθείας,

2.14 εἰς ὃ καὶ ἐκάλεσεν ὑμᾶς διὰ τοῦ εὐαγγελίου ἡμῶν, εἰς περιποίησιν δόξης τοῦ κυρίου ἡμῶν Ἰησοῦ χριστοῦ.

2.15 ἄρα οὖν, ἀδελφοί, στήκετε, καὶ κρατεῖτε τὰς παραδόσεις ἃς ἐδιδάχθητε εἴτε διὰ λόγου εἴτε δι᾽ ἐπιστολῆς ἡμῶν. 2.16 αὐτὸς δὲ ὁ κύριος ἡμῶν Ἰησοῦς χριστὸς καὶ ὁ θεὸς ὁ πατὴρ ἡμῶν, ὁ ἀγαπήσας ἡμᾶς καὶ δοὺς παράκλησιν αἰωνίαν καὶ ἐλπίδα ἀγαθὴν ἐν χάριτι, 2.17 παρακαλέσαι τὰς καρδίας ὑμῶν καὶ στηρίξαι ἐν παντὶ ἔργῳ καὶ λόγῳ ἀγαθῷ.

3.1 Τὸ λοιπὸν προσεύχεσθαι, ἀδελφοί, περὶ ἡμῶν, ἵνα ὁ λόγος τοῦ κυρίου τρέχῃ καὶ δοξάζηται καθὼς καὶ πρὸς ὑμᾶς, 3.2 καὶ ἵνα ῥυσθῶμεν ἀπὸ τῶν ἀτόπων καὶ πονηρῶν ἀνθρώπων· οὐ γὰρ πάντων ἡ πίστις.

3.3 πιστὸς δέ ἐστιν ὁ κύριος, ὃς στηρίξει ὑμᾶς καὶ φυλάξει ἀπὸ τοῦ πονηροῦ.

3.4 πεποίθαμεν δὲ ἐν κυρίῳ ἐφ᾽ ὑμᾶς, ὅτι ἃ παραγγέλλομεν καὶ ποιεῖτε καὶ ποιήσετε.

3.5 ὁ δὲ κύριος κατευθύναι ὑμῶν τὰς καρδίας εἰς τὴν ἀγάπην τοῦ θεοῦ καὶ εἰς τὴν ὑπομονὴν τοῦ χριστοῦ.

3.6 παραγγέλλομεν δὲ ὑμῖν, ἀδελφοί, ἐν ὀνόματι τοῦ κυρίου ἡμῶν Ἰησοῦ χριστοῦ, στέλλεσθαι ὑμᾶς ἀπὸ παντὸς ἀδελφοῦ ἀτάκτως περιπατοῦντος καὶ μὴ κατὰ τὴν παράδοσιν ἣν παρελάβοσαν παρ᾽ ἡμῶν.

3.7 αὐτοὶ γὰρ οἴδατε πῶς δεῖ μιμεῖσθαι ἡμᾶς, ὅτι οὐκ ἠτακτήσαμεν ἐν ὑμῖν 3.8 οὐδὲ δωρεὰν ἄρτον ἐφάγομεν παρά τινος, ἀλλὰ ἐν κόπῳ καὶ μόχθῳ νυκτὸς καὶ ἡμέρας ἐργαζόμενοι πρὸς τὸ μὴ ἐπιβαρῆσαί τινα ὑμῶν· 3.9 οὐχ ὅτι οὐκ ἔχομεν

from a beginning to/into salvation in/by consecration
of spirit and faith from truth,

2.14   to/for which also he called ye through the
good message from us, in/for acquisition/gaining
fame/glory from our Lord Jesus, the anointed (one).

2.15   Therefore then, brothers, ye stand firm,
and hold ye fast the traditions which ye were taught
either through a saying/word or through an epistle/
letter from us.   2.16 And our Lord Jesus himself, the
anointed (one), and the God our father, the (one)
having loved us and having given eternal consolation/
encouragement and a good hope by/in grace,   2.17 may
he encourage/console your hearts and may he estab-
lish/confirm ye in every good work and saying/word.

3.1   Pray ye *for* the rest/remaining (time),
brothers, about us, in order that the reasoning/saying
from the Lord may run and may be glorified/given
repute as also with/to ye,   3.2 and that we might be
rescued/delivered from the unusual/improper and evil
men/humans; for the faith is not of all (men).

3.3   But the Lord is faithful, who will estab-
lish/confirm ye and will guard/keep *ye* from the evil
(one).

3.4   And we have trusted in the Lord to/upon ye,
because what (things) we order/command, ye both do/
make and will do.

3.5   And may the Lord direct your hearts into the
agape of God and into the patience/endurance of the
anointed (one).

3.6   *And* we charge/command to ye, brothers, by
the name of our Lord Jesus, the anointed (one), *for* ye
to keep yourselves away from every brother walking
idly/in idleness and not according to the tradition
which ye received from us.

3.7   For ye yourselves know how it is necessary
to imitate/emulate us, because we were not idle among
ye   3.8 neither ate we a free loaf from anyone, but by
labor and toil night and day, working toward the
(thing) not to burden anyone of ye;   3.9 not that we
do not have authority, but in order that we might of
ourselves give an example to ye in/for the (thing) to

ἐξουσίαν, ἀλλ᾽ ἵνα ἑαυτοὺς τύπον δῶμεν ὑμῖν εἰς τὸ μιμῖσθαι ἡμᾶς.

3.10 καὶ γὰρ ὅτε ἦμεν πρὸς ὑμᾶς, τοῦτο παρηγγέλλομεν ὑμῖν, ὅτι εἴ τις οὐ θέλει ἐργάζεσθαι μηδὲ ἐσθιέτω. 3.11 ἀκούομεν γάρ τινας περιπατοῦντας ἐν ὑμῖν ἀτάκτως, μηδὲν ἐργαζομένους ἀλλὰ περιεργαζομένους· 3.12 τοῖς δὲ τοιούτοις παραγγέλλομεν καὶ παρακαλοῦμεν ἐν κυρίῳ Ἰησοῦ χριστῷ ἵνα μετὰ ἡσυχίας ἐργαζόμενοι τὸν ἑαυτῶν ἄρτον ἐσθίωσιν.

3.13 ὑμεῖς δέ, ἀδελφοί, μὴ ἐγκακήσητε καλοποιοῦντες. 3.14 εἰ δέ τις οὐχ ὑπακούει τῷ λόγῳ ἡμῶν διὰ τῆς ἐπιστολῆς, τοῦτον σημιοῦσθαι, μὴ συναναμίγνυσθαι αὐτῷ, ἵνα ἐντραπῇ· 3.15 καὶ μὴ ὡς ἐχθρὸν ἡγεῖσθε, ἀλλὰ νουθετῖται ὡς ἀδελφόν.

3.16 αὐτὸς δὲ ὁ κύριος τῆς εἰρήνης δώῃ ὑμῖν τὴν εἰρήνην διὰ παντὸς ἐν παντὶ τρόπῳ. ὁ κύριος μετὰ πάντων ὑμῶν. 3.17 ὁ ἀσπασμὸς τῇ ἐμῇ χειρὶ Παύλου, ὅ ἐστιν σημῖον ἐν πάσῃ ἐπιστολῇ· οὕτως γράφω. 3.18 ἡ χάρις τοῦ κυρίου ἡμῶν Ἰησοῦ χριστοῦ μετὰ πάντων ὑμῶν.

Πρὸς Θεσσαλονίκεις Β΄

imitate/emulate us.

3.10   For even when we were with/near ye, we charge/ordered this to ye, that if anyone wants/wishes not to work, neither let him eat.   3.11 For we hear *of* some walking among ye in idleness/not working/unruly, working *for* nothing but being busybodies/gossipers; 3.12 and to those such (ones) we charge/command and we beseech in/by *the* Lord Jesus, the anointed (one), that working with silence/quietness they may eat the loaf/- bread of themselves.

3.13   And ye, brothers, grow ye not weary/do not lose heart doing good.   3.14   And if anyone obeys not/is not obedient to the saying/word from us through the epistle/letter, signify ye especially this (one), not to mingle together with him, that he might be shamed;   3.15 but consider ye not as an enemy, but admonish ye *him* as a brother.

3.16   And may the Lord of the peace himself give the peace to ye through every (thing) and in every manner. The Lord *be* with ye all.   3.17 The saluta- tion/greeting from Paul in/by my hand, which is a sign in every epistle/letter; so I write.   3.18 The grace of our Lord Jesus, the anointed (one) *be* with ye all.

To Thessalonians

This is the Sinaitic New Testament, book of Hebrews.

1.1 Πολυμερῶς καὶ πολυτρόπως πάλαι ὁ θεὸς λαλήσας τοῖς πατράσιν ἐν τοῖς προφήταις 1.2 ἐπ' ἐσχάτου τῶν ἡμερῶν τούτων ἐλάλησεν ἡμῖν ἐν υἱῷ, ὃν ἔθηκεν κληρονόμον πάντων, δι' οὗ καὶ ἐποίησεν τοὺς αἰῶνας·

1.3 ὃς ὢν ἀπαύγασμα τῆς δόξης καὶ χαρακτὴρ τῆς ὑποστάσεως αὐτοῦ, φέρων τε τὰ πάντα τῷ ῥήματι τῆς δυνάμεως αὐτοῦ, καθαρισμὸν τῶν ἁμαρτιῶν ποιησάμενος ἐκάθισεν ἐν δεξιᾷ τῆς μεγαλωσύνης ἐν ὑψηλοῖς,

1.4 τοσούτῳ κρίττων γενόμενος τῶν ἀγγέλων ὅσῳ διαφορώτερον παρ' αὐτοὺς κεκληρονόμηκεν ὄνομα.

1.5 τίνι γὰρ εἶπέν ποτε τῶν ἀγγέλων, «υἱός μου εἶ σύ, ἐγὼ σήμερον γεγέννηκά σε;» καὶ πάλιν, «ἐγὼ ἔσομαι αὐτῷ εἰς πατέρα, καὶ αὐτὸς ἔσται μοι εἰς υἱόν;»

1.6 ὅταν δὲ πάλιν εἰσαγάγῃ τὸν πρωτότοκον εἰς τὴν οἰκουμένην, λέγει, «καὶ προσκυνησάτωσαν αὐτῷ πάντες ἄγγελοι θεοῦ.»

1.7 καὶ πρὸς μὲν τοὺς ἀγγέλους λέγει, « ὁ ποιῶν τοὺς ἀγγέλους αὐτοῦ πνεύματα, καὶ τοὺς λιτουργοὺς αὐτοῦ πυρὸς φλόγα·» 1.8 πρὸς δὲ τὸν υἱόν, « ὁ θρόνος σου, ὁ θεός, εἰς τὸν αἰῶνα τοῦ αἰῶνος, καὶ ἡ ῥάβδος τῆς εὐθύτητος ῥάβδος τῆς βασιλείας σου. 1.9 ἠγάπησας δικαιοσύνην καὶ ἐμίσησας ἀδικίαν· διὰ τοῦτο ἔχρισέν σε ὁ θεός, ὁ θεός σου, ἔλαιον ἀγαλλιάσεως παρὰ τοὺς μετόχους σου»

1.10 καί, «σὺ κατ' ἀρχάς, κύριε, τὴν γῆν ἐθεμελίωσας, καὶ ἔργα τῶν χειρῶν σού εἰσιν οἱ οὐρανοί· 1.11 αὐτοὶ ἀπολοῦνται, σὺ δὲ διαμένεις· καὶ πάντες ὡς ἱμάτιον παλαιωθήσονται, 1.12 καὶ ὡσεὶ περιβόλαιον ἑλίξεις αὐτούς,» ὡς ἱμάτιον «καὶ ἀλλαγήσονται· σὺ δὲ ὁ αὐτὸς εἶ καὶ τὰ ἔτη σου οὐκ ἐκλίψουσιν.»

1.13 πρὸς τίνα δὲ τῶν ἀγγέλων εἴρηκέν ποτε, «κάθου ἐκ

1.1 God, having spoken in past times in many parts and many manners/ways to the fathers by the prophets, 1.2 over *the* last of these days he spoke to us by a son, whom he put/placed a heir of all, through whom he also made the ages;

1.3 who being a shining light of the glory/fame and an image of his essence/reality and bearing/bringing all the (things) by the word of his power, having made himself pure/clean from the sins/faults, he sat at *the* right of the greatness in high places/among exalted (ones),

1.4 having become himself so much better from the messengers/angels in as much as he has inherited a more excellent name/calling.

1.5 For to which of the messengers/angels did he say at some time: YOU, YOU ARE MY SON; I, I HAVE GENERATED YOU TODAY? And again: I, I SHALL BE TO HIM IN/FOR A FATHER, AND HE, HE WILL BE TO ME IN/FOR A SON?

1.6 And whenever he might again bring in the firstborn into the inhabited earth/Roman Empire, he says: AND LET ALL MESSENGERS/ANGELS OF GOD WORSHIP TO HIM.

1.7 And indeed to/toward the messengers/angels he says: THE (ONE) MAKING HIS MESSENGERS/ANGELS SPIRITS AND HIS LITURGISTS/PUBLIC SERVANTS A FLAME OF FIRE; 1.8 but to/toward the son: YOUR THRONE, GOD, *is* IN/FOR THE AGE OF THE AGE, AND THE STAFF/ROD OF THE EQUITY/IMMEDIACY *is* A STAFF OF HIS KINGDOM. 1.9 (YOU) HAVING LOVED JUSTICE AND HAVING HATED INJUSTICE; BECAUSE OF THIS GOD ANOINTED YOU, YOUR GOD, AN OIL OF EXULTATION FROM BESIDE YOUR COMPANIONS;

1.10 and: YOU, LORD, DOWN FROM/BY *the* BEGINNINGS HAVING FOUNDED THE EARTH, AND THE SKIES/HEAVENS ARE WORKS OF YOUR HANDS; 1.11 THESE WILL PERISH OF THEMSELVES, BUT YOU, YOU ARE STAYING ON; AND ALL WILL BECOME OLD/AGED AS A GARMENT/CLOAK, 1.12 AND YOU WILL FOLD THEM UP LIKE A COVERING/CLOAK, AND THEY WILL BE CHANGED as a garment; AND YOU, YOU ARE THE SAME AND THE YEARS OF YOU WILL NOT END/FAIL.

1.13 But to which of the messengers/angels has he said at some time: YOU SIT OUT OF MY RIGHT

δεξιῶν μου ἕως ἂν θῶ τοὺς ἐχθρούς σου ὑποπόδιον τῶν ποδῶν σου;» 1.14 οὐχὶ πάντες εἰσὶν λιτουργικὰ πνεύματα εἰς διακονίαν ἀποστελλόμενα διὰ τοὺς μέλλοντας κληρονομεῖν σωτηρίαν;

2.1 Διὰ τοῦτο περισσοτέρως δεῖ προσέχιν ἡμᾶς τοῖς ἀκουσθῖσιν, μήποτε παραρυῶμεν.

2.2 εἰ γὰρ ὁ δι᾽ ἀγγέλων λαληθεὶς λόγος ἐγένετο βέβαιος, καὶ πᾶσα παράβασις καὶ παρακοὴ ἔλαβεν ἔνδικον μισθαποδοσίαν, 2.3 πῶς ἡμεῖς ἐκφευξόμεθα τηλικαύτης ἀμελήσαντες σωτηρίας; ἥτις, ἀρχὴν λαβοῦσα λαλεῖσθαι διὰ τοῦ κυρίου, ὑπὸ τῶν ἀκουσάντων εἰς ἡμᾶς ἐβεβαιώθη, 2.4 συνεπιμαρτυροῦντος τοῦ θεοῦ σημίοις τε καὶ τέρασι καὶ ποικίλαις δυνάμεσιν καὶ πνεύματος ἁγίου μερισμοῖς κατὰ τὴν αὐτοῦ θέλησιν.

2.5 οὐ γὰρ ἀγγέλοις ὑπέταξεν τὴν οἰκουμένην τὴν μέλλουσαν, περὶ ἧς λαλοῦμεν.

2.6 διεμαρτύρατο δέ πού τις λέγων, «τί ἐστιν ἄνθρωπος ὅτι μιμνήσκῃ αὐτοῦ, ἢ υἱὸς ἀνθρώπου ὅτι ἐπισκέπτῃ αὐτόν; 2.7 ἠλάττωσας αὐτὸν βραχύ τι παρ᾽ ἀγγέλους, δόξῃ καὶ τιμῇ ἐστεφάνωσας αὐτόν », καὶ κατέστησας αὐτὸν ἐπὶ τὰ ἔργα τῶν κειρῶν σου, 2.8 « πάντα ὑπέταξας ὑποκάτω τῶν ποδῶν αὐτοῦ.» ἐν τῷ γὰρ ὑποτάξαι αὐτῷ τὰ πάντα οὐδὲν ἀφῆκεν αὐτῷ ἀνυπότακτον. νῦν δὲ οὔπω ὁρῶμεν αὐτῷ τὰ πάντα ὑποτεταγμένα·

2.9 τὸν δὲ «βραχύ τι παρ᾽ ἀγγέλους ἠλαττωμένον» βλέπομεν Ἰησοῦν διὰ τὸ πάθημα τοῦ θανάτου «δόξῃ καὶ τιμῇ ἐστεφανωμένον,» ὅπως χάριτι θεοῦ ὑπὲρ παντὸς γεύσηται θανάτου.

2.10 ἔπρεπεν γὰρ αὐτῷ, δι᾽ ὃν τὰ πάντα καὶ δι᾽ οὗ τὰ πάντα, πολλοὺς υἱοὺς εἰς δόξαν ἀγαγόντα τὸν ἀρχηγὸν τῆς

(ONES)/(at my right hand) UNTIL I WOULD PUT/PLACE YOUR ENEMIES A FOOTSTOOL OF/FROM YOUR FEET? 1.14 Are they not all public serving/liturgistic spirits, being sent forth into a ministry/service because of those being about to inherit salvation?

2.1 Because of this it is necessary for us to heed/attend more abundantly to the (things) having been heard, lest then we might fall aside/away.
2.2 For if the logos/saying/word having been spoken through messengers/angels became reliable/firm, and every transgression and disobedience received a deserved/just penalty/punishment, 2.3 how shall we, we ourselves escape, having neglected/disregarded so great a salvation? Which, having received/took a beginning to be spoken through the Lord, it was established/confirmed to/for us by those having heard, 2.4 being testified to with both signs and wonders from God, also various/manifold powers and by portions/parts from a holy spirit according to his will/wish.
2.5 For to messengers/angels he subjected not the inhabited earth/empire, the (one) being about to come, about which we speak.
2.6 But a certain one solemnly testified, saying: WHAT IS A MAN/HUMAN THAT YOU SHOULD REMEMBER HIM, OR A SON OF A MAN THAT YOU SHOULD VISIT/CARE FOR HIM? 2.7 YOU MADE HIM SOMETHING A LITTLE LESS ALONGSIDE MESSENGERS/ANGELS, YOU CROWNED HIM WITH GLORY/FAME AND HONOR, AND YOU SET HIM OVER THE WORKS OF YOUR HANDS, 2.8 YOU PUT IN SUBJECTION ALL (THINGS) UNDERNEATH HIS FEET. FOR IN/BY THE (THING) *for* ALL THE (THINGS) TO BE SUBJECTED TO/FOR HIM, HE LEFT OUT NOTHING UNSUBJECTED TO HIM. BUT NOW WE SEE ALL THE (THINGS) NOT YET HAVING BEEN SUBJECTED TO HIM.
2.9 But we see the (one), HAVING BEEN MADE SOMETHING A LITTLE LESS ALONGSIDE MESSENGERS, Jesus, because of the suffering of the death, HAVING BEEN CROWNED WITH GLORY/FAME AND HONOR, that by grace from God in behalf of every (one) he might taste of death.
2.10 For it was proper/fitting for him, because of whom all things *are* and through whom all things *are*, to complete through sufferings the leader/origi-

σωτηρίας αὐτῶν διὰ παθημάτων τελιῶσαι.

2.11 ὅ τε γὰρ ἁγιάζων καὶ οἱ ἁγιαζόμενοι ἐξ ἑνὸς πάντες· δι' ἣν αἰτίαν οὐκ ἐπαισχύνεται ἀδελφοὺς αὐτοὺς καλεῖν, 2.12 λέγων,

«ἀπαγγελῶ τὸ ὄνομά σου τοῖς ἀδελφοῖς μου, ἐν μέσῳ ἐκκλησίας ὑμνήσω σε»

2.13 καὶ πάλιν, «ἐγὼ ἔσομαι πεποιθὼς ἐπ' αὐτῷ·» καὶ πάλιν, «ἰδοὺ ἐγὼ καὶ τὰ παιδία ἅ μοι ἔδωκεν ὁ θεός.»

2.14 ἐπεὶ οὖν τὰ παιδία κεκοινώνηκεν αἵματος καὶ σαρκός, καὶ αὐτὸς παραπλησίως μετέσχεν τῶν αὐτῶν, ἵνα διὰ τοῦ θανάτου καταργήσῃ τὸν τὸ κράτος ἔχοντα τοῦ θανάτου, τοῦτ' ἔστιν τὸν διάβολον, 2.15 καὶ ἀπαλλάξῃ τούτους, ὅσοι φόβῳ θανάτου διὰ παντὸς τοῦ ζῆν ἔνοχοι ἦσαν δουλίας. 2.16 οὐ γὰρ δήπου ἀγγέλων ἐπιλαμβάνεται, ἀλλὰ σπέρματος Ἀβραὰμ ἐπιλαμβάνεται.

2.17 ὅθεν ὤφειλεν κατὰ πάντα τοῖς ἀδελφοῖς ὁμοιωθῆναι, ἵνα ἐλεήμων γένηται καὶ πιστὸς ἀρχιερεὺς τὰ πρὸς τὸν θεόν, εἰς τὸ ἱλάσκεσθαι τὰς ἁμαρτίας τοῦ λαοῦ·

2.18 ἐν ᾧ γὰρ πέπονθεν αὐτὸς πιρασθίς, δύναται τοῖς πιραζομένοις βοηθῆσαι.

3.1 Ὅθεν, ἀδελφοὶ ἅγιοι, κλήσεως ἐπουρανίου μέτοχοι, κατανοήσατε τὸν ἀπόστολον καὶ ἀρχιερέα τῆς ὁμολογίας ἡμῶν Ἰησοῦν, 3.2 πιστὸν ὄντα τῷ ποιήσαντι αὐτὸν ὡς καὶ Μωσῆς ἐν ὅλῳ τῷ οἴκῳ αὐτοῦ. 3.3 πλείονος γὰρ οὗτος δόξης παρὰ Μωϋσῆν ἠξίωται καθ' ὅσον πλείονα τιμὴν ἔχει τοῦ οἴκου ὁ κατασκευάσας αὐτόν. 3.4 πᾶς γὰρ οἶκος κατασκευάζεται ὑπό τινος, ὁ δὲ πάντα κατασκευάσας θεός. 3.5 καὶ Μωϋσῆς μὲν πιστὸς ἐν ὅλῳ τῷ οἴκῳ αὐτοῦ ὡς θεράπων εἰς μαρτύριον τῶν

nator of their salvation having led many sons into glory/fame/reputation.

2.11 For both the (one) setting apart/sanctifying and those being set apart/sanctified *are* all from one; because of which cause he is not ashamed to call them brothers, 2.12 saying:

I SHALL ANNOUNCE YOUR NAME TO MY BROTHERS, IN THE MIDST OF AN ASSEMBLY I SHALL SING HYMNS *for* YOU;

2.13 and again: I, I SHALL HAVE TRUSTED UPON HIM; and again: BEHOLD, I AND THE CHILDREN THAT GOD GAVE TO ME.

2.14 Therefore, when the children have partaken of blood and flesh, he himself also partook/shared in the same way from the same (things), that through the death he might render useless/null the (one) holding the dominion/power of the death, this (one) is the devil, 2.15 and he might set free these (ones), as many as by fear of death were to live through all the *time* involved in slavery. 2.16 For of course he does not take hold of messengers/angels, but he takes hold of seed of Abraham.

2.17 From where he was owing/obligated according to all (things) to be likened to the brothers, in order that he might become a merciful and faithful high priest *for* the (things) to/near God, for the (thing) to atone for the faults/sins of the people;

2.18 for in what he has suffered, having been tested, he is able to help those being tempted/tested.

3.1 From where, brothers, saints/holy (ones), sharers/partakers of a heavenly calling, consider ye the apostle and high priest of our profession/confession, Jesus, 3.2 being faithful to the (one) having made him as also *was* Moses in/with his whole house. 3.3 For this (one) has been deemed worthy of greater/more fame/glory than Moses by as much as the (one) having prepared/erected it has more/greater honor from/than the house. 3.4 For every house *is* prepared/erected/furnished by someone, but the (one) having furnished/preparedall (things) is God. 3.5 And Moses indeed *was* faithful in/with his whole house/household as a servant/therapist in/for a testimony of the

λαληθησομένων, 3.6 χριστὸς δὲ ὡς υἱὸς ἐπὶ τὸν οἶκον αὐτοῦ·

οὗ οἶκός ἐσμεν ἡμεῖς, ἐὰν τὴν παρρησίαν καὶ τὸ καύχημα τῆς ἐλπίδος μέχρι τελοὺς βέβαιαν κατάσχωμεν. 3.7 διό, καθὼς λέγει τὸ πνεῦμα τὸ ἅγιον, «σήμερον ἐὰν τῆς φωνῆς αὐτοῦ ἀκούσητε, 3.8 μὴ σκληρύνητε τὰς καρδίας ὑμῶν ὡς ἐν τῷ πιρασμῷ, κατὰ τὴν ἡμέραν τοῦ πειρασμοῦ ἐν τῇ ἐρήμῳ, 3.9 οὗ ἐπίρασαν οἱ πατέρες ὑμῶν ἐν δοκιμασίᾳ καὶ εἶδον τὰ ἔργα μου 3.10 τεσσεράκοντα ἔτη· διὸ προσώχθισα τῇ γενεᾷ ταύτῃ καὶ εἶπον, ἀεὶ πλανῶνται τῇ καρδίᾳ· αὐτοὶ δὲ οὐκ ἔγνωσαν τὰς ὁδούς μου· 3.11 ὡς ὤμοσα ἐν τῇ ὀργῇ μου, εἰ εἰσελεύσονται εἰς τὴν κατάπαυσίν μου.»

3.12 βλέπετε, ἀδελφοί, μήποτε ἔστε ἔν τινι ὑμῶν καρδία πονηρὰ ἀπιστίας ἐν τῷ ἀποστῆναι ἀπὸ θεοῦ ζῶντος, 3.13 ἀλλὰ παρακαλεῖτε ἑαυτοὺς καθ’ ἑκάστην ἡμέραν, ἄχρις οὗ τὸ «σήμερον» καλεῖται, ἵνα μὴ σκληρυνθῇ τις ἐξ ὑμῶν ἀπάτῃ τῆς ἁμαρτίας·

3.14 μέτοχοι γὰρ τοῦ χριστοῦ γεγόναμεν, ἐάνπερ τὴν ἀρχὴν τῆς ὑποστάσεως μέχρι τέλους βεβαίαν κατάσχωμεν,

3.15 ἐν τῷ λέγεσθαι, «σήμερον ἐὰν τῆς φωνῆς αὐτοῦ ἀκούσητε, μὴ σκληρύνητε τὰς καρδίας ὑμῶν ὡς ἐν τῷ παραπικρασμῷ.» 3.16 τίνες γὰρ ἀκούσαντες παρεπίκραναν; ἀλλ’ οὐ πάντες οἱ ἐξελθόντες ἐξ Ἐγύπτου διὰ Μωϋσέως;

3.17 τίσιν δὲ «προσώχθισεν τεσσεράκοντα ἔτη;» οὐχὶ τοῖς ἁμαρτήσασιν, ὧν τὰ κῶλα ἔπεσεν ἐν τῇ ἐρήμῳ;

3.18 τίσιν δὲ «ὤμοσεν μὴ εἰσελεύσεσθαι εἰς τὴν κατάπαυσιν αὐτοῦ» εἰ μὴ τοῖς ἀπιθήσασιν;

3.19 καὶ βλέπομεν ὅτι οὐκ ἠδυνήθησαν εἰσελθῖν δι’ ἀπιστίαν.

4.1 Φοβηθῶμεν οὖν μήποτε καταλιπομένης ἐπαγγελίας εἰσελθῖν εἰς τὴν κατάπαυσιν αὐτοῦ δοκῇ τις ἐξ ὑμῶν ὑστερηκέναι·

(things) going to be spoken, 3.6 but the anointed (one) as a son over his household.

of whom we, we are a house/household, if we might hold fast the confidence and the triumph of the hope, firm until *the* end. 3.7 Wherefore, as the holy spirit says: IF YE MIGHT HEAR HIS VOICE TODAY, 3.8 HARDEN YE NOT YOUR HEARTS AS IN THE EMBITTERMENT/REBELLION, THROUGH/TO THE DAY OF THE TRYING/TEMPTATION IN THE DESERT/WILDERNESS, 3.9 WHERE OUR FATHERS WERE TRIED/ TEMPTED IN/BY A PROVING AND THEY SAW MY WORKS 3.10 *for* FORTY YEARS; WHEREFORE I WAS ANGRY/PROVOKED TO/BY THIS GENERATION AND I SAID: THEY ARE ALWAYS LED ASTRAY IN THE HEART; AND THESE (ONES) THEY KNEW THE ROADS/ WAYS/PATHS OF ME; 3.11 AS I SWORE IN MY ANGER, IF THEY THEMSELVES WILL ENTER INTO MY REST/REPOSE.

3.12 See ye, brothers, that there will not be in anyone of ye an evil heart of unbelief/disobedience in/by the (thing) to withdraw from a living God, 3.13 but I beseech ye of yourselves by each day, as far as which (time) it is being called the day, that anyone out of ye be not hardened by deceit from the sin.

3.14 For we have become partakers/sharers of the anointed (one), if indeed we might hold fast the beginning of the reality/assurance, firm until *the* end.

3.15 In/by the (thing) to be said: IF YE MIGHT HEAR HIS VOICE TODAY, HARDEN YE NOT YOUR HEARTS AS IN THE EMBITTERMENT/REBELLION. 3.16 For *are* some *of those* having heard embittered? But *were* not all those having come forth out of Egypt through Moses?

3.17 But with/to whom WAS HE ANGRY/PROVOKED *for* FORTY YEARS? *Was it* not those having sinned, of whom the corpses fell in the desert/wilderness?

3.18 And to/for whom SWORE HE NOT TO ENTER INTO HIS REST/REPOSE except the (ones) having disobeyed/ disbelieved?

3.19 And we see that they were not able to enter because of unbelief/disobedience.

4.1 Therefore, let us fear lest *for* a promise being left behind to enter into his rest/repose anyone out of ye may seem to have lacked/been deficient;

4.2 καὶ γὰρ ἐσμεν εὐηγγελισμένοι καθάπερ κἀκεῖνοι, ἀλλ' οὐκ ὠφέλησεν ὁ λόγος τῆς ἀκοῆς ἐκείνους, μὴ συγκεκερασμένος τῇ πίστι τοῖς ἀκούσασιν.

4.3 εἰσερχόμεθα οὖν εἰς τὴν κατάπαυσιν οἱ πιστεύσαντες, καθὼς εἴρηκεν, «Ὡς ὤμοσα ἐν τῇ ὀργῇ μου, εἰ εἰσελεύσονται εἰς τὴν κατάπαυσίν μου,»

καίτοι τῶν ἔργων ἀπὸ καταβολῆς κόσμου γενηθέντων. 4.4 εἴρηκεν γάρ που περὶ τῆς ἑβδόμης οὕτως,

«καὶ κατέπαυσεν ὁ θεὸς ἐν τῇ ἡμέρᾳ τῇ ἑβδόμῃ ἀπὸ πάντων τῶν ἔργων αὐτοῦ·» 4.5 καὶ ἐν τούτῳ πάλιν, «εἰ εἰσελεύσονται εἰς τὴν κατάπαυσίν μου.»

4.6 ἐπεὶ οὖν ἀπολείπεται τινὰς εἰσελθεῖν εἰς αὐτήν, καὶ οἱ πρότερον εὐαγγελισθέντες οὐκ εἰσῆλθον δι' ἀπίθιαν, 4.7 πάλιν τινὰ ὁρίζει ἡμέραν, «σήμερον,» ἐν Δαυεὶδ λέγων μετὰ τοσοῦτον χρόνον, καθὼς προείρηται, «σήμερον ἐὰν τῆς φωνῆς αὐτοῦ ἀκούσητε, μὴ σκληρύνητε τὰς καρδίας ὑμῶν.»

4.8 εἰ γὰρ αὐτοὺς Ἰησοῦς κατέπαυσεν, οὐκ ἂν περὶ ἄλλης ἐλάλει μετὰ ταῦτα ἡμέρας. 4.9 ἄρα ἀπολείπεται σαββατισμὸς τῷ λαῷ τοῦ θεοῦ· 4.10 ὁ γὰρ εἰσελθὼν εἰς τὴν κατάπαυσιν αὐτοῦ καὶ αὐτὸς κατέπαυσεν ἀπὸ τῶν ἔργων αὐτοῦ ὥσπερ ἀπὸ τῶν ἰδίων ὁ θεός.

4.11 σπουδάσωμεν οὖν εἰσελθεῖν εἰς ἐκείνην τὴν κατάπαυσιν, εἵνα μὴ ἐν τῷ αὐτῷ τις ὑποδείγματι πέσῃ τῆς ἀπιθίας. 4.12 ζῶν γὰρ ὁ λόγος τοῦ θεοῦ καὶ ἐνεργὴς καὶ τομώτερος ὑπὲρ πᾶσαν μάχαιραν δίστομον καὶ διϊκνούμενος ἄχρι μερισμοῦ ψυχῆς καὶ πνεύματος, ἁρμῶν τε καὶ μυελῶν, καὶ κριτικὸς ἐνθυμήσεων καὶ ἐννοιῶν καρδίας· 4.13 καὶ οὐκ ἔστιν κτίσις ἀφανὴς ἐνώπιον αὐτοῦ, πάντα δὲ γυμνὰ καὶ τετραχηλισμένα τοῖς ὀφθαλμοῖς αὐτοῦ, πρὸς ὃν ἡμῖν ὁ λόγος.

4.14 ἔχοντες οὖν ἀρχιερέα μέγαν διεληλύθα τοὺς οὐρανούς,

4.2   for we also have been evangelized even as they also, but the saying/logos/word profited/gained not those of the hearing/report, having not been mixed together in the faith to/for the (ones) having heard/listened.

4.3   Therefore we ourselves, the (ones) having believed/obeyed enter into the rest/repose as he has said: AS I SWORE IN MY ANGER: IF THEY WILL THEMSELVES ENTER INTO MY REST/REPOSE,

and yet having been generated from the works from the beginning of a world. 4.4   For he has thus said somewhere about/concerning the seventh: AND GOD RESTED IN/ON THE SEVENTH DAY FROM ALL HIS WORKS;   4.5 and again in/by this: IF THEY WILL ENTER INTO MY REST/REPOSE.

4.6   Therefore, since it is void/nought *for* some to enter into it, and those formerly having been evangelized went not in because of disobedience/unbelief,   4.7 again he defines/appoints a certain day, today, saying in/by David after so much time, as he has said before: IF YE MIGHT HEAR HIS VOICE TODAY, HARDEN YE NOT YOUR HEARTS.

4.8   For if Jesus refreshed/rested them, he would not be speaking about another day after these (things).   4.9 Then a sabbath observance/rest is void/nought to/for the people of God;   4.10 for the (one) having entered into his rest/repose even he, he rested from his works just as God from those his own.

4.11   Therefore we might be diligent to enter into that rest/repose, in order that anyone might not fall in/by the same example/copy of the unbelief/disobedience.   4.12 For the logos/word/reasoning of/from God is living, both active/effective and sharper over/beyond every double-edged sword, and passing through/penetrating as far as/until a separation of life/soul and spirit, both from joints and marrows, and able to judge from thoughts and notions/intents of a heart;   4.13 and there is not a creature invisible before him, but all (things) *are* naked and having been wounded/layed open to his eyes, to/with whom the logos/word/reason *is* to/for us.

4.14   Having then a great high priest, having

Ἰησοῦν τὸν υἱὸν τοῦ θεοῦ, κρατῶμεν τῆς ὁμολογίας·

4.15 οὐ γὰρ ἔχομεν ἀρχιερέα μὴ δυνάμενον συνπαθῆσαι ταῖς ἀσθενίαις ἡμῶν, πεπιρασμένον δὲ κατὰ πάντα καθ' ὁμοιότητα χωρὶς ἁμαρτίας. 4.16 προσερχώμεθα οὖν μετὰ παρρησίας τῷ θρόνῳ τῆς χάριτος, ἵνα λάβωμεν ἔλεος καὶ χάριν εὕρωμεν εἰς εὔκαιρον βοήθειαν. 5.1 πᾶς γὰρ ἀρχιερεὺς ἐξ ἀνθρώπων λαμβανόμενος ὑπὲρ ἀνθρώπων καθίσταται τὰ πρὸς τὸν θεόν, ἵνα προσφέρῃ δῶρά τε καὶ θυσίας ὑπὲρ ἁμαρτιῶν, 5.2 μετριοπαθεῖν δυνάμενος τοῖς ἀγνοοῦσι καὶ πλανωμένοις, ἐπεὶ καὶ αὐτὸς περίκειται ἀσθένιαν, 5.3 καὶ δι' αὐτὴν ὀφείλει καθὼς περὶ τοῦ λαοῦ οὕτως καὶ περὶ ἑαυτοῦ προσφέρειν περὶ ἁμαρτιῶν. 5.4 καὶ οὐχ ἑαυτῷ τις λαμβάνει τὴν τιμήν, ἀλλὰ καλούμενος ὑπὸ τοῦ θεοῦ, καθώσπερ καὶ Ἀαρών. 5.5 οὕτως καὶ ὁ χριστὸς οὐχ ἑαυτὸν ἐδόξασεν γενηθῆναι ἀρχιερέα, ἀλλ' ὁ λαλήσας πρὸς αὐτόν, «υἱός μου εἶ σύ, ἐγὼ σήμερον γεγέννηκά σε» 5.6 καθὼς καὶ ἐν ἑτέρῳ λέγει, «σὺ ἱερεὺς εἰς τὸν αἰῶνα κατὰ τὴν τάξιν Μελχισέδεκ.» 5.7 ὃς ἐν ταῖς ἡμέραις τῆς σαρκὸς αὐτοῦ, δεήσεις τε καὶ ἱκετηρίας πρὸς τὸν δυνάμενον σῴζειν αὐτὸν ἐκ θανάτου μετὰ κραυγῆς ἰσχυρᾶς καὶ δακρύων προσενέγκας καὶ εἰσακουσθεὶς ἀπὸ τῆς εὐλαβείας, 5.8 καίπερ ὢν υἱὸς ἔμαθεν ἀφ' ὧν ἔπαθεν τὴν ὑπακοήν· 5.9 καὶ τελειωθεὶς ἐγένετο πᾶσιν τοῖς ὑπακούουσιν αὐτῷ αἴτιος σωτηρίας αἰωνίου, 5.10 προσαγορευθεὶς ὑπὸ τοῦ θεοῦ ἀρχιερεὺς κατὰ τὴν τάξιν Μελχισέδεκ. 5.11 περὶ οὗ πολὺς ἡμῖν ὁ λόγος καὶ δυσερμήνευτος λέγειν, ἐπεὶ νωθροὶ γεγόνατε ταῖς ἀκοαῖς. 5.12 καὶ γὰρ ὀφείλοντες εἶναι διδάσκαλοι διὰ τὸν χρόνον, πάλιν χρίαν ἔχετε

gone through the skies/heavens, Jesus the son of God, let us hold fast from the profession/confession.
4.15 For we have not a high priest being not able to suffer with our weaknesses, but (one) having been tried/tested/tempted/proved according to all (things) in our likeness without sin. 4.16 Therefore, we may be approaching/coming near with confidence/ boldness to the throne of the gift/grace, in order that we might receive mercy and we might find favor/ grace in timely help. 5.1 For every high priest being taken/received out of men constituted/set in behalf of men/humans *for* the (things) with/toward God, in order that he offer both gifts and sacrifices in behalf of men/humans, 5.2 being able to suffer due measure for those being unaware/ignorant and being led astray, since also he himself is beset *with* weaknesses, 5.3 and because of it he owes *it*, as concerning the people so also concerning himself, to offer/bring forward concerning faults/sins. 5.4 And anyone takes not the honor/price for himself, but being called by God, even as Aaron *was*. 5.5 So also the anointed (one) glorified/made of reputation not himself to be generated a high priest, but the (one) having spoken to him: YOU, YOU ARE MY SON; I, I HAVE GENERATED YOU TODAY; 5.6 as also he says in another/different: YOU *are* A PRIEST IN THE AGE ACCORDING TO THE ORDER OF MELCHISEDEC, 5.7 who in the days of his flesh, having brought forward both petitions/entreaties and supplications/prayers with strong outcry and tears to the (one) being able to save him out of death and having been heard from the reverence/devout service, 5.8 although being a son, he learned the obedience from what (things) he suffered; 5.9 and having been completed/finished, he became/was generated a cause/reason of eternal salvation for all those obeying/listening to him, 5.10 having been named/declared by God a high priest according to the order of Melchisedec. 5.11 About the logos/word of whom for us to say much and hard to interpret, since ye have become blunted/- dull (ones) to the hearings/reports. 5.12 For also owing *it* to be teachers through the time, ye again have a need of the (thing) *for* someone to teach ye the

τοῦ διδάσκειν ὑμᾶς τινὰ τὰ στοιχῖα τῆς ἀρχῆς τῶν λογίων τοῦ θεοῦ, καὶ γεγόνατε χρείαν ἔχοντες γάλακτος, οὐ στερεᾶς τροφῆς. 5.13 πᾶς γὰρ ὁ μετέχων γάλακτος ἄπειρος λόγου δικαιοσύνης, νήπιος γάρ ἐστιν· 5.14 τελείων δέ ἐστιν ἡ στερεὰ τροφή, τῶν διὰ τὴν ἕξιν τὰ αἰσθητήρια γεγυμνασμένα ἐχόντων πρὸς διάκρισιν καλοῦ τε καὶ κακοῦ. 6.1 διὸ ἀφέντες τὸν τῆς ἀρχῆς τοῦ χριστοῦ λόγον ἐπὶ τὴν τελειότητα φερώμεθα, μὴ πάλιν θεμέλιον καταβαλλόμενοι μετανοίας ἀπὸ νεκρῶν ἔργων, καὶ πίστεως ἐπὶ θεόν, 6.2 βαπτισμῶν διδαχῆς, ἐπιθέσεώς τε χειρῶν, ἀναστάσεώς τε νεκρῶν, καὶ κρίματος αἰωνίου. 6.3 καὶ τοῦτο ποιήσομεν ἐάνπερ ἐπιτρέπῃ ὁ θεός. 6.4 ἀδύνατον γὰρ τοὺς ἅπαξ φωτισθέντας, γευσαμένους τε τῆς δωρεᾶς τῆς ἐπουρανίου καὶ μετόχους γενηθέντας πνεύματος ἁγίου 6.5 καὶ καλὸν γευσαμένους θεοῦ ῥῆμα δυνάμεις τε μέλλοντος αἰῶνος, 6.6 καὶ παραπεσόντας, πάλιν ἀνακαινίζειν εἰς μετάνοιαν, ἀνασταυροῦντας ἑαυτοῖς τὸν υἱὸν τοῦ θεοῦ καὶ παραδιγματίζοντας. 6.7 γῆ γὰρ ἡ πιοῦσα τὸν ἐπ᾽ αὐτῆς ἐρχόμενον πολλάκις ὑετόν, καὶ τίκτουσα βοτάνην εὔθετον ἐκείνοις δι᾽ οὓς καὶ γεωργεῖται, μεταλαμβάνει εὐλογίας ἀπὸ τοῦ θεοῦ· 6.8 ἐκφέρουσα δὲ ἀκάνθας καὶ τριβόλους ἀδόκιμος καὶ κατάρας ἐγγύς, ἧς τὸ τέλος εἰς καῦσιν.

6.9 πεπείσμεθα δὲ περὶ ὑμῶν, ἀγαπητοί, τὰ κρίσσονα καὶ ἐχόμενα σωτηρίας, εἰ καὶ οὕτως λαλοῦμεν· 6.10 οὐ γὰρ ἄδικος ὁ θεὸς ἐπιλαθέσθαι τοῦ ἔργου ὑμῶν καὶ τῆς ἀγάπης ἧς ἐνεδείξασθε εἰς τὸ ὄνομα αὐτοῦ, διακονήσαντες τοῖς ἁγίοις καὶ διακονοῦντες. 6.11 ἐπιθυμοῦμεν δὲ ἕκαστον ὑμῶν τὴν αὐτὴν ἐνδείκνυσθαι σπουδὴν πρὸς τὴν πληροφορίαν τῆς ἐλπίδος ἄχρι τέλους, 6.12 ἵνα μὴ νωθροὶ γένησθε,

μειμηταὶ δὲ τῶν διὰ πίστεως καὶ μακροθυμίας

elements from the beginning of the sayings/reasonings
of God, and ye have become having a need of milk, not
of firm/solid food. 5.13 For every one partaking/-
sharing from milk *is* unacquainted with a logos/saying
of justness, for he is an infant; 5.14 but the firm/-
solid food is of/from complete/mature (ones), of those
through the practice/exercise of having the faculties
having been trained toward distinction/discriminating
both of good and of bad. 6.1 Wherefore leaving the
saying/word from the beginning of the anointed (one),
we may be brought to the completion/maturity, not
again laying down for ourselves a foundation of repentance from dead works, and of faith to/on God, 6.2
from a teaching/doctrine of baptisms, and of laying on
of hands, and of a resurrection from dead (ones), and
of eternal judgment. 6.3 And we do this if indeed God
may permit. 6.4 For it is impossible *for* those once
having been enlightened, and having tasted themselves
of the heavenly gift and having been generated par-
takers/sharers from/of a holy spirit, 6.5 and having
themselves tasted a beautiful word of/from God and
powers of an age being about to come, 6.6 and having
fallen away, to renew again in repentance, crucifying
for/to themselves the son of God and making a shameful
example. 6.7 For the earth/land having drunk the rain
coming often upon it, and bearing vegetation suitable
to/for those through whom it is even/also farmed, it
partakes of/shares a blessing from God; 6.8 But
bringing forth thorns and thistles *is* rejected/unap-
proved and near an execration/curse, of which the end
is in burning.

6.9 But concerning ye, beloved (ones), we have
been persuaded *for* the better (things) and having
salvation, if even we so speak. 6.10 For God *is* not
unjust to forget/neglect the work of ye and the agape
which ye displayed in his name, having served/minis-
tered to the saints and serving/waiting on *them*. 6.11
But we desire earnestly *for* each of ye to display the
same diligence/eagerness to/with the full assurance of
the hope until an end, 6.12 that ye might not become
blunted/dull (ones),
but imitators of those inheriting the promises

κληρονομούντων τὰς ἐπαγγελίας.

6.13 τῷ γὰρ ᾿Αβραὰμ ἐπαγγιλάμενος ὁ θεός, ἐπεὶ κατ᾽ οὐδενὸς εἶχεν μείζονος ὀμόσαι, «ὤμοσεν καθ᾽ ἑαυτοῦ,» 6.14 λέγων, «εἰ μὴν εὐλογῶν εὐλογήσω σε καὶ πληθύνων πληθυνῶ» σε· 6.15 καὶ οὕτως μακροθυμήσας ἐπέτυχεν τῆς ἐπαγγελίας. 6.16 ἄνθρωποι γὰρ κατὰ τοῦ μείζονος ὀμνύουσιν, καὶ πάσης αὐτοῖς ἀντιλογίας πέρας εἰς βεβαίωσιν ὁ ὅρκος· 6.17 ἐν ᾧ περισσότερον βουλόμενος ὁ θεὸς ἐπιδεῖξαι τοῖς κληρονόμοις τῆς ἐπαγγελίας τὸ ἀμετάθετον τῆς βουλῆς αὐτοῦ ἐμεσίτευσεν ὅρκῳ, 6.18 ἵνα διὰ δύο πραγμάτων ἀμεταθέτων, ἐν οἷς ἀδύνατον ψεύσασθαι τὸν θεόν, ἰσχυρὰν παράκλησιν ἔχωμεν οἱ καταφυγόντες κρατῆσαι τῆς προκιμένης ἐλπίδος· 6.19 ἣν ὡς ἄγκυραν ἔχομεν τῆς ψυχῆς, ἀσφαλῆ τε καὶ βεβαίαν καὶ εἰσερχομένην εἰς τὸ ἐσώτερον τοῦ καταπετάσματος, 6.20 ὅπου πρόδρομος ὑπὲρ ἡμῶν εἰσῆλθεν Ἰησοῦς, κατὰ τὴν τάξιν Μελχεισέδεκ ἀρχιερεὺς γενόμενος εἰς τὸν αἰῶνα.

7.1 Οὗτος γὰρ ὁ «Μελχεισέδεκ, βασιλεὺς Σαλήμ, ἱερεὺς τοῦ θεοῦ τοῦ ὑψίστου,» ὃς «συναντήσας ᾿Αβραὰμ ὑποστρέφοντι ἀπὸ τῆς κοπῆς τῶν βασιλέων» καὶ «εὐλογήσας αὐτόν,» 7.2 ᾧ καὶ «δεκάτην ἐμέρισεν ἀπὸ πάντων» «᾿Αβραάμ,»

πρῶτον μὲν ἑρμηνευόμενος βασιλεὺς δικαιοσύνης ἔπειτα δὲ καὶ «βασιλεὺς Σαλήμ,» ὅ ἐστιν βασιλεὺς εἰρήνης, 7.3 ἀπάτωρ, ἀμήτωρ, ἀγενεαλόγητος, μήτε ἀρχὴν ἡμερῶν μήτε ζωῆς τέλος ἔχων, ἀφωμοιωμένος δὲ τῷ υἱῷ τοῦ θεοῦ, μένει ἱερεὺς εἰς τὸ διηνεκές.

7.4 θεωρεῖτε δὲ πηλίκος οὗτος ᾧ καὶ δεκάτην ᾿Αβραὰμ ἔδωκεν ἐκ τῶν ἀκροθινίων ὁ πατριάρχης. 7.5 καὶ οἱ μὲν ἐκ τῶν υἱῶν Λευεὶ τὴν ἱερατίαν λαμβάνοντες ἐντολὴν ἔχουσιν ἀποδεκατοῦν τὸν λαὸν κατὰ τὸν νόμον, τοῦτ᾽ ἔστιν τοὺς

through faith and patience/steadfastness.

6.13   For God, himself having promised to Abraham, since he had by no one a greater (thing) to swear, HE SWORE BY HIMSELF, 6.14 saying: SURELY BLESSING/SPEAKING WELL OF I SHALL BLESS YOU AND MULTIPLYING/INCREASING I SHALL MULTIPLY YOU; 6.15 and so having been patient/steadfast he obtained the promise. 6.16 For men/humans swear according to/by the greater (thing), and the oath *is* for them a limit/bound of every (one) in/for confirmation; 6.17 in/by which God being willing to demonstrate more abundantly to the heirs of the promise the unchangeableness of his will/purpose guaranteed by an oath, 6.18 in order that through two unchangeable matters/works, in/by which *it is* impossible *for* God himself to lie, we may have a strong consolation *for* those having run away to take hold of the faith being layed before us; 6.19 which we have/hold as an anchor of the life/soul, both safe and secure and entering into the innermost from/ of the veil/curtain, 6.20 where in behalf of us a forerunner, Jesus, went in, having become a priest according to the order of Melchisedec into/for the age.

7.1   For this (one), MELCHISEDEC, A KING OF SALEM, A PRIEST OF THE HIGH GOD, who HAVING MET ABRAHAM RETURNING FROM THE SLAUGHTER OF THE KINGS AND HAVING BLESSED/SPOKEN WELL OF HIM, 7.2 to whom also ABRAHAM BESTOWED A TENTH FROM ALL (THINGS), firstly being indeed interpreted/translated a king of justice and then also A KING OF SALEM, which is a king of peace, 7.3 without father, without mother, without a genealogy, neither a beginning of days nor having an end of life, but having been caused to resemble the son of God, a priest abiding in the continuous/uninterrupted.

7.4   And behold ye how great this (one) *was* to whom Abraham the patriarch gave a tenth out of the spoils/booty. 7.5 And indeed those out of the sons of Levi receiving/taking the priesthood have a command/ rule to receive a tenth from the people according to the law, this *tenth* is *for* their brothers, although

ἀδελφοὺς αὐτῶν, καίπερ ἐξεληλυθότας ἐκ τῆς ὀσφύος Ἀβραάμ· 7.6 ὁ δὲ μὴ γενεαλογούμενος ἐξ αὐτῶν δεδεκάτωκεν Ἀβραάμ, καὶ τὸν ἔχοντα τὰς ἐπαγγελίας εὐλόγηκεν. 7.7 χωρὶς δὲ πάσης ἀντιλογίας τὸ ἔλαττον ὑπὸ τοῦ κρείττονος εὐλογεῖται. 7.8 καὶ ὧδε μὲν δεκάτας ἀποθνήσκοντες ἄνθρωποι λαμβάνουσιν, ἐκεῖ δὲ μαρτυρούμενος ὅτι ζῇ. 7.9 καὶ ὡς ἔπος εἰπεῖν, δι᾿ Ἀβραὰμ καὶ Λευεὶ ὁ δεκάτας λαμβάνων δεδεκάτωται, 7.10 ἔτι γὰρ ἐν τῇ ὀσφύϊ τοῦ πατρὸς ἦν ὅτε συνήντησεν αὐτῷ Μελχισέδεκ. 7.11 εἰ μὲν οὖν τελείωσις διὰ τῆς Λευειτικῆς ἱερωσύνης ἦν, ὁ λαὸς γὰρ ἐπ᾿ αὐτῆς νενομοθέτηται, τίς ἔτι χρεία κατὰ τὴν τάξιν Μελχισέδεκ ἕτερον ἀνίστασθαι ἱερέα καὶ οὐ κατὰ τὴν τάξιν Ἀαρὼν λέγεσθαι; 7.12 μετατιθεμένης γὰρ τῆς ἱερωσύνης ἐξ ἀνάγκης καὶ νόμου μετάθεσις γίνεται. 7.13 ἐφ᾿ ὃν γὰρ λέγεται ταῦτα φυλῆς ἑτέρας μετέσχηκεν, ἀφ᾿ ἧς οὐδεὶς προσέσχηκεν τῷ θυσιαστηρίῳ· 7.14 πρόδηλον γὰρ ὅτι ἐξ Ἰούδα ἀνατέταλκεν ὁ κύριος ἡμῶν, εἰς ἣν φυλὴν περὶ ἱερέων οὐδὲν Μωϋσῆς ἐλάλησεν.

7.15 καὶ περισσότερον ἔτι κατάδηλόν ἐστιν, εἰ κατὰ τὴν ὁμοιότητα Μελχεισέδεκ ἀνίσταται ἱερεὺς ἕτερος, 7.16 ὃς οὐ κατὰ νόμον ἐντολῆς σαρκίνης γέγονεν ἀλλὰ κατὰ δύναμιν ζωῆς ἀκαταλύτου, 7.17 μαρτυρεῖτε γὰρ ὅτι «σὺ ἱερεὺς εἰς τὸν αἰῶνα κατὰ τὴν τάξιν Μελχισέδεκ.»

7.18 ἀθέτησις μὲν γὰρ γίνεται προαγούσης ἐντολῆς διὰ τὸ αὐτῆς ἀσθενὲς καὶ ἀνωφελές, 7.19 οὐδὲν γὰρ ἐτελείωσεν ὁ νόμος, ἐπεισαγωγὴ δὲ κρίττονος ἐλπίδος, δι᾿ ἧς ἐγγίζομεν τῷ θεῷ.

7.20 καὶ καθ᾿ ὅσον οὐ χωρὶς ὁρκωμοσίας, οἱ μὲν γὰρ χωρὶς ὁρκωμοσίας εἰσὶν ἱερεῖς γεγονότες, 7.21 ὁ δὲ μετὰ

having come forth out of the loin of Abraham; 7.6 but also the (one) being not generated/having no genealogy out of them Abraham has given a tenth, and he has praised/blessed the (one) having the promises. 7.7 And without every dispute/contradiction, the lesser/ lower is praised/blessed by the better. 7.8 And indeed here dying men/humans receive tenths/tithes, but also there being testified that he lives. 7.9 And so to speak a word, through Abraham even Levi, the (one) receiving tenths/tithes has been tithed, 7.10 for he was still in the loin of the father when Melchisedec met with him. 7.11 Then if indeed an ending/completion was through the Levitical priesthood, for to/on/by it the people has been furnished/endowed with law, why *is* still a need *for* another/different priest to arise according to the order of Melchisedec and not to be said/called according to the order of Aaron? 7.12 For the priesthood, from being changed, it becomes also out of necessity *for* a change of law. 7.13 for *he* upon/to whom these (things) is/are said has partaken of another/different tribe, from which no one has attended to the sacrificial altar; 7.14 for *it is* clear/evident that our Lord has risen up out of Juda, in which tribe Moses spoke nothing about/concerning priests.

7.15 And more excessively it is still very clear, if another/different priest arises according to the likeness of Melchisedec, 7.16 who became/came into being not according to a law of fleshy command/ order, but according to a power of indestructible/indissoluble life, 7.17 for it was testified: YOU *are* A PRIEST INTO/FOR THE AGE ACCORDING TO THE ORDER OF MELCHISEDEC.

7.18 For indeed there becomes an annulment/a setting aside of preceding/previous command/order/ rule because of the (thing) of it *being* weak and unprofitable, 7.19 for the law finished/completed nothing, but also the bringing on of a better hope, through which we draw near to God.

7.20 And be as much as not without an oath/taking an oath, for indeed they have become without taking an oath, 7.21 but also the (he) with/after

ὁρκωμοσίας διὰ τοῦ λέγοντος πρὸς αὐτόν, «ὤμοσεν κύριος, καὶ οὐ μεταμεληθήσεται, σὺ ἱερεὺς εἰς τὸν αἰῶνα,» 7.22 κατὰ τοσοῦτο καὶ κρείττονος διαθήκης γέγονεν ἔγγυος Ἰησοῦς. 7.23 καὶ οἱ μὲν πλείονές εἰσιν γεγονότες ἱερεῖς διὰ τὸ θανάτῳ κωλύεσθαι παραμένειν· 7.24 ὁ δὲ διὰ τὸ μένειν αὐτὸν εἰς τὸν αἰῶνα ἀπαράβατον ἔχει τὴν ἱερωσύνην· 7.25 ὅθεν καὶ σῴζειν εἰς τὸ παντελὲς δύναται τοὺς προσερχομένους δι' αὐτοῦ τῷ θεῷ, πάντοτε ζῶν εἰς τὸ ἐντυγχάνειν ὑπὲρ αὐτῶν.

7.26 τοιοῦτος γὰρ ἡμῖν ἔπρεπεν ἀρχιερεύς, ὅσιος, ἄκακος, ἀμίαντος, κεχωρισμένος ἀπὸ τῶν ἁμαρτωλῶν, καὶ ὑψηλότερος τῶν οὐρανῶν γενόμενος· 7.27 ὃς οὐκ ἔχει καθ' ἡμέραν ἀνάγκην, ὥσπερ οἱ ἀρχιερεῖς, πρότερον ὑπὲρ τῶν ἰδίων ἁμαρτιῶν θυσίας ἀναφέρειν, ἔπειτα τῶν τοῦ λαοῦ· τοῦτο γὰρ ἐποίησεν ἐφάπαξ ἑαυτὸν προσενέγκας.

7.28 ὁ νόμος γὰρ ἀνθρώπους καθίστησιν ἀρχιερεῖς ἔχοντας ἀσθένειαν, ὁ λόγος δὲ τῆς ὁρκωμοσίας τῆς μετὰ τὸν νόμον υἱὸν εἰς τὸν αἰῶνα τετελειωμένον.

8.1 Κεφάλαιον δὲ ἐπὶ τοῖς λεγομένοις, τοιοῦτον ἔχομεν ἀρχιερέα, ὃς ἐκάθισεν ἐν δεξιᾷ τοῦ θρόνου τῆς μεγαλωσύνης ἐν τοῖς οὐρανοῖς, 8.2 τῶν ἁγίων λιτουργὸς καὶ τῆς σκηνῆς τῆς ἀληθινῆς, ἣν ἔπηξεν ὁ κύριος, οὐκ ἄνθρωπος.

8.3 πᾶς γὰρ ἀρχιερεὺς εἰς τὸ προσφέρειν δῶρά τε καὶ θυσίας καθίσταται· ὅθεν ἀναγκαῖον ἔχειν τι καὶ τοῦτον ὃ προσενέγκῃ.

8.4 εἰ μὲν οὖν ἦν ἐπὶ γῆς, οὐδ' ἂν ἦν ἱερεύς, ὄντων τῶν προσφερόντων κατὰ νόμον τὰ δῶρα· 8.5 οἵτινες ὑποδίγματι καὶ σκιᾷ λατρεύουσιν τῶν ἐπουρανίων,

καθὼς κεχρημάτισται Μωϋσῆς μέλλων ἐπιτελεῖν τὴν σκηνήν, «ὅρα» γάρ, φησίν, «ποιήσῃς πάντα κατὰ τὸν τύπον τὸν

taking an oath through the (one) saying to him: *The* LORD SWORE, AND HE WILL NOT CHANGE *his* MIND: YOU *are* A PRIEST INTO/FOR THE AGE, 7.22 according to so much also Jesus has become a guarantee of a better covenant. 7.23 And they indeed have become many priests because of the (thing) to be prevented by death to continue/remain; 7.24 but also the (he), because of the (thing) *for* him to abide into/for the age, he has/holds the permanent priesthood; 7.25 from where also he is able to save in the entirety those coming near to God through him, always living in/to the (thing) to intercede in behalf of them.

7.26 For such a high priest was also fitting for us, holy, not/without bad, unstained, having been separated from the sinners, and having become higher from/than the skies/heavens; 7.27 who has not a necessity day by day, even as the high priests, firstly in behalf of the sins his own to offer sacrifices, then of those of the people; for this he did at one time, having offered up himself.

7.28 For the law constitutes/sets men having weakness *as* priests, but the saying/word of the oath taking, from the (one) after the law, *sets* a son having been finished/completed into/for the age.

8.1 And a summary over the (things) being said: We have such a high priest, who sat in/by *the* right of the throne of the majesty in the heavens, 8.2 a public servant/minister of the holy (things) and of the true tabernacle, which the Lord set up, not a man/human.

8.3 For every high priest is constituted in/to the (thing) to offer both gifts and sacrifices; from where *is* a necessity *for* this (one) to have something which he might offer.

8.4 Then if indeed he were on earth, he would not be a priest, being of those offering the gifts according to law; 8.5 who they serve/worship a copy/example and a shadow of the heavenly (things),

as Moses has been taught/warned being about to complete the tabernacle/tent, for he says: SEE, YOU WILL MAKE/DO ALL (THINGS) ACCORDING TO THE IMAGE/TYPE

δειχθέντα σοι ἐν τῷ ὄρει·» 8.6 νυνὶ δὲ διαφορωτέρας τέτυχε λιτουργίας, ὅσῳ καὶ κρείττονός διαθήκης ἐστιν μεσίτης, ἥτις ἐπὶ κρίττοσιν ἐπαγγελίαις νενομοθέτηται.

8.7 εἰ γὰρ ἡ πρώτη ἐκείνη ἦν ἄμεμπτος, οὐκ ἂν δευτέρας ἐζητεῖτο τόπος· 8.8 μεμφόμενος γὰρ αὐτοὺς λέγει, « ἰδοὺ ἡμέραι ἔρχονται, λέγει κύριος, καὶ συντελέσω ἐπὶ τὸν οἶκον Ἰσραὴλ καὶ ἐπὶ τὸν οἶκον Ἰούδα διαθήκην καινήν, 8.9 οὐ κατὰ τὴν διαθήκην ἣν ἐποίησα τοῖς πατράσιν αὐτῶν ἐν ἡμέρᾳ ἐπιλαβομένου μου τῆς χειρὸς αὐτῶν ἐξαγαγεῖν αὐτοὺς ἐκ γῆς Αἰγύπτου, ὅτι αὐτοὶ οὐκ ἐνέμιναν ἐν τῇ διαθήκῃ μου, κἀγὼ ἠμέλησα αὐτῶν, λέγει κύριος.

8.10 ὅτι αὕτη ἡ διαθήκη ἣν διαθήσομαι τῷ οἴκῳ Ἰσραὴλ μετὰ τὰς ἡμέρας ἐκίνας, λέγει κύριος, διδοὺς νόμους μου εἰς τὴν διάνοιαν αὐτῶν, καὶ ἐπὶ καρδίας αὐτῶν ἐπιγράψω αὐτούς, καὶ ἔσομαι αὐτοῖς εἰς θεὸν καὶ αὐτοὶ ἔσονταί μοι εἰς λαόν. 8.11 καὶ οὐ μὴ διδάξωσιν ἕκαστος τὸν πολίτην αὐτοῦ καὶ ἕκαστος τὸν ἀδελφὸν αὐτοῦ, λέγων, γνῶθι τὸν κύριον, ὅτι πάντες εἰδήσουσίν με ἀπὸ μικροῦ ἕως μεγάλου αὐτῶν. 8.12 ὅτι ἵλεως ἔσομαι ταῖς ἀδικίαις αὐτῶν, καὶ τῶν ἁμαρτιῶν αὐτῶν οὐ μὴ μνησθῶ ἔτι.»

8.13 ἐν τῷ λέγειν « κενὴν» πεπαλαίωκε τὴν πρώτην· τὸ δὲ παλαιούμενον καὶ γηράσκον ἐγγὺς ἀφανισμοῦ.

9.1 Εἶχε μὲν οὖν καὶ ἡ πρώτη δικαιώματα λατρίας τό τε ἅγιον κοσμικόν. 9.2 σκηνὴ γὰρ κατεσκευάσθη ἡ πρώτη ἐν ᾗ ἥ τε λυχνία καὶ ἡ τράπεζα καὶ ἡ πρόθεσις τῶν ἄρτων, ἥτις λέγεται ἅγια·

9.3 μετὰ δὲ τὸ δεύτερον καταπέτασμα σκηνὴ ἡ λεγομένη ἅγια ἁγίων, 9.4 χρυσοῦν ἔχουσα θυμιατήριον καὶ τὴν κιβωτὸν

HAVING BEEN SHOWN TO YOU ON/AT THE MOUNTAIN; 8.6 but now he has obtained a more excellent public ministry/ service, in as much as he is also a mediator of a better covenant, which has been enacted upon better promises.

8.7 For if that first (one) were without fault, a place he would not be seeking from/of a second; 8.8 for finding fault for/*with* them, he says: BEHOLD, DAYS ARE COMING, SAYS THE LORD, AND I SHALL COMPLETE/ACCOMPLISH A NEW COVENANT OVER/UPON THE HOUSE OF ISRAEL AND THE HOUSE OF JUDA, 8.9 NOT ACCORDING TO THE COVENANT WHICH I MADE WITH THEIR FATHERS IN A DAY OF MY HAVING TAKEN THE HAND OF THEM TO LEAD/BRING THEM FORTH OUT OF A LAND/EARTH OF EGYPT, BECAUSE THEY CONTINUED NOT IN/WITH MY COVENANT, AND I, I DISREGARDED/NEGLECTED THEM, SAYS *the* LORD.

8.10 BECAUSE THIS *is* THE COVENANT WHICH I SHALL COVENANT WITH THE HOUSE OF ISRAEL AFTER THOSE DAYS, SAYS *the* LORD, GIVING LAWS FROM ME INTO THE MIND/ THOUGHT OF THEM, AND I SHALL INSCRIBE THEM UPON THEIR HEARTS, AND I SHALL BE FOR THEM IN/FOR A GOD AND THEY WILL BE OF ME IN/FOR A PEOPLE. 8.11 AND BY NO MEANS MIGHT THEY TEACH EACH (ONE) HIS FELLOW TOWNSMAN AND EACH (ONE) HIS BROTHER, SAYING: KNOW YOU THE LORD, BECAUSE ALL (MEN) WILL KNOW ME FROM A LITTLE (ONE) UNTIL A GREAT (ONE) OF THEM/(THE LEAST TO THEIR GREATEST). 8.12 BECAUSE I SHALL BE MERCIFUL FOR/TO THEIR INJUSTICES, AND BY NO MEANS MIGHT I STILL BE REMINDED OF THEIR FAULTS/SINS.

8.13 By the (thing) to say: A new (one), he has declared the first obsolete/old; and the (thing) being declared obsolete also is aging near *to be* an invisible (thing).

9.1 Then indeed the first/former (one) had just rules of worship/service and the adorned/decorated holy (place). 9.2 For the first (one) a tent/tabernacle was prepared/erected in which was both a lampstand and the table and laying before/setting forth of the loaves, which is called holy (things/loaves);

9.3 and after the second veil/curtain *was* the tent being called: Holy of holies, 9.4 having/holding

τῆς διαθήκης περικεκαλυμμένην πάντοθεν χρυσίῳ, ἐν ᾗ στάμνος χρυσῆ ἔχουσα τὸ μάννα καὶ ἡ ῥάβδος Ἀαρὼν ἡ βλαστήσασα καὶ αἱ πλάκες τῆς διαθήκης, 9.5 ὑπεράνω δὲ αὐτῆς χερουβὶν δόξης κατασκιάζοντα τὸ ἱλαστήριον· περὶ ὧν οὐκ ἐν ἔστιν νῦν λέγειν κατὰ μέρος.

9.6 τούτων δὲ οὕτως κατεσκευασμένων, εἰς μὲν τὴν πρώτην σκηνὴν διὰ παντὸς εἰσίασιν οἱ ἱερεῖς τὰς λατρείας ἐπιτελοῦντες, 9.7 εἰς δὲ τὴν δευτέραν ἅπαξ τοῦ ἐνιαυτοῦ μόνος ὁ ἀρχιερεύς, οὐ χωρὶς αἵματος, ὃ προσφέρει ὑπὲρ ἑαυτοῦ καὶ τῶν τοῦ λαοῦ ἀγνοημάτων,

9.8 τοῦτο δηλοῦντος τοῦ πνεύματος τοῦ ἁγίου, μήπω πεφανερῶσθαι τὴν τῶν ἁγίων ὁδὸν ἔτι τῆς πρώτης σκηνῆς ἐχούσης στάσιν,

9.9 ἥτις παραβολὴ εἰς τὸν καιρὸν τὸν ἐνεστηκότα, καθ᾿ ἣν δῶρά τε καὶ θυσίαι προσφέρονται μὴ δυνάμεναι κατὰ συνίδησιν τελιῶσαι τὸν λατρεύοντα, 9.10 μόνον ἐπὶ βρώμασιν καὶ πόμασιν καὶ διαφόροις βαπτισμοῖς, δικαιώματα σαρκὸς μέχρι καιροῦ διορθώσεως ἐπικείμενα.

9.11 χριστὸς δὲ παραγενόμενος ἀρχιερεὺς τῶν μέλλων τῶν ἀγαθῶν διὰ τῆς μείζονος καὶ τελειοτέρας σκηνῆς οὐ χειροποιήτου, τοῦτ᾿ ἔστιν οὐ ταύτης τῆς κτίσεως, 9.12 οὐδὲ δι᾿ αἵματος τράγων καὶ μόσχων διὰ δὲ τοῦ ἰδίου αἵματος, εἰσῆλθεν ἐφάπαξ εἰς τὰ ἅγια, αἰωνίαν λύτρωσιν εὑράμενος. 9.13 εἰ γὰρ τὸ αἷμα τράγων καὶ ταύρων καὶ σποδὸς δαμάλεως ῥαντίζουσα τοὺς κεκοινωμένους ἁγιάζει πρὸς τὴν τῆς σαρκὸς καθαρότητα, 9.14 πόσῳ μᾶλλον τὸ αἷμα τοῦ χριστοῦ, ὃς διὰ πνεύματος αἰωνίου ἑαυτὸν προσήνεγκεν ἄμωμον τῷ θεῷ, καθαριεῖ τὴν συνείδησιν ἡμῶν ἀπὸ νεκρῶν ἔργων εἰς τὸ λατρεύειν θεῷ ζῶντι.

9.15 καὶ διὰ τοῦτο διαθήκης καινῆς μεσίτης ἐστίν, ὅπως

a golden altar and the ark of the covenant, having
been covered about from all directions/sides with
gold, in which *were* a gold pot having/holding the
manna and the staff/rod of Aaron, the (one) having
budded, and the tablets of the covenant, 9.5 and
above/over it *were* cherubim of glory/fame overshadowing the place/means of conciliation, about which it is
not now/presently to speak down from a part/in detail.

9.6 And thus from these (things) having been
prepared, the priests indeed were entering into the
first tent on account of every ending/accomplishing *of*
the services/rites/duties, 9.7 but also only the high
priest *entered* into the second *tent* at one time of the
year, not without blood, which he offers in behalf of
himself and of the ignorances of the people,

9.8 this (thing), being made clear from the holy
spirit, the road/way of the holy (ones)/saints not yet
to have been manifested from the first/former tent/
tabernacle still having a standing,

9.9 which *was* a parable to/for the time/season
having been present, according to which both gifts and
sacrifices are offered being not able according to
conscience for the one worshiping/serving to com-
plete/finish, 9.10 only on/over foods and drinks and
different dippings/washings, just rules from/of flesh
being pressed upon until a time of a change in form.

9.11 But the anointed (one), having arrived a
high priest of the good (things) being about to become
through the greater and more complete tent/tabernacle
not made by hand, this is not of this creation, 9.12
nor through blood of goats and bullocks/calves, but
through the blood his own/his own blood, he entered
once/at one time into the holies, having found eternal
redemption/release. 9.13 For if the blood of goats
and bulls and ashes of a heifer, being sprinkled *for*
those having been defiled, sanctifies to/toward the
cleanness of the flesh, 9.14 by how much more the
blood of the anointed (one), who through an eternal
spirit offered himself without fault/blame to God,
will cleanse our conscience from dead works in/for the
(thing) to serve/worship to/for a living God.

9.15 And because of this he is a mediator of a

θανάτου γενομένου εἰς ἀπολύτρωσιν τῶν ἐπὶ τῇ πρώτῃ διαθήκῃ παραβάσεων τὴν ἐπαγγελίαν λάβωσιν οἱ κεκλημένοι τῆς αἰωνίου κληρονομίας.

9.16 ὅπου γὰρ διαθήκη, θάνατον ἀνάγκη φέρεσθαι τοῦ διαθεμένου· 9.17 διαθήκη γὰρ ἐπὶ νεκροῖς βεβαία, ἐπεὶ μήποτε ἰσχύι ὅτε ζῇ ὁ διαθέμενος.

9.18 ὅθεν οὐδ᾽ ἡ πρώτη χωρὶς αἵματος ἐνκεκένισται·

9.19 λαληθείσης γὰρ πάσης ἐντολῆς κατὰ τὸν νόμον ὑπὸ Μωϋσέως παντὶ τῷ λαῷ, λαβὼν τὸ αἷμα τῶν μόσχων καὶ τῶν τράγων μετὰ ὕδατος καὶ ἐρίου κοκκίνου καὶ ὑσσώπου αὐτό τε τὸ βιβλίον καὶ πάντα τὸν λαὸν ἐράντισεν, 9.20 λέγων, τοῦτο «τὸ αἷμα τῆς διαθήκης ἧς ἐνετίλατο πρὸς ὑμᾶς ὁ θεός·»

9.21 καὶ τὴν σκηνὴν δὲ καὶ πάντα τὰ σκεύη τῆς λιτουργίας τῷ αἵματι ὁμοίως ἐράντισεν. 9.22 καὶ σχεδὸν ἐν αἵματι πάντα καθαρίζεται κατὰ τὸν νόμον, καὶ χωρὶς αἱματεκχυσίας οὐ γίνεται ἄφεσις.

9.23 ἀνάγκη οὖν τὰ μὲν ὑποδίγματα τῶν ἐν τοῖς οὐρανοῖς τούτοις καθαρίζεσθαι, αὐτὰ δὲ τὰ ἐπουράνια κρείττοσι θυσίαις παρὰ ταύτας.

9.24 οὐ γὰρ εἰς χιροποίητα εἰσῆλθεν ἅγια χριστός, ἀντίτυπα τῶν ἀληθινῶν, ἀλλ᾽ εἰς αὐτὸν τὸν οὐρανόν, νῦν ἐμφανισθῆναι τῷ προσώπῳ τοῦ θεοῦ ὑπὲρ ἡμῶν· 9.25 οὐδ᾽ ἵνα πολλάκις προσφέρῃ ἑαυτόν, ὥσπερ ὁ ἀρχιερεὺς εἰσέρχεται εἰς τὰ ἅγια κατ᾽ ἐνιαυτὸν ἐν αἵματι ἀλλοτρίῳ, 9.26 ἐπεὶ ἔδει αὐτὸν πολλάκις παθεῖν ἀπὸ καταβολῆς κόσμου·

νυνὶ δὲ ἅπαξ ἐπὶ συντελείᾳ τῶν αἰώνων εἰς ἀθέτησιν τῆς ἁμαρτίας διὰ τῆς θυσίας αὐτοῦ πεφανέρωται.

9.27 καὶ καθ᾽ ὅσον ἀπόκειται τοῖς ἀνθρώποις ἅπαξ

new covenant, that from a death having happened to/for redemption of the transgressions upon/against the first covenant, those having been called/invited might take/receive the promise of the eternal inheritance.

9.16 For where a covenant *exists*, *is* a necessity *for* death of the one covenanting to be brought/offered; 9.17 for a covenant over/to dead (ones) *is* firm/sure, since it never is strong when the (one) having covenanted is living.

9.18 From where neither the first has been dedicated without blood;

9.19 for every command having been spoken by Moses to all the people according to the law, having taken the blood of the bullocks and the goats with water and red wool and hyssop, he sprinkled/purified both the scroll itself and all the people, 9.20 saying: This *is* THE BLOOD OF THE COVENANT WHICH GOD ENJOINED/CHARGED TO YE.

9.21 And both the tent/tabernacle and all the vessels/instruments of the liturgy/public service he likewise sprinkled/purified with the blood. 9.22 And in/by blood, almost all (things) are cleansed/purified according to the law, and without shedding of blood, forgiveness/remission becomes not.

9.23 Therefore a necessity *is* indeed *for* the copies/examples of the (things) in the skies/heavens to be cleansed/purified by these (things), but also for the heavenly (things) themselves by better sacrifices from/than these (things).

9.24 For the anointed (one) went not into holies made by hand, types/substitutes of the true (things), but into the sky/heaven itself, now to be manifested before the face of God in behalf of us; 9.25 nor that he should offer himself often, even as the high priest enters into the holies year by year with blood belonging to another, 9.26 since it was necessary *for* him to suffer often from foundation of a world;

but now at one time/once to/against completion of the ages he has been manifested/made clear to/for a setting aside of the sin through his sacrifice. 9.27 And in as much as it has been reserved/layed up for the men once to die, but after this (thing) a judg-

ἀποθανεῖν, μετὰ δὲ τοῦτο κρίσις, 9.28 οὕτως καὶ ὁ χριστός, ἅπαξ προσενεχθεὶς εἰς τὸ πολλῶν ἀνενεγκεῖν ἁμαρτίας, ἐκ δευτέρου χωρὶς ἁμαρτίας ὀφθήσεται τοῖς αὐτὸν ἀπεκδεχομένοις εἰς σωτηρίαν.

10.1 Σκιὰν γὰρ ἔχων ὁ νόμος τῶν μελλόντων ἀγαθῶν, οὐκ αὐτὴν τὴν εἰκόνα τῶν πραγμάτων, κατ' ἐνιαυτὸν ταῖς αὐταῖς θυσίαις αὐτῶν ἃς προσφέρουσιν εἰς τὸ διηνεκὲς οὐδέποτε δύναται τοὺς προσερχομένους τελιῶσαι·

10.2 ἐπεὶ οὐκ ἂν ἐπαύσαντο προσφερόμεναι, διὰ τὸ μηδεμίαν ἔχιν ἔτι συνίδησιν ἁμαρτιῶν τοὺς λατρεύοντας ἅπαξ κεκαθαρισμένους;

10.3 ἀλλ' ἐν αὐταῖς ἀνάμνησις ἁμαρτιῶν κατ' ἐνιαυτόν, 10.4 ἀδύνατον γὰρ αἷμα τράγων καὶ ταύρων ἀφαιρῖν ἁμαρτίας. 10.5 διὸ εἰσερχόμενος εἰς τὸν κόσμον λέγει, «θυσίαν καὶ προσφορὰν οὐκ ἠθέλησας, σῶμα δὲ κατηρτίσω μοι·

10.6 ὁλοκαυτώματα καὶ περὶ ἁμαρτίας οὐκ εὐδόκησας. 10.7 τότε εἶπον, ἰδοὺ ἥκω, ἐν κεφαλίδι βιβλίου γέγραπται περὶ ἐμοῦ, τοῦ ποιῆσαι, ὁ θεός, τὸ θέλημά σου.» 10.8 ἀνώτερον λέγων ὅτι «θυσίας καὶ προσφορὰς» καὶ «ὁλοκαυτώματα καὶ περὶ ἁμαρτίας οὐκ ἠθέλησας οὐδὲ εὐδόκησας,» αἵτινες κατὰ νόμον προσφέρονται, 10.9 «τότε» εἴρηκεν, «ἰδοὺ ἥκω τοῦ ποιῆσαι τὸ θέλημά σου.»

ἀναιρεῖ τὸ πρῶτον ἵνα τὸ δεύτερον στήσῃ·

10.10 ἐν ᾧ θελήματι ἡγιασμένοι ἐσμὲν διὰ τῆς προσφορᾶς τοῦ σώματος Ἰησοῦ χριστοῦ ἐφάπαξ.

10.11 καὶ πᾶς μὲν ἱερεὺς ἔστηκεν καθ' ἡμέραν λιτουργῶν καὶ τὰς αὐτὰς πολλάκις προσφέρων θυσίας, αἵτινες οὐδέποτε δύνανται περιελεῖν ἁμαρτίας.

10.12 οὗτος δὲ μίαν ὑπὲρ ἁμαρτιῶν προσενέγκας θυσίαν εἰς

ment, 9.28 thus also the anointed (one), having been offered once in/for the (thing) to bear/carry sins of many, he will be seen/visible from a second (time) without a sin to those awaiting/earnestly expecting him in salvation.

10.1 For the law, holding/having a shadow of the good (things) being about to come, not the image itself of the matters/works/practical things, is never able by the same sacrifices which they offer year by year in the continual (rites) to mature/complete/perfect the (ones) coming near;
10.2 when would not they have ceased being offered, because of the (thing) *for* those worshiping once/at one time having been cleansed to have nothing/no conscience of sins?
10.3 But in them *is* a remembrance/reminder of sins year by year/by a year/annually, 10.4 for *it is* impossible *for* blood of goats and bulls to take away/forgive sins. 10.5 Wherefore, entering into the world, he says: SACRIFICE AND OFFERING YOU WANTED NOT, BUT YOU PREPARED YOURSELF A BODY FOR ME;
10.6 AND CONCERNING SINS, YOU WERE NOT WELL PLEASED WITH WHOLE BURNT OFFERINGS. 10.7 THEN I SAID: BEHOLD, I HAVE COME, IN A HEADING/CHAPTER OF A SCROLL IT HAS BEEN WRITTEN ABOUT ME, OF THE (THING) TO DO, GOD, YOUR WILL. 10.8 More above saying that YOU WANTED NOT, NEITHER WERE YOU WELL PLEASED WITH SACRIFICES AND OFFERING and BURNT OFFERINGS, EVEN CONCERNING SIN, which are being offered according to the law, 10.9 then he has said: BEHOLD, I HAVE COME FROM THE (THING) TO DO YOUR WILL.
He takes up/away the first in order that he might establish/set up the second;
10.10 in/by which will we have been sanctified/set apart through the offering of the body of Jesus, the anointed (one), at one time/once.
10.11 And indeed every priest has stood day by day serving/ministering publicly and offering often/many times the same sacrifices, which are never able to remove sins.
10.12 But also this (one) having offered one

τὸ διηνεκὲς ἐκάθισεν ἐν δεξιᾷ τοῦ θεοῦ,

10.13 τὸ λοιπὸν ἐκδεχόμενος ἕως τεθῶσιν οἱ ἐχθροὶ αὐτοῦ ὑποπόδιον τῶν ποδῶν αὐτοῦ· 10.14 μιᾷ γὰρ προσφορᾷ τετελίωκεν εἰς τὸ διηνεκὲς τοὺς ἁγιαζομένους.

10.15 μαρτυρεῖ δὲ ἡμῖν καὶ τὸ πνεῦμα τὸ ἅγιον· μετὰ γὰρ τὸ εἰρηκέναι, 10.16 «αὕτη ἡ διαθήκη ἣν διαθήσομαι» πρὸς αὐτοὺς «μετὰ τὰς ἡμέρας ἐκείνας, λέγει κύριος, διδοὺς νόμους μου ἐπὶ καρδίας αὐτῶν, καὶ ἐπὶ τὴν διάνοιαν αὐτῶν ἐπιγράψω αὐτούς, 10.17 καὶ τῶν ἁμαρτιῶν αὐτῶν καὶ τῶν ἀνομιῶν αὐτῶν οὐ μὴ μνησθήσομαι ἔτι.»

10.18 ὅπου δὲ ἄφεσις τούτων, οὐκέτι προσφορὰ περὶ ἁμαρτίας.

10.19 ἔχοντες οὖν, ἀδελφοί, παρρησίαν εἰς τὴν εἴσοδον τῶν ἁγίων ἐν τῷ αἵματι Ἰησοῦ, 10.20 ἣν ἐνεκαίνισεν ἡμῖν ὁδὸν πρόσφατον καὶ ζῶσαν διὰ τοῦ καταπετάσματος, τοῦτ' ἔστιν τῆς σαρκὸς αὐτοῦ, 10.21 καὶ ἱερέα μέγαν ἐπὶ τὸν οἶκον τοῦ θεοῦ, 10.22 προσερχώμεθα μετὰ ἀληθινῆς καρδίας ἐν πληροφορίᾳ πίστεως, ῥεραντισμένοι τὰς καρδίας ἀπὸ συνειδήσεως πονηρᾶς καὶ λελουσμένοι τὸ σῶμα ὕδατι καθαρῷ· 10.23 κατέχωμεν τὴν ὁμολογίαν τῆς ἐλπίδος ἀκλινῆ, πιστὸς γὰρ ὁ ἐπαγγειλάμενος· 10.24 καὶ κατανοῶμεν ἀλλήλους εἰς παροξυσμὸν ἀγάπης καὶ καλῶν ἔργων, 10.25 μὴ ἐγκαταλίποντες τὴν ἐπισυναγωγὴν ἑαυτῶν, καθὼς ἔθος τισίν, ἀλλὰ παρακαλοῦντες, καὶ τοσούτῳ μᾶλλον ὅσῳ βλέπετε ἐγγίζουσαν τὴν ἡμέραν.

10.26 ἑκουσίως γὰρ ἁμαρτανόντων ἡμῶν μετὰ τὸ λαβεῖν τὴν ἐπίγνωσιν τῆς ἀληθείας, οὐκέτι περὶ ἁμαρτιῶν ἀπολίπεται θυσία,

10.27 φοβερὰ δέ τις ἐκδοχὴ κρίσεως καὶ πυρὸς ζῆλος ἐσθίειν μέλλοντος τοὺς ὑπεναντίους.

sacrifice in behalf of sins sat in the continual/un-
ending (time) at *the* right *hand* of God,

10.13 *for* the remaining (time)/henceforth await-
ing expectantly until the enemies of him might be put
a footstool of his feet; 10.14 for in/by one sacrifice he has completed/finished into the uninterrupted
(time) the (ones) being sanctified/set apart.

10.15 And the holy spirit also testifies for us;
for after the (thing) to have been said: 10.16 THIS
is THE COVENANT WHICH I SHALL COVENANT WITH THEM AFTER
THOSE DAYS, SAYS *the* LORD: GIVING MY LAWS, I SHALL
INSCRIBE THEM UPON THEIR HEARTS AND UPON THEIR MINDS,
10.17 AND BY NO MEANS SHALL I STILL REMEMBER THEIR
SINS AND THEIR LAWLESSNESSES/VIOLATIONS.

10.18 And where *there is* forgiveness/remission
of these, *there is* no longer an offering concerning
sin.

10.19 Therefore, brothers, having confidence/
boldness in/for the entering of the holies/holy
(ones)/saints by the blood of Jesus, 10.20 which he
initiated/instituted for us a newly made and living
way/road through the veil/curtain, this (one) is his
flesh, 10.21 and a great priest over the house/house-
hold of God, 10.22 we may ourselves come near with a
true heart in/with full assurance/certainty from
faith, the hearts having been purified/sprinkled from
an evil conscience and the body having been bathed
in/with clean/pure water; 10.23 we may hold fast the
profession/confession of the unwavering hope, for the
(one) having promised *is* faithful; 10.24 and we may/
should consider one another in/for an encouragement/a
stirring up of agape and of good works, 10.25 forsak-
ing not the coming together of ourselves, as *is* a
custom for some, but urging/encouraging, and in/by so
much more as ye see the day drawing near.

10.26 For of/from us sinning intentionally/de-
liberately after the (thing) to receive the recogni-
tion/full knowledge of the truth, there is no longer
left a sacrifice concerning sins,

10.27 but a certain fearful awaiting/expecting
of judgment and of a jealous fire being about to eat
the adversaries/opponents.

10.28 ἀθετήσας τις νόμον Μωϋσέως χωρὶς οἰκτιρμῶν ἐπὶ δυσὶν ἢ τρισὶν μάρτυσιν ἀποθνῄσκει· 10.29 πόσῳ δοκεῖτε χείρονος ἀξιωθήσεται τιμωρίας ὁ τὸν υἱὸν τοῦ θεοῦ καταπατήσας, καὶ τὸ αἷμα τῆς διαθήκης κοινὸν ἡγησάμενος ἐν ᾧ ἡγιάσθη, καὶ τὸ πνεῦμα τῆς χάριτος ἐνυβρίσας; 10.30 οἴδαμεν γὰρ τὸν εἰπόντα, «ἐμοὶ ἐκδίκησεις, ἐγὼ ἀνταποδώσω» καὶ πάλιν, «κρινεῖ κύριος τὸν λαὸν αὐτοῦ.» 10.31 φοβερὸν τὸ ἐμπεσῖν εἰς χῖρας θεοῦ ζῶντος.

10.32 ἀναμιμνῄσκεσθε δὲ τὰς πρότερον ἡμέρας, ἐν αἷς φωτισθέντες πολλὴν ἄθλησιν ὑπεμείνατε παθημάτων, 10.33 τοῦτο μὲν ὀνιδισμοῖς τε καὶ θλίψεσιν θεατριζόμενοι, τοῦτο δὲ κοινωνοὶ τῶν οὕτως ἀναστρεφομένων γενηθέντες· 10.34 καὶ γὰρ τοῖς δεσμοῖς μου συνεπαθήσατε, καὶ τὴν ἁρπαγὴν τῶν ὑπαρχόντων ὑμῶν μετὰ χαρᾶς προσεδέξασθε, γινώσκον ἔχειν ἑαυτοὺς κρίσσονα ὕπαρξιν καὶ μένουσαν.

10.35 μὴ ἀποβάλητε οὖν τὴν παρρησίαν ὑμῶν, ἥτις ἔχει μεγάλην μισθαποδοσίαν,

10.36 ὑπομονῆς γὰρ ἔχετε χρίαν ἵνα τὸ θέλημα τοῦ θεοῦ ποιήσαντες κομίσασθαι τὴν ἐπαγγελίαν. 10.37 ἔτι γὰρ «μικρὸν ὅσον ὅσον,» ὁ «ἐρχόμενος ἥξει καὶ οὐ χρονίσει· 10.38 ὁ δὲ δίκαιός μου ἐκ πίστεως ζήσεται,» καὶ «ἐὰν ὑποστίληται, οὐκ εὐδοκεῖ ἡ ψυχή μου ἐν αὐτῷ.»

10.39 ἡμεῖς δὲ οὐκ ἐσμὲν ὑποστολῆς εἰς ἀπώλιαν, ἀλλὰ πίστεως εἰς περιποίησιν ψυχῆς.

11.1 Ἔστιν δὲ πίστις ἐλπιζομένων ὑπόστασις, πραγμάτων ἔλεγχος οὐ βλεπομένων. 11.2 ἐν ταύτῃ γὰρ ἐμαρτυρήθησαν οἱ πρεσβύτεροι.

11.3 πίστι νοοῦμεν κατηρτίσθαι τοὺς αἰῶνας ῥήματι θεοῦ,

10.28   Anyone having set aside/annulled a law of Moses dies without compassions on two or three witnesses;   10.29 by how much think ye *that ye* will be deemed worthy of worse punishment the one having trampled down/despised the son of God, and having regarded *as* common the blood of the covenant by which he was sanctified, and having insulted the spirit of the gift/grace?   10.30 For we know the (one) having said: FOR ME *is* VENGEANCE/VENGEANCE IS MINE;   I,   I SHALL REPAY; and again: *The* LORD WILL JUDGE HIS PEOPLE.   10.31 A terrible (thing) *is* the (thing) to fall into hands of a living God.

10.32   But remember ye the former days, in which having been enlightened ye endured a much struggle of/from sufferings,   10.33 this (thing) indeed both reproaches and oppressions/afflictions being exposed, but also this (thing), having been generated sharers/partners of those so living.   10.34 For even in the bonds of me ye suffered together, and ye accepted with joy the seizure/snatching away of your possessions, knowing *for* yourselves to have a better and abiding possession.

10.35   Therefore, throw ye not away your confidence/free speech, which holds/has a great recompense/reward.

10.36   For ye have a need of endurance/patience in order that having done the will of God ye might obtain the promise.   10.37 For yet A VERY LITTLE *time*, the (one) COMING WILL COME AND HE WILL NOT TARRY/LINGER;   10.38 BUT MY JUST (ONE) WILL LIVE OUT OF/FROM FAITH,   and IF HE MIGHT WITHDRAW, MY LIFE/SOUL IS NOT WELL PLEASED IN/BY HIM.

10.39   But we, we are not of/from withdrawal into destruction, but of faith in gaining/saving of a soul/life.

11.1   But faith is the assurance/essence of (things) being hoped *for*, a conviction of things/matters not being seen.   11.2 For by this the elders were made witnesses/given a testimony.

11.3   By faith we understand the ages to have been framed/united by a word from God, in that the

391

εἰς τὸ μὴ ἐκ φαινομένων τὸ βλεπόμενον γεγονέναι.

11.4 πίστι πλείονα θυσίαν Ἄβελ παρὰ Κάϊν προσήνεγκεν τῷ θεῷ, δι' ἧς ἐμαρτυρήθη εἶναι δίκαιος, μαρτυροῦντος ἐπὶ τοῖς δώροις αὐτοῦ τοῦ θεοῦ, καὶ δι' αὐτῆς ἀποθανὼν ἔτι λαλεῖ.

11.5 πίστει Ἐνὼχ μετετέθη τοῦ μὴ ἰδεῖν θάνατον, καὶ «οὐχ ηὑρίσκετο διότι μετέθηκεν αὐτὸν ὁ θεός» πρὸ γὰρ τῆς μεταθέσεως μεμαρτύρηται «εὐαρεστηκέναι τῷ θεῷ,»

11.6 χωρὶς δὲ πίστεως ἀδύνατον εὐαρεστῆσαι, πιστεῦσαι γὰρ δεῖ τὸν προσερχόμενον τῷ θεῷ ὅτι ἔστιν καὶ τοῖς ἐκζητοῦσιν αὐτὸν μισθαποδότης γείνεται.

11.7 πίστει χρηματισθεὶς Νῶε περὶ τῶν μηδέπω βλεπομένων εὐλαβηθεὶς κατεσκεύασεν κιβωτὸν εἰς σωτηρίαν τοῦ οἴκου αὐτοῦ, δι' ἧς κατέκρινε τὸν κόσμον, καὶ τῆς κατὰ πίστιν δικαιοσύνης ἐγένετο κληρονόμος.

11.8 πίστι καλούμενος Ἀβραὰμ ὑπήκουσεν ἐξελθεῖν εἰς τόπον ὃν ἤμελλεν κληρονομίαν λαμβάνιν, καὶ ἐξῆλθεν μὴ ἐπιστάμενος ποῦ ἔρχεται.

11.9 πίστι παρῴκησεν εἰς γῆν τῆς ἐπαγγελίας ὡς ἀλλοτρίαν, ἐν σκηναῖς κατοικήσας μετὰ Ἰσαὰκ καὶ Ἰακὼβ τῶν συγκληρονόμων τῆς ἐπαγγελίας τῆς αὐτῆς· 11.10 ἐξεδέχετο γὰρ τὴν τοὺς θεμελίους ἔχουσαν πόλιν, ἧς τεχνίτης καὶ δημιουργὸς ὁ θεός.

11.11 πίστι καὶ αὐτὴ Σάρρα δύναμιν εἰς καταβολὴν σπέρματος ἔλαβεν καὶ παρὰ καιρὸν ἡλικίας, ἐπεὶ πιστὸν ἡγήσατο τὸν ἐπαγγειλάμενον·

11.12 διὸ καὶ ἀφ' ἑνὸς ἐγεννήθησαν, καὶ ταῦτα νενεκρωμένου, καθὼς τὰ ἄστρα τοῦ οὐρανοῦ τῷ πλήθει καὶ ὡς ἡ ἄμμος ἡ παρὰ τὸ χῖλος τῆς θαλάσσης ἡ ἀναρίθμητος.

11.13 κατὰ πίστιν ἀπέθανον οὗτοι πάντες, μὴ κομισάμενοι

(thing) not being seen to have become not out of/from visible/manifest (things).

11.4 By faith Abel offered a greater sacrifice to God from/than Cain, through which he was given a testimony to be a just (one), from God testifying/witnessing at/over his gifts, and through it having died he still speaks.

11.5 By faith Enoch was removed from the (thing) not to see death, and HE WAS NOT FOUND BECAUSE GOD REMOVED HIM; for before the removal he had been given a testimony *for him* TO HAVE BEEN WELL PLEASING TO/FOR GOD,

11.6 but without faith *it is* impossible to be well pleasing, for it is necessary *for* the (one) coming near to God to believe that he is and *that* he becomes a rewarder to/for those seeking him out.

11.7 By faith Noah, having been instructed about the (things) not yet being seen, being reverent/devout, he prepared an ark to/for salvation/deliverance of his house/household, through which he condemned the world, and he became a heir of the justice/justness according to faith.

11.8 By faith Abraham, being called to go forth to a place which he was about to receive *for* an inheritance, he obeyed and went forth/out, not understanding where he goes.

11.9 By faith he sojourned in a land of the promise as a foreigner, having dwelt in tents with Isaac and Jacob of the fellow heirs of the same promise; 11.10 for he awaited the city having the foundations, of which God *is* a/*the* craftsman/designer and builder.

11.11 By faith also Sarah herself received power/ability into/for conception of seed even from/beyond a season of age, since she deemed/considered faithful the (one) having promised;

11.12 wherefore they were generated even from one, and these (things) having been dead, as the stars of the sky/heaven for the multitude, and as the sand along the shore of the sea, the innumerable.

11.13 These all died according to faith, not having obtained the promises, but having seen and

τὰς ἐπαγγελίας, ἀλλὰ πόρρωθεν αὐτὰς ἰδόντες καὶ ἀσπασάμενοι, καὶ ὁμολογήσαντες ὅτι ξένοι καὶ παρεπίδημοί εἰσιν ἐπὶ τῆς γῆς· 11.14 οἱ γὰρ τοιαῦτα λέγοντες ἐμφανίζουσιν ὅτι πατρίδα ἐπιζητοῦσιν. 11.15 καὶ εἰ μὲν ἐκείνης ἐμνημόνευον ἀφ' ἧς ἐξέβησαν, εἶχον ἂν καιρὸν ἀνακάμψαι· 11.16 νῦν δὲ κρίττονος ὀρέγονται, τοῦτ' ἔστιν ἐπουρανίου. διὸ οὐκ ἐπεσχύνεται αὐτοὺς ὁ θεὸς θεὸς ἐπικαλεῖσθαι αὐτῶν, ἡτοίμασεν γὰρ αὐτοῖς πόλιν.

11.17 πείστι προσενήνοχεν Ἀβραὰμ τὸν Ἰσὰκ πιραζόμενος, καὶ τὸν μονογενῆ προσέφερεν ὁ τὰς ἐπαγγελίας ἀναδεξάμενος, 11.18 πρὸς ὃν ἐλαλήθη ὅτι «ἐν Ἰσὰκ κληθήσεταί σοι σπέρμα,» 11.19 λογισάμενος ὅτι καὶ ἐκ νεκρῶν ἐγίρειν δυνατὸς ὁ θεός· ὅθεν αὐτὸν καὶ ἐν παραβολῇ ἐκομίσατο. 11.20 πείστι περὶ μελλόντων εὐλόγησεν Ἰσαὰκ τὸν Ἰακὼβ καὶ τὸν Ἡσαῦ.

11.21 πίστι Ἰακὼβ ἀποθνήσκων ἕκαστον τῶν υἱῶν Ἰωσὴφ εὐλόγησεν, καὶ «προσεκύνησεν ἐπὶ τὸ ἄκρον τῆς ῥάβδου αὐτοῦ.»

11.22 πίστι Ἰωσὴφ τελευτῶν περὶ τῆς ἐξόδου τῶν υἱῶν Ἰσραὴλ ἐμνημόνευσεν, καὶ περὶ τῶν ὀστέων αὐτοῦ ἐνετίλατο.

11.23 πίστι Μωϋσῆς γεννηθεὶς ἐκρύβη τρίμηνον ὑπὸ τῶν πατέρων αὐτοῦ, διότι εἶδον ἀστῖον τὸ παιδίον, καὶ οὐκ ἐφοβήθησαν τὸ διάταγμα τοῦ βασιλέως.

11.24 πίστι Μωϋσῆς μέγας γενόμενος ἠρνήσατο λέγεσθαι υἱὸς θυγατρὸς Φαραώ, 11.25 μᾶλλον ἑλόμενος συγκακουχῖσθαι τῷ λαῷ τοῦ θεοῦ ἢ πρόσκαιρον ἔχειν ἁμαρτίας ἀπόλαυσιν, 11.26 μίζονα πλοῦτον ἡγησάμενος τῶν Αἰγύπτου θησαυρῶν τὸν ὀνειδισμὸν τοῦ χριστοῦ, ἀπέβλεπεν γὰρ εἰς τὴν μισθαποδοσίαν. 11.27 πίστει κατέλιπεν Αἴγυπτον, μὴ φοβηθεὶς τὸν θυμὸν τοῦ βασιλέως, τὸν γὰρ ἀόρατον ὡς ὁρῶν ἐκαρτέρησεν.

11.28 πίστι πεποίηκεν τὸ πάσχα καὶ τὴν πρόσχυσιν τοῦ

having greeted them from afar, and having confessed that they are strangers and sojourners on the land; 11.14 for those saying such (things) emphasize/make clear that they seek for a fatherland/home country. 11.15 And if indeed they were remembering that from which they came out, they would be having a time to return; 11.16 but also now they aspire to a better (one), this (one) is of a heavenly (one). Wherefore God is not ashamed of them, to be called a god of them/their god, for he prepared a city for them.

11.17 By faith Abraham, being tested, has offered Isaac; and the (one) having received the promises was offering up the only generated son, 11.18 to whom it was spoken that in/by Isaac a seed will be called for you, 11.19 having reasoned/reckoned that God was able to raise up (one) even out of dead (ones); from where also he obtained him by a parable. 11.20 By faith also Isaac blessed/spoke well of Jacob and Esau about (things) being about to come. 11.21 By faith Jacob, dying, blessed/spoke well of each of the sons of Joseph, and HE WORSHIPED UPON THE END OF HIS STAFF/STICK.

11.22 By faith Joseph, finishing/dying, remembered about the exodus of the sons of Israel, and he gave orders concerning his bones.

11.23 By faith Moses, having been generated, was hidden for three months by his fathers, because they saw that the child was well-formed/beautiful, and feared not the decree/ordinance of the king.

11.24 By faith Moses, having become great, denied/refused to be called a son of a daughter of Pharaoh, 11.25 rather having chosen to be mistreated/ill-treated with the people of God than temporarily to have pleasure from sin/fault. 11.26 having thought the reproach/abuse of the anointed (one) greater than wealth from the treasures/storehouses of Egypt, for he was looking away to the recompense/reward. 11.27 By faith he left Egypt, having not feared the wrath of the king, for he bore patiently/endured as seeing/beholding the invisible/unseen (one).

11.28 By faith he has made the passover and the pouring/sprinkling of the blood, that the (one) de-

αἵματος, ἵνα μὴ ὁ ὀλοθρεύων τὰ πρωτότοκα θίγῃ αὐτῶν. 11.29 πίστι διέβησαν τὴν ἐρυθρὰν Θάλασσαν ὡς διὰ ξηρᾶς γῆς, ἧς πεῖραν λαβόντες οἱ Αἰγύπτιοι κατεπόθησαν.

11.30 πίστι τὰ τείχη Ἰερειχὼ ἔπεσαν κυκλωθέντα ἐπὶ ἑπτὰ ἡμέρας.

11.31 πίστει Ῥαὰβ ἡ πόρνη οὐ συναπώλετο τοῖς ἀπιθήσασιν, δεξαμένη τοὺς κατασκόπους μετ᾽ εἰρήνης.

11.32 καὶ τί ἔτι λέγω; ἐπιλείψι με γὰρ διηγούμενον ὁ χρόνος περὶ Γεδεών, Βαράκ, Σαμψών, Ἰεφθάε, Δαυείδ τε καὶ Σαμουὴλ καὶ τῶν προφητῶν,

11.33 οἳ διὰ πίστεως κατηγωνίσαντο βασιλείας, εἰργάσαντο δικαιοσύνην, ἐπέτυχον ἐπαγγελιῶν, ἔφραξαν στόματα λεόντων, 11.34 ἔσβεσαν δύναμιν πυρός, ἔφυγον στόματα μαχαίρης, ἐδυναμώθησαν ἀπὸ ἀσθενείας, ἐγενήθησαν ἰσχυροὶ ἐν πολέμῳ, παρεμβολὰς ἔκλιναν ἀλλοτρίων· 11.35 ἔλαβον γυναῖκες ἐξ ἀναστάσεως τοὺς νεκροὺς αὐτῶν·

ἄλλοι δὲ ἐτυμπανίσθησαν, οὐ προσδεξάμενοι τὴν ἀπολύτρωσιν, ἵνα κρίττονος ἀναστάσεως τύχωσιν·

11.36 ἕτεροι δὲ ἐνπεγμῶν καὶ μαστίγων πῖραν ἔλαβον, ἔτι δὲ δεσμῶν καὶ φυλακῆς· 11.37 ἐλιθάσθησαν, ἐπιράσθησαν, ἐπρίσθησαν, ἐν φόνῳ μαχαίρης ἀπέθανον, περιῆλθον ἐν μηλωταῖς, ἐν αἰγίοις δέρμασιν, ὑστερούμενοι, θλιβόμενοι, κακουχούμενοι, 11.38 ὧν οὐκ ἦν ἄξιος ὁ κόσμος, ἐπὶ ἐρημίαις πλανώμενοι καὶ ὄρεσι καὶ σπηλαίοις καὶ ταῖς ὀπαῖς τῆς γῆς.

11.39 καὶ οὗτοι πάντες μαρτυρηθέντες διὰ τῆς πίστεως οὐκ ἐκομίσαντο τὴν ἐπαγγελίαν, 11.40 τοῦ θεοῦ περὶ ἡμῶν κρῖττόν τι προβλεψαμένου, ἵνα μὴ χωρὶς ἡμῶν τελιωθῶσιν.

12.1 Τοιγαροῦν καὶ ἡμῖς, τοσοῦτον ἔχοντες περικείμενον

stroying should not touch/harm the firstborn (ones) of them. 11.29 By faith they went through the red sea as through/across dry land, which the Egyptians, having taken a trial/chance were drowned/swallowed up.

11.30 By faith the walls of Jericho fell, having been marched around on/for seven days.

11.31 By faith Rahab the prostitute perished not with the (ones) having disobeyed/disbelieved, having received the spies with peace.

11.32 And what may I yet say? For the time will fail/leave me relating/recounting about Gideon, Barak, Sampson, Jephthae, both David and Samuel and from the prophets,

11.33 who through faith subdued/conquered kingdoms, worked justice/justness, obtained promises, stopped mouths of lions, 11.34 extinguished a power from fire, escaped mouths/(edges) of a sword, were strengthened from weaknesses, were generated/became strong (ones) in/by war/battle, they wore away armies of foreigners/other tribes; 11.35 women received their dead out of/from a resurrection;

but others were beaten to death, having not themselves accepted the deliverance/release in order that they might obtain from a better resurrection;

11.36 and others/different (ones) took/received a trial/test from mockings and scourgings, and further from bonds and prison; 11.37 they were stoned, they were tried/tempted, they were sawn asunder/to pieces, they died from a sword in/by murder, they went about in sheepskins/with sheep, in goat skins, being deficient/in want, being oppressed (ones), being maltreated (ones), 11.38 of whom the world was not worthy, being led astray on/over both mountains and caves and the caverns of the land/earth.

11.39 And all these, having been testified *for* through the faith, obtained not the promise, 11.40 from God having foreseen something better concerning us, in order that they might be finished/completed without us.

12.1 For that very reason we also, having such a cloud of testimonies/witnesses lying around for us,

ἡμῖν νέφος μαρτύρων, ὄγκον ἀποθέμενοι πάντα καὶ τὴν εὐπερίστατον ἁμαρτίαν, δι' ὑπομονῆς τρέχωμεν τὸν προκείμενον ἡμῖν ἀγῶνα, 12.2 ἀφορῶντες εἰς τὸν τῆς πίστεως ἀρχηγὸν καὶ τελειωτὴν Ἰησοῦν,

ὃς ἀντὶ τῆς προκειμένης αὐτῷ χαρᾶς ὑπέμεινεν σταυρὸν αἰσχύνης καταφρονήσας, ἐν δεξιᾷ τε τοῦ θρόνου κεκάθικεν.

12.3 ἀναλογίσασθε γὰρ τὸν τοιαύτην ὑπομεμενηκότα ὑπὸ τῶν ἁμαρτωλῶν εἰς ἑαυτοὺς ἀντιλογίαν, ἵνα μὴ κάμητε ταῖς ψυχαῖς ὑμῶν ἐκλυόμενοι. 12.4 οὔπω μέχρις αἵματος ἀντικατέστητε πρὸς τὴν ἁμαρτίαν ἀνταγωνιζόμενοι, 12.5 καὶ ἐκλέλησθε τῆς παρακλήσεως, ἥτις ὑμῖν ὡς υἱοῖς διαλέγεται, «υἱέ μου, μὴ ὀλιγώρει παιδίας κυρίου, μηδὲ ἐκλύου ὑπ' αὐτοῦ ἐλεγχόμενος· 12.6 ὃν γὰρ ἀγαπᾷ κύριος παιδεύει, μαστιγοῖ δὲ πάντα υἱὸν ὃν παραδέχεται.»

12.7 εἰς παιδίαν ὑπομένετε· ὡς υἱοῖς ὑμῖν προσφέρεται ὁ θεός· τίς γὰρ υἱὸς ὃν οὐ παιδεύει πατήρ; 12.8 εἰ δὲ χωρίς ἐστε παιδίας ἧς μέτοχοι γεγόνασι πάντες, ἄρα νόθοι καὶ οὐχ υἱοί ἐστε.

12.9 εἶτα τοὺς μὲν τῆς σαρκὸς ἡμῶν πατέρας εἴχομεν παιδευτὰς καὶ ἐνετρεπόμεθα· οὐ πολὺ δὲ μᾶλλον ὑποταγησόμεθα τῷ πατρὶ τῶν πνευμάτων καὶ ζήσομεν;

12.10 οἱ μὲν γὰρ πρὸς ὀλίγας ἡμέρας κατὰ τὸ δοκοῦν αὐτοῖς ἐπέδευον, ὁ δὲ ἐπὶ τὸ συμφέρον εἰς τὸ μεταλαβεῖν τῆς ἁγιότητος αὐτοῦ.

12.11 πᾶσα δὲ παιδία πρὸς μὲν τὸ παρὸν οὐ δοκεῖ χαρᾶς εἶναι ἀλλὰ λύπης, ὕστερον δὲ καρπὸν εἰρηνικὸν τοῖς δι' αὐτῆς γεγυμνασμένοις ἀποδίδωσιν δικαιοσύνης.

12.12 διὸ τὰς παρειμένας χῖρας καὶ τὰ παραλελυμένα γόνατα ἀνορθώσατε, 12.13 καὶ τροχιὰς ὀρθὰς ποιεῖτε τοῖς ποσὶν ὑμῶν, ἵνα μὴ τὸ χωλὸν ἐκτραπῇ, ἰαθῇ δὲ μᾶλλον.

having thrust away every weight/burden and the easily ensnaring sin, through endurance we may run the race being pre-set/layed out for us, 12.2 looking away to the prince/founder and finisher of the faith, Jesus,

who instead of the joy being pre-set/layed out for him, he endured, having contemned/despised a cross of shame, and he has sat at *the* right *hand* of God.

12.3 For consider ye the (one) having endured in himself such contradiction/dispute by/under the sinners, that ye might not tire out, being wearied in your lives/souls. 12.4 Ye resisted not yet until blood, striving with the sin/fault, 12.5 and ye have forgotten of/from the entreaty, which he discusses/reasons with ye as with sons: MY SON, MAKE NOT SMALL DISCIPLINE FROM*the* LORD, NEITHER FAINT BEING REPROVED BY HIM; 12.6 FOR WHOM *the* LORD LOVES HE DISCIPLINES/TRAINS, AND HE SCOURGES EVERY SON WHOM HE APPROVES/RECEIVES.

12.7 Endure ye in training/chastising; God is offering/bearing to/with ye as to/with sons; for what son *is there* whom a father *does* not discipline? 12.8 But if ye are without discipline/training of which all have become sharers/partakers, then ye are spurious (ones)/bastards and not sons.

12.9 Then we indeed had the fathers of our flesh *for* correctors/trainers and we respected *them*; but shall we not be much more subject to the father of the spirits, and we shall live?

12.10 For they indeed disciplined/corrected *us* to/with a few days according to the (thing) seeming *good* to them, but the (he) to the mutual benefit in the (thing) to share/partake of his sanctity.

12.11 Indeed every correction/discipline to/at the present (time) seems not to be of joy but of pain/grief, but also it gives back afterwards a peaceful fruit/product of justice/justness to the (ones) having been trained.

12.12 Wherefore straighten ye the hands having hung helplessly and the knees having been weakened/para-lyzed. 12.13 and make ye straight paths/tracks for your feet, that the lame might not be turned aside, but rather they might be healed.

12.14 εἰρήνην διώκετε μετὰ πάντων, καὶ τὸν ἁγιασμόν, οὗ χωρὶς οὐδὶς ὄψεται τὸν κύριον,

12.15 ἐπισκοποῦντες μή τις ὑστερῶν ἀπὸ τῆς χάριτος τοῦ θεοῦ, μή τις ῥίζα πικρίας ἄνω φύουσα ἐνοχλῇ καὶ διὰ ταύτης μιανθῶσιν οἱ πολλοί,

12.16 μή τις πόρνος ἢ βέβηλος ὡς Ἠσαῦ, ὃς ἀντὶ βρώσεως μιᾶς ἀπέδοτο τὰ πρωτοτόκια ἑαυτοῦ. 12.17 ἴστε γὰρ ὅτι καὶ μετέπειτα θέλων κληρονομῆσαι τὴν εὐλογίαν ἀπεδοκιμάσθη, μετανοίας γὰρ τόπον οὐχ εὗρεν, καίπερ μετὰ δακρύων ἐκζητήσας αὐτήν. 12.18 οὐ γὰρ προσεληλύθατε ψηλαφωμένῳ καὶ κεκαυμένῳ πυρὶ καὶ γνόφῳ καὶ ζόφῳ καὶ θυέλλῃ 12.19 καὶ σάλπιγγος ἤχῳ καὶ φωνῇ ῥημάτων, ἧς οἱ ἀκούσαντες παρῃτήσαντο μὴ προστεθῆναι αὐτοῖς λόγον· 12.20 οὐκ ἔφερον γὰρ τὸ διαστελλόμενον, «κἂν θηρίον θίγῃ τοῦ ὄρους, λιθοβοληθήσεται» 12.21 καί, οὕτω φοβερὸν ἦν τὸ φανταζόμενον, Μωϋσῆς εἶπεν, «ἔκφοβός εἰμι» καὶ ἔντρομος. 12.22 ἀλλὰ προσεληλύθατε Σιὼν ὄρει καὶ πόλει θεοῦ ζῶντος, Ἰερουσαλὴμ ἐπουρανίῳ, καὶ μυριάσιν ἀγγέλων, πανηγύρει 12.23 καὶ ἐκκλησίᾳ πρωτοτόκων ἀπογεγραμμένων ἐν οὐρανοῖς, καὶ κριτῇ θεῷ πάντων, καὶ πνεύμασι δικαίων τετελιωμένων, 12.24 καὶ διαθήκης νέας μεσίτῃ Ἰησοῦ, καὶ αἵματι ῥαντισμοῦ κρῖττον λαλοῦντι παρὰ τὸν Ἄβελ.

12.25 βλέπετε μὴ παραιτήσησθε τὸν λαλοῦντα· εἰ γὰρ ἐκεῖνοι οὐκ ἐξέφυγον ἐπὶ γῆς παραιτησάμενοι τὸν χρηματίζοντα, πολὺ μᾶλλον ἡμεῖς οἱ τὸν ἀπ' οὐρανῶν ἀποστρεφόμενοι·

12.26 οὗ ἡ φωνὴ τὴν γῆν ἐσάλευσεν τότε, νῦν δὲ ἐπήγγελται λέγων, «ἔτι ἅπαξ ἐγὼ σίσω» οὐ μόνον «τὴν γῆν»

12.14 Pursue ye peace with all, also the sanctification, without which no one will see/observe the Lord,

12.15 overseeing lest anyone *be* lacking from the gift/grace from God, lest a certain root of bitterness/animosity growing up may trouble/disturb and through this the many might be defiled/stained,

12.16 lest a certain male prostitute/whoremonger or a common/unholy (one) like Esau, who gave away the firstborn (rights) of/from himself instead of/for one eating/meal. 12.17 For ye know that afterwards, also wanting/wishing to inherit the blessing, he was rejected, for he found not a place from/of repentance, although he was seeking for it with tears. 12.18 For ye have not come near to being touched/felt, and having been burned by fire, also in a thick cloud and in darkness and by/in windstorm 12.19 and by a sound from a trumpet and by a voice of words, which the (ones) having heard pleaded *for* not a saying/word to be added to them; 12.20 for they carried/bore not the (thing) being charged/commanded: IF EVEN A BEAST OF THE MOUNTAIN MIGHT TOUCH/HANDLE, IT WILL BE STONED; 12.21 and, so fearful was the (thing) being visible/appearing, Moses said: I AM TERRIFIED and trembling. 12.22 But ye have come near to a mountain of Zion and to a city of a living God, to a heavenly Jerusalem, and to myriads of messengers/angels, to a solemn gathering 12.23 and to an assembly of firstborns having been enrolled/registered in heavens/skies, and to a judge, to a God of all, and to spirits of just (ones) having been finished/completed, 12.24 and to Jesus, a mediator of a new covenant, and to a blood of cleansing/purifying, speaking a better (thing/-covenant) from/than the (one) of Abel.

12.25 See ye *that* ye refuse not the (one) speaking; for if those escaped not from the (thing) of having refused the (one) instructing/warning upon earth/land, much more we, the (ones) being turned away from the (one) from heavens/skies;

12.26 from whom the voice/sound shook the land/earth then, but now he has promised, saying: YET/STILL AT ONE TIME/ONCE I, I SHALL SHAKE not THE EARTH only,

ἀλλὰ καὶ «τὸν οὐρανόν.» 12.27 τὸ δέ, «ἔτι ἅπαξ» δηλοῖ τὴν τῶν σαλευομένων μετάθεσιν ὡς πεποιημένων, ἵνα μίνῃ τὰ μὴ σαλευόμενα. 12.28 διὸ βασιλείαν ἀσάλευτον παραλαμβάνοντες ἔχωμεν χάριν, δι᾿ ἧς λατρεύωμεν εὐαρέστως τῷ θεῷ μετὰ εὐλαβίας καὶ δέους· 12.29 καὶ γὰρ ὁ θεὸς ἡμῶν πῦρ καταναλίσκον. 13.1 ἡ φιλαδελφία μενέτω. 13.2 τῆς φιλοξενίας μὴ ἐπιλανθάνεσθε, διὰ ταύτης γὰρ ἔλαθόν τινες ξενίσαντες ἀγγέλους.

13.3 μιμνήσκεσθαι τῶν δεσμίων ὡς συνδεδεμένοι, τῶν κακουχουμένων ὡς καὶ αὐτοὶ ὄντες ἐν σώματι.

13.4 τίμιος ὁ γάμος ἐν πᾶσιν καὶ ἡ κοίτη ἀμίαντος, πόρνους γὰρ καὶ μοιχοὺς κρινεῖ ὁ θεός.

13.5 ἀφιλάργυρος ὁ τρόπος· ἀρκούμενοι τοῖς παροῦσιν· αὐτὸς γὰρ εἴρηκεν, «οὐ μή σε ἀνῶ οὐδ᾿ οὐ μή σε ἐγκαταλείπω» 13.6 ὥστε θαρροῦντας ἡμᾶς λέγειν, «κύριος ἐμοὶ βοηθός, καὶ οὐ φοβηθήσομαι· τί ποιήσει μοι ἄνθρωπος;»

13.7 μνημονεύετε τῶν ἡγουμένων ὑμῶν, οἵτινες ἐλάλησαν ὑμῖν τὸν λόγον τοῦ θεοῦ, ὧν ἀναθεωροῦντες τὴν ἔκβασιν τῆς ἀναστροφῆς μιμεῖσθαι τὴν πίστιν.

13.8 Ἰησοῦς χριστὸς ἐχθὲς καὶ σήμερον ὁ αὐτός, καὶ εἰς τοὺς αἰῶνας. 13.9 διδαχαῖς ποικίλαις καὶ ξέναις μὴ παραφέρεσθε· καλὸν γὰρ χάριτι βεβαιοῦσθε τὴν καρδίαν, οὐ βρώμασιν, ἐν οἷς οὐκ ὠφελήθησαν οἱ περιπατοῦντες.

13.10 ἔχομεν θυσιαστήριον ἐξ οὗ φαγεῖν οὐκ ἔχουσιν ἐξουσίαν οἱ τῇ σκηνῇ λατρεύοντες. 13.11 ὧν γὰρ εἰσφέρεται ζώων τὸ αἷμα περὶ ἁμαρτίας εἰς τὰ ἅγια διὰ τοῦ ἀρχιερέως, τούτων τὰ σώματα κατακαίεται ἔξω τῆς παρεμβολῆς.

13.12 διὸ καὶ Ἰησοῦς, ἵνα ἁγιάσῃ διὰ τοῦ ἰδίου αἵματος

but also THE SKY/HEAVEN.   12.27 But the (thing): YET ONCE, it makes clear/plain the removal of the (things) being shaken as from (things) having been made, in order that the (things) being not shaken might abide/ remain.   12.28 Wherefore we might have/hold an unsha- kable kingdom, receiving *it* by/from grace, through which we may serve/worship well-pleasing to/for God with reverence/pious awe and *for* gods;   12.29 for our God *is* also a consuming fire.   13.1 Let the brotherly love abide/remain.   13.2 Of the hospitality forget ye not, for because of this some were unaware of having entertained angels/messengers.

13.3   Be ye reminded of the prisoners as *if* having been fellow prisoners, of those being ill- treated as yourselves also being in a body.

13.4   The wedding/marriage *is* honorable among all and the bed/sex undefiled/unstained, for God will judge whoremongers and adulterers.

13.5   The manner/way is without love of money/ silver; ye being satisfied with the (things) being present; for he, he has said: BY NO MEANS MIGHT I SEND YOU UP NOR BY NO MEANS MIGHT I FORSAKE/ABANDON YOU; 13.6 so as *for* us, being of good cheer, to say: *The* LORD IS A HELPER FOR/TO ME, AND I SHALL NOT FEAR; WHAT WILL A MAN/HUMAN DO TO ME?

13.7   Remember ye those leading/governing ye, who spoke to ye the   saying/logos/word of God, of whom viewing ye the result/outcome of the conduct/behavior, imitate/emulate ye the faith.

13.8   Jesus the anointed (one) *is* the same yes- terday and today, and/also into/for the ages.   13.9 Be ye not carried away by various and strange/foreign doctrines/teachings; for *it is* good *for* the heart to be established/confirmed by grace, not by foods, in/by which those walking were not benefited/profited.

13.10   We have an altar from which the (ones) serving/worshiping in the tent/tabernacle have not a right/authority to eat.   13.11 For the blood of what animals concerning sins is brought in into the hol- ies/holy (places) through the high priest, of these the bodies are burned outside the camp.

13.12   Wherefore even/also Jesus, in order that

τὸν λαόν, ἔξω τῆς πύλης ἔπαθεν. 13.13 τοίνυν ἐξερχώμεθα πρὸς αὐτὸν ἔξω τῆς παρεμβολῆς, τὸν ὀνειδισμὸν αὐτοῦ φέροντες· 13.14 οὐ γὰρ ἔχομεν ὧδε μένουσαν πόλιν, ἀλλὰ τὴν μέλλουσαν ἐπιζητοῦμεν.

13.15 δι’ αὐτοῦ οὖν ἀναφέρωμεν θυσίαν αἰνέσεως διὰ παντὸς τῷ θεῷ, τοῦτ’ ἔστιν καρπὸν χειλέων ὁμολογούντων τῷ ὀνόματι αὐτοῦ. 13.16 τῆς δὲ εὐποιΐας καὶ κοινωνίας μὴ ἐπιλανθάνεσθε, τοιαύταις γὰρ θυσίαις εὐαρεστῖται ὁ θεός.

13.17 Πείθεσθε τοῖς ἡγουμένοις ὑμῶν καὶ ὑπείκετε, αὐτοὶ γὰρ ἀγρυπνοῦσιν ὑπὲρ τῶν ψυχῶν ὑμῶν ὡς λόγον ἀποδώσοντες, ἵνα μετὰ χαρᾶς τοῦτο ποιῶσιν καὶ μὴ στενάζοντες, ἀλυσιτελὲς γὰρ ὑμῖν τοῦτο.

13.18 προσεύχεσθε περὶ ἡμῶν, πεποίθαμεν γὰρ ὅτι καλὴν συνίδησιν ἔχομεν, ἐν πᾶσιν καλῶς θέλοντες ἀναστρέφεσθαι. 13.19 περισσοτέρως δὲ παρακαλῶ τοῦτο ποιῆσαι ἵνα τάχειον ἀποκατασταθῶ ὑμῖν.

13.20 ὁ δὲ θεὸς τῆς εἰρήνης, ὁ ἀναγαγὼν ἐκ νεκρῶν τὸν ποιμένα τῶν προβάτων τὸν μέγαν ἐν αἵματι διαθήκης αἰωνίου, τὸν κύριον ἡμῶν Ἰησοῦν, 13.21 καταρτίσαι ὑμᾶς ἐν παντὶ ἀγαθῷ εἰς τὸ ποιῆσαι τὸ θέλημα αὐτοῦ, ποιῶν ἐν ἡμῖν τὸ εὐάρεστον ἐνώπιον αὐτοῦ διὰ Ἰησοῦ χριστοῦ, ᾧ ἡ δόξα εἰς τοὺς αἰῶνας τῶν αἰώνων· ἀμήν.

13.22 παρακαλῶ δὲ ὑμᾶς, ἀδελφοί, ἀνέχεσθε τοῦ λόγου τῆς παρακλήσεως, καὶ γὰρ διὰ βραχέων ἐπέστιλα ὑμῖν.

13.23 γεινώσκετε τὸν ἀδελφὸν ἡμῶν Τιμόθεον ἀπολελυμένον, μεθ’ οὗ ἐὰν τάχιον ἔρχηται ὄψομαι ὑμᾶς. 13.24 ἀσπάσασθαι πάντας τοὺς ἡγουμένους ὑμῶν καὶ πάντας τοὺς ἁγίους. ἀσπάζονται ὑμᾶς οἱ ἀπὸ τῆς Ἰταλίας. 13.25 ἡ χάρις μετὰ πάντων ὑμῶν. αμην.

Πρὸς Ἑβραίους

he might sanctify/set apart the people through his own blood, he suffered outside the gate. 13.13 So now we may go forth in/with him outside the camp, bearing/ carrying his reproach/disgrace/reviling; 13.14 for we have not an abiding city here, but we will seek for the (one) being about to come.

13.15 Therefore through/because of him we may offer up a sacrifice of praise through every (thing) to God, this is a product/fruit from lips confessing to/for/in his name. 13.16 But of the well-doing and fellowship, forget/neglect ye not, for with such sacrifices God is well pleased.

13.17 Obey ye your leaders/governors and be ye subject, for they watch in behalf of your lives/souls as *if* rendering an account/word, that with joy they may do this and not groaning, for this *is* disastrous/ without profit for ye.

13.18 Pray ye about/concerning us, for we have persuaded that we have a good conscience, wanting/ wishing to be well behaving in every (thing). 13.19 And more abundantly/especially I beseech *ye* to do this in order that I might more quickly be restored to/for ye.

13.20 And the God of peace, the (one) having led/brought back from/out of dead (ones) the shepherd of the sheep, the great (one) of an eternal covenant in/by blood, Jesus our Lord, 13.21 may he fit/mend ye in every good (thing) to/for the (thing) to do his will, doing in/by us the (thing) well pleasing before him through Jesus the anointed (one), to/for whom *be* the glory/fame into/for the ages of the ages; truly.

13.22 But I beseech ye, brothers, endure ye from the saying/word of the beseeching/exhortation, for also through few *words* I sent a letter to/for ye.

13.23 Ye know our brother Timothy, having been released, with whom if I may come quickly I shall see ye. 13.24 Greet ye all the (ones) leading/governing of ye and all the saints. Those from Italy greet/sal- ute ye. 13.25 The grace *be* with all of ye.

Truly.

To Hebrews

This is the Sinaitic New Testament, book of 1 Timothy.

1.1 Παῦλος ἀπόστολος χριστοῦ Ἰησοῦ κατ' ἐπαγγελίαν θεοῦ σωτῆρος ἡμῶν καὶ κυρίου Ἰησοῦ χριστοῦ τῆς ἐλπίδος ἡμῶν 1.2 Τιμοθέῳ γνησίῳ τέκνῳ ἐν πίστι· χάρις, ἔλεος, ἰρήνη ἀπὸ θεοῦ πατρὸς καὶ χριστοῦ Ἰησοῦ τοῦ κυρίου ἡμῶν.

1.3 καθὼς παρεκάλεσά σε προσμεῖναι ἐν Ἐφέσῳ πορευόμενος εἰς Μακαιδονίαν, ἵνα παραγγίλῃς τισὶν μὴ ἑτεροδιδασκαλῖν 1.4 μηδὲ προσέχειν μύθοις καὶ γενεαλογίαις ἀπεράντοις, αἵτινες ἐκζητήσεις παρέχουσι μᾶλλον ἢ οἰκονομίαν θεοῦ τὴν ἐν πίστει·

1.5 τὸ δὲ τέλος τῆς παραγγελίας ἐστὶν ἀγάπη ἐκ καθαρᾶς καρδίας καὶ συνειδήσεως ἀγαθῆς καὶ πίστεως ἀνυποκρίτου,

1.6 ὧν τινες ἀστοχήσαντες ἐξετράπησαν εἰς ματαιολογίαν, 1.7 θέλοντες εἶναι νομοδιδάσκαλοι, μὴ νοοῦντες μήτε ἃ λέγουσιν μήτε περὶ τίνων διαβεβαιοῦνται.

1.8 οἴδαμεν δὲ ὅτι καλὸς ὁ νόμος ἐάν τις αὐτῷ νομίμως χρῆται,

1.9 εἰδὼς τοῦτο, ὅτι δικαίῳ νόμος οὐ κῖται, ἀνόμοις δὲ καὶ ἀνυποτάκτοις, ἀσεβέσι καὶ ἁμαρτωλοῖς, ἀνοσίοις καὶ βεβήλοις, πατρολῴαις καὶ μητρολῴαις, ἀνδροφόνοις, 1.10 πόρνοις, ἀρσενοκοίταις, ἀνδραποδισταῖς, ψεύσταις, ἐπιόρκοις, καὶ εἴ τι ἕτερον τῇ ὑγιαινούσῃ διδασκαλίᾳ ἀντίκειται, 1.11 κατὰ τὸ εὐαγγέλιον τῆς δόξης τοῦ μακαρίου θεοῦ, ὃ ἐπιστεύθην ἐγώ.

1.12 χάριν ἔχω τῷ ἐνδυναμώσαντί με χριστῷ Ἰησοῦ τῷ κυρίῳ ἡμῶν, ὅτι πιστόν με ἡγήσατο θέμενος εἰς διακονίαν, 1.13 τὸ πρότερον ὄντα βλάσφημον καὶ διώκτην καὶ ὑβριστήν· ἀλλὰ

1.1   Paul, an apostle of the anointed Jesus, according to a command from God our savior and from *the* Lord Jesus, the anointed (one), our hope,   1.2 to Timothy, a true child in/by faith: Grace, mercy, peace from God *our* father and from the anointed (one), Jesus our Lord.

1.3   As I besought you to remain/stay in Ephesus, *me* going into Macedonia, in order that you might charge certain persons not to teach differently   1.4 nor to heed/give attention to myths/stories/tales and to endless genealogies, which offers/occasions diligent investigations/seekings for rather than the work/responsibility from God in/by faith.

1.5   But the end of the charge/command is agape out of a clean/pure heart and a good conscience and out of unhypocritical/unpretended/sincere faith,

1.6   from which (things) some having missed the mark turned aside into vain disputes/discussions,   1.7 wanting/wishing to be teachers of the law, not minding/understanding either what (things) they say nor about/concerning what (things) they emphatically assert/declare.

1.8   And we know that the law *is* good if anyone uses/employs it lawfully/according to legal rules,

1.9   having been knowing this, that a law is not laid down for a just (one), but for lawless (ones) and rebellious (ones), for irreverent/impious and sinful (ones), for unholy and unreligious/common (ones), for father murderers and mother murderers, for man murderers,   1.10 for whoremongers/male prostitutes, for homosexuals/sodomites, for slave dealers/kidnappers, for liars, for perjurers, and if any other/different (thing) is set against the teaching being sound/healthy,   1.11 according to the good message/gospel from the fame/glory of the happy/blessed God, *with* which I, I was entrusted.

1.12   I have thanks for the (one) having strengthened me, the anointed (one), Jesus our Lord, because he reckoned me faithful, having placed/put (me) into a service/ministry,   1.13 being the former blasphemer/reviler and pursuer/prosecutor and mistreater; but I was shown/received mercy, because being ignorant I did

ἠλεήθην, ὅτι ἀγνοῶν ἐποίησα ἐν ἀπιστίᾳ, 1.14 ὑπερεπλεόνασεν δὲ ἡ χάρις τοῦ κυρίου ἡμῶν μετὰ πίστεως καὶ ἀγάπης τῆς ἐν χριστῷ Ἰησοῦ.

1.15 πιστὸς ὁ λόγος καὶ πάσης ἀποδοχῆς ἄξιος, ὅτι χριστὸς Ἰησοῦς ἦλθεν εἰς κόσμον ἁμαρτωλοὺς σῶσαι· ὧν πρῶτός εἰμι ἐγώ,

1.16 ἀλλὰ διὰ τοῦτο ἠλεήθην, ἵνα ἐν ἐμοὶ πρώτῳ ἐνδίξηται Ἰησοῦς χριστὸς τὴν ἅπασαν μακροθυμίαν, πρὸς ὑποτύπωσιν τῶν μελλόντων ἀγαθῶν πιστεύειν ἐπ᾽ αὐτῷ εἰς ζωὴν αἰώνιον.

1.17 τῷ δὲ βασιλεῖ τῶν αἰώνων, ἀφθάρτῳ, ἀοράτῳ, μόνῳ θεῷ, τιμὴ καὶ δόξα εἰς τοὺς αἰῶνας τῶν αἰώνων· ἀμήν.

1.18 ταύτην τὴν παραγγελίαν παρατίθεμαί σοι, τέκνον Τιμόθεε, κατὰ τὰς προαγούσας ἐπὶ σὲ προφητείας, ἵνα στρατεύῃ ἐν αὐταῖς τὴν καλὴν στρατείαν, 1.19 ἔχων πίστιν καὶ ἀγαθὴν συνίδησιν, ἥν τινες ἀπωσάμενοι περὶ τὴν πίστιν ἐναυάγησαν· 1.20 ὧν ἐστιν Ὑμέναιος καὶ Ἀλέξανδρος, οὓς παρέδωκα τῷ Σατανᾷ ἵνα παιδευθῶσι μὴ βλασφημῖν.

2.1 Παρακαλῶ οὖν πρῶτον πάντων ποιεῖσθαι δεήσεις, προσευχάς, ἐντεύξεις, εὐχαριστίας, ὑπὲρ πάντων ἀνθρώπων, 2.2 ὑπὲρ βασιλέων καὶ πάντων τῶν ἐν ὑπεροχῇ ὄντων, ἵνα ἤρεμον καὶ ἡσύχιον βίον διάγωμεν ἐν πάσῃ εὐσεβίᾳ καὶ σεμνότητι. 2.3 τοῦτο καλὸν καὶ ἀπόδεκτον ἐνώπιον τοῦ σωτῆρος ἡμῶν θεοῦ, 2.4 ὃς πάντας ἀνθρώπους θέλει σωθῆναι καὶ εἰς ἐπίγνωσιν ἀληθείας ἐλθῖν.

2.5 εἷς γὰρ θεός, εἷς καὶ μεσίτης θεοῦ καὶ ἀνθρώπων, ἄνθρωπος χριστὸς Ἰησοῦς, 2.6 ὁ δοὺς ἑαυτὸν ἀντίλυτρον ὑπὲρ πάντων, τὸ μαρτύριον καιροῖς ἰδίοις·

2.7 εἰς ὃ ἐτέθην ἐγὼ κῆρυξ καὶ ἀπόστολος ἀλήθειαν λέγω

(things) in/by unbelief, 1.14 but the grace of our Lord superabounded with faith and agape, the (one) in the anointed Jesus.

1.15 The saying/word/logos is faithful and worthy of every acceptance: that the anointed Jesus came into a world to save sinners; of whom I, I am first,

1.16 but because of this I was shown/received mercy, in order that in me first Jesus, the anointed (one), might demonstrate all the patience/steadfastness, to/toward an example/type of the good (ones) being about to come to believe on him into/for eternal life.

1.17 And to/for the king of the ages, to/for the undecayable, unseen, only God, *be* honor and fame/glory into/for the ages of the ages; truly.

1.18 I put/lay this very charge to you, child Timothy, according to the preceding prophecies to/on you, in order that in/by them you might soldier/battle the good soldiering/battle, 1.19 having/holding faith and good conscience, which some (persons) having rejected/thrust away were shipwrecked/made shipwreck concerning the faith; 1.20 of whom is/are Hymenaius and Alexander, whom I delivered over/betrayed to Satan in order that they might be trained/disciplined not to revile/blaspheme.

2.1 I beseech therefore, first of all, *for* petitions, prayers, supplications/intercessions, thanksgivings to be made in behalf of all men, 2.2 in behalf of kings and all those being in prominence/excellence, in order that we may lead a tranquil and quiet life in/with every reverence/piety and dignity. 2.3 This is good and acceptable before the savior of us/our savior, God, 2.4 who wants/wishes for all men/humans to be saved and to come to/into a full knowledge/recognition of truth.

2.5 For one *is* God, and one *is* a mediator of God and of men/humans, a man, the anointed Jesus, 2.6 the (one) having given himself a ransom in behalf of all, the testimony for its own times/seasons;

2.7 in/for which I, I was put/placed a herald/

ἐν χριστῷ, οὐ ψεύδομαι   διδάσκαλος ἐθνῶν ἐν γνῶσι καὶ ἀληθείᾳ.

2.8 βούλομαι οὖν προσεύχεσθαι τοὺς ἄνδρας ἐν παντὶ τόπῳ, ἐπαίροντας ὁσίους χῖρας χωρὶς ὀργῆς καὶ διαλογισμοῦ·

2.9 ὡσαύτως γυναῖκας ἐν καταστολῇ κοσμίῳ μετὰ αἰδοῦς καὶ σωφροσύνης κοσμῖν ἑαυτάς, μὴ ἐν πλέγμασιν καὶ χρυσῷ ἢ μαργαρίταις ἢ ἱματισμῷ πολυτελεῖ, 2.10 ἀλλ᾽ ὃ πρέπει γυναιξὶν ἐπαγγελλομέναις θεοσέβειαν, δι᾽ ἔργων ἀγαθῶν.

2.11 γυνὴ ἐν ἡσυχίᾳ μανθανέτω ἐν πάσῃ ὑποταγῇ· 2.12 διδάσκιν δὲ γυναικὶ οὐκ ἐπιτρέπω, οὐδὲ αὐθεντεῖν ἀνδρός, ἀλλ᾽ εἶναι ἐν ἡσυχίᾳ.

2.13 Ἀδὰμ γὰρ πρῶτος ἐπλάσθη, εἶτα Εὔα· 2.14 καὶ Ἀδὰμ οὐκ ἠπατήθη, ἡ δὲ γυνὴ ἐξαπατηθεῖσα ἐν παραβάσει γέγονεν. 2.15 σωθήσεται δὲ διὰ τῆς τεκνογονίας, ἐὰν μίνωσιν ἐν πίστι καὶ ἀγάπῃ καὶ ἁγιασμῷ μετὰ σωφροσύνης.

3.1   Πιστὸς ὁ λόγος· εἴ τις ἐπισκοπῆς ὀρέγεται, καλοῦ ἔργου ἐπιθυμεῖ. 3.2 δῖ οὖν τὸν ἐπίσκοπον ἀνεπίλημπτον εἶναι, μιᾶς γυναικὸς ἄνδρα, νηφάλιον, σώφρονα, κόσμιον, φιλόξενον, διδακτικόν, 3.3 μὴ πάροινον, μὴ πλήκτην, ἀλλὰ ἐπιεικῆ, ἄμαχον, ἀφιλάργυρον, 3.4 τοῦ ἰδίου οἴκου καλῶς προϊστανόμενον, τέκνα ἔχοντα ἐν ὑποταγῇ μετὰ πάσης σεμνότητος·

3.5 εἰ δέ τις τοῦ ἰδίου οἴκου προστῆναι οὐκ οἶδεν, πῶς ἐκκλησίας θεοῦ ἐπιμελήσεται;

3.6 μὴ νεόφυτον, ἵνα μὴ τυφωθεὶς εἰς κρίμα ἐμπέσῃ τοῦ διαβόλου. 3.7 δεῖ δὲ καὶ μαρτυρίαν καλὴν ἔχιν ἀπὸ τῶν ἔξωθεν, ἵνα μὴ εἰς ὀνιδισμὸν ἐμπέσῃ καὶ παγίδα τοῦ διαβόλου.

preacher and an apostle -- I say/speak truth in/by the anointed (one); I *do* not lie -- a teacher of ethnics in/by knowledge and truth.

2.8 Therefore, I wish/will *for* the men/males to pray in every place, lifting up holy hands without anger and disputing/arguing.

2.9 Similarly/likewise *for* women to adorn/decorate/order themselves in/with orderly clothing with modesty and sobriety, not with braiding and gold or pearls or very costly clothing, 2.10 but what is fitting/proper *for* women declaring themselves reverent for god, through good works.

2.11 Let a woman learn in silence with/in every subjection; 2.12 but I permit not a woman/wife to teach nor to exercise authority over a man/husband, but to be in silence.

2.13 For Adam was formed first, then Eve; 2.14 and Adam was not deceived, but the woman having been deceived has come to be in transgression. 2.15 But she will be saved through the (thing) of childbearing, if they might abide/remain in faith and agape and sanctification/consecration.

3.1 The saying/word *is* faithful: If anyone strives/longs for an overseership/bishopric, he desires a good work. 3.2 It is necessary then *for* the overseer to be irreproachable, a man of one woman, temperate in wine, of sound mind, respectable, hospitable, skillful in teaching, 3.3 not addicted to wine/a drunkard, not a striker, but kind/yielding, without strife/fighting, without love of money/silver, 3.4 presiding well over his own house, having children in subjection with every dignity/respect/seriousness.

3.5 But if anyone knows not to preside over his own house, how will he take care of an assembly of God?

3.6 Not newly planted/a neophyte, lest being inflated/puffed up he might fall into a judgment from the devil. 3.7 And it is necessary also to have a good testimony from those outside, in order that he might not fall into reproach/disgrace and a snare of the devil.

3.8 διακόνους ὡσαύτως, μὴ διλόγους, μὴ οἴνῳ πολλῷ προσέχοντας, μὴ αἰσχροκερδεῖς, 3.9 ἔχοντας τὸ μυστήριον τῆς πίστεως ἐν καθαρᾷ συνειδήσει. 3.10 καὶ οὗτοι δὲ δοκιμαζέσθωσαν πρῶτον, εἶτα διακονίτωσαν ἀνέγκλητοι ὄντες.

3.11 γυναῖκας ὡσαύτως σεμνάς, μὴ διαβόλους, νηφαλίους, πιστὰς ἐν πᾶσιν. 3.12 διάκονοι ἔστωσαν μιᾶς γυναικὸς ἄνδρες, τέκνων καλῶς προϊστάμενοι καὶ τῶν ἰδίων οἴκων·

3.13 οἱ γὰρ καλῶς διακονήσαντες βαθμὸν ἑαυτοῖς καλὸν περιποιοῦνται καὶ πολλὴν παρρησίαν ἐν πίστι τῇ ἐν χριστῷ Ἰησοῦ.

3.14 ταῦτά σοι γράφω, ἐλπίζων ἐλθῖν πρὸς σὲ τάχιον· 3.15 ἐὰν δὲ βραδύνω, ἵνα εἰδῇς πῶς δεῖ ἐν οἴκῳ θεοῦ ἀναστρέφεσθαι, ἥτις ἐστὶν ἐκκλησία θεοῦ ζῶντος, στῦλος καὶ ἑδραίωμα τῆς ἀληθίας. 3.16 καὶ ὁμολογουμένως μέγα ἐστὶν τὸ τῆς εὐσεβείας μυστήριον· ὃς ἐφανερώθη ἐν σαρκί, ἐδικαιώθη ἐν πνεύματι, ὤφθη ἀγγέλοις, ἐκηρύχθη ἐν ἔθνεσιν, ἐπιστεύθη ἐν κόσμῳ, ἀνελήμφθη ἐν δόξῃ.

4.1 Τὸ δὲ πνεῦμα ῥητῶς λέγει ὅτι ἐν ὑστέροις καιροῖς ἀποστήσονταί τινες τῆς πίστεως, προσέχοντες πνεύμασιν πλάνοις καὶ διδασκαλίαις δαιμονίων, 4.2 ἐν ὑποκρίσει ψευδολόγων, κεκαυστηριασμένων τὴν ἰδίαν συνίδησιν, 4.3 κωλυόντων γαμεῖν, ἀπέχεσθαι βρωμάτων ἃ ὁ θεὸς ἔκτισεν εἰς μετάλημψιν μετὰ εὐχαριστίας τοῖς πιστοῖς καὶ ἐπεγνωκόσι τὴν ἀλήθιαν. 4.4 ὅτι πᾶν κτίσμα θεοῦ καλόν, καὶ οὐδὲν ἀπόβλητον μετὰ εὐχαριστίας λαμβανόμενον, 4.5 ἁγιάζεται γὰρ διὰ λόγου θεοῦ καὶ ἐντεύξεως.

4.6 ταῦτα ὑποτιθέμενος τοῖς ἀδελφοῖς καλὸς ἔσῃ διάκονος

3.8 Similarly/likewise *for* servants/waiters/deacons: Not double- tongued/two-faced, not being addicted to much wine, not fond of shameful gain, 3.9 having/holding the mystery (religion) of the faith in/with a clean/pure conscience. 3.10 And let these also be proved/tried first, then let them minister/ serve, being irreproachable.

3.11 Similarly/likewise *for* women, *being* serious/respectable, not devils/slanderers, temperate in wine, faithful in all (things). 3.12 Let servants/ waiters be men of one woman, presiding well *over*/of children and their own houses.

3.13 For those having ministered/served well acquire for themselves a good rank/standing and much free speech/confidence in/by faith, the (one) in the anointed Jesus.

3.14 I write these (things) to you, hoping to come to you quickly/soon; 3.15 but if I might be slow/delay, in order that you might know how it is necessary to behave in a house of God, which is an assembly of a living God, a pillar and a mainstay/ foundation of the truth. 3.16 And confessedly great is the mystery (religion) of the reverence/piety: (One) who was made plain/visible in flesh, was vindicated in/by a spirit, was seen by messengers/angels, was heralded/preached among ethnics, was believed in a world, was taken up in glory/fame.

4.1 And the spirit says explicitly/expressly that in later times some (persons) will withdraw from the faith, giving heed to deceitful spirits and to teachings/doctrines of/from demons, 4.2 from false reasoners in/by pretense/hypocrisy, having been seared/branded *for* her/*their* own conscience, 4.3 forbidding to marry, *teaching* to abstain from foods which God created to/for partaking with/after thanksgiving by the faithful/believing (ones) and (ones) having recognized/come to know the truth. 4.4 Because every creature/creation of/from God is good, and nothing being received with/after thanksgiving *is* to be thrown away, 4.5 for it is being sanctified/consecrated through a saying/word from God and prayer.

4.6 Recommending/laying down these (things)

χριστοῦ Ἰησοῦ, ἐντρεφόμενος τοῖς λόγοις τῆς πίστεως καὶ τῆς καλῆς διδασκαλίας ᾗ παρηκολούθηκας· 4.7 τοὺς δὲ βεβήλους καὶ γραώδεις μύθους παραιτοῦ. γύμναζε δὲ σεαυτὸν πρὸς εὐσέβιαν· 4.8 ἡ γὰρ σωματικὴ γυμνασία πρὸς ὀλίγον ἐστὶν ὠφέλιμος, ἡ δὲ εὐσέβεια πρὸς πάντα ὠφέλιμός ἐστιν, ἐπαγγελίαν ἔχουσα ζωῆς τῆς νῦν καὶ τῆς μελλούσης.

4.9 πιστὸς ὁ λόγος καὶ πάσης ἀποδοχῆς ἄξιος· 4.10 εἰς τοῦτο γὰρ κοπιῶμεν καὶ ἀγωνιζόμεθα, ὅτι ἠλπίκαμεν ἐπὶ θεῷ ζῶντι, ὅς ἐστιν σωτὴρ πάντων ἀνθρώπων, μάλιστα πιστῶν.

4.11 παράγγελλε ταῦτα καὶ δίδασκε. 4.12 μηδίς σου τῆς νεότητος καταφρονίτω, ἀλλὰ τύπος γίνου τῶν πιστῶν ἐν λόγῳ, ἐν ἀναστροφῇ, ἐν ἀγάπῃ, ἐν πίστι, ἐν ἁγνίᾳ. 4.13 ἕως ἔρχομαι πρόσεχε τῇ ἀναγνώσει, τῇ παρακλήσει, τῇ διδασκαλίᾳ. 4.14 μὴ ἀμέλει τοῦ ἐν σοὶ χαρίσματος, ὃ ἐδόθη σοι διὰ προφητείας μετὰ ἐπιθέσεως τῶν χειρῶν τοῦ πρεσβυτερίου.

4.15 ταῦτα μελέτα, ἐν τούτοις ἴσθι, ἵνα σου ἡ προκοπὴ φανερὰ ᾖ πᾶσιν. 4.16 ἔπεχε σεαυτῷ καὶ τῇ διδασκαλίᾳ· ἐπίμενε αὐτοῖς· τοῦτο γὰρ ποιῶν καὶ σεαυτὸν σώσεις καὶ τοὺς ἀκούοντάς σου. 5.1 πρεσβυτέρῳ μὴ ἐπιπλήξῃς, ἀλλὰ παρακάλει ὡς πατέρα, νεωτέρους ὡς ἀδελφούς, 5.2 πρεσβυτέρας ὡς μητέρας, νεωτέρας ὡς ἀδελφὰς ἐν πάσῃ ἁγνίᾳ.

5.3 χήρας τίμα τὰς ὄντως χήρας. 5.4 εἰ δέ τις χήρα τέκνα ἢ ἔκγονα ἔχει, μανθανέτωσαν πρῶτον τὸν ἴδιον οἶκον εὐσεβῖν καὶ ἀμοιβὰς ἀποδιδόναι τοῖς προγόνοις, τοῦτο γάρ ἐστιν ἀπόδεκτον ἐνώπιον τοῦ θεοῦ. 5.5 ἡ δὲ ὄντως χήρα καὶ μεμονωμένη ἤλπικεν

to/for the brothers, you will be a good servant/minis-
ter/deacon of the anointed Jesus; being sustained/
nourished by the sayings/words of the faith and from/
of the good teaching which you have followed closely;
4.7 but (you) refuse the common/unhallowed and old
womanish myths/tales. And (you) train/exercise yourself toward reverence/piety; 4.8 for the body is
benefited with a little exercise/training, but the
reverence/piety is beneficial/useful to/toward all
(things), having a promise of life, of the present
(one) and the (one) being about to come.

4.9 The saying/word *is* faithful and worthy of
every acceptance; 4.10 for in this we toil/labor and
struggle, because we had hoped upon a living God, who
is a savior of all men/humans, especially of believing
(ones).

4.11 You charge/command and teach these
(things). 4.12 Let no one contemn/despise your youth,
but you become an example/type of the believing (ones)
in logic/word, in conduct/behavior, in agape, in
faith, in chastity. 4.13 Until I come, you attend to
the reading, to the beseeching/comforting, to the
teaching. 4.14 Do not neglect the gift (of grace) in
you, which was given to you through a prophecy with/
after laying on of the hands of the presbytery/body of
elders.

4.15 Take care *for* these (things), be with/in/by
these (things), in order that your progress may be
clear/plain to all. 4.16 Take heed for yourself and
for the teaching; continue in them; for doing this you
will save both yourself and those hearing you. 5.1
You should not rebuke an elder, but comfort/console
him as a father, youths/young men as brothers, 5.2
elder (women) as mothers, young (women) as sisters
in/with every purity/chastity.

5.3 Honor widows, the (ones) really *being* widows. 5.4 But if a certain widow has children or
grandchildren/descendants, let them first learn to
respect/revere their own house/household and to re-
pay/recompense requitals to the parents/forefathers,
for this is acceptable before/in the sight of God.
5.5 But the (one) really *being* a widow and having

ἐπὶ τὸν θεὸν καὶ προσμένει ταῖς δεήσεσιν καὶ ταῖς προσευχαῖς νυκτὸς καὶ ἡμέρας· 5.6 ἡ δὲ σπαταλῶσα ζῶσα τέθνηκεν. 5.7 καὶ ταῦτα παράγγελλε, ἵνα ἀνεπίλημπτοι ὦσιν.

5.8 εἰ δέ τις τῶν ἰδίων καὶ μάλιστα οἰκίων οὐ προνοεῖ, τὴν πίστιν ἤρνηται καὶ ἔστιν ἀπίστου χείρων. 5.9 χήρα καταλεγέσθω μὴ ἔλαττον ἐτῶν ἑξήκοντα γεγονυῖα, ἑνὸς ἀνδρὸς γυνή, 5.10 ἐν ἔργοις καλοῖς μαρτυρουμένη, εἰ ἐτεκνοτρόφησεν, εἰ ἐξενοδόχησεν, εἰ ἁγίων πόδας ἔνιψεν, εἰ θλιβομένοις ἐπήρκεσεν, εἰ παντὶ ἔργῳ ἀγαθῷ ἐπηκολούθησεν. 5.11 νεωτέρας δὲ χήρας παραιτοῦ· ὅταν γὰρ καταστρηνιάσωσιν τοῦ χριστοῦ, γαμῖν θέλουσιν, 5.12 ἔχουσαι κρίμα ὅτι τὴν πρώτην πίστιν ἠθέτησαν· 5.13 ἅμα δὲ καὶ ἀργαὶ μανθάνουσιν, περιερχόμεναι τὰς οἰκίας, οὐ μόνον δὲ ἀργαὶ ἀλλὰ καὶ φλύαροι καὶ περίεργοι, λαλοῦσαι τὰ μὴ δέοντα. 5.14 βούλομαι οὖν νεωτέρας γαμῖν, τεκνογονεῖν, οἰκοδεσποτῖν, μηδεμίαν ἀφορμὴν διδόναι τῷ ἀντικειμένῳ λοιδορίας χάριν· 5.15 ἤδη γάρ τινες ἐξετράπησαν ὀπίσω τοῦ Σατανᾶ. 5.16 εἴ τις πιστὴ ἔχει χήρας, ἐπαρκείσθω αὐταῖς, καὶ μὴ βαρείσθω ἡ ἐκκλησία, ἵνα ταῖς ὄντως χήραις ἐπαρκέσῃ.

5.17 οἱ καλῶς προεστῶτες πρεσβύτεροι διπλῆς τιμῆς ἀξιούσθωσαν, μάλιστα οἱ κοπιῶντες ἐν λόγῳ καὶ διδασκαλίᾳ· 5.18 λέγει γὰρ ἡ γραφή, «βοῦν ἀλοῶντα οὐ φιμώσεις·» καί, ἄξιος ὁ ἐργάτης τοῦ μισθοῦ αὐτοῦ.

5.19 κατὰ πρεσβυτέρου κατηγορίαν μὴ παραδέχου, ἐκτὸς εἰ μὴ ἐπὶ δύο ἢ τριῶν μαρτύρων.

5.20 τοὺς ἁμαρτάνοντας ἐνώπιον πάντων ἔλεγχε, ἵνα καὶ οἱ λοιποὶ φόβον ἔχωσιν. 5.21 διαμαρτύρομαι ἐνώπιον τοῦ θεοῦ καὶ χριστοῦ Ἰησοῦ καὶ τῶν ἐκλεκτῶν ἀγγέλων, ἵνα ταῦτα

been left alone has hoped on God and continues with the petitions and the prayers night and day; 5.6 but the (one) living luxuriously has died living. 5.7 And you charge/command these (things), in order that they may be above reproach.

5.8 But if anyone from those his own and especially from a household provides not himself, he has denied the faith and he is worse than an unbeliever. 5.9 Let a widow be numbered/enrolled, having become not less than sixty years, a woman of one man, 5.10 being witnessed/testified *for* by good works, if she reared children, if she was hospitable, if she washed feet of saints, if she relieved (ones) being oppressed, if she followed after every good work. 5.11 But refuse younger widows; for when they might grow wanton against the anointed (one), they want/wish to marry, 5.12 having a judgment because they annulled/set aside the first faith; 5.13 and at the same time they also learn *to be* idle/not working, wandering around the houses, and not only idle/not working, but *to be* tattlers/gossips and busybodies, speaking the (things) not proper/falling short. 5.14 Therefore I wish/will *for* younger (widows) to marry, to bear children, to keep/mistress a house, to give nothing on account of/for the sake of an occasion of abuse/reproach to/for the (one) opposing; 5.15 for already some turned aside after Satan. 5.16 If a certain believing (woman) has widows, let her/them relieve/assist them/themselves, and let the assembly be not burdened, in order that it might relieve those really *being* widows.

5.17 Let the elders having presided well be considered worthy of a double honor/value, especially those toiling in/by reasoning/speech and teaching; 5.18 for the writing says: YOU WILL NOT MUZZLE A THRESHING OX; and, a worker/laborer is worthy of his wage/reward.

5.19 Accept you not an accusation against an elder, unless/except upon two or three witnesses.

5.20 Reprove you the (ones) having sinned before all, in order that the rest/others also may have fear. 5.21 I solemnly testify before God and the anointed Jesus and the chosen messengers/angels, that you might

φυλάξης χωρὶς προκρίματος, μηδὲν ποιῶν κατὰ πρόσκλισιν. 5.22 χεῖρας ταχέως μηδενὶ ἐπιτίθει, μηδὲ κοινώνει ἁμαρτίαις ἀλλοτρίαις· σεαυτὸν ἁγνὸν τήρει.

5.23 μηκέτι ὑδροπότει, ἀλλὰ οἴνῳ ὀλίγῳ χρῶ διὰ τὸν στόμαχον καὶ τὰς πυκνάς σου ἀσθενείας.

5.24 τινῶν ἀνθρώπων αἱ ἁμαρτίαι πρόδηλοί εἰσιν, προάγουσαι εἰς κρίσιν, τισὶν δὲ καὶ ἐπακολουθοῦσιν· 5.25 ὡσαύτως καὶ τὰ ἔργα τὰ καλὰ πρόδηλα, καὶ τὰ ἄλλως ἔχοντα κρυβῆναι οὐ δύναται.

6.1 Ὅσοι εἰσὶν ὑπὸ ζυγὸν δοῦλοι, τοὺς ἰδίους δεσπότας πάσης τιμῆς ἀξίους ἡγείσθωσαν, ἵνα μὴ τὸ ὄνομα τοῦ θεοῦ καὶ ἡ διδασκαλία βλασφημῆται. 6.2 οἱ δὲ πιστοὺς ἔχοντες δεσπότας μὴ καταφρονίτωσαν, ὅτι ἀδελφοί εἰσιν· ἀλλὰ μᾶλλον δουλευέτωσαν, ὅτι πιστοί εἰσιν καὶ ἀγαπητοὶ οἱ τῆς εὐεργεσίας ἀντιλαμβανόμενοι.

ταῦτα δίδασκε καὶ παρακάλει. 6.3 εἴ τις ἑτεροδιδασκαλεῖ καὶ μὴ προσέρχεται ὑγιαίνουσι λόγοις, τοῖς τοῦ κυρίου ἡμῶν Ἰησοῦ χριστοῦ, καὶ τῇ κατ' εὐσέβιαν διδασκαλίᾳ, 6.4 τετύφωται, μηδὲν ἐπιστάμενος, ἀλλὰ νοσῶν περὶ ζητήσεις καὶ λογομαχίας, ἐξ ὧν γίνεται φθόνος, ἔρις, βλασφημίαι, ὑπόνοιαι πονηραί, 6.5 διαπαρατριβαὶ διεφθαρμένων ἀνθρώπων τὸν νοῦν καὶ ἀπεστερημένων τῆς ἀληθείας, νομιζόντων πορισμὸν εἶναι τὴν εὐσέβιαν. 6.6 ἔστιν δὲ πορισμὸς μέγας ἡ εὐσέβεια μετὰ αὐταρκείας· 6.7 οὐδὲν γὰρ εἰσηνέγκαμεν εἰς τὸν κόσμον, ὅτι οὐδὲ ἐξενεγκεῖν τι δυνάμεθα· 6.8 ἔχοντες δὲ διατροφὰς καὶ

guard/keep these (things) without prejudgment, doing nothing according to pre- inclination. 5.22 Lay hands on no one quickly, neither share/fellowship in others' sins; keep yourself pure/clean.

5.23 Drink you water no longer, but use/employ a little wine because of the stomach and your frequent weaknesses/illnesses.

5.24 The sins of some/certain men/humans are clear/manifest beforehand, going before/preceding into judgment, but some also follow after; 5.25 similarly/likewise the works, the good (ones) *are* clear/plain beforehand, and the (ones) having/holding otherwise are not able to be hidden/concealed.

6.1 As many slaves as are under a yoke, let them deem/think their own masters worthy of each/every honor/value, that the name of God and the teaching may not be reviled/blasphemed. 6.2 And let not the (ones) having believing/faithful masters despise *them*, because they are brothers; but rather let them serve as slaves, because the (ones) receiving in return the good service/energy are faithful/believing and beloved (ones).

You teach and beseech/exhort these (things). 6.3 If anyone teaches another/different (doctrine) and consents/agrees not to sayings/words being sound/healthy, to those from our Lord Jesus, the anointed (one), and to the teaching according to reverence/piety, 6.4 he has been inflated/puffed up, understanding nothing, but being diseased about/around discussions/arguments and battles of words, out of which becomes envy, strife, revilings/blasphemies, evil suspicions, 6.5 constant irritations/rubbings/disputes from men having been corrupted *in* the mind and having been robbed/deprived/defrauded of the truth, from supposing/thinking *for* the reverence/piety to be a means of gain/profit. 6.6 But the religion/reverence/piety with self-sufficiency/contentment is a great means of gain; 6.7 for we have carried/brought nothing evident/manifest into the world, because neither are we able to carry anything out of *it*; 6.8 but having foods/sustenance and coverings/shelters/clothing, we shall be satisfied

σκεπάσματα, τούτοις ἀρκεσθησόμεθα. 6.9 οἱ δὲ βουλόμενοι πλουτῖν ἐμπίπτουσιν εἰς πειρασμὸν καὶ παγίδα καὶ ἐπιθυμίας πολλὰς ἀνοήτους καὶ βλαβεράς, αἵτινες βυθίζουσι τοὺς ἀνθρώπους εἰς ὄλεθρον καὶ ἀπώλιαν·

6.10 ῥίζα γὰρ πάντων τῶν κακῶν ἐστιν ἡ φιλαργυρία, ἧς τινες ὀρεγόμενοι ἀπεπλανήθησαν ἀπὸ τῆς πίστεως καὶ ἑαυτοὺς περιέπειραν ὀδύναις ποικίλαις πολλαῖς.

6.11 σὺ δέ, ὦ ἄνθρωπε θεοῦ, ταῦτα φεῦγε· δίωκε δὲ δικαιοσύνην, εὐσέβιαν, πίστιν, ἀγάπην, ὑπομονήν, πραϋπαθίαν.

6.12 ἀγωνίζου τὸν καλὸν ἀγῶνα τῆς πίστεως, ἐπιλαβοῦ τῆς αἰωνίου ζωῆς, εἰς ἣν ἐκλήθης καὶ ὡμολόγησας τὴν καλὴν ὁμολογίαν ἐνώπιον πολλῶν μαρτύρων. 6.13 παραγγέλλω σοι ἐνώπιον θεοῦ τοῦ ζῳοποιοῦντος τὰ πάντα καὶ Ἰησοῦ χριστοῦ τοῦ μαρτυρήσαντος ἐπὶ Ποντίου Πιλάτου τὴν καλὴν ὁμολογίαν, 6.14 τηρῆσαί σε τὴν ἐντολὴν ἄσπιλον ἀνεπίλημπτον μέχρι τῆς ἐπιφανείας τοῦ κυρίου ἡμῶν χριστοῦ Ἰησοῦ, 6.15 ἣν καιροῖς ἰδίοις δίξει ὁ μακάριος καὶ μόνος δυνάστης, ὁ βασιλεὺς τῶν βασιλευόντων καὶ κύριος τῶν κυριευόντων, 6.16 ὁ μόνος ἔχων ἀθανασίαν, φῶς οἰκῶν ἀπρόσιτον, ὃν εἶδεν οὐδεὶς ἀνθρώπων οὐδὲ ἰδεῖν δύναται· ᾧ τιμὴ καὶ τὸ κράτος αἰώνιον· ἀμήν.

6.17 τοῖς πλουσίοις ἐν τῷ νῦν αἰῶνι παράγγελλε μὴ ὑψηλαφρονῖν μηδὲ ἠλπικέναι ἐπὶ πλούτου ἀδηλότητι, ἀλλ᾽ ἐπὶ θεῷ τῷ παρέχοντι ἡμῖν πάντα πλουσίως εἰς ἀπόλαυσιν, 6.18 ἀγαθοεργεῖν, πλουτῖν ἐν ἔργοις καλοῖς, εὐμεταδότους εἶναι, κοινωνικούς, 6.19 ἀποθησαυρίζοντας ἑαυτοῖς θεμέλιον καλὸν εἰς τὸ μέλλον, ἵνα ἐπιλάβωνται τῆς ὄντως ζωῆς.

6.20 ὦ Τιμόθεε, τὴν παραθήκην φύλαξον, ἐκτρεπόμενος τὰς

with these (things).   6.9 But those wishing/planning
to become/be rich fall into temptation and a trap/
snare and many useless/unwise/unprudent and harmful
desires, which sink to the bottom/drown the men/humans
in ruin and destruction;

6.10 for the love of money/silver is a root of
all the bad/evil (things), of which some aspiring to
were led astray from the faith and pierced themselves
through with many varied pains/sorrows/griefs.

6.11 But you, o man of God, you flee these
(things); but you pursue justice, reverence/piety,
faith, agape, endurance/patience, gentleness/meek-
ness.

6.12 Struggle/fight you the good struggle/fight
of the faith, take you hold on the eternal life,
to/for which you were called and confess you the good
confession before many witnesses.   6.13 I charge/com-
mand to you before God, the (one) making alive all the
(things), and Jesus the anointed (one), the (one)
having testified/witnessed the good confession to
Pontius Pilate, 6.14 for you to keep the command
without spot, without reproach, until the coming/ap-
pearance/epiphany of our Lord, the anointed Jesus,
6.15 which the happy/blessed and only sovereign/power-
ful (one) will show in his own seasons/times, the king
of those reigning as kings and Lord of those being
lords, 6.16 the only (one) having immortality, inhabiting an unapproachable light, whom no one from
men/humans saw nor is able to see; to whom be honor
and the eternal dominion; truly.

6.17 Charge/command you to the rich (ones) in
the present age not to be high minded nor to have set
hope upon the uncertainty of wealth/riches, but upon/
to God, the (one) offering to us all (things) abun-
dantly/richly to/for enjoyment/repose, 6.18 to work
good, to be rich in/by good works, to be liberal/ready
to share, social/beneficent, 6.19 storing/hoarding up
for themselves a good foundation to/for the (thing)
being about to come, in order that they might take
hold of the reality of life.

6.20 O Timothy, guard the deposit, turning yourself from/out of the worldly/common chatter/empty talk

βεβήλους κενοφωνίας καὶ ἀντιθέσεις τῆς ψευδωνύμου γνώσεως, 6.21 ἥν τινες ἐπαγγελλόμενοι περὶ τὴν πίστιν ἠστόχησαν. ἡ χάρις μεθ᾽ ὑμῶν. ἀμήν.

Πρὸς Τιμοθέον Α΄

and opposition/opposing thesis of the (thing) falsely called knowledge, 6.21 which some being promised missed the mark/deviated concerning the faith. The grace *be* with ye. Truly.

To Timothy 1

This is the Sinaitic New Testament, book of 2 Timothy.

1.1 Παῦλος ἀπόστολος χριστοῦ Ἰησοῦ διὰ θελήματος θεοῦ κατ᾽ ἐπαγγελίας ζωῆς τῆς ἐν χριστῷ Ἰησοῦ 1.2 Τιμοθέῳ ἀγαπητῷ τέκνῳ· χάρις, ἔλεος, ἰρήνη ἀπὸ θεοῦ πατρὸς καὶ κυρίου Ἰησοῦ χριστοῦ τοῦ κυρίου ἡμῶν.

1.3 χάριν ἔχω τῷ θεῷ, ᾧ λατρεύω ἀπὸ προγόνων ἐν καθαρᾷ συνιδήσι, ὡς ἀδιάλειπτον ἔχω τὴν περὶ σοῦ μνίαν ἐν ταῖς δεήσεσίν μου νυκτὸς καὶ ἡμέρας, 1.4 ἐπιποθῶν σε ἰδεῖν, μεμνημένος σου τῶν δακρύων, ἵνα χαρᾶς πληρωθῶ,

1.5 ὑπόμνησιν λαβὼν τῆς ἐν σοὶ ἀνυποκρίτου πίστεως, ἥτις ἐνῴκησεν πρῶτον ἐν τῇ μάμμῃ σου Λωΐδι καὶ τῇ μητρί σου Εὐνίκῃ, πέπισμαι δὲ ὅτι καὶ ἐν σοί.

1.6 δι᾽ ἣν αἰτίαν ἀναμιμνήσκω σε ἀναζωπυρεῖν τὸ χάρισμα τοῦ θεοῦ, ὅ ἐστιν ἐν σοὶ διὰ τῆς ἐπιθέσεως τῶν χιρῶν μου·

1.7 οὐ γὰρ ἔδωκεν ἡμῖν ὁ θεὸς πνεῦμα δειλίας, ἀλλὰ δυνάμεως καὶ ἀγάπης καὶ σωφρονισμοῦ.

1.8 μὴ οὖν ἐπεσχυνθῇς τὸ μαρτύριον τοῦ κυρίου ἡμῶν μηδὲ ἐμὲ τὸν δέσμιον αὐτοῦ, ἀλλὰ συνκακοπάθησον τῷ εὐαγγελίῳ κατὰ δύναμιν θεοῦ, 1.9 τοῦ σώσαντος ἡμᾶς καὶ καλέσαντος κλήσει ἁγίᾳ, οὐ κατὰ τὰ ἔργα ἡμῶν ἀλλὰ κατὰ ἰδίαν πρόθεσιν καὶ χάριν, τὴν δοθῖσαν ἡμῖν ἐν χριστῷ Ἰησοῦ πρὸ χρόνων αἰωνίων, 1.10 φανερωθεῖσαν δὲ νῦν διὰ τῆς ἐπιφανείας τοῦ σωτῆρος ἡμῶν χριστοῦ Ἰησοῦ, καταργήσαντος μὲν τὸν θάνατον φωτίσαντος δὲ ζωὴν καὶ ἀφθαρσίαν διὰ τοῦ εὐαγγελίου, 1.11 εἰς ὃ ἐτέθην ἐγὼ κῆρυξ καὶ ἀπόστολος καὶ διδάσκαλος. 1.12 δι᾽ ἣν αἰτίαν καὶ ταῦτα πάσχω,

ἀλλ᾽ οὐκ ἐπαισχύνομαι, οἶδα γὰρ ᾧ πεπίστευκα, καὶ πέπισμαι ὅτι δυνατός ἐστιν τὴν παραθήκην μου φυλάξαι εἰς ἐκίνην τὴν ἡμέραν.

1.13 ὑποτύπωσιν ἔχε ὑγιαινόντων λόγων ὧν παρ᾽ ἐμοῦ

1.1   Paul an apostle of the anointed (one), Jesus, through *the* will of God according to a promise of life, the (one) in the anointed Jesus,   1.2 to Timothy, a beloved child; grace, mercy, peace from God *the* father and the anointed (one), Jesus our Lord.

1.3   I have thanks/grace to/for God, whom I serve/worship from my forefathers/parents with a clean/pure conscience, as I have/hold the constant memory/remembrance about you in my supplications night and day,   1.4 longing earnestly to see you, having called to mind/remembered your tears, in order that I might be filled of/from joy,

1.5   having taken a remembrance of the unpretentious/sincere faith in you, which dwelt first in your grandmother Lois and in your mother Eunice, and I have been persuaded that also in you.

1.6   Through which cause I remind you to revive the fire *for* the gift from   God, which is   in   you through the laying on of my hands;

1.7   For God gave not a spirit of cowardice/timidness to us, but of power and agape and somberness/self-control/seriousness.

1.8   Therefore you should not be ashamed *for* the testimony of our Lord neither *for* me the prisoner of him, but suffer evil together with/for the good message/gospel according to power/strength from God,   1.9 from the (one) having saved us and having called *us* to a holy calling, not according to our works but according to his own purpose and grace, the (one) having been given to us in/by the anointed Jesus, before eternal times,   1.10 but having been made clear now through the advent/appearance/coming of our savior, the anointed Jesus, having indeed abolished/rendered null the death and also having lightened life and immortality through the good message/gospel,   1.11 into/for which I, I was pleased/appointed a herald/preacher and an apostle and a teacher.   1.12 Because of which cause/reason I also   suffer   these   (things),

but I am not ashamed, for I know whom I have believed, and I have been persuaded that he is able to guard/ keep my deposit in/to that day.

1.13 You have a model/example/standard, sayings/-

ἤκουσας ἐν πίστει καὶ ἀγάπῃ τῇ ἐν χριστῷ Ἰησοῦ·

1.14 τὴν καλὴν παραθήκην φύλαξον διὰ πνεύματος ἁγίου τοῦ ἐνοικοῦντος ἐν ἡμῖν.

1.15 οἶδας τοῦτο, ὅτι ἀπεστράφησάν με πάντες οἱ ἐν τῇ Ἀσίᾳ, ὧν ἐστιν Φύγελος καὶ Ἑρμογένης.

1.16 δῴη ἔλεος ὁ κύριος τῷ Ὀνησιφόρου οἴκῳ, ὅτι πολλάκις με ἀνέψυξεν καὶ τὴν ἅλυσίν μου οὐκ ἐπαισχύνθη, 1.17 ἀλλὰ γενόμενος ἐν Ῥώμῃ σπουδαίως ἐζήτησέν με καὶ εὗρεν 1.18 δῴη αὐτῷ ὁ κύριος εὑρεῖν ἔλεος παρὰ κυρίου ἐν ἐκείνῃ τῇ ἡμέρᾳ καὶ ὅσα ἐν Ἐφέσῳ διηκόνησεν, βέλτιον σὺ γινώσκεις.

2.1 Σὺ οὖν, τέκνον μου, ἐνδυναμοῦ ἐν τῇ χάριτι τῇ ἐν χριστῷ Ἰησοῦ, 2.2 καὶ ἃ ἤκουσας παρ᾽ ἐμοῦ διὰ πολλῶν μαρτύρων, ταῦτα παράθου πιστοῖς ἀνθρώποις, οἵτινες ἱκανοὶ ἔσονται καὶ ἑτέρους διδάξαι.

2.3 συγκακοπάθησον ὡς καλὸς στρατιώτης χριστοῦ Ἰησοῦ. 2.4 οὐδεὶς στρατευόμενος ἐμπλέκετε ταῖς τοῦ βίου πραγματίαις, ἵνα τῷ στρατολογήσαντι ἀρέσῃ· 2.5 ἐὰν δὲ καὶ ἀθλῇ τις, οὐ στεφανοῦται ἐὰν μὴ νομίμως ἀθλήσῃ.

2.6 τὸν κοπιῶντα γεωργὸν δεῖ πρῶτον τῶν καρπῶν μεταλαμβάνιν. 2.7 νόει ὃ λέγω· δώσει γάρ σοι ὁ κύριος σύνεσιν ἐν πᾶσιν.

2.8 μνημόνευε Ἰησοῦν χριστὸν ἐγηγερμένον ἐκ νεκρῶν, ἐκ σπέρματος Δαυίδ, κατὰ τὸ εὐαγγέλιόν μου· 2.9 ἐν ᾧ κακοπαθῶ μέχρι δεσμῶν ὡς κακοῦργος, ἀλλὰ ὁ λόγος τοῦ θεοῦ οὐ δέδεται.

2.10 διὰ τοῦτο πάντα ὑπομένω διὰ τοὺς ἐκλεκτούς, ἵνα καὶ

reasonings being healthy/whole, which you heard from me in faith and agape, the (one) in the anointed (one), Jesus;

1.14   guard/keep you the good deposit/store through a holy spirit, the (one) dwelling in us.

1.15   You know this, that all the (ones) in Asia were turned away from me, of whom is Phygelus and Hermogenes.

1.16   May the Lord give mercy to the house of Onesiphorus, because he refreshed me often and he was not shamed/disgraced *for* my chain,   1.17 but having become/happened to be in Rome, he sought me earnestly/eagerly and he found *me*;   1.18 may the Lord give to him to find mercy from *the* Lord in that day. And as many (things) as he served/ministered in Ephesus, you, you know very well/better.

2.1   Therefore you, my child, be you strengthened in/by the grace/gift, the one in the anointed Jesus, 2.2 And what (things) you heard from me through many testimonies/witnessings, you entrust these (things) to faithful men, who will be able also to teach others/ different (ones).

2.3   Suffer you evil together/bear with evil patiently as a good soldier of the anointed Jesus. 2.4 No one serving as a soldier is entangled/involved in the matters of everyday life, in order that he might please the (one) having enlisted *him*;   2.5 and if also anyone competes, he is not crowned/wreathed a victor unless he may compete lawfully.

2.6   It is necessary *for* the laboring/toiling farmers to partake first of the fruits/products.   2.7 Consider what I say; for the Lord will give to you insight/understanding in all (things).

2.8   Remember you Jesus, the anointed (one), having been raised up out of dead (ones)/*from the dead*, from a seed of David, according to the good message from me;   2.9 in/for which I suffer evil as far as bonds like a criminal, but the logos/saying/ word of God has not been bound.

2.10   Because of this I endure all (things) on account of the chosen (ones), in order that they also

αὐτοὶ σωτηρίας τύχωσιν τῆς ἐν χριστῷ Ἰησοῦ μετὰ δόξης αἰωνίου.

2.11 πιστὸς ὁ λόγος· εἰ γὰρ συναπεθάνομεν, καὶ συνζήσομεν· 2.12 εἰ ὑπομένομεν, καὶ συνβασιλεύσομεν· εἰ ἀρνησόμεθα, κἀκεῖνος ἀρνήσεται ἡμᾶς· 2.13 εἰ ἀπιστοῦμεν, ἐκῖνος πιστὸς μένει, ἀρνήσασθαι γὰρ ἑαυτὸν οὐ δύναται. 2.14 ταῦτα ὑπομίμνησκε, διαμαρτυρόμενος ἐνώπιον τοῦ θεοῦ μὴ λογομαχεῖν, ἐπ' οὐδὲν χρήσιμον, ἐπὶ καταστροφῇ τῶν ἀκουόντων.

2.15 σπούδασον σεαυτὸν δόκιμον παραστῆσαι τῷ θεῷ, ἐργάτην ἀνεπέσχυντον, ὀρθοτομοῦντα τὸν λόγον τῆς ἀληθείας.

2.16 τὰς δὲ βεβήλους κενοφωνίας περιΐστασο· ἐπὶ πλεῖον γὰρ προκόψουσιν ἀσεβείας, 2.17 καὶ ὁ λόγος αὐτῶν ὡς γάγγραινα νομὴν ἕξι· ὧν ἐστιν Ὑμέναιος καὶ Φίλητος, 2.18 οἵτινες περὶ τὴν ἀλήθιαν ἠστόχησαν, λέγοντες ἀνάστασιν ἤδη γεγονέναι, καὶ ἀνατρέπουσιν πίστιν τήν τινων.

2.19 ὁ μέντοι στερεὸς θεμέλιος τοῦ θεοῦ ἕστηκεν, ἔχων τὴν σφραγῖδα ταύτην·

«ἔγνω κύριος τοὺς ὄντας αὐτοῦ,» καί, ἀποστήτω ἀπὸ ἀδικίας πᾶς ὁ ὀνομάζων τὸ ὄνομα κυρίου.

2.20 ἐν μεγάλῃ δὲ οἰκίᾳ οὐκ ἔστιν μόνον σκεύη χρυσᾶ καὶ ἀργυρᾶ ἀλλὰ καὶ ξύλινα καὶ ὀστράκινα, καὶ ἃ μὲν εἰς τιμὴν ἃ δὲ εἰς ἀτιμίαν·

2.21 ἐὰν οὖν τις ἐκκαθάρῃ ἑαυτὸν ἀπὸ τούτων, ἔσται σκεῦος εἰς τιμήν, ἡγιασμένον, εὔχρηστον τῷ δεσπότῃ, εἰς πᾶν ἔργον ἀγαθὸν ἡτοιμασμένον.

2.22 τὰς δὲ νεωτερικὰς ἐπιθυμίας φεῦγε, δίωκε δὲ δικαιοσύνην, πίστιν, ἀγάπην, εἰρήνην μετὰ τῶν ἐπικαλουμένων τὸν κύριον ἐκ καθαρᾶς καρδίας.

2.23 τὰς δὲ μωρὰς καὶ ἀπεδεύτους ζητήσις παραιτοῦ, εἰδὼς

might obtain salvation, the (one) in/by the anointed Jesus, with eternal/everlasting glory/fame.

2.11 The saying/word is faithful: for if we died together/with *him*, also we shall live together/with *him*; 2.12 if we endure, we shall also reign together/with *him*; if we shall deny *him*, that (one) shall deny us; 2.13 if wedisbelieve, that (one) abides/remains faithful, for he is not able to deny himself. 2.14 You recall these (things), solemnly testifying/witnessing *them* before God, not to fight with words, useful to nothing/no purpose, to/on overthrowing/destruction of those hearing.

2.15 Be diligent/eager to set/present yourself approved to God, a worker without shame, guiding straight the saying/word of the truth.

2.16 But avoid the common/irreligious vain babblings/utterances; for they will progress/advance to/upon more irreverence/impiety, 2.17 and their saying/reasoning will have *it* as a spreading gangrene; of whom are/is Hyemaeus and Philetus, 2.18 who failed/missed concerning the truth, saying *for* *the* resurrection to have happened already, and they overturn/ruin the faith of some.

2.19 However, the firm foundation of God has stood, having/holding this seal/security:

The LORD KNEW THOSE BEING OF/FROM HIM, and: Let every one calling upon the name of *the* Lord stand away/apart from injustice/unjustness.

2.20 And in a large/great house *there* is not only gold and silver vessels/objects but also wood and pottery, and indeed some in/for honor but also some in/for dishonor;

2.21 therefore, if anyone might cleanse/purify himself from these, he will be a vessel/object in honor, having been sanctified/set apart, highly useful for the master, having been prepared to/for every good work.

2.22 But flee (you) the youthful desires, and you pursue justice/justness, faith, agape, peace with those calling upon the Lord out of a clean/pure heart.

2.23 But you refuse the foolish and uninformed/uneducated/unlearned questions, knowing that they

ὅτι γεννῶσι μάχας· 2.24 δοῦλον δὲ κυρίου οὐ δεῖ μάχεσθαι, ἀλλὰ ἤπιον εἶναι πρὸς πάντας, διδακτικόν, ἀνεξίκακον, 2.25 ἐν πραΰτητι πεδεύοντα τοὺς ἀντιδιατιθεμένους, μήποτε δώῃ αὐτοῖς ὁ θεὸς μετάνοιαν εἰς ἐπίγνωσιν ἀληθείας, 2.26 καὶ ἀνανήψωσιν ἐκ τῆς τοῦ διαβόλου παγίδος, ἐζωγρημένοι ὑπ' αὐτοῦ εἰς τὸ ἐκείνου θέλημα.

3.1 Τοῦτο δὲ γίνωσκε, ὅτι ἐν ἐσχάταις ἡμέραις ἐνστήσονται καιροὶ χαλεποί· 3.2 ἔσονται γὰρ ἄνθρωποι φίλαυτοι, φιλάργυροι, ἀλαζόνες, ὑπερήφανοι, βλάσφημοι, γονεῦσιν ἀπιθεῖς, ἀχάριστοι, ἀνόσιοι, 3.3 ἄσπονδοι, διάβολοι, ἀκρατεῖς, ἀνήμεροι, ἀφιλάγαθοι, 3.4 προδόται, προπετεῖς, τετυφωμένοι, φιλήδονοι μᾶλλον ἢ φιλόθεοι, 3.5 ἔχοντες μόρφωσιν εὐσεβίας τὴν δὲ δύναμιν αὐτῆς ἠρνημένοι· καὶ τούτους ἀποτρέπου.

3.6 ἐκ τούτων γάρ εἰσιν οἱ ἐνδύνοντες εἰς τὰς οἰκίας καὶ αἰχμαλωτίζοντες γυναικάρια σεσωρευμένα ἁμαρτίαις, ἀγόμενα ἐπιθυμίαις ποικίλαις, 3.7 πάντοτε μανθάνοντα καὶ μηδέποτε εἰς ἐπίγνωσιν ἀληθίας ἐλθεῖν δυνάμενα.

3.8 ὃν τρόπον δὲ Ἰάννης καὶ Ἰαμβρῆς ἀντέστησαν Μωϋσεῖ, οὕτως καὶ οὗτοι ἀνθίστανται τῇ ἀληθείᾳ, ἄνθρωποι κατεφθαρμένοι τὸν νοῦν, ἀδόκιμοι περὶ τὴν πίστιν· 3.9 ἀλλ' οὐ προκόψουσιν ἐπὶ πλεῖον, ἡ γὰρ ἄνοια αὐτῶν ἔκδηλος ἔσται πᾶσιν, ὡς καὶ ἡ ἐκίνων ἐγένετο.

3.10 σὺ δὲ παρηκολούθησάς μου τῇ διδασκαλίᾳ, τῇ ἀγωγῇ, τῇ προθέσει, τῇ πίστι, τῇ μακροθυμίᾳ, τῇ ἀγάπῃ, τῇ ὑπομονῇ, 3.11 τοῖς διωγμοῖς, τοῖς παθήμασιν,

οἷά μοι ἐγένετο ἐν Ἀντιοχίᾳ, ἐν Εἰκονίῳ, ἐν Λύστροις, οἵους διωγμοὺς ὑπήνεγκα· καὶ ἐκ πάντων με ἐρρύσατο ὁ κύριος.

generate fights/quarrels; 2.24 and it is not necessary *for* a slave of the Lord to fight, but to be gentle toward all, skillful in teaching, bearing evil patiently, 2.25 in gentleness training/instructing the (ones) opposing/resisting, maybe God may give to them repentance in knowledge of truth, 2.26 and they might return to soberness out of the snare/trap of the devil, having been taken captive by him into the will of that (one).

3.1 And know you this, that in *the* last days hard/trying times will present themselves; 3.2 for the men/humans will be lovers of themselves, lovers of money, braggarts, arrogant (ones), slanderers/blasphemers, disobedient *to* parents, unthankful, unholy, 3.3 irreconcilable/implacable, devilish slanderers, without self-control, brutal, without love of good (ones), 3.4 betrayers/traitors, rash/reckless, having been conceited, lovers of pleasure/pleasure lovers more/rather than lovers of God/God lovers, 3.5 having a form of reverence/piety but denying the power of it; and (you) turn away from these.
3.6 For out of these are the (ones) sneaking/entering into the houses and leading captive silly women having been laden with sins, being led by various/manifold desires, 3.7 always learning but never being able to come into an understanding/a recognition of truth.
3.8 And which manner Jannes and Jambres opposed Moses, so also these oppose/resist truth, men/humans having been corrupted against the mind, unapproved/rejected concerning the faith; 3.9 but they will not advance upon/to more, for their ignorance/folly/foolishness will be very clear to all, as even/also the (folly) of those became.
3.10 But you, you have followed my teaching closely, in the conduct, in the purpose, in the faith, in the patience, in the agape, in the endurance, 3.11 in the prosecution, in the sufferings,
which happened to me in Antioch, in Iconium, in Lystra, what prosecutions I bore up under; and the Lord delivered/rescued me out of all.

3.12 καὶ πάντες δὲ οἱ θέλοντες ζῆν εὐσεβῶς ἐν χριστῷ Ἰησοῦ διωχθήσονται· 3.13 πονηροὶ δὲ ἄνθρωποι καὶ γόητες προκόψουσιν ἐπὶ τὸ χεῖρον, πλανῶντες καὶ πλανώμενοι.

3.14 σὺ δὲ μένε ἐν οἷς ἔμαθες καὶ ἐπιστώθης, εἰδὼς παρὰ τίνων ἔμαθες, 3.15 καὶ ὅτι ἀπὸ βρέφους ἱερὰ γράμματα οἶδας, τὰ δυνάμενά σε σοφίσαι εἰς σωτηρίαν διὰ πίστεως τῆς ἐν χριστῷ Ἰησοῦ. 3.16 πᾶσα γραφὴ θεόπνευστος καὶ ὠφέλιμος πρὸς διδασκαλίαν, πρὸς ἐλεγμόν, πρὸς ἐπανόρθωσιν, πρὸς παιδίαν τὴν ἐν δικαιοσύνῃ, 3.17 ἵνα ἄρτιος ᾖ ὁ τοῦ θεοῦ ἄνθρωπος, πρὸς πᾶν ἔργον ἀγαθὸν ἐξηρτισμένος.

4.1 Διαμαρτύρομαι ἐνώπιον τοῦ θεοῦ καὶ χριστοῦ Ἰησοῦ, τοῦ μέλλοντος κρίνιν ζῶντας καὶ νεκρούς, καὶ τὴν ἐπιφάνειαν αὐτοῦ καὶ τὴν βασιλείαν αὐτοῦ· 4.2 κήρυξον τὸν λόγον, ἐπίστηθι εὐκαίρως ἀκαίρως, ἔλεγξον, παρακάλεσον, ἐπιτίμησον, ἐν πάσῃ μακροθυμίᾳ καὶ διδαχῇ.

4.3 ἔσται γὰρ καιρὸς ὅτε τῆς ὑγιαινούσης διδασκαλίας οὐκ ἀνέξονται, ἀλλὰ κατὰ τὰς ἰδίας ἐπιθυμίας ἑαυτοῖς ἐπισωρεύσουσιν διδασκάλους κνηθόμενοι τὴν ἀκοήν, 4.4 καὶ ἀπὸ μὲν τῆς ἀληθίας τὴν ἀκοὴν ἀποστρέψουσιν, ἐπὶ δὲ τοὺς μύθους ἐκτραπήσονται. 4.5 σὺ δὲ νῆφε ἐν πᾶσιν, κακοπάθησον, ἔργον ποίησον εὐαγγελιστοῦ, τὴν διακονίαν σου πληροφόρησον.

4.6 ἐγὼ γὰρ ἤδη σπένδομαι, καὶ ὁ καιρὸς τῆς ἀναλύσεώς μου ἐφέστηκεν. 4.7 τὸν καλὸν ἀγῶνα ἠγώνισμαι, τὸν δρόμον τετέλεκα, τὴν πίστιν τετήρηκα· 4.8 λοιπὸν ἀπόκειταί μοι ὁ τῆς δικαιοσύνης στέφανος, ὃν ἀποδώσει μοι ὁ κύριος ἐν ἐκίνῃ τῇ ἡμέρᾳ, ὁ δίκαιος κριτής, οὐ μόνον δὲ ἐμοὶ ἀλλὰ καὶ πᾶσι τοῖς ἠγαπηκόσι τὴν ἐπιφάνειαν αὐτοῦ.

3.12 And also all those wanting/wishing to live piously/reverently in the anointed Jesus will be prosecuted; 3.13 but evil men/humans and jugglers/diviners will advance/progress to the worse, deceiving and being deceived.

3.14 But you abide/remain in what (things) you learned and were persuaded of, knowing from whom you learned, 3.15 and that from a baby you have known sacred literature/letters, the (ones) being able to make you wise into salvation/deliverance through faith, the (faith) in the anointed Jesus. 3.16 Every writing *is* God-breathed and useful/profitable toward teaching, toward reproof, toward improvement, toward the training/correction in justice/justness, 3.17 in order that the man of God may be proficient, having been furnished/equipped toward every good work.

4.1 I solemnly testify before God and the a-nointed Jesus, the (one) being about to judge living (ones) and dead (ones), both *for/concerning* his ap-pearance/coming and his kingdom; 4.2 you herald/preach the reasoning/saying/word, be earnest/urgent timely/opportunely without season; reprove, beseech/exhort, rebuke/warn, in/with every patience/steadfast-ness and doctrine/teaching.

4.3 For a time/season will be when they will not permit/endure sound/healthy teaching, but according to their own desires they will heap up teachings for themselves pleasing *to* the ear/*for* the hearing, 4.4 and indeed they will turn away from the hearing of the truth, and also they will be turned aside to the myths/tales/legends. 4.5 But you, you be sober in all (things), suffer evil, do the work of an evangelist/gospel preacher, fulfill/render full your service/ministry.

4.6 For I, I am already offered up, and the time of my dissolution/death has come upon *me*. 4.7 I have struggled the good struggle, I have finished the course/career, I have kept the faith; 4.8 the crown of justice is henceforth reserved for me, which the Lord will render to me in/on that day, the just judge, and not only to me, but also to all those having loved

4.9 σπούδασον ἐλθῖν πρός με ταχέως· 4.10 Δημᾶς γάρ με ἐγκατέλιπεν ἀγαπήσας τὸν νῦν αἰῶνα, καὶ ἐπορεύθη εἰς Θεσσαλονίκην, Κρήσκης εἰς Γαλατίαν, Τίτος εἰς Δαλματίαν· 4.11 Λουκᾶς ἐστιν μόνος μετ᾽ ἐμοῦ.

Μᾶρκον ἀναλαβὼν ἄγε μετὰ σεαυτοῦ, ἔστιν γάρ μοι εὔχρηστος εἰς διακονίαν. 4.12 Τυχικὸν δὲ ἀπέστιλα εἰς Ἔφεσον. 4.13 τὸν φελόνην ὃν ἀπέλιπον ἐν Τρῳάδι παρὰ Κάρπῳ ἐρχόμενος φέρε, καὶ τὰ βιβλία, μάλιστα τὰς μεμβράνας.

4.14 Ἀλέξανδρος ὁ χαλκεὺς πολλά μοι κακὰ ἐνεδίξατο· ἀποδώσει αὐτῷ ὁ κύριος κατὰ τὰ ἔργα αὐτοῦ· 4.15 ὃν καὶ σὺ φυλάσσου, λίαν γὰρ ἀντέστη τοῖς ἡμετέροις λόγοις. 4.16 ἐν τῇ πρώτῃ μου ἀπολογίᾳ οὐδείς μοι παρεγένετο, ἀλλὰ πάντες με ἐνκατέλιπον· μὴ αὐτοῖς λογισθίη·

4.17 ὁ δὲ κύριός μοι παρέστη καὶ ἐνεδυνάμωσέν με, ἵνα δι᾽ ἐμοῦ τὸ κήρυγμα πληροφορηθῇ καὶ ἀκούσωσιν πάντα τὰ ἔθνη, καὶ ἐρύσθην ἐκ στόματος λέοντος.

4.18 ρύσετέ με ὁ κύριος ἀπὸ παντὸς ἔργου πονηροῦ καὶ σώσει εἰς τὴν βασιλείαν αὐτοῦ τὴν ἐπουράνιον, ᾧ ἡ δόξα εἰς τοὺς αἰῶνας τῶν αἰώνων· ἀμήν.

4.19 ἄσπασαι Πρίσκαν καὶ Ἀκύλαν καὶ τὸν Ὀνησιφόρου οἶκον. 4.20 Ἔραστος ἔμινεν ἐν Κορίνθῳ, Τρόφιμον δὲ ἀπέλιπον ἐν Μιλήτῳ ἀσθενοῦντα. 4.21 σπούδασον πρὸ χειμῶνος ἐλθεῖν. ἀσπάζετέ σε Εὔβουλος καὶ Πούδης καὶ Λίνος καὶ Κλαυδία καὶ οἱ ἀδελφοὶ πάντες. 4.22 ὁ κύριος μετὰ τοῦ πνεύματός σου. ἡ χάρις μεθ᾽ ὑμῶν. ἀμήν.

Πρὸς Τιμοθέον Β΄

his coming/appearance.

4.9 You be diligent to come to me quickly/soon; 4.10 for Demas abandoned/forsook me, loving the present age, and he proceeded to Thessalonika, Crescens to Galatia, Titus to Dalmatia; 4.11 only Luke is with me.

Having taken/received Mark, bring (him) with yourself, for he is very useful to me in service/ministry. 4.12 And/also I sent Tychicus to Ephesus. 4.13 Coming, you bring the cloak which I left in Troas with Carpus, also the scrolls, especially the parchments/writing skins.

4.14 Alexander the coppersmith displayed many evils to me; the Lord will give back to him according to his works; 4.15 whom also you, you watch, for he greatly opposed our sayings/reasonings/words. 4.16 No one happened along/became beside *for* me in/at my first defense, but all (men) abandoned/forsook me; may it not be accounted to them;

4.17 but the Lord stood beside me and strengthened me, in order that through me the heralding/preaching might be fulfilled/accomplished and all the ethnics might hear, and I was rescued/delivered out of a lion's mouth.

4.18 The Lord will rescue me from every evil work and he will save *me* in his heavenly kingdom, to whom *be* the fame/glory into/for the ages of the ages. Truly.

4.19 Greet you Prisca and Aquila and the house/household of Onesiporus. 4.20 Erastus remained/stayed in Corinth, and I left Trophimus ailing/being sick in Meletus. 4.21 You hasten/be diligent to come before winter/foul weather. Eubulus, and Pudens and Limus and Claudia and all the brothers greets/salutes you. 4.22 The Lord *be* with your spirit. The grace *be* with ye. Truly.

To Timothy

413

ΠΡΟΣ ΤΙΤΟΝ

This is the Sinaitic New Testament, book of Titus.

1.1 Παῦλος δοῦλος θεοῦ, ἀπόστολος δὲ Ἰησοῦ χριστοῦ κατὰ πίστιν ἐκλεκτῶν θεοῦ καὶ ἐπίγνωσιν ἀληθείας τῆς κατ᾽ εὐσέβειαν 1.2 ἐπ᾽ ἐλπίδι ζωῆς αἰωνίου, ἣν ἐπηγγείλατο ὁ ἀψευδὴς θεὸς πρὸ χρόνων αἰωνίων, 1.3 ἐφανέρωσεν δὲ καιροῖς ἰδίοις τὸν λόγον αὐτοῦ ἐν κηρύγματι ὃ ἐπιστεύθην ἐγὼ κατ᾽ ἐπιταγὴν τοῦ σωτῆρος ἡμῶν θεοῦ, 1.4 Τίτῳ γνησίῳ τέκνῳ κατὰ κοινὴν πίστιν· χάρις καὶ εἰρήνη ἀπὸ θεοῦ πατρὸς καὶ χριστοῦ Ἰησοῦ τοῦ σωτῆρος ἡμῶν.

1.5 τούτου χάριν ἀπέλιπόν σε ἐν Κρήτῃ, ἵνα τὰ λίποντα ἐπιδιορθώσῃ καὶ καταστήσῃς κατὰ πόλιν πρεσβυτέρους, ὡς ἐγώ σοι διεταξάμην, 1.6 εἴ τίς ἐστιν ἀνέγκλητος, μιᾶς γυναικὸς ἀνήρ, τέκνα ἔχων πιστά, μὴ ἐν κατηγορίᾳ ἀσωτίας ἢ ἀνυπότακτα. 1.7 δεῖ γὰρ τὸν ἐπίσκοπον ἀνέγκλητον εἶναι ὡς θεοῦ οἰκονόμον, μὴ αὐθάδη, μὴ ὀργίλον, μὴ πάροινον, μὴ πλήκτην, μὴ αἰσχροκερδῆ, 1.8 ἀλλὰ φιλόξενον, φιλάγαθον, σώφρονα, δίκαιον, ὅσιον, ἐγκρατῆ, 1.9 ἀντεχόμενον τοῦ κατὰ τὴν διδαχὴν πιστοῦ λόγου, ἵνα δυνατὸς ᾖ καὶ παρακαλεῖν ἐν τῇ διδασκαλίᾳ τῇ ὑγιαινούσῃ καὶ τοὺς ἀντιλέγοντας ἐλέγχειν. 1.10 εἰσὶν γὰρ πολλοὶ ἀνυπότακτοι, ματαιολόγοι καὶ φρεναπάται, μάλιστα οἱ ἐκ τῆς περιτομῆς, 1.11 οὓς δεῖ ἐπιστομίζειν, οἵτινες ὅλους οἴκους ἀνατρέπουσιν διδάσκοντες ἃ μὴ δῖ αἰσχροῦ κέρδους χάριν. 1.12 εἶπέν τις ἐξ αὐτῶν, ἴδιος αὐτῶν προφήτης, Κρῆτες ἀεὶ ψεῦσται, κακὰ θηρία, γαστέρες ἀργαί. 1.13 ἡ μαρτυρία αὕτη ἐστὶν ἀληθής.

δι᾽ ἣν αἰτίαν ἔλεγχε αὐτοὺς ἀποτόμως, ἵνα ὑγιαίνωσιν ἐν τῇ πίστι, 1.14 μὴ προσέχοντες Ἰουδαϊκοῖς μύθοις καὶ ἐντολαῖς

1.1   Paul, a slave of God and an apostle of Jesus, the anointed (one), according to/by faith of chosen (ones) from God/God's chosen (ones) and recognition of the truth according to reverence/piety   1.2 upon/to a hope of eternal life, which the unlying God promised before eternal times,   1.3 but he made clear/plain his saying/reasoning/word in their own times/seasons in/by a proclamation which I, I was entrusted *with* according to an injunction/order from our savior, God,   1.4 to Titus, a generated child according to a common faith: Grace and peace from God *the* father and the anointed Jesus, our savior.

1.5   On account of this I left you in Crete in order that you yourself might set in order the (things) lacking/being deficient, and might appoint elders by/in every city, as I, I commanded to you, 1.6 if anyone is irreproachable/blameless, a man of one woman, having faithful/believing children, not in accusation of wild dissipation/revelry/extravagance or non- subject/rebellious.   1.7 For it is necessary *for* the overseer/guardian/bishop to be irreproachable as a manager of God, not self-willed/stubborn, not quick to anger, not drunken/addicted to wine, not a striker, not fond of dishonest/shameful gain,   1.8 but hospitable, a lover of good, serious/sensible, just, devout, self-controlled/temperate,   1.9 paying attention/taking interest according to the teaching of the faithful reasoning/word, in order that he may be able both to beseech/exhort in/by the healthy/sound teaching and to reprove/convict the contradicting (ones).   1.10 For there are many non- subject/independent/rebellious (ones), vain reasoners and seducers/deceivers, especially those from/out of the circumcision,   1.11 of whom it is necessary to muzzle the mouths, who overturn/destroy entire houses/households, teaching things which it is not necessary, for the sake of shameful gain. 1.12 A certain one of them, their own prophet, said: Creteans *are* always liars, evil beasts, lazy/idle gluttons.   1.13 This testimony/witness is true.

Through which cause/reason reprove you them severely, in order that they may be healthy/whole for/in the faith,   1.14 not giving heed to Judean

ἀνθρώπων ἀποστρεφομένων τὴν ἀλήθιαν.

1.15 πάντα καθαρὰ τοῖς καθαροῖς· τοῖς δὲ μεμιαμμένοις καὶ ἀπίστοις οὐδὲν καθαρόν, ἀλλὰ μεμίανται αὐτῶν καὶ ὁ νοῦς καὶ ἡ συνίδησις.

1.16 θεὸν ὁμολογοῦσιν εἰδέναι, τοῖς δὲ ἔργοις ἀρνοῦνται, βδελυκτοὶ ὄντες καὶ ἀπιθεῖς καὶ πρὸς πᾶν ἔργον ἀγαθὸν ἀδόκιμοι.

2.1 Σὺ δὲ λάλει ἃ πρέπι τῇ ὑγιαινούσῃ διδασκαλίᾳ.

2.2 πρεσβύτας νηφαλίους εἶναι, σεμνούς, σώφρονας, ὑγιαίνοντας τῇ πίστι, τῇ ἀγάπῃ, τῇ ὑπομονῇ.

2.3 πρεσβύτιδας ὡσαύτως ἐν καταστήματι ἱεροπρεπῖς, μὴ διαβόλους μηδὲ οἴνῳ πολλῷ δεδουλωμένας, καλοδιδασκάλους, 2.4 ἵνα σωφρονίζωσι τὰς νέας φιλάνδρους εἶναι, φιλοτέκνους, 2.5 σώφρονας, ἁγνάς, οἰκουργούς ἀγαθάς, ὑποτασσομένας τοῖς ἰδίοις ἀνδράσιν, ἵνα μὴ ὁ λόγος τοῦ θεοῦ βλασφημῆται. 2.6 τοὺς νεωτέρους ὡσαύτως παρακάλει σωφρονεῖν· 2.7 περὶ πάντα σεαυτὸν τύπον παρεχόμενος καλῶν ἔργων, ἐν τῇ διδασκαλίᾳ ἀφθορίαν, σεμνότητα, 2.8 λόγον ὑγιῆ ἀκατάγνωστον, ἵνα ὁ ἐξ ἐναντίας ἐντραπῇ μηδὲν ἔχων λέγειν περὶ ἡμῶν φαῦλον.

2.9 δούλους ἰδίοις δεσπόταις ὑποτάσσεσθαι ἐν πᾶσιν, εὐαρέστους εἶναι, μὴ ἀντιλέγοντας, 2.10 μὴ νοσφιζομένους, ἀλλὰ πᾶσαν πίστιν ἐνδικνυμένους ἀγαθήν, ἵνα τὴν διδασκαλίαν τὴν τοῦ σωτῆρος ἡμῶν θεοῦ κοσμῶσιν ἐν πᾶσιν. 2.11 ἐπεφάνη γὰρ ἡ

415

myths/tales and commands of men rejecting/turning away from the truth.

1.15   All (things) are clean/pure to the clean/ pure (ones); but to those having been stained/defiled and to unfaithful (ones) nothing is clean/pure, but both the mind and the conscience of them have been stained/defiled.

1.16   They profess to know God, but they deny him in/by the/*their* works, being abominable and disobedient (ones) and to/toward every good work *being* unapproved/rejecting (ones).

2.1   But you, you speak what (things) are proper/fitting for the healthy/sound teaching.

2.2   *For* older (men) to be sober/temperate in wine, honorable, prudent/thoughtful/sound-minded, healthy/sound (ones) in/for the faith, in the agape, in the patience/endurance.

2.3   Similarly *for* older (women) *to be* in/by behavior worthy of reverence/proper in the temple, not devilish/slanderous (ones) nor having been enslaved by much wine, good/beautiful teachers,   2.4 in order that they may make the young (females) to be lovers of men, lovers of children,   2.5 sober- minded/of sound mind pure/chaste (ones), good housekeepers/workers of the house, being submissive/subordinate to their own men, that the reason/saying/word of   God be not reviled/ blasphemed.   2.6 Similarly *for* the younger (men), you beseech *them* to be sober-minded;   2.7 concerning all (things) offering/exhibiting yourself an example of good works, in/by the teaching *for* incorruptibility, dignity,   2.8 healthy/sound irreprehensible reasoning, in order that the (one) out of opposition/the opponent might be shamed, having nothing vile/evil to say about us.

2.9   *For* slaves to be subject to their own masters in all (things), to be well-pleasing/satisfying, not contradicting/disputing,   2.10 not embezzling/ misappropriating, but *for* every (thing) exhibiting/ showing good faith, in order that they might set in order/adorn the teaching from our savior, God, in all (things).   2.11 For the saving grace of/from God was

χάρις τοῦ θεοῦ σωτήρος πᾶσιν ἀνθρώποις, 2.12 πεδεύουσα ἡμᾶς ἵνα ἀρνησάμενοι τὴν ἀσέβειαν καὶ τὰς κοσμικὰς ἐπιθυμίας σωφρόνως καὶ δικαίως καὶ εὐσεβῶς ζήσωμεν ἐν τῷ νῦν αἰῶνι, 2.13 προσδεχόμενοι τὴν μακαρίαν ἐλπίδα καὶ ἐπιφάνειαν τῆς δόξης τοῦ μεγάλου θεοῦ καὶ σωτῆρος ἡμῶν Ἰησοῦ χριστοῦ,

2.14 ὃς ἔδωκεν ἑαυτὸν ὑπὲρ ἡμῶν ἵνα λυτρώσηται ἡμᾶς ἀπὸ πάσης ἀνομίας καὶ καθαρίσῃ ἑαυτῷ λαὸν περιούσιον, ζηλωτὴν καλῶν ἔργων. 2.15 ταῦτα λάλει καὶ παρακάλει καὶ ἔλεγχε μετὰ πάσης ἐπιταγῆς· μηδίς σου περιφρονείτω.

3.1 Ὑπομίμνησκε αὐτοὺς ἀρχαῖς ἐξουσίαις ὑποτάσσεσθαι, πιθαρχῖν, πρὸς πᾶν ἔργον ἀγαθὸν ἑτοίμους εἶναι, 3.2 μηδένα βλασφημῖν, ἀμάχους εἶναι, ἐπιεικεῖς, πᾶσαν ἐνδικνυμένους πραότητα πρὸς πάντας ἀνθρώπους.

3.3 ἦμεν γάρ ποτε καὶ ἡμεῖς ἀνόητοι, ἀπιθεῖς, πλανώμενοι, δουλεύοντες ἐπιθυμίαις καὶ ἡδοναῖς ποικίλαις, ἐν κακίᾳ καὶ φθόνῳ διάγοντες, στυγητοί, μεισοῦντες ἀλλήλους. 3.4 ὅτε δὲ ἡ χρηστότης καὶ ἡ φιλανθρωπία ἐπεφάνη τοῦ σωτῆρος ἡμῶν θεοῦ, 3.5 οὐκ ἐξ ἔργων τῶν ἐν δικαιοσύνῃ ἃ ἐποιήσαμεν ἡμεῖς ἀλλὰ κατὰ τὸ αὐτοῦ ἔλεος ἔσωσεν ἡμᾶς διὰ λουτροῦ παλινγενεσίας καὶ ἀνακαινώσεως πνεύματος ἁγίου, 3.6 οὗ ἐξέχεεν ἐφ' ἡμᾶς πλουσίως διὰ Ἰησοῦ χριστοῦ τοῦ σωτῆρος ἡμῶν, 3.7 ἵνα δικαιωθέντος τῇ ἐκείνου χάριτι κληρονόμοι γενηθῶμεν κατ' ἐλπίδα ζωῆς αἰωνίου. 3.8 πιστὸς ὁ λόγος,

καὶ περὶ τούτων βούλομαί σε διαβεβαιοῦσθαι, ἵνα φροντίζωσιν καλῶν ἔργων προΐστασθαι οἱ πεπιστευκότες θεῷ.

made manifest/plain for all men/humans, 2.12 training/disciplining us that having denied ourselves the impiety/irreverence and the worldly desires, we might live prudently and justly and reverently/respectfully in the present age, 2.13 awaiting/expecting the happy/blessed hope and an appearance/epiphany of/from the fame/glory of the great God and savior of us, Jesus the anointed (one),

2.14 who gave himself in behalf of us in order that he might ransom/release us from every lawlessness and might cleanse/purify a peculiar/special people for himself, zealous of good works. 2.15 You speak and beseech and reprove/convict these (things) with every authority/command; let no one from/of you despise/disregard *these things*.

3.1 You remind them to be submissive/subject to rulers, to be obedient to authorities, to be ready/ prepared toward/with every good work, 3.2 to revile/ blaspheme no one, to be without fighting/quarreling, yielding/gentle (ones), to display every abiding kindness to/toward all men/humans.

3.3 For we, we also were then ignorant (ones), disobedient/unbelieving, being led astray/deceived, serving as slaves to desires and varied/various pleasures, spending time in badness/evil and envy, hating one another. 3.4 But when the kindness and the love for men/humans of our savior, God, was made clear/ plain, 3.5 not out of works, the (ones) which we, we did in/with justice, but according to his mercy he saved us through a washing of regeneration and renewal from/of a holy spirit, 3.6 which he poured out upon us abundantly through Jesus, the anointed (one), our savior, 3.7 in order that having been vindicated/justified by the grace of that (one) we might become heirs by/according to a hope of eternal life. 3.8 The saying/word *is* faithful,

and concerning these (things) I will/wish *for* you to affirm confidently, in order that the (ones) having believed in God may be careful/think carefully of good works to set before themselves.

These (things) are good and profitable for the

ταῦτά ἐστιν καλὰ καὶ ὠφέλιμα τοῖς ἀνθρώποις· 3.9 μωρὰς δὲ ζητήσις καὶ γενεαλογίας καὶ ἔριν καὶ μάχας νομικὰς περιΐστασο, εἰσὶν γὰρ ἀνωφελεῖς καὶ μάταιοι. 3.10 αἱρετικὸν ἄνθρωπον μετὰ μίαν καὶ δευτέραν νουθεσίαν παραιτοῦ, 3.11 εἰδὼς ὅτι ἐξέστραπται ὁ τοιοῦτος καὶ ἁμαρτάνει, ὢν αὐτοκατάκριτος.

3.12 ὅταν πέμψω Ἀρτεμᾶν πρὸς σὲ ἢ Τυχικόν, σπούδασον ἐλθεῖν πρός με εἰς Νεικόπολιν, ἐκεῖ γὰρ κέκρικα παραχιμάσαι.

3.13 Ζηνᾶν τὸν νομικὸν καὶ Ἀπολλῶν σπουδαίως πρόπεμψον, ἵνα μηδὲν αὐτοῖς λίπῃ. 3.14 μανθανέτωσαν δὲ καὶ οἱ ἡμέτεροι καλῶν ἔργων προΐστασθαι εἰς τὰς ἀναγκαίας χρίας, ἵνα μὴ ὦσιν ἄκαρποι.

3.15 ἀσπάζονταί σε οἱ μετ᾽ ἐμοῦ πάντες. ἄσπασαι τοὺς φιλοῦντας ἡμᾶς ἐν πίστι. ἡ χάρις μετὰ πάντων ὑμῶν.

Πρὸς Τίτον

men/humans; 3.9 but keep yourselves from/avoid foolish questionings/arguments and genealogies and strifes and legal fightings/quarrels, for they are unprofitable and vain/empty/fallacious. 3.10 You avoid a factious/heretical man/human after one and a second admonition/warning, 3.11 knowing that the such has been turned inside out/perverted, being self-condemned.

3.12 Whenever I might sent Artemas or Tychicus to you, you hasten to come to me in Nicopolis, for I have decided to winter there.

3.13 You send forward hastily Zenas the lawyer and Apollos, in order that nothing may be lacking for them. 3.14 And let the (ones) belonging to us learn to practice diligently of good works in/for the necessary needs, that they may not be unfruitful/unproductive.

3.15 All the (ones)/those with me greet you. Greet/salute you the (ones)/those loving us in faith. The grace *be* with ye all.

To Titus

This is the Sinaitic New Testament, book of Philemon.

1.1 Παῦλος δέσμιος χριστοῦ Ἰησοῦ καὶ Τιμόθεος ὁ ἀδελφὸς Φιλήμονι τῷ ἀγαπητῷ καὶ συνεργῷ ἡμῶν 1.2 καὶ Ἀπφίᾳ τῇ ἀδελφῇ καὶ Ἀρχίππῳ τῷ συνστρατιώτῃ ἡμῶν καὶ τῇ κατ' οἶκόν σου ἐκκλησίᾳ· 1.3 χάρις ὑμῖν καὶ εἰρήνη ἀπὸ θεοῦ πατρὸς ἡμῶν καὶ κυρίου Ἰησοῦ χριστοῦ.

1.4 εὐχαριστῶ τῷ θεῷ μου πάντοτε μνίαν σου ποιούμενος ἐπὶ τῶν προσευχῶν μου, 1.5 ἀκούων σου τὴν ἀγάπην καὶ τὴν πίστιν ἣν ἔχεις πρὸς τὸν κύριον Ἰησοῦν καὶ εἰς πάντας τοὺς ἁγίους, 1.6 ὅπως ἡ κοινωνία τῆς πίστεώς σου ἐνεργὴς γένηται ἐν ἐπιγνώσι παντὸς ἀγαθοῦ τοῦ ἐν ὑμῖν εἰς χριστόν Ἰησοῦν·

1.7 χαρὰν γὰρ πολλὴν ἔσχον ἐπὶ τῇ ἀγάπῃ σου, ὅτι τὰ σπλάγχνα τῶν ἁγίων ἀναπέπαυται διὰ σοῦ, ἀδελφέ.

1.8 διό, πολλὴν ἐν χριστῷ παρρησίαν ἔχων ἐπιτάσσιν σοι τὸ ἀνῆκον, 1.9 διὰ τὴν ἀγάπην μᾶλλον παρακαλῶ, τοιοῦτος ὢν ὡς Παῦλος πρεσβύτης, νυνὶ δὲ καὶ δέσμιος χριστοῦ Ἰησοῦ

1.10 παρακαλῶ σε περὶ τοῦ ἐμοῦ τέκνου, ὃν ἐγέννησα ἐν τοῖς δεσμοῖς Ὀνήσιμον, 1.11 τόν ποτέ σοι ἄχρηστον νυνὶ δὲ καὶ σοὶ καὶ ἐμοὶ εὔχρηστον, 1.12 ὃν ἀνέπεμψά σὺ δέ, αὐτόν, τοῦτ' ἔστιν τὰ ἐμὰ σπλάγχνα· 1.13 ὃν ἐγὼ ἠβουλόμην πρὸς ἐμαυτὸν κατέχιν, ἵνα ὑπὲρ σοῦ μοι διακονῇ ἐν τοῖς δεσμοῖς τοῦ εὐαγγελίου, 1.14 χωρὶς δὲ τῆς σῆς γνώμης οὐδὲν ἠθέλησα ποιῆσαι, ἵνα μὴ ὡς κατὰ ἀνάγκην τὸ ἀγαθόν σου ᾖ ἀλλὰ κατὰ ἑκούσιον. 1.15 τάχα γὰρ διὰ τοῦτο ἐχωρίσθη πρὸς ὥραν ἵνα αἰώνιον αὐτὸν ἀπέχῃς, 1.16 οὐκέτι ὡς δοῦλον ἀλλὰ ὑπὲρ δοῦλον, ἀδελφὸν ἀγαπητόν, μάλιστα ἐμοί, πόσῳ δὲ μᾶλλον σοὶ καὶ ἐν σαρκὶ καὶ ἐν κυρίῳ.

1.17 εἰ οὖν με ἔχεις κοινωνόν, προσλαβοῦ αὐτὸν ὡς ἐμέ. 1.18 εἰ δέ τι ἠδίκησέν σε ἢ ὀφίλει, τοῦτο ἐμοὶ ἐλλόγα· 1.19 ἐγὼ Παῦλος ἔγραψα τῇ ἐμῇ χειρί, ἐγὼ ἀποτίσω· ἵνα μὴ λέγω σοι ὅτι

1.1 Paul, a prisoner of the anointed Jesus, and Timothy the brother to the beloved Philemon and our fellow worker, 1.2 and to Apphia the sister and to Archippus our fellow soldier and to the assembly down from/at/by your house; 1.3 grace to ye and peace from God our father and *the* Lord Jesus, the anointed (one).

1.4 I give thanks to my God always, making mention of you on/at my prayers, 1.5 hearing of/from you the agape and the faith which you have with/toward the Lord Jesus and to/for all the saints, 1.6 so that the fellowship of your faith might become effective in recognition/knowledge of every good (thing), of the (thing) with/by us in the anointed Jesus;

1.7 For I had much joy over the agape of you because the compassions of the saints have been refreshed through you, brother.

1.8 Wherefore, having much confidence/freedom of speech in the anointed (one) to enjoin upon you the proper thing, 1.9 because of the agape I beseech/exhort more, such a one being old/aging as Paul, and now also a prisoner of the anointed Jesus,

1.10 I beseech you concerning my child, whom I generated in the bonds, Onesimus, 1.11 the (one) *being* useless to you then, but now *is* highly useful both to you and to me, 1.12 whom I sent back, and you, you take him to yourself; this is my compassions; 1.13 whom I, I planned to retain with/near myself, that in behalf of you he might minister to/wait on me in the bonds of the good message/gospel, 1.14 but I wanted not to do nothing without your mind/decision, that the good (thing) from you might not be by/down from a necessity but according to a free will. 1.15 For perhaps because of this he was withdrawn toward a time/hour that you might receive him eternally, 1.16 no longer as a slave but above/beyond a slave, a beloved brother, especially to/for me, and by how much more for you, both in flesh and in *the* Lord.

1.17 Therefore if you have/hold me a partner, you accept him as me. 1.18 And if he owes or he did anything unjust *for* you, you account this to me: 1.19 I, Paul, I wrote with my hand; I, I will repay; that I

καὶ σεαυτόν μοι προσοφίλεις.

1.20 ναί, ἀδελφέ, ἐγώ σου ὀναίμην ἐν κυρίῳ· ἀνάπαυσόν μου τὰ σπλάγχνα ἐν χριστῷ.

1.21 πεποιθὼς τῇ ὑπακοῇ σου ἔγραψά σοι, εἰδὼς ὅτι καὶ ὑπὲρ ἃ λέγω ποιήσεις.

1.22 ἅμα δὲ καὶ ἑτοίμαζέ μοι ξενίαν, ἐλπίζω γὰρ ὅτι διὰ τῶν προσευχῶν ὑμῶν χαρισθήσομαι ὑμῖν.

1.23 ἀσπάζεταί σε Ἐπαφρᾶς ὁ συναιχμάλωτός μου ἐν χριστῷ Ἰησοῦ, 1.24 Μᾶρκος, Ἀρίσταρχος, Δημᾶς, Λουκᾶς, οἱ συνεργοί μου.

1.25 ἡ χάρις τοῦ κυρίου Ἰησοῦ χριστοῦ μετὰ τοῦ πνεύματος ὑμῶν. ἀμήν.

Πρὸς Φιλήμονα

may not say to you that you also owe besides yourself to me.

1.20 Yes, brother, I, I may have joy from you in *the* Lord, you refresh/rest my compassions/concerns in *the* Lord.

1.21 Having trusted for your obedience I wrote to you, knowing also that you will do above/beyond what (things) I say.

1.22 And at the same time you also prepare for me a guest room, for I hope that through the prayers of ye I shall be given freely to ye.

1.23 Epaphras, my fellow captive in the anointed Jesus, greets you; 1.24 *also* Mark, Aristarchus, Demas, *and* Luke, my fellow workers/helpers.

1.25 The grace of the Lord Jesus, the anointed (one), *be* with the spirit of ye. Truly.

To Philemon

This is the Sinaitic New Testament, book of Acts.

1.1 Τὸν μὲν πρῶτον λόγον ἐποιησάμην περὶ πάντων, ὦ Θεόφιλε, ὧν ἤρξατο ὁ Ἰησοῦς ποιεῖν τε καὶ διδάσκιν 1.2 ἄχρι ἧς ἡμέρας ἐντιλάμενος τοῖς ἀποστόλοις διὰ πνεύματος ἁγίου οὓς ἐξελέξατο ἀνελήμφθη· 1.3 οἷς καὶ παρέστησεν ἑαυτὸν ζῶντα μετὰ τὸ παθεῖν αὐτὸν ἐν πολλοῖς τεκμηρίοις, δι’ ἡμερῶν τεσσεράκοντα ὀπτανόμενος αὐτοῖς καὶ λέγων τὰ περὶ τῆς βασιλείας τοῦ θεοῦ.

1.4 καὶ συναλιζόμενος παρήγγειλεν αὐτοῖς ἀπὸ Ἱεροσολύμων μὴ χωρίζεσθαι, ἀλλὰ περιμένιν τὴν ἐπαγγελίαν τοῦ πατρὸς ἣν ἠκούσατέ μου· 1.5 ὅτι Ἰωάννης μὲν ἐβάπτισεν ὕδατι, ὑμεῖς δὲ ἐν πνεύματι βαπτισθήσεσθαι ἁγίῳ οὐ μετὰ πολλὰς ταύτας ἡμέρας.

1.6 οἱ μὲν οὖν συνελθόντες ἠρώτων αὐτὸν λέγοντες, κύριε, εἰ ἐν τῷ χρόνῳ τούτῳ ἀποκαθιστάνεις τὴν βασιλείαν τῷ Ἰσραήλ;

1.7 εἶπεν δὲ πρὸς αὐτούς, οὐχ ὑμῶν ἐστιν γνῶναι χρόνους ἢ καιροὺς οὓς ὁ πατὴρ ἔθετο ἐν τῇ ἰδίᾳ ἐξουσίᾳ· 1.8 ἀλλὰ λήμψεσθαι δύναμιν ἐπελθόντος τοῦ ἁγίου πνεύματος ἐφ’ ὑμᾶς, καὶ ἔσεσθέ μου μάρτυρες ἔν τε Ἰερουσαλὴμ καὶ ἐν πάσῃ τῇ Ἰουδαίᾳ καὶ Σαμαρίᾳ καὶ ἕως αἰσχάτου τῆς γῆς.

1.9 καὶ ταῦτα εἰπὼν βλεπόντων αὐτῶν ἐπήρθη, καὶ νεφέλη ὑπέλαβεν αὐτὸν ἀπὸ τῶν ὀφθαλμῶν αὐτῶν.

1.10 καὶ ὡς ἀτενίζοντες ἦσαν εἰς τὸν οὐρανὸν πορευομένου αὐτοῦ, καὶ ἰδοὺ ἄνδρες δύο παριστήκισαν αὐτοῖς ἐν ἐσθήσεσι λευκαῖς, 1.11 οἳ καὶ εἶπαν, ἄνδρες Γαλιλαῖοι, τί ἑστήκατε βλέποντες εἰς τὸν οὐρανόν; οὗτος ὁ Ἰησοῦς ὁ ἀναλημφθεὶς ἀφ’ ὑμῶν εἰς τὸν οὐρανὸν οὕτως ἐλεύσεται ὃν τρόπον ἐθεάσασθαι αὐτὸν πορευόμενον εἰς τὸν οὐρανόν.

1.12 τότε ὑπέστρεψαν εἰς Ἰερουσαλὴμ ἀπὸ ὄρους τοῦ καλουμένου ἐλεῶνος, ὅ ἐστιν ἐγγὺς Ἰερουσαλὴμ σαββάτου ἔχον ὁδόν. 1.13 καὶ ὅτε εἰσῆλθον, εἰς τὸ ὑπερῷον ἀνέβησαν οὗ ἦσαν καταμένοντες, ὅ τε Πέτρος καὶ Ἰωάννης καὶ Ἰάκωβος καὶ Ἀνδρέας, Φίλιππος καὶ Θωμᾶς, Βαρθολομέος καὶ Μαθθαῖος,

1.1 I made indeed the first/former account/word about all (things), O Theophilus, which Jesus began both to do and to teach 1.2 until a day *on* which he was taken up, having commanded through a holy spirit to the apostles whom he chose; 1.3 to whom he also presented himself living, after the (thing) *for* him to suffer, by many proofs, having been visible to them through forty days and speaking/saying the (things) concerning the kingdom of God.

1.4 And having eaten together he charged to them not to desert/depart from Jerusalem, but to wait for the promise of the father which ye heard from me: 1.5 because John indeed baptized in/with water, but ye, ye will be baptized in/with a holy spirit not many days after these (things).

1.6 Then they indeed having gone together were asking him, saying: Lord, if/whether in this time, will you restore the kingdom to Israel?

1.7 But he said to them: It is not of ye to know times or seasons which the father himself placed in/by his own authority; 1.8 but ye will receive power from the holy spirit having come upon ye, and ye will be my witnesses both in Jerusalem and in all Judea and Samaria and until/as far as a last (place) of the land/earth.

1.9 And having said these (things), from them looking on/watching, he was taken up, and a cloud received him from the eyes of them.

1.10 And as they were gazing into the sky/heaven from him going, and behold two men had stood beside them in white clothing/apparel, 1.11 and the (they) said: Galilean men, why have ye stood seeing/looking into the sky/heaven? This Jesus, the (one) having been taken up from ye into the sky/heaven, will thus come *in* a manner which ye beheld him going into the sky/heaven.

1.12 Then they returned to Jerusalem from a mountain, the (one) being called/named from an olive grove, which is near Jerusalem, having a sabbath's road/way. 1.13 And when they entered *her* they ascended to the upper room where they were waiting, and Peter and John and James and Andrew, Philip and Tho-

Ἰάκωβος Ἁλφαίου καὶ Σίμων ὁ ζηλωτὴς καὶ Ἰούδας Ἰακώβου.

1.14 οὗτοι πάντες ἦσαν ὁμοθυμαδὸν προσκαρτεροῦντες τῇ προσευχῇ σὺν γυναιξὶν καὶ Μαριὰ τῇ μητρὶ τοῦ Ἰησοῦ καὶ τοῖς ἀδελφοῖς αὐτοῦ.

1.15 καὶ ἐν ταῖς ἡμέραις ταύταις ἀναστὰς Πέτρος ἐν μέσῳ τῶν ἀδελφῶν εἶπεν

ἦν τε ὄχλος ὀνομάτων ἐπὶ τὸ αὐτὸ ὡσεὶ ἑκατὸν εἴκοσι,

1.16 ἄνδρες ἀδελφοί, ἔδει πληρωθῆναι τὴν γραφὴν ἣν προεῖπεν τὸ πνεῦμα τὸ ἅγιον διὰ στόματος Δαυὶδ περὶ Ἰούδα τοῦ γενομένου ὁδηγοῦ τοῖς συλλαβοῦσιν Ἰησοῦν, 1.17 ὅτι κατηριθμημένος ἦν ἐν ἡμῖν καὶ ἔλαχεν τὸν κλῆρον τῆς διακονίας ταύτης. 1.18 οὗτος μὲν οὖν ἐκτήσατο χωρίον ἐκ μισθοῦ τῆς ἀδικίας, καὶ πρηνὴς γενόμενος ἐλάκησεν μέσος, καὶ ἐξεχύθη πάντα τὰ σπλάγχνα αὐτοῦ. 1.19 καὶ γνωστὸν ἐγένετο πᾶσι τοῖς κατοικοῦσιν Ἰερουσαλήμ, ὥστε κληθῆναι τὸ χωρίον ἐκεῖνο τῇ διαλέκτῳ αὐτῶν Ἁκελδαμάχ, τοῦτ' ἔστιν, χωρίον αἵματος. 1.20 γέγραπται γὰρ ἐν βίβλῳ ψαλμῶν, «γενηθήτω ἡ ἔπαυλις αὐτοῦ ἔρημος καὶ μὴ ἔστω ὁ κατοικῶν ἐν αὐτῇ,» καί, «Τὴν ἐπισκοπὴν αὐτοῦ λαβέτω ἕτερος.»

1.21 δῖ οὖν τῶν συνελθόντων ἡμῖν ἀνδρῶν ἐν παντὶ χρόνῳ ᾧ εἰσῆλθεν καὶ ἐξῆλθεν ἐφ' ἡμᾶς ὁ κύριος Ἰησοῦς, 1.22 ἀρξάμενος ἀπὸ τοῦ βαπτίσματος Ἰωάννου ἄχρι τῆς ἡμέρας ἧς ἀνελήμφθη ἀφ' ἡμῶν, μάρτυρα τῆς ἀναστάσεως αὐτοῦ σὺν ἡμῖν γενέσθαι ἕνα τούτων. 1.23 καὶ ἔστησαν δύο, Ἰωσὴφ τὸν καλούμενον Βαρσαββᾶν, ὃς ἐπεκλήθη Ἰοῦστος, καὶ Ματθίαν. 1.24 καὶ προσευξάμενοι εἶπαν, σὺ κύριε, καρδιογνῶστα πάντων, ἀνάδειξον ὃν ἐξελέξω ἐκ τούτων τῶν δύο ἕνα 1.25 λαβεῖν τὸν κλῆρον τῆς διακονίας ταύτης καὶ ἀποστολῆς, ἀφ' ἧς παρέβη Ἰούδας πορευθῆναι εἰς τὸν τόπον τὸν ἴδιον. 1.26 καὶ ἔδωκαν κλήρους αὐτοῖς, καὶ ἔπεσεν ὁ κλῆρος ἐπὶ Ματθίαν, καὶ

421

mas, Bartholomew and Matthew, James of Alphaeus and Simon the zealot, and Judas of James.

1.14 All these were unanimously/of one accord attending constantly to the prayer with women and Mary the mother of Jesus and the brothers of him.

1.15 And in those days Peter, having stood up in the midst of the brothers, spoke,

and there was a crowd of names/named (ones) at the same (place), about a hundred twenty:

1.16 Men, brothers, it was necessary *for* the writing to be fulfilled which the holy spirit spoke before through David's mouth concerning Judas, the (one) having become a guide for those having taken Jesus, 1.17 because he had been numbered/had belonged among us and obtained the portion/share of this service/ministry. 1.18 Then this (one) indeed acquired a possession/land piece out of a reward from the injustice, and having become prostrate/headlong he burst open in the middle, and all his bowels/compassions were poured out. 1.19 And it became known to all those inhabiting Jerusalem, so as *for* that land piece to be called Aceldamach in their dialect, this is: a possession/land piece of blood. 1.20 For it has been written in a scroll of psalms: LET HIS HOMESTEAD BECOME DESERTED AND LET NOT THE (ONE) BE DWELLING IN/ON HER/*it*. and: LET ANOTHER/DIFFERENT RECEIVE HIS VISITATION/OFFICE.

1.21 Therefore it is necessary of all the men having gone with us in/by every time in which the Lord Jesus came in and went out to/for us, 1.22 having begun from John's baptism until the day of which he was taken up from us, *for* one of these to become a witness with us of his resurrection. 1.23 And they stood/set two, Joseph the (one) being called Barsabbas, who was also called Justus, and Matthias. 1.24 And having themselves prayed, they said: You, Lord, knower of all hearts, show/demonstrate whom you choose out of these, one from the two 1.25 to receive the portion/share of this service/ministry and of an apostle, from which Judas turned aside to go into his own place. 1.26 And they gave lots/dice to them, and the lot fell on Matthias, and he was reckoned/account-

συνκατεψηφίσθη μετὰ τῶν ἕνδεκα ἀποστόλων.

2.1 Καὶ ἐν τῷ συμπληροῦσθαι τὴν ἡμέραν τῆς πεντηκοστῆς ἦσαν πάντες ὁμοῦ ἐπὶ τὸ αὐτό. 2.2 καὶ ἐγένετο ἄφνω ἐκ τοῦ οὐρανοῦ ἦχος ὥσπερ φερομένης πνοῆς βιαίας καὶ ἐπλήρωσεν ὅλον τὸν οἶκον οὗ ἦσαν καθήμενοι· 2.3 καὶ ὤφθησαν αὐτοῖς διαμεριζόμεναι γλῶσσαι ὡσεὶ πυρός, καὶ ἐκάθισεν ἐφ᾽ ἕνα ἕκαστον αὐτῶν, 2.4 καὶ ἐπλήσθησαν πάντες πνεύματος ἁγίου, καὶ ἤρξαντο λαλῖν ἑτέραις γλώσσαις καθὼς τὸ πνεῦμα ἐδίδου ἀποφθέγγεσθαι αὐτοῖς.

2.5 ἦσαν δὲ εἰς Ἰερουσαλὴμ κατοικοῦντες, ἄνδρες εὐλαβεῖς ἀπὸ παντὸς ἔθνους τῶν ὑπὸ τὸν οὐρανόν· 2.6 γενομένης δὲ τῆς φωνῆς ταύτης συνῆλθε τὸ πλῆθος καὶ συνεχύθη, ὅτι ἤκουσεν ἕκαστος τῇ ἰδίᾳ διαλέκτῳ λαλούντων αὐτῶν. 2.7 ἐξίσταντο δὲ ἅπαντες καὶ ἐθαύμαζον λέγοντες, οὐχ ἰδοὺ ἅπαντες οὗτοί εἰσιν οἱ λαλοῦντες Γαλιλαῖοι; 2.8 καὶ πῶς ἡμῖς ἀκούομεν ἕκαστος τῇ ἰδίᾳ διαλέκτῳ ἡμῶν ἐν ᾗ ἐγεννήθημεν; 2.9 Πάρθοι καὶ Μῆδοι καὶ Ἐλαμῖται, καὶ οἱ κατοικοῦντες τὴν Μεσοποταμίαν, Ἰουδαίαν τε καὶ Καππαδοκίαν, Πόντον καὶ τὴν Ἀσίαν, 2.10 Φρυγίαν τε καὶ Παμφυλίαν, Αἴγυπτον καὶ τὰ μέρη τῆς Λιβύης τῆς κατὰ Κυρήνην, καὶ οἱ ἐπιδημοῦντες Ῥωμαῖοι, 2.11 Ἰουδαῖοί τε καὶ προσήλυτοι, Κρῆτες καὶ Ἄραβες, ἀκούομεν λαλούντων αὐτῶν ταῖς ἡμετέραις γλώσσαις τὰ μεγαλεῖα τοῦ θεοῦ.

2.12 ἐξίσταντο δὲ πάντες καὶ διηπόρουντο, ἄλλος πρὸς ἄλλον λέγοντες, τί θέλοι τοῦτο εἶναι; 2.13 ἕτεροι δὲ διαχλευάζοντες ἔλεγον ὅτι γλεύκους μεμεστωμένοι εἰσίν.

2.14 σταθεὶς δὲ ὁ Πέτρος σὺν τοῖς ἕνδεκα ἐπῆρεν τὴν φωνὴν αὐτοῦ καὶ ἀπεφθέγξατο αὐτοῖς, ἄνδρες Ἰουδαῖοι καὶ οἱ κατοικοῦντες Ἰερουσαλὴμ πάντες, τοῦτο ὑμῖν γνωστὸν ἔστω καὶ ἐνωτίσασθαι τὰ ῥήματά μου. 2.15 οὐ γὰρ ὡς ὑμεῖς ὑπολαμβάνεται οὗτοι μεθύουσιν, ἔστιν γὰρ ὥρα τρίτη τῆς ἡμέρας,

ed with the eleven apostles.

2.1 And in the (thing)/at the (time) *for* the day of the fiftieth/pentecost to be fulfilled, they were all together to/on the same (place/*festival*). 2.2 And there suddenly became/happened a sound out of the sky/heaven as of a violent wind being carried and it filled up the entire house/building where they were being seated; 2.3 and tongues as of fire being divided were made visible to them, and it sat on each one of them, 2.4 and they were all filled from a holy spirit, and they began to speak in other/different languages as the spirit was giving to be declared/spoken out by them.
2.5 And there were dwelling in Jerusalem reverent men from every ethnic/nation of those under the sky/heaven; 2.6 and from this sound having become/happened, the multitude came together and was confounded, because each (one) was hearing (one) speaking in his own dialect. 2.7 And they were all being amazed and were marveling/wondering, saying: Behold, are not all these, the (ones) speaking, Galileans? 2.8 And how *do* we, each of us, hear in his own dialect in which we were born/generated? 2.9 Parthians and Medes and Elamites, and those inhabiting Mesopotamia, both Judea and Cappadocia, Pontus and Asia, 2.10 both Phrygia and Pamphylia, Egypt and the parts of Libya down from Cyrene, and the Romans being abroad/away from home, 2.11 both Judeans and proselytes/converts, Cretans and Arabians, we hear from them speaking the majestic (things) of God in our own languages.
2.12 And they all were being amazed and perplexed, saying other to other/one to another: What may this want/wish to be? 2.13 But others/different (ones), through deriding/mocking, were saying that they had been made drunk from sweet/cheap wine.
2.14 But Peter, having stood with the eleven, lifted up his voice and spoke out to them: Men, Judeans and all those inhabiting Jerusalem, let this be known to ye, give ye ear/pay attention *for* my words. 2.15 For *it is* not as ye, ye suppose *that* these are drunk, for it is *the* third hour of the day, 2.16 but

422

2.16 ἀλλὰ τοῦτό ἐστιν τὸ εἰρημένον διὰ τοῦ προφήτου Ἰωήλ,

2.17 «καὶ ἔσται» ἐν ταῖς ἐσχάταις ἡμέραις, λέγει ὁ θεός, «ἐκχεῶ ἀπὸ τοῦ πνεύματός μου ἐπὶ πᾶσαν σάρκα, καὶ προφητεύσουσιν οἱ υἱοὶ ὑμῶν καὶ αἱ θυγατέρες ὑμῶν, καὶ οἱ νεανίσκοι ὑμῶν ὁράσεις ὄψονται, καὶ οἱ πρεσβύτεροι ὑμῶν ἐνυπνίοις ἐνυπνιασθήσονται· 2.18 καί γε ἐπὶ τὰς δούλας μου καὶ ἐπὶ τοὺς δούλους μου ἐν ταῖς ἡμέραις ἐκίναις ἐκχεῶ ἀπὸ τοῦ πνεύματός μου,» καὶ προφητεύσουσιν. 2.19 «καὶ δώσω τέρατα ἐν τῷ οὐρανῷ» ἄνω «καὶ» σημεῖα «ἐπὶ τῆς γῆς» κάτω, «αἷμα καὶ πῦρ καὶ ἀτμίδα καπνοῦ· 2.20 ὁ ἥλιος μεταστραφήσεται εἰς σκότος καὶ ἡ σελήνη εἰς αἷμα πρὶν ἐλθῖν ἡμέραν κυρίου τὴν μεγάλην καὶ ἐπιφανῆ. 2.21 καὶ ἔσται πᾶς ὃς ἂν ἐπικαλέσηται τὸ ὄνομα κυρίου σωθήσεται.»

2.22 ἄνδρες Ἰσδραηλεῖτε, ἀκούσατε τοὺς λόγους τούτους· Ἰησοῦν τὸν Ναζωραῖον, ἄνδρα ἀποδεδιγμένον ἀπὸ τοῦ θεοῦ εἰς ὑμᾶς δυνάμεσι καὶ τέρασι καὶ σημίοις οἷς ἐποίησεν δι' αὐτοῦ ὁ θεὸς ἐν μέσῳ ὑμῶν, καθὼς αὐτοὶ οἴδαται, 2.23 τοῦτον τῇ ὡρισμένῃ βουλῇ καὶ προγνώσει τοῦ θεοῦ ἔκδοτον διὰ χειρὸς ἀνόμων προσπήξαντες ἀνείλατε, 2.24 ὃν ὁ θεὸς ἀνέστησεν λύσας τὰς ὠδεῖνας τοῦ θανάτου, καθότι οὐκ ἦν δυνατὸν κρατῖσθαι αὐτὸν ὑπ' αὐτοῦ· 2.25 Δαυὶδ γὰρ λέγει εἰς αὐτόν, «προορώμην τὸν κύριόν μου ἐνώπιόν μου διὰ παντός, ὅτι ἐκ δεξιῶν μού ἐστιν ἵνα μὴ σαλευθῶ. 2.26 διὰ τοῦτο ηὐφράνθη μου ἡ καρδία καὶ ἠγαλλιάσατο ἡ γλῶσσά μου, ἔτι δὲ καὶ ἡ σάρξ μου κατασκηνώσει ἐφ' ἐλπίδι· 2.27 ὅτι οὐκ ἐγκαταλίψεις τὴν ψυχήν μου εἰς ᾅδην, οὐδὲ δώσεις τὸν ὅσιόν σου ἰδεῖν διαφθοράν. 2.28 ἐγνώρισάς μοι ὁδοὺς ζωῆς, πληρώσεις με εὐφροσύνης μετὰ τοῦ προσώπου σου.»

2.29 ἄνδρες ἀδελφοί, ἐξὸν εἰπεῖν μετὰ παρρησίας πρὸς ὑμᾶς περὶ τοῦ πατριάρχου Δαυίδ, ὅτι καὶ ἐτελεύτησεν καὶ ἐτάφη καὶ τὸ μνῆμα αὐτοῦ ἔστιν ἐν ἡμῖν ἄχρι τῆς ἡμέρας ταύτης·

2.30 προφήτης οὖν ὑπάρχων, καὶ εἰδὼς ὅτι ὅρκῳ «ὤμοσεν αὐτῷ» ὁ θεὸς «ἐκ καρποῦ τῆς ὀσφύος αὐτοῦ καθίσε ἐπὶ τὸν

this is the (thing) having been spoken through the prophet Joel:

2.17 AND IT WILL BE in the last days, says God, I SHALL POUR OUT FROM THE SPIRIT OF ME/MY SPIRIT UPON EVERY FLESH, AND YOUR SONS AND YOUR DAUGHTERS WILL PROPHESY, AND YOUR YOUTHS WILL SEE VISIONS, AND YOUR ELDERS WILL BE CAUSED TO DREAM IN DREAMS/SLEEPINGS; 2.18 AND I SHALL EVEN POUR OUT FROM MY SPIRIT IN THOSE DAYS UPON MY WOMEN SLAVES AND UPON MY MEN SLAVES, and they will prophesy. 2.19 AND I SHALL GIVE WONDERS IN THE SKY/HEAVEN above AND signs UPON THE EARTH below, BLOOD AND FIRE AND VAPOR OF SMOKE; 2.20 THE SUN WILL BE TRANSFORMED INTO DARKNESS AND THE MOON INTO BLOOD BEFORE *for* THE GREAT AND SPLENDID DAY OF THE LORD TO COME. 2.21 AND IT WILL BE *that* EVERY (ONE) WHO EVER MIGHT CALL UPON THE NAME OF *the* LORD WILL BE SAVED.

2.22 Men, Israelites, hear ye these sayings/ words: Jesus the Nazarene, a man having been shown/at-tested from God to ye by powers and wonders and signs which God did through him in the midst of ye, as ye yourselves know, 2.23 ye took up/killed this (one) given up, having been fixed by the will and foreknow-ledge of God, having affixed through a hand of lawless (ones), 2.24 whom God raised up, having loosed the pains of the death, because it was not possible *for* him to be held by it; 2.25 for David says to him: I WAS FORESEEING MY LORD BEFORE ME THROUGH EVERY (THING), BECAUSE HIS IS OUT OF MY RIGHT (ONES)/AT MY RIGHT HAND LEST I BE SHAKEN. 2.26 BECAUSE OF THIS MY HEART WAS ENCOURAGED AND MY TONGUE EXALTED, AND EVEN MY FLESH WILL ALSO DWELL UPON A HOPE; 2.27 BECAUSE YOU WILL NOT ABANDON MY SOUL/LIFE IN HADES, NOR WILL YOU GIVE YOUR PIOUS/DEVOUT (ONE) TO SEE DECAY/CORRUP-TION. 2.28 YOU MADE KNOWN TO ME PATHS/WAYS OF LIFE, YOU WILL FILL ME FROM GLADNESS WITH YOUR FACE.

2.29 Men, brothers, being permitted to speak with confidence/plainness to ye about the patriarch David, that he both died and was buried and his grave is among us until this day;

2.30 being/existing therefore a prophet, and knowing that by an oath God SWORE TO HIM OUT OF THE FRUIT OF HIS LOIN TO SIT UPON HIS THRONE, 2.31 having

423

θρόνον αὐτοῦ,» 2.31 προϊδὼν ἐλάλησεν περὶ τῆς ἀναστάσεως τοῦ χριστοῦ ὅτι «οὔτε ἐνκατελίφθη εἰς ᾅδην οὔτε» ἡ σὰρξ αὐτοῦ «εἶδεν διαφθοράν.» 2.32 τοῦτον τὸν Ἰησοῦν ἀνέστησεν ὁ θεός, οὗ πάντες ἐσμεν ἡμεῖς μάρτυρες. 2.33 τῇ δεξιᾷ οὖν θεοῦ ὑψωθεὶς τήν τε ἐπαγγελίαν τοῦ πνεύματος τοῦ ἁγίου λαβὼν παρὰ τοῦ πατρὸς ἐξέχεεν τοῦτο ὃ ὑμεῖς βλέπετε καὶ ἀκούετε. 2.34 οὐ γὰρ Δαυὶδ ἀνέβη εἰς τοὺς οὐρανούς, λέγει δὲ αὐτός, «εἶπεν ὁ κύριος τῷ κυρίῳ μου, κάθου ἐκ δεξιῶν μου 2.35 ἕως ἂν θῶ τοὺς ἐχθρούς σου ὑποπόδιον τῶν ποδῶν σου.»

2.36 ἀσφαλῶς οὖν γινωσκέτω πᾶς οἶκος Ἰσραὴλ ὅτι καὶ κύριον αὐτὸν καὶ χριστὸν ἐποίησεν ὁ θεός, τοῦτον τὸν Ἰησοῦν ὃν ὑμεῖς ἐσταυρώσατε. 2.37 ἀκούσαντες δὲ κατενύγησαν τὴν καρδίαν, εἰπόντες πρὸς τὸν Πέτρον καὶ τοὺς λοιποὺς ἀποστόλους, τί ποιήσωμεν, ἄνδρες ἀδελφοί; 2.38 Πέτρος δὲ πρὸς αὐτούς, μετανοήσατε, φησίν, καὶ βαπτισθήτω ἕκαστος ὑμῶν ἐπὶ τῷ ὀνόματι Ἰησοῦ χριστοῦ εἰς ἄφεσιν τῶν ἁμαρτιῶν ὑμῶν, καὶ λήμψεσθαι τὴν δωρεὰν τοῦ ἁγίου πνεύματος· 2.39 ὑμῖν γάρ ἐστιν ἡ ἐπαγγελία καὶ τοῖς τέκνοις ὑμῶν καὶ πᾶσι τοῖς εἰς μακρὰν ὅσους ἂν προσκαλέσητε κύριος ὁ θεὸς ἡμῶν. 2.40 ἑτέροις τε λόγοις πλίοσιν διεμαρτύρατο, καὶ παρεκάλει αὐτοὺς λέγων, σώθηται ἀπὸ τῆς γενεᾶς τῆς σκολιᾶς ταύτης. 2.41 οἱ μὲν οὖν ἀποδεξάμενοι τὸν λόγον αὐτοῦ ἐβαπτίσθησαν, καὶ προσετέθησαν ἐν τῇ ἡμέρᾳ ἐκίνη ψυχαὶ ὡσεὶ τρισχίλιαι.

2.42 ἦσαν δὲ προσκαρτεροῦντες τῇ διδαχῇ τῶν ἀποστόλων καὶ τῇ κοινωνίᾳ, τῇ κλάσι τοῦ ἄρτου καὶ ταῖς προσευχαῖς. 2.43 ἐγίνετο δὲ πάσῃ ψυχῇ φόβος, πολλά δε τέρατα καὶ σημῖα διὰ τῶν ἀποστόλων ἐγίνετο ἐν Ἰερουσαλὴμ φόβος τε ἦν μέγας ἐπὶ πάντας. 2.44 καὶ πάντες δὲ οἱ πιστεύσαντες ἦσαν ἐπὶ τὸ αὐτὸ καὶ εἶχον ἅπαντα κοινά, 2.45 καὶ τὰ κτήματα καὶ τὰς ὑπάρξεις ἐπίπρασκον καὶ διεμέριζον αὐτὰ πᾶσιν καθότι ἄν τις χρίαν

foreseen he spoke about the resurrection of the a-
nointed (one), that HE WAS NEITHER ABANDONED IN HADES
NOR HIS FLESH SAW DECAY/DESTRUCTION/DECOMPOSITION.
2.32 God raised up this Jesus, of which we ourselves
are all witnesses. 2.33 Therefore, having been exalted
to the right of God and having received the promise of
the holy spirit from the father, he poured out this
which ye yourselves see and hear. 2.34 For David did
not ascend into the skies/heavens, but he himself
says: THE LORD SAID TO MY LORD: SIT OUT OF MY RIGHT
(ONES)/AT MY RIGHT (HAND) 2.35 UNTIL I WOULD PUT/
PLACE YOUR ENEMIES A FOOTSTOOL OF YOUR FEET.

2.36 Securely then, let all *the* house of Israel
know that God made him both a lord and the anointed
(one), this Jesus whom ye, ye crucified. 2.37 And
having listened they were pierced *to* the heart, saying
to Peter and the remaining apostles: What should we
do, men, brothers? 2.38 And Peter to them: Repent ye,
he says, and let each (one) of ye be baptized on the
name of Jesus, the anointed (one), into/for forgive-
ness/remission of your faults/sins, and ye will receive the gift of/from the holy spirit; 2.39 for the
promise is for ye and your children and for all those
in a far (place), as many as the Lord our God would
summon/call to. 2.40 And he solemnly testified with
many other/different sayings/words, and was exhorting
them, saying: Be ye saved/delivered from this crook-
ed/perverse generation. 2.41 Then indeed the (ones)
having welcomed the saying/word from him were baptized, and there were added on that day about three
thousand souls/lives.

2.42 And they were attending/adhering constantly
to the doctrine of the apostles and to the fellowship,
to the breaking of the loaf, and to the prayers. 2.43
And a fear became to/came about for every soul/life,
and many wonders and signs came about through the
apostles in Jerusalem, and a great fear was over/upon
all. 2.44 And all the (ones) having believed were
also at the same (place) and having/holding all
(things) common, 2.45 both the land pieces and the
goods/existing things they were selling and distributing them to all according as anyone would have a need;

εἶχεν· 2.46 καθ’ ἡμέραν τε προσκαρτεροῦντες ὁμοθυμαδὸν ἐν τῷ ἱερῷ, κλῶντές τε κατ’ οἶκον ἄρτον, μετελάμβανον τροφῆς ἐν ἀγαλλιάσει καὶ ἀφελότητι καρδίας, 2.47 αἰνοῦντες τὸν θεὸν καὶ ἔχοντες χάριν πρὸς ὅλον τὸν λαόν. ὁ δὲ κύριος προσετίθει τοὺς σωζομένους καθ’ ἡμέραν ἐπὶ τὸ αὐτό.

3.1 Πέτρος δὲ καὶ Ἰωάννης ἀνέβαινον εἰς τὸ ἱερὸν ἐπὶ τὴν ὥραν τῆς προσευχῆς τὴν ἐνάτην. 3.2 καί τις ἀνὴρ χωλὸς ἐκ κοιλίας μητρὸς αὐτοῦ ὑπάρχων ἐβαστάζετο, ὃν ἐτίθουν καθ’ ἡμέραν πρὸς τὴν θύραν τοῦ ἱεροῦ τὴν λεγομένην ὡραίαν τοῦ αἰτῖν ἐλεημοσύνην παρὰ τῶν εἰσπορευομένων εἰς τὸ ἱερόν· 3.3 ὃς ἰδὼν Πέτρον καὶ Ἰωάννην μέλλοντας εἰσιέναι εἰς τὸ ἱερὸν ἠρώτα ἐλεημοσύνην λαβῖν. 3.4 ἀτενίσας δὲ Πέτρος πρὸς αὐτὸν σὺν τῷ Ἰωάννῃ εἶπεν, Βλέψον εἰς ἡμᾶς. 3.5 ὁ δὲ ἐπεῖχεν αὐτοῖς προσδοκῶν τι παρ’ αὐτῶν λαβῖν.

3.6 εἶπεν δὲ Πέτρος, ἀργύριον καὶ χρυσίον οὐκ ὑπάρχει μοι, ὃ δὲ ἔχω τοῦτό σοι δίδωμι· ἐν τῷ ὀνόματι Ἰησοῦ χριστοῦ τοῦ Ναζωραίου περιπάτει. 3.7 καὶ πιάσας αὐτὸν τῆς δεξιᾶς χειρὸς ἤγειρεν αὐτόν· παραχρῆμα δὲ ἐστερεώθησαν αἱ βάσις αὐτοῦ καὶ τὰ στασφυδρά, 3.8 καὶ ἐξαλλόμενος ἔστη καὶ περιεπάτει, καὶ εἰσῆλθεν σὺν αὐτοῖς εἰς τὸ ἱερὸν περιπατῶν καὶ ἁλλόμενος καὶ αἰνῶν τὸν θεόν. 3.9 καὶ εἶδεν πᾶς ὁ λαὸς αὐτὸν περιπατοῦντα καὶ αἰνοῦντα τὸν θεόν, 3.10 ἐπεγίνωσκον δὲ αὐτὸν ὅτι αὐτὸς ἦν ὁ πρὸς τὴν ἐλαιημοσύνην καθήμενος ἐπὶ τῇ ὡραίᾳ πύλην τοῦ ἱεροῦ, καὶ ἐπλήσθησαν θάμβους

καὶ ἐκστάσεως ἐπὶ τῷ συμβεβηκότι αὐτῷ. 3.11 κρατοῦντος δὲ αὐτοῦ τὸν Πέτρον καὶ τὸν Ἰωάννην συνέδραμεν πᾶς ὁ λαὸς πρὸς αὐτοὺς ἐπὶ τῇ στοᾷ τῇ καλουμένῃ Σολομῶντος ἔκθαμβοι. 3.12 ἰδὼν δὲ ὁ Πέτρος ἀπεκρίνατο πρὸς τὸν λαόν, ἄνδρες Ἰσδραηλῖται, τί θαυμάζετε ἐπὶ τούτῳ, εἰ ἡμῖν τί ἀτενίζεται ὡς

2.46 and day by day attending constantly with one accord in the *outer* temple, and breaking a loaf by *the* house/house by house, they were sharing/partaking of food with exultation and simplicity of heart, 2.47 praising God and having grace/favor toward all the people. And the Lord was adding those being saved day by day to the same (thing).

3.1 But Peter and John were going up to the *outer* temple on/at the hour of the prayer, the ninth (hour). 3.2 And a certain man, existing/being lame from his mother's belly/womb was being carried, whom they were putting day by day near the door of the *outer* temple, the (one) being called Beautiful from the (thing) to ask charity from those going into the *outer* temple, 3.3 who having seen Peter and John being about to enter into the *outer* temple, he was asking to receive charity. 3.4 And Peter having gazed toward him with John said: Look you to us. 3.5 And the (he) gave heed to them, expecting to receive something from them.
3.6 But Peter said: Silver and gold do not exist for me, but what I have, this I give to you; in the name of Jesus, the anointed (one) from Nazareth, walk. 3.7 And having seized him from the right hand, he raised him; and immediately his feet and ankle bones were strengthened, 3.8 and leaping about, he stood and was walking, and he went in with them into the *outer* temple, walking and leaping and praising God. 3.9 And all the people saw him walking and praising God, 3.10 and they were recognizing him that he himself was the (one) being seated for the charity at the Beautiful gate of the *outer* temple, and were filled from wonder
and astonishment at the (thing) having happened to him. 3.11 And from him holding fast Peter and John, all the people ran together to them at the porch/colonnade being called Solomon's/of Solomon, utterly astonished. 3.12 And having seen, Peter answered to the people: Men, Israelites, why do ye wonder at/marvel over this (one), or why do ye gaze at us from the (thing) for him to walk as *if* by our own

ἰδίᾳ δυνάμι ἢ εὐσεβείᾳ πεποιηκόσιν τοῦ περιπατεῖν αὐτόν; 3.13 «ὁ θεὸς Ἀβραὰμ καὶ ὁ θεὸς Ἰσαὰκ καὶ ὁ θεὸς Ἰακώβ, ὁ θεὸς τῶν πατέρων ἡμῶν,» ἐδόξασεν τὸν παῖδα αὐτοῦ Ἰησοῦν, ὃν ὑμεῖς μὲν παρεδώκατε καὶ ἠρνήσασθε κατὰ πρόσωπον Πιλάτου, κρίναντος ἐκίνου ἀπολλύειν· 3.14 ὑμεῖς δὲ τὸν ἅγιον καὶ δίκαιον ἠρνήσασθε, καὶ ᾐτήσασθαι ἄνδρα φονέα χαρισθῆναι ὑμῖν, 3.15 τὸν δὲ ἀρχηγὸν τῆς ζωῆς ἀπεκτίνατε, ὃν ὁ θεὸς ἤγειρεν ἐκ νεκρῶν, οὗ ἡμῖς μάρτυρές ἐσμεν. 3.16 καὶ ἐπὶ τῇ πίστι τοῦ ὀνόματος αὐτοῦ τοῦτον ὃν θεωρεῖτε καὶ οἴδαται ἐστερέωσεν τὸ ὄνομα αὐτοῦ, καὶ ἡ πίστις ἡ δι' αὐτοῦ ἔδωκεν αὐτῷ τὴν ὁλοκληρίαν ταύτην ἀπέναντι πάντων ὑμῶν. 3.17 καὶ νῦν, ἀδελφοί, οἶδα ὅτι κατὰ ἄγνοιαν ἐπράξατε, ὥσπερ καὶ οἱ ἄρχοντες ὑμῶν· 3.18 ὁ δὲ θεὸς ἃ προκατήγγιλεν διὰ στόματος πάντων τῶν προφητῶν παθῖν τὸν χριστὸν αὐτοῦ ἐπλήρωσεν οὕτως.

3.19 μετανοήσαται οὖν καὶ ἐπιστρέψαται πρὸς τὸ ἐξαλιφθῆναι ὑμῶν τὰς ἁμαρτίας, 3.20 ὅπως ἂν ἔλθωσιν καιροὶ ἀναψύξεως ἀπὸ προσώπου τοῦ κυρίου καὶ ἀποστίλῃ τὸν προκεχειρισμένον ὑμῖν χριστόν, Ἰησοῦν, 3.21 ὃν δῖ οὐρανὸν μὲν δέξασθαι ἄχρι χρόνων ἀποκαταστάσεως πάντων ὧν ἐλάλησεν ὁ θεὸς διὰ στόματος τῶν ἁγίων ἀπ' αἰῶνος αὐτοῦ προφητῶν.

3.22 Μωσῆς μὲν εἶπεν ὅτι «προφήτην ὑμῖν ἀναστήσει κύριος ὁ θεὸς ὑμῶν ἐκ τῶν ἀδελφῶν ὑμῶν ὡς ἐμέ· αὐτοῦ ἀκούσεσθε κατὰ πάντα ὅσα ἂν λαλήσῃ» πρὸς ὑμᾶς. 3.23 «ἔσται δὲ πᾶσα ψυχὴ ἥτις ἐὰν μὴ ἀκούσῃ τοῦ προφήτου ἐκείνου ἐξολοθρευθήσεται ἐκ τοῦ λαοῦ.» 3.24 καὶ πάντες δὲ οἱ προφῆται ἀπὸ Σαμουὴλ καὶ τῶν καθεξῆς οἱ ἐλάλησαν καὶ κατήγγιλαν τὰς ἡμέρας ταύτας. 3.25 ὑμεῖς ἐστε οἱ υἱοὶ τῶν προφητῶν καὶ τῆς διαθήκης ἧς διέθετο ὁ θεὸς πρὸς τοὺς πατέρας ὑμῶν, λέγων πρὸς Ἀβραάμ, «καὶ ἐν τῷ σπέρματί σου ἐνευλογηθήσονται πᾶσαι αἱ πατριαὶ τῆς γῆς.» 3.26 ὑμῖν πρῶτον ἀναστήσας ὁ θεὸς τὸν

power or piety/reverence we are having done *it*? 3.13 THE GOD OF ABRAHAM AND THE GOD OF ISAAC AND THE GOD OF JACOB, THE GOD OF OUR FATHERS, he glorified his boy Jesus, whom ye, indeed ye delivered over and denied by *the* face of Pilate, from that (one) having judged/decided to release (him); 3.14 but ye, ye denied the holy and just (one), and ye requested *for* a man, a murderer, to be given freely to ye, 3.15 but ye killed the prince/founder of the life, whom God raised out of dead (ones), of which we, we are witnesses. 3.16 And on the faith of his name, the name of him made firm/strong this (one) whom ye behold and know, and the faith through him gave this wholeness to him before all of ye. 3.17 And now, brothers, I know that ye acted/practiced according to ignorance, even as your rulers *did* also; 3.18 but God thus fulfilled (things) which he declared beforehand through *the* mouth of all the prophets *for* the anointed (one) from him to suffer.

3.19 Therefore, repent ye and turn ye to/toward the (thing) *for* your sins/faults to be erased/wiped out, 3.20 in order that times of rest/relief might come from a face/*the* countenance of the Lord and he might send forth the (one) having been hand picked beforehand for ye, the anointed (one), Jesus, 3.21 whom it is necessary indeed *for* heaven to receive until times/seasons of restoration of all (things) which God spoke through *the* mouth of his holy prophets from an era/age.

3.22 Moses indeed said: THE LORD YOUR GOD WILL RAISE UP A PROPHET LIKE ME FOR YE OUT OF YOUR BROTHERS; YE WILL HEAR FROM HIM ACCORDING TO ALL (THINGS) WHATEVER HE MIGHT SPEAK to ye. 3.23 AND IT WILL BE *that* EVERY SOUL/LIFE WHO MIGHT NOT LISTEN/HEAR FROM THAT PROPHET WILL BE UTTERLY DESTROYED OUT OF THE PEOPLE. 3.24 And also all the prophets from Samuel and the (ones) in order/one after another who spoke and proclaimed these days. 3.25 Ye, ye are the sons of the prophets and of the covenant/testament which God made/arranged with/to our fathers, saying to Abraham: AND IN/BY YOUR SEED ALL THE FAMILIES OF THE LAND/EARTH WILL BE BLESSED. 3.26 God, having first

426

παῖδα αὐτοῦ ἀπέστιλεν αὐτὸν εὐλογοῦντα ὑμᾶς ἐν τῷ ἀποστρέφιν ἕκαστον ἀπὸ τῶν πονηριῶν ὑμῶν.

4.1 Λαλούντων δὲ αὐτῶν πρὸς τὸν λαὸν ἐπέστησαν αὐτοῖς οἱ ἱερεῖς καὶ ὁ στρατηγὸς τοῦ ἱεροῦ καὶ οἱ Σαδδουκαῖοι, 4.2 διαπονούμενοι διὰ τὸ διδάσκειν αὐτοὺς τὸν λαὸν καὶ καταγγέλλιν ἐν τῷ Ἰησοῦ τὴν ἀνάστασιν τὴν ἐκ νεκρῶν, 4.3 καὶ ἐπέβαλον αὐτοῖς τὰς χῖρας καὶ ἔθεντο εἰς τήρησιν εἰς τὴν αὔριον· ἦν γὰρ ἑσπέρα ἤδη. 4.4 πολλοὶ δὲ τῶν ἀκουσάντων τὸν λόγον ἐπίστευσαν, καὶ ἐγενήθη ἀριθμὸς τῶν ἀνδρῶν χιλιάδες πέντε.

4.5 ἐγένετο δὲ ἐπὶ τὴν αὔριον συναχθῆναι αὐτῶν τοὺς ἄρχοντας καὶ τοὺς πρεσβυτέρους καὶ τοὺς γραμματεῖς εἰς Ἰερουσαλήμ 4.6 καὶ Ἄννας ὁ ἀρχιερεὺς καὶ Καϊάφας καὶ Ἰωάννης καὶ Ἀλέξανδρος καὶ ὅσοι ἦσαν ἐκ γένους ἀρχιερατικοῦ 4.7 καὶ στήσαντες αὐτοὺς ἐν τῷ μέσῳ ἐπυνθάνοντο, ἐν ποίᾳ δυνάμι ἢ ἐν ποίῳ ὀνόματι τοῦτο ποιήσατε ὑμῖς;

4.8 τότε Πέτρος πλησθὶς πνεύματος ἁγίου εἶπεν πρὸς αὐτούς, ἄρχοντες τοῦ λαοῦ καὶ πρεσβύτεροι, 4.9 εἰ ἡμῖς σήμερον ἀνακρινόμεθα ἐπὶ εὐεργεσίᾳ ἀνθρώπου ἀσθενοῦς, ἐν τίνι οὗτος σέσωται, 4.10 γνωστὸν ἔστω πᾶσιν ὑμῖν καὶ παντὶ τῷ λαῷ Ἰσραὴλ ὅτι ἐν τῷ ὀνόματι Ἰησοῦ χριστοῦ τοῦ Ναζωραίου, ὃν ὑμῖς ἐσταυρώσατε, ὃν ὁ θεὸς ἤγειρεν ἐκ νεκρῶν, ἐν τούτῳ οὗτος παρέστηκεν ἐνώπιον ὑμῶν ὑγιής. 4.11 οὗτός ἐστιν «ὁ λίθος ὁ ἐξουθενηθὶς ὑφ'» ὑμῶν «τῶν οἰκοδόμων, ὁ γενόμενος εἰς κεφαλὴν γωνίας.»

4.12 καὶ οὐκ ἔστιν ἐν ἄλλῳ οὐδενὶ ἡ σωτηρία, οὐδὲ γὰρ ἕτερον ὄνομά ἐστιν ὑπὸ τὸν οὐρανὸν τὸ δεδομένον ἐν ἀνθρώποις ἐν ᾧ δεῖ σωθῆναι ἡμᾶς.

4.13 θεωροῦντες δὲ τὴν τοῦ Πέτρου παρρησίαν καὶ Ἰωάννου, καὶ καταλαβόμενοι ὅτι ἄνθρωποι ἀγράμματοί εἰσιν καὶ ἰδιῶται, ἐθαύμαζον ἐπεγίνωσκόν τε αὐτοὺς ὅτι σὺν τῷ

raised up for ye his boy, he sent him forth blessing ye in/by the (thing) *for* each (one) to turn away from the evils of ye/your evils.

4.1 And from them speaking to the people, the priests and the military commander and the Sadducees of the *outer* temple came upon them, 4.2 being greatly disturbed because of the (thing) *for* them to teach the people and to proclaim the resurrection out of dead (ones) in/by Jesus, 4.3 and they put the hands upon them and put (them) in prison to/*until* the morrow; for it was already evening. 4.4 But many of those having heard the saying/word believed, and *the* number of the men was caused to become five thousand.

4.5 And it came about on the morrow *for* the leaders and the elders and the scribes of them to be gathered in Jerusalem, 4.6 and Annas the high priest and Caiaphas and John and Alexander and as many as were from a priestly race/kind, 4.7 and having stood them in the midst, they were inquiring: By what power or by/in which name did ye, ye do this (thing)?

4.8 Then Peter, having been filled from a holy spirit, said to them: Leaders and elders of the people, 4.9 if we, we are being examined/judged over good work/energy of an infirm man, by which this (one) has been saved, 4.10 let it be known to ye all and to all the people of Israel that in/by the name of Jesus, the anointed (one), the Nazarene whom ye, ye crucified, whom God raised out of dead (ones), by this (name) this (one) has stood before ye whole/healthy. 4.11 This is THE STONE HAVING BEEN DESPISED/REJECTED IN CONTEMPT BY ye THE BUILDERS, THE (ONE) HAVING BECOME/BEEN MADE INTO A HEAD OF A CORNER.

4.12 And the salvation/deliverance is not in/by any/no other, for neither is there another/different name under the sky/heaven, the (name) having been given among men, in/by which it is necessary *for* us to be saved.

4.13 And beholding the boldness of Peter and John, and having themselves apprehended that they are unlettered and unlearned/illiterate and ignorant, they were wondering and they were recognizing/coming to

Ἰησοῦ ἦσαν· 4.14 τόν τε ἄνθρωπον βλέποντες σὺν αὐτοῖς ἑστῶτα τὸν τεθεραπευμένον οὐδὲν εἶχον ἀντειπῖν.

4.15 κελεύσαντες δὲ αὐτοὺς ἔξω τοῦ συνεδρίου ἀπελθεῖν συνέβαλλον πρὸς ἀλλήλους 4.16 λέγοντες, τί ποιήσωμεν τοῖς ἀνθρώποις τούτοις; ὅτι μὲν γὰρ γνωστὸν σημεῖον γέγονεν δι' αὐτῶν πᾶσι τοῖς κατοικοῦσιν Ἰερουσαλὴμ φανερόν, καὶ οὐ δυνάμεθα ἀρνῖσθαι· 4.17 ἀλλ' ἵνα μὴ ἐπὶ πλεῖον διανεμηθῇ εἰς τὸν λαόν, ἀπιλησώμεθα αὐτοῖς μηκέτι λαλῖν ἐπὶ τῷ ὀνόματι τούτῳ μηδενὶ ἀνθρώπων. 4.18 καὶ καλέσαντες αὐτοὺς παρήγγιλαν τὸ καθόλου μὴ φθέγγεσθαι μηδὲ διδάσκειν ἐπὶ τῷ ὀνόματι τοῦ Ἰησοῦ.

4.19 ὁ δὲ Πέτρος καὶ Ἰωάννης ἀποκριθέντες εἶπον πρὸς αὐτούς, εἰ δίκαιόν ἐστιν ἐνώπιον τοῦ θεοῦ ὑμῶν ἀκούειν μᾶλλον ἢ τοῦ θεοῦ, κρίναται, 4.20 οὐ δυνάμεθα γὰρ ἡμεῖς ἃ εἴδαμεν καὶ ἠκούσαμεν μὴ λαλῖν. 4.21 οἱ δὲ προσαπιλησάμενοι ἀπέλυσαν αὐτούς, μηδὲν εὑρίσκοντες τὸ πῶς κολάσωνται αὐτούς, διὰ τὸν λαόν, ὅτι πάντες ἐδόξαζον τὸν θεὸν ἐπὶ τῷ γεγονότι· 4.22 ἐτῶν γὰρ ἦν πλειόνων τεσσεράκοντα ὁ ἄνθρωπος ἐφ' ὃν ἐγεγόνει τὸ σημῖον τοῦτο τῆς ἰάσεως.

4.23 ἀπολυθέντες δὲ ἦλθον πρὸς τοὺς ἰδίους καὶ ἀπήγγιλαν ὅσα πρὸς αὐτοὺς οἱ ἀρχιερῖς καὶ οἱ πρεσβύτεροι εἶπαν.

4.24 οἱ δὲ ἀκούσαντες ὁμοθυμαδὸν ἦραν φωνὴν πρὸς τὸν θεὸν καὶ εἶπαν, δέσποτα, σὺ ὁ ποιήσας τὸν οὐρανὸν καὶ τὴν γῆν καὶ τὴν θάλασσαν καὶ πάντα τὰ ἐν αὐτοῖς, 4.25 ὁ τοῦ πατρὸς ἡμῶν διὰ πνεύματος ἁγίου στόματος Δαυὶδ παιδός σου εἰπών,

«ἱνατί ἐφρύαξαν ἔθνη καὶ λαοὶ ἐμελέτησαν καινά; 4.26 παρέστησαν οἱ βασιλεῖς τῆς γῆς καὶ οἱ ἄρχοντες συνήχθησαν ἐπὶ τὸ αὐτὸ κατὰ τοῦ κυρίου καὶ κατὰ τοῦ χριστοῦ αὐτοῦ.»

4.27 συνήχθησαν γὰρ ἐπ' ἀληθείας ἐν τῇ πόλι ταύτῃ ἐπὶ τὸν ἅγιον παῖδά σου Ἰησοῦν, ὃν ἔχρισας, Ἡρώδης τε καὶ

know them that they were with Jesus; 4.14 and seeing the man having stood with them, the (one) having been treated/healed, they were having nothing to say against *it*.

4.15 And having commanded *for* them to go away outside the council/Sanhedrin, they were conferring to/with one another, 4.16 saying: What should we do to these men? For that a known sign indeed has happened through them *is* clear/manifest to all those dwelling in Jerusalem, and we are not able to deny *it*; 4.17 but in order that it might not be spread around over more/excessively to the people, we should/let us threaten to them no longer to speak on this name to no one of men. 4.18 And having called them, they charged *them* the (thing) not to speak out at all nor to teach on the name of Jesus.

4.19 But Peter and John, answering, said to them: Judge/decide ye if it is just before God to hear from ye more/rather than from God, 4.20 for we, we are not able not to speak (things) which we heard and saw. 4.21 And the (they) having added threats, released them, not finding the (thing) how they might punish them, on account of the people, because all were glorifying/praising God over the (thing) having happened; 4.22 for the man on whom this sign came about was more than forty years from the healing/cure. 4.23 And having been released they went to their own and reported what things the high priests and the elders said to them.

4.24 And the (they), having heard, of one accord they lifted up a voice/sound to God and said: Master, you *are* the (one) having made the sky/heaven and the land/earth and the sea and all the (things) in them, 4.25 the (one) of our father having spoken through a holy spirit from *the* mouth of David your boy:

WHY DID ETHNICS/NATIONS BE INSOLENT/HAUGHTY AND PEOPLES THOUGHT/MEDITATED IN VAIN? 4.26 THE KINGS OF THE EARTH/LAND STOOD BY/HELPED AND THE LEADERS/RULERS WE GATHERED UPON THE SAME (THING) AGAINST THE LORD AND AGAINST HIS ANOINTED (ONE).

4.27 For on a truth they were gathered in this city against your holy boy Jesus, whom you anointed,

Πόντιος Πιλᾶτος σὺν ἔθνεσιν καὶ λαοῖς Ἰσραήλ, 4.28 ποιῆσαι ὅσα ἡ χίρ σου καὶ ἡ βουλή σου προώρισεν γενέσθαι. 4.29 καὶ τὰ νῦν, κύριε, ἔπιδε ἐπὶ τὰς ἀπιλὰς αὐτῶν, καὶ δὸς τοῖς δούλοις σου μετὰ παρρησίας πάσης λαλῖν τὸν λόγον σου, 4.30 ἐν τῷ τὴν χῖρά σου ἐκτείνιν σε ἰς ἴασιν καὶ σημῖα καὶ τέρατα γείνεσθαι διὰ τοῦ ὀνόματος τοῦ ἁγίου παιδός σου Ἰησοῦ. 4.31 καὶ δεηθέντων αὐτῶν ἐσαλεύθη ὁ τόπος ἐν ᾧ ἦσαν συνηγμένοι, καὶ ἐπλήσθησαν πάντες τοῦ ἁγίου πνεύματος, καὶ ἐλάλουν τὸν λόγον τοῦ θεοῦ μετὰ παρρησίας.

4.32 τοῦ δὲ πλήθους τῶν πιστευσάντων ἦν καρδία καὶ ψυχὴ μία, καὶ οὐδὲ εἷς τι τῶν ὑπαρχόντων αὐτῷ ἔλεγεν ἴδιον εἶναι, ἀλλ' ἦν αὐτοῖς ἅπαντα κοινά. 4.33 καὶ δυνάμι μεγάλη ἀπεδίδουν τὸ μαρτύριον οἱ ἀπόστολοι τῆς ἀναστάσεως Ἰησοῦ χριστοῦ τοῦ κυρίου, χάρις τε μεγάλη ἦν ἐπὶ πάντας αὐτούς. 4.34 οὐδὲ γὰρ ἐνδεής τις ἦν ἐν αὐτοῖς· ὅσοι γὰρ κτήτορες χωρίων ἢ οἰκιῶν ὑπῆρχον, πωλοῦντες ἔφερον τὰς τιμὰς τῶν πιπρασκομένων 4.35 καὶ ἐτίθουν παρὰ τοὺς πόδας τῶν ἀποστόλων· διεδίδετο δὲ ἑκάστῳ καθότι ἄν τις χρίαν εἶχεν.

4.36 Ἰωσὴφ δὲ ὁ ἐπικληθεὶς Βαρναβᾶς ἀπὸ τῶν ἀποστόλων, ὅ ἐστιν μεθερμηνευόμενον υἱὸς παρακλήσεως, Λευίτης, Κύπριος τῷ γένει, 4.37 ὑπάρχοντος αὐτῷ ἀγροῦ πωλήσας ἤνεγκεν τὸ χρῆμα καὶ ἔθηκεν πρὸς τοὺς πόδας τῶν ἀποστόλων.

5.1 Ἀνὴρ δέ τις Ἀνανίας ὀνόματι σὺν Σαμφίρῃ τῇ γυναικὶ αὐτοῦ ἐπώλησεν κτῆμα 5.2 καὶ ἐνοσφίσατο ἀπὸ τῆς τιμῆς, συνειδύης καὶ τῆς γυναικός, καὶ ἐνέγκας μέρος τι παρὰ τοὺς πόδας τῶν ἀποστόλων ἔθηκεν.

5.3 εἶπεν δὲ ὁ Πέτρος, Ἀνανία, διὰ τί ἐπλήρωσεν ὁ Σατανᾶς τὴν καρδίαν σου ψεύσασθαί σε τὸ πνεῦμα τὸ ἅγιον

both Herod and Pontius Pilate with ethnics and peoples of Israel, 4.28 to do whatever (things) your hand and your purpose/will preappointed/predetermined to happen. 4.29 And *for* the present (things), Lord, look upon their threats, and give to your slaves to speak your saying/word with all boldness/free speech, 4.30 by the (thing) *for* you to stretch out your hand in/for healing and *for* signs and wonders to happen through the mouth of your holy boy/servant Jesus. 4.31 And from them having petitioned, the place in which they had been gathered was shaken, and they were all filled up from the holy spirit, and they were speaking the saying/word from God with boldness/courage.

4.32 And there was one heart and soul/life of the multitude of those having believed, and not one was saying *for* anything of the goods/possessions for him to be his own, but all (things) were common to them. 4.33 And with great power the apostles were giving out the testimony of the resurrection of Jesus, the anointed (one) of the Lord, and a great grace/favor was upon them all. 4.34 For neither was anyone impoverished among them; for as many as were being owners of lands or houses, selling *them*, they were bringing the prices of the (things) being sold 4.35 and they were putting *it* beside the feet of the apostles; and they were distributing to each (one) according as anyone would have a need.

4.36 And Joseph, the (one) having been called Barnabas from the apostles, which is, being translated, a son of consolation, a Levite, a Cypriot by the race, 4.37 from a field existing for him/being possessed by him, having sold *it*, he brought the money and put *it* near the feet of the apostles.

5.1 But a certain man, Ananias by name, with Sapphira his woman sold a land piece/possession 5.2 and misappropriated from the price, of the woman also having been aware of *it*, and having brought some part, he put it beside the feet of the apostles. 5.3 And Peter said: Ananias, why did Satan fill up your heart *for* you to lie to/deceive the holy spirit and to misappropriate from the price of the

καὶ νοσφίσασθαι ἀπὸ τῆς τιμῆς τοῦ χωρίου; 5.4 οὐχὶ μένον σοὶ ἔμενεν καὶ πραθὲν ἐν τῇ σῇ ἐξουσίᾳ ὑπῆρχεν; τί ὅτι ἔθου ἐν τῇ καρδίᾳ σου τὸ πρᾶγμα τοῦτο; οὐκ ἐψεύσω ἀνθρώποις ἀλλὰ τῷ θεῷ. 5.5 ἀκούων δὲ ὁ Ἀνανίας τοὺς λόγους τούτους πεσὼν ἐξέψυξεν· καὶ ἐγένετο φόβος μέγας ἐπὶ πάντας τοὺς ἀκούοντας.

5.6 ἀναστάντες δὲ οἱ νεώτεροι συνέστιλαν αὐτὸν καὶ ἐξενέγκαντες ἔθαψαν.

5.7 ἐγένετο δὲ ὡς ὡρῶν τριῶν διάστημα καὶ ἡ γυνὴ αὐτοῦ μὴ ἰδυῖα τὸ γεγονὸς εἰσῆλθεν. 5.8 ἀπεκρίθη δὲ πρὸς αὐτὴν Πέτρος, εἰπέ μοι, εἰ τοσούτου τὸ χωρίον ἀπέδοσθαι; ἡ δὲ εἶπεν, ναί, τοσούτου.

5.9 ὁ δὲ Πέτρος πρὸς αὐτήν, τί ὅτι συνεφωνήθη ὑμῖν πειράσαι τὸ πνεῦμα κυρίου; ἰδοὺ οἱ πόδες τῶν θαψάντων τὸν ἄνδρα σου ἐπὶ τῇ θύρᾳ καὶ ἐξοίσουσίν σε. 5.10 ἔπεσεν δὲ παραχρῆμα πρὸς τοὺς πόδας αὐτοῦ καὶ ἐξέψυξεν· εἰσελθόντες δὲ οἱ νεανίσκοι εὗρον αὐτὴν νεκράν, καὶ ἐξενέγκαντες ἔθαψαν πρὸς τὸν ἄνδρα αὐτῆς.

5.11 καὶ ἐγένετο φόβος μέγας ἐφ᾽ ὅλην τὴν ἐκκλησίαν καὶ ἐπὶ πάντας τοὺς ἀκούοντας ταῦτα.

5.12 διὰ δὲ τῶν χιρῶν τῶν ἀποστόλων ἐγίνετο σημῖα καὶ τέρατα πολλὰ ἐν τῷ λαῷ· καὶ ἦσαν ὁμοθυμαδὸν ἅπαντες ἐν τῇ Στοᾷ Σαλομῶντος. 5.13 τῶν δὲ λοιπῶν οὐδὶς ἐτόλμα κολλᾶσθαι αὐτοῖς, ἀλλ᾽ ἐμεγάλυνεν αὐτοὺς ὁ λαός· 5.14 μᾶλλον δὲ προσετίθεντο πιστεύοντες τῷ κυρίῳ πλήθη ἀνδρῶν τε καὶ γυναικῶν, 5.15 ὥστε καὶ εἰς τὰς πλατίας ἐκφέρειν τοὺς ἀσθενῖς καὶ τιθέναι ἐπὶ κλιναρίων καὶ κραβάττων, ἵνα ἐρχομένου Πέτρου κἂν ἡ σκιὰ ἐπισκιάσῃ τινὶ αὐτῶν. 5.16 συνήρχετο δὲ καὶ τὸ πλῆθος τῶν πέριξ πόλεων Ἰερουσαλήμ, φέροντες ἀσθενῖς καὶ ὀχλουμένους ὑπὸ πνευμάτων ἀκαθάρτων, οἵτινες ἐθεραπεύοντο ἅπαντες.

5.17 ἀναστὰς δὲ ὁ ἀρχιερεὺς καὶ πάντες οἱ σὺν αὐτῷ, ἡ οὖσα αἵρεσις τῶν Σαδδουκαίων, ἐπλήσθησαν ζήλου 5.18 καὶ ἐπέβαλον τὰς χῖρας ἐπὶ τοὺς ἀποστόλους καὶ ἔθεντο αὐτοὺς ἐν

field? 5.4 Remaining, was it not remaining for you and being sold it was existing in your own authority? Why did you put this matter/deed in your heart? You lied not to men but to God. 5.5 And Ananias, hearing these sayings/words, having fallen, he breathed his last/expired; and a great fear became over/upon all those hearing.

5.6 And having arisen, the youths/young men wrapped him and having carried *him* out they buried *him*.

5.7 And an interval of about three hours came about, and his woman came in not knowing the (thing) having happened. 5.8 And Peter answered to her/took it up with her: Say to me, if of so much ye sold the country/land? And the (she) said: Yes, of so much.

5.9 And Peter to her: Why was it agreed for ye to try/tempt the spirit of *the* Lord? Behold, the feet of those having buried your man *are* at the door and they will carry you out. 5.10 And she fell immediately near his feet and breathed her last/expired; and having come in, the youths found her dead, and having carried *her* out, they buried *her* near her man.

5.11 And a great fear became over/upon the whole assembly and upon all those hearing these (things).

5.12 And through the hands of the apostles many signs and wonders happened among the people; and they were all of one accord/mind in the porch/colonnade of Solomon. 5.13 And no one of the rest were daring to be joined with them, but the people magnified them; 5.14 and more were being added, multitudes of both men and women believing in the Lord, 5.15 so as even to bring out into the streets the ailing (ones) and to place *them* upon pallets and mattresses, in order that if even the shadow of Peter coming might fall upon someone of them. 5.16 And the multitude was also being gathered from the cities round about Jerusalem, bringing ailing (ones) and (ones) being tormented by unclean spirits, who were all being treated/healed.

5.17 But having risen up, the high priest and all those with him, the sect being of the Pharisees, they were filled from jealousy 5.18 and threw the hands upon the apostles and put them in public custo-

τηρήσει δημοσίᾳ.

5.19 ἄγγελος δὲ κυρίου διὰ νυκτὸς ἀνοίξας τὰς θύρας τῆς φυλακῆς ἐξαγαγών τε αὐτοὺς εἶπεν, 5.20 πορεύεσθε καὶ σταθέντες λαλεῖτε ἐν τῷ ἱερῷ τῷ λαῷ πάντα τὰ ῥήματα τῆς ζωῆς ταύτης.

5.21 ἀκούσαντες δὲ εἰσῆλθον ὑπὸ τὸν ὄρθρον εἰς τὸ ἱερὸν καὶ ἐδίδασκον. παραγενόμενος δὲ ὁ ἀρχιερεὺς καὶ οἱ σὺν αὐτῷ συνεκάλεσαν τὸ συνέδριον καὶ πᾶσαν τὴν γερουσίαν τῶν υἱῶν Ἰσραήλ, καὶ ἀπέστιλαν εἰς τὸ δεσμωτήριον ἀχθῆναι αὐτούς. 5.22 οἱ δὲ παραγενόμενοι ὑπηρέται οὐχ εὗρον αὐτοὺς ἐν τῇ φυλακῇ, ἀναστρέψαντες δὲ ἀπήγγιλον 5.23 λέγοντες ὅτι Τὸ δεσμωτήριον εὕρομεν κεκλισμένον ἐν πάσῃ ἀσφαλείᾳ καὶ τοὺς φύλακας ἑστῶτας ἐπὶ τῶν θυρῶν, ἀνοίξαντες δὲ ἔσω, οὐδένα εὕρομεν.

5.24 ὡς δὲ ἤκουσαν τοὺς λόγους τούτους ὅ τε στρατηγὸς τοῦ ἱεροῦ καὶ οἱ ἀρχιερεῖς, διηπόρουν περὶ αὐτῶν τί ἂν γένοιτο τοῦτο.

5.25 παραγενόμενος δέ τις ἀπήγγιλεν αὐτοῖς ὅτι ἰδοὺ οἱ ἄνδρες οὓς ἔθεσθαι ἐν τῇ φυλακῇ εἰσὶν ἐν τῷ ἱερῷ ἑστῶτες καὶ διδάσκοντες τὸν λαόν. 5.26 τότε ἀπελθὼν ὁ στρατηγὸς σὺν τοῖς ὑπηρέταις ἦγεν αὐτούς, οὐ μετὰ βίας, ἐφοβοῦντο γὰρ τὸν λαόν, μὴ λιθασθῶσιν. 5.27 ἀγαγόντες δὲ αὐτοὺς ἔστησαν ἐν τῷ συνεδρίῳ. καὶ ἐπηρώτησεν αὐτοὺς ὁ ἀρχιερεὺς 5.28 λέγων, οὐ παραγγελίᾳ παρηγγίλαμεν ὑμῖν μὴ διδάσκιν ἐπὶ τῷ ὀνόματι τούτῳ; καὶ ἰδοὺ ἐπληρώσαται τὴν Ἰερουσαλὴμ τῆς διδαχῆς ὑμῶν, καὶ βούλεσθαι ἐπαγαγεῖν ἐφ' ἡμᾶς τὸ αἷμα τοῦ ἀνθρώπου τούτου.

5.29 ἀποκριθεὶς δὲ Πέτρος καὶ οἱ ἀπόστολοι εἶπαν, πιθαρχεῖν δῖ θεῷ μᾶλλον ἢ ἀνθρώποις. 5.30 ὁ δὲ θεὸς τῶν πατέρων ἡμῶν ἤγειρεν Ἰησοῦν, ὃν ὑμεῖς διεχιρίσασθε κρεμάσαντες ἐπὶ ξύλου· 5.31 τοῦτον ὁ θεὸς ἀρχηγὸν καὶ σωτῆρα ὕψωσεν τῇ δεξιᾷ αὐτοῦ, τοῦ δοῦναι μετάνοιαν τῷ Ἰσραὴλ καὶ ἄφεσιν ἁμαρτιῶν. 5.32 καὶ ἡμεῖς ἐσμεν μάρτυρες τῶν ῥημάτων

dy/in keeping publicly/in common prison.

5.19 But a messenger/angel from *the* Lord opened the doors of the prison through/during *the* night, and having led them out, he said: 5.20 Be ye going, and having been stood in the *outer* temple speak ye all the words of this life to the people.

5.21 And having heard, they went in by the dawn into the *outer* temple and were teaching. But having arrived, the high priest and those with him called together the council and all the senate/council of elders of the sons of Israel, and they sent to the prison/jail *for* them to be brought. 5.22 But having gone, the assistants/servants did not find them in the prison, and having returned they reported, 5.23 saying: We found the jail having been shut with every security and the guards having stood at the doors, but having opened *it* we found no one inside.

5.24 And as they heard these words, both the commander of the *outer* temple and the high priests, they were in doubt/perplexed about them, what this (thing) may be.

5.25 And having come, someone announced to them: Behold, the men whom ye put in the prison have been standing in the *outer* temple and teaching the people. 5.26 Then, having gone, the commander with the assistants/servants brought them, not with violence, for they were fearing the people, lest they might be stoned. 5.27 And having brought them, they stood in the council. And the high priest questioned them, 5.28 saying: Did not we charge to ye with a command not to teach on this name? And behold, ye filled up Jerusalem of/from your doctrine, and ye plan/plot to bring the blood of this man upon us.

5.29 And answering, Peter and the apostles said: It is necessary to obey for God rather than for men/ humans. 5.30 The God of our fathers raised up Jesus, whom ye laid hands on violently, having hung *him* upon a tree; 5.31 God exalted this (one), a leader/prince and a savior, to the right (hand) of him, from the (thing) to give repentance and remission/forgiveness of sins/faults to Israel. 5.32 And we, we are witnesses of these words/things, and the holy spirit which

τούτων, καὶ τὸ πνεῦμα τὸ ἅγιον ὃ ἔδωκεν ὁ θεὸς τοῖς πιθαρχοῦσιν αὐτῷ. 5.33 οἱ δὲ ἀκούσαντες διεπρίοντο καὶ ἐβουλεύοντο ἀναιλεῖν αὐτούς.

5.34 ἀναστὰς δέ τις ἐν τῷ συνεδρίῳ Φαρισαῖος ὀνόματι Γαμαλιήλ, νομοδιδάσκαλος τίμιος παντὶ τῷ λαῷ, ἐκέλευσεν ἔξω βραχὺ τοὺς ἀνθρώπους ποιῆσαι,

5.35 εἶπέν τε πρὸς αὐτούς, ἄνδρες Ἰσδραηλῖται, προσέχετε ἑαυτοῖς ἐπὶ τοῖς ἀνθρώποις τούτοις τί μέλλεται πράττειν. 5.36 πρὸ γὰρ τούτων τῶν ἡμερῶν ἀνέστη Θευδᾶς, λέγων εἶναί τινα ἑαυτόν, ᾧ προσεκλίθη ἀνδρῶν ἀριθμὸς ὡς τετρακοσίων· ὃς ἀνῃρέθη, καὶ πάντες ὅσοι ἐπίθοντο αὐτῷ διελύθησαν καὶ ἐγένοντο εἰς οὐδέν. 5.37 μετὰ τοῦτον ἀνέστη Ἰούδας ὁ Γαλιλαῖος ἐν ταῖς ἡμέραις τῆς ἀπογραφῆς καὶ ἀπέστησεν λαὸν ὀπίσω αὐτοῦ· κἀκῖνος ἀπώλετο, καὶ πάντες ὅσοι ἐπίθοντο αὐτῷ διεσκορπίσθησαν. 5.38 καὶ τὰ νῦν λέγω ὑμῖν, ἀπόστηται ἀπὸ τῶν ἀνθρώπων τούτων καὶ ἄφετε αὐτούς· ὅτι ἐὰν ᾖ ἐξ ἀνθρώπων ἡ βουλὴ αὕτη ἢ τὸ ἔργον τοῦτο, καταλυθήσεται· 5.39 εἰ δὲ ἐκ θεοῦ ἐστιν, οὐ δυνήσεσθαι καταλῦσαι αὐτούς· μήποτε καὶ θεομάχοι εὑρεθῆτε. ἐπίσθησαν δὲ αὐτῷ, 5.40 καὶ προσκαλεσάμενοι τοὺς ἀποστόλους δείραντες παρήγγιλαν μὴ λαλῖν ἐπὶ τῷ ὀνόματι τοῦ Ἰησοῦ καὶ ἀπέλυσαν. 5.41 οἱ μὲν οὖν ἐπορεύοντο χαίροντες ἀπὸ προσώπου τοῦ συνεδρίου ὅτι κατηξιώθησαν ὑπὲρ τοῦ ὀνόματος ἀτιμασθῆναι· 5.42 πᾶσάν τε ἡμέραν ἐν τῷ ἱερῷ καὶ κατ' οἶκον οὐκ ἐπαύοντο διδάσκοντες καὶ εὐαγγελιζόμενοι τὸν χριστόν, Ἰησοῦν.

6.1 Ἐν δὲ ταῖς ἡμέραις ταύταις πληθυνόντων τῶν μαθητῶν ἐγένετο γογγυσμὸς τῶν Ἑλληνιστῶν πρὸς τοὺς Ἑβραίους, ὅτι παρεθεωροῦντο ἐν τῇ διακονίᾳ τῇ καθημερινῇ αἱ χῆραι αὐτῶν. 6.2 προσκαλεσάμενοι δὲ οἱ δώδεκα τὸ πλῆθος τῶν μαθητῶν εἶπον, οὐκ ἀρεστόν ἐστιν ἡμᾶς καταλίψαντας τὸν λόγον τοῦ

God gave to the (ones) obeying him/persuading for him. 5.33 And the (those) having heard were being cut to the quick and they were conspiring/consulting to kill them.

5.34 But having stood up in the council, a certain Pharisee by name of Gamaliel, a teacher of the law honored by all the people, urged/ordered to make the men outside a short (time),

5.35 and he said to them: Men, Israelites, take heed/be careful for yourselves what ye are being about to do/practice against these men. 5.36 For before these days Theudas rose up, saying *for* himself to be someone, to whom a number of men were inclined/attached, about four hundred; who was killed, and all, as many as were persuaded by him were scattered and they became to/for nothing. 5.37 After this, Judas the Galilean rose up in the days of the enrollment/registration and withdrew/drew away a people after him; and that (one) perished, and all, as many as were persuaded by him were scattered. 5.38 And the (things) I say now to ye: Stand ye away from these men and leave them alone; because if this will/counsel or this work be from men, it will be destroyed; 5.39 but if it is from God, ye will not be able to destroy them -- lest ye be found even fighting against God. And they were persuaded by him, 5.40 and having called/summoned the apostles, having beat them, they charged (them) not to speak on the name of Jesus and released them. 5.41 Then the (they) were going/departing from *the* face of the council, rejoicing indeed because they were deemed worthy to be dishonored; 5.42 and every day, in the *outer* temple and house to house, they were not resting/ceasing, teaching and proclaiming the anointed Jesus.

6.1 And in those days, from multiplying/increasing the learners/pupils, there became a murmuring/grumbling of the Hellenists toward/against the Hebrews, because their widows were being overlooked in the daily ministry/serving tables. 6.2 And the twelve, having called for the multitude of the learners/pupils, were saying: It is not pleasing/agreeable

432

θεοῦ διακονεῖν τραπέζαις· 6.3 ἐπισκέψασθαι δέ, ἀδελφοί, ἄνδρας ἐξ ὑμῶν μαρτυρουμένους ἑπτὰ πλήρεις πνεύματος καὶ σοφίας, οὓς καταστήσομεν ἐπὶ τῆς χρίας ταύτης· 6.4 ἡμεῖς δὲ τῇ προσευχῇ καὶ τῇ διακονίᾳ τοῦ λόγου προσκαρτερήσομεν. 6.5 καὶ ἤρεσεν ὁ λόγος ἐνώπιον παντὸς τοῦ πλήθους, καὶ ἐξελέξαντον Στέφανον, ἄνδρα πλήρης πίστεως καὶ πνεύματος ἁγίου, καὶ Φίλιππον καὶ Πρόχορον καὶ Νικάνορα καὶ Τίμωνα καὶ Παρμενᾶν καὶ Νικόλαον προσήλυτον Ἀντιοχέα, 6.6 οὓς ἔστησαν ἐνώπιον τῶν ἀποστόλων, καὶ προσευξάμενοι ἐπέθηκαν αὐτοῖς τὰς χεῖρας. 6.7 καὶ ὁ λόγος τοῦ θεοῦ ηὔξανεν, καὶ ἐπληθύνετο ὁ ἀριθμὸς τῶν μαθητῶν ἐν Ἰερουσαλὴμ σφόδρα, πολύς τε ὄχλος τῶν ἱερέων ὑπήκουον τῇ πίστει. 6.8 Στέφανος δὲ πλήρης χάριτος καὶ δυνάμεως ἐποίει τέρατα καὶ σημῖα μεγάλα ἐν τῷ λαῷ.

6.9 ἀνέστησαν δέ τινες ἐκ τῆς συναγωγῆς τῶν λεγομένων Λιβερτίνων καὶ Κυρηναίων καὶ Ἀλεξανδρέων καὶ τῶν ἀπὸ Κιλικίας καὶ Ἀσίας συζητοῦντες τῷ Στεφάνῳ, 6.10 καὶ οὐκ ἴσχυον ἀντιστῆναι τῇ σοφίᾳ καὶ τῷ πνεύματι ᾧ ἐλάλει.

6.11 τότε ὑπέβαλον ἄνδρας λέγοντες ὅτι ἀκηκόαμεν αὐτοῦ λαλοῦντος ῥήματα βλάσφημα ἅ εἰς Μωϋσῆν καὶ τὸν θεόν· 6.12 συνεκίνησάν τε τὸν λαὸν καὶ τοὺς πρεσβυτέρους καὶ τοὺς γραμματεῖς, καὶ ἐπιστάντες συνήρπασαν αὐτὸν καὶ ἤγαγον εἰς τὸ συνέδριον, 6.13 ἔστησάν τε μάρτυρας ψευδεῖς λέγοντες, ὁ ἄνθρωπος οὗτος οὐ παύεται λαλῶν ῥήματα κατὰ τοῦ τόπου τοῦ ἁγίου καὶ τοῦ νόμου· 6.14 ἀκηκόαμεν γὰρ αὐτοῦ λέγοντος ὅτι Ἰησοῦς ὁ Ναζωραῖος οὗτος καταλύσει τὸν τόπον τοῦτον καὶ ἀλλάξει τὰ ἔθη ἃ παρέδωκεν ἡμῖν Μωϋσῆς. 6.15 καὶ ἀτενίσαντες εἰς αὐτὸν πάντες οἱ καθεζόμενοι ἐν τῷ συνεδρίῳ εἶδον τὸ πρόσωπον αὐτοῦ ὡσεὶ πρόσωπον ἀγγέλου.

7.1 Εἶπεν δὲ ὁ ἀρχιερεύς, εἰ ταῦτα οὕτως ἔχει; 7.2 ὁ δὲ ἔφη, ἄνδρες ἀδελφοὶ καὶ πατέρες, ἀκούσατε. ὁ θεὸς τῆς δόξης

for us to serve/minister to/wait on tables, having abandoned/left the reasoning/word of God; 6.3 but ye inspect/examine, brothers, seven men out of ye, being witnessed to, full of spirit and wisdom, who we shall appoint/set over this need; 6.4 but we, we shall attend constantly/adhere to the prayer and the service/ministry of the reasoning/word. 6.5 And the saying/logic/word was pleasing before the multitude, and they chose/elected Stephen, a man full of faith and of a holy spirit, and Philip and Prochorus and Nicanor and Timon and Parmenas and Nicolaus, a proselyte/convert from Antioch, 6.6 whom they stood before the apostles, and having prayed, they placed the hands on them. 6.7 And the reasoning/word of God was increasing, and the number of the learners/pupils was being multiplied exceedingly in Jerusalem, and a much crowd of the priests were obedient to the faith. 6.8 And Stephen, full of grace and power, did wonders and great signs among the people.

6.9 But some out of the congregation/synagogue rose/stood up, of those being called Freedmen and Cyrenians and Alexandrians and of those from Cilicia and Asia, disputing/arguing with Stephen, 6.10 and they were not able to resist/stand against the wisdom and the spirit with which he was speaking.

6.11 Then they instigated/suborned men, saying: We have heard of him speaking words which *are* slanderous/blasphemous to Moses and God; 6.12 and they stirred up the people and the elders and the scribes, and having come upon/against *him*, they seized him and led him to the council/Sanhedrin, 6.13 and they stood/appointed false witnesses, saying: This man ceases not speaking words against the holy place and the law; 6.14 for we have heard of him saying this Jesus, the Nazarene, will destroy this place and will change the customs which Moses delivered for us. 6.15 And having gazed to him, all those sitting in the council saw his face as a face of an angel/messenger. 7.1 And the high priest said, if/whether he has/holds these (things) so? 7.2 And the (he) was saying: Men, brothers and fathers, hear ye: The God of the fame/glory was made visible to our father Abraham, being in

ὤφθη τῷ πατρὶ ἡμῶν Ἀβραὰμ ὄντι ἐν τῇ Μεσοποταμίᾳ πρὶν ἢ κατοικῆσαι αὐτὸν ἐν Χαρράν, 7.3 «καὶ εἶπεν πρὸς αὐτόν, ἔξελθε ἐκ τῆς γῆς σου καὶ ἐκ τῆς συγγενίας σου, καὶ δεῦρο εἰς τὴν γῆν ἣν ἄν σοι δίξω.» 7.4 τότε ἐξελθὼν ἐκ γῆς Χαλδαίων κατώκησεν ἐν Χαρράν. κἀκεῖθεν μετὰ τὸ ἀποθανῖν τὸν πατέρα αὐτοῦ μετώκισεν αὐτὸν εἰς τὴν γῆν ταύτην εἰς ἣν ὑμεῖς νῦν κατοικῖτε, 7.5 καὶ οὐκ ἔδωκεν αὐτῷ κληρονομίαν ἐν αὐτῇ οὐδὲ βῆμα ποδός, καὶ ἐπηγγίλατο «δοῦναι αὐτὴν εἰς κατάσχεσιν αὐτῷ, ναὶ τῷ σπέρματι αὐτοῦ μετ' αὐτόν,» οὐκ ὄντος αὐτῷ τέκνου. 7.6 ἐλάλησεν δὲ αὐτῷ ὁ θεὸς ὅτι «ἔσται τὸ σπέρμα σοῦ πάροικον ἐν γῇ ἀλλοτρίᾳ, καὶ δουλώσουσιν αὐτὸ καὶ κακώσουσιν ἔτη τετρακόσια· 7.7 καὶ τὸ ἔθνος ᾧ ἐὰν δουλεύσωσιν κρινῶ ἐγώ,» ὁ θεὸς εἶπεν, «καὶ μετὰ ταῦτα ἐξελεύσονται καὶ λατρεύσουσίν μοι ἐν τῷ» τόπῳ «τούτῳ.» 7.8 καὶ ἔδωκεν αὐτῷ διαθήκην περιτομῆς· καὶ οὕτως ἐγέννησεν τὸν Ἰσαὰκ καὶ περιέτεμεν αὐτὸν τῇ ἡμέρᾳ τῇ ὀγδόῃ, καὶ Ἰσαὰκ τὸν Ἰακώβ, καὶ Ἰακὼβ τοὺς δώδεκα πατριάρχας. 7.9 καὶ οἱ πατριάρχαι ζηλώσαντες τὸν Ἰωσὴφ ἀπέδοντο εἰς Αἴγυπτον· καὶ ἦν ὁ θεὸς μετ' αὐτοῦ, 7.10 καὶ ἐξίλατο αὐτὸν ἐκ πασῶν τῶν θλίψεων αὐτοῦ, καὶ ἔδωκεν αὐτῷ χάριν καὶ σοφίαν ἐναντί Φαραὼ βασιλέως Αἰγύπτου, καὶ κατέστησεν αὐτὸν ἡγούμενον ἐπ' Αἴγυπτον καὶ ἐφ' ὅλον τὸν οἶκον αὐτοῦ. 7.11 ἦλθεν δὲ λιμὸς ἐφ' ὅλην τὴν Αἴγυπτον καὶ Χανάαν καὶ θλῖψεις μεγάλη, καὶ οὐχ εὕρισκον χορτάσματα οἱ πατέρες ἡμῶν. 7.12 ἀκούσας δὲ Ἰακὼβ ὄντα σιτία εἰς Αἴγυπτον ἐξαπέστιλεν τοὺς πατέρας ἡμῶν πρῶτον· 7.13 καὶ ἐν τῷ δευτέρῳ ἀνεγνωρίσθη Ἰωσὴφ τοῖς ἀδελφοῖς αὐτοῦ, καὶ φανερὸν ἐγένετο τῷ Φαραὼ τὸ γένος αὐτοῦ. 7.14 ἀποστίλας δὲ Ἰωσὴφ μετεκαλέσατο Ἰακὼβ τὸν πατέρα αὐτοῦ καὶ πᾶσαν τὴν συγγένειαν ἐν ψυχαῖς ἑβδομήκοντα πέντε, 7.15 καὶ κατέβη Ἰακὼβ εἰς Αἴγυπτον. καὶ ἐτελεύτησεν αὐτὸς καὶ οἱ πατέρες ἡμῶν, 7.16 καὶ μετετέθησαν εἰς Συχὲμ καὶ ἐτέθησαν ἐν τῷ μνήματι ᾧ ὠνήσατο Ἀβραὰμ τιμῆς ἀργυρίου παρὰ τῶν υἱῶν Ἐμμὼρ ἐν Συχέμ. 7.17 καθὼς δὲ ἤγγιζεν ὁ χρόνος τῆς ἐπαγγελίας ἧς

Mesopotamia before which (time) *for* him to dwell in Charran, 7.3 AND HE SAID TO HIM: GO YOU FORTH OUT OF YOUR LAND AND OUT OF YOUR KINDRED/FAMILY, AND COME INTO THE LAND WHICH I WOULD GIVE TO YOU. 7.4 Then having gone forth out of a land of *the* Chaldees he dwelt in Charran. And from there, after the (thing) *for* his father to die, he (God) removed him to this land in which ye, ye now dwell, 7.5 and he gave not an inheritance to him in her/*it*, nor a space of a foot, and he himself promised TO GIVE HER/*it* TO HIM INTO/FOR A POSSESSION, YES, TO HIS SEED AFTER HIM, from a child not being for him. 7.6 And God spoke to him: YOUR SEED WILL BE A STRANGER/ALIEN IN A LAND BELONGING TO ANOTHER, AND THEY WILL ENSLAVE IT AND MISTREAT *it/them for* FOUR HUNDRED YEARS; 7.7 AND I, I SHALL JUDGE WHICH EVER ETHNIC/NATION THEY MIGHT SERVE AS SLAVES, God said, AND AFTER THESE (THINGS) THEY WILL COME FORTH AND WILL SERVE/WORSHIP TO ME IN THIS place. 7.8 And he gave to him a covenant of circumcision; and so he generated/begat Isaac and he circumcised him on the eighth day, and Isaac Jacob, and Jacob the twelve patriarchs. 7.9 And the patriarchs, having been jealous, they sold Joseph into Egypt; and God was with him, 7.10 and he delivered him out of all his afflictions/oppressions, and he gave grace/favor and wisdom to him before Pharaoh king of Egypt, and he appointed him being a governor over Egypt and over his entire/whole house/household. 7.11 But a famine and a great affliction/tribulation came over all Egypt and Canaan, and our fathers were not finding grasses/sustenance. 7.12 And Jacob, having heard *of* wheat being in Egypt, sent forth our fathers first; 7.13 and on the second *time* Joseph was made known to his brothers, and his race/kind became manifest/known to Pharaoh. 7.14 And having sent *them* forth, Joseph called/summoned Jacob his father and all the relatives in seventy-five souls/lives, 7.15 and Jacob went down to Egypt and died, himself and our fathers, 7.16 and they were moved/transferred to Sychem and were placed in the tomb which Abraham bought of/for a price of silver from the sons of Emmor in Sychem. 7.17 And as the time of the promise which God professed to Abraham

ὁμολόγησεν ὁ θεὸς τῷ Ἀβραάμ, ηὔξησεν ὁ λαὸς καὶ ἐπληθύνθη ἐν Αἰγύπτῳ, 7.18 ἄχρις οὗ «ἀνέστη βασιλεὺς ἕτερος ἐπ᾽ Αἴγυπτον ὃς οὐκ ᾔδει τὸν Ἰωσήφ.» 7.19 οὗτος κατασοφισάμενος τὸ γένος ἡμῶν ἐκάκωσεν τοὺς πατέρας τοῦ ποιεῖν τὰ βρέφη ἔκθετα αὐτῶν εἰς τὸ μὴ ζῳογονεῖσθαι. 7.20 ἐν ᾧ καιρῷ ἐγεννήθη Μωϋσῆς, καὶ ἦν ἀστεῖος τῷ θεῷ· ὃς ἀνετράφη μῆνας τρεῖς ἐν τῷ οἴκῳ τοῦ πατρός· 7.21 ἐκτεθέντος δὲ αὐτοῦ ἀνείλατο αὐτὸν ἡ θυγάτηρ Φαραὼ καὶ ἀνεθρέψατο αὐτὸν ἑαυτῇ εἰς υἱόν. 7.22 καὶ ἐπεδεύθη Μωϋσῆς ἐν πάσῃ σοφίᾳ Αἰγυπτίων, ἦν δὲ δυνατὸς ἐν λόγοις καὶ ἔργοις αὐτοῦ. 7.23 ὡς δὲ ἐπληροῦτο αὐτῷ τεσσερακονταετὴς χρόνος, ἀνέβη ἐπὶ τὴν καρδίαν αὐτοῦ ἐπισκέψασθαι τοὺς ἀδελφοὺς αὐτοῦ τοὺς υἱοὺς Ἰσραήλ. 7.24 καὶ ἰδών τινα ἀδικούμενον ἠμύνατο καὶ ἐποίησεν ἐκδίκησιν τῷ καταπονουμένῳ πατάξας τὸν Αἰγύπτιον. 7.25 ἐνόμιζεν δὲ συνιέναι τοὺς ἀδελφοὺς ὅτι ὁ θεὸς διὰ χειρὸς αὐτοῦ δίδωσι σωτηρίαν αὐτοῖς, οἱ δὲ οὐ συνῆκαν. 7.26 τῇ τε ἐπιούσῃ ἡμέρᾳ ὤφθη αὐτοῖς μαχομένοις καὶ συνήλλασσεν αὐτοὺς εἰς εἰρήνην εἰπών, ἄνδρες, ἀδελφοί ἐστε· ἱνατί ἀδικεῖτε ἀλλήλους; 7.27 ὁ δὲ ἀδικῶν τὸν πλησίον ἀπώσατο αὐτὸν εἰπών, «τίς σε κατέστησεν ἄρχοντα καὶ δικαστὴν ἐφ᾽ ἡμῶν; 7.28 μὴ ἀναλεῖν με σὺ θέλεις ὃν τρόπον ἀνεῖλες ἐχθὲς τὸν Αἰγύπτιον;»

7.29 ἔφυγεν δὲ Μωϋσῆς ἐν τῷ λόγῳ τούτῳ, καὶ ἐγένετο πάροικος ἐν γῇ Μαδιάμ, οὗ ἐγέννησεν υἱοὺς δύο. 7.30 καὶ πληρωθέντων ἐτῶν τεσσεράκοντα «ὤφθη αὐτῷ ἐν τῇ ἐρήμῳ τοῦ ὄρους» Σινᾶ «ἄγγελος ἐν φλογὶ πυρὸς βάτου.»

7.31 ὁ δὲ Μωϋσῆς ἰδὼν ἐθαύμαζεν τὸ ὅραμα· προσερχομένου δὲ αὐτοῦ κατανοῆσαι ἐγένετο φωνὴ κυρίου, 7.32 «ἐγὼ ὁ θεὸς τῶν πατέρων σου, ὁ θεὸς Ἀβραὰμ καὶ Ἰσαὰκ καὶ Ἰακώβ.»

ἔντρομος δὲ Μωϋσῆς γενόμενος οὐκ ἐτόλμησεν κατανοῆσαι. 7.33 «εἶπεν δὲ αὐτῷ ὁ κύριος, λῦσον τὸ ὑπόδημα τῶν ποδῶν

drew near, the people increased/grew and were multiplied in Egypt, 7.18 until which *time* ANOTHER/DIFFERENT KING ROSE UP OVER EGYPT WHO DID NOT KNOW JOSEPH. 7.19 This (one), having dealt craftily *with* our race, mistreated the fathers from the (thing) to make their babies abandoned to/for the (thing) not to be preserved alive. 7.20 In which time Moses was generated/born, and he was fair to God, who was nourished three months in the house of the father; 7.21 and from him having been abandoned, Pharaoh's daughter took him up and raised him into/as a son for herself. 7.22 And Moses was trained/disciplined in every wisdom of Egyptians, and he was powerful in his reasonings/words and works. 7.23 But when a time/period of forty years was being completed for him, it came upon his heart to visit/inspect his brothers, the sons of Israel. 7.24 And having seen someone being wronged, he defended *him* and made/did punishment for the (one) being oppressed, having struck down/smote the Egyptian. 7.25 And he supposed *for* the brothers to understand that God gives salvation/deliverance to them through his hand, but the (they) did not understand. 7.26 And on the next day, he was seen by them fighting and he was reconciling them to peace, having said: Men, ye are brothers; why do ye wrong one another? 7.27 But the (one) wronging the neighbor rejected him, saying: WHO APPOINTED YOU A RULER AND A JUDGE OVER US? 7.28 YOU, DO YOU WANT TO KILL ME IN WHICH MANNER YOU KILLED THE EGYPTIAN YESTERDAY?

7.29 And Moses fled at this saying/word, and became an exile in a land of Midian, where he generated/begat two sons. 7.30 And from forty years having been completed A MESSENGER/ANGEL WAS SEEN BY HIM IN THE WILDERNESS/DESERT OF THE MOUNTAIN Sinai IN A FLAME OF FIRE FROM A BUSH.

7.31 And Moses, having seen, was wondering at the sight/vision; and from him (his) coming near to consider it/think it over, there became a voice from *the* Lord: 7.32 I *am* THE GOD OF YOUR FATHERS, THE GOD OF ABRAHAM AND ISAAC AND JACOB.

But having become trembling, Moses dared not to consider/notice *it*. 7.33 AND THE LORD SAID TO HIM:

σου, ὁ γὰρ τόπος ἐφ᾽ ᾧ ἕστηκας γῆ ἁγία ἐστίν.

7.34 ἰδὼν εἶδον τὴν κάκωσιν τοῦ λαοῦ μου τοῦ ἐν Αἰγύπτῳ, καὶ τοῦ στεναγμοῦ αὐτῶν ἤκουσα, καὶ κατέβην ἐξελέσθαι αὐτούς· καὶ νῦν δεῦρο ἀποστίλω σε εἰς Αἴγυπτον.» 7.35 τοῦτον τὸν Μωϋσῆν, ὃν ἠρνήσαντο εἰπόντες, «τίς σε κατέστησεν ἄρχοντα καὶ δικαστήν» ἐφ᾽ ἡμων; τοῦτον ὁ θεὸς ἄρχοντα καὶ λυτρωτὴν δικάστην ἀπέσταλκεν ἐν χειρὶ ἀγγέλου τοῦ ὀφθέντος αὐτῷ ἐν τῇ βάτῳ. 7.36 οὗτος ἐξήγαγεν αὐτοὺς ποιήσας τέρατα καὶ σημῖα ἐν γῇ Αἰγύπτῳ καὶ ἐν ἐρυθρᾷ θαλάσσῃ καὶ ἐν τῇ ἐρήμῳ ἔτη τεσσεράκοντα.

7.37 οὗτός ἐστιν ὁ Μωϋσῆς ὁ εἶπας τοῖς υἱοῖς Ἰσραήλ, «προφήτην ὑμῖν ἀναστήσι ὁ θεὸς ἐκ τῶν ἀδελφῶν ὑμῶν ὡς ἐμέ.» 7.38 οὗτός ἐστιν ὁ γενόμενος ἐν τῇ ἐκκλησίᾳ ἐν τῇ ἐρήμῳ μετὰ τοῦ ἀγγέλου τοῦ λαλοῦντος αὐτῷ ἐν τῷ ὄρι Σινᾶ καὶ τῶν πατέρων ἡμῶν, ὃς ἐδέξατο λόγια ζῶντα δοῦναι ἡμῖν, 7.39 ᾧ οὐκ ἠθέλησαν ὑπήκοοι γενέσθαι οἱ πατέρες ἡμῶν ἀλλὰ ἀπώσαντο καὶ ἐστράφησαν καὶ ἐν ταῖς καρδίαις αὐτῶν εἰς Αἴγυπτον, 7.40 εἰπόντες τῷ Ἀαρών, «ποίησον ἡμῖν θεοὺς οἳ προπορεύσονται ἡμῶν· ὁ γὰρ Μωϋσῆς οὗτος, ὁ ἄνθρωπος ὃς ἐξήγαγεν ἡμᾶς ἐκ γῆς Αἰγύπτου, οὐκ οἴδαμεν τί ἐγένετο αὐτῷ.» 7.41 καὶ ἐμοσχοποίησαν ἐν ταῖς ἡμέραις ἐκείναις καὶ ἀνήγαγον θυσίαν τῷ εἰδώλῳ, καὶ εὐφραίνοντο ἐν τοῖς ἔργοις τῶν χειρῶν αὐτῶν. 7.42 ἔστρεψεν δὲ ὁ θεὸς καὶ παρέδωκεν αὐτοὺς λατρεύειν τῇ στρατιᾷ τοῦ οὐρανοῦ, καθὼς γέγραπται ἐν βίβλῳ τῶν προφητῶν, «μὴ σφάγια καὶ θυσίας προσηνέγκατέ μοι ἔτη τεσσεράκοντα ἐν τῇ ἐρήμῳ, οἶκος Ἰσραήλ; 7.43 καὶ ἀνελάβετε τὴν σκηνὴν τοῦ Μολὸχ καὶ τὸ ἄστρον τοῦ θεοῦ ὑμῶν Ραιφάν, τοὺς τύπους οὓς ἐποιήσατε» προσκυνῖν αὐτοῖς· «καὶ μετοικιῶ ὑμᾶς ἐπέκινα» Βαβυλῶνος.

7.44 ἡ σκηνὴ τοῦ μαρτυρίου ἦν τοῖς πατράσιν ἡμῶν ἐν τῇ ἐρήμῳ, καθὼς διετάξατο ὁ λαλῶν τῷ Μωϋσῇ ποιῆσαι αὐτὴ κατὰ τὸν τύπον ὃν ἑωράκει, 7.45 ἣν καὶ εἰσήγαγον διαδεξάμενοι οἱ πατέρες ἡμῶν μετὰ Ἰησοῦ ἐν τῇ κατασχέσει τῶν ἐθνῶν ὧν

LOOSE THE SANDALS FROM YOUR FEET, FOR THE PLACE ON
WHICH YOU HAVE STOOD IS HOLY GROUND.
7.34 HAVING BEHELD, I SAW THE BAD TREATMENT OF
MY PEOPLE, THE (ONE) IN EGYPT, AND I HEARD OF/FROM
THEIR GROAN, AND I CAME DOWN TO TAKE THEM OUT; AND NOW
COME, I SHALL SEND YOU TO EGYPT. 7.35 This Moses,
whom they denied, saying: WHO APPOINTED YOU A RULER
AND A JUDGE OVER US? God has sent this (one) a ruler/
leader and a redeemer/deliverer, a judge by hand of a
messenger, of the (one) having been seen by him in the
bush. 7.36 This (one) led them out, doing wonders and
signs in *the* land of Egypt and in/at the red sea and
in the desert/wilderness *for* forty years.
7.37 This (one) is Moses, the (one) having said
to the sons of Israel: GOD WILL RAISE UP OUT OF YOUR
BROTHERS A PROPHET LIKE ME. 7.38 This (one) is the
(one) having become in the assembly in the desert with
the messenger, the (one) speaking to him on the mountain Sinai and *with* our fathers, who received living
oracles to give to ye, 7.39 to whom our fathers did
not want to become obedient, but they rejected/repuls-
ed *him* and turned also with/in their hearts to Egypt,
7.40 saying to Aaron: MAKE YOU GODS FOR US WHICH WILL
GO BEFORE US; FOR THIS MOSES, THE MAN WHO LED US FORTH
OUT OF *the* LAND OF EGYPT, WE KNOW NOT WHAT HAPPENED TO
HIM. 7.41 And they made a calf in those days and they
brought a sacrifice to the idol, and they were rejoicing in the works of their hands. 7.42 And God turned
and delivered them up to serve/worship for the host of
the sky/heaven, as it has been written in a scroll of
the prophets: DID YE NOT OFFER SLAIN (THINGS) AND
OFFERINGS/SACRIFICES TO ME *for* FORTY YEARS IN THE
WILDERNESS/DESERT, HOUSE OF ISRAEL? 7.43 AND YE TOOK
UP THE TENT OF MOLOCH AND THE STAR OF YOUR GOD RAPHAN,
THE FORMS/STATUES WHICH YE MADE to worship/kneel down
to them; AND I SHALL DEPORT YE BEYOND Babylon.
7.44 The tent/tabernacle of the testimony was
for our fathers in the desert/wilderness, as the (one)
speaking to Moses ordered to make it according to the
sample/model which he had seen, 7.45 which having
been received in turn our fathers also brought in with
Jesus (Joshua) in the possession of the ethnics/na-

ἐξῶσεν ὁ θεὸς ἀπὸ προσώπου τῶν πατέρων ἡμῶν ἕως τῶν ἡμερῶν Δαυίδ, 7.46 ὃς εὗρεν χάριν ἐνώπιον τοῦ θεοῦ καὶ ἠτήσατο εὑρῖν σκήνωμα τῷ οἴκῳ Ἰακώβ. 7.47 Σαλομῶν δὲ ᾠκοδόμησεν αὐτῷ οἶκον. 7.48 ἀλλ' οὐχ ὁ ὕψιστος ἐν χιροποιήτοις κατοικῖ·

καθὼς ὁ προφήτης λέγει, 7.49 «ὁ οὐρανός μοι θρόνος, ἡ δὲ γῆ ὑποπόδιον τῶν ποδῶν μου· ποῖον οἶκον οἰκοδομήσετέ μοι, λέγι κύριος, ἢ τίς τόπος τῆς καταπαύσεώς μου; 7.50 οὐχὶ ἡ χείρ μου ἐποίησεν ταῦτα πάντα;» 7.51 σκληροτράχηλοι καὶ ἀπερίτμητοι ταῖς καρδίαις ὑμῶν καὶ τοῖς ὠσίν, ὑμεῖς ἀεὶ τῷ πνεύματι τῷ ἁγίῳ ἀντιπίπτεται, ὡς οἱ πατέρες ὑμῶν καὶ ὑμῖς. 7.52 τίνα τῶν προφητῶν οὐκ ἐδίωξαν οἱ πατέρες ὑμῶν; καὶ ἀπέκτιναν τοὺς προκαταγγίλαντας περὶ τῆς ἐλεύσεως τοῦ δικαίου οὗ νῦν ὑμεῖς προδόται καὶ φονῖς ἐγένεσθαι, 7.53 οἵτινες ἐλάβετε τὸν νόμον εἰς διαταγὰς ἀγγέλων, καὶ οὐκ ἐφυλάξατε. 7.54 ἀκούοντες δὲ ταῦτα διεπρίοντο ταῖς καρδίαις αὐτῶν καὶ ἔβρυχον τοὺς ὀδόντας ἐπ' αὐτόν. 7.55 ὑπάρχων δὲ πλήρης πίστεως καὶ πνεύματος ἁγίου ἀτενίσας εἰς τὸν οὐρανὸν εἶδεν δόξαν θεοῦ καὶ Ἰησοῦν ἑστῶτα ἐκ δεξιῶν τοῦ θεοῦ, 7.56 καὶ εἶπεν, ἰδοὺ θεωρῶ τοὺς οὐρανοὺς διηνοιγμένους καὶ τὸν υἱὸν τοῦ ἀνθρώπου ἐκ ἑστῶτα δεξιῶν τοῦ θεοῦ. 7.57 κράξαντες δὲ φωνῇ μεγάλῃ συνέσχον τὰ ὦτα αὐτῶν, καὶ ὥρμησαν ὁμοθυμαδὸν ἐπ' αὐτόν, 7.58 καὶ ἐκβαλόντες ἔξω τῆς πόλεως ἐλιθοβόλουν. καὶ οἱ μάρτυρες ἀπέθεντο τὰ ἱμάτια αὐτῶν παρὰ τοὺς πόδας νεανίου καλουμένου Σαύλου. 7.59 καὶ ἐλιθοβόλουν τὸν Στέφανον ἐπικαλούμενον καὶ λέγοντα, κύριε Ἰησοῦ, δέξαι τὸ πνεῦμά μου. 7.60 θεὶς δὲ τὰ γόνατα ἔκραξεν φωνῇ μεγάλῃ, κύριε, μὴ στήσῃς αὐτοῖς τὴν ἁμαρτίαν ταύτην. καὶ τοῦτο εἰπὼν ἐκοιμήθη. 8.1 Σαῦλος δὲ ἦν συνευδοκῶν τῇ ἀναιρέσι αὐτοῦ. ἐγένετο δὲ ἐν ἐκίνῃ τῇ ἡμέρᾳ διωγμὸς μέγας ἐπὶ τὴν ἐκκλησίαν

tions whom God expelled from *the* face of our fathers until the days of David, 7.46 who found grace/favor before God and himself asked to find a tent/tabernacle for the house of Jacob. 7.47 But Solomon built a house for him. 7.48 But the most high does not dwell in (things) made by hand;

as the prophet says: 7.49 THE SKY/HEAVEN *is* A THRONE FOR ME, AND THE EARTH *is* A FOOTSTOOL OF MY FEET; WHAT SORT OF HOUSE WILL YE BUILD FOR ME, SAYS *the* LORD, OR WHAT *is* A PLACE OF MY REST/REPOSE? 7.50 DID NOT MY HAND MAKE ALL THESE (THINGS)? 7.51 Stiff-necked/stubborn and uncircumcised (ones) in your hearts, even to the ears, ye, ye always resist against the holy spirit; as your fathers, ye also. 7.52 Which of the prophets did your fathers not pursue/persecute? And they killed the (ones) having proclaimed before-hand about the advent/coming of the just (one) of whom ye, ye now became betrayers and murderers, 7.53 who took/received the law in ordinances of messengers/ angels, and guarded/kept *it* not. 7.54 But hearing these (things), they were being cut to their hearts and they were gritting/gnashing the teeth at him. 7.55 But being/existing full of faith and a holy spirit, having gazed into the sky/heaven, he saw glory/fame of God and Jesus having stood out of right (ones)/at *the* right *hand* of God, 7.56 and he said: Behold, I see the skies/heavens having been opened and the son of the man having stood out of right (ones)/at *the* right *hand* of God. 7.57 And having cried out with a great sound/voice, they stopped/held together their ears, and rushed of one accord/unanimously upon him, 7.58 and having thrown *him* outside the city they were stoning *him*. And the witnesses put off their garments beside the feet of a young man being called Saul. 7.59 And they were stoning Stephen, himself calling upon *God* and saying: Lord Jesus, receive/take my spirit/the spirit from me. 7.60 And having put *down* the knees, he cried out in a great voice: Lord, place not this sin/failure to them. And having said this he was put to sleep. 8.1 And Saul was consenting to the killing of him. And there became a great prosecution in that day upon/against the assembly among the Jeru-

τὴν ἐν Ἱεροσολύμοις· καὶ πάντες διεσπάρησαν κατὰ τὰς χώρας τῆς Ἰουδαίας καὶ Σαμαρίας πλὴν τῶν ἀποστόλων. 8.2 συνεκόμισαν δὲ τὸν Στέφανον ἄνδρες εὐλαβεῖς καὶ ἐποίησαν κοπετὸν μέγαν ἐπ᾿ αὐτῷ. 8.3 Σαῦλος δὲ ἐλυμαίνετο τὴν ἐκκλησίαν κατὰ τοὺς οἴκους εἰσπορευόμενος, σύρων τε ἄνδρας καὶ γυναῖκας παρεδίδου εἰς φυλακήν.

8.4 οἱ μὲν οὖν διασπαρέντες διῆλθον εὐαγγελιζόμενοι τὸν λόγον. 8.5 Φίλιππος δὲ κατελθὼν εἰς τὴν πόλιν τῆς Σαμαρίας ἐκήρυσσεν αὐτοῖς τὸν χριστόν. 8.6 προσεῖχον δὲ οἱ ὄχλοι τοῖς λεγομένοις ὑπὸ τοῦ Φιλίππου ὁμοθυμαδὸν ἐν τῷ ἀκούειν αὐτοὺς καὶ βλέπιν τὰ σημῖα ἃ ἐποίει· 8.7 πολλοὶ γὰρ τῶν ἐχόντων πνεύματα ἀκάθαρτα βοῶντα φωνῇ μεγάλῃ ἐξήρχοντο, πολλοὶ δὲ παραλελυμένοι καὶ χωλοὶ ἐθεραπεύθησαν· 8.8 ἐγένετο δὲ πολλὴ χαρὰ ἐν τῇ πόλι ἐκείνῃ.

8.9 ἀνὴρ δέ τις ὀνόματι Σίμων προϋπῆρχεν ἐν τῇ πόλι μαγεύων καὶ ἐξιστάνων τὸ ἔθνος τῆς Σαμαρίας, λέγων εἶναί τινα ἑαυτὸν μέγαν, 8.10 ᾧ προσεῖχαν πάντες ἀπὸ μικροῦ ἕως μεγάλου λέγοντες, οὗτός ἐστιν ἡ δύναμις τοῦ θεοῦ ἡ καλουμένη μεγάλη. 8.11 προσεῖχον δὲ αὐτῷ διὰ τὸ ἱκανῷ χρόνῳ ταῖς μαγίαις ἐξεστακέναι αὐτούς. 8.12 ὅτε δὲ ἐπίστευσαν τῷ Φιλίππῳ εὐαγγελιζομένῳ περὶ τῆς βασιλίας τοῦ θεοῦ καὶ τοῦ ὀνόματος Ἰησοῦ χριστοῦ, ἐβαπτίζοντο ἄνδρες τε καὶ γυναῖκες. 8.13 ὁ δὲ Σίμων καὶ αὐτὸς ἐπίστευσεν, καὶ βαπτισθεὶς ἦν προσκαρτερῶν τῷ Φιλίππῳ, θεωρῶν τε σημῖα καὶ δυνάμις μεγάλας γεινομένας ἐξίστατο.

8.14 ἀκούσαντες δὲ οἱ ἐν Ἱεροσολύμοις ἀπόστολοι ὅτι δέδεκται ἡ Σαμάρια τὸν λόγον τοῦ θεοῦ ἀπέστιλαν πρὸς αὐτοὺς Πέτρον καὶ Ἰωάννην, 8.15 οἵτινες καταβάντες προσηύξαντο περὶ αὐτῶν ὅπως λάβωσιν πνεῦμα ἅγιον· 8.16 οὐδέπω γὰρ ἦν ἐπ᾿ οὐδενὶ αὐτῶν ἐπιπεπτωκός, μόνον δὲ βεβαπτισμένοι ὑπῆρχον εἰς

salemites; and they all were scattered/dispersed according to/throughout the countries of Judea and Samaria, except the apostles. 8.2 And devout men buried Stephen and made a great mourning/lamentation over him. 8.3 And Saul was damaging/destroying the assembly, going into house by house/entering throughout the houses, dragging both men and women, he was delivering *them* to prison.

8.4 Then indeed the (ones) having been scattered went through/about, themselves announcing/preaching the reason/saying/word. 8.5 And Philip, having gone down to the city of Samaria, was heralding/preaching the anointed (one) to them. 8.6 And the crowds were heeding to the (things) being said by Philip, with one accord in the (thing) *for* them to hear and to see the signs which he was doing. 8.7 For many of those having unclean spirits, crying with a great voice, were coming out, and many having been paralyzed and lame (ones) were treated/healed; 8.8 and much joy came about in that city.

8.9 And a certain man by name of Simon was formerly in the city practicing magic and amazing the ethnic/nation of Samaria, saying *for* himself to be someone great, 8.10 to whom all from small until great gave heed, saying: This (one) is the power of God, the (power) being called great. 8.11 And they were giving heed to him because of the (thing) *for* them to be amazed/astonished by the magics for a considerable time. 8.12 But when they believed for Philip announcing/preaching about the kingdom of God and the name of Jesus, the anointed (one), both men and women were being baptized. 8.13 And Simon himself also believed, and having been baptized he was adhering/attending constantly to Philip, and beholding/observing signs and great powers coming about, he was himself amazed.

8.14 And the apostles, having heard among Jerusalemites that Samaria has received the saying/word of God, sent Peter and John to them, 8.15 who having gone down prayed concerning them that they might receive a holy spirit; 8.16 for it had not yet fallen upon anyone of them, but they had only been baptized

τὸ ὄνομα τοῦ κυρίου Ἰησοῦ. 8.17 τότε ἐπετίθεσαν τὰς χῖρας ἐπ' αὐτούς, καὶ ἐλάμβανον πνεῦμα ἅγιον. 8.18 ἰδὼν δὲ ὁ Σίμων ὅτι διὰ τῆς ἐπιθέσεως τῶν χιρῶν τῶν ἀποστόλων δίδοται τὸ πνεῦμα, προσήνεγκεν αὐτοῖς χρήματα 8.19 λέγων, δότε κἀμοὶ τὴν ἐξουσίαν ταύτην ἵνα ᾧ ἐὰν ἐπιθῶ τὰς χῖρας λαμβάνῃ πνεῦμα ἅγιον. 8.20 Πέτρος δὲ εἶπεν πρὸς αὐτόν, τὸ ἀργύριόν σου σὺν σοὶ εἴη εἰς ἀπώλιαν, ὅτι τὴν δωρεὰν τοῦ θεοῦ ἐνόμισας διὰ χρημάτων κτᾶσθαι. 8.21 οὐκ ἔστιν σοι μερὶς οὐδὲ κλῆρος ἐν τῷ λόγῳ τούτῳ, ἡ γὰρ καρδία σου οὐκ ἔστιν εὐθῖα ἔναντι τοῦ θεοῦ.

8.22 μετανόησον οὖν ἀπὸ τῆς κακίας σου ταύτης, καὶ δεήθητι τοῦ κυρίου εἰ ἄρα ἀφεθήσεταί σοι ἡ ἐπίνοια τῆς καρδίας σου· 8.23 εἰς γὰρ χολὴν πικρίας καὶ σύνδεσμον ἀδικίας ὁρῶ σε ὄντα.

8.24 ἀποκριθεὶς δὲ ὁ Σίμων εἶπεν, δεήθητε ὑμῖς ὑπὲρ ἐμοῦ πρὸς τὸν κύριον ὅπως μηδὲν ἐπέλθῃ ἐπ' ἐμὲ ὧν εἰρήκατε. 8.25 οἱ μὲν οὖν διαμαρτυρόμενοι καὶ λαλήσαντες τὸν λόγον τοῦ κυρίου ὑπέστρεφον εἰς Ἱεροσόλυμα, πολλάς τε κώμας τῶν Σαμαριτῶν εὐηγγελίζοντο.

8.26 ἄγγελος δὲ κυρίου ἐλάλησεν πρὸς Φίλιππον λέγων, ἀνάστηθι καὶ πορεύου κατὰ μεσημβρίαν ἐπὶ τὴν ὁδὸν τὴν καταβαίνουσαν ἀπὸ Ἱερουσαλὴμ εἰς Γάζαν· αὕτη ἐστὶν ἔρημος. 8.27 καὶ ἀναστὰς ἐπορεύθη·

καὶ ἰδοὺ ἀνὴρ Αἰθίοψ εὐνοῦχος δυνάστης Κανδάκης βασιλίσσης Αἰθιόπων, ὃς ἦν ἐπὶ πάσης τῆς γάζης αὐτῆς, ὃς ἐληλύθει προσκυνήσων εἰς Ἱερουσαλήμ, 8.28 ἦν τε ὑποστρέφων καὶ καθήμενος ἐπὶ τοῦ ἅρματος αὐτοῦ καὶ ἀνεγίνωσκεν τὸν προφήτην Ἡσαΐαν. 8.29 εἶπεν δὲ τὸ πνεῦμα τῷ Φιλίππῳ, πρόσελθε καὶ κολλήθητι τῷ ἅρματι τούτῳ. 8.30 προσδραμὼν δὲ ὁ Φίλιππος ἤκουσεν αὐτοῦ ἀναγινώσκοντος Ἡσαΐαν τὸν προφήτην, καὶ εἶπεν, ἆρά γε γινώσκεις ἃ ἀναγινώσκεις; 8.31 ὁ δὲ εἶπεν, πῶς γὰρ ἂν δυναίμην ἐὰν μὴ τις ὁδηγήσει με; παρεκάλεσέν τε τὸν Φίλιππον ἀναβάντα καθίσε σὺν αὐτῷ. 8.32 ἡ δὲ περιοχὴ τῆς γραφῆς ἣν ἀνεγίνωσκεν ἦν αὕτη· «ὡς πρόβατον

in the name of the Lord Jesus. 8.17 Then they laid the hands upon them, and they were receiving a holy spirit. 8.18 And Simon, having seen that the spirit is given through the laying on of the apostles' hands, he offered money to them, 8.19 saying: Give ye to me also this authority, in order that on whom ever I might lay on the hands he might receive a holy spirit. 8.20 But Peter said to him: May your silver be with you in destruction, because you supposed/thought to acquire the gift of God through money. 8.21 There is not a part for you nor a lot/share in this saying/word, for your heart is not straight before God.

8.22 Repent therefore from this your badness/wickedness, and petition from the Lord whether the thought of your heart will be forgiven for you; 8.23 for I see you being in a gall of bitterness and a bond of unjustness.

8.24 And answering, Simon said: Ye, petition ye in behalf of me to the Lord that nothing of (things) which you have spoken might come upon me. 8.25 Then indeed they, having testified solemnly and having spoken the saying/word of the Lord, they were returning to Jerusalem, and they were evangelizing many villages of the Samaritans.

8.26 And a messenger/angel from *the* Lord spoke to Philip, saying: Rise up and go along south on the road going down from Jerusalem to Gaza; this is a desert. 8.27 And having risen up, he was gone;

and behold a man, an Ethiopian eunuch, a courtier of Candace, queen of Ethiopians, who was over all her treasury, who had come going to worship in Jerusalem, 8.28 and he was returning and sitting upon his chariot, and he was reading the prophet Esaias. 8.29 And the spirit said to Philip: Go near and be joined to this chariot. 8.30 And having run to *it*, Philip heard from him reading Esaias the prophet, and he said: Do you indeed know/understand what (things) you are reading? 8.31 And the (he) said: For how could I be able unless someone will guide me? And he beseeched Philip, having come up, to sit with him. 8.32 And the portion of the writing which he was reading was this: HE WAS LED AS A SHEEP TO A SLAUGHTER, AND *he was*

ἐπὶ σφαγὴν ἤχθη, καὶ ὡς ἀμνὸς ἐναντίον τοῦ κίραντος αὐτὸν ἄφωνος, οὕτως οὐκ ἀνύγει τὸ στόμα αὐτοῦ. 8.33 ἐν τῇ ταπινώσει «ἡ κρίσις αὐτοῦ ἤρθη· τὴν γενεὰν αὐτοῦ τίς διηγήσεται; ὅτι αἴρεται ἀπὸ τῆς γῆς ἡ ζωὴ αὐτοῦ.»

8.34 ἀποκριθεὶς δὲ ὁ εὐνοῦχος τῷ Φιλίππῳ εἶπεν, δέομαί σου, περὶ τίνος ὁ προφήτης λέγει τοῦτο; περὶ ἑαυτοῦ ἢ περὶ ἑτέρου τινός;

8.35 ἀνοίξας δὲ ὁ Φίλιππος τὸ στόμα αὐτοῦ καὶ ἀρξάμενος ἀπὸ τῆς γραφῆς ταύτης εὐηγγελίσατο αὐτῷ τὸν Ἰησοῦν. 8.36 ὡς δὲ ἐπορεύοντο κατὰ τὴν ὁδόν, ἦλθον ἐπί τι ὕδωρ, καὶ φησὶν ὁ εὐνοῦχος, ἰδοὺ ὕδωρ· τί κωλύει με βαπτισθῆναι; 8.38 καὶ ἐκέλευσεν στῆναι τὸ ἅρμα, καὶ κατέβησαν ἀμφότεροι εἰς τὸ ὕδωρ ὅ τε Φίλιππος καὶ ὁ εὐνοῦχος, καὶ ἐβάπτισεν αὐτόν. 8.39 ὅτε δὲ ἀνέβησαν ἐκ τοῦ ὕδατος, πνεῦμα κυρίου ἥρπασεν τὸν Φίλιππον, καὶ οὐκ εἶδεν αὐτὸν οὐκέτι ὁ εὐνοῦχος· ἐπορεύετο γὰρ τὴν ὁδὸν αὐτοῦ χαίρων. 8.40 Φίλιππος δὲ εὑρέθη εἰς Ἄζωτον, καὶ διερχόμενος εὐηγγελίζετο τὰς πόλις πάσας ἕως τοῦ ἐλθῖν αὐτὸν εἰς Καισάριαν.

9.1 Ὁ δὲ Σαῦλος, ἔτι ἐμπνέων ἀπιλῆς καὶ φόνου εἰς τοὺς μαθητὰς τοῦ κυρίου, προσελθὼν τῷ ἀρχιερεῖ 9.2 ᾐτήσατο ἐπιστολὰς παρ' αὐτοῦ εἰς Δαμασκὸν πρὸς τὰς συναγωγάς, ὅπως ἄν τινας εὕρῃ ὄντας τῆς ὁδοῦ, ἄνδρας τε καὶ γυναῖκας, δεδεμένους ἀγάγῃ εἰς Ἰερουσαλήμ. 9.3 ἐν δὲ τῷ πορεύεσθαι ἐγένετο αὐτὸν ἐγγίζειν τῇ Δαμασκῷ, ἐξέφνης τε αὐτὸν περιήστραψεν φῶς ἐκ τοῦ οὐρανοῦ, 9.4 καὶ πεσὼν ἐπὶ τὴν γῆν ἤκουσεν φωνὴν λέγουσαν αὐτῷ, Σαοὺλ Σαούλ, τί με διώκεις; 9.5 εἶπεν δέ, τίς εἶ, κύριε; ὁ δέ εἶπεν, ἐγώ εἰμι Ἰησοῦς ὃν σὺ διώκεις· 9.6 ἀλλὰ ἀνάστηθι καὶ εἴσελθε εἰς τὴν πόλιν, καὶ λαληθήσεται σοι ὅ τί σε δεῖ ποιεῖν. 9.7 οἱ δὲ ἄνδρες οἱ συνοδεύοντες αὐτῷ ἱστήκεισαν ἐνεοί, ἀκούοντες μὲν τῆς φωνῆς μηδένα δὲ θεωροῦντες. 9.8 ἠγέρθη δὲ Σαῦλος ἀπὸ τῆς γῆς, ἠνεῳγμένων δὲ τῶν ὀφθαλμῶν αὐτοῦ οὐδὲν ἔβλεπεν· χειραγωγοῦντες δὲ αὐτὸν εἰσήγαγον εἰς

DUMB/SILENT AS A LAMB BEFORE THE (ONE) HAVING SHEARED HIM/*it*, THUS HE OPENS NOT HIS MOUTH. 8.33 HIS JUDG-MENT WAS TAKEN AWAY IN/BY THE HUMILIATION; WHO WILL RELATE/DECLARE HIS GENERATION? BECAUSE HIS LIFE IS TAKEN FROM THE EARTH/LAND.

8.34 And answering, the eunuch said to Philip: I beg of you, about whom does the prophet say this? About himself or about some other/different?

8.35 And having opened his mouth and having begun from this writing, Philip announced/preached Jesus to him. 8.36 And as they were going along the road, they came to some water, and the eunuch says: Behold/look, water; what hinders me to be baptized? 8.38 And he ordered *for* the chariot to stop, and they both went down to the water, both Philip and the eunuch, and he baptized him. 8.39 And when they went up out of the water, a spirit from *the* Lord snatched Philip away, and the eunuch saw him not any more; for he was going his way/road rejoicing. 8.40 But Philip was found in Azotus, and going through, he was evangelizing all the cities until the (thing) *for* him to come to Caesarea.

9.1 But Saul, still breathing threat and murder to the learners/pupils of the Lord, having gone to the high priest, 9.2 he requested letters from him to the congregations/synagogues in Damascus, so that if he might find some being of the way, both men and women, he might bring *them*, having been bound, to Jerusalem. 9.3 But in the (thing) *for* him to go, it happened/came about *for him* to draw near to Damascus, and suddenly a light out of the sky/heaven shone around him, 9.4 and having fallen to the ground/earth, he heard a voice saying to him: Saul, Saul, why do you prosecute me? 9.5 And he said: Who are you, lord? And the (he) said: I, I am Jesus whom you, you prosecute; 9.6 but rise up and enter into the city, and it will be spoken to you what it is necessary *for* you to do. 9.7 And the men going/traveling with him had stood speechless, hearing indeed the voice but seeing no one/nothing. 9.8 And Saul was raised up from the ground, but from his eyes having been opened he saw nothing; and being

Δαμασκόν. 9.9 καὶ ἦν ἡμέρας τρῖς μὴ βλέπων, καὶ οὐκ ἔφαγεν οὐδὲ ἔπιεν.

9.10 ἦν δέ τις μαθητὴς ἐν Δαμασκῷ ὀνόματι Ἀνανίας, καὶ εἶπεν πρὸς αὐτὸν ἐν ὁράματι ὁ κύριος, Ἀνανία. ὁ δὲ εἶπεν, ἰδοὺ ἐγώ, κύριε. 9.11 ὁ δὲ κύριος πρὸς αὐτόν, ἀναστὰς πορεύθητι ἐπὶ τὴν ῥύμην τὴν καλουμένην εὐθῖαν καὶ ζήτησον ἐν οἰκίᾳ Ἰούδα Σαῦλον ὀνόματι Ταρσέα· ἰδοὺ γὰρ προσεύχεται, 9.12 καὶ ἶδεν ἄνδρα Ἀνανίαν ὀνόματι εἰσελθόντα καὶ ἐπιθέντα αὐτῷ τὰς χεῖρας ὅπως ἀναβλέψῃ.

9.13 ἀπεκρίθη δὲ Ἀνανίας, κύριε, ἤκουσα ἀπὸ πολλῶν περὶ τοῦ ἀνδρὸς τούτου, ὅσα κακὰ τοῖς ἁγίοις σου ἐποίησεν ἐν Ἰερουσαλήμ· 9.14 καὶ ὧδε ἔχει ἐξουσίαν παρὰ τῶν ἀρχιερέων δῆσαι πάντας τοὺς ἐπικαλουμένους τὸ ὄνομά σου.

9.15 εἶπεν δὲ πρὸς αὐτὸν ὁ κύριος, πορεύου, ὅτι σκεῦος ἐκλογῆς ἐστίν μοι οὗτος τοῦ βαστάσαι τὸ ὄνομά μου ἐνώπιον ἐθνῶν τε καὶ βασιλέων υἱῶν τε Ἰσραήλ· 9.16 ἐγὼ γὰρ ὑποδίξω αὐτῷ ὅσα δεῖ αὐτὸν ὑπὲρ τοῦ ὀνόματός μου παθεῖν.

9.17 ἀπῆλθεν δὲ Ἀνανίας καὶ εἰσῆλθεν εἰς τὴν οἰκίαν, καὶ ἐπιθεὶς ἐπ' αὐτὸν τὰς χῖρας εἶπεν, Σαοὺλ ἀδελφέ, ὁ κύριος ἀπέσταλκέν με, Ἰησοῦς ὁ ὀφθείς σοι ἐν τῇ ὁδῷ ᾗ ἤρχου, ὅπως ἀναβλέψῃς καὶ πλησθῇς πνεύματος ἁγίου. 9.18 καὶ εὐθέως ἀπέπεσαν ἀπὸ τῶν ὀφθαλμῶν αὐτοῦ ὡς λεπίδες, ἀνέβλεψεν δέ, καὶ ἀναστὰς ἐβαπτίσθη, 9.19 καὶ λαβὼν τροφὴν ἐνίσχυσεν.

ἐγένετο δὲ μετὰ τῶν ἐν Δαμασκῷ μαθητῶν ἡμέρας τινάς, 9.20 καὶ εὐθέως ἐν ταῖς συναγωγαῖς ἐκήρυσσεν τὸν Ἰησοῦν ὅτι οὗτός ἐστιν ὁ υἱὸς τοῦ θεοῦ.

9.21 ἐξίσταντο δὲ πάντες οἱ ἀκούοντες καὶ ἔλεγον, οὐχ οὗτός ἐστιν ὁ πορθήσας εἰς Ἰερουσαλὴμ τοὺς ἐπικαλουμένους τὸ ὄνομα τοῦτο, καὶ ὧδε εἰς τοῦτο ἐληλύθει ἵνα δεδεμένους αὐτοὺς ἀγάγῃ ἐπὶ τοὺς ἀρχιερεῖς;

led by hand, they led him into Damascus. 9.9 And he was seeing not *for* three days, and he did not eat nor drink.

9.10 And a certain learner/pupil was in Damascus, by name of Ananias, and the Lord said to him in a vision: Ananias! And the (he) said: Behold I, Lord. 9.11 And the Lord to him: Having risen up, go you to the street being called Straight and seek in a house of Judas a Tarsian, Saul by name; for behold, he prays, 9.12 and he saw a man, Ananias by name, having come in and placed the hands on him in order that he might receive sight.

9.13 But Ananias answered: Lord, I heard about this man from many, how many bad (things) he did to your saints in Jerusalem; 9.14 and he has authority here from the high priests to bind all those calling upon your name.

9.15 But the Lord said to him: You go, because this (one) is a tool/vessel of choice for me of the (thing) to carry/bear my name both before ethnics/nations, also *before* kings and sons of Israel; 9.16 for I, I shall show to him how many (things) it is necessary *for* him to suffer in behalf of my name.

9.17 And Ananias went away and entered into the house, and having laid the hands upon him, he said: Brother Saul, the Lord has sent me, Jesus, the (one) having been seen by you on the road by which you came, so that you might receive sight and be filled from a holy spirit. 9.18 And immediately (things) like scales fell away from his eyes, and he received *his* sight/saw again, and having risen up he was baptized, 9.19 and having received food, he was strong.

And he became with the learners/pupils in Damascus *for* some days, 9.20 and at once he was heralding/preaching Jesus in the congregations/synagogues that this (one) is the son of God.

9.21 And all those hearing were astounded/amazed, and they were saying: Is not this (one) the (one) having pillaged those calling upon this name in Jerusalem, and he had come here in this/for the same, that he might bring them having been bound to the high priests?

9.22 Σαῦλος δὲ μᾶλλον ἐνεδυναμοῦτο καὶ συνέχυννε τοὺς Ἰουδαίους τοὺς κατοικοῦντας ἐν Δαμασκῷ, συμβιβάζων ὅτι οὗτός ἐστιν ὁ χριστός. 9.23 ὡς δὲ ἐπληροῦντο ἡμέραι ἱκαναί, συνεβουλεύσαντο οἱ Ἰουδαῖοι ἀνελεῖν αὐτόν· 9.24 ἐγνώσθη δὲ τῷ Σαύλῳ ἡ ἐπιβουλὴ αὐτῶν. παρετηροῦντο δὲ καὶ τὰς πύλας ἡμέρας τε καὶ νυκτὸς ὅπως αὐτὸν ἀνέλωσιν· 9.25 λαβόντες δὲ οἱ μαθηταὶ αὐτοῦ νυκτὸς διὰ τοῦ τίχους καθῆκαν αὐτὸν χαλάσαντες ἐν σφυρίδι. 9.26 παραγενόμενος δὲ εἰς Ἰερουσαλὴμ ἐπίραζεν κολλᾶσθαι τοῖς μαθηταῖς· καὶ πάντες ἐφοβοῦντο αὐτόν, μὴ πιστεύοντες ὅτι ἐστὶν μαθητής.

9.27 Βαρναβᾶς δὲ ἐπιλαβόμενος αὐτὸν ἤγαγεν πρὸς τοὺς ἀποστόλους, καὶ διηγήσατο αὐτοῖς πῶς ἐν τῇ ὁδῷ εἶδεν τὸν κύριον καὶ ὅτι ἐλάλησεν αὐτῷ, καὶ πῶς ἐν Δαμασκῷ ἐπαρρησιάσατο ἐν τῷ ὀνόματι τοῦ Ἰησοῦ. 9.28 καὶ ἦν μετ' αὐτῶν εἰσπορευόμενος καὶ ἐκπορευόμενος εἰς Ἰερουσαλήμ, παρρησιαζόμενος ἐν τῷ ὀνόματι τοῦ κυρίου, 9.29 ἐλάλει τε καὶ συνεζήτει τε πρὸς τοὺς Ἑλληνιστάς· οἱ δὲ ἐπεχίρουν ἀνελεῖν αὐτόν. 9.30 ἐπιγνόντες δὲ οἱ ἀδελφοὶ κατήγαγον αὐτὸν εἰς Καισάριαν καὶ ἐξαπέστιλαν αὐτὸν εἰς Ταρσόν.

9.31 ἡ μὲν οὖν ἐκκλησία καθ' ὅλης τῆς Ἰουδαίας καὶ Γαλιλαίας καὶ Σαμαρίας εἶχεν εἰρήνην, οἰκοδομουμένη καὶ πορευομένη τῷ φόβῳ τοῦ κυρίου, καὶ τῇ παρακλήσει τοῦ ἁγίου πνεύματος ἐπληθύνετο.

9.32 ἐγένετο δὲ Πέτρον διερχόμενον διὰ πάντων κατελθῖν καὶ πρὸς τοὺς ἁγίους τοὺς κατοικοῦντας ἐν Λύδδα. 9.33 εὗρεν δὲ ἐκεῖ ἄνθρωπόν τινα ὀνόματι Αἰνέαν ἐξ ἐτῶν ὀκτὼ κατακείμενον ἐπὶ κραβάττου, ὃς ἦν παραλελυμένος. 9.34 καὶ εἶπεν αὐτῷ ὁ Πέτρος, Αἰνέα, ἰαταί σε Ἰησοῦς χριστός· ἀνάστηθι καὶ στρῶσον σεαυτῷ. καὶ εὐθέως ἀνέστη. 9.35 καὶ εἶδον αὐτὸν πάντες οἱ κατοικοῦντες Λύδδα καὶ τὸν Σαρῶνα, οἵτινες ἐπέστρεψαν ἐπὶ τὸν κύριον.

9.36 ἐν Ἰόππῃ δέ τις ἦν μαθήτρια ὀνόματι Ταβιθά, ἡ διερμηνευομένη λέγεται Δορκάς· αὕτη ἦν πλήρης ἀγαθῶν ἔργων

9.22   But Saul was being more empowered and he was confounding the Judeans dwelling in Damascus, demonstrating that this (one) is the anointed (one). 9.23 And since considerable days were being used up/filled, the Judeans were themselves plotting together to kill him; 9.24 but their plot was known to Saul. And they were watching him closely, also the gates, both day and night so that they might kill him; 9.25 but having taken *him*, the learners/pupils of him let him down through the wall *at* night, having lowered *him* in a basket. 9.26 And having arrived in Jerusalem, he was trying to be joined to the learners/pupils; and they all were fearing him, not believing that he is a learner/pupil.

9.27   But Barnabas, having taken hold of him, led him to the apostles, and he related to them how he saw the Lord on the road and that he spoke to him, and how he spoke boldly in Damascus in the name of Jesus. 9.28 And he was going in and going out with them in Jerusalem, speaking freely/boldly in the name of the Lord, 9.29 he was both speaking and disputing to/with the Hellenists; and they were attempting to kill him. 9.30 But having known *it*, the brothers brought him down to Caesarea and they sent him forth to Tarsus.

9.31   Then indeed the assembly had peace throughout all Judea and Galilee and Samaria, being built/edified and going in the fear of the Lord, and being multiplied/increased by the consolation/comforting of the holy spirit.

9.32   And it came about *for* Peter to come down, passing through all (lands) even to the saints dwelling in Lydda. 9.33 And he found a certain man there by name of Aeneas, from eight years lying down on a mattress, who had been paralyzed. 9.34 And Peter said to him: Aeneas, Jesus, the anointed (one) heals you; rise up and spread/make *the bed* for yourself. And he rose up immediately. 9.35 And all those inhabiting Lydda and Saron were seeing him, who turned to the Lord.

9.36   And in Joppa there was a certain learner/pupil by name of Tabitha, which being translated is called Dorcas; this (woman) was full of good works and

καὶ ἐλαημοσυνῶν ὧν ἐποίει. 9.37 ἐγένετο δὲ ἐν ταῖς ἡμέραις ἐκίναις ἀσθενήσασαν αὐτὴν ἀποθανῖν· λούσαντες δὲ ἔθηκαν αὐτὴν ἐν ὑπερῴῳ.

9.38 ἐγγὺς δὲ οὔσης Λύδδας τῇ Ἰόππῃ οἱ μαθηταὶ ἀκούσαντες ὅτι Πέτρος ἐστὶν ἐν αὐτῇ ἀπέστιλαν δύο ἄνδρας πρὸς αὐτὸν παρακαλοῦντες, μὴ ὀκνήσῃς διελθῖν ἕως ἡμῶν. 9.39 ἀναστὰς δὲ Πέτρος συνῆλθεν αὐτοῖς· ὃν παραγενόμενον ἀνήγαγον εἰς τὸ ὑπερῷον, καὶ παρέστησαν αὐτῷ πᾶσαι αἱ χῆραι κλέουσαι καὶ ἐπιδικνύμεναι χιτῶνας καὶ ἱμάτια ὅσα ἐποίει μετ' αὐτῶν οὖσα ἡ Δορκάς. 9.40 ἐκβαλὼν δὲ ἔξω πάντας ὁ Πέτρος καὶ θεὶς τὰ γόνατα προσηύξατο, καὶ ἐπιστρέψας πρὸς τὸ σῶμα εἶπεν, Ταβιθά, ἀνάστηθι. ἡ δὲ ἤνοιξε τοὺς ὀφθαλμοὺς αὐτῆς, καὶ ἰδοῦσα τὸν Πέτρον ἀνεκάθισεν. 9.41 δοὺς δὲ αὐτῇ χεῖρα ἀνέστησεν αὐτήν, φωνήσας δὲ τοὺς ἁγίους καὶ τὰς χήρας παρέστησεν αὐτὴν ζῶσαν.

9.42 γνωστὸν δὲ ἐγένετο καθ' ὅλης τῆς Ἰόππης, καὶ ἐπίστευσαν πολλοὶ ἐπὶ τὸν κύριον. 9.43 ἐγένετο δὲ ἡμέρας ἱκανὰς μῖναι ἐν Ἰόππῃ παρά τινι Σίμωνι βυρσεῖ.

10.1 Ἀνὴρ δέ τις ἐν Καισαρίᾳ ὀνόματι Κορνήλιος, ἑκατοντάρχης ἐκ σπείρης τῆς καλουμένης Ἰταλικῆς, 10.2 εὐσεβὴς καὶ φοβούμενος τὸν θεὸν σὺν παντὶ τῷ οἴκῳ αὐτοῦ, ποιῶν ἐλεημοσύνας πολλὰς τῷ λαῷ καὶ δεόμενος τοῦ θεοῦ διὰ παντός, 10.3 εἶδεν ὁράματι φανερῶς ὡσὶ περὶ ὥραν ἐνάτην τῆς ἡμέρας ἄγγελον τοῦ θεοῦ εἰσελθόντα πρὸς αὐτὸν καὶ εἰπόντα αὐτῷ, Κορνήλιε. 10.4 ὁ δὲ ἀτενίσας αὐτῷ καὶ ἔμφοβος γενόμενος εἶπεν, τί ἐστιν, κύριε; εἶπεν δὲ αὐτῷ, αἱ προσευχαί σου καὶ αἱ ἐλεημοσύναι σου ἀνέβησαν εἰς μνημόσυνον ἔμπροσθεν τοῦ θεοῦ. 10.5 καὶ νῦν πέμψον ἄνδρας εἰς Ἰόππην καὶ μετάπεμψαι Σίμωνά ὃς ἐπικαλῖται Πέτρος· 10.6 οὗτος ξενίζεται παρά τινι Σίμωνι βυρσεῖ, ᾧ ἐστιν οἰκία παρὰ θάλασσαν. 10.7 ὡς δὲ ἀπῆλθεν ὁ ἄγγελος ὁ λαλῶν αὐτῷ, φωνήσας δύο τῶν οἰκετῶν καὶ στρατιώτην εὐσεβῆ τῶν προσκαρτερούντων αὐτῷ, 10.8 καὶ ἐξηγησάμενος ἅπαντα αὐτοῖς ἀπέστιλεν αὐτοὺς εἰς τὴν Ἰόππην.

of charities which she was doing. 9.37 And it came about in those days *for* her, having been sick, to die; and having washed *her* they put her in an upper room.

9.38 And from Lydda being near to Joppa, the learners/pupils, having heard that Peter is in her/it, sent two men to him beseeching *him*: Do not delay to come as far as/until us. 9.39 And having risen up Peter went with them; whom having arrived, they led to the upper room, and all the widows stood beside him weeping and showing to *him* tunics and clothing which Dorcas was making, being with them. 9.40 And Peter, having put all outside and having put down the knees, he prayed, and having turned toward the body he said: Tabitha, rise up. And she opened her eyes, and having seen Peter, she sat up. 9.41 And having given a hand to her, he raised her up, and having called the saints and the widows, he presented her living.

9.42 And it became known throughout all Joppa, and many believed on the Lord. 9.43 And it happened *for him* to stay considerable days in Joppa with a certain Simon, a tanner.

10.1 And *there was* a certain man in Caesarea, Cornelius by name, a centurion out of a cohort being called Italian, 10.2 and reverent/pious, fearing God with all his house, doing/making many charities for the people and asking from God through every (thing), 10.3 he saw clearly in a vision, about *the* ninth hour of the day, *there was* a messenger/angel from God having come in near him and having said to him: Cornelius. 10.4 And the (he) having gazed at him and having become afraid, he said: What is it, lord/Lord? And he said to him: Your prayers and your charities went up in/for a memorial before God. 10.5 And now, you send men to Joppa and summon Simon who is also called Peter; 10.6 this (one) is a guest with a certain Simon, an tanner, for whom a house is beside a lake/sea. 10.7 And when the messenger/angel speaking to him went away, having called two of the domestic servants and a devout/pious soldier of those attending constantly to him, 10.8 and having explained all to them, he sent them to Joppa.

10.9 τῇ δὲ ἐπαύριον ὁδοιπορούντων αὐτῶν καὶ τῇ πόλει ἐγγιζόντων ἀνέβη Πέτρος ἐπὶ τὸ δῶμα προσεύξασθε περὶ ὥραν ἕκτην. 10.10 ἐγένετο δὲ πρόσπινος καὶ ἤθελεν γεύσασθε· παρασκευαζόντων δὲ αὐτῶν ἐγένετο ἐπ' αὐτὸν ἔκστασις, 10.11 καὶ θεωρῖ τὸν οὐρανὸν ἀνεῳγμένον καὶ καταβαῖνον σκεῦός τι ὡς ὀθόνην μεγάλην τέσσαρσιν ἀρχαῖς καθιέμενον ἐπὶ τῆς γῆς, 10.12 ἐν ᾧ ὑπῆρχεν πάντα τὰ τετράποδα καὶ ἑρπετὰ τῆς γῆς καὶ πετινὰ τοῦ οὐρανοῦ.

10.13 καὶ ἐγένετο φωνὴ πρὸς αὐτόν, ἀναστάς, Πέτρε, θῦσον καὶ φάγε. 10.14 ὁ δὲ Πέτρος εἶπεν, μηδαμῶς, κύριε, ὅτι οὐδέποτε ἔφαγον πᾶν κοινὸν καὶ ἀκάθαρτον. 10.15 καὶ φωνὴ πάλιν ἐκ δευτέρου πρὸς αὐτόν, ἃ ὁ θεὸς ἐκαθάρισεν σὺ μὴ κοίνου. 10.16 τοῦτο δὲ ἐγένετο ἐπὶ τρείς, καὶ εὐθὺς ἀνελήμφθη τὸ σκεῦος εἰς τὸν οὐρανόν. 10.17 ὡς δὲ ἐν ἑαυτῷ διηπόρει ὁ Πέτρος τί ἂν εἴη τὸ ὅραμα ὃ εἶδεν, ἰδοὺ οἱ ἄνδρες οἱ ἀπεσταλμένοι ὑπὸ τοῦ Κορνηλίου διερωτήσαντες τὴν οἰκίαν τοῦ Σίμωνος ἐπέστησαν ἐπὶ τὸν πυλῶνα, 10.18 καὶ φωνήσαντες ἐπυνθάνοντο εἰ Σίμων ὁ ἐπικαλούμενος Πέτρος ἐνθάδε ξενίζεται.

10.19 τοῦ δὲ Πέτρου διενθυμένου περὶ τοῦ ὁράματος εἶπεν τὸ πνεῦμα αὐτῷ, ἰδοὺ ἄνδρες τρῖς ζητοῦντές σε· 10.20 ἀλλὰ ἀναστὰς κατάβηθι καὶ πορεύου σὺν αὐτοῖς μηδὲν διακρινόμενος, ὅτι ἐγὼ ἀπέσταλκα αὐτούς. 10.21 καταβὰς δὲ Πέτρος πρὸς τοὺς ἄνδρας εἶπεν, ἰδοὺ ἐγώ εἰμι ὃν ζητεῖτε· τίς ἡ αἰτία δι' ἣν πάρεστε; 10.22 οἱ δὲ εἶπαν, Κορνήλιος ἑκατοντάρχης, ἀνὴρ δίκαιος καὶ φοβούμενος τὸν θεὸν μαρτυρούμενός τε ὑπὸ ὅλου τοῦ ἔθνους τῶν Ἰουδαίων, ἐχρηματίσθη ὑπὸ ἀγγέλου ἁγίου μεταπέμψασθαί σε εἰς τὸν οἶκον αὐτοῦ καὶ ἀκοῦσαι ῥήματα παρὰ σοῦ.

10.23 εἰσκαλεσάμενος οὖν αὐτοὺς ἐξένισεν. τῇ δὲ ἐπαύριον ἀναστὰς ἐξῆλθεν σὺν αὐτοῖς, καί τινες τῶν ἀδελφῶν τῶν ἀπὸ Ἰόππης συνῆλθον αὐτῷ. 10.24 τῇ δὲ ἐπαύριον εἰσῆλθαν εἰς τὴν Κεσάρειαν· ὁ δὲ Κορνήλιος ἦν προσδοκῶν αὐτούς,

10.9 And on the morrow, from them traveling by road and drawing near to the city, Peter went up on the roof to pray about *the* sixth hour. 10.10 And he became hungry and was wanting to taste/eat; and from them preparing *it* an amazement/ecstasy became over him, 10.11 and he beholds the sky/heaven having been opened and a certain vessel coming down like a great linen cloth, being lowered by four corners to the earth, 10.12 on/in which were existing all the quadrupeds and reptiles of the earth and birds of the sky/heaven.

10.13 And a voice became to him: Having risen up, Peter, sacrifice/slaughter and eat. 10.14 But Peter said: Certainly not, Lord, because I never ate every (thing) common and unclean. 10.15 And a voice again, from a second *time, said* to him: What (things) God cleansed, you, you deem not unclean. 10.16 And this happened for three times, and at once the vessel was taken up into the sky/heaven. 10.17 And as Peter was doubting/at a loss in himself what ever the vision which he saw may be, behold, the men having been sent by Cornelius, having asked for the house of Simon, stood at the portal/vestibule, 10.18 and having called out, they were inquiring if Simon, the (one) also being called Peter is being a guest here.

10.19 And from Peter pondering about the vision, the spirit said to him: Behold, three men *are* seeking you; 10.20 but having risen up, you go down and travel with them, doubting nothing, because I myself have sent them. 10.21 And having descended, Peter said to the men: Behold, I, I am *the one* whom ye seek; what is the reason on account of which ye have come? 10.22 And the (they) said: Cornelius, a centurion, a just man and fearing God, and being witnessed for by the entire ethnic/nation of the Judeans, was directed by a holy messenger/angel to summon you to his house and to hear words from you.

10.23 Then having called/invited them in, he lodged/spent the night. And having risen up on the morrow, he went with them, and some of the brothers from Joppa went with him. 10.24 And on the morrow they entered into Caesarea; and Cornelius was waiting

444

συνκαλεσάμενος τοὺς συγγενεῖς αὐτοῦ καὶ τοὺς ἀναγκαίους φίλους.

10.25 ὡς δὲ ἐγένετο τοῦ εἰσελθῖν τὸν Πέτρον, συναντήσας αὐτῷ ὁ Κορνήλιος πεσὼν ἐπὶ τοὺς πόδας προσεκύνησεν. 10.26 ὁ δὲ Πέτρος ἤγειρεν αὐτὸν λέγων, ἀνάστηθι· καὶ ἐγὼ αὐτὸς ἄνθρωπός εἰμι. 10.27 καὶ συνομιλῶν αὐτῷ εἰσῆλθεν, καὶ εὑρίσκει συνεληλυθότας πολλούς, 10.28 ἔφη τε πρὸς αὐτούς, ὑμεῖς ἐπίστασθαι ὡς ἀθέμιτόν ἐστιν ἀνδρὶ Ἰουδαίῳ κολλᾶσθαι ἢ προσέρχεσθαι ἀλλοφύλῳ· κἀμοὶ ἔδειξεν ὁ θεὸς μηδένα κοινὸν ἢ ἀκάθαρτον λέγειν ἄνθρωπον· 10.29 διὸ καὶ ἀναντιρρήτως ἦλθον μεταπεμφθείς. πυνθάνομε οὖν τίνι λόγῳ μετεπέμψασθαί με;

10.30 καὶ ὁ Κορνήλιος ἔφη, ἀπὸ τετάρτης ἡμέρας μέχρι ταύτης τῆς ὥρας ἤμην τὴν ἐνάτην προσευχόμενος ἐν τῷ οἴκῳ μου, καὶ ἰδοὺ ἀνὴρ ἔστη ἐνώπιόν ἐμοῦ ἐν ἐσθῆτι λαμπρᾷ 10.31 καὶ φησίν, Κορνήλιε, εἰσηκούσθη σου ἡ προσευχὴ καὶ αἱ ἐλεημοσύναι σου ἐμνήσθησαν ἐνώπιον τοῦ θεοῦ. 10.32 πέμψον οὖν εἰς Ἰόππην καὶ μετακάλεσαι Σίμωνα ὃς ἐπικαλεῖται Πέτρος· οὗτος ξενίζεται ἐν οἰκίᾳ Σίμωνος βυρσέως παρὰ θάλασσαν. 10.33 ἐξαυτῆς οὖν ἔπεμψα πρὸς σέ, σύ τε καλῶς ἐποίησας παραγενόμενος. νῦν οὖν πάντες ἡμεῖς ἐνώπιον τοῦ θεοῦ πάρεσμεν ἀκοῦσαι πάντα τὰ προστεταγμένα σοι ὑπὸ τοῦ κυρίου.

10.34 ἀνοίξας δὲ Πέτρος τὸ στόμα εἶπεν, ἐπ᾽ ἀληθείας καταλαμβάνομαι ὅτι οὐκ ἔστιν προσωπολήμπτης ὁ θεός, 10.35 ἀλλ᾽ ἐν παντὶ ἔθνι ὁ φοβούμενος αὐτὸν καὶ ἐργαζόμενος δικαιοσύνην δεκτὸς αὐτῷ ἐστιν. 10.36 τὸν λόγον ὃν ἀπέστιλεν τοῖς υἱοῖς Ἰσραὴλ εὐαγγελιζόμενος εἰρήνην διὰ Ἰησοῦ χριστοῦ οὗτός ἐστιν πάντων κύριος 10.37 ὑμεῖς οἴδατε, τὸ γενόμενον ῥῆμα καθ᾽ ὅλης τῆς Ἰουδαίας, ἀρξάμενος ἀπὸ τῆς Γαλιλαίας μετὰ τὸ βάπτισμα ὃ ἐκήρυξεν Ἰωάννης, 10.38 Ἰησοῦν τὸν ἀπὸ Ναζαρέθ, ὡς ἔχρισεν αὐτὸν ὁ θεὸς πνεύματι ἁγίῳ καὶ δυνάμει, ὃς διῆλθεν εὐεργετῶν καὶ ἰώμενος πάντας τοὺς καταδυναστευομένους ὑπὸ τοῦ διαβόλου, ὅτι ὁ θεὸς ἦν μετ᾽ αὐτοῦ. 10.39 καὶ ἡμεῖς μάρτυρες πάντων ὧν ἐποίησεν ἔν τε τῇ

for them, having called his relatives and close/intimate friends together.

10.25 And as it happened from the (thing) *for* Peter to enter, having met him, Cornelius worshiped to him, having fallen at the feet. 10.26 But Peter raised him, saying: Stand up; I, I myself am also a man. 10.27 And he entered talking with him, and he finds many having come together, 10.28 and he was saying to them: Ye, ye understand how unlawful it is for a Judean man to be joined or to come near to a foreigner/one of another tribe; and God showed to me to call no man common or unclean; 10.29 wherefore, having been summoned, I indeed came undeniably. Therefore I inquire, for what reason sent ye for me?

10.30 And Cornelius was saying: From the fourth day *ago* until this hour/time I was praying the ninth *hour* in my house, and behold, a man stood in front of me in shining apparel, 10.31 and he says: Cornelius, your prayer was heard and your charities were remembered before God. 10.32 Send therefore to Joppa and send for/summon Simon, who is also called Peter; this (one) lodges/is a guest in a house of Simon a tanner beside a lake/sea. 10.33 Therefore, I sent immediately to/for you, and you, you did well, having arrived/come. Now therefore we, we all are present before God to hear all the (things) having been ordered/prescribed to you by the Lord.

10.34 And having opened the mouth, Peter said: On a truth I perceive that God is not one showing partiality, 10.35 but in every ethnic/nation, the (one) fearing him and working justice/justness is acceptable to him; 10.36 the saying/word which he sent to the sons of Israel, announcing/preaching peace through Jesus the anointed (one) -- this (one) is Lord of all -- 10.37 ye, ye know the word/saying having become throughout all Judea, beginning from Galilee after the baptism which John heralded/preached, 10.38 Jesus, the (one) from Nazareth, how God anointed him with a holy spirit and power, who went about working good and healing all those being oppressed/dominated by the devil, because God was with him. 10.39 And we *are* witnesses of all which he did, both in the country

χώρα τῶν Ἰουδαίων καὶ ἐν Ἱερουσαλήμ· ὃν καὶ ἀνῖλαν κρεμάσαντες ἐπὶ ξύλου. 10.40 τοῦτον ὁ θεὸς ἤγειρεν ἐντῇ τρίτῃ ἡμέρᾳ καὶ ἔδωκεν αὐτὸν ἐμφανῆ γενέσθαι, 10.41 οὐ παντὶ τῷ λαῷ ἀλλὰ μάρτυσι τοῖς προκεχιροτονημένοις ὑπὸ τοῦ θεοῦ, ἡμῖν, οἵτινες συνεφάγομεν καὶ συνεπίομεν αὐτῷ μετὰ τὸ ἀναστῆναι αὐτὸν ἐκ νεκρῶν· 10.42 καὶ παρήγγιλεν ἡμῖν κηρύξαι τῷ λαῷ καὶ διαμαρτύρασθαι ὅτι αὐτός ἐστιν ὁ ὡρισμένος ὑπὸ τοῦ θεοῦ κριτὴς ζώντων καὶ νεκρῶν. 10.43 τούτῳ πάντες οἱ προφῆται μαρτυροῦσιν, ἄφεσιν ἁμαρτιῶν λαβῖν διὰ τοῦ ὀνόματος αὐτοῦ πάντα τὸν πιστεύοντα εἰς αὐτόν.

10.44 ἔτι λαλοῦντος τοῦ Πέτρου τὰ ῥήματα ταῦτα ἐπέπεσε τὸ πνεῦμα τὸ ἅγιον ἐπὶ πάντας τοὺς ἀκούοντας τὸν λόγον. 10.45 καὶ ἐξέστησαν οἱ ἐκ περιτομῆς πιστοὶ ὅσοι συνῆλθαν τῷ Πέτρῳ, ὅτι καὶ ἐπὶ τὰ ἔθνη ἡ δωρεὰ τοῦ ἁγίου πνεύματος ἐκκέχυται· 10.46 ἤκουον γὰρ αὐτῶν λαλούντων γλώσσαις καὶ μεγαλυνόντων τὸν θεόν. τότε ἀπεκρίθη Πέτρος, 10.47 μήτι τὸ ὕδωρ δύναται κωλῦσαί τις τοῦ μὴ βαπτισθῆναι τούτους οἵτινες τὸ πνεῦμα τὸ ἅγιον ἔλαβον ὡς καὶ ἡμεῖς; 10.48 προσέταξεν δὲ αὐτοῖς ἐν τῷ ὀνόματι Ἰησοῦ χριστοῦ βαπτισθῆναι. τότε ἠρώτησαν αὐτὸν ἐπιμεῖναι ἡμέρας τινάς. 11.1 Ἤκουσαν δὲ οἱ ἀπόστολοι καὶ οἱ ἀδελφοὶ οἱ ὄντες κατὰ τὴν Ἰουδαίαν ὅτι καὶ τὰ ἔθνη ἐδέξαντο τὸν λόγον τοῦ θεοῦ.

11.2 ὅτε δὲ ἀνέβη Πέτρος εἰς Ἱερουσαλήμ, διεκρίνοντο πρὸς αὐτὸν οἱ ἐκ περιτομῆς 11.3 λέγοντες ὅτι εἰσῆλθες πρὸς ἄνδρας ἀκροβυστίαν ἔχοντας καὶ συνέφαγες αὐτοῖς. 11.4 ἀρξάμενος δὲ Πέτρος ἐξετίθετο αὐτοῖς καθεξῆς λέγων,

11.5 ἐγὼ ἤμην ἐν πόλι Ἰόππῃ προσευχόμενος καὶ εἶδον ἐν ἐκστάσι ὅραμα, καταβαῖνον σκεῦός τι ὡς ὀθόνην μεγάλην τέσσαρσιν ἀρχαῖς καθιεμένην ἐκ τοῦ οὐρανοῦ, καὶ ἦλθεν ἄχρι ἐμοῦ· 11.6 εἰς ἣν ἀτενίσας κατενόουν καὶ εἶδον τὰ τετράποδα τῆς γῆς καὶ τὰ θηρία καὶ τὰ ἑρπετὰ καὶ τὰ πετινὰ τοῦ οὐρανοῦ.

of the Judeans and in Jerusalem; whom they indeed killed/took up, having hung *him* on a tree/wood. 10.40 God raised this (one) on the third day and he gave *it for* him to become visible/manifest, 10.41 not to all the people but to witnesses, to those having been hand picked beforehand by God, to us, who ate and drank with him after the (thing) *for* him to rise up out of dead (ones); 10.42 and he charged/commanded to us to herald/preach to the people and to testify solemnly that this (one) is the (one) having been determined/appointed by God, *being* a judge of living (ones) and of dead (ones). 10.43 All the prophets testify/witness for/to this (one), *for* every/each (one) believing in him to receive forgiveness/remission of sins/faults through his name.

10.44 From Peter still speaking these words, the holy spirit fell upon all those hearing the saying/word. 10.45 And the faithful (ones) from the circumcision, as many as went with Peter, were astounded, because the gift of the holy spirit was also poured out upon the ethnics; 10.46 for they were hearing them speaking in languages and magnifying God. Then Peter answered: 10.47 Not anyone is able to hinder/prevent the water of the (thing) for these not to be baptized, who received the holy spirit even as we, *is he*? 10.48 And he ordered for them to be baptized in the name of Jesus, the anointed (one). Then they asked him to stay some days. 11.1 And the apostles and the brothers, those being throughout Judea, heard that the ethnics also received the saying/word of God.

11.2 But when Peter went up to Jerusalem, those from the circumcision were disputing toward/with him, 11.3 saying: You went in to/with men having uncircumcision and you ate with them. 11.4 But Peter, having began, was explaining to them in order, saying:

11.5 I, I was in *the* city Joppa praying and I saw a vision in astonishment/ecstasy, a certain vessel was coming down like a great linen cloth, having been lowered out of the sky/heaven by four corners, and it came as far as me; 11.6 into which having gazed I was perceiving/considering, and I saw quadrupeds and the wild beasts and the reptiles of the earth and the

11.7 ἤκουσα δὲ καὶ φωνῆς λεγούσης μοι, ἀναστάς, Πέτρε, θῦσον καὶ φάγε. 11.8 εἶπον δέ, μηδαμῶς, κύριε, ὅτι κοινὸν ἢ ἀκάθαρτον οὐδέποτε εἰσῆλθεν εἰς τὸ στόμα μου. 11.9 ἀπεκρίθη δὲ φωνὴ ἐκ δευτέρου ἐκ τοῦ οὐρανοῦ, ἃ ὁ θεὸς ἐκαθάρισεν σὺ μὴ κοίνου. 11.10 τοῦτο δὲ ἐγένετο ἐπὶ τρίς, καὶ ἀνεσπάσθη πάλιν ἅπαντα εἰς τὸν οὐρανόν. 11.11 καὶ ἰδοὺ ἐξαυτῆς τρῖς ἄνδρες ἐπέστησαν ἐπὶ τὴν οἰκίαν ἐν ᾗ ἦμεν, ἀπεσταλμένοι ἀπὸ Καισαρίας πρός ἐμέ. 11.12 εἶπεν δὲ τὸ πνεῦμά μοι συνελθῖν αὐτοῖς μηδὲν διακρίναντα. ἦλθον δὲ σὺν ἐμοὶ καὶ οἱ ἓξ ἀδελφοὶ οὗτοι, καὶ εἰσήλθομεν εἰς τὸν οἶκον τοῦ ἀνδρός· 11.13 ἀπήγγειλεν δὲ ἡμῖν πῶς εἶδεν τὸν ἄγγελον ἐν τῷ οἴκῳ αὐτοῦ σταθέντα καὶ εἰπόντα, ἀπόστιλον εἰς Ἰόππην καὶ μετάπεμψαι Σίμωνα τὸν ἐπικαλούμενον Πέτρον, 11.14 ὃς λαλήσι ῥήματα πρὸς σὲ ἐν οἷς σωθήσῃ σὺ καὶ πᾶς ὁ οἶκός σου.

11.15 ἐν δὲ τῷ ἄρξασθαί με λαλῖν ἐπέπεσε τὸ πνεῦμα τὸ ἅγιον ἐπ᾽ αὐτοὺς ὥσπερ καὶ ἐφ᾽ ἡμᾶς ἐν ἀρχῇ. 11.16 ἐμνήσθην δὲ τοῦ ῥήματος τοῦ κυρίου ὡς ἔλεγεν, Ἰωάννης μὲν ἐβάπτισεν ὕδατι, ὑμεῖς δὲ βαπτισθήσεσθαι ἐν πνεύματι ἁγίῳ.

11.17 εἰ οὖν τὴν ἴσην δωρεὰν δέδωκεν αὐτοῖς ὁ θεὸς ὡς καὶ ἡμῖν πιστεύσασιν ἐπὶ τὸν κύριον Ἰησοῦν χριστόν, ἐγὼ τίς ἤμην δυνατὸς κωλῦσαι τὸν θεόν;

11.18 ἀκούσαντες δὲ ταῦτα ἡσύχασαν καὶ ἐδόξασαν τὸν θεὸν λέγοντες, ἄρα καὶ τοῖς ἔθνεσιν ὁ θεὸς τὴν μετάνοιαν εἰς ζωὴν ἔδωκεν. 11.19 οἱ μὲν οὖν διασπαρέντες ἀπὸ τῆς θλίψεως τῆς γενομένης ἐπὶ Στεφάνῳ διῆλθον ἕως Φοινίκης καὶ Κύπρου καὶ Ἀντιοχίας, μηδενὶ λαλοῦντες τὸν λόγον εἰ μὴ μόνον Ἰουδαίοι.

11.20 ἦσαν δέ τινες ἐξ αὐτῶν ἄνδρες Κύπριοι καὶ Κυρηναῖοι, οἵτινες ἐλθόντες εἰς Ἀντιόχιαν ἐλάλουν καὶ πρὸς τοὺς Ἕλληνάς, εὐαγγελιζόμενοι τὸν κύριον Ἰησοῦν. 11.21 καὶ ἦν χεὶρ κυρίου μετ᾽ αὐτῶν,

πολύς τε ἀριθμὸς ὁ πιστεύσας ἐπέστρεψεν ἐπὶ τὸν κύριον. 11.22 ἠκούσθη δὲ ὁ λόγος εἰς τὰ ὦτα τῆς ἐκκλησίας τῆς οὔσης ἐν

birds of the sky/heaven.   11.7 And I also heard a voice saying to me: Having risen up, Peter, slay and eat.   11.8 But I said: Certainly not, Lord, because a common or unclean (thing) never entered into my mouth. 11.9   And a voice answered from a second *time* out of the sky/heaven: What (things) God cleansed, you, you call not common.   11.10 And this happened thrice over, and all was drawn up again into the sky/heaven.   11.11 And behold, three men immediately stopped/stood at the house in which I was, having been sent from Caesarea to me.   11.12 And the spirit said to me to go with them,   doubting/questioning   nothing.   And   these   six brothers also went with me, and we entered into the house of the man;   11.13 and he reported to us how he saw a messenger/angel in his house, having stood and having said: Send to Joppa and summon Simon, the (one) also being called Peter,   11.14 who will speak words to you in/by which you and all your house will be saved.

11.15   And in/at the *time for* me to begin to speak, the holy spirit fell upon them just as also upon us in the beginning.   11.16 And I was reminded of the word of the Lord when he was saying: John indeed baptized in/with water, but ye, ye will be baptized in/with a holy spirit.

11.17   Therefore, if God gave the equal gift to them even as to us, having believed on the Lord Jesus, the anointed (one), I, why was I able to hinder God?

11.18   And having heard these (things) they were quiet and glorified God, saying: Then God also gave the repentance into life to the ethnics.   11.19 Then indeed the (those) having been scattered from the affliction having happened to Stephen went through as far as/until Phoenicia and Cyprus and Antioch, speaking the saying/word to no one except to Judeans only.

11.20   And some (men) out of them *were* Cypriots and Cyrenians, who having come to Antioch were speaking also to the Greeks, announcing/preaching the Lord Jesus.   11.21 And *the* hand of *the* Lord was with them,

and a much number having believed turned to the Lord.   11.22 And the saying/word/account about them was heard in the ears of the assembly being in Jerusa-

Ἰερουσαλὴμ περὶ αὐτῶν, καὶ ἐξαπέστιλαν Βαρναβᾶν ἕως Ἀντιοχείας· 11.23 ὃς παραγενόμενος καὶ ἰδὼν τὴν χάριν τὴν τοῦ θεοῦ ἐχάρη καὶ παρεκάλει πάντας τῇ προθέσει τῆς καρδίας προσμένιν τῷ κυρίῳ, 11.24 ὅτι ἀνὴρ ἦν ἀγαθὸς καὶ πλήρης πνεύματος ἁγίου καὶ πίστεως. καὶ προσετέθη ὄχλος ἱκανὸς τῷ κυρίῳ.

11.25 ἐξῆλθεν δὲ εἰς Ταρσὸν ἀναζητῆσαι Σαῦλον, 11.26 καὶ εὑρὼν ἤγαγεν εἰς Ἀντιόχιαν.

ἐγένετο δὲ αὐτοῖς καὶ ἐνιαυτὸν ὅλον συναχθῆναι ἐν τῇ ἐκκλησίᾳ καὶ διδάξαι ὄχλον ἱκανόν, χρηματίσαι τε πρώτως ἐν Ἀντιοχίᾳ τοὺς μαθητὰς χριστιανούς.

11.27 ἐν ταύταις δὲ ταῖς ἡμέραις κατῆλθον ἀπὸ Ἱεροσολύμων προφῆται εἰς Ἀντιόχιαν·

11.28 ἀναστὰς δὲ εἷς ἐξ αὐτῶν ὀνόματι Ἅγαβος ἐσήμανεν διὰ τοῦ πνεύματος λιμὸν μεγάλην μέλλιν ἔσεσθαι ἐφ' ὅλην τὴν οἰκουμένην· ἥτις ἐγένετο ἐπὶ Κλαυδίου.

11.29 τῶν δὲ μαθητῶν καθὼς εὐπορῖτό τις ὥρισαν ἕκαστος αὐτῶν εἰς διακονίαν πέμψαι τοῖς κατοικοῦσιν ἐν τῇ Ἰουδαίᾳ ἀδελφοῖς· 11.30 ὃ καὶ ἐποίησαν ἀποστίλαντες πρὸς τοὺς πρεσβυτέρους διὰ χειρὸς Βαρναβᾶ καὶ Σαύλου.

12.1 Κατ' ἐκεῖνον δὲ τὸν καιρὸν ἐπέβαλεν ὁ βασιλεὺς Ἡρῴδης τὰς χῖρας κακῶσαί τινας τῶν ἀπὸ τῆς ἐκκλησίας. 12.2 ἀνῖλεν δὲ Ἰάκωβον τὸν ἀδελφὸν Ἰωάννου μαχαίρῃ. 12.3 ἰδὼν δὲ ὅτι ἀρεστόν ἐστιν τοῖς Ἰουδαίοις προσέθετο συλλαβῖν καὶ Πέτρον, ἦσαν δὲ ἡμέραι τῶν ἀζύμων, 12.4 ὃν καὶ πιάσας ἔθετο εἰς φυλακήν, παραδοὺς τέσσαρσιν τετραδίοις στρατιωτῶν φυλάσσειν αὐτόν, βουλόμενος μετὰ τὸ πάσχα ἀναγαγῖν αὐτὸν τῷ λαῷ. 12.5 ὁ μὲν οὖν Πέτρος ἐτηρῖτο ἐν τῇ φυλακῇ· προσευχὴ δὲ ἦν ἐκτενῶς γινομένη ὑπὸ τῆς ἐκκλησίας πρὸς τὸν θεὸν περὶ αὐτοῦ.

lem, and they sent out Barnabas as far as Antioch; 11.23 who having arrived and seen the grace/favor of God was cheered, and he was exhorting all with the purpose of the heart to remain with the Lord, 11.24 because he was a good man and full of a holy spirit and of faith. And a considerable crowd was added for the Lord.

11.25 And he went forth to Tarsus to seek for Saul, 11.26 and having found *him* he brought *him* to Antioch.

And it happened for them also to be gathered *for* a whole year with/in the assembly and to teach a considerable crowd, and *for* the learners/pupils to bear the name Christians for the first time in/at Antioch.

11.27 And in those days prophets came down from Jerusalem to Antioch;

11.28 and having risen up one out of them by name of Agabus predicted/signified through the spirit *for* a great famine to be about to come over all the empire/inhabited earth; which happened upon/at the *time* of Claudius.

11.29 And as anyone of the learners/pupils were being prosperous they determined/appointed each of them into/for a service/table ministry to send to the brothers dwelling in Judea; 11.30 which indeed they did, having sent *it* to the elders through *the* hand of Barnabas and Saul.

12.1 But at that time, the king Herod laid the hands on some of those from the assembly to treat *them* badly. 12.2 And he killed James the brother of John with a sword. 12.3 And having seen that it is pleas-ing to the Judeans he added *it* to seize Peter also (and *the* days were of the unleavened *bread*), 12.4 whom having arrested also, he was put in prison, having delivered *him* to four squads of four soldiers to guard him, planning to bring him up to the people after the Passover. 12.5 Therefore Peter was indeed being kept in the prison; but prayer was becoming/hap-pening constantly to God from the assembly concerning him.

12.6 ὅτε δὲ ἤμελλεν προσαγεῖν αὐτὸν ὁ Ἡρώδης, τῇ νυκτὶ ἐκείνῃ ἦν ὁ Πέτρος κοιμώμενος μεταξὺ δύο στρατιωτῶν δεδεμένος ἁλύσεσιν δυσίν, φύλακές τε πρὸ τῆς θύρας ἐτήρουν τὴν φυλακήν. 12.7 καὶ ἰδοὺ ἄγγελος κυρίου ἐπέστη, καὶ φῶς ἔλαμψεν ἐν τῷ οἰκήματι· πατάξας δὲ τὴν πλευρὰν τοῦ Πέτρου ἤγειρεν αὐτὸν λέγων, ἀνάστα ἐν τάχει. καὶ ἐξέπεσαν αὐτοῦ αἱ ἁλύσεις ἐκ τῶν χειρῶν. 12.8 εἶπεν τὲ ὁ ἄγγελος πρὸς αὐτόν, ζῶσαι καὶ ὑπόδησαι τὰ σανδάλιά σου. ἐποίησεν δὲ οὕτως. καὶ λέγι αὐτῷ, περιβαλοῦ τὸ ἱμάτιόν σου καὶ ἀκολούθι μοι. 12.9 καὶ ἐξελθὼν ἠκολούθι, καὶ οὐκ ᾔδι ὅτι ἀληθές ἐστι τὸ γινόμενον διὰ τοῦ ἀγγέλου, ἐδόκι δὲ ὅραμα βλέπιν. 12.10 διελθόντες δὲ πρώτην φυλακὴν καὶ δευτέραν ἦλθαν ἐπὶ τὴν πύλην τὴν σιδηρᾶν τὴν φέρουσαν εἰς τὴν πόλιν, ἥτις αὐτομάτη ἠνύγη αὐτοῖς, καὶ ἐξελθόντες προῆλθον ῥύμην μίαν, καὶ εὐθέως ἀπέστη ὁ ἄγγελος ἀπ᾽ αὐτοῦ. 12.11 καὶ ὁ Πέτρος ἐν ἑαυτῷ γενόμενος εἶπεν, νῦν οἶδα ἀληθῶς ὅτι ἐξαπέστιλεν κύριος τὸν ἄγγελον αὐτοῦ καὶ ἐξείλατό με ἐκ χειρὸς Ἡρώδου καὶ πάσης τῆς προσδοκίας τοῦ λαοῦ τῶν Ἰουδαίων. 12.12 συνιδών τε ἦλθεν ἐπὶ τὴν οἰκίαν τῆς Μαρίας τῆς μητρὸς Ἰωάννου τοῦ ἐπικαλουμένου Μάρκου, οὗ ἦσαν ἱκανοὶ συνηθροισμένοι καὶ προσευχόμενοι. 12.13 κρούσαντος δὲ αὐτοῦ τὴν θύραν τοῦ πυλῶνος προσῆλθε παιδίσκη ὑπακοῦσαι ὀνόματι Ῥόδη· 12.14 καὶ ἐπιγνοῦσα τὴν φωνὴν τοῦ Πέτρου ἀπὸ τῆς χαρᾶς οὐκ ἤνυξε τὸν πυλῶνα, εἰσδραμοῦσα δὲ ἀπήγγιλεν ἑστάναι τὸν Πέτρον πρὸ τοῦ πυλῶνος. 12.15 οἱ δὲ πρὸς αὐτὴν εἶπαν, μαίνῃ. ἡ δὲ διϊσχυρίζετο οὕτως ἔχειν. οἱ δὲ ἔλεγον, ὁ ἄγγελός ἐστιν αὐτοῦ. 12.16 ὁ δὲ Πέτρος ἐπέμενε κρούων· ἀνοίξαντες δὲ εἶδον αὐτὸν καὶ ἐξέστησαν. 12.17 κατασίσας δὲ αὐτοῖς τῇ χιρὶ σιγᾶν διηγήσατο πῶς ὁ κύριος αὐτὸν ἐξήγαγεν ἐκ τῆς φυλακῆς, εἶπέν τε, ἀπαγγίλατε Ἰακώβῳ καὶ τοῖς ἀδελφοῖς

12.6   But when Herod was about to bring him forward, in that night Peter was sleeping between two soldiers, having been bound with two chains, and guards before the door were keeping the prison.   12.7 And behold, a messenger/angel from *the* Lord stood by *him*, and a light shone in the building; and having struck Peter's side, he awakened/raised him, saying: Rise up with speed/haste. And the chains fell off from the hands   12.8 And the messenger/angel said to him: Gird yourself and tie on your sandals. And then he did. And he says to him: Put on your garment/cloak and follow with me.   12.9 And having gone forth, he was following, and he knew not that the (thing) happening through the messenger/angel is true, but he was supposing to see a vision.   12.10 But having gone past/ through *the* first and second prison/guard, they came to the iron gate leading to the city, which was opened automatically for them, and having gone out they went forward one street, and the messenger/angel immediately departed from him.   12.11 And Peter, having become in himself, said: Now I know truly that *the* Lord sent forth his messenger/angel and himself took me out from *the* hand of Herod and from every expectation of the people of the Judeans.   12.12 And having understood, he went to the house of Mary the mother of John, the (one) being called Mark, where considerable (ones) had been gathered together and praying.   12.13 And from him having knocked, a maidservant, Rhoda by name, approached the door of the vestibule/gate to listen;   12.14 and having recognized Peter's voice, from the joy she opened not the gate/vestibule, but having run in, she announced/reported *for* Peter to have stood before the gate.   12.15 But the (they) said to her: You are mad. But the (she) was insisting to have *it* so. And they were saying: It is the messenger/angel of/from him.   12.16 But Peter was continuing knocking; and having opened *up* they were seeing him and they were amazed.   12.17 And having motioned to them with the hand to be quiet, he related/narrated how the Lord brought him forth out of the prison, and he said: Report/announce ye these (things) to James and the brothers. And having gone out he was gone to

ταῦτα. καὶ ἐξελθὼν ἐπορεύθη εἰς ἕτερον τόπον.

12.18 Γενομένης δὲ ἡμέρας ἦν τάραχος οὐχ ὀλίγος ἐν τοῖς στρατιώταις, τί ἄρα ὁ Πέτρος ἐγένετο. 12.19 Ἡρῴδης δὲ ἐπιζητήσας αὐτὸν καὶ μὴ εὑρὼν ἀνακρίνας τοὺς φύλακας ἐκέλευσεν ἀπαχθῆναι, καὶ κατελθὼν ἀπὸ τῆς Ἰουδαίας εἰς Καισάριαν διέτριβεν. 12.20 ἦν δὲ θυμομαχῶν Τυρίοις καὶ Σιδωνίοις· ὁμοθυμαδὸν δὲ παρῆσαν πρὸς αὐτόν, καὶ πίσαντες Βλάστον τὸν ἐπὶ τοῦ κοιτῶνος τοῦ βασιλέως ᾐτοῦντο εἰρήνην, διὰ τὸ τρέφεσθαι αὐτῶν τὴν χώραν ἀπὸ τῆς βασιλικῆς. 12.21 τακτῇ δὲ ἡμέρᾳ ὁ Ἡρῴδης ἐνδυσάμενος αἰσθῆτα βασιλικὴν καθίσας ἐπὶ τοῦ βήματος ἐδημηγόρει πρὸς αὐτούς· 12.22 ὁ δὲ δῆμος ἐπεφώνει, θεοῦ φωνὴ καὶ οὐκ ἀνθρώπου. 12.23 παραχρῆμα δὲ ἐπάταξεν αὐτὸν ἄγγελος κυρίου ἀνθ' ὧν οὐκ ἔδωκε τὴν δόξαν τῷ θεῷ, καὶ γενόμενος σκωληκόβρωτος ἐξέψυξεν.

12.24 ὁ δὲ λόγος τοῦ θεοῦ ηὔξανεν καὶ ἐπληθύνετο. 12.25 Βαρναβᾶς δὲ καὶ Σαῦλος ὑπέστρεψαν εἰς Ἰερουσαλὴμ πληρώσαντες τὴν διακονίαν, συνπαραλαβόντες Ἰωάννην τὸν ἐπικαλούμενον Μᾶρκον. 13.1 ἦσαν δὲ ἐν Ἀντιοχᾳ κατὰ τὴν οὖσαν ἐκκλησίαν προφῆται καὶ διδάσκαλοι ὅ τε Βαρναβᾶς καὶ Συμεὼν ὁ καλούμενος Νίγερ, καὶ Λούκιος ὁ Κυρηναῖος, Μαναήν τε Ἡρῴδου τοῦ τετραάρχου σύντροφος καὶ Σαῦλος.

13.2 λειτουργούντων δὲ αὐτῶν τῷ κυρίῳ καὶ νηστευόντων εἶπεν τὸ πνεῦμα τὸ ἅγιον, ἀφορίσατε δή μοι τὸν Βαρναβᾶν καὶ τὸν Σαῦλον εἰς τὸ ἔργον ὃ προσκέκλημαι αὐτούς. 13.3 τότε νηστεύσαντες καὶ προσευξάμενοι καὶ ἐπιθέντες τὰς χῖρας αὐτοῖς ἀπέλυσαν.

13.4 αὐτοὶ μὲν οὖν ἐκπεμφθέντες ὑπὸ τοῦ ἁγίου πνεύματος κατῆλθον εἰς Σελεύκιαν, ἐκεῖθέν τε ἀπέπλευσαν εἰς Κύπρον, 13.5 καὶ γενόμενοι ἐν Σαλαμῖνῃ κατήγγελλον τὸν λόγον τοῦ θεοῦ ἐν ταῖς συναγωγαῖς τῶν Ἰουδαίων· εἶχον δὲ καὶ Ἰωάννην ὑπηρέτην.

another/different place.

12.18 And from day having become, there was not a little consternation among the soldiers, what Peter then/indeed became. 12.19 But Herod, having searched for him and not having found *him*, having examined the guards, he ordered *them* to be led away, and having gone down from Judea to Caesarea, he was staying *there*. 12.20 And he was being very angry with Tyrians and Sidonians; and of one accord they were present to/near him, and having persuaded Blastus, the (one) over the king's bed chamber, they were asking peace, because of the (thing) for their country to be fed/ sustained from the royalty. 12.21 And on the appointed day Herod, having been dressed *with* royal clothing, having sat upon the tribunal/judgment seat, he was delivering a public address to them; 12.22 and the populace was crying out: A voice of a god and not of a man. 12.23 But immediately a messenger/angel from *the* Lord smote him because he gave not the fame/glory to God, and having become eaten by worms, he breathed his last/expired.

12.24 And the saying/word of God was increasing and being multiplied. 12.25 But Barnabas and Saul returned to Jerusalem, having completed the service/ ministry, having taken along John, the (one) also being called Mark. 13.1 And there were prophets and teachers according to the assembly being in Antioch, including Barnabas and Simeon, the one being called Niger, and Lucius the Cyrenian and Manaen, a foster brother of Herod the tetrarch, and Saul.

13.2 And from them serving publicly/doing the liturgy for the Lord and fasting, the holy spirit said: Now separate/appoint ye for me Barnabas and Saul to the work which I have called them. 13.3 Then, having fasted and prayed, and having laid the hands on them, they released/dismissed (them).

13.4 Then these, having indeed been sent out by the holy spirit, went down to Seleucia, and they sailed away from there to Cyprus, 13.5 and having become in Salamis, they were proclaiming the saying/ word of God in the congregations of the Judeans; and they were also having John, an assistant.

13.6 διελθόντες δὲ ὅλην τὴν νῆσον ἄχρι Πάφου εὗρον ἄνδρα τινὰ μάγον ψευδοπροφήτην Ἰουδαῖον ᾧ ὄνομα Βαριησοῦ, 13.7 ὃς ἦν σὺν τῷ ἀνθυπάτῳ Σεργίῳ Παύλῳ, ἀνδρὶ συνετῷ. οὗτος προσκαλεσάμενος Βαρναβᾶν καὶ Σαῦλον ἐπεζήτησεν ἀκοῦσαι τὸν λόγον τοῦ θεοῦ· 13.8 ἀνθίστατο δὲ αὐτοῖς Ἐλύμας ὁ μάγος, οὕτως γὰρ μεθερμηνεύεται τὸ ὄνομα αὐτοῦ, ζητῶν διαστρέψαι τὸν ἀνθύπατον ἀπὸ τῆς πίστεως. 13.9 Σαῦλος δέ, ὁ καὶ Παῦλος, πλησθεὶς πνεύματος ἁγίου ἀτενίσας εἰς αὐτὸν 13.10 εἶπεν, ὦ πλήρης παντὸς δόλου καὶ πάσης ῥᾳδιουργίας, υἱὲ διαβόλου, ἐχθρὲ πάσης δικαιοσύνης, οὐ παύσῃ διαστρέφων τὰς ὁδοὺς τοῦ κυρίου τὰς εὐθίας; 13.11 καὶ νῦν ἰδοὺ χὶρ κυρίου ἐπὶ σέ, καὶ ἔσῃ τυφλὸς μὴ βλέπων τὸν ἥλιον ἄχρι καιροῦ. παραχρῆμά τε ἔπεσεν ἐπ' αὐτὸν ἀχλὺς καὶ σκότος, καὶ περιάγων ἐζήτι χιραγωγούς. 13.12 τότε ἰδὼν ὁ ἀνθύπατος τὸ γεγονὸς ἐπίστευσεν ἐκπλησσόμενος ἐπὶ τῇ διδαχῇ τοῦ κυρίου. 13.13 ἀναχθέντες δὲ ἀπὸ τῆς Πάφου οἱ περὶ Παῦλον ἦλθον εἰς Πέργην τῆς Παμφυλίας· Ἰωάννης δὲ ἀποχωρήσας ἀπ' αὐτῶν ὑπέστρεψεν εἰς Ἱεροσόλυμα.

13.14 αὐτοὶ δὲ διελθόντες ἀπὸ τῆς Πέργης παρεγένοντο εἰς Ἀντιόχειαν τὴν Πισιδίαν, καὶ ἐλθόντες εἰς τὴν συναγωγὴν τῇ ἡμέρᾳ τῶν σαββάτων ἐκάθισαν.

13.15 μετὰ δὲ τὴν ἀνάγνωσιν τοῦ νόμου καὶ τῶν προφητῶν ἀπέστιλαν οἱ ἀρχισυνάγωγοι πρὸς αὐτοὺς λέγοντες, ἄνδρες ἀδελφοί, εἴ τίς ἐστιν ἐν ὑμῖν λόγος παρακλήσεως πρὸς τὸν λαόν, λέγετε. 13.16 ἀναστὰς δὲ Παῦλος καὶ κατασίσας τῇ χειρὶ εἶπεν·

ἄνδρες Ἰσδραηλῖται καὶ οἱ φοβούμενοι τὸν θεόν, ἀκούσατε. 13.17 ὁ θεὸς τοῦ λαοῦ τούτου Ἰσραὴλ ἐξελέξατο τοὺς πατέρας ἡμῶν, καὶ τὸν λαὸν ὕψωσεν ἐν τῇ παροικίᾳ ἐν γῇ Αἰγύπτου, καὶ μετὰ βραχείονος ὑψηλοῦ ἐξήγαγεν αὐτοὺς ἐξ αὐτῆς, 13.18 καὶ ὡς τεσσερακονταετῆ χρόνον ἐτροποφόρησεν

13.6 And having gone through the entire island until Paphos they found a man, a certain wise man/magician, a Judean false prophet, for whom *was* a name of Barjesus, 13.7 who was with the proconsul Sergius Paulus, an intelligent man. This (one), having called to Barnabas and Saul, sought/wished to hear the reason/saying/word of God; 13.8 But Elymas the magician/wise man was being opposed to them, for so is his name interpreted/translated, seeking to pervert/mislead the proconsul from the faith. 13.9 But Saul, the (one) also *being* Paul, having been filled from/of a holy spirit, having gazed into him, 13.10 said: O (one) full of every deceit and every crime/villainy, son of a devil, enemy of every justice/justness, will you not stop perverting/distorting the straight roads/ways of the Lord? 13.11 And now behold, *the* hand of *the* Lord *is* upon you, and you will be blind, not seeing the sun, until a season/time. And immediately a mistiness and darkness fell upon/over him, and leading around/going about he was seeking hand-leaders. 13.12 Then the proconsul, having seen the (thing) having happened, believed, being astonished/amazed at the teaching/doctrine of the Lord. 13.13 And having set sail from Paphos, the (those) around Paul went to Perga of Pamphylia; and John, having departed/withdrew from them, returned to Jerusalem.

13.14 And they, having gone through from Perga, arrived in Antioch, the Pisidian (one), and having gone into the congregation/synagogue on the day of the sabbaths, they sat down.

13.15 And after the reading from the law and the prophets, the congregation leaders sent to them, saying: Men, brothers, if there is anyone among ye *having* a saying/word of exhortation to the people, ye speak. 13.16 And Paul, having risen up and motioned with the hand, he said:

Men, Israelites and those fearing God, hear ye. 13.17 The God of this people Israel himself chose our fathers, and he exalted the people in the stay/sojourn in *the* land of Egypt, and with a high arm he led them forth out of her, 13.18 and he endured/put up with them *for* about forty years time in the desert/wilder-

αὐτοὺς ἐν τῇ ἐρήμῳ, 13.19 καὶ καθελὼν ἔθνη ἑπτὰ ἐν γῇ Χανάαν κατεκληρονόμησεν τὴν γῆν αὐτῶν 13.20 ὡς ἔτεσι τετρακοσίοις καὶ πεντήκοντα. καὶ μετὰ ταῦτα ἔδωκεν κριτὰς ἕως Σαμουὴλ προφήτου. 13.21 κἀκεῖθεν ᾐτήσαντο βασιλέα, καὶ ἔδωκεν αὐτοῖς ὁ θεὸς τὸν Σαοὺλ υἱὸν Κείς, ἄνδρα ἐκ φυλῆς Βενιαμείν, ἔτη τεσσεράκοντα. 13.22 καὶ μεταστήσας αὐτὸν ἤγειρεν τὸν Δαυὶδ αὐτοῖς εἰς βασιλέα, ᾧ καὶ εἶπεν μαρτυρήσας, «εὗρον Δαυὶδ» τὸν τοῦ Ἰεσσαί, «ἄνδρα κατὰ τὴν καρδίαν μου,» ὃς ποιήσει πάντα τὰ θελήματά μου. 13.23 τούτου ὁ θεὸς ἀπὸ τοῦ σπέρματος κατ᾽ ἐπαγγελίαν ἤγαγεν τῷ Ἰσραὴλ σωτῆρα Ἰησοῦν, 13.24 προκηρύξαντος Ἰωάννου πρὸ προσώπου τῆς εἰσόδου αὐτοῦ βάπτισμα μετανοίας παντὶ τῷ λαῷ Ἰσραήλ.

13.25 ὡς δὲ ἐπλήρου Ἰωάννης τὸν δρόμον, ἔλεγεν, τί ἐμὲ ὑπονοεῖται εἶναι; οὐκ εἰμὶ ἐγώ· ἀλλ᾽ εἰδοὺ ἔρχετε μετ᾽ ἐμὲ οὗ οὐκ εἰμὶ ἄξιος τὸ ὑπόδημα τῶν ποδῶν λῦσε. 13.26 ἄνδρες ἀδελφοί, υἱοὶ γένους Ἀβραὰμ καὶ οἱ ἐν ὑμῖν φοβούμενοι τὸν θεόν, ἡμῖν ὁ λόγος τῆς σωτηρίας ταύτης ἐξαπεστάλη. 13.27 οἱ γὰρ κατοικοῦντες ἐν Ἰερουσαλὴμ καὶ οἱ ἄρχοντες αὐτῶν τοῦτον ἀγνοήσαντες καὶ τὰς φωνὰς τῶν προφητῶν τὰς κατὰ πᾶν σάββατον ἀναγινωσκομένας κρίναντες ἐπλήρωσαν, 13.28 καὶ μηδεμίαν αἰτίαν θανάτου εὑρόντες ᾐτήσαντο Πιλᾶτον ἀναιρεθῆναι αὐτόν· 13.29 ὡς δὲ ἐτέλεσαν πάντα τὰ περὶ αὐτοῦ γεγραμμένα, καθελόντες ἀπὸ τοῦ ξύλου ἔθηκαν εἰς μνημεῖον. 13.30 ὁ δὲ θεὸς ἤγειρεν αὐτὸν ἐκ νεκρῶν· 13.31 ὃς ὤφθη ἐπὶ ἡμέρας πλίους τοῖς συναναβᾶσιν αὐτῷ ἀπὸ τῆς Γαλιλαίας εἰς Ἰερουσαλήμ, οἵτινες εἰσιν νῦν μάρτυρες αὐτοῦ πρὸς τὸν λαόν. 13.32 καὶ ἡμεῖς ὑμᾶς εὐαγγελιζόμεθα τὴν πρὸς τοὺς πατέρας ἐπαγγελίαν γενομένην, 13.33 ὅτι ταύτην ὁ θεὸς ἐκπεπλήρωκεν τοῖς τέκνοις ἡμῶν ἀναστήσας Ἰησοῦν, ὡς καὶ ἐν τῷ ψαλμῷ γέγραπται τῷ δευτέρῳ, «υἱός μου εἶ σύ, ἐγὼ σήμερον γεγέννηκά σε.» 13.34 ὅτι δὲ ἀνέστησεν αὐτὸν ἐκ νεκρῶν μηκέτι μέλλοντα ὑποστρέφιν εἰς διαφθοράν, οὕτως εἴρηκεν ὅτι δώσω «ὑμῖν τὰ

ness, 13.19 and having overthrown seven ethnics/nations in *the* land of Canaan, he gave as an inheritance the land of them, 13.20 about four hundreds and fifty years. And after these (things) he gave judges until Samuel a prophet. 13.21 And from there (him) they asked *for* a king, and God gave Saul, a son of Cis, to them, a man out of *the* tribe of Benjamin, *for* forty years. 13.22 And having removed him, he raised up David into a king for them, to whom he said, having witnessed: I FOUND DAVID the (one) of Jesse, A MAN ACCORDING TO MY HEART, who will do all my wants/wishes. 13.23 From the seed of this (one) God brought a savior, Jesus, according to the promise, 13.24 from John having heralded/preached, before the coming of his face, a baptism of repentance for all the people of Israel.

13.25 And when John was completed the course, he was saying: What do ye suppose to be? I, I am not; but behold, one comes after me, of whom I am not worthy to loose the sandals from the feet. 13.26 Men, brothers, sons of *the* race of Abraham and the (ones) among ye fearing God, the saying word of this salvation was sent forth to us. 13.27 For the (those) dwelling in Jerusalem and their leaders/rulers, having not known this (one) and the voices of the prophets being read throughout every sabbath, they fulfilled *them* having judged *him*, 13.28 and having found no reason/cause of death, they asked Pilate *for* him to be killed; 13.29 and as they finished/completed all the (things) having been written concerning him, having taken *him* down from the tree/wood, they placed *him* in a tomb. 13.30 But God raised him out of dead (ones); 13.31 who was manifested/made visible over many days to those having come up with him from Galilee to Jerusalem, who are now his witnesses to the people. 13.32 And we ourselves announce/preach *for* ye the promise having become to the fathers, 13.33 because God has fulfilled *it* to/for our children, having raised Jesus up, as it has also been written in the second psalm: YOU, YOU ARE MY SON; I, I HAVE GENERATED YOU TODAY. 13.34 And because he raised him up out of dead (ones), no longer being about to return in corruption/decaying, thus he

ὅσια Δαυὶδ τὰ πιστά.» 13.35 διότι καὶ ἐν ἑτέρῳ λέγει, «οὐ δώσεις τὸν ὅσιόν σου εἰδῖν διαφθοράν.» 13.36 Δαυὶδ μὲν γὰρ ἰδίᾳ γενεᾷ ὑπηρετήσας τῇ τοῦ θεοῦ βουλῇ ἐκοιμήθη καὶ προσετέθη πρὸς τοὺς πατέρας αὐτοῦ καὶ εἶδεν διαφθοράν, 13.37 ὃν δὲ ὁ θεὸς ἤγειρεν οὐκ εἶδεν διαφθοράν.

13.38 γνωστὸν οὖν ὑμῖν ἔστω, ἄνδρες ἀδελφοί, ὅτι διὰ τούτου ὑμῖν ἄφεσις ἁμαρτιῶν καταγγέλλεται, ἀπὸ πάντων ὧν οὐκ ἠδυνήθητε ἐν νόμῳ Μωϋσέως δικαιωθῆναι 13.39 ἐν τούτῳ πᾶς ὁ πιστεύων δικαιοῦται.

13.40 βλέπετε οὖν μὴ ἐπέλθῃ τὸ εἰρημένον ἐν τοῖς προφήταις, 13.41 «εἴδετε, οἱ καταφρονηταί, καὶ θαυμάσετε καὶ ἀφανίσθητε, ὅτι ἔργον ὃ ἐγὼ ἐργάζομε ἐγὼ ἐν ταῖς ἡμέραις ὑμῶν,» ἔργον «ὃ οὐ μὴ πιστεύσηται ἐάν τις ἐκδιηγῆται ὑμῖν.» 13.42 Ἐξιόντων δὲ αὐτῶν παρεκάλουν εἰς τὸ μεταξὺ σάββατον λαληθῆναι αὐτοῖς τὰ ῥήματα ταῦτα.

13.43 λυθίσης δὲ τῆς συναγωγῆς ἠκολούθησαν πολλοὶ τῶν Ἰουδαίων καὶ τῶν σεβομένων προσηλύτων τῷ Παύλῳ καὶ τῷ Βαρναβᾷ, οἵτινες προσλαλοῦντες αὐτοῖς ἔπιθον αὐτοὺς προσμένιν τῇ χάριτι τοῦ θεοῦ. 13.44 τῷ δὲ ἐρχομένῳ σαββάτῳ σχεδὸν πᾶσα ἡ πόλις συνήχθη ἀκοῦσαι τὸν λόγον τοῦ κυρίου. 13.45 ἰδόντες δὲ οἱ Ἰουδαῖοι τοὺς ὄχλους ἐπλήσθησαν ζήλου καὶ ἀντέλεγον τοῖς ὑπὸ Παύλου λαλουμένοις βλασφημοῦντες.

13.46 παρρησιασάμενοί τε ὁ Παῦλος καὶ ὁ Βαρναβᾶς εἶπαν, ὑμῖν ἦν ἀναγκαῖον πρῶτον λαληθῆναι τὸν λόγον τοῦ θεοῦ· ἐπειδὴ ἀπωθῖσθαι αὐτὸν καὶ οὐκ ἀξίους κρίνεται ἑαυτοὺς τῆς αἰωνίου ζωῆς, ἰδοὺ στρεφόμεθα εἰς τὰ ἔθνη. 13.47 οὕτω γὰρ ἐντέταλται ἡμῖν ὁ κύριος, «τέθικά σαι εἰς φῶς ἐθνῶν τοῦ εἶναί σε εἰς σωτηρίαν ἕως ἐσχάτου τῆς γῆς.»

has said: I SHALL GIVE TO YE THE SACRED (THINGS), THE FAITHFUL (THINGS) OF DAVID. 13.35 Because he also says in another/different: YOU WILL NOT GIVE THE SACRED (ONE) TO SEE DECAY/CORRUPTION. 13.36 For David, having indeed served in his own generation for the purpose/will of God, fell asleep and was added to his fathers and he saw decaying/corruption. 13.37 But *the one* whom God raised saw not decaying/corruption.

13.38 Therefore, let it be known to ye, men, brothers, that remission/forgiveness of sins/faults through this (one) is proclaimed to ye, from all (things) from which ye were not able to be justified by a law of Moses, 13.39 every one believing is justified by this (one).

13.40 See ye/be careful therefore lest the (thing) having been spoken by the prophets might come upon *ye*, 13.41 SEE/BEHOLD YE, THE SCOFFERS/DESPISERS, AND MARVEL YE AND DISAPPEAR, BECAUSE I, I WORK A WORK WHICH I *have* IN YOUR DAYS, a work WHICH YE BY NO MEANS MIGHT BELIEVE IF SOMEONE RELATES IT IN DETAIL TO YE. 13.42 And from them going out they were exhorting to/for the (thing) for these words to be spoken to them between the sabbath.

13.43 And from the congregation having been loosed many of the Judeans and the pious/reverent proselytes/converts followed with Paul and Barnabas, who speaking beforehand to them were persuading them to continue in the grace/favor of God. 13.44 And on the coming sabbath, almost all the city was gathered to hear the reason/saying/word of the Lord. 13.45 But the Judeans, having seen the crowds, were filled up from jealousy and were speaking against the (things) being spoken by Paul, slandering/blaspheming.

13.46 And having themselves spoken boldly, Paul and Barnabas said: It was first necessary for the saying/word of God to be spoken to ye; since ye reject him and judge yourselves not worthy of the eternal life, behold we are turned to the ethnics. 13.47. For thus the Lord himself commanded to us: I HAVE PLACED YOU INTO/FOR A LIGHT OF ETHNICS, FROM THE (THING) *for* YOU TO BE INTO/FOR DELIVERANCE/SALVATION UNTIL *the* LAST (PART) OF THE LAND/EARTH.

13.48 ἀκούοντα δὲ τὰ ἔθνη ἔχαιρον καὶ ἐδόξαζον τὸν λόγον τοῦ κυρίου, καὶ ἐπίστευσαν ὅσοι ἦσαν τεταγμένοι εἰς ζωὴν αἰώνιον·

13.49 διεφέρετο δὲ ὁ λόγος τοῦ κυρίου καθ᾽ ὅλης τῆς χώρας. 13.50 οἱ δὲ Ἰουδαῖοι παρώτρυναν τὰς σεβομένας γυναῖκας τὰς εὐσχήμονας καὶ τοὺς πρώτους τῆς πόλεως καὶ ἐπήγιραν διωγμὸν ἐπὶ τὸν Παῦλον καὶ Βαρναβᾶν, καὶ ἐξέβαλον αὐτοὺς ἀπὸ τῶν ὁρίων αὐτῶν.

13.51 οἱ δὲ ἐκτιναξάμενοι τὸν κονιορτὸν τῶν ποδῶν ἐπ᾽ αὐτοὺς ἦλθον εἰς Ἰκόνιον, 13.52 οἱ δὲ μαθηταὶ ἐπληροῦντο χαρᾶς καὶ πνεύματος ἁγίου.

14.1 Ἐγένετο δὲ ἐν Εἰκονίῳ κατὰ τὸ αὐτὸ εἰσελθεῖν αὐτοὺς εἰς τὴν συναγωγὴν τῶν Ἰουδαίων καὶ λαλῆσαι οὕτως ὥστε πιστεῦσαι Ἰουδαίων τε καὶ Ἑλλήνων πολὺ πλῆθος. 14.2 οἱ δὲ ἀπιθήσαντες Ἰουδαῖοι ἐπήγιραν καὶ ἐκάκωσαν τὰς ψυχὰς τῶν ἐθνῶν κατὰ τῶν ἀδελφῶν.

14.3 ἱκανὸν μὲν οὖν χρόνον διέτριψαν παρρησιαζόμενοι ἐπὶ τῷ κυρίῳ τῷ μαρτυροῦντι ἐπὶ τῷ λόγῳ τῆς χάριτος αὐτοῦ, διδόντος σημῖα καὶ τέρατα γείνεσθαι διὰ τῶν χιρῶν αὐτῶν. 14.4 ἐσχίσθη δὲ τὸ πλῆθος τῆς πόλεως, καὶ οἱ μὲν ἦσαν σὺν τοῖς Ἰουδαίοις οἱ δὲ σὺν τοῖς ἀποστόλοις. 14.5 ὡς δὲ ἐγένετο ὁρμὴ τῶν ἐθνῶν τε καὶ Ἰουδαίων σὺν τοῖς ἄρχουσιν αὐτῶν ὑβρίσαι καὶ λιθοβολῆσαι αὐτούς, 14.6 συνιδόντες κατέφυγον εἰς τὰς πόλεις τῆς Λυκαονίας Λύστραν καὶ Δέρβην καὶ τὴν περίχωρον, 14.7 κἀκεῖ εὐαγγελιζόμενοι ἦσαν. 14.8 καί τις ἀνὴρ ἀδύνατος ἐν Λύστροις τοῖς ποσὶν ἐκάθητο, χωλὸς ἐκ κοιλίας μητρὸς αὐτοῦ, ὃς οὐδέποτε περιεπάτησεν. 14.9 οὗτος οὐκ ἤκουσεν τοῦ Παύλου λαλοῦντος· ὃς ἀτενίσας αὐτῷ καὶ ἰδὼν ὅτι ἔχει πίστιν τοῦ σωθῆναι 14.10 εἶπεν μεγάλῃ φωνῇ, ἀνάστηθι ἐπὶ τοὺς πόδας σου ὀρθός. καὶ ἥλατο καὶ περιεπάτει. 14.11 οἵ τε ὄχλοι εἰδόντες ὃ ἐποίησεν Παῦλος ἐπῆραν τὴν φωνὴν αὐτῶν Λυκαονιστὶ λέγοντες,

13.48 And hearing, the ethnics were rejoicing and glorifying the saying/word of the Lord, and as many as had been appointed/disposed into/for life eternal believed;

13.49 And the saying/word of the Lord was being carried throughout the whole country. 13.50 But the Judeans incited the reverent women, the prominent (ones) and the first (men) of the city and raised up a prosecution/persecution against Paul and Barnabas, and they threw them out from their borders.

13.51 But the (they) having shaken off the dust from the feet against them, they went to Iconium, 13.52 and the learners/pupils were filled from/of joy and a holy spirit.

14.1 And it happened in Iconium by the thing *for* them to enter into the congregation of the Judeans and to speak thus so as *for* a much multitude to believe, both of Judeans and of Greeks. 14.2 But the Judeans having disbelieved incited/aroused and embittered the souls/lives of the ethnics against the brothers.

14.3 Then *for* a considerable time they indeed continued speaking boldly on/for the Lord for the (thing) witnessing to/for the saying/word of his grace/favor, of giving signs and wonders to come about through their hands. 14.4 And the multitude of the city was split, and some were with the Judeans and others with the apostles. 14.5 And as there became a hostile movement, both of the ethnics and of Judeans with their leaders/rulers to mistreat/insult and to stone them, 14.6 having perceived *it*, they fled/- escaped to the cities of Lycaonia, Lystra and Derbe, and the surrounding country, 14.7 and there they were preaching the good message. 14.8 And a certain man in Lystra, *being* powerless in the feet, was sitting, lame from his mother's belly/womb, who never walked. 14.9 This (one) heard/listened not from Paul speaking; who having gazed at him and having seen that he has faith of the (thing) to be saved, 14.10 he said in a great voice: Stand upright on your feet. And he leaped up and was walking. 14.11 And the crowds, having seen what Paul did, lifted up their voice in Lycaonian,

οἱ θεοὶ ὁμοιωθέντες ἀνθρώποις κατέβησαν πρὸς ἡμᾶς· 14.12 ἐκάλουν τε τὸν Βαρναβᾶν Δία, τὸν δὲ Παῦλον Ἑρμῆν, ἐπιδὴ αὐτὸς ἦν ὁ ἡγούμενος τοῦ λόγου. 14.13 ὅ τε ἱερεὺς τοῦ Διὸς τοῦ ὄντος πρὸ τῆς πόλεως ταύρους καὶ στέμματα ἐπὶ τοὺς πυλῶνας ἐνέγκας σὺν τοῖς ὄχλοις ἤθελεν θύειν.

14.14 ἀκούσαντες δὲ οἱ ἀπόστολοι Βαρναβ καὶ Παῦλος, διαρρήξαντες τὰ ἱμάτια αὐτῶν ἐξεπήδησαν εἰς τὸν ὄχλον, κράζοντες 14.15 καὶ λέγοντες, ἄνδρες, τί ταῦτα ποιεῖτε; καὶ ἡμεῖς ὁμοιοπαθεῖς ἐσμεν ὑμῖν ἄνθρωποι, εὐαγγελιζόμενοι ὑμᾶς ἀπὸ τούτων τῶν ματαίων ἐπιστρέφιν ἐπὶ θεὸν τὸν ζῶντα ὃς ἐποίησεν τὸν οὐρανὸν καὶ τὴν γῆν καὶ τὴν θάλασσαν καὶ πάντα τὰ ἐν αὐτοῖς· 14.16 ὃς ἐν ταῖς παρῳχημέναις γενεαῖς ἴασεν πάντα τὰ ἔθνη πορεύεσθε ταῖς ὁδοῖς αὐτῶν· 14.17 καίτοι οὐκ ἀμάρτυρον αὐτὸν ἀφῆκεν ἀγαθουργῶν, οὐρανόθεν ὑμῖν διδοὺς ὑετοὺς καὶ καιροὺς καρποφόρους, ἐμπιπλῶν τροφῆς καὶ εὐφροσύνης τὰς καρδίας ὑμῶν. 14.18 καὶ ταῦτα λέγοντες μόλις κατέπαυσαν τοὺς ὄχλους τοῦ μὴ θύειν αὐτοῖς.

14.19 ἐπῆλθαν δὲ ἀπὸ Ἀντιοχίας καὶ Ἰκονίου Ἰουδαῖοι, καὶ πίσαντες τοὺς ὄχλους καὶ λιθάσαντες τὸν Παῦλον ἔσυρον ἔξω τῆς πόλεως, νομίζοντες αὐτὸν τεθνηκέναι.

14.20 κυκλωσάντων δὲ τῶν μαθητῶν αὐτὸν ἀναστὰς εἰσῆλθεν εἰς τὴν πόλιν. καὶ τῇ ἐπαύριον ἐξῆλθεν σὺν τῷ Βαρναβᾷ εἰς Δέρβην. 14.21 εὐαγγελισάμενοί τε τὴν πόλιν ἐκείνην καὶ μαθητεύσαντες ἱκανοὺς ὑπέστρεψαν εἰς τὴν Λύστραν καὶ εἰς Ἐικόνιον καὶ εἰς Ἀντιόχιαν, 14.22 ἐπιστηρίζοντες τὰς ψυχὰς τῶν μαθητῶν, παρακαλοῦντες ἐνμένιν τῇ πίστει, καὶ ὅτι διὰ πολλῶν θλίψεων δεῖ ἡμᾶς εἰσελθῖν εἰς τὴν βασιλείαν τοῦ θεοῦ. 14.23 χειροτονήσαντες δὲ αὐτοῖς κατ' ἐκκλησίαν πρεσβυτέρους προσευξάμενοι μετὰ νηστιῶν παρέθεντο αὐτοὺς τῷ κυρίῳ εἰς ὃν πεπιστεύκισαν. 14.24 καὶ διελθόντες εἰς τὴν Πισιδίαν ἦλθον εἰς τὴν Παμφυλίαν, 14.25 καὶ λαλήσαντες εἰς τὴν Πέργη τὸν λόγον

saying: The gods came down to us, having been made like men; 14.12 and they were calling Barnabas Zeus, and Paul Hermes, since he himself was the leader of the saying/word. 14.13 And the priest of Zeus, of the (one) being before the city, having brought bulls and wreaths to the gates, was wanting/wishing to sacrifice with the crowds.

14.14 But having heard, the apostles Barnabas and Paul, having torn their garments, rushed out into the crowd, crying out 14.15 and saying: Men, why do ye these (things)? We, we also are men similar to/the same as ye, announcing/proclaiming a good message *for* ye to turn from these vanities to a living God, who made the sky/heaven and the earth and the sea and all the (things) in them; 14.16 who in the generations having passed allowed all the ethnics to go in the ways/roads of themselves; 14.17 and yet he left not himself without witness/testimony doing good, from heaven giving rains and fruitful seasons for us, filling our hearts from food and good cheer. 14.18 And saying these (things) they scarcely stopped the crowds from the (thing) not to sacrifice to them.

14.19 And Judeans from Antioch and Iconium came upon (them), both having persuaded the crowds and having stoned Paul, they were dragging him outside the city, supposing *for* him to have died.

14.20 But from the learners/pupils having surrounded him, having risen up, he entered into the city. And on the morrow he went forth with Barnabas to Derbe. 14.21 And having evangelized/proclaimed the good message *in* that city, having made considerable learners/pupils, they returned to Lystra and to Iconium and to Antioch, 14.22 strengthening the souls/lives of the learners/pupils, exhorting *them* to persevere in the faith, and that it is necessary *for* us to enter into the kingdom of God through many oppressions/afflictions. 14.23 And having hand picked/appointed elders for them according to/for each assembly, having prayed with fastings, they commended them/set them apart to/for the Lord in whom they believed. 14.24 And having passed through into Pisidia they went to Pamphylia, 14.25 and having spoken

455

τοῦ κυρίου κατέβησαν εἰς Ἀττάλιαν.

14.26 κἀκεῖθεν ἀπέπλευσαν εἰς Ἀντιόχειαν, ὅθεν ἦσαν παραδεδομένοι τῇ χάριτι τοῦ θεοῦ εἰς τὸ ἔργον ὃ ἐπλήρωσαν.

14.27 παραγενόμενοι δὲ καὶ συναγαγόντες τὴν ἐκκλησίαν ἀνήγγελλον ὅσα ὁ θεὸς ἐποίησεν μετ' αὐτῶν καὶ ὅτι ἤνυξεν τοῖς ἔθνεσιν θύραν πίστεως. 14.28 διέτριβον δὲ χρόνον οὐχ ὀλίγον σὺν τοῖς μαθηταῖς.

15.1 Καί τινες κατελθόντες ἀπὸ τῆς Ἰουδαίας ἐδίδασκον τοὺς ἀδελφοὺς ὅτι ἐὰν μὴ περιτμηθῆτε τῷ ἔθνι τῷ Μωϋσέως, οὐ δύνασθαι σωθῆναι. 15.2 γενομένης δὲ στάσεως καὶ ζητήσεως οὐκ ὀλίγης τῷ Παύλῳ καὶ τῷ Βαρναβᾷ πρὸς αὐτοὺς ἔταξαν ἀναβαίνιν Παῦλον καὶ Βαρναβᾶν καί τινας ἐξ αὐτῶν ἄλλους πρὸς τοὺς ἀποστόλους καὶ πρεσβυτέρους εἰς Ἰερουσαλὴμ περὶ τοῦ ζητήματος τούτου.

15.3 οἱ μὲν οὖν προπεμφθέντες ὑπὸ τῆς ἐκκλησίας διήρχοντο τήν τε Φοινίκην καὶ Σαμάριαν ἐκδιηγούμενοι τὴν ἐπιστροφὴν τῶν ἐθνῶν, καὶ ἐποίουν χαρὰν μεγάλην πᾶσι τοῖς ἀδελφοῖς. 15.4 παραγενόμενοι δὲ εἰς Ἰερουσαλὴμ παρεδέχθησαν ὑπὸ τῆς ἐκκλησίας καὶ τῶν ἀποστόλων καὶ τῶν πρεσβυτέρων, ἀνήγγιλάν τε ὅσα ὁ θεὸς ἐποίησεν μετ' αὐτῶν. 15.5 ἐξανέστησαν δέ τινες τῶν ἀπὸ τῆς αἱρέσεως τῶν Φαρισαίων πεπιστευκότες, λέγοντες ὅτι δεῖ περιτέμνειν αὐτοὺς παραγγέλλιν τε τηρῖν τὸν νόμον Μωϋσέως.

15.6 συνήχθησαν δὲ οἱ ἀπόστολοι καὶ οἱ πρεσβύτεροι εἰδῖν περὶ τοῦ λόγου τούτου.

15.7 πολλῆς δὲ ζητήσεως γενομένης ἀναστὰς Πέτρος εἶπεν πρὸς αὐτούς, ἄνδρες ἀδελφοί, ὑμεῖς ἐπίστασθαι ὅτι ἀφ' ἡμερῶν ἀρχαίων ἐν ὑμῖν ἐξελέξατο ὁ θεὸς διὰ τοῦ στόματός μου ἀκοῦσαι τὰ ἔθνη τὸν λόγον τοῦ εὐαγγελίου καὶ πιστεῦσαι· 15.8 καὶ ὁ καρδιογνώστης θεὸς ἐμαρτύρησεν αὐτοῖς δοὺς τὸ πνεῦμα τὸ ἅγιον καθὼς καὶ ἡμῖν, 15.9 καὶ οὐθὲν διέκρινεν μεταξὺ ἡμῶν

the word/saying of the Lord in Perga, they went down to Attalia.

14.26 And from there they set sail to Antioch, from where they had been commended/set apart by the grace/gift of God into/for the work which they accomplished.

14.27 And having arrived and having gathered the assembly they were reporting what things God did with them and that he opened a door of faith for the ethnics. 14.28 And they were staying not a little time with the learners/pupils.

15.1 And some, having come down from Judea were teaching the brothers: Unless ye might be circumcised by the custom of Moses, ye are not able to be saved. 15.2 And from not a little strife and debate having happened for/to Paul and Barnabas near/with them, they arranged for Paul and Barnabas and some out of them to go up to the apostles and elders in Jerusalem concerning this question/issue.

15.3 Then the (they), indeed having been sent forward by the assembly, were going through both Phoenicia and Samaria relating in detail the conversion of the ethnics, and they were making a great joy for all the brothers. 15.4 And having arrived in Jerusalem, they were welcomed by the assembly and the apostles and the elders, and they reported what things God did with them. 15.5 But some of those having believed from the sect of the Pharisees stood up/out, saying: It is necessary to circumcise them and to charge/command them to keep the law of Moses.

15.6 And the apostles and the elders were gathered to see about this saying/word.

15.7 And from much discussion having happened, having risen up, Peter said to them: Men, brothers, ye yourselves understand that from days of old among ye God chose for the ethnics to hear the saying/word of the good message/gospel from my mouth and to believe; 15.8 and God, the (one) knowing hearts, testified/witnessed, having given the holy spirit to them even as to us, 15.9 and he distinguished nothing between both us and them, having cleansed their hearts for the

τε καὶ αὐτῶν, τῇ πίστι καθαρίσας τὰς καρδίας αὐτῶν. 15.10 νῦν οὖν τί πιράζετε τὸν θεόν, ἐπιθεῖναι ἐπὶ τὸν τράχηλον τῶν μαθητῶν ὃν οὔτε οἱ πατέρες ἡμῶν οὔτε ἡμῖς ἰσχύσαμεν βαστάσαι; 15.11 ἀλλὰ διὰ τῆς χάριτος τοῦ κυρίου Ἰησοῦ πιστεύομεν σωθῆναι καθ᾽ ὃν τρόπον κἀκεῖνοι.

15.12 ἐσίγησεν δὲ πᾶν τὸ πλῆθος, καὶ ἤκουον Βαρναβᾶ καὶ Παύλου ἐξηγουμένων ὅσα ἐποίησεν ὁ θεὸς σημῖα καὶ τέρατα ἐν τοῖς ἔθνεσιν δι᾽ αὐτῶν. 15.13 μετὰ δὲ τὸ σιγῆσαι αὐτοὺς ἀπεκρίθη Ἰάκωβος λέγων, ἄνδρες ἀδελφοί, ἀκούσαταί μου. 15.14 Συμεὼν ἐξηγήσατο καθὼς πρῶτον ὁ θεὸς ἐπεσκέψατο λαβῖν ἐξ ἐθνῶν λαὸν τῷ ὀνόματι αὐτοῦ. 15.15 καὶ τούτῳ συμφωνοῦσιν οἱ λόγοι τῶν προφητῶν, καθὼς γέγραπται, 15.16 «μετὰ ταῦτα ἀναστρέψω καὶ ἀνοικοδομήσω τὴν σκηνὴν Δαυὶδ τὴν πεπτωκυῖαν, καὶ τὰ κατεσκαμμένα αὐτῆς ἀνοικοδομήσω καὶ ἀνορθώσω αὐτήν, 15.17 ὅπως ἂν ἐκζητήσωσιν οἱ κατάλοιποι τῶν ἀνθρώπων τὸν κύριον, καὶ πάντα τὰ ἔθνη ἐφ᾽ οὓς ἐπικέκληται τὸ ὄνομά μου ἐπ᾽ αὐτούς, λέγει κύριος ὁ ποιῶν ταῦτα» 15.18 γνωστὰ ἀπ᾽ αἰῶνος.

15.19 διὸ ἐγὼ κρίνω μὴ παρενοχλεῖν τοῖς ἀπὸ τῶν ἐθνῶν ἐπιστρέφουσιν ἐπὶ τὸν θεόν, 15.20 ἀλλὰ ἐπιστῖλαι αὐτοῖς τοῦ ἀπέχεσθαι τῶν ἀλισγημάτων τῶν εἰδώλων καὶ τῆς πορνίας καὶ τοῦ πνικτοῦ καὶ τοῦ αἵματος· 15.21 Μωϋσῆς γὰρ ἐκ γενεῶν ἀρχαίων κατὰ πόλιν τοὺς κηρύσσοντας αὐτὸν ἔχει ἐν ταῖς συναγωγαῖς κατὰ πᾶν σάββατον ἀναγινωσκόμενος. 15.22 τότε ἔδοξε τοῖς ἀποστόλοις καὶ τοῖς πρεσβυτέροις σὺν ὅλῃ τῇ ἐκκλησίᾳ ἐκλεξαμένους ἄνδρας ἐξ αὐτῶν πέμψαι εἰς Ἀντιόχιαν σὺν τῷ Παύλῳ καὶ Βαρναβᾷ, Ἰούδαν τὸν καλούμενον Βαρσαββᾶν καὶ Σιλᾶν, ἄνδρας ἡγουμένους ἐν τοῖς ἀδελφοῖς, 15.23 γράψαντες διὰ χειρὸς αὐτῶν,

οἱ ἀπόστολοι καὶ οἱ πρεσβύτεροι ἀδελφοὶ τοῖς κατὰ τὴν Ἀντιόχιαν καὶ Συρίαν καὶ Κιλικίαν ἀδελφοῖς τοῖς ἐξ ἐθνῶν χαίρειν.

15.24 ἐπιδὴ ἠκούσαμεν ὅτι τινὲς ἐξ ἡμῶν ἐξελθόντες

faith.   15.10 Therefore, why do ye now test/try God, to place a yoke upon the neck of the learners which neither our fathers nor we ourselves were able to bear?   15.11 But we believe to be saved through the grace/gift of the Lord Jesus, by which manner those also.

15.12 And all the multitude was silent, and they were hearing Barnabas and Paul relating whatever signs and wonders God did through them among the ethnics. 15.13 And after the (thing) for them to be silent, James answered, saying: Men, brothers, hear ye from me.   15.14 Simeon himself   related/explained also as God himself visited to take out of ethnics a people for his name.   15.15 And the sayings/words of the prophets agree with this, even as it has been written: 15.16 AFTER THESE (THINGS) I SHALL RETURN AND REBUILD/ RESTORE THE TENT OF DAVID, THE (ONE) HAVING FALLEN, AND THE (THINGS) OF HER/*it* HAVING BEEN OVERTHROWN, I SHALL RETURN AND REBUILD AND RESTORE HER/*it*,   15.17 SO THAT THE REST OF THE MEN/HUMANS MIGHT SEEK OUT/SEARCH FOR THE LORD, AND ALL THE ETHNICS/NATIONS ON/TO WHOM MY NAME HAS BEEN CALLED/INVOKED TO THEM, SAYS *the* LORD, THE (ONE) DOING THESE (THINGS)   15.18 known from an age.

15.19   Wherefore I, I judge not to vex/trouble for those of the ethnics turning to God,   15.20 but to send a letter to them of the (thing) to abstain from the pollutions of the idols and the prostitution and the strangled (thing) and the blood;   15.21 for Moses, from past/ancient generations, has those heralding him city by city, being read in the congregations on every sabbath.   15.22 Then it seemed *good* to the apostles and the elders with the whole/entire assembly, having chosen men out of them to send to Antioch with Paul and Barnabas, Judas the (one) being called Barsabbas and Silas, men being leaders among the brothers, 15.23 having written through their hand:

The apostles and the elder brothers/brother elders to the brothers out of ethnics/nations through- out Antioch and Syria and Cilicia, to greet/greeting.

15.24 Since we heard that some having gone forth from us troubled ye with sayings/words upsetting your

ἐτάραξαν ὑμᾶς λόγοις ἀνασκευάζοντες τὰς ψυχὰς ὑμῶν, οἷς οὐ διεστιλάμεθα, 15.25 ἔδοξεν ἡμῖν γενομένοις ὁμοθυμαδὸν ἐκλεξαμένους ἄνδρας πέμψαι πρὸς ὑμᾶς σὺν τοῖς ἀγαπητοῖς ἡμῶν Βαρναβᾷ καὶ Παύλῳ, 15.26 ἀνθρώποις παραδεδωκόσι τὰς ψυχὰς αὐτῶν ὑπὲρ τοῦ ὀνόματος τοῦ κυρίου ἡμῶν Ἰησοῦ χριστοῦ. 15.27 ἀπεστάλκαμεν οὖν Ἰούδαν καὶ Σιλᾶν, καὶ αὐτοὺς διὰ λόγου ἀπαγγέλλοντας τὰ αὐτά. 15.28 ἔδοξεν γὰρ τῷ πνεύματι τῷ ἁγίῳ καὶ ἡμῖν μηδὲν πλέον ἐπιτίθεσθαι ὑμῖν βάρος πλὴν τούτων τῶν ἐπάναγκαις, 15.29 ἀπέχεσθαι εἰδωλοθύτων καὶ αἵματος καὶ πνικτῶν καὶ πορνείας· ἐξ ὧν διατηροῦντες ἑαυτοὺς εὖ πράξετε. ἔρρωσθαι.

15.30 οἱ μὲν οὖν ἀπολυθέντες κατῆλθον εἰς Ἀντιόχειαν, καὶ συναγαγόντες τὸ πλῆθος ἐπέδωκαν τὴν ἐπιστολήν· 15.31 ἀναγνόντες δὲ ἐχάρησαν ἐπὶ τῇ παρακλήσει. 15.32 Ἰούδας τε καὶ Σιλᾶς, καὶ αὐτοὶ προφῆται ὄντες, διὰ λόγου πολλοῦ παρεκάλεσαν τοὺς ἀδελφοὺς καὶ ἐπεστήριξαν· 15.33 ποιήσαντες δὲ χρόνον ἀπελύθησαν μετ' εἰρήνης ἀπὸ τῶν ἀδελφῶν πρὸς τοὺς ἀποστίλαντας ἑαυτούς.

15.35 Παῦλος δὲ καὶ Βαρναβᾶς διέτριβον ἐν Ἀντιοχείᾳ διδάσκοντες καὶ εὐαγγελιζόμενοι μετὰ καὶ ἑτέρων πολλῶν τὸν λόγον τοῦ κυρίου.

15.36 μετὰ δέ τινας ἡμέρας εἶπεν πρὸς Βαρναβᾶν Παῦλος, ἐπιστρέψαντες δὴ ἐπισκεψώμεθα τοὺς ἀδελφοὺς κατὰ πόλιν πᾶσαν ἐν αἷς κατηγγίλαμεν τὸν λόγον τοῦ κυρίου, πῶς ἔχουσιν. 15.37 Βαρναβᾶς δὲ ἐβούλετο συμπαραλαβῖν καὶ τὸν Ἰωάννην τὸν καλούμενον Μᾶρκον· 15.38 Παῦλος δὲ ἠξίου τὸν ἀποστάντα ἀπ' αὐτῶν ἀπὸ Παμφυλίας καὶ μὴ συνελθόντα αὐτοῖς εἰς τὸ ἔργον μὴ συνπαραλαμβάνιν τοῦτον.

15.39 ἐγένετο δὲ παροξυσμὸς ὥστε ἀποχωρισθῆναι αὐτοὺς ἀπ' ἀλλήλων, τόν τε Βαρναβᾶν παραλαβόντα τὸν Μᾶρκον ἐκπλεῦσαι εἰς Κύπρον. 15.40 Παῦλος δὲ ἐπιλεξάμενος Σιλᾶν ἐξῆλθεν παραδοθεὶς τῇ χάριτι τοῦ κυρίου ὑπὸ τῶν ἀδελφῶν,

souls/lives, to whom we did not give charge/command, 15.25 it seemed *good* to us, having become of one accord to send men having been chosen/elected to ye with our beloved (ones) Barnabas and Paul, 15.26 men having given up their lives/souls in behalf of the name of our Lord Jesus, the anointed (one). 15.27 We have therefore sent Judas and Silas, and them through a saying/word announcing/reporting the same (things). 15.28 For it seemed *good* to the holy spirit and to us to put upon ye no burden more than these necessary things: 15.29 To abstain from (things) sacrificed to idols and from blood and (things) strangled and prostitution/unchastity, from which keeping yourselves, ye will practice well. Farewell/be ye strong.

15.30 Then the (they) indeed having been dismissed went down to Antioch, and having gathered the multitude they delivered the letter; 15.31 and having read *it* publicly they rejoiced over the exhortation. 15.32 Both Judas and Silas, and these/those being prophets, exhorted and strengthened the brothers through much speaking/reasoning, 15.33 and having done a time, they were dismissed with peace from the brothers to those having sent themselves.

15.35 But Paul and Barnabas stayed on in Antioch, teaching and evangelizing/proclaiming the word/saying of the Lord with many others/different (ones) also.

15.36 And after some days Paul said to Barnabas: Having turned to *it* now/returning (one trip) now, let us visit the brothers at every city in which we proclaimed the word/saying/reason of the Lord, how they hold *it*. 15.37 And Barnabas was planning to take along also John, the (one) being called Mark; 15.38 but Paul thought *it* best not to take along this (one), the (one) having withdrawn from them from Pamphylia and not having gone with them in the work.

15.39 And there became a sharp disagreement so as *for* them to separate from one another, and *for* Barnabas, having taken Mark along, to sail away to Cyprus. 15.40 But Paul, having chosen Silas, went forth, having been commended by the brothers for/in the grace of the Lord, 15.41 and he went through

15.41 διήρχετο δὲ τὴν Συρίαν καὶ Κιλικίαν ἐπιστηρίζων τὰς ἐκκλησίας. 16.1 κατήντησεν δὲ εἰς Δέρβην καὶ εἰς Λύστραν. καὶ ἰδοὺ μαθητής τις ἦν ἐκεῖ ὀνόματι Τιμόθεος, υἱὸς γυναικὸς Ἰουδαίας πιστῆς πατρὸς δὲ Ἕλληνος, 16.2 ὃς ἐμαρτυρεῖτο ὑπὸ τῶν ἐν Λύστροις καὶ Ἰκονίου ἀδελφῶν. 16.3 τοῦτον ἠθέλησεν ὁ Παῦλος σὺν αὐτῷ ἐξελθῖν, καὶ λαβὼν περιέτεμεν αὐτὸν διὰ τοὺς Ἰουδαίους τοὺς ὄντας ἐν τοῖς τόποις ἐκίνοις, δεῖσαν γὰρ ἅπαντες ὅτι Ἕλλην ὁ πατὴρ αὐτοῦ ὑπῆρχεν. 16.4 ὡς δὲ διεπορεύοντο τὰς πόλεις, παρεδίδοσαν αὐτοῖς φυλάσσιν τὰ δόγματα τὰ κεκριμένα ὑπὸ τῶν ἀποστόλων καὶ πρεσβυτέρων τῶν ἐν Ἱεροσολύμοις.

16.5 αἱ μὲν οὖν ἐκκλησίαι ἐστερεοῦντο τῇ πίστι καὶ ἐπερίσσευον τῷ ἀριθμῷ καθ' ἡμέραν.

16.6 διῆλθον δὲ τὴν Φρυγίαν καὶ Γαλατικὴν χώραν, κωλυθέντες ὑπὸ τοῦ ἁγίου πνεύματος λαλῆσαι τὸν λόγον ἐν τῇ Ἀσίᾳ· 16.7 ἐλθόντες δὲ κατὰ τὴν Μυσίαν ἐπίραζον εἰς τὴν Βιθυνίαν πορευθῆναι, καὶ οὐκ ἴασεν αὐτοὺς τὸ πνεῦμα Ἰησοῦ· 16.8 παρελθόντες δὲ τὴν Μυσίαν κατέβησαν εἰς Τρῳάδα. 16.9 καὶ ὅραμα διὰ τῆς νυκτὸς τῷ Παύλῳ ὤφθη, ἀνὴρ Μακαιδών τις ἦν ἑστὼς καὶ παρακαλῶν αὐτὸν καὶ λέγων, διαβὰς εἰς Μακεδονίαν βοήθησον ἡμῖν. 16.10 ὡς δὲ τὸ ὅραμα εἶδεν, εὐθέως ἐζητήσαμεν ἐξελθῖν εἰς Μακαιδονίαν, συμβιβάζοντες ὅτι προσκέκληται ἡμᾶς ὁ θεὸς εὐαγγελίσασθαι αὐτούς.

16.11 ἀναχθέντες δὲ ἀπὸ Τρῳάδος εὐθυδρομήσαμεν εἰς Σαμοθρᾴκην, τῇ δὲ ἐπιούσῃ εἰς Νέαν Πόλιν, 16.12 κἀκεῖθεν εἰς Φιλίππους, ἥτις ἐστὶν πρώτη τῆς μερίδος Μακαιδονίας πόλις, κολωνία. ἦμεν δὲ ἐν ταύτῃ τῇ πόλει διατρίβοντες ἡμέρας τινάς.

16.13 τῇ τε ἡμέρᾳ τῶν σαββάτων ἐξήλθομεν ἔξω τῆς πύλης παρὰ ποταμὸν οὗ ἐνομίζεν προσευχὴν εἶναι, καὶ καθίσαντες ἐλαλοῦμεν ταῖς συνελθούσαις γυναιξίν.

16.14 καί τις γυνὴ ὀνόματι Λυδία, πορφυρόπωλις πόλεως Θυατείρων σεβομένη τὸν θεόν, ἤκουεν, ἧς ὁ κύριος διήνυξεν τὴν

Syria and Cilicia strengthening/confirming the assemblies. 16.1 And he arrived in/came to Derbe and to Lystra. And behold, a certain learner/pupil was there, Timothy by name, a son of a faithful Judean woman and a Greek father, 16.2 who was being witnessed by the brothers in Lystra and Iconium. 16.3 Paul wanted this (one) to go forth with him, and having taken *him* he circumcised him because of the Judeans being in those places, for they all knew that his father was a Greek. 16.4 And as they were going through the cities, they delivered to them to observe/keep the rules/decrees having been judged *good* by the apostles and elders from those among Jerusalemites.

16.5 Then the assemblies were indeed being strengthened for/in the faith and were growing in the count/number day by day.

16.6 And they went through the Phrygian and Galatian country, having been forbidden by the holy spirit to speak the saying/word in Asia; 16.7 but having gone down along Mysia, they were trying to be gone into Bithynia, and the spirit from Jesus did not allow them; 16.8 but having gone through Mysia they went down to Troas. 16.9 And through/during the night, a vision was manifested to Paul, a certain Macedonian man had stood and beseeched him and said: Having come over into Macedonia, help us. 16.10 And since he saw the vision, we immediately sought to go forth to Macedonia, concluding that God has called us to proclaim the good message/gospel *for* them.

16.11 And having set sail from Troas, we ran a straight course to Samothracia, and on the next day to Neapolis, 16.12 and from there to Philippi, which is a first city of the part of Macedonia, a colony. And we were staying in this city *for* some days.

16.13 And on the day of the sabbaths we went forth outside the gate beside a river where he was supposing to be a prayer (place), and having sat down we were speaking to the women having come together.

16.14 And a certain woman, Lydia by name, a dealer in purple cloth from *the* city of Thyatira, reverencing/respecting God, was listening, of whom the Lord opened up the heart to take heed for the (things)

καρδίαν προσέχειν τοῖς λαλουμένοις ὑπὸ τοῦ Παύλου. 16.15 ὡς δὲ ἐβαπτίσθη καὶ ὁ οἶκος αὐτῆς, παρεκάλεσεν λέγουσα, εἰ κεκρίκατέ με πιστὴν τῷ κυρίῳ εἶναι, εἰσελθόντες εἰς τὸν οἶκόν μου μένετε· καὶ παρεβιάσατο ἡμᾶς. 16.16 ἐγένετο δὲ πορευομένων ἡμῶν εἰς τὴν προσευχὴν παιδίσκην τινὰ ἔχουσαν πνεῦμα πύθωνα ὑπαντῆσαι ἡμῖν, ἥτις ἐργασίαν πολλὴν παρεῖχεν τοῖς κυρίοις αὐτῆς μαντευομένη. 16.17 αὕτη κατακολουθοῦσα τῷ Παύλῳ καὶ ἡμῖν ἔκραζε λέγουσα, οὗτοι οἱ ἄνθρωποι δοῦλοι τοῦ θεοῦ τοῦ ὑψίστου εἰσίν, οἵτινες καταγγέλλουσιν ὑμῖν ὁδὸν σωτηρίας. 16.18 τοῦτο δὲ ἐποίει ἐπὶ πολλὰς ἡμέρας. διαπονηθεὶς δὲ Παῦλος καὶ ἐπιστρέψας τῷ πνεύματι εἶπεν, Παραγγέλλω σοι ἐν ὀνόματι Ἰησοῦ χριστοῦ ἐξελθεῖν ἀπ' αὐτῆς· καὶ ἐξῆλθεν αὐτῇ τῇ ὥρᾳ. 16.19 ἰδόντες δὲ οἱ κύριοι αὐτῆς ὅτι ἐξῆλθεν ἡ ἐλπὶς τῆς ἐργασίας αὐτῶν ἐπιλαβόμενοι τὸν Παῦλον καὶ τὸν Σιλᾶν εἵλκυσαν εἰς τὴν ἀγορὰν ἐπὶ τοὺς ἄρχοντας, 16.20 καὶ προσαγαγόντες αὐτοὺς τοῖς στρατηγοῖς εἶπαν,

οὗτοι οἱ ἄνθρωποι ἐκταράσσουσιν ἡμῶν τὴν πόλιν Ἰουδαῖοι ὑπάρχοντες, 16.21 καὶ καταγγέλλουσιν ἔθη ἃ οὐκ ἔξεστιν ἡμῖν παραδέχεσθαι οὐδὲ ποιεῖν Ῥωμαίοις οὖσιν. 16.22 καὶ συνεπέστη ὁ ὄχλος κατ' αὐτῶν, καὶ οἱ στρατηγοὶ περιρήξαντες αὐτῶν τὰ ἱμάτια ἐκέλευον ῥαβδίζειν, 16.23 πολλάς τε ἐπιθέντες αὐτοῖς πληγὰς ἔβαλον εἰς φυλακήν, παραγγίλαντες τῷ δεσμοφύλακι ἀσφαλῶς τηρῖν αὐτούς· 16.24 ὃς παραγγελίαν τοιαύτην λαβὼν ἔβαλεν αὐτοὺς εἰς τὴν ἐσωτέραν φυλακὴν καὶ τοὺς πόδας ἠσφαλίσατο αὐτῶν εἰς τὸ ξύλον.

16.25 κατὰ δὲ μεσονύκτιον Παῦλος καὶ Σιλᾶς προσευχόμενοι ὕμνουν τὸν θεόν, ἐπηκροῶντο δὲ αὐτῶν οἱ δέσμιοι· 16.26 ἄφνω δὲ σισμὸς ἐγένετο μέγας ὥστε σαλευθῆναι τὰ θεμέλια τοῦ δεσμωτηρίου, ἠνοίχθησαν δὲ παραχρῆμα αἱ θύραι πᾶσαι, καὶ πάντων τὰ δεσμὰ ἀνέθη. 16.27 ἔξυπνος δὲ γενόμενος ὁ δεσμοφύλας καὶ ἰδὼν ἀνεῳγμένας τὰς θύρας τῆς φυλακῆς, σπασάμενος μάχαιραν ἤμελλεν ἑαυτὸν ἀναιρεῖν, νομίζων

being spoken by Paul. 16.15 And when she was baptized and her house/household, she beseeched *us* saying: If ye have judged me to be faithful to the Lord, having entered into my house, ye abide/stay *there*; and she prevailed upon us. 16.16 And from us going to the prayer (place), it happened *for* a certain maidservant having a spirit of divination to meet with us, who was bringing much business/profit to her lords practicing soothsaying/giving oracles. 16.17 This (girl), following with Paul and us, was crying out, saying: These men are slaves of the most high God, who proclaim to ye a way/road of salvation. 16.18 And she was doing this over/for many days. But Paul, having been annoyed and having turned to the spirit, he said: I charge/command for you to come out from her in *the* name of Jesus, the anointed (one); and it came out in that very/the same hour. 16.19 But her lords, having seen that the hope of their business/profit went out, having taken hold of Paul and Silas, they dragged them into the market to the rulers/leaders, 16.20 and having brought them to the commanders, they said:

These men, being Judeans, agitate/disturb our city/are troubling our city, 16.21 and they proclaim customs which it is not lawful for us to receive nor to do, being Romans. 16.22 And the crowd rose up together against them, and the commanders, having torn off their garments, were ordering to flog *them*/beat with rods/staffs. 16.23 and having laid many blows on them, they threw *them* into prison, having charged the jailer to keep them securely; 16.24 who having received such a charge, he threw them into the more inner prison and secured their feet in the wood/tree/*stocks*.

16.25 And praying at/about midnight, Paul and Silas were singing hymns *for* God, and the prisoners were hearing from them; 16.26 and suddenly a great earthquake happened so as *for* the foundations of the jail to be shaken, and all the doors were opened at once, and the bonds of all were unfastened. 16.27 But the jailer, having become out of sleep/awakened and having seen the doors of the prison having been opened, having drawn his sword was being about to kill

ἐκπεφευγέναι τοὺς δεσμίους.

16.28 ἐφώνησεν δὲ φωνῇ μεγάλῃ Παῦλος λέγων, μηδὲν πράξῃς σεαυτῷ κακόν, ἅπαντες γάρ ἐσμεν ἐνθάδε. 16.29 αἰτήσας δὲ φῶτα εἰσεπήδησεν, καὶ ἔντρομος γενόμενος προσέπεσεν τῷ Παύλῳ καὶ τῷ Σιλᾷ, 16.30 καὶ προαγαγὼν αὐτοὺς ἔξω ἔφη, κύριοι, τί με δεῖ ποιεῖν ἵνα σωθῶ; 16.31 οἱ δὲ εἶπαν, Πίστευσον ἐπὶ τὸν κύριον Ἰησοῦν, καὶ σωθήσῃ σὺ καὶ ὁ οἶκός σου. 16.32 καὶ ἐλάλησαν αὐτῷ τὸν λόγον τοῦ κυρίου σὺμ πᾶσι τοῖς ἐν τῇ οἰκίᾳ αὐτοῦ. 16.33 καὶ παραλαβὼν αὐτοὺς ἐν ἐκίνῃ τῇ ὥρᾳ τῆς νυκτὸς ἔλουσεν ἀπὸ τῶν πληγῶν, καὶ ἐβαπτίσθη αὐτὸς καὶ οἱ αὐτοῦ ἅπαντες παραχρῆμα, 16.34 ἀναγαγών τε αὐτοὺς εἰς τὸν οἶκον αὐτοῦ παρέθηκεν τράπεζαν, καὶ ἠγαλλιάσατο πανοικεὶ πεπιστευκὼς τῷ θεῷ.

16.35 ἡμέρας δὲ γενομένης ἀπέστιλαν οἱ στρατηγοὶ τοὺς ῥαβδούχους λέγοντες, ἀπόλυσον τοὺς ἀνθρώπους ἐκείνους. 16.36 ἀπήγγιλεν δὲ ὁ δεσμοφύλαξ τοὺς λόγους τούτους πρὸς τὸν Παῦλον, ὅτι ἀπέσταλκαν οἱ στρατηγοὶ ἵνα ἀπολυθῆτε· νῦν οὖν ἐξελθόντες πορεύεσθε εἰς ἰρήνην.

16.37 ὁ δὲ Παῦλος ἔφη πρὸς αὐτούς, δίραντες ἡμᾶς δημοσίᾳ ἀκατακρίτους, ἀνθρώπους Ῥωμαίους ὑπάρχοντας, ἔβαλον εἰς φυλακήν· καὶ νῦν λάθρα ἡμᾶς ἐκβάλλουσιν; οὐ γάρ, ἀλλὰ ἐλθόντες αὐτοὶ ἡμᾶς ἐξαγαγέτωσαν. 16.38 ἀπήγγιλάν τε τοῖς στρατηγοῖς οἱ ῥαβδοῦχοι τὰ ῥήματα ταῦτα. ἐφοβήθησαν δὲ ἀκούσαντες ὅτι Ῥωμαῖοί εἰσιν, 16.39 καὶ ἐλθόντες παρεκάλεσαν αὐτούς, καὶ ἐξαγαγόντες ἠρώτων ἀπελθῖν ἀπὸ τῆς πόλεως. 16.40 ἐξελθόντες δὲ ἀπὸ τῆς φυλακῆς εἰσῆλθον πρὸς τὴν Λυδίαν, καὶ ἰδόντες παρεκάλεσαν τοὺς ἀδελφοὺς καὶ ἐξῆλθαν.

17.1 Διοδεύσαντες δὲ τὴν Ἀμφίπολιν καὶ τὴν Ἀπολλωνίαν ἦλθον εἰς Θεσσαλονίκην, ὅπου ἦν συναγωγὴ τῶν Ἰουδαίων. 17.2 κατὰ δὲ τὸ εἰωθὸς τῷ Παύλῳ εἰσῆλθεν πρὸς αὐτοὺς καὶ ἐπὶ σάββατα τρία διελέξατο αὐτοῖς ἀπὸ τῶν γραφῶν, 17.3 διανοίγων καὶ παρατιθέμενος ὅτι τὸν χριστὸν ἔδει παθῖν καὶ

himself, supposing *for* the prisoners to have escaped.

16.28 But Paul called out in a great voice, saying: Do not a bad (thing) to yourself, for we are all here. 16.29 And having asked for lights, he rushed in, and having become trembling, he fell before Paul and Silas. 16.30 and having brought them outside, he was saying: Lords, what is it necessary *for* me to do in order that I might be saved? 16.31 And the (they) said: Believe on the Lord Jesus, and you will/may be saved, you and your house. 16.32 And they spoke the saying/reason/word of the Lord to him with all those in his house. 16.33 And having taken/received them in that hour of the night, he washed from the blows/wounds, and he was baptized, he and all those of him/his at once/immediately, 16.34 and having brought them up to his house, he set a table before them, and they rejoiced greatly with all the household having believed in God.

16.35 And from it having become day, the commanders sent the lictors/policemen, saying: Release those men. 16.36 And the jailer reported/announced these words to Paul: The commanders have sent (men) in order that ye might be released; therefore, going out now, go ye in peace.

16.37 But Paul was saying to them: Having beaten us in public without a proper trial, being Roman men, they threw *us* into prison; and now they put us out secretly? For not *so*, but having come themselves, let them bring us out. 16.38 And the lictors/policemen reported these words to the commanders. And they were terrified, having heard that they are Romans, 16.39 and having come, they comforted/entreated them, and having brought them out, they were asking *them* to depart from the city. 16.40 And having gone forth from the prison, they went in to Lydia, and having seen the brothers, they exhorted *them* and went forth.

17.1 And having traveled through Amphipolis and Apollonia they went to Thessalonica, where there was a congregation of the Judeans. 17.2 And according to custom with Paul, we went in to/with them and on three sabbaths he reasoned/argued with them from the writings, 17.3 explaining and setting forth/showing that

ἀναστῆναι ἐκ νεκρῶν, καὶ ὅτι οὗτός ἐστιν Ἰησοῦς χριστός, ὃν ἐγὼ καταγγέλλω ὑμῖν. 17.4 καί τινες ἐξ αὐτῶν ἐπίσθησαν καὶ προσεκληρώθησαν τῷ Παύλῳ καὶ τῷ Σιλᾷ, τῶν τε σεβομένων Ἑλλήνων πλῆθος πολὺ γυναικῶν τε τῶν πρώτων οὐκ ὀλίγαι.

17.5 ζηλώσαντες δὲ οἱ Ἰουδαῖοι καὶ προσλαβόμενοι τῶν ἀγοραίων τινὰς ἄνδρας πονηροὺς καὶ ὀχλοποιήσαντες ἐθορύβουν τὴν πόλιν, καὶ ἐπιστάντες τῇ οἰκίᾳ Ἰάσονος ἐζήτουν αὐτοὺς προαγαγεῖν εἰς τὸν δῆμον. 17.6 μὴ εὑρόντες δὲ αὐτοὺς ἔσυρον Ἰάσονα καί τινας ἀδελφοὺς ἐπὶ τοὺς πολιτάρχας, βοῶντες ὅτι οἱ τὴν οἰκουμένην ἀναστατώσαντες οὗτοι καὶ ἐνθάδε πάρεισιν, 17.7 οὓς ὑποδέδεκται Ἰάσων· καὶ οὗτοι πάντες ἀπέναντι τῶν δογμάτων Καίσαρος πράσσουσι, βασιλέα ἕτερον λέγοντες εἶναι Ἰησοῦν. 17.8 ἐτάραξαν δὲ τὸν ὄχλον καὶ τοὺς πολιτάρχας ἀκούοντας ταῦτα, 17.9 καὶ λαβόντες τὸ ἱκανὸν παρὰ τοῦ Ἰάσονος καὶ τῶν λοιπῶν ἀπέλυσαν αὐτούς. 17.10 οἱ δὲ ἀδελφοὶ εὐθέως ἐξέπεμψαν διὰ νυκτὸς τόν τε Παῦλον καὶ τὸν Σιλᾶν εἰς Βέροιαν, οἵτινες παραγενόμενοι εἰς τὴν συναγωγὴν τῶν Ἰουδαίων ἀπήεσαν. 17.11 οὗτοι δὲ ἦσαν εὐγενέστεροι τῶν ἐν Θεσσαλονίκῃ, οἵτινες ἐδέξαντο τὸν λόγον μετὰ πάσης προθυμίας, καθ' ἡμέραν ἀνακρίνοντες τὰς γραφὰς εἰ ἔχοι ταῦτα οὕτως.

17.12 πολλοὶ μὲν οὖν ἐξ αὐτῶν ἐπίστευσαν, καὶ τῶν Ἑλληνίδων γυναικῶν τῶν εὐσχημόνων καὶ ἀνδρῶν οὐκ ὀλίγοι. 17.13 ὡς δὲ ἔγνωσαν οἱ ἀπὸ τῆς Θεσσαλονίκης Ἰουδαῖοι ὅτι καὶ ἐν τῇ Βεροίᾳ κατηγγέλη ὑπὸ τοῦ Παύλου ὁ λόγος τοῦ θεοῦ, ἦλθον κἀκεῖ σαλεύοντες καὶ ταράσσοντες τοὺς ὄχλους. 17.14 εὐθέως δὲ τότε τὸν Παῦλον ἐξαπέστιλαν οἱ ἀδελφοὶ πορεύεσθαι ἕως ἐπὶ τὴν θάλασσαν·

ὑπέμινάν τε ὅ τε Σιλᾶς καὶ ὁ Τιμόθεος ἐκεῖ. 17.15 οἱ δὲ καθιστῶντες τὸν Παῦλον ἤγαγον ἕως Ἀθηνῶν, καὶ λαβόντες ἐντολὴν πρὸς τὸν Σιλᾶν καὶ τὸν Τιμόθεον ἵνα ὡς τάχιστα ἔλθωσιν πρὸς αὐτὸν ἐξῄεσαν.

it was necessary for the anointed (one) to suffer and to rise up out of dead (ones), and that this (one) is Jesus, the anointed (one), whom I, I proclaim to ye. 17.4 And some out of them were persuaded and were attached/joined with Paul and Silas, both a much multitude of the reverent Greeks and not a few of the first women.

17.5 But the Judeans, having become jealous and having taken aside some evil men of the market crowd/ rabble, and having made a crowd/mob, they were disturbing the city, and having come upon the house of Jason, they were seeking/asking to bring them forward to the populace/public. 17.6 But not having found them, they were dragging Jason and some brothers to the politarchs/magistrates, crying that these/those, the (ones) having upset the empire/inhabited earth, are also present here, 17.7 whom Jason has welcomed/ received; and all these practice contrary to the decrees of Caesar, saying *for* Jesus to be another/different king. 17.8 And they stirred up/troubled the crowd and the politarchs hearing these (things), 17.9 and having taken the pledge/bond from Jason and the rest (others), they released them. 17.10 And the brothers immediately through/during night sent out both Paul and Silas to Beroea, who having arrived, they went away into the congregation of the Judeans. 17.11 And these were more noble-minded than those in Thessalonica, who received the saying/reason/word with all willingness, examining the writings day by day whether these may hold/have *it* so.

17.12 Therefore many out of them indeed believed, both of the decent Greek women and of men not a few. 17.13 But when the Judeans from Thessalonica learned/knew that the saying/word of God was also proclaimed in Beroea by Paul, they went there also, shaking and troubling/stirring up the crowds. 17.14 And immediately at that time the brothers sent Paul out to go until/as far as to the sea/lake;

and both Silas and Timothy stayed there. 17.15 And the (ones) conducting Paul brought him until Athenians, and having received a command to Silas and Timothy that as quickly they should come to him, they

17.16 ἐν δὲ ταῖς Ἀθήναις ἐκδεχομένου αὐτοῦ τοῦ Παύλου, παρωξύνετο τὸ πνεῦμα αὐτοῦ ἐν αὐτῷ θεωροῦντος κατίδωλον οὖσαν τὴν πόλιν.

17.17 διελέγετο μὲν οὖν ἐν τῇ συναγωγῇ τοῖς Ἰουδαίοις καὶ τοῖς σεβομένοις καὶ ἐν τῇ ἀγορᾷ κατὰ πᾶσαν ἡμέραν πρὸς τοὺς παρατυγχάνοντας. 17.18 τινὲς δὲ καὶ τῶν Ἐπικουρίων καὶ Στοϊκῶν φιλοσόφων συνέβαλλον αὐτῷ, καί τινες ἔλεγον, τί ἂν θέλοι ὁ σπερμολόγος οὗτος λέγειν; οἱ δέ, ξένων δαιμονίων δοκεῖ καταγγελεὺς εἶναι· ὅτι τὸν Ἰησοῦν καὶ τὴν ἀνάστασιν εὐηγγελίζετο. 17.19 ἐπιλαβόμενοί τε αὐτοῦ ἐπὶ τὸν Ἄριον πάγον ἤγαγον, λέγοντες, δυνάμεθα γνῶναι τίς ἡ καινὴ αὕτη ἡ ὑπὸ σοῦ λαλουμένη διδαχή; 17.20 ξενίζοντα γάρ τινα εἰσφέρεις εἰς τὰς ἀκοὰς ἡμῶν· βουλόμεθα οὖν γνῶναι τίνα θέλει ταῦτα εἶναι. 17.21 Ἀθηναῖοι δὲ πάντες καὶ οἱ ἐπιδημοῦντες ξένοι εἰς οὐδὲν ἕτερον ηὐκέρουν ἢ λέγειν τι ἢ ἀκούειν τι καινότερον.

17.22 σταθεὶς δὲ Παῦλος ἐν μέσῳ τοῦ Ἀρίου πάγου εἶπεν, ἄνδρες Ἀθηναῖοι, κατὰ πάντα ὡς δισιδαιμονεστέρους ὑμᾶς θεωρῶ· 17.23 διερχόμενος γὰρ καὶ ἀναθεωρῶν τὰ σεβάστα ὑμῶν εὗρον καὶ βωμὸν ἐν ᾧ ἐπεγέγραπτο, ἀγνώστῳ θεῷ. ὃ οὖν ἀγνοοῦντες εὐσεβεῖτε, τοῦτο ἐγὼ καταγγέλλω ὑμῖν. 17.24 ὁ θεὸς ὁ ποιήσας τὸν κόσμον καὶ πάντα τὰ ἐν αὐτῷ, οὗτος οὐρανοῦ καὶ γῆς ὑπάρχων κύριος οὐκ ἐν χιροποιήτοις ναοῖς κατοικεῖ 17.25 οὐδὲ ὑπὸ ἀνθρωπίνων χιρῶν θεραπεύεται προσδεόμενός τινος, αὐτὸς διδοὺς πᾶσι ζωὴν καὶ πνοὴν καὶ τὰ πάντα· 17.26 ἐποίησέν τε ἐξ ἑνὸς πᾶν ἔθνος ἀνθρώπων κατοικῖν ἐπὶ παντὸς προσώπου τῆς γῆς,

ὁρίσας προστεταγμένους καιροὺς καὶ τὰς ὁροθεσίας τῆς κατοικίας αὐτῶν, 17.27 ζητεῖν τὸν θεὸν εἰ ἄρα γε ψηλαφήσειεν αὐτὸν καὶ εὕροιεν, καίτοι γε οὐ μακρὰν ἀπὸ ἑνὸς ἑκάστου ἡμῶν ὑπάρχοντα. 17.28 ἐν αὐτῷ γὰρ ζῶμεν καὶ κινούμεθα καὶ

departed.

17.16 And from Paul waiting for him among the Athenians, his spirit was provoking/urging in him, observing/beholding the city being full of idols.

17.17 Therefore he was indeed reasoning in the congregation with the Judeans and the reverent (ones), and in/at the market throughout every day with/to those happening to be present. 17.18 But also some of the Epicurean and Stoic philosophers conferred with him, and some were saying: What ever may this babbler/chatterer want/wish to say? And the (others): He seems to be a proclaimer of strange/foreign demons; because he was announcing/preaching Jesus and the resurrection. 17.19 And having taken hold of him they brought him to the Areopagus, saying: Are we able to know what this new doctrine being spoken by you *is*? 17.20 For you are bringing startling things into our hearings; we are purposing therefore to know what these things want to be. 17.21 And all Athenians and the sojourning strangers were having time/opportunity in/for nothing other than to say something or to hear something newer.

17.22 And having been stood in the midst of the Areopagus, Paul said: Men, Athenians, I behold/perceive *for* ye *to be* very religious according to/by all (things); 17.23 for going through and closely observing the (things) of your reverence/worship, I also found an altar on which had been inscribed: To An Unknown God. What therefore ye reverence without knowing, this I, I proclaim to ye. 17.24 The God having made the world and all the (things) in it, this (one) being Lord of heaven and earth dwells not in handmade temples 17.25 nor is he having need of anything served/treated by human hands, he himself giving to every (one) life and breath and all things; 17.26 and he made from one every ethnic/nation of men to dwell upon every face of the land/earth,

having defined pre-arranged seasons and the boundaries of their habitation, 17.27 to seek God if at least you might feel about/for him and they may find *him* , and indeed being/existing not far from each one of us. 17.28 For we live in/by him and we are

463

ἐσμέν, ὡς καί τινες τῶν καθ᾽ ὑμᾶς ποιητῶν εἰρήκασιν, τοῦ γὰρ καὶ γένος ἐσμέν. 17.29 γένος οὖν ὑπάρχοντες τοῦ θεοῦ οὐκ ὀφίλομεν νομίζειν χρυσιῷ ἢ ἀργύρῳ ἢ λίθῳ, χαράγματι τέχνης καὶ ἐνθυμήσεως ἀνθρώπου, τὸ θῖον εἶναι ὅμοιον. 17.30 τοὺς μὲν οὖν χρόνους τῆς ἀγνοίας ὑπεριδὼν ὁ θεὸς τὰ νῦν παραγγέλλει τοῖς ἀνθρώποις πάντας πανταχοῦ μετανοεῖν, 17.31 καθότι ἔστησεν ἡμέραν ἐν ᾗ μέλλει κρίνιν τὴν οἰκουμένην ἐν δικαιοσύνῃ ἐν ἀνδρὶ ᾧ ὥρισεν, πίστιν παρασχὼν πᾶσιν ἀναστήσας αὐτὸν ἐκ νεκρῶν.

17.32 ἀκούσαντες δὲ ἀνάστασιν νεκρῶν οἱ μὲν ἐχλεύαζον, οἱ δὲ εἶπαν, ἀκουσόμεθά σου περὶ τούτου καὶ πάλιν. 17.33 οὕτως ὁ Παῦλος ἐξῆλθεν ἐκ μέσου αὐτῶν. 17.34 τινές δὲ ἄνδρες κολληθέντες αὐτῷ ἐπίστευσαν, ἐν οἷς καὶ Διονύσιος ὁ Ἀρεοπαγίτης καὶ γυνὴ ὀνόματι Δάμαρις καὶ ἕτεροι σὺν αὐτοῖς. 18.1 μετὰ ταῦτα χωρισθεὶς ἐκ τῶν Ἀθηνῶν ἦλθεν εἰς Κόρινθον. 18.2 καὶ εὑρών τινα Ἰουδαῖον ὀνόματι Ἀκύλαν, Ποντικὸν τῷ γένι, προσφάτως ἐληλυθότα ἀπὸ τῆς Ἰταλίας καὶ Πρίσκιλλαν γυναῖκα αὐτοῦ διὰ τὸ διατεταχέναι Κλαύδιον χωρίζεσθαι πάντας τοὺς Ἰουδαίους ἀπὸ τῆς Ῥώμης, προσῆλθεν αὐτοῖς, 18.3 καὶ διὰ τὸ ὁμότεχνον εἶναι ἔμενεν παρ᾽ αὐτοῖς καὶ ἠργάζετο· ἦσαν γὰρ σκηνοποιοὶ τῇ τέχνῃ.

18.4 διελέγετο δὲ ἐν τῇ συναγωγῇ κατὰ πᾶν σάββατον, ἔπιθέν τε Ἰουδαίους καὶ Ἕλληνας. 18.5 ὡς δὲ κατῆλθον ἀπὸ τῆς Μακαιδονίας ὅ τε Σιλᾶς καὶ ὁ Τιμόθεος, συνείχετο τῷ λόγῳ ὁ Παῦλος, διαμαρτυρόμενος τοῖς Ἰουδαίοις εἶναι τὸν χριστόν Ἰησοῦν.

18.6 ἀντιτασσομένων δὲ αὐτῶν καὶ βλασφημούντων ἐκτιναξάμενος τὰ ἱμάτια εἶπεν πρὸς αὐτούς, Τὸ αἷμα ὑμῶν ἐπὶ τὴν κεφαλὴν ὑμῶν· καθαρὸς ἐγώ· ἀπὸ τοῦ νῦν εἰς τὰ ἔθνη πορεύσομαι. 18.7 καὶ μεταβὰς ἐκεῖθεν εἰσῆλθεν εἰς οἰκίαν τινὸς ὀνόματι Τίτου Ἰούστου σεβομένου τὸν θεόν, οὗ ἡ οἰκία ἦν

also being moved, even as some of your poets have said: For we are also a race/kind of the (him). 17.29 Therefore, being a race/kind of God, we owe *it* to think not *for* the divine (thing) to be like/similar to gold or silver or stone, to a thing from a craft/skill and an idea of a man. 17.30 Indeed, therefore, God, having overlooked the times of ignorance, the (things) he now commands to all the men everywhere *is* to repent, 17.31 because he set a day in which he is about to judge the empire/inhabited earth with justness by a man whom he appointed, having offered a faith for all, having raised him up out of dead (ones).

17.32 And having heard a resurrection of dead (ones), some were scoffing/sneering, but others said: We ourselves will also hear from you again about/concerning this. 17.33 So Paul went out from the midst of them. 17.34 And some men having been joined to him believed, among whom *were* both Dionysius the Areopagite and a woman, Damaris by name, and others/different (ones) with them. 18.1 After these (things), having departed from the Athenians, he went to Corinth. 18.2 And having found a certain Judean, Aquila by name, Pontus by the race/kind, recently having come from Italy, and Priscilla his woman, because of the (thing) for Claudius having commanded/ordered *for* all the Judeans to depart from Rome, he went to them, 18.3 and because of the (thing) to be of like trade, he staged with them and they were working; for they were tentmakers by the trade/craft.

18.4 And he was reasoning in the congregation on every sabbath, and he was persuading Judeans and Greeks. 18.5 And when both Silas and Timothy came down from Macedonia, Paul was being absorbed in the reasoning/word, solemnly testifying to the Judeans *for* Jesus to be the anointed (one).

18.6 And from them opposing and blaspheming/reviling *him*, having shook off the garment, he said to them: The blood of ye *is* upon the head of ye; I *am* clean; from now/the present (time) I shall go to the ethnics. 18.7 And having removed from there, he entered into a house of a certain Titius, by name of Justus, reverencing God, of whom the house was being

συνομοροῦσα τῇ συναγωγῇ. 18.8 Κρίσπος δὲ ὁ ἀρχισυνάγωγος ἐπίστευσεν τῷ κυρίῳ σὺν ὅλῳ τῷ οἴκῳ αὐτοῦ, καὶ πολλοὶ τῶν Κορινθίων ἀκούοντες ἐπίστευον καὶ ἐβαπτίζοντο. 18.9 εἶπεν δὲ ὁ κύριος ἐν νυκτὶ δι' ὁράματος τῷ Παύλῳ, μὴ φοβοῦ, ἀλλὰ λάλει καὶ μὴ σιωπήσῃς, 18.10 διότι ἐγώ εἰμι μετὰ σοῦ καὶ οὐδὶς ἐπιθήσεταί σοι τοῦ κακῶσέ σε, διότι λαός ἐστί μοι πολὺς ἐν τῇ πόλι ταύτῃ. 18.11 ἐκάθισεν δὲ ἐνιαυτὸν ἕνα καὶ μῆνας ἓξ διδάσκων ἐν αὐτοῖς τὸν λόγον τοῦ θεοῦ.

18.12 Γαλλίωνος δὲ ἀνθυπάτου ὄντος τῆς Ἀχαΐας κατεπέστησαν ὁμοθυμαδὸν οἱ Ἰουδαῖοι τῷ Παύλῳ καὶ ἤγαγον αὐτὸν παρὰ τὸ βῆμα, 18.13 λέγοντες ὅτι παρὰ τὸν νόμον ἀναπείθει οὗτος τοὺς ἀνθρώπους σέβεσθαι τὸν θεόν. 18.14 μέλλοντος δὲ τοῦ Παύλου ἀνοίγιν τὸ στόμα εἶπεν ὁ Γαλλίων πρὸς τοὺς Ἰουδαίους, εἰ μὲν ἦν ἀδίκημά τι ἢ ῥαδιούργημα πονηρόν, ὦ Ἰουδαῖοι, κατὰ λόγον ἂν ἀνεσχόμην ὑμῶν· 18.15 εἰ δὲ ζητήματά ἐστιν περὶ λόγου καὶ ὀνομάτων καὶ νόμου τοῦ καθ' ὑμᾶς, ὄψεσθε αὐτοί· κριτὴς ἐγὼ τούτων οὐ βούλομαι εἶναι. 18.16 καὶ ἀπήλασεν αὐτοὺς ἀπὸ τοῦ βήματος. 18.17 ἐπιλαβόμενοι δὲ πάντες Σωσθένην τὸν ἀρχισυνάγωγον ἔτυπτον ἔμπροσθεν τοῦ βήματος· καὶ οὐδὲν τούτων τῷ Γαλλίωνι ἔμελλεν. 18.18 ὁ δὲ Παῦλος ἔτι προσμίνας ἡμέρας ἱκανὰς τοῖς ἀδελφοῖς ἀποταξάμενος ἐξέπλει εἰς τὴν Συρίαν, καὶ σὺν αὐτῷ Πρίσκιλλα καὶ Ἀκύλας, κειράμενος ἐν Κενχραιαῖς τὴν κεφαλήν, εἶχεν γὰρ εὐχήν. 18.19 κατήντησαν δὲ εἰς Ἔφεσον, κἀκείνους κατέλιπεν ἐκεῖ, αὐτὸς δὲ εἰσελθὼν εἰς τὴν συναγωγὴν διελέξατο τοῖς Ἰουδαίοις. 18.20 ἐρωτώντων δὲ αὐτῶν ἐπὶ πλείονα χρόνον μεῖναι οὐκ ἐπένευσεν, 18.21 ἀλλὰ ἀποταξάμενος καὶ εἰπών, πάλιν ἀνακάμψω πρὸς ὑμᾶς τοῦ θεοῦ θέλοντος, ἀνήχθη ἀπὸ τῆς Ἐφέσου· 18.22 καὶ κατελθὼν εἰς Καισάριαν, ἀναβὰς καὶ ἀσπασάμενος τὴν ἐκκλησίαν, κατέβη εἰς Ἀντιόχειαν, 18.23 καὶ ποιήσας χρόνον τινὰ ἐξῆλθεν, διερχόμενος καθεξῆς τὴν

next to the congregation/synagogue. 18.8 And Crispus, the congregation leader believed in the Lord with
his whole house, and many of the Corinthians hearing/
listening were believing and being baptized. 18.9 And
the Lord said/spoke to Paul through a vision at night:
Fear not, but speak and be not silent, 18.10 because
I, I am with you and no one will set upon you from the
(thing) to treat you bad, because much people is/*are*
for me in this city. 18.11 And he sat/remained for
one year and six months, teaching the reason/word/say-
ing of God among them.

18.12 And from Gallio being proconsul of Achaia,
the Judeans unanimously rose up against Paul and they
brought him beside/in the presence of the judgment
seat, 18.13 saying that this (one) persuades/induces
the men to reverence/worship God beside/apart from the
law. 18.14 And of Paul being about to open the mouth,
Gallio said to the Judeans: If indeed it was *for* some
wrong or an evil crime, O Judeans, I would bear with
ye according to a saying/word; 18.15 but if it is
for questions concerning a saying/word and names and
the law according to ye, ye yourselves will see *to it*;
I, I wish/plan not to be a judge of these (things).
18.16 And he drove them away from the tribunal/judg-
ment seat. 18.17 But all, having taken hold of Sosthenes the congregationleader, they were beating *him*
before the tribunal; and nothing of these (things) was
being a care to Gallio. 18.18 But Paul, having still
remained/continued *for* considerable days, having bid
farewell to the brothers, he sailed away to Syria, and
Priscilla and Aquila *were* with him, having shorn the
head in Cenchrea, for he was having a vow/oath. 18.19
And they arrived in Ephesus, and he left them there,
but himself having entered into the congregation, he
reasoned/disputed with the Judeans. 18.20 And from
them asking *him* to remain over/for more time, he
consented not. 18.21 but having bid farewell and
having said: I shall return to ye again, from God
being willing, he set sail from Ephesus; 18.22 and
having gone down to Caesarea, having gone up and
greeted the assembly, he went down to Antioch, 18.23
and having done a certain time, he went out, going in

465

Γαλατικὴν χώραν καὶ Φρυγίαν, στηρίζων πάντας τοὺς μαθητάς.

18.24 Ἰουδαῖος δέ τις Ἀπολλῶς ὀνόματι, Ἀλεξανδρεὺς τῷ γένει, ἀνὴρ λόγιος, κατήντησεν εἰς Ἔφεσον, δυνατὸς ὢν ἐν ταῖς γραφαῖς. 18.25 οὗτος ἦν κατηχημένος τὴν ὁδὸν τοῦ κυρίου, καὶ ζέων τῷ πνεύματι ἐλάλει καὶ ἐδίδασκεν ἀκριβῶς τὰ περὶ τοῦ Ἰησοῦ, ἐπιστάμενος μόνον τὸ βάπτισμα Ἰωάννου. 18.26 οὗτός τε ἤρξατο παρρησιάζεσθαι ἐν τῇ συναγωγῇ· ἀκούσαντες δὲ αὐτοῦ Πρίσκιλλα καὶ Ἀκύλας προσελάβοντο αὐτὸν καὶ ἀκριβέστερον αὐτῷ ἐξέθεντο τὴν ὁδὸν τοῦ θεοῦ.

18.27 βουλομένου δὲ αὐτοῦ διελθεῖν εἰς τὴν Ἀχαΐαν προτρεψάμενοι οἱ ἀδελφοὶ ἔγραψαν τοῖς μαθηταῖς ἀποδέξασθαι αὐτόν· ὃς παραγενόμενος συνεβάλετο πολὺ τοῖς πεπιστευκόσιν διὰ τῆς χάριτος· 18.28 εὐτόνως γὰρ τοῖς Ἰουδαίοις διακατηλέγχετο δημοσίᾳ ἐπιδικνὺς διὰ τῶν γραφῶν εἶναι τὸν χριστὸν, Ἰησοῦν.

19.1 Ἐγένετο δὲ ἐν τῷ τὸν Ἀπολλῶ εἶναι ἐν Κορίνθῳ Παῦλον διελθόντα τὰ ἀνωτερικὰ μέρη κατελθῖν εἰς Ἔφεσον καὶ εὑρῖν τινας μαθητάς, 19.2 εἶπέν τε πρὸς αὐτούς, εἰ πνεῦμα ἅγιον ἐλάβετε πιστεύσαντες; οἱ δὲ πρὸς αὐτόν, ἀλλ' οὐδ' εἰ πνεῦμα ἅγιον ἔστιν ἠκούσαμεν. 19.3 ὁ δὲ εἶπέν, εἰς τί οὖν ἐβαπτίσθητε; οἱ δὲ εἶπαν, εἰς τὸ Ἰωάννου βάπτισμα.

19.4 εἶπεν δὲ Παῦλος, Ἰωάννης ἐβάπτισεν βάπτισμα μετανοίας, τῷ λαῷ λέγων εἰς τὸν ἐρχόμενον μετ' αὐτὸν ἵνα πιστεύσωσιν, τοῦτ' ἔστιν εἰς τὸν Ἰησοῦν. 19.5 ἀκούσαντες δὲ ἐβαπτίσθησαν εἰς τὸ ὄνομα τοῦ κυρίου Ἰησοῦ· 19.6 καὶ ἐπιθέντος αὐτοῖς τοῦ Παύλου χῖρας ἦλθε τὸ πνεῦμα τὸ ἅγιον ἐπ' αὐτούς, ἐλάλουν τε γλώσσαις καὶ ἐπροφήτευον. 19.7 ἦσαν δὲ οἱ πάντες ἄνδρες ὡσεὶ δώδεκα. 19.8 εἰσελθὼν δὲ εἰς τὴν συναγωγὴν ἐπαρρησιάζετο ἐπὶ μῆνας τρῖς διαλεγόμενος καὶ

order through the Galatian country and Phrygia, strengthening/confirming all the learners/pupils.

18.24 And a certain Judean, Apollos by name, an Alexandrian by the race/kind, a learned/eloquent man, arrived in Ephesus, being powerful/able in/with the writings. 18.25 This (one) was instructing/revealing the way/road of the Lord, and boiling/being fervent in the spirit, he was speaking and teaching accurately the (things) concerning Jesus, understanding only the baptism of John. 18.26 And this (one) began to speak boldly/freely in the congregation. And having heard from him, Priscilla and Aquila took him aside and more accurately set forth/explained the way/road of God to him.

18.27 And of him planning to go through into Achia, being encouraged, the brothers wrote to the learners/pupils to welcome him; who having arrived he contributed much/gave much assistance to those having believed through the grace/favor; 18.28 for he was vigorously refuting to the Judeans in public, demonstrating through the writings *for* Jesus to be the anointed (one).

19.1 And it happened in the (time) *for* Apollos to be in Corinth *for* Paul, having gone through the upper/inland parts, to go down into Ephesus and to find some learners/pupils, 19.2 and he said to them: If having believed, did ye receive a holy spirit? And the (they) to him: But we did not hear if there is a holy spirit. 19.3 And the (he) said: Then in what were ye baptized? And the (they) said: In the baptism of John.

19.4 And Paul said: John baptized a baptism of repentance, saying to the people that they should believe in the (one) coming after him, this is in Jesus. 19.5 And having heard, they were baptized in the name of the Lord Jesus. 19.6 And from Paul laying hands on them, the holy spirit came over/upon them, and they were speaking in languages and prophesying. 19.7 And all the men were about twelve. 19.8 And having entered into the congregation, he was speaking boldly/freely over/for three months, reasoning and

πίθων τὰ περὶ τῆς βασιλείας τοῦ θεοῦ. 19.9 ὡς δέ τινες ἐσκληρύνοντο καὶ ἠπίθουν κακολογοῦντες τὴν ὁδὸν ἐνώπιον τοῦ πλήθους, ἀποστὰς ἀπ' αὐτῶν ἀφώρισεν τοὺς μαθητάς, καθ' ἡμέραν διαλεγόμενος ἐν τῇ σχολῇ Τυράννου. 19.10 τοῦτο δὲ ἐγένετο ἐπὶ ἔτη δύο, ὥστε πάντας τοὺς κατοικοῦντας τὴν Ἀσίαν ἀκοῦσαι τὸν λόγον τοῦ κυρίου, Ἰουδαίους τε καὶ Ἕλληνας. 19.11 Δύναμίς τε οὐ τὰς τυχούσας ὁ θεὸς ἐποίει διὰ τῶν χιρῶν Παύλου, 19.12 ὥστε καὶ ἐπὶ τοὺς ἀσθενοῦντας ἀποφέρεσθαι ἀπὸ τοῦ χρωτὸς αὐτοῦ σουδάρια ἢ σιμικίνθια καὶ ἀπαλλάσσεσθαι ἀπ' αὐτῶν τὰς νόσους, τά τε πνεύματα τὰ πονηρὰ ἐκπορεύεσθαι.

19.13 ἐπεχίρησαν δέ τινες καὶ τῶν περιερχομένων Ἰουδαίων ἐξορκιστῶν ὀνομάζειν ἐπὶ τοὺς ἔχοντας τὰ πνεύματα τὰ πονηρὰ τὸ ὄνομα τοῦ κυρίου Ἰησοῦ λέγοντες, ὁρκίζω ὑμᾶς τὸν κύριον Ἰησοῦν ὃν Παῦλος κηρύσσει. 19.14 ἦσαν δέ τινες Σκευᾶ Ἰουδαίου ἀρχιερέως ἑπτὰ υἱοὶ τοῦτο ποιοῦντες.

19.15 ἀποκριθὲν δὲ τὸ πνεῦμα τὸ πονηρὸν εἶπεν αὐτοῖς, τὸν μὲν Ἰησοῦν γινώσκω καὶ τὸν Παῦλον ἐπίσταμαι, ὑμεῖς δὲ τίνες ἐστέ; 19.16 καὶ ἐφαλόμενος ὁ ἄνθρωπος ἐπ' αὐτοὺς ἐν ᾧ ἦν τὸ πνεῦμα τὸ πονηρὸν κατακυριεύσας ἀμφοτέρων ἴσχυσεν κατ' αὐτῶν, ὥστε γυμνοὺς καὶ τετραυματισμένους ἐκφυγεῖν ἐκ τοῦ οἴκου ἐκείνου.

19.17 τοῦτο δὲ ἐγένετο γνωστὸν πᾶσιν Ἰουδαίοις τε καὶ Ἕλλησιν τοῖς κατοικοῦσιν τὴν Ἔφεσον, καὶ ἐπέπεσεν φόβος ἐπὶ πάντας αὐτούς, καὶ ἐμεγαλύνετο τὸ ὄνομα τοῦ κυρίου Ἰησοῦ.

19.18 πολλοί τε τῶν πεπιστευκότων ἤρχοντο ἐξομολογούμενοι καὶ ἀναγγέλλοντες τὰς πράξεις αὐτῶν. 19.19 ἱκανοὶ δὲ τῶν τὰ περίεργα πραξάντων συνενέγκαντες τὰς βίβλους κατέκεον ἐνώπιον πάντων· καὶ συνεψήφισαν τὰς τιμὰς αὐτῶν καὶ εὗρον ἀργυρίου μυριάδας πέντε. 19.20 οὕτως κατὰ κράτος τοῦ κυρίου ὁ λόγος ηὔξανεν καὶ ἴσχυσεν. 19.21 ὡς δὲ ἐπληρώθη ταῦτα, ἔθετο ὁ Παῦλος ἐν τῷ πνεύματι διελθὼν τὴν Μακαιδονίαν

persuading the (things) concerning the kingdom of God. 19.9 But as some were being hardened and were disobey-ing, speaking against the road/way before the multi-tude, having withdrawn from them, he separated/set apart the learners/pupils, reasoning daily in the school of Tyrannus. 19.10 And thus happened over/for two years, so as *for* all those inhabiting Asia to hear the saying/word of the Lord, both Judeans and Greeks. 19.11 And God did/made powers, not the ordinary (things), through the hands of Paul, 19.12 so as even *for* handkerchiefs or aprons to be brought away from his skin to/upon the sick (ones) *for* diseases to depart from them, and *for* the evil spirits to be going out.

19.13 But also some of the Judeans, going about being exorcists, attempted to name/call on the name of the Lord Jesus over those having the evil spirits, saying: I adjure/implore ye *by* the Lord Jesus whom Paul heralds/preaches. 19.14 And there were seven sons of a certain Sceva, a Judean high priest, doing this.

19.15 And answering, the evil spirit said to them: I indeed know Jesus and I understand Paul, but ye, who are ye? 19.16 And the man in whom the evil spirit was, having leaped upon them, having become lord/master of both, he was strong/prevailed against them, so as to flee out of that house naked and having been wounded.

19.17 And this became known to all, both Judeans and Greeks, to those inhabiting Ephesus, and fear fell upon them all, and the name of the Lord Jesus was being magnified.

19.18 And many of those having believed were coming, confessing and reporting their practices. 19.19 And considerable (men) from those having prac-ticed the curious (things)/magic, having brought the scrolls, they were burning *them* before all; and they counted up the prices/values of them and they found five myriads of silver. 19.20 So through power/might the saying/word of the Lord was growing and was strong. 19.21 And when these (things) were finished, Paul set himself in/by the spirit, having gone through

καὶ Ἀχαΐαν πορεύεσθαι εἰς Ἱεροσόλυμα, εἰπὼν ὅτι μετὰ τὸ γενέσθαι με ἐκεῖ δεῖ με καὶ Ῥώμην ἰδεῖν.

19.22 ἀποστίλας δὲ εἰς τὴν Μακαιδονίαν δύο τῶν διακονούντων αὐτῷ, Τιμόθεον καὶ Ἔραστον, αὐτὸς ἐπέσχεν χρόνον εἰς τὴν Ἀσίαν. 19.23 ἐγένετο δὲ κατὰ τὸν καιρὸν ἐκῖνον τάραχος οὐχ ὀλίγος περὶ τῆς ὁδοῦ.

19.24 Δημήτριος γάρ τις ὀνόματι, ἀργυροκόπος, ποιῶν ναοὺς ἀργυροῦς Ἀρτέμιδος παρείχετο τοῖς τεχνίταις οὐκ ὀλίγην ἐργασίαν, 19.25 οὓς συναθροίσας καὶ τοὺς περὶ τὰ τοιαῦτας ἐργάτας εἶπεν, ἄνδρες, ἐπίστασθαι ὅτι ἐκ ταύτης τῆς ἐργασίας ἡ εὐπορία ἡμῖν ἐστιν, 19.26 καὶ θεωρεῖτε καὶ ἀκούετε ὅτι οὐ μόνον Ἐφέσου ἀλλὰ σχεδὸν πάσης τῆς Ἀσίας ὁ Παῦλος οὗτος μετέστησεν ἱκανὸν ὄχλον, λέγων ὅτι οὐκ εἰσὶν θεοὶ οἱ διὰ χειρῶν γινόμενοι. 19.27 οὐ μόνον δὲ τοῦτο κινδυνεύει ἡμῖν τὸ μέρος εἰς ἀπελεγμὸν ἐλθεῖν, καὶ τὸ τῆς μεγάλης θεᾶς Ἀρτέμιδος ἱερὸν εἰς οὐθὲν λογισθῆναι, μέλλειν τε καὶ καθαιρεῖσθαι τῆς μεγαλιότητος αὐτῆς, ἣν ὅλη ἡ Ἀσία καὶ ἡ οἰκουμένη σέβεται. 19.28 ἀκούσαντες δὲ καὶ γενόμενοι πλήρις θυμοῦ ἔκραζον λέγοντες, μεγάλη ἡ Ἄρτεμις Ἐφεσίων. 19.29 καὶ ἐπλήσθη ἡ πόλις τῆς συγχύσεως, ὥρμησάν τε ὁμοθυμαδὸν εἰς τὸ θέατρον συναρπάσαντες Γάϊον καὶ Ἀρίσταρχον Μακαιδόνας, συνεκδήμους Παύλου.

19.30 Παύλου δὲ βουλομένου εἰσελθῖν εἰς τὸν δῆμον οὐκ εἴων αὐτὸν οἱ μαθηταί· 19.31 τινὲς δὲ καὶ τῶν Ἀσιαρχῶν, ὄντες αὐτῷ φίλοι, πέμψαντες πρὸς αὐτὸν παρεκάλουν μὴ δοῦναι ἑαυτὸν εἰς τὸ θέατρον. 19.32 ἄλλοι μὲν οὖν ἄλλο τι ἔκραζον, ἦν γὰρ ἡ ἐκκλησία συγκεχυμένη, καὶ οἱ πλείους οὐκ ᾔδεισαν τίνος ἕνεκα συνεληλύθισαν.

19.33 ἐκ δὲ τοῦ ὄχλου συνεβίβασαν Ἀλέξανδρον, προβαλόντων αὐτὸν τῶν Ἰουδαίων· ὁ δὲ Ἀλέξανδρος κατασίσας

Macedonia and Achaia, to go to Jerusalem, having said: After the (thing) *for* me to become there, it is necessary *for* me also to see Rome.

19.22 And having sent two of those serving/ministering with him, Timothy and Erastus, into Macedonia, he himself stopped *for* a time in Asia. 19.23 And there became through/about that time not a little trouble concerning the way/road.

19.24 For a certain (one), Demetrius by name, a silversmith, making silver temples of Artemis was providing not a little work/business for the craftsmen, 19.25 whom having gathered also the workers about such things, he said: Men, understand ye that our living/prosperity is from this business/work, 19.26 ye both behold and hear that this Paul removed/misled a considerable crowd, not only from Ephesus but nearly all of Asia, saying that the (things) coming about through hands are not gods. 19.27 And not only this is in danger, the part for us to come into disrepute, *but* also *for* the temple of the great goddess Artemis to be reckoned/accounted to/for nothing, and also to be about to be destroyed/pulled down from her majesty/greatness, whom all Asia and the empire/inhabited earth respects/reverences. 19.28 But having heard and having become full of wrath, they were crying out, saying: Great *is* Artemis of Ephesians. 19.29 And the city was filled from the confusion, and they rushed with one accord into the theater, having snatched/dragged away Gaius and Aristarchus, Macedonians, traveling companions of Paul.

19.30 And of Paul planning to go into the populace/public/mob, the learners/pupils were not allowing him. 19.31 But also some of the Asiarchs, being friends with him, having sent to him, they were beseeching *him* not to give himself in the theater. 19.32 Then others indeed were crying out something other, for the assembly had been confused, and the most/majority knew not on account of what they had gathered.

19.33 And they instructed Alexander, one out of the crowd, from the Judeans having put him forward; and Alexander, having raised/waved the hand, was

τὴν χεῖρα ἤθελεν ἀπολογεῖσθαι τῷ δήμῳ. 19.34 ἐπιγνόντες δὲ ὅτι Ἰουδαῖός ἐστιν φωνὴ ἐγένετο μία ἐκ πάντων ὡς ἐπὶ ὥρας δύο κραζόντων, μεγάλη ἡ Ἄρτεμις Ἐφεσίων.

19.35 καταστίλας δὲ ὁ γραμματεὺς τὸν ὄχλον φησίν, ἄνδρες Ἐφέσιοι, τίς γάρ ἐστιν ἀνθρώπων ὃς οὐ γινώσκι τὴν Ἐφεσίων πόλιν νεωκόρον οὖσαν τῆς μεγάλης Ἀρτέμιδος καὶ τοῦ διοπετοῦς; 19.36 ἀναντιρρήτων οὖν ὄντων τούτων δέον ἐστὶν ὑμᾶς κατεσταλμένους ὑπάρχιν καὶ μηδὲν προπετὲς πράσσειν. 19.37 ἠγάγετε γὰρ τοὺς ἄνδρας τούτους οὔτε ἱεροσύλους οὔτε βλασφημοῦντας τὴν θεὸν ἡμῶν. 19.38 εἰ μὲν οὖν Δημήτριος καὶ οἱ σὺν αὐτῷ τεχνῖται ἔχουσιν πρός τινα λόγον, ἀγοραῖοι ἄγονται καὶ ἀνθύπατοί εἰσιν· ἐγκαλείτωσαν ἀλλήλοις. 19.39 εἰ δέ τι περὶ ἑτέρων ἐπιζητεῖται, ἐν τῇ ἐννόμῳ ἐκκλησίᾳ ἐπιλυθήσεται. 19.40 καὶ γὰρ κινδυνεύομεν ἐγκαλῖσθαι στάσεως περὶ τῆς σήμερον, μηδενὸς αἰτίου ὑπάρχοντος, περὶ οὗ οὐ δυνησόμεθα ἀποδοῦναι λόγον περὶ τῆς συστροφῆς ταύτης. καὶ ταῦτα εἰπὼν ἀπέλυσε τὴν ἐκκλησίαν.

20.1 Μετὰ δὲ τὸ παύσασθαι τὸν θόρυβον μεταπεμψάμενος ὁ Παῦλος τοὺς μαθητὰς καὶ παρακαλέσας, καὶ ἀσπασάμενος ἐξῆλθεν πορεύεσθαι εἰς Μακαιδονίαν. 20.2 διελθὼν δὲ τὰ μέρη ἐκεῖνα καὶ παρακαλέσας αὐτοὺς λόγῳ πολλῷ ἦλθεν εἰς τὴν Ἑλλάδα, 20.3 ποιήσας τε μῆνας τρεῖς γενομένης ἐπιβουλῆς αὐτῷ ὑπὸ τῶν Ἰουδαίων μέλλοντι ἀνάγεσθαι εἰς τὴν Συρίαν ἐγένετο γνώμης τοῦ ὑποστρέφιν διὰ Μακεδονίας. 20.4 συνείπετο δὲ αὐτῷ Σώπατρος Πύρρου Βεροιεὸς, Θεσσαλονικαίων δὲ Ἀρίσταρχος καὶ Σεκοῦνδος, καὶ Γάϊος Δερβαῖος καὶ Τιμόθεος, Ἀσιανοὶ δὲ Τυχικὸς καὶ Τρόφιμος. 20.5 οὗτοι δὲ προσελθόντες ἔμεινον ἡμᾶς ἐν Τρῳάδει· 20.6 ἡμεῖς δὲ ἐξεπλεύσαμεν μετὰ τὰς ἡμέρας τῶν ἀζύμων ἀπὸ Φιλίππων, καὶ ἤλθομεν πρὸς αὐτοὺς εἰς τὴν Τρῳάδα ἀπὸ ἡμερῶν πέντε, ὅπου διετρίψαμεν ἡμέρας ἑπτά. 20.7 ἐν δὲ τῇ μιᾷ τῶν σαββάτων συνηγμένων ἡμῶν κλάσαι

wanting to make a defense to the public/mob. 19.34 But knowing that he is a Judean, there became one voice from all over/for about two hours, crying loudly: Great *is* Artemis of Ephesians.

19.35 And the scribe, having quieted the crowd, says: Men, Ephesians, for who is there of men who knows not the city of Ephesians being temple keeper of the great Artemis and of the (thing) fallen from heaven? 19.36 Therefore, from these (things) being undeniable it is needful/proper to exist having been quieted and to practice nothing rash. 19.37 For ye brought these men, *being* neither temple robbers nor blaspheming your God. 19.38 Therefore, if indeed Demetrius and the craftsmen with him have an account/a word to anyone, there are court sessions and proconsuls; let them bring charges against one another. 19.39 But if ye seek for anything further, it will be settled in the lawful assembly. 19.40 For we are also in danger to be accused of insurrection concerning the (thing) today, it being not from a cause, about which we shall not be able to give from an account/reason concerning this commotion. And having said these (things) he dismissed the assembly.

20.1 And after the (thing) *for* the uproar to cease, Paul, having summoned the learners/pupils and exhorted/consoled *them*, and having taken leave he went out to go to Macedonia. 20.2 And having gone through those parts and having exhorted/consoled them by much reasoning/speaking he went to Greece, 20.3 and having done three months, a plot having become to/against him by the Judeans, being about to set sail to Syria, he became of a mind of/for the (thing) to return through Macedonia. 20.4 And Sopater of Pyrrhus a Beroean was accompanying with him, and Aristarchus and Secundus of Thessalonians, and Gaius a Derbaean and Timothy, and Asians Tychicus and Trophimus. 20.5 And these, having drawn near, were waiting for us in Troas; 20.6 and we, having sailed out from Philippi after the days of the unleavened (loaves), and we went to them in Troas from five days, where we continued/spent seven days.

20.7 And from us having been gathered on the

ἄρτον ὁ Παῦλος διελέγετο αὐτοῖς, μέλλων ἐξιέναι τῇ ἐπαύριον, παρέτινέν τε τὸν λόγον μέχρι μεσονυκτίου. 20.8 ἦσαν δὲ λαμπάδες ἱκαναὶ ἐν τῷ ὑπερῴῳ οὗ ἦμεν συνηγμένοι· 20.9 καθεζόμενος δέ τις νεανίας ὀνόματι Εὔτυχος ἐπὶ τῆς θυρίδος, καταφερόμενος ὕπνῳ βαθεῖ διαλεγομένου τοῦ Παύλου ἐπὶ πλῖον, κατενεχθεὶς ἀπὸ τοῦ ὕπνου ἔπεσεν ἀπὸ τοῦ τριστέγου κάτω καὶ ἤρθη νεκρός. 20.10 καταβὰς δὲ ὁ Παῦλος ἐπέπεσεν αὐτῷ καὶ συμπεριλαβὼν εἶπεν, μὴ θορυβεῖσθε, ἡ γὰρ ψυχὴ αὐτοῦ ἐν αὐτῷ ἐστιν. 20.11 ἀναβὰς δὲ καὶ κλάσας τὸν ἄρτον καὶ γευσάμενος ἐφ’ ἱκανόν τε ὁμιλήσας ἄχρι αὐγῆς οὕτως ἐξῆλθεν. 20.12 ἤγαγον δὲ τὸν παῖδα ζῶντα, καὶ παρεκλήθησαν οὐ μετρίως.

20.13 ἡμεῖς δὲ προελθόντες ἐπὶ τὸ πλοῖον ἀνήχθημεν ἐπὶ τὴν ῎Ασσον, ἐκεῖθεν μέλλοντες ἀναλαμβάνιν τὸν Παῦλον, οὕτως γὰρ διατεταγμένος ἦν μέλλων αὐτὸς πεζεύειν. 20.14 ὡς δὲ συνέβαλλεν ἡμῖν εἰς τὴν ῎Ασσον, ἀναλαβόντες αὐτὸν ἤλθομεν εἰς Μιτυλήνην, 20.15 κἀκεῖθεν ἀποπλεύσαντες τῇ ἐπιούσῃ κατηντήσαμεν ἄντικρυς Χίου, τῇ δὲ ἑτέρᾳ παρεβάλομεν εἰς Σάμον, τῇ δὲ ἐχομένῃ ἤλθομεν εἰς Μίλητον· 20.16 κεκρίκει γὰρ ὁ Παῦλος παραπλεῦσαι τὴν ῎Εφεσον, ὅπως μὴ γένηται αὐτῷ χρονοτριβῆσαι ἐν τῇ ᾿Ασίᾳ, ἔσπευδεν γὰρ εἰ δυνατὸν εἴη αὐτῷ τὴν ἡμέραν τῆς πεντηκοστῆς γενέσθαι εἰς ῾Ιερουσαλήμ.

20.17 ἀπὸ δὲ τῆς Μιλήτου πέμψας εἰς ῎Εφεσον μετεκαλέσατο τοὺς πρεσβυτέρους τῆς ἐκκλησίας. 20.18 ὡς δὲ παρεγένοντο πρὸς αὐτὸν εἶπεν αὐτοῖς, ὑμεῖς ἐπίστασθαι ἀπὸ πρώτης ἡμέρας ἀφ’ ἧς ἐπέβην εἰς τὴν ᾿Ασίαν πῶς μεθ’ ὑμῶν τὸν πάντα χρόνον ἐγενόμην, 20.19 δουλεύων τῷ κυρίῳ μετὰ πάσης ταπινοφρόσύνης καὶ δακρύων καὶ πιρασμῶν τῶν συμβάντων μοι ἐν ταῖς ἐπιβουλαῖς τῶν ᾿Ιουδαίων· 20.20 ὡς οὐδὲν ὑπεστιλάμην τῶν συμφερόντων τοῦ μὴ ἀναγγῖλαι ὑμῖν καὶ διδάξαι ὑμᾶς δημοσίᾳ καὶ κατ’ οἴκους, 20.21 διαμαρτυρόμενος ᾿Ιουδαίοις τε

one/first (day) of the sabbaths to break a loaf, Paul was reasoning/debating with them, being about to depart on the morrow, and he was prolonging the saying/word until midnight. 20.8 and sufficient lamps were in the upper room where we had been assembled. 20.9 And a certain youth, Eutychus by name, is sitting on the window, being overcome by a deep sleep from Paul's reasoning over more *time*, having been overcome from the sleep, he fell down from the third floor and was taken up dead. 20.10 But having gone down, Paul fell on him and having embrace *him* he said: Fear ye not, for his soul/life is in him. 20.11 And having gone up and broke the loaf and having tasted *it* himself, and having conferred over a considerable *time* until daybreak, he thus went out. 20.12 And they brought the boy living, and they were comforted not moderately/greatly.

20.13 And we, having gone before to the ship, we set sail to Assos, *for* Paul being about to be taken up/aboard from there, for thus it had been arranged, he himself being about to go by land. 20.14 And when he was put with us in Assos, having taken him up/aboard, we went to Mitylene, 20.15 and having sailed away from there we arrived opposite Chios on the following day, and we crossed over on the other/different to Samos, and by the holding we came to Miletus. 20.16 For Paul had decided to sail past Ephesus, so as not becoming for him to delay in Asia, for he was hasting if it may be possible for him to become in Jerusalem *for* the day of the Pentecost (festival).

20.17 And having sent from Miletus to Ephesus, he called to himself the elders of the assembly. 20.18 And when they came to him, he said to them: Ye, ye understand from a first day from which I set foot in Asia, how I myself became with ye all the time, 20.19 serving as a slave for the Lord with every humility and tears and trials/temptations having happened to me in/by the plots/conspiracies of the Judeans, 20.20 as I kept back/silent none of the beneficial things from the (thing) not to announce/report to ye and to teach ye in public and from house to house, 20.21 testifying solemnly to both Judeans and

καὶ Ἕλλησι τὴν εἰς θεὸν μετάνοιαν καὶ πίστιν εἰς τὸν κύριον ἡμῶν Ἰησοῦν χριστοῦν.

20.22 καὶ νῦν ἰδοὺ δεδεμένος ἐγὼ τῷ πνεύματι πορεύομε εἰς Ἰερουσαλήμ, τὰ ἐν αὐτῇ συναντήσοντά μοι μὴ εἰδώς, 20.23 πλὴν ὅτι τὸ πνεῦμα τὸ ἅγιον κατὰ πόλιν διαμαρτύρεταί μοι λέγον ὅτι δεσμὰ καὶ θλίψις με μένουσιν. 20.24 ἀλλ' οὐδενὸς λόγου ποιοῦμαι τὴν ψυχὴν τιμίαν ἐμαυτῷ ὡς τελιώσω τὸν δρόμον μου καὶ τὴν διακονίαν ἣν ἔλαβον παρὰ τοῦ κυρίου Ἰησοῦ, διαμαρτύρασθαι τὸ εὐαγγέλιον τῆς χάριτος τοῦ θεοῦ. 20.25 καὶ νῦν ἰδοὺ ἐγὼ οἶδα ὅτι οὐκ ὄψεσθε τὸ πρόσωπόν μου ὑμεῖς πάντες ἐν οἷς διῆλθον κηρύσσων τὴν βασιλείαν. 20.26 διότι μαρτύρομαι ὑμῖν ἐν τῇ σήμερον ἡμέρᾳ ὅτι καθαρός εἰμι ἀπὸ τοῦ αἵματος πάντων, 20.27 οὐ γὰρ ὑπεστιλάμην τοῦ μὴ ἀναγγῖλαι πᾶσαν τὴν βουλὴν τοῦ θεοῦ ὑμῖν. 20.28 προσέχετε ἑαυτοῖς καὶ παντὶ τῷ ποιμνίῳ, ἐν ᾧ ὑμᾶς τὸ πνεῦμα τὸ ἅγιον ἔθετο ἐπισκόπους, ποιμένιν τὴν ἐκκλησίαν τοῦ θεοῦ, ἣν περιεποιήσατο διὰ τοῦ αἵματος τοῦ ἰδίου.

20.29 ἐγὼ οἶδα ὅτι εἰσελεύσονται μετὰ τὴν ἄφιξίν μου λύκοι βαρῖς εἰς ὑμᾶς μὴ φιδόμενοι τοῦ ποιμνίου, 20.30 καὶ ἐξ ὑμῶν αὐτῶν ἀναστήσονται ἄνδρες λαλοῦντες διεστραμμένα τοῦ ἀποσπᾶν τοὺς μαθητὰς ὀπίσω αὐτῶν. 20.31 διὸ γρηγορῖται, μνημονεύοντες ὅτι τριετίαν νύκτα καὶ ἡμέραν οὐκ ἐπαυσάμην μετὰ δακρύων νουθετῶν ἕνα ἕκαστον. 20.32 καὶ τὰ νῦν παρατίθεμαι ὑμῖν τῷ θεῷ καὶ τῷ λόγῳ τῆς χάριτος αὐτοῦ τῷ δυναμένῳ οἰκοδομῆσαι καὶ δοῦναι τὴν κληρονομίαν ἐν τοῖς ἡγιασμένοις πᾶσιν. 20.33 ἀργυρίου ἢ χρυσίου ἢ ἱματισμοῦ οὐδενὸς ἐπεθύμησα· 20.34 αὐτοὶ γινώσκετε ὅτι ταῖς χρίαις μου καὶ τοῖς οὖσι μετ' ἐμοῦ ὑπηρέτησαν αἱ χῖρες αὗται.

20.35 πάντα ὑπέδειξα ὑμῖν ὅτι οὕτως κοπιῶντας δεῖ ἀντιλαμβάνεσθαι τῶν ἀσθενούντων, μνημονεύειν τε τῶν λόγων τοῦ κυρίου Ἰησοῦ ὅτι αὐτὸς εἶπεν,

μακάριόν ἐστιν μᾶλλον διδόναι ἢ λαμβάνιν. 20.36 καὶ

Greeks the repentance to God and faith in our Lord Jesus, the anointed (one).

20.22 And now behold I, having been bound by the spirit, I go to Jerusalem, not knowing the (things) going to happen to me in her/*it*, 20.23 except that the holy spirit witnesses solemnly to me from city to city saying that bonds and oppression/afflictions wait *for* me. 20.24 But I make not the soul/life precious for myself, as/when I might finish my course and the service/ministry which I received from the Lord Jesus, to solemnly testify the good message/gospel of the grace/gift of God. 20.25 And now behold, I, I know that ye, ye all will not see my face among (those) whom I went through heralding/preaching the kingdom. 20.26 Therefore, I testify to ye today, in the day that I am clean from the blood of all; 20.27 for I kept not back/was not silent from the (thing) not to announce/report all the purpose/will of God to ye. 20.28 Take heed for yourselves and all the flock, in which the holy spirit placed overseers/bishops, to shepherd/tend the assembly of God, which he acquired/obtained through his own blood.

20.29 I know not that after my departure grievous wolves will come in to ye not refraining from/sparing the flock, 20.30 and men will rise up out of ye yourselves speaking (things) having been distorted from the (thing) to draw the learners/pupils away after themselves. 20.31 Wherefore watch ye, remembering that *for* three years I ceased/rested not night and day admonishingeach one with tears. 20.32 And the (things) I now entrust to ye for the Lord and for the saying/word of his grace for the (thing) being able to build/edify and to give the inheritance among all those having been sanctified/set apart. 20.33 I did not desire silver or gold or clothing from anyone; 20.34 ye yourselves know that these hands served/attended to the needs for those being with me.

20.35 I showed all (things) to ye that so laboring it is necessary to be helpers of the ailing (ones), and from the sayings/words of the Lord Jesus that he himself said/spoke:

It is more happy to give than to receive. 20.36

ταῦτα εἰπὼν θὶς τὰ γόνατα αὐτοῦ σὺν πᾶσιν αὐτοῖς προσηύξατο. 20.37 ἱκανός τε κλαυθμὸς ἐγένετο πάντων, καὶ ἐπιπεσόντες ἐπὶ τὸν τράχηλον τοῦ Παύλου κατεφίλουν αὐτόν, 20.38 ὀδυνώμενοι μάλιστα ἐπὶ τῷ λόγῳ ᾧ εἰρήκει ὅτι οὐκέτι μέλλουσιν τὸ πρόσωπον αὐτοῦ θεωρῖν.

προέπεμπον δὲ αὐτὸν εἰς τὸ πλοῖον. 21.1 ὡς δὲ ἐγένετο ἀναχθῆναι ἡμᾶς ἀποσπασθέντας ἀπ' αὐτῶν, εὐθυδρομήσαντες ἤλθομεν εἰς τὴν Κῶ, τῇ δὲ ἑξῆς εἰς τὴν Ῥόδον, κἀκεῖθεν εἰς Πάταρα· 21.2 καὶ εὑρόντες πλοῖον διαπερῶν εἰς Φοινίκην ἐπιβάντες ἀνήχθημεν. 21.3 ἀναφάναντες δὲ τὴν Κύπρον καὶ καταλιπόντες αὐτὴν εὐώνυμον ἐπλέομεν εἰς Συρίαν, καὶ κατήλθομεν εἰς Τύρον, ἐκεῖσε γὰρ τὸ πλοῖον ἦν ἀποφορτιζόμενον τὸν γόμον.

21.4 ἀνευρόντες δὲ τοὺς μαθητὰς ἐπεμίναμεν αὐτοῦ ἡμέρας ἑπτά, οἵτινες τῷ Παύλῳ ἔλεγον διὰ τοῦ πνεύματος μὴ ἐπιβαίνιν εἰς Ἱεροσόλυμα. 21.5 ὅτε δὲ ἐγένετο ἡμᾶς ἐξαρτίσαι τὰς ἡμέρας, ἐξελθόντες ἐπορευόμεθα προπεμπόντων ἡμᾶς πάντων σὺν γυναιξὶ καὶ τέκνοις ἔξω τῆς πόλεως,

καὶ θέντες τὰ γόνατα ἐπὶ τὸν αἰγιαλὸν προσευξάμενοι 21.6 ἀπησπασάμεθα ἀλλήλους, καὶ ἀνέβημεν εἰς τὸ πλοῖον, ἐκεῖνοι δὲ ὑπέστρεψαν εἰς τὰ ἴδια. 21.7 ἡμεῖς δὲ τὸν πλοῦν διανύσαντες ἀπὸ Τύρου κατηντήσαμεν εἰς Πτολεμαΐδα, καὶ ἀσπασάμενοι τοὺς ἀδελφοὺς ἐμίναμεν ἡμέραν μίαν παρ' αὐτοῖς.

21.8 τῇ δὲ ἐπαύριον ἐξελθόντες ἤλθομεν εἰς Καισάριαν, καὶ εἰσελθόντες εἰς τὸν οἶκον Φιλίππου τοῦ εὐαγγελιστοῦ ὄντος ἐκ τῶν ἑπτὰ ἐμείναμεν παρ' αὐτῷ. 21.9 τούτῳ δὲ ἦσαν θυγατέρες τέσσαρες παρθένοι προφητεύουσαι.

21.10 ἐπιμενόντων δὲ αὐτῶν ἡμέρας πλίους κατῆλθέν τις ἀπὸ τῆς Ἰουδαίας προφήτης ὀνόματι Ἅγαβος, 21.11 καὶ ἐλθὼν πρὸς ἡμᾶς καὶ ἄρας τὴν ζώνην τοῦ Παύλου δήσας ἑαυτοῦ τοὺς πόδας καὶ τὰς χῖρας εἶπεν,

τάδε λέγι τὸ πνεῦμα τὸ ἅγιον, τὸν ἄνδρα οὗ ἐστιν ἡ ζώνη

And having said these (things), having put (down) his knees, he prayed with them all.   20.37 And there became/took place considerable weeping from all, and having fallen upon Paul's neck, they were fervently kissing him,   20.38 being especially pained over the saying/word which he had said, that no longer were they being about to see/behold his face.

And they were escorting him to the ship.   21.1 And it became/happened *for* us to set sail, having departed from them, having set a straight course we went to Cos, and on the next day to Rhodes, and from there to Patara;   21.2 and having found a boat crossing over to Phoenice, having embarked, we set sail. 21.3 And having sighted Cyprus and having left her behind on the left, we were sailing to Syria, and we went down to Tyre, for there the ship was unloading the cargo.

21.4 And having located his learners/pupils who was speaking to Paul through the spirit not to embark/set foot in Jerusalem, we remained/stayed seven days.   21.5 But when it became/came about *for* us to fit out/accomplish the days, having gone out, we were traveling from all escorting us with women and children outside the city,

and having put *down* the knees upon the seashore, having prayed,   21.6 we were taking leave of one another, and we embarked in the ship, and those (men) returned to their own (things).   21.7 But we, having completed the sailing voyage from Tyre, we arrived in Ptolemais, and having greeted the brothers, we stayed one day with them.

21.8   And having gone forth on the morrow, we went to Caesarea, and having entered into the house of Philip, the (one) being an evangelist out of the seven, we stayed with him.   21.9 And to/for this (one) four daughters were prophesying maidens.

21.10 And from them staying more days, a certain prophet, Agabus by name, came down from Judea,   21.11 and having come to us and having taken Paul's belt, having bound of himself the feet and the hands, he said:

The holy spirit says these (things): Thus the

472

αὕτη οὕτως δήσουσιν ἐν Ἰερουσαλὴμ οἱ Ἰουδαῖοι καὶ παραδώσουσιν εἰς χῖρας ἐθνῶν. 21.12 ὡς δὲ ἠκούσαμεν ταῦτα, παρεκαλοῦμεν ἡμῖς τε καὶ οἱ ἐντόπιοι τοῦ μὴ ἀναβαίνιν αὐτὸν εἰς Ἰερουσαλήμ.

21.13 τότε ἀπεκρίθη ὁ Παῦλος καὶ εἶπεν, τί ποιεῖτε κλέοντες καὶ συνθρύπτοντές μου τὴν καρδίαν; ἐγὼ γὰρ οὐ μόνον δεθῆναι ἀλλὰ καὶ ἀποθανῖν εἰς Ἰερουσαλὴμ ἑτοίμως ἔχω ὑπὲρ τοῦ ὀνόματος τοῦ κυρίου Ἰησοῦ. 21.14 μὴ πιθομένου δὲ αὐτοῦ ἡσυχάσαμεν εἰπόντες, τοῦ κυρίου τὸ θέλημα γεινέσθω.

21.15 μετὰ δὲ τὰς ἡμέρας ταύτας ἐπισκευασάμενοι ἀνεβαίνομεν εἰς Ἱεροσόλυμα· 21.16 συνῆλθον δὲ καὶ τῶν μαθητῶν ἀπὸ Καισαρίας σὺν ἡμῖν, ἄγοντες παρ' ᾧ ξενισθῶμεν Ἰάσονί τινι Κυπρίῳ, ἀρχαίῳ μαθητῇ. 21.17 Γενομένων δὲ ἡμῶν ἰς Ἱεροσόλυμα ἀσμένως ἀπεδέξαντο ἡμᾶς οἱ ἀδελφοί.

21.18 τῇ τε ἐπιούσῃ εἰσῄει ὁ Παῦλος σὺν ἡμῖν πρὸς Ἰάκωβον, πάντες τε παρεγένοντο οἱ πρεσβύτεροι. 21.19 καὶ ἀσπασάμενος αὐτοὺς ἐξηγεῖτο καθ' ἓν ἕκαστον ὧν ἐποίησεν ὁ θεὸς ἐν τοῖς ἔθνεσιν τῆς διακονίας αὐτοῦ. 21.20 οἱ δὲ ἀκούσαντες ἐδόξασαν τὸν θεόν, εἶπάν τε αὐτῷ, θεωρῖς, ἀδελφέ, πόσαι μυριάδες εἰσὶν τῶν πεπιστευκότων, καὶ πάντες ζηλωταὶ τοῦ νόμου ὑπάρχουσιν· 21.21 κατηχήθησαν δὲ περὶ σοῦ ὅτι ἀποστασίαν διδάσκις ἀπὸ Μωϋσέως τοὺς κατὰ τὰ ἔθνη πάντας Ἰουδαίους, λέγων μὴ περιτέμνιν αὐτοὺς τὰ τέκνα μηδὲ τοῖς ἔθεσιν περιπατῖν. 21.22 τί οὖν ἐστιν; πάντως δεῖ συνελθεῖν πλῆθος ἀκούσονται ὅτι ἐλήλυθας. 21.23 τοῦτο οὖν ποίησον ὅ σοι λέγομεν· εἰσὶν ἡμῖν ἄνδρες τέσσαρες εὐχὴν ἔχοντες ἐφ' ἑαυτῶν. 21.24 τούτους παραλαβὼν ἁγνίσθητι σὺν αὐτοῖς καὶ δαπάνησον ἐπ' αὐτοῖς ἵνα ξυρήσονται τὴν κεφαλήν, καὶ γνώσονται πάντες ὅτι ὧν κατήχηνται περὶ σοῦ οὐδέν ἐστιν, ἀλλὰ στοιχεῖς καὶ αὐτὸς φυλάσσων τὸν νόμον. 21.25 περὶ δὲ τῶν πεπιστευκότων ἐθνῶν ἡμεῖς ἐπεστίλαμεν κρίναντες φυλάσσεσθαι αὐτοὺς τό τε εἰδωλόθυτον καὶ αἷμα καὶ πνικτὸν καὶ πορνίαν.

Judeans in Jerusalem will bind the man of whom this belt is, and they will deliver him up into hands of ethnics. 21.12 And when we heard these (things), both we and the residents were exhorting/beseeching from the (thing) *for* him not to go up to Jerusalem.

21.13 Then Paul answered and said: What do ye, weeping and breaking my heart? For I, I hold readily not only to be bound but also to die in Jerusalem in behalf of the name of the Lord Jesus. 21.14 And from him not being persuaded we kept silence, having said: Let the will of the Lord come about.

21.15 And after these days, having prepared ourselves, we were going up to Jerusalem; 21.16 and (some) of the learners/pupils from Caesarea went with us, bringing Jason, a certain Cypriot, an old learner/pupil with whom we might be lodged. 21.17 And from us having become in Jerusalem, the brothers received us gladly.

21.18 And on the next day Paul was going in with us to James, and all the elders arrived. 21.19 And having greeted them, he was relating one by one each (thing) which God did among the ethnics from the service/ministry of him. 21.20 And the (they) having heard, they glorified God, and they said to him: You behold, brother, how many myriads there are of those having believed, and they are all zealots of the law. 21.21 And they were informed/instructed about you that you teach all the Judeans according to/throughout the ethnics/nations apostacy from Moses, telling them not to circumcise the children nor to walk in the customs. 21.22 What therefore is it? It is certainly necessary to come together, a multitude will hear that you have come. 21.23 Therefore, you do this which we say to you: There are four men for us holding a vow upon themselves. 21.24 Having received these, be purified with them and pay to them in order that they will shave the head, and all will know that there is nothing of which they were informed about you, but you agree with and *are* yourself guarding/keeping the law. 21.25 And concerning the ethnics having believed, we ourselves instructed by letter *for* them to guard/keep *from* both the thing sacrificed to idols and blood and

473

21.26 τότε ὁ Παῦλος παραλαβὼν τοὺς ἄνδρας, τῇ ἐχομένῃ ἡμέρᾳ σὺν αὐτοῖς ἁγνισθεὶς εἰσῄει εἰς τὸ ἱερόν, διαγγέλλων τὴν ἐκπλήρωσιν τῶν ἡμερῶν τοῦ ἁγνισμοῦ ἕως οὗ προσηνέχθη ὑπὲρ ἑνὸς ἑκάστου αὐτῶν ἡ προσφορά.

21.27 ὡς δὲ ἔμελλον αἱ ἑπτὰ ἡμέραι συντελῖσθαι, οἱ ἀπὸ τῆς Ἀσίας Ἰουδαῖοι θεασάμενοι αὐτὸν ἐν τῷ ἱερῷ συνέχεον πάντα τὸν ὄχλον καὶ ἐπέβαλον ἐπ᾽ αὐτὸν τὰς χῖρας, 21.28 κράζοντες, ἄνδρες Ἰσδραηλεῖται, βοηθῖται· οὗτός ἐστιν ὁ ἄνθρωπος ὁ κατὰ τοῦ λαοῦ καὶ τοῦ νόμου καὶ τοῦ τόπου τούτου πάντας πανταχῇ διδάσκων, ἔτι τε καὶ Ἕλληνας εἰσήγαγεν εἰς τὸ ἱερὸν καὶ κεκοίνωκεν τὸν ἅγιον τόπον τοῦτον. 21.29 ἦσαν γὰρ προεωρακότες Τρόφιμον τὸν Ἐφέσιον ἐν τῇ πόλει σὺν αὐτῷ, ὃν ἐνόμιζον ὅτι εἰς τὸ ἱερὸν εἰσήγαγεν ὁ Παῦλος.

21.30 ἐκινήθη τε ἡ πόλις ὅλη καὶ ἐγένετο συνδρομὴ τοῦ λαοῦ, καὶ ἐπιλαβόμενοι τοῦ Παύλου εἷλκον αὐτὸν ἔξω τοῦ ἱεροῦ, καὶ εὐθέως ἐκλίσθησαν αἱ θύραι. 21.31 ζητούντων τε αὐτὸν ἀποκτῖναι ἀνέβη φάσις τῷ χιλιάρχῳ τῆς σπίρης ὅτι ὅλη συγχύννεται Ἰερουσαλήμ, 21.32 ὃς ἐξαυτῆς παραλαβὼν στρατιώτας καὶ ἑκατοντάρχας κατέδραμεν ἐπ᾽ αὐτούς· οἱ δὲ ἰδόντες τὸν χιλίαρχον καὶ τοὺς στρατιώτας ἐπαύσαντο τύπτοντες τὸν Παῦλον. 21.33 τότε ἐγγίσας ὁ χιλίαρχος ἐπελάβετο αὐτοῦ καὶ ἐκέλευσε δεθῆναι ἁλύσεσι δυσί, καὶ ἐπυνθάνετο τίς εἴη καὶ τί ἐστιν πεποιηκώς. 21.34 ἄλλοι δὲ ἄλλο τι ἐπεφώνουν ἐν τῷ ὄχλῳ·

μὴ δυναμένου δὲ αὐτοῦ γνῶναι τὸ ἀσφαλὲς διὰ τὸν θόρυβον ἐκέλευσεν ἄγεσθαι αὐτὸν εἰς τὴν παρεμβολήν. 21.35 ὅτε δὲ ἐγένετο ἐπὶ τοὺς ἀναβαθμούς, συνέβη βαστάζεσθαι αὐτὸν ὑπὸ τῶν στρατιωτῶν διὰ τὴν βίαν τοῦ ὄχλου, 21.36 ἠκολούθι γὰρ τὸ πλῆθος τοῦ λαοῦ κράζοντες, αἶρε αὐτόν.

21.37 μέλλων τε εἰσάγεσθαι εἰς τὴν παρεμβολὴν ὁ Παῦλος

strangled and prostitution.

21.26   Then Paul, having taken the men, on the next day having been purified with them, he was entering into the *outer* temple, giving notice of the completion of the days of the purification until which *time* the offering might be offered in behalf of each one of them.

21.27   And when the seven days were about to be finished, the Judeans from Asia having seen/observed him in the *outer* temple were stirring up all the crowd and they laid the hands upon him,   21.28 crying out: Men, Israelites, help *us*! This (one) is the man, the (one) teaching all (men) everywhere against the people and the law and this place, and yet he also brought Greeks into the *outer* temple and has made this holy place common.   21.29   For they had previously seen Trophimus, an Ephesian, in the city with him, whom they were supposing that Paul brought into the *outer* temple.

21.30   And the whole city was aroused and there became a running together of the people, and having taken hold of Paul, they were dragging him outside the *outer* temple, and immediately the doors were closed. 21.31 And seeking to kill him, information came up to the captain/chiliarch of the cohort/band of soldiers that all Jerusalem is in confusion,   21.32 who immediately, having taken soldiers and centurions, he ran to/against them; and the (they), having seen the captain and the soldiers, they stopped beating Paul. 21.33 Then having drawn near the captain laid hold of him and ordered to be bound with two chains, and he was inquiring who he may be and what he has done. 21.34 But others among the crowd were calling out something other;

and from him not being able to know the certainty because of the uproar he ordered *for* him to be brought to the camp/fort.   21.35 And when he became on the stairs, it happened *for* him to be carried by the soldiers because of the violence of the crowd,   21.36 for the multitude of the people were following, crying out: Take him away/destroy/kill him!

21.37   And being about to be brought into the

474

λέγει τῷ χιλιάρχῳ, εἰ ἔξεστίν μοι εἰπεῖν τι πρός σέ; ὁ δὲ ἔφη, Ἑλληνιστὶ γινώσκις; 21.38 οὐκ ἄρα σὺ εἶ ὁ Αἰγύπτιος ὁ πρὸ τούτων τῶν ἡμερῶν ἀναστατώσας καὶ ἐξαγαγὼν εἰς τὴν ἔρημον τοὺς τετρακισχιλίους ἄνδρας τῶν σικαρίων;

21.39 εἶπεν δὲ ὁ Παῦλος, ἐγὼ ἄνθρωπος μέν εἰμι Ἰουδαῖος, Ταρσεὺς τῆς Κιλικίας, οὐκ ἀσήμου πόλεως πολίτης· δέομαι δέ σου, ἐπίτρεψόν μοι λαλῆσαι πρὸς τὸν λαόν. 21.40 ἐπιτρέψαντος δὲ αὐτοῦ ὁ Παῦλος ἑστὼς ἐπὶ τῶν ἀναβαθμῶν κατέσισε τῇ χειρὶ τῷ λαῷ·

πολλῆς δὲ σιγῆς γενομένης προσεφώνησεν τῇ Ἑβραΐδι διαλέκτῳ λέγων, 22.1 ἄνδρες ἀδελφοὶ καὶ πατέρες, ἀκούσατέ μου τῆς πρὸς ὑμᾶς νυνὶ ἀπολογίας 22.2 ἀκούσαντες δὲ ὅτι τῇ Ἑβραΐδι διαλέκτῳ προσεφώνει αὐτοῖς μᾶλλον παρέσχον ἡσυχίαν.

καὶ φησίν 22.3 ἐγώ ἀνήρ εἰμι Ἰουδαῖος, γεγεννημένος ἐν Ταρσῷ τῆς Κιλικίας, ἀνατεθραμμένος δὲ ἐν τῇ πόλει ταύτῃ, παρὰ τοὺς πόδας Γαμαλιὴλ πεπαιδευμένος κατὰ ἀκρίβιαν τοῦ πατρῴου νόμου, ζηλωτὴς ὑπάρχων τοῦ θεοῦ καθὼς πάντες ὑμεῖς ἐστε σήμερον· 22.4 ὃς ταύτην τὴν ὁδὸν ἐδίωξα ἄχρι θανάτου, δεσμεύων καὶ παραδιδοὺς εἰς φυλακὰς ἄνδρας τε καὶ γυναῖκας, 22.5 ὡς καὶ ὁ ἀρχιερεὺς μαρτυρῖ μοι καὶ πᾶν τὸ πρεσβυτέριον· παρ' ὧν καὶ ἐπιστολὰς δεξάμενος πρὸς τοὺς ἀδελφοὺς εἰς Δαμασκὸν ἐπορευόμην ἄξων καὶ τοὺς ἐκεῖσε ὄντας δεδεμένους εἰς Ἰερουσαλὴμ ἵνα τιμωρηθῶσιν.

22.6 ἐγένετο δέ μοι πορευομένῳ καὶ ἐγγίζοντι τῇ Δαμασκῷ περὶ μεσημβρίαν ἐξαίφνης ἐκ τοῦ οὐρανοῦ περιαστράψαι φῶς ἱκανὸν περὶ ἐμέ, 22.7 ἔπεσά τε εἰς τὸ ἔδαφος καὶ ἤκουσα φωνῆς λεγούσης μοι, Σαοὺλ Σαούλ, τί με διώκεις; 22.8 ἐγὼ δὲ ἀπεκρίθην καὶ εἶπα, τίς εἶ, κύριε; εἶπέν τε πρός με, ἐγὼ εἰμι Ἰησοῦς ὁ Ναζωραῖος ὃν σὺ διώκεις. 22.9 οἱ δὲ σὺν ἐμοὶ ὄντες τὸ μὲν φῶς ἐθεάσαντο τὴν δὲ φωνὴν οὐκ ἤκουσαν τοῦ λαλοῦντός μοι. 22.10 εἶπον δέ, τί ποιήσω, κύριε; ὁ δὲ κύριος εἶπεν πρός με, ἀναστὰς

camp/fort, Paul says to the captain: If it is lawful/permitted for me to say something to you? And the (he) was saying: You know in Greek? 21.38 Then you, you are not the Egyptian, the (one) before these days having revolted and having led the four thousand men of the Sicarii out into the desert?

21.39 And Paul said: I, I am indeed a man, a Judean, a Tarsian of Cilicia, not a citizen of an obscure city; and I beg of you, permit/allow for me to speak to the people. 21.40 And from him having allowed *it*, Paul, having stood on the stairs, motioned with the hand to the people;

and from much silence having become, he addressed *them* in the Hebrew dialect, saying: 22.1 Men, brothers and fathers, hear ye now of my defense to ye -- 22.2 And having heard that he was speaking to them in the Hebrew dialect they offered more quietness.

And he says: -- 22.3 I, I am a Judean man, having been generated/born in Tarsus of Cilicia, and having been reared in this/the same city, beside the feet of Gamaliel, having been trained/disciplined according to accuracy of the ancestral law, being a zealot of God even as all ye yourselves are today; 22.4 who prosecuted this way until death, binding and delivering up to prisons both men and women, 22.5 as even the high priest testifies for me and all the presbytery/body of elders, from whom also having received letters to the brothers in Damascus, I was going *there* willing to bring also those being in that place, having been bound, to Jerusalem in order that they might by punished. 22.6 And it happened to me, traveling and drawing near to Damascus, about noon/midday, *for* a considerable light to flash/shine around me, 22.7 and I fell to the ground and I heard a voice saying to me: Saul, Saul, why to you pursue/prosecute me? 22.8 And I, I answered and said: Who are you, lord? And he said to me: I, I am Jesus, the Nazarene whom you, you pursue/prosecute. 22.9 And the (they)/those being with me indeed beheld the light but they heard not the voice of the (one) speaking to me. 22.10 And I said: What should I do, Lord? And the Lord said to me: Having risen up, you go into Damascus, and there it

πορεύου εἰς Δαμασκόν, κἀκῖ σοι λαληθήσεται περὶ πάντων ὧν τέτακταί σοι ποιῆσαι. 22.11 ὡς δὲ οὐκ ἐνέβλεπον ἀπὸ τῆς δόξης τοῦ φωτὸς ἐκείνου, χειραγωγούμενος ὑπὸ τῶν συνόντων μοι ἦλθον εἰς Δαμασκόν.

22.12 Ἀνανίας δέ τις, ἀνὴρ εὐλαβὴς κατὰ τὸν νόμον, μαρτυρούμενος ὑπὸ πάντων τῶν κατοικούντων Ἰουδαίων, 22.13 ἐλθὼν πρός ἐμὲ καὶ ἐπιστὰς εἶπέν μοι, Σαοὺλ ἀδελφέ, ἀνάβλεψον· κἀγὼ αὐτῇ τῇ ὥρᾳ ἀνέβλεψα εἰς αὐτόν. 22.14 ὁ δὲ εἶπεν, ὁ θεὸς τῶν πατέρων ἡμῶν προεχειρίσατό σε γνῶναι τὸ θέλημα αὐτοῦ καὶ ἰδῖν τὸν δίκαιον καὶ ἀκοῦσαι φωνὴν ἐκ τοῦ στόματος αὐτοῦ, 22.15 ὅτι ἔσῃ μάρτυς αὐτῷ πρὸς πάντας ἀνθρώπους ὧν ἑώρακας καὶ ἤκουσας. 22.16 καὶ νῦν τί μέλλεις; ἀναστὰς βάπτισαι καὶ ἀπόλουσαι τὰς ἁμαρτίας σου ἐπικαλεσάμενος τὸ ὄνομα αὐτοῦ.

22.17 ἐγένετο δέ μοι ὑποστρέψαντι ἰς Ἰερουσαλὴμ καὶ προσευχομένου μου ἐν τῷ ἱερῷ γενέσθαι με ἐν ἐκστάσι 22.18 καὶ ἰδὸν αὐτὸν λέγοντά μοι, σπεῦσον καὶ ἔξελθε ἐν τάχι ἐξ Ἰερουσαλήμ, διότι οὐ παραδέξονταί σου μαρτυρίαν περὶ ἐμοῦ. 22.19 κἀγὼ εἶπον, κύριε, αὐτοὶ ἐπίστανται ὅτι ἐγὼ ἤμην φυλακίζων καὶ δέρων κατὰ τὰς συναγωγὰς τοὺς πιστεύοντας ἐπὶ σέ· 22.20 καὶ ὅτε ἐξεχύννετο τὸ αἷμα Στεφάνου τοῦ μάρτυρός σου, καὶ αὐτὸς ἤμην ἐφεστὼς καὶ συνευδοκῶν καὶ φυλάσσων τὰ ἱμάτια τῶν ἀναιρούντων αὐτόν. 22.21 καὶ εἶπεν πρός με, πορεύου, ὅτι ἐγὼ εἰς ἔθνη μακρὰν ἐξαποστελῶ σε.

22.22 ἤκουον δὲ αὐτοῦ ἄχρι τούτου τοῦ λόγου καὶ ἐπῆραν τὴν φωνὴν αὐτῶν λέγοντες, αἶρε ἀπὸ τῆς γῆς τὸν τοιοῦτον, οὐ γὰρ καθῆκεν αὐτὸν ζῆν. 22.23 κραυγαζόντων δὲ αὐτῶν καὶ ῥιπτούντων τὰ ἱμάτια καὶ κονιορτὸν βαλλόντων εἰς τὸν ἀέραν, 22.24 ἐκέλευσεν ὁ χιλίαρχος εἰσάγεσθαι αὐτὸν εἰς τὴν παρεμβολήν, εἴπας μάστιξιν ἀνετάζεσθαι αὐτὸν ἵνα ἐπιγνῷ δι' ἣν αἰτίαν οὕτως ἐπεφώνουν αὐτῷ.

will be spoken to you concerning all (things) which have been appointed for you to do. 22.11 And since I was not seeing from the glory of that light, being led by the hand by those being with me, I went into Damascus.

22.12 And a certain Ananias, a devout/reverent man according to the law, being attested by all the Judeans dwelling *there*, 22.13 having come to me and stood over (me), he said to me: Saul, brother, look up/see again; and I at the same hour looked up to him. 22.14 And the (he) said: The God of our fathers pre-appointed you/hand picked you beforehand to know his will and to see the just (one) and to hear a voice out of his mouth, 22.15 because you will be a witness for him to all men/humans of (things) which you have seen and heard. 22.16 And what are you about to do now? Having risen up, be baptized and wash away your sins/faults, having called upon his name.

22.17 And it happened to me, having returned to Jerusalem and from my praying in the *outer* temple, *for* me to become in ecstasy/a trance 22.18 and I saw him speaking to me: You hasten and go forth with speed out of Jerusalem, because they will not receive/accept a testimony from you about me. 22.19 And I, I said: Lord, they themselves understand that I myself was imprisoning and beating those believing on you throughout the congregations; 22.20 and when the blood of Stephen, your witness, was being poured out, even I myself had stood by and was consenting and guarding/keeping the garments of those killing him. 22.21 And he said to me: You go, because I, I shall send you out to ethnics afar/afar to ethnics.

22.22 And they were hearing from him until this saying/word, and they lifted up their voice, saying: Take away/destroy/kill the (one) such from the land/earth, for it is not fitting *for* him to live. 22.23 And from them shouting and tearing the garments asunder and throwing dust into the air, 22.24 the captain ordered *for* him to be brought into the camp/fort, having said *for* him to be examined by scourgings in order that he might learn on account of what cause/reason they were thus shouting against him.

22.25 ὡς δὲ προέτιναν αὐτὸν τοῖς ἱμᾶσιν εἶπεν πρὸς τὸν ἑστῶτα ἑκατόνταρχον ὁ Παῦλος, εἰ ἄνθρωπον Ῥωμαῖον καὶ ἀκατάκριτον ἔξεστιν ὑμῖν μαστίζειν; 22.26 ἀκούσας δὲ ὁ ἑκατοντάρχης προσελθὼν τῷ χιλιάρχῳ ἀπήγγιλεν λέγων, τί μέλλεις ποιεῖν; ὁ γὰρ ἄνθρωπος οὗτος Ῥωμαῖός ἐστιν.

22.27 προσελθὼν δὲ ὁ χιλίαρχος εἶπεν αὐτῷ, λέγε μοι, σὺ Ῥωμαῖος εἶ; ὁ δὲ ἔφη, ναί. 22.28 ἀπεκρίθη δὲ ὁ χιλίαρχος, ἐγὼ πολλοῦ κεφαλαίου τὴν πολιτίαν ταύτην ἐκτησάμην. ὁ δὲ Παῦλος ἔφη, ἐγὼ δὲ καὶ γεγέννημαι. 22.29 εὐθέως οὖν ἀπέστησαν ἀπ' αὐτοῦ οἱ μέλλοντες αὐτὸν ἀνετάζειν· καὶ ὁ χιλίαρχος δὲ ἐφοβήθη ἐπιγνοὺς ὅτι Ῥωμαῖός ἐστιν καὶ ὅτι αὐτὸν ἦν δεδεκώς.

22.30 τῇ δὲ ἐπαύριον βουλόμενος γνῶναι τὸ ἀσφαλὲς τὸ τί κατηγορῖται ὑπὸ τῶν Ἰουδαίων ἔλυσεν αὐτόν, καὶ ἐκέλευσεν συνελθεῖν τοὺς ἀρχιερεῖς καὶ πᾶν τὸ συνέδριον, καὶ καταγαγὼν τὸν Παῦλον ἔστησεν εἰς αὐτούς.

23.1 Ἀτενίσας δὲ τῷ συνεδρίῳ ὁ Παῦλος εἶπεν, ἄνδρες ἀδελφοί, ἐγὼ πάσῃ συνιδήσει ἀγαθῇ πεπολίτευμαι τῷ θεῷ ἄχρι ταύτης τῆς ἡμέρας. 23.2 ὁ δὲ ἀρχιερεὺς Ἀνανίας ἐπέταξε τοῖς παρεστῶσιν αὐτῷ τύπτιν αὐτοῦ τὸ στόμα. 23.3 τότε πρὸς αὐτὸν ὁ Παῦλος εἶπεν, τύπτιν σε μέλλει ὁ θεός, τοῖχε κεκονιαμένε· καὶ σὺ κάθῃ κρίνων με κατὰ τὸν νόμον, καὶ παρανομῶν κελεύεις με τύπτεσθαι; 23.4 οἱ δὲ παρεστῶτες εἶπαν, τὸν ἀρχιερέα τοῦ θεοῦ λοιδορεῖς; 23.5 ἔφη τε ὁ Παῦλος, οὐκ ᾔδιν, ἀδελφοί, ὅτι ἐστὶν ἀρχιερεύς· γέγραπται γὰρ ὅτι «ἄρχοντα τοῦ λαοῦ σου οὐκ ἐρῖς κακῶς.»

23.6 γνοὺς δὲ ὁ Παῦλος ὅτι τὸ ἓν μέρος ἐστὶν Σαδδουκαίων τὸ δὲ ἕτερον Φαρισαίων ἔκραζεν ἐν τῷ συνεδρίῳ, ἄνδρες ἀδελφοί, ἐγὼ Φαρισαῖός εἰμι, υἱὸς Φαρισαίων· περὶ ἐλπίδος καὶ ἀναστάσεως νεκρῶν ἐγὼ κρίνομαι.

23.7 τοῦτο δὲ αὐτοῦ εἰπόντος ἐγένετο στάσις τῶν

22.25 But as they stretched him out with the thongs, Paul said to the centurion having stood by: Is it lawful for ye to scourge/whip a man *being* a Roman and uncondemned? 22.26 And having heard, the centurion having gone to the captain reported *it*, saying: What are you about to do? For this man is a Roman.

22.27 And having come near, the captain said to him: Say to me, you, are you a Roman? And the (he) was saying: Yes. 22.8 And the captain answered: I acquired this citizenship from a much heading/listing/sum of money. And Paul was saying: But I *am* even having been born. 22.29 Then immediately those being about to examine/whip him stood away from him, and even the captain was afraid, having learned that he is a Roman and that/because he had bound him.

22.30 And on the morrow being purposed/minded to know the certainty what *is* the thing he is being accused *of* by the Judeans he loosed him, and he ordered *for* the high priests and all the council to gather, and having broughtPaul down, he set/stood *him* in/for them.

23.1 And having gazed at the council, Paul said: Men, brothers, I have conducted my life with every good conscience for God until this day. 23.2 But the high priest, Ananias, ordered to those standing beside him to strike his mouth. 23.3 Then Paul said to him: God is about to strike/smite you, O wall having been whitewashed; and you, you sit judging me according to the law, and being contrary to law, you order *for* me to be struck? 23.4 And those standing by said: Do you revile God's high priest? 23.5 And Paul was saying: I knew not, brothers, that he is a high priest; for it has been written: A RULER/LEADER OF YOUR PEOPLE WILL NOT SPEAK BADLY.

23.6 And Paul, having known that the one part was of Sadducees but the other/different of Pharisees, cried out in the council: Men, brothers, I, I am a Pharisee, a son of Pharisees; I am being judged concerning a hope and resurrection of dead (ones).

23.7 And from him having said this, there became a discord/striving from/*between* the Sadducees and

Σαδδουκαίων καὶ Φαρισαίων, καὶ ἐσχίσθη τὸ πλῆθος. 23.8 Σαδδουκαῖοι μὲν γὰρ λέγουσιν μὴ εἶναι ἀνάστασιν μήτε ἄγγελον μήτε πνεῦμα, Φαρισαῖοι δὲ ὁμολογοῦσιν τὰ ἀμφότερα.

23.9 ἐγένετο δὲ κραυγὴ μεγάλη, καὶ ἀναστάντες τινὲς τῶν γραμματέων τοῦ μέρους τῶν Φαρισαίων διεμάχοντο πρὸς ἀλλήλους λέγοντες, οὐδὲν κακὸν εὑρίσκομεν ἐν τῷ ἀνθρώπῳ τούτῳ· εἰ δὲ πνεῦμα ἐλάλησεν αὐτῷ ἢ ἄγγελος 23.10 πολλῆς δὲ γινομένης στάσεως φοβηθὶς ὁ χιλίαρχος μὴ διασπασθῇ ὁ Παῦλος ὑπ᾽ αὐτῶν ἐκέλευσεν τὸ στράτευμα καταβὰν ἁρπάσαι αὐτὸν ἐκ μέσου αὐτῶν, ἄγειν τε εἰς τὴν παρεμβολήν.

23.11 τῇ δὲ ἐπιούσῃ νυκτὶ ἐπιστὰς αὐτῷ ὁ κύριος εἶπεν, θάρσει, ὡς γὰρ διεμαρτύρω τὰ περὶ ἐμοῦ εἰς Ἰερουσαλὴμ οὕτω σε δεῖ καὶ εἰς Ῥώμην μαρτυρῆσαι.

23.12 γενομένης δὲ ἡμέρας ποιήσαντες συστροφὴν οἱ Ἰουδαῖοι ἀνεθεμάτισαν ἑαυτοὺς λέγοντες μήτε φαγῖν μήτε πίειν ἕως οὗ ἀποκτίνωσιν τὸν Παῦλον. 23.13 ἦσαν δὲ πλείους τεσσεράκοντα οἱ ταύτην τὴν συνωμοσίαν ποιησάμενοι· 23.14 οἵτινες προσελθόντες τοῖς ἀρχιερεῦσι καὶ τοῖς πρεσβυτέροις εἶπαν, ἀναθέματι ἀνεθεματίσαμεν ἑαυτοὺς μηδενὸς γεύσασθε ἕως οὗ ἀποκτίνωμεν τὸν Παῦλον. 23.15 νῦν οὖν ὑμεῖς ἐμφανίσατε τῷ χιλιάρχῳ σὺν τῷ συνεδρίῳ ὅπως καταγάγῃ αὐτὸν εἰς ὑμᾶς ὡς μέλλοντας διαγινώσκιν ἀκριβέστερον τὰ περὶ αὐτοῦ·

ἡμεῖς δὲ πρὸ τοῦ ἐγγίσαι αὐτὸν ἕτοιμοί ἐσμεν τοῦ ἀνελεῖν αὐτόν. 23.16 ἀκούσας δὲ ὁ υἱὸς τῆς ἀδελφῆς Παύλου τὴν ἐνέδραν παραγενόμενος καὶ εἰσελθὼν εἰς τὴν παρεμβολὴν ἀπήγγιλεν τῷ Παύλῳ. 23.17 προσκαλεσάμενος δὲ ὁ Παῦλος ἕνα τῶν ἑκατονταρχῶν ἔφη, τὸν νεανίαν τοῦτον ἀπάγε πρὸς τὸν χιλίαρχον, ἔχει γάρ τι ἀπαγγῖλαί αὐτῷ. 23.18 ὁ μὲν οὖν παραλαβὼν αὐτὸν ἤγαγε πρὸς τὸν χιλίαρχον καὶ φησίν, ὁ δέσμιος Παῦλος προσκαλεσάμενός με ἠρώτησεν τοῦτον τὸν

Pharisees, and the multitude was split/divided. 23.8 For on one hand Sadducees say *for* a resurrection not to be, neither a messenger/angel nor a spirit, but on the other hand, Pharisees confess both things.

23.9 And there became a great shouting/clamor, and having risen up, some of the scribes from the part of the Pharisees were fighting/contending with one another, saying: We find nothing bad in this man; and if/whether a spirit or a messenger/angel spoke to him -- . 23.10 And from much strife becoming, the captain, having feared lest Paul might be torn apart by them, he ordered the soldiers having come down to snatch him out of the midst of them, and to bring *him* into the camp/fort.

23.11 And having stood over him on the following night, the Lord said: Be of good cheer, for as you testified solemnly the (things) about me in Jerusalem, so it is necessary *for* you also to testify/witness in Rome.

23.12 And from it having become day, having made a plot/conspiracy, the Judeans bound themselves with an oath, saying neither to eat nor to drink until which *time* they might kill Paul. 23.13 And the (those) having made this plot/conspiracy were more than forty; 23.14 who having come near to the high priests and the elders, they said: We bound ourselves by an oath to taste of nothing until which *time* we might kill Paul. 23.15 Therefore ye now, ye make known/emphasize to the captain with the council so that he might bring him down to/for ye as being about to determine more accurately the (things) about him;

and we, before the (thing) *for* him to draw near, we are ready/prepared from the (thing) to kill him. 23.16 But having heard the ambush/treachery, the son of Paul's sister, having become beside/arrived and having come into the camp/fort, he reported *it* to Paul. 23.17 And having called to one of the centurions, Paul was saying: Lead this youth away to the captain, for he has something to report to him. 23.18 Then the (he) indeed having taken him along, he brought/led *him* to the captain and says: The prisoner Paul, having called to me, he requested to bring this

478

νεανίσκον ἀγαγεῖν πρὸς σέ, ἔχοντά τι λαλῆσαί σοι. 23.19 ἐπιλαβόμενος δὲ τῆς χιρὸς αὐτοῦ ὁ χιλίαρχος καὶ ἀναχωρήσας κατ᾽ ἰδίαν ἐπυνθάνετο, τί ἐστιν ὃ ἔχις ἀπαγγεῖλαί μοι; 23.20 εἶπεν δὲ ὅτι οἱ Ἰουδαῖοι συνέθεντο τοῦ ἐρωτῆσαί σε ὅπως αὔριον τὸν Παῦλον καταγάγῃς εἰς τὸ συνέδριον ὡς μέλλον τι ἀκριβέστερον πυνθάνεσθαι περὶ αὐτοῦ. 23.21 σὺ οὖν μὴ πισθῇς αὐτοῖς· ἐνεδρεύουσι γὰρ αὐτὸν ἐξ αὐτῶν ἄνδρες πλείους τεσσεράκοντα, οἵτινες ἀνεθεμάτισαν ἑαυτοὺς μήτε φαγῖν μήτε πιεῖν ἕως οὗ ἀνέλωσιν αὐτόν, καὶ νῦν εἰσιν ἕτοιμοι προσδεχόμενοι τὴν ἀπὸ σοῦ ἐπαγγελίαν. 23.22 ὁ μὲν οὖν χιλίαρχος ἀπέλυσε τὸν νεανίσκον παραγγίλας μηδενὶ ἐκλαλῆσαι ὅτι ταῦτα ἐνεφάνισας πρός ἐμέ.

23.23 καὶ προσκαλεσάμενος τινὰς δύο τῶν ἑκατονταρχῶν εἶπεν, ἑτοιμάσατε στρατιώτας διακοσίους ὅπως πορευθῶσιν ἕως Καισαρίας, καὶ ἱππεῖς ἑβδομήκοντα καὶ δεξιολάβους διακοσίους, ἀπὸ τρίτης ὥρας τῆς νυκτός, 23.24 κτήνη τε παραστῆσαι ἵνα ἐπιβιβάσαντες τὸν Παῦλον διασώσωσι πρὸς Φήλικα τὸν ἡγεμόνα, 23.25 γράψας ἐπιστολὴν ἔχουσαν τὸν τύπον τοῦτον· 23.26 Κλαύδιος Λυσίας τῷ κρατίστῳ ἡγεμόνι Φήλικι χαίρειν. 23.27 τὸν ἄνδρα τοῦτον συλλημφθέντα ὑπὸ τῶν Ἰουδαίων καὶ μέλλοντα ἀναιρεῖσθε ὑπ᾽ αὐτῶν ἐπιστὰς σὺν τῷ στρατεύματι ἐξειλάμην, μαθὼν ὅτι Ῥωμαῖός ἐστιν· 23.28 βουλόμενός τε ἐπιγνῶναι τὴν αἰτίαν δι᾽ ἣν ἐνεκάλουν αὐτῷ κατήγαγον εἰς τὸ συνέδριον αὐτῶν· 23.29 ὃν εὗρον ἐγκαλούμενον περὶ ζητημάτων τοῦ νόμου αὐτῶν, μηδὲν δὲ ἄξιον θανάτου ἢ δεσμῶν ἔχοντα ἔγκλημα. 23.30 μηνυθίσης δέ μοι ἐπιβουλῆς εἰς τὸν ἄνδρα ἔσεσθαι, ἐξαυτῶν ἔπεμψα πρὸς σέ, παραγγίλας καὶ τοῖς κατηγόροις λέγιν αὐτοὺς ἐπὶ σοῦ.

ἔρρωσο.

23.31 οἱ μὲν οὖν στρατιῶται κατὰ τὸ διατεταγμένον αὐτοῖς ἀναλαβόντες τὸν Παῦλον ἤγαγον διὰ νυκτὸς εἰς τὴν

youth to you, having something to speak to you. 23.19 And having taken his hand and having withdrawn privately, the chiliarch/captain was inquiring: What is it which you have to report to me? 23.20 And he said: The Judeans agreed/decided of the (thing) to ask you that tomorrow you might bring Paul down to the council as being about to inquire more accurately something about him. 23.21 Then you, you be not persuaded by them; for more than forty men from them lie in ambush for him, who bound themselves by an oath neither to eat nor to drink until which *time* they might destroy him, and they are ready/prepared now, waiting for the promise from you. 23.22 Then the chiliarch indeed dismissed the youth, having charged *him* to speak out to no one that you revealed these (things) to me.

23.23 And having summoned a certain two/pair of the centurions, he said: Prepare ye two hundred soldiers so that they might go/travel as far as Caesarea, and seventy horsemen and two hundred spearmen, from a third hour of the night, 23.24 and pack animals to stand by, in order that having caused Paul to mount, they might bring *him* safely through to Felix the governor, 23.25 having written a letter having this type/pattern: 23.26 Claudias Lysias to the most excellent governor Felix to greet/greeting. 23.27 This man, having been seized by the Judeans and being about to be destroyed by them, having come against *them* with the army/armed force, I took *him* out, having learned that he is a Roman; 23.28 and consulting/willing to learn/know fully the cause/reason on account of which they were bringing a charge against him I brought him down to their council; 23.29 whom I found being accused about questions/issues of their law, but having no charge worthy of death or bonds. 23.30 And from it having been made known to me of a plot/conspiracy to be to/against the man, I sent *him* immediately to you, having also charged/commanded to the accusers *for* them to say it at/in your presence.

Farewell.

23.31 Then indeed the soldiers, according to the (thing) having been appointed to them, having taken up Paul, they brought him through *the* night to Antipat-

Ἀντιπατρίδα· 23.32 τῇ δὲ ἐπαύριον ἐάσαντες τοὺς ἱππεῖς ἀπέρχεσθε σὺν αὐτῷ ὑπέστρεψαν εἰς τὴν παρεμβολήν· 23.33 οἵτινες εἰσελθόντες εἰς τὴν Καισάριαν καὶ ἀναδόντες τὴν ἐπιστολὴν τῷ ἡγεμόνι παρέστησαν καὶ τὸν Παῦλον αὐτῷ.

23.34 ἀναγνοὺς δὲ καὶ ἐπερωτήσας ἐκ ποίας ἐπαρχείας ἐστὶν καὶ πυθόμενος ὅτι ἀπὸ Κιλικίας, 23.35 διακούσομέ σου, ἔφη, ὅταν καὶ οἱ κατήγοροί σου παραγένωνται· κελεύσας ἐν τῷ πραιτωρίῳ τοῦ Ἡρῴδου φυλάσσεσθαι αὐτόν.

24.1 Μετὰ δὲ πέντε ἡμέρας κατέβη ὁ ἀρχιερεὺς Ἀνανίας μετὰ πρεσβυτέρων τινῶν καὶ ῥήτορος Τερτύλλου τινός, οἵτινες ἐνεφάνισαν τῷ ἡγεμόνι κατὰ τοῦ Παύλου. 24.2 κληθέντος δὲ αὐτοῦ ἤρξατο κατηγορεῖν ὁ Τέρτυλλος λέγων, πολλῆς εἰρήνης τυγχάνοντες διὰ σοῦ καὶ διορθωμάτων γινομένων τῷ ἔθνι τούτῳ διὰ τῆς σῆς προνοίας, 24.3 πάντῃ τε καὶ πανταχοῦ ἀποδεχόμεθα, κράτιστε Φῆλιξ, μετὰ πάσης εὐχαριστίας. 24.4 ἵνα δὲ μὴ ἐπὶ πλεῖόν σε ἐνκόπτω, παρακαλῶ ἀκοῦσαί σε ἡμῶν συντόμως τῇ σῇ ἐπιεικίᾳ. 24.5 εὑρόντες γὰρ τὸν ἄνδρα τοῦτον λοιμὸν καὶ κινοῦντα στάσις πᾶσι τοῖς Ἰουδαίοις τοῖς κατὰ τὴν οἰκουμένην πρωτοστάτην τε τῆς τῶν Ναζωραίων ἑρέσεως, 24.6 ὃς καὶ τὸ ἱερὸν ἐπίρασεν βεβηλῶσαι, ὃν καὶ ἐκρατήσαμεν, 24.8 παρ᾽ οὗ δυνήσῃ αὐτὸς ἀνακρίνας περὶ πάντων τούτων ἐπιγνῶναι ὧν ἡμεῖς κατηγοροῦμεν αὐτοῦ. 24.9 συνεπέθεντο δὲ καὶ οἱ Ἰουδαῖοι φάσκοντες ταῦτα οὕτως ἔχειν.

24.10 ἀπεκρίθη τε ὁ Παῦλος νεύσαντος αὐτῷ τοῦ ἡγεμόνος λέγειν, ἐκ πολλῶν ἐτῶν ὄντα σε κριτὴν τῷ ἔθνι τούτῳ ἐπιστάμενος εὐθύμως τὰ περὶ ἐμαυτοῦ ἀπολογοῦμαι, 24.11 δυναμένου σου ἐπιγνῶναι ὅτι οὐ πλείους εἰσίν μοι ἡμέραι δώδεκα ἀφ᾽ ἧς ἀνέβην προσκυνήσων εἰς Ἱερουσαλήμ, 24.12 καὶ οὔτε ἐν τῷ ἱερῷ εὗρόν

ris;   23.32 and having allowed the horsemen with him
to depart, they returned to the camp/fort on the
morrow;   23.33 who having entered into Caesarea and
having delivered the letter to the governor, they also
presented Paul to him.

23.34   And having read *it* and asked from what
province he is, and having learned that *he is* from
Cilicia,   23.35 he was saying: I shall give a hearing
of you whenever your accusers might also arrive;
having ordered *for* him to be guarded/kept in Herod's
praetorium/palace guard.

24.1   And after five days the high priest Ananias
came down with some elders and a public speaker, a
certain Tertullus, who enlightened/made a report to
the governor against Paul.   24.2 And from him having
been called *for*, Tertullus began to accuse *him* saying:
From much peace being obtained through you, and from
reforms becoming for this ethnic/nation through your
foresight,   24.3 both in every (thing) and from everywhere we receive gladly, most excellent Felix, with
every thanksgiving/gratitude.   24.4 But in order that
I may not hinder/weary you over more *time*, I beseech
for you to hear/listen briefly from us by your graci-
ousness.   24.5 For having found this man a pest and
stirring up strife with all the Judeans throughout the
empire/inhabited earth, and a ringleader of a sect of
the Nazarenes,   24.6 who also tried to make the temple
common/desecrate the temple, whom we also seized/
arrested,   24.8 from whom you yourself will be able to
know fully,   having   examined *him* about all these
(things) of which we, we are accusing of him.   24.9
And having joined in, the Judeans *were* also asserting
to have/hold these (things) so.

24.10   And from the governor having nodded to him
to speak, Paul answered: Understanding *for* you being
from many years a judge for this ethnic/nation, I
defend myself cheerfully *for* the (things) concerning
myself,   24.11   from you being able to fully know that
there are not more than twelve days for me from which
time I went up *for* worshiping to Jerusalem,   24.12 And
they found me neither in the *outer* temple discussing

με πρός τινα διαλεγόμενον ἢ ἐπίστασιν ποιοῦντα ὄχλου οὔτε ἐν ταῖς συναγωγαῖς οὔτε κατὰ τὴν πόλιν, 24.13 οὐδὲ παραστῆσαι δύνανταί σοι περὶ ὧν νυνὶ κατηγοροῦσίν μου. 24.14 ὁμολογῶ δὲ τοῦτό σοι ὅτι κατὰ τὴν ὁδὸν ἣν λέγουσιν αἵρεσιν οὕτως λατρεύω τῷ πατρῴῳ θεῷ, πιστεύων πᾶσι τοῖς κατὰ τὸν νόμον καὶ τοῖς ἐν τοῖς προφήταις γεγραμμένοις, 24.15 ἐλπίδα ἔχων πρὸς τὸν θεόν, ἣν καὶ αὐτοὶ προσδέχονται, ἀνάστασιν μέλλιν ἔσεσθαι δικαίων τε καὶ ἀδίκων. 24.16 ἐν τούτῳ καὶ αὐτὸς ἀσκῶ ἀπρόσκοπον συνίδησιν ἔχειν πρὸς τὸν θεὸν καὶ τοὺς ἀνθρώπους διὰ παντός.

24.17 δι' ἐτῶν δὲ πλειόνων ἐλεημοσύνας ποιήσων εἰς τὸ ἔθνος μου παρεγενόμην καὶ προσφοράς, 24.18 ἐν αἷς εὖρόν με ἡγνισμένον ἐν τῷ ἱερῷ, οὐ μετὰ ὄχλου οὐδὲ μετὰ θορύβου· 24.19 τινὲς δὲ ἀπὸ τῆς Ἀσίας Ἰουδαῖοι, οὓς ἔδει ἐπὶ σοῦ παρεῖναι καὶ κατηγορεῖν εἴ τι ἔχοιεν πρὸς ἐμέ 24.20 ἢ αὐτοὶ οὗτοι εἰπάτωσαν τί εὖρον ἀδίκημα στάντος μου ἐπὶ τοῦ συνεδρίου 24.21 ἢ περὶ μιᾶς ταύτης φωνῆς ἧς ἐκέκραξα ἐν αὐτοῖς ἑστὼς ὅτι Περὶ ἀναστάσεως νεκρῶν ἐγὼ κρίνομαι σήμερον ὑφ' ὑμῶν.

24.22 ἀνεβάλετο δὲ αὐτοὺς ὁ Φῆλιξ, ἀκριβέστερον εἰδὼς τὰ περὶ τῆς ὁδοῦ, εἴπας, ὅταν Λυσίας ὁ χιλίαρχος καταβῇ διαγνώσομαι τὰ καθ' ὑμᾶς, 24.23 διαταξάμενος τῷ τοντάρχῃ τηρῖσθαι αὐτὸν ἔχιν τε ἄνεσιν καὶ μηδένα κωλύειν τῶν ἰδίων αὐτοῦ ὑπηρετῖν αὐτῷ.

24.24 μετὰ δὲ ἡμέρας τινὰς παραγενόμενος ὁ Φῆλιξ σὺν Δρουσίλλῃ τῇ ἰδίᾳ γυναικὶ αὐτοῦ οὔσῃ Ἰουδαίᾳ μετεπέμψατο τὸν Παῦλον καὶ ἤκουσεν αὐτοῦ περὶ τῆς εἰς χριστὸν Ἰησοῦν πίστεως. 24.25 διαλεγομένου δὲ αὐτοῦ περὶ ἐγκρατίας καὶ δικαιοσύνης καὶ τοῦ κρίματος τοῦ μέλλοντος ἔμφοβος γενόμενος ὁ Φῆλιξ ἀπεκρίθη, τὸ νῦν ἔχον πορεύου, καιρὸν δὲ μεταλαβὼν μετακαλέσομαί σε· 24.26 ἅμα καὶ ἐλπίζων ὅτι χρήματα δοθήσεται

with anyone or making a pressure/onset of a crowd, nor in the congregations nor throughout the city, 24.13 neither are they able to prove to you concerning (things) of which they are now accusing of me. 24.14 But I confess this to you, that according to the way/road which they call a sect/heresy I thus serve/ worship for the ancestral God, believing all the (things) according to the law and the (things) having been written by the prophets, 24.15 having a hope toward God, which these (men) also expect/wait for, *for* a resurrection to be about to be of both just (ones) and unjust (ones). 24.16 In/by this I also myself practice to have a clear conscience toward God and the men through all (time). 24.17 And through many years *for* making charities and offerings in/for my ethnic/race I became present/arrived, 24.18 among which they found me, having been purified, in the *outer* temple, not with a crowd nor with an uproar; 24.19 but certain Judeans from Asia, whom it was necessary to be present before you and to accuse if they may have anything to/with me. 24.20 Or let these themselves say what injustice/wrong they found from me having stood before the council, 24.21 or about this one voice/sound which I cried out having stood among them, that about a resurrection of dead (ones) I, I am being judged by ye today.

24.22 But Felix postponed them/put them off, *for* knowing more exactly the (things) concerning the way, having said: Whenever Lysias the chiliarch might come down I shall decide determine the (things) of ye; 24.23 having ordered for the centurion to keep him and to have relaxation/liberty and to forbid no one of those his own to serve/assist for him.

24.24 And after some days Felix, having arrived with Drusilla, his own woman being a Judean, he sent for Paul and heard from him concerning the faith in the anointed Jesus. 24.25 And from him reasoning about self- control/temperance and justice/justness and the judgment being about to come, having himself become afraid, Felix answered: You go, holding the present (thing), but having shared a time I shall call you to me; 24.26 at the same time hoping also that

481

αὐτῷ ὑπὸ τοῦ Παύλου· διὸ καὶ πυκνότερον αὐτὸν μεταπεμπόμενος ὡμίλει αὐτῷ.

24.27 διετίας δὲ πληρωθίσης ἔλαβεν διάδοχον ὁ Φῆλιξ Πόρκιον Φῆστον· θέλων τε χάριτα καταθέσθαι τοῖς Ἰουδαίοις ὁ Φῆλιξ κατέλιπεν τὸν Παῦλον δεδεμένον.

25.1 Φῆστος οὖν ἐπιβὰς τῇ ἐπαρχίᾳ μετὰ τρῖς ἡμέρας ἀνέβη εἰς Ἱεροσόλυμα ἀπὸ Καισαρίας, 25.2 ἐνεφάνισάν τε αὐτῷ οἱ ἀρχιερεῖς καὶ οἱ πρῶτοι τῶν Ἰουδέων κατὰ τοῦ Παύλου, καὶ παρεκάλουν αὐτὸν 25.3 αἰτούμενοι χάριν κατ' αὐτοῦ ὅπως μεταπέμψηται αὐτὸν εἰς Ἱερουσαλήμ, ἐνέδραν ποιοῦντες ἀνελεῖν αὐτὸν κατὰ τὴν ὁδόν.

25.4 ὁ μὲν οὖν Φῆστος ἀπεκρίθη τηρῖσθαι τὸν Παῦλον εἰς Καισάριαν, ἑαυτὸν δὲ μέλλιν ἐν τάχει ἐκπορεύεσθαι· 25.5 οἱ οὖν ἐν ὑμῖν, φησίν, δυνατοὶ καταβάντες εἴ τί ἐστιν ἐν τῷ ἀνδρὶ ἄτοπον κατηγορίτωσαν αὐτοῦ. 25.6 διατρίψας δὲ ἐν αὐτοῖς οὐ πλείους ἡμέρας ὀκτὼ ἢ δέκα, καταβὰς εἰς Κεσάριαν, τῇ ἐπαύριον καθίσας ἐπὶ τοῦ βήματος ἐκέλευσεν τὸν Παῦλον ἀχθῆναι. 25.7 παραγενομένου δὲ αὐτοῦ περιέστησαν αὐτὸν οἱ ἀπὸ Ἱεροσολύμων καταβεβηκότες Ἰουδαῖοι, πολλὰ καὶ βαρέα αἰτιώματα καταφέροντες ἃ οὐκ ἴσχυον ἀποδῖξαι, 25.8 τοῦ Παύλου ἀπολογουμένου ὅτι οὔτε εἰς τὸν νόμον τῶν Ἰουδαίων οὔτε εἰς τὸ ἱερὸν οὔτε εἰς Καίσαρά τι ἥμαρτον.

25.9 ὁ Φῆστος δὲ θέλων τοῖς Ἰουδαίοις χάριν καταθέσθαι ἀποκριθεὶς τῷ Παύλῳ εἶπεν, θέλεις εἰς Ἱεροσόλυμα ἀναβὰς ἐκεῖ περὶ τούτων κριθῆναι ἐπ' ἐμοῦ; 25.10 εἶπεν δὲ ὁ Παῦλος, ἐπὶ τοῦ βήματος Καίσαρός ἑστώς εἰμι, οὗ με δεῖ κρίνεσθαι. Ἰουδαίους οὐδὲν ἠδίκηκα, ὡς καὶ σὺ κάλλιον ἐπιγινώσκεις. 25.11 εἰ μὲν οὖν ἀδικῶ καὶ ἄξιον θανάτου πέπραχά τι, οὐ παραιτοῦμε τὸ ἀποθανῖν· εἰ δὲ οὐδέν ἐστιν ὧν οὗτοι κατηγοροῦσίν μου, οὐδείς

money will be given to him by Paul; wherefore also sending for him more frequently he was conversing with him.

24.27 And from two years having been completed Felix received a successor, Porcius Festus; and wanting/wishing to do a favor for the Judeans, Felix left Paul having been bound.

25.1 Then Festus, having come to the province/prefect, after three days he went up to Jerusalem from Caesarea, 15.2 and the high priests and the first (men) of the Judeans enlightened/informed to him against Paul, and they were beseeching him 25.3 asking *for* a grace/favor against him so that he might dispatch him to Jerusalem, making an ambush to destroy/kill him along the road/way.

25.4 Then indeed Festus answered *for* Paul to be kept in Caesarea, and *for* himself being about to go forth with quickness; 25.5 then let the able (ones) among ye, he says, having gone down, bring a charge against him if there is anything improper in the man. 25.6 And having stayed among them not more than eight or ten days, having gone down to Caesarea, on the morrow having sat upon the judgment seat, he ordered *for* Paul to be brought. 25.7 And from him having arrived, the Judeans having come down from Jerusalem stood around him, and bringing many grievous charges against *him* which they were not being able to prove, 25.8 from Paul defending himself: I sinned neither to/against the law of the Judeans nor to/against the *outer* temple nor anything to/against Caesar.

25.9 But Festus, wanting to do a grace/favor for the Judeans, replying to Paul, he said: Do you want, having gone up to Jerusalem, to be judged before me there concerning these (things)? 25.10 But Paul said: I am standing at the judgment seat of Caesar, where it is necessary *for* me to be judged. I have done no injustice/wrong *to* Judeans, as even/also you, you know very well. 25.11 Therefore, if I indeed do wrong and have practiced anything worthy of death, I refuse not the (thing) to die; but if there is nothing of (things) which these (men) accuse me of, no one is

με δύναται αὐτοῖς χαρίσασθαι· Καίσαρα ἐπικαλοῦμαι.

25.12 τότε ὁ Φῆστος συλλαλήσας μετὰ τοῦ συμβουλίου ἀπεκρίθη, Καίσαρα ἐπικέκλησαι, ἐπὶ Καίσαρα πορεύσῃ.

25.13 ἡμερῶν δὲ διαγενομένων τινῶν Ἀγρίππας ὁ βασιλεὺς καὶ Βερνίκη κατήντησαν εἰς Καισάριαν ἀσπασάμενοι τὸν Φῆστον.

25.14 ὡς δὲ πλείους ἡμέρας διέτριβον ἐκεῖ, ὁ Φῆστος τῷ βασιλεῖ ἀνέθετο τὰ κατὰ τὸν Παῦλον λέγων, ἀνήρ τίς ἐστιν καταλελιμμένος ὑπὸ Φήλικος δέσμιος, 25.15 περὶ οὗ γενομένου μου εἰς Ἱεροσόλυμα ἐνεφάνισαν οἱ ἀρχιερεῖς καὶ οἱ πρεσβύτεροι τῶν Ἰουδαίων, αἰτούμενοι κατ᾽ αὐτοῦ καταδίκην· 25.16 πρὸς οὓς ἀπεκρίθην ὅτι οὐκ ἔστιν ἔθος Ῥωμαίοις χαρίζεσθαί τινα ἄνθρωπον πρὶν ἢ ὁ κατηγορούμενος ἔχοι κατὰ πρόσωπον τοὺς κατηγόρους τόπον τε ἀπολογίας λάβοι περὶ τοῦ ἐγκλήματος. 25.17 συνελθόντων οὖν αὐτῶν ἐνθάδε ἀναβολὴν μηδεμίαν ποιησάμενος τῇ ἑξῆς καθίσας ἐπὶ τοῦ βήματος ἐκέλευσα ἀχθῆναι τὸν ἄνδρα· 25.18 περὶ οὗ σταθέντες οἱ κατήγοροι οὐδεμίαν αἰτίαν ἔφερον ὧν ἐγὼ ὑπενόουν πονηρῶν, 25.19 ζητήματα δέ τινα περὶ τῆς ἰδίας δισιδαιμονίας εἶχον πρὸς αὐτὸν καὶ περὶ τινος Ἰησοῦ τεθνηκότος, ὃν ἔφασκεν ὁ Παῦλος ζῆν.

25.20 ἀπορούμενος δὲ ἐγὼ τὴν περὶ τούτων ζήτησιν ἔλεγον εἰ βούλοιτο πορεύεσθαι εἰς Ἱεροσόλυμα κἀκεῖ κρίνεσθαι περὶ τούτων. 25.21 τοῦ δὲ Παύλου ἐπικαλεσαμένου τηρηθῆναι αὐτὸν εἰς τὴν τοῦ Σεβαστοῦ διάγνωσιν, ἐκέλευσα τηρῖσθαι αὐτὸν ἕως οὗ ἀναπέμψω αὐτὸν πρὸς Καίσαρα. 25.22 Ἀγρίππας δὲ πρὸς τὸν Φῆστον, ἐβουλόμην καὶ αὐτὸς τοῦ ἀνθρώπου ἀκοῦσαι. αὔριον, φησίν, ἀκούσῃ αὐτοῦ. 25.23 τῇ οὖν ἐπαύριον ἐλθόντος τοῦ Ἀγρίππα καὶ τῆς Βερνίκης μετὰ πολλῆς φαντασίας καὶ εἰσελθόντων εἰς τὸ ἀκροατήριον σύν τε χιλιάρχοις καὶ ἀνδράσι

able to grant me to them as a favor; I call upon/appeal to Caesar.

25.12 Then Festus, having talked with the council, answered: You have appealed to Caesar, you will go to Caesar.

25.13 And from some days having elapsed, Agrippa the king and Bernice arrived in Caesarea, having greeted Festus.

25.14 And as they were staying there more days, Festus communicated to the king the things against Paul, saying: There is a certain man, a prisoner having been left behind by Felix, 25.15 about whom, from me having become in Jerusalem, the high priests and the elders of the Judeans enlightened/informed *me*, asking *for* condemnation/sentence against him; 25.16 to whom I answered that it is not a custom for Romans to freely grant a certain man before the (one) being accused may have the accusers face to face and may take/receive a place/time of defense/reply concerning the charge/accusation. 25.17 Then from them having come together in that place/there having made no postponement, on the next (day) having sat upon the judgment seat, I ordered *for* the man to be brought; 25.18 concerning whom the accusers, having been stood, were bringing no reason/cause which I was supposing of evil (things), 25.19 but they were holding to him certain questions/issues about their own religion and about a certain Jesus having died, whom Paul was asserting/claiming to live.

25.20 But I, being in doubt about the seeking/investigation of these (things), I was saying whether he may wish to go to Jerusalem and to be judged there concerning these (things). 25.21 But from Paul having appealed *for* him to be kept to/for the decision of Augustus, I ordered *for* him to be in keeping until which *time* I might send him to Caesar. 25.22 And Agrippa to Festus: I myself was also planning/wishing to hear from the man. Tomorrow, he says, you will hear from him. 25.23 Therefore, on the morrow, from Agrippa and Bernice having come with much pomp/pageantry and having entered into the audience room with both chiliarchs and the most prominent men of the

τοῖς κατ᾽ ἐξοχὴν τῆς πόλεως, καὶ κελεύσαντος τοῦ Φήστου ἤχθη ὁ Παῦλος.

25.24 καὶ φησιν ὁ Φῆστος, Ἀγρίππα βασιλεῦ καὶ πάντες οἱ συνπαρόντες ἡμῖν ἄνδρες, θεωρεῖτε τοῦτον περὶ οὗ ἅπαν τὸ πλῆθος τῶν Ἰουδαίων ἐνέτυχόν μοι ἔν τε Ἱεροσολύμοις καὶ ἐνθάδε, βοῶντες μὴ δεῖν αὐτὸν ζῆν μηκέτι. 25.25 ἐγὼ δὲ κατελαβόμην μηδὲν ἄξιον θανάτου αὐτὸν πεπραχέναι, αὐτοῦ δὲ τούτου ἐπικαλεσαμένου τὸν Σεβαστὸν ἔκρινα πέμπιν. 25.26 περὶ οὗ ἀσφαλές τι γράψαι τῷ κυρίῳ οὐκ ἔχω· διὸ προήγαγον αὐτὸν ἐφ᾽ ὑμῶν καὶ μάλιστα ἐπὶ σοῦ, βασιλεῦ Ἀγρίππα, ὅπως τῆς ἀνακρίσεως γενομένης σχῶ τί γράψω· 25.27 ἄλογον γάρ μοι δοκεῖ πέμποντα δέσμιον μὴ καὶ τὰς κατ᾽ αὐτοῦ αἰτίας σημᾶναι.

26.1 Ἀγρίππας δὲ πρὸς τὸν Παῦλον ἔφη, ἐπιτρέπεταί σοι περὶ σεαυτοῦ λέγειν. τότε ὁ Παῦλος ἐκτίνας τὴν χῖρα ἀπελογῖτο, 26.2 περὶ πάντων ὧν ἐγκαλοῦμαι ὑπὸ Ἰουδαίων, βασιλεῦ Ἀγρίππα, ἥγημαι ἐμαυτὸν μακάριον ἐπὶ σοῦ μέλλων σήμερον ἀπολογῖσθαι, 26.3 μάλιστα γνώστην ὄντα σε πάντων τῶν κατὰ Ἰουδαίους ἐθῶν τε καὶ ζητημάτων· διὸ δέομαι μακροθύμως ἀκοῦσαί μου.

26.4 τὴν μὲν οὖν βίωσίν μου τὴν ἐκ νεότητος τὴν ἀπ᾽ ἀρχῆς γενομένην ἐν τῷ ἔθνι μου ἔν τε Ἱεροσολύμοις ἴσασι πάντες οἱ Ἰουδαῖοι, 26.5 προγινώσκοντές με ἄνωθεν, ἐὰν θέλωσι μαρτυρῖν, ὅτι κατὰ τὴν ἀκριβεστάτην αἵρεσιν τῆς ἡμετέρας θρησκίας ἔζησα Φαρισαῖος. 26.6 καὶ νῦν ἐπ᾽ ἐλπίδι τῆς εἰς τοὺς πατέρας ἡμῶν ἐπαγγελίας γενομένης ὑπὸ τοῦ θεοῦ ἕστηκα κρινόμενος, 26.7 εἰς ἣν τὸ δωδεκάφυλον ἡμῶν ἐν ἐκτενείᾳ νύκτα καὶ ἡμέραν λατρεῦον ἐλπίζι καταντῆσαι· περὶ ἧς ἐλπίδος ἐγκαλοῦμαι ὑπὸ Ἰουδαίων, βασιλεῦ. 26.8 τί ἄπιστον κρίνεται παρ᾽ ὑμῖν εἰ ὁ θεὸς νεκροὺς ἐγείρει;

26.9 ἐγὼ μὲν οὖν ἔδοξα ἐμαυτῷ πρὸς τὸ ὄνομα Ἰησοῦ τοῦ

city, and from Festus having ordered *it*, Paul was led *in*.

25.24 And Festus says: King Agrippa and all the men being present with us, behold ye this (one) about whom all the multitude of the Judeans, both in Jerusalem and here, appealed to me, crying *for* it no longer to be necessary *for* him to live. 25.25 But I comprehended *for* him to have practiced nothing worthy of death, but from this (one) himself having appealed to Augustus, I judged to send *him*. 25.26 About whom I have not anything sure/certain to write; wherefore I brought him forward before/to ye, and especially before/to you, king Agrippa, so that from the examination having come about, I might have something *that* I might write; 25.27 for it seems unreasonable to me, sending a prisoner and not to designate/signify the accusations against him.

26.1 And Agrippa was saying to Paul: It is permitted for you to speak about yourself. Then Paul, having stretched out the hand, was defending himself: 26.2 Concerning all (things) of which I am accused by Judeans, king Agrippa, I consider myself happy/blessed being about to defend myself before/to you, 26.3 *for* you being especially knowledgeable, both of all the customs according to Judeans and of questions/issues; wherefore I beg *you* to hear from me patiently. 26.4 Then indeed, it having become my daily/manner of life from a youth from the beginning/first, *both* in my ethnic/nation and in Jerusalem I have known all the Judeans, 26.5 knowing me before from above, if they may want to testify, that I lived a Pharisee according to the most accurate sect/heresy of our religion. 26.6 And now, on a hope from a promise having become to/for our fathers by God, I have stood *here* being judged, 26.7 into which our twelve tribes, serving/worshiping in perseverance night and day, hopes to attain/reach; concerning which hope I am accused by Judeans, O king. 26.8 Why is it judged unbelievable/unfaithful by ye if God raises up dead (ones)?

26.9 Then indeed I, I thought it to be necessary

Ναζοραίου δεῖν πολλὰ ἐναντία πρᾶξαι· 26.10 ὃ καὶ ἐποίησα ἐν Ἱεροσολύμοις, καὶ πολλούς τε τῶν ἁγίων ἐγὼ ἐν φυλακαῖς κατέκλισα τὴν παρὰ τῶν ἀρχιερέων ἐξουσίαν λαβών, ἀναιρουμένων τε αὐτῶν κατήνεγκαν ψῆφον, 26.11 καὶ κατὰ πάσας τὰς συναγωγὰς πολλάκις τιμωρῶν αὐτοὺς ἠνάγκαζον βλασφημεῖν, περισσῶς τε ἐμμενόμενος αὐτοῖς ἐδίωκον ἕως καὶ εἰς τὰς ἔξω πόλεις. 26.12 ἐν οἷς πορευόμενος εἰς τὴν Δαμασκὸν μετ' ἐξουσίας καὶ ἐπιτροπῆς τῆς τῶν ἀρχιερέων 26.13 ἡμέρας μέσης κα' τὴν ὁδὸν εἶδον, βασιλεῦ, οὐρανόθεν ὑπὲρ τὴν λαμπρότητα τοῦ ἡλίου περιλάμψαν με φῶς καὶ τοὺς σὺν ἐμοὶ πορευομένους·

26.14 πάντων τε καταπεσόντων ἡμῶν εἰς τὴν γῆν ἤκουσα φωνὴν λέγουσαν πρός με τῇ Ἑβραΐδι διαλέκτῳ, Σαοὺλ Σαούλ, τί με διώκεις; σκληρόν σοι πρὸς κέντρα λακτίζειν. 26.15 ἐγὼ δὲ εἶπον, τίς εἶ, κύριε; ὁ δὲ κύριος εἶπεν, ἐγώ εἰμι Ἰησοῦς ὃν σὺ διώκεις. 26.16 ἀλλὰ ἀνάστηθι καὶ στῆθι ἐπὶ τοὺς πόδας σου· εἰς τοῦτο γὰρ ὤφθην σοι, προχειρίσασθαί σε ὑπηρέτην καὶ μάρτυρα ὧν τε εἶδες ὧν τε ὀφθήσομέ σοι, 26.17 ἐξερούμενός σε ἐκ τοῦ λαοῦ καὶ ἐκ τῶν ἐθνῶν, εἰς οὓς ἐγὼ ἀποστέλλω σε 26.18 ἀνῦξαι ὀφθαλμοὺς αὐτῶν, τοῦ ἐπιστρέψαι ἀπὸ σκότους εἰς φῶς καὶ τῆς ἐξουσίας τοῦ Σατανᾶ ἐπὶ τὸν θεόν, τοῦ λαβεῖν αὐτοὺς ἄφεσιν ἁμαρτιῶν καὶ κλῆρον ἐν τοῖς ἡγιασμένοις πίστι τῇ εἰς ἐμέ.

26.19 ὅθεν, βασιλεῦ Ἀγρίππα, οὐκ ἐγενόμην ἀπιθὴς τῇ οὐρανίῳ ὀπτασίᾳ, 26.20 ἀλλὰ τοῖς ἐν Δαμασκῷ πρῶτόν τε καὶ Ἱεροσολύμοις, πᾶσάν τε τὴν χώραν τῆς Ἰουδαίας καὶ τοῖς ἔθνεσιν ἀπήγγελλον μετανοεῖν καὶ ἐπιστρέφιν ἐπὶ τὸν θεόν, ἄξια τῆς μετανοίας ἔργα πράσσοντας. 26.21 ἕνεκα τούτων με Ἰουδαῖοι συλλαβούμενοι ὄντα ἐν τῷ ἱερῷ ἐπιρῶντο διαχιρίσασθαι.

for myself to practice many (things) contrary to the name of Jesus the Nazarene; 26.10 which I also did in Jerusalem, and I even shut up many of the saints in prisons, having received the authority from the high priests, and of them being destroyed/killed, I cast a pebble/vote against *them*, 26.11 and often punishing them through all the congregations I compelled *them* to slander/blaspheme, and being mad beyond measure a-gainst them, I was pursuing/prosecuting also until in the cities outside (Judea). 26.12 In which going to Damascus with authority and the commission from the high priests, 26.13 about mid day along the road, I saw, O king, a light from heaven above/beyond the brightness of the sun, shining around me and those going with me;

26.14 and from all of us having fallen down to the earth/ground, I heard a voice speaking to me in the Hebrew dialect: Saul, Saul, why do you pursue/ prosecute me? *It is* hard for you to kick to/toward goads. 26.15 And I, I said: Who are you, lord? And the Lord said: I, I am Jesus whom you, you pursue/ prosecute. 26.16 But you rise up and stand on your feet; for I was manifested to you in/for this, to choose/select you a servant/assistant and a witness of (things) which you saw and (things) which will be seen by you, 26.17 delivering you out of/from the people and out of/from the ethnics, to whom I, I send you 26.18 to open their eyes, from the (thing) to turn around from darkness to light and from the authority of Satan to God, from the (thing) *for* them to receive forgiveness/remission of sins/faults and a portion/ share among those having been set apart/sanctified by faith, the (one)in me.

26.19 From where, king Agrippa, I became not disobedient to the heavenly vision, 26.20 but first to those in Damascus and also to Jerusalemites, and all the country of Judea, and to the ethnics I an-nounced the message to repent and to turn around to God, practicing works worthy of the repentance. 26.21 On account of these (things), Judeans being in the *outer* temple, having seized me, were trying to kill me by hands.

26.22 ἐπικουρίας οὖν τυχὼν τῆς ἀπὸ τοῦ θεοῦ ἄχρι τῆς ἡμέρας ταύτης ἕστηκα μαρτυρόμενος μικρῷ τε καὶ μεγάλῳ, οὐδὲν ἐκτὸς λέγων ὧν τε οἱ προφῆται ἐλάλησαν μελλόντων γίνεσθαι καὶ Μωϋσῆς, 26.23 εἰ παθητὸς ὁ χριστός, εἰ πρῶτος ἐξ ἀναστάσεως νεκρῶν φῶς μέλλι καταγγέλλειν τῷ τε λαῷ καὶ τοῖς ἔθνεσιν. 26.24 ταῦτα δὲ αὐτοῦ ἀπολογουμένου ὁ Φῆστος μεγάλῃ τῇ φωνῇ φησιν, μαίνῃ, Παῦλε· τὰ πολλά σε γράμματα εἰς μανίαν περιτρέπει.

26.25 ὁ δὲ Παῦλος, οὐ μαίνομε, φησίν, κράτιστε Φῆστε, ἀλλὰ ἀληθίας καὶ σωφροσύνης ῥήματα ἀποφθέγγομαι. 26.26 ἐπίσταται γὰρ περὶ τούτων ὁ βασιλεύς, πρὸς ὃν καὶ παρρησιαζόμενος λαλῶ· λανθάνιν γὰρ αὐτὸν τι τούτων οὐ πίθομαι οὐθέν, οὐ γάρ ἐστιν ἐν γωνίᾳ πεπραγμένον τοῦτο.

26.27 πιστεύεις, βασιλεῦ Ἀγρίππα, τοῖς προφήταις; οἶδα ὅτι πιστεύεις.

26.28 ὁ δὲ Ἀγρίππας πρὸς τὸν Παῦλον, ἐν ὀλίγῳ με πίθεις χριστιανὸν ποιῆσαι. 26.29 ὁ δὲ Παῦλος, εὐξαίμην ἂν τῷ θεῷ καὶ ἐν ὀλίγῳ καὶ ἐν μεγάλῳ οὐ μόνον σὲ ἀλλὰ καὶ πάντας τοὺς ἀκούοντάς μου σήμερον γενέσθαι τοιούτους ὁποῖος κἀγώ εἰμι, παρεκτὸς τῶν δεσμῶν τούτων.

26.30 ἀνέστη τε ὁ βασιλεὺς καὶ ὁ ἡγεμὼν ἥ τε Βερνίκη καὶ οἱ συγκαθήμενοι αὐτοῖς, 26.31 καὶ ἀναχωρήσαντες ἐλάλουν πρὸς ἀλλήλους λέγοντες ὅτι οὐδὲν θανάτου ἢ δεσμῶν ἄξιον τι πράσσει ὁ ἄνθρωπος οὗτος. 26.32 Ἀγρίππας δὲ τῷ Φήστῳ ἔφη, ἀπολελύσθαι ἐδύνατο ὁ ἄνθρωπος οὗτος εἰ μὴ ἐπεκέκλητο Καίσαρα.

27.1 Ὡς δὲ ἐκρίθη τοῦ ἀποπλεῖν ἡμᾶς εἰς τὴν Ἰταλίαν, παρεδίδουν τόν τε Παῦλον καί τινας ἑτέρους δεσμώτας ἑκατοντάρχῃ ὀνόματι Ἰουλίῳ σπείρης Σεβαστῆς. 27.2 ἐπιβάντες δὲ πλοίῳ Ἀδραμυττηνῷ μέλλοντι πλεῖν εἰς τοὺς κατὰ τὴν Ἀσίαν τόπους ἀνήχθημεν, ὄντος σὺν ἡμῖν Ἀριστάρχου Μακαιδόνος

26.22 Therefore having obtained/gained from the assistance/help from God until this day, I have stood witnessing to small and great, saying nothing besides (things) which both the prophets and Moses spoke *of* being about to become/happen, 26.23 that the anointed (one) *is* a sufferer, that he is about to become a first resurrection out of dead (ones) to proclaim a light for both the people and the ethnics. 26.24 And from him having answered/defended these (things), Festus says with a great voice: You are mad, Paul; the many letters/much writing drives/turns you insane/to madness.

26.25 But Paul says: I am not mad, most excellent Festus, but I speak out words of truth and from mental soundness. 26.26 For the king understands about these (things), to whom I also am speaking freely; for I am not persuaded *for* him to be unaware of nothing of these (things), for this is not having been practiced in a corner.

26.27 Do you, King Agrippa, believe in the prophets? I know that you believe.

26.28 And Agrippa to Paul: In/by a little you are persuading to make me a Christian. 26.29 And Paul: I would pray to God *that* both in little and in great, not only *for* you but also *for* all those hearing from me today, to become like such as even I myself am, except for these bonds/chains.

26.30 Both the king and the governor rose up, and Bernice and those sitting with them, 26.31 and having departed, they were speaking to one another, saying: This man is something! He practices nothing worthy of death or bonds. 26.32 And Agrippa was saying to Festus: This man was being able to have been released, except he had appealed to Caesar.

27.1 And since it was judged/decided from the (thing) *for* us to sail away to Italy, they were delivering both Paul and some other/different prisoners to a centurion, Julius by name, from a cohort of Augustan/an Augustan cohort. 27.2 And having embarked in an Adramyttian ship being about to sail to the places down from Asia, we set sail, from Aristarchus a Mace-

Θεσσαλονικέως· 27.3 τῇ τε ἑτέρᾳ κατήχθημεν εἰς Σιδῶνα, φιλανθρώπως τε ὁ Ἰούλιος τῷ Παύλῳ χρησάμενος ἐπέτρεψε πρὸς τοὺς φίλους πορευθέντι ἐπιμελίας τυχεῖν. 27.4 κἀκεῖθεν ἀναχθέντες ὑπεπλεύσαμεν τὴν Κύπρον διὰ τὸ τοὺς ἀνέμους εἶναι ἐναντίους,

27.5 τό τε πέλαγος τὸ κατὰ τὴν Κιλικίαν καὶ Παμφυλίαν διαπλεύσαντες κατήλθαμεν εἰς Λύσραν τῆς Λυκίας. 27.6 κἀκεῖ εὑρὼν ὁ ἑκατοντάρχης πλοῖον Ἀλεξανδρῖνον πλέον εἰς τὴν Ἰταλίαν ἐνεβίβασεν ἡμᾶς εἰς αὐτό.

27.7 ἐν ἱκαναῖς δὲ ἡμέραις βραδυπλοοῦντες καὶ μόλις γενόμενοι κατὰ τὴν Κνίδον, μὴ προσεῶντος ἡμᾶς τοῦ ἀνέμου, ὑπεπλεύσαμεν τὴν Κρήτην κατὰ Σαλμώνην, 27.8 μόλις τε παραλεγόμενοι αὐτὴν ἤλθομεν εἰς τόπον τινὰ καλούμενον καλοὺς λιμένας, ᾧ ἐγγὺς πόλις ἦν Λασσαία. 27.9 ἱκανοῦ δὲ χρόνου διαγενομένου καὶ ὄντος ἤδη ἐπισφαλοῦς τοῦ πλοὸς διὰ τὸ καὶ τὴν νηστίαν ἤδη παρεληλυθέναι, παρῄνει ὁ Παῦλος 27.10 λέγων αὐτοῖς, ἄνδρες, θεωρῶ ὅτι μετὰ ὕβρεως καὶ πολλῆς ζημίας οὐ μόνον τοῦ φορτίου καὶ τοῦ πλοίου ἀλλὰ καὶ τῶν ψυχῶν ἡμῶν μέλλειν ἔσεσθαι τὸν πλοῦν.

27.11 ὁ δὲ ἑκατοντάρχης τῷ κυβερνήτῃ καὶ τῷ ναυκλήρῳ μᾶλλον ἐπίθετο ἢ τοῖς ὑπὸ Παύλου λεγομένοις.

27.12 ἀνευθέτου δὲ τοῦ λιμένος ὑπάρχοντος πρὸς παραχειμασίαν οἱ πλίονες ἔθεντο βουλὴν ἀναχθῆναι ἐκεῖθεν, εἴ πως δύναιντο καταντήσαντες εἰς Φοίνικα παραχειμάσαι, λειμένα τῆς Κρήτης βλέποντα κατὰ λίβα καὶ κατὰ χῶρον.

27.13 ὑποπνεύσαντες δὲ νότου δόξαντες τῆς προθέσεως κεκρατηκέναι, ἄραντες ἆσσον παρελέγοντο τὴν Κρήτην. 27.14 μετ᾽ οὐ πολὺ δὲ ἔβαλεν κατὰ ταύτης ἄνεμος τυφωνικὸς ὁ καλούμενος εὐρακύλων· 27.15 συναρπασθέντος δὲ τοῦ πλοίου

donian from Thessalonica being with us; 27.3 and on the other/different/next day we were brought down in Sidon, and Julius, having treated *him* kindly, permitted for Paul, going to the friends, to obtain care/attention. 27.4 And having set sail from there, we sailed by the lee *of* Cyprus because of the (thing) *for* the winds to be opposite/contrary,

27.5 and having sailed through the open sea down from Cilicia and Pamphylia, we came down to Lystra (Myra) of Lycia. 27.6 And there, having found an Alexandrian ship sailing to Italy, the centurion embarked us in it.

27.7 And navigating slowly in/on considerable days and scarcely having become down from Cnidus, from the winds not permitting us, we sailed under the lee *of* Crete down from Salmone, 27.8 and scarcely moving along her/*it* we came to a certain place being called Fair Havens, which was near a city, Lasaea. 27.9 But from considerable time having elapsed and the voyage now being unsafe/uncertain, because of the (thing) *for* the fast/starving already to have enfeebled (them), Paul was advising/recommending, 27.10 saying to them: Men, I behold/perceive that the voyage is being about to be with injury and much damage/loss, not only of the cargo and the ship, but also of our souls/lives.

27.11 But the centurion was being persuaded by the steersman and the ship master rather than by the (things) being said by Paul.

27.12 But from the harbor being unfavorable to/for wintering, the most/majority set a purpose/will to set sail from there, if somehow they may be able, having reached *it*, to winter in Phoenix, a port/harbor of Crete looking toward/(sailing first) southwest and *then* toward northwest.

27.13 And from a south wind blowing gently, having seemed to have attained the purpose, having taken up (anchor), they were coasting/drifting nearer Crete. 27.14 And after not much *time*, a violent/hurricane wind being called Euraquila/a northeast wind thrust/beat against this (one)/herself; 27.15 and from the ship having been seized violently and not being able to look/face directly against the wind,

καὶ μὴ δυναμένου ἀντοφθαλμῖν τῷ ἀνέμῳ ἐπιδόντες ἐφερόμεθα. 27.16 νησίον δέ τι ὑποδραμόντες καλούμενον Καῦδα ἰσχύσαμεν μόλις περικρατῖς γενέσθαι τῆς σκάφης, 27.17 ἣν ἄραντες βοηθίαις ἐχρῶντο ὑποζωννύντες τὸ πλοῖον· φοβούμενοί τε μὴ εἰς τὴν Σύρτιν ἐκπλέσωσιν, χαλάσαντες τὸ σκεῦος, οὕτως ἐφέροντο. 27.18 σφοδρῶς δὲ χειμαζομένων ἡμῶν τῇ ἑξῆς ἐκβολὴν ἐποιοῦντο, 27.19 καὶ τῇ τρίτῃ αὐτόχειρες τὴν σκευὴν τοῦ πλοίου ἔριψαν. 27.20 μήτε δὲ ἡλίου μήτε ἄστρων ἐπιφαινόντων ἐπὶ πλείονας ἡμέρας, χειμῶνός τε οὐκ ὀλίγου ἐπικειμένου, λοιπὸν περιηρεῖτο πᾶσα ἐλπὶς τοῦ σῴζεσθαι ἡμᾶς. 27.21 πολλῆς τε ἀσιτίας ὑπαρχούσης τότε σταθὶς ὁ Παῦλος ἐν μέσῳ αὐτῶν εἶπεν, ἔδει μέν, ὦ ἄνδρες, πιθαρχήσαντάς μοι μὴ ἀνάγεσθαι ἀπὸ τῆς Κρήτης κερδῆσέ τε τὴν ὕβριν ταύτην καὶ τὴν ζημίαν. 27.22 καὶ τὰ νῦν παραινῶ ὑμᾶς εὐθυμῖν, ἀποβολὴ γὰρ ψυχῆς οὐδεμία ἔσται ἐξ ὑμῶν πλὴν τοῦ πλοίου· 27.23 παρέστη γάρ μοι ταύτῃ τῇ νυκτὶ τοῦ θεοῦ οὗ εἰμι ἐγώ, ᾧ καὶ λατρεύω, ἄγγελος 27.24 λέγων, μὴ φοβοῦ, Παῦλε· Καίσαρί σε δεῖ παραστῆναι, καὶ ἰδοὺ κεχάρισταί σοι ὁ θεὸς πάντας τοὺς πλέοντας μετὰ σοῦ. 27.25 διὸ εὐθυμεῖται, ἄνδρες· πιστεύω γὰρ τῷ θεῷ ὅτι οὕτως ἔσται καθ' ὃν τρόπον λελάληταί μοι. 27.26 εἰς νῆσον δέ τινα δεῖ ἡμᾶς ἐκπεσεῖν.

27.27 ὡς δὲ τεσσαρεσκαιδεκάτη νὺξ ἐγένετο διαφερομένων ἡμῶν ἐν τῷ Ἀδρίᾳ, κατὰ μέσον τῆς νυκτὸς ὑπενόουν οἱ ναῦται προσάγειν τινὰ αὐτοῖς χώραν. 27.28 καὶ βολίσαντες εὗρον ὀργυιὰς εἴκοσι, βραχὺ δὲ διαστήσαντες καὶ πάλιν βολίσαντες εὗρον ὀργυιὰς δεκαπέντε· 27.29 φοβούμενοι δὲ μή που κατὰ τραχεῖς τόπους ἐμπέσωμεν, ἐκ πρύμνης ῥίψαντες ἀγκύρας

having given over we were being carried out of position. 27.16 And having run under the lee of a certain little island being called Clauda we were scarcely able to become in control of the skiff/lifeboat, 27.17 which, having taken up, they were employing for helps under-girding the ship; and fearing lest they might sail away into Syrtis (Bay), having lowered the implement/tackle, they were thus being borne *along*. 27.18 And from us being exceedingly storm-tossed on the next (day) they were doing a jettisoning/throwing out, 27.19 and on the third (day) they threw off the equipment/tackle/gear with their own hands. 27.20 And from neither sun nor stars appearing over many days, and from not a little foul weather pressing against (us), every hope of the (thing) *for* us to be saved was finally being taken away. 27.21 And from much abstinence, Paul having then stood in the midst of them, said: It was indeed necessary, O men, not having obeyed to me not to set sail from Crete, to gain both this injury/disaster and the damage/loss. 27.22 And the (things) I now recommend *for* ye to be of good cheer, for there will be no throwing away of souls/ lives from ye, but of the ship; 27.23 for a messenger/angel from the God of whom I myself am, for whom I also serve, stood beside me this night, 27.24 saying: Fear not, Paul; it is necessary *for* you to stand at/beside Caesar, and behold, God has granted to you all those sailing with you. 27.25 Wherefore, be ye cheerful, men; for I believe by God that it will be so according to *the* way which it was spoken to me. 27.26 But it is necessary *for* us to fall off/drift off course to a certain island.

27.27 And as it became the fourteenth night of us being driven about in the Adria/Adriatic Sea, about *the* middle of the night the sailors were suspecting for them to be approaching some country/land. 27.28 And having taken soundings, they found twenty fathoms (120 feet), and having gone a little *time* and again having taken a sounding they found fifteen fathoms; 27.29 and fearing lest we might fall in/run aground somewhere against rough places, having thrown down four anchors out of the stern, they were longing for

τέσσαρες ηὔχοντο ἡμέραν γενέσθαι. 27.30 τῶν δὲ ναυτῶν ζητούντων φυγεῖν ἐκ τοῦ πλοίου καὶ χαλασάντων τὴν σκάφην εἰς τὴν θάλασσαν προφάσει ὡς ἐκ πρῴρης μελλόντων ἀγκύρας ἐκτίνειν, 27.31 εἶπεν ὁ Παῦλος τῷ ἑκατοντάρχῃ καὶ τοῖς στρατιώταις, ἐὰν μὴ οὗτοι μίνωσιν ἐν τῷ πλοίῳ, ὑμεῖς σωθῆναι οὐ δύνασθε.

27.32 τότε ἀπέκοψαν οἱ στρατιῶται τὰ σχοινία τῆς σκάφης καὶ ἴασαν αὐτὴν ἐκπεσεῖν. 27.33 ἄχρι δὲ οὗ ἡμέρα ἔμελλεν γείνεσθαι παρεκάλει ὁ Παῦλος ἅπαντας μεταλαβεῖν τροφῆς λέγων, τεσσαρεσκαιδεκάτην σήμερον ἡμέραν προσδοκῶντες ἄσιτοι διατελεῖται, μηθὲν προσλαβόμενοι· 27.34 διὸ παρακα-- ὑμᾶς μεταλαβεῖν τροφῆς, τοῦτο γὰρ πρὸς τῆς ὑμετέρας σωτηρίας ὑπάρχει· οὐδενὸς γὰρ ὑμῶν θρὶξ ἐκ τῆς κεφαλῆς ἀπολεῖται. 27.35 εἴπας δὲ ταῦτα καὶ λαβὼν ἄρτον εὐχαρίστησας τῷ θεῷ ἐνώπιον πάντων καὶ κλάσας ἤρξατο ἐσθίειν. 27.36 εὔθυμοι δὲ γενόμενοι πάντες καὶ αὐτοὶ μεταλάβαν τροφῆς. 27.37 ἤμεθα δὲ αἱ πᾶσαι ψυχαὶ ἐν τῷ πλοίῳ διακόσιαι ἑβδομήκοντα ἕξ. 27.38 κορεσθέντες δὲ τροφῆς ἐκούφιζον τὸ πλοῖον ἐκβαλλόμενοι τὸν σῖτον εἰς τὴν θάλασσαν. 27.39 ὅτε δὲ ἡμέρα ἐγένετο, τὴν γῆν οὐκ ἐπεγίνωσκον, κόλπον δέ τινα κατενόουν ἔχοντα αἰγιαλὸν εἰς ὃν ἐβουλεύοντο εἰ δύναιντο ἐξῶσαι τὸ πλοῖον. 27.40 καὶ τὰς ἀγκύρας περιελόντες εἴων εἰς τὴν θάλασσαν, ἅμα ἀνέντες τὰς ζευκτηρίας τῶν πηδαλίων, καὶ ἐπάραντες τὸν ἀρτέμωνα τῇ πνεούσῃ κατεῖχον εἰς τὸν αἰγιαλόν. 27.41 περιπεσόντες δὲ εἰς τόπον διθάλασσον ἐπέκειλαν τὴν ναῦν, καὶ ἡ μὲν πρῷρα ἐρείσασα ἔμεινεν ἀσάλευτος, ἡ δὲ πρύμνα ἐλύτο ὑπὸ τῆς βίας τῶν κυμάτων. 27.42 τῶν δὲ στρατιωτῶν βουλὴ ἐγένετο ἵνα τοὺς δεσμώτας ἀποκτίνωσιν, μή τις ἐκκολυβήσας διαφύγῃ· 27.43 ὁ δὲ ἑκατοντάρχης βουλόμενος διασῶσαι τὸν Παῦλον ἐκώλυσεν

it to become day.   27.30 And of/from the sailors
seeking to flee/escape from the ship and having lowered the skiff/lifeboat into the sea by a pretense as
being about to stretch out anchors from *the* prow,
27.31 Paul said to the centurion and to the soldiers:
Unless these remain/stay in/with the ship, ye yourselves are not able to be saved.

27.32 Then the soldiers cut off the ropes of the
skiff and allowed her/*it* to fall off.   27.33 And
until which *time* it was about to become day, Paul was
exhorting all to partake of food, saying: Today is *the*
fourteenth day ye continue/complete waiting/expecting
without eating, having taken nothing;   27.34 wherefore, I call upon ye to partake of food, for this is
toward/for your salvation/deliverance; for of no one
of ye will a hair perish from the head.   27.35 And
having said these (things) and having taken a loaf,
having given thanks to God before all and having
broken *it*, he began to eat.   27.36 And all these,
having become cheerful, they partook of food.   27.37
And we, all the souls/lives in the ship were two
hundred seventy-six.   27.38 And having been filled
from food, they were lightening the ship, throwing the
wheat into the sea.   27.39 And when it became day,
they were not recognizing the land, but they were
noticing a certain bay/inlet/bosom having a beach/
shore into which they were planning to beach the ship
if they may be able.   27.40 And having removed the
anchors, they were allowing *them* into the sea, at the
same time having unfastened the bands from the rud-
ders, and having raised the fore sail to the breeze,
they were holding/heading down to the beach.   27.41
And having fallen/come around to a place (sand bar/
reef) with sea on both sides they drove/ran the ship
aground, and on one hand the prow having jammed fast
remained unshakable/immovable, but on the other the
stern was being destroyed by the force/violence of the
waves.   27.42 And the purpose/will of the soldiers
became that they should kill the prisoners lest anyone
having swam out might escape;   27.43 but the centurion, deciding/purposing to deliver/save Paul forbade
them from the plan/purpose, and he ordered *for* those

αὐτοὺς τοῦ βουλήματος, ἐκέλευσέν τε τοὺς δυναμένους κολυμβᾶν ἀπορίψαντας πρώτους ἐπὶ τῆς γῆς ἐξιέναι, 27.44 καὶ τοὺς λοιποὺς οὓς μὲν ἐπὶ σανίσιν οὓς δὲ ἐπί τινων τῶν ἀπὸ τοῦ πλοίου· καὶ οὕτως ἐγένετο πάντας διασωθῆναι ἐπὶ τὴν γῆν. 28.1 καὶ διασωθέντες τότε ἐπέγνωμεν ὅτι Μελίτη ἡ νῆσος καλεῖται. 28.2 οἵ δε βάρβαροι παρεῖχαν οὐ τὴν τυχοῦσαν φιλανθρωπίαν ἡμῖν, ἅψαντες γὰρ πυρὰν προσελάμβοντο πάντας ἡμᾶς διὰ τὸν ὑετὸν τὸν ἐφεστῶτα καὶ διὰ τὸ ψῦχος. 28.3 συστρέψαντος δὲ τοῦ Παύλου φρυγάνων πλῆθος καὶ ἐπιθέντες ἐπὶ τὴν πυράν, ἔχιδνα ἀπὸ τῆς θέρμης ἐξελθοῦσα καθῆψε τῆς χιρὸς αὐτοῦ. 28.4 ὡς δὲ εἶδον οἱ βάρβαροι κρεμάμενον τὸ θηρίον ἐκ τῆς χιρὸς αὐτοῦ, πρὸς ἀλλήλους ἔλεγον, πάντως φονεύς ἐστιν ὁ ἄνθρωπος οὗτος ὃν διασωθέντα εἰς θαλάσσης ἡ δίκη ζῆν οὐκ ἴασεν. 28.5 ὁ μὲν οὖν ἀποτινάξας τὸ θηρίον εἰς τὸ πῦρ ἔπαθεν οὐδὲν κακόν· 28.6 οἱ δὲ προσεδόκων αὐτὸν μέλλιν πίμπρασθαι ἢ καταπίπτιν ἄφνω νεκρόν. ἐπὶ πολὺ δὲ αὐτῶν προσδοκώντων καὶ θεωρούντων μηδὲν ἄτοπον εἰς αὐτὸν γεινόμενον, μεταβαλλόμενοι ἔλεγον αὐτὸν εἶναι θεόν.

28.7 ἐν δὲ τοῖς περὶ τὸν τόπον ἐκῖνον ὑπῆρχε χωρία τῷ πρώτῳ τῆς νήσου ὀνόματι Ποπλίῳ, ὃς ἀναδεξάμενος ἡμᾶς τρῖς ἡμέρας φιλοφρόνως ἐξένισεν.

28.8 ἐγένετο δὲ τὸν πατέρα τοῦ Ποπλίου πυρετοῖς καὶ δυσεντερίῳ συνεχόμενον κατακεῖσθαι, πρὸς ὃν ὁ Παῦλος εἰσελθὼν καὶ προσευξάμενος ἐπιθὶς τὰς χῖρας αὐτῷ ἰάσατο αὐτόν.

28.9 τούτου δὲ γενομένου καὶ οἱ λοιποὶ οἱ ἐν τῇ νήσῳ ἔχοντες ἀσθενείας προσήρχοντο καὶ ἐθεραπεύοντο, 28.10 οἳ καὶ πολλαῖς τιμαῖς ἐτίμησαν ἡμᾶς καὶ ἀναγομένοις ἐπέθεντο τὰ πρὸς τὰς χρείας.

28.11 μετὰ δὲ τρῖς μῆνας ἀνήχθημεν ἐν πλοίῳ παρακεχειμακότι ἐν τῇ νήσῳ Ἀλεξανδρίνῳ, παρασήμῳ Διοσκούροις. 28.12 καὶ καταχθέντες εἰς Συρακούσας ἐπεμείναμεν

being able to swim, first having thrown (themselves) off, to go out to the land, 27.44 and *for* the rest *of* whom some on boards *of* whom others on some of the (things) from the ship; and so all happened to be brought safely to the land. 28.1 And having been brought safely through, we learned then that the island is called Melita. 28.2 And the barbarians/non-Greeks showed to us not the ordinary kindness/hospitality, for having lit a fire, they welcomed us all because of the rain coming on and because of the cold. 28.3 And from Paul having gathered a multitude of sticks and having put *them* on the fire, a snake/viper having come out from the heat fastened/seized on his hand. 28.4 And when the barbarians/foreigners saw the beast hanging from his hand, they were saying to one another: This man is surely a murderer, whom having been saved/delivered in/*from the* sea, the justice/vengeance allowed not to live. 28.5 Then the (he) on one hand having shaken off the beast into the fire he suffered nothing bad; 28.6 but the (they) on the other were expecting *for* him to be about to be swollen or to suddenly fall down dead. But from them waiting/expecting for much *time* and beholding nothing becoming unusual/out of place in him, having changed their minds, they were saying *for* him to be a god.

28.7 And in the (parts) around that place were existing lands for the first (man) of the island, Publius by name, who having himself welcomed us, he entertained *us* hospitably *for* three days.

28.8. It happened *for* the father of Publius to be lying down, being seized by fevers and dysentery, to/for whom Paul, having entered and having prayed himself, having placed the hands on him, he healed him.

28.9 And from this having happened, the rest on the island having sicknesses were also coming near and being treated/healed, 28.10 who also honored us with many honors/valuables, and for *our* setting sail, they placed the (things) near the hands.

28.11 And after three months we were embarked in an Alexandrian ship having spent the winter at the island, with a sign/flag for Dioscuri. 28.12 And

ἡμέρας τρῖς, 28.13 ὅθεν περιελόντες κατηντήσαμεν εἰς Ῥήγιον. καὶ μετὰ μίαν ἡμέραν ἐπιγενομένου νότου δευτερέοι ἤλθομεν εἰς Ποτιόλους, 28.14 οὗ εὑρόντες ἀδελφοὺς παρεκλήθημεν παρ' αὐτοῖς ἐπιμεῖναι ἡμέρας ἑπτά· καὶ οὕτως εἰς τὴν Ῥώμην ἤλθαμεν. 28.15 κἀκεῖθεν οἱ ἀδελφοὶ ἀκούσαντες τὰ περὶ ἡμῶν ἦλθαν εἰς ἀπάντησιν ἡμῖν ἄχρι Ἀππίου Φόρου καὶ Τριῶν Ταβερνῶν, οὓς ἰδὼν ὁ Παῦλος εὐχαριστήσας τῷ θεῷ ἔλαβεν θάρσος. 28.16 Ὅτε δὲ εἰσήλθομεν εἰς Ῥώμην, ἐπετράπη τῷ Παύλῳ μένιν καθ' ἑαυτὸν σὺν τῷ φυλάσσοντι αὐτὸν στρατιώτῃ. 28.17 ἐγένετο δὲ μετὰ ἡμέρας τρεῖς συνκαλέσασθαι αὐτὸν τοὺς ὄντας τῶν Ἰουδαίων πρώτους· συνελθόντων δὲ δὲ αὐτῶν ἔλεγεν πρὸς αὐτούς, λέγων, ἄνδρες ἀδελφοί, οὐδὲν ἐναντίον ποιήσας τῷ λαῷ ἢ τοῖς ἔθεσι τοῖς πατρῴοις δέσμιος ἐξ Ἱεροσολύμων παρεδόθην εἰς τὰς χῖρας τῶν Ῥωμαίων, 28.18 οἵτινες ἀνακρίναντές με ἐβούλοντο ἀπολῦσαι διὰ τὸ μηδεμίαν αἰτίαν θανάτου ὑπάρχειν ἐν ἐμοί· 28.19 ἀντιλεγόντων δὲ τῶν Ἰουδαίων ἠναγκάσθην ἐπικαλέσασθαι Κέσαρα, οὐχ ὡς τοῦ ἔθνους μου ἔχων τι κατηγορεῖν. 28.20 διὰ ταύτην οὖν τὴν αἰτίαν παρεκάλεσα ὑμᾶς ἰδῖν καὶ προσλαλῆσαι, ἕνεκεν γὰρ τῆς ἐλπίδος τοῦ Ἰσδραὴλ τὴν ἅλυσιν ταύτην περίκειμαι. 28.21 οἱ δὲ πρὸς αὐτὸν εἶπαν, ἡμῖς οὔτε γράμματα κατὰ σοῦ ἐδεξάμεθα ἀπὸ τῆς Ἰουδαίας, οὔτε παραγενόμενός τις τῶν ἀδελφῶν ἀπήγγιλεν ἢ ἐλάλησέν τι περὶ σοῦ πονηρόν.

28.22 ἀξιοῦμεν δὲ ἀκοῦσαι παρὰ σοῦ ἃ φρονῖς, περὶ μὲν γὰρ τῆς αἱρέσεως ταύτης γνωστὸν ἡμῖν ἐστιν ὅτι πανταχοῦ ἀντιλέγεται. 28.23 ταξάμενοι δὲ αὐτῷ ἡμέραν ἦλθον πρὸς αὐτὸν εἰς τὴν ξενίαν πλείονες, οἷς ἐξετίθετο διαμαρτυράμενος τὴν βασιλείαν τοῦ θεοῦ πίθων τε αὐτοὺς περὶ τοῦ Ἰησοῦ ἀπό τε τοῦ νόμου Μωϋσέως καὶ τῶν προφητῶν ἀπὸ πρωῒ ἕως ἑσπέρας. 28.24 καὶ οἱ μὲν ἐπίθοντο τοῖς λεγομένοις, οἱ δὲ ἠπίστουν· 28.25

having been brought down to Syracuse, we stayed *there* three days, 28.13 from where having sailed around, we arrived at Rhegium. And after one day, from a south wind having come about, on the second we went to Puteoli, 28.14 where having found brothers, we were invited to stay with them *for* seven days; and thus we went to Rome. 28.15 And from there the brothers, having heard the (things) about us, came to a meeting with us until as far as Appii Forum and Three Taverns, whom having seen, Paul, having given thanks to God, took courage. 28.16 And when we went into Rome, it was permitted for Paul to abide/stay by himself with the soldier guarding him. 28.17 And it came about after three days *for* him to call together those being first (men) of the Judeans; and from them having gathered he was speaking to them, saying: Men and brothers, having done nothing contrary to the people or the ancestral customs, I was delivered a prisoner out of Jerusalem into the hands of the Romans, 28.18 who having examined me were planning/deciding to release *me* because of the (thing) to be no cause/reason of death in me; 28.19 but from the Judeans opposing/speaking against *me*, I was compelled to appeal to Caesar, not as my ethnic/nation having anything to charge/accuse. 28.20 Then on account of this cause/reason I summoned ye to see and to speak to, for on account of the hope of Israel I am bound *by* this chain. 28.21 And the (they) said to him: We ourselves received neither writing/letters from Judea against you, nor did anyone of/from the brothers having arrived report or speak anything evil about you.

28.22 But we think it best to hear from you what (things) you think, for indeed it is known to us concerning this sect/heresy that it is opposed/spoken against everywhere. 28.23 And having arranged a day with him, they came to him in the lodging place many *times/for* more *time*, to whom testifying solemnly he was setting forth/explaining the kingdom of God, and persuading them about Jesus, both from the law of Moses and the prophets, from early morning until evening. 28.24 And the (they) indeed/some were being persuaded by the (things) being said, but others were

491

ἀσύμφωνοι δὲ ὄντες πρὸς ἀλλήλους ἀπελύοντο,

εἰπόντος τοῦ Παύλου ῥῆμα ἓν ὅτι καλῶς τὸ πνεῦμα τὸ ἅγιον ἐλάλησεν διὰ Ἠσαΐου τοῦ προφήτου πρὸς τοὺς πατέρας ὑμῶν 28.26 λέγων, «πορεύθητι πρὸς τὸν λαὸν τοῦτον καὶ εἰπόν, ἀκοῇ ἀκούσετε καὶ οὐ μὴ συνῆτε, καὶ βλέποντες βλέψετε καὶ οὐ μὴ ἴδητε· 28.27 ἐπαχύνθη γὰρ ἡ καρδία τοῦ λαοῦ τούτου, καὶ τοῖς ὠσὶν αὐτῶν βαρέως ἤκουσαν, καὶ τοὺς ὀφθαλμοὺς αὐτῶν ἐκάμμυσαν· μήποτε ἴδωσιν τοῖς ὀφθαλμοῖς καὶ τοῖς ὠσὶν ἀκούσωσιν καὶ τῇ καρδίᾳ συνῶσιν καὶ ἐπιστρέψωσιν, καὶ ἰάσομαι αὐτούς.»

28.28 γνωστὸν οὖν ἔστω ὑμῖν ὅτι τοῖς ἔθνεσιν ἀπεστάλη τοῦτο τὸ σωτήριον τοῦ θεοῦ· αὐτοὶ καὶ ἀκούσονται. 28.30 ἐνέμινεν δὲ διετίαν ὅλην ἐν ἰδίῳ μισθώματι, καὶ ἀπεδέχετο πάντας τοὺς εἰσπορευομένους πρὸς αὐτόν, 28.31 κηρύσσων τὴν βασιλείαν τοῦ θεοῦ καὶ διδάσκων τὰ περὶ τοῦ κυρίου Ἰησοῦ χριστοῦ μετὰ πάσης παρρησίας ἀκωλύτως.

Πράξεις Ἀποστόλων

disbelieving; 28.25 and being in disagreement with one another, they were being released/gone away

from Paul having said one thing/word: That the holy spirit spoke well through Isaias the prophet to the fathers of ye, 28.26 saying: GO YOU TO THIS PEOPLE AND SAY (ONCE): IN HEARING, YE WILL HEAR AND BY NO MEANS MIGHT YE UNDERSTAND, AND SEEING YE WILL SEE/LOOK AND BY NO MEANS MIGHT YE PERCEIVE/BEHOLD; 28.27 FOR THE HEART OF THIS PEOPLE WAS MADE GROSS/ DULL, AND THEY HEARD/LISTENED WITH DIFFICULTY/HARDNESS OF HEARING IN THEIR EARS, AND THEY CLOSED THEIR EYES; LEST PERCHANCE THEY MIGHT BEHOLD WITH THE EYES, AND THEY MIGHT HEAR WITH THE EARS, AND THEY MIGHT UNDER- STAND IN THE HEART AND THEY MIGHT TURN AROUND AND I MYSELF SHALL HEAL THEM.

28.28 Therefore, let it be known to ye that this deliverance/salvation of/from God was sent to the ethnics; and those, they will hear. 28.30 And he lived/stayed a whole two year period in his own hired/rented quarters, and he welcomed all those coming in to him, 28.31 heralding/preaching the kingdom of God and teaching the (things) concerning the Lord Jesus, the anointed (one), with boldness/free speech, without hindrance.

Practices of Apostles

ΙΑΚΩΒΟΥ

This is the Sinaitic New Testament, book of James.

1.1 Ἰάκωβος θεοῦ καὶ κυρίου Ἰησοῦ χριστοῦ δοῦλος ταῖς δώδεκα φυλαῖς ταῖς ἐν τῇ διασπορᾷ χαίρειν.

1.2 πᾶσαν χαρὰν ἡγήσασθαι, ἀδελφοί μου, ὅταν πιρασμοῖς περιπέσηται ποικίλοις, 1.3 γινώσκοντες ὅτι τὸ δοκίμειον ὑμῶν τῆς πίστεως κατεργάζεται ὑπομονήν· 1.4 ἡ δὲ ὑπομονὴ ἔργον τέλιον ἐχέτω, ἵνα ἦτε τέλιοι καὶ ὁλόκληροι, ἐν μηδενὶ λειπόμενοι. 1.5 εἰ δέ τις ὑμῶν λείπεται σοφίας, αἰτίτω παρὰ τοῦ διδόντος θεοῦ πᾶσιν ἁπλῶς καὶ μὴ ὀνιδίζοντος, καὶ δοθήσεται αὐτῷ. 1.6 αἰτείτω δὲ ἐν πίστι, μηδὲν διακρινόμενος, ὁ γὰρ διακρινόμενος ἔοικεν κλύδωνι θαλάσσης ἀνεμιζομένῳ καὶ ῥιπιζομένῳ· 1.7 μὴ γὰρ οἰέσθω ὁ ἄνθρωπος ἐκεῖνος ὅτι λήμψεταί παρὰ τοῦ κυρίου, 1.8 ἀνὴρ δίψυχος, ἀκατάστατος ἐν πάσαις ταῖς ὁδοῖς αὐτοῦ. 1.9 καυχάσθω δὲ ὁ ἀδελφὸς ὁ ταπινὸς ἐν τῷ ὕψει αὐτοῦ, 1.10 ὁ δὲ πλούσιος ἐν τῇ ταπινώσει αὐτοῦ, ὅτι ὡς ἄνθος χόρτου παρελεύσεται. 1.11 ἀνέτιλεν γὰρ ὁ ἥλιος σὺν τῷ καύσωνι καὶ ἐξήρανεν τὸν χόρτον, καὶ τὸ ἄνθος αὐτοῦ ἐξέπεσεν καὶ ἡ εὐπρέπια τοῦ προσώπου αὐτοῦ ἀπώλετο· οὕτως καὶ ὁ πλούσιος ἐν ταῖς πορίαις αὐτοῦ μαρανθήσεται. 1.12 μακάριος ἀνὴρ ὃς ὑπομένι πειρασμόν, ὅτι δόκιμος γενόμενος λήμψεται τὸν στέφανον τῆς ζωῆς, ὃν ἐπηγγίλατο τοῖς ἀγαπῶσιν αὐτόν. 1.13 μηδὶς πιραζόμενος λεγέτω ὅτι ὑπὸ θεοῦ πειράζομαι· ὁ γὰρ θεὸς ἀπείραστός ἐστιν κακῶν, πειράζει δὲ αὐτὸς οὐδένα. 1.14 ἕκαστος δὲ πιράζετε ὑπὸ τῆς ἰδίας ἐπιθυμίας ἐξελκόμενος καὶ δελεαζόμενος· 1.15 εἶτα ἡ ἐπιθυμία συλλαβοῦσα τίκτει ἁμαρτίαν, ἡ δὲ ἁμαρτία ἀποτελεσθεῖσα ἀποκύει θάνατον. 1.16 μὴ πλανᾶσθαι, ἀδελφοί μου ἀγαπητοί. 1.17 πᾶσα δόσις ἀγαθὴ καὶ πᾶν δώρημα τέλειον ἄνωθέν ἐστιν, καταβενον ἀπὸ τοῦ πατρὸς τῶν φώτων, παρ' ᾧ οὐκ ἔστιν παραλλαγὴ ἢ τροπῆς ἀποσκίασμα. 1.18 βουληθὶς ἀπεκύησεν ἡμᾶς λόγῳ ἀληθίας, εἰς τὸ εἶναι ἡμᾶς

1.1   James, a slave of God and *the* Lord, Jesus the anointed (one), to the twelve tribes, to greet those in the dispersion.

1.2   Ye count/reckon *it* all joy, my brothers, when ye might fall in various temptations/trials,   1.3 knowing that the proving of your faith works endurance/patience;   1.4 and let the patience have a finished work, in order that ye may be complete and whole (ones), lacking in nothing.   1.5 But if anyone of ye lacks wisdom, let him ask from God, the (one) giving to all liberally and reproaching not, and it will be given to him.   1.6 But let him ask in faith, doubting nothing, for the (one) doubting is likened to a wave of a sea, being wind driven and thrown down;   1.7 for let that man not suppose that he will receive/take from the Lord,   1.8 a two-souled/double-lifed man, unstable in all his ways/roads.   1.9 But let the humble/lowly brother triumph in/by his height,   1.10 and the rich (one) in/by his humility, because he will pass away as a blossom of grass.   1.11 For the sun rose with the scorching heat and withered the grass, and the blossom of it fell out and the comeliness of its face/appearance perished/was destroyed; so also the rich (one) will be faded in his goings/ventures.   1.12   Happy *is* a man who endures temptation/trial because, having been proven/approved he will take/receive the crown of the life, which he promised to those loving him.   1.13 Let no one being tried/tested say: I am tempted/tested from God; for God is untempted from evil (things), and he, he tempts/tests no one.   1.14 But each (one) is being tempted/tried by the (thing) of his own desire being drawn out and being lured/enticed.   1.15 Then the desire having conceived/apprehended gives birth to sin/a fault, and the sin/fault, having been completed, generates death.   1.16   Be ye not deceived/led astray, my beloved brothers.   1.17 Every good giving and every complete/mature gift is from above, coming down from the father of the lights, from whom there is not a change/variation or a shadow of/from turning.   1.18 Having purposed/planned, he brought us forth with a saying of truth, for the (thing) of us to be a certain first-

ἀπαρχήν τινα τῶν αὐτοῦ κτισμάτων. 1.19 ἴστω, ἀδελφοί μου ἀγαπητοί. ἔστω δὲ πᾶς ἄνθρωπος ταχὺς εἰς τὸ ἀκοῦσαι, βραδὺς εἰς τὸ λαλῆσαι, βραδὺς εἰς ὀργήν· 1.20 ὀργὴ γὰρ ἀνδρὸς δικαιοσύνην θεοῦ οὐκ ἐργάζεται. 1.21 διὸ ἀποθέμενοι πᾶσαν ῥυπαρίαν καὶ περισσίαν κακίας ἐμπραΰτητι δέξασθαι τὸν ἔμφυτον λόγον τὸν δυνάμενον σῶσαι τὰς ψυχὰς ὑμῶν.

1.22 γείνεσθε δὲ ποιηταὶ λόγου καὶ μὴ μόνον ἀκροαταὶ παραλογιζόμενοι ἑαυτούς. 1.23 ὅτι εἴ τις ἀκροατὴς λόγου ἐστὶν καὶ οὐ ποιητής, οὗτος ἔοικεν ἀνδρὶ κατανοοῦντι τὸ πρόσωπον τῆς γενέσεως αὐτοῦ ἐν ἐσόπτρῳ· 1.24 κατενόησεν γὰρ ἑαυτὸν καὶ ἀπελήλυθεν καὶ εὐθέως ἐπελάθετο ὁποῖος ἦν. 1.25 ὁ δὲ παρακύψας εἰς νόμον τέλειον τὸν τῆς ἐλευθερίας καὶ παραμίνας, οὐκ ἀκροατὴς ἐπιλησμονῆς γενόμενος ἀλλὰ ποιητὴς ἔργου, οὗτος μακάριος ἐν τῇ ποιήσει αὐτοῦ ἔσται.

1.26 εἴ τις δοκεῖ θρησκὸς εἶναι, μὴ χαλιναγωγῶν γλῶσσαν αὐτοῦ ἀλλὰ ἀπατῶν καρδίαν αὐτοῦ, τούτου μάταιος ἡ θρησκία. 1.27 θρησκία καθαρὰ καὶ ἀμίαντος παρὰ τῷ θεῷ καὶ πατρὶ αὕτη ἐστίν, ἐπισκέπτεσθε ὀρφανοὺς καὶ χήρας ἐν τῇ θλίψει αὐτῶν, ἄσπιλον ἑαυτὸν τηρῖν ἀπὸ τοῦ κόσμου. 2.1 ἀδελφοί μου, μὴ ἐν προσωπολημψίαις ἔχετε τὴν πίστιν τοῦ κυρίου ἡμῶν Ἰησοῦ χριστοῦ τῆς δόξης. 2.2 ἐὰν γὰρ εἰσέλθῃ εἰς συναγωγὴν ὑμῶν ἀνὴρ χρυσοδακτύλιος ἐν αἰσθῆτι λαμπρᾷ, εἰσέλθῃ δὲ καὶ πτωχὸς ἐν ῥυπαρᾷ αἰσθῆτι, 2.3 καὶ ἐπιβλέψηται ἐπὶ τὸν φοροῦντα τὴν ἐσθῆτα τὴν λαμπρὰν καὶ εἴπητε, σὺ κάθου ὧδε καλῶς, καὶ τῷ πτωχῷ εἴπητε, σὺ στῆθι ἐκεῖ ἢ κάθου ὑπὸ τὸ ὑποπόδιόν μου, 2.4 οὐ διεκρίθηται ἐν ἑαυτοῖς καὶ ἐγένεσθαι κριταὶ διαλογισμῶν πονηρῶν; 2.5 ἀκούσατε, ἀδελφοί μου ἀγαπητοί. οὐκ ὁ θεὸς ἐξελέξατο τοὺς πτωχοὺς τῷ κόσμῳ πλουσίους ἐν πίστι καὶ κληρονόμους τῆς θασιλίας ἧς ἐπηγγείλατο τοῖς ἀγαπῶσιν αὐτόν; 2.6 ὑμεῖς δὲ ἠτιμάσατε τὸν

fruit of the creations/creatures from/of him. 1.19 Let us stand, my beloved brothers. But let every man/human be quick in the (thing) to hear/listen, slow in the (thing) to speak, slow to/in anger; 1.20 for anger of/from a man works not justness/justice of God. 1.21 Wherefore, putting away every filthy (thing) and abundance/excess of evil/malice in lowliness/gentleness receive ye the implanted saying/word/logos, the (one) being able to save your souls/lives.

1.22 And become ye doers/makers of logos/reason/word and not only listeners, misreasoning/misleading yourselves. 1.23 Because if anyone is a hearer of a reason/saying/word and not a doer, this (one) is likened to a man perceiving the face of his generation in a mirror; 1.24 for he understood/perceived himself and has departed, and immediately he disregarded/forgot of what sort he was. 1.25 But the (one) having looked into the complete law of the liberty/freedom and having remained/abided, becoming not a hearer of neglect but a doer of work, this (one) will be happy in/with his doing/making.

1.26 If anyone seems/thinks to be religious, not bridling his tongue but deceiving his heart, the religion of this (one) is empty/vain. 1.27 Religion, pure and undefiled with the God and father, is this: To visit/look after orphans and widows in their oppression/affliction, to keep himself without blemish from the world. 2.1 My brothers, not in/by partialities have ye the faith from our Lord Jesus, the anointed (one) of the fame/reputation/glory. 2.2 For if one might enter into your congregation, a goldfingered man in splendid clothing, and also one might enter, a poor (one) in filthy clothing, 2.3 and ye will look upon the (one) wearing the splendid clothing and ye might say: You, you sit well here, and ye might say to the poor (one): You, you stand there or sit beneath my footstool, 2.4 did ye not discriminate among yourselves, and ye became judges of evil reasonings? 2.5 Ye listen/hear, my beloved brothers. Elected/chose not God the poor (ones) in the world, rich (ones) in faith and heirs of the kingdom which he promised to those loving him? 2.6 But ye, ye dishon-

πτωχόν. οὐχ οἱ πλούσιοι καταδυναστεύουσιν ὑμῶν, καὶ αὐτοὶ ἕλκουσιν ὑμᾶς εἰς κριτήρια; 2.7 οὐκ αὐτοὶ βλασφημοῦσιν τὸ καλὸν ὄνομα τὸ ἐπικληθὲν ἐφ' ὑμᾶς; 2.8 εἰ μέντοι νόμον τελεῖτε βασιλικὸν κατὰ τὴν γραφήν, «ἀγαπήσεις τὸν πλησίον σου ὡς σεαυτόν,» καλῶς ποιεῖται· 2.9 εἰ δὲ προσωπολημπτῖται, ἁμαρτίαν ἐργάζεσθαι, ἐλεγχόμενοι ὑπὸ τοῦ νόμου ὡς παραβάται.

2.10 ὅστις γὰρ ὅλον τὸν νόμον τηρήσῃ, πταίσῃ δὲ ἐν ἑνί, γέγονεν πάντων ἔνοχος. 2.11 ὁ γὰρ εἰπών, «μὴ μοιχεύσῃς,» εἶπεν καί, «μὴ φονεύσῃς·» εἰ δὲ οὐ μοιχεύεις, φονεύεις δέ, γέγονας παραβάτης νόμου. 2.12 οὕτως λαλεῖτε καὶ οὕτω ποιεῖτε ὡς διὰ νόμου ἐλευθερίας μέλλοντες κρίνεσθαι. 2.13 ἡ γὰρ κρίσις ἀνέλεος τῷ μὴ ποιήσαντι ἔλεος· κατακαυχᾶται ἔλεος κρίσεως. 2.14 Τί τὸ ὄφελος, ἀδελφοί μου, ἐὰν πίστιν λέγῃ τις ἔχειν, ἔργα δὲ μὴ ἔχῃ; μὴ δύναται ἡ πίστις σῶσαι αὐτόν; 2.15 ἐὰν ἀδελφὸς ἢ ἀδελφὴ γυμνοὶ ὑπάρχωσιν καὶ λειπόμενοι τῆς ἐφημέρου τροφῆς, 2.16 εἴπῃ δέ τις αὐτοῖς ἐξ ὑμῶν, ὑπάγεται ἐν ἰρήνῃ, θερμαίνεσθαι καὶ χορτάζεσθαι, μὴ δῶτε δὲ αὐτοῖς τὰ ἐπιτήδια τοῦ σώματος, τί τὸ ὄφελος; 2.17 οὕτως καὶ ἡ πίστις, ἐὰν μὴ ἔχῃ ἔργα, νεκρά ἐστιν καθ' ἑαυτήν. 2.18 ἀλλ' ἐρῖ τις, σὺ πίστιν ἔχεις κἀγὼ ἔργα ἔχω. δῖξόν μοι τὴν πίστιν σου χωρὶς τῶν ἔργων, κἀγώ σοι δείξω ἐκ τῶν ἔργων μου τὴν πίστιν. 2.19 σὺ πιστεύεις ὅτι εἷς ἐστιν ὁ θεός; καλῶς ποιεῖς· καὶ τὰ δαιμόνια πιστεύουσιν καὶ φρίσσουσιν.

2.20 θέλεις δὲ γνῶναι, ὦ ἄνθρωπε καινέ, ὅτι ἡ πίστις χωρὶς τῶν ἔργων νεκρά ἐστιν; 2.21 Ἀβραὰμ ὁ πατὴρ ἡμῶν οὐκ ἐξ ἔργων ἐδικαιώθη, ἀνενέγκας Ἰσαὰκ τὸν υἱὸν αὐτοῦ ἐπὶ τὸ θυσιαστήριον; 2.22 βλέπεις ὅτι ἡ πίστις συνήργει τοῖς ἔργοις αὐτοῦ καὶ ἐκ τῶν ἔργων ἡ πίστις ἐτελειώθη, 2.23 καὶ ἐπληρώθη ἡ γραφὴ ἡ λέγουσα, «ἐπίστευσεν δὲ Ἀβραὰμ τῷ θεῷ, καὶ ἐλογίσθη αὐτῷ εἰς δικαιοσύνην,» καὶ φίλος θεοῦ ἐκλήθη. 2.24 ὁρᾶτε ὅτι

ored the poor (one). Do not the rich (ones) tyrannize ye, and these, they drag ye into tribunals/courts? 2.7 Do not they, they slander/blaspheme the good name, the (one) bestowed upon ye? 2.8 If indeed ye complete/finish a royal law according to the writing: YOU WILL LOVE YOUR NEIGHBOR AS YOURSELF, ye do well; 2.9 but if ye show partiality, ye work a sin/fault, being reproved by the law as transgressors.

2.10 For *the one* who might keep the entire law, but might stumble in one, has become guilty of all. 2.11 For the (one) saying : YOU MAY NOT DO ADULTERY, he said also: YOU MAY NOT MURDER; and if you do not adultery, but you murder, you have become a transgressor of law. 2.12 Thus ye speak and thus ye do as being about to be judged through a law of freedom. 2.13 for the judgment *will be* without mercy for the (one) not having made/did mercy; mercy triumphs over/boasts against judgment. 2.14 What *is* the benefit, my brothers, if anyone may say/claim to have faith, but may not have works? The faith is not able to save him! 2.15 If a brother or a sister are existing named and lacking from the daily food, 2.16 and anyone out of ye may say to them: Depart/ye go away in peace, be ye warmed and filled, but ye might not give to them the necessities of the body, what is the benefit? 2.17 So also the faith, if it may not have works, is dead by itself. 2.18 But someone will say: You, you have faith and I, I have works. You show to me your faith without the works, and I shall show to you the faith out of my works. 2.19 You, you believe that one is God? You do well; even the demons believe and they shudder.

2.20 But *do* you want to know, O vain/empty man, that the faith without the works is dead? 2.21 Was not our father Abraham vindicated out to works, offering up his son Isaac upon the altar? 2.22 You see that the faith worked together with his works, and the faith was completed/matured out of/from the works, 2.23 and the writing was fulfilled, the (one) saying: AND ABRAHAM BELIEVED/OBEYED GOD AND IT WAS ACCOUNTED TO HIM IN/FOR JUSTICE/JUSTNESS, and he was called a friend of God. 2.24 Ye see that out of/from works a

ἐξ ἔργων δικαιοῦται ἄνθρωπος καὶ οὐκ ἐκ πίστεως μόνον.

2.25 ὁμοίως δὲ καὶ Ῥαὰβ ἡ πόρνη οὐκ ἐξ ἔργων ἐδικαιώθη, ὑποδεξαμένη τοὺς ἀγγέλους καὶ ἑτέρα ὁδῷ ἐκβαλοῦσα; 2.26 ὥσπερ γὰρ τὸ σῶμα χωρὶς πνεύματος νεκρόν ἐστιν, οὕτως καὶ ἡ πίστις χωρὶς ἔργων νεκρά ἐστιν.

3.1 Μὴ πολλοὶ διδάσκαλοι γίνεσθε, ἀδελφοί μου, εἰδότες ὅτι μεῖζον κρίμα λημψόμεθα. 3.2 πολλὰ γὰρ πταίομεν ἅπαντες. εἴ τις ἐν λόγῳ οὐ πταίει, οὗτος τέλειος ἀνήρ, δυνάμενος χαλιναγωγῆσαι καὶ ὅλον τὸ σῶμα.

3.3 εἰ δὲ τῶν ἵππων τοὺς χαλινοὺς εἰς τὰ στόματα βάλλομεν εἰς τὸ πίθεσθαι αὐτοὺς ἡμῖν, καὶ ὅλον τὸ σῶμα αὐτῶν μετάγομεν. 3.4 ἰδοὺ καὶ τὰ πλοῖα, τηλικαῦτα ὄντα καὶ ὑπὸ ἀνέμων σκληρῶν ἐλαυνόμενα, μετάγεται ὑπὸ ἐλαχίστου πηδαλίου ὅπου ἡ ὁρμὴ τοῦ εὐθύνοντος βούλεται· 3.5 οὕτως καὶ ἡ γλῶσσα μικρὸν μέλος ἐστὶν καὶ μεγάλα αὐχεῖ. ἰδοὺ ἡλίκον πῦρ ἡλίκην ὕλην ἀνάπτι· 3.6 καὶ ἡ γλῶσσα πῦρ, ὁ κόσμος τῆς ἀδικίας, ἡ γλῶσσα καθίσταται ἐν τοῖς μέλεσιν ἡμῶν, ἡ σπιλοῦσα ὅλον τὸ σῶμα καὶ φλογίζουσα τὸν τροχὸν τῆς γενέσεως ἡμῶν καὶ φλογιζομένη ὑπὸ τῆς γεέννης. 3.7 πᾶσα γὰρ φύσις θηρίων τε καὶ πετινῶν ἑρπετῶν τε καὶ ἐναλίων δαμάζεται καὶ δεδάμασται τῇ φύσει τῇ ἀνθρωπίνῃ· 3.8 τὴν δὲ γλῶσσαν οὐδεὶς δύναται δαμάσαι ἀνθρώπων· ἀκατάστατον κακόν, μεστὴ ἰοῦ θανατηφόρου. 3.9 ἐν αὐτῇ εὐλογοῦμεν τὸν κύριον καὶ πατέρα, καὶ ἐν αὐτῇ καταρώμεθα τοὺς ἀνθρώπους τοὺς καθ᾽ ὁμοίωσιν θεοῦ γεγονότας· 3.10 ἐκ τοῦ αὐτοῦ στόματος ἐξέρχεται εὐλογία καὶ κατάρα. οὐ χρή, ἀδελφοί μου, ταῦτα οὕτως γίνεσθαι. 3.11 μήτι ἡ πηγὴ ἐκ τῆς αὐτῆς ὀπῆς βρύει τὸ γλυκὺ καὶ τὸ πικρόν; 3.12 μὴ δύναται, ἀδελφοί μου, συκῆ ἐλέας ποιῆσαι ἢ ἄμπελος σῦκα; οὕτως οὐδὲ ἁλυκὸν γλυκὺ ποιῆσαι ὕδωρ.

man is justified and not from faith alone.

2.25 And similarly, was not Rahab the prostitute vindicated out of/from works, welcoming/entertaining the messengers and putting them out by a different way? 2.26 For as the body is dead without a spirit/breath, so also is the faith dead without/apart from works.

3.1 Become ye not many teachers, my brothers, knowing that we shall receive a greater judgment. 3.2 For many (things) we all stumble/fall. If anyone stumbles/trips not in/by a saying/word, this (one) *is* a complete/mature man, being able also to bridle/control the whole body.

3.3 But if we place/put the bits into the mouths of the horses to/for the (thing/purpose) *for* them to obey us, we direct/guide their whole body. 3.4 Behold also the ships/boats, being so great and being driven by violent winds, it is guided/steered by a least rudder where the impulse of the (one) steering wills/wants; 3.5 so also the tongue is a little member, but it boasts great (things). Behold how large a fire kindles/lights how great a wood; 3.6 and the tongue *is* a fire, the world of the injustice, the tongue is constituted in/among our members, the (one) blemishing the entire body and setting aflame the course/career of our generation/becoming, and being set aflame by the hell. 3.7 For every species, both of beasts and of birds, both of reptiles and of sea creatures is tamed and has been tamed by the human species; 3.8 but no one of men/humans is able to tame the tongue; an unstableevil, full of death-dealing poison. 3.9 With it we praise the Lord and father, and with it we curse the men/humans, those having become according to a likeness of God; 3.10 out of the same mouth comes forth praise and execration/-cursing. It is not proper, my brothers, *for* these (things) to become so. 3.11 The fountain/spring emits not the sweet and the bitter out of the same hole, *does it*? 3.12 My brothers, a fig tree is not able to make olives or a vine figs, *are they*? So neither *is able* to make salt water sweet.

3.13 τίς σοφὸς καὶ ἐπιστήμων ἐν ὑμῖν; δειξάτω ἐκ τῆς καλῆς ἀναστροφῆς τὰ ἔργα αὐτοῦ ἐν πραΰτητι σοφίας. 3.14 εἰ δὲ ζῆλον πικρὸν ἔχετε καὶ ἐριθίαν ἐν ταῖς καρδίαις ὑμῶν, μὴ κατακαυχᾶσθαι κατὰ τῆς ἀληθίας καὶ ψεύδεσθαι. 3.15 οὐκ ἔστιν αὕτη ἡ σοφία ἄνωθεν κατερχομένη, ἀλλὰ ἐπίγιος, ψυχική, δαιμονιώδης· 3.16 ὅπου γὰρ ζῆλος καὶ ἐριθία, ἐκεῖ κακαταστασία καὶ πᾶν φαῦλον πρᾶγμα. 3.17 ἡ δὲ ἄνωθεν σοφία πρῶτον μὲν ἁγνή ἐστιν, ἔπειτα ἰρηνική, ἐπιεικής, εὐπειθής, μεστὴ ἐλέους καὶ καρπῶν ἀγαθῶν, ἀδιάκριτος, ἀνυπόκριτος· 3.18 καρπὸς δὲ ὁ δικαιοσύνης ἐν εἰρήνῃ σπίρεται τοῖς ποιοῦσιν εἰρήνην. 4.1 πόθεν πόλεμοι καὶ πόθεν μάχαι ἐν ὑμῖν; οὐκ ἐντεῦθεν, ἐκ τῶν ἡδονῶν ὑμῶν τῶν στρατευομένων ἐν τοῖς μέλεσιν ὑμῶν; 4.2 ἐπιθυμεῖτε, καὶ οὐκ ἔχετε· φονεύετε καὶ ζηλοῦτε, καὶ οὐ δύνασθαι ἐπιτυχεῖν· μάχεσθε καὶ πολεμεῖτε. καὶ οὐκ ἔχετε διὰ τὸ μὴ αἰτῖσθαι ὑμᾶς· 4.3 αἰτῖτε καὶ οὐ λαμβάνετε, διότι κακῶς αἰτῖσθαι, ἵνα ἐν ταῖς ἡδοναῖς ὑμῶν κατὰ δαπανήσητε. 4.4 μοιχαλείδες, οὐκ οἴδατε ὅτι ἡ φιλία τοῦ κόσμου τούτου ἔχθρα ἐστιν τῷ θεῷ; ὃς ἐὰν οὖν βουληθῇ φίλος εἶναι τοῦ κόσμου, ἐχθρὸς τοῦ θεοῦ καθίσταται. 4.5 ἢ δοκεῖται ὅτι κενῶς ἡ γραφὴ λέγει, Πρὸς φθόνον ἐπιποθεῖ τὸ πνεῦμα ὃ κατῴκισεν ἐν ἡμῖν; 4.6 μίζονα δὲ δίδωσιν χάριν· διὸ λέγει, «ὁ θεὸς ὑπερηφάνοις ἀντιτάσσεται, ταπινοῖς δὲ δίδωσιν χάριν.» 4.7 ὑποτάγητε οὖν τῷ θεῷ· ἀντίστητε δὲ τῷ διαβόλῳ, καὶ φεύξετε ἀφ' ὑμῶν· 4.8 ἐγγίσατε τῷ θεῷ, καὶ ἐγγιεῖ ὑμῖν. καθαρίσατε χεῖρας, ἁμαρτωλοί, καὶ ἁγνίσατε καρδίας, δίψυχοι. 4.9 ταλαιπωρήσατε καὶ πενθήσατε κλαύσατε· ὁ γέλως ὑμῶν εἰς πένθος μετατραφήτω καὶ ἡ χαρὰ εἰς κατήφιαν. 4.10 ταπινώθητε οὖν ἐνώπιον κυρίου, καὶ ὑψώσει ὑμᾶς. 4.11 μὴ καταλαλεῖται ἀλλήλων, ἀδελφοί· ὁ καταλαλῶν ἀδελφοῦ ἢ κρίνων τὸν ἀδελφὸν αὐτοῦ καταλαλεῖ νόμου καὶ κρίνι νόμον· εἰ δὲ νόμον κρίνις, οὐκ εἶ ποιητὴς νόμου

FROM JAMES

3.13 Who is wise and understanding among ye? Let him show from the good conduct his works in consideration/meekness of wisdom. 3.14 But if ye hold bitter jealousy and rivalry/contention in your hearts, boast ye and lie ye not against the truth. 3.15 This is not the wisdom from above coming down, but earthly, natural, demon-like; 3.16 for where jealousy and contention *are*, there *is* instability and every vile matter/thing. 3.17 But the wisdom from above is indeed pure first, then peaceable, yielding, well persuaded, full of mercy and of good fruits, without doubt, without pretense; 3.18 but the fruit of justness/justice is sown in peace for those making peace. 4.1 From where *are* wars and from where *are* quarrels among ye? Not from here, out of the pleasures of ye, of those soldiering/fighting in your members? 4.2 Ye desire, but ye have not; ye murder and ye are jealous, and ye are not able to obtain; ye fight and ye make war. And ye have not because of the (thing) of ye to ask not, 4.3 ye ask but ye receive not, because ye ask badly, in order that ye may spend freely on/in your pleasures/enjoyments. 4.4 Adulteresses, know ye not that the love/friendship of this world is enmity/hostility to God? Therefore, who ever might wish/will to be a friend of the world, is constituted an enemy of God. 4.5 Or think ye that vainly/emptily the writing says: The spirit which dwelt in/among ye yearns toward envy/spite? 4.6 But he gives a greater/more grace; wherefore, it says: GOD RESISTS/OPPOSES HAUGHTY/PROUD (ONES), BUT HE GIVES GRACE/FAVOR TO THE HUMBLE (ONES). 4.7 Therefore be ye subject/obedient to God; but ye resist/stand against the devil, and he will flee from ye; 4.8 draw ye near to God, and he will draw near to ye. Cleanse ye hands, sinners, and purify hearts, two-lived/double- souled (ones). 4.9 Be ye distressed and mourn, weep ye; let your laughter be turned into grief/mourning and the joy into dejection. 4.10 Be ye humbled therefore before the Lord, and he will exalt ye. 4.11 Speak ye not against/slander not one another, brothers; the (one) slandering/speaking against a brother or judging his brother, he slanders law and judges law; and if you judge law, you are not a doer

497

ἀλλὰ κριτής. 4.12 εἷς ἐστιν ὁ νομοθέτης καὶ κριτής, ὁ δυνάμενος σῶσαι καὶ ἀπολέσαι· σὺ δὲ τίς εἶ, ὁ κρίνων τὸν πλησίον;

4.13 ἄγε νῦν οἱ λέγοντες, σήμερον ἢ αὔριον πορευσόμεθα εἰς τήνδε τὴν πόλιν καὶ ποιήσομεν ἐκεῖ ἐνιαυτὸν καὶ ἐμπορευσόμεθα καὶ κερδήσομεν· 4.14 οἵτινες οὐκ ἐπίστασθε τὸ τῆς αὔριον ποία ἡ ζωὴ ὑμῶν. — ἡ πρὸς ὀλίγον φαινομένη, ἔπειτα καὶ ἀφανιζομένη 4.15 ἀντὶ τοῦ λέγιν ὑμᾶς, ἐὰν ὁ κύριος θελήσῃ, καὶ ζήσομεν καὶ ποιήσομεν τοῦτο ἢ ἐκῖνο. 4.16 νῦν δὲ κατακαυχᾶσθε ἐν ταῖς ἀλαζονίαις ὑμῶν· ἄπασα καύχησεις τοιαύτη πονηρά ἐστιν. 4.17 εἰδότι οὖν καλὸν ποιεῖν καὶ μὴ ποιοῦντι, ἁμαρτία αὐτῷ ἐστιν.

5.1 Ἄγε νῦν οἱ πλούσιοι, κλαύσατε ὀλολύζοντες ἐπὶ ταῖς ταλαιπωρίαις ὑμῶν ταῖς ἐπερχομέναις ὑμῖν. 5.2 ὁ πλοῦτος ὑμῶν σέσηπεν καὶ τὰ ἱμάτια ὑμῶν σητόβρωτα γέγονεν,

5.3 ὁ χρυσὸς ὑμῶν καὶ ὁ ἄργυρος κατίωται, καὶ ὁ ἰὸς αὐτῶν εἰς μαρτύριον ὑμῖν ἔστε καὶ φάγετε τὰς σάρκας ὑμῶν ὡς πῦρ· ἐθησαυρίσατε ἐν ἐσχάταις ἡμέραις. 5.4 ἰδοὺ ὁ μισθὸς τῶν ἐργατῶν τῶν ἀμησάντων τὰς χώρας ὑμῶν ὁ ἀφυστερημένος ἀφ' ὑμῶν κράζει, καὶ αἱ βοαὶ τῶν θερισάντων εἰς τὰ ὦτα κυρίου Σαβαὼθ εἰσεληλύθασιν. 5.5 ἐτρυφήσατε ἐπὶ τῆς γῆς καὶ ἐσπαταλήσατε, ἐθρέψατε τὰς καρδίας ὑμῶν ἐν ἡμέρᾳ σφαγῆς. 5.6 κατεδικάσατε, ἐφονεύσατε τὸν δίκαιον. οὐκ ἀντιτάσσεται ὑμῖν.

5.7 μακροθυμήσατε οὖν, ἀδελφοί, ἕως τῆς παρουσίας τοῦ κυρίου. ἰδοὺ ὁ γεωργὸς ἐκδέχεται τὸν τίμιον καρπὸν τῆς γῆς, μακροθυμῶν ἐπ' αὐτῷ ἕως ἂν λάβῃ καρπὸν πρόϊμον καὶ ὄψιμον.

5.8 μακροθυμήσατε οὖν καὶ ὑμεῖς, στηρίξατε τὰς καρδίας ὑμῶν, ὅτι ἡ παρουσία τοῦ κυρίου ἤγγικεν. 5.9 μὴ στενάζετε κατὰ ἀλλήλων, ἀδελφοί, ἵνα μὴ κριθῆτε· ἰδοὺ ὁ κριτὴς πρὸ τῶν

of law but a judge.   4.12 One is the lawgiver and
judge, the (one) being able to save and to destroy;
but you, who are you, the (one) judging the neighbor?
    4.13   Come now, those saying: Today or tomorrow
we shall go into this city and we shall do/make a year
there and we shall trade/be merchants and we shall
gain/profit;   4.14 who/which ye understand not the
(thing) of tomorrow, what your life *may be*; -- with
the appearing *for* a little (time), then also disap-
pearing;   4.15 instead of the (thing) *for* ye to say:
If the Lord might will/want, we shall both live and do
this or that.   4.16 But now ye boast/triumph in/with
your arrogances/prides;   all   such   boasting   is   evil.
4.17 Therefore, for *the one* knowing to do good but not
doing, for him it is a fault/sin/failure.

    5.1   Come now, the rich (ones), lament ye, crying
aloud   over   your   difficulties/hardships,   for   those
coming upon ye.   5.2 The rich (one)/wealth of ye has
rotted and your garments have become moth-food,
    5.3   your gold and the silver has been tarnished
and the rust/poison of them will be in/for a testimony
for ye and they will eat/devour the fleshes of ye as a
fire;   ye   accumulated   stores/treasures   in/for   last
days.   5.4 Behold, the reward/wages of the workers
having   reaped   your   lands/fields/regions,   the   (one)
being kept back from (them) by ye cries out, and the
outcries from those having reaped have gone in to the
ears of *the* Lord of Saboath.   5.5 Ye lived in luxury
upon the land/earth and ye lived wantonly/riotously,
ye gorged your hearts in a day of slaughter.   5.6 Ye
condemned, ye murdered the just (one), he is not opposed to ye.
    5.7   Therefore, be ye patient, brothers, until
the coming of the Lord. Behold, the farmer awaits the
precious fruit/product from the land, being patient
over it until he would/might receive a product/pro-
duce, the early and late.
    5.8   Therefore even/also ye, be ye patient/stead-
fast, fix ye firmly your hearts, because the coming of
the Lord has drawn near.   5.9 Groan ye not against one
another, brothers, that ye might not be judged; be-

IAKΩBOY

θυρῶν ἕστηκεν. 5.10 ὑπόδειγμα λάβετε, ἀδελφοί μου, τῆς καλοκαγαθίας καὶ τῆς μακροθυμίας τοὺς προφήτας, οἳ ἐλάλησαν ἐν ὀνόματι κυρίου. 5.11 ἰδοὺ μακαρίζομεν τοὺς ὑπομίναντας· τὴν ὑπομονὴν Ἰὼβ ἠκούσατε, καὶ τὸ τέλος κυρίου εἴδετε, ὅτι πολύσπλαγχνός ἐστιν ὁ κύριος καὶ οἰκτείρμων.

5.12 πρὸ πάντων δέ, ἀδελφοί μου, μὴ ὀμνύετε, μήτε τὸν οὐρανὸν μήτε τὴν γῆν μήτε ἄλλον τινὰ ὅρκον· ἤτω δὲ ὁ λόγος ὑμῶν τὸ ναὶ ναὶ καὶ τὸ οὒ οὔ, ἵνα μὴ ὑπὸ κρίσιν πέσητε. 5.13 κακοπαθεῖ τις ἐν ὑμῖν; προσευχέσθω· εὐθυμεῖ τις; ψαλλέτω. 5.14 ἀσθενεῖ τις ἐν ὑμῖν; προσκαλεσάσθω τοὺς πρεσβυτέρους τῆς ἐκκλησίας, καὶ προσευξάσθωσαν ἐπ᾽ αὐτὸν ἀλίψαντες αὐτὸν ἐλαίῳ ἐν τῷ ὀνόματι τοῦ κυρίου· 5.15 καὶ ἡ εὐχὴ τῆς πίστεως σώσει τὸν κάμνοντα, καὶ ἐγερεῖ αὐτὸν ὁ κύριος· κἂν ἁμαρτίας ᾖ πεποιηκώς, ἀφεθήσεται αὐτῷ.

5.16 ἐξομολογῖσθαι οὖν ἀλλήλοις τὰς ἁμαρτίας καὶ εὔχεσθαι ὑπὲρ ἀλλήλων, ὅπως ἰαθῆτε. πολὺ ἰσχύει δέησις δικαίου ἐνεργουμένη. 5.17 Ἡλίας ἄνθρωπος ἦν ὁμοιοπαθὴς ἡμῖν, καὶ προσευχῇ προσηύξατο τοῦ μὴ βρέξαι, καὶ οὐκ ἔβρεξεν ἐπὶ τῆς γῆς ἐνιαυτοὺς τρῖς καὶ μῆνας ἕξ· 5.18 καὶ πάλιν προσηύξατο, καὶ ὁ οὐρανὸς ἔδωκεν τὸν ὑετὸν καὶ ἡ γῆ ἐβλάστησεν τὸν καρπὸν αὐτῆς.

5.19 ἀδελφοί μου, ἐάν τις ἐν ὑμῖν πλανηθῇ ἀπὸ τῆς ὁδοῦ τῆς ἀληθίας καὶ ἐπιστρέψῃ τις αὐτόν, 5.20 γινωσκέτω ὅτι ὁ ἐπιστρέψας ἁμαρτωλὸν ἐκ πλάνης ὁδοῦ αὐτοῦ σώσει ψυχὴν αὐτοῦ ἐκ θανάτου καὶ καλύψει πλῆθος ἁμαρτιῶν.

Ἐπιστολὴ Ἰακώβου

hold, the judge stands before the doors.   5.10 Take/ receive ye, my brothers, an example from the good and suffering and the patience *of* the prophets, who spoke in *the* name of *the* Lord.   5.11 Behold, we consider happy the (ones) enduring; ye heard the endurance of Job, and ye say the end of the Lord, that the Lord is very compassionate and merciful/pitiful.

5.12 But before all (things), my brothers, swear ye not, neither *for* the sky/heaven nor the earth/land nor any other oath; but let be the saying/speech of ye: The yes, yes and the no, no, that ye might fall not under judgment.   5.13 *Does* anyone among ye suffer evil? Let him pray; *Is* anyone cheerful? Let him sing a psalm.   5.14 *Is* anyone among ye weak/sick? Let him call the elders of the assembly, and let them pray over him, having anointed him with olive oil in/by the name of the Lord;   5.15 and the prayer of the faith will save the (one) being exhausted, and the Lord will raise him; and if he be having done sins/failures, it will be forgiven for him.

5.16   Therefore confess/admit ye to one another the sins/faults and pray ye in behalf of one another, that ye might be healed. A petition from a just one strengthens greatly, being effective.   5.17 Elias was a man for us of the same nature, and in prayer he prayed of/from the (thing) to rain not, and it rained not upon the land *for* three years and six months; 5.18 and again he prayed, and the sky gave the rain and the land produced her fruit/produce.

5.19   My brothers, if anyone among ye might be led astray from the way/road of the truth and someone might turn him back, 5.20 let him know that the (one) turning back/returning a sinner out of the deception/ wandering from his way/road, he saves his life/soul out ot death and he covers a multitude of sins/faults.

A Letter from James

ΠΕΤΡΟΥ Α΄

This is the Sinaitic New Testament, book of 1 Peter.

1.1 Πέτρος ἀπόστολος Ἰησοῦ χριστοῦ ἐκλεκτοῖς παρεπιδήμοις διασπορᾶς Πόντου, Γαλατείας, Καππαδοκείας, Ἀσίας, καὶ Βιθυνίας, 1.2 κατὰ πρόγνωσιν θεοῦ πατρός, ἐν ἁγιασμῷ πνεύματος, εἰς ὑπακοὴν καὶ ῥαντισμὸν αἵματος Ἰησοῦ χριστοῦ· χάρις ὑμῖν καὶ εἰρήνη πληθυνθίη.

1.3 εὐλογητὸς ὁ θεὸς καὶ πατὴρ τοῦ κυρίου ἡμῶν Ἰησοῦ χριστοῦ, ὁ κατὰ τὸ πολὺ αὐτοῦ ἔλεος ἀναγεννήσας ἡμᾶς εἰς ἐλπίδα ζῶσαν διὰ ἀναστάσεως Ἰησοῦ χριστοῦ ἐκ νεκρῶν, 1.4 εἰς κληρονομίαν ἄφθαρτον καὶ ἀμάραντον καὶ ἀμίαντον, τετηρημένην ἐν οὐρανῷ εἰς ὑμᾶς 1.5 τοὺς ἐν δυνάμι θεοῦ φρουρουμένους διὰ πίστεως εἰς σωτηρίαν ἑτοίμην ἀποκαλυφθῆναι ἐν καιρῷ ἐσχάτῳ. 1.6 ἐν ᾧ ἀγαλλιᾶσθε, ὀλίγον ἄρτι εἰ δέον ἐστὶν λυπηθέντες ἐν ποικίλοις πιρασμοῖς, 1.7 ἵνα τὸ δοκίμον ὑμῶν τῆς πίστεως πολυτιμότερον χρυσίου τοῦ ἀπολλυμένου, διὰ πυρὸς δὲ δοκιμαζομένου, εὑρεθῇ εἰς ἔπενον καὶ δόξαν καὶ τιμὴν ἐν ἀποκαλύψει Ἰησοῦ χριστοῦ. 1.8 ὃν οὐκ ἰδόντες ἀγαπᾶτε, εἰς ὃν ἄρτι μὴ ὁρῶντες πιστεύοντες δὲ ἀγαλλιᾶσθαι χαρᾷ ἀνεκλαλήτῳ καὶ δεδοξασμένῃ, 1.9 κομιζόμενοι τὸ τέλος τῆς πίστεως ὑμῶν σωτηρίαν ψυχῶν. 1.10 Περὶ ἧς σωτηρίας ἐξεζήτησαν καὶ ἐξηραύνησαν προφῆται οἱ περὶ τῆς εἰς ὑμᾶς χάριτος προφητεύσαντες, 1.11 ἐραυνῶντες εἰς τίνα ἢ ποῖον καιρὸν ἐδήλου τὸ ἐν αὐτοῖς πνεῦμα χριστοῦ προμαρτυρόμενον τὰ εἰς χριστὸν παθήματα καὶ τὰς μετὰ ταῦτα δόξας· 1.12 οἷς ἀπεκαλύφθη ὅτι οὐχ ἑαυτοῖς ὑμῖν δὲ διηκόνουν αὐτά, ἃ νῦν ἀνηγγέλη ὑμῖν διὰ τῶν εὐαγγελισαμένων ὑμᾶς ἐν πνεύματι ἁγίῳ ἀποσταλέντι ἀπ᾽ οὐρανοῦ, εἰς ἃ ἐπιθυμοῦσιν ἄγγελοι παρακύψαι. 1.13 διὸ ἀναζωσάμενοι τὰς ὀσφύας τῆς διανοίας ὑμῶν, νήφοντες, τελίως ἐλπίσατε ἐπὶ τὴν φερομένην ὑμῖν χάριν ἐν ἀποκαλύψει Ἰησοῦ χριστοῦ. 1.14 ὡς τέκνα ὑπακοῆς, μὴ συσχηματιζόμενοι ταῖς

1.1   Peter, an apostle of Jesus, the anointed (one), to the chosen sojourners of the dispersion of Pontus, of Galatia, of Cappadocia, of Asia, and of Bithynia,   1.2 according to foreknowledge of God *the* father, by sanctification of spirit, in obedience and a sprinkling from blood of Jesus, the anointed (one); may grace and peace be multiplied to ye.

1.3   The God and father of our Lord Jesus the anointed (one) *be* praised, the (one) having regenerated us according to his much mercy into a living hope through resurrection out of dead (ones) of Jesus the anointed (one),   1.4 into an inheritance immortal and unfading and undefiled, having been kept in heaven to/for us,   1.5 the (ones) being guarded by power from God through faith into a salvation ready to be revealed in/at *the* last time.   1.6 In which ye exult, grieving a little *time* now if necessary in various temptations/tryings,   1.7 in order that the quality of your faith, much more valuable *than* the perishing gold, and being proved/tested through fire, might be found in praise and fame/glory and honor in/at a revelation of/from Jesus the anointed (one).   1.8   Whom ye love, not having seen, in whom not now seeing, but believing, ye exult with/in joy unspeakable and having been glorified/made of reputation,   1.9   receiving back the end from your faith: salvation of souls/lives.   1.10 Concerning which salvation, the prophets, those prophesying about the grace to/for ye, they sought out and searched out,   1.11 searching to/for what or what sort of time the spirit of the anointed (one) made known to them forewitnessing the sufferings to/for the anointed (one) and the glories/fames after these – (things);   1.12 to whom it was revealed that not for themselves but for ye they served the same, which now were announced to ye through those having evangelized ye by/in a holy spirit having been sent from heaven, in/for which (things) messengers/angels desire to look into.   1.13 Wherefore, be ye girding up your loins of your mind, being serious, ye hope completely on the grace being brought to ye in a revelation from Jesus the anointed (one).   1.14   As children of obedience, not fashioning yourselves according to the former

πρότερον ἐν τῇ ἀγνοίᾳ ὑμῶν ἐπιθυμίαις, 1.15 ἀλλὰ κατὰ τὸν καλέσαντα ὑμᾶς ἅγιον καὶ αὐτοὶ ἅγιοι ἐν πάσῃ ἀναστροφῇ γενήθητε, 1.16 διό γέγραπται «ἅγιοι ἔσεσθαι, διότι ἐγὼ ἅγιος.» 1.17 καὶ εἰ πατέρα ἐπικαλεῖσθαι τὸν ἀπροσωπολήμπτως κρίνοντα κατὰ τὸ ἑκάστου ἔργον, ἐν φόβῳ τὸν τῆς παροικίας ὑμῶν χρόνον ἀναστράφητε, 1.18 εἰδότες ὅτι οὐ φθαρτοῖς, ἀργυρίῳ ἢ χρυσίῳ ἐλωυτρώθητε ἐκ τῆς ματαίας ὑμῶν ἀναστροφῆς πατροπαραδότου, 1.19 ἀλλὰ τιμίῳ αἵματι ὡς ἀμνοῦ ἀμώμου καὶ ἀσπίλου χριστοῦ, 1.20 προεγνωσμένου μὲν πρὸ καταβολῆς κόσμου, φανερωθέντος δὲ ἐπ' ἐσχάτου τῶν χρόνων δι' ὑμᾶς 1.21 τοὺς δι' αὐτοῦ πισττεύοντας εἰς θεὸν τὸν ἐγείραντα αὐτὸν ἐκ νεκρῶν καὶ δόξαν αὐτῷ δόντα, ὥστε τὴν πίστιν ὑμῶν καὶ ἐλπίδα εἶναι εἰς θεόν. 1.22 τὰς ψυχὰς ὑμῶν ἡγνικότες ἐν τῇ ὑπακοῇ τῆς ἀληθίας εἰς φιλαδελφίαν ἀνυπόκριτον, ἐκ καθαρᾶς καρδίας ἀλλήλους ἀγαπήσατε ἐκτενῶς, 1.23 ἀναγεγεννημένοι οὐκ ἐκ σπορᾶς φθαρτῆς ἀλλὰ ἀφθάρτου, διὰ λόγου ζῶντος θεοῦ καὶ μένοντος· 1.24 διότι «πᾶσα σὰρξ ὡς χόρτος, καὶ πᾶσα δόξα αὐτῆς ὡς ἄνθος χόρτου· ἐξηράνθη ὁ χόρτος, καὶ τὸ ἄνθος ἐξέπεσεν· 1.25 τὸ δὲ ῥῆμα κυρίου μένει εἰς τὸν αἰῶνα.»

τοῦτο δέ ἐστιν τὸ ῥῆμα τὸ εὐαγγελισθὲν εἰς ὑμᾶς. 2.1 ἀποθέμενοι οὖν πᾶσαν κακίαν καὶ πάντα δόλον καὶ ὑποκρίσεις καὶ φθόνους καὶ πάσας καταλαλιάς, 2.2 ὡς ἀρτιγέννητα βρέφη τὸ λογικὸν ἄδολον γάλα ἐπιποθήσατε, ἵνα ἐν αὐτῷ αὐξηθῆτε εἰς σωτηρίαν, 2.3 εἰ ἐγεύσασθαι ὅτι χρηστὸς ὁ κύριος. 2.4 πρὸς ὃν προσερχόμενοι, λίθον ζῶντα, ὑπὸ ἀνθρώπων μὲν ἀποδεδοκιμασμένον παρὰ δὲ θεῷ ἐκλεκτὸν ἔντιμον, 2.5 καὶ αὐτοὶ ὡς λίθοι ζῶντες ἐπ' οἰκοδομεῖσθαι οἶκος πνευματικὸς ἱς ἱεράτευμα ἅγιον, ἀνενέγκαι θυσίας εὐπροσδέκτους Τῷ θεῷ διὰ

desires in your ignorance, 1.15 but according to the holy (one) having called ye, become ye holy (ones)/ saints yourselves in every conduct/behavior, 1.16 because it has been written: YE WILL BE SAINTS/HOLY (ONES), BECAUSE I *am* HOLY/A HOLY (ONE)/SAINT. 1.17 And if ye call upon *the* father, the (one) judging without partiality according to the work of each (one), conducting yourselves in fear *for* the time of your exile/sojourning, 1.18 knowing that not for mortal/perishable (things), for silver or gold, were ye redeemed out of your vain/fallacious way of life delivered from *your* fathers, 1.19 but with precious blood as from an unblemished and unspotted lamb, from the anointed (one), 1.20 from having been read/known indeed before foundation of a world, and having been made clear at the last of the time because of ye, 1.21 the (ones) through him being believers in God, the (one) having raised him out of dead (ones) and having given glory/fame to him, so as *for* the faith and hope of ye to be in God. 1.22 Having purified your lives/souls by the obedience of the truth into unpretended/unhipocritic brotherly love, love ye one another constantly out of/from a pure/clean heart, 1.23 having been regenerated, not out of mortal ruin, but from immortal, through a saying/word from a living and abiding God; 1.24 because EVERY FLESH *is* AS GRASS, AND EVERY FAME/REPUTATION OF IT AS A BLOSSOM OF GRASS; THE GRASS WAS WITHERED/DRIED, AND THE BLOSSOM FELL OUT/AWAY; 1.25 BUT THE WORD OF *the* LORD ABIDES INTO/FOR THE AGE.

And this is the word, the (one) having been evangelized to ye. 2.1 Therefore, putting away every malice and every treachery and pretenses and spites/ envies and every slander/evil speech, 2.2 as now-born infants desire ye earnestly the rational, unadulterated milk in order that by it ye might grow into salvation, 2.3 if ye tasted that the Lord *is* kind/useful. 2.4 To whom coming near, a living stone, having been rejected indeed by men but from God chosen, valuable/ respected, 2.5 also these as living stones being built a spiritual house into a holy priesthood, to offer sacrifices well-pleasing to God through Jesus

Ἰησοῦ χριστοῦ. 2.6 διότι περιέχει ἐν γραφῇ, «ἰδοὺ τίθημι ἐν Σιὼν λίθον ἀκρογωνιαῖον ἐκλεκτὸν ἔντιμον, καὶ ὁ πιστεύων ἐπ᾽ αὐτῷ οὐ μὴ καταισχυνθῇ.» 2.7 ὑμῖν οὖν ἡ τιμὴ τοῖς πιστεύουσιν· ἀπιστοῦσιν δὲ «λίθος ὃν ἀπεδοκίμασαν οἱ οἰκοδομοῦντες οὗτος ἐγενήθη εἰς κεφαλὴν γωνίας» 2.8 καὶ «λίθος προσκόμματος καὶ πέτραν σκανδάλου» οἳ προσκόπτουσιν τῷ λόγῳ ἀπιθοῦντες, εἰς ὃ καὶ ἐτέθησαν. 2.9 ὑμεῖς δὲ «γένος ἐκλεκτόν, βασίλιον ἱεράτευμα, ἔθνος ἅγιον, λαὸς εἰς περιποίησιν, ὅπως τὰς ἀρετὰς ἐξαγγίληται» τοῦ ἐκ σκότους ὑμᾶς καλέσαντος εἰς τὸ θαυμαστὸν αὐτοῦ φῶς· 2.10 οἵ ποτε οὐ λαὸς νῦν δὲ λαὸς θεοῦ, οἱ οὐκ ἠλεημένοι νῦν δὲ ἐλεηθέντες.

2.11 ἀγαπητοί, παρακαλῶ ὡς παροίκους καὶ παρεπιδήμους ἀπέχεσθαι τῶν σαρκικῶν ἐπιθυμιῶν, αἵτινες στρατεύονται κατὰ τῆς ψυχῆς· 2.12 τὴν ἀναστροφὴν ὑμῖν ἐν τοῖς ἔθνεσιν ἔχοντες καλήν, ἵνα, ἐν ᾧ καταλαλοῦσιν ὑμῶν ὡς κακοποιῶν, ἐκ τῶν καλῶν ἔργων ἐποπτεύοντες δοξάσωσιν τὸν θεὸν ἐν ἡμέρᾳ ἐπισκοπῆς. 2.13 ὑποτάγητε πάσῃ ἀνθρωπίνῃ κτίσει διὰ τὸν κύριον· εἴτε βασιλεῖ ὡς ὑπερέχοντι, 2.14 εἴτε ἡγεμόσιν ὡς δι᾽ αὐτοῦ πεμπομένοις εἰς ἐκδίκησιν κακοποιῶν ἔπαινον δὲ ἀγαθοποιῶν· 2.15 ὅτι οὕτως ἐστὶν τὸ θέλημα τοῦ θεοῦ, ἀγαθοποιοῦντας φιμοῦν τὴν τῶν ἀφρόνων ἀνθρώπων ἀγνωσίαν· 2.16 ὡς ἐλεύθεροι, καὶ μὴ ὡς ἐπικάλυμμα ἔχοντες τῆς κακίας τὴν ἐλευθερίαν, ἀλλ᾽ ὡς θεοῦ δοῦλοι. 2.17 πάντες τιμήσατε, τὴν ἀδελφότητα ἀγαπᾶτε, τὸν θεὸν φοβεῖσθαι, τὸν βασιλέα τιμᾶτε. 2.18 οἱ οἰκέται ἐν παντὶ φόβῳ ὑποτασσόμενοι τοῖς δεσπόταις ὑμῶν, οὐ μόνον τοῖς ἀγαθοῖς καὶ ἐπιεικέσιν ἀλλὰ καὶ τοῖς σκολιοῖς. 2.19 τοῦτο γὰρ χάρις εἰ διὰ συνίδησιν θεοῦ ὑποφέρει τις λύπας πάσχων ἀδίκως. 2.20 ποῖον γὰρ κλέος εἰ ἁμαρτάνοντες καὶ κολαφιζόμενοι ὑπομενεῖτε; ἀλλ᾽ εἰ ἀγαθοποιοῦντες καὶ πάσχοντες ὑπομενεῖτε, τοῦτο χάρις παρὰ θεῷ. 2.21 εἰς τοῦτο γὰρ

the anointed (one). 2.6 Because it is contained in a writing: BEHOLD, I LAY/PLACE IN ZION A STONE, A CHOSEN PRECIOUS CORNERSTONE, AND THE (ONE) BELIEVING ON HIM/it WILL BY NO MEANS BE SHAMED. 2.7 Therefore, the honor is for ye, for the (ones) believing; but for ye unbelieving, A STONE WHICH THE (ONES) BUILDING REJECT-ED, THIS (ONE) WAS MADE TO BECOME A HEAD CORNERSTONE 2.8 and A STONE OF STUMBLING AND A ROCK OF OFFENSE; who, disobeying, they stumble in/at the saying, to which also they were appointed. 2.9 But ye *are* A CHOSEN RACE/KIND, A ROYAL PRIESTHOOD, A HOLY ETHNIC/NATION, A PEOPLE FOR PRESERVING, SO THAT YE MAY RE-PORT/PROCLAIM THE VIRTUES of the (one) having called ye out of darkness into his wonderful light; 2.10 who *were* then not a people but *are* now a people of God, those not having been pitied but now having received mercy/being pitied.

2.11 Beloved (ones), I beseech *ye* as sojourners and aliens/foreigners to abstain from the fleshy de-sires, which soldier/battle against the life/soul; 2.12 holding your behavior good among the ethnics/nations, in order that, by what they speak against ye as evildoers, observing from your good works they glorified God in a day of visitation. 2.13 Be ye subject to every human creation/order through the Lord; whether to a king as being superior, 2.14 or to governors as being sent through him for punishment of evildoers and lauding of well-doers; 2.15 because so/this is the will of God, doing good to silence/quiet the ignorance of the foolish men; 2.16 as free (ones), and not holding the freedom/liberty as a co-vering over the evil, but as slaves of God. 2.17 Honor ye all (men), love ye the brotherhood, fear ye God, honor ye the king. 2.18 The domestic servants, having been subjected in every (thing) with fear to your masters, not only to those good and kindly (ones) but also to the perverse/crooked (ones). 2.19 For this is grace/favor if, because of conscience from God, anyone bears griefs of suffering unjustly. 2.20 For what *is* fame/credit if ye will endure sinning and being buffeted *by fists*? But if ye will endure doing good and suffering, this *is* grace with God. 2.21 For

ἐκλήθητε, ὅτι καὶ ὁ χριστὸς ἔπέθανεν ὑπὲρ ὑμῶν, ὑμῖν ὑπολιμπάνων ὑπογραμμὸν ἵνα ἐπακολουθήσητε τοῖς ἴχνεσιν αὐτοῦ· 2.22 ὃς «ἁμαρτίαν οὐκ ἐποίησεν οὐδὲ ηὑρέθη δόλος ἐν τῷ στόματι αὐτοῦ·» 2.23 ὃς λοιδορούμενος οὐκ ἀντελοιδόρει, πάσχων οὐκ ἠπίλει, παρεδίδου δὲ τῷ κρίνοντι δικαίως· 2.24 ὃς τὰς ἁμαρτίας ἡμῶν αὐτὸς ἀνήνεγκεν ἐν τῷ σώματι αὐτοῦ ἐπὶ τὸ ξύλον, ἵνα ταῖς ἁμαρτίαις ἀπογενόμενοι τῇ δικαιοσύνῃ ζήσωμεν· οὗ τῷ μώλωπι ἰάθητε. 2.25 ἦτε γὰρ ὡς πρόβατα πλανώμενοι, ἀλλ᾽ ἐπιστράφητε νῦν ἐπὶ τὸν ποιμένα καὶ ἐπίσκοπον τῶν ψυχῶν ὑμῶν.

3.1 Ὁμοίως γυναῖκες ὑποτασσόμεναι τοῖς ἰδίοις ἀνδράσιν, ἵνα καὶ εἴ τινες ἀπιθοῦσιν τῷ λόγῳ διὰ τῆς τῶν γυναικῶν ἀναστροφῆς ἄνευ λόγου κερδηθήσονται 3.2 ἐποπτεύσαντες τὴν ἐν φόβῳ ἁγνὴν ἀναστροφὴν ὑμῶν. 3.3 ὧν ἔστω οὐκ ὁ ἔξωθεν ἐμπλοκῆς τριχῶν καὶ περιθέσεως χρυσίων ἢ ἐνδύσεως ἱματίων κόσμος, 3.4 ἀλλ᾽ ὁ κρυπτὸς τῆς καρδίας ἄνθρωπος ἐν τῷ ἀφθάρτῳ τοῦ πραέως καὶ ἡσυχίους πνεύματος, ὅ ἐστιν ἐνώπιον τοῦ θεοῦ πολυτελές. 3.5 οὕτως γάρ ποτε καὶ αἱ ἅγιαι γυναῖκες ἐκόσμουν ἑαυτάς αἱ ἐλπίζουσαι ἐπὶ τὸν θεόν, ὑποτασσόμεναι τοῖς ἰδίοις ἀνδράσιν, 3.6 ὡς Σάρρα ὑπήκουσεν τῷ Ἀβραάμ, κύριον αὐτὸν καλοῦσα· ἧς ἐγενήθητε τέκνα ἀγαθοποιοῦσαι καὶ μὴ φοβούμεναι μηδεμίαν πτόησιν.

3.7 οἱ ἄνδρες ὁμοίως συνοικοῦντες κατὰ γνῶσιν, ὡς ἀσθενεστέρῳ σκεύει τῷ γυναικείῳ ἀπονέμοντες τιμήν, ὡς καὶ συνκληρονόμοις ποικίλης χάριτος ζωῆς, εἰς τὸ μὴ ἐνκόπτεσθαι τὰς προσευχὰς ὑμῶν. 3.8 τὸ δὲ τέλος πάντες ὁμόφρονες, συμπαθεῖς, φιλάδελφοι, εὔσπλαγχνοι, ταπινόφρονες, 3.9 μὴ ἀποδιδόντες κακὸν ἀντὶ κακοῦ ἢ λοιδορίαν ἀντὶ λοιδορίας, τοὐναντίον δὲ εὐλογοῦντες, ὅτι εἰς τοῦτο ἐκλήθητε ἵνα εὐλογίαν κληρονομήσητε. 3.10 «ὁ» γὰρ «θέλων ζωὴν ἀγαπᾶν καὶ ἰδῖν

to this (thing) ye were called, because the anointed
(one) even died in behalf of ye, leaving behind an
example for ye that ye might follow in his footsteps;
2.22 who DID NOT A SIN NEITHER WAS A DECEIT FOUND IN
HIS MOUTH; 2.23 Who being abused, he abused not/
answered not in return/abusively, suffering he was not
threatening, but he was delivering for/to the one
judging justly; 2.24 who himself bore up the faults/
sins of us in/with his body upon the wood/tree, in
order that having died to the sins/faults we might
live for the justness/justice; of/from whom ye were
healed by the wound/blow. 2.25 For ye were being led
astray/deceived like sheep, but now ye were returned
to the shepherd and overseer/guardian/bishop of your
lives/souls.

3.1 Similarly, women, having been subjected to
their/your own men, that even if some disobey the
logos/word/saying, they will be gained through the
behavior of the women without a saying/word/logos,
3.2 observing your pure conduct/behavior in/with
fear. 3.3 Of whom let it be not the braiding of hairs
from without and from wearing of gold or from dressing
with a world of clothing/decorative clothing, 3.4 but
the hidden man from the heart in the immortality of
the meekness and quietness of spirit, which is very
valuable before/in the sight of God. 3.5 For then
indeed the holy/saintly women were so adorning themselves, the (ones) hoping upon God, being subjected to
their own men, 3.6 as Sarah obeyed for Abraham,
calling him lord; of whom ye were generated children,
doing good and not fearing any intimidation/terror.
3.7 The men likewise, dwelling together according to knowledge, as with a weaker vessel, assigning
honor to the woman, as joint-heirs diversified from a
grace/gift of life, in the (thing) *for* your prayers
not to be hindered. 3.8 And the end all *be* of like
minds, sympathies, brotherly loves, compassions, hu-
milities, 3.9 repaying not evil for evil or abusing
for abusing, but on thecontrary praising, because
to/for this ye were called in order that ye might
inherit praise/a blessing. 3.10 For THE (ONE) WANTING

ἡμέρας ἀγαθὰς παυσάτω τὴν γλῶσσαν αὐτοῦ ἀπὸ κακοῦ καὶ χίλη τοῦ μὴ λαλῆσαι δόλον, 3.11 ἐκκλινάτω ἀπὸ κακοῦ καὶ ποιησάτω ἀγαθόν, ζητησάτω ἰρήνην καὶ διωξάτω αὐτήν. 3.12 ὅτι ὀφθαλμοὶ κυρίου ἐπὶ δικαίους καὶ ὦτα αὐτοῦ εἰς δέησιν αὐτῶν, πρόσωπον δὲ κυρίου ἐπὶ ποιοῦντας κακά.» 3.13 καὶ τίς ὁ κακώσων ὑμᾶς ἐὰν τοῦ ἀγαθοῦ ζηλωταὶ γένησθαι; 3.14 ἀλλ' εἰ καὶ πάσχοιτε διὰ δικαιοσύνην, μακάριοι ἔσται. τὸν δὲ φόβον αὐτῶν μὴ φοβηθῆται μηδὲ ταραχθῆτε, 3.15 κύριον δὲ τὸν χριστὸν ἁγιάσατε ἐν ταῖς καρδίαις ὑμῶν, ἕτοιμοι ἀεὶ πρὸς ἀπολογίαν παντὶ τῷ αἰτοῦντι ὑμᾶς λόγον περὶ τῆς ἐν ὑμῖν ἐλπίδος, 3.16 ἀλλὰ μετὰ πραΰτητος καὶ φόβου, συνίδησιν ἔχοντες ἀγαθήν, ἵνα ἐν ᾧ καταλαλοῦσιν ὑνῶν ὡς κακοποίων κατεσχυνθῶσιν οἱ ἐπηρεάζοντες ὑμῶν τὴν ἀγαθὴν ἐν χριστῷ ἀναστροφήν. 3.17 κρῖττον γὰρ ἀγαθοποιοῦντας, εἰ θέλοι τὸ θέλημα τοῦ θεοῦ, πάσχειν ἢ κακοποιοῦντας. 3.18 ὅτι χριστὸς ἅπαξ περὶ ἁμαρτιῶν ὑπὲρ ἡμῶν ἀπέθανεν, δίκαιος ὑπὲρ ἀδίκων, ἵνα ὑμᾶς προσαγάγῃ τῷ θεῷ, θανατωθεὶς μὲν σαρκεὶ ζωοποιηθεὶς δὲ πνεύματι·

3.19 ἐν ᾧ καὶ τοῖς ἐν φυλακῇ πνεύμασιν πορευθεὶς ἐκήρυξεν, 3.20 ἀπιθήσασίν ποτε ὅτε ἀπεξεδέχετο τὴν τοῦ θεοῦ μακροθυμίαν ἐν ἡμέραις Νῶε κατασκευαζομένης κιβωτοῦ, εἰς ἣν ὀλίγοι, τοῦτ' ἔστιν ὀκτὼ ψυχαί, διεσώθησαν δι' ὕδατος. 3.21 ὃ καὶ ὑμᾶς νῦν ἀντίτυπον σῴζει βάπτισμα, οὐ σαρκὸς ἀπόθεσις ῥύπου ἀλλὰ συνειδήσεως ἀγαθῆς ἐπερώτημα εἰς θεόν, δι' ἀναστάσεως Ἰησοῦ χριστοῦ, 3.22 ὅς ἐστιν ἐν δεξιᾷ θεοῦ, πορευθεὶς εἰς οὐρανόν, ὑποταγέντων αὐτῷ ἀγγέλων καὶ ἐξουσιῶν καὶ δυνάμεων. 4.1 χριστοῦ οὖν παθόντος ὑπὲρ ὑμῶν σαρκὶ καὶ ὑμεῖς τὴν αὐτὴν ἔννοιαν ὁπλίσασθε, ὅτι ὁ παθὼν σαρκὶ πέπαυται ἁμαρτίας, 4.2 εἰς τὸ μηκέτι ἀνθρώπων ἐπιθυμίαις ἀλλὰ θελήματι θεοῦ τὸν ἐπίλοιπον ἐν σαρκὶ βιῶσαι χρόνον. 4.3

TO LOVE LIFE AND TO SEE GOOD DAYS, LET HIM CEASE/STOP HIS TONGUE FROM EVIL AND LIP FROM THE (THING) TO SPEAK NOT DECEIT, 3.11 AND LET HIM TURN ASIDE FROM EVIL AND LET HIM DO/MAKE GOOD, LET HIM SEEK PEACE AND PURSUE IT. 3.12 BECAUSE EYES OF THE LORD *are* UPON JUST (ONES) AND HIS EARS TO THEIR PETITION, AND A FACE OF *the* LORD *is* AGAINST DOING EVIL/BAD (THINGS). 3.13 And who *is* the (one) harming ye if to become zealots of the good? 3.14 But if indeed ye should suffer because of justness, happy (ones) ye will be. But fear ye not the fear of them, neither be ye troubled, 3.15 but sanctify ye *the* lord, the anointed (one), in your hearts, *being* ready (ones) always to/with a defense for every one asking ye a saying/reason/word concerning the hope in ye; 3.16 but with gentleness and fear, having a good conscience, that in what they speak against ye as evildoers, those harassing the good conduct of ye in/for the anointed (one), they might be shamed/ashamed. 3.17 For *it is* better doing good, if the will of God might wish to suffer, than doing evil. 3.18 Because the anointed (one) died once in behalf of our sins, a just (one) in behalf of unjust (ones), in order that he might lead ye to God, having been put to death in flesh but having been made alive in spirit;

3.19 by which even having gone to the spirits in prison, he heralded/preached 3.20 to those having disobeyed then when the patience of God waited expectantly in days of Noe's ark being prepared, in which a few, this was eight souls/lives, were saved through water. 3.21 Which antitype, baptism, also saves us now, not a removal of filth from flesh but an appeal to God from a good conscience, through resurrection of Jesus the anointed (one), 3.22 who is by/at *the* right *hand* of God, having gone into heaven, from angels and authorities and powers having been subjected to him. 4.1 Therefore, the anointed (one), having suffered in behalf of us in flesh, also ye, ye equip yourselves *with* the same mind, because the (one) having suffered in flesh has ceased from sin, 4.2 to/for the (thing) of men no longer to subsist/consume goods in/by desires *for* the remaining time in flesh, but by a will/

ἀρκετὸς γὰρ ὁ παρεληλυθὼς χρόνος τὸ βούλημα τῶν ἐθνῶν κατιργάσθε, πεπορευμένους ἐν ἀσελγίαις, ἐπιθυμίαις, οἰνοφλυγίαις, κώμοις, πότοις, καὶ ἀθεμίτοις εἰδωλολατρίαις. 4.4 ἐν ᾧ ξενίζονται μὴ συντρεχόντων ὑμῶν εἰς τὴν αὐτὴν τῆς ἀσωτίας ἀνάχυσιν, βλασφημοῦντες· 4.5 οἳ ἀποδώσουσιν λόγον τῷ ἑτοίμως ἔχοντι κρῖναι ζῶντας καὶ νεκρούς. 4.6 εἰς τοῦτο γὰρ καὶ νεκροῖς εὐηγγελίσθη ἵνα κριθῶσι μὲν κατὰ ἀνθρώπους σαρκὶ ζῶσι δὲ κατὰ θεὸν πνεύματι. 4.7 πάντων δὲ τὸ τέλος ἤγγικεν. σωφρονήσατε οὖν καὶ νήψατε εἰς προσευχάς· 4.8 πρὸ πάντων τὴν εἰς ἑαυτοὺς ἀγάπην ἐκτενῆ ἔχοντες, ὅτι ἀγάπη καλύψει πλῆθος ἁμαρτιῶν· 4.9 φιλόξενοι εἰς ἀλλήλους ἄνευ γογγυσμοῦ· 4.10 ἕκαστος καθὼς ἔλαβεν χάρισμα, εἰς ἑαυτοὺς αὐτὸ διακονοῦντες ὡς καλοὶ οἰκονόμοι ποικίλης χάριτος θεοῦ. 4.11 εἴ τις λαλεῖ, ὡς λόγια θεοῦ· εἴ τις διακονεῖ, ὡς ἐξ ἰσχύος ἧς χορηγεῖ ὁ θεός· ἵνα ἐν πᾶσιν δοξάζητε ὁ θεὸς διὰ Ἰησοῦ χριστοῦ, ᾧ ἐστιν ἡ δόξα καὶ τὸ κράτος εἰς τοὺς αἰῶνας τῶν αἰώνων· ἀμήν.

4.12 ἀγαπητοί, μὴ ξενίζεσθε τῇ ἐν ὑμῖν πυρώσει πρὸς πειρασμὸν ὑμῖν γινομένῃ ὡς ξένου ὑμῖν συμβαίνοντος, 4.13 ἀλλὰ καθὸ κοινωνεῖτε τοῖς τοῦ χριστοῦ παθήμασιν χαίρετε, ἵνα καὶ ἐν τῇ ἀποκαλύψει τῆς δόξης αὐτοῦ χαρῆτε ἀγαλλιώμενοι. 4.14 εἰ ὀνιδίζεσθαι ἐν ὀνόματι χριστοῦ, μακάριοι, ὅτι τὸ τῆς δόξης καὶ τῆς δυναμέως αὐτοῦ καὶ τὸ τοῦ θεοῦ πνεῦμα ἐφ᾽ ὑμᾶς ἀναπαύεται. 4.15 μὴ γάρ τις ὑμῶν πασχέτω ὡς φονεὺς ἢ κλέπτης ἢ κακοποιὸς ἢ ὡς ἀλλοτριεπίσκοπος· 4.16 εἰ δὲ ὡς χριστιανός, μὴ αἰσχυνέσθω, δοξαζέτω δὲ τὸν θεὸν ἐν τῷ ὀνόματι τούτῳ. 4.17 ὅτι ὁ καιρὸς τοῦ ἄρξασθαι τὸ κρίμα ἀπὸ τοῦ οἴκου τοῦ θεοῦ· εἰ δὲ

purpose of God. 4.3 For the time having passed by *was* enough to have worked out the will/purpose of the ethnics, those having gone in revelings, desires, intoxications/drunks, carousings, drinkings, and wanton idolatries. 4.4 In/with which they are astonished from ye not running with *them* in the same stream/flood of the dissipation/riotous living, slandering/blaspheming; 4.5 who will give an accounting to the (one) holding readily to judge living and dead (ones). 4.6 For indeed to/for this thing a good message was announced to dead (ones), that they might indeed be judged according to men in flesh, but they might live according to God in spirit. 4.7 And the end of all (things) has drawn near. Therefore, be ye soberminded/serious and sober in prayers; 4.8 before all (things) holding constantly the agape in yourselves, because agape covers a multitude of faults/sins; 4.9 *be* hospitable (ones) to one another without grumbling; 4.10 even as each (one) received a gift/grace, serv-ing/waiting on it to yourselves as good managers of a varied gift from God. 4.11 If anyone speaks, as ora-cles/sayings from God; if anyone serves, as from a strength which God supplies; that in all (things) God may be glorified/made of reputation through Jesus the anointed (one) for whom *is* the fame/glory and the dominion/might into the ages of the ages; truly.

4.12 Beloved (ones), be ye not surprised by the fiery ordeal becoming among ye toward a temptation/ testing for ye as a strange (thing) happening to ye, 4.13 but rejoice ye because ye participate in the sufferings of the anointed (one), in order that ye might also rejoice in/at the revelation of his fame/ glory, exulting. 4.14 If ye are reviled in *the* name of the anointed (one), *ye are* happy, because the (thing) of the fame/glory and of his power, and the spirit of God rests upon ye. 4.15 For let not anyone of ye suffer as a murderer or a thief or a criminal/ evildoer or as a busybody/gossipper; 4.16 but if as a Christian, let him not be shamed, but let him glorify/acknowledge God by/in this name. 4.17 Because the time of the (thing) *for* the judgment to begin from the house of God; and if first from us, what *is* the end of

πρῶτον ἀφ' ἡμῶν, τί τὸ τέλος τῶν ἀπιθούντων τῷ λόγῳ τοῦ θεοῦ εὐαγγελίῳ; 4.18 καὶ «εἰ ὁ δίκαιος μόλις σώζεται, ὁ ἀσεβὴς καὶ ὁ ἁμαρτωλὸς ποῦ φανεῖτε;» 4.19 ὥστε καὶ οἱ πάσχοντες κατὰ τὸ θέλημα τοῦ θεοῦ πιστῷ κτίστῃ παρατιθέσθωσαν τὰς ψυχὰς αὐτῶν ἐν ἀγαθοποιΐᾳ.

5.1 Πρεσβυτέρους τοὺς οὖν ἐν ὑμῖν παρακαλῶ ὁ συνπρεσβύτερος καὶ μάρτυς τῶν τοῦ χριστοῦ παθημάτων, ὁ καὶ τῆς μελλούσης ἀποκαλύπτεσθαι δόξης κοινωνός· 5.2 ποιμάναται τὸ ἐν ὑμῖν ποίμνιον τοῦ θεοῦ, ἐπισκοποῦντες μὴ ἀναγκαστῶς ἀλλὰ ἑκουσίως κατὰ θεόν, μηδὲ αἰσχροκερδῶς ἀλλὰ προθύμως, 5.3 μηδ᾽ ὡς κατακυριεύοντες τῶν κλήρων ἀλλὰ τύποι γινόμενοι τοῦ ποιμνίου· 5.4 καὶ φανερωθέντος τοῦ ἀρχιποίμαινος κομιεῖσθαι τὸν ἀμαράντινον τῆς δόξης στέφανον.

5.5 ὁμοίως δέ, νεώτεροι, ὑποτάγητε τοῖς πρεσβυτέροις. πάντες δὲ ἀλλήλοις τὴν ταπινοφροσύνην ἐνκομβώσασθαι, ὅτι « ὁ θεὸς ὑπερηφάνοις ἀντιτάσσεται, ταπινοῖς δὲ δίδωσιν χάριν.»

5.6 ταπινώθητε οὖν ὑπὸ τὴν κραταιὰν χεῖραν τοῦ θεοῦ, ἵνα ὑμᾶς ὑψώσῃ ἐν κερῷ, 5.7 πᾶσαν τὴν μέριμναν ὑμῶν ἐπιρίψαντες ἐπ᾽ αὐτόν, ὅτι αὐτῷ μέλει περὶ ὑμῶν.

5.8 νήψατε, γρηγορήσατε. ὁ ἀντίδικος ὑμῶν διάβολος ὡς λέων ὠρυόμενος περιπατῖ ζητῶν τινα καταπεῖν·

5.9 ᾧ ἀντίστητε στερεοὶ τῇ πίστι, εἰδότες τὰ αὐτὰ τῶν παθημάτων τῇ ἐν τῷ κόσμῳ ὑμῶν ἀδελφότητι ἐπιτελεῖσθε.

5.10 ὁ δὲ θεὸς πάσης χάριτος, ὁ καλέσας ὑμᾶς εἰς τὴν αἰώνιον αὐτοῦ δόξαν ἐν χριστῷ, ὀλίγον παθόντας αὐτὸς καταρτίσει, στηρίξει, σθενώσι, θεμελιώσει. 5.11 αὐτῷ ἡ δόξα καὶ τὸ κράτος εἰς τοὺς αἰῶνας τῶν αἰώνων· ἀμήν.

5.12 διὰ Σιλουανοῦ ὑμῖν τοῦ πιστοῦ ἀδελφοῦ, ὡς λογίζομαι, δι᾽ ὀλίγων ἔγραψα, παρακαλῶν καὶ ἐπιμαρτυρῶν

those disobeying the saying/word of God, the good message? 4.18 And IF THE JUST (ONE) IS HARDLY SAVED, WHERE WILL THE IMPIOUS AND THE SINNER APPEAR? 4.19 So as also those suffering according to the will of God, let the lives/souls of them be committed in well-doing for a faithful creator.

5.1 Therefore I beseech the elders among ye, the fellow-elder and witness of the sufferings of the anointed (one), the sharer also of the glory/fame being about to be revealed; 5.2 shepherd/tend ye the flock of God among ye, overseeing *them*, not compulsively but voluntarily according to God, nor for dishonorable gain but eagerly/willingly, 5.3 nor as being lord over the lots/*dice* but becoming types/examples of the flock; 5.4 and from the chief shepherd having been manifested/made visible ye will receive back the unfading crown/wreath of the glory/fame.

5.5 And likewise, younger (ones), be ye subjected to the elders. And all ye put on humility for one another, because GOD OPPOSES HAUGHTY/ARROGANT (ONES), BUT HE GIVES GRACE/FAVOR TO HUMBLE (ONES).

5.6 Be ye humbled therefore under the mighty hand of God, that he might exalt ye in a season/at a time, 5.7 throwing all your worry/anxiety upon him, because it is a care to him concerning ye.

5.8 Be ye sober, watch ye. Your adversary, a/*the* devil, walks around as a lion, seeking someone to devour;

5.9 whom ye resist/oppose, *being* steadfast (ones) in the faith, knowing the same (things) from the sufferings to be completed/accomplished by your brotherhood in the world.

5.10 And the God of every gift/grace, the (one) having called ye to his eternal glory with/in the anointed (one), having suffered a little himself, he will fit/mend, establish, strengthen, and lay the foundation. 5.11 For him *is* the glory/fame and the dominion/might into the ages of the ages; truly.

5.12 Through Silvanus the faithful brother to ye, as I reckon, because of/through a few (words) I wrote, encouraging and testifying this to be a true

ταύτην εἶναι ἀληθῆ χάριν τοῦ θεοῦ· εἰς ἣν στῆτε. 5.13 ἀσπάζετε ὑμᾶς ἡ ἐν Βαβυλῶνι ἐκκλησία συνεκλεκτὴ καὶ Μᾶρκος ὁ υἱός μου. 5.14 ἀσπάσασθε ἀλλήλους ἐν φιλήματι ἀγάπης. εἰρήνη ὑμῖν πᾶσιν τοῖς ἐν χριστῷ Ἰησοῦ. ἀμήν.

Πέτρου Α΄

gift/grace/favor from God; in which stand ye. 5.13 The assembly, the fellow-elect (one) in Babylon, and Mark my son salutes/greets ye. 5.14 Greet/salute ye one another by a kiss of agape. Peace to ye, to all those in the anointed Jesus. Truly.

From Peter 1

This is the Sinaitic New Testament, book of 2 Peter.

1.1 Συμεὼν Πέτρος δοῦλος καὶ ἀπόστολος Ἰησοῦ χριστοῦ τοῖς ἰσότιμον ἡμῖν λαχοῦσιν πίστιν εἰς δικαιοσύνην τοῦ κυρίου ἡμῶν καὶ σωτῆρος Ἰησοῦ χριστοῦ·

1.2 χάρις ὑμῖν καὶ εἰρήνη πληθυνθίη ἐν ἐπιγνώσι τοῦ θεοῦ καὶ Ἰησοῦ χριστοῦ τοῦ κυρίου ἡμῶν. 1.3 ὡς τὰ πάντα ἡμῖν τῆς θίας δυνάμεως αὐτοῦ τὰ πρὸς ζωὴν καὶ εὐσέβιαν δεδωρημένης διὰ τῆς ἐπιγνώσεως τοῦ καλέσαντος ἡμᾶς ἰδίᾳ δόξῃ καὶ ἀρετῇ, 1.4 δι' ὧν τὰ τίμια ἡμῖν καὶ μέγιστα ἐπαγγέλματα δεδώρηται, ἵνα διὰ τούτων γένησθε θείας φύσεως κοινωνοί, ἀποφυγόντες τὴν ἐν τῷ κόσμῳ ἐπιθυμίαν φθορᾶς. 1.5 καὶ αὐτὸ δὲ τοῦτο σπουδὴν πᾶσαν παρεισενέγκαντες ἐπιχορηγήσατε ἐν τῇ πίστι ὑμῶν τὴν ἀρετήν, ἐν δὲ τῇ ἀρετῇ τὴν γνῶσιν, 1.6 ἐν δὲ τῇ γνώσι τὴν ἐγκράτιαν, ἐν δὲ τῇ ἐγκρατίᾳ τὴν ὑπομονήν, ἐν δὲ τῇ ὑπομονῇ τὴν εὐσέβειαν, 1.7 ἐν δὲ τὴν εὐσεβίᾳ τὴν φιλαδελφίαν, ἐν δὲ τῇ φιλαδελφίᾳ τὴν ἀγάπην. 1.8 ταῦτα γὰρ ὑμῖν ὑπάρχοντα καὶ πλεονάζοντα οὐκ ἀργοὺς οὐδὲ ἀκάρπους καθίστησιν εἰς τὴν τοῦ κυρίου ἡμῶν Ἰησοῦ χριστοῦ ἐπίγνωσιν·

1.9 ᾧ γὰρ μὴ πάρεστιν ταῦτα, τυφλός ἐστιν μυωπάζων, λήθην λαβὼν τοῦ καθαρισμοῦ τῶν πάλαι αὐτοῦ ἁμαρτημάτων. 1.10 διὸ μᾶλλον, ἀδελφοί, σπουδάσατε ἵνα διὰ τῶν καλῶν ἔργον βεβαίαν ὑμῶν τὴν κλῆσιν καὶ ἐκλογὴν ποιεῖσθαι· ταῦτα γὰρ ποιοῦντες οὐ μὴ πτέσητέ ποτε· 1.11 οὕτως γὰρ πλουσίως ἐπιχορηγηθήσεται ὑμῖν εἴσοδος εἰς τὴν αἰώνιον βασιλίαν τοῦ κυρίου ἡμῶν καὶ σωτῆρος Ἰησοῦ χριστοῦ. 1.12 διὸ μελλήσω ἀεὶ περὶ τούτων ὑπομιμνήσκιν ὑμᾶς, καίπερ ἰδότας καὶ ἐστηριγμένους ἐν τῇ παρούσῃ ἀληθίᾳ. 1.13 δίκαιον δὲ ἡγοῦμαι, ἐφ' ὅσον εἰμὶ ἐν τούτῳ τῷ σκηνώματι, διεγίριν ὑμᾶς ἐν τῇ ὑπομνήσει, 1.14 εἰδὼς ὅτι ταχεινή ἐστιν ἡ ἀπόθεσις τοῦ

1.1 Simeon Peter a slave and apostle of Jesus, the anointed (one), to those having attained equally precious faith with us in justice/justness from our Lord and savior Jesus, the anointed (one).
1.2 Grace to ye and may peace be multiplied in/by a full knowledge of God and of Jesus the anointed (one), our Lord. 1.3 As all the (things) *are* for us from his divine power, the (things) toward life and piety having been given through the full knowledge/recognition of the (thing) of having called us to his own glory/fame and virtue, 1.4 through which he has given to us the precious and great promises, that through these ye might become sharers/partakers of a divine nature, escaping the desire of corruption in the world. 1.5 But also *for* this (thing) bring in every diligence, support ye the virtue in/by your faith, and by/with the virtue *is* the mind/knowledge, 1.6 and in/by the knowledge *is* the self-control/ temperance, and in/by the self-control *is* the endurance/patience, and in/by the endurance *is* the piety/reverence, 1.7 and in/by the reverence *is* the brotherly love, and in/by the brotherly love *is* the agape. 1.8 For these (things) existing and abounding in ye, not idle/lazy (ones) nor unproductive (ones) constitutes/sets into the full knowledge of our Lord Jesus, the anointed (one);
1.9 for *the one* in whom these (things) *are* not present, he is blind, being short-sighted, being forgetful of the cleansing from his sins of past times. 1.10 Wherefore rather, brothers, be ye diligent/eager that through the good work(s) to make firm your calling and choice/election; for by no means might ye stumble once/when doing these (things); 1.11 for so will it be furnished/granted abundantly for ye, entrance into the eternal kingdom of our Lord and savior Jesus, the anointed (one). 1.12 Wherefore, I will always be about to remind ye concerning these (things), though having been known and remaining established in the present truth. 1.13 And I think it just, for as long as I am in this covering/skin, to arouse ye by the reminder, 1.14 knowing that the putting off of my covering/shell/skin is soon, --

σκηνώματός μου, — Ἰησοῦς χριστὸς ἐδήλωσέν μοι· 1.15 σπουδάζω δὲ καὶ ἑκάστοτε ἔχειν ὑμᾶς μετὰ τὴν ἐμὴν ἔξοδον τὴν τούτων μνήμην ποιεῖσθαι. 1.16 οὐ γὰρ σεσοφισμένοις μύθοις ἐξακολουθήσαντες ἐγνωρίσαμεν ὑμῖν τὴν τοῦ κυρίου ἡμῶν Ἰησοῦ χριστοῦ δύναμιν καὶ παρουσίαν, ἀλλ’ ἐπόπται γενηθέντες τῆς ἐκείνου μεγαλειότητος. 1.17 λαβὼν γὰρ παρὰ τοῦ θεοῦ πατρὸς τιμὴν καὶ δόξαν φωνῆς ἐνεχθίσης αὐτῷ τοιᾶσδε ὑπὸ τῆς μεγαλοπρεποῦς δόξης, οὗτός ἐστιν ὁ υἱός μου ὁ ἀγαπητός, εἰς ὃν ἐγὼ εὐδόκησα 1.18 καὶ ταύτην τὴν φωνὴν ἡμεῖς ἠκούσαμεν ἐκ τοῦ οὐρανοῦ ἐνεχθεῖσαν σὺν αὐτῷ ὄντες ἐν τῳ ὄρι τῷ ἁγίῳ. 1.19 καὶ ἔχομεν βεβαιότερον τὸν προφητικὸν λόγον, ᾧ καλῶς ποιεῖται προσέχοντες ὡς λύχνῳ φαίνοντι ἐν αὐχμηρῷ τόπῳ, ἕως οὗ ἡ ἡμέρα διαυγάσῃ καὶ φωσφόρος ἀνατίλῃ ἐν ταῖς καρδίαις ὑμῶν· 1.20 τοῦτο πρῶτον γινώσκοντες, ὅτι πᾶσα προφητία γραφῆς ἰδίας ἐπιλύσεως οὐ γίνεται· 1.21 οὐ γὰρ θελήματι ἀνθρώπου ἠνέχθη ποτέ προφητεία, ἀλλὰ ὑπὸ πνεύματος ἁγίου φερόμενοι ἐλάλησαν ἅγιοι θεοῦ ἄνθρωποι.

2.1 Ἐγένοντο δὲ καὶ ψευδοπροφῆται ἐν τῷ λαῷ, ὡς καὶ ἐν ὑμῖν ἔσονται ψευδοδιδάσκαλοι, οἵτινες παρισάξουσιν αἱρέσεις ἀπωλίας, καὶ τὸν ἀγοράσαντα αὐτοὺς δεσπότην ἀρνούμενοι, ἐπάγοντες ἑαυτοῖς ταχινὴν ἀπώλιαν. 2.2 καὶ πολλοὶ ἐξακολουθήσουσιν αὐτῶν ταῖς ἀσελγίαις, δι’ οὓς ἡ ὁδὸς τῆς ἀληθίας βλασφημηθήσεται· 2.3 καὶ ἐν πλεονεξίᾳ πλαστοῖς λόγοις ὑμᾶς ἐμπορεύσονται· οἷς τὸ κρίμα ἔκπαλαι οὐκ ἀργεῖ, καὶ ἡ ἀπώλεια αὐτῶν οὐ νυστάζει. 2.4 εἰ γὰρ ὁ θεὸς ἀγγέλων ἁμαρτησάντων οὐκ ἐφίσατο, ἀλλὰ σιροῖς ζόφου ταρταρώσας παρέδωκεν εἰς κρίσιν κολαζομένους τηρῖν, 2.5 καὶ ἀρχαίου κόσμου οὐκ ἐφίσατο, ἀλλὰ ὄγδοον Νῶε δικαιοσύνης κήρυκα ἐφύλαξεν, κατακλυσμὸν κόσμῳ ἀσεβῶν ἐπάξας, 2.6 καὶ πόλις

Jesus, the anointed (one) made *it* clear to me;   1.15
but I shall be diligent also to make ye to hold/have,
after my departure, the reminder of these things.
1.16 For not following myths having been cleverly
devised, we made known to ye the power and assurance/
confidence of our Lord, Jesus the anointed (one), but
having become eyewitnesses of the majesty of that
(one).   1.17 For receiving honor and fame/glory from
God the father, a voice such as this being carried to
him by the majestic glory/reputation: This (one) is my
beloved son, in whom I, I was well pleased, -- 1.18
and the same voice we, we heard being borne/carried
out of the sky/heaven, being with him on the holy
mountain.   1.19 And we hold more firm the prophetic
saying, to which ye do well heeding as to a lamp shining in a murky place, until which *time* the day dawns
and a morning star might rise in your hearts;   1.20
knowing this first, that every prophecy of a writing
becomes not of/from its own liberation/solution,   1.21
for prophecy was not once brought/borne by a will of
man, but holy men of God spoke, being borne/brought by
a holy spirit.

2.1   But there also came to be false/lying prophets among the people, as even among ye there will be
lying teachers, who will bring in stealthily sects/
choices/denominations/heresies of destruction,   even
denying the master having bought them, bringing swift
destruction for/to themselves.   2.2 And many follow-
ed/pursued the wanton orgies/unlawful excesses of
them, because of whom the way of the truth will be
slandered/blasphemed;   2.3 and in greediness with
fabricated sayings they will make trade/barter/mer-
chandise of ye; for whom the judgment of old lingers
not, and the destruction of them sleeps/slumbers not.
2.4 For if God refrained not from sinning messengers/
angels, but consigning to Tartarus he delivered *them*
to pits of gloom to confine/keep to/for judgment,   2.5
And he refrained not from *the* ancient world, but he
protected *the* eighth, Noe, a herald of justice, bringing a flood upon a world of impious/irreverent (ones),
2.6 and having reduced them to ashes, he condemned *the*

Σοδόμων καὶ Γομόρρας τεφρώσας καταστροφῇ κατέκρινεν, ὑπόδιγμα μελλόντων ἀσεβέιν τεθικώς, 2.7 καὶ δίκαιον Λὼτ καταπονούμενο ὑπὸ τῆς τῶν ἀθέσμων ἐν ἀσελγίᾳ ἀναστροφῆς ἐρρύσατο· 2.8 βλέμματι γὰρ καὶ ἀκοῇ ὁ δίκαιος ἐγκατοικῶν ἐν αὐτοῖς ἡμέραν ἐξ ἡμέρας ψυχὴν δικαίαν ἀνόμοις ἔργοις ἐβασάνιζεν· 2.9 οἶδεν κύριος εὐσεβεῖς ἐκ πιρασμοῦ ῥύεσθαι, ἀδίκους δὲ εἰς ἦραν κρίσεως κολαζομένους τηρῖν, 2.10 μάλιστα δὲ τοὺς ὀπίσω σαρκὸς ἐν ἐπιθυμίᾳ μιασμοῦ πορευομένους καὶ κυριότητος καταφρονοῦντας. τολμηταί, αὐθάδις, δόξας οὐ τρέμουσιν βλασφημοῦντες, 2.11 ὅπου ἄγγελοι ἰσχύει καὶ δυνάμι μίζονες ὄντες οὐ φέρουσιν κατ᾽ αὐτῶν παρὰ κυρίῳ βλάσφημον κρίσιν. 2.12 αὐτοὶ δέ, ὡς ἄλογα ζῷα γεγεννημένα φυσικὰ εἰς ἅλωσιν καὶ φθοράν, ἐν οἷς ἀγνοοῦντες βλασφημοῦσιν, ἐν τῇ φθορᾷ αὐτῶν καὶ φθαρήσονται, 2.13 ἀδικούμενοι μισθὸν ἀδικίας· ἡδονὴν ἡγούμενοι τὴν ἐν ἡμέρᾳ τρυφήν, σπίλοι καὶ μῶμοι ἐντρυφῶντες ἐν ταῖς ἀπάταις αὐτῶν συνευωχούμενοι ὑμῖν, 2.14 ὀφθαλμοὺς ἔχοντες μεστοὺς μοιχαλίας καὶ ἀκαταπαύστους ἁμαρτίαις, δελεάζοντες ψυχὰς ἀστηρίκτους, καρδίαν γεγυμνασμένην πλεονεξίας ἔχοντες, κατάρας τέκνα, 2.15 καταλείποντες εὐθεῖαν ὁδὸν ἐπλανήθησαν, ἐξακολουθήσαντες τῇ ὁδῷ τοῦ Βαλαὰμ τοῦ Βοσόρ, ὃς μισθὸν ἀδικίας ἠγάπησεν 2.16 ἔλεγξειν δὲ ἔσχεν ἰδίας παρανομίας· ὑποζύγιον ἄφωνον ἐν ἀνθρώπου φωνῇ φθεγξάμενον ἐκώλυσεν τὴν τοῦ προφήτου παραφρονίαν. 2.17 οὗτοί εἰσιν πηγαὶ ἄνυδροι καὶ ὁμίχλαι ὑπὸ λέλαπος ἐλαυνόμεναι, οἷς ὁ ζόφος τοῦ σκότους τετήρηται. 2.18 ὑπέρογκα γὰρ ματαιότητος φθεγγόμενοι δελεάζουσιν ἐν ἐπιθυμίαις σαρκὸς ἀσελγίαις τοὺς ὀλίγως ἀποφεύγοντας τοὺς ἐν πλάνῃ ἀναστρεφομένους, 2.19 ἐλευθερίαν αὐτοῖς

cities of Sodom and Gomorra by an overthrowing, having set/made an example of (those) being about to live impiously/irreverently,   2.7 and he delivered a just (one), Lot, being oppressed by the conduct in wanton orgies of the lawless (ones);   2.8 for in/by seeing and hearing, the just (one) dwelling among them day by day was tormenting a just life/soul with lawless works;   2.9 *The* Lord knows to rescue/deliver reverent/pious (ones) out of temptations/testings,   but to keep unjust (ones) being punished in a day of judgment,   2.10 and especially the (ones) going after flesh in a desire of defiling and despising lordship/ dominion. Self-satisfied darers, they tremble not, reviling/blaspheming glories/reputations,   2.11 where messengers/angels being of greater strength and power they bring not a slanderous judgment from the Lord against them.   2.12 But they, as natural animals having been generated without reason for/into capture and depravity, they slander/blaspheme in what things being ignorant of, by their ruin/decay they will also be ruined/decayed,   2.13 (ones) receiving unjust wages of injustice; regarding the luxury in a day *to be* pleasure/enjoyment, spotted and blemished (ones) reveling/living luxuriously in their deceits, feasting together with ye,   2.14 having eyes full of an adulteress and unresting/unceasing in sins, luring/entrapping instable lives/souls, having a heart having been trained/exercised from greediness/greed, children of execration/a curse,   2.15 leaving behind/forsaking a straight road/way, they were deceived/misled, following in/on the way/road of Balaam, the (one) of Beor, who loved wages of injustice, 2.16 and he had a reproof of/from her own transgression; a dumb/senseless donkey speaking with/in a man's voice he detained the madness of the prophet.   2.17 These are springs/ wells without water and mists being driven by a windstorm, for whom the gloom of the darkness has been kept.   2.18 For declaring haughty (things) of vain learning they lure/entrap in desires of flesh for revelries/extravagances those barely escaping from the (ones) conducting themselves in deceit/error,   2.19 promising freedom, freedom to those, being slaves of

ἐπαγγελλόμενοι, αὐτοὶ δοῦλοι ὑπάρχοντες τῆς φθορᾶς· ᾧ γάρ τις ἥττηται, τούτῳ δεδούλωται. 2.20 εἰ γὰρ ἀποφυγόντες τὰ μιάσματα τοῦ κόσμου ἐν ἐπιγνώσει τοῦ κυρίου ἡμῶν καὶ σωτῆρος Ἰησοῦ χριστοῦ τούτοις δὲ πάλιν ἐμπλακέντες ἡττῶνται, γέγονεν αὐτοῖς τὰ ἔσχατα χείρονα τῶν πρώτων. 2.21 κρῖσσον γὰρ ἦν αὐτοῖς μὴ ἐπεγνωκέναι τὴν ὁδὸν τῆς δικαιοσύνης ἢ ἐπιγνοῦσιν εἰς τὰ ὀπίσω ἀνακάμψαι ἀπο τῆς παραδοθίσης αὐτοῖς ἁγίας ἐντολῆς. 2.22 συμβέβηκεν αὐτοῖς τὸ τῆς ἀληθοῦς παροιμίας, «κύων ἐπιστρέψας ἐπὶ τὸ ἴδιον ἐξέραμα,» καί, ὗς λουσαμένη εἰς κυλισμὰ βορβόρου.

3.1 Ταύτην ἤδη, ἀγαπητοί, δευτέραν ὑμῖν γράφω ἐπιστολήν, ἐν αἷς διεγείρω ὑμῶν ἐν ὑπομνήσι τὴν εἰλικρινῆ διάνοιαν, 3.2 μνησθῆναι τῶν προειρημένων ῥημάτων ὑπὸ τῶν ἁγίων προφητῶν καὶ τῆς τῶν ἀποστόλων ὑμῶν ἐντολῆς τοῦ κυρίου καὶ σωτῆρος· 3.3 τοῦτο πρῶτον γινώσκοντες, ὅτι ἐλεύσονται ἐπ᾿ ἐσχάτων τῶν ἡμερῶν ἐν ἐμπεγμονῇ ἐμπέκται κατὰ τὰς ἰδίας αὐτῶν ἐπιθυμίας πορευόμενοι 3.4 καὶ λέγοντες, ποῦ ἐστιν ἡ ἐπαγγελία τῆς παρουσίας αὐτοῦ; ἀφ᾿ ἧς γὰρ οἱ πατέρες ἐκοιμήθησαν, πάντα οὕτως διαμένει ἀπ᾿ ἀρχῆς κτίσεως.

3.5 λανθάνει γὰρ αὐτοὺς τοῦτο θέλοντας, ὅτι οὐρανοὶ ἦσαν ἔκπαλαι καὶ γῆ ἐξ ὕδατος καὶ διὰ ὕδατος συνεστῶσα τῷ τοῦ θεοῦ λόγῳ, 3.6 δι᾿ ὧν ὁ τότε κόσμος ὕδατι κατακλυσθεὶς ἀπώλετο· 3.7 οἱ δὲ νῦν οὐρανοὶ καὶ ἡ γῆ τῷ αὐτοῦ λόγῳ τεθησαυρισμένοι εἰσὶν πυρί, τηρούμενοι εἰς ἡμέραν κρίσεως καὶ ἀπωλείας τῶν ἀσεβῶν ἀνθρώπων. 3.8 ἓν δὲ τοῦτο μὴ λανθανέτω ὑμᾶς, ἀγαπητοί, ὅτι μία ἡμέρα παρὰ κυρίου ὡς χίλια ἔτη καὶ χίλια ἔτη ὡς ἡμέρα μία. 3.9 οὐ βραδύνει κύριος τῆς ἐπαγγελίας, ὥς τινες βραδύτητα ἡγοῦνται, ἀλλὰ μακροθυμεῖ δι᾿ ὑμᾶς, μὴ βουλόμενός τινας ἀπολέσθαι ἀλλὰ πάντες εἰς μετάνοιαν χωρῆσαι. 3.10 ἥξει δὲ ἡ ἡμέρα κυρίου ὡς κλέπτης, ἐν ᾗ οὐρανοὶ μὲν

the decay/corruption themselves; for to whom anyone has succumbed, to this (one) he has been enslaved. 2.20 For if having escaped the defilements of the world by knowing our Lord and savior Jesus, the a-nointed (one), and having again been entangled in them, they have been defeated, the last (things) have become worse for these than the first.   2.21 For it was better for them not to have known the way/road of the justice/justness than having known to return to the (things) behind from the holy command having been delivered to them.   2.22 The (thing) from the true proverb has happened to them: A DOG RETURNING TO ITS OWN VOMIT, and, a sow having washed herself to wallow-ings of mud.

3.1 Already/now, beloved (ones), I write to ye this second letter, in which I wake up your sincere mind by a reminder,   3.2 to remember the words having been previously spoken by the holy prophets and the command from the apostles of the Lord and savior;   3.3 knowing this first, that mockers will come to/on the last days, going in ridiculing according to their own desires   3.4 and saying: Where is the promise of his coming? For from which *time* the fathers fell asleep (died), all (things) so remains from *the* beginning of creation.

3.5 For this is hidden for those wanting that heavens/skies were of old and land out of water and through water having been held together by the rea-son/logos/word of god,   3.6 through which the world once perished by water, having been flooded;   3.7 but now the heavens and the earth for the same reason are having been stored up for fire, being kept in/for a day of judgment and destruction of the irreverent/im-pious men.   3.8 But this one (thing), let it not be hidden/ignored, brothers, that one day beside/with *the* Lord *is* as a thousand years and a thousand years *is* as one day.   3.9 *The* Lord is not slow of/from the prom-ise, as some regard slowness, but he is patient/for-bearing because of us, not willing/purposing *for* any-one to perish, but *for* all to yield in repentance. 3.10 But the day of *the* Lord will come as a thief, in

ρυζηδὸν παρελεύσονται, στοιχεῖα δὲ καυσούμενα λυθήσεται, γῆ καὶ τὰ ἐν αὐτῇ ἔργα εὑρεθήσεται. 3.11 τούτων οὖν πάντων λυομένων ποταποὺς δεῖ ὑπάρχειν ὑμᾶς ἐν ἁγίαις ἀναστροφαῖς καὶ εὐσεβείαις, 3.12 προσδοκῶντας καὶ σπεύδοντας τὴν παρουσίαν τῆς τοῦ θεοῦ ἡμέρας, δι᾽ ἣν οὐρανοὶ πυρούμενοι λυθήσονται καὶ στοιχῖα καυσούμενα τήκεται. 3.13 καινοὺς δὲ οὐρανοὺς καὶ κενὴν γῆν κατὰ τὰ ἐπαγγέλματα αὐτοῦ προσδοκῶμεν, ἐν οἷς δικαιοσύνη κατοικεῖ. 3.14 διό, ἀγαπητοί, ταῦτα προσδοκῶντες σπουδάσατε ἄσπιλοι καὶ ἀμώμητοι αὐτῷ εὑρεθῆναι ἐν εἰρήνῃ, 3.15 καὶ τὴν τοῦ κυρίου ἡμῶν μακροθυμίαν σωτηρίαν ἡγεῖσθαι, καθὼς καὶ ὁ ἀγαπητὸς ἡμῶν ἀδελφὸς Παῦλος κατὰ τὴν δοθεῖσαν αὐτῷ σοφίαν ἔγραψεν ὑμῖν, 3.16 ὡς καὶ ἐν πάσαις ταῖς ἐπιστολαῖς λαλῶν ἐν αὐταῖς περὶ τούτων, ἐν αἷς ἐστιν δυσνόητά τινα, ἃ οἱ ἀμαθεῖς καὶ ἀστήρικτοι στρεβλοῦσιν ὡς καὶ τὰς λοιπὰς γραφὰς πρὸς τὴν ἰδίαν αὐτῶν ἀπώλειαν. 3.17 ὑμεῖς οὖν, ἀγαπητοί, προγινώσκοντες φυλάσσεσθαι ἵνα μὴ τῇ τῶν ἀθέσμων πλάνῃ συναπαχθέντες ἐκπέσητε τοῦ ἰδίου στηριγμοῦ, 3.18 αὐξάνετε δὲ ἐν χάριτι καὶ γνώσι τοῦ κυρίου ἡμῶν καὶ σωτῆρος Ἰησοῦ χριστοῦ. αὐτῷ ἡ δόξα καὶ νῦν καὶ εἰς ἡμέραν αἰῶνος. ἀμήν.

Πέτρου Β΄

which *the* skies/heavens on one hand will pass away with a rushing sound, and elements/fundamentals being burned will be destroyed, and land/earth and the works in/on it will be discovered/found *out*. 3.11 Then all these (things), being destroyed, it is necessary what sort of (men) *for* ye to be/exist in holy/set apart ways of life/behaviors and reverences/pieties, 3.12 expecting and desiring earnestly the coming of the day of God, through which skies/heavens being set on fire will be destroyed, and elements/fundamentals being burned will be melted. 3.13 But we await expectantly *for* new skies/heavens and a new earth according to his promise, one in/on which justice/justness dwells. 3.14 Wherefore, beloved (ones), expecting/awaiting these (things) be ye diligent to be found spotless and blameless (ones) by/for him in peace, 3.15 and consider ye the patience/forbearance of our Lord *is* salvation, as also our beloved brother Paul wrote to ye, according to the wisdom having been given to him, 3.16 as also in all the epistles, speaking in them concerning these (things), in which *there* are some (things) hard to understand, which the unlearned and unstable (ones) distort/pervert, as also the remaining/rest of the writings, toward their own destruction. 3.17 Therefore ye, beloved (ones), knowing beforehand, ye guard/watch lest, being led astray in/by the deceit/deception of the lawless/unrestrained (ones), ye might fall away from your own firmness/ standing, 3.18 but grow/increase ye in grace and knowledge of our Lord and savior Jesus, the anointed (one). To him *be* the fame/glory, both now and in a/*the* day of eternity. Truly.

From Peter 2

This is the Sinaitic New Testament, book of 1 John.

1.1 Ὁ ἦν ἀπ' ἀρχῆς, ὃ ἀκηκόαμεν, ὃ ἑωράκαμεν τοῖς ὀφθαλμοῖς ἡμῶν, ὃ ἐθεασάμεθα καὶ αἱ χεῖρες ἡμῶν ἐψηλάφησαν, περὶ τοῦ λόγου τῆς ζωῆς 1.2 καὶ ἡ ζωὴ ἐφανερώθη, καὶ ἑωράκαμεν καὶ μαρτυροῦμεν καὶ ἀπαγγέλλομεν ὑμῖν τὴν ζωὴν τὴν αἰώνιον ἥτις ἦν πρὸς τὸν πατέρα καὶ ἐφανερώθη ἡμῖν 1.3 ὃ ἀκηκόαμεν ἑωράκαμεν καὶ ἀπαγγέλλομεν καὶ ὑμῖν, ἵνα καὶ ὑμῖς κοινωνίαν ἔχηται μεθ' ἡμῶν. καὶ ἡ κοινωνία δὲ ἡ ἡμετέρα ὑμῶν μετὰ τοῦ πατρὸς καὶ μετὰ τοῦ υἱοῦ αὐτοῦ Ἰησοῦ χριστοῦ. 1.4 καὶ ταῦτα γράφομεν ἡμεῖς ἵνα ἡ χαρὰ ἡμῶν ἦ πεπληρωμένη. 1.5 καὶ ἔστιν αὕτη ἡ ἀγγελία ἣν ἀκηκόαμεν ἀπ' αὐτοῦ καὶ ἀναγγέλλομεν ὑμῖν, ὅτι ὁ θεὸς φῶς ἐστιν καὶ σκοτία ἐν αὐτῷ οὐκ ἔστιν οὐδεμία. 1.6 ἐὰν εἴπωμεν ὅτι κοινωνίαν ἔχομεν μετ' αὐτοῦ καὶ ἐν τῷ σκότι περιπατῶμεν, ψευδόμεθα καὶ οὐ ποιοῦμεν τὴν ἀλήθιαν· 1.7 ἐὰν δὲ ἐν τῷ φωτὶ περιπατῶμεν ὡς αὐτός ἐστιν ἐν τῷ φωτί, κοινωνίαν ἔχομεν μετ' ἀλλήλων καὶ τὸ αἷμα Ἰησοῦ τοῦ υἱοῦ αὐτοῦ καθαρίζει ἡμᾶς ἀπὸ πάσης ἁμαρτίας. 1.8 ἐὰν εἴπωμεν ὅτι ἁμαρτίαν οὐκ ἔχομεν, ἑαυτοὺς πλανῶμεν καὶ ἡ ἀλήθεια οὐκ ἔστιν ἐν ἡμῖν.

1.9 ἐὰν ὁμολογῶμεν τὰς ἁμαρτίας ἡμῶν, πιστός ἐστιν καὶ δίκαιος ἵνα ἀφῇ ἡμῖν τὰς ἁμαρτίας ἡμῶν καὶ καθαρίσῃ ἡμᾶς ἀπὸ πάσης ἀδικίας. 1.10 ἐὰν εἴπωμεν ὅτι οὐκ ἡμαρτήκαμεν, ψεύστην ποιοῦμεν αὐτὸν καὶ ὁ λόγος αὐτοῦ οὐκ ἔστιν ἐν ἡμῖν.

2.1 Τεκνία μου, ταῦτα γράφω ὑμῖν ἵνα μὴ ἁμάρτητε. καὶ ἐάν τις ἁμάρτῃ, παράκλητον ἔχομεν πρὸς τὸν πατέρα, Ἰησοῦν χριστὸν δίκαιον· 2.2 καὶ αὐτὸς ἱλασμός ἐστιν περὶ τῶν ἁμαρτιῶν ἡμῶν, οὐ περὶ τῶν ἡμετέρων δὲ μόνον ἀλλὰ καὶ περὶ ὅλου τοῦ κόσμου. 2.3 καὶ ἐν τούτῳ γινώσκομεν ὅτι ἐγνώκαμεν αὐτόν, ἐὰν τὰς ἐντολὰς αὐτοῦ τηρῶμεν.

2.4 ὁ λέγων ὅτι ἔγνωκα αὐτόν, καὶ τὰς ἐντολὰς αὐτοῦ μὴ τηρῶν, ψεύστης ἐστίν, καὶ ἡ ἀλήθεια τοῦ θεοῦ οὐκ ἔστιν· 2.5 ὃς δ' ἂν τηρῇ αὐτοῦ τὸν λόγον, ἀληθῶς ἐν τούτῳ ἡ ἀγάπη τοῦ

1.1   What was from *the* beginning, what we have
heard, what we have seen with our eyes, what we beheld
and our hands touched, concerning the logos/word of
life -- 1.2 And the life was manifested, and we have
seen and we testify and we announce to ye the eternal
life which was with the father and was manifested to
us -- 1.3 What we have heard we have seen and we announce also to ye, that ye also may have fellowship
with us. And also our fellowship *is* with the father
and with his son Jesus, the anointed (one).   1.4 And
these (things) we, we write that our joy may be having
been fulfilled.   1.5 And this is the announcement
which we have heard from him and we announce to ye,
that God is light and there is not any darkness in
him.   1.6 If we might say that we have fellowship with
him, but in the darkness we may continue walking, we
lie and we do not the truth.   1.7 But if we may walk
in the light as he, he is in the light, we have fellowship with one another and the blood of his son
Jesus cleanses us from every fault/sin.   1.8 If we
might say that we have not a fault/sin, we deceive
ourselves and the truth is not in us.
      1.9   If we may confess our faults/sins, he is
faithful and just that he may forgive us our faults/
sins and he may cleanse us from every injustice.   1.10
If we may say that we have not sinned, we make him a
liar and the logos/word/reason or him/his word is not
in us.

      2.1   My little children, I write these (things)
to ye in order that ye may not fail/sin. But if someone might sin, we have a paraclete with the father,
Jesus, the anointed just (one);   2.2 and he is a means
of atonement concerning our faults/sins; but not concerning those of us only, but also concerning the
entire world.   2.3 And by this we know that we have
known him (and continue knowing), if we should keep
the commands from him/his commands.
      2.4   The (one) saying that he has known him and
not keeping his commands is a liar, and the truth of
God is not *in him*;   2.5 but who ever may keep his
logos/word, the agape of God truly has been matured in

θεοῦ τετελείωται. ἐν τούτῳ γινώσκομεν ὅτι ἐν αὐτῷ ἐσμεν· 2.6 ὁ λέγων ἐν αὐτῷ μένιν ὀφίλει καθὼς ἐκεῖνος περιεπάτησεν καὶ αὐτὸς οὕτως περιπατεῖν.

2.7 ἀγαπητοί, οὐκ ἐντολὴν καινὴν γράφω ὑμῖν, ἀλλ᾽ ἐντολὴν παλαιὰν ἣν εἴχετε ἀπ᾽ ἀρχῆς· ἡ ἐντολὴ ἡ παλαιά ἐστιν ὁ λόγος ὃν ἠκούσατε. 2.8 πάλιν ἐντολὴν καινὴν γράφω ὑμῖν, ὅ ἐστιν ἀληθὲς καὶ ἐν αὐτῷ καὶ ἐν ὑμῖν, ὅτι ἡ σκοτία παράγεται καὶ τὸ φῶς τὸ ἀληθινὸν ἤδη φαίνει. 2.9 ὁ λέγων ἐν τῷ φωτὶ εἶναι καὶ τὸν ἀδελφὸν αὐτοῦ μεισῶν ψεύστης ἐστιν καὶ ἐν τῇ σκοτίᾳ ἐστὶν ἕως ἄρτι. 2.10 ὁ ἀγαπῶν τὸν ἀδελφὸν αὐτοῦ ἐν τῷ φωτὶ μένει, καὶ σκάνδαλον οὐκ ἔστιν ἐν αὐτῷ· 2.11 ὁ δὲ μισῶν τὸν ἀδελφὸν αὐτοῦ ἐν τῇ σκοτίᾳ ἐστὶν καὶ ἐν τῇ σκοτίᾳ περιπατεῖ, καὶ οὐκ οἶδεν ποῦ ὑπάγει, ὅτι ἡ σκοτία ἐτύφλωσεν τοὺς ὀφθαλμοὺς αὐτοῦ.

2.12 γράφω ὑμῖν, τεκνία, ὅτι ἀφέωνται ὑμῖν αἱ ἁμαρτίαι διὰ τὸ ὄνομα αὐτοῦ. 2.13 γράφω ὑμῖν, πατέρες, ὅτι ἐγνώκατε τὸν ἀπ᾽ ἀρχῆς. γράφω ὑμῖν, νεανίσκοι, ὅτι νενικήκατε τὸ πονηρόν.

2.14 ἔγραψα ὑμῖν, παιδία, ὅτι ἐγνώκατε τὸν πατέρα. ἔγραψα ὑμῖν, πατέρες, ὅτι ἐγνώκατε τὸν ἀπ᾽ ἀρχῆς. ἔγραψα ὑμῖν, νεανίσκοι, ὅτι ἰσχυροί ἐστε καὶ ὁ λόγος τοῦ θεοῦ ἐν ὑμῖν μένει καὶ νενικήκατε τὸν πονηρόν. 2.15 μὴ ἀγαπᾶτε τὸν κόσμον μηδὲ τὰ ἐν τῷ κόσμῳ. ἐάν τις ἀγαπᾷ τὸν κόσμον, οὐκ ἔστιν ἡ ἀγάπη τοῦ πατρὸς ἐν αὐτῷ· 2.16 ὅτι πᾶν τὸ ἐν τῷ κόσμῳ, ἡ ἐπιθυμία τῆς σαρκὸς καὶ ἡ ἐπιθυμία τῶν ὀφθαλμῶν καὶ ἡ ἀλαζονία τοῦ βίου, οὐκ ἔστιν ἐκ τοῦ πατρὸς ἀλλ᾽ ἐκ τοῦ κόσμου ἐστίν. 2.17 καὶ ὁ κόσμος παράγεται καὶ ἡ ἐπιθυμία αὐτοῦ, ὁ δὲ ποιῶν τὸ θέλημα τοῦ θεοῦ μένει εἰς τὸν αἰῶνα.

2.18 παιδία, ἐσχάτη ὥρα ἐστίν, καὶ καθὼς ἠκούσατε ὅτι ἀντίχριστος ἔρχεται, καὶ νῦν ἀντίχριστοι πολλοὶ γεγόνασιν· ὅθεν γινώσκομεν ὅτι ἐσχάτη ὥρα ἐστίν.

2.19 ἐξ ἡμῶν ἐξῆλθον, ἀλλ᾽ οὐκ ἦσαν ἐξ ἡμῶν· εἰ γὰρ

this (one). By this we know that we are in him.   2.6
The (one) saying to abide in him owes *it*, as that
(one) walked, so also to walk himself.

2.7 Beloved (ones), I write not a new command to
ye, but an old command which ye had from the beginning; the old command is the logos/word/reason which
ye heard.   2.8 Again, I write a new command to ye,
which is true both in him and in ye, because the darkness is passed and the true light already/now shines.
2.9 The (one) saying to be in the light and hating his
brother is a liar and he is in the darkness until now.
2.10 The (one) loving his brother abides in the light,
and an offense is not in him;   2.11 but the (one)
hating his brother is in the darkness and he walks in
the dark-ness, and he knows not where he goes, because
the darkness blinded his eyes.

2.12 I write to ye, little children, because for
ye the faults/sins have been forgiven through his
name,   2.13 I write to ye, fathers, because ye have
known the (one) from the beginning. I write to ye,
young (ones), because ye have overcome the evil
(thing).

2.14 I wrote to ye, children, because ye have
known the father. I wrote to ye, fathers, because ye
have known the (one) from the beginning. I wrote to
ye, young (ones) because ye are strong (ones) and the
logos/word of God abides in ye and ye have overcome
the evil (one).   2.15 Ye may love not the world nor
the (things) in the world. If anyone loves the world,
the agape of the father is not in him,   2.16 because
every thing in the world, the desire of the flesh, and
the desire of the eyes and the pride of the *means/
goods of* life, is not from the father but it is from
the world.   2.17 And the world is passing by and the
desire of it, but the (one) doing the will of God
abides into the age.

2.18 Children, it is a last hour, and as ye
heard that an antichrist comes, even now many anti-
christs have become; from which we know that it is a
last hour.

2.19 They went out from us, but they were not of
us; for if they were of us, they would have remained

ἦσαν ἐξ ἡμῶν, μεμενήκισαν ἂν μεθ᾽ ἡμῶν· ἀλλ᾽ ἵνα φανερωθῶσιν ὅτι οὐκ εἰσὶν πάντες ἐξ ἡμῶν. 2.20 καὶ ὑμῖς χρῖσμα ἔχετε ἀπὸ τοῦ ἁγίου, καὶ οἴδαται πάντες. 2.21 οὐκ ἔγραψα ὑμῖν ὅτι οὐκ οἴδατε τὴν ἀλήθιαν, ἀλλ᾽ ὅτι οἴδαται αὐτήν, καὶ ὅτι πᾶν ψεῦδος ἐκ τῆς ἀληθίας οὐκ ἔστιν. 2.22 τίς ἐστιν ὁ ψεύστης εἰ μὴ ὁ ἀρνούμενος ὅτι Ἰησοῦς οὐκ ἔστιν ὁ χριστός; οὗτός ἐστιν ὁ ἀντίχριστος, ὁ ἀρνούμενος τὸν πατέρα καὶ τὸν υἱόν. 2.23 πᾶς ὁ ἀρνούμενος τὸν υἱὸν οὐδὲ τὸν πατέρα ἔχει· ὁ ὁμολογῶν τὸν υἱὸν καὶ τὸν πατέρα ἔχει. 2.24 ὑμῖς ὃ ἀκηκόατε ἀπ᾽ ἀρχῆς ἐν ὑμῖν μενέτω· ἐὰν ἐν ὑμῖν μίνῃ ὃ ἀκηκόατε ἀπ᾽ ἀρχῆς, καὶ ὑμῖς ἐν τῷ πατρὶ καὶ ἐν τῷ υἱῷ μενεῖτε. 2.25 καὶ αὕτη ἐστὶν ἡ ἐπαγγελία ἣν αὐτὸς ἐπηγγίλατο ἡμῖν, τὴν ζωὴν τὴν αἰώνιον. 2.26 ταῦτα δὲ ἔγραψα ὑμῖν περὶ τῶν πλανώντων ὑμᾶς. 2.27 καὶ ὑμῖς τὸ χρῖσμα ὃ ἐλάβετε ἀπ᾽ αὐτοῦ μένει ἐν ὑμῖν, καὶ οὐ χρίαν ἔχετε ἵνα τις διδάσκῃ ὑμᾶς· ἀλλ᾽ ὡς τὸ αὐτοῦ χρῖσμα πνεῦμα διδάσκει ὑμᾶς περὶ πάντων, καὶ ἀληθῆς ἐστιν καὶ οὐκ ἔστιν ψεῦδος, καὶ καθὼς ἐδίδαξεν ὑμᾶς, μένετε ἐν αὐτῷ. 2.28 --, ἵνα ἐὰν φανερωθῇ σχῶμεν παρρησίαν καὶ μὴ αἰσχυνθῶμεν ἐν τῇ παρουσίᾳ αὐτοῦ ἀπ᾽ αὐτοῦ.

2.29 ἐὰν εἰδῆτε ὅτι δίκαιός ἐστιν, γινώσκετε ὅτι καὶ πᾶς ὁ ποιῶν τὴν δικαιοσύνην ἐξ αὐτοῦ γεγέννηται. 3.1 εἴδετε ποταπὴν ἀγάπην δέδωκεν ἡμῖν ὁ πατὴρ ἵνα τέκνα θεοῦ κληθῶμεν· καὶ ἐσμέν. διὰ τοῦτο ὁ κόσμος οὐ γινώσκει ἡμᾶς ὅτι οὐκ ἔγνω αὐτόν.

3.2 ἀγαπητοί, νῦν τέκνα θεοῦ ἐσμεν, καὶ οὔπω ἐφανερώθη τί ἐσόμεθα. οἴδαμεν ὅτι ἐὰν φανερωθῇ ὅμοιοι αὐτῷ ἐσόμεθα, ὅτι ὀψόμεθα αὐτὸν καθὼς ἐστιν. 3.3 καὶ πᾶς ὁ ἔχων τὴν ἐλπίδα ταύτην ἐπ᾽ αὐτῷ ἁγνίζι ἑαυτὸν καθὼς ἐκῖνος ἁγνός ἐστιν. 3.4 πᾶς ὁ ποιῶν τὴν ἁμαρτίαν καὶ τὴν ἀνομίαν ποιεῖ, καὶ ἡ ἁμαρτία ἐστὶν ἡ ἀνομία. 3.5 καὶ οἴδαμεν ὅτι ἐκεῖνος ἐφανερώθη ἵνα τὰς ἁμαρτίας ἡμῶν ἄρῃ, καὶ ἁμαρτία οὐκ ἔστιν ἐν αὐτῷ. 3.6 πᾶς ὁ ἐν αὐτῷ μένων οὐχ ἁμαρτάνι· πᾶς ὁ ἁμαρτάνων οὐχ

with us; but *they went* in order that it might be clear that all were not of us. 2.20 And ye, ye have an anointing from the holy (one), and all *them* ye know. 2.21 I wrote not to ye because ye know not the truth, but because ye know it, and because every lie is not from the truth. 2.22 Who is the liar except the (one) denying that Jesus is not the anointed (one)? This (one) is the antichrist, the (one) denying the father and the son. 2.23 Every one denying the son neither has the father; the (one) confessing the son has also the father. 2.24 What ye, ye heard from the beginning, let it abide in ye; if what ye heard from the beginning, might abide in ye; ye, ye will abide both in the father and in the son. 2.25 And this is the promise which he, he promised to us: The eternal life. 2.26 But I wrote these (things) to ye concerning those deceiving ye. 2.27 And ye, the anointing which ye received from him abides in ye, and ye have not a need that anyone *else* should teach ye; but as the anointing from his spirit teaches ye; concerning all (things), it is both true and is not a lie, and according as it taught ye, abide ye in him/by it, 2.28 --, in order that if it be made clear we might have courage and we should not be ashamed of/from it in/at his coming/advent.

2.29 If ye may have known that he is just, know ye that also every one doing the justness/justice has been generated from him. 3.1 See ye what kind of agape the father has given to us that we might be called children of God; and we are. Because of this the world knows not us, because it knew not him.

3.2 Beloved (ones), we are now children of God, but it was not yet made clear what we shall be. We know that if it were made clear, we shall be like him, because we shall view him as he is. 3.3 And every one having this hope upon him purifies himself as that (one) is pure. 3.4 Every one making the fault/sin makes also the lawlessness, and the sin is the lawlessness. 3.5 And we know that that (one) was manifested in order that he might take up our sins, but there is not a sin in him. 3.6 Every one abiding in him sins not continually; every one sinning continual-

ἑώρακεν αὐτὸν οὐδὲ ἔγνωκεν αὐτόν.

3.7 τεκνία, μηδεὶς πλανάτω ὑμᾶς· ὁ ποιῶν τὴν δικαιοσύνην δίκαιός ἐστιν, καθὼς ἐκεῖνος δίκαιός ἐστιν· 3.8 ὁ ποιῶν τὴν ἁμαρτίαν ἐκ τοῦ διαβόλου ἐστίν, ὅτι ἀπ’ ἀρχῆς ὁ διάβολος ἁμαρτάνι. εἰς τοῦτο ἐφανερώθη ὁ υἱὸς τοῦ θεοῦ, ἵνα λύσῃ τὰ ἔργα τοῦ διαβόλου. 3.9 πᾶς ὁ γεγεννημένος ἐκ τοῦ θεοῦ ἁμαρτίαν οὐ ποιεῖ, ὅτι σπέρμα αὐτοῦ ἐν αὐτῷ μένει· καὶ οὐ δύναται ἁμαρτάνιν, ὅτι ἐκ τοῦ θεοῦ γεγέννηται. 3.10 ἐν τούτῳ φανερά ἐστιν τὰ τέκνα τοῦ θεοῦ καὶ τὰ τέκνα τοῦ διαβόλου· πᾶς ὁ μὴ ποιῶν δικεοσύνην οὐκ ἔστιν ἐκ τοῦ θεοῦ, καὶ ὁ μὴ ἀγαπῶν τὸν ἀδελφὸν αὐτοῦ. 3.11 ὅτι αὕτη ἐστὶν ἡ ἐπαγγελία ἣν ἠκούσαται ἀπ’ ἀρχῆς, ἵνα ἀγαπῶμεν ἀλλήλους· 3.12 οὐ καθὼς Κάϊν ἐκ τοῦ πονηροῦ ἦν καὶ ἔσφαξεν τὸν ἀδελφὸν αὐτοῦ· καὶ χάριν τίνος ἔσφαξεν αὐτόν; ὅτι τὰ ἔργα αὐτοῦ πονηρὰ ἦν, τὰ δὲ τοῦ ἀδελφοῦ αὐτοῦ δίκαια. 3.13 καὶ μὴ θαυμάζετε, ἀδελφοί, εἰ μισῖ ὑμᾶς ὁ κόσμος. 3.14 ἡμεῖς οἴδαμεν ὅτι μεταβεβήκεν ἐκ τοῦ θανάτου εἰς τὴν ζωήν, ὅτι ἀγαπῶμεν τοὺς ἀδελφούς ἡμῶν· ὁ μὴ ἀγαπῶν μένει ἐν τῷ θανάτῳ. 3.15 πᾶς ὁ μισῶν τὸν ἀδελφὸν αὐτοῦ ἀνθρωποκτόνος ἐστίν, καὶ οἴδατε ὅτι πᾶς ἀνθρωποκτόνος οὐκ ἔχει ζωὴν αἰώνιον ἐν ἑαυτῷ μένουσαν. 3.16 ἐν τούτῳ ἐγνώκαμεν τὴν ἀγάπην, ὅτι ἐκεῖνος ὑπὲρ ἡμῶν τὴν ψυχὴν αὐτοῦ ἔθηκεν· καὶ ἡμῖς ὀφείλομεν ὑπὲρ τῶν ἀδελφῶν τὰς ψυχὰς θεῖναι. 3.17 ὃς δ’ ἂν ἔχῃ τὸν βίον τοῦ κόσμου καὶ θεωρῇ τὸν ἀδελφὸν αὐτοῦ χρίαν ἔχοντα καὶ κλίσῃ τὰ σπλάγχνα αὐτοῦ ἀπ’ αὐτοῦ, πῶς ἡ ἀγάπη τοῦ θεοῦ μένει ἐν αὐτῷ;

3.18 τεκνία, μὴ ἀγαπῶμεν λόγῳ καὶ γλώσσῃ ἀλλὰ ἐν ἔργῳ καὶ ἀληθίᾳ. 3.19 καὶ ἐν τούτῳ γνωσόμεθα ὅτι ἐκ τῆς ἀληθείας ἐσμέν, καὶ ἔκπροσθεν αὐτοῦ πείσομεν τὰς καρδίας ἡμῶν 3.20 ὅτι ἐὰν καταγινώσκῃ ἡμῶν ἡ καρδία, ὅτι μείζων ἐστὶν ὁ θεὸς τῆς καρδίας ἡμῶν καὶ γινώσκι πάντα.

3.21 ἀγαπητοί, ἐὰν ἡ καρδία ἡμῶν μὴ καταγινώσκῃ ἡμῶν, παρρησίαν ἔχομεν πρὸς τὸν θεόν, 3.22 καὶ ὃ ἐὰν αἰτώμεθα

ly has not seen him nor has he known him.

3.7 Little children, let no one deceive ye; the (one) doing the justness/justice is just, even as that (one) is just. 3.8 The (one) making/doing the fault/sin is from the devil, because from the beginning the devil continually sins. In this (thing) the son of God was manifested, in order that he might destroy the works of the devil. 3.9 Every one having been generated from God makes not a sin, because his seed abides in him; and he is not able to sin, because he has been generated from God. 3.10 By this (thing) are the children of God clear, also the children of the devil; every one doing not justice is not of God, also the (one) not loving his brother. 3.11 Because this is the promise/message which ye heard from the beginning, that we should love one another; 3.12 not as Cain was out of the evil (one) and slew his brother; and for the sake of what he slew him? Because his works were evil, but those of his brother *were* just. 3.13 And wonder/marvel ye not, brothers, if the world hates ye. 3.14 We, we know that we have passed from the death into the life, because we love our brothers; the one not loving remains in the death. 3.15 Every one hating his brother is a man-killer, and ye know that every man-killer has not eternal life abiding in himself. 3.16 By this (thing) we have known the agape, because that (one) in behalf of us put down his life; and we, we owe it in behalf of the brothers to put *down* the lives *our own*. 3.17 And who ever may have the goods/means of life from the world and may behold his brother having a need and might shut his compassions from him, how abides the agape of God in him?

3.18 Little children, we may not love by a word/logos and a language but be work and truth. 3.19 And by this (thing) we shall know that we are from the truth, and from before him we shall persuade our hearts 3.20 that if our hearts condemn (us) that God is greater than our heart and he knows all (things). 3.21 Beloved (ones), if our heart may not condemn us, we have a confidence with/boldness toward God, 3.22 and what ever we may be asking we receive from him,

λαμβάνομεν ἀπ᾽ αὐτοῦ, ὅτι τὰς ἐντολὰς αὐτοῦ τηρῶμεν καὶ τὰ ἀρεστὰ ἐνώπιον αὐτοῦ ποιοῦμεν. 3.23 καὶ αὕτη ἐστὶν ἡ ἐντολὴ αὐτοῦ, ἵνα πιστεύσωμεν τῷ ὀνόματι τοῦ υἱοῦ αὐτοῦ Ἰησοῦ χριστοῦ καὶ ἀγαπῶμεν ἀλλήλους, καθὼς ἔδωκεν ἐντολὴν ἡμῖν. 3.24 καὶ ὁ τηρῶν τὰς ἐντολὰς αὐτοῦ ἐν αὐτῷ μένει καὶ αὐτὸς ἐν αὐτῷ· καὶ ἐν τούτῳ γινώσκομεν ὅτι μένει ἐν ἡμῖν, ἐκ τοῦ πνεύματος οὗ ἔδωκεν ἡμῖν. 4.1 ἀγαπητοί, μὴ παντὶ πνεύματι πιστεύετε, ἀλλὰ δοκιμάζετε τὰ πνεύματα εἰ ἐκ τοῦ θεοῦ ἐστιν, ὅτι πολλοὶ ψευδοπροφῆται ἐξεληλύθασιν εἰς τὸν κόσμον. 4.2 ἐν τούτῳ γινώσκετε τὸ πνεῦμα τοῦ θεοῦ· πᾶν πνεῦμα ὃ ὁμολογεῖ Ἰησοῦν χριστὸν ἐν σαρκὶ ἐληλυθότα ἐκ τοῦ θεοῦ ἐστιν, 4.3 καὶ πᾶν πνεῦμα ὃ μὴ ὁμολογεῖ τὸν Ἰησοῦν χριστὸν ἐν σαρκὶ ἐληλυθότα ἐκ τοῦ θεοῦ οὐκ ἔστιν· καὶ τοῦτό ἐστιν τὸ τοῦ ἀντιχρίστου, ὅτι ἀκηκόαμεν ὅτι ἔρχεται, καὶ νῦν ἐν τῷ κόσμῳ ἐστὶν ἤδη. 4.4 ὑμεῖς ἐκ τοῦ θεοῦ ἐστε, τεκνία, καὶ νενικήκατε αὐτούς, ὅτι μείζων ἐστὶν ὁ ἐν ὑμῖν ἢ ὁ ἐν τῷ κόσμῳ. 4.5 αὐτοὶ ἐκ τοῦ κόσμου εἰσίν· διὰ τοῦτο ἐκ τοῦ κόσμου λαλοῦσιν καὶ ὁ κόσμος αὐτῶν ἀκούει. 4.6 ἡμεῖς ἐκ τοῦ θεοῦ ἐσμεν· ὁ γινώσκων τὸν θεὸν ἀκούει ἡμῶν, ὃς οὐκ ἔστιν ἐκ τοῦ θεοῦ οὐκ ἀκούει ἡμῶν. ἐκ τούτου γινώσκομεν τὸ πνεῦμα τῆς ἀληθείας καὶ τὸ πνεῦμα τῆς πλάνης. 4.7 ἀγαπητοί, ἀγαπῶμεν ἀλλήλους, ὅτι ἡ ἀγάπη ἐκ τοῦ θεοῦ ἐστιν, καὶ πᾶς ὁ ἀγαπῶν ἐκ τοῦ θεοῦ γεγέννηται καὶ γιγνώσκει τὸν θεόν. 4.8 ὁ μὴ ἀγαπῶν οὐκ ἔγνωκεν, ὅτι ὁ θεὸς ἀγάπη ἐστίν. 4.9 ἐν τούτῳ ἐφανερώθη ἡ ἀγάπη τοῦ θεοῦ ἐν ἡμῖν, ὅτι τὸν υἱὸν αὐτοῦ τὸν μονογενῆ ἀπέσταλκεν ὁ θεὸς εἰς τὸν κόσμον ἵνα ζήσωμεν δι᾽ αὐτοῦ. 4.10 ἐν τούτῳ ἐστὶν ἡ ἀγάπη τοῦ θεοῦ, οὐχ ὅτι ἡμεῖς ἠγάπησεν τὸν θεόν, ἀλλ᾽ ὅτι αὐτὸς ἠγάπησεν ἡμᾶς καὶ ἀπέσταλκεν τὸν υἱὸν αὐτοῦ ἱλασμὸν περὶ τῶν ἁμαρτιῶν ἡμῶν.

4.11 ἀγαπητοί, εἰ οὕτως ὁ θεὸς ἠγάπησεν ἡμᾶς, καὶ ἡμεῖς ὀφίλομεν ἀλλήλους ἀγαπᾶν. 4.12 θεὸν οὐδεὶς πώποτε τεθέαται· ἐὰν ἀγαπῶμεν ἀλλήλους, ὁ θεὸς ἐν ἡμῖν μένει καὶ ἡ ἀγάπη αὐτοῦ τετελειωμένη ἐν ἡμῖν ἐστιν. 4.13 ἐν τούτῳ γινώσκομεν ὅτι ἐν αὐτῷ μένομεν καὶ αὐτὸς ἐν ἡμῖν, ὅτι ἐκ τοῦ πνεύματος αὐτοῦ

because we keep his commands and we do the (things) pleasing in the sight of him. 3.23 And this is his command: That we should believe in the name of his son Jesus, the anointed (one), and we should love one another, as he gave a command to us. 3.24 And the (one) keeping the commands of him abides in him and he in him; and by this (thing) we know that he abides in us, from the spirit which he gave to us. 4.1 Beloved (ones), believe ye not every spirit, but prove/test ye the spirits if/whether they are from God, because many lying prophets have gone out into the world. 4.2 By this (thing) ye know the spirit from God: Every spirit which confesses Jesus the anointed (one) having come in flesh is from God, 4.3 and every spirit which confesses not Jesus, the anointed (one), having come in flesh is not from God; and this (spirit) is the (one) from the antichrist, because we heard that he comes, and now he is already in the world. 4.4 Ye, ye are of God, little children, and ye have overcome them, because the (one) with ye is greater than the (one) in the world. 4.5 They are of the world; because of this, they speak of the world and the world hears them. 4.6 We, we are of God: the (one) knowing God hears us; *the one* who is not of God hears not us. From this we know the spirit of the truth and the spirit of the deceit. 4.7 Beloved (ones), we should love one another, because the agape is from God, and every one loving has been generated from God and he knows God. 4.8 The (one) not loving has not known *him*, because God is agape. 4.9 By this (thing) the agape of God was made plain in us, that God has sent his only-generated son into the world in order that we might live through him. 4.10 In this is the agape of God, not that we, we loved God, but because he, he loved us and he has sent his son, a means of atonement concerning our faults/sins.

4.11 Beloved (ones), if God so loved us, we, we owe it/are obligated to love one another. 4.12 No one has ever beheld God; if we would love one another, God abides in us and the agape of him is having been completed/matured in us. 4.13 By this (thing) we know that we abide in him and he in us, because out of/from

517

δέδωκεν ἡμῖν. 4.14 καὶ ἡμεῖς τεθεάμεθα καὶ μαρτυροῦμεν ὅτι ὁ πατὴρ ἀπέσταλκεν τὸν υἱὸν σωτῆρα τοῦ κόσμου. 4.15 ὃς ἂν ὁμολογήσῃ ὅτι Ἰησοῦς ἐστιν ὁ υἱὸς τοῦ θεοῦ, ὁ θεὸς ἐν αὐτῷ μένι καὶ αὐτὸς ἐν τῷ θεῷ. 4.16 καὶ ἡμῖς ἐγνώκαμεν καὶ πεπιστεύκαμεν τὴν ἀγάπην ἣν ἔχει ὁ θεὸς ἐν ἡμῖν. ὁ θεὸς ἀγάπη ἐστίν, καὶ ὁ μένων ἐν τῇ ἀγάπῃ ἐν τῷ θεῷ μένι καὶ θεὸς ἐν αὐτῷ μένι. 4.17 ἐν τούτῳ τετελείωται ἡ ἀγάπη μεθ᾽ ἡμῶν ἐν ἡμῖν, ἵνα παρρησίαν ἔχομεν ἐν τῇ ἀγάπῃ τῆς κρίσεως, ὅτι καθὼς ἐκεῖνός ἐστιν καὶ ἡμεῖς ἐσόμεθα ἐν τῷ κόσμῳ τούτῳ. 4.18 φόβος οὐκ ἔστιν ἐν τῇ ἀγάπῃ, ἀλλ᾽ ἡ τελεία ἀγάπη ἔξω βάλλει τὸν φόβον, ὅτι ὁ φόβος κόλασιν ἔχει, ὁ δὲ φοβούμενος οὐ τετελείωται ἐν τῇ ἀγάπῃ. 4.19 ἡμῖς ἀγαπῶμεν τὸν θεόν, ὅτι αὐτὸς πρῶτος ἠγάπησεν ἡμᾶς. 4.20 ἐάν τις εἴπῃ ἀγαπῶ τὸν θεόν, καὶ τὸν ἀδελφὸν αὐτοῦ μεισῇ, ψεύστης ἐστίν· ὁ γὰρ μὴ ἀγαπῶν τὸν ἀδελφὸν αὐτοῦ ὃν ἑώρακεν, τὸν θεὸν ὃν οὐχ ἑώρακεν οὐ δύνατε ἀγαπᾶν. 4.21 καὶ ταύτην τὴν ἐντολὴν ἔχομεν ἀπ᾽ αὐτοῦ, ἵνα ὁ ἀγαπῶν τὸν θεὸν ἀγαπᾷ καὶ τὸν ἀδελφὸν αὐτοῦ. 5.1 πᾶς ὁ πιστεύων ὅτι Ἰησοῦς ἐστιν ὁ χριστὸς ἐκ τοῦ θεοῦ γεγέννηται, καὶ πᾶς ὁ ἀγαπῶν τὸν γεννήσαντα ἀγαπᾷ καὶ τὸν γεγεννημένον ἐξ αὐτοῦ. 5.2 ἐν τούτῳ γινώσκομεν ὅτι ἀγαπῶμεν τὰ τέκνα τοῦ θεοῦ, ὅταν τὸν θεὸν ἀγαπῶμεν καὶ τὰς ἐντολὰς αὐτοῦ τηρῶμεν.

5.3 αὕτη γάρ ἐστιν ἡ ἀγάπη τοῦ θεοῦ, ἵνα τὰς ἐντολὰς αὐτοῦ τηρῶμεν· καὶ αἱ ἐντολαὶ αὐτοῦ βαρεῖαι οὐκ εἰσίν, 5.4 ὅτι πᾶν τὸ γεγεννημένον ἐκ τοῦ θεοῦ νικᾷ τὸν κόσμον· καὶ αὕτη ἐστὶν ἡ νίκη ἡ νικήσασα τὸν κόσμον, ἡ πίστις ἡμῶν. 5.5 τίς δέ ἐστιν ὁ νεικῶν τὸν κόσμον εἰ μὴ ὁ πιστεύων ὅτι Ἰησοῦς ἐστιν ὁ υἱὸς τοῦ θεοῦ; 5.6 Οὗτός ἐστιν ὁ ἐλθὼν διὰ ὕδατος καὶ αἵματος καὶ πνεύματος, Ἰησοῦς χριστός· οὐκ ἐν τῷ ὕδατι μόνον ἀλλ᾽ ἐν τῷ ὕδατι καὶ ἐν τῷ αἵματι· καὶ τὸ πνεῦμά ἐστιν τὸ μαρτυροῦν, ὅτι τὸ πνεῦμά ἐστιν ἡ ἀλήθεια. 5.7 ὅτι οἱ τρεῖς εἰσιν οἱ μαρτυροῦντες, 5.8 τὸ πνεῦμα καὶ τὸ ὕδωρ καὶ τὸ αἷμα, καὶ οἱ τρεῖς εἰς τὸ ἕν εἰσιν. 5.9 εἰ τὴν μαρτυρίαν τῶν ἀνθρώπων

the spirit of him he has given to us. 4.14 And we, we have beheld and we testify that the father has sent the son, a savior of the world. 4.15 Who ever might confess that Jesus is the son of God, God abides in him and he in God. 4.16 And we, we have known and we have believed the agape which God holds in us. God is agape, and the (one) abiding in the agape abides in God and God abides in him. 4.17 In this the agape has been completed with us, in us in order that we *may* have confidence in the agape at the judgment, because even as that (one) was, also we, we shall be in this world. 4.18 Fear is not in the agape, but the mature agape throws the fear outside, because the fear has a punishment, and the (one) fearing has not been matured in the agape. 4.19 We, we love God, because he, he loved us first. 4.20 If anyone might say: I love God, but may be hating his brother, he is a liar; for the (one) not loving his brother whom he has seen, he is not able to love God whom he has seen not. 4.21 And this command we have from him, that the (one) loving God should love also his brother. 5.1 Every one believing that Jesus is the anointed (one) has been generated from God, and every one loving the (one) having been generated loves also that/the (thing) having been generated out of/from him. 5.2 By this we know that we love the children of God, when we love God and we may keep the commands from him.

5.3 For this is the agape of God, that we keep the commands from him; and the commands from him are not heavy (ones), 5.4 because every thing having been generated out of God overcomes the world; and this is the victory, the (one) overcoming the world: The faith of us/our faith. 5.5 And who is the (one) overcoming the world except the (one) believing that Jesus is the son of God? 5.6 This is the (one) coming through water and blood and spirit: Jesus, the anointed (one); not by the water only, but by the water and the blood; and the spirit is the (one) testifying, because the spirit is the truth. 5.7 Because these three are those testifying: 5.8 The spirit and the water and the blood, and these three are in the one/for the one (thing). 5.9 If we receive the testimony from the

λαμβάνομεν, ἡ μαρτυρία τοῦ θεοῦ μείζων ἐστίν, ὅτι αὕτη ἐστὶν ἡ μαρτυρία τοῦ θεοῦ, ὅτι μεμαρτύρηκεν περὶ τοῦ υἱοῦ αὐτοῦ. 5.10 ὁ πιστεύων εἰς τὸν υἱὸν τοῦ θεοῦ ἔχει τὴν μαρτυρίαν ἐν ἑαυτῷ· ὁ μὴ πιστεύων τῷ θεῷ ψεύστην πεποίηκεν αὐτόν, ὅτι οὐκ ἐπίστευκεν εἰς τὴν μαρτυρίαν ἣν μεμαρτύρηκεν ὁ θεὸς περὶ τοῦ υἱοῦ αὐτοῦ. 5.11 καὶ αὕτη ἐστὶν ἡ μαρτυρία, ὅτι ζωὴν αἰώνιον ἔδωκεν ἡμῖν ὁ θεός, καὶ αὕτη ἡ ζωὴ ἐν τῷ υἱῷ αὐτοῦ ἐστιν. 5.12 ὁ ἔχων τὸν υἱὸν ἔχει τὴν ζωήν· ὁ μὴ ἔχων τὸν υἱὸν τοῦ θεοῦ τὴν ζωὴν οὐκ ἔχει. 5.13 ταῦτα ἔγραψα ὑμῖν ἵνα εἰδῆτε ὅτι ζωὴν αἰώνιον ἔχετε, τοῖς πιστεύουσιν εἰς τὸ ὄνομα τοῦ υἱοῦ τοῦ θεοῦ. 5.14 καὶ αὕτη ἐστὶν ἡ παρρησία ἣν ἔχομεν πρὸς αὐτόν, ὅτι ἐάν τι αἰτώμεθα κατὰ τὸ θέλημα αὐτοῦ ἀκούει ἡμῶν. 5.15 καὶ ἐὰν ἴδωμεν ὅτι ἀκούει ἡμῶν ὃ ἐὰν αἰτώμεθα, οἴδαμεν ὅτι ἔχομεν τὰ αἰτήματα ἃ ᾐτήκαμεν ἀπ' αὐτοῦ.

5.16 ἐάν τις ἴδῃ τὸν ἀδελφὸν αὐτοῦ ἁμαρτάνοντα ἁμαρτίαν μὴ πρὸς θάνατον, αἰτήσι, καὶ δώσει αὐτῷ ζωήν, τοῖς ἁμαρτάνουσιν μὴ πρὸς θάνατον.

ἔστιν ἁμαρτία πρὸς θάνατον· οὐ περὶ ἐκείνης λέγω ἵνα ἐρωτήσῃ. 5.17 πᾶσα ἀδικία ἁμαρτία ἐστίν, καὶ ἔστιν ἁμαρτία οὐ πρὸς θάνατον. 5.18 οἴδαμεν ὅτι πᾶς ὁ γεγεννημένος ἐκ τοῦ θεοῦ οὐχ ἁμαρτάνι, ἀλλ' ὁ γεννηθεὶς ἐκ τοῦ θεοῦ τηρῖ αὐτόν, καὶ ὁ πονηρὸς οὐχ ἅπτεται αὐτοῦ. 5.19 οἴδαμεν ὅτι ἐκ τοῦ θεοῦ ἐσμεν, καὶ ὁ κόσμος ὅλος ἐν τῷ πονηρῷ κεῖται. 5.20 οἴδαμεν δὲ ὅτι ὁ υἱὸς τοῦ θεοῦ ἥκει, καὶ δέδωκεν ἡμῖν διάνοιαν ἵνα γινώσκομεν τὸν ἀληθινόν· καὶ ἐσμὲν ἐν τῷ ἀληθινῷ, ἐν τῷ υἱῷ αὐτοῦ Ἰησοῦ χριστῷ. οὗτός ἐστιν ὁ ἀληθινὸς θεὸς καὶ ζωὴ αἰώνιος. 5.21 τεκνία, φυλάξατε ἑαυτὰ ἀπὸ τῶν εἰδώλων.

Ἰωάννου Α΄

men/humans, the testimony from God is greater, because this is the testimony from God: that he has testified about his son. 5.10 The (one) believing in the son of God has the testimony in him; the (one) not believing in God has made him a liar, because he has believed not in the testimony which God testified about his son. 5.11 And this is the testimony: That God gave eternal life to us, and this is the life in the son of him. 5.12 The (one) having the son has the life; the (one) not having the son of God has not the life. 5.13 These (things) I wrote to ye that ye may know that ye have life eternal, for those believing in the name of the son of God. 5.14 And this is the confidence which we have toward him, that if we may ask anything according to his will, he hears us. 5.15 And if we might know that he hears us, what ever we may ask, we know that we have/hold the requests which we have asked from him.

5.16 If anyone might see his brother sinning a sin not toward/to death, let him ask, and he will give to him life, to those sinning not toward/to death.

There is a sin toward/to death; I speak not concerning that (one) that he might question/ask. 5.17 Every injustice is a fault/sin, and a fault/sin is not toward/to death. 5.18 We know that every one having been generated from God sins not, but the (one) being generated from God keeps himself, and the evil (one) takes not hold of him. 5.19 We know that we are from God, and the whole world is reclined by the evil (one). 5.20 And we know that the son of God is come, and he has given to us a mind that we know the true (one); and we are in the true (one), in his son Jesus, the anointed (one). This (one) is the true God and life eternal. 5.21 Little children, guard/keep ye yourselves from the idols.

From John 1

This is the Sinaitic New Testament, book of 2 John.

1.1 Ὁ πρεσβύτερος ἐκλεκτῇ κυρίᾳ καὶ τοῖς τέκνοις αὐτῆς, οὓς ἐγὼ ἀγαπῶ ἐν ἀληθίᾳ, καὶ οὐκ ἐγὼ μόνος ἀλλὰ καὶ πάντες οἱ ἐγνωκότες τὴν ἀλήθειαν, 1.2 διὰ τὴν ἀλήθειαν τὴν μένουσαν ἐν ἡμῖν, καὶ μεθ' ἡμῶν ἔσται εἰς τὸν αἰῶνα. 1.3 ἔσται μεθ' ἡμῶν χάρις ἔλεος εἰρήνη παρὰ θεοῦ πατρός, καὶ παρὰ κυρίου Ἰησοῦ χριστοῦ τοῦ υἱοῦ τοῦ πατρός, ἐν ἀληθείᾳ καὶ ἀγάπῃ. 1.4 ἐχάρην λίαν ὅτι εὕρηκα ἐκ τῶν τέκνων σου περιπατοῦντας ἐν ἀληθείᾳ, καθὼς ἐντολὴν ἐλάβον παρὰ τοῦ πατρός. 1.5 καὶ νῦν ἐρωτῶ σε, κυρία, οὐχ ὡς ἐντολὴν καινὴν γράφων σοι ἀλλὰ ἐντολὴν ἣν εἴχομεν ἀπ' ἀρχῆς, ἵνα ἀγαπῶμεν ἀλλήλους. 1.6 καὶ αὕτη ἐστὶν ἡ ἀγάπη, ἵνα περιπατῶμεν κατὰ τὰς ἐντολὰς αὐτοῦ· ἵνα αὕτη καθὼς ἐστιν ἡ ἐντο αὐτοῦ, ἵνα καθὼς ἠκούσατε ἀπ' ἀρχῆς, ἵνα ἐν αὐτῇ περιπατήσητε. 1.7 ὅτι πολλοὶ πλάνοι ἐξῆλθον εἰς τὸν κόσμον, οἱ μὴ ὁμολογοῦντες Ἰησοῦν χριστὸν ἐρχόμενον ἐν σαρκί· οὗτός ἐστιν ὁ πλάνος κ' ἀντίχριστος. 1.8 βλέπετε ἑαυτούς, ἵνα μὴ ἀπολέσητε ἃ εἰργάσασθαι ἀλλὰ μισθὸν πλήρη ἀπολάβητε. 1.9 πᾶς ὁ προάγων καὶ μὴ μένων καὶ μὴ ἐν τῇ διδαχῇ τοῦ χριστοῦ θεὸν οὐκ ἔχει· ὁ μένων ἐν τῇ διδαχῇ, οὗτος καὶ τὸν πατέρα καὶ τὸν υἱὸν ἔχει. 1.10 εἴ τις ἔρχεται πρὸς ὑμᾶς καὶ ταύτην τὴν διδαχὴν οὐ φέρι, μὴ λαμβάνετε αὐτὸν εἰς οἰκίαν καὶ χαίρειν αὐτῷ μὴ λέγετε· 1.11 ὁ λέγων γὰρ αὐτῷ χαίρειν κοινωνεῖ τοῖς ἔργοις αὐτοῦ τοῖς πονηροῖς. 1.12 πολλὰ ἔχων ὑμῖν γράφειν οὐκ ἐβουλήθην διὰ χάρτου καὶ μέλανος, ἀλλὰ ἐλπίζω γενέσθαι πρὸς ὑμᾶς καὶ στόματι πρὸς στόμα λαλῆσαι, ἵνα ἡ χαρὰ ἡμῶν πεπληρωμένη ᾖ. 1.13 ἀσπάζετε σε τὰ τέκνα τῆς ἀδελφῆς σου τῆς ἐκλεκτῆς.

Ἰωάννου Β΄

1.1   The elder to an elect lady and to her children, whom I, I love in truth, and not I alone but also all those having known the truth,   1.2 because of the truth, the (one) abiding in us, and it will be with us into the age.   1.3   Grace, mercy, peace will be with us from God *the* father, and from *the* Lord Jesus, the anointed (one), the son of the father, in truth and agape. 1.4 I rejoiced greatly because I have found those of your children walking in truth, according to a command we received from the father. 1.5 And now I ask you, lady, not as writing a new command to you, but a command which we had from *the* beginning, that we should love one another.   1.6 And this is the agape, that we should walk according to the commands of him; that this is as his command, that even as ye heard from *the* beginning, that in this we should walk.   1.7 Because many deceivers went out into the world, those not confessing Jesus, the anointed (one), coming in flesh; this is the deceiver and antichrist.   1.8 Ye see of yourselves, that ye might not lose *that* which ye worked, but a full reward ye might receive.   1.9 Every one going forward and remaining not, even not in the teaching of the anointed (one), has not God; the (one) abiding in the teaching/doctrine, this (one) has both the father and the son.   1.10 If anyone comes to us and brings not this, the teaching/doctrine, ye receive him not into a house and ye say not to him to rejoice/speak not to greet for him;   1.11 for the (one) saying to him to rejoice shares in common the evil works of him.   1.12 Having many things to write to you, I purposed not through grass/paper and ink, but I hope to become with you and to speak mouth to mouth, that our joy, having been fulfilled, may be.   1.13 The children of your sister, the elect (woman), greets you.

From John 2

This is the Sinaitic New Testament, book of 3 John.

1.1 Ὁ πρεσβύτερος Γαΐῳ τῷ ἀγαπητῷ, ὃν ἐγὼ ἀγαπῶ ἐν ἀληθίᾳ. 1.2 ἀγαπητέ, περὶ πάντων εὔχομέ σε εὐοδοῦσθε καὶ ὑγιαίνειν, καθὼς εὐοδοῦταί σου ἡ ψυχή. 1.3 ἐχάρην λίαν ἐρχομένων ἀδελφῶν καὶ μαρτυρούντων σου τῇ ἀληθείᾳ, καθὼς σὺ ἐν ἀληθείᾳ περιπατεῖς. 1.4 μιζοτέραν τούτων οὐκ ἔχω χαράν, ἵνα ἀκούω τὰ ἐμὰ τέκνα ἐν ἀληθείᾳ περιπατοῦντα. 1.5 ἀγαπητέ, πιστὸν ποιεῖς ὃ ἐὰν ἐργάσῃ εἰς τοὺς ἀδελφοὺς καὶ τοῦτο ξένους, 1.6 οἳ ἐμαρτύρησάν σου τῇ ἀγάπῃ ἐνώπιον ἐκκλησίας, οὓς καλῶς ποιήσεις προπέμψας ἀξίως τοῦ θεοῦ· 1.7 ὑπὲρ γὰρ τοῦ ὀνόματος ἐξῆλθαν μηδὲν λαμβάνοντες ἀπὸ τῶν ἐθνικῶν. 1.8 ἡμεῖς οὖν ὀφίλομεν ὑπολαμβάνιν τοὺς τοιούτους, ἵνα συνεργοὶ γινώμεθα τῇ ἐκ ἀληθείᾳ. 1.9 ἔγραψά τι τῇ ἐκκλησίᾳ· ἀλλ' ὁ φιλοπρωτεύων αὐτῶν Διοτρέφης οὐκ ἐπιδέχεται ἡμᾶς. 1.10 διὰ τοῦτο, ἐὰν ἔλθω, ὑπομνήσω αὐτοῦ τὰ ἔργα ἃ ποιεῖ, λόγοις πονηροῖς φλοιαρῶν ἡμᾶς· καὶ μὴ ἀρκούμενος ἐπὶ τούτοις οὔτε αὐτὸς ἐπιδέχετε τοὺς ἀδελφοὺς καὶ τοὺς βουλομένους κωλύει καὶ τῆς ἐκκλησίας ἐκβάλλει. 1.11 ἀγαπητέ, μὴ μιμοῦ τὸ κακὸν ἀλλὰ τὸ ἀγαθόν. ὁ ἀγαθοποιῶν ἐκ τοῦ θεοῦ ἐστιν· ὁ κακοποιῶν οὐχ ἑώρακεν τὸν θεόν. 1.12 Δημητρίῳ μεμαρτύρηται ὑπὸ πάντων καὶ ὑπὸ αὐτῆς τῆς ἀληθίας· καὶ ἡμεῖς δὲ μαρτυροῦμεν, καὶ οἶδας ὅτι ἡ μαρτυρία ἡμῶν ἀληθής ἐστιν. 1.13 πολλὰ εἶχον γράψαι σοι, ἀλλ' οὐ θέλω διὰ μέλανος καὶ καλάμου σοι γράφειν· 1.14 ἐλπίζω δὲ εὐθέως ἰδεῖν σε, καὶ στόμα πρὸς στόμα λαλήσαμεν. 1.15 εἰρήνη σοι. ἀσπάζονταί σε οἱ φίλοι. ἀσπάσαι τοὺς φίλους κατ' ὄνομα.

1.1 The elder to Gaius the beloved, whom I, I love in truth. 1.2 Beloved (one), concerning all (things), I wish *for* you to succeed and to be healthy, even as your life/soul succeeds. 1.3 I rejoiced greatly from brothers coming and testifying of you in the truth, just as you, you walk in truth. 1.4 I have not a joy greater than these (things), that I hear *about* my children walking in truth. 1.5 Beloved (one), what ever you may work, you do faithfully to the brothers and this (thing) to strangers, 1.6 which they witness of you in the agape before an assembly, whom you will do well sending forward worthily from God; 1.7 for in behalf of the name they went out, taking nothing from the ethnics. 1.8 Therefore, we are obligated to welcome such as them in order that we may become co-workers for the truth. 1.9 I wrote something to the assembly, but the (one) of them loving to be first, Deotrephes, receives us not. 1.10 Because of this, if I may come, I shall remember his works that he does, prating *on* us with evil reasonings/words; and not being satisfied on these, he himself receives not the brothers; he even forbids those being willing and puts *them* out of the assembly. 1.11 O beloved, imitate not the bad but the good. The (one) doing good is from God; the one doing evil has not seen God. 1.12 Demetrius has been witnessed by all and by the truth herself/*itself*; and we, we also testify, and you know that our testimony is true. 1.13 I had many (things) to write to you, but I wish not through ink and pen to write to you; 1.14 but I hope to see you soon, and we shall speak mouth to mouth. 1.15 Peace *be* to you. The friends greet you. Greet the friends by name.

From John 3

This is the Sinaitic New Testament, book of Jude.

1.1 Ἰούδας Ἰησοῦ χριστοῦ δοῦλος, ἀδελφὸς δὲ Ἰακώβου, τοῖς ἐν θεῷ πατρὶ ἠγαπημένοις καὶ Ἰησοῦ χριστῷ τετηρημένοις κλητοῖς· 1.2 ἔλεος ὑμῖν καὶ εἰρήνη καὶ ἀγάπη πληθυνοί ῇ. 1.3 ἀγαπητοί,

πᾶσαν σπουδὴν ποιούμενος τοῦ γράφειν ὑμῖν περὶ τῆς κοινῆς ἡμῶν σωτηρίας καὶ ζωῆς ἀνάγκην ἔσχον γράφιν ὑμῖν παρακαλῶν ἐπαγωνίζεσθαι τῇ ἅπαξ παραδοθείσῃ τοῖς ἁγίοις πίστι. 1.4 παρεισέδυσαν γάρ τινες ἄνθρωποι, οἱ καὶ πάλαι προγεγραμμένοι εἰς τοῦτο τὸ κρίμα, ἀσεβεῖς, τὴν τοῦ θεοῦ ἡμῶν χάριν μετατιθέντες εἰς ἀσέλγιαν καὶ τὸν μόνον δεσπότην καὶ κύριον ἡμῶν Ἰησοῦν χριστὸν ἀρνούμενοι. 1.5 ὑπομνῆσαι δὲ ὑμᾶς βούλομαι, εἰδότας ὑμᾶς πάντα, ὅτι κύριος ἅπαξ λαὸν ἐκ γῆς Αἰγύπτου σώσας τὸ δεύτερον τοὺς μὴ πιστεύσαντας ἀπώλεσεν, 1.6 ἀγγέλους τε τοὺς μὴ τηρήσαντας τὴν ἑαυτῶν ἀρχὴν ἀλλὰ ἀπολιπόντας τὸ ἴδιον οἰκητήριον εἰς κρίσιν μεγάλης ἡμέρας δεσμοῖς ἀϊδίοις ὑπὸ ζόφον τετήρηκεν· 1.7 ὡς Σόδομα καὶ Γόμορρα καὶ αἱ περὶ αὐτὰς πόλεις, τὸν ὅμοιον τρόπον τούτοις ἐκπορνεύσασαι καὶ ἀπελθοῦσαι ὀπίσω σαρκὸς ἑτέρας, πρόκινται δεδῖγμα πυρὸς αἰωνίου δίκην οὐκ ἔχουσιν. 1.8 ὁμοίως μέντοι καὶ οὗτοι ἐνυπνιαζόμενοι σάρκα μὲν μιαίνουσιν, κυριότητας δὲ ἀθετοῦσιν, δόξας δὲ βλασφημοῦσιν. 1.9 ὁ δὲ Μιχαὴλ ὁ ἀρχάγγελος, ὅτε τῷ διαβόλῳ διακρινόμενος διελέγετο περὶ τοῦ Μωϋσέως σώματος, οὐκ ἐτόλμησεν κρίσιν ἐπενεγκεῖν βλασφημίας, ἀλλ᾽ εἶπεν, ἐπιτιμήσαι σοι ὁ κύριος.

1.10 οὗτοι δὲ ὅσα μὲν οὐκ οἴδασιν βλασφημοῦσιν, ὅσα δὲ φυσικῶς ὡς τὰ ἄλογα ζῷα ἐπίστανται, ἐν τούτοις φθείρονται. 1.11 οὐαὶ αὐτοῖς, ὅτι τῇ ὁδῷ τοῦ Κάϊν ἐπορεύθησαν, καὶ τῇ πλάνῃ τοῦ Βαλαὰμ μισθοῦ ἐξεχύθησαν, καὶ τῇ ἀντιλογίᾳ τοῦ Κόρε ἀπώλοντο. 1.12 οὗτοί εἰσιν οἱ ἐν ταῖς ἀγάπαις ὑμῶν σπιλάδες συνευωχούμενοι ἀφόβως, ἑαυτοὺς ποιμαίνοντες, νεφέλαι

1.1 Jude, a slave of Jesus the anointed (one), and a brother of James, to the called (ones) having been loved by God *the* father and having been kept for Jesus the anointed (one).   1.2 Mercy to ye, may both peace and agape be multiplied.   1.3 Truly beloved (ones),

making all haste of the (thing) to write to ye concerning our common salvation and life, I had a necessity to write to ye appealing *to ye* to contend for the faith once having been delivered to the saints.   1.4 For certain men crept in, even those long ago having been pre-written into this judgment, impious (ones), perverting the grace of our God into wantonness and denying our only master and Lord, Jesus the anointed (one).   1.5 But I purpose to remind ye, ye having known all, that *the* Lord once having saved a people out of *the* land of Egypt, the second (thing): He destroyed the (ones) not believing,   1.6 and *for* angels, the (ones) not having kept their position but having left from their assigned dwelling, he has kept under gloom in everlasting bonds to a judgment of a great day;   1.7 even as Sodom and Gomorra and the cities around them, *in* the like manner to those being given to prostitution and going away after different flesh, but they are set forth *as* an example: Have they not a sentence of eternal fire?   1.8 Likewise, truly, these dreaming (men) also defile flesh, and they despise lordships, and they revile dignitaries. 1.9 But the archangel Michael, when reasoning with the devil he was contending about the body of Moses, he presumed not to bring upon a judgment of reproach, but he said: May the Lord rebuke to you.

1.10   And these (men) indeed revile what they know not, but what they understand naturally as the animals without reason, by these (things) they are corrupted.   1.11 Woe to them, because they went on the road of Cain, and they were abandoned to the error of the reward of Balaam and they perished in the dispute of Korah.   1.12 These (men) are grumblers, fault-finders, those going according to their *own* desires, the reefs in your love feasts, feasting together fearlessly, feeding themselves, clouds without water,

ἄνυδροι πάντι ἀνέμῳ παραφερόμεναι, δένδρα φθινοπωρινὰ ἄκαρπα δὶς ἀποθανόντα ἐκριζωθέντα, 1.13 ἄγρια κύματα θαλάσσης ἐπαφρίζοντα τὰς ἑαυτῶν αἰσχύνας, ἀστέρες πλανῆται οἷς ὁ ζόφος τοῦ σκότους εἰς αἰῶνα τετήρηται. 1.14 προεπροφήτευσεν δὲ καὶ τούτοις ἕβδομος ἀπὸ Ἀδὰμ Ἐνὼχ λέγων, ἰδοὺ ἦλθεν ὁ κύριος ἐν μυριάσιν ἁγίων ἀγγέλων, 1.15 ποιῆσαι κρίσιν κατὰ πάντων καὶ ἐλέγξαι πᾶσαν ψυχὴν περὶ πάντων τῶν ἔργων ὧν ἠσέβησαν καὶ περὶ πάντων τῶν σκληρῶν λόγων ὧν ἐλάλησαν κατ' αὐτοῦ ἁμαρτωλοὶ ἀσεβεῖς. 1.16 οὗτοί εἰσιν γογγυσταί, μεμψίμυροι, κατὰ τὰς ἐπιθυμίας ἑαυτῶν πορευόμενοι, καὶ τὸ στόμα αὐτῶν λαλεῖ ὑπέρογκα, θαυμάζοντες πρόσωπα ὠφελείας χάριν.

1.17 ὑμεῖς δέ, ἀγαπητοί, μνήσθητε τῶν ῥημάτων τῶν προειρημένων ὑπὸ τῶν ἀποστόλων τοῦ κυρίου ἡμῶν Ἰησοῦ χριστοῦ· 1.18 ὅτι ἔλεγον ὑμῖν Ἐπ' ἐσχάτου τοῦ χρόνου ἔσονται ἐμπῑκται κατὰ τὰς ἐπιθυμίας ἑαυτῶν πορευόμενοι τῶν ἀσεβειῶν. 1.19 οὗτοί εἰσιν οἱ ἀποδιορίζοντες, ψυχικοί, πνεῦμα μὴ ἔχοντες. 1.20 ὑμεῖς δέ, ἀγαπητοί, ἐποικοδομοῦντες ἑαυτοὺς τῇ ἁγιωτάτῃ ὑμῶν πίστι, ἐν πνεύματι ἁγίῳ προσευχόμενοι, 1.21 ἑαυτοὺς ἐν ἀγάπῃ θεοῦ τηρήσατε, προσδεχόμενοι τὸ ἔλεος τοῦ κυρίου ἡμῶν Ἰησοῦ χριστοῦ εἰς ζωὴν αἰώνιον.

1.22 καὶ οὓς μὲν ἐλεᾶτε διακρινομένους, 1.23 οὓς δὲ σώζετε ἐκ πυρὸς ἁρπάζοντες, οὓς δὲ ἐλεᾶτε ἐν φόβῳ, μισοῦντες καὶ τὸν ἀπὸ τῆς σαρκὸς ἐσπιλωμένον χιτῶνα. 1.24 τῷ δὲ δυναμένῳ φυλάξαι ὑμᾶς ἀπτέστους καὶ στῆσαι κατενώπιον τῆς δόξης αὐτοῦ ἀμώμους ἐν ἀγαλλιάσι, 1.25 μόνῳ θεῷ σωτῆρι ἡμῶν διὰ Ἰησοῦ χριστοῦ τοῦ κυρίου ἡμῶν δόξα μεγαλωσύνη κράτος καὶ ἐξουσία πρὸ παντὸς τοῦ αἰῶνος καὶ νῦν καὶ εἰς τοὺς αἰῶνας· ἀμήν.

being carried along by every wind, autumn trees without fruits, dying twice, having been uprooted, 1.13 wild waves of a sea foaming upon the disgraces of themselves, straying stars for whom the gloom of the darkness has been kept in/for an age. 1.14 And even Enoch, a seventh (one) from Adam, prophesied to these (men) saying: Behold, the Lord came with myriads of holy messengers/angels, 1.15 to do/make judgment upon all and to reprove every soul about all the works which they impiously/irreverently did and concerning all the hard things which impious sinners spoke against him. 1.16 These (men) are grumblers, fault-finders, going according to the desires of themselves, and the mouth of them speaks boastful things, faces marveling for the sake of gain/profit.

1.17 But ye, beloved, be ye mindful of the words having been spoken before by the apostles of our Lord Jesus, the anointed (one); 1.18 because they said to ye at the last of time *there* will be mockers, *those* going according to the desires of the irreverent/impious things of themselves. 1.19 These are those making divisions, natural/soulish (ones), not having a spirit. 1.20 But ye, beloved (ones), building yourselves up in your most holy faith, praying by a holy spirit, 1.21 keep ye yourselves in *the* agape of God, expecting the mercy of our Lord Jesus, the anointed (one), into eternal life.

1.22 And indeed pity ye some doubting (ones), 1.23 but save ye some, snatching *them* out of fire, and pity ye some with fear, hating even the tunic having been spotted/stained from the flesh. 1.24 And to the (one) being able to guard/keep ye without stumbling and to stand *ye* in the presence of his glory without blame in extreme joy, 1.25 to *the* only God our savior through Jesus, the anointed (one), or Lord, *be* glory, greatness/majesty, dominion, and authority before all the age, both now and into the ages; truly.

Jude

ΑΠΟΚΑΛΥΨΙΣ ΙΩΑΝΝΟΥ

This is the Sinaitic New Testament, book of Revelation.

1.1 Ἀποκάλυψις Ἰησοῦ χριστοῦ, ἣν ἔδωκεν αὐτῷ ὁ θεός, δεῖξαι τοῖς δούλοις αὐτοῦ ἃ δεῖ γενέσθαι ἐν τάχει, καὶ ἐσήμανεν ἀποστείλας διὰ τοῦ ἀγγέλου αὐτοῦ τῷ δούλῳ αὐτοῦ Ἰωάννῃ, 1.2 ὃς ἐμαρτύρησεν τὸν λόγον τοῦ θεοῦ καὶ τὴν μαρτυρίαν Ἰησοῦ χριστοῦ, ὅσα ἶδεν.

1.3 μακάριος ὁ ἀναγινώσκων καὶ οἱ ἀκούοντες τὸν λόγον τῆς προφητίας καὶ τηροῦντες τὰ ἐν αὐτῇ γεγραμμένα, ὁ γὰρ καιρὸς ἐγγύς.

1.4 Ἰωάνης ταῖς ἑπτὰ ἐκκλησίαις ταῖς ἐν τῇ Ἀσίᾳ· χάρις ὑμῖν καὶ εἰρήνη ἀπὸ ὁ ὢν καὶ ὁ ἦν καὶ ὁ ἐρχόμενος, καὶ ἀπὸ τῶν ἑπτὰ πνευμάτων τῶν ἐνώπιον τοῦ θρόνου αὐτοῦ, 1.5 καὶ ἀπὸ Ἰησοῦ χριστοῦ,

ὁ μάρτυς ὁ πιστός, ὁ πρωτότοκος τῶν νεκρῶν καὶ ὁ ἄρχων τῶν βασειλέων τῆς γῆς. τῷ ἀγαπῶντι ἡμᾶς καὶ λύσαντι ἡμᾶς ἐκ τῶν ἁμαρτιῶν ἡμῶν ἐν τῷ αἵματι αὐτοῦ 1.6 καὶ ἐποίησεν ἡμᾶς βασιλείαν, ἱερεῖς τῷ θεῷ καὶ πατρὶ αὐτοῦ αὐτῷ ἡ δόξα καὶ τὸ κράτος εἰς τοὺς αἰῶνας τῶν αἰώνων· ἀμήν. 1.7 ἰδοὺ ἔρχεται μετὰ τῶν νεφελῶν, καὶ ὄψονται αὐτὸν πᾶς ὀφθαλμὸς καὶ οἵτινες αὐτὸν ἐξεκέντησαν, καὶ κόψονται ἐπ᾽ αὐτὸν πᾶσαι αἱ φυλαὶ τῆς γῆς. ναί, ἀμήν.

1.8 ἐγώ εἰμι τὸ ἄλφα καὶ τὸ ὦ, ἀρχῇ καὶ τέλος, λέγει κύριος ὁ θεός, ὁ ὢν καὶ ὁ ἦν καὶ ὁ ἐρχόμενος, ὁ παντοκράτωρ.

1.9 ἐγὼ Ἰωάννης, ὁ ἀδελφὸς ὑμῶν καὶ συγκοινωνὸς ἐν τῇ θλίψι καὶ βασιλείᾳ καὶ ὑπομονῇ ἐν Ἰησοῦ, ἐγενόμην ἐν τῇ νήσῳ τῇ καλουμένῃ Πάτμῳ διὰ τὸν λόγον τοῦ θεοῦ καὶ διὰ τὴν μαρτυρίαν Ἰησοῦ. 1.10 ἐγενόμην ἐν πνεύματι ἐν τῇ κυριακῇ ἡμέρᾳ, καὶ ἤκουσα ὀπίσω μου φωνὴν μεγάλην ὡς σάλπιγγος 1.11 λεγούσης, ὃ βλέπεις γράψον εἰς τὸ βιβλίον καὶ πέμψον ταῖς ἑπτὰ ἐκκλησίαις, εἰς Ἔφεσον καὶ εἰς Πέργαμον καὶ εἰς Θυάτειρα καὶ εἰς Ζμύρναν καὶ εἰς Φιλαδέλφιαν καὶ εἰς Λαοδίκειαν καὶ εἰς Σάρδις. 1.12 καὶ ἐπέστρεψα βλέπειν τὴν φωνὴν ἥτις ἐλάλει μετ᾽

1.1 A revelation from Jesus the anointed (one), which God gave to him, to show to his slaves what (things) it is necessary to happen in quickness, and having sent through his messenger, he signified *them* to his slave John, 1.2 who testified *for* the saying/ word from God and the testimony of Jesus the anointed (one), as many things as he saw.

1.3 Happy *is* the (one) reading and the (ones) hearing from the saying of the prophecy and keeping/ treasuring the (things) having been written in it, for the time/season *is* near.

1.4 John, to the seven assemblies in Asia (Turkey): Grace to ye and peace from the (one) being and the (one) *who* was and the (one) coming, and from the seven spirits before the throne of him, 1.5 and from Jesus the anointed (one),

the faithful witness, the firstborn from the dead (ones), and the ruler of the kingdoms of the earth. To the (one) loving us and having loosed us from our faults/sins in/by his blood, -- 1.6 and he made us a kingdom, priests for God and his father -- , for him *is* the fame/glory and the dominion/might into the ages of the ages; truly. 1.7 Behold, he comes with the clouds, and every eye will behold/observe him and/ even/also (those) who pierced him, and all the tribes of the earth will lament/wail upon/to/over him. Yes, truly.

1.8 I, I am the alpha and the omega, the beginning and end, says the Lord God, the (one) *who* is being and was being and is coming, the almighty/ruler of all.

1.9 I John, the brother of ye and a sharer in the affliction and kingdom and endurance in Jesus, I came/happened to be on the island being called Patmos because of the saying/word of/from God and because of the testimony of Jesus. 1.10 I became in/with a spirit in/on the Lord's day, and I heard a great voice from behind me, as from a trumpet/megaphone, 1.11 saying: What you see you write on/in the scroll and you send *it* to the seven assemblies, to Ephesus and to Pergamum and to Thyatira and to Smyrna and to Philadelphia and to Laodicea and to Sardis. 1.12 And

ἐμοῦ· καὶ ἐπιστρέψας εἶδον ἑπτὰ λυχνίας χρυσᾶς, 1.13 καὶ μέσον τῶν ἑπτὰ λυχνιῶν ὅμοιον υἱὸν ἀνθρώπου, ἐνδεδυμένον ποδήρη καὶ περιεζωσμένον πρὸς τοῖς μασθοῖς ζώνην χρυσᾶν· 1.14 ἡ δὲ κεφαλὴ αὐτοῦ καὶ αἱ τρίχες λευκαὶ ὡς ἔριον λευκόν, ὡς χιών, καὶ οἱ ὀφθαλμοὶ αὐτοῦ ὡς φλὸξ πυρός, 1.15 καὶ οἱ πόδες αὐτοῦ ὅμοιοι χαλκολιβάνῳ ὡς ἐν καμίνῳ πεπυρωμένῳ, καὶ ἡ φωνὴ αὐτοῦ ὡς φωνὴ ὑδάτων πολλῶν, 1.16 καὶ ἔχων ἐν τῇ δεξιᾷ χειρὶ αὐτοῦ ἀστέρας ἑπτά, καὶ ἐκ τοῦ στόματος αὐτοῦ ρομφαία δίστομος ὀξεῖα ἐκπορευομένη, καὶ ἡ ὄψις αὐτοῦ φαίνει ὡς ὁ ἥλιος ἐν τῇ δυνάμει αὐτοῦ. 1.17 καὶ ὅτε εἶδον αὐτόν, ἔπεσα εἰς τοὺς πόδας αὐτοῦ ὡσὶ νεκρός· καὶ ἐπέθηκεν τὴν δεξιὰν αὐτοῦ ἐπ᾽ ἐμὲ λέγων, μὴ φοβοῦ· ἐγώ εἰμι ὁ πρῶτος καὶ ὁ ἔσχατος, 1.18 καὶ ὁ ζῶν, καὶ ἐγενόμην νεκρὸς καὶ ἰδοὺ ζῶν εἰμι εἰς τοὺς αἰῶνας τῶν αἰώνων, καὶ ἔχω τὰς κλεῖς τοῦ θανάτου καὶ τοῦ ᾅδου. 1.19 γράψον οὖν ἃ εἶδες καὶ ἃ εἰσὶν καὶ ἃ μέλλει γενέσθαι μετὰ ταῦτα. 1.20 τὸ μυστήριον τῶν ἑπτὰ ἀστέρων οὓς εἶδες ἐπὶ τῆς δεξιᾶς μου, καὶ τὰς ἑπτὰ λυχνίας τὰς χρυσᾶς· οἱ ἑπτὰ ἀστέρες ἄγγελοι τῶν ἑπτὰ ἐκκλησιῶν εἰσιν, καὶ αἱ ἑπτὰ λυχνίαι ἑπτὰ ἐκκλησίαι εἰσίν.

2.1 Τῷ ἀγγέλῳ τῆς ἐν Ἐφέσῳ ἐκκλησίας γράψον· τάδε λέγει ὁ κρατῶν τοὺς ἑπτὰ ἀστέρας ἐν τῇ δεξιᾷ αὐτοῦ, ὁ περιπατῶν ἐν μέσῳ τῶν ἑπτὰ λυχνιῶν τῶν χρυσῶν· 2.2 οἶδα τὰ ἔργα σου καὶ τὸν κόπον σου καὶ τὴν ὑπομονήν σου, καὶ ὅτι οὐ δύνῃ βαστάσαι κακούς, καὶ ἐπίρασας τοὺς λέγοντας ἑαυτοὺς ἀποστόλους καὶ οὐκ εἰσίν, καὶ εὗρες αὐτοὺς ψευδεῖς· 2.3 καὶ ὑπομονὴν ἔχις, καὶ ἐβάστασας διὰ τὸ ὄνομά μου, καὶ οὐ κεκοπίασας. 2.4 ἀλλὰ ἔχω κατὰ σοῦ ὅτι τὴν ἀγάπην σου τὴν πρώτην ἀφῆκες. 2.5 μνημόνευε οὖν πόθεν πέπτωκες, καὶ μετανόησον καὶ τὰ πρῶτα ἔργα ποίησον· εἰ δὲ μή, ἔρχομαί σοι

I turned to see the voice which was speaking with me; and having turned, I saw seven gold lampstands, 1.13 and in the midst of the lampstands *was one* like a son of a man, having been clothed *to* a foot and having been girded near the breasts *with* a gold girdle/belt; 1.14 and his head and the hairs *were* white as wool *and* white as snow, and his eyes *were* as a flame of fire, 1.15 and his feet *were* like polished bronze, as having been fired in a furnace, and his voice *was* as a sound from many waters, 1.16 and holding seven stars in his right hand, and a sharp double-edged sword was going out of his mouth, and his face shines as the sun with its power. 1.17 And when I saw him, I fell to his feet, being as a dead (one); and he put his right (hand) on me, saying: Fear you not; I, I am the first and the last, 1.18 and the (one) living, I also became a dead (one) and behold, I am living into/*for* the ages of the ages, and I hold/have the keys of the death and the Hades. 1.19 Therefore, you write what (things) you saw and what (things) are and what (things) are about to happen after these (things). 1.20 The mystery of the seven stars which you saw on the right of me, and the seven gold lampstands: The seven stars are messengers/angels from the seven assemblies, and the seven lampstands are seven assemblies.

2.1 To the messenger/angel from the assembly in Ephesus, you write: These things says the (one) grasping the seven stars in his right (hand), the (one) walking in the midst of the seven gold lampstands: 2.2 I know your works and the toil of you/your toil and your endurance, and that you are not able to bear/stand bad (ones), and tested those calling themselves apostles but they are not, and you found them *to be* liars; 2.3 and you have endurance/patience, and *this* you carried/bore because of my name, and you have not grown weary. 2.4 But I hold *it* against you that you left your first agape. 2.5 You remember therefore from where you have fallen, and you repent and you make/do the first works; but if not, I come to you and I shall move your

καὶ κινήσω τὴν λυχνίαν σου ἐκ τοῦ τόπου αὐτῆς, ἐὰν μὴ μετανοήσῃς. 2.6 ἀλλὰ τοῦτο ἔχεις, ὅτι μισεῖς τὰ ἔργα τῶν Νικολαϊτῶν, ἃ κἀγὼ μισῶ. 2.7 ὁ ἔχων οὖς ἀκουσάτω τί τὸ πνεῦμα λέγει ταῖς ἐκκλησίαις. τῷ νικῶντι δώσω φαγεῖν ἐκ τοῦ ξύλου τῆς ζωῆς, ὅ ἐστιν ἐν τῷ παραδίσῳ τοῦ θεοῦ. 2.8 καὶ τῷ ἀγγέλῳ τῆς ἐν Ζμύρνῃ ἐκκλησίας γράψον·

τάδε λέγει ὁ πρῶτος καὶ ὁ ἔσχατος, ὃς ἐγένετο νεκρὸς καὶ ἔζησεν· 2.9 οἶδά σου τὰ ἔργα καὶ τὴν θλῖψιν καὶ τὴν πτωχίαν, ἀλλὰ πλούσιος εἶ, καὶ τὴν βλασφημίαν τὴν ἐκ τῶν λεγόντων Ἰουδαίους εἶναι ἑαυτούς, καὶ οὐκ εἰσὶν ἀλλὰ συναγωγὴ τοῦ Σατανᾶ. 2.10 μηδὲν φοβοῦ ἃ μέλλεις πάσχειν. ἰδοὺ μέλλει βάλλειν ἐξ ὑμῶν ὁ διάβολος εἰς φυλακὴν ἵνα πιρασθῆται, καὶ ἕξετε θλῖψιν ἡμερῶν δέκα. γίνου πιστὸς ἄχρι θανάτου, καὶ δώσω σοι τὸν στέφανον τῆς ζωῆς. 2.11 ὁ ἔχων οὖς ἀκουσάτω τί τὸ πνεῦμα λέγει ταῖς ἐκκλησίαις. ὁ νικῶν οὐ μὴ ἀδικηθῇ ἐκ τοῦ θανάτου τοῦ δευτέρου. 2.12 καὶ τῷ ἀγγέλῳ τῆς ἐν Περγάμῳ ἐκκλησίας γράψον· τάδε λέγει ὁ ἔχων τὴν ῥομφαίαν τὴν δίστομον τὴν ὀξεῖαν· 2.13 οἶδα ποῦ κατοικεῖς, ὅπου ὁ θρόνος τοῦ Σατανᾶ, καὶ κρατεῖς τὸ ὄνομά μου, καὶ οὐκ ἠρνήσω τὴν πίστιν μου ἐν ταῖς ἡμέραις ἐν ταῖς Ἀντιπᾶς ὁ μάρτυς μου ὁ πιστός, ὃς ἀπεκτάνθη παρ' ὑμῖν, ὅπου ὁ Σατανᾶς κατοικεῖ. 2.14 ἀλλ' ἔχω κατὰ σοῦ ὀλίγα, ὅτι ἔχεις ἐκεῖ κρατοῦντας τὴν διδαχὴν Βαλαάμ, ὃς ἐδίδασκεν τὸν Βαλὰκ βαλεῖν σκάνδαλον ἐνώπιον τῶν υἱῶν Ἰσραήλ, φαγεῖν εἰδωλόθυτα καὶ πορνεῦσαι· 2.15 οὕτως ἔχεις καὶ σὺ κρατοῦντας τὴν διδαχὴν τῶν Νικολαϊτῶν ὁμοίως. 2.16 μετανόησον· εἰ δὲ μή, ἔρχομαί σοι ταχύ, καὶ πολεμήσω μετ' αὐτῶν ἐν τῇ ῥομφαίᾳ τοῦ στόματός μου. 2.17 ὁ ἔχων οὖς ἀκουσάτω τί τὸ πνεῦμα λέγι ταῖς ἐκκλησίαις. τῷ νικῶντι δώσω ἐκ τοῦ μάννα τοῦ κεκρυμμένου, καὶ ψῆφον λευκὴν καὶ ἐπὶ τὴν

lampstand out of its place, unless you might repent. 2.6 But you hold/have this (thing), that you hate the works of the Nicolaitans, which even/also I, I hate. 2.7 The (one) having an ear, let him hear what the spirit says to the assemblies. To the (one) overcoming, I shall give to eat from the tree of the life, which is in the paradise of God. 2.8 And to the messenger/angel of the assembly in Smyrna, you write:

These things says the first and the last, who became dead and lived *again*; 2.9 I know of you the works and the affliction and the poverty, but you are rich, and the slander/blasphemy, the (one) from those saying of themselves to be Judeans, but they are not but a congregation/synagogue from/of Satan. 2.10 Fear you nothing which you are about to suffer. Behold, I am about to throw the devil out of ye into a prison in order that ye might be tried/tested, and ye will have affliction *for* ten days. You become faithful until death, and I shall give to you the crown/wreath of the life. 2.11 The (one) having an ear, let him hear what the spirit says to the assemblies. The (one) overcoming by no means will be wronged from the second death. 2.12 And to the messenger/angel of the assembly in Pergamum, you write: These things says the (one) holding the sharp, double-edged sword: 2.13 I know where you live, where the throne of Satan *is*, and you hold fast the name of me, and you denied not the faith of me in the days, in those of Antipas, my witness, the faithful (one), who was killed with/beside ye, where Satan lives/dwells. 2.14 But I hold a few (things) against you, because you have there those holding fast the doctrine/teaching of Balaam, who taught Balak to throw/put a stumbling block/offense before the sons of Israel, to eat things sacrificed to idols and to consort with prostitutes; 2.15 So you, you have also those holding fast the doctrine/teaching of the Nicolaitans likewise. 2.16 You repent; and if not, I come to you quickly, and I shall make war with them by the sword from my mouth. 2.17 The (one) having an ear, let him hear what the spirit says to the assemblies. To the (one) overcoming I shall give out of the manna having been hidden, and

ψῆφον ὄνομα καινὸν γεγραμμένον ὃ οὐδεὶς οἶδεν εἰ μὴ ὁ λαμβάνων. 2.18 καὶ τῷ ἀγγέλῳ τῆς ἐν Θυατείροις ἐκκλησίας γράψον· τάδε λέγει ὁ υἱὸς τοῦ θεοῦ, ὁ ἔχων τοὺς ὀφθαλμοὺς αὐτοῦ ὡς φλὸξ πυρός, καὶ οἱ πόδες αὐτοῦ ὅμοιοι χαλκολιβάνῳ· 2.19 οἶδά σου τὰ ἔργα καὶ τὴν ἀγάπην καὶ τὴν πίστιν καὶ τὴν διακονίαν καὶ τὴν ὑπομονήν σου, καὶ τὰ ἔργα σου τὰ ἔσχατα πλείονα τῶν πρώτων. 2.20 ἀλλ᾿ ἔχω κατὰ σοῦ πολὺ ὅτι ἀφεῖς τὴν γυναῖκα Ἰεζάβελ, ἡ λέγουσα αὐτὴν προφῆτιν εἶναι, καὶ διδάσκει καὶ πλανᾷ τοὺς ἐμοὺς δούλους πορνεῦσαι καὶ φαγεῖν εἰδωλόθυτα. 2.21 καὶ ἔδωκα αὐτῇ χρόνον ἵνα μετανοήσῃ, καὶ οὐ θέλι μετανοῆσαι ἐκ τῆς πορνίας ταύτης. 2.22 ἰδοὺ βάλλω αὐτὴν εἰς κλίνην, καὶ τοὺς μοιχεύοντας μετ᾿ αὐτῆς εἰς θλῖψιν μεγάλην, ἐὰν μὴ μετανοήσουσιν ἐκ τῶν ἔργων αὐτῆς· 2.23 καὶ τὰ τέκνα αὐτῆς ἀποκτενῶ ἐν θανάτῳ· καὶ γνώσονται πᾶσαι αἱ ἐκκλησίαι ὅτι ἐγώ εἰμι ὁ ἐρευνῶν νεφροὺς καὶ καρδίας, καὶ δώσω ὑμῖν ἑκάστῳ κατὰ τὰ ἔργα ὑμῶν. 2.24 ὑμῖν δὲ λέγω τοῖς λοιποῖς τοῖς ἐν Θυατείροις, ὅσοι οὐκ ἔχουσιν τὴν διδαχὴν ταύτην, οἵτινες οὐκ ἔγνωσαν τὰ βαθὴ τοῦ Σατανᾶ, ὡς λέγουσιν, οὐ βάλω ἐφ᾿ ὑμᾶς ἄλλο βάρος· 2.25 πλὴν ὃ ἔχεται κρατήσατε ἄχρι οὗ ἂν ἥξω. 2.26 καὶ ὁ νικῶν καὶ ὁ τηρῶν ἄχρι τέλους τὰ ἔργα μου, δώσω αὐτῷ ἐξουσίαν ἐπὶ τῶν ἐθνῶν, 2.27 καὶ ποιμανῖ αὐτοὺς ἐν ῥάβδῳ σιδηρᾷ, ὡς τὰ σκεύη τὰ κεραμικὰ συντρίβεται, 2.28 ὡς κἀγὼ εἴληφα παρὰ τοῦ πατρός μου, καὶ δώσω αὐτῷ τὸν ἀστέρα τὸν πρωϊνόν. 2.29 ὁ ἔχων οὖς ἀκουσάτω τί τὸ πνεῦμα λέγι ταῖς ἐκκλησίαις. 3.1 καὶ τῷ ἀγγέλῳ τῆς ἐν Σάρδεσιν ἐκκλησίας γράψον· τάδε λέγει ὁ ἔχων τὰ ἑπτὰ πνεύματα τοῦ θεοῦ καὶ τοὺς ἑπτὰ ἀστέρας· οἶδά σου τὰ ἔργα, ὅτι ὄνομα ἔχεις ὅτι ζῆς, καὶ νεκρὸς εἶ. 3.2 γίνου γρηγορῶν, καὶ στήριζον τὰ λοιπὰ ἃ ἔμελλον ἀποθανῖν, οὐ γὰρ εὕρηκά σου τὰ ἔργα πεπληρωμένα ἐνώπιον

a white pebble and on the pebble a new name having been written which no one has known except the (one) receiving *it*. 2.18 And to the messenger/angel of the assembly in Thyatira, you write: These things says the son of God, the (one) having his eyes as a flame of fire, and his feet like to polished brass: 2.19 I know of you the works and the agape and the faith and the service/ministry and your patience/endurance, and your works, the last (things) more than the first. 2.20 But I hold much against you because you let the woman Jezebel, the (one) saying *of* herself to be a prophetess, and she teaches and deceives/leads astray my slaves to indulge in prostitution and to eat things sacrificed to idols. 2.21 And I gave to her a time that she might repent, but she wants not to repent from this prostitution. 2.22 Behold, I throw her into a bed, and those having done adultery with her into a great affliction, unless they will repent out of/from the works of her; 2.23 And I shall kill the children of her in a death; and all the assemblies will know that I, I am the (one) searching/examining kidneys and hearts, and I shall give to ye, to each (one), according to your works. 2.24 But I say to ye, to the remaining (ones) in Thyatira, as many as hold not this doctrine/teaching, who knew not the deep things of Satan, since/as they say: I put not another burden upon ye; 2.25 however, what ye have hold ye fast until which *time* I might come. 2.26 Both the (one) overcoming and the (one) keeping/guarding until the ends of my works, I shall give to him authority on/over the ethnics, 2.27 and he will shepherd/tend them with an iron rod, as the pottery vessels are broken, 2.28 and as I, I have received from my father, also I shall give the morning star to him. 2.29 The (one) having an ear, let him hear what the spirit says to the assemblies. 3.1 And to the messenger/angel of the assembly in Sardis, you write: These things says the (one) holding the seven spirits of God and the seven stars: I know your works, that you have/hold a name because you live, but you are dead. 3.2 Be you watching, and fix firmly the remaining (things) which were about to die, for I have

τοῦ θεοῦ μου· 3.3 μνημόνευε πῶς εἴληφας καὶ ἤκουσας, καὶ τήρει, καὶ μετανόησον. ἐὰν οὖν μὴ γρηγορήσῃς μετανοήσῃς, ἥξω ἐπὶ σέ ὡς κλέπτης, καὶ οὐ μὴ γνῷς ἡ οἵαν ὥραν ἥξω ἐπὶ σέ. 3.4 ἀλλὰ ἔχις ὀλίγα ὀνόματα ἐν Σάρδεσιν ἃ οὐκ ἐμόλυναν τὰ ἱμάτια αὐτῶν, καὶ περιπατήσουσιν μετ' ἐμοῦ ἐν λευκοῖς, ὅτι ἄξιοί εἰσιν. 3.5 ὁ νικῶν οὕτως περιβαλεῖται ἐν ἱματίοις λευκοῖς, καὶ οὐ μὴ ἐξαλείψω τὸ ὄνομα αὐτοῦ ἐκ τῆς βίβλου τῆς ζωῆς, καὶ ὁμολογήσω τὸ ὄνομα αὐτοῦ ἔμπροσθεν τοῦ πατρός μου καὶ ἐνώπιον τῶν ἀγγέλων αὐτοῦ. 3.6 ὁ ἔχων οὖς ἀκουσάτω τί τὸ πνεῦμα λέγει ταῖς ἐκκλησίαις. 3.7 καὶ τῷ ἀγγέλῳ τῆς ἐν Φιλαδελφείᾳ ἐκκλησίας γράψον· τάδε λέγει ὁ ἀληθινός, ὁ ἅγιος, ὁ ἔχων τὴν κλῖν τοῦ Δαυίδ, καὶ ἀνύγων καὶ οὐδὶς κλίσει, καὶ κλείων καὶ οὐδὶς ἀνύξει· 3.8 οἶδά τὰ ἔργα σου ἰδοὺ δέδωκα ἐνώπιόν σου θύραν ἠνεῳγμένην, ἣν οὐδεὶς δύναται κλεῖσαι ὅτι μικρὰν ἔχεις δύναμιν, καὶ ἐτήρησάς μου τὸν λόγον, καὶ οὐκ ἠρνήσω τὸ ὄνομά μου. 3.9 ἰδοὺ δέδωκα ἐκ τῆς συναγωγῆς τοῦ Σατανᾶ, τῶν λεγόντων ἑαυτοὺς Ἰουδαίους εἶναι, καὶ οὐκ εἰσὶν ἀλλὰ ψεύδονται· ἰδοὺ ποιήσω αὐτοὺς ἵνα ἥξουσιν καὶ προσκυνήσουσιν ἐνώπιον τῶν ποδῶν σου, καὶ γνῶσῃ ὅτι ἐγὼ ἠγάπησά σε. 3.10 ὅτι ἐτήρησας τὸν λόγον τῆς ὑπομονῆς μου, κἀγώ σε ἐκ τῆς ὥρας τοῦ πιρασμοῦ τῆς μελλούσης ἔρχεσθε ἐπὶ τῆς οἰκουμένης ὅλης πιράσαι τοὺς κατοικοῦντας ἐπὶ τῆς γῆς. 3.11 ἔρχομαι ταχύ· κράτι ὃ ἔχις, ἵνα μηδὶς λάβῃ τὸν στέφανόν σου. 3.12 ὁ νικῶν ποιήσω αὐτὸν στῦλον ἐν τῷ ναῷ τοῦ θεοῦ μου, καὶ ἔξω οὐ μὴ ἐξέλθῃ, καὶ γράψω ἐπ' αὐτὸν τὸ ὄνομα τοῦ θεοῦ μου καὶ τὸ ὄνομα τῆς πόλεως τοῦ θεοῦ μου, τῆς καινῆς Ἰερουσαλήμ, ἡ καταβαίνουσα ἐκ τοῦ οὐρανοῦ ἀπὸ τοῦ θεοῦ μου, καὶ τὸ ὄνομά μου τὸ καινόν. 3.13 ὁ ἔχων οὖς ἀκουσάτω τί τὸ πνεῦμα

not found from you the works having been fulfilled
before my God; 3.3 you remember how you have received
and heard, and you kept, and you repented. If
therefore you might not watch, I shall come upon you
as a thief, and by no means might you know what
hour/time I shall come upon you. 3.4 But you have a
few names in Sardis which polluted not their garments,
and they will walk with me in white (ones), because
they are worthy. 3.5 The (one) overcoming will be so
clothed in white garments, and by no means shall I
erase/blot out his name out of the scroll of life, and
I shall profess/confess his name before my father and
in the sight of his messengers/angels. 3.6 The (one)
having an ear let him hear what the spirit says to the
assemblies. 3.7 And to the messenger/angel of the
assembly in Philadelphia, you write: These things says
the true (one), the holy (one), the (one) having the
key from David, both opening and no one will close,
and closing and no one opens: 3.8 I know your works
--. Behold, I have given before you a door, having
been opened, which no one is able to close --, because
you hold a little power, and you kept my logos/saying/
word, and you denied not my name. 3.9 Behold, I have
given out of/from the congregation/synagogue of Satan,
from those saying of themselves to be Judeans, and
they are not, but they lie; behold, I shall make them
that they will come and worship before my feet, and
they will know that I, I loved you. 3.10 Because you
kept the logos/saying of my endurance, I also *shall
keep* you out of the hour/time of the proving/testing
being about to come upon the entire Roman
Empire/inhabited house, to prove those dwelling upon
the earth. 3.11 I am coming quickly; you hold fast
what you have, in order that no one might take/receive
your crown/wreath. 3.12 The (one) overcoming, I
shall make him a pillar/steeple in the *inner* temple of
my God, and by no means will he go forth outside, and
I shall write on him the name of my God and the name
of the city of my God, of the new Jerusalem, the (one)
coming down out of the sky/heaven from my God, and the
name of me, the new (one). 3.13 The (one) having an
ear let him hear what the spirit says to the

λέγι ταῖς ἐκκλησίαις. 3.14 καὶ τῷ ἀγγέλῳ τῆς ἐν Λαοδικίᾳ ἐκκλησίας γράψον· τάδε λέγει ὁ ἀμήν, ὁ μάρτυς ὁ πιστὸς καὶ ὁ ἀληθινός, καὶ ἡ ἀρχὴ τῆς ἐκκλησίας τοῦ θεοῦ· 3.15 οἶδά σου τὰ ἔργα, ὅτι οὔτε ψυχρὸς οὔτε ζεστός. ὄφελον ψυχρὸς ἦς ἢ ζεστός. 3.16 ὅτι οὕτως χλιαρὸς καὶ οὔτε ζεστὸς εἶ οὔτε ψυχρός, μέλλω σε ἐμέσαι ἐκ τοῦ στόματός μου. 3.17 ὅτι λέγεις πλούσιός εἰμι καὶ πεπλούτηκα καὶ οὐδὲν ὃς χρίαν ἔχω, καὶ οὐκ οἶδας ὅτι ταλαίπωρος εἶ καὶ ἐλεεινὸς καὶ πτωχὸς καὶ τυφλὸς καὶ γυμνός, 3.18 συμβουλεύω σοι ἀγοράσαι παρ' ἐμοῦ χρυσίον πεπυρωμένον ἐκ πυρὸς ἵνα πλουτήσῃς, καὶ ἱμάτια λευκὰ ἵνα περιβάλῃ καὶ μὴ φανερωθῇ ἡ αἰσχύνη τῆς γυμνότητός σου, καὶ κολλύριον ἐνχρῖσαι τοὺς ὀφθαλμούς σου ἵνα βλέπῃς. 3.19 ἐγὼ ὅσους ἂν φιλῶ ἐλέγχω καὶ παιδεύω· ζήλωσον οὖν καὶ μετανόησον. 3.20 ἰδοὺ ἕστηκα ἐπὶ τὴν θύραν καὶ κρούω· ἐάν τις ἀκούσῃ τῆς φωνῆς μου καὶ ἀνοίξω τὴν θύραν, καὶ εἰσελεύσομαι πρὸς αὐτὸν καὶ διπνήσω μετ' αὐτοῦ καὶ αὐτὸς μετ' ἐμοῦ. 3.21 ὁ νικῶν δώσω αὐτῷ καθίσαι μετ' ἐμοῦ ἐν τῷ θρόνῳ μου, ὡς κἀγὼ ἐνίκησα καὶ ἐκάθισα μετὰ τοῦ πατρός μου ἐν τῷ θρόνῳ αὐτοῦ. 3.22 ὁ ἔχων οὖς ἀκουσάτω τί τὸ πνεῦμα λέγει ταῖς ἐκκλησίαις. 4.1 μετὰ ταῦτα ἶδον, καὶ ἰδοὺ θύρα ἠνεῳγμένη ἐν τῷ οὐρανῷ, καὶ ἰδοὺ ἡ φωνὴ ἡ πρώτη ἣν ἤκουσα ὡς σάλπιγγος λαλούσαν μετ' ἐμοῦ λέγων, ἀνάβα ὧδε, καὶ δίξω σοι ἃ δῖ γενέσθαι μετὰ ταῦτα. 4.2 εὐθέως ἐγενόμην ἐν πνεύματι· καὶ ἰδοὺ θρόνος ἔκειτο ἐν τῷ οὐρανῷ, καὶ ἐπὶ τὸν θρόνον καθήμενος, 4.3 καὶ ὁ καθήμενος ὅμοιος ὁράσει λίθῳ ἰάσπιδι καὶ σαρδίῳ, καὶ ἶρεις κυκλόθεν τοῦ θρόνου ὅμοιος ὁράσι σμαραγδίνῳ. 4.4 καὶ κυκλόθεν τοῦ θρόνου θρόνους εἴκοσι τέσσαρες, καὶ πρεσβυτέρους καθημένους περιβεβλημένους ἐν λευκοῖς, καὶ ἐπὶ τὰς κεφαλὰς αὐτῶν στεφάνους χρυσοῦς. 4.5 καὶ ἐκ τοῦ θρόνου ἐκπορεύονται

assemblies.   3.14 And to the messenger/angel of the
assembly in Laodicea, you write: These things says the
true (one)/truly, the faithful and true witness, and
the beginning/ruler of the creation of God: 3.15 I
know the works of you, that *you are* neither cold nor
hot. I would that you was being cold or hot.   3.16 So,
because you are lukewarm and neither hot nor cold, you
are about to be vomited from my mouth.   3.17 Because
you say: I am rich and I have become wealthy and *there
is* nothing which I have a need, and you know not that
you are wretched and pitiable and poor and blind and
naked,   3.18 I advise for you to buy from me gold
having been tried from fire, in order that you might
become rich, and white garments, in order that you
might be clothed and the shame of your nakedness might
not be shown, and eye salve to anoint/rub in your eyes
in order that you may see.   3.19 I, I would love as
many   as   I   convict/reprove   and   train/chastise;
therefore, you be zealous and repent.   3.20 Behold, I
have stood at the door and I am knocking; if anyone
might hear my voice/sound and will open the door, I
shall both go in to him and I shall dine with him and
he with me.   3.21 The (one) overcoming, I shall give
to him to sit with me in/on my throne, as even I, I
overcame and sat with my father in/on his throne.
3.22 The (one) having an ear, let him hear what the
spirit says to the assemblies.   4.1   After these
(things) I looked/saw, and behold, a door having been
opened in the sky/heaven, and behold the voice, the
first (one) which I heard as from a trumpet/bullhorn,
speaking with me, saying: Come up here, and I shall
show to you what (things) it is necessary to happen
after these (things).   4.2 Immediately, I became in a
spirit; and behold, a throne was being placed in the
sky/heaven, and upon the throne *was one* sitting,   4.3
and the (one) sitting *was* a vision like to a stone, to
a jasper and to a sardius,   and   a   halo/rainbow *was*
round about the throne, a vision like to an emerald.
4.4 And all around the throne *I saw* twenty-four
thrones, and *I saw* elders having been sat, having been
dressed in white (things), and upon their heads *I saw*
gold crowns/wreaths.   4.5 And out from the throne

ἀστραπαὶ καὶ φωναὶ καὶ βρονταί· καὶ ἑπτὰ λαμπάδες πυρὸς καιόμεναι ἐνώπιον τοῦ θρόνου, ἅ εἰσιν τὰ ἑπτὰ πνεύματα τοῦ θεοῦ, 4.6 καὶ ἐνώπιον τοῦ θρόνου ὡς θάλασσα ὑαλίνη ὁμοία κρυστάλλῳ. καὶ ἐν μέσῳ τοῦ θρόνου καὶ κύκλῳ τοῦ θρόνου τέσσαρα ζῷα γέμοντα ὀφθαλμῶν ἔμπροσθεν καὶ ὄπισθεν· 4.7 καὶ τὸ ζῷον τὸ πρῶτον ὅμοιον λέοντι, καὶ τὸ δεύτερον ζῷον ὅμοιον μόσχῳ, καὶ τὸ τρίτον ζῷον ἔχον τὸ πρόσωπον ὡς ὅμοιον ἀνθρώπῳ, καὶ τὸ τέταρτον ζῷον ὅμοιον ἀετῷ πετομένῳ. 4.8 καὶ τὰ τέσσαρα ζῷα, ἓν ἕκαστον αὐτῶν ἔχον ἀνὰ πτέρυγας ἕξ, κυκλόθεν καὶ ἔσωθεν γέμουσιν ὀφθαλμῶν· καὶ ἀνάπαυσιν οὐκ ἔχουσιν ἡμέρας καὶ νυκτὸς λέγοντες,

ἅγιος ἅγιος ἅγιος κύριος ὁ θεὸς ὁ παντοκράτωρ, ὁ ἦν καὶ ὁ ὢν καὶ ὁ ἐρχόμενος. 4.9 καὶ ὅταν δώσωσιν τὰ ζῷα δόξαν καὶ τιμὴν καὶ εὐχαριστίαν τῷ καθημένῳ ἐπὶ τῷ θρόνῳ, τῷ ζῶντι εἰς τοὺς αἰῶνας τῶν αἰώνων, ἀμήν, 4.10 καὶ πεσοῦνται οἱ εἴκοσι τέσσαρες πρεσβύτεροι ἐνώπιον τοῦ καθημένου ἐπὶ τοῦ θρόνου καὶ προσκυνήσουσιν τῷ ζῶντι εἰς τοὺς αἰῶνας τῶν αἰώνων, ἀμήν, καὶ βαλοῦσιν τοὺς στεφάνους αὐτῶν ἐνώπιον τοῦ θρόνου λέγοντες, 4.11 ἄξιος εἶ, κύριε, ὁ κύριος καὶ ὁ θεὸς ἡμῶν, λαβεῖν τὴν δόξαν καὶ τιμὴν καὶ τὴν δύναμιν, ὅτι σὺ ἔκτισας τὰ πάντα, καὶ διὰ τὸ θέλημά σου ἦσαν καὶ ἐκτίσθησαν. 5.1 καὶ εἶδον ἐπὶ τὴν δεξιὰν τοῦ καθημένου ἐπὶ τοῦ θρόνου βιβλίον γεγραμμένον ἔμβροσθεν καὶ ὄπισθεν, κατεσφραγισμένον σφραγῖσιν ἑπτά. 5.2 καὶ εἶδον ἄγγελον κηρύσσοντα ἰσχυρὸν ἐν φωνῇ μεγάλῃ, τίς ἄξιος ἀνοῖξε τὸ βιβλίον καὶ λῦσαι τὰς σφραγῖδας αὐτοῦ; 5.3 καὶ οὐδεὶς ἐδύνατο ἐν τῷ οὐρανῷ οὐτὲ ἐπὶ τῆς γῆς — ἀνοῖξε τὸ βιβλίον οὔτε βλέπειν αὐτό. 5.4 καὶ ἔκλεον πολὺ ὅτι οὐδεὶς ἄξιος εὑρέθη ἀνοῖξαι τὸ βιβλίον οὔτε βλέπειν αὐτό. 5.5 καὶ εἷς ἐκ τῶν πρεσβυτέρων λέγει μοι, μὴ κλαῖε· ἰδοὺ ἐνίκησεν ὁ λέων ἐκ τῆς

comes lightnings and sounds and thunders; and seven lamps of fire burning before the throne, which are the seven spirits of God, 4.6 and before the throne as a glassy sea like to a crystal. And in the midst of the throne and around the throne *were* four living (things) being full of eyes from before and from behind; 4.7 and the first living (thing/creature) *was* like to a lion, and the second living (thing) was similar to a calf, and the third living (thing) had the face as (one) similar to a man, and the fourth living (thing) was similar to a flying eagle. 4.8 And the four living (things), each one of them held up six wings, from all around and from within they are full of eyes; and they have not a repose/rest of day and of night, saying:

Holy, holy, holy *is* the Lord, the God, the almighty/ruler of all, the *one who* was being and the (one) being and the (one) coming. 4.9 And whenever the living (things) might give fame/glory and honor and thanksgiving to the (one) sitting upon the throne, to the (one) living into the ages of the ages, truly, 4.10 the twenty-four elders will also fall down before the (one) sitting upon the throne and they will worship the (one) living into the ages of the ages, and truly, they will throw their crowns/wreaths before the throne, saying: 4.11 You are worthy, Lord, the lord and God of us, to receive/take the fame/glory and honor and the power, because you, you created all (things), and because of your purpose/will they were and they were created. 5.1 And I saw, on/at the right of the (one) sitting upon the throne, a scroll having been written before and from behind/(front and back), having been sealed with seven seals. 5.2 And I saw a strong messenger/angel heralding in a great voice: Who *is* worthy to open the scroll and to loose the seals from it? 5.3 And no one was able *to* in the sky/heaven, not upon the earth/land, to open the scroll nor to view/look at it. 5.4 And I wept much, because no one worthy was found to open the scroll nor to view it. 5.5 And one out of the elders says to me: Weep you not; behold, the lion out of the tribe of Juda, the root from David, overcame to open the scroll

φυλῆς Ἰούδα, ἡ ῥίζα Δαυίδ, ἀνοῖξαι τὸ βιβλίον καὶ λῦσαι τὰς ἑπτὰ σφραγῖδας αὐτοῦ. 5.6 καὶ εἶδον ἐν μέσῳ τοῦ θρόνου καὶ τῶν τεσσάρων ζώων καὶ ἐν μέσῳ τῶν πρεσβυτέρων ἀρνίον ἑστηκὼς ὡς ἐσφαγμένον, ἔχων κέρατα ἑπτὰ καὶ ὀφθαλμοὺς ἑπτά, οἵ εἰσιν τὰ ἑπτὰ πνεύματα τοῦ θεοῦ ἀπεσταλμένα εἰς πᾶσαν τὴν γῆν. 5.7 καὶ ἦλθεν καὶ εἴληφεν ἐκ τῆς δεξιᾶς τοῦ καθημένου ἐπὶ τοῦ θρόνου. 5.8 καὶ ὅτε ἔλαβεν τὸ βιβλίον, τὰ τέσσαρα ζῷα καὶ οἱ εἴκοσι τέσσαρες πρεσβύτεροι ἔπεσν ἐνώπιον τοῦ ἀρνίου, ἕκαστος ἔχοντες κιθάραν καὶ φιάλας χρυσεᾶς γεμούσας θυμιαμάτων, ἃ εἰσιν προσευχαὶ τῶν ἁγίων. 5.9 καὶ ᾄδουσιν ᾠδὴν καινὴν λέγοντες, ἄξιος εἶ λαβῖν τὸ βιβλίον καὶ ἀνοῖξαι τὰς σφραγῖδας αὐτοῦ, ὅτι ἐσφάγης καὶ ἠγόρασας τῷ θεῷ ἡμᾶς ἐν τῷ αἵματί σου ἐκ πάσης φυλῆς καὶ γλώσσης καὶ λαοῦ καὶ ἔθνους, 5.10 καὶ ἐποίησας αὐτοὺς τῷ θεῷ ἡμῶν βασιλίαν καὶ ἱεράτεαν, καὶ βασιλεύσουσιν ἐπὶ τῆς γῆς. 5.11 καὶ εἶδον, καὶ ἤκουσα ὡς φωνὴν ἀγγέλων πολλῶν κύκλῳ τοῦ θρόνου καὶ τῶν ζώων καὶ τῶν πρεσβυτέρων, καὶ ἦν ὁ ἀριθμὸς αὐτῶν μυριάδες μυριάδων καὶ χιλιάδες χιλιάδων, 5.12 λέγοντες φωνῇ μεγάλῃ, ἄξιόν ἐστιν τὸ ἀρνίον τὸ ἐσφαγμένον λαβῖν τὴν δύναμιν καὶ πλοῦτον καὶ σοφίαν καὶ ἰσχὺν καὶ τιμὴν καὶ δόξαν καὶ εὐλογίαν. 5.13 καὶ πᾶν κτίσμα τό ἐν τῷ οὐρανῷ καὶ ἐπὶ τῆς γῆς καὶ τά ἐν τῆς θαλάσσης, καὶ τὰ ἐν αὐτοῖς πάντα, καὶ ἤκουσα λέγοντας, τῷ καθημένῳ ἐπὶ τοῦ θρόνῳ καὶ τῷ ἀρνίῳ ἡ εὐλογία καὶ ἡ τιμὴ καὶ ἡ δόξα καὶ τὸ κράτος εἰς τοὺς αἰῶνας τῶν αἰώνων. 5.14 καὶ τὰ τέσσαρα ζῷα ἔλεγον, ἀμήν· καὶ οἱ πρεσβύτεροι ἔπεσαν καὶ προσεκύνησαν. 6.1 καὶ εἶδον ὅτε ἤνυξεν τὸ ἀρνίον μίαν ἐκ τῶν ἑπτὰ σφραγίδων, καὶ ἤκουσα ἑνὸς ἐκ τῶν τεσσάρων ζώων λεγόντων ὡς φωνὴν βροντῆς, ἔρχου. 6.2 καὶ ἴδε καὶ εἶδον, καὶ ἰδοὺ ἵππος λευκός, καὶ ὁ καθήμενος ἐπ' αὐτὸν ἔχων τόξον, καὶ ἐδόθη αὐτῷ στέφανος, καὶ ἐξῆλθεν νικῶν καὶ ἐνικήσεν. 6.3 καὶ ὅτε ἤνυξεν τὴν σφραγῖδα τὴν δευτέραν, ἤκουσα τοῦ δευτέρου ζώου λέγοντος, ἔρχου. 6.4 καὶ ἴδε καὶ

and to loose the seven seals of it. 5.6 And I saw, in the midst of the throne and of the four living (things) and in the midst of the elders, a lamb having been stood as having been slain, having seven horns and seven eyes, which are the seven spirits of God having been sent away into all the earth/land. 5.7 And he came and has taken out of the right (hand) of the (one) sitting upon the throne. 5.8 And when he received the scroll, the four living (things) and the twenty-four elders fell *down* before the lamb, each (one) having a lyre and golden bowls being full of incense offerings, which are prayers from the saints. 5.9 And they sing a new song, saying: You are worthy to receive the scroll and to open its seals, because you was slain and you bought us with/by your blood, out of every tribe and tongue and people and ethnic/nation, 5.10 and you made them a kingdom and a priesthood for our God, and they will reign on/over the earth/land. 5.11 And I saw, and I heard as a sound of many messengers/angels around the throne and the living (things) and the elders, and the number of them was myriads of myriads and thousands of thousands, 5.12 saying in/with a great voice: Worthy is the lamb, the (one) having been slain, to receive the power and wealth and wisdom and strength and honor and fame/glory/reputation and praise. 5.13 And every creature which *is* in the sky/heaven and upon the earth and the (things) in the sea, even the (things) in them all, also I heard them saying: To the (one) sitting upon the throne and to the lamb *be* the praise and the honor and the fame/glory and the power/dominion into the ages of the ages. 5.14 And the four living (things) said: Truly/so be it; and the elders fell *down* and worshiped. 6.1 And I saw when the lamb opened one out of the seven seals, and I heard one out of the four living (things) saying as a sound of thunder: You come. 6.2 And behold! I also saw, and behold, a white horse and the (one) sitting upon it having a bow, and a crown/wreath was given to him, and he went forth overcoming, and he conquered/overcame. 6.3 And when he opened the second seal, I heard the second living (thing) saying: You come. 6.4 And

531

ῖδον καὶ ἰδοὺ ἐξῆλθεν ἄλλος ἵππος πυρρός, καὶ τῷ καθημένῳ ἐπ' αὐτὸν ἐδόθη αὐτῷ λαβεῖν τὴν εἰρήνην ἐκ τῆς γῆς καὶ εἵνα ἀλλήλους σφάξωσιν, καὶ ἐδόθη αὐτῷ μάχαιρα μεγάλη. 6.5 καὶ ὅτε ἤνυξε τὴν σφραγῖδα τὴν τρίτην, ἤκουσα τοῦ τρίτου ζῴου λέγοντος, ἔρχου. καὶ ἴδε καὶ εἶδον, καὶ ἰδοὺ ἵππος μέλας, καὶ ὁ καθήμενος ἐπ' αὐτὸν ἔχων ζυγὸν ἐν τῇ χιρὶ αὐτοῦ. 6.6 καὶ ἤκουσα ὡς φωνὴν ἐν μέσῳ τῶν τεσσάρων ζῴων λέγουσαν, χοῖνιξ σίτου δηναρίου, καὶ τρῖς χοίνικες κριθῶν δηναρίου· καὶ τὸ ἔλαιον καὶ τὸν οἶνον μὴ ἀδικήσῃς. 6.7 καὶ ὅτε ἤνυξεν τὴν σφραγῖδα τὴν τετάρτην, ἤκουσα φωνὴν τοῦ τετάρτου ζῴου λέγοντος, ἔρχου. 6.8 καὶ ἴδε καὶ εἶδον, καὶ ἰδοὺ ἵππος χλωρός, καὶ ὁ καθήμενος ἐπάνω αὐτοῦ ὄνομα αὐτῷ θάνατος, καὶ ὁ ᾅδης ἠκολούθι αὐτῷ· καὶ ἐδόθη αὐτοῖς ἐξουσία ἐπὶ τὸ τέταρτον τῆς γῆς, ἀποκτεῖναι ἐν ῥομφαίᾳ καὶ λιμῷ καὶ θανάτῳ καὶ ὑπὸ τῶν θηρίων τῆς γῆς. 6.9 καὶ ὅτε ἤνοιξεν τὴν σφραγῖδα, εἶδον ὑποκάτω τοῦ θυσιαστηρίου τὰς ψυχὰς τῶν ἀνθρώπων τῶν ἐσφαγμένων διὰ τὸν λόγον τοῦ θεοῦ καὶ διὰ τὴν μαρτυρίαν ἣν εἶχον. 6.10 καὶ ἔκραξαν φωνῇ μεγάλῃ λέγοντες, ἕως πότε, ὁ δεσπότης ὁ ἅγιος καὶ ἀληθινός, οὐ κρίνεις καὶ ἐκδικῆς εἰς τὸ αἷμα ἡμῶν ἐκ τῶν κατοικούντων ἐπὶ τῆς γῆς; 6.11 καὶ ἐδόθη αὐτοῖς ἐκάστῳ στολὴ λευκή, καὶ ἐρέθη αὐτοῖς ἵνα ἀναπαύσωνται ἔπι χρόνον μικρόν, ἕως πληρωσῶσιν καὶ οἱ σύνδουλοι αὐτῶν καὶ οἱ ἀδελφοὶ αὐτῶν οἱ μέλλοντες ἀποκτέννεσθαι ὡς καὶ αὐτοί. 6.12 καὶ εἶδον ὅτε ἤνυξεν τὴν σφραγῖδα τὴν ἕκτην, καὶ σισμὸς μέλας ἐγένετο, καὶ ὁ ἥλιος μέλας ἐγένετο ὡς σάκκος τρίχινος, καὶ ἡ σελήνη ὅλη ἐγένετο ὡς αἷμα, 6.13 καὶ οἱ ἀστέρες τοῦ οὐρανοῦ ἔπεσαν ἐπὶ τὴν γῆν, ὡς συκῆ βάλλουσα τοὺς ὀλύνθους αὐτῆς ἀπὸ ἀνέμου μεγάλου σιομένη, 6.14 καὶ ὁ οὐρανὸς ἀπεχωρίσθη ὡς βιβλίον ἑλισσόμενος, καὶ πᾶν

behold! Also I saw/watched, and behold, another horse, a red (one), went forth, and to the (one) sitting upon it, it was given to him to take the peace out of the land/earth in order that they might slaughter one another, and a large sword/weapon was given to him. 6.5 And when he opened the third seal, I heard from the third living (thing) saying: You come. And behold! I also saw, and behold, a black horse, and the (one) sitting upon it *was* holding a balance/scale in his hand. 6.6 And I heard as a voice in the midst of the four living (things), saying: A choenix/quart of wheat from a denarius, and three choenixes/quarts of barley from a denarius; and you might spoil not the olive oil and the wine. 6.7 And when he opened the fourth seal, I heard a voice from the fourth living (thing), saying: You come. 6.8 And behold! I also saw, and behold, a yellow/pale green horse and the (one) sitting above/over it, a name for him *was* death, and the Hades followed with him; and an authority/a power was given to them against/over the fourth of the earth, to kill with a sword and famine and death and by the wild beasts of the earth. 6.9 And when he opened the -- seal, I saw underneath the altar the souls/lives of the men, of the (ones) having been slain because of the word/logos/reason/saying from God and because of the testimony which they had/held. 6.10 And they cried out with a great voice/sound, saying: Until when, the master, the holy and true (one), do you not judge and avenge to/for our blood out of/from those dwelling upon the earth? 6.11 And a white robe was given to them, to each (one), and it was spoken to them that they will rest for a little time, until their fellow slaves and their brothers, those being about to be killed even as they *were*, might be fulfilled. 6.12 And I saw when he opened the sixth seal, and a great earthquake happened, and the sun became black as sackcloth made of hair, and the entire moon became as blood, 6.13 and the stars fell from the sky/heaven upon/to the earth, as a fig tree having thrown its unripened figs, shaking from a great wind, 6.14 and the sky/heaven was swept aside as a scroll being rolled up, and every mountain and hill

ὄρος καὶ βουνὸς ἐκ τῶν τόπων ἐκινήθησαν. 6.15 καὶ οἱ βασιλεῖς τῆς γῆς καὶ οἱ μεγιστᾶνες καὶ οἱ χιλίαρχοι καὶ οἱ πλούσιοι καὶ οἱ ἰσχυροὶ καὶ πᾶς δοῦλος καὶ πᾶς ἐλεύθερος ἔκρυψαν ἑαυτοὺς εἰς τὰ σπήλεα καὶ εἰς τὰς πέτρας τῶν ὀρέων· 6.16 καὶ λέγουσιν τοῖς ὄρεσιν καὶ ταῖς πέτραις, πέσετε ἐφ᾽ ἡμᾶς καὶ κρύψετε ἐφ᾽ ἡμᾶς ἀπὸ προσώπου τοῦ καθημένου ἐπὶ τῷ θρόνῳ καὶ ἀπὸ τῆς ὀργῆς τοῦ ἀρνίου, 6.17 ὅτι ἦλθεν ἡ ἡμέρα ἡ μεγάλη τῆς ὀργῆς αὐτῶν, καὶ τίς δύναται σταθῆναι; 7.1 καὶ μετὰ τοῦτο ἴδον τέσσαρας ἀγγέλους ἑστῶτας ἐπὶ τὰς τέσσαρας γωνίας τῆς γῆς, κρατοῦντας τοὺς τέσσαρας ἀνέμους τῆς γῆς, ἵνα μὴ πνεύσῃ ἄνεμος ἐπὶ τῆς γῆς μήτε ἐπὶ τῆς θαλάσσης μήτε ἐπὶ πᾶν δένδρον. 7.2 καὶ εἶδον ἄλλον ἄγγελον ἀναβαίνοντα ἀπὸ ἀνατολῆς ἡλίου, ἔχοντα σφραγῖδα θεοῦ ζῶντος, καὶ ἔκραξεν φωνῇ μεγάλῃ τοῖς τέσσαρσιν ἀγγέλοις οἷς ἐδόθη αὐτοῖς ἀδικῆσαι τὴν γῆν καὶ τὴν θάλασσαν, 7.3 λέγων, μὴ ἀδικήσετε τὴν γῆν μήδε τὴν θάλασσαν μήδε τὰ δένδρα ἄχρις σφραγίσωμεν τοὺς δούλους τοῦ θεοῦ ἡμῶν ἐπὶ τῶν μετώπων αὐτῶν. 7.4 καὶ ἤκουσαν τὸν ἀριθμὸν τῶν ἐσφραγισμένων, ἑκατὸν τεσσεράκοντα χιλιάδες, ἐσφραγισμένοι ἐκ πάσης φυλῆς υἱῶν Ἰσραήλ· 7.5 ἐκ φυλῆς Ἰούδα δώδεκα χιλιάδες ἐσφραγισμένοι, ἐκ φυλῆς Ῥουβὴν δώδεκα χιλιάδες, 7.6 ἐκ φυλῆς Ἀσὴρ δώδεκα χιλιάδες, ἐκ φυλῆς Νεφθαλὶ δώδεκα χιλιάδες, ἐκ φυλῆς Μανασσῆ δώδεκα χιλιάδες, 7.7 ἐκ φυλῆς Λευεὶ δώδεκα χειλιάδες, ἐκ φυλῆς Ἰσσαχὰρ δώδεκα χιλιάδες, 7.8 ἐκ φυλῆς Ζαβουλὼν δώδεκα χιλιάδες, ἐκ φυλῆς Βενιαμὶν δώδεκα χειλιάδες, ἐκ φυλῆς Ἰωσὴφ δώδεκα χειλιάδες ἐσφραγισμένοι.

7.9 μετὰ ταῦτα ἴδον, καὶ ἰδοὺ ὄχλος πολύς, ὃν ἀριθμῆσαι αὐτὸν οὐδὶς ἐδύνατο, ἐκ παντὸς ἔθνους καὶ φυλῶν καὶ λαῶν καὶ γλωσσῶν, ἑστῶτες ἐνώπιον τοῦ θρόνου καὶ ἐνώπιον τοῦ ἀρνίου, περιβεβλημένους στολὰς λευκάς, καὶ φοίνικες ἐν ταῖς χερσὶν αὐτῶν· 7.10 καὶ κράζουσιν φωνῇ μεγάλῃ λέγοντες, ἡ σωτηρία τῷ

were moved out of the places. 6.15 And the kings of
the land/earth and the magistrates and the commanders
and the rich (ones) and the strong (ones) and every
slave and every free (one), they concealed/hid
themselves in the caves and in the rocks of the
mountains; 6.16 and they say to the mountains and to
the rocks: Fall ye upon us and hide ye us from the
face/countenance of the (one) sitting upon the throne
and from the anger/indignation of the lamb, 6.17
because the great day of their anger/indignation came,
and who is able to be stood? 7.1 And after this I
saw four messengers/angels having been stood upon the
four corners of the earth, holding fast the four winds
of the land/earth, in order that a wind might not
blow/breathe upon the land nor upon the sea nor upon
every tree. 7.2 And I saw another messenger/angel
going up from the rising of a sun, having a seal of a
living God, and he cried out with a great voice to the
four messengers/angels to whom it was given to them to
spoil/mistreat the land and the sea, 7.3 saying:
Spoil/harm ye not the land nor the sea nor the trees
until we might seal the slaves of our God upon their
foreheads. 7.4 And I heard the number of those having
been sealed, a hundred forty -- thousands, having been
sealed out of every tribe of sons of Israel. 7.5 Out
of a tribe of Juda twelve thousands having been
sealed, from a tribe of Reuben twelve thousands -- ,
7.6 from a tribe of Aser twelve thousands, from a
tribe of Nephthalim twelve thousands, from a tribe of
Manasse twelve thousands, -- , 7.7 from a tribe of
Levi twelve thousands, from a tribe of Issachar twelve
thousands, 7.8 from a tribe of Zabulon twelve
thousands, from a tribe of Benjamin twelve thousands,
from a tribe of Joseph twelve thousands having been
sealed.
　　　　7.9 After these (things) I saw/looked and
behold, a much crowd, which no one was able to number
it, out of every ethnic/nation and from tribes and
from peoples and from tongues/languages, having been
stood before the throne and before the lamb, having
been clothed *with* white robes, and palms *were* in their
hands; 7.10 and they cry out in/with a great voice,

θεῷ ἡμῶν τῷ καθημένῳ ἐπὶ τῷ θρόνῳ καὶ τῷ ἀρνίῳ. 7.11 καὶ πάντες οἱ ἄγγελοι ἱστήκισαν κύκλῳ τοῦ θρόνου καὶ τῶν πρεσβυτέρων καὶ τῶν τεσσάρων ζῴων, καὶ ἔπεσαν ἐνώπιον τοῦ θρόνου ἐπὶ τὰ πρόσωπα αὐτῶν καὶ προσεκύνησαν τῷ θεῷ, 7.12 λέγοντες, ἀμήν· ἡ εὐλογία καὶ ἡ δόξα καὶ ἡ σοφία καὶ ἡ εὐχαριστία καὶ ἡ τιμὴ καὶ ἡ δύναμις καὶ ἡ ἰσχὺς τῷ θεῷ ἡμῶν εἰς τοὺς αἰῶνας τῶν αἰώνων· ἀμήν.

7.13 καὶ ἀπεκρίθη εἷς τῶν πρεσβυτέρων λέγων μοι, οὗτοι οἱ περιβεβλημένοι τὰς στολὰς τὰς λευκὰς τίνες εἰσὶν καὶ πόθεν ἦλθον; 7.14 καὶ εἴρηκα αὐτῷ, κύριέ μου, σὺ οἶδας. καὶ εἶπέν, οὗτοί εἰσιν οἱ ἐρχόμενοι ἐκ τῆς θλίψεως τῆς μεγάλης, καὶ ἔπλυναν τὰς στολὰς αὐτῶν καὶ ἐλεύκαναν αὐτὰς ἐν τῷ αἵματι τοῦ ἀρνίου. 7.15 διὰ τοῦτό εἰσιν ἐνώπιον τοῦ θρόνου τοῦ θεοῦ, καὶ λατρεύουσιν αὐτῷ ἡμέρας καὶ νυκτὸς ἐν τῷ ναῷ αὐτοῦ, καὶ ὁ καθήμενος ἐπὶ τοῦ θρόνου σκηνώσει ἐπ᾽ αὐτούς. 7.16 οὐ πινάσουσιν οὐδὲ διψάσουσιν ἔτι, οὐδὲ μὴ πέσῃ ἐπ᾽ αὐτοὺς ὁ ἥλιος ἔτι οὐδὲ πᾶν καῦμα, 7.17 ὅτι τὸ ἀρνίον τὸ ἀνὰ μέσον τοῦ θρόνου ποιμανεῖ αὐτούς, καὶ ὁδηγήσει αὐτοὺς ἐπὶ ζωῆς πηγὰς ὑδάτων· καὶ ἐξαλίψει ὁ θεὸς πᾶν δάκρυον ἀπὸ τῶν ὀφθαλμῶν αὐτῶν. 8.1 καὶ ὅτε ἤνοιξεν τὴν σφραγῖδα τὴν ἑβδόμην, ἐγένετο σιγὴ ἐν τῷ οὐρανῷ ὡς εἰμιώριον. 8.2 καὶ ἴδον τοὺς ἑπτὰ ἀγγέλους οἳ ἐνώπιον τοῦ θεοῦ ἐστήκασιν, καὶ ἐδόθησαν αὐτοῖς ἑπτὰ σάλπιγγες. 8.3 καὶ ἄλλος ἄγγελος ἦλθεν καὶ ἐστάθη ἐπὶ τοῦ θυσιαστηρίου ἔχων λιβανωτὸν χρυσοῦν, καὶ ἐδόθη αὐτῷ θυμιάματα πολλὰ ἵνα δώσει ταῖς προσευχαῖς τῶν ἁγίων πάντων ἐπὶ τὸ θυσιαστήριον τὸ χρυσοῦν ἐνώπιον τοῦ θρόνου. 8.4 καὶ ἀνέβη ὁ καπνὸς τῶν θυμιαμάτων ταῖς προσευχαῖς τῶν ἁγίων ἐκ χιρὸς τοῦ ἀγγέλου ἐνώπιον τοῦ θεοῦ. 8.5 καὶ εἴληφεν ὁ ἄγγελος τὸν λιβανωτόν, καὶ ἐγέμισεν αὐτὸν ἐκ τοῦ πυρὸς τοῦ θυσιαστηρίου καὶ ἔβαλεν εἰς τὴν γῆν· καὶ ἐγένοντο βρονταὶ καὶ

saying: The salvation *be* for our God, for the (one) sitting upon the throne, and for the lamb. 7.11 And all the messengers/angels had been stood around the throne and the elders and the four living (things), and they fell *down* before the throne upon their faces and they worshiped to God, 7.12 saying: Truly, the praise and the fame/glory and the wisdom and the thanksgiving and the honor and the power and the strength *is* to/for our God into the ages of the ages; truly.

7.13 And one of the elders answered, saying to me: These, the (ones) having been clothed with the white robes, who are they and from where came they? 7.14 And I have said to him: My lord, you, you know. And he said: These, they are the (ones) coming out of the great affliction/tribulation, and they washed their robes and whitened them in/with the blood of the lamb. 7.15 Because of this they are before the throne of God, and they serve/worship for him day and night in the *inner* temple of him, and the (one) sitting upon the throne will spread a tent/shelter over them. 7.16 They will not hunger nor thirst still, neither might fall not the sun on them still, not every heat, 7.17 because the lamb, the (one) in the midst of the throne, will shepherd/feed them, and he will guide/lead them to fountains of waters of life; and God will wipe out every tear from their eyes. 8.1 And when he opened the seventh seal, a silence became in the sky/heaven about a half hour. 8.2 And I saw the seven messengers/angels who were stood before God, and seven trumpets were given to them. 8.3 And another messenger/angel came and stood upon the altar having a golden senser, and many incense offerings were given to him in order that he will give *them* with the prayers to all the saints upon the altar, the golden (one) before the throne. 8.4 And the smoke from the incense offerings ascended/rose with the prayers of the saints from a hand of the messenger before God. 8.5 And the messenger has taken the censer, and he filled it out of the fire from the altar and he threw *it* to the earth; and there happened/became thunders and sounds/voices and lightnings and an earthquake.

φωναὶ καὶ ἀστραπαὶ καὶ σεισμός. 8.6 καὶ οἱ ἑπτὰ ἄγγελοι ἔχοντες τὰς ἑπτὰ σάλπιγγας ἡτοίμασαν αὐτοὺς ἵνα σαλπίσωσιν. 8.7 καὶ ὁ πρῶτος ἐσάλπισεν· καὶ ἐγένετο χάλαζα καὶ πῦρ μεμιγμένον ἐν αἵματι, καὶ ἐβλήθη εἰς τὴν γῆν· καὶ τὸ τρίτον τῆς γῆς κατεκάη, καὶ τὸ τρίτον τῶν δένδρων κατεκάη, καὶ πᾶς χόρτος χλωρὸς κατεκάη. 8.8 καὶ ὁ δεύτερος ἐσάλπισεν· καὶ ὡς ὄρος μέγα πυρὶ καιόμενον ἐβλήθη εἰς τὴν θάλασσαν· καὶ ἐγενήθη τὸ τρίτον τῆς θαλάσσης αἷμα, 8.9 καὶ ἀπέθανε τὸ τρίτον μέρος τῶν κτισμάτων τῶν ἐν τῇ θαλάσσῃ, τὰ ἔχοντα ψυχήν, καὶ τὸ τρίτον τῶν πλοίων διεφθάρησαν.

8.10 καὶ ὁ τρίτος ἄγγελος ἐσάλπισεν· καὶ ἔπεσεν ἐκ τοῦ οὐρανοῦ ἀστὴρ μέγας καιόμενος ὡς λαμπάς, καὶ ἔπεσεν ἐπὶ τὸ τρίτον τῶν ποταμῶν καὶ ἐπὶ τὰς πηγὰς τῶν ὑδάτων. 8.11 καὶ τὸ ὄνομα τοῦ ἀστέρος λέγεται Ἄψινθος. καὶ ἐγένετο τὸ τρίτον τῶν ὑδάτων εἰς ἄψινθον, καὶ πολλοὶ τῶν ἀνθρώπων ἀπέθανον ἐκ τῶν ὑδάτων, ὅτι ἐπικράνθησαν.

8.12 καὶ ὁ τέταρτος ἄγγελος ἐσάλπισεν· καὶ ἐπλήγη τὸ τρίτον τοῦ ἡλίου καὶ τὸ τρίτον τῆς σελήνης καὶ τὸ τρίτον τῶν ἀστέρων, ἵνα σκοτισθῇ τὸ τρίτον αὐτῶν καὶ ἡ ἡμέρα μὴ φάνῃ τὸ τρίτον αὐτῆς, καὶ ἡ νὺξ ὁμοίως. 8.13 καὶ εἶδον, καὶ ἤκουσα ἀετοῦ πετομένου ἐν μεσουρανήματι λέγοντος φωνῇ μεγάλῃ, οὐαὶ οὐαὶ οὐαὶ τοὺς κατοικοῦντας ἐπὶ τῆς γῆς ἐκ τῶν λοιπῶν φωνῶν τῆς σάλπιγγος τῶν τριῶν ἀγγέλων τῶν μελλόντων σαλπίζειν.

9.1 Καὶ ὁ πέμπτος ἄγγελος ἐσάλπισεν· καὶ εἶδον ἀστέρα ἐκ τοῦ οὐρανοῦ πεπτωκότα εἰς τὴν γῆν, καὶ ἐδόθη αὐτῷ ἡ κλὶς τοῦ φρέατος τῆς ἀβύσσου. 9.2 καὶ ἤνοιξεν τὸ φρέαρ τῆς ἀβύσσου, καὶ ἀνέβη καπνὸς ἐκ τοῦ φρέατος ὡς καπνὸς καμίνου μεγάλης, καὶ ἐσκοτίσθη ὁ ἥλιος καὶ ὁ ἀὴρ ἐκ τοῦ καπνοῦ τοῦ φρέατος. 9.3 καὶ ἐκ τοῦ καπνοῦ ἐξῆλθον ἀκρίδες εἰς τὴν γῆν, καὶ

8.6 And the seven messengers/angels holding the seven trumpets prepared themselves that they might trumpet. 8.7 And the first (one) trumpeted; and there became hail and fire, having been mixed with blood, and it was thrown to the earth; and the third (part) of the earth/land was burned up, and the third (part) of the trees was burnt up, and every yellow/pale green grass was burnt up. 8.8 And the second (one) trumpeted; and as a large mountain burning with fire, it was thrown into the sea; and the third (part) of the sea was caused to become blood, 8.9 and the third part of the creatures in the sea, the (things) having a soul/life, they died, and the third (part) of the boats/ships were destroyed.

8.10 And the third messenger/angel trumpeted; and a large star fell out of the sky/heaven, burning as a lamp, and it fell on the third (part) of the rivers and on the springs/fountains of the waters. 8.11 And the name of the star is said Wormwood. And the third (part) of the waters became/were turned into wormwood, and many of the men died from the waters, because they were made bitter/embittered.

8.12 And the fourth messenger/angel trumpeted; and the third (part) of the sun was struck and the third (part) of the moon and the third (part) of the stars, in order that the third (part) of them might be darkened and the day might not appear *for* the third (part) of it, and the night similarly. 8.13 And I saw, and I heard an eagle/vulture flying in mid sky/heaven, saying with a great voice: Woe, woe, woe *for* those having dwelt upon the earth, out of the sounds from the trumpets of the three messengers/angels, of those being about to trumpet.

9.1 And the fifth messenger/angel trumpeted; and I saw a star out of the sky having fallen to the earth, and the key/bolt of the shaft/pit of the abyss was given to it. 9.2 And it opened the pit/shaft of the abyss, and smoke ascended out of the pit as smoke from a great furnace, and the sun and the air were darkened from the smoke of/from the pit. 9.3 And locusts/grasshoppers went forth out of the smoke into

ἐδόθη αὐτοῖς ἐξουσία ὡς ἔχουσιν ἐξουσίαν οἱ σκορπίοι τῆς γῆς. 9.4 καὶ ἐρρέθη αὐτοῖς ἵνα μὴ ἀδικήσωσιν τὸν χόρτον τῆς γῆς οὐδὲ πᾶν — δένδρον, εἰ μὴ τοὺς ἀνθρώπους οἵτινες οὐκ ἔχουσιν τὴν σφραγῖδαν τοῦ θεοῦ ἐπὶ τῶν μετώπων. 9.5 καὶ ἐδόθη αὐτοῖς ἵνα μὴ ἀποκτίνωσιν αὐτούς, ἀλλ' ἵνα βασανισθήσονται μῆνας πέντε· καὶ ὁ βασανισμὸς αὐτῶν ὡς βασανισμὸς σκορπίου, ὅταν πέσῃ ἄνθρωπον. 9.6 καὶ ἐν ταῖς ἡμέραις ἐκείναις ζητήσουσιν οἱ ἄνθρωποι τὸν θάνατον καὶ οὐ μὴ εὑρήσουσιν αὐτόν, καὶ ἐπιθυμήσουσιν ἀποθανῖν καὶ φύγῃ ὁ θάνατος ἀπ' αὐτῶν. 9.7 καὶ τὰ ὁμοιώματα τῶν ἀκρίδων ὅμοιοι ἵπποις ἡτοιμασμένοις εἰς πόλεμον, καὶ ἐπὶ τὰς κεφαλὰς αὐτῶν ὡς στέφανοι ὅμοιοι χρυσῷ, καὶ τὰ πρόσωπα αὐτῶν ὡς πρόσωπα ἀνθρώπων, 9.8 καὶ εἶχαν τρίχας ὡς τρίχας γυναικῶν, καὶ οἱ ὀδόντες αὐτῶν ὡς λεόντων ἦσαν, 9.9 καὶ εἶχαν θώρακας ὡς θώρακας σιδηροῦς, καὶ ἡ φωνὴ τῶν πτερύγων αὐτῶν ὡς φωνὴ ἁρμάτων ἵππων πολλῶν τρεχόντων εἰς πόλεμον. 9.10 καὶ ἔχουσιν οὐρὰς ὁμοίοι σκορπίοις καὶ κέντρα, καὶ ἐν ταῖς οὐραῖς αὐτῶν ἡ ἐξουσία αὐτῶν ἀδικῆσαι τοὺς ἀνθρώπους μῆνας πέντε. 9.11 ἔχουσιν ἑαυτῶν τὸν βασιλέα τὸν ἄγγελον τῆς ἀβύσσου· ᾧ ὄνομα αὐτῷ Ἑβραϊστὶ Ἀβαδδὼν καὶ ἐν τῇ Ἑλληνιδῖ ἔχι ὄνομα Ἀπολλύων. 9.12 οὐαὶ ἡ μία ἀπῆλθεν· ἰδοὺ ἔρχεται ἔτι δύο οὐαὶ μετὰ ταῦτα. 9.13 ὁ ἕκτος ἄγγελος ἐσάλπισεν· καὶ ἤκουσα φωνὴν μίας ἐκ τῶν κεράτων τοῦ θυσιαστηρίου τοῦ χρυσοῦ τοῦ ἐνώπιον τοῦ θεοῦ, 9.14 λέγοντα τῷ ἕκτῳ ἀγγέλῳ, ὁ ἔχων τὴν σάλπιγγα, λῦσον τοὺς τέσσαρες ἀγγέλους τοὺς δεδεμένους ἐπὶ τῷ ποταμῷ τῷ μεγάλῳ Εὐφράτῃ. 9.15 καὶ ἐλύθησαν οἱ τέσσαρες ἄγγελοι ἡτοιμασμένοι εἰς τὴν ὥραν καὶ μῆνα καὶ ἐνιαυτόν, ἵνα μὴ ἀποκτίνωσιν τὸ τρίτον τῶν ἀνθρώπων. 9.16 καὶ ὁ ἀριθμὸς τῶν στρατευμάτων τοῦ ἱππικοῦ δύο μυριάδων μυριάδας· ἤκουσα τὸν ἀριθμὸν αὐτῶν. 9.17 καὶ οὕτως εἶδον τοὺς ἵππους ἐν τῇ ὁράσει καὶ τοὺς καθημένους ἐπάνω αὐτῶν, ἔχοντας θώρακας πυρίνους καὶ ὑακινθίνους καὶ θυώδεις· καὶ αἱ κεφαλαὶ τῶν ἵππων ὡς κεφαλαὶ λεόντων, καὶ ἐκ

the land, and an authority was given to them as
scorpions of the land/earth have an authority/power.
9.4 And it was spoken to them that they should
spoil/harm not the grass of the land, neither every --
tree, except the men/humans who have not the seal of
God upon the foreheads. 9.5 And it was given to them
that they should not kill them, but that they should
be tormented *for* five months; and their torment *is* as
a torment from a scorpion, whenever it might sting a
man/human. 9.6 And in those days the men/humans will
seek death and by no means will they find it, and they
will desire to die but the death flees from them. 9.7
And the likenesses/shapes of the locusts/grasshoppers
are similar to horses having been readied/prepared for
war, and upon their heads as crowns/wreaths similar to
gold, and their faces as/like faces of men/humans,
9.8 and they had hairs as hairs of women, and their
teeth were as from lions, 9.9 and they had
breastplates as/like iron breastplates, and the sound
of their wings *was* as a sound of chariots, of many
horses running to war/battle. 9.10 And they have
tails like scorpions and goads/stings, and their
authority/power *is* to harm/mistreat the men/humans
with their tails *for* five months. 9.11 They have of
themselves the king, the messenger/angel of the abyss;
a name for him in Hebrew *is* Abaddon, and in the Greek
he has a name, Apollyon. 9.12 The one woe went away;
behold, there comes yet two woes after these (things).
9.13 The sixth messenger/angel trumpeted; and I heard
a voice out of one of the horns of the golden altar,
of the (one) before God, 9.14 saying to the sixth
messenger/angel, the (one) having the trumpet: You
loose the four messengers/angels, those having been
bound at the great river Euphrates. 9.15 And the four
messengers/angels, having been prepared, were loosed
in the/*that* hour both *for* a month and a year, that
they might kill the third (part) of the men/humans.
9.16 And the number of the soldiers of the horses *was*
two myriads of myriads; I heard the number of them.
9.17 And thus I saw the horses in the vision and those
sitting above/over them, having fiery and hyacinth and
sulfurous breastplates; and the heads of the horses

τῶν στομάτων αὐτῶν ἐκπορεύεται πῦρ καὶ καπνὸς καὶ θῖον. 9.18 ἀπὸ τῶν πληγῶν τούτων ἀπεκτάνθησαν τὸ τρίτον τῶν ἀνθρώπων, ἐκ τοῦ πυρὸς καὶ τοῦ καπνοῦ καὶ τοῦ θείου τοῦ ἐκπορευομένου ἐκ τῶν στομάτων αὐτῶν. 9.19 ἡ γὰρ ἐξουσία τῶν ἵππων ἐν τῷ στόματι αὐτῶν ἐστιν καὶ ἐν ταῖς οὐραῖς αὐτῶν· αἱ γὰρ οὐραὶ αὐτῶν ὅμοιαι ὄφεσιν, ἔχουσαις κεφαλάς, καὶ ἐν αὐταῖς ἀδικοῦσιν. 9.20 καὶ οἱ λοιποὶ τῶν ἀνθρώπων, οἳ οὐκ ἀπεκτάνθησαν ἐν ταῖς πληγαῖς αὐτῶν ταύταις, οὐδὲ μετενόησαν ἐκ τῶν ἔργων τῶν χιρῶν αὐτῶν, ἵνα μὴ προσκυνήσουσιν τὰ δαιμόνια καὶ τὰ ἴδωλα τὰ χρυσαῖα καὶ τὰ ἀργυρᾶ καὶ τὰ χαλκεᾶ καὶ τὰ ξύλινα καὶ τὰ λίθινα, ἃ οὔτε βλέπειν δύνανται οὔτε ἀκούειν οὔτε περιπατεῖν, 9.21 καὶ οὐ μετενόησαν ἐκ τῶν φόνων αὐτῶν οὔτε ἐκ τῶν φαρμάκων αὐτῶν οὔτε ἐκ τῆς πορνίας αὐτῶν οὔτε ἐκ τῶν κλεμμάτων αὐτῶν. 10.1 καὶ εἶδον ἄλλον ἄγγελον ἰσχυρὸν καταβαίνοντα ἐκ τοῦ οὐρανοῦ, περιβεβλημένον νεφέλην, καὶ ἡ ἶρις ἐπὶ τῆς κεφαλῆς αὐτοῦ, καὶ τὸ πρόσωπον αὐτοῦ ὡς ὁ ἥλιος, καὶ οἱ πόδες αὐτοῦ ὡς στῦλοι πυρός, 10.2 καὶ ἔχων ἐν τῇ χειρὶ αὐτοῦ βιβλαρίδιον ἠνεῳγμένον. καὶ ἔθηκεν τὸν πόδα αὐτοῦ τὸν δεξιὸν ἐπὶ τῆς θαλάσσης, τὸν δὲ εὐώνυμον ἐπὶ τῆς γῆς, 10.3 καὶ ἔκραξεν φωνῇ μεγάλῃ ὥσπερ λέων μυκᾶτε. καὶ ὅτε ἔκραξεν, ἐλάλησαν αἱ ἑπτὰ βρονταὶ ταῖς ἑαυτῶν φωναῖς. 10.4 καὶ ὅσα ἐλάλησαν αἱ ἑπτὰ βρονταί, ἔμελλον γράφειν· καὶ ἤκουσα φωνὴν ἐκ τοῦ οὐρανοῦ λέγουσαν, σφράγισον ὅσα ἐλάλησαν αἱ ἑπτὰ βρονταί, καὶ μὴ αὐτὰ γράψῃς. 10.5 καὶ ὁ ἄγγελος ὃν εἶδον ἑστῶτα ἐπὶ τῆς θαλάσσης καὶ ἐπὶ τῆς γῆς ἦρεν τὴν χεῖρα αὐτοῦ τὴν δεξιὰν εἰς τὸν οὐρανὸν 10.6 καὶ ὤμοσεν ἐν τῷ ζῶντι εἰς τοὺς αἰῶνας τῶν αἰώνων, ὃς ἔκτισεν τὸν οὐρανὸν καὶ τὰ ἐν αὐτῷ καὶ τὴν γῆν καὶ τὰ ἐν αὐτῇ καὶ τὴν θάλασσαν καὶ τὰ ἐν αὐτῇ, ὅτι χρόνος οὐκέτι ἔσται, 10.7 ἀλλ' ἐν ταῖς ἡμέραις τῆς φωνῆς τοῦ ἀγγέλου τοῦ ἑβδόμου, ὅταν μέλλῃ σαλπίζειν, καὶ ἐτελέσθη τὸ μυστήριον τοῦ θεοῦ, ὡς εὐηγγέλισεν

were as heads of lions, and fire and smoke and sulphur goes forth out of their mouths. 9.18 From these plagues the third (part) of the men/humans were killed, from the fire and the smoke and the sulphur, from *that* going forth out of their mouths, 9.19 for the authority/power of the horses is in their mouths and in their tails; for their tails are similar to serpents having heads, and they spoil/harm with them. 9.20 And the rest of the men/humans, who were not killed by these their plagues, they not even repented from the works of their hands, in order that they will not worship the demons and the idols, the gold (things) and the silver (things) and the copper (things) and the wood (things) and the stone (things), which are neither able to see nor to hear nor to walk, 9.21 and they repented not from their murders nor from their enchantments nor from their prostitution/unchastity nor from their thefts. 10.1 And I saw another strong messenger/angel descending out of the sky/heaven, having been dressed *with* a cloud, and the halo/rainbow *was* upon his head, and his face *was* as/like the sun, and his feet *were* as pillars of fire, 10.2 and holding in his hand a little scroll having been opened. And he place his right foot upon the sea and the left upon the land, 10.3 and he cried out with a great sound/voice even as a lion roars. And when he cried out, the seven thunders spoke the sounds of themselves. 10.4 And I was about to write whatever the seven thunders spoke; and I heard a voice out of the sky/heaven saying: You seal/secure whatever the seven thunders spoke, but you may not write them. 10.5 And the messenger/angel whom I saw having stood upon the sea and upon the land lifted his right hand to/into the sky/heaven 10.6 and he swore by the (one) living into the ages of the ages, who created the sky and the (things) in it and the earth/land and the (things) in her/*it* and the sea and the (things) in her/*it*, that time will be no longer, 10.7 but in the days of the voice/sound of the seventh angel/messenger, whenever he may be about to trumpet, and the mystery of God was finished as he heralded the good message/gospel *for* the slaves of himself and *for*

τοὺς ἑαυτοῦ δούλους καὶ τοὺς προφήτας. 10.8 καὶ ἡ φωνὴ ἣν ἤκουσα ἐκ τοῦ οὐρανοῦ, πάλιν λαλοῦσαν μετ' ἐμοῦ καὶ λέγουσαν, ὕπαγε λάβε τὸ βιβλαρίδιον τὸ ἠνεῳγμένον ἐν τῇ χειρὶ τοῦ ἀγγέλου τοῦ ἑστῶτος ἐπὶ τῆς θαλάσσης καὶ ἐπὶ τῆς γῆς. 10.9 καὶ ἀπῆλθον πρὸς τὸν ἄγγελον λέγων αὐτῷ δοῦναί μοι τὸ βιβλίον. καὶ λέγει μοι, λάβε αὐτὸ καὶ κατάφαγε αὐτό, καὶ πικρανεῖ σου τὴν κοιλίαν, ἀλλὰ ἐν τῷ στόματί σου ἔσται γλυκὺ ὡς μέλι. 10.10 καὶ ἔλαβον τὸ βιβλίον ἐκ τῆς χειρὸς τοῦ ἀγγέλου καὶ κατέφαγον αὐτό, καὶ ἦν ἐν τῷ στόματί μου ὡς μέλι γλυκύ· καὶ ὅτε ἔφαγον αὐτό, ἐπικράνθη ἡ κοιλία μου. 10.11 καὶ λέγουσίν μοι, δεῖ σε πάλιν προφητεῦσαι ἐπὶ λαοῖς καὶ ἔθνεσιν καὶ γλώσσαις καὶ βασιλεῦσιν πολλοῖς. 11.1 καὶ ἐδόθη μοι κάλαμος ὅμοιος ῥάβδῳ, λέγων, ἔγειρε καὶ μέτρησον τὸν ναὸν τοῦ θεοῦ καὶ τὸ θυσιαστήριον καὶ τοὺς προσκυνοῦντας ἐν αὐτῷ. 11.2 καὶ τὴν αὐλὴν τὴν ἔσωθεν τοῦ ναοῦ καὶ ἔκβαλε ἔξωθεν καὶ μὴ αὐτὴν μετρήσῃς, ὅτι ἐδόθη τοῖς ἔθνεσιν, καὶ τὴν πόλιν τὴν ἁγίαν πατήσουσιν μῆνας τεσσεράκοντα δύο. 11.3 καὶ δώσω τοῖς δυσὶν μάρτυσίν μου, καὶ προφητεύσουσιν ἡμέρας χιλίας διακοσίας ἑξήκοντα περιβεβλημένοι σάκκους. 11.4 οὗτοί εἰσιν αἱ δύο ἐλαῖαι καὶ αἱ δύο λυχνίαι ἐνώπιον τοῦ κυρίου τῆς γῆς ἑστῶτες. 11.5 καὶ εἴ τις θέλει αὐτοὺς ἀδικῆσαι, πῦρ ἐκπορεύεται ἐκ τοῦ στόματος αὐτῶν καὶ κατεσθίει τοὺς ἐχθροὺς αὐτῶν· καὶ εἴ τις θελήσῃ ἀδικῆσαι αὐτούς, οὕτως δεῖ αὐτὸν ἀποκτανθῆναι. 11.6 οὗτοι ἔχουσιν ἐξουσίαν κλεῖσαι τὸν οὐρανόν, ἵνα μὴ ὑετὸς βρέχῃ τὰς ἡμέρας τῆς προφητείας αὐτῶν, καὶ ἐξουσίαν ἔχουσιν ἐπὶ τῶν ὑδάτων στρέφειν αὐτὰ εἰς αἷμα καὶ πατάξαι τὴν γῆν ἐν πάσῃ πληγῇ ὁσάκις ἐὰν θελήσωσι. 11.7 καὶ ὅταν τελέσωσιν τὴν μαρτυρίαν αὐτῶν, τὸ θηρίον τὸ ἀναβαῖνον ἐκ τῆς ἀβύσσου ποιήσει μετ' αὐτῶν πόλεμον καὶ νικήσει αὐτοὺς καὶ ἀποκτενεῖ αὐτούς. 11.8 καὶ τὰ πτώματα αὐτῶν ἐπὶ τῆς πλατίας τῆς πόλεως τῆς μεγάλης, ἥτις καλεῖται πνευματικῶς Σόδομα καὶ Αἴγυπτος,

the prophets. 10.8 And the voice which I heard out of the sky/heaven *was* again speaking with me and saying: You go, receive you the little scroll, the (one) having been opened in the hand of the messenger/angel, of the (one) having stood upon the sea and upon the land. 10.9 And I went to the messenger/angel, saying to him to give to me the scroll. And he says to me: You take it and you eat/consume it, and it will embitter your belly, but in your mouth it will be sweet as honey. 10.10 And I took the scroll out of the hand of the messenger/angel and devoured/consumed it, and it was sweet as honey in my mouth, and when/after I ate it, my belly was embittered. 10.11 And they say to me: It is necessary *for* you to prophesy again to/before peoples and ethnics and tongues/languages and to many kings. 11.1 And a staff similar to a rod was given to me, saying: You rise and measure the *inner* temple of God and the altar and those worshiping in it. 11.2 And the court (yard) from within the *inner* temple, and put you outside and you may not measure it, because it was given to/for the ethnics/nations, and they will tread down the holy city *for* forty-two months. 11.3 And I shall give *it* to my two witnesses, and they will prophesy a thousand two hundred sixty days, having been clothed *with* sackcloth. 11.4 These are the two olive trees and the two lampstands having stood before the lord/Lord of the land/earth. 11.5 And if anyone wants to mistreat/wrong them, fire goes forth out of the mouth of them and devours their enemies; and if anyone might want to mistreat/wrong them, it is thus necessary *for* him to be killed. 11.6 These have authority to shut the sky/heaven, in order that it may not rain *for* the days of their prophecy, and they have authority/power upon/over the waters, to turn them into blood and to smite the earth with every plague as often as they would want. 11.7 And whenever they might finish their testimony/witnessing, the wild beast, the (one) ascending out of the abyss, will make war/a fight with them and will overcome/conquer them and will kill them. 11.8 And their corpses *will be* upon the broad street of the great city, which is spiritually called

ὅπου καὶ ὁ κύριος αὐτῶν ἐσταυρώθη. 11.9 καὶ βλέπουσιν ἐκ τῶν φυλῶν καὶ λαῶν καὶ γλωσσῶν καὶ ἐθνῶν τὸ πτῶμα αὐτῶν ἡμέρας τρεῖς καὶ ἥμισυ, καὶ τὰ πτώματα αὐτῶν οὐκ ἀφίουσιν τεθῆναι εἰς μνήματα. 11.10 καὶ οἱ κατοικοῦντες ἐπὶ τῆς γῆς χαίρουσιν ἐπ' αὐτοῖς καὶ εὐφραίνονται, καὶ δῶρα πέμψουσιν ἀλλήλοις, ὅτι οὗτοι οἱ προφῆται οἱ δύο ἐβασάνισαν τοὺς κατοικοῦντας ἐπὶ τῆς γῆς. 11.11 καὶ μετὰ τὰς τρῖς ἡμέρας καὶ ἥμισου πνεῦμα ζωῆς ἐκ τοῦ θεοῦ εἰσῆλθεν εἰς αὐτούς, καὶ ἔστησαν ἐπὶ τοὺς πόδας αὐτῶν, καὶ φόβος μέγας ἔπεσεν ἐπὶ τοὺς θεωροῦντας αὐτούς. 11.12 καὶ ἤκουσαν φωνῆς μεγάλης ἐκ τοῦ οὐρανοῦ λεγούσης αὐτοῖς, ἀνάβατε ὧδε· καὶ ἀνέβησαν εἰς τὸν οὐρανὸν ἐν τῇ νεφέλῃ, καὶ ἐθεώρησαν αὐτοὺς οἱ ἐχθροὶ αὐτῶν. 11.13 καὶ ἐν ἐκίνῃ τῇ ὥρᾳ ἐγένετο σισμὸς μέγας, καὶ τὸ δέκατον τῆς πόλεως ἔπεσεν, καὶ ἀπεκτάνθησαν ἐν τῷ σισμῷ ὀνόματα ἀνθρώπων χιλιάδες ἑπτά, καὶ οἱ λοιποὶ ἐνφόβω ἐγένοντο καὶ ἔδωκαν δόξαν τῷ θεῷ τοῦ οὐρανοῦ. 11.14 ἡ οὐαὶ ἡ δευτέρα παπῆλθεν· ἰδοὺ ἔρχεται ἡ οὐαὶ ἡ τρίτη ταχύ. 11.15 καὶ ὁ ἕβδομος ἄγγελος ἐσάλπισεν· καὶ ἐγένοντο φωναὶ μεγάλαι ἐν τῷ οὐρανῷ λέγουσαι, ἐγένετο ἡ βασιλία τοῦ κόσμου τοῦ κυρίου ἡμῶν καὶ τοῦ χριστοῦ αὐτοῦ, καὶ βασιλεύσει εἰς τοὺς αἰῶνας τῶν αἰώνων. ἀμήν. 11.16 καὶ εἴκοσι τέσσαρες πρεσβύτεροι οἱ ἐνώπιον τοῦ θεοῦ οἱ καθήται ἐπὶ τοὺς θρόνους αὐτῶν καὶ ἔπεσαν ἐπὶ τὰ πρόσωπα αὐτῶν καὶ προσεκύνησαν τῷ θεῷ 11.17 λέγοντες, εὐχαριστοῦμέν σοι, κύριος ὁ θεὸς ὁ παντοκράτωρ, ὁ ὢν καὶ ὁ ἦν, ὅτι εἴληφας τὴν δύναμίν σου τὴν μεγάλην καὶ ἐβασίλευσας· 11.18 καὶ τὰ ἔθνη ὠργίσθησαν, καὶ ἦλθεν ἡ ὀργή σου καὶ ὁ καιρὸς τῶν νεκρῶν κριθῆναι καὶ δοῦναι τὸν μισθὸν τοῖς δούλοις σου τοῖς προφήταις καὶ τοῖς ἁγίοις καὶ φοβουμένοις τὸ ὄνομά σου, τοὺς μικροὺς καὶ τοὺς μεγάλους, καὶ διαφθεῖραι τοὺς διαφθείροντας τὴν γῆν. 11.19 καὶ ἠνοίγη ὁ ναὸς τοῦ θεοῦ ἐν τῷ οὐρανῷ, καὶ ὤφθη ἡ κιβωτὸς τῆς διαθήκης τοῦ

Sodom, and Egypt, where also their lord was crucified. 11.9 And *some* out of the tribes and peoples and tongues and ethnics, they see their corpse three and a half days, and they allow/let not their corpses to be placed into tombs. 11.10 And those dwelling upon the earth rejoice upon/over them and they are gladdened, and they will send gifts to one another, because these, the two prophets, tortured/tormented those dwelling upon the earth. 11.11 And after the three and a half days, a spirit/breath of life from God entered into them, and they stood on their feet, and a great fear/terror fell upon those beholding them. 11.12 And they heard a great voice out of the sky/heaven saying to them: Ascend ye here; and they ascended into the sky in/on the cloud, and their enemies beheld/viewed them. 11.13 And in/at that very hour/time there became a great shaking/earthquake, and the tenth (part) of the city fell, and seven thousands names of men/humans were killed in the earthquake, and the rest (others) became in fear and they gave glory/fame to the God of the sky/heaven. 11.14 The second woe passed by; behold, the third woe comes quickly. 11.15 And the seventh messenger/angel trumpeted; and there became great voices in the sky saying: The kingdom of the world became from our Lord and from his anointed (one), and he will reign into the ages of the ages. Truly. 11.16 And the twenty four elders, the (ones) before God, those *who* sit upon their thrones, even they fell upon their faces and worshiped God, 11.17 saying: We give thanks to you, Lord, the God, the ruler of all/the almighty, the (one) being and the (one) *who* was being, because you have received your power, the great (one), and you reigned/ruled; 11.18 and the ethnics were angered, and your anger came, also the time for the dead (ones) to be judged to give the reward/wages to your slaves, to the prophets, and to the saints and to those fearing your name, *for* the small (ones) and the great (ones), and to destroy/corrupt those corrupting the earth. 11.19 And the *inner* temple of God was opened in the sky/heaven, and the ark of the covenant of God was seen in his *inner* temple; and there came to

θεοῦ ἐν τῷ ναῷ αὐτοῦ· καὶ ἐγένοντο ἀστραπαὶ καὶ φωναὶ καὶ βρονταὶ καὶ σεισμὸς καὶ χάλαζα μεγάλη. 12.1 καὶ σημῖον μέγα ὤφθη ἐν τῷ οὐρανῷ, γυνὴ περιβεβλημένη τὸν ἥλιον, καὶ ἡ σελήνη ὑποκάτω τῶν ποδῶν αὐτῆς, καὶ ἐπὶ τῆς κεφαλῆς αὐτῆς στέφανος ἀστέρων δώδεκα, 12.2 καὶ ἐν γαστρὶ ἔχουσα, καὶ κράζει ὠδίνουσα καὶ βασανιζομένη τεκεῖν. 12.3 καὶ ὤφθη ἄλλο σημῖον ἐν τῷ οὐρανῷ, καὶ ἰδοὺ δράκων πυρρός μέγας, ἔχων κεφαλὰς ἑπτὰ καὶ κέρατα δέκα καὶ ἐπὶ τὰς κεφαλὰς αὐτοῦ ἑπτὰ διαδήματα, 12.4 καὶ ἡ οὐρὰ αὐτοῦ σύρι τὸ τρίτον τῶν ἀστέρων τοῦ οὐρανοῦ καὶ ἔβαλεν αὐτοὺς εἰς τὴν γῆν. καὶ ὁ δράκων ἔστηκεν ἐνώπιον τῆς γυναικὸς τῆς μελλούσης τεκεῖν, ἵνα ὅταν τέκῃ τὸ τέκνον αὐτῆς καταφάγῃ. 12.5 καὶ ἔτεκεν υἱόν, ἄρρενα, ὃς μέλλει ποιμένιν πάντα τὰ ἔθνη ἐν ῥάβδῳ σιδηρᾷ· καὶ ἡρπάγη τὸ τέκνον αὐτῆς πρὸς τὸν θεὸν καὶ πρὸς τὸν θρόνον αὐτοῦ. 12.6 καὶ ἡ γυνὴ ἔφυγεν εἰς τὴν ἔρημον, ὅπου ἔχι ἐκεῖ τόπον ἡτοιμασμένον ἀπὸ τοῦ θεοῦ, ἵνα ἐκεῖ τρέφουσιν αὐτὴν ἡμέρας χιλίας διακοσίας ἑξήκοντα. 12.7 καὶ ἐγένετο πόλεμος ἐν τῷ οὐρανῷ, ὁ Μιχαὴλ καὶ οἱ ἄγγελοι αὐτοῦ πολεμῆσαι μετὰ τοῦ δράκοντος. καὶ ὁ δράκων ἐπολέμησεν καὶ οἱ ἄγγελοι αὐτοῦ, 12.8 καὶ οὐκ ἴσχυσαν πρὸς αὐτόν, οὐδὲ τόπος εὑρέθη αὐτῶν ἔτι ἐν τῷ οὐρανῷ. 12.9 καὶ ἐβλήθη ὁ δράκων ὁ μέγας, ὄφις ὁ ἀρχαῖος, ὁ καλούμενος διάβολος ὁ Σατανᾶς, ὁ πλανῶν τὴν οἰκουμένην ὅλην, ἐβλήθη εἰς τὴν γῆν, καὶ οἱ ἄγγελοι αὐτοῦ μετ' αὐτοῦ ἐβλήθησαν. 12.10 καὶ ἤκουσα φωνὴν μεγάλην ἐν τῷ οὐρανῷ λέγουσαν, ἄρτι ἐγένετο ἡ σωτηρία καὶ ἡ δύναμις καὶ ἡ βασιλία τοῦ θεοῦ ἡμῶν καὶ ἡ ἐξουσία τοῦ χριστοῦ αὐτοῦ, ὅτι ἐβλήθη ὁ κατήγορος τῶν ἀδελφῶν ἡμῶν, ὁ κατηγορῶν αὐτῶν ἐνώπιον τοῦ θεοῦ ἡμῶν ἡμέρας καὶ νυκτός. 12.11 καὶ οὗτοι ἐνίκησαν αὐτὸν διὰ τὸ αἷμα τοῦ ἀρνίου καὶ διὰ τὸν λόγον τῆς μαρτυρίας αὐτῶν, καὶ οὐκ ἠγάπησαν τὴν ψυχὴν αὐτῶν ἄχρι θανάτου. 12.12 διὰ τοῦτο εὐφρένεσθε, οὐρανοὶ καὶ οἱ κατοικοῦντες ἐν αὐτοῖς· οὐαὶ εἰς τὴν γῆν καὶ τὴν θάλασσαν, ὅτι κατέβη ὁ

be/happened lightnings and sounds and thunders and an earthquake and a great hailstorm. 12.1 And a great sign was seen in the sky/heaven, a woman having been dressed *with* the sun, and the moon *was* beneath her feet, and a crown/wreath of twelve stars was upon her head, 12.2 and she has in a belly (pregnancy), and she cries out, suffering birthpains and being tortured to give birth. 12.3 And another sign was seen in the sky/heaven, and behold, a great red serpent/dragon, having seven heads and ten horns, and seven crowns *were* upon his heads. 12.4 and his tail drags/draws the third (part) of the stars from the sky/heaven, and he throws them to the earth. And the dragon/serpent was standing before the woman, the (one) about to give birth, in order that when she might birth her child, he might devour *it*. 12.5 And she birthed a son, a male, who is about to shepherd all the ethnics with an iron rod; and the child was snatched away from her to God and to his throne. 12.6 And the woman fled into the desert/wilderness, where she has there a place having been prepared from God, in order that they will feed/sustain her there a thousand two hundred sixty days. 12.7 And a war/fight happened in the sky/heaven, Michael and his messengers/angels to make war with the dragon/serpent. And the dragon and his messengers/angels made war, 12.8 and they prevailed not with/against him, neither was their place still found in the sky. 12.9 And he was thrown *out*, the great dragon, the old serpent, the (one) being called the devil, Satan, the (one) deceiving the entire empire/inhabited earth, he was thrown to the earth and his messengers/angels were thrown *out* with him. 12.10 And I heard a great voice in the sky saying: Now became the salvation and the power and the kingdom of our God and the authority of his anointed (one), because the accuser of our brothers was thrown *out*, the (one) accusing them before our God day and night. 12.11 And these overcame him through the blood of the lamb and through the reasoning/saying of their testimony, and they loved not their soul/life until death. 12.12 Because of this be ye gladdened, skies/ heavens and the (ones) dwelling in them; woe to the

διάβολος πρὸς ὑμᾶς ἔχων θυμόν, εἰδὼς ὅτι ὀλίγον καιρὸν ἔχει. 12.13 καὶ ὅτε εἶδεν ὁ δράκων ὅτι ἐβλήθη εἰς τὴν γῆν, ἐξεδίωκεν τὴν γυναῖκα ἥτις ἔτεκεν τὸν ἄρσενα. 12.14 καὶ ἐδόθησαν τῇ γυναικὶ δύο πτέρυγες ἀετοῦ τοῦ μεγάλου, ἵνα πέτηται εἰς τὴν ἔρημον εἰς τόπον αὐτῆς, ὅπου τρέφεται ἐκεῖ καιρὸν καὶ κερούς καὶ ἥμισυ καιροῦ ἀπὸ προσώπου τοῦ ὄφεως. 12.15 καὶ ἔβαλεν ὁ ὄφις ἐκ τοῦ στόματος αὐτοῦ ὀπίσω τῆς γυναικὸς ὕδωρ ὡς ποταμόν, ἵνα αὐτὴν ποταμοφόρητον ποιήσῃ. 12.16 καὶ ἐβοήθησεν ἡ γῆ τῇ γυναικί, καὶ ἤνοιξεν ἡ γῆ τὸ στόμα αὐτῆς καὶ κατέπιε τὸν ποταμὸν ὃν ἔβαλεν ὁ δράκων ἐκ τοῦ στόματος αὐτοῦ. 12.17 καὶ ὠργίσθη ὁ δράκων ἐπὶ τῇ γυναικί, καὶ ἀπῆλθεν πόλεμον ποιῆσαι μετὰ τῶν ἐπὶ λοιπῶν τοῦ σπέρματος αὐτῆς, τῶν τηρούντων τὰς ἐντολὰς τοῦ θεοῦ καὶ ἐχόντων τὴν μαρτυρίαν Ἰησοῦ· 12.18 καὶ ἐστάθη ἐπὶ τὴν ἄμμον τῆς θαλάσσης. 13.1 καὶ εἶδον ἐκ τῆς θαλάσσης θηρίον ἀναβαῖνον, ἔχον κέρατα δέκα καὶ κεφαλὰς ἑπτά, καὶ ἐπὶ τῶν κεράτων αὐτοῦ διαδήματα δέκα, καὶ ἐπὶ τὰς κεφαλὰς αὐτοῦ ὀνόμα βλασφημίας. 13.2 καὶ τὸ θηρίον ὃ εἶδον ἦν ὅμοιον παρδάλι, καὶ οἱ πόδες αὐτοῦ ὡς ἄρκου, καὶ τὸ στόμα αὐτοῦ ὡς στόμα λεόντων. καὶ ἔδωκεν αὐτῷ ὁ δράκων τὴν δύναμιν αὐτοῦ καὶ τὸν θρόνον αὐτοῦ καὶ ἐξουσίαν μεγάλην. 13.3 καὶ μίαν ἐκ τῶν κεφαλῶν αὐτοῦ ὡς ἐσφαγμένην εἰς θάνατον, καὶ ἡ πληγὴ τοῦ θανάτου αὐτοῦ ἐθεραπεύθη. καὶ ἐθαυμάσεν ὅλη ἡ γῆ ὀπίσω τοῦ θηρίου, 13.4 καὶ προσεκύνησαν τῷ δράκοντι ὅτι ἔδωκεν τὴν ἐξουσίαν τῷ θηρίῳ, καὶ προσεκύνησαν τῷ θηρίῳ λέγοντες, τίς ὅμοιος τῷ θηρίῳ, καὶ τίς δύναται πολεμῆσαι μετ᾽ αὐτοῦ; 13.5 καὶ ἐδόθη αὐτῷ στόμα λαλοῦν μεγάλα καὶ βλασφημίας, καὶ ἐδόθη αὐτῷ ἐξουσία ποιῆσαι ὁ θέλιε μῆνας τεσσεράκοντα δύο. 13.6 καὶ ἤνοιξε τὸ στόμα αὐτοῦ εἰς βλασφημίας πρὸς τὸν θεόν, βλασφημῆσαι τὸ ὄνομα αὐτοῦ καὶ τὴν σκηνὴν αὐτοῦ, τοὺς ἐν τῷ οὐρανῷ σκηνοῦντες. 13.7 καὶ ἐδόθη αὐτῷ ποιῆσαι πόλεμον μετὰ τῶν ἁγίων καὶ νικῆσαι αὐτούς, καὶ ἐδόθη αὐτῷ ἐξουσία ἐπὶ

land and the sea, because the devil descended to/near ye having wrath, knowing that he has little time. 12.13 And when the dragon/serpent saw that he was thrown to the earth, he pursued/persecuted the woman who birthed the male. 12.14 And two wings of/from the great vulture/eagle were given to the woman, in order that she might fly to her place in the desert, where she is nourished/sustained there *for* a season and seasons and a half season from the face of the serpent. 12.15 And the serpent threw out of his mouth waters as a river behind the woman, that he might make her swept away by a river. 12.16 And the land/earth helped the woman, and the land opened her mouth and swallowed the river which the dragon threw out of his mouth. 12.17 And the dragon was angered upon/at the woman, and he went away to make a war with the remaining (ones), upon her seed, *with* those keeping the commands of God and having the testimony of Jesus; 12.18 and he was stood upon the sand/shore of the sea. 13.1 And a wild beast going up out of the sea, having ten horns and seven heads, and ten crowns *were* upon its horns, and a name of slander/blasphemy *was* upon its heads. 13.2 And the beast which I saw was like a leopard, and its feet as a bear, and its mouth as a mouth of lions. And the dragon gave to it his power and his throne and great authority. 13.3 And one out of its heads *was* as having been slain to death, but the blow/wound of its death was healed. And the entire land/earth wondered/marveled behind/after the beast, 13.4 and they worshiped to/for the dragon/serpent because he gave the authority to the beast, and they worshiped to the beast, saying: Who *is* like to the beast, and who is able to fight/make war with it? 13.5 And a mouth was given to it, speaking great (things), even slanders/blasphemies, and authority was given to it to do what it will *for* forty-two months. 13.6 And it opened its mouth in slanderings/ blasphemies toward God, to slander/blaspheme his name and his tent/tabernacle, the (ones) tenting/taber- nacling in the sky/heaven. 13.7 And it was given to it to make a fight/war with the saints and to conquer/overcome them, and authority was given to it

πᾶσαν φυλὴν καὶ λαὸν καὶ γλῶσσαν καὶ ἔθνος. 13.8 καὶ προσκυνήσουσιν αὐτῷ πάντες οἱ κατοικοῦντες ἐπὶ τῆς γῆς, ὧν οὐ γέγραπται τὰ ὀνόματα αὐτῶν ἐν τῷ βιβλῷ τῆς ζωῆς τοῦ ἀρνίου τοῦ ἐσφαγμένου ἀπὸ καταβολῆς κόσμου. 13.9 εἴ τις ἔχει οὖς ἀκουσάτω. 13.10 εἴ τις εἰς αἰχμαλωσίαν, ὑπάγει· εἴ τις ἐν μαχαίρᾳ ἀποκτείνει, δεῖ αὐτὸν ἐν μαχαίρᾳ ἀποκτανθῆναι. ὧδέ ἐστιν ἡ ὑπομονὴ καὶ ἡ πίστις τῶν ἁγίων. 13.11 καὶ εἶδον ἄλλο θηρίον ἀναβαῖνον ἐκ τῆς γῆς, καὶ εἶχεν κέρατα δύο ὅμοια ἀρνίῳ, καὶ ἐλάλει ὡς δράκων. 13.12 καὶ τὴν ἐξουσίαν τοῦ πρώτου θηρίου πᾶσαν ποιεῖ ἐνώπιον αὐτοῦ. καὶ ποιεῖ τὴν γῆν καὶ τοὺς ἐν αὐτῇ κατοικοῦντας προσκύνιν τὸ θηρίον τὸ πρῶτον, οὗ ἐθεραπεύθη ἡ πληγὴ τοῦ θανάτου αὐτοῦ. 13.13 καὶ ποιεῖ σημῖα μεγάλα, ἵνα καὶ πῦρ ποιῇ καταβαίνειν ἐκ τοῦ οὐρανοῦ εἰς τὴν γῆν ἐνώπιον τῶν ἀνθρώπων. 13.14 καὶ πλανᾷ τοὺς κατοικοῦντας ἐπὶ τῆς γῆς διὰ τὰ σημῖα ἃ ἐδόθη αὐτῷ ποιῆσαι ἐνώπιον τοῦ θηρίου, λέγων τοῖς κατοικοῦσιν ἐπὶ τῆς γῆς καὶ ποιῆσαι εἰκόνα τῷ θηρίῳ ὃ ἔχει πληγὴς τῆς μαχαίρης καὶ ἔζησεν. 13.15 καὶ ἐδόθη αὐτῷ δοῦναι πνεῦμα τῇ εἰκόνι τοῦ θηρίου, ἵνα καὶ λαλήσῃ ἡ εἰκὼν τοῦ θηρίου καὶ ποιήσει ὅσοι ἂν μὴ προσκυνήσουσιν τῇ εἰκόνι τοῦ θηρίου ἀποκτανθῶσιν. 13.16 καὶ ποιεῖ πάντας, τοὺς μικροὺς καὶ μεγάλους, καὶ τοὺς πτωχοὺς καὶ τοὺς πλουσίους, καὶ τοὺς ἐλευθέρους καὶ τοὺς δούλους, ἵνα δῶσιν αὐτοῖς χάραγμα ἐπὶ τῆς χειρὸς αὐτῶν τῆς δεξιᾶς ἢ ἐπὶ τὸ μέτωπον αὐτῶν, 13.17 καὶ ἵνα μή τις δύνηται ἀγοράσαι ἢ πωλῆσαι εἰ μὴ ὁ ἔχων τὸ χάραγμα τοῦ θηρίου ἢ τὸ ὄνομα αὐτοῦ ἢ τὸν ἀριθμὸν τοῦ ὀνόματος αὐτοῦ. 13.18 ὧδε ἡ σοφία ἐστίν· ὁ ἔχων νοῦν ψηφισάτω τὸν ἀριθμὸν τοῦ θηρίου, ἀριθμὸς γὰρ ἀνθρώπου ἐστίν· ἑξακόσια ἑξήκοντα ἕξ. 14.1 καὶ εἶδον, καὶ ἰδοὺ τὸ ἀρνίον ἑστὸς ἐπὶ τὸ ὄρος Σιών, καὶ μετ᾽ αὐτοῦ ἑκατὸν τεσσεράκοντα τέσσαρες χιλιάδες ἔχουσαι τὸ ὄνομα αὐτοῦ καὶ τὸ ὄνομα τοῦ πατρὸς αὐτοῦ γεγραμμένον ἐπὶ τῶν

upon/against every tribe and people and tongue and ethnic/nation. 13.8 And all those dwelling upon the earth will worship to/for it, of whom their names have not been written in the scroll of the life of the lamb, of the (one) having been slain from the foundation of a world. 13.9 If anyone has an ear let him hear. 13.10 If anyone *be* in captivity, he goes/departs; if anyone kills with a sword, it is necessary *for* him to be killed with a sword. Here is the patience/endurance and the faith of the saints. 13.11 And I saw another wild beast ascending out of the earth, and it had two horns like to a lamb, and it spoke as a dragon. 13.12 And it makes/does all the authority of the first beast before it. And it makes the earth/land and those dwelling in her/*it* to worship the first beast, of which was healed the blow/stroke of its death. 13.13 And it does/makes great signs, in order that it might even/also make fire to come down/descend out of the sky to the land before the men/humans. 13.14 And it deceives those dwelling upon the earth because of the signs which was given to it to do before the beast, saying to those dwelling upon the earth to make also an image of the beast which has a blow/stroke from the sword and lived. 13.15 And it was given to it to give breath/a spirit to the image of the beast, in order that the image of the beast might speak, and it will make as many as would not worship the image of the beast *that* they might be killed. 13.16 And it makes all, the small (ones) and great (ones), and the poor (ones) and the rich (ones), and the free (ones) and the slaves, that they might give to them a stamp upon their right hand or upon their forehead, 13.17 even that anyone be not able to buy or to sell except the (one) having the stamp of the beast or its name or the number of its name. 13.18 Here is the wisdom. The (one) having a mind, let him count the number of the beast, for it is a number of a man/human: -- six hundred sixty-six. 14.1 And I saw, and behold, the lamb having stood upon the mountain of Zion, and with him *were* a hundred forty-four thousands having his name and the name of his father having been written upon their foreheads,

μετώπων αὐτῶν. 14.2 καὶ ἤκουσα φωνὴν ἐκ τοῦ οὐρανοῦ ὡς φωνὴν ὑδάτων πολλῶν καὶ ὡς φωνὴν βροντῆς μεγάλης, καὶ ἡ φωνὴ ἣν ἤκουσα ὡς κιθαρῳδῶν κιθαριζόντων ἐν ταῖς κιθάραις αὐτῶν. 14.3 καὶ ᾄδουσιν ᾠδὴν καινὴν καὶ ἐνώπιον τοῦ θρόνου καὶ ἐνώπιον τῶν τῶν τεσσάρων ζῴων καὶ ἐνώπιον τῶν πρεσβυτέρων· καὶ οὐδεὶς ἐδύνατο μαθεῖν τὴν ᾠδὴν εἰ μὴ αἱ ἑκατὸν τεσσεράκοντα τέσσαρες χιλιάδες, οἱ ἠγορασμένοι ἀπὸ τῆς γῆς. 14.4 οὗτοί εἰσιν οἳ μετὰ γυναικῶν οὐκ ἐμολύνθησαν, παρθένοι γάρ εἰσιν. οὗτοι ἀκολουθοῦντες τῷ ἀρνίῳ ὅπου ἂν ὑπάγῃ. οὗτοι ἠγοράσθησαν ἀπὸ τῶν ἀνθρώπων ἀπαρχὴ τῷ θεῷ καὶ ἐν τῷ ἀρνίῳ, 14.5 καὶ ἐν τῷ στόματι αὐτῶν οὐχ εὑρέθη ψεῦδος· ἄμωμοι γάρ εἰσιν. 14.6 καὶ εἶδον ἄλλον ἄγγελον πετόμενον ἐν μεσουρανήματι, ἔχοντα εὐαγγέλιον αἰώνιον εὐαγγελίσασθε ἐπὶ τοὺς καθημένους ἐπὶ τῆς γῆς καὶ ἐπὶ πᾶν ἔθνος καὶ φυλὴν καὶ γλῶσσαν καὶ λαόν, 14.7 ἐν φωνῇ μεγάλῃ, Φοβήθητε τὸν θεὸν καὶ δότε αὐτῷ δόξαν, ὅτι ἦλθεν ἡ ὥρα τῆς κρίσεως αὐτοῦ, καὶ προσκυνήσατε τῷ ποιήσαντι τὸν οὐρανὸν καὶ τὴν γῆν καὶ τὴν θάλασσαν καὶ πηγὰς ὑδάτων.

14.8 καὶ ἄλλος ἄγγελος δεύτερος ἠκολούθησεν λέγων, ἔπεσεν Βαβυλὼν ἡ μεγάλη, ἐκ τοῦ οἴνου τοῦ θυμοῦ τῆς πορνίας αὐτῆς πεπότικαν πάντα τὰ ἔθνη. 14.9 καὶ ἄλλος ἄγγελος ἠκολούθησεν τρίτος αὐτοῖς λέγων ἐν φωνῇ μεγάλῃ, εἴ τις προσκυνεῖ τὸ θηρίον καὶ τὴν εἰκόνα αὐτοῦ, καὶ λαμβάνι χάραγμα ἐπὶ τῷ μετώπῳ αὐτοῦ ἢ ἐπὶ τὴν χεῖρα αὐτοῦ, 14.10 καὶ αὐτὸς πίεται ἐκ τοῦ οἴνου τοῦ θυμοῦ τοῦ θεοῦ τοῦ κεκερασμένου ἀκράτου ἐν τῷ ποτηρίῳ τῆς ὀργῆς αὐτοῦ, καὶ βασανισθήσεται ἐν πυρὶ καὶ θείῳ ἐνώπιον ἀγγέλων ἁγίων καὶ ἐνώπιον τοῦ ἀρνίου. 14.11 καὶ ὁ καπνὸς τοῦ βασανισμοῦ αὐτῶν εἰς αἰῶνας τῶν αἰώνων ἀναβαίνει, καὶ οὐκ ἔχουσιν ἀνάπαυσιν ἡμέρας καὶ νυκτός, οἱ προσκυνοῦντες τὸ θηρίον καὶ τὴν εἰκόνα αὐτοῦ, καὶ εἴ τις λαμβάνει τὸ χάραγμα τοῦ ὀνόματος αὐτοῦ. 14.12 ὧδε ἡ ὑπομονὴ τῶν ἁγίων ἐστίν, τῶν τηρούντων τὰς

14.2 And I heard a sound out of the sky/heaven as a sound of many waters and as a sound of great thunder, and the sound which I heard *was* as from harpers/lyrists harping/playing with/on their harps/lyres. 14.3 and they sing a new song, both before the throne and before the four living (things), also before the elders; and no one was able to learn the song except the hundred forty-four thousands, those having been bought/redeemed from the earth/land. 14.4 These are *the ones* who were not defiled with women, for they are chaste (ones)/virgins. These *are ones* following the lamb where ever he may go. These were purchased/redeemed from the men/humans, a first-fruit for God and in/by the lamb, 14.5 and in the mouth of them a lie was not found; for they are blameless. 14.6 And I saw another messenger/angel flying in midsky, having an eternal good message/gospel to preach/evangelize to those sitting upon the land and to every ethnic/nation and tribe and tongue/language and people, 14.7 *saying* in a great voice: Fear ye God and ye give glory/fame to him, because the hour/time of his judgment came, and ye worship to the (one) having made the sky/heaven and the land and the sea and springs of waters.

14.8 And another, a second messenger/angel followed, saying: The great Babylon fell; out of/from the wine of the wrath from her prostitution she has made all the ethnics to drink. 14.9 And another messenger/angel, a third (one), followed them, saying in a voice: If anyone worships the beast and its image, and receives a stamp upon/on his forehead or on his hand, 14.10 he, he will also drink out of/from the wine of the wrath of God, of the (one) having been mixed undiluted in the cup from his anger, and he will be tortured tormented in fire and sulphur before holy messengers/angels and before the lamb. 14.11 And the smoke from their torment ascends into/for ages of the ages, and they have not a rest/repose day and night, those worshiping the beast and its image, and if anyone receives/takes the stamp of its name. 14.12 Here is the endurance/patience of the saints, of those keeping the commands/decrees of God and the faith of

ἐντολὰς τοῦ θεοῦ καὶ τὴν πίστιν Ἰησοῦ. 14.13 καὶ ἤκουσα φωνῆς λεγούσης ἐκ τοῦ οὐρανοῦ, γράψον· μακάριοι οἱ νεκροὶ οἱ ἐν κυρίῳ ἀποθνήσκοντες ἀπ' ἄρτι. ναί, λέγει τὸ πνεῦμα, ἵνα ἀναπαήσονται ἐκ τῶν κόπων αὐτῶν· τὰ γὰρ ἔργα αὐτῶν ἀκολουθεῖ μετ' αὐτῶν. 14.14 καὶ ἰδοὺ νεφέλη λευκή, καὶ ἐπὶ τὴν νεφέλην καθήμενον ὅμοιον υἱὸν ἀνθρώπου, ἔχον ἐπὶ τῆς κεφαλῆς αὐτοῦ στέφανον χρυσοῦν καὶ ἐν τῇ χειρὶ αὐτοῦ δρέπανον ὀξύ. 14.15 καὶ ἄλλος ἄγγελος ἐξῆλθεν ἐκ τοῦ ναοῦ αὐτοῦ, κράζων ἐν φωνῇ μεγάλῃ τῷ καθημένῳ ἐπὶ τῆς νεφέλης, πέμψον τὸ δρέπανόν σου καὶ θέρισον, ὅτι ἦλθεν ἡ ὥρα τοῦ θερισμοῦ, ὅτι ἐξηράνθη ὁ θερισμὸς τῆς γῆς. 14.16 καὶ ἔβαλεν ὁ καθήμενος ἐπὶ τῆς νεφέλης τὸ δρέπανον αὐτοῦ ἐπὶ τὴν γῆν, καὶ ἐθερίσθη ἡ γῆ. 14.17 καὶ ἄλλος ἄγγελος ἐξῆλθεν ἐκ τοῦ ναοῦ τοῦ ἐν τῷ οὐρανῷ, ἔχων καὶ αὐτὸς δρέπανον ὀξύ.

14.18 καὶ ἄλλος ἄγγελος ἐξῆλθεν ἐκ τοῦ θυσιαστηρίου, ἔχων ἐξουσίαν ἐπὶ τοῦ πυρός, καὶ ἐφώνησεν φωνῇ μεγάλῃ τῷ ἔχοντι τὸ δρέπανον τὸ ὀξὺ λέγων, πέμψον τὸ δρέπανόν σου τὸ ὀξὺ καὶ τρύγησον τοὺς βότρυας τῆς ἀμπέλου τῆς γῆς, ὅτι ἤκμασαν αἱ σταφυλαὶ αὐτῆς. 14.19 καὶ ἔβαλεν ὁ ἄγγελος τὸ δρέπανον αὐτοῦ ἐπὶ τῆς γῆς, καὶ ἐτρύγησεν τὴν ἄμπελον τῆς γῆς καὶ ἔβαλεν εἰς τὴν ληνὸν τοῦ θυμοῦ τοῦ θεοῦ τὴν μεγάλην. 14.20 καὶ ἐπατήθη ἡ ληνὸς ἔξω τῆς πόλεως, καὶ ἐξῆλθεν αἷμα ἐκ τῆς ληνοῦ ἄχρι τῶν χαλινῶν τῶν ἵππων ἀπὸ σταδίων χιλίων ἑξακοσίων. 15.1 καὶ εἶδον ἄλλο σημῖον ἐν τῷ οὐρανῷ μέγα καὶ θαυμαστόν, ἀγγέλους ἑπτὰ ἔχοντας πληγὰς ἑπτὰ τὰς ἐσχάτας, ὅτι ἐν αὐταῖς ἐτελέσθη ὁ θυμὸς τοῦ θεοῦ. 15.2 καὶ εἶδον ὡς θάλασσαν ὑαλίνην μεμιγμένην πυρί, καὶ τοὺς νικῶντας ἐκ τοῦ θηρίου καὶ τῆς εἰκόνος αὐτοῦ καὶ ἐκ τοῦ ἀριθμοῦ τοῦ ὀνόματος αὐτοῦ ἑστῶτας ἐπὶ τὴν θάλασσαν τὴν ὑαλίνην, ἔχοντας κιθάρας κυρίου τοῦ θεοῦ. 15.3 καὶ ᾄδοντας τὴν ᾠδὴν Μωϋσέως τοῦ δούλου τοῦ θεοῦ καὶ τὴν ᾠδὴν τοῦ ἀρνίου λέγοντες, μεγάλα

Jesus.   14.13 And I heard a voice out of the
sky/heaven saying: You write: Happy are the dead
(ones), those dying in the Lord from now/this time.
Yes, says the spirit, in order that they will
rest/refresh out of/from their labors; for their works
follow after them.   14.14 And behold, a white cloud,
and upon the cloud *was one* sitting like a son of man,
having a gold crown/wreath on his head and a sharp
scythe/sickle in his hand.   14.15 And another
messenger/angel went forth out of his *inner* temple,
crying out in a great voice to the (one) sitting upon
the cloud: You send your scythe and reap, because the
time/hour of the harvest came, because the
harvest/crop of the land was dried/withered.   14.16
And the (one) sitting upon the cloud put/thrust his
scythe upon/over the land/earth, and the land was
harvested/reaped.   14.17 And another messenger/angel
went forth out of the *inner* temple, from the (one) in
the sky/heaven, having also himself a sharp scythe.
        14.18 And another messenger/angel went forth out
of/from the altar, having an authority over/upon the
fire, and he shouted with a great voice to the (one)
having the sharp scythe, saying: Send your sharp
scythe and you gather the bunches from the vine of the
land/earth, because its grapes are matured/ripened.
14.19 And the messenger/angel put his scythe to/upon
the land/earth, and he gathered/picked the vine of the
land/earth and he put *it* into the great winepress of
the wrath of God.   14.20 And the winepress was
trampled outside the city, and blood went forth out of
the winepress as far asthe bridles of the horses, from
a thousand six hundred stadia.   15.1   And I saw
another sign in the sky/heaven, great and marvelous,
seven messengers/angels having the last seven
plagues, · because in/by them the wrath of God was
finished/completed.   15.2 And I saw as a glassy sea
having been mixed with fire, and those
overcoming/surviving from the beast and its image and
from the number of its name, having stood upon the
glassy sea, holding harps/lyres from the Lord God,
15.3 and singing the song of Moses the slave of God
and the song of the lamb, saying: Great and marvelous

καὶ θαυμαστὰ τὰ ἔργα σου, κύριε ὁ θεὸς ὁ παντοκράτωρ· δίκαιαι καὶ ἀληθιναὶ αἱ ὁδοί σου, βασιλεὺς τῶν ἐθνῶν. 15.4 τίς σε οὐ φοβηθῇ, κύριε, καὶ δοξάσῃ τὸ ὄνομά σου; ὅτι μόνος ὅσιος, ὅτι πάντα τὰ ἔθνη ἥξουσιν καὶ προσκυνήσουσιν ἐνώπιόν σου, ὅτι δικαιώματά ἐνώπιον σου ἐφανερώθησαν. 15.5 καὶ μετὰ ταῦτα εἶδον, καὶ ἠνύγη ὁ ναὸς τῆς σκηνῆς τοῦ μαρτυρίου ἐν τῷ οὐρανῷ, 15.6 καὶ ἐξῆλθον οἱ ἑπτὰ ἄγγελοι ἔχοντες τὰς ἑπτὰ πληγὰς ἐκ τοῦ ναοῦ, ἐνδεδυμένοι καθαροὺς λίνους λαμπροὺς καὶ περιεζωσμένοι περὶ τὰ στήθη ζώνας χρυσᾶς. 15.7 καὶ ἓν ἐκ τῶν τεσσάρων ζῴων ἔδωκεν τοῖς ἑπτὰ ἀγγέλοις φιάλας χρυσᾶς γεμούσας τοῦ θυμοῦ τοῦ θεοῦ τοῦ ζῶντος εἰς τοὺς αἰῶνας τῶν αἰώνων ἀμήν. 15.8 καὶ ἐγεμίσθη ὁ ναὸς καπνοῦ ἐκ τῆς δόξης τοῦ θεοῦ καὶ ἐκ τῆς δυνάμεως αὐτοῦ, καὶ οὐδεὶς ἠδύνατο εἰς τὸν ναὸν εἰσελθεῖν ἄχρι τελεσθῶσιν αἱ ἑπτὰ πληγαὶ τῶν ἑπτὰ ἀγγέλων. 16.1 καὶ ἤκουσα φωνῆς μεγάλης ἐκ τοῦ ναοῦ λεγούσης τοῖς ἑπτὰ ἀγγέλοις, ὑπάγετε καὶ ἐκχέετε τὰς ἑπτὰ φιάλας τοῦ θυμοῦ τοῦ θεοῦ εἰς τὴν γῆν. 16.2 καὶ ἀπῆλθεν ὁ πρῶτος καὶ ἐξέχεεν τὴν φιάλην αὐτοῦ εἰς τὴν γῆν· καὶ ἐγένετο ἕλκος κακὸν καὶ πονηρὸν ἐπὶ τοὺς ἀνθρώπους τοὺς ἔχοντας τὸ χάραγμα τοῦ θηρίου καὶ τοὺς προσκυνοῦντας τὴν εἰκόνα αὐτοῦ. 16.3 καὶ ὁ δεύτερος ἐξέχεεν εἰς τὴν φιάλην αὐτοῦ εἰς τὴν θάλασσαν· καὶ ἐγένετο αἷμα ὡσι νεκροῦ, καὶ πᾶσα ψυχὴ ζῶσα ἀπέθανεν, ἐπὶ τῆς θαλάσσης. 16.4 καὶ ὁ τρίτος ἐξέχεεν τὴν φιάλην αὐτοῦ εἰς τοὺς ποταμοὺς καὶ τὰς πηγὰς τῶν ὑδάτων· καὶ ἐγένετο αἷμα. 16.5 καὶ ἤκουσα τοῦ ἀγγέλου τῶν ὑδάτων λέγοντος, δίκαιος εἶ, ὁ ὢν καὶ ὁ ἦν, ὁ ὅσιος, ὅτι ταῦτα ἔκρινας, 16.6 ὅτι αἵματα ἁγίων καὶ προφητῶν ἐξέχεαν, καὶ αἷμα ἔδωκας αὐτοῖς πιεῖν· ὅ περ ἄξιοί εἰσιν. 16.7 καὶ ἤκουσα τοῦ θυσιαστηρίου λέγοντος, ναί, κύριε ὁ θεὸς ὁ παντοκράτωρ, ἀληθιναὶ καὶ δίκαιαι αἱ κρίσις σου. 16.8 καὶ ὁ τέταρτος ἄγγελος ἐξέχεεν τὴν φιάλην αὐτοῦ ἐπὶ τὸν ἥλιον· καὶ ἐδόθη αὐτῷ

are your works, Lord, the God, and the Almighty; the roads/ways of you *are* just and true, a king of the ethnics. 15.4 Who might not fear you, Lord, and might glorify your name? Because *you* alone *are* holy, because all the ethnics will come and will worship before you, because your just deeds were manifested/made clear before you. 15.5 And after these (things) I saw/looked, and the *inner* temple of the tent/tabernacle of the testimony was opened in the sky/heaven, 15.6 And the seven messengers/angels having the seven plagues came/went forth out of the *inner* temple, having been clothed in bright, clean linens and having been girded around the breasts *with* gold belts/girdles. 15.7 And one out of the four living (things) gave gold bowls to the seven messengers/angels, being filled from the wrath of God, the (one) living into the ages of the ages, truly. 15.8 And the *inner* temple was full of smoke from the glory/reputation of God and from his power, and no one was able to enter into the *inner* temple until the seven plagues from the seven messengers/angels might be finished/completed. 16.1 And I heard a great voice out of the *inner* temple saying to the seven messengers/angels: Go ye and pour out the seven bowls of the wrath of God into the land/earth. 16.2 And the first (one) went away and poured out his bowl in the land/earth; and there became a bad and evil boil/sore upon the men having the stamp of the beast and those worshiping its image. 16.3 And the second (one) poured out his cup into the sea; and it became blood as from a dead (one), and every soul living died, *the things* upon the sea. 16.4 And the third (one) poured out his bowl in the rivers and the springs of the waters; and it became blood. 16.5 And I heard from the messenger/angel of the waters saying: You are just, the (one) being and the *one who* was, the holy (one), because you judged these (things), 16.6 because they shed bloods of saints and prophets, also you have given blood to them to drink; they are worthy. 16.7 And I heard from the altar saying: Yes, Lord, the almighty God, true and just *are* your judgments. 16.8 And the fourth messenger/angel poured out his bowl upon the sun; and it was given to

καυματίσαι τοὺς ἀνθρώπους πυρί. 16.9 καὶ ἐκαυματίσθησαν οἱ ἄνθρωποι καῦμα μέγα, καὶ ἐβλασφήμησαν τὸ ὄνομα τοῦ θεοῦ τοῦ ἔχοντος τὴν ἐξουσίαν ἐπὶ τὰς πληγὰς ταύτας, καὶ οὐ μετενόησαν δοῦναι αὐτῷ δόξαν.

16.10 καὶ ὁ πέμπτος ἐξέχεεν τὴν φιάλην αὐτοῦ ἐπὶ τὸν θρόνον τοῦ θηρίου· καὶ ἐγένετο ἡ βασιλεία αὐτοῦ ἐσκοτισμένη, καὶ ἐμασῶντο τὰς γλώσσας αὐτῶν ἀπὸ τοῦ πόνου, 16.11 καὶ ἐβλασφήμησαν τὸν θεὸν τοῦ οὐρανοῦ ἐκ τῶν πόνων αὐτῶν, καὶ οὐ μετενόησαν. 16.12 καὶ ὁ ἕκτος ἐξέχεεν τὴν φιάλην αὐτοῦ ἐπὶ τὸν ποταμὸν τὸν μέγαν τὸν Εὐφράτην· καὶ ἐξηράνθη τὸ ὕδωρ αὐτοῦ, ἵνα ἑτοιμασθῇ ἡ ὁδὸς τῶν βασιλέων τῶν ἀπὸ ἀνατολῆς ἡλίου. 16.13 καὶ ἐδόθη ἐκ τοῦ στόματος τοῦ δράκοντος καὶ ἐκ τοῦ στόματος τοῦ θηρίου καὶ ἐκ τοῦ στόματος τοῦ ψευδοπροφήτου πνεύματα τρία ἀκάθαρτα εἰ ὥσει βάτραχοι· 16.14 εἰσὶν γὰρ πνεύματα δαιμονίων ποιοῦντα σημεῖα, ἐκπορεύεσθαι εἰς τοὺς βασιλεῖς τῆς οἰκουμένης ὅλης, συναγαγεῖν αὐτοὺς εἰς τὸν πόλεμον τῆς ἡμέρας τῆς μεγάλης τοῦ θεοῦ τοῦ παντοκράτορος. 16.15 ἰδοὺ ἔρχομαι ὡς κλέπτης. μακάριος ὁ γρηγορῶν καὶ τηρῶν τὰ ἱμάτια αὐτοῦ, ἵνα μὴ γυμνὸς περιπατῇ καὶ βλέπωσιν τὴν ἀσχημοσύνην αὐτοῦ. 16.16 καὶ συνήγαγον αὐτοὺς εἰς τόπον τὸν καλούμενον Ἑβραϊστὶ Ἀρμαγεδών. 16.17 καὶ ὁ ἕβδομος ἐξέχεεν τὴν φιάλην αὐτοῦ ἐπὶ τὸν ἀέρα· καὶ ἐξῆλθεν φωνὴ μεγάλη ἐκ τοῦ ναοῦ τοῦ θεοῦ λέγουσα, γέγονεν. 16.18 καὶ ἐγένοντο βρονταὶ καὶ ἀστραπαὶ καὶ φωναὶ καὶ, καὶ σισμὸς ἐγένετο μέγας οἷος οὐκ ἐγένετο ἀφ' οὗ ἄνθρωποι ἐγένοντο ἐπὶ τῆς γῆς τηλικοῦτος σισμὸς οὕτω μέγας. 16.19 καὶ ἐγένετο ἡ πόλις ἡ μεγάλη εἰς τρία μέρη, καὶ αἱ πόλις τῶν ἐθνῶν ἔπεσαν. καὶ Βαβυλὼν ἡ μεγάλη ἐμνήσθη ἐνώπιον τοῦ θεοῦ τοῦ δοῦναι αὐτῇ ποτήριον οἴνου τοῦ θυμοῦ τῆς ὀργῆς. 16.20 καὶ πᾶσα νῆσος ἔφυγεν, καὶ ὄρη οὐχ εὑρέθησαν. 16.21 καὶ χάλαζα μεγάλη ὡς ταλαντιαία καταβαίνει ἐκ τοῦ οὐρανοῦ ἐπὶ τοὺς ἀνθρώπους· καὶ ἐβλασφήμησαν οἱ ἄνθρωποι τὸν θεὸν ἐκ τῆς πληγῆς τῆς χαλάζης, ὅτι μεγάλη ἐστὶν ἡ πληγὴ αὐτῆς σφόδρα. 17.1 καὶ ἦλθεν εἷς τῶν ἑπτὰ ἀγγέλων τῶν ἐχόντων τὰς ἑπτὰ

him to burn/scorch the men/humans with fire. 16.9 And the men/humans were scorched *with* a great heat, and they reviled/blasphemed the name of God, of the (one) having the authority over/upon these plagues, and they repented not to give fame/glory to him.

16.10 And the fifth (one) poured out his bowl upon the throne of the beast; and its kingdom became darkened, and they gnawed their tongues from the pain, 16.11 and they reviled/blasphemed the God of the sky/heaven from their pains, and they repented not. 16.12 And the sixth (one) poured out his bowl upon the great river Euphrates; and its water was dried up/out, in order that the road/way of the kings might be prepared, of the (ones) from *the* rising of a/*the* sun. 16.13 And it was given, out of the mouth of the dragon and out of the mouth of the beast and out of the mouth of the lying prophet, three unclean spirits as frogs; 16.14 for they are spirits of demons making/doing signs, to go forth to the kings of the entire empire/inhabited earth, to gather them to/for the war/fight of the great day of the almighty God. 16.15 Behold, I come as a thief. Happy is the (one) both watching and keeping his garments, that he may not walk naked and they see his shame. 16.16 And they gathered them into a place being called in Hebrew: Harmagedon. 16.17 And the seventh (one) poured out his bowl upon/against the air; and a great voice came forth out of the *inner* temple of God, saying: It has happened. 16.18 And there became thunders and lightnings and sounds/voices, and a great earthquake happened such as happened not from a *time* which men/humans came to be on the earth, such an earthquake so great. 16.19 And the great city came to be in three parts, and the cities of the ethnics fell. And the great Babylon was remembered before God to give to her a cup of wine from the wrath of the anger. 16.20 And every island fled/ran away, and mountains were not found. 16.21 And a great hailstorm about a talentweight came down out of the sky upon the men; and the men slandered/blasphemed God from the plague of the hailstorm, because the plague of it was exceedingly great. 17.1 And one of the seven messengers/angels,

φιάλας, καὶ ἐλάλησεν μετ᾽ ἐμοῦ λέγων, δεῦρο, δίξω σοι τὸ κρίμα τῆς πόρνης τῆς μεγάλης τῆς καθημένης ἐπὶ ὑδάτων πολλῶν, 17.2 μεθ᾽ ἧς ἐποίησαν πορνίαν οἱ βασιλεῖς τῆς γῆς, καὶ ἐμεθύσθησαν οἱ κατοικοῦντες τὴν γῆν ἐκ τοῦ οἴνου τῆς πορνίας αὐτῆς. 17.3 καὶ ἀπήνεγκέν με εἰς ἔρημον ἐν πνεύματι. καὶ εἶδον γυναῖκα καθημένην ἐπὶ θηρίον κόκκινον, γέμοντα ὀνόματα βλασφημίας, ἔχον τὰ κεφαλὰς ἑπτὰ καὶ κέρατα δέκα. 17.4 καὶ ἡ γυνὴ ἦν περιβεβλημένη πορφυροῦν καὶ κόκκινον, καὶ κεχρυσωμένη χρυσῷ καὶ λίθῳ τιμίῳ καὶ μαργαρίταις, ἔχουσα ποτήριον χρουσοῦν ἐν τῇ χειρὶ αὐτῆς γέμον βδελυγμάτων καὶ τὰ ἀκάθαρτα τῆς πορνίας αὐτῆς καὶ τῆς γῆς, 17.5 καὶ ἐπὶ τὸ μέτωπον αὐτῆς ὄνομα γεγραμμένον, μυστήριον, Βαβυλὼν ἡ μεγάλη, ἡ μήτηρ τῶν πορνῶν καὶ τῶν βδελυγμάτων τῆς γῆς. 17.6 καὶ εἶδαν τὴν γυναῖκα μεθύουσαν τοῦ αἵματος τῶν ἁγίων καὶ ἐκ τοῦ αἵματος τῶν μαρτύρων Ἰησοῦ. καὶ ἐθαύμασα θαῦμα μέγα εἰδὼν αὐτήν. 17.7 καὶ εἶπέν μοι ὁ ἄγγελος, διὰ τί ἐθαύμασας; ἐγὼ σοι ἐρῶ τὸ μυστήριον τῆς γυναικὸς καὶ τοῦ θηρίου τοῦ βαστάζοντος αὐτήν, τοῦ ἔχοντος τὰς ἑπτὰ κεφαλὰς καὶ τὰ δέκα κέρατα· 17.8 τὸ θηρίον ὃ εἶδες ἦν καὶ οὐκ ἔστιν, καὶ μέλλει ἀναβαίνιν ἐκ τῆς ἀβύσσου, καὶ εἰς ἀπώλιαν ὑπάγειν· καὶ θαυμάσονται οἱ κατοικοῦντες ἐπὶ τῆς γῆς, ὧν οὐ γέγραπται τὰ ὀνόματα ἐπὶ τὸ βιβλίον τῆς ζωῆς ἀπὸ καταβολῆς κόσμου, βλεπόντων τὸ θηρίον ὅτι ἦν καὶ οὐκ ἔστιν καὶ παρέστε. 17.9 ὧδε ὁ νοῦς ὁ ἔχων σοφίαν. αἱ ἑπτὰ κεφαλαὶ ἑπτὰ ὄρη εἰσίν, ὅπου ἡ γυνὴ κάθηται ἐπ᾽ αὐτῶν. καὶ ἑπτὰ βασιλεῖς εἰσιν· 17.10 οἱ πέντε ἔπεσαν, ὁ εἷς ἔστιν, ὁ ἄλλος οὔπω ἦλθεν, καὶ ὅταν ἔλθῃ ὀλίγον αὐτὸν μίνε δεῖ. 17.11 καὶ τὸ θηρίον ὃ ἦν καὶ οὐκ ἔστιν, οὗτος ὁ ὄγδοός ἐστιν καὶ ἐκ τῶν ἑπτά ἐστιν, καὶ εἰς ἀπώλιαν ὑπάγει. 17.12 καὶ τὰ δέκα καίρατα ἃ εἶδες δέκα βασιλεῖς εἰσιν, οἵτινες βασιλίαν οὔπω ἔλαβον, ἀλλὰ ἐξουσίαν ὡς βασιλεῖς βαμίαν ὥραν λαμβάνουσιν μετὰ τοῦ θηρίου. 17.13 οὗτοι μίαν γνώμην ἔχουσιν, καὶ τὴν

of those having/holding the seven bowls, came, and he spoke with me, saying: Come, I shall show to you the judgment of the great harlot/prostitute, of the (one) sitting upon many waters, 17.2 with whom the kings of the land made/did prostitution, and those dwelling *on* the land were made drunk from the wine of her prostitution. 17.3 And he led me away into a desert (place) in/by a spirit. And I saw a woman sitting upon a red beast, being filled with names of blasphemy, having seven heads and ten horns. 17.4 And the woman was clothed *in* purple and red, and having been adorned with gold and precious stone and pearls, holding a gold cup in her hand being filled from abominations and the unclean (things) of her prostitution and the land/earth. 17.5 And upon her forehead *was* a name having been written, a mystery: The great Babylon, the mother of the prostitutes and of the abominations of the land/earth. 17.6 And I saw the woman being drunk from the blood of the saints and from the blood of the witnesses of Jesus. And seeing her, I wondered a great wonder. 17.7 And the messenger/angel said to me: Why *did* you wonder/marvel? I, I shall say to you the mystery of the woman and the beast carrying her, of the (one) having the seven heads and the ten horns; 17.8 the beast that you saw was but is not, and it is about to ascend out of the abyss, and to go into/to destruction; and those dwelling upon the earth/land will wonder, of whom the names has not been written upon the scroll of the life from foundation of a world, seeing the beast that was but is not and *again* is present. 17.9 Here *is* the mind having wisdom: The seven heads are seven mountains, where the woman sits upon them. And they are seven kings; 17.10 the five fell, the one is, the other came not yet, and when he might come, it is necessary *for* him to stay a little (time). 17.11 And the beast which was but is not, this (one) is the eighth, and it is out of the seven, and it goes into destruction. 17.12 And the ten horns that you saw are ten kings, who not yet took/received a kingdom, but they receive authority as kings *for* one hour/time with/after the beast. 17.13 These have/hold one mind/judgment, and they give their power and

δύναμιν καὶ τὴν ἐξουσίαν αὐτῶν τῷ θηρίῳ διδόασιν. 17.14 οὗτοι μετὰ τοῦ ἀρνίου πολεμήσουσιν, καὶ τὸ ἀρνίον νικήσι αὐτούς, ὅτι κύριος κυρίων ἐστὶν καὶ βασιλεὺς βασιλέων, καὶ οἱ μετ' αὐτοῦ κλητοὶ καὶ ἐκλεκτοὶ καὶ πιστοί. 17.15 καὶ λέγει μοι, ταῦτα τὰ ὕδατα ἃ εἶδες, οὗ ἡ πόρνη κάθηται, καὶ λαοὶ καὶ ὄχλοι εἰσὶν καὶ ἔθνη καὶ γλῶσσαι. 17.16 καὶ τὰ δέκα κέρατα ἃ εἶδες καὶ τὸ θηρίον, οὗτοι μισήσουσιν τὴν πόρνην, καὶ ἠρημωμένην ποιήσουσιν αὐτὴν καὶ γυμνήν, καὶ τὰς σάρκας αὐτῆς φάγονται, καὶ αὐτὴν κατακαύσουσιν πυρί· 17.17 ὁ γὰρ θεὸς ἔδωκεν εἰς τὰς καρδίας αὐτῶν ποιῆσαι τὴν γνώμην αὐτοῦ, καὶ ποιῆσε μίαν γνώμην καὶ δοῦναι τὴν βασιλίαν αὐτῶν τῷ θηρίῳ, ἄχρι τελεσθήσονται οἱ λόγοι τοῦ θεοῦ. 17.18 καὶ ἡ γυνὴ ἣν εἶδες ἔστιν ἡ πόλις ἡ μεγάλη ἡ ἔχουσα βασιλείαν ἐπὶ τῶν βασιλείων τῆς γῆς.

18.1 Μετὰ ταῦτα εἶδον ἄλλον ἄγγελον καταβαίνοντα ἐκ τοῦ οὐρανοῦ, ἔχοντα ἐξουσίαν μεγάλην, καὶ ἡ γῆ ἐφωτίσθη ἐκ τῆς δόξης αὐτοῦ. 18.2 καὶ ἔκραξεν ἰσχυρᾷ φωνῇ λέγων, ἔπεσεν Βαβυλὼν ἡ μεγάλη, καὶ ἐγένετο κατοικητήριον δαιμονίων καὶ φυλακὴ παντὸς πνεύματος ἀκαθάρτου καὶ φυλακὴ παντὸς ὀρνέου ἀκαθάρτου καὶ μεμισημένου, 18.3 ὅτι ἐκ τοῦ οἴνου τοῦ θυμοῦ τῆς πορνίας αὐτῆς πεπτώκασιν πάντα τὰ ἔθνη, καὶ οἱ βασιλεῖς τῆς γῆς μετ' αὐτῆς ἐπόρνευσαν, καὶ οἱ ἔμποροι τῆς γῆς μετ'αὐτῆς ἐπόρνευσαν ἐκ τῆς δυνάμεως τοῦ στρήνους αὐτῆς ἐπλούτησαν. 18.4 καὶ ἤκουσα ἄλλην φωνὴν ἐκ τοῦ οὐρανοῦ λέγουσαν, ἐξέλθαται, ὁ λαός μου, ἐξ αὐτῆς, ἵνα μὴ συγκοινωνήσητε ταῖς ἁμαρτίαις αὐτῆς, καὶ ἐκ τῶν πληγῶν αὐτῆς ἵνα μὴ λάβητε· 18.5 ὅτι ἐκολλήθησαν αὐτῆς αἱ ἁμαρτίαι ἄχρι τοῦ οὐρανοῦ, καὶ ἐμνημόνευσεν ὁ θεὸς τὰ ἀδικήματα αὐτῆς. 18.6 ἀπόδοτε αὐτῇ ὡς καὶ αὐτὴ ἀπέδωκεν, διπλώσατε τὰ διπλᾶ κατὰ τὰ ἔργα αὐτῆς· ἐν τῷ ποτηρίῳ ᾧ ἐκέρασεν κεράσατε

authority to the beast. 17.14 These will make war/fight with the lamb, and the lamb will overcome/conquer them, because he is Lord of lords and King of kings, and those with him *are* called and elect/chosen and faithful (ones). 17.15 And he says to me: These waters that you saw, where the prostitute sits, they are both peoples and crowds and ethnics/nations and tongues/languages. 17.16 And the ten horns that you saw and the beast, these will hate the prostitute, and they will make her having been desolated and naked, and they will eat the fleshes of her, and they will burn her up in fire; 17.17 for God gave into/to their hearts to do/make his judgment/mind, and to do/make one judgment/mind and to give their kingdom to the beast, until the sayings/words/reasonings of God will be completed/finished. 17.18 And the woman whom you saw is the great city holding a kingdom upon/over the kings of the land/earth.

18.1 After these (things) I saw another messenger/angel coming down out of the sky/heaven, having great authority, and the land was lightened from his glory. 18.2 And he cried out in a strong voice, saying: She fell, the great Babylon, and she became a dwelling place of demons and a prison of every unclean spirit and a prison of every unclean and hated bird, 18.3 because out of the wine of the wrath from her prostitution all the ethnics/nations have drunk, and the kings of the land/earth did prostitution with her, and the merchants of the earth/land did prostitution with her, they became rich from the power of her luxury/sensuality. 18.4 And I heard another voice out of the sky/heaven, saying: Come ye out, my people, out of her, that ye might not share in her sins/faults, and out of her plagues that ye might not receive *them*; 18.5 because her faults/sins were joined together as far as the sky/heaven, and God remembered her unjust deeds. 18.6 Repay ye to her as also she, she repaid; double ye the two-fold (things) according to her works; in the cup which she mixed, mix ye double for her; 18.7

αὐτῇ διπλοῦν· 18.7 ὅσα ἐδόξασεν αὐτὴν καὶ ἐστρηνίασεν, τοσοῦτον δότε αὐτῇ βασανισμὸν καὶ πένθος. ὅτι ἐν τῇ καρδίᾳ αὐτῆς λέγει ὅτι κάθημε βασίλισσα, καὶ χήρα οὐκ εἰμί, καὶ πένθος οὐ μὴ εἴδω· 18.8 διὰ τοῦτο ἐν μιᾷ ἡμέρᾳ ἥξουσιν αἱ πληγαὶ αὐτῆς, θάνατος καὶ πένθος καὶ λιμός, καὶ ἐν πυρὶ κατακαυθήσεται· ὅτι ἰσχυρὸς ὁ θεὸς ὁ κύριος ὁ κρίνας αὐτήν. 18.9 καὶ κλαύσονται καὶ κόψονται ἐπ᾿ αὐτὴν οἱ βασιλεῖς τῆς γῆς οἱ μετ᾿ αὐτῆς πορνεύσαντες καὶ στρηνιάσαντες, ὅταν ἴδωσιν τὸν καπνὸν τῆς πυρώσεως αὐτῆς, 18.10 ἀπὸ μακρόθεν ἑστηκότες διὰ τὸν φόβον τοῦ βασανισμοῦ αὐτῆς, λέγοντες, οὐαὶ οὐαί, ἡ πόλις ἡ μεγάλη, Βαβυλὼν ἡ πόλις ἡ ἰσχυρά, ὅτι μιᾷ ὥρᾳ ἦλθεν ἡ κρίσις σου. 18.11 καὶ οἱ ἔμποροι τῆς γῆς σου κλαίουσιν καὶ πενθοῦσιν ἐπ᾿ αὐτήν, ὅτι τὸν γόμον αὐτῶν οὐδεὶς ἀγοράζει οὐκέτι, 18.12 γόμον χρυσοῦ καὶ ἀργύρου καὶ λίθου τιμίου καὶ μαργαριτῶν καὶ βυσσίνων καὶ πορφύρας καὶ σιρικοῦ καὶ κοκκίνου, καὶ πᾶν ξύλον θύϊνον καὶ πᾶν σκεῦος ἐλεφάντινον καὶ πᾶν σκεῦος ἐκ ξύλου τιμιωτάτου καὶ χαλκοῦ καὶ σιδήρου, 18.13 καὶ κινναμώμου καὶ ἄμωμον καὶ θυμιάματα καὶ μύρον καὶ λίβανον καὶ οἶνον καὶ ἔλαιον καὶ σεμίδαλιν καὶ σῖτον καὶ κτήνη καὶ πρόβατα, καὶ ἵππων καὶ ῥεδῶν καὶ σωμάτων, καὶ ψυχὰς ἀνθρώπων. 18.14 καὶ ἡ ὀπώρα σου τῆς ἐπιθυμίας τῆς ψυχῆς ἀπῆλθεν ἀπὸ σοῦ, καὶ πάντα τὰ λιπαρὰ καὶ λαμπρὰ ἀπώλοντο ἀπὸ σοῦ, καὶ οὐκέτι οὐ μὴ αὐτὰ εὑρήσουσιν. 18.15 οἱ ἔμποροι τούτων, οἱ πλουτήσαντες ἀπ᾿ αὐτῆς, ἀπὸ μακρόθεν στήσονται διὰ τὸν φόβον τοῦ βασανισμοῦ αὐτῆς, κλαίοντες καὶ πενθοῦντες, 18.16 λέγοντες, οὐαὶ οὐαί, ἡ πόλις ἡ μεγάλη, ἡ περιβεβλημένη βύσσινον καὶ πορφυροῦν καὶ κόκκινον, καὶ κεχρυσωμένον ἐν χρυσῷ καὶ λίθῳ τιμίῳ καὶ μαργαρίτῃ, 18.17 ὅτι μιᾷ ὥρᾳ ἠρημώθη ὁ τοσοῦτος πλοῦτος. καὶ πᾶς κυβερνήτης καὶ πᾶς ὁ ἐπὶ τὸν τόπον πλέων καὶ ναῦται καὶ ὅσοι τὴν θάλασσαν ἐργάζονται ἀπὸ μακρόθεν ἔστησαν 18.18 καὶ

whatever (things) she glorified *for* her and lived in luxury, give ye so much torture and grief to her. Because she says to her heart: I sit a queen, and I am not a widow, and I shall by no means see grief; 18.8 because of this in one day her plagues will come, death and grief and famine, and she will be burned up in fire; because strong *is* God, the Lord judging her. 18.9 And the kings of the land will lament and wail over her, those having done prostitution and having lived in luxury with her, whenever they might see the smoke of her burning, 18.10 standing from afar because of the fear of her torture, saying: Woe, woe, the great city, Babylon the strong city, because your judgment came in/at one hour/time. 18.11 And the merchants from your earth/land weep and mourn over her, because no one buys their wares any more/no longer, 18.12 wares of gold and of silver and of valuable stone and of pearls and of fine linen and of purple (things) and of silk and of red/scarlet, and every thyine tree/wood and every ivory vessel/implement and every vessel/implement of valuable wood and of brass and of iron, 18.13 and cinnamon and spice and incenses and ointment/perfume and of frankincense and wine and olive oil and flour and wheat and pack animals and sheep, and of horses and of carriages and of bodies, and souls/lives of men/humans. 18.14 And the season/dog days of the desire of your soul/life went away from you, and all the costly luxuries and shining/bright (things) perished from you, and by no means will they find them no/any longer. 18.15 The merchants of these (things), those having been rich from her, they will stand themselves from afar because of the fear of her torture/torment, weeping and mourning, 18.16 saying: Woe, woe, the great city, the (one) having been dressed in fine linen and purple and scarlet/red, and having been adorned/gilded in with gold and valuable stone and pearl, 18.17 because in/at one hour/time the wealth so great was laid waste. And every steersman/pilot and every one sailing to the place and seamen and as many as work the sea, they stood from afar 18.18 and cried out, seeing the smoke

ἔκραζον βλέποντες τὸν καπνὸν τῆς πυρώσεως αὐτῆς λέγοντες, τίς ὁμοία τῇ πόλι τῇ μεγάλῃ; 18.19 καὶ ἔβαλον χοῦν ἐπὶ τῆς κεφαλῆς αὐτῶν καὶ ἔκραζον κλαίοντες καὶ πενθοῦντες, λέγοντες, οὐαί, ἡ πόλις ἡ μεγάλη, ἐν ᾗ ἐπλούτησαν πάντες οἱ ἔχοντες τὰ πλοῖα ἐν τῇ θαλάσσῃ ἐκ τῆς τιμιότητος αὐτῆς, ὅτι μιᾷ ὥρᾳ ἠρημώθη. 18.20 εὐφραίνου ἐπ' αὐτῇ, οὐρανοί, καὶ οἱ ἅγιοι καὶ οἱ ἀπόστολοι καὶ οἱ προφῆται, ὅτι ἔκρινεν ὁ θεὸς τὸ κρίμα ὑμῶν ἐξ αὐτῆς.

18.21 καὶ ἦρεν εἷς ἄγγελος ἰσχυρὸς ὡς λίθον μέγαν καὶ ἔβαλεν εἰς τὴν θάλασσαν λέγων, ὅτι οὕτως ὁρμήματι βληθήσεται Βαβυλὼν ἡ μεγάλη πόλις, καὶ οὐ μὴ εὑρεθῇ ἔτι ἐν αὐτῇ. 18.22 φωνὴ κιθαρῳδῶν καὶ μουσικῶν καὶ αὐλητῶν καὶ σαλπιγγῶν οὐ μὴ ἀκουσθῇ ἐν σοὶ ἔτι, καὶ πᾶς τεχνίτης πάσης τέχνης οὐ μὴ εὑρεθῇ ἐν σοὶ ἔτι, 18.23 καὶ φῶς λύχνου οὐ μὴ φάνῃ ἐν σοὶ ἔτι,

καὶ φωνὴ νυμφίου καὶ νύμφης οὐ μὴ ἀκουσθῇ ἐν σοὶ ἔτι· ὅτι οἱ ἔμποροί σου ἦσαν οἱ μεγιστᾶνες τῆς γῆς, ὅτι ἐν τῇ φαρμακίᾳ σου ἐπλανήθησαν πάντα τὰ ἔθνη, 18.24 καὶ ἐν αὐτῇ αἷμα προφητῶν καὶ ἁγίων εὑρέθη καὶ πάντων τῶν ἐσφαγμένων ἐπὶ τῆς γῆς.

19.1 Μετὰ ταῦτα ἤκουσα ὡς φωνὴν μεγάλην ὄχλου πολλοῦ ἐν τῷ οὐρανῷ λεγόντων, ἀλληλουϊά· ἡ σωτηρία καὶ ἡ δόξα καὶ ἡ δύναμις τοῦ θεοῦ ἡμῶν, 19.2 ὅτι ἀληθιναὶ καὶ δίκαιαι αἱ κρίσεις αὐτοῦ· ὅτι ἔκρινεν τὴν πόρνην τὴν μεγάλην ἥτις ἔφθειρεν τὴν γῆν ἐν τῇ πορνίᾳ αὐτῆς, καὶ ἐξεδίκησεν τὸ αἷμα τῶν δούλων αὐτοῦ ἐκ χιρὸς αὐτῆς. 19.3 καὶ δεύτερον εἴρηκαν, ἀλληλουϊά· καὶ ὁ καπνὸς αὐτῆς ἀναβαίνει εἰς τοὺς αἰῶνας τῶν αἰώνων.

19.4 καὶ ἔπεσαν οἱ πρεσβύτεροι οἱ εἴκοσι τέσσαρες καὶ τὰ τέσσαρα ζῷα, καὶ προσεκύνησαν τῷ θεῷ τῷ καθημένῳ ἐπὶ τῷ θρόνῳ, λέγοντες, ἀμήν, ἀλληλουϊά.

from her burning, saying: Who/what is like to the great city? 18.19 And they threw dust upon their heads and cried out, weeping and mourning, saying: Woe, the great city, in/by which all those having ships in/on the sea were rich out of her costly (things), because in/at one hour/time she was laid waste. 18.20 Be you gladdened over her, heaven/sky, also the saints and the apostles and the prophets, because God judged the judgment of ye out of her.

18.21 And one strong/mighty messenger/angel lifted up as a great stone and *it* into the sea, saying: Thus with a rush will be thrown the great city Babylon, and by no means might it be found still in her. 18.22 A sound from harpists and musicians and flutists and trumpeters by no means might be heard in you still, and every craftsman of every trade by no means might be found in you still/yet, 18.23 and light from a lamp by no means might still shine in you,

and a voice of a bridegroom and a bride by no means might be heard in you yet/still; because your merchants were the great (ones) of the land/earth, because all the ethnics/nations were deceived/led astray by your enchantment, 18.24 and in her was found blood from prophets and saints and from all those having been slain/slaughtered upon the land/earth.

19.1 After these (things) I heard as a sound/voice from a much crowd in the sky/heaven saying: Halleluia! The salvation and the fame/glory and the power of our God, 19.2 because his judgments *are* true and just; because he judged the great prostitute who corrupted the land with her prostitution/unchastity, and he avenged the blood of his slaves out of/from her hand. 19.3 And they said a second (time): Halleluia! And the smoke from her ascends into/for the ages of the ages.

19.4 And the twenty-four elders and the four living (things) fell *down* and they worshiped to God, to the (one) sitting upon the throne, saying: Truly, halleluia!

19.5 καὶ φωνὴ ἐξῆλθεν ἐκ τοῦ θρόνου λέγουσα,

αἰνεῖται τῷ θεῷ ἡμῶν, πάντες οἱ δοῦλοι αὐτοῦ, οἱ φοβούμενοι αὐτόν, οἱ μικροὶ καὶ οἱ μεγάλοι. 19.6 καὶ ἤκουσα ὡς φωνὴν ὄχλου πολλοῦ καὶ ὡς φωνὴν ὑδάτων πολλῶν καὶ ὡς φωνὴν βροντῶν ἰσχυρῶν λεγούσων, ἀλληλουϊά, ὅτι ἐβασίλευσεν ὁ θεὸς ὁ κύριος ἡμῶν ὁ παντοκράτωρ. 19.7 χαίρωμεν καὶ ἀγαλλιῶμεν, καὶ δώσωμεν τὴν δόξαν αὐτῷ, ὅτι ἦλθεν ὁ γάμος τοῦ ἀρνίου, καὶ ἡ γυνὴ αὐτοῦ ἡτοίμασεν ἑαυτήν· 19.8 καὶ ἐδόθη αὐτῇ ἵνα περιβάληται βύσσινον λαμπρὸν καθαρόν, τὸ γὰρ βύσσινον τὰ δικαιώματα τῶν ἁγίων ἐστίν. 19.9 καὶ λέγει μοι, γράψον· μακάριοι οἱ εἰς τὸ δῖπνον τοῦ γάμου τοῦ ἀρνίου κεκλημένοι. καὶ λέγι μοι, οὗτοι οἱ λόγοι ἀληθινοί εἰσιν τοῦ θεοῦ. 19.10 καὶ ἔπεσα ἔμπροσθεν τῶν ποδῶν αὐτοῦ προσκυνῆσαι αὐτῷ. καὶ λέγει μοι, ὅρα μή· σύνδουλός σού εἰμι καὶ τῶν ἀδελφῶν σου τῶν ἐχόντων τὴν μαρτυρίαν Ἰησοῦ· τῷ θεῷ προσκύνησον. ἡ γὰρ μαρτυρία Ἰησοῦ ἐστιν τὸ πνεῦμα τῆς προφητίας. 19.11 καὶ εἶδον τὸν οὐρανὸν ἠνεῳγμένον, καὶ ἰδοὺ ἵππος λευκός, καὶ ὁ καθήμενος ἐπ’ αὐτὸν πιστὸς καλούμενος καὶ ἀληθινός, καὶ ἐν δικαιοσύνῃ κρίνει καὶ πολεμῖ. 19.12 οἱ δὲ οἱ ὀφθαλμοὶ αὐτοῦ φλὸξ πυρός, καὶ ἐπὶ τὴν κεφαλὴν αὐτοῦ διαδήματα πολλά, ἔχων ὀνόματα γεγραμμένα ἃ οὐδὶς οἶδεν ἡ μὴ αὐτός, 19.13 καὶ περιβεβλημένος ἱμάτιον περιρερανμένον αἵματι, καὶ κέκληται τὸ ὄνομα αὐτοῦ ὁ λόγος τοῦ θεοῦ. 19.14 καὶ τὰ στρατεύματα ἐν τῷ οὐρανῷ ἠκολούθι αὐτῷ ἐφ’ ἵπποις λευκοῖς, ἐνδεδυμένοι βύσσινον λευκὸν καθαρόν. 19.15 καὶ ἐκ τοῦ στόματος αὐτοῦ ἐκπορεύεται ῥομφαία ὀξεῖα, ἵνα ἐν αὐτῇ πατάξει τὰ ἔθνη, καὶ αὐτὸς ποιμανεῖ αὐτοὺς ἐν ῥάβδῳ σιδηρᾷ· καὶ αὐτὸς πατεῖ τὴν ληνὸν τοῦ οἴνου τῆς ὀργῆς τοῦ θυμοῦ τοῦ θεοῦ τοῦ παντοκράτορος. 19.16 καὶ ἔχει ἐπὶ τὸ ἱμάτιον καὶ τὸν μηρὸν αὐτοῦ ὄνομα γεγραμμένον· βασιλεὺς βασιλέων καὶ κύριος κυρίων. 19.17 καὶ εἶδον ἄλλον ἄγγελον ἑστῶτα ἐν τῷ ἡλίῳ, καὶ

19.5 And a voice came out of the throne, saying: Praise ye to our God, all the slaves of him, the (ones) fearing him, the small (ones) and the great (ones). 19.6 And I heard as a sound/voice from a much crowd and as a sound from many waters and as a sound from strong thunders, saying: Halleluia! Because God our Lord, the almighty/ruler of all, reigns. 19.7 Let us rejoice and let us exult, and we shall give the fame/glory to him, because the marriage of the lamb came, and his woman prepared herself; 19.8 And it was given to her in order that she might be clothed *with* shining clean linen, for the fine linen is the just deeds of the saints/holy (ones). 19.9 And he says to me: You write: Happy *are* those having been called/invited to the dinner of the marriage of the lamb. And he says to me: These are the true sayings/words/reasonings of God. 19.10 And I fell *down* before his feet to worship him. And he says to me: You see not; I am your fellow slave and from your brothers, those having the testimony/witness of Jesus; you worship to God. For the witness from Jesus is the spirit from/of the prophecy. 19.11 And I saw the sky/heaven having been opened, and behold a white horse, and the (one) sitting upon it being called faithful and true, and in justness he judges and fights. 19.12 And his eyes *are/were* a flame of fire, and upon his head *are/were* many crowns, having names having been written which no one knows except himself, 19.13 and having been clothed *with* a garment having been dipped in blood, and his name has been called the logos/reason/word of God. 19.14 And the armies in the sky/heaven followed with him on white horses, having been dressed *in* fine linen, white and clean/pure. 19.15 And a sharp sword goes forth out of his mouth, in order that he will smite the ethnics/nations with it, and he, he will shepherd/tend them with an iron rod; and he, he treads the winepress of the wine of the anger from the wrath of God, the almighty/ruler of all. 19.16 And he has on the garment and a name having been written *on* his thigh: King of kings and Lord of lords. 19.17 And I saw another messenger/angel having stood in the sun, and

551

ἔκραξεν ἐν φωνῇ μεγάλῃ λέγων πᾶσιν τοῖς ὀρνέοις τοῖς πετομένοις ἐν μεσουρανήματι, δεῦτε συνάχθητε εἰς τὸ δῖπνον τὸ μέγα τοῦ θεοῦ, 19.18 ἵνα φάγηται σάρκας βασιλέων καὶ σάρκας χιλιάρχων καὶ σάρκας ἰσχυρῶν καὶ σάρκας ἵππων καὶ τῶν καθημένων ἐπ' αὐτοῖς καὶ σάρκας πάντων ἐλευθέρων τε καὶ δούλων καὶ μικρῶν καὶ τῶν μεγάλων. 19.19 καὶ ἶδον τὸ θηρίον καὶ τοὺς βασιλεῖς τῆς γῆς καὶ τὰ στρατεύματα αὐτῶν συνηγμένα ποιῆσαι τὸν πόλεμον μετὰ τοῦ καθημένου ἐπὶ τοῦ ἵππου καὶ μετὰ τοῦ στρατεύματος αὐτοῦ. 19.20 καὶ ἐπιάσθη τὸ θηρίον καὶ μετ' αὐτοῦ ὁ ψευδοπροφήτης ὁ ποιήσας τὰ σημῖα ἐνώπιον αὐτοῦ, ἐν οἷς ἐπλάνησεν τοὺς λαβόντας τὸ χάραγμα τοῦ θηρίου καὶ τοὺς προσκυνοῦντας τῇ εἰκόνι αὐτοῦ· ζῶντες ἐβλήθησας οἱ δύο εἰς τὴν λίμνην τοῦ πυρὸς τῆς κεομένης ἐν θίῳ. 19.21 καὶ οἱ λοιποὶ ἀπεκτάνθησαν ἐν τῇ ῥομφαίᾳ τοῦ καθημένου ἐπὶ τοῦ ἵππου τῇ ἐξελθούσῃ ἐκ τοῦ στόματος αὐτοῦ, καὶ πάντα τὰ ὄρνεα ἐχορτάσθησαν ἐκ τῶν σαρκῶν αὐτῶν. 20.1 καὶ εἶδον ἄγγελον καταβαίνοντα ἐκ τοῦ οὐρανοῦ, ἔχοντα τὴν κλῖν τῆς ἀβύσσου καὶ ἅλυσιν μεγάλην ἐν τῇ χειρὶ αὐτοῦ. 20.2 καὶ ἐκράτησεν τὸν δράκοντα, τὸν ὄφιν τὸν ἀρχαῖον, ὅ ἐστιν ὁ διάβολος καὶ ὁ Σατανᾶς, καὶ ἔδησεν αὐτὸν —, 20.3 — εἰς τὴν ἄβυσσον καὶ ἔκλισεν καὶ ἐσφράγισεν ἐπάνω αὐτοῦ ἵνα μὴ πλανήσει ἔτι τὰ ἔθνη ἄχρι τελεσθῇ τὰ χίλια ἔτη· μετὰ ταῦτα δεῖ αὐτὸν λυθῆναι μικρὸν χρόνον. 20.4 καὶ εἶδον θρόνους, καὶ ἐκάθισαν ἐπ' αὐτούς, καὶ κρίμα ἐδόθη αὐτοῖς, καὶ τὰς ψυχὰς τῶν πεπελεκισμένων διὰ τὴν μαρτυρίαν Ἰησοῦ καὶ διὰ τὸν λόγον τοῦ θεοῦ, εἴτινες οὖν προσεκύνησαν τὸ θηρίον οὐδὲ τὴν εἰκόνα αὐτοῦ καὶ οὐκ ἔλαβον τὸ χάραγμα ἐπὶ τὸ μέτωπον καὶ ἐπὶ τὴν χεῖρα αὐτῶν· καὶ ἔζησαν καὶ ἐβασίλευσαν μετὰ τοῦ χριστοῦ χίλια ἔτη. 20.5 —αὕτη ἡ ἀνάστασις ἡ πρώτη. 20.6 μακάριος καὶ ἅγιος ὁ ἔχων μέρος ἐν τῇ ἀναστάσι τῇ πρώτῃ· ἐπὶ τούτων ὁ δεύτερος θάνατος οὐκ ἔχει ἐξουσίαν, ἀλλ' ἔσονται ἱερεῖς καὶ τοῦ

he cried out with a great voice saying to all the birds flying in mid-sky/mid-heaven: Ye come, gather ye to the great dinner/supper of God, 19.18 in order that ye might eat fleshes of kings and fleshes of chiliarchs/captains and fleshes of strong/mighty (ones) and fleshes of horses and of those sitting upon them and fleshes of all (men), both free (ones) and slaves, both small and great (ones). 19.19 And I saw the beast and the kings of the land/earth and their armies, having been gathered to make the fight/war with the (one) sitting upon the horse and with his armies. 19.20 And the beast was seized, and with it the lying/false prophet, the (one) having done the signs before it, by which he deceived/led astray those having taken/received the stamp of the beast and those worshiping the image of it; the two were thrown living into the lake of the fire burning in/with sulphur. 19.21 And the rest (others) were killed by the sword of the (one) sitting upon the horse, by the (one) going forth out of his mouth, and all the birds were filled/satisfied out of/from their fleshes. 20.1 And I saw a messenger/angel coming down out of the sky/heaven, holding the key/bolt of the abyss and a great chain in his hand. 20.2 And he grasped the dragon, the ancient serpent, which is the devil and Satan, and he bound him, -- 20.3 -- into the abyss and he closed and made *it* secure over him in order that he should not still deceive the ethnics/nations until the thousand years might be completed/finished; after these (things) it is necessary *for* him to be loosed a little time. 20.4 And I saw thrones, and they sat upon them, and the judgment was given to them, and the souls/lives of those having been beheaded because of the testimony of Jesus and because of the saying/word from God, who then worshiped *not* the beast nor the image of it and they took/received not the stamp upon the forehead and on the hand; and they lived and they reigned with the anointed (one) a thousand years. 20.5 This *is* the first resurrection. 20.6 Happy and holy *is* the (one) having a part in the first resurrection; upon/over these the second death has not authority, but they will be priests, both of God and

θεοῦ καὶ τοῦ χριστοῦ, καὶ βασιλεύσουσιν μετ' αὐτοῦ τὰ χίλια ἔτη.

20.7 καὶ ὅταν τελεσθῇ τὰ χίλια ἔτη, λυθήσεται ὁ Σατανᾶς ἐκ τῆς φυλακῆς αὐτοῦ, 20.8 καὶ ἐξελεύσεται πλανῆσαι πάντα τὰ ἔθνη ἐν ταῖς τέτρασι γωνίαις τῆς γῆς, τὸν Γὼγ καὶ Μαγώγ, καὶ συναγαγεῖν αὐτοὺς εἰς τὸν πόλεμον, ὧν ὁ ἀριθμὸς αὐτῶν ὡς ἡ ἄμμος τῆς θαλάσσης. 20.9 καὶ ἀνέβησαν ἐπὶ τὸ πλάτος τῆς γῆς καὶ ἐκύκλωσαν τὴν παρεμβολὴν τῶν ἁγίων καὶ τὴν πόλιν τὴν ἠγαπημένην. καὶ κατέβη πῦρ ἀπὸ τοῦ θεοῦ ἐκ τοῦ οὐρανοῦ καὶ κατέφαγεν αὐτούς· 20.10 καὶ ὁ διάβολος ὁ πλανῶν αὐτοὺς ἐβλήθη εἰς τὴν λίμνην τοῦ πυρὸς καὶ τοῦ θίου, ὅπου τὸ θηρίον καὶ ὅπου ὁ ψευδοπροφήτης, καὶ βασανισθήσονται ἡμέρας καὶ νυκτὸς εἰς τοὺς αἰῶνας τῶν αἰώνων.

20.11 καὶ εἶδον θρόνον μέγαν λευκὸν καὶ τὸν καθήμενον ἐπάνω αὐτοῦ, οὗ ἀπὸ τοῦ προσώπου ἔφυγεν ἡ γῆ καὶ ὁ οὐρανός, καὶ τόπος οὐχ εὑρέθη αὐτοῖς. 20.12 καὶ εἶδον τοὺς νεκρούς, τοὺς μεγάλους καὶ τοὺς μικρούς, ἑστῶτας ἐνώπιον ἐπὶ τοῦ θρόνου, καὶ βιβλία ἠνεώχθη· καὶ ἄλλο βιβλίον ἠνεώχθη, ὅ ἐστιν τῆς ζωῆς· καὶ ἐκρίθησαν οἱ νεκροὶ ἐκ τῶν γεγραμμένων ἐν τοῖς βιβλοῖς κατὰ τὰ ἔργα αὐτῶν. 20.13 καὶ ἔδωκεν ἡ θάλασσα τοὺς νεκροὺς τοὺς ἐν αὐτῇ, καὶ τὰ θάνατος καὶ ὁ ᾅδης ἔδωκαν τοὺς νεκροὺς τοὺς ἐν αὐτοῖς, καὶ κατεκρίθησαν ἕκαστος κατὰ τὰ ἔργα αὐτῶν. 20.14 καὶ ὁ θάνατος καὶ ὁ ᾅδης ἐβλήθησαν εἰς τὴν λίμνην τοῦ πυρός. καὶ οὗτος ὁ δεύτερός θάνατος ἐστιν, ἡ λίμνη τοῦ πυρός. 20.15 καὶ εἴ τις οὐχ εὑρέθη ἐν τῇ βίβλῳ τῆς ζωῆς γεγραμμένος ἐβλήθη εἰς τὴν λίμνην τοῦ πυρός. 21.1 καὶ εἶδον οὐρανὸν κενὸν καὶ γῆν κενήν· ὁ γὰρ πρῶτος οὐρανὸς καὶ ἡ πρώτη γῆ ἀπῆλθαν, καὶ ἡ θάλασσα οὐκ ἔστιν ἔτι. 21.2 καὶ τὴν πόλιν τὴν ἁγίαν Ἰερουσαλὴμ κενὴν εἶδον καταβαίνουσαν ἐκ τοῦ οὐρανοῦ ἀπὸ τοῦ θεοῦ, ἡτοιμασμένην ὡς νύμφην κεκοσμημένην τῷ ἀνδρὶ αὐτῆς. 21.3 καὶ ἤκουσα φωνῆς μεγάλης ἐκ τοῦ θρόνου λεγούσης, ἰδοὺ ἡ σκηνὴ τοῦ θεοῦ μετὰ τῶν ἀνθρώπων, καὶ

of the anointed (one), and they will reign with him the thousand years.

20.7 And when the thousand years might be completed, Satan will be loosed out of his prison, 20.8 and he will go forth to deceive all the ethnics/nations in the four corners of the earth, Gog and Magog, also to gather them to/for the war/fight, of whom their number *is* as the sand of the sea, 20.9 and they went up over the breadth of the land and encircled/marched around the camp of the saints and the city, the (one) having been loved. And fire came down from God out of the sky and devoured them; 20.10 and the devil, the (one) deceiving them was thrown into the lake of the fire and the sulphur, where the beast and where the lying/false prophet *are/were*, and they will be tormented/tortured day and night into/for the ages of the ages.

20.11 And I saw a great white throne and the (one) sitting upon it, from the face of whom the earth and the sky fled, and a place was found not for them. 20.12 And I saw the dead (ones), the great (ones) and the small (ones) having stood before *the one* upon the throne, and books/scrolls were opened; and another scroll was opened, which is of the life; and the dead (ones) were judged out of the (things) having been written in the scrolls, according to their works. 20.13 And the sea gave the dead (ones) in it, and the (things/places) death and Hades gave the dead (ones) in them, and they were condemned, each one according to their works. 20.14 And death and Hades were thrown into the lake of the fire. And this is the second death, the lake of the fire. 20.15 And if anyone was not found having been written in the scroll of life, he was thrown into the lake of the fire. 21.1 And I saw a new sky/heaven and a new earth; for the first sky/heaven and the first earth passed away, and the sea is not still/yet. 21.2 And I saw the holy city, a new Jerusalem, descending/coming down out of the sky/heaven from God, having been prepared as a bride having been adorned for her man. 21.3 And I heard a great voice out of the throne saying: Behold, the tent/tabernacle of God *is* with the men/humans, and he

σκηνώσει μετ' αὐτῶν, καὶ αὐτοὶ λαοὶ αὐτοῦ ἔσονται, αὐτὸς ὁ θεὸς ἔσται μετ' αὐτῶν, 21.4 καὶ ἐξαλίψει πᾶν δάκρυον ἐκ τῶν ὀφθαλμῶν αὐτῶν, καὶ θάνατος οὐκ ἔσται ἔτι, οὔτε κραυγὴ οὔτε πένθος οὐκ ἔσται· ὅτι τὰ πρῶτα ἀπῆλθεν. 21.5 καὶ εἶπεν ὁ καθήμενος ἐπὶ τῷ θρόνῳ, ἰδοὺ κενὰ ποιῶ πάντα. καὶ λέγει μοι, γράψον, ὅτι οὗτοι οἱ λόγοι πιστοὶ καὶ ἀληθινοί εἰσιν. 21.6 καὶ λέγεί μοι, γέγοναν. ἐγὼ τὸ ἄλφα καὶ τὸ ὦ, ἡ ἀρχὴ καὶ τὸ τέλος. ἐγὼ τῷ διψῶντι δώσω ἐκ τῆς πηγῆς τοῦ ὕδατος τῆς ζωῆς δωρεάν. 21.7 ὁ νικῶν κληρονομήσι ταῦτα, καὶ ἔσομαι αὐτῷ θεὸς καὶ αὐτὸς ἔσται μοι υἱός. 21.8 τοῖς δὲ διλοῖς καὶ ἀπίστοις καὶ ἐβδελυγμένοις καὶ φονεῦσει καὶ πόρνοις καὶ φαρμάκοις καὶ εἰδωλολάτραις καὶ πᾶσιν τοῖς ψευδέσιν τὸ μέρος αὐτῶν ἐν τῇ λίμνῃ τῇ καιομένῃ πυρὶ καὶ θίῳ, ὅ ἐστιν ὁ θάνατος ὁ δεύτερος. 21.9 καὶ ἦλθεν εἷς ἐκ τῶν ἑπτὰ ἀγγέλων τῶν ἐχόντων τὰς ἑπτὰ φιάλας, τῶν γεμόντων τῶν ἑπτὰ πληγῶν τῶν ἐσχάτων, καὶ ἐλάλησεν μετ' ἐμοῦ λέγων, δεῦρο, δίξω σοι τὴν νύμφην τὴν γυναῖκα τοῦ ἀρνίου. 21.10 καὶ ἀπήνεγκέν με ἐν πνεύματι ἐπὶ ὄρος μέγα καὶ ὑψηλόν, καὶ ἔδιξέν μοι τὴν πόλιν τὴν ἁγίαν Ἰερουσαλὴμ καταβαίνουσαν ἐκ τοῦ οὐρανοῦ ἀπὸ τοῦ θεοῦ, 21.11 ἔχουσαν τὴν δόξαν ἀπὸ τοῦ θεοῦ· ὁ φωστὴρ αὐτῆς ὅμοιος λίθῳ τιμιωτάτῳ, ὡς λίθῳ ἰάσπιδι κρυσταλλίζοντι· 21.12 ἔχοντι τῖχος μέγα καὶ ὑψηλόν, ἔχουσα πυλῶνας δώδεκα, καὶ ἐπὶ τοὺς πυλῶνας ἀγγέλους δώδεκα, καὶ ὀνόματα αὐτῶν γεγραμμένα ἅ ἐστιν τῶν δώδεκα φυλῶν υἱῶν Ἰσραήλ· 21.13 ἀπὸ ἀνατολῆς πυλῶνες τρεῖς, καὶ ἀπὸ βορρᾶ πυλῶνες τρεῖς, καὶ ἀπὸ νότου πυλῶνες τρεῖς, καὶ ἀπὸ δυσμῶν πυλῶνες τρεῖς· 21.14 καὶ τὸ τῖχος τῆς πόλεως ἔχον θεμελίους δώδεκα, καὶ ἐπ' αὐτῶν δώδεκα ὀνόματα τῶν δώδεκα ἀποστόλων τοῦ ἀρνίου. 21.15 καὶ ὁ λαλῶν μετ' ἐμοῦ εἶχεν μέτρον καλάμου χρυσοῦν, ἵνα μετρήσῃ τὴν πόλιν καὶ τοὺς πυλῶνας αὐτῆς καὶ τὸ τῖχος αὐτῆς. 21.16 καὶ ἡ πόλις τετράγωνος κεῖται, καὶ τὸ μῆκος ὅσον τὸ πλάτος. καὶ ἐμέτρησεν

will tent/dwell with them, and they will be his peoples; God himself will be with them, 21.4 and he will wipe off/away every tear out of their eyes, and death will not be yet/still, neither clamor nor grief will not be *yet*; because the first (things) passed away. 21.5 And the (one) sitting upon the throne said: Behold, I make all (things) new. And he says to me: You write, because these sayings/words are faithful and true (ones). 21.6 And he says to me: It has happened/become. I *am* the alpha and the omega, the beginning and the end. I, I shall give freely to the (one) thirsting out of the spring of the water of the life. 21.7 The (one) overcoming will inherit these (things), and I shall be a God to him and he, he will be my son. 21.8 But for the (ones) timid and unfaithful and having become detestable, and murderers and whoremongers/male prostitutes and magicians and idolaters and all the liars, their part *will be* in the lake burning with fire and sulphur, which is the second death. 21.9 And one came out of the seven messengers/angels holding the seven bowls, the (ones) being filled from the seven last plagues, and he spoke with me saying: Come, I shall show to you the bride, the woman of the lamb. 21.10 And he brought me in/by spirit to a great and high mountain, and he showed to me the holy city Jerusalem coming down/descending out of the sky/heaven from God, 21.11 having the fame/glory from God; the light of it *was* like a very costly stone, as to a jasper stone, being clear as crystal; 21.12 having a great and high wall, having twelve gates, and upon/at the gates *were* twelve messengers/angels, and names of them having been written, which are from the twelve tribes of/from sons of Israel; 21.13 From east three gates, and from north three gates, and from south three gates and from west three gates; 21.14 and the wall of the city having twelve foundations, and on them twelve names of the twelve apostles of the lamb. 21.15 And the (one) speaking with me held a measure, a golden reed/staff, in order that he might measure the city and her gates and her walls. 21.16 And the city lies foursquare, and the length *is* as much as the width. And he

τὴν πόλιν τῷ καλάμῳ ἐπὶ σταδίων δώδεκα χιλιάδων· τὸ μῆκος καὶ τὸ πλάτος καὶ τὸ ὕψος αὐτῆς ἴσα ἐστίν. 21.17 καὶ ἐμέτρησεν τὸ χῖλος αὐτῆς ἑκατὸν τεσσεράκοντα τεσσάρων πηχέων, μέτρον ἀνθρώπου, ὅ ἐστιν ἀγγέλου. 21.18 καὶ ἡ ἐνδώμησις τοῦ τίχους αὐτῆς εἴασπις, καὶ ἡ πόλις χρυσίον καθαρὸν ὅμοιον ὑάλῳ καθαρῷ. 21.19 οἱ θεμέλιοι τοῦ τίχους τῆς πόλεως παντὶ λίθῳ τιμίῳ κεκοσμημένοι· ὁ θεμέλιος ὁ εἷς ἴασπις, καὶ ὁ δεύτερος σάπφιρος, καὶ ὁ τρίτος χαλκηδών, ὁ τέταρτος σμάραγδος, 21.20 ὁ πέμπτος σαρδόνυξ, ὁ ἕκτος σάρδιον, ὁ ἕβδομος χρυσόλιθος, ὁ ὄγδοος βήρυλλος, ὁ ἔνατος τοπάζιον, ὁ δέκατος χρυσόπρασος, ὁ ἑνδέκατος ὑάκινθος, ὁ δωδέκατος ἀμέθυστος. 21.21 καὶ οἱ δώδεκα πυλῶνες δώδεκα μαργαρεῖται, ἀνὰ εἷς ἕκαστος τῶν πυλώνων ἦν ἐξ ἑνὸς μαργαρίτου. καὶ ἡ πλατῖα τῆς πόλεως χρυσίον καθαρὸν ὡς ὕαλος διαυγής. 21.22 καὶ ναὸν οὐκ εἶδον ἐν αὐτῇ, ὁ γὰρ κύριος ὁ θεὸς ὁ παντοκράτωρ ναὸς αὐτῆς ἐστιν, καὶ τὸ ἀρνίον. 21.23 καὶ ἡ πόλις οὐ χρίαν ἔχει τοῦ ἡλίου οὐδὲ τῆς σελήνης, ἵνα φαίνωσιν ἐν αὐτῇ, ἡ γὰρ δόξα τοῦ θεοῦ ἐφώτισεν αὐτήν, καὶ ὁ λύχνος αὐτῆς τὸ ἀρνίον. 21.24 καὶ περιπατήσουσιν τὰ ἔθνη διὰ τοῦ φωτὸς αὐτῆς· καὶ οἱ βασιλεῖς τῆς γῆς φέρουσιν τὴν δόξαν αὐτῶν εἰς αὐτήν· 21.25 καὶ οἱ πυλῶνες αὐτῆς οὐ μὴ κλεισθῶσιν ἡμέρας, νὺξ γὰρ οὐκ ἔστε ἐκεῖ· 21.26 καὶ οἴσουσιν τὴν δόξαν καὶ τὴν τιμὴν τῶν ἐθνῶν εἰς αὐτήν. 21.27 καὶ οὐ μὴ εἰσέλθωσιν εἰς αὐτὴν πᾶν κοινὸν καὶ ὁ ποιῶν βδέλυγμα καὶ ψεῦδος, εἰ μὴ οἱ γεγραμμένοι ἐν τῷ βιβλίῳ τῆς ζωῆς τοῦ οὐρανοῦ. 22.1 καὶ ἔδιξέν μοι ποταμὸν ὕδατος ζωῆς λαμπρὸν ὡς κρύσταλλον, ἐκπορευόμενον ἐκ θρόνου τοῦ θεοῦ καὶ τοῦ ἀρνίου. 22.2 ἐν μέσῳ τῆς πλατίας αὐτῆς καὶ τοῦ ποταμοῦ ἔνθεν καὶ ἔνθεν καὶ ποιοῦν καρποὺς δώδεκα, κατὰ μῆνα ἕκαστον ἀποδιδοῦς τοὺς καρποὺς αὐτοῦ, καὶ τὰ φύλλα τῶν ξύλων εἰς θεραπείαν ἐθνῶν. 22.3 καὶ πᾶν κατάθεμα οὐκ ἔσται ἔτι. καὶ θρόνος τοῦ θεοῦ καὶ τοῦ ἀρνίου ἐν αὐτῇ ἔσται,

measured the city with the staff/reed at twelve thousand stadia (about 1379 miles); the length and the width and the height of her are equal. 21.17 And he measured the wall of her a hundred forty-four cubits, a measure of a man, which is from a messenger/angel. 21.18 And the material/construction of her wall *was* jasper, and the city *was* pure gold similar to clean/pure glass. 21.19 The foundation of the wall of the city having been decorated with every precious stone; the one foundation jasper, and the second sapphire, and the third chalcedony, the fourth emerald, 21.20 the fifth sardonyx, the sixth sardius, the seventh chrysolite, the eighth beryl, the ninth topaz, the tenth chrysoprasus, the eleventh hyacinth, the twelfth amethyst. 21.21 And the twelve gates *were* twelve pearls, each one singly of the gates was from one pearl. And the broad street of the city *was* pure gold, as transparent glass. 21.22 And I saw not an *inner* temple in her, for the Lord, the God, the almighty/ruler of all is her *inner* temple, and/also the lamb. 21.23 And the city has not a need of the sun nor of the moon, that they might shine in her, for the fame/glory of God enlightened/lighted her, and the lamp of her is the lamb. 21.24 And the ethnics will walk about through her light; and the kings of the land/earth bring their fame/glory into her; 21.25 and by no means may her gates be closed of day, for a night will not be there; 21.26 and they will bring the fame/glory and the honor of the ethnics into her. 21.27 and by no means might enter into her every common (thing) and the (one) doing/making an abomination and a lie, except those having been written in the scroll of the life from the sky/heaven. 22.1 And he showed to me a river of water of life bright as a crystal, going forth out of a throne of God and of the lamb. 22.2 In the midst of its broad street and of the river from here/this place and hereafter/this time and making twelve fruits, according to each month giving back its fruits/ products, and the leaves being from a tree *are* for healing ethnics. 22.3 And every cursed (thing) will not be yet/still. And a throne of God and of the lamb

καὶ οἱ δοῦλοι αὐτοῦ λατρεύσουσιν αὐτῷ, 22.4 καὶ ὄψονται τὸ πρόσωπον αὐτοῦ, καὶ τὸ ὄνομα αὐτοῦ καὶ ἐπὶ τῶν μετώπων αὐτῶν. 22.5 καὶ νὺξ οὐκ ἔσται ἔτι, καὶ οὐκ ἔχουσιν χρείαν φωτὸς λύχνου καὶ φωτὸς ἡλίου, ὅτι κύριος ὁ θεὸς φωτίει ἐπ' αὐτούς, καὶ βασιλεύσουσιν εἰς τοὺς αἰῶνας τῶν αἰώνων. 22.6 καὶ εἰπέν μοι, οὗτοι οἱ λόγοι πιστοὶ καὶ ἀληθινοί,

καὶ ὁ κύριος, ὁ θεὸς τῶν πνευμάτων τῶν προφητῶν, ἀπέστιλεν τὸν ἄγγελον αὐτοῦ δῖξαι τοῖς δούλοις αὐτοῦ ἃ δῖ γενέσθαι ἐν τάχει. 22.7 καὶ ἰδοὺ ἔρχομαι ταχύ.

μακάριος ὁ τηρῶν τοὺς λόγους τῆς προφητίας τοῦ βιβλίου τούτου. 22.8 κἀγὼ Ἰωάννης ὁ βλέπων καὶ ἀκούων ταῦτα. καὶ ὅτε ἤκουσα καὶ ἔβλεψα, ἔπεσα προσκυνῆσαι ἔμπροσθεν τῶν ποδῶν τοῦ ἀγγέλου τοῦ δικνύντός μοι ταῦτα. 22.9 καὶ λέγει μοι, ὅρα μή· σύνδουλός σού εἰμι καὶ τῶν ἀδελφῶν σου τῶν προφητῶν καὶ τῶν τηρούντων τοὺς λόγους τοῦ βιβλίου τούτου· τῷ θεῷ προσκύνησον. 22.10 καὶ λέγει μοι, μὴ σφραγίσῃς τοὺς λόγους τῆς προφητείας τοῦ βιβλίου τούτου, ὁ καιρὸς γὰρ ἐγγύς ἐστιν. 22.11 ὁ ἀδικῶν ἀδικησάτω ἔτι, καὶ ὁ ῥυπαρὸς ῥυπανθήτω ἔτι, καὶ ὁ δίκαιος δικαιοσύνην ποιησάτω ἔτι, καὶ ὁ ἅγιος ἁγιασθήτω ἔτι. 22.12 ἰδοὺ ἔρχομαι ταχύ, καὶ ὁ μισθός μου μετ' ἐμοῦ, ἀποδοῦναι ἑκάστῳ ὡς τὸ ἔργον ἐστὶν αὐτοῦ. 22.13 ἐγὼ τὸ ἄλφα καὶ τὸ ὦ, ὁ πρῶτος καὶ ὁ ἔσχατος, ἡ ἀρχὴ καὶ τὸ τέλος. 22.14 μακάριοι οἱ πλύνοντες τὰς στολὰς αὐτῶν, ἵνα ἔσται ἡ ἐξουσία αὐτῶν ἐπὶ τὸ ξύλον τῆς ζωῆς καὶ τοῖς πυλῶσιν εἰσέλθωσιν εἰς τὴν πόλιν. 22.15 ἔξω οἱ κύνες καὶ οἱ φάρμακοι καὶ οἱ πόρνοι καὶ οἱ φονεῖς καὶ οἱ εἰδωλολάτραι καὶ πᾶς ποιῶν καὶ φιλῶν ψεῦδος. 22.16 ἐγὼ Ἰησοῦς ἔπεμψα τὸν ἄγγελόν μου μαρτυρῆσαι ὑμῖν ταῦτα ἐπὶ ταῖς ἐκκλησίαις. ἐγὼ εἰμι ἡ ῥίζα καὶ τὸ γένος Δαυίδ, ὁ ἀστὴρ ὁ λαμπρὸς ὁ πρωϊνός. 22.17 καὶ πνεῦμα καὶ νύμφη λέγουσιν, ἔρχου. καὶ ὁ ἀκούων εἰπάτω, ἔρχου. καὶ ὁ διψῶν ἐρχέσθω, ὁ

will be in her, and his slaves will do service for
him, 22.4 and they will see his face, and his name
will be upon their foreheads. 22.5 And a night will
not be still/yet and they have not a need of light
from a lamp and light from a sun, because the Lord God
sheds light on them, and they will reign into/for the
ages of the ages. 22.6 And he said to me: These
words/sayings *are* faithful and true (ones),

and the Lord, the God of the spirits of the
prophets, he sent his messenger/angel to show to his
slaves what (things) it is necessary to happen in
quickness. 22.7 And behold, I come quickly.

Happy *is* the (one) keeping the sayings/words of
the prophecy from this scroll. 22.8 And I, John, *am*
the (one) seeing and hearing these (things). And when
I heard and saw, I fell *down* to worship before the
feet of the messenger/angel, of the (one) showing to
me these (things). 22.9 And he says to me: You see
not; I am a fellow slave of you and of your brothers,
from the prophets and those keeping the sayings/words
of this scroll/book; worship you for/to God. 22.10
And he says to me: You may not seal/secure the sayings
of the prophecy of this scroll, for the time is near.
22.11 The (one) being unjust, let him be unjust still,
and the filthy (one), let him be filthy still, and the
just (one), let him do/make justice still, and the
holy (one), let him be holy still. 22.12 Behold, I
come quickly, and my wage/reward *is* with me, to pay to
each as his work is. 22.13 I *am* the alpha and the
omega, the first and the last, the beginning and the
end. 22.14 Happy *are* those washing their robes, in
order that their authority will be over the tree of
the life and they may enter by the gates into the
city. 22.15 Outside *are* the dogs and the enchanters
and the whoremongers/male prostitutes and the
murderers and the idolaters and every (one) making and
loving a lie/falsehood. 22.16 I, Jesus, I sent my
messenger/angel to witness/testify to ye these
(things) to the assemblies. I, I am the root and the
kind/race of David, the bright/shining morning star.
22.17 And a spirit and a bride say: You come. And the
(one) hearing, let him say: You come. And the (one)

θέλων λαβέτω ὕδωρ ζωῆς δωρεάν.

22.18 μαρτυρῶ ἐγὼ παντὶ τῷ ἀκούοντι τοὺς λόγους τῆς προφητείας τοῦ βιβλίου τούτου· ἐάν τις ἐπιθήσει ἐπ' αὐτά, ἐπιθήσι ἐπ' αὐτὸν ὁ θεὸς τὰς πληγὰς τὰς γεγραμμένας ἐν τῷ βιβλίῳ τούτῳ· 22.19 καὶ ἄν τις ἀφέλῃ ἀπὸ τῶν λόγων τουτῶν τοῦ βιβλίου τῆς προφητίας ταύτης, ἀφελῖ ὁ θεὸς τὸ μέρος αὐτοῦ ἀπὸ τοῦ ξύλου τῆς ζωῆς καὶ ἐκ τῆς πόλεως τῆς ἁγίας, τῶν γεγραμμένων ἐν τῷ βιβλίῳ τούτῳ. 22.20 λέγι ὁ μαρτυρῶν ταῦτα, ναί, ἔρχομαι ταχύ. ἔρχου, κύριε Ἰησοῦ. 22.21 ἡ χάρις τοῦ κυρίου Ἰησοῦ μετὰ τῶν ἁγίων. ἀμήν.

Ἀποκάλιψις Ἰωάννου

thirsting, let him come, the (one) wanting, let him take/receive water of life freely.

22.18   I, I testify to every one hearing the sayings/words of the prophecy from this scroll; if anyone will lay/put/add upon/to them, God will lay/put/add upon/to him the plagues having been written in this scroll,   22.19 and if anyone might send away/dismiss from these words/sayings from the scroll of this prophecy, God will send away/dismiss his part from the tree of the life and out of the holy city, of the (things) having been written in this scroll. 22.20 The (one) testifying these (things) says: Yes, I come quickly. You come, Lord Jesus.   22.21 The grace/favor of the Lord Jesus *be* with the saints. Truly.

A Revelation of John

ΒΑΡΝΑΒΑ ΕΠΙΣΤΟΛΗ

This is the Sinaitic New Testament, book of Barnabas.

1.1 Χαίρετε, υἱοὶ καὶ θυγατέρες, ἐν ὀνόματι κυρίου τοῦ ἀγαπήσαντος ἡμᾶς, ἐν εἰρήνῃ.

1.2 μεγάλων μὲν ὄντων καὶ πλουσίων τῶν τοῦ θεοῦ δικαιωμάτων εἰς ὑμᾶς, ὑπέρ τι καὶ καθ' ὑπερβολὴν ὑπερευφρένομε ἐπὶ τοῖς μακαρίοις καὶ ἐνδόξοις ὑμῶν πνεύμασιν· οὕτο ἔμφυτον τῆς δωρεᾶς πνευματικῆς χάριν εἰλήφαται. 1.3 διὸ καὶ μᾶλλον συγχαίρω ἐμαυτῷ ἐλπίζων σωθῆναι, ὅτι ἀληθῶς βλέπω ἐν ὑμῖν ἐκκεχυμένον ἀπὸ τοῦ πλουσίου τῆς ἀγαπῆς κυρίου πνεῦμα εφ' ὑμᾶς. οὕτω με ἐξέπληξεν ἐπὶ ὑμῶν ἡ ἐπιποθήτη ὄψις ὑμῶν. 1.4 πεπισμένος οὖν τοῦτο καὶ συνιδὼς ἐμαυτῷ, ὅτι ἐν ὑμῖν λαλήσας πολλὰ ἐπίσταμαι ὅτι ἐμοὶ συνώδευσεν ἐν ὁδῷ δικαιοσύνης κύριος, καὶ πάντως ἀναγκάζομε κἀγὼ εἰς τοῦτο, ἀγαπᾶν ὑμᾶς ὑπὲρ τὴν ψυχήν μου, ὅτι μεγάλη πίστις καὶ ἀγάπη ἐγκατοικεῖ ἐν ὑμῖν ἐλπίδει ζωῆς αὐτοῦ. 1.5 λογισάμενος οὖν τοῦτο, ὅτι ἐὰν μελήσῃ μοι περὶ ὑμῶν τοῦ μέρος τι μεταδοῦναι αφ' οὗ ἔλαβον, ὅτι ἔσται μοι τοιούτοις πνεύμασιν ὑπηρετήσαντι εἰς μισθόν, ἐσπούδασα κατὰ μικρὸν ὑμῖν πέμπειν, ἵνα μετὰ τῆς πίστεως ὑμῶν τελίαν ἔχηται τὴν γνῶσιν. 1.6 τρία οὖν δόγματά ἐστιν κυρίου· ζωῆς πίστις ἐλπίς, ἀρχὴ καὶ τέλος ἡμῶν· καὶ δικεοσύνη, κρίσεως ἀρχὴ καὶ τέλος· ἀγάπη εὐφροσύνη καὶ ἀγαλλιάσεως ἔργων ἐν δικαιοσύναι μαρτυρία. 1.7 ἐγνώρισεν γὰρ ὑμῖν ὁ δεσπότης διὰ τῶν προφητῶν τὰ παρεληλυθότα καὶ τὰ ἐνεστῶτα, καὶ τῶν μελλόντων δοὺς ἀπαρχὰς ἡμῖν γεύσεως, ὧν τὰ καθ' ἕκαστα βλέποντες ἐνεργύμενα, καθὼς ἐλάλησεν, ὀφίλομεν πλουσιώτερον καὶ ὑψηλότερον προσάγειν τῷ φόβῳ αὐτοῦ. 1.8 ἐγὼ δὲ οὐχ ὡς διδάσσκαλος, ἀλλ' ὡς εἷς ἐξ ὑμῶν ὑποδίξω ὀλίγα, δι' ὧν ἐν τοῖς παροῦσιν εὐφρανθήσεσθε. 2.1 ἡμερῶν οὖν οὐσῶν πονηρῶν καὶ

1.1 Greetings, sons and daughters, in *the* name of the Lord, of the (one) having loved us, in peace.

1.2 Being indeed from greatness and richness of the just regulations/requirements of God to/for ye, in behalf of what also *is* against/beyond excess, I rejoice exceedingly over your happy and glorious spirits; this implanted grace of the spiritual gift ye have received. 1.3 Wherefore I also rejoice rather/more in myself, having hope to be saved, because I truly see in ye a spirit having been poured out upon ye from the richness/abundance of the agape of *the* Lord. Thus your desired vision/sight/appearance amazed me at/over ye. 1.4 Being persuaded then *of* this and being conscious for myself, that having spoken among ye I understand much because *the* Lord traveled with me on/in the road/way of justness, and I, I am wholly compelled in this, to love ye over/above my life/soul, because great faith and agape dwells/lives in ye for hope of/from his life. 1.5 Therefore having accounted/reckoned this, that if it be a care to me concerning ye of the (thing) to impart/share a part from that which I received, because having served/ministered for such spirits will be to me for a reward, I hastened to send to ye down from/after a little (time), in order that with the faith of ye, ye might have complete/mature knowledge. 1.6 Then there are three decrees/dogmas of the Lord: Faith *is* a hope of life, your beginning and end; and justice/justness, the beginning and end of judgment; agape, from cheerfulness and extreme joy *is* in/by a witness/testimony to be justified from works. 1.7 For the lord/master made known to us through the prophets the (things) being past and the (things) being present, and having given first-fruits to us from a taste of the (things) about to become/happen, which things having seen being worked according to each/one-by-one/in order, even as he spoke we are obligated to offer a richer and more exalted *offering* in the fear of him. 1.8 But I, I shall show/exhibit a few (things), not as a teacher but as one out of ye, through which ye will be gladdened/cheered in the present (time). 2.1 Therefore from days being evil and the (one) working having the

αὐτοῦ τοῦ ἐνεργοῦντος ἔχοντος τὴν ἐξουσίαν, ὀφίλομεν ἑαυτοῖς προσέχοντες ἐκζητεῖν τὰ δικαιώματα κυρίου. 2.2 τῆς οὖν πίστεως ἡμῶν εἰσιν βοηθοὶ φόβος ὑπομονή, τὰ δὲ συμμαχοῦντα ἡμῖν μακροθυμία καὶ ἐγκράτια· 2.3 τούτων μενόντων τὰ πρὸς κύριον ἁγνῶς, συνευφρένονται αὐτοῖς σοφία, σύνεσις, ἐπιστήμη, γνῶσις. 2.4 πεφανέρωκεν γὰρ ἡμῖν διὰ πάντων τῶν προφητῶν, ὅτι οὔτε θυσιῶν οὔτε ὁλοκαυτωμάτων οὔτε προσφορῶν χρῄζει, λέγων ὅτε μέν· 2.5 τί μοι πλῆθος τῶν θυσιῶν ὑμῶν; λέγει κύριος. πλήρης εἰμὶ ὁλοκαυτωμάτων, καὶ στέαρ ἀρνῶν καὶ αἷμα ταύρων καὶ τράγων οὐ βούλομε, οὐδ᾽ ἂν ἔρχησθε ὀφθῆναί μοι. τίς γὰρ ἐξεζήτησεν ταῦτα ἐκ τῶν χιρῶν ὑμῶν; πατῖν μου τὴν αὐλὴν οὐ προσθήσεσθαι. οὐδε ἐὰν φέρηται σεμίδαλιν, μάταιον· θυμίαμα βδέλυγμά μοί ἐστιν· τὰς νεομηνίας ὑμῶν καὶ τὰ σάββατα οὐκ ἀνέχομαι. 2.6 ταῦτα οὖν κατήργησεν, ἵνα ὁ καινὸς νόμος τοῦ κυρίου ἡμῶν Ἰησοῦ χριστοῦ, ἄνευ ζυγοῦ ἀνάγκης ὤν, μὴ ἀνθρωποποίητον ἔχῃ τὴν προσοράν.

2.7 λέγει δὲ πάλιν πρὸς αὐτούς· μὴ ἐγὼ ἐνετιλάμην τοῖς πατράσιν ὑμῶν ἐκπορευομένοις ἐκ γῆς Αἰγύπτου, προσενέγκαι μοι ὁλοκαυτώματα καὶ θυσίας; 2.8 ἀλλ᾽ ἢ τοῦτο ἐνετειλάμην αὐτοῖς· ἕκαστος ὑμῶν κατὰ τοῦ πλησίον ἐν τῇ καρδίᾳ ἑαυτοῦ κακίαν μὴ μνησικακίτω, καὶ ὅρκον ψευδῆ μὴ ἀγαπᾶται. 2.9 αἰσθάνεσθαι οὖν ὀφίλομεν, μὴ ὄντες ἀσύνετοι, τὴν γνώμην τῆς ἀγαθωσύνης τοῦ πατρὸς ἡμῶν, ὅτι ἡμῖν λέγει, θέλων ἡμᾶς μὴ ὁμοίως πλανωμένους ἐκείνοις ζητῖν, πῶς προσάγωμεν αὐτῷ. 2.10 ἡμῖν οὖν οὕτως λέγει· θυσία τῷ θεῷ καρδία συντετριμμένη, ὀσμὴ εὐωδίας τῷ κυρίῳ καρδία δοξάζουσα τὸν πεπλακότα αὐτήν. ἀκριβεύεσθαι οὖν ὀφίλομεν, ἀδελφοί, περὶ τῆς σωτηρίας ἡμῶν, ἵνα μὴ ὁ πονηρὸς παρείσδυσιν πλάνης ποιήσας ἐν ἡμῖν

authority of himself, we are obligated/indebted, taking heed for ourselves, to seek out the just things/requirements/deeds of *the* Lord 2.2 Fear *and* patience then are helpers of our faith, and patience/ steadfastness and self-control/temperance *are* the weapons/allies/helpers for us. 2.3 From these (things) remaining purely the (things) of *the* Lord: wisdom, insight, understanding and knowledge, they rejoice with them. 2.4 For he has made plain/manifested to us through all the prophets, that he has a need neither of sacrifices nor of whole burnt-offerings nor of gifts/oblations, saying when on one hand: 2.5 WHAT TO ME *is* A MULTITUDE OF YOUR SACRIFICES? SAYS *the* LORD; I AM FULL OF WHOLE BURNT-OFFERINGS, AND I WISH/WANT NOT FAT OF LAMBS AND BLOOD OF BULLS AND GOATS, NOR IF YE MAY COME TO APPEAR TO/FOR ME. FOR WHO HAS SOUGHT THESE (THINGS) OUT OF/FROM YOUR HANDS? YE WILL NOT CONTINUE TO TREAD MY COURT-YARD. NOR IF YE MAY BRING FINE FLOUR, *it is* EMPTY/VAIN; INCENSE IS A DETESTABLE THING TO ME; I ENDURE NOT YOUR NEW MOONS AND THE SABBATHS. 2.6 He abolished then these (things) in order that the new law from our Lord Jesus, the anointed (one), being without a yoke of necessity, may have the gift/offering/oblation not made by man.

2.7 And again he says to them: DID NOT I COMMAND TO YOUR FATHERS, COMING FORTH OUT OF A LAND OF EGYPT, TO BRING/OFFER WHOLE BURNT-OFFERINGS AND SACRIFICES TO ME? 2.8 BUT I COMMANDED MORE THIS TO THEM: LET EACH (ONE) OF YE NOT REMEMBER EVIL AGAINST THE NEIGHBOR IN THE HEART OF HIMSELF, AND LOVE YE NOT A FALSE OATH. 2.9 Therefore we are obligated to perceive, being not senseless (ones), the judgment/decision from the goodness of our father, because he speaks to us, wanting/wishing not *for* us likewise to seek for those leading astray, how we might offer to him. 2.10 Then he speaks thus to us: A SACRIFICE FOR THE LORD *is* A HEART HAVING BEEN BROKEN, an odor of fragrance to the Lord *is* a heart glorifying the (one) having made it. Then we are obligated to inquire accurately, brothers, concerning our salvation, in order that the evil (one) may not stealthily slip in a deceitful doing in/among

ἐκσφενδονήσῃ ἡμᾶς ἀπὸ τῆς ζωῆς ἡμῶν. 3.1 λέγει οὖν πάλιν περὶ τούτων πρὸς αὐτούς· ἱνατί μοι νηστεύεται, λέγει κύριος, ὡς σήμερον ἀκουσθῆναι κραυγῇ τὴν φωνὴν ὑμῶν; οὐ ταύτην τὴν νηστίαν ἐγὼ ἐξελεξάμην, λέγει κύριος, οὐκ ἄνθρωπον ταπινοῦντα τὴν ψυχὴν αὐτοῦ, 3.2 οὐδ' ἂν κάμψηται ὡς κρίκον τὸν τράχηλον ὑμῶν καὶ σάκκον καὶ σποδὸν ὑποστρώσηται, οὐδ' οὕτως καλέσεται νηστείαν δεκτήν. 3.3 πρὸς ἡμᾶς δὲ λέγει· ἰδοὺ αὕτη νυστία, ἣν ἐγὼ ἐξελεξάμην, λέγει κύριος· οὐκ ἄνθρωπον ταπινοῦντα τὴν ψυχὴν αὐτοῦ, ἀλλὰ λύε πᾶν σύνδεσμον ἀδικίας, διάλυε στραγγαλιὰς βιαίων συναλλαγμάτων, ἀπόστελλε τεθραυσμένους ἐν ἀφέσει καὶ πᾶσαν ἄδικον συγγραφὴν διάσπα. διάθρυπτε πινῶσιν τὸν ἄρτον σου, καὶ γυμνὸν ἐὰν εἴδῃς περίβαλε· ἀστέγους εἴσαγε εἰς τὸν οἶκον σου, καὶ ἐὰν ἴδῃς ταπινόν, οὐχ ὑπερόψῃ αὐτόν, οὐδὲ ἀπὸ τῶν οἰκίων τοῦ σπέρματός σου. 3.4 τότε ῥαγήσεται πρώιμον τὸ φῶς σου, καὶ τὰ ἱμάτα σου ταχέως ἀνατελεῖ, καὶ προπορεύσεται ἔμπροσθέν σου ἡ δικαιοσύνη, καὶ ἡ δόξα τοῦ θεοῦ περιστελεῖ σε. 3.5 τότε βοήσεις, καὶ ὁ θεὸς ἐπακούσεταί σου, ἔτι λαλοῦντός σου ἐρῖ· ἰδοὺ πάρειμι· ἐὰν ἀφέλῃς ἀπὸ σοῦ σύνδεσμον καὶ χειροτονίαν καὶ ῥῆμα γογγυσμοῦ, καὶ δῷς πινῶντι τὸν ἄρτον σου ἐκ ψυχῆς σου καὶ ψυχὴν τεταπεινωμένην ἐλεήσεις. 3.6 εἰς τοῦτο οὖν, ἀδελφοί, ὁ μακρόθυμος προβλέψας, ὡς ἐν ἀκεραιοσύνῃ πιστεύσει ὁ λαός, ὃν ἡτοίμασεν ἐν τῷ ἠγαπημένῳ αὐτοῦ, προεφανέρωσεν γὰρ ἡμῖν περὶ πάντων, εἵνα μὴ προσρησσώμεθα ὡς ἐπήλυτοι τῷ ἐκίνων νόμῳ 4.1 δεῖ οὖν ἡμᾶς περὶ τῶν ἐνεστώτων ἐπιπολὺ ἐραυνῶντας ἐκζητῖν τὰ δυνάμενα ἡμᾶς σώζειν. φύγωμεν οὖν τελείως ἀπὸ πάντων τῶν ἔργων τῆς ἀνομίας, μήποτε καταλάβῃ

us *and* may *not* sling us out from our life. 3.1 Then he says/speaks again to them concerning these (things): WHY FAST YE FOR ME, SAYS *the* LORD, SINCE THE VOICE OF YE IS TO BE HEARD TODAY IN A CLAMOR/OUTCRY? I, I CHOSE NOT THIS FAST, SAYS *the* LORD, NOT A MAN/HUMAN HUMBLING HIS SOUL/LIFE, 3.2 NOR IF YE MAY BOW/BEND THE NECK OF YE AS A HOOP/RING AND YE MAY SPREAD SACKCLOTH AND ASHES UNDERNEATH, YE WILL NOT CALL *it* THUS AN ACCEPTABLE FAST. 3.3 But he says to us: BEHOLD, THIS *is* A FAST WHICH I, I CHOSE, SAYS *the* LORD: NOT A MAN/HUMAN HUMBLING HIS SOUL/LIFE, BUT LOOSE EVERY BOND OF/FROM INJUSTICE, UNTIE KNOTS/STRANGLE HOLDS OF FORCED AGREEMENTS, SEND AWAY THOSE HAVING BEEN CRUSHED IN FORGIVENESS/RELEASE, AND TEAR UP/IN PIECES EVERY UNJUST DOCUMENT/ACCOUNT. BREAK/-SHARE YOUR LOAF/BREAD FOR/WITH HUNGRY (ONES), AND IF YOU MIGHT SEE A NAKED (ONE) CLOTH (HIM); BRING/LEAD THE WANDERING/HOMELESS (ONES) INTO YOUR HOUSE, AND IF YOU MAY SEE A HUMBLE/LOWLY (ONE), BE NOT/LOOK NOT SUPERIOR TO/ABOVE/OVER HIM, NOR FROM THE HOUSEHOLDS OF YOUR SEED. 3.4 THEN YOUR LIGHT WILL BREAK FORTH EARLY/IN THE MORNING, AND YOUR GARMENTS WILL RISE UP QUICKLY, AND THE JUSTICE/JUSTNESS OF YOU WILL GO BEFORE YOU, AND THE FAME/GLORY/EXPECTATION FROM GOD WILL CLOTHE/SURROUND YOU. 3.5 THEN YOU WILL CRY AND GOD WILL LISTEN/HEARKEN *to* YOU, FROM YOU YET SPEAKING, HE WILL SPEAK: BEHOLD, I AM HERE; IF YOU MIGHT SEND AWAY/LEAVE BONDAGE FROM YOU, ALSO LIFTING UP THE HAND/VIOLENCE AND A WORD OF GRUMBLING/WHISPERING, AND YOU MAY GIVE YOUR LOAF/BREAD TO HUNGRY (ONES) OUT OF/FROM YOUR SOUL/LIFE AND YOU MAY PITY/HAVE MERCY ON A LIFE/SOUL HAVING BEEN HUMBLED/DEPRESSED. 3.6 In this then, brothers, the patient (one) foresaw, as/since the people believe in purity, whom he prepared in the (one) having been loved of him, for he made plain/manifested to us beforehand concerning all (things), that we may not be shipwrecked as proselytes to the law of those/them. 4.1 Then it is necessary for us, searching carefully concerning the present (things), to seek out the (things) being able to save us. Then let us flee completely from all the works of the lawlessness, lest the works of the lawlessness

ἡμᾶς τὰ ἔργα τῆς ἀνομίας· καὶ μισήσωμεν τὴν πλάνην τοῦ νῦν καιροῦ, ἵνα εἰς τὸν μέλλοντα ἀγαπηθῶμεν. 4.2 μὴ δῶμεν τῇ ἑαυτῶν ψυχῇ ἄνεσιν, ὥστε ἔχιν αὐτὴν ἐξουσίαν μετὰ ἁμαρτωλῶν καὶ πονηρῶν αυντρέχιν, μήποτε ὁμοιωθῶμεν αὐτοῖς. 4.3 τὸ τέλιον σκάνδαλον ἤγγικεν, περὶ οὗ γέγραπται, ὡς Ἐνὼχ λέγει. εἰς τοῦτο γὰρ ὁ δεσπότης συντέτμηκεν τοὺς καιροὺς καὶ τὰς ἡμέρας, ἵνα ταχύνῃ ὁ ἠγαπημένος αὐτοῦ καὶ ἐπὶ τὴν κληρονομίαν ἥξει. 4.4 λέγει δὲ οὕτως καὶ ὁ προφήτης· βασιλεῖαι δέκα ἐπὶ τῆς γῆς βασιλεύσουσιν, καὶ ἐξαναστήσεται ὄπισθεν αὐτῶν μικρὸς βασιλεύς, ὃς ταπινώσει τρῖς ὑφ' ἓν τῶν βασιλέων. 4.5 ὁμοίως περὶ τοῦ αὐτοῦ λέγι Δανιήλ· καὶ εἶδον τὸ τέταρτον θηρίον πονηρὸν καὶ ἰσχυρὸν καὶ χαλεπώτερον παρὰ πάντα τὰ θηρία τῆς γῆς, καὶ ὡς ἐξ αὐτοῦ ἀνέτιλεν δέκα κέρατα, καὶ ἐξ αὐτῶν μικρὸν κέρας παραφυάδιον, καὶ ὡς ἐταπίνωσεν ὑφ' ἓν τρία τῶν μεγάλων κεράτω. 4.6 συνιέναι οὖν ὀφίλεται. ἔτι δὲ καὶ τοῦτο ἐρωτῶ ὑμᾶς ὡς εἷς ἐξ ὑμῶν ὤν, ἰδείως δὲ καὶ πάντας ἀγαπῶν ὑπὲρ τὴν ψυχήν μου, προσέχειν νῦν ἑαυτοῖς καὶ μὴ ὁμοιοῦσθαί τισιν ἐπισωρεύοντες ταῖς ἁμαρτίαις ὑμῶν λέγοντας, ὅτι ἡ διαθήκη. 4.7 ἡμῶν μέν· ἀλλ' ἐκῖνοι οὕτως εἰς τέλος ἀπώλεσαν αὐτὴν λαβόντος ἤδη τοῦ Μωϋσέως. λέγει γὰρ ἡ γραφή· καὶ ἦν Μωϋσῆς ἐν τῷ ὄρι νηστεύων ἡμέρας τεσσαράκοντα καὶ νύκτας τεσσαράκοντα, καὶ ἔλαβεν τὴν διαθήκην ἀπὸ τοῦ κυρίου, πλάκας λιθίνας γεγραμμένας τῷ δακτύλῳ τῆς χειρὸς τοῦ κυρίου. 4.8 ἀλλὰ ἐπιστραφέντες ἐπὶ τὰ εἴδωλα ἀπώλεσαν αὐτήν. λέγει γὰρ οὕτως κύριος. Μωσῆ Μωσῆ, κατάβηθι τὸ τάχος, ὅτι ἠνόμησεν ὁ λαός σου, οὓς ἐξήγαγες ἐκ γῆς Αἰγύτου, καὶ συνῆκεν Μωσῆς καὶ ἔριψεν τὰς δύο πλάκας ἐκ τῶν χειρῶν αὐτοῦ· καὶ συνετρίβη αὐτῶν ἡ διαθήκη, ἵνα ἡ τοῦ ἠγαπημένου Ἰησοῦ ἐγκατασφραγισθῇ εἰς τὴν καρδίαν ἡμῶν ἐν ἐλπίδι τῆς πίστεως αὐτοῦ. 4.9 πολλὰ δὲ θέλων γράφειν, οὐχ ὡς διδάσκαλος, ἀλλ' ὡς

might overtake us; and let us hate the deceit of the present time/season, in order that we may be loved in the (time) being about to come. 4.2 May we not give liberty to the life/soul of ourselves, so as to have authority/a right to run together with sinners and evil (ones), lest we might be made like them. 4.3 The complete offense/stumbling block has drawn near, about which it has been written, as Enoch says: For to this (thing) the lord/master has cut short the times/ seasons and the days, in order that the (one) being loved of him may hasten and will come to the inheritance. 4.4 And the prophet also says thus: TEN KING-DOMS WILL RULE/REIGN UPON THE EARTH, AND A LITTLE KING WILL RAISE UP FROM BEHIND/AFTER THEM, WHO WILL HUMBLE THREE OF THE KINGS UNDER ONE. 4.5 Daniel says like-wise concerning the same: AND I SAW THE FOURTH BEAST, EVIL AND STRONG, AND MORE VIOLENT BESIDE/FROM ALL THE BEASTS OF THE EARTH, AND HOW TEN HORNS AROSE OUT OF IT, AND A LITTLE OFFSHOOT HORN OUT OF THEM, AND HOW IT HUMBLED THREE OF THE GREAT HORNS UNDER ONE. 4.6 Ye are obligated/indebted to understand. But yet I also ask ye this, as being one out of/of ye, and even especially loving all *ye* above/over my soul/life, to take heed now for yourselves and to be not made like some, heaping up their sins/faults, saying that *it is* the covenant. 4.7 *It is* indeed ours/of us; but in an end they thus lost/destroyed it from the (thing) of Moses now/already having received *it*. For the writing says: AND MOSES WAS ON THE MOUNTAIN FASTING FORTY DAYS AND FORTY NIGHTS, and he received the covenant from the Lord, tablets/plaques of stone having been written by the finger of the hand of the Lord. 4.8 But having turned to the idols they lost/destroyed it. For thus says *the* Lord: Moses, Moses, GO YOU DOWN *with* THE SPEED, BECAUSE YOUR PEOPLE BROKE THE LAW, *those* WHOM YOU LED FORTH OUT OF A LAND OF EGYPT, and Moses under-stood and he threw the two tablets/plaques out of his hands; and the covenant of them was broken, in order that the covenant of the (one) having been loved, Jesus, might be sealed/secured in the heart of us/our heart in/by a hope of the faith from him. 4.9 And wanting/wishing to write many (things)/much, not as a

πρέπι ἀγαπῶντι ἀφ᾽ ὧν ἔχομεν μὴ ἐλλίπειν, γράφειν ἐσπούδασα, διὸ περίψημα ὑμῶν. προσέχωμεν ἐν ταῖς ἐσχάταις ἡμέραις· οὐδὲν γὰρ ὠφελήσει ἡμᾶς ὁ πᾶς χρόνος τῆς πίστεως ἡμῶν, ἐὰν μὴ νῦν ἐν τῷ ἀνόμῳ καιρῷ καὶ τοῖς μέλλουσιν σκανδάλοις, ὡς πρέπει υἱοῖς θεοῦ, ἀντιστῶμεν, ἵνα μὴ ἐχῇ παρίσδυσιν ὁ μέλας. 4.10 φύγωμεν ἀπὸ πάσης ματαιότητος, μισήσωμεν τελίως τὰ ἔργα τῆς πονηρίας ὁδοῦ. μὴ καθ᾽ ἑαυτούς ἐνδύνοντες μονάζεται ὡς ἤδη δεδικαιωμένοι, ἀλλ᾽ ἐπὶ τὸ αὐτὸ συνερχόμενοι συνζητεῖτε περὶ τοῦ κοινῇ συμφέροντος. 4.11 λέγει γὰρ ἡ γραφή· οὐαὶ οἱ συνετοὶ ἑαυτοῖς καὶ ἐνώπιον ἑαυτῶν ἐπιστήμονες. γενώμεθα πνευματικοί, γενώμεθα ναὸς τέλειος τῷ θεῷ. ἐφ᾽ ὅσον ἐστὶν ἐν ἡμῖν, μελετῶμεν τὸν φόβον τοῦ θεοῦ καὶ φυλάσσιν ἀγωνιζώμεθα τὰς ἐντολὰς αὐτοῦ, ἵνα ἐν τοῖς δικαιώμασιν αὐτοῦ εὐφρανθῶμεν. 4.12 ὁ κύριος ἀπροσωπολήμπτως κρινεῖ τὸν κόσμον. ἕκαστος καθὼς ἐποίησεν κομιεῖται. ἐὰν ᾖ ἀγαθός, ἡ δικαιοσύνη αὐτοῦ προηγήσεται αὐτοῦ· ἐὰν ᾖ πονηρός, ὁ μισθὸς τῆς πονηρίας ἔμπροσθεν αὐτοῦ· 4.13 ἵνα μήποτε ἐπαναπαυόμενοι ὡς κλητοὶ ἐπικαθυπνώσωμεν ταῖς ἁμαρτίαις ἡμῶν, καὶ ὁ πονηρὸς ἄρχων λαβὼν τὴν καθ᾽ ἡμῶν ἐξουσίαν ἀπώσηται ἡμᾶς ἀπὸ τῆς βασιλίας τοῦ κυρίου. 4.14 ἔτι δὲ κἀκῖνο, ἀδελφοί μου, νοεῖται· ὅταν βλέπεται μετὰ τηλικαῦτα σημῖα καὶ τέρατα γεγονότα ἐν τῷ Ἰσραήλ, καὶ οὕτως ἐγκαταλελῖφθαι αὐτούς· προσέχωμεν, μήποτε, ὡς γέγραπται, πολλοὶ κλητοί, ὀλίγοι δὲ ἐκλεκτοὶ εὑρεθῶμεν. 5.1 εἰς τοῦτο γὰρ ὑπέμινεν ὁ κύριος παραδοῦναι τὴν σάρκα εἰς καταφθοράν, ἵνα τῇ ἀφέσει τῶν ἁμαρτιῶν ἁγνισθῶμεν, ὅ ἐστιν ἐν τῷ αἵματι τοῦ ῥαντίσματος αὐτοῦ.

teacher, but I was diligent to write as is proper *for* (one) loving not to leave off from *that* which we have, wherefore an offscouring of ye *it is.* Let us take heed in the last days; for all the time of our faith will benefit/profit us nothing, unless we might resist now, in the time/season for the lawless (one), and in the offenses about to come, as is proper for sons of God, in order that the black (one) may not have an opportunity. 4.10 Let us/we should flee from every vanity/vain thing, let us/we should hate completely the works of the road/way of evil. Live ye not alone putting on/clothing according to yourselves, as already having been justified, but coming together, seek/discuss ye on/for the (thing) concerning the common benefit/expedient. 4.11 For the writing says: WOE BE *for* THOSE WISE/PRUDENT FOR THEMSELVES AND BEING MAS-TERS/WELL-VERSED BEFORE THEMSELVES. We should be spiritual (ones), we should become a complete/mature *inner* temple for God. For as much as it is in us, we should pay attention to/carefully consider the fear of God and we should be contending/striving earnestly to guard/keep the commands from him, in order that we might be gladdened/cheered up in/by his just acts/decrees. 4.12 The Lord will judge/judges the world impartially/without partiality. Each (one) will receive/get back even/according as he did. If it/he be good, the justice/justness of him will precede/go before him; if it/he be evil, the reward/wages of/from the evil *is* before him; 4.13 let us/we should never fall asleep in our sins/faults in order that resting as called/invited (ones), and the evil ruler, having taken/received the authority against us, might thrust us away from the kingdom of the Lord. 4.14 And yet consider ye this also, my brothers: Whenever ye see, after such signs and wonders had happened in Israel, even so *for* them to be left behind/abandoned; we should take heed lest we might be found, as it has been written: many *are* called, but few chosen. 5.1 For to this (thing) the Lord endured to deliver over the flesh into/for destruction, in order that we might be purified by the forgiveness/remission of the faults/sins, which is from the sprinkling/purifying

5.2 γέγραπται γὰρ περὶ αὐτοῦ ἃ μὲν πρὸς τὸν Ἰσραήλ, ἃ δὲ πρὸς ἡμᾶς, λέγει δὲ οὕτως· ἐτραυματίσθη διὰ τὰς ἀνομίας ἡμῶν καὶ μεμαλάκισται διὰ τὰς ἁμαρτίας ἡμῶν· τῷ μώλωπι αὐτοῦ ἡμῖς ἰάθημεν· ὡς πρόβατον ἐπὶ σφαγὴν ἤχθη, καὶ ὡς ἀμνὸς ἄφωνος ἐναντίον τοῦ κίραντος αὐτόν. 5.3 οὐκοῦν ὑπερευχαριστῖν ἀφίλομεν τῷ χυρίῳ, ὅτι καὶ τὰ παρεληλυθότα ἡμῖν ἐγνώρισεν καὶ ἐν τοῖς ἐνεστῶσιν ἡμᾶς ἐσόφισεν, καὶ εἰς τὰ μέλλοντα οὐκ ἐσμὲν ἀσύνετοι.

5.4 λέγει δὲ ἡ γραφή· οὐκ ἀδίκως ἐκτίνεται δίκτυα πτερωτοῖς. τοῦτο λέγι, ὅτι δικαίως ἀπολῖται ἄνθρωπος, ὃ ἔχων ὁδοῦ δικαιοσύνης γνῶσιν ἑαυτὸν εἰς ὁδὸν σκότους ἀποσυνέχει.

5.5 ἔτι δὲ καὶ τοῦτο, ἀδελφοί μου· εἰ ὁ κύριος ὑπέμινεν παθεῖν περὶ τῆς ψυχῆς ἡμῶν, ὢν παντὸς τοῦ κόσμου κύριος ᾧ εἶπεν ὁ θεὸς ἀπὸ καταβολῆς κόσμου· ποιήσωμεν ἄνθρωπον κατ' ἰκόνα καὶ καθ' ὁμοίωσιν ἡμετέραν· πῶς οὖν ὑπέμινεν ὑπὸ χιρὸς ἀνθρώπων παθεῖν; 5.6 μάθεται. οἱ προφῆται, ἀπ' αὐτοῦ ἔχοντες τὴν χάριν, εἰς αὐτὸν ἐπροφήτευσαν· αὐτὸς δέ, εἵνα καταργήσει τὸν θάνατον καὶ τὴν ἐκ νεκρῶν ἀνάστασιν δείξει, ὅτι ἐν σαρκὶ ἔδει αὐτὸν φανερωθῆναι, ὑπέμεινεν, 5.7 ἵνα καὶ τοῖς πατράσιν τὴν ἐπαγγελίαν ἀποδῷ, καὶ αὐτὸς ἑαυτῷ τὸν λαὸν τὸν κενὸν ἑτοιμάζων ἐπιδείξει ἐπὶ τῆς γῆς ὤν, ὅτι τὴν ἀνάσται αὐτὸς ποιήσας κρινῖ. 5.8 πέρας γέ τοι διδάσκων τὸν Ἰσραὴλ καὶ τηλικαῦτα τέρατα καὶ σημῖα ποιῶν ἐκήρυσσεν, καὶ ὑπερηγάπησα αὐτόν. 5.9 ὅτε δὲ τοὺς ἰδίους ἀποστόλους τοὺς μέλλοντας κηρύσσιν τὸ εὐαγγέλιον αὐτοῦ ἐξελέξατο, ὄντας ὑπὲρ πᾶσαν ἁμαρτίαν ἀνομωτέρους, ἵνα δείξῃ, ὅτι οὐκ ἦλθεν καλέσαι δικαίους, ἀλλὰ ἁμαρτωλούς, τότε ἐφανέρωσεν ἑαυτὸν εἶναι υἱὸν θεοῦ. 5.10 εἰ γὰρ μὴ ἦλθεν ἐν σαρκί, οὐδ' ἂν πως οἱ ἄνθρωποι

by/in the blood of him.

5.2 For it has been written about him, some (things) to Israel, and some/other (things) to us, and thus it says: HE WAS WOUNDED BECAUSE OF OUR LAWLESS- NESS/INIQUITIES AND BRUISED BECAUSE OF OUR FAULTS/ SINS; WE, WE ARE HEALED BY HIS BLOWS/STRIPES; HE WAS LED AS A SHEEP TO A SLAUGHTER, AND DUMB/SILENT AS A LAMB BEFORE ITS SHEARER. 5.3 Therefore we are indebt- ed/obligated to give great thanks to the Lord, because he both gave knowledge to us from the past things and he gave wisdom *for* us in the present things, and in the (things) being about to come we are not without insight.

5.4 And the writing says: NOT UNJUSTLY HE STRET- CHES OUT NETS FOR BIRDS. This says that a man perished justly, who having a road/way of justice he holds himself to a road/way of darkness.

5.5 But still/yet even this, my brothers: If the Lord endured to suffer concerning the soul/life of us, being Lord of all the world, to whom God said from foundation of a world: WE SHOULD/LET US MAKE A MAN ACCORDING TO OUR IMAGE AND LIKENESS; how then endured he to suffer by a hand of men? 5.6 Learn ye: The prophets, having the grace/favor from him, they pro- phesied in/for him; and he, in order that he might destroy the death and show/demonstrate the resurrec- tion out of dead (ones), because it was being necessa- ry *for* him to be made plain/manifested in flesh, he endured, 5.7 in order that he might even give back/ restore the promise to/for the ancestors, and himself preparing the new people for himself, he might show *while* being on the earth that he, having made the resurrection, will judge *it*. 5.8 And besides teaching Israel and doing/making such wonders and signs, he preached/heralded and he loved it exceedingly. 5.9 But when he chose out his own apostles, the (ones) being about to herald/preach his good message/gospel, being more wicked/lawless beyond/above every fault/ sin, in order that he might show that he came not to call just (ones), but sinners, then he made clear/man- ifested himself to be a son of God. 5.10 For if he came not in flesh, in no way could the men/humans

563

ἐσώθησαν βλέποντες αὐτόν, ὅτε τὸν μέλλοτα μὴ εἶναι ἥλιον, ἔργον τῶν χιρῶν αὐτοῦ ὑπάρχοντα, ἐμβλέποντες οὐκ ἰσχύουσιν εἰς τὰς ἀκτῖνας αὐτοῦ ἀντοφθαλμῆσαι; 5.11 οὐκοῦν ὁ υἱὸς τοῦ θεοῦ ἐν σαρκὶ ἦλθεν, ἵνα τὸ τέλειον τῶν ἁμαρτιῶν ἀνακεφαλαιώσῃ τοῖς διώξασιν ἐν θανάτῳ τοὺς προφήτας αὐτοῦ. 5.12 οὐκοῦν εἰς τοῦτο ὑπέμινεν. λέγει γὰρ ὁ θεὸς τὴν πληγὴν τῆς σαρκὸς αὐτοῦ ὅτι ἐξ αὐτῶν· ὅταν πατάξωσιν τὸν ποιμένα ἑαυτῶν, τότε ἀπολεῖται τὰ πρόβατα τῆς ποίμνης. 5.13 αὐτὸς δὲ ἠθέλησεν οὕτω παθεῖν· ἔδει γάρ, ἵνα ἐπὶ ξύλου πάθῃ. λέγει γὰρ ὁ προφητεύων ἐπ' αὐτῷ. φεῖσέ μου τῆς ψυχῆς ἀπὸ ῥομφαίας, καί· καθήλωσόν μου τὰς σάρκας, ὅτι συναγωγὴ πονηρευομένων ἐπανέστησάν μοι. 5.14 καὶ πάλιν λέγει· ἰδού, τέθεικά μου τὸν νῶτον εἰς μάστιγας, τὰς δὲ σειαγόνας μου εἰς ῥαπίσματα. τὸ δὲ πρόσωπόν μου ἔθηκα ὡς στερεὰν πέτραν. 6.1 ὅτε οὖν ἐποίησεν τὴν ἐντολήν, τί λέγει; τίς ὁ κρινόμενός μοι; ἀντιστήτω μοι· ἢ τίς ὁ δικαιούμενός μοι; ἐνγισάτω τῷ παιδὶ κυρίου. 6.2 οὐαὶ ὑμῖν, ὅτι ὑμῖς πάντες ὡς ἱμάτιον παλαιωθήσεσθαι, καὶ σὴς καταφάγεται ὑμᾶς.

καὶ πάλιν λέγει ὁ προφήτης, ἐπὶ ὡς λίθος ἰσχυρὸς ἐτέθη εἰς συντριβήν· ἰδού, ἐμβαλῶ εἰς τὰ θεμέλια Σιὼν λίθον πολυτελήν, ἐκλεκτόν, ἀκρογωνιέον, ἔντιμον. 6.3 εἶτα τί λέγει; καὶ ὁ πιστεύων εἰς αὐτὸν ζήσεται εἰς τὸν αἰῶνα. ἐπὶ λίθον οὖν ἡμῶν ἡ ἐλπίς; μὴ γένοιτο· ἀλλὰ εἰπεὶ ἐν ἰσχύϊ τέθεικεν τὴν σάρκαν αὐτοῦ κύριος. λέγει γάρ· καὶ ἔθηκέν με ὡς στερεὰν πέτραν. 6.4 λέγει δὲ πάλιν ὁ προφήτης· λίθον ὃν ἀπεδοκίμασαν οἱ οἰκοδομοῦντες, οὗτος ἐγενήθη εἰς κεφαλὴν γωνίας. καὶ πάλιν λέγει· αὕτη ἐστὶν ἡ ἡμέρα ἡ μεγάλη καὶ θαυμαστή, ἣν ἐποίησεν ὁ κύριος. 6.5 ἁπλούστερον ὑμῖν γράφω, ἵνα συνίετε· ἐγὼ περίψημα τῆς ἀγάπης ὑμῶν. 6.6 τί οὖν λέγει πάλιν ὁ προφήτης; περιέσχεν με συναγωγὴ

seeing him be saved, when the (one) not being about to be a sun, an existing work from his hands, considering they are not able to look directly into its rays. 5.11 Therefore the son of God came in flesh, in order that he might head up the completion of the sins/faults for the (ones) having prosecuted/pursued his prophets in/by death. 5.12 Accordingly, he endured in this (thing). For God says that out of/from them *is* the blow/plague of his flesh: Whenever they might SMITE THE SHEPHERD OF THEMSELVES, THEN THE SHEEP OF THE FLOCK WILL PERISH/BE DESTROYED. 5.13 And he, he wanted/wished to so suffer; for it was being necessary that he should suffer upon a tree. For the (one) prophesying says to him: Spare my soul/life from a sword, and: Nail my fleshes, because a congregation of evil (ones/men) rose up against me. 5.14 And again he says: BEHOLD, I HAVE PUT/PLACED MY BACK TO/FOR SCOURGES/WHIPS, AND MY CHEEKS TO/FOR SLAPS/BLOWS, AND/BUT I HAVE PUT/PLACED MY FACE/COUNTENANCE AS A FIRM/STEADFAST ROCK. 6.1 Therefore, when he made the command, what says he/it? WHO *is* THE (ONE) JUDGING ME? LET HIM OPPOSE ME; OR, WHO *is* THE (ONE) JUSTIFYING ME? LET HIM DRAW NEAR TO the child/boy of *the* Lord. 6.2 Woe to ye, because YE ALL WILL BECOME/BE MADE OLD AS A GARMENT, AND A MOTH WILL DEVOUR YE.

And again the prophet says: HE WAS PLACED THERE AS A STRONG STONE IN/FOR CRUSHING; BEHOLD, I SHALL PLACE A PRECIOUS STONE IN THE FOUNDATIONS OF ZION, A CHOICE (ONE)/CHOSEN OUT, A CHIEF CORNERSTONE, RENOWNED/HONORED. 6.3 What says he next? And the (one) believing in him will live into the age. Then is the hope of us upon a stone? May it not become so! But he says/means the Lord put/placed his flesh in strength/power. For he says: AND HE HAS PLACED ME AS A FIRM/STABLE ROCK. 6.4 And again the prophet says: A STONE WHICH THOSE BUILDING REJECTED, THIS (ONE) WAS GENERATED INTO A HEAD KEYSTONE/CORNERSTONE. And again he says: THIS IS THE GREAT AND WONDERFUL DAY WHICH THE LORD MADE. 6.5 I write more simply to ye, in order that ye may understand; I, I am most humble from the agape of ye. 6.6 What then says the prophet again? AN EVIL- DOING CONGREGATION ENCOMPASSED ME, THEY SUR-

πονηρευομένων, ἐκύκλωσάν με ὡσὶ μέλισσαι κηρίον, καί· ἐπὶ τὸν ἱματισμόν μου ἔβαλον κλῆρον. 6.7 ἐν σαρκὶ οὖν αὐτοῦ μέλλοντος φανεροῦσθαι καὶ πάσχειν, προεφανερώθη τὸ πάθος. λέγει γὰρ ὁ προφήτης ἐπὶ τὸν Ἰσραήλ· οὐαὶ τῇ ψυχῇ αὐτῶν, ὅτι βεβούλευνται βουλὴν πονηρὰν καθ᾽ ἑαυτῶν, εἰπόντες· δήσωμεν τὸν δίκαιον, ὅτι δύσχρηστος ἡμῖν ἐστίν. 6.8 τί λέγει ὁ ἄλλος προφήτης Μωσῆς αὐτοῖς; ἰδού, τάδε λέγει κύριος ὁ θεός· εἰσέλθαται εἰς τὴν γῆν τὴν ἀγαθήν, ἣν ὤμοσεν κύριος τῷ Ἀβραὰμ καὶ Ἰσὰκ καὶ Ἰακώβ, καὶ κατακληρονομήσατε αὐτήν, γῆν ῥέουσαν γάλα καὶ μέλι. 6.9 τί δὲ λέγει ἡ γνῶσις; μάθετε. ἐλπίσαται, φησίν, ἐπὶ τὸν ἐν σαρκὶ μέλλοντα φανεροῦσθαι ὑμῖν Ἰησοῦν. ἄνθρωπος γὰρ γῆ ἐστιν πάσχουσα· ἀπὸ προσώπου γὰρ τῆς γῆς ἡ πλάσις τοῦ Ἀδὰμ ἐγένετο. 6.10 τί οὖν λέγει· εἰς τὴν γῆν τὴν ἀγαθήν, γῆν ῥέουσαν γάλα καὶ μέλι; εὐλογητὸς ὁ κύριος ἡμῶν, ἀδελφοί, ὁ σοφίαν καὶ νοῦν θέμενος ἐν ἡμῖν τῶν κρυφίων αὐτοῦ· λέγει γὰρ ὁ προφήτης παραβολὴν κυρίου· τίς νοήσει, εἰ μὴ σοφὸς καὶ ἐπιστήμων καὶ ἀγαπῶν τὸν κύριον αὐτοῦ; 6.11 ἐπὶ οὖν ἀνακαινίσας ἡμᾶς ἐν τῇ ἀφέσει τῶν ἁμαρτιῶν, ἐποίησεν ἡμᾶς ἄλλον τύπον, ὡς παιδίων ἔχειν τὴν ψυχήν, ὡς ἂν δὴ ἀναπλάσσοντος αὐτοῦ ἡμᾶς. 6.12 λέγει γὰρ ἡ γραφὴ περὶ ἡμῶν, ὡς λέγει τῷ υἱῷ· ποιήσωμεν κατ᾽ εἰκόνα καὶ καθ᾽ ὁμοίωσιν ἡμῶν τὸν ἄνθρωπον, καὶ ἀρχέτωσαν τῶν θηρίων τῆς γῆς καὶ τῶν πετεινῶν τοῦ οὐρανοῦ καὶ τῶν ἰχθύων τῆς θαλάσσης.

καὶ εἶπεν κύριος, ἰδὼν τὸ καλὸν πλάσμα ἡμῶν· αὐξάνεσθε καὶ πληθύνεσθε καὶ πληρώσαται τὴν γῆν. ταῦτα πρὸς τὸν υἱόν. 6.13 πάλιν σοι ἐπιδείξω, πῶς πρὸς ἡμᾶς λέγει κύριος. δευτέραν πλάσιν ἐπ᾽ ἐσχάτων ἐποίησεν. λέγει δὲ κύριος· ἰδού, ποιῶ τὰ ἔσχατα ὡς τὰ πρῶτα. εἰς τοῦτο οὖν ἐκήρυξεν ὁ προφήτης· εἰσέλθαται εἰς γῆν ῥέουσαν γάλα καὶ μέλι καὶ κατακυριεύσατε

ROUNDED ME AS BEES *do* A HONEYCOMB, and: THEY THREW A LOT FOR MY GARMENT. 6.7 Therefore, from him being about to make an appearance and to suffer, the passion was made plain beforehand. For the prophet says to/against Israel: WOE TO THE SOUL/LIFE OF THEM, FOR THEY HAVE PLOTTED AN EVIL PLOT AGAINST/ACCORDING TO THEMSELVES, SAYING: WE SHOULD/LET US BIND THE JUST (ONE), BECAUSE HE IS AN ANNOYANCE/DISADVANTAGE TO US. 6.8 What says the other prophet, Moses, to them? BEHOLD, THE LORD GOD SAYS THESE (THINGS): ENTER YE INTO THE GOOD LAND, WHICH *the* LORD SWORE TO ABRAHAM AND ISAAC AND JACOB, AND INHERIT YE IT, A LAND FLOWING *with* MILK AND HONEY. 6.9 But what says the knowledge? Learn ye. Hope ye, he says, upon the (one) being about to make an appearance to ye in flesh, Jesus. For a man/human is a land suffering; for the molding/creation of Adam came to be from a face of the land/earth. 6.10 What then says/means: Into the good land, a land flowing *with* milk and honey? Praised/blessed *be* our Lord, brothers, the (one) having put in us wisdom and an understanding of the secrets of him; for the prophet says/speaks a parable from *the* Lord: Who will comprehend, except a wise (one) both knowing/understanding and loving his Lord? 6.11 Therefore, since he renewed us in/by the forgiveness of the faults/sins, he made us another example/type, like to have the soul/life of children, as if truly having transformed us from himself. 6.12 For the writing says concerning us, as it/he says to the son: LET US MAKE THE MAN ACCORDING TO AN IMAGE AND LIKENESS/SHAPE OF US, AND LET THEM RULE/BE CHIEF OF THE BEASTS OF THE LAND AND THE BIRDS OF THE SKY/HEAVEN AND THE FISHES OF THE SEA.

And *the* Lord said, having beheld our beautiful creation: Grow/increase ye and multiply and fill up the land. These (things) to the son. 6.13 Again I shall show to you how *the* Lord speaks to us. He made a second forming/creation upon last (ones). And the Lord says: Behold, I make the last (things) as/like the first (things). To/for this then the prophet heralded/preached: ENTER YE INTO A LAND FLOWING *with* MILK AND HONEY, be ye lords of/over it. 6.14 Then behold,

αὐτῆς. 6.14 ἴδε οὖν, ἡμῖς ἀναπεπλάσμεθα, καθὼς πάλιν ἐν ἑτέρῳ προφήτῃ λέγει· ἰδού, λέγει κύριος, ἐξελῶ τούτων, τουτέστιν ὧν προέβλεπεν τὸ πνεῦμα κυρίου, τὰς λιθίνας καρδίας καὶ ἐμβαλῶ σαρκίνας· ὅτι αὐτὸς ἐν σαρκὶ ἔμελλεν φανεροῦσθαι καὶ ἐν ἡμῖν κατοικεῖν. 6.15 ναὸς γὰρ ἅγιος, ἀδελφοί μου, τῷ κυρίῳ τὸ κατοικητήριον ἡμῶν τῆς καρδίας. 6.16 λέγει γὰρ κύριος πάλιν· καὶ ἐν τίνι ὀφθήσομε τῷ κυρίῳ τῷ θεῷ μου καὶ δοξασθήσομαι; ἐξομολογήσομαί σοι ἐν ἐκκλησίᾳ ἀδελφῶν μου, καὶ ψαλῶ σοι ἀνάμενσον ἐκκλησίας ἁγίων. οὐκοῦν ἡμεῖς ἐσμέν, οὓς εἰσήγαγεν εἰς τὴν γῆν τὴν ἀγαθήν. 6.17 τί οὖν τὸ γάλα καὶ τὸ μέλι; ὅτι πρῶτον τὸ παιδίον μέλιτι, εἶτα γάλακτι ζωοποιεῖται· οὕτως οὖν καὶ ἡμῖς τῇ πίστι τῆς ἐπαγγελίας καὶ τῷ λόγῳ ζωοποιούμενοι ζήσομεν κατακυριεύοντες τῆς γῆς. 6.18 προειρήκαμεν δὲ ἐπάνω. καὶ αὐξανέσθωσαν καὶ πληθυνέσθωσαν καὶ ἀρχέτωσαν τῶν ἰχθύων. τίς οὖν ὁ δυνάμενος ἄρχιν θηρίων ἢ ἰχθύων ἢ πετινῶν τοῦ οὐρανοῦ; αἰσθάνεσθαι γὰρ ὀφίλομεν, ὅτι τὸ ἄρχειν ἐξουσίας ἐστίν, ἵνα τις ἐπιτάξας κυριεύσει. 6.19 εἰ οὖν οὐ γείνεται τοῦτο νῦν, ἄρα ἡμῖν εἴρηκεν, πότε· ὅταν καὶ αὐτοὶ τελιωθῶμεν κληρονόμοι τῆς διαθήκης κυρίου γενέσθαι. 7.1 οὐκοῦν νοεῖται, τέκνα εὐφροσύνης, ὅτι πάντα ὁ καλὸς κύριος προεφανέρωσεν ἡμῖν, ἵνα γνῶμεν, ᾧ κατὰ πάντα εὐχαριστοῦντες ὀφίλομεν αἰνῖν. 7.2 εἰ οὖν ὁ υἱὸς τοῦ θεοῦ, ὢν κύριος προεφανέρωσεν ἵνα γνῶμεν ᾧ κατὰ πάντα εὐχαριστοῦντες καὶ μέλλων κρίνιν ζῶντας καὶ νεκρούς, ἔπαθεν ἵνα ἡ πληγὴ αὐτοῦ ζωοποιήσι ἡμᾶς· πιστεύσομεν, ὅτι ὁ υἱὸς τοῦ θεοῦ οὐκ ἠδύνατο παθεῖν εἰ μὴ δι' ἡμᾶς. 7.3 ἀλλὰ καὶ σταυρωθεὶς ἐποτίζετο ὄξει καὶ χολῇ. ἀκούσατε, περὶ τούτου πεφανέρωκαν οἱ ἱερῖς τοῦ ναοῦ. γεγραμμένης ἐντολῆς· ὃς ἂν μὴ νηστεύσῃ τὴν νηστίαν, θανάτῳ

we, we have been reformed, even as he/it says again in/by a different prophet: Behold, says *the* Lord: I SHALL TAKE OUT FROM THESE, this means/that is whom the spirit of *the* Lord foresaw, THE STONE HEARTS AND I SHALL EMPLACE FLESHY (ONES); because he, he was about to become visible/manifest in flesh and to dwell among us. 6.15 For, my brothers, the habitation of/from the heart of us *is* a holy *inner* temple for the Lord. 6.16 For *the* Lord says again: AND IN/BY WHAT SHALL I BE SEEN BY THE LORD MY GOD AND SHALL BE GLORIFIED? I SHALL CONFESS TO/FOR YOU IN AN ASSEMBLY OF MY BRO-THERS, AND I SHALL SING HYMNS FOR YOU IN THE MIDST OF AN ASSEMBLY OF SAINTS. Therefore we, we are *those* whom he led into the good land. 6.17 What then *is* the milk and the honey? Because the child is first made alive with honey, afterwards with milk; thus/so therefore we also, we shall live in/by the faith of the promise and the saying/word being made alive, being lords of/over the land. 6.18 And we have foretold above: ALSO LET THEM INCREASE/GROW AND LET THEM MULTIPLY AND LET THEM RULE OVER THE FISHES. Then who is the (one) being able to rule over the beasts or the fishes or the birds of the sky/heaven? For we are obligated to perceive that the (thing) to rule *is* authority, in order that some-one will be lord over/for decrees. 6.19 Therefore, if this happens not now, then he has said to us when/at what time; even whenever we might complete/finish ourselves to become heirs of the covenant of *the* Lord. 7.1 Consider ye therefore, children of gladness, that the good Lord made all (things) clear to us before-hand, that we should know to whom we are obligated to praise, giving thanks according to all (things). 7.2 If therefore the son of God, being a lord revealed beforehand, that we may know to whom *we are* giving thanks according to all (things), and being about to judge living (ones) and dead (ones), he suffered in order that his sound/plague might make us alive; we should believe that the son of God was not able to suffer except because of us. 7.3 But also, being crucified, he was given sour wine and gall to drink. Listen/hear ye, the priests of the *inner* temple have revealed/made plain this, from a command having been

ἐξολεθρευθήσετε, ἐνετίλατο κύριος, αὐτ' ἐπὶ καὶ αὐτὸς ὑπὲρ τῶν ἡμετέρων ἁμαρτιῶν ἔμελλεν τὸ σκεῦος τοῦ πνεύματος προσφέριν θυσίαν, ἵνα καὶ ὁ τύπος ὁ γενόμενος ἐπὶ Ἰσαὰκ τοῦ προσενεχθέντος ἐπὶ τὸ θυσίαν τελεσθῆναι. 7.4 τί οὖν λέγει ἐν τῷ προφήτῃ; καὶ φαγέτωσαν ἐκ τοῦ τράγου τοῦ προσφερομένου τῇ νηστίᾳ ὑπὲρ πασῶν τῶν ἁμαρτιῶν. προσέχεται ἀκριβῶς· καὶ φαγέτωσαν οἱ ἱερεῖς μόνοι πάντες τὸ ἔντερον ἄπλυτον μετὰ ὄξους. 7.5 πρὸς τί; ἐπιδὴ ἐμὲ ὑπὲρ ἁμαρτιῶν μέλλοντα τοῦ λαοῦ μου τοῦ κενοῦ προσφέριν τὴν σάρκαν μου μέλλεται ποτίζειν χολὴν μετὰ ὄξους, φάγεται ὑμῖς μόνοι, τοῦ λαοῦ νηστεύοντος καὶ κοπτομένου ἐπὶ σάκκου καὶ σποδοῦ. ἵνα δίξῃ, ὅτι δεῖ αὐτὸν πολλὰ παθεῖν ὑπ' αὐτῶν. 7.6 ἃ ἐνετίλατο, προσέχεται· λάβετε δύο τράγους καλοὺς καὶ ὁμοίους καὶ προσενέγκαται, καὶ λαβέτω ὁ ἱερεὺς τὸν ἕνα εἰς ὁλοκαύτωμα τὸν ἕνα ὑπὲρ ἁμαρτιῶν. 7.7 τὸν δὲ ἕνα τί ποιήσωσιν; ἐπικατάρατος, φησίν, ὁ εἷς. προσέχετε, πῶς ὁ τύπος τοῦ Ἰησοῦ φανεροῦται· 7.8 καὶ ἐμπτύσαται πάντες καὶ κατακεντήσαται καὶ περίθεται τὸ ἔριον τὸ κόκκινον περὶ τὴν κεφαλὴν αὐτοῦ, καὶ οὕτως εἰς ἔρημον βληθήτω. καὶ ὅταν γένηται οὕτως, ἄγει ὁ βαστάζων τὸν τράγον εἰς τὴν ἔρημον καὶ ἀφερῖ τὸ ἔριον καὶ ἐπιτίθησιν αὐτὸ ἐπὶ φρύγανον τὸ λεγόμενον ραχήλ, οὗ καὶ τοὺς βλαστοὺς εἰώθαμεν τρώγειν ἐν τῇ χώρᾳ εὑρίσκοντες· οὕτω μόνης τῆς ραχοῦς οἱ καρποὶ γλυκεῖς εἰσιν. 7.9 τί οὖν τοῦτο ἐστιν; προσέχετε· τὸν μὲν ἕνα ἐπὶ τὸ θυσιαστήριον, τὸν δὲ ἕνα ἐπικατάρατον, καὶ ὅτι τὸν ἐστεφανωμένον ἐπικατάρατον; ἐπιδὴ ὄψονται αὐτὸν τότε τῇ ἡμέρᾳ τὸν ποδήρη ἔχοντα τὸν κόκκινον περὶ τὴν σάρκα καὶ ἐροῦσιν· οὐχ οὗτός ἐστιν, ὅν ποτε ἡμῖς ἐσταυρώσαμεν καὶ ἐξουθενήσαμεν ἐμπτύσαντες; ἀληθῶς οὗτος ἦν, ὁ τότε λέγων ἑαυτὸν υἱὸν τοῦ θεοῦ εἶναι. 7.10 πῶς γὰρ ὅμοιος ἐκείμῳ; εἰς τοῦτο ὁμοίους τοὺς τράγους, καλούς, ἴσους, ἵνα ὅταν

written: Who ever may not fast the fasting, he will be utterly destroyed to death, *the* Lord commanded this there and he himself was about to offer the vessel from the spirit, a sacrifice in behalf of our sins, in order that the type/example having become on/by Isaac, of the (one) having been offered to/for the sacrifice to be finished/completed.   7.4 What then says he by/in the prophet? And let them eat from the goat being offered for the fast in behalf of all the sins. Attend to *it* carefully, and let only the priests eat all the entrails unwashed with sour wine/vinegar.   7.5 To/for what? Since/because I am about to offer my flesh in behalf sins of my new people, ye are about to give gall with sour wine for me to drink, only ye, ye will eat, from the people fasting and mourning on sackcloth and ashes, in order that he/it may show that it is necessary *for* him to suffer much by/under them. 7.6 Attend ye to what was commanded: TAKE YE TWO GOOD AND SIMILAR GOATS AND OFFER YE THEM, AND LET THE PRIEST TAKE THE ONE TO/FOR A BURNT OFFERING, THE ONE IN BEHALF OF SINS.   7.7 But what should they do *with* the one (other)? He says: THE ONE IS BEING CURSED OVER. Take ye heed how the type/example of Jesus is made clear/manifested;   7.8 and all ye spit upon *it* and goad against *it* and bind the scarlet wool around its head, and so let it be thrown into a desert/desolate (place). And whenever it may become so, the (one) bearing the goat into the desert brings *it* and takes away the wool and puts it upon a brushwood, the (one) being called Rachel, of which also we are accustomed to eat/chew the shoots, finding *them* in the country; thus only the fruits from the Rachel are sweet.   7.9 Then what is this? Take ye heed: The one indeed *is* upon/for the altar, but also the one (other) is accursed, and that the (one) being crowned is accursed, since they will see him then on the day, having the long scarlet robe around the flesh, and they will say: Is not this *the one* whom when we, we crucified and despised, having spit on *him*? Truly he was this (one), the (one) saying then *of* himself to be a son of God. 7.10   For how *is he* similar to that (one)? In this like the goats, good/beautiful, equal/alike, in order

εἴδωσιν αὐτὸν τότε ἐρχόμενον, ἐκπλαγῶσιν ἐπὶ τῇ ὁμοιότητι τοῦ τράγου. οὐκοῦν εἶδε τὸν τράγον τὸν τύπον τοῦ μέλλοντος πάσχειν Ἰησοῦ. 7.11 τί δέ, ὅτι τὸ ἔριον μέσον τῶν ἀκανθῶν τιθέασιν; τύπος ἐστὶν τοῦ Ἰησοῦ τῇ ἐκκλησίᾳ θέμενος, ὅτι ὃς ἐὰν θέλῃ τὸ ἔριον ἆραι τὸ κόκκινον, ἐδεῖ αὐτὸν πολλὰ παθῖν διὰ τὸ εἶναι φορερὰν τὴν ἄκανθαν, καὶ θλιβέντα κυριεῦσαι αὐτοῦ. οὕτω, φησίν, οἱ θέλοντές με ἰδῖν καὶ ἅψασθαί μου τῆς βασιλείας ὀφίλουσιν θλιβέντες καὶ παθόντες λαβεῖν με. 8.1 τίνα δὲ δοκῖται τύπον εἶναι, ὅτι ἐντέταλται τῷ Ἰσραὴλ προσφέριν δάμαλιν τοὺς ἄνδρας, ἐν οἷς εἰσὶν ἁμαρτίαι τέλιαι, καὶ σφάξαντας κατακαίειν, καὶ ἔριν τότε τὰ παιδία σποδὸν καὶ βάλλιν εἰς ἄγγη καὶ περιτιθέναι τὸ ἔριον τὸ κόκκινον ἐπὶ ξύλον εἶδε πάλιν ὁ τύπος ὁ τοῦ σταυροῦ καὶ τὸ ἔριον τὸ κόκκινον καὶ τὸ ὕσσωπον, καὶ οὕτως ῥαντίζειν τὰ παιδία καθ' ἕνα τὸν λαόν, ἵνα ἁγνίζωνται ἀπὸ τῶν ἁμαρτιῶν; 8.2 νοεῖται, πῶς ἐν ἁπλότητι λέγεται ὑμῖν. ὁ μόσχος ὁ Ἰησοῦς ἐστίν, οἱ προσφέροντες ἄνδρες ἁμαρτωλοὶ οἱ προσενέγκαντες αὐτὸν ἐπὶ τὴν σφαγήν. εἶτα οὐκέτι ἄνδρες, οὐκέτι ἁμαρτωλῶν ἡ δόξα. 8.3 οἱ ῥαντίζοντες παῖδες οἱ εὐαγγελισάμενοι ὑμῖν τὴν ἄφεσιν τῶν ἁμαρτιῶν καὶ τὸν ἁγνισμὸν τῆς καρδίας, οἷς ἔδωκεν τοῦ εὐαγγελίου τὴν ἐξουσίαν οὖσιν δεκάδυο εἰς μαρτύριον τῶν φυλῶν ὅτι δεκάδυο φυλαὶ τοῦ Ἰσραήλ, εἰς τὸ κηρύσσειν. 8.4 διὰ τί δὲ τρεῖς παῖδες οἱ ῥαντίζοντες; εἰς μαρτύριον Ἀβραάμ, Ἰσάκ, Ἰακώβ, ὅτι οὗτοι μεγάλοι τῷ θεῷ. 8.5 ὅτι δὲ τὸ ἔριον ἐπὶ τὸ ξύλον; ὅτι ἡ βασιλεία Ἰησοῦ ἐπὶ ξύλου, καὶ ὅτι οἱ ἐλπίζοντες ἐπ' αὐτὸν ζήσονται εἰς τὸν αἰῶνα. 8.6 διὰ τί δὲ ἅμα τὸ ἔριον καὶ τὸ ὕσσωπον; ὅτι ἐν τῇ βασιλείᾳ αὐτοῦ ἡμέραι ἔσονται ῥυπαραὶ καὶ πονηραί, ἐν αἷς

that whenever they might see him coming then, they will be astounded at the similarity/likeness of/from the goat. Therefore, behold the goat, the type example of the (one) being about to suffer, Jesus. 7.11 But why then *do* they put the wool in the middle of the horns? It is an example of Jesus being placed in the assembly, because who ever may want/wish to take away the scarlet wool, it is necessary *for* him to suffer much through the (thing) *for* the thorn to be terrible, and from him being afflicted to become lord. Thus, he says: Those wanting to see me and to touch/contact my kingdom are obligated to receive me through oppressing and suffering. 8.1 But what suppose/think ye to be an example/type, that it has been commanded to Israel *for* the men/males, in whom are complete sins/faults, to offer a heifer, and slaughtering *it*, to burn it up, and then *for* the children to take ashes and to put *them* into vessels and to bind the scarlet/red wool on wood/a tree, behold again the type/example of the cross and the scarlet wool, and the hyssop; and thus *for* the children to sprinkle/cleanse the people one by one, in order that they may be purified from the sins? 8.2 Think ye over how he speaks to ye in simplicity. The calf is Jesus, the sinful men offering *it are* the (ones) having brought him to the slaughter. Afterwards *there are* no longer men, no longer the glory of sin-ners/sins. 8.3 The boys sprinkling/purifying *are* the (ones) having announced/preached to us the forgive-ness/remission of the sins/faults, and the cleans-ing/purification of the heart, to whom he gave the right/authority of the good message/gospel, *there* being twelve in/for a testimony/witness from the tribes, because *there are* twelve tribes of Israel, in/for the (thing) to preach. 8.4 But why *are* three boys the (ones) sprinkling/purifying? In/for a testi-mony *for* Abraham, Isaac, *and* Jacob, because they *were* great (ones) for God. 8.5 And why *was* the wool on the wood/tree? Because the kingdom of Jesus *is* on a tree/wood, and because the (ones) hoping on him will live in/into the age. 8.6 But why *are/were* the wool and the hyssop together? Because there will be foul and evil days in his kingdom, in/by which we, we shall

ἡμεῖς σωθησόμεθα· ὅτι ὁ ἀλγῶν σάρκα διὰ τοῦ ῥύπου τοῦ ὑσσύπου ἰᾶται. 8.7 καὶ διὰ τοῦτο οὕτως γενόμενα ἡμῖν μέν ἐστιν φανερά, ἐκείνοις δὲ σκοτεινά, ὅτι ἡ οὐκ ἤκουσαν φωνῆς κυρίου. 9.1 λέγει γὰρ πάλιν περὶ τῶν ὠτίων, πῶς περιέτεμεν ἡμῶν τὴν καρδίαν. λέγει κύριος ἐν τῷ προφήτῃ· εἰς ἀκοὴν ὠτίου ὑπήκουσάν μου. καὶ πάλιν λέγει· ἀκοῇ ἀκούσονται οἱ πόρρωθεν, ἃ ἐποίησα γνώσονται. καί· περιτμήθητι, λέγει κύριος, τὰς καρδίας ὑμῶν. 9.2 καὶ πάλιν λέγει· ἄκουε Ἰσραήλ, ὅτι τάδε λέγει κύριος ὁ θεός σου. τίς ἐστιν ὁ θέλων ζῆσαι εἰς τὸν αἰῶνα; ἀκοῇ ἀκουσάτω τῆς φωνῆς τοῦ παιδός μου.

9.3 καὶ πάλιν λέγει· ἄκουε οὐρανέ, καὶ ἐνωτίζου γῆ, ὅτι κύριος ἐλάλησεν ταῦτα εἰς μαρτύριον. καὶ πάλιν λέγει· ἀκούσατε λόγον κυρίου, ἄρχοντες τοῦ λαοῦ τούτου.

καὶ πάλιν λέγει· ἀκούσατε, τέκνα, φωνῆς βοῶντος ἐν τῇ ἐρήμῳ. οὐκοῦν περιέτεμεν ἡμῶν τὰς ἀκοάς, ἵνα ἀκούσωμεν λόγον καὶ μὴ μόνον πιστεύσωμεν ἡμῖς. 9.4 ἀλλὰ καὶ ἡ περιτομή, ἐφ᾽ ᾗ πεποίθασιν, κατήργηται. περιτομὴν γὰρ εἴρηκεν οὐ σαρκὸς γενηθῆναι· ἀλλὰ παρέβησαν, ὅτι ἄγγελος πονηρὸς ἔσφαξεν αὐτούς. 9.5 λέγει πρὸς αὐτούς· τάδε λέγει κύριος ὁ θεὸς ὑμῶν ὧδε εὑρίσκω ἐντολήν· μὴ σπείρηται ἐπ᾽ ἀκάνθαις, περιτμήθητι τῷ θεῷ ὑμῶν. καὶ τί λέγει; περιτμήθητι τὴν σκληροκαρδίαν ὑμῶν, καὶ τὸν τράχηλον ὑμῶν οὐ σκληρυνεῖτε. λάβε πάλιν· ἰδού, λέγει κύριος, πάντα τὰ ἔθνη ἀκροβυστίαν, ὁ δὲ λαὸς οὗτος ἀπερίτμητος καρδίας. 9.6 ἀλλ᾽ ἐρῖς· καὶ μὴν περιτέτμηται ὁ λαὸς εἰς σφραγῖδα. ἀλλὰ καὶ πᾶς Σύρος καὶ Ἄραψ καὶ πάντες οἱ ἱερεῖς τῶν εἰδώλων. ἄρα οὖν κἀκεῖνοι ἐκ τῆς διαθήκης αὐτῶν εἰσίν; ἀλλὰ καὶ οἱ Αἰγύπτιοι ἐν περετομῇ εἰσί. 9.7 μάθετε οὖν,

be saved; because the (one) suffering pain in flesh is healed through the foulness of the hyssop. 8.7 And because of this, (things) having so happened are indeed plain to us, but darkened to them, because they heard not a sound/voice from *the* Lord. 9.1 For he speaks/says again concerning/about the ears, how he circumcised the heart of us. *The* Lord says by the prophet: THEY OBEYED ME IN A REPORT/HEARING FROM AN EAR. And again he says: THOSE FROM AFAR WILL HEAR IN/BY A REPORT, THEY WILL KNOW WHAT (THINGS) I DID. And *the* Lord says: CIRCUMCISE YE YOUR HEARTS. 9.2 And again he says: Listen, Israel, because *the* Lord your God says these (things): Who is the (one) wanting/ wishing to live into the age? Let him listen to a report from the voice of my boy.

9.3 And again he says: LISTEN, SKY/HEAVEN, AND HEARKEN, EARTH/LAND, BECAUSE *the* LORD SPOKE THESE (THINGS) IN/FOR A TESTIMONY. And again he says: HEAR YE A SAYING/ORACLE/WORD FROM *the* Lord, (MEN) RULING THIS PEOPLE.

And again he says: Hear ye, children, FROM A VOICE CRYING IN THE DESERT/WILDERNESS. Therefore he circumcised the hearings/reports of us, in order that we might hear a saying/oracle/word and we, we might not believe alone, 9.4 but also the circumcision, on which they trusted, might be abolished. For he has said *of* circumcision not to happen from flesh, but they turned aside because an evil messenger/angel deceived/misled them. 9.5 He says to them: *The* LORD YOUR GOD SAYS THESE (THINGS) -- I find a command here: YE MAY NOT SOW UPON THORNY (PLACES), BE YE CIRCUMCISED FOR YOUR GOD. And what says he? BE YE CIRCUMCISED *for* YOUR HARDNESS OF HEART, AND HARDEN YE NOT YOUR NECK. Take/receive *it* again: BEHOLD, SAYS *the* LORD, ALL THE ETHNICS *are* UNCIRCUMCISED, BUT THIS PEOPLE *is* UNCIR-CUMCISED OF/FROM HEART. 9.6 But you will say: Surely the people are being circumcised in/for a seal/securi-ty. But even/also every Syrian and Arab and all the priests of the idols. Therefore then are those also from the covenant of them? But even the Egyptians are among *the* circumcision. 9.7 Learn ye then, children of agape, about all (things), because Abraham, the

τέκνα ἀγάπης, περὶ πάντων, ὅτι Ἀβραάμ, πρῶτος περιτομὴν δούς, ἐν πνεύματι πλουσίως προβλέψας εἰς τὸν Ἰησοῦν περιέτεμεν, λαβὼ τριῶν γραμμάτων δόγματα. 9.8 λέγει γάρ· καὶ περιέτεμεν Ἀβραὰμ ἐκ τοῦ οἴκου αὐτοῦ ἄνδρας δεκαοκτὼ καὶ τριακοσίους. τὶς οὖν ἡ δοθῖσα αὐτῷ γνῶσις; μάθετε, ὅτι τοὺς δεκαοκτὼ πρώτους, καὶ διάστημα ποιήσας λέγει τριακοσίους. τὸ δεκαοκτὼ ἔχεις Ἰησοῦν. ὅτι δὲ ὁ σταυρὸς ἐν τῷ τριακοστῷ ἤμελλεν ἔχιν τὴν χάριν, λέγει καὶ τριακοσίους. δηλοῖ οὖν τὸν μέν Ἰησοῦν ἐν τοῖς δυσὶν γράμμασιν, καὶ ἐν τῷ ἑνὶ τὸν σταυρόν. 9.9 οἶδεν ὅτι τὴν ἔμφυτον δωρεὰν τῆς διαθήκης αὐτοῦ θέμενος ἐν ἡμῖν. οὐδεὶς γνησιώτερον ἔμαθεν ἀπ' ἐμοῦ λόγον· ἀλλά, ὅτι ἄξιοί ἐστε ὑμεῖς.

10.1 Ὅτι δὲ Μωσῆς εἶπεν· οὐ φάγεσθε χοῖρον οὔτε ἀετὸν οὔτε ὀξύπτερον οὔτε κόρακα οὔτε ἰχθήν, ὃς οὐκ ἔχει λεπίδα ἐν ἑαυτῷ, τρία ἔλαβεν ἐν τῇ συνέσει δόγματα. 10.2 πέρας γέ τοι λέγει αὐτοῖς ἐν τῷ δευτερονομίῳ· καὶ διαθήσομαι πρὸς τὸν λαὸν τοῦτον τὰ δικαιώματά μου. ἄρα οὖν οὐκ ἔστιν ἐντολὴ θεοῦ τὸ μὴ τρώγειν, Μωϋσῆς δὲ ἐν πνεύματι ἐλάλησεν. 10.3 τὸ οὖν χοιρίον πρὸς τοῦτο εἶπεν· οὐ κολληθήσῃ, φησίν, ἀνθρώποις τοιούτοις, οἵτινές εἰσιν ὅμοιοι χοίρων· τουτέστιν ὅταν σπαταλῶσιν, ἐπιλανθάνονται τοῦ κυρίου, ὅταν δὲ ὑστεροῦνται, ἐπιγινώσκουσιν τὸν κύριον, ὡς καὶ ὁ χοῖρος ὅταν τρώγει τὸν κύριον οὐκ οἶδεν, ὅταν δὲ πινᾷ κραυγάζει, καὶ λαβὼν πάλιν σιωπᾷ. 10.4 οὔτε φάγῃ τὸν ἀετὸν οὐδὲ τὸν ὀξύπτερον οὐδὲ τὸν ἰκτῖνα οὔτε τὸν κόρακα· οὐ μή, φησίν, κολληθήσῃ οὐδὲ ὁμοιωθήσῃ ἀνθρώποις τοιούτοις, οἵτινες οὐκ οἴδασιν διὰ κόπου καὶ ἱδρῶτος ἑαυτοῖς πορίζειν τὴν τροφήν, ἀλλὰ ἁρπάζουσιν τὰ ἀλλότρια ἐν ἀνομίᾳ αὐτῶν καὶ περιτηροῦσιν ἐν ἀκεραιοσύνῃ περιπατοῦντες καὶ περιβλέπονται, τίνα ἐκδύσωσιν διὰ τὴν

first (one) having given circumcision, he circumcised looking abundantly forward in/by spirit to Jesus, having received decrees/rules/doctrines from/of three letters. 9.8 For it says: AND ABRAHAM CIRCUMCISED THREE HUNDRED AND EIGHTEEN MEN OUT OF HIS HOUSEHOLD. What then *was* the knowledge having been given to him? Learn ye that eighteen *are* the first, and having made an interval, he says three hundred. The eighteen -- you have Jesus. And because the cross was about to have the grace in/by the three hundred, he says also three hundred. Therefore he indeed shows Jesus by the two letters, and the cross by the one, 9.9 because he knew *the one* having himself placed/put the implanted gift of his covenant in/among us. No one learned a more becoming reasoning/saying/word from me; but that ye, ye are worthy (ones).

10.1 And because Moses said: YE WILL NOT EAT SWINE, NOR A VULTURE, NOR A HAWK, NOR A CROW, NOR A FISH WHICH HAS NOT SCALES ON ITSELF, he received/took three decrees in/by the insight/understanding. 10.2 Furthermore he says to them in the second law: AND I SHALL COVENANT MY JUST ORDINANCES TO/WITH THIS PEOPLE. So therefore, the (thing) to eat not is not a command from God, but Moses spoke in/by a spirit. 10.3 Therefore, he said the swine toward this: You will not associate, he says, with such men who are like swine/pigs; that is, whenever they live luxuriously/wantonly, they forget the Lord, but whenever they are deficient/lacking, they recognize the Lord, as even/also the pig, whenever he chews/eats, knows not the lord, but whenever it may hunger it cries out, and having received/taken it is quiet/silent again. 10.4 NEITHER SHOULD YOU EAT THE VULTURE NOR THE HAWK NOR THE KITE NOR THE CROW; by no means, he means/says, should you join or be like such men/humans, who know not to provide the food for themselves through labor/toil and sweat, but they plunder/seize the (things) belonging to others in/by their lawlessness, and they keep walking and looking around, *as* in innocence, *for* whom they might strip through the greediness, even as these birds alone provide not the food for themselves, but

πλεονεξίαν, ὡς καὶ τὰ ὄρνεα ταῦτα μόνα ἑαυτοῖς οὐ πορίζει τὴν τροφήν, ἀλλὰ ἀργὰ καθήμενα ἐκζητεῖ, πῶς ἀλλοτρίας σάρκας φάγῃ, ὄντα λοιμὰ τῇ πονηρίᾳ αὐτῶν. 10.5 καὶ οὐ φάγῃ, φησίν, σμύρναν οὐδὲ πωλύπαν οὐδὲ σηπίαν· οὐ μὴ φάγωσιν, οὐ μή, φυσίν, ὁμοιωθήσῃ ἀνθρώποις τοιούτοις, οἵτινες εἰσὶν ἀσεβεῖς εἰς τέλος καὶ κεκριμένοι ἤδη τῷ θανάτῳ, ὡς καὶ ταῦτα τὰ ἰχθύδια μόνα ἐπικατάρατα τὰ ἐν τῷ βυθῷ νήχεται, μὴ κολυμβῶντα ὡς καὶ τὰ λοιπά, ἀλλὰ ἐν τῇ γῇ κάτω τοῦ βυθοῦ κατοικῖ. 10.6 ἀλλὰ καὶ τὸν δασύποδα οὐ μὴ φάγῃ. πρὸς τί; οὐ μὴ γένῃ, παιδοφθόρος οὐδὲ ὁμοιωθήσῃ τοῖς τοιούτοις, ὅτι ὁ λαγωὸς κατ' ἐνιαυτὸν πλεονεκτῖ τὴν ἀφόδευσιν· ὅσα γὰρ ἔτη ζῇ, τοσαύτας ἔχει τρύπας. 10.7 ἀλλ' οὐδὲ τὴν ὕεναν φάγῃ· οὐ μή, φησίν, γένῃ μοιχὸς οὐδὲ φθορεὺς οὐδέ ὁμοιωθήσῃ τοῖς τοιούτοις. πρὸς τί; ὅτι τὸ ζῷον τοῦτο παρ' ἐνεαυτὸν ἀλλάσσει τὴν φύσιν καὶ ποτὲ μὲν ἄρρεν, ποτὲ θῆλυ γείνεται. 10.8 ἀλλὰ καὶ τὴν γαλῆν ἐμίσησεν καλῶς. οὐ μή, φησίν, γενηθῇς τοιοῦτος, οἵους ἀκούομεν ἀνομίας ποιοῦντας ἐν τῷ σώματι δι' ἀκαθαρσίαν, οὐδὲ ταῖς τὴν ἀνομίαν ποιούσαις ἐν τῷ στόματι. καὶ ἀκαθαρσία κολλήθησει τὸ γὰρ ζῷον τοῦτο τῷ στόματι κύει. 10.9 περὶ μὲν τῶν βρωμάτων λαβὼν Μωϋσῆς τρία δόγματα οὕτως ἐν πνεύματι ἐλάλησεν· οἱ δὲ κατ' ἐπιθυμίαν τῆς σαρκὸς ὡς περὶ βρώσεως προσεδέξαντο. 10.10 λαμβάνι δὲ τῶν αὐτῶν τριῶν δογμάτων γνῶσιν Δαυεὶδ καὶ λέγει· μακάριος ἀνήρ, ὃς οὐκ ἐπορεύθη ἐν βουλῇ ἀσεβῶν, καθὼς καὶ οἱ ἰχθύες πορεύονται ἐν σκότι εἰς τὰ βάθη· καὶ ἐν ὁδῷ ἁμαρτωλῶν οὐκ ἔστη, καθὼς οἱ δοκοῦντες φοβῖσθαι τὸν κύριον ἁμαρτάνουσιν ὡς οἱ χοῖροι, καὶ ἐπὶ καθέδραν λοιμῶν οὐκ ἐκάθισεν, καθὼς τὰ πετινὰ καθήμενα εἰς ἁρπαγήν, ἔχε τελίως καὶ περὶ τῆς βρώσεως. 10.11 πάλιν λέγει Μωϋσῆς· φάγεσθε πᾶν διχηλοῦν καὶ μαρυκούμενον. τί λέγει; ὅτι τὴν τροφὴν λαμβάνων

571

sitting idly it seeks out how it might eat flesh
belonging to another, being pestilent in their evil.
10.5 And, he says, you should/might not eat a lamprey
nor a polypus nor a cuttlefish; by no means might they
eat, by no means, he says/means be like such men/hu-
mans, who are impious/irreverent in/for an end and
having been already judged for the death, even as
these fishes alone are accursed, the (ones) floating
in the deep, not swimming also like the rest/others,
but living on the land/earth beneath the deep.   10.6
But also/even the rabbit/hare you should by no means
eat. For what/why? By no means should you become a
child corrupter, be not like those such, because the
hare increases year by year/by a time *that* he grows a
new anus. For he has/lives as many years as he has so
many burrow-holes.   10.7 But you should not eat the
hyena; by no means he says/means, may you become an
adulterer nor a corrupter nor be like those such. For
what/why? Because this living (thing) changes the
nature year by year, even becoming a male at one time,
a female at another time.   10.8 But also he hated well
the weasel. By no means, he says/means, you may not
become such, of what sort we heard doing lawlessness
in the body because of uncleanliness, nor to/with
those (women) doing the lawlessness/lawless (thing)
in/by the mouth. And it is associated with uncleanness, for this living creature/animal gives birth by
the mouth.   10.9 Moses, having indeed received these
decrees/ordinances about the foods, he so spoke in/by
a spirit, but they also received *them* as concerning
food according to the desire of the flesh.   10.10 But
David receives knowledge of the same three decrees,
and he says: HAPPY IS A MAN WHO WENT NOT IN A COUNSEL
OF IRREVERENT/IMPIOUS (ONES), even as the fishes go in
darkness into the deep (places/waters); AND HE STOOD
NOT IN/ON THE WAY/ROAD OF SINNERS, as those seeming to
fear the Lord, they sin as/like the pigs/swine; AND HE
SAT NOT UPON A SEAT OF PESTILENT/SCORNFUL (MEN), as
the birds sitting in/for plunder/pillage; you also
hold completely concerning the food.   10.11 Again,
Moses says: EAT YE EVERY (THING) DIVIDING HOOF AND
CHEWING CUD. What says he? That *the (one)* receiving/

οἶδεν τὸν τρέφοντα αὐτὸν καὶ ἐπ' αὐτῷ ἀναπαυόμενος εὐφρένεσθαι δοκεῖ. καλῶς εἶπεν βλέπων τὴν ἐντολήν. τὶ οὖν λέγει; κολλᾶσθαι μετὰ τῶν φοβουμένων τὸν κύριον, μετὰ τῶν μελετούντων ὃ ἔλαβον διάσταλμα ῥήματος ἐν τῇ καρδίᾳ, μετὰ τῶν λαλούντων τὰ δικαιώματα κυρίου καὶ τηρούντων, μετὰ τῶν εἰδότων, ὅτι ἡ μελέτη ἐστὶν ἔργον εὐφρονσύνης, καὶ ἀναμαρυκωμένον τὸν λόγον τοῦ κυρίου. τὶ δὲ τὸ διχηλοῦν; ὅτι καὶ ὁ δίκαιος ἐν τούτῳ τῷ κόσμῳ περιπατῖ καὶ τὸν ἅγιον αἰῶνα ἐκδέχεται. βλέπετε, πῶς ἐνομοθέτησεν Μωϋσῆς καλῶς. 10.12 ἀλλὰ πόθεν ἐκείνοις ταῦτα νοῆσαι ἢ συνιέναι; ἡμεῖς δὲ δικαίως νοήσαντες τὰς ἐντολὰς δικαίως λαλοῦμεν, ὡς ἠθέλησεν ὁ κύριος. διὰ τοῦτο περιέτεμεν τὰς ἀκοὰς ἡμῶν καὶ τὰς καρδίας, ἵνα συνιῶμεν ταῦτα. 11.1 ζητήσωμεν ταῦτα, εἰ ἐμέλησεν τῷ κυρίῳ προεφανερῶσεν περὶ τοῦ ὕδατος καὶ περὶ τοῦ σταυροῦ. περὶ μὲν τοῦ ὕδατος γέγραπται ἐπὶ τὸν Ἰσραήλ, πῶς τὸ βάπτισμα τὸ φέρον ἄφεσιν ἁμαρτιῶν οὐ μὴ προσδέξονται, ἀλλ' ἑαυτοῖς οἰκοδομήσουσιν. 11.2 λέγει γὰρ ὁ προφήτης· ἔκστηθι οὐρανέ, καὶ ἐπὶ τούτῳ πλῖον φριξάτω ἡ γῆ, ὅτι δύο καὶ πονηρὰ ἐποίησεν ὁ λαὸς αὖτος· ἐμὲ ἐγκατέλιπον, πηγὴν ζωῆς, καὶ ἑαυτοῖς ὤρυξαν βόθρον θανάτου. 11.3 μὴ πέτρα ἔρημός ἐστιν τὸ ὄρος τὸ ἅγιόν μου Σεινᾶ; ἔσεσθαι γὰρ ὡς πετινοῦ νοσσοὶ ἀνιπτάμενοι νοσσιᾶς ἀφηρημένοι. 11.4 καὶ πάλιν λέγει ὁ προφήτης· ἐγὼ πορεύσομαι ἔμπροσθέν σου καὶ ὄρη ὁμαλιῶ καὶ πύλας χαλκᾶς συντρίψω καὶ μοχλοὺς σιδηροὺς συνκλάσω, καὶ δώσω σοι θησαυροὺς σκοτούς, ἀποκρύφους, ἀοράτους, ἵνα γνῶσιν ὅτι ἐγὼ κύριος ὁ θεός. 11.5 καί· κατοικήσεις ἐν ὑψηλῷ σπηλαίῳ πέτρας ἰσχυρᾶς. καί· τὸ ὕδωρ αὐτοῦ πιστόν· βασιλέα μετὰ δόξης ὄψεσθε, καὶ ἡ ψυχὴ ὑμῶν μελετήσει φόβον κυρίου. 11.6 καὶ πάλιν ἐν ἄλλῳ προφήτῃ

taking the food knows the (one) nourishing/feeding him, and resting on him he seems to rejoice/cheer. Seeing the command, he spoke well. What then says he? To associate/join with those fearing the Lord, with those meditating in the heart the meaning of *the* word which they received, with those speaking the just things/ordinances of the Lord and keeping *them*, with those knowing that the meditation is a work of gladness/good cheer, and ruminating/thinking again and again the reason/word/saying of the Lord. But what *is* the divided hoof? That the just (one) walks both in the world and expects/awaits the holy age. See ye how well Moses enacted law.   10.12 But from where to perceive or to understand those things? But we, having justly/rightly perceived the commands, we speak justly/right, as the Lord wanted/wished. Because of this he circumcised the hearings/reports and the hearts of us, in order that we might understand these (things).   11.1 We should seek/inquire to the Lord *for* these (things), if he cared for he made clear beforehand concerning the water and concerning the cross. Indeed, about the water, it has been written to/upon Israel how by not means will they accept/ submit to the baptism bringing forgiveness of sins, but they will build up for themselves.   11.2 For the prophet says: BE ASTOUNDED, SKY/HEAVEN, AND LET THE LAND/EARTH SHUDDER MORE AT THIS, BECAUSE THIS PEOPLE DID TWO EVILS; THEY DESERTED/ABANDONED ME, A SPRING OF LIFE, AND THEY DUG A PIT OF DEATH FOR THEMSELVES. 11.3 IS NOT MY HOLY MOUNTAIN SINAI A DESERT/DESOLATE ROCK? FOR YE WILL BE LIKE A BIRD, FLUTTERING YOUNG (ONES), FROM YOUNG (ONES) BEING UNFASTENED *from nest.* 11.4 And again the prophet says: I SHALL GO BEFORE YOU AND I SHALL MAKE MOUNTAINS LEVEL AND I SHALL BREAK/ CRUSH GATES OF BRONZE, AND I SHALL SHATTER BARS OF IRON, AND· I SHALL GIVE STORES/TREASURES FOR YOU FROM DARKNESS, SECRET, INVISIBLE (ONES), IN ORDER THAT THEY MAY KNOW THAT I *am* THE LORD GOD.   11.5 Also: YOU WILL DWELL IN A LOFTY CAVE OF STRONG ROCK. And: HIS WATER *is* FAITHFUL; YE WILL SEE A KING WITH GLORY/FAME, AND THE SOUL/LIFE OF YE WILL TAKE CARE *for* FEAR of *the* Lord.   11.6 And again he says in/by another prophet:

572

λέγει· καὶ ἔσται ὁ ταῦτα ποιῶν ὡς τὸ ξύλον τὸ πεφυτευμένον παρὰ τὰς διεξόδους τῶν ὑδάτων, ὃ τὸν καρπὸν αὐτοῦ δώσει ἐν καιρῷ αὐτοῦ, καὶ τὸ φύλλον αὐτοῦ οὐκ ἀπορυήσεται, καὶ πάντα, ὅσα ἂν ποιῇ, κατευοδωθήσεται. 11.7 οὐχ οὕτως οἱ ἀσεβεῖς, οὐχ οὕτως, ἀλλ’ ἢ ὡς ὁ χνοῦς, ὃν ἐκρίπτει ὁ ἄνεμος ἀπὸ προσώπου τῆς γῆς. διὰ τοῦτο οὐκ ἀναστήσονται οἱ ἀσεβεῖς ἐν κρίσει οὐδὲ ἁμαρτωλοὶ ἐν βουλῇ δικαίων, ὅτι γινώσκι κύριος ὁδὸν δικαίων, καὶ ὁδὸς ἀσεβῶν ἀπολῖται. 11.8 αἰσθάνεσθαι, πῶς τὸ ὕδωρ καὶ τὸν σταυρὸν ἐπὶ τὸ αὐτὸ ὥρισεν. τοῦτο γὰρ λέγι· μακάριοι, οἱ ἐπὶ τὸν σταυρὸν ἐλπίσαντες κατέβησαν εἰς τὸ ὕδωρ, ὅτι τὸν μὲν μισθὸν λέγει ἐν καιρῷ αὐτοῦ· τότε, φησίν, ἀποδώσω. νῦν δὲ ὃ λέγει· τὰ φύλλα οὐκ ἀπορυήσεται, τοῦτο λέγει· ὅτι πᾶν ῥῆμα, ὃ ἐὰν ἐξελεύσεται ἐξ ὑμῶν διὰ τοῦ στόματος ὑμῶν ἐν πίστι καὶ ἀγάπῃ, ἔσται καὶ ἐπιστροφὴν καὶ ἐλπίδα πολλοῖς. 11.9 καὶ πάλιν ἕταιρος προφήτης λέγει. καὶ ἦν ἡ γῆ τοῦ Ἰακὼβ ἐπαινουμένη παρὰ πᾶσαν τὴν γῆν. τοῦτο λέγει· τὸ σκεῦος τοῦ πνεύματος αὐτοῦ δοξάζει. 11.10 εἶτα τί λέγει; καὶ ἦν ποταμὸς ἕλκων ἐκ δεξιῶν, καὶ ἀνέβαινεν ἐξ αὐτοῦ δένδρα ὡραῖα· καὶ ὃς ἂν φάγῃ ἐξ αὐτῶν, ζήσεται εἰς τὸν αἰῶνα. 11.11 ὅτι ἡμεῖς μὲν καταβαίνομεν εἰς τὸ ὕδωρ γέμοντες ἁμαρτιῶν καὶ ῥύπου, καὶ ἀναβαίνομεν καρποφοροῦντες ἐν τῇ καρδίᾳ καὶ τὸν φόβον καὶ τὴν ἐλπίδαν εἰς τὸν Ἰησοῦν ἐν τῷ πνεύματι ἔχοντες. καὶ ὃς ἂν φάγῃ ἀπὸ τούτων, ζήσεται εἰς τὸν αἰῶνα, τοῦτο λέγει· ὃς ἄν, φησίν, ἀκούσῃ τούτων λαλουμένων καὶ πιστεύσει, ζήσεται εἰς τὸν αἰῶνα. 12.1 ὁμοίως πάλιν περὶ τοῦ σταυροῦ ὁρίζει ἐν ἄλλῳ προφήτῃ λέγων ὅτι· καὶ πότε ταῦτα συντελεσθήσεται; λέγει κύριος· ὅταν ξύλον κλιθῇ καὶ ἀναστῇ, καὶ ὅταν ἐκ ξύλου αἷμα στάξῃ.

AND THE (ONE) DOING THESE (THINGS) WILL BE LIKE THE TREE BEING PLANTED BESIDE THE PASSAGES/COURSES OF THE WATERS, WHICH WILL GIVE ITS FRUIT IN/AT ITS SEASON/TIME, AND THE LEAF OF IT WILL NOT FADE, AND ALL (THINGS) WHATEVER HE WOULD DO WILL PROSPER/BE PROSPERED. 11.7 *For* THE IRREVERENT/IMPIOUS (ONES) *it is* NOT SO, NOT THUS, BUT (THEY) BE AS THE DUST/CHAFF WHICH THE WIND DRIVES AWAY FROM *the* FACE OF THE LAND/EARTH. BECAUSE OF THIS THE IMPIOUS/IRREVERENT (ONES) WILL NOT THEMSELVES RISE UP IN JUDGMENT, NOR SINNERS IN A COUNCIL OF JUST (ONES), BECAUSE *the* LORD KNOWS THE WAY/ROAD OF JUST (ONES), AND THE WAY OF IMPIOUS/IRREVERENT (ONES) WILL PERISH. 11.8 Perceive ye how he defined/appointed the water and the cross to/for the same (thing). For he says this: Happy (ones), who having hoped on the cross, they went down into the water, because he indeed speaks *for* the reward/wages in its season/at its time; then at one time he says: I shall repay. But now, what he says: THE LEAVES WILL NOT FADE, he says/means this: that every word, which if it may come forth out of ye through the mouth of ye in/by faith and agape, will be both a turning and a hope to/for many. 11.9 And again, another/different prophet says: And the land of Jacob was being praised/commended from all the land/earth. He says/means this: He glorifies the implement/utensil of his spirit. 11.10 What says he next? AND A RIVER WAS FLOWING OUT OF RIGHT (ONES), AND BEAUTIFUL TREES WERE GROWING OUT OF IT; AND WHO EVER MIGHT EAT FROM THEM, HE WILL LIVE in/into the age. 11.11 -- because we, we indeed go down in the water being full of sins and foulness, and we come up producing fruit in the heart, having/holding both the fear and the hope in Jesus by the spirit. And who ever might eat from these, he will live into the age, this he says: Who ever, he says/means, might hear of these (things) being spoken and will believe, he will live into the age. 12.1 Likewise, he again defines/determines about the cross in/by another prophet, saying: AND WHEN WILL THESE (THINGS) BE ACCOMPLISHED/FINISHED TOGETHER? THE LORD SAYS: WHENEVER A TREE MIGHT BE FELLED AND ARISE, AND WHENEVER BLOOD MIGHT DRIP/TRICKLE OUT OF A TREE. Again

ἔχεις πάλιν περὶ τοῦ σταυροῦ καὶ τοῦ σταυροῦσθαι μέλλοντος. 12.2 λέγει δὲ πάλιν τῷ Μωϋσῇ, πολεμουμένου τοῦ Ἰσραὴλ ὑπὸ τῶν ἀλλοφύλων, καὶ ἵνα ὑπομνήσει αὐτοὺς πολεμουμένους, ὅτι διὰ τὰς ἁμαρτίας αὐτῶν παρεδόθησαν εἰς θάνατον· λέγει εἰς τὴν καρδίαν Μωσέως τὸ πνεῦμα, ἵνα ποιήσῃ τύπον τοῦ σταυροῦ τοῦ μέλλοντος πάσχειν, ὅτι, ἐὰν μή, φησίν, ἐλπίσωσιν ἐπ' αὐτῷ, εἰς τὸν αἰῶνα πολεμηθήσονται. τίθησιν οὖν Μωϋσῆς ἓν ἐφ' ἓν ὅπλον ἐν μέσῳ τῆς πυγμῆς, καὶ ὑψηλότερος σταθὶς πάντων ἐξέτινεν τὰς χῖρας, καὶ οὕτως πάλιν ἐνίκα ὁ Ἰσραήλ. εἶτα, ὁπόταν καθῖλεν, ἐθανατοῦντο. 12.3 πρὸς τί; ἵνα γνῶσιν ὅτι οὐ δύνανται σωθῆναι, ἐὰν μὴ ἐπ' αὐτῷ ἐλπίσωσιν.

12.4 καὶ πάλιν ἐν ἑτέρῳ προφήτῃ λέγει· ὅλην τὴν ἡμέραν ἐξεπέτασα τὰς χεῖράς μου πρὸς λαὸν ἀπιθῆ καὶ ἀντιλέγοντα ὁδῷ δικαίᾳ μου.

12.5 πάλιν Μωσῆς ποιεῖ τύπον τοῦ Ἰησοῦ, ὅτι δῖ αὐτὸν παθεῖν, καὶ αὐτὸς ζωοποιήσει, ὃν δόξουσιν ἀπολωλεκέναι, ἐν σημίῳ πίπτοντος τοῦ Ἰσραήλ, ἐποίησεν γὰρ κύριος πάντα ὄφιν δάκνιν αὐτούς, καὶ ἀπέθνησκον ἐπιδὴ ἡ παράβασις διὰ τοῦ ὄφεως ἐν Εὔᾳ ἐγένετο, ἵνα ἐλέγξῃ αὐτούς, ὅτι διὰ τὴν παράβασιν αὐτῶν εἰς θλῖψιν θανάτου παραδοθήσονται. 12.6 πέρας γέ τοι αὐτὸς Μωϋσῆς ἐντιλάμενος· οὐκ ἔστιν ὑμῖν οὔτε χωνευτὸν οὔτε γλυπτὸν εἰς θεὸν ὑμῖν, αὐτὸς ποιεῖ, ἵνα τύπον τοῦ Ἰησοῦ δείξει. ποιεῖ οὖν Μωϋσῆς χαλκοῦν ὄφιν καὶ τίθησιν ἐνδόξως καὶ κηρύγματι καλῖ τὸν λαόν. 12.7 ἐλθόντες οὖν ἐπὶ τὸ αὐτὸ ἐδέοντο Μωσέως, ἵνα περὶ αὐτῶν ἀνενέγκῃ δέησιν περὶ τῆς ἰάσεως αὐτῶν.

εἶπεν δὲ Μωσῆς πρὸς αὐτούς· ὅταν, φησίν, δηχθῇ τις ὑμῶν, ἐλθέτω ἐπὶ τὸν ὄφιν τὸν ἐπὶ τοῦ ξύλου ἐπικείμενον καὶ ἐλπισάτω

you have *it/here* about the cross and the (one) being about to be crucified. 12.2 And he says again to Moses, from Israel being warred upon by those of another tribe, and that he reminds them being warred upon that they were delivered over to death because of their sins/faults; the spirit says/speaks to the heart of Moses that he should make a type/example of the cross of the (one) being about to suffer, because, he says/means, unless they might hope on him, they will be warred against into the age. Therefore, Moses placed a weapon one over one/one on another in the midst of the fight, and having stood higher than all, he stretched out the hands, and thus Israel again was conquering. Then, whenever he let them down, they were being killed. 12.3 For what/why? In order that they might know that they are not able to be saved/delivered, except they might hope on him.

12.4 And again in/by another/different prophet, he says: I STRETCHED FORTH MY HANDS THE WHOLE DAY TO A DISOBEDIENT PEOPLE, EVEN *a people* SPEAKING AGAINST MY JUST WAY.

12.5 Again Moses makes a type/example of Jesus, that it is necessary *for* him to suffer, and he, he will give life, whom they will suppose to have destroyed, in/by a sign of Israel falling, for *the* Lord made every serpent to bite them, and they were dying since the transgression happened/came about in/by Eve through the serpent, in order that he might punish/convict them, because they will be delivered/handed over into an affliction/oppression of death because of their transgression. 12.6 And furthermore, Moses himself, having commanded: IT IS NOT FOR YE, NEITHER MOLTEN METAL NOR CARVED (THING) INTO A GOD FOR YE; he, he makes (one), in order that he will show/demonstrate a type/example of Jesus. Therefore, Moses makes a bronze/brass serpent and puts/places *it* in *a place of* honor and calls the people by a herald/proclamation. 12.7 Then having come to/upon the same, they were beseeching Moses, that he might offer a supplication about them concerning the healing of them.

But Moses said to them: Whenever, he says, anyone of ye might be bitten, let him come to the serpent,

πιστεύσας, ὅτι αὐτὸς ὢν νεκρὸς δύναται ζωοποιῆσαι, καὶ παραχρῆμα σωθήσεται. καὶ οὕτως ἐποίουν. ἔχεις πάλιν καὶ ἐν τούτοις τὴν δόξαν τοῦ Ἰησοῦ, ὅτι ἐν αὐτῷ πάντα καὶ εἰς αὐτόν. 12.8 τί λέγει πάλιν Μωϋσῆς Ἰησοῦ, υἱῷ Ναυή, ἐπιθεὶς αὐτῷ τοῦτο τὸ ὄνομα, ὄντι προφήτῃ, ἵνα μόνον ἀκούσῃ πᾶς ὁ λαός; ὅτι ὁ πατὴρ πάντα φανεροῖ περὶ τοῦ υἱοῦ Ἰησοῦ. 12.9 λέγει οὖν Μωϋσῆς Ἰησοῦ, υἱῷ Ναυή, ἐπιθεὶς τοῦτο ὄνομα, ὁπότε ἔπεμπεν αὐτὸν κατάσκοπον τῆς γῆς· λάβε βιβλίον εἰς τὰς χῖρὰς σου καὶ γράψον, ἃ λέγει κύριος, ὅτι ἐκκόψεις ἐκ ῥιζῶν τὸν οἶκον πάντα τοῦ Ἀμαλὴκ ὁ υἱὸς τοῦ θεοῦ ἐπ' ἐσχάτων τῶν ἡμερῶν. 12.10 εἶδε πάλιν Ἰησοῦς, οὐχὶ υἱὸς ἀνθρώπου, ἀλλὰ υἱὸς τοῦ θεοῦ, τύπῳ δὲ ἐν σαρκὶ φανερωθείς. ἐπὶ οὖν μέλλουσιν λέγειν, ὅτι χριστὸς υἱὸς Δαυείδ ἐστιν, αὐτὸς ὁ προφητεύει Δαυείδ, φοβούμενος καὶ συνίων τὴν πλάνην τῶν ἁμαρτωλῶν· εἶπεν κύριος τῷ κυρίῳ μου· κάθου ἐκ δεξιῶν μου, ἕως ἂν θῶ τοὺς ἐχθρούς σου ὑποπόδιον τῶν ποδῶν σου.

12.11 καὶ πάλιν λέγει οὕτως Ἡσαΐας· εἶπεν κύριος τῷ χριστῷ μου κυρίῳ, οὗ ἐκράτησεν τῆς δεξιᾶς αὐτοῦ, ἐπακοῦσε ἔμπροσθεν αὐτοῦ ἔθνη, καὶ ἰσχὺν βασιλέων διαρρήξω. εἶδε, πῶς Δαυεὶδ λέγει αὐτὸν κύριον, καὶ υἱὸν θεοῦ. 13.1 ἴδωμεν δὲ εἰ οὗτος ὁ λαὸς κληρονομεῖ εἰ ὁ πρῶτος, καὶ ἡ διαθήκη εἰς ἡμᾶς ἢ εἰς ἐκίνους. 13.2 ἀκούσατε οὖν περὶ τοῦ λαοῦ τί λέγει ἡ γραφή· ἐδεῖτο δὲ Ἰσαὰκ περὶ Ῥεβέκκας τῆς γυναικὸς αὐτοῦ, ὅτι στῖρα ἦν· καὶ συνέλαβεν. εἶτα ἐξῆλθεν Ῥεβέκκα πυθέσθαι παρὰ κυρίου, καὶ εἶπεν κύριος πρὸς αὐτήν· δύο ἔθνη ἐν τῇ γαστρί σου καὶ δύο λαοὶ ἐν τῇ κοιλίᾳ σου, καὶ ὑπερέξει λαὸς λαοῦ καὶ ὁ μείζων δουλεύσει τῷ ἐλάσσονι. 13.3 αἰσθάνεσθαι ὀφίλεται, τίς ὁ Ἰσαὰκ καὶ τίς ἡ Ῥεβέκκα, καὶ ἐπὶ τίνων δέδιχεν, ὅτι μείζων ὁ

the (one) being placed upon the wood/tree, and let him hope, having believed that he, being dead, he is able to make alive/impart life, and immediately he will be saved. And so/thus they did. And in these (things) you have again the fame/glory of Jesus, because all (things) *are* by/in him and in/for him. 12.8 Again, why says Moses to Jesus, a son of Naue, giving to him this name, for being a prophet, that all the people might hear *him* only? Because the father was making plain all (things) concerning Jesus the son. 12.9 Therefore, Moses says to Jesus, a son of Naue, having given this name, when he sent him scouting/viewing closely the land: YOU TAKE A SCROLL IN YOUR HANDS AND WRITE WHAT (THINGS) *the* LORD SAYS, BECAUSE/THAT YOU, THE SON OF GOD, WILL CUT OUT FROM ROOTS ALL THE HOUSE-HOLD OF AMALEK ON/AGAINST THE LAST DAYS. 12.10 You see again Jesus, not a son of a man, but a son of God, and being revealed in flesh for a type/example. There-fore, since they are about to say that the anointed (one) is a son of David, David himself prophesies, fearing and understanding the deceit/error/straying of the sinners: *The* LORD SAID TO MY LORD: YOU SIT OUT OF/FROM MY RIGHT (ONES), UNTIL I WOULD PUT/LAY YOUR ENEMIES A FOOTSTOOL OF YOUR FEET.

12.11 And again Isaias speaks thus: *The* LORD SAID TO THE ANOINTED (ONE), MY LORD, OF WHOM HE GRASP-ED HIS RIGHT (HAND): ETHNICS/NATIONS WILL HEAR/LISTEN BEFORE HIM, AND I SHALL BREAK ASUNDER A STRENGTH/MIGHT OF KINGS. You see how David says/calls him *the* Lord, and/also a son of God. 13.1 But let us see if this people or the first/former (people) inherits, and *if/whether* the covenant *is* to us or to those. 13.2 Then hear ye what the writing says about the people: AND ISAAC WAS SUPPLICATING/ENTREATING ABOUT REBECCA HIS WOMAN, BECAUSE SHE WAS BARREN; AND SHE CONCEIVED. THEN REBECCA WENT OUT TO INQUIRE FROM *the* LORD, AND *the* LORD SAID TO HER: TWO ETHNICS/NATIONS *are* IN YOUR BELLY AND TWO PEOPLES IN YOUR WOMB, AND A PEOPLE/*one* WILL RISE ABOVE/EXCEL FROM A PEOPLE/*the other*, AND THE GREATER/OLDER WILL SERVE AS A SLAVE TO THE LESSER/YOUNGER. 13.3 Ye are obligated to perceive who Isaac *is* and who Rebecca *is*, and to whom he has shown that

λαὸς οὗτος ἢ ἐκεῖνος. 13.4 καὶ ἐν ἄλλῃ προφητίᾳ λέγει φανερώτερον ὁ Ἰακὼβ πρὸς Ἰωσὴφ τὸν υἱὸν αὐτοῦ, λέγων· ἰδού, οὐκ ἐστέρησέν με κύριος τοῦ προσώπου σου· προσάγαγέ μοι τοὺς υἱούς σου, ἵνα εὐλογήσω αὐτούς. 13.5 καὶ προσήγαγεν Ἐφραὶμ καὶ Μανασσῆ, θέλων τὸν Ἐφραὶμ ἵνα εὐλογηθῇ, ὅτι πρεσβύτερος ἦν· ὁ γὰρ Ἰωσὴφ προσήγαγεν εἰς τὴν δεξιὰν χεῖρα τοῦ πατρὸς Ἰακώβ. εἶδεν δὲ Ἰακὼβ τύπον τῷ πνεύματι τοῦ λαοῦ τοῦ μεταξύ· καὶ τί λέγει; καὶ ἐποίησεν Ἰακὼβ ἐναλλὰξ τὰς χῖρας αὐτοῦ καὶ ἐπέθηκεν τὴν δεξιὰν ἐπὶ τὴν κεφαλὴν Μανασσῆ, τοῦ δευτέρου καὶ νεωτέρου, καὶ εὐλόγησεν αὐτόν. καὶ εἶπεν Ἰωσὴφ πρὸς Ἰακώβ· μετάθες σου τὴν δεξιὰν ἐπὶ τὴν κεφαλὴν Ἐφραίμ, ὅτι πρωτότοκός μου υἱός ἐστιν. καὶ εἶπεν Ἰακὼβ πρὸς Ἰακώβ· οἶδα, τέκνον, οἶδα· ἀλλ' ὁ μίζων δουλεύσει τῷ ἐλάσσονι, καὶ οὗτος δὲ εὐλογηθήσεται. 13.6 βλέπετε, ἐπὶ τίνων ἔθεικεν, τὸν λαὸν τοῦτον εἶναι πρῶτον καὶ τῆς διαθήκης κληρονόμον. 13.7 εἰ οὖν ἔτι καὶ διὰ τοῦ Ἀβραὰμ ἐμνήσθη, ἀπέχομεν τὸ τέλειον τῆς γνώσεως ἡμῶν. τί οὖν λέγει τῷ Ἀβραάμ, ὅτε μόνος πιστεύσας ἐτέθη εἰς δικαιοσύνην; ἰδού, τέθεικά σε, Ἀβραάμ, πατέρα ἐθνῶν τῶν πιστευόντων τῶν δι' ἀκροβυστίαν τῷ θεῷ. 14.1 ναί. ἀλλὰ εἴδωμεν, εἰ ἡ διαθήκη, ἣν ὤμοσεν δοῦναι τοῖς πατράσιν δοῦναι τῷ λαῷ, εἰ δέδωκεν. δέδωκεν· αὐτοὶ δὲ οὐκ ἐγένοντο ἄξιοι λαβεῖν διὰ τὰς ἁμαρτίας αὐτῶν. 14.2 λέγει γὰρ ὁ προφήτης· καὶ ἦν Μωϋσῆς νηστεύων ἐν ὄρι Σινᾶ, τοῦ λαβεῖν τὴν διαθήκην κυρίου πρὸς τὸν λαόν, ἡμέρας τεσσεράκοντα καὶ νύκτας τεσσεράκοντα. καὶ ἔλαβεν Μωϋσῆς παρὰ κυρίου τὰς δύο πλάκας τὰς γεγραμμένας τῷ δακτύλῳ τῆς χειρὸς κυρίου ἐν πνεύματι· καὶ λαβὼν Μωσῆς κατέφερεν πρὸς τὸν λαὸν δοῦναι.

14.3 καὶ εἶπεν κύριος πρὸς Μωσῆν. Μωσῆ Μωσῆ, κατάβηθι τὸ τάχος, ὅτι ὁ λαός σου, ὃν ἐξήγαγες ἐκ γῆς

this people is greater than that.   13.4 And in another
prophecy, Jacob says/speaks more plainly to Joseph his
son, saying: BEHOLD, *the* LORD DEPRIVED ME NOT OF YOUR
FACE; BRING TO ME YOUR SONS, THAT I MAY BLESS THEM.
13.5 And he brought forward Ephraim and Manasses,
wanting/wishing that Ephraim may be blessed, because
he was elder; for Joseph brought *him* forward to the
right hand of the father Jacob. But Jacob saw a type/
example of the next people in/by the spirit; and what
says he/it? And Jacob did crosswise his hands, and he
placed the right upon the head of Manasses, the second
and younger, and he blessed him. And Joseph said to
Jacob: Change your right upon the head of Ephraim,
because he is my firstborn son. And Jacob said to
Jacob (Joseph): I know, child, I know; but the greater
(one) will serve as a slave to the lesser (one), and
even/also this (one) will be blessed.   13.6 See ye
upon whom he has put the (thing) for this people to be
first and heir of the covenant.   13.7 Therefore, if it
was still remembered   also through/on account of
Abraham, we received the completeness of our knowledge. What then says he to Abraham, when having
believed alone, it was put/placed in justice/justness?
Behold, I have placed you, Abraham, a father of eth-
nics/nations, of those believing in God through uncircumcision.   14.1   Yes. But we should see/observe if
the covenant which he swore to give to the ancestors
to give to the people, if he has given *it*. He has
given *it*; but they became not worthy themselves to
receive *it* because of their sins/faults.   14.2 For the
prophet says: AND MOSES WAS FASTING ON A MOUNTAIN,
SINAI,   FROM   THE   (THING)   TO   RECEIVE/TAKE   THE   COVENANT
OF/FROM   *the*   LORD   TO   THE   PEOPLE,   FORTY   DAYS   AND   FORTY
NIGHTS.   AND   MOSES   RECEIVED   FROM   *the*   LORD   THE   TWO
PLAQUES/STONE   TABLETS   HAVING   BEEN   WRITTEN   BY   A   FINGER
OF *the* LORD'S HAND in/by a spirit; and having received
them, Moses carried them down to give *them* to the
people.
     14.3   And *the* Lord said to Moses: Moses, Moses,
go you down *with* the speed, because your people whom
you led forth out of a land of Egypt, they broke the
law. And Moses understood that they made molten images

Αἰγύπτου, ἠνόμησεν. καὶ συνῆκεν Μωσῆς, ὅτι ἐποίησαν ἑαυτοῖς χωνεύματα, καὶ ἔρρειψεν ἐκ τῶν χιρῶν, καὶ συνετρίβησαν αἱ πλάκες τῆς διαθήκης κυρίου. 14.4 Μωσῆς μὲν ἔλαβεν, αὐτοὶ δὲ οὐκ ἐγένοντο ἄξιοι. πῶς δὲ ἡμῖς ἐλάβομεν, μάθετε. Μωσῆς θεράπων ὢν ἔλαβεν. οὗτος δὲ κύριος ἡμῖν ἔδωκεν εἰς λαὸν κληρονομίας, δι' ἡμᾶς ὑπομίνας. 14.5 ἐφανερώθη δέ, ἵνα κἀκῖνοι τελειωθῶσιν τοῖς ἁμαρτήμασιν, καὶ ἡμῖς διὰ τοῦ κληρονομοῦντος διαθήκην κυρίου Ἰησοῦ λάβωμεν, ὃς εἰς τοῦτο ἡτοιμάσθη, ἵνα αὐτὸς φανίς, τὰς ἤδη δεδαπανημένας ἡμῶν καρδίας τῷ θανάτῳ καὶ παραδεδομένας τῇ τῆς πλάνης ἀνομίᾳ λυτρωσάμενος ἐκ τοῦ σκότους, διάθηται ἐν ἡμῖν διαθήκην λόγῳ. 14.6 γέγραπται γάρ, πῶς αὐτῷ ὁ πατὴρ ἐντέλλεται, λυτρωσάμενον ἡμᾶς ἐκ τοῦ σκότους ἑαυτῷ ἑτοιμάσε λαὸν ἅγιον. 14.7 λέγει οὖν ὁ προφήτης· ἐγὼ κύριος, ὁ θεός σου, ἐκάλεσά σε ἐν δικαιοσύνῃ καὶ κρατήσω τῆς χιρός σου καὶ ἰσχύσω σε, καὶ ἔδωκά σε εἰς διαθήκην γένους, εἰς φῶς ἐθνῶν ἀνοῖξε ὀφθαλμοὺς τυφλῶν καὶ ἐξαγαγεῖν ἐκ δεσμῶν πεπεδημένους καὶ ἐξ οἴκου φυλακῆς καθημένους ἐν σκότι. γινώσκομεν οὖν, πόθεν ἐλυτρώθημεν. 14.9 πάλιν ὁ προφήτης λέγει· πνεῦμα κυρίου ἐπ' ἐμέ, οὗ εἵνεκεν ἔχρισέν με εὐαγγελίσασθαι πτωχοῖς, ἀπέσταλκέν με ἰάσασθαι τοὺς συντετριμμένους τὴν καρδίαν, κηρῦξαι αἰχμαλώτοις ἄφεσιν καὶ τυφλοῖς ἀνάβλεψιν, καλέσε ἐνιαυτὸν κυρίου δεκτὸν καὶ ἡμέραν ἀνταποδόσεως, παρακαλέσε πάντας τοὺς πενθοῦντας.

14.8 πάλιν ὁ προφήτης λέγει· ἰδού, τέθεικά σε εἰς φῶς ἐθνῶν, τοῦ εἶναί σε εἰς σωτηρίαν ἕως ἐσχάτου τῆς γῆς,

οὕτως λέγει κύριος ὁ λυτρωσάμενός σε θεὸς Ἰσραήλ. 15.1

for themselves, and he threw *them* down out of the hands, and the plaques of the covenant of *the* Lord were broken. 14.4 Moses indeed received *it*, but they themselves became not worthy. But how we, we received *it*, learn ye. Moses, being a servant/therapist, received *it*, but *the* Lord himself gave *it* to us, to a people of inheritance, having endured because of us. 14.5 And it was manifested/made plain that those also might be ended/finished to the sins; and we, we might receive *it* through Jesus, the (one) inheriting a covenant of *the* Lord, who was prepared to/for this (thing), in order that he, having appeared, having delivered/redeemed out of the darkness our hearts already having been spent/expended to the death, and having been delivered over to the lawlessness of the deceit/error/straying, he may covenant/arrange a covenant with us by a reasoning/word. 14.6 For it has been written how the father enjoins/commands it, having redeemed/delivered us out of the darkness, he prepared a holy/consecrated people for himself. 14.7 Then the prophet says: I *am* THE LORD YOUR GOD, I CALLED YOU IN JUSTNESS AND I SHALL HOLD FAST YOUR HAND AND I SHALL STRENGTHEN YOU, AND I GAVE YOU IN/FOR A COVENANT OF A RACE/KIND, IN/FOR A LIGHT OF ETHNICS, TO OPEN EYES OF BLIND (ONES) AND TO LEAD FORTH OUT OF BONDS THOSE HAVING BEEN BOUND AND OUT OF A HOUSE OF PRISON THOSE SITTING IN DARKNESS. Then we know from where we were released/redeemed/ransomed. 14.9 Again the prophet says: A SPIRIT FROM *the* LORD *is* UPON ME, WHO ANOINTED ME ON ACCOUNT OF TO ANNOUNCE A GOOD MESSAGE TO POOR (ONES), HE SENT ME TO HEAL THOSE HAVING BEEN BROKEN/BRUISED *in* THE HEART, TO HERALD/PREACH FORGIVENESS/REMISSION TO CAPTIVES/PRISONERS OF WAR AND RECOVERY OF SIGHT TO BLIND (ONES), TO CALL AN ACCEPTABLE YEAR/TIME OF *the* LORD AND A DAY OF RECOMPENSE, TO CONSOLE/COMFORT ALL THE (ONES)/THOSE MOURNING/GRIEVING.

14.8 Again the prophet says: BEHOLD, I HAVE PLACED YOU IN/FOR A LIGHT OF ETHNICS, FROM THE (THING) *for* YOU TO BE IN/FOR A DELIVERANCE UNTIL THE LAST/END OF THE LAND/EARTH, THUS SAYS *the* LORD GOD OF ISRAEL, THE (ONE) HAVING REDEEMED/RANSOMED YOU. 15.1 And

ἔτι οὖν καὶ περὶ τοῦ σαββάτου γέγραπται ἐν τοῖς δέκα λόγοις, ἐν οἷς ἐλάλησεν ἐν τῷ ὄρι Σινᾶ πρὸς Μωσῆν κατὰ πρόσωπον· καὶ ἁγιάσαται τὸ σάββατον κυρίου χερσὶν καθαραῖς καὶ καρδίᾳ καθαρᾷ. 15.2 καὶ ἐν ἑταίρῳ λέγει· ἐὰν φυλάξωσιν οἱ υἱοί μου τὸ σάββατον, τότε ἐπιθήσω τὸ ἔλεός μου ἐπ᾽ αὐτούς. 15.3 τὸ σάββατον λέγει ἐν ἀρχῇ τῆς κτίσεως·

καὶ ἐποίησεν ὁ θεὸς ἐν ἓξ ἡμέραις τὰ ἔργα τῶν χιρῶν αὐτοῦ, καὶ συνετέλεσεν ἐν τῇ ἡμέρᾳ τῇ ἑβδόμῃ καὶ κατέπαυσεν αὐτὴν καὶ ἡγίασεν αὐτήν. 15.4 προσέχετε, τέκνα, τί λέγει τὸ συνετέλεσεν ἐν ἓξ ἡμέραις. τοῦτο λέγει, ὅτι ἐν ἑξακισχιλίοις ἔτεσιν συντελέσι κύριος τὰ σύμπαντα· ἡ γὰρ ἡμέρα παρ᾽ αὐτῷ σημαίνι χίλια ἔτη. αὐτὸς δέ μοι μαρτυρεῖ λέγων·

ἰδού, ἡμέρα κυρίου ἔσται ὡς χίλια ἔτη οὐκοῦν, τέκνα, ἐν ἓξ ἡμέραις, ἐν τοῖς ἑξακισχιλίοις ἔτεσεν συντελεσθήσεται τὰ σύμπαντα. 15.5 καὶ κατέπαυσεν τῇ ἡμερα τῇ ἑβδόμῃ. τοῦτο λέγει· ὅταν ἐλθὼν ὁ υἱὸς αὐτοῦ καταργήσει τὸν καιρὸν καὶ κρινῖ τοὺς ἀσεβεῖς καὶ ἀλλάξει τὸν ἥλιον καὶ τοὺς ἀστέρας καὶ τὴν σελήνην, τότε καλῶς καταπαύσεται ἐν ἡμέρα τῇ ἑβδόμῃ. 15.6 πέρας γέ τοι λέγει· ἁγιάσεις αὐτὴν χερσὶν καθαραῖς καὶ καρδίᾳ καθαρᾷ. εἰ οὖν ἦν ὁ θεὸς ἡμέραν ἡγίασεν νῦν τις δύναται ἁγιάσαι καθαρὸς ὢν τῇ καρδίᾳ, ἐν πᾶσιν πεπλανήμεθα. 15.7 εἴδε οὖν ἄρα τότε καλῶς καταπαυόμενοι ἁγιάσομεν αὐτήν, ὅτε δυνησόμεθα αὐτοὶ δικαιωθέντες καὶ ἀπολαβόντες τὴν ἐπαγγελίαν, μηκέτι οὔσης τῆς ἀνομίας, καινῶν δὲ γεγονότων πάντων ὑπὸ τοῦ κυρίου· τότε δυνησόμεθα αὐτὴν ἁγιάσε, αὐτοὶ ἁγιασθέντες πρῶτον. 15.8 πέρας γέ τοι λέγει αὐτοῖς· τὰς νεομηνίας ὑμῶν καὶ

then it has further been written in the ten sayings/reasonings/words, in those spoken to Moses face to face on the mountain, Sinai: AND DEDICATE/SET YE APART THE SABBATH OF *the* LORD WITH CLEAN HANDS AND A CLEAN/PURE HEART. 15.2 And in/by another/different (one) he says: If my sons might guard/keep the sabbath, then I shall put/lay my mercy upon them. 15.3 He says/means the sabbath in the beginning of the creation:

AND GOD DID/MADE THE WORKS OF HIS HANDS IN SIX DAYS, AND HE COMPLETED/FINISHED/ENDED (THEM) TOGETHER IN/ON THE SEVENTH DAY AND HE CEASED/RESTED *on* IT AND DEDICATED IT/SET IT APART. 15.4 Take ye heed, children, what it says/means, the (thing): He completed together in six days. This (thing) he says, that in six thousand years *the* Lord will complete/finish all things together; for the day from/with him signifies a thousand years. And he himself testifies/witnesses to me, saying:

BEHOLD, A DAY OF/FROM *the* LORD WILL BE ABOUT A THOUSAND YEARS. Therefore, children, in six days, in the six thousand years, all things will be completed/ended together. 15.5 And he rested on the seventh day. He says/means this: Whenever his son, having come, he will pull down/destroy the time/season, and he will judge the impious/irreverent (ones), and he will change/alter the sun and the stars and the moon, then he will truly rest on/in the seventh day. 15.6 Furthermore he says: You will sanctify it/set it apart with clean hands and a clean/pure heart. If then anyone may now be able to sanctify a day which God sanctified/set apart, being pure in heart, we are having been deceived in all (things). 15.7 You see then, at that time resting well, we shall sanctify it/set it apart, when we ourselves shall be able, having been justified and having received back the promise, no longer being of the lawlessness, but *from* all (things) having become new by the Lord; then we shall be able to consecrate/sanctify it, ourselves having been consecrated first. 15.8 Furthermore, he says to them: I ENDURE NOT THE NEW MOONS/SECULAR FESTIVALS AND THE SABBATHS OF YE. Observe ye how he says/means: The present sabbaths *are* not accepted, but

ΒΑΡΝΑΒΑ ΕΠΙΣΤΟΛΗ

τὰ σάββατα οὐκ ἀνέχομαι. ὁράται, πῶς λέγει; οὐ τὰ νῦν σάββατα δεκτά, ἀλλὰ ὃ πεποίηκα, ἐν ᾧ καταπαύσας τὰ πάντα ἀρχὴν ἡμέρας ὀγδόης ποιήσω, ὅ ἐστιν ἄλλου κόσμου ἀρχήν. 15.9 διὸ καὶ ἄγομεν τὴν ἡμέραν τὴν ὀγδόην εἰς εὐφροσύνην, ἐν ᾗ καὶ ὁ κύριος ἡμῶν Ἰησοῦς ὁ χριστὸς ἀνέστη ἐκ νεκρῶν καὶ φανερωθεὶς ἀνέβη εἰς οὐρανούς. 16.1 ἔτι δὲ καὶ περὶ τοῦ ναοῦ ἐρῶ ὑμῖν, ὡς πλανώμενοι οἱ ταλαίπωροι εἰς τὴν οἰκοδομὴν ἤλπισαν, καὶ οὐκ ἐπὶ τὸν θεὸν αὐτῶν τὸν ποιήσαντα αὐτούς, ὡς ὄντα οἶκον θεοῦ. 16.2 σχεδὸν εἰς τὰ ἔθνη ἀφιέρωσαν γὰρ αὐτὸν ἐν τῷ ναῷ. ἀλλὰ πῶς λέγει κύριος καταργῶν αὐτόν, μάθεται· τίς ἐμέτρησεν τὸν οὐρανὸν σπιθαμῇ ἢ τὴν γῆν δρακεί; οὐκ ἐγώ; λέγει κύριος· ὁ οὐρανός μοι θρόνος, ἡ δὲ γῆ ὑποπόδιον τῶν ποδῶν μου· ποῖον οἶκον οἰκοδομήσεταί μοι, ἢ τίς τόπος τῆς καταπαύσεώς μου;

ἐγνώκαται, ὅτι ματαία ἡ ἐλπὶς αὐτῶν. 16.3 πέρας γέ τοι πάλιν λέγει· ἰδού, οἱ καθελόντες τὸν ναὸν τοῦτον αὐτοὶ οἰκοδομήσουσιν αὐτόν. 16.4 διὰ γὰρ τὸ πολοιμῖν αὐτοὺς καθῃρέθη ὑπὸ τῶν ἃ ἐχθρῶν· νῦν καὶ αὐτοὶ καὶ οἱ τῶν ἐχθρῶν ὑπηρέται ἀνοικοδομήσωσιν αὐτόν. 16.5 πάλιν ὡς ἔμελλεν ἡ πόλις καὶ ὁ λαὸς καὶ ο ναὸς Ἰσραὴλ παραδίδοσθαι, ἐφανερώθη. λέγει γὰρ ἡ γραφή·

καὶ ἔσται ἐπ' ἐσχάτων τῶν ἡμερῶν, καὶ παραδώσει κύριος τὰ πρόβατα τῆς νομῆς καὶ τὴν μάνδραν καὶ τὸν πύργον αὐτῶν εἰς καταφθοράν. καὶ ἐγένετο καθ' ἃ ἐλάλησεν κύριος. 16.6 ζητήσωμεν δέ, εἰ ἔστιν ναὸς θεοῦ. ἔστιν, ὅπου αὐτὸς λέγει ποιεῖν καὶ καταρτίζειν. γέγραπται γάρ· καὶ ἔσται, τῆς ἑβδομάδος συντελουμένης οἰκοδομηθήσεται ναὸς θεοῦ ἐνδόξως ἐπὶ τῷ ὀνόματι κυρίου. 16.7 εὑρίσκω οὖν ὅτι ἔστιν ναός. πῶς οὖν οἰκοδομηθήσεται ἐπὶ τῷ ὀνόματι κυρίου, μάθεται.

the one which I have made, in which having rested, I shall make all the (things), beginning from *the* eighth day, which is from the beginning of another world. 15.9 Wherefore even we bring the eighth day in rejoicing/gladness, on which also our Lord Jesus, the anointed (one), arose out of dead (ones) and having been manifested/made visible (or plain) he went up into *the* skies/heavens. 16.1 And yet I shall also say/speak to ye concerning the *inner* temple, as straying/being misled the (ones) enduring hardship hoped in the building, and not upon their God, the (one) having made them, as being a house/home of God. 16.2 For they almost clothed/invested him to/for the ethnics in the *inner* temple. But learn ye how *the* Lord speaks, having abolished it: WHO MEASURED THE SKY/HEAVEN WITH A SPAN/HAND BREADTH OR THE LAND/EARTH WITH A HAND SPREAD? *Have* NOT I? *The* Lord says: THE SKY/HEAVEN *is* A THRONE FOR ME, AND THE EARTH/LAND *is* A FOOTSTOOL FOR MY FEET; WHAT SORT OF A HOUSE WILL YE BUILD FOR ME, OR WHAT *is* A PLACE OF MY REST/REPOSE?

Ye know that the hope of them *is* empty/vain. 16.3 Furthermore, he says again: BEHOLD, THOSE DESTROYING THIS *inner* TEMPLE, THEY THEMSELVES WILL BUILD IT. 16.4 For because of the (thing) *for* them to make war, it was destroyed by the enemies; and now they, even the servants/assistants of the enemies, will build it up. 16.5 Again it was made plain/manifested when the city and the people and the *inner* temple of Israel were about to be delivered over. For the writing says:

AND IT WILL BE AT/BEFORE THE LAST DAYS, *the* LORD WILL BOTH DELIVER OVER THE SHEEP(S) OF THE PASTURE AND THE SHEEPFOLD AND THEIR TOWER/FORTRESS INTO/FOR DESTRUCTION. And it happened according to what *the* Lord spoke. 16.6 But let us seek/inquire if there is an *inner* temple of God. There is, where it/he says *for* himself to make and to mend/perfect *it*. For it has been written: And it will be, from the week/seventh (day) being ended/finished, an *inner* temple of God will be built gloriously upon the name of *the* Lord. 16.7 I find therefore that there is an *inner* temple. Then learn ye how it will be built upon the name of

πρὸ τοῦ ἡμᾶς πιστεῦσαι τῷ θεῷ ἦν ἡμῶν τὸ κατοικητήριον τῆς καρδίας φθαρτὸν καὶ ἀσθενές, ὡς ἀληθῶς οἰκοδομητὸς ναὸς διὰ χιρός, ὅτι ἦν πλήρις μὲν εἰδωλολατρίας καὶ ἦν οἶκος δαιμονίων διὰ τὸ ποιεῖν, ὅσα ἦν ἐναντία τῷ θεῷ. 16.8 οἰκοδομηθήσεται δὲ ἐπὶ τῷ ὀνόματι κυρίου. προσέχετε δέ, ἵνα ὁ ναὸς τοῦ θεοῦ ἐνδόξως οἰκοδομηθῇ. πῶς, μάθεται. λαβόντες τὴν ἄφεσιν τῶν ἁμαρτιῶν καὶ ἐλπίσαντες ἐπὶ τὸ ὄνομα ἐγενόμεθα κενοί, πάλιν ἐξ ἀρχῆς κτιζόμενοι· διὸ ἐν τῷ κατοικητηρίῳ ἡμῶν ἀληθῶς ὁ θεὸς κατοικεῖ ἐν ἡμῖν. 16.9 πῶς; ὁ λόγος αὐτοῦ τῆς πίστεως, ἡ κλῆσις τῆς ἐπαγγελίας,

ἡ σοφία τῶν δικαιωμάτων, αἱ ἐντολαὶ τῆς διδαχῆς,

αὐτὸς ἐν ἡμῖν προφητεύων, αὐτὸς ἐν ἡμῖν κατοικῶν,

τοῖς τῷ θανάτῳ δεδουλωμένοις ἀνύγων ἡμῖν τὴν θύραν τοῦ ναοῦ,

ὅ ἐστιν στόμα, μετάνοιαν διδοὺς ἡμῖν, εἰσάγει εἰς τὸν ἄφθαρτον ἢ ναόν. 16.10 ὁ γὰρ ποθῶν σωθῆναι βλέπει οὐκ εἰς τὸν ἄνθρωπον, ἀλλὰ εἰς τὸν ἐν αὐτῷ κατοικοῦντα καὶ λαλοῦντα, ἐπ᾽ αὐτῷ ἐκπλησσόμενος, ἐπὶ τῷ μηδέποτε μήτε τοῦ λέγοντος τὰ ῥήματα ἀκηκοέναι ἐκ τοῦ στόματος μήτε αὐτός ποτε ἐπιτεθυμηκέναι ἀκούειν. τοῦτό ἐστιν πνευματικὸς ναὸς οἰκοδομούμενος τῷ κυρίῳ. 17.1 ἐφ᾽ ὅσον ἦν ἐν δυνατῷ καὶ ἁπλότητι δηλῶσε ὑμῖν, ἐλπίζει μου ἡ ψυχὴ τῇ ἐπιθυμίᾳ μου μὴ παραλελοιπέναι τι τῶν ἀνηκόντων εἰς σωτηρίαν. 17.2 ἐὰν γὰρ περὶ τῶν ἐνεστώτων ἢ μελλόντων γράφω ὑμῖν, οὐ μὴ νοήσηται διὰ τὸ ἐν παραβολαῖς κεῖσθε. ταῦτα μὲν οὕτως.

18.1 Μεταβῶμεν δὲ καὶ ἐφ᾽ ἑτέραν γνῶσιν καὶ διδαχήν. ὁδοὶ δύο εἰσὶν διδαχῆς καὶ ἐχουσίας, ἤ τοῦ φωτὸς καὶ ἡ τοῦ

the Lord.

Before the (thing) for us to believe in God the habitation of the heart of us was mortal and weak, like an *inner* temple having been built through a hand, because it was indeed full of idolatry and it was a house of demons because of the (thing) to do whatever was opposed/contrary to God.   16.8 But it will be built upon the name of *the* Lord. And ye take heed that the *inner* temple of God may be built gloriously. Learn ye how: Having received the forgiveness/remission/ sending away of the sins/faults and having hoped on the name, we became new (men), being created again from the beginning. Wherefore, God truly dwells in us, in our habitation/dwelling place.   16.9 How? His saying/word/reason/logos of/from the faith, the invitation/calling of/from the promise,

the wisdom of/from the just acts, the commands of/from the teaching/doctrine,

(he) himself prophesying in/by us, (he) himself dwelling in us,

the (ones) having been enslaved to the death, opening to us the door of the *inner* temple,

which is a mouth, giving repentance to us, he brings/leads into the immortality being an *inner* temple.   16.10 For the (one) longing to be saved he sees/looks not into/to the man, but into/to the (one) dwelling and speaking in him, being amazed over/at him, at the (thing) never, neither from the (thing) to have heard the words being spoken from the mouth nor (he) himself at any time to have desired to hear. This is a spiritual *inner* temple being built for the Lord. 17.1   On/for as much as it was in/by ability and simplicity to make plain to ye, my life/soul hopes in/by my desire not to have weakened anything of the (things) pertaining to deliverance/salvation.   17.2 For if I write to ye about the (things) being present or being about to come, by no means may ye perceive because of the (thing) to be set/put in parables. These (things) *are* indeed so.

18.1   But let us move also to another/different knowledge and doctrine/teaching. There are two ways/

σκότους. διαφορὰ δὲ πολλὴ τῶν δύο ὁδῶν. ἐφ' ἧς μὲν γάρ εἰσιν τεταγμένοι φωταγωγοὶ ἄγγελοι τοῦ θεοῦ, ἐφ' ἧς δὲ ἄγγελοι τοῦ Σατανᾶ. 18.2 καὶ ὁ μέν ἐστιν κύριος ἀπὸ αἰώνων καὶ εἰς τοὺς αἰῶνας, ὁ δὲ ἄρχων καιροῦ τοῦ νῦν τῆς ἀνομίας.

19.1 Ἡ οὖν ὁδὸς τοῦ φωτός ἐστιν τοιαύτη· ἐάν τις θέλων ὁδὸν ὁδεύειν ἐπὶ τὸν ὡρισμένον τόπον, σπεύσῃ τοῖς ἔργοις αὐτοῦ. ἔστιν οὖν ἡ δοθῖσα ἡμῖν γνῶσις τοῦ περιπατῖν ἐν ταύτῃ τοιαύτη. 19.2 ἀγαπήσεις τὸν ποιήσαντά σε, φοβηθήσῃ τόν σε πλάσαντα, δοξάσεις τόν σε λυτρωσάμενον ἐκ θανάτου· ἔσῃ ἁπλοῦς τῇ καρδίᾳ καὶ πλούσιος τῷ πνεύματι· οὐ κολληθήσῃ μετὰ προευομένων ἐν ὁδῷ θανάτου,

μισήσεις πᾶν, ὃ οὐκ ἔστιν ἀρεστὸν τῷ θεῷ, μισήσεις πᾶσαν ὑπόκρισιν·

οὐ μὴ ἐγκαταλίπῃς ἐντολὰς χυρίου. 19.3 οὐχ ὑψώσεις σεαυτόν, ἔσῃ δὲ ταπινόφρων κατὰ πάντα· οὐκ ἀρῖς ἐπὶ σεαυτὸν δόξαν. οὐ λήμψῃ βουλὴν πονηρὰν κατὰ τοῦ πλησίον σου, οὐ δώσεις τῇ ψυχῇ σου θράσος. 19.4 οὐ πορνεύσεις, οὐ μοιχεύσεις, οὐ παιδοφθορήσεις. οὐ μή σου ὁ λόγος τοῦ θεοῦ ἐξέλθῃ ἐν ἀκαθαρσίᾳ τινῶν. οὐ λήμψῃ πρόσωπον ἐλέγξε τινὰ ἐπὶ παραπτώματι.

ἔσῃ πραΰς, ἔσῃ ἡσύχιος, ἔσῃ τρέμων τοὺς λόγους οὓς ἤκουσας. οὐ μνησικακήσεις τῷ ἀδελφῷ σου. 19.5 οὐ μὴ διψυχήσεις, πότερον ἔσται ἢ οὔ. οὐ μὴ λάβῃς ἐπὶ ματαίῳ τὸ ὄνομα κυρίου. ἀγαπήσεις τὸν πλησίον σου ὑπὲρ τὸν ἐχθρόν σου

581

roads of/for teaching/doctrine and authority, either of the light or also of the darkness. And *there is* a much difference of/from the two ways/roads. For upon/over which on the one hand light giving messengers/angels from God are having been appointed, but *over* which on the other *are* messengers/angels of Satan. 18.2 And the (one) indeed is Lord from ages even into the ages, but the *other* also *is* a ruler of the present (time) of the lawlessness.

19.1 Therefore the way/road of the light is such as this/like this: If anyone be wanting/wishing to journey/travel a way/road to the place having been appointed, he should be diligent in his works. Then the knowledge is having been given to us of the (thing) to walk in such as this (way). 19.2 You will love the (one) having made you; you should fear the (one) having molded/formed you, you will glorify the (one) having redeemed you out of death; you should be simple/sound in the heart and rich in the spirit; you should not join/associate with (ones) going on a road/way of death;

you will hate every (thing) which is not pleasing to God, you will hate every pretense/hypocrisy;

by no means might you forsake commands of *the* Lord. 19.3 You will not exalt yourself, but you should be humble minded in respect to all (things); you will not take fame/glory upon yourself. You may not receive/take an evil plan/counsel against your neighbor, you will not give arrogance to your soul/life. 19.4 You will not do prostitution, you will not do adultery, you will not do sodomy/be homosexual. By no means might the saying/word of God go out from you in uncleanliness of certain sorts. You may not receive/take a face to reprove someone over a trespass.

You should be gentle/meek, you should be quiet/silent, you should be standing in awe/trembling *for* the sayings/words which you heard. You will not remember malice/bear a grudge to your brother. 19.5 By no means may you be doubtful/double-minded, whether it will be or not. BY NO MEANS MAY YOU TAKE/RECEIVE THE NAME OF *the* LORD ON THE BASIS OF VANITY. You will love

581

τὴν ψυχήν σου. οὐ φονεύσεις τέκνον ἐν φθορᾷ, οὐδὲ πάλιν γεννηθὲν ἀποκτενεῖς. οὐ μὴ ἄρῃς τὴν χεῖρά σου ἀπὸ τοῦ υἱοῦ σου ἢ ἀπὸ τῆς θυγατρός σου, ἀλλὰ ἀπὸ νεότητος διδάξεις φόβον θεοῦ. 19.6 οὐ μὴ γένῃ ἐπιθυμῶν τὰ τοῦ πλησίον σου, οὐ μὴ γένῃ πλεονέκτης. οὐδὲ κολληθήσῃ ἐκ ψυχῆς σου μετὰ ὑψηλῶν, ἀλλὰ μετὰ ταπινῶν καὶ δικαίων ἀναστραφήσῃ.

τὰ συμβαίνοντά σοι ἐνεργήματα ὡς ἀγαθὰ προσδέξῃ, εἰδὼς ὅτι ἄνευ θεοῦ οὐδὲν γείνεται. 19.7 οὐκ ἔσῃ διγνώμων οὐδὲ γλωσσώδης, ὑποταγὴ κυρίοις ὡς τύπῳ θεοῦ αἰσχύνῃ καὶ φόβῳ· οὐ μὴ ἐπιτάξῃς δούλῳ σου ἢ παιδίσκῃ ἐν πικρίᾳ, τοῖς ἐπὶ τὸν αὐτὸν θεὸν ἐλπίζουσιν, μή ποτε οὐ μὴ φοβηθήσονται τὸν ἐπ' ἀμφοτέροις θεόν· ὅτι οὐκ ἦλθεν κατὰ πρόσωπον καλέσε, ἀλλ' ἐφ' οὓς τὸ πνεῦμα ἡτοίμασεν. 19.8 κοινωνήσεις ἐν πᾶσιν τῷ πλησίον σου καὶ οὐκ ἐρεῖς ἴδια εἶναι· εἰ γὰρ ἐν τῷ ἀφθάρτῳ κοινωνοί ἐστε, πόσῳ μᾶλλον ἐν τοῖς φθαρτοῖς; οὐκ ἔσῃ πρόγλωσσος· παγὶς γὰρ τὸ στόμα θανάτου. ὅσον δύνασε, ὑπὲρ τῆς ψυχῆς σου ἁγνεύσις. 19.9 μὴ γείνου πρὸς μὲν τὸ λαβεῖν ἐκτίνων τὰς χῖρας, πρὸς δὲ τὸ δοῦναι συσπῶν. ἀγαπήσεις ὡς κόρην τοῦ ὀφθαλμοῦ σου πάντα τὸν λαλοῦντά σοι τὸν λόγον κυρίου. 19.10 μνησθήσῃ ἡμέραν κρίσεως νυκτὸς καὶ ἡμέρας, καὶ ἐκζητήσεις καθ' ἑκάστην ἡμέραν τὰ πρόσωπα τῶν ἁγίων, ἢ διὰ λόγου κοπίων καὶ πορευόμενος εἰς τὸ παρακαλέσε καὶ μελετῶν εἰς τὸ σῶσαι ψυχὴν τῷ λόγῳ, ἢ διὰ τῶν χιρῶν σου ἐργάσῃ εἰς λύτρον ἁμαρτιῶν σου. 19.11 οὐ διστάσεις δοῦναι οὐδὲ διδοὺς γογγύσει· γνώσῃ δέ, τὶς ὁ τοῦ μισθοῦ καλὸς ἀνταποδότης. φυλάξεις ἃ παρέλαβες, μήτε

your neighbor above your enemy *and* your soul/life. You will not murder a child in/by corruption, neither will you kill again from having been generated/born. By no means might you take away your hand from your son or from your daughter, but you will teach *them* fear of God from *their* youth. 19.6 By no means may you be desiring the (things) of your neighbor, by no means may you be a greedy/covetous (one). You may not be joined/associated out of your life/soul with high/exalted (ones), but you should live/conduct yourself with humble (ones) and just (ones).

You may receive the effective (things)/workings befalling/happening to you as good, knowing that nothing happens/becomes without God. 19.7 You may/should not be double-minded nor talkative, *in* submission to *the* Lord as a type of God in modesty/shame and fear; by no means might you charge upon your slave or maidservant in anger/bitterness, upon/against those hoping on the same God, lest then they might by no means fear the God over both; because he came not to call according to a face/by partiality, but to *those* whom the spirit prepared. 19.8 You will share in all (things) with your neighbor, and you will not say to be your own; for if ye are fellows in the undecayable/immortal (things), how much more in the mortal/decayable (things)? You will not be hasty in speech/talkative; for the mouth *is* a trap/snare of death. So far as to be able, be pure in behalf of your soul/life. 19.9 Be you not, on one hand, stretching forth the hands to the (thing) to take/receive, but, on on the other, closing *them* to the (thing) to give. You will love AS/LIKE AN APPLE OF YOUR EYE every one speaking to you the saying/word of *the* Lord. 19.10 You will be reminded of a day of judgment night and day, and you will seek out each day the faces of the saints, either toiling on account of a saying/word and going to/for the (thing) to exhort/comfort and having a care to/for the (thing) to save a life/soul by the saying/word, or you might work through/*with* your hands in/for a ransom of your sins/faults. 19.11 You will not hesitate to give nor grumble *about* giving; but you will know who *is* the good paymaster of the wage/

προσθὶς μήτε ἀφαιρῶν. εἰς τέλος μισήσεις πονηρόν. καὶ κρινεῖς δικαίως. 19.12 οὐ ποιήσεις σχίσμα, εἰρηνεύσεις μαχομένους συναγαγών. ἐξομολογήσει ἐν ἁμαρτίαις σου. οὐ προσήξεις ἐπὶ προσευχὴν ἐν συνειδήσει πονηρᾷ. αὕτη ἐστὶν ἡ ὁδὸς τοῦ φωτός. 20.1 ἡ δὲ τοῦ μέλανος ὁδός ἐστιν σκολιὰ καὶ κατάρας μεστή. ὁδὸς γάρ ἐστιν θανάτου αἰωνία μετὰ τιμωρίας, ἐν ᾗ ἐστιν τὰ ἀπολλύντα τὴν ψυχὴν αὐτῶν·

εἰδωλολατρεία, θρασύτης, ὕψος δυνάμεως, ὑπόκρισις, διπλοκαρδία, μοιχεία, φόνος, ἁρπαγή, ὑπερηφανία, παράβασις, δόλος, κακία, αὐθάδια, φαρμακία, ἀφοβία θεοῦ· 20.2 διῶκται τῶν ἀγαθῶν, μισοῦντες ἀλήθιαν, ἀγαπῶντες ψεύδη, οὐ γινώσκοντες μισθὸν δικαιοσύνης, οὐ κολλώμενοι ἀγαθῷ, οὐ κρίσει δικαίᾳ, χήρᾳ καὶ ὀρφανῷ οὐ προσέχοντες, ἀγρυπνοῦντες οὐκ εἰς φόβον θεοῦ, ἀλλὰ ἐπὶ τὸ πονηρόν, ὧν μακρὰν καὶ πόρρω πραΰτης καὶ ὑπομονή, ἀγαπῶντες μάταια, ὅτ' ἢ τὰ διώκοντες ἀνταπόδομα, οὐκ ἐλεῶντες πτωχόν, οὐ πονοῦντες ἐπὶ καταπονουμένῳ, εὐχερῖς ἐν καταλαλίᾳ, οὐ γινώσκοντες τὸν ποιήσαντα αὐτούς, φονῖς τέκνων, φθορῖς πλάσματος θεοῦ, ἀποστρεφόμενοι τὸν ἐνδεόμενον, καὶ καταπονοῦντες τὸν θλιβόμενον, πλουσίων παράκλητοι, πενήτων ἄνομοι κριταί, πανταμάρτητοι. 21.1 καλόν ἐστιν μαθόντα τὰ δικαιώματα τοῦ κυρίου, ὅσα γέγραπται, ἐν τούτοις περιπατεῖν. ὁ γὰρ ταῦτα ποιῶν ἐν τῇ βασιλείᾳ τοῦ θεοῦ δοξασθήσεται· ὁ ἐκεῖνα ἐκλεγόμενος μετὰ τῶν ἔργων αὐτοῦ συναπολῖται. διὰ τοῦτο ἀνάστασις, διὰ τοῦτο ἀνταπόδομα. 21.2 ἐρωτῶ τοὺς ὑπερέχοντας,

reward. YOU WILL GUARD/KEEP WHAT (THINGS) YOU RECEIV-
ED, NEITHER MIGHT YOU ADD, NOR TAKING AWAY. To *the* end
you will hate evil. And YOU WILL JUDGE JUSTLY.   19.12
You will not make divisions/splits, having assembled
them you will make peace/reconcile fighting/quarreling
(ones). You will confess in your sins. You will not
come/approach to prayer in/with an evil conscience.
This is the road/way of the light.   20.1 But the
way/road of the black (one) is crooked/perverse and
full of cursing. For it is a road/way of death, eternal with/after punishment, in which are the (things)
destroying the soul/life of them/their soul/life:

Idolatry, arrogance, high from power, pretense/
hypocrisy, double-heartedness, adultery, murder,
robbery/plunder, haughtiness/pride, transgression,
fraud, malice, willfulness, sorcery/enchantment,
fearlessness of God;   20.2 prosecutors of the good
(ones), (ones) hating truth, (ones) loving a lie,
(ones) not knowing a reward of justice/justness,
(ones) not cleaving to/associating with good, not
in/by just judgment, not heeding attending to a widow
and orphan, not watching/being alert in fear of God,
but to/for the evil, from whom gentleness and pati-
ence/endurance *are* far away and distant, (ONES) LOVING
VANITY, (ONES) PURSUING THE ACQUITTALS/RECOMPENSES,
(ones) not pitying a poor (one), (ones) not laboring
to/for the (one) being worked down, (ones) being prone
to slander/vowing by speaking against, (ones) knowing
not the (one) having made them, murderers of children,
corrupters of God's molding, (ones) turning away the
needy/entangled (one), and (ones) working down *to
exhaustion* the (one) being oppressed, intercessors/ad-
vocates of rich/wealthy (ones), lawless judges of
poor/needy (ones), (ones) steeped in sin.   21.1 It is
good *for* those having learned the just deeds/decrees
of the Lord, as many as has been written, to walk
in/by them. For the (one) doing these (things) will be
glorified/given repute in the kingdom of god;   the
(one) choosing those *other* (things) will perish together with his works. Because of this *there is* a resurrection, because of this *there is* recompense/acquit-
tal.   21.2 I ask those being in high positions, if ye

εἴ τινά μου γνώμης ἀγαθῆς λαμβάνεται συμβουλίαν· ἔχετε μεθ᾽ ἑαυτῶν εἰς οὓς ἐργάσησθε τὸ καλόν· μὴ ἐνλίπητε. 21.3 ἐγγὺς ἡ ἡμέρα ἐν ᾗ συναπολῖται πάντα τῷ πονηρῷ· ἐγγὺς ὁ κύριος καὶ ὁ μισθὸς αὐτοῦ. 21.4 ἔτι καὶ ἔτι ἐρωτῶ ὑμᾶς· ἑαυτῶν γείνεσθαι νομοθέται ἀγαθῶν, ἑαυτῶν μένετε σύμβουλοι πιστοί, ἄραται ἐξ ὑμῶν παρρησίαν ὑπόκρισιν. 21.5 ὁ δὲ θεός, ὁ τοῦ παντὸς κόσμου κυριεύων, δῴη ὑμῖν σοφίαν, σύνεσιν, ἐπιστήμην, γνῶσιν τῶν δικαιωμάτων αὐτοῦ, ὑπομονήν. 21.6 γίγνεσθε δέ, ἐκζητοῦντες τί ζητῖ κύριος ἀφ᾽ ὑμῶν, καὶ ποιεῖται ἵνα εὑρεθῆται ἐν ἡμέρᾳ κρίσεως. 21.7 εἰ δὲ τί ἐστιν ἀγαθοῦ μνία, μνημονεύεταί μου μελετῶντες ταῦτα, ἵνα καὶ ἡ ἐπιθυμία καὶ ἡ ἀγρυπνία εἴς τι ἀγαθὸν χωρήσῃ. ἐρωτῶ ὑμᾶς, χάριν αἰτούμενος. 21.8 ἕως ἔτι τὸ καλὸν σκεῦός ἐστιν μεθ᾽ ὑμῶν, μὴ ἐνλίπηται μηδενὶ ἑαυτῶν, ἀλλὰ συνεχῶς ἐκζητῖται ταῦτα καὶ ἀναπληροῦνται πᾶσαν ἐντολήν· ἔστιν γὰρ ἄξια. 21.9 διὸ μᾶλλον ἐσπούδασα γράψε ἀφ᾽ ὧν ἠδυνήθην, εἰς τὸ εὐφρᾶναι ὑμᾶς. σώζεσθαι, ἀγάπης τέκνα καὶ ἰρήνης. ὁ κύριος τῆς δόξης καὶ πάσης χάριτος μετὰ τοῦ πνεύματος ὑμῶν.

Ἐπιστολὴ Βαρνάβα

take/receive some advice/consultation from my good mind/judgment; ye have/hold with yourselves (those) in/for whom ye might work the good; may ye not fail. 21.3 The day *is* near in which every (one) in/with the evil/evil (one) will be destroyed; THE LORD AND HIS REWARD/WAGES *is* NEAR. 21.4 I ask yet and still/again and again *for* ye to become lawgivers/legislators of good (things) from yourselves, remain/abide ye faithful counselors of yourselves, take away/remove ye out of ye/yourselves outspoken pretense/bold hypocrisy. 21.5 But God, the (one) being Lord of the whole world, may he give wisdom to ye, insight, understanding, knowledge of his just deeds/decrees, patience/endurance. 21.6 And become ye (ones) seeking out/for what *the* Lord seeks/desires from ye, and/even making ye (yourselves) that ye might be found in a day of judgment. 21.7 And if there is a certain recollection of good, remember ye my having a care *for* these (things), that both the desire and the watching you might regard in/for something good. I ask ye, requesting a favor/grace. 21.8 As long as the beautiful vessel/good tool is with ye, fail ye not in anything of yourselves, but seek ye out these (things) continually and fulfill ye every command; for *they are*/it is worthy. 21.9 Wherefore I was more diligent to write from being able in/for the (thing) to gladden/cheer ye. Ye *are* saved/safe, children of agape and peace. The Lord of the glory/fame and every favor/gift/grace *be* with the spirit of ye.

An Epistle of Barnabas

This is the Sinaitic New Testament, book of The Shepherd.

ΟΡΑΣΙΣ Α΄

1.1 Ὁ θρέψας με πέπρακέν με Ῥόδῃ τινὶ εἰς Ῥώμην. μετὰ πολλὰ ἔτη ταύτην ἀνεγνωρισάμην καὶ ἠρξάμην αὐτὴν ἀγαπᾶν ὡς ἀδελφήν. 1.2 μετὰ χρόνον τινὰ λουομένην εἰς τὸν ποταμὸν τὸν Τίβεριν εἶδον καὶ ἐπέδωκα αὐτῇ τὴν χεῖρα καὶ ἐξήγαγον αὐτὴν ἐκ τοῦ ποταμοῦ. ταύτης οὖν ἰδὼν τὸ κάλλος διελογιζόμην ἐν τῇ καρδίᾳ μου λέγων· μακάριος ἤμην, εἰ τοιαύτην γυναῖκα εἶχον καὶ τῷ κάλλει καὶ τῷ τρόπῳ. μόνον τοῦτο ἐβουλευσάμην, ἕτερον δὲ οὐδὲ ἕν. 1.3 μετὰ χρόνον τινα πορευομένου οὗ μου εἰς Κώμας καὶ δοξάζοντος τὰς κτίσεις τοῦ θεοῦ, ὡς μεγάλαι καὶ ἐκπρεπεῖς καὶ δυνατοί εἰσιν, περιπατῶν ἀφύπνωσα. καὶ πνεῦμά με ἔλαβεν καὶ ἀπήνεγκέν με δι᾽ ἀνοδίας τινός, δι᾽ ἧς ἄνθρωπος οὐκ ἐδύνατο ὁδεῦσαι· ἦν δὲ ὁ τόπος κρημνώδης καὶ ἀπερρηγὼς ἀπὸ τῶν ὑδάτων. διαβὰς οὖν τὸν ποταμὸν ἐκῖνον ἦλθον εἰς τὰ ὁμαλὰ καὶ τιθῶ τὰ γόνατα καὶ ἠρξάμη προσεύχεσθαι τῷ θεῷ καὶ ἐξομολογεῖσθαί μου τὰς ἁμαρτίας. 1.4 προσευχομένου δέ μου ἠνύγη ὁ οὐρανός, καὶ βλέπω τὴν γυναῖκα ἐκίνην, ἣν ἐπεθύμησα, ἀσπαζομένην με ἐκ τοῦ οὐρανοῦ, λέγουσαν· Ἑρμᾶ χαῖρε. 1.5 βλέψας δὲ εἰς αὐτὴν λέγω αὐτῇ· κυρία, τί σὺ ὧδε ποιεῖς; ἡ δὲ ἀπεκρίθη μοι· ἀνελήμφθην, ἵνα σου τὰς ἁμαρτίας ἐλέγξω πρὸς τὸν κύριον. 1.6 λέγω αὐτῇ· νῦν σύ μου ἔλεγχος εἶ; οὔ, φησίν, ἀλλὰ ἄκουσον τὰ ῥήματα, ἅ σοι μέλλω λέγειν. ὁ θεὸς ὁ ἐν τοῖς οὐρανοῖς κατοικῶν καὶ κτίσας ἐκ τοῦ μὴ ὄντος τὰ ὄντα καὶ πληθύνας καὶ αὐξήσας ἕνεκεν τῆς ἁγίας ἐκκλησίας αὐτοῦ ὀργίζεταί σοι, ὅτι ἥμαρτες εἰς ἐμέ. 1.7 ἀποκριθεὶς αὐτῇ λέγω· εἰς σὲ ἥμαρτον; ποίῳ τόπῳ ἢ πότε σοι αἰσχρὸν ῥῆμα ἐλάλησα; οὐ πάντοτέ σε ὡς θεὰν ἡγησάμην; οὐ πάντοτέ σε ἐνετράπην ὡς ἀδελφήν; τί μου καταψεύδῃ, ὦ γύναι, τὰ πονηρὰ ταῦτα καὶ ἀκάθαρτα; 1.8 γελάσασά μοι λέγει· ἐπὶ τὴν καρδίαν σου ἀνέβη ἡ

VISION 1

1.1 The (one) having reared me has sold me as a slave to a certain Rhoda in Rome. After many years I recognized/came to know her and began to love her as a sister. 1.2 After some time I saw her bathing in the Tiber River, and I gave the hand to her and led her forth out of the river. Then, having seen the beauty of her I reasoned in my heart, saying: I was being happy if I had such a woman, both in the beauty and the manner. I willed/intended only this, and *there was* not one other/different (thing). 1.3 After some time from which of me going into Cumae and glorifying the creations of God, as/since they are greatnesses and remarkable/outstanding (things) and powers, walking *along* I fell asleep. And a spirit took me and led me away through a certain place without roads, through which a man was not able to travel; but the place was steep/precipitous and broken from the waters. Then having passed through that river, I came to the level ground/(place) and I placed the knees *down* and began to pray to God and to confess my sins. 1.4 And from me praying, the sky/heaven was opened, and I see that woman whom I desired, greeting me out of the sky/heaven, saying: Greetings/rejoice, Hermas. 1.5 And having looked to her, I say to her: Lady, what are you, you doing here? And the (lady) answered/replied to me: I was taken up in order that I shall expose/reprove your sins/faults to the Lord. 1.6 I say to her: You, are you now reproving me? No, she said, but hear the words which I am about to say to you. God, the (one) dwelling in the skies/heavens and having created the (things) being from/out of the (thing) not being and having multiplied and increased for the sake of his holy assembly, is angry with you, because you sinned to/against me. 1.7 Answering, I say to her: I sinned/did I sin to/against you? At/in what place or when spoke I a shameful word to you? Did I not always consider/esteem you as a goddess? Did not I always regard/revere you as a sister? Why *do* you lie against me, O lady, these wicked and unclean things? 1.8 Having laughed, she says to me: The desire of the evil

ἐπιθυμία τῆς πονηρίας. ἢ οὐ δοκεῖ σοι ἀνδρὶ δικαίῳ πονηρὸν πρᾶγμα εἶναι, ἐὰν ἀναβῇ αὐτοῦ ἐπὶ τὴν καρδίαν ἡ πονηρὰ ἐπιθυμία; ἁμαρτία γέ ἐστιν, καὶ μεγάλη, φησίν. ὁ γὰρ δίκαιος ἀνὴρ δίκαια βουλεύεται. ἐν τῷ οὖν δίκαια βουλεύεσθαι αὐτὸν κατορθοῦται ἡ δόξα αὐτοῦ ἐν τοῖς οὐρανοῖς καὶ εὐκατάλλακτον ἔχι τὸν κύριον ἐν παντὶ πράγματι αὐτοῦ· οἱ δὲ πονηρὰ βουλευόμενοι ἐν ταῖς καρδίαις αὐτῶν θάνατον καὶ αἰχμαλωτισμὸν ἑαυτοῖς ἐπισπῶνται, μάλιστα οἱ τὸν αἰῶνα τοῦτον περιποιούμενοι καὶ γαυριῶντες ἐν τῷ πλούτῳ αὐτῶν καὶ μὴ ἀντεχόμενοι τῶν ἀγαθῶν τῶν μελλόντων. 1.9 μετανοήσουσιν αἱ ψυχαὶ αὐτῶν, οἵτινες οὐκ ἔχουσιν ἐλπίδα, ἀλλὰ ἑαυτοὺς ἀπεγνώκασιν καὶ τὴν ζωὴν αὐτῶν. ἀλλὰ σὺ προσεύχου πρὸς τὸν θεόν, καὶ ἰάσεται τὰ ἁμαρτήματά σου καὶ ὅλου τοῦ οἴκου σου καὶ πάντων τῶν ἁγίων.

2.1 Μετὰ τὸ λαλῆσαι αὐτὴν τὰ ῥήματα ταῦτα ἐκλείσθησαν οἱ οὐρανοί· κἀγὼ ὅλος ἤμην πεφρικὼς καὶ λυπούμενος. ἔλεγον δὲ ἐν ἐμαυτῷ· ἡ αὕτη μοι ἡ ἁμαρτία ἀναγράφεται, πῶς δυνήσομαι σωθῆναι; ἢ πῶς ἐξιλάσομαι τὸν θεὸν περὶ τῶν ἁμαρτιῶν μου τῶν τελείων; ἢ ποίοις ῥήμασιν ἐρωτήσω τὸν κύριον, ἵνα ἱλατεύσητέ μοι; 2.2 ταῦτά μου συμβουλευομένου καὶ διακρίνοντος ἐν τῇ καρδίᾳ μου, βλέπω κατέναντί μου καθέδραν λευκὴν ἐξ ἐρίων χιονίνων γεγονυῖαν μεγάλην· καὶ ἦλθεν γυνὴ πρεσβύτεις ἐν ἱμαρισμῷ λαμπροτάτῳ, ἔχουσα βιβλίον εἰς τὰς χῖρας, καὶ ἐκάσθισεν μόνη καὶ ἀσπάζεταί μαι. Ἑρμᾶ, χέραι. κἀγὼ λυπούμενος καὶ κλαίων εἶπον· κυρία, χαῖρε. 2.3 καὶ εἶπέν μοι· τί στυγνός, Ἑρμᾶ; ὁ μακρόθυμος ὁ ἀστομάχητος, ὁ πάντοτε γελῶν, τὶ οὕτω κατηφὴς τῇ ἰδέᾳ καὶ οὐχ ἱλαρός; κἀγὼ εἶπον αὐτῇ· ὑπὸ γυναικὸς ἀγαθωτάτης λεγούσης, ὅτι ἥμαρτον εἰς αὐτήν. 2.4 ἡ δὲ ἔφη· μηδαμῶς ἐπὶ τὸν δοῦλον τοῦ θεοῦ τὸ πρᾶγμα τοῦτο. ἀλλὰ

came up upon your heart. Or does it seem not to you to be an evil deed/thing for a just man, if the evil desire might come up upon his heart? It is indeed a sin and a great (one), she said. For the just man gives just counsel. Therefore, in/by the (thing) *for* him to counsel/plan justness, his fame/glory/repute is made worthy/set upright in the skies/heavens, and the Lord has/holds favor/acceptance in every deed/thing of him. But those purposing/planning evil (things) in their hearts draw death and captivity to/for themselves, especially those acquiring/preserving this age for themselves both priding themselves/taking pride in their wealth and not holding firmly/taking interest in the good (things) about to come. 1.9 The souls of them will repent, seeing that/since they have not hope, but they have hanged/abandoned themselves and the life of them. But you, you pray to God, AND HE WILL HEAL YOUR SINFUL DEEDS, both of your whole house and of all the saints.

2.1   After the (thing) *for* her to speak these words, the skies/heavens were closed, and I, I was wholly shuddering and being grieved. And I was saying in myself: This sin is recorded/registered to me, how shall I be able to be saved? Or how shall I atone *for* God concerning my completed sins? Or with what words might I ask/entreat the Lord, in order that he might atone/make pardon for me? 2.2 From me reasoning/consulting and doubting these (things) in my heart, I see before me a white seat/chair having become great out of snow white wools; and a woman being old came, in a shining/bright garment, holding a scroll in the/*her* hands, and she sat alone and greets me: Rejoice/greetings, Hermas. And I, being grieved and weeping, I said: Greetings, Lady.   2.3 And she said to me: Why *are you* gloomy/downcast, Hermas? The (one) having been patient, the (one) having been peaceable, the (one) always laughing, why *are you* dejected/downcast in form/aspect and not cheerful? And I, I said to her: By a most good woman saying that I sinned to/against her. 2.4 And the (she) was saying: By no means *be* this deed/matter upon the slave of God. But certainly *it*

πάντως ἐπὶ τὴν καρδίαν σου ἀνέβη περὶ αὐτῆς. ἔστιν μὲν τοῖς δούλοις τοῦ θεοῦ ἡ τοιαύτη βουλὴ ἁμαρτίαν ἐπιφέρουσα· πονηρὰ γὰρ βουλὴ καὶ ἔκπληκτος εἰς πάνσεμνον πνεῦμα καὶ ἤδη δεδοκιμασμένον, ἐὰν ἐπιθυμήσῃ πονηρὸν ἔργον, καὶ μάλιστα Ἑρμᾶς ὁ ἐγκρατής, ὁ ἀπεχόμενος πάσης ἐπιθυμίας πονηρᾶς καὶ πλήρης πάσης ἁπλότητος καὶ ἀκακίας μεγάλης. 3.1 ἀλλ᾽ οὐχ ἵνεκα τούτου ὀργείζεταί σοι ὁ θεός, ἀλλ᾽ ἵνα τὸν οἶκόν σου τὸν ἀνομήσαντα εἰς τὸν κύριον καὶ εἰς ὑμᾶς τοὺς γονεῖς αὐτῶν ἐπιστρέψῃς. ἀλλὰ φιλότεκνος ὢν οὐκ ἐνουθέτις σου τὸν οἶκον, ἀλλὰ ἀφῆκες αὐτὸν καταφθαρῆναι, διὰ τοῦτό σοι ὀργείζεται ὁ κύριος· ἀλλὰ ἰάσεταί σου πάντα τὰ προγεγονότα πονηρὰ ἐν τῷ οἴκῳ σου· διὰ γὰρ τὰς ἐκείνων ἁμαρτίας καὶ ἀνομήματα σὺ κατεφθάρης ἀπὸ τῶν βιωτικῶν πράξεων. 3.2 ἀλλ᾽ ἡ πολυσπλαγχία τοῦ κυρίου ἠλέησέν σε καὶ τὸν οἶκόν σου καὶ ἰσχυραποιῆσί σαι καὶ θεμελιῶσί σαι ἐν τῇ δόξῃ αὐτοῦ. σὺ μόνον μὴ ῥαθυμήσῃς, ἀλλὰ εὐψύχει καὶ εἰσχυροποίει σου τὸν οἶκον. ὡς γὰρ ὁ χαλκεὺς σφυροκοπῶν τὸ ἔργο αὐτοῦ περιγίνετε τοῦ πράγματος οὗ θέλι, οὕτω καὶ ὁ λόγος ὁ καθημερινὸς ὁ δίκαιος περιγείνεται πάσης πονηρίας. μὴ διαλίπῃς οὖν νουθετῶν σου τὰ τέκνα. οἶδα γάρ, ὅτι, ἐὰν μετανοήσουσιν ἐξ ὅλης καρδίας αὐτῶν, ἐνγραφήσονται εἰς τὰς βίβλους τῆς ζωῆς μετὰ τῶν ἁγίων. 3.3 μετὰ τὸ παῆναι αὐτῆς τὰ ῥήματα ταῦτα λέγει μοι· θέλις ἀκοῦσε μου ἀναγεινωσκούσης; λέγω κἀγώ· θέλω, κυρία. λέγει μοι· γενοῦ ἀκροατὴς καὶ ἄκουε τὰς δόξας τοῦ θεοῦ. ἤκουσα μελάλως καὶ θαυμαστῶς, ὃ οὐκ ἴσχυσα μνημονεῦσαι· πάντα γὰρ τὰ ῥήματα ἔκφρικτα, ἃ οὐ δύνατε ἄνθρωπος βαστάσαι. τὰ οὖν ἔσχατα ῥήματα ἐμνημόνευσα· ἦν γὰρ ἡμῖν σύμφορα καὶ ἥμερα· 3.4 ἰδού, ὁ θεὸς τῶν δυνάμαιων, ὃν ἀγαπῶ, δυνάμει κραταιᾷ καὶ τῇ

came to/upon your heart concerning her. It is indeed the such purpose/will bringing a sin/fault to/upon the slaves of God; for *it is* an evil and frightful/shocking purpose/will to/for a revered spirit, also having been proven/tested already, if (one) might desire an evil work, and especially *for* Hermas, the self-controlled/temperate (one), the (one) abstaining/holding away from every evil desire, and *being* full of every sincerity/generosity and of great innocence.

3. 1 But God is not angry with you on account of this, but in order that you might turn around your household, the (one) having been lawless to the Lord and to ye their parents. But being a child lover, you rebuke/correct not your household, but you allowed it to be corrupt/unclean. Because of this the Lord is angry with you; but he will heal for you all the previous evil happenings in your household; for through the sins and lawless (things) of those you, you were corrupted from practicing the (things) of daily life. 3. 2 But the great compassion of the Lord pitied you and your household and will make you strong and will found/establish you in/by the fame/glory of him. You, only you may not be unconcerned, but be courageous and strengthen your household. For as the coppersmith hammering his work becomes master of the thing/work which he wants, so also the just logos/reason/word repeated daily overcomes/becomes master of every evil (thing). Therefore, *do* not leave/cease from admonishing/correcting your children. For I know that if they might repent from their whole heart, they will be recorded/registered in the scrolls of the life with the saints. 3. 3 After the (thing) *for* her to cease these words, she says to me: Do you want to hear my reading? And I, I say: I want *to,* Lady. She says to me: Become a listener and hear the fame/glory of God. I heard greatly and wonderfully, which I was not able to remember; for all the words were frightful, which a man/human is not able to bear. I remembered, then the last words, for they were agreeable/beneficial and mild to us. 3. 4 Behold, the God of the powers, whom I love, by power, dominion/might and his great insight/

μεγάλῃ συνέσει αὐτοῦ κτίσας τὸν κόσμον καὶ τῇ ἐνδόξῳ βουλῇ περιθεὶς τὴν εὐπρέπιαν τῇ κτίσι αὐτοῦ καὶ τῷ ἰσχυρῷ ῥήματι πήξας τὸν οὐρανὸν καὶ θεμελιώσας τὴν γῆν ἐπὶ ὑδάτων καὶ τῇ ἰδίᾳ σοφίᾳ καὶ προνοίᾳ κτίσας τὴν ἁγίαν ἐκκλησίαν αὐτοῦ, ἣν καὶ ηὐλόγησεν, ἰδού, μεθιστάνι τοὺς οὐρανούς, καὶ τὰ ὄρη καὶ τοὺς βουνοὺς καὶ τὰς θαλάσσας, καὶ πάντα ὁμαλὰ γείνεται τοῖς ἐκλεκτοῖς αὐτοῦ, ἵνα ἀποδῷ αὐτοῖς τὴν ἐπαγγελίαν, ἣν ἐπηγγείλατο μετὰ πολλῆς δόξης καὶ χαρᾶς, ἐὰν τηρήσωσιν τὰ νόμιμα τοῦ θεοῦ, ἃ παρέλαβον ἐν μεγάλῃ πίστει. 4.1 ὅτε οὖν ἐτέλεσεν ἀναγινώσκουσα καὶ ἠγέρθη ἀπὸ τῆς καθέδρας, ἦλθαν τέσσαρες νεανίαι καὶ ἦραν τὴν καθέδραν καὶ ἀπῆλθον πρὸς τὴν ἀνατολήν. 4.2 προσκαλεῖται δέ μαι καὶ ἥψατο τοῦ στήθους μου καὶ λέγι μοι· ἤρεσέν σοι ἡ ἀνάγνωσίς μου; καὶ λέγω αὐτῇ κυρία, ταῦτά μοι τὰ ἔσχατα ἀρέσκι, τὰ δὲ πρότερα καλεπὰ καὶ σκληρά. ἡ δὲ ἔφη μοι λέγουσα· ταῦτα τὰ ἔσχατα τοῖς δικαίοις, τὰ δὲ πρῶτα τοῖς ἔθνεσιν καὶ τοῖς ἀποστάταις.

4.3 λαλούσης αὐτῆς μετ᾽ ἐμοῦ δύο τινὲς ἄνδραις ἐφάνησαν καὶ ἦραν αὐτὴν τῶν ἀγκώνων καὶ ἀπῆλθαν, ὅπου ἡ καθέδρα, πρὸς τὴν ἀνατολήν. ἱλαρὰ δὲ ἀπῆλθεν καὶ ὑπάγουσα λέγει· ἀνδρίζου, Ἑρμᾶ.

ΟΡΑΣΙΣ Β΄

1.1 Πορευομένου μου εἰς Κώμας κατὰ τὸν καιρόν, ὃν καὶ πέρυσι, περιματῶν ἀνεμνήσθην τῆς περυσινῆς ὁράσεως, καὶ πάλιν με ἔρι πνεῦμα καὶ ἀποφέρει εἰς τὸν αὐτὸν τόπον, ὅπου καὶ πέρυσι. 1.2 ἐλθὼν οὖν εἰς τὸν τόπον τιθῶ τὰ γόνατα καὶ ἠρξάμην προσεύχεσθε τῷ κυρίῳ καὶ δοξάζειν αὐτοῦ τὸ ὄνομα, ὅτι με ἄξιον ἡγήσατο καὶ ἐγνώρισέν μοι τὰς ἁμαρτίας μου τὰς πρότερον.

1.3 μετὰ δὲ τὸ ἐγερθῆνε με ἀπὸ τῆς προσευχῆς βλέπω

understanding having created the world, and for the honorable purpose having placed the beauty around his creation, and by the strong word having fixed the sky/heaven and founded the land/earth upon waters, and having created his holy assembly by his own wisdom and forethought/innate knowledge, which he also blessed. Behold, he removes/changes the skies/heavens and the mountains and the hills and the seas, and all (things/places) are becoming level for his chosen (ones), in order that he might give back/discharge to them the promise which he himself promised with much glory/fame and joy, if they might observe/keep the laws of God, which they received in great faith. 4.1 Then, when she finished reading and was raised from the seat/chair, four youths came and took up the seat and went away toward the east. 4.2 And she summoned me and touched of my chest and she says to me: Was my reading pleasing to you? And I say to her: Lady, these last things are pleasing to me, but the former things *are* violent/difficult and severe/hard. And the (she) was speaking to me, saying: These last things *are* for the just (ones), but the first things *are* for the ethnics and the apostates/withdrawn (ones).

4.3 From her speaking with me two certain men appeared and took her up from the arms and went away, where the seat *went*, toward the east. But she went away cheerfully and, departing, she says: *You* be a man, Hermas.

VISION 2

1.1 From my going to Cumae according to the season which also *I was* last year, walking *along* I was reminded of the vision of last year, and a spirit takes me up and carries *me* away to the same place where also *I went* last year. 1.2 Then, having come into the place, I put *down* the knees and began to pray to the Lord and to glorify his name, because he considered me worthy and made known to me my former sins/faults.

1.3 But after the (thing) *for* me to be raised

ἀπέναντί μου τὴν πρεσβυτέραν, ἣν καὶ πρότερον ἑωράκειν, περιπατοῦσαν καὶ ἀναγεινώσκουσαν βιβλαρίδιον, καὶ λέγει μοι· δύνῃ ταῦτα τοῖς ἐκλεκτοῖς τοῦ θεοῦ ἀναγγεῖλαι; λέγω αὐτῇ· κυρία, τοσαῦτα μνὴ μνημονεύσαι οὐ δύναμαι· δὸς δέ μοι τὸ βιβλίδιον, εἵνα μεταγράψωμαι αὐτό. λάβε, φησίν, καὶ ἀποδώσις μοι. 1.4 ἔλαβον ἐγώ, καὶ εἴς τινα τόπον τοῦ ἀγροῦ ἀναχωρήσας μετεγραψάμην πάντα πρὸς γράμμα· οὐχ ηὕρισκον γὰρ τὰς συλλαβάς. τελέσαντος οὖν τὰ γράμματα τοῦ βιβλιδίου ἐξαίφνης ἡρπάγη μου ἐκ τῆς χιρὸς τὸ βιβλίδιον· ὑπὸ τίνος δὲ οὐκ ἶδον. 2.1 μετὰ δὲ δέκα καὶ πέντε ἡμέρας νηστεύσαντός μου καὶ πολλὰ ἐρωτήσαντος τὸν κύριον ἀπεκαλύφθη μοι ἡ γυῶσεις τῆς γραφῆς. ἦν δὲ γεγραμμένα ταῦτα· 2.2 τὸ σπέρμα σου, Ἑρμᾶ, ἠθέτησαν εἰς τὸν θεὸν καὶ ἐβλασφήμησαν εἰς τὸν κύριον καὶ προέδωκαν τοὺς γονεῖς αὐτῶν ἐν πονηρίᾳ μεγάλῃ καὶ ἤκουσαν προδόται γονέων καὶ προδόντες οὐκ ὠφελήθησαν, ἀλλὰ ἔτι προσέθηκαν ταῖς ἁμαρτίαις αὐτῶν τὰς ἀσελγίας καὶ συνφυρμοὺς πονηρίας, καὶ οὕτως ἐπλήσθησαν αἱ ἀνομίαι αὐτῶν. 2.3 ἀλλὰ γνώρισον ταῦτα τὰ ῥήματα τοῖς τέκνοις σου πᾶσιν καὶ τῇ συμβίῳ σου τῇ μελλούσῃ ἀδελφῇ· καὶ γὰρ αὕτη οὐκ ἀπέχεται τῆς γλώσσης, ἐν ᾗ πονηρεύεται· ἀλλὰ ἀκούσασα τὰ ῥήματα ταῦτα ἀφέξετε καὶ ἕξεις ἔλεος. 2.4 μετὰ τὸ γνωρίσε σαι ταῦτα τὰ ῥήματα αὐτοῖς, ἃ ἐνετίλατό μοι ὁ δεσπότης ἵνα σοι ἀποκαλυφθῇ, τότε ἀφίενται αὐτοῖς αἱ ἁμαρτίαι πᾶσαι, ἃς πρότερον ἥμαρτον, καὶ πᾶσιν τοῖς ἁγίοις τοῖς ἁμαρτήσασιν μέχρι ταύτης τῆς ἡμέρας, ἐὰν ἐξ ὅλης τῆς καρδίας μετανοήσουσιν καὶ ἄρωσιν ἀπὸ τῆς καρδίας αὐτῶν τὰς διψυχίας. 2.5 ὤμοσεν γὰρ ὁ δεσπότης κατὰ τῆς δόξης αὐτοῦ ἐπὶ τοὺς ἐκλεκτοὺς αὐτοῦ· ἐὰν ὡρισμένης τῆς ἡμέρας ταύτης ἐπὶ ἁμαρτήσεις γένηται, μὴ ἔχειν αὐτοὺς σωτηρίαν· ἡ γὰρ μετάνοια τοῖς δικαίοις ἔχι τέλος· πεπλήρωνται αἱ ἡμέραι μεγανοίας πᾶσιν

from the prayer, I see the elder/aged (woman) before me, *the one* which I had also seen formerly, walking and reading a little scroll, and she says to me: Are you able to announce/report these (things) to the chosen (ones) of God? I say to her: Lady, I am not able to remember so much; but give you the little scroll to me, that I may copy it. Take *it* she said, and give it back to me. 1.4 I, I took *it* and having withdrawn to a certain place of the field I copied all to a letter; for I was not finding the syllables. Then, having finished/completed the letters/writing of the little scroll, the little scroll was snatched suddenly out of my hand; but I saw not by whom. 2.1 But after fifteen days of my having fasted and having questioned/beseeched the Lord many (times), the know-ledge of the writing was revealed to me. And these (things) were having been written: 2.2 The seed/off-spring of you, Hermas, have set aside/made void to God and they slandered/blasphemed to the Lord and repaid/gave back to their parents in/with great evilness and they heard/listened to betrayers of parents and having betrayed they were not profited, but they have yet added the wanton/revelous (things) and wicked immoral-ities/sexual mingling to their sins, and thus their lawlessnesses/lawless deeds were multiplied. 2.3 But you make known these words to all your children and to your fellow-liver/(female) companion, the (one) about to become a sister; for she also holds not away/back the tongue by which she does evil; but having heard these words she will leave/relax *it* and you will have mercy. 2.4 After the (thing) *for* you to make known these words to them, which the master commanded to me in order that I might reveal *them* to you, then all the sins/faults are forgiven for them, which they formerly sinned, and/also for all the saints having sinned until this day, if they might repent from the whole heart and might remove the double-minds from the heart of them. 2.5 For the master swore to his chosen (ones) by/according to his reputation/fame/glory; If, from having appointed this day, you shall sin against *it*, it becomes not *for* them to have salvation; for the repentance for the just (ones) has an end; the days of

τοῖς ἁγίοις· καὶ τοῖς δὲ ἔθνεσιν μετάνοιά ἐστιν ἕως ἐσχάτης ἡμέρας. 2.6 ἐρεῖς οὖν τοῖς προηγουμένοις τῆς ἐκκλησίας, ἵνα κατορθώσωνται τὰς ὁδοὺς αὐτῶν ἐν δικαιοσύνῃ, ἵνα ἀπολάβωσιν ἐκ πλήρους τὰς ἐπαγγελίας μετὰ πολλῆς δόξης. 2.7 ἐνμίνατε οὖν οἱ ἐργαζόμενοι τὴν δικαιοσύνην καὶ μὴ διψυχήσητε, εἴνα γένηται ὑμῶν ἡ πάροδος μετὰ τῶν ἀγγέλων τῶν ἁγίων. μακάριοι ὑμῖς, ὅσοι ὑπομένεται τὴν θλῖψιν τὴν ἐρχομένην τὴν μεγάλην καὶ ὅσοι οὐκ ἀρνήσονται τὴν ζωὴν αὐτῶν. 2.8 ὤμοσεν γὰρ κύριος κατὰ τοῦ υἱοῦ αὐτοῦ, τοὺς ἀρνησαμένους τὸν χριστὸν αὐτῶν ἀπεγνωρίσθαι ἀπὸ τῆς ζωῆς αὐτῶν, τοὺς νῦν μέλλοντας ἀρνῖσθαι ταῖς ἐρχομέναις ἡμέραις· τοῖς δὲ πρότερον ἀρνησαμένοις, διὰ τὴν πολυσπλαγχνίαν ἵλεως ἐγένετο αὐτοῖς. 3.1 σὺ δέ, Ἑρμᾶ, μηκέτι μνησικακήσῃς τοῖς τέκνοις σου μηδὲ τὴν ἀδελφήν σου ἐάσῃς, ἵνα καθαρισθῶσιν ἀπὸ τῶν προτέρων ἁμαρτιῶν αὐτῶν. παιδευθήσοντε γὰρ παιδείᾳ δικαίᾳ, ἐὰν σὺ μὴ μνησικακήσῃς αὐτοῖς. ἡ μνησικακία θάνατον κατεργάζεται. σὺ δέ, Ἑρμᾶ, μεγάλας θλίψεις ἔσχες ἰδιωτικὰς διὰ τὰς παραβάσις τοῦ οἴκου σου, ὅτι οὐκ αἰμέλησέν σοι περὶ αὐτῶν· ἀλλὰ παρενεθυμήθης καὶ ταῖς πραγματείαις σου συνανεφύρης ταῖς πονηραῖς· 3.2 ἀλλὰ σώζι σε τὸ μὴ ἀποστῆναί σε ἀπὸ θεοῦ ζῶντος καὶ ἡ ἁπλότης σου καὶ ἡ πολλὴ ἐγκράτια· ταῦτα σέσωκέν σαι, ἐὰν ἐνμίνῃς, καὶ πάντας σώζεις τοὺς τὰ τοιαῦτα ἐργαζομένους καὶ πορευομένους ἐν ἀκακίᾳ καὶ ἁπλότητι. οὗτοι κατισχύσουσιν πάσης πονηρίας καὶ παραμενοῦσιν εἰς ζωὴν αἰώνιον. 3.3 μακάριοι πάντες οἱ ἐργαζόμενοι τὴν δικαιοσύνην. οὐ διαφθαρήσονται ἕως αἰῶνος.

repentance have been fulfilled/filled up for all the saints; but also for the ethnics repentance is until a last day. 2.6 Therefore you will say to the leaders of the assembly that they should set straight their ways in justice/justness, in order that they might receive the promises out of full (things) with much glory/fame. 2.7 Therefore ye persevere/continue, the (ones) working the justice/justness, and ye may not be double-minded, in order that the passing of ye may become with the messengers/angels, the holy (ones). Ye *are* happy (ones), as many as endure the oppression/ tribulation, the great (one) coming, and as many as will deny not their soul/life. 2.8 For the Lord swore by/down from his son *for* those having denied their anointed (one) to be unknown from the life of them, *for* those now being about to deny *him* in the coming days; but to the (ones) formerly having denied, mercy/favor happened/became for them   through the great compassion. 3.1 But you, Hermas, you may no longer remember/bear a grudge against your children nor may you allow your sister *to*, in order that they might be cleansed from their former sins/faults. For they will be trained/corrected in/with just disci- pline/correction/training, if you, you will not remember evil against them. The remembrance of evil/ grudgebearing works out death. But you, Hermas, you had great afflictions of your own because of the transgressions of your household, because it was not a care to you concerning them. But you also involved/ busied yourself in/with your evil affairs/ matters/(things); 3.2 but the (thing) *for* you not to draw back/withdraw from a living God, both your simplicity/sincerity and your great/much self-control/ temperance; these (things) have saved you, if you might continue in/abide by *them*, and they will save all the (ones) working such things and going/ journeying in innocence/lack of evil intent and simplicity/sincerity. These will overpower/predomi- nate over every evil (thing) and will continue/abide in eternal life. 3.3 Happy (ones) *are* all the (ones) working the justice/justness. They will not decay/rot until/as long as eternity/an age.

3.4 ἐρῖς δὲ Μαξίμῳ· εἰδοῦ, θλῖψις ἔρχεται· ἐάν σοι φανῇ, πάλιν ἄρνησαι. ἐγγὺς κύριος τοῖς ἐπιστρεφομένοις, ὡς γέγραπται ἐν τῷ Ἑλδὰδ καὶ Μωδάτ, τοῖς προφητεύσασιν ἐν τῇ ἐρήμῳ τῷ λαῷ.

4.1 Ἀπεκαλύφθη δέ μοι, ἀδελφοί, κοιμωμένῳ ὑπὸ νεανίσκου εὐειδεστάτου λέγοντός μοι· τὴν πρεσβυτέραν, παρ᾿ ἧς ἔλαβες τὸ βιβλίδιον, τίνα δοκῖς εἶναι; ἐγὼ φησίν· τὴν Σίβυλλαν. πλανᾶσαι, φησίν, οὐκ ἔστιν. τὶς οὖν ἐστιν; φημί. ἡ ἐκκλησία, φησίν. εἶπον αὐτῷ· διατὶ οὖν πρεσβυτέρα; ὅτι φησίν, πάντων πρώτη ἐκτίσθη· διὰ τοῦτο πρεσβυτέρα· καὶ διὰ ταύτην ὁ κόσμος κατηρτίσθη.

4.2 μετέπειτα δὲ ὅρασιν εἶδον ἐν τῷ οἴκῳ μου. ἦλθεν ἡ πρεσβυτέρα καὶ πρώτησέν με, εἰ ἤδη τὸ βιβλίον δέδωκα τοῖς πρεσβυτέροις. ἠρνησάμην δεδωκέναι. καλῶς, φησίν, πεποίηκας· ἔχω γὰρ ῥήματα προσθῖναι. ὅταν οὖν ἀποτελέσω τὰ ῥήματα πάντα, διὰ σοῦ γνωρισθήσεται τοῖς ἐκλεκτοῖς πᾶσιν. 4.3 γράψεις οὖν δύο βιβλαρίδια καὶ μέμψεις ἐν Κλήμεντι καὶ ἐν Γραπτῇ. πέμψι οὖν Κλήμης εἰς τὰς ἔξω πόλις, ἐκίνῳ γὰρ ἐπιτέτρεπται· Γραπτὴ δὲ νουθετήσει τὰς χήρας καὶ τοὺς ὀρφανούς. σὺ δὲ ἀναγνώσῃ εἰς ταύτην τὴν πόλιν μετὰ τῶν πρεσβυτέρων τῶν προϊσταμένων τῆς ἐκκλησίας.

ΟΡΑΣΙΣ Γ΄

1.1 Ἣν εἶδον, ἀδελφοί, τοιαύτη. 1.2 νηστεύσας πολλάκις καὶ δεηθεὶς τοῦ κυρίου, εἵνα μοι φανερώσῃ τὴν ἀποκάλυψιν, ἥν μοι ἐπηγγείλατο δῖξε διὰ τῆς πρεσβυτέρας,

αὐτῇ τῇ νυκτί μοι ὦπται ἡ πρεσβυτέρα καὶ εἶπέν μοι· ἐπὶ οὕτως ἐνδεὴς εἶ καὶ σπουδαῖος ἱς τὸ γνῶνε πάντα, ἐλθὲ εἰς τὸν ἀγρόν, ὅπου χονδρίζεις, καὶ περὶ ὥραν πένπτην ἐμφανισθήσομέ

591

3.4 But you will say to Maximus: Behold, an affliction/oppression comes; if it might appear to you to refuse/deny again. *The* Lord *is* near to the (ones)/those turning to *him*, as it has been written in the *writing* Eldad and Modat, by those having prophesied to the people in the desert/wilderness.

4.1 And it was revealed to me, brothers, in sleeping, by a good-looking youth, saying to me: The elder/old lady from whom you received the little scroll, who/what seems she to be? I, I say: The Sibyl. You are deceived, he says, she is not. Then who is she? I say. The assembly/(church), he says. I said to him: Then why elderly/an old (woman)? Because, he says, she was created before all (things); because of this (she) *is* older/elderly; and the world was fitted/mended through/because of her.
4.2 And afterwards I saw a vision in my house. The aged/old (lady) came and asked me if I had already given the scroll to the elders. I denied to have given *it*. She says: You have done well, for I have words to add. Therefore, whenever I shall complete all the words, it will be made known to all the chosen (ones) through you. 4.3 Therefore you will write two little scrolls and send one to Clement and one to Grapte. Then Clement will send *it* to the outside cities, for it has been entrusted to that (one); and Grapte will admonish/warn the widows and the orphans. But you, you will read *it* in this city with the elders managing/having been set before the assembly.

VISION 3

1.1 What/(that) which I saw, brothers, *is* such: 1.2 Having often fasted and entreated of the Lord that he might make plain for me the revelation which he himself promised to show to me through the old lady,

in this night the old lady appears to me and said to me: Since you are so indigent/needy and zealous/eager in/for the (thing) to know all (things), go into the field where you make groats, and around *the* fifth hour I shall appear to you and show to you what

591

σοι καὶ δίξω σοι, ἃ δεῖ σε εἰδῖν. 1.3 πρώτησα αὐτὴν λέγων· κυρία, εἰς ποῖον τόπον τοῦ ἀγροῦ; ὅπου, θησίν, θέλεις. ἐξελεξάμην τόπον καλὸν ἀνακεχωρηκότα. πρὶν δὲ λαλῆσαι αὐτῇ καὶ εἰπεῖν τὸν τόπον, λέγει μοι· ἥξω ἐκῖ, ὅπου θέλεις. 1.4 ἐγενόμην οὖν, ἀδελφοί, εἰς τὸν ἀγρὸν καὶ συνεψήφισα τὰς ὥρας καὶ ἦλθον εἰς τὸν τόπον, ὅπου διεταξάμην αὐτῇ ἐλθεῖν, καὶ βλέπω συμψέλιον κίμενον ἐλεφάντινον, καὶ ἐπὶ τοῦ συμψελίου ἔκιτο κερβικάριον λινοῦν καὶ ἐπάνω λέντιον ἐξηπλωμένον λινοῦν καρπάσιον. 1.5 ἰδὼν ταῦτα κίμενα καὶ μηδένα ὄντα ἐν τῷ τόπῳ ἔκθαμβος ἐγενόμην, καὶ ὡσεὶ τρόμος με ἔλαβεν καὶ αἱ τρίχες μου ὀρθαί· καὶ ὡσεὶ φρίκη μοι προσῆλθεν μόνου μου ὄντος. ἐν ἐμαυτῷ οὖν γενόμενος καὶ μνησθεὶς τῆς δόξης τοῦ θεοῦ καὶ λαβὼν θάρσος, θεὶς τὰ γόνατα ἐξωμολογούμην τῷ κυρίῳ πάλιν τὰς ἁμαρτίας μου. 1.6 -- καὶ ἁψαμένη μου λέγει· Ἑρμᾶ, παῦσε περὶ τῶν ἁμαρτιῶν σου πάντα αἰρωτῶν· ἐρώτα καὶ περὶ δικαιοσύνης, ἵνα λάβῃς μέρος τι ἐξ αὐτῆς τὸν οἶκόν σου. 1.7 καὶ ἐξεγείρει με τῆς χιρὸς καὶ ἄγι με πρὸς τὸ συμψέλιον καὶ λέγει τοῖς νεανίσκοις· ὑπάγεται καὶ οἰκοδομῖται. 1.8 καὶ μετὰ τὸ ἀναχωρῆσαι τοὺς νιανίσκους καὶ μόνων ἡμῶν γεγονότων λέγει μοι· κάθισον ὧδε. λέγω αὐτῇ· κυρία, ἄφες τοὺς πρεσβυτέρους πρῶτον καθίσαι. ὅ σοι λέγω, φησίν, κάθισον. 1.9 θέλοντος οὖν μου καθίσαι εἰς τὰ δεξιὰ μέρη οὐκ εἴασέν με, -- εἰς τὰ δεξιὰ μέρη καθίσαι, λέγι μοι· λυπῇ, Ἑρμᾶ; ὁ εἰς τὰ δεξιὰ μέρη τόπος ἄλλων ἐστίν, τῶν ἤδη εὐαρεστηκότων τῷ θεῷ καὶ παθόντων εἵνεκά μου τοῦ ὀνόματος· σοὶ δὲ πολλὰ λίπει εἵνα μετ' αὐτῶν καθίσῃς· ἀλλὰ ὡς μένις τῇ ἁπλότητί σου, μῖνον, καὶ καθιῇ μετ' αὐτῶν καὶ ὅσοι ἐὰν ἐργάσωνται τὰ ἐκίνων ἔργα καὶ ὑπενέγκωσιν, ἃ καὶ ἐκῖνοι ὑπήνεγκαν. 2.1 τί, φημί, ὑπήνεκκαν; ἄκουε, φησίν· μάστιγας, φυλακάς, θλίψεις μεγάλας, σταυρούς,

(things) it is necessary *for* you to see. 1.3 I asked her, saying: Lady, in what place of the field? She says: Where you wish/want. I chose/picked out a beautiful, secluded place. But before *for me* to speak to her and to say the place, she says to me: I shall be there, where you wish/want. 1.4 Then I became/am, brothers, in the field, and I counted/kept track of the hours and I went to the place where I arranged for her to come, and I see a bench made of ivory being set down/placed *there*, and a linen pillow was being placed on the bench and over/above a linen *cover*, a fine linen cloth being spread out. 1.5 Having seen these (things) being placed but no one being in the place I became astonished utterly, and as a trembling took me my hairs also stood erect; and (something) like a shudder came to me, from me being alone. Then having become in myself and recalling/remembering the fame/glory of God and having taken courage, having put down the knees, I again confessed all my sins/faults to the Lord. -- 1.6 -- And having touched me, she says: Hermas, *you are* to cease asking about all your sins/faults; ask also about justness, in order that you might receive some part out of her/it in/for your household. 1.7 And she raises me up from the hand and leads me to the bench and says to the youths: Ye depart and build. 1.8 And after the (thing) *for* the youths to depart and of us becoming alone, she says to me: (You) sit here. I say to her: Lady, allow (you) *for* the elders to sit first. She said: What I say to you, sit. 1.9 Then from me wanting to sit in the right (hand) parts, she allowed me not, -- to sit in the right (hand) parts, she says to me: *Do* you grieve, Hermas? The (one) to/in the right parts is a place of others, of those already having been acceptable to God and having suffered on account of my name. But for you, you are much deficient that you might sit with them; but as you abide/continue in your simplicity/sincerity, abide you, and you may sit with them and as many as would work the works/deeds of those and might bear up under what (things) those also have born up under. 2.1 What, I say, did they bear up under? Listen, she says: scourgings, imprisonments, great

θηρία εἴνεκεν τοῦ ὀνόματος· διὰ τοῦτο ἐκίνων ἐστὶν τὰ δεξιὰ μέρη τοῦ ἀγιάσματος καὶ ὃς ἐὰν πάθῃ διὰ τὸ ὄνομα· τῶν δὲ λοιπῶν τὰ ἀρειστερὰ μέρη ἐστιν. ἀλλὰ ἀμφοτέρων, καὶ τῶν ἐκ δεξιῶν καὶ τῶν ἀριστερῶν καθημένων, τὰ αὐτὰ δῶρα καὶ αἱ αὐταὶ ἐπαγγελίαι· μόνον ἐκῖνοι ἐκ δεξιῶν κάθηνται καὶ ἔχουσιν δόξαν τινά. 2.2 σὺ δὲ κατεπιθυμῖς καθίσαι ἐκ δεξιῶν μετ' αὐτῶν, ἀλλὰ τὰ ὑστερήματά σου πολλά. καθαρισθήσῃ δὲ ἀπὸ τῶν ὑστερρημάτων σου· καὶ πάντες οἱ μὴ διψυχοῦνταις καθαρισθήσονται ἀπὸ πάντων τῶν ἀμαρτημάτων εἰς ταύτην τὴν ἡμαίραν. 2.3 ταῦτα εἴπασσα ἤθελεν ἀπελθεῖν· πεσὼν δὲ αὐτῆς πρὸς τοὺς πόδας ἠρώτησα αὐτὴν κατὰ τοῦ κυρίου, ἵνα μοι ἐπιδίξῃ ὃ ἐπηγγείλατο ὅραμα. 2.4 ἡ δὲ πάλιν ἐπελάβετό μου τῆς χιρὸς καὶ ἐγίρι με καὶ καθίζει ἐπὶ τὸ συμψέλιον ἐξ εὐωνύμων· ἐκαθέζετο δὲ καὶ αὐτὴ ἐκ δεξιῶν. καὶ ἐπάρασα ῥάβδον τινὰ λαμπρὰν λέγι μοι· βλέπις μέγα πρᾶγμα; λέγω αὐτῇ κυρία, οὐδὲν βλέπω. λέγει μοι· σύ, ἰδού, οὐχ ὁρᾷς κατέναντί σου πύργον μέγαν οἰκοδομούμενον ἐπὶ ὑδάτων λίθοις τετραγώνοις λαμπροῖς; 2.5 ἐν τετραγώνῳ δὲ ᾠκοδομῖτο ὁ πύργος ὑπὸ τῶν ἓξ νεανίσκων τῶν ἐληλυθότων μετ' αὐτῆς· ἄλλαι δὲ μυριάδες ἀνδρῶν παρέφερον λίθους, οἱ μὲν ἐκ τοῦ βυθοῦ, οἱ δὲ ἐκ τῆς γῆς, καὶ ἐπεδίδουν τοῖς ἓξ νεανίσκοις· ἐκῖνοι δὲ ἐλάμβανον καὶ ᾠκοδόμουν. 2.6 τοὺς μὲν ἐκ τοῦ βυθοῦ λίθους ἑλκομένους πάντας οὕτως ἐτίθεσαν εἰς τὴν οἰκοδομήν· ἡρμοσμένοι γὰρ ἦσαν καὶ συνεφώνουν τῇ ἀρμογῇ μετὰ τῶν ἑτέρων λίθων· καὶ οὕτως ἐκολλῶντο ἀλλήλοις, ὥστε τὴν ἀρμογὴν αὐτὴν μὴ φένεσθε. ἐφένετο δὲ ἡ οἰκοδομὴ τοῦ πύργου ὡς ἐξ ἑνὸς λίθον ᾠκοδομημένη. 2.7 τοὺς δὲ ἕτερος λίθους τοὺς φερομένους ἀπὸ τῆς ξηρᾶς τοὺς μὲν ἀπέβαλλον, τοὺς δὲ ἐτίθουν

oppressions/afflictions, crucifixions, wild beasts on account of the name/Name; because of this the right (hand) parts of the sanctuary is of them and who ever might suffer because of the name; but the left (hand) parts is of the rest/others. But of both, both of those out of right (ones)/on the right and those out of left (ones)/on the left sitting, *are* the same gifts and the same promises; only those out of right (ones)/on the right, they sit and they have some fame/glory. 2.2 But you, you desire *down* to sit out of right (ones)/at the right with them, but your deficiencies *are* many. But you will be purified/cleansed from your deficiencies; and all the (ones) not being double-minded will be cleansed from all the sins/faults to this day. 2.3 Having said these (things) she was wanting to go away; but having fallen near her feet, I petitioned her according to/by the Lord that she might show to me a vision which she herself promised. 2.4 And the (she) again took hold of my hand and raises me and seats *me* on the bench out of left (ones)/on the left; but she herself sat out of right (ones)/on the right. And having lifted up a certain bright/shining rod, she says to me: See you a great thing? I say to her: Lady, I see nothing. She says to me: You, behold, *do* you not observe before you a great fortress/tower being built from waters upon shining four-cornered stones? 2.5 And the tower/fortress was being built in/with four corners by the six youths/young men having come with her; but other myriads of men were bringing stones, some out of the deep, others out of/from the land, and they were giving *them* to the six young men; and those were receiving/taking and building, 2.6 They were thus putting all the stones on one hand being dragged out of the deep into the building, for they were having been formed/shaped and were fitting together in the joints with the other/different stones; and so they were uniting/fitting with one another so as *for* the joint itself not to be visible/evident. And the building of the fortress/tower appeared as being built out of one stone. 2.7 But *for* the other/different stones, the (ones) being carried from the dry (land),

εἰς τὴν οἰκοδομήν· ἄλλους δὲ κατέκοπταν καὶ ἐτίθουν μακρὰν ἀπὸ τοῦ πύργου. 2.8 -- ἔκιντο, καὶ οὐκ ἐχρῶντο αὐτοῖς ἐπὶ τὴν οἰκοδομήν· ἦσαν γάρ τινες ἐξ αὐτῶν ἐψωριακότες, ἕτεροι δὲ σχισμὰς ἔχοντες, ἄλλοι δὲ κεκολοβωμένοι, ἄλλοι δὲ λευκοὶ καὶ στρογγύλοι, μὴ ἁρμόζοντες εἰς τὴν οἰκοδομήν. 2.9 ἔβλεπον δὲ ἑτέρους λίθους ῥιπτομένους μακρὰν ἀποὺ τοῦ πύργου καὶ ἐρχομένους εἰς τὸ αὐτὸ καὶ μὴ μένοντας ἐν τῇ ὁδῷ, ἀλλὰ κυλιομένους εἰς τὴν ἀνοδίαν· ἑτέρους δὲ ἐπὶ πῦρ ἐνπίπτοντας καὶ καιομένους· ἑτέρους δὲ πίπτοντας ἐγγὺς ὑδάτων καὶ μὴ δυναμένους κυλισθῆνε εἰς τὸ ὕδωρ, καίπερ θελόντων κυλισθῆναι καὶ ἐλθῖν εἰς τὸ ὕδωρ. 3.1 δίξασά μοι ταῦτα ἤθελεν ἀποτρέχειν. λέγω αὐτῇ· κυρία, τί μοι ὄφελος ταῦτα ἑωρακότι καὶ μὴ γινώσκοντι, τί ἐσιν τὰ πράγματα; ἀποκριθῖσά μοι λέγει·

πανοῦργο οἱ ἄνθροπος, θέλων γεινώσκειν τὰ περὶ τὸν πύργον. ναί, φημί, κυρία, ἵνα τοῖς ἀδελφοῖς ἀναγείλω καὶ ἀκούσαντες γεινώσκωσιν τὸν κύριον ἐν πολλῇ δόξῃ. 3.2 ἔφη· ἀκούσονται μὲν πολλοί· ἀκούσαντες δέ τινες ἐξ αὐτῶν χαρήσονται,

τινὲς δὲ κλαύσονται· ἀλλὰ καὶ αὗτοι, ἐὰν ἀκούσωσιν καὶ μετανοήσωσιν, καὶ αὐτοὶ χαρήσονται. ἄκουαι οὖν τὰς παραβολὰς τοῦ πύργου· ἀποκαλύψω γάρ σοι πάντα. καὶ μηκαίτι μοι κόπους πάρεχε περὶ ἀποκαλύψεως· αἱ γὰρ ἀποκαλύψεις αὗται τέλος ἔχουσιν· πεπληρωμέναι γάρ εἰσιν. ἀλλ' οὐ παύσῃ αἰτούμενος ἀποκαλύψεις· ἀνεδὴς γὰρ εἶ.

3.3 ὁ μὲν πύργος, ὃν βλέπεις οἰκοδομούμενον, ἐγώ εἰμι ἡ ἐκκλησία, ἡ ὀφθεῖσά σοι καὶ νῦν καὶ τὸ πρότερον·

ὃ ἂν οὖν θελήσῃς, ἐπερώτα περὶ τοῦ πύργου, καὶ

they were casting/laying some aside, some others they were putting into the building; but they struck/cut down others and were placing *them* far from the fortress/tower. 2.8 They were lying/laying and they were not using them upon/for the building, for some out of them were being rough, and others/different having splits/divisions, and others were having been cut short, and others *were* white and round, not fitting together/being compatible in the building. 2.9 And I was seeing other/different stones being thrown down far from the fortress/tower and coming to the same but not remaining in/on the road, but rolling into the place with no roads; and others/different falling in/upon a fire and being burned; but others having fallen near waters and not being able to be rolled into the water, although wanting/wishing to be rolled and to go into the water. 3.1 Having shown these (things) to me she was wanting to run away. I say to her: Lady, what benefit *are* these (things) to me, seeing and not knowing/understanding what the practical things/matters are? Answering to me, she says:

A man/human who *is* cunning/crafty, wanting to know the (things) about the fortress/tower. I say: Yes, Lady, that/in order that I may report to the brothers, and having heard, they may know the Lord in much fame/glory. 3.2 She was saying: Many indeed will hear, and having heard some out of them will rejoice,

but some will lament/wail; but even these, if they might hear/listen and repent, these also will rejoice. Therefore, hear you the parables of the fortress/tower; for I shall reveal all to you. And no longer offer/render trouble to me concerning revelation; for these revelations have an end, for they are having been fulfilled. But you/yourself may not cease asking/requesting revelations; for you are bold/shameless.

3.3 Indeed, the fortress/tower which you see being built, *is* I, I am the assembly, the (one) having appeared to you both now and the former (time):

Therefore what ever you might want, (you) ask about the fortress/tower, and I shall reveal it to

ἀποκαλύψω σοι, εἵνα χαρῇς μετὰ τῶν ἁγίων. 3.4 λέγω αὐτῇ·
κυρία, ἐπὶ ἅπαξ ἄξιόν με ἡγήσω τοῦ πάντα μοι ἀποκαλύψαι,
ἀποκάλυψον. ἡ δὲ λέγει· ὃ ἐὰν δέχητέ σοι ἀποκαλυφθῆναι,
ἀποκαλυφθήσεται. μόνον ἡ καρδία σου περὶ τὸν θεὸν ἤτω καὶ
μὴ διψυχήσεις, ὃ ἂν εἴδῃς. 3.5 ἐπηρώτησα αὐτήν· διατὶ ὁ πύργος
ἐπὶ ὑδάτων ᾠκοδόμηται, κυρία; εἶπά σοι, φησίν, καὶ τὸ
πρότερον, καὶ ἐκζητῖς ἐπιμελῶς· ἐκζητῶν οὖν εὑρίσκεις τὴν
ἀλήθιαν. διατὶ οὖν ἐπὶ ὑδάτων ᾠκοδόμηται ὁ πύργος, ἄκουε· ὅτι
ἡ ζωὴ ὑμῶν διὰ ὕδατος ἐσώθη καὶ σωθήσεται. τεθεμελίωται δὲ ὁ
πύργος τῷ ῥήματι τοῦ παντοκράτορος καὶ ἐνδόξου ἀνόματος,
κρατῖτε δὲ ὑπὸ τῆς ἀοράτου δυνάμεως τοῦ δεσπότου. 4.1
ἀποκριθεὶς λέγω αὐτῇ· κυρία, μεγάλως καὶ θαυμαστῶς ἔχει τὸ
πρᾶγμα τοῦτο· οἱ δὲ νεανίσκοι οἱ ἓξ οἱ οἰκοδομοῦνταις, τίνες
εἰσίν, κυρία; οὗτοί εἰσιν οἱ ἅγιοι ἄγγελοι τοῦ θεοῦ οἱ πρῶτοι
κτισθέντες, οἷς παρέδωκεν ὁ κύριος πᾶσαν τὴν κτίσιν αὐτοῦ
αὔξειν καὶ οἰκοδομεῖν καὶ δεσπόζειν τῆς κτίσεως πάσης· διὰ
τούτων τελεσθήσεται ἡ οἰκοδομὴ τοῦ πύργου. 4.2 οἱ δὲ ἕτεροι οἱ
παραφέρον τοὺς λίθους, τίνες εἰσίν; καὶ αὐτοὶ ἅγιοι ἄγγελοι τοῦ
θεοῦ· οὗτοι δὲ οἱ ἓξ ὑπερέχοντες αὐτούς εἰσιν· συντελεσθήσετε
οὖν ἡ οἰκοδομὴ τοῦ πύργου, καὶ πάντες ὁμοῦ εὐφρανθήσονται
κύκλῳ τοῦ πύργου καὶ δοξάσουσιν τὸν θεόν, ὅτι ἐτελέσθη ἡ
οἰκοδομὴ τοῦ πύργου. 4.3 ἐπηρώτησα αὐτὴν λέγων· κυρία,
ἤθελον γνῶνε τῶν λίθων τὴν ἔξοδον καὶ τὴν δύναμιν αὐτῶν,
ποταμή ἐστιν. ἀποκριθῖσά μοι λέγει· οὐχ ὅτι σὺ ἐκ πάντων
ἀξιώτερος εἶ, ἵνα σοι ἀποκαλυφθῇ. ἄλλοι γάρ σου πρότεροί
εἰσιν καὶ βελτιόνές σου, οἷς ἔδι ἀποκαλυφθῆναι τὰ ὁράματα
ταῦτα· ἀλλ' ἵνα δοξασθῇ τὸ ὄνομα τοῦ θεοῦ, ἀπεκαλύφθη καὶ

you, in order that you might rejoice with the saints.
3.4 I say to her: Lady, since at one time you will
regard me worthy of the (thing) to reveal all to me,
you reveal. And the (she) says: What ever may be
possible to be revealed to you, it will be revealed.
Only *let* your heart be around/about God and be not
double-souled/minded, what ever you might see. 3.5 I
asked her: Why *was* the fortress/tower built upon
waters, Lady? She said: I spoke to you also the former
(time), and you seek out diligently; seeking out, then
you find/are finding the truth. Therefore, you hear
why the fortress/tower was built on waters: Because
the life of ye was saved through water and it will be
saved. And the fortress/tower has been founded by the
word of the almighty and of an honored/glorious name,
and it is strengthened/held fast by the unseen power
of the master. 4.1 Answering, I say to her: Lady, he
holds this thing/matter greatly and wonderfully/
marvelously; but who are the six young men, lady, the
(ones) building *it*? These are the holy messengers/an-
gels from God, the first (ones) having been created,
to whom the Lord handed over/delivered up all his
creation to increase and to build and to master all
the creation; the building of the fortress/tower will
be finished/completed through them. 4.2 But who are
the others, the (ones) carrying the stones? These also
are holy messengers/angels from God; but these, the
six (men) are being held above/superior to them;
therefore, the building of the fortress/tower will be
finished/completed, and all will be glad/rejoice
together around the fortress/tower and they will
glorify God, because the building of the fortress/tow-
er was finished/completed. 4.3 I asked her, saying:
Lady, I was wanting/wishing to know the exodus/going
out of the stones and the power of them, what sort it
is. Answering to me she says: *It is* not because you,
you out of all are more worthy, that it might be
revealed to you; for others preceding/more former than
you are even better than you, to whom it was being
proper to reveal these visions; but in order that the
name of God might be glorified, *to you* it was revealed
and it will be revealed because of the double-

ΠΟΙΜΗΝ

ἀποκαλυφθήσεται διὰ τοὺς διψύχους, τοὺς διαλογειζομένους ἐν ταῖς καρδίαις αὐτῶν, —— . λέγε αὐτοῖς, ὅτι ταῦτα πάντα ἐστὶν ἀληθῆ καὶ οὐθὲν ἔξωθέν ἐστιν τῆς ἀληθίας, ἀλλὰ πάντα ἰσχυρὰ καὶ βέβαια καὶ τεθεμελιωμένα ἐστίν. 5.1 ἄκουε νῦν περὶ τῶν λίθων τῶν ὑπαγόντων εἰς τὴν οἰκοδομήν. οἱ μὲν οὖν λίθοι οἱ τετράγωνοι καὶ λευκοὶ καὶ συμφωνοῦντες ταῖς ἁρμογαῖς αὐτῶν, οὗτοί εἰσιν οἱ ἀπόστολοι καὶ ἐπίσκοποι καὶ διδάσκαλοι καὶ διάκονοι οἱ πορευθέντες κατὰ τὴν σεμνότητα τοῦ θεοῦ καὶ ἐπισκοπήσαντες καὶ διδάξαντες καὶ διακονήσαντες ἁγνῶς καὶ σεμνῶς τοῖς ἐκλεκτοῖς τοῦ θεοῦ, οἱ μὲν κεκοιμημένοι, οἱ δὲ ἔτι ὄντες· καὶ πάντοται αὐτοῖς συμφωνήσαντες καὶ ἐν ἑαυτοῖς εἰρήνην ἔσχαν τὸ ἐν τῇ οἰκοδομῇ τοῦ πύργου αυμφωνοῦσιν αἱ ἁρμογαὶ αὐτῶν. 5.2 οἱ δὲ ἐκ τοῦ βυθοῦ ἑλκόμενοι καὶ ἐπιτειθέμενοι καὶ συμφῶ ταῖς ἁρμογαῖς αὐτῶν μετὰ τῶν αἰτέρων λίθων τῶν ἤδη οἰκοδομουμένων, τίνες εἰσίν; οὗτοί εἰσιν οἱ παθόντες ἕνεκεν τοῦ ὀνόματος τοῦ θεοῦ. 5.3 τοὺς δὲ ἑτέρους λίθους τοὺς φερομένους ἀπὸ τῆς ξηρᾶς θέλω γνῶναι, τίνες εἰσείν, κυρία. ἔφη· τοὺς μὲν εἰς τὴν οἰκοδομὴν ὑπάγοντας καὶ μὴ λατομουμένους, τούτους ὁ κύριος ἐδοκίμασεν, ὅτι ἐπορεύθησαν ἐν τῇ εὐθύτητι τοῦ κυρίου καὶ κατωρθώσαντο τὰς ἐντολὰς αὐτοῦ. 5.4 οἱ δὲ ἀγόμενοι καὶ τιθέμεμοι εἰς τὴν οἰκοδομήν, τίνες εἰσίν; νέοι εἰσὶν ἐν τῇ πίστι καὶ πιστοί, νουθετοῦνται δὲ ὑπὸ τῶν ἀγγέλων εἰς τὸ ἀγαθοποιεῖν, διότι εὑρέθη ἐν αὐτοῖς πονηρία. 5.5 οὓς δὲ ἀπέβαλλον καὶ ἐρίπτουν, τίνες εἰσίν; οὗτοί εἰσιν ἡμαρτηκότες καὶ θέλοντες μετανοῆσαι· διὰ τοῦτο μακρὰν οὐκ ἀπερίφησαν ἔξω τοῦ πύργου, ὅτι εὔχρηστοι ἔσονται εἰς τὴν

minded/two-faced (ones), the (ones) disputing/contending/pondering in their hearts. Say you to them that all these (things) are true and nothing from outside is of/from the truth, but all (these) are strong and stable/firm and having been founded/established. 5.1 Hear you now about the stones, the (ones) going into the building. Therefore, the stones (on one hand), the four-cornered (ones) and white (ones) and (ones) agreeing/fitting together in their joints, these are the apostles and overseers/bishops and teachers and servants/ministers/waiters having gone before according to the dignity/reverence of God and having overseen/served as bishops and taught and served/ministered sincerely and honorably to/for the chosen (ones) of God, some indeed having fallen asleep, but also some being *alive* still, and having always agreed/fit together to/for themselves and they had peace in/among themselves *for* the (thing): the joints/joinings of them agree/fit together in the building of the fortress/tower. 5.2 But who are the (ones) being dragged out of the deep and being placed upon and agreeing/harmonizing in their joints with the other/different stones, with those already being built? These, they are the (ones) having suffered on account of the name of God. 5.3 And I want to know, lady, who are the other/different stones, the (ones) being carried/brought from the dry (land)? She was saying: *For* those indeed going into the building and not being hewed/cut to shape, the Lord approved them, because they went/traveled in the rightness/correctness of the Lord and they set straight/successfully concluded the commands from him. 5.4 But who are the (ones) being led/brought and placed/put into the building? They are new/young and faithful (ones) in the faith. But they are being admonished/warned by the messengers/angels in the (thing) to do good, because evil/wickedness was found in them. 5.5 But (those) whom they were casting down and throwing away, who are they? These are they having sinned and wanting to repent; because of this they are not cast far outside the fortress/tower, because they will be highly useful in the building, if they might/should repent. Therefore, the (ones) being

οἰκοδομήν, ἐὰν μετανοήσωσιν. οἱ οὖν μέλλοντες μετανοεῖν, ἐὰν μετανοήσουσιν, ἰσχυροὶ ἔσονται ἐν τῇ πίστι, ἐὰν νῦν μετανοήσωσιν, ἐν ᾧ οἰκοδομῖται ὁ πύργος. ἐὰν δὲ τελεσθῇ ἡ οἰκοδομή, οὐκέτι ἔχουσιν τόπον, ἀλλ' ἔσονται ἔκβολοι· μόνον δὲ τοῦτο ἔχουσιν, παρὰ τῷ πύργῳ κῖσθαι. 6.1 τοὺς δὲ κατακοπτομένους ἀπὸ τοῦ πύργου θέλις γνῶναι; οὗτοί εἰσιν οἱ υἱοὶ τῆς ἀνομίας· ἐπίστευσαν δὲ ἐν ὑποκρίσι, καὶ πᾶσα πονηρία οὐκ ἀπέστη ἀπ' αὐτῶν· διὰ τοῦτο οὐκ ἔχουσιν σωτηρίαν, ὅτι οὐκ εἰσὶν εὔχρηστοι εἰς οἰκοδομὴν διὰ τὰς πονηρίας αὐτῶν. διὰ τοῦτο συνεκόπησαν καὶ πόρρω ἀπερίθησαν διὰ τὴν ὀργὴν τοῦ κυρίου, ὅτι παρώργισαν αὐτόν. 6.2 τοὺς δὲ ἑτέρους, οὓς ἑώρακας πολλοὺς κιμένους, μὴ ὑπάγοντας εἰς τὴν οἰκοδομήν, οὗτοι οἱ μὲν ἐψωριακότες εἰσίν, οἱ ἐγνωκότες τὴν ἀλήθειαν, μὴ ἐπιμένοντες δὲ ἐν αὐτῇ. 6.3 οἱ δὲ τὰς σχισμὰς ἔχοντες, τίνες εἰσίν; οὗτοί εἰσιν οἱ κατ' ἀλλήλων ἐν ταῖς καρδίαις ἔχοντες καὶ μὴ εἰρηνεύονταις ἐν ἑαυτοῖς, ἀλλὰ πρόσωπον ἰρήνης ἔχοντες, ὅταν δὲ ἀπ' ἀλλήλων ἀποχωρήσωσιν, αἱ πονηρίαι αὐτῶν ἐν ταῖς καρδίαις ἐμμένουσιν· αὗται οὖν αἱ σχισμαί εἰσιν, ἃς ἔχουσιν οἱ λίθοι. 6.4 οἱ δὲ κεκολοβωμένοι, οὗτοί εἰσιν πεπιστευκότες μὲν καὶ τὸ πλεῖον μέρος ἔχουσιν ἐν τῇ δικαιοσύνῃ, τινὰ δὲ μέρη ἔχουσιν τῆς ἀνομίας· διὰ τοῦτο κολοβοὶ καὶ οὐχ ὁλοτελῖς εἰσιν. 6.5 οἱ δὲ λευκοὶ καὶ στρογγύλοι καὶ μὴ ἁρμόζοντες εἰς τὴν οἰκοδομήν, τίνες εἰσιν, κυρία; ἀποκριθῖσά μοι λέγει· ἕως πότε μωρὸς εἶ καὶ ἀσύνετος, καὶ πάντα ἐπερωτᾷς καὶ οὐδὲν νοεῖς; οὗτοί εἰσιν ἔχοντες μὲν πίστιν, ἔχοντες δὲ καὶ πλοῦτον αὐτῶν καὶ διὰ τὰς πραγματείας ἀπαρνοῦντε τὸν κύριον αὐτῶν. 6.6 καὶ ἀποκριθεὶς αὐτῇ λέγω· κυρία, πότε οὖν εὔχρηστοι ἔσονται εἰς τὴν οἰκοδομήν; ὅταν,

about to repent, if they will repent, will be strong
(ones) in the faith; if they might/should repent now,
in *the time* which the tower/fortress is being built.
But if the building be completed/finished, they no
longer have a place, but they will be thrown out; and
they have only this: to lie beside the fortress/
tower. 6.1 And *do* you want/wish to know *who are* the
(ones) being broken up from the tower/fortress? These,
they are the sons of the evilness/lawlessness; but
they believed by pretense/in hypocrisy, and every
evil/wickedness departed/withdrew not from them;
because of this they have not deliverance/salvation,
because they are not useful/serviceable in/for building because of the evils/wickednesses of them. Because
of this they were cut out together and cast far away
because of the anger of the Lord, because they provok-
ed him to anger. 6.2 But *for* the others, of whom you
have seen many laying, not going into the building,
these are indeed the (ones) having decayed, the (ones)
having known the truth, but not having abided in/by
her/it. 6.3 But who are the (ones) having the
splits/divisions? These are the (ones) holding (grud-
ges) against one another in the hearts and not making
peace among themselves, but having a face/appearance
of peace, but whenever they might depart from one
another, their evils/wickednesses perseveres/remains
in the hearts; these then are the splits which the
stones have. 6.4 And the (ones) having been cut
short, these are they having believed indeed and
have/hold the greater part in the justness/justice,
but they have/hold some part of lawlessness; because
of this they are mutilated/cut short and not wholly
complete. 6.5 And the white (ones) and round (ones)
also not fitting/harmonizing into the building, who
are they, lady? Answering to me, she says: Until when
are you foolish and senseless, both questioning all
(things) and understanding nothing? These are they
having faith on one hand, but also having their
wealth, and they deny/renounce their Lord because of
the works/matters/things. 6.6 And answering I say to
her: Lady, then when will they be serviceable/useful
in/for the building? She says: Whenever the wealth

φησίν, περικοπῇ αὐτῶν ὁ πλοῦτος ὁ ψυχαγωγῶν αὐτούς, τότε εὔχρηστοι ἔσονται τῷ θεῷ. ὥσπερ γὰρ ὁ λίθος ὁ στρογγύλος, ἐὰν μὴ περικοπῇ καὶ ἀποβάλῃ ἐξ αὐτοῦ τι, οὐ δύναται τετράγωνος γενέσθαι, οὕτω καὶ οἱ πλουτοῦνταις ἐν τούτῳ τῷ αἰῶνι, ἐὰν μὴ περικοπῇ αὐτῶν ὁ πλοῦτος, οὐ δύνανται τῷ κυρίῳ εὔχρηστοι γενέσθαι. 6.7 ἀπὸ σεαυτοῦ πρῶτον γνῶθι· ὅτε ἐπλούτις, ἄχρηστος ἦς, νῦν δὲ εὔχρυστος εἶ καὶ ὠφέλιμος τῇ ζωῇ. εὔχρηστοι γείνεσθε τῷ θεῷ. 7.1 τοὺς δὲ ἑτέρους λίθους, οὓς εἶδες μακρὰν ἀπὸ τοῦ πύργου ῥιπτομένους καὶ πίπτοντας εἰς τὴν ὁδὸν καὶ κυλιομένους ἐκ τῆς ὁδοῦ εἰς τὰς ἀνοδίας· οὗτοί εἰσιν οἱ πεπειστευκότες μέν, ἀπὸ δὲ τῆς διψυχίας αὐτῶν ἀφίουσιν τὴν ὁδὸν αὐτῶν τὴν ἀληθινήν· δοκοῦντες οὖν βελτίονα ὁδὸν δύνασθε εὑρῖν, πλανῶντε καὶ ταλαιπωροῦσιν περιπατοῦνταις ἐν ταῖς ἀνοδίαις. 7.2 οἱ δὲ πίπτοντες εἰς τὸ πῦρ καὶ κεόμενοι, οὗτοί εἰσιν οἱ εἰς τέλος ἀποστάντες τοῦ θεοῦ τοῦ ζῶντος, καὶ οὐκέτι αὐτοῖς ἀνέβη ἐπὶ τὴν καρδίαν τοῦ μετανοῆσαι διὰ τὰς ἐπιθυμίας τῆς ἀσελγείας αὐτῶν καὶ τῶν πονηριῶν ὧν ἠργάσαντο. 7.3 τοὺς δὲ ἑτέρους τοὺς πίπτοντας ἐγγὺς τῶν ὑδάτων καὶ μὴ δυναμένους κυλισθῆναι εἰς τὸ ὕδωρ, τίνες εἰσίν; οὗτοί εἰσειν οἱ τὸν λόγον ἀκούσαντες καὶ θέλοντες βαπτισθῆναι εἰς τὸ ὄνομα τοῦ κυρίου· εἶτα ὅταν αὐτοῖς ἔλθῃ εἰς μνίαν ἡ ἁγνότης τῆς ἀληθίας, μετανοοῦσιν καὶ πορεύονται πάλιν ὀπίσω τῶν ἐπιθυμιῶν αὐτῶν τῶν πονηρῶν.

7.4 ἐτέλεσεν οὖν τὴν ἐξήγησιν τοῦ πύργου. 7.5 ἀνεδευσάμενος ἔτι αὐτὴν ἐπηρώτησα, εἰ ἄρα πάντες οἱ λίθοι οὗτοι οἱ ἀποβεβλημένοι καὶ μὴ ἁρμόζοντες εἰς τὴν οἰκοδομὴν τοῦ πύργου, εἰ ἔστιν αὐτοῖς μετάνοια καὶ ἔχουσιν τόπον εἰς τὸν πύργον τοῦτον. ἔχουσιν, φησίν, μετάνοιαν, ἀλλὰ εἰς τοῦτον τὸν πύργον οὐ δύνανται ἁρμόσαι· 7.6 ἑτέρῳ δὲ τόπῳ ἁρμόσουσιν πολὺ ἐλάττονι, καὶ τοῦτο ὅταν βασανίσθωσιν καὶ ἐκπληρώσωσειν

598

leading their life/soul may be cut off from them, then they will be serviceable/useful to/for God. For just as a round stone is not able to become four-cornered, unless something might be cut off and thrown away from it, so also the (ones) being rich/wealthy in this age, unless the wealth may be cut off from them, they are not able to become serviceable/useful for the Lord. 6.7 Know you first from yourself: When you were being rich, you were unkind, but now you are useful and profitable for the life. Become ye serviceable for God. 7.1 But *for* the other stones, which you saw being thrown/cast down far from the tower and falling in the road and rolling out of the road into the places with no roads: These are the (ones) having indeed believed, but from their double-mind they leave the true road/way; thinking then to be able to find a better road/way, they wander/stray and be miserable, walking in the places with no roads. 7.2 And the (ones) falling into the fire and being burned, these are the (ones) in *the* end having stood/withdrawn from the living God, and no longer to them it came upon the heart *from* the (thing) to repent, because of the desires of their revelries/parties and the evils/wickednesses which they worked. 7.3 And who are the others/different (ones) falling near the waters and not being able to be rolled into the water? These are the (ones) having heard the saying/word and wanting/wishing to be baptized in the name of the Lord; then whenever the purity of the truth might come to them in a memory, they will repent and/but they go/travel again after their desires of the evils/wickednesses. 7.4 Then she finished the narrative of the fortress/tower. 7.5 Being still impudent, I asked her if consequently all these stones, the (ones) having been thrown away and not having fit together/harmonized in the building of the tower, if repentance is for them and they have a place in this tower. She says: They have repentance, but they are not able to fit together in this tower/fortress; 7.6 but they will fit together in another/different place being much lower/lesser, and this whenever they might be tormented and might have filled out/completed the days of/

τὰς ἡμέρας τῶν ἁμαρτιῶν. καὶ διὰ τοῦτο μετατεθήσονται, ὅτι μετέλαβον τοῦ ῥήματος τοῦ δικαίου. καὶ τότε αὐτοῖς συμβήσεται μετατεθῆναι ἐκ τῶν βασάνων αὐτῶν, διὰ τὰ ἔργα ἃ εἰρπάσαντο πονηρά. ἐὰν δὲ μὴ ἀναβῇ ἐπὶ τὴν καρδίαν αὐτῶν, οὐ σῴζονται διὰ τὴν σκηροκαρδίαν αὐτῶν. 8.1 ὅτε οὖν ἐπαυσάμην ἐρωτῶν αὐτὴν περὶ πάντων τούτων, λέγει μοι· θέλις ἄλλο ἰδεῖν; κατεπίθυμος ὢν τοῦ θεάσασθαι περιχαρὴς ἐγενόμην τοῦ ἰδῖν. 8.2 βλέψασά μοι ὑπεμειδίασεν καὶ λέγει μοι· βλέπις ἑπτὰ γυναῖκας κύκλῳ τοῦ πύργου; βλέπω, φημί, κυρία. ὁ πύργος ὑπὸ τούτων βαστάζεται κατ᾽ ἐπιταγὴν τοῦ κυρίου. 8.3 ἄκουε νῦν τὰς ἐνεργείας αὐτῶν. ἡ μὲν πρώτη αὐτῶν, ἡ κρατοῦσα τὰς χῖρας, πίστις καλῖται· διὰ ταύτην σῴζονται οἱ ἐκλεκτοὶ τοῦ θεοῦ. 8.4 ἡ δὲ ἑτέρα, ἡ περιεζωσμένη καὶ ἀνδριζομένη, ἐνκράτια καλῖται· αὕτη θυγάτηρ ἐστὶν τῆς πίστεως. ὃς ἂν οὖν ἀκολουθήσῃ αὐτῇ, μακάριος γείνεται ἐν τῇ ζωῇ αὐτοῦ, ὅτι πάντων τῶν πονηρῶν ἔργων ἀφέξεται, καὶ πάσης ἐπιθυμίας πονηρᾶς, καὶ κληρονομήσῃ ζωὴν αἰώνιον. 8.5 αἱ δὲ ἕτεραι, κυρία, τίνες εἰσίν; θυγατέρες ἀλλήλων εἰσὶν καλοῦνται δὲ ἡ μὲν ἁπλότης, ἡ δὲ ἐπιστήμη, ἡ δὲ ἀκακία, ἡ δὲ σεμνότις, ἡ δὲ ἀγάπη. ὅταν οὖν τὰ ἔργα τῆς μητρὸς μητρὸς αὐτῶν πάντα ποιής, δύνασαι ζῆσαι. 8.6 ἤθελον, φημί, γνῶναι, κυρία, τίς τίνα δύναμιν ἔχει αὐτῶν. ἄκουε, φησίν, τὰς δυνάμις, ἃς ἔχουσιν.

8.7 κρατοῦνται δὲ ἀλλήλων αἱ δυνάμις αὐτῶν καὶ ἀκολουθοῦσιν ἀλλήλαις, καθὼς καὶ γεγεννημαίναι εἰσίν. ἐκ τῆς πίστεως γεννᾶται ἐνκράτεια, ἐκ τῆς ἐνκατίας ἁπλότης, ἐκ τῆς ἁπλότητος ἀκακία, ἐκ τῆς ἀκακίας σεμνότης, ἐκ τῆς σεμνότητος ἐπιστήμη, ἐκ τῆς ἐπιστήμης ἀγάπη. τούτων τὰ ἔργα ἁγνὰ καὶ

from the sins. And because of/through this they will
be removed/transformed, because they received/partook
of the just word. And then it will come about for them
to be removed/changed out of their torments, because
of the evil works which they seized/snatched. But if
it may not come upon/to their heart, they will not be
saved because of their hard heart. 8.1 Then when I
stopped asking her about all these (things), she says
to me: *Do* you want to see another? Being desirous of
the (thing) to behold *it*, I became very glad of the
(thing) to see *it*. 8.2 Having looked at me, she
smiled and says to me: *Do* you see seven women around
the tower? I say: I see, lady. The tower is borne/car-
ried by them according to an injunction from the Lord.
8.3 Hear you now the workings/energies/efficiencies of
them. The first one of them, the (one) clasping/grasp-
ing the hands, is called faith; the chosen (ones) of
God are saved through her. 8.4 And the other (one)
being girded around and appearing like a man, is
called self-control/temperance; she is a daughter of
the faith. Who ever, then, might follow her, he
becomes happy in/with his life, because he will
abstain/hold away from all the evil works, and every
evil desire, and he might inherit eternal life. 8.5
But who are the others/different (ones), lady? They
are daughters of one another and they are called, the
one, simplicity/sincerity, another understanding,
another innocence, another dignity/reverence, the
other agape. Whenever, then, you might do all the
works of the mother, their mother, you are able to
live. 8.6 I say: I was wanting to know, lady,
who/which of them holds/has certain/what powers. Hear
you, she says, the powers which they have.

8.7 Then powers are corroborated/held fast *by*
one another, and they follow one another, just as they
are also having been generated/born. Self control is
generated out of the faith, sincerity/simplicity out
of the temperance/self-control, innocence out of
simplicity/sincerity, dignity/reverent respect out of
the innocence, understanding out of the dignity/
respect, agape out of/from the understanding. The
words of them are pure and respectable/honorable and

σεμνὰ καὶ θῖά ἐστιν. 8.8 ὃς ἂν οὖν δουλεύσῃ ταύταις καὶ ἰσχύσῃ κρατῆσαι τῶν ἔργων αὐτῶν, ἐν τῷ πύργῳ ἕξι τὴν κατοίκησιν μετὰ τῶν ἁγίων τοῦ θεοῦ. 8.9 ἐπηρώτων δὲ αὐτὴν περὶ τῶν καιρῶν, εἰ ἤδη συντελιά ἐστιν. ἡ δὲ ἀνέκραγε φωνῇ μεγάλῃ λέγουσα· ἀσύνεται ἄνθρωπαι, οὐχ ὁρᾷς τὸν πύργον ἔτι οἰκοδομοῦμενον; ὡς ἐὰν οὖν συντελεσθῇ ὁ πύργος οἰκοδομούμενον, ὁ ἔχι τέλος. ἀλλὰ ταχὺ ἐποικοδομηθήσεται. μηκέτι μαι ἐπερώτα μηδέν· ἀρκετή σοι ἡ ὑπόμνησις αὕτη καὶ τοῖς ἁγίοις καὶ ἡ ἀνακαινώσεις τῶν πνευμάτων ὑμῶν. 8.10 ἀλλ' οὐ σοὶ μόνῳ ἀπεκαλύφθη, ἀλλ' ἵνα πᾶσιν δηλώσεις αὐτά, 8.11 μετὰ τρῖς ἡμέρας, νοῆσέ σε γὰρ δεῖ πρῶτον. Ἑρμᾶ, τὰ ῥήματα ταῦτα, ἅ σοι μέλλω λέγειν, λαλῆσαι αὐτὰ εἰς τὰ ὦτα τῶν ἁγίων, εἶνα ἀκούσαντες αὐτὰ καὶ ποιήσανταις καθαρισθῶσιν ἀπὸ τῶν πονηριῶν αὐτῶν καὶ σὺ δὲ μετ' αὐτῶν. 9.1 ἀκούσατέ μου, τέκνα· ἐγὼ ὑμᾶς ἐξέθρεψα ἐν πολλῇ ἁπλότητι καὶ ἀκακίᾳ καὶ σεμνότητι διὰ τὸ ἔλεος τοῦ κυρίου τοῦ ἐφ' ὑμᾶς στάξαντος τὴν δικαιοσύνην, ἵνα δικαιωθῆται καὶ ἁγιασθῆτε ἀπὸ πάσης πονηρίας καὶ ἀπὸ πάσης σκολιότητος· ὑμῖς δὲ οὐ θέλεται παῆνε ἀπὸ τῆς πονηρίας ὑμῶν. 9.2 νῦν οὖν ἀκούσατέ μου καὶ εἰρηνεύεται ἐν ἑαυτοῖς καὶ ἐπισκέπτεσθαι ἀλλήλους καὶ ἀντιλαμβάνεσθαι ἀλλήλων, καὶ μὴ μόνοι τὰ κτίσματα τοῦ θεοῦ μεταλαμβάνετε ἐκ καταχύματος, ἀλλὰ μεταδίδοται καὶ τοῖς ὑστερημένοις· 9.3 οἱ μὲν γὰρ ἀπὸ τῶν πολλῶν ἐδεσμάτων ἀσθένιαν τῇ σαρκὶ ἐπισπῶνται καὶ λύμενι τὴν σάρκα αὐτῶν· τῶν δὲ μὴ ἐχόντων ἐδέσματα λυμαίνεται ἡ σὰρξ διὰ τὸ μὴ ἔχειν τὸ ἀρκετὸν τῆς τροφῆς, καὶ διαφθείρετε τὸ σῶμα αὐτῶν. 9.4 αὕτη οὖν ἡ ἀσυνκρασία βλαβερὰ ὑμῖν τοῖς ἔχουσι καὶ μὴ μεταδιδοῦσιν τοῖς ὑστερουμένοις. 9.5 βλέπετε τὴν κρίσιν τὴν ἐπερχομένην. οἱ ὑπερέχοντες οὖν ἐκζητεῖται τοὺς πινῶντας, ἕως

godly. 8.8 Therefore, who ever would slave for them
and be strong to lay hold of/adhere to their works, he
will have the dwelling (place) in the tower with the
saints of God/God's holy (ones). 8.9 And I was questioning her about the times/seasons, if there is
already a completion, butthe (she) cried out in a
great voice, saying: Senseless man/human, are you not
seeing/perceiving the tower still being built? As if
then the tower being built may be completed, which has
an end. But it will be built up quickly; no longer ask
me nothing; this reminder and the renewing of your
spirits *is* sufficient/enough for you and for the
saints. 8.10 But it is not revealed for you only, but
in order that you might show it to all them, 8.11
after three days, for it is necessary *for* you to
perceive *it* first. Hermas, these words which I am
about to say to you, to speak them in/to the ears of
the saints, in order that having heard and done them,
they might be cleansed from their evils, and also you
with them. 9.1 Hear ye from me, children: I, I
reared ye in/with much sincerity and innocence and
dignity/respect through the mercy of the Lord, the
(one) having instilled the justness/justice upon ye,
in order that ye may be justified and consecrated/
sanctified from every evil and from every crooked/per-
verse (thing); but ye, ye want/wish not to cease from
your evil/wickedness. 9.2 Now, therefore, hear ye
from me and be at peace among yourselves and care for
one another and help ye one another, and not for ye
only partake/receive ye the created (things) of God
out of abundance, but share/impart ye also with/to the
(ones) lacking; 9.3 for some are sowing sickness in
the flesh from the many (things) being eaten and are
violently mistreating/injuring their flesh, but the
flesh of others not having eatings is maltreated/in-
jured because of the (thing) not to have the sufficiency of the food, and their body is being destroyed.
9.4 Then this (thing), the lack of sharing, is harmful
for ye, the (ones) having and not sharing with/giving
to (ones) lacking. 9.5 See/view ye the judgment being
expected/awaited. Therefore let ye the (ones) having
excess/abundance seek out the (ones) hungering, since

οὔπω ὁ πύργος τελέσθη· μετὰ γὰρ τὸ τελεσθῆναι τὸν πύργον θελήσεται ἀγαθοποιεῖν, καὶ οὐχ ἕξετε τόπον. 9.6 βλέπετε οὖν ὑμεῖς οἱ γαυριώμενοι ἐν τῷ πλούτῳ ὑμῶν, μήποτε στενάξουσιν οἱ ὑστερούμενοι καὶ ὁ στεναγμὸς αὐτῶν ἀναβήσεται πρὸς τὸν κύριον καὶ ἐκκλεισθήσεσθαι μετὰ τῶν ἀγαθῶν ὑμῶν ἔξω τῆς θύρας τοῦ πύργου. 9.7 νῦν οὖν ὑμῖν λέγω τοῖς προηγουμένοις τῆς ἐκκλησίας καὶ τοῖς πρωτοκαθεδρίγαις· μὴ γείνεσθαι ὅμοιοι τοῖς φαρμακοῖς. οἱ φαρμακοὶ μὲν οὖν τὰ φάρμακα ἑαυτῶν εἰς τὰς πυξίδας βαστάζουσιν, ὑμῖς δὲ τὸ φάρμακον ὑμῶν καὶ τὸν ἰὸν εἰς τὴν καρδίαν. 9.8 ἐνεσκιρωμένοι ἐστὲ καὶ οὐ θέλεται καθαρίσαι τὰς καρδίας ὑμῶν καὶ συνκεράσαι ὑμῶν τὴν φρόνησιν ἐπὶ τὸ αὐτὸ ἐν καθαρᾷ καρδίᾳ, ἵνα σχῆτε ἔλεος παρὰ τοῦ βασιλέως τοῦ μεγάλου. 9.9 βλέπετε οὖν, τέκνα, μήποται αὗται αἱ διχοστασίαι αὗται ὑμῶν ἀποστερήσουσιν τὴν ζωὴν ὑμῶν. 9.10 πῶς ὑμῖς παιδεύειν θέλεται τοὺς ἐκλεκτοὺς κυρίου, αὐτοὶ μὴ ἔχοντες παιδίαν; παιδεύετε οὖν ἀλλήλους καὶ εἰρηνεύεται ἐν αὐτοῖς ἵνα κἀγὼ κατέναντι τοῦ πατρὸς ἱλαρὰ σταθεῖσα λόγον ἀποδῶ ὑπὲρ ὑμῶν πάντων τῷ κυρίῳ ὑμῶν.

10.1 Ὅτε οὖν ἐπαύσατο μετ' ἐμοῦ λαλοῦσα, ἦλθον οἱ ἓξ νεανίσκοι οἱ οἰκοδομοῦντες καὶ ἀπήνεγκαν αὐτὴν πρὸς τὸν πύργον, καὶ ἄλλοι τέσσαρες ἦραν τὸ συμψέλιον καὶ ἀπήνεγκαν καὶ αὐτὸ πρὸς τὸν πύργον. τούτων τὸ πρόσωπον οὐκ εἶδον, ὅτι ἀπεστραμμένοι ἦσαν.

10.2 ὑπάγουσαν δὲ αὐτὴν ἠρώτων, ἵνα μοι ἀποκαλύψῃ περὶ τῶν τριῶν μορφῶν, ἐν αἷς μοι ἐνεφανίσθη. ἀποκριθῖσά μοι λέγει· περὶ τούτων ἕτερον δῖ σαι ἐπερωτῆσαι, ἵνα σοι ἀποκαλυφθῇ. 10.3 ὤφθη δέ μοι, ἀδελφοί, τῇ μὲν πρώτῃ ὁράσι τῇ περσυνῇ λίαν πρεσβυτέρα καὶ ἐν καθέδρᾳ καθημένη. 10.4 τῇ δὲ

the fortress/tower is not yet finished, for after the (thing) *for* the tower to be completed ye will want/wish to do good, and ye will not have a place/opportunity. 9.6 Then see ye, ye, the (ones) boasting/glorying in your wealth/riches, lest the ones lacking groan and their groaning will go up to the Lord and ye will be shut out with your good (things) outside the door of the fortress/tower. 9.7 Therefore I say now to ye, to the (ones) leading/governing the assembly and to the (ones) taking the chief seats: Become ye not like the sorcerers. Then the sorcerers indeed carry the enchantment of themselves in the boxes, but ye, *ye carry* the enchantment/magic potion and the poison/rust of ye in the heart. 9.8 Ye are having been hardened and ye want/wish not to cleanse your hearts and to unite/combine the thinking of ye upon the same/thing in/with a clean heart, in order that they might form/have mercy from the great king. 9.9 Therefore, see/beware ye, children, lest these same dissensions/divisions of ye might defraud/rob your life/the life from ye. 9.10 Ye, how do ye wish/want to teach/train the chosen (ones) of the Lord, yourselves having not teaching/training? Therefore teach/train/correct ye one another and be ye at peace among yourselves in order that I also, standing cheerfully before the father, I might give a word/reasoning in behalf of ye to our Lord.

10.1 Then, when she ceased speaking with me, the six young men, the (ones) building, came and carried her away to the tower, and four others took up the bench and carried it away also to the tower. I saw not the face of these, because they were turned away.
10.2 But departing, I was asking her that she might reveal to me concerning the three forms in which she was manifested to me. Answering to me she says: Concerning these (things), it is necessary for you to ask another/different (one) in order that it might be revealed to you. 10.3 And she was seen be me, brothers, in the first vision in the last year a very old/aged (woman) and sitting in a chair. 10.4 But in the other/different vision she had the younger face,

ἑτέρα ὁράσι τὴν μὲν ὄψιν νεωτέραν εἶχεν, τὴν δὲ σάρκα καὶ τὰς τρίχας πρεσβυτέρας, καὶ ἑστηκυῖά μοι ἐλάλει· ἱλαρωτέρα δὲ ἦν τὸ πρόσοπον. 10.5 τῇ δὲ τρίτῃ ὁράσι ὅλη νεωτέρα καὶ κάλλι ἐκπρεπεστάτη, μόνας δὲ τὰς τρίχας πρεσβυτέρας εἶχεν· ἱλαρὰ δὲ εἰς τέλος ἦν καὶ ἐπὶ συμψελίου καθημένη. 10.6 περὶ τούτων περίλουπος ἤμην λίαν τοῦ γνῶναί με τὴν ἀποκάλυψιν ταύτην, καὶ βλέπω τὴν πρεσβυτέραν ἐν ὁράματι τῆς νυκτὸς λέγουσάν μοι. πᾶσα ἐρῶτησεις ταπινοφροσύνης χρῄζει. νήστευσον οὖν, καὶ λήμψῃ ὃ αἰτῖς παρὰ τοῦ κυρίου. 10.7 ἐνήστευσα οὖν μίαν ἡμέραν, καὶ αὐτῇ τῇ νυκτί μοι ὤφθη νεανίσκος καὶ λέγι μοι· τί σὺ ὑπὸ χῖρα αἰτῖς ἀποκαλύψεις ἐν δεήσει; βλέπε, μήποτε πολλὰ αἰτούμενος βλάψῃς σου τὴν σάρκα. 10.8 ἀρκοῦσίν σοι αἱ ἀποκαλύψεις αὗται. μήτι δύνῃ ἰσχυροτέρας ἀποκαλύψεις ὧν ἑώρακας ἰδεῖν; 10.9 ἀποκριθεὶς αὐτῷ λέγω· κύριε, τοῦτο μόνον αἰτοῦμαι, περὶ τῶν τριῶν μορφῶν τῆς πρεσβυτέρας ἵνα ἀποκαλύψεις ὁλοτελὴς γένηται. ἀποκριθεὶς μοι λέγει· μέχρι τίνος ἀσύνετοί ἐστε; ἀλλ’ αἱ διψυχίαι ὑμῶν ἀσυνέτους ὑμᾶς ποιοῦσιν καὶ τὸ μὴ ἔχιν τὴν καρδίαν ὑμῶν πρὸς τὸν κύριον. 10.10 ἀποκριθεὶς αὐτῷ πάλιν εἶπον· ἀλλ’ ἀπὸ σοῦ, κύριε, ἀκριβέστερον αὐτὰ γνωσόμεθα. 11.1 ἄκουε, φησίν, περὶ τῶν μορφῶν ὧν ἐπιζητεῖς. 11.2 τῇ μὲν πρώτῃ ὁράσι διατὶ πρεσβυτέρα ὤφθη σοι καὶ ἐπὶ καθέδραν καθημένη; ὅτι τὸ πνεῦμα ὑμῶν πρεσβύτερον καὶ ἤδη μεμαραμμένον καὶ μὴ ἔχον δύναμιν ἀπὸ τῶν μαλακιῶν ὑμῶν καὶ διψυχιῶν· 11.3 ὥσπερ γὰρ οἱ πρεσβύτεροι, μηκέτι ἔχοντες ἐλπίδαν τοῦ ἀνανεῶσαι, οὐδὲν ἄλλο προσδοκῶσιν εἰ μὴ τὴν κοίμησιν αὐτῶν, οὕτως καὶ ὑμεῖς μαλακισθέντες ἀπὸ τῶν βιωτικῶν πραγμάτων παρεδώκατε ἑαυτοὺς εἰς τὰς ἀκηδίας καὶ οὐκ ἐπερίψατε ἑαυτῶν τὰς μερίμνας ἐπὶ τὸν κύριον· ἀλλὰ ἐθραύσθη ὑμῶν ἡ διάνοια καὶ ἐπαλεώθητε ταῖς λύπαις ὑμῶν. 11.4 διατὶ οὖν ἐν καθέδρᾳ ἐκάθητο, ἤθελον γνῶναι, κύριε. ὅτι

but the flesh and the hairs *were* old/elderly, and she spoke to me standing: but the face/countenance was more cheerful. 10.5 But in the third vision *she was* all young and remarkably beautiful, and she had only the hairs old/elderly; and she was cheerful in/to *the* end and sitting upon a bench/couch. 10.6 Concerning these (things) I was being exceedingly sad from the (thing) *for* me to know this revelation, and I see the elder (lady) in a vision of the night saying to me: Every request has need of modesty/humility. You fast, therefore, and you might receive what you ask from the Lord. 10.7 Then I fasted one day, and in the same night a young man was seen by me and he says to me: Why *do* you, by hand/agency, you ask *for* revelations in a petition? See/look/take care lest asking many things you might harm your flesh. 10.8 These revelations *are* enough/sufficient for you. Are you not able to see stronger/mightier revelations than *those* which you have seen? 10.9 Answering to him, I say: Lord, sir, I myself ask only this (thing), concerning/about the three forms of the elder (lady), in order that it might become finished/completed revelations. Answering to me he says: Until what (time) are ye senseless/foolish (ones)? But the double-minds of ye makes ye senseless (ones), and the (thing) not to have the heart of ye toward/to the Lord. 10.10 Answering to him, I spoke again: But from you, Lord/sir, we shall know them more accurately. 11.1 Hear you, he says, about the forms which you seek for. 11.2 Why, in the first vision, was she seen by you an elder lady and sitting upon a chair? Because the spirit of ye *is* old and already having faded out and not having power from the softnesses and double-minds of ye; 11.3 for just as the elders/aged (ones), having no longer a hope of the (thing) to be renovated, they wait for nothing else except the sleep of them/their sleep, so also ye, being softened/weakened from the matters of daily life, ye gave yourselves up to the indifferences/apathies and ye off-scoured not the burden/cares of yourselves upon the Lord; but the mind/understanding of ye was crushed and ye were made old by your griefs/sorrows. 11.4 Then I am wanting to know,

---

πᾶς ἀσθενὴς εἰς καθέδραν καθέζεται διὰ τὴν ἀσθένιαν αὐτοῦ, ἵνα συνκρατηθῇ ἡ ἀσθένια τοῦ σώματος αὐτοῦ. ἔχις τὸν τύπον τῆς πρώτης ὁράσεως. 12.1 τῇ δὲ δευτέρᾳ ὁράσι εἶδες αὐτὴν ἑστηκυῖαν καὶ τὴν ὄψιν νεωτέραν ἔχουσαν καὶ ἱλαρωτέραν παρὰ τὸ πρότερον, τὴν δὲ σάρκα καὶ τὰς τρίχας πρεσβυτέρας. ἄκουε, φησίν, καὶ ταύτην τὴν παραβολήν· 12.2 ὅταν πρεσβύτερός τις, ἴδη ἀφελπικῶς ἑαυτὸν διὰ τὴν ἀσθένιαν αὐτοῦ καὶ τὴν πτωχότητα, οὐδὲν ἕτερον προσδέχεται εἰ μὴ τὴν ἡμέραν τῆς ἐσχάτης ζωῆς αὐτοῦ· εἶτα ἐξέφνης κατελίφθη αὐτῷ κληρονονία, ἀκούσας δὲ ἐξεγέρθη καὶ περιχαρὴς γενόμενος ἐνεδύσατο τὴν ἰσχύν· καὶ οὐκαίτι ἀνακεῖται, ἀλλὰ ἔστηκεν, καὶ ἀνανεοῦτο αὐτοῦ τὸ πνεῦμα τὸ ἤδη ἐφθαρμένον ἀπὸ τῶν προτέρων αὐτοῦ πράξεων, καὶ οὐκέτι κάθηται, ἀλλὰ ἀνδρίζεται· οὕτως καὶ ὑμῖς, ἀκούσαντες τὴν ἀποκάλυψιν, 12.3 ὅτι ἐσπλαγχίσθη ἐφ᾽ ὑμᾶς καὶ ἀνενεώσατο τὰ πνεύματα ὑμῶν καὶ ἀπέθεσθαι τὰς μαλακίας ὑμῶν, καὶ προσῆλθεν ὑμῖν ἐσχυρότης καὶ ἐδυναμώθητε ἐν τῇ πίστι, ναὶ ἰδὼν ὁ κύριος τὴν ἰσχυροποίησιν αὐτῶν ἐχάρη· καὶ διὰ τοῦτο ἐδήλωσεν ὑμῶν τὴν οἰκοδομὴν τοῦ πύργου καὶ ἕτερα δηλώσει, ἐὰν ἐξ ὅλης καρδίας εἰρηνεύεται ἐν ἑαυτοῖς. 13.1 τῇ δὲ τρίτῃ ὁράσει εἶδες αὐτὴν νεωτέραν καὶ καλὴν καὶ ἱλαρὰν καὶ καλὴν τὴν μορφὴν αὐτῆς· 13.2 ὡς ἐὰν γάρ τινι λυπουμένῳ ἔλθῃ ἀγγελία ἀγαθή τις, εὐθὺς ἐπελάθετο τῶν προτέρων λυπῶν καὶ οὐδὲν ἄλλο προσδέχεται εἰ μὴ τὴν ἀγγελίαν, ἣν ἤκουσεν, καὶ ἰσχυραποιεῖται λοιπὸν εἰς τὸ ἀγαθὸν καὶ ἀνανεοῦται αὐτοῦ τὸ πνεῦμα διὰ τὴν χαράν, ἣν ἔλαβεν· οὕτως καὶ ὑμῖς ἀνανέωσιν ἰλήφατε τῶν πνευμάτων ὑμῶν ἰδόντες ταῦτα τὰ ἀγαθά. 13.3 καὶ ὅτι ἐπὶ συμψελίου εἶδες καθημένην, ἰσχυρὰ ἡ θέσεις, ὅτι τέσσαρες πόδας ἔχι τὸ συμψέλιον καὶ ἰσχυρῶς ἔστηκεν· καὶ γὰρ ὁ κόσμος διὰ τεσσάρων στοιχίων κρατεῖται. 13.4 οἱ οὖν μετανοήσαντες ὁλοτελῶς νέοι ἔσονται καὶ τεθεμελιωμένοι, ἐξ ὅλης καρδίας

Lord/sir, why she was sittingin a chair. Because every sick/weak (one) sits in a chair because of the sickness/weakness of him, in order that the sickness/weakness of his body might be supported. You have the type/pattern of the first vision. 12.1 But in the second vision you saw her standing and having the younger face and more cheerful from/than the former (time), but the flesh and the hairs were old. You hear, he says, this parable also: 12.2 Whenever anyone is old, he despairs already of himself because of his weakness and poverty, he expects/awaits nothing different except the day of his last life; then an inheritance was suddenly left to him, and having heard he was raised up and having become very glad he put on the strength; and he no longer lies down, but has stood up, and his spirit, the (one) already having been corrupted from his former practices, is renewed, and he sits no longer, but behaves like a man; so also ye, having heard the revelation, 12.3 because he had compassion on ye and renewed your spirits and ye put away the softnesses/weaknesses of ye, and strength came to ye and ye were strengthened/made powerful in the faith; yes, having seen/beheld the strengthening of them, the Lord rejoiced; and because of this he showed of/to ye the building of the tower and he will show other (things), if ye be at peace in yourselves out of/from a whole heart. 13.1 But in the third vision you saw her younger and beautiful and cheerful and her form was beautiful; 13.2 for as if a certain good message may come to someone grieving, he immediately forgot the former sorrows/griefs and he expects/receives nothing else except the message which he heard, and he is strengthened henceforth in/for the good and his spirit is renewed because of the joy which he received; so ye also, ye received a renewal of your spirits, having seen these good things. 13.3 And that you saw her sitting on a bench/couch, the position is strong/secure, because the bench has four feet and it has stood strongly/securely; for the world is also held fast/retained through four elements/rudiments. 13.4 Therefore, the (ones) having repented will be wholly young and having been founded/estab-

μετανοήσαντες. ἀπέχεις ὁλοτελῆ τὴν ἀποκάλυψιν· μηκέτι μηδὲν αἰτήσῃς, ἐάν τι δὲ δέῃ, ἀποκαλυφθήσεταί σοι.

ΟΡΑΣΙΣ Δ΄

1.1 Ἣν εἶδον, ἀδελφοί, μετὰ ἡμέρας εἴκοσι τῆς προτέρας ὁράσεως τῆς γενομένης. 1.2 ὑπῆγον εἰς ἀγρὸν τῇ ὁδῷ τῇ καμπανῇ. ἀπὸ τῆς ὁδοῦ τῆς δημοσίας ἐστὶν δὲ ὡσεὶ στάδια δέκα· ῥᾳδίως δὲ ὁδεύεται ὁ τόπος. 1.3 μόνος οὖν περιπατῶν ἀξιῶν τὸν κύριον, ἵνα τὰς ἀποκαλύψεις καὶ τὰ ὁράματα, ἅ μοι ἔδειξεν διὰ τῆς ἁγίας ἐκκλησίας αὐτοῦ, τελειώσῃ, ἵνα μοι ἰσχυραποιήσῃ καὶ δῷ τὴν μετάνοιαν τοῖς δούλοις αὐτοῦ τοῖς ἐσκανδαλισμένοις, ἵνα δοξασθῇ τὸ ὄνομα αὐτοῦ τὸ μέγα καὶ ἔνδοξον, ὅτι με ἄξιον ἡγήσατο τοῦ δεῖξέ μοι τὰ θαυμάσια αὐτοῦ. 1.4 καὶ δοξάζοντός μου καὶ εὐχαριστοῦντος αὐτῷ, ὡς ἦχος φωνῆς μοι ἀπεκρίθη· μὴ διψυχήσεις, Ἑρμᾶ. ἐμαυτῷ ἠρξάμην διαλογίζεσθαι καὶ λέγειν· ἐγὼ τί ἔχω διψυχῆσαι, οὕτω τεθεμελιωμένος ὑπὸ τοῦ κυρίου καὶ ἰδὼν ἔνδοξα πράγματα; 1.5 καὶ προσέβην μικρόν, ἀδελφοί, καὶ ἰδού, βλέπω κονιορτὸν ὡς εἰς τὸν οὐρανὸν καὶ ἠρξάμην λέγειν ἐν ἐμαυτῷ· μήποτε κτήνη ἔρχοντε καὶ κονιορτὸν ἐγίρωσιν; οὕτω γὰρ ἦν ἀπ᾿ ἐμοῦ ὡς ἀπὸ σταδίου. 1.6 γεινομένου μίζονος καὶ μίζονος κονιορτοῦ ὑπενόησα εἶναι τι θεῖον· μικρὸν ἐξέλαμψεν ὁ ἥλιος κιὰ ἰδού, βλέπω θηρίον μέγιστον ὡσεὶ κῆτός τι, καὶ ἐκ τοῦ στόματος αὐτοῦ ἀκρίδες πύριναι ἐξεπορεύοντο· ἦν δὲ τὸ θηρίον τῷ μήκι ὡσεὶ ποδῶν ρ΄, τὴν δὲ καιφαλὴν εἶχεν ὡσεὶ καιράμου. 1.7 καὶ ἠρξάμην κλαίειν καὶ ἐρωτᾶν τὸν κύριον, εἵνα με λυτρώσηται ἐξ αὐτοῦ· καὶ ἐπανεμνήσθην τοῦ ῥήματος οὗ ἀκηκόειν· μὴ διψυχήσεις, Ἑρμᾶ. 1.8 ἐνδυσάμενος οὖν, ἀδελφοί, τὴν πίστιν τοῦ κυρίου καὶ μνησθεὶς ὧν ἐδίδαξέν με μεγαλίων,

lished, having repented out of a whole heart. You have received the entire revelation; no longer ask nothing, but if something be necessary, it will be revealed to you.

VISION 4

1.1 That which I saw, brothers, after twenty days from the former vision having become. 1.2 I was going to a field on the road to Campana. And the place is about ten stadia (6070 feet) from the public road, and easily traveled. 1.3 Then walking alone petitioning the Lord, that he might complete the revelations and the visions which he showed to me through his holy assembly, in order that he might strengthen me and give the repentance to his slaves, the (ones) having been caused to stumble, that his great and honorable name might be glorified/honored, because he considered me worthy of the (thing) to show his marvels/wonders to me. 1.4 And *from* me glorifying and giving thanks to him, I was answered as a tone/sound of a voice to me: Be not double-minded, Hermas. I began to reason in myself and to say: I, why have I to be double-minded, having thus been founded by the Lord and having seen glorious deeds/things? 1.5 And I approached a little *further*, brothers, and behold, I see dust as in/to the sky/heaven, and I began to say in myself: Perhaps cattle are coming and they raise dust? For this/it was about a stadium (about 607 feet) from me. 1.6 From dust having become greater and greater I supposed it to be some sulphur; the sun shone forth a little and behold, I see a great beast like some/a certain sea monster, and fiery locusts were going forth out of its mouth; and the beast was about a hundred of feet/steps in the length, and it held/had the head as of pottery. 1.7 And I began to weep and to ask the Lord that he might deliver me from it; and I remembered/was reminded of the word which I had heard: Be not double-minded, Hermas. 1.8 Therefore, brothers, having put on the faith of the Lord and having remembered from great (things) which he taught me, having taken courage, I gave myself to the beast. And so the beast was

θαρσήσας εἰς τὸ θηρίον ἐμαυτὸν ἔδωκα. οὕτω δὲ ἤρχετο τὸ
θηρίον ῥοίζω ὥστε δύνασθαι αὐτὸ πόλιν λουμάναι. 1.9 ἔρχομε
ἐγγὺς αὐτοῦ, καὶ τὸ τηλικοῦτο κῆτος ἐκτίνι αὐτὸ χαμαὶ καὶ
οὐδὲν εἰ μὴ τὴν γλῶσσαν προέβαλλεν καὶ ὅλως οὐκ ἐκινήθη,
μέχρεις ὅτε ὑπαρῆλθον αὐτό· 1.10 εἶχεν δὲ τὸ θηρίον ἐπὶ τῆς
καιφαλῆς χρώματα τέσσερα· μέλαν, εἶτα πυροειδὲς καὶ αἱματῶδες,
εἶτα χρυσοῦν, εἶτα λευκόν. 2.1 μετὰ δὲ τὸ παρελθεῖν με τὸ
θηρίον καὶ προελθῖν ὡσεὶ πόδας λ΄, ἰδού, ὑπαντᾷ μοι παρθένος
κεκοσμημένη ὡς ἐκ νυμφῶνος ἐκπορευομένη, ὅλη ἐν λευκοῖς καὶ
ὑποδήμασιν λευκοῖς, κατακεκαλυμμένη ἕως τοῦ μετώπου, ἐν
μίτρα δὲ ἦν ἡ κατακάλυψεις αὐτῆς· εἶχεν δὲ τὰς χῖρας λευκάς.
2.2 ἔγνων ἐγὼ ἐκ τῶν προτέρων ὁραμάτων, ὅτι ἡ ἐκκλησία ἐστίν,
καὶ ἱλαρώτερος ἐγενόμην. ἀσπάζεταί με λέγουσα· χέρε σύ,
ἄνθρωπε. καὶ ἐγὼ αὐτὴν ἀντεσπασάμην· κυρία, χέραι. 2.3
ἀποκριθῖσά μοι λέγει· οὐδέν σοι ἀπήντησεν; λέγω αὐτῇ κυρία,
τηλικοῦτο θηρίον, δυνάμενον λαοὺς διαφθεῖραι· ἀλλὰ τῇ δυνάμι
τοῦ κυρίου καὶ τῇ πολυσπλαγχίᾳ αὐτοῦ ἐξέφυγον αὐτό. 2.4
καλῶς ἐξέφυγες, φησίν, ὅτι τὴν μέριμνάν σου ἐπὶ τὸν θεὸν
ἐπέριψας καὶ τὴν καρδίαν σου ἤνοιξας πρὸς τὸν κύριον,
πιστεύσας, ὅτι δι᾽ οὐδενὸς δύνῃ σωθῆναι εἰ μὴ διὰ τοῦ ἁγίου
μεγάλου καὶ ἐνδόξου ὀνόματος. διὰ τοῦτο ἀπέστειλεν τὸν
ἄγγελον αὐτοῦ τὸν ἐπὶ τῶν θηρίων ὄντα, οὗ τὸ ὄνομά ἐστιν
Θεγρεί, καὶ ἐνέφραξεν τὸ στόμα αὐτοῦ, εἵνα μή σε λυμάνῃ.
μεγάλην θλῖψιν ἐκπέφευγας διὰ τὴν πίστιν σου καὶ ὅτι τηλικοῦτο
θηρίον ἰδὼν οὐκ ἐδιψύχησας· 2.5 ὕπαγε οὖν καὶ ἐξήγησαι τοῖς
ἐκλεκτοῖς τοῦ κυρίου τὰ μεγαλεῖα αὐτοῦ καὶ εἰπὲ αὐτοῖς, ὅτι τὸ
θηρίον τοῦτο τύπος ἐστὶν θλίψεως τῆς μελλούσης τῆς μεγάλης· ἐὰν
οὖν προετοιμάσησθαι καὶ μετανοήσητε ἐξ ὅλης καρδίας ὑμῶν
πρὸς τὸν κύριον, δυνήσεσθε ἐκφυγεῖν αὐτήν, ἐὰν ἡ καρδία ὑμῶν
γένηται καθαρὰ καὶ ἄμωμος καὶ τὰς λοιπὰς τῆς ζωῆς ἡμαίρας

coming in a rush so as *for* it to be able to destroy a city.   1.9 I come near from it, and the sea monster *being* so great stretches itself on the ground and it put forth nothing except the tongue and it was not moved at all until when I passed it by;   1.10 and the beast had four colors on the head; black, then the color of flame and of blood, then golden, then white. 2.1 And after the (thing) *for* me to pass by the beast and to go about thirty feet/steps, behold, a maiden met me having been adorned as (one) coming forth out of a bridal chamber, all in white (things) and wearing white sandals, having been veiled until the forehead, and her (head) covering was with a snood/turban; but she had white hands (hairs). 2.2 I, I knew from the former visions that she is the assembly/(church), and I became more cheerful. She greets me, saying: You, you rejoice/greeting *for* you, O man. And I myself greeted her: You rejoice/greetings, lady.   2.3 Answering to me, she says: Did nothing meet you? I say to her: Lady, such a great beast, being able to destroy peoples; but by the power of the Lord and the great compassion of him, I escaped it.   2.4 You escaped well, she says, because you put your cares upon God and you opened your heart to the Lord, believing that (one) may be able to be saved through nothing except through the holy, great, and glorious name. Because of this he sent his messenger/angel, the (one) being over the beasts, of whom the name is Thegri, and he shut the mouth of it, in order that it   might not injure/ harm you. You have escaped a great affliction through your faith and because, having seen so great a beast, you were not double-minded;   2.5   you go, therefore, also to tell to the chosen (ones) of the Lord the great (things) of him, and say to them that this beast is a type/example of the great affliction/tribulation/oppression being about to come; if then ye might be prepared beforehand and ye might repent to the Lord with the whole heart of ye/your whole heart, ye will be able to escape it, if the heart of ye might become clean/pure and without blame and ye might slave blamelessly for the Lord the rest of your days of the life/the remaining days of your life. Having thrown

ΠΟΙΜΗΝ

ὑμῶν δουλεύσητε τῷ κυρίῳ ἀμέμπτως. ἐπιρίψαντες τὰς μερίμνας ὑμῶν ἐπὶ τὸν κύριον, καὶ αὐτὸς κατορθώσι αὐτάς. 2.6 πιστεύσατε τῷ κυρίῳ, οἱ δίψυχοι, ὅτι πάντα δύναται καὶ ἀποστρέφι τὴν ὀργὴν αὐτοῦ ἀφ' ὑμῶν καὶ ἐξαποστέλλει μάστιγας ὑμῖν τοῖς διψύχοις. οὐαὶ τοῖς ἀκούσασιν τὰ ῥήματα ταῦτα καὶ παρακούσασιν· ἑρετώτερον ἦν αὐτοῖς τὸ μὴ γεννηθῆναι. 3.1 ἠρώτησα αὐτὴν περὶ τῶν τεσσάρων χρωμάτων ὧν εἶχεν τὸ θηρίον εἰς τὴν καιφαλήν. ἡ δὲ ἀποκριθεῖσα μοι λέγει· πάλιν περίεργος εἶ περὶ τοιούτων πραγμάτων. ναί, φημί, κυρία· γνώρισόν μοι, τί ἐστιν ταῦτα. 3.2 ἄκουε, φησίν· τὸ μὲν μέλαν οὗτος ὁ κόσμος ἐστίν, ἐν ᾧ κατοικῖται· 3.3 τὸ δὲ πυρροϊδὲς καὶ αἱματώιδες, ὅτι δεῖ κόσμον τοῦτον δι' αἵματος καὶ πυρὸς ἀπόλλυσθαι· 3.4 τὸ δὲ χρυσσοῦν μέρος ὑμεῖς ἐστε οἱ ἐκφυγόνταις τὸν κόσμον τοῦτον. ὥσπερ γὰρ τὸ χρυσίον δοκιμάζεται διὰ τοῦ πυρὸς καὶ εὔχρησον γείνεται, οὕτως καὶ ὑμῖς δοκιμάζεσθαι οἱ κατοικοῦντες ἐν αὐτοῖς. οἱ οὖν μίναντες καὶ πυρωθέντες ὑπ' αὐτῶν καθαρισθήσεσθε. ὥσπερ χρυσίον ἀποβάλλι τὴν σκωρίαν αὐτοῦ, οὕτω καὶ ὑμῖς ἀποβαλεῖται πᾶσαν λύπην καὶ στενοχωρίαν, καὶ καθαρισθήσεσθε καὶ χρήσιμοι ἔσεσθαι εἰς τὴν οἰκοδομὴν τοῦ πύργου. 3.5 τὸ δὲ λευκὸν μέρος ὁ αἰὼν ὁ ἐπερχόμενος, ἐν ᾧ κατοικοῦσιν οἱ ἐκλεκτοὶ τοῦ θεοῦ· — εἰς ζωὴν αἰώνιον. 3.6 σὺ οὖν μὴ διαλίπῃς λαλῶν εἰς τὰ ὦτα τῶν ἁγίων. ἔχετε τύπον τῆς θλίψεως τῆς ἐρχομένης μεγάλης. ἐὰν δὲ ὑμῖς θελήσητε, οὐδὲν ἔσται. μνημονεύετε τὰ προγεγραμμένα. 3.7 ταῦτα εἴπασα ἀπῆλθεν, καὶ οὐκ ἶδον, ποίῳ τόπῳ ἀπῆλθεν· νέφος γὰρ ἐγένετο· κἀγὼ ἐπεστράφην εἰς τὰ ὀπίσω φοβηθείς, δοκῶν ὅτι τὸ θηρείον ἔρχεται.

ΑΠΟΚΑΛΥΨΙΣ Ε΄

1.1 Προσευξαμένου μου ἐν τῷ οἴκῳ καὶ καθίσαντος εἰς τὴν κλίνην εἰσῆλθεν ἀνήρ τις ἔνδοξος τῇ ὄψι, σχήματι ποιμενικῷ,

your cares/burdens upon the Lord, he himself will also set them straight. 2.6 Ye believed in the Lord, the double-minded (ones), because he is powerful *for* all (things) and he turns away his anger from ye and he sends forth scourges to ye, the double-minded (ones). Woe to the (ones)/those having heard these words and having disregarded *them*; the (thing) not to be born was better for them. 3.1 I questioned her about the four colors which the beast had in the head. And the (she), answering to me, she says: Again you are curious about such matters. Yes, lady, I say: Make known to me what is these (things). 3.2 You hear, she says: The black is indeed this world, in which ye dwell; 3.3 and the color of fire and of blood because it is necessary *for* this world to be destroyed through blood and fire; 3.4 and ye, ye are the golden part, the (ones) having fled/escaped this world. For even as the gold is proved/tested through the fire and becomes useful/valuable, so also ye, the (ones) dwelling among them, ye are tested. Therefore ye, the (ones) remaining and burning, will be cleansed/purified by them. Even as gold puts away the slag/dross of it/its slag, so also ye, ye will be useful (ones) in the building of the tower. 3.5 But the white part *is* the expected/awaited age, in which the chosen (ones) of God *will dwell* in eternal life. 3.6 Therefore you, you may not cease speaking to the ears of the saints. Ye have a type/example of the oppression/affliction, the great (one) coming. But if ye, ye might wish/want, it will be nothing. Remember ye the (things) having been written before. 3.7 Having said these (things), she went away, and I saw not to what place she went; for there became a cloud; and I, I turned to the (things) behind, fearing, supposing that the beast comes.

REVELATION 5

1.1 From having been praying in my house and having sat in the bed, a certain man came in/entered, *being* honorable/glorious in the appearance, in fashion/form like a shepherd, wearing a white animal

περικίμενος δέρμα λευκὸν καὶ πήραν ἔχων ἐπὶ τῶν ὤμων καὶ ῥάβδον εἰς τὴν χῖραν. καὶ ἠσπάσατό μαι, κἀγὼ ἀντεσπασάμην αὐτόν. 1.2 καὶ εὐθὺς παρεκάθισέν μοι καὶ λέγει μοι· ἀπεστάλην ὑπὸ τοῦ σεμνοτάτου ἀγγέλου, ἵνα μετὰ σοῦ οἰκήσω τὰς λοιπὰς ἡμέρας τῆς ζωῆς σου. 1.3 ἔδοξα ἐγώ, ὅτι πάρεστιν ἐκπιράζων με, καὶ λέγω αὐτῷ· σὺ γὰρ τίς εἶ; ἐγὼ γάρ, φημί, γεινώσκω, ᾧ παρεδόθην. λέγει μοι· οὐκ ἐπιγεινώσκεις με; οὔ, φημί. ἐγώ, φησίν, εἰμὶ ὁ ποιμήν, ᾧ παρεδόθη. 1.4 ἔτι λαλοῦντος αὐτοῦ ἠλλοιώθη ἡ εἰδέα αὐτοῦ, καὶ ἐπέγνων αὐτόν, ὅτι ἐκίνος ἦν, ᾧ παρεδόδην, καὶ εὐθὺς συνεχύθην καὶ φόβος με ἔλαβεν καὶ ὅλος συνεκόπην ἀπὸ τῆς λύπης, ὅτι οὕτως αὐτῷ ἀπεκρίθην πονηρῶς καὶ ἀφρόνως. 1.5 ὁ δὲ ἀποκριθείς μοι λέγει· μὴ συγχύννου, ἀλλὰ ἰσχυροποιοῦ ἐν τὲς ἐντολαῖς μου αἷς σοι μέλλω ἐντέλλεσθε. ἐπεστάλην γάρ, φησίν, ἵνα ἃ εἶδες πρότερον πάντα σοι πάλιν δίξω, αὐτὰ τὰ καιφάλεα τὰ ὄντα ὑμῖν σύμφορα.

πρῶτον πάντων τὰς ἐντολάς μου γράψον καὶ τὰς παραβολάς· τὰ δὲ ἕτερα, καθώς σοι δίξω, οὕτως γράψεις· διὰ τοῦτο, φησίν, ἐντέλλομέ σοι πρῶτον γράψε τὰς ἐντολὰς καὶ παραβολάς, ἵνα ὑπὸ χῖρα ἀναγεινώσκῃς αὐτὰ καὶ δυνηθῇς φυλάξε αὐτάς. 1.6 ἔγραψα οὖν τὰς ἐντολὰς καὶ παραβολάς, καθὼς ἐνετίλατό μοι. 1.7 ἐὰν οὖν ἀκούσαντες αὐτὰς φυλάξητε καὶ ἐν αὐταῖς πορευθῆται καὶ ἐργάσησθαι αὐτὰς ἐν καθαρᾷ καρδίᾳ, ἀπολήμψεσθε ἀπὸ τοῦ κυρίου, ὅσα ἐπηγγείλατο ὑμῖν· ἐὰν δὲ ἀκούσαντες μὴ μετανοήσηται, ἀλλ' ἔτι προσθῆται ταῖς ἁμαρτίαις ὑμῶν, ἀπολήμψεσται παρὰ τοῦ κυρίου τὰ ἐναντία. ταῦτά μοι οὕτως ἔγραψε ὁ ποιμὴν ὁ ἐνετίλατο, ὁ ἄγγελος τῆς μετανοίας.

skin and having a traveling bag/knapsack upon the shoulders and a staff/rod in the hand. And he greeted me, and I greeted him back. 1.2 And at once he sat down with me and he says to me: I was sent by the most venerable messenger/angel, that I might live/dwell with you the remaining days of your life. 1.3 I, I thought that he is present *for* trying/tempting me, and I say to him: For you, who are you? For I, I *may* say: I know to whom I was delivered over. He says to me: Do you not recognize me? No, I say. I, he says, I am the shepherd to whom it/he/you was handed over. 1.4 From him yet speaking, his appearance was changed and I recognized him, that he was that (one) to whom I was handed over and I was confused/confounded and fear took me and I was entirely buried from the sorrow/grief, because I answered him so wickedly and foolish-ly. 1.5 But the (he) answering to me, he says: Be not confused, but be made strong by the commands from me which I am about to command to you. For I was sent, he says, in order that I might show again to you all (things) which you saw formerly; they *are* the head/principle things being brought together for ye.

First of all, you write the commands and the parables from me; and the other/different (things), as I show to you, so you write; because of this, he says, I command you first to write the commands and parables, that by/under hand you may read them and be able to guard/keep them. 1.6 Therefore I wrote the commands and parables just as he commanded to me. 1.7 Then if, having heard them, ye might guard/keep *them* and ye might proceed/travel in/by them and work them with a clean/pure heart, ye will receive from the Lord as much as/whatever he promised to ye; but if, having heard, ye might not repent, but ye might still add to your sins/faults, ye will receive the opposite/contrary (things) from the Lord. The shepherd thus commanded me to write these (things), *being* the messenger/angel of the repentance.

ΠΟΙΜΗΝ

ΕΝΤΟΛΗ Α΄

1.1 Πρῶτον πάντων πίστευσον, ὅτι εἷς ἐστὶν ὁ θεός, ὁ τὰ πάντα κτίσας καὶ καταρτίσας καὶ ποιήσας ἐκ τοῦ μὴ ὄντος εἰς τὸ εἶναι τὰ πάντα καὶ πάντα χωρῶν, μόνος δὲ ἀχώρητος ὤν. 1.2 πίστευσον οὖν αὐτῷ καὶ φοβήθητει αὐτόν, φοβηθεὶς δὲ ἐγκράτευσε. ταῦτα φύλαξε, καὶ ἀποβαλῖς πᾶσαν πονηρίαν ἀπὸ σεαυτοῦ καὶ ἐνδύσῃ πᾶσαν ἀρετὴν δικαιοσύνης καὶ ζήσῃς τῷ θεῷ, ἐὰν φυλάξῃς τὴν ἐντολὴν ταύτην.

ΕΝΤΟΛΗ Β΄

1.1 Λέγει μοι· ἁπλότητα ἔχε καὶ ἄκακος γείνου, καὶ ἔσῃ ὡς τὰ νήπια τὰ μὴ γινώσκοντα τὴν πονηρίαν τὴν ἀπολλύουσαν τὴν ζωὴν τῶν ἀνθρώπων. 1.2 πρῶτον μὲν μηδενὸς καταλάλει μηδὲ ἡδέως ἄκουαι καταλαλοῦντος· εἰ δὲ μή, καὶ σὺ ὁ ἀκούων ἔνοχος εἶ τῆς ἁμαρτίας τοῦ καταλαλοῦντος, ἐὰν πιστεύσῃς τῆς καταλαλίας ᾗ ἂν ἀκούσῃς· πιστεύσας καὶ σὺ αὐτὸς ἕξεις κατὰ τοῦ ἀδελφοῦ σου· οὕτως οὖν ἔνοχος ἔσῃ τῆς ἁμαρτίας τοῦ καταλαλοῦντος. 1.3 πονηρὰ καταλαλιά· ἀκατάστατον δαιμόνιόν ἐστιν, μηδέποτε εἰρηνεῦον, ἀλλὰ πάντοτε ἐν διχοστασίαις κατοικοῦν. ἀπέχου οὖν ἀπ᾽ αὐτοῦ, καὶ εὐθηνίαν πάντοται ἕξεις μετὰ πάντων. 1.4 ἔνδυσε δὲ τὴν σεμνότητα, ἐν ᾗ οὐδὲν πρόσκομμά ἐστιν πονηρόν, ἀλλὰ πάντα ἱλαρὰ καὶ ὁμαλά. ἐργάζου τὸ ἀγαθὸν καὶ ἐκ τῶν κόπων σου ὧν ὁ θεὸς δίδωσίν σοι πᾶσιν ὑστερουμένοις δίδου ἁπλῶς, μὴ διστάζων, τίνι δῷς ἢ τίνι μὴ δῷς. πᾶσιν δίδου· πᾶσιν γὰρ ὁ θεὸς δίδοσθε θέλι ἀπὸ τῶν ἰδίων δωρημάτων. 1.5 οἱ οὖν λαμβάνοντες ἀποδώσουσι λόγον τῷ θεῷ, διατὶ ἔλαβον καὶ εἰς τί· οἱ μὲν γὰρ λαμβάνοντες ἀπθλιβόμενοι οὐ δικασθήσονται, οἱ δὲ ἐν ὑποκρίσει

COMMAND 1

1.1 First of all, you believe that God is one, the (one) having created and fitted and made all things out of the (thing) not being into the (thing) for all things to be and all being contained/limited, but he alone being uncontained. 1.2 Believe then in him and fear him, and having feared, control yourself. guard/keep these (things), and put away every evil (thing)/wickedness from yourself and put on every virtue of justice/justness, and you will live for God if you might guard/keep this command.

COMMAND 2

1.1 He says to me: Have sincerity and become innocent/without bad, and you will be like the infants not knowing the wickedness/evil destroying the life of the men/humans. 1.2 First, indeed, speak against no one, neither hear gladly (one) speaking against/slandering, otherwise you also, the (one) hearing, you are guilty of the sin of the (ones) speaking against/slandering, if you might believe the evil speaking which you would hear; having believed, you, you also will have/hold *it* against your brother; so therefore, you will be guilty of the sin of the (one) speaking evil. 1.3 Evil speaking *is* wicked; it is an unstable demon, never being at peace, but always dwelling/living in dissensions/strifes. Therefore, you abstain from it, and you will always have well-being with all. 1.4 And put on the dignity/gravity, in which there is no evil stumbling block/offense, but all (things) *are* cheerful and smooth/level. Work the good and out of your labors which God gives to you, give generously to all *those* lacking/being deficient, not doubting to whom you may give or give not. Give to all; for God wants/wishes to give to all from his own gifts. 1.5 Then the (ones) receiving will give back/render an account to God, why they received *it* and to/for what; for indeed the (ones) receiving from being oppressed will not be punished, but the (ones) receiving in/by pretense/

λαμβάνονταις τίσσουσιν δίκην. 1.6 ὁ οὖν διδοὺς ἀθῷός ἐστιν· ὡς γὰρ ἔλαβεν παρὰ τοῦ κυρίου τὴν διακονίαν τελέσαι, ἁπλῶς αὐτὴν ἐτέλεσεν, μηθὲν διακρίνων, τίνι δῷ ἢ μὴ δῷ. ἐγένετο οὖν ἡ διακονία αὕτη ἁπλῶς τελεσθεῖσα ἔνδοξος παρὰ τῷ θεῷ. ὁ οὖν οὕτως ἁπλῶς διακονῶν τῷ θεῷ ζήσεται. 1.7 -- -αντος.

ΕΝΤΟΛΗ Γ΄

1.1 Πάλιν μοι λέγει· ἀλήθειαν ἀγάπα καὶ πᾶσα ἀλήθεια, ἐκ τοῦ στόματός σου ἐκπορευέσθω, ἵνα τὸ πνεῦμα. ὃ ὁ θεὸς κατῴκισεν ἐν τῇ σαρκὶ ταύτῃ, ἀληθὲς εὑρεθῇ παρὰ πᾶσιν ἀνθρώποις, καὶ οὕτως δοξασθήσεται ὁ κύριος ὁ ἐν σοὶ κατοικῶν, ὅτι ὁ κύριος ἀληθινὸς ἐν παντὶ ῥήματι καὶ οὐδὲν παρ' αὐτῷ ψεῦδος. 1.2 οἱ οὖν ψευδόμενοι ἀθετοῦσι τὸν κύριον καὶ γίνονται --. 1.5 -- -τάτου ψεύσματος ζήσεται τῷ θεῷ.

ΕΝΤΟΛΗ Δ΄

1.1 Ἐντέλλομέ σοι, φησίν, φυλάσσειν τὴν ἁγνίαν, μὴ ἀναβαινέτω σου ἐπὶ τὴν καρδίαν περὶ γυναικὸς ἀλλοτρίας ἢ περὶ πορνίας τινὸς ἢ περὶ τοιούτων τινῶν ὁμοιωμάτων πονηρῶν. τοῦτο γὰρ ποιῶν μεγάλην ἁμαρτίαν ἐργάζῃ. τῆς δὲ σῆς μνημονεύων πάντοται γυναικὸς οὐδέποτε διαμαρτήσεις. 1.2 ἐὰν γὰρ αὕτη ἡ ἐνθύμησεις ἐπὶ καρδίαν σου ἀναβῇ, διαμαρτήσεις, καὶ ἐὰν ἕτερα οὕτως πονηρά, ἁμαρτίαν ἐργάζῃ· ἡ γὰρ ἐνθύμησις αὕτη θεῷ δούλῳ ἁμαρτία μεγάλη ἐστίν· ἐὰν δέ τις ἐργάσηται τὸ ἔργον τὸ πονηρὸν τοῦτο, θάνατον ἑαυτῷ ἐργάζεται. 1.3 βλέπε οὖν σύ· ἀπέχου ἀπὸ τῆς ἐθυμήσεως ταύτης· ὅπου γὰρ σεμνότης κατοικῖ, ἐκῖ ἀνομία οὐκ ὀφίλει ἀναβαίνειν ἐπὶ καρδίαν ἀνδρὸς δικαίου. 1.4 λέγω αὐτῷ· κύριε, ἐπίτρεψόν μοι ὀλίγα ἐπερωτῆσέ σαι. λέγε, φησίν. κύριε, φημί, ἡ γυναῖκα ἔχων τις πιστὴν ἐν κυρίῳ καὶ

hypocrisy will pay/incur a penalty/punishment. 1.6 Therefore, the (one) giving is innocent; for as he received the service/ministry from the Lord to finish, he finished it sincerely, doubting nothing to whom he may give or give not. Therefore this service/ministry, having been finished sincerely, became honorable/glorious with/beside God. Therefore, the (one) so serving sincerely will live with/for God. 1.7 -- unstained.

COMMAND 3

1.1 Again he says to me: Love truth and let all truth go/proceed out of your mouth, in order that the spirit which God dwelled/inhabited in this flesh might be found true by all men/humans, and so/thus the Lord dwelling in you will be glorified, because the Lord *is* true in every word and nothing *is* a lie with/beside him. 1.2 Therefore those lying themselves annul/violate the Lord and they become -- . 1.5 -- most *evil* (thing) of lying will live for God.

COMMAND 4

1.1 I command to you, he says, to guard/keep the chastity; let it not go up from you upon the heart about another's woman or about certain prostitutions or about some such evil (things) of like form. For doing this (thing) you work a great sin. But always remembering your woman, you will never miss the mark/sin. 1.2 For if this thought/reflection may arise upon your heart, you will sin, and if thus other/different evils, you work/do sin; for this thought/reflection is a great sin for a slave of God; and if anyone might work this evil work/deed, he works death for himself. 1.3 Therefore you, you see/beware, abstain from this desire, for where dignity/reverence dwells, lawlessness is not obliged there to come upon a just man's heart. 1.4 I say to him: Lord/sir, allow me to ask you a few (things). Speak, he says. Lord/sir, I say, the woman having a certain (man) faithful

ταύτην εὕρῃ ἐν μοιχίᾳ τινεί, ἆρα ἁμαρτάνει ὁ ἀνὴρ συνζῶν μετ᾽ αὐτῆς; 1.5 ἄχρι τῆς ἀγνοίας, φησίν, οὐκ ἁμαρτάνι· ἐὰν δὲ γνοῖ ὁ ἀνὴρ τὴν ἁμαρτίαν αὐτῆς καὶ μὴ μετανοήσῃ ἡ γυνή, ἀλλ᾽ ἐπιμένῃ τῇ πορνίᾳ αὐτῆς καὶ συνζῇ ὁ ἀνὴρ μετ᾽ αὐτῆς, ἔνοχος γείνεται τῆς ἁμαρτίας αὐτῆς καὶ κοινωνὸς τῆς μοιχίας. 1.6 τί οὖν, φημί, κύριε, ποιήσῃ ὁ ἀνήρ, ἐὰν ἐπιμίνῃ τῷ πάθι τούτῳ ἡ γυνή; ἀπολυσάτω, φησίν, αὐτὴν καὶ ὁ ἀνὴρ ἐφ᾽ ἑαυτῷ μενέτω· ἐὰν δὲ ἀπολύσας τὴν γυναῖκα ἑτέραν γαμήσῃ, καὶ αὐτὸς μοιχᾶται. 1.7 ἐὰν οὖν, φημί, κύριε, μετὰ τὸ ἀπολυθῆναι τὴν γυναῖκα μετανοήσῃ ἡ γυνὴ καὶ θελήσῃ ἐπὶ τὸν ἑαυτῆς ἄνδρα ὑποστρέψαι, οὐ παραδεχθήσεται; 1.8 καὶ μήν, φησίν, ἐὰν μὴ παραδέξηται αὐτὴν ὁ ἀνήρ, ἁμαρτάνει καὶ μεγάλην ἁμαρτίαν ἑαυτῷ ἐπισπᾶται, ἀλλὰ δεῖ παραδεχθῆναι τὸν ἡμαρτηκότα καὶ μετανοοῦντα, μὴ ἐπὶ πολὺ δέ· τοῖς γὰρ δούλοις τοῦ θεοῦ μετάνοιά ἐστιν μία. διὰ τὴν μετάνοιαν οὖν οὐκ ὀφείλει γαμεῖν ὁ ἀνὴρ αὐτῆς. αὕτη ἡ πράξεις ἐπὶ γυναικὶ καὶ ἀνδρὶ κεῖται. 1.9 οὐ μόνον, φησίν, μοιχία ἐστίν, ἐάν τις τὴν σάρκαν ἑαυτοῦ μιάνῃ, ἀλλὰ καὶ ὃς ἂν τὰ ὁμοιώματα ποιῇ τοῖς ἔθνεσιν, μοιχᾶται. ὥστε καὶ ἐν τοῖς τοιούτοις ἔργοις ἐὰν ἐμμένῃ τις καὶ μὴ μετανοῇ, ἀπέχου ἀπ᾽ αὐτοῦ καὶ μὴ συνζῆθι αὐτῷ· εἰ δὲ μή, καὶ σὺ μέτοχος εἶ τῆς ἁμαρτίας αὐτοῦ. 1.10 διὰ τοῦτο προσετάγη ὑμῖν ἐφ᾽ ἑαυτοῖς μένειν, εἴτε ἀνὴρ εἴτε γυνή· δύναται γὰρ ἐν τοῖς τοιούτοις μετάνοια εἶναι. 1.11 ἐγὼ οὖν, φησίν, οὐ δίδωμι ἀφορμήν, ἵνα αὕτη ἡ πρᾶξις οὕτως συντελῆται, ἀλλὰ εἰς τὸ μηκέτι ἁμαρτάνειν τὸν ἡμαρτηκότα. περὶ δὲ τῆς προτέρας ἁμαρτίας αὐτοῦ ἔστιν ὁ δυνάμενος ἴασιν δοῦναι· αὐτὸς γάρ ἐστιν ὁ ἔχων πάντων τὴν ἐξουσίαν. 2.1 ἠρώτησα δὲ αὐτὸν λέγων· κύριε, ἐπὶ ὁ κύριός μου ἄξιόν με ἡγήσατο, ἵνα μετ᾽ ἐμοῦ

in *the* Lord and he might find this (one)/her in some
adultery, then *does* the man living with her sin? 1.5
He says: As long as from the ignorance, he sins not;
but if the man might know the sin/fault of her and the
woman might not repent, but might continue/persevere
in her prostitution and the man may live with her, he
becomes guilty of her sin and a partner/companion of
the adultery. 1.6 I say: Then what, lord/sir, might/
should the man do, if the woman might continue in this
passion? Let him dismiss/release her, he says, and let
the man abide by himself; but if, having released/dis-
missed the woman, he might marry another/different
(woman), he himself also does adultery. 1.7 I say:
Lord/sir, then if after the (thing) *for* the (thing)
for the woman to be released/dismissed, the woman
might repent and want/wish to return to the man of
herself, will/should she not be received/accepted?
1.8 Certainly, he says, if the man might not receive/
accept her, he sins and draws a great sin upon himself, but it is necessary *for* the (one) having sinned
and having repented to be received/accepted, but not
for much (many times) for to the slaves of God, there
is one repentance. Therefore her man is not obligat-
ed/ought not to marry because of the repentance. This
is the practice/mode of action laid out upon/for a
woman and a man. 1.9 He says: It is not only adultery
if someone may stain/defile the flesh of himself, but
also who ever may do similar things to the ethnics, he
does adultery, so that also if anyone might perse-
vere/abide in such works and might not repent, avoid/
abstain from him and live not with him; otherwise you,
you are also a partaker/sharer of his sin/fault. 1.10
Because of this it was enjoined/commanded to ye to
abide by yourselves, whether a man or a woman; for
repentance is able to be in those such/the such
(things). 1.11 Then he says: I, I give not an occasion that this practice/act may thus be completed/fin-
ished together, but in/for the (thing) *for* the (one)
having sinned to sin no longer. And concerning his
former sin, there is the (one) being able to give
healing/a cure; for he himself is the (one) having/
holding the authority of all. 2.1 But I questioned

πάντοται κατοικῆς, ὀλίγα μου ῥήματα ἔτι ἀνάσχου, ἐπὶ οὐ συνίω οὐδὲν καὶ ἡ καρδία μου πεπώρωται ἀπὸ τῶν προτέρων μου πράξεων· συνέτισόν με, ὅτι λίαν ἄφρων εἰμὶ καὶ ὅλως οὐδὲν νοῶ. 2.2 ἀποκριθείς μοι λέγει· ἐγώ, φησίν, ἐπὶ τῆς μετανοίας εἰμὶ καὶ πᾶσιν τοῖς μετανοοῦσιν σύνεσιν δίδωμι. ἢ οὐ δοκεῖ σοι, φησίν, αὐτὸ τοῦτο τὸ μετανοῆσαι σύνεσιν εἶναι; τὸ μετανοῆσε, φησίν, σύνεσίς ἐστιν μεγάλη· συνίει γὰρ ὁ ἀνὴρ ὁ ἁμαρτήσας, ὅτι πεποίηκεν τὸ πονηρὸν ἔμπροσθεν τοῦ κυρίου καὶ ἀναβαίνει ἐπὶ τὴν καρδίαν αὐτοῦ ἡ πρᾶξεις, ἣν ἔπραξεν, καὶ μετανοεῖ καὶ οὐκέτι ἐργάζεται τὸ πονηρόν, ἀλλὰ τὸ ἀγαθὸν πολυτελῶς ἐργάζεται καὶ ταπινοῖ τὴν ἑαυτοῦ ψυχὴν καὶ βασανίζει, ὅτι ἥμαρτεν. βλέπεις οὖν, ὅτι ἡ μετάνοια σύνεσίς ἐστιν μεγάλη. 2.3 διὰ τοῦτο οὖν, φημί, κύριε, ἐξακριβάζομαι παρὰ σοῦ πάντα· πρῶτον μέν,

Thus ends "The Shepherd" in Codex Sinaiticus, except for one small fragment. This is the only incomplete book in the New Testament portion of that Codex, but this is by no means the end of "The Shepherd of Hermas". The reader can read the remainder in English in any edition of "The Lost Books of the Bible". For both Greek and English, the writer recommends The Loeb Classical Library, volume number 25, "Apostolic Fathers II", Harvard University Press.

him, saying: Lord/sir, since my Lord considered me worthy that you might always dwell with me, allow you yet a few of my words, since I *do* not understand nothing and my heart has been hardened from my former practices/acts; understand you me, because I am very foolish and I actually perceive/know nothing.   2.2 Answering to me, he says: I, he says, I am over the repentance and I give insight/understanding to all the (ones) repenting. Or seems it not to you, he says, *for* this very thing, to repent, to be insight? The (thing) to repent, he says,   is   great insight/understanding; for the man having sinned understands that he has done the evil (thing) before the Lord, and the act/practice which he did/practiced comes upon his heart, and he repents and no longer works the evil, but he works the good lavishly and he humbles the soul/life of himself and torments *it*, because he missed the mark/sinned. You see, then, that the repentance is a great insight/understanding.   2.3 Then because of this I say: Lord/sir, I enquire exactly all (things) from you; first, indeed,

Thus ends "The Shepherd" in Codex Sinaiticus, except for one small fragment. This is the only incomplete book/scroll in the New Testament portion of that Codex, but this is by no means the end of "The Shepherd of Hermas". The reader can read the remainder in English in any edition of "The Lost Books of the Bible". For both Greek and English, the writer recommends The Loeb Classical Library, volume number 25, "Apostolic Fathers II", Harvard University Press.

Old Testament Order

APPENDIX I: INDEX OF QUOTATIONS

New Testament Order

Matthew

1.23	Is 7.14
	Is 8.8,10 (Gr)
2.6	Mic 5.2
2.15	Ho 11.1
2.18	Jr 13.11
3.3	Is 40.3
4.4	Dt 8.3
4.6	Ps 91.11-12
4.7	Dt 6.16
4.10	Dt 6.13
4.15-16	Is 9.1-2
5.21	Ex 20.13
	Dt 5.17
5.27	Ex 20.14
	Dt 5.18
5.31	Dt 24.1
5.33	Lv 19.12
	Nu 30.2
5.38	Ex 21.24
	Lv 24.20
	Dt 19.21
5.43	Lv 19.18
8.17	Is 53.4
9.13	Ho 6.6
10.35	Mic 7.6
11.10	Mal 3.1
12.7	Ho 6.6
12.18.21	Is 42.1-4
12.40	Jon 1.17
13.14-15	Is 6.9-10
13.35	Ps 78.2
15.4a	Ex 20.12
	Dt 5.16
15.4b	Ex 21.17
15.8-9	Is 29.13 (Gr)
18.16	Dt 19.15
19.4	Gn 1.27
	5.2
19.5	Gn 2.24
19.7	Dt 24.1
19.18-19	Ex 20.12-16
	Dt 5.16-20
19.19	Lv 19.18
21.5	Is 62.11
	Zch 9.9
21.9	Ps 118.25-26
21.13	Is 56.7
21.16	Ps 8.3 (Gr)
21.42	Ps 118.22.23
22.24	Dt 25.5
22.32	Ex 3.6,15
22.37	Dt 6.5
22.39	Lv 19.18
22.44	Ps 110.1
23.39	Ps 118.26
24.30	Dn 7.13
26.31	Zch 13.7
26.64a	Ps 110.1
26.64b	Dn 7.13
27.9-10	Zch 11.12-13
27.46	Ps 22.1

Mark

1.2	Mal 3.1
1.3	Is 40.3
4.12	Is 6.9-10
7.6-7	Is 29.13 (Gr)
7.10a	Ex 20.12
	Dt 5.16
7.10b	Ex 21.17
10.4	Dt 24.1,3
10.6	Gn 1.27
	5.2
10.7-8	Gn 2.24
10.19	Ex 20.12-16
	Dt 5.16.20
11.9-10	Ps 118.25-26
11.17	Is 56.7

Mark (cont.)

12.10-11	Ps 118.22-23
12.19	Dt 25.5
12.26	Ex 3.6,15
12.29-30	Dt 6.4-5
12.31	Lv 19.18
12.32a	Dt 6.4
12.32b	Dt 4.35
	Is 45.21
12.33a	Dt 6.5
12.33b	Lv 19.18
12.36	Ps 110.1
13.26	Dn 7.13
14.27	Zch 13.7
14.62a	Ps 110.1
14.62b	Dn 7.13
15.34	Ps 22.1

Luke

2.23	Ex 13.2,12,15
2.24	Lv 12.8
3.4-6	Is 40.3-5
4.4	Dt 8.3
4.8	Dt 6.13
4.10-11	Ps 91.11-12
4.12	Dt 6.16
4.18-19	Is 61.1-2
7.27	Mal 3.1
8.10	Is 6.9
10.27a	Dt 6.5
10.27b	Lv 19.18
13.35	Ps 118.26
18.20	Ex 20.12-16
	Dt 5.16-20
19.38	Ps 118.26
19.46	Is 56.7
20.17	Ps 118.22
20.28	Dt 25.5
20.37	Ex 3.6
20.42-43	Ps 110.1

21.27	Dn 7.13
22.37	Is 53.12
22.69	Ps 110.1
23.30	Ho 10.8
23.46	Ps 31.5

John

1.23	Is 40.3
2.17	Ps 69.9
6.31	Ps 78.24
6.45	Is 54.13
10.34	Ps 82.6
12.13	Ps 118.25-26
12.15	Zch 9.9
12.38	Is 53.1
12.40	Is 6.10
13.18	Ps 41.9
15.25	Ps 35.19
	69.4
19.24	Ps 22.18
19.36	Ex 12.46
	Nu 9.12
19.37	Zch 12.10

Acts

1.20a	Ps 69.25
1.20b	Ps 109.8
2.17-21	Jl 2.28-32
2.25-28	Ps 16.8-11
2.30	Ps 132.11
2.31	Ps 16.10
2.34-35	Ps 110.1
3.13	Ex 3.6,15
3.22	Dt 18.15-16
3.23a	Dt 18.19
3.23b	Lv 23.29
3.25	Gn 22.18
	26.4
4.11	Ps 118.22
4.25-26	Ps 2.1-2
7.3	Gn 12.1

Hebrews (cont.)

1.7	Ps 104.4
1.8-9	Ps 45.6-7
1.10-12	Ps 102.25-27
1.13	Ps 110.1
2.6-8	Ps 8.4-6 (Gr)
2.12	Ps 22.22
2.13a	Is 8.17 (Gr)
2.13b	Is 8.18
3.7-11	Ps 95.7-11
3.15	Ps 95.7-8
4.3	Ps 95.11
4.4	Gn 2.2
4.7	Ps 95.7-8
5.5	Ps 2.7
5.6,10	Ps 110.4
6.13-14	Gn 22.16-17
7.1-2	Gn 14.17-20
7.17-21	Ps 110.4
8.5	Ex 25.40
8.8-12	Jr 31.31-34
9.20	Ex 24.8
10.5-7	Ps 40.6-8
10.16-17	Jr 31.33-34
10.30	Dt 32.35-36
10.37.38	Is 26.20 (Gr)
	Hab 2.3-4 (Gr)
11.15	Gn 5.24
11.18	Gn 21.12
11.21	Gn 47.31 (Gr)
12.5-6	Pr 3.11-12
12.20	Ex 19.12-13
12.21	Dt 9.19
12.26	Hg 2.6
13.5	Dt 31.6,8
13.6	Ps 118.6

James

2.8	Lv 19.18
2.11	Ex 20.13-14
	Dt 5.17-18

2.23	Gn 15.6
4.6	Pr 3.34 (Gr)

1 Peter

1.16	Lv 19.2
1.24-25	Is 40.6-8
2.6	Is 28.16
2.7	Ps 118.22
2.8	Is 8.14
2.9a	Is 43.20
2.9b	Ex 19.6
	Is 61.66
2.9c	Ex 19.2
2.9d	Is 43.91
2.22	Is 53.9
3.10-12	Ps 34.12-16
3.14	Is 8.12-13
4.18	Pr 11.31 (Gr)
5.5	Pr 3.34 (Gr)

2 Peter

2.22	Pr 26.11

Jude

14, 15	1 Enoch 1.9
15	1 Enoch 27.2

Barnabas

2.5	Is. 1.11-13
2.7	Jr. 7.22-23
2.8	Zech. 8.17
2.10	Ps. 51.17
3.1-2	Is. 58.4-5
3.3-5	Is. 58.6-10
4.4	Dan. 7.24
4.5	Dan. 7.7-8
4.7	Ex. 34.28
4.8	Ex. 32.7
4.11	Is. 5.21

Abbreviations commonly used in the ancient manu-scripts. Most pertain to diety, and all of this list are used in the Codex Sinaiticus:

Christ/anointed	X̄Σ̄, X̄Ȳ, X̄N̄, X̄Ω̄, X̄P̄Ȳ
David	Δ̄Λ̄Δ̄
father	Π̄H̄P̄, Π̄P̄Σ̄, Π̄P̄Ī, Π̄P̄Ā, Π̄Ē P̄, Π̄P̄Ā Σ̄, Π̄P̄Ω̄N̄
God	Θ̄Σ̄, Θ̄Ȳ, Θ̄N̄, Θ̄Ω̄, Θ̄Ē
heaven(s)/Heaven	O̅Y̅N̅O̅Σ̅, O̅Y̅N̅O̅Y̅, O̅Y̅N̅O̅N̅, O̅Y̅N̅O̅I̅Σ̅, O̅Y̅N̅O̅I̅, O̅Y̅N̅Ω̅N̅, O̅Y̅N̅Ω̅
Israel	Ī H̄ Λ̄, K̄Σ̄Λ̄, Ī Σ̄H̄Λ̄
Jerusalem	Ī H̄ Λ̄ M̄
Jesus	Ī Σ̄, Ī Ȳ, Ī N̄, Ī H̄Ȳ
Lord/lord/sir	K̄Σ̄, K̄Ȳ, K̄N̄, K̄Ω̄, K̄Ē, K̄Ω̄N̄
man (mankind)	A̅N̅O̅Σ̅, A̅N̅O̅Y̅, A̅N̅O̅N̅, A̅N̅Ω̅, A̅N̅Ē, A̅N̅O̅I̅, A̅N̅Ω̅N̅, A̅N̅O̅I̅Σ̅, A̅N̅O̅Y̅Σ̅
mother	M̄H̄P̄, M̄P̄Σ̄, M̄P̄Ī, M̄P̄Ā
final "N"	as T̄Ω̄ for TΩN/των
savior	Σ̄P̄Ī, Σ̄P̄Σ̄
son	Ȳ Σ̄, Ȳ Ȳ, Ȳ N̄, Ȳ Ω̄, Ȳ Ē
spirit/Spirit	Π̄N̄Ā, Π̄N̄Σ̄, Π̄H̄Ī

Numerals are often spelled out, but sometimes abbreviated in the standard way in Greek, as:

One	(1)	Ā	Nine	(9)	Θ̄
Two	(2)	B̄	Ten	(10)	Ī
Three	(3)	Γ̄	Eleven	(11)	Ī Ā
Four	(4)	Δ̄	Twelve	(12)	Ī B̄
Five	(5)	Ē	Thirty	(30)	Λ̄
Six	(6)	ς̄	Sixty	(60)	ξ̄
Seven	(7)	Z̄	Hundred	(100)	P̄
Eight	(8)	H̄			

APPENDIX III

Liturgical/Eccles. Word	Literal Meaning, from Greek
advocate, Comforter	paraclete
Amen	truly
angel	messenger
bishop	overseer
Christ	the anointed (one)
church	assembly, ecclesia
covetousness	greediness
deacon	servant, minister, waiter
disciple	learner, pupil, student
do (from πράσσω)	practice
doctors of law	scribe, secretary, clerk
fornication	prostitution, unchastity
Gentiles	ethnics, nations
glorify	exalt, acknowledge
glory	fame, reputation
gospel/good news	good message, well message
heathen	ethnics, nations
heaven	sky
husband	man
Joshua	Jesus
Jews	Judeans
Lord	sir, mister, lord
lust	desire
mammon	money, wealth, property
mansions	rooms, abodes
pastor	shepherd
perfect	complete, mature, finished
righteous	just
righteousness	justice, justness
Scripture(s)	writing(s)
servant (from δοῦλος)	slave
steward	manager, foreman
stewardship	responsibility, managerial work
synagogue	congregation
tempt	try, prove, test
testament	covenant
wife	woman

APPENDIX III

Following is a sample list of English "synonyms" used by most translators to translate the same Greek word:

chief priest/high priest	ἀρχιερεύς
come/go	ἔρχομαι
desire/lust	ἐπιθυμία
do/make	ποιέω
heaven/sky	οὐρανός
interpret/translate	διερμηνεύω
man/husband	ἀνήρ
pagan/heathen/Gentiles/nations	ἔθνη
publican/tax gatherer	τελώνης
road/way/Way	ὁδός
soul/life	ψηχή
take/receive	λαμβάνω
woman/wife	γυνή

John 1.38-2.17:
Courtesy The British Library, London.

St. Katerina on Mt. Sinai:
Courtesy The British Library, London.